Annual Subscription for Two Parts
Ordinary paper, 21/- net; hand-made paper, 42/- net

Each Part to Non-Subscribers
Ordinary paper, 15/- net; hand-made paper,

THE
ENGLISH DIALECT
DICTIONARY

EDITED BY

JOSEPH WRIGHT, M.A., Ph.D., D.C.L.

PROFESSOR OF COMPARATIVE PHILOLOGY IN THE UNIVERSITY OF OXFORD

PARTS XI AND XII

HA—JINKETING

LONDON: PUBLISHED BY HENRY FROWDE, AMEN CORNER, E.C.
(PUBLISHER TO THE ENGLISH DIALECT SOCIETY)
OXFORD: 116 HIGH STREET
NEW YORK: G. P. PUTNAM'S SONS

THE
ENGLISH DIALECT DICTIONARY

THE

ENGLISH DIALECT

DICTIONARY

BEING, THE

COMPLETE VOCABULARY OF ALL DIALECT WORDS STILL IN USE, OR KNOWN
TO HAVE BEEN IN USE DURING THE LAST TWO HUNDRED YEARS

*FOUNDED ON THE PUBLICATIONS OF THE ENGLISH DIALECT SOCIETY AND ON A LARGE
AMOUNT OF MATERIAL NEVER BEFORE PRINTED*

EDITED BY

JOSEPH WRIGHT, M.A., Ph.D., D.C.L.

PROFESSOR OF COMPARATIVE PHILOLOGY IN THE UNIVERSITY OF OXFORD

VOLUME III. H–L

LONDON: PUBLISHED BY HENRY FROWDE, AMEN CORNER, E.C.

(PUBLISHER TO THE ENGLISH DIALECT SOCIETY)

OXFORD: 116 HIGH STREET

NEW YORK: G. P. PUTNAM'S SONS

1902

𝕺𝔵𝔣𝔬𝔯𝔡

PRINTED BY HORACE HART

AT THE UNIVERSITY PRESS

NOTE

THE ENGLISH DIALECT DICTIONARY *is printed at the expense of* JOSEPH WRIGHT, *M.A.*
of Langdale House, Park Town, Oxford.

SELECT BIBLIOGRAPHICAL LIST

REPRESENTED BY NUMBERS

N.I.[1] = Antrim and Down.—A Glossary of Words in use in the Counties of Antrim and Down. By W. HUGH PATTERSON. E. D. S., 1880.

Bnff.[1] = Banffshire.—The Dialect of Banffshire. By Rev. W. GREGOR, 1866.

Brks.[1] = Berkshire.—A Glossary of Berkshire Words and Phrases. By Major B. LOWSLEY. E. D. S., 1888.

Cai.[1] = Caithness.—MS. Collection of Caithness Words. By D. NICOLSON.

Cmb.[1] = Cambridgeshire.—MS. Collection of Cambridgeshire Words. By J. W. DARWOOD.

Chs.[1] = Cheshire.—Glossary of Words used in the County of Chester. By R. HOLLAND. E. D. S., 1884–6.

Chs.[2] = Cheshire.—An Attempt at a Glossary of some Words used in Cheshire. By ROGER WILBRAHAM, 1826.

Chs.[3] = Cheshire.—A Glossary of Words used in the Dialect of Cheshire. By E. LEIGH, 1877.

s.Chs.[1] = Cheshire.—The Folk-Speech of South Cheshire. By TH. DARLINGTON. E. D. S., 1887.

Cor.[1] = Cornwall.—Glossary of Words in use in Cornwall. By Miss M. A. COURTNEY and T. Q. COUCH. E. D. S., 1880.

Cor.[2] = Cornwall.—The Ancient Language and the Dialect of Cornwall. By F. W. P. JAGO, 1882.

Cor.[3] = Cornwall.—MS. Collection of Cornish Words. By T. C. PETER.

Cum.[1] = Cumberland.—A Glossary of Words and Phrases pertaining to the Dialect of Cumberland. By W. DICKINSON. E. D. S., 1878–81.

Cum.[2] = Cumberland.—The Dialect of Cumberland. By R. FERGUSON, 1873.

Cum.[3] = Cumberland.—The Folk-Speech of Cumberland and some Districts adjacent. By A. C. GIBSON, 1869.

Cum.[4] = Cumberland.—A Glossary of the Words and Phrases pertaining to the Dialect of Cumberland. By W. DICKINSON. Re-arranged, illustrated, and augmented by quotations, by E. W. PREVOST, 1899.

Der.[1] = Derbyshire.—Pegge's Derbicisms, edited by TH. HALLAM and W. W. SKEAT. E. D. S., 1894.

Der.[2] = Derbyshire.—An Attempt at a Derbyshire Glossary. By JOHN SLEIGH, 1865.

nw.Der.[1] = Derbyshire.—MS. Collection of North-West Derbyshire Words. By T. HALLAM.

Dev.[1] = Devonshire.—Glossary to 'A Dialogue in the Devonshire Dialect,' by a Lady. By J. F. PALMER, 1837.

Dev.[2] = Devonshire.—MS. Collection of North Devonshire Words. By W. H. DANIELS.

Dev.[3] = Devonshire.—MS. Collection of Devonshire Words. By MRS. SARAH HEWETT.

Dev.[4] = Devonshire.—A Glossary of Devonshire Plant Names. By Rev. HILDERIC FRIEND. E.D.S., 1882.

nw.Dev.[1] = Devonshire.—The Dialect of Hartland, Devonshire. By R. PEARSE CHOPE. E. D. S., 1891.

Dor.[1] = Dorsetshire.—Poems of Rural Life, in the Dorset Dialect; with a Dissertation and Glossary, 1848. By W. BARNES.

Dur.[1] = Durham.—A Glossary of Provincial Words used in Teesdale in the County of Durham. 1849.

e.Dur.[1] = Durham.—A List of Words and Phrases in every-day use by the natives of Hetton-le-Hole. By Rev. F. M. T. PALGRAVE. E. D. S., 1896.

w.Dur.[1] = Durham.—Walks in Weardale. By W. H. SMITH (ed. 1885).

e.An.[1] = East Anglia.—The Vocabulary of East Anglia. By R. FORBY, 1830. Second Edition, considerably enlarged, by W. RYE. E. D. S., 1895.

e.An.[2] = East Anglia.—The Vocabulary of East Anglia. By Rev. W. T. SPURDENS. E. D. S., 1879.

Ess.[1] = Essex.—A Glossary of the Essex Dialect. By R. S. CHARNOCK, 1880.

Glo.[1] = Gloucestershire.—A Glossary of Dialect and Archaic Words used in the County of Gloucester. By J. DRUMMOND ROBERTSON. E. D. S., 1890.

Glo.[2] = Gloucestershire.—A Glossary of the Cotswold (Gloucestershire) Dialect. By Rev. R. W. HUNTLEY, 1868.

Hmp.[1] = Hampshire.—A Glossary of Hampshire Words and Phrases. By Rev. Sir W. H. COPE, Bart. E. D. S., 1883.

I.W.[1] = Hampshire.—Isle of Wight Words. By Major H. SMITH and C. ROACH SMITH. E. D. S., 1881.

I.W.[2] = Hampshire.—A Dictionary of the Isle of Wight Dialect, and of Provincialisms used in the Island. By W. H. LONG, 1886.

Hrf.[1] = Herefordshire.—A Glossary of Provincial Words used in Herefordshire and some of the adjoining Counties. [By Sir G. C. LEWIS], 1839.

Hrf.[2] = Herefordshire.—Herefordshire Glossary. By FRANCIS T. HAVERGAL, 1887.

Ken.[1] = Kent.—A Dictionary of the Kentish Dialect and Provincialisms in use in the County of Kent. By W. D. PARISH and W. F. SHAW. E. D. S., 1887.

Ken.[2] = Kent.—An Alphabet of Kenticisms. By SAMUEL PEGGE. E. D. S., 1876.

Lakel.[1] = Lakeland.—Lakeland and Iceland. By T. ELLWOOD. E. D. S., 1895.

Lakel.[2] = Lakeland.—Lakeland Words. By B. KIRKBY, 1898.

Lan.[1] = Lancashire.—A Glossary of the Lancashire Dialect. By J. H. NODAL and G. MILNER. E. D. S., 1875–82.

n.Lan.[1] = Lancashire.—A Glossary of the Words and Phrases of Furness (North Lancashire). By J. P. MORRIS, 1869.

ne.Lan.[1] = Lancashire.—A Glossary of the Dialect of the Hundred of Lonsdale. By R. B. PEACOCK. London Phil. Soc. Trans., 1869.

e.Lan.[1] = Lancashire.—A Glossary of Rochdale-with-Rossendale Words and Phrases. By H. CUNLIFFE, 1886.

m.Lan.[1] = Lancashire.—A Blegburn Dickshonary. By J. BARON, 1891.

s.Lan.[1] = Lancashire.—The Folk-Speech of South Lancashire. By F. E. TAYLOR, 1901.

Lei.[1] = Leicestershire.—Leicestershire Words. Phrases, and Proverbs. By A. BENONI EVANS. E.D.S., 1881.

Lin.[1] = Lincolnshire.—Provincial Words and Expressions current in Lincolnshire. By J. E. BROGDEN, 1866.

n.Lin.[1] = Lincolnshire.—A Glossary of Words used in the Wapentakes of Manley and Corringham, Lincolnshire. By EDWARD PEACOCK. E.D.S., First Edition, 1877; Second Edition, 1889.

sw.Lin.[1] = Lincolnshire.—Glossary of the Words in use in South-West Lincolnshire. By Rev. R. E. G. COLE. E.D.S., 1886.

Nrf.[1] = Norfolk.—Great Yarmouth and Lowestoft. By J. G. NALL, 1866.

Nhp.[1] = Northamptonshire.—Glossary of Northamptonshire Words and Phrases. By A. E. BAKER, 1854.

Nhp.[2] = Northamptonshire.—The Dialect and Folk-Lore of Northamptonshire. By THOMAS STERNBERG, 1851.

N.Cy.[1] = North Country.—A Glossary of North Country Words. By J. T. BROCKETT, 1846.

N.Cy.[2] = North Country.—A Collection of English Words, 1691. By JOHN RAY. E.D.S., 1874.

Nhb.[1] = Northumberland.—Northumberland Words. A Glossary of Words used in the County of Northumberland. By R. O. HESLOP. E.D.S., 1892-4.

Not.[1] = Nottinghamshire.—MS. Collection of Nottinghamshire Words. By THOMAS A. HILL.

Not.[2] = Nottinghamshire.—MS. Collection of Nottinghamshire Words. By HORACE WALKER.

Not.[3] = Nottinghamshire.—MS. Collection of Nottinghamshire Words. By R. L. ABBOTT.

Oxf.[1] = Oxfordshire.—Oxfordshire Words. By Mrs. PARKER. E.D.S., 1876, 1881.

Rut.[1] = Rutlandshire.—Rutland Words. By Rev. CHRISTOPHER WORDSWORTH. E.D.S., 1891.

S.&Ork.[1] = Shetland and Orkneys.—An Etymological Glossary of the Shetland and Orkney Dialect. By T. EDMONDSTON, 1866.

Shr.[1] = Shropshire.—Shropshire Word-Book, a Glossary of Archaic and Provincial Words, &c., used in the County. By G. F. JACKSON, 1879.

Shr.[2] = Shropshire.—Salopia Antiqua. By C. H. HARTSHORNE. London, 1841.

w.Som.[1] = Somersetshire.—The West Somerset Word-Book. A Glossary of Dialectal and Archaic Words and Phrases used in the West of Somerset and East of Devon. By F. T. ELWORTHY. E.D.S., 1886.

Stf.[1] = Staffordshire.—An Attempt towards a Glossary of the Archaic and Provincial Words of the County of Stafford. By CHARLES H. POOLE, 1880.

Stf.[2] = Staffordshire.—MS. Collection of Staffordshire Words. By T. C. WARRINGTON and A. POPE.

Suf.[1] = Suffolk.—Suffolk Words and Phrases. By E. MOOR, 1823.

Sur.[1] = Surrey.—Surrey Provincialisms. By GRANVILLE LEVESON-GOWER. E.D.S., 1876, 1893.

Sus.[1] = Sussex.—A Dictionary of the Sussex Dialect. By W. D. PARISH, 1875.

Sus.[2] = Sussex.—A Glossary of the Provincialisms in use in the County of Sussex. By W. D. COOPER, 1853.

Warwickshire.—Warwickshire Glossary. By T. SHARP. Ed. J. O. HALLIWELL, 1865. = **War.[1]**

Warwickshire.—A Warwickshire Word-Book. By G. F. NORTHALL. E.D.S., 1896. = **War.[2]**

Warwickshire.—MS. Collection of Warwickshire Words. By E. SMITH. = **War.[3]**

Warwickshire.—Glossary of Warwickshire Dialect. By G. MILLER, 1898. = **War.[4]**

Warwickshire.—South Warwickshire Words. By Mrs. FRANCIS. E.D.S., 1876. = **s.War.[1]**

Westmoreland.—MS. Collection of Westmoreland Words. By W. H. HILLS and Dr. JUST. = **Wm.[1]**

Westmoreland and Cumberland.—Dialogues, Poems, Songs, and Ballads, by various writers, in the Westmoreland and Cumberland Dialects. Published by J. R. SMITH, 1839. = **Wm. & Cum.[1]**

Wexford.—A Glossary, with some Pieces of Verse, &c. By JACOB POOLE, 1867. = **Wxf.[1]**

Wiltshire.—A Glossary of Words used in the County of Wiltshire. By G. E. DARTNELL and E. H. GODDARD. E.D.S., 1893. = **Wil.[1]**

Wiltshire.—A Glossary of Provincial Words and Phrases in use in Wiltshire. By J. Y. AKERMAN, 1842. = **Wil.[2]**

Worcestershire.—A Glossary of West Worcestershire Words. By Mrs. CHAMBERLAIN. E.D.S., 1882. = **w.Wor.[1]**

Worcestershire.—South-East Worcestershire Words. A Glossary of Words and Phrases used in South-East Worcestershire. By JESSE SALISBURY. E.D.S., 1894. = **se.Wor.[1]**

Worcestershire.—Upton-on-Severn Words and Phrases. By ROBERT LAWSON. E.D.S., 1884. = **s.Wor.[1]**

Yorkshire.—A Glossary of the Cleveland Dialect. By Rev. J. C. ATKINSON, 1868. Additions to the above. E.D.S., 1876. = **n.Yks.[1]**

Yorkshire.—A Glossary of Words used in the neighbourhood of Whitby. By F. K. ROBINSON. E.D.S., 1876. = **n.Yks.[2]**

Yorkshire.—A Glossary of Words used in Swaledale, Yorkshire. By Captain JOHN HARLAND. E.D.S., 1873. = **n.Yks.[3]**

Yorkshire.—Wit, Character, Folklore, and Customs of the North Riding of Yorkshire. By R. BLAKEBOROUGH, 1898. = **n.Yks.[4]**

Yorkshire.—Yorkshire Folk-Talk. By M. C. F. MORRIS, 1892. = **ne.Yks.[1]**

Yorkshire.—A Glossary of Words used in Holderness in the East Riding of Yorkshire. By F. Ross, R. STEAD, and TH. HOLDERNESS. E.D.S., 1877. = **e.Yks.[1]**

Yorkshire.—A Glossary of Words pertaining to the Dialect of Mid-Yorkshire. By C. CLOUGH ROBINSON. E.D.S., 1876. = **m.Yks.[1]**

Yorkshire.—The Dialect of Craven, in the West Riding of the County of York. By W. CARR, 1828. = **w.Yks.[1]**

Yorkshire.—A Glossary of Words used in the neighbourhood of Sheffield. By S. O. ADDY. E.D.S., 1888-90. = **w.Yks.[2]**

Yorkshire.—A Glossary of the Dialect of Almondbury and Huddersfield. By ALFRED EASTHER. E.D.S., 1883. = **w.Yks.[3]**

Yorkshire.—The Hallamshire Glossary. By J. HUNTER, 1829. = **w.Yks.[4]**

Yorkshire.—The Dialect of Leeds, and its Neighbourhood . . . . . to which is added a copious Glossary. By C. C. ROBINSON, 1861. = **w.Yks.[5]**

Where no authority is given for plant-names, the information has been obtained from A Dictionary of English Plant-Names, by J. Britten and R. Holland. E.D.S., 1878-86.

LIST OF WORDS FOR THE PRESENT KEPT BACK
FROM THE WANT OF FURTHER INFORMATION

HAAS, *v.* Meaning unknown (Suf.).

HAASLIG, *sb.* Meaning unknown (Sh.I.).

HACK-A-THRAW, *adj.* Meaning unknown (s.Sc.).

HACKEN-CROOK, *sb.* Meaning unknown (Lan.).

HACKING, *vbl. sb.* In phr. *hacking and heeling.* Meaning unknown (Som.).

HADYEDS, *adj.* or *sb.* (?). Meaning unknown (Ayr.).

HAIL, *v.* In phr. *to hail a hundred,* a weaving term (Edb.).

(?) **HAINI** or **HAIM**, *sb.* A hand (Lin.).

HAIVINGS, *sb. pl.* Shallows in a river (Not.).

HALE, *sb.* A land measure (Sus.).

HALF-BAG-MAUND, *sb.* Meaning unknown (Som.).

HALLAN-SHACKER, *sb.* A hare (Dev.).

HALPER-POT, *sb.* Meaning unknown (Lan.).

HALT-WO, *int.* A wagoner's call to his team to go to the off-side of the road (Sus.).

HALVANS, *sb.* Inferior ore (n.Cy.).

HAMCH, *sb.* The hip-joint (Nhb.).

HAMIL, *sb.* A handle (Som.).

HAND, *sb.* Meaning unknown (Sh.I.).

HANNA-PAGE, *sb.* Meaning unknown (Nrf.).

HANNIE, *sb.* Meaning unknown (Cum.).

HAN-SPAN, *adv. Obs.* Very heartily (?) (Nhb.).

HATEN, *adj.* Meaning unknown (Wm.).

HAUM, *sb.* Meaning unknown (Wil.).

HAUTECKING, *adj.* Meaning unknown (Dev.).

HAVER, *v.* To toast before the fire (Bwk.).

HAWK-TREE, *sb.* An oak-tree (?) (Wm.).

HAY, *v.* Meaning unknown (Dev.).

HEADSET, *sb.* Meaning unknown (Abd.).

HEAL-HA'DIN or **·MAKIN'**, *sb.* Salvation (Sc.).

HEARF, *sb.* Health (Som.).

HEAUVELESS, *adj.* Meaning unknown (Sc.).

HEELIN', *vbl. sb.* Meaning unknown (Dev.).

HEEL-SCAT, *sb.* Meaning unknown (Slg.).

HEFF, *sb.* Meaning unknown (Dev.).

HEFTERT, *adv.* After (n.Cy.).

HEINT, *pret.* Saw, observed (Ir.).

HELM, *v.* To turn, govern, guide (Edb.).

HEN, *adj.* Old (Chs.).

HEPPER, *sb.* A young salmon (Wal.).

HERBRY, *sb.* Meaning unknown (Inv.).

HERONIOUS, *adj.* Meaning unknown (Ayr.).

HERTA, *adj.* Female (Sh.I.).

HETHOR-DRAYKIN, *sb.* Meaning ·unknown (Nhb.).

HEUCH, *sb.* Meaning unknown (Sc.).

HEVER, *sb.* The hemlock (Hrf.).

HEVICAIRIES, *int.* An exclamation of surprise, &c. (Sc.)

HICE, *int.* 'Keep still!' (Hrf.).

HICKERTY-PICKERTY, *adv.* A nonsense formula used by mummers (Chs.).

HIE, *v.* (?) Meaning unknown (Der.).

HIERTIEING, *vbl. sb.* Meaning unknown (Sc.).

HILDING, *sb.* Meaning unknown (Bdf.).

HILLY HO! *phr.* A hunting or trumpet cry (?) (Sc.).

HIM, *v.* To believe (Som.).

HINN, *v.* Meaning unknown (Dev.).

HIP-HOUSE, *sb.* A lone house (Dor.).

HIPSY DIXY, *phr.* Of evidence : trumped up, faked (Dur.).

HISHER or **ISHER**, *adj.* and *adv.* Higher (n.Yks., w.Yks.).

HITCH, *sb.* Monthly Agents [*sic*] (Wil.).

HIVE, *v.* Meaning unknown (Sur.).

HJUD, *v.* (?). Meaning unknown (Sh.I.).

HO, *sb.* (?). Cover (Sc.).

HO, *pron.* Her (Cum.).

HOBLINS, *adv.* Meaning unknown (Cum.).

HOCKEDOCK, *sb.* An aqueduct (Cmb.).

HOCKER, *v.* To seek (w.Yks.).

HOCKLER-OCKLER, *sb.* A hawking greengrocer (w.Yks.).

HOCKY-VOCKSY, *sb.* A head constable's staff (Dev.).

HODLE-MAKENSTER, *sb.* Meaning unknown (Sc.).

(?) **HODYCOLVONY** or **HODYCOLOONY**, *sb.* Meaning unknown (Ir.).

HOGANSTORE, *sb.* Meaning unknown (w.Cy.).

HOG-PIPES, *sb. pl.* Meaning unknown (Chs.).

HOLLEN, *sb.* Meaning unknown (Per.).

HOLLY-GALONE or **HOLLY-GOLONE**, *sb.* Eau-de-Cologne (Nrf.).

HOMI-OMRIE, *sb.* A hotch-potch, miscellany (Sc.).

HOOF, *sb.* An acre (Lin.).

HOO-FLOO, *adj.* Meaning unknown (w.Cy.).

HOOT, *sb.* or *adj.* (?). Meaning unknown (Rnf.).

HOPE, *sb.* A short street (Dev.).

HORNSHOTTLE, *adj.* Meaning unknown (Rnf.).

HORNSTRING, *v.* Meaning unknown (Oxf.).

HORRORSCUP, *sb.* A horoscope (Lan.).

HORSE-CRIPPLE, *sb.* Meaning unknown (Gall.).

HORSE-HOOD, *adv.* In kind [*sic*] (Dev.).

HOTTENPOT or **HOT-IN-POT**, *sb.* A Hottentot (w.Ir., I.W.).

HOUG, *sb.* A hold upon, grasp of (Rnf.).

HOUNDINGS, *sb. pl.* The housings of harness, covering the collar (e.An.).

HOWF, *sb.* Meaning unknown (s.Sc.).

HOWSTER, *sb.* The knot, *Tringa canutus* (dial. unknown).

HOX, *int.* In phr. *hox an' frog,* an exclamation (Stf.).

HUDDLINGS, *sb. pl.* Meaning unknown (Lei.).

HULBIRT, *sb.* Meaning unknown (Sh.I.).

HULET, *sb.* Meaning unknown (Hmp.).

HULL, *sb.* Meaning unknown (Sus.).

HULLET, *sb.* Meaning unknown (w.Yks.).

HUMBLE, *v.* To humble oneself, demean oneself (dial. unknown).

HUMLY-BUSH, *sb.* Meaning unknown (w.Yks.).

HUMP, *sb.* The thigh (w.Yks.).

HUNDEN, *sb.* The 'hooding' of a flail (Nhb.).

HUNDER-STONE, *sb.* A thunderbolt (Wil.).

HUNKEY, *adj.* Meaning unknown (Sh.I.).

HUNKIN, *sb.* Meaning unknown (Cor.).

HURD, *sb.* Meaning unknown (Sh.I.).

HURMS, *sb. pl.* Meaning unknown (Lan.).

HURST-RIGG, *sb.* Meaning unknown (Sc.).

HUSSING, *prp.* Meaning unknown (Abd.).

HUTS, *sb. pl.* The loppings of trees (?) (dial. unknown).

HWOAZIN, *sb.* Rosin (Cum.).

HYHUMPUS, *sb.* Meaning unknown (Lan.).

HYPLOCK, *adj.* Meaning unknown (Gall.).

ICEE-WILLEE, *sb.* A sandling (Cor.).

ICKET, *sb.* Meaning unknown (w.Yks.).

IDDLINS, *sb. pl.* Meaning unknown (Der.).

ILILUK, *sb.* Meaning unknown (Ir.).

ILL-SANTAFIED, *ppl. adj.* Meaning unknown (Sh.I.).

ILOAN, *sb.* An island (Wxf.).

IMPISITIN, *sb.* Meaning unknown (Sur.).

INAIRT, *adj.* Meaning unknown (Fif.).

INCOMING GROUND, *phr.* The downhill part of a journey (Hmp. ?).

INDE, (?). Meaning unknown (Frf.).

INGLE-SAVE, *sb.* Meaning unknown (Edb.).

INGLIFIED, *ppl. adj.* Learned (Ant.).

INISITIJITTY, *sb.* A little, ridiculous person (War.).

INNERS, *sb. pl.* In phr. *to be in one's inners,* meaning unknown (Sh.I.).

INPLAY, *sb.* Meaning unknown (Sh.I.).

INSKIN, *adj.* Close, intimate (Mid.).

INTAKE, *sb.* Meaning unknown (Yks.).

INTHREATHMENT, *sb.* Meaning unknown (Sh.I.).

INVENTIONARY, *sb.* An inventory (Sus.).

INYARY, *sb.* Diarrhœa (Sh.I.).

ITHE-SAY, *sb.* Telridge hay [*sic*] (Der.).

JAAKE, v. or sb. (?). Meaning unknown (Per.).
JAGE, sb. A violent motion (w.Yks.).
JAGGERS, sb. In phr. by jaggers, an expletive (Ess.).
JAKE-EASY, adj. Meaning unknown (Lnk.).
JANNOCK, sb. A buttress or support against a wall (Nhp.).
JARGE, sb. A jug (Yks.).
(?) **JAUK** or **AUK,** v. Of shoes : to be too large for the foot, not to fit closely (Abd.).
JELLING, adj. Jovial (w.Yks.).
JIB, v. To move restlessly (Dev.).
JIG, sb. A measure of yarn (?) (Frf.).
JILLY-WOW, sb. A witch (Stf.).
JIMRIE-COSIE, sb. Meaning unknown (Abd.).
JINGLER, sb. Meaning unknown (w.Yks.).
JISSICK, sb. A tickling cough (Suf.).
JIZE, sb. In phr. jize be here, an expletive (Abd.).
JOE, sb. An agricultural instrument (?) (Bck.).
JOKIM, sb. Meaning unknown (Rnf.).
JOOPIE, sb. Meaning unknown (Sh.I.).
JOT, sb. Meaning unknown (Wil.).
JOWEY, adj. Meaning unknown (Lan. or Slang).
JUGLER, sb. Meaning unknown (Lei.).
JUMCTURER, sb. A great-coat (Rxb.).
JUNKIT, adj. Meaning unknown (Ayr.).
JU-UM, adj. Empty (n.Cy.).

KAAN, v. Meaning unknown (Sh.I.).
KAKER, sb. Meaning unknown (Per.).
KALTS, sb. pl. The game of quoits (Shr.).
KANN, sb. Fluor-spar (Cor.).
KARKEN, v. Meaning unknown (Lan.).
KATE, sb. A public-house (e.Yks.).
KATLET, sb. Meaning unknown (Sc.).
KAVEL, sb. Meaning unknown (Sh.I.).
KECK, sb. Success, luck (w.Yks.).
KECKER, sb. An overseer at a coal-mine (n.Cy.).
KEEL, sb. Meaning unknown (Dur.).
KEEL, v. Meaning unknown (Dmb.).
KEEPS, sb. pl. Meaning unknown (Frf.).
KELD, v. To thump (Nhb.).
KELSHIE, adj. Meaning unknown (Frf.).
KEMBING, sb. A utensil used in brewing (Lin.).
KENNEN, v. To know (Ir.).
KEOSTREL, sb. A karl (sic) (Cum., Wm.).
KESTERN, adj. Cross, contentious (n.Cy.).
KETT, v. Meaning unknown (Lth., Hdg.).
KETTLE, sb. Meaning unknown (Ir.).
KIAAR, sb. Meaning unknown (Sh.I.).
KIFT, sb. Meaning unknown (Ayr.).
KILHAB, v. Meaning unknown (Slk.).
KILLEMS-OUT, sb. pl. Marbles (Nrf.).
KILLSIMMER, sb. Meaning unknown (Sh.I.).
KINCH, sb.[1] Meaning unknown (Frf.).
KINCH, sb.[2] Meaning unknown (Edb.).
KINDER-MAKER, sb. Meaning unknown (Sc.).
KING'S TAW, phr. Meaning unknown (w.Ir.).
KINSH, sb. Meaning unknown (Sc.).
KIPES, sb. pl. Meaning unknown (Frf.).
KISHY, adj. Thick, stiff, pasty (w.Yks.).
KJAEKSIE, adj. Meaning unknown (Sh.I.).
KJIMPIN', ppl. adj. Meaning unknown (Sh.I.).

KJÖDEE, sb. Meaning unknown (Sh.I.).
KLEEPIE STONES, phr. Meaning unknown (Sh.I.).
KNAKS, sb. pl. In phr. to take the knaks, meaning unknown (Edb.).
KNALTER, v. To know (Lan.).
KNAUM, v. Meaning unknown (Lnk.).
KNAVE, v.[1] To gnaw or bite (Lan.).
KNAVE, v.[2] Meaning unknown (Nhp.).
KNEE, sb. Meaning unknown (Nrf.).
KNERRY, v. To nay [sic] (Stf.).
KNETTER, v. Meaning unknown (n.Yks.).
KNITTAL, sb. Meaning unknown (Abd.).
KNOCKIE, adj. Meaning unknown (Sc.).
KNOCK-SO, sb. Meaning unknown (Sh I.).
KORSIS, sb. pl. Meaning unknown (Sh.I.).
KRACHT, sb. Wickedness, craft (Sc.).
KRAEK, sb. Meaning unknown (Sh.I.).
KRIKKETY, sb. Meaning unknown (Lan.).
KROGIK EE'D, phr. Meaning unknown (Sh.I.).
KULLIE FOR BULLIE, phr. Meaning unknown (Sh.I.).
KYRST, sb. A wood (Oxf.).

LAANGER, sb. A disease of cows (?) (Sh.I.).
LAAVER, sb. Meaning unknown (Sh.I.).
LAEGA, sb. Meaning unknown (Sh.I.).
LAFT, v. To look for (Cum.).
LAG, sb. Meaning unknown (Slg.).
LAIGGENS, sb. pl. Meaning unknown (Slk.).
LAIR, adj. Meaning unknown (Gall.).
LALE, adj. Meaning unknown (Wm.).
LANCROCK, (?). A word occurring in a Shrovetide rhyme ; meaning unknown (Dev.).
LANT, sb. Meaning unknown (Lan.).
LAP, v. To cry (Yks.).
LAP-MESSIN, sb. A term applied to a dog (Sh.I.).
LAPPERTAGE, sb. Obs. Meaning unknown (Wor.).
LARCH, v. Meaning unknown (Dev.).
LARE, adj. In phr. as lare do so and so, as lief do so and so (?) (Dor.).
LASAVRAN, sb. Meaning unknown (Pem.).
LASHIGILLAVERY, sb. A superfluity, esp. of food (n.Cy.).
LASSY, adj. Last (n.Yks.).
LAUG, sb. or adj. (?). Meaning unknown (Sh.I.).
LAUGHER, sb. Meaning unknown (Yks.).
LAUK URROW, phr. Meaning unknown (w.Yks.).
LAUMINGK, prp. Meaning unknown (Chs.).
LAVEER, v. To linger, procrastinate (Sh.I.).
LAVER, sb. The remainder (n.Cy.).
LAX, sb. A part (Som.).
LAY ACROSS, phr. Meaning unknown (War.).
LAY IN LEAD, phr. Meaning unknown (Sh.I.).
LEACHT, sb. A large-sized kistvaen (Dev., Cor.).
LEAD-RECORDER, sb. Meaning unknown (w.Yks.).
LEAR, v. To lean (n.Cy.).
LEAREN-TUB, sb. The vessel in which meal and water are mingled before being baked into oatcake (w.Yks.).
LECTURE, sb. A speech, cry, warning (Hnt. ?).
LEE, adj. Meaning unknown (Sc.).

LEEVE, sb. Meaning unknown (Sh.I.).
LEG, sb. In phr. a leg of raan, meaning unknown (Sh.I.).
LEGIM, adv. In phr. to ride legim or on legim, to ride astride (Rxb.).
LENNOCKMORE, adj. Meaning unknown (Slk.).
LENTEN, pp. Allowed, let (Per.).
LENTOR, sb. Meaning unknown (Ir.).
LETCH, sb. Meaning unknown (Ayr.).
LICKFALADITY, adv. With full force (Lin.).
LICKY-HOW, int. An exclamation (Cor.).
LIDDALES, adj. Out of anything, esp. out of provisions (Sh.I.).
LIE, v. In phr. to lie out; meaning unknown (Sh.I.).
LIFT-HAUSE, sb. The left hand (Rxb.).
LIFTING, ppl. adj. Applied to cattle; meaning unknown (Sh.I.).
LIGH, adj. Meaning unknown (Lan.).
LIGHT, sb. (?). Meaning unknown (Ir.).
LIGS, sb. pl. ' Ley ' (Yks.).
LIN, v. Meaning unknown (Sh.I.).
LING, sb. In phr. the ling of one's life ; meaning unknown (Wxf.).
LING, v. Meaning unknown (Lan.).
LINGER, sb. Meaning unknown (Wxf.).
LINITY, sb. Meaning unknown (Sh.I.).
LINKS, sb. pl. Meaning unknown (Sh.I.).
LIP, sb. or adj. (?). In phr. to be lip, to begin lip; meaning unknown (Sh.I.).
LITTER, adj. Meaning unknown (Dev.).
LÖ, adj. Meaning unknown (Sh.I.).
LOAK-HEN, sb. Meaning unknown (Nrf.).
LOBBYSTHROWL, sb. Goitre (Der.).
LOCK, sb. Meaning unknown (Lth.).
LOCKER STRAE, phr. Meaning unknown (Abd.).
LODGE, adj. Meaning unknown (Sh.I.).
LOKKER, v. To curl (Sc.).
LONE, adj. Long (Nhb.).
LOOG, v. (?). Meaning unknown (Sh.I.).
LOOMENT, sb. Obscurity (Dev.).
LOON, sb. Meaning unknown (Ayr.).
LORNE, sb. Meaning unknown (Sh.I.).
LOSEN, v. To look (Wor.).
LOSES, sb. pl. Meaning unknown (Lan.).
LOTHER, sb. Meaning unknown (Ken.).
LOUNDSING, prp. Lingering (Cmb.).
LOVE-SPOKEN, ppl. adj. Meaning unknown (Bnff.).
LOYST, v. Meaning unknown (Lan.).
LUCKER, adj. Loose, flabby (Ken.).
LUCKING-MILL, sb. A fulling-mill (Ken.).
LUCKS, sb. pl. Meaning unknown (w.Yks.).
LUCKY-PROACH, sb. The father-lasher, Cottus bubalis (Fif.).
LUELY, adv. A fray (Sc.).
LUFES, sb. pl. The ears of a toad (n.Cy.).
LUMSTHROWL, adj. Goitre (Der.).
LUNDGATE, sb. Meaning unknown (n.Yks.).
LURDER, sb. An awkward, lazy, worthless person (Sc.).
LURE, sb. The palm of the hand (n.Cy., Nhb.).
LUSCH, sb. A wish, desire (Som.).
LUSKEE, sb. Meaning unknown (Rxb.).
LYERON, sb. Meaning unknown (Som.).
LYINS, sb. pl. Meaning unknown (Sh.I.).
LYLSIE-WULSIE, sb. Linsey-woolsey (Cld.).
LYMPHAD, sb. A galley (Sc.).
LYTHING, vbl. sb. Softening, soothing (Abd.).

j

H

HA, *adj.* Sc. Also in form **hi.** [Not known to our correspondents.] In phr. *ha year olds,* cattle eighteen months old. s.Sc. Morton *Cyclo. Agric.* (1863).

HA, *int.* Dev. An exclamation of indignation and contempt. Grose (1790) *MS. add.* (M.)

HA, HAA, see Hay, *sb.*[1], Haw, *sb.*[1], *int.*[1], How, *sb.*[1], *adv., int.*

HAABER, HAABUCK, HAACK, see Habber, Hawbuck, Hawk, *v.*[1].

HAAF, *sb.*[1] and *v.* Sc. Lakel. Also in forms **haave** Sc. (Jam.); **haf(f** Sh.I.; **halve, hauve** Sc. (Jam.) [hāf, hāv.] 1. *sb.* The open sea, the deep-sea fishing-ground.

Sh.I. Mony a day he made for da haaf whin aulder men shook dir heids, an' widna lave da beach, Clark *Gleams* (1898) 33 ; They had had a hard week at the 'haf,' Burgess *Tang* (1898) 8 ; (W.A.G.); (Coll. L.L.B.) ; **S. & Ork.**[1]

Hence **Haafing,** *vbl. sb.* deep-sea fishing; also used *fig.* Sh.I. Da days o' haafin i' da saxern is by, I faer, *Sh. News* (Sept. 10, 1898).

2. *Comp.* (1) **Haaf-boat,** a boat suitable for deep-sea fishing; (2) **-eel,** the conger-eel, *Conger vulgaris* ; (3) **-fish,** the great seal, *Phoca barbata* ; (4) **-fishing,** deep-sea fishing ; (5) **-lines,** the lines used in deep-sea fishing ; (6) **-man,** a fisherman engaged in the deep-sea fishing ; (7) **-seat,** a deep-sea fishing-ground.

(1) **Sh.I.** The old haf boat measured from 18 to 20 feet of keel, the stems bending outwards in a graceful curve, so as to give a length of some 26 feet over all. The breadth of beam was 6 to 7 feet, and the depth of the hold 27 inches. The boat was divided into six compartments, viz. fore-head, fore-room, mid-room, oost-room, shott, burrik or kannie, Spence *Flk-Lore* (1899) 127. **S. & Ork.**[1] (2) **Nai.** Haaf-eel, a name given to the common conger in the Moray Firth, Day *Brit. Fishes* (1880–4) II. 251. (3) **Sh.I.** Our boat was visited by one of the large seals of the country (*Phoca barbata*), named by the natives a Haaf-fish, because it usually appears at that remote distance from the main coast, Hibbert *Desc. Sh. I.* (1822) 166, ed. 1891 ; (Coll. L.L.B.) ; **S. & Ork.**[1] (4) **Sh.I.** As good . . . as ever rowed . . . to the haaf-fishing, Scott *Pirate* (1821) ii. **S. & Ork.**[1] (5) **Sh.I.** The haf lines were also set during aevaliss [unsettled] weather, Spence *ib.* 131. (6) **Sh.I.** Doo canna tak' hit a' rightly in, no bein' a haaf man dysel, *Sh. News* (July 3, 1897) ; The signs in heaven above were the special study of the hafman, Spence *ib.* 115. (7) **Sh.I.** One of these ancient sinker stones was lifted on a fish hook at a haf seat off the north part of Unst, Spence *ib.* 129.

3. Phr. *to go to haaf* or *haaves,* to go out to the deep-sea fishing. **S. & Ork.**[1], Or.I. (Jam.)

4. A large pock-net used in fishing. Also in *comp.* **Haaf-net.**

Abd. Lady Kigie who had a lodging in the Chanonry, and a hannet [half-net] upon Don, Turreff *Antiq. Gleanings* (1859) 64. Dmf. *Agric. Surv.* 603 (Jam.) ; A few nights after his marriage he was standing with a halve-net, Cromek *Remains* (1810) 305. Gall. A standing net placed within water-mark to prevent the fishes from returning with the tide (Jam.). Wgt. These [fish] are taken betwixt Wigton and the Ferrieton ; some in the halfe-net ; some in cups fixt on the sands, Fraser *Wigtown* (1877) 88. **Lakel.**[1] **Cum.** Two [sturgeons] were taken last week with the haaf net . . . Mr. —— was lucky enough to secure another [sturgeon] in his haaf, *Carlisle Pat.* (June 28, 1889) 5 ; **Cum.**[2] It consists of a pock-net fixed to a kind of frame, which, whenever a fish strikes against it, is hauled out of the water ; **Cum.**[4] A net used on the Solway, which consists of a pock-net fixed on a frame of wood,

being kept open by a cross-bar fixed at right angles to the pole held by the fisherman standing in the water.

Hence (1) **Haaf-bawk,** *sb.* the pole attached to a ' haaf-net' whereby it is raised out of the water ; (2) **Ha'netsman,** *sb.* a fisherman who shares in a ' haaf-net.'

(1) **Cum.**[4] (2) **Sc.** We swam owre the Dee . . . the ha'netsman, Main, Wad charge us across to the Brick Kilns again, Anderson *Rhymes* (1867) 78.

5. *v.* To fish with a ' haaf' or pock-net.

s.Sc. (Jam.) Dmf. A second mode of fishing, called ' haaving ' or ' hauling,' is standing in the stream, either at the flowing or ebbing of the tide, with a pock net fixed to a kind of frame, consisting of a beam, 12 or 14 feet long, having three small sticks or rungs fixed into it. Whenever a fish strikes against the net, they, by means of the middle rung, instantly haul up the mouth of the net above water, *Statist. Acc.* II. 16 (*ib.*). **Lakel.**[1] So used by fishermen of the Solway, both on Scottish and Cumbrian side. **Cum.**[4]

[Sw. *haf,* the sea ; Dan. and Norw. dial. *hav* (Aasen) ; ON. *haf.*]

HAAF, *sb.*[2] n.Yks.[2] A haven, port.

HAAF, HAAFURE, see Heaf, *sb.*[1], Haugh, Haaver.

HAAG, *sb.* and *v.* Sh.I. [hāg.] 1. *sb.* Thrift, economy.

Du's nae hāg i' dy haand Jakobsen *Norsk in Sh.* (1897) 36; **S. & Ork.**[1]

2. *v.* To use sparingly.

Skeek signifies to use sparingly, and is similar in meaning to the words hain and haag, Spence *Flk-Lore* (1899) 207.

[Norw. dial. *hag,* order, management (Aasen) ; ON. *hagr,* state, condition.]

HAAG, see Hag, *sb.*[2]

HAAGLESS, *adj.* Sh.I. Limitless, boundless. See **Hag-mark.**

What's twenty year ta dee or me ? Hit's no a knuckle o wir towes Set oot upon a haagless sea Ta flot, or sink for want o bowes, Junda *Klingrahool* (1898) 51.

HAAGLET, *sb.* Sh.I. In phr. *it's come back to its auld haaglet,* said of an animal that has strayed, and returned to its old pasture. **S. & Ork.**[1]

[Cp. ON. *hagi,* a pasture, *hag-lendi,* pasture land (Vigfusson).]

HAAK, see Hake, *v.,* Hawk, *sb.*[2], *v.*[1]

HAAL, *sb.* Cai.[1] [hāl.] A hold, support, used esp. in connexion with children learning to walk.

' To stan' at 'e haal.' To stand at a chair or such like. ' To gang at 'e haal, or by the haal.' To move from chair to chair, or from one support to another, but not to venture to cross an open space.

[Cp. Norw. dial. and ON. *halla,* to lean with the body, to swerve (Aasen).]

HAALLIGET, *adj.* Cai.[1] Disreputable, violent, light-headed.

[Cp. Norw. dial. *haalig,* bad, also *haadleg,* shameful, disgraceful (Aasen) ; ON. *hāðuligr,* disgraceful, contemptible (Vigfusson).]

HAALYAN, HAAM, see Hallion, Haulm.

HAANYAL, HAAP(E, see Hanniel, Hap, *v.*[3]

HAAP, *v.* Nhp.[1] Of cattle : to eat, to bite close to the ground.

HAAR, *sb.*[1] Sc. Nhb. Dur. Yks. Lan. Lin. Also in forms **aar** n.Lin.[1] ; **har** N.Cy.[1] Nhb.[1] Dur. e.Yks. n.Lin.[1] ; **harr** Frf. Fif. N.Cy.[1] Dur. n.Yks.[1][2][4] m.Yks.[1] Lin. ; **haur** Ayr. Lth. ; **hear, here** Lan. [(h)ār, h)ar.] 1. A cold sea-fog or mist ; a drizzling rain or fog. Cf. harl(e, *sb.*[2]

B

Sc. On the face of the water, where the haar lay, STEVENSON *Catriona* (1893) xxi. **Cai.**[1] Abd. A frosty haar filled Noran valley, M‘KENZIE *Sketches* (1894) iii; Not common (G.W.). **Frf.** Nor harr nor cluds Forebodit rain, SANDS *Poems* (1833) 70. **Per.** The morn brings sleet And haar and hail together, SPENCE *Poems* (1898) 18. **Fif.** That's a nasty haar come on, ROBERTSON *Provost* (1894) 67. **Ayr.** When the haur hings on the hill, AINSLIE *Land of Burns* (ed. 1892) 13. **Lth.** A strange—a new man—Strode beside them in the haur, LUMSDEN *Sheep-head* (1892) 316. **Gall.** It came upon the land suddenly as the ' haar ' that in the autumn drives up the eastern valleys from the sea, CROCKETT *Moss-Hags* (1895) xxii. **N.Cy.**[1] A Northern harr Brings drought from far, *Prov.* **Nhb.**[1], **Dur.** (K.) n.Yks.[1]; n.Yks.[2] Mist with small rain. So good in a morning for vegetation. ' A northern harr Brings fine weather from far '; n.Yks.[4] **e.Yks.** MARSHALL *Rur. Econ.* (1788). m.Yks.[1] **Lan.** GROSE (1790) *MS. add.* (C.) Lin. SKINNER (1671); RAY (1691); MILLER & SKERTCHLY *Fenland* (1878) iv. n.Lin. SUTTON *Wds.* (1881); Still current, but rare. It seems always to include the idea of cold (E.P.); n.Lin.[1] **se.Lin.** The harr was very heavy in the marshes this mornin' (T.H.R.).

2. A cold easterly wind; also in *comb.* **Easterly haar.**
Sig. In the months of April and May, easterly winds, commonly called Haars, usually blow with great violence, NIMMO *Stirlingshire* (1777) 438 (JAM.). **Cld.** The cold damp called Easterly-hars, so prevalent on the east coast, seldom arrive here, *Agric. Surv.* 4 (*ib.*). **Fif.** Their topsails strutting with the vernal harr, TENNANT *Anster* (1812) 23, ed. 1871 ; This parish [St. Andrews] is well acquainted with the cold, damp easterly winds, or haar of April and May, *Statist. Acc.* XIII. 197.

Hence **Haary** or **Haury,** *adj.* of wind : cold, keen, biting. **Sc.** Tho' Envy's haury blastin' breath, WILSON *Poems* (1822) 56. **Sh.I.** A haary wind blaws keen an cauld Across da voe, JUNDA *Klingrahool* (1898) 22.

3. Hoar-frost, rime.
Per., Cld. (JAM.) Lan. GROSE (1790) *MS. add.* (C.) ; TIM BOBBIN *View Dial.* (ed. 1806) *Gl.*
[1. Cp. Du. dial. (Zaansche) *harig,* ' dampig, mistig, met scherpen damp of nevel vervuld ' (BOEKENOOGEN). 2. MDu. *hare,* a keen cold wind (VERDAM) ; Du. *haere,* a keen wind (KILIAN) ; WFlem. *harie,* a cold wind which frequently blows in March and April (DE BO) ; cp. Fr. *un temps haireux,* cold and damp weather. 3. Du. *haere,* night frost (KILIAN).]

HAAR, *sb.*[2] and *v.* Sc. Lin. Also in forms **har** n.Lin.[1]; **haur** Sc. (JAM.) 1. *sb.* A cough. n.Lin.[1]
2. An impediment in speech ; a huskiness in the throat.
Lnk. (JAM.) **e.Lth., Rxb.** This is *gen.* applied to some impediment in the throat, which makes [it] necessary for a person as it were to cough up his words, before he can get them rightly articulated (*ib.*).
3. *v.* To speak thickly and hoarsely. Lnk. (JAM.)

HAAS, see **Halse,** *sb.*[1]

HAAVE, *adj. Obs.* Sc. Pale, wan.
Abd. The third was an auld, wizen'd, haave coloured carlen, FORBES *Jrn.* (1742) 14 ; The tither was a haave colour'd smeerless tapie, *ib.* 17.
[OFr. *hâve,* ' pâle ' (HATZFELD).]

HAAVE, see **Haaf,** *sb.*[1], **Hauve,** *v.*[1], **Haw,** *sb.*[1]

HAAVER, *sb.* n.Cy. Yks. Written **haafure** n.Cy. (HALL.) ; **haavre** n.Yks.[2] A fisherman's line, used in the deep-sea fishing, to which the ' snoods,' each terminating in a hook, are appended. Cf. **haaf,** *sb.*[1] **4.**
n.Cy. (HALL.) n.Yks.[1] ; n.Yks.[2] The fisherman's lines stretched horizontally, and furnished with suspended rows of baited hooks, for catching the larger sea-fish in deep water.

HAAVER, HAAZE, see **Halver, Haw,** *sb.*[1]

HAB, *sb.*[1] *Obs.* Nhb. A halbert.
The Scottish habs were stout and true, *Bishoprick Garl.* (1834) 34.

HAB, *sb.*[2] Glo.[1] [æb.] The woof, yarn woven across the warp. See **Abb.**
When the weavers in their glory stood, The chain and hab was very good ; But when the chain was very bad, They cursed the chain, and damned the hab.

HAB, *adv.* and *sb.*[3] Nhb. Yks. Lin. Also Som. Dev. Also written **ab** n.Yks. sw.Lin.[1] [h)ab, æb.] 1. *adv.* In *comb.* **Hab-nab,** anyhow, in random fashion.
Nhb. His wardrobe, got up quite habnab, Was second-hand, WILSON *Tippling Dominie* ; Nhb.[1]
2. *sb.* Phr. (1) *hab or nab,* (*a*) get or lose, hit or miss ;

(*b*) by hook or by crook ; (*a*) *habs and nabs,* little by little, piecemeal ; in one way and another.
(1, *a*) **w.Som.**[1] In a market, a buyer pretending to walk off, says : ' Then you 'ont take no less ! ' (*Seller*) ' No, I 'ont, not one varden.' (*Buyer*) ' Then I'll ab-m—hab or nab ! ' **nw.Dev.**[1] (*b*) **w.Yks.** He'll hev it awther bi hab or nab, *Prov.* in *Brighouse News* (Sept. 14, 1889). (*a*) **n.Yks.** He did by abs an' nabs (I.W.). **e.Yks.**[1] Anything done in odd moments or at intervals of leisure, not continuously, is said to be done by habs-an-nabs. **n.Lin.**[1] ' I've scratted it together by habs an' nabs.' Said of rent. **sw.Lin.**[1] We've gotten our hay by abs and nabs—a load nows and thens. They had to finish the church by abs and nabs.
[1. Cyphers, astral characters . . . set down hab-nab, at random, BUTLER *Hud.* (1664) II. iii. 990.]

HAB-, see **Hob,** *sb.*[2]

HA-BA, *sb.* Yks. Also written **aah-ba, a-ba, a-bay.** [e·-be, ea·-bea.] A roar of laughter ; a shout, blatant cry ; a hullabaloo.
w.Yks. But if ide a been thear, ah sud set up a a-ba, TOM TREDDLEHOYLE *Bairnsla Ann.* (Mar. 1854); Tha's making a girt a-bay about nowt (F.K.); What ar ta makkin that gert aah-ba for ! BANKS *Whfld. Wds.* (1865) ; w.Yks.[6] Sehr up a gurt hâa-bâa.

HABAKER, HABBAD, see **Half, Aye but.**

HABBER, *sb.* and *v.* Sc. Irel. Also in form **haaber** Ant. [ha·ber.] 1. *sb.* A person who stammers in speaking or speaks thickly ; a clumsy clown.
Bnff.[1] Commonly used with the notion of stupidity. Ant. GROSE (1790) *MS. add.* (C.)
Hence (1) **Habbergaw,** *sb.* (*a*) hesitation, suspense ; (*b*) an objection ; (2) **Habberjock,** *sb.* (*a*) a turkey-cock ; (*b*) a big, stupid person who speaks thickly.
(1) **n.Sc.** (JAM.) (2, *a*) **Bnff.**[1] (*b*) *ib.* He's a stoopid habber-jock o' a cheel.
2. The act of snarling or growling like a dog.
n.Sc. (JAM.) **Abd.** Fell death had came to see them An' gi'en a habber, Wi' solemn air, TARRAS *Poems* (1804) 12 (*ib.*).
3. *v.* To stutter, stammer. Sc. (JAM.) **4.** To snarl, growl. n.Sc. (*ib.*)

HABBERDYN-FISH, *sb. Obs.* Sc. n.Cy. That kind of cod which is usually salted ; barrelled cod.
Sc. Dried cod fish, at that period known by the name of Habberdyn fish, PENNANT *Tour Sc.* (ed. 1790) 138. **n.Cy.** GROSE (1790) *MS. add.* (M.)
[Habberdine fish, *Asellus salitus,* BARET (1580) s.v. *Fish.* ME. *haburdenne,* Accts.(1370), see ROGERS *Agric. and Prices* I. 616. Fr. *habordean* and *labordean,* an haberdine (COTGR.). MDu. *habourdaen,* also *laberdaen* (VERDAM). Prob. fr. the Basque district *le Labourd, Lapurdum* (the old name for Bayonne), see FRANCK (s.v. *Labberdaan*).]

HABBERNAB, see **Hobnob.**

HABBIE, *adj.* Lth. (JAM.) [Not known to our correspondents.] Stiff in motion.

HABBIE-GABBIE, *v.* Sh.I. To throw money, &c., among a crowd to be scrambled for. S. & Ork.[1]

HABBLE, *sb.* and *v.* Sc. [ha·bl.] 1. *sb.* A difficulty, perplexity, quandary ; 'fix.' See **Hobble,** *sb.* 9.
Sc. An' ayne got into a fair habble, HUNTER *J. Armiger's Revenge* (1897) xi. **Slg.** You've put [him] in a habble, TAYLOR *Poems* (186a) 17. **Ayr.** When whiles in a habble Be manly and clean, WHITE *Jottings* (1879) 290. **Lnk.** I hae gotten mysel' into a bonny habble ! GORDON *Pyotshaw* (1885) 74. **e.Lth.** Man, yon was an awfu' habble to be in, HUNTER *J. Inwick* (1895) 28.
2. Confusion, tumult, hubbub ; a squabble, quarrel.
Abd. Cripples ne'er were made for habbles, SHIRREFS *Sale Catal.* (17—) 21. **Cld.** (JAM.) **Rnf.** We'll aft be plung'd into a habble, TANNAHILL *Poems* (1807) 44, ed. 1817. **Ayr.** (J.M.), **Ayr., Lth.** (JAM.) **Lth.** Morosely by a glowing fire, I retrospect the habble, LUMSDEN *Sheep-head* (1892) 50. **Peb.** He has got into a habble with a neighbour (A.C.). **Rxb.** (JAM.)
Hence **Habblesheuf,** *sb.* an uproar, tumult, confusion. Ayr. (J.M.)
3. *v.* To confuse, reduce to a state of perplexity ; to stammer, speak or act confusedly ; to gabble, talk fast ; to wrangle, quarrel.
Sc. To habble a lesson, to say it confusedly (JAM.). **Slk.** Are we to be habbled out o' house and hadding ! HOGG *Tales* (1838) 323, ed. 1866. **Rxb.** Some trump the fauts o' ither fonk, Some habblin on religion, A. SCOTT *Poems* (ed. 1808) 145.

Hence (1) **Habbler**, *sb.* one who causes or delights in a squabble ; (2) **Habbling**, (*a*) *sb.* confusion, hubbub; wrangling, confused speaking ; (*b*) *ppl. adj.* given to petty quarrelling.

(1) Cld. (JAM.) (*a, a*) Fif. Sic habblin' an' gabblin, Ye never heard nor saw, DOUGLAS *Poems* (1806) 121. Edb. They're here Wi' habblin, a' wi' ane anither, An' a' asteer, LIDDLE *Poems* (1821) 43. (*b*) Bnff.[1]

4. To snap at anything as a dog does.

Sc. Also used to denote the growling noise made by a dog when eating voraciously (JAM.).

Hence **Habble**, *sb.* the act of snapping. Sc. (*ib.*)

HABBLE, see **Hobble**, *v.*[1]

HABBLIE, *adj.* Sc. (JAM.) Of cattle : having big bones, ill-set.

HABBOCRAWS, *int.* Sc. A shout used to frighten the crows from the corn-fields.

a.Sc. HISLOP *Anecdote* (1874) 343. Gall. He believed himself among the rooks, and started up, roaring, with outspread arms, habbocraws, to the astonishment of the holy congregation, MACTAGGART *Encycl.* (1824) 249, ed. 1876.

HABEEK-A-HA, *int.* Sc. A cry given as a signal that a marble, bool, &c., is to be scrambled for.

Per. When a bool tirled oot o' oor pooch to the flure, It was put in a roond penny spunk-box secure, Till it got rovin' fu, then—I min' o't sae weel—Twas ' habeek-a-ha ' at auld Jenny's Schule, EDWARDS *Strathearn Lyrics* (1889) 35. [In Abd. this used to be called a ' logan.' The master pitched in succession each forfeited ' bool ' among the scholars out of doors (A.W.).]

HABER-, see **Haver**, *sb.*[2]

HABERDASH, *sb.* Sc. Small wares, miscellaneous articles.

Abd. There will be sold ... a quantity of haberdash, an' gin ony body wants to ken what that is, its piggery, PAUL *Aberdeenshire* (1881) 46.

[Ther haberdashe, Ther pylde pedlarye, *Papist. Exhort.* (c. 1550) (NARES).]

HABERDASHER, *sb. Obs.* n.Cy. Yks. Fig. A schoolmaster.

n.Cy. (HALL.) w.Yks.[1] A haberdasher of nouns and pronouns.

HABERSCHON, *sb. Obs.* Sc. A jacket of mail or scale armour, an habergeon.

Ayr. All armed for battle, full of zeal, In haberschons and caps of steel, BOSWELL *Poet. Wks.* (1811) 89., ed. 1871.

[Helmys and hawbyrschownys, BARBOUR *Bruce* (1375) XI. 130.]

HABILIMENTS, *sb. pl.* Sc. Outfit.

a.Sc. The form ' bulyments' is still used in parts of the north to mean any kind of ragged unshapely clothing, particularly a beggar's; and ' habiliments,' outfit. Both words, however, are employed with a somewhat ludicrous meaning, FRANCISQUE-MICHEL *Sc. Lang.* (1882) 70.

HABIT, *v.* Yks. Lin. [a·bit.] To accustom.

n.Yks.[2], w.Yks. (C.C.R.) Lin. He's habited his sen to tekkin' doctor's stuff while he's clean wore oot his i'side, *Lin. N. & Q.* (Oct. 1891) 251.

[O y'are a shrewd one ; and so habited In taking heed, CHAPMAN *Odysseys* (1615) *v.*[1]]

HABIT, *prep.* Stf.[1] [Not known to our correspondents.] In the place of.

HABIT AND REPUTE, *phr.* Sc. Held and reputed to be so and so, repr. legal Lat. *habitus et reputatus.*

Baff. Most of them depone that the pannels [prisoners] were habit and repute Egyptians, GORDON *Chron. Keith* (1880) 39. Per. A general allegation of her being habite and repute a witch, SPOTTISWOODE *Miscell.* (1844) II. 61. [If the person ... be habit and repute a thief—i.e. one who notoriously makes or helps his livelihood by thieving, BELL *Dict. Law Scotl.* (1861).]

HABIT-SARK, *sb.* Sc. A woman's riding-shirt.

Per. A habit-sark ... O'erspread a breast, perhaps o' virtue proof, DUFF *Poems*, 81 (JAM.).

HABLIMENTS, *sb. pl.* Yks. [a·bliments.] Habiliments, vestments.

n.Yks.[1] ' Noo ye've getten yer habliments on, Ah'll awa' an' knoll t'bell ;' the clerk to the clergyman about to officiate at a funeral, of the surplice, scarf, &c.

HACHEE, *adj. Obs.* Irel. Cross, ill-tempered.

Wxf.[1] Fartoo zo hachee ! [Why so ill-tempered !], 84.

HACHEL, *sb.* Sc. [hã·χl.] A sloven, slut.

Ayr. A gipsy's character, a hachel's slovenliness, and a waster's want are three things [&c.], GALT *Sir A. Wylie* (1822) xlix.

HACK, *sb.*[1] and *v.*[1] Var. dial. uses in Sc. Irel. and Eng. Also in forms ack Stf.[2] se.Wor.[1]; **haike** Cum. ; **hake** Fif.; hauk Lth. (JAM.) n.Cy. (K.); hawk Sc. (JAM.) Nhb.[1]; heck w.Yks.[5]; hick Nhb.[1] Cor.[1]; hjuk Sh.I.; hock Nrf. Hmp.[1] [h]ak, æk.] **1.** *sb.* A kind of pickaxe or mattock used in agricultural employments ; see below.

n.Cy. BAILEY (1721) ; GROSE (1790) ; (K.) ; N.Cy.[1]; N.Cy.[2] A mattock made only with one and that a broad end. Nhb. Shovels, hacks, spades, &c., RICHARDSON *Borderer's Table-bk.* (1846) V. 277 ; Nhb.[1] Dur.[1] An implement of two kinds : one is called a pick, having one end pointed, and the other rather broader. The other kind is called a mattock, one end of which is axe-shaped, and the other end like the broad end of the pick. Lakel.[1] Cum.[1] A pickaxe having points about an inch in width ; Cum.[4] s.Wm. (J.A.B.) n.Yks. They [turnips] are pulled up by a peculiar drag, or ' hack' as it is provincially called, *Jrn. R. Agric. Soc.* (1848) IX. ii; n.Yks.[1]; n.Yks.[2] Half a mattock ; a pickaxe with one arm ; n.Yks.[3][4] e.Yks. MARSHALL *Rur. Econ.* (1788). m.Yks.[1] A kind of pickaxe, or mattock, without the blade end. w.Yks. WILLAN *List Wds.* (1811) ; (J.T.) ; w.Yks.[12], Lan.[1] n.Lan. (W.S.) ; n.Lan.[1] April wi' his hack an' bill, Sets a flow'r on iv'ry hill, *Local Rhyme.* e.Lan.[1] Chs.[1] ; Chs.[2] A gorse hack. s.Chs.[1] A kind of mattock used to stock or pull up gorse. nw.Der.[1] s.Not. The turnip hack is a kind of mattock with either one or two blades (J.P.K.). w.Dev. A one ended mattock, MARSHALL *Rur. Econ.* (1796). Cor. A digging instrument, the same as the biddix or beat-axe (q.v.), and used in Zennor for cutting turves (J.W.).

2. A heavy tool or pickaxe used by miners ; see below.

Nhb., Dur. GREENWELL *Coal Tr. Gl.* (1849). e.Dur.[1] A heavy pick, weighing about 7 lbs., with head about 18 in. in length. There are var. kinds, e.g. Tommy hack (round head and chisel point), Jack hack (round head and sharp point), Pick hack (sharp head and chisel point). Der. MANLOVE *Lead Mines* (1653) *Gl.* Shr.[1] A small pick used in getting coal.

Hence **Hack-ave**, *sb.* the handle of a ' hack.' Shr.[1]

3. A large hoe.

w.Yks. *Hlfx. Courier* (May 8, 1897) ; (J.T.) ; w.Yks.[2]; w.Yks.[5] A kind of hoe with a long blade.

4. A pronged instrument or mattock used for dragging dung from a cart ; see below. *Gen.* in *comb.* **Muck-hack**.

Cai.[1] Bnff., Rnf. They loosen all the ground completely with a hack, an instrument with a handle of about 4 or 5 feet long, and two iron prongs like a fork but turned inwards, *Statist. Acc.* XIX. 534 (JAM.). Lth. (JAM.) Nhb.[1] A muck fork, having 3 or 4 tines or teeth, which are bent at a right angle to the handle. It is used for drawing litter out of cattle lairs and similar places, and is sometimes called a drag. The above is called a ' teeming hack,' as it is used in emptying [teeming]. There is also a ' filling hack,' which is like a four or five pronged fork bent at the neck to an angle of 45 degrees with the shank. Both teeming and filling hacks are used when working among manure.

5. An axe for dressing stone.

Lin. STREATFEILD *Lin. and Danes* (1884) 334. n.Lin.[1]

6. A mark, notch ; a deep cut, a fissure. Also used *fig.*

Sc. Ye may pit a hack i' the post the day [To-day has been a red-letter day with you], *Prov.* (G.W.) Elg. Ca' in the crook a hack again, TESTER *Poems* (1865) 160. Abd. I sud set up my bonnet a hack fan I gaed owre to Clinkstyle this time, ALEXANDER *Johnny Gibb* (1871) xliii. Lnk. Stamp'd in fire upon the broo, Were figures three, in unco hacks, *Deil's Hallowe'en* (1856) 42.

7. A cut, wound, gash. Also used *fig.*

Edb. Aft the hack o' honour shines In bruiser's face wi' broken lines, FERGUSSON *Poems* (1773) 206, ed. 1785; Geordy's men cou'd not withstand The hacks o' their claymores, LIDDLE *Poems* (1821) 238. n.Cy. (K.) Cum. Wi' nowther haike nor quarrel, GILPIN *Sngs.* (1866) 282.

8. A chap or crack in the skin of the hands or feet caused by exposure to cold and wet.

Sc. (JAM.), Cai.[1] Fif. Skelbs and hacks needed tender handling, COLVILLE *Vernacular* (1899) 18. Ayr. Mittens on her hands after she has creeshed them weel with saim for the hacks, SERVICE *Dr. Duguid* (ed. 1887) 161. Nhb.[1] A surface fissure or chap in the skin produced by cold or work. A deeper fissure than a hack is called a ' keen.'

9. An indentation or hollow made in ice to keep the feet steady in ' curling.'

B 2

Sc. A longitudinal hollow is made to support the foot, close by the tee, and at right angles with a line drawn from one end of the rink to the other. This is called a hack or hatch, *Act. of Curling,* 6 (JAM.). Ayr. Tees, hogscores, and hacks, or triggers [were] made, while busy sweepers cleared the rinks of anything that might impede the progress of the stones, JOHNSTON *Kilmallie* (1891) II. 109. Peb. He strains its wished-for road to trace The hack and tee between, *Lintoun Green* (1685) 38, ed. 1817.

10. A ridge of earth thrown up by ploughing or hoeing.
Hrt. The ground which was fallowed in April is stirred (in May) into hacks, ELLIS *Mod. Husb.* (1750) III. i.

11. A row of half-made hay.
Bdf. When the grass was hagled it is disposed in hacks (J.W.B.); Both clover and grass is powerfully acted upon by the sun and wind when in the state of hacks, BATCHELOR *Agric.* (1813) 443. Sur.[1] A thin row in which hay is laid to dry after being shaken out, and before it is got into wider rows, which are called ' windrows.'

12. The heart, liver, and lights of a pig. Cf. hackamuggie.
Cha.[18] s.Cha.[1] Goa·tū Longg·liz ūn aas·k ūm fār ū pig·z aak [Go to Longley's an' ask 'em for a pig's hack]. Shr.[1] *Obsol.*
Hence (1) Hacelet-pie, sb. a dish composed of the heart, liver, and lights of a pig baked in a pie. War.[2]; (2) Hack-fat, sb. the fat obtained from cleaning the intestines of a pig. nw.Der.[1] 13. A hard, dry cough. Cum.[4], Stf.[2]

14. *Fig.* Phr. *hack and sweep,* a complete upturn; a scene, commotion.
Abd. Gin the French officers begin to blab on ane anither, then we'll get hack an' sweep (G.W.).

15. *v.* To chop, cut up; to cut roughly or unevenly.
Sc. If I was gaen to be an elder, we couldna get a bit stick hackit on Sabbath, *Jokes,* 1st S. (1889) 38. Sh.I. Shū hjukid a sleesh or 'twa aff a roond lof, *Sh. News* (Oct. 29, 1898). Abd. Maidens and widows . . . Made mony an errand wi' bog fir to hack, ANDERSON *Rhymes* (1867) 20. Frf. Instead of . . . hacking his face, for he was shaving at the time, BARRIE *Thrums* (1889) xvi. Cld. (JAM.), n.Cy. (J.W.) Shr.[1] Now, 'ack them garrits, an' get the bif an' bacon up fur the men's dinner; Shr.[2] Oxf.[1] *MS. add.* Hmp.[1] w.Som.[1] To hack a joint. A good gate hacked all abroad.
Hence (1) Hack-clog, sb. a chopping-block; (2) Hacket, ppl. adj., fig. cutting, biting, severe, caustic; (3) Hacket kail, phr. chopped kail or cabbage; (4)—flesh, phr. a carrion charm for doing injury to a neighbour's beasts; see below; (5) Hacking, sb. a pudding or sausage made of the chopped interiors of sheep or pigs; (6) Hacking-block, sb. a block of wood used for cutting meat upon; (7) -iron, sb. an inverted chisel put into an anvil when the blacksmith wishes to cut anything off; (8) -knife, sb. a chopper, cleaver; (9) -stock, (10) -trough, see (6); (11) Hack-meat, sb. mincemeat; (12) -pudding, sb., see (5); (13) -saw, sb. a saw used by smiths and others for cutting iron; (14) -spyel, sb. a useless joiner or cartwright; (15) Hackster, sb., fig. a butcher, cut-throat; (16) Hack-stock, see (6); (17) Hackum kail, phr., see (3).
(1) n.Yks.[2] (2) Dmb. Out on you, bawdron! wi' your hacket tongue, SALMON *Gowodean* (1868) 71. (3) Sc. To feast me wi' caddels And guid hackit kail, CHAMBERS *Sngs.* (1829) I. 2; Noganes full of hackit kaile, MAIDMENT *Ballads* (1844) 13, ed. 1868. (4) ne.Sc. One mode of an enemy's working evil among a neighbour's cattle was to take a piece of carrion, cut the surface of it into small pieces, and bury it in the dunghill, or put it over the lintel of the door. Such carrion was called 'hackit-flesh,' GREGOR *Flk-Lore* (1881) 184. (5) N.Cy.[1] Nhb. A pudding made in the maw of a sheep or hog (K.). Cum.[1] A mincemeat and fruit pudding, used till lately for the family breakfast on Christmas day. Wm. & Cum.[1] Wi' sweet minch'd-pyes and hackins feyne, 171. Lan. HARLAND & WILKINSON *Flk-Lore* (1867) 216. (6) e.Yks. NICHOLSON *Flk-Sp.* (1889) 65; e.Yks.[1] (7) w.Yks.[2] (8) e.Yks. NICHOLSON *Flk-Sp.* (1889) 65. Cha.[1] (9) Cal.[1] (10) e.Yks. The trough or block on which the work is performed is a hacking-trough, or hacking-block, NICHOLSON *Flk-Sp.* (1889) 65. (11) e.Yks. ib.; e.Yks.[1] (12) Cum. On the morn of Christmas-day the people breakfast early on hack-pudding, a mess made of sheep's heart, chopped with suet and sweet fruits, HUTCHINSON *Hist. Cum.* (1794) I. 555. (13) n.Wil. An old scythe-blade, or a piece of one, with the edge jagged into teeth, set in a handle, and used for sawing through iron bars or rods, &c. (G.E.D.). w.Som.[1] There idn nort better vor a hack-zaw-n a old zive [scythe]. (14) Nhb.[1] (15) Sc. A crew of bloody Irish rebels, and desperat [*sic*] hacksters, CRAU-

FURD *Hist. Edb.* (1808) 155 (JAM.). n.Yks.[2] (16) Sc. (JAM.) (17) Dmb. Good hackum kail twice laid, SALMON *Gowodean* (1868) 108.

16. Of the skin: to chap, become cracked through cold.
Sc. To plout her hands through Hawkey's caff-cog, is a hateful hardship for Mammy's Pet, and will hack a' her hands, GRAHAM *Coll. Writings* (1883) II. 148. Cai.[1], Cld. (JAM.) Ayr. There's nae frost to hack them [the hands] in the simmer time, SERVICE *Dr. Duguid* (ed. 1887) 161.
Hence (1) Hacked or Hackit, ppl. adj. cracked, chapped through cold; (2) Hacking, vbl. sb. the chapping of hands or feet through cold.
(1) Sc. His wee, hackit heelies are hard as the airn, THOM *Rhymes* (1844) 140. Frf. His hackit hands to heat, JAMIE *Emigrant's Family* (1853) 106. Per. For festerin' finger or sair hackit heel, EDWARDS *Strathearn Lyrics* (1889) 34. Fif. A day's durg brings nae regret, nor sair backs, nor hackit feet, ROBERTSON *Provost* (1894) 188. Rnf. The lass wi' hakit hands and feet, McGILVRAY *Poems* (ed. 1862) 48. Ayr. Who tied up my wee hackit taes in the winter time! SERVICE *Dr. Duguid* (ed. 1887) 16. Lnk. The wee stumpy legs ance hacket an' blae, NICHOLSON *Idylls* (1870) 70. N.I.[1], N.Cy.[1] Nhb. Lassis, wi' hackt heels an' hans, *Keelman's Ann.* (1869) 25. Dur.[1] Applied to the hands when frostbitten, or to the heels or instep when very rough. Cum.[14] (2) Ayr. A hushion . . . worn on the legs of women and boys at country work to keep their legs frae hacking—what refinement calls chapping or gelling, HUNTER *Studies* (1870) 29.

17. To work with a pickaxe.
Cum. RICHARDSON *Talk* (1876) 2nd S. 43; Cum.[4], s.Wm. (J.A.B.), w.Yks. (R.H.H.)

18. To dig with a mattock, so as to break the clods.
Glo.[1] w.Som.[1] The term rather implies digging ground which has already been turned up with a spade. 'Spit it [the ground] up rough, and after 't have a lied a bit, take and hack it back.' Dev. To break clods with a mattock, after seed has been sown, to avoid harrowing, *Horae Subsecivae* (1777) 197; MORTON *Cyclo. Agric.* (1863). nw.Dev.[1], Cor.[12]
Hence (1) hack and hail, phr. digging and thatching; hard work; (2) Hackynex, sb. a tool for digging.
(1) n.Dev. A beat'th mun all vor hack an' hail, ROCK *Jim an' Nell* (1867) st. 42. (2) Cor.[2]

19. To hoe or loosen the earth round potatoes, preparatory to earthing them up; to hoe.
se.Wor.[1] Wil.[1] This is done with a 'tater-hacker,' an old three-grained garden-fork, which by bending down the tines or 'grains' at right angles to the handle has been converted into something resembling a rake, but used as a hoe. Dor. DARTNELL & GODDARD *Wds.* (1893). Dev.[2] I've been hackin' tittie voors all day. Cor.[1] To hack tetties.

20. To cut peas, beans, vetches, &c., with a hook; to dress a hedge-breast or a gutter with a sickle.
Cum.[4], Oxf.[1] Brks. I be gwain pea-'acking next week (W.H.E.); Brks.[1] w.Mid. The haulm is raised with a stick or old hook held in the left hand, and severed with the hook that is wielded in the right hand. 'You can go and hack that pea-haulm when you have done this hoeing' (W.P.M.). Hmp. To harvest beans, the reapers using two hooks, one wherewith to cut, and the other, an old one, wherewith to pull up the halm, WISE *New Forest* (1883) 288; (W.H.E.); Hmp.[1], Wil. (W.H.E.)
Hence (1) Hacked, ppl. adj. of a path or track: cleared, made passable; (2) Hack-hook, sb. a curved knife with a long handle, used for cutting tares or peas, or for trimming hedges.
(1) Nhp. A keeper pointed out to me a recently cleared path which he described as the 'hacked way,' *N. & Q.* (1878) 5th S. ix. 575. (2) Sm.[1] Hmp. HOLLOWAY.

21. To uproot turnips, &c., with a turnip-hack.
s.Not. It is done after the upper part of the root has been gnawed off by the sheep, in order to make the remainder available. 'He's bruck 'is 'ack, 'ackin them tunnips' (J.P.K.). Dor. The swede-field in which she and her companion were set hacking, HARDY *Tess* (1891) xliii.

22. To throw up earth in ridges by ploughing or hoeing.
Hrt. Combing is also called hacking and are synonymous names for one and the same operation, ELLIS *Mod. Husb.* (1750) VIII. 36.

23. To rake up hay into rows.
Not. Is the hay hacked in? (J.H.B.) Lei.[1] Nhp.[1] The grass, as it falls from the mower's scythe, is called a swathe, which is tedded or spread over the whole surface of the meadow; it is next hacked, or separated into small rows. War. LEWIS *Gl.* (1839).

s.Wor.[1] Bdf. (J.W.B.); Spread the swarths about the ground, and afterwards hack it into small rows, BATCHELOR *Agric.* (1813) 429. w.Mid. When you have done shaking out these windrows, you may go and hack in over yonder (W.P.M.). Sus.[1]

Hence **Hack-rake**, *v.* to rake the hay together after it has been spread out to dry. se.Wor.[1]

24. To win everything at games of marbles, &c.

Cum. When we'd hacked the lads aw roun us, ANDERSON *Ballads* (1805) 111, ed. 1808; *Gl.* (1851).

25. With *at*: to imitate. Yks. (HALL.), w.Yks.[1]

26. To hesitate; to hesitate in speech; to stammer, stutter. Cf. **hacker**, *v.* 2.

Nhb.[1] He hicked at forst, but they gat him to gan on. n.Yks.[2], Shr.[2], e.An.[1] Nrf. How that man did hack (W.R.E.); (E.M.)

Hence (1) **Hacka**, *sb.* a nervous hesitation in speaking. Wil.[1]; (2) Hocker, *sb.* one who stammers. Nrf. (E.M.)

27. Phr. (1) *to hack and har*, (2) *— and haw* or *hew*, (3) *— and hammer* or *hommer*, to hum and haw; to hesitate or stammer in speech.

(1) Oxf.[1] (2) War.[28] se.Wor.[1] Why doesn't spell the words, an' nat stond 'ackin' an' haowin' athattens! Glo. *Horae Subsecivae* (1777). (3) Shr.[2] Hacks and hammers at his words. Oxf.[1] Dwunt stan u ak'in un om·uurin dhaa·r [Dwun't stan' a 'ackin' an' 'om-merin' thar]. LW. (J.D.R.)

28. Of the teeth : to chatter. Cf. **hacker**, *v.* 4.

Lan. Meh teeth hackut imeh yed agen, TIM BOBBIN *View Dial.* (1740) 23; Lan.[1], e.Lan.[1] nw.Der.[1] Thy teeth hacks i' thy yead. Dev. (HALL.)

29. To snap at with the mouth.

s.Chs.[1] Dh)uwd saay)z got·n pigz, bŭr ah dóo daayt óo i)nŭ góo·in taak· tóo ŭm rey·ti, fŭr óo aak·s aat' ŭm wenev·ŭr dhi kŭmn klóos ŭp tóo ŭr [Th' owd sal's gotten pigs, bur ah do daft hoo inna gooin' tak to 'em reightly, fur hoo hacks at 'em whenever they com'n cloose up to her].

30. To cough frequently and distressingly; to cough in a hard, dry manner. Cf. **hacker**, *v.* 5.

Stf.[2] Used almost entirely in the phr. ' to cough and ack.' sw.Lin.[1] He has been hacking like that all night. War. *Leamington Courier* (Mar. 6, 1897); War.[3] He hacks so at night; War.[4], s.War.[1], e.An.[1], Sus.[1]

Hence **Hacking** or **Hicking**, *ppl. adj.* of a cough : hard, dry.

n.Yks.[2] sw.Lin.[1] He has such a hacking cough. s.Lin. (T.H.R.), Nhp.[1], Brks.[1], Hnt.(T.P.F.), e.An.[1] Nrf. I fare to have sich a hacking cough (W.R.E.). Cor.[1]

HACK, *sb.*[2] Var. dial. uses in Sc. Irel. and Eng. Also in forms ack- Chs.[1]; eck w.Yks.; haek Sh.I.; haik Bnff.[1] Frf. Ayr. Lth.; hake Abd. Lth.; heck Or.I. Cai.[1] Per. Rnf. Ant. N.Cy.[1] Nhb.[1] Dur.[1] Lakel.[1] Cum.[14] Wm. n.Yks.[12] ne.Yks.[1] e.Yks.[1] m.Yks.[1] w.Yks.[12345] Lan.[1] n.Lan.[1] ne.Lan.[1] Der.[1] Not.[28] n.Lin.[1] sw.Lin.[1] Nhp.[1] Hrf. e.An.[1] [h]ak, æk, h)ek.] **1.** A rack or manger to hold fodder for horses or cattle in a stable.

Sc. (G.W.), Or.I. (S.A.S.), Bnff.[1] Ayr. [He] mounted into the hack, and hid himself among the hay, GALT *Gilhaize* (1823) iv. n.Cy. BAILEY (1721); GROSE (1790); (K.); N.Cy.[12] Nhb. MORTON *Cyclo. Agric.* (1863); Nhb.[1], Dur.[1], Cum.[24], n.Yks.(T.S.), n.Yks.[124], ne.Yks.[1] e.Yks. MARSHALL *Rur. Econ.* (1788) ; e.Yks.[1] w.Yks. T'stable lad went in wi a pale ov watter ta put ontut eck, reddy fer use, *Yksman. Comic Ann.* (1878) 21 ; Horses owt ta be weel fettald dahn and fodderd wi oats and beans and t'heck filled wi good sweet hay, Tom TREDDLEHOYLE *Bairnsla Ann.* (1873) 45 ; w.Yks.[12345], ne.Lan.[1], Not.[28], s.Not.(J.P.K.), Der.[2] Lin. GROSE (1790). n.Lin.[1] We mun hev them hecks mended e' th' coo staables, th' beäs' waaste the'r fother theäre shaameful. sw.Lin.[1], s.Lin. (T.H.R.) Hrf. The young horses and brood mares [are fed] in hecks under a shade, *Reports Agric.* (1793-1813) 25. Nrf. (HALL.)

Hence **Heckstower**, *sb.* a rack-staff. Yks. (HALL.)

2. Phr. (1) *hack and harbour*, food and shelter; (2) *— and manger*, free quarters, plenty, abundance, esp. in phr. *to live at hack and manger.*

(1) n.Yks.[1] ' To eat one out of heck and harbour,' ot a poor man's family with good appetites ; n.Yks.[2] ' Cleared out of heck and harbour,' destitute both of food and shelter. (2) Sc. Maintained puir Davie at heck and manger maist feck o' his life, SCOTT *Waverley* (1814) lxiv. Cai.[1] Bnff. The marauding Bully, who had been living at haik and manger, GORDON *Chron. Keith* (1880) 143. Abd. At hake and manger, Jane and ye sall live, Ross

Helenore (1768) 124, ed. 1812. w.Sc. The members of Presbytéry had often lived at heck and manger in their houses, MACDONALD *Settlement* (1869) 17, ed. 1877. Per. She'll hae her run o' heck an' manger sae lang as she lives, IAN MACLAREN *Brier Bush* (1895) 296. Rnf. They that live at heck an' manger Sigh vainly for ' the little stranger,' YOUNG *Pictures* (1865) 166. Ayr. Ne'er-do-well dyvours and licht limmers who leeved at heck and manger, SERVICE *Dr. Duguid* (ed. 1887) 74 ; Wasting baith at heck and manger wi' bardie leddies, GALT *Sir A. Wylie* (1822) xvii. Slk. Her ladyship . . . was bred at the same heck an' manger as oursels, HOGG *Tales* (1838) 80, ed. 1866. Nhb. (R.O.H.), w.Yks.[1] sw.Lin.[1] ' He lives at heck and manger,' said of one who has free quarters, the run of his teeth.

3. A crib for fodder from which animals are fed in the open air. Also in *comb.* **Stand-hack.**

Lth. Sparred boxes for holding fodder for sheep, MORTON *Cyclo. Agric.* (1863). Dur.[1] A four-sided rack (raised some height from the ground) of wood bars for holding straw in a fold-yard. e.Yks. (Miss A.), e.Yks.[1] m.Yks.[1] A moveable rack, sometimes placed on a trestle ; at other times, having fixed supports. w.Yks. He pickt five or six [recruits] aght at renks at wor az knock-kneed az a stand heck, Tom TREDDLEHOYLE *Bairnsla Ann.* (1853) 43 ; w.Yks.[2], s.Not. (J.P.K.) Lin. STREATFEILD *Lin. and Danes* (1884) 337.

4. A wooden frame on which fish are hung to dry.

Sc. An' hing ye up like herrin' on a hake, ALLAN *Lilts* (1874) 71 ; (JAM.) Sh.I. Ye sall get dem [herrings] as I get dem, uncle, an' a hack ta Sibbie, *Sh. News* (Aug. 13, 1898). Bnff.[1] Three pieces of wood nailed together in the shape of a triangle and filled with small spikes on which to hang fish.

5. That part of a spinning-wheel armed with teeth, by which the spun thread is conducted to the ' pirn.'

Frf. I wish you would take your arm off the haik, BARRIE *Tommy* (1896) 128. Lth. (JAM.) ; Fringe-hake, a small loom on which females work their fringes (*ib.*). Gall. MACTAGGART *Encycl.* (1824) 259, ed. 1876. Ant. An elliptical bow of wood, the arms of which extend in the direction of the bobbin-spindle, and have their edges set with crooked teeth, made of iron wire, to direct the thread equally over the spool or bobbin of the common spinning wheel, GROSE (1790) *MS. add.* (C.)

6. A wooden frame or rack on which cheeses are hung to dry.

Sc. A wooden frame, suspended from the roof, containing different shelves, for drying cheeses (JAM.). Cai.[1] Abd. A hake was frae the rigging hanging fu' O' quarter kebbocks, Ross *Helenore* (1768) 83, ed. 1812.

7. An open kind of cupboard suspended from the wall. Bnff.[1]

8. A slightly raised bank or wall on which bricks are set up to dry before going into the kiln.

Glo.[1] Mid. Rye straw is used by brickmakers, to cover their hacks, MIDDLETON *View Agric.* (1798) 418. w.Mid. Newly made bricks, before being baked, are placed to dry in rows, called ' hacks ' (W.P.M.). Sus. (F.E.S.), Wil.[1] Som. JENNINGS *Obs. Dial. w.Eng.* (1845) ; W. & J. *Gl.* (1873). w.Som.[1] The rain come avore we'd agot time vor to cover em, and spwoiled the wole hack o' bricks.

Hence **Hackstead**, *sb.* the place where bricks are laid out to dry in a brick-garth.

N.Cy.[1] Nhb.[1] *Obs.* Chs.[1] Acksted, a foundation of sods for the drying wall in a brickfield.

9. *pl.* The bottom or hard bricks of an undried brick wall. n.Yks. (I.W.)

10. A hatch ; a half-door or hatch-door ; a small gate or wicket.

n.Cy. GROSE (1790) ; *Trans. Phil. Soc.* (1858) 160 ; (K.) ; N.Cy.[2] Lakel.[2] Cum.[2]; Cum.[4] An iron heck with bars about five inches apart was fixed to the bridge, *Carlisle Pat.* (Aug. 31, 1894) 3. Cum., Wm. The hatch or gate between a barn and cowhouse, NICOLSON (1677) *Trans. R. Lit. Soc.* (1868) IX. n.Yks.[1] When a door is made to open in two parts, the upper half which fastens with a latch, is the Heck. The lower part fastens with a bolt or bolts, and is sometimes called Half-heck; n.Yks.[2] w.Yks. THORESBY *Lett.* (1703) ; HUTTON *Tour to Caves* (1781) ; WILLAN *List Wds.* (1811); w.Yks.[24], Lan.[1], n.Lan.[1], ne.Lan.[1], Der.[1] Lin. BAILEY (1721). Nhp.[1], e.An.[1] Nrf. MARSHALL *Rur. Econ.* (1787).

11. *Comb.* (1) **Heck-door**, the door between the kitchen of a farm-house and the stable or farm-yard ; (2) **-stake**, the door-stake or night-bar ; (3) **-stead**, the doorway ; (4) **-stead fat**, a facetious name for water ; see below ; (5)

-stower or -staver, the portable beam across the middle of the hatchway ; (6) -way, see (3).

(1) s.Sc. (JAM.) Ayr. The cattle ... *gen.* entered by the same door with the family, .. turning the contrary way by the heck-door to the byre or stable, *Agric. Surv.* 114 (JAM.). w.Yks.² (2, 3) n.Yks.² (4) *ib.* 'Hecksteead fat,' a facetious term in the country for water ; it being usual in farm-houses to keep a supply in ' pankins ' in the passage, or recessed behind the door. ' If you'll stay tea, you shall have a cake knodden wi' hecksteead fat,' which implies a cake made of flour and water only ; but in the good nature of hospitality, the cakes turn out to be as rich as butter and currants can make them. (5) *ib.* s.Yks. Trees . . . will serve for . . . heckstowers, BEST *Rur. Econ.* (1641) 121. n.Lin.¹ s.Lin. Two o' the heck-stavvers 's brok (T.H.R.). (6) n.Yks.²

12. Phr. *to bark at the heck*, to be kept waiting at the door. Cum. (M.P.), Cum.¹⁴

13. The inner door between the entry and the 'house-place' or kitchen.

n.Cy. (J.L.) (1783). Nhb.¹ Cum. A door, half of rails, or what is called in the south a ' hatch,' in old farm-houses opened from the entry, between the mill-doors, to the hallan (M.P.). n.Yks.¹ ' Steck t'heck, bairn,' latch or fasten the inner door. ne.Yks.¹ It blaws cau'd ; steck t'heck. e.Yks. MARSHALL *Rur. Econ.* (1788).

14. *Comp.* (1) Heck-door, the inner door of a house only partly panelled and the rest latticed ; (2) -stead, the site or place of the inner door between the entry and the ' house-place ' or kitchen.

(1) N.Cy.¹, Nhb.¹ Cum. LINTON *Lake Cy.* (1864) 305. (2) n.Yks.¹ We'll noo gan thruff [through] t'heck-stead inti' t'kitchen.

15. A weather-board at a barn door to keep out the rain.

Lan. You pull your faces as long as a barn door 'eck, ELLIS *Pronunc.* (1889) V. 356.

16. A latch.

n.Cy. GROSE (1790). Wm. The girl unsneck'd the raddle heck, HUTTON *Bran New Wark* (1785) l. 372 ; When gust bi gust blew up the heck, WHITEHEAD *Leg.* (1859) 13. m.Yks.¹ Steck t'heck [drop the latch]. Steck t'door, and don't let t'heck go down. w.Yks.²

17. A kind of screen forming a passage ; see below.

s.Dur. Still found in some old farm-house kitchens when the door and fireplace both occur on one side of the room. ' She threshed me a-back o' t'heck.' ' He placed the besom-shank where it always stood, namely, a'-back-ed-heck ' (J.E.D.). Wm. The mell-door opened into the Heck, a narrow passage six feet long, and leading into the house, *Lonsdale Mag.* (1822) III. 249 ; The passage [heck] was separated from the house by a partition of old oak, and only seldom of stone. This partition was frequently carved and bore the date, and the builder's name ; and was denominated the heck. In houses of the most ancient date, this heck reached to the first beam of the upper story, where a huge octagonal post formed its termination, *ib.* 251 ; Drest in a shroud wi noiseless step Up t'heck com gliden in, WHITEHEAD *Leg.* (1859) 14, ed. 1896 ; As dark as a heck [the unlighted passage found in many of the older class of farm-houses) (B.K.).

18. The tail-board or movable board at the back of a cart. Also in *comp.* Heck-board. Cf. hawk, *sb.*⁴

N.Cy.¹, Nhb.¹, Cum.², Dur.¹, s.Dur. (J.E.D.) Wm. (J.M.) ; (E.C.) s.Wm. (J.A.B.), ne.Lan.¹, Not.², Nhp.¹

19. A wooden grating or fence set across a stream to catch fish or to obstruct their passage ; a swinging fence where a wall crosses a stream.

Sc. To require the said proprietors and tenants . . . to put proper hecks on the tail-races of their canals, to prevent salmon or grilse from entering them, *Abd. Jrn.* (Aug. 9, 1820) (JAM.). s.Sc. Speaks o' hecks (a new invention) 'Cross dam an' ditch, WATSON *Bards* (1859) 53. Wgt. The Scavengers are . . . to keep the ayvors sunk, runners and iron hecks thereon always clear and clean, FRASER *Wigtown* (1877) 81. s.Dur. (J.E.D.), Lakel.¹ Cum. Sat and screecht on t'watter heck, DICKINSON *Cumbr.* (1876) 256. e.Yks. The best and readyest way of keepinge up the water is to set downe broade and close doore or coupelynges against some heck or bridge, BEST *Rur. Econ.* (1641) 18. w.Yks. *Leeds Merc. Suppl.* (July 11, 1896) ; LUCAS *Stud. Nidderdale* (c. 1882) Gl.

20. A shuttle in a drain. n.Lin.¹

21. A hedge.

Lin. KENNETT *Par. Antiq.* (1695) ; (K.) n.Lin.¹ Rare. ' It ewsed to stan' up by yon heck yonder agaān th' beāch tree.'

[The forms in all their meanings may be referred to OE. *hec(c,* also *hæc(c* (SWEET). 10. Of paradys he opened þe hekke, *Minor Poems* (Vernon MS.) (c. 1350) xxiv. 231.]

HACK, *sb.*² and *v.*² Suf. Wil. Som. Also in form hock Wil.¹ 1. *sb.* In *comp.* Hack-horse, a hackney, roadster. w.Som.¹ Tis a useful sort of a hack-horse [aak-au's] like, but I 'ont zay he've a-got timber 'nough vor to car you.

2. A hardworking man ; a drudge. Suf. (HALL.), e.Suf. (F.H.)

3. *v.* To ride on horseback along the road.

w.Som.¹ I've a-knowed th' old man hack all the way to Horner, to meet, .. and hack home again arterwards.

4. Phr. *to hack about*, (1) to scamper, ride hard ; to give a horse no breathing time or rest ; (2) to treat a thing carelessly, drag it through the mud.

(1) w.Som.¹ Ter'ble fuller to ride ; I wid'n let-n hack about no 'oss o' mine vor no money. (2) Wil.¹ ' Now dwoan't 'ee gwo a-hocken on your new vrock about.' The usual form in s.Wil. is Hack-about.

5. To work hard.

e.Suf. He hacks that poor fellow dreadfully. Mind yow don't hack yowrsell to dead (F.H.).

HACK, *sb.*⁴ Yks. e.An. [ak, æk.] Havoc, injury, damage. Also in *comp.* Hackwark, and used *advb.*

n.Yks.² ' They made mair hack than mends,' there was more injury done than good effected. w.Yks. (J.W.) e.An.¹ A flock of sheep playing hack. Birds play hack with fruit trees. e.Suf. To play hack, to frolic. To play hack with, to spoil, injure (F.H.).

HACK, *sb.*⁵ e.Dur.¹ Filth, dirt.

Aa canna get the hack off tha.

HACK, *v.*³ ? *Obs.* Sc. To hawk, sell by peddling.

Edb. It's hack'd frae town to town abuse't, An' house to house, LIDDLE *Poems* (1821) 80.

HACK, see Hag(g, *sb.*², Hake, *sb.*³, Heck, *v.*², Howk.

HACKAMUGGIE, *sb.* Sh.I. The stomach of a fish stuffed with a hash of meat, ' sounds,' and liver. S. & Ork.¹ Cf. hack, *sb.*¹ 12.

HACKASING, *prp.* Chs. Lin. Hrf. Also in forms accussin Chs.¹ ; hakussing n.Lin.¹ [a·k-, æ·kəsin.] Disputing, wrangling ; moving about violently as people do when in anger ; doing work in a violent or angry way. Also used as *sb.* Cf. yackaz.

Chs.¹ Nah then ! no accussin. n.Lin.¹ I could see sum'ats was wrong as soon as I went in ; she was puttin' dinner things by, an' hakussin' aboot all th' time. Hrf.² What are yer hackasing at ?

HACK-BERRY, see Hag-berry.

HACKBOLT, *sb.* Cor. The greater shearwater, *Puffinus major.*

Cor. RODD *Birds* (1880) 314. Sc.I. In the Scilly islands, where they are called Hackbolts, they are said to be yet more frequent, JOHNS *Birds* (1862) 601 ; SWAINSON *Birds* (1885) 212.

HACK-CLAY, *sb.* Nhb.¹ A whitish sort of clay, found in Northumberland moors.

It is tough, unctuous, of a whitish (colour), and like rotten clay (or) like that of the decomposed granite kind found in Cornwall.

HACKEN, *sb.* Lakel.² A term of disgust.

T'gurt brossen hacken wad eat tell he dud hissel a mischief.

HACKER, *sb.* Lin. War. Wor. Shr. Rdn. Glo. Wil. Dor. [a·kə(r), æ·kə(r).] 1. A chopper or hedging-hook used by hedgers, &c. ; a bill-hook.

War. (E.A.P.), War.², æ.Wor.¹ Shr.¹ A short, strong, slightly curved implement of a peculiar kind, for chopping off the branches of fallen trees, &c. ' Axe, hacker, mittins, and other small tools,' *Auctioneer's Catal.* (1870) ; Shr.² An axe usually taken to cut up cordwood ; it is from 2 to 2½ pounds weight, almost straight, and set in a wooden handle. Rdn.², Glo.¹

2. An instrument used in ' hacking ' potatoes ; a hoe.

Wil.¹ Also known as a Tomahawk. n.Wil. An instrument made out of an old three-grained fork, used for ' hacking ' potatoes. Not much used nowadays (E.H.G.). Dor. To grub up the lower or earthy half of the root with a hooked fork called a ' hacker,' HARDY *Tess* (1891) xliii ; BARNES *Gl.* (1863).

3. A person who dresses stone. n.Lin.¹

HACKER, *v.* Var. dial. uses in Sc. and Eng. Also written hakker Cum.¹ Wil.¹ ; and in forms accer e.Yks. ; acker Lan.¹ ; akker Nhp.² ; ecker Ken.¹ ; hicker w.Som.¹ ; ocker Lan. [(h)a·kə(r, æ·kə(r).] 1. To hack in cutting ; to cut or chop small.

s.Sc. (JAM.) Slk. An his throat was a' hackered an' ghastly was he, HOGG *Poems* (ed. 1865) 65.

2. *Fig.* To hesitate in speech; to stammer, stutter. Cf. hack, *v.*[1] **26.**

Cum. He drank and he hakkert and sang, Dickinson *Cumbr.* (1875) 292; Cum.[1] He hakkers an' gits nin on wid his talk; Cum.[4] n.Yks.[2] He began to hacker on. ne.Yks.[1] He hackered an' stammered. e.Yks. What's thah accering at? (R.M.); e.Yks.[1] What is thi hackerin an stammerin aboot? Lan. He ockers, an' stutters, an' tries to tell th' tale, Standing *Echoes* (1885) 11; Lan.[1] He ackers and haffles: he's lyin'. s.Chs.[1] A weaker term than 'stammer.' Soa·ŭn Soa·)z ŭ gŭd spee·kŭr, oa·ni ey aak·ŭrz ŭ bit, naat· tŭ kau· it staam·ŭrin [So and So's a good speaker, on'y he hackers a bit, nat to caw it stammerin']. Lin. Streatfeild *Lin. and Danes* (1884) 334. n.Lin. An' soa Aamos scrats his heäd, an' hackers a time or two, Peacock *Tales* (1890) and S. 11; n.Lin.[1] s.Lin. He hackers that had when he speaks it's grievous to hear him (T.H.R.). Brks.[1] One is said to 'hacker and stammer' when answering disjointedly on account of having no excuse or explanation forthcoming. s.Cy. Grose (1790). Ken. (G.B.), Ken.[1] Sus. Hackerin a bit she says, 'I've a mort o' pettigues, Mus Ladds,' Jackson *Southward Ho* (1894) I. 200; Sus.[1], Hmp. (J.R.W.), Hmp.[1], I.W.[12] Som. W. & J. *Gl.* (1873).

Hence (1) **Hackering**, (*a*) *vbl. sb.*, (*b*) *ppl. adj.* stuttering, stammering; (2) **Hackery**, *adv.* in a stammering, stuttering manner.

(1, *a*) n.Yks.[2] s.Lin. What wi' Ted's hackering and Jim's grimaaces I ommoäst split mi sides wi' laughin' (T.H.R.). e.An.[1] Nrf. Cozens-Hardy *Broad Nrf.* (1893) 88. (*b*) Cum.[4] Sad hakkeran wark they maade o' ther neamen, *W. C. T.* (July 9, 1898) 8, col. 2. (2) n.Yks.[2] He talks quite hackery.

3. To shuffle, hesitate.

n.Lin.[1] He'll be hackerin' aboot wi' foäks till he gets his sen atween th' foher walls o' Ketton prison.

4. To shake or tremble with anger, fear, cold, &c.; to chatter with cold. Cf. hack, *v.*[1] **28.**

Nhp.[2], Glo.[1] Wil. Our maester's got the ager! How a hackers and bivers, Akerman *Tales* (1853) 55; Slow *Gl.* (1892); Wil.[12] Dor. Barnes *Gl.* (1863). Som. W. & J. *Gl.* (1873); Sweetman *Wincanton Gl.* (1885). w.Som.[1] Why's 'n yeat thy zul, and neet bide there hickerin? This here wind 'll make anybody hickery wi' the cold.

5. To cough. Cf. hack, *v.*[1] **30.**

Lan.[1] He ackers and spits.

HACKER-BERRY, see **Hag-berry.**

HACKET, *v.*[1] and *sb.* Oxf. Brks. Sus. Wil. Also in forms heccat- Brks.[1]; heckut- Oxf.[1]; hicket- Wil.[1] [æ·kət, e·kət.] **1.** *v.* To cough in a hard, dry manner; to hack.

Sus. He hackets so with his cough (G.A.W.).

Hence **Hacketing** or **Heckuting**, *ppl. adj.* of a cough : dry, hard, 'hacking.'

Oxf.[1] Uur a got u naa·sti ek·utin kau·f, un uu)y shuodnt uon·duur if uur went in u dikluuy·n wun u dhaiz yuur daiz ['Er a got a naasty 'eckutin cough, an' I shouldn't öönder if 'er went in a decline one of thase yer days]. Sus. A hacketing cough (G.A.W.).

2. *sb.* A short, dry, wearing cough. In *pl.* form. Brks.[1]

Hence **Heccatty** or **Hicketty**, *adj.* of a cough : short, dry, 'hacking.' Brks.[1], Wil.[1]

HACKET, *v.*[2] Som. Also in form hecket-. [æ·kət.] To hop on one leg; to play 'hop-scotch.' Cf. heck, *v.*[2] hick.

Som. W. & J. *Gl.* (1873). w.Som.[1] I've a-squat my voot, eens I be a-foc'd, otherways to bide still, or else to hackety 'pon tother.

Hence (1) **Hackety**, (2) **Hackety-oyster**, (3) **Heckity-bed**, *sb.* the game of 'hop-scotch.'

(1) w.Som.[1] Sometimes called 'ik·utee-aak·utee.' 'Come on, Bill! lets play to hackety!' (2) Som. W. & J. *Gl.* (1873). (3) Som. Sweetman *Wincanton Gl.* (1885).

HACKIT, see **Hawkit.**

HACKLE, *sb.*[1] and *v.*[1] Yks. Lan. Chs. Der. Nhp. War. Wor. Shr. Hrf. Glo. Oxf. Brks. Hrt. Ess. Sur. Sus. Hmp. I.W. Wil. Dor. Also in forms ackle w.Yks. Hmp.; aikle s.Chs.[1]; heckle n.Yks.[1] [a·kl, æ·kl.] **1.** *sb.* The natural covering of an animal, wool, feathers, &c.; clothing, covering, clothes. Also used *fig.*

n.Yks.[1] 'He has a good hackle on his back; he does not shame his keeper;' of one who is stout and well-looking; n.Yks.[3] Substance about the person, as flesh, clothing. Property in general; n.Yks.[4] ne.Yks.[1] 'A good hackle' implies good-looking, well-cared-for. 'He's got a good hackle ov his back.' e.Yks.[1] He's

getten a rare hackle on his back [he is very fat]. Hrt. The slug slipped his outer skin, or what we call his hackle, Ellis *Mod. Husb.* (1750) III. ii. 116; The serpent sheds his skin or hackle every year, *ib.* 112. Ess. *Trans. Arch. Soc.* (1863) II.185; (W.W.S.)

2. A cone-shaped covering of straw placed over bee-hives to protect them from cold and wet.

e.Yks.[1] *MS. add.* (T.H.) Der.[2], nw.Der.[1] War. *Leamington Courier* (Mar. 6, 1897); War.[24], s.War.[1], s.Wor.[1], Shr.[1], Hrf.[12] Glo. The covering of a beehive made of reed or halm, *Horae Sub-secivae* (1777) 197; Glo.[1], Brks.[1], Sus.[1], Hmp. (W.M.E.F.), Hmp.[1], I.W.[1] Wil. Britton *Beauties* (1825); Wil.[1] Hackle, and sometimes Shackle, are used at Deverill, while elsewhere in s.Wil. Bee-hackle is the word employed. Dor.[1]

3. The straw covering of the apex of a rick.

Hrf.[1], Hmp.[1] Wil. Britton *Beauties* (1825); Wil.[1]

4. A covering of inverted sheaves spread over the tops of others to protect them from the wet.

Hrf.[12] Sur.[1] Sometimes in harvesting, esp. in wet weather, they make a covering which they place over the sheaves, and this they call a hackle.

5. A stook of beans, *gen.* consisting of three sheaves, set up together in a field.

s.Wor.[1] Glo. (A.B.); Beans are usually 'set up in what are termed hackles—singlets of unusual size,' Marshall *Rur. Econ.* (1789) I. 151; Glo.[1], n.Wil. (G.E.D.)

6. Hay gathered into a small row.

War. A smaller row than a swath; windrow is seven or eight hackles put into one for carting, *Leamington Courier* (Jan. 30, 1897); War.[2] To rake newly made hay into rows or hackles.

7. *v.* To dress, put on one's best clothes; to equip, get ready, put in order; to do anything tidily and well.

n.Yks.[1]; n.Yks.[4] Sha's hackled hersel wiv all t'gewgaws 'at sha's gitten. w.Yks. Come, hackle tha, *Prov.* in *Brighouse News* (Aug. 10, 1889); Hackle thi frock waist up, *Yks. Wkly. Post* (May 9, 1896); w.Yks.[1] Come, lass, git thysel hackled; w.Yks.[2] He's gone to hackle the horse; w.Yks.[2] A witness at a trial said, 'Deceased hardly knew how to hackle a child.' ne.Lan.[1] s.Chs.[1] 'Ye mun begin an' aikle naї,' was the signal given by an old dame who kept a school near Wrenbury that lessons were over for the day.

8. To fit well, be well adapted to.

m.Yks.[1] A garment hackles well to a person's back; and a new servant to the duties of an old one. 'She hackles well to her work, however.' w.Yks. A new servant doing unaccustomed work well is said to ackle well to his work, *Leeds Merc. Suppl.* (Apr. 11, 1891); That coat hackles well (C.C.R.).

9. To turn the soil lightly; to dress or harrow the ground.

n.Yks.[12]; n.Yks.[4] Thoo mun just hackle aboot t'reeats. m.Yks.[1]

10. *Fig.* To correct, chastise.

n.Yks.[2] I'll hackle thy back for thee. w.Yks.[2] Au nivver knew a man so hackled i' mi' lauf.

11. To cover bee-hives with 'hackles' or straw coverings.

War.[2] Shr.[1] It's gettin' time to 'ackle 'an' clicket the bees—theer'll be a snow afore long.

12. To cover outstanding corn by placing inverted sheaves over the 'mow,' so as to protect it from the wet.

War.[2], s.Wor.[1] Shr.[1] I 'spect the glass is gweïn down, fur they'n begun to 'ackle the corn i' the lung leasow.

Hence **Hackling-sheaves**, *sb. pl.* inverted sheaves placed over outstanding corn. Shr.[1]

13. To gather hay into small rows.

War. Morton *Cyclo. Agric.* (1863); War.[23]; War.[4] Feyther, baint us to hackle the hay this afternoon? s.War.[1] Oxf.[1] To rake hay into rows after it has been 'tedded': usually called to hackle in, or up.

Hence **Hackling**, *sb.* hay gathered into small rows; see below.

Nhp.[1] Three hatchels or hacklings thrown together into one broad row or swathe, are termed a win-row or windrow (s.v. Hack).

14. To bind beans and set them up in stooks. Wor. (W.C.B.)

[1. OE. *hacele*, a cloak (Ælfric); Goth. *hakuls*, OHG. *hachul*, 'cuculla' (Graff).]

HACKLE, *sb.*[2] and *v.*[2] Var. dial. uses in Sc. and Eng. Also written haccle Chs.[1]; and in forms eckle w.Yks. Nhp.[1]; ekkle w.Yks.; heckle Sc. (Jam.) Lnk. N.Cy.[1] Nhb.[1] Dur. (K.) Cum.[1] n.Yks. w.Yks.[245] Chs.[1] Der.[2] nw.Der.[1] Not. [h)a·kl, h)e·kl, æ·kl.] **1.** *sb.* The crest or neck feathers of a cock or bird.

Nhb.[1] Dur. The heckle of a fighting cock (K.). Cum.[1] Cum.,

Wm. The word heckle in a cock's feathers is probably used when the plumage falls in points of varied colour (M.P.). **w.Yks.**[128], **Der.**[2], nw.**Der.**[1], **Nhp.**[1], War.[8], I.W.[1] **Dev.** *Reports Provinc.* (1885) 96.

2. Fig. Temper, dander, esp. in phr. *to get* or *set up one's heckle.*

n.Yks. Dunnot thee be so ready to set up the heckle agin, *Why John (Coll. L.L.B.)* **w.Yks.** He's a short-tempered thing, he gets his eckle up with nout (M.N.) ; Settin' up his ekkle an' hinderin' boath father and son, *Yksman. Comic Ann.* (1880) 43 ; **w.Yks.**[2] Don't set up your heckle at me ; **w.Yks.**[8] ; **w.Yks.**[6] He's nowt to be sticking up his heckle abart, soa let him hod his noise ! **Nhp.**[1] 'To set up your eckles,' is to give yourself airs, to rouse your spirit. **Mid.** They have such a knack of setting one another's hackles up, **Blackmore** *Kit* (1890) II, x. **Dev.** The girl's got her hackle up, poor plucky little minx ! **Stooke** *Not Exactly*, xii. **n.Dev.** Zo ott's this hackle vor ! **Rock** *Jim an' Nell* (1867) st. 7. **nw.Dev.**[1] I rack'n he'd a-got his hackle up, had'n a, think ?

Hence (1) **Hackled**, *adj.* peevish, cross-grained, angry ; (2) **Heckle-tempered**, *adj.* short-tempered, hasty, touchy.

(1) **n.Cy.** (**Hall.**) **Chs.** A hackled cow has short horns (K.). **n.Dev.** Till wan day, tachy, hackled, forth, **Rock** *Jim an' Nell* (1867) st. 81. (2) **Chs.**[18]

3. An angler's artificial fly, usually made from the neck feather of a cock ; the long piece of gut at the end of a line, together with the artificial fly attached. Also in *comp.* **Hackle-fly.**

Lnk. I'll do my best, I think I'll try the heckle, **Stewart** *Twa Elders* (1886) 143. **N.Cy.**[1] **Nhb.** The fishers they try Wi' hackle an' fly, **Richardson** *Borderer's Table-bk.* (1846) VIII. 184 ; **Nhb.**[1] 'The bonny reed heckle,' usually made from the red feathers of a cock. Another artificial fly is the black heckle or Blaewing. **w.Som.**[1] The flies themselves severally are never so called, but the name is used for the whole apparatus, gut and flies together. A feather from a fowl's neck, suitable for making an artificial fly. 'Our Jim can dress a hackle way anybody.'

4. The hair or bristles on a dog's back.

Nhb. Up came the other hounds quickly with raised hackles, **Armstrong** *Otter Hunting* (1879) ; **Nhb.**[1] **Not.** He set his heckles up, as if he'd fly at me. They were running to kill their fox, with all their heckles up (L.C.M.). [**Mayer** *Sptsmn's Direct.* (1845) 142.]

5. The mane of a hog. **Wil.** **Britton** *Beauties* (1825) ; **Wil.**[12]

6. pl. The ears of barley and oats. Also in phr. *in hackle*, in ear.

War. The oats are in hackle, *Leamington Courier* (Jan. 30, 1897) ; **War.**[2] ; **War.**[4] Cut your oats when they hackles is green, if your 'd save the King and Queen.

Hence **Hackle**,*v.*of oats,&c. : to form large heads or ears. **War.**[2] When oats form large heads of corn they are said to hackle well.

7. The stickleback, *Gasterosteus trachurus.* Dev. (**Hall.**) [**Satchell** (1879).]

8. v. To look angry or indignant ; to grumble, dispute. **Cum. Linton** *Lake Cy.* (1864) 305. **Chs.** *Sheaf* (1878) I. 60 ; **Chs.**[1] **Der. Grose** (1790) *MS. add.* (P.) ; **Der.**[2], nw.**Der.**[1]

[1. Take the hackel of a cock or capons neck, **Walton** *Angler* (1653) 110 ; The wynges of the drake & of the redde capons hakyll, *Treatise of Fysshynge* (c. 1425), ed. Satchell, 34.]

HACKLE, *sb.*[8] Nhp. See below.

O'er the flood the hackle swarms, **Clare** *Remains* (1873) 160 ; The coarse bits of twitch left after raking hay, which would readily float if the field were flooded. When the floods are severe, they bring down on their surface a sort of scum of bits of grass stalks and light bits of grass (W.D.S.).

HACKLE, *v.*[8] and *sb.*[4] Brks. Hmp. Wil. [**æˑkl.**]

1. v. To conspire, agree together. Wil.[1], Brks.[1], Hmp.[1]
2. sb. A conspiracy, cabal.

Brks.[1] Labourers are said to be 'all of a hackle' when making agreement together to get higher wages or shorter time for work.
[2. If a majority of the old hackle come in again, *Norris Papers* (c. 1700), Chetham Soc. (1846) 74.]

HACKLE, *v.*[4] Wil. [**æˑkl.**] To rattle, re-echo.

Wil.[1] n.**Wil.** How them guns do hackle to-night, don 'em ! (E.H.G.) [Cp. Norw. dial. *hakla*, to give a crackling sound (**Aasen**).]

HACKLE, *v.*[5] Som. Amer. To haggle, chaffer.

w.Som.[1] They'd bide and hackly [haaˑklee] for an hour about twopence. [**Amer.** *Dial. Notes* (1896) I. 379.]

HACKLE, *v.*[6] Midl. Lin. [**aˑkl.**] To draw from the earth by the roots ; to dig. Cf. **hack**, *v.*[1] 18.

Midl. To 'hackle turneps,' to pull them up with a little two-pronged hack, **Marshall** *Rur. Econ.* (1796) II. **Lin.**[1]

HACKLE, *v.*[7] Lan. Glo. e.An. [**aˑkl**, **æˑkl.**] **1.** To shackle or tether animals to prevent their running away.

e.An.[1] **Suf.** The fastening is usually made of hair, with an eye at one end and a toggle round the other, round the fetlocks of a cow to prevent her kicking when milked, **Rainbird** *Agric.* (1819) 294, ed. 1849 ; **Suf.**[1], e.**Suf.** (F.H.)

Hence **Hackled**, *pp., fig.* hampered or inconvenienced from scarcity of money. e.**Lan.**[1]

2. A gamekeeper's term : to interlace the hind-legs of game for convenience of carriage by houghing the one and slitting the sinew of the other. Glo.[12]

HACKLE, *v.*[8] and *sb.*[5] Mid. Som. **1. v.** To apply oneself to anything ; to undertake with energy. Also with *to*. Cf. **hackle**, *v.*[1] 8.

w.Mid. 'He's got a lot of sons, but they're no good for the business—they won't hackle.' 'There's plenty of work about ; but the drunken rascals won't hackle to it' (W.P.M.).
2. sb. A good job. Som. W. & J. *Gl.* (1873).
3. Phr. *just one's hackle*, exactly suitable, just what one likes. Cf. **hackle**, *v.*[1] 8.

w.Mid. 'That bit o' fat pork's jest his 'ackle.' 'That there job seems to be jest his hackle' (W.P.M.).

HACKLE, see **Heckle**, *sb.*
HACKLE-BERRY, *sb.* N.I.[1] A growth on a horse's leg. Also called **Angle-berry** (q.v.).

HACKLED, *ppl. adj.* Cum. See below. Cf. **hackle**, *v.*[7]

Cum.[4] The exact meaning of hackled has passed out of recollection ; I suggest that 'plaited' was intended. 'Halters of hemp both heads and shanks ; But some were made of hackled seives,' *Carlisle Pat.* (May 13, 1870).

HACKLEY, *sb.* Irel. The perch, *Perca fluviatilis.*

s.Don. So called from the sharp points on the dorsal fin, **Simmons** *Gl.* (1890).

HACKLING, *ppl. adj.* Chs. Lin. Glo. Som. [**aˑk-, æˑklin.**] Of a cough : dry, hard, 'hacking.'

Chs.[1] Oo's getten sitch a hacklin cough ; **Chs.**[3] sw.**Lin.**[1] He has that nasty hackling cough and raising. **Glo.** (J.S.F.S.), **Som.** (F.A.A.)

HACKMAL, *sb.* Som. Dev. Cor. Also in forms ack-mal n.Dev. ; ackymal Dev. Cor. ; ekky-mal Cor.[8] ; ekky-mowl Cor.[128] ; hack-mull n.Dev. ; hacky-mal(l w.Som.[1] nw.Dev.[1] Cor. ; hakkimal Cor. ; heckamall Dev. ; hecke-mal Dev.[1] ; heck-mall Dev. ; heckymal Dev. Cor.[8] ; hekkymal Cor.[1] ; hick-mall Cor.[12] ; hickymal s.Dev. ; uckmaul Dev. [**æˑkmæl.**] **1.** The common tomtit or blue titmouse, *Parus caeruleus.* See **Hag-mal**(l.

w.Som.[1] We 'ant a got no gooseberries de year, the hacky-mals eat all the bud. **Dev.** There's a hackmal's nest out in a hole in the awpel tree, **Hewett** *Peas. Sp.* (1892) ; The heck-mall, a busy bird, and fond of making himself comfortable, **Bray** *Desc. Tamar and Tavy* (1836) I. 319 ; A hok, ur kit's, no mor tel granny, Than enny heckymal, ur ranny, Es to a gooze vur zize like, **Daniel** *Bride of Scio* (1842) 187 ; He'll go snuggle into the straw like a heckamall in a rick, **Baring-Gould** *J. Herring* (1888) 23 ; **Dev.**[1] **n.Dev.** Tie a bullbagger to tha tree, l zeed tha ackmals thare, **Rock** *Jim an' Nell* (1867) st. 5 ; Fox *Kingsbridge* (1874) ; (E.H.G.) nw.**Dev.**[1], s.**Dev.** (F.W.C.) **Dev.**, Cor. From the strong pecks which it deals with its bill are derived the names hickmall, hackmall, &c., **Swainson** *Birds* (1885) 34. s.**Dev.**, e.**Cor.** (Miss D.) Cor. (J.W.) ; **Rodd** *Birds* (1880) 314 ; Cor.[128]

2. The great titmouse, *Parus major.* Dev. **Swainson** *ib.* 34.

HACKNEY, *sb.* and *v.* Sc. Lan. Der. Lei. Shr. Hrf. Som. Dev. Also in forms agney e.**Lan.**[1] ; hocknie S. & Ork.[1] [**h)aˑkni, æˑkni.**] **1. sb.** A saddle-horse ; an easy-paced, lady's horse.

Sc. His hackney will be set up with the day's work, and now he has no fresh horse, **Scott** *Bride of Lam.* (1819) vi. **Sh.I.** (*Coll.* L.L.B.) ; **S.** & Ork.[1], e.**Lan.**[1] nw.**Der.**[1] **Shr.**[1] 'Whad ! han'ee got two 'ackneys ?' 'Aye, that's a spon new un fur the Missis.' **Shr.**, **Hrf.** **Bound** *Provinc.* (1876). **Som.** The servan' chap was going for to let out the 'ackney, **Ellis** *Pronunc.* (1889) V. 152.

2. *Comp.* **Hackney-saddle,** a riding-saddle; the ordinary saddle on which a man (not a woman) rides.

Lan. I got my two mares and set the saddle on the little one for a load and the hackney saddle on the great one to ride on, WALKDEN *Diary* (ed. 1866) 66. nw.Der.[1] w.Som.[1] This is a relic of the time when the pack-saddle was commonest, and hence the riding-saddle had to be distinguished. If spoken of as an equipment for a saddle horse, we always say a [bruy·dl-n-zad·l] bridle and saddle, but if the saddle only were spoken of, we say : Kaar een dh-aa·kn·ee-zad·l-n ae·un u dùe·d [carry in the hackney-saddle and have it mended], to distinguish it from the cart or the gig saddle. nw.Dev.[1]

3. *v.* Of horses : to ride quietly, to use as a saddle-horse.

Lei.[1] A'll dew very well to droive, but a een't seafe to 'ackney no loonger.

HACKSEY-LOOKED, *adj.* Sh. & Or.I. Also in form **hackrey-** (JAM.). Having a coarse visage, gruff ; pitted with small-pox. (JAM.), S. & Ork.[1]

HACK-SLAVER, *v.* and *sb.* n.Cy. Cum. Yks. Lan. Der. Lin. e.An. Also written **hack-slavver** n.Yks. ; and in form **keck-** w.Yks.[1] **1.** *v.* To cut roughly.

n.Yks. What's t'use ov hack-slavverin on i' that way ? (I.W.)

2. To stammer and splutter like a dunce at his lesson. Used in *prp.* e.An.[1]

3. *sb.* A sloven ; an idle, dissolute, good-for-nothing man.

n.Cy. GROSE (1790). Cum. LINTON *Lake Cy.* (1864) 304. n.Yks.[2] e.Yks.[1] What can lass meean bl takkin wi sike a hack-slavver as that ? w.Yks. A hasty slovenly fellow, both in habit and deed ; but it has a peculiar respect to speaking ill, naturally or morally, THORESBY *Lett.* (1703) ; He's a great idle hackslavver (L.M.S.) ; w.Yks.[1][2], Lan.[1], e.Lan.[1], nw.Der.[1] n.Lin.[1] He's a love-begot an' a real hackslaver.

HACKUM-PLACKUM, *adv.* Sc. Nhb. In equal shares ; in exchange or barter.

Tev. Each paying an equal share, as of a tavern-bill (JAM.). Nhb. (HALL.)

HACK-WOOD, *sb.* Nhb. Cum. Wm. The bird-cherry, *Prunus Padus.* See **Hag-berry.**

Nhb.[1] Hack-wood is a name for the shrub itself, and hacker, hack, and hagberry are names for the fruit. Cum., Wm. (B. & H.)

HACKY, *sb.* Nhb. Also in form **whacky** (q. v.). [ha·ki.] A prostitute ; a term of great contempt.

In a brawl in the streets of Newcastle (1888) one woman was heard to call after another, ' Hacky, hacky, hacky !' ' Whacky' was formerly the contemptuous term applied by natives of Newcastle to their neighbours on the south side of the Tyne. ' He's nowt but a Durham whacky' (R.O.H.).

HACKY-MAL(L, see **Hackmal.**

HADABAND, *sb.* Sh.I. Also in form **hadiband.** A wooden band fastening securely the ribs of a boat.

The main division between the rooms [compartments of a sixern] was the fastabaands, or haddabaands, Sh. *News* (Oct. 21, 1899) ; Da boat wis filled ta da hadabaands, SPENCE *Flk-Lore* (1899) 250 ; S. & Ork.[1]

HADDABAT, *sb.* Lin. [a·dəbat.] The common bat.

MILLER & SKERTCHLY *Fenland* (1878) xii.

HADDAG, HADDEN, see **Haddie, Have, Hold.**

HADDER, *sb.*[1] Sc. Nhb. Cum. Wm. Yks. e.An. Also in form **hedder** Sc. n.Cy. Nhb.[1] Cum.[14] Wm. e.An. [h]a·də(r, h]e·də(r.] **1.** Var. kinds of heather or ling, esp. *Calluna vulgaris, Erica tetralix,* and *E. cinerea.*

Sh.I. I's' tak dy haand in mine, An wale for da saftest hedder, JUNDA *Klingrahool* (1898) 26. n.Cy. GROSE (1790) ; (K.) ; N.Cy.[2] Nhb. *Reports Agric.* (1793-1813) 20 ; Nhb.[1] A house thatched with ' hedder and straw to gedders, or meadow thake and hadder to gedders,' Dec. 14, 1505, WELFORD *Hist. Newcastle,* 22. Cum. Skiddaw stack its hedder up, RICHARDSON *Talk* (1876) and S. 14. Cum., Wm. *N. & Q.* (1873) 4th S. xi. 40. w.Yks. You mun mind your dresses w'en you get to the hadder (F.P.T.). e.Cy., e.An. (B. & H.)

Hence (1) **Hedder-faced,** *adj.* rough-faced, unshaven ; (2) **Heddery** or **Hedry,** *adj.* heathery ; *fig.* rough, shaggy.

(1) Cum. He's nobbet a hedder-feac'd mazlin, ANDERSON *Ballads* (ed. 1840) 24 ; Whea's the hether-feac'd chap ? *ib.* 111 ; Cum.[1] (2) Abd. Afore he us'd to bare his hedry pow, Where'er we met, SHIRREFS *Poems* (1790) 87.

2. *Comp.* (1) **Hedder-grey,** (2) **-linty,** the twite or rock lintie, *Linota flavirostris.* Cum.[4]

[They lay upon the ground, as the redshanks do on hadder, BURTON *Anat. Mel.* (1621), ed. 1896, III. 220; With peittis, with turuis, and mony turse of hedder, *Sat. Poems* (c. 1570), ed. Cranstoun, I. 222 ; Full feill fagaldys in to the dyk thai cast, Hadyr and hay bond, *Wallace* (1488) xi. 898.}

HADDER, *sb.*[2] and *v.* Dur. Lakel. Cum. Yks. Also in forms **hater** Wm.[1] ; **hather, heather** Lakel.[2] [h]a·dar.] **1.** *sb.* A fine rain or drizzle ; a heavy mist or bank of fog.

s.Dur. (J.E.D.) Lakel.[2] T'party at assd knew neea mair ner a fiul what hadder meant, an' they set off withoot top cooats, an' come back wet throo, an' gaan on aboot this hadder. Cum.[1] Cum., n.Yks. *N. & Q.* (1882) 6th S. v. 55. Wm.[1] It's a sign o' bad weather when them hater things cum up Sand.

Hence **Haddery,** *adj.* drizzling.

Cum. Auld Skiddaw, lap't i' heddery duds, RICHARDSON *Talk* (1876) and S. 13 ; It's a haddery day, SULLIVAN *Cum. and Wm.* (1857) 81.

2. A state of perspiration ; sweat.

Lakel.[2] Fouk at sweets a lot 'll say, ' Ah's o' in a hather.' Cum.[4]

3. *v.* To drizzle, rain finely.

s.Dur. It hadders and rains (J.E.D.). Lakel.[2] Nay, it'll rain nin, nut it marry ; it may hadder a bit. Cum. It keeps haddering and raining, SULLIVAN *Cum. and Wm.* (1857) 81 ; Cum.[1] It hadders and rains on ; Cum.[4] n.Yks. It hadders and rofiks, *N. & Q.* (1882) 6th S. v. 55.

Hence **Heatheran,** *sb.* a heavy mist. Lakel.[2]

HADDIE, *sb.* Sc. Also in forms **haadie** Ayr. ; **haddag** Cai.[1] ; **haddo.** [ha·di.] **1.** The haddock, *Morrhua aeglefinus* ; also used *attrib.*

Sc. A gill of brandy ower bread after the haddies, SCOTT *Antiquary* (1816) v ; Can ye tell me, minister, how mony hooks it taks to bait a fifteen score haddie line? DICKSON *Auld Min.* (1892) 192. ne.Sc. We're nae decin' muckle at the haddies eynoo ony gate, *Gordonhaven* (1887) 76. Cai.[1] Per. The ale-wife's fairin—Ait cakes, saut haddies, and red herrin', SPENCE *Poems* (1898) 169. w.Sc. They catch speldings an' finnan haddies there, MACDONALD *Settlement* (1869) 99, ed. 1877. Ayr. Haadics and whiteys ! SERVICE *Dr. Duguid* (ed. 1887) 88. Lnk. Mr. Sawdust then came up to them, smiling like a ' boilt baddy,' GORDON *Pyotshaw* (1885) 133. Lth. Mussels pickled nice wi' broo; And haddies caller at last carting, MACNEILL *Poet. Wks.* (1801) 171, ed. 1856. Edb. After a rizzard haddo, we had a jug of toddy, MOIR *Mansie Wauch* (1828) xi. Slk. ' I, for one, eat no fish for a twelvemonth.' ' Oh! the puir harmless haddies !' CHR. NORTH *Noctes* (ed. 1856) III. 219. [SATCHELL (1879).]

2. *Comp.* **Haddo-breeks,** the roe of the haddock. Rxb. (JAM.)

HADDIGAUD, see **Harry-gaud.**

HADDIN, *sb.* N.I.[1] [ha·din.] A ' hallan ' or partition wall in a cottage facing the door.

In [it] is the triangular or other shaped ' spy-hole.'

HADDISH, *sb.* Obsol. Sc. Also in form **haddies-** Ags. (JAM.) A measure of any dry grain ; also in *comp.* **Haddies-cog.**

Abd. The haddish is one-third of a peck. By Decree Arbitral— one peck of meal to the miller, and one haddish to the under-miller, *Proof regarding the Mill of Inverramsay* (c. 1814) (JAM.); According to others a fourth of a peck (JAM.). Ags. Formerly used for meting out the meal appropriated for supper to the servants. It contained the fourth part of a peck (*ib.*).

HADDLE, *v.* Glo. To throw out shoots from the root. Cf. **addle,** *v.*[2] **4.**

In March they are again grited, and sometimes tumped, or moulded close round, to make them haddle out, or throw forth side shoots, MARSHALL *Review* (1818) II. 457.

HADDLE, HADDLIN, HADDO, see **Addle,** *v.*[1], **Head-land, Haddie.**

HADDOCK, *sb.*[1] Sc. Also Som. Dev. Cor. Also in form **haddick** Sh.I. n.Dev. Cor.; **haddik** Sh.I. **1.** In *comp.* **Haddock-sand,** grounds much frequented by haddocks.

Sh.I. If da Government hed been mair stricter . . . dey'd been less raikin' o' wir haandlin' gruid an haddick saands, *Sh. News* (Apr. 2, 1898) ; A galleon belonging to the famous Spanish Armada, which sank on a haddock-sand near Reawick Head, HIBBERT *Desc. Sh. I.* (1822) 196, ed. 1891 ; The moonbeams sparkled on the waters of the ' Haddik Saand,' BURGESS *Lowra Biglan* (1896) 23.

c

2. Phr. *as deaf as a haddock*, very deaf. Cf. **addick.**

w.Som.[1] We seldom hear ' deaf as a post' or any other than ' so deef's a 'addick.' n.Dev. Tha'rt so deeve as a haddick, *Exm. Scold.* (1746) l. 129. Dev., Cor. Common, ELWORTHY *Wd-bk.* (1888). Cor. I was as deef as a haddock, TREGELLAS *Tales* (1868) 8.

3. A term of contempt for any one.

Dmf. The most insignificant haddock in nature—a dirty, greasy, cockney apprentice, CARLYLE *Lett.* (1831).

HADDOCK, *sb.*[2] Irel. Yks. Also written **haddok** Wxf.[1]   **1.** A shock of corn consisting of a varying number of sheaves, a ' hattock.'

Yks. Ten or twelve sheaves set upright in a double row, MORTON *Cyclo. Agric.* (1863) (s.v. Stook) ; Of six sheaves (G.R.). n.s.Yks.[1] Of eight sheaves. Sometimes distinguished from a stook by not having two additional sheaves on the top as a precaution against rain. m.Yks.[1] Commonly twelve.

2. *pl.* Imperfectly threshed heads of corn left after winnowing. Wxf.[1]

HADDY-DADDY, see **Hoddy-doddy.**

HADE, *sb.*[1] Rut. Lei: Nhp. War. Wor. Oxf. Also in forms **aid** Wor. ; **haid** Lei.[1] [ēd.] A ' headland ' or strip of land at the side of an arable field upon which the plough turns.

Rut.[1] A term in field mensuration. ' 6 rodes with hades at both ends. 2 Landes 4 ro. with hades,' *Terrier* (1635). Lei.[1] Nhp.[1] A small piece of greensward or grass at the head or end of arable land. A word that has gradually fallen into disuse, since the inclosure of open fields. War. The word occurs in the Holbech Estate Book (1770). It is still in common use (A.L.M.). Wor. (E.S.) Oxf. *Obs.* The description of certeine arable landes some of them havinge hades of meadow and grasse grounde lieinge in the Southe fielde of Einsham, *Map* (in Corpus Christi Coll. Oxon, 1615).

Hence **Hade-ley,** a ' headland.'

War. Item one other section of land called a hade ley, *Terrier of Fenny Compton Glebe* (1587) ; (A.L.M.) Lei.[1] The upper ' land ' in a grass field, the lower one being called the ' foot-ley.' Both as a rule run at right angles to the rest of the ' lands ' in a field. In the New Close a hadley and footeleay butting north and south, the Town Hill furlong west, the Constable's piece east, *Terrier of Claybrook Glebe* (1698).

[Horses may be teddered vpon leys, balkes, or hades, FITZHERBERT *Husb.* (1534) 15. Norw. dial. *hadd* (pl. *haddir*), a slope, an incline, rising ground, esp. on the side of a hayfield (AASEN, s.v. *Hall*) ; ON. *hallr*, a slope, hill, cp. *halla*, to slope (VIGFUSSON) ; OHG. *halden*, ' inclinare ' (GRAFF).]

HADE, *sb.*[2] and *v.* Nhb. Dur. Stf. Der. Also written **haid** Nhb. ; and in form **aid** w.Yks.[1] Stf.[1] [h)ēd.]   **1.** *sb.* Mining term : the slope or inclination of a dike with the seam in a coal-pit ; the inclination of a vein of lead or ore, a sloping vein.

N.Cy.[1] By it the character of a trouble is determined. Nhb. The haids of the several Slip Dykes . . . were ascertained, BUDDLE *Trans. Nat. Hist. Soc. Nhb. and Dur.* (1831) I. 296 ; Nhb.[1] Nhb., Dur. The slope or inclination of the leader of a dyke, GREENWELL *Coal Tr. Gl.* (1849). w.Yks. BAINES *Yks. Past* (1870) 20 ; w.Yks.[1] A lodge or vein going downwards, N. or S. out of the perpendicular line. Stf.[1] Der. MANLOVE *Lead Mines* (1653) *Gl.* ; *Eng. Gl. Mining Terms* (1830).

2. *v.* Of a vein of ore : to incline, dip.

w.Yks. BAINES *Yks. Past* (1870) 22 ; (T.T.) Der. MAWE *Mineralogy* (1802) *Gl.* ; Veins upon an east and west point generally hade or slope towards the south and north; and south veins towards the west, MANDER *Miners Gl.* (1824) ; Where any shaft or turn descends like the side of a house or like the descent of a steep hill it is said to hade, TAPPING *Gl. to Manlove* (1851).

Hence **Hading,** *sb.* a sloping vein.

Der. MANDER *Miners Gl.* (1824). nw.Der.[1]

[1. The same word as **Hade,** *sb.*[1]]

HADE, see **Heed, Hide,** *v.*[2]

HADEN, *adj. Obs.* Yks. w.Cy. Also in forms **headen, heiden** w.Yks.   Obstinate, headstrong ; ugly. Cf. **heady.**

w.Yks. HUTTON *Tour to Caves* (1781). w.Cy. (HALL.) [GROSE (1790).]

HADES, *sb.* e.Lan.[1] A place between or behind hills and out of sight. Cf. **hade,** *sb.*[1]

HADGE-, see **Hedge-.**

HADICK, *sb.* Sh.I. A hat. *(Coll.* L.L.B.)

HAE, HAED, HAEF, see **Have, How,** *adv.*, **Haet, Half.**

HAEG, HAEL, see **Hag,** *sb.*[2]**, Hale,** *adj.*

HAELTY, *adv.* Sh.I. In phr. *ill haelty eetim*, nothing whatever, ' deil a thing.'

Da men is aye best aff, haelty ill eetim dey hae ta dö bit tak aff der kjaep [cap], an' set dem til, *Sh. News* (Sept. 3, 1898) ; Common (J.I.).

HAEM, HAEMILT, see **Hame,** *sb.*[1]**, Hamald.**

HAEMONY, *sb.* Glo. The lemon-scented agrimony, *Agrimonia Eupatoria.*

It is, I believe, sold to this day in Bristol market under the name of Haemony, *Monthly Pckt.* (1863) V. 467 in (B. & H.).

HAEN, see **Hain,** *v.*[1]

HAENKS, *v.* Sh.I. [hēnks.] With *up* : to hitch or pull up.

I haenksd up me breeks—dis laskit strops is a curse, whin a body is carryin' a burdeen, *Sh. News* (June 4, 1898).

HAERST, HAESTIS, see **Harvest, Hastis.**

HAET, *vbl. phr.* and *sb.* Sc. Irel. n.Cy. Amer. Also written **hait** Sc. N.I.[1] ; **hate** Sc. s.Don. ; and in forms **haed** Sc. ; **haeit** Sh.I. ; **haid** Sc. (JAM.) ; **head** e.Fif.

1. *vbl. phr.* : *Deil haet,* the Devil have it ! *Fiend haet,* the Fiend have it ! used as a strong negative, equivalent to ' Devil a bit.'

Sc. Diel haet o' me kens, SCOTT *Midlothian* (1818) xvi. Sh.I. Da deil haeit ye got for a second cup but da sam' as wal wattir, *Sh. News* (Feb. 12, 1898). Frf. [He] swore the fient haed mair He'd draw that day, MORISON *Poems* (1790) 18. Per. Wi' deil haet but a tongue an' slavers To start anew on, HALIBURTON *Ochil Idylls* (1891) 89. Fif. For de'il haet mair hae I to say, TENNANT *Papistry* (1827) 103. e.Fif. Stanes, stanes! and scraps o' auld eiron l· feint head else, LATTO *Tam Bodkin* (1864) v. Ayr. It was sae blunt, Fient haet o't wad hae pierc'd the heart, BURNS *Doctor Hornbook* (1785) st. 17. Lnk. Fint hate ye gie them bot wee pickles o' pease-meal, GRAHAM *Writings* (1883) II. 297. Edb. Deil hait we do will e'er content them! MACNEILL *Bygane Times* (1811) 17. Peb. On holidays ye did me ride For deil hate else but shew, AFFLECK *Poet. Wks.* (1836) 60. Rxb. De'il haet was left but runts an' stibble, RUICKBIE *Wayside Cottager* (1807) 108. n.Cy. *Border Gl.* (Coll. L.L.B.)

2. *sb.* Phr. *Deil a haet, Fient a haet, Deuce a haet,* Devil a bit.

Abd. Some thousan' pounds, for fint a hait, Is nae bad notion, COCK *Strains* (1810) II. 90. Rnf. The deuce a haet they could be call'd But words and rhyme, McGILVRAY *Poems* (ed. 1862) 160. Lnk. The deil a hate o' wark she's done the day, BLACK *Falls of Clyde* (1806) 173. Lth. Fient the haet o' them was soun', SMITH *Merry Bridal* (1866) 12. Slk. Feint a haet he minds, HOGG *Tales* (1838) 364, ed. 1866. N.I.[1]

3. A whit, atom, anything, the smallest thing that can be conceived, *gen.* in negative sentences.

Inv. ' That's a haet,' it is of no consequence. Used esp. in a contemptuous sense (H.E.F.). Kcb. What haet cared they for fortune's gifts l ELDER *Borgue* (1897) 16. Uls. I haven't a haet. I didn't do a haet (M.B.-S. . s.Don. Half-penny worth; a small quantity, SIMMONS *Gl.* (1890). [Amer. Didn't get a hate, *Dial. Notes* (1896) I. 389.]

4. Phr. (1) *haid nor maid,* nothing at all ; (2) *neither ocht nor hate,* neither one thing nor another.

(1) Ags. Used to denote extreme poverty. ' There is neither haid nor maid in the house ' (JAM.). (2) Sc. (*ib.*)

HAEV, *sb.* Cai.[1] A small hand-basket used by fishermen to carry bait.

[Norw. dial. *haav*, a fisherman's basket (AASEN).]

HAEVER, see **Eaver,** *sb.*[2]

HAFER, *v.* Suf.[1] To act or speak in an unsettled, unsteady manner from love or idleness, not necessarily from immorality. *Gen.* in *prp.*   ' A go haferen about.'

HAFER, HAF(F, see **Halver, Haaf,** *sb.*[1]

HAFFANT, *sb.* Sh.I. Also in form **haffin.** A paramour. S. & Ork.[1]

HAFFER, *v.*[1] e.Yks.[1] To speak stammeringly or hesitatingly. Cf. **haffle, haver,** *v.*[1]

HAFFER, *v.*[2] Som. Also written **halfer.** [ā·fə(r).] To make a noise like the bursting of a pod.

She told me that [formerly] the youth of both sexes used to assemble under the tree [Glastonbury Thorn] at midnight on Christmas Eve, in order to hear the bursting of the buds, .. and she added, 'As they comed out, you could hear 'um haffer,' *N. & Q.* (1866) 3rd S. ix. 34. **n.Som.** As they [buds] comed out you could hear 'um halfer, Timbs *Thoughts for Times and Seasons*, 9.

HAFFER, see **Halver**.

HAFFET, *sb.* Sc. Irel. Nhb. Cum. Wm. Also written haffat Abd.; haffit Sc. S. & Ork.[1] Nhb. [ha·fət, -ɪt.]

1. The temple; side of the face; *gen.* in *pl.*; also used *attrib.*

Sc. The grey locks that straggled ... down his weather-beaten 'haffets,' Scott *Midlothian* (1818) xlii. **Sh.I.** Da first ane o' da tribe o' dem 'at mak's for dark'nin' wir door, sall geng oot wi' haet haffits, *Sh. News* (Mar. 5, 1898). **S. & Ork.[1]** **Elg.** Guldroch's cleuks Your haffits weel will claw, Couper *Poetry* (1804) II. 70. **Abd.** Her hand she had upon her haffat laid, Ross *Helenore* (1768) 27, ed. 1812. **Per.** Men bow'd wi' toil an' age—wi' haffets auld an' thin, Nicoll *Poems* (ed. 1843) 226. **Dmb.** Your haffits dressing clout for clout, Salmon *Gowodean* (1868) 78. **Ked.** Wi' haffet locks as white 's a daisy, Burness *Garron Ha'* (c. 1796) l. 10. **Rnf.** And screed till the sweat fa' in beads frae his haffet, Tannahill *Poems* (1807) 257, ed. 1817. **Lnk.** Her haffet locks hang waving on her cheek, Ramsay *Gentle Shep.* (1725) 23, ed. 1783. **Lth.** Dark wave her haffet locks owre her white brow, Macneill *Poet. Wks.* (1801) 212, ed. 1856. **Edb.** A runkled brow, sunburnt haffits, and two sharp piercing eyes, Moir *Mansie Wauch* (1828) xx. **Bwk.** Set the stoor about your haffets, Henderson *Pop. Rhymes* (1856) 79. **Dmf.** O haffet locks look weel whan they're bleach'd like the snaw, Cromek *Remains* (1810) 116. **Gall.** Mess Hairry ... had keeled ower Black Coskery wi' ae stroke o' his oak clickie on the haffets, Crockett *Standard Bearer* (1898) 124. **Keb.** Whase haffet a Kilmarnock hood Kept warm an' snug, Davidson *Seasons* (1789) 64. **n.Cy.** *Border Gl.* (Coll. L.L.B.); **n.Cy.[1], Nhb.[1], Cum.[4]** **Wm. & Cum.[1]** Seylin sweats their haffets bathe, 172.

Hence **Haffet-clawing**, *vbl. sb.* face-scratching. **Lnk.** The fierce haffet-clawin o' an enraged woman, Murdoch *Readings* (ed. 1895) I. 121.

2. *pl.* Locks of hair, *gen.* growing on the temples. **Abd.** Haffets whiter than the snaw Down ower yer happy temples thinly fa', Still *Cottar's Sunday* (1845) 159. **Frf.** The carle ... Wi' his haffets as white as the snaw, Watt *Poet. Sketches* (1880) 115. **Fif.** Your haffets white an' a' that, Douglas *Poems* (1806) 169. **Ayr.** His lyart haffets wearing thin an' bare, Burns *Cotter's Sat. Night* (1785) st. 14. **Slk.** Time had now grizzled his haffets wi' snaw, Hogg *Poems* (ed. 1865) 67. **Rxb.** Till the arm waxes weak and the haffet grows grey, Riddell *Poet. Wks.* (1871) I. 118. **N.I.[1]**

3. *pl.* The jaws; the under-sides of the jaw. **Nhb.** The lugs o' hippocrissy hingin owor thor haffits, Chater *Tyneside Alm.* (1869) 46; **Nhb.[1]**

4. *Phr.* (1) *I'll gie you a haffit, and I'll scum your chafts to you*, I will give you a blow on the cheek; (2) *I'll take my hand from your haffet*, I will give you a blow on the cheek; (3) *to kaim down one's haffits*, to give one a complete drubbing.

(1) **Lth.** (Jam.) (2) **Sc.** Kelly *Prov.* (1721) 396. (3) **Abd.** Then they may Gallia's braggers trim, An' down their haffits kaim, Tarras *Poems* (1804) 139 (Jam.).

[1. Wnfreindlie eild had thus besprent My heid and halfettis baith with camus hair, Douglas *Eneados* (1513), ed. 1874, II. 248. OE. *healfhéafod*, the front part of the head (Ælfric).]

HAFFICK, *sb.* Sus. Tangle, confusion, rubbish, litter. Bricklayers use the word in connection with the rubbish or litter lying about. 'What a haffick you are making.' 'We must clear away the haffick' (F.W.L.); (E.E.S.); Not often heard now. An old gardener looking at a flower-border said, 'Here's fire an' all of a baffic' (G.A.W.).

HAFFIGRAPH, *sb.* *Obs.* n.Yks.[2] Also written halfigraph. Half the breadth of an engraved line. 'It came to a haffigraph,' within a hair of the quantity required.

HAFFINS, see **Halfins**.

HAFFLE, *sb.* Nhb. [ha·fl.] A rag tied round an injured finger; a finger-poke. Cf. hovel, *sb.*[2] A finger-glove used to protect a quarryman's skin. Also used by stone-wallers (G.M.); **Nhb.[1]**

HAFFLE, *v.* Nhb. Dur. Cum. Wm. Yks. Lan. Chs. Der. Not. Nrf. Also in forms hawfle n.Yks.[2]; heffle Dur. Cum.[14] Wm.; hiffle Cum.[14] [h)a·fl, he·fl.] 1. To hesitate, speak confusedly, falter, stammer; to prevaricate, quibble.

n.Cy. Grose (1790); **N.Cy.[1]** **Nhb.** He wis hafflin (R.O.H.).

---

n.Dur. He heffled an' talked an' could git nowt out (J.E.D.). **Cum.** I's tryin to hiffle oot o' nowt, Gwordie Greenup *Anudder Batch* (1873) 7; **Cum.[14]** **Wm.** It's nea use hafflin en leein aboot it, Taylor *Sketches* (1882a) 13; 'What are you heflin about!' when a person does not get on with their work (A.T.), **n.Yks.[12]**; **n.Yks.[4]** Deean't haffle leyke that, bud speeak plain. He awlus haffles on that mich, whahl neeabody ho'ds ti owt he sez. **m.Yks.[1]** **w.Yks.** Thow'lt haffle and jest while fowk pine to death, Snowden *Web of Weaver* (1896) 46. **Lan.** He haffled at that, Walkden *Diary* (ed. 1866) 113. **n.Lan.[1], ne.Lan.[1] Chs.[1]; Chs.[3]** Haffle, and yore dun for. **Der.[1], Not.** (J.H.B.)

Hence (1) **Haffle**, *sb.* hesitation; (2) **Haffling**, *sb.* confused talk; (3) **Haffling**, *ppl. adj.*, (4) **Haffly**, *adj.* hesitating, indecisive; prevaricating.

(1) **Lan.** Becose thou's no 'casion t'mak any haffle about it, Brierley *Waverlow* (1863) 85, ed. 1884. (2) **N.Cy.[1]** **Cum.** Asteed a payan om meh, adoot enny mair hifflin, Sargisson *Joe Scoap* (1881) 110. **Wm.** After a full four hoors wer spent I' hifflin, hafflin —shifflin shafflin ... I nailt him at last, *Spec. Dial.* (1872a) pt. i. 43. (3) **n.Yks.[2]** **w.Yks.** He's a haffling speyker (J.B.). **Lan.[1]** We'll ha' noan o' thi hafflin' wark here. (4) **n.Yks.** He's nobbut a haffly talker (I.W.).

2. *Comb.* (1) **Haffle-caffle**, to falter, vacillate, act with indecision. **w.Yks.[2]**; (2) **·maffle**, to speak unintelligibly, stammer. **w.Yks.[1]**

3. *Phr.* (1) *haffle and caffle*, to shilly-shally; (2) *haffling and jaffling*, chattering, gossiping; (3) *— shaffling*, confused, prevaricating.

(1) **nw.Der.[1]** **Not.** The doctor, he haffled and caffled, he didn't rightly know what war wrong wi' her himself (L.C.M.); **Not.[1]** (2) **Nrf.** The goodwife may be 'haffling and jaffling' with a neighbour, Rye *Hist. Nrf.* (1885) xv. (3) **w.Yks.** I make nought of haffling and shaffling tales that keep part back, Snowden *Web of Weaver* (1896) 1; 'What are tə afflin' an' shafflin' abaht; get forrəd wi' thi teal (J.R.). **Chs.[1]**

4. Of a horse: when pawing the ground. **Der.[1]** Ée aaf'lz ŭlŭng(g· [he haffles along].

[1. Du. *haffelen*, to fumble, to dawdle; to mumble; also used of old people who eat their food with difficulty (Beets).]

HAFFLIN, *sb.* Sc. Also in form halfin Abd. (Jam.) A plane used by carpenters.

Sc. Still in use. It is in size between the hand-plane and the large finishing plane (G.W.); (Jam.) **Abd.** The plane that is used after the 'Scrub' or 'Foreplane' and before the 'Jointer' (*ib.*).

HAFFLING, see **Halfling**.

HAFT, *sb.*[1] and *v.* Var. dial. uses in Sc. Irel. and Eng. Also in forms hart Hmp. w.Som.[1] nw.Dev.[1]; heft Sc. (Jam.) S. & Ork.[1] Cai.[1] Nhb.[1] Dur.[1] Cum.[14] Wm. n.Yks.[14] n.Lan.[1] Not.[1] Lin.[1] n.Lin.[1] sw.Lin.[1] Nhp.[1] Bdf. e.An.[1] Suf.[1] Hmp.[1] [h)aft, æft, h)eft.] 1. *sb.* A handle, esp. of a knife or small tool.

Sc. Cripple Archy ... strak like a Turk wi' the heft o' a hammer, *MS. Poem* (Jam.). **Sh.I.** Turnin' a pancake wi' da heft o' a iron spūne, *Sh. News* (Apr. 2, 1898). **S. & Ork.[1], Cai.[1] Ayr.** As muckle ... as wou'd made a heft to a kail gully, Ainslie *Land of Burns* (ed. 1892) 78. **Ant.** Grose (1790) *MS. add.* (C.) **N.Cy.[1] Nhb.** 'Frae the sword, the heuk heft, and the gallace may the Lord deliver us!' viz. from war, shearing, and the gallows, Dixon *Whittingham Vale* (1895) 277. **Dur.[1], Cum.[14] Wm.** Theear's a heft ta put te bleead in, Clarke *Jonny Shippard's Journa* (ed. 1870) 15; As t'shapless form a gully waved Wi' bleudy bleayde an heft, Whitehead *Leg.* (1859) 14, ed. 1896. **n.Yks.[12]; n.Yks.[4]** T'knife's gitten a grand heft tul 't. **ne.Yks.[1]**; **e.Yks.[1], w.Yks.[24], n.Lan.[1] Chs.[1]** Chs. men never say 'handle,' but always 'haft.' **Not.[1], (J.P.K.), n.Lin.[1], sw.Lin.[1], s.Lin.** (T.H.R.) **Nhp.[1]** When all is gone, and none left, Turn the blade into the haft. **s.Wor.** (H.K.), **Rdn.[1], Brks.[1], Bdf.** (J.W.B.), **e.An.[1], Suf.[1], Hmp.[1] Som.** I went up to cut a straight ... stick for a good haft, Raymond *Men o' Mendip* (1898) vii. **w.Som.[1]** Thick wid'n be a bad knive, neef's had [if thou hadst] a new hart an' a new blade to un. Haft not so common as hart. **Dev.[1], nw.Dev.[1]**

Hence (1) **Hafted**, *ppl. adj.* fitted with a handle; (2) **Heft**, *sb., fig.* a portion, part; (3) **Heft-end**, *sb., fig.* the beginning, commencement.

(1) **Per.** Bra' knives, hafted wi' bane, Nicol *Poems* (1766) 48. **n.Cy.** (J.W.) **Dor.** All the broken-hafted speädes, Barnes *Poems* (1869-70) 67. (2) **n.Yks.[4]** Thoo's nobbut gitten a heft on 't, sha's kept t'main on t'back. (3) **Sc.** Once more he tackled the subject by the 'heft end,' Ford *Thistledown* (1891) 111.

2. *Comp.* **Heft-pipe,** a temporary handle used in grinding razors and forks.

w.Yks. Bil Heftpoip [a Sheffield grinder], BYWATER *Sheffield Dial.* (1839) 4.

3. The right-hand side of a band of reapers. Also in phr. *haft and point,* the outermost party on each side in a field of reapers.

Sc. MORTON *Cyclo. Agric.* (1863). Dmf. (JAM.)

4. *Phr.* (1) *by the haft,* a common oath ; (2) *down i' t'heft,* weakly, despondent, 'down in the mouth'; (3) *dunna waste a fresh haft on an ould blade,* don't throw good money after bad ; (4) *every knife of his'n has a golden haft,* everything he undertakes turns out well ; (5) *fulfilled to the heft,* fulfilled thoroughly ; (6) *heft or blade,* any part ; (7) *like heft and blade,* close companions ; (8) *loose i' t'heft,* dissolute, dishonest, untrustworthy ; (9) *to be done to t'heft,* to be worn out by toil ; (10) *to have both heft and blade to hadd,* to have things entirely under one's own control ; (11) *to have nee heft t'one's hand,* to be unthrifty, extravagant ; (12) *to hold one in the heft,* to be a match for one ; (13) *to stick to the haft,* not to desert.

(1) nw.Der.¹ [The cross of the sword-heft or handle was frequently sworn by, *N. & Q.* (1899) 9th S. iv. 355.] (2) m.Yks.¹ (3, 4) Chs.² (5) Ayr. The Scriptural text was fulfilled to the heft, LAING *Poems* (1894) 111. (6) Ayr. He'll not get either heft or blade o' my vote for sic a trifle, GALT *Lairds* (1826) xxxiv. (7) Ked. They had been like heft an' blade The feck o' baith their lives, GRANT *Lays* (1884) 56. (8) w.Yks. *Leeds Merc. Suppl.* (Feb. 2, 1895). w.Yks.² He's a bit loose i' t'heft ! (9) w.Yks.¹ (10) Abd. (JAM.); Ye had, In your ain hand to hadd, baith heft and blade, Ross *Helenore* (1768) 90, ed. 1812. (11) Nhb. (R.O.H.) (12) w.Yks.¹ (13) Per. The Highland Clans stuck to the haft, MONTEATH *Dunblane* (1835) 107, ed. 1889.

5. *v.* To fit with, supply with ; *gen.* in *pass.*

S. & Ork.¹ n.Yks. He was hefted wi plenty o' lads (I.W.). ne.Yks.¹ e.Yks.¹ Bill's hefted up wi munney. Betty hoose is hefted up wi muck, MS. *add.* (T.H.)

6. To hold fast, beset, encumber ; *gen.* in *pass.*

n.Yks.¹ Ah doo'ts he'll find hissel' sair hefted wiv her ; n.Yks.² Hefted with a large family.

[For *fig.* use in the sense of a pretext, see **Heft,** *sb.*⁸]

HAFT, *sb.*² Stf. A little island or raised bank in a pond on which water-fowl build their nests.

The Hafts or Islands in the pooles, PLOT *Sif.* (1686) 232 ; (K.); Stf.¹

HAFT, see **Heft,** *sb.*², *v.*⁴

HAFTER, *sb.* Obs. N.Cy.² A wrangler, caviller.

[*Vitiligator,* an hafter, a wrangler, a quarreller, GOULDMAN (1678) ; so BARET (1580).]

HAFTY, *adj.* Cum. Yks. Also in form **hefty** Cum.⁴ e.Yks. [h]a'fti.] Saucy, pert ; handy, active. See **Haft,** *sb.*¹

Cum.⁴ n.Yks. He's hafty at his work (I.W.). n. & e.Yks. Still fairly common in N. &. E. Ridings (R.S.). e.Yks. (Miss A.)

HAG, *sb.*¹ Sc. n.Cy. Wm. Yks. Lan. War. Glo. Ken. Sur. Sus. I.W. Wil. Dor. Som. Dev. Cor. Also in forms **haig** Cai.¹ ; **heg** Ken.¹ [h]ag, æg.] **1.** An evil spirit or infernal being in female form; also applied to the fairies or pixies ; a witch.

n.Yks. (T.S.), Ken.¹, I.W.¹, w.Som.¹

Hence **Hagging,** *vbl. sb.* practising the arts of a witch. n.Yks.²

2. *Comb.* (1) **Hag-begagged,** bewitched ; (2) **-bone,** the shoulder-bone or blade of a sheep ; (3) **-'s pence,** old coins found in the ground ; (4) **-ride,** to bewitch; to inflict with nightmare; also used *fig.* and *gen.* in *pp.*; (5) **-stone,** a stone with a hole in it, used as a charm against witches ; (6) **-track,** a 'fairy-ring' or circle of coarse green grass found in meadows and on downs.

(1) Dev. Thereaway, every land save feyther's was called hagbegagged, to keep us childer in proper bounds belike, MADOX-BROWN *Yeth-hounds* (1876) 252. (2) Som. Witches were believed to ride upon these and consequently it was necessary to burn them (W.F.R.). (3) Ken.¹ (4) Sc. The thought of the dead men hag-rode my spirits, STEVENSON *Catriona* (1893) iii. Edb. Hag-rid wi' conscience, gout, an' spleen, LEARMONT *Poems* (1791) 58. n.Cy. *Denham Tracts* (ed. 1895) II. 86. Sus. This unhappy man, he said, was hag-ridden, HEATH *Eng. Peas.* (1893) 191. Sus.¹

Wil.¹ Dor. Souls above us, your face is as if you'd been hag-rode, HARDY *Tess* (1891) 424, ed. 1895 ; Dor.¹ The nightmare is attributed to the supernatural presence of a witch or hag by whom one is ridden in sleep. Som. Abraham was hag-rod every night of his life about two 'in marnen,' RAYMOND *Love and Quiet Life* (1894) 205 ; (W.F.R.) w.Som.¹ Also applied to horses which often break out into a sweat in the stable, and are said to have been hag-rided, or pixy-rided. The belief is quite common that the pixies come and ride the horses round the stable in the night. Most farm stable-doors have a rusty horseshoe nailed, sometimes to the threshold, generally on the inside of the lintel, to keep off the pixies. Dev. Hag-ridden, entangled (HALL.). Cor. There was the Vicar with inflated cheeks and a hag-ridden stare, 'Q.' *Troy Town* (1888) ix. (5) Lan. A hag-stone, penetrated with a hole, and attached to the key of the stable, preserved the horse from being ridden by the witch, HARLAND & WILKINSON *Flk-Lore* (1867) 72 ; THORNBER *Hist. Blackpool* (1837) 100 ; A hag-stone with a hole through, tied to the key of the stable-door, protects the horses, and if hung up at the bed's head, the farmer also, *N. & Q.* (1851) 1st S. iii. 56. (6) Sur. Many a large 'ring' or 'hag-track' may be seen in lonely spots, JENNINGS *Field Paths* (1884) 67. Sus. Most interesting objects . . . upon the South Downs are the numerous fairy-rings or 'hag-tracks,' LOWER *South Downs* (1854) 154 ; Sus.¹ Supposed to be tracks of hags or witches who have danced there at night.

3. *Fig.* A violent, ill-tempered woman, a scold ; an ugly, dirty woman. Cai.¹, Lan. (S.W.), War.², Glo.¹

[L. Blue meagre hag, or stubborn unlaid ghost, MILTON *Comus* (1634) 434.]

HAG, *sb.*² n.Cy. Yks. Lan. Chs. Der. Brks. Bck. Hrt. Ken. Sus. Hmp. I.W. Som. Dev. Also in forms **aag** w.Yks. ; **ag-** Brks.¹ Sus.¹ ; **aga** Ken. Hmp. Wil. ; **agg** Bck. ; **aght** Dev. ; **ague** Chs.² ; **aig, haag** w.Yks. ; **haeg** w.Yks. Chs. ; **haga** I.W. ; **hagga** Brks.¹ ; **haghe** n.Cy. w.Yks.² Der.¹ nw.Der.¹ ; **hague** w.Yks.¹ Lan.¹ ne.Lan.¹ Chs.¹ ; **haig** w.Yks.⁴ ² Lan.¹ e.Lan.¹ Chs.¹ ; **haigh** w.Yks.²² ; **hoeg** Chs.² [ĕg, e̯ag, æg.] **1.** A haw, the fruit of the hawthorn, *Crataegus Oxyacantha* ; *gen.* in *pl.* Also in *comp.* Hag-berry.

n.Cy. BAILEY (1721). w.Yks. Us lads kept blawin' aags at one another, *Leeds Merc. Suppl.* (Apr. 4, 1891) ; Getting stuff to eat —haegs and epps, SNOWDEN *Web of Weaver* (1896) 6; w.Yks.¹² ⁴ ⁴ ⁵, Lan. (S.W.), Lan.¹, ne.Lan.¹, e.Lan.¹ Chs. *Science Gossip* (1865) 198 ; Chs.¹ ², Der.¹, nw.Der.¹ Brks. Gl. (1852) ; Brks.¹, Ken. (W.H.E.), Hmp. (J.R.W.), (W.H.E.), Hmp.¹, Wil. (W.H.E.), I.W. (B. & H.) Dev. GROSE (1790) *MS. add.* (C.) [RAY (1691).]

Hence (1) **Agarves** or **Hag-haws,** (2) **Agasses** or **Hagasses,** (3) **Agogs,** *sb. pl.* haws, the fruit of the hawthorn ; (4) **Haggises,** *sb. pl.* hips, the fruit of the dog-rose, *Rosa canina.*

(1) Sus.¹ (2) Sus. (R.P.C.), Hmp. (J.R.W.) (3) Brks.¹ (4) Hmp.¹

2. The hawthorn, *Crataegus Oxyacantha.* Lan.¹

3. *Comp.* (1) **Hag-blossom,** the blossom of the hawthorn ; (2) **-bush,** the hawthorn ; (3) **-leaf,** (4) **-paper,** the great mullein, *Verbascum Thapsus*; (5) **-rope(s,** the wild clematis, *Clematis Vitalba* ; (6) **-taper,** see (4) ; (7) **-thorn,** (8) **-tree,** see (2).

(1) w.Yks. (D.L.) Lan. Wilt ha' this bit o' hague-blossom ? BRIERLEY *Irkdale* (1865) iv. (2) w.Yks. (S.P.U.) (3, 4) Bck. *Science Gossip* (1869) 26. (5) Som. *N. & Q.* (1877) 5th S. viii. 358 ; W. & J. Gl. (1873). w.Som.¹ (6) Hrt. ELLIS *New Experiments* (1750) 22. (7) w.Som.¹, Dev.⁴ (8) w.Yks. (S.P.U.)

[1. A form of lit. E. *haw,* OE. *haga,* the fruit of the hawthorn ; cp. LG. *hagdoorn,* 'Crataegus oxyacantha' (BERGHAUS).]

HAG, *sb.*³ n.Cy. Nhb. Yks. Also Cor. [h]ag, æg.] A thick white mist or fog.

n.Cy.¹ Nhb. *Gent. Mag.* (1794), ed. Gomme ; Nhb.¹, Wm. (J.H.) n.Yks. A frost hag (T.S.) ; n.Yks.¹ Such as sometimes occurs coincidently with frost: whence frost-hag ; n.Yks.²⁴, m.Yks.¹, Cor.²

Hence **Haggy,** *adj.* misty from the frost. n.Yks.²

HAG, *sb.*⁴ n.Cy. Nhb. Lan. [h]ag.] The paunch, belly. See **Haggis, 3.**

n.Cy. GROSE (1790). Nhb.¹ Lan. GROSE (1790) *MS. add.* (C.) ; Lan.¹

HAG, *sb.*⁵ ? *Obs.* Bdf. Som. Idle disorder.

Bdf. You have got the hag, BATCHELOR *Anal. Eng. Lang.* (1809) 136. Som. (HALL.)

HAG, v.[1] and sb.[6] Sc. Irel. Nhb. Dur. Cum. Wm. Yks. an. Der. Not. Lin. Rut. Lei. Nhp. War. Wor. Shr. Brks. mp. Wil. Also written **hagg** Sc. War. Shr.[2]; and in rms ag N.Cy.[1] Nhb.[1] w.Yks. Not.[1]; ag Brks.[1] Hmp. 'il.[1] [h]ag, æg.] 1. v. To hew, chop; to cut down th an axe; to hack, cut clumsily or roughly.

Sc. That chief sin, that he should have a hand in hagging and shing at Christ's kirk, STEVENSON Catriona (1893) xv. Fif. Wi' eir swords them hash't and hagget, TENNANT Papistry (1827) x. Dmb. I doot I've haggit the feck o' my chin awa', CROSS sruption (1844) xiv. Ayr. Let him swurl his glaive [sword] wi' his micht, and hag the heid o't aff at ance, SERVICE Notandums 890) 125. Lnk. They may hag and hew my body as they ease, WODROW Ch. Hist. (1721) IV. 112, ed. 1828. Gall. The agoons are . . . haggin' them doon, CROCKETT Moss-Hags (1895) N.I.[1] I hagged a wheen o' sticks. Ant. Ballymena Obs. 892). N.Cy.[1], Nhb.[1], Dur.[1] Cum. Begon to hag his way through eurr, DICKINSON Lamplugh (1856) 9; (M.P.); Cum.[2] Toald kler hoond bed hagg't it off afooar he meäd a fleeght on't, 71. m. He teeak it intle his heead it heed hagg it doon, Spec. Dial. 877) pt. i. 25; (M.P.) n.Wm. (B.K.), s.Wm. (J.A.B.), n.Yks.[8], Yks.[1] w.Yks. WILLAN List Wds. (1811); w.Yks.[1] They hagged nice birk for't yusterneet, ii. 290; w.Yks.[2], ne.Lan.[1] Not.[1] Don't g the meat that road. Lin. STREATFEILD Lin. and Danes (1884) 4. n.Lin.[1] Doän't hag thý meät 'e that how, lad. sw.Lin.[1] Of odmen: 'They started hagging last week.' Nhp.[1] War. B'ham Wy. Post (June 10, 1893); War.[1 2 3], Shr.[2] Brks.[1] What be at aggin the me-at like that ther, 'twunt go hafe zo vur. Hmp.[1] l. SLOW Gl. (1892); Wil.[1]

Hence (1) **Hagger**, sb. (a) one who uses a hatchet, one mployed to fell trees; (b) a coal-hewer; (2) **Haggit**, l. adj. notched, jagged; (3) **Hagman**, sb. one who gains is living by felling and selling wood; a woodcutter.

(1, a) Lakel.[2] A man mun deea o' at ivver he can fer hissel; he un hag-an'-trail his awn. (2) Cum.[1] (3) Cum. 'Gaun on like a an haggin rice,' great progress made in a short time, N. & Q. 871) 5th S. ii. 71. Cum., Wm. 'Ga'un on, like a man haggin' ce,' was sometimes used in a comic way, as indicating a swift earance by a hungry or hasty person at table (M.P.).

3. Comp. (1) **Hag-block**, (2) **-clog**, a chopping-block, large block of wood, used to chop firewood, &c. on; a part f a tree-stem; (3) **-iron** or **Haggon**, a blacksmith's hisel; (4) **-stock**, see (2).

(1) Wgt. Hughie's shop was well stocked with visitors; so much that he could scarcely get the use of his hag-block, FRASER Vigtown (1877) 375. (2) Gall. I could hear him at the hag-clog where we cut the branches and wood into billets to go into the reat fireplace, CROCKETT Raiders (1894) xxxv. n.Cy. HOLLOWAY. un.[1] n.Wm. Tak it ta t'hag-clog ta chop (B.K.). n.Yks.[1 2 4] s.Yks.[1], w.Yks.[2] (3) Rxb. A chisel on which the blacksmith cuts f the nails from the rod or piece of iron of which they are made Yks.[1], w.Yks.[2] An inverted cbisel which a blacksmith puts f the anvil when he wishes to cut anything off. (4) Lakel.[2], Cum.[1] w.Yks.[1] (J.A.B.) ne.Lan.[1] As foul as t'hagstock.

4. To use the rake in haymaking with a peculiar sharp ction. Lei.[1] Cf. **hack**, v.[1] 23.

5. Fig. To bungle, mangle any business.

Sc. But let them hag and hash on, for they will make no cleanly ork neither in state nor church, WALKER Remark. Passages 1727) 80 (JAM.).

6. sb. A stroke with a sharp and heavy instrument, hack; a notch, mark; esp. in phr. to give the hallen, r post, a hag, to make a mark in remembrance of a otable event, to 'chalk up' an event. Cf. hack, sb.[1] 6.

Ayr. I'm sure the post should get a hag when we hear o' him oming wi' hundreds o' pounds in his pouch, GALT Entail (1823) xi. Lnk. 'He may strike a hag i' the post,' a proverbial phr. pplied to one who has been very fortunate (JAM.). Cum. A very

complimentary speech to a rare or notable visitor: 'We mun give t'hallen a hag as ye're cum't' (M.P.).

7. A clearing or cutting down of timber; a cutting in a wood.

N.Cy.[1] Nhb. The number of trees in the oak wood have been considerably diminished. A great hag in 1802-3 thinned them, HARDY Hist. Bwk. Natur. Club, VIII. 401; (R.O.H.); Nhb.[1], Cum. (M.P.)

8. An allotment of timber for felling, a certain portion of wood marked off to be cut down.

Sc. The derk hag, which had somewhat puzzled him in the butler's account of his master's avocations, . . was simply a portion of oak copse which was to be felled that day, SCOTT Waverley (1814) x; There is to be exposed for sale by public roup, —a hag of wood, consisting of oak, beech and birch, all in one lot, Edb. Even. Courant (Mar. 26, 1803) (JAM.). Cld. Woods that are extensive are divided into separate lots called hags, one of which is appointed to be cut annually, Agric. Surv. 137 (ib.). Dmb. They [the oak woods] are of such extent as to admit of their being properly divided into 20 separate hags or parts, one of which may be cut every year, Statist. Acc. XVII. 244 (ib.). Nhb.[1], ne.Lan.[1] War. The separate portions [of a fall of timber] so divided are called each man's hagg, BAKER Gl. (1854). Shr.[1] When a wood is to be cut down, a number of men range themselves at the edge of the wood at about forty yards apart, then they start, proceeding in straight lines through the wood, hewing down the underwood, and hacking the outer bark of the trees with their 'hackers' as they go along; shouting to each other in the meanwhile, in order to keep their respective distances, till they reach the farther limit. The lines thus cleared form the boundaries of the hag apportioned to each man to fell; Shr.[2]

9. A lot of about 100 ash or willow poles.

War.[4] The ould Colonel, he got 50 hags of poles off a quarter acre, and sold them for three pounds a hag.

10. Brushwood, hedge, low bushy wood cut for firewood.

Sc. The lesser branches used for fire-wood after the trees are felled for carpentering, sometimes Auld hag (JAM.); Give me some of that hag, MILLER My Schools (1879) iv. Frf. The fresh young sprouts, that took the place of the old tangled 'hagg,' after the purifying flames had passed over it, INGLIS Ain Flk. (1895) 15. ne.Yks.[1] Wor. In common use in connexion with the divisions of underwood, N. & Q. (1887) 7th S. iii. 35.

Hence (1) **Hag-road**, (2) **-way**, sb. a path or way cut through the undergrowth of a wood.

(1) Der. We mun cut a hag-rooad thro t'underbrush, maister, N. & Q. (1878) 5th S. ix. 515. (2) s.Lin. Used by keepers, beaters, and sportsmen to signify the narrow winding paths that are cut through the undergrowth of a wood to allow the shooters to get at the game, ib. (1886) 7th S. ii. 366. Rut. ib. (1878) 5th S. ix. 68; Rut.[1] Used by the beaters when engaged in driving game.

11. Comp. (1) **Hag-snar(e**, the stub left in the ground from which coppice-wood has been cut; the stump of a tree; (2) **-staff**, a rod used to mark the boundary of a fall of timber; (3) **-wood**, a copse or wood fitted for having a regular cutting of trees in it.

(1) n.Yks.[1 2 4] ne.Yks.[1] At Linton-on-Ouse there are two contiguous fields called 'Thag' and 'Snahry clooas.' e.Yks. MARSHALL Rur. Econ. (1796) II. 324. n.Lin.[1] The perpendicular end or stump of the thorn at the surface of the ground after the upper portion has been partially divided and laid horizontally. (2) ne.Lan.[1] War. BAKER Gl. (1854). (3) Bwk. Ancient oak forests . . . which have grown into a kind of copse, or what is termed in Scotland hag-woods, Agric. Surv. 33ª (JAM.).

12. Phr. clear the hag, clear all out of the way. Gall. MACTAGGART Encycl. (1824) 251, ed. 1876.

[1. Degrader une forest, to hagge, or fell it all down, COTGR.; Ɖai . . . hurlit Ɖurgh the hard maile, hagget the lere, Dest. Troy (c. 1400) 10023. ON. höggva, to hew.]

HAG, v.[2] Lin. Hmp. Dev. [ag, æg.] 1. To pull, draw; to drag out.

Lin. (R.E.C.) s.Lin. Hag your money out (l.W.). s.Hmp. Tripped him up . . . wi' hagging at a rope, VERNEY L. Lisle (1870) xxv. Dev. Missis, I've abin awver tü Mr. Broom's, an' 'ad out my tüthe, an' 'e hagged tü 'n zo I thort 'e 'd abroked my jaw, HEWETT Peas. Sp. (1892).

2. To rob, take.

Lin. There was a nest there, but some one has hagged it (R.E.C.).

HAG, v.[3] Nhb.[1] [hag.] Of the moon: to wane.

HAG, *adj.* Dev. [æg.] Haggard.

She looks very hag since her trouble, *Reports Provinc.* (1889).

HAGA, see Hag, *sb.*²

HAG·A·BAG, *sb.* *Obs.* Sc. 1. A stout linen fabric, huckaback.

n.Sc. Properly cloth made wholly of tow for the use of the kitchen (JAM.). Baff. Thro' lawn hagabag her breast did keek, TAYLOR *Poems* (1787) 76. Lnk. Clean hag-a-bag I'll spread upon his board, RAMSAY *Gentle Shep.* (1725) 37, ed. 1783.

2. Refuse of any kind. n.Sc. (JAM.)

HAG·ABOUT, *sb.* Yks. [a·g·əbȧt.] An idle, lounging fellow.

w.Yks. He wor what is knone be that strong, but foorcibul wurd, a hag-a-baate, TIFFAMY *Yks. Tyke's Ann.* (1872) 35.

HAG·A·KNOWE, *sb.* Lan. Also written haggoknow. An ungainly blockhead.

Wot could we do wi sitch haggoknows as these i' Bowton ? STATON *B. Shuttle*, 34 ; Sit to deawn, thae gawmbless hag-a-knowe, or aw'll kom thi yure for tho, WAUGH *Ben an' th' Bantam*, v ; Lan.¹

HAGAL, HAGALEF, see Haggle, *sb.*¹, Hogalif.

HAGASTED, *adj.* Sh.I. Familiarized with a particular place by a long stay in it. S. & Ork.¹

HAG·BERRY, *sb.* Sc. Nhb. Dur. Cum. Wm. Yks. Lan. e.Cy. Hmp. Also in forms eck-berry Cum.¹ ; egg-Cum.¹ n.Yks.¹ w.Yks.¹ ; hack- Sc. (JAM.) Nhb.¹ e.Cy. Hmp. ; hacker- Nhb.¹ ; heck- N.Cy.¹ Nhb.¹ Lakel.¹ Dur.¹ Cum.¹ Wm.n.n.Yks. m.Yks.¹ w.Yks.¹ ; heg- Nhb.¹ Cum. Wm. ; hic- Wm. 1. The fruit and tree of the bird-cherry, *Prunus Padus*.

Per. On the banks of the Lunan, there is a shrub here called the hack-berry . . . that carries beautiful flowers which are succeeded by a cluster of fine blackberries, *Statist. Acc.* IX. 239 (JAM.). Lnk. While hagberry and bourtree bushes shelter the gardens from intrusive sheep, FRASER *Whaups* (1895) i. N.Cy.¹, Nhb.¹, Lakel.¹, Dur.¹, s.Dur. (J.E.D.) Cum. From its growth in hedges ; though children at Langwathby used to say, 'We caw them hegberries because they heg our teeth,' i. e. set the teeth on edge (B. & H.) ; Cum.¹ Wm. (J.H.) ; The heckberry trees . . . caught and emphasised the golden rays, WARD *R. Elsmere* (1888) 28, 11th ed. n.Yks. (W.H.), n.Yks.¹⁴, ne.Yks.¹ w.Yks. WILLAN *List Wds.* (1811) ; (J.T.) ; w.Yks.¹, Lan.¹, ne.Lan.¹, e.Cy., Hmp. (B. & H.)

2. The wild service, *Pyrus torminalis.* m.Yks.¹

[1. Dan. *hæggebær*, Norw. dial. *hæggjebær* (AASEN) ; ON. *heggr*, the bird-cherry (VIGFUSSON).]

HAGDOWN, *sb.* I.Ma. The greater shearwater, *Puffinus major.* SWAINSON *Birds* (1885) 212.

HAGEL, see Haggle, *v.*²

HAGER, *sb.* Cor.² Ugly, deformed, rough ; fierce, cruel, evil.

[OCor. *hager* (WILLIAMS).]

HAGERY, *adj.* Sh.I. Also in form haegry. Of worsted : rough, short in the fibre.

Dey widna luk at him [it] becaas dey tought he wis made o' hagery wirsit, *Sh. News* (June 12, 1897) ; 'Lass, I tinks hit's [worsted] haegry !' . . 'Haegry!.. Hit's a corne o' lambs 'oo', man, an' hit wis awful short,' *ib.* (Oct. 8, 1898).

HAGES, *sb.* Sc. A disguised form of the word 'Jesus,' used in petty oaths.

Lnk. By hages! Jean, it's weel kent aboot the raws that ye wear the breeks, GORDON *Pyotshaw* (1885) 21.

HAGESTER; see Hagister.

HAG(G, *sb.*¹ Nhb. Cum. Wm. Yks. Lan. Lin. Shr. [h)ag.] A wooded enclosure ; a wood, copse.

n.Cy. At Aukland Castle, the park was formerly called the Hagg (K.) ; N.Cy.¹ *Gen.* one into which cattle are admitted. Nhb.¹ Cum.¹ A woody place intermixed with grass land. A wooded hill. Wm. (J.H.), n.Yks.¹²⁴ e.Yks. Originally, perhaps, the woodland set apart, by the lord of the soil, for fuel for his tenants ; many woods yet retain the name of hags, and one wood, in Sinnington, that of ' poor folks hags,' MARSHALL *Rur. Econ.* (1796). m.Yks.¹ w.Yks.¹ A hanging wood ; w.Yks.² A hag of hollin was the holly trees growing upon a certain portion of ground in the commons of the manor of Sheffield ; w.Yks.⁴, Lan.¹, ne.Lan.¹ Lin. (W.W.S.). Used only as a proper name for a wood (R.E.C.). Shr.¹ There is a farm called the Hag a few miles south of Bridgnorth, in the parish of Highley ; Shr.²

[He led me over holts and hags, FAIRFAX *Tasso* (1600)

viii. xli. A form of OE. *haga*, an enclosure (EARLE *Charters*), lit. E. *haw.*]

HAG(G, *sb.*² Sc. Nhb. Cum. Wm. Yks. Lin. Rut. Nhp. e.An. Also in form hack Sc. (JAM.) [h)ag, æg.] 1. A rock or cliff ; an abrupt, cliffy prominence.

Nhb.¹ n.Yks.¹ ; n.Yks.² Built on the face of the hag ; n.Yks.⁴, m.Yks.¹

2. Wild, broken ground ; rocky moorland ; a common, waste.

Gall. Down heuchs and craigs—and glens and hags, As fast as he cud flee, MACTAGGART *Encycl.* (1824) 24, ed. 1876 ; Hags—Rocky moor ground ; Rocky, mossy, black wilds, *ib.* 251. n.Yks.¹ Such as may be met with in boggy, and therefore uncultivated, lands. w.Yks. The strongest nag that crosses th' hagg Wi' wots to Fullod mill, SENIOR *Smithy Rhymes* (1882a) 46 ; w.Yks.¹²

3. A piece of soft bog in a moor or morass ; a break in a 'moss' or bog from which peats have been cut. Also called Moss-hag, Peat-hag, and in *comp.* Hag-moss.

Sc. Tearing thro' moss and hagg, SCOTT *Abbot* (1820) xvii ; That part in mosses which is naturally or artificially cut, hollowed, hagged, or hacked ; naturally by water runlets forming hollows, and artificially by, among other means, the cutting and removal of peat, *N. & Q.* (1874) 5th S. ii. 253. Per. The murky flag Flaps on Turftenant's rushy hag, SPENCE *Poems* (1898) 189. Dmb. I had made sure To find him in the hag o' Coars-Neuk Moor, SALMON *Gowodean* (1868) 49. Slg. The summit and back part is a deep muir ground, interspersed with moss hags, *Statist. Acc.* XV. 317 (JAM.). Ayr. Sendin' the stuff o'er muirs an' hags Like drivin' wrack, BURNS *Ep. to J. Lapraik* (Sept. 13, 1785) st. 2. Lnk. Now a splash would be heard, followed by a roar, as some luckless wight fell into a moss hagg, FRASER *Whaups* (1895) 119. Edb. A deep peat moss, broken into hags and hillocks, PENNECUIK *Wks.* (1715) 116, ed. 1815. Peb. Wi' a divot's weight Ta'en from mossy hag, *Lintoun Green* (1685) 39, ed. 1817. Slk. I was crossing frae Loch Ericht fit to the heid o' Glenorchy, and got in among the hags, CHR. NORTH *Noctes* (ed. 1856) II. 405. Rxb. *N. & Q.* (1874) 5th S. ii. 115. Dmf. Instead o' hag moss beat wi' sleet, Were miles on miles, rich holms o' wheat, SHAW *Schoolmaster* (1899) 369. Kcb. 'Mang our clints and hags and rashy bogs Chiels do appear would claw a fallow's lugs, ELDER *Borgue* (1897) 33. N.Cy.¹ Nhb. Right yaul they hag ower bagg and syke, GRAHAM *Moorland Dial.* (1826) 5 ; (R.O.H.) Cum. (M.P.), Wm. (J.H.), n.Yks.²⁸ Lin. STREATFEILD *Lin. and Danes* (1884) 334. n.Lin.¹ Ther's many a hoss hes been lost e' them peät moor hags. sw.Lin.¹ If you get into one of them hags, there is no getting out.

Hence Haggy, *adj.* full of 'hags,' rough, broken, boggy.

Dmb. The fec o't thrivin' moss and haggie wood, SALMON *Gowodean* (1868) 70. Lnk. He thocht he had yet tae cross A haggy, benty, splashy moss, THOMSON *Musings* (1881) 62. n.Yks.⁴ Lin. A bad highway is said to be 'strange and haggy,' *N. & Q.* (1874) 5th S. i. 311. Nhp.¹ Applied to any coarse rough uneven ground. Most used in a woodland district. e.An.¹ Suf. Applied to the broken and uneven surface of the soil when in a moist state, RAINBIRD *Agric.* (1819) 294, ed. 1849. e.Suf. (F.H.)

4. A water-hollow or channel, wet in winter and dry in summer. Sc. *N. & Q.* (1874) 5th S. ii. 253.

5. A muddy hollow, a deep hole in a rut.

Lin. *N. & Q.* (1873) 5th S. i. 311. sw.Lin.¹ The road was full of hags.

6. A stiff clump of coarse grass ; an islet of grass in the midst of a bog.

Sc. He led a small and shaggy nag, That through a bog, from hag to hag, Could bound like stag, SCOTT *Last Minstrel* (ed. 1847) c. iv. st. 5. Rut.¹ 'How did you get on with the mowing ?' 'Very well, sir, if it wunt for them hags ; they do turn the scythe so.'

[8. (The castle) es hy sett apon a cragg Gray and hard, widuten hagg, *Cursor M.* (c. 1340) 9886.]

HAG(G, *sb.*³ Fif. [hag.] 1. A stall-fed ox. MORTON *Cyclo. Agric.* (1863). 2. One who tends fat cattle. COLVILLE *Vernacular* (1899) 19.

HAG(G, *v.*¹ and *sb.*⁴ Sc. Irel. Yks. Lan. Chs. Der. Not. Lin. Lei. Nhp. War. Shr. Glo. Oxf. Brks. Bdf. Ken. Sus. Wil. Som. Dev. Cor. Also in forms ag m.Yks.¹ w.Som.¹ ; agg w.Yks. Lan.¹ Chs.¹²³ Der. n.Lin.¹ Nhp.¹ Glo. Bdf. Sus. Wil.¹ Dev.¹ Cor.¹ [h)ag, æg.] 1. *v.* To incite, urge ; to try to persuade ; to 'egg' ; to excite to quarrel ; to provoke, irritate.

w.Yks. Lucas *Stud. Nidderdale* (c. 1882) 229. **Chs.** She keeps agging me for t'buy it. They kept agging them on to fight (E.M.G.) ; **Chs.¹²⁸** Lei.¹ Doon't ye hagg him on. **Sus.** Holloway. **Wil.¹** n.Dev. Grose (1790) ; *Monthly Mag.* (1808) II. 421. Cor. Thomas *Randigal Rhymes* (1895) *Gl.* ; Cor.¹

2. To worry, tease ; to ' gnag ' at.

Wxf. And my ould thief of a measther, tattheration to him ! hagging, hagging, till he'll have the very flesh wasted off of our bones, Kennedy *Banks Boro* (1867) 243. **m.Yks.¹ w.Yks.** Shoe was a roof kind iv a woman, an' 'er 'usband wor fair hagged to 'is graive (F.P.T.). **Lan.¹** Thae'rt aulus aggin' at mi. **Der.** Yo keep aggin and teasin', Ward *David Grieve* (1892) I. viii. **Lin.** He said he was only agging me, *N. & Q.* (1880) 6th S. ii. 485. **sw.Lin.¹** I've hagged at her such a mess o' times about it. **War.** The old lady and all the family hagged me to death, *Times* (Dec. 19, 1889) 6, col. 6. **Shr.²** Glo. Baylis *Illus. Dial.* (1870) ; (F.H.) **Bdf.** (J.W.B.) **w.Som.¹** Her'll ag anybody out o' their life, her will. **Dev.¹** Iv her was to begin to aggie way en there wid be no hod, 5. **n.Dev.** Thy skin oll vlagged with nort bet agging, *Exm. Scold.* (1746) l. 75.

3. To haggle, dispute, argue.

Nhp.¹, War.², Glo.¹ Dev. When they beginn'th tū haggee I turns tail and urn'th 'ome, Hewett *Peas. Sp.* (1892).

4. To fatigue, tire out, ' fag.'

m.Yks.¹ I was sore hagged with going. Hagging at it [toiling at it]. **w.Yks.²** Shoo fair hags hersen. He wur fair hagged up. **e.Lan.¹** Not. I'm hagged to death (J.H.B.). **sw.Lin.¹** I'm quiet hagged out. It bothers me, and hags me to dead. **Lei.¹** I've walked all the way, and don't want to come again, it's so hagging. It's very haggin' when you'n no servants. **Nhp.¹²** Wil.¹ Her've a had a lot to contend wi' to-year, and her's hagged to death wi't aal.

Hence (1) **Hagged** or **Haggit**, *ppl. adj.* tired, worn out ; harassed, careworn, thin ; (2) **Haggey**, *adj.*, (3) **Hagging**, *ppl. adj.* tiring, fatiguing.

(1) Sc. Wi' haggit ee, and haw as death, The auld spae-man did stand, Jamieson *Pop. Ballads* (1806) I. 235. **w.Yks.¹, Chs.¹⁸** nw.Der.¹ **s.Lin.** How hagged the poor o'd wench looked (T.H.R.). **Shr.¹** Poor Nancy Poppet looks despert 'aggit, as if 'er worked 'ard an' far'd 'ard. Oxf.¹ *MS. add.* **Brks.¹** Thee look'st hagged at times, and folk 'll see't, and talk about thee afore long, Hughes *T. Brown Oxf.* (1861) xviii ; Brks.¹ **Ken.** Why dis here wall It looks sa old and hagged, Masters *Dick and Sal* (c. 1821) st. 48 ; **Ken.¹** ' They did look so very old and hagged ' ; spoken of some maiden ladies. **n.Wil.** He looks sort o' hagged, dwont ee ! (E.H.G.) (2) **Nhp.²** ' A haggey road,' i. e. one that is tiring to the horses. (3) **Nhp.¹** It was a hagging job for the horse, he had such a heavy load to draw.

5. In *pass.* with *about* : to be buffeted about, treated unkindly.

w.Yks. Nout macks ma war mad ner ta see tway at a poor fellah is agged abaht if he appears ta be dahn a bit, *Bill Hoylhus Ends Alm.* (1873).

6. *sb.* A worry, trouble, burden ; a difficulty.

Chs.¹ If one tries to persuade another against his will it would be said, ' I got him to go at last but I'd a regular hag with him.' **s.Chs.¹** n.Lin.¹ ' That's a soor agg ' is a common expression to indicate a teasing circumstance. **sw.Lin.¹** The child's a great hag to her. It's a hag, carrying it all that way.

Hence **Hag-stop**, *sb.* weariness ; a stoppage, dilemma.

Lin.¹ I never had such a hag-stop before.

7. A task, job, an allotted portion of work ; esp. in phr. *to work by the hag,* to do piece-work in contradistinction to day-work.

n.Cy. (Hall.), Lan.¹ **ne.Lan.¹** I wark be t'hag, an' net be t'day. **Chs.¹²⁸ s.Chs.¹** They'n tayn the wheeat by hagg an they bin gooin' to butty o'er it (s.v. Butty). **nw.Der.¹** A rough hag ; a tough hag, Nhp.¹ An allotted portion of manual labour on the soil ; as digging, draining, embanking, &c. ' Have you done your agg !' Shr.¹ I'm on'y doin' a bit of a 'ag fur owd Tummas ; **Shr.²** On by the hagg. Glo.¹

Hence (1) **Hag-master**, *sb.* an overseer or contractor ; (2) -work, *sb.* piece-work.

(1) Chs.¹², s.Chs.¹ Nhp.¹ One who contracts for the completion of a specific work or portion of work, at a stipulated price, employing others to execute it under his superintendence. (2) Chs.¹², s.Chs.¹, Shr.²

8. One who does another's tasks, a drudge.

w.Yks. Ah think thi nont [aunt] is 't'hag fer ye o' (B.K.). **e.Lin.** A place or situation which is hard to fill to the employer's satisfaction, is called a hag's plaάce (J.C.W.).

HAG(G, *sb.⁵* Wm. Yks. [h]ag.] A hedge or fence. See Hay, *sb.²*

Wm. (J.H.) **e.Yks.** Cole *Place Names* (1879) 33.

HAG(G, *v.²* Sc. Also in form **haig** (Jam.). [hag.] Of cattle : to butt with the head, to fight.

Mry. You may see the elf-bull haiging with the strongest bull or ox in the herd, *N. Antiq.* (1814) 404 (Jam.). Bnff.¹

Hence **Haggin,** *ppl. adj.* given to butting with the head. **Bnff.¹** She's a haggin' brute o' a coo, that.

HAGG, HAGGA, see Hag, *v.,* Hag, *sb.²*

HAGGADAY, *sb.* Yks. Lin. Nrf. Also in form hago-day Nrf. [h]a'gədē.] 1. A latch to a door or gate.

Yks. (Hall.) **n.Lin.¹** A haggaday is frequently put upon a cottage door on the inside, without anything projecting outwards by which it may be lifted. A little slit is made in the door, and the latch can only be raised by inserting therein a nail or slip of metal. ' Old men alus calls them wooden snecks wheáre you hev to put yer finger thrif a roond hoάle e' th' door to oppen 'em, haggadays.'

2. A sanctuary ring-knocker.

Nrf. Jessopp *Hist. of St. Gregory's Church* (1886) 10 ; In the church of St. Gregory, Norwich, is a large antique knocker for use by persons seeking sanctuary. This is called a ' hagoday,' *N. & Q.* (1894) 8th S. vi. 188.

[1. An haguday, *vectes, Cath. Angl.* (1483).]

HAGGAGE, *sb.* Som. Dev. Also written **hagage** Dev. ; **hageg-** n.Dev. [æ·gidg.] A term of reproach for a woman, a ' baggage ' ; an untidy, slatternly woman.

w.Som.¹ Dev. Dawnt 'a' nort tū zay tū thickee slammicking gert haggage ! Hewett *Peas. Sp.* (1892). **n.Dev.** *Horae Subsecivae* (1777) 197 ; What disyease than ya gurt haggage, *Exm. Scold.* (1746) l. 27. nw.Dev.¹

Hence (1) **Hagegy,** *adj.* untidy, slovenly ; loose ; (2) **Haggaging,** (a) *adj.,* see (1) ; (b) *sb.* a term of reproach for a woman.

(1) n.Dev. If ha lov'th jakes, why let un beckon Hagegy Bess, Rock *Jim an' Nell* (1867) st. 89. (2, a) w.Som.¹ Dev. A chittering, raving, rixy, lonching, haggaging moil, Madox-Brown *Dwale Bluth* (1876) bk. i. i ; A servant-girl describes another girl as ' very good to work, but very hagagin',' *Reports Provinc.* (1891) ; Dev.¹ The very daps of her mother,—another such a haggagen, maundering, hawk-a-mouth'd trub, 7 ; Dev.² Jane Ley's a cruel haggagin' body. n.Dev. A buzzom-chuck'd haggaging moyle, *Exm. Crishp.* (1746) l. 502. (b) Dev. Calling her could witch an' haggaging as they did ... had crossed her mind a bit, Madox-Brown *Yeth-hounds* (1876) 251.

HAGGAN, *sb. Obs.* Cum. A kind of pudding ; see below. Cf. **haggis.**

Sometimes fruit, suet, and the minced entrails of a sheep, and sometimes only oatmeal, suet, and sugar boiled in the large gut of a sheep (J.L.) (1783).

HAGGAR, *adj.* Yks. [Not known to our correspondents.] Wild, untamed. (Hall.)

HAGGARD, *sb.* Sc. Irel. I.Ma. Cth. Pem. ? w.Cy. Also in forms **haggart** Sc. (Jam.) Wxf. I.Ma. Pem. ; **hag-yard** Sc. N.I.¹ [h]a·gəd, -әt.] A stack-yard.

Gall. Mactaggart *Encycl.* (1824) 251, ed. 1876. Keb., Wgt. (Jam.) Ir. The master wasn't in the haggard, Carleton *Fardorougha* (1836) 78. **N.I.¹** Uls. An enclosed place near the farm-house (M.B.-S.). Lns. The corn [was] all safe in the haggard, Croker *Leg.* (1862) 242. Wxf. A haggart with hay-ricks and corn-stacks, Kennedy *Evenings Duffrey* (1869) 62. I.Ma. Searched ... every place on the farm, and the haggart and pokin every stack, Brown *Doctor* (1887) 70 ; They crossed the haggard, .. she scattering great handfuls of oats, Caine *Manxman* (1894) pt. ii. viii. Cth. (W.W.S.), Pem. (E.D.) **s.Pem.** Laws *Little Eng.* (1888) 420. ? w.Cy. (Hall.)

Hence **Haggard-mows,** *sb.* mows in the stack-yard, not in the field. Cth. (W.W.S.)

[ON. *hey-garðr,* a stack-yard (Vigfusson).]

HAGGART, *sb.* Lth. (Jam.) [Not known to our correspondents.] An old useless horse.

HAGGEL, HAGGEN, see Haggle, *sb.¹,* *v.¹²,* Hoggan, *sb.¹*

HAGGER, *v.¹* and *sb.¹* Sc. [ha·gər.] 1. *v.* To cut roughly and unevenly, to hack, mangle. Bch., s.Sc. (Jam.) See Hack, *v.¹*

Hence (1) **Haggeran,** *vbl. sb.* the act of cutting in a rough manner. Bnff.¹ ; (2) **Hagger'd,** *ppl. adj.* unevenly cut, mangled, full of notches. Bch., s.Sc. (Jam.)

2. *sb.* A large cut, esp. one with a ragged edge.

Bnff.[1] 'A've gien ma finger a great hagger wee a knife.' 'He took a bullax and ga' the tree a hagger half-through.'

Hence **Haggeral,** *sb.* a very large cut ; an open, festering sore. *ib.*

HAGGER, *v.*[2] and *sb.*[2] n.Cy. Nhb. Yks. Also written **haggar** N.Cy.[1] ; and in form **heggr** Nhb. [h)a·gə(r.]

1. *v.* To 'beggar' ; in games 'of marbles, &c. : to win all an opponent's marbles, &c., to 'clear out.' *Gen.* used in *pp.*

Nhb. In Hexham when a boy has lost all his marbles or cherry-stones, he is said to be heggr'd, *N. & Q.* (1871) 4th S. viii. 304 ; *ib.* 407 ; Nhb.[1] He wis fair hagger't.

2. *sb. pl.* A term in marbles ; see below.

Nhb. The loser [in a game of marbles] usually asks the winner to give him one back for his heggrs, *N. & Q.* (1871) 4th S. viii. 304.

3. *Comb.* Hagger-maker's shop, a public-house. N.Cy.[1], Nhb.[1], Yks. (HALL.)

HAGGER, *v.*[3] and *sb.*[3] Ags. (JAM.) [Not known to our correspondents.] **1.** *v.* To rain gently. **2.** *sb.* A fine small rain.

HAGGER, *v.*[4] Wil.[1] [æ·gə(r.] Of the teeth : to chatter with cold. Cf. hacker, *v.* 4.

HAGGERDASH, *sb.* and *adv.* Sc. Also in form **haggerdecash** Ags. (JAM.) **1.** *sb.* Disorder ; a broil. Lnk. (JAM.) **2.** *adv.* In confusion, in a disorderly state, topsy-turvy. Ags., Cld. (*ib.*)

HAGGERIN, *ppl. adj.* Lth. (JAM.) [Not known to our correspondents.] In phr. *haggerin and swaggerin*, in an indifferent state of health ; *fig.* unprosperous in business.

HAGGERSNASH, *sb.* and *adj.* Sc. [Not known to our correspondents.] **1.** *sb.* Offals. n.Sc. (JAM.) **2.** *Fig.* A spiteful person. Ayr. (*ib.*) **3.** *adj.* Spiteful, sharp.

Ayr. I maun lea' them to spaing athort their tapseltirie taun-trums an' haggersnash pilgatings upo' some hairum-skairum rattle-scull, *Edb. Mag.* (Apr. 1821) 351 (*ib.*).

HAGGERTY, *adj.* Sc. Also written **haggarty** Frf. [ha·gərti.] In *comb.* (1) **Haggerty-tag,** in an untidy, ragged manner ; (2) **-tag-like,** (3) **-taggerty,** ragged, tattered, ragamuffin.

(1, a) n.Sc. (JAM.) (3) *ib.* Frf. This haggarty-taggarty Egyptian, BARRIE *Minister* (1891) xiv.

HAGGILS, *sb. pl.* Fif. (JAM.) In phr. *in the haggils*, in trammels.

HAGGIS, *sb.* and *v.* Sc. Nhb. Cum. Yks. Lan. War. Shr. Glo. Also in forms **haggas** Nhb. n.Yks. ; **haggass(e** Nhb. ; **haggies** Sc. Lan. ; **haggise** Sc. ; **haggish** Sc. N.Cy.[1] Nhb.[1] Cum. ; **haggus** n.Cy. Lan.[1] Glo.[1] ; **heygus** Lan.[1] [h)a·gis, æ·gis.] **1.** *sb.* A dish, *gen.* consisting of the lungs, heart, and liver of a sheep, minced with suet, onions, &c., and cooked in a sheep's maw.

Sc. It ill sets a haggis to be roasted, RAMSAY *Prov.* (1737) ; I hope he'll get a haggis to his dinner, SCOTT *Bride of Lam.* (1819) xviii. Bch. Like an ill-scraped haggis, FORBES *Jrn.* (1742) 2. Abd. I left my mither To cook the haggis, COCK *Strains* (1810) I. 120. w.Sc. Gif a' your hums and ha's were hams and haggises, the parish o' Kippen needna fear a dearth, CARRICK *Laird of Logan* (1835) 172. Dmb. A table bent wi' cheer . . . Haggis aboon and mutton at the foot, SALMON *Gowodean* (1868) 108. Rnf. [I] set some haggis down afore, I trow the smell o't didna shore, PICKEN *Poems* (1813) I. 62. Ayr. Not forgetting the savoury sonsy haggis, GALT *Entail* (1823) vii. Lnk. On the haggies Elspa spares nae cost, RAMSAY *Gentle Shep.* (1725) 44, ed. 1783. Lth. A sonsey haggis, reeking, rose Fu' proudly in the centre, BRUCE *Poems* (1813) II. 65. Edb. A haggis fat Weel tottled in a seything pat, FERGUSSON *Poems* (1773) 186, ed. 1785. Bwk. Mountalban for a haggis ; Lamington for tea, HENDERSON *Pop. Rhymes* (1856) 23. Slk. If I would . . . take a share of a haggis wi' them, HOGG *Tales* (1838) 151, ed. 1866. Rxb. A very singular superstition in regard to this favourite dish prevails in Rxb. and perhaps in other southern counties. As it is a nice piece of cookery to boil a haggis, without suffering it to burst in the pot and run out, the only effectual antidote known is nominally to commit it to the keeping of some male who is generally supposed to bear antlers on his brow. When the cook puts it into the pot, she says, 'I gie this to—such a one—to keep' (JAM.) ; A good fat haggies, if his purse can spare it, RUICKBIE *Wayside Cottager* (1807) 73. Dmf. Mony a haggis that reeked an' swat,

THOM *Jock o' Knowe* (1878) 39. Wgt. It was only a haggish, an A think ee needna mak' sae muckle din aboot it. FRASER *Wigtown* (1877) 363. n.Cy. *Border Gl.* (Coll. L.L.B.) ; N.Cy.[1] Nhb. GROSE (1790) ; Like the first puffe of a haggasse, RICHARDSON *Borderer's Table-bk.* (1846) VI. 309 ; Nhb.[1] Tripe minced small. Cum. Sometimes fruit, suet, and the minced entrails of a sheep, and sometimes only oatmeal, suet, and sugar, boiled in the large gut of a sheep. It was till lately the common custom to have this dish to breakfast every Christmas day, and some part of the family sat up all night to have it ready at an early hour. It is now used at dinner on the same day (J.L.) (1783) ; We'd stew'd geuse and haggish, ANDERSON *Ballads* (ed. 1808) 173 ; Cum.[1] A pudding of mincemeat for eating with potatoes on Christmas day. Lan. Her food . . . was haggis, made of boil'd groats, mixed with thyme or parsley, HARLAND & WILKINSON *Flk-Lore* (1867) 207 ; Lan.[1] Pottage made of herbs e.Lan.[1] A pudding of herbs.

2. *Comp.* (1) **Haggis-bag,** the maw of a sheep in which the haggis is cooked ; *fig.* a windbag, a contemptuous term for anything ; (2) **-feast,** a feast or meal consisting of haggis ; (3) **-fed,** fed upon haggis ; (4) **-headed,** soft-headed, foolish, stupid ; (5) **-heart,** a soft, cowardly heart ; (6) **-kail,** the water in which a haggis is cooked ; (7) **-meat,** minced and seasoned tripe ; (8) **-supper,** a supper consisting of haggis ; (9) **-wife,** a woman who sells minced and seasoned tripe.

(1) Sc. It is more like an empty haggis-bag than ony thing else, *Blackw. Mag.* (Sept. 1819) 677 (JAM.). Dmb. 'Principles ! haggis bags !' exclaimed the lady, CROSS *Disruption* (1844) v. (2) Nhb. Aw'd suener hev a haggish feast, Or drink wi' skipper Morgan, ALLAN *Tyneside Sngs.* (1891) 333. (3) Ayr. But saith the rustic, haggis-fed, BURNS *To a Haggis* (1787) st. 7. (4) Edb. Bring haggis-headed William Younger, PENNECUIK *Wks.* (1715) 412, ed. 1815. (5) Edb. His haggis heart it fills Wi' grief, FORBES *Poems* (1812) 40. (6) Bnff. Wi' puddin broe or haggies kail, Or something maks a battin meal, TAYLOR *Poems* (1787) 52. (7) Nhb. Aw got tired o' sellin' haggish meat, BAGNALL *Sngs.* (c. 1850) 26 ; Ov sheep's feet then we hev a feed, An' haggish meat an' aw, man, *ib.* 23 ; Nhb.[1] (8) Sc. A wis at a haggis supper that nicht, *Jokes*, and S. (1889) 36. (9) Nhb. Whaiv haggish wives wi' tubs an' knives, ROBSON *Evangeline* (1870) 343.

3. The paunch, belly. Cf. **hag,** *sb.*[4]

Lnk. John goes to the amry and lays to the haggies, till his ain haggies cou'd had nae mair, GRAHAM *Writings* (1883) II. 210. Feb. Ned wi' his haggise toom Sall's stringless coats, as fast 's he dow, Geed back, *Lintoun Green* (1685) 62, ed. 1817. n.Cy. GROSE (1790). Lan. *ib.* MS. add. (C.) ; Lan.[1]

4. The smaller entrails or 'chitterlings' of a calf. War.[2], Shr.[1], Glo.[1]

5. Phr. *to cool one's haggas*, to beat one soundly.

n.Cy. GROSE (1790). n.Yks. Ile coul thy haggas, bitch, if I begin, MERITON *Praise Ale* (1684) l. 76 ; (K.)

6. *Fig.* A term of contempt applied to a lumpish, unwieldy person ; a soft, 'pudding-headed' person ; a 'baggage.'

Dmf. The lazy haggises! CARLYLE *Lett.* (1886) II. 28. N.Cy.[1], Nhb.[1]

7. *v.* In boxing : to bruise, cut up, 'do for' ; *fig.* to scatter, spread abroad.

Nhb. Come up to the Scratch ! or, the Pitman haggish'd, ROBSON *Sngs. of Tyne* (1849) 281 ; So wishing trade may brisker be, An' fuels aw haggished owre the sea, *ib.* 295 ; By gox, 'fore aw's duen ye'll be haggished eneuf, *ib. Evangeline* (1870) 347 ; Nhb.[1]

[1. Haggas a podyng, *caliette de mouton*, PALSGR. (1530) ; Hagws of a schepe. Take the roppis with þe talowe & parboyle hem ; þan hakke hem smal, *Cookery Bk.* (c. 1430), ed. Austin, 39.]

HAGGLE, *sb.*[1] Chs. Hmp. I.W. Wil. Dor. Dev. Cor. Also written **hagal** I.W. ; **haggel** Cor. ; **haggil** Hmp.[1] ; **hagl·** Cor. ; and in forms **agald** Wil.[1] ; **aggle** Dev. nw.Dev.[1] ; **agle** Chs. Cor.[12] ; **awgl·** Cor.[12] ; **haigle** n.Dev. ; **hail, hayel** Dor. ; **orgl·** Cor.[1] [a·gl, æ·gl.] A haw, the fruit of the hawthorn, *Crataegus Oxyacantha* ; also in *comp.* **Haggle-berry.** See **Hag,** *sb.*[2] Cf. **eggle-berry.**

Chs. (B. & H.), Hmp.[1], n.Hmp. (J.R.W.), I.W., Wil.[1] Dor. *w.Gazette* (Feb. 15, 1889) 7, col. 1. Dev. A farmer informs me that the saying : 'Many aggles, Many cradles,' is frequently added to the better-known sayings : 'Many nits, Many pits ; Many slones, Many groans,' *Reports Provinc.* (1893) ; *Horae Subsecivae* (1777) 198. n.Dev. Sloans, bullans, and haigles be about, ROCK *Jim an' Nell*

367) st. 12.   nw.Dev.[1]   Cor. Housen and shops so thick as haggel, REGRLLAB *Tales* (1867) 67; Cor.[128]

Hence (1) **Hagglan, Aglon, Awglon,** or **Orglon,** *sb.* a aw; (2) -tree, *sb.* a hawthorn tree.

(1) Cor. Her lips were red as hagglons, THOMAS *Randigal Rymes* (1895) 11; Cor.[12] (2) Cor. The lizamamoo and the ggas grew under the hagglan-tree, THOMAS *Randigal Rhymes* 895) 15.

HAGGLE, *sb.*[2]   Sh.I.   [ha·gl.]   A subordinate division- ark between districts.   S. & Ork.[1]

HAGGLE, *v.*[1] and *sb.*[3]   Var. dial. and colloq. uses in . Irel. and Eng.   Also written haggel Cum.[2]; hagil Sc. AM.); hagle Lan. Glo.; and in forms aggle w.Yks.[5] an. Nhp.[1] Bdf. n.Bck. Wil.[1]; haigel Sc.; haigle Sc. hb.[1]; heggle Sus.[1]   [h)a·gl, æ·gl.]   l. *v.* To cut awk- ardly or unevenly, to hack, mangle; to bungle.   See ag, *v.*[1]

Fif. (JAM.) Ayr. They may learn at the college to haggle aff a r leg, GALT *Sir A. Wylie* (1822) ciii. Ant. GROSE (1790) *MS.* d. (C.) Cum.[1] Cum.[2] An' he haggelt an' cot at his pultess- each't po', 162. n.Yks.[14] w.Yks. THORESBY *Lett.* (1703) ;. Yks.[24]; w.Yks.[5] ' Luke how thah's aggled that loaf!'   Cloth is ggled ' when the knives of the cutting-machine, or rather the ller on which the knives are fixed, pimp and cut the cloth at ort distances till it is re-arranged. ne.Lan.[1], Chs.[1] s.Chs.[1] Yi m)û aag'l dhû cheyz; taak·it streyt ûfoa·r yi [Ye munna haggle e cheise; tak it streight afore ye]. Not. (J.H.B.), Not.[1], Lin.[1], Lin.[1], Nhp.[1]   Shr.[1] Dunna yo' 'aggle the mate i' that way—I nna bar to see it; Shr.[2]   Glo. BAYLIS *Illus. Dial.* (1870); *Horae ubsecivae* (1777) 198.   Oxf.[1] *MS. add.* Bdf. To cut unevenly, as joint of meat or a loaf of bread (J.W.B.).   Wil. They took out eir knives and haggled the skin off, JEFFERIES *Bevis* (1882) vii; Wil.[1]

Hence (1) **Haggled,** *ppl. adj.* hacked, mangled, mutilated;) **Hagglin,** *ppl. adj.* rash, incautious; (3) **Haggly,** *adj.* ugh, unevenly cut.

(1) Gall. I see thee, little loch. Thou art clear this morning. hou art red at even, and there is a pile of haggled meat by thee, ROCKETT *Raiders* (1894) xiv.   (2) Fif. A hagglin' gomrel (JAM.).) Cld. (JAM.), s.Chs.[1]

2. To dispute, cavil, argue; *esp.* to dispute the terms f a bargain; to chatter; to quarrel, bicker.

Sc. To use a great deal of useless talk in making a bargain, SIB- ALD *Gl.* (JAM.) Abd. Sandy Mutch would not ' haggle ' over a few hillings, ALEXANDER *Ain Flk.* (1882) 107.   Cai.[1]   Per. It wes for ve's sake a' haggled an' schemed, IAN MACLAREN *Auld Lang Syne* 895) 157.   Slk. I . . . baidna langer to haigel, HOGG *Tales* (1838) to, ed. 1866.   N.I.[1], Dur.[1], Cum.[1]   n.Yks. Thoo's allus haggling nd scouding (T.S.); n.Yks.[124], m.Yks.[1]   w.Yks. Their isn't a ainute's peace i' t'house—they're always haggling and jaggling bout something (H.L.); LUCAS *Stud. Nidderdale* (c. 1882) 229; . Yks.[1]   Lan. He's always aggling about something not worth a arthing (S.W.).   ne.Lan.[1], Chs.[1], Not. (W.H.B.), Not.[1], Lin.[1], Lin.[1]   s.Lin. Them two'll haggle ovver nowt by the hour if obody stops 'em (T.H.R.).   War. (J.R.W.); War.[4] What a mon ou be ! you'll haggle for the last farding.   m.Wor. Don't haggle ay more about it (J.C.).   se.Wor. Shr.[1] Yo' wanten to 'aggle, un'ee—yo' bin al'ays ready for cross-pladin'; Shr.[2]   Glo. Wall, ve bided thur and haggled a smart while, BUCKMAN *Darke's Sojourn* 1890) 140; BAYLIS *Illus. Dial.* (1870).   Brks.[1] Sometimes also it used in the sense of ' to hesitate in reply.'   ' A haggled a good bit avoor a'd tell I wher a'd a-bin.'   s.Bck. (A.C.), e.An.[2], Sus.[3], imp.[1]   Dev. *Horae Subsecivae* (1777) 198.   Cor. Mrs. Tucker used p haggle with everybody, PARR *Adam and Eve* (1880) III. 235.

Hence (1) **Haggling,** (*a*) *sb.* a dispute, argument; a pro- onged bargaining; (*b*) *ppl. adj.* vexatious, trying, weari- ome; (2) **Hagil-bargain,** *sb.* one who is difficult to come o terms with in making a bargain, a ' stickler.'

(1, *a*) Frf. ' The chairge is saxpence, Davit,' he shouted.   Then haggling ensued, BARRIE *Licht* (1888) ii.   n.Yks.[2], se.Wor.[1]   (*b*) nff.[1] A term applied by fishermen and sailors to weather, in which he wind dies away during daytime, and springs up towards evening. us.[1]   (*a*) Rxb. SIBBALD *Gl.* (1802) (JAM.).

3. To tease, worry, harass; to over-work, fatigue, re out.

Cum.[1], n.Yks.[14] ne.Lan.[1]   War.[4] What are you haggling our Bess r! Oxf. I get quite haggled, Sir, by the close of the day (W.F.R.); xf.[1] Often applied to energetic preachers. ' 'Ow 'a did 'aggle 'isself.'

Hence **Haggled,** *ppl. adj.* wearied, harassed, worn out. nw.Lin.[1] Poor things, how baggled they look !

VOL. III.

---

4. To advance with difficulty; to do anything with much obstruction, to struggle.

Bwk., Rxb. To carry with difficulty anything that is heavy, cum- bersome, or entangling (JAM.).   Rxb. I hae mair than I can haigle wi'.   My lade is sae sad I can scarcely haigle (*ib.*).   Nhb. Aa could hardly get haigl't through (R.O.H.); Nhb.[1] Here she comes haiglin wi a greet bunch o' sticks.   Lan. Hagglin at th' seck to get hissel out, WAUGH *Old Cronies* (1875) iv.

5. *sb.* A mild dispute; the process of bargaining. s.Wor.[1], Glo. (A.B.)

[1. Suffolk first died : and York, all haggled over, Comes to him, SHAKS. *Hen. V,* IV. vi. 11.   **2.** *Harceler,* to haggle, huck, hedge, or paulter long in the buying of a commodity, COTGR.   **3.** We are so harassed and haggled out in this business, CROMWELL *Lett.* (Aug. 20, 1648).]

HAGGLE, *v.*[2] and *sb.*[4]   n.Cy. Yks. Pem.   Also written hagel s.Pem.; haggel e.Yks.; hagle s.Pem.; and in forms aggle e.Yks.; hag· m.Yks.[1] (h)a·gl.]   1. *v.* To hail.

n.Cy. GROSE (1790); (K.)   n.Yks.[1]; n.Yks.[2] It beeath haggl'd and snaw'd. ne.Yks.[1] It haggled heavy t'last neet. e.Yks. It haggled 't morn, COLES *Place Names* (1879) 30; (Miss A.); e.Yks.[1] We moont gan oot just yit, it's beginnin te haggle.   m.Yks.[1] [RAY (1691).]

2. *sb.* Hail, a hailstone; also in *comp.* **Haggle-stone, Hag-stone.**

e.Yks. (R.M.); Haggles doon wide chimla clatthered, *Yks. Dial.* (1887) 35; MORRIS *Flk-Talk* (1892).   m.Yks.[1]   s.Pem. There is a shower of hagles a comin' (W.M.M.); LAWS *Little Eng.* (1888) 420.

HAGGLE-CART, *sb.*   Oxf.   [æ·g l-kât.]   A horse and cart let out on hire to do rough work or odd jobs; also used *attrib.* and *vb.*

' Haggle-cart man,' a person whose services may be hired for any kind of carting work required of him.   ' Haggle-cart men ' and ' haggle-cart work ' are common terms in Oxford (G.O.): We are to distribute the work equally amongst the haggle-cart men in Oxford, *Oxf. Times* (Jan. 7, 1899) 3; Oxf.[1] Ea goes [guez] to haggle-cart, *MS. add.*

HAGGLER, *sb.*   Lon. Hmp. I.W. Wil. Dor.   Also written hagler Hmp.[1] Dor.   [æ·gla(r).]   1. A pedlar, huckster; a ' middle-man.'   Cf. higgler.

Lon. In Billingsgate the 'forestallers' or middlemen,.. as regards means, are a far superior class to the ' hagglers ' (the forestallers of the green markets), MAYHEW *Lond. Labour* (1851) I. 67.   Wil. SLOW *Gl.* (1892).   Dor. I be plain Jack Durbeyfield the haggler, HARDY *Tess* (1891) 4; An you do know young Jimmey Brown the hagler, *Eclogue* (1862) 26; Dor.[1] One who buys up poultry to sell again.

2. The upper servant of a farm.   Hmp.[1], I.W.[12]

HAGGLE-TOOTH, *sb.*   Som. Dev.   A tooth belonging to the second set which appears prematurely through the gum and projects.   Dev.[1]   Cf. aigle, 4.

Hence **Haggle-toothed,** *adj.* having prominent or pro- jecting teeth.

w.Som.[1] Ag-l-tèo·thud.   Dev. *Horae Subsecivae* (1777) 198. n.Dev. Wey zich a whatnozed haggle-tooth'd . . . theng as thee art, *Exm. Scold.* (1746) l. 58.

HAGGOKNOW, see Hag-a-knowe.

HAGGRIE, *sb.*   Bnff.[1]   [ha·grl.]   An unseemly mass. It is very often spoken of food badly cooked and served up in an untidy way.

HAGHOG, *sb.*   Obs.   Rut.[1]   A hedgehog. Paid for a haghog, 2d., *Chwarden's Accts.* (1790).

HAGHT, *sb.*   Ant.   A voluntary cough to remove mucus from the throat.   *Ballymena Obs.* (1892).

HAGH YE, *phr.*   Obsol.   Cum.[1]   Listen, hark ye.

HAGIL, HAGLE, see Haggle, *v.*[12], Hauchle.

HAGISTER, *sb.*   Lin. Ken.   Also written hageater, haggister Ken.; and in form eggiste Lin. Dor.   The mag- pie, *Pica rustica.*

Lin. A gamekeeper's word, *N. & Q.* (1899) 9th S. iv. 357; (T.H.)   Ken. RAY (1691); (K.); I took up a libbet to holl at a hageater that sat in the pea gratten, GROSE (1790); I hove a libbit at the hagister, LEWIS *I. Tenet* (1736) (s.v. Libbit); Ken.[12]

[EFris. âkster, ekster, hâkster, heister, ' pica' (KOOLMAN); Du. *aakster* (more commonly *ekster*), the magpie (DE VRIES).]

D

HAGLY-CRAB, *sb.* Hrf. A variety of apple.

Nature has endued some apple trees, such as the redstreak, .. with the power of maturing their fruits earlier in the season than others, such as the hagly crab, golden pippin, MARSHALL *Review* (1818) II. 289.

HAGMAHUSH, *sb.* Sc. An awkward sloven; also used *attrib.*

Abd. O laddy! ye're a hagmahush; yer face is barkid o'er wi' smush, BEATTIE *Parings* (1801) 5, ed. 1873; Most commonly applied to a female (JAM.).

HAG-MAL(L, *sb.* Som. 1. The titmouse, *Acredula rosea. N. & Q.* (1877) 5th S. viii. 358; W. & J. *Gl.* (1873).
2. A sloven, slattern.

W. & J. *Gl.* (1873). w.Som.[1] Her's a purty old beauty, her is —a rigler old hag-mall [hag-maa·l].

HAGMAN-HEIGH, see Hogmany.

HAG-MARK, *sb.* Sh.I. A boundary stone, a stone set up to indicate the line of division between separate districts; also called Hag-stane.

JAKOBSEN *Norsk in Sh.* (1897) 117; (*Coll.* L.L.B.); **S. & Ork.**[1]

HAGMENA, see Hogmany.

HAG-NAIL, *sb.* Suf. Same as Agnail (q.v.).

HAGODAY, see Haggaday.

HAGRI, *sb.* Sh.I. In phr. *to ride the hagri*, see below.

There is an old Shetland expression : ' to ride de hagri '—'hagri' being an O.N. hag(s)reið: skattald-ride. In former times neighbouring proprietors used to ride in company around their skattald-boundaries in order to inspect the marches, or put up new march-stones, and thus prevent future disputes. Every year, when this was done, they took with them a boy, the son of some crofter, residing on one or other of the properties. At every march-stone they came to, the boy got a flogging: this, it was thought, made him remember the place ever after. For every year this ' hagri ' or skattald-riding was done, a different boy was selected to accompany the proprietors and receive the floggings, JAKOBSEN *Dial.* (1897) 109.

HAG-STONE, see Haggle, *sb.*[4] 2.

HAGUE, *sb.* and *v.* N.Cy.[1] [hēg.] 1. *sb.* The inclination of a dike with the seam in a coal-pit. Cf. hade, *sb.*[2]
2. *v.* To incline, slope. ' She hagues sare to the south.'

HAGUE, see Hag, *sb.*[2]

HAGWESH, *sb.* Cum.[1] Ruin, bankruptcy. Cf. bagweah.

HAGWIFE, *sb.* Sc. A midwife.

Lnk. I maun hae a hagwife or my mither dee, for truly she's very frail, GRAHAM *Writings* (1883) II. 208.

HAG-WORM, *sb.* Nhb. Dur. Cum. Wm. Yks. Lan. Lin. Also written hag-wurm Cum.[2]; and in forms ag-worm w.Yks.; -worrum e.Yks.[1]; haggom n.Yks.[2]; hag-worrum e.Yks.[1] [h]a·g-werm, -wōm.] 1. The adder or viper, *Pelias berus.*

n.Cy. Ah's as crazy as a hag-worm ower yon nag o' oors (B.K.). Nhb. RICHARDSON *Borderer's Table-bk.* (1846) VIII. 15; (R.O.H.) Lakel.[1] Cum. ' What thinks teh they fand iv his stomach?' ' Mebby a hag-worm,' SARGISSON *Joe Scoap* (1881) 99; Cum.[2] An t'fat rwoastit oot o beath hagwurms an eela, 161; Cum.[4] Wm. A hagworm will bite fra the clint, HUTTON *Bran New Wark* (1785) l. 407. s.Wm. (J.A.B.) Yks. GROSE (1790). n.Yks.[124] e.Yks. MARSHALL *Rur. Econ.* (1788); e.Yks.[1] w.Yks. LUCAS *Stud. Niddardale* (c. 1882) Gl.; HUTTON *Tour to Caves* (1781). Lin. STREATFEILD *Lin. and Danes* (1884) 334; Lin.[1] n.Lin.[1] *Obsol.*
2. The common snake, *Coluber natrix*; also used generically for snakes of any kind.

N.Cy.[1], Cum.[4] n.Yks. *Science Gossip* (1882) 161; n.Yks.[2] Often, though wrongly, applied to the common harmless snake ; n.Yks.[2] ne.Yks.[1] Used generically rather than specifically. m.Yks.[1] Applied to all kinds of snakes, which are rarely found out of woods. w.Yks. WILLAN *List Wds.* (1811). Lan.[1] n.Lan.[1]
3. The blind-worm, *Anguis fragilis.*

Nhb. It is affirmed that the bite of the hag-worm ... is much more deadly, RICHARDSON *Borderer's Table-bk.* (1846) VIII. 15; Nhb.[1] Dur.[1] A worm of a brown mottled colour, the belly being lighter. It is about a foot in length, and an inch in diameter. Cum. HUTCHINSON *Hist. Cum.* (1794) I. App. 54; Cum.[4] w.Yks. Yan 'ud amost think ye'd swallowed a hagworm, *Jabez Oliphant* (1870) bk. I. v; w.Yks.[1]
4. *Comp.* (1) Hagworm-flower, the star-wort, *Stellaria holostea*; (2) -stones, perforated fragments of the grey alum shale found on Whitby beach.

(1) Yks. (B. & H.) (2) n.Yks.[2] The round holes were traditionally supposed to be due to the sting of the adder.
[L ON. *högg-ormr*, a viper (VIGFUSSON).]

HAG-YARD, see Haggard.

HAH, HAHL, HAHM, HAHNSER, see I, Hale, *v.*[1], Haulm, Heronsew.

HA-HO, *sb.* Irel. Also in form hi-how N.I.[1] The hedge-parsley, *Anthriscus sylvestris.*

N.I.[1] Of the parts of the stem between the joints children make ' pliffers ' to ' pluff ' hawstones through. Children also make ' scouts,' i. e. squirts, of the stem of this plant. An instrument for producing a noise is also made. ' When we were wee fellows we used to make horns of the hi-how.' Ldd. (B. & H.)

HAHO, see Haihow.

HAICHES, *sb.* Sc. Also written haichess Abd. (JAM.); haichus Rxb. (JAM.) Force, impetus ; a heavy fall, the noise made by the falling of a heavy body.

n.Sc. (JAM.), Abd. (*ib.*) Frf. [She] Mistook a fit for a' her care, An' wi' a haiches fell, MORISON *Poems* (1790) 25. Rxb. (JAM.)

HAID, see Hade, *sb.*[12], Hide, *v.*[2]

HAID-CORN, *sb.* Nhb. The plants of wheat in winter. (HALL.), Nhb.[1] Cf. hard-corn.

HAIFER, *v.* ? *Obs.* e.An. To toil, labour. (HALL.), e.An.[1]

HAIFTY-KAIFTY, *adj.* w.Yks.[2] Also in form hefty-kefty. Wavering, undecided. Cf. havey-cavey.

HAIG, HAIGEL, see Hag, *sb.*[12], Hagg, *v.*, Haggle, *v.*[1]

HAIGH, *sb.* Sc. Wm. A precipice ; a hillside.

Per. Syne a great haigh they row'd him down, DUFF *Poems*, 87 (JAM.). Wm. GIBSON *Leg.* (1877) 93.

HAIGH, *v.* Lan. Chs. Also written hay. To raise, lift up, heave ; to take the top earth off gravel.

Lan.[1] A farmer at Flixton had fetched some gravel and complained of his pay, saying, ' I had to hay it as well.' Chs.[1]; Chs.[2] Hay it up.
[Nu sket shall illc an dale beon All hejhedd upp and filledd, *Ormulum* (c. 1200) 9204.]

HAIGH, HAIGLE, see Hag, *sb.*[2], Haggle, *sb.*[1], *v.*[1]

HAIG-RAIG, *adj.* Wil. [e·g·rēg.] Bewildered.

SLOW *Gl.* (1892); Wil.[1] (s.v. Hag-rod).

HAIGRIE, *sb.* Sh.I. Also in forms haegrie; hegrie S. & Ork.[1] (JAM.) [hē·gri.] The heron, *Ardea cinerea.*

The ... heron (haigrie) ... might surely have been scheduled ... [for] protection, *Sh. News* (Jan. 14, 1899); Gazin' aboot him laek a howlin' haegrie, STEWART *Tales* (1892) 256 ; (W.A.G.); SWAINSON *Birds* (1885) 144 ; EDMONSTON *Zetl.* (1809) II. 266 (JAM.). [Norw. dial. *hegre*, a heron (AASEN) ; ON. *hegri.*]

HAIHOW, *sb.* n.Cy. Shr. Also in forms haho n.Cy.; high hoe Shr. The green woodpecker, *Gecinus viridis.*

n.Cy. *Poetry Provinc. in Cornh. Mag.* (1865) XII. 35. Shr. Its loud, laughing note has caused it to be called High hoe or Hai how, SWAINSON *Birds* (1885) 100; Shr.[1] [Pinard, Heighaw or Woodpecker, COTGR.]

HAIK(E, HAIKED, see Hack, *sb.*[12], Hake, *sb.*[8], *v.*, Hawkit.

HAIL, *sb.*[1] Sc. Irel. [hēl.] Small shot, pellets.

Edb. They canna eithly miss their aim, The wail o' hail they use for game, LIDDLE *Poems* (1821) 69. N.I.[1] Sparrow hail. ' The whole charge of hail went into his back.'
[*Postes*, big hail-shot for herons, geese, and other such great fowl, COTGR.]

HAIL, *v.*[1] Sc. Som. Cor. [h]ēl.] To shout; to roar, cry.

Frf. They hailed doon to see if ony o' the inmates were alive, WILLOCK *Rosetty Ends* (1886) 72, ed. 1889. Som. *Trans. Phil. Soc.* (1858) 159; (HALL.) Cor. The souls of the drowned sailors ... haunt these spots, and the ' calling of the dead ' has frequently been heard... Many a fisherman has declared he has heard the voices of dead sailors ' hailing their own names,' HUNT *Pop. Rom. w.Eng.* (1865) 366, ed. 1896.

HAIL, *v.*[2] and *sb.*[2] Sc. Nhb. Cum. Also written hale Sc. Nhb.[1] Cum.[14] [hēl.] 1. *v.* To drive the ball to the goal ; to win the goal. Cf. dool, *sb.*[2] 3.

Edb. When the ball is driven to the enemy's boundary it is ' hailed ' (D.M.R.). Cum.[1]; Cum.[4] The ball went ' down ' very soon and did not stop until hailed in the harbour.

Hence Haler, *sb.* a ' goal ' or ' win ' in the game of ' shinny ' or ' shinty.' Cum.[4]

2. Phr. (1) *hail the ball*, (2) — *the dool* or *dools*, a term used in football or other similar games, meaning to win a goal, drive the ball through the goal ; to win the mark, be victorious.
(1) Sc. (JAM.) Abd. The ba' spel's won And we the ba' ha'e hail'd, SKINNER *Poems* (1809) 51. Nhb. The dawn will be cheery, When death 'hails' the ba! PROUDLOCK *Borderland Muse* (1896) 248; We haled the baa safe i' the chorch porch [the goal], DIXON *Shrove-tide Customs*, 6; Nhb.¹ Cum. Others start to hale the ball (E.W.P.). (2) See DOOL, *sb.*² 3.
3. *sb.* The call announcing the winning stroke at shinty and some other ball games ; the act of driving the ball to the boundary.
Sc. (JAM.), Cai.¹ Edb. The cry of 'hail' is raised at the game of shinty when the ball is driven through the enemy's goal (D.M.R.).
4. The goal at shinty, football, &c. ; the 'goal' scored.
Sc. The struggle is, which party will drive the ball to their 'hail,' *Chambers' Information* (ed. 1842) s.v. Shinty ; The haila is wun, TARRAS *Poems* (1804) 66 (JAM.). Abd. The hail at 'shinty,' and the dell at 'hunty' and 'kee how,' CADENHEAD *Bon Accord* (1853) 192. Edb. The goal at shinty is known as 'the hails,' and a goal won is a 'hail' (D.M.R.). Dmf. (JAM., s.v. Han'-an-hail). Nhb.¹ ' To kick hale ' is to win the game. Cum. A hail at feut-bo between t'scheulhoose an' t'low stump, SARGISSON *Joe Scoap* (1881) 2 ; Cum.⁴
5. *pl.* A game of ball somewhat resembling ' shinty ' or hockey ; see below.
Lth. Great was the variety of games played with the ball, both by boys and girls, from ' shintie ' and ' hails ' to ' stot-ba ' and ' bannets,' STRATHESK *More Bits* (ed. 1885) 32. Edb. At the Edb. Academy there is a game called 'haila,' which is akin to hockey, only it is played with the flat wooden rackets called ' clackens,' and the manner of playing is different (D.M.R.).
6. The place for playing off the ball at hockey and similar games. Sc. Also used in *pl.* (JAM.)
7. *Comp.* (1) Hail-ball, a boys' game ; see below ; also called Han-an'-hail (q.v.) ; (2) -lick, the last blow or kick of the ball, which wins the game at football, &c.
(1) Dmf. Two goals called ' hails ' or ' dules ' are fixed on. . . The two parties then place themselves in the middle between the goals or 'dules,' and one of the persons, taking a soft elastic ball about the size of a man's fist, tosses it into the air, and as it falls strikes it with his palm towards his antagonist. The object of the game is for either party to drive the ball beyond the goal which lies before them, while their opponents do all in their power to prevent this (JAM., s.v. Han'-an-hail). (2) Knr. (JAM.)

HAIL, *int.* Yks. Also written hale. [ēl.] A cry used to drive away geese.
n.Yks. ' Hale,' be off wi' ye, opposed to ' Abbey, abbey, abbey,' a summons to come (R.H.H.). e.Yks. (Miss A.)

HAIL, HAILL, see Ail, *sb.*², Hale, *sb.*¹, *adj., v.*¹², Heal, *v.*²

HAILY, *sb.* Brks. Also written haighly. [Not known to our other correspondents.] [ē·li.] An onset, onrush. (J.C.K.)

HAIM, HAIMALD, see Hame, *sb.*¹², Hain, *v.*¹, Hamald.

HAIN, *sb.*¹ Sc. [hēn.] A haven, place of refuge.
Ags. The East Hain (Jam.). Frf. The hind comes in, if hain he win, LOWSON *Guidfollow* (1890) 242.

HAIN, *sb.*² Chs. [ēn.] Hatred, malice. (HALL.), Chs.¹⁸
[Fr. *haine*, hatred.]

HAIN, *v.*¹ and *sb.*⁴ Var. dial. uses in Sc. Irel. and Eng. Also written haain Brks.¹ I.W.¹²; haen Abd. Ant.; hane Sc. (JAM.); hayn s.Wor.¹ Oxf.¹ Hmp.¹; hayne Glo.¹ Som. Cor.¹²; and in forms haim Glo.¹²; hein Frf.; hen- Nhb.¹ [hēn.] **1.** *v.* To enclose, surround by a hedge ; to shut up or preserve grass land from cattle, &c., with a view to a crop of hay. Also with *up*.
Gall. (JAM.) Nhb. (J.H.) Nhb.¹ A grass field kept back from pasture till late in summer is said to be hained. Nhp.¹ ' Have you hained your land ? ' i.e. have you excluded cattle from the field, in order that the grass may grow ? Nhp.², War. (J.R.W.) Wor. Old turf keeping for sale. This keeping is very fresh, having been winter hained, *Evesham Jrn.* (May 14, 1898). s.Wor.¹ Glo. (J.S.F.S.); MARSHALL *Rur. Econ.* (1789) I ; Gl. (1851); Glo.¹² Oxf. When the cattle are taken off, and the fences made up, the meadows are hayned (K.); *N. & Q.* (1884) 6th S. ix. 390; Oxf.¹, Hmp.¹ I.W.¹ Don't thee dreyve the cattle into that meead, caas 'tes haain'd up; I.W.² Wil. They make a practice of haining up their meadows as early as possible, MARSHALL *Review* (1818) II. 489; BRITTON *Beauties* (1825); Wil.¹ Dor.¹ The meäd wer winter-häined. Som. His plan is to winter hayne fifteen acres, *Reports Agric.* (1793-

1813) 114 ; (W.F.R.); JENNINGS *Obs. Dial. w.Eng.* (1825) ; SWEETMAN *Wincanton Gl.* (1885). Cor.¹²
Hence **Hained**, *ppl. adj.* (1) of grass : preserved for hay, not used as pasture ; (2) of ground : enclosed, preserved from pasturage for a season. Also used *fig.*
(1) Sc. That the bees may feed on the flowers of the heath and late meadows or hain'd, that is kept grass, MAXWELL *Bee-Master* (1747) 55 (JAM.) ; We'll thrive like hainet girss in May, CHAMBERS *Sngs.* (1829) II. 517. w.Eng. MORTON *Cyclo. Agric.* (1863). (2) Sc. (JAM.) Abd. Hawkies twa, Whilk o'er the craft to some hained rig she leads, STILL *Cottar's Sunday* (1845) 18. Frf. Transferred to a man who is plump and well grown. ' Ye've been on the hain'd rig ' (JAM.). s.Sc. In sheep-farms, hained ground means, that which is reserved for a particular purpose, such as to pasture the lambs after they are weaned, or for the purpose of making hay from, *N. & Q.* (1856) and S. ii. 157. Ayr. Wi' tentie care I'll flit thy tether To some hain'd rig, BURNS *To his Auld Mare*, st. 18. Slk. That's the hained grund like, HOGG *Tales* (1838) 23, ed. 1866. Keb. Now weir an' fence o' wattl'd rice The hained fields inclose, DAVIDSON *Seasons* (1789) 51. n.Cy. *N. & Q.* (1856) and S. ii. 157.
2. To protect or preserve from harm ; to shield, exculpate.
Frf. Hain them weel, and deil the fear But on ye'll get, SANDS *Poems* (1833) 24. Rnf. Wha wadna up an' rin To hain a weel pay'd skin ? FINLAYSON *Rhymes* (1815) 57. Ayr. Be hain'd wha like, there was no excuse for him, HUNTER *Studies* (1870) 96. Lak. The guidwife, to hain her table, Spread a coverin' white as snaw, NICHOLSON *Kilwuddie* (ed. 1895) 52. Edb. Hain the life o' mony a brave ane, CRAWFORD *Poems* (1798) 91. e.Dur.¹
3. To husband, economize, use sparingly ; to save up, hoard, lay by.
Sc. It is well hain'd, that is hain'd off the belly, KELLY *Prov.* (1721) 182 ; Kail hains bread, RAMSAY *Prov.* (1737) ; We hain our little hates, and are niggards of the love that would begin Heaven for us even here, KEITH *Bonnie Lady* (1897) 73. Sh.I. Dey [bones] wir weel hained, for we haed naethin' troo da voar, I may say, bit just maet an' watter, STEWART *Tales* (1892) 249. Cai.¹ Ked. Bare an' aits in sheaves or taits, Weel haint the simmer through, GRANT *Lays* (1884) 3. Abd. I wyte her squeelin's nae been hain't, *Good-wife* (1867) st. 13. Frf. Come, hain your siller, pick an' eat, BEATTIE *Arnha* (c. 1820) 16, ed. 1882. Per. I cut the bread thick to hain the butter, FERGUSSON *Vill. Poet.* (1897) 121. s.Sc. A man among men he For catching the soveran and haining the penny ! ALLAN *Poems* (1887) 65. Rnf. Some hae routh to spen' an' hain, NEILSON *Poems* (1877) 27. Ayr. Ye're no to hain your ability in the business, GALT *Sir A. Wylie* (1822) xxviii ; (J.M.) Lnk. You needna hain the jeel [jelly] for there's twa dizzen pats, CHR. NORTH *Noctes* (ed. 1856) IV. 98. Rxb. The French Their lead an' powther hae nae hain'd, A. SCOTT *Poems* (ed. 1808) 142. Gall. What Highlan' han' its blade would hain ! NICHOLSON *Poet. Wks.* (1814) 178, ed. 1897. Wgt. A thrifty bit wife wha his weekly wage hains, FRASER *Poems* (1885) 177. N.I.¹ Ant. ' Haen your kitchen,' that is save your soup, beef, or whatever else you have got to eat with your potatoes, *Ballymena Obs.* (1892). N.Cy.¹ Haining a new suit of clothes. Nhb. The gear I hain, he just destroys, PROUDLOCK *Borderland Muse* (1896) 339 ; Nhb.¹ A man hains his food or drink to make it go as far as possible. Dur. GIBSON *Up-Weardale Gl.* (1870). Cum. We'll not give yae pleace a' our gift An' hain nought for anither, *Sngs.* (1866) 239 ; Cum.⁴, s.Wor. (H.K.)
Hence (1) **Hained**, *ppl. adj.* (a) saved up, hoarded, preserved from use ; freq. in *comb.* Weel-hained ; (b) *fig.* preserved, kept in store ; (2) **Hained-up**, *ppl. adj.*, see (1, a) ; (3) **Hainer**, *sb.* one who saves anything from being worn or expended ; (4) **Haining**, (a) *ppl. adj.* thrifty, saving, frugal, penurious ; (b) *sb.* economy, frugality, saving ; parsimony ; (5) **Hainings**, *sb. pl.* earnings, savings.
(1, a) Sc. The long-hained silver is paid over the counter, KEITH *Prus* (1895) 159. Abd. I maun yield my weel-hained gear to deck yon modern wa's, CADENHEAD *Bon Accord* (1853) 187. Per. She puts on her weel-hain'd tartan plaid, NICOLL *Poems* (ed. 1843) 94. Dmb. It's no my weel-hained pickle siller that's to keep him up ony langer to play the fule, CROSS *Disruption* (1844) l. Ayr. Wha waste your weel-hain'd gear on damn'd new Brigs and Harbours ! BURNS *Brigs of Ayr* (1787) l. 173. Edb. Hain'd multer hads the mill at ease, FERGUSSON *Poems* (1773) 150, ed. 1785. Dmf. Our guidwife coft a snip white coat, Wi' monie a weel hained buttergroat, CROMEK *Remains* (1810) 90. n.Cy. *Border Gl.* (Coll. L.L.B.) Nhb. Auld Bella's well hain'd china ware, PROUDLOCK *Borderland*

D 2

Muse (1896) 338. (*b*) **Sc.** Hain'd men I will ye not heark I AYTOUN *Ballads* (ed. 1861) I. 91. (2) **Sc.** It's fair pizen, It's naething but the bained-up syndings o' the glesses, KEITH *Bonnie Lady* (1897) 29. (3) **Cld.** He's a gude hainer o' his claise. He's an ill hainer o' his siller (JAM.). (4, *a*) **Sh.I.** Der ower hainin ta spend mair is dey can help, *Sh. News* (Aug. 19, 1899). **Baff.[1] Elg.** Jeems, though he's hainin', keeps a gey decent dram, TESTER *Poems* (1865) 133. **Ayr.** Being of a haining disposition, SERVICE *Notandums* (1890) 9. (*b*) **Sh.I.** Lang want, dey say, is nae bread hainin, *Sh. News* (July 9, 1898). **Abd.** That's an unco haenin o' the strae, ALEXANDER *Johnny Gibb* (1871) xxxvii. **Ayr.** A spirit of scarting and haining that I never could abide, SERVICE *Dr. Duguid* (ed. 1887) 25. **Lnk.** Our John was aye a great man for hainin', ROY *Generalship* (ed. 1895) 2. (5) **Ayr.** My lawful jointure and honest hainings, GALT *Entail* (1823) lii.

4. Phr. (1) *hain the charge*, to save expense; to grudge, be penurious; (2) — *the road*, to save a journey.

(1) **Sc.** If my dear wife should hain the charge As I expect she will, CHAMBERS *Sngs.* (1829) II. 487. (2) **Edb.** If ye'd stay'd at hame, and cooked, And hain'd the road, LIDDLE *Poems* (1821) 27.

5. To save or spare exertion, trouble, &c.

Sc. (JAM.) **Sh.I.** I could a haind my trouble, *Sh. News* (July 2, 1898). **Inv.** To hain one's self in a race, not to force one's self at first (H.E.F.). **Bch.** They are so hain'd, they grow so daft, FORBES *Dominie* (1785) 42. **Abd.** Swankies they link aff the pot To hain their joes, KEITH *Farmer's Ha'* (1774) st. 60. **Ayr.** Flit in tethers needless nags That us'd to hain us, MUIR *Poems* (1818) 13. **Ayr.** Sic hauns as you sud ne'er be faikit, Be hain'd wha like, BURNS 2nd *Ep. to Davie.* **e.Lth.** I'm suir ye dinna hain yoursel, sir, HUNTER *J. Inwick* (1895) 134. **Dmf.** Wha toiled sae sair tae hain me, QUINN *Heather* (1863) 245. **Gall.** You know I havena sought to hain you in the hottest of the harvest; neither have I urged you on, NICHOLSON *Hist. Tales* (1843) 324. **N.I.[1]** Ye hained yersel' the day. **Nhb.[1]** A man takes work easily and hains himself in order that his strength may endure to the end of the day.

Hence **Hained,** *ppl. adj.* (1) well-preserved, not wasted by bodily fatigue or exertion ; (2) *fig.* chaste.

(1) **Nhb.[1]** A man who has gone through a long life and presents a fresh appearance is said to be ' weel hained.' (2) **Sc.** ' Well-hained,' not wasted by venery (JAM.).

6. With *on* : to grudge the expense of a bargain ; to grudge one's pains or trouble.

After aa've myed the bargain aa hen'd on't (R.O.H.) ; **Nhb.[1]** ' He seun henned on't,' he soon gave it up or tired of doing it.

7. With *from* or *off* : to abstain or hold aloof from.

Slg. I am sorry he has been so long hained from Court, BRUCE *Sermons* (1631) 20, ed. 1843. **Dmf.** Us 'ool hain aff vrom taaykin' any notice on't vor a daay or two, praps a wunt do't no moor. **W.F.R.**).

8. To cease raining.

Sh.I. Da rain hained an' da wind banged ta wast wi' a perfect gyndagooster, SPENCE *Flk-Lore* (1899) 250 ; *ib.* 119.

9. *sb.* A field shut up for hay ; an enclosure.

Hrf. (W.W.S.), **Hrf.[1] Glo.** LEWIS *Gl.* (1839) ; **Glo.[1] Wil.** BRITTON *Beauties* (1825). **Som.** Mr. H., speaking of an egg he had found on another person's land, said, ' I had no right to it ; it wasn't my hain ' (W.F.R.).

[1. Norw. dial. *hegna*, to fence in, enclose (AASEN) ; so ON. *hegna* (VIGFUSSON). **3.** In Seytoun he remaned, Whair wyne and aill was nothing hayned, *Sat. Poems* (1583), ed. Cranstoun, I. 372.]

HAIN, *v.*[3] **Lin.** To possess.

(HALL.) ; *Trans. Phil. Soc.* (1858) 159.

HAIN, *v.*[3] **e.An.** Also in forms **heigh'n** e.An.[12] ; **heign, heig'n** Nrf. ; **heyne** Suf. ; **highen** Nrf. [ēn.] To raise, heighten, esp. to raise in price.

e.An.[1] Invariably applied to the increase of prices, wages, &c. ; **e.An.[2]** Flour is hain to-day a penny a stun. **Nrf.** Yow would a larfed . . . tu see that old hussy [a cow] hain up her buttuck. **Man and Nat.** (1895) 66 ; Master said . . . he should heig'n the whole of his men on Saturday night, SPILLING *Molly Miggs* (1873) 8 ; I'm afeard that flour will be hained again next week (W.R.E.) ; A bricklayer speaks of heigning a wall, COZENS-HARDY *Broad Nrf.* (1893) 15 ; (W.H.Y.) ; GROSE (1790). **e.Nrf.** To hain the rent, the rick, the ditch, MARSHALL *Rur. Econ.* (1787). **w.Nrf.** Everythin' is heighen'd 'cept wages t'yaar, ORTON *Beeston Ghost* (1884) 7. **Suf.** RAVEN *Hist. Suf.* (1895) 262.

[I have spoke with Borges that he shuld heyne the price of the mershe, *Paston Let.* (1465) II. 176 ; Heynyn, *exalto, elevo, Prompt.*]

HAIN, *v.*[4] **Ess.** [ēn.] To drive away.

Trans. Arch. Soc. (1863) II. 185 ; (W.W.S.)

HAIN, *v.*[5] **Som. Dev.** Also written **hayne** Dev. ; and in forms **ain** w.Som.[1] ; **aine** Som. ; **hend, hen(n** Som. Dev. ; **yean** Dev.[1] ; **yen** Dev.[12] n.Dev. nw.Dev.[1] [ēn, en, jen.] To throw, fling, esp. to throw stones, &c.

Som. JENNINGS *Obs. Dial. w.Eng.* (1825) ; W. & J. *Gl.* (1873) ; *Monthly Mag.* (1814) II. 126. **w.Som.[1]** Dhu bwuuyz bee ai'neen stoa·unz tu dhu duuks [The boys are throwing stones at the ducks]. **Dev.** Ef 2o be thee dissent be quiet, I'll henn thease gert cob tū thy heyde ! HEWETT *Peas. Sp.* (1892) ; Don't you hayne stwones, there ! PULMAN *Sketches* (1842) 103, ed. 1871 ; MOORE *Hist.* (1829) I. 354 ; Still most commonly applied to throwing stones, though not always, *Reports Provinc.* (1889) ; **Dev.[1]** Whan a had greep'd down a wallige of muss, a . . . yean'd et away, 2 ; Witherly up with his voot and yand over the tea-kittle, *ib.* 4 ; **Dev.[2]** n.Dev. Yen ma thick Cris'mus brawn, ROCK *Jim an' Nell* (1867) st. 1 ; Tha henst along thy Torn, *Exm. Scold.* (1746) l. 255. nw.Dev.[1] Yen 'n away.

[Our giwes him ladde wiþþoute þe toun and henede him wiþ stones, þe *Holy Rode* (c. 1300) 263. OE. *hǣnan*, to stone (*John* x. 32).]

HAIN, see Hine.

HAINBERRIES, *sb.* **Sc.** Raspberries, the fruit of *Rubus Idaeus.* Cf. **hindberry.**

Sc. Haw-burs an hainberries grow bonnilie, EDWARDS *Mod. Poets.* 3rd S. 396. **Rxb.** (JAM.)

HAINCH, *sb.* and *v.* **Sc.** Irel. n.Cy. Nhb. Lakel. Written **hainsh** Rnf. ; also in forms **hench** Sc. Ant. Cum.[4] ; **henge** Nhb.[1] ; **hinch** Sc. Inv. Bnff.[1] Per. N.I.[1] s.Don.

1. *sb.* The haunch.

Sc. (JAM.) **Gall.** The upper han' at last he has gat, And reel'd thee on thy hench fu' flat, MACTAGGART *Encycl.* (1824) 501, ed. 1876. **N.I.[1]** The corn was that short a Jinny Wran might ha' sat on her hinches an' picked the top pickle off. **Ant.** GROSE (1790) *MS. add.* (C.) **s.Don.** SIMMONS *Gl.* (1890). **N.Cy.[1] Nhb.** In constant *gen.* use (R.O.H.).

2. *Comp.* (1) **Hench-bane,** the haunch-bone ; (2) **-deep,** up to the haunches ; (3) **-hoops,** *obs.,* hoops over which skirts were draped ; (4) **-knots,** bunches of ribbons worn on the hips ; (5) **-vent,** a triangular bit of linen, a gore.

(1) **Inv.** (H.E.F.) **Gall.** A cleg that nips him on the hench bane, CROCKETT *Raiders* (1894) xlvi. (2) **Sh.I.** Da fans o' snaw wis lyin' hench deep, *Sh. News* (Feb. 5, 1898). **Per.** In scutter holes hinchdeep I've been Wi' dirt a' mestered to the e'en, SPENCE *Poems* (1898) 165. (3) **Ayr.** Her twa sisters, in their hench-hoops with their fans in their hands, GALT *Entail* (1823) i. (4) **Edb.** CHAMBERS *Trad. Edb.* II. 59. (5) **Gall.** (JAM.)

3. A term in wrestling ; see below.

Cum.[4] Fallen into disuse among modern wrestlers ; it is the equivalent of the ' half-buttock.' The wrestler turns in as for a ' buttock ' and pulls his opponent across his haunch instead of over his back as in the ' buttock.' ' He was an excellent striker with the right leg, effective with the hench, and clever also at hyping,' *Wrestling,* 142.

4. *v.* To throw by resting the arm on the thigh, to throw under the leg or haunch ; to jerk, fling. Also used *fig.*

Bnff.[1] Rnf. Natural Fools to rank an' power She hainshes undeservin', PICKEN *Poems* (1813) I. 147. **Ayr.** He was the best at hainching a stane, young or auld, that I ever saw, SERVICE *Dr. Duguid* (ed. 1887) 42. **Gall.** There were few places . . . from which I could not reach an erring youth with pebble cunningly ' henched,' CROCKETT *Raiders* (1894) xii. **N.I.[1]** To throw stones by bringing the hand across the thigh. **Ant.** Hoo far can you throw a stane by henchin' it ! A henched it to him, *Ballymena Obs.* (1892) ; GROSE (1790) *MS. add.* (C.) **Uls.** (M.B.-S.) **s.Don.** SIMMONS *Gl.* (1890). **N.Cy.[1] Nhb.[1]** To throw a stone by striking the hand against the haunch bone and throwing it with high trajectory. **Cum.[4]**

[1. King James . . . strukne in the hench or he was war . . . dies, DALRYMPLE *Leslie's Hist. Scotl.* (1596) II. 81.]

HAINE, *sb.* w.Yks.[3] The same as Ain (q.v.).

HAINER, *sb.* e.An.[1] [Not known to our correspondents.] The master who holds or sustains the expenses of the feast.

HAINGLE, *v.* and *sb.* **Sc.** [hē·ŋgl.] **1.** *v.* To go about in a feeble, languid way ; to hang about, loiter, wander about aimlessly.

Sc. They haingled frae folk to folk, WADDELL *Ps.* (1871) cv. 13 ;

(Jam.) s.Flf. To haingle aboot through the streets o' a big city, Latto *Tam Bodkin* (1864) xviii.

2. *sb.* A lout, booby, an awkward fellow.

Sc. I'll gar ye—ye wilycart haingle; an ye gie me sic a fright. *St. Patrick* (1819) (Jam.).

3. *pl.* The influenza.

Abs. From hanging so long about those who are afflicted with it, often without positively assuming the form of a disease (Jam.).

4. Phr. *to hae the haingles,* to be in a state of ennui. *ib.*

HAINING, *sb.* Sc. Nhb. Yks. Lan. Der. Glo. Brks. Also in form **haning** Abd. [h)ē·nin.] The preserving of grass for cattle ; protected grass ; any fenced field or enclosure ; a separate place for cattle. See **Hain,** *v.*[1]

Abd. As haining water'd with the morning dew, Ross *Helenore* (1768) 140, ed. Nimmo ; Any field where the grass or crop is protected from being eaten up, cut, or destroyed, whether inclosed or not (Jam.). Nhb. A company of hay-makers, whose work in the adjacent haining had been interrupted, *Denham Tracts* (ed. 1895) II. 208; Nhb.[1] w.Yks. Lucas *Stud. Nidderdale* (c. 1882) Gl. Lan. Davies *Races* (1856) 268. Der. The laying or shutting up meadows for hay is called hayning, Glover *Hist.* (1829) I. 203. Glo.[1] Brks. We present that no owner or occupier of land in Northcroft has a right to hitch, enclose, or feed any of the lands there from the usual time of hayning to the customary time of breaking, *Rec. Court Leet* (1830) in *Newbury Wkly. News* (Feb. 16, 1888); Brks.[1]

Hence (1) **Haining-ground,** *sb.* an outlet for cattle ; (2) **-time,** *sb.* cropping-time, while the fields or crops are enclosed in order to keep out cattle.

(1) Lan.[1] (2) Ayr. Vnles the samyn guddis be sufficientlie tedderit in hanyng tyme, *Burgh Rec. Prestwick* (Oct. .2, 1605) (Jam. *Suppl.*).

HAINING, *adj.* Obs. Yks. Of the weather : cold, drizzly.

w.Yks. In 1871 I was just able to rescue the word from oblivion. . . . Since then I have not found anyone who knows it, Lucas *Stud. Nidderdale* (c. 1882) Gl.

HAINISH, *adj.*[1] Hrt. Ess. Also in form **ainish** Hrt. [ē·niʃ.] **1.** Unpleasant, used esp. of the weather, showery, rainy. Cf. **hayness.**

Ess. *Monthly Mag.* (1814) I. 498 ; *Trans. Arch. Soc.* (1863) II. 185 ; Gl. (1851) ; Ess.[1]

2. Awkward, ill-tempered.

Hrt. He was such an ainish old man (G.H.).

[1. Prob. a form of lit. E. *heinous.*]

HAINISH, *adj.*[2] Pem. Also written **haynish.** [ē·niʃ.] Greedy, ravenous ; craving for a thing.

s.Pem. Laws *Little Eng.* (1888) 420 ; So, man, yea'l be very haynish, yea'l get the whole haws (W.M.M.).

HAINRIDGE, see **Henridge.**

HAIPS, *sb.* Sc. Yks. Lan. Also in form **haip** Fif. A sloven.

Fif. She jaw'd them, misca'd them For clashin' claikin' haips, Douglas *Poems* (1806) 125. w.Yks. (Hall.), w.Yks.[1], ne.Lan.[1]

HAIR, *sb.* and *v.* Var. dial. forms and uses in Sc. Irel. and Eng. **I.** Dial. forms : (1) Haar, (2) Har, (3) Hear(r, (4) Heear, (5) Heer, (6) Heere, (7) Hewr, (8) Huer, (9) Hure, (10) Ure, (11) Yar, (12) Yare, (13) Year, (14) Yor, (15) Yur, (16) Yure.

(1) S. & Ork.[1] w.Yks. His haar he ne'er puts comb in, Twisleton *Poems* (c. 1867) I. 6. Glo. *Horae Subsecivae* (1777) 197. (2) Oxf.[1] (3) Cum. It wad ha keep't me a noor lang to swort up me heärr, *Willy Wattle* (1870) 7 ; Cum.[1] (4) Wm. T'heear a mi heead steead an end, *Spec. Dial.* (1885) pt. iii. 3. (5) Der.[1], nw.Der.[1] Lin. Long and black ma heer was then, *Monthly Pckt.* (Apr. 1862) 377. (6) Ken. (G.B.) (7) Lan. Meh hewr war clottert wi' gore, Ainsworth *Witches* (ed. 1849) *Introd.* iii. (8) w.Yks.[1] (9) n.Cy. Grose (1790). Lan. Till it come to meh hure, Tim Bobbin *View Dial.* (1740) 17 ; Lan.[1], Chs.[1,2], nw.Der.[1] (10) Lan. Noane hauve us mich ure oppo his faze us sum o yo chaps han, Ormerod *Felley fro Rachde* (1864) ii. (11) Cum.[1] ; Cum.[3] A scwore of as bonnie Galloway Scots as iver hed yär o' t'ootside on them, 32. Wm. T'red en yalla tale wi' o t'yar ont, Robison *Aald Tales* (1882) 9. n.Lan.[1], se.Wor.[1] Shr.[1] The child mun'äve'er yar cut short, I doubt. Hrf.[2], Oxf.[1] (12) Brks. His yead did grawy above his yare, Hughes *Scour. White Horse* (1859) vii. (13) n.Wil. Yer yeär uz lik a vlock o' gwoäts, Kite *Sng. Sol.* (1860) iv. 1. (14) Wor. Allies *Antiq. Flk-Lore* (1840) 366, ed. 1852. (15) Cum.[1] Glo. Hev thi yur cut, *Roger Plowman,* 29. (16) Lan.[1], s.Lan.[1], m.Lan.[1], Chs.[1,2,3], s.Chs.[1], nw.Der.[1]

II. Dial. uses. **1.** *sb.* In *comb.* (1) Hair-beard, the field woodrush, *Luzula campestris* ; (2) -bell, the foxglove, *Digitalis purpurea* ; (3) -breed, a hair-breadth, a very narrow margin ; (4) -breeds, little by little, by slow degrees ; (5) -charm, see below ; (6) -hung or -hanged, hanging by the hair ; (7) -kaimer, a hairdresser ; (8) -knife, a knife used in freeing butter from hairs ; (9) -line, (*a*) a fishing-line made of hair ; (*b*) a kind of cloth with very fine stripes ; (10) -pitched, (*a*) bald ; (*b*) having rough, unbrushed hair or coat ; (11) -scaup, the crown of the head ; (12) -shagh, -shard, or -shaw,(13) -shorn-lip,a cleft lip ; a hare-lip ; (14) -sit, a scented mucilaginous preparation for keeping the hair in place ; (15) -sore, (*a*) when the skin of the head is sore from any cause, as from a cold ; (*b*) *fig.* touchy, ready to take offence ; (16) -teemsey, a fine sieve, with a grating of hair-cloth, used for sifting fine flour, &c. ; (17) -tether, a tether made of hair ; (18) -weed, the greater dodder, *Cuscuta europaea,* or the lesser dodder, *C. Epithymum.*

(1) Nhp.[1] This plant, being one of the harbingers of spring, and *gen.* making its appearance in mild, genial weather, has originated the following prophetic adage : ' When the hair-beard appear The shepherd need not fear.' (2) Ir. *Science Gossip* (1870) 135. (3) n.Yks.[2] ; n.Yks.[4] He 'scaped wiv his leyfe, bud it war nobbut byv a hair-breed. m.Yks.[1], n.Lin.[1] (4) n.Yks.[1] ; n.Yks.[4] We're bodduming what tha did byv hair-breeds. Willie mends, bud it's nobbut byv hair-breeds. (5) Sh.I. Peggy still breathing threatenings and slaughter against Sarah o' Northouse for abstracting her butter profit, and against himself for not being more expert in obtaining the hair-charm from the said Sarah's cow ; for in this important enterprise he had failed, owing to that wide-awake individual coming upon him just at the moment he was in the act of applying the shears to Crummie's side, Stewart *Tales* (1892) 54. (6) Lnk. Absalom's lyfe, hayre-hung, betwene two trees, Lithgow *Poet. Rem.* (ed. 1863) Sc. *Welcome* ; Proud Absalom was hair-hangd on a tree, *ib.* Gushing *Teares.* (7) Edb. Hair-kaimers, crieshy gizy-makers, Fergusson *Poems* (1773) 174, ed. 1785. (8) Sc. (Jam.) (9, *a*) Sc. Wi' hair-lines, and lang wands whuppin the burns, Leighton *Words* (1869) 17. Lnk. There's a haill saxpince worth o' hair-line and gut, Gordon *Pyotshaw* (1885) 116. (*b*) w.Yks. (J.M.) (10, *a*) Cor.[1] ' Hair-pitched ould hermit,' term of reproach ; Cor.[2] (*b*) Cor. The cow would go round the fields bleating and crying as if she had lost her calf ; she became hair-pitched, and pined away to skin and bone, Hunt *Pop. Rom.* w.*Eng.* (1865) 109, ed. 1896; Thomas *Randigal Rhymes* (1895) Gl. ; A person covered with loose hairs shed by a horse, &c. is said to be hair-pitched (M.A.C.) ; Cor.[2] It indicates the state of the hair when from the over-dryness of the skin it sticks up irregularly and cannot be smoothed. (11) n.Yks.[2] (12) Sc. A hair-shagh urisum and grim, Drummond *Muckomachy* (1846) 7. Abd. He has a hairshard (G.W.). Per. He has a hairshaw (*ib.*). Gall. (A.W.) (13) s.Chs.[1] (14) n.Yks.[2] (15, *a*) Chs.[1] It may sometimes be naturally tender ; at any rate yure-sore is looked upon as a real and almost incurable disease ; Chs.[2] (*b*) Chs.[1] (16) Nhb.[1] (17) Sc. Supposed to be employed in witch-craft (Jam.). (18) Bdf. Dodder, hell-weed, or devil's-guts (*Cuscuta Europaea*) is called hale-weed, hair-weed, and beggar-weed in this neighbourhood, Batchelor *Agric.* (1813) 325. Hrt. Ellis *Mod. Husb.* (1750) IV. ii. Nrf. We could never cut the hair-weed, Emerson *Son of Fens* (1892) 103.

2. Phr. (1) *hair and head, an' that's all,* said of one without brains or sense ; (2) *— and lime,* see below ; (3) *— about,* an expression used to describe the hair when it is changing to grey ; (4) *— of the head clock,* a clock hanging to the wall, with weights and pendulum exposed ; (5) *in her hair,* in full dress; (6) *a dog of a different hair,* a person or thing of a different kind ; (7) *to a hair,* exactly ; (8) *to find or have a hair in the neck,* (*a*) to find fault with ; (*b*) to experience a difficulty or annoyance ; (9) *to have hair on one's head,* to be clever, cautious, or wise ; (10) *to lug the hair,* to pull the hair ; (11) *to miss every hair of his head,* to miss any one very much ; (12) *to stand upon a hair,* to be within a very little, to be ' touch and go ' with ; (13) *to take one's hair off,* to surprise greatly ; (14) *a hair needed to make a cable or a tether,* to exaggerate greatly, make much of a trifle ; (15) *hilt or hair,* absolutely nothing ; used with a *neg.*

(1) n.Yks.[2] (s.v. Heead). (2) n.Yks. At old farm houses, when

saltfish was eaten to dinner, they took what was spared, picked out the bones, and hashed it up for supper with potatoes, and pepper and salt. This was called hair and lime (I.W.). (3) Ant. (W.H.P.) (4) w.Yks. (S.P.U.) (5) Wxf. They speak of a lady going to an evening party 'in her hair,' meaning 'in full dress' (J.S.). (6) Lan. Nawe Bright's a dog of a different yure, BRIERLEY *Old Radicals*, 11. (7) s.Sc. It's nowther birsslet by the sun owr sair, Nor starv't aneath a winter sky, But rightt' a hair, T. SCOTT *Poems* (1793) 349. Dmb. I've seen a place that'll fit us to a vera hair, CROSS *Disruption* (1844) vi. Edb. Whate'er disease he didna care, J— could cure them to a hair, FORBES *Poems* (1812) 85. n.Cy. (J.W.) Lan. Hoo [she] knows th' temper o' my inside to a yure, WAUGH *Snowed-up*, i ; Lan.[1] Nhp.[1] To suit you to a hair. (8, *a*) Sc. To hold another under restraint by having the power of saying or doing something that would give pain (JAM.). s.Sc. Your husband was a maist worthy man. Though a barber, nae man ever fand a hair i' his neck, WILSON *Tales* (1836) III. 67. (*b*) Per. 'That's a hair in yer neck.' Something to make you think about, a difficult point for you (G.W.). Lak. It wad hae been a gey sair hair i' her neck for mony, mony a lang day, GORDON *Pyotshaw* (1885) 40. (9) Fif. (JAM.) (10) Chs.[1] Aw'll lug thy yure for thee. (11) s.Wor.[1] 35. (12) Sh.I. Hit juist stüde apon a hair 'at wir coortin' didna caese dair an' dan, *Sh. News* (Nov. 26, 1898). (13) e.Suf. That takes my hair off (F.H.). (14) Sc. A' he wanted was a hair To mak' a tether, FORD *Thistledown* (1891) 205. Sh.I. Der among wis 'at only need a hair ta mak' a tedder, *Sh. News* (May 7, 1898). Abd. Imagined by folk that ken't nae better, an' when they got a hair would mak' a tether o't, *Deeside Tales* (1872) 141. Per. Clear of all this clachan rabble Who with one hair can make a cable, SPENCE *Poems* (1898) 168. Dmb. Rummaged through the hoose for a hair to mak' a tether o't, CROSS *Disruption* (1844) xxviii. Rnf. Just gie him a hair to mak a tether, He needs nae mair, WEBSTER *Rhymes* (1835) 107. Ayr. When once she found a hair, She soon a tether made, WHITE *Jottings* (1879) 178. Edb. You only wanted but a hair As a pretext to mak a tether, LIDDLE *Poems* (1821) 134. (15) Dmb. If never hilt or hair o't had been seen or heard tell o' wha wad ha'e been to blame but yoursel ? CROSS *Disruption* (1844) xxviii.

3. A filament of flax or hemp ; a sixth of a hank of yarn.
S. & Ork.[1] Ayr. A heap o' seven heere yarn, GALT *Entail* (1823) lxxx.

4. A very small portion or quantity of anything ; a trifle, the smallest possible amount.
Sc. A hair of meal, a few grains (JAM.) ; They seemed all a hair set back and gave various answers, STEVENSON *Catriona* (1893) xvii. Sh.I. Some got a hair o 'oo', an' som' got what he ca'd sax-penny rivlins, *Sh. News* (Mar. 4, 1899). Per. An elder o' the kirk, an' . . . fient a hair the waur o' that, WILLOCK *Rosetty Ends* (1886) 95, ed. 1889. Per. There wasna the hair o' a stroke on it, *Sandy Scott* (1897) 65. Rnf. I proffer'd a hair o' my sneeshin, WEBSTER *Rhymes* (1835) 82. Edb. N' excrescence left t' improve 't a hair, Sae weel's ye've done it, LIDDLE *Poems* (1821) 136. Gall. MACTAGGART *Encycl.* (1824) 251, ed. 1876. N.I.[1] 'No a hair feared,' not a bit afraid. N.Cy.[1] A hair of salt. A hair of meal. Nhb.[1] Sur.[1] I've never been a hair's malice with him.

5. The corn-spurrey, *Spergula arvensis*. Cum.[1]
6. A hair-cloth used in the cider-press. Gen. in *pl.* s.Wor.[1], Shr.[1], Hrf.[2], Glo. (A.B.) **7.** The cloth on the oast above the fire, upon which the hops are dried. Ken.[1], Sur.[1]
8. *v.* Phr. *to hair butter*, to free butter of hairs, &c. by passing a knife through it in all directions.
Pmb. A large knife . . . was repeatedly passed through it [butter] in all directions, that hairs and other impurities might be removed. . . . This practice, then universal, was called hairing the butter, *Agric. Surv.* 81 (JAM.).

HAIRED, *ppl. adj.* Sc. Having a mixture of white and red or white and black hairs. Fif. (JAM.)
HAIREN, *adj.* Sc. Also e.An. w.Cy. Dev. Written harren e.An.[1] Made of hair.
S. & Ork.[1], Cai.[1] Buff. They took a hairen tether and hanged him, KEITH *Leg. Strathisla* (1851) 77. Abd. (JAM.) e.An.[1] 'A harren brum,' is a hair broom. w.Cy. (J.W.) Dev. In explaining to me the harness of pack-saddles, T.C. said that 'a hairen gease' completely encircled the body of the animal. This peculiar form of gease (girth) was made partly of hair webbing and partly of rope, the two parts respectively passing under the belly and over the saddle on the back, *Reports Provinc.* (1893).
HAIRIF, *sb.* In *gen.* dial. use in Eng. Also in forms airess w.Yks. ; aireve Midl. ; airif Lin. ; airup Yks. ;

areas w.Yks. ; eerif s.Chs.[1] ; eriff, erith s.Not.[1] ; errif(f Chs.[18] Stf.[2] Not.[1] Rut.[1] Lei.[1] ; haireve Glo.[1] ; hairough e.Yks.[1] Midl. Lei.[1] ; hairrough n.Yks.[2] ; hairup e.Yks.[1] ; harif(f N.Cy.[2] n.Yks.[2] e.Yks.[1] Not. sw.Lin.[1] Glo.[1] ; hariffe Shr.[1] ; harrup Yks. ; hayriff sw.Lin.[1] War.[23] s.Wor.[1] se.Wor.[1] Rdn. Dev.[6] ; heiriff(e Nhp.[1] ; herif(f Chs.[1] Midl. Stf.[2] War.[2] Hmp.[1] ; herrif Not. [h]arrif, ērif, e'rif.]
1. The goose-grass, *Galium Aparine*.
n.Cy. GROSE (1790) ; N.Cy.[2], Yks. (B. & H.), n.Yks.[2] e.Yks. MARSHALL *Rur. Econ.* (1788) ; e.Yks.[1], w.Yks. (B. & H.), Chs.[13], s.Chs.[1] Midl. MARSHALL *Rur. Econ.* (1796) II ; *Science Gossip* (1869) 26. Stf. *Reports Agric.* (1793-1813) 95 ; Stf.[2] Not. YOUNG *Annals Agric.* (1784-1815) XXIII. 151 ; (W.H.S.) ; Not.[1], s.Not. (J.P.K.), n.Lin.[1] sw.Lin.[1] We call that hariff ; when we were childer, we used to flog our tongues wi' it, to make them bleed. Rut.[1] The crop wur half erriff. Lei.[1], Nhp.[1], War.[23], s.Wor.[1], se.Wor.[1], Shr.[1], Hrf. (B. & H.), Rdn. (B. & H.) Glo. MARSHALL *Rur. Econ.* (1789) I ; *Science Gossip* (1876) 167 ; Glo.[1], Hmp.[1]
2. The meadow-sweet, *Spiraea Ulmaria*. Dev.[4]
[**1.** *Rubea minor*, hayrive, Sin. *Barth.* (c. 1350) 37. OE. *hægerife* (*Leechdoms*).]

HAIRLY, HAIRM, see Hardleys, Harm, *v.*
HAIR-MOULD, *sb.* Sc. Mouldiness which appears on bread, &c., caused by dampness. Also used *attrib.*
Sc. (JAM.) Buff. On hair-mould bannocks fed, TAYLOR *Poems* (1787) 3. Edb. I vow my hair-mould milk would poison dogs, FERGUSSON *Poems* (1773) 108, ed. 1785.
[*Mucor*, hery mowldnes : *vitium panis, açor potus, rancor carnis*, DUNCAN *Etym.* (1595).]
HAIRN,HAIROUGH,HAIRSE,HAIRSHIP,HAIRUP, see Harden, *v.*, Hairif, Hearse, Hership.
HAIRY, *adj.* Var. dial. uses in Sc. Irel. and Eng. Written harey N.I.[1] **1.** Comp. (1) Hairy-bind, the greater dodder, *Cuscuta europaea* ; (2) -brotag, any very large, hairy caterpillar ; (3) -bummler, a name given to several kinds of crabs ; (4) -granfer, (5) -hoobit, -Hubert, or -oobit, see (2) ; (6) -hutcheon, a sea-urchin ; (7) -man, the larva of the tiger-moth ; (8) -milner, see (2) ; (9) -moggans, hose without feet ; (10) -palmer, (11) -tailor, see (2) ; (12) -wig, the earwig ; (13) -worm, see (2).
(1) Hrt. ELLIS *Mod. Husb.* (1750) IV. ii. (2) Cai.[1] (3) Buff.[1] (4) Cor. (M.A.C.) (5) Buff. He lifted up his hand to wipe something off his cheek. It was a hairy oobit, SMILES *Natur.* (ed. 1893) 191 ; The hairy-oubits hid frae view, SHELLEY *Flowers* (1868) 56. Nhb. If you throw a hairy worm, in the North called Hairy-Hubert, over your head, and take care not to look to see where it alights, you are sure to get something new before long, BROCKIE *Leg.* 140 ; Nhb.[1] Sometimes applied to a showy, helpless character. (6) Rxb. (JAM.) (7) e.Yks. *Nature Notes*, No. 4. w.Yks. (W.M.E.F.) (8) w.Wor.[1] (9) Fif. (JAM.) (10) w.Som.[1] Ae-uree paar mur. (11) Shr.[1] (12) Ken. (G.B.) (13) Nhb.[1], Cum.[4], n.Yks. (I.W.), n.Yks.[4] s.Yks.[1] MS. *add.* (T.H.)
2. Clever, sharp, capable ; cunning.
N.I.[1] Wmh. If it is proposed to send a boy on business to a fair, &c. it will be said, 'O, he is not hairy enough for that' (E.M.) ; You'd want to be very hairy to catch fish (M.S.M.).
3. Flighty, light-headed.
Nhb. In my recollection every one shaved some part of his face, except imbeciles or lunatics. Hence probably the term (M.H.D.).
HAISER, *v.* Sc. Irel. Also written haisre, haisre Sc. (JAM. *Suppl.*) ; haizer Sc. (JAM.) ; and in form hazerd N.I.[1] [hē'zer.] To dry clothes in the open air. See Haze, *v.*[4], Hazle, *v.*
Sc. (JAM. *Suppl.*) Abd. Our clothes are out 'haiserin.' Fresh air and sunlight are required to haiser recently-washed clothes (G.W.).
Hence **Haizert** or **Hazerded,** *ppl. adj.* half-dried, surface-dried.
Ayr. (JAM.) N.I.[1] Them clothes are not dry at all ; they're only hazerded.
HAISK, HAISLE, see Hask, *adj.*, Hazle, *v.*
HAISS, *adj.* Sc. Also written hess (JAM.). [hēs.] Hoarse. (JAM.), Cai.[1] Cf. hose, *adj.*
[OE. *hās*, hoarse ; cp. OHG. *heis*, 'raucus' (GRAFF).]
HAIST, see Harvest.
HAISTER, *v.* and *sb.* Sc. Cum. Wm. Also written haster Cum. Wm. ; hayster Cum.[1] [hē'ster.] **1.** *v.* To

anything hurriedly or in a slovenly manner; to act or speak without consideration.

Rxb. Applied to bread, when ill-toasted. Any work ill done, and in a hurried way, is also said to be haister'd (Jam.). Cum.⁴ Food put into a quick oven may be overcooked and spoiled; it is an haister't.

Hence **Haistering**, *ppl. adj.* careless, slovenly.

Rxb. 'A haisterin' hallock,' a careless or slovenly gillflirt (Jam.).

3. To fatigue with hard work; to pull about roughly; to annoy.

Cum. Young Martha Todd was haister't sair By rammish Wully Garr'as, Gilpin *Sngs.* (1866) 281; Cum.²⁴

Hence **Haister'd**, *pp.* roughly treated, harassed by cold; of the skin: roughened, chapped.

Cum.¹; Cum.⁴ An animal severely pinched by hunger and cold haister't. 'Yon nag's o' hastered.' Wm. Mi feeace is o' hēstәr'd i' t'helm wind (B.K.).

3. *sb.* One who speaks or acts confusedly. In *pl.* form. xb. (Jam.)

4. A slovenly woman; confusion, hodge-podge.

Slk. (*ib.*) Rxb. Sometimes applied to a great dinner confusedly set down (*ib.*).

5. A surfeit. Linton *Lake Cy.* (1864) 305; Cum.⁴

HAISTER, *sb.* Shr. (Hall.) The same as Astre (q.v.).

HAIT, *int.* and *v.* In *gen.* dial. use in Sc. and Eng. Also written hayt n.Yks.¹ Not.¹ Lei.¹ War.² Wil.; and in forms ait Chs.¹; ate, hate Chs.¹; heet Shr.¹; height .Yks. e.Yks.¹ s.Lan. nw.Der.¹ n.Lin.¹ Shr. Hrf. Suf.¹; heit n.Cy. s.Chs.¹ nw.Der.¹ Rut.¹ Nhp.¹² Shr.¹ Suf.¹ Dev.; het s.Wor. Glo.¹ Oxf.¹; hett w.Yks.¹; hite Nhb.¹ Wm. Yks.; hout Glo.; huyt s.Dur.; hyte Lth. n.Yks.¹; yate w.Yks.² Nhp.² [hȳt, eat, eit, it.] **1.** *int.* A call to horses or other animals to go on.

Wm. A sheep dog is urged to the furthermost point of the field by the shepherd calling out to it, 'Hite away! Hite away roond!' (B.K.) s.Lan. (W.H.T.) Rut.¹ Heit! Jack! s.Pem. Used fifty years ago in urging the bullocks (W.M.M.). Glo. A carter's phrase to encourage his horse, *Horae Subsecivae* (1777) 179. Dev. *ib.*

2. A call to the horse to go to the left.

Nhb.¹ Yks. For 'gee' and 'ob,' the carters say 'hite' and 'ree' (K.). n.Yks.¹ The old word of command to the horses in a team is the plough to turn towards the driver, or to the left. w.Yks.¹², e.An.¹, Ess. (H.H.M.)

Hence (1) **Haito** or **Hayto**, *sb.* a child's name for a horse; (2) **Hait-wo**, *int.* a call to horses to go to the left; (3) **Heighty-osa**, *sb.*, see (1); (4) **Highty**, *int.*, see (2).

(1) Wil.¹ n.Wil. Look at the haitos then! (E.H.G.) (2) e.An.¹, Wil.¹ (3) e.Yks.¹ (4) n.Cy. Dartnell & Goddard *Wds.* (1893).

3. A call to the horse to go to the right or off-side, away from the carter.

Chs. (E.M.G.), Chs.¹ s.Chs.¹ Heit off. nw.Der.¹ Not. Height again (E.P.); Not.¹ n.Lin.¹ Obsol. Lei.¹ Nhp.¹ A command to the filler, or shaft-horse, to go from the driver; Nhp.² A word addressed to the second horse in a team. War.², s.Wor. (H.K.) Shr.¹ (s.v. Waggoner's Words). Shr., Hrf. Bound *Provinc.* (1876). Glo.¹ Het off! Oxf.¹ Het up. e.Suf. (F.H.) Hmp. Formerly at harvest suppers, a song was sung in praise of the head carter, the chorus of which was, 'With a heit, with a ree, with a who, with gee,' Holloway.

4. *Phr.* (1) *neither hait nor ree*, neither one side nor the other; used *fig.* of a wilful person who will go his own way; (2) *always of hite or of shite*, said of a person with an uncertain, uneven temper.

(1) n.Cy. He will neither heit nor ree, Grose (1790). Nhb.¹ She wou'd neither byte nor ree. n.Yks. Thou'l neither height nor ree, Meriton *Praise Ale* (1684) l. 415. (2) Wm. (B.K.)

5. *v.* To urge or egg on; to urge on a horse.

Lth. He hyted, he huppit—in vain, O! He ferlied what gaured his horse stand like a stock, Ballantine *Poems* (1856) 114. s.Dur. He was always huyten' me on (J.E.D.).

[1. His thought said *haight*, his sillie speache cryed *ho*, Gascoigne *Dan Bartholmew* (1576), ed. Hazlitt, I. 136; The carter smoot, and cryde, as he were wood, Hayt, Brok! hayt, Scot! what spare ye for the stones? Chaucer . T. D. 1543. 2. Cp. Sw. dial. *håjt*, a cry to the ox or horse to turn to the left (Rietz, s.v. *hit*).]

HAIT, see **Haet**.

HAITCH, *sb.* Ken. Sus. [ētʃ.] A slight, passing shower. Sus.¹²

Hence **Haitchy**, *adj.* misty. Ken. (Holloway), Sus.¹²

[A form and special use of *ache*, *sb.*¹, used in the sense of a sudden and intermittent attack.]

HAITH, *int.* Sc. Irel. Also in form heth. [hēp, hep.] An exclamation of surprise, &c., 'faith.' Cf. **hegs**.

Sc. Heth she's o'er gently brought up to be a poor man's penny worth, Graham *Writings* (1883) II. 55. Sh.I. True in heth! *Sh. News* (Nov. 19, 1898); As for paecable neebors, guid heth, I tink we're no been sae ill dat wy ava, Burgess *Sketches* (2nd ed.) ii. n.Sc. Haith, an' if she's guid eneuch for Andrew, she's guid eneuch for the likes o' us, Gordon *Carglen* (1891) 197. Cai.¹ Abd. Haith! Cordy slunk awa', Cadenhead *Bon Accord* (1853) 248; Heth that's capital, Alexander *Johnny Gibb* (1871) xxxix. Frf. Heth, I mind she was a rael bad yin when I wis a wee lassie, Inglis *Ain Flk.* (1895) xii. Per. Haith I am doild, because 'tis so, That she is high and I am mean, Nicol *Poems* (1766) 34. Fif. Haith, I'd gang mysel' if he would dae that, Robertson *Provost* (1894) 23; Heth! I'm sair eneuch fashed wi' police tax ... withoot haeing mair rent to pey, McLaren *Tibbie* (1894) 17. s.Sc. Haith, we'll be as merry as we can, Wilson *Tales* (1836) II. 214. Rnf. Till, haith! the younker courage took, Young *Pictures* (1865) 10. Ayr. Haith, lad, ye little ken about it, Burns *Twa Dogs* (1786) l. 149. Lnk. But haith I'll cheat my joe in that, Lemon *St. Mungo* (1844) 37. Lth. Haith, mony a tryst I've seen us hae, Smith *Merry Bridal* (1866) 40. Edb. Haith, you mith do meikle ill, Crawford *Poems* (1798) 89. Peb. Haith, our wives will a' be here, Affleck *Poet. Wks.* (1836) 123. Dmf. An', haith! wi' me she's kindlie grown, Cromek *Remains* (1810) 37. Gall. If a minister thinks na muckle o' himself—haith, they will e'en jaloose that he kens best, Crockett *Standard Bearer* (1898) 119. N.I.¹ 'Heth no.' 'Heth aye.' Haith an' soul, but you won't.' 'Heth i,' faith yes. Ant. Heth I won't (S.A.B.).

HAITSUM, HAIVER, see **Hatesum**, *adj.*, **Haver**, *v.*¹

HAIVER, *sb.* Sc. Cmb. Also written **hever** Cmb.; and in forms **aiver** Lth.; **haivrel, haverel** Sc. (Jam.); **haveron** Gall. A cart-foal, after he has been gelded.

Lnk., Lth., e.Lth. (Jam.) Gall. Mactaggart *Encycl.* (1824). Cmb. Grose (1790) *MS. add.* (P.)

[ON. *hafr*, a buck, OE. *hæfer* (*Leechdoms*).]

HAIVER, HAIVEREL, see **Haver**, *v.*¹, **Haverel**.

HAIVERY, *adj.* Cor. [ē‑v(ә)ri.] 1. Miserly, greedy of money. Cor.¹² **2.** Envious. Cor.²

HAIVES, *sb. pl.* Sc. ? Hoofs.

If ye look yoursel', ye'll see she's fair into the haives, Ochiltree *Redburn* (1895) v.

HAIVING, *prp.* Cor.² The same as Eving, s.v. Eve, *v.*

HAIVINS, HAIZER, HAIZART, see **Havings, Haiser, Hazard**.

HAIZY, *adj.* Nhb. [hē·zi.] Hasty, excitable.

She's a kind o' haizy body (R.O.H.); Nhb.¹

HAKE, *sb.*¹ Bdf. Nrf. Ken. Cor. [ēk.] Phr. (1) *as dry as a hake*, very thirsty; (2) *a hake-shaped cloud*, a cloud in shape like the fish hake; (3) *who whipped the hake?* prov. saying; see below.

(1) Nrf. (E.M.) Ken. Kennett *Par. Antiq.* (1695). (2) Bdf. The hake-shaped cloud, if pointing east and west, indicates rain: if north and south, more fine weather, Swainson *Weather Flk-Lore* (1873) 204. (3) Cor. It is not improbable that the saying applied to the people of one of the Cornish fishing-towns, of 'Who whipped the hake!' may be explained by the following :— 'Lastly, they are persecuted by the hakes, who (not long sithence) haunted the coast in great abundance; but now being deprived of their wonted bait, are much diminished, verifying the proverb, "What we lose in hake we shall have in herring,"' Carew *Survey*, 34; Annoyed with the hakes, the seiners may, in their ignorance, have actually served one of those fish as indicated, Hunt *Pop. Rom. w.Eng.* (1865) 370, ed. 1896.

HAKE, *sb.*² Dur. Wm. Yks. Nhp. War. e.An. Also in forms **heaik** Dur.; **heeak** Wm. [h)ēk, h)iәk.] 1. A hook of any kind.

Dur. Heaicks 'n' creaiks 're as rank ez pint pots in a public house, Egglestone *Betty Podkins' Lett.* (1877) 9. Wm. She meead ersel saartan a gittan haald a Bobby Beetham, aedther be heeak er creeak, *Spec. Dial.* (1880) pt. ii. 19. n.Yks.², e.An.¹ Nrf. Rye *Hist. Nrf.* (1885) xv.

2. A pot-hook; a hook built into the chimney to hang a pot or 'boiler' on.

Nhp.[1] Not freq. **War.**[2] An adjustable hook and rack; through the holes of the latter the hook could be hung at a higher or lower position over the fire, as desired. **e.An.**[1]; **e.An.**[2] Now chiefly used for a kind of gate which swings over the kitchen fire, or another utensil which hangs down the chimney, both used for suspending pots and boilers. **Nrf.** 'As black as a hake,' very black (E.M.); **Cozens-Hardy** Broad Nrf. (1893) 17. **w.Nrf.** I'd ha put the hakes on her, if she'd ben my missus, **Orton** Beeston Ghost (1884) 4. **Suf.** On went the boilers till the hake Had much ado to bear 'em, Suf. Garl. (1818) 339; **Cullum** Hist. Hawsted (1813). **e.Suf.** A dentated iron bar, suspended in a chimney, on which pots or kettles are hung. Another kind has, instead of teeth, holes. A pin, projecting from another piece of iron, fits into any of these holes. This second piece of iron has a hook at the bottom, from which a kettle or pot is suspended over the fire. ' As black as the hake up of the chimney.' Said of anything very black or dirty (F.H.).

3. The dentated iron head of a plough.

Nrf. Grose (1790); The iron on a plough to which the ' pundle tree' is attached, Arch. (1879) VIII. 170. **e.Nrf.** **Marshall** Rur. Econ. (1787). **Suf.** Morton Cyclo. Agric. (1863); **Rainbird** Agric. (1819) 294, ed. 1849; Suf.[1], e.Suf. (F.H.)

[1. Norw. dial. hake, a hook (Aasen); so ON. haki (Vigfusson).]

HAKE, sb.[2] Cum. Wm. Lan. Also in forms aik Wm.[1]; hack Wm.; haike Wm. & Cum.[1] [h]ēk.] **1.** A merry meeting; a rustic dance or gathering.

Lakel.[2] Cum. We agreed amang oorsels to stop an' see t'end o' t'hake, **Richardson** Talk (1876) 5; The arrival of the young hopeful was, in former times, duly celebrated by a series of 'hakes,' of a highly amusing and jovial character, Lonsdale Mag. (July 1866) 23; **Cum.**[18] Wm. A'll tell yu some o' t'haeks an' stirs, **Wilson** Kitty Kirkis, 102; It hap'n'd ta be ther Auld-wife-Hayke, **Blezard** Sngs. (1848) 17; Wm.[1] Village dances in the Lake District were formerly often called Auld-wife aiks, being frequently got up by some elderly female in order to raise a small fund, &c.

2. A stir, turmoil, tumult.

Wm. & Cum.[1] Wi' nowther haike nor quarrel, 207. **n.Lan.** They ... feight an' fratch, an' meakk cruel hakes, **Piketah** Forness Flk. (1870) 23.

HAKE, sb.[4] Cum.[124] [hēk.] A lean horse or cow.

HAKE, sb.[5] Cor. Also in form ache. A large comfortless room or place. Cf. ache, sb.[2]

A great hake of a house, **Thomas** Randigal Rhymes (1895) Gl.; How can you sit in such a hake of a room? (M.A.C.)

HAKE, v. and sb.[6] Sc. and n. counties to Lin. Nhp. Also Hrf. e.An. Also in forms ache m.Yks.[1] Hrf.; aik e.Yks.; ake e.Yks.[1]; haak n.Lin.[1]; haig Ayr. (Jam.); haik Sc. (Jam.) Sh.I. Bnff.[1] Abd. Cum. w.Yks.; heeak n.Yks.[24] [h]ēk, iək.] **1.** v. To wander about aimlessly and idly; to loiter, lounge; to hang about with intent to eavesdrop; to sneak. Also with about.

Sc. Haikin throw the country (Jam.). **Bnff.**[1] To roam in an unsettled manner over the pasture; as, ' That coo winna sattle : she haiks on.' **N.Cy.**[12] **Nhb.**[1] Wm. Maunders abaut fra hause to hause, haking and slinging, **Hutton** Bran New Wark (1785) l. 461; Ise net gaan ta hev ya gaan gadden off tat fairs an haken aboot it rowads et neets an sec like, **Taylor** Sketches (1882) 17. **m.Yks.**[1] To hang about pryingly, to sneak, or aim at getting at information, &c., in an underhand way; n.Yks.[4] e.Yks. He was akin about all day lang; an all fo nowt, **Nicholson** Flk-Sp. (1889) 50; Thoo's allus ganning aiking about (R.M.); e.Yks.[1], m.Yks.[1] w.Yks.[1] He leeads a filthy peyl ... wi' his prancin an hakin about, ii. 305. **Lan.** **Harland & Wilkinson** Flk-Lore (1867) 216. **ne.Lan.**[1] **n.Lin.** **Sutton** Wds. (1881). **sw.Lin.**[1] She'd as well been at school as haking about. I don't like my bairns haking about.

Hence (1) Haikan, vbl. sb. continued wandering about in an idle manner; (2) Haiker, sb. an animal that has a habit of wandering over the pasture or of straying from it; (3) Haiking or Haking, (a) ppl. adj. wandering, loitering; idle, lounging; worthless; (b) see (1); (4) Haiking about, phr. having the habit of wandering in an idle manner or of roaming over pasture.

(1, 2) Bnff.[1] (3, a) s.Sc. Can Lizzy hae gane oot wi' that haikin' callant, Jamie Rib[1] **Wilson** Tales (1896) IV. 356. **w.Yks.** 'A haking fellow,' an idle loiterer, **Thoresby** Lett. (1703); **Hutton**

Tour to Caves (1781); w.Yks.[4] Lin. **Thompson** Hist. Boston (1856) 708. n.Lin.[1] (b) Sc. He gaed awa gey wearied wi' haikin, **Edwards** Mod. Poets, 7th S. 53. (4) Bnff.[1] He'll niver get on; he's sic a haikin'-aboot hypal.

2. To hanker or gape after. n.Cy. **Bailey** (1721).

3. To drag or carry from one place to another with little purpose; to tramp, trudge; esp. with about or up and down.

Sh.I. Shü wid hae wiz gaun haikin' as muckle hay i' da bul o' a maishie as ye wid fling in a kishie for a hen ta lae in, Sh. News (Sept. 3, 1898). **Abd.** Haikin' thro' the feedles the tae time, an' in'o the byres the neist, **Alexander** Ain Flk. (1882) 151. **s.Sc.** ' To haik up and down, to haik about,' to drag from one place to another to little purpose, conveying the idea of fatigue caused to the person who is thus carried about, or produced by the thing that one carries. ' What needs ye haik her up and down throw the haill town ! ' ' What needs you weary yourself, haiking about that heavy big-coat whare'er ye gang ? ' (Jam.) **Lakel.**[2] Ah's fair doon sto'ed wi' haken aboot efter yon ducks an' things. Ye wad hake yan aboot wi' ye as lang as ivver yan could trail. **s.Yks.**[1] To do anything unnecessarily or with more labour than is requisite. **e.An.**[1] Often joined with ' hatter.' ' He has been haking and hattering all day long.' **Nrf.** I am that tired, I don't know what to do with myself. I've been haking about all day (W.R.E.).

4. To tease, worry, importune; to pester or worry with questions, &c.; to persecute, hurry on.

Wm. Such as he would hake the life out of a toad (B.K.). n.Yks.[1]; n.Yks.[2] They hake my very heart out; n.Yks.[4] ne.Yks.[1] Hake 'em away [urge them on almost faster than they can go]. m.Yks.[1] c.Hrf. Ther bent no boy or girl either as aches I, but'l be the worse for't, Why John (Coll. L.L.B.)

5. To tire, distress, applied to land.

Cum.[1] It indicates exhaustion from over-cropping; **Cum.**[2]; **Cum.**[4] T'field hes been fairly haket ta deeth; what can it grow ?

6. To beat, batter, drive or knock out of one's way; to butt with the horns or head.

Sc. He swore he wad lay my back laigh on the plain, But I haikit him weel, **Ballantine** Whistle Binkie (1878) II. 3 (Jam. Suppl.). **Cum.**[12]; **Cum.**[4] T'cows used to hake yan anudder till t'beals were summat awful to hear.

7. To kidnap, carry off by force.

Sc. They'll haik ye up and settle ye bye, **Scott** Minstrelsy (1802) III. 127, ed. 1848. **Edb.** Still used in the same sense by the boys of the High School of Edinburgh (Jam.).

8. sb. An idle, lounging fellow; an animal that wanders in an unsettled manner over the pasture, or strays over it. Gen. in pl. form.

Bnff.[1], Abd. (G.W.), Cld. (Jam.), w.Yks.[1] Lin. Always associated with the idea of idleness, **Streatfeild** Lin. and Danes (1884) 334. **s.Lin.** What a gre't hulkin' hakkes the feller is. **sw.Lin.**[1] **Nhp.**[1] The use of this word is confined to the n. part of the county.

Hence Hakesing, ppl. adj. tramping idly about. sw.Lin.[1]

9. A greedy, grasping person ; a miser ; a pertinacious asker or beggar.

Wm. (B.K.) n.Yks.[1]; n.Yks.[2] ' A mischievous heeak,' an annoyer. ' A greedy hake,' a grasper; n.Yks.[4], m.Yks.[1]

10. A forward, tattling woman.

Abd. (Jam.) **Ayr.** A female, whose chief delight is to fly from place to place, telling tales concerning her neighbours (ib.).

[2. Du. haken, to long for (Hexham). 3. He haikit to that hall, For to wit gif Wymondis wynnyng was thair, Rauf Coilʒear (c. 1475) 642, in Sc. Allit. Poems (1897) 103.]

HAKE, int. n.Cy. Cum. Written haike n.Cy. (Hall.) [hēk.] An expression of defiance.

n.Cy. (Hall.) **Cum.**[2] Hake for a fight! Cum.[4]

HAKE, see Hack, sb.[2], Hawk, v.[1]

HAKED, sb. Obs. Hnt. Cmb. w.Cy. A large pike, Esox lucius

Hnt. Pikes of a great bigness taken in Ramsey Mere, **Blount** (1681). **Cmb.** (Hall.) **w.Cy.** **Skinner** (1671). [**Satchell** (1879).] [OE. hacod, a pike (Ælfric); cp. G. hecht.]

HAKEL, HAKUSSING, see Hickwall, Hackasing.

HAL, sb. and v. Yks. Lan. Also in form al Lan. [al.] **1.** sb. A fool, a jester ; a silly person.

m.Yks.[1] **w.Yks.** Sum drucken owd hals at hed been on t'spree Com singin like mad up t'street, **Preston** Poems (1864) 31; Standin at house ends makin hals o' thersenns, Saunierer's Satchel (1877) 23; w.Yks.[2] He's acting the hal agean; w.Yks.[6]

Gurt idle hal ! Lan. Mak a hal o' somebory else ; for yo sha'not make one o' him no moor, WAUGH *Besom Ben*, 19a ; Troyin to may a hal on im, SCHOLES *Tim Gamwattle* (1857) 4.

2. *v.* To banter ; to worry or bother.

w.Yks. (S.W.) Lan. Let's ha noane o' thy allin', BRIERLEY *Adventures* (1881) 39. e.Lan. She keeps allin her to go (H.M.). sw.Lan. What's thaa allin abaat ? (*ib.*)

[1. The same word as *Hal*, the familiar form for *Henry* (*Harry*).]

HAL, HALA, see Hale, *sb.*², Hallow, *sb.*¹

HALA, *adv.* Lan. [Not known to our correspondents.] Pretty well. THORNBER *Hist. Blackpool* (1837) 108.

HALAH, see Heloe.

HAL-AN-TOW, *sb.* Cor. Also written ha.lan.tow. A pleasure party on May 8.

The Hal-an-tow are privileged to levy contributions on strangers coming into the town, *Flk-Lore Jrn.* (1886) IV. 231 ; The Hal-an-tow, or party of servants and their friends, go on 8th of May (Flora-day or Faddy) to breakfast in the country and return laden with boughs . J.W.) ; With ha-lan-tow, rumble, O! *Helstone Furry-Day Sng.* in DIXON *Sngs. Eng. Peas.* (1846) 168, ed. 1857.

HALBERDIER, *sb.* Sc. A person armed with a halberd, esp. a member of a civic guard carrying a halberd as a badge of office ; a Town's Sergeant.

Escorted by Donald, our stout halberdier, In solemn procession, owerbye to the kirk, VEDDER *Poems* (1842) 302.

HALBERT, *sb.* Sh.I. A tall, thin person. S. & Ork.¹

HALCH, see Halsh.

HALCUP, *sb.* Hmp. The marsh-marigold or kingcup, *Caltha palustris* ; *gen.* in *pl.* (J.R.W.), Hmp.¹

HALD, see HOLD, *v.*

HALE, *sb.*¹ Yks. Not. Lin. Suf. Ess. s.Cy. Dev. Cor. Also written hail w.Yks.² ; haile e.Yks. Lin.¹ sw.Lin.¹ ; and in forms hail nw.Dev.¹ ; hall Suf. Dev. [ēl, eəl.]

1. One of the two handles of a plough or wheelbarrow ; *gen.* in *pl.*

n.Yks.¹ Usually in the form Plough-hales ; n.Yks.⁴, ne.Yks.¹ e.Yks. The things ... ommast throppled thersens ower hales ov a hickin-barra, NICHOLSON *Flk-Sp.* (1889) 34 ; e.Yks.¹, m.Yks.¹, w.Yks.², Not.², s.Not. (J.P.K.) Lin. STREATFEILD *Lin. and Danes* (1884) 335. Lin.¹ The hailes flew up and caught me on the gob. n.Lin.¹ To be sold by auction . . . 30 plough hales, *Stamford Merc.* (Sept. 20, 1867). n.Lin. Lay bo'd o' th' plough haäls and let's see what soört o' a furrer yah can cut (T.H.R.). sw.Lin.¹ Dev. The sole-piece or chip, showing the splay of the two hails or handles, together with the share and cradle-pins, MOORE *Hist. Dev.* (1809) I. 296 ; *Horae Subsecivae* (1777) 199. nw.Dev.¹ The left-hand or stouter handle of a timbern zole. Cor. The part of a wooden plough, to which the handles, beam and foot are attached, THOMAS *Randigal Rhymes* (1895) Gl.

2. An instrument for hanging a pot over a fire ; a 'trammel.'

Suf. RAY (1691) ; (K.) Ess. BAILEY (1721) ; Gl. (1851) ; Ess.¹ s.Cy. GROSE (1790).

3. A rake used for raking loose stones or pebbles from a brook.

Dev. Like a dung rake, with several strong teeth, *Horae Subsecivae* (1777) 199 ; GROSE (1790) MS. add. (M.)

[1. *Le manche d'une charruå,* a plough-tail, or handle ; the plough-hale, COTGR. Norw. dial. and Dan. *hale,* the tail ; ON. *hali,* the tail of cattle (VIGFUSSON).]

HALE, *sb.*² Lan. Lin. Mid. Also in form hal Lan. [ēl.] 1. A piece of flat alluvial land by the side of a river ; a sand-bank. See Haugh. Cf. eale.

Lan. *N. & Q.* (1870) 4th S. v. 570. n.Lin.¹ An angular pasture in the township of East Butterwick, adjoining Bottesford Beck on the North, is called Butterwick Hale. It has been used from an early period as a rest for the high-land water in flood time, until it could flow into the Trent.

2. A triangular corner of land, a 'gair' ; a bank or strip of grass, separating lands in an open field.

Lin. STREATFEILD *Lin. and Danes* (1884) 335. n.Lin.¹ Mid. There is a piece of low land in Tottenham between the High Cross and the railway station called Tottenham Hale, or more commonly the Hale, *N. & Q.* (1868) 4th S. ii. 405.

HALE, *sb.*³ e.An. [ēl.] A heap of anything, a mangold clamp ; a long range or pile of bricks set out to dry in the open air before being burned.

VOL. III.

e.An.¹ Nrf. A mangold hale (E.M.) ; Potatoes, roots, &c. buried in heaps are said to be in hales (U.W.).

HALE, *v.*¹ Sc. Nhb. Cum. Yks. Lin. Dor. Also written hail Sc. Nhb.¹ sw.Lin.¹ [h]ēl, h)eəl.] 1. To pour or empty out, as water from a vessel by inclining it to one side ; to bale. Cf. heel, *v.*²

n.Yks. Thah neeam is as ointment haled out, ROBINSON *Sng. Sol.* (1860) i. 3 ; n.Yks.¹ ; n.Yks.² Hale me out another cup ; n.Yks.⁴, ne.Yks.¹, m.Yks.¹ Lin. Hale out the water, THOMPSON *Hist. Boston* (1856) 708 ; Lin.¹ Dor. *Gl.* (1851).

2. To flow, run down in a large stream ; to pour.

Sc. Drops of blude frae Rose the Red Came hailing to the groun', CHILD *Ballads* (1886) II. 418 ; 'It's hailin on' or 'down' is commonly used with respect to a heavy rain (JAM.). Abd. They are posting on whate'er they may Baith het and meeth, till they are haling down, ROSS *Helenore* (1768) 79, ed. 1812. Lnk. Facht when they were kiss'd or huggit, Till the sweat cam' hailin' doon, NICHOLSON *Kilwuddie* (ed. 1895) 96. Nhb.¹ Az rout [wrought] till the sweet hailed off us. Cum.² Lin. The sweat hales of'n me o' nights, STREATFEILD *Lin. and Danes* (1884) 335. sw.Lin.¹ The sweat hailed offen him.

[1. Norw. dial. *halla,* to incline or tilt a vessel (AASEN) ; so Icel. (ZOEGA) ; ON. *halla,* to lean or turn sideways. 2. The teris began fast to hale owre hir chekis, BELLENDEN *Livy* (1533), ed. 1822, 101.]

HALE, *v.*² *sb.*⁴ Sc. Nhb. Cum. Yks. Lan. Wor. Shr. Hrt. e.An. Hmp. w.Cy. Wil. Som. Cor. Also written hail S. & Ork.¹ Cum.⁸ e.Yks. ; haill Abd. ; hayl Lan. ; and in form ally Wor. [h)ēl, h)eəl.] 1. *v.* To haul ; to draw forcibly, pull ; to drag along ; to load.

Sh.I. Hails wi' an easy tow, an' comes ashore wi' forty wys o' white fish, STEWART *Tales* (1892) 14. Abd. There blind zeall to the Couenant did so haill them on to their own destruction, TURREFF *Antiq. Gleanings* (1859) 57. Per. That stead Where yee did hail your shaft unto the head, FORD *Harp* (1893) 3. Gall. As the Dominie and I were haled away, CROCKETT *Grey Man* (1896) 305. n.Cy. (J.L.) (1783). Nhb.¹ Cum.³ ; Cum.⁵ hail't Jonathan out fray amang them. e.Yks. Soe need they not to trouble themselves with hailinge on soe much ait once, BEST *Rur. Econ.* (1641) 50. Shr.² Confined to the river side and chiefly to men or horses drawing small or large craft on the Severn against the stream. Hmp. GROSE (1790) *MS. add.* (M.) Wil. (K.M.G.) Som. Plough-men have been haleing bells, HERVEY *Wedmore Chron.* (1887) I. 79. w.Cor. ' I can neither hale them nor häve [heave] them.' Said by an old woman with rheumatism in her feet (M.A.C.).

Hence (1) Haler or Hayler, *sb.* one who works or does anything energetically and effectively ; (2) Hale-to, *sb.* the movement of a rake in raking up grain, &c. ; (3) Haling-muff, *sb.* a mitten used by fishermen to protect their hands when hauling the lines into the boat ; (4) -way, *sb.* a towing-path ; cf. hauling-path, s.v. Haul, *v.*¹ ; (5) Halster, *sb.* one who tows a barge alongside a river by means of a rope.

(1) Cum.¹² Lan. He is a hayler at it, R. PIKETAH *Forness Flk.* (1870) 38. (2) Hrt. A man with one motion or hale-to on each side of him will rake up a parcel of grain in a trice, ELLIS *Mod. Husb.* (1750) V. ii. (3) S. & Ork.¹ (4) Cmb. *N. & Q.* (1860) 2nd S. ix. 51. (5) w.Cy. (HALL.)

2. To carry on the trade of a carrier, to cart, carry.

Wor. E've got a 'oss an' cart ... an' does allyin', *Vig. Mon.* in *Berrow's Jrn.* (Mar. 9, 1895) 4, col. 3 ; It's him as bin allying on this road (H.K.). Wil. (K.M.G.)

3. To breathe heavily, pant ; to inhale ; also in phr. *to hale for breath.*

Suf. e.An. *Dy. Times* (1892) ; (C.T.) e.Suf. (F.H.)

4. *sb.* A haul of fish.

Sh.I. I can mind wis takin' forty o' him [turbot], grit an' sma', apo' ae hail i' da deep water, *Sh. News* (July 10, 1897) ; Efter we set aff fir a mornin' hail, I lays me doon i' da fore-head i' da bight o' da sail, STEWART *Tales* (1892) 243.

[1. Halyn or drawyn, *traho, Prompt.* ; What that on may hale, that other let, CHAUCER *Parl. Foules,* 151. OFr. *haler,* 'tirer' (LA CURNE).]

HALE, *adj.* and *sb.*⁵ Sc. Nhb. Dur. Cum. Wm. Yks. Lan. Also ? Ken. ? Dor. ? Som. Also written hail Sc. Bnff.¹ Nhb.¹ Dor. ; haill Sc. ; hayl Wm. ; and in forms haal w.Yks.¹ ; hael Sh.I. Nhb.¹ ; heaal Cum. ; heal Sc. w.Yks.¹ ; heale Cum. Wm. ; heall Cum.¹ ; heeal(l Wm.

E

n.Yks.²⁴ ne.Yks.¹ e.Yks.¹; heyel Nhb.¹; hiyal Wm.; hyal Dur.¹ n.Lan.; hyel(l N.Cy.¹ Nhb.¹; yal n.Yks.² ne.Yks.¹ [h]ēl, h]eəl, hil, hiəl.] 1. adj. Free from injury; safe, sound, unhurt.

Sc. It's good sleeping in a haill skin, Scott Bride of Lam. (1819) vi. Sh.I. Get me . . . my sea-brecks, An' see dey're hale afore, Stewart Tales (1892) 92. Bch. Paris . . . gart me wish I were awa' While I had a hale skin, Forbes Ulysses (1785) 21. Kcd. Pantaloons and guid black breeks, If they be hale and hae the steeks, Jamie Muss (1844) 45. Frf. His hyde, they said, was heal an' sound, Piper o' Peebles (1794) 16. Rnf. Ye [a pair of shoes] did right weel whan ye war hale, Picken Poems (1813) I. 33. Ayr. Lord, remember singing Sannock, Wi' hale-breeks, saxpence, an' a bannock, Burns Lett. to J. Tennant, l. 47. Dmf. Routh o' potatoes—champit an' hale I' their ragged jackets, Thom Jock o' Knowe (1878) 39. Peb. With bonnet black, too, old, but hale, Lintoun Green (1685) 37, ed. 1817. n.Cy. Border Gl. (Coll. L.L.B.)

Hence (1) Hale-headit, adj. unhurt ; whole and entire; (2) -hearted, adj. of unbroken spirit; (3) -hide, see (1); (4) -scart, adj. without a scratch, unhurt, wholly safe ; also used fig.; (5) -skinnt, adj. having a whole skin without sores or disease.

(1) Sc., Abd. (Jam.) (2) Edb. Bronze-browed, ruddy-cheeked, and hale-hearted as I am, Ballantine Gaberlunzie (ed. 1875) 12. (3) Bch. But he gaed aff hale-hide frae you For a' your windy voust, Forbes Ajax (1785) 28. (4) Sc. Symon and Janet his dame, Halescart frae the wars without skaithing, Chambers Sngs. (1829) II. 347. Ayr. Lord, let us a' aff haill-scart at the last if aiblins it be within t'e compass o' Thy power! Service Dr. Duguid (ed. 1887) 21. Rxb. In spite o' dool, haith here we're hale-scart yet, A. Scott Poems (ed. 1808) 159. (5) Buff.¹ We canna be our thankfou' it w'ir hail-skinnt, fin we see yon peer thing a' our wee cruels.

2. Healthy, sound, vigorous ; health-giving, wholesome.

Sc. Broken bread makes hail bairns, Ramsay Prov. (1737). Sh.I. An' you an' I be hael an' weel, Stewart Tales (1892) 244. Elg. Donald's still in Donald's trews, Hale, weel, an' livin', Tester Poems (1865) 97. Abd. Hale be your heart, my canty Cock, Cock Strains (1810) I. 125. Kcd. The Piper is dune out, Although he be baith hale and stout, Jamie Muse (1844) 104. Frf. Young guidmen, fond, stark an' hale, Morison Poems (1790) 16. Per. As hale and hearty as a three-year-auld buirn, Sandy Scott (1897) 21. Fif. Men ferdy-limb'd and swank and hale, Tennant Papistry (1827) 92. Dmb. His thrifty wife, tho' heal and leal, Whiles canna bake for want o' meal, Taylor Poems (1827) 70. Rnf. Ane may be hale, an' weel in health the day, Picken Poems (1813) I. 21. Ayr. We maun hae a little more of your balsamic advice, to make a' heal among us, Galt Provost (1822) xlvi. Lnk. Three hale and healthy bairnies, Wardrop J. Mathison (1881) 97. Lth. I ferlie gin in palace, or in lordly ha', Their hearts are a' as hale, as in our cot sae sma', Ballantine Poems (1856) 148. Edb. Wholesome, hale, historic food, Forbes Poems (1812) 6. Dmf. Tak ye a lassie tight and heal, Shennan Tales (1831) 61. Nhb. For we are hale an' hearty baith, Coquetdale Sngs. (1852) 59. Ken.² Hale weather. Dor. Barnes Gl. (1863). Som. I did nev'r see her look more hale an' dapper than her do just now, Leith Lemon Verbena (1895) 6.

3. Phr. (1) hale an' a-hame, quite at home, in one's element ; in good spirits; (2) — and fere, in perfect health, strong, healthy; (3) to be hale o' mair, to recover, to get over (an illness, &c.).

(1) Lak. He's [Cupid] hale an' a-hame amang touslin' an' kissin', Watson Poems (1853) 50. (2) Per. Spunky, hale, an' fere, Gleg —he kens his bis'ness, Stewart Character (1857) 67. Slg. It was sturdy, hale, an' fier, Wi' sock an' couter bright an' clear, Muir Poems (1818) 8. Ayr. As lang's we're hale and fier, Burns Ep. to Davie (1784) st. 2. Edb. Thinking to . . . look baith hail an' fier, Till at the lang-run Death dirks in, Fergusson Poems (1773) 199, ed. 1785. Gall. I hae tooted it owre in nogginfus now for mair than a hunner year, and am tae fore yet hale and fear, Mactaggart Encycl. (1824) 4, ed. 1876. (3) Sh.I. If puir Girzzie is gotten her endin' strake ta day, he's a job 'at A'll no be hale o' mair, ta da grave, Sh. News (Aug. 28, 1897).

4. Whole, entire, complete. Also used advb.

Sc. However the haill hive was ower mony for me at last, Scott Nigel (1822) iii. Sh.I. We wid a bed da hael trave o' da bairns ower, bit da skûle lay i' da hill, Burgess Sketches (2nd ed.) 111. Cai.¹ Buff. The bare and simple name of MacGregor made that hail clan to presume on their power, Gordon Chron. Keith (1880) 96. Abd. I cured the hale complainin' gang For nought ava,

---

Cadenhead Bon Accord (1853) 159. Frf. The hail night thro', Sands Poems (1833) 44. Per. For twa hale hours he preached, Cleland Inchbrachen (1883) 11, ed. 1887. Fif. Great baps and scones were swallow'd hail, Tennant Papistry (1827) 53. Rnf. Afore the hail assembl'd rout, Wi' scornfu' hiss deride ye, Picken Poems (1813) I. 109. Ayr. The haill clanjamphrey of the toon and kintra-side, Service Dr. Duguid (ed. 1887) 68. Lnk. I was half crazy made wi' their clavers, An' hale wi' her twa lauchin' een, Nicholson Idylls (1870) 76. Lth. Through a' the hale parish, Ballantine Poems (1856) 2. Edb. The hale house thought she had followed my faither, Ballantine Gaberlunzie (ed. 1875) 231. Peb. Tho' ye seek the hale creation, Affleck Poet. Wks. (1836) 84. Gall. Able in a het contention For to outwit a hale convention, Lauderdale Poems (1796) 211. Kcb. A sonsier pair ye wadna seen In a' the hale warl' wide, Armstrong Ingleside (1890) 41. N.Cy.¹ Nhb. Gan finely clad the hyell year roun', Wilson Pitman's Pay (1843) 33 ; Nhb.¹, Dur.¹ Cum. T'wad shem the heale parish, Rayson Misc. Poems (1858) 56 ; Aa cud trot am about for a heall day, Dickinson Joe and Geol. (1866) 6. Wm. Meh hayl fraym iz affected, Blezard Sngs. (1848) ; The Armstrangs an Hardens, an aw' the heale gang, Whitehead Leg. (1859) 7 ; Thoos geean an spilt a heeal meeal a new milk, Spec. Dial. (1885) pt. iii. 6. n.Yks.²⁴, ne.Yks.¹ e.Yks. Marshall Rur. Econ. (1788). w.Yks.¹ Thank God for 'em, wi' or haal heart, ii. 312. n.Lan. There was a hyal famaly on um, Lonsdale Mag. (Jan. 1867) 270.

Hence (1) Haellens, adv. certainly, completely; (2) Hailly or Halelie, adv. wholly, utterly ; (3) Haleumlie or Helimly, adv., see (1); (4) Yalseeal, adj. wholesale, plentiful.

(1) Sh.I. Ta tell da truth I haellens tought Sibbie wis noo geen juist far enough wi' trying mi patience, Sh. News (May 15, 1897). (2) Fif. The sinfu' bodies o' the Elie Were spain'd frae image-worship hailly, Tennant Papistry (1827) 12. Slg. A fear to devour them halelie at the last, Bruce Sermons (1631) iv, ed. 1843. w.Yks.¹ Gie thersels haally to'th' sarvice, ii. 323. (3) Abd. For fan I saw you, I thought haleumlie That ye wad never speak again to me, Ross Helenore (1768) 13, ed. 1812 ; O yon dreadfu' crack I haleumlie thought wad ha been our wrack, ib. 81. (4) n.Yks. They gat them by yalseeal (I.W.).

5. Comb. (1) Hael-an-hadden, entire, complete; (2) Hale-head, in phr. to go hale-head errand, to go on express or sole purpose; (3) -lot, a considerable number, a 'whole lot '; (4) -oot drinks, a toast ; see below ; (5) -ruck, the sum total of a person's property ; (6) -water, a heavy fall of rain ; (7) -wheel, in wholesale fashion, in quick succession ; (8) -wort, the whole number or amount.

(1) Sh.I. In aess o hael-an-hadden worls, Burgess Rasmie (1892) 6a. (2) Cai.¹ (3) e.Yks.¹ The' was a heeal-lot o' fooaks there. (4) Sc. Here Allan studied and practised Hy-Jinks, and once at least fell a victim to the game of 'haill oot drinks,' Haliburton Puir Auld Scot. (1887) 59. Per. 'Hail oot drinks! come what will empty your glasses.' The chairman at a dinner-party gave out this toast, and on this account became intoxicated, and fell a victim to the game of 'hail oot drinks' (G.W.). (5) Rxb. (Jam.) (6) Sc. The rain, which fell almost in hale water, as we say, has washed away half the school-master's kail-yard, Glenfergus (1820) I. 203 (Jam.). N.Cy.¹ Nhb.¹ In a thunder shower the rain is said to be comin' doon hail (or hyel) watter. Cum. Just heaal watter cumman slap doon ontah yan eh gegginfuls, Sargisson Joe Scoap (1881) '200 ; Cum.¹ Wm. 'Is't rainen when ye com in!' 'Aye, is't, ebben doon hiyal watter, as yan says' (B.K.). (7) Abd. He had been sen'in' them to Lunnon b' the dizzen ilka ither ouk, hale-wheel, this file, Alexander Ain Flk. (1882) 121. (8) Slk. I wish ye be nae the deil's bairns, the halewort o' ye! Hogg Tales (1838) 51, ed. 1866 ; If he made weel through wi' his hides mayhap he wad pay the hale wort, ib. Perils of Man (1822) III. 283 (Jam.).

6. sb. Health, comfort, welfare. Cf. heal, sb.¹

Abd. Health and hale, Cock Strains (1810) I. 81. Ayr. My hale and weal I'll tak a care o't, Burns To Mitchell (1795) st. 5.

7. The whole, the whole amount or number ; the sum-total.

Sc. I adhere to all and haill upon all perils whatsomever, Thomson Cloud of Witnesses (1714) 391, ed. 1871. Ayr. Half o' the hale dung aff their feet, Then is a victory complete, Boswell Poet. Wks. (1816) 166, ed. 1871. Lth. The hale o' his pack he has now on his back, Macneill Poet. Wks. (1801) 217, ed. 1856. Wgt. The ban' cheers the haill o' the streets roun' an' roun', Fraser Poems (1885) 51. Cum. I'll try to be happy the hale o' the day, Gilpin Ballads (1874) 17a. ne.Yks.¹ Ah've deean t'heeal on't.

8. Phr. in hale, altogether, the whole sum.

Edb. Gied ye in a shoeing bill, 'Twas twenty shillings sax in hale,

LIDDLE *Poems* (1821) 110. **Pcb.** My tocher's fifty pound in hale, AFFLECK *Post. Whs.* (1896) 81.

9. Whole coal, as distinguished from coal that has been partly worked.

Nhb. Though still they're i' the hyell a' hewin', WILSON *Pitman's Pay* (1843) 59 ; Nhb.¹

[1. Þou sal baþ sounde & hale come of þis ship to lande, *Cursor M.* (c. 1300) 24888. OE. *hāl*, safe (*Matt.* x. 22).]

HALE, see **Hal, Hall,** *sb.*¹ ², **Heal,** *v.*², **Hell,** *sb.*

HALEHEEAM, *sb.* e.Yks.¹ [ē·liəm.] An heirloom. Awd creddle's [cradle's] been a haleheeam I family fo' ginerations.

HALER, see **Heloe.**

HALESOME, *adj.* Sc. Nhb. Cum. Yks. Also in forms **haalsome** w.Yks.¹ ; **halsome** Sc. ; **healesome** Cum. ; **healsome** m.Yks.¹ ; **heealsome** n.Yks.² ; **helsum** Nhb.¹ [h]ē·l-, h)iə·lsəm.] Wholesome, healthful, sound.

Sc. Naebody shall persuade me, that it's either halesome or prudent, SCOTT *Rob Roy* (1817) xviii. **Abd.** They now rejoicin' taste its halesome bree, STILL *Cottar's Sunday* (1845) 22 ; Keep her . . . as white and clean in thy een, as she is fair and halesome in oors, MACDONALD *D. Elginbrod* (1863) I. 6. **Frf.** Clean halesome ale, tho' sma', MORISON *Poems* (1790) 46. **Per.** Get a howp in ilka cheek O' halesome livin', HALIBURTON *Horace* (1886) 29. **Fif.** Share our halesome country cheer, DOUGLAS *Poems* (1806) 102. **Dmb.** Thou finds upon the grass Sweet halesome dew, TAYLOR *Poems* (1827) 84. **Rnf.** Yer lot the Bard envies, Sae halsome near the water, PICKEN *Poems* (1813) II. 11. **Ayr.** Whether it was the halsome dreid thereof, or whether it was that I was but wee, SERVICE *Dr. Duguid* (ed. 1887) 30. **Lnk.** A halesome heart and guileless mind, HUNTER *Poems* (1884) 22. **Edb.** A' the thrang in a sang Should join wi' halesome heart, M°DOWALL *Poems* (1839) 226. **Dmf.** Help that was halesome slid frae a' han' The ee o' the gleggest never saw, THOM *Jock o' Knowe* (1878) 45. **Gall.** Halesome breezes from the thorn Refresh the swain, LAUDERDALE *Poems* (1796) 53. **Wgt.** Fed on the halesome Scottish fare, FRASER *Poems* (1885) 231. **Nhb.¹** Aa leev'd there oncy a few weeks, 'cas aa fund it not helsum. **Cum.** An' when the healesome supper's duin' The toilin' day his task hes duin, GILPIN *Ballads* (1874) 152. n.Yks.², e.Yks.¹, m.Yks.¹, w.Yks.¹

HALESTONE, *sb.* *Obs.* n.Cy. (HALL) Wm. (K.) A flint or firestone.

HALEWARE, *sb.* Sc. Also written **hailwair** (JAM.) ; **hailwur, halewar.** [hē·lwĕr.] The whole, the whole number or company ; the whole assortment of things.

Bch. He . . . Gar'd the hale-ware o' us trow That he was gane clean wud, FORBES *Ajax* (1785) 5. **s.Sc.** They'd . . . burn the verra earth about their lugs, An' end the haleware and themselves at ance, T. SCOTT *Poems* (1793) 367. **Gall.** The verra last shot that was fired . . . carried awa' the halewar o' their steerin' gear, CROCKETT *Raiders* (1894) x ; The haleware o't seemed to be gran plowable lan', MACTAGGART *Encycl.* (1824) 307, ed. 1876. **Kcb.** Aft ye kink an' skirl like mad, And laird it ower the hailwur, ARMSTRONG *Ingleside* (1890) 143.

HALEWOOD PLUM, *phr.* Chs.¹ A red plum.

Formerly much cultivated in nw.Chs. and greatly esteemed for preserving. It is becoming more scarce, but may still be bought in Warrington market ; and there are several trees of it in the neighbourhood of Norton and Frodsham.

HALF, *sb.*, *adj.*, *adv.* and *v.* Var. dial. uses in Sc. Irel. Eng. and Amer. Also in forms **avv** Hrt. ; **awf** e.Yks.¹ ; **haaf** Suf. Cor.² ; **haat** Nhp.¹ ; **haef** Cum. sw.Lin.¹ ; **haf** Sc. Cum.¹⁴ ; **hafe** Cum.⁸ Lan. s.Chs.¹ Not.² Brks.¹ ; **haff** Sc. ; **hauf** Sc. Bnff.¹ Nhb. Lakel.² Cum. e.Yks.¹ w.Yks.¹ ² ne.Lan.¹ s.Stf. ; **hauv** nw.Der.¹ ; **hauve** Lan. ; **hawf** Nhb. Cum. n.Yks.² e.Yks. w.Yks. ; **hawve** Lan. e.Lan.¹ ; **hayf** Flt. ; **hef** N.I.¹ ; **hoaf** Cum.⁵ w.Yks. ; **hofe** Cum.¹ ⁴ Wm. Yks. Lan. ; **oaf** n.Yks.¹ [hāf, h)ŏf, h)oəf.]

1. *sb.* In phr. (1) *by halfs,* half, partially ; (2) *by the half,* by half, considerably ; (3) *the half of,* half of.

(1) **Bnff.** I see by hafs ye're only wise ; Gang to the ant, an' lear some mair, TAYLOR *Poems* (1787) 32. (2) **w.Yks.** Ha felt mesen bigger be t'hoaf, *A Six Days' Aght,* 5. **Lan.** But more by the hauve nor these, are like, HARLAND *Lyrics* (1866) 88. (3) **Yks.** More than t'hauf on't is nought but idle talk, TAYLOR *Miss Miles* (1890) xviii. **w.Yks.¹** Whether thou's ivver doon taa hauf o' what our parson hes tell'd the . . . to do ? ii. 352. **Lan.** We'n nobbut cleared t'one hafe o' one mough, KAY-SHUTTLEWORTH *Scarsdale* (1860) II. 212 ; But aw couldn't tell th' hawve 'at aw feel, HARLAND

Lyrics (1866) 307 ; Nivver med th' hove o' th' noise, DONALDSON *Larnin to Sing* (1886).

2. A portion, division, piece.

w.Ir. Dish iv delf . . . bruk in three halves, LOVER *Leg.* (1848) I. 202.

3. *pl.* Equal shares, an exclamation used by children to claim half of anything found by another ; also used *advb.* in equal shares.

w.Yks.¹ In order, however, to deprive the other of his supposed right the finder will cry out : ' Ricket, racket, finnd it, tackit, And nivver give it to the aunder [owner].' **sw.Lin.¹** We went haves at it. **Oxf.** (G.O.), **Hnt.** (T.P.F.)

4. Phr. *to halves,* of animals : to be put out to fold on terms of partnership ; see below. Cf. **halver,** *sb.* **2.** See **Crease,** *sb.*³

Dev. Ewes to Halves.—W. Lewis, Templeton, is prepared to put out any number of ewes on the most favourable terms yet heard of, *Tiverton Gazette* (Aug. 11, 1896). The system is for the owner, as above, to provide the ewes for another man to keep until a certain date, to be agreed on when the ewes return to their owner, and the 'crease' is divided as may be agreed, *Reports Provinc.* (1897).

5. *pl.* The allotments on Corfe Common. Dor. (C.W.)

6. *adj.* In *comb.* (1) **Half-acre** or **Habaker,** a small field or allotment ; also used *fig.,* see below ; (2) **-amon,** the game of hop, skip, and a jump ; (3) **-a-nicker,** (4) **-a-thick-'un,** half a sovereign ; (5) **-a-tram,** one of two men that manage a tram in a mine ; (6) **-bushel,** a measure of beer : four gallons ; (7) **-clinks,** in phr. *to go half-clinks,* to go shares ; (8) **-cousin,** first cousin once removed ; (9) **-crease,** half the increase in value of stock ; to put out bees to feed ; see **Crease,** *sb.*³ ; (10) **-dole** (**-dooal**), entitled to a part only of the profits of any concern ; (11) **-draw,** in digging : half the depth of the tool used ; (12) **-fallow,** light ploughing, not of the usual depth ; to plough lightly ; (13) **-fool,** stupid, ignorant, half-witted ; (14) **-fou,** half a bushel ; (15) **-gable,** a gable common to two houses ; used *fig.* in phr. *to big half-gable with some one* ; (16) **-gam,** assisting to accomplish anything ; (17) **-groape,** a state of half-feeling, half-seeing ; (18) **-hack** or **-heck,** the lower half of a door divided into two parts ; (19) **-hammer,** see (2) ; (20) **-hatch nail,** a particular kind of nail ; (21) **-horn,** (*a*) *obs.,* a horn slit lengthways and nailed to the end of a staff ; see below ; (*b*) a half-pint of ale or beer ; (22) **-knack,** partial, half-and-half ; half-trained ; (23) **-lade,** a large straw basket or ' cassie ' ; (24) **-laugh,** any action done by halves, or half-heartedly ; (25) **-loaf,** in phr. *to leap,* or *loup, at the half-loaf,* a custom among reapers ; see below ; *fig.* to snatch at small boons ; to be content with a dependent or humble position ; (26) **-manor,** having land in partnership between two ; (27) **-mark** (or **-merk**) **bridal,** in phr. *to tye the haf-merk bridal band,* to be married clandestinely ; (28) **-mark kirk** or church, the place where clandestine marriages are celebrated ; (29) **-mark** (or **-merk**) **marriage,** a clandestine marriage ; (30) **-mark-marriage kirk,** see (28) ; (31) **-marrow,** (*a*) a spouse, a husband or wife ; a yoke-fellow, mate ; (*b*) a lad or boy serving his apprenticeship ; one of two boys working together ; (32) **-moon flask,** a flask formerly used in smuggling ; (33) **-mutchkin,** half a pint ; (34) **-nabs,** good-for-nothing, neither one thing nor another ; (35) **-natural,** a fool ; (36) **-nothing,** (37) **-nowt** or **-nought,** a very small sum, little or nothing, anything beneath consideration ; a worthless person ; also used *attrib.* ; (38) **-oaf moulsin,** see (35) ; (39) **-one** or **Hef yin,** (*a*) a half-glass of whisky ; (*b*) a term in golfing : see below ; (40) **-parson,** a deacon ; (41) **-piece crock,** the ordinary deep-shaped dairy crock ; (42) **-pint,** to drink ; (43) **-reacher,** a pitchfork of more than ordinary length ; (44) **-scale** (**-akeeal**), of manure : half the usual quantity spread on the surface of ground ; (45) **-sea,** tipsy ; (46) **-shaft,** *obs.,* the water-shaft in a colliery ; (47) **-shoon,** old shoes with the toes cut off ; (48) **-sir,** a churl, a miser ; (49) **-snacks,** in phr. *to go half-snacks,* see (7) ; (50) **-stuff,** a term of depreciation applied to persons ; (51) **-swing plough,** a plough in which the mould-board is a fixture ; (52) **-tester,** a bed with a canopy ; (53) **-timer,** a child who works half the day at a factory ; (54) -tiner, in phr. *half-tiner, half-winner,* one who shares half the loss or half the gain of anything ; (55) -ware, a mixture of peas and beans sown together ; (56) -water, half-way between the boat and the bottom of the sea ; (57) -wit, an idiot, a natural ; (58) -work, the time when the day's work is half done ; the middle of a shift ; half-time employment through bad trade ; (59) -yard coal, coal of about half a yard in thickness ; (60) -year meads, meadows of which one person has the hay and another the right to 'after-shear.'

(1) Sc. ' Half acres bears good corn.' Alluding to the half acre given to the herd, and commonly spoken in gaming, when we are but half as many as our antagonists, KELLY *Prov.* (1721) 143 ; I ordaine my husband to infeft Wm. my eldest sone in the house and Zairdiss barne, and twa half aikeris of land, LITHGOW *Poet. Rem.* (ed. 1863) xxxiv. Oxf. ' Habaker' is a term employed in certain fields between Oxford and Yarnton, known as the ' Lot Meadows' (G.O.) ; A habaker is half a lot : an acre is a lot. An acre or lot is sometimes three or four acres : the habaker, two or two and a half, STAPLETON *Four Oxf. Parishes* (1893) 309. Hrt. CUSSANS *Hist. Hrt.* (1879-1881) III. 321. [Amer. When the score of one side in a game is half that of the other, a common remark of encouragement is ' a half acre raises good corn if it's hoed well' ; often merely the phrase half acre is used alone, *Dial. Notes* (1896) I. 397.] (2) Ken.¹² (3) w.Yks.² Nrf. When I chucks the half-a-nicker in the broad, yer should ha' seen him look ! PATTERSON *Man and Nat.* (1895) 99. (4) w.Yks.² Lon. I only had ' half a thick 'un' for my trouble, *The People* (Aug. 25, 1889) 13, col. 4. (5) Nhb. Aw neist to half-a-tram was bun', But gat a marrow gruff and sour, WILSON *Pitman's Pay* (1843) 32 ; Nhb.¹ (6) Sur. (T.S.C.) (7) e.Suf. (F.H.) (8) Sc. ' Sophy,' an orphan half-cousin . . . was now Alick Welsh's good and amiable wife, MRS. CARLYLE *Lett.* (1883) II. 231. n.Cy. (J.W.), e.Suf. (F.H.) (9) Dev.² Wanted, a score of sheep to graze. Terms, half crease. Cor.¹ Half the increase, when the owner has half the honey, and the person who takes care of the bees the other half. (10) n.Yks.² A hawf-dooal man. (11) Nrf. That ain't deep enough. We shall have to get another half-draw out, EMERSON *Son of Fens* (1892) 205. (12) s.Wor.(H.K.) (13) w.Som.¹ *Gen.* used with fellow or some word expressing person. ' I never widn ha nort to zay to no jis aa-feol fuul-'ur-z ee-' [half-fool fellow as he]. (14) Sc. I brought a half-fou of gude red goud Out o'er the sea wi' me, SCOTT *Minstrelsy* (1802) I. 301, ed. 1848. Lnk., Rxb. (JAM.) (15) Rnf. The heresy of Arminianism, which he described as an attempt ' tae big hauf-gable wi' the Lord,' GILMOUR *Pen Flk.* (1873) 25. (16) Nhb. (R.O.H.) (17) w.Yks. Well, I woked on an' on in a soart of a hofe groape, HALLAM *Wadsley Jack* (1866) ix. (18) Nhb.¹ Cum. LINTON *Lake Cy.* (1864) 305. e.An.¹, Nrf. (W.W.S.) (19) e.An.¹ One boy challenges another to ' go the half-hammer.' Nrf. (W.W.S.) e.Suf. To come or go on the half-hammer, with a hop, skip, and jump (F.H.). Suu.¹ (20) nw.Dev.¹ A rectangular rose-headed hand-made nail—a ins. long. A hatch nail is 3 ins. long. (21, *a*) Sur. The shepherds of the Downs hereabouts use, what they call a half-horn, i. e. a horn slit lengthways, and nailed to the end of a staff, as long as the shepherds crooks, with which they can hurl a stone a great way, and so keep their sheep within due bounds. This instrument is seen in some pictures and hangings, but is not in use anywhere else, *England's Gazetteer* (1778) (s.v. Hedley). (*b*) Oxf. Let's go in and have a half-horn (G.O.). (22) Dev. ' I can't nivver zill no butter in town now, there's zo many half-knack farmers about '—meaning that there were so many tradesmen and others who kept a few cows, but did not make their living out of farming, *Reports Provinc.* (1897). (23) Or.I. So called because two of these baskets when filled and slung on a pack-saddle form a load for a pony (JAM. *Suppl.*). (24) Nhp.¹ None of your half-laughs for me. (25) Sc. To live honourably abroade and with credit then to encroach . . . on their friends at home, as . . . leaping at the half loafe, while as others through vertue live nobly abroade, MONRO *Exped.* (1637) pt. i. 36 (JAM.). Rxb. Still used. This is half a loaf which happens to exceed the number of loaves allotted for the reapers ; which being divided the one is thrown up for a scramble among the women and the other among the men (JAM.). (26) Gall. MACTAGGART *Encycl.* (1824). (27) Sc. HERD *Coll. Sngs.* (1776) *Gl.* Lnk. Since ye are content to tye The haff mark bridal band wi' me, RAMSAY *Poems* (1800) I. 309 (JAM.). (28) Sc. To gae to the half-mark kirk, to go to be married clandestinely. The name seems to have arisen from the price of the ceremony (JAM.). (29) Sc. Making a half-merk marriage wi' Simon Mucklebackit, SCOTT *Antiquary* (1816) xxxix. (30) Sc. (JAM.) (31, *a*) Sc. GROSE (1790) *MS. add.* (C.) ; Come awa hame to thy hauf-marrow,

GRAHAM *Writings* (1883) II. 37. Frf. Provost Binnie has an 'ee aifter him as a hauf-marrow tae his bonnie dother, LOWSON *John Guidfollow* (1890) 34 ; Lady Crawford, the wicked Teegur Earl Beardie's half-marrow, *ib.* 60. Keb. Plead with your harlot-mother, who hath been a treacherous half-marrow to her husband Jesus, RUTHERFORD *Lett.* (1765) pt. i. ep. 123 (JAM.). (*b*) N.Cy.¹ A middle-sized lad, two such being needed in coal pits to ' put' a corf of coals equal to a man. Nhb. One of two boys who manage a tram, of about equal age, WILSON *Pitman's Pay* (1843) *Gl.* ; Nhb.¹ Nhb., Dur. One of two boys putting together, NICHOLSON *Coal Tr. Gl.* (1888). n.Yks.¹ ; n.Yks.² Two halfmarrows make one whole man ; n.Yks.⁴ (32) Per. She seldom travelled without a wee drap slung about her person, which was often contained in a half-moon flask, almost encircling her huge body, MONTEATH *Dunblane* (1835) 87, ed. 1887. (33) Sc. He might have staid to take a half-mutchkin extraordinary with his crony the hostler, SCOTT *Antiquary* (1816) i. e.Fif. Four sooks ! Haigh that wad be ae half-mutchkin, LATTO *Tam Bodkin* (1864) vii. (34) Nhb.¹ (35) N.I.¹ (36) Sc. It sold for half-nothing, *Scoticisms* (1787) 61. (37) Nhb. Shanks full o' mawks, and half-nowt cheese, WILSON *Pitman's Pay* (1843) 10 ; He bowt the cuddy for half-nowt. The farmers hez ne crops noo-a-days, an' what they hev they get half-nowt for (R.O.H.). n.Yks.¹ Ah'd ding tha' au'd heead aff fur hauf-nowght, Ah wad ; n.Yks.² I gat it for hawf nowt ; n.Yks.⁴ It's nobbut a hauf-nowt when it's deean. T'father's i' prison an' t'lad's a hauf-nowt. e.Yks.¹ Ah sell'd m¹ wots for hawf nowt, *MS. add.* (T.H.) w.Yks. (J.W.) (38) Hrt.² (39, *a*) N.I.¹ (*b*) Sc. A handicap of a stroke deducted every second hole (JAM. *Suppl.*). (40) Wor. One of them there half-parsons (H.K.). (41) N.I.¹ (42) Cor. Two miners . . . had . . . been . . . ' half-pinting' in the publichouse, HUNT *Pop. Rom. w.Eng.* (1865) 217, ed. 1896. (43) s.Chs.¹ Used to hand up hay to the top of a stack which is approaching completion. (44) n.Yks.² We put a hawf-skeeal o' mannishment upon t'land. (45) Per. Hoarse elder John sat at his knee, In proper trim—more than half-sea, SPENCE *Poems* (1898) 86. (46) Nhb. Mr. G. C. Greenwell writes : ' Query ; is this not when in an inundation the water has risen to half the depth of the shaft ?' (R.O.H.) ; Nhb.¹ *Compleat Collier* (1708) 21. (47) Nhb. Wi' half-shoon at maw bait poke hung, WILSON *Pitman's Pay* (1843) 30 ; Nhb.¹ Nhb., Dur. There is my hoggars, likewise my half shoon, *Bishoprick Garl.* (1784) 54, ed. 1834. (48) Ir. None of your beggarly half-sirs, CARLETON *Traits Peas.* (ed. 1843) I. 15. Wxf. A big solemn prig of a half-sir of a farmer, KENNEDY *Banks of Boro* (1867) 159. (49) e.Suf. (F.H.) (50) Dev. *Reports Provinc.* (1888) 85. (51) Suu.¹ (52) Oxf.¹ *MS. add.* (53) w.Yks. The law fixes a limit of age, and a standard of education below which children are not allowed to work all day in factories. A ' half-timer' is generally one who has not fulfilled the required conditions (F.J.N.) ; a large proportion of these children were under instruction as ' half-timers,' CUDWORTH *Worstedopolis* (1888) 52. Chs.¹ (54) Keb. Be half tiner, half winner with my Master, RUTHERFORD *Lett.* (1660) No. 182. (55) Hrt. If Vale farmers should sow beans and pease together (or what the Valemen call half ware), ELLIS *Mod. Husb.* (1750) I. ii. (56) S. & Ork.¹ (57) Chs.¹ ; Chs.² Our Raphe's a pratty toidy scollard ; but as for Dick, poor chap, he's a hafe-wit. (58) Nhb. But, then, at half wark aw was duin, WILSON *Pitman's Pay* (1843) 30 ; Nhb.¹ Nhb., Dur. NICHOLSON *Coal Tr. Gl.* (1888). (59) Nhb.¹ *Gen.* good coal, and better than the three-quarter coal, yet being so low to work in (or that of small thickness), it is scarce worth while to work it, J. C. *Compleat Collier* (1708) 16. (60) Dor. MARSHALL *Review* (1817) V. 261.

7. *Comb.* in names of birds, fishes, or plants : (1) Half-bird, (*a*) the widgeon, *Mareca penelope* ; (*b*) the whimbrel, *Numenius phaeopus* ; (2) -callo, see (1, *b*) ; (3) -curlew, (*a*) see (1, *b*) ; (*b*) the bar-tailed godwit, *Limosa Lapponica* ; (4) -duck, see (1, *a*) ; (5) -fish, the salmon-cock or graveling, *Salmo salar* ; (6) -fowl, any wild fowl other than the mallard, esp. the teal, *Querquedula crecca*, and the widgeon, *Mareca penelope* ; (7) -smart, the yellow bedstraw, *Galium verum* ; (8) -snipe, the jack-snipe, *Limnocryptes gallinula* ; (9) -web, (*a*) the red-necked phalarope, *Phalaropus hyperboreus* ; (*b*) the grey phalarope, *P. lobatus* ; (10) -whaup, see (3, *b*) ; (11) -wood, (*a*) the woody nightshade, *Solanum Dulcamara* ; (*b*) the clematis or honesty, *Clematis Vitalba.*

(1, *a*) Lin. As it only fetches half the price of a mallard or brent goose it is known to the fenners as a half bird, SMITH *Birds* (1887) 482. (*b*) Nrf. SWAINSON *Birds* (1885) 199. (2) Nrf. The whimbrel or ' half-callo,' in habits, custom, and appearance much resembles the curlew, EMERSON *Birds* (ed. 1895) 305. (3, *a*) Nrf. SWAINSON *ib.* 199. [The whimbrel very closely resembles the curlew, but is . . .

very considerably smaller in size, YARRELL *Birds* (ed. 1845) II. 583.] (b) Nrf. SWAINSON *ib.* 198. (4) *ib.* 154. (5) **Sus.** In the river Tees we take notice but of two distinctions of size, viz. a salmon cock, which some call a half fish, RAY *Corres.* (1677) 127. [SATCHELL (1879).] (6) **e.An.¹** Nrf. COZENS-HARDY *Broad Nrf.* (1893) 45. (7) Bck. *Science Gossip* (1891) 119. (8) SWAINSON *ib.* 193. Oxf. APLIN *Birds* (1889) 214. (9) Or.I. SMITH *Birds* (1887) 452. S. & Ork.¹ (10) Frf. SWAINSON *ib.* 198. (11, a) War.⁵, Wor. (B. & H.), a.War. (H.K.) (b) Glo.¹

8. adv. In *comb.* (1) **Half away,** mad; (2) **— back,** an exclamation used to direct horses to turn to the left; (3) **·baked,** (a) foolish, silly, weak of intellect; raw, inexperienced; (b) a foolish fellow; (4) **— baptize,** to baptize privately; (5) **·baptized,** see (3, a); (6) **·char,** (a) doing things by halves, slightly or badly done; (b) see (3, b); (7) **·christened,** see (3, a); (8) **·cocked,** half-drunk; (9) **·cow'd,** bent, stooping; also used *fig.*; (10) **— enough,** ? half as much again; (11) **·gaited,** limping, weak of gait; (12) **·gate(s** or **·gait,** half-way; (13) **·going,** the right of pasturage upon the Fell for a certain number of sheep within defined limits; (14) **·gone,** (a) see (3, a); (b) about the middle period of pregnancy; (15) **·lang leather,** a ladder of medium length; (16) **·lang ploo,** a plough with medium metals; (17) **·middling,** in poor health, indifferent in health; (18) **·mounted gentleman,** a yeoman, small proprietor of land; (19) **·named,** privately baptized; (20) **·nethered,** nearly perished with cold; (21) **·old,** middle-aged; (22) **— right,** see (3, a); (23) **·roads,** see (12); (24) **·rock,** a foolish fellow; half-witted; (25) **·rocked** or **·rockton,** see (3, a); (26) **·sarkit,** half-clothed; (27) **·saved,** also in phr. *not half-saved,* (28) **·scraped,** (29) **·shaked,** (30) **·shanny,** (31) **·shaved,** see (3, a); (32) **·shaven,** ? without ceremony; (33) **·skim,** made of milk skimmed once only; (34) **·slew'd,** see (8); (35) **·soaked,** see (3, a); (36) **·sprung,** see (8); (37) **·strain,** (a) see (3, a); (b) mongrel; (38) **·strained,** (a) see (3, a); (b) in phr. *half-strained gentry,* 'shabby-genteel' persons, those who have difficulty in keeping up appearances; (39) **— there,** see (3, a); (40) **·thick,** (a) see (3, a); (b) see (3, b); (c) half-fat; a half-fattened animal; (41) **— tidy,** pretty well; (42) **·waxed,** half-grown; (43) **·ways,** half, partly.

(1) **N.I.¹** (a) Dur.¹ (3, a) n.Cy. (B.K.) **Nhb.** The proposition was a half-baked one, WATSON *Hist. Lit. and Phil. Soc.* (1897) 134. n.Yks.¹⁴, w.Yks.², ne.Lan.¹, s.Chs.¹ nw.Der.¹ Having had only half sleep or rest. n.Lin.¹ sw.Lin.¹ He talks like a man hāef-baked. War.²; War.⁴ Yer mount expect too much of him; he were only half-baked when he were born. w.Wor. I warn't half-baked, nor borned isterday, S. BEAUCHAMP *Grantley Grange* (1874) I. 76. Oxf.¹ MS. *add.* Wil. (G.E.D.), (E.H.G.), Wil.¹, Som. (J.S.F.S.) n.Dev. KINGSLEY *Westward Ho!* (1855) I. 91, in PEACOCK *Gl.* (1889). Cor. A fine, bowerly woman, but a bit ha'f-baked in her wits; put in wi' the bread, as they say, an' tuk out wi' the cakes, 'Q.' *Troy Town* (1888) xi; Cor.¹²⁸ (b) Der.⁸ (4) s.Wor.¹, Hrf.², Glo. (A.B.) Oxf.¹ MS. *add.* Ken.¹ Ken., Sus. *N. & Q.* (1893) 8th S. iv. 275. **Sus.¹** If you please, sir, will you be so good as to half-baptize the baby? (5) Sus.¹ You must have been half-baptized to water those flowers when the sun was full on them. (6, a) s.Chs.¹ It)s terrǐbl ai'f-chaa'r wuurk tū aa tóo aawts ūt gy'et'in ū job labyk dhaat doin [It's terrible hafe-char work to ha' two outs at gettin' a job like that done]. nw.Der.¹ (b) Der.², nw.Der.¹ (7) n.Lin.¹ (8) Nhb. Half-cock'd and canty, hyem we gat, WILSON *Pitman's Pay* (1843) 54; Nhb.¹ I.W.² All on 'em was abaut half cocked. (9) n.Yks.² 'A poor hawf-cow'd fellow,' one whom his wife rules. (10) Dev. They say Bradninch bells are half-enough more than Thorverton bells, *Reports Provinc.* (1889). (11).w.Yks. Thear he goaze wi his hauf-gaited legs an a smile on his poor thin face, TOM TREDDLEHOYLE *Bairnsla Ann.* (1873) 6a. (12) Sc. I wud be verie happy—verie weel-pleased to meet him half-gates, *Glenfergus* (1820) III. 291 (JAM.). Sh.I. I'm mair as half-gaets up da voe, JUNDA *Klingrahool* (1898) 52. Abd. When he was about half gates up the wood he had got some plan in his head, *Deeside Tales* (1872) 121. Per. When ance we're in the battle's din We'll find we're half gate thro', HALIBURTON *Ochil Idylls* (1891) 44. e.Fif. His coat was o' many colours an' hang doon half-gaits till 'a heels, LATTO *Tam Bodkin* (1864) xiv. Gall. Wi' whiskers half-gate o'er his face, NICHOLSON *Poet. Whs.* (1814) 47, ed. 1897. (13) Cum. Attached to most of the Fell dale farms (J.Ar.). (14, a) w.Yks. He is abaht hauf gooan, *Leeds Merc.*

Suppl. (Nov. 11, 1893). (b) Sc. (JAM.), Cai.¹ (15) Nhb. (R.O.H.) (16) Nhb.¹ A 'lang-ploo' is a plough with a long mould board. A 'short-ploo' is a short metalled one. A half-lang is between the two. (17) w.Yks. Ah'm nobbut just abaht hauf-middlin, *Yks. Wkly. Post* (Feb. 15, 1896). (18) Ir. A sturdy half-mounted gentleman, BARRINGTON *Sketches* (1830) I. xii ; In those days the common people, ideally separated the gentry... into three classes. . . I. Half-mounted gentlemen. . . The first-named class formed the only species of independent yeomanry then existing in Ireland, *ib.* (19) Hrf.¹, Glo.¹ (20) n.Yks.² (21) Abd. Drink soon wad mak' him daz'd and doited ere ha'f auld, SHIRREFS *Poems* (1790) 42. (22) Cum. Ye munna trust him, he's nobbet hofe-reet (E.W.P.); They say he is nobbet hawf reet, GILPIN *Sngs.* (1866) 310; Cum.¹⁴ Lan. He wos nobbut hofe reet, R. PIKETAH *Forness Flk.* (1870) 34. (23) Sc. (JAM.) (24) n.Yks.² Nrf. COZENS-HARDY *Broad Nrf.* (1893) 58. (25) N.Cy.¹ Half-rocked-innocent. Nhb. The Biship o' Jarra is a hawf rockt un, *Keelman's Ann.* (1869) 23 ; Nhb.¹ Cum. They're what ah may co hofe rockt mak o' whoke, SARGISSON *Joe Scoap* (1881) 129; Cum.³ He was yan o' t'hafe-rock't mak was Wiffy, 27. Wm. Thaer folk browt him up bi cannel-leet; turned him oot a hofe rocked 'un, *Spec. Dial.* (1880) pt. ii. 42. n.Yks.¹; n.Yks.⁴ It's nobbut a hauf-rocked thing foor onnybody ti deea. ne.Yks.¹, e.Yks.¹ w.Yks. He wor one o' them harmless, gawmless, hauf-rockt, sleeveless, dateless creeturs, *Yksman. Comic Ann.* (1881) 27; w.Yks.¹², ne.Lan.¹, e.Lan.¹, nw.Der.¹ Lin.¹ Take no notice of Aunt, she's half-rocked. n.Lin.¹, sw.Lin.¹, e.An.¹ Cmb.¹ Why he's only a poor half-rocked sort of fellow. Nrf. (E.M.), e.Suf. (F.H.) (26) Ayr. While here, half-mad, half-fed, half-sarkit, Is a' the amount, BURNS *Vision,* st. 5. (27) sw.Lin.¹ He's a poor half-saved sort of creature. War.² Shr., Hrf. BOUND *Provinc.* (1876). Hrf. DUNCUMB *Hist. Hrf.* (1804-1812) ; Hrf.¹, Glo.¹ Mid. 'When spiders go thrumming, there is wild weather coming,' came clumsily into my half-saved mind, BLACKMORE *Kit* (1890) II. iv. Wil.¹ Som. Used as 'not half-saved' (W.F.R.); *Monthly Mag.* (1814) II. 126. w.Som.¹ Poor bwoy, you can't 'spect much vrom he—he idn 'boo half a-saved. Dev. PULMAN *Sketches* (1842) 101, ed. 1871. nw.Dev.¹ Cor. For he was but half-saaved, TREGELLAS *Tales* (1868) 49 ; Cor.¹² (28) n.Cy. (B.K.) (29) Chs.¹ (30) Ess.¹ (31) n.Cy. (B.K.) (32) w.Yks. You're to bring Peggy, and come hawf shavven, DIXON *Craven Dales* (1881) 175. (33) Dor. Half-skim cheese, BARNES *Gl.* (1863). (34) e.Yks.¹, w.Yks. (J.W.) (35) s.Chs.¹ a.Stf. He acts soo haulf soaked folks never thinkin he's gettin the better on 'em, but he is, PINNOCK *Blk. Cy. Ann.* (1895). War. NORTHALL *Wd. Bk.* (1896) (s.v. Half-saved). w.Wor.¹, ne.Wor.¹ Shr.¹ That chap looks as if 'e wuz on'y 'afe-soaked. (36) Oxf. (G.P.) (37) Som. W. & J. *Gl.* (1873). (38, a) s.Chs.¹ Shr.¹ I think the Maister wuz to blame to trust a 'afe-strained auf like 'im, ōōth a sperited 'orse; Shr.² Hrf.² She's a half-strained donkey. (b) Dev. *Reports Provinc.* (1877) 131. (39) n.Yks.¹ Puir silly gomerill ! He's nobbut hauf-there. n.Lin.¹ (40, a) e.Cum. (C.W.D.), w.Yks.²⁵, Flt. (T.K.J.) (b) Nhb. Ah larned thee hoo to dae thy reckonin'—an' it's mair nor a haufthick like thee deserves, S. *Tynedale Stud.* (1896) v. Cum. Haufthicks leyke his-sell, STAGG *Misc. Poems* (ed. 1807) 89; Cum.¹; Cum.³ Thou's rayder a hoaf-thick, but m'appen I may, 39. Wm. Enny gomeless hofe-thick mae deea ya ill turn fer anudther, *Spec. Dial.* (1880) pt. ii. 8. w.Yks. Does ta meean to tell me 'at tha'd noa moor respect for thisen nor to wed a hawfthick like Alick ! HARTLEY *Clock Alm.* (1877) 31. Lan. Waw, hoo says, theaw hawve-thick, that's th' angelica percil, STATON *Loominary* (c. 1861) 31. s.Chs.¹, nw.Der.¹ (c) Cum.¹⁴, w.Yks.¹² ne.Lan.¹ 'She's nobbut hauf-thick,' not fat enough for a butcher. (41) Ess. 'How do you like yourself in your new place?' 'Oh, half tidy!' (H.M.M.) (42) Nhb.¹ A half-waxed lad. (43) Lnk. I'm half-ways git'en to tak' your part, An' half-ways to abuse ye, MURDOCH *Doric Lyre* (1873) 68.

9: Phr. (1) *half and between,* neutral, neither one thing nor the other; (2) *— and half,* (a) see (1); (b) half-witted; (c) tipsy, half-intoxicated; (3) *— half,* with numerals: half-past such and such an hour; (4) *— a-two,* almost in two pieces, cracked, in half; (5) *— too much,* too much by half; (6) *not to half do anything,* to do anything thoroughly or very much; (7) *to be half-past five with anything,* to be all up with anything, be 'finished,' 'done for'; (8) *to kill half a beast a week,* see below; (9) *to lose half the way of anybody,* not to be able to keep up with any one, to run or walk half as fast as.

(1) Rnf. Take the Radical side, And nae mair be a half-and-between, M°GILVRAY *Poems* (ed. 186a) 280. (2, a) Cld. (JAM.) (b) Not.⁵ Nobbut 'afe an' 'afe. (c) Dmf. Big John M'Maff . . .

Turned, though the chiel was half and half, His head away, MAYNE *Siller Gun* (1808) st. 74. **Gall.** Our wooer wasna happy, Though fully half and half wi' nappy, NICHOLSON *Poet. Wks.* (1814) 44, ed. 1897. **Wor.** 'Were you drunk at the time?' 'Well, I'll tell you what it is, gentlemen, I was half-an'-half, *Evesham Jrn.* (Dec. 25, 1897'. (3) **Sc.** (A.W.) **Nhp.**[1] 'What's o'clock, Bill?' 'Haat arter ten.' **Nrf.** We started to get our dinners at half arter twelve, EMERSON *Son of Fens* (1892) 136. **Suf.** Haaf arter three, *e.An. Dy. Times* (1892). **Som.** At half-aater zix, AGRIKLER *Rhymes* (1872) 106. (4) **n.Cy.** (J.W.), **War.**[2], **Oxf.**[1] **Brks.**[1] The led o' the box be hafe-atwo an' wunt stan' no mendin'. **Hrt.** I'll cut it half in two and use one piece here (G.H.G.). (5) **Guer.** It's half too much (G.H.G.). (6) **s.Stf.** I daint hauf enj'y myself, PINNOCK *Blk. Cy. Ann.* (1895). (7) **Glo.** It was all half-past five with the bicycle (S.S.B.). (8) **w.Yks.** (J.W.) **Lin.** A man said of a butcher who had risen in the world, 'He was in a poor way when he fo'st comed here, nobbut ewest to kill hauf a beast a week.' The common and appropriate phr. for a butcher who joins weekly with another in purchasing a beast for slaughter (E.P.). (9) **Nhb.** Alice followed as fast as she could, but lost half the way of Edward, *The Long Pack* (c. 1728) in *N. & Q.* (1888) 7th S. vi. 148.

10. Followed by numerals in speaking of the time of day : half-past the preceding hour.
Sc. 'What's o'clock?' 'Half six,' or half-past five, *Scoticisms* (1787) 42 ; Tell Geordie, wull ye, to bid Else come down to the byre at half aicht, SWAN *Gates of Eden* (1895) i. **Sh. & Or.I.** Comber (J.M.). **Frf.** Jess looked quickly at the clock. 'Half fower!' she said excitedly, BARRIE *Thrums* (1889) iii. **Per.** He gaed tae bed at half twa and wes oot in the fields by four, IAN MACLAREN K. *Carnegie* (1896) 154.

11. *v.* To halve, divide into two equal parts, to share; in sheep-marking : to cut off half the ear.
Banf.[1] **Lth.** 'To hauf and snake,' to divide. **Esp.** applied to a tavern bill or lauwin, as 'We'll hauf and snake,' we shall pay equal shares (JAM.). **Lakel.**[2] Hauf a hig off. **e.Suf.** (F.H.) **Cor.** And haafey wîth waun, DANIEL *Poems*.

12. With *down* : to half-plough, plough lightly; also called **Halfen down.**
w.Som.[1] To make a kind of half ploughing, by which a shallow sod is turned upside down upon the adjacent unmoved sod. A very common operation, when it is desired only to rot the surface growth without burying it deeply.

HALFENDEAL, *sb.* Som. Dev. A half part of anything, a moiety ; also used *attrib.*
Som. A halfendeal garment is one composed of two different materials, *N. & Q.* (1852) 1st S. vi. 184; W. & J. *Gl.* (1873). **w.Som.**[1] The word rather implies a division by counting, although it is used occas. with reference to division by measure only, as of liquids, cheese, &c. 'I let'n had a full halfen deal, same's off we was to share and share alike.' **nw.Dev.**[1] Now *obs.*, but common in old leases in the phr. 'moiety or halfendeal.'
[He . . . neme þat halfendele, LAȝAMON (c. 1275) 7093. OE. (*þone*) *healfan dǽl*, the half part.]

HALFER, see Halver, Haffer, *v.*[2]

HALFING, *sb.* Dev. The custom of collecting birds' eggs to string together for use at the sports held on the 29th of May.
The children go about in parties, six or seven together, halfing, as they call it. This custom is nothing more than to collect as many birds' eggs as they can against garland day, BRAY *Desc. Tamar and Tavy* (1836) II. lett. 30; GROSE (1790) *MS. add.* (M.)

HALFLIN, see **Haffin.**

HALFLIN(G, *sb.* and *adj.* Sc. Cum. Yks. Lan. Also in forms **haaflan** Cld.; **haaflang** Sc. (JAM.); **hafflin** Sc. n.Yks.[2]; **haflin** Sc. Cum.[1]; **half-lang, hauflin** Sc.; **hawflin** Cum. n.Yks.[2]; **hoafen** ne.Lan.[1]; **hoaflin** Cum.[1] 1. *sb.* A half-grown boy, a stripling, a boy employed upon a farm or in a stable ; a hobbledehoy.
Or.I. An' thus unto the halfin' she sed, *Orcad. J. Gilpin*, st. 55, in ELLIS *Pronunc.* (1889) V. 809. **Cai.**[1] **Abd.** The dress of boys or haflins was a leather cap trimmed with cat's fur, a very short blue sey coat, and corduroy trousers, ANDERSON *Rhymes* (1867) 207. **Frf.** He had ordered the hauflin' to saddle the shilt, WATT *Poet. Sketches* (1880) 81. **Per.** Send a haflin for some medicine, IAN MACLAREN *Brier Bush* (1894) 233. **Fif.** To snotter or to slaver was no less objectionable in the callant, the loon, or the haflin, COLVILLE *Vernacular* (1899) 17. **s.Sc.** Who was horse-herd, what was in those days called hauflin, upon a neighbouring farm,

WILSON *Tales* (1839) V. 340. **Dmb.** Wi' daffin' haflins, gayest o' the gay, SALMON *Gowodean* (1868) 30. **Lnk.** I see the coonter-louper chiels, The hafflin warehoose clerks, COGHILL *Poems* (1890) 18. **e.Lth.** Owre the lugs in love, and breesting up like a halflin' to Miss Jessie, MUCKLEBACKIT *Rhymes* (1885) 179.
2. A half-witted person, a fool.
Cai.[1], **Sth.** (JAM.) **Cum.** Tou's nobbet a hawflin bworn, ANDERSON *Ballads* (ed. 1808) 105; *Gl.* (1851); **Cum.**[1], **n.Yks.**[2], **ne.Lan.**[1]
3. *adj.* Half-grown, youthful.
Sc. He wears a tousie wig that micht set a haflin laddie, KEITH *Indian Uncle* (1896) 4. **Per.** Johnny was for speed unmatched, An' halflin hares had often catched, SPENCE *Poems* (1898) 197. **w.Sc.** Amongst the servants of our Scottish farmers, there is the 'little man,' or hauflin callan, CARRICK *Laird of Logan* (1835) 83. **Ayr.** Proud o' the height o' some bit half-lang tree, BURNS *Brigs of Ayr* (1787) l. 43. **Lnk.** I was but a hauflin' chiel O' seventeen simmers, COGHILL *Poems* (1890) 68. **Lth.** His minnie in her bafflin days, Had met his faither's ardent gaze, SMITH *Merry Bridal* (1866) 7. **Edb.** Some outlandish half'lin creatures Nae o' God's mak, LEARMONT *Poems* (1791) 1. **Dmf.** Halflin swankies blithely turn Tae sport wi' them they lo'e, REID *Poems* (1894) 57. **Gall.** More like a halfling lassie than a douce mother, CROCKETT *Cleg Kelly* (1896) 276.

HALFLINS, *adv.* and *adj.* Sc. Nhb. Cum. Also written **halfens** Nhb.; and in forms **haffins** Edb.; **hafflins** Sc. n.Cy.; **haflin** Sc. (JAM. *Suppl.*); **haftins** Sc. Cum.[1]; **hallens** Abd.; **hallins** n.Sc. (JAM.); **hauflins, havlins** Sc.; **hoaflins** Cum.[1] 1. *adv.* Half, partially ; nearly.
Sc. She haflins showed a rosie cheek, CUNNINGHAM *Sngs.* (1813) 52. **Elg.** 'It's serious,' says I, somehoo halflins winkin, TESTER *Poems* (1865) 133. **Abd.** I think nae sae, she says' and haflins leugh, Ross *Helenore* (1768) 73, ed. 1812. **Frf.** I'm baith cripple an' hafflins blind, BEATTIE *Arnha* (c. 1800) 21, ed. 1882. **Fif.** A show'r o' beams, That halflins blindet, wi' their sheen, TENNANT *Papistry* (1827) 9. **Dmb.** Halflins clad He frae their cruel hands in anguish flew, SALMON *Gowodean* (1868) 27. **Rnf.** Wi' a face haflins wae, haflins glad, WEBSTER *Rhymes* (1835) 85. **Ayr.** While Jenny hafflins is afraid to speak, BURNS *Cottar's Sat. Night* (1785) st. 7. **Lnk.** Mayhap you'll think I halflins ken You're frae the bonnie banks o' Ayr, PARKER *Misc. Poems* (1859) 51. **Lth.** In a dooer, ha'flings sleeping, Sad he saw, wi' hallow ee, Mally, BRUCE *Poems* (1813) II. 120. **Edb.** When the company had hafflins met, MOIR *Mansie Wauch* (1828) ix. **Slk.** I halflins thought to speed, Hogg *Tales* (1838) 358, ed. 1866. **Rxb.** They [birds] haflins tame do seek for food an' bield, A. SCOTT *Poems* (ed. 1808) 110. **Dmf.** Halflins droon The laich seep-sabbin' o' the burn doon by, REID *Poems* (1894) 20. **Gall.** He hurkled ben and hauflins fell asleep, MACTAGGART *Encycl.* (1824) 116, ed. 1876. **n.Cy.** *Border Gl.* (Coll. L.L.B.) **Nhb.** I've haflens rued o' Mr. Bell! GRAHAM *Morai. Dial.* (1826) 8. **Cum.**[1] When 'tis carded, row'd and spun, Then the work is haflins done, *Sng. of Tarry Woo.*
Hence **Haflin(s)-wise,** *adv.* partly, in a slight measure; reluctantly, half-heartedly.
Sc. She haflin-wise consented (JAM. *Suppl.*). **Ayr.** Altho' his carnal wit an' sense Like hafflins-wise o'ercomes him At times that day, BURNS *Holy Fair* (1785) st. 17.
2. Half-way; mid-way ; in equal shares.
Sc. West the gate To auld Kilmeny—it slants hafflins hame, LEIGHTON *Wds.* (1869) 19. **Abd.** Hallens to anything, near by it, SHIRREFS *Poems* (1790) *Gl.* Ha'flins has life's pirnie reeled, an' something mair, MORISON *Poems* (1790) 117. **Rnf.** Though haflins backward, thus I must commence, WEBSTER *Rhymes* (1835) 198. **Ayr.** An' win' o' doctrine hafflins mixt, SILLAR *Poems* (1789) 59. **Edb.** Patricks [partridges] skiming o'er the mead, And haflins rin to meet their bride, LIDDLE *Poems* (1821) 170. **Gall.** MACTAGGART *Encycl.* (1824). **Cum.**[1]
3. *adj.* Half, partial.
Rnf. For me, I hae a halflins swither, Howe'er Sectarians girn at ither, FINLAYSON *Rhymes* (1815) 98. **Lnk.** A halflins thaw is come at last, HAMILTON *Poems* (1865) 103. **Edb.** Wi' Habby Graeme, the haflins fool, *Tint Quey* (1796) 17.
4. Half-grown, young.
Sc. My father was then a hafflins callant, SCOTT *Redg.* (1824) Lett. xi. **Lnk.** The hafflins man himself is likely to be in a state of discontent, FRASER *Whaups* (1895) ix. **Edb.** A touzy ragged halflins callant of thirteen, MOIR *Mansie Wauch* (1828) x.
[1. Than vp I lenyt, halflingis in affrey, DUNBAR *Thistle and Rose* (c. 1510) 187.]

HALFPENNY, *sb.* Sc. Cum. Yks. Lan. ? Nrf. Dev. Cor. Also in forms **awpenny** Yks.; **awpney** w.Yks.;

'penny Fif. Cor.; hapmy Dev.; happenny Cor.; hau·ny w.Yks.¹; hawpney w.Yks.¹; hawpny w.Yks.¹ n.¹; ho'penny Cum.¹ 1. In *comp.* (1) Halfpenny-bit, ·alfpenny; (2) -deevils, a kind of sweetmeat or cake; ·piece, see (1); (4) -slit, an ear-mark given to pigs or eep [not known to our other correspondents].

(1) Dev. Canst gie me tū hapmy bits vur a penny! Hewett s. *Sp.* (1892). (2) Fif. There were such special aids to friend·p as 'clack'... the 'gundy' of Edinburgh youth, 'pawrlies,' 'ha'penny deevils,' Colville *Vernacular* (1899) 14. (3) Yks. He owes ma ivvery awpney piece Fur twenty pund a ·e, Preston *Poems* (1864) 16; w.Yks.¹ He cares nut a haupenny se what expense an trouble he puts other foak tull, ii. 298. a.Aw'll lend 'em nowt, not a hawp'ny piece, Doherty *N. Barlow* 84) 38. (4) ¹ Nrf. (W.W.S.)

Phr. (1) *halfpenny head and a fardin tail*, applied to ything of which the parts do not correspond, one being ·ch better than another. Cum.¹; (2) *to have*, or *keep*, 's hand on one's halfpenny, to be mean, stingy; to look ·r one's own interests. w.Yks.¹, ne.Lan.¹

pl. Savings, a fortune.

w.Cor. 'She has bra' happunce, I can tell ee.' Small savings are ·n spoken of as 'little ha'pence.' 'I should like to have her 'e ha'pence' (M.A.C.).

HALFPENNY-WORTH, *sb.* Sc. Irel. Yks. Lin. Brks. V. Also in forms aapoth Lin.; hapeth I.W.¹; ha·rth Ir.; happorth Lnk.; hauaporth w.Yks.⁸; hawporth Yks.¹; hawpworth n.Yks.; yeppath Brks.¹ [h]ā·pəp, ·əp.] 1. In *phr. to lose a hog*, or *ewe, for a halfpenny·rth of tar*, to be penny wise and pound foolish, to be so ·ring in little things as to risk things of value.

s.Yks. Let's nut loase an hogg for a hawpworth of tarr, Meriton ·ise *Ale* (1684) l. 195. w.Yks.¹ Dunnot loaz t'yow for a haw·th o' tar.

A very small quantity.

·nk. Not a wan in Towe-Rowe knows a happorth about me, ·rdoch *Readings* (ed. 1895) I. 32. Ir. A grand baste—but no porth o' use, Barlow *Bogland* (1892) 7, ed. 1893. Lin. A mowt a ·n owd Joanes. as 'ant nor a 'aȧpoth o' sense, Tennyson *N. Far·r, Old Style* (1864) st. 13. Brks.¹ A yent got a yeppath o' zense.

An article of little value; a bargain; a good-for·thing or clownish fellow.

w.Yks.⁸ A clownish, ridiculous person, is 'nobbut a hauaporth!' ·e who commits a great mistake is stigmatized as being 'a gurt ·aporth!' A newly-bought joint of meat turning out to be ·gotty, is 'a rum hauaporth!' An eccentric-spoken man who · occupied a pulpit, is 'a queer hauaporth!' to the listener. w.¹ That chap's a bad hapeth.

HALFY, *sb.* nw.Dev.¹ [æ·fi.] A fool, a half-witted ·rson. Cf. halflin(g, 2.

HALGAVER COURT, *phr.* Cor. See below.

The people of Bodmin had an old custom of assembling . . . on ·lgaver Moor in . . . July, and electing a 'Mayor of Misrule,' the punishment of petty offenders. . . . When these mates meet ·h any raw serving-man or other young master, who may serve · deserve to make pastime, they cause him to be solemnly ·ested for his appearance before the Mayor of Halgaver, who · is charged with wearing one spur, or wanting a girdle, or some ·ch like felony, and . . . judgment is given in formal terms, and ·ecuted in some one ungracious prank or other. Hence is sprung · proverb, when we see one slovenly apparelled, to say 'He ·all be presented in Halgaver Court,' Hunt *Pop. Rom. w.Eng.* 865) 402–3, ed. 1896.

HALGH, HALIDAY, HALIER, see Haugh, Holiday, ·lier.

HALIFAX, *sb.* Yks. Lin. Oxf. Cor. Amer. In *phr. go to ·lifax*, a mild substitute for a direction to go to a place ·t to be named to ears polite. Cf. Hecklebirnie, Hexham, ·ll.

w.Yks. (J.W.) n.Lin. Well known in these parts, *N. & Q.* ·75) 5th S. iv. 154; n.Lin.¹, Oxf. (G.O.) s.Cor. Very common ·out Looe, fifty years ago, *N. & Q.* (l. c.) [Amer. Common, ·al. *Notes* (1896) I. 382.]

HALIKELD, *sb.* Obs. Yks. A holy well. See Keld. ·a.Yks. The pins cast into the halikeld, Atkinson *Moorl. Parish* 91) 132.

HALINAS, *sb. pl.* w.Yks. In the rag-trade: coarse ·hite blankets from Hungary, Roumania, &c. (M.F.)

HALISH, *adj.* Cor. Also in form allish. Pale, sickly in appearance, weak, ailing.

Thomas *Randigal Rhymes* (1895) *Gl.*; Cor.¹ She's a poor halish creetur; Cor.²

HALISON, *sb.* Sc. ? A saying.

Abd. Sweeter bliss Than faith in this glad Halison, 'The e'enin' brings a' Hame,' Edwards *Mod. Poets*, 1st S. 66.

HALIWERK-FOLK, *sb.* Obs. Dur. Also written Halywerc folk. People who held their lands by the service of defending the body, relics, and territory of St. Cuthbert.

Surtees *Hist. Dur.* I. xv, xvi, in Brockett *Gl.* (1846); They pleaded . . . that they were Haliwerke folkes, and held their lands to defend the Corps of Saint Cuthbert, Camden *Brit.* (1610) 736; Halyworkfolk, Bailey (1721).

[A contam. form of the older *Haliwares folc*, the people of the holy man (Cuthbert); see *Feodarium Prioratus Dunelm.* (Surtees) (*passim*) (N.E.D.).]

HALL, *sb.*¹ and *int.* Sc. Nhb. Dur. Yks. Lan. Stf. Suf. Ken. Sus. Cor. Also in forms ha' Sc.; haa Nhb.¹; haal Cor.⁸; hal· N.Cy.¹ Ken.¹; hale Cor.; haw Sc. Stf.; ho' Lan. [hā, ǫl, ǫəl.] 1. *sb.* A house, home; a farm-house or cottage.

Cai.¹ The chief farm in a township. Elg. The calves prance round the ha', Couper *Poetry* (1804) I. 113. Abd. My wee bit cantie ha' Peeps out frae 'mid a wreath o' snaw, Still *Cottar's Sunday* (1845) 144. Kcd. To see . . . His father's ha' and youthful hame, Jamie *Muse* (1844) 14. Frf. Her smile was the sunshine that lichtit oor ha', Watt *Poet. Sketches* (1880) 81. Nae mair I'll see my faither's ha', Barr *Poems* (1861) 99. Ayr. Noo I am moor'd in my ain cosie ha', White *Jottings* (1879) 176. Lth. She's the star o' his heart an' his ha', man, Ballantine *Poems* (1856) 86. Bwk. *Monthly Mag.* (1814) I. 31. Edb. Lang mat your ha' be stow'd wi' blessin's rife! Learmont *Poems* (1791) 194. Lan. I' th' ho an' cottage ingill, Kay-Shuttleworth *Scarsdale* (1860) II. 215.

2. The principal room of a house, the parlour; also in *comp.* Hall-chamber.

Sc. A' that's said in the kitchen shou'd na be tauld in the ha', Ramsay *Prov.* (1737). Cor. I knawed un by Mally, Phelleps' pictur of un in her hall, Tregellas *Tales* (1865) 33; Ai wud·nt . . . tres'n in âur eel tjeem·ba bái asel·f [I wouldn't trust him in our hall-chamber by himself], Ellis *Pronunc.* (1889) V. 172; Cor.⁸ w.Cor. They cal'n a pare-lar, forsuth; why a es but a good hale and make the most of'n, Bottrell *Trad.* 3rd S. 60.

Hence *not to remember from the haal to the hetch, phr.* to have a bad memory. Cor.⁸

3. The kitchen of a farm-house, the principal living-room; also called Farmer's ha'.

Abd. In winter's nights, whae'er has seen The farmer's Ha' convene Finds a' thing there to please his een, Keith *Farmer's Ha'* (1774) st. 1. s.Sc. Blithe at night was ilka one In the auld snug ha' o' Little Billy, Watson *Border Bards* (1859) 7. Lnk. Glad tidings in the Farmer's ha' Is terror to the weavers, Watson *Poems* (1853) 3.

4. The country justices' room where they hold their court. e.Suf. (F.H.)

5. *Comb.* (1) Hall-bible, a large family-bible; (2) -clay, potter's earth; (3) -corn beer, a certain quantity of barley paid by the tenants of Amble to the lord of the manor; (4) -en', the end or side of a house; (5) -farm, a farm specially attached to a manor-house and not rented to a tenant; (6) -farmer, one who works a farm for the lord of the manor [not known to our correspondents]; (7) -folk, servants; kitchen-folk; (8) -garth, a hall-yard, an open enclosure pertaining to a hall; (9) -house, (a) a manor-house, the residence of the landed proprietor; (b) a large house, a farmer's house in contradistinction to that of a cottar; (10) -maiden, a maidservant in a farmer's house; (11) -neuk, a corner in a hall or large living-room; (12) -rig, the first ridge in a field cut in harvest.

(1) Sc. The large Bible, formerly appropriated for family-worship and which lay in the Ha' or principal apartment (Jam.). Ayr. The big ha' bible was accordingly removed by Mrs. Walkinshaw from the shelf, Galt *Entail* (1823) xix. Lnk. The muckle ha'-bible was brocht frae the bole, Nicholson *Kilwuddie* (ed. 1895) 144. Gall. It's in your hand o' write that the name o' Janet Geddes stands in the big ha' Bible, Crockett *Raiders* (1894) xxxiii.

(2) **Rxb.** A tough blue clay, so called because used by the peasantry to whiten the walls of their houses (Jam.). (3) **Nhb.[1]** Formerly for the use of the monastic cell there. (4) **Dmf.** What step is that by our ha' en'? Cromek *Remains* (1810) 75. (5) **Lan.** If yo'n tae me on booard at t'Ho fearm, Kay-Shuttleworth *Scarsdale* (1860) II. 215; The hall-farm is almost invariably farmed by the owner or the tenant of the hall, retained for the use of the household. In cases where the tenant of the hall does not require it, the hall-farm is sometimes let to an adjoining farm-tenant on the estate. Usually it is principally grazing ground (S.W.). **e.Suf.** (F.H.) (6) **Suf.** Even this happened in the practice of a hall-farmer, Marshall *Review* (1811) III. 449. (7) **Ayr.** Tho' the gentry first are stechin Yet ev'n the ha' folk fill their pechan, Burns *Twa Dogs* (1786) l. 61, 62. (8) **m.Yks.[1]** (s.v. Garth). (9, *a*) **Sh.I.** I was just seeking you that you may gang after him to the hall-house, for, to my thought, he is far frae weel, Scott *Pirate* (1822) vii. **Twd.** They shall pay a plack yearly, if demanded from the hole in the back wall of the Hall-house, *Notes to Pennecuik's Desc. Twd.* (1815) 161 (Jam.). **Edb.** Rinning about the Laird's ha' house, Macneill *Bygane Times* (1811) 43. **Dmf.** The talk in the ha' hoose, the talk in the manse, Thom *Jock o' Knowe* (1878) 32. **Dur.[1]**, **Stf.** (K.) (*b*) **Sc.** I've a ha'-house, I hae baith goods an' gear, *Shepherd's Wedding* (1789) 11; A house large enough to possess a dining-room (H.W.). **Abd.** The cottage built on an inferior scale differed in no other respect from the farmer's or ha'-house, *Statist. Acc.* XXI. 242 (Jam.). **Gall.** In yon ha' house, ayont the fell, Whar rural peace and pleasure dwell, Nicholson *Poet. Wks.* (1814) 39, ed. 1897. **Keb.** The hailoo rais'd forth frae the ha'-house swarm, Davidson *Seasons* (1789) 27 (Jam.). **Nhb.[1]** It is always distinguished from the 'hinds' hooses,' as the hinds' cottages are called. (10) **Nhb.[1]** In contradistinction to a hind's maiden. (11) **Sc.** A leddy sits in our hall-neuk, Scott *Bride of Lam.* (1819) xiv. (12) **Lth.** Thus denominated, because it is cut down by the domestics on the farm, i.e. the members of the farmer's family. It is deemed the post of honour and given to them, as they are *gen.* the most expert and careful reapers. The other reapers are understood to keep always a little behind those who have this honourable station, which is therefore also called the foremost rig (Jam.). **Edb.** The ha-rig rins fu' fast awa, *Har'st Rig* (1794) 11, ed. 1801. **Rxb.** (Jam.) **6.** *int.* An exclamation used by the master or mistress of a house to keep order at an entertainment. w.Yks.[2]

[6. A hall, a hall! give room! and foot it, girls! Shaks. *R. & J.* I. v. 28.]

HALL, sb.[2] Som. Cor. Also written **haul** Som.; and in form **hale** Cor. The fruit and tree of the hazel, *Corylus Avellana*; *gen.* in *comp.* Hall-nut. Som., Cor. (B. & H.), Cor.[12] See **Halse, sb.[2]**

HALL, sb.[3] Dev. Cor. Also written **hawl** Dev. (Hall.) In *comp.* (1) Hall-eve, the eve of Ash Wednesday; (2) -Monday, the day before Shrove Tuesday; (3) -night, see (1); (4) -Sunday, the Sunday before Shrove-tide; (5) -Tuesday, Shrove Tuesday. Cf. hallow, sb.[1]

(1) Dev. ' His nose smells of Hall Eve,' i.e. has the smell of good meat yet in it, *Horae Subsecivae* (1777) 199. (2) Cor. On the day termed ' Hall ' Monday, which precedes Shrove Tuesday, about the dusk of the evening it is the custom for boys . . . to prowl about the streets with short clubs, and to knock loudly at every door, running off to escape detection on the slightest sign of a motion within. If, however, no attention be excited, and especially if any article be discovered negligently exposed, or carelessly guarded, then the articles are carried away; and on the following morning are seen displayed in some conspicuous place, to expose the disgraceful want of vigilance supposed to characterise the owner, *Reports R. Instit.* (1842) in Quiller-Couch *Hist. Polperro* (1871) 151; Cor.[12] e.Cor. *Flk-Lore Jrn.* (1886) IV. 129. (3, 4) Dev. *Horae Subsecivae* (1777) 199. (5) Dev. (Hall.)

HALL, v. Yks. [al.] To shout, halloo.
w.Yks. When fowk o' ivry side on him is hallin an' shaatin, *Yksman.* (1880) 214; In ordinary use about Bradford (S.P.U.).

HALL, HALLA, see Hale, sb.[1], Hallow, sb.[1]

HALLAK, sb. Sc. A hillock.
Per. Frae hallak to hallak I haapit, My heart was as light as a strae, Duff *Poems* 133 (Jam.).

HALLAN, sb.[1] *Obsol.* Sc. Irel. Nhb. Dur. Cum. Wm. Lan. Also written **hallen** Sc. N.Cy.[1] Nhb.[1] Cum. Wm.; **hallon** Sc. n.Cy.; and in forms **halland** Sc.; **hollan** Sc. N.I.[1]; **hollen** N.Cy.[2]; **hollin** N.Cy.[1] Nhb.[1] [ha·lən, ho·lən.] **1.** A partition-wall in a cottage between the door and the fire to keep off draughts, a screen;

the space within the partition, a porch, lobby, or passage; also used *attrib.* Cf. **haddin.**

Sc. In old cottages, an inner wall built between the fire-place and the door, and extending backwards as far as is necessary to shelter the inner part of the house from the air of the door, when it is opened. It is *gen.* composed of stone and clay to the height of the side walls and brace. At this height the mud or cat and clay wall begins and is carried up to the chimney top. The term is sometimes applied to a partition of this kind extending to the opposite wall, but the first seems to be the original sense (Jam.): When we had passed the hallan we entered a well-sized apartment, Scott *Redg.* (1824) Lett. iv. **ne.Sc.** Matthew got up an' stept out to the hallan to put on his big coat, Grant *Keckleton*, 41. **Elg.** Hawky ahint the hallan maint And routed aft and sair, Couper *Poetry* (1804) II. 57. **Baff.** I hat the hallen A thump fu' sicker, Taylor *Poems* (1787) 62. **Frf.** The usual hallan, or passage, divided the but from the ben, Barrie *Tommy* (1896) xi. **Per.** The latch o' the hallan was lifted in haste, Stewart *Character* (1857) 23. **s.Sc.** Auld barn-man Davie sang wi' glee, And canty by the hallan was he, Watson *Bards* (1859) 9. **Dmb.** If death cam' tirlin' at the hallan door, Salmon *Gowodean* (1868) 34. **Rnf.** An' jinken 'bout the hallan wa', Allan *Poems* (1836) 14. **Ayr.** Thou need na jouk behint the hallan, A chiel sae clever, Burns *Past. Poetry*, st. 6. **Lnk.** Your niece . . . was laid Down at your hallon-side, Ramsay *Gentle Shep.* (1725) 66, ed. 1783. **Lth.** Lassie steek the hallan door, Bruce *Poems* (1813) II. 177. **Edb.** He out o'er the halland flings his een, Fergusson *Poems* (1773) 161, ed. 1785. **Bwk.** Honest Tibby, at whose fireside, inside her hollan wa', we sat, Henderson *Pop. Rhymes* (1856) 91. **Slk.** I got the back o' the hallan to keep, Hogg *Tales* (1838) 36a, ed. 1866. **Dmf.** Ance poortith came in 'yont our hallan to keek, Cromek *Remains* (1810) 51. **Gall.** Mid-walls through cottages, composed of cross-bars, and overlaid with straw plastered with clay, called cat clay, Mactaggart *Encycl.* (1824) 251, ed. 1876. **Keb.** Draw doon the blind, An' steek to the hallan door, Armstrong *Ingleside* (1890) 78. **N.I.[1]** In cottages a wall called the ' hollan ' is built to screen the hearth from the observation of any one standing at the threshold, but in order to allow a person within to see who approaches the door, a small hole, usually triangular, . . is made in the hollan (s.v. Spy-hole). **Uls.** Sit down on that furm by the hollan' An' I'll brisk up the fire in a jiffey, *Uls. Jrn. Arch.* (1858) 45. **n.Cy.** Grose (1790); N.Cy.[1] Often made of wickerwork, plastered with clay, running from front door of cottage to within the width of a door of the back wall; N.Cy.[2] A wall about 2½ yds. high. To this wall on the side next to the hearth is annexed a sconce or screen of wood or stone. **Nhb.** Rouse, leave your lanely hallens, Proudlock *Borderland Muse* (1896) 262; Nhb.[1] Against this hallen it was common for the cow to stand. **Dur.[1]** **Cum.** Sae by the hallan softly creep, Anderson *Ballads* (ed. 1808) 49; Some o' th' hallan, or th' mell deers, Their geylefat guts war clearan, Stagg *Misc. Poems* (ed. 1805) 198. **Cum., Wm.** A partition, from the cross passage of old farm or country houses, which formed a screen for some distance, to the fireside of the chief family room. The hallan was usually finished with stone coins, or with wood if not altogether of stone. The master's seat was often within the hallan, and bright things hung upon its wall (M.P.). **Wm.** A passage nearly four feet broad led to the other side of the building, where, in front was the back, on the left the down house door, and on the right the mell door, *Lonsdale Mag.* (1822) III. 248. **ne.Lan.[1]**

2. *Comp.* (1) Hallan-drop, a mixture of soot and water falling from the sides of a chimney; (2) -pin, a pin fixed upon the hallan for the purpose of hanging game or hats, &c., upon; (3) -post, the post at the extremity of the sconce; (4) -stone, the threshold, doorstep.

(1) Cum. They hed to watch for t'hallen drops, Richardson *Talk* (1871) 57, ed. 1876; Cum.[4] Wm. *Manners of Wm.* (1847) 13; Under this smoky dome, which in moist weather was continually shedding a black sooty lee, called the hallan drop, sat the family, *Lonsdale Mag.* (1822) III. 249; Black sooty lye rising in damp weather from joints of meat swung up to dry in the chimney, Brockett *Gl.* (1846). (2) n.Cy. (J.L.) (1783). ne.Lan.[1] (3) ne.Lan.[1] (4) Keb. The ducks had drate Upo' the hallan-stane, Davidson *Seasons* (1789) 7.

3. A house, dwelling, cottage.
Sc. The Lord himsel ever-mair ettles it for his hallan, Waddell *Psalms* (1871) lxviii. 16. **Abd.** See ye yon bit canty hallan Jam'd against the broomy brae! Still *Cottar's Sunday* (1845) 29. **Ked.** There was yet the drouthy callan, That wadna leave the vintner's hallan Ava that day, Jamie *Muse* (1844) 113. **Frf.** Hinds,

plewmen, lairds, and cottar callans, That frae their spences, ha's, and hallans, Did congregate, TENNANT *Papistry* (1827) 71. Rnf. A dark smeeky hallan was ance a' our dwallin', YOUNG *Pictures* (1865) 125. Lnk. Aye the first to greet the mornin', In the hallan first asteer, NICHOLSON *Idylls* (1870) 29.

4. The division between two horse or cow stalls. Cum.[14]

5. A buttress built against a weak wall to prevent it from falling. Gall. MACTAGGART *Encycl.* (1824) 251.

6. The space above the cross-beams of the couples of a house. Or.I. (S.A.S.) 7. A seat of turf at the outside of a cottage. Ayr. BURNS *Gl.* (JAM.)

HALLAN, *sb.*[2] Wor. I.W. Cor. Also written allan-Cor.[8]; and in forms allens· Cor.; hollan I.W.[1]; hollon s.Wor. [æ·lən.] 1. In *comp.* (1) Hallan-apple, a large apple given to each member of the family at All-Hallows-tide; also called Hallan; (2) ·cakes, cakes baked for All Hallows Day; (3) ·day, All Hallows Day; (4) ·market, the market held on All Hallows Eve; (5) ·night, All Hallows Eve; (6) ·summer, St. Luke's summer or an Indian summer, a spell of fine weather about All Hallows Day.

(1) Cor. Fruiterers of Penzance display large apples, known locally as 'Allens' apples, *Flk-Lore Jrn.* (1886) IV. 110; Cor.[18] (2) I.W.[1] (3, 4, 5) Cor.[8] At St. Ives the custom is still kept up of providing children with a large apple (Allan apple) on Allan-night (the eve of Allhallows day--called Allan day). The market held on Allan-night is called Allan-market. (6) s.Wor. (H.K.)

[*Hallan-* is for *Hallantide* (q.v.).]

HALLAN, *sb.*[8] N.Cy.[1] Nhb.[1] [ha·lən.] The young of the coal-fish when about five inches long.

HALLAND, see Hallow, *sb.*[1]

HALLANSHAKER, *sb.* Sc. Nhb. Cum. Also written halan-, halin- Sc.; hallen- Sc. N.Cy.[1] Nhb.[1]; and in form hellenshaker Sc. [ha·lənʃakər.] A ragged fellow, a vagabond or beggar; a knave, rascal; also used *attrib.*

Sc. I, and a wheen hallenshakers like mysell . . . built this bit thing here, SCOTT *Antiquary* (1816) iv. Sh.I. A very hallanshaker loon, *ib. Pirate* (1822) v. Bch. Staakin about like a hallen-shaker, FORBES *Jrn.* (1742 15. Frf. 'Only a puir gypsy your honour.' . . .'Only a wandering hallenshaker,' BARRIE *Minister* (1891) xiii. Rnf. Tho' something halanshaker-like, Ye'll may be own that I Some feelings hae, WEBSTER *Rhymes* (1835) 207. Ayr. Some hallen-shakers nearer hame, THOM *Amusements* (1812) 17. Lnk. Nodding to Jouks of Hallenshaker, RAMSAY *Poems* (1721) 211. Lth. Ye fell clootyraker! ye vile halanshaker, SMITH *Merry Bridal* (1866) 10. Edb. It sets him weel, the bloodthirsty Gehazi, the halanshaker ne'er-do-weel! MOIR *Mansie Wauch* (1828) xxvii. Slk. Great muckle hallanshaker cuff, HOGG *Tales* (1838) 78, ed. 1866. Peb. You, ye hellenshaker villain! AFFLECK *Poet. Wks.* (1836) 127. N.Cy.[1] Nhb.[1] Obs. Cum. LINTON *Lake Cy.* (1864) 304; Cum.[4]

Hence **Hallanshaker-looking**, *adj.* ragged, unkempt, like a tramp.

Edb. He was a wauf, hallanshaker-looking chield, MOIR *Mansie Wauch* (1828) xiv.

[Sic knavis and crakkaris. Sic halland schekkaris, DUNBAR *Poems* (c. 1510), ed. Small, II. 83.]

HALLANTIDE, *sb.* Irel. I.Ma. Lin. Nhp. Wor. Shr. Glo. Bck. Hrt. I.W. Wil. Som. Cor. Also in forms hallon- n.Lin.[1] Nhp.[2]; hollan- I.Ma. I.W.[1]; holland- Ir. Glo. Bck. Hrt. The season of All Saints, the first week of November. See All-hallow(s.

Ir. Holland-tide at the Big House, KENNEDY *Evenings Duffrey* (1869) 91. I.Ma. I have not seen her since hollantide (S.M.); I don't think it's ten years since he died—ten would it be, hollantide? BROWN *Doctor* (1887) 130. n.Lin.[1] Obs. Nhp.[2] From Michaelmas to Hallon-tide was the old rule for the period of sowing wheat. s.Wor. (H.K.) Shr.[1] Obsol. Glo. Last night were Hollantide eve, and where the wind is at Hollandtide it will stick best part of the winter, GIBBS *Cotswold Vill.* (1898) 388; Glo.[1] Bck. If ducks do slide at Hollandtide, At Christmas they will swim; If ducks do swim at Hollandtide, At Christmas they will slide, *Flk-Lore Rec.* (1881) IV. 128; *N. & Q.* (1874) 5th S. i. 383. Hrt. *Reports Agric.* (1793-1813) 28. I.W.[1] Wil. BRITTON *Beauties* (1825); Wil.[1] Som. JENNINGS *Obs. Dial. w.Eng.* (1825); W. & J. *Gl.* (1873). w.Som.[1] 'Twas a ter'ble hard winter tho—I mind 'twas nort but vrost and snow vrom Hallantide [aa·luntuy·d] gin Can'lmas. Cor.[12] [Set trees at All Hallo'ntide, and command them to prosper, SWAINSON *Weather Flk-Lore* (1873) 143.]

[At Hallontide, slaughter time entereth in, and then doth the husbandmans feasting begin, TUSSER *Husb.* (1580) 55.]

HALLE, HALLEDGE, HALLEGE, HALLENS, see Hallow, *sb.*[1], Harriage, Halflins.

HALLENS, *sb. pl. Obs.* Abd. In phr. *to go by the hallens*, to go by holds as a child. SHIRREFS *Poems* (1709) *Gl.* Cf. haal.

HALLI-, see Holy.

HALLIBLASH, *sb.* n.Cy. Lan. Der. Also written hallyblash Lan. [(h)a·liblaʃ.] A great blaze. See Blash, *sb.*[2]

n.Cy. GROSE (1790). Lan. I'st ha set th' how leath on a halli-blash, TIM BOBBIN *View Dial.* (1740) 17; Aw'd mak a' hally-blash ov every factory i' Englandshire, BRIERLEY *Irkdale* (1865) 7, ed. 1868; Lan.[1] Der. He and his loike 'll mak a halliblash of us aw soon, WARD *David Grieve* (1892) III. bk. x.

HALLIDAY, see Holiday.

HALLIE, *sb.* Abd. (JAM.) Also in form hallyie. Romping diversion.

HALLIER, see Halyear, Haulier.

HALLIHOE, *sb.* Cor. Also written hallyhoe Cor.[2] The skipper fish, *Scomberesox saurus.* Cor.[12] [SATCHELL (1879).]

HALLINES, *sb.* Nhb.[1] Also written haliness. [ha·linəs.] A Sunday holiday walk.

HALLINS, see Halflins.

HALLION, *sb.* Sc. Irel. Nhb. Cum. Also in forms haalyan Cai.[1]; hullion Sc. Ir. [ha·liən.] 1. A clown, a clumsy fellow; a good-for-nothing idle scamp, a sloven, a rascal.

Sc. We're just takin' tem doon to Stirling—ta curst hallions tat ta are, FORD *Thistledown* (1891) 319; FRANCISQUE-MICHEL *Sc. Lang.* (1882) 179. e.Fif. Man, ye're a rammelsome hallion, LATTO *Tam Bodkin* (1864) vi. Ayr. An' tirl the hallions to the birses, BURNS *Address to Beelsebub,* l. 36. Gall. Brave hallions twa, Laird Nurgle and Laird Nabble, MACTAGGART *Encycl.* (1824) 80, ed. 1876. Kcb. But should some rustic hallion see thee here In thy luxuriant pastime, DAVIDSON *Seasons* (1789) 26. N.I.[1] Ant. *Ballymena Obs.* (1892); A fat, dirty, untidy woman (W.H.P.). N.Cy.[1] Nhb. No man wou'd have thought any hallion Could ever have acted the thing, RITSON *Garl.* (1810) 61; And byeth tar and feather the hallion that dar', WILSON *Poems* (1843) 128; Nhb.[1], Cum.[1]

2. A gentleman's servant out of livery; an inferior servant employed to do odd jobs. Abd., Rxb. (JAM.)

3. An overbearing, quarrelsome woman of vulgar manners. Bwk. (*ib.*)

HALLIOR, *sb.* ? *Obs.* Sc. In phr. *the moon is in the hallior*, the moon is in her last quarter, is much in the wane.

Abd. It is a saying among our people, whenever they mistake one object for two, that the moon is in the hallior, or clouded, and at such times they are winnel-skewed, or their eyes deceive them, PENROSE *Jrn.* (1815) III. 83 (JAM.).

HALLIRACKIT, *adj.* Abd. (G.W.) Giddy, hare-brained.

HALLIRAKUS, *sb.* Sc. A giddy, hare-brained person; also used *attrib.*

Abd. Fat keeps that hallirakus scum, The tailor, 'at he winna come, BEATTIE *Parings* (1803) 28, ed. 1873. Abd., Rnf. (JAM.)

HALLOCK, *v., sb.* and *adj.* Sc. Nhb. Cum. Wm. Yks. Der. Also written hallok· Sc.; and in forms allack e.Yks.[1] w.Yks.; halic· Sc.; hallach Sc. Bnff.[1]; hallack Yks. w.Yks.[5] nw.Der.[1]; hallak· Sc. Wm. w.Yks.; hal-lich Sc. (JAM.) Bnff.[1]; hallic(k Sc.; hallik Sc. (JAM.) m.Yks.[1] w.Yks.; haluck· Sc.; hollock w.Yks.[2]; hollok w.Yks. [h]a·lək.] 1. *v.* To behave in a foolish, noisy way. See Halok. Bnff.[1], Cld., Lth. (JAM.)

Hence (1) **Hallachan**, *sb.* noisy, foolish conduct; (2) **Hallachin**, *ppl. adj.* noisy, foolish. *ib.*

2. To idle away time; to loiter, loaf, play. *Gen.* with *about.*

Cum.[4] Wm. He wad rayder hallak aboot t'public hoose ner work (B.K.). n.Yks.[4] If he isn't risting up agaain a wall, he'll be hallocking sumwheear. ne.Yks.[1] He gans hallockin' aboot frev hoos ti hoos. e.Yks.[1] w.Yks. He's hollocking abeat, *Hlfx. Courier* (May 15, 1897); Two texts, sich as a mannyfactrer wod like to see hung up i' t'miln to stare at his hands when they wor allackin asteead o' workin', *Yksman.* (Oct. 1898) 362; w.Yks.[2] He's always hollocking about with a parcel of idle fellows; w.Yks.[5], nw.Der.[1]

Hence (1) **Hallacker**, *sb.* an idle fellow; (2) **Hallacking**, (*a*) *sb.* a foolish person; (*b*) *ppl. adj.* idle, lazy, trifling, loitering.

(1) w.**Yks.** He is a hallocker abaht, *Leeds Merc. Suppl.* (Oct. 21, 1893). (2, *a*) m.**Yks.**¹ w.**Yks.** HAMILTON *Nugae Lit.* (1841) 354. (*b*) **Wm.** A gurt hallaken thing—she wad gang oot any fashion (B.K.). n.**Yks.**¹ w.**Yks.** Tha'd turn aght a idle hallockin' haand, HARTLEY *Clock Alm.* (1878) 47; w.**Yks.**⁵ *Gen.* coupled with 'stoit.' ' A gurt hallacking stoit.'

3. To tease, worry, bully.

n.**Yks.** Thoo'l hallock me to death (T.S.); n.**Yks.**² They hallock'd me an end [urged me forward].

Hence (1) **Hallocked**, *ppl. adj.* teased, harassed. n.Yks.¹; (2) **Hallocking**, *ppl. adj.* teasing, bullying; boisterous, rough, rude. n.Yks.², w.Yks. (J.W.)

4. *sb.* A tall, lazy, ungainly fellow; a rough, uncouth person. Also called **Hallacks**.

Cum.⁴ w.**Yks.**⁵ Goa wesh thee faace thou gurt hallacks!

5. A tiring affair, as a lengthy journey.

n.**Yks.**² It's a lang hallock.

6. *adj.* Crazy. Abd. (JAM.)

HALLOCKIT, *ppl. adj.* Sc. Nhb. Also in forms hal(l)ach'd Abd.; -aket Edb.; -egirt Sh.I.; -icat Frf. -ickit Lth. Gall.; -icut Per.; -igate Nhb.¹; -igit S. & Ork.¹ Nhb.¹; -uckit Sc. Bnff. Rnf.; hullockit Ayr. [haˈlǝkit.] Wild, romping; light, giddy; crazy, half-witted; also as *sb.* a noisy, restless person; a romp, a hoyden. See **Hallock**, *v.*

Sc. And shangy-mou'd halucket Meg, HERD *Coll. Sngs.* (1776) II. 25. **Sh.I.** Ance upon a day I wis light-hearted an' hallegirt enough, STEWART *Tales* (1892) 52. **S. & Ork.**¹ **Bnff.** Let poets crack o' fragrant brose, . . . They're halucket, Commen' me to a haggis, TAYLOR *Poems* (1787) 144. **Abd.** Hallach'd and damish'd, and scarce at her sell, ROSS *Helenore* (1768) 23, ed. 1812. A muckle halicat bruit o' the mastiff breed, WILLOCK *Rosetty Ends* (1886) 134, ed. 1889. **Per.** He's hallicut an' wild, he's gane ower his mither's thoomb, FORD *Harp* (1893) 151. w.**Sc.** A hair-brained hallica't hissey, CARRICK *Laird o' Logan* (1835) 91. e.**Frf.** John M'Brian's auldest dochter, a daft ram-stam hollokit quean, LATTO *Tam Bodkin* (1864) xxiv. **Rnf.** Quo' Lizzy to halucket Jannock, WEBSTER *Rhymes* (1835) 85. **Ayr.** (J.M.); The snash and impiddence of hullockit haverals and thochtless fules. SERVICE *Dr. Duguid* (ed. 1887) 114. **Lth.** Hallickit Meg frae Fisherraw, SMITH *Merry Bridal* (1866) 5. **Edb.** Wi's reefart-nosed, blae-cheeked wife, Hallaket Jess, the tawpy, *Carlop Grœn* (1793) 128, ed. 1817. **Gall.** MACTAGGART *Encycl.* (1824). **Nhb.**¹ A greet halligit lass.

HALLOE, HALLON, see Hallow, *sb.*², Hallan, *sb.*¹

HALLOO, see Hallow, *adj.*

HALLOP, *v.* and *sb.* Sc. [haˈlǝp.] **1.** *v.* To frisk about, to be precipitate in one's movements. Fif. (JAM.)

Hence (1) **Halloper**, *sb.* one who is giddy or precipitate. *ib.*; (2) **Hallopin**, *ppl. adj.* unsteady, unsettled, foolish. *ib.* **2.** *sb.* A hasty, precipitate person.

Gall. Black Jock wad to a neebor farm To get mair aid the hallop, MACTAGGART *Encycl.* (1824) 499, ed. 1876.

HALLOW, *sb.*¹ Sc. Irel. n.Cy. Nhb. Lan. Wal. Wor. e.An. Som. Also in forms hala- Sh.I.; halla- Sc. ne.Lan.¹; halle- N.Cy.¹; hollow- Ir. Wal. Wor. [Sc. and n.Cy. haˈla.] In *comb.* (1) Hallow-day, (*a*) All Saints' or All Hallows' Day; (*b*) a holiday; (2) -een or -eve(n, the eve of All Saints' Day; also called **Halloween-night**; (3) -een bleeze, a bonfire kindled on Halloween; (4) -fair, a fair held in the beginning of November; (5) -fire, see (3); (6) -market, a market held on All Saints' Day; (7) -mas, All Saints' Day; the season of All Hallows, the first week of November; also used *attrib.*; (8) -masrade, the name given to the general assembly of witches and 'warlocks' supposed to have been held at this time; (9) -tide night, see (2).

(1, *a*) **Sc.** (JAM.) **Ayr.** There would be ither words amang your win' afore auld Halla'-day, AINSLIE *Land of Burns* (ed. 1892) 28. **Slk.** It was on ane hallow-day, HOGG *Poems* (ed. 1865) 367. (*b*) e.**An.**¹, e.**Suf.** (F.H.) (2) **Sc.** It was believed that if, on Hallowe'en, any person should go round one of these [fairy] hillocks nine times, contrary to the course of the sun, a door would open, by which he would be admitted into the realms of fairyland, FORD *Thistledown* (1891) 263; To haud Halloween, to observe the childish or superstitious rites appropriated to this evening (JAM.). **Sh.I.** 'Auld Halloween' and taking in the sheep from the fields occurred generally about the same time, STEWART *Tales* (1892) 78. **Cai.**¹ **Abd.** It was i' the go-hairst, weel on to Halloween, *Deeside Tales* (1872) 91. e.**Sc.** From Hallowe'en to Hogmanay, and the year was at an end, SETOUN *Sunshine* (1895) 2. **Per.** Heath, broom, and dressings of flax are tied upon a pole. This faggot is then kindled; one takes it upon his shoulders and running bears it round the village; a crowd attend. When the first faggot is burnt out, a second is bound to the pole and kindled in the same manner as before. Numbers of these blazing faggots are often carried about together and when the night happens to be dark they form a splendid illumination. This is Halloween, *Statist. Acc.* V. 84, 85 (JAM.). w.**Sc.** For several days before Hallowe'en, boys and youths collected wood and conveyed it to the most prominent places on the hill sides in their neighbourhood. . . After dark on Hallowe'en, these heaps were kindled. . . At the beginning of this century men as well as boys took part, and when the fire was ablaze, all joined hands and danced round the fire; . . . as these gatherings generally ended in drunkenness and rough and dangerous fun, the ministers set their faces against the observance, and so the practice was discontinued by adults and relegated to school boys, NAPIER *Flk-Lore* (1879) 179–80. **Rnf.** Whether it was on hallowe'en . . . She couldna, 'twas sae lang since syne, Just be exact, WEBSTER *Rhymes* (1835) 23. **Ayr.** Hallowe'en among us is a dreadfu' night! witches and warlocks, and a' lang-nebbit things, hae a power and a dominion unspeakable on Hallowe'en, GALT *Gilhaize* (1823) xvii; It was Halloween: . . the wee callans were at it already, rinning aboot wi' their fause-faces on and their bits o' turnip lanthrons in their haun, SERVICE *Notandums* (1890) 40. **Lnk.** The serio-comic drama acted by our peasant fathers on Halloween nicht, with its absurd, yet amusing, and sometimes fatal superstitious observances, HAMILTON *Poems* (1865) 184. **Dmf.** This song was his favourite, and he usually sung it at Halloweens, at Kirk-suppers, and other trystes, CROMEK *Remains* (1810) 19. **Gall.** When those creatures called 'Gian Carlins' wont to meet with any one alone on Hallowe'en night, they stuffed it with beer awns and butter, MACTAGGART *Encycl.* (1824) 58, ed. 1876. s.**Ir.** Of a Hollow-eve night he'd find more gold, CROKER *Leg.* (1862) 327. n.**Cy.** Hey how for Hallowe'en When all the witches are to be seen, *Denham Tracts* (ed. 1895) II. 79; N.Cy.¹, Nhb.¹, ne.Lan.¹ (3) **Sc.** In some parts of Sc. it is customary on this evening for young people to kindle fires on the tops of hills or rising grounds. A fire of this kind they call a Halloween blaze (JAM.). (4) **Sc.** (*ib.*) **Lth.** 'Mang Hallow-fair's wild noisy brattle Thou'st foughten mony a weary battle, BALLANTINE *Poems* (1856) 66. **Edb.** At Hallow-fair, where browsters rare Keep gude ale, FERGUSSON *Poems* (1773) 131, ed. 1785; The bard, wha sang o' Hallow-fair, *New Year's Morning* (1792) 7. (5) **Sc.** Now the Hallow-fire when kindled is attended by children only, *Statist. Acc.* XXI. 145 (JAM.). (6) **Fif.** Daddie's gane to Hallow-market, DOUGLAS *Poems* (1806) 84. (7) **Sh.I.** At Hallowmas I commenced my duties as a teacher, STEWART *Tales* (1892) 57; The Hallowmass roup, or cattle sale, was going to come off shortly, NICOLSON *Aithstin' Hedder* (1898) 9. **Cai.**¹ **Ayr.** As bleak-faced Hallowmass returns, BURNS *Twa Dogs* (1786) l. 123. **Lth.** When Hallowmas swept bleak the plain, A fleet of ships stood o'er the Forth, LUMSDEN *Sheep-head* (1892) 33. **Edb.** At Hallowmas, whan nights grow lang, FERGUSSON *Poems* (1773) 131, ed. 1785. **Dmf.** Sung the season's dying lay, When hallowmas was past, SHENNAN *Tales* (1837) 149. s.**Wor.** (H.K.) w.**Som.**¹ We always reckons to pay our Michaelmas rent to Hallowmas [t-auˈlurmus]. (8) **Sc.** (JAM.) **Dmf.** The peasantry . . . were wont to date their age from them; thus: 'I was christened o' the Sunday after Tibbie Fleucher's Hallowmass Rade,' CROMEK *Remains* (1810) 276. (9) **Wal.** Pastimes of Hallow Eve are still kept up in Wales on 'Hollowtide Night'—the name by which it is there known, *Monthly Pckt.* (Dec. 1863) 678.

[For explanation of *Hallow* see All-hallow(s.]

HALLOW, *sb.*² Sh.I. Also written **halloe**. A bunch of straw or hay tied round the middle with a rope twisted of the same material. Also called **Hallow-twist**.

Haes doo plenty o' hallows fir da kye's supper, daa? *Sh. News* (Mar. 11, 1899); Makkin' da strae up in hallows reddy ta lay afore da baess, *ib.* (Nov. 26, 1898); Du'll gie dem a halloe tweeat every twa, JUNDA *Klingrahool* (1898) 24; S. & Ork.¹

HALLOW, *adj.*, *adv.*, *sb.*³ and *v.* Sc. Yks. Also in form halloo n.Yks.⁵ **1.** *adj.* Hollow, sunken.

Cai.¹ **Abd.** Sometimes also the flesh is sunk in and hallow, Bell's *Trial of Witchcraft* in LAW *Memor.* (1818) *Pref.* 32 (JAM.). **Rnf.** Phoebus, glowin' fallow, Has owre the wastlan' hills shot hallow, YOUNG *Pictures* (1865) 167.

2. *adv.* Completely, surpassingly, 'hollow.' n.Yks.[2] (s.v. Hollow.)

3. *sb.* A hollow; valley.

Sh.I. Snipe call frae the flossy hallow, BURGESS *Sketches* (2nd ed.) 80. Cai.[1] Raf. There was Tam that wins down in the hallow, WEBSTER *Rhymes* (1835) 4; Lth. O'er green knowe and flowery hallow, Till they reached the cot-house door, MACNEILL *Poet. Wks.* (1801) 163, ed. 1856.

4. *v.* To make hollow. Cai.[1], Abd. (JAM.)

HALL'S DOG, *phr.* Nrf. In saying *as lazy as Hall's dog*.

'As lazy as Hall's dog': he was so lazy he used to lean up against the wall to bark (E.M.).

HALLUM, *sb.* Lth. (JAM.) [Not known to our correspondents.] The woody part of flax.

HALLY, HALLY·LOO, see Holy, Holyrood.

HALLYOCH, *sb.* Sc. A strange gabbling noise, esp. that heard when listening to a strange tongue.

Gall. A club of Manxmen together are said to haud an unco gabbie labbie o' a hallyoch wi' ither, MACTAGGART *Encycl.* (1824) 252, ed. 1876.

HALM, see Haulm.

HALMOT, *sb.* Obs. n.Cy. Ken. Sus. Also in form halimote Sus. The court of the lord of a manor, held in the hall, a court-baron ; also called Halmot·court.

N.Cy.[1], Ken.[1] Sus. The Court Baron of Brighton manor was known by this name in the 17th century (F.E.S.).

[OE. *heall-gemōt*, a hall-meeting.]

HALOK, *sb.* Obs. s.Sc. (JAM.) Also, written haloc ; and in forms hailick, hallik. A light, thoughtless girl, a giddy young woman.

[Hutit be the halok lase a hunder ʒeir of eild ! DUNBAR *Tua Mariit Wem.* (1508) 465.]

HALO(W, see Heloe.

HALPED, *ppl. adj.* I.W. Crippled. (HALL.)

HALPISH, *sb.* Obs. Wxf.[1] Hardship.

HALSE, *sb.[1]* and *v.* Sc. Nhb. Cum. Wm. Yks. Lan. Also written hals Sc.; and in forms haas Cai.[1]; hass Sc. N.Cy.[2] Nhb.[1]; hause Sc. N.Cy.[12] Nhb.[1] Lakel.[1] Cum. Wm. n.Yks.[124] m.Yks.[1] w.Yks. Lan. ne.Lan.[1]; haws(e Sc. Cum.[1] Wm. n.Yks.; hawze n.Cy.; heise Cum.[1]; hoce Cum.[1]; horse w.Yks.; hose N.Cy.[2] Cum. w.Yks. [hȧs, has, h)ǫs.] **1.** *sb.* The neck.

Sc. She bare a horn about her halse, AYTOUN *Ballads* (ed. 1861) I. 29. Sh.I. What the lad has round his halse, SCOTT *Pirate* (1822) v. Or.I. Awaa gied Gilpin, hās ar nokht [Awa' gied Gilpin, hass or naught], *Oread. J. Gilpin,* st. 25, in ELLIS *Pronunc.* (1889) V. 806. N.Cy.[1] Nhb. *Denham Tracts* (ed. 1892) 288 ; Nhb.[1] Cum. *Gl.* (1851). Wm. *Applsby Monthly Messenger* (Apr. 1891) ; (K.) n.Yks.[14] Hence Hausin, *adj.* belonging to the neck.

Wm. Fine lin' shirt wie a girt hausin ruffel, WHEELER *Dial.* (1790) 56.

2. *Comp.* (1) Hause-band, a collar, necklace ; (2) -bane, the collar-bone ; (3) -lock, the wool growing on the neck of a sheep.

(1) N.Cy.[1] There's silk in your white hause-band, *Old Sng.* Nhb.[1] (2) Sc. Ye'll pick out his white hause-bane, And I'll pick out his bonny blue een, SCOTT *Minstrelsy* (1802) II. 360, ed. 1848. Dmf. The wecht o't maun tell on his white hause-bane, REID *Poems* (1894) 97. Gall. That rise beneath the chin and throat, MACTAGGART *Encycl.* (1824) 257, ed. 1876. (3) Bch. Right weel we wat they're hashlock oo, The best 'at e'er was creesh't, TARRAS *Poems* (1804) 94 (JAM.). Ayr. I coft a stane o' haslock woo', BURNS *The cardin' o'i,* st. 1. Lnk. A tartan plaid spun o' good hawslock woo, RAMSAY *Gentle Shep.* (1725) I. i. Edb. Her breasts are whiter than the snow, .. Softer than hauss-locks of the ew, PENNECUIK *Helicon* (1720) 160.

3. The throat, gullet, windpipe.

Sh.I. (*Coll.* L.L.B.) Cai.[1] Elg. Shame and despair roar't in his hause, COUPER *Poetry* (1804) II. 88. Bnff. Tell them either to grow wise, Or cut their hawses, TAYLOR *Poems* (1787) 191. Abd. The deevil o' drink has me by the hause, MACDONALD *Sir Gibbie,* vi. Rnf. With bread and cheese their bellies cram, And synde their hauses with a dram, M'GILVRAY *Poems* (ed. 186a) 39. Ayr. It was to be expecket, considering the spark in my hass, that the first use I would mak o' the freedom o' the Reformation would be to quench it, GALT *Gilhaise* (1823) v. Lnk. Stoups a Froth aboon the hause, RAMSAY *Poems* (1721) 30. e.Lth. As if a haill regent tattie had gotten into and stuck fast in my hause, MUCKLEBACKIT

Rhymes (1885) 173. Edb. A gill comes in, he weets his hause, BALLANTINE *Gaberlunzie* (ed. 1875) 206. Dmf. Nae caller streams To weet their hasses, MAYNE *Siller Gun* (1808) 92. Gall. If one part of the oath fell to hindering the other and fighting in his hass, it was not his fault, CROCKETT *Moss-Hags* (1895) xxxiv. n.Cy. GROSE (1790); N.Cy.[12] Nhb.[1] Cum. Twea or three let-downs o' yell Suon set their hawses free, STAGG *Misc. Poems* (ed. 1805) 132; *Gl.* (1851); Cum.[1] n.Yks. She'l macke them late their teeth, naunt, in their hawse, MERITON *Praise Ale* (1684) l. 604 ; n.Yks.[1]; n.Yks.[2] 'A brave hause,' a wide gullet or good swallow ; a loud voice ; n.Yks.[4], m.Yks.[1] w.Yks. HUTTON *Tour to Caves* (1781).

4. *Phr.* (1) *the pap of the hass,* the uvula ; cf. **hask,** *sb.[2]* ; (2) *to be butter in the black dog's hause,* to be past recovery ; to be no help for anything ; (3) *to go down,* or *into, the wrong hause,* of food, &c. : to go down the wrong way in the throat.

(1) Sc. Gapin' as if ye had a barley awn sticking in the pap o' yer hass, OCHILTREE *Redburn* (1895) v; I'm fash'd wi' an unco kittlin' i' the paup o' my hass, FORD *Thistledown* (1891) 116 ; It's an unco kittlin' in the paup o' the hass, DICKSON *Auld Precentor* (1894) 62. (2) Sc. It wad hae been butter in the black dog's hause, SCOTT *Antiquary* (1816) xxxviii ; (JAM.) Ayr. It was like butter in the black dog's hause for Jenny to get haud of a hole in my coat like this, SERVICE *Dr. Duguid* (ed. 1887) 103. (3) Sc. When a particle of food or drop of liquid goes into the windpipe, it is vulgarly said that it has gone into the wrang hause (JAM.). Cai.[1] Ayr. Something gaed doon the wrang hass, and sic a fit o' hoastin' cam on, SERVICE *Notandums* (1890) 28. Edb. She was suffocated, the foul air having gone down her wrong hause, MOIR *Mansie Wauch* (1828) xix. N.Cy.[1]

5. A rope to tie round a horse's neck in place of a halter. Cum.[1]

6. That part of a chimney where the smoke passes out of sight.

Cum. Used by old people, *N. & Q.* (1878) 5th S. x. 273.

7. A defile, a narrow passage between mountains ; a narrow connecting ridge.

Sc. A storm is coming down from the Cairn-brae-hawse and we shall have nothing but a wild night, *Lights and Shadows* (1822) 114 (JAM.). Dmf. Atween aud Mennock-hass There is a cosy biel', REID *Poems* (1894) 133. Gall. Over there by the halse of the pass, CROCKETT *Bog-Myrtle* (1895) 295. Lakel.[1] Used of the passes over the lower fells which separate the valleys of Lakeland, as Scatoller Hause. Cum. Haws out o' number, nae country can bang, ANDERSON *Ballads* (1805) 106; Cum.[1] w.Yks. HUTTON *Tour to Caves* (1781). ne.Lan.[1]

8. A shallow in a river. Mry. *Agric. Surv. Gl.* (JAM.)

9. *v.* To embrace, hug, take in the arms.

Sc. He hawsed, he kissed her, And ca'd her his sweet, CHAMBERS *Sngs.* (1829) I. 2. a.Sc. Nae blythsume wean has she To halse hir necke, WATSON *Bards* (1859) 111. Ayr. As he halsit her in the parks by the Boag, SERVICE *Dr. Duguid* (ed. 1887) 253. Keb. To come nigh ... and hause him, and embrace him, RUTHERFORD *Lett.* (1660) No. 69. n.Cy. GROSE (1790); N.Cy.[2] Lan. 'An' are yo hausin' too?' said Sally, BRIERLEY *Cast upon World* (1886) 290. Hence Hawse and, *phr.* a nursery term meaning 'kiss me and I am pleased.' Gall. MACTAGGART *Encycl.* (1824) 273, ed. 1876.

[1. Wiþ a rughe skyn ho heled his hals, *Cursor M.* (c. 1300) 3677. OE. *heals.* 3. Hals, throte, *guttur, Prompt.* 9. I halse one, I take hym aboute the necke, *je accolle,* PALSGR. (1530) ; Come halse me, the myrth of our morne, *York Plays* (c. 1400) 445.]

HALSE, *sb.[2]* Irel. Som. Dev. Also in forms alla Dev.[4] n.Dev.; alse' Dev.; hawlse Wxf.[1] [ōls, ȧls.] **1.** The hazel, *Corylus Avellana.* Also used *attrib.* Cf. **hall,** *sb.[2]*

Wxf.[1] Som. A halse coppice, W. & J. *Gl.* (1873); *N. & Q.* (1877) 5th S. viii. 358. w.Som.[1] Dev. A man said he had put 'an 'alse 'andle' into his hammer, *Reports Provinc.* (1877) 131 ; For the bottom of the basket he would lay hands on hedge willow or halse, or any other 'old stuff,' *Longman's Mag.* (Oct. 1897) 509 ; Dev.[4]

Hence Halsen, *adj.* made of hazel.

Som. If they didn' chain thik there poor fakket up under they halsen withes so as he couldn' bust, RAYMOND *Sam and Sabina* (1894) 25. w.Som.[1] A hazel-rod is always a 'halsen stick.' n.Dev. In that part of Devonshire which skirts the south-east of Dartmoor, the prevalent equivalent for hazel wood is ' 'alsen 'ood,' *N. & Q.* (1874) 5th S. ii. 204.

2. *Comp.* (1) **Halse-bushes,** (*a*) hazel-bushes; (*b*) the common alder, *Alnus glutinosa*; (2) -**nut,** a hazel-nut.

(1, *a*) Dev.⁴ (*b*) n.Dev. (*a*) n.Dev. 'A did es halse-nits theeve, Rock *Jim an' Nell* (1867) st. 112.

3. The wych-elm, *Ulmus montana.* w.Som. (B. & H.)

HALSEN, *v.* and *sb.* Hmp. Dor. Som. Dev. Cor. Also in forms **ausney** Dor. Som. n.Dev.; **halzen** Dev.; **hawsen** Som.; **hazen** Dor.¹; **hiessen** s.Hmp. Dor.¹; **housen** Som.; **oseny** e.Som.; **osney** Dur. Som. [ā·lzən, ǭ·zən.]

1. *v.* To predict, divine, conjecture; to forebode evil, anticipate bad news; to speak evil.

s.Hmp. Now don't ye hiessenny like that, Verney *L. Lisle* (1870) xiv. Dor. (W.C.); Haynes *Voc.* (c. 1730) in *N. & Q.* (1883) 6th S. vii. 366; Dor.¹ ''T'll rāin avore night.' 'There, don't ye hiessenny,' *Gl.* Som. Don't 'e houseny (E.N.); W. & J. *Gl.* (1873); *Monthly Mag.* (1814) II. 126. e.Som. W. & J. *Gl.* (1873). w.Som.¹ You never don't hear her zay no good by nobody, but her'll halseny [aa·lznee, rarely pron. oa·znee] all the day long 'bout everybody. Dev.¹ As zoon as you halseny I'm about to break my meend—whip sissa ! you be ago, 34. n.Dev. I ausney zich a' farra', Rock *Jim an' Nell* (1867) st. 60.

Hence **Halsening,** *vbl. sb.* predicting or speaking evil.

e.Som. W. & J. *Gl.* (1873). w.Som.¹ Dev. Concerning the general morality of [her] conduct no amount of 'halzening' could be considered as an exaggeration, Madox-Brown *Dwale Bluth* (1876) bk. i. v. 102. n.Dev. Oll vor . . . halzening, or cuffing a tale, *Exm. Scold.* (1746) l. 298; In phr. 'hoaling and halzening,' picking holes, and suggesting the worst that can happen, *Horae Subsecivae* (1777) 213. Cor. At Little Colan, . . . on Palm Sunday, Carew says: 'Sought at our Lady Nant's well . . . to fore knowe . . . fortune . . . resorted with a palme crosse . . . and an offring. The offring fell to the priest's share . . . a foolish conceite of this "halsening,"' *Flk-Lore Jrn.* (1886) IV. 229.

2. *sb.* A guess. n.Dev. *Handbk.* (ed. 1877) 258.

[1. Cp. OHG. *heilisōn,* 'augurari,' *heilisāri,* 'augur, aruspex' (Graff), cogn. w. ON. *heill,* an omen, auspice, foreboding (Vigfusson). We may also cp. ME. *halsien,* to adjure (Chaucer *C. T.* B. 1835).]

HALSER, *sb.* Sc. A hawser.

Fif. Fix'd are the halsers to the folk-clad shores, Tennant *Anster* (1812) 40, ed. 1815.

[*Alsaniére,* a halsier in a ship, Florio; With well-wreath'd halsers hoise Their white sails, Chapman *Odysseys* (1615) 11. 609.]

HALSH, *v.* and *sb.* Sc. Nhb. Yks. Lan. Chs. Der. War. Bdf. Also in forms **halch** Nhb. w.Yks.² Lan.¹ ne.Lan.¹; **hilch** War.; **holsh** Bdf. [h]alʃ.] **1.** *v.* To fasten, tie; to knot, noose, loop, twist.

w.Yks. T'bobbins bin halshed i' t'windin hoile (W.C.S.); w.Yks.¹²; w.Yks.⁵ Halsh that band up. Lan. A taugh clooas line halshed round their throttles, Clegg *Sketches* (1895) 398; Halsh those two poles t'gether (S.W.). ne.Lan.¹, m.Lan.¹ Chs.¹ To tie a rope in a peculiar way round timber or stone which is to be hoisted; Chs.⁸ Halsh the rope. ne.Der.¹, War. (J.R.W.) Bdf. Batchelor *Anal. Eng. Lang.* (1809) 135.

2. To embrace. Cf. **halse,** *sb.*¹ **9.**

Nhb. He halched him right curteouslie, Richardson *Borderer's Table-bk.* (1846) VI. 51. w.Yks.¹

3. *sb.* A noose, loop, or a slip-knot; a twist, turn. Also in *comp.* **halsh-knot.**

w.Sc. Margaret Reid, . . suspect of witchcraft, confessed she put a woman newlie delivered, thrice through a green halshe, Napier *Flk-Lore* (1879) 131. w.Yks.⁸ Scatcherd *Hist. Morley* (1830) *Gl.*; (J.T.); Banks *Whfld. Wds.* (1865); w.Yks.⁸, Lan.¹, e.Lan.¹, m.Lan.¹, Chs.³

[1. Quat gome so is gorde with þis grene lace, While he hit hade hemely halched aboute þer is no haþel vnder heuen to hewe hym þat myȝt, *Gawayne* (c. 1360) 1852.]

HALT, *sb.*¹ Sc. Bck. Dev. **1.** A defect.

Ayr. When he spies in me a halt, Me secretly to tell the fault, Fisher *Poems* (1790) 67.

2. Rheumatism.

Dev. Hunt *Pop. Rom. w.Eng.* (1865) 412, ed. 1896.

3. In sheep : the foot-rot.

Bck. Ellis *Mod. Husb.* (1750) IV. i.

HALT, *sb.*² Som. Animal deposit. (Hall.)

HALT, *v.* Yks. Not. [olt.] To hesitate.

w.Yks. Duant olt so mitð (J.W.). s.Not. He halted an' halted;

at last he said he'd goo (J.P.K.). [How long halt ye between two opinions ? Bible 1 *Kings* xviii. 21.]

HALTER, *sb.* and *v.* Sc. Yks. Chs. Shr. Nrf. Dor. Som. Dev. Also in forms **auter** Shr.¹; **awter** Chs.¹; **hauter** s.Chs.¹; **helter** ne.Yks.¹ [ǭ·lta(r), ǭ·tə(r).] **1.** *sb.* In phr. (1) *as mad as a tup in a halter,* (2) *to play the halter,* to inflict punishment; (3) *what the halter,* an exclamation, 'what the deuce.'

(1) Shr.¹ It is commonly said of a person in impotent rage that he is 'as mad as a tup in a 'auter.' (2) Chs.¹ (3) s.Chs.¹

2. *Comp.* (1) **Halter-path,** a bridle-path, horse-road; (2) -**shank,** a cart-rope.

1) Dor. *Gl.* (1851); Dor.¹ w.Som.¹ There are still many of these left in the Hill district where, since my recollection, pack-horses were the chief mode of transit. Across a farm of my own is a very ancient [au·ltur paa·th], called 'Hart's Path,' which was never wide enough for two horses to walk abreast. (2) ne.Yks.¹ A long halter shank or cart rope is attached.

3. A hair noose for catching trout and eels. nw.Dev.¹

4. A bridle. Nrf. (F.H.)

5. *v.* To bridle; to bridle a colt for the first time. Also used *fig.*

Sc. Ony hale-hearted halsome hissie, that wants to halter a good husband, Graham *Writings* (1883) II. 154; He halters the black mare, *ib.* 32. w.Som.¹ I had'n a rough colt never haltered. 'I bought an Exmoor pony for twenty-three shillings. . . When haltered . . . for the first time in his life, he proved to be two years old,' Collyns, 156.

Hence **Heltering,** *vbl. sb.* the act of 'breaking in' a young colt or filly. ne.Yks.¹

HALTON SHIELDS, *phr.* Nhb. In phr. *like the man at Halton Shields* ; see below.

Nhb.¹ Common a while ago. This celebrated personage set off on a journey, and, after travelling laboriously all night, found himself at his own back door next morning, Bruce *Handbk. to Roman Wall* (1884) 57.

HALTS, *sb. pl.* Cum. Wm. Also in form **holts** Wm. Wicker hampers; see below.

Cum. Halts, a pair of strong wicker hampers which were joined by a pack saddle, and hung across a horse's back, Linton *Lake Cy.* (1864) 304. Wm. The turf or peat was conveyed from the mosses in halts, *Manners, &c. of Wm.* (1847) 34 ; In the dales bordering upon Yorkshire, the women often carried dung in holts . . . on their shoulders to the fields, Briggs *Remains* (1825) 210.

HALTUGONGA, *int.* Sh.I. Also written **haltagongi;** and in form **altagongi.** An expression used by fishermen to check the running of a halibut that has been hooked.

When the halibut was running with such force, that it was feared that it might break the line, the Unst fishermen would cry after it : 'Haltagongi,' or 'altagongi,' which means 'stop running.' . . Said in English this would have no effect on the fish, but said in Norn it was thought to be effectual and to stop the fish, Jakobsen *Dial.* (1897) 29 ; S. & Ork.¹

HALUCK, see Hallock.

HALVANS, *sb. pl.* Dev. Cor. **1.** Half produce of labour, given instead of wages. Cor.¹

Hence **Halvaner,** *sb.* one who receives half the produce of his labour.

Cor. Boath tutwork men and tributers And halvaners, I say, Tregellas *Tales* (1865) 17 ; Cor.¹²

2. In mining : refuse of the lode after the ore is separated from the rock ; inferior ore.

Dev., Cor. In constant use (R.O.H.). Cor.¹² [Weale.]

Hence **Halvanner,** *sb.* a miner whose earnings are gained by dressing or cleaning the refuse or poorest quality of tin-stone. Cor.⁸

HALVE, *v.*¹ Lakel. Also in form **hauve** Lakel.² Of sheep : to mark by cutting away half the top of the ear.

Cum. Every shepherd's flock hes some variety in ear-marking. . . We cut one-half of a top of the ear clean away, and we call it under or upper halving, *Helvellyn in Cornh. Mag.* (Oct. 1890) 387.

Hence **Hauved,** *adj.* of a sheep : marked in such a way. Lakel.²

HALVE, *v.*² Som. Also in form **helve.** To turn over, turn upside down. W. & J. *Gl.* (1873).

HALVE, see Haaf, *sb.*¹, **Haw,** *sb.*¹

HALVED, *ppl. adj.* Sc. (Jam. *Suppl.*) Golfing term: see below.

Applied to a match which results in a drawn game. Also applied to a hole when each party takes the same number of strokes to play it.

HALVER, *sb.*, *adj.* and *v.* Sc. n.Cy. Nhb. Yks. Chs. Also in forms **haaver** Sc. S. & Ork.[1] Bnff.[1]; **hafer** s.Chs.[1]; **haffer** Gall.; **halfer** Sc. (Jam.) N.Cy.[1]; **haver** Sh.I. Abd. [h]ā·vər, ǭ·və(r.] 1. *sb.* *Obs.* One who has a moiety or half of anything, a sharer, partner.

Kcb. Christ will have joy and sorrow haivers of the life of the saints . . . as the night and day are kindly partners and halvers of time, Rutherford *Lett.* (1660) No. 245.

2. A half, an equal share or portion; *gen.* in *pl.*, esp. in phr. *to go halvers*, to go shares; *in halvers*, in partnership.

Sc. Halvers gang I wi' a' that fear thee, Waddell *Psalms* (1871) cxi. 63. Sh.I. With this view he gave to them in 'halvers' certain mare ponies. This is in accordance with a custom of the county under which the owner of a pony gives to another as custodier a *pro indiviso* right in the animal. . . The custodier is bound to keep and feed the animal, and is entitled to receive in joint property with the original owner of the pony one-half of all stock the produce or descendants of said animal, or one-half of the pony or ponies while in his possession, *Sh. News* (July 16, 1898); They had a considerable number of sheep and ponies—some of which were held in halvers with the neighbours, Clark *Gleams* (1898) 52; S. & Ork.[1] Cai.[1] 'To go haavers.' 'In haavers.' Ayr. Will she let me go halver? Galt *Entail* (1823) xxv. Gall. I'll rin haffers wi' the bed O' Wattie the killman, Mactaggart *Encycl.* (1824) 297, ed. 1876. w.Yks. Let's go halvers wi' this (S.K.C.).

3. *pl.* An exclamation used by children to claim half the value of any treasure found by another; also in phr. *haavers and shaivers*.

Sc. The beggar exclaimed, like a Scotch schoolboy, when he finds anything, 'Nae halvers and quarters, hale o' mine ain, and nane o' my neighbour's,' Scott *Antiquary* (1816) xxiii; Nae bunchers, nor halvers, But a' my ain, Chambers *Pop. Rhymes* (ed. 1870) 145; When one of a party unexpectedly finds a piece of money or other article of value, the first in calling halfers is supposed to have a right to share to that extent with the finder (Jam. *Suppl.*). Per. (G.W.) Lth. Haavers and shaivers. If one who sees another find anything exclaims in this language, he is entitled to the moiety of what is found. If he who is finder uses these terms before any other, he is viewed as having the sole right to the property (Jam.); The phr. more fully is 'haavers and shaivers, and hale o' mine ain.' This is pronounced indiscriminately by the finder and by one who claims a share (*ib.*). e.Lth. Gin the lairds could see an inch afore their nose, they wad be glad to cry haavers raither than tine a', Hunter *J. Inwick* (1895) 89. N.Cy.[1] If, however, the finder be quick, he exclaims 'No halfers—findee keepee, lossee seekee,' which destroys the claim, and gives him the sole right to the property. Nhb.[1] Another formula is: 'Ne halfers; ne quarters; ne pin points; Nyen o' me neybors; aall me aan.' s.Chs.[1]

4. *adj.* Of cattle or stock: held in partnership.

Sh.I. Admits that defender has in his possession the 'halvers' stock specified, *Sh. News* (July 16, 1898); I fan a' 'at we hed comin' dat wye—aless dy grey ha'vers yow, mam. *ib.* (Apr. 1, 1899).

5. *v.* To divide into equal shares, to halve; to possess in partnership with any one.

S. & Ork.[1], Cai.[1], Bnff.[1] Abd. Cut an' ha'ver the roast, Alexander *Johnny Gibb* (1871) xl; (Jam.)

Hence **Halvert**, *ppl. adj.* cut in two, divided in half.

Abd. Nae mair deed nor a halvert worm, Macdonald *Malcolm* (1875) I. 4.

HALY, see Holy.

HALY-CALY, *v.* Cor.[12] To throw things to be scrambled for.

HALYEAR, *sb.* *Obs.* Sc. Also written **hallier** (Jam.); and in form **hellzier** Abd. A half-year.

n.Sc. (Jam.) Abd. Three hellzier [halyear, ed. 1789 (Jam.)] younger she than dindy was, Ross *Helenore* (1768) 14, ed. 1812.

HAM, *sb.*[1] and *v.*[1] Sc. Cum. Yks. Lan. Chs. Lin. Som. Dev. Also in forms **hame** Dmf.; **hom** e.Lan.[1] s.Chs.[1] [h]am, æm.] 1. *sb.* The thigh; the part of the leg immediately behind the knee.

Frf. Roll down the sweaty crowds with wearied legs and hams, Tennant *Anster* (1812) 32, ed. 1871. Cum. He slap't his ham, Gilpin *Sngs.* (1866) 202. w.Yks.[1], e.Lan.[1], s.Chs.[1], n.Lin.[1]

Hence **Hamkin**, *sb.* the hock of a pig. n.Lin.[1]

2. *Comp.* **Hame-blade**, *sb.* ham-bone.

Dmf. Sometimes a bane like a hame-blade, Hawkins *Poems* (1841) V. 25.

3. *Phr.* **ham o' pork**, the joint, as distinguished from meat.

w.Som.[1] It is nearly invariable to speak of 'dressing a ham o' pork,' while the same speaker would say, 'Thank 'ee, I'll have a little bit o' ham.' Dev. They'd a-dressed a ham o' pork and a gurt piece o' beef, *Reports Provinc.* (1885) 96.

4. Wrestling term: see below.

Cum.[4] The action differs from 'catching the heel' by the attack being made behind the knee of the opponent, instead of behind his ankle.

5. *v.* To salt the hind-quarters of beef, pork, or mutton, and hang them up to be smoked.

Twd. To ham the leg of a sheep (Jam.). Gall. He's hung upon a nag [pin] to be ham'd to the reekiest neuk o' hell, Mactaggart *Encycl.* (1824) 175, ed. 1876.

HAM, *sb.*[2] Not. Nhp. Glo. Sus. Wil. Dor. Som. Dev. Also written **hamm**; and in form **homm** Glo. [am, æm.] 1. Flat, low-lying pasture land near a stream or river. Cf. holm, *sb.*[1] 2.

Nhp.[1] An inclosed level pasture. Glo. A common or marsh land, Baylis *Illus. Dial.* (1870); Glo.[1] A considerable tract of ground along the Severn, adjoining the City of Gloucester, and owned by the Freemen of the City, is known as 'The Ham.' Sus.[1] Wil. A narrow strip of ground by the side of a river, Davis *Agric.* (1813); Wil.[1] Dor. The meadow behind East Holme Church is called 'The Hams' (C.W.). Som. Ave you bin down in ham, Thomas, o' late? Jennings *Dial. w. Eng.* (1869) 141. w.Som.[1] The word rather implies land subject to be flooded, but yet rich, and by no means swampy or wet land. Dev. That ham's a long way from the farm, *Reports Provinc.* (1884) 19; The stile of the little ham, Blackmore *Christowell* (1881) xxvi; Dev.[1], nw.Dev.[1]

Hence **Hammings**, *sb. pl.* shallow parts of a river broken up by islands where the water flows rapidly. Not. (W.J.R.)

2. A stinted common pasture for cows.

Glo. Grose (1790); Marshall *Rur. Econ.* (1789, II; *Gl.* (1851).

[1. A hamme or a little plot of ground by the Thames side . . . beset with many willow trees or osiers, William *Ductor* (1617). OE. *hamm*, a pasture or meadow enclosed with a ditch (*Eardulf's Charter*, 875). Cp. Du. *hamme* van *Wilgen*, a place planted with willowes (Hexham); LG. *ham*, 'eine Wiese' (Berghaus).]

HAM, *sb.*[8] *Obs.* Som. Old calamine pits. W. & J. *Gl.* (1873).

HAM, *v.*[2] Bdf. [æm.] To cut and trim a hedge. (J.W.B.)

HAM, *v.*[8] Dur. [ham.] To repeat.

e.Dur.[1] He ham'd it o'er and o'er.

HAM, see Haulm.

HAMALD, *adj.*, *v.* and *sb.* Sc. n.Cy. Nhb. Also in forms **haemilt** Slk.; **haimald** Sc. (Jam.); **haimelt** Sh.I.; **hameald** Sc.; **hameil** Lth. Edb. Slk. n.Cy.; **hamel** Abd.; **hameld** Sc.; **hamelt** Lnk. Edb. Peb.; **hamhald** Sc. (Jam.); **hamil** Abd.; **hamilt** Frf. Per. Lth.; **hammal** Cai.[1]; **hammel** Elg. Per.; **hyemmelt** Nhb.[1] [ha·ml(d.] 1. *adj.* Homely, domestic, household. Cf. hamert; see Home.

Sc. Herd *Coll. Sngs.* (1776) Gl. Cai.[1] Hame is hammal [there is no place like home]. Elg. Former times, and hammel news Steal aff the hour and mair, Couper *Poetry* (1804) I. 117; A mair hammel carl there couldna weel been, Watt *Poet.* (June 25, 1898). Abd. Simple, honest, hamel fowk, Alexander *Ain Flk.* (1882) 82. Frf. A hoosie mair hamilt than braw, Watt *Poet. Sketches* (1880) 67. Per. Buckled up their hammell'd gear, Monteath *Dunblane* (1835) 116, ed. 1887. Lnk. Our auld hamelt tongue . . . is deein', Hamilton *Poems* (1865) 196. Lth. O ken ye auld Janet's bit hamilt made biggin'? Ballantine *Poems* (1856) 46. Edb. Nae herds on Yarrow's bonny braes . . . Delight to chaunt their hameil lays, Fergusson *Poems* (1773) II. 129, ed. 1785. Peb. To send some hamelt, rustic lays, To your sweet muse, Nicol *Poems* (1805) I. 93. Slk. The gude auld haemilt blude that rins in her veins, Hogg *Tales* (1898) 80, ed. 1866; Our grumblin' reachin' some folk's ears Of hameil brulies rais'd their fears, *ib.* Sc. *Pastorals* (1801) 15 (Jam.). n.Cy. *Border Gl.* (Coll. L.L.B.)

2. Home-made ; home-grown, home-bred as opposed to foreign.

Sc. Haimilt claith is that which has been spun at home and given out to be wrought, as distinguished from what has been purchased in the piece, although the latter should be the manufacture of the country. This is also called haimilt-made (JAM.). **Elg.** He wore . . . a hammel-spun coat, *Abd. Wkly. Free Press* (June 25, 1898). **Edb.** I am hameil . . . I'm na frae Turkey, Italy, or France, FERGUSSON *Poems* (1773) 182, ed. 1785.

3. Tame, domestic, as opposed to wild.

Sc. Lang lean makes hameald cattel, RAY *Prov.* (1678) 382; HENDERSON *Prov.* (1832) 82, ed. 1881. **Abd.** Critic or bard or hamil kine, SKINNER *Poems* (1809) 179 (JAM.). **Nhb.**[1]

4. *v.* To domesticate.

Lth. A beast is said to be haimilt when, after a change, it becomes accustomed to the pasture to which it is sent (JAM.).

5. *sb.* A 'haaf-word' for wife.

Sh.I. The common name for 'wife' was haimelt or hjaimelt, because she sat at home, while her husband was at the haaf, JAKOBSEN *Dial.* (1897) 28 ; SPENCE *Flk-Lore* (1899) 121.

[1. Cariand to Italy Thair vincust hammald goddis and Ilion, DOUGLAS *Eneados* (1513), ed. 1874, II. 26. Norw. dial. *heimholl*, homely (AASEN) ; ON. *heimoll* (*heimull*, *heimili*), also *heimhollr* (FRITZNER) ; cp. *heimold* (*-ild*), right of possession (VIGFUSSON) ; see Brogh and Hammer.]

HAMBLE, *v.* Sc. Yks. Lan. Der. Nhp. War. Also in forms hampie w.Yks. ; hamel w.Yks.[1] ; hamle w.Yks.[1] Nhp.[1]; hammle Slk. e.Yks.[1] ne.Lan.[1]; haumpus nw.Der.[1]; hawmple Lan.[1]; hawmpo Lan. ; homble w.Yks. Der.[2]; homple w.Yks. e.Lan.[1] ; humple Slk. Rxb. ; oample Lan. [a'm(b)l.] To limp, halt, walk feebly or awkwardly ; to stumble. Cf. himple.

Rxb. Then humpled be out in a hurry, A. SCOTT *Poems* (ed. 1808) 218. **e.Yks.**[1] Poor awd fellow ! he can hardly hammle alang. **w.Yks.** I wor as wake as a cheild. I hombled on till I got to Camblesworth, HALLAM *Wadsley Jack* (1866) xvi ; **w.Yks.**[14] **Lan.** He hawmples in his walk, like a lame duck, WAUGH *Hermit Cobbler* (1876) 6 ; I mede o' shift to hawmpo owey cwt o' th' huzzy o'bit, PAUL BOBBIN *Sequel* (1819) 41; **Lan.**[1] ne.Lan.[1] e.Lan.[1] s.Lan. BAMFORD *Dial.* (1854). Der.[1] ; Der.[2] He goes hombling along. nw.Der.[1], Nhp.[1] War. (J.R.W.)

Hence Hammlin, *ppl. adj.* limping, shambling ; feeble.

Slk. Sir David's trusty hound wi' humpling back, HOGG *Poems* (ed. 1865) 63. **e.Yks.**[1] **w.Yks.** Astride hir homblin mare, SENIOR *Smithy Rhymes* (1882) 35 ; Every bunion hez a tendency to stop t'progress o' poor homplin pilgrims, *Dewsbre Olm.* (1881) 7. **Lan.** That hawmpoin tyke Hal wur wi' um, TIM BOBBIN *View Dial.* (1740) 14 ; He wur nobbut a hawmplin' mak of a walker at th' best, WAUGH *Chim. Corner* (1874) 116, ed. 1879.

HAMBURGH, *sb.* Irel. Yks. Lan. Lin. Gmg. Pem. Dev. Also in forms hamaron Wxf.[1]; hambrah Pem. ; hamburgher Lin.[1]; hamrach Gmg. Pem. ; hawmbark Lan. ; hanaborough Dev. ; hanniber n.Dev. ; hannibur Dev.[2]; homber w.Yks.[2] **1.** The collar of a draught-horse, *gen.* made of reed or straw, a 'bargham.'

Wxf.[1] *Obs.* **w.Yks.**[2] **Lan.** His wig . . . leet like a hawmbark on his shilders, TIM BOBBIN *View Dial.* (1740) 25 ; **Lan.**[1] **s.Lan.** PICTON *Dial.* (1865). **Gmg.** COLLINS *Gower Dial.* in *Trans. Phil. Soc.* (1848-50) IV. 222. **Pem.** JAGO *Gl.* (1882) 102. **Dev.** *Horae Subsecivae* (1777) 201. **n.Dev.** Bobby 'th vaught 'e . . . Haimses, a banniber, a vell, ROCK *Jim an' Nell* (1867) st. 67.

2. *pl. Fig.* Arm-holes.

Lin. (HALL.) ; **Lin.**[1] The waistcoat pinches me in the hamburghers.

3. A large scarf or comforter. Dev.[8]

4. A straw-mat used in brewing to rest the pan upon.

s.Pem. Bring 'ere the hambark, we moost task off the pan, 'tis boilin' (W.M.M.).

[1. Than muste he haue his horses or mares or both his hombers or collers, FITZHERBERT *Husb.* (1534) 14 ; *Epyphium*, an hamborwe, *Trin. Coll. MS.* (c. 1450) in Wright's *Voc.* (1884) 580. *Hame*, sb.[2] + -*borwe* (*-berwe*), OE. -*beorg(e*, protection.]

HAME, *sb.*[1] In *gen.* dial. use in Sc. Irel. and Eng. Also in forms aime Ken.[1]; ame e.Yks. Not. Suf. Ken. ; eame War.[2] s.War.[1] ; eyam Not. s.Hmp. ; haam n.Yks.[2] w.Yks.[1] n.Lin.[1] s.Lin. Hmp. Som.; haayme Brks.[1]; haem Sc. (JAM.); haim Inv. Abd. Nhb.[1] e.Yks.[1]; hairm n.Lin.[1] ; ham Lan. Sus.[12] w.Dev. ; hamm n.Yks. ; haum

e.Lan.[1] w.Wor.[1] ; hawm Lan.[1] Chs.[1] Dev. ; heam N.Cy.[1] Cum. w.Yks. Der. Dor. ; heeam n.Yks.[4] e.Yks.[1] ; heme Chs.[18]; hem Inv. Elg. N.I.[1] Ken.[1] ; hemm Ant. ; heyam Dur.[1] Not. Hmp. ; heyem Nhb.[1]; hiam Wm. ; home Chs.[1] War. se.Wor.[1] Shr.[1] Hrf.[2] ; holme w.Wor.[1] ; hyem Nhb.[1] ; yam n.Yks.[2] e.Yks.[1] ; *pl.* aimses Dev. ; hameses Hrf. Glo.[12] w.Som.[1] Dev. ; hamses nw.Dev.[1] ; heamsies Som. [h)ēm, h)iəm, īm.] **1.** *pl.* The two curved pieces of wood or metal resting on the collar of a draughthorse, to which the traces are attached. Cf. bargham.

Sc. A pair of hames and brechom fine, RAMSAY *Tea-Table Misc.* (1724) I. 175, ed. 1871. Inv. (H.E.F.) **Elg.** The hems were taen aff, an' the halter made fest, *Abd. Wkly. Free Press* (June 25, 1898). **Abd.** Gin ye slack the haims . . . the beasts 'll be throu' wi' their feed, ALEXANDER *Ain Flk.* (1882) 195. **N.I.**[1], **Wxf.**[1], **N.Cy.**[1] **Nhb.**[1] The two pieces of crooked wood or bent iron hinged at the bottom and held together with a strap atop. They are passed round the collar of a horse, and are furnished with an eye in each side to which are attached the chains to draw the load. Dur.[1], **s.Dur.** (J.E.D.), Wm. (B.K.) **Cum.** Rigreape, braugham, pair o' heams, GILPIN *Sngs.* (1866) 201. **n.Yks.** Neither traces, hames, nor baurghwans to finnd, MERITON *Praise Ale* (1684) l. 93 ; **n.Yks.**[124], **ne.Yks.**[1], **e.Yks.**[1] **w.Yks.** HUTTON *Tour to Caves* (1781) ; **w.Yks.**[2] **Lan.** GROSE (1790) *MS. add.* (C.) **e.Lan.**[1], **Chs.**[123], **Der.**[2], **nw.Der.**[1], **Not.** (L.C.M.), (J.H.B.), **Not.**[128], **n.Lin.**[1] **s.Lin.** What a unheppen looby to put that hoss's haäms on i' that how (T.H.R.). **sw.Lin.**[1], **Rut.**[1], **Lei.**[1], **Nhp.**[1] **War.** *Leamington Courier* (Mar. 6, 1897); **War.**[2], **s.War.**[1], **w.Wor.**[1], **s.Wor.** (H.K.), **se.Wor.**[1], **Shr.**[1], **Hrf.**[12], **Glo.** (J.S.F.S.), **Glo.**[12], **Oxf.**[1], **Brks.**[1], **Bdf.** (J.W.B.), **w.Mid.** (W.P.M.) **Nrf.** *Arch.* (1879) VIII. 170. **Suf.** (F.H.), **Ken.** (H.M.), **Ken.**[1], **Hmp.**[1], **I.W.**[1], **Wil.**[1] **Dor.** BARNES *Gl.* (1863). **Som.** A horsecollar and a pair o' hamses, RAYMOND *Sam and Sabina* (1894) 107 ; W. & J. *Gl.* (1873). **w.Som.**[1] In the dial. there is no *sing.* To denote one of the separate parts, it is necessary to say, 'one o' the sides o' th' hameses,' or 'one o' th' hameces' [ae·umsez]. **Dev.** The hames is very loose, *Reports Provinc.* (1884) 19 ; Where's ta put tha aimses tü ! HEWETT *Peas. Sp.* (1892) 46. nw.Dev.[1]

Hence (1) *Hame and chain-maker, phr.* a maker of harness ; (2) Hamed, *ppl. adj.* yoked.

(1) **Lan.**[1] Common in Manchester. (2) **Glo.** The horse being harnassed or hamed, MARSHALL *Review* (1818) II. 439.

2. *Comb.* (1) Hame-blade, the half of a horse-collar ; (2) -houghed, having houghs shaped like a 'hame' ; (3) -rough, (4) -stick, one of a pair of 'hames' ; (5) -stick ring, a ring attached to the 'hame,' through which the rein passes ; (6) -stick strap, the strap which fastens the 'hame' ; (7) -tree, (8) -ward, see (4); (9) -wood, the 'hames.'

(1, Lth. (JAM.) (2) Sc. A term applied to a horse when it is straiter above than below the hough; from the resemblance of its hind legs to a pair of hames (*ib.*); She was lang-toothed an' blench-lippit, Haem-houghed an' haggis-fittit, *Edb. Monthly Mag.* (June 1817) 238 (JAM.). (3) Chs. (K.) (4) Nhb.[1] (5, 6) Nhb. (R.O.H.) (7, 8) w.Dev. MARSHALL *Rur. Econ.* (1796). (9) Ken.[1], Sus.[12]

3. A horse-collar ; a circle of straw rope often used to fasten the head of a sheep to its fore-leg to prevent its straying. Cor.[12]

[1. LG. *ham*, ein Joch, Kummet, der Pferde (BERGHAUS); MDu. *hame*, a leather or wooden yoke for horses (VERDAM).]

HAME, *sb.*[2] and *v.*[1] Lin. Suf. Also written haim se.Lin. [ēm.] **1.** *sb.* Steam from boiling water ; warm vapour as from heated horses, slaked lime, &c.

Lin.[1] This hame has scauded me. **e.Lin.** Used also of the damp and moist feeling of an empty house opened out again (G.G.W.). **se.Lin.** In *gen.* use near the sea-coast. 'The wesh'us is white with haim out o' the boiler.' 'Ho'd yer he'd in the haim from a baison o' hot waäter' (T.H.R.). **Suf.** The hame is coming out of the kettle (F.H.).

2. *v.* To steam.

Suf. If your throat is sore, you can't do better than hame it. The kettle begins to hame (F.H.).

[1, 2. Norw. dial. *eim*, steam, *eimbaat*, a steamboat ; *eima*, to steam (AASEN) ; ON. *eimr*, reek, vapour (VIGFUSSON).]

HAME, *sb.*[3] Hmp. [ēm.] A small piece, in *phr. all to hame*, all to bits.

The glass is all to hame, WISE *New Forest* (1883) 283 ; Hmp.[1]

[EFris. *ham*, 'Biss, Bissen, Stück' (KOOLMAN).]

HAME, *v.*[2] Som. [ēm.] To have sexual intercourse. W. & J. *Gl.* (1873).

[OE. *hǣman*, ' concumbere, coire, nubere ' (B.T.).]

HAME, see Ham, *sb.*[1], Haulm, Home.

HAMEART, *adv.* Sc. Yks. Also in forms **hamewarts** Fif. ; **hamedards** w.Yks. [hē·mərt.] Homeward ; also used *attrib.* Cf. **hamert**, *adj.*

Fif. Hamewarts bairn and wife, and man, Helter-skelter they skelpt and ran, TENNANT *Papistry* (1827) 222. Rnf. Sir Guy is forced to . . . tak' the hameart gate [way], THOMSON *Leddy May* (1883) 3. Lnk. Hameart he gaed that nicht, COGHILL *Poems* (1890) 78. w.Yks. Breakfast dune, they mud hamedards start, DIXON *Slaadburn Faar* (1871) 16.

HAMEL, HAMELT, HAMEL-TREE, see Hamble, Hamald, Hample-tree.

HAMEREST, *sb.* Sh.I. Also in form **hamerist.** [hē·mrest.] The commonage adjoining enclosed land.

Da mais o' wir paets wis apo' da hamerist, *Sh. News* (May 22, 1897) ; S. & Ork.[1]

[Norw. dial. *heimrast*, the nearest grass-land to the enclosed land (AASEN) ; ON. *heim-röst.*]

HAMERT, *adj.* Sc. Nhb. Also written **haimart** Rnf. ; **haimert** Frf. ; **hamart** Sc. (JAM.) ; **hame'art** Dmb. Ayr. ; and in forms **hame-at** Ayr. ; **hameit, hamet** Per. ; **hameward** Fif. Nhb. ; **hamewart** Ayr. ; **hamit** Frf. [hē·mart.] 1. Belonging to home, home-grown, home-made, homekeeping ; also used *advb.* Cf. **hameart.**

Sc. Cleedin guid o' hamert mak', EDWARDS *Mod. Poets*, 8th S. 307. Frf. Weel twisted oot o' haimert woo', BEATTIE *Arnha* (c. 1820) 15, ed. 1882 ; Nane but hamit linjet [flax-seed] sawn, *Piper of Peebles* (1794). Per. Roll'd up like a witch in a hameitspun plaidie, FORD *Harp* (1893) 147 ; The gude auld times O' hearty rants and hamet rhymes, HALIBURTON *Puir Auld Scotland* (1887) 164. Fif. It was hameward wisdom, the wisdom that likes to brood oure a cog o' guid stiff parritch, ROBERTSON *Provost* (1894) 128. e.Fif. On his lower shanks, he had a pair o' coarse ribbit hamert-wrocht blue stockins, LATTO *Tam Bodkin* (1864) iii. Dmb. The yarn in grist is a' alike, Tho' hame'art spun, TAYLOR *Poems* (1827) 58. Rnf. Stegh the loun weel wi' haimart gear, PICKEN *Poems* (1813) I. 129. Ayr. Nane o' our hamewart gentry, GALT *Lairds* (1826) xxii ; An auld-fashion'd man, a hame'art gentleman who has never seen the world, *ib.* xxvi ; The homespun, or ' hame-at-made ' articles, were the pride of every housewife, WHITE *Jottings* (1879) 36. Lnk. Scrimp her o' her bit and brat, That hameward agriculture May thrive, WATSON *Poems* (1853) 5. Dmf. He's haimert-made and genuine, SHAW *Schoolmaster* (1899) 334. Nhb. Obs. I will no longer submit to his hameward country ways, *Lett. from Corbridge* (1775) (R.O.H.).

Hence **Haimartness**, *sb.* childish attachment to home. Sc. (JAM.)

2. Condescending in manner, not haughty.

Ags. A person of rank is hameart who is courteous (JAM.). Dmf. The hamert heart was donnert dung, REID *Poems* (1894) 260.

HAMFLEETS, *sb. pl. Obs.* Glo. Cloth buskins to defend the legs from dirt, 'sheenstrads.'

Horae Subsecivae (1777) 201 ; *Gl.* (1851) ; Glo.[1] Hame-leets [sic].

HAM-GAMS, *sb. pl.* Lei.[1] [æ·m-gæmz.] Antics, tricks. A's bin at some o' his hamgams agen.

HAMIE, *adj. Obs.* Sc. Suggestive of home, domestic. Edb. I . . . ripet a' my shallow pow For hamie lays, CRAWFORD *Poems* (1798) 47.

HAMIL, *sb.* n.Cy. Nhb. Lan. Chs. Sus. Also written **hamel** e.Lan.[1]; **hammil** Lan.[1]; **hammill** n.Cy. ; and in form **hemmel** Nhb. e.Sus. [a·ml, h]e·ml.] 1. A hamlet, village.

n.Cy. GROSE (1790). Nhb. 'Tween Foxstane hemmils an' the Peels, PROUDLOCK *Borderland Muse* (1896) 84. Lan. Aw know o' that country-side, . . . hill an' dale, . . . hamil an' road-side heawse, WAUGH *Yeth-Bobs* (1869) i ; Lan.[1], e.Lan.[1] e.Sus. HOLLOWAY.

2. *Comp.* **Hamil-sconce**, *fig.* the light of the village or hamlet, the village Solomon.

Lan. Owd Jeremy at tat time wur look't on as th' hammel's skonse amung 'em e Juda, WALKER *Plebeian Pol.* (1795) 58, ed. 1801 ; A schoolmaster, who was looked up to by his neighbours as a kind of ' hamel-scoance,' or lanthorn of the village, WAUGH *Old Cronies* (1875) iii ; Lan.[1], Chs.[18]

[1. The hamell of Aynsworth [in Lan.], *Exam. Cokeye More* (c. 1514) in Chetham Soc. (1855) XXXVII. 11. OFr. *hamel*, ' hameau ' (LA CURNE).]

HAMIL(T, see Hamald.

HAMLET, *sb.* Yks. [a·mlit.] Phr. *play Hamlet with*, to play ' the deuce ' with ; to give one a ' good blowing up.'

w.Yks. Aw cud like to see thee wed ta nobbut one, Shoo'd play Hamlet wi' thee, HARTLEY *Clock Alm.* (1874) 43 ; Bai gou lad ! wen ta gets uam ɓel bi amlit ta pleə. Mi muɓo pleəd amlit wi im fə stopin ət lat ət nit (J.W.).

HAMLIN, *sb.* Sc. (JAM. *Suppl.*) Also in form **hamlan.** [Not known to our correspondents.] A cross, wile, trick.

HAMMAL, HAMMEL, see Hamald, Hemmel, *sb.*[3]

HAMMER, *sb.*[1] and *v.*[1] Var. dial. uses in Sc. Irel. and Eng. Also in forms **haumer** Abd. ; **hawmer** Bnff.[1] ; **hommer** Lan. I.Ma. s.Chs.[1] nw.Der.[1] ; **homber** Shr.[1] [h]a·mə(r, æ·mə(r).] 1. *sb.* In *comb.* (1) Hammer-axe, an implement with a hammer on one side and an axe on the other ; (2) -bate, a dappled spot on a horse ; (3) -bleat, the snipe, *Gallinago caelestis* ; (4) -clawed, like the claws of a nail-hammer ; (5) -dressed, stone faced with a pick or pointed hammer ; (6) -flush, sparks from an anvil ; (7) -hay, rough hay as in moors or waste ground ; (8) -head, a dull, stupid fellow ; (9) -heel, the portion of the face of the hammer next the head ; (10) -man, (*a*) a blacksmith, a worker in iron, tin, or other metals ; a member of the blacksmiths' guild ; (*b*) in coal-mining : see below ; (11) -nose, the portion of the hammer-face opposite the ' heel' ; (12) -spots, the dappled appearance of a horse ; (13) -tacking, dawdling, working in a half-hearted manner ; (14) -thrower, a man who throws the sledge-hammer in athletic sports ; (15) -toe, a malformation of the toe.

(1) N.Cy.[1], Nhb.[1] (2) Dev. Maister, he's as full of hammerbates as can be, *Reports Provinc.* (1897). (3) Cum. Na mair you'll hear the hammerbleats, DICKINSON *Lit. Rem.* (1888) 161 ; Cum.[14], m.Yks.[1], ne.Lan.[1] (4) Nhb.[1] A tail coat is still called a ' hammerclaad cwoat.' (5) Nhb.[1], w.Yks. (J.W.), nw.Der.[1] (6) Fif. Frae the blacksmith's study rush Sae thick the sparks and hammerflush, TENNANT *Papistry* (1827) 205. (7) n.Yks. That's what I call hammer hay (J.W.). (8) w.Yks.[5] (9) Nbb.[1] (10, *a*) Sc. The hammermen of Edinburgh are to my mind afore the warld for making stancheons, ring-bolts [&c.], SCOTT *Midlothian* (1818) xxix. Elg. A hammerman's but black at best, TESTER *Poems* (1865) 1. Abd. These were the hammermen, headed by Vulcan sitting shivering in an iron car, ANDERSON *Rhymes* (1867) 214. Frf. Robert Hepburn, hammerman, LOWSON *Guidfollow* (1890) 265. Ayr. One Thomas Sword, the deacon of the hammermen, GALT *Gilhaize* (1823) iv. Gall. He . . . was buried there in state by the hammer-men, which body would not permit the Earl of Selkirk to lay his head in the grave, merely because his Lordship was not one of their incorporated tribe, MACTAGGART *Encycl.* (1824) 68, ed. 1876. Dev. The stamping of this impression by a hammer is coining the tin, and the man who does it is called the hammer-man, BRAY *Desc. Tamar and Tavy* (1836) I. 118. (*b*) Dev. When the holers have finished their operations, a new set of men, called hammermen, or drivers, enter the works. These fall, or force down, large masses of coal, by means of long and sharp iron wedges, GLOVER *Hist. Der.* (1829) I. 58. (11) Nhb.[1] When a hand hammer is held up by the helve, and the flat disc of its ' face' placed opposite to the observer, the upper portion of the disc is the ' nose,' and the lower, or portion towards the helve, is the ' heel.' (12) Nrf. (A.G.) (13) nw.Dev.[1] ' They've bin hammer-tackin' about yur all day, but I doan' zim they've got ort to shaw vor'L ' ' Ot b'ee hammer-tackin' about yur vor ! ' (14) Abd. I have seen him do a feat which would put the best hammer-thrower to the blush, ANDERSON *Rhymes* (1867) 194. (15) e.Suf. (F.H.)

2. Phr. (1) *as dead as a hammer*, quite dead ; (2) *hammer and block*, (3) —, *block, and Bible*, (4) —, *block, and study*, a boys' game ; see below ; (5) — *and pincers*, (6) —*and pinsons*, the noise made by a horse when the hind-leg strikes the fore-leg ; (7) — *and tongs*, (*a*) high words ; also in phr. *to go at a thing hammer and tongs*, to dispute or do violently ; (*b*) curling term ; see below ; (8) *the hammer of it*, the pith of a message ; the principal cause of anything ; (9) *to go at a thing hammer and pinsons*, to set about a thing with determination and force.

(1) n.Cy. (J.W.) Lan. As deed as a hommer, LAYCOCK *Sngs.* (1866) 32. Brks.[1] I chucked my stick at that ther rat an' killed un as ' dead as a hammer.' (2) Abd. At the 'Hammer and the Block' deal mony a sturdy blow, CADENHEAD *Bon Accord* (1853) 189 ; One boy had to prostrate himself on his hands and knees, with his pos-

teriors protruding, while four boys took another boy, one at each arm, and one at each leg, and bearing him, with his face upward, used him as a battering-ram against the other boy, posteriors to posteriors. It was a punishment rather than a game ; but, when not carried to an extreme, created a deal of rather cruel fun (W.C.). **Lan.** Another party engaged in the games of . . . hop-scotch, hammer and block, THORNBER *Hist. Blackpool* (1837) 90 ; Those glorious English games of cricket, 'hammer and block,' BRIERLEY *Irkdale* (1865) 67, ed. 1868. (3) **N.I.** Each of the three objects is represented by a boy. (4) **Gall.** A fellow lies on all fours, this is the block ; one steadies him before, this is the study [anvil] ; a third is made a hammer of, and swung by the boys against the block, MACTAGGART *Encycl.* (1824) 252, ed. 1876. (5) **Cum.** (M.P.), **w.Yks.** (W.C.S.), **w.Yks.¹**, **Chs.¹ ⁸**, **Nhp.¹** (6) **n.Lin.¹** (7, *a*) **Ayr.** They would go at it again, hammer and tangs, for anither hour, SERVICE *Dr. Duguid* (ed. 1887) xxii. **w.Yks.** *Hlfx. Courier* (May 8, 1897). **Chs.¹** 'Falling out hammer and tongs' is a very common expression ; **Chs.² Nhp.¹** When a person is relating his falling out with some one, it is common to say among the lower orders, 'Oh, we got up to hammer and tongs.' **War.⁸** 'They went at it hammer and tongs,' they scolded each other unceasingly. Also used as equivalent to rough, unscientific fighting. **Oxf.¹** *MS. add.* **Sus., Hmp.** 'To live hammer and tongs' is said of married people who seldom agree, HOLLOWAY. (*b*) **Abd., Per.** At curling a common order is, 'Come up an' gie the stane hammer and tangs' (G.W.). (8) **Ess.** Ay, that's the hammer on't (C.W.D.). (9) **Shr.¹** The constable parted 'em wunst, but they watchen 'im away, an' then wenten 'omber an' pinsons at it again.

3. A blow with a hammer.

Frf. I decided to gang oot an' gie't a hammer on, WILLOCK *Rosetty Ends* (1886) 37, ed. 1889.

4. The fist ; a blow with the fist ; also in phr. *the hammer o' death.*

w.Yks.¹ When a person is quarrelling with another, whom he wishes to intimidate, he will hold up his fist in a menacing attitude, and say, 'See, here's t'hammer o'deeoth.' **ne.Lan.¹ e.Suf.** To give one a hammer (F.H.).

5. Clumsy, noisy walking or working ; a clumsy, noisy person or worker.

Bnff.¹ The hawmer he keeps up an' doon the chaamer's nae bearable. **Ayr.** My bonie maid, before ye wed Sic clumsy-witted hammers, BURNS *Willie Chalmers*, st. 5.

6. *v.* To thrash ; to beat continuously with a stick.

Sc. (A.W.) **Nhb.** Wor sowldiers hammered the beggars. Come on, aa'll hammer aall the three on ye (R.O.H.) ; **Nhb.¹ n.Yks.** Ah hammered him weel (T.S.). **e.Yks.** Next tahm he diz it, Ah'll hammer him weel, NICHOLSON *Flk-Sp.* (1889) 26 ; **e.Yks.¹ w.Yks.** He hammered David for long enough, *Eng. Illus. Mag.* (Mar. 1896) 592 ; **w.Yks.²** A boy said to his schoolfellow, 'Which o' thee and me can hammer?' i.e. fight best. **Lan.** They're hardly a lad i' o' th' village bur what Bobby had hommert oather at one toime or another, MELLOR *Mick Owdem* (1867) 8. **m.Lan.¹ LMa.** Had to hommer him—that was all, BROWN *Indiaman* (1889) 149. **s.Chs.¹** Ahy)] om-ŭr yü iv ahy)kn gy'et wurt ŭ yŭ [I'll hommer yō if I con get howt o' yō]. **Not.¹ Lei.¹** 'Did you hear me talk about hammering anyone?' asked by a prisoner on trial for shooting a toll-keeper. **Oxf.** (G.O.) **Hnt.** (T.P.F.)

Hence **Hammering**, *sb.* a thrashing.

Sc. Gi'e ower, ye loons, wi' throwin' stanes, Or haith ye's get a hammerin', VEDDER *Poems* (1842) 119. **Yks.** (J.W.) **Lan.** Yo desarved a good hommerin' . . . for usin' a poor chap so, WOOD *Hum. Sketches,* 6. **Midl.** Ye'll remember the hammering Exeter gev him, BARTRAM *People of Clopton* (1897) 53. **War.⁸** He gave me such a hammering (E.S.). **Oxf.** (G.O.), **e.Suf.** (F.H.)

7. Phr. *hammered up,* at a loss for words.

w.Yks.⁵ A bashful and very nervous young man gets into a bonnet-shop somehow (say during a shower), and is 'hammer'd up clean,' finding himself in that most interesting predicament of having nothing to say !

8. To practise laboriously ; to labour.

Nhb. Aw hammer on till efternuin Wi' weary byens and empty wyem, WILSON *Pitman's Pay* (1843) 9. **Lan.** Dun yo' know the time th' owd lad's hommerin' at ? *Longman's Mag.* (Apr. 1897) 553.

9. To walk or work in a noisy, clumsy way ; to stumble.

Cai.¹ Bnff.¹ 'The muckle fabrick o' a cheel cam hawmerin' ben the fleer, an' knockit our the bairn.' 'He wiz hawmerin' wee a spawd at the back o' a dyke.' **Abd.** Aw haumer't into the kitchie upo' the mistress an' him speakin', ALEXANDER *Johnny Gibb* (1871) xvi. **Ayr.** Stumpin on his ploughman's shanks, He in the parlour hammer'd, BURNS *Interview with Dacre* st. 4.

Hence (1) **Hawmerer**, *sb.* a big, awkward person, with unwieldy feet ; one who is clumsy and noisy at work ; (2) **Hawmerin,** *ppl. adj.* big and clumsy.

Bnff.¹ (1) {One} who makes much noise in walking, and is apt to trample on what comes in the way. (2) He's a hawmerin' cheel. A cudna bide the sicht o' 'im aboot the toon for a servan.

HAMMER, *sb.²* **Sh.I.** Also in form **haamar.** A large mass of stone or rock jutting out, *gen.* from the side of a hill.

There was scarcely a spot that was not called by some appropriate name of Norse origin, such beautifully characteristic names as . . . Gulla Hammar (the yellow rocks), SPENCE *Flk-Lore* (1899) 176 ; JAKOBSEN *Dial.* 1897) 80 ; **S. & Ork.¹**

[ON. *hamarr*, a hammer-shaped crag (VIGFUSSON).]

HAMMER, *v.²* Sc. n.Cy. Nhb. Yks. Lin. [h)a·mə(r).] To stammer, hesitate in speaking.

Sc. (A.W.), **N.Cy.¹ Nhb.** Aw hammer'd out lyem excuse, WILSON *Pitman's Pay* (1843) 49. **n.Yks.¹** The two words hammer and stammer are frequently joined together in use ; **n.Yks.² ⁴, e.Yks.¹, m.Yks.¹, w.Yks.¹,** n.Lin.¹

HAMMER-BAND, *sb.* **Cum.** A manner of yoking ; used *attrib.* ; also used *fig.*

Cum.¹ Uphill work, constant pull on the shoulders. In old times the horse was yoked to the cart by ropes from the shoulders to iron or willow or hazel rings sliding on the shafts, held by a pin. This was hammer-band yoking ; **Cum.⁴** *Obs.* No iron staps, nor shoulder links, For all had hammer bands, *Carlisle Patr.* (May 13, 1870).

HAMMERGAG, *v.* and *sb.* Der. Not. Wor. Suf. Also in form **ammergag** s.Not. w.Wor.¹ [a·magag.] **1.** *v.* To stammer, speak with difficulty. Der.², Not.

2. To scold ; to argue.

s.Not. Yer can't get away frum 'im ; 'e'll stand ammergagging for a hour (J.P.K.). **w.Wor.¹** 'Ow 'im an' er do quar'l, to be sure. You can 'ear 'em thraow the wall, 'ammergaggin' awaay from marnin' till night.

3. *sb.* A boisterous noise. **e.Suf.** (F.H.)

HAMMERGAW, *v.* Sc. To argue pertinaciously.

Ayr. Ye may spend the evening o' your days in lown felicity ; and hammergaw frae morning to night wi' the advocates about corn-laws, GALT *Lairds* (1826) xxxv.

HAMMER-SCAPPLE, *sb.* *Obs.* n.Cy. Yks. A niggardly person who attempts to drive a hard bargain. n.Cy. HOLLOWAY. **w.Yks.¹⁵**

HAMMERY, *sb.* **Cum.** [Not known to our correspondents.] People who live by working with the hammer ; used *attrib.*

Carlisle possesses eight craft guilds, namely, the Weavers, the Smiths, &c., or all that live by the Hammery Art, FERGUSON *Hist. Cum.* (1890) xiii.

HAMMICK, see **Hommock.**

HAMMIL, *v.* Chs. [a·mil, a·ml.] To ill-treat, abuse ; to overwork.

s.Chs. God Awmighty's hammil'd me, DARLINGTON *Ruth,* i. 21 ; **s.Chs.¹** A henpecked husband was said to be 'Aam·ild widh iz weyf' [hammiled with his weife].

Hence **Hammilled**, *ppl. adj.* ill-treated, abused.

s.Chs.¹ An overworked servant maid is called 'a poor hammilled thing.'

[OE. *hamelian,* to maim, mutilate (*Chron.*).]

HAMMIL, see **Hummel,** *adj.*

HAMMIT, *adj.* Sc. (JAM.) Also in form **hammot.** [Not known to our correspondents.] Plentiful ; used of corn growing close, but short in the straw ; also applied to corn with many grains on one stalk, or of potatoes growing thickly on one stem.

[Dan. dial. *hammel,* yielding, productive, fruitful, used of corn having many grains ; *hammelt* (adv.) (MOLBECH).]

HAMMOCK, *sb.¹* Sc. [ha·mək.] A bed. Also used *fig.*

Sc. Mony a crone was laid on her last hammack, For want o' eggs, to fill her cravin' stamack, STEWART *Character* (1857) 188. **Elg.** I'll e'en pop in my hammock, TESTER *Poems* (1865) 130. **Abd.** She warms them weel, an' pits them to their hammock, BEATTIE *Parings* (1801) 40, ed. 1873. **Rnf.** Lord . . . bless thee . . . Wi' couthy wife and cozie hammock, WEBSTER *Rhymes* (1835) 108.

HAMMOCK, *sb.²* e.Suf. The fist ; a blow with the fist. (F.H.) See **Hammer,** *sb.¹* **4.**

HAMMOCK, HAMMUT, see Hommock, Emmet.

HAMMY, sb. n.Cy. Nhb. Also written hammie N.Cy.[1] [ha·mi.] 1. A sheepish, cowardly person.

N.Cy.[1] Nhb. Tho' Gurty sairly run her rig, An' shameful used er Hammy, ROBSON *Evangeline* (1870) 353; Nhb.[1]

2. A cock that will not fight. N.Cy.[1], Nhb.[1]

HAMP, sb.[1] Obs. Yks. A kind of smock-frock.

n.Yks. Gin Hob mun hae nowght but a hardin' hamp, He'll oom nae mair, nowther to berry nor stamp. . . Obs. forty years go. . . The hamp was a smockfrock-like article of raiment, athered in somewhat about the middle, and coming some little ay below the knee, ATKINSON *Moorl. Parish* (1891) 56; n.Yks.[1] hamp and a hood! Then Hobbie again 'll dee nae mair good.

[Dan. dial. *hempe*, a peasant's frock, 'toga rustica' MOLBECH).]

HAMP, v. and sb.[2] Sc. Lan. Wor. Also in forms aumpe Lan.; omp Wor. [hamp.] 1. v. To halt in alking; to limp. Cf. himp, v.

Twd. (JAM.) Lan. *Trans. Phil. Soc.* (1858) 160. s.Wor. A cow omped along on three legs, *Vig. Mon.* in *Berrow's Jrn.* (1896).

2. To stammer, speak or read hesitatingly.

Cld., Lth. (JAM.) Rxb. Ye mind auld stories I can hamp but t, A. SCOTT *Poems* (ed. 1808) 31; If ye 'bout it hamp and hay . . . e soon will fin' A wilfu' man maun hae his way, RIDDELL *Poet. Wks.* (ed. 1871) I. 5. Gall. How it came, I scarce can tell, I learnt wee to hamp an' spell, LAUDERDALE *Poems* (1796) 80.

Hence **Hamper,** sb. one who cannot read fluently. Cld. (JAM.)

3. sb. A halt in walking. Twd. (JAM.)

4. A stutter.

Slk. He got through the saxteenth o' Romans without a hamp, HOGG *Tales* (1838) 366, ed. 1865.

HAMPER, sb. Chs.[1] [a·mpə(r).] A measure of six ecks.

Apples, pears, plums, damsons, and gooseberries are generally old wholesale by the hamper. So also are potatoes, especially ew potatoes, which are always sent to market in these hampers. . . Each hamper holds half a load of potatoes, that is six pecks r scores of twenty-ones pounds to the score (a long score).

HAMPER, v.[1] Sc. Yks. Chs. Der. Not. Lin. Lei. War. hr. Glo. Oxf. Brks. e.An. Ken. Wil. Som. Also in forms mper Wil.; homper Not.[1] War.[2]; omper Lei.[1] Oxf.[1] h]a·mpə(r, æ·mpə(r).] 1. To hinder, impede; to em- arrass, burden; to puzzle; freq. in *pp.* In *gen.* colloq. use.

Gall. For topling clubs, Oh! let them be, Or Sawny lad, ye'll amper me, LAUDERDALE *Poems* (1796) 82. n.Yks.[1]; n.Yks.[4] ich've been hampered wi' all maks an' manders o' things. m.Yks.[2] ha.[1] To burden with debt. Not.[1] n.Lin.[1] She can't go oot taastie ickin', she's so hamper'd wi' bairns. I'm well enif if it warn't r this here cough that hampers me. Lei.[1] Mr. — is a streenge erson, a doos 'omper one so. Shr.[1] God 'elp the poor ôôman— r'll be despertly 'ompered ôôth them two twins. Glo. BAYLIS *lus. Dial.* (1870). Oxf.[1] 'Er 'usband's dead and left her hampered i' six children, *MS. add.* e.An.[1] I 'ont be hampered up along o' ou. Nrf. I'm hampered to get hold of my breath, COZENS-HARDY *road Nrf.* (1893) 88. e.Suf. He's hampered to get his breath F.H.). Ess. Who are in the warld well to do, They onny shud a' cubs; Who's nut, lore! how he's hampered up, CLARK *J. Noakes* 1839) st. 19. Wil. SLOW *Gl.* (1892).

Hence (1) **Hamper,** sb. confusion, entanglement; per- lexity; (2) **Hampered,** *ppl. adj.* beset with difficulties; arassed, troubled; (3) **Hamperment,** sb., see (1).

(1) Ess. An entangled skein is said to be 'all in a hamper'; as That's in sich a hamper, I shall niver git it out no more' (W.W.S.). Wil. When the horses in a team get all into confusion, or a ball f string is in a harl, this would be a case of 'aal in a hamper' G.E.D.). (2) n.Yks.[1]; n.Yks.[2] 'A sair hamper'd family,' borne own with difficulties. w.Yks. Troubled with (as toothache) (J.T.). w.Der.[1] War.[2] (3) Glo.[1], n.Wil. (G.E.D.)

2. To hesitate. e.Suf. (F.H.)

3. To infest with vermin; to choke with dirt. *Gen.* in *pp.* n.Yks.[12]; n.Yks.[4] Them to'nips leeak a bit hampered wi' t'fly. s.Yks.[1] w.Yks. We're sairly hampered wi' rats, *Yks. Wkly. Post* 1883). Chs.[1] Yo never seed sitch a place i' your loif, it were aw ampered up wi dirt.

4. To injure, disarrange, throw out of gear.

Oxf.[1] A lock is said to be 'hampered' when out of repair so hat the key cannot work it, *MS. add.* Brks.[1] Ken. (G.B.); en.[1] The door is hampered. Wil. SLOW *Gl.* (1892).

5. To coerce; to bridle a colt for the first time.

w.Som.[1] Aay boa·ut dhik poa·nee au·l ruuf, uvoa·r u wuz dv·ur u-aam·purd [I bought that pony in a wild state, before he was ever bridled]. Ees! un u puur·dee jau·b wee-d u-gau·t vur tu aam·pur-n ! [Yes! and a pretty job we had to bridle him!]

6. To punish by legal procedure.

w.Yks. They could be hampered for selling lottery-tickets (S.K.C.).

7. *Comp.* **Hamper-logged,** overborne, persuaded.

War. *B'ham Wkly. Post* (June 10, 1893); War.[2] A witness at a late assize at Warwick used this word in the sense of being overborne or persuaded by his wife, saying that he was 'quite hamperlogged by her.'

HAMPER, v.[2] Yks. Der. [a·mpə(r).] To beat.

w.Yks.[1]; w.Yks.[5] Bin hampering thuh agean!—wah thah sud 'a' hamper'd him then—mun, thah's big herniff to heit him! nw.Der.[1]

HAMPER-CLOT, sb. n.Cy. [Not known to our corre- spondents.] A ploughman. (HALL.)

HAMPEROR, sb. w.Wor.[1] A hamper.

HAMPHIS, v. Obs. Sc. To surround; to hem in, to confine.

Sc. Agast the Sothroun stood astound, Syne hamphised him, pele-mele, ane and a', JAMIESON *Pop. Ballads* (1806) II. 175. Abd. Out gush'd her eyn . . . Sae hamphis'd was she atween glee and wae, Ross *Helenore* (1768) 67, ed. 1812; A band of Keltrin hamphis'd all our braes, *ib.* 109.

HAMPLE-TREE, sb. Hrt. e.An. Also in form hamel-. [æ·mpl-tri.] The bar by which a horse draws a plough or carriage. *Gen.* in *pl.*

Hrt. ELLIS *Mod. Husb.* (1750) I. 141. e.An.[12]

HAMPOT, sb. Shr. Also in form ampot. [æ·mpət.] A hamper.

Shr.[1] Poor Dick ôôd think it a poor Chris'mas if 'e didna 'ave 'is ampot; Shr.[2]

HAMRACH, see Hamburgh.

HAMREL, sb. Sc. An awkward person; one who stumbles often in walking.

Abd. Ye never saw sic a hamrel as oor laddie is; yesterday he fell owre my honey pig an' brak it a' to smash. Not uncommon (G.W.). Slk. (JAM.)

HAM-SAM, adv. Sc. Yks. Lan. Also written hamm-samm Wm. & Cum.[1]; and in forms ham- scram Wm.; him-sam Dur. [h]a·m-sam.] Irregularly, confusedly; hastily; in confusion or disorder.

Dur. 'Re mixt up ham-sam wu froaks, clockers n' eels, EGGLE- STONE *Betty Podkin's Lett.* (1877) 9; GIBSON *Up-Weardale Gl.* (1870). s.Dur. Things was all thrawn in ham-sam (J.E.D.). Cum. She'd pack't them [clothes] eh sec a hurry, teuh, at they wur oa ham-sam, SARGISSON *Joe Scoap* (1881) 11; *Gl.* (1851); Cum.[4] Wm. & Cum.[1] An' sat hamm-samm togither, 201. Wm. Then reayve their clwoaks to screeds ham-scram, WHITEHEAD *Leg.* (1859) 8, ed. 1896; He put his tools in his box ham-sam (B.K.). n.Yks. He went at t'wark ham-sam (T.W.); n.Yks.[24] m.Yks.[1] To lay anything hamsam, is to heap together. n.Lan.[1], ne.Lan.[1]

HAMSH, v. Sc. In form humsh Abd. To eat noisily and hastily or in a voracious manner. See Hanch, v. 2.

Sc. (JAM.) Abd. Common. 'Ye sudna humsh up yer sweeties that wye; gie them time to melt i' ye mou'' (G.W.). Ags. (JAM.) Per. Well known. 'Humsh yer apple' (G.W.).

HAMSHACKLE, v. Sc. n.Cy. Nhb. Yks. Lan. Nhp. War. Also in form homshackle e.Lan.[1] [h]a·m[akl.] To fasten the head of an animal to one of its fore-legs to pre- vent its straying; also used *fig.*

Sc. Some job that would hamshackle him at least until the Courts rose, SCOTT *Redg.* (1824) i. N.Cy.[1], Nhb.[1], n.Yks.[14], ne.Yks.[1], Lan.[1], Nhp.[1], War.[2]

Hence **Homshackled,** *ppl. adj.* fettered by having the head tied to the fore-leg. e.Lan.[1]

HAMSHOCH, sb. and adj. Sc. Also written ham- schoch, -shogh (JAM.); and in forms hamsheugh, haum- ahoch Sc. [ha·mʃəx.] 1. sb. A sprain or contusion in the leg; a severe bruise, esp. when accompanied by a wound; a severe laceration of the body. Fif., Ayr. (JAM.)

2. A misfortune, an untoward accident; a disturbance.

Sc. The hamsheughs were very great until auld uncle Rabby came into redd them, GRAHAM *Writings* (1883) II. 16. Knr. Wat ye na that we're gaun straught the gate we pactioned about, afore thir hamshoghs dang a' our plans heels-o'er-head? *St. Patrick* (1819) II. 77 (JAM.).

G

3. A harsh and unmannerly intermeddling in any business. Fif. (Jam.)

4. *adj.* Much bruised, often referring to a contusion accompanied with a wound. (*ib.*)

5. Severe, censorious, as applied to critics.

Sc. Thae haumshoch bodies o' critics get up wi' sic lang-nebbit gallehooings, *Edb. Mag.* (Apr. 1821) 351 (Jam.). Ayr. (*ib.*)

HAMSTERS, *sb. pl.* Lan. [a'mstəz.] A kind of knee-breeches; lit. a covering for the 'hams.'

His hamsters of dark kerseymere, grey at the knees, Bamford *Radical* (1840) I. 51; Wi' stockins deawn, unteed his shoon, His hamsters loosely hung, Ridings *Muse* (1845) 6; Lan.[1]

HAMSTRAM, *sb.* Sc. Difficulty.

Abd. Wi' great hamstram they thriml'd thro' the thrang, Ross *Helenore* (1768) 94, ed. 1812.

HAN, *sb.* *Obs.* w.Yks.[1] The sound made by men while cleaving wood.

[Fr. *han*, the groan, or forced, and sigh-like voice, wherewith wood-cleavers, &c. keep time to their strokes (Cotgr.).]

HANBURY, see Anbury.

HANBY, *adj.* n.Cy. [Not known to our correspondents.] Wanton, unruly. Holloway.

HANCE, *v.* Not. Rut. Lei. Also written hanse Lei.[1] [ans, æns.] To give one 'handsel' or earnest-money.

Not.[1], Rut.[1] Lei.[1] I hope, ma'am, you'll hance me.

HANCER, see Heronsew.

HANCH, *sb.*[1] Som. Dev. Also written anch Dev. [ænʃ.] The upright part of a gate to which the hinges are attached.

w.Som.[1] Thick piece'll mak a very good head, but he id'n stiff enough for a hanch. We be bound vor to drow another piece o' oak vor zome more gate-stuff. There's a plenty o' larras a-cut out, but we be short o' heads an' [an·shez] hanches. Dev. Sometimes called the 'hanging head.' 'Some larch lars and oak anches will last as long as anything,' *Reports Provinc.* (1883) 86.

Hence **Hanching**, *sb.* carpentering term : the part left outside the end mortices in the side of a door, sash, or other frame.

w.Som.[1] The sarsh was too long; vore he'd fit, fo'ced to cut away all the hanching.

HANCH, *v.* and *sb.*[2] Sc. Irel. Nhb. Cum. Yks. Lan. Chs. Stf. Nhp. War. Glo. Oxf. Wil. Som. Dev. Also written hansh n.Lan.[1] Chs.[1]; and in forms ansh e.Lan.[1]; aunch Stf.[2]; haunch Nhb.[1] Nhp.[1] Glo.[1,2] Oxf.[1]; haunsh Sc. (Jam.) [h)anʃ, ænʃ, ǭnʃ.] **1.** *v.* To bite, snap at with the teeth as a dog does. Also used *fig.*

Sc. Esp. applied to the action of a dog, when seizing anything thrown to him, and apparently including the idea of the noise made by his jaws when he snaps at it (Jam.); A number greedily haunsht at the argument, Baillie *Lett.* (1776) I. 200 (*ib.*). Ant. *Ballymena Obs.* (1892). Nhb. (J.M.M.); Nhb.[1] He fair haunched at me. The dog haunched at me. Cum. T'policeman pot t'beuck up tull his gob, an hancht it, as if he was gaan teh tak a lump oot on't, Sargisson *Joe Scoap* (1881) 37; Cum.[4] Also to threaten to bite as does a really good-natured horse. 'Quiet will ta! hanchin on like that.' n.Yks. (I.W.); (T.S.) ne.Yks.[1] That dog o' yours hanched at ma when ah tried ti clap him. e.Yks. Dog hansht at im, buod e cuodn't ger 'od on im [the dog snatched at him, but he could not get hold of him] (Miss A.); e.Yks.[1] Lan. No bitin'! Anybody ut hanches shall have a tooth drawn! Brierley *Cast upon World* (1886) 36; Yerin 'em hanch an' arre at us, Clegg *Sketches* (1895) 397; At Bolton the word is in common use; in use in Preston and Ashton-under-Lyne, but not so common as it was (S.W.); Davies *Races* (1856) 275; Lan.[1], n.Lan.[1], e.Lan.[1] Chs.[1] If a dog's mad, he'll hansh at anything that's near him. s.Chs.[1] Ahy dü)nū lahyk)th lŏoks ū dhaat· dog; ey aan·sht aat· mi veri saav·ich jūs dhen [I dunna like th' looks o' that dog; he hanshed at me very savage jus' then].

Hence (1) **Hanch-apple**, *sb.* the game of 'snap-apple'; see below; (2) **Hanching-night**, *sb.* Halloween.

(1) Lan. Davies *Races* (1856) 275; Lan.[1] The game of snap-apple, which consists in biting at an apple floating in water or suspended by a cord. It is usually played at Halloween. (2) Cum.[4] Hanchin' neet takes its name from the game of 'Bob-apple,' when with hands behind the back, the players hanched at an apple suspended from the ceiling by a string.

2. To eat greedily or voraciously as a dog or pig does.

Slk. (Jam.) Gall. To eat like a swine, Mactaggart *Encycl.* (1824) 252, ed. 1876; His sillar up in meat he'd hanch, *ib.* 135.

Hence **Hanshun**, *sb.* a savage grunt; a greedy way of feeding like a pig. Nhb.[1]

3. To seize, snatch; to take hold of roughly; to handle roughly or unkindly.

ne.Yks.[1] m.Yks.[1] What are ye hanching and clicking at, there! If thou hanches in that way, I'll—! Stf.[2] Dunner ōnsh dhat babi ədhatnz; puər litl thing.

Hence **Aunching**, *ppl. adj.* unkindly treated or handled.

Stf.[2] Wel, iz weifs betər of nā ərz jed, fər ər ad ə ōnahin loif wi im.

4. Of a cow or bull: to thrust or gore with the horns.

e.Yks.[1] Bull hanch'd at mā wiv his hoorns, bud Ah got oot of his way. Nhp.[1] When a cow has been tossing a beast, it is said 'she has been haunching it.' If a person were gored to death by a beast, it would be said, 'He's got haunched.' War. (J.R.W.), Glo.[1,2] Oxf.[1] If dhee guost in aa·wuld Dan'l Braa·ynz klaaw·s iz buol ul au·rnch dhu [If thee gu'st in awuld Dan'l Braain's claaos, 'is bull 'll 'aunch tha]. Wil.[1] n.Wil. Common (E.H.G.). Som. W. & J. Gl. (1873). w.Som.[1] Less commonly used than horch (q.v.). Dev.[2]

5. *sb.* A voracious snap or snatch; an attempt to bite from behind.

Sc. (Jam.) N.I.[1] The dog made a hanch at me. n.Yks.[4]

[1. Som hanchyd of the heued, *Wars Alex.* (c. 1450) 774. Fr. *hancher*, to snatch at with the teeth (Cotgr.).]

HANCHMAN, see Henchman.

HANCHUM-SCRANSHUM, *sb.* Lin. Also written anshum- n.Lin.[1] [a·njəm-skranʃəm.] Bewilderment, confusion, disorder. Also used *attrib.*

A scramble for food at a table where there is a scarcity; any scene of confusion, Thompson *Hist. Boston* (1856) 698; Lin.[1] Provisions were scarce, and to get at it I never saw such hanchum-scranshum work in my life. n.Lin.[1] Ther' was a deāl o' anshum-scranshum wark at Smith's saale along o' th' auksoneer not causin' folks to stan' e' a ring.

HANCLE, *sb.* Sc. n.Cy. Nhb. Also written hankle Sc. [ha·ŋkl.] A handful; a great deal, considerable quantity or amount. See Hantle.

Sc. Just like a hankle folks, they think they're right enough if they go to kirk on Sunday, Calder *Presbyt. Eloq.* (1694) 155, ed. 1847. n.Cy. (W.T.), N.Cy.[1], Nhb.[1]

HAND, *sb.* and *v.* Var. dial. uses in Sc. Irel. Eng. and Amer. Also in forms an- Nhp.[1] Oxf.[1] Dev.; haand Sh.I.; han Sc. (Jam.) Cai.[1] N.I.[1] Nhb.[1] Dur.[1] Lakel.[12] Cum.[14] e.Yks.[1] w.Yks. Suf.[1] Dev.; hant Lan.; haun Ayr. Lnk.; hond w.Yks. Lan.[1] s.Stf. [h)an(d, ænd, ond.] **1.** *sb.* In *comb.* (1) Hand-ball, the game of rounders; (2) -barrow, a barrow or kind of large tray on legs, with four projecting handles, carried by the hands; (3) -beast, the horse a ploughman directs with his left hand; (4) -beat, to cut off the turf, &c. with a mattock, in order to burn it and so render the land arable; see Burn-beat; (5) -beating, the process of preparing land by 'burn-beating' (q.v.); (6) -bellows, a small pair of bellows; (7) -bill, a bill-hook or hedging-hook; (8) -bind, a grip in wrestling; (9) -blomary, *Obs.*, a smelting furnace; (10) -board, a tea-tray; (11) -bolts, handcuffs; (12) -bound, (*a*) fully occupied, very busy; (*b*) hampered, put to inconvenience; (13) -box, the lower handle of a sawyer's long pit-saw; also called Box; (14) -braid or -breed, a hand's breadth; (15) -breadth, a measure of 3 inches, sometimes used loosely for 'hand'; (16) -brush, a brush used for domestic cleaning purposes; (17) -burying, a walking funeral, in which the body is carried by hand; (18) -canter, a quick canter; (19) -carrying, see (17); (20) -'s-chare, light household work; a very small piece of work, an odd job; (21) -clap, a moment, short space of time; (22) -cled, gloved; (23) -cloth, (*a*) a towel; (*b*) a pocket-handkerchief; (24) -clout or -cloot, see (23, *a*); (25) -cold, cold enough to chill the hands; (26) -croppers, *obs.*, workmen who formerly cropped or cut the raised fibres on the face of cloth, by hand; (27) -darg, handiwork, labour, toil; what is gained by labour; (28) -drist, to separate corn from the chaff, &c., after it is threshed, by rubbing it between the hands; (29) -fast, (*a*) to betroth; to pledge; to shake hands over a bargain; also used *attrib.*; (*b*) able to hold tight; also used *fig.*; (30) -fasting or -fisting, *obs.*, a betrothal; see below; (31) -fill, to separate the small from the large coal in a mine; (32) -flower, the wallflower, *Cheiranthus Cheiri*; (33) ·frandie, a hand-rick or small stack of corn, no higher than can be reached with the hand ; (34) ·ful, (a) a heavy charge or task ; a burden, responsibility ; (b) a few ; a small quantity ; (35) ·gear, any working arrangement of machinery, which is moved by hand ; (36) ·gloves, gloves ; (37) ·going or ·gying, reported from one to another ; (38) ·greeping·hook, *obs.*, a hook formerly used by women for cutting wheat ; (39) ·grip, a grasp of the hand ; (40) ·gun, a pistol ; a pop-gun ; (41) ·habble, see below ; (42) ·haill, hand-whole, fit for all one's work ; (43) ·hap, a chance, hazard ; (44) ·hats, a kind of glove, made of thick felt, covering only the palm of the hand and the fingers ; (45) ·hawk, a plasterer's tool on which he lays the plaster ; (46) ·hold, a firm grasp with the hand ; anything that may be grasped or taken hold of with the hand ; (47) ·hollow, a term used in the game of 'hop-scotch' or 'hitchy-dabber' ; see below ; (48) ·hook, tanning term : a short iron hook, fixed in a cross-handle of wood, with which tanners move the wet hides ; (49) ·hoven-bread, oatmeal bread kneaded very stiffly and with very little leaven ; (50) ·huts, small stacks built by hand, by a person standing on the ground ; (51) ·idle, idle, having nothing to occupy the hands ; (52) ·irons, flat-irons for laundry work ; (53) ·ladder, a light ladder, easily carried by hand ; (54) ·lass, a windlass ; the handle of a windlass ; (55) ·leather, a partial leather covering for the hands of shoemakers, brick-fillers, &c. ; (56) ·led, led by the hand ; (57) ·less, awkward, clumsy ; awkward in using the hands ; (58) ·line, (a) a fishing-line for taking fish from the bottom of deep water ; also used *attrib.* ; (b) fishing with a hand-line ; (59) ·making, making or manufacturing by hand as opposed to machinery ; (60) ·meag, a tool used to mow peas, brake, &c. ; (61) ·mow, a small stack of hay or corn ; (62) ·ock, see (45) ; (63) ·offer, a gift ; (64) ·pannier, a small hand-basket ; (65) ·pat, ready at hand, convenient ; off-hand, fluent ; (66) ·payment, a beating ; (67) ·picked, used of large coals or coke filled by hand without using a shovel ; (68) ·pin, a wooden pin used for the purpose of wringing hanks ; (69) ·pins, the handles of a scythe ; (70) ·plane, a smoothing-plane ; (71) ·promise, a betrothal, troth-plight ; (72) ·prop, a walking-stick ; (73) ·putter, a person who 'puts' or pushes a barrow without the assistance of a pony, in a coal-mine ; (74) ·rackle, careless, acting without consideration ; active, ready ; (75) ·raising, the process of raising the surface of cloth, &c. by hand-cards ; (76) ·reel, an old reel or machine, used for winding and numbering the hanks of yarn ; (77) ·rest, the right-hand or slighter handle of a 'timbern zole' ; (78) ·ride or ·rode, a term used by shepherds in sheep-breeding ; see below ; (79) ·running, consecutively, continuously, in uninterrupted succession ; (80) ·saw, in phr. *to have a voice like the sharpening of a handsaw*, to have a harsh, disagreeable voice ; (81) ·scroo, a rick of sheaves such as can be built by hand from the ground : (82) ·seller, see below ; (83) ·shaking, (a) a correction, punishment ; a close engagement, grappling ; (b) an interference, intermeddling ; (84) ·sheckles, see (11) ; (85) ·shoes, gloves ; (86) ·smooth, quite level, as smooth as the palm of the hand, without obstacle, uninterruptedly ; (87) ·spaik or ·spoke, a handspike, a piece of wood with handles, used esp. for carrying the dead to the place of interment ; (88) ·spike, a wooden lever, shod with iron ; (89) ·spring, a street-arab's acrobatic performance ; (90) ·staff or ·stave, (a) the handle of a flail ; (b) see (72) ; (91) ·staff-cap, the swivel that joins the handle and swingle of a flail ; (92) ·stick, see (90, a) ; (93) ·stir, (a) a very small distance ; a slight movement ; (b) the smallest possible amount of labour ; (94) ·stocking, a mitten ; (95) ·stone, a small stone, a pebble ; (96) ·strike, (a) a blow with the hand ; (b) a strong piece of wood used as a lever to a windlass ; (97) ·stroke, see (93, b) ; (98) ·tethers, (a) see (11) ; (b) pursuits requiring constant attention ; (99) ·thief, one who steals with the hands ; (100) ·tied, (a) unable to leave a job in which one is engaged ; (b) hand-clasped ; (101) ·ties, (a) see (11) ; (b) see (98, b) ; (102) ·tillage, artificial

manure spread on the land with the hand ; (103) ·tree, *obs.*, the top piece of the 'going part' of a hand-loom ; (104) ·turn or ·'s turn, a single act of doing a piece of work ; (105) ·wailed or ·waled, remarkable, distinguished in whatever way ; carefully selected ; (106) ·wave, to 'streek' a measure of grain by striking it with the hand in order to give good measure ; (107) ·waving, a mode of measuring grain by striking it with the hand ; (108) ·wed, weeded by hand ; (109) ·('s while, a little while ; (110) ·woman, a midwife ; (111) ·wrist, the wrist ; (112) ·write, handwriting, penmanship ; (113) ·wrought, fabricated by hand.

(1) Sc. Ye may walk in't very near three hours a-day, and play at pitch-and-toss, and hand-ba', and what not, Scott *Guy M.* (1815) xliv. e.Dur.[1] More commonly called 'roondies.' Played by girls with shells ('williks') and a ball, whilst these words are recited :— 'Set a cup upon a rock, Chalk me one a pot. One, two, three, four, One at a time,' &c. 'One up,' &c. (2) Gall. Mactaggart *Encycl.* (1824). æ.Wor.[1] A barrow or carriage without a wheel, but with a pair of handles at each end, by which to carry it. w.Som.[1] In constant use by gardeners for carrying flowers, &c. ; also in quarries for carrying stones. (3) Gall. Mactaggart *Encycl.* (1824). (4) Dev. To hand-beat, to cut off the surface of the earth or spine with a hough, which is otherwise done with a spade, and sometimes with a breast-plough, and even with a paring-plough, drawn with horses, in order for sweating or burning, Grose (1790) *MS. add.* (M.) (5) w.Som.[1] The act of digging up with a mattock old weedy and furzy turf (which is too full of roots to be ploughed) for the purpose of burning it, and so rendering the land arable. n.Dev. Whare they be shooling o' beat, handbeating or anglebowing, *Exm. Scold.* (1746) l. 197. w.Dev. Chipping off the sward with a beating-axe, Marshall *Rur. Econ.* (1796) I. 142. (6) Sc. I'll bring a pair o' han'-bellows, Sc. *Haggis*, 60. (7) n.Cy. (J.W.), s.Not. (J.P.K.) Lin. Come out here with the handbills and brattle all the willows anywhere nigh, Fenn *Dick o' the Fens* (1888) iv. (8) Sh.I. Dey wir nae buttin i' da haandbind I tink, an' hit wis as weel for Geordie, *Sh. News* (May 7, 1898). (9) Hrf. Iron ore was discovered in the sandy district of Wormelow hundred as early as the time of the Romans in Britain, and many of the hand-blomaries used by them have been met with on Peterslow Common, Marshall *Review* (1818) II. 303. (10) e.Lan.[1], Chs.[1], s.Chs.[1] (11) Hmp. (J.R.W.), Hmp.[1] (12, a) Lth. How may hand-bound minnie get Her tottums clad sae gaily ! Ballantine *Poems* (1856) 276. (b) Nhb.[1] An old bird fancier, when asked how he was getting on, replied, 'Middlin ! Aa's fair handbun for the want o' a Jack' (jackdaw). (13) Wil.[1] (14) Frf. He perceived a nitch in it, some more than a hand-brode from the hilt, Lowson *Guidfollow* (1890) 282. e.Fif. Cuttin' the legs o' them a hand-breed ower short, Latto *Tam Bodkin* (1864) viii. Ayr. Ae limpin leg a hand-breed shorter, Burns *Willie's Wife*, st. 3 ; I went out from his presence a hand-breid heicher in my own estimation, Service *Dr. Duguid* (ed. 1887) 89. Lnk. Pouther up her hair, An' stick her newest kame abune't, A hand-braid high an' mair, Murdoch *Doric Lyre* (1873) 93. Nhb.[1], Cum.[14], s.Yks.[1], w.Yks.[1], e.Lan.[1], n.Lin.[1], Nhp.[1] (15) Shr.[1] A rather loose expression, signifying approximately rather than exactly, *Introd.* 93. (16) w.Mid. They have a handle about a foot long, which is cut from the same piece of wood as the back. This is about 4 in. square, except that the end farthest away from the handle is slightly rounded like a cricket-bat (W.P.M.). (17) n.Yks.[2] (18) Ayr. They drove at a fine 'han' canter' down the Kyle Stewart, Ainslie *Land of Burns* (ed. 1892) 49. (19) n.Yks.[2] Many of the old inhabitants had an aversion to be hearsed, choosing rather to be 'carried by hand and sung before,' as it was the mode of their families in time past ; and in the suspensary manner of 'hand-carrying' with the hold of linen towels passing beneath the coffin, we still see women borne by women, as men by men, &c., *Introd.* 9. (20) n.Not. Oh, my sister ! she niver does a hand's-chare for me (J.P.K.). s.Lin. *Obs.* (T.H.R.) Lei.[1] I have no one to do a hand's-chare for me. Nhp.[1] 'She wont do a hands-chare,' is a common mode of complaint against an indolent, inactive person; Nhp.[2], War.[3] (21) Cai.[1] Gall. They would get husbands in a handclap, Mactaggart *Encycl.* (1824) 302, ed. 1876. (22) n.Yks.[2] (23, a) Lakel.[1], Cum.[4] (b) Lakel.[2] (24) n.Cy. Grose (1790). Dur.[1], Lakel.[12], Cum.[14] n.Yks.[1] w.Yks. Muder, ev yo' seen t'hand-clout ? A want to wipe thees things (W.H.); n.Yks.[124], ne.Yks.[1] e.Yks. Marshall *Rur. Econ.* (1788). m.Yks.[1] w.Yks. Leuk fer t'clean hancloot an' all, Blackah *Poems* (1867) 10 ; w.Yks.[18], nw.Der.[1], n.Lin.[1] (25) Ken.[1] There was a frost down in the bottoms, for I was right-down hand-cold as I come up to the great house. (26) w.Yks. The ire of the hand-croppers in this district were directed against a machine termed

a frame, PEEL *Luddites* (1870) 9. (27) **Sc.** (JAM. *Suppl.*) **Ayr.** Nought but his han' darg, to keep Them right an' tight, BURNS *Twa Dogs* (1786) l. 77. (28) **S. & Ork.**[1] (29, *a*) **Sc.** Endeavour to have in mind the love of your espousals, when ye and Christ were hand-fasted, THOMSON *Cloud of Witnesses* (1714) 254, ed. 1871; This Isobel was but handfast with him, and deceased before the marriage, ANDREWS *Bygone Ch. Life* (1899) 210; That gentlewoman had confess'd to himself she was handfast before she came out of England, SPOTTISWOODE *Miscell.* (1844) I. 107. **Nbb.**[1] **Obs.** Lakel.[2] **n.Yks.**[2] 'A handfast lot,' unionists. Handfasted, pledged. (*b*) **Ken.**[1] 'Old George is middlin' handfast to-day' (said of a good catch at cricket). **Dev.**[1] When a was bad a was so handyfast that a widn't suffer her out o' es sight neart or day, 40. (30) **Sc.** It was not until more than twenty years after the Reformation that the custom of 'handfasting,' which had come down from old Celtic times, fell into disrepute, and consequent disuse. By this term was understood cohabitation for a year, the couple being then free to separate, unless they agreed to make the union permanent, ANDREWS *Bygone Ch. Life* (1899) 210; Among the various customs now *obs.* the most curious was that of 'handfisting.' . . In the upper part of Eskdale . . . was held an annual fair, where multitudes of each sex repaired. The unmarried looked out for mates, made their engagements by joining hands, or by handfisting, went off in pairs, cohabited till the next annual return of the fair . . . and then were at liberty to declare their approbation or dislike of each other. If each party continued constant, the handfisting was renewed for life, PENNANT *Tour* (1772) 91, 92 (JAM.). **Slk.** We hae comed far . . . for a preevat but honest hand-fasting, HOGG *Tales* (1838) 368, ed. 1866. **Dmf.** At that fair it was the custom for the unmarried persons of both sexes to choose a companion . . . with whom they were to live till that time next year. This was called hand-fasting, *Statist. Acc.* XII. 615 (JAM.). **N.Cy.**[2], **Nhb.** (K.) (31) **Nhb.** To separate the small from the large coals in the mine, the latter being filled by the hand into the tub or corf, and the former thrown to the side of the working-place, or filled separately as required (R.O.H.). **Nhb.**, **Dur.** GREENWELL *Coal Tr. Gl.* (ed. 1888). (32) **w.Yks.** LEES *Flora* (1888) 137. (33) **Fif.** (JAM.) (34, *a*) **Cai.**[1] Unfeeling or selfish persons who have to attend to one in severe or protracted illness, sometimes say that 'he is a sair hanfu'.' **Sh.I.** If he's [it's] no a haandfoo 'at folk haes wi' dem frae da first fael is lifted an' fil [till] der i' da paet-neuk, dan, dan! *Sh. News* (Aug. 13, 1898). **Ked.** Years the bailie hed been dowie, Lang an unco han'fu' till her, GRANT *Lays* (1884) 45. **Per.** I leave ye wi' a heavy handfu', but oh, woman, lean on Him to whom naething's a burden, JACQUES *Herd Laddie*, 24. **Lnk.** Watty left wi' sic a han'fu', What to dae, losh! couldna see, NICHOLSON *Idylls* (1870) 28. **Ayr.** He had been long a heavy handful, having been for years but, as it were, a breathing lump of mortality, GALT *Provost* (1822) viii. **Nhb.** 'He has a handful' (of work or anxiety). When any person is bedridden and helpless, they are said to be a 'heavy handfa' to those in whose care they are (R.O.H.). **Yks.** (J.W.) **sw.Lin.**[1] You are well aware I have a handful wi' the boys. **Rut.**[1] He's quite a handful, you're sure! **War.**[2] You'll find that lad a rare handful. **s.Wor.**[1] 'Our 'Liza's wonderful took up uv that chap o' hern, but if they gets married he'll be a handful, I reckon. **Glo.** (A.B.) **Oxf.**[1] *MS. add.* **Ken.**[1] To have a handful is to have as much as a person can do and bear. 'Mrs. S. says she has a sad handful with her mother.' **Sur.** (L.J.Y.) (*b*) **Fif.** I stood for a handfu' o' minutes afore I steppit aneath the trees, ROBERTSON *Provost* (1894) 22. (35) **Nhb.** (R.O.H.) (36) **Cor.**[1] What! begging with hand-gloves on! (37) **n.Yks.**[2] (38) **nw.Dev.**[1] It was about half the length of an ordinary reap-hook (q.v.), and was used in the right hand whilst the wheat was greeped [gripped] with the left. About six greeps or handfuls were made into one sheaf. (39) **n.Yks.**[2] (40) **Sc.** Jockey and his mither cam hame together, cheek for chow, cracking like twa hand-guns, GRAHAM *Writings* (1883) II. 31. (41) **Rxb.** Business that is done quickly, summarily, without any previous plan, or without loss of time, is said to be done hand-habble. It often includes the idea of something haughty or imperious in the mode of acting (JAM.). (42) **Per.** The man that sits, as I do here, Haund-haill, an' neither slow to steer Nor quick to live, HALIBURTON *Ochil Idylls* (1891) 40. (43) **Fif.** At handhap, by chance (JAM.). (44) **Nhb.** These were formerly made at Corbridge for the teazers at glass works, who wore hand-hats to protect their hands in holding the hot pokers and tools used in their work. *Obsol.* (R.O.H.); **Nhb.**[1] s.v. Hawk. **e.An.**[1] (46) **n.Yks.**[1] Ah couldn't ho'd mah handho'd, strahve as I moud; **n.Yks.**[2] 'Tak good hand-hod,' take firm hold; **n.Yks.**[4] It 'ez a good hand-ho'd ti't. **e.Yks.**[1] Hez thå getten a good handhod, for if thoo hez'nt it'll slip away fre thå. **Lin.** STREATFEILD *Lin. and Danes* (1884) 335. **n.Lin.**[1] I darn't climb noå higher,

ther's naather hand-hohd nor foot-hohd for one. **Ken.**[1] 'Tis a plaguey queer job to climb up there, there an't no hand-hold. (47) **e.Dur.**[1] Used by girls when playing the game of 'hitchy-dabber' (hopscotch). Often the 'dabber' gets so near the line that a girl cannot insert the breadth of her hand between, in which case she must give up the 'dabber' to her opponent to play. (48) **Cha.**[1] (49) **N.Cy.**[2], **Lan.** (K.) (50) [A dry moment should be seized to put 2 or 3 stooks into what are called hand-huts in the field, that is, small stacks built by hand, by a person standing on the ground, STEPHENS *Farm Bk.* (ed. 1849) II. 372.] (51) **Sc.** I am hand-idle like yourself, minister, KEITH *Bonnie Lady* (1897) 79. **Sh.I.** A'm gaein ta spin a treed o' wirset. I can say A'm haand idle for da want o' hit, *Sh. News* (Feb. 12, 1898). **N.I.**[1] They're hand idle for want o' their tools. (52) **e.Yks.** (S.K.C.) (53) **Wgt.** Jamie's quarters were in the loft, to which a hand-ladder led, FRASER *Wigtown* (1877) 229. (54) **Shr.**[12] (55) **n.Yks.** (I.W.) (56) **n.Yks.**[2] 'A hand-led bairn,' a child just beginning to walk. (57) **Sc.** Being a lonely man, and used to fend for himself, . . . the schoolmaster was not as handless as might be supposed, KEITH *Bonnie Lady* (1897) 69; A handless taupie, a woman who exerts herself in so slovenly a way, that she still lets her work fall out of her hands (JAM.). **Cai.**[1] **Buff.** Hundreds of times we have tasted beef tea . . . cooked by handless dawdles, which an Irish pig would disgorge, GORDON *Chron. Keith* (1880) 75. **Frf.** He is most terribly handless, BARRIE *M. Ogilvy* (1896) 128. **Rnf.** Curse her for a hanless gab, YOUNG *Pictures* (1865) 162. **Ayr.** Wha wad keep the handless coof That couldna labour lea! BURNS *O can ye labour lea?* **Lnk.** Ane and a' were puir feckless han'less creaturs, their fingers were a' thooms as the saying is, FRASER *Whaups* (1895) 173. **e.Lth.** I peety ony man wha gets ane o' the thowless, han'-less tawpies, HUNTER *J. Inwick* (1895) 148. **Cum.**[14] (58, *a*) **Sh.I.** Formerly sinkers were made of klamal or soap-stone, instead of lead as at present, and to this day fishermen speak of the haandline stane or lead stane, a remnant of the ancient practice, SPENCE *Flk-Lore* (1899) 129. **Cai.**[1] A hand-line is wrought vertically from a boat. The hooks are at the end. It is run to the bottom, and then drawn back a fathom or so. (*b*) **Sh.I.** They had been off at the handline, and on their return one evening after dark were recounting the day's adventures to the old man, SPENCE *Flk-Lore* (1899) 22. (59) **Frf.** The days o' hand-makin' are aboot past an' dune noo, WILLOCK *Rosetty Ends* (1886) 2, ed. 1889. (60) **Nrf.** I want you to make me a hand-meag, EMERSON *Son of Fens* (1892) 96. (61) **Som.** (W.F.R.) (62) **Dev.** *Reports Provinc.* (1889). (63) **n.Yks.**[2] (64) **Glo.** GROSE (1790) *MS. add.* (M.) (65) **Nhp.**[1] He told it me as hand-pat as could be; **Nhp.**[2], **War.**[2] **Wor.** Another illustration comes hand-pat, *Evesham Jrn.* (Jan. 30, 1897). **Oxf.**[1] Uur'd dhû wul stoo'ri uz an'pat uz cuod bee ['Er 'd (she had) the wul stoory as anpat as could be]. **Bdf.** BATCHELOR *Anal. Eng. Lang.* (1809) 135. **Dor.** He had it all handpat, BARNES *Gl.* (1863). **Som.** I've hitch un up on chimbley-crook, han'pat again he's wanted, RAYMOND *Men o' Mendip* (1898) i. **Dev.** Got et han'pat, PULMAN *Sketches* (1842) 109, ed. 1871. (66) **Abd.** (JAM.) (67) **Nhb.**, **Dur.** NICHOLSON *Coal Tr. Gl.* (1888). (68) **w.Yks.** Usually from 18 to 24 inches long, and *gen.* made of *lignum vitae* (R.S.). (69) **nw.Dev.**[1] (70) **Sc.** (JAM.) (71) **Ir.** But Molly says, 'I'd his handpromise, an' shure he'll meet me agin,' TENNYSON *To-morrow* (1885). (72) **Sc.** Wha negleckit to bring your hand-prap? O whaur i' the warld's your bane-headit staff! STEWART *Character* (1857) 27. (73) **Nhb.**[1] **Nhb.**, **Dur.** NICHOLSON *Coal Tr. Gl.* (1888). [*Reports Mines.*] (74) **Slk.** The hand-rackle Homes, the dorty Dumbars, HOGG *Perils of Man* (1822) III. 19 (JAM.). **Rxb.** He's as hand-rackle a fallow as in a' the parish (JAM.). (75) **w.Yks.** (J.M.) (76) **Gall.** MACTAGGART *Encycl.* (1824). (77) **nw.Dev.**[1] (78) **Not.** A word used by flock-owners or their men when in the autumn the ewes are put to the ram; it really means that instead of the ewes running with the ram he is kept up and the ewes brought to him and put in stocks, to be served (W.L.H.); **Not.**[2] (79) **Lakel.**[2], **Cum.**[14] **n.Yks.** (T.S.); **n.Yks.**[1] He stopped away three weeks hand-running and nivver went til his work at all; **n.Yks.**[4] He's ta'en fowr prizes han'-running. **ne.Yks.**[1] We've had three decaths i' t'toon three tahms han'-runnin'. **w.Yks.** Shoo fetched her husband hooam twenty-one nights, hand-running, TOM TREDDLEHOYLE *Bairnsla Ann.* (1852) 10; **w.Yks.**[1]; **w.Yks.**[2] He won six games hand-running; **w.Yks.**[3] **Lan.**[1] He'd feight the whole lot on 'em, hond-running, as easy as ninepence. **e.Lan.**[1], **m.Lan.**[1], **Stf.**[1], **nw.Der.**[1], **Not.**[1] **s.Not.** I've hit that post five times hand-running (J.P.K.). **n.Lin.** Th' sho't-horn coo hed three roånd cauves hand-runnin' (M.P.); **n.Lin.**[1] Ther' was six deaths from that feåver hand-running. **Lei.**[1], **Nhp.**[1], **War.**[3] **Bck.**, **Bdf.** I fell down three times, hand-running (J.W.B.). **Hnt.** (T.P.F.) (80) **N.I.**[1] (81) **Cai.**[1] (82) **Lon.** The sellers of tins, who carry them under their arms, or in any way on a round, apart from the use of a vehicle, are known as hand-sellers, MAYHEW *Lond. Labour* (1851) I. 354. (83, *a*) **Slk.** Fain wad I hae had a handshaking wi' them, HOGG *Brownie of Bodsbeck* (1818) (JAM.). **Nhb.** 'Aa gav him a hanshakin,' I corrected him severely (M.H.D.). (*b*) **Rxb.** I wad like naething better than to hae a handshakin' wi' that business (JAM.). (84) **Nhb.** (85) **s.Sc.** The skin of the goat that furnishes soft hand-shoes, as they call gloves in the Pictish counties of Scotland, WILSON *Tales* (1836) III. 142. (86) **e.An.** He ate it up hand-smooth. **Suf.**[1], **e.Suf.** (F.H.) (87) **Sc.** The coffin was carried out on hand-spaiks, HUNTER *J. Armiger's Revenge* (1897) xv. **Sh.I.** Da men wis fix'd da twa fowereen staangs 'at Geordie Moad wis taen frae da banks fir haandspaiks, *Sh. News* (Jan. 7, 1899). **e.Lth.** It took four-an-twenty men wi' han'-spaiks to lift him doun the avenue, HUNTER *J. Inwick* (1895) 74. **Gall.** The old freet . . . that those who fall when at the handspake aneath the corpse, will soon be the corpse themsell, MACTAGGART *Encycl.* (1824) 263, ed. 1876. **Nhb.**[1], **n.Lin.**[1], **Suf.**[1] (88) **w.Yks.**[1] **Wil.** SLOW *Gl.* (1892). (89) **Lon.** I'd even begin tumbling when I went out on errands, doing hand-spring, and starts-up (that's laying on your back and throwing yourself up), MAYHEW *Lond. Labour* (ed. 1861) III. 104. (90, *a*) **Sc.** (JAM.), **Cai.**[1] **Gall.** The swoople on the end of the handstaff being whirled round on the barn-floor by the barnman, MACTAGGART *Encycl.* (1824) 49, ed. 1876. **N.I.**[1] (s.v. Flail.) **Cum.** We fit up a flail Wi' handstaff, and soople, and cappin, DICKINSON *Cumbr.* (1875) 230; **Cum.**[1 4] **Wm.** I brokken mi handstaff (B.K.). **n.Yks.**[1 2 4], **ne.Yks.**[1], **w.Yks.**[1], **Cha.**[1], **s.Cha.**[1], **nw.Der.**[1], **s.Not.** (J.P.K.), **n.Lin.**[1] **Nhp.**[1] Anstiff, a corruption of handstaff; the handle of a flail. **Shr.**[2], **Hrf.**[2] **Glo.** The labourer held the handstaff in both hands, swung it over his head, and brought the swingle down horizontally, GIBBS *Cotswold Vill.* (1898) 385. **Bdf.** BATCHELOR *Anal. Eng. Lang.* (1809) 135. **e.An.**[1] **Suf.** RAINBIRD *Agric.* (1819) 294, ed. 1849; **Suf.**[1], **e.Suf.** (F.H.), **Ken.**[1], **Wil.**[1], **Som.** (W.F.R.) **Dev.** Ansteeve, the handle of a flail, HEWETT *Peas. Sp.* (1892) 46. **nw.Dev.**[1] (*b*) **Per.** Hoastin' on their haund-staffs, And crynin' wi' the cauld, HALIBURTON *Ochil Idylls* (1891) 59. (91) **e.An.**[1] (92) **War.**[2], **s.Wor.**[1] **w.Som.**[1] It is a round, straight piece of very tough ash, so shaped as to leave a projecting ring of wood at the top. Over this comes the capel (q.v.), which is hollowed out to fit this ring, and turns easily upon it without coming off from the handstick. (93, *a*) **w.Yks.** Nay lass, sh'm noan gooin ta move a hand stir, TOM TREDDLEHOYLE *Bairnsla Ann.* (1896) 4. **n.Lin.**[1] I've heärd them saay as has been e' Lunnun, that th' roäk's ofens soä thick theäre 'at you can't seä a handstir afoore you, reight e' th' middle o' th' daay. (*b*) **w.Yks.**[5] ' Come, come, my lass, we've nivver done a hand-stir yet—get t'shool an' be cindering t'hearth up ! ' ' Hands-turn ' implies less of action than ' handsstir.' **n.Lin.**[1] Here you are clartin' aboot an' not a handstir of wark dun yet. (94) [*Poetry Provinc. in Cornh. Mag.* (1865) XII. 40.] (95) **Sc.** Formerly used for a small stone or one that could be easily lifted and thrown by the hand, in contradistinction from one which required much greater exertion (JAM.). **Wgt.** In this moor, and not far from the tomb, are great heaps of small hand-stones, which the country people call Cairnes, FRASER *Wigtown* (1877) 196. (96, *a*) **Sc.** Flycht is called flyting in French 'melle,' quhilk sumtimes is conjoined with hand-streikes, SKENE *Difficult Wds.* (1681) 87. (*b*) **Shr.**[2] (97) **Yks.** (J.W.) **n.Lin.**[1] ' I'd hardly struck a hand-stroäk when doon she cums.' Said by a man who had felled a rotten tree. (98) **n.Yks.**[2] (99) **Sh.I.** Of slanderers it is said : ' Ye may lock afore a haand t'ief, but no afore a tongue t'ief,' SPENCE *Flk-Lore* (1899) 229. (100, *a*) **Nhb.**[1] (*b*) **Som.** From the balconies above did hand-tied lovers lean and sigh, RAYMOND *Tryphena* (1895) 23. (101) **n.Yks.**[2] (102) **w.Yks.** Bone-dust, or as it is called, hand-tillage, is used to a great extent for twenty miles around Sheffield, MARSHALL *Review* (1808) I. 386. (103) **w.Yks.** The weaver's left hand rested on this for the purpose of giving the necessary backward and forward motion to the siey (J.T.); (S.P.U.) (104) **Sc.** I would do a hand's-turn myself, and blithely, KEITH *Bonnie Lady* (1897) 67. **Sh.I.** Dü ye tink 'at we'd grudged your maet if ye'd nivver be duin' a haand's turn? *Sk. News* (Oct. 30, 1897). **Per.** A useless body, hardly able to do a hand's turn, FERGUSSON *Vill. Poet* (1897) 62. **Dmb.** Keep baith yoursel and me without doin a han's turn of wark, CROSS *Disruption* (1844) ix. **Lnk.** She's a rale wee leddy yon, and canna dae a han's turn, FRASER *Whaups* (1895) 94. **Gall.** The shilpit pulin' brat that never did a hand's turn in her life, CROCKETT *Standard Bearer* (1898) 200. **N.I.**[1] He hasn't done a hand's turn these six months. **Nhb.** Aa henna dyun a hands-turn thi day (R.O.H.); **Nhb.**[1], **e.Dur.**[1] **Cum.**[1] He will n't set to ya hand's turn ; **Cum.**[4] **n.Yks.** I haint duan a 'single hand's tonn for a fotnith (T.S.); **n.Yks.**[1] 'Ah's nivver decan a hand-to'n sen Marti'mas' ; spoken by a person incapaci-

tated by illness ; **n.Yks.**[4] Sha's that lazy 'at sha wean't deea a hand-to'n foor hersen let alean foor onnybody else. **ne.Yks.**[1] **w.Yks.**[1] ; **w.Yks.**[5] ' Come, gi'e us a hand-turn wi't lad ! '—lend us your assistance here. **Lan.**[1], **Nhp.**[1] **War.**[3] Not a hand's-turn would be put for'ad to help anybody ; **War.**[8] **Nrf.** She niver offered to dew a hand's tu'n, but stood garpin an starin just like numb chance (E.M.). **Suf.** ' He gave her a hand's turn,' a help with hand labour (e.g. in digging) (C.L.F.). (105) **Sc.** Often used in a bad sense ; as ' a hand-wail'd waster,' a mere prodigal (JAM.). **Ayr.** My hand-waled curse keep hard in chase, BURNS *Ep. to Maj. Logan* (Oct. 30, 1786) st. 7. **Lnk.** Sic wordy, wanton, hand-wail'd ware, RAMSAY *Poems* (ed. 1733) 112. (106) **Nhb.**[1] To streek a measure of corn with the hand by waving or passing the fingers over it to leave good measure. **e.Yks.** When they hand-wave (the corne), they draw (it) lightly aboute in the bushell with theire hand, BEST *Rur. Econ.* (1641) 104. [Not striked, but heaped, or at least hand-waved, so that the full allowance will weigh even more than this, STEPHENS *Farm Bk.* (ed. 1849) I. 311.] (107) **Abd.** They are measured by hand-waving, i.e. they are stroked by the hand about 4 inches above the top of the firlot, *Statist. Acc.* II. 533 (JAM.). (108) Not. You'll have to get all them nettles hand-wed, afore you can make a job of it (L.C.M.). **sw.Lin.**[1] It'll be sooner all hacked up than hand-wed. (109) **Slk.**, **Peb.** (JAM.), **Nhp.**[1] (110) **Dev.** (HALL.) (111) **Glo.**[1], **Sus.** (F.A.A.) **w.Hmp.** I sprained my hand-wrist (H.C.M.B.). **Wil.**[1], **n.Dor.** (S.S.B.) **Som.** He dragged me all up the court by the hand-wristes (S.K.L.); (W.F.R.) **w.Som.**[1] Aay-v u-kuut' mee an'rús [I have cut my wrist]. **Dev.** Poor little Clara West 'ath a-valled down pin tap tha ice an' brawked 'er 'and-wrist, HEWETT *Peas. Sp.* (1892). (112) **Sc.** Albeit it wanted a subscription, yet by the handwrite, and the style, and the purpose, I knew it tobe yours, WODROW *Soc. Sel. Biog.* (1847) I. 95. **Cai.**[1] **Lnk.** Adhered to your preaching book, and declared the same to be your own hand-write, WODROW *Ch. Hist.* (1721) IV. 448, ed. 1848. **Keb.** His hand-writ and his seal, RUTHERFORD *Lett.* (1660) No. 284. **N.I.**[1] Whose hand-write is that ! (113) **n.Yks.**[2]

2. Phr. (*a*) *sing.* (1) *Hand and hail*, a game ; see below ; (2) — *awhile*, now and then ; (3) — *for nieve*, side by side, cheek by jowl ; abreast ; also used *fig.* ; (4) — *in gully*, a small half-circle just within a large ring, from which a boy, in a game of marbles, shoots or 'lobs' until he knocks one out ; (5) — *in the pie*, concern or interference in a matter ; (6) — *of writ* or *write*, handwriting, penmanship ; (7) — *over fist*, with all possible haste or speed, hand over hand ; (8) — *over head*, (*a*) indiscriminately, inconsiderately, without calculating consequences ; (*b*) in confusion or disorder, pell-mell, confusedly ; (*c*) used of hemp-dressing when the coarse is not separated from the fine part ; (9) — *to nieve*, hand to hand, singly opposed ; (10) *ahin the hand*, in arrears, in debt ; (11) *ahint the —*, after the event ; (12) *at no —*, on no account ; (13) *at one —*, at one time ; (14) *behind* or *behint —*, (*a*) see (10) ; (*b*) in secret, in an underhand way ; (15) *by —*, (*a*) past, done with ; (*b*) out of the way ; (16) *fae —*, not at hand ; (17) *in —*, in charge ; going on ; (18) *off —*, at once, without deliberation ; (19) *off one's —*, of one's own accord ; (20) *off the —*, fed by the hand ; (21) *out of —*, (*a*) forthwith, immediately ; without delay ; (*b*) reckless, off-hand, rough and ready ; (*c*) applied to a child when first able to walk alone ; (*d*) finished, completed ; (22) *with the —*, easily done ; (23) *any hand afore*, ready and prepared for any undertaking ; (24) *the back of my hand to*, an ungracious farewell ; a mild rejection or repulse ; (25) *at every hand's turn*, every moment, on every occasion ; (26) *there's my hand*, an expression of sincere conviction ; (27) *to bear hand at*, (*a*) to blame, hold one guilty of a thing ; (*b*) to owe a grudge to, bear malice against ; (28) *to be on the mending hand*, to improve in health, be convalescent ; (29) *to buy by hand*, to estimate the value of anything without weighing it ; (30) *to give a hand*, to help, assist ; (31) *to give in hand*, to give into a person's hand ; (32) *to have a full hand*, to have plenty of work ; (33) *to hold the hand*, to keep in a state of expectation ; to carry on correspondence with opposite parties in a clandestine manner ; (34) *to keep in hand*, to keep in reserve ; to be tedious in executing ; (35) *to lend a hand*, see (30) ; (36) *to make a hand of*, (*a*) to spoil, waste, destroy ; (*b*) to make a good business or profit out of ; (*c*) to impose upon, make a profit out of a person ; (*d*) to make a handle out of, *fig.* to make a cause of quarrel ; (37) *to make the safest hand of it*, to make a sure job of it ; (38) *to put hand to paper*, to write ; to commit oneself by writing ; (39) *to put anything by hand*, to go through with it ; (40) *to put hand in* or *to oneself*, to commit suicide ; (41) *to put in hand*, (42) *to put to the hand*, to begin work, commence a job ; (43) *to take a hand at*, to make fun of ; to mislead purposely ; (44) *to take by the hand*, to marry ; (45) *to take through hand*, to take to task ; (46) *one's own hand*, one's own doing, of one's own accord.

(1) Dmf. Two goals, called ' hails ' or ' dules,' are fixed on : .. the two parties then place themselves between the goals or ' dules,' and one of the persons, taking a soft elastic ball, about the size of a man's fist, tosses it into the air, and as it falls strikes it with his palm towards his antagonists. . . As soon as the ball is ' gowf't,' that is struck away, the opposite party attempt to intercept it in its fall. This is called ' keppan' the ba'.' If they succeed in this attempt, the person who does so is entitled to throw the ball with all his might towards his antagonists (Jam.). (2) Nhb.¹ (3) Cai.¹ Rnf. Han'-for-nieve, the hawkies stan', Picken *Poems* (1788) 53 (Jam.). Lnk. Haun for nieve awa' fu' proud They tak the road thegither, Watson *Poems* (1853) 42. e.Lth. No' a frien' to lippen to, an' the Irish han'-for-nieve wi' oor enemies, Hunter *J. Inwick* (1895) 77. (4) Oxf.¹ *MS. add.* (5) Edb. Has our folk nae hand i' the pye, Like the ither lads that bides o'er by! Liddle *Poems* (1821) 205. n.Cy. (J.W.) (6) Sc. Div ye think naebody can read hand o' writ but yoursell? Scott *Antiquary* (1816) xv. Abd. Ken ye that han' o' wreet! Macdonald *Malcolm* (1875) III. 250. Dmb. I ...soon learn'd a han'some hand o' write, Taylor *Poems* (1827) 102. Ayr. A well-written letter in a fair hand of write, Galt *Ann. Parish* (1821) i. Gall. It's in your hand o' write that the name o' Janet Geddes stands in the big ha' Bible, Crockett *Raiders* (1894) xxxiii. (7) Gall. Tossing it ower their thrapples hand ower fist, *ib. Standard Bearer* (1898) 118. Cor. Watty pulled in hand over fist ; and in came the lead sinker over the notch, ' Q.' *Wandering Heath* (1895) 82. (8, *a*) Gall. Drovers in purchasing [large herds] will sometimes take the good, and leave the bad ; this is called ' shooting ' : others will take the lot as it is ; this is buying them hand owre head, Mactaggart *Encycl.* (1824) 250, ed. 1876. N.I.¹ One with another, an expression used in selling, and meaning the putting an average value on a number of things that differ in value. ' Now how much a piece will you say for them, if I take the whole lot hand over head!' n.Cy. (J.W.), Lakel.², Not.¹, Lei.¹, Nhp.¹ Glo.² 16. e.An.¹ w.Som.¹ They be bound vor to go wrong (i. e. come to grief) ; can't go on hand-over-head like that there, very long. (*b*) n.Yks. They are mixed hand ower heead (I.W.). w.Yks.⁵ ' A lot o' fellahs cam running hand-ower-head through t'passage [entry] an' ommast pick'd muh darn.' ' Here they come, hand-ower-head.' s.Lin. When a went to see her she was hand-over-head cleaning her room (F.H.W.). (*c*) e.An.¹ (9) Gall. (Jam.) Keb. Some han' to nieve Wi' manly pith o' arm, beyond the mark, Far fling the pond'rous mell, Davidson *Seasons* (1789) 87. (10) Abd. (Jam.) (11) Slk. Folk are a' wise ahint the hand, Hogg *Tales* (1838) 321, ed. 1866. (12) Sc. ' But father,' said Jenny, .. ' suldna I cry on you!' ' At no hand, Jenny,' Scott *Old Mortality* (1816) iii. (13) w.Wor.¹ Sam's a very good lad to me now, but at one 'and I thaowt 'e'd never do no good, to 'isself nar no one else. (14, *a*) Cai.¹ (*b*) Cai.¹, Cld. (Jam.) (15, *a*) Sc. Applied to any work that is already done, or any hardship that has been sustained (Jam.). Cai.¹ (*b*) n.Sc. Applied to a person, at times in relation to marriage (Jam.) ; When she's by hand and awa', Ross *Sng.* (*ib.*) (17) Sc. (Jam.) (18) Nhp.¹ (19) Ayr. I was aye for our ane to mak' that proposal to you, but it has come better aff your haun, Hunter *Studies* (1870) 39. (20) Sh.I. Sha'll no foster twa lambs 'ithoot somtin' aff o' da haand, alto' he [it] is da end o' Aapril, *Sh. News* (May 7, 1898). (21, *a*) Ayr. When he asked her, she married him oot of haun, Service *Dr. Duguid* (ed. 1887) 9. Nhp.¹ w.Som.¹ You might depend, sir, I'll do un vor ee, right out o' hand. (*b*) Ayr. I would not juist insist upon such a hasty and out of hand manner of treatment, Service *Dr. Duguid* (ed. 1887) 123. (*c*) Nhp.¹ (*d*) Nhp.¹ I've got the job out of hand at last. w.Som.¹ The job shall be a-put out o' hand in a proper, workmanship manner. (22) N.I.¹ ' It's doon the hill, an' wi' the han' :' said of a thing that is easily done. This expression is taken from ploughing experience. When a man is ploughing across a sloping place, and has difficulty in getting the earth to lie back, he would say it was ' again the han' :' if otherwise he would say it was ' wi' the han' (s.v. Wi' the han'). (23) w.Yks.¹ (24) Sh.I. Da back o' my haand baith ta dem an' der laws, *Sh. News*

(Apr. 2, 1898). Cai.¹ 'E back o' my han' t'ye, I am done with you. Lnk. The back o' my hand to ye, Annie, Murdoch *Doric Lyrs* (1873) 91. (25) s.Ir. He wasn't in the forge at that present, —but was expected at every hand's turn, Lover *Leg.* (1848) II. 417. (26) Edb. There's my hand she'll tire, and soon sing dumb, Fergusson *Poems* (1773) 107, ed. 1785. (27, *a*) n.Yks.¹ ; n.Yks.⁴ Ah beear him at hand foor all sha knaws aboot what wa did ay Sallie's. (*b*) n.Yks.¹ ; n.Yks.² ' I'll bear thee at hand for't,' I will owe you a grudge in the matter ; n.Yks.⁴ It war nowt bud a dirty trick, an' Ah s'all awlus beear him at hand for't. (28) Nhp.¹ w.Wor.¹ The fever's made 'im mighty weak, but 'e's on the mendin 'and now. s.Wor. (H.K.), se.Wor.¹ (29) Chs.¹ The expression is chiefly used in buying fat pigs. s.Chs.¹ Oxf.¹ *MS. add.* (30) Sh.I. He had been in the habit of going south to sail, and coming home again every year in time to give the 'old folks' a hand with the harvest, Nicholson *Aithstin' Hodder* (1898) 7. Per. It's no a tracer to gie ye a hand at a brae, *Sandy Scott* (1897) 17. Lnk. John had come hame raither sooner than usual, just to gie a bit han', Roy *Generalship* (ed. 1895) 7. n.Cy. (J.W.) Ken. Give us a hand with this, will you! (D.W.L.) (31) Lin. An' a towd ma my sins, an's toithe were due, an' I gied it in hond, Tennyson *N. Farmer, Old Style* (1864) st. 3. (32) w.Wor.¹ (33) Sc. The Admiral Hamilton ... held both the king and them in hand for his own ends, not yet known, Spalding *Hist. Sc.* (1792) I. 182 (Jam.). (34) Nhp.¹ (35) Gall. He ne'er was sweir a han' to len', Nicholson *Poet. Wks.* (1814) 52, ed. 1897. w.Yks. Tha'll suarly len' a helpin' hand To lift her off o' t'plat, Preston *Poems* (ed. 1881) 8. n.Lin.¹ I alus lend 'em a hand when ther'sonything goäs wrong. Nhp.¹, Oxf. (G.O.) (36. *a*) N.I.¹ If you let the chile get the book he'll make a hand of it. w.Yks. (E.G.) Lan. Freq. heard, *N. & Q.* (1886) 7th S. i. 517. e.An.¹ ' He has made a hand of all he had,' he has wasted his whole property. Suf. Children make a hand of a proper lot of boots, *Macmillan's Mag.* (Sept. 1889) 358. (*b*) s.Not. ' I med a hand on't,' or ' a good hand out of it ' (J.P.K.). (*c*) s.Chs.¹ Ahy mŭn noa' ŭbuw·t)th maa·rkits d)foa·r ahy sel ; ahy dŭ)nŭ waan·t bi mai·d ŭ aan·d on [I mun know abowt th' markets afore I sell : I·dunna want be made a hand on]. s.Not. He ollus tries to mek a hand on yer (J.P.K.). (*d*) Lei. Endeavouring to urge me to say something he might take hold of to make a hand of, *MS. Acct. of matters in dispute betw. Thornton and Bosworth* (1796). (37) Sur.¹ (38) Nhb. There is still a very common dread amongst some old people that evil may ensue from their writing anything. Great caution is therefore always exercised in the matter. ' He wis not one to put hand to paper '—to commit himself (R.O.H.) ; Nhb.¹ (39) Sc. (Jam.) (40) Sc. Hislop *Anecdote* (1874) 634. Or.I. Belus being much discouraged and broken in spirit, despairing of life, put hand in himself, and became his own executioner, Brand *Hist.* (1721) 14 (Jam.). Cai.¹ (41) Nhp.¹ (42) Ayr. He is very anxious to put to his haun', Service *Dr. Duguid* (ed. 1887) 163. Cai.¹ N.I.¹ There, don't mind him ; he's only takin' a han' at you. (44) Sh.I. Trial an' hardship is been her lot, objeck, frae day 'at shŭ took Aandrew Tulloch bi da haand, *Sh. News* (Feb. 5, 1898). (45) Sc. (Jam.) (46) Nhb. He just took it up at his aan hand (R.O.H.).

(*b*) *pl.* (1) **Hands up**, a term in curling : cease sweeping ; (2) *among hands*, (3) *atween* —, in the intervals of other engagements, between whiles ; (4) *between* —, in the meantime ; (5) *first* —, early, at the beginning ; (6) *through* —, in hand ; discussed, done with, settled ; (7) *to be in hands with*, (*a*) to possess in a certain way ; (*b*) to be in a state of courtship with ; (8) *to be no great hands*, not to be anything very good or remarkable ; (9) *to have no hands with*, to have nothing to do with, have no dealings or connexion with ; (10) *to lay hands on*, to baptize ; (11) *to put in one's hands*, (12) *to put out one's hands*, to help oneself at table.

(1) Ayr. I carena though ye're twa ells short—Hands up—there's walth o' pouther, Boswell *Poet. Wks.* (ed. 1871) 196. (2) Gall. Little jobs are sometimes done amang hans ; that is to say, they are done without, in any shape, retarding the large job, Mactaggart *Encycl.* (1824) 8, ed. 1876. n.Cy. (J.W.) (3) Sc. (Jam.) (4) Per. The carles did baith rant and roar, And delt some knoits between-hands, Nicol *Poems* (1766) 48. n.Cy. (J.W.) (5) Sur.¹ They didn't get much of a shoot first hands. (6) Ayr. Haith! we'se hae mony an auld ploy through hauns again! Service *Notandums* (1890) 3. (7, *a*) Sc. (Jam.) (*b*) Sc. He's in hands wi' Jean ; do ye think they'll mak it out? (*ib.*) (8) Stf. I'm no great hands of a traveller, Murray *Joseph's Coat* (1882) 38. (9) Glo. 'Ee did et yer see, and I didn't 'a no 'ands wi' ut, Buckman *Darke's Sojourn* (1890) iv ; Glo.¹ I won't have no hands wi ye. Wil.¹ I shan't hae no hands wi't. (10) Sc. This daft divine Shall ne'er lay hands on

rn o' yours and mine, LEIGHTON *Wds.* (1869) 13. (11) Sh.I. bin we wir set wis in, I says, ' Gud bliss wis, men. Pit in your ands an' begin,' *Sh. News* (Sept. 18, 1897). (12) Gall. (A.W.)

. *Fig.* A workman, servant ; an employé in a factory mill. In *gen.* colloq. use.

rfl. One of the old ' wrichts ' had several apprentices and even ew journeyman ' hands,' INGLIS *Ain Flk.* (1895) 39. Per. This a the way they do wi' hired hands where I come frae, *Sandy* ott (1897) 10. n.Yks.[2] An individual. A helper. ' Good hand, od hire, good servant, good wages. w.Yks. Dun yo ever speak fur th' honds ! *Warty Rhymes* (1894) 18 ; (F.J.N.) ; w.Yks.[6] In.[1] Women and children who work upon a farm. The labourers d servant ' chaps ' are not hands. s.Oxf. The 'ands are busy 'eshin' now most days, jest the last o' my barley, ROSEMARY *ilterns* (1895) 39.

. An adept, clever performer.

Sh.I. Doo's da haand fir borin' even gengs, *Sh. News* (Apr. 29, 99). Abd. He was nae han' at bargain-makin' an' that, ALEX-DER *Ain Flk.* (1882) 16. Per. Gin there wasna a better hand I uld hae to do my endeavour, *Sandy Scott* (1897) 56. Ayr. He's a eat han' for splorin' about his punctuality in ordinary transactions, JNTER *Studies* (1870) 283. n.Cy. (J.W.) n.Yks. ' She is a good nd,' she is a clever needlewoman (T.S.). s.Stf. He was a g'lar hond at carvin', PINNOCK *Blk. Cy. Ann.* (1895). Nhp.[1] A d hand at that work. Oxf. (G.O.) Nrf. You grind the scythes. ou're a better hand on it than I am, EMERSON *Son of Fens* 8ga) 248. Sus. HOLLOWAY.

. Handwriting ; signature.

Rnf. I doot it's no dune for improvin' his haun, NEILSON *Poems* 877) 48. Nhp.[1] Put your hand to this receipt.

. A handling, feel when handled.

WiL Corn has a good hand when it is dry and slippery in the ck : a bad hand when damp ahd rough, DAVIS *Agric.* (1813) ; WiL[1] . *Fig.* Anything difficult to manage, a 'handful'; esp. in 1r. *a great hand.*

Cmb. He's been a great hand to me sin' he's been ill (M.J.B.). as. ' A great hand,' a good deal of trouble, as the trouble of inging up a delicate child (S.P.H.). Ess. Well, sir, children e a hand (A.S.P.) ; Mother's a great hand (S.P.H.). Sur.[1] It's very great hand to have so many sick people. Sus.[1] I was a rible hand to mother all the time I was down with the titus-fever.

. Business, performance, job.

Ayr. A bonnie haun ye had made o't, GALT *Provost* (1826) xxxiii. b. See what a bonny hand ye'll mak o't ! *Tint Quey* (1796) 15. all. He makes a bad hand o' himself, i. e. he abuses himself .W.). n.Cy. (J.W.) Nrf., Suf., Hmp. HOLLOWAY.

. The horse that walks on the left-hand side in a team, opposed to the ' fur' or ' furrow' horse.

Ayr. My han' afore's a gude auld has-been, BURNS *Inventory* 786) l. 8 ; My han' ahin's a weel gaun fillie, *ib.* l. 10. e.Lth. e couldna fit him wrang In whatna yoke ye bade him gang . . . ollowing or leadin', hand or fur, MUCKLEBACKIT *Rhymes* (1885) . N.I.[1] The horse that walks on the unploughed land is said to ' in the han' ' ; the other horse is called the ' fur horse ' (s.v. 'i' the han').

.O. Direction ; neighbourhood.

Abd. Nearer han' hame, at Marnoch, ALEXANDER *Johnny Gibb* 871) xiii. Nhb. Ever as mony cheps fre Rothbury hand came , OLIVER *Rambles in Nhb.* (1835) 156 ; (R.O.H.) ; Nhb.[1] akel.[2] He co's off o' Kendal hand bi' t'twang on him. Cum.[1] e's gone toward Ireby and that hand ; Cum.[4] n.Yks.[2] I went wer te Kirby hand. w.Yks. (J.W.) Lan. They moight get th' b done gradely nigher hant than Gratna Green, BANKS *Forbidden* 885) xxv.

1. A shoulder of pork, when cut as a joint without the ade-bone. *Gen.* in phr. *a hand of pork.*

N.I.[1] A ham made from the fore-leg of a pig. s.Don. SIMMONS . (1890). Not. (J.H.B.), Lin. (W.W.S.), Nhp.[1], War.[2][3] Oxf.[1] S. *add.* Hnt. (T.P.F.), e.An.[1], e.Suf. (F.H.), w.Som.[1]

2. The fore upright of a gate.

Nhb.[1] ' Hand and har,' front and back uprights.

3. A measure for water-cress.

Lon. We buy the water-cresses by the ' hand.' One hand will make out five halfpenny bundles, MAYHEW *Lond. Labour* (1851) I. 150.

4. *v.* Phr. (1) *to hand about,* to escort a lady ; (2) — *out,* distribute ; (3) — *up,* to summon, bring up before a agistrate ; (4) — *me down,* any article purchased second-and or ready made ; any odd-looking garment ; (5) -*me-wn looking,* worthless, good-for-nothing in appearance.

(1) Nrf. We met several young couples out for a walk. ' Dash it, master, they fare to be a-handing 'em about to-night ' (W.R.E.). (2) n.Lin.[1] Ey, Miss, it's Loord 'at hands oot iv'rything 'e riches an' poverty, an' sickness an' health. (3) Suf. If you do . . . I'll hand you up before the justice, STRICKLAND *Old Friends* (1864) 9. (4) Dmb. Och try nae mair a han-me-down, But tryst ta braw new clock, TAYLOR *Poems* (1827) 110. N.I.[1] Whar did ye get that auld hand ma doon of a coat? Nhp. *N. & Q.* (1878) 5th S. ix. 263. [Amer. *Kansas Univ. Quar.* (1892) l.] (5) Lak. Ye've maybe heard o' the braw troot that a lang-haired han'-me-doon looking creatur' pented on the shutter o' the box-bed in the Gledshaw kitchen, FRASER *Whaups* (1895) 188.

15. To sign. e.An.[1] They made me hand a paper.

16. To act as second in a fight either between men or cocks. s.Don. SIMMONS *Gl.* (1890). WiL[1] n.WiL I'll hand 'e, if you be gwain to fight un (E.H.G.).

Hence **Hander** or **Handler**, *sb.* (1) a second in a fight ; (2) the adviser of a competitor in a ploughing-match.

(1) Nhb. A famous ' handler ' who died not long ago had but to make his appearance at the [church] door, and the usually long sermon, and prayer almost as long, were abridged, the sleepy congregation . . . would be seen making for a well-known rendezvous, where mains were often fought on Sunday afternoons, *Longman's Mag.* (Feb. 1897) 331. n.Lin.[1], sw.Lin.[1], Hrf.[1] WiL BRITTON *Beauties* (1825) ; WiL[1] n.WiL Who's agwain to be hander thun ! (E.H.G.) (2) Gall. Every competitor has a friend, a ploughman, to help and advise him during the competition, who is called a ' hander.' The friend walks beside the competitor, and is of special service in the opening up of the first furrow, and at the ends of each furrow (A.W.).

HANDECHAMP, *sb.* ? *Obs.* w.Yks. Also in form **handerhamp** (HALL). A ruffle. (HALL.), w.Yks.[1]

HANDED, *ppl. adj.* Sc. Nhb. Chs. Nhp. 1. In phr. (1) *handed·squares,* salt-making term : squares of salt such as are commonly hawked about the streets. Chs.[1] ; (2) *well handed,* clever at particular work. Nhb.[1] ; (3) *to swop even-handed,* to exchange without profit. Yks. (J.W.), Nhp.[1]

2. Hand in hand.

Flf. One summer eve, as in delightful walk, Handed, they past down Thirdpart's avenue, TENNANT *Anster* (1812) 105, ed. 1871.

HANDEL, *sb.* Sc. Light refreshment taken before breakfast, a snack of food.

Slg. First cut our handel, weel ye ken our due, Good routh o' bread and cheese and whiskey blue, GALLOWAY *Luncarty* (1804) 25.

HANDERMENT, *sb.* Cor.[2] Obstruction, delay, hin-drance.

HANDERSOME, *adj.* n.Yks.[2] w.Yks.[1] ne.Lan.[1] [a'ndəsəm.] Handy ; inclined to meddle, meddling.

[Handersome, *factiosus,* LEVINS (1570).]

HANDING, *prp.* War. Glo. Oxf. Brks. WiL Also in forms **handen·** Glo. ; **handson·** Glo.[1] In *comp.* (1) **Handing-point,** (2) -**post,** a sign-post, finger-post.

(1) Glo. (S.S.B.) (2) War.[3] Glo. A bit further along you'll come to a 'andin post (E.S.) ; You'll see a handen post at road end (A.J.M.) ; Glo.[1] Oxf.[1] *MS. add.* Brks. Quite commonly spoken and written. WiL[1]

HANDKERCHIEF, *sb.* Var. dial. forms in Sc. and Eng.

I. Dial. forms : (1) **Ankatcher,** (2) **Ankercher,** (3) **Ankitcher,** (4) **Hancheker,** (5) **Hancurchor,** (6) **Han-cutcher,** (7) **Handkecher,** (8) **Handkercher,** (9) **Hand-kerchy,** (10) **Handkertcher,** (11) **Handketcher,** (12) **Hangecher,** (13) **Hangkecher,** (14) **Hangkicher,** (15) **Hangkitcher,** (16) **Hankcher,** (17) **Hankecher,** (18) **Hankercher,** (19) **Hankerchir,** (20) **Hankershor,** (21) **Hanketcher,** (22) **Hankicher,** (23) **Hankisher,** (24) **Han-kitch,** (25) **Hankitchor,** (26) **Hanksher,** (27) **Hankutcher,** (28) **Hanky,** (29) **Hankycher,** (30) **Hanshaker,** (31) **Henkicher,** (32) **Henkitch,** (33) **Ontcher.**

(1) Not.[6] (2) s.War.[1] Dev. 'E tuk out ez 'ankercher, BURNETT *Stable Boy* (1888) xi. (3) War.[2], se.Wor.[1] (4) nw.Der.[1] (5) Nhb. (R.O.H.) (6) w.Yks.[1] (7) Lan. WESTALL *Birch Dene* (1889) I. 299. Dev. *Reports Provinc.* (1887) 8. (8) n.Lin.[1], sw.Lin.[1] Midl. Common (E.S.). War.[2] Shr.[1] Ang·kur'chur'. Cor. A clane handkercher, *Longman's Mag.* (Feb. 1893) 380. (9) w.Yks. Polish it up wi' his handkerchy, HARTLEY *Clock Alm.* (1878) 7. (10) Not. (J.H.B.) (11) N.I.[1] (12) s.Lan.[1] (13) w.Som.[1] Ang·kechur. (14) m.Lan.[1] Som. JENNINGS *Obs. Dial. w.Eng.* (1825). (15) Oxf.[1] (16) Cor.[1] (17) Cum.[6] His white hankecher, a. Cha.[1], nw.Der.[1]

(18) Ir. Corners of 'hankerchers,' BARLOW *Idylls* (1892) ii. Cum. That reed check hankercher, *Mary Drayson* (1872) 23. w.Yks.[2], War.[4], Brks.[1], Sur.[1] Som. A white pocket-han'kercher, RAYMOND *Sam and Sabina* (1894) 34. (19) w.Yks. Spread yer hankerchir o' t'top on't, BRONTË *Wuthering Hts.* (1847) xiii. (20) Nhb. (R.O.H.) (21) Lan. An owd hanketcher, CLEGG *Reaund bi th' Derby* (1890) 9. (22) w.Yks. Yhs. Wbly. Post (Apr. 10. 1897). I.W.[1] Som. Their white 'hankichers,' RAYMOND *Men o' Mendip* (1898) xiii. (23) Cum.[1] (24) s.Chs.[1] Aangk'ich. (25) Nhb. (R.O.H.) (26) Cor. She took un out of the hanksher, HIGHAM *Dial.* (1866) 6. (27) Dur.[1], Cum.[1], n.Yks. (T.S.) (28) Sh.I. She had tied in the corner of her hanky, BURGESS *Sketches* (2nd ed.) 29. e.Sc. I've tied my hanky round it, SETOUN *R. Urquhart* (1896) xix. Frf. The pupils had to bring handkerchiefs to the Dovecot, which led to its being called the Hanky School, BARRIE *Tommy* (1896) 157. Fif. Ane o' Stewart's tippence-happeny Union Jack hankies, MᶜLAREN *Tibbie* (1894) 14. Oxf. (W.D.), Sur. (L.J.Y.) (29) Lon. MAYHEW *Prisons* (1862) 424. (30) Chs.[1] Shr.[1] An'shukur. (31) w.Yks. BANKS *Whfld. Wds.* (1865). (32) s.Chs.[1] (33) se. Wor.[1]

II. Dial. use. In *comp.* Handkerchief-dance, a country dance performed with handkerchiefs.

Oxf.[1] Som. They had 'Hunt the squirrel' and the handkerchief dance, RAYMOND *Men o' Mendip* (1898) xiii.

HANDLE, *sb.* and *v.* Var. dial. uses in Sc. Irel. and Eng. Also written handel Sh.I.; and in forms han'le Ayr. N.I.[1]; hannel Cum.[14]; hann'l n.Yks.[4] [h]a·n(d)l, æ·n(d)l.]

1. *sb.* In phr. *to make a handle of anything,* to endeavour to turn a thing to one's own advantage or to another's discredit.

Sc. (A.W.), Nhp.[1] Nrf. To represent a subject matter more to the disadvantage or discredit of a person than the circumstance will really admit; to exaggerate, though frequently in a jocular way; to banter; to ridicule (W.W.S.).

2. *Comp.* Handle-dish, a hand-cup, a bowl with a handle. Sus. (S.P.H.), Sus.[1]

3. A hand, esp. the hand of a clock or watch.

w.Yks. Da muant leok wi' t'anlz ə t'tlok. Av brokən litl anl ə mi wotš (J.W.); T'meter hannels, BINNS *Orig.* (1889) 5.

4. Fishing tackle or gear. Also in form handlin.

Sh.I. I' da time 'at I got me handel tagedder, Girzzie leepid da bait, an' lightin' me pipe awa' I gengs, *Sh. News* (Oct. 2, 1897); My sntids an' handlin rex me doon, Dey're dere upo' da lame, STEWART *Tales* (1892) 92.

5. A large pail or tub. Also in *comb.* Milk-hannel.

Cum.[1]; Cum.[4] A tub larger than a 'geggin,' wider at the bottom than the top, but with a proportionately shorter stave-handle; used for collecting the milk in the byre, or for carrying water from a spring; it was carried on the head.

6. *v.* To secure, get hold of, esp. to receive or get money from; to touch.

Knr. 'Handle the dust,' to receive money (JAM.). Ayr. Ne'er a bawbee hae I yet han'let o' the price, GALT *Gilhaize* (1823) i. Gall. It canna be proven that ever I handled a plack o' the price, CROCKETT *Anna Mark* (1899) lii. n.Cy. (J.W.) s.Not. If they ain't allus handlin' on yer, they wain't be civil to yer (J.P.K.). n.Lin.[1] Times is strannge an' bad, I niver handled soä little money as I hev this last year. I weänt hev you bairns han'lin bull, he'll be stabbin' on you. Oxf. (G.O.)

7. To put an arm round a girl's waist.

Brks.[1] In love making, where the swain may not have flow of language, he may sometimes attempt to put his arm round the girl's waist; this is called 'handlin' on her,' and would probably be met by the command to 'Adone now,' or a more decided 'Gie out!'

8. To use, employ, make use of, not necessarily with the hands; esp. in phr. *to handle the feet.*

N.I.[1] 'Handle yer feet,' make good use of your legs. n.Lin.[1] An old woman who was lame said, 'I can't han'le my feet so well as I wessd to could.' Ess.[1]

9. To deal with, treat, manage; to afflict with illness, &c. *Gen.* in *pass.*

Ayr. Tightly he did the guager han'le, The mair he shuck the fallow by the throat, BOSWELL *Poet. Wks.* (1816) 148, ed. 1871. n.Yks.[1] He's been desper't'ly sair hannled wi' t'fever. A chap's lahk t'be parlously hannled gif he gits intiv t'haands o' thae low-wers (lawyers); n.Yks.[2] I was varry sair hannel'd that bout; n.Yks.[4] Tha hann'ld t'lad varry badly. Sha's varra kittlish an' bad ti hann'l. ne.Yks.[1] He's very queerly hannl'd. w.Yks. (J.W.)

10. To drag up a curling-stone by the handle.

Sc. It is said of a stone that has not pith, 'handle't' (G.W.); Big Andra fairly felled his stane, Handle 'im a hog or I'm mistaen, *R. Caled. Curling Club Ann.* (1886–7).

11. To hurry, exert oneself. N.I.[1]

HANDLEBERRY, HANDLER, see Angleberry, *sb.*[1], Hand, *v.* 16.

HANDLING, *sb.* Sc. Not. Also in forms haandling Sh.I.; hannlin' Lnk. **1.** A business, affair; a position of trust, stewardship; interference, intermeddling.

Sc. He wad fain hae a handling in that affair (JAM.). Sh.I. (K.L.I.) w.Sc. A discussion, altercation, quarrel (*ib. Suppl.*). Gall. Me wi' the care o' yer grau'faither— sic a handling, him nae better nor a bairn, CROCKETT *Sunbonnat* (1895) iv. Keb. He giveth him no handling or credit, only he intrusteth him with common errands, wherein he cannot play the knave, RUTHERFORD *Lett.* (1660) No. 106.

2. An entertainment, party, meeting, gathering.

w.Sc. A merry-making, a meeting of friends or opponents for discussion; a soirée is often called a tea-hanlan (JAM. *Suppl.*). Dmb. Thae gangrel folk At ilka han'lin' aye afore the clock, SALMON *Gowodean* (1868) 68. Ayr. We are providing for a handling, GALT *Legatees* (1820) viii. Lnk. I proposed to John that we should hae a kind o' hannlin' by way o' beatin the house, ROY *Generalship* (ed. 1895) 6. Dnf. I had only been yinst in her house since she settled, and that was at a promiscuous tea handling, SHAW *Schoolmaster* (1899) 329.

3. A boat-hook.

Not. (J.H.B.). A species of boat-hook with two prongs at the end instead of a hook, used for propelling a boat across a river (W.H.S.).

HANDLUM, *adj.* w.Som.[1] Awkward, clumsy of hand.

Uur-z dh-an·lums maa·yd dv·ur aay zee·d; uur-ul tae·ur ubroa·ud moo·ur cloa·m-un ur wae·ujez kau·ms tüe [She is the handlumest girl I ever saw; she will tear abroad more crockery than her wages come to].

HANDMAN, *sb.* Obs. ? Dev. A man-servant.

She, .. in imitation of the patriarchs of old, went to bed to the handman, because her consort was stricken in years, SHEBBEARE *Matrimony* (1754) II. 245, ed. 1766.

HANDSALE, see Auncel.

HANDSEL, *sb.* and *v.* In *gen.* dial. use in Sc. Irel. and Eng. Also in forms ansel(l e.Yks.[1] w.Yks. Chs.[2] Der.[2] nw.Der.[1] Not. Dev.; anstil Chs.[1]; hansel(l Sc. (JAM.) N.I.[1] Nhb. Dur.[1] s.Dur. Cum.[14] Wm. n.Yks.[14] e.Yks.[1] w.Yks.[2] Lan.[1] Chs.[13] s.Chs.[1] nw.Der.[1] Not.[1] n.Lin.[1] sw.Lin.[1] Lei.[1] War.[2] Shr.[1] Hrf. e.An.[2] Suf.[1] Sus.[1] Hmp. Dor. [h]a·nsal, æ·nsl.] **1.** *sb.* A gift conferred at a particular season or on the commencement of a new undertaking to confer luck; an auspicious beginning; a good omen. Also used *attrib.*

Sc. The first thing ye'll get for your handsel in the morning will be a sonsie breakfast, FORD *Thistledown* (1891) 322; Her new year's hansel for to gie, DONALD *Poems* (1867) 249. Sh.I. The first house to be visited was Braefield, where they were hopeful of getting a good 'hansel,' CLARK *Gleams* (1898) 150. ne.Sc. When one put on a piece of new dress, a coin of the realm called hansel, had to be put into one of the pockets. When one put on a piece of new dress, a kiss was given to and taken from the wearer, and was called the 'beverage o' the new claes.' When a boy or girl wearing a piece of new dress entered a neighbour's house something was given as hansel, GREGOR *Flk-Lore* (1881) 31. Abd. When the christening was over, the old minister put a half-crown into the baby's breast for 'hansel,' ALEXANDER *Ain Flk.* (1882) 25. Per. Gie the student his degree, The advocat' his hansel fee, HALIBURTON *Ochil Idylls* (1891) 135. Fif. Granny, gie's oor hansel, It's new-year's day, DOUGLAS *Poems* (1806) 68. Dmb. By and by ... To gi'e us a' our hansel time about. SALMON *Gowodean* (1868) 70. Raf. Whan buskit oot in braw new claes, Auld grannie's hansel's never miss't, NEILSON *Poems* (1877) 16. Ayr. Ye'll no guess what the Gudeman has in his pouch to gie them for hansel to their matrimony, GALT *Entail* (1823) xx; A blast o' Janwar win' Blew hansel in on Robin, BURNS *There was a Lad*, st. 2. Lnk. Ye're bringin' us ben A hansel o' fortune for a', New Year! WRIGHT *Life* (1897) 75. Edb. Auld-nick may gie't for them its handsel, LEARMONT *Poems* (1791) 164. Nhb. 'A hansel penny' is usually put into the pocket of any new garment to hansel it and the formula repeated, 'Health to weer, strength to teer, an money to buy another' (R.O.H.). w.Yks. I must buy something for ansel (H.F.S.). Lan. Money given when anything new is undertaken, Thornber *Hist. Blackpool* (1837); Lan.[1] A gift given to the first purchaser. s.Hmp. I've brought a parcel. . . T'aint often as a handsel comes to the Woodhouse, Verney *L. Lisle* (1870) vii. Dor. Something given to a young woman at her wedding towards house-keeping is called a ' good-handsel' in the vale of Blackmore, Barnes *Gl.* (1863); A goodish hansel come Behind her pretty soon, *ib. Poems* (1869–70) 3rd S. 72.

2. *Comp.* (1) **Handsel·e'en**, the eve of the first Monday of the New Year; (2) ·**Monday**, the first Monday of the New Year; *Auld Handsel Monday*, the first Monday of the year, Old Style; (3) ·**Tuesday**, the first Tuesday of the New Year; (4) ·**wife**, the woman who distributes the ' handsel' or gifts at a marriage.

(1) Lth. One hansel-e'en, on begging bound, He trudged the rural district round, M°Neill *Preston* (c. 1895) 9. (2) Bch. It was deemed unlucky to spend money in any form on hansel Monandy, Gregor *Flb-Lore* (1881) 164. e.Sc. Hansel Monday's comin' on, We'll get pies and porter, Setoun *Sunshine* (1895) 1. Per. As brisk a morn's I've seen For mony a Hansel-Munonday, Ford *Harp* (1893) 385. w.Sc. Hansell Monday, on which occasion practices similar to those of Yule were observed, Napier *Flb-Lore* (1879) 155. Fif. For one to propose the substitution of New Year's Day for Auld Handsel-Monday as the winter festival was to invite contemptuous ostracism, Robertson *Provost* (1894) 53. Clc. On the evening of Handsel Monday, as it is called, some of his neighbours came to make merry with him, *Statist. Acc.* XV. 201 n. (Jam.) s.Sc. All our fun of Beltane, Halloween, Hogmanay, and Hanselmonday are gone, Wilson *Tales* (1839) V. 65. Ayr. I was sitting on Hansel Monday by myself, Galt *Ann. Parish* (1821) xxxvi. Lnk. We renounce . . . New-year's day, and Hansel-monday, Wodrow *Ch. Hist.* (1721) III. 351, ed. 1828. Lth. Auld Hansel Monday comes again Wi' routhy mirth an' cheer, Lumsden *Sheep-head* (1892) 35. Edb. Auld Handsel Monday. A day set apart, by the common people in this country, for feasting and drinking, *Auld Handsel Monday* (1792) 17. Ir. The first Monday in the year, when formerly a present or hansel was given by a master or mistress to the servants, and by fathers or mothers to children. Anything that comes into your possession that day indicates luck, such as a child, calf, lamb, or money. If you receive on Hansel Monday you will be sure to be lucky the rest of the year, *Flb-Lore Rec.* (1881) IV. 107. N.I.[1] Nhb. At the Trinity House, Newcastle, on Hansel-Monday every free brother who answers to his name is entitled to five shillings in money, quarter a pound of tobacco, a glass of wine, and as much bread and cheese and ale as he pleases (R.O.H.). Lakel.[2] It is customary to make children and servants a present. Chs.[1] (3) Edb. My barrel . . . has na gotten sic a fill Sin fu' on Handsel-Teysday, Fergusson *Poems* (1773) 168, ed. 1785. (4) Or.I. *Gen.* the bride's mother (Jam. *Suppl.*).

3. The first money received in the day for the sale of goods; also the first purchaser.

Sc. Grose (1790) *MS. add.* (C.) Edb. A bareheaded lassie, hoping to be hansel, threw down twopence, Moir *Mansie Wauch* (1828) vi. Nhb. (R.O.H.) Dur. Thus, fishwomen and hucksters generally spit upon the hansel, i. e. the first money they receive, Henderson *Flb-Lore* (1879) i. s.Dur. Now gie us a hansel, a've selt nowt te-day—just gie us a hansel for luck (J.E.D.). Lakel.[1], Cum.[14] n.Wm. Giv us a hansel (B.K.). n.Yks. (W.H.); n.Yks.[1]; n.Yks.[2] ' There's handsel this morning,' says the sales-man, as he shows the coin to the bystanders for the first thing he has sold. e.Yks.[1] w.Yks.[2] Hawkers and pedlars who go round from house to house say, ' Please give me hansel, missis '; w.Yks.[5] ' I've not taken a handsel to-day.' On receiving a handsel, the recipient sometimes turns it over and spits on it ' for luck.' Lan. Hansell (they say) is always lucky when well wet [i. e. with spittle]. Harland & Wilkinson *Flb-Lore* (1867) 70. Chs. I have given you a good ansel, *Chs. N. & Q.* (1881) I. 82; Chs.[1] ' Gi me a hansel this morning.' There is a sort of idea that it brings good luck; Chs.[3] s.Cha.[1] Gy'i)mi ŭ aan·sl, ŭn it)l gy'i)mi gŭd lŭk. Der.[2], nw.Der.[1] Not. (J.H.B.); Not.[1] Ah've sold nowt yet, won't yer gie me a hansel? sw.Lin.[1] Won't you give us a hansel? i. e. make a first purchase of our wares. Nhp.[1] The first money received in the day, by small tradesmen or hawkers, is commonly called ' taking handsell '; and many superstitiously spit upon it, to pro-pitiate good luck. Shr.[1] Bless yo', Missis, tak' summat off me jest fur 'ansel; I've carried my basket all mornin' an' never soud a crock. Thank yo', Missis, I'll spit on this, an' 'ope it'll be lucky. Shr., Hrf. Bound *Provinc.* (1876). Cth. (W.W.S.) Lon. Grose (1790) *MS. add.* (M.) e.An.[12] Nrf. You are intreated by an itinerant hawker to give him a hansell, Cozens-Hardy *Broad Nrf.* (1893)

71. e.Suf. (F.H.) Sus.[1] The market women have a custom of kissing the first coin, spitting on it, and putting it in a pocket by itself for luck. Dev. The good luck, which the foolish Devonshire market women spit upon, or kiss, and then put into their purse or pocket, *Horae Subsecivae* (1777) 202. Cor.[1] When a man is well paid for any chance job early in the day, he says ' that's a good hansel.'

4. A piece of bread given before breakfast; a morning lunch. Gall. (Jam.); Mactaggart *Encycl.* (1824). N.I.[1]

5. Guerdon, reward; also ironically, a punishment, a smack of the hand.
Sh.I. Contentmint is da hansel o da sage, Burgess *Rasmie* (1892) 22. w.Yks. Ah'll gi' tha a good handsell if tha doesn't be quiet (J.J.B.).

6. A handful. w.Yks. Gi' us a handsell o' beans (S.K.C.).

7. The earnest given on completion of a bargain; the bargain itself.
Sc. (Jam.) Dur.[1] Seldom used. e.Yks. Thompson *Hist. Welton* (1869) 172. w.Yks. (F.M.L.), Not.[1], sw.Lin.[1], LeL[1] Dev. *Horae Subsecivae* (1777) 202; Hewett *Peas. Sp.* (1892) 46.

8. The first use or trial of anything.
Nhb. (R.O.H.), Dur.[1] Cum. Ferguson *Northmen* (1856) 214; Cum.[4], n.Yks.[1] w.Yks. Scatcherd *Hist. Morley* (1874) *Gl.* ; *Leeds Merc. Suppl.* (1884); w.Yks.[1] Chs. *Sheaf* (1879) I. 182. nw.Der.[1], n.Lin.[1] sw.Lin.[1] He is taking hansel of it. Shr., Hrf. Bound *Provinc.* (1876). Som. Sweetman *Wincanton Gl.* (1885).

9. *v.* To give money or a present to celebrate a new undertaking, &c.; to inaugurate, celebrate for the first time, esp. by drinking.
Sc. Was there a birth in the family, the dram had to circulate to handsel the young Scot, Ford *Thistledown* (1891) 123. Abd. Your dock's in order now, I ween, Ye'se get it hansell'd by a queen, Cadenhead *Bon Accord* (1853) 147. Per. Juist tae hansel her new kist, Ian Maclaren *Auld Lang Syne* (1895) 278. Fif. Well, I wish you success, and to handsel your new adventure I will not charge you anything for these, Robertson *Provost* (1894) 82. Ayr. Before he had begun to levy ' black mail,' as he named it, I hansel'd him with a penny, Hunter *Studies* (1870) 135. Lnk. Ilka guidwife her doon-lyin' Hansell'd wi' the barley bree, Nicholson *Kilwuddie* (ed. 1895) 50. Rxb. Come, neibour Tam, we'll take a glass To hansel the new year, Wilson *Poems* (1824) 17. Keb. Some tippling chiels gaed to the tent To hansel Leezy Waldron, Davidson *Seasons* (1789) 73. N.I.[1] The first purchase made from a dealer bansels him, brings luck. Cum.[4] The gift of a coin to the wearer of a new suit of clothes, hansels or makes that suit lucky. n.Yks.[4] Whya, thoo'll be lyke ti' han'sel t'new hoss, wa's want a glass apiece. w.Yks.[4] The first buyer in a shop newly opened hansels it. e.An.[1] To put the first coin into a collection.

Hence **Hanselling**, *vbl. sb.* the inauguration, first use or celebration.
Dmf. The fits of ague-fever you had at first were a severe intro-duction, . . I can hope now it was only the hanselling of you in your new climate, Carlyle *Unpubl. Lett.* (1853) in *Atlantic Monthly* (1898) 685.

10. *Ironically.* To give something unpleasant; to punish with a blow. w.Yks. (S.P.U.), (J.J.B.)

11. To pay earnest-money on a bargain. Also used *fig.*
Fif. [He] was the neist man whase shaven crown was hansel'd wi' a swap, Tennant *Papistry* (1827) 194. n.Yks.[4] Ah'll pay the summat noo ti han'sel t'job. w.Yks. (F.M.L.), Not.[1], LeL[1] War.[3] I said I'd go—but he didn't hansel me [I have promised to go (to a situation as servant) but I am not bound to fulfil my promise]. Dev. Tellee whot 'tez, min, thee shedstūa-anselled 'n wi' a shilling, an' made zure aw 'un, Hewett *Peas. Sp.* (1892).

12. To try or use a thing for the first time; to test, prove.
Sc. It's exactly a fortnight this day syne ye handselled it for the first time, Dickson *Kirk Beadle* (ed. 1892) 99; He that invented the Maiden first hansel'd her, Henderson *Prov.* (1832) 118, ed. 1881. Lnk. Gazed at the maister to see if he was going to ' hansel the new clogs with a licking,' Fraser *Whaups* (1895) vi. Edb. The unfortunate earl was the first himself that handselled that merciless Maiden, which proved so soon after his own executioner, Pennecuik *Wks.* (1715) 191, ed. 1815. Dmf. I'll be yere blythe bridegroom and hansel the sark, Cromek *Remains* (1810) 112. Keb. It is a long time since Abel first handseled the cross, and had it laid upon his shoulder, Rutherford *Lett.* (1660) No. 239. Nhb. [The new assembly rooms] were opened and ' a very numerous and brilliant company' gathered to hansel them, Watson *Hist. Lit. Phil. Soc. Newc.* (1897) 34; Aa'll not hansel the coat till the

morn (R.O.H.). **Dur.** It's partly . . . to handsel our new kitchen, *Longman's Mag.* (Oct. 1896) 579 ; **Dur.**[1], **Cum.** (J.Ar.), **Cum.**[14] **n.Yks.**[1] ; **n.Yks.**[2] Ah've han'sel'd t'new reaper ti-daay. **ne.Yks.**[1] Ah handsel'd mah new dhriss last Sunda. **e.Yks.**[1] Ah sal ansel m! new bonnet o' Sunday. **w.Yks.** LUCAS *Stud. Nidderdale* (c. 1882) Gl. ; I ansell'd the tea-pot yesterday (H.F.S.); **w.Yks.**[2] I've not hand-selled my new plough. **Lan.**[1], **n.Lan.** (C.W.D.), **Cha.**[1], **Not.**[1] **n.Lin.**[1] I'm gooin' to hansel that new plew. **sw.Lin.**[1], **Lei.**[1] **Shr.**[1] I never sid sich a time fur wet ; I thought to 'ansel my new bonnet o' Wissun-Sunday, but it raȳned all daȳ lung. **Shr., Hrf.** BOUND *Provinc.* (1876). **Suf.**[1] First wearing a new coat, gown, or any-thing else is hanselling it. **e.Suf.** To hansel a brewing-tub. To hansel an oven is to heat it very thoroughly, when first built, for the purpose of drying it, not in order to bake in it. Except in these connexions, not used here (F.H.). **Sus.**[12] **Dor.** Here, Jenny, .. hansell, wi' zome tidy tea, The zilver pot, BARNES *Poems* (1869–70) 3rd S. 100. **Dev.** To prove the goodness of a thing by the trial of a part, as when we say, to hansell a pasty or gammon of bacon—to have the maidenhead or first use of anything—to hansell a new knife in a good plum pudding, *Horae Subsecivae* (1777) 202. **Cor.**[1]

13. To be the first purchaser.
w.Yks. Ye've hansil'd meh, BANKS *Whfld. Wds.* (1865). **n.Lan.**[1] **Not.** I've just anselled (J.H.B.).

[1. God giue the guid prosperitie . . . In hansell of this guid new ȝeir, DUNBAR *New Years Gift* (c. 1510) 16, ed. Small, II. 256. 5. Some . . . were be-hote hansell, if þey helpe wold, *Rich. Redeless* (1399) IV. 91. 7. I have taken handsel, *Mercimonii primitias accepi*, COLES (1679).]

HANDSOME, *adj.* Sc. Yks. Not. Lei. Dor. Dev. Cor. [h]a'nsəm, æ·nsəm.] **1.** Very good ; elegant in person ; good-looking, used of inanimate things.
Sc. Not applied to the face. She's a very handsome woman, but far frae being bonny (JAM.). **Dmb.** I gade to learn at the night school, Soon learn'd a han'some han' o' write, TAYLOR *Poems* (1827) 102. **w.Yks.** It's a better roäd ner t'other, but it's nut as handsome (F.P.T.). **Dev.** She gave me such a handsome cup o' tea, *Reports Provinc.* (1891).

2. Honourable, noble ; good, giving good quality or measure.
Not.[1], **Lei.**[1] **Dor.** A handsome man, one who keeps good strong beer (W.C.) ; My mother told me that she had heard guests say to her father when they tasted his beer, ' Mr. Boswell, you are very handsome ' (W.G.B.-S.) ; (A.C.)

3. Of the weather : fine, good, bright.
Sh.I. It's still very necessitous, an very handsome wedder, BURGESS *Tang* (1898) 5a. **w.Yks.** Eh ! Miss, but it is a handsome day (F.P.T.). **w.Cor.** It's some handsome weather. Common (M.A.C.).

4. Thorough, complete. Also used *advb.*
Cor.[2] A handsome service, a church service not shortened, includ-ing the Litany. ' To do a thing hïandsome ' is to do it thoroughly.

HANDTOGGERS, *sb. pl.* Dev.[2] The handles fixed on the snead of a scythe.

HANDY, *sb.*[1], *adj.* and *adv.* Var. dial. uses in Sc. Irel. and Eng. Also written **handl-** Sc. (JAM.) Cai.[1]; and in forms **haand-de-** Sh.I. ; **hanni-** Cai.[1]; **hany** Nhb.; **han'y** Ayr. ; **haunie** Per. [h]a·ndi, æ·ndi]. **1.** *sb.* and *adj.* In *comp.* (1) **Handy-bandy,** (2) **-croopen,** a game; see below ; (3) **-cuffs,** (a) blows with the fist, fisticuffs ; (b) handcuffs, manacles ; (4) **-dandy,** (a) see (1) ; (b) on the alert ; (5) **-grips,** close quarters, grappling ; (6) **-man,** one who has no trade in particular, but does a little at several ; (7) **-might,** strength of hand, main force ; (8) **-paddy,** a winch, traversing on temporary rails, employed to raise heavy weights at large buildings ; (9) **-pandy,** see (1) ; (10) **-pungy,** a fight with the fists ; (11) **-stone,** a small stone, one that can be thrown with the hand ; (12) **-warp,** *obs.,* a kind of cloth, formerly made in Essex ; (13) **-workman,** a mechanic ; a tool-handler.

(1) **s.Cha.**[1] A person conceals an object in one of his two closed hands, and invites his companion to tell which hand contains the object in the following words : ' Handy-Bandy, sugar-candy, Which hand wun yö have ! ' (a) **Sh.I.** They amused themselves with such games as hunt-de-slipper, wads, and haand-de-kroopin, SPENCE *Flk-Lore* (1899) 190 ; **S. & Ork.**[1] A game in which one of the players turns his face to the wall, his hand resting upon his back ; he must continue in this position until he guesses who struck his hand, when the striker takes his place. (3, a) **Sc.** (JAM.) **Cai.**[1]

To come to handicuffs, to come to blows. **w.Yks.**[1] (b) **w.Yks.**[1] (4, a) **Nhb.**[1], **w.Yks.**[2] **Lan.**[1] Common. Something being hidden in one hand, both are presented by the player to his opponent with the words, ' Handy-dandy, sugar candy, which hand is it in!' **Glo.** A game, ' when by nimbly changing hands, and slipping a piece of money from one hand into the other, the guesser is at a loss, which hand to fix upon, tho' he thinks he saw its place, *Horae Subsecivae* (1777) 200. **Hmp.** To play at handy dandy, and guess which is the justice, which is the thief. A sort of slight of hand, when by exchanging hands nimbly, and slipping the thing from one hand to another, the guesser is often deceived, and at a loss what hand to fix upon. There is a . . . way of playing it, by two persons putting their hands one above the other, and then raising them and replacing them with rapidity ; used among children, GROSE (1790) *MS. add.* (M.) **Dev.**[5] (b) **m.Yks.**[1] ' He's handy-dandy with him,' said of one who is a match for another in sharpness. (5) **Sh.I.** He'd been blied if dey'd come in haandie-grips, *Sh. News* (Oct. 23, 1897). **Cai.**[1] **Slk.** We canna come to handygrips wi' him, HOGG *Tales* (1838) 46, ed. 1866. **Keb.** Certainly my light is dim, when it cometh to handy-grips, RUTHER-FORD *Lett.* (1660) No. 108. (6) **Oxf.**[1] *MS. add.* (7) **Abd.** Seean' nae way for the laird out o' his difficulty but by handy micht, *Deeside Tales* (1872) 121. (8) [It is very handy for the masons and is almost invariably worked by Irishmen, *N. & Q.* (1853) 1st S. viii. 508.] (9) **w.Yks.**[5] A child's game, in which something is changed from one hand to the other, and guesses are made as to which hand contains it. **Cha.**[1] The one who conceals the object says—' Handy Pandy, sugary candy, Guess which hand it's in ; Right hand or left hand, Guess which hand it's in.' **Shr.** BURNE *Flk-Lore* (1883) 531 ; **Shr.**[1] (10) **s.Cha.**[1] Wi)an sey ū bit ū aan'di-pŭngg·i naay [We s'n sey a bit o' handy-pungy na!]. (11) **Fif.** The hedge sparrow and the yite jinked the handy-stone, COLVILLE *Vernacular* (1899) 8. (12) **Ess.** (HALL.), **Ess.**[1] (13) **n.Yks.**[2]

2. *adj.* Skilful, dexterous, clever-handed ; apt, clever ; useful.
Sh.I. I was always a handy man, BURGESS *Tang* (1898) 87. **Elg.** I wat she is a handy wife, Oor wife Bell, TESTER *Poems* (1865) 106. **Lnk.** You find Doghip handy, I suppose, GORDON *Pyotshaw* (1885) 233. **Edb.** Cou'd Prick-the-louse but be sae handy As mak the breeks and claise to stand ay, FERGUSSON *Poems* (1773) 201, ed. 1785. **Dmf.** Ye gleg, handy craftsmen, that toil for yer bread, QUINN *Heather* (1863) 143. **Nhb.** (W.G.) **Dur.**[1] A handy lad. **Wm.** He's handy wi' a pen (B.K.). **n.Yks.**[1] A despert handy chap wiv a specad ; **n.Yks.**[4] He's a varra handy chap. **I.Ma.** The doctor was that handy about him the ould chap couldn' do without him, BROWN *Doctor* (1887) 94, ed. 1891. **nw.Der.**[1] **a.Not.** ' You'll hev to be handy how you get 'em,' said A to B, who meant ' snaking ' some grafts from a choice, well-watched apple-tree (J.P.K.). **Nhp.**[1] **Glo.** What a handy girl Mary is (A.B.) ; **Glo.**[2] **Oxf.**[1] *MS. add.* **Brks.**[1] He be a handy zart o' chap. **e.An.**[2] A clever workman is ' a handy fellow.' **Hmp.**[1] **Wil.** SLOW *Gl.* (1892) ; BRITTON *Beauties* (1825). **Dor.** Abel be wonderful handy about the place, *Longman's Mag.* (Nov. 1898) 50. **w.Som.**[1] I 'sure 'ee, he's a rare fuller to work, and he's a'andy 's a gimblet. **Dev.** 'Tis true that pegs be vury handy crayters, SALMON *Ballads* (1899) 50.

3. Good, sound ; suitable, seemly.
Abd. The beast's as soun' 's ever a beast was ; and there's nae a handier creatur i' the market, ALEXANDER *Ain Flk.* (1882) 102. **Fif.** Gin ye angry grow, or glowr, That winna be sae handy, DOUGLAS *Poems* (1806) 69.

4. *adv.* Of place : near by, adjacent to, close at hand.
Sc. (A.W.) **s.Ir.** How should you know that I was here so handy to you ! CROKER *Leg.* (1862) 289. **n.Cy.** (J.W.) **Cum.** His house is handy to his office (E.W.P.) ; **Cum.**[4] His house is very handy to his office. **Yks.** (J.W.), **Not.** (L.C.M.), **Not.**[1] **n.Lin.**[1] Oor chech stan's soä nice an' handy that I mostlin's goä theäre e'steäd o' to chapil. **Lei.**[1] 'Weer's Higgam !' ' Whoy, joost 'andy to Stooke.' **Nhp.**[12] **War.**[2] The farm lies very handy. **Glo.** (J.S.F.S.) ; I says to her 'as 'er'd ought to go to the churchyard of the parish as 'er's now in, as it is so much handier, yer see, BUCKMAN *Darke's Sojourn* (1890) xi ; **Glo.**[12], **Oxf.** (G.O.) **Brks.**[1] A little me-ad lez handy to the house. **Sur.**[1] **Sus.** HOLLOWAY. **Wil.** SLOW *Gl.* (1892) ; **Wil.**[1] Handy home. ' I be zo hard o' hirin', I caan't hire nothen, wi'out I comes handier to 'ee,' *ib.* 211. **n.Wil.** 'Tis handy 'Vize ; It's near Devizes] (E.H.G.). **Som.** Handy her last end, RAYMOND *Men o' Mendip* (1898) i ; JENNINGS *Obs. Dial. w.Eng.* (1825). **w.Som.**[1] Her do live up handy Taun'on. **Dev.** He said the stones were very handy for him, BRAY *Desc. Tamar and Tavy* (1836) I. 248. **Cor.** And ef the sai [sea] es handy by, In the ' Fisheries ' we will fish, FORFAR *Poems* (1885) 10.

5. Of time : near to, approaching, nearly.

Hmp. How old is she !—Oh, she's handy upon twelve (M.C.H.B.). I.W. Pretty handy twelve o'clock (J.D.R.); I.W.[1], Wil.[1]   s Wil. Handy ten o'clock, *Monthly Mag.* (1814) II. 114. w.Som.[1] They did'n come home gin handy one o'clock. Come, Soce! I zim 'tis handy dinner-time. Dev. Christmas Day being so handy to Sunday this year (H.S.H.).

6. Almost, very nearly, near about.

War. *Leamington Courier* (Mar. 6, 1897); War.[2] s.War.[1] That bit o' garden ground is handy to 20 pole. Hrf.[1] Handy a mile. Oxf.[1] Dhat dhaa'r pig waiz aan·di ten skor [That thar pig weighs handy ten scor]. Wil.[1] A gied un vower days' work, or handy. Dev. The game was preserved, but the keeper lived handy two mile from here, MORTIMER *Tales Moors* (1895) 265; Handy two thousand feet auver the zea, *ib.* 290.

7. Easily, readily, without trouble.   Also used *attrib.*

Ayr. When climbing o'er the Hadyer Hill, It wasna han'y wark, man, *Ballads and Sngs.* (1846) I. 94 ; Oaths come oot far owre handy when folk get a drap o' whisky, JOHNSTON *Glenbuckie* (1889) 16. Wgt. Onything they get ower handy they think nae gear aboot, FRASER *Wigtown* (1877) 364. n.Cy. (J.W.) War.[3] It is a good bit of ground, it works so handy.

8. Readily, quickly.

n.Cy. (J.W.)   Not. Look handy (L.C.M.) ; Be handy, be quick (J.H.B.) ; (W.H.S.)   Nhp.[2]

9. Officious ; over-busy with one's hands.

n.Cy. (J.W.)   s.Not. Don't be so handy with your marking ; I can mark for myself (J.P.K.). Oxf. (G.O.)

HANDY, *sb.*[2] Sc. Nhb. Cum. Also in form **hannie** Lnk. Cum.[12] [**ha'ndi, ha'ni.**] **1.** A small tub with a handle used for carrying water, milk, &c. ; a milking-pail.

Per. Women used to milk the cows into handies before pails were used for this purpose. The handy is seldom seen now (G.W.). Lnk. Bring the twa milk hannies, WATT *Poems* (1827) 59. N.Cy.[1] Small wooden cylindrical vessel made of staves hooped together, one being longer than the rest and serving as a handle. Nhb. (W.G.) ; Lyave the watter oot wi' the handy, lass (R.O.H.) ; Nhb.[1] Cum.[1] ; Cum.[4] A small tub of cylindrical form having a long handle ; elsewhere called Piggin. [A handy formed like a miniature milk-pail, STEPHENS *Farm Bk.* (ed. 1849) I. 528.]

2. *Comp.* (1) **Handie-full,** the fill of a milk-pail ; (2) **-kit,** a tub or pail having a long handle.

(1) Lnk. I had gane into the milkhouse... to teem a hannie-fu' o' milk, *Edb. Mag.* (Dec. 1818) 503 (JAM.). (2) Cum.[14]

3. A wooden dish for holding food.

s.Sc. I flang the hannie frae me, *Edb. Mag.* (Dec. 1818) 503 (JAM.) ; Thus denominated because it has an ear or hand for holding by (JAM.).

HANE, see **Hain,** *v.*[1]

HANG, *v.* and *sb.* Var. dial. uses in Sc. Irel. Eng. and Amer. Also in forms **ang-** Cor.[12] ; **hange-** Der. [(h)aŋ, eŋ, æŋ.] **1.** *v.* Gram. forms. **1.** *Present Tense :* (1) **Ank,** (2) **Haing,** (3) **Heng,** (4) **Hong.** [For additional examples see II below.] See **Hing.**

(1) Ess.[1] (2) Arg. Haing the meishachan, where first I felt love's mainglin' smart, COLVILLE *Vernacular* (1899) 6. (3) n.Yks.[4], w.Yks.[2], s.Chs.[1]   Sus. What dey heng a thousan bucklers on, LOWER *Sng. Sol.* (1860) iv. 4. (4) Lan. Furst he chops off his woife's heaod, and then hongs aw t'priests, AINSWORTH *Witches* (ed. 1849) Introd. iii. Cor.[2]

2. *Preterite :* (1) **Henged,** (2) **Unged.**

(1) w.Yks. A've a singin bird heng'd at t'haase top, ECCLES *Sngs.* (1862) 24. (2) w.Som. Uung·d, *Athenaeum* (Feb. 26, 1898).

3. *pp.* (1) **Hangen,** (2) **Hangit,** (3) **Henged,** (4) **Unged,** (5) **Ungen.**

(1) e.Yks.[1] (2) Sc. Do not talk of a rape to a chiel whase father was hangit, RAMSAY *Prov.* (1737). Nhb. Weel fangit—syne hangit, we'se see them a', DIXON *Whittingham Vale* (1895) 193 ; (R.O.H.) (3) w.Yks. Be heng'd to yer meter hannels ! BINNS *Orig.* (1889) No. i. 5. (4) w.Som. U-ung·d, *Athenaeum* (Feb. 26, 1898). (5) s.Chs.[1] Ŭngn, 81.

II. *Dial. uses.* **1.** *v.* In *comb.* (1) **Hang-a-balk,** a gallows-bird, one ripe for the gallows ; (2) **-back,** hesitation, hanging back ; (3) **-bench,** a piece of timber forming part of the ' stow ' in a mine ; (4) **-bow,** the hanging-post of a gate, to which the hinges are attached ; (5) **-by,** a hanger-on ; (6) **-choice,** no difference, one as bad as the other ; ' Hobson's choice ' ; (7) **-dog,** (*a*) a worthless fellow, a reprobate ; (*b*) villainous, bad ; (8) **-dog-like,** see

(7, *b*) ; (9) **-dog look,** a villainous or vile expression ; also used *attrib.* in form **-dog-looking** ; (10) **-fair,** a public execution ; also called **Hanging-fair** (q. v.) ; (11) **-gallows,** (*a*) see (1) ; (*b*) see (7, *b*) ; (12) **-gallows-look,** see (9) ; (13) **-lock,** a padlock ; (14) **-mad,** riotous tumult, boisterous frolic ; also used *attrib.* ; (15) **-net,** a species of net ; see below ; (16) **— on,** mining term : a call from the banksman to the onsetter, after any stop, to recommence work ; (17) **-post,** see (4) ; (18) **-sleeve,** a dangler ; an officious but unmeaning suitor ; (19) **-such,** (20) **-trace,** see (1) ; (21) **-(s-tree,** see (4).

(1) Nhb.[1] (*a*) Som. There'd be no hang-back about John Winterhead, once his mind was made up, RAYMOND *Men o' Mendip* (1898) xi. (*g*) Der. Hading Hang-bench muttering in his sleeve, FURNESS *Medicus* (1836) 31 ; Hange-benches, turntree, and coes, MANLOVE *Lead Mines* (1653) l. 268. (4) nw.Dev.[1] Formerly it used to project considerably above the gate, the upper part being curved towards the head and secured at its end to a diagonal cross-piece. Cor. The hang-bow and millyer [the hinge] was all that was left of the gate, THOMAS *Randigal Rhymes* (1895) 6. (5) w.Yks.[2] (6) Nhb.[1] Chs.[1] ' Am nor oi a better bye than Johnny, grandmother ! ' ' Aw dunna know ; you're both so nowt, that it's hang choice between you.' s.Chs.[1] (7, *a*) n.Yks.[4] [The man is not a reprobate—not a hang-dog, JEFFERIES *Hodge* (1880) II. 195.] (*b*) Buff.[1] He canna be gueede, he hiz sic a hang-dog face. [Look at his hang-dog air, DICKENS *Mutual Friend* (1865) bk. 1. xii.] (8) Buff.[1] A widna like t'meet yon lad i' the dark ; he hiz as hingum-tringum, hang-dog-like a leuck 's iver I saw. (9) Lakel.[2] n.Yks.[4] Deean't gan aboot wiv a hang-dog leeak o' thi feeace leyke that. e.Yks.[1], n.Lin.[1] w.Som.[1] Me, gwain to have thick hangdog-looking fuller ! —why, I widn be a zeed in a ten-acre field way un. (10) Wil.[1] ' Hang-fair at 'Vize,' formerly treated as a great holiday. *Obs.* The Pleasure Fair at Warminster, on August 11, is known as ' Hang-Fair,' perhaps from the hanging of two murderers there on that day in 1813. Dor. The innkeeper supposed her some harum-skarum young woman who had come to attend ' hang-fair ' next day, HARDY *Wessex Tales* (1888) I. 111. Som. They told the grim story of that day ... How there were thousands at Hang-fair, RAYMOND *Men o' Mendip* (1898) ii ; (W.F.R.); W. & J. *Gl.* (1873). (11, *a*) Nhb.[1] Cum. That furst fella's a real Yankee, an a regular hang-gallas, SARGISSON *Joe Scoap* (1881) 211. n.Yks. (T.S.), w.Yks.[15], War. (J.R.W.) Wil. Where's the money I put in th' zack, you hang-gallus ! AKERMAN *Tales* (1853) 55; Snow *Gl.* (1892) ; Wil.[1] Som. SWEETMAN *Wincanton Gl.* (1885). w.Som.[1] ' I calls'n a proper hang-gallus—why I widn be a zeed in a ten-acre field way un.' Very commonly used to express repugnance at association or contact with any one. s.Dev., e.Cor. (Miss D.) (*b*) I.W.[2] He's a hang-gallus rascal. Dor. A hang-gallows rogue, BARNES *Gl.* (1863). Som. That hang-gallis fellow Standerwick, RAYMOND *Men o' Mendip* (1898) viii ; A hang-gallise fellow, JENNINGS *Dial. w.Eng.* (1869). w.Som.[1] You hang-gallis oseburd, tid'n good I catch thee. Who's thick there hang-gallis fuller ! Cor.[1] You angallish dog, you ; Cor.[2] (12) Lakel.[2], e.Yks.[1], w.Yks.[1], Lin.[1] Dev.[2] Bill Jones 'th a-got a 'ang-gallious loke in 'es face that mak'th me creem tü lüke at 'n. (13) Nhb.[1] Still used, but probably *obsol.* (14) m.Yks.[1] Employed occas. as an *adj.* and commonly as a *sb.* (15) Dmf. Hang-nets are larger in the mesh than any other nets, and are stretched upright between stakes of about ten feet long, placed at regular distances of about eight feet, *Agric. Surv.* 605 (JAM.). e.An.[1] (s.v. Hay-net). (16) Nhb., Dur. NICHOLSON *Coal Tr. Gl.* (1888). (17) Chs.[1] ; Chs.[3] In contradistinction to the ' clap post,' against which the gate shuts. (18, 19) s.An.[1] (20) m.Yks.[1] Aye, he's a hang-trace, as aud Betty says by such like. (21) Hrf.[2]

2. *Phr.* (1) *to hang at,* to take one's time at ; (2) *— by,* to cling to, be on the side of ; (3) *—for,* to be desirous or anxious for ; (4) *— for rain,* to threaten rain ; (5) *— idly,* of a sheep : to be ill ; (6) *— in hand,* to be dull of sale ; (7) *— in the band,* to remain unsold ; (8) *— in the bell-ropes,* said of a couple in the interval elapsing between the calling of their banns in church and the wedding ; also of one who has been deserted after publication of the banns ; (9) *— in the wind,* (*a*) to subsist on uncertainty, await events ; used *attrib.* ; (*b*) to put off, delay, postpone ; (10) *— on the bough,* to remain unmarried ; (11) *— on the slack rope,* to be lazy ; (12) *— on to,* to scold ; (13) *— out,* to loiter or stop about a place ; (14) *— to,* to have an inclination or affection for ; (15) *— together,* to just be alive and nothing more ; (16) *— up,* (*a*) to bring in debt ; (*b*) to hinder or delay ; to foil, prevent ; used in *pp.* ; (*c*) to leave off work ;

(17) — *up a field*, to take the cattle off a field and give it a long rest, so as to freshen up the pasture ; (18) — *up the hat*, (*a*) to be very intimate in a house ; to be an accepted suitor ; (*b*) of a man when married : to go and live in his wife's house ; (19) — *up by one leg*, see below ; (20) — *the a–e*, to loiter, hold back ; (21) — *the baker*, to become bankrupt, be out of materials for work ; (22) — *the fiddle behind the door*, to leave one's good humour behind one ; (23) — *the lip*, to pout, look sullen ; (24) — *the stump*, see below ; (25) *be hang ye or to ye*, an exclamation ; (26) *what did ye hang your father for*, see below ; (27) *Guy heng !* see (25) ; (28) *to hang out the broomstick*, to angle for a husband.

(1) w.Wor. [He] want to hang at it, S. BEAUCHAMP *Grantley Grange* (1874) II. 56. (2) s.Oxf. Them lawyers allus 'angs by the rich folks, ROSEMARY *Chilterns* (1895) 61. (3) n.Lin.¹ Well Mary Ann, thoo can do as ta likes, bud I hang for ye goin' to Mrs. —— plaace ; its a knawn good un. (4) w.Yks. (J.W.) n.Lin.¹ It's been hangin' for raain three or foher daays but noän cums. (5) Nrf. When a sheep 'hang idly,' as they say here in their sing-song provincialism, the knowing dog will never touch it—they seem to discern that the sheep is ill, EMERSON *Yarns* (1891) 116. (6) Nhp.¹, Hnt. (T.P.F.) (7) w.Yks.² A house or a farm is said ' to hang i' t'band a long time ' if it does not sell when it is offered for sale, and when for a considerable time no purchaser can be found. (8) s.Chs.¹, nw.Der.¹ Wor. If, after the publication of banns, the marriage does not come off, the ' deserted one ' is said to be hung in the bell-ropes, *N. & Q.* (1867) 3rd S. xii. 139. (9, *a*) Cum.⁴ The company consists of the ' well-to-do ' and the hang-i'-th'-win' class, BURN *Rosenthal*, 13. (*b*) Gall. She seldom saw them happy, Matches that hang long i' win, NICHOLSON *Poet. Wks.* (1814) 114, ed. 1897. (10) Sc. Ye impident woman ! It's easy seen why ye were left hingin' on the bough, KEITH *Indian Uncle* (1896) 5. (11) w.Cor. He rarely does anything, he's very fond of hanging on the slack rope (M.A.C.). (12) e.An.¹ I'll hang on to him properly when I catch him. (13) Mid. Don't hang out here, stops business, BLACKMORE *Kit* (1890) I. xvi. (14) s.Chs.¹ Oo wūz widh ūz fūr ū men·i ē·ūr, ūn it)s lahyk ūz iv ōo)z au·viz ūngn tōo ūz [Hoo was with us for a many 'ear, an' it's like as if hoo's auvays hungn to us]. (15) S. & Ork.¹ Yea, lamb, he's just hanging together. Cai.¹ (16, *a*) w.Som.¹ A man having a bill brought in unexpectedly for goods ordered on his account by his wife or servant, would say : ' I'm darned if I'll be a hanged up like this here.' This phr. is most likely the same in origin as ' chalk up '—viz. from the score due to a publican being written on a slate and hung up, the more primitive method having been to chalk it on the back of the door. It is easy to see how the expression might get to be applied to a more systematic debit. (*b*) Ken.¹ ' He is quite hung up,' so circumstanced that he is hindered from doing what otherwise he would. Sur.¹ To be delayed or hindered, as in hay-making or harvest, from bad weather or want of hands. Sus.¹ I was so hung up for time all last week I couldn't come. (*c*) [Amer. A mower, when rain was coming on : ' I reckon we'll have to hang up for all day, *Dial. Notes* (1896) I. 372.] (17) Wil.¹ n.Wil. After a farmer has turned his cattle out and ' fed ' a field, he will say, ' We'll hang up that field ' (E.H.G.). (18, *a*) Ayr. Ye have only to gang doon and hang up your hat, JOHNSTON *Glenbuckie* (1889) 220. n.Yks.⁴ Ah can hang mah hat up yonder when Ah've a mahnd teea. s.Stf. It was known . . . that Snelling ' hung his hat up '—that is the local phrase—at the abode of Ephraim Shorthouse, whose daughter Cecilia was grown to a marriageable age, MURRAY *John Vale* (1890) xvii. Brks.¹ (*b*) Sc. (A.W.) w.Som.¹ When a man marries and goes home to the wife's house to live, he is said to ' hang up his hat.' The phr. is an everyday one, perfectly well understood by every one. It is a bantering and rather depreciatory saying. (19) Wil. Though the wheat grew very luxuriantly during the winter, the March winds, particularly after frost, frequently blew the earth away from the plant, and left it (as the Wiltshire phrase is) ' hung up by one leg,' *Agric.* 50. (20) w.Yks.¹ [My lads, I am told you hang an a—se. I have gone to sea thirty years man and boy, and never saw English sailors afraid before, SMOLLETT *R. Random* (1748) lxv.] (21) Cum.⁴ (22) Ir. No man 'ill know berther how to hang his fiddle behind the door, CARLETON *Fardorougha* (1836) 21 ; The old midwives believed that if a man was brutal or unkind (e. g. hung his fiddle behind the door) when a child was born to him they could transfer all the pain of child-bearing to him, *ib. note*. (23) nw.Der.¹ (24) Nhp.¹ A term amongst hedgers and ditchers when they hang small thorns on the stumps of the lower table of a newly laid hedge ; to prevent animals biting the young shoots in the spring and summer. (25) N.I.¹ O behang t'ye for a fool. n.Yks.² (26) Brks.¹ Children run after cock turkeys calling,

' What d'ye hang yer vather wi',' to get the reply ' Holter, holter, holter ' (s.v. Come back). (27) I.Ma. Guy heng ! The woman's mad, CAINE *Manxman* (1894) I. iii. (28) Oxf. (G.O.)

3. Of mortar : to cling, hold together.
Lon. A walling builder told me that ' mac ' was us good as the best sand ; it made the mortar ' hang,' and without either that or sand, the lime would ' brittle ' away, MAYHEW *Lond. Labour* (ed. 1861) II. 199.

4. Coal-mining term : to incline or dip. See Hing, *v.* II. 6. Nhb.¹ Nhb., Dur. GREENWELL *Coal Tr. Gl.* (1849).

5. To stand ; to incline or stand on a slope.
N.I.¹ Hangin' on my feet all day. e.Suf. ' That are hill du hang wholly heavy,' is very steep (F.H.).

6. To fix a gate or door in its place by crooks or hinges.
Yks. (J.W.), n.Lin.¹ Ess.¹ ' Ank that gate ' for ' hang or shut that gate.' w.Som.¹ Technically a carpenter hangs a door or gate when he fits it to its place, fixes the hinges, and makes it open and shut properly.

7. Of a scythe : to set it in its ' snead ' or handle.
N.I.¹ Nrf. I take my old Fanny—we allust call our scythes arter our wives—and hung her, EMERSON *Son of Fens* (1892) 131. w.Som.¹ Thy zive id'n a-hang vitty, the toer o' un's a cocked up to much. nw.Der.¹

8. *sb.* Phr. (1) *hang lit on it !* may hanging befall it ; an imprecation ; (2) *the hang !* an expletive.
(1) Lakel.², n.Yks.², m.Yks.¹ (2) Don. What the hang did ye call her ! MACMANUS *Oiney Kittach* in *Century Mag.* (Oct. 1899 955.

9. A snare for catching rabbits, hares, &c.
Nhb. I'm no sae laith to see them spang An' wam'le, fast tied wi' a 'hang,' PROUDLOCK *Borderland Muse* (1896) 341 ; Nhb.¹ A noose made of very fine wire or hair. n.Yks. T'hare was catcht in a hang (I.W.). Chs.¹², s.Chs.¹

10. A crop of fruit.
e.An.¹ A good tidy hang of apples. Nrf. We've got a rare hang of plums t'year (W.R.E.). Suf. (R.E.L.), Suf.¹, e.Suf. (F.H.)

11. A declivity, slope. Cf. hanger, 5, hanging, *sb.* 4.
e.An.¹ e.Suf. The hang of a hill (F.H.).

HANGALL, see Hankle, *v.*

HANGE, *sb.* Hrf. Glo. Hmp. I.W. Wil. Dor. Som. Dev. Cor. Also written **hanje** Dev. ; and in forms **henge** Hmp.¹ I.W.¹ Wil.¹ Som. Dev. ; **hinge** Hrf.¹ Glo.¹² Hmp.¹ Wil.¹ Dor.¹ Cor.⁸ ; **inge** Glo.¹ [æng, eng, ing.] The pluck or liver, lungs and heart of any animal.
Hrf.¹ Glo. LEWIS *Gl.* (1839) ; Glo.¹² Hmp. A sheep's head and henge. A pig's henge (J.R.W.) ; Hmp.¹, I.W.¹ Wil. SLOW *Gl.* (1892) ; ' Peg's henge,' pig's fry or ' inwards ' (K.M.G.) ; BRITTON *Beauties* (1825) ; Wil.¹ The heart, liver, and lungs of a sheep or pig. In some parts of s.Wil. used only of the latter. w.Cy. GROSE (1790). Dor.¹ Som. JENNINGS *Obs. Dial. w.Eng.* (1825) ; (W.F.R.) w.Som.¹ In dressing sheep, the head is usually left attached by the windpipe ; this is always called a ' sheep's head and hange ' [anj]. A calf or pig always has the head separated ; hence one hears only of a ' calf's hange,' or a ' pig's hange.' Dev. Butchers sell ' sheep's-head and hange ' for a few pence, HEWETT *Peas. Sp.* (1892) ; *Reports Provinc.* (1877) 132 ; Dev.¹ Why if es could ha' but a sheep's head and hange es should ha' the virst cut o't, 44. n.Dev. GROSE (1790). nw.Dev.¹, s.Dev. (F.W.C.), Cor.¹²³ w.Cor. The tinner's wife put all the pork left at home in salt, except the beans, and saved them to make a good pie the Feasten Sunday. She made the hinges and other things serve them till then, BOTTRELL *Trad.* 3rd S. 69.

Hence **Hanjed**, *ppl. adj.* used as a term of abuse.
n.Dev. What's me-an by that, ya long-hanjed meazle, *Exm. Scold.* (1746) l. 30 ; A long hanjed creature, *Horae Subsecivae* (1777) 201. [Et sol' pro j Calvishede cum le henge ad paschetyde proiantacula iiijᵈ, *Chw. Acc.* (1494) S. *Edmund Sarum* (ed. 1896) 43.]

HANGED, *ppl. adj.* Sc. Cum. Chs. Also in form **hangit** Sc. Cum.⁴ 1. In *comb.* (1) Hanged-faced, having a look that seems to point to the gallows ; (2) — hay, hay hung on the steelyard to be weighed, previous to selling ; (3) -like, shamefaced, hang-dog like.
(1) Rxb. (JAM.) (2) Chs.¹ ; Chs.² (s.v. Doe) ; Chs.³ ' Hanged hay never does cattle,' i. e. bought hay does not pay. ' Slung hay ' is another version, and like ' hanged hay,' refers to the mode of weighing. (3) Sc. Applied to one who is out of countenance or knows not what excuse to make for his conduct. It is said that he looks very hangit-like (JAM.). Cum.⁴ At last he turn't oot, bit hang't like, RICHARDSON *Talk* (1871) 1st S. 24.

2. Cursed, damned.

e.Fif. He paid the siller wi' hangit ill-will, Latto *Tam Bodkin* (1864) xv. Lak. It's a lee! It's a hangit lee, she's gaun to marry oor Jossie! Gordon *Pyotshaw* (1885) 41.

HANGEDLY, adv. Cum. Yks. Reluctantly, unwillingly; despondently, as though being led to the gallows.

Cum. The lave tho' hang'dly follow him Wi' nea uncommon spead, Stagg *Misc. Poems* (ed. 1807) 40. n.Yks.[1]; n.Yks.[2] He left heeam varry hangedly; n.Yks.[24], ne.Yks.[1] w.Yks.[1] He gangs vara hangedly.

HANGER, sb. Nhb. Yks. Oxf. Nrf. Ken. Sus. Hmp. I.W. w.Cy. Dor. Also in form anjur- I.W.[2] **1.** A hook or link by which a pot or kettle is suspended over the fireplace.

Oxf.[1] *MS. add.* w.Cy. Hung a black kettle over it [fire] on a veritable pothook and hanger, *Longman's Mag.* (Apr. 1898) 543; The old iron 'hangers' for pots are very common, *ib.* (Nov. 1896, 64.

2. Comp. Anjur-dogs, andirons at the side of a hearth to support the logs, and with hooks for the spit to run on. I.W.[2]

3. A hinge. See Hinger, 3.

Nhb.[1] As *gen.* used on field or garden gates. w.Cor. I bought new hangers for my desk. Shall I put new hangers to this door? (M.A.C.)

4. *pl.* Fungi hanging to old logs. Nrf. (P.H.E.)

5. A hanging wood on the side of a hill. Cf. hang, *sb.* 1.

w.Yks. The Jay . . . occurs in some of the large falls, or hangers, in Airedale, Lucas *Stud. Nidderdale* (c. 1882) 143. Ken.[1], Sus.[12] Hmp. The naked part of the Hanger is now covered with thistles, White *Selborne* (1789) 301, ed. 1853; (J.R.W.); (H.E.); Hmp.[1] These hangers are woods on the sides of very steep hills. The trees and underwood hang, in some sort, instead of standing on it. Hence these places are called hangers, Cobbett *Rur. Rides*, 87. Dor. Barnes *Gl.* (1863).

HANGEREL, sb. Sc. Nhb. Cum. Wm. Yks. Also in forms hangarel(l Sc. (Jam.) Cum.[14]; hangerill n.Yks.; hangrell Gall. Wm. & Cum.[1] [(h)a·nərəl.] **1.** A stick in a butcher's shop, on which the carcase of a pig or other animal is suspended, a 'cambrel.' N.Cy.[1], Nhb.[1]

2. An implement of the stable, upon which bridles, halters, &c., are hung; a stick or post on which anything is hung.

Sc. Commonly a stout branch of a tree with a number of knots left on, *Gl. Sibb.* (Jam.) Gall. They [liggetts] are hung on what is termed a hangrell, Mactaggart *Encycl.* (1824) 316, ed. 1876.

3. *Fig.* A lazy, idle, good-for-nothing person; a hanger-on. Also used *attrib.*

Cum.[14] Wm. & Cum.[1] A hangrell gang Com' with a bensil owr the sea, 168. n.Yks.[2]

HANGIE, sb. Sc. Nhb. [ha·ŋi.] **1.** A hangman.

Sc. Gin hangie would gie them a dip through his trap door, Ford *Thistledown* (1891) 312. Frf. There he stood till hangie got Beneath his lug the ugly knot, Sands *Poems* (1833) 109. Lak. Vild hangy's taz, Ramsay *Poems* (1721) 36; Ilk ane saw auld Hangie's helter Owre his head aboot to fa', Nicholson *Kilwuddie* (ed. 1895) 76. Nhb. The hangey . . . that trims wor neckornowt suit in this life, Chater *Tyneside Alm.* (1869) 21.

2. The devil.

Cai.[1] Ayr. Hear me, auld Hangie, for a wee, An' let poor damned bodies be, Burns *Address Deil* (1785) st. 2.

3. A drift-net. See hang, 9. The use of the hangie or drift-net on the waters of the Tay, *Scottish Leader* (Mar. 11, 1889) 5.

HANGING, *ppl. adj.* and *sb.* Var. dial. uses in Sc. Irel. Eng. and Colon. Also written hangen War. Dor.[1]

1. *ppl. adj.* in *comp.* (1) Hanging-bout, an execution, hanging; (2) — coal, a common sort of coal; (3) — cover, a wood on the slope of a hill; (4) -fair, see (1); (5) — field, a field on a slope; (6) — gale, a payment of rent allowed to lie in arrear; see Gale, *sb.*[2]; (7) — gate, a bar hung across a small stream to prevent any one passing it; (8) — geranium, the geranium, *Saxifraga sarmentosa*; (9) -head, the upright part of a gate, to which the hinges are attached; (10) -house, a shed under a continuation of the roof of a house; (11) — level, an uninterrupted declivity; an inclined plane; (12) — market, see below; (13) -on, mining term; a place in the shaft where tubs are taken out and put in; (14) -post, see (9); (15) -side, the high side of a drift in a colliery, driven on the level of an inclined stratum; (16) -wall, an overhanging wall; the wall or side in a mine over the regular vein; (17) -wood, see (3).

(1) n.Yks.[2] (2) Stf.[1] (3) War. The hounds were 'run through a hanging cover,' *B'ham Dy. Gazette* (Feb. 18, 1899) *Hunting Notes.* (4) Som. W. & J. *Gl.* (1873). w.Som.[1] Jack and Liz be gwain to be married next Thuzday, 'cause there's gwain to be a hanging fair to Taunton thick morning, and they must lost a day's work, so they be gwain there fust, vor a bit of a spree. (5) e.Suf. (F.H.) (6) N.I.[1] On some estates it is customary to allow one gale of rent to lie always in arrear. This is called the hanging gale. Myo. They owed but six months' rent with the hanging gale, *Times* (Nov. 13, 1880). (7) Lak. Below the hanging gate on Barncluith burn, Patrick *Plants* (1831) 191. (8) Wil.[1] From the way in which it is usually suspended in a cottage window. (9) w.Som.[1] (10) Dor. Barnes *Gl.* (1863). (11) Nhp.[1], e.An.[1] Nrf., Sus. Holloway. (12) Lon. It was a hanging market that day—that is to say, things had been dear, and the costers couldn't pay the price for them, Mayhew *Lond. Labour* (1851) I. 64. (13) Nhb., Dur. Nicholson *Coal Tr. Gl.* (1888). (14) Wil.[1] Freq. heard, although 'har' is much more commonly used. w.Som.[1] Thick piece mid do vor a vallin post, but he id'n good 'nough vor a hangin-post. nw.Dev.[1] The back is hinged to the hangin'-poss by crooks an' eyes, and the head is usually fastened to the vallin'-poss by a hapse and stape. (15) Nhb. (G.C.G.) (16) nw.Der.[1], Nhp.[1] [Aus. What we thought was the 'hanging-wall' caved in, and showed us the true reef again, Vogan *Blk. Police* (1890) vii.] (17) Nhp.[1], War.[2], e.Suf. (F.H.)

2. Phr. (1) *hanging bone villain*, a term of abuse; (2) — *sort of way*, wavering between illness and health.

(1) w.Ir. Oh, the hangin' bone villian! Lover *Leg.* (1848) I. 199. (2) Chs.[1]

3. *sb. pl.* The hinges or apparatus on which a door, gate, &c., is made to swing.

w.Som.[1] The hook and eye or hook and twist are the common forms of gate hangings. '(You) can put wiren hangings to thick box, neef 'ee mind to.' nw.Dev.[1]

4. The sloping side of a hill; the steep wooded side of a hill. Cf. hanger, 5.

Nhp.[1] 'It lies on the hangings,' on the side of a hill. Brks.[1] E'll vind moor partridges on the hangin' yander 'n anywher. Hmp. (J.R.W.), Wil.[1] n.Wil. I see dree foxes up in th' hanging (E.H.G.). Dor. Barnes *Gl.* (1863); Dor.[1] My little zummer-leäze da stratch all down the hangen, 141.

5. A hillside field.

War. (J.R.W.) Wil. Slow *Gl.* (1892); Wil.[1] Som. Sweetman *Wincanton Gl.* (1885).

HANGLE, sb. Lan. Glo. Brks. Wil. Som. Also in forms angle Lan.; hangler Wil.[1] [a·ŋl, æ·ŋl.] **1.** The iron rack or pot-hook on which a kettle, &c., is suspended over the fire. Gen. in *pl.*

Glo. (J.S.F.S.) Brks. *Gl.* (1852); Brks.[1], Wil.[1] Som. Jennings *Obs. Dial. w.Eng.* (1825); W. & J. *Gl.* (1873); (W.F.R.); (F.A.A.) w.Som.[1] In farm-houses and places where wood only is burnt, a bar of iron is placed across the chimney, six or seven feet from the ground; from this are hung iron hooks so made as to lengthen or shorten at will, and on these are hung the various pots and kettles over the fire. These hooks are sometimes called hangles, or 'a pair o' angles,' but oftener 'chimbly crooks.'

2. A door-hinge.

Lan. The gate drooping from its angles, Brierley *Layrock* (1864) III. 36; In Saddleworth and its neighbourhood the word 'angle' is very commonly used to denote a door-hinge, *Manch. City News* (Feb. 29, 1896).

HANGMAN, sb. Der. Nhp. War. Shr. Som. In phr. *hangman's wages*, (1) thirteen pence halfpenny; (2) money paid beforehand for work.

(1) nw.Der.[1], Nhp.[1] War.[2] Rarely heard now. w.Som.[1] The tradition is that in the time of good King George, or 'Farmer George,' as he is still called, the hangman, himself a reprieved convict, received the clothes of the condemned and thirteen pence half-penny for each culprit. The price of a box of pills is still facetiously spoken of as hangman's wages. (2) Shr.[1]

HANGMENT, sb. n.Cy. Cum. Yks. Lan. Chs. Der. Not. War. Also Som. Also in forms engmond, engmont w.Yks.; hangman w.Yks.[2]; hangmet w.Yks.; hangmut e.Lan.[1]; hengment, hengmondt w.Yks. [(h)a·ŋment, e·ŋment, æ·ŋment.] **1.** A hanging, execution; entanglement.

n.Yks.[2] w.Som.[1] I thort I never should'n a-got droo they there brimmles, 'twas jish hangment's never you behold. They do zay how thick there fuller's a-let off, zo there 'ont be no hangment to Taun'on thease year.

2. The devil, deuce, used as an oath in var. phr., esp. *what the hangment.* Also in *pl.*

Cum. What the hangment is ta maapen aboot noo ? *Willy Wattle* (1870) 3; **Cum.**[14] **Yks.** The haangment tak that hangrick, FETHER- STON *T. Goorkrodger* (1870) 137. **n.Yks.** (I.W.); What the hangment is t'fellow gain to diu ? (W.H.) **e.Yks.**[1] Hangment tiv it, says Ah. **w.Yks.** I couldn't imagine whot the engmond wor t'matter wi' um, *Yksman.* (1880) 198; Nah then, hah leng are ye bahn ta keep me waiten ? Whot the hengmondt ! HARTLEY *Clock Alm.* (1874) 7 ; Whear the hengments hes teh been ? (Æ.B.); (S.P.U.); **w.Yks.**[12] ; **w.Yks.**[3] A woman who turned in her toes put her shoes, by mistake, on the wrong feet and exclaimed, ' Why what the hangman do I ail ? I used to twang, but now I shale.' **Lan.** What the hangment ails 'em ? CLEGG *Sketches* (1895) 7 ; **Lan.**[1], **n.Lan.**[1], **e.Lan.**[1] **War.**[3] What the hangment is that fellow doing?

3. Phr. (1) *to play the hangment*, (*a*) to be very much en- raged ; (*b*) to injure, play havoc or the mischief with ; (2) *shame and hangment*, an oath or exclamation.

(1, *a*) **N.Cy.**[1] **Cum.**[1] ' He'll play the hangment wid ye,' he will be very severe; **Cum.**[4] **n.Yks.** Yon fellow a'l play the hangment wi' me if a doant tack him some brass (W.H.). **w.Yks.** He varry oft, in his tantrums, plays the engmond wi' hizzen, *Yksman.* (July 1878) 52; Thare wor t'hengment ta play, *Pudsey Alm.* (1894) ; **w.Yks.**[1] He wor hotterin mad, an play'd t'hangment, ii. 304. **ne.Lan.** I mun know naa, lass, or there'll be th' hangments to play, MATHER *Idylls* (1895) 259. **nw.Der.**[1] (*b*) **e.Yks.**[1] This dbry weather's playin hangment wi tonnops [turnips]. **Chs.**[1] It's played the hangment with me. **Not.**[2] He played hangment (or the hangment) with it. (2) **Cum.**[3] What the sham' an hangment d'ye mean be that ! *Yan o' t' Elect*; **Cum.**[4]

HANGY, *adj.* Cum. Brks. Suf. **1.** Of soil : sticky, wet, clayey. Cf. clung, **5.**

Brks.[1] **e.An.**[1] ; **e.An.**[2] Clayey soil, when wet, is hangy. **e.Suf.** (F.H.)

2. Poorly, dull through incipient illness. **Cum.**[4] (s. v. Hingy).

HANGY-BANGY, *sb.* Nhb.[1] A big, lazy fellow ; a good-for-nothing.

HANK, *sb.*[1] and *v.* Var. dial. uses in Sc. Irel. and Eng. Also in forms **ank** Bdf. ; **henk** w.Yks. ; **hink** Ken.[13] ; **honk** m.Lan.[1] s.Lan. [h]**ank, enk.**] **1.** *sb.* A rope or coil ; a knot, loop. Also used *fig.*

Sc. Her hanks of raven hair, CUNNINGHAM *Sngs.* (1813) 28 ; I have cast a double hank about the round world since I last heard of a soft morning, SCOTT *St. Ronan* (1824) xv. **Ayr.** The broom- covered knowes Took a hank on this heart I ne'er can unlowse, AINSLIE *Land of Burns* (ed. 1892) 208. **N.I.**[1] **Cum.**[8] Though thy hair were hanks o' gowd, *Sng. Waukrife Minnie.* **ne.Yks.**[1], **m.Yks.**[1]

2. A skein or measure of cotton, thread, wool, &c. Also used *fig.*

Sc. It taks twa hanks o' thread, HISLOP *Anecdote* (1874) 259. **Abd.** I'm ganin' ower to the toon to buy a few hanks o' worset, MACDONALD *Sir Gibbie*, xxii. **Per.** Hanks o' thread, FORD *Harp* (1893) 210. **Ayr.** Richt or wrang ye maun leeze out the tangled hank for yoursel', JOHNSTON *Glenbuckie* (1889) 50. **Lnk.** Coft the yarn in hanks, WATSON *Poems* (1853) 85. **Gall.** At every 'hank' it [the chack reel] winds, it gives a ' chack ' or clack, MACTAGGART *Encycl.* (1824) 130, ed. 1876. **N.I.**[1] A measure of linen yarn. **Uls.** A ravelled hank, an intricate piece of business (M.B.-S.). **N.Cy.**[1] To make a ravelled hank, to put anything into confusion. **Nhb.** A ravelled hank is a tangled skein, and the word is *fig.* applied for a confused state (R.O.H.). **Dur.**[1], **Lakel.**[2] **Cum.**[1] **Cum.**[2] When the worsted hanks she wound, 180 ; **Cum.**[4] A skein of thread or yarn, composed of 12 cuts. **Wm.** Hod us this hank o' wursit (B.K.). **n.Yks.**[1] ; **n.Yks.**[2] A knot or clump of worsted consisting of so many skeins. ' They're boun te mak a cotter'd hank on't,' an entangled business of it. **e.Yks.** MARSHALL *Rur. Econ.* (1796). **m.Yks.**[1] Two or more skeins of cotton, silk, worsted, or thread of any kind. **w.Yks.** The standard hank of worsted is 560 yards in length (F.R.); **w.Yks.**[3] Thread, &c. in course of preparation, wound upon a large cylinder. A hank of wool or cotton is 840 yards, of worsted 560. Six hanks make one bunch in cotton and worsted, four in woollen ; **w.Yks.**[5], **n.Lan.**[1] **s.Lan.** BAMFORD *Dial.* (1854). **Chs.**[1] A term used in flax-dressing. **nw.Der.**[1], **Not.**[1] **Lin.** A hank of woollen yarn consists of seven lees, MARSHALL *Review* (1811) III. **n.Lin.**[1], **Glo.** (A.B.), **Glo.**[2], **Oxf.** (G.O.) **e.An.**[1] A small quantity of twine, yarn, &c., not rolled in a ball, but

doubled over in lengths, is called a hank. **Ken.** LEWIS *I. Tenet* (1736); **Ken.**[1]; **Ken.**[2] A hank of silk. **w.Som.**[1]

3. Phr. (1) *to be in a hank*, (2) *to get* or *have things in a hank*, to be in a state of perplexity or trouble ; to get one's circumstances involved ; (3) *to have, hold,* or *keep the hank in one's own hand*, to be master of the situation ; to hold one's own.

(1) **n.Yks.**[1] (2) **n.Yks.**[14] (3) **Sc.** Hangie aye keeps the hank in his ain hand, FORD *Thistledown* (1891) 312. **ne.Sc.** I believed that I had the hank o' circumstances fairly in my han', an' cud win' the thread just as I wished, GRANT *Kechleton*, 14. **Abd.** Which meeting enabled the goodwife to get ' the hank ' sufficiently in her ain hand, without the appearance, as she thought, of seizing it too openly, ALEXANDER *Ain Flk.* (1882) 173. **Ayr.** Keep your ain han' at your ain hank, Nor fash wi' fremmit matters, AINSLIE *Land of Burns* (ed. 1892) 92. **Uls.** 'To keep the hank in your own hand.' *Prov.* Do not abandon any advantage you possess, from custom of buyer and seller seizing hold of a hank, latter retaining it, or handing it over according to issue of bargain, *Uls. Jrn. Arch.* (1857) V. 106. **Cum.**[4] She had t'hank in her awn hand, FARRALL *Betty Wilson* (1886) 127.

4. A cluster, collection of things ; a gang, confederacy, assemblage.

Nhp.[1] They are all of a hank. **War.** (HALL.) **Som.** 'There's such a hank wi' em al' ' would be said where it was impossible to lay blame on the right person. Mark Beauchamp tells me that he has lived for 35 years ' in the hank o' houses' (W.F.R.).

5. Dealings with, connexion. Also in *pl.* in phr. *to have hanks with.* Used always with a *neg.*

War. (J.R.W.) **Oxf.**[1] Us be fren's now, but at one time, I öödn't aa no hank wi'n, *MS. add.* **Wil.** SLOW *Gl.* (1892) ; **Wil.**[1] I won't ha' no hank wi' un. **Dor.** He would never again have hanks with any young woman, except the girl he intended to marry (C.K.P.). **Som.** I never had noo hank in mathymaticks or astronomy, AGRIKLER *Rhymes* (1872) 55; W. & J. *Gl.* (1873). **w.Som.**[1] Her said how her wid'n ha no hanks way un. Also applied to animals *gen.* I have heard people warned, moreover, ' not to have no hanks ' with a certain horse, or with an undesir- able bargain. **Dev.** A coachman, whose horse had run away, said to his master afterwards, ' I'll have no more hank with 'im,' *Reports Provinc.* (1897). **nw.Dev.**[1]

6. A loop for fastening a door or gate.

n.Cy. GROSE (1790). **Nhb.** (R.O.H.) **n.Yks.**[1] ; **n.Yks.**[2] A rope- loop for fastening a gate to the post, in lieu of a latch or a hook; **n.Yks.**[4] **e.Yks.** MARSHALL *Rur. Econ.* (1788). **Nhp.**[1], **War.**[2], **e.An.**[1], **Suf.**[1], **e.Suf.** (F.H.)

7. Hold, influence, esp. in phr. *to have a hank over one,* to have an advantage over one.

Sc. ' You abuse your advantages, madam,' he said, ' and act as foolishly in doing so, as I did in affording you such a hank over me,' SCOTT *Redg.* (1824) xix. **n.Yks.**[1] To have one in hank. To have, or have placed, a person in such circumstances that he is in a state of perplexity, trouble, or anxiety ; or that he is unable to extricate himself. **Hrf.**[2] And a couldna get a hank on him. **Glo.**[1] If I'd a done that, I should have given him a hank over me. **Ken.**[1] We say a man has a hank on another ; or, he has him entangled in a skein or string ; **Ken.**[2], **Hmp.** (J.R.W.) **Som.** Mothers will say that the other boys have such a hank upon their own particular boys (W.F.R.). **Dev.**[1] A wid trounce me if a cou'd ha' any hank upon me, 43.

8. Phr. (1) *to break the hank of a thing*, to overcome the principal difficulty ; (2) *to keep a good hank upon your horse*, to have a good hold of the reins.

(1) **Bdf.** ' To break the ank ' or ' hank ' of a thing has the same meaning as ' to break the neck ' of it. It may denote properly to break the bondage which a task imposes,—the hold which it has upon one (J.W.B.). (2) **N.Cy.**[1]

9. A habit, custom, practice.

N.Cy.[1], **Nhb.**[1] **Cum.** (H.W.) ; **Cum.**[1] He hes a hank o' gangan out at neets ; **Cum.**[4] **w.Yks.**[1] Shoe's gitten a sad hank o' runnin out at neets.

10. A fall or ' chip ' in wrestling.

Lakel.[2] **Cum.**[4] C— tried the click and turned it into the hank. **11.** A hook, something to hang a thing upon ; a handle.

w.Yks. Aw'll put this parkin' i' this pot up'o t'henk, *Yksman. Comic Ann.* (1880) 11. **Som.** (HALL.)

12. *v.* To make up into coils or skeins.

Sh.I. He found the cow's tethers hanging hanked, BURGESS *Tang* (1898) 157; He bankit his tail ower his elbik, *ib. Rasmie*

(1890) 17. **N.Cy.**[1], **Cum.**[4], **n.Yks.**[2] **w.Yks.**[3] 'Hank,' or 'skein-thread,' so called because looped together in certain lengths, or 'hanked' together. 'Hank us that,' loop me that.

Hence **Hanking**, *vbl. sb.* the process of putting yarn or worsted into 'hanks' or skeins.

w.Yks. (J.M.); BANKS *Whfld. Wds.* (1865).

13. To fasten, secure, tie up; to fasten with a loop. Also used *fig.*

Sc. A man is said to be hankit, when he has so engaged himself to a woman, that he cannot recede without breach of faith, and loss of character (JAM.). **Lth.** We both jumped from the trap, hanked the nag to the nearest tree, LUMSDEN *Sheep-head* (1892) 204. **Edb.** A bonny flae . . . Had a' the night been hankit Fast by the left foot muckle tae, FORBES *Poems* (1812) 98. **Nhb.** Hank them chines on (R.O.H.). **Dur.**[1], **Lakel.**[1], **Cum.**[14] **Wm.** Ther chaps al hank thersells onta tha, *Spec. Dial.* (1885) pt. iii. 16. **n.Yks.**[1] To fasten or 'hang' a horse: as, by passing his bridle, or halter, over a gate, a hook, or what not; **n.Yks.**[2] To tie up with a bandage; **n.Yks.**[3][4] **ne.Yks.**[1] To hank a band, i. e. fasten or secure a band. **e.Yks.** THOMPSON *Hist. Welton* (1869) 170. **w.Yks.**[1], Der.[2], **nw.Der.**[1] **n.Lin.** Then owd woman teks clock-waaight, an' cat-gut band, . . an' hanks it roond tooth, PEACOCK *Tales* (1886) 98. **s.Wor.** To overcast [in sewing] (H.K.). **Nrf.** Hank up the gate, COZENS-HARDY *Broad Nrf.* (1893) 3. **e.Suf.** Hank up, to fasten a door or gate with a hook (F.H.).

14. To tie anything so tight, as to leave the impression of the cord; to gall with a rope or cord; to hold a horse in tight, check him by drawing bridle.

Sc. The neck is said to be hankit when a necklace is tied too strait (JAM.). **n.Yks.**[1]

15. To walk arm in arm with; to link arms.

Nhb. Hank your airm through mine (R.O.H.).

Hence **Hanking-arms**, *vbl. sb.* the act of walking arm in arm.

Lan. They had risen to the dignity of 'hankin'-arms,' although they had not quite mastered the difficulty of keeping in step with each other, ALMOND *Watercresses*, 28.

16. To associate with; to act or agree with; to keep company with.

w.Yks. A man is hanked with another in an evil undertaking, *Leeds Merc. Suppl.* (June 6, 1896); **w.Yks.**[2] Au wonder haa he could hank wi' sich folk. **Som.** There was one Abraham Urch, and William did use to hanky wi' he (W.F.R.). **Dev.** If anything good in my heart had a place I could hank it wi' thee and thy workin's could trace, PULMAN *Sketches* (1842) 71, ed. 1871.

17. Wrestling term: see below.

Cum. (H.W.); **Cum.**[4] When wrestling the left leg is put forward and between the legs of the opponent, thus catching his right. At the same time the body is thrown back, and the opponent turns under. This is considered to be a beaten man's 'chip,' and not a good one, and to avoid it the 'click' or 'back-heel' is employed. My informant 'liked weel to be hankt, he has sic a lang leg, and generally fellt them 'at triet it.' 'J— was hanked, S— trying the inside click.'

18. To catch or hang anything on to a hook.

Edb. Her coats upon a lang nail hanket, *Tint Quey* (1796) 20. **Wm.** Hank t'kettle on t'creuk (B.K.). **w.Yks.**[2] Two bow-legged knife-grinders met on a footpath. One of them said to the other, 'Nah, moind, owd lad, or we shall hank.' He meant that his leg might, unless he took care, be hooked or fastened to his friend's leg. His foot hankt in a three-legged stool, *Takin' th' New Year in* (1888) 14. **m.Lan.**[1] To honk yo'r cooat sleeve on a nail. **s.Lan.** Honk it on, BAMFORD *Dial.* (1854). **Not.**[1]

19. To long for, desire earnestly. Cf. **hanker**, *v.* 5.

Cum. (W.K.), **Chs.**[3] **Lin.** In agro Linc. usurpatur pro inclinatione et propensione animi, SKINNER (1671). **w.Som.**[1] He do hank arter her sure-lie!

[1. As he [Laocoon] etlis thair hankis to have rent, DOUGLAS *Eneados* (1513), ed. 1874, II. 80. ON. *hönk* (gen. *hankar*), a hank, coil, skein (VIGFUSSON). 11. Da. *hank*, handle of a basket, ear of a pot. 13. Thair navy can thai ankir fast and hank, DOUGLAS *Eneados*, III. 88.]

HANK, *sb.*[2] Sc. Also in form **haank**, **haanka** Sh.I.

1. The leeside of a boat.

Sh.I. I see da black lump o' da boat noo. Shö's juist baerin' apo' wir haank yonder, *Sh. News* (Feb. 4, 1899); He laid da peerie taft across da haanks o' da foreeven, an' set him [it] up, *ib.* (June 3, 1899); 'Takkin' her up in hank,' pulling strongly on the leeside to lie nearer the line (J.L.).

2. *Comp.* **Hank-oarsman**, the rower who sits near the helmsman. Bnff.[1]

HANKER, *v.* and *sb.*[1] Sc. Nhb. Cum. Wm. Yks. Lan. Chs. Der. War. Wor. Oxf. Brks. Ess. Dor. Also in form onker se.Wor.[1] [h]a'ŋkə(r, æ'ŋkə(r).] 1. *v.* To entangle in, become fastened on.

Cum.[4] When a rope is dragged along the ground, it may be hankered round a stone or stake. If a girl was taking linen off the hedge where it had been put to dry and it got fixed to the thorns she would say it was hankered.

2. Phr. *hanker the heel*, wrestling term: to trip up one's antagonist by planting one's foot behind his. **Cum.**[4] See Back-heel.

3. To loiter, linger about; to dally, tarry, stop.

Sc. Bonny, bonny stanes come pirlin' [moving], And hanker juist when they reach the tee, *R. Caled. Curling Club Ann.* (1887–88) 377. **Ayr.** We know they would not stay nor hanker Till it was quite overthrown, LAING *Poems* (1894) 46. **Edb.** He sees her aft, an' winna bide away, But hankers i' my house the li'e-lang day, LEARMONT *Poems* (1791) 296. **Wm.** A hankert aboot an dud, an eftre a bit whaa sud a see bet Tommy his varra sell, *Spec. Dial.* (1865) 17. **w.Yks.** I hanker abaght t'public hoose, *Leeds Herald* (Jan. 1862). **Lan.** THORNBER *Hist. Blackpool* (1837) 108. **Oxf.** (G.O.) **Brks.** I used to hanker round the kitchen, or still room, HUGHES *Scour. White Horse* (1858) viii.

4. To hesitate, ponder, esp. to hesitate in speaking.

Rnf. Willie hankered awee this morning, I think, but there is nae wonner, for he got unco near the throne whiles, GILMOUR *Pen Flk.* (1873) 46. **Ayr.** He hums and he hankers, BURNS *What can a Young Lassie do*, st. 2; Ne'er hanker lang, when tempted sair, WHITE *Jottings* (1879) 148. **Lnk.** Ilka day she hankered owre't, I bothered her the mair, ORR *Laigh Flichts* (1882) 35. **Nhb.** He kinda hankert i' the middle o'hees speech (R.O.H.); **Nhb.**[1]

5. To desire, covet, long for. Also with *after.*

e.Sc. Her heart hankers after the pots, SETOUN *Sunshine* (1895) 276. **Cum.** Auld Skiddaw lang hed hanker't sair Itsel to be t'Fell king, RICHARDSON *Talk* (1876) and S. 13; Thoo knows it's thee he hankers efter, GWORDIE GREENUP *Yance a Year* (1873) 6; **Cum.**[4] Yks. (J.W.) **Lan.** Ye won't hanker after a fire again, GASKELL *M. Barton* (1848) v. **Chs.**[1] Der. Art tha hankerin after a trade? WARD *David Grieve* (1892) I. iv. **War.** There's many another man 'ud hanker more than he does, GEO. ELIOT *S. Marner* (1861) 133. **se.Wor.**[1] **Nrf.** John is a kind a' hankering arter Mary (W.W.S.).

Hence (1) **Hankering**, (*a*) *sb.* a strong desire, a longing; (*b*) *ppl. adj.* longing, desirous; (2) **Hankersome**, *adj.* uneasy, discontented, envious.

(1, *a*) **Sc.** Hankering and hinging on is a poor trade, RAMSAY *Prov.* (1737). **Cum.**[1] He still hez a hankeran' for her. **Yks.** (J.W.) **Chs.**[1] An yo getten a sope o' red port wine as yo'd give my mother; oo's been ta'en bad in her bowels, and oo has sitch a hankerin for a sope o' red port wine. **Brks.** *Gl.* (1852); **Brks.**[1] **Ess.** Oathers had A hank'rin' arter Mary, CLARK *J. Noakes* (1839) st. 29. (*b*) **Dor.** In a hankering tone, HARDY *Trumpet-Major* (1880) iii. (2) **Wm.** Yan mae be hankersem an bad anuff, *Spec. Dial.* (1880) pt. ii. 7.

6. *sb.* Phr. *there's the hanker*, there's the rub. **Cum.**[4]

7. Inclination, longing, desire.

Lan. There's hanker i' every condition, HARLAND *Lyrics* (1866) 296. **Dor.** She has not shown a genuine hanker for anybody yet, HARDY *Laodicean* (ed. 1896) bk. iii. 273.

8. Hesitation, doubt, regret.

Rnf. As one who laughs at social wit, And laughs without a hanker, McGILVRAY *Poems* (ed. 1862) 93.

HANKER, *sb.*[2] Yks. An open clasp or buckle. See Anchor, *sb.* **e.Yks.** Still in use, though not usual (R.S.). **m.Yks.**[1] [Cp. ON. *hanki*, the hoop or clasp of a chest.]

HANKIE, *sb.* Dmf. (JAM.) A bucket narrower at the top than the bottom, with an iron handle, used in carrying water.

HANKLE, *v.* and *sb.*[1] Sc. Nhb. Dur. Cum. Wm. Yks. Lan. Lin. Also written **hanckle** n.Cy. Dur.[1]; and in forms **ankel** n.Yks.; **ankle** e.Yks.[1] **w.Yks.**; **enkle** w.Yks.; **hangall** Rnf.; **henkl** S. & Ork.[1]; **henkle** n.Yks.[4] **w.Yks.**[5] [h)a'ŋkl, h)e'ŋkl.] 1. *v.* To entangle, twist together. Also used *fig.*

n.Cy. GROSE (1790). **Nhb.**[1], **Dur.**[1], **Cum.**[14] **Wm.** His booat in her crin'lin' did hankle, BLEZARD *Sngs.* (1868) 17. **n.Yks.** He gat hankled amang t'briers (I.W.); n.Yks.¹; n.Yks.⁴ Ah've gitten t'kite sadly hankled. ne.Yks.¹ It's a dree job; they're all seea hankled tigither. e.Yks.¹, m.Yks.¹ w.Yks. WILLAN *List Wds.* (1811); (R.H.H.); w.Yks.¹; w.Yks.⁵ 'Luke what that barn's done!—goan an' lowsed t'skein off o' t'chairs an' henkled it awal on a heap !' 'Hankled' is very rarely heard; it is always 'henkled.' Lan. You may get hankled among the bushes, BRIGGS *Remains* (1825) 48; Lan.¹ n.Lan. (C.W.D.); Fishing-nets are said to be ankled when they have become twisted together (W.H.H.); n.Lan.¹ n.Lin. All his munny as he should ha' gotten's hankled up wi' th' farm, PEACOCK *Tales* (1890) and S. 50; n.Lin.¹

Hence **Hankled**, *ppl. adj.* twisted, entangled. Nhb.¹, m.Yks.¹

2. *Fig.* To entangle in some pursuit or proceeding; to associate with, be connected with; to inveigle, entice, decoy. *Gen.* with *in* or *on.*

Ruf. We are so far involved and hangalled . . . that I am at a loss what to wish were done, WODROW *Corresp.* (ed. 1842) I. 243. s.Dur. 'He's gitten hankled in.' An expression often used in connexion with courtship, where the connexion is not considered desirable (J.E.D.). Wm. He gat hankled on wi' a lot at nivver did neea dow an' nivver will (B.K.); Thae trie o mannars a waes to tice fooak an git em hankalt in ta treeat em, *Spec. Dial.* (1885) pt. iii. 26. n.Yks. He hankled on wiv a woman (I.W.) ; Him as hankled him on! ATKINSON *Last* (1870) xxvi; n.Yks.¹ They hankled him on intiv t'matter ; n.Yks.² ' They hankled him on,' drew him in to be one of their set; n.Yks.⁴ Ah weean't be hankied on wi' neea sike leyke carryings on. ne.Yks.¹ Ah is vexed at oor Tom's gitten hankled in wi sike a rafflin lot. e.Yks.¹ Ah's varry sorry she's getten hankled wi sike a slither-pooak as him. w.Yks. He's getten ankled on wi' a low lot (S.K.C.); If tha gets henkled on with that low lot, thall soon loss both credit and character (M.N.). n.Lin.¹ He's a honest chap his sen, bud he's gotten hankled in wi' a strannge lot o' rogues. sw.Lin.¹ He has got so hankled amongst them.

Hence **Hankled**, *pp.*, *fig.* habituated, accustomed to. n.Yks.²

3. To wind up a fishing-line, rope, &c., into a coil; to 'work' in hemp.

Sc. To fasten by tight tying (JAM.); Wha hankle the hemp sae fine, WADDELL *Isaiah* (1879) xix. 19. Sh.I. I hankl'd up Staarna's teddir an' hang him [it] ower da kneebi o' da klibber, *Sh. News* (Aug. 13, 1898); Shū hankl'd aff a lock o' wirsit aff o' a clue at wis lyin' in her lap, *ib.* (July 23) ; S. & Ork.¹

4. To greatly desire; to 'hanker' after. n.Yks.⁴

Hence **Hankling**, (1) *vbl. sb.* a hankering, craving after ; (2) *ppl. adj.* desirous of, having a craving or desire for.

(1) Cum.² n.Yks.⁴ Ah awlus hed a hankling foor Tom's meer. Neea, wa didn't bargain, bud Ah've a gert hankling foor't. e.Yks.¹ (2) n.Yks.²

5. To loiter, linger, wait about. Cf. **hanker,** *v.* 3.

Lan. So tha'st no cageon ston' hanklin' theere, HARLAND *Lyrics* (1866) 137; A young man seeking the favour of a young woman with whom he is in love, goes hanklin about her house on all possible occasions (S.W.).

6. *sb.* A tangle, twist.

Lakel.² A hank o' wusset 'll o' gang intul a hankle when ye're windin' it. Wm. Hod on ! Thoos garn ta hev mi threed o in a hankle (B.K.).

HANKLE, *sb.²* Cai.¹ The ancle.

[*Hec cavilla,* a hankyl, *Pict. Voc.* (c. 1475) in Wright's *Voc.* (1884) 751. Cp. the obs. Sc. *hanckleth,* an ancle. Thair cotes war syd evin to the hanckleth, DALRYMPLE *Leslie's Hist. Scotl.* (1596) I. 94. See **Ancliff.**]

HANKLE, see **Hancle.**

HANKTELO, *sb.* *Obs.* s.Cy. Slang. [Not known to our correspondents.] A silly fellow. (HALL.)

[Hanktelo, a silly fellow, a meer codshead, B. E. *Dict. Cant. Crew* (1690) (FARMER).]

HANKY-PANKY, *sb.* and *v.* Yks. Lan. Stf. Lin. Hrf. Som. Slang. Also in forms **anky-pranky** Stf.²; **henky-penky** Lan.¹ **1.** *sb.* Trickery, underhand dealing, shuffling. Also used *attrib.*

w.Yks. An if aw catch him onny hanky panky tricks wi' me aw'll repooart him, HARTLEY *Seets Yks. and Lan.* (1895) iii; w.Yks.² He's full of his hanky-panky tricks! Lan.¹ Now mi lad— none o' thi henky-penky here; stand up fair. Stf.² Let's 'ave none o' yer anky-prankies here. Th' lad's good at th' bottom, but 'e's such a anky-pranky sort of a chap. s.Stf. If you try to come any hankypanky dodge with me, MURRAY *Rainbow Gold* (1886)

262. n.Lin.¹ Noo goä stright, lets hev noä hanky-panky-wark this time. Hrf.² None of your hanky-panky. w.Som.¹ I told'n he was a vrong directed wi me; I zeed droo his hanky-panky in a minute. Slang. Hanky-panky, legerdemain, whence trickery, any manner of double-dealing or intrigue, FARMER.

2. *v.* To humbug, cheat, trick ; to be up to tricks.

Stf.² I gien th' lad sack at last, fur 'e was anky-prankying a' the dee thro.

Hence **Hanky-pankying,** *vbl. sb.* humbugging, cheating, tricking.

Lan. No hanky-pankyin' wi'out belungin' to us, BRIERLEY *Irh-dale* (1868) 71.

HANNEL, *sb.* Lim. A blow given to the head of one pegging-top by the spike of another. SIMMONS *Gl.* (1890).

HANNEL, HANNI(E, see **Handle, Handy,** *sb.¹²*

HANNIEL, *sb.* and *v.* Sc. Nhb. Cum. Wm. Yks. Lan. Also written **haniel** Sc. (JAM.) Slk. Nhb.; **hanyel** Sc. (JAM.); **hanziel** Bch.; and in forms **haanyal** Cai.¹; **hunniel** n.Cy. w.Yks. ne.Lan.¹; **hynail** Edb. [h]a'niəl, h]a'njl.] **1.** *sb.* A greedy dog ; a covetous, greedy person. Slk. (JAM.) n.Cy. GROSE (1790). w.Yks. HUTTON *Tour to Caves* (1781). ne.Lan.¹

2. A long, hungry-looking fellow.

Cum. Thoo hofe-starv't leuckan hanniel thoo, SARGISSON *Joe Scoap* (1881) 209; We'd hay-cruiks, and hen-tails, and hanniels, ANDERSON *Ballads* (1805) 170, ed. 1808; Shem o' them! thur peer country hanniels, That slink into Carel to feeght, *ib.* 47, ed. 1840; Cum.¹

3. A lout ; a lazy, awkward, good-for-nothing fellow; a worthless, mischievous person ; a *gen.* term of abuse.

Cai.¹ Edb. Tam Pucker's sic anither hynail ; And vends about diurnal scandal, LEARMONT *Poems* (1791) 66. Slk. Sae little kend the haniel about fencing that . . . he held up his sword-arm to save his head, HOGG *Tales* (1838) 7, ed. 1866. Rxb. A lazy haniel (JAM.) n.Cy. (J.L.) (1783). Nhb. Ah'll tie yer legs ye haniel, ye, if ye diven't larn to behave, CLARE *Rise of River* (1897) 51; ' Ye greet hanniel, ye, what are ye dein' here!' Spoken to a lazy idler (R.O.H.); Nhb.¹ Cum.⁴ A waggish man, to be looked down on, but with deference. A girt lang hanniel. Wm. (J.H.)

4. *Comb.* **Haniel slyp,** an uncouthly-dressed person; an ugly fellow.

Bch. (JAM.); In came sik a rangel o' gentles an' a liethry o' hanziel slyps at their tail, FORBES *Jrn.* (1742) 17.

5. *v.* To have a jaded appearance from extreme fatigue.

Lnk. To gang hanyellin, to walk with the appearance of slovenliness and fatigue (JAM.).

HANNIER, *sb.* *Obs.* Yks. A cross, teasing person. w.Yks. WATSON *Hist. Hlfx.* (1775) 539; *Leeds Merc. Suppl.* (Mar. 1, 1884) 8 ; w.Yks.⁴

HANNIES, *sb. pl.* Sc. Oatcakes.

Edb. May ye'r board be ay weel said'd Wi' Adie hannies, FORBES *Poems* (1812) 88 ; ' Oat-cakes,' called so from a baker of that name in Dalkeith, famed for baking them, *ib. note.*

HANNIWING, *sb.* Sc. A term of contempt.

Frf. But ha! ye hanniwings, look there! SANDS *Poems* (1833) 88.

HANNY, *v.* Lan. ? *Obs.* To dispute, argue.

He couldn't allow us to stond hannyin theere, un obstructin th' passage, STATON *B. Shuttle,* 70 ; A friend writes that 'hannying and yinnying ' formerly meant ' harring and jarring' in an alehouse in argument or dispute, but it is not known to me (S.W.).

HANOVER, *sb.* Lin. Suf. Used in exclamations or mild oaths; see below. Cf. **Halifax, Hull,** &c.

s.Lin. ' Go to Hanover.' ' What the Hanover do I care about it ' (T.H.R.). e.Suf. ' Go to Hanover and hoe turnips.' Said to date from the time of the Georges, who were very unpopular in the east, if not elsewhere. Still in popular use (F.H.).

HANS, *sb.* *Obs.* Sc. Yks. Cant. In phr. *Hans in Kelder,* an unborn child ; a toast formerly drunk to the health of the expected infant.

Per. Syne pauky Steen drank to the bride, Come, lass, your hans on kelder, NICOL *Poems* (1766) 49. n.Yks. An old lady, long dead, whose childhood was passed in Whitby, told me that she remembered at dessert sometimes this toast being drunk. . . She found from Yorkshire friends that it was a custom to gather a knot of very intimate friends together, for a take-leave party, at a house where hospitalities would necessarily be suspended till the christening day, *N. & Q.* (1868) 4th S. i. 181; n.Yks.² Cant. Hans-ein-kelder, Jack in the box, the child in the womb, or a health to it, B.E. *Dict. Cant. Crew* (1690) (FARMER).

[Du. *Hans in Kelder*, lit. Jack in cellar, an unborn child; cp. the Swabian toast, *Hänschen im Keller soll leben*, ' dies sagt man bei dem Gesundheit-trinken auf eine schwangere Frau ' (BIRLINGER); EFris. *hänsken in de keller* (KOOLMAN); Bremen dial. *hänsken im keller* (*Wtb.*).]

HANSE, HANSEL(L, see **Hance, Handsel.**

HANSEL, *sb.* Hmp. [æ·nsl.] The handle of a flail.
An implement consisting of two sticks loosely joined together; one, the hansel, held in the hand, and the other joined to it, the zwingel, descending with a dull thud upon the wheat-ears, GRAY *Heart of Storm* (1891) II. 175.

HANSER, HANT, see **Heronsew, Haunt.**

HANTERIN, *sb.* Sc. Written **hantrin** e.Lth. A moment, short space of time. Also used *attrib.* See **Aunterin.**
Cai.¹ I'll be at yer han' in a hanterin. Boid [wait] ye a hanterin. e.Lth. At hantrin, north, south, or wast—At hantrin times grow dull an' dour, MUCKLEBACKIT *Rhymes* (1885) 9a.

HANTIC(K, see **Antic.**

HANTINGS, *sb. pl.* n.Cy. (HALL.) Dev.¹ The handles which fix on to the snead of a scythe.

HANTLE, *sb.* Sc. Irel. and n. counties to War. Wor. Shr. Also written **hantel** Sc. Cum.⁴; and in forms **antel** n.Stf.; **antle** n.Lin.¹; **handtle** Chs.⁹⁸; **hontle** w.Yks.² Lan.¹ Chs.¹ s.Stf. nw.Der.¹; **ontle** se.Wor.¹ [h]a·ntl, o·ntl.]
1. A handful.
Cum.⁴, Lakel.² n.Yks. A hantle o' morr is mah weel-beluvved unto me, ROBINSON *Whitby Sng. Sol.* (1860) i. 13. w.Yks.² Lan. A hontle o' wot corks feel intot, TIM BOBBIN *View Dial.* (1740) 25; Lan.¹, Chs.¹²⁸ s.Chs.¹ Dhi sen ey mai·z ŭ aan·tl ŭ mŭn·i ev·ri faer-dee [They sen hey mays a hantle o' money every fair-dee]. n.Stf. (A.P.) s.Stf. Gie us a hontle o parsley, PINNOCK *Blk. Cy. Ann.* (1895). Der.², nw.Der.¹, Lei.¹ Nhp.¹ It is customary to say, ' a good hantle,' whenever the quantity exceeds a common handful; Nhp.², War.², se.Wor.¹ Shr.¹ I'll scaud a 'antle o' 'ops an' bind it to the mar's leg—it'll bring the swellin' down.
2. *Fig.* A tussle, hand to hand fight; a scuffle; as much as one can manage.
s.Stf. Yo'fl find yo'n got a hontle wi' him when he's growed up, PINNOCK *Blk. Cy. Ann.* (1895). Der. You'd a sore hantle wi' him bytimes an all tales be true, VERNEY *Stone Edge* (1868) xviii. Lei.¹ ' Ah cain't tell ye what a hantle ah hed wi' him : ' said a woman of a violent old man, disordered in mind. Nhp.², War.²
3. A large quantity or amount; a great deal. Freq. used in *pl.* Also used *attrib.*
Sc. Ye'll be a hantle better by it, STEVENSON *Catriona* (1893) xiv; There's a hantle bogles about it, SCOTT *Guy M.* (1815) i. Sh.I. A bed, ta luck daecent, needs a hantle o' attention, CLARK *Gleams* (1898) 19. Bnff. Hantels o' folk dinna get that, GORDON *Chron. Keith* (1880) 321. ne.Sc. He didna weel understand hantles o' oor words, GRANT *Kechleton*, 97. e.Sc. Man, ye're a hantle waur yoursel', SETOUN *Sunshine* (1895) 226. Bch. He makes a hantle rout an' din, But brings but little woo', FORBES *Ulysses* (1785) 35. nw.Abd. A hantle widna min' the leyk o' his [us], *Goodwife* (1867) st. 43. Kcd. Forks an' futtles were to hantles Leems nae handlet ilka day, GRANT *Lays* (1884) 72. Frf. I would a hantle rather waur my money on Elspeth, BARRIE *Tommy* (1896) 223. Per. That says a hantle About a licht heart in a sorrow-proof mantle, STEWART *Character* (1857) 71. Fif. I'm gaun back to't a hantle sicht puirer than I left it, MELDRUM *Margrédel* (1894) 231. e.Fif. She had a mind o' her ain aboot a hantle o' things, LATTO *Tam Bodkin* (1864) viii. Dmb. If I hadna better reasons a hantle to gar me steer my feathers, CROSS *Disruption* (1844) ii. Ayr. A hantle o' ither courtly glammer that's no worth a repetition, GALT *Provost* (1822) vii; (J.M.) Lnk. Hantles wba tipple do miscarry, WATT *Poems* (1827) 51. e.Lth. We'll be a hantle better off nor them, HUNTER *J. Inwick* (1895) 172. Edb. A hantle graces roun' her lip Sat sweet as dew on lily's dreep, LEARMONT *Poems* (1791) 27. Slk. A hantle bigger wi' nothing ye'll say the nicht, CHR. NORTH *Noctes* (ed. 1856) III. 35. Rxb. Mischanters I hae met a hantle, A. SCOTT *Poems* (ed. 1808) 46. Gall. Possest wi' a hantle o' jaw, LAUDERDALE *Poems* (1796) 74. Kcb. I've a weel-stockit hame o' my ain, Wi' horses an' kye, an' a hantle o' siller, ARMSTRONG *Ingleside* (1890) 150. Ir. The hantle of money them dhrainin' works come to is untould, BARLOW *Kerrigan* (1894) 113. N.Cy.¹ Nhb. Aa've getten a hantle o' caud. Fishermen's creels are aye a hantle bigger wi' thinkin o' them (R.O.H.); Nhb.¹ Cum. Still ha'e a hantel left yet, ANDERSON *Ballads* (1805) 94, ed. 1815; Cum.² A hantle o' ye hae turn't oot to be deuks, 181; Cum.⁴ n.Yks.¹; n.Yks.² A hantle o' money. m.Yks.¹

Hence **Antling,** *sb.* with *neg.* not any amount (of knowledge), no inkling.
Lin. Rare (E.P.). n.Lin.¹ I ha'nt noā antlin' wheāre he is noo, bud he did tell me his wife ewsed him that bad he should slot off to 'Merikay.

[1. *Hand + -tle* (suff.); this is a common suff. in the Chs. and Shr. dials.; cp. **apperntle.** It is prob. an equiv. of *-ful*; see s.Chs.¹ (gram. 57) and Shr.¹ (gram. xliii).]

HANTRIN, see **Hanterin.**

HANTS, *adj.* Wil. Used in *comb.* with sheep and horses; see below.
They were called with them hants sheep; they were a sort of sheep that never shelled their teeth, but always had their lambs-teeth without shedding them, and thrusting out two broader in their room every year. . . There were such a sort of horses called hants horses, that always shewed themselves to be six years old, LISLE *Husbandry* (1757) 360, 361; Wil.¹

HANTY, *adj. Obs.* Sc. Also in form **haunty** Abd.
1. Convenient, handy.
Abd. SHIRREFS *Poems* (1890) *Gl.* Rnf. Thou wast the hantiest biel, in truth, That e'er I saw, PICKEN *Poems* (1788) 180 (JAM.). Lnk. RAMSAY *Gentle Shep.* (1725) *Gl.*, Scenary ed.
2. Not troublesome, often applied to a beast.
Sc. (JAM.) Rnf. ' Hanty,' manageable with ease, PICKEN *Poems* (1788) *Gl.*
3. Handsome.
Sc. Lizie they think far mair banty, GALLOWAY *Poems* (1788) 214 (JAM.). Abd. SHIRREFS *Poems* (1890) *Gl.* Lnk. RAMSAY *Gentle Shep.* (1725) *Gl.*, Scenary ed.

HANVAYGE, *v.* Sh.I. To look or wait about for.
We hanvayged aboot fir maistlins an ooer, bit never saw da bow again, SPENCE *Flk-Lore* (1899) 248.

HANYADU, *int.* Sh.I. A call to a bird to come and pick up food thrown to it from a boat. S. & Ork.¹

HANYEL, HAOLEGHEY, see **Hanniel, Holghe.**

HAP, *v.*¹, *sb.*¹ and *adv.* Var. dial. uses in Sc. Irel. and Eng. [(h)ap, æp.] **1.** *v.* To happen, chance, befall.
Abd. May sic like hap to Uncle Tam, ANDERSON *Rhymes* (1867) 62. Frf. Wyle well for gin ye hap to rue, What can be worse ? MORISON *Poems* (1790) 81. Fif. If unaware you hap to lose your body's well-adjusted poise, TENNANT *Anster* (1812) 71, ed. 1871. Rnf. Hap what micht, 'Twad aiblins mak' a fen', YOUNG *Pictures* (1865) 10. Ayr. Erch lest the gentle fouk should hap To hear or see, FISHER *Poems* (1790) 68. Lnk. They . . . spak' o' deaths that late had been, An' some wad maybe hap bedeen, MURDOCH *Doric Lyre* (1873) 9. Edb. How haps it, say, that mealy bakers . . . Shou'd a' get leave? FERGUSSON *Poems* (1773) 174, ed. 1785. Nhb.¹ Aa'll be there o' Monday as it haps. n.Yks.¹ Hap what hap may; n.Yks.⁴ If nowt s'u'd hap ti stop ma, Ah s' cum. e.Yks.¹ Happen, *pp.* of to hap. n.Lin.¹ If it haps to raain I shan't goā. Ken. How haps you don't know ! (G.B.) ; Ken.¹ Som. Not knowing anything at all o' what had happed, RAYMOND *Men o' Mendip* (1898) vii. w.Som.¹ Cor. It canna be ondone what ha' happ'd, BARING-GOULD *Curgenven* (1893) xxi.
2. With *on* or *upon*: to come upon by chance, light on; to meet with.
e.Yks. Black Morris . . . managed to hap on Lucy Blyth, WRAY *Nestleton* (1876) 54. Cha.¹ If yo're goin to th' fair may be yo'n hap on our Jim, for he's gone an hour sin. Sur. N. & Q. (1874) 5th S. i. 517; Sur.¹ Maybe you'll hap upon him in the wood. w.Som.¹ By good luck I hap 'pon the very man. Very common. Cor. I happed once on a manuscript account book of a white witch or charmer, QUILLER-COUCH *Hist. Polperro* (1871) 148.
3. *sb.* Chance, fortune, fate ; luck ; esp. in phr. *by*) *good, great, &c., hap,* by good luck.
Sc. Better hap at court than good service, RAMSAY *Prov.* (1737) ; Hanging gangs by hap, FERGUSON *Prov.* (1641) 14. Per. I wish naething but good betide, Or be your hap, NICOL *Poems* (1766) 59. Fif. Guid hap, their dinner then was laid Upon the tables lang and braid, Wi' damask napery owrspread, TENNANT *Papistry* (1827) 99. Gall. Yet it was far out of my hap to help it, CROCKETT *Moss-Hags* (1895) xvii. Wxf.¹ n.Yks.¹ In Clevel. the word is usually qualified, as in ' ill hap,' ' strange hap ' ; but we also say ' by what hap,' or the like ; n.Yks.² Lan. DAVIES *Races* (1856) 233. ne.Lan.¹ Sur. Apropos of the happy stoppage of the fire on a common, a woman said, ' You know, Sir, luck is God's hap,' N. & Q. (1880) 6th S. i. 239. w.Som.¹ By good hap we jis meet'n eens he was a comin out. n.Dev. And nif by gurt hap tha dest zey mun at oll, Exm. *Scold.* (1746) l. 267.

I ·

4. An event, occurrence, esp. an ill event, a misfortune, accident. Also in form **hapment.**

Lnk. Belyve the lang-legged Tailor chap Cam' canny back to learn the hap, MURDOCH *Doric Lyre* (1873) 30. **m.Yks.**[1] Hapment. **n.Lin.**[1] A sore hap. [But mark the hap! a cow came by And up the thistle eat, HALLIWELL *Rhymes* (1842) 47, ed. 1886.]

5. *Comp.* (1) **Hap-luck,** chance, *gen.* used *advb.* haphazard, without premeditation ; (2) **-stumble,** a chance stumble.

(1) **Nhp.**[1]; **Nhp.**[2] He did it hap-luck. (2) **Sc.** Such hap-stumble as this into pure nonsense, PITCAIRN *Assembly* (1766) v.

6. *adv.* Perhaps, perchance. Cf. **haps.**

Lan. DAVIES *Races* (1856) 233. **Ess.** (S.P.H.), **Ken.** (W.F.S.) **Sur.** *N. & Q.* (1874) 5th S. i. 517 ; **Snr.**[1], **Sus.** (S.P.H.), **Sus.**[1]

HAP, *v.*[2] and *sb.*[2] In *gen.* dial. use in Sc. Irel. and n. counties to Der. Not. Lin. ; also Nhp. e.An. Also written **happ** Wm. w.Yks.[4]; **happe** N.Cy.[2]; and in forms **ap** n.Yks. Lin.[1] sw.Lin.[1]; **haup** Rxb. ; **heap** Lin. [h)ap.]

1. *v.* To cover, enwrap ; to envelop, surround ; also with *up, in.*

Per. The snaws o' time May hap your forehead high, HALIBURTON *Ochil Idylls* (1891) 127. **Lnk.** The mists that had happit the nicht Row'd up frae the glens, HAMILTON *Poems* (1865) 23. **Slk.** She lay her lane All happed wi' flowers, HOGG *Poems* (ed. 1865) 35. **Dmf.** Wi' some sweet lass beside ye, when the gloamin' haps the glen, REID *Poems* (1894) 6. **Cum.** T'poor sheep In t'snowdrifts war hapt up, RICHARDSON *Talk* (1871) 131, ed. 1876. **Wm.** Sno' that haps the frozen poles, WHITEHEAD *Leg.* (1859) 8. **n.Yks.**[2] All white and happ'd up ; snowed over. **w.Yks.** (J.W.) **n.Lin.**[1] It was hapt 'e a peåce o' broon paaper.

2. To cover up for the sake of warmth ; to wrap ; to tuck up in bed ; also with *down, in, up.*

Sc. I took my cloak to her and sought to hap her in the same, STEVENSON *Catriona* (1893) xxiii. **Sh.I.** Her dimity coat, an' her pepper an' saut mantle, wid hap ye weel, STEWART *Tales* (1892) 33. **ne.Sc.** Littlens wull tak' caulds, herd an' hap them hoo ye like, GRANT *Kackleton,* 95. **Cai.**[1] **Baff.** His head an' hands he maunna hap, For fear a beagle should him slap, TAYLOR *Poems* (1787) 35. **Bch.** I hae ... gloves likewise, to hap the hand Of fremt an' sib, FORBES *Shop Bill* (1785) 13. **Abd.** Hap it weel wi' strae an' keep awa' the caul (W.M.). **Kcd.** His ridin' coat Happin' half the buckskin breeches, GRANT *Lays* (1884) 81. **Frf.** Watch ower your little sister by day and hap her by night, BARRIE *Tommy* (1896) 117. **Per.** Mistress Hoo 'ill hap ye round, for we maunna let ye come tac ony ill the first day ye'r oot, IAN MACLAREN *Brier Bush* (1895) 167. **Fif.** Hose an' shoon, an' sarks an' coats To hap, an' keep them hale, DOUGLAS *Poems* (1806) 41. **s.Sc.** Hap her white breast wi' my little wee wing, WATSON *Bards* (1859) 13. **Rnf.** His head aneath the claes he haps, PICKEN *Poems* (1813) I. 120. **Ayr.** The worthy man happing us with his plaid, we soon fell asleep, GALT *Gilhaize* (1823) xxvi. **Lnk.** Nae lordly ermine his shouthers may hap, LEMON *St. Mungo* (1844) 82. **Edb.** Our wife handed us out a pair of blankets to hap round me, MOIR *Mansie Wauch* (1828) xiii. **Rxb.** While ae auld blanket Can hap us baith, RUICKBIE *Wayside Cottager* (1807) 175. **Dmf.** Here's a dud to hap its head, CROMEK *Remains* (1810) 30. **Gall.** Then we happed him up, CROCKETT *Moss-Hags* (1895) vii. **Wgt.** A happit up the prawtas wi' strae, FRASER *Wigtown* (1877) 364. **N.I.** (M.B.-S.) ; *N. & Q.* (1873) 4th S. vii. 480 ; **N.I.**[1] **Uls.** *Uls. Jrn. Arch.* (1858) VI. 361. **n.Don.** SIMMONS *Gl.* (1890). **n.Cy.** GROSE (1790) ; **N.Cy.**[12] **Nhb.** There ! Thoo's weel happed up, and reet too, it's vara caud, CLARE *Love of Lass* (1890) II. 127. **Dur.** It will be very cold, mind hap y'rself up well (A.B.) ; **Dur.**[1] **s.Dur.** Mind ye hap him in well (J.E.D.). **Cum.** She happ'd her up, Aw wished her weel, ANDERSON *Ballads* (ed. 1808) 14 ; **Cum.**[1] She hap't o' t'barns at bed time. **Wm.** (C.W.D.) ; Thick leather jerkins hap'd their sides, WHITEHEAD *Lyvennet* (1859) 4. **s.Wm.** (J.A.B.) **n.Yks.** They pulled some more ling to hap themselves withal, ATKINSON *Moorl. Parish* (1891) 381 ; **n.Yks.**[123]; **n.Yks.**[4] Noo ya mun hap up well. It's a cau'd neeet. **ne.Yks.**[1] Thoo mun hap thysen weel ; it's varry cau'd. **e.Yks.**[1], **m.Yks.**[1] **w.Yks.** (F.M.L.) ; His mother happed him up i' two blankets (S.P.U.) ; **w.Yks.**[1234]; **w.Yks.**[5] Am weel hap'd up, ah sal tak no harm a' t'outside, whativver ah chonce in. **Lan.** (S.W.) ; The old fellow stopped now and then to hap her up and see if she wanted anything, WAUGH *Chim. Corner* (1874) 80, ed. 1879 ; **Lan.**[1], **ne.Lan.**[1] **Chs.**[1] Put him to bed, and put plenty of hillin on him, an hap him up warm. **Der.**[1], **nw.Der.**[1] Not. It's very cold, but she's well happed up (L.C.M.) ; (J.H.B.) **s.Not.** Hap the child up well from the co'd (J.P.K.). **Lin.** Hap him up wi' cloes (J.C.W.) ; They're all happed up warm

in their roons, FENN *Dick o' the Fens* (1888) iii. **n.Lin.** 'At's obligated to hap itsen doon as soon as coud weather sets in, PEACOCK *Tales* (1890) and S. 59 ; **n.Lin.**[1] **s.Lin.** She's happing the young chickens up as carefully as she would her own babby (T.H.R.). **sw.Lin.**[1] **Nhp.** His universal care Who hapt thee down, CLARE *Village Minst.* (1821) II. 206; **Nhp.**[1] Only adopted in the Northern part of the county. **e.An.**[1] **Nrf.** HOLLOWAY.

Hence (1) **Happed** or **Happit,** *ppl. adj.* covered, wrapt up, furnished with wrappings or clothes ; (2) **Happing,** *sb.* a covering, wrapping, a coverlet ; *pl.* clothes, esp. bedclothes ; (3) **Happing-kist,** *sb.* a linen-chest ; (4) **-sheets,** *sb. pl.* bed-coverings.

(1) **Sc.** GROSE (1790) *MS. add.* (C.) **Abd.** Scantily happet, Bell Skene wi' her twa bairnies lay, ANDERSON *Rhymes* (1867) 143. **Frf.** His backie ill happit, au's feetie ill shod, WATT *Poet. Sketches* (1880) 15. **Per.** A wee auld man, warm-happit in a cloak, STEWART *Character* (1857) 181. **Lnk.** Beds weel happit, sheets like snaw, NICHOLSON *Kilwuddie* (ed. 1895) 87. **Dmf.** Bonny wee bairns, a' weel happ'd and fu', SHENNAN *Tales* (1831) 155. **n.Cy.** *Border Gl.* (*Coll.* L.L.B.) **w.Yks.** Weel hapt up abaht t'neck, BANKS *Wkfld. Wds.* (1865). (2) **Sc.** And ye'll mak' a bed o' green rashes, Likewise a happing of gray, AYTOUN *Ballads* (ed. 1861) I. 282. **e.Sc.** On a sharp frosty morning ... thatch roofs have a look of cosiness and warmth, hanging over the houses like a thick winter happing fringed at the eaves, SETOUN *R. Urquhart* (1896) ii. **Rnf.** An' cozie the happin o' the farmer's bed, THOM *Rhymes* (1844) 72. **Ayr.** My gray plaid, my cauld winter's warm happin', BOSWELL *Poet. Wks.* (1801) 21, ed. 1871. **Edb.** Throwing awa siller on your nick-nack feckless happins, BALLANTINE *Gaberlunzie* (ed. 1875) 23. **Gall.** A twig o' hazel's a' her happin', To hatch her young, NICHOLSON *Poet. Wks.* (1814) 96, ed. 1897. **N.Cy.**[1], **Nhb.**[1], **Dur.**[1], **s.Dur.** (J.E.D.) **Cum.** T'fella at poot t'happin off, SARGISSON *Joe Scoap* (1881) 155 ; A happin tied on t'top on't, *Willy Wattle* (1870) 3 ; **Cum.**[1] **Wm.** Three par a blankets an twoa happins, WHEELER *Dial.* (1790) 62 ; (A.C.) **s.Wm.** (J.A.B.), **n.Yks.**[124] **ne.Yks.**[1] A'e ya happins eneeaf? **e.Yks.** Bed appin (Miss A.) ; **e.Yks.**[1] **m.Yks.**[1] Bed-happing. **w.Yks.** We've na happin o' that bed (J.T.F.) ; (J.T.) ; **w.Yks.**[1]; **w.Yks.**[5] Ah've nivver hed hâaf happing eniff this winter. **ne.Lan.**[1] **s.Not.** It's co'd abed now for them as 'asn't plenty o' happins (J.P.K.). **Lin.** BROOKES *Tracts Gl.* ; **Lin.**[1] The nights being cold we require more appin. **n.Lin.**[1] I've knawn farm hooses, a many, wheåre sarvant chaps bed niver enif happin' o' the'r beds. **s.Lin.** See that he's plenty happing ower him : it's fretzin' co'd (T.H.R.). **Nhp.**[1], **e.An.**[1] (3) **n.Yks.**[2] A large chest for linen, seen hereabouts in old family houses. Some are pannelled and carved ; and in raised figures bear dates within the 17th century. (4) *ib.*

3. To clothe, dress ; also with *up.*

Frf. She was naturally a bonny bit kimmer rather than happit up to the nines, BARRIE *Minister* (1891) vi. **Per.** I'll hap ye an' fend ye, an' busk ye, an' tend ye, FORD *Harp* (1893) 164. **Fif.** I sall hae you happit well, DOUGLAS *Poems* (1806) 84. **Lnk.** Lasses a' weel hapt wi' druggit, NICHOLSON *Kilwuddie* (ed. 1895) 26. **Rxb.** Paper, In whilk my muse here boots to haup her, A. SCOTT *Poems* (ed. 1808) 17. **n.Yks.**[28], **w.Yks.** (J.T.)

4. *Comp.* (1) **Hap-gear,** clothing of all sorts ; (2) **-harlot,** a coarse coverlet ; (3) **-warm,** a warm, substantial covering or article of dress ; also used *attrib.*

(1) **n.Yks.**[2] (2) **N.Cy.**[1] A servant's coverlet. **e.An.**[1] (3) **ne.Sc.** The tailor ... plied his needle and thread ... till the webs had become hapwarms fit to defend the coldest blast, GREGOR *Flk-Lore* (1881) 58. **Baff.**[1] That quyte o' yours is a gueede hap-warm. **Edb.** Ye'll bring up after us, your master's trotcozy an' hapwarm, BALLANTINE *Gaberlunzie* (ed. 1875) 328. **n.Cy.** *Border Gl.* (*Coll.* L.L.B.)

5. To cover over ; to bury, cover with earth ; to cover with earth or straw as a protection from cold or wet, to thatch ; also with *down, in, over, up.*

Sc. And my luve's briest is happit 'Neath cauld drifts o' snaw, *Ballads* (1885) 65. **Elg.** The carle sees the last ruck-head Hapt in baith saif and braw, COUPER *Poetry* (1804) I. 188. **e.Sc.** Better be happed with the eternal silence of the hills than drowned in the din of the streets, SETOUN *R. Urquhart* (1896) i. **Abd.** Stacks wi' thack an' rape war happit licht, *Guidman Inglismaill* (1873) 27. **Per.** My babe sleeps in yon kirkyard Happed owre wi' clammy clay, SPENCE *Poems* (1898) 48. **e.Fif.** The solace o' my granfaither's solitary oors, after he had happit my grannie i' the mools, LATTO *Tam Bodkin* (1864) xi. **Dmf.** Our wee hoose, new happit, brushed and clean, SALMON *Gowodean* (1868) 37. **Rnf.** The cauld clay haps the Rose of Elderslie, FRASER *Chimes* (1853) 82. **Ayr.**

It wasna till they had gotten them a' safely hame and the hole happit up, that they really kent what they had, SERVICE *Notandums* (1890) 67. Lnk. To-day auld Wullie Gaw has been happing somebody up, FRASER *Whaups* (1895) i. Lth. Green's the sod that haps the grave O' mony a Cannygoshan! SMITH *Merry Bridal* (1866) 38. Slk. I digged a grave, and laid him in, And happ'd him with the sod sae green, BORLAND *Yarrow* (1890) 54. Rxb. Ance I'm happit wi' the truff I ken I'll need nae mair, WILSON *Poems* (1824) 21. Dmf. Tae me wad been doubly kin' . . . Had he me happ'd some dyke behin' There tae remain, QUINN *Heather* (1863) 74. Nhb. Gae hap him up i' his lang hame Sin' Billie's dead, DONALDSON *Poems* (1809) 62. Cum. He's been happed up many a long year (J.Ar.). n.Yks. They've gitten t'muck an' taties all hapt nicely in (W.H.); n.Yks.¹ To cover, by placing straw and earth over potatoes, earth over the dead, and the like. 'All.'s dune, now: thou mun hap him oop.' To a sexton after the graveservice was completed ; n.Yks.² 'I should like to see thee happ'd up,' an ill wish—to see you in your grave; n.Yks.⁴ Ah've just happ'd Willie's grave up. ne.Yks.¹ Then you've gitten poor au'd Willie happed up at last. e.Yks. To cover; as the seed with soil, MARSHALL *Rur. Econ.* (1788) ; e.Yks.¹ We happ'd awd woman up quite comfortably I chetch-yard, last Monday. Der.² ' He's now't good for till he's happed up,' said of a miserly churl. nw.Der.¹ Not.⁸ Well happed down, well covered in. s.Not. Ah just 'apped the taters up wi' a little earth (J.P.K.). Lin.¹ It will not be long before you'll have her to hap up. n.Lin. I wasn't goin' to hev him happ'd awaay i' a parish coffin, PEACOCK *Taales* (1890) and S. 56 ; n.Lin.¹ Noo then, get them taaties happed doon, it'll freeze to-neet like smack. sw.Lin.¹ They happed the stack up. Our potatoes are well apped up. So you've happed poor old Charley up. Nhp. When I, Hapt in the cold dark grave, Can heed it not, CLARE *Village Minst.* (1821) l. 173.

Hence (1) **Happing**, *sb.* thatch, straw or earth used as a covering ; (2) **Happing-up**, *sb.* a burial.

(1) n.Lin.¹ Covering, such as . . . earth on a potatoe pie. sw.Lin.¹ We're short of happing, to hap the stacks with. (2) Cum. Coniston . . . was obliged to send all its deceased to Ulverston for interment, and Christian happing up, LINTON *Lake Cy.* (1864) 265.

6. To hide, conceal, cover away, to 'hush up' ; also *intr.* to hide oneself.

Sc. Man, doctor, I ha'e happit mony a faut o' yours, an' I think ye micht thole ane o' mine, FORD *Thistledown* (1891) 98. e.Sc. What way will ye seek to rake up what I've happit awa for years? SETOUN *R. Urquhart* (1896) xxvii. Ayr. Ye maun be cowards, whan ye hap By dykebacks, sheughs, and ditches, *Ballads and Sngs.* (1847) II. 113. n.Yks.² 'They got it happed up,' the matter was silenced ; n.Yks.⁴ Let's hap t'job up noo an' saay neea mair aboot it. w.Yks. (J.W.) n.Lin.¹ Thaay maay try as thaay like ther's nol happin' a thing o' that soort up e' theåse daays.

7. To shelter, shield, protect.

Sc. The moonlight, they say, is no just canny . . . and ye should be happit and sained from its influence, COBBAN *Andaman* (1895) xxiv. Bch. Syne slouch behind my doughty targe, That yon day your head happit, FORBES *Ajax* (1785) 9. Ked. My auld biggin', That mony year has happed me Up to the very riggin', JAMIE *Muse* (1844) 32. Frf. Dear cottie ye cou'd tell . . . How many ills on me befel, When ye did hap my tally, Yon rantin night, MORISON *Poems* (1790) 85. Per. Wi' Dives' craps to ca' oor ain, A' hoosed an' happit frae the rain, HALIBURTON *Ochil Idylls* (1891) 29. Ayr. Jamaica bodies, use him weel, An' hap him in a cozie biel, BURNS *On a Sc. Bard*, st. 9. Edb. They scoug frae street an' field, An' hap them in a lyther bield, FERGUSSON *Poems* (1773) 130, ed. 1785.

8. To smooth down, press lightly ; to pat soil with the back of a spade ; in salt-making : to smooth the lump salt.

Lan.¹, Chs.¹² nw.Der.¹ To press slightly the soil in garden beds with a spade after the seeds are sown.

Hence **Happer**, *sb.* salt-making term : a small wooden spade or paddle used to smooth lump salt. Chs.¹

9. To make up a fire, to stack or heap it up so as to keep it in.

Sc. It's time I should hap up the wee bit gathering turf, as the fire is ower low, SCOTT *Monastery* (1820) iv ; I'll maybe find the fire black out, though I had happit it so as to last the whole day, WHITEHEAD *Daft Davie* (1876) 149, ed. 1894. Cum.⁴, Yks. (J.W.)

10. *sb.* A covering or wrap of any kind ; a coverlet, rug ; a thick outer garment, dress, clothing ; also used *fig.*

Sc. Mak's cosie the hap o' a theekit cot bed, ALLAN *Lilts* (1874) 357. Shl. Shü laid aff her hap an' axd for a drap o' mylk, *Sh. News* (May 14, 1898). Abd. The hairst was ta'en in, and the rucks got a hap, ANDERSON *Rhymes* (1867) 124. Frf. They were sair in

want o' a puckle needfu' haps in the day-time, WILLOCK *Rosetty Ends* (1886) 25, ed. 1889. Per. I met her by the burnie's flow, Aneath the hap o' e'enin', EDWARDS *Strathearn Lyrics* (1889) 43. Ayr. I'd be mair vauntie o' my hap, Douce hingin' owre my curple, BURNS *Answer to Verses* (1787) st. 5. Lnk. The plaided hap o' auld warl' ways, MURDOCH *Doric Lyre* (1873) 8. Lth. [He] wons upon the hill-tap, In peat-biggit shieling wi' thin theekit hap, BALLANTINE *Poems* (1856) 98. e.Lth. Swathed up in mufflers, mittens, haps and hose, MUCKLEBACKIT *Rhymes* (1885) 167. Edb. Winter's caulds, baith keen and snell, Freeze on the hap o'er muir an' fell, GLASS *Cal. Parnassus* (1812) 40. Ked. When Criffel wears a hap, Skiddaw wots well o' that, SWAINSON *Weather Flk-Lore* (1873) 206. N.I.¹ n.Cy. *Border Gl.* (Coll. L.L.B.); N.Cy.¹ Nhb.¹ ' Put a hap on the bed,' means put an extra covering on it. Dur.¹ Cum. A hap mear or less is nowt in our house, RIGBY *Midsummer to Martinmas* (1891) i. Wm. Have you put plenty of hap on? (B.K.) n.Yks.¹ ' Have you plenty o' haps?' ' Aye, Ah's tweea shawls an' mah thick cloak, forby t'roog' ; n.Yks.² Rare good haps ; n.Yks.⁴ m.Yks.¹ They may manage for a bit of scran [food], but they've scarcely a rag of hap. w.Yks.¹ Gimme plenty o' hap. Lan. To doff his winter-hap, WAUGH *Heather* (ed. Milner) II. 26 ; Thae's a terrible lot o' hap abeawt tho', *ib. Snowed-up*, ii. ne.Lan.¹ Der. 'Ha' ye got plenty o' haps!' .. ' Tis main cold,' VERNEY *Stone Edge* (1868) xxv.

11. A heavy fall of snow.

n.Yks. [He] would be matched to get home again; for it was safe there was going to be a ' hap,' ATKINSON *Moorl. Parish* (1891) 349.

[**1.** The peaple sawe thame [the opinions] happit al, and coloured with fair wourdes, DALRYMPLE *Leslie's Hist. Scotl.* (1596) II. 466. **2.** I pray þe Marie happe hym warme, *York Plays* (c. 1400) 144.]

HAP, *v.*⁸ and *int.* Sc. Irel. Lei. Dev. Also in forms **haap** Sc. Lei.¹ ; **haape** n.Dev.; **hape** Frf. ; **haup** Sc. (JAM.) [h]ap, h[ĕ]p.] **1.** *v.* Of horses or yoke-cattle : to turn to the right away from the driver.

Sc. STEPHENS *Farm Bk.* (ed. 1849) I. 160 ; It is opposed to wynd, which signifies to turn to the left or towards the driver (JAM.).

2. Phr. (1) *to hap or wynd*, (*a*) to make draught cattle turn to the right or left ; (*b*) to turn one way or another at another's will, to be tractable ; (*a*) *haup weel, rake weel*, try every way, rather than be disappointed.

(1, *a*) Abd. But he could make them turn or veer, And hap or wynd them by the ear, MESTON *Poet. Wks.* (1723) 16. (*b*) Frf. How bless'd is he that to his mind Has got a wifie . . . That to his wish will hape or winde, Soothing each care, MORISON *Poems* (1790) 79. s.Sc. Ye'll neither hap nor wyn—neither dance nor haud the caunle, WILSON *Tales* (1839) V. 234 ; We say of a stubborn person : ' He will neither haup nor wynd ' (JAM.). (*a*) Fif. A phr. borrowed from ploughing. The lit. meaning is: If the horse will not go to the right hand, let him take the opposite direction (*ib.*).

3. To stop, keep back ; to check, balk.

Dev. A farmer, speaking of some encroaching neighbours, said, ' They'd have it all, nif did'n hape 'em a bit,' *Reports Provinc.* (1889). n.Dev. *Horae Subsecivae* (1777) 197; Nif vauther dedn't ha-ape tha, *Exm. Scold.* (1746) l. 51.

4. *int.* A call to a horse to turn to the right ; also with *off, up*.

St. (JAM.); MORTON *Cyclo. Agric.* (1863). w.Sc. ' Haup up ' is only applied to [cattle], *N. & Q.* (1856) and S. i. 439. s.Sc. 'Hap, Bassie, hap,' and smacking his whip the horse increased his speed, WILSON *Tales* (1839) V. 13. Ayr. Just gies his naigs a hap or gee, An' canny drives around it, AINSLIE *Land of Burns* (ed. 1892) 217. Lnk. By their answerin' our ca'—Hap, wyne, wo back, or step awa', WATSON *Poems* (1853) 25. Bwk. *Monthly Mag.* (1814) I. 31. N.I.¹

5. A call for cows.

Lei.¹ When I wus a b'y they'd use to call the cows with a 'haap,' now they call 'em·wi' a ' hoop.'

HAP, *v.*⁴ Sc. [hap.] In phr. *hap weel, w)rap weel*, come of it what will, whatever be the result, hit or miss. Cf. hap, *v.*⁸ **2.**

Cai.¹ Slk. Whilk makes me half and mair afraid, .. But hap weel, rap weel, I will send it, Hogg *Poems* (1801) I. 91 (JAM.). Rxb. I carena, I'll do it, hap weel, rap weel (*ib.*). Gall. MACTAGGART *Encycl.* (1824). Ked. Hap weel an' wrap weel, I'll ax her ower hame, ARMSTRONG *Ingleside* (1890) 219.

HAP, *v.*⁵ w.Yks. [ap.] **1.** Of animals : to lap, suck up. (J.B.), (J.W.) **2.** To dry or mop up a wet place. (J.W.)

I 2

HAP, *sb.*[3] *Obs.* Sc. Cum. An instrument for scraping up sea-ooze to make salt with.

Dmf. His first care is to collect the sleech proper for his purpose; this he effects by means of an implement named a hap, a kind of sledge drag furnished with a sharp edge at that part which touches the ground, and drawn by a single horse, *Agric. Surv.* 527 (Jam.). Cum.[4] A sledge-drag or scraper, drawn by a horse, used for collecting the surface-leech on the salt-bed, *Solway*, 44.

HAP, see Hip, *sb.*[1], Hop, *v.*[2]

HAPE, *sb.* Sc. A halfpenny.

Lnk. Dae ye want the Citeez [Citizen]? Evenin' or Weekly? It's only a hape, Nicholson *Idylls* (1870) 106.

HAPE, see Hap, *v.*[8], Heap, *sb.*[1]

HAPLY, *adv. Obs.* Chs. Der. Also in form **happely** Chs.[2] Perhaps. Chs.[18] Der. Grose (1790) *MS. add.* (P.) [He came, if haply he might find any thing thereon, Bible *Mark* xi. 13.]

HAPP, HAPPA, see Hap, *v.*[2], Hap ye.

HAPPE, *v. Obs.* n.Cy. To encourage or set on a dog. Grose (1790).

HAPPEN, *v.*[1] and *sb.*[1] Var. dial. uses in Sc. and Eng.

1. *v.* To befall, happen to ; to become of. Also used in *pass.*

Slg. Some dreadful dool shall happen us, Towers *Poems* (1885) 56. Edb. The fate That soon will happen Kirk or State, Crawford *Poems* (1798) 38. Lth. Has anything happened Hootsman ? Lumsden *Sheep-head* (1892) 311. w.Yks. If owt happens me tha mun lewk after aar Lizzie, *Spec. Dial.* s.Not. Ah've bin lookin for th' mester i' th' shop. What's appened im? (J.P.K.) Lei.[1] A's 'appened very lucky to get independent.

2. To incur, meet with (an accident, &c.); to have anything occur to one ; occas. with *of*.

e.Dur.[1] He happened it [it happened to him]. She happened a bad accident. n.Yks. Ah happen'd a accident (T.S.); n.Yks.[1] ' Puir gell ! she's happ'n'd a misfort'n ;' had, or going to have, an illegitimate child. ' Ah seen a hare liggin, an' Ah happ'n'd (t') misfort'n te knap't o' t'heead'; n.Yks.[4] ne.Yks.[1] Ah's happen'd a bad accident. w.Yks. He'd happened t'accident at his wark, *Yksman. Comic Ann.* (1878) 42. n.Lin. Whativer's matter noo ? Has Jack happen'd owt ? Peacock *Tales* (1886) 61; n.Lin.[1] He happen'd an accident up o' Magin Moor ; his herse flung him and brok two on his ribs. sw.Lin.[1] They've never happened owt yet. They were down together, but they happened nothing. Cmb. He happened of an accident (W.W.S.). Suf. (C.L.F.)

3. With *of, on, in,* or *with*: to come upon by chance, fall in with, light upon.

Per. Ance we happen'd on a stell, High up amang the Ochils, Haliburton *Ochil Idylls* (1891) 13. Ayr. Gif that ye Coud happen on a loving wife, She might a comfort to ye be, Fisher *Poems* (1790) 154. Gall. She happen't on a frien' To help her in the time o' need, Lauderdale *Poems* (1796) 68. n.Cy. (J.W.), ne.Lan.[1] s.Chs.[1] Iv yd aap'n-n ûpûn aa·r Joa·j, tel im th)mes·tûr)z bin waan·tin im [If yô happen'n upon ahr Geo'ge, tell him th' mester's bin wantin him]. Not. I happened on him just agen the miln (L.C.M.); The difficulty of happening on a policeman, Prior *Renie* (1895) 61 ; Not.[1] Lin.[1] n.Lin.[1] I happen'd on her just agean Bell-hoᴅle. sw.Lin.[1] I happened on him last market. Rut.[1] I thought I'd ask the doctor to call in next door, if I should happen on him to-day or to-morrow. Lei.[1] Nhp. The restless hogs will happen on the prize, Clare *Shep. Calendar* (1827) 74 ; Nhp.[1] I couldn't happen on him no where. War.[3], Hnt. (T.P.F.) Nrf. I used to go up the road and happen in with some boys, Emerson *Son of Fens* (1892) 18 ; I happened with him at mine [at my house], Cozens-Hardy *Broad Nrf.* (1893) 63 ; I had just happened of him up a tree when you began to halloa, Haggard *Col. Quaritch* (1888) I. xii. Suf. I happened o' he at Ipstich (C.G.B.). e.Suf. I happened with him at the inn (F.H.).

4. With *along*: to come by chance, to arrive unexpectedly.

Sur.[1] Sus.[1] Master Tumptops, he's a man as you'll notice mostly happens-along about anyone's dinner-time.

5. Phr. *to happen right*, to agree together, ' hit it off.'

s.Not. ' How did you get on with him ? ' ' Oh, sometimes we happened right, an' sometimes we didn't' (J.P.K.)

6. *Comp.* (1) **Happen-chance**, a matter of casual occurrence. n.Yks.[2]; (2) ·**clash**, an accidental blow or fall. *ib.* ; (3) ·**keease**, see (1). *ib.*

7. *sb.* An accident, occurrence.

w.Wor. That were a baddish happen, S. Beauchamp *N. Hamilton* (1875) II. 133.

HAPPEN, *v.*[2] Som. To rattle, make a cracking sound. See **Happer.**

What I don't like about coke is its happening on al' the while when you first put it on (W.F.R.).

HAPPEN, *sb.*[2] Ayr. (Jam.) The path trodden by cattle, esp. on high grounds.

HAPPENING, *sb.* and *ppl. adj.* Sc. Yks. Also Dev.

1. *sb.* An event, occurrence.

Gall. I could not find it in my heart to tell him of the happening, Crockett *Grey Man* (1896) 189. w.Yks. I could take more pleasure in telling such young doings without meaning ... nor in jumping out into the quick and strong flood of happenings that came after, Snowden *Web of Weaver* (1896) 17. Dev. Tidings and happenings new and old, Salmon *Ballads* (1899) 6 ; Before the final coorious happening, there was a fire in a croft of auld Applebird's, Phillpotts *Bill Vogwell in Blk. and White* (June 27, 1896) 824.

2. *ppl. adj.* Casual, chance, occasional.

Per. Mrs. So and So was here to-day, but it was only a happening call (G.W.). Lnk. If it wasna for a happening visitor looking in at orra times, Fraser *Whaups* (1895) xii.

HAPPEN(S, *adv.* and *conj.* n.Cy. Cum. Wm. Yks. Lan. Chs. Stf. Der. Not. Lin. Lei. Nhp. War. Wor. Shr. Glo. Also written **happance** w.Yks. ; and in forms **'appen** Lan. m.Lan.[1] Der. ; **hap'm** Cum.[4]; **oppen** Der. 1. *adv.* Perhaps, possibly, may be.

n.Cy.[1], Cum.[4] Wm. ' Will you lend me a book ? ' ' Happen I have not got one ' (B.K.) ; Said he was happen rader better ner good, *Ald Smiler*, 19. n.Yks.[2]; n.Yks.[4] ' Wilt ta cum ? ' ' Happen Ah may.' ne.Yks.[1] Happen Bill 'll cum whom [home] next week. m.Yks.[1] w.Yks. Yo! happance think this a queer idea a mine, Tom Treddlehoyle *Thowts* (1845) 11 ; w.Yks.[1] I spreead taable claath—happen nut scea simmit as they'd been used tull, ii. 299; w.Yks.[24]; w.Yks.[5] Happen ah sal an' happen ah sahn't. Lan. That friend's happen slander'd yoa o' at he could, Harland *Lyrics* (1866) 223; Our Jacob's got something on his mind. . . He's appen fallen in love, Hamerton *Wenderholme* (1869) xv; Lan.[1], ne.Lan.[1] e.Lan.[1] The cheapest is happen not the best. m.Lan.[1], Chs.[123] Stf. Happen your husband tied ye off marryin' afore he died ? *Cornh. Mag.* (Jan. 1894) 38. n.Stf. Happen ye'd get something to think on, Geo. Eliot *A. Bede* (1859) I. 8. Der. It's 'oppen two moil fro' here, Hall *Hathersage* (1896) i ; 'Appen thou be'st, and 'appen thou baint, Le Fanu *Uncle Silas* (1865) I. 298; Der.[2], nw.Der.[1] Not. (J.H.B.); If he speaks to you, you can 'appen be deaf, Prior *Renie* (1895) 60. Lin. Happen sea-bank broke to show folk as fen warn't niver meant to be drained, Fenn *Dick o' the Fens* (1888) iii. n.Lin.[1] Happen I maay cum doon o' Sunda' at neet, bud I'm not sewer. s.Lin. Happen he may arter all (T.H.R.). sw.Lin.[1] Happens, I may-It was a good job, happen, as she did go. Lei.[1] ' Do you think she's gone home? ' ' 'Appen.' Nhp.[1] War. They'd happen has died, if they'd been fed, Geo. Eliot *Floss* (1860) I. 42; War.[12] ; War.[3] 'Ave a go at a ship, master; appen yo might 'it a ship [sheep].' A sarcasm launched at me by a shepherd who had seen me miss my game in two successive shots ; War.[4] Happen I may light upon it when I goes a milking. s.War.[1], s.Wor. (H.K.), s.Wor.[1], se.Wor.[1] Shr.[1] 'Appen I shall be theer. Glo.[1]

2. *conj.* In case, lest, perchance.

n.Yks.[1] Ah'll think, happen Ah gans. ne.Yks.[1] Ah'll waæt happen sha cums. w.Yks. (J.W.)

HAPPER, *v.* Hmp. Wil. Dor. Som. To fall with a heavy sound ; to rattle down, patter ; to crackle ; *gen.* with *down*.

Hmp. Of an apple falling from a tree, ' Didn't it happer down ? ' (W.H.E.) Wil. You can hear the rain now. It's happering down. *ib.* ; Wil.[1] To come down smartly, as hail, or leaves in autumn. Dor. An' orcha'd apples, red hall round, Have all a happer'd down. Barnes *Poems* (1863) 78. Som. Till tha snaw happer'd down and cover'd tha groun, Agrikler *Rhymes* (1872) 110; Sweetman *Wincanton Gl.* (1885); W. & J. Gl. (1873); Jennings *Obs. Dial. w.Eng.* (1825). w.Som.[1] How that there 'ood do happery !

Hence (1) **Happering**, (a) *vbl. sb.* the snapping or crackling of an ember in a fire ; (b) *ppl. adj.* pattering, rattling coming down like hail ; (2) **Happery**, *adj.* crackling, apt to snap or crackle.

(1, a) Wil. *N. & Q.* (1881) 6th S. iv. 106. (b) Dor. At the feast, I do mind very well, all the vo'ks Wer a-took in a happeren show'r, Barnes *Poems* (1863) 111. (2) w.Som.[1] Vir [fir] tops baint much o' viring, they be so happery.

HAPPER, see Hopper, *sb.*[1]

HAPPINCH, *sb.* Chs. The lapwing, *Vanellus vulgaris. Science Gossip* (1865) 36.

HAPPIT, see **Hoppet**, *v.*

HAPPLE, *v.* Sc. [Not known to our correspondents.] To trickle, roll down. See Hop, *v.*² 6.

Edb. The sa't tears ran happlin' owr my cheek, LEARMONT *Poems* (1791) 325.

HAPPY, *adj.* Sc. Irel. n.Cy. Nhb. Yks. Chs. Lei. Nhp. War. Cor. [(h)a·pi, æ·pi.] 1. In phr. (1) *Happy by lucky*, at a venture, at all hazards, by chance ; (2) — *family*, a variety of stonecrop, *Sedum* ; (3) *-go-long*, an easy-going person ; (4) *-go-lucky*, (*a*) see (1) ; (*b*) see (3) ; (*c*) chance, accident ; (5) — *man be his dole*, a good wish, an expression of goodwill.

(1) Nhp.¹ He has taken that bit o' ground happy by lucky, he's chanced it. (2) Chs.¹ Frequently grown in cottage windows; Chs.² The buds and flowers, though on different stalks, all nestle together. (3) Nhb. (R.O.H.) (4, *a*) Cai.¹ Rxb. Happy-go-lucky, I'll venture (JAM.). s.Don. He could not ride a bicycle, but he said he would try happy go lucky (D.A.S.). Lin.¹, n.Lin.¹ (*b*) Lei.¹ A good fellow of a reckless random disposition. War.² (*c*) n.Yks. It's happy-go-lucky whether you get them or nut (I.W.). m.Yks.¹ The well-known phrase 'happy-go-lucky' has more of a meaning to northern than southern ears. Cor. After that went recklessly . . . and finally abandoned the exercise of . . . reason for happy-go-lucky, BARING-GOULD *Gaverocks* (1887) i. (5) n.Cy. GROSE (1790) *MS. add.* (P.)

2. Lucky, fortunate, boding good fortune.

Bnff. There are happy and unhappy days for beginning any undertaking. . . There are also happy and unhappy feet. Thus they wish bridegrooms and brides a happy foot, *Statist. Acc.* XIV. 541 *n.* (JAM.)

HAPRICK, *sb.* Sh.I. Also written **happrick**. [ha·prik.] Panniers or baskets slung over a horse's back.

A auld osmal lūikin' auld maid, wi' a mooth laek a horse happrick, STEWART *Tales* (1892) 35 ; S. & Ork.¹ Two cazzies united by a band laid over a horse's back for carrying manure.

HAPS, *adv.* Sc. n.Cy. Ess. Ken. [haps, æps.] Perhaps, perchance. See Hap, *adv.* 6.

Edb. If yer morals dinna men' Ye'll haps be scau'ded at the en', LIDDLE *Poems* (1821) 58. n.Cy. *Border Gl.* (Coll. L.L.B.) Ess. An', haps, near ov a-fire, CLARK *J. Noakes* (1839) st. 170 ; Ess.¹ Ken. Aps he may. Aps he be (W.G.P.).

[It may haps be objected, CALLIS *Stat. Sewers* (ed. 1647) 94 (N.E.D.).]

HAPS, see **Hasp**, *sb.*¹

HAP-SHACKLE, *v.* and *sb.* Sc. Lan. Also in form **hop-shackle** Sc. Lan.¹ [ha·p-, h)o·p-ʃakl.] 1. *v.* To bind together the feet of cattle so as to prevent them from straying. Slk., Gall. (JAM.)

Hence **Hap-shackled**, *ppl. adj.* fettered, cumbered, hobbled.

Ayr. Thou now has got thy daddie's chair, Nae hand-cuff'd, mizzl'd, nap-shackl'd Regent, BURNS *Elegy on the Year 1788* (1789) l. 34 ; Jeanie stood like ane hapshackl'd, AINSLIE *Land of Burns* (ed. 1892) 188. Gall. An horse is said to be so when an hind and fore foot are confined by a rope fixed to them ; this is to hinder them to 'hop' or 'leap,' MACTAGGART *Encycl.* (1824) 253, ed. 1876. Lan. 'Thou walks as if thou were hop-shackle't!' 'Thou'd be hop-shackle't too, if thou'd as mony corns o' thi toes as I have,' WAUGH *Chim. Corner* (1874) 17, ed. 1879 ; Lan.¹

2. *sb.* A ligament for confining a horse or cow; a shackle, fetter ; also used *fig.*

Ayr. No creatures in a crib, no horses in hapshackles, AINSLIE *Land of Burns* (ed. 1892) 139. Slk. An intelligent correspondent from Ettrick Forest informs me that he never saw the operation of hapshackling performed otherwise than by fastening the hapshackle round the fore feet of the animal (JAM.); I have got this matrimonial hap-shackle off and am free, HOGG *Tales* (1838) 282, ed. 1866. Gall. (JAM.)

HAPSHER, *adv.* Lakel. Cum. In forms **hapsha** Lakel.² Cum. ; **hapshy** Cum.¹ In *comp.* (1) **Hapsher-hapsher**, (2) **-rapsher**, **rapsha**, or **-rapshy**, haphazard, at random.

(1) Cum. (J.W.O.) (2) Lakel.² Cum. (J.W.O.); Bit ah sed, just hapsha-rapsha, sez ah, SARGISSON *Joe Scoap* (1881) 140 ; Cum.¹

HAP YE, *phr.* Obs. n.Cy. Also in forms **happa** N.Cy.² ; **happe**. 1. What think you ? do you think so ? GROSE (1790), (K.), N.Cy.² 2. Thank you. BAILEY (1721).

HAR, *int.* Nhb. Dur. Yks. e.An. Also in form **arr**, **aar** e.An. 1. A call of the carter to a horse to come to the left or near side.

e.An. The rustic teamman's address to his horse when he wants it to turn into a gateway to the left is something of this kind, 'Cup bear, har, hate wa' holt' (H.C.H.). Nrf. RAINBIRD *Agric.* (1819) 302, ed. 1849.

2. A word of command addressed to a plough-horse to turn to the right.

Yks. The horses are trained when young to turn to the right on hearing this word (G.W.W.).

3. Phr. *har away*, be off! come along. Cf. hay·ree.

Nhb. (H.M.) e.Dur.¹ Haa·wee·u, haa·ru·wee·u, haru ('harra') wee·u. The shibboleth of this county, heard every day and almost every five minutes.

HAR, see **Haar**, *sb.*¹, **Have**, **Her**.

HARASS, *sb.* Lin. Sur. [aɹəs.] Difficulty, great trouble.

Sur.¹ 'It's a harass to get them up they hills.' Speaking of carting building materials on to the hill.

Hence **Harassment**, *sb.* a worry, trouble, harassed condition.

n.Lin.¹ Dr. P. he says to me, 'Mrs. D.,' he says, 'it's ovver-harassment o' th' liver 'at yer sufferin' from.' s.Lin. (T.H.R.)

HARBER, *sb.* e.An.¹ Suf.¹ e.Suf. (F.H.) Also written **harbur**, and in form **arbour** Suf.¹ [ā·bə(r).] The hornbeam or hard-beam, *Carpinus Betulus*. Also in *comp.* **Harber-tree**.

HARBIN(E, *sb.* Or.I. A young coal-fish of about two years old, *Merlangus carbonarius.*

The piltock of Shetland is the kuth of Orkney, which the following year is distinguished in the latter place as harbines, or two-year-old kuths, HIBBERT *Desc. Sh. I.* (1822) 25, ed. 1891 ; S. & Ork.¹ [SATCHELL (1879).]

HARBOUR, *sb.* and *v.* Sc. Nhb. Cum. Wm. Yks. Chs. Lin. Wor. Pem. Glo. Oxf. Som. Dev. Cor. Also written **harbar** s.Pem. ; and in form **herbour** Sc. 1. *sb.* A shelter, refuge.

Edb. It is said, as a harbour and rallying point, to have been much resorted to by the Covenanters, PENNECUIK *Wks.* (1715) 127, ed. 1815. n.Yks.⁴ Wa mun finnd a harbour sumwhere whahl t'shooer's ower'd. w.Yks. (J.W.) n.Lin.¹ It power'd doon wi' raain an' ther' was noä harbour to find noä wheäre. w.Som.¹ Kau·m soa·us ! lat-s goo t-aar·bur [Come matas ! let's take shelter]. The word 'shelter' is unknown.

Hence (1) **Harberance**, *sb.* **Harberie**, *sb.* harbourage, shelter ; (3) **Harbourless**, *adj.* without shelter or refuge.

(1) Nhb.¹ Thor's a lot o' rattins this year ; the rough stubbles is been a grand harberance for them. (2) Sc. He that is ill of his harberie, is good of his way kenning, RAY *Prov.* (1678) 370. (3) Lnk. Soam I harbourless, LITHGOW *Poet. Rem.*, ed. 1863 (*Passionado*).

2. Lodging, house-room ; a house, home ; a room, place of entertainment, place of reception.

Sc. He kept them up till I had neither house nor harbour, KIRKTON *Ch. Hist.* (1817) 274. Per. Wha'l' herbour freers ? an' the gudeman fra hame ? HALIBURTON *Dunbar* (1895) 95. Lakel.¹ Turned out of 'huse and harbour.' Cum.⁴ Wm. Cheated aut ot hause and harbour, HUTTON *Bran New Wark* (1785) l. 312. n.Yks.¹; n.Yks.⁴ Seea lang ez it's cleean, Ah decant mahnd, bud Ah mun 'ev a harbour foor t'neet. w.Yks. (J.W.) Chs.¹ My word! but this is a wyndy harbour. A wood-fent's a regular harbour for rottens. n.Lin.¹ Thaay was to'n'd oot i'to th' streät, an' noä harbour was to be gotten for 'em noäwheäres, soä I let 'em lig e' my barn. sw.Lin.¹ His sister gives him harbour, but he finds himself. There's no harbour at D, so they've ta'en a house at H. There's no other harbour to be got. Oxf. (G.O.), w.Som.¹

Hence (1) **Harbourage**, *sb.* stopping-place, entertainment ; (2) **Harbouration**, *sb.* a collection, lodgement ; a collection of anything unpleasant.

(1) w.Som.¹ Noa· aa·rbureej yuur! [No shelter here !] is the usual reply to a tramp. I heard a bleak moor described as 'lig u dai·zaa·rt, u-dhaew·t aj·, aew·z, ur aa·rbureej ' [like a desert, without hedge, house, or harbourage]. (2) Chs.¹ ; Chs.² Oi ne'er seed sich a harbouration o' dirt as that is. s.Chs.¹ Mahy sai·ks ūlahy·v! wot ū aa·rbūrai·shūn ū rüb·ich dhūr iz i dhū aays [My sakes alive ! what a harbouration o' rubbitch there is i' the haïse].

3. The place where a deer lies or has been lying ; the bed of a deer.

w.Som.¹ An old stag always tries to find a young deer to turn out of his harbour. **n.Dev.** When he [the stag] has settled himself down he is said to be ' in harbour,' JEFFERIES *Red Deer* (1884) vi.

Hence **Harbourage,** *sb.* a covert, lair, hiding-place.

w.Som.¹ The deer made for Bollam Wood, but there was no harbourage there.

4. *v.* To give shelter to; to hide; to entertain, give house-room to.

Ayr. We had committed the unpardonable sin against the prelacy of harbouring our minister and his destitute family, GALT *Gilhaize* (1823) xvii. **n.Yks.⁴** *Gen.* used in a derogatory sense. ' Sha's neeawaays neyce whaw sha harbours.' ' Tha'd harbour tha devil if tha thowt tha c'u'd mak owt byv it.' **w.Yks.** (J.W.) **Chs.¹** He harbours aw th' poachers i' th' country; **Chs.³,** n.Lin.¹, Oxf. (G.O.) **Glo.¹** Her says she won't harbour the dog in the parlour. **w.Som.¹** 'Tis a place where they do harbour thieves and all sorts o' rough car'iturs. **Cor.** And 'cused me for harbren hes booay to my house, TREGELLAS *Tales* (1860) 5.

Hence **Harberous,** *adj.* hospitable, affording shelter.

Sc. He liberal was and harberous, ROGERS *Three Reformers* (1819) 114.

5. To pet, spoil, make much of.

s.Pem. Ye'v alwiz been harbarin' this child, an' naw a's spoilt (W.M.M.).

6. *Phr.* **to harbour laze,** to induce or encourage laziness.

s.Wor. PORSON *Quaint Wds.* (1875) 20.

7. To dwell in a place; to haunt, frequent.

n.Cy. (J.W.) **Chs.¹** Rats harbour in a barn. Partridges harbour amongst turnips; **Chs.³** They harbour there continually. **Glo.²** **w.Som.¹** The police kept watch on the places he was known to harbour. Her told em how he did'n harboury there.

8. Of a deer or stag: to have a lair; to haunt, frequent.

w.Som.¹ To ascertain by tracking, or other means, that the deer is harbouring or laired in a particular spot or covert. **n.Dev.** If a man could steal a view of 'un, . . where he harbours, WHYTE-MELVILLE *Katerfelto* (1875) xv.

9. To track a stag to its lair.

w.Som.¹ **n.Dev.** To use woodman's language, he had fairly ' harboured his deer,' WHYTE-MELVILLE *Katerfelto* (1875) xvi ; A guinea is paid for each stag ' harboured' successfully, JEFFERIES *Red Deer* (1884) vi.

Hence **Harbourer,** *sb.* hunting term : a man whose duty it is to track out a stag's lair or ' harbour.'

w.Som.¹ The harbourer . . . is as important an officer in the establishment of a pack of hounds kept for hunting the wild deer as the huntsman himself. Indeed it would be well if every huntsman was to serve a novitiate as harbourer. It unfortunately happens that every under-keeper and loiterer about the haunts of the wild deer, thinks he can act as harbourer, COLLYNS, 76. **Dev.** The harbourer having reported a ' warrantable deer ' in Parsonage Wood, *Mem. Rev. J. Russell* (1883) xii. **n.Dev.** He has earned an unchallenged right to call himself the most skilful ' Harbourer ' in the west, WHYTE-MELVILLE *Katerfelto* (1875) xvi.

[**1.** I was a straunger and nedy of harboure, UDALL *Erasm. Par.* (1548) *Matt.* xxv. **2.** An harbar, *hospicium,* Cath. *Angl.* (1483).]

HARBY, HARCELET, see Herb, Haslet.

HARD, *adj., adv.* and *sb.* Var. dial. uses in Sc. Irel. Eng. and Colon. Also in forms **haad** e.Yks.¹; **hahd** e.Yks.; **hurd** Cmb. **1.** *adj.* and *adv.* In *comb.* (1) **Hard-backed,** miserly, stingy, noted for driving hard bargains ; (2) **-batch,** grape-wine ; see below; (3) **-bitten one,** a hard taskmaster; (4) **-bound,** constipated ; (5) **-bowed,** said of flax when the seed has formed ; (6) **-bread,** oatcake ; (7) **-buttons,** a boys' game ; see below ; (8) **— cake,** (9) **— cheese,** hard treatment, a hard lot, ' hard lines ' ; (10) **-core,** brick, rubbish, or refuse used to make foundations; (11) **-corn,** wheat and rye, as opposed to barley and oats ; (12) **-dick,** a pudding made only of flour and water ; (13) **— does,** see (9) ; (14) **-dumpling,** see (12) ; (15) **— eating,** dry food and corn, as opposed to grass; also called **Hard-food** ; (16) **-faced,** (a) impudent, obstinate, brazen-faced ; (b) obstinate in making a bargain ; (c) close-grained, hard in texture ; (17) **-favoured,** stern-faced ; coarse-featured ; (18) **-fish,** dried or salt fish ; (19) **-fist,** a miserly person ; (20) **-fisted,** covetous ; (21) **-fruit,** stone-fruit, plums, &c. ; (22) **-gait,** a hard road ; used *fig.* in *prov.*; see below ; (23) **-gob,** white metal ; (24) **-grain,** a present of wheat or money made to children at Christmas ;

(25) **— grass,** var. species of sedge or *Carex* ; (26) **-ground man,** a workman employed in driving rock other than coal ; (27) **-haddled,** hard-earned ; see Addle, *v.²* ; (28) **-handed,** stingy, niggardly, close-fisted ; (29) **— hap,** misfortune, adversity ; (30) **-head,** hardihood; (31) **-headed,** (a) unyielding, stubborn ; (b) shrewd, ' cute ' ; (32) **-hearted,** heart-breaking, distressing ; (33) **-hewer,** a stone-mason ; (34) **-hodden** or **-holden,** tightly held ; at a loss, embarrassed ; hard put to it ; (35) **-horn,** tightly ; (36) **-iron** or **Hardine,** (a) the black knapweed, *Centaurea nigra* ; also called **Hardhead** (q.v.) ; (b) the corn-crowfoot, *Ranunculus arvensis* ; (c) the spreading halbert-leaved orache, *Atriplex hastata* ; (37) **-matched,** hardly able ; (38) **— matter,** difficult ; (39) **— meat,** see (15) ; (40) **-melched,** of a cow: difficult to milk ; (41) **-mouthed,** obstinate, stubborn ; (42) **-nap,** a shrewd, clever fellow ; (43) **-ooined,** badly treated, over-worked ; see Hoin, *v.* ; (44) **-pin't,** said of grass when eaten off close to the bare ground ; (45) **-pushed,** hard put to it ; (46) **-race,** calcareous concretionary matter formed round fossilized bones, found in brick-earth; (47) **-sailing,** trouble, misfortune ; (48) **-set,** (a) scarcely able, hardly, with difficulty ; hard-pressed, in difficulties, straits ; (b) hungry ; (c) to overdo ; (49) **-setten,** said of eggs sat upon until nearly the date of hatching ; (50) **-stocking,** land on which more stock is pastured than it can properly nourish ; (51) **-thistle,** the creeping plume-thistle, *Carduus arvensis* ; (52) **-tree,** close-grained wood ; (53) **— water,** spring water as distinguished from rain or soft water ; (54) **— weight,** a trifle short of the weight named ; (55) **— wheat,** bearded wheat, *Triticum durum* ; (56) **— wood,** (a) oak and ash as distinguished from fir, willow, beech, &c. ; (b) firewood in logs or brands as distinguished from faggot-wood or ' wood ' simply ; (57) **-wood trees,** deciduous trees (with the exception of oak), not of the fir tribe ; (58) **-woolled one,** see (3) ; (59) **— word,** (a) abuse ; scandal ; (b) a blunt refusal ; (c) a pass-word or sign.

(1) **n.Yks.** He's a hard-backed un (T.S.). (2) **s.Hmp.** Do you fetch that bottle of hard-batch (wine made from the outdoor grapes), VERNEY *L. Lisle* (1870) vi. (3) **w.Wor.** A hard-bitten un as be no mon's friend, S. BEAUCHAMP *N. Hamilton* (1875) I. 3. (4) **Chs.¹** (5) **N.I.¹** (6) **n.Ir.** She bakit aboot three griddle fu's o' hard breid, LYTTLE *Paddy McQuillan,* 18. **Lan.** Wi'n yo have hard brade or loaf-brade ! WAUGH *Awd Bodle,* 250. (7) **Lon.** Several boys place one button each close together on a line. The game consists in hitting a particular button out of this line without touching the others. This is *gen.* played in London streets, GOMME *Games* (1894) 190. (8) **n.Lin.¹, Lei.¹, War.³** (9) **e.Yks.¹** It's hard cheese when yan awn bayns tons ther backs o' yan, *MS. add.* (T.H.) **w.Yks.²** To be turned off the premises where several generations of a family have lived and died, would be ' hard-cheese.' A criminal may deserve his twenty-one years' sentence of transportation, nevertheless it is ' hard cheese to the poor fellah ! ' Not.¹, **n.Lin.¹, Lei.¹, Oxf.** (G.O.) (10) **Lon.** The phrase ' hard-core ' seems strictly to mean all such refuse matter as will admit of being used as the foundation of roads, buildings, &c., MAYHEW *Lond. Labour* (ed. 1861) II. 281. (11) **N.Cy.¹, Nhb.¹ Dur.¹** Wheat or maslin, when growing, as distinguished from barley and oats. **Stf.** (K.) (12) **Sus.¹** (13) **Yks.** (J.W.) **n.Lin.¹** It's hard-does for a man and his wife and bairns to be thrawn oot o' wark wi'oot warnin'. **Glo.** These 'ere times with hard doos fur farmers, and wi' the 'cheenery and zo on, BUCKMAN *Darke's Sojourn* (1890) x. **Oxf.¹** *MS. add.* (14) **n.Yks.** (I.W.) (15) **Sc.** (A.W.) **Myo.** I'd like the white mare tuk off the grash an' gave some hard'atin' for a few days, STOKER *Snake's Pass* (1891) vi. (16, a) **Chs.³** I have heard a bold horse called ' a regular hard-faced one.' **s.Chs.¹** Ŭ tae·rbl aa·rd-fai·st wensh [A terr'ble hard-faced wench]. (b) **Chs.¹** (c) *ib.* Timber which is hard and difficult to work is said to be hard-faced. An apple of so close a texture that you can scarcely get your teeth through it would be called hard-faced. (17) **Ayr.** A stalwart, hard-favoured, grey-haired man-at-arms, GALT *Gilhaise* (1823) i. **Cum.¹⁴** (18) **Sc.** Indiscriminately given to cod, ling, and torsk, salted and dried (JAM.) ; *Scoticisms* (1787) 38. **Or.I.** PETERKIN *Notes* (1822) App. 32. **Cai.¹** (19) **s.Lin.** Ha'e you hired yer sen to an o'd hard-fist like her ! (T.H.R.) (20) **Nhp.¹** (21) **Ken.¹** (22) **Sc.** ' The hare maun come to the hard gait,' matters must take their course. *Gen.* addressed to those who appear wilful, and are determined to take their own way apparently against their interest (JAM.). (23)

w.Yks. *Leeds Merc. Suppl.* (Nov. 4, 1893); w.Yks.² (24) ne.Lan.¹ (25) Stf. Various sorts of seg grasses, provincially hard grass, iron grass, carnation grass, *Reports Agric.* (1798–1813) 27. (26) [*Reports Mines.*] (27) w.Yks. Dunnot be fooils goin an spendin boath yer time an yer hard-haddled cash at a jerry-shop, *Dewsbre Olm.* (1878) 3. (28) n.Sc. (JAM.) (29) Cum. Then hard hap have I, GILPIN *Ballads* (1874) 52. (30) w.Cy. (HALL.) (31, *a*) Cai.¹, Slk. (JAM.) (*b*) Nhb. (R.O.H.) (32) Sh.I. Is dis wadder iver gaun ta shange, Magnus! He's [it's] truly been a hard-heartid time dis while, as iver I mind, I tink, *Sh. News* (June 11, 1898). (33) Ken.¹² (34) Lakel.² Ah was hard hodden ta keep mi tongue atween mi teeth an' keep frae tellen mi mind streck oot. n.Yks.² ' I was hard-hodden frae laughing,' with difficulty I refrained from it. w.Yks. I have never seen a man so hard holden as he was, SNOWDEN *Web of Weaver* (1896) ii. (35) Sc. With his eyes shut hardhorn, *Magopico* (ed. 1836) 29. (36, *a*) Lan. (B. & H.), Chs.¹², Stf. (B. & H.), s.Not. (J.P.K.) (*b*) n.Cy. (HALL.) Midl. MARSHALL *Rur. Econ.* (1796) II. Der.², nw.Der.¹, Lei.¹ (*c*) Lei.¹ (37) n.Yks.² That wall's hard-match'd to stand. (38) Oxf.¹ *MS. add.* nw.Dev.¹ 'Tis hard matter to git about. (39) e.Yks. Maketh goodes fall sharply to their hard meate, BEST *Rur. Econ.* (1641) 76. (40) s.Chs.¹ (41) Cor. You loose-jaw! hard-mouth'd, chuckle-headed kna-ave, FORFAR *Poems* (1885) 47. (42) Hrf.² (43) w.Yks. And all the while this lovin' wife, Hard-ooined although shoo be, CUDWORTH *Dial. Sketches* (1884) 107. (44) Cum.⁴ (45) Sc. (A.W.), n.Cy. (J.W.), Oxf. (G.O.) w.Som.¹ We was terrible hard-pushed to get em a-dood in time. (46) Ken. It is called ' Hard race ' by the workmen . . . at the large brickyard near Erith, RAMSAY *Rock Specimens* (186a) 180. (47) e.Yks.¹ Poor awd Mally ; sha's had nowt bud hard-salin all her life-tahm, *MS. add.* (T.H.) (48, *a*) Sc. (A.W.) n.Yks. Ah's hard-set to dua 't (T.S.) ; T'parson was hard-set [to keep from laughing], TWEDDELL *Clevel. Rhymes* (1875) 35 ; n.Yks.¹²; n.Yks.⁴ Ah wur hardset ti git t'job deean i' tahm. ne.Yks.¹ Ah lay he'll be hard-set ti a'e deean afoor neet. e.Yks.¹ Ah's haad-set ti live o' that wage. .m.Yks.¹ w.Yks. Shoo wir hard-set to do sich a thing as that, HARTLEY *Clock Alm,* (1886) 44 ; w.Yks.¹² Lan.¹ He's hard-set, aw con tell thi—eawt o' wark an' his woife deawn wi' twins. e.Lan.¹, Not.¹ n.Lin.¹ We shall most on us be hard set if theäse prices hohds on a year or two longer. sw.Lin.¹ They're often hardset for a meal. Lei.¹ Nhp.¹ He is hard set to maintain his family. War.³, Hnt. (T.P.F.) Dev.³ He's hardzet to pay his rent. (*b*) w.Yks.² War.³ He is so hard set he will eat anything offered to him. (*c*) m.Yks.¹ Take him to the field with thee, and don't hardset him, now. (49) Cum. (J.Ar.), Cum.⁴ (50) s.Wil. I have known the principle of hard-stocking carried to an injurious length, MARSHALL *Review* (1817) V. 224. (51) e.An. (B. & H.) (52) Kcd. O get to me a cloak of cloth, A staff of good hard tree, MAIDMENT *Garl.* (1824) 30, ed. 1868. (53) Lakel.² Spring watter 'at jikes when ye wesh in 't. n.Lin.¹, Oxf. (G.O.) (54) e.Yks.¹ Twea pund, hahd weight, *MS. add.* (T.H.) Sus. I weighted a carp . . . and it proved 2 lbs. hard weight, MARCHANT *Diary* (1714–28) in *N. & Q.* (1879) 5th S. xi. 247. (55) Som. (W.F.R.) (56, *a*) Kcd. The whole of this is thickly planted with deciduous trees, or what is here called hard wood ; its distinction from the evergreens or firs, whose timber is comparatively softer and of less value, *Agric. Surv.* 343 (JAM.). Slg. Upwards of 200,000 trees of various kinds, but chiefly of hard wood, that is oak and ash, *ib.* 220. n.Lin.¹, w.Som.¹ (*b*) w.Som.¹ To be sold, about 100 cords of hard wood, in lots to suit purchasers, *Advt.* nw.Dev.¹ (57) Cum.⁴, w.Yks.¹ (58) Nrf. COZENS-HARDY *Broad Nrf.* (1893) 35. (59, *a*) Sc. Hard words break no bones (A.W.). Myo. Again he burst out at me . . . he would send the hard word round the country about me and my leman ! STOKER *Snake's Pass* (1891) xvi. Lakel.² He gat t'hard-word frae t'maister. Cum.⁴ (*b*) Wm. Ah assed him for a shillin', an' he gev mi t'hard-word at yance (B.K.). (*c*) Ir. So I gives Jack the hard word, CARLETON *Traits Peas.* (ed. 1843) I. 78.

2. Phr. (1) *hard about,* (2) — *again,* (3) — *at hand,* (4) — *by,* near, close to ; (5) — *enough,* sure enough, without doubt, certainly ; (6) — *laid on,* much oppressed or burdened with work, sickness, &c. ; (7) — *on,* (*a*) see (4); (*b*) nearly, almost, approaching to ; (*c*) hard at work, in full swing ; (*d*) fast asleep ; (8) — *to,* see (4) ; (9) — *upon,* see (7, *b*) ; (10) — *a-gallop,* galloping very fast ; (11) — *and fast,* (*a*) safely secured, immovable ; (*b*) vigorously, with great energy ; with eagerness or determination ; (*c*) see (5) ; (*d*) see (7, *d*) ; (12) — *and heather bred,* hardy, possessed of great vigour and activity ; (13) — *and sharp,* (*a*) scarcely, hardly, with difficulty, barely ; (*b*) cruelly, harshly ; (*c*) to

a nicety, just right ; (*d*) slightly short in the required weight or size ; (14) — *in the mouth,* stubborn, obstinate ; (15) — *of belief,* dubious, doubtful ; (16) — *of the feather,* used in reference to fighting cocks, fully grown and not soft-feathered ; (17) *to get it hard,* to find it a difficult matter ; (18) *to be at hard canny,* to have a struggle to make both ends meet ; (19) *to be in hard earnest,* to be in sober, downright earnest ; (20) *to have the hard drop in one,* to be penurious, miserly.

(1) w.Yks. It's hard about yonder clump of trees (C.C.R.). (2) Lakel.² It's hard again t'fell sides. Cum.⁴ Ye'll finnd t'hoose hard agean t'stayshin. n.Wm. Your stick is hard again your nief (B.K.). (3) Som. I was . . . thinken', mabbee, o' thik good-bye as was hard at hand, LEITH *Verbena* (1895) 99. (4) Abd. Hard by the house o' Robie Mill, FORBES *Shop Bill* (1785) 14. e.Yks.¹ w.Yks.⁵ Hard by t'owd church. Der.², nw.Der.¹ n.Lin. Yalthrup is hard by Bottesford (E.P.). Oxf. (G.O.) (5) n.Yks.²; n.Yks.⁴ He'll tell tha what he thinks, hard eaneeaf. w.Yks. (Æ.B.); w.Yks.⁵ ' I can du it hard eniff.' A man repairs a clock, and says, when he has concluded his task, ' Thear, it al go hard eniff now.' n.Lin. He'll goä hard enif if thoo nobbud axes him (M.P.). (6) Cum.¹⁴ w.Yks.¹; w.Yks.⁵ A lad sent to work at the factory when very young is ' hard-laid on.' A man emaciated in appearance by illness has ' bin hard Mad on, poor fellah !' n.Lin.¹, Nhp.¹ (7, *a*) Lakel.² s.Lin. You'll be hard on it when you reach the next cross roads (T.H.R.). (*b*) Cum.⁴ It'll be hard on till nect or we git heam. Wm. It'll be hard on ta ten mile ta Penrith (B.K.). Lei.¹ It's six o'clock, hard on. War.² Hard upon three months ; War.³ (*c*) Not.¹ Lei.¹ Ah'n bin aard on all dee. Shay's aard on at th' o'd man from mornin' to noight an' noight till mornin'. War.³, Oxf. (G.O.) (*d*) w.Yks. ' Is t'barn asleep ?' ' Ay, he's hard on ' (Æ.B.). (8) Cum. I wad fain a seen't cum hard tull us, *Borrowdale Lett.* in *Lonsdale Mag.* (Feb. 1867) 309. (9) Slk. It is hard upon the gloamin', HOGG *Tales* (1838) 68, ed. 1866. Nhp.¹ Hard upon eighty. Hmp. ' How far is it to Christchurch !' ' Oh, it's hard upon a mile ' (H.C.M.B.). Som. Hard upon thirty year have I a-bin clerk, RAYMOND *Love and Quiet Life* (1894) 107. (10) nw.Dev.¹ He raud roun' the corner 'ard-a-gallop. (11, *a*) n.Yks.² (*b*) n.Cy. Yah, ye mun hit it hard an' fast as weel, ta mack a wage (B.K.). Chs. GROSE (1790) *MS. add.* (M.) (*c*) n.Yks.² It is so, hard and fast. (*d*) n.Cy. Ah was hard an fast asleep (B.K.). w.Yks. (Æ.B.) (12) Nhb. ' Hard and heather-bred ' ran the ancient North-Tyne slogan ; 'hard and heather-bred—yet—yet—yet,' PEASE *Tales* (1899) 5 ; The slogan is actually ' Hard a—d ' (in allusion to constant training in the saddle) ' and heather-bred, yit, yit, yit !' (R.O.H.) (13, *a*) w.Yks. Ah catched t'train, but it wor hard and sharp (J.T.) ; w.Yks.¹ Hesto mesur, naa matters, it's nobbud hard and sharp. n.Lin.¹ I did catch th' traain, bud it was hard an' sharp, she was movin' when I got in. s.Cy. HOLLOWAY. w.Som.¹ Ees, mum, we was there, but 'twas hard and sharp ; the train was jis pon comin' eens we stapt. (*b*) Ayr. Ne'er grudge an' carp Tho' fortune use you hard an' sharp, BURNS *Ep. J. Lapraik* (Apr. 21, 1785) st. 8. w.Yks.¹ Not often used in this sense. (*c*) w.Yks.⁵ A shop-keeper who gives standing weight and not a draw, manages matters ' hard an' sharp.' A policeman who lays his hand upon the shoulder of a man stepping into a railway carriage, as the train is beginning to move, is ' hard an' sharp upon his customer,' or, the capture is a ' hard an' sharp ' one,—done to a nicety. (*d*) Wm. He sez ther's a steean o' taties e that pooak, but they'll be hard an' sharp seea many (B.K.). n.Yks.² s.Yks.¹ There was hard an' sharp of a bushel of them, *MS. add.* (T.H.) (14) Glo. Noa, thay 'oodn't 'gree to't, not they. ' Ye be dalled hard in the mouth,' says Willum, BUCKMAN *Darke's Sojourn* (1890) iv. (15) n.Yks. (T.S.) Cum.¹ (17) Wmh. Did you get it hard to pay your rint? (S.A.B.) (18) n.Yks.² A person is said to be at hard canny, who has to struggle ' to make ends meet.' (19) s.Dur. He's in hard-earnest (J.E.D.). (20) Ir. An' would stand his treat as well as another ; but now see what he is ! . . It was . . . no aisy matther to get him into a trate ; . . . he had always the hard drop in him, CARLETON *Fardorougha* (1848) *Introd.* 11.

3. *adj.* Hardy, enduring ; not sensitive to pain ; daring, bold, resolute.

Cum.¹ He's as hard as a fell teädd ; Cum.⁴ n.Yks.¹ He's bodden a vast ; he wur a desput hard man iv's yowth. ' Thae's hard lahtle chaps ; they heed it na mair an nowght ' ; of some young boys who had had several teeth out without a cry or a wry face. s.Yks. As hahd as a grund tooad, NICHOLSON *Flh-Sp.* (1889) 19. w.Yks. (C.C.R.) ; ' It al mack uz hard, this will,' answered Polly, TOM TREDDLEHOYLE *Bairnsla Ann.* (185a) 43. s.Chs.¹ Aa·r yüng

Ben)z ûz aa·rd ûz nee·lz; yŏ mi rûn û pin in·tû im ûn ey wû)n·û shuwt [Ahr young Ben's as hard as neels; yŏ may run a pin into him an' hey wunna showt]. nw.Der.[1]

Hence **Hardness**, *sb.* strength, applied to the voice.

n.Lin.[1] 'I shooted wi' all my hardness,' that is, I called as loud as I could.

4. Big, strong, robust, well-grown; growing, full-grown.
s.Cy. (HALL) LW.[1] 'He's a gurt hard bwoy,' he's a strong robust lad; I.W.[2] Dor. The youngest son hizzelf a hard bwoy o' nine, *Why John* (*Coll.* L.L.B.); A 'hard boy' means a boy of such an age and stoutness as to be able to do almost or quite a man's work, a boy from 16 to 19 years of age (O.P.C.); BARNES *Gl.* (1863). Som. Hard people, adults, JENNINGS *Obs. Dial.* w.Eng. (1895); Full grown, as hard stock or sheep. Hardboy, a boy of about 13 years old, W. & J. *Gl.* (1873); (W.F.R.) w.Som.[1] The word does not mean full-grown—it rather means growing. A 'hard boy' is a most common description of a strong lad, fit to work. So we hear of a 'hard colt,' 'hard slips' (young pigs of either sex), a 'hard maid'—this means a strong, growing lass.

Hence **Hardish**, *adj.* strong, robust, well-grown.
Wil. When I wur up a ardish bwoy, *Rhymes*, 5th S. 136; (G.E.D.) Dor.[1] When I wer up a hardish lad, 254. Som. When he was up a hardish lad, and without thought, RAYMOND *Love and Quiet Life* (1894) 207; Joseph Pierce! whom he had known from the first—who was up a hardish lad when he was a child, *ib. Men o' Mendip* (1898) iii.

5. Close-fisted, grasping, penurious, miserly; covetous.
Per. We a' ken ye for a hard thrifty body at winna spend yer ain, gin ye can finger ither folks, CLELAND *Inchbracken* (1883) 60, ed. 1887. Ayr. As he grew up he was counted a hard man, SERVICE *Notandums* (1890) 9. Lnk. I'm surely no so desperate hard as a' that, ROY *Generalship* (ed. 1895) 120. Ir. I was never much acquainted with the Donovans. I'm tould they're a hard pack, that loves the money, CARLETON *Fardorougha* (1848) i. N.I.[1] n.Yks.[4] He's a hard un ti bargain wi'. w.Yks. THORESBY *Lett.* (1703); w.Yks.[4]

6. Of spirits: strong, undiluted, raw.
Abd. Ye're maybe jist as weel nae to meddle wi' the hard stuff till your beard's a bit langer, GREIG *Logie o' Buchan* (1899) 10. Ir. You must put a grain o' shugar an' a dhrop o' bilin' wather to it. It may do very well hard for the servants, CARLETON *Fardorougha* (1848) i. N.I.[1] [Aus. To those who are used to it cool bitter beer goes well in any kind of weather. Anything is better than 'the confounded hard stuff! BOLDREWOOD *Colon. Reformer* (1890) I. viii.]

Hence **Hard**, *sb.* whisky, esp. in phr. *the hard.*
Inv. (H.E.F.) Lnk. Ne'er a sup o' saft or hard to drink But ginger, lemonade, an' sic-like trash, COGHILL *Poems* (1890) 129.

7. Of ale or beer: sour, acid, sharp.
Sc. (A.W.) Lakel.[2] This yal's as hard as a whinstun. Cum.[1] Wm. T'leetnin' turned t'yal hard (B.K.). n.Yks.[1], w.Yks.[1], Chs.[1], s.Chs.[1] Der.[2], nw.Der.[1] n.Lin.[1] This aale o' yours is uncommon bard. s.Lin. The aâle's gone that hard the men saâ' they weânt drink eny moore on it (T.H.R.). Nhp.[1] The beer is hard. War.[2], Hnt. (T.P.F.) w.Som.[1] Good hard cider's best to work by.

8. Half-drunk. Yks. (HALL), w.Yks.[4]

9. A term used in fitting in joinery, masonry, &c.; see below.
Cai.[1] Having certain inequalities of surface which prevent close contact at parts. At such places the surfaces are said to be hard, i. e. something must be pared off to make a perfect fit. Abd. When two pieces of wood, &c. that are to be fitted together, are close at one place and not at another, they are said to be hard where they thus come into contact (JAM.).

Hence **Hard**, *sb.* the place where two pieces of wood join too closely together. Abd. (*ib.*)

10. Convex as opposed to concave.
w.Som.[1] In planing a true surface, any convex part is said to be hard; if concave, 'slack.' uw.Dev.[1] Used in mow-making in the sense of convex. 'I rim the moo's purty hard jis' yur,' i. e. certain sheaves project at this point.

11. *adv.* Of the wind: fiercely, strongly.
Sc. (A.W.) Lakel.[2] When t'wind blows hard frae Stowgill eyast. Cum.[4], Yks. (J.W.)

12. Tightly, firmly, securely.
Sh.I. He put on his waescot, an' tied da tow o' his left rivlin a corn harder, *Sh. News* (Aug. 7, 1897). e.Yks. NICHOLSON *Flk-Sp.* (1889) 66.

13. Quickly, very fast.
n.I.[1] Now run hard. e.Yks. NICHOLSON *Flk-Sp.* (1889) 66

w.Yks. (J.W.) n.Lin.[1] Th' gress'll graw hard enif noo this sup o' raain's cum'd. ns.Wor. He allus goes as 'ard as 'e can tear (J.W.P.). Cor. Then I up on my horse and galloped away as hard as I could, BARING-GOULD *Vicar* (1876) vi.

14. Loudly, out loud; aloud.
Dev. A farmer, on being asked to read through a document before signing it, said to me, 'Must I read it hard?' *Reports Provinc.* (1897); Speak harder for I can't hear you, *ib.* (1884) 20; 'Whot's Bet blazing about now, then!' 'Aw, I dawn't know; 'tez the likes ov she tû holly za 'ard's 'er can,' HEWETT *Peas. Sp.* (1892) 53; Dev.[1] Than telling to hizzell, and bamby out hard, a. nw.Dev.[1] Spaik harder; I can't yur ee.

15. Much.
n.Yks.[4] It ficked that hard, whahl Ah c'u'dn't ho'd it. w.Yks. (J.W.) Chs.[3] Oo fretted very hard.

16. *Obs.* Too.
Hrf. 'Hard high,' too high. 'Hard low,' too low, RAY (1691) *MS. add.* (J.C.) 101.

17. *sb. Fig.* Difficulty, hardship, esp. in phr. *to come through the hard*, to encounter difficulties, experience adverse fortune.
Sc. (JAM.) Abd. A plain North-country bard, Who fain would cripple thro' the hard, SHIRREFS *Sale Catal.* (1795) 3. Lnk. The bits o' bairns run a great risk o' coming through the hard, ROY *Generalship* (ed. 1895) 73.

Hence **Hardship**, *sb.* a difficulty, strait.
Sh.I. He was tellin me what a hardship he was in fir meal dis year, afore he got it aff da eart. STEWART *Tales* (1892) 17.

18. *pl.* That part of boiled food which sticks to the pot; thin, hard cakes that come off the sides of a pot in which porridge, &c. has been prepared. Also in form **hardens.** Lnk. (JAM.)

19. *pl.* The calx of coal from a forge; very hard iron cinders. e.An.[1], Suf.[1], e.Suf. (F.H.)

20. A firm foreshore or gravelly landing-place in a harbour or creek; a wharf, landing-place.
Nhb. The 'Brotherly Love' wis lyin on the hard at Alum House Ham (R.O.H.); Nhb.[1] Ess. Under the cliff was a good beach, termed a 'hard,' BARING-GOULD *Mehalah* (1885·3. Hmp.[1] Cor. Tarring of boats on the hard, PEARCE *Inconsequent Lives*, 22. [At four minutes to three the Cambridge crew left the Leander hard, *Standard* (Mar. 28, 1887) 3.]

21. A hard patch of land in a marsh; land bordering the turf-moor marshes. Also used *attrib.*
Nhp.[2] Applied in the fenny districts to those patches of land which, from superior elevation, or other causes, remain hard and dry during the winter season. Cmb. Leaving the hurds of Denny Abbey upon the east, *Reports Agric.* (1793–1813) 129. Brt. That warn't no swamp mash, but a hard mash, EMERSON *Son of Fens* (1892) 197; The swan dearly loves a 'hard' covered with weed, *ib. Birds* (ed. 1895) 215; (P.H.E.) [It consists of a flat, interspersed with small elevations and hills, which, to distinguish from the flat are called hard lands, STEPHENS *Farm Bk.* (ed. 1849) I. 490.]

22. The stoned part of a road as distinguished from the sides.
Lin. The middle of a road is ... called 'the hard' to distinguish it from the sides, which are not stoned. There was a trial at Lincoln assizes concerning certain encroachments ... made on a highway. .. One chief matter in dispute was whether land had been taken in within fifteen feet of the middle of the 'hard.' The 'hard' is sometimes used to distinguish a raised footpath from the rest of the highway. This however is uncommon, *N. & Q.* (1881) 6th S. iv. 98. n.Lin.[1]

23. A small marble. Som. (HALL)

24. *pl.* Torches made of rags dipped in tar.
Sc. When rags dipped in tar are employed [as torches] they are called Hards, probably from the French, SCOTT *Guy M.* (1815) xxvi, *note.*

HARD, see Earth, *sb.*[1], Herd, *sb.*
HARDAH, *sb.* Cor.[12] Elvan rock.
HARDEN, *sb.* Sc. Nhb. Dur. Cum. Wm. Yks. Not. Lin. Lei. War. Wor. Shr. Hrf. Also in forms **hardest** Sh.I.; **hardin** Sc. (JAM.) Abd. Lakel.[2] n.Yks. w.Yks.[2]; **harding** n.Yks.[14] ne. Yks.[1] m.Yks.[1] w.Yks.[5]; **hardow** Sh.I.; **haren** Nhb.[1]; **harn** Sc. (JAM.) Cai.[1] N.Cy.[1] Nhb.[1] n.Yks.[124] m.Yks.[1]; **harran** e.Fif.; **harren** N.Cy.[1]; **hearn** Nhb.[1]; **herden** se.Wor.[1] Shr.[1]; **hurden** Lei.[1] War.[28] Wor. Shr.[1] Hrf.[2] [(h)a·rdən, harn, h)ä·din.] 1. Very coarse cloth made

m the refuse or 'hards' of flax and hemp; sack-cloth. so used *attrib.* and *fig.* See **Hards.**

Sh.I. Before the introduction of cotton goods, linen and hardow re the only bed and body material in the house. Hardow cloth s made from lint, very imperfectly dressed, a great portion of rind still adhering to the fibre, *Sh. News* (Aug. 7, 1897). **nd.Sc.** th regard to the weather, the saw is: 'A harn Monanday cks a linen week,' GREGOR *Flk-Lore* (1881) 149. CaI.¹ Bnff. llowses, Harns, Beet Hose . . . were ingeniously arranged, RDON *Chron. Keith* (1880) 74. Abd. His hardin sark as white 's driven snaw, *Guidman Inglismaill* (1873) 32. Frf. His bare ows were seen through his frockie o' harn, WATT *Poet. Sketches* 80) 54. Per. Seyin' sowens and spinnin' harn, SPENCE *Poems* 98) 142. e.Per. As coorse as Coupar harn (W.A.C.). FIf. m—For harden to be jumps to them, £3 10s. 0d., ANDREWS *gone Ch. Life* (1899) 189. Dmb. Weel fed wi' brose and sarked harn, SALMON *Gowodean* (1868) 12. Ayr. Her cutty sark o' isley harn, BURNS *Tam o' Shanter* (1790) l. 171. Lnk. A good ck of harn and linen cloth, HAMILTON *Poems* (1865) 201. Edb. ne'er wad gat mair leave to skip On skin or harn, LIDDLE *ms* (1821) 51. Slk. A strong harn shirt, clean as a lily, CHR. RTH *Noctes* (ed. 1856) II. 337. n.Cy. GROSE (1790); N.Cy.¹ b. BRAND *Pop. Antiq.* (ed. 1870) I. 208; Nhb.¹ Sometimes applied a coarse thread. Dur.¹ Lakel.¹ Very rough and coarse linen ed in the last century for jackets and overcoats; Lakel.² n.Yks. bit ə kuərs harden maks giud ruf tŭilis (W.H.); n.Yks.¹; n.Yks.² wide-setten harn appron,' a rough apron of open texture; Yks.⁴ ne.Yks.¹ Wheer's my au'd hard'n appron? e.Yks.¹, Yks.¹ w.Yks. Hawkin harden o' ther awn manifacter, LUCAS *ud. Nidderdale* (c. 188ə) 217; A rough harden apron is much ed by cottage housewives to cover up the dress, while working T.); w.Yks.¹²; w.Yks.⁵ A finer kind of canvass, of which wels, aprons for house-work, and 'brats,' too, sometimes, are de, &c. s.Not. (J.P.K.) Lin. THOMPSON *Hist. Boston* (1856)); Lin.¹, sw.Lin.¹, Lei.¹ War.² Flower [flour] of England, fruit Spain, Met together in a storm of rain, A hempen shirt, and a rden cravat, If you're a wise man, tell me that, *Old Riddle.* s. A plum-pudding; War.³ Wor. An undergarment, called in the ntry language a 'hurden,'or 'hoggen' shirt, made of the coarsest he hemp, *Wil. Arch. Mag.* XXVI. 7. ne.Wor. (J.W.P.), se.Wor.¹ r.¹ The waiver's maden a nice piece o' 'uckaback of the 'erden rn—it'll do mighty well for the men's tablecloths. Hrf.²A hurden ther is better than a golden father [a rough hard-working mother].

Hence **Harn'd,** *adj.* made of strong coarse linen. Rnf. He took his weel harn'd weddin' sark, BARR *Poems* (1861) 50.

Comp. (1) **Harden-** or **Harn-brat,** a long pinafore or ter garment made of 'harden' or coarse hempen cloth; -**cloth,** a coarse hempen cloth used in wrapping bales, .; (3) -**gown,** a sackcloth or coarse linen garment worn a penitent's gown; see below; (4) -**jacket,** (*a*) a loose d light jacket worn over the shirt when stripped for rk; (*b*) a top shirt made of coarse linen; (5) -**kytle,** a se jacket worn by girls when employed in tending ttle or in outdoor work; (6) -**pock** or -**poke,** a bag or ck made of coarse cloth; (7) -**sark,** (*a*) a coarse linen hempen shirt; (*b*) a kind of overall made of coarse en; (8) -**wab,** a web of coarse cloth.

(1) Lakel.² m.Yks.¹ A harding brat, hempen pinafore; or a g outer garment of the kind, with or without sleeves, and only n in town districts. (a) Cum. The Cumberland clergyman in mer times received as part of his remuneration a 'sark of rden cloth,' SULLIVAN *Cum. and Wm.* (1857) 87; Cum.⁴ Not much ed now. Wm. Shirts of this cloth were apt to make too free the skin, from their natural inflexibility. To render them a de more tractable and kindly, they were taken to some neighbour- brook, where there was a battling stone : . . being steeped in water, were laid in folds upon the stone, and beat with a ttling wad, *Lonsdale Mag.* (1822) III. 291. (3) Sc. An offender, 'ged to perform a public penance on this [repentance] stool, as first clothed in an appropriate habit, the Scottish representa- e of the traditional white sheet, which consisted of a cloak of arse linen, known as the 'harden goun,' the 'harn goun,' or e 'sack goun,' ANDREWS *Bygone Ch. Life* (1899) 111; The acken sark' had a variety of names, such as the 'harden gown,' e 'sack gown,' the 'harn gown,' and 'the linen.' Each parish supposed to have one of these habits, GRAHAM *Writings* 38g). (4, 5) Cum.¹⁴ (6) Per. (W.A.C.) e.FIf. Drawin' frae s oxter pouch a dirty harran-poke, LATTO *Tam Bodkin* (1864) iv. 2. The mice charmed the harden poke and let out the chisels, LLER & SKERTCHLY *Fenland* (1878) iv. (7, *a*) Sc. The hard

VOL. III.

harn sark plaid clash between his legs like a wet dish clout, GRAHAM *Writings* (1883) II. 37; The whole front of his pure white harn sark, OCHILTREE *Redburn* (1895) ii. Sh.I. Perhaps very few people living in this Diamond Jubilee Year, have ever seen a hardest sark, *Sh. News* (Aug. 7, 1897). Or.I. The limpet bro' began to rin Atween his harn sark an' his skin, *Pasty Toral* (1880) l. 100, in ELLIS *Pronunc.* (1889) V. 800. Ked. Wi' naething save his harn sark Upon his dreepin' back, GRANT *Lays* (1884) 4. (*b*) Dur.¹, Lakel.¹ Cum. Originally the Westcote priest had been paid by 'clog-shoon, harden-sark, whittle-gait, and guse-gait,' LINTON *Lizzie Lorton* (1867) xiv. (8) w.Sc. Every sparge that gaed frae my fit was like a harn-wab, CARRICK *Laird of Logan* (1835) 162.

3. The tarred tow or oakum used for caulking the seams of ships. Nhb.¹

HARDEN, *v.* and *adj.* Sc. Irel. Nhb. Cum. Yks. Lan. Stf. Lin. War. Shr. Hrf. Oxf. Brks. Also in forms **hairn** Cum.¹⁴; **harn** N.I.¹ Uls. Cum.¹⁴; **haurn** Sc. (JAM.); **hurden** War.²⁴ s.War.¹ Oxf. Brks. **1.** *v.* To be obdurate, incorrigible. Used in *pass.*

m.Yks.¹ A mother will exclaim, on observing a toddling child dip- ping its fingers in a cream-bowl, 'He's hardened to the haft.' s.Stf. Yo' ca' talk him o'er, he's tu hardened, PINNOCK *Blk. Cy. Ann.* (1895).

Hence **Hardened,** *ppl. adj.* used as a term of reproach. m.Yks.¹ Very common in opprobrium. 'Thou harden'd thief.' w.Yks. (J.W.), Oxf. (G.O.)

2. To encourage, incite, urge on. *Gen.* with *on* or *up.* Also used *reflex.*

n.Yks. Thoo harden'd om on (T.S.); n.Yks.¹ 'He hardened him on tiv it'; of a person reluctant or afraid to act, but encouraged by another to the venture. 'Poor lahtle chap! he ommost brak' out when tahm caen' te gan i' airnest; but he hardened hissel' oop an niver grat nae mair an nowght; n.Yks.²; n.Yks.⁴ Ah deean't leyke t'job, bud Ah s'all a'e ti harden mysel til 't. ne.Yks.¹ He hardened hissen up at last. He's awlus hardenin' 'em on intiv a mischief. e.Yks. When lads was fightin, Tom harden'd 'em on all he could, NICHOLSON *Flk-Sp.* (1889) 66. w.Yks. They're ready enough abaht hard'nin 'em on, BANKS *Wkfld. Wds.* (1865); w.Yks.² Lan. Hardenin me on to make a bigger foo of misel, CLEGG *Sketches* (1895) 472. sw.Lin.¹ They harden one another on. George kep' hardening on him on to come.

3. To roast on the embers; to toast bread on a griddle. Sc. Oh to be haurning bread at my aunt's hearthstane, *Blackw. Mag.* (May 1820) 165 (JAM.). Bwk. Knuckled Cakes . . . haurned, or havered [toasted] on the decayed embers of the fire, HENDER- SON *Pop. Rhymes* (1856) 66. Slk. She . . . has a gift at haurning bread, HOGG *Tales* (1838) 282, ed. 1866. Dmf. Knuckled cakes, made of meal, warm from the mill, haurned on the decayed embers of the fire, and smeared with honey, CROMEK *Remains* (1810) 337; A common term in Nithsdale (JAM.). N.I.¹ Uls. Hardening bread, cooking it against the mudyarn before the fire, or on a griddle, *Uls. Jrn. Arch.* (1853-1862) V. 99.

4. To dry or air clothes, &c., by holding them to the fire, or by hanging them out in the open air.

Cum.¹⁴, ne.Lan.¹ Shr.¹ Mind as yo' 'ard'n them things afore yo' putten 'em away; Shr.² Shr., Hrf. BOUND *Provinc.* (1876). Oxf. 'Harden' is com. used on days which are not good for dry- ing. 'I think I will hang the clothes out: if it don't dry it will harden them.' Clothes are not dry when hardened : just the worst of the wet taken out of them. The drying is completed by hanging them in front of a fire (G.O.); Oxf.¹ 'Ang the things out, Nancy; if it dun't wet um 'll 'arden, *MS. add.*

5. Of the weather : to clear up and become settled after rain. *Gen.* with *out* or *up.*

Cai.¹ Bnff.¹ We've hid eneuch o' rain noo. A howp it'll harden up. n.Yks.¹ I think it will harden out innoo (I.W.); n.Yks.¹ 'It's to be hoped 't will harden out'; said when a rainy fit in harvest-time appeared to be likely to give way to fair weather; n.Yks.² 'The day will harden out,' the rain will keep off. 'We want t'weather te harden up a bit,' to become dry; n.Yks.⁴ It's neea ewse to'ning t'hay, whahl it hardens up a bit. ne.Yks.¹ It'll a'e ti harden oot afoor wa git onny matters o' sun. w.Yks. (C.C.R.), w.Yks.⁵

Hence *Hardening of the drouth, phr.* a continuance or settlement of dry weather.

Cld. This term is used by country people, when, during a time of drouth, a dull threatening day has become clear and settled : 'It was jist a hardenin' o' the drouth' (JAM.).

6. Of prices : to advance, grow dear, heighten. Sc. (A.W.) n.Cy. BAILEY (1721); GROSE (1790); N.Cy.¹; N.Cy.² 'The market hardens,' things grow dear. Nhb.¹ w.Yks.¹ T'corn

K

rayther hardens; w.Yks.⁵ 'Wheat's hard'ning agean ah reckon,'— getting up again I suppose.

7. *adj. Comb.* (1) Harden-face, a bold, brazen-faced person; (2) -faced, (*a*) impertinent, brazen-faced; hard-hearted; (*b*) of the weather: threatening, lowering, gloomy, unsettled.

(1) m.Yks.¹ (2, *a*) n.Yks.² 'A harden-faced fellow,' a delinquent without showing signs of repentance. m.Yks.¹ Thou harden'-faced brute!—thou's no pity in thee! Lin. STREATFEILD *Lin. and Danes* (1884) 336. n.Lin.¹ A harden-faaced huzzy. s.Lin. Yah'd better mind, or I'll gi'e you a taäste o' my strap, yah young harden-faaced rascal. He's a harden-faäced skin-flint (T.H.R.). (*b*) n.Yks.¹; n.Yks.² The sky looks a harden-faced look; n.Yks.⁴, m.Yks.¹

8. Of the weather: windy, drying; cold, bleak.

War. *Leamington Courier* (Mar. 13, 1897); War.²⁴ s.War.³ It's hurden weather now. Oxf. It is such hurden weather (M.A.R.). Brks. (W.H.Y.)

HARDENING, *vbl. sb.* Chs.¹ Same as Basoning (q.v.).

HARDENS, *sb. pl.* Bdf. Small pieces of sward at the ends of ploughed land, on which the horses turn.

BATCHELOR *Anal. Eng. Lang.* (1809) 135.

HARDESS, *sb.* Irel. The hard-twisted and gummed silk thread used for netting. Ant. GROSE (1790) *MS. add.* (C.)

HARDEST, see Harden, *sb.*

HARDFULLY, *adv.* Cum. Industriously.

Cum.¹ He gits his leevin reet hardfully; Cum.⁴

HARD-HEAD(S, *sb.* Var. dial. uses in Sc. Irel. and Eng. 1. A boys' game; see below. Cf. hardy-nut.

w.Yks. Two lads have each a chestnut, or a cork, strung on a string, and take alternate turns at striking at each other's chestnut with a view to breaking it (H.L.).

2. A hard felt hat.

Der. The miller's Sunday hard-head was on its proper hook, CUSHING *Voe* (1888) II. iii.

3. A hard cinder found in furnaces. Also called crozzil (q.v.). w.Yks.² 4. The refuse of tin after smelting. Cor.¹²

5. A small coin of mixed metal.

Sc. An ancient Scotch coin value three pennies Scotch or one farthing Engl. (*De Cardonnel's Numism. Scotiae*), GROSE (1790) *MS. add.* (C.) Ayr. Bonnet Pieces. Testoons, Hard Heads or Non Sunts, and Bawbees, SERVICE *Notandums* (1890) 68.

6. The grey gurnard, *Trigla gurnardus.*

Fif. NEILL *Fishes* (1810) 14 (JAM.). [SATCHELL (1879).]

7. A kind of sea-scorpion, prob. the fatherlasher, *Cottus scorpius.*

Fif. *Scorpius major nostras*; our fishers called it Hard-head, SIBBALD *Hist. Fif.* (1803) 128 (JAM.).

8. The lake-trout, *Salmo lacustris.*

Cum. We conjecture that this is the fish called in the Lakes of Derwent, Bassenthwaite, &c., Hard Head, HUTCHINSON *Hist. Cum.* (1794) I. 460; Cum.¹ Cum.⁴ A large (out-grown) kind of trout found in the Esk, Irt, Mite, Bleng and Calder rivers. It has also been caught in Wastwater.

9. The black knapweed, *Centaurea nigra.*

Nhb.¹ Called also 'horse-nobs.' Cum.⁴, w.Yks. (W.M.E.F.), w.Yks.¹, ne.Lan.¹, Chs.¹, s.Chs.¹, n.Lin.¹, Wor. (J.R.W.) Shr. Why it brings nowt but snizzle grass and hardyeds, *Science Gossip* (1870) 227; Shr.¹ The hard globose heads of *Centaurea nigra*, black Knapweed. s.Pem. (W.M.M.), Glo.¹, Wil.¹ Wil., Dor. Hard-heads . . . is at Lyneham and Whitchurch given to the Knapweeds, *Sarum Dioc. Gazette* (Jan. 1891) 14, col. 2. Dor. (G.E.D.), Cor.¹²

10. The greater knapweed, *Centaurea Scabiosa.* Glo.¹

11. The plantain, *Plantago major* and *P. lanceolata.*

w.Yks. (W.M.E.F.) ne.Lan.¹ The seed-heads of plantain. Wor. (J.R.W.) Wil. Spear-plantain . . . the Hawkchurch name of the plant [is] Hard-heads, *Sarum Dioc. Gazette* (Jan. 1891) 14, col. 2. Dor. (G.E.D.), Dev.⁴, Cor.¹²

12. The sneeze-wort, *Achillea Ptarmica.* Ayr. *Agric. Surv.* 675 (JAM.).

13. The scabious, *Scabiosa Succisa.* Lan.¹ 14. The corn-cockle, *Lychnis Githago.* Nhb. (B. & H.) 15. The cow-parsnip, *Heracleum Sphondylium.* Glo.¹

16. A large, sour apple.

Lakel.² Sowen gurt apples, an' as hard as granite.

HARDISHE, *sb. Obs.* Wxf.¹ A thing.

O hardishe o' anoor [One thing or another].

HARDISHREW, -STRAW, -STROW, HARDLE, see Harvest-shrew, Harl.

HARDLEYS, *adv.* Sc. Nhb. Cum. Yks. Also written hardlies Sc. (JAM. *Suppl.*) Nhb.¹; hardlys Nhb. m.Yks.¹; and in forms hadleys n.Cy. (HALL.); hairly, harleys Cum.¹⁴ Hardly, scarcely. Cf. hardlings.

Sc. (JAM. *Suppl.*) n.Cy. (HALL.), N.Cy.¹ Nhb. Thoo's hardlys sae mazed, efther arl, or thoo wouldn't could ha' thowt on, *S. Tyne-dale Stud.* (1896) *Robbie Armstrong*; Nhb.¹ He'd hardlies getten there when it happened. Ye's hardlies catch the train, aa doot. Cum. He hardleys can grease his awn clogs, ANDERSON *Ballads* (1805) 92; Cum.¹; Cum.⁴ Tekin to keepin' another man's bairn, when he can arlies keep hissel, *Rosenthal*, 15. m.Yks.¹ I was that tired I could hardlys step a foot.

HARDLINGS, *adv.* n.Cy. Dur. Lakel. Cum. Yks. Stf. Not. Lin. Also in forms ardlins Yks.; haadlins e.Yks.¹; hadlins n.Cy. (HALL.); hardlins Dur.¹ Lakel.² n.Yks.² e.Yks. w.Yks.¹ Stf. Not. n.Lin. [h]a·rd, h]ä·dlinz.] Hardly, scarcely.

n.Cy. (HALL.), Dur.¹, Lakel.² Cum. Ah'm hardlings worth savin'; Ah ken that, CLARK *Rise of River* (1897) 199; My hand can hardlins find it, GILPIN *Pop. Poetry* (1875) 55. n.Yks. Noo, my lad, thoo asn't ardlins iver seen ony partridges this mornin ommost! FRANK *Fishing* (1894) 30; Ah hardlins knew how te git yam efter't, TWEDDELL *Clevel. Rhymes* (1875) 36; n.Yks.¹²⁴, ne.Yks.¹ e.Yks. His ayms began ti wahk, whahl he cud hardlins bahd, NICHOLSON *Flk-Sp.* (1889) 36; e.Yks.¹ Ah can haadlins crammle [crawl] alang. w.Yks. Aw can hardlins beleeve mi awn een, HARTLEY *Cloch Alm.* (1874) *Pref.*; Ha doant naw ha foaks cud help it ardlins, ROGERS *Nan Bunt* (1899) 2; w.Yks.¹; w.Yks.⁵ Av hardlings gotten 't done yet. Its hardlings the thing; hamsumivver lehr it goa! Stf. I can hardlins move about at times, FLETCHER *Wapentake* (1895) 29; Common near New-castle (J.T.). Not. I hardlins ever go out (J.H.B.). Lin. I laughed till I could hardlings caw, BROWN *Lit. Laur.* (1890) 48; (J.T.F.) n.Lin. He hardlin's knaws if cauves is born wi' horns, PEACOCK *Tales* (1886) 77; n.Lin.² Ther's hardlin's time to catch th' packit noo.

HARDLY, *adj.* Yks. Lan. Hardy, robust, strong; hard.

w.Yks. She was a very hardly woman, she used to come and scold at my mother when she was laid up with her headache and say, 'What, gurning [crying, sbirking] again' (E.L.); (C.C.R.) Lan. Being of a fresh complexion and not very hardly, 'twas much to be questioned whether the cittie aire would agree with her, *Life A. Martindale* (1685) 6, ed. 1845.

HARDOW, see Harden, *sb.*

HARDS, *sb. pl.* Sc. Yks. Chs. Midl. Stf. Der. Not. Lin. Lei. War. Wor. Shr. Hrf. Rdn. e.An. Also in forms herdes Shr.¹; herds nw.Der.¹ War.² w.Wor.¹ se.Wor.¹ Hrf.²; huerds Chs.¹; hurds Yks. Stf. (K.) Lei.¹ War.²³ s.Wor. Shr.¹ Rdn.¹ Nrf. [hardz, h]ädz, ŭdz.] The coarse refuse of flax or hemp, tow; the worked fibre of flax or hemp. Rarely in *sing.*

Sc. (JAM.), Cai.¹ Kcd. She held the herd on the beam, And gar'd the treddles ply, JAMIE *Muse* (1844) 135. Yks. (K.) w.Yks. Rags from closely woven cloth, that is of the hind *gen.* worn by men (M.F.); w.Yks.²⁴ Chs.¹ Now called yerds. Midl., Stf. (K.) nw.Der.¹, Not.², n.Lin.¹, Lei.¹ War.²⁸, w.Wor.¹, s.Wor. (H.K.), se.Wor.¹ Shr. The small pieces of coarse matted linen used to stuff mattresses, the refuse of flax or hemp, the unravelling of twine, BOUND *Provinc.* (1876); Shr.¹ *Obsol.* Hrf.², Rdn.¹, e.An.¹ Nrf. GROSE (1790).

[Hyrdys or herdys of flax or hempe, *stuppa, Prompt.*; A sukkenye That not of hempene herdes was, CHAUCER *R. Rose*, 1233. OE. *heordan (Corpus Gl.*)]

HARDY, *adj.* and *sb.* Sc. Irel. Nhb. Dur. Cum. Yks. Stf. 1. *adj.* In *comb.* (1) Hardy-earnest, downright earnest; (2) -nut, a boys' game; see below.

(1) s.Dur. He's in hardy-carnest (J.E.D.). (2) Nhb.¹ A boyish game played with nuts pierced with a hole for a string. Each alternately aims a blow at his opponent's nut so as to break it.

2. Strong, robust, of a strong constitution; brave, enduring.

Abd. Mary was never jist fat you wud ca' unco hardy, ALEXANDER *Ain Flk.* (1882) 34. Frf. 'Ay, she's hardy,' agreed the town, 'but it's better, maybe, for hersel', BARRIE *Tommy* (1896) 368. w.Yks. Applied to one who is resolute and intrepid, or inured to fatigue (C.C.R.).

Hence Hardiness, *sb.* bravery, endurance.

Fif. Eschew the feats and wark divine O' hardiness and weir, TENNANT *Papistry* (1827) 172.

3. Frosty. Sc. (A.W.) N.I.¹ It's a hardy mornin'. 4. *sb. pl.* Broken stones, used as road metal.

N.I.¹ 'Nappin' hardies,' breaking stones.

5. A clay marble having a bright surface. Cum.⁴

6. A tool used in making nails by hand.

s.Stf. Somebry had stole my hardy soo I couldner work, PIN-ROCK *Blk. Cy. Ann.* (1895).

7. A fixed, shouldered chisel, placed upright in a square hole in a blacksmith's anvil, upon which he cuts hot iron.

Nhb.[1] Dur. GIBSON *Up-Weardale Gl.* (1870). w.Yks.[2]

HARDY-MOUSE, *sb.* Nhp.[1] The shrew-mouse, *Mus araneus.* See Harvest-shrew.

HARE, *sb.*[1] Var. dial. uses in Sc. Irel. and Eng. Also in form ar· Shr.[1] 1. In *comb.* (1) Hare-bell, (*a*) the wild hyacinth, *Scilla nutans;* (*b*) the bluebell, *Campanula rotundifolia;* (2) -bouk, the body of a hare; (3) ·'s-foot, the cotton-grass, *Eriophorum vaginatum;* (4) ·'s-foot clover, the trefoil, *Trifolium arvense;* (5) ·'s-foot fern, the Killarney fern, *Trichomanes radicans;* (6) -gate, an opening in a hedge, sufficient for the passage of hares; (7) -hole, a pitfall dug in the run of a hare; (8)·'s-meat, the wood-sorrel, *Oxalis Acetosella;* (9)-nut, the earth-nut, *Bunium flexuosum;* (10) -parsley, the cow-parsley, *Anthriscus sylvestris;* (11) pied, resembling the colour of a hare; (12) -scaled, having a cleft or hare-lip ; (13) -scart, (14) -sha, (15) -shard, (16) shaw, (17) -ahed, (18) -shie, (19) -shore, a hare-lip; (20) shorn or -shawn, (21) -shotten, see (12); (22) -skart, see 19); (23) -smoot, see (6); (24) -snickle, a trap for hares. (1, *a*) Ldd. (B. & H.), Dev.[4] (*b*) Abd. The daisy white and harebells blue, CADENHEAD *Bon Accord* (1853) 111. Per. The modest primrose set in green, And bonnie harebell blue, EDWARDS *Strathearn Lyrics* (1889) 50. Rnf. The bonnie harebell, that's fan'd by the breeze, ALLAN *Poems* (1836) 78. Bwk. The hinmaist hare-bell rings a knell For faded comrades, ance sae blue, CHISHOLM *Poems* (1879) 35. Gall. Harebells blooming bonnie, O, NICHOLSON *Poet. Wks.* (1814) 18a, ed. 1897. ne.Yks., w.Chs. (B. & H.) Lan. *N. & Q.* (1869) 4th S. iii. 469. (2) s.Sc. The poor man cou'd have ment a meal Wi' a hare-bouk or sa'mon tail, T. SCOTT *Poems* (1793) 329. (3) w.Yks. LEES *Flora* (1888) 457. (4) w.Som.[1] (5) Cor. (6) Lan. The hedge on each side was full of holes and 'hare-gates,' and tunnels, and runs, WAUGH *Chim. Corner* (1874) 5, ed. 1879; Lan.[1] 'He knows both th' hare an' th' hare-gate,' i. e. he knows both the hare, and the way the hare runs—a proverbial saying commonly applied to a person who is supposed to be thoroughly acquainted with any particular matter. (7) Ir. There was Mrs. Rooney up to her arm-pits in a hare-hole, *Paddiana* (ed. 1848) I. 86. (8) Cor.[12] (9) Wxf.[1] Zim dellen harnothès w'aar nize [Some digging earth-nuts with their noses], 86. w.Yks. He'll use it for diggin' up harenuts, HARTLEY *Lundun*, 93 ; THORESBY *Lett.* (1703) ; w.Yks.[24], e.Lan.[1] Dor. Hares are fond of its green leaves, w.*Gasette* (Feb. 15, 1889) 7, col. 1. (10) Som. Sprinklen' the hare parsley with dewdrops, LEITH *Verbena* (1895) 98. (11) Dev. Hare-pied in colour, *Mem. Rev. J. Russell* (1883) 283. (12) w.Yks.[8] (13) N.I.[1] Ant. *Ballymena Obs.* (1892). (14) Nhb. I cursed the deep scheeming o' hare-sha'-lip'd Nan, PROUD-LOCK *Borderland Muse* (1896) 35. (15, 16) Sc. (JAM.) (17) Nhb.[1] (18) Sc. He tell'd me too that my wee namedochter had gotten a harshie lip, WHITEHEAD *Daft Davie* (1876) 221, ed. 1894. (19) ne.Wor.[1] (20) e.Lan.[1] Chs.[1] Oi could na mak aht a word he said, for he's hare-shawn. Not.[1], Lei.[1], War.[2], Shr.[1] (21) Shr. If a hare crosses the path of a woman with child, she must instantly stoop down and tear her shift, or her child will have a hare-lip—an ' ar-shotten ' lip, as it is called in the Clun Forest neighbour-hood, BURNE *Flk-Lore* (1883) 213; Shr.[1] (22) Rnf. (JAM.) (23) n.Yks.[2] (24) w.Yks. Patridge-nets, hare-snickles, burd-caiges, pumils, &c., TOM TREDDLEHOYLE *Thowts* (1845) 39.

2. Phr. (1) *to make a hare of a man*, to get the better of, overcome in argument, &c.; (2) *not to care whether the dog catch the hare or the hare catch the dog*, said of a person who is utterly thoughtless or reckless of consequences.

(1) Ir. If you had hard Mat and Frahzer the other evening at it. What a hare Mat made of him ! CARLETON *Traits Peas.* (ed. 1843) I. 272. (2) w.Yks.[1]

HARE, *sb.*[2] Irel. Der. 1. The last handful of growing corn cut at harvest. Also called churn (q.v.).

N.I.[1] Der.[1] The finishing the cutting of the corn they call getting the hare. *Obs.*

2. *Comp.* Hare-supper, a supper given to the servants and labourers when the harvest is got in. Der.[12], nw.Der.[1]

HARE, *v. Obs.* Oxf. s.Cy. To tease, harass, make wild; to frighten.

Oxf. You hared me out of my wits (K.). s.Cy. RAY (1691); GROSE (1790). [To hare one, *perterrefacio*, COLES (1679).]

HARE-HUNT, *sb.* Dev. See below.

A stag and a hare hunt are the rude means employed by a village community for maintaining its standard of morals or expressing its disapprobation of petticoat rule. . . The hare-hunt, now extinct, was intended to ridicule the man who submitted to a rough woman's tongue, BARING-GOULD *Red Spider* (1887) xxiv ; The hunt ends with the stag or hare, one or the other, being fagged out, and thrown at the door of the house whose inmates' conduct has occasioned the stag or hare hunt. . . If the hunt be that of a hare the pretence is—or was— made of knocking it on the head, *ib.* xxvi.

HAREY, see Hairy.

HARFISH, *sb.* Pem. [ā·fiʃ.] The razor-fish, *Ensis siliqua.* s.Pem. LAWS *Little Eng.* (1888) 420.

HARG, *v.* Hmp.[1] Same as Argue, *v.* (q.v.)

HARIE, see Harry, *sb.*[1]

HARIGALD, *sb.* Sc. In phr. *Head and harigald money;* see below.

They [the colliers and salters] esteemed the interest taken in their freedom to be a mere decree on the part of the proprietors to get rid of what they called head and harigald money, payable to them when a female of their number, by bearing a child, made an addition to the live stock of their master's property, SCOTT *Redg.* (1824) xxi, note E.

HARIGALDS, *sb. pl.* Sc. Also in forms haricles (JAM.) Ayr.; harigals Ayr.; harigells Edb.; harragles Dmb.; harrigals Gall. [haˈri-, haˈraglz.] 1. The viscera or pluck of an animal.

Sc. He that never eats flesh thinks harigalds a feast, RAMSAY *Prov.* (1737); The dowg's awa' wi' the head and harrigals, HISLOP *Anecdote* (1874) 168. Dmb. Ye're no rinnin the same risk o' getting a swurd in yer kyte or a ball through yer harragles, CROSS *Disruption* (1844) xxxvii. Ayr. The head and harigals of the sheep ... were served up, GALT *Entail* (1823) vii ; Wha likit could gang for the rest o' the stot, The heid, feet, an' haricles, LAING *Poems* (1894) 110. Gall. May they burn back and front, ingate and out-gate, hide, hair, and harrigals, CROCKETT *Standard Bearer* (1898) 301.

2. *Fig.* Locks of hair.

Sc. Used metaph. and ludicrously; being applied to the tearing of one's hair, a rough handling, &c. (JAM.) Lnk. I think I've towzl'd his harigalds a wee, RAMSAY *Gentle Shep.* (1725) 87, ed. 1783. Edb. Madge ance Bauldy sent away With touzled harigells, *Carlop Green* (1793) 111, ed. 1817. Slk. Scowder their harigalds, De'ils wi' a bleery, HOGG *Tales* (1838) 17, ed. 1866.

HARISHER, *sb.* Nhb.[1] A large quantity; used to express number in disarrangement.

HARK, *v.* and *sb.*[1] Sc. Irel. Lakel. Cum. Yks. Stf. Not. Lin. Lei. War. Wor. Shr. Wal. Hrt. Nrf. Ken. Som. Dev. Cor. Amer. Also in forms ack w.Yks.[2]; ak Hrt.; heark Wor. [h)ark, āk.] 1. *v.* To listen, hearken.

Frf. To his master's council harkit, An' wagged his tail, SMART *Rhymes* (1834) 118. Ayr. Had I to guid advice but harkit, BURNS *Vision*, st. 5. Lakel.[2] Harks-ta at that noo, is that thunner! Cum. *Gl.* (1851). n.Yks. 'Harks theh,' listen, pay attention (T.S.); n.Yks.[4] 'Hark ya,' hear you! listen! ne.Yks.[1] 'Hark yer,' sometimes repeated, as 'just fancy that.' w.Yks.[2] Ack thee, Tom, what's that! Lin. Hark at him ! . . . young squire ar'n't going to eat any more bacon, 'cause it's cruel to kill the pigs, FENN *Dick o' the Fens* (1888) vii. Hrt. Seldom used except in the imperative, CUSSANS *Hist. Hrt.* (1879–81) III. 320. Som. Speak her will, an' it d' be thy bounden duty t'hark t'her, LEITH *Verbena* (1895) 78. w.Som.[1] I cant never abear to hark to jis stuff. Don't you harky to he. Cor.[1] I wouldn't hark to her nonsense.

Hence (1) Harker, *sb.* a listener ; (2) Harky, *int.* listen, hark !

(1) Sc. Still commonly used in the prov. ' Harkers never heard a gude word of themselves' (JAM.). (2) w.Yks. (C.C.R.), Ken. (G.B.), Ken.[1]

2. *Phr.* *hark the robbers*, a children's game ; see below.

Ir. The Belfast version is practically the same [as the Deptford one] except that the verses are not sung as a dialogue, but by all the players together, and the prisoner, when caught, has the choice of sides, by being asked 'Which will you have, a golden apple or golden pear!' GOMME *Games* (1894) 197. w.Yks. *ib.* 196. Shr. The first six verses are sung by the alternate parties, who advance and retire tramping their feet, at first, to imitate the robbers. The last verse is sung altogether going round in a ring, *ib.* 198. Nrf. Two girls take hold of hands, and another, the prisoner, stands between them. The rest form themselves into a line opposite, and advance and retreat while singing the first verse, the gaolers singing the next verse, and so on alternately, *ib.* **Ken.** In the Deptford version two girls join hands, holding them up as an arch for the other players to tramp through. The first two verses are sung first by one and then by the other of the two girls. At the finish of these the girl then going through the arch is stopped, and the third, fourth, and fifth verses are sung by the two girls alternately. Then finally both girls sing the last verse, and the child is sent as prisoner behind one or other of the two girls. . . The two sides thus formed then proceeded to tug against each other, and the strongest side wins the game, *ib.* 197; In the Shipley version, the children form themselves into two lines, while two or three, representing the robbers, swagger along between them. When the robbers sing the last verse they should have attained the end of the lines of children, as during the parley they were safe; having pronounced the defiance they run away. The children in the lines rush after them, and should catch them and put them in prison, *ib.* 198. [For further details see GOMME *ib.* 192-199.]

3. To look out; to make inquiries. **Stf.[1]** Cf. **hearken.**

4. To smell.

s.**Wal.** I was once invited by a South Wales collier to ' Hark that smell !' (T.C.P.)

5. With *back*: to retrace one's steps; to go back and try again.

n.**Yks.[4]**, w.**Yks.[2]**, **Not.[1]**, **Lei.[1]** **War.** My memory harks back, *Midl. Counties Herald* (Dec. 31, 1896); **War.[2]** **Wor.** You've read too fur, you must hark back a bit (J.W.P.). w.**Som.[1]** The phr. is taken from hunting talk, when if the hounds lose the scent they are made to hark-back, i. e. go back to a spot where they had the scent, and try to get it again; in fox-hunting more *gen.* they have to ' hark-forard.' **Dev.** Hark back, Tancred ! Tarquin ! Tarquin ! hark back ! WHYTE-MELVILLE *Katerfelto* (1875) xxii; We must hark back a good many years, O'NEILL *Dimpses* (1893) 61. [*Amer. Dial. Notes* (1896) I. 389.]

6. To whisper; to guess. Cf. **hearken.**

Sc. Bob harked in the young laird's lug, PENNECUIK *Collection* (1787) 44. **Sh.I.** I laached, an harkit ' Tanks,' BURGESS *Rasmie* (1892) 25. **Cai.[1]** **Bch.** Then whispering low to me she harked, FORBES *Dominie* (1785) 38. **Fif.** Tho' I hark it in your lug, Ye needna tak' offence, DOUGLAS *Poems* (1806) 51. **Edb.** He said to me,—it's bawdy, I had best hark it, PENNECUIK *Tinklarian* (ed. 1810) 6. **Cum.** While to a corner snug I git, And kiss and hark wi' Sally, RELPH *Misc. Poems* (1743) 118 ; Fwok harkt an' guesst an' guesst agean, GILPIN *Sngs.* (1866) 278; **Cum.[4]** *Obsol.*

Hence **Harking,** *vbl. sb.* a whispering.

Sh.I. Yon's da end o' your harkin' i' Friday night, *Sh. News* (May 29, 1897).

7. *sb.* Phr. *on the hark*, on the watch, look out, *qui vive.*

Wor. The dog has been on the heark for you for some time (W.A.S.).

8. A whisper; a secret wish or desire.

Slk. Take heart till I tell you the hark of my mind, HOGG *Poems* (ed. 1865) 287. **Rxb.** (JAM.) **Gall.** To crown a' his hopes in a hurry, She haflins said aye in a hark, NICHOLSON *Poet. Wks.* (1814) 195, ed. 1897.

HARK, *sb.[2]* **Ess.** [Not known to our other correspondents.] In phr. *to come down with a hark*, to come down with a run, to fall suddenly.

An old woman who had had a fall, said, ' I came down with a hark' (S.P.H.).

HARKANY, *sb.* e.**An.[1]** [Not known to our correspondents.] A job. ' I have finished my harkany.'

HARKAUDIENCE, *sb.* n.**Lin.[1]** An accordion.

HARKIE, *sb.* **Sh.I.** [ha‧rki.] A pig; a boar-pig.

JAKOBSEN *Norsk in Shetl.* (1897) 91 ; **S. & Ork.[1]**

[Cogn. w. Norw. dial. *hark*, a rattling sound in the throat, a grunt (AASEN).]

HARKLE, *v.* **Nhp.[1]** Also in form **hartle.** To make an incision in one hind-leg of a hare or rabbit, that the other may be insinuated for the purpose of suspension. See **Harl,** *v.* 3 ; cf. **hock,** *v.[1]* **5.**

HARL, *v.* and *sb.* **Lin. Oxf. Brks. Hmp. I.W. Wil. Dor. Som.** Also in forms **hardle** Wil.[1] **Som. Dor.** ; **haul** Hmp.[1]; **horl** I.W. [āl, ā‧dl.] **1.** *v.* To entangle; to become knotted or entangled. Also with *up.*

. **Brks.** *Gl.* (1852); **Brks.[1]**, **Hmp.** (J.R.W.), **Hmp.[1]** **I.W.** Also to be crowded up by superabundance of anything, so that one hardly knows how to get out of the tangle (J.D.R.); **I.W.[1]**; **I.W.[2]** The keert rope es all harled up. **Wil.[1]** **Dor.** BARNES *Gl.* (1863); *Gl.* (1851).

2. *Fig.* To be in a state of confusion or perplexity. Also with *up.*

I.W. In the vain attempt to be in five places at once, .. the landlady became ' that harled,' as she expressed it, GRAY *Annesley* (1889) I. 240 ; I'm that harled up with so many about, *ib. Dean Maitland,* 107. **Dor.** (G.E.D.)

3. To couple the hind-legs of a rabbit by threading one leg through the ham-string of the other. Cf. **harkle.**

n.**Lin.[1]** w.**Cy.** GROSE (1790). **Wil.** The keeper's boy . . . has imbibed all the ways of the woods, and is an adept at everything, from ' harling' a rabbit upwards. . . It is done by passing the blade of the knife between the bone of the thigh and the great sinew—where there is nothing but skin—and then thrusting the other foot through the hole made. The rabbit . . . can then be conveniently carried by the loop thus formed, or slung on a stick, JEFFERIES *Gamekeeper* (1887) 35 ; **Wil.[1]**

4. *sb.* A confused, tangled mass; an entanglement; a state of confusion.

Brks.[1] If 'e dwoant mind thee 'ooll get that string in a harl. **Hmp.** That thread of silk is all in a harl, HOLLOWAY; **Hmp.[1]** ' It's all in a haul.' Spoken of entangled yarn. cotton, &c. **LW.** (J.D.R.); **I.W.[1]**; **I.W.[2]** I never vound things in such a harl in my life. **Wil.** BRITTON *Beauties* (1825) ; SLOW *Gl.* (1892); **Wil.[1]** The thread be aal in a harl. His hair is all in a harl. **Som.** SWEETMAN *Wincanton Gl.* (1885).

5. *Fig.* A state of great excitement.

n.**Lin.[1]** Jimmy H—— is e'such 'n a harl as niver was aboot this. here jewbilee.

6. A couple and a half of hounds ; three hounds, beagles, &c. Oxf. (K.), (HALL.)

7. The hock of a sheep; the hough of a cow or cart-horse.

Hmp. WISE *New Forest* (1883) 283 ; (H.E.) ; **Hmp.[1]**

Hence **Harlens,** *sb. pl.* the hock-joints of a cow.

I.W.[2] The wold cows got stuck in the keert loose up over their harlens.

[1. Þe hasel & þe haȝ-þorne were harled al samen, *Gawaine* (c. 1360) 744.]

HARLAN, *sb.* **Irel.** The fresh-water duck, the pintail, *Dafila acuta.* Wxf. SWAINSON *Birds* (1885) 155.

HARL(E, *sb.[1]* **Sc. Nhb. Wm. Yks. Chs. Der.** Also Cor. Also in forms **herle** Der.[2] nw.Der.[1]; **hurle** Cor.[12] [harl, āl.] **1.** The filament of flax ; the reed or brittle stem of flax separated from the filament.

n.**Sc.** These broken pieces of straw, hanging in a great measure loose upon the harle or flax, MAXWELL *Sel. Trans.* (1743) 331 (JAM.). **Mry.** *Gl. Surv.* (JAM.) **Cor.[1]** As dry as hurle ; Cor.[2] [In the natural state the fibres of the harl are attached firmly . . . to each other, STEPHENS *Farm Bk.* (ed. 1849) II. 324.]

2. The side-fibre of a peacock's tail feather, used for dubbing flies in angling; the feathery part of a quill-pen.

Slk. Ye ken little about the Kirby bends, gin ye think the peacock's harl and the tinsy hae slipped frae your jaws, CHR. NORTH *Noctes* (ed. 1856) III. 301. **Nhb.[1]** Particularly applied to that of the tail feathers of a peacock when employed in giving an irridescent appearance to the bodies of artificial flies, in which case it is called ' peacock harle.' **Wm.** (J.H.), **Der.[2]**, nw.**Der.[1]**

3. Hair, wool.

w.**Yks.[1]** His harl sticks up, for au t'ward, like an urchin back, ii. 289.

4. A small portion of hay or straw.

s.**Chs.[1]** Taak‧ dhŭ os‧-ree‧k in‧tŏ)th fuur ee‧-feyld, ŭn mahynd yi ree‧kn ev‧ri aa‧rl on it ŭp [Tak the hoss-reek (horse-rake) into th' fur hee-feild, an' min ye reeken every harl on it up].

[1. EFris. *harl, harrel,* a filament of flax (KOOLMAN) ; so LG. (BERGHAUS), MLG. (SCHILLER-LÜBBEN, s.v. *Herle*).]

HARL(E, *sb.[2]* n.**Cy. Lin.** [āl.] A mist, a fog or drizzle coming up with the tide from the sea. See **Haar,** *sb.[1]*

n.**Cy.** (K.) ; BAILEY (1721); GROSE (1790); **N.Cy.[2]** **Lin.[1]** I saw the harle on the 3rd June last. sw.**Lin.[1]** There was a kind of harle came up. I think it's no-but a sea-harle.

HARL(E, *v.* and *sb.[2]* Var. dial. uses in Sc. Irel. Nhb. Also Glo. ? Som. Also written **harri** Sh.I.; and in form **haurl** Sc. (JAM.) Nhb.[1] [harl, āl.] **1.** *v.* To drag, pull, tug ; to trail along the ground ; to haul.

Sc. It's an unco thing that decent folk should be harled through the country this gate, SCOTT *Old Mortality* (1816) xiii. **Cai.[1]** **Abd.** Strauchtway they harle him 'fore the royal chair, *Guidman Inglis-*

maill (1873) 58. **Kod.** [He] ceased to speak, began a-snorin', Was by Knappy harl'd to bed, GRANT *Lays* (1884) 41. **Fif.** Some haurl'd at cart and barrow trams, TENNANT *Papistry* (1827) 53. **e.Fif.** They harled me awa to a laigh bit hoosie, LATTO *Tam Bodkin* (1864) vii. **Slg.** The horses harl'd them thro' the water, MUIR *Poems* (1818) 11. **Dmb.** It wadna be lang o' being haurled through my fingers if it were kent I had it, CROSS *Disruption* (1844) xviii. **Rnf.** Bess . . . harl't out my very hair, WILSON *Watty* (1792) 5. **Ayr.** I haurled the whole lot of the dishes to the flure, SERVICE *Notandums* (1890) 28. **Lth.** He harl'd her bits o' things awa, SMITH *Merry Bridal* (1866) 193. **Rnf.** Others mind ye o' a rat, Harl't thro' the dirt in teeth o' cat, BARR *Poems* (1861) 33. **Lnk.** Wha lets her laddies harl me doun the stair? NICHOLSON *Idylls* (1870) 88. **Edb.** Harling them away to the college, MOIR *Mansie Wauch* (1828) x. **Peb.** Ilka buik except the bible, Frae the house you've harl'd for drink, AFFLECK *Poet. Wks.* (1836) 132. **Slk.** Matthew Ford harled him into the shallow, HOGG *Tales* (1838) 150, ed. 1866. **Rxb.** It harles the whole heart out o' her, RIDDELL *Poet. Wks.* (ed. 1871) II. 342. **Dmf.** Sad wights Wi' ribs baith black an' blae Were harlit hame, MAYNE *Siller Gun* (1808) 8. **Gall.** I'll come doon and harl ye in mysel', CROCKETT *Cleg Kelly* (1896) 202. **n.Cy.** *Border Gl.* (*Coll.* L.L.B.) **Nhb.** They harled her through the paddock-peul, RITSON *N. Garl.* (1810) 54. †**Som.** Whenever they'd a chaance the neighbours was harlen' an' car'ren' down to moor, LEITH *Verbena* (1895) 43.

Hence (1) **Harlin**, (2) **Harlin-favour**, *sb.* some degree of affection, a *penchant*, inclination towards; (3) **Haurl-a-hame**, *adj.* selfish, grasping.

(1) **Sc.** Wha for the bardies has a harlin, NICOL *Poems* (1805) I. 120 (JAM.). (2) **Bch.** I canna say bat I had a kirnen wi' her an' a kine o' harlin favour for her, FORBES *Jrn.* (1742) 7. (3) **Rnf.** On his [the devil's] haurl-a-hame manner were a' agree't quite, NEILSON *Poems* (1877) 112.

2. *intrans.* To drag, trail, draw with difficulty; also used *fig.*

Sc. Amang such rugh rigs, highs an' hows as I hae to harl through, GRAHAM *Writings* (1883) II. 43 ; To move onward with difficulty, implying the idea of feebleness (JAM.) ; To draw oneself by griping or violent means (*ib.*). **Abd.** For cadgers . . . Maun ay be harlin in their trade [must talk 'shop'], SKINNER *Poems* (1809) 40. **Frf.** Hameward, hoolie, they gaed haurlin', WATT *Poet. Sketches* (1880) 23. **Dmf.** The cauld snell blast o' the uncivil warld, Through whilk sae lang thin-cled I've harl'd, THOM *Jock o' Knowe* (1878) 26.

3. Phr. (1) *to harl about*, to move about feebly ; to crawl, creep ; (2) *— away*, to drive away, drive off ; (3) *— ower*, to overhaul, examine, look into.

(1) **Sc.** Lat them harl about for meat till eat, WADDELL *Ps.* (1871) lix. 15 ; To harle about, to go from place to place. It *gen.* conveys the idea of inconstancy, of feebleness, or of some load or incumbrance (JAM.). **Cai.**[1] (2) **ne.Glo.** I think he've harled George away ; the lad often said as he'd run away, and I think he've done it now, *Household Wds.* (1885) 142. (3) **Sc.** They'll just harl ower a' thir petitions, pick out my name, and the like o' me, Sc. *Haggis*, 32.
4. To scrape or take together ; to peel, come off in pieces. Also used *fig.* and *intrans.*

Sc. (JAM.) **Rnf.** A wedge o' broun saip would be better, To harl the dirt aff her hide, BARR *Poems* (1861) 118. **Ayr.** Till skin in blypes cam haurlin Aff's nieves that night, BURNS *Halloween* (1785) st. 23. **Gall.** To harl the pow is to scratch the head (A.W.). **Nhb.**[1] To harle the road.

5. To roughcast a wall with lime.

Sc. An old turreted house in Huxter Row was being newly harled, HISLOP *Anecdote* (1874) 382. **Sh.I.** The walls were harried with systematic regularity, CLARK *Gleams* (1898) 221. **Cai.**[1] **Inv.** HERD *Coll. Sngs.* (1776) Gl. **Bnff.** When the walls were 'harled,' it was always left untouched, GORDON *Chron. Keith* (1880) 35. **Abd.** The ruins of the ancient church have actually been 'harled,' SMILES *Natur.* (1893) 135.

Hence (1) **Harled**, *ppl. adj.* roughcast with lime ; (2) **Harling**, *vbl. sb.* the act of roughcasting with lime, &c. ; lime or roughcasting ; (3) *Joint harl, phr.* to point walls.

(1) **Sc.** Droning psalms in a gray harled kirk, KEITH *Indian Uncle* (1896) 256 ; Its harled walls tinged with green towards their base, HUNTER *J. Armiger's Revenge* (1897) iv. **Gall.** That grey kirk of rough harled masonry, CROCKETT *Stickit Min.* (1893) 236. (2) **n.Sc.** Face the work all over with mortar thrown against it with a trowel, which they call harling, *Lett. from Gentleman* (1754) I. 65 (JAM.). **Gall.** They are set without lime under the harling, CROCKETT *Grey Man* (1896) 30. (3) **Cai.**[1]

6. *sb.* The act of dragging or trailing.

Sc. Of a paralytic person, it is said, 'He has a harle with the left leg' (JAM.).
7. A haul, a collection, that which is gathered together ; money or property obtained by dishonourable means. Also used *fig.*

Sc. He gat a harle of siller (JAM.) ; The time was when I could hae taen a harle o' onything that was gaun, FORD *Thistledown* (1891) 242. **Rnf.** O' rhymes he gather'd sic a harl', FINLAYSON *Rhymes* (1815) 165. **Ayr.** I had a bit haurl o' fifty pounds to carry me on for the next winter, SERVICE *Dr. Duguid* (ed. 1887) 69. **Lnk.** She's fond to git a haurl O' warldly wealth, and pomp, and glory, RODGER *Poems* (1838) 140, ed. 1897.
8. A small quantity of anything ; anything obtained with difficulty and on rare occasions.

Sc. See if I cannae get a little harle of justice out of the 'military man notoriously ignorant of the law,' STEVENSON *Catriona* (1893) ix. **Cai.**[1] A small quantity of any substance composed of loose particles, e. g. meal, salt, &c. **Fif.** Gie's a harle o' meal (JAM.). **e.Fif.** See ! there's a wee harlie o' sugar to put i' yer gab, LATTO *Tam Bodkin* (1864) viii. **s.Sc.** Indeed, ouy haurl o' health I had was aye about meal-times, *Blackw. Mag.* (Jan. 1821) 400 (JAM.). **Ayr.** Ony harl of health he has is aye about meal-time, GALT *Sir A. Wylie* (1822) lx.
9. A drag or mud-rake used for scraping a road, &c. ; an instrument for raking or drawing together soft manure.

Rxb. Used esp. in the cow-house (JAM.). **Nhb.**[1] A kind of scraper with a long handle. [The men should each take a mud hoe or harle, STEPHENS *Farm Bk.* (ed. 1849) I. 470.]
10. A slattern ; a big, untidy, coarse, cross-grained person ; a rough field-labourer.

Rnf. She maun be a tasteless haurl 'Twad face the gleg e'e o' the warl', An' cause gie to its bitter gab To curse her for a hanless drab, YOUNG *Pictures* (1865) 162. **Ayr.** Ane of them . . . was a great muckle haurl of a dirty fum, SERVICE *Dr. Duguid* (ed. 1887) 169. **Dmf.** SHAW *Schoolmaster* (1899) 349. **Gall.** MACTAGGART *Encycl.* (1824). **N.I.**[1] **Ant.** A rough worker, who will do a lot but do it badly, *Ballymena Obs.* (1892).
11. A mixture of lime and sand, used for roughcasting or coating the outside of a building. Also used *fig.*

Sc. Plastered with harl, COBBAN *Andaman* (1895) i. **Sh.I.** The gable was white, for the 'harl' had been picked off in the spring, BURGESS *Tang* (1898) 23. **e.Lth.** An' the way he splairges ye wi' butter—layin't on in clauts an' harles, HUNTER *J. Inwick* (1895) 93. [1. The hors him harland behynd the woid cart, DOUGLAS *Eneados* (1513), ed. 1874, II. 48; Hii harlede him out of churche, *R. Glouc.* (c. 1300) fo. 151 b.]

HARLE, *sb.* Sh. & Or.I. Nrf. [harl, ǎl.] **1.** The goosander, *Mergus merganser*. Also in *comp.* **Harle-duck.**
S. & Ork.[1] Or.I. The goosander, the harle of this country, remains with us constantly, BARRY *Hist.* (1805) 302 (JAM.).
2. The red-breasted merganser, *Mergus serrator*. Also in *comp.* **Harle-duck.** Cf. **earl-duck.** Or.I. SWAINSON *Birds* (1885) 164.
3. The grey duck or gadwall, *Chaudelasmus streperus*.
Nrf. COZENS-HARDY *Broad Nrf.* (1893) 45.
[L Fr. *harle* or *herle*, a merganser, see BELON *Hist. de la nature des Oyseaux* (1555) 164, in NEWTON & GADOW (1896) 407 ; *Harle* (*herle*), a kind of sheldrake (COTGR.).]

HARLED, *ppl. adj.* n.Cy. Yks. [arld, ǎld.] Mottled, speckled, as cattle.
n.Cy. GROSE (1790). **n.Yks.**[1 2 4] **e.Yks.** MARSHALL *Rur. Econ.* (1788). **w.Yks.**[1] 'Shoe's a feaful hask harl'd an' ; that is, the cow has harsh hair, always an unfavourable symptom of fattening.

HARLED, *adj.* Wil. In *comb.* **Well-harled,** of oats : well-eared. DAVIS *Agric.* (1813) ; **Wil.**[1]

HARLEY, *sb.* Frf. The swift, *Cypselus apus*. SWAINSON *Birds* (1885) 96.

HARLEY-HARTHER, *int.* Nrf. A call to horses to go to the left. *Arch.* (1879) VIII. 170.

HARLICAN, *sb.* Dor. [ǎ'likən.] A term of abuse. Bring on that water, you idle young harlican ! HARDY *Jude* (1896) pt. i. i.

HARLIKINS, *sb. pl.* Sh.I. Tight pantaloons opening behind, worn by children. S. & Ork.[1]

HARLIN, *adj.* Cum. Difficult, close ; exhausting, severe.
Cum. An' monie a harlin reace they hed, STAGG *Misc. Poems* (ed. 1807) 3 ; **Cum.**[4]

HARLOCK, sb. Ess. The charlock, *Sinapis arvensis*. (W.W.S.)

HARM, sb. Glo. w.Cy. Som. [ärm.] **1.** Any contagious or epidemic disease, not distinguished by a specific name; a fever.

Glo. (J.S.F.S.), w.Cy. (HALL.) Som. JENNINGS *Obs. Dial. w.Eng.* (1895); (F.A.A.)

2. The distemper in dogs.

w.Som.[1] In buying a young dog it is usual to ask, ' Have 'er had the harm ? '

HARM, v. Sc. Yks. Lan. Also in forms **aam** Lan.[1]; **ahm** e.Lan.[1]; **hairm** Cld. (JAM.); **hirm** w.Sc. (JAM. *Suppl.*) [harm, ärm.] **1.** To fret, grumble ; to be peevish or ill-natured. Or.I. (JAM. *Suppl.*), w.Sc. (*ib.*) Hence **Harming**, sb. fretfulness, peevishness, grumbling. Or.I. (*ib.*)

2. To dwell upon a trifling fault or misfortune, continually upbraiding the defaulter or sufferer. Hence (1) **Hairmer**, sb. one who acts in this manner ; (2) **Hairming**, vbl. sb. the act of continually dwelling upon a fault, &c. Cld. (JAM.)

3. To mock or imitate in speaking ; to mimic. Also with *at* and *after*.

Yks. (HALL.) [Not known to our correspondents.] Lan. I connaw be angurt ot tee . . . os lung os to boh harms after other fok, TIM BOBBIN *View Dial.* (ed. 1806) 67 ; Lan.[1] A person repeating another's words in an ironical manner is said to be ' aamin ' after him. e.Lan. In use to-day (S.W.) ; At one time a very common word and is still used, though not so frequently as formerly. Used in connection with the affix ' at.' ' He wor aamin' at me,' *Manch. City News* (Jan. 4, 1896) ; e.Lan.[1] s.Lan. Commonly used in the neighbourhood of Oldham and district when I was a boy. Thus, if a boy mocked another, the one mocked would say, ' He keeps aamin' after me,' *Manch. City News* (Jan. 4, 1896) ; *Obsol.* (F.E.T.)

[1. LG. *harmen un karmen*, ' härmen und wehklagen, sich ängstlich quälen ' (BERGHAUS). **2, 3.** Norw. dial. *herma*, to repeat anything ; to ape, to mimic (AASEN).]

HARM, see Haulm.

HARMING, sb. Pem. Harm, hurt, injury.

a.Pem. He'll keep us from all harmin' (W.M.M.).

HARMLESS, adj. Sc. Sur. Sus. **1.** *Obs.* Unharmed, safe, secure.

Abd. That he, his men, tenants, and servants, should be harmless and skaithless in their bodies, SPALDING *Hist. Sc.* (1792) I. 43.

2. Fair to both parties, just.

Sur.[1] If you make twenty-eight shillings of the pig it will be a harmless price between buyer and seller.

3. See below.

Sus. ' Our Rosie be a very harmless child.' . . . The remark merely means that she has a certain friendly and winning way with her that goes straight to people's hearts and makes her a favourite everywhere, O'REILLY *Stories* (1880) I. 233-4.

HARMLY, adj. n.Yks.[2] Hurtful, harmful ; annoying.

HARMONY, sb. e.Suf. Uproar, noise, disturbance. (F.H.)

HARMSUMIVVER, HARN, see Howsomever, Harden, Hern.

HARN, sb. Sc. Nhb. Cum. Wm. Yks. Lan. Also in forms **hairn** Edb. Bwk. Dmf. Nhb.[1]; **harran** Sh.I. e.Fif.; **harren** Fif.; **haurn** Lnk. Gall.; **hern** Sc. [harn, hern, än.] **1.** pl. Brains. Also used fig.

Sc. Kilmadie barns, Where many shot were thro' the herns, GRAHAM *Writings* (1883) I. 152; It will knock its harns out, SCOTT *Antiquary* (1816) xv. Sh.I. If he had blown the ' harrans ' out of his old 'moorit' sheep, BURGESS *Sketches* (2nd ed.) 25. Or.I. (S.A.S.) Abd. For fear I shou'd hae gotten my harns kleckit out, FORBES *Jrn.* (1742) 16. Abd. Ye may comfort yersel' that they warna dishes wi' harns i' them, MACDONALD *Malcolm* (1875) I. 248. Frf. My lugs and harns wi' rage maist bizzin', SANDS *Poems* (1833) 121. Per. Johnnie's harns grew dazed and giddie, SPENCE *Poems* (1898) 287. Fif. The harrens o' the clerk Were sae commovit wi' the werk O' harnessin' and weir, TENNANT *Papistry* (1827) 126. e.Fif. A cockit pistol in his neive ready to blaw oot my harus, LATTO *Tam Bodkin* (1864) vii. Ayr. Till our harns are spattered at the bottom o' the well o' despair, GALT *Entail* (1823) lxxviii. Lnk. Oot fell the haurns o' my muckle meal-pock, NICHOLSON *Idylls* (1870) 104. Lth. There's naething here our harns to daver, MACNEILL *Poet. Whs.* (1801) 173, ed. 1856. e.Lth. He was sittin amang his buiks . . . howkin his harns for a sermon,

HUNTER *J. Inwick* (1895) 44. Edb. If harns and pens can do 't aright, LIDDLE *Poems* (1821) 114. Bwk. Ance we get another Willie We'll knock out auld Willie's hairns, *Denham Tracts* (ed. 1892) I. 171. Dmf. Their heads had aye mair hair than hairns, SHAW *Schoolmaster* (1899) 371. Gall. Wi' frothy haurns and goarling baird, MACTAGGART *Encycl.* (1824) 333, ed. 1876. n.Cy. BAILEY (1721) ; N.Cy.[1] Nhb.[1] Nearly out of use except by old people. Cum. RAY (1691) ; GROSE (1790) ; Cum.[4] Cum., Wm. NICOLSON (1677) *Trans. R. Lit. Soc.* (1868) IX. Yks. ' Ile ding out your harns, Ile beat out your brains (K.). n.Yks.[2] w.Yks. THORESBY *Lett.* (1703) ; w.Yks.[1] Pash'd an bray'd his harnes out, ii. 303 ; w.Yks.[4], ne.Lan.[1]

Hence **Harnless**, adj. brainless.

Sh.I. A harnliss snül, BURGESS *Rasmie* (1892) 92. n.Yks.[2]

2. *Comp.* **Harn-pan**, the brain-pan, skull.

Sc. In the pingle or the pan, Or the haurnpan o' man, FORD *Thistledown* (1891) 961 ; Weize a brace of balls through his harnpan, SCOTT *Rob Roy* (1817) xxxiii. Cai.[1] Abd. He sware he'd gar their harnpans ring, SKINNER *Poems* (1809) 16. Frf. Quit, or I'll brak' your harn pan, MORISON *Poems* (1790) 25. e.Fif. Oonless he has within his harran-pan the stuff philosophers are made of, LATTO *Tam Bodkin* (1864) xxvi. Rnf. Leeze me on the harn pan, WEBSTER *Rhymes* (1835) 155. Ayr. We think his harnpan's surely dunklet, GALT *Sir A. Wylie* (1822) ciii; (J.M.) Lnk. I spat by turns on ilka loof, Haw'd first my harn-pan, syne my loof, COGHILL *Poems* (1890) 66. e.Lth. He didna think there was anither harn-pan in the pairish wad ha stude it, HUNTER *J. Inwick* (1895) 241. Edb. A hag sailt i' his toom hairn-pans Awa' to France, LEARMONT *Poems* (1791) 24. Slk. ' This to thy harnpan,' said Gabriel, drawing his sword, HOGG *Tales* (1838) 660, ed. 1866. Gall. His haurn pan was aye sae fu', MACTAGGART *Encycl.* (1824) 189, ed. 1876. Nhb.[1], w.Yks.[1], ne.Lan.[1]

[1. My harnis trimblit besily, DOUGLAS *Pal. Hon.* (1501), ed. 1874, 78 ; He the hed till harnys claf, BARBOUR *Bruce* (1375) XII. 56. OE. *hærnes* (*Chron.* an. 1137). **2.** It . . . persit the harnpan, DOUGLAS *Eneados* (1513) II. 252.]

HARNESS, sb. Sc. Nhb. Yks. Brks. e.An. Sus. Dor. Som. Aus. [har-, ä·nis.] **1.** In *comp.* (1) **Harness-cask**, a receptacle on board ship, where the meat, after being taken out of the pickle-cask, is kept ready for use ; (2) **-lid**, a lid or covering to a ' harness-cask ' ; (3) **-plaid**, a special kind of plaid ; see below ; (4) **-tack**, a swinging cross-tree in a stable on which harness is hung.

(1) Abd. One that has a lid, guarded by a rim which comes a small way down on the outside of the vessel (JAM.) ; Some thieves . . . breaking open a harness cask . . . stole about a cwt. of beef, Abd. *Jrn.* (Dec. 2, 1818) (*ib.*). Nhb. It is an upright cask with straight, tapering sides, narrowing to the top, which closes with a hinged lid and padlock. A brass or iron hoop surrounds the former, and is made wider than the thickness of the lid, so as to overlap the head of the castle (R.O.H.); Nhb.[1] [Aus. The steer was cut up and salted and in the harness-cask soon after sunrise, BOLDREWOOD *Robbery* (1888) I. ii.] (2) Abd. (JAM.) (3) Sc. She had just taken off her bonnet and harness-plaid, OCHILTREE *Redburn* (1895) vi. w.Sc. Until very recent times no Scotswoman was considered respectably married unless her trousseau included a plaid of specially fine manufacture fit to appear in at kirk or market. It, with the bonnet, was a badge of marriage, hence the term ' harness ' denoting the yoke. Paisley was famous for harness plaids (G.W.). (4) Brks.[1]

2. Weaving term : the ' heald ' or arrangement of loops of twine, by which the threads of the warp are changed in position at every passage of the shuttle.

w.Yks. It enables a much larger pattern to be woven than is possible with plain gear (J.M.). w.Som.[1] It is adjusted into the loom along with the warp to which it belongs.

3. The apparatus required for making cider.

Dor. BARNES *Gl.* (1863). Som. (W.F.R.)

4. Leather defences for the hands and legs of hedgers, to protect them from the thorns. e.An.[12]

5. Temper, humour.

s.Cy. (HALL.) Sus. ' He is in a pretty harness,' he is in a rare bad humour, HOLLOWAY ; Sus.[1] Master's in purty good harness this morning ; Sus.[2]

HARNISHIN, sb. N.I.[1] Harness.

HARNSA, HARNSER, HARNSEY, see Heronsew.

HARP, sb.[1] and v.[1] Sc. Irel. Nhb. Cum. Yks. Lan. Der. Not. Lin. Lei. Nhp. Wor. Oxf. Brks. Hnt. Nrf. Sus. Hmp. I.W. Also in forms **hirp** Rnf.; **yerp** e.Lth. [harp, äp.]

1. *sb. Obs.* An Irish shilling. Also in *comb.* **Harp-shilling.**
Ir. *N. & Q.* (1885) 6th S. xi. 296. **N.I.**[1] Equal only to 9*d.* sterling money.

2. Phr. *Head or harp,* head or tail.
Ant. The reverse of Irish copper coins formerly bore a harp. 'Head or harp,' the call in playing pitch and toss (W.H.P.).

3. An instrument used in sifting or 'riddling.'
Sc. The mason sets his harp upon en', An' harls the fire-hoose gable, **Murray** *Spring* in *Blk. and White* (Apr. 18, 1896) 490. **Dmf.** Evidently suggested by the shape of the instrument used in riddling or separating sand and gravel, which is of an oblong shape, containing wires enclosed in a wooden frame, **Shaw** *Schoolmaster* (1899) 349. [A portable screen or harp for riddling and depositing the stones, **Stephens** *Farm Bk.* (ed. 1849) II. 637.]

4. That part of a mill which separates the 'dust' of grain or meal from the 'shilling.'
Sc. An instrument for cleansing grain, a kind of 'searce' (**Jam.**). **Cai.**[1] The wire-cloth frame by which grain or meal is sifted in the various processes of milling. **Abd.** (**Jam.**)

5. *v.* To constantly dwell on one topic, refer constantly to an unpleasant subject; to grumble. *Gen.* with *on,* esp. in phr. *to harp on one string.* In *gen.* colloq. use.
Cai.[1] **Rnf.** I hae a richt to hirp an' murn [mourn] Oure that death-dealin' blast, **Young** *Pictures* (1865) 13. **e.Lth.** He had been guzzling toddy and yerping about Spiritual Freedom with a Free Church tailor, **Mucklebackit** *Rhymes* (1885) 141. **Edb.** 'I'se tell ye what' That harps, whate'er ye, 'I'se tell ye what, and there's that in't,' *Carlop Green* (1793) 125, ed. 1817. **N.Cy.**[1] **Nhb.** He kept harp, harpin on till as wis fair sick o' hearin 't (R.O.H.). **Cum.**[1] **n.Yks.**[4] Sha nivver let's t'thing dee, sha's awlus harping on aboot it. **e.Yks.** **Thompson** *Hist. Welton* (1869) 170; **e.Yks.**[1] *MS. add.* (T.H.) **w.Yks.** Aw, be heng'd to that tale; he's allus harpin' o' that string (Æ.B.). **Lan.** (S.W.), **nw.Der.**[1], **Not.**[1], **n.Lin.**[1] **Lei.**[1] Shay aarped o' seein 'im again so mooch. **Nhp.**[1], **s.Wor.** (H.K.) **Oxf.**[1] Ther you be agen, 'arp, 'arp, 'arp, *MS. add.* **Brks.**[1], **Hnt.** (T.P.F.) **Nrf.** You continue to harp upon the same string (W.W.S.). **Sus.**, **Hmp.** **Holloway.** **I.W.**[1]

6. Phr. *to harp against a person,* to insinuate to his disadvantage.
n.Cy. **Grose** (1790). **w.Yks.** **Hutton** *Tour to Caves* (1781).

7. To riddle or sift with a 'harp.' Abd. (**Jam.**)
HARP, *v.*[2] and *sb.*[2] Wor. Also written **arp.** [ặp.]

1. *v.* To listen to, hearken, pay attention.
s.Wor. Folks talks but I doesn't harp. Folks wuz alistenin' an' 'arpin' hiver so, an' a didn't 'ear nothin' (H.K.); A on't 'arp 'owever 'ardly noane on 'em, *Vig. Mon.* in *Berrow's Jrn.* (1896) xvii.

2. *sb.* Phr. *all of a harp,* all on the *qui vive.*
s.Wor. A knaowed as summat ar another wuz agate, an' a wuz a' ov a 'arp (H.K.)

HARPEN, *v.* **Nrf.** With *on*: to encourage, cheer on to fight.
John and Tom were quarrelling and Will harpen'd them on till he got them to fight (W.W.S.).

HARPER, *sb.* **Sc.** In *comb.* **Harper crab,** the crab, *Cancer varius Gesneri.* Also called **Tammie Harper.**
Fif. **Sibbald** *Hist. Fif.* (1803) 132 (**Jam.**, s.v. Tammie Harper).

HARPING, *adj.* **Nrf.** In *comb.* **Harping Johnny,** the orpine, *Sedum Telephium.* (B. & H.)

HARPLEAT, *sb.* **Wxf.**[1] A snipe, 'bleater.'

HARPOON, *v.* Irel. In phr. *to harpoon a bottle-nose,* to make a gross mistake.
I harpooned a bottle-nose, **Lever** *Con Cregan* (1849-50) xiv.

HAR(R, *sb.* **Sc.** Irel. **Nhb.** Dur. **Cum.** **Wm.** **Yks.** **Lan.** Also Mid. e.An. Hmp. Wil. Som. Also in forms **harl**· n.Yks.; **haur** Sc. (**Jam.**); **haw**· Nhb.[1]; **her** Hmp. [har, ă(r).] **1.** The upright part of a gate or door to which the hinges are fastened.
Sh.I. We took a door aff da harrs, **Clark** *Gleams* (1898) 106. **S. & Ork.**[1], **Dmf.** (**Jam.**), **N.Cy.**[1] **Nhb.** The back and breast of a gate are called the back har and fore har (J.H.); **Nhb.**[1] **Dur.** The hole in a stone in which the spindle of a door or gate resteth (K.). **Cum.**[1] **Wm.** A door-harr (K.). **w.Mid.** (W.P.M.), **Hmp.** (H.C.M.B.) **Wil.**[1] We wants some more heads and hars cut out. **Som.** (W.F.R.); **W. & J.** *Gl.* (1873).

2. *Comp.* **Har-tree,** the strong end of a gate to which the bars are secured.
Nhb.[1], **Dur.**[1], **s.Dur.** (J.E.D.), **Cum.**[1] **n.Yks.** The bars are *gen.* made either of fir or ash, and the harltree and head, of oak or

---

ash, **Tuke** *Agric.* (1800) 98; **n.Yks.**[4], **ne.Yks.**[1] **e.Yks.** **Marshall** *Rur. Econ.* (1796) I. 192. **w.Yks.**[2], **ne.Lan.**[1], **e.An.**[12]

3. A hinge, joint. Used *fig.*
Dmf. To ruse one's arse out o' har, to praise a person till he be too much elated (**Jam.**). **Wxf.**[1] Ingsaury neileare (pidh ?) his niz outh o' harr, 100.

4. The shank of a button. **Wxf.**[1]
[1. Ther nas no dore that he nolde heve of harre, **Chaucer** *C. T. A.* 550. OE. *heorr,* a hinge; cp. Du. *harre aen een deure,* the post and hinge of a doore or a gate (**Hexham**).]

HARR, see Haar, *sb.*[1], Hurr, *v.*[2]

HARRAGE, *sb.* **Sc.** Also in forms **arage, arrage, aryage, auarage, average, harriage** (**Jam.**). **1.** Service due by tenants, in men and horses, to their landlords, 'average.'
This custom is not entirely abolished in some parts (**Jam.**).

2. Phr. *arage (and) carriage,* a service in carts and horses.
'Arage and carriage' is a phr. still commonly used in leases (**Jam.**); Regular payment of mail-duties, kain, arriage, carriage, **Scott** *Midlothian* (1818) viii. **Per.** With harrage, carriage, them he still molests, **Nicol** *Poems* (1766) 75.
[1. Arage, vtherwaies Average, from *Averia,* quhilk signifies ane beast... Average signifies service, quhilk the tennent aucht to his master be horse or cariage of horse, **Skene** *Expos.* (ed. 1641) 9. 2. I am maid ane slaue of my body to ryn and rashe in arrage & carriage, *Compl. Scoll.* (1549) 125. In Law Lat. *cum Avaragiis & Cariagiis, Indenture* (1371), in **Skene** (*l.c.*). See Average.]

HARRAGLES, HARRIGALS, see Harigalds.

HARRAGRAF, *sb.* **Sc.** A curling term: see below.
Slg. Men that are not usually taken out to matches are called the harragraf of the Kippen Curling Club. As far as I am aware it is not known in surrounding clubs (G.W.).

HARRAN, see Harden, *sb.,* Harn.

HARRAS, see Harvest.

HARRASKAP, *sb.* **Sh.I.** Character. S. & Ork.[1]

HARRAST, *sb.* Der.[2] nw.Der.[1] *Fig.* Delight.

HARRAST, HARREST, see Harvest.

HARREN, see Hairen, Harden, *sb.,* Harn.

HARRIAGE, *sb.* **Nhp.** e.An. Wil. Dev. Also in forms **halledge** Wil.; **hallege, harrige** Wil.[1]; **harwich** e.An.[1]; **herridge** n.Dev. **1.** A disturbance; a bustle, fuss.
Wil.[1] Occasionally used of a disturbance of some sort, as 'What a hallege!' what a row. **n.Dev.** Yer's a brave briss an' herridge, **Rock** *Jim an' Nell* (1867) st. 191.

2. A moving, tumultuous assemblage of rough people; a rabble. Cf. **haurrage.**
Wil. *N. & Q.* (1881) 6th S. iv. 106; **Wil.**[1] Harrige seems to be the original form of the word, and is still occasionally heard; but for at least seventy years it has been more commonly pronounced as hallege. Not used in s.Wil. 'Be you a-gwain down to zee what they be a-doing at the Veast?' 'No, *I* bean't a-gwain amang such a hallege as that!'

3. Confusion, disorder.
Nhp.[1], **e.An.**[1] 'They are all up at harriage.' In the south part of Suf. the phrase, 'He is gone to Harwich,' means he is gone to rack and ruin. **Wil.**[1] Were a load of top and lop, intended to be cut up for firewood, shot down clumsily in a yard gateway, it would be said, 'What a hallege you've a-got there, blocking up the way!' It sometimes appears to mean rubbish, as when it is applied to the mess and litter of small broken twigs and chips left on the ground after a tree has been cut and carried.
[Prob. conn. w. ME. *harageous,* violent (*Morte Arthur*); OFr. *orageux,* stormy (**Hatzfeld**).]

HARRIAL, *sb.* ? *Obs.* Cum.[14] The payment of the best live beast or dead chattel of a deceased tenant to the lord of whom he held, a 'heriot.'
[Herrezelda is the best aucht, oxe, kowe, or uther beast quhilk ane husbandman... hes in his possession, the time of his decease, quhilk aucht and suld be given to his Landis-lord, **Skene** *Expos.* (ed. 1641). The same word as OE. *heregield,* the tribute paid to the (Danish) host (*Charter of Cnut,* an. 1018).]

HARRIDGE, *sb.* Lakel. Yks. Also written **harredge** w.Yks. [(h)a·ridg.] The angular edge of anything; the turned edge of a sharp knife ; also used *fig.* a sharp edge to one's appetite. See **Arris.**

Lakel.[2] **Wm.** He could put an harridge on a scythe. Ah've neea harridge fer mi tea (B.K.). **Yks.** (HALL.), e.**Yks.**[1], w. **Yks.** (J.J.B.)

HARRIGE, HARRIGOAD, see **Harriage, Harry-gaud.**

HARRIMAN, *sb.* Shr. A lizard, newt. (HALL.), Shr.[2]

HARRISH, *v.* and *sb.* Irel. Nhb. Dur. Cum. Yks. Lan. Wor. Also written **harish** Irel. [h]a·riʃ.] 1. *v.* To harass, worry, torment, trouble ; to ravage ; to drive about.

Ir. The poor woman was so harished, CARLETON *Traits Peas.* (ed. 1843) 95. **Nhb.**[1], **Dur.**[1], **Cum.**[1] n.**Yks.**[1] Ah's harrished nearlings te decad by's ragally gannin's on ; n.**Yks.**[4], w.**Yks.**[1] **Lan.** They mun be harrish't, an' parish't, an' hamper't, an' pincer't, an' powler't abot th' cowd world, WAUGH *Chim. Corner* (1874) 141, ed. 1879; Oyned an' harrished whol life were a ruebargain, CLEGG *Sketches* (1895) 397; **Lan.**[1], e.**Lan.**[1] s.**Wor.** They cattle bean't harrished about (H.K.).

Hence **Harrishin',** *vbl. sb.* violent invasion, 'harrying.' Cum.[14]

2. To starve with cold. w.**Yks.**[3] He harrished his colts.

Hence **Harrishing,** *ppl. adj.* cold and stormy. w.Yks. (W.A.S.)

8. *sb.* Distress, worry, annoyance, trouble.

n.**Yks.**[1] It's been a sair harrish tiv' 'im ; n.**Yks.**[4] It's a bit of a harrish, but then wa s' git ower't sumhoo.

HARRISH, see **Harsh.**

HARRISON, *sb.* Chs.[1] [a·risən.] In phr. *Harrison's pippin,* a variety of apple ; see below.

Only seen in old orchards, and probably could not now be obtained from any nurseryman. It is large and handsome, a first-class table-fruit, and a fairly good cooking apple.

HARRO, *int.* and *v.* Sc. Also in forms **hary** ; **hirro** (JAM.), Cai.[1] **1.** *int.* Hurrah, huzza !

Sc. (JAM.) **Fif.** 'Harro!' the folk o' Caryl [Crail] cry'd: 'Hurra!' the Anster folk reply'd ; 'Harro!' cry'd wife and man, TENNANT *Papistry* (1827) 58.

2. An exclamation of surprise ; an outcry for help.

Sc. FRANCISQUE-MICHEL *Sc. Lang.* (1882) 168. **Cai.**[1]

3. *v.* To hurrah, huzza, halloo. **Sc.** (JAM.)

HARROOST, HARROST, see **Harvest.**

HARROW, *sb.*[1] and *v.* Var. dial. uses in Sc. and Eng. [ha·rə.] **1.** *sb.* In *comp.* (1) **Harrow-bills,** the ribs of a wooden harrow ; (2) **-breeth,** the breadth of a harrow as shown by the mark on the land over which it has been dragged ; (3) **-bull** or **-bulls,** the longitudinal beams of a wooden harrow in which the iron teeth are inserted ; (4) **-plough,** a plough used for killing weeds in the dressing of turnips, &c. ; (5) **-rest,** the rest-harrow, *Ononis arvensis;* (6) **-shaikle,** the shackle by which a pair of harrows are linked together ; (7) **-sheth,** the transverse framework of a harrow ; (8) **-slaying,** the destruction of grass-seeds by rain, before they have struck root, when the mould has been too much pulverized ; (9) **-teeth,** the iron teeth of a harrow ; used *fig.* ; (10) **-tines** or **-tynes,** the iron teeth of a harrow ; (11) **-tree,** the piece of wood by which the harrow is yoked.

(1) **Cum.**[4] (2) **Nhb.**[1] (3) **Nhb.**[1], **Cum.**[14], e.**Yks.**[1] n.**Lin.** You'd hcv no more thought about them papers then a hosshoe hes about a harrow-bull, PEACOCK *J. Markenfield* (1874) I. 114; n.**Lin.**[1] (4) **Lth.** (JAM., s.v. Fotch-plough.) (5) n.**Lin.**[1] (6, 7) **Nhb.**[1] (8) **Sc.** The mould . . . will be in danger of being washed from the grain, if rain comes before it strikes root fully ; which in that case will malt, then be scorched by the sun, and killed ; which is . . . called harrow-slaying, MAXWELL *Sel. Trans.* (1743) 251 (JAM.). (9) **Dmb.** It'll mak' nae difference if the Doctor gets me under the harrow-teeth o' the law, CROSS *Disruption* (1844) vi. w.**Yks.** 'All of you masters,' as the toad said to the harrow-teeth, *Prov.* in *Brighouse News* (July 23, 1887). (10) ne.**Sc.** At times a bundle or two of harrow-tynes to dry and harden, GREGOR *Flk-Lore* (1881) 51. [The plough-irons new-laid –the harrow-tines new-laid, sharpened, and firmly fastened, STEPHENS *Farm Bk.* (ed. 1849) I. 504.] (11) **Nhb.**[1]

2. Phr. (1) *to live* or *to lead a life like a toad under a harrow,* to suffer from ill-treatment or ill-usage ; (2) *to pass the harrow,* see below; (3) *to trail a light harrow,* to be a bachelor ; to have a small family, have few worries or cares ; (4) *to clear the harrows,* to get one's object, attain

one's desire ; (5) *to have one leg over the harrows,* to break loose, become unmanageable ; (6) *to run away with the harrows,* (*a*) to be in too great a hurry ; (*b*) to carry off the prize ; to acquire superiority ; (7) *to run off with the harrows,* (*a*) to go too fast ; to carry things too far ; (*b*) see (5) ; (8) *to see* or *hear how the harrows are going,* to see how matters are progressing.

(1) **Sc.** (A.W.), **Dur.**[1], n.**Yks.**[2] (2) **Sh.I.** Passin' the harrow ... was a performance seldom practised, except by some person of a 'deil-may-care' disposition. . . This was supposed to unfold the future, even the spirit world ; and the person who had the hardihood to 'go i' da harrow' never revealed what they either saw or heard, and always warned others not to try such a trick. . . Three harrows were placed, some distance apart, outside the open fodder door of an old barn, and at the hour of midnight a person went blindfold into the yard, and passed back foremost over each harrow in turn, thence through the barn window, and at the end of the journey he was supposed to fall into a sort of trance and hear and see unutterable things, SPENCE *Flk-Lore* (1899) 194. (3) n.**Yks.** Neea, neea, he's nane married. He still trails a leeght harrow, ATKINSON *Moorl. Parish* (1891) 35 ; n.**Yks.**[2] He trails a light harrow, his hat covers his family ; n.**Yks.**[4], w.**Yks.**[1] (4) Ayr. O, for a cot. a wee bit grun', An' twa three lads, that trade in fun, To be my marrows, Then, let the warld lose or win, I've clear'd the harrows, AINSLIE *Land of Burns* (ed. 1892) 215. (5) **Sc.** A phr. borrowed from an unruly horse or ox (JAM.); She has her leg ower the harrows now . . . stop her wha can, SCOTT *Old Mortality* (1816) viii. (6, *a*) **Sc.** Applied to those who do not reason fairly (JAM.). **Dmb.** Hooly, freends, hooly ! Ye mauna rin awa' wi' the harrows that way, CROSS *Disruption* (1844) xxxix. e.**Lth.** Ye're rinnin awa wi' the harrows noo, HUNTER *J. Inwick* (1895) 79. (*b*) **Ayr.** (JAM.) (7, *a*) **Sc.** That's a wheen blethers, Will ! an it's aye your way to run aff wi' the harrows, *Cracks about Kirk* (1843) I. 3. (*b*) **Rnf.** Twad be a guid joke if a rough kintry chiel Soud rin aff wi' the harrows, PICKEN *Poems* (1813) II. 192. (8) **Ayr.** We was curious too, ye ken, just to hear hoo the harrows were gaun, noo that Robert Simpson has been left the rough o' the siller, JOHNSTON *Glenbuckie* (1889) 74.

8. *pl.* The longitudinal bars of a harrow. Wil. DAVIS *Agric.* (1813) ; Wil.[1]

4. *v.* *Fig.* With *up* : to arouse, stir up.

Edb. To harrow up the Juler's rage, LEARMONT *Poems* (1791) 166.

5. To harass, distress, fatigue greatly. *Gen.* used in *pp.*

Lin. (HALL.) n.**Lin.** 1 was fair arra'd wi' it all (M.P.) ; SUTTON *Wds.* (1881) ; n.**Lin.**[1] sw.**Lin.**[1] It's fit to harrow one to dead. I was harrowed, taking up after my husband in one of them closen.

6. To be beaten, overcome, brought to a standstill ; to be obstructed by an impediment or obstacle. *Gen.* in *pp.*

e.**Yks.**[1] Ah thowt Ah could lowzen this knot, but Ah's boon tl be harrow'd. **Glo.**[1] He was goin to the station with all them things, and was reglar harrowed, and had to get a man to help carry them.

HARROW, *sb.*[2] Dor. The hinder upright timber of a gate by which it is hung to its post, the 'harr.'

The one in the middle, between the harrow and the head, is the middle spear, BARNES *Gl.* (1863). (C.W.)

[Ye harrow of a gate, *Acc. St. John's Hosp. Canterbury* (1528) (N.E.D.).]

HARROW-GOOSE, *sb.* Irel. [Not known to our correspondents.] A large bird (?).

N.I.[1] HARRIS *Hist. Dwn.* (1744).

HARROWSTER, *sb.* Sc. A spawned haddock.

ne.**Sc.** The saying about the spawned haddock, harrowster or kameril, is that it is not good till it gets three dips in the May flood, GREGOR *Flk-Lore* (1881) 146. **Bnff.**[1]

HARRUP, HARRUST, see **Hairif, Harvest.**

HARRY, *sb.*[1] Var. dial. uses in Sc. Irel. and Eng. Also in forms **hairey** Lnk. ; **harie** Sc. (JAM.) ; **herry** Yks.; **horry** se.Wor.[1] [h]a·ri.] **1.** In *comp.* (1) **Harry-banning,** the stickleback, *Gasterosteus trachurus;* (2) — **behint,** always last or behindhand ; (3) — **Denchman,** the hooded crow, *Corvus cornix;* (4) — **Hurcheon** or **Hutcheon,** a children's game ; see below ; also called **Curcuddie** (q.v.) ; (5) **-long-legs,** the cranefly or daddy-long-legs, *Tipula gigantea* ; (6) **-purcan,** the game of 'blind man's buff' ; (7) — **Whistle,** a name given to the second finger ; (8) — **Wibel,** a name given to the thumb.

(1) n.Cy. (HALL.) (2) **Cum.**[14] (3) e.**An.**[1] **Nrf.** *Arch.* (1879)

VIII. **170.** (4) n.Sc. The game called Harry Hurcheon ... is a grotesque kind of dance, performed in a shortened posture, sitting on one's hams, with arms akimbo, the dancers forming a circle of independent figures, CHAMBERS *Pop. Rhymes* (1890) 139 ; The name of a play among children, in which they hop round in a ring, sitting on their hams (JAM.). (5) e.Lan.[1] Chs.[1] Occasionally, but daddy-long-legs is more common. s.Chs.[1], nw.Der.[1], Not.[1], s.Not. (J.P.K.), Lei.[1], Nhp.[1], War.[12], se.Wor.[1] Shr.[1] 'Arry, 'Arry-lung legs, Couldna say 'is prars ; Kecht 'im by the lef' leg, An throwed 'im down stars, *Children's Doggerel Verse.* Hnt. (T.P.F.) (6) Per. (G.W.) (7, 8) w.Yks.[2] Well known in the neighbourhood of Sheffield (s.v. Fingers).

2. The devil, esp. in *comb.* **Old Harry, Lord Harry,** &c.
Sc. (JAM.) Per. I'll play old Harry wi ye (G.W.). Lnk. By the livin' hairey, if I could win ower tae them I wad gi'e them something tae lauch at, WARDROP *J. Mathison* (1881) 44. Dmb. (A.S.-P.) Wmh. By the lord Harry (*ib.*). Yks. Herry with long nails, the Devil (K.). w.Yks.[2] A girl said that her rubbing-stones in the kitchen were 'as hard as Old Harry.' Lan. I wundurt what i' th' neme o' owd harry, wurt' do weh meh, PAUL BOBBIN *Sequel* (1819) 17 ; I'm fettlet now, by the Lord Harry ! BURNETT *Haworth's* (1887) xxxvi. Nrf. Yow'd maake peaace ᵂith owd Harry hisself ! A.B.K. *Wright's Fortune* (1885) 55.

3. Phr. *to play harry over any one,* to beat or punish severely. N.Cy.[1], Yks. (J.W.)

4. A countryman, rude boor ; an opprobrious term applied to a woman.
Fif. The severest criticism of conduct indeed was directed to the frailer sex, progressively characterized by the epithets—'gilpy,' 'besom,' 'hizzie,' 'harry,' 'randy,' 'limmer,' COLVILLE *Vernacular* (1899) 18. w.Yks. (HALL.), w.Yks.[1]

5. The youngest and smallest pig in a litter. Also in *comb.* **Harry pig.**
Hrt. You call 'em Harries, we call 'em cads at my home (G.H.G.). Hrt., Cmb., Ken., Wil. Common (J.W.B.).

6. The male of any species of animal. e.Lan.[1]

7. The remainder of the porridge left in the dish after every one has been supplied.
Lakel.[2] When t'poddish hes been sarra'd oot, an' ther's some left, that's Harry. Wm. Barley me t'harry [a hungry lad's method of claiming more than his share] (B.K.).

HARRY, *sb.*[2] and *v.*[1] Sc. Yks. Also in form **ary** e.Yks.
1. *sb.* A harrow.
Sc. Ye're like Burns, surely, ye've pickit it up . . . at the ploo, an' the harries, SWAN *Gates of Eden* (1895) vii.

2. *v.* *Obs.* To harrow, turn up the soil for the destruction of weeds.
e.Yks. Christmasse, when men shoulde beginne to fallowe and ary, BEST *Rur. Econ.* (1641) 76.

HARRY, *v.*[2] Sc. Nhb. Dur. Cum. Wm. Yks. Lan. I.Ma. Der. Nhp. War. Also in forms **hairry** ne.Sc. ; **hairy** Fif. ; **herrie** Bnff.[1] ; **herry** Sc. Cai.[1] N.Cy.[2] Nhb. Lakel.[1] Cum. Wm. I.Ma. [(h)a'ri, h)e'ri.] **1.** To rob, plunder, pillage, used esp. of robbing birds' nests.
ne.Sc. They hairry folk biggin kirks and payin' steepin's, *Gordonhaven* (1887) 86. Bnff. Thae to herry Wha simply trust the h—born rogues, TAYLOR *Poems* (1787) 10. Abd. It was no use people herryin' themsel's an' throwin' awa gweed siller upon 'im, ALEXANDER *Ain Flk.* (1882) 96. Frf. Think shame of yoursel', lassie, for harrying birds' nests, BARRIE *Tommy* (1896) 169. Per. Be sure he's herryin' craws' nests, FORD *Harp* (1893) 152. Fif. Peeseweet, peesesweet, hairy my nest and gar me greet, COLVILLE *Vernacular* (1899) 12. s.Sc. Did the rascal harry ye oot and oot ! WILSON *Tales* (1839) V. 18. Dmb. To herry Halket on the Tyesday night, SALMON *Gowodean* (1868) 14. Lnk. Herrying nests in the wuds, FRASER *Whaups* (1895) xii. s.Lth. Thae locus' beas' that cam up in a michty swarm . . . an' herried the haill land o' Israel, HUNTER *J. Inwick* (1895) 89. Edb. Herryin' linties, yites an' kays, FORBES *Poems* (1812) 104. Slk. As for pyats an' the like, I used to herry them without compunction, CHR. NORTH *Noctes* (ed. 1856) III. 4. Gall. To harry their houses and gear, CROCKETT *Standard Bearer* (1898) 52. Wgt. The Bailie wad travel frae Wigtown tae Burrowhead tae harry a piet's nest, FRASER *Wigtown* (1877) 263. n.Cy. GROSE (1790) ; *Border Gl.* (*Coll. L.L.B.*) ; N.Cy.[12] Nhb. Thoo'l't take care o' me ! Thoo winnot let her harry me again, that gate ! CLARE *Love of Lass* (1890) I. 216 ; The word survives in constant use as applied to the pillage of birds' nests, &c. (R.O.H.) Dur. GIBSON *Up-Weardale Gl.* (1870). Lakel.[1] Cum. A hive, owr ventersome wad herry,

RELPH *Misc. Poems* (1747) 60 ; There was a corbie's nest in the hee plantin but it was harried lang syne (J.Ar.) ; *Gl.* (1851) ; Cum.[1] ; Cum.[4] Refers *gen,* to birds' nests. Cum., Wm. NICOLSON (1677) *Trans. R. Lit. Soc.* (1868) IX. e.Yks. THOMPSON *Hist. Welton* (1869).

Hence (1) **Harried,** *ppl. adj.* plundered, robbed, pillaged ; (2) **Harryer** or **Herrier,** *sb.* a robber ; a rifler of birds' nests ; (3) **Harrying** or **Herrying,** (*a*) *ppl. adj.* robbing, plundering ; (*b*) *vbl. sb.* the act of robbing or plundering ; (4) **Harry-net,** *sb.* a net, used to catch or retain fish of a small size ; (5) **Herrial** or **Herrieal,** *sb.* that which causes loss or ruin ; *fig.* a great expense ; (6) **Herriement,** see (3, *b*) ; (7) **Herry-water,** *sb.* (*a*) see (4) ; (*b*) a selfish person who takes all he can get.
(1) Lnk. Like a lanely herrit ane [bird] Nae biding place I've here, LEMON *St. Mungo* (1844) 18. Dmf. I lookit roun At oor herrit nest, REID *Poems* (1894) 128. Gall. Like a bird out of a harried nest, CROCKETT *Standard Bearer* (1898) 226. (2) Per. He had repeatedly foiled parties of Highland harryers, MONTEATH *Dunblane* (1835) 19, ed. 1888. Ayr. Quate, retired, and oot o' the herriers' ken, SERVICE *Notandums* (1890) 51. Slk. When I was a laddie, I was an awfu'.herrier, CHR. NORTH *Noctes* (ed. 1856) III. 3. (3, *a*) Gall. Like bees from a byke upon a company of harrying boys, CROCKETT *Standard Bearer* (1898) 314. (*b*) Ayr. The nests would be weel worth the herryin', SERVICE *Dr. Duguid* (ed. 1887) 262. (4) n.Sc. (JAM.) (5) Bnff.[1] It's a perfit herrieal t' ha'e t' keep sae mony servan's. Abd. They're sic a herrial, that buiks, ALEXANDER *Johnny Gibb* (1871) x. (6) Fif. Kirk-spulyie, herriement, and raid, Gaed on mair fast than ever, TENNANT *Papistry* (1827) 210. Ayr. The herryment and ruin of the country, BURNS *Brigs of Ayr* (1787) l. 171. (7, *a*) Sc. (JAM.) (*b*) Cai.[1] The phr. refers to such as would clear all the fish out of a stream by dragging it with a net, thus leaving none to the angler.

2. To harass, oppress, despoil, ruin ; to hunt or drive off ; to drag or carry off. *Gen.* with *off* or *out.*
Sc. They have come to herry us out of house and ha', SCOTT *Leg. Mont.* (1818) iv. Kcd. We're herrit, wife ! we're herrit clean ! Faur, faur's the fusky pig ! GRANT *Lays* (1884) 6. Per. Noo ye wud harry [hunt] me aff again, IAN MACLAREN *K. Carnegie* (1896) 217. Dmb. Be harried out like gipsy horde at e'en, SALMON *Gowodean* (1868) 24. Ayr. The avenger coming to herry you out o' house and hame, GALT *Lairds* (1826) xiv. Lnk. The bairns o' yer bairns . . . Will be harry't wi' taxes, an' put to the horn, HAMILTON *Poems* (1865) 46. Kcb. We'll be harried out o' house an' ha' in a crack, ELDER *Borgue* (1897) 28. w.Yks. The divil's harried off his soul, BRONTË *Wuthering Hts.* (1847) xxxiv. Lan. When owd Holte and t'Ratchda 'torney ud a harried me off yon bit of waste, KAY-SHUTTLEWORTH *Scarsdale* (1860) III. 74 ; Harry them o' fro' their feythers graves an' owd whoams, *ib.* I. 191.

3. To harass, tease, worry, bother ; to overdo, urge, impel, hurry on. Also used *fig.*
Wm. (E.C.), n.Yks.[2], e.Yks.[1] w.Yks. Ben wor one o' them poor miln hands 'at hed been ' harrud off,' *Yksman.* (1880) 139. Lan. An oi wunnot harry a poor man wi' law, KAY-SHUTTLEWORTH *Scarsdale* (1860) III. 74 ; Yo' dunnot harry me wi' talk, BURNETT *Lowrie's* (1877) vii. I.Ma. The short seas berryin her, BROWN *Yarns* (1881) 265, ed. 1889. nw.Der.[1] War.[1] When a number of workmen are employed together, and one supplies another with such a load as he is unable to convey in time to the next, he is said to harry the man, and the person thus harried or overladen is turned out of the party ; War.[2]

Hence (1) **Harried,** *ppl. adj.* overdone, wearied, jaded ; harassed ; (2) **Harry,** *int,* see below ; (3) **Harrying,** *ppl. adj.* worrying, harassing, wearying.
(1) Nhb. Aa'm fairly herryt oot, man, wi' carryin' that poke o' yets up thame lang granery stairs (R.O.H.). Lakel.[1] Ah's fairly harried. Ye've harried mi' wi' meat. s.Yks.[1] s.Lin. A farm labourer on being asked how he is or how he feels after a hard day's work, usually answers ' I'm harrad ' (T.H.R.). (*a*) Nhp.[1] A jeering interjectional imperative, used when a labourer or navigator is overladen and cannot wheel his barrow (for instance) along : his fellow-workmen then cry out ' harry ! harry ! ' (3) n.Yks.[2] A harrying sort of a body.

HARRY-GAUD, *sb.* and *v.* n.Cy. Nhb. Yks. Nrf. Also written **harrigaud** Yks. ; **harrygawd** n.Cy. ; and in forms **haddigaud** N.Cy.[1] Nhb.[1] ; **harrigoad** n.Yks.[2] m.Yks.[1] ; **harrygaud, -gad** Nhb.[1] ; **-goad** e.Yks.[1] ; **-goat** Nhb.[1] **-guard** N.Cy.[1] [h)a'rigŏd, -goəd.] **1.** *sb.* *Obsol.* A wild wanton girl or child ; a run-about, flighty or good-for-nothing person. Also used *fig.* and *attrib.*

L

n.Cy. Grose (1790) ; (K.); Bailey (1721); N.Cy.[1,2], Nhb.[1] Yks. She's a wonderful sensible young body, is Letty, noan o' yer harrygauds, Farquhar *Frankheart*, 199. n.Yks. When Ah'd getten t'awd harrigooad . . . tonn'd out o' t'gardin', Tweddell *Cleval. Rhymes* (1875) 48 ; n.Yks.[2] 'A harrigood wind,' a rushing mighty wind. ' A coarse harrigoad fellow.' ne.Yks.[1] Whau's them harry-gauds 'at gans shootin' an' beealin an' gaapin i t'toon ? m.Yks.[1] Nrf. Holloway.

2. A master of labour, who is continually goading on his workmen to greater exertion. e.Yks.[1]

3. *v.* To go about in a wild, flighty manner ; to ramble, roam about.

Yks. Mind thou comes yam i' good time, an' dinnet gan harri-gaudin' about (T.K.). m.Yks.[1] Freq. used towards grown children. ' Where's thou been harrygoading while [till] now ?'

HARRYWIG, see Earwig.

HARSH, *adj.* Nhb. Dur. Yks. Chs. Stf. Der. Rut. Nhp. War. Glo. Hnt. Hmp. I.W. Wil. Som. Also in forms ash Stf.[1] Rut. ; harrish Nhb.[1]; hash Dur.[1] w.Yks.[1] nw.Der.[1] Nhp.[1] War.[3] Glo.[1] Hnt. Hmp.[1] I.W.[12] Wil. w.Som.[1] [aʃ, h)aʃ, æʃ.] 1. Of the wind or weather: piercing, bitter, cold, severe. Cf. hask, *adj.*[1]

Nhb. The wun's varry harrish (R.O.H.) ; Nhb.[1], Dur.[1] w.Yks.[1] It is hash and cold. Chs.[1] The opposite to ' melsh ' (q.v.). s.Chs.[1] It's û aa·rsh weynd bloa·in tüdee—mai·z dhû ae·r snai·ch [It's a harsh weind blowin' to-dee—mays the air snaitch]. Stf.[1] Ash wind, east wind. Rut. I have a bad cold, and am hoast all through them ash winds, *N. & Q.* (1876) 5th S. v. 363. Nhp.[1] It's a very hash wind. Glo.[1] Applied to the east wind Hnt. (T.P.F.) n.Wil. Used commonly in the expression used of March weather: ' Tis vurry hash dryin'' (E.H.G.).

2. Unpleasant, rough ; parched, dry ; not pliable.

nw.Der.[1] Nhp.[1] My hands are very hash. War.[3] It is very 'ash and dry [speaking of arable land]. Hmp.[1] That rope's too hash. Wil. Britton *Beauties* (1825). w.Som.[1] Chiefly applied to texture or material, to denote want of softness. The word would not be applied to conduct. ' This yer cloth don't han'le soft enough, 'tis too hash ; I be safe t'ont wear.'

3. Vigorous, energetic, hasty, impetuous.

s.Chs.[1] Yoa wüd'·nû thingk· ûz Ben ûd gy'et sû eksahy·tid ; bût ey)z aa·rsh wen ey gy'ets ûgy'ai·t [Yo wudna think as Ben 'ud get sô excited ; but he's harsh when he gets agate]. I.W.[1]; I.W.[2] Don't ee be too hash wi' that colt.

HARSK, see Hask, *adj.*[1]

HARSLEM, *sb.* Ken.[1] [ä·zləm.] An asylum.

When he got to settin' on de hob and pokin' de fire wid's fingers, dey thought 'twas purty nigh time dey had him away to de harslem.

HARSLET, HARST, HARSY, see Haslet, Harvest, Haw, *sb.*[1]

HART, *sb.* and *v.* n.Cy. Yks. Also Hmp. Dor. Also written heart Hmp.[1] 1. *sb.* In *comb.* (1) Hart-berries, the whortle-berry, *Vaccinium myrtillus* ; (2) {s claver or clover, *obs.*, the melilot, *Melilotus officinalis.*

(1) Dor. Barnes *Gl.* (1863); *N. & Q.* (1877) 5th S. viii. 45. (2) n.Cy. Grose (1790); (K.); Bailey (1721); N.Cy.[3], Yks. (B. & H.)

2. *v.* Phr. *to go harting,* to gather whortle- or bilberries. Hmp.[1]

HART, HARTISTRAW, HARTLE, see Haft, *sb.*[1], Harvest-shrew, Harkle.

HARTOGS, *sb. pl.* War. See below.

I dote on what are called ' hartogs '—that is, good clothes that are gone to the bad—or at any rate are a long way past their best, *Midl. C. Herald* (Sept. 15, 1898).

HARTS, see Ort.

HARUM, *adj.* Nhp.[1] [ē·rəm.] Untidy, slovenly.

HARVE, *sb.*[1] and *v.* Dev. Cor. [ä·v.] 1. *sb.* A harrow.

Dev. Morton *Cyclo. Agric.* (1863). s.Dev., e.Cor. (Miss D.) Cor. Thomas *Randigal Rhymes* (1895) *Gl.* ; Cor.[12]

2. *v.* To harrow.

Cor. So I ploughed—and harvey'd, Thomas *Randigal Rhymes* (1895) 6 ; Cor.[2]

[2. ME. *harwen,* to harrow (*P. Plowman*).]

HARVE, *sb.*[2] Ess. A close or small piece of land near a house ; a 'haw.' *Gl.* (1851) ; Ess.[1]

HARV(E, HARVER, see Hanve, *v.*[1], However.

HARVEST, *sb.* and *v.* Var. dial. forms and uses in Sc. Irel. and Eng. I. Dial. forms : (1) Arrest, (2) Aurrust,

(3) Haerst, (4) Hairst, (5) Haist, (6) Harest, (7) Har'est, (8) Harras, (9) Harrast, (10) Harrest, (11) Harrist, (12) Harroost, (13) Harrost, (14) Harrust, (15) Harst, (16) Har'st, (17) Harvis, (18) Harwust, (19) Hearesth, (20) Hearst. [For further examples see II. below.]

(1) Glo.[1], w.Som.[1] Dev. I've a mind tu bide till arter 'ay-arrest, Phillpotts *Dartmoor* (1896) 144. (2) Wor. Grose (1790). (3) Rnf. After haerst. our kirn cam' roun', Picken *Poems* (1813) I. 127. (4) Sc. (Jam.), Cai.[1], Bnff.[1] Nhb. There's going to be a good hairst, White *Nhb.* (1859) 62. (5) Mry. (Jam.) (6) n.Dev. How dedst thee stertlee upon the Zess last harest, *Exm. Scold.* (1746) l. 32. (7) w.Yks.[2] Som. 'Tis handy enough to get in the har'est just so well, Raymond *Men o' Mendip* (1898) viii. (8) Som. Jennings *Obs. Dial. w.Eng.* (1825). (9) Der.[2], nw.Der.[1], Shr.[2] (10) Yks. (K.\, Glo.[1] Wil. Britton *Beauties* (1825). w.Som.[1] Dev. Za zune's the harrest is avver, Hewett *Peas. Sp.* (1892). n.Dev. Grose (1790). (11) Gall. (A.W.) Nhb. The hindor-end o' barley harrist, Robson *Bk. Ruth* (1860) xi. 23. (12) Shr.[1] .13. Der.[1] (14) w.Yks.[2] (15) Sc. (Jam.) (16) Edb. Our eldin's driven, an' our har'st is owr, Fergusson *Poems* (1773) 110, ed. 1785. Bwk. The earliest ha'rst that e'er was seen, Henderson *Pop. Rhymes* (1856) 19. n.Cy. *Border Gl.* (*Coll. L.L.B.*) Cum.[1] (17) w.Yks. (J.W.) I.Ma. The Docthor must come with him for harvis, Brown *Doctor* (1887) 46. (18) Don. To sport it in the Glenties harwust fair, Macmanus *Maguire in Harper's Mag.* (Jan. 1900) 212. (19) Wxf.[1] (20) Rnf. The hearst on us is drawing, Webster *Rhymes* (1835) 3.

II. Dial. uses. 1. *sb.* In *comp.*(1) Harvest-beef, butcher's meat, eaten in harvest, whether beef or mutton ; (2) -beer, strong, twelve-month-old ale ; (3) -bell, a bell rung daily during harvest at the parish church ; (4) -bottle, a small cask or barrel with handles in which beer or cider is carried to the fields at harvest-time ; (5) -bug, the lady-bird, *Coccinella septempunctata* ; (6) -cart, the cart carrying the last load of harvest ; (7) -dam, harvest-home ; (8) -day, a day during harvest ; (9) -drink, (*a*) thin ale brewed for harvest ; (*b*) see (2) ; (10) -ears, deaf-ears ; see below ; (11) -folks, workers engaged as harvesters ; (12) -gearing or -gears, the rails fixed on a cart for carrying hay or corn ; (13) -gloves, special sheepskin gloves used in binding corn into sheaves ; (14) -goose, (*a*) a goose pro-vided at a harvest-supper ; (*b*) a young goose fed on stubble ; (15) -hog, a young sheep that is smeared at the end of harvest, when it ceases to be a lamb ; (16) -home, (*a*) the feast given by a farmer at the conclusion of the harvest ; (*b*) winter ; (17) -hummard, a beetle very pre-valent at harvest-time ; (18) -lady, the second reaper in the row, who takes the place of the principal reaper, on his occasional absence ; (19) -lice, the fruits of the common agrimony, *Agrimonia Eupatoria,* and the goose-grass, *Galium Aparine* ; (20) -lily, the great bindweed, *Convol-vulus sepium* ; (21) -load, the last load carried in harvest ; (22) -loaf, a large loaf, placed on the altar at a harvest-festival, and afterwards divided amongst the poorest villagers ; (23) -lord, the principal reaper, who goes first and whose motions regulate those of his followers ; (24) -maiden, a figure formed of a sheaf, which surmounted the last load of grain brought home ; (25) -man, (*a*) a worker only employed at harvest-time ; (*b*) a kind of spider with very long legs ; the cranefly, *Tepula gigantea* ; (26) -Monday, the Monday occurring about four weeks before the anticipated commencement of the local harvest ; (27) -moon, the September moon ; (28) -play, the holidays of a school during the time of harvest ; the autumn holi-days ; (29) -queen, the belle of the harvest-home dance ; (30) -rig, (*a*) the harvest-field or field on which reaping goes on ; (*b*) the couple, man and woman, who reap together in harvest ; (31) -roup, the sale by auction held at a harvest-fair ; (32) -schelley, a variety of *Salmo lavaretus* ; (33) -shearers, workers at the harvest ; (34) -vaicance, see (28) ; (35) -wet or -whet, a beer frolic at the commencement of harvest.

(1) Nrf. Grose (1790). e.Nrf. Marshall *Rur. Econ.* (1787). e.Suf. I'm fatting this bullock for harvest-beef (F.H.). (2) Shr.[1] (3) e.Yks. The ancient custom of ringing the harvest bell daily during harvest at the parish church, Driffield, was begun yesterday. The first bell is rung at five in the morning, and the evening bell at eight. The parish clerk has performed this duty for fifty years,

he having just completed his jubilee in that office, *Dy. Mail* (Aug. 23, 1898). (4) **War.** (J.R.W.) (5) **Cum.** In one or two localities, notably at Skinburness (E.W.P.). (6) **s.Not.** It used to be decorated with ash boughs, and the boys of the village rode in it singing their traditional songs; while of the bystanders some threw water at them, others scrambled apples. ' Mester [so and so] es got 'is corn, Well shorn, well mawn, Never bulled ower, yet never stuck fast, And 'is 'arvest cart's comin home at last,' *Flk. Sng.* (J.P.K.) **Nhp.**[1] **Oxf.**[1] *MS. add.* **Hnt.** (T.P.F.) (7) **Yks.** (HALL.) ; (K.) (8) **Ayr.** A hairst day, wi' the mist lying thick i' the glen, JOHNSTON *Glenbuckie* (1889) 58. **Som.** When zummertime is passin An harras dās be vine, JENNINGS *Obs. Dial. w.Eng.* (1825) 129. (9, *a*) **w.Som.**[1] It is usually thin stuff, and ' fresh ' or new. ' I be very zorry, zir, we 'ant nort in house but harrest-drink, and you widn care much about that, I reckon.' (*b*) **Shr.**[1] ' They'n got some o' the best owd beer at Goff's o' Wes'ley as ever I tasted.' 'Aye, they wun al'ays noted fur good 'arrŏost-drink.' (10) **Nhp.**[1] ' You've got your harvest cars on, I can't make you hear.' This expression may have arisen from the custom of hooting loudly in the harvest field, to those who are at a distance. (11) **Dmf.** The hairst folks gaun a-field, THOM *Jock o' Knows* (1878) 3. (12) **Chs.**[1]; **Chs.**[2] Thrippows the harvest-geers of carts and waggons, which are moveable and put on only when hay or corn is to be carried (s.v. Thrippows). **s.Chs.**[1] The harvest-gearing consists of front and back thrippas (s.v. Cart). (13) **nw.Dev.**[1] (14, *a*) **Shr.** The great aim, and the chief subject of self-congratulation, is that all the corn should be safely ' lugged ' or ' carried ' . . . without overthrowing a single load. The penalty for overthrowing, used, in the old times, to be the loss of the goose at the harvest-supper. Whatever other good things there might be, this, which was otherwise the labourer's due, was forfeited if a load was overthrown, BURNE *Flk-Lore* (1883) 375 ; **Shr.**[1] (*b*) **Ir.** (W.J.K.) (15) **Sc.** (JAM.) (16, *a*) **Nhb.**, **Dur.** Of which our Harvest Home and Mell Supper in the north are the only remains, BRAND *Pop. Antiq.* (ed. 1777) 305. **n.Lin.**[1], **Oxf.**[1], **Brks.**[1] **Bdf.** Hickely, hockely, harvest home! Three plum-puddings are better than none, Want some water and can't get none.' (J.W.B.) (*b*) **Sc.** *Monthly Mag.* (1798) II. 435. (17) **Lin.**[1] (18) **Lin.**[1] **e.An.**[1] The second reaper in the row, who does not seem to have been ever so regularly greeted by the title, except on the day of harvest-home. **e.Suf.** (F.H.) (19) **Hmp.** WISE *New Forest* (1883) 283 ; The fruits of both species are covered with small hooks, by which they cling to the clothes (B. & H.); **Hmp.**[1] (20) **Sur.** (B. & H.) (21) **Nhp.**[2] (22) **Hmp.** (W.M.E.F.) (23) **Lin.** THOMPSON *Hist. Boston* (1856) 709 ; **Lin.**[1], **e.An.**[1], **e.Suf.** (F.H.) (24) **Sc.** A sweet and winsome lassie was Mary Campbell. . . No harvest maiden or other merrymaking was complete without her, SWAN *Gates of Eden* (1895) iv. (25, *a*) **Hrt.** A month's man, or, as we call it, a harvestman, ELLIS *Mod. Husb.* (1750) I. vi. (*b*) **n.Lin.**[1] **Nhp.**[2] One of those insects which superstition protects from wanton injury. Their abundance is supposed to denote a dry harvest. **Ess.** *N. & Q.* (1853) 1st S. vii. 152. **Wil.**[1] **Dor.** BARNES *Gl.* (1863) ; *N. & Q.* (1877) 5th S. viii. 45. (26) **n.Sc.** Certain days known as ' feein' Friday,' ' hairst Monday,' and such like. . . . ' Hairst Monday ' occurring about four weeks before the anticipated commencement of the local harvest, GORDON *Carglen* (1891) 66. (27) **Sc.** I notice that the hairst munes a' rin vera like the seed anes, OCHILTREE *Redburn* (1895) ii. **Sh.I.** Glower an' glower till ivery ee wis laek a hairst mūn, STEWART *Tales* (1892) 252. **Frf.** They baith slaid awa' in the bricht hair'st-mune, *Longman's Mag.* (Feb. 1893) 439. **Fif.** Like a raw O' hairst-moons down the table, TENNANT *Papistry* (1827) 24. **Lnk.** Ye micht glower through the reek at the bonny hairst mune, HAMILTON *Poems* (1865) 150. **Ayr.** Weel do I like the braid hairst moon, *Ballads and Sngs.* (1847) II. 109. **Gall.** We may know by the sublime science of Astronomy—' That the Harrist Moon Rises nine nights alike soon,' MACTAGGART *Encycl.* (1824) 254, ed. 1876. **s.Sc.**, **e.Yks.** Lan. HARLAND & WILKINSON *Flk-Lore* (1867) 250. (28) **Sc.** (H.E.F.) **Abd.** Mr. Peterkin was wont, when the hairst play came, to hire himself out as a raker, ALEXANDER *Johnny Gibb* (1871) ix. (29) **Edb.** Thus to be placed at e'en, An' be amang that happy band, The dautit harvest queen, MᶜDOWALL *Poems* (1839) 218 ; The chiel the harst queen's heart has won, *ib.* 222. (30, *a*) **Sc.** Will ye gang out and see the hairst-rig ? (JAM.) **Fif.** There never was sic chaft-blade blatter On hairst-rigs or on crafts, TENNANT *Papistry* (1827) 116. **Ayr.** No courtier ever showed more gallantry towards the fair sex than did the youths on the hairst-rig, WHITE *Jottings* (1879) 48. **Kcb.** So unlike auld Millha' on the hairst rig, ELDER *Borgue* (1897) 31. (*b*) **Cld.** (JAM.) (31) **Sh.I.** Dey hed a cow . . . an dey were of a mind to sell her at da Hairst Roup for da rent, BURGESS *Lowra Biglan* (1896) 55. (32)

Cum. In the autumnal months, a larger species weighing from seven to twenty ounces, is taken (but in smaller quantities) along with the trout, &c. These are of a much superior quality, and are denominated Harvest Schelley, HUTCHINSON *Hist. Cum.* (1794) I. 463. (33) **Slk.** Country maidens, such as ewe-milkers, . . har'st-shearers, HOGG *Tales* (1838) 359, ed. 1866. (34) **e.Fif.** As impatient . . . as any thochtless schule-laddie ever was for the hairst-vaicance, LATTO *Tam Bodkin* (1864) xxii. (35) **Nrf.** (E.M.)

2. Phr. (1) *back of harvest*, after the harvest ; (2) *head of harvest*, the most important part of the harvest when the grain is all cut ; (3) *tail of harvest*, the end or finish of the harvest ; (4) *a hog in harvest*, a young sheep that is smeared at the end of harvest, when it ceases to be a lamb ; also called **Harvest-hog** (q.v.) ; (5) *just your harvest*, just what suits you, just what you like ; (6) *to owe one a day in harvest*, to owe one a good turn ; '(7) *as welcome as frost in harvest*, very inopportune ; (8) *to take a harvest*, to engage oneself as a harvest-labourer.

(1) **Shr.**[1] ' Wen's yore wakes, Tum ! ' ' Oh, back o' 'arrŏost ' ; **Shr.**[2] At the back o' quern harrast. (2) **Abd.** Gin ye hed seen 'im as I did, i' the vera heid o' hairst gyaun stoitin' aboot amo' the stooks at'a leasure, ALEXANDER *Ain Flk.* (1882) 67. (3) **Kcd.** It fell aboot the tail o' hairst. . . The craps were maistly i' the yard, GRANT *Lays* (1884) 52. (4) **Sc.** The central dish was a yearling lamb, called ' a hog in har'st,' roasted whole, SCOTT *Waverley* (1814) xx. **s.Sc.** Ask a thief, what's the best mutton, he'll answer ' a hog's the better mutton in harst,' meaning that a young sheep, called a hog, can be eaten sooner after being killed than one that's older (JAM.). (5) **Glo.** (S.S.B.) (6) **Sc.** The morn's a new day and Lord Evandale awes ye a day in har'st, SCOTT *Old Mortality* (1816) xxxii ; ' Aye, you owe him a day in hairst.' ' I owe him my wife. No harvest day will ever pay for that,' KEITH *Bonnie Lady* (1897) 207. (7) **s.Sc.** Aboot as welcome as frost i' hairst, I trow, SNAITH *Fierceheart* (1897) 65. (8) **Abd.** The geet being now six months old, was spean't, and Baubie ' took a hairst,' ALEXANDER *Ain Flk.* (1882) 227. **Frf. Gen.** said of persons who have other occupations in the village, and who take the opportunity to make some extra money in harvest-time (W.A.C.).

3. The autumn crop of any kind, not restricted to wheat.

Bdf. This term implies all the fruits of autumn, including beans. Clover, however. is not included, as it comes later in the year (J.W.B.).

4. Autumn.

Sc. *Monthly Mag.* (1798) II. 435 ; I was in London last harvest, *Scoticisms* (1787) 45. **Sh.I.** Mi Uncle Lowrie 'at deed da year afore last i da hairst, BURGESS *Sketches* (and ed.) 88. **Per.** Our summer's short, our hairst is cauld, MONTEATH *Dunblane* (1835) 108, ed. 1887.

5. v. To work in the harvest-field, gather in the corn.

Bnff.[1] They wir hairstin' a' the ook. **n.Cy.** (J.W.) **Shr.**[2] My mon's gwun a harrasting. **Ken.**[1] ' Where's Harry ? ' ' Oh ! he's harvesting 'long with his father ' ; **Ken.**[2] **w.Som.**[1] He bin to work along vor Mr. Bird harrestin, but now he ant a got nort to do.

Hence (1) **Hairstan, Harresting**, or **Harroosting**, *vbl. sb.* the act of getting in the corn or harvest ; (2) **Harvester**, *sb.* (*a*) a worker employed to assist in getting in the harvest ; (*b*) a harvest-bug or small insect, prevalent about harvest-time.

(1) **Bnff.**[1] **Shr.**[1] Our Dick's gwun 66th Jack Sankey an' a lot on 'em down tŏert Atchaman' Emstrey a-'arrŏostin'. **w.Som.**[1] We cant 'tend to no such jobs as that there, while the harrestin's about. (2, *a*) **Ken.**[1][2] (*b*) **n.Lin.**[1], **War.**[3], **Brks.**[1]

HARVEST-SHREW, *sb.* **Stf. War. Wor. Shr. Hrf. Glo. Oxf. Wil.** Also in forms **artishrew** Glo.[12] ; **artishow** Shr.[1] ; **artisrobe** m.Wor. ; **artistrow** Glo.[1] ; **hardi-shraow** se.Wor.[1] ; **hardishrew** Stf.[1] w.Wor.[1] ; **hardistraw** w.Wor.[1] Hrf.[2] ; **hardistrew** s.Wor. ; **hardistrow** s.Wor.[1] ; **hardy-shrew** Glo. ; **hartistraw** Glo.[1] ; **harvest-row** Wil.[1] ; **harvest-shrow** Oxf. ; **harvest-trow** Wil.[1] The shrew or harvest-mouse, *Mus minimus.* Cf. **ard-srew**.

Stf. (K.), **Stf.**[1], **War.**[3], m.Wor. (J.C.), w.Wor.[1], a.Wor. (H.K.), a.Wor.[1], se.Wor.[1], **Shr.**[1], **Hrf.** (W.W.S.), **Hrf.**[2] **Glo.** *Horae Subsecivae* (1777) 203 ; **Glo.**[12] **Oxf.** (G.E.D.) ; *Scienca Gossip* (1882) 165. **Wil.** BRITTON *Beauties* (1825) ; **Wil.**[1] **n.Wil.** The nests of the ' Harvest Trow '—a still smaller mouse, seldom seen except in summer, JEFFERIES *Wild Life* (1879) 186 ; T'can' a mouse—'tis a Harvest-row (E.H.G.).

HARWICH, see Harriage.

HASE, *sb.* e.An. [ēz.] The liver, heart, and lights of a pig; these parts seasoned, wrapped up in the omentum, and roasted. e.An.[1], Nrf. (HALL.) Cf. **haslet.**

HASE, HASEL, see Haze, *v.*[1], Hazel, *sb.*[1]

HASH, *sb.*[1] Nhb. Lan. [h), af.] 1. A sheep's lights boiled, then minced small and stewed with onions. Nhb.[1]

2. *Comp.* **Hash-pudding,** a large dumpling eaten at sheep-shearing; a mess made of sheep's heart chopped with suet and sweet fruits. ne.Lan.[1]

HASH, *sb.*[2] and *v.* Sc. Irel. Nhb. Cum. Yks. Not. War. Hnt. Also in form **ash** n.Yks. [(h)af, æf.] 1. *sb.* A mess, muddle; a confused mass; disorder in money matters.

Bnff.[1] The death or the aul ooman made a hash nae ordinar amo' them : she keepit thim a' thegeethir. He's a' till a hash. His maitters are a' in a hash. Abd. We gave them such a volley this time that they did not come to close quarters. A great hash o' them fell, and the rest galloped off, *Deeside Tales* (1872) 87. Per. You'll see a hash ere a' be dune, FORD *Harp* (1893) 346. n.Cy. (J.W.), Not.[2]

2. Careless, wasteful use ; destruction.

Bnff.[1] There's an awfu' hash aboot that fairm-toon : ilky bodie haiks through a' thing.

Hence (1) **Hash-loch,** *sb.* waste, refuse; (2) ·**mash,** *adv.* slap-dash; (3) ·**metram,** *adv.* in a state of disorder, topsy-turvy ; (4) **Hashrie,** *sb.* destruction from carelessness.

(1) Gall. MACTAGGART *Encycl.* (1824) 256, ed. 1876. (2) Lnk. I've done war deeds than dash your heads Hash-mash against the hallen, WATT *Poems* (1827) 65. (3) Sc. (JAM.) (4) Rxb. *(ib.)*

3. A noise, tumult ; strife, rioting ; ribald talk, nonsense.

Bnff.[1] The tail . . . o' the market wiz a real hash ; the lads wir a' lickin' ane anither aboot thir lasses. Ther's an unco hash amo' the freens aboot the old bodie's siller. Abd. Ye began wi' sic a hash, And fear'd my bairn, BEATTIE *Parings* (1801) 43, ed. 1873. Nhb. (R.O.H.)

4. *Phr. to settle one's hash,* to overcome a person completely. In *gen.* slang use.

Sh.I. Tak' de tedder an' gie da grice a gud slaag or twa ower his lugs. Dat'll settle his hash, *Sh. News* (Nov. 6, 1897). Nhb. Their hash was sattled, So off we rattled, ALLAN *Tyneside Sngs.* (ed. 1891) 96; (R.O.H.). Cum.[4] Lword Nelson settlt t'French ther hash at sea, SARGISSON *Joe Scoap* (1881) 105. n.Yks. Ah'll sattle your ash for you, if you don't be quiet (I.W.). War.[2] The pack very sharply settled his hash [killed the fox], *B'ham Dy. Gazette* (Feb. 18, 1899).

5. A heavy fall of rain.

Sh.I. Gūd keep a' frae a hash o' weet i' da tatties, *Sh. News* (Oct. 22, 1898).

Hence **Hashy,** *adj.* wet, sleety, slushy.

Lth., Bwk. A hashy day (JAM.). Nhb.[1] After snow begins to melt upon the ground it is, more especially if rain be falling, ' hashy walking.' The sea agitated by short turbulent waves is termed hashy.

6. A wasteful, slovenly person ; one who talks nonsense, a fool; a scamp; also used as a term of endearment for a boy.

Sc. ' What was I wanting to say ?' answered Jenny . . . ' Ye muckle hash !' SCOTT *Old Mortality* (1816) xxviii ; There he sat, a muckle, fat, white hash of a man, STEVENSON *Catriona* (1893) xv. Cai.[1] Fif. Time . . . leaveth nocht to modern hashes But idle tales and empty clashes, TENNANT *Papistry* (1827) 214. e.Fif. ' Ye may say sae,' remarkit anither smyaterin hash, as she tane a hearty sook o' the buttersaps, LATTO *Tam Bodkin* (1864) ii. Slg. Wha jeering snash, An' ca' me tentless, fretfu' hash, MUIR *Poems* (1818) 25. s.Sc. He's a spiritless hash—and no little 's the disgrace he's like to bring upon us a', WILSON *Tales* (1836) II. 163. Cld. (JAM.) Dmb. A young man was thought a wicked hash That had seduced a virtuous lass, TAYLOR *Poems* (1827) 90. Rnf. Crappie, the other night, poor hash ! Wi' hunger, took sae sair a brash, PICKEN *Poems* (1813) I. 61. Ayr. A poor doylt druken hash, BURNS *Sc. Drink* (1786) st. 15. Lnk. Clear the house of mony a hash Wi' empty brains, MUIR *Minstrulsy* (1816) 67. Lth. [I] feel—ye hash, wi' a' your duds on, For you attractions like a loadstone, MACNEILL *Poet. Wks.* (1801) 47, ed. 1856. Edb. 'Tis no in poortith, or in cash, To curb a genius, change a hash, McDOWALL *Poems* (1839) 33. Bwk. Wha e'er believe Betty's tales are a' silly hashes, HENDERSON *Pop. Rhymes* (1856) 98. Peb. The nauseous mixture fell Wi' jaws upon the sprawling hash, Maist choak'd wi' th' taste and smell, *Lintoun Green* (1685) 62, ed. 1817. Slk. Oh ! hoo I hate to hear a hash insist—insistin that

you shall tell a story, CHR. NORTH *Noctes* (ed. 1856) IV. 269. Gall. In truth ilk worthy hash In estimation high is held By big Sir Balderdash, MACTAGGART *Encycl.* (1824), ed. 1876. N.I.[1], n.Cy. (HALL.), N.Cy.[1] Nhb. Ye greet blubberin hash (R.O.H.) ; This ye sud let some chiel done for ye, My boasting hash, DONALDSON *Poems* (1801) 215. Cum.[4] Tho' ye was rash, I'll scorn to wrang ye, senseless hash, *Daft Bargain,* l. 17.

Hence (1) **Hash-a-pie,** *sb.* a lazy, slovenly, greedy fellow; (2) **Hashly,** *adv.* in a slovenly manner ; (3) **Hashy,** *adj.* slovenly, careless, destructive.

(1) Sc. (JAM.) (2) Lnk. In hoden grey right hashly clad, RAMSAY *Poems* (1721) II. 388, ed. 1800 ·*ib.*.·. (3) Sc. (JAM.), Cai.[1]

7. *v.* To slash, hack ; also used *fig.*

Sc. Hagging and hashing at Christ's kirk, STEVENSON *Catriona* (1893) xv. Per. All raging there in blood, they hew'd and hash'd, FORD *Harp* (1893) 6. Ayr. They hack'd and hash'd, while braid-swords clash'd, BURNS *Battle of Sheriffmuir,* st. 2. Edb. Sortin' sairs an' broken banes Whan hash't an' smash't wi' coals an' stanes, FORBES *Poems* (1812) 86. Rxb. A broom-stick take, and hash and smash, And all the ware to pieces dash, WILSON *Poems* (1824) 37.

8. To spoil, damage, destroy, make a mess of.

Sc. To hash grain, to injure it by careless reaping (JAM.) ; Ye're in your right to ask for my authority to interfere . . .—to hash, may be, other folks' weft, COBBAN *Andaman* (1895) xiii. Cai.[1] To hash one's clothes. To hash the material in which one works. Edb. Winter's sour, Whase floods did erst their mailin's produce hash, FERGUSSON *Poems* (1773) 162, ed. 1785. Not.[1]

Hence **Hashing,** *ppl. adj.* wasteful, destructive ; overflowing, as of a flood.

Bnff.[1] He's a hashin' servan' : he blaads mair nor he's worth. Edb. Hashin', splashin', white or gray, O'er the dam-head, FORBES *Poems* (1812) 99.

9. To bruise, ill-treat.

Lnk. How unfeelin' wretches will Poor brutes torment an' hash, an' kill, WATT *Poems* (1827) 11. Nhb.[1] The horse was gye sair hashed.

10. To grind corn partially. Nhb.[1] Hence **Hashed,** *ppl. adj.* crushed. *ib.*

HASH, *sb.*[3] Som. A rash on the skin. (W.F.R.)

HASHIE, *adj.* Sc. ? Rough, coarse.

Edb. Characters with deformed legs, and thrawn necks, and blind eyes, and hashie lips, MOIR *Mansie Wauch* (1828) xii.

HASHINESS, *sb.* Sc. Carelessness in dress, slovenliness. See **Hash,** *sb.*[2]

Fif. The elder sister, fikey and perjink, was severe on a younger brother's hashiness, COLVILLE *Vernacular* (1899) 17.

HASHTER, *sb.* and *v.* Ayr. (JAM.) Also in form **hushter.** [ha·ʃtər.] 1. *sb.* Work ill-arranged or executed in a slovenly manner. 2. *v.* To work in a hurried, slovenly, and wasteful manner. Hence **Hashtered,** *ppl. adj.* hurried.

HASHY, *sb.* Sc. Also in form **hassie** Lth. (JAM.) [ha·ʃi.] 1. A mess, muddle, confusion ; noise, riot ; also used *attrib.*

Bnff.[1] It is somewhat more emphatic than hash. Cld., Lth. (JAM.) 2. An old sermon preached over again.

Peb. Being often abroad in the service of God He dealt out his hashies at hame, AFFLECK *Poet. Wks.* (1836) 104; Ye've gien him a call to oppose Dr. Hall; He'll feed you wi' hashies belyve. *ib.* 105.

[1. Fr. *hachis,* a hachey or hachee, minced meat (COTGR.).]

HASK, *adj.*[1], *sb.*[1] and *v.* In *gen.* dial. use in Sc. Irel. and Eng. Also written **haske** Cum.[1] w.Yks.[2]; and in forms **arsk** w.Yks.[2]; **ask** ne.Yks.[1] e.Yks.[1] w.Yks.[2345] Lan.[1] m.Lan.[1] Chs.[1] Stf.[12] nw.Der.[1] n.Lin.[1] sw.Lin.[1] War.[2]; **aske** Cum.[1]; **asp** e.Yks.[1]; **haisk** Slk. Dmf. (JAM.) ; **harsk** n.Yks.[2]; **harske** w.Yks.[1]; **hoak** Chs.[1] ; **yask** s.Chs.[1] [(h)ask.] 1. *adj.* Of the weather: dry, parching, piercingly cold.

n.Cy. GROSE (1790); N.Cy.[1] Nhb.[1] A hask wind is keen and parching. Cum. (J.Ar.), s.Wm. (J.A.B.), n.Yks. (R.H.H.), ne.Yks.[1] w.Yks.[1]; w.Yks.[5] Damp and unsettled. n.Lan. (W.S.); n.Lan.[1] A keen frosty wind is said to be ' varra hask.' ne.Lan.[1], m.Lan.[1] Chs. Th' snow lay thick upo' th' ground, an' th' hask wind kept moanin' an' wailin', CROSTON *Enoch Crump* (1887) 8; Chs.[1] A cold, dry east wind is said to be a hosk wind; Chs.[3] Stf.[2] Its veri ask ðis mornin, ð winds got raind toð lst. Der.[2]

nw.Der.[1] It's a eest wind; it's very 'ask en drey. Not.[8] Lin. STREATFEILD *Lin. and Danes* (1884) 265. **sw.Lin.**[1] How ask and parched I am !—Oh, it's the weather, and the ask winds, and that.

Hence (1) **Haskiness,** *sb.* dryness and insipidity of food; the parched condition of land ; (2) **Haskish,** *adj.* dry, harsh ; (3) **Haskness,** *sb.* dryness, harshness ; (4) **Hasky,** *adj.* dry, parched.

(1) n.Yks.[2] (2) w.Yks. (Æ.B.) (3) w.Yks.[3] (4) Sc. GROSE (1790) *MS. add.* (C.) Gall. For her he shook the hasky strae, NICHOLSON *Poet. Wks.* (1814) 137, ed. 1897. **N.I.**[1], Cav. (M.S.M.) **n.Yks.** Them turnips teeasts hasky (I.W.) ; n.Yks.[4] w.Yks. *Leeds Merc. Suppl.* (May 30, 1891); w.Yks.[24] Chs. Old people frequently speak of dry, piercing winds, as asky weather; and dry, cold, windy weather is often spoken of as asky weather, *Sheaf* (1879) I. 271 ; Chs.[1], s.Chs.[1], Stf.[1], Not. (L.C.M.) Shr.[1] 'Ard an' 'asky land.

2. Rough to the touch ; stiff, unyielding ; hard, brittle and difficult to work ; also used *advb.*

Bwk., Rxb. (JAM.), N.Cy.[1] Nhb.[1] Hask is also applied to the sense of feeling when anything from its touch appears unpleasantly dry or hard. Coarse worsted is hask to the feeling. 'Hask coal' is very hard, brittle coal ; or coal that is ' winded,' or woody in texture. Dur. GIBSON *Up-Weardale Gl.* (1870); Dur.[1] s.Dur. Spoken of any material with a coarse surface. ' It feels varra hask' (J.E.D.). Lakel.[2] It maks yan's hands hask to howk amang lime. Cum. Of a horse's coat, without gloss, harsh and rough to the touch (J.Ar.) ; A dry, aske weeping—no tears, DALBY *Mayroyd* (1880) III. 49; Cum.[1] Your cow hez a hask hide on her. n.Yks.[1] ; n.Yks.[2] ' As harsk as sawcum,' as sawdust; spoken of bread. As hask as chopped hay ' ; n.Yks.[24] ne.Yks.[1] T'grass is bad ti cut, it's varra ask at t'boddum. e.Yks. Deficient in moisture ; spoken more particularly of food, as bread, MARSHALL *Rur. Econ.* (1788) ; e.Yks.[1], m.Yks.[1] His skin's varry ask, t'doctor says (J.R.) ; ' It handles ask,' might be said of wool if dried too quickly on a stove, *Leeds Merc. Suppl.* (May 30, 1891) ; w.Yks.[1] 'Hask grass,' rough, coarse grass. Also rigid or harsh to the touch, as ' This cow handles vara hask' ; w.Yks.[3] It's varry ask and drau, and hasn't natur in it it owt to have; w.Yks.[4] Not. ' It made my hair hask' or ' my hair became hask' (W.H.S.). n.Lin.[1] Strong clay land when baked by the sun is said to be very ask. 'You ha'nt anuther bit o' land . . . oht like as ask as th'top end o' th' Wood Cloäs is. sw.Lin.[1] 'That cloth is stiff to work I' ' Yes, it's hask, it's very hask.' War.[2] Lon. Then it always feels hask to the hand, MAYHEW *Lond. Labour* (1851) I. 443. Hmp. (H.C.M.B.)

Hence **Hasky,** *adj.* harsh, rough, coarse, unyielding ; also used *fig.* and *advb.*

s.Don. Stony ground hard to dig is called hasky (D.A.S.). n.Yks.[4] ne.Yks.[1] T'bread's that asky Ah can't eeat it. w.Yks.[2] The hands of bricklayers are said to be hasky when they are covered with lime and dry. s.Chs.[1] We say, when a person has heard something unpleasant, ' It went daayn ver'i aas'ki widh im' [It went daïn very hasky with him]. Not. (L.C.M.), Not.[1] Lei.[1] The skin is dry and hasky. Nhp.[2] A person affected with a severe scorbutic affection described her face as 'very hasky.'

3. Bitter, sour, tart, harsh to the taste.

e.Yks. NICHOLSON *Flk-Sp.* (1889) 66 ; e.Yks.[1] Give us another lump o' secagur [sugar], teea's se hask. w.Yks. *Leeds Merc. Suppl.* (May 30, 1891); w.Yks.[2] Said of sour plums, &c. n.Lin. SUTTON *Wds.* (1881) ; n.Lin.[1] The äale's as ask as whig. s.Lin. I can't eät sloes, they're so hask i' yer mouth (T.H.R.)

Hence **Hasky,** *adj.* harsh, bitter ; *fig.* ill-natured, harsh, severe.

s.Don. A man who is unkind to his children and severe with them is called a hasky father (D.A.S.). Cav. Mrs. Brady is a hasky neighbour (M.S.M.). Lan.[1] This ale has an asky taste.

4. Dry, husky, hoarse.

Nhb. A hask cough (R.O.H.). s.Lan.[1] Not. She seems to have such a hask cough on her (L.C.M.).

Hence **Hasky,** *adj.* husky.

Sc. GROSE (1790) *MS. add.* (C.) N.I.[1], w.Yks.[24], Stf.[1], Shr.[1]

5. A sharp, biting wind. Not. (W.H.S.)

6. Dryness ; sharpness, crispness, as in cotton. w.Yks. (J.W.), w.Yks.[2]

7. A hoarse, dry cough ; a cough to which animals, esp. calves, are subject, caused by worms in the windpipe. Cf. **husk,** *sb.*[1]

Nhb. (R.O.H.), Chs.[1] s.Chs.[1] Iv óo wüz mai'kin dhaat· aas·k, óo)d aav· ü óos on ür [If hoo was makin' that hask, hoo'd have a hoose on her ; of a cow]. Dhaat· ky'aay)z got·n ü naas·ti aas·k [That caf's gotten a nasty hask]. Shr.[1] 'E's gotten sich a 'ask on 'im. Wil. LISLE *Husbandry* (1757) 343 ; Wil.[1], Som. (W.F.R.)

---

8. *v.* To emit a short, dry cough ; to clear the throat; to make a noise as a dog does when anything sticks in its throat.

Ayr. Spettin an' haskin (F.J.C.). Dmf., Slk. (JAM.), Nhb. (R.O.H.), Chs.[1] s.Chs.[1] Dhée·ûr dhaa sits, baas·kin ün yaas·kin [Theer tha sits, baskin' an' yaskin']. Aa·rkn üt dhaat· ky'aat· yaas·kin ; püt ür thróo)th win·dû, els óo)l bi sik i)dh aays [Hearken at that cat yaskin' ; put her through th' window, else hoo'll be sick i' th' haise].

Hence **Hasked,** *ppl. adj.* dry, parched.

m.Yks.[1] The throat is said to be hasked when parched.

HASK, *sb.*[2] Sh.I. A haze on the horizon foreboding wind. See **Ask,** *sb.*[2]

A skubby hask hings, icet-gray, JUNDA *Klingrahool* (1898) 22 ; JAKOBSEN *Norsk in Sh.* (1897) 69.

HASK, *adj.*[2] Not. Written **ask.** [Not known to our other correspondents.] Foolish, not quite right in the head. (J.S.J.)

HASK, *sb.*[3] Sc. Nhb. [hask.] The throat, the soft palate. Ayr. (F.J.C.) Nhb.[1] ' Pap o' the hask ' is the uvula.

[Cp. *haskwort,* a name given by Lyte to the halswort (G. *halskraut*), also called throatwort, the *Campanula Trachelium* (N.E.D.).]

HASKETS, *sb. pl.* Dor. Also written **hasketts.** Hazel and maple bushes ; brushwood.

Whether the inhabitants of the parish of Tollard Farnham, in the county of Dorset, have the right to cut and take fagots or haskets of the underwood growing upon . . . the common, KELLY *Law Reports* (1878) *Exch. Div.* III. 363; *w. Gazette* (Feb. 15, 1889) 7.

HASKIN, *sb.* Hmp. An inferior kind of cheese. (J.R.W.)

HASKING, see **Huskin(g.**

HASKY, *adj.* n.Sc. (JAM.) **1.** Rank, strong, luxuriant, applied to growing corn or vegetables ; also to a man.

'A hasky carl,' a big raw-boned man.

2. Coarse to the taste, unpalatable ; dirty, applied to work ; slovenly, applied to a person.

HASLE, *sb.* Ess. Sus. [Not known to our other correspondents.] [æ·sl.] An iron to hang pots on over the fire. (P.R.)

HASLE, see **Hay,** *sb.*[1], **Hazle,** *sb.*[1]

HASLET, *sb.* Sc. Chs. Lin. Nhp. War. Wor. Shr. Hrf. Glo. Brks. Suf. Ken. Hmp. I.W. Wil. Also written **hasslet** Glo.[1] ; and in forms **acelet** Chs. Brks.[1] ; **acelot** Ken.[1] ; **aislet** Ken. ; **arslet** Ken.[1] ; **aslat** w.Wor.[1] se.Wor.[1] Shr.[2] Hrf.[2] Glo. Ken.; **azlitse.** Wor.[1]; **harcelets.** Wor.[1] Glo. Ken.[12]; **harslet** Chs.[1] Lin. War.[2] Shr.[1] Glo.[1] e.Suf. Ken.[1] Hmp. Wil. ; **hastelet** e.Suf. ; **hauslet** Sc. (JAM. *Suppl.*) [ä·slit, a·zlit, æ·zlit.] **1.** The liver, lights, &c. of a pig ; occas. of a cow, sheep, or other animal. Cf. **haste,** *sb.*

Sc. (JAM. *Suppl.*) Slk. Hook the haslet of the hind, HOGG *Queer Bk.* (1832) 36. Chs. The liver and lights of a cow, sheep, or pig, *Sheaf* (1884) III. 195 ; Chs.[1] War.[2] w.Wor.[1], se.Wor.[1], Shr.[12] Hrf.[2], Glo.[1], Suf.[1], e.Suf. (F.H.), Ken.[1], Hmp.[1] I.W. Reserving the lebb, pluck, and haslet, MONCRIEFF *Dream* (1863) l. 36; I.W.[1] Also, the edible parts of a calf's viscera; I.W.[2], Wil. (G.E.D.)

2. A dish made of the entrails or trimmings of a pig ; also used of griskin.

Lin. The minced meat prepared for sausages ; inclosed and cooked in the caul of the hog, THOMPSON *Hist. Boston* (1856) 709 ; Lin.[1] s.Lin. Savoury pig cheer made like a sausage about six inches in thickness. A favourite Lin. dish (T.H.R.). Nhp.[1] The small pieces cut off, in trimming the hams and flitches of a singed pig ; these cuttings are made into pork pies, or haslet-pies, as they are called, and it is customary in many villages for the farmers' wives to send one of these pies, with some pig's puddings, as presents to their neighbours. In some places the griskin is termed haslit. w.Wor.[1] A dish composed of these parts [liver, &c. of a pig] wrapped in the caul, and baked with sage and onions. s.Wor.[1] Shr.[1] Obsol. The heart, liver, and lights of a pig taken out entire—with the wind-pipe attached. ' We shanna a to bwile the pot o' Friday, theer'll be the 'aslet for the men's dinners.' Glo. (A.B.), Brks.[1] Ken.[1] ; Ken.[2] They mix some fat bits and lean of the pork, and roast all together. s.Hmp. The heart and lights or lungs of a hog, all mixed up and boiled together, HOLLOWAY.

[1. He britnes out þe brawen . . . & hatȝ out þe hastlette, *Gawayne* (c. 1360) 1612. Fr. (Norm. dial.) *hâtelet,* 'région des côtes du porc ; côtelette appartenant à cette région ' (MOISY).]

HASLIG, *sb.* Sh.I. The wool on the neck of a sheep. Cf. halse-lock, s.v. Halse, *sb.*[1]

I turn'd her [a ewe] up an' begood ta roo her haslig, *Sh. News* (Jan. 13, 1900).

HASLING-PIECES, *sb. pl.* w.Som.[1] [ā·slin-pìsiz.] Upright pieces of wood fixed from the floor to the roof in an attic, to form the sides of a room, and to which the laths and plaster are attached.

HASP, *sb.*[1] and *v.* In *gen.* dial. use in Sc. Irel. Eng. and Nfld. Also in forms **apse** Oxf. Wil. Dev.; **asp** Not.[2]; **esp** Cum.[1] Not.[2]; **haps** Glo.[1] Brks.[1] Ken.[2] Sur.[1] Sus.[1] Hmp.[1] Wil.[1] Dor.[1] Som. Dev. Cor.[12a] Nfld.; **hapse** Brks. Ken.[1] Sus. Hmp. I.W.[1] w.Som.[1] Dev. Cor.[1]; **heps** Cor.[12]; **hesp** Sc. N.Cy.[1] Nhb. Dur.[1] Lakel.[12] Cum.[12] n.Yks.[124] ne.Yks.[1] e.Yks.[1] m.Yks.[1] w.Yks.[12] n.Lan.[1] ne.Lan.[1] Not. n.Lin.[1] sw.Lin.[1] [h)asp, h)esp; æps, āps.] 1. *sb.* A latch; a fastening for a door, gate, or window, *gen.* consisting of a loop and staple; a clasp for the lid of a box, which falls into the lock; a clasp or buckle.

Or.I. (S.A.S.) Ayr. You might have disappointed him [a caller]; you had the hasp in your hand, HUNTER *Studies* (1870) 197. Gall. He undid the hasp of the creaking front door of the manse, CROCKETT *Stickit Min.* (1893) 230. Wgt. Shut him in and fixed the hasp which rendered Jamie's exit equally impracticable for the time being, FRASER *Wigtown* (1877) 352. Dwn. The black-smith placed the hasp of the door upon the iron staple, LYTTLE *Betsy Gray* (1894) 17. N.Cy.[1], Nhb. (R.O.H.), Dur.[1], Lakel.[2], Cum.[2] n.Yks.[1] The button which turns on a central pivot and so clasps or fastens a window, &c., is specially indicated; n.Yks.[24], ne.Yks.[1], e.Yks.[1], m.Yks.[1] w.Yks. One of the staple trades of Leeds is the manufacture of hasps and catches, *Yksman.* (1881) 197; w.Yks.[12], n.Lan.[1], Chs.[1], nw.Der.[1], Not.[123], s.Not. (J.P.K.) n.Lin. SUTTON *Wds.* (1881); n.Lin.[1] s.Lin. Ah must laa' in some new hesps . . . or ah s'll be hevin' the gaīts all undone [left open] (T.H.R.). sw.Lin.[1] Shr.[1] I lost the kay, an' didna like to break the 'asp, so I knocked a bwurd out o' the bottom; Shr.[2], Glo.[1], Oxf. (J.E.) Brks. (M.J.B.); Brks.[1] The withy tie used to secure hurdles to 'vawle staaykes' or to each other. Suf.[1] Ken. (K.); Ken.[1] The hasp [of the gate] is gone; Ken.[2] Sur.[1] Sus. (K.), Sus.[1] Hmp.[1], I.W.[1] Wil. The fastening of a pair of braces, &c. In fact, the word is applied to almost any kind of fastening (G.E.D.); Suow Gl. (1892); Wil.[1] Dor. (C.W.), Dor.[1] Som. Christopher stood dumbfounded, with his hand on the hapse, RAYMOND *Sam and Sabina* (1894) 109; JENNINGS *Obs. Dial. w.Eng.* (1825). w.Som.[1] Th' hapse o' the gate's a-tor'd, an all the bullicks be a-go to road. s.Dev. (Miss D.) Cor. She slammed the haps agen my hand, TREGELLAS *Tales, Betty White,* 77; Cor.[12]

2. *Phr.* (1) *to be all buckled with one hasp,* not to be better than one another; (2) *to be made to ride the hasp,* to be brought before one's superiors and reprimanded.

(1) Ayr. They are a' buckled wi' ae hasp, JOHNSTON *Glenbuckie* (1889) 211. (2) Cor.[1]

3. A short half-door within the whole door often seen in country shops. Also used *fig.*

Cor.[1] The lower half is kept shut, the top open. There is *gen.* a bell fastened to it to give notice of a customer. 'She has more tongue than teeth, she had better keep a heps before her mouth'; Cor.[1]

4. The tendril of a vine or climbing plant. Sur. *Trans. Phil. Soc.* (1854) 83.

5. *v.* To fasten the latch of a door, gate, or window; to secure by hitching a thing round another; to fasten up a box.

Sc. (JAM.) Ayr. While's the purse that's hespet steeve, Tines a' its gatherings oot, *Ballads and Sngs.* (1847) II. 61. N.Cy.[1] Nhb. Hasp the door, or window (R.O.H.). Cum. LINTON *Lake Cy.* (1864) 305. m.Yks.[1] w.Yks. To fasten by a catch, but not a lock (J.T.). ne.Lan.[1], nw.Der.[1] Not.[1]; Not.[2] Esp the door, I tell ye, if yo doan't want to be blown up chimbley. s.Not. (J.P.K.), Lin. (W.W.S.) sw.Lin.[1] Just hesp yon gate. Shr.[1] Brks. Gl. (1852); Brks.[1], Ken.[1] Hapse the gate after you! Wil.[1] n.Wil. Why don'ee haps the door? (E.H.G.) Som. JENNINGS *Dial. w.Eng.* (1869) Gl. w.Som.[1] Mind an hapse the door arter ee, you do 'most always lef-m onhapsed. Dev. Apsen thickee geat there, or us chell 'ave the cows awl awver the place avore marning, HEWETT *Peas. Sp.* (1892). n.Dev. Well, Giles tha hatch as well may hapse, ROCK *Jim an' Nell* (1867) st. 14. Cor. THOMAS *Ran-digal Rhymes* (1895) Gl. [Nfld. (G.P.)]

Hence **Hasped**, *ppl. adj.* fastened up, secured.

Dev. You see, he was never yewsed to be apsed up, *Reports Provinc.* (1891).

6. To catch hold as a tendril does. Sur. *Trans. Phil. Soc.* (1854) 83.

HASP, *sb.*[2] Sc. Also in form **hesp.** [hasp, hesp.] 1. A hank of yarn, worsted, or flax; *gen.* a definite quantity, the fourth part of a spindle.

Sh.I. Hendry wis haddin' a hesp o' wirsid, BURGESS *Sketches* (2nd ed.) 72. Cai.[1] Bnff. The frequent 'charms' were a 'hesp of yarn,' with which some dementit old woman had hanged herself, GORDON *Chron. Keith* (1880) 61. Kcd. His pirns an' clews, an' worset hesps, [were] Beclairtit i' the glaur, GRANT *Lays* (1884) 8. Fif. About thirty years ago . . . a hesp or slip . . . was thought a sufficient day's work for a woman, *Statist. Acc.* VI. 43 (JAM.). Slg. Twisted hard like ony hesp O' hempen thread, MUIR *Poems* (1818) 14. s.Sc. I could neither mak' the parritch - nor wash, nor spin, nor mak' up a hasp o' yarn to please her, WILSON *Tales* (1839) V. 58. Rnf. To beet the hesp o' yarn, ALLAN *Poems* (1696) 113. Ayr. Anither kimmer would say her dochter was in bairn-bed, and she was tell't to tak her withershins nine times through a hesp o' unwatered yarn, to tak the cat through't sungates aboot as mony times again, and baudrons would hae the pains, SERVICE *Notandums* (1890) 100. Lnk. She could not finish her hasp or hank of yarn that night, HAMILTON *Poems* (1865) 209. Edb. Providence seems a ravel'd hasp. PENNECUIK *Helicon* (1790) 26.

2. *Phr.* (1) *to have a ravelled hasp,* to be in a difficulty; (2) *to make a ravelled hasp,* to put a thing into confusion; (3) *to redd* or *wind a ravelled hasp,* to restore order, put things right.

(1) Sc. Ye have gotten a revel'd hesp o't, RAMSAY *Prov.* (1737). (2) Sc. (JAM.) (3) Sc. Left us a tangled hesp to wind, SCOTT *Redg.* (1824) Lett. xi. Abd. Gin mammy miss, again, her bairn, 'Twill be a hesp o' ravel'd yarn, We winna redd, COCK *Strains* (1810' I. 119. Dmb. There's plenty o' the raveled hasp M'Corkle left to redd yet, CROSS *Disruption* (1844) xxxvii. e.Lth. It was a raivelled hasp he had to redd, HUNTER *J. Inwick* (1895) 32.

[1. Haspis of silke, *Dest. Troy* (c. 1400) 3899. Du. *haspe,* a haspe or a reele; *haspen,* to hasple or to reele up thred or yarne (HEXHAM); Norw. dial. *hespa,* a hank or skein of yarn (AASEN).]

HASPAL, *sb.* Sc. Yks. Also written **haspill** w.Yks.[5]; **hasple** Dmf. (JAM.); and in forms **aspill, espill** w.Yks.[6] [h)a·spl.] 1. A sloven; a clownish-mannered person; a silly fellow.

Dmf. A sloven, with his shirt-neck open (JAM.). Gall. MAC-TAGGART *Encyl.* (1824). w.Yks. SCATCHERD *Hist. Morley* (1830) 168, ed. 1874; w.Yks.[6]

2. An overgrown boy, a 'haspenald' (q.v.). w.Yks.[6]

[Tirol. dial. *haspel,* 'alberner Mensch' (SCHÖPF); Swab. dial. *haspele,* 'eine sich übereilende Person' (BIRLINGER); cp. Bavar. dial. *hispel,* 'alberner Mensch' (SCHMELLER).]

HASPAT, *sb. Obs.* n.Cy. A stripling, a youth between man and boy. (K.), GROSE (1790), N.Cy.[2]

[*Half + spaut* (a youth), q.v.]

HASPENALD, *sb. Obs.* n.Cy. Yks. Also in form **haspenal** n.Cy. A youth between man and boy; an overgrown boy; also in *comp.* **Haspenald-lad, -tike.**

n.Cy. (K.); GROSE (1790); N.Cy.[2] w.Yks. SCATCHERD *Hist. Morley* (1830) 169, ed. 1874; w.Yks.[1] Hee's waxen a gay, leathe-wake, fendible, whelkin, haspenald tike, ii. 289; w.Yks.[6]

HASPERT, *sb.* w.Yks.[1] ne.Lan.[1] Also in form **hespert** ne.Lan.[1] [a·spət.] A rough, uncultivated fellow.

HASPIN, *sb.*[1] Sc. n.Cy. Cum. Lan. Also written **haspan** s.Sc. (JAM.) [h)a·spin.] 1. A stripling. Cf. **haspat, haspenald.**

s.Sc. A raw haspan of a callan! *Blackw. Mag.* (May 1820) 164 (JAM.). n.Cy. (HALL.)

2. An idle fellow, doing nothing but lounging about.

Cum. LINTON *Lake Cy.* (1864) 305. ne.Lan.[1]

HASPIN, *sb.*[2] n.Cy. Lakel. Cum. Yks. Lan. Also in form **hespin** Lakel.[1] Cum.[4] [h)a·spin, h)e·spin.] A close-fisted person, a miser; a greedy and over-reaching man.

n.Cy. GROSE (1790). Lakel.[1] An ole hespin. Cum.[4] w.Yks. HUTTON *Tour to Caves* (1781). ne.Lan.[1]

HASS, see **Halse**, *sb.*[1]

HASSBILES, *sb. pl.* Or.I. A skin-disease peculiar to infancy, which produces patches of dry scab on the head. (J.G.), (JAM.) See **Halse**, *sb.*[1] 1.

HASSENS, *sb. pl.* Sh.I. Also written **hassings** ; **hassins** S. & Ork.[1] 1. The bottom boards of a boat next to the stern. (*Coll.* L.L.B.), S. & Ork.[1] 2. *Comb.* **Hassins-fore-and-aft**, the boards that adjoin the keel about one-third of its length. S. & Ork.[1]

HASSICK, HASSIE, HASSING, see **Hussock, Hashy, Hassens**.

HASSLE, *v.* Cum. Also written **hassel**. [ha·sl.] To hack at ; to cut with a blunt knife and with a sawing motion.

At week ould beard to hassel and hack Wid razor as blunt as a saw, DICKINSON *Cumbr.* (1878) 238 ; A razor meaad oot of an oald hand saw eh t'tudder, was shaven oa t'feaace on em... When he'd hasselt at em till bleudd began teh cum, SARGISSON *Joe Scoap* (1881) 199 ; **Cum.**[4]

HASSLIN-TOOTH, see **Axle-tooth**.

HASSOCK, *sb.* In *gen.* dial. use in Sc. and Eng. Also written **hassack** Lin. Nhp.[2] s.Pem. ; **hassick** Bch. I.W.[1] Dor.[1] ; and in forms **assock** s.Not ; **hazzick** Brks.[1] ; **hossock** n.Yks.[4] ; **hussick** Sh.I. ; **hussock** Gall. n.Yks.[1] ne.Yks.[1] w.Yks.[1] ne.Lan.[1] Nhp.[1] ; **huzzick, huzzock** s.Chs.[1] [h]a·sǝk, æ·sǝk, u·sǝk.] 1. A tuft of coarse grass, *gen.* growing in boggy places ; a tuft of sedges, reeds, or rushes. Also used *attrib.*

N.Cy.[1] **Nhb.** Rounded tufts of grass in the fields, especially those of the *Carex paniculata*, Linn., are called hassocks (R.O.H.). **Cum.** Who should come up but Robbie Atkinson leading hassocks, CAINE *Hagar* (1887) III. 159. **n.Yks.**[1] Large tufts of coarse grass growing in boggy places in low pastures, or carrs, often nearly or quite two feet high and twelve or fifteen inches in diameter in the dry, pillar-like growth of root and stem above which the herbage flourishes ; **n.Yks.**[4], **ne.Yks.**[1], **w.Yks.**[1] **Lan.** Son John went to th' fell for a double load of hassocks, WALKDEN *Diary* (ed. 1866) 28 ; Wanting some hassock turf to top our stack with ... Son John led me 4 double loads home, *ib.* 30. **Chs.** *Sheaf* (1883) III. 16 ; **Chs.**[1] The grass which forms hassocks is chiefly *Aira caespitosa* ; the sedges are *Carex caespitosa* and *C. paniculata* ; **Chs.**[2] **Midl.** Close under the bank, in the middle of a large clump of ' hassock ' grass, a moorhen has formed her nest, *Cornh. Mag.* (Aug. 1892) 149. **s.Not.** All them 'assocks wants diggin up (J.P.K.). **Lin.** MILLER & SKERTCHLY *Fenland* (1878) vi. **n.Lin.**[1], **Rut.**[1], **Lei.**[1], **Nhp.**[1][2], **War.**[2] **s.Pem.** The moor is covered with hassack, we must boorn it (W.M.M.). **Hnt.** (T.P.F.) **e.An.**[1] These hassocks in bogs, were formerly taken up with a part of the soil, matted together with roots, shaped, trimmed, and dressed, a sufficient part of their shaggy and tufted surface being left, to make kneeling much easier than on the pavement of the church, or the bare boarded floor of a pew. **Suf.** RAINBIRD *Agric.* (1819) 301, ed. 1849 ; In these fens the original surface is rough and unequal from the great tufts of rushes, &c., called hassocks, MARSHALL *Review* (1811) III. 289. **e.Suf.** (F.H.), **Sur.**[1] **Hmp.** The hassocks or carex form a very marked feature, WHITE *Selborne* (1788) 20, ed. 1853 ; A field in which the grass is tangled is said to be 'all of a hassock ' (H.C.M.B.) ; **Hmp.**[1], **I.W.**[1], **Dor.**[1] **Dev.** With much difficulty I could step from one hassock to another in laying out the drains, VANCOUVER *Agric.* (1807) 286, ed. 1813 ; (R.P.C.)

Hence **Hassocky** or **Huzzicky**, *adj.* of grass : coarse, sedgy, matted together ; of land : abounding in hassocks. **s.Chs.**[1] Applied to hay, matted together and mouldy, the result of its being got together in bad condition. Not.[1], n.Lin.[1], Lei.[1], Nhp.[1] **Hnt.** A sort of coarse bad hassocky grass, MARSHALL *Review* (1814) IV. 419.

2. *Fig.* A ' shock ' of hair.

Sc. His ain shaggy hassock of hair, SCOTT *Rob Roy* (1817) xxxiv. **Sh.I.** (*Coll.* L.L.B.) **Bch.** The tither wis a haave colour'd smeer-less tapie wi' a great hassick o' hair hingin in twa pennerets about her haffats, FORBES *Jrn.* (1742) 17. **Gall.** His eyes shining from under his hassock of grey hair, CROCKETT *Grey Man* (1896) xlix ; MACTAGGART *Encycl.* (1824).

Hence **Hassock-head**, *sb.* a shock head ; a bushy and entangled growth of coarse hair. e.An.[1], e.Suf. (F.H.) 3. An ant-hill. Rut.[1], Lei.[1] Hence **Hassock-hoeing**, *vbl. sb.* taking off the tops of ant-hills with a hoe. Rut.[1] 4. The surface-layer of turf, with heath, &c. upon it, cut about three inches thick ; rotted sward such as appears when a field is reploughed, and the grass of last year exposed to view.

s.Sc. A large round turf of peat-moss, in form of a seat, and used as such (JAM.). **Wm.** A thick square of peaty or rushy sod set behind the hearth fire (J.H.). **Chs.**[1], **s.Chs.**[1]

Hence **Hassock-spade**, *sb.* a tool used to get turfs from the surface of a bog, made in the form of a crescent, and fixed to a long handle, curved at the lower end. Chs.[1] 5. Anything growing in a thick, matted state ; a thick, wooded shaw or little wood.

Brks.[1] A wood usually of Scotch firs with much coarse rank grass. **Sus.**[1][2]

6. The soft calcareous sandstone which separates the beds of ragstone in Kent, used in building the interior walls of churches ; stone-chippings used instead of gravel for paths.

Ken. The calcareous sandstones in the Hythe beds are locally termed hassock, RUTLEY *Stud. Rocks* (1879) XIV. 281 ; (W.F.S.) ; This stone comes from the Kentish Rag quarries. . . It is called ' hassock ' and ' calk-stone ' by the workmen, RAMSAY *Rock Spec.* (1862) 153.

Hence **Hassocky**, *adj.* stony. Sur.[1] 7. A large pond. Ken.[1] 8. *Fig.* A large, coarse woman. w.Yks.[1], ne.Lan.[1]

[1. OE. *hassuc*, coarse grass, a place where such grass grows (B.T.).]

HASTARD, *adj.* Sc. (JAM.) [Not known to our correspondents.] Irascible.

HASTE, *sb.* Suf. The heart, liver, lungs, or lights of an animal, esp. of a pig. Cf. **hase, haslet**.

Suf.[1] **e.Suf.** ' Hâste ' one hears from the old here, but their juniors have not taken it up (F.H.).

Hence **Hastelings**, *sb. pl.* a pig's ' haste.' e.Suf. (F.H.)

[OFr. *haste*, ' broche, viande cuite à la broche, échinée de porc ' (LA CURNE).]

HASTE, *v.* Sc. Irel. Lakel. Also written **haiste** Ayr. ; and in form **heest** Sc. [hēst.] 1. To make haste, *gen.* in *imp.*

Sc. Heest ye, man, and let me gang, GREY *Misanthrope's Heir* (1897) i. **Fif.** Heest ye an' get tea ready, an' I'll set aff the nicht, ROBERTSON *Provost* (1894) 49. **Ayr.** Haste ye fast, for I want to have a choice o' beasts, JOHNSTON *Kilmallie* (1891) I. 76. **Lnk.** Come, laddie, heest ye, bring the liquor ben, COGHILL *Poems* (1890) 128. **Ant.** (W.H.P.)

Hence **Haster**, *sb.* a violent storm of rain.

Lakel.[2] When it's comen down a regular haster ye know what ta deea.

2. In phr. *to haste one's ways*, to hasten one's steps, to look sharp.

Ayr. Haiste ye're ways ... but the house to the scullery, GALT *Lairds* (1826) xxxviii.

HASTELET, see **Haslet**.

HASTENER, *sb.* Nhb. Yks. Der. Not. Lei. Nhp. War. Shr. Oxf. [h]ē·sən(r.] 1. A semicircular screen lined with tin, placed behind meat roasting before the fire, to keep the cold air off and hasten the cooking by reflected heat.

Nhb.[1], **w.Yks.**[2], **nw.Der.**[1], **Not.**[1], **Lei.**[1], **Nhp.**[1][2], **War.**[2][3], **Oxf.** (G.O.)

2. A long funnel-shaped tin vessel which can be thrust deeply into the fire, used for warming ale, &c. War.[2], Shr.[1]

HASTER, *sb.*[1] Dur. Yks. Lan. Lin. Also written **haister** w.Yks. n.Lan.[1] [h]ē·stǝ(r.] A ' hastener,' a Dutch-oven.

Dur.[1] **w.Yks.** Reight at top end wor a haister-looking thing like wot's put before t'fire when a piece a beef iz rostin, TOM TREDDLEHOYLE *Fr. Exhebishan* (1856) 99 ; **w.Yks.**[2] Shoo tumbled backards, and nockt haster uppat beef an t'beef into assnook ; **w.Yks.**[3][4], **n.Lan.**[1], **n.Lin.**[1]

[Cp. OFr. *hasteur*, ' rôtisseur ' (LA CURNE).]

HASTER, *sb.*[2] n.Cy. A surfeit. (HALL.)

HASTER, *v.* Sc. Also in form **hasther** Rnf. To hurry, to drive to work ; to fluster.

Rnf. Ne'er fash your thume although your bairns Be hasthered like a nigger, BARR *Poems* (1861) 158. **Peb.** But Meg wi' the sight, was quite hastered, NICOL *Poems* (1805) II. 160 (JAM.).

HASTERED, *ppl. adj.* Lakel.[2] Having the skin roughened by contact with the weather, or disease.

HASTERN, *adj.* ? Obs. n.Sc. (JAM.) Also in form **hastered**. Early, soon ripe. See **Hastings**.

Hastern aits, early oats.

HASTINGS, *sb. pl.* Suf. Sus. [ē·stinz.] An early variety of pea, *Pisum sativum* ; also used for green peas.

Suf. A day or two since I heard the cry ' Green Hastings.' . .

When a boy, fifty years ago, it was the usual cry for green peas, *Science Gossip* (Aug. 1878) in (B. & H.). e.Suf. (F.H.) Sus. *N. & Q.* (1884) 6th S. ix. 403.

[As loud as one that sings his part T' a wheel-barrow, or turnip-cart, Or your new nick'd nam'd old invention To cry green hastings, BUTLER *Hud.* (1664) *Ep. to Sidrophel,* 22.]

HASTIS, *adj.* and *adv.* Dev. Cor. Also written **haestis** Cor.[2] [ē-stis.] 1. *adj.* Hasty, hurried.

Cor. Ef tha arn't hastis thee shust hire tha hole, J. TRENOODLE *Spec. Dial.* (1846) 23 ; Cor.[1]

2. Sudden. Cor.[1] Hastis news.

3. *adv.* Hurriedly, hastily; impatiently.

Dev. That I got all hastis To zee a gaarden vul o' bastes, DANIEL *Bride of Scio* (1842) 185. Cor.[2]

4. *Comb.* **Haestis-go-thurra,** diarrhœa. *ib.*

HASTREL, *sb.* Rxb. (JAM.) [Not known to our correspondents.] A confused person, one who is always in haste.

HASTY, *sb.* Sc. Also in form **heasty** Sth. The murrain which attacks cattle.

Cai. The most formidable of these distempers is called the murrain (provinc. hasty), because the animal dies soon after it is seized with it. The symptoms are these : the animal swells, breathes hard, a great flow of tears from its eyes ; it lies down, and in some cases is dead in the course of a few hours, *Agric. Surv.* 200 (JAM.). Sth. The disease called murrain, or heasty, prevailed among the black cattle of this county when the vallies were covered with wood ; since these woods have decayed, this distemper is little known, *ib.* 101.

HASTY, *adj.* Var. dial. uses in Sc. and Eng. Also written **haasty** w.Yks.; **haaysty** Brks.[1]; and in forms **eeasty** n.Yks.; **heasty** Abd.; **hyeaty** Nhb.[1] 1. In *comp.* (1) Hasty-betty, the tin frame of a meat-jack ; cf. hastener ; (2) -brose, (3) -Dick, (4) -pudding or -poddish, oatmeal porridge ; a pudding *gen.* made of milk and flour, see below ; (5) -Rogers, the common nipplewort, *Lapsana communis* ; (6) -whittle, an iron skewer heated red-hot for the purpose of burning a hole through a piece of wood.

(1) w.Yks. T'cat ligs i' t'hasty-betty (W.M.E.F.) ; Th' cat wor sittin' o'th' Hasty Betty wi' it feet tucked under it, purrin', HARTLEY *Clock Alm.* (1887) 28. (2) Abd. Heasty-brose, which . . . are rather tough to swallow, RUDDIMAN *Sc. Parish* (1828) 133, ed. 1889. (3) Oxf.[1] (4) n.Cy. (HALL.) Nhb. Breakfast, every day—hasty pudding and one gill of milk, MACKENZIE *Hist. Newcastle* (1827) 541 ; Nhb.[1], Dur.[1] Lakel.[2] Thick poddish and treacle. Cum. With hot hasty pudding see some cramm'd, GILPIN *Sngs.* (1866) 268 ; Cum.[4] Thick pottage,—a dish which almost universally formed the breakfast, and often the supper ; it consisted of oatmeal boiled with water to a thick pulp, and was eaten along with butter, milk, treacle or beer. n.Yks. Pudding made of watmeeal [oatmeal], water, and salt (sometimes called gulls) (W.H.). w.Yks. Scotch oatmeal which has been ground over again so as to be nearly as fine as flour, boiled smooth and eaten with milk or treacle, LUCAS *Stud. Nidderdale* (c. 1882) iv ; Flour or wheat or oats boiled in water or milk, poured on a plate, and eaten with treacle, or into a basin of milk, BANKS *Whfld. Wds.* (1865) ; w.Yks.[1] Cha. Oat meal boiled with water or milk into hasty pudding, MARSHALL *Review* (1818) II. 110. a.Lin. Milky puddings, such as are made of pearl-barley, arrowroot, &c. ' It's a poor dinner y'r'll ha'e to-day ; we've nobbud haasty-puddin' and co'd meat' (T.H.R.). Brks.[1] A pudding of boiled dough ; sugar and butter, or else treacle, being usually added when eating. (5) Dev. *Science Gossip* (1873) 263. (6) Cum.[4]

2. Heavy, violent, *gen.* used of rain. Also used *adub.*

Glo. What hasty rain (A.B.). Ken.[1] It did come down hasty, an' no mistake. Sur. The rain cluttered down hasty (T.S.C.). Sus. The rain was not so hasty as it had been, *N. & Q.* (1882) 6th S. vi. 447; The rain come down terr'ble hasty surelye, *ib.* (1883) 6th S. vii. 155.

HASUM-JASUM, see Aizam-jazam.

HAT, *sb.*[1] and *v.* Var. dial. uses in Sc. and Eng. Also in form at Not. Oxf.[1] w.Som.[1] 1. *sb.* In *comp.* (1) Hat-bat, applied *gen.* to all bats, esp. *Plecotus auritus* and *Vespertilio noctula* ; (2) -body, the foundation of which a hat is made ; (3) -birret, (4) -brinks, (5) -bruarts, (6) -flipe, the brim or edge of a hat or cap ; (7) -sheaf or -shav, the covering sheaf of a corn-stook.

(1) Not. (W.H.S.) s.Not. The boys sometimes bring bats down by throwing up their hats at them. ' At-bat, come under my 'at.

I'll give you a slice of bacon ; And when we brew and when we bake, I'll give you a chin-cake' (J.P.K.). Lei.[1], Shr.[1][2] (2) Cha.[1] (3) Cum. I can mind of the old people speaking of the hat birret. The hat birret was broad and worn soft (E.W.P.). (4) s.Not. 'Er 'at-brinks wor all tunned up (J.P.K.). sw.Lin.[1] The puppies tore his hat-brinks off (s.v. Brink). (5) w.Yks.[1], e.Lan.[1] Cha. RAY (1691). nw.Der.[1] (6) n.Yks.[2] (7) Cum.[1]

2. *Phr.* (1) *an old hat,* (*a*) an old person ; (*b*) the prize supposed to be won by a person telling a great lie ; (2) *as queer as Dick's hat-band,* very queer ; see also Dick, *sb.*[1] **2** (2) ; (3) *a three-cocked hat,* a kind of tart ; (4) *hat-full of feathers,* (*a*) the nest of the long-tailed titmouse, *Acredula rosea* ; (*b*) the nest of the willow-wren, *Phylloscopus trochilus* ; (5) *hats in holes,* a boys' game, see below ; (6) *to carry a lot under one's hat,* to be crafty, sly ; (7) *to give any one a hat,* to touch one's hat in salutation.

(1, *a*) Cum. If thou wast ane o' t'lads I'd say sum auld hats ower t'hill had been efter thee : but thou's not sae daft as to letten thysel' be guided i' thy years, LINTON *Lizzie Lorton* (1867) xxiii ; I believe this is a mere local allusion and could only be understood by a small coterie to whom the coining of the word was known. There are hundreds of such-like words coined in Cum. (J.A.) (*b.* w.Yks.[1] When he is suspected to be guilty of it [a great lie], it is common to say, ' Here's my oud hat for the.' (a w.Yks. As queer as Dick's hatband, 'at went nine times raand an' wodn't tee, Prov. in *Brighouse News* (July 23, 1887). Lin. THOMPSON *Hist. Boston* (1856) 733. (3) w.Yks.[1] Currants or preserves inclosed in a thin crust or triangular paste or pasty. (4, *a*) Shr. Rupert . . . discovered the . . . nest of . . . the long-tailed tit. . . Inside, it was so full of fine soft feathers, that it quite justified the name it bears among the country lads of a ' hat full of feathers,' DAVIES *Rambles Sch. Field-Club* (1875) xviii ; Shr.[1] (*b*) Shr.[1] (5) w.Som.[1] The players range their hats in a row against a wall, and each boy in turn pitches a ball from a line at some twenty-five feet distance into one of the hats. The boy into whose hat it falls has to seize it and throw it at one or other of the others, who all scamper off when the ball is ' packed in.' If he fails to hit, he is out and takes his cap up. The boy whose cap is left at the last has to ' cork ' the others—that is, to throw the ball at their bent backs, each in turn stooping down to take his punishment. (6) e.Suf. (F.H.) (7) Sc. He contented his politeness with ' giving him a hat,' touching, that is, his bonnet, in token of salutation, and so left the shop. SCOTT *Nigel* (1822) ii.

3. *v.* To cover a stook of corn with some of the sheaves. Cf. **hattock,** *sb.*[1]

w.Som.[1] To doubly cap-stitch—i. e. to set up the sheaves in a large stook and to cover down the top with a kind of thatch made of some of the sheaves with the ear downwards. This method is very common in ' lappery ' seasons, and it prevents the corn from sprouting, while at the same time it allows the wind to pass through, and so dry the straw. Dev. A hat is much larger than a ' cap-stitch,' but not so large as a ' wind-mow.' ' I reckoned to a-car'd thick piece o' wheat, but he idn't ardly fit, not eet, zo I told em to go and hat'n up,' *Reports Provinc.* (1884) 19.

HAT, *sb.*[2] Brks. Hmp. Nfld. A small clump or ring of trees; any small irregular mass of trees.

Brks.[1] Hmp. The term hat is still in use for a little wood crowning a hill, DE CRESPIGNY & HUTCHINSON *New Forest* (1895) 113 ; Hmp.[1] E. g. the ' Dark hats,' near Lyndhurst. [Nfld. A hat of trees, PATTERSON *Trans. Amer. Flk-Lore Soc.* (1894).]

HAT, *sb.*[3] Lin. A narrow clearing in a wood, in which at a battue sportsmen are placed separately to shoot game crossing it. (J.C.W.)

HAT, see Heat, Hit, Hurt.

HATCH, *sb.*[1] In *gen.* dial. use in Sc. and Eng. Also in form **hetch** ne.Yks.[1] [h)atʃ, ætʃ, etʃ.] 1. A door filling only the lower half of the doorway.

Nhp.[1], War.[3], Hrf.[1], Glo.[12] Oxf.[1] A broad piece of wood placed across the entrance to a barn, &c., to prevent the cattle passing through. Brks.[1] An opening which may be closed by a wooden slide or door, used for passing articles through by hand. n.An.[2], Sus.[1] Hmp.[1] The buttery-hatch, in old halls, was a half-door, with a ledge on the top. Wil. BRITTON *Beauties* (1825) ; Wil.[1] ' Barn-hatch,' a low board put across the door, over which you must step to enter. Gen. applied to the half doors frequent in shops. Dor. The childern all did run an' poke Their heads vrom hatch or door, an' shout, BARNES *Poems* (1869-70) 3rd S. 102. w.Som.[1] Often in cottages called the half-hatch. ' I zeed th' old man a Zunday hon I passéd, 'cause he was a stood a lookin out over the hatch.'

Dev. Shũt tha hatch, Sallie, that tha wet midden come in, Hewett *Peas. Sp.* (1892); Dev.[1] The half-door of cot-houses; also a sliding-pannel to answer the same purpose. nw.Dev.[1] The doors in a barn are usually made in halves, called half batches, and distinguished as top-hatch and bottom-hatch. In cottages, the hatch corresponds to the bottom-hatch, but there is an ordinary or full-length door as well. A trap-door is called trap-hatch. s.Dev. Fox *Kingsbridge* (1874). Cor. There was to the front door of this house, a hatch, which is a half-door, that is kept closed when the whole door behind it is open, and it then serves as a guard against the intrusion of dogs, hogs, and ducks, while air and light are freely admitted, Hunt *Pop. Rom. w.Eng.* (ed. 1896) 95. [It's good to have a hatch before the door, Ray *Prov.* (1678) 152.]

2. *Comp.* (1) Hatch-door, a wicket or half-door; (2) -hole, a trap-door; (3) -way, (a) an opening used for pitching into a barn or hay-loft; (b) the sliding panel to a box-bed.

(1) Sc. He retired into his shop and shut the hatch-door, Scott *Nigel* (1822) xxvi. Glo. (A.B.) (2) e.Fif. She disturbed the repose of the barrel, causin' it to tak its flicht doon through the hatchhole as aforesaid, Latto *Tam Bodkin* (1864) xxii. (3, a) Nhp.[1] (b) Sc. Waverley had repeatedly drawn open . . . the hatchway of his cage, Scott *Waverley* (1814) xxxvii.

3. A small gate or wicket, *gen.* leading into a garden or put across a narrow road.

Nhb.[1] Near a wicket or hatch at Cockmount Hill. Chs. Shut the hatch after yow (E.F.); Chs.[1] s.Chs.[1] Dhū foa·ks i Sol·ūp dũn)ũ tau·k reyt Ingg·lish; dhai kau·n ū aach· ũ wik·it [The folks i' Sollop dunna talk reight English; they cawn a hatch a wicket]. Shr. Ellis *Pronunc.* (1889) V. 454. e.An.[1] Ess.[1] Ken.[1] A half-hatch is where a horse may pass, but not a cart; Ken.[2] Sus. Perhaps entrance to a forest or wood, *N. & Q.* (1887) 7th S. iii. 192; Sus.[1] Hmp.[1] *Gen.* a gate dividing parishes or manors. Wil.[1] Dor. Paid James Elby for mending the hatches, 3d., *Tyneham Overseers' Acc.* (June 10, 1753); (C.W.); An' leānes wi' here an' there a hatch, Barnes *Poems* (1879) 40. Som. I was not allowed to go out into the road, but watched them from the garden-hatch (W.F.R.); She stood at the hatch watching her aunt out of sight, Raymond *Tryphena* (1895) 36.

Hence **Hatch-gate**, *sb.* a gate at the junction of parishes or manors. Brks.[1]

4. The flood-gate of a water-meadow; a sluice; a dam or mound to keep back water.

n.Wil. The farmers lower down the brook pull up the hatches to let the flood pass, Jefferies *Wild Life* (1879) 107. Dor. (C.W.), Cor. (K.), Cor.[1]

5. Salt-making term: the door of a furnace. Chs.[1]

6. The portion of a window that opens on hinges. War.[2]

7. The latch of a door.

Chs.[1] Dunna bowt th' durr, lave it o'th hatch, and then thi fayther can come in when he's a mind an we'n go to blanket fair [bed]. Suf.[1]

8. A hen-coop. War.[2]   **9.** The back part of a wagon which lets down for the contents to be taken out. ne.Yks.[1], e.Yks. (Miss A.) Cf. hack, *sb.*[2] 18.

HATCH, *sb.*[2] n.Lin.[1] [atʃ.] The sharp-pointed end of a mason's hammer.

HATCH, *sb.*[3] and *v.*[1] Glo. Wil. [ætʃ.] **1.** *sb.* The row into which grass is raked after being 'tedded,' a line of raked-up hay, a 'wallow.' Cf. hack, *sb.*[1] 11.

Glo.[1] Three or four hatches are then raked into a 'double hatch'; two, or sometimes three, of these double hatches make a 'bray.' Wil.[1] n.Wil. Grass is first mown; then it is 'tedded,' i. e. spread, then it is raked up into lines, 'hatches,' or 'wallows,' which may be either single hatches or double hatches (E.H.G.).

2. *v.* To rake the 'tedded' hay into small rows ready for cocking; freq. used with *up* or *in.*

Glo. Lewis *Gl.* (1839); Glo.[1], Wil.[1], n.Wil. (E.H.G.)

HATCH, *v.*[2] and *sb.*[4] Hmp. I.W. [ætʃ.] **1.** *v.* To hook on; with *in* or *on* : to harness. Hmp. (H.E.), I.W.[1]

2. To tear a thing by catching it on something. I.W. (J.D.R.), I.W.[1]

3. *sb.* A tear in a garment caused by catching it on some projecting object.

Hmp. (H.C.M.B.) I.W. (J.D.R.); I.W.[2] I've maade a middlen half hatch in my breeches . . . gitten over that wattle hurdle.

HATCH, *v.*[3] Sur. Sus. Hmp. I.W. [ætʃ.] To scrape the bark from the tree, after the 'rinding' is over, in order

VOL. III.

to free the bark from lichen; to dress the bark for the tanner.

Sur.[1] Sus. Faggoting the lop and scraping and hatching the bark are different operations, Heath *Eng. Peas.* (1893) 183; (S.P.H.); Sus.[1], Hmp.[1]

Hence **Hatch-hook**, *sb.* the kind of bill-hook used for chopping oak-bark small for the tanner. Hmp.[1], I.W.[1]

HATCH, *v.*[4] Ken. Sus. [ætʃ.] To prepare for; to develop a disease; freq. with *up* ; used *trans.* and *intr.*

Ken.[1] I think it's hatching up for snow. She's hatching up a cold. Sus.[1] I think she's hatching the measles.

HATCH(·, see **Hawch, Hotch,** *v.*

HATCHEL, *sb.*[1] e.Lan.[1] [a·tʃl.] A hatchet; a mason's dressing-hammer.

HATCHEL, *sb.*[2] and *v.*[1] *Obs.* Chs. Nhp. Shr. Also in form **hetchel** Shr.[1]   **1.** *sb.* An instrument for dressing hemp or flax. Chs.[1], Nhp.[1], Shr.[1]

2. *v.* To comb flax or hemp with a 'hatchel.'

Chs.[1] [*Serancer*, to hatchel flax, &c., to comb, or dress it on an iron comb, Cotgr.]

HATCHEL, *sb.*[3] and *v.*[2] Nhp. Sus. [æ·tʃl.] **1.** *sb.* A small row or cock of cut grass. Also in *comp.* **Hatchel-cock.**

Nhp.[1] The grass . . . is next hacked, or separated into small rows ; in the evening it is put into small cocks, sometimes called hatchel-cocks, or toddle-cocks, or wads. Three hatchels or hacklings, thrown together into one broad row or swathe, are termed a win-row, or windrow (s.v. Hack); Nhp.[2]

2. *v.* To rake cut grass into small rows. Nhp.[2], Sus.[1]

HATCHEL, *v.*[3] Fif. (Jam.) [Not known to our correspondents.] To shake in crying. See **Hotch.**

HATCHELOR, *sb.* e.Lan.[1] Stone squared and bedded for walling in even courses, ashlar.

HATCHER, *sb.* Nrf. The hedge-sparrow, *Accentor modularis.*

This . . . little bird goes in the Broadland by the name of the 'Hatcher,' perhaps because he sometimes 'hatches off' the lazy cuckoo's egg, Emerson *Birds* (ed. 1895) 54.

HATCHET, *sb.*[1] Dev. Cor. In phr. *to sling the hatchet,* to be lazy.

Dev.[3] Sometimes, but very rarely, heard. Dev., Cor. *N. & Q.* (1869) 4th S. iv. 254.

HATCHET, *sb.*[2] Shr. Dev. Also written **atchett.** **1.** A hurdle hung on a beam across a stream to keep back cattle. *Reports Provinc.* (1891).

2. A low garden gate. Shr. Ellis *Pronunc.* (1889) V. 454. Cf. **hatch,** *sb.*[1] 3.

HATCHET-PIECE, *sb.* Sus. A 'paūl' or division of tenantry land of irregular shape.

Sus.[1] (s.v. Tenantry-acre); Sus.[2] (s.v. Paul).

HATCH-HORN, see **Acorn.**

HATCH-NAIL, *sb.* nw.Dev.[1] A rectangular, rose-headed, hand-made nail 3 inches long; a half-hatch nail is 2 inches long.

HATE, see **Halt, Height, Hot.**

HATEABLE, *adj.* Sh.I. Hateful, odious.

Der [weasels] hateable things, *Sh. News* (Nov. 25, 1899).

HATELY, *adj.* Lan. [ē·tli.] Bad-tempered, hateful; showing hate.

Lan.[1], e.Lan.[1] e.Lan. Dunno be so hately, Bamford *Dial.* (1854).

HATER, see **Hadder,** *sb.*[2]

HATESUM, *adj.* Sc. n.Cy. Also written hait- (Jam. *Suppl.*). [h)ē·tsəm.] Unkind, hateful, hated. Sc. (Jam. *Suppl.*), Cai.[1], n.Cy. (J.W.)

[This haitsum lyfe, Douglas *Eneados* (1513), ed. 1874, IV. 22.]

HATHA, *int.* n.Lan. Hark, listen! (C.W.D.) [Repr. lit. E. *hark thou !*]

HATHA, see **Hither.**

HATHE, *sb.* Dor. Som. [ēð.] A thick covering; *gen.* in phr. *to be in a hathe,* to be thickly covered with the pustules of the small-pox or other eruptive disease ; to be matted closely together.

Dor. Barnes *Gl.* (1863). Som. Jennings *Obs. Dial. w.Eng.* (1825) *Gl.* ; W. & J. *Gl.* (1873).

HATHER, see **Hadder,** *sb.*[2] **Heather.**

M

HATHERN, *sb.* Som. The hand-rail to stairs.

I first catched a hold o' the hathern, so I jissy saved I (W.F.R.).

HATHISH, *sb.* Sc. A small dry measure; four in a peck; also used *attrib.*

ne.Sc. The new tenant came along with a friend went from farm to farm and got a peck or two from this one, . . a hathish cogful from the next one, GREGOR *Flk-Lore* (1881) 178; *ib. Gl.*

HATKIN, see Hutkin.

HATREDANS, HATT, see Aitredan, Hit.

HATTED KIT(T, *phr.* Sc. A preparation of milk, &c., with a creamy top.

Sc. He has spilt the hatted kitt that was for the master's dinner, SCOTT *Bride of Lam.* (1819) xi. Lnl. A wooden bowlful of sour cream (JAM.). [Hatted kit is one of the pleasantest preparations of milk. Make 2 quarts of new milk scalding hot, and pour upon it quickly 4 quarts of fresh butter-milk; let it stand, without stirring, till it becomes cold and firm; then take off the hat or upper part, drain it in a hair-sieve, put it into a shape for half an hour, turn it into a dish, and serve with cream and sugar, STEPHENS *Farm Bk.* (1855) II. 299.]

HATTER, *sb.*[1] Sc. Nhb. Yks. In phr. *like a hatter*, used as an intensive, in the sense of vigorously, boldly, &c.

Sc. When tyrant Death grim o'er him stood He faced him like a hatter, FORD *Thistledown* (1891) 327. Per. I birl'd my tip'ce [twopence] like a hatter, STEWART *Character* (1857) 44. Slg. Where'er he spies a washing tub, He rins like ony hatter, TOWERS *Poems* (1885) 161. Lnk. Ye maun rin like a hatter. . . Bring up twa pails fou o' clear caller water, HAMILTON *Poems* (1865) 133. Nhb. Off like a hatter, to fight like a hatter (R.O.H.). w.Yks. (J.W.)

HATTER, *v.* and *sb.*[2] Sc. Nhb. Dur. Yks. Nhp. Bdf. e.An. Ken. Also in form atter w.Yks. m.Yks.[1] [ha'tə(r, æ'tə(r).] 1. *v.* To shake; to shake up as on a rough road. Cf. hotter, *v.*

N.Cy.[1] I'm all hattered to pieces. Nhb. The road wis that bad, see ye!—Aw wis aall hattered to bits (R.O.H.). Dur. GIBSON *Up-Weardale Gl.* (1870); Dur.[1]

2. To harass, vex, ill-treat; to exhaust with fatigue.

Sc. This hatters and chatters My very soul with care, TRAIN *Poet. Reveries* (1806) 49 (JAM.). Sh.I. Doo'll hae to pit somtin in his [pig] nose if hit wis bit a muckle preen!. . Hit'll hatter him, Girzzie, *Sh. News* (Sept. 2, 1899); (*Coll.* L.L.B.); S. & Ork.[1] Abd. I've hattered a' my hand wi' the saw (G.W.). e.An.[1] Ken. A horse by too much riding; or a utensil by too much lending, is hatter'd about (K.).

Hence (1) **Hattered**, *ppl. adj.* badly treated; exhausted or wearied; (2) **Hattering**, *ppl. adj.* harassing, tiring.

(1) Sh.I. A poor hattered ting o' bairn (K.I.); S. & Ork.[1] Nhp.[1] (2) Bdf. Your's must be a hattering life (J.W.B.).

3. To fret, make a fuss.

Nhp.[1] She's always scolding and hattering about.

4. To mix or confuse things; to throw into disorder, to entangle, knot.

n.Yks. Twomen atters t'berrytrees wi' their cleeas (I.W.); n.Yks.[4], m.Yks.[1]

5. To be in a confused but moving state. Dmf. (JAM.)

6. To gather, to collect in crowds. Fif. (*ib.*) 7. To speak thick and confusedly. Slk. (*ib.*)

8. *sb.* A jumble, confused crowd; a knot or tangle. Cf. hatter[1].

Sc. Amang a perfect hatter of unkent faces, Sc. *Haggis*, 156; A hatter of stanes, a heap of stones; a hatter of berries, a large cluster or great quantity crowded together (JAM.). w.Sc. Buy B——! what would I do wi' B——! it's naething but a hatter of peat-pots frae the one end to the other, CARRICK *Laird of Logan* (1835) 84. Fif. In their criticisms they resented all corruptions or conglomerations of ornamental styles. The latter they scornfully designated 'a hatter o' nonsense,' ROBERTSON *Provost* (1894) 84. n.Yks. T'thread was raffled [tangled] all in a hard atter (I.W.).

Hence **Hatery** or **Hatry**, (1) *adj.* dishevelled, entangled; (2) *sb.* a confused jumble.

(1) Sc. A hatry hesp, a hank of yarn that is tangled or disordered (JAM.). n.Sc. A hatry head when the hair has not been combed out for a long time (*ib.*). (2) Per. Whatna hatery hae we here! (G.W.)

9. Phr. *to be a' in a hatter*, said of the face, &c., when entirely covered with any eruption, as small-pox.

Sc. I wish you saw my a——, its a' in ae hatter, GRAHAM *Writings* (1883) II. 232. Cai.[1], Dmf. (JAM.)

HATTER-CROPPER, see Attercop.

HATTEREL, *sb.* Sc. Irel. Yks. Also written **hateral** Ayr.; **hatteral**(l Bnff.[1] Ayr.; and in forms **hatrel** Sc. (JAM.); **hattrel** Bnff.; **hitteril** w.Yks.[1] [ha·t(ə)rl.] 1. A large quantity; a miscellaneous collection, jumble. See Hatter, *sb.*[2] 8.

Bnff. A 'hattrel' of poor cots belonging to the glebe, GORDON *Chron. Keith* (1880) 270; Bnff.[1] A large quantity of small stones lying together, not in heaps, but spread over a space. 'Ye'll niver get a crap aff o' that lan': it's naething bit a hatteral o' stanes.' Ayr. My heid seems to be in a perfect hatterall of confusion, SERVICE *Notandums* (1890) 8; He threeps that the body is no his wife's, and ca's it a hateral o' clay and stones, GALT *Entail* (1823) xxxv. N.I.[1] A hatterel o' weans.

2. A collection of sores in any part of the body; a series of scabs running into one another.

Sc. (JAM.) N.I.[1] 'He's all in a hatterel,' i. e. his body is all over sores. Ant. *Ballymena Obs.* (1892). w.Yks.[1] My legs 're all of a hitteril.

HATTER-FLITTER, *sb.* Cor. Also in form **hatter-flight**. The jack-snipe, *Limnocryptes gallinula*.

They be wild as hatter-flights, BARING-GOULD *Curgenven* (1893) xi; Cor.[12]

HATTERN, *sb.* n.Yks.[2] Clothing of all kinds.

[I haue here a hatir to hyde hym, *York Plays* (c. 1400) 267. OE. *hæteru*, clothes.]

HATTIL, see Hottle, *sb.*[1]

HATTING OWER THE BONNETS, *phr.* Sc. The name of a game.

Lnk. When we were deeply engaged in a game of 'hatting ower the bonnets,' FRASER *Whaups* (1895) iii.

HATTLE, *adj.* n.Cy. Yks. Chs. Also Ken. 1. Wild, skittish, mischievous; uncertain in temper; *gen.* used of a skittish cow.

n.Cy. BAILEY (1721). Yks., Chs. (P.R.) Chs. Tie the hattle ky by the horn, RAY (1691); Chs.[123] s.Chs.[1] Yoa· mûn mahynd dhaat· ky·aay; óo)z û aat·l beg·ûr [Yo mun mind that cat; hoo's a hattle beggar]. Ken. (P.R.)

2. *Comb.* **Hattle-tempered**, quick-tempered, 'touchy.'

s.Chs.[1] Yû· aa·rdli daa·rn spee·k tû)th mon—ey)z sô aat·ltem·pûrd [Yô hardly darn (dare) speak to th' mon—hey's sô hattle-tempered].

[The same as ME. *hatel*, hateful, fierce. Povert is hatel good, CHAUCER *C. T.* D. 1195 (Corpus MS.). OE. *hatol*, 'odiosus,' *Kentish Glosses* (c. 870), in Wright's *Voc.* (1884) 70.]

HATTOCK, *sb.*[1] and *v.* Nhb. Cum. Wm. Yks. Lan. Chs. Stf. Shr. Also in forms **attock** Yks. n.Stf.; **huttock** N.Cy.[1] Nhb.[1] [ha·tək.] 1. *sb.* A shock of standing sheaves of corn, the tops of which are protected by two sheaves laid along them in such a way as to carry off rain; the two covering sheaves, 'hood-sheaves,' 'hooders.'

n.Cy. A shock containing 12 sheaves of corn, BAILEY (1721); N.Cy.[1] 10 sheaves of corn, set two and two upright and two 'hoods,' one at each end, to cover them; N.Cy.[2] Nhb.[1] A pile of corn sheaves, made of twelve sheaves, ten of which are set upright, two and two together, whilst two are laid on the top as hood or covering sheaves. Cum. Ten sheaves are a hattock and twelve a stook, MORTON *Cyclo. Agric.* (1863) (s.v. Haddock). Wm. Ten sheaves of corn, eight set upright and two placed for hoods or covers (J.H.). s.Wm. (J.A.B.) n.Yks. A man, or stout boy, following to tie up the sheaves, which are set up in 'stooks' or 'attocks' by the men, in the evening, TUKE *Agric.* (1800) 120. w.Yks. A pile of four sheaves (S.K.C.); w.Yks.[1] A shock of corn containing ten sheaves. Lan. THORNBER *Hist. Blackpool* (1837); Lan.[1], ns.Lan.[1], e.Lan.[1] Chs. By custom is paid y[e] 11th, and not y[e] 10th, Hattock or Rider of Corn, GASTRELL *Notitia Cestriensis* (c. 1707) in Cheth. Soc. (1845) VIII. 164; A stack of corn, consisting of five or more sheaves, as it stands in the field before carrying (E.F.); Chs.[1] We wanten a good wynd as 'll blow th' attocks o'er, afore th' curn 'll be ready to lead. s.Chs.[1] n.Stf. Ten sheaves of corn (J.T.). Shr.[1] Sheaves of corn inverted over the 'mow' to protect it from wet. The two end sheaves of the 'mow,' which consists of eight sheaves, are taken as hattocks for the remaining six.

2. *v.* To cover reaped corn in the field with sheaves. Shr.[1]

[1. A der. of ON. *höttr* (gen. *hattar*), a cowl or hood; cp. Sw. dial. *hatt*, the covering of a corn-rick (RIETZ).]

HATTOCK, sb.[2] Chs.[18] [a·tək.] A hole in the roof where owls harbour.

HATTREL, sb. w.Sc. (JAM.) [Not known to our correspondents.] The core or flint of a horn.

HATTY, sb. Sc. Nhb. Lakel. Also written **hattie** Sc. [ha·ti.] 1. A game of leap-frog; see below.

Nhb.[1] A game at leap-frog where each boy leaves his cap on the back as he leaps over. The boy who 'makes the back' is called 'hatty.' If a boy causes a cap to slip off as he leaps he becomes 'hatty.'

2. A game with pins.

Gall. A game with preens on the crown of a hat; two or more play; each lay[s] on a pin, then with the hand they strike the side of the hat, time about, and whoever makes the pins, by a stroke, cross each other, lift[s] those so crossed, MACTAGGART Encycl. (1824) 255, ed. 1876.

3. Comp. Hatty-cap, a boys' game; see below.

Lakel. A game at ball with hats for 'motty.' The hats or caps are placed in a row and the ball thrown towards them; if it alights in one and remains there the lad it belongs to must mind the motty (B.K.).

HAU, HAUBER, see How, adv.[1], Haver, sb.[2]

HAUCH, see Haugh, Hawk, v.[1]

HAUCHEE-PAUCHEE, sb. Dev.[1] A term applied to potatoes when boiled to a mash, a 'hodge-podge.'

HAUCHLE, v. Sc. Irel. Also in forms **haghle** Lth. Rxb. (JAM.); **haughie** N.I.[1] [hā·χl, hŏ·χl.] To walk lamely or with difficulty, to hobble, drag the feet along the ground.

Lak. To walk as those do who are carrying a heavy burden (JAM.). Lth. (ib.) e.Lth. What needs ye gang hauchlin an' hirplin alang, like crupple Dick upon a stick? HUNTER J. Inwick (1895) 14. Rxb. (JAM.), N.I.[1]

Hence (1) **Hauchal**, sb. a deformed or crippled person; (2) **Hauchlin**, ppl. adj. (a) hobbling, limping, shambling; (b) slovenly.

(1) Ayr. He had a long square body and short legs, with a deformity about the houghs that earned for him the name of the hauchal, JOHNSTON Kilmallie (1891) II. 141. (2, a) Hauchlin Pate, the village drummer, got a job from the auctioneer, ib. I. 1. (b) Rnf. (JAM.)

HAUCHS, sb. pl. Ags. (JAM.) The three points at which the upper part of a ploughshare is divided and by which it clasps in the wood.

HAUD, sb. Sc. [Not known to our correspondents.] A squall. Mry. Gl. Surv. (JAM.)

HAUD, see Hold, v., sb.

HAUEN, sb. Cor. Also written **hawn**. A harbour, haven.

The common word for haven, as meaning a harbour. Our fishermen say their boats are out in the hawn, as distinguished from being at the piers, N. & Q. (1854) 1st S. x. 319; The harbour of Polperro, locally termed the hauen, QUILLER-COUCH Hist. Polperro (1871) 30; Cor.[1]

HAUF, see Half, How, sb.[1], Howf(f.

HAUFISH, HAUFLIN, HAUFLINS, HAUGAW, see Awvish, Halflin(g, Halflins, Hawgaw.

HAUGH, sb. Sc. Nhb. Dur. Cum. Wm. Yks. Lan. Also written **hawgh** n.Cy. Wm.; and in forms **ha'** Sc.; **haaf** Nhb.[1]; **halgh** Lan.; **hauch** Sc.; **haulgh** Lan.; **haw** Dur. n.Yks.[2] [Sc. hāχ.] 1. Low-lying, level ground by the side of a river; also used fig. and attrib. Cf. hale, sb.[2]

Sc. The margin of the brook ... displayed a narrow meadow, or haugh, as it was called, which formed a small washing-green, SCOTT Waverley (1814) ix; In a lythe, cantie hauch in a cottage, JAMIESON Pop. Ballads (1806) I. 292. Mry. Gi'e me the land where Lossie pours By haugh and flowery mead, HAY Lintie (1851) 45. Bnff. More particularly when wandering amongst the delightful haughs of Grandholm, SMILES Natur. (1876) ix. Abd. The prisoner ... set off wildly over the adjacent haugh, Deeside Tales (1872) 77. Kcd. The Feugh cam' rairin' doon fae Birse, An' swept the haughs o' Stra'an, GRANT Lays (1884) 2. Frf. The village commonage ... running down on one side to the haughs bordering the North Esk, INGLIS Ain Flk. (1895) 68. Per. It wes the haugh field of aits, IAN MACLAREN K. Carnegie (1896) 19. Slg. (JAM.) Rnf. In flow'ry dells, and haughs, and glades, Where streamlets rin, M'GILVRAY Poems (ed. 1862) 151. Ayr. Let busky wheat the haughs adorn, BURNS Sc. Drink (1786) st. 3. Lnk. Howes,

an' haughs, an' laigh lyin' leas Were a' like lochs, or ragin' seas, THOMSON Musings (1881) 55. e.Lth. Auld clover riggs! thy cleuchs and craigs, Green haughs an' winding river, MUCKLEBACKIT Rhymes (1885) 13. Edb. Thou's aften dander'd wi' the musie Down burnie's haughs, LIDDLE Poems (1821) 135. Peb. Ilk to the green haugh hies, Lintoun Green (1685) 21, ed. 1817. Slk. And rounde onne Ettrickis baittle haughis, HOGG Poems (ed. 1865) 84. Rxb. The bairns was laughin' an' scratchin' among the saughs doun i' the haugh, ELLIS Pronunc. (1889) V. 714. Dmf. Her glance she cast Ower holm an' haugh, THOM Jock o' Knowe (1878) 13. Gall. By Skeldon haughs, CROCKETT Grey Man (1896) 93. n.Cy. Border Gl. (Coll. L.L.B.); A green plot in a valley (K.); N.Cy.[1] Nhb. Oer the gay daisied haughs will I roam, RICHARDSON Borderer's Table-bk. (1846) VII. 78; Low-lying spreads of loam, sand, or gravel which form the lowest ground of the river valleys which are still flooded from time to time, or which, although they may have for years kept above water, may yet conceivably still be flooded in unusual seasons. Such are most of the haughs of Northumberland, LEBOUR Geol. Nhb. and Dur. (ed. 1886) 9; Nhb.[1], Dur.(K.) s.Dur. The Haughs at Egglestone is a pasture, very smooth and flat, the river Tees flowing on one side (J.E.D.). Cum.[1] Wm. Cuckoos love to change to mare sunny hawghs, HUTTON Bran New Wark (1785) l. 42. n.Yks. ATKINSON Whitby (1894) 80; n.Yks.[2] Lan. N. & Q. (1870) 4th S. v. 570. ne.Lan.[1]

2. Comp. (1) Ha'-bink, the bank of a 'haugh' overhanging a stream; (2) Haugh-grund, (3) -land, low-lying ground by the side of a stream or river.

(1) Sc. Ha' binks are sliddery, RAMSAY Prov. (1737). (2) Lnk. The haugh-ground is gen. ploughed 3, and sometimes 4 years, for oats, and then allowed to lie as long in natural grass, Statist. Acc. XII. 34 (JAM.). e.Lth. As guid a bit o' haugh-grund for crappin as there was in the pairish, HUNTER J. Inwick (1895) 161. (3) Fif. The corn-craik scraiched among the 'skellochs' in the haughland, COLVILLE Vernacular (1899) 13. Rxb. His haid fields o' haughland corn On flood-red tumbling waves are borne, A. SCOTT Poems (1811) 19 (JAM.).

[1. Amid the hawchis, and euery lusty vaill, DOUGLAS Eneados (1513), ed. 1874, IV. 168; The hawch (v.r. halche) of lyntoun-le, BARBOUR Bruce (1375) XVI. 336. OE. healh, in the place-name 'on Strēones hēale' (Chron. an. 680).]

HAUGH, see Haw, int.[1], Hawk, v.[1], Hough, sb.[1], How, sb.[1]

HAUGHENDOLE, sb. Obs. or obsol. Lan. Also in forms **aghendole** Lan. e.Lan.[1]; **haughendo** Lan.[1]; **nackendole** Lan.; **nackleton, naghendal, naghendole, naghleton** e.Lan.[1] A half part or half measure; a meal-measure of 8 or 8½ lb.; the quantity of meal usually taken for kneading at one time.

Trans. Phil. Soc. (1858) 164; There seems to have been some uncertainty about the use of this word, but properly it means a dole of eight pounds (J.D.); Lan.[1] e.Lan. Iohn Device ... did covenant with the said Anne [Chattox] that if she would hurt neither of them, she should yearely have one aghendole of meale, POTTS Discoverie of Witches (1613) sign. E 4; Still in use in Little Harwood, in the district of Pendle, Chet. Soc. (1845) VI. note; Still used about Padiham, and denotes a batch (sufficient for one baking) of meal for oatcakes (S.W.); Now almost obs. in those parts of Lan. where it was formerly known, N. & Q. (1852) 1st S. vi. 9; e.Lan.[1] The quantity supposed to have been doled out weekly by the Saxon employer to each of his manservants.

[The same as ME. ey3tyndele, mesure, 'satum' (Prompt.).]

HAUGHLE, see Hauchle.

HAUGHTY, adj. Obs. e.An. In phr. haughty weather, windy weather.

s.An.[1] Nrf. GROSE (1790). e.Nrf. MARSHALL Rur. Econ. (1787).

HAUGO, see Hogo.

HAUGULL, sb. ? Obs. Sc. (JAM.) A cold damp wind blowing from the sea during summer. ne.Sc.

Hence **Haugullin'**, adj. of the weather: drizzling, cold and damp. Fif.

[Norw. dial. havgula and havgul, a wind blowing from the sea, esp. the wind which blows into the fjords in the afternoon in warm weather; hav, the sea + gul (also gula), a steady wind, ON. haf + gol (Icel. gola), a breeze (AASEN).]

HAUK, HAUKA, see Hack, sb.[1], Hawk, v.[1], Howk, v.[1], Hawgaw.

HAUKUM-PLAUKUM, adj. Bwk. (JAM.) [Not known to our correspondents.] Equal in every way.

M 2

HAUK-WALK, sb. Obs. Lan. A path across Chat Moss.

In the course of an important trial at the Liverpool Assizes some forty years ago, involving the ownership of a portion of the well-known Chat Moss, mention was made of certain roads or paths across the Moss which bore the name of Hauk-walks, *N. & Q.* (1878) 5th S. x. 118.

HAUL, v.[1] and sb.[1] Sc. Nhb. Lin. Wor. Shr. Hrf. Glo. Sus. Dor. Som. Dev. Also written **hall** Nhb. [h]ǭl.]

1. v. To draw a vehicle; to tow, to tug a vessel up stream. Cf. **hale**, v.[2]

Shr.[2] Confined to the river side and chiefly applied to men or horses drawing small or large craft on the Severn against the stream (s.v. Hale). Glo.[2] Dor. He drove his ekkipage hisself, and it was always hauled by four beautiful white horses, HARDY *Laodicean* (ed. 1896) bk. i. v. Som. They hauled the waggon home beside the rick, RAYMOND *Tryphena* (1895) 14.

Hence (1) **Hauling-horse**, sb. a horse used for towing; (2) ·**path**, sb. a tow-path.

(1) n.Lin.[1] (2) *ib.* The occupiers of land ... where there is no hauling-path are authorized to discharge all persons trespassing thereon, *Ancholme Navigation Notice* (Oct. 6, 1874).

2. Phr. *to haul upon the right tow*, to say the right thing. Sh.I. Dooaye hauls ipoda richt tow, BURGESS *Sketches* (2nd ed.) 76.

3. Comp. **Haul-to**, a three-pronged dung-rake. w.Dev. MARSHALL *Rur. Econ.* (1796).

4. To carry on the trade of a carrier, to cart, carry. Cf. **hale**, v.[2] 2.

Nhb. A sledge of wood, halled all along the barrow-way to the pit shaft, J.C. *Compleat Collier* (1708) 36. se.Wor.[1] (s.v. Haulier). Shr.[1] 1805, Dec. 7th, hawling load coals to the workhouse, 1–0–0, *Par. Acc., Much Wenlock.* Hrf.[1] Glo. MARSHALL *Rur. Econ.* (1789); Gl. (1851); Glo.[1] Som. I'll be glad to haul for you if you've got any goods lying at the station (W.F.R.).

5. To throw. e.Sus. Haul up that stick, HOLLOWAY.

6. sb. A large quantity or amount.

Bnff.[1] Thir uncle's dead. an' left thim a haul o' siller. The coo jist gees hauls o' milk. Cld. (JAM.) Gall. Never had any great haul of sense, CROCKETT *Grey Man* (1896) 2.

HAUL, sb.[2] Yks. [ǭl.] A small inlet or recess into which boats from the beach are drawn up for safety.

n.Yks.[2] We put her into a bit of a haul.

HAUL, v.[2] Ken. [ǭl.] To shout. (G.B.), Ken.[1]

[EFris. *hallen*, ' hallen, schallen, tönen ' (KOOLMAN); so LG. (BERGHAUS).]

HAUL, see **Hall**, sb.[2], **Hold**, v., **Hole**, sb.[1]

HAULD, HAULGH, see **Hold**, v., **Haugh**.

HAULIER, sb. Wor. Shr. Hrf. Glo. Oxf. Dor. Som. Also in forms **allier** s.Wor.[1]; **hallier** s.Wor.[1] Hrf.[1] Glo.; **hallyer** se.Wor.[1] [ǭ·liə(r), ǭ·ljə(r).] A person whose business is to do ' hauling,' with horse and cart for hire; a carrier, carter. Cf. **haul**, v.[1] 4.

Wor. (J.W.) s.Wor. (H.K.); s.Wor.[1] One who draws coal, timber, bricks, &c. se.Wor.[1] Shr.[1] I've bin to Philips the 'aulier to axe 'im w'en 'e can fatch me a loöäd o' cöäl from the Cut-w'arf. Hrf.[1] Glo. MARSHALL *Rur. Econ.* (1789); BAVLIS *Illus. Dial.* (1870); Glo.[1], Oxf. (G.O.) Dor. Dewy and Son, tranters and hauliers... Furniture, coals, potatoes, live and dead stock, removed to any distance on the shortest notice, HARDY *Greenwd. Tree* (1872) pt. iv. vii. w.Som.[1]

HAULIN, see **Hawlin**.

HAULING, vbl. sb. Sc. A method of fishing by means of a pock-net; see below.

Dmf. A second mode of fishing, called haaving or hauling, is standing in the stream, either at the flowing or ebbing of the tide, with a pock-net fixed to a kind of frame consisting of a beam 12 or 14 ft. long, having three small sticks or rungs fixed into it. Whenever a fish strikes against the net they, by means of the middle rung, instantly haul up the mouth of the net above water, *Statist. Acc.* II. 16 (JAM., s.v. Haave).

HAULING-HOME, sb. Irel. The bringing home of the bride, the wedding day; also called *the hauling-home day.*

Ir. On the marriage the father of the bride gives a feast, after which the husband stops with her a few days; then he returns home, and on the seventh day comes with his friends to haul her home, when he gives a feast. In some places, however, the hauling home takes place on the marriage day, *Flk-Lore Rec.* (1881) IV. 110. Wxf. Such a well-looking young girl as Miss

Mary there, that ... could bring about seventy or eighty pounds with her on the day of the Hauling Home, KENNEDY *Banks Boro* (1867) 158; To provide a good chest of linen for the hauling home day, *ib. Evenings Duffrey* (1869) 204.

HAULKET, see **Hawkit**.

HAULLY, sb. Obs. Sc. A ' hauling,' rough handling.

Edb. They ae puir fuddl'd chiel did hook, An' gied him a rough haully To the guard that morn, *New Year's Morning* (1792) 12.

HAULM, sb. and v. Var. dial. uses in Sc. Irel. Yks. Midl. e., s. and w. counties. Also written **hawlm** Lin.[1] s.Cy.; and in forms **arm** e.Hmp.; **aum** Lei.[1]; **awm** Nrf.; **elam**, **ellam** Hmp.; **ellum** Brks.[1]; **elm** Hmp.[1] Wil.[1]; **haam** Oxf.[1] Brks.[1] I.W.[1] Wil.[1]; **hahm** Suf.[1]; **halm** Nhp.[2] War.[4] Wor. Hrf.[1] Bdf. Nrf. Ken.[1] Hmp.[1]; **ham** War.[2] Glo.[1] I.W. Wil.[1]; **hame** Ken.[1] Dor.[1]; **harm** Nrf. Suf.; **haulin** Stf.[1] Not.[1]; **haum** n.Lin.[1] Hrf. Sus.[2]; **hawhm** Suf.[1]; **hawme** e.Yks.[1]; **hellam** w.Yks.; **hellum** w.Som.[1] Dev.; **helm** w.Yks. Glo.[1] Hrt. Ken.[12] s.Cy. Hmp.[1] Wil.[1] Som.; **horm** Bdf.; **ullum** w.Som.[1]; **yalm** Glo.[1]; **yelben** Nhp.[1]; **yelham** Hrt.; **yellom** Suf. Ess. Sus.; **yelm** Nhp.[12] Lei.[1] Oxf.[1] Brks.[1] Bdf. Hrt. e.An.[1] Suf. Sus. Wil.[1]; **yelven** Nhp.[1]; **yolm** Glo.[1]; **yullum** Suf. [ǭm, ām, elm, jelm.] **1.** sb. Straw, stubble; the dried stalks of peas, beans, &c.

Sc. (A.W.) w.Yks. LUCAS *Stud. Nidderdale* (c. 1882) 258. Stf.[1] Lin.[1] Peas-straw. n.Lin.[1] The straw of beans, peas, tares. Nhp.[1] Wheat stubble for thatching; the gathering of which, after the harvest, in the neighbourhood of Northampton, is called ' peeking the haulm '; in other parts of the county, the same operation is called ' bagging the haulm '; Nhp.[2] War.[2]; War.[4] Wha'at be yer a putting that halm on the roof for? It's full of mullock. Shr.[1] Hrf. COOPER *Gl.* (1853). Glo. (A.B.); GROSE (1790); Glo.[2] Oxf.[1] Applied to the straw of white crops only. Brks.[1] Bdf. (J.W.B.); Cutting of the haulm, or wheat stubble, costs about 1s. 6d. per acre, BATCHELOR *Agric.* (1813) 108. Hrt. The straw, helm, &c. with which the cattle are littered, MARSHALL *Review* (1817) V. 14. Hnt. (T.P.F.), Nrf. (A.G.) Suf. RAINBIRD *Agric.* (1819) 296, ed. 1849; Suf.[1] The stubble of wheat. It is raked together in heaps by women generally at 16d. or 18d. an acre. If done before it be a little frosted it is man's work with a scythe. s.Cy. RAY (1691); GROSE (1790). Ken. (G.B.), Ken.[12] War.[1] The straw of peas, tares, beans, potatoes, but never used of white crops in this district; Sus.[12], I.W.[1] Wil. BRITTON *Beauties* (1825). Dev.[18]

Hence (1) **Haulm-rick**, sb. a rick consisting of the stubble or straw of vetches, peas, beans, &c.; (2) ·**wall**, sb. a wall made of haulm or stubble.

(1) Brks.[1] The ' Haam ' rick in the Vale of Brks. is of bean or wheat straw, and there they do not usually speak of a ' vetch haam rick' as in the hill part of the county. (2) Ess. And hid them in the ditches or the haulm walls, HEYGATE *Poems* (1870) 187.

2. A stubble-stack. War.[4], s.War.[1]

3. Straw made ready for thatching; bundles or handfuls of straw prepared and laid ready for the thatcher.

Nhp. *N. & Q.* (1880) 6th S. i. 330; Nhp.[12] Lei.[1] As much corn in the straw as can be embraced in both arms. Brks.[1] Bdf. (J.W.B.); BATCHELOR *Anal. Eng. Lang.* (1809) 147. Hrt. (H.G.); ELLIS *Cy. Hswf.* (1750) 231. e.An.[1] Suf. (C.T.); RAINBIRD *Agric.* (1819) 302, ed. 1849. Ess. (H.M.M.) s.Cy. A straw of wheat or rye unbruised, bound in bundles for matching, RAY (1691). Sus. A narrow flat bundle of thatch drawn for fixing to a roof (F.E.); (F.A.A.) Hmp. (H.E.); A handful of thatch. Three elams make a bundle, 20 bundles 1 score, 4 scores 1 ton, WISE *New Forest* (1883) 282; Hmp.[1] w.Cy. The best unbroken straw for thatching, MORTON *Cyclo. Agric.* (1863). Wil. He is attended by a man to carry up the ' yelms,' JEFFERIES *Wild Life* (1879) 124; Wil.[1] n.Wil. Long straws selected for thatching (W.C.P.). Som. Straw prepared for thatching by having the ears cut off (W.F.R.); (F.A.A.); JENNINGS *Obs. Dial. w.Eng.* (1825).

Hence (1) **Helm-sheaf**, sb. a sheaf of straw ready for use in thatching; (2) **Yelm-** or **Elm-stock**, sb. a forked stick used for carrying straw for thatching.

(1) Som. Properly a helm-sheaf is the length of the strand, 5½ ft. round (W.F.R.). (2) Wil. SLOW *Gl.* (1892); Wil.[1]

4. The stalk of certain cultivated plants, esp. of potatoes, peas, or beans; the green, unripened stalks of cereals.

Sc. (A.W.) Ir. But we swore it was merely a heap of haulms rottin', BARLOW *Bogland* (1892) 20, ed. 1893; [Of potatoes] Ne'er a big crop you'll get under that heigth of haulms, *ib. Lisconnel* (1895) 104. w.Yks. All around me the young growths were showing purple haulms or green leaf, Snowden *Web of Weaver* (1896) xiii; The ries [sticks] for peas, &c. (J.T.) s.Chs.[1] Not used of the stalk of any kind of corn. Not.[1] n.Lin. An' lets him hev . . . taatie-haums, Peacock *Tales and Rhymes* (1886) 69. n.Lin.[1] The stalks of rape and turnips. The stalk of flax and hemp. Lei.[1], War.[23], Wor. (W.C.B.), Shr.[1] Hrf.[1] That part of the vegetable above the ground. Rdn. Morgan *Wds.* (1881). Glo. Beans . . . are very short in the haulm, *Evesham Jrn.* (July 18, 1896); Used chiefly of potatoes (J.A.B.); Glo.[1] ' Tater hams,' ' peas' hams,' &c. Bdf. (J.W.B.) Nrf. The disease begin to show itself among them taturs, Sir; hadn't we better cut the harms off? (W.R.E.) Snf. Rainbird *Agric.* (1819) 294. ed. 1849; Suf.[1] The risps of potatoes and of pease . . . as well as the remnant of beans, when they have been cut by the sickle. Ken.[1], ne.Ken. (H.M.), Hmp.[1] e.Hmp. They be ready for diggin' now their arms be died off (W.M.E.F.), I.W. (J.D.R.) Wil. Slow *Gl.* (1892); Wil.[1], Dor.[1] Som. W. & J. *Gl.* (1873). w.Som.[1] Not used to denote straw of any kind. A coarse kind of stalk is implied: if clover has been left to ripen its seed, the stalk becomes rank, and after the seed has been thrashed out, the residuum is always ' clover hellum.' Dev. Us 'ad best ways burn up awl tha bellums and rubbage that's lying about, Hewitt *Peas. Sp.* (1892).

5. The husk of corn or of peas, beans, &c., chaff; the beard of barley.

Not. (J.H.B.), Lin.[1], n.Lin.[1] Nrf. *Trans. Phil. Soc.* (1855) 32. Suf. (W.W.S.)

6. The fruit of the hawthorn, *Crataegus Oxyacantha*, esp. in phr. *haulms and figs*, hips and haws. Ken.[1]

7. *v.* To cut off the ears of wheat previous to threshing; to prepare straw for thatching and lay it in bundles ready for the thatcher.

Glo. To cut the ears from the stems of wheat, previous to thrashing, Marshall *Rur. Econ.* (1789); Baylis *Illus. Dial.* (1870); Glo.[1] To comb off the flag, and then to cut off the ears. Oxf.[1] Women sometimes yelm, but they do not thatch. Brks.[1] Bdf. This operation consists in throwing water over the straw and drawing it forcibly under one's foot (J.W.B.). e.An. To lay straw in convenient quantities to be used by the thatcher, or for the chaff-cutter, Morton *Cyclo. Agric.* (1863); e.An.[1] Suf. Rainbird *Agric.* (1819) 302, ed. 1814. Ess. The wheat stubbles are haulmed immediately after harvest, Marshall *Review* (1811) I. 481. Hmp.[1] Wil. Two or three women are busy ' yelming,' i.e. separating the straw, selecting the longest and laying it level and parallel, damping it with water, and preparing it for the yokes, Jefferies *Wild Life* (1879); Wil.[1], Som. (W.F.R.)

Hence (1) Haulming, *vbl. sb.* the process of preparing straw for thatching; (2) Yelbener, *sb.* one who prepares straw for the thatcher.

(1) Bdf. Which, added to the cutting, makes the whole expense of haulming as. 3d. per acre, Batchelor *Agric.* (1813) 108. n.Wil. (W.C.P.) (2) Nhp.[1]

8. To pull up stubble.

e.Yks. Wee have beene forced to hawme wheat and rye stubble and therewith to thatch our stacks, Best *Rur. Econ.* (1642) 60.

9. To reap peas or beans with a hook. s.Not. (J.P.K.)

[1. Halm or stobyl, *stipula*, Prompt. ON. *halmr*, straw (Vigfusson). 4. OE. *healm*, stem of grass, stalk of a plant (B.T.).]

HAULM, see Hawm, *sb.*

HAULY-CAULY, *sb.* Mid. Slang. Also in forms auly-cauly, auly-crauly w.Mid.; hawley-auley Slang. The name of a game at ball; see below.

w.Mid. One player throws the ball upon the sloping roof of a building, at the same time calling out, ' Hauly-cauly (boy's name).' If the boy named can catch the ball before it touches the ground he throws it up again and calls upon someone else to do likewise; but if not, he picks it up and throws it at one of the others, who scatter to avoid being hit. Any boy he may hit has to pay a penalty, which he incurs himself if he misses. At the end of the game those who have incurred penalties must place one of their hands against the wall and allow one of the others to throw at it once for each penalty they have incurred. Formerly very popular in this neighbourhood (W.P.M.). Slang. A game played in Commoners [Winchester College]. It was played with a red india-rubber ball. As far as I know the game consisted in the boy who got possession of the ball selecting another boy whom he tried to hit with it, the object of the latter being either to escape the ball when thrown at him, or to catch it, Shadwell *Wykehamical Slang* (1859–1864).

HAUM, see Hame, *sb.*[1], Haulm.

HAUMER, HAUMPUS, HAUMSHOCH, see Hammer, *sb.*[1], Hamble, Hamshoch.

HAUNCH, *v.*[1] Lin. To fondle, pet. (Hall.)

HAUNCH, *v.*[2] Lakel.[2] To throw. See Hainch, *v.* 4.

HAUNCH, see Hanch, *v.*

HAUNGE, *v.* Lin. To hover about waiting to seize anything that turns up. Cf. hanch, *v.*

m.Lin. That greedy hulks of a feller was haunging about at the club feast waitin' for owt he could laä' hands on (T.H.R.).

HAUNGE, HAUNIE, see Hunch, *sb.*[1], Handy, *sb.*[1]

HAUNT, *v.* and *sb.* Sc. Nhb. Dur. Cum. Yks. Chs. Der. Not. Hmp. Som. Also in form hant Sc. (Jam. *Suppl.*) N.Cy.[1] Nhb.[1] e.Dur.[1] Cum. n.Yks.[4] e.Yks. [h]ǫnt, h]änt, h]ant.] 1. *v.* To accustom, habituate; used *refl.*, or in *pass.* to become accustomed to.

Nhb. We let her oot ower suin; afore she'd getten hanted (R.O.H.); As wasn't reet hanted wid, an hadn't getten the way, Haldane *His Other Eye* (1880) 3; Nhb.[1] Cum.[4] ' To be haunted to a place,' said principally in reference to cattle. n.Yks.[12] ne.Yks.[1] Ah s'all nivver git hanted ti t'job. e.Yks.[1] He'll seean get maisther o' deeahin on't, if he'll hant his-sen tiv it, *MS. add.* (T.H.) m.Yks.[1]

2. To practise. Sc. Francisque-Michel *Lang.* (1882) 366.

3. To frequent, resort to; to visit frequently, to pester with one's company.

s.Sc. The blaeberry bank where we haunted langsyne, Watson *Bards* (1859) 7. Lnk. They observed the bulk of them so immoral and profane, that they were ashamed to haunt their company, Wodrow *Ch. Hist.* (1721) I. 335, ed. 1828. Rxb. Canty we might be, Did nae she haunt me like a de'il About my dear rappee, Wilson *Poems* (1824) 20. Cum. It hantit o' round about Scallow beck steann, Dickinson *Scallow Beck* (1866) l. 8. n.Yks.[2] He haunts t'yal-house; n.Yks.[4] He's awlus sumwheear nigh at hand, Ah's fairly hanted wi' t'lad. s.Chs.[1] A person is haunted with a subject when he has it continually brought before his notice. nw.Der.[1] Said of an ailment or disease, which attacks any one periodically. s.Not. 'E uster to reglar haunt me; ah hed to fall out wee 'im (J.P.K.).

Hence Hauntskip, *sb.* a place of resort.

Abd. The evil spirit took up a hauntskip in the folk's peat neuk, Milne *Sngs.* (1871) 89.

4. To cause animals to resort to a certain spot.

Hmp.[1] To haunt pigs or cattle in the New Forest, is to accustom them to repair to a certain spot, by throwing down beans or fodder there when they are first turned out.

5. To provide a haunt for.

Ayr. For haunting drucken groups, On Sabbath days, Fisher *Poems* (1790) 66.

6. *sb.* A custom, practice, habit.

Sc. Ye'll ne'er turn an auld cat fra ill hants (Jam. *Suppl.*). N.Cy.[1] ' At your aud hants,' at your old habits. Nhb. Aa'd getten canny inte the hant o' weerin' me new blinker, Haldane *His Other Eye* (1880) 6; Nhb.[1] e.Dur.[1] He has a nasty hant of doing that. n.Yks.[12], ne.Yks.[1] e.Yks. He's getten a hant o' scrattin' his heead when he's talkin' ti yan, *Leeds Merc. Suppl.* (Nov. 4, 1893); Os az gotten a hant o she-in [The horse has got a trick of shying] (Miss A.). m.Yks.[1] s.Chs.[1] Ahy)shl aav' wai·n ŭm of ekspek·tin thing·z brau·t ŭm frŭm maa·rkit, els dhi)n gy'et ŭ au·nt on it [I shall have wane 'em off expectin' things brought 'em from market, else they'n get a haunt on it]. Som. They have such a haunt of mooching (W.F.R.).

7. *Obs.* Phr. *to get haunt of*, to go among.

e.Yks. They shoulde not gette haunt of the wheate and rye, Best *Rur. Econ.* (1641) 72.

HAUNTY, *adj.* Sc. n.Cy. Nhb. Stf. Nhp. War. Wor. Glo. Also in form hanty N.Cy.[12] Nhb.[1] Wanton, unruly; full of spirit, mettlesome; excited, frisky, *gen.* used of horses.

n.Cy. Bailey (1721); Grose (1790); N.Cy.[1]; N.Cy.[2] Spoken of a horse or the like when provender pricks him. Nhb.[1] Stf. Northall *Flk-Phr.* (1894). s.Stf. I should think yo'm haunty, olliprancin' about like that, Pinnock *Blk. Cy. Ann.* (1895). Nhp.[1] Playful, without being vicious; applied almost exclusively to cows. War. E'ham *Wkly. Post* (June 10, 1893); War.[1] As applied to a horse, it conveys the idea of his being so from overfeeding and too much rest. Not synonymous with restive; War.[23] Wor., Glo. Northall *Flk-Phr.* (1894).

HAUNTY, see Hanty.

HAUP, v. Obs. Sc. To limp.

He cam hauping on ae foot, KINLOCH Ballads (1827) 19.

HAUP, HAUPS, HAUR, see Hap, v.[2,8], Hawps, Haar, sb.[1,2], Har(t.

HAURK, v. Sc. In imp. used by huntsmen as an encouragement to the foxhounds; see below.

Gall. A term much used by Sc. fox-hunters when the hounds find the scent of Reynard in one of his keeps, or challenge him. The hunter . . . bawls down to 'Haurk to him, haurk to him, ye wee blasties'; so in defiance of the tusks of the fox they seize on and drag out the crafty villain, MACTAGGART Encycl. (1824).

HAURL, HAURN, see Harl(e, v., Harden, v.

HAURRAGE, sb. Sc. A blackguard crew of people. Cf. harriage.

Sc. FRANCISQUE-MICHEL Lang. (1882) 179. Gall. MACTAGGART Encycl. (1824).

HAUSE, HAUSLET, see Halse, sb.[1], Hawse, v.[1], Haslet.

HAUSS-SPANG, sb. Or.I. An iron rod of a plough.

[It] surrounds the beam and handle of the Orcadian plough at the place where the one is morticed into the other (JAM.); S. & Ork.[1]

HAUST, see Hoast, sb.[1]

HAUT, v.[1] and sb. Sc. 1. v. To limp; to hop. Cld., Slk. (JAM.)

1. sb. Hauter, sb. one who can hop. Cld. (ib.)

2. sb. The act of limping, a hop. Cld. (ib.)

3. Phr. (1) haut, stap, an' loup, a hop, skip, and a jump; (2) — stride and loup, a very short distance, a 'step.'

(1) ib. (2) Slk. It's nae gate ava to Gorranberry, a mere haut-stride and loup, HOGG Tales (1838) 619, ed. 1866.

HAUT, v.[2] Obs. Sc. To gather with the fingers, as one collects stones with a garden-rake; in phr. to haut the kirn, to take off all the butter.

Slk. He steal't the key, and hautit the kirn, HOGG Jacobite Relics (ed. 1874) I. 96; (JAM.)

HAUT, see Holt, sb.[1], Hot(t.

HAUTER, HAUV(E, see Halter, Half, Halve.

HAUVE, sb. Stf. Hrf. Rdn. [ǭv.] The haft or handle of an axe or pick.

n.Stf. (J.T.), Hrf.[1] Rdn. MORGAN Wds. (1881).

HAUVE, v.[1] Yks. Der. Not. Lin. Also written hawve Lin.[1]; and in forms aauve, arv(e Yks.[1]; auve w.Yks.[2] s.Not. Lin.; awve sw.Lin.[1]; haave n.Yks.; half Yks.; harv n.Yks.[14] ne.Yks.[1]; harve n.Yks.[2]; hoave e.Yks.[1]; horve nw.Der.[1] Not.[2]; howve Der.[1]; orve w.Yks.[2] Not.[2] [ǭv.] Of horses: to turn to the left towards the driver; gen. used as an int.: a carter's or ploughman's command to his team. Also used fig.

Yks. 'Aauve the cum hither,' followed by the name of the horse which the driver wishes to bear towards himself on the left (G.W.W.); MORTON Cyclo. Agric. (1863). n.Yks. Gen. used in full form, 'Haave, come here !' (R.H.H.); n.Yks.[1] Replaces the older word 'hait' ; n.Yks.[2] 'She will nowther jee nor harve,' will not turn one way or the other; said of a stubborn woman (s.v. Jee) ; n.Yks.[4], ne.Yks.[1], e.Yks.[1], w.Yks.[12] Der.[1] In modified use. nw.Der.[1] Not. (J.H.B.) Not.[2] In rare use. The more common word is 'boc'; Not.[2] 'Orve again. s.Not. Gen. used with some adv., as 'up', 'ower,' 'again,' 'then' (J.P.K.). Lin. BROWN Lit. Laur. (1890) 64 ; n.Lin. SUTTON Wds. (1881) ; n.Lin.[1] sw.Lin.[1] They have to take care in awving and gee-ing [turning round at the end of the furrows in ploughing].

Hence Hoave-gee or -gee wohop, int. a call to a horse to go straight forward. e.Yks.[1]

HAUVE, v.[2] Yks. Lin. Also written hawve e.Yks.; hoave n.Yks.[14] e.Yks.[1]; hove e.Yks.[1] w.Yks.; oave m.Yks.[1] [ǭv.] 1. To stare, to gaze vacantly or in astonishment. See Awf.

Yks. What are ye hauvin' an' gauvin' at ? MACQUOID Doris Barugh (1877) xxxiii. n.Yks.[1] ; n.Yks.[2] What are you hauving at ? n.Yks.[4], m.Yks.[1], n.Lin.[1]

Hence (1) Hauven, sb. a lout, a coarse rude fellow; (2) Hauvenish, adj. loutish; (3) Hauving, ppl. adj. simple-witted, foolish, clownish; (4) -gam, sb. a stupid person; (5) Hauviah, adj., see (3); (6) Hauvison, (7) Hauvy, (8) Hauvy-gauvy, sb. a simpleton; a clownish, awkward person.

(1, 2) n.Lin.[1] (3) n.Yks.[1], m.Yks.[1] (4) e.Yks.[1] (5) n.Yks.[14] w.Yks. He's up to o sooarts o hoveish wark. It's nobbut one ov

his hoviah speyks [i.e. remarks] (D.L.); w.Yks.[1] (6) n.Yks.[2], m.Yks.[1] (7) m.Yks.[1] (8) n.Yks. (T.S.), n.Yks.[12,4], ne.Yks.[1] e.Yks. What a hawvy-gawvy Sammy-Codlin sooat ov a chap oor Jack is, NICHOLSON Flk-Sp. (1889) 90 ; e.Yks.[1] MS. add. (T.H.) m.Yks.[1], w.Yks.[26]

2. To walk blunderingly or stupidly.

e.Yks.[1] Giles hoav'd inti wrang shop, an' Roger hoav'd efter him.

HAUVE, HAUVER, see Haaf, sb.[1], Haver, sb.[2]

HAUX, v. Hrf.[2] To stroll.

Where are you hauxing off to ?

HAV, see Haw, sb.[1]

HAVAGE, sb. Dev. Cor. Also written haveage. [æ·vidg.] Race, lineage, family stock.

Dev. Both the father and mother being pure North-Devoners, and claiming descent from two good old county families, they were proud of the 'haveage' to which they belonged, Mem. Rev. J. Russell (1883) vi ; Dev.[1] Her come vrom a good havage—the very daps of her mother, 7. n.Dev. 'E'm too good haveage vor'n by haff, ROCK Jim an' Nell (1867) st. 87. sw.Dev.[1] He kom'th of a good havage. Cor. I'd like my old bones to be carr'd home to Carne, an' laid to rest 'long wi' my haveage, 'Q.' Troy Town (1888) xix ; A comprehensive word, applied to the lineage of a person; his family, and companions with whom it is natural for him to associate. It thus marks the race from which he has sprung and his station in society, N. & Q. (1854) 1st S. x. 318–9 ; The havage of my family wain't be easy for to find, J. TRENOODLE Spec. Dial. (1846) 9 ; Cor.[1] The children of a family of ill repute are said to be 'o' bad havage'; Cor.[2]

HAVANCE, sb. Obs. Sc. Dev. Also written havence Frf. Manners, behaviour. Cf. havings.

Frf. Now ilka lad does taunt her wi' her havence, MORISON Poems (1790) 151. Dev. GROSE (1790); (HALL.)

HAVE, v. and sb. Var. dial. forms and uses in Sc. Irel. Eng. and Amer. I. Dial. forms. 1. Indicative Mood, Present Tense. i. Simple Affirmative.

Sc. As hæ or hæv, hey hæs, wey hæ or hev; contracted forms : as've, hey's, wey've, MURRAY Dial. (1873) 219; Hez, ELLIS Pronunc. (1889) 684. Sh.I. The ill-vicked coo haes short horns, SPENCE Flk-Lore (1899) 229; A'm heard o' nae rot yit, Sh. News (Oct. 7, 1899); Da tatties . . . is been laek braed, ib.; Ye're shürely brunt dis broth folk, ib. (Dec. 16, 1899); Dere am I lost mi coont, ib. [For other dial. uses of 'be' for 'have,' see Be, VIII. 4.] Doo haes, shü's tell'd, ye hae, ib.; Ye 'a, ib. (Aug. 27, 1898). Or.I. Du hiz, ELLIS ib. 796. Cai.[1] I hiv; he, hid his; we, &c. hiv; 'e man his; 'e men hiv. Bnff.[1] He hiz as . . bang-dog-like a leuck's iver I saw (s.v. Hang-dog); He's taen, ib. 21. e.Sc. I've been feeared for this, SETOUN R. Urquhart (1896) xxv; The loon an' you's been aye haein bits o' sharries, ib. viii; Hae, hiv [have], his [has] (G.W.). Frf. I hiv or hae; he, it his; we, &c. hiv or hae ; the man his a hoose ; the men hiv hooses (J.B.). w.Frf., e.Per. Ai'v, emph. ai hęv; 'e, ət hęz, emph. hl, ęt hęz ; wə, &c. hęv, emph. wl hev ; 5ə men hęz or hęv husəz (W.A.C.). n.Ayr. I ha'e or hiv; he his; we, &c. hae or hiv (J.F.). Rxb. Iv [you have], ELLIS ib. 714; haez, ib. 717; Oo've [we have] nae need o' sodgers' claes, MURRAY Hawick Sngs. (1890) 31. Dmf. We hae goods, SHENNAN Tales (1891) 43. Wgt. I've, I hiv or hae ; thou'st ; he his, he's ; we've, we, &c. hiv or hae ; they hiv or hae houses (A.W.). Ant. A hae ; he haes ; we, &c. hae (W.J.K.). n.Ldd. I hive; he, it hes; we, &c. hive or hev (A.J.T.). Wxf.[1] Obs. Cha, for ich ha [I have]. n.Cy. I han, GROSE (1790) ; N.Cy.[1] Hes, han pl. Nhb. Simple : Aa'v, thoo'st, hee'z, it'z; stressed : aa he' or hev ; thoo, he, it hez. Simple : We, &c. 'v ; stressed : we, &c. he' or hev ; the men he' hooza. The forms he' and hev are used, the former when a consonant follows—' Aa he' nowt to gi' ye'; the latter when it is followed by a vowel or 'h' mute—' Aa hev on'y sixpence; aa hev 'im noo' (R.O.H.); Hest [hast], ib. ; Whot isnt gyud that the minister hes? RICHARDSON Borderer's Table-bk. (1846) VIII. 201 ; The hens, poor things, hes nowt, ROBSON Evangeline (1870) 320. Dur. A he, hev; dhū, hi hez ; wi hev; hi hest [he has it], ELLIS ib. 618; Dur.[1] Hev, hez. Cum. Ye that hae gear, ANDERSON Ballads (ed. 1840) 57; Cum.[1] Ah hev, I ha' ; Cum.[2] I've nit sēa offen hed, 3; Thou's cheatit them, ib. 40 ; I's sworry it hes, ib. 42 ; We've summat else to deu, 1. e.Cum. Ah hev; thoo, he, it hes ; we, &c. hev (J.A.). s.Cum. I hev; thou, he, it hez; we, &c. hev; the men hev or hez houses (J.P.). Cum., Wm. Av, az [I have], ELLIS ib. 569. Wm. I hae gitten a swoap, WHEELER Dial. (1790) 113, ed. 1821; Sall hes hort her heel, ib. 112. n.Wm. I heve or heh; thou, he, it hez; we, &c. 've ; the men hev or hez houses (B.K.). s.Wm. I hev or hes ; thoo, he, it hes; we, &c. hev. Also the abbreviated forms 's, 've ;

I's gitten ; thoo's, he's, we've, ye've, they've gitten (J.M.). n.Yks. Ah hev a paper, Castillo *Poems* (1878) 42 ; Az [I have], Ellis *ib.* 504 ; A'v ə lot ə biznis (W.H.) ; Thou hez meead my heart glad ! Tweddell *Clevel. Rhymes* (1875) 34 ; It's ommest deed away, *ib.* 2 ; Yah hea neea wealth, *ib.* 42 ; n.Yks.[1] Ah's bin chassin' t'harras, '95 ; Thou's getten a sair clash, *ib.* 102 ; He's getten t'farm, *ib.* 29 ; They've getten fairly agate, *ib.* 3 ; n.Yks.[2] Hae, hev [have] ; hez [has]. ne.Yks.[1] Ah a'e, ev, *or* 've ; thoo ez, es, *or* 'z ; he ez *or* 'z ; we, &c. a'e, ev, *or* 've, 30. e.Yks. Az *or* av dian [I have done], Ellis *ib.* 504 ; I 'ev, (e') ; thoo, he, it 'ez ; we, &c. 'ev (e') ; the men 'ev, e', *or* 'ez houses (R.S.) ; Hey [has], Marshall *Rur. Econ.* (1788) ; e.Yks.[1] I hev *or* hez ; thoo, he hez ; we, &c. hev. m.Yks.[1] Aa ev ; dhoo, ey ez ; wey, &c. ev ; aa· ez· is freq. heard for ' I have', *Introd.* 47. w.Yks. Aiv, av, iv ; ŏaz ; Iz ; wiv ; yiv ; ŏeav, ŏev, Wright *Gram. Wndhll.* (1892) 154 ; The plural forms wiv, &c. are only used in comb. with personal pronouns, in other cases we use ez, əz, z, z, just as in the second and third pers. s., *ib.* 156 ; At hez him near two hands in height, Lucas *Stud. Nidderdale* (c. 1882) 258 ; We'n a wooden ax somewhere, *Gossips*, 18 ; Here yo'n been spendin all, *ib.* 12 ; Ahr voines hae tender grapes, Rogers *Sng. Sol.* (1860) ii. 15 ; w.Yks.[1] I've [I have] ; ha, hay, hev *or* hey [have] ; hes [has] ; han [they have] ; w.Yks.[2] I ha but sixpence ; they han ; w.Yks.[3] We han him. Much used for *pl.* ; w.Yks.[4] Han *pl.* ; w.Yks.[5] He's gotten't ; he hes tu. Lan.I'nbeencleanagain, Kay-Shuttleworth *Scarsdale* (1860) I. 94 ; I han got no money, Gaskell *M. Barton* (1848) vi ; He's etten all t'goose, Waugh *Heather* (ed. Milner) I. 90 ; ' Han' *gen.* becomes shortened into ''n,' when preceded by the personal pronouns. We'n better i' th' heawse. Yo'n, they'n, Gaskell *Lectures Dial.* (1854) 25 ; Yoan hameh [have my] sneeze urn, Tim Bobbin *View Dial.* (1740) 99 ; Theer yo' han him pinned, Brierley *Old Radicals*, 6 ; Lan.[1] Han *pl.* ; we'n, we'en, yo'n. e.Lan.[1] Han *pl.* se.Lan. Aw've ; theaw'st *or* theaw's ; he, it 's ; we, &c. 'n *or* han ; th' mon's getten a héawse ; th' men have getten heawses (F.E.T.). s.Lan. Aw've ; thea's *or* thea has ; he's ; we, &c. 've *or* we han ; th' mon's getten a house (S.W.) ; Ez, əz [has], Ellis *ib.* 332 ; Ov dun [I have done], *ib.* 333. I.Ma. I hev, I've ; thou, he, we, &c. hev (E.G.) ; Iz [has], Ellis *ib.* 360a. w.I.Ma. Oi, thou, he, we, &c. 've ; it hev ; the man have a house ; the men hev hooses (G.K.). Chs. Ye an heerd it mony a time, Croston *Enoch Crump* (1887) 7 ; Chs.[1] We'n, yo'n ; Chs.[2] They han ; Chs.[3] Han *pl.* e.Chs.[1] Aaz·, ənd and 3rd *sg.*, *pl.* aan· : Ahy'v got'n ŭ ky'aay [I have got a cow], *ib.* 71. Stf. 'z [has], Ellis *ib.* 473 ; win biu, *ib.* 478 : you bin, *ib.* 477. n.Stf. Thy poor feyther... as I'n washed for, Geo. Eliot *A. Bede* (1859) I. 155 ; Oi av, ŏei ast, ei as ; wei, &c. an *or* av (T.C.W.). a.Stf. I've, thee'st, he's ; we ha(ve)n *or* we'n ; yo', they han *or* 'n ; the mon's got a house (G.T.L.). Der.I'v dun, Ellis *ib.* 429 ; 'z [has], *ib.* 427 ; Der.[1] Han *pl.* nw.Der.[1] Ha'n *pl.* Not. Ai ev tə gjiv ; iz [he has] got it, Ellis *ib.* 449 ; Han (J.H.B.). s.Not. I hev, 've, hae, ha, a ; he, it hez *or* 's ; we, &c. hev, 've, hae, ha, a (J.P.K.). Lin. Thou's rode of 'is back, Tennyson *Owd Rod* (1889). n.Lin. I hev, ha', *or* I've ; thoo, he, it hes ; we, &c. hev *or* 've ; th' man's a hoose ; th' man hes a hoose ; th' men hev *or* hes hooses. In all cases the ' h' is silent unless emphasis is thrown on the word. The verb often varies in sound before certain words—e.g. ' We hettá (*or* hattá) goa' for ' we hev tá goa' (M.P.). m.Lin. Ai ə dun, Ellis *ib.* 304. s.Lin. Hiz [he has] gotn, *ib.* 298. Rut. Iz gon, *ib.* 255. Lei. Aiv dun, *ib.* 465 ; 'z [has], *ib.* 473 ; My brother always haves his supper with us (C.E.) ; Lei.[1] *Emph.* I hev *or* han ; thee has *or* hast ; he, we have, hev, *or* han. *Unemph.* I've, I hae, hea, I'n ; thee's *or* thee'st ; he's, he've, he hae, he hea, he'n ; we've, we hae, hea, we'n, 30. Nhp. I am got a bad cold, *or* I are got a bad cold ; the men are got housen (C.A.M.). [For other dial. uses of ' be' for ' have,' see Be, VIII. 4.] I bin [has been], Ellis *ib.* 216 ; 'z bin, *ib.* 217 ; Nhp.[1] I ha'. n.Nhp. Iz [has] ; aiv [I have], *ib.* 213. War. I've *or* I hay ; thee'st ; he, it 's *or* hay ; we, &c. 've *or* hay. The aspirate was only used by the educated few. ' I am' was also frequently used for ' I have'—I'm done my work (E.S.) ; War.[1] Han *pl.* Ween bin to market, *ib. Pref.* 15 ; You'n done it, *ib.* 16 ; War.[2] Han *pl.* nw.War. I've, I 'ave ; he's, he 'as ; we've, we 'ave ; yo've, yŏ 'ave, yŏ'n ; they've, they 'ave ; the mon's a (got) 'ouse ; the men 'ave (got) 'ouses (G.T.N.). e.War. Oin dun, Ellis *ib.* 465. m.Wor. Hi *or* A 'ave, 've, 'a, 's ; thee 'ast, 'st ; E *or* A 'aves, 'ave, 'a ; 't 'ave ; us 'ave, 'as, 've, 's ; you 'as, 's, 'a' ; thahy *or* A 'as, 've, 's ; the mon 'ave *or* a 'ouse ; the men a 'ousen (H.K.). w.Wor.[1] I 'ave *or* 'a ; thee'st, 'ast ; 'e, 'a, *or* a'e ; us 'as *or* 'ave ; you 'ave *or* a ; thaay 'as, *Introd.* 26. Shr. 'z [has], Ellis *ib.* 473 ; Shr.[1] I've *or* I han ; thee'st ; we, yo han *or* 'n ; they han *or* a'n *or* 'n, *Gram. Outlines*, 58. Hrf. He a-done it now ; he have then ; her have (J.B.) ; Ii ə dun [I have done], Ellis *ib.* 70 ; 'z [has], *ib.*

176 ; Dhai əv dən [they have done], *ib.* 177 ; Hrf.[1] Han *pl.* s.Wal. Johnnie George have lost more in her than he do know, *Longman's Mag.* (Dec. 1899) 144. Pem. Həv əgon [has gone], Ellis *ib.* 32. Glo. Mebbe I 'ev time to tell 'e, Gissing *Vill. Hampden* (1890) I. i ; I ha' zeed its full length, *ib. Both of this Parish* (1889) I. 98 ; I, he, it a ; thees't a ; we, &c. a (H.S.H.) ; Iz *or* Iz bin [he has been], Ellis *ib.* 66. Oxf. I has *or* haves ; he, it have *or* haves ; we, &c. has *or* haves ; Tom have come home from school ; we haves eggs for brekfust (G.O.) ; I av *or* ae ; thee 'ast ; 'ee, it 'av *or* a ; we, &c. 'av *or* aa ; th' man 'a got a 'ouse ; th' men 'a got some 'ousen. Aa for 'av is not used before a vowel (A.P.) ; I hath a been thinking, Blackmore *Cripps* (ed. 1895) xix ; 'z [has], Ellis *ib.* 93 ; They has a cart (M.R.). Brks. The squire hev promised, Hughes *Scour. White Horse* (1859) iv ; Brks.[1] I hev *or* has ; thee *or* 's hast, has, hev, *or* hevs ; he hev, hevs, *or* has ; we *or* us hev ; thaay, them, *or* um hev, hevs, *or* has, 8. Bdf. Uy hev [I have], Batchelor *Anal. Eng. Lang.* (1809) 157 ; Iv gon [has gone], Ellis *ib.* 94 ; 'z [has], *ib.* 206 ; Iz [has], *ib.* 207 ; Jiu ə bin [you have been], *ib.* 208. Hrt. Oi ə dun [I have done] ; Ez [has], *ib.* 198 ; I gon [has gone], *ib.* 200. Hnt. 'z [has], *ib.* 211. Cmb. I 'av, I've ; 'e 'az, 'e'z (W.W.S.) ; He haves the book (W.M.B.) ; 'z gon [has gone], Ellis *ib.* 249. Nrf. Ai hæ dun [I have done], *ib.* 273 ; Iz gon [has gone], *ib.* 263 ; Miss Woodhouse have had it, Mrs. A. Godwin *Latt.* (1805) in *W. Godwin* (1876) II. 195. e.Nrf. I ha' ;,he, it ha' *or* have ; we, &c. ha' (M.C.H.B.). Suf. Ai ə dun [I have done], Ellis *ib.* 280 ; His [he has] (C.G.B.) ; Suf.[1] Mr. Johnson he have two sons. n.Suf. 'z [has], Ellis *ib.* 278. e.Suf. He, it hĕv ; we, &c. hĕv (F.H.). w.Suf. He have (C.L.F.). Ess. He hev, *or* in shortened form ' ha' *or* ' a' (H.H.M.) ; Iz gon [has gone], Ellis *ib.* 293. n.Ken. Ai ə dun [I have done], *ib.* 137. e.Ken. Iz [has], *ib.* 142. Sur. I be glad I'se said summat, Bickley *Sur. Hills* (1890) I. xii ; I has fits, *ib.* x ; Whaät he an givun, he an givun, *ib.* III. xvi ; We ha' no minister, Jennings *Field Paths* (1884) 64 ; They must ha' lain here. That must ha' rotted away, *ib.* 69. Sus. He *or* her have (R.B.). w.Sus. I, thee, he, we, &c. hev (E.E.S.). Hmp. I don't think she have (W.M.E.F.) ; Iz [has], Ellis *ib.* 105. n.Hmp. Oi 'as ; thou 'ast ; 'e, she has ; we 'ave *or* 'as ; you, they 'ave. The verb ' to get' used after ' to have' in a sentence of any length (E.H.R.). s.Hmp. ' They have,' ' we have,' when used as auxiliaries, are often changed into ' they'm' and ' we'm.' ' They'm bought a cow' (H.W.E.). I.W. He've (J.D.R.). Wil. Həv [has], Ellis *ib.* 58 ; *emph.* Zhŭ əvz'n [she has him] ; *unemph.* Irz ·got'n [she's got him], *ib.* 47. n.Wil. I've, thee'st, he have *or* 've ; we've, you've, they've *or* ha' ; the man have a got a house ; the men ha' got housen (E.H.G.) ; Th' king ha' vot m' into hiz cheammurs, Kite *Sng. Sol.* (1860) i. 4. s.Wil. Oi ha', thee'st, her've *or* have ; us ha', you've, thaai've (C.V.G.). Dor. Chave [I have], Haynes *Voc.* (c. 1730) in *N. & Q.* (1883) 6th S. vii. 366 ; I've, he've ; we, &c. 've, Barnes *Gl.* (1863) 25 ; I've a got, thee's a got, he've a got (H.J.M.) ; Həv əgon [has gone] ; John hə [John has], Ellis *ib.* 76. Som. 'Ch'ave [I have], W. & J. *Gl.* (1873) ; Hav əgon [has gone], Ellis *ib.* 85. w.Som. Aay·u z-zoa·id ; dhee·s u-toa·dird ; ee·dh *or* ee·v u-wuy·pd ; wee, &c. 'v u-shaud', Elworthy *Gram.* (1877) 57. Dev. Chave un ! Chave un ! Jet gae on now reart an tha whult, Madox-Brown *Dwale Bluth* (1876) bk. i. iv ; I ha put auf ma cote, Baird *Sng. Sol.* (1860) v. 3 ; Thow ist duv's eyes, *ib.* iv. 1 ; Tha king ith brort ma inta es chimbers, *ib.* i. 4 ; Cuvert 'ath a-doffed his wings, Salmon *Ballads* (1899) 76. n.Dev. I've ; thee'st ; he, it hath *or* he'th ; us ha' ; you, they 've ; the man's a-got a 'ouze ; the men hev a-got 'ouzes (R.P.C.) ; And chave an over arrant to tha mun, *Exm. Crtshp.* (1746) l. 396 ; *Obs.* Use in text prob. exaggerated, *ib. Gl.* e.Dev. Th' zun hev a-tann'd me, Pulman *Sng. Sol.* (1860) i. 6. s.Dev. Hez [has], Ellis *ib.* 162. Cor. 'z [has], *ib.* 166 ; Iz, *ib.* 169 ; The best custom we ha' got, Forfar *Pentowan* (1859) i ; Cor.[2] I haave a ben ; thee'st, a haave, we haave, *or* wee've, 61 ; Cor.[3] *Gen.* used with ' got.' I have got a book. w.Cor. Have is com.hav'. In the last generationit was pronounced hǎve (M.A.C.).

ii. Simple Negative.

Sc. I haena fund Miss Clara, Scott *St. Ronan* (1824) xxxvii ; He hasna a divot-cast of land, *ib. Midlothian* (1818) xii ; They havena sae mickle, *ib. Leg. of Mont.* (1818) iii. Sh.I. If shū's no tell'd, *Sh. News* (Dec. 16, 1899). Cai.[1] I hivna ; he, hid hisna ; we, &c. hivna. Bnff. Hinna [have not], Ellis *ib.* 779. Abd. I haena ; he, it hasna ; we, &c. haena (G.W.) ; Ai hi)ne, Ellis *ib.* 769 : I suppose ye hinna jist a lot o' siller, Greig *Logie o' Buchan* (1899) 203. Frf. I hivna *or* hinna ; he, it hisna ; we, &c. hivna *or* hinna (J.B.) ; We hivena been sic a short time acquaint, Lowson *Guidfollow* (1890) 30. w.Frf. e.Per. Ai hęvnä, hənä ; 'e, ət hęznä ; wə, &c. hęvnä, hənä ; also dęznä hē ; ŏə men hęznä husəz (W.A.C.). w.Sc. Henna and hinna [have not] represent the com. pronun. (JAM. *Suppl.*) **Rnf.** Some puir creatures haena where to lay their heads, A. WILSON *Poems* (1816) 321, ed. 1876 (JAM. *Suppl.*). n.Ayr. I hae nae (*pron.* hinney); he his nae; we, &c. hae nae (J.F.). **Lnk.** I hinna the power, WARDROP *J. Mathison* (1881) 36. **Wgt.** I, we, &c. hinna, haena, hivna; thou'st not; he, it hisna (A.W.). **Ant.** I, we, &c. haenae *or* hae not; he haesnae. ' I have not ' would be rendered ' A haenae ' and ' A bae not ' according as the question required. ' Have you six-pence? ' ' No, I haenae ony mony.' ' Have you got your break-fast? ' ' I hae not.' And so of some others (W.J.K.). **N.Cy.**[1] Henna, hanna [have not]. **Nhb.** *Simple*: Aa hevn't; Aa henna; thoo, he, it hezn't; we, &c. hevn't. *Stressed*: Aa've not; thoo's not; he'z not; it'z not; we, &c. 've not. Used as follows. *Absolute*: ' Aa hevn't.' When followed by a phr. beginning with a consonant: ' Aa henna,' e.g. ' Aa henna seen him.' *Phrasal*, when a vowel follows: ' Aa hennit,' e.g. ' Aa hennit a penny ' (R.O.H.) ; I hev not a boat, ALLAN *Tyneside Sngs.* (1891) 8 ; A keahm hes-int been int this twe months, BEWICK *Tyneside Tales* (1850) 10; They hennet te touch the', ROBSON *Bk. Ruth* (1860) xi. 9. **Dur.** A hev'nt, henət, henə; dhu, he hez'nt, ELLIS *ib.* 618. **Cum.** I hae nea power, BURN *Ballads* (1877) 6a ; There hes-na gaen a month, *ib.* 7 ; **Cum.**[1] Hevvent, hennet [have not]. c.**Cum.** Ah hevent ; thou, he, it hessent; we, &c. hevvent (J.A.). n.**Wm.** I hev'nt; thou,. he, it hezzant; we, you hevvant; they hevvant *or* hezzant; the men hevvant *or* hezzant. When emphasis is required, ' Ah've, we've, &c. nut ' is substituted (B.K.). s.**Wm.** I hevn't *or* hesn't; thou, he, it hesn't; we, &c. hevn't (J.M.). n.**Yks.** Ah aint neea mair te say, TWEDDELL *Clevl. Rhymes* (1875) 8 ; Ah essent patience, *ib.* 37; We aint mitch trade, *ib.* 19 ; Tha hevvent deed, CASTILLO *Poems* (1878) 25 ; Thoo ezent tried (W.H.) ; Hezzent [has not]; hennut [have not] (T.S.) ; n.**Yks.**[1] Ah hevn't strucken a bat, 32 ; n.**Yks.**[4] ' Hennet ' [have not] should be written ' a'e nut.' ne.**Yks.**[1] Ah a'e n't ; thoo, he ez n't; we a'e n't *or* we ev n't ; you, they a'e n't, 30. e.**Yks.** I, we, &c. ain't; thoo, 'e, it ezn't; the men ain't *or* ez'nt houses (R.S.) ; Ah a'e nut *or* 'ev nut ; thoo, he, it 'es nut; we, &c. a'e nut (M.C.F.M.); e.**Yks.**[1] Ah hain't nivver thried; haan't [have not]. m.**Yks.**[1] Besides the com. neg. 'evu'nt,' there is an additional form ' en'ut.' ' Aa· ez·u'nt' [I have] is freq. heard, *Introd.* 47. w.**Yks.** I havvant a penny, BURNLEY *Yks. Stories Retold*, 146 ; Ah hevn't goan, *Yksman.* (1888) 223, col. 2; Tha hessan't long to live, *Keighley News* (Mar. 16, 1889) 7, col. 7 ; If she'y hezzant, LUCAS *Stud. Nidderdale* (c. 1882) 34; Ai, a, i evnt ; ɔ̃t, tḷ, tə ɛrnt, WRIGHT *Gram. Wndhll.* (1892) 154 ; w.**Yks.**[1] Hanno [have not] ; I hennət doon wi' the yet, *ib.* ii. 336 ; w.**Yks.**[5] Hen't [hasn't]. **Lan.** He has no, BRIERLEY *Layrock* (1864) v ; Yo' hanna seen, ACKWORTH *Clog Shop Chron.* (1896) 279. s.**Lan.**[1] Hannot (Roch-dale), harnd (Rossendale) [have not]. se.**Lan.** Aw've no' *or* aw hannot; theawst no' *or* theaw hasno; he, it's no', *or* he hasno'; we, &c. hanno' *or* hannot (F.E.T.). s.**Lan.** Awve not *or* I hanna *or* hannot ; thea, he, it hasna *or* hasn't; we, &c. hanna *or* hannot (S.W.) ; I, &c. hanno, BAMFORD *Dial.* (1854). I.**Ma.** I hev'n; thou hev'n; he hev'n; they hev'n; the men hev'n housses (E.G.). **Chs.** Nay I han'not, CROSTON *Enoch Crump* (1887) 7; They surely hanno' bin berryin' somebody wick, *ib.* 12; **Chs.**[1] Hanna *or* hanner [have not]; **Chs.**[2] Hannah; **Chs.**[3] Hanna. s.**Chs.**[1] Ahy aa)nū ; Dhū aa·(nō bin, 92. n.**Stf.** Oi ano; Dhei astnə; ei, it asnə; we, &c. ano *or* anna (T.C.W.). s.**Stf.** I ha'nt; thee has'nt ; he ha't *or* han't; we ha' *or* han't (G.T.L.) ; Ai et [I have not], ELLIS *ib.* 461. **Der.** Ye hanna suppered up thae five new heifers, VERNEY *Stone Edge* (1868) viii. nw.**Der.**[1] Hanna. **Not.** He aint *or* haint got it (J.H.B.). n.**Not.** I haint *or* hevn't ; he, it haint, hesn't, *or* hesna; we, &c. hain't *or* hevn't. ' Hesna ' is undoubtedly some-times used by the old ; it may be an introduction, but I have found it in central parts of the district (J.P.K.). n.**Lin.** I hevn't *or* ha'nt ; thoo, he, it hesn't; we, &c. hevn't *or* ha'nt; th' man's not a hoose; th' men hesn't noa hooses (M.P.). s.**Lin.** I haěnt; thou, he, it hesn't; we, &c. haěnt (T.H.R.). **Lei.** [The use of ' be ' instead of ' have ' is] very common. I'm not brought my paper. He is'nt got none (C.E.). [For other dial. uses of ' be ' for ' have,' see **Be,** VIII. 4.] **Lei.**[1] I haven't, hevn't, havena, hanna, *or* I hannot, hain't, hean't, 31. **Nhp.**[1] Hanna [have not]. She ha'n't got it. It hassant done no hurt. **War.** I hanna seen my mate yet, WHITE *Wrekin* (1860) xxiv ; Thee hanna roggled to be such a good wench, *B'ham Wkly. Post* (Apr. 29, 1899) ; **War.**[2] Han not, *pl.* Now confined to remote hamlets; replaced by ' ain't ' and ' arn't,' which are employed with a *sing.* *or* *pl.* pron. ; **War.**[3] I, thee, he, it haint; we, &c. harn't; I aint been ; I hent been a naughty girl ; **War.**[5] I harnt got it. nw.**War.** I ain't, arn't, 'annut (rare) ; Yo, he, it, we ain't, arn't (G.T.N.). **Wor.** I 'ant got the money, *Evesham Jrn.* (Nov. 18, 1899). m.**Wor.** I 'an't ; thou 'ast *or* 'st not ; he, it 'ave, 've not, 'an't ; we 'ave, 've, 'as,

'an't ; you 'as, 's, 'an't ; they 'as, 've, 's, 'an't (H.K.) ; No he h'ant *or* aant (J.C.). w.**Wor.**[1] I 'anna *or* 'avna ; thee 'asna ; 'e 'anna *or* 'asna ; us, yer 'anna *or* 'avna ; thaay 'anna *or* 'asna, *Introd.* 26. **Shr.** They hanna got nothing to do (A.J.M.) ; **Shr.**[1] I hanna ; thee has'na ; A, 'e, *or* 'er hanna ; we, &c. hanna, *Gram. Outlines*, 58 ; **Hrf.**[2] Hanna [has not]; havena [have not]. s.**Wal.** You ain't got no spirit, *Longman's Mag.* (Dec. 1899) 144. **Glo.** I han't; thee hastn't; he, it, we, you hant; they hant *or* hanna (H.S.H.); I'sn't carried a pall afore, GISSING *Both of this Par.* (1889) I. 104 ; Ye ent zeed the last of I, *ib. Vill. Hampden* (1890) III. iv. **Oxf.** I ain't *or* ent ; thou, he, it ain't ; we ain't *or* ent ; you, they ain't. An't is sometimes used ; e.g. 'I'll be jiggered if some young uns an't bin in my garden ' (G.O.) ; I aa·nt ; thee 'asn't ; Ee, it aan't; us *or* we, &c.,um, *or* they aan't; th' menaan't got no' ouzen(A.P.); I, &c. 'an't got; the man 'an't got a house (M.R.) ; I han't no patience with thee, BLACKMORE *Cripps* (ed. 1895) ii. **Brks.** Hæænt got [has not], ELLIS *ib.* 97 ; **Brks.**[1] Haint *or* hev'nt [have not] ; I, he ent, aint, hev'nt, *or* yent; thee *or* 'e hasn't *or* hevn't, *ib.* 10. **Bdf.** Uy he nu [I have not], BATCHELOR *Anal. Eng. Lang.* (1809) 154. **Hrt.** Ent [have not], ELLIS *ib.* 199. **Cmb.** I 'av'n't *or* I ain't ; 'e 'avn't *or* 'e ain't (W.W.S.). e.**Nrf.** I, &c. haint (M.C.H.B.). **Suf.** I, &c. ha'nt ; aint [has not] (C.G.B.) ; **Suf.**[1] Heent [has *or* have not] ; 'A heent got a wad ta sah. e.**Suf.** He haint (F.H.) ; Hint got [has not got], ELLIS *ib.* 279. **Ess.** I hant (H.H.M.). **Ken.** I ain't done it yet. He ain't got none (D.W.L.). **Sur.** I ain't got nōne, lăd, but I ainna wi' in a drop, BICKLEY *Sur. Hills* (1890) I. i ; Thou has'na faither, *ib.* II. xv ; They as hanna enou' for theysen, *ib.* i. **Sus.** He *or* her have not (R.B.). w.**Sus.** I aint ; thee ănt; he, &c. aint (E.E.S.). **Hmp.** Hǎnt got [has not] got, ELLIS *ib.* 97. n.**Hmp.** Oi 'avnt ; thou 'asnt ; he 'asnt ; we, &c. 'avnt (E.H.R.). s.**Hmp.** I ain't [ěnt] ; they ain't [ěnt] (J.B.P.). w.**Cy.** Yent [you have not] no need, *Cornh. Mag.* (Dec. 1895) 601. n.**Wil.** I haa'n't a keep'd, KITE *Sng. Sol.* (1860) I. 6 ; I ha'nt ; thee hass'nt ; he ha'nt; we, &c. ha'nt ; the man ha'nt got no house ; the men ha'nt got no housen (E.H.G.). **Dor.** The man ha'nt got ar a house (H.J.M.) ; **Dor.**[1] Hassen [hast not]. w.**Som.** Aay aa·n ; dhee as-n ; Ee (*or* ai) aa·n (*or* aa·th-n); wee aa·n, ELWORTHY *Gram.* (1877) 57; w.**Som.**[1] I han't; thee has'n; he han't *or* hath'n; we, &c. hant. Often written ' ant.' **Dev.** I be zartin that thee ant, SALMON *Ballads* (1899) 64. n.**Dev.** I ha'nt *or* heb'm ; thee hass'n; he hath'n, han't, *or* heb'm ; it han't *or* tan't; us, &c. ha'nt *or* heb'm (R.P.C.). nw.**Dev.**[1] Ant.

iii. Simple Interrogative.

Sc. Hæv-aa ! hæs-hey ! hæ-wey ! MURRAY *Dial.* (1873) 219. **Sh.I.** Heas doo mair levin ! *Sh. News* (Nov. 4, 1899) ; Is doo ! [hast thou ?] *ib.* (Dec. 16, 1899). **Cai.**[1] Hiv I, we, ye, wey ! his he ! **Abd.** His 't hae you *or* [hive] ye ! (G.W.) **Frf.** Hiv I ! his he ! his 't ! hiv we ! &c. (J.B.) w.**Frf.,** e.**Per.** Hev ə ! hez 'e *or* 't ! hęv we ! &c. (W.A.C.) n.**Ayr.** Hae *or* hiv I ! his 'e ! hae we *or* ye ! hiv *or* hae they ! (J.F.) **Rxb.** Hae I ! [have you ?] ELLIS *ib.* 714. **Wgt.** Hiv *or* hae I ! his he ! hiv *or* hae we ! &c. (A.W.) **Ant.** Hae a ! haes he ! haes we ! &c. (W.J.K.) **Nhb.** Hev aa ! hesta *or* hez tha ! hez 'ee ! hest ! he' we ! &c. Hez ony on ye getten deun ! (R.O.H.) ; What hasta been daein'! CLARE *Love of Lass* (1890) I. 6 ; Where hest te been, ma canny hinny ! *Old Sng., Ma Canny Hinny*; How monny bayrnes hes thee muther now ! BEWICK *Tyneside Tales* (1850) 11 ; Ha' ye heard ! OLIVER *Local Sngs.* (1844) 6 ; **Nhb.**[1] Hev, the emphatic form . . . used . . . when the word following begins with an open vowel *or* **h** mute. **Cum.** Hesta a job frat Castle foke ! *Poll Bk. Whitehaven* (1832) 35 ; What heste got to say ageăn it ! DICKINSON *Cumbr.* (1876) 41. e.**Cum.** Hev ah ! hesta ! hes he ! hes it *or* hes't ! hev we ! hev ya, they ! *or* ha' ya, they ! (J.A.) s.**Cum.** Hev I, we, you, they ! hez thou, he, it ! hev *or* hez the men houses ! (J.P.) **Wm.** What hesta deean weet cheeses ! *Spec. Dial.* (1885) pt. iii. 6. n.**Wm.** Heve *or* heh, I, we ! &c.; hez he, it ! heve *or* hest the men houses ! hest gone ten ! hest [has the] coo cauved ! (B.K.) s.**Wm.** Hev I *or* hes I ! hes ta, he, it ! hev we ! &c. (J.M.) **Yks.** You're not been wanting to go long, han yo ! GASKELL *Sylvia* (1863) I. xii. n.**Yks.** Ez-ta gitten the lesson off ! Weea hez te there ! (W.H.) ; Weea hez te there ! TWEDDELL *Clevl. Rhymes* (1875) 16 ; Hasta, has-thah, *or* hez theh ! hey-yah! (T.S.) ; n.**Yks.**[2] Hae ye hitten on yet ! 95. ne.**Yks.**[1] Ev ah ! es ta ! ez a ! A'e wá ! &c., 30. e.**Yks.** 'Ev ah ! 'ez thoo ! 'ez 'e, it ! 'ev *or* 'e we ! (R.S.) ; 'Ev ah ! 'es tá ! *or* a'e thoo ! 'es he, it ! a'e wá ! &c. (M.C.F.M.) ; e.**Yks.**[1] Hes-tă *or* hez-thă. w.**Yks.** Hezta gotten owt nice ! *Bradford Life*, 198 ; Evi ! eatə ! ezə ! e we ! WRIGHT *Gram. Wndhll.* (1892) 155; Ez oni on jə oni on jə ! (J.W.); Han yo ony moorweft ! (D.L.) ; An ye ! (S.P.U.) ; w.**Yks.**[1] Hasto ! Ha ye onny ! w.**Yks.**[2] Asta *or* astow ; w.**Yks.**[5] Hes tuh gotten that to-dǎay ! **Lan.** Hasta bin axin him for brass ! CLEGG *David's Loom*

(1894) i; Whatever hasto bin doin', lad! Waugh *Hermit Cobbler*, iii; Who hes! *ib. Heather* (ed. Milner) I. 90; Hanney fawn eawt withur, measter! Tim Bobbin *View Dial.* (ed. 1806) 16; An they been sellin' a mill! Hamerton *Wenderholme* (1869) lxiv; Lan.[1] Thae's never browt o' that lumber wi' thi', asto! ne.Lan. What han yo done wi' hira! Mather *Idylls* (1895) 221; Wots to gjetn! Ellis *ib.* 553. e.Lan.[1] se.Lan. Have aw! hast' *or* hasto! has he, it! han we! &c. (F.E.T.) s.Lan. Hanni! [have you!] Bamford *Dial.* (1854). I.Ma. Hev I! &c., throughout (E.G.). w.I.Ma. Hev oi, he, it! have thaa! hev we, thee! have yea! (G.K.) Chs.[1] Hasta! han yo! s.Chs.[1] Aas't bin! 90. Oo'u)z bin! *ib.* 66; Aaz 60 uurt ûr! [has she hurt herself!] *ib.* 69; Aan) yû! *ib.* 72. Stf. Wior æ bin! [where hast thou been!] Ellis *ib.* 478. n.Stf. Av oi! ast 6ei! as ei, it! an wei! &c. (T.C.W.) s.Stf. Han' I, we, yo', they! has 't! (G.T.L.) Der.[1] Hasto! [hast thou all !] Der.[2] Ha'n ! *pl.* Not. Hae yer got it! (J.H.B.) s.Not. Hev a *or* hae a! hasta! hes 'e, it! hev *or* hae we! &c. Hasta almost entirely addressed to children and fast dying out (J.P.K.). Lin. Wheer 'asta beän! Tennyson *N. Farmer, Old Style* (1864) st. 1. n.Lin. Es ta 't rääke! Es thî fayther gon' 6ôt! (J.P.F.); Hev I! Hes tâ *or* tha! hes he, it! hev wê! hev *or* ha' yê! hev *or* ha' thaay *or* th'! (M.P.); n.Lin.[1] Hast ta gotten thŷ dinner! Lei. Hev yu bin dheer! Am I! (C.E.); Lei.[1] Ow hev ye! Nhp.[1] What ha' ye got theere! Han y' got any 'taters! War.[2] Ha [hay] I, thee. he, we! &c. nw.War. 'Ave I, we, yo! 'As *or* a', 'e, it! (G.T.N.) s.War. An jo! Ellis *ib.* 487. m.Wor. Ave *or* 'a hi! 'ast *or* 'ast thou! ave 'e *or* a! ave 't! a 't! *pl.* Ave *or* a'! (H.K.) s.Wor. Hast! [hast thou !] Porson *Quaint Wds.* (1895) 7. Shr. An jo dun! Ellis *ib.* 476; Shr.[1] Have I! hast 'ee! has a! *pl.* han! *Gram. Outlines*, 59. Glo. Ha I, he, we! &c.: hast! (H.S.H.) Oxf. 'Av I! 'ast! 'ast thee! av a! av ee! *pl.* 'Av *or* a'! (A.P.); Wo's bin o düin! [what hast thou been doing!] Ellis *ib.* 196; Have it bin seen to! (G.O.); 'Ave ee! 'ave em! (M.R.) Cmb. 'Ave I! 'av ee! &c. (W.W.S.) Nrf. Hay you got the guy rope! Rye *Hist. Nrf.* (1885) xv. e.Nrf. Have he, it! ha' we! &c. (M.C.H.B.) Suf. Have he, that! (C.G.B.) e.Suf. Hêv he, it! (F.H.) Sur. What ah 'ee sent they hope ovĕr there fur! Bickley *Sur. Hills* (1890) I. i. Sus. Have ee [thou]! have he, it! (R.B.) w.Sus. Hev I, he, it, we! &c.; hes thee! (E.E.S.) n.Hmp. 'ave oi! 'ast a! 'ave 'e! 'ave un! 'ave we! 'ave 'e! 'ave they! (E.H.R.) Wil. Hast! [have you !] Slow *Gl.* (189a). n.Wil. Hast thee! have he, it! (E.H.G.). s.Wil. H've oi! hast thee! h've ee *or* her *or* ur! h've us! &c. (C.V.G.) Dor. 'v I a got! (H.J.M.) Som. Hæst dhi lukt! Ellis *ib.* 90. w.Som. Uv aay! us thee! uv uur! &c., Elworthy *Gram.* (1877) 58. n.Dev. Hev I! bast! hath a! hev us! &c. (R.P.C.); Av! [have you] got eni! Ellis *ib.* 160. Cor.[2] Hasta! w.Cor. Hast-ee *or* hav'-ee! sometimes hab'-ee! In com. use (M.A.C.).

iv. Interrogative Negative.

Sc. Havena I been telling ye! Scott *Midlothian* (1818) xviii. Cai.[1] Hivna I! hisna he! his'nt 'id! hivna we! &c. Abd. Haena *or* hivna I! &c. (G.W.) Frf. Hiv I no! his he no! his't no! hiv we, &c. no! hinna the man a hoose! hinna the men hooses! (J.B.) w.Frf., e.Per. Hçv 9 nô! hçs 'e nô! hçz 't nô! hçv wo, &c. nô! dçz 6ə man nô hê a hus! div 6ə men nô hê hooses! (W.A.C.) Raf. Hinna ye heard, man, o' Barrochan Jean! Tannahill *Poems* (1807) 204, ed. 1817. n.Ayr. Hae *or* hiv I not! his he not! hiv *or* hae we, &c. not! (J.F.) Wgt. Hivna, hinna, *or* haena I, we, you! &c.; his he na! his na he! (A.W.) Ant. Hae A no! haes he no! hae we, &c. no! (W.J.K.) Nhb. Hev aa not! [hevn't aa!] hez thoo not! [hezn't thoo!] hez 'ee not! [hezn't 'ee!] he' we, *or* not! [hevn't we, ye!] he' they not! [he'na they !] The pronoun is almost invariably used at the end of the phr., e. g. 'Hevn't aa!' (R.O.H.) e.Cum. Hevent ah! hement thoo, he, it! hevn't we! hevvent ya, thaey! (J.A.) s.Cum. Hev I, we, you, they, not! hez thou, he, it not! hev *or* hez not the men houses! (J.P.) n.Wm. Hevvant I! hezzant thoo, he, it! hevvant we! &c. Hezzant freq. used for the *pl.* 'hevvant,' e. g. 'Hezzant oor lads come!' (B.K.) s.Wm. Hevn't I *or* hesn't I! hes te nut *or* hesn'te! hes he nut *or* hesn't he! hes 't nut *or* hesn' 't! hevn't t'men! Also Hev I nut *or* hes I not! when emphasis is required (J.M.). n.Yks. Has'nt ah! (T.S.) e.Yks. 'Ain't ah! 'ezn't thoo, 'e, it! 'ain't we! &c. (R.S.); A'en't ah! a'en't *or* 'ean't thoo! 'esn't he, it! a'en't wa! &c. (M.C.F.M.) w.Yks. Evnt I! eznt ta! eznt 9! evnt wo! &c. (J.W.); w.Yks.[1] Hesn't he! hent! [has not!] Lan. Hannot yo yerd! Clegg *David's Loom* (1894) iii; Han tey not t'murrain! Kay-Shuttleworth *Scarsdale* (1860) I. 36. se.Lan. Hannot aw! hastno'! hasno' he! hanno' *or* hannot we! (F.E.T.) s.Lan. Hastono'! Bamford *Dial.* (1854); Havn't *or* hannot I! hastn't *or* hasn't to! hasn't he! hanna *or* hannot we! &c. (S.W.) I.Ma. Haven'

he got the tools to his hand! Brown *Doctor* (1887) 2; Hev'n I! &c. (E.G.) s.Chs.[1] Aan't! [haven't *or* hasn't !] 77. n.Stf. The gentry says 'hevn't you!'—the people about here says 'hanna yey!' Geo. Eliot *A. Bede* (1859) I. 19; Avno *or* ano oi! astno 6ei! asno *or* avo ei! ano wei! &c. (T.C.W.) s.Stf. Han't I, he, we! hasn't thee! (G.T.L.) s.Not. Hevn't *or* hain't a! hesn't a! hesn't *or* hain't e! hevn't *or* hain't we! &c. (J.P.K.) n.Lin. Ev'nt I, we! &c.; has'nt e! (J.P.F.); Hevn't *or* ha'n't I! hesn't thoo, he! hevn't *or* ha'n't we, thaay! (M.P.) s.Lin. Haent I! hesn't he! *pl.* hev (T.H.R.). Lei. Is'nt he! (C.E.) War.[2] Haint I, thee, he! harnt we! &c. nw.War. Ain't, arn't I! &c. (G.T.N.) m.Wor. 'An't I, thee! 'an't *or* 'aven't e! an't we! &c. (H.K.) w.Wor.[1] 'Anna I! 'astna thee! 'ant 'e, us! 'anna yû, thaay! *Introd.*, 26. Shr.[1] Hannad-I! has'na thee! hannad-a, 'e! hanna we, yo! hannad-a *or* they! *Gram. Outlines*, 59. Hrf.[2] Hanna ye! Glo. Han't I, he, we! &c.; hasn't thee! (H.S.H.) Oxf. Aint *or* ent I, thou! &c.; aint *or* ent we! &c. (G.O.); Aa'nt I! asn't! asn't thee! aa'nt ee! aa'nt us! &c. (A.P.) Cmb. 'Av'nt *or* ain't I! ain't 'e, we! &c. (W.W.S.) e.Nrf. Haint I! &c. (M.C.H.B.) Suf. Ha'nt I! &c. (C.G.B.) e.Suf. Haint he! haint it! (F.H.) w.Sus. Aint I! &c. (E.E.S.) Hmp. Haint you got it! (H.C.M.B) n.Hmp. 'aint 'oi! 'asnt 'a! 'aint 'e! 'asnt I ut! 'aint we! 'avn't 'e! 'aint they! (E.H.R.) n.Wil. Han't I! hassn't thee! han't he, we, they! hav'en ee! (E.H.G.) s.Wil. Harnt thee got nare on! *Monthly Mag.* (1814) II. 114; Ha'n't oi! hasn't thee! ha'n't her *or* ur, we! &c. (C.V.G.) Dor. Ha'nt I a got! (H.J.M.) Som. Han't er! *Monthly Mag.* (1814) II. 127. w.Som. Aa'n aay! as-n! aa'n ur! aa'n wee! Elworthy *Gram.* (1877) 58. n.Dev. Han't *or* heb'm I! hass'n! hath'n a! hant *or* heb'm us, ee' m, *or* nim! (R.P.C.) [Amer. Haint they cut a thunderin' swarth! Lowell *Biglow Papers* (1848) 45.]

2. Indicative Mood, Past Tense. i. Simple Affirmative.

Sc. Hæd. *Contracted*: Aa'd, yee'd, &c., Murray *Dial.* (1873) 219. Sh.I. I telt my midder da draem I haed, Spence *Flk-Lore* (1899) 241; Doo'd been helpin, *Sh. News* (Oct. 7, 1899); A body hed, *ib.*; Ye hed, *ib.*; William's folk 'id been, *ib.*; I wis noticed da shows, *ib.* (Dec. 16, 1899); They wis gotten a wab, *ib.* [For other uses of 'be' for 'have' see Be, VIII. 4.] Or.I. Ξ mûr hed fàn, Ellis *ib.* 79a. Cai.[1] I hid, he hid *or* he'd; we, &c. hid *or* 'd. Suf.[1] They hid a great aff-lat, 7. Abd. Ye hed me o' the steel, Alexander *Johnny Gibb* (1871) iv; A hid (A.W.). Frf. I, he, we, &c. hid (J.B.). w.Frf., e.Per. Ξ, 'e, we, &c. hed (W.A.C.). n.Ayr. I, he, we, &c. hud (J.F.). Rxb. Id [you had], Ellis *ib.* 714. Wgt. I hæed, hid, hed; thou'dst; he, we, &c. haed, hid, hed. Haen occurs (A.W.). Nhb. *Simple*: Ha'd, thou'dst, he'd, it id, we'd, &c. *Stressed* (rarely): Ha hed, thou hedst; he, it hed; we, &c. hed. In the stressed forms 'had,' 'hadst' are almost invariable, but 'hed' [*pron.* like head] is also heard (R.O.H.); The kinsman thìt Booz hid spok' on, Robson *Bk. Ruth* (1860) iv. 1. Cum. Sum thowt 'at ah'd chowkt'mesel, *Jos and Landlord*, 7; Cum.[1] Hed; Cum.[3] A queer hammer he hed wid him, 3; I'd tel't them me-sel, *ib.* 8. e.Cum. Ah, &c. hed (J.A.). n.Wm. I, &c. hed. Freq. abbreviated as Ah'd, thoo'd, &c. (B.K.) s.Wm. I hed, thou hedst *or* hed; he, we, &c. hed. Abbreviated forms also used, as 'I'd gitten' (J.M.). se.Yks.[1] Ah ed *or* ad; thoo ed, &c. *or* adst; he, we, &c. ed *or* ad, 30. e.Yks. Ah 'ed, thoo 'edst; he, we, &c. 'ed. 'Ad is often used instead of 'ed (M.C.F.M.); I, thoo, &c. 'ad *or* 'ed. The 'a' is the usual broad Holderness 'aa' (R.S.). m.Yks.[1] Aa ed *or* aad·; dhoo· ed, aad· *or* edst', adst·; ey, we, &c. ed· *or* aad·, *Introd.* 47. w.Yks. Ai, a, i ed *or* aid, ad, ed; 6ă, tă, tə ed *or* ăăd, tăd, tad; ï, ə əd *or* ïd, ad; wï, wə ed *or* wïd, wəd, Wright *Gram. Wndhll.* (189a) 155; Ardly hed Ah darken'd t'doar, Preston *Poems, &c.* (1864) 4; It ud been on t'table fer sum meyt, *Yksman.* (1888) 223; w.Yks.[1] Eed [I had]. Lan. Shou hed fill'd her brat, Harland & Wilkinson *Flk-Lore* (1867) 60; Yo hadden âm, Kay-Shuttleworth *Scarsdale* (1860) I. 61; Lan.[1] Wi'dd'n [we had], yo'dd'n, you'd [you had]. ne.Lan.[1] Hed. se.Lan. Aw'd; theawdst *or* theaw'd; he, we, &c. 'd (F.E.T.). s.Lan. Aw'd *or* aw had, thea'd *or* thea had; we'd *or* we had, they'd *or* they had (S.W.); Hadn [we had], Bamford *Dial.* (1854); Idd'n [you had] money (J.A.P.). I.Ma. I, thou, &c. hed (E.G.). w.I.Ma. Oi, &c. 'd (G.K.). s.Chs.[1] Oi'd; Chs.[23] Aw'd. s.Chs.[1] Ahy)d ů bin dhée-ŭr [I had (have) been there], 79; Dhaa aad·st, *ib.* 76; Wì)d lost ïm, *ib.* 135. n.Stf. Oi ad, 6ei adst; ei, we, &c. ad (T.C.W.). s.Stf. I'd, the'd'st; he, we, &c. 'd. They say 'used to ha' a house' instead of 'had a house' (G.T.L.). Der. We hadden to brussen thee wee, Howitt *Rur. Life* (1838) I. 150. nw.Der.[1] Ee'd [he had], *unemph.* s.Not. I, he, &c. hed *or* 'd (J.P.K.). n.Lin. I, &c. hed *or* 'd (M.P.); I, &c. ed (J.P.F.). s.Lin. Hed in each case, *sing.* and *pl.* (T.H.R.). Lei.[1] I hed; *unemph.* I'd, 30. War.[2] I'd, thee'dst, he'd, it 'ud; we, &c. 'd.

nw.War. I, yo', &c. 'd, 'ad (G.T.N.). m.Wor. I 'ad; thou 'adst, 'dst ; he, we, &c. 'ad (H.K.). w.Wor.¹ I 'ad, thee 'adst ; e, us, &c. 'ad, *Introd.* ᵆ6. s.Wal. She wass not marry [had not married] him, *Longman's Mag.* (Dec. 1899) 147. Shr.¹ I'd ; thee had'st ; A'd, 'e'd, ᵒr 'er'd ; we, yo, a, ᵒr they hadden, *Gram. Outlines*, 58. Glo. I'd ; theeudst ; he, we, &c. 'd (H.S.H.). Oxf. I'd ; thou'dst ; he, we, &c. 'd (G.O.) ; I 'ad ; thee adst, th' adst ; ee 'ad ; we, &c. 'ad (A.P.). Brks.¹ A'd tell I wher a'd a-bin. Cmb. I'd, 'e'd, that 'ad, that 'd (W.W.S.). **Ess.** He h'd (H.H.M.). w.Sus. I hed, thee hedst ; he, we, &c. hed (E.E.S.). n.Hmp. Oi 'ad, thou 'adst ; we, &c. 'ad ; the man 'ad a 'ouse (E.H.R.). Wil. Hæd, Ellis *ib.* 48. n.Wil. I'd, thee had, he'd, we'd (E.H.G.). s.Wil. Oi'd, theed'st, her'd ᵒr ur'd ; us, &c. 'd (C.V.G.). Dor. I'd, thou'dst ; he, &c. 'd, Barnes *Gl.* (1863) 25 ; Chad [I had¹, Haynes *Voc.* (c. 1730) in *N. & Q.* (1883) 6th S. vii. 366. Som. 'Ch'ad [I had], W. & J. *Gl.* (1873). w.Som. Aay-d ᵒr aay ad¹, dhee-ds ᵒr dhee ad·s, dhai-d ᵒr dhai ad¹, Elworthy *Gram.* (1877) 58. n.Dev. Chad [I had] et in my meend, *Exm. Scold.* (1746) l. 244 ; I, thee, he'd ; I'ad [it had¹; us 'ad ; you, they 'd ; the men 'ad a-got 'ouzes (R.P.C.). Cor. I'd ben killed, Forfar *Pentowan* (1889) i ; Cor.² I haad, thee haad ᵒr theed, thay haad. w.Cor. Hîd sîd [he had seen] ; wi hæd, Ellis *ib.* 172. [Amer. All the mischief hed been done, Lowell *Biglow Papers* (1848) 29.]

ii. Simple Negative.

Sc. She hadna ridden half thro' the town Jamieson *Pop. Ballads* (1806) I. 70 ; Hædna, Murray *Dial.* (1873) 219. Cai.¹ I, he, &c. hidna. Bnff.¹ A'hidna hid some rumgumshion (s.v. Gulliegaw). Abd. I, &c. hadna ᵒr hidna (G.W.) ; She hedna a pig teem, Alexander *Johnny Gibb* (1871) vi. Frf. I, &c. hidna (J.B.). w.Frf., e.Per. 3 &c. hędnâ (W.A.C.). n.Ayr. I, &c. hudnae (J.F.). Wgt. I, he, &c. hidna, haedna, hedna ; thou'dst not (A.W.). Ant. A, &c. hadnae (W.J.K.). Nhb. *Simple :* Thoo hadn't ; stressed : Aa, thoo, &c. 'd not. Ah hadna tell'd (R.O.H.). Cum.¹ Hednt ; Cum.⁴ I hedn't woak't far, 4. e.Cum. Ah, &c. heddent (J.A.). s.Cum. I, &c. hed not (J.P.). n.Wm. I, &c. heddant (B.K.). s.Wm. I, &c. hedn't (J.P.). n.Yks. Ah haddent patience wiv em, Tweddell *Clevel. Rhymes* (1875) 49 ; Thaddent been for her, *ib.* 24. e.Yks. I, &c. 'adnt ᵒr 'ednt (R.S.) ; Ah, &c. 'ed nut (M.C.F.M.). w.Yks. Two .. hedn't t'chonce, Binns *Orig.* (1889) No. i. 3 ; A ednt (J.W.) ; w.Yks.⁵ Hen't owt to du. se.Lan. Aw hadno', theaw hadstno' ᵒr hadno' ; he, &c. hadno' (F.E.T.). s.Lan. Aw hadno ; he, we, &c. hadna ᵒr 'd not (S.W.). I.Ma. I, &c. hed'n (E.G.). Chs.¹ Hadna. s.Chs.¹ Dhaa aad·s)nû [thou hadst not], 78. n.Stf. Oi adno, ðei adstno ; el, we, &c. adna (T.C.W.). s.Not. I, &c. hedn't (J.P.K.). n.Lin. I, &c. hedn't (M.P.) ; I, &c. ednt (J.P.F.). s.Lin. I, &c. hedn't (T.H.R.). War.³ I, &c. haddunt. We hadna gone more than a mile. nw.War. I, &c. 'adn't (G.T.N.). m.Wor. A adn't, thee adn'st ; he ᵒr us, &c. adn't (H.K.). w.Wor.¹ I'adna, thee 'adstna, 'e 'adna ; us, &c. 'adna ᵒr adn't, *Introd.* ᵆ6. Shr.¹ I hadna, thee hadsna, we hadna, *Gram. Outlines*, 58. Glo. Theeusn't (H.S.H.). Oxf. I, &c. 'adn't ; th' men aan't got no ouzen (A.P.). Cmb. I, &c. 'adn't (W.W.S.). Ess. I hent (H H M.) ; Ess.¹ Hant. n.Ken. Shî sed'nt, Ellis *ib.* 138. Sur. We hadna forgot it, Bickley *Sur. Hills* (1890) I. iv. w.Sus. I hed'nt, thee had'nst ; he, we, &c. hed'nt (E.E.S.). n.Hmp. Oi 'adnt, thou 'adnst ; e, we, &c. 'adnt (E.H.R.). n.Wil. I had'n (E.H.G.). s.Wil. Theeds't not (C.V.G.). Som. I hadden a-pearted vrom um long, Baynes *Sng. Sol.* (1860) iii. 4. w.Som. Aay ad·n, dhai ad·n, Elworthy *Gram.* (1877) 59. n.Dev. I, &c. had'n (R.P.C.).

iii. Simple Interrogative.

Cai.¹ Hid I ? &c. Frf. Hid I ? &c. (J.B.) w.Frf., e.Per. Hęd ᵊ ? &c. (W.A.C.). n.Ayr. Hud I ? &c. (J.F.) Wgt. Haed, hid, hed I ? &c. (A W.) Nhb. Hadsta ? (R.O.H.) c.Cum. Hed ah ? &c. (J.A.) n.Wm. Hed I ? &c. (B.K.) s.Wm. Hed I ? hedst' te ᵒr hed te ? hed he ? &c. (J.M.) n.Yks. Hed he been fallin' oot wi' onny-body ? Tweddell *Clevel. Rhymes* (1875) 84, ed. 1892. e.Yks. 'Ad ah ? &c. (R.S.) ; 'Ed ah ? &c. (M.C.F.M.). w.Yks. Edi ? edwa ? Wright *Gram. Wndhll.* (1892) 155. Lan. What ud becomn o' thee ? Brierley *Layrock* (1864) vi. se.Lan. Hadst ᵒr hadsto ? (F.E.T.). I.Ma. Hed I ? &c. (E.G.) n.Stf. Ad oi ? adst thei ? ad ei ? &c. (T.C.W.) s.Not. Hed a ? &c. (J.P.K.) n.Lin. Ed I ? &c. (J.P.F.) ; Hed I ? hed thâ ? hed he ? hed hê ? &c. (M.P.) s.Lin. Hed I ? &c. (T.H.R.) nw.War. 'Ad I ? &c. (G.T.N.) m.Wor. Ad I ? adst thee ? ad he ? &c. (H.K.) Shr.¹ Hadden we ? *Gram. Outlines*, 59. Oxf. 'Ad I ? adst ? adst thee ? 'ad ee ? &c. (A.P.) Cmb. 'Ad I ? &c. (W.W.S.) w.Sus. Hed I ? hedst thee ? had un ? &c. (E.E.S.) n.Hmp. 'ad 'oi ? 'adst' a ? 'ad 'e ? &c. (E.H.R.) I.W.¹ How many had'st got ? s.Wil. H'd oi ? h'dst thee ? h'd her ᵒr ur ? &c. (C.V.G.) w.Som. Ud aay ? ud-s dhee ? ud yùe ? Elworthy *Gram.* (1877) 59. Dev. Hadda [had he] ? White *Cyman's Conductor* (1701) 127.

iv. Interrogative Negative.

Sh.I. Wir ye haed na maet frae ye got your brakwist ? *Sh. News* (Dec. 9, 1899). [For other uses of 'be' for 'have' see Be, VIII. 4.] Cai.¹ Hid'nt I ? &c. Abd. Hedna I ? &c. (G.W.) Frf. Hid I no ? &c. (J.B.) w.Frf., e.Per. Hęd ᵊ no ? &c. (W.A.C.) n.Ayr. Hud I not ? &c. (J.F.) Wgt. Haed I no ? haed na I ? &c. (A.W.) Nhb. Hadsta not ? (R.O.H.) Cum.¹ Hednt ? c.Cum. Heddent ah ? &c. (J.A.) s.Cum. Hed I not ? &c. (J.P.) s.Wm. Heddant I ? &c. (B.K.) s.Wm. Hed I nut ᵒr hedn't I ? &c. (J.M.) e.Yks. 'Edn't ah ? &c. (M.C.F.M.) ; 'Adnt ah ? &c. (R.S.) w.Yks. Ednt i ? ednt ta ? ednt wa ? (J.W.) se.Lan. Hadno' aw ? hadstno'? hadno' he ? &c. (F.E.T.) w.I.Ma. Hed'n oi ? &c. (G.K.) n.Stf. Adnə oi ? adstnə ðei ? adnə ei ? &c. (T.C.W.) s.Stf. Hadn't thee ? (G.T.L.) s.Not. Hedn't a ? &c. (J.P.K.) n.Lin. Hedn't I ? &c. (M.P.) ; Ed'nt I ? &c. (J.P.K.) s.Lin. Hedn't I to'd you how it 'ud be ? Hedn't they it back i' the'r oên coin ? (T.H.R.) War.⁵ Haddunt I ? &c. nw.War. 'Adn't I ? &c. (G.T.N.) m.Wor. Adn't I ? &c. (H.K.) w.Wor.¹ 'Adna I ? 'adna ᵒr 'adstna thee ? 'adna 'e ? 'adna ᵒr 'adn't us ? 'adstna yû ? 'adna thay ? *Introd.* ᵆ6. Shr.¹ Hadnad I ? had'sna thee ? hadna we ? hadnad-a ? ᵒr hadna they ? *Gram. Outlines*, 59. Glo. Hadn'tst? (H.S.H.) Oxf. 'Adn't I ? 'adnst thee ? 'adn't ee ? &c. (A.P.) Cmb. 'Adn't I ? &c. (W.W.S.) w.Sus. Hed'nt I ? hed'nst thee ? had'nt-un ? hed we, ye not ? hed'nt they ? (E.E.S.) n.Hmp. 'Adn't oi ? 'adn'st a ? 'adn't 'e ? &c. (E.H.R.) n.Wil. Had'n I ? &c. (E.H.G.) s.Wil. H'dn't oi ? hadden th' man got nar a house ? (C.V.G.) Som. Had'n er ? *Monthly Mag.* (1814) 127. w.Som. Ad·n aay ? Elworthy *Gram.* (1877) 59. n.Dev. Had'n I ? &c. (R.P.C.)

3. Imperative Mood, Affirmative and Negative.

Sc. Hæ ᵒr hæv, Murray *Dial.* (1873) 219. Sh.I. Hae, *Sh. News* (Dec. 16, 1899). Abd. *neg.* Let na him ha'e, let's no hae, hinna ye (G.W.). Frf. Hae, *neg.* dinna hae, dinna lat 'm hae ᵒr lat 'm no hae (J.B.). w.Frf., e.Per. Hê, *neg.* danâ hê. The imperative 'he' is only used in handing a thing to a person. Otherwise 'tak' would be employed. The negative (danâ hê) is used more freely, but here also 'danâ tak' would often be substituted (W.A.C.). n.Ayr. Hae ᵒr hiv (J.F.). Wgt. Hae, *neg.* dunna hae, hiv (A.W.). Ant. Hae you, *neg.* hae nae (W.J.K.). Nhb. He' ᵒr hev, *neg.* henna ᵒr hennot, let 'm not he' ᵒr hev, henna ye (R.O.H.). c.Cum. Hev, *neg.* dooant hev, dooant you hev (J.A.). s.Cum. Hev (J.P.). s.Wm. Heve, *neg. sg.* hevvant, *pl.* heve ᵒr hevvant (B.K.). s.Wm. Thoo hev, ye hev ᵒr hev ye (J.M.). ne.Yks.¹ Ev ᵒr a'e. e.Yks. Ev, *neg.* dawn't ev (R.S.) ; Ev ᵒr a'e, *neg.* 'ev nut ᵒr a'e nut (M.C.F.M.) ; e.Yks.¹ He't [have it]. m.Yks.¹ Ev. w.Yks. Ev əm [have them], et [have it] (J.W.) ; w.Yks.¹ Hab at him, ii. 305. Lan.¹ God a mercy ! I. se.Lan. Ha', *neg.* dunno' (ᵒr dunnot) ha' (F.E.T.). I.Ma. Hev, *neg.* dunt hev ; dunt lerr-us hev (E.G.). n.Stf. Av, *neg.* donə av, donə you av (T.C.W.). s.Stf. Han thee, han yo, *neg.* do have, han't yo' (G.T.L.). s.Not. Hev ᵒr hae, *neg.* don't hev ᵒr hae (J.P.K.). n.Lin. Hev ᵒr ha', *neg.* dôan't hev ᵒr ha' noâ ᵒr hev noâ (M.P.). n.Lin.¹ A', I. s.Lin. Hev (T.H.R.). War.³ Ha [hay], *neg.* harnt thee, harnt yu. nw.War. 'Ave, *neg.* 'a' no. Don't yo 'ave (G.T.N.). m.Wor. A, *neg.* don't a (H.K.). w.Wor.¹ Adna oi. Glo. Ha, *neg.* don't ha (H.S.H.). Oxf. Ha' done (G.O.) ; Ast, as't thee, 'av ee, 'av you ; *neg. sg.* asn't, aan't thee, *pl.* aan't ee (A.P.). Brks.¹ Hev thee ᵒr do thee hev. e.Nrf. Do you have, *neg.* don't you have (M.C.H.B.). Sur. Ha'e some now, sir, Bickley *Sur. Hills* (1890) III. xvi. w.Sus. Hev, *neg.* hev nout ᵒr none (E.E.S.). Hmp.¹ U' dun [have done], I. n.Hmp. Hast 'a, hav 'e (E.H.R.). I.W.¹ A done [u' dun·]! n.Wil. Ha', *neg.* dwont ee ha ! (E.H.G.) s.Wil. Hant 'e (C.V.G.). w.Som. Aa·û sau·m aay tuul·êe [have some I tell thee], Elworthy *Gram.* (1877) 60. n.Dev. Ha ! *neg.* don't ee ha ! (R.P.C.) w.Dev.¹ Hab. [The 3rd pers. *sg.* and 1st and 3rd pers. *pl.* are formed with 'Let' and the *inf.* (q.v.) as in lit. English.]

4. Infinitive Mood.   i. Present.

Sc. Hæ ᵒr hæv, Murray *Dial.* (1873) 219 ; Haif, Gross (1790) *MS. add.* (C.) Sh.I. I could a haind my trouble, *Sh. News* (July 2, 1898) ; May he hae, *ib.* (Dec. 7, 1899). Cai.¹ Hiv ᵒr hae. Bnff. He, Ellis *ib.* 779 ; Buff.¹ A 'wid like t'hae an attle at it, 8. Abd. Dher wod ə bin, Ellis *ib.* 771 ; Wha is to ha'e the lad, Shirrefs *Poems* (1790) 32. Frf. Hae (J.B.). w.Frf., e.Per. To hê (W.A.C.). Ayr. Hêv ᵒr hiv, he ᵒr hî, Ellis *ib.* 742. n.Ayr. Hae ᵒr hiv (J.F.). Edb. What wad a sens'd your waefu' warblin's better, Learmont *Poems* (1791) 218. Rxb. Hæv, Ellis *ib.* 316. Wgt. Hae (A.W.). N.I.¹ Ha' (s.v. Haen). Ant. Hae (W.J.K.). n.Cy. Haigh (Hall.). Nhb. Else how wad aw heh been heer, Bewick *Tyneside Tales* (1850) 15 ; Ye should ha' keept him here to lade, Clare *Love of Lass* (1890) I. 7 ; As a verb transitive there is a carefully marked distinction between 'he' [heh] and 'hev' ; the former being used only before a consonant or the semi-vowels *y* and *w*; the latter most commonly before a vowel. ' Ye may be this or he what ye like; but if ye hev ony gumption, or hev a care for yorsel, ye'll let them abee' (R.O.H.); He'd [have it]; he' ta [have to], sometimes hev ta *or* hefta, *ib.*; Nhb.¹ He, heh, hae, hev. As an auxiliary verb, 'have' is *gen.* shortened to a mere *v* sound : ' Aa've been there.' When emphasis is required the aspirated form is used. —Hev, the emphatic form of the verb 'have.' Used also when the word following begins with an open vowel or *h* mute, *ib.* Dur.¹ Hev. Cum. Tha mud ha thout reet, *Borrowdale Lett. in Lonsdale Mag.* (Feb. 1867) 312 ; Cum.¹ Ha', hay, hev ; Cum.³ Does té think I'd ha'e thee, than ! 40. Wm. Ah'll hey the noo (F.P.T.); Yan mud ha thought, WHITEHEAD *Leg.* (1859) 13 ; T'mistress . . . sed a mud hae mi poddish, *Spec. Dial.* (1885) pt. iii. 5. n.Wm. Hev (B.K.). s.Wm. Hev (J.M.). n.Yks. What misery ya'll ha' te bahd, TWEDDELL *Clevel. Rhymes* (1875) 55 ; Will thah he' mah ! *ib.* 85 ; Our awd man 'ell be seeaf te hea t'kettle aboil, *ib.* 39 ; He'l etta [have to] du 't. He'l evta [have to] gan (W.H.); n.Yks.¹ Thou s' ha'e, *Pref.* 42 ; n.Yks.² Hev *or* hae. ne.Yks.¹ Ti a'e *or* ev. e.Yks. *Gen.* speaking 'ev is used before a vowel and a'e before a consonant. Thoo'll ev it. Thoo'll ae ti cum. Before *y* a'e is *gen.* used (M.C.F.M.) ; e.Yks.¹ He' is used before consonants ; before vowels it becomes 'hev.' m.Yks.¹ Tu' ev. w.Yks. Ev, e, weak form ɒv, ə, WRIGHT *Gram. Wndhll.* (1892) 154 ; Very com. It was one of the very best things which could of happened (M.F.); I mun he' thah, HOWSON *Cur. Craven* (1850) 116 ; It 'ud ha' taen a duzzen on us, CUDWORTH *Dial.-Sketches* (1884) 2 ; He'd hetta [have to] cum ageean, *ib.* 98 ; w.Yks.¹ Hab, hae, hay, hey, hev ; hett *or* hay 't [have it] ; witto hett ! w.Yks.⁵ Witta he't to morn ! Lan. Oi'll hae nae moor loives to anser for, KAY-SHUTTLEWORTH *Scarsdale* (1860) II. 300 ; Haigh *or* hay, WILBRAHAM *Gl.* (1826) ; Let's hev a look, BANKS *Manch. Man* (1876) ii ; As luck wou'd height, TIM BOBBIN *View Dial.* (ed. 1806) 18 ; I'll heyt too, *ib.* 48 ; I wadn't hetha [have thee] to try, EAVESDROPPER *Vill. Life* (1869) 21. n.Lan.¹ I'd 'a geen my silver watch. ne.Lan.¹ Ha. e.Lan.¹ Ha, used before consonants. se.Lan. Hae. The common form before a consonant, but before a vowel, especially 'a,' the word 'have' is frequently used, as : ' Aw'll ha' mi dinner,' ' Aw'll have a pint ov ale' (F.E.T.). I.Ma. It'd ha' puzzled him to do that, BROWN *Yarns* (1881) 206, ed. 1889. w.I.Ma. Hev (G.K.). Chs.¹ Oi'd a gen im a clout, 1 ; Chs.³ Hay *or* haigh. s.Chs.¹ Yǒ)n aa góòǔ [Yǒ'n ha' gooa]. Chiefly used before consonants in preference to aav'.—Tǒ̀ aav· dhǔr tóòth drau·n, *ib.* 79. n.Stf. Av (T.C.W.). e.Stf. È, ELLIS *ib.* 444. s.Stf. Ha [have] has a broad ' aa ' sound between ' eh ' and ' her,' but no distinct equivalent [G.T.L.). Der. Av, ELLIS *ib.* 324; Der.¹ Wil·t ae' ǔ dlass' ǔ jin'? [Wilt ha a glass o' gin ?] Der.² I'll ha' it (s.v. Rap-ring). nw.Der.¹ Wil't he't *or* he' it? Not. Har (L.C.M.). s.Not. (H)ə, hev, but (h)ei when emphatic (J.P.K.) ; Who'd ha' thought it? PRIOR *Renie* (1895) 306. Rut. Ev, ELLIS *ib.* 256. Lin.¹ Hev. n.Lin. Ev (J.P.F.) ; n.Lin.¹ Hev. s.Lin. Id a [he would have], ELLIS *ib.* 298. Lei. Ê, e, ev, ELLIS *ib.* 489 ; Lei.¹ Han. Nhp. Ev, ELLIS *ib.* 254 ; Nhp.¹ Ha't *or* het [have it] ; Nhp.² Har. War.¹ A unemphatic form ; War.² Ha ; War.³ You shall hev it to play with. Let's ha [hay] it. nw.War. Ave (G.T.N.). m.Wor. A' *or* 'av (H.K.). Shr.¹ I shall a, *Gram. Outlines*, 58. Hrf. To av, ELLIS *ib.* 177. s.Wal. She'd a died, *Longman's Mag.* (Dec. 1899) 144. Glo. To s, ELLIS *ib.* 66; Abben *or* hab, *Gl.* (1851) ; Glo.² Hae, 10. Oxf. It must ha' bin layin' here all the time (G.O.) ; Oxf.¹ H'at [have it], *MS. add.* Brks.¹ Ha, 2. Brks.² Hev, *or* ev, *ib.* 190. Bdf. Ă, *ib.* 209. Hrt. Æv *or* ev, *ib.* 199. Nrf. Hev, *ib.* 264 ; He shan't bet [have it] any longer (W.W.S.) ; He'd a jabbed my eyes out, EMERSON *Birds* (ed. 1895) 205. Suf. The final *v* is often dropped. He mah'nt do as he hè done. You shan't het [have it] (C.T.) ; Suf.¹ Yow mought as well 'a dunt, 3. e.Suf. Hev (F.H.). Ess. He may ha, *or* hev, wished to see 't (H.H.M.); Ess.¹ Ha, hev, heve ; Ha' at [have it], *ib.* Sur. I shall ha' a pain, BICKLEY *Sur. Hills* (1890) I. 1 ; A regular pension at once loike we used to 'un, *ib.* viii. w.Sus. Hev, *unemph.* 'a (E.E.S.). Hmp. Heəv, ELLIS *ib.* 104. n.Hmp. Ave (E.H.R.). I.W. Squire Rickman 'll hae a powerful weight of hay, GRAY *Annesley* (1889) II. 122; I.W.¹ I'll hey zum on't ; I.W.² Let's hay't. Wil. To hè, ELLIS *ib.* 49 ; Wil.¹ Hae. n.Wil. Ye . . . must haā a thousan', KITE *Sng. Sol.* (1860) viii. 12 ; Ha (E.H.G.). Dor. Hou se [How are you] going haven [have it] cooked, John ! *Flk-Lore Rec.* (1880) VIII. pt. i. 111. Som. Ev, ELLIS *ib.* 90. w.Som.¹ U ; ae·u, *or* hae·u, emph. ; aa *or* haa emph. before negative. The *v* is only sounded before a vowel—and not always even then. I'ont [u] ha none o' this yer nonsense. Dev. Thee may 'av loved, SALMON *Ballads* (1899) 63; Dawnt 'ă' nort tǔ zay tǔ thickee slammicking gert haggage ! HEWETT *Peas. Sp.* (1892). n.Dev. Ae'n [ha'] (R.P.C.);

To ǣ, ELLIS *ib.* 161. w.Cor. Hæv, *ib.* 173 ; I c'd hav *or* ha', done et for ee (M.A.C.).

ii. Past. See II. 1.

Sc. It wad a tane thee *or* ony body to hane them greed again, GRAHAM *Writings* (1883) II. 9. Bch. An' wad hae gien twice forty pennies to had the gowan ouer my feet again, FORBES *Jrn.* (1742) 15. Slg. Katie's mither should haen meal, Yet fient a bag cam' near, TOWERS *Poems* (1885) 173. Ayr. The shop-hander wou'd ha'en her to tak' some new-fangled thing, AINSLIE *Land of Burns* (ed. 1892) 152. w.Yks. Ai out tə ed it dun bi nā (J.W.).

5. Participles. i. Present.

Sc. Hæan', hævan', MURRAY *Dial.* (1873) 219. Sh.I. Folk is haein', *Sh. News* (Dec. 16, 1899). Cai.¹ Hivan. The *prp.* is in 'an' and the *vbl. sb.* in 'in.' This distinction is clear in Cai. but gets confused in the counties across the Moray Firth. Abd. Haein (G.W.). Frf. What's the use o' their haeing a policeman ! BARRIE *Minister* (1891) iv. w.Frf., e.Per. He'an (W.A.C.). n.Ayr. Haein (J.F.). Lnk. Ye're no worth the ha'en for't a', THOMSON *Musings* (1881) 45. Dmf. At haeing tae haud on by the Laird as weel, THOM *Jock o' Knowe* (1878) 14. Wgt. Hae-in (A.W.). Ant. Haeen (W.J.K.). Nhb. He'vin (R.O.H.). Dur. My mother hevin' gi'en to Aucklan' Flooer Show, EGGLESTONE *Betty Podkin's Visit* (1877) 3. c.Cum. Hevn (J.A.). s.Cum. Hevin (J.P.). n.Wm. Hevven (B.K.). s.Wm. Heven (J.M.). n.Yks.² Hevving. ne.Yks.¹ Evvin. e.Yks. Evvin (M.C.F.M.). m.Yks.¹ Evin. w.Yks. Ah intend hevvin' a reyt ride aht, BINNS *Orig.* (1889) 4 ; Hevin (S.K.C.) ; Evin, WRIGHT *Gram. Wndhll.* (1892) 155. se.Lan. Havvin (F.E.T.). s.Lan. Havin (S.W.). I.Ma. It's gud hevin' the pockat full. It's gud dhè be hevin' (E.G.). w.I.Ma. Hev'n (G.K.). Chs.¹ Hebbon ; Chs.³ He's not much worth hebbon. n.Stf. Avin (T.C.W.). s.Not. Hevin (J.P.K.). n.Lin. Evin (J.P.F.) ; Hevin (M.P.). s.Lin. Evin (T.H.H.). War.³ He'in. nw.War. Avin, a-avin (G.T.N.). m.Wor. Avin (H.K.). Brks.¹ A-hevin'. e.Suf. Hevin (F.H.). w.Sus. Heven (E.E.S.). n.Hmp. 'Aven (E.H.R.). n.Wil. Havin (E.H.G.). n.Dev. Ha'-in' (R.P.C.).

ii. Past.

Sc. Hæed, MURRAY *Dial.* (1873) 219 ; Haen (JAM.). Sh.I. A'm hed, *Sh. News* (Dec. 16, 1899) ; If I hed hedden da laer an' fine wirds o' some graand learned man, STEWART *Tales* (1892) 261. Cai.¹ Hid. Bnff.¹ A hidna hid (s.v. Gulliegaw). Abd. Hed (G.W.) ; I've haen to flit afore noo, ALEXANDER *Johnny Gibb* (1871) xxvi. Frf. You'd haen but sma' cause to laugh, SANDS *Poems* (1833) 87. w.Frf., e.Per. Hèn (W.A.C.). Per. I'se haen the run o' a lad, *Sandy Scott* (1897) 18. Ayr. That fain wad a haen him, BURNS *There's a Youth*, st. 2. n.Ayr. Haed (J.F.). Lnk. That leg or this micht ha'e ha'en the gout, THOMSON *Leddy May* (1883) 103. Dmf. I might a ha'en a wife, SHENNAN *Tales* (1891) 62. Wgt. Haed and haen (A.W.). N.I.¹ I should ha' haen them things home in the cart. Nhb. Haven't Ah hed eneugh from her? CLARE *Love of Lass* (1890) I. 107 ; He'd hadden the same trouble. He'd a heven a litter o' yits six (R.O.H.). Cum.¹ Hed, *Pref.* 10. n.Wm. We hed hed oor tea (B.K.). s.Wm. Hed (J.M.). ne.Yks.¹ Ed *or* ad. e.Yks. Hed (M.C.F.M.). m.Yks.¹ Ed *or* aad. w.Yks. I wish we could 'a' hadden Mr. B. 'ere to-neght (F.P.T.) ; The barn hasn't had a door to it for the last twelve month, *Flk-Lore Jrn.* (1883) I. 379 ; Ed, əd, d, WRIGHT *Gram. Wndhll.* (1892) 155. Lan. We'n hed a tidy time on't, HARLAND *Lyrics* (1866) 304. ne.Lan.¹ Hedden. w.I.Ma. Hed (G.K.). n.Stf. Ad (T.C.W.). s.Not. Hed (J.P.K.). n.Lin. Ed (J.P.F.) ; Hed (M.P.). s.Lin. (T.H.H.) War. Hed (E.S.). m.Wor. 'Ad (H.K.). Shr.¹ Ad, *Gram. Outlines*, 58. Brks.⁵ A-had. w.Sus. Hed (E.E.S.). n.Dev. Ad (R.P.C.).

II. Idiomatic uses. 1. Cases in which *have* is omitted. See L 4. ii.

Sh.I. Da sam' as hit been [as if it had been] gruul, *Sh. News* (Dec. 16, 1899) ; If I'd kent you, I'd [I should have] slippid da eggs i' da tae-kettle, *ib.* (Oct. 7, 1899) ; Da clock been dumb [The clock has been dumb], *ib.* Edb. If her ye'd gien a Hawick gill, She might been leal, LIDDLE *Poems* (1821) 29. e.Yks.¹ The auxiliary ' have ' is freq. omitted, as ' Ah fun ' for ' Ah've fun,' 7. w.Yks. A faiv on əm [I have five of them] ; ðe guən uəm [they have gone home] ; wi or wə funt [we have found it], but wi or wə fant [we found it], WRIGHT *Gram. Wndhll.* (1892) 154.

2. *Have* used redundantly.

e.Yks.¹ If he'd he' geean. w.Yks. (J.W.) War.² Sometimes redundant, as ' If I'd ha' sin [seen] him, I'd ha' gin him a piece o' my mind.' Suf. If he hadn't ha' hit he harder than what he did (C.G.B.).

3. Followed by a direct object and *pp.* : see below.

Ir.¹ ' I am sorry I have kept your book so long.' ' It is no matter: I had it read.' That woman has me annoyed. She has my heart broke (G.M.H.).

N 2

4. *Have* used for *be.*

Rut.[1] Has is often used where we should use 'is.' Lei.[1] Both as a substantive and auxiliary verb. Yo've a loyar [you are a liar]. Whoy, oi hevn't. Well, an' ou hev ye? Oi hevn't not quoite so well to-dee, 21. Sur. What ah'ee sent they hops over there fur, if it hanna to make good aäle wi'? BICKLEY *Sur. Hills* (1890) I. i.

5. *Had* used instead of *would.*

I.Ma. Nelly had ha' took and went over the mountains like a shot, BROWN *Yarns* (1881) 276, ed. 1889.

III. Dial. uses. **1.** *v.* In *comb.* with *prep.*, *adv.*, &c. (1) *to have agean*, to have objections to, be opposed to ; (2) — *at* or *hab-at*, to attack, assail ; *fig.* to set to, to go at any-thing, to undertake vigorously ; (3) — *off*, to have know-ledge of, be acquainted with, to learn ; (4) — *on*, to make fun of, chaff, tease, to deceive in order to make fun of ; (5) — *over*, (*a*) to transmit, transfer ; (*b*) to discuss the character of, to talk over.

(1) w.Yks. What hes tu agean drinking? SNOWDEN *Web of Weaver* (1896) iv. (2) Edb. As lang as I can wag my wing I will have at you wi' my sting, CRAWFORD *Poems* (1798) 57 ; Wi' ram-race we'll ha'e at them, GLASS *Cal. Parnassus* (1812) 42. Cum.[1] A mower said to his grass, 'Tea and whay a feckless day! An' will n't pay I'll bet a crown ; But beef and breid, hev at thy heid, An good strang yal, an' I'll awash thee down.' w.Yks.[1] Brks.[1] I me-ans to hev at killin' down thaay rabbuts avoor long, see me a-yettin all the young kern. Sur.[1] We'll have at that job next. (3) Cum. He hes mair off ner many an oalden, GWORDIE GREENUP *Yance a Year* (1873) 9 ; Wo' betide ... yan 'at hedn't his tasks off, FARRALL *Betty Wilson* (1886) 35 ; He'd nobbet a single letter off, SILPHEO *Billy Brannan* (1885) 4. Wm. Willie ... hed a gae bit off, fer he went tel skooal tel t'maester sed he cud laarn him neea fardther, *Spec. Dial.* (1880) pt. ii. 3. (4) w.Yks. Aw've known chaps 'at's tell'd ther wives things abaat thersen just to have 'em on a bit, HARTLEY *Clock Alm.* (1896) 25 ; Don't believe 'em, they're nobbut hevin' tha on (S.K.C.) ; w.Yks.[2] ; w.Yks.[5] 'They are nobbut having him on.' Sometimes they say, 'having him on for the mug,' the meaning of the last words of which is not quite clear. Lan. It looks as if somebuddy wur havin me on, STATON *Loominary* (c. 1861) 117. ne.Lan. I were nobbut hevin' her on a bit, MATHER *Idylls* (1895) 46. s.Not. I took no notice ; I saw he was only trying to have me on (J.P.K.). Colloq. (A.B.C.) (5, *a*) Abd. The rental was given up by virtue of ilk heritor's oath ... and had over by Mr. Thomas Gordon ... to the Master of Forbes' lodging, SPALDING *Hist. Sc.* (1792) I. 254 (JAM.). (*b*) Oxf. They've been having you over finely at the meeting to-night (G.O.).

2. Phr. (1) *have a care of us*, an exclamation of surprise ; (2) — *done* or *a-done*, cease, stop, be quiet ; (3) *to have a come*, to go by, pass ; (4) — *as lief*, to have as soon, as willingly ; (5) — *drink*, to be slightly intoxicated but not drunk ; (6) — *fault to*, to find fault with ; (7) — *for to*, to be obliged to, to have to ; (8) — *had something to do*, to have been fated to do something ; (9) — *ill doing something*, to do something with difficulty ; (10) — *it*, to allow, believe anything ; (11) — *it to say*, to have been known to say ; (12) — *liefer*, to have rather, sooner ; (13) — *mind* (*of*, to remember, call to mind ; (14) — *no hands with*, to have no hand in, to have nothing to do with ; (15) — *no nay*, to take no denial ; (16) — *one on the stick*, to 'take in,' deceive, chaff ; (17) — *one's limbs*, to have the use of one's limbs, to walk ; (18) — *other oats to thresh*, to have other things to do, to have something else in hand ; (19) — *ought*, in *p.t.* ought ; freq. in *neg.* ; (20) — *share*, to share, to partake of anything ; (21) — *speech*, to talk ; (22) — *the heels of*, to excel, surpass, have the best of ; (23) — *the needle*, to be in a disagreeable mood ; (24) *to be well had*, to be well off ; (25) *one must have to do something*, one is obliged to, must do something ; (26) *not to have need*, not to need to, ought not to ; in *p.t.* ; (27) *had I wist*, *addiwissen*, or *heddiwissen*, had I known ; also in phr. *to be sent about addiwissen*, to be sent on a fool's errand.

(1) Edb. Have a care of us! all the eggs in Smeaton dairy might have found resting-places for their doups in a row, MOIR *Mansie Wauch* (1828) iii. (2) n.Lin.[1] A' dun wi' thee, 1. w.Wor.[1] A done, ööl ee! Oxf. (G.O.) Brks.[1] (s.v. Hand). Hmp.[1] 1. I.W.[1] Adone, I tell 'ee. Dev. Have-a-done wi' that noise there, will ee? PULMAN *Sketches* (1842) 103, ed. 1871. (3) Ess. Here, good alive, jes let me

---

hev a come, DOWNE *Ballads* (1895) 25. (4) Sc. (A.W.), n.Cy. (J.W.) Oxf. I'd as lief be hanged (G.O.). (5) Cha.[1] (6) Sc. I have no fault to him, *Monthly Mag.* (1798) II. 437 ; MITCHELL *Scotticisms* (1799) 44. (7) w.Som. Aay shèo·d-n muuch luyk vur t·ae·d vur t·ae·u·r [I should not much like to be obliged to have her], ELWORTHY *Gram.* (1877) 60. (8) Sc. 'He had ha'en that to do,' commonly used as a kind of apology for crime (JAM.). (9) Frf. Mother, you are lingering so long at the end, I have ill waiting for you, BARRIE *M. Ogilvy* (1896) x. (10) Brks.[1] I tawld 'un I zin't myzell, but a oodn't ha't. (11) I.W. He've had it to say of me (J.D.R.) ; I.W.[1] (12) n.Cy. (J.W.) Oxf. I had liever him than me (G.O.). (13) Sh.I. Ye shūrely a' mind what a soss we wir in last year, *Sh. News* (Aug. 27, 1898). N.I.[1] I had no mind of it. Have you mind of that, Sam? (14) Glo. 'Ee did et yer see, and I didn't 'a no 'ands wi' ut, BUCKMAN *Darke's Sojourn* (1890) iv. Wil.[1] I shan't hae no hands wi't. (15) s.Not. Followed by—but, but what, but why. 'They'd have no pay but why ah moot stay a day longer' (J.P.K.). (16) w.Yks. (J.W.) Lan. I began o' thinkin' hoo're havin' me on th' stick, *Ab-o'-th'-Yate's Xmas Dinner* (1886) 7. (17) Nrf. Two or t'ree had their limbs ; they was getting well, EMERSON *Son of Fens* (1892) 71. (18) w.Yks. Thah's other oats to thresh, PRESTON *Poems* (1881) 9 ; (J.W.) (19) w.Yks.[2] Hen't owt to du! Not.[1], Rut.[1], Lei.[1] Nhp.[1] He had'nt ought to ha' dun it. War.[13], Hnt. (T.P.F.) Ken. You had ought to go. You hadn't ought to do that (D.W.L.) ; Ken.[1] He hadn't ought to go swishing along as that, no-how. (20) I.Ma. 'I'm going in to dinner, come and "have share."' 'Not to-day, I have promised to "have share" at home' (S.M.) ; Before they went in the father kindly invited me to go in with them to breakfast and 'have share, RYDINGS *Tales* (1895) 12. (21) Suf. (C.G.B.) (22) Sc. The leddies had the heels of the beaux in the matter of dancing, *Sc. Haggis*, 157. Frf. For expressiveness I maun say I think ' dam ' has the heels o't, MELDRUM *Margrédel* (1894) 151. (23) Oxf. He'll have the needle if he gets on that job (G.O.). (24) Ayr. We're weel had that's in aff the hight, At this bra' meikle ingle, FISHER *Poems* (1790) 78. (25) Nrf. He found the first bird's egg, so he must have to shew me that, EMERSON *Son of Fens* (1892) 4. (26) n.Yks.[2] 'You hadn't need try,' you certainly ought not to attempt it. e.Yks.[1] Used to denote the non-necessity of doing anything, esp. when attended with risk. ' He hadn't-need let him he' brass, for if he diz he'll nivver see it ni mare.' w.Yks. (J.W.) (27) N.Cy.[1] Nearly obs., but still retained by some old persons. Nhb.[1], n.Yks.[2] s.Yks. To be sent about addiwissen. Nearly obs., MARSHALL *Rur. Econ.* (1788). w.Yks. Beware of 'had I wist,' *Prov. in Brighouse News* (Aug. 10, 1889). ne.Lan.[1]

3. *Comp.* **Have-been** or **Has-been**, (1) a person, animal, or thing, formerly serviceable but now past its prime, worn out, or decrepit ; (2) an ancient rite or custom, an antiquity.

(1) Ayr. My han' afore's a gude auld has-been, BURNS *Inventory* (1786) l. 8. n.Cy. (J.W.), Lakel.[2] n.Yks. An seah like all other gud oade hez-beens, it wer naa'd intav onny lumber hooal to git it oot o't rooad, *Nidderdill Olm.* (1873) *J. Bullitt.* e.Yks.[1] Poor awd fella ! a good awd hes-been, bud he's deean for noo. w.Yks.[1] s.Cha.[1] Of a cow : Ůr)z Q gůd uwd aar·bin [Her's a good owd has-bin]. n.Lin.[1] It stan's to reåson at yung college-gentlemen like you knaws a vast sight moore then a worn-oot hes-been like me. War.[2] One of the has-beens. Shr.[1] 'Er's a good owd 'as bin' was remarked of a sometime beauty who had lost all pretension to be considered sych. (2) Sc. Gude auld has-beens should aye be uphauden, *Blackw. Mag.* (Sept. 1829) 660 (JAM.). n.Lin.[1] 'That's a fine ohd hes-been isn't it,' said ßf an old carved chair.

4. *Reflex.* To have for oneself.

Wor. I must 'ave me a bit o' bacca, corn't go on else (H.K.).

5. To have enough, have sufficient.

Lak. Our bairns cam' thick ... And somehow or ither, we aye had to gie them, RODGER *Poems* (1838) 7, ed. 1897.

6. To understand, comprehend ; to have a knowledge of.

Sc. I have no Gaelic, STEVENSON *Catriona* (1893) ii. Abd. I hae ye now (JAM.). Cum.[1], w.Yks.[1], Nhp.[1]

7. To take, bear, carry ; to lead.

n.Sc. He had her on to gude greenwood Before that it was day, BUCHAN *Ballads* (1828) I. 95, ed. 1875. Abd. I'm feared it's mony ance Lords Havin' my love to the clay, MAIDMENT n.Cy. *Garl.* (1824) 4, ed. 1868 ; He is had to Aberdeen and warded in the tolbooth, SPALDING *Hist. Sc.* (1792) I. 126 (JAM.). n.Cy. (J.W.). Nhp.[1] He had his things away. War.[23], Hnt. (T.P.F.) ; Oxf. (G.O.) Lan.[1] ; Ken.[1] Have the horse to the field. Sus.[1] I shall have him down to his grandmother while I go haying.

8. To surpass, be superior to, to have the better of.

Nhb. Bob hez thee at lowpin and flingin, At the bool, football, clubby, and swingin, Selkirk *Bob Cranky* (1843). **Cum.**¹ 'He hez tha now,' he is thy master. **Yks.** (J.W.)

9. To give birth to.

Nhb. Thaw dowtor-o'-law hes had 'im, Robson *Bk. Ruth* (1860) iv. 15. **Yks.** (J.W.) **Nrf.** She's the chice un o' her as had her, Gillett *Sng. Sol.* (1860) vi. 9.

10. To behave.

w.Yks. Hãve yoursen, Lucas *Stud. Nidderdale* (c. 1882) Gl. **Som.** Jennings *Obs. Dial. w.Eng.* (1825).

11. Used in *imper.* as an exclamation when anything is held out towards another, meaning 'take this.'

Sc. Hae, wear it for my sake, Jamieson *Pop. Ballads* (1806) I. 30. 'Hae.' 'Lat's see.' 'Hae,' *Sh. News* (Oct. 7, 1899). **Cai.**¹ Abd. Hae lassie, Alexander *Johnny Gibb* (1871) vii. **w.Frf.**, **e.Per.** The imper. '*hæ*' is only used in handing a thing to a person (W.A.C.). **w.Sc.** Hae, puir body, .. there's a neivefu' out o' my ain pock, Carrick *Laird of Logan* (1835) 35. **Dmf.** Hae! there's airle-pennies twa or three, Cromek *Remains* (1810) 80. **Ayr.** Hae, there's my haun', Burns *To Mr. J. Kennedy*, st. 5; Hae, .. that will help a wee to put you right, Hunter *Studies* (1870) 166.

Hence (1) *Hae boy, rin boy mak's a good lad*, (2) — *lad and run lad*, (3) — *will make a deaf man hear, or a deaf man hears hae*, *prov.*, see below.

(1) **Sh.I.** Give a boy food and clothing and keep him from idle-ness, and he will grow up to be useful, Spence *Flk-Lore* (1899) 215. (2) **Sc.** Give ready-money for your service and you will be sure to be ready served, Kelly *Prov.* (1721) 131. (3) Hae will make a deaf man hear, *ib.* 133. **Cai.**¹ A deaf man hears hae.

12. *sb.* Property, possessions, wealth. Also in *pl.*

Sc. *Gl. Sibb.* (1802) (Jam.). Abd. And pray the Lord may ever gie you Baith hae and heal, Skinner *Poems* (ed. 1809) 37; (Jam.).

HAVE, HAVEER, see **Haw,** *sb.*¹, **Heave, Haver,** *sb.*⁴

HAVEING, *sb.* Chs.¹² Also written *having* Chs.⁴ Cleaning corn by throwing it against the wind.

HAVEL, *sb.*¹ e.An.¹ The slough of a snake. [The same word as **avel** (the beard of barley).]

HAVEL, *sb.*² e.An. [æ·vl.] In phr. *havel and slaie* or *slea*, part of the fittings of a weaver's loom. e.An.¹, Nrf. (W.W.S.)

[ON. *hafald*, the perpendicular thrums that hold the weft (Vigfusson).]

HAVEL, see **Avel, Haviler.**

HAVELESS, *adj.* Sc. Lin. Also written **haiveless** Abd.; **haiviess** Bnff.¹ Wasteful, incompetent; slovenly, ill-mannered, unrefined.

Bnff.¹ Abd. He's a haiveless man, Alexander *Johnny Gibb* (1871) xix ; A vigorous fellow ... whose habits might be not incorrectly described by the word 'haiveless,' *ib. Ain Flk.* (1882) 209. **n.Lin.**¹ A haveless chap that's run'd thrif three fo'tuns. She's as haaveless a bairn as lives. [Poor, having nothing (K.).]

HAVER, *sb.*¹ Obs. Sc.Lakel. A nowner, a possessor.

Or.I. Patrick Earl of Orkney, and all other havers, keepers, and detainers of the castles, Peterkin *Notes* (1822) *App.* 62. Abd. Her at all hazards we intend to claim And on the havers fix the riesing[*sic*]blame, Ross *Helenore* (1768) 132, ed. 1812. **Flf.** Truethis for the Covenant gainers not to be printed, except the printer, haver, and reader, Row *Ch. Hist.* (1650) 443, ed. 1842. **Lak.** The havers of the said book are ordained to bring in and deliver the same, Woddrow *Ch. Hist.* (1721) II. 4, ed. 1828. **Wgt.** They further ordain intimation to be made to all havers of geese in the place, Fraser *Wigtown* (1877) 42.

2. A person of parsimonious habits. Lakel.¹

HAVER, *sb.*² Sc. Nhb. Dur. Cum. Wm. Yks. Lan. Lin. Also written **havre** Cum.; **havver** Cum.¹ Wm. n.Yks.²⁴ e.Yks. m.Yks.¹ w.Yks.¹ Lin.; and in forms **aver-** w.Yks. ; **haber-** n.Cy. Nhb.¹; **hauber-** Sc. n.Cy.; **hauver-** Sc. [h)a·və(r.] 1. Oats, *Avena sativa*. Also used *attrib.*

Slk. (Jam.) **Dmf.** We seldom hear o' guid Scotch kale Or Scottish haver brose, McVittie *In Memoriam* (1893) 191. **n.Cy.** (K.) **Nhb.** She beggars me with haver and hey, Ritson *N. Garl.* (1810) *Ecky's Marv.* **Lakel.**¹² Cum. Aw their lock of havver thresh't an' deetit,Richardson *Talk* (1876) and S. 154; If you gang to see your havver in May You'll come weepin away, But if you gang in June, You'll come back in a different tune, *Prov.* (E.W.P.); **Cum.**¹ The common name. **Wm.** We'd faer crops o havver, *Spec. Dial.* (1885) 3. **Yks.** Ray (1691). n.Yks.¹²⁴ e.Yks. In mowing of haver; ... unlesse your oates be exceedinge ranke and stronge, Best *Rur. Econ.* (1641) 48; Marshall *Rur. Econ.*

(1788) ; **e.Yks.**¹ *Obs., MS. add.* (T.H.) m.Yks.¹ **w.Yks.** A pair o' gooid spurs to a borrowed horse Is better nor a peck o' haver, *Prov.* in *Brighouse News* (July 23, 1887); A field of havver(R.H.H.); **w.Yks.**¹⁴, **Lan.**¹

2. *Comb.* (1) **Haver-bannock**, a thick cake or bannock made of oatmeal ; (2) **-bread,** (3) **-cake,** oatcake or bread, esp. a large, round, thin cake made of oatmeal, baked on a griddle, and dried; (4) **-cake lads,** name of a regiment of soldiers; see below; (5) **-cake rack,** the rack hung from the ceiling on which oatcake is put to dry; (6) **-cracknels,** cracknels or biscuits made of oatmeal ; (7) **-grust,** oats that have gone through the first stage of preparation at the mill; (8) **-jannock,** see (3) ; (9) **-kist,** an oatmeal chest ; (10) **-malt,** malt formerly made from oats ; (11) **-meal,** oatmeal ; also used *attrib.* ; (12) **-natel** or **-nettle, see** (3) ; (13) **-riddle,** an oat-sieve ; (14) **-sack,** a bag hung at a horse's mouth containing his oats ; a bag for carrying oatmeal ; (15) **-shaff,** an oat-sheaf; (16) **-stack,** a stack of oats ; (17) **-straw,** the straw of oats ; (18) **-stubble,** the stubble of oats.

(1) **Slk.** (Jam.) Cum. Hard havver bannock so thick, Dickinson *Cumbr.* (1876) 238; Havver-bannock pleases Dick, Anderson *Ballads* (1805) 94; **Cum.**¹ Wm. Havver bannock, cald dumplin, Wheeler *Dial.* (1790) 114, ed. 1821. (2) n.Cy. Grose (1790); **N.Cy.**¹ **Lakel.**² It is of various names : thick, thin, riddle, clap, girdle, squares, snaps, or treacle parkin, according to its preparation, which is various. Cum. A wooden trencher filled with fresh crisp 'havre bread,' Linton *Lizzie Lorton* (1867) xii. Wm. Her mudder used ta ga oot ta day-wark sec as weshin an bakin haver-bread, Taylor *Sketches* (1882) 3 ; (A.T.) **s.Wm.** (J.A.B.) **Yks.** Browis is maãde o' havver-breãd an' drip (F.P.T.). n.Yks.² **w.Yks.** Reykka bitta havverbread off t'fleyk wilta ! *Leeds Sat. Jrn.* (1895) *Xmas No.* 3; Willan *List Wds.* (1811); **w.Yks.**¹² **Lan.** Stew weel thicken't wi' crisp haver-brade, Waugh *Heather* (ed. Milner) II. 199 ; **Lan.**¹, **n.Lan.**¹ (3) **N.Cy.**¹, **Nhb.**¹, **Dur.**¹, **n.Yks.**²⁴, ne.Yks.¹ **w.Yks.** Peggy hed hauf a stone a soft havver-cake lapt raand hur waist ta keep it moist, Tom Treddlehoyle *Bairnsla Ann.* (1881) 42 ; **w.Yks.**¹ Th' girt fonlin didn't ken what havver-cake wor, ii. 300; **w.Yks.**²³⁴⁵, **Lan.**¹ (4) **w.Yks.** The 33rd Regiment had its establishment completed in the neighbourhood of Leeds and Halifax. .. The regiment was known in the service as ' the Aver-cake Lads.' The origin of the name was in the fact that the recruiting sergeants were wont to carry a piece of aver-cake on the point of their swords as an offer to the ' lads ' of good cheer in His Majesty's service, *Yks. Wkly. Post* (1883); **w.Yks.**¹ Recruits from the northern counties, where oat cakes are generally used, are denominated havver-cake lads. And the serjeant of a recruiting party, in order to tempt men to enlist, hoisted an oat cake on the point of his sword, and with a stentoric voice exclaimed, ' Hey for't havver cake lads' ; **w.Yks.**³ The 33rd Reg. rejoices in the title ' Havercake Lads.' **Lan.**¹ The country people used to pride themselves on the name of the Havercake Lads. A regiment raised in Lancashire during the war bore this name, Waugh *Sketches* (1865) 128. (5) **w.Yks.** Shoo mud as weel ha' tawked to a havercake rack, Hartley *Clock Alm.* (1888) 21. (6) **w.Yks.** Putting haver cracknels in my pocket, Snowden *Web of Weaver* (1896) 193. (7) **Lakel.**² (8) **Sc.**, **n.Cy.** Blount (1681). **n.Cy.** Bailey (1721); (P.R.) **w.Yks.** Banks *Whfld. Wds.* (1865). (9) **Nhb.**¹ (10) **w.Yks.** Thou's lang a-coming, thou braids of haver-maut, Meriton *Praise Ale* (1684) l. 54. **w.Yks.**¹ (11) **Sc.** Francisque-Michel *Lang.* (1882) 424. **s.Sc.** (Jam.) **Rxb.** O whar got ye that haver-meal bannock ! *Sng., Bonny Dundee* (Jam.). **n.Cy.** Grose (1790) ; **N.Cy.**¹, **Nhb.**¹, **Dur.**¹ **Lakel.**² Havermeal-pooak, a wallet that a beggar carries wi' him to put his meal in when he gits eny gien. **Cum.**¹ Wm. A dubbler of haver-meal, Hutton *Bran New Wark* (1785) l. 403. n.Yks.¹²³⁴, m.Yks.¹ **w.Yks.** One or two meals a day ... composed of 'Havermeil,' Binns *Vill. to Town* (1882) 70 ; Hutton *Tour to Caves* (1781); **w.Yks.**¹⁵ **n.Lin.**¹ *Obsol.* (12) **Nhb.**¹ (13) **Yks.** (K.) (s.v. Riddle). **n.Yks.** Pegg, whores our haver-riddle! Meriton *Praise Ale* (1684) l. 167. (14) **Flf.**, **Rxb.** (Jam.) **N.Cy.**¹, **Nhb.**¹ **Lakel.** A sack for the oatmeal that is for domestic use, and is therefore kept clean (B.K.). (15) n.Yks.² (16) n.Yks. It's him that brack down'th railes to'th haver-stacks, Meriton *Praise Ale* (1684) l. 358. (17) **Dmf.** They had to hurkle down on a heap o' haver straw, *Blackw. Mag.* (Nov. 1800) 146 (Jam.). **Dur.**¹ **w.Yks.** Th' stee i' our heigh laithe, cleeam'd up againt' black havver-strea moo, ii. 286. (18) **e.Yks.** If the haver stubbles be allmost done, then wee give them [the sheepe] the barley stubbles, Best *Rur. Econ.* (1641) 27.

3. Wild, self-sown oats, *Avena fatua* and *Bromus secalinus*. **n.Cy.** Morton *Cyclo. Agric.* (1863). **e.Yks.** (Miss A.) **Lin.**

THOMPSON *Hist. Boston* (1856) 709. n.Lin. SUTTON *Wds.* (1881) ; n.Lin.[1], sw.Lin.[1]

4. *Comp.* **Haver-grass,** several kinds of oat-grass, esp. *Avena elatior* and *Bromus mollis.* Cum.[1]

[1. Norw. dial. *havre*, oats (AASEN), Sw. *hafre* (WIDEGREN); cp. EFris. *hafer* (KOOLMAN). 8. *Aveneron*, wild oats, haver, or oat-grass, COTGR.]

HAVER, *sb.*[3] Shr. The lower part of a barn-door ; a hurdle. BOUND *Provinc.* (1876) ; Shr.[3]

HAVER, *sb.*[4] Dur. War. Wor. Som. Also in forms **haveer** War.; **havering** Dur.; **havier** Wor.; **hevior** w.Som.[1] A castrated stag.

Dur. (K.) ; (HALL.) War. Mr. Lucy used to feed a haveer, that is, a red deer stag, with his horns cut off, MORDAUNT & VERNEY *Hunt* (1896) I. 253. Wor. A stag that is to be chased by the Royal Buckhounds. 'The Royal Paddocks produced two fine haviers' (H.K.). w.Som.[1] Met at Cot Bridge at ten o'clock; tried the Arlington Coverts for the hevior [aev·iur], *Rec. N. D. Stag-hounds,* 43. [Haviour bucks, YOUNG *Annals Agric.* (1784–1815) XXXIX. 558.]

[Prob. the same word as *aver, sb.*]

HAVER, *v.* and *sb.*[5] Sc. Irel. Nhb. Cum. Also ? Ken. Also written **haiver** Sc. Cai.[1] Bnff.[1] ; and in form ? **aver** Gall. [hē·vər.] **1.** *v.* To talk in a foolish, incoherent manner ; to talk nonsense.

Sc. He just havered on about it, SCOTT *Antiquary* (1816) xliv ; Toots, man, ye're haiverin' nonsense, FORD *Thistledown* (1891) 144. Cal.[1] e.Sc. Donal' havers o' rain ower a plug o' baccy, SETOUN *R. Urquhart* (1896) iv. Abd. Ye're aye haverin aboot something, ALEXANDER *Ain Flk.* (1882) 155 ; A man 'at in ane o' his gran'est verses cud haiver aboot the birth o' a yoong airthquauck ! Iosh ! MACDONALD *Sir Gibbie* (1879) 4. Frf. Dinna haver, lassie, you're blethering, BARRIE *Tommy* (1896) 57. Per. Yammerin' and haverin' like a starling, IAN MACLAREN *Brier Bush* (1895) 176. w.Sc. Hoot, toot ! gudeman, ye're haverin' noo, CARRICK *Laird of Logan* (1835) 234. Ayr. He continued to haver with him, till the ale was ready, GALT *Gilhaize* (1823) v. Lnk. They tell me he havered awfu' nonsense, FRASER *Whaups* (1895) xiv. Lth. Next morn I met her aunt . . . And soon we fell a-havering, M⁴NEILL *Preston* (c. 1895) 82. Slk. When the doited auld body begins haverin about himsel, he's deaf to a' thing else, CHR. NORTH *Noctes* (ed. 1856) III. 54. Gall. They were self-respectin' men, an' nae ranters haiverin' oot o' their heids, CROCKETT *Stickit Min.* (1893) 102. N.Cy.[1] Nhb. When sitting cosy wi' his dearie, To joke and haver, STRANG *Earth Fiend* (1892) 3. Cum. FERGUSSON *Northmen* (1856) ; Hiding away o' neuks an' corners, an' whisper-ing an' havering, LINTON *Silken Thread* (1880) 277 ; Cum.[14] [Sentimental persons have been havering this week about the execution of one of the Crewe murderers, *Sat. Review* (1890) 428, col. 1.]

Hence (1) **Havered,** *ppl. adj.* spoken at random or desultorily ; (2) **Haverer,** *sb.* a foolish talker ; (3) **Havering,** *ppl. adj.* chattering, nonsense-talking, nonsensical.

(1) Edb. I tak' my station An' hears ilk haver'd hale oration, FORBES *Poems* (1812) 5. (2) Arg. Go in-bye, haverer, and—oh, my heart ! MUNRO *Lost Pibroch* (1896) 185. (3) Sc. Gae 'wa, ye haverin cuddie, *Jokes* (1889) 2nd S. 57. Frf. Oh haud yer tongue, ye haiverin eediot, INGLIS *Ain Flk.* (1895) 172. Ayr. Toddling home from the town-hall wi' goggling een and havering idiots, GALT *Provost* (1822) xliii. Edb. Ye're a pair of havering idiots, MOIR *Mansie Wauch* (1828) xxiii. Gall. ? Averin, MACTAGGART *Encycl.* (1824) 35, ed. 1876.

2. To hesitate and make much ado about doing anything ; to be lazy at work.

Bnff.[1] Ye needna be haiverin' that wye aboot gain' haim [escort-ing home] wee the lassie. The hail height o' the day, he did naething but haiver at 's wark.

3. *sb. pl.* Foolish talk, chatter, nonsense. Rarely in *sing.*

Sc. Dinna deave the gentleman wi' your havers, SCOTT *Redg.* (1824) Lett. x ; A long palaver is nothing but a blether or a haver, LEIGHTON *Wds.* (1869) 5. Sh.I. Ta tak up da half o' da time wi' my ain clash an' havers, STEWART *Tales* (1892) 37. Cai.[1] Bnff. Ye're sure in jest, Gie o'er sic havers, TAYLOR *Poems* (1787) 64. Abd. They interrupt 'im wi' a' kin' o' haivers, ALEXANDER *Johnny Gibb* (1871) xviii. Frf. Tell us not to talk havers when we chide her, BARRIE *M. Ogilvy* (1896) 87. Per. Ye'll no mind the havers of an auld dominie, IAN MACLAREN *Brier Bush* (1895) 27. Fif. It's a' platform havers, M⁴LAREN *Tibbie* (1894) 84. Dmb. I've seen a gude deal in the 'Witness' and ither papers about Non-intrusion

and sic like havers, CROSS *Disruption* (1844) ii. Ayr. Wi' claivers an' haivers Wearing the day awa, BURNS *Answer to Verses* (1787) st. 1. Lnk. I haena the time for sic havers, NICHOLSON *Idylls* (1870) 65. Edb. To show his wares an' town-bred airs, An' hae a haver wi' the lasses, MACLAGAN *Poems* (1851) 315. Slk. Hush your havers, CHR. NORTH *Noctes* (ed. 1856) III. 47. Dmf. The turn o' nicht when havers fail, REID *Poems* (1894) 30. Gall. The town's fouk wi' their havers About him raise sic lies and clavers, NICHOLSON *Poet. Wks.* (1814) 61, ed. 1897. Keb. They never talked naething but haivers, ARMSTRONG *Ingleside* (1890) 149. Wgt. The haivers o' some Councillors dinna meet the approval o' decent fowk generally, FRASER *Wigtoun* (1877) 186. Ant. (W.H.P.), N.Cy.[1] Nhb. Hoots, man ; ye've come to t'wrang customer wi' havers like yon, S. *Tynedale Stud.* (1896) No. vi; A rambling or wandering story (R.O.H.) ; an auld wives' haver, DONALDSON *Poems* (1809) 134; Nhb.[1], Cum.[4] ? Ken. You are talking havers, *N. & Q.* (1852) 1st S. v. 306.

Hence **Havers,** *int.* nonsense, rubbish.

Sc. Havers ! that is what no mortal man can do, STEEL *Rowans* (1895) 201. Frf. Havers! I'm no' to be catched with chaff, BARRIE *M. Ogilvy* (1896) 78. Per. Havers, man, ye dinna mean tae say they pack beds and tables in boxes, IAN MACLAREN *K. Carnegie* (1896) 163. Gall. Hoots, haivers; I'll never believe that, CROCKETT *Bog-Myrtle* (1895) 200. Cum. Havers ! The lass hasn't a full thousand, LINTON *Silken Thread* (1880) 290.

4. A piece of folly or nonsense ; a whim, piece of foolish-ness.

Abd. Fat haiver's this 't ye've ta'en i' yer heid noo! ALEXANDER *Johnny Gibb* (1871) xvi. Per. To ca' your crackit quaver Melodious noo is juist a haver, HALIBURTON *Horace* (1886) 53. Frf. Dinna fash yoursels. It's juist a haver o' the grieve's, BARRIE *Lichts* (1888) x. Fif. What kind o' haver is this noo ! ROBERTSON *Provost* (1894) 124 ; A' men o' sense will ca't a haver Throughout a' Fife, DOUGLAS *Poems* (1806) 37. ■ Sc. Be na angry at this haver, T. SCOTT *Poems* (1793) 362. Rnf. Whilk at the best is but a haiver O' rhymin' ware, CLARK *Rhymes* (1842) 96. Lnk. To splutter some disjointed haver, *Deil's Hallowe'en* (1856) 48. Lth. Fu' lang had he bruipled aboot her, And mony a haver had said, M⁴NEILL *Preston* (c. 1895) 85.

5. A stupid, chattering person ; a lazy, idle fellow. Also in *pl.* form.

Bnff.[1] He's a mere haiver wee 's wark. Per. Puir Mr. Peattie o' Muirton is juist a holy haver—He's a puir, bletherin body, FER-GUSSON *Vill. Poet* (1897) 25. Nhb.[1] A havers is an incoherent or garrulous person.

6. Hesitation accompanied with a great fuss ; a person who hesitates. Also in *pl.* form.

Bnff.[1] Nae mair o' yir haivers. Awa ye go an' deet at ance, an' hae deen wee't. He's a mere haiver o' a cheel.

HAVER, HAVERDEPAZE, see Aver, *sb.,* Halver, Haviour, Avoirdupois.

HAVERDRIL, *sb.* Chs.[1] The daffodil, *Narcissus Pseudo-narcissus.*

HAVEREL, *sb.,* *adj.* and *v.* Sc. Irel. Nhb. Cum. Yks. Also Nrf. Also written **haiverel** Cai.[1] N.I.[1] ; **haiverll** Nhb.[1]; **haivrel** Lth.; **haverall** Sc.; **haveril** Sc. Ant. N.Cy.[1] Nhb.[1] Yks. Nrf.; **haverill** n.Yks.[2]; **havrel** Sc. Nhb.[1] Cum.[1]; **hav'ril** Cum. ; and in forms ? **aivrill** Bnff.[1]; **bovrel** Cum.[1] [h]ē·vərl, h)ē·v·rl.] **1.** *sb.* A stupid, half-witted person ; a talkative, garrulous person ; a fool. See Haver, *v.*

Sc. It was. only the New Inn, and the daft havrels, that they caa'd the Company, that she misliked, SCOTT *St. Ronan* (1824) xv. Cal.[1], Bnff.[1] Abd. To screen wi' palaver some haverel's miscarriage, CADENHEAD *Bon Accord* (1853) 213. Per. Ilka daft-like clash at ony donnart haverel may set rinnin', CLELAND *Inchbracken* (1883) 186. w.Sc. Sit down, ye hungry haveral that ye are, CARRICK *Laird of Logan* (1835) 86. Fif. It's surely no canny for an auld, doited haverel to be the first the bairn should meet, ROBERTSON *Provost* (1894) 57. e.Fif. Spak' not only for hersel' but for anither half-score o' ordinary haverils, LATTO *Tam Bodkin* (1864) xxix. Ayr. He . . . will no fail to take the law o' [him] for a haveral, GALT *Entail* (1823) viii. Lth. Gley'd Sawnie, the haivrel, he met me yestreen, MACNEILL *Poet. Wks.* (1801) 207, ed. 1856. e.Lth. I thocht him little better nor an auld haveril, HUNTER *J. Inwick* (1895) 40. Dmf. A lump of an old woman, half haveral, half genius, CARLYLE *Lett.* (Aug. 30, 1843). Gall. Though mony a haverall they hae bred, MACTAGGART *Encycl.* (1824) 40, ed. 1876. Wgt. Whun there's nae gossipin' haverils tae hear us, FRASER

Wigtown (1877) 348. n.Ir. (D.A.S.), **N.I.**[1] Ant. *Ballymena Obs.* (1892); (W.H.P.) n.Cy. *Border Gl.* (*Coll.* L.L.B.); **N.Cy.**[1] **Nhb.** Loodly the haverils war tawkin, ALLAN *Tyneside Sngs.* (ed. 1891) 488; **Nhb.**[1] **Cum.** A wutless bit hav'ril, RAYSON *Misc. Poems* (1858) 62; **Cum.**[1] **Yks.** This missis he's getten is nobbut a haveril, MACQUOID *Doris Barugh* (1877) viii. **n.Yks.**[2] Nrf. *Arch.* (1879) VIII. 170.

Hence (1) **Haveral-hash**, *sb.* a silly, nonsensical person; a fool; (2) **Haverelism**, *sb.* a habit of foolish, nonsensical talking.

(1) **Lnk.** A haveral-hash, wi' head as saft as a cahoutchie ba', NICHOLSON *Idylls* (1870) 121. (2) **Ayr.** Jenny had more of a thorough-going haverelism about her, GALT *Lairds* (1806) i.

2. *adj.* Foolish, silly, nonsensical; talking foolishly.

Sh.I. Blinkin' her een wi' delicht whin some haveril chap wis makin' a fuil o' her, STEWART *Tales* (1892) 35. Per. You're wrang in your guessing, you haverel lout, STEWART *Character* (1857) 19. **Dmb.** It's no a right kind o' luve ye have for me ava, butt just a haveral notion, CROSS *Disruption* (1844) xxxii. Rnf. Ca'd me a hav'rel tyke, PICKEN *Poems* (1813) I. 194. **Ayr.** Poor hav'rel Will fell aff the drift, BURNS *Halloween* (1785) st. 4. **Lnk.** Gae wa, gae wa, ye hav'rel sheep! WATSON *Poems* (1853) 15. **Edb.** Ye've lear'd to crack sae crouse, ye haveril Scot, FERGUSSON *Poems* (1773) 183, ed. 1785. **Peb.** Her haveral daughter ... Stood near, *Lintoun Green* (1685) 61, ed. 1817. **Slk.** But haverel Meg, as they called her, HOGG *Tales* (1838) 73, ed. 1866. **Gall.** I ... cursed my life Wi' tap o' a' things maist unchancy—A haverel wife, NICHOLSON *Poet. Wks.* (1814) 155, ed. 1897. **N.I.**[1] **Nhb.** A haverill tyke kept by the family . . . as a fool, *Denham Tracts* (ed. 1892) I. 273.

3. *v.* To talk nonsense; to make a fool of; to chaff.

Ayr. Some ne'er-do-weel clerks were seen gaffawing and haverelling with Jeanie, GALT *Provost* (1822) xxxviii. **Nhb.** Aw yence was hav'rel'd i' my day, ROBSON *Bards of Tyne* (1849) 151.

HAVEREL, see **Haiver**.

HAVEREN, *sb.* Sc. A sloven. HERD *Coll. Sngs.* (1776) Gl.

HAVERING, HAVERON, see **Haver,** *sb.*[4], **Haiver**.

HAVERN, *adj.* Bdf. Same as **Avern** (q.v.).

HAVEY-CAVEY, *adv.* and *adj.* Cum. Yks. Lan. Der. Not. Lin. Nhp. Also in forms eyvy-keyvy w.Yks.; havey-quavey sw.Lin.[1]; havey-scavey Lakel.[2] Cum.; havy-akavy Cum.[1]; heavely-keavely Der.[1] nw.Der.[1]; heavy-ceavy Yks.; heevy-skeevy Cum.; heighvy-keighvy Lan.; heivy-keivy w.Yks.[1] Nhp.[1]; heyvy-keyvy e.Lan.[1]; hevy-skevy Cum.[1]; hivie-skivy Lin.; hivy-skivy e.Yks.[1]; hivy-skyvy n.Lin.[2] [h)ē·vi-kē·vi, ei·vi-kei·vi.] **1.** *adv.* Unsteady, trembling in the balance; uncertain, undetermined, doubtful, wavering, precarious. Also used *attrib.*

Yks. It was heavy ceavy whether I came or not (M.N.). **w.Yks.** Tweddin' question remained heivy-keivy in his mind fur sum months, HARTLEY *Clock Alm.* (1874) 40; That miln chimli lewks rayther eyvy-keyvy (Æ.B.); **w.Yks.**[1]; **w.Yks.**[2] A young man who was very ill was said to be in a very havey-cavey state, tottering between life and death. **Lan.** Sich heighvy-keighvy pickhawms, CLEGG *Sketches* (1895) 397. **e.Lan.**[1], **Der.**[2], **nw.Der.**[1] **Not.** GROSE (1790). **Nhp.**[1] Confined to the n. part of the county.

2. All in confusion, 'higgledy-piggledy'; helter-skelter. Lakel.[2] Throw them in havey-scavey. **Cum.** All havey skavey and kelavey, ANDERSON *Ballads* (ed. 1808) 14; Now heevy skeevy off they set to the kurk, STAGG *Misc. Poems* (ed. 1807) 7; *Gl.* (1851); Cum.[1], **e.Yks.**[1] w.Yks. Mi heead's all eyvy-keyvy this mornin' (Æ.B.). **Lin.** The bull is turned out of the Alderman's house, and then hivie skivy, tag and rag, men, women, and children . . . running after him with their bull clubs, BUTCHER *Survey* (1717) 77, in BRAND *Pop. Antiq.* (ed. 1813) I. 483. **n.Lin.**[1]

3. *Phr.* *to be on the havey-quavey,* to be on the inquiry, questioning and doubting. Also used as *v.*

sw.Lin.[1] I've been rather on the havey-quavey after a little place at Eagle. We've been havey-quaveying after it some time.

4. *adj.* Drunken.

w.Yks.[1] Because a person in this state is on the equipoise.

HAVIER, see **Haver,** *sb.*[4]

HAVIL, *sb.* Irel. A temporary structure made of wooden standards for a cart-shed, and covered with a stack of hay on the top. Ant. *Ballymena Obs.* (1892).

HAVILER, *sb.* Lon. Ken. Sus. Also in forms **havel** Sus.; **havill** Lon. A small kind of crab. Cf. **heaver,** *sb.*[1] **Lon.** A small species [of crab] ... known by the French as *l'Etrille*, and called in some parts of our country grubbin, or -crabbin, .. in London havill, *Illus. Lond. News* (1857) 70. **Ken.**

COOPER *Gl.* (1853). **Sus.** GROSE (1790); The male is a 'Jack Havel' and the female a 'Jenny Havel' (F.E.S.); **Sus.**[12]

HAVING, *ppl. adj.* and *sb.* Sc. Irel. Yks. Chs. Der. War. Also in form hevving n.Yks.[2] **1.** *ppl. adj.* Greedy, acquisitive; miserly, penurious.

w.Ir. A gosthering, spending, having brood they are and always have been, LAWLESS *Grania* (1892) I. pt. ii. ii. **s.Cha.**[1] Der. A' talked o' his back-rent; . . he's a very having man, VERNEY *Stone Edge* (1868) xxi. **nw.Der.**[1] War. Mrs. Deane . . . was proud and having enough, GEO. ELIOT *Floss* (1860) I. 93. [An avaricious person is very 'having,' JEFFERIES *Hdgrow.* (1889) 188.]

2. *sb. pl.* Possessions.

Dmf. (JAM.), Yks. (C.C.R.) **n.Yks.**[2] I wad nowther hev him nor his hevvings.

3. *pl.* Dress, garments.

Abd. Ye'll tak this angel sweet And dress with havins for your mistress meet, Ross *Helenore* (1768) 126, ed. 1812.

HAVINGS, *sb. pl. Obs.* or *obsol.* Sc. Also written haivens, haivins, havens, havins. Manners, behaviour. Cf. havance.

Sc. I think the Quaker has smitten me with his ill-bred havings, SCOTT *Redg.* (1824) xx. **Abd.** Ye've fairly tint a' sense o' shame; Ye're haivens, lad's, uncommon, COCK *Strains* (1810) II. 64. **Frf.** Excuse The havins of a hamely muse, BEATTIE *Arnha* (c. 1820) 45, ed. 1882. Rnf. A rebuke from the mothers for our want of havens would calm us down, GILMOUR *Pen Flk.* (1873) 29. **Ayr.** To pit some havins in his breast, BURNS *Death of Poor Mailie*, l. 46; (J.M.) **Lnk.** A rattle-skull, Wha's neither mense nor havens, WATT *Poems* (1827) 67. **Lth.** Wha wad gar the lasses wait, That had o' havins ony? BRUCE *Poems* (1813) II. 63. **Edb.** Forgie The little 'havin's that ye see i' me, LEARMONT *Poems* (1791) 312. **Rxb.** What ! has the wretch nae havins better? A. SCOTT *Poems* (ed. 1808) 45.

[The merie speiche, fair hauingis, hie renoun Of thame, DOUGLAS *Pal. Hon.* (1501), ed. 1874, 44.]

HAVIOUR, *sb.* Sc. Yks. Chs. Also in form haver w.Yks.[24] Chs.[123] [h)ē·vjə(r, h)ē·və(r.] Behaviour; *pl.* manners, *gen.* used in a good sense.

Abd. SHIRREFS *Poems* (1790) Gl. **Lnk.** RAMSAY *Gentle Shep.* (1725) Gl., Scenary ed. **w.Yks.**[2] THOREEBY *Lett.* (1703); **n.Yks.**[2] He's no havers at all; **w.Yks.**[4] **Chs.**[12]; **Chs.**[3] To be on one's haviours, is to be on one's good behaviour. **s.Chs.**[1] Naay, dhen, yi mŭn bey ŭpon· yŭr ai·vyŭr wel dhŭ mes·tŭr)z ŭbuw·t [Naï, then, ye mun bey upon yur haviour whel the mester's abowt].

[Her heavenly haveour, her princely grace, SPENSER *Sh. Kal.* (1579) IV. 66.]

HAVLINS, see **Halflins.**

HAVOC, *sb.* Sc. Also Som. **1.** Waste.

w.Som.[1] Very common. Zee what havoc you be makin way the hay; there 'tis a-littered all the way in from the rick.

2. *Comp.* Havoc-burds, large flocks of small birds which fly about the fields after harvest.

Gall. They are of different sorts, though all of the linnet tribe. 'Whunlinties' form the greatest number, MACTAGGART *Encycl.* (1824) 256, ed. 1876.

HAVVER, see **Haver,** *sb.*[2], **However.**

HAW, *sb.*[1] Var. dial. forms and uses in Sc. and Eng.

I. Dial. forms: (1) **Ah,** (2) **Ahzy,** (3) **Airsen,** (4) **Awsen,** (5) **Haa,** (6) **Haave,** (7) **Haaze,** (8) **Haiv,** (9) **Halve,** (10) **Harsy,** (11) **Harve,** (12) **Hav,** (13) **Have,** (14) **Hawse,** (15) **Hawsen,** (16) **Hawve,** (17) **Hay,** (18) **Howe.** See **Hag,** *sb.*[2]

(1, 2) Oxf. (G.O.), Oxf.[1] (3) Glo.[1] Fat airsens. (4) Glo. (S.S.B.) (5) **Nhb.** Mony hips, mony haas, Mony blaas, mony snaas, *Old prov.* (R.O.H.); **Nhb.**[1], **Cum.**[1], **Ess.** (W.W.S.) (6) Dev. Th' vish be za thick as hâives, PULMAN *Sketches* (1842) 101, ed. 1871. (7) **Ken.** (G.B.), **Ken.**[1] (8) **w.Som.**[1] We be gwain to have a hard winter, the haivs be so plenty. (9) **Ken.** (G.B.), **Ken.**[1] **Som.** FRIEND *Gl.* (1882a). **Dev.**[4] (10) **Ess.** (B. & H.) (11) **n.Ess.**, **Ken.**[1] (12) Dor.[1] (13) **Ken.** (W.F.S.) **Dor.** *w.Gazette* (Feb. 15, 1889) 7, col. 1. **Dev.**[4] (14) **Glo.** (S.S.B.); **Bayle** *Illus. Dial.* (1870). (16) **sw.Wor.**[1] (17) **s.Not.** Let's gether some hays from the hedge (J.P.K.). **Nhp.**[2] (18) **Shr.**[2], **Suf.**[1]

II. Dial. meanings. 1. In *comp.* (1) **Haw-berry,** the fruit of the hawthorn, *Crataegus Oxyacantha,* a haw; (2) **buss,** a hawthorn-tree; (3) **-gaw,** see (1); (4) **-stones,** the hard 'stones' or seeds contained in the haw; (5) **-tree,** see (2).

(1) **Edb.** Whar the red hips and hawberries hing In clusters, MACLAGAN *Poems* (1851) 20. **Chs.**[1]; **Chs.**[2] There is a legend that for several days before the Battle of Blore Heath, there arose each morning out of the foss, three mermaids, who announced 'Ere yet the Hawberry assumes its deep red, Embued shall this heath be with blood nobly shed.' (a) **Dmf.** We had nae sutten lang aneath the haw-buss, till we heard the loud laugh of fowk riding, CROMEK *Remains* (1810) 298. (3) **Sur.** (4) **Gall.** Bluchtans... are hollowed [mugwort] tubes; boys blow haw-stones and what not out of them: hence the name, MACTAGGART *Encycl.* (1824) 76, ed. 1876; Well known. When I was a boy we used to blow stones from the hawthorn berries from the hedges; the tubes or blow-pipes we used were made of bore-tree (S.R.C.). (5) **Ayr.** Busking our bonny hawtree, AINSLIE *Land of Burns* (ed. 1892) 175. **Lnk.** Yon bonnie haw-tree That blossoms aye fairer, LEMON *St. Mungo* (1844) 43. **Lth.** Sweet bloom'd the bonny spray O' the haw-tree, BRUCE *Poems* (1813) II. 93. **Dmf.** 'Side the green haw-tree, CROMEK *Remains* (1810) 51. **Nhb.**[1] **Glo.** Those are the awsen-trees then (S.S.B.).

2. Phr. *a haw year,* a year in which haws abound.
Sc. A haw year A snaw year, CHEALES *Prov. Flk-Lore,* 22. **Cum.**[4]

3. The hawthorn-tree, *Crataegus Oxyacantha.*
Slk. Sweetly blows the haw an' the rowan tree, HOGG *Poems* (ed. 1865) 412. **Dmf.** Thocht cam' thick as drift at Yule Aneth that hoary haw, REID *Poems* (1894) 59.

4. A hip, the fruit of the dog-rose, *Rosa canina.*
Dor. *w. Gazette* (Feb. 15, 1889) 7, col. 1.

HAW, *sb.*[2] Shr. e.An. Ken. Hmp. Dor. Dev. Also in form hav Dor.[1] Dev.[4] n.Dev. (HALL.) [ọ.] The ear of oats. See Aw, *sb.*
e.An.[1] Suf. *Science Gossip* (1883) 113. e.Suf. (F.H.), Ken., Hmp. (B. & H.) Dor.[1] The woats be out in háv. Dev.[4], n.Dev. (HALL.)
Hence **Hawed,** *adj.,* see below.
Shr.[2] When oats are well headed, having shot their heads from the stem and begun to swell and ripen, they are said to be hawed. The term is not applied to any other kind of grain. n.Dev. Oats when planted are said to be haved (HALL.).

HAW, *sb.*[3] *Obs.* or *obsol.* Yks. Nhp. Brks. Suf. Ess. Ken. 1. A small piece of land adjoining a house, a close; a small yard or enclosure.
Yks. *Leeds Merc. Suppl.* (July 11, 1896). **Ken.** RAY (1691); A hemp-haw, a bean-haw (K.); LEWIS *I. Tenet* (1736); By some the houses themselves are called haws (P.R.); **Ken.**[12]

2. A small wood or coppice; a dwelling enclosed by woods; a depression in a wood.
Nhp.[1]; **Nhp.**[2] Used in conjunction with some other word. Swine-haw, West-haw, &c. **Brks.**[1], e.Suf. (F.H.)

[1. Ther was a polcat in his hawe, CHAUCER *C. T.* c. 855. OE. *haga,* an enclosure (EARLE *Charters, Gl.*).]

HAW, *sb.*[4] Lan.[1] [ọ.] In phr. *all of a haw,* all on one side, out of the perpendicular.
HAW, *adj.* *Obs.* or *obsol.* Sc. Also in form hawes Sh.I. Of a bluish-grey or pale-green colour; livid, pale, wan.
Sc. Wi' haggit ee, and haw as death, The auld spae-man did stand, JAMIESON *Pop. Ballads* (1806) I. 236; Like moonshine on the icy loch, Thin, cauld, and haw to see, *ib.* 242. **Sh.I.** He's wrate a sicht mair, an' apo' boonie hawee blue paper tū, *Sh. News* (May 15, 1897). n.Sc. Thro' and thro' the bonny ship's side He saw the green haw sea, CHILD *Ballads* (1885) II. 28. **Abd.** Twa shepherds... as haw as death, Ross *Helenore* (1768) 22, ed. 1812. **Per.** His eyes turn'd as a sullid glass, And like haw clay his hands and face, SMITH *Poems* (1714) 5, ed. 1853.
[Crownit with garlandis all of hair see hewis, DOUGLAS *Eneados* (1513), ed. 1874, II. 122. OE. *hæwi,* also *hǽwi,* azure (SWEET *O.E.T.* 596).]

HAW, *int.*[1] Dur. Cum. Yks. Lan. Chs. Der. Lei. Nhp. War. Wor. Shr. Glo. Oxf. Som. Dev. Also in forms au Lei.[1]; aw w.Yks. Chs.[1] ne.Der.[1] w.Wor.[1] se.Wor.[1] Glo.[1] Dev.[2]; awe Oxf.[1]; ha e.Dur.[1] ne.Lan.[1]; haa Cum.[1]; hah w.Yks. ne.Lan.[1]; haugh s.Lan. [họ, h]ā.] 1. A call to horses or cattle to turn to the left, towards the driver.
Cum.[1] (s.v. Ho). w.Yks. (H.V.), w.Yks.[2], ne.Lan.[1], s.Lan. (W.H.T.) **Chs.** MORTON *Cyclo.* (1863) (s.v. Horses); **Chs.**[1], nw.Der.[1], Lei.[1] **Nhp.**[1] Used to all the horses in a team, except the fore-horse. **War.**[2] w.Wor.[1] Aw! aw! a call to cows. se.Wor.[1] **Shr.**[1] To the pin-horse and shafter, with a rise of pitch on the latter part of the vowel (s.v. Waggoners' Words); **Shr.**[2], w.Som.[1] **Dev.** *Horae Subsecivae* (1777) 179. nw.Dev.[1] [Aw makes Dun draw, RAY *Prov.* (ed. 1678) 95.]

---

2. Comb. (1) **Haw-back,** a call to horses or cattle to turn back; (2) -come 'ere, a call to horses to turn completely round to the left; (3) -waay, -wee, or -woy, a call to horses to turn to the left, towards the driver; (4) -whoop or -woop, (a) see (3); (b) a call to horses to go on; (5) -woe, see (3); (6) -wut or awitt, (a) see (3); (b) a call made to attract the attention of cows.
(1) **Oxf.**[1] When a carter has a team and waggon in a road too narrow to turn, he shuts out all the horses but the thiller, and 'backs' him by taking hold of the 'mullin' and pushing him backwards, and says to the horse 'Awe back,' *MS. add.* w.Som.[1] (2) **Chs.**[1] (3) e.Dur.[1] w.Yks. The Wilsden form is 'Aw-wee!' *Leeds Merc. Suppl.* (June 20, 1891). (4, a) **Shr.**[1] (b) **Glo.**[1] (5) w.Yks. (H.V.) (6, a) **Oxf.**[1] (b) **Dev.**[2]

HAW, *int.*[2] Yks. Lin. Ken. [ọ.] An exclamation of surprise or contempt.
w.Yks. Haw! t'wife says tha'rt hungry, BINNS *Orig.* (1889) No. i. 2; w.Yks.[2] 'Can one du it!' 'Haw aye' (s.v. How). n.Lin.[1] Jaanie Smith hes gotten fine i' her talk; .. when ony body says oht to her she duzn't saay 'haw' as we do; she says, 'Well, you 'atonish me.' **Ken.** Look haw look (K.).

HAW, see Hall, *sb.*[1] Har(r, Haugh, Ho, *v.,* How, *sb.*[1], *adv.*
HAWBAW, *sb.* Yks. Lin. Also in form hawby Yks. [ọ·bọ, -bl.] 1. A stupid, clumsy fellow, a lout; a coarse, vulgar lad. Cf. hawbuck.
w.Yks.[2] n.Lin. Never mind the shavings, you silly hawbaw, PEACOCK *M. Heron* (1872) II. 114; n.Lin.[1]

2. Impudence; pert, saucy speaking.
m.Lin. If ah've eny moore o' y'r haw baw ah s'll mek you laugh tothor side o' y'r imperdent young faäce (T.H.R.).

HAWBOY, *sb.* Yks. A wooden double-reed wind instrument of high pitch; a hautboy.
e.Yks. When they tooted the hawboy, an Billy ga mooth, NICHOLSON *Flk-Sp.* (1889) 40.
[Fr. *hautbois,* 'instrument à vent, qui donne des sons clairs d'une grande douceur' (HATZFELD).]

HAWBUCK, *sb.* In *gen.* dial. and colloq. use in Eng. and Amer. Also in forms aubuck n.Yks. m.Yks.; haabuck Nhb.[1]; hobuck Cum.[4]; hoe-buck w.Yks.[1] [h]ọ·-, h]ā·buk, -bǝk.] A clumsy fellow, lout; a country bumpkin, a 'chaw-bacon'; a noisy, rough, turbulent young man. Cf. hawbaw.
Nhb.[1] Cum. For fear some hawbuck tek't i' his head To brake us weel, STAGG *Misc. Poems* (ed. 1807) 146; **Cum.**[4] **Wm.** En' than, a girt hawbuck, away did he sneak, BLEZARD *Sngs.* (1848) 35. n.Yks. Onybody ma see 'at yon's a cuntry aubuck (W.H.); n.Yks.[12], ne.Yks.[1] e.Yks. He's a great haw-buck (Miss A.); e.Yks.[1], m.Yks. (W.P.), m.Yks.[1] w.Yks. Lunnon fowks owt not to want tu mak country hawbecks on us, TOM TREDDLEHOYLE *Bairnsla Ann.* (1852) 46; w.Yks.[1235] Lan.[1], n.Lan.[1], ne.Lan.[1] s.Lin. SUTTON *Wds.* (1881); n.Lin.[1], Lei.[1], Nhp.[1] War.[2] A young man, who in dress or manners imitated in some degree the rank above him, or who affected some foppishness. I have only heard it applied to young farmers or yeomen, or the sons of rural tradesmen. Hmp.[1], w.Som.[1] n.Dev. Sorrow is making a hawbuck of me, KINGSLEY *Westward Ho* (1855) 47, ed. 1889. [*Amer. Dial. Notes* (1896) I. 418.]

HAWCH, *v.* Glo. Som. Dev. Also in forms hatch-Dev.[3]; hoach Glo. [ǫtʃ.] 1. To eat badly; to make a loud noise with the lips or mouth in eating.
w.Som.[1] Where's thee larn thy manners? Why's-n shut thy girt trap, not bide and hauchy, like a girt fat pig. n.Dev. When tha com'st to good tackling, thee unt poochee and hawchee, *Exm. Scold.* (1746) l. 188; *Horae Subsecivae* (1777) 206.

2. Phr. *to hoach and haw,* to hawk and spit.
Glo. *Horae Subsecivae* (1777) 206; GROSE (1790) *MS. add.* (M.)

3. Comb. (1) **Hawch-(a)-mouth,** (a) one who 'hawks' and spits, *fig.* a foul-mouthed, blustering person, one who talks indecently; also used *attrib.*; (b) one who makes much noise in eating; (2) **Hawch-mouthed,** coarse, vulgar, or profane in speech, blustering, bullying.
(1, a) **Glo.** GROSE (1790) *MS. add.* (M.) w.Som.[1] **Dev.**[2] Not in present use, but in years gone by it was a word commonly used at and in the neighbourhood of Parracombe. It really meant a person who talked incessantly in a coarse, vulgar manner, using obscene and offensive language, mingled with foul epithets. n.Dev. A gottering hawchamouth theng, *Exm. Scold.* (1746) l. 187; *Horae Subsecivae* (1777) 206; GROSE (1790). (b) w.Som.[1] (a)

w.Som.[1] He! you never did'n come 'cross a more rougher, hawchemoutheder, cussin, girt bully in all your born days. **Dev.** I 'opes our Anna Maria won't graw up sich a hatchmouthed maid as Amy Keslake is, HEWETT *Peas. Sp.* (1890a); 'E weer that hatchmouthed that volks shivered tu 'ear 'im talk, PHILLPOTTS *Dartmoor* (1895) 196, ed. 1896.

HAWDOD, *sb.* *Obs.* Yks. The blue cornflower, *Centaurea Cyanus.* See **Haw,** *adj.*

Yks. 8th May, 1730. He also told me that in the fields in summer, there grows a flower call'd hawdods, which with a touch will bend down as if they had broken, HOBSON *Diary* (Surtees Soc.) 296 in (B. & H.). We know of no plant having this peculiarity (B. & H.). [Hawdod hath a blewe floure, and a fewe lytle leaves, and have fyve or syxe braunches floured on the top and groweth commonly in rye upon leane grounde, FITZHERBERT *Husbandry* (1534).]

HAWFER, HAWFISH, see **Aver,** *sb.,* **Awvish.**

HAWFLE, HAWFLIN, see **Haffle,** *v.,* **Halflin(g.**

HAW-GAW, *sb.* Sc. (JAM. *Suppl.*) Also written haugaw; and in form hauka. [Not known to our correspondents.] A rag or refuse gatherer, a midden-raker.

HAWGH, see **Haugh, Hawk,** *v.*[1]

HAWICK GILL, *phr.* Sc. A measure of ale or spirits, containing half an English pint. See **Gill,** *sb.*[7] **2.**

Sc. And weel she loo'd a Hawick gill, HERD *Coll. Sngs.* (1776) II. 18; A Hawick gill is a double gill, so named from the town of Hawick, *ib. Gl.* **s.Sc.** Bring 's a Hawick gill, An' here's to Hawick's bonnie lasses! WATSON *Bards* (1859) 121. **Lth.** Come hostess, bring 's a Hawick gill, An' to his health a glass I'll fill, BRUCE *Poems* (1813) II. 133. **Edb.** If her ye'd gien a Hawick gill, She might been leal, LIDDLE *Poems* (1821) 29.

HAWING, *ppl. adj.* ? *Obs.* Sc. Resounding, guiding, directing.

When they chance to mak a brick Loud sound their hawing cheers, A. SCOTT *Poems* (1805) 54 (JAM.).

HAWK, *sb.*[1] Sh.I. Or.I. Irel. Wm. Der. Lin. e.An. Also in form **halk-** S. & Ork.[1] 1. In *comb.* (1) **Hawk's-bill bramble,** the blackberry, *Rubus fruticosus* ; (2) **-'s cud,** the cast of a hawk, a pellet of undigested food thrown up by a hawk ; (3) **-hen,** a hen formerly demanded from each house for the support of the royal hawks ; (4) **-spaun,** a tall, ungainly woman ; (5) **-studyin,** the steady hovering of hawks over their prey before pouncing upon it.

(1) **e.An.** (B. & H.) (2) **Der.** *Cornh. Mag.* (1865) XII. 41. (3) **Sh.I.** To feed these birds [hawks for the use of the King], a hen was demanded from every house ; or (as it is called) from every 'reek,' under the name of hawk-hens, HIBBERT *Desc. Sh. I.* (1822) 134, ed. 1891 ; I know the meaning of scat and wattle and hawkhen, SCOTT *Pirate* (1822) ii. **S. & Ork.**[1] Hens falling to be contributed for support of royal hawks when falconers went to Orkney to procure hawks, payable and paid down to 1838 and 1839. **Or.I.** With xxiiij cunningis tantum skynnis for Sandisend, and xxiiij halk hennis, PETERKIN *Rentals* (1820) 11 (JAM.). (4) **n.Lin.**[1] (5) **Gall.** MACTAGGART *Encycl.* (1824) (JAM.).

2. *Phr.* (1) *as hungry as a hawk,* very hungry. **Ant.** *Ballymena Obs.* (1892) ; (2) *between buzzard and hawk,* neither good nor bad, nondescript. **Der.**[2], nw.Der.[1]

HAWK, *sb.*[2] Nhb. Cum. Wm. Yks. Also in forms **haak** Nhb.[1]; **howk** Nhb.[1] **Lakel.**[2] **Cum.**[4] **Wm.** [h)ŏk, **hǎk.**] 1. Among animals : a disease of the eye ; *gen.* in *pl.*

Nhb. Of the eye in horses. It is a film or cataract, which may be removed (R.O.H.) ; 'The howks,' on a pig's eye, is an inflammation of the front external covering of the eyeball, *ib.* ; **Nhb.**[1] **Cum.**[4] An inflammation of the *membrana nictitans* of pigs. **Wm.** Affecting the eyes of store pigs in which a formation comes over the eyes. ' Can thou tak t'howks of our pig !' (B.K.) **n.Yks.**[2] ' Oor pig's gitten hawks i' t'een,' a filminess on the eyes ; removed with a sharp awl. [ARMITAGE *Cattle* (1882) 184.]

2. A disease of the skin, urticaria.

Lakel.[2] A disease amongst cattle and swine, followed in the former case by sudden death unless the animal is bled. **Cum.** A swelling of the 'chafts' of cattle (J.W.O.) ; **Cum.**[4] In cattle, more commonly known here as blains, and seen about eyes, ears, neck and vulva, and other parts of thickened skin ; in the horse the attack comes on suddenly and appears as elastic patchy swellings all over the body (J.H.).

VOL. III.

Hence **Hawk't,** *ppl. adj.* suffering from the disease 'hawks.' Cum.[4]

HAWK, *sb.*[3] Cum. Wm. Nhp. Lon. Also in form **hawky** Cum.[4] Wm. [h)ŏk.] 1. The board used by a mason or plasterer to hold mortar ; a bricklayer's hod. Cum.[4], Wm. (B.K.), Nhp.[1]

2. A mason's labourer, the man or boy who carries the hod. Also in *comp.* **Hawk-boy.**

Cum.[4] What was he onyway !—nobbut a hawky, settin hissel oop ! **Wm.** He's gitten a job as hawky (B.K.). **Nhp.**[1] A boy engaged to furnish a hawk with mortar, and carry it to his master for use. **Lon.** Was a 'hawk-boy,' he said, at the plasterer's trade, MAYHEW *Prisons of Lond.* (1862) 424.

HAWK, *sb.*[4] Sus.[1] A rail at the back of a wagon. See **Hack,** *sb.*[2] **18.**

The corresponding rail [to the fore-summer or top rail in front of a wagon] at the back (s.v. Fore-summer).

HAWK, *v.*[1] and *sb.*[5] In *gen.* dial. and colloq. use in Sc. and Eng. Also written **hauk** n.Lin.[1] Wil. Dor.[1]; **hawck** Elg. ; and in forms **awk** s.Pem. ; **haack** Cum. ; **haak** Nhb.[1] Cum.[1]; **hake** m.Yks.[1]; **hauch** Cai.[1] Bnff.[1] Cld. (JAM.); **haugh** Frf. ; **hawgh** Sc. (JAM.); **hooak** e.Yks.[1]; **ock-** w.Yks.[2]; **howk** Nhb. ; **oke** s.Pem. [h)ŏk, h)āk, Sc. also hăx.] 1. *v.* To clear the throat from phlegm ; to cough ; to spit. Cf. **hawch.**

Sc. (JAM.), Cal.[1] Bnff.[1] **s.Sc.** The pipe it gars ye hawk and spit, ALLAN *Poems* (1887) 93. Cld. (JAM.) **e.Lth.** Pechin an' hawkin an' hoastin like an auld wife, HUNTER *J. Inwick* (1895) 27. **N.Cy.**[1], **Nhb.** (W.G.), **Nhb.**[1] **Cum.** Cough't an haackt an neezt a few times, SARGISSON *Joe Scoap* (1881) 129 ; He startit teh haak an cough as if he was makken ruddy fer anudder brust, *ib.* 240 ; **Cum.**[1], **e.Yks.**[1], **m.Yks.**[1] **w.Yks.** *Sheffield Indep.* (1874). **Lan.** DAVIES *Races* (1856) 233. **ne.Lan.**[1], **n.Lin.**[1], **War.** (J.R.W.), **Shr.**[2] **s.Pem.** A's awking his throat tremendous (W.M.M.). **Hnt.** (T.P.F.), **Suf.** (C.T.), **Suf.**[1] **Ken.** (G.B.) ; **Ken.**[1] He was hawking and spetting for near an hour after he first got up. **Sus.** HOLLOWAY. **Wil.** SLOW *Gl.* (1892). **Dor.**[2] The men did hauk an' spet, 208. **Som.** SWEETMAN *Wincanton Gl.* (1885).

Hence **Hauchan,** *sb.* the mucus expelled in clearing the throat. Bnff.[1]

2. *Comb.* (1) **Hawk-a-mouth,** (2) **Hawk-a-mouthed,** continually ' hawking ' and spitting ; *fig.* foul-mouthed, scolding ; cf. **hawch-(a)-mouth,** s.v. **Hawch** ; (3) **Ock-slaver,** one who foams at the mouth. Cf. **hack-slaver,** *sb.* **3.**

(1) **Dev.** Hawk-a-mouth-trub [a scold], BOWRING *Lang.* (1866) I. pt. v. 36. (2) **Dev.**[1] The very daps of her mother—another such a haggagen, maundering, hawk-a-mouth'd trub, 7. (3) **w.Yks.**[2]

3. To expel anything from the throat by force of the breath ; *gen.* with *up.*

Cai.[1] **Bnff.**[1] A bit beef stack in's craig ; but he seen haucht it up. Cld. (JAM.)

4. To gargle. s.Pem. (W.M.M.) **5.** To hesitate, to ' hum and haw,' to make much ado before doing anything. Also with *about.* Cai.[1], Bnff.[1], Cld. (JAM.) Hence (1) *Hawking and swappin,* *phr.* failing in prosperity, in poor worldly circumstances. Rxb. (JAM.) ; (2) *— and swaupin,* *phr.* (*a*) in a state of hesitation or irresolution ; (*b*) in an indifferent state of health or prosperity. Lth. (*ib.*)

6. To seek or wish for in vain.

s.Chs.[1] If a person asks another for something, which the latter is not disposed to give, he tells the former he ' mun hawk for it.'

7. *sb.* An effort to clear the throat, the sound made in clearing the throat.

Elg. I had not even given a hawck when I felt a little heat on my cheek, COUPER *Tourifications* (1803) I. 123. **Frf.** Ilk friend and crony prin their mou, Or gies a cough or sober haugh, For fear o' lattin out a haugh, SANDS *Poems* (1833) 98. m.Yks.[1]

HAWK, *v.*[2] Nhp.[1] To carry anything about unnecessarily and with labour.

She hawked her things up all the way to London, and didn't want them when she'd done. ' How you hawk that child about,' when one child is trying to carry another that is too heavy for its strength.

HAWK, see **Hack,** *sb.*[1], **Hock,** *sb.*[1]

HAWKATHRAW, *sb.* Rxb. (JAM.) [Not known to our correspondents.] A country wright or carpenter.

O

HAWKERY-PAWKERY, *sb.* Yks. Deceit, unfairness, trickery, hocus-pocus.

n.Yks. They take care to see that there be no hawkerypawkery about burning the house (I.W.).

HAWKEY, *sb.* Sus. A boys' game resembling hockey; see below.

w.Sus. Played by several boys on each side with sticks. . . In a piece of ground with a fence at each end a line is drawn across the middle of the ground from one side to the other; one party stands on one side of the line, and the opposite party on the other; and neither must over-step this boundary; but they are allowed to reach over as far as their bats will permit to strike the ball. The object is to strike the ball to the further end, to touch the fence of the opposing party's side, when the party so striking the ball scores one, and supposing nine to be the game, the party obtaining that number first of course wins the game, HOLLOWAY.

Hence **Hawkey-bat,** *sb.* the stick used in the game of 'hawkey.' *ib.*

HAWKEY, HAWKIE, see Hockey, *sb.*[1]

HAWKIE, *sb.* Sc. Nhb. Cum. Also written **hauky** Rnf.; and in form **hokey** Cum. [hǫ·ki, hā·ki.] 1. A white-faced cow; freq. used as a general or pet name for a cow; also used *fig.* Cf. **hawkit.**

Sc. Nae mair the hawkies thou shalt milk, RAMSAY *Tea-Table Misc.* (1724) I. 213, ed. 1871; Pbroo, pbroo! my bonnie cow, Pbroo, hawkie! ho, hawkie! CHAMBERS *Sngs.* (1829) II. 515. Elg. Hawky ahint the hallan main't, COUPER *Poetry* (1804) II. 57. Baff. She gaed an' milkit Hawkie, TAYLOR *Poems* (1787) 65. Abd. Ca' hawkie throw the water: Hawkie was a wyllie beast, An' hawkie wad no wade the water, BEATTIE *Parings* (1801) 62, ed. 1873. Frf. A scull, made up o' Hawkie's hair, MORISON *Poems* (1790) 22. Per. A mighty whang aff a cream kebbuck made frae the produce of her favourite Hawky, STEWART *Character* (1857) *Introd.* 73. Slg. Hawkey now, weel sair'd wi' food, TENNANT *Papistry* (1827) 112. Slg. Poor Hawkie's sisterhood That on the mountains chew'd their cud, MUIR *Poems* (1818) 18. Dmb. Hawkie and Brakie met a sudden death, TAYLOR *Poems* (1847) 56. Rnf. Hawkie no more the gate can leap, MᶜGILVRAY *Poems* (ed. 1862) 301. Ayr. An' dawtit, twal-pint Hawkie's gaen As yell's the Bill, BURNS *Add. to Deil* (1785) st. 10. Lnk. Effie's love an' Hawkie's milk will Mak' thee soon a stout wee wean, NICHOLSON *Idylls* (1870) 29. e.Lth. As a 'cow's keep' was a portion of nearly every ploughman's wage, there was always an abundance of the 'soupe that hawkie does afford,' MUCKLEBACKIT *Rhymes* (1885) 149. Edb. Her hireling damsels bids Glour thro' the byre, and see the hawkies bound, FERGUSSON *Poems* (1773) 164. ed. 1785. Slk. Our wee bit hawkie, twice had raised the hungry croon, HOGG *Poems* (ed. 1865) 92. Dmf. Hawky will starve in the cauld winter day, SHENNAN *Poems* (1831) 155. Gall. They...blamed her wee Hawkie wi' things she ne'er saw, KERR *Maggie o' the Moss* (ed. 1891) 40. n.Cy. *Border Gl.* (Coll. L.L.B.) Nhb. My hearty service to your dame, And likewise to your Hawkie; She'll grease the bread to cram our wame, DONALDSON *Poems* (1809) 79; Nhb.[1] A *gen.* pet-name for the cow. Cum. LINTON *Lake Cy.* (1864) 305; Cum.[4] An Dick ran on before Wi' hawkie in a string, GILPIN *Sngs.* 15.

2. A bull or cow having a white face; also used *attrib.*

Cum. Saul o't'Ho, wad talk aboot nowt bit Lampla' hokey bulls, DICKINSON *Lamplugh* (1856) 8; Cum.[4] Formerly they had an inferior breed of cattle in Swindale, near Shap, and the term 'Swindale hawkie' continues to this day as applicable to a person of inferior mental capacity. The old long-horned breed had many of them white faces.

3. The bald coot, *Fulica atra.*

Per. The coot bears on his forehead a shield pure white in colour... We called it the Hawkie in my boyhood, SWORD *Bird Coll.* (1894) 175.

4. *Fig.* A stupid, clumsy fellow.

Baff. Be gane frae me, ye dozent hawkie, Gae hame an' wooe some country gawkie, TAYLOR *Poems* (1787) 57.

5. A slang name for a whore.

Rnf. Haun for nieve the haukies staun, PICKEN *Poems* (1813) I. 96.

6. *Comp.* **Hawkie-buis,** a place of punishment for ill-behaving people. Cum. (M.P.)

HAWKIT, *adj.* Sc. Also written **haukit, hawket**; and in forms **hackit, haiked, halkit, haulket, hawked.** 1. Of animals: having a white face. Cf. **hawkie.**

Sc. As the hackit greyhound bitch now! SCOTT *Abbot* (1820) xviii; I'll sell my rokely and my tow, My gude grey mare and hawket cow, CHAMBERS *Sngs.* (1829) I. 157. Cai.[1]

Baff., Abd. MORTON *Cyclo. Agric.* (1863). Abd. Upo' a' fours, Like ony haulket hummel doddy stirk, *Guidman Inglismaill* (1873) 30. Frf. She likes him just as weel I'll swear, As I do our gray hawkit mare, MORISON *Poems* (1790) 112. Fif. Forby her cow an' hawkit stirk, DOUGLAS *Poems* (1806) 95. Rnf. Ane halkit cow, worth twentie punds Scots money, HECTOR *Judic. Rec.* (1876) 45. Lth. The hawkit Crummie chew'd her cude, SMITH *Merry Bridal* (1866) 187. Slk. To spare me a lamb for a hawked ewe, HOGG *Tales* (1838) 404, ed. 1866.

2. *Fig.* Stupid, foolish.

Abd. We want Carnegie's councils now, that hawket, lucky chiel, ANDERSON *Rhymes* (1867) 189; Some rattle-scull, I wad, like Geordy Will, Or haukit Ned, . . twa, that I kenna whilk's the greatest fool, SHIRREFS *Poems* (1790) 87; (JAM.)

HAWKY, *adj.* Hrt. Of the nature of a hawk, greedy, voracious.

Gravel is of a hawky voracious nature, ELLIS *Pract. Farmer* (1750) 98.

HAWL, HAWLE, HAWLM, HAWLSE, see **Hall,** *sb.*[3], **Hole,** *sb.*[1], **Haulm, Halse,** *sb.*[2]

HAWLSE, *v.* Obs. Wxf.[1] To lay a spirit. See **Halsen.**

HAWM, *sb.* Yks. Lan. Chs. Der. Also in forms **ame** Chs.[18]; **aulm** Der.[2] nw.Der.[1]; **awm** Chs.[1]; **hame** Chs.; **haulm** Der.[2] nw.Der.[1]; **haum** Lan.; **helm** w.Yks. Der.[2] [ǫm, ǫǝm.] A haft, the handle of an axe, hammer, spade, &c.; a pick-shaft.

w.Yks. Try if we cant drahve un inte t'helm, *Spec. Dial.* 24. Lan. Bat . . . shaped out of a pick-haum, BRIERLEY *Cotters*, xxv. e.Lan.[1] Chs. Not a'that'ns—put the head of the axe hame jed down, *Sheaf* (1878) I. 82; Chs.[1]; Chs.[2] Th' axe ame's broke. Der. GROSE (1790) *MS. add.* (P.); Der.[2], nw.Der.[1]

[Tirol. dial. *hālm,* 'stiel' (SCHÖPF); MHG. *halme, halm,* 'handhabe, stiel' (LEXER).]

HAWM, *v.*[1] Sc. Yks. Chs. Der. Not. Lin. Also written **haum** w.Yks.[2] nw.Der.[1] Lin.; and in forms **aum** Not.; **awm** w.Yks.[2] Chs.[18] Not.[128] Lin. sw.Lin.[1] [h)ǫm.] 1. To waste time, to be idle; to move about aimlessly, to loiter, lounge; to stand gaping and staring; to do work in a slovenly manner.

Baff.[1] w.Yks.[2] Look at him how he's hawming; he wants nowt to do to-day! Chs.[1]; Chs.[2] What are ye awming at! Not. (W.H.S.); Not.[1]; Not.[2] That idle chap is awmin' about doing note. He's drunk and awmin' all ower d'rooad; Not.[2] s.Not. 'What's that chap awmin about that 'ow for! Is 'e drunk!' 'What are yer doing awming about theer! Get on with yer work' (J.P.K.). Lin. He was awming about wi' the bairn, and let her fall of her elbow (R.E.C.); (J.C.W.); They hawmed and pawted just like cats, BROWN *Lit. Laur.* (1890) 49; MILLER & SKEERTCHLY *Fenland* (1878) iv; Lin.[1], n.Lin.[1] sw.Lin.[1] Dont stand awming there.

Hence **Haumgobbard,** *sb.* a silly, clownish fellow. w.Yks. GROSE (1790); w.Yks.[6]

2. To set about a thing, to begin, move, attempt. w.Yks.[2], nw.Der.[1]

HAWM, *v.*[2] Lin. To shackle, clog, hamper.

Clear hawmed up wi' wattle guiders, i.e. by the collars pressing his cheeks, BROWN *Lit. Laur.* (1890) 50, *footnote.*

HAWM(E, see **Hame,** *sb.*[1], **Haulm.**

HAWMEL(L, *sb.* Obs. Ken. A small close or paddock.

Lewis *I. Tenet* (1736); GROSE (1790); Ken.[1]

[Haw, *sb.*[2] + *mel,* OE. *mǣl,* a measure, freq. in comps., e.g. *dægmǣl, fōl-mǣl.*]

HAWMER, HAWMPLE, HAWMPO, see **Hammer,** *sb.*[1], **Hamble.**

HAWMUS, *sb.* Lin.[1] In phr. *all of a hawmus,* all of a heap. 'She stood all of a hawmus.' Cf. **almous, 2.**

HAWN, *sb.* Cor. [Not known to our correspondents.] An oven. (J.W.) [A pron. of ME. *oven,* OE. *ofen.*]

HAWN, see **Hauen, Hean,** *sb.*[1]

HAWNIE, *sb.* Sc. A milk-vessel, made of wood.

Lth. The cooper had before him milk dishes of all kinds—leglins, cogs, hawnies, &c., STRATHESK *More Bits* (ed. 1885) 109; The 'hawnie' had a handle, and is used largely in the feeding of calves (A.W.).

HAWPS, *sb.* Yks.[15] ne.Lan.[1] Also written **haupa** ne.Lan.[1] [ǫps.] A tall, awkward person. Cf. **awp(s,** *sb.*[2] **2.**

HAWS(E, see **Halse,** *sb.*[1]

HAWSE, v.¹ Lan. Also written **hause**. To prepare ; to attempt, try ; to offer. See **Oss.**

If he hauses t'be obstropilous, he shall smell at this timber, BRIERLEY *Waverlow* (1863) 216, ed. 1884 ; It wer th' furrest thaut e' maw yed us evvur aw shud hause fur to may onuther, ORMEROD *Felley fro Rachde* (1851) *Pref.* 7, ed. 1864 ; Dun yoa think aw wur hawsin t'steight it ! STATON *B. Shuttle*, 61 ; As Pee wur hawsin t'bid Patty good neet, *ib. Loominary* (c. 1861) 95.

HAWSE, v.² Lan. With *up* : to raise, lift or poke up.

Then come the opportunity—to give her kitchen fire one of her favorite ' hawsins up,' DONALDSON *Tooth Drawin'*, 7.

[Bomilcar . . . having sea-roume, halsed up sailes, HOLLAND *Livy* (1600) 568. Fr. *hausser*, to raise (COTGR.) ; OFr. *haucier, halcier* (HATZFELD).]

HAWSE, v.³ Pem. To gossip. s.Pem. LAWS *Little Eng.* (1888) 420.

HAWSE, see Haw, sb.¹

HAWSEMAN, sb. Nrf. One of the crew of a fishing-boat.

Used by wherry-men on the broads (E.G.P.); The master, mate, hawseman, wheelman, net-roper, and me, lived aft in the cabin (of the herring fishing-boat), EMERSON *Son of Fens* (1892) 58 ; One of the crew of a fishing boat, i.e. a boat engaged in catching herrings by drifting with nets. He is a superior member of the crew and stands forward when shooting the nets. When the nets are hauled the hawseman again goes forward and casts off the rope and lets go the 'tizzard' (a rope from the ship to the warp). When the nets are pulled alongside he unbends the seizings and passes them to the net-roper. After that the hawse-man helps to salt the herrings in the wings (P.H.E.).

HAWSEN, sb. Sh.I. The curved board near the bow or stern of a fishing-boat.

'Ye see,' William answer'd, pointin' ta da hawsen, 'whaur yon rive is,' *Sh. News* (Dec. 17, 1898); Second or third from the keel (J.I.).

HAWSEN, HAWST, see Halsen, Haw, sb.¹, Hazen, Hoast, sb.¹

HAWTANE, adj. *Obs.* Sc. Haughty. GROSE (1790) *MS. add.* (C.)

[Swa hawtane and dispitous, BARBOUR *Bruce* (1375) I. 196. Fr. *hautain*, haughty (COTGR.).]

HAWTH, sb. Sus. Also in form hoth Sus.¹ [ọp.]

1. Gorse or furze, *Ulex europaeus.* Also in *comp.* Hawth-bush.

(S.P.H.); LOWER *S. Downs* (1854) 152; He would throw himself backwards into a hawth-bush, *ib. Stray Leaves* (1862) 92; Sus.¹ 'Tis very poor ground, it wont grow naun but heath and hoth.

2. A heath.

Old people still call Hayward's Heath ' Heward's Hawth ' (W.D.P.).

HAWTHERY, adj. N.I.¹ Untidy, tossed. Cf. huthery.

HAWTHORN, sb. *Obs.* Dev. Also written haw-thern n.Dev. A kind of hook or pin cut out of an erect board and used to hang a coat, &c., upon. *Horae Subsecivae* (1777) 206. n.Dev. GROSE (1790).

HAWTHORN-DEAN, sb. Sc. Yks. Also written Hawthorn Dene w.Yks.² A species of apple.

Edb. The Hawthorndean, or White Apple of Hawthorndean, derives its name from the romantic seat in Midlothian of the poet and historian Drummond, NEILL *Hortic. Encycl.* (1817) 109 (JAM.). w.Yks.²

HAWVE, see Half, Hauve, v.¹², Haw, sb.¹

HAWVISH, adj. Lan. [ọ·viʃ.] Undecided, indefinite. See **Awvish, adv. 2.**

Let's ha' no moore o' thi hawvish tawk, WOOD *Hum. Sketches*, 26.

HAWY, adv. Sc. (JAM.) Heavily.

HAWZE, HAWZEN, see Halse, sb.¹, Hoze(e, Hazen.

HAY, sb.¹ and **v.¹** Var. dial. uses in Sc. Irel. and Eng. Also written ha Som. ; hey Lan. **1.** sb. In *comp.* (1) Hay-band, (a) a rope of twisted hay used to bind a truss, or to fasten thatch on a stack ; (b) a rope of hay twisted round the leg to keep it dry ; (2) -bank, a loose piece of wood placed above the stalls in a cow-house to hold hay ; (3) -bay, a place on the ground-floor for keeping hay ; (4) -bird, a name given to var. birds which build their nests of hay : (a) the blackcap, *Sylvia atricapilla*; (b) the willow-warbler, *Phylloscopus*

trochilus ; (c) the wood-warbler, *P. sibilatrix* ; (5) -bog, a damp hay-meadow ; (6) -bote, the right of cutting a specified quantity of hay from the property of another ; (7) -box, a hayloft ; (8) -brew, a decoction of hay ; (9) -builder, the chiff-chaff, *Phylloscopus rufus*; also the willow-wren, *P. trochilus* ; (10) -carrying, the hay-harvest ; (11) -chamber, a hayloft ; a room over a stable ; (12) -chat, (a) see (4, a); (b) the whinchat, *Pratincola rubetra*; cf. **hay, sb.²** 5 (2) ; (13) -cock, a much larger heap of haythan a 'footcock'; (14) -crome, a hay-rake, *obs.* ; *fig.* ' pot-hooks '; (15) -crook, a long rod with a barbed head used to draw samples of hay out of a stack ; *fig.* a long, lank, hungry-looking man ; also ' pot-hooks'; (16) -fog, aftermath ; (17) -folk, haymakers ; (18) -fow, a hay-fork ; (19) -gang, the gangway leading from the barn or hayloft to the cow-stalls ; (20) -goaf or -goffe, a haystack ; (21) -goak, the haystack as it stands pared round in use ; (22) -grass, (a) see (16) ; (b) the grass of tilled land ; (23) -green, the ragwort, *Senecio Jacobaea* ; (24) -heck, a rack for holding hay ; (25) -home, the last day of the hay-harvest ; (26) -jack, (a) see (4, a) ; (b) the reed-sparrow, *Emberiza schoeniclus* ; (27) -knife, a knife used for cutting hay in the stack ; (28) -makers, the name given to a particular country dance ; (29) -mow, (a) a haystack ; hay stored up under cover ; (b) the barn or loft in which hay is stored ; (30) -net, a net hung on to the collar of a horse, in which hay is placed ; (31) -neuk, the stall or crib where the hay for immediate consumption is put when brought in from the outside stack ; (32) -pike, a circular pile of hay pointed at the top ; (33) -pines, hay-seeds ; (34) -plant, the sweet woodruff, *Asperula odorata* ; (35) -pook, (36) -quile, a hay-cock ; (37) -riff, a pernicious weed with very small seeds ; (38) -scent, the scented fern, *Nephrodium Oreopteris* ; (39) -seed, the meadow soft-grass, *Holcus lanatus*; also in phr. *not to have the hay-seed out of one's hair*, not to have outgrown one's youthful ' greenness '; (40) -sel(e or Hasle, the season of making hay ; the hay-harvest ; (41) -shakers, the quaking-grass, *Briza media* ; (42) -silver, a tithe-charge of one shilling an acre upon mown land ; (43) -sow, a large, oblong stack of hay ; (44) -spade, a sharp heart-shaped spade for cutting hay ; (45) -stang, a hay-pole ; (46) -sweep, a large sled used to carry the hay ; (47) -tallat, see (7) ; (48) -tea, a decoction made by pouring boiling water on hay, sometimes used for rearing calves ; (49) -tedder, a haymaking machine ; (50) -tenter, a haymaker as distinguished from a mower ; (51) -tenting, haymaking ; (52) -tick, the whitethroat, *Sylvia cinerea*; cf. **hay, sb.²** 5 (6) ; (53) -tier, one who cuts hay out of a rick and makes it up into trusses ; (54) -tit, (a) see (52) ; (b) see (4, b) ; (c) the sedge-warbler, *Acrocephalus phragmites* ; (55) -trusser, see (53) ; (56) -worker, a haymaker.

(1, a) Lan.¹ Here, lass, tee this on for mo. It looks like a haybant, when aw tee it for mysel, BRIERLEY *Owd Blanket* (1867) i. Cha.¹ n.Lin.¹ Sixty years ago it was almost universal, now it is rarely seen. (b) They became, however, to be considered as a mark of extreme poverty and consequently dropped out of use, *ib.* Som. Worn by shepherds in snowy weather. Still used (F.W.W.). Cor.² (a) n.Yks. (T.S.), n.Yks.¹⁴, ne.Yks.¹ Lan. Iz een streek foyar loik o wild cat's on o hey-bawk, SCHOLES *Tim Gamwattle* (1857) vii. (3) w.Wor.¹ (4, a) Nhp.¹ (b) Sc. SWAINSON *Birds* (1885) 26. Nhp.¹ (c) w.Yks. SWAINSON *ib.* 27. (5) Dmf. She left the hay-bog in a fit of despair, SHENNAN *Tales* (1831) 155. (6) Cum.¹ (7) Lan. Ther's a hay-boax theere ut I've bin in afore, BRIERLEY *Out of Work* (1885) iii. (8) Ayr. That lassock has biled the tea till it's like hay-broo, SERVICE *Dr. Duguid* (ed. 1887) 228. (9) Sur. ' That's where we see them 'ere little hay-builders.'.. Chiff-chaffs and willow wrens the boy meant, *Times* (Dec. 7, 1894) 13, col. 5. (10) Som. Thic night at Squire Reeve's when we made an end o' Hā-corrin, JENNINGS *Obs. Dial. w.Eng.* (1825) 127. (11) n.Yks. Wld [we had] better ev ə bit ə he it [in the] bēchemar radi fort [for the] hossiz [horses] wen thə kum in fra wāk [work] (W.H.). s.Yks.¹ *MS. add.* (T.H.) (12, a) Nhp. SWAINSON *ib.* 24; Nhp.¹ (b) Nhb.¹ (13) Wil.¹ (14) e.An.¹ The characters scrawled by an awkward penman are likened to ' hay-cromes and pitchforks '; as they more *gen.* are to ' pot-hooks.' e.Suf. (F.H.) (15) Cum. Like a laal scholar larnen teh mak strokes, an heucks an hay-creucks, SARGISSON *Joe*

Scoap (1881) 102; We'd hay-cruiks and hen-tails and hanniels, And nattlers that fuddle for nought, ANDERSON *Ballads* (ed. 1808) 170; **Cum.**[4] That's a cruikt un! I think it is leyke a hay-cruik, SILPHEO *Billy Brannan*, 5. **Wm.** & **Cum.**[1], **Wm.** (B.K.) (16) **Sth.** The paleys (young weak and stunted lambs) are ... sent directly to the hay-fog, *Farm Reports* (1832) 80. (17) **Kcb.** The layerock that rise ... Frae the mead an' the feet o' the hay-folk, ARMSTRONG *Ingleside* (1890) 177. (18) **Gall.** I'll learn ye to stick hay-fows into decent folk, CROCKETT *Cleg Kelly* (1896) 298. (19) **Cum.**[1] (20) **e.An.**[1], **Ess.** (W.W.S.) (21) **n.Yks.**[2] 'T wind's whemml'd t'hay-gooak ower,' overturned it. (22, *a*) **Som.** (W.F.R.); W. & J. *Gl.* (1873). (*b*) *ib.* (23) **Cum.**[4] (24) **Yks.** An put hur intul a hay-heck it far corner at laith, *Dewsbre Olm.* (1865) 8. (25) **Oxf.**[1] *MS. add.* **Wil.**[1] It was the last day of the hay-harvest—it was 'hay-home' that night, JEFFERIES *Wil. Labourer*. (26, *a*) **Nhp.** SWAINSON *ib.* 24. **Nhp.**[1] (*b*) **e.An.**[1], **e.Suf.** (F.H.), **Suf.**[1] (27) **Per.** When a' thing gaed dune, Willie seized the hay-knife, FORD *Harp* (1893) 189. **Wgt.** Gen. part of the blade of an old scythe (A.W.). **w.Yks.** (W.H.) (28) **Sc.** Neither the haymakers nor the soldier's joy formed part of the entertainment, *Sc. Haggis*, 158. **Edb.** Nae stupid waltz or gallopad Frae Italy or France, But to the merry hay-makers, The roof an' rafters ring, M'DOWALL *Poems* (1890) 217. (29, *a*) **Nhb.** (R.O.H.) **w.Yks.** He'd set th' haymoo o' fire, HARTLEY *Puddin'* (1876) 233. **Lan.** I'll goo into quarantine upon some hay-moof, BRIERLEY *Out of Work* (1885) 1; They climbed through the round hole on to the top of the hay-mough, KAY-SHUTTLEWORTH *Scarsdale* (1860) II. 167; **Lan.**[1], **e.Lan.**[1] **Mid.** Or frighten Giles from kissing Gillian behind the hay-mow, BARTRAM *People of Clopton* (1897) 8. **War.**[3] A distinction is drawn nowadays by speaking of any crop stacked in barns or under cover as a mow, while any stacked out of doors is a rick. **Som.** AGRIKLER *Rhymes* (1872) 21. (*b*) **Nhb.** (R.O.H.) **Cum.** If you would see the midday siesta of these birds, climb up into some hay-mow. There, in an angle of the beam, you will see their owlships, WATSON *Nature Wdcraft.* (1890) i. **Yks.** At six to the hay-mow hie ye all, HONE *Table-bk.* (1827) I. 73. **w.Yks.** Lan. He's sprain't his anclif a bit, wi' jumpin' off th' hay-moo yesterday, WAUGH *Ben an' th' Bantam* (1866) ii; **Lan.**[1] (30) **War.**[3] (31) **Gall.** I ... spoke to her as I used to do in the hay-neuk at Partou, CROCKETT *Raiders* (1894) xxiii; It is gen. the only clean place in the byre, and is often patronized by tramps, who enter without leave, as well as by lovers among the farm servants (S.R.C.). (32) **n.Yks.**[2] (33) **Glo.** Hay dust, such as the ails and beards of corn, *Horae Subsecivae* (1777) 206. (34) **Ldd.** (B. & H.) (35) **w.Som.**[1] The usual word—hay-cock is seldom heard. **Dev.** Now tha rain's awver yu'd better draw they hay-pooks abroad, HEWETT *Peas. Sp.* (1892). **n.Dev.** Why dedst thee, than, tell me o' the Zess, or it of the Hay-pook! *Exm. Scold.* (1746) l. 88. **nw.Dev.**[1] (36) **Der.**[2], **nw.Der.**[1] (37) **Shr.**[2] (38) **Cum.** (B. & H.) (39) **e.Yks.** MARSHALL *Rur. Econ.* (1796) II. 104. **I.Ma.** Ould! He hasn't the hayseed out of his hair, CAINE *Deemster* (1887) 6, ed. 1889. (40) **Cum.**[4] Yan o' t'measte important seasons o' t'year wid t'farmer was haysel or haytime, C. Pacq. (Aug. 17, 1893) 6, col. 1. **e.An.**[1] *N. & Q.* (1879) 5th S. xi. 194; **e.An.**[1] **Nrf.** Wanted, a good thatcher for haysel and harvest, *Norwich Merc.* (July 6, 1889) 1, col. 2. **Suf.** I always fare so busy in haysel (M.E.R.); **Suf.**[1], **e.Suf.** (F.H.) **Ess.** An' 'twas the time ov haysel, CLARK *J. Noakes* (1839) st. 43; (H.H.M.); When it is too dry for swedes or mangolds it is delightful weather for the haysel, HURNARD *Setting Sun*; (W.W.S.); **Ess.**[1] **Dev.** There had been dry weather for the haysel, BARING-GOULD *Red Spider* (1887) xxxv. **Cor.** A day of days for the haysel ... The air was fragrant with hay, p. *Gaverocks* (1887) xxxvii. (41) **Cha.**[12] (42) **Der.** ADDY *Gl.* (1891). (43) **Sc.** (JAM., s.v. Sow); Tak' a ride on your hay-soo! *Hislop Anecdote* (1874) 106. **Frf.** A thecker fell aff a hay-soo he was workin' at, an' crackit his pow, WILLOCK *Rosetty Ends* (1886) 67, ed. 1889. (44) **Edb.** Alexander Bailie of Culens ... had borrowed a shearing hay spade from the Author, PENNECUIK *Wks.* (1715) 361, ed. 1815. **n.Yks.** A'l tel ya wat, this hēspiad iznt [is not] vara shāp [sharp] (W.H.). **e.Yks.** A common hay-spade turned up at both sides, MARSHALL *Review* (1808) l. 513. **n.Lin.**[1] (45) **Lan.** Armed with hay-forks and hay-stangs, *Neddy's Courtship* (1888) 8. (46) **n.Yks.** In several parts of the N. Riding a hay-sweep is used for readily collecting the hay together, when intended to be stacked in the field, TUKE *Agric.* (1800) 88. (47) **Dev.** Forced to dress in the hay-tallat, BLACKMORE *Lorna Doone* (1869) xix. (48) **Ken.**[1] (49) **w.Mid.**, **Sur.** Lot 70. A Howard's Hay-tedder (W.P.M.). (50) **Cha.**[12] (51) **Lan.** (S.W.) (52) **Shr.** They stopped and found a whitethroat's nest—what the country lads call a 'hay-tick's,' DAVIES *Rambles Sch. Field-club* (1881) iv; **Shr.**[1] This bird, when alarmed, flics about the tall

grass uttering a 'tick-ing' sound, from which it gets its name. (53) **Oxf.**[1] *MS. add.* (54, *a*) **Shr.**, **Oxf.** SWAINSON *ib.* 29. (*b*) **Lin.** (HALL.), **Lin.**[1] (*c*) **Oxf.** SWAINSON *ib.* 23. (55) **s.Wor.**[1], **Glo.** (A.B.) **Dor.** The hay trusser. which he obviously was, nodded with some superciliousness, HARDY *Mayor of Casterbridge* (ed. 1895) 4. (56) **Slk.** Country maidens such as ewe-milkers, hay-workers, HOGG *Tales* (1838) 359, ed. 1866.

2. Phr. (1) *hay abouts*, an order given in drill; see below; (2) *to make sweet hay*, see below.

(1) **Hrt.** The *gen.* acknowledged tradition respecting raw recruits training for the Hrt. Militia is that they were generally found to be ignorant concerning which was the right and left when marching, so that a hay-band was fastened to the right leg and a straw band to the left, that they should be able to distinguish the difference, and instead of the words, 'right,' 'left' being used during drilling the sergeant called out, 'Hay-band,' 'Straw-band.' Hence the term Hay-abouts, *Hrt. Merc.* (June 23, 1888). (2) **Dev.** The field rang with laughter, and occasional screams, as a man twisted a cord of hay, cast the loop round a girl's neck, drew her head towards him and kissed her face. That is called 'the making of sweet hay,' BARING-GOULD *Red Spider* (1887) xxii.

3. The hay-harvest.

Ayr. Some to fee for hay and hairst, *Ballads and Sngs.* (1846) I. 95; Thro' hay, an' thro' hairst, sair we toil it, AINSLIE *Land of Burns* (ed. 1892) 246. **Edb.** It's wearin' on now to the tail o' May, An' just between the beer-seed and the hay, FERGUSSON *Poems* (1773) 109, ed. 1785.

4. *v.* Of newly-cut grass : to become hay, to dry.

s.Not. It don't hay a deal to-day. Them first swaths has hayed a deal sin mornin (J.P.K.). **Nhp.**[1] In the process of hay-making, when the weather is dull and heavy, 'the grass hays badly'; if fine and drying, 'it hays well.' Not applied to corn. According to Holloway *Provinc.* the term is current in Hmp. for both corn and grass. **Lin.**[1] Its haying nistly, if it nobbut hohds fine we can leäd o' Tuesda'. **Hnt.** (T.P.F.)

Hence **Haying**, *sb.* the hay-harvest.

s.Oxf. Through the haying she stayed at home, for her mother was in the hay-field working all day, ROSEMARY *Chilterns* (1895) 53. **Ken.** They're going to begin haying soon (D.W.L.).

HAY, *sb.*[2] In gen. dial. use in Irel. and Eng. Also written hey **Wxf.**[1] **w.Yks.**[4] **Lan.** **e.An.**[1] **n.Dev.**; and in form hye **Wxf.**[1]; *pl.* haies **n.Yks.**[2]; hayes **Wil.**[1]; haze **Dor.** 1. A hedge, fence ; a boundary.

n.Yks.[1] Enclosure fences, often doing duty as boundaries, in which sense the word exists in several local names; **n.Yks.**[2] Ridges of land as district boundaries. 'Scalby haies,' the limits of Whitby Strand in that direction. **w.Yks.**[3] **e.An.**[1] More particularly a clipped quickset hedge. Commonly pron. as if it were in the *pl.* **Nrf.** A clipt hedge, MARSHALL *Rur. Econ.* (1787). **Suf.** RAINBIRD *Agric.* (1819) 294, ed. 1849; **Suf.**[1], **e.Suf.** (F.H.) **2.** A place fenced round, an enclosure ; freq. in *pl.*

Wxf.[1] A garden, field, enclosure, e.g. 'Church hey,' a church-yard. 'Barach-hey,' a barley-field. **Nhb.**[1] Hays or inclosures, HODGSON *Nhb.* II. iii. 89. **Lan.** Cut the last of my wheat and the beans that grew in my little hey, WALKDEN *Diary* (ed. 1866) 40. **Gmg.** A small plot of ground attached to a dwelling, COLLINS *Gow. Dial.* in *Trans. Phil. Soc.* (1848–50) IV. 222. **Hnt.** (T.P.F.) **Wil.**[1] Used as a termination, as Calf-Hayes. **Dor.** Ewe haze, cow haze, MORTON *Cyclo. Agric.* (1863). **Som.** HERVEY *Wedmore Chron.* (1887) I. 385. **Cor.** The churchyard was called the church-hay, *N. & Q.* (1854) 1st S. x. 319.

3. A small wood, coppice, or plantation.

Cha.[1] Freq. in place-names—as Hall o' th' Hay, a farm at Kingsley. **Nhp.**[1] A small wood near the village of Sywell is called 'Sywell Hay.' **Shr.**[1] We'n seventeen 'ays about 'ere, an' we cut'n [thin] one every 'ear.

Hence **Haystall**, *sb.* a small portion of wood on the outskirts of a large wood. Hrf. (HALL.) Glo. *Horae Subsecivae* (1777) 207.

4. *pl.* Flat plains, esp. those covered with ling. Stf. (K.), Stf.[1]

5. *Comp.* (1) **Hay-boot** or -**bote**, *obs.*, the right of cutting as much wood within an enclosure as is necessary to repair the surrounding hedge; (2) -**chat**, (3) -**chick**, the whitethroat, *Sylvia cinerea*; (4) -**gob**, climbing buckwheat, *Polygonum convolvulus*; (5) -**hoa**, the ground-ivy, *Nepeta Glechoma*; (6) -**jack**, see (3); (7) -**maiden**, (*a*) see (4); (*b*) a wild flower of the mint-tribe.

(1) **n.Lin.**[1] [KENNETT *Par. Antiq.* (1695).] (2) **n.Yks.**[4], **ne.Lan.**[1],

Nhp.[1] Oxf. APLIN *Birds* (1889) 214. (3) ne.Lan.[1] (4) War. *B'ham Wkly. Post* (June 10, 1893) ; War.[1] A name given . . . because it mats other herbs together by twisting round them ; War.[28] (5) Hmp.[1] (6) e.An.[1] Nrf. COZENS-HARDY *Broad Nrf.* (1893) 45 ; The Greater Whitethroat, or ' Hay-jack,' as he is locally called, is by no means uncommon, EMERSON *Birds* (ed. 1895) 27. Nrf., Suf. SWAINSON *Birds* (1885) 23. Suf. (G.E.D.) e.Suf. e.An. *Dy. Times* (1892). (7, *a*) Cum. LINTON *Lake Cy.* (1864) 305. Glo.[1] Grass ivy. Dor. (C.W.) Som. JENNINGS *Obs. Dial. w.Eng.* (1825) ; (W.F.R.) Dev. BOWRING *Lang.* (1866) I. pt. v. 17: Dev.[1] n.Dev. Us foun', In a heymaiden bush, These corniwillins, ROCK *Jim an' Nell* (1867) st. 193. Cor. THOMAS *Randigal Rhymes* (1895) Gl. (*b*) Dor. Used for making a medicinal liquor, ' hay-maiden tea,' BARNES *Gl.* (1863) ; Dor.[1]

[1. Ther is neither busk nor hay In May, that it nil . . . been . . . with new leves wreen, CHAUCER *R. Rose*, 54 ; Þou fordide his haies mare and lesse (=destruxisti omnes sepes ejus), *Ps.* (c. 1290) lxxxviii. 41, ed. Surtees Soc. OE. *hege*, 'sepes' (ÆLFRIC) ; cp. OFr. *haie*, hedge (*R. Rose*, 50).]

HAY, *int.* Cum. Yks. Lan. Der. Glo. Hmp. Also in form he Glo. Hmp. [h)ē.] An exclamation, *gen.* interrogative.

Cum. Will ta ivver dee it aggan ? hay ! CHRISTIAN *Sailor Lad* (1880) 3 ; Cum.[1], Yks. (J.W.) Lan. Hay! dew have him dew, ACKWORTH *Clog Shop Chron.* (1896) 271. Der.[2] Hay! it wor grand, lads, that ale wor (s.v. Grand). Glo., Hmp. GROSE (1790) *MS. add.*

HAY, see Haigh, *v.*, Haw, *sb.*[1]

HAY-BAY, *sb.* Lakel. Cum. Yks. Also written hey-bey Wm. & Cum.[1] w.Yks. ; and in form heyba w.Yks.[1] [h)ē·-bē.] A hubbub, uproar ; a commotion, disturbance.

Lakel.[1] At times used to signify a ' discussion with sticks' ; Lakel.[2] He kickt up a gurt hay-bay aboot his money. Cum. Fadder's been kickan up sec hay-bays, SARGISSON *Joe Scoap* (1881) 7 ; Aa! what a hay-bay! 'twas just like the battle of Watterlew, ANDERSON *Ballads* (1805) 124, ed. 1881 ; Cum.[4] Wm. & Cum.[1] Tom hed sec a hruoly An' hey-bey wi' his weyfe, 179. n.Yks. He was in sike a haybay. They come [to the tailor] wiv a greeat haybay (I.W.) ; n.Yks.[24] w.Yks. They set up sich hey-beys as war nivver heerd afore ner sin, DIXON *Craven Dales* (1881) 178 ; w.Yks.[1] Mackin a feaful heyba, ii. 288.

HAY-BREDE, *sb.* n.Yks.[2] The ledge on the fore-front of a wagon upon which the driver sits.

HAYDIGEES, *sb. pl.* Som. Dev. Also in forms high-degrees, highdigees w.Som.[1] High spirits ; merriment, roystering.

Som. From that they ' fell a-romping, and to pretty highdigees,' RAYMOND *Men o' Mendip* (1898) xvi ; JENNINGS *Obs. Dial. w.Eng.* (1825). w.Som.[1] When I come on by the house, there was pretty highdigees [aa·ydijee·z, aa·ydigree·z] gwain on, sure 'nough. Dev. MOORE *Hist. Dev.* (1829) I. 354. n.Dev. Tho' thee'rt in desperd haydigees, ROCK *Jim an' Nell* (1867) st. 62.

[The same word as older E. *hay-de-guy* or *hay-de-guise*, the name of a particular kind of ' hay' or dance. By wells and rills, in meadowes greene, We nightly dance our hey-day-guise, *Robin Good-fellow* (c. 1580) 102, in Percy's *Reliques* (ed. 1887) III. 204.]

HAYEL, *sb.* Dev. Cor. [Not known to our other correspondents.] The windpipe. (Miss D.)

HAYEL, see Haggle, *sb.*[1]

HAYLUNSH, *sb.* Bdf. A headlong fall.

(HALL.); BATCHELOR *Anal. Eng. Lang.* (1809) 135.

HAYMENT, *sb.* Obs. Chs. Shr. Also written hey-ment Shr.[1] A fence or boundary.

Chs.[1] Shr.[1] The parishioners of Myddle answeared that the brooke was whoaly in the parish of Baschurch, and was the hay-ment or fence of the men of Baschurch parish, betweene their lands, and the lands in Myddle parish, GOUGH *Hist. Myddle* (1770) 10, 11 ; Agreed at a vestry meeting held for the parish of Clun, the 24th day of May 1755, for the repairs of the church and the churchyard wall or hayments.

**HAYN(E, see Hain, *v.*[18]

HAYNESS, *adj.* Cum. Horrible, dreadful, terrible ; also used *advb.* Cf. hainish, *adj.*[1] 1.

Cum.[4] ' Hayness fine' ; ' hayness dirty.' Ah was wokent up be a hayness ruck-shin gaan forret ower me heid, SARGISSON *Joe Scoap* (1881) 200.

[The same word as lit. E. *heinous.*]

HAY-NET, *sb.* Nhp. e.An. Ken. [ē·-net.] A net for catching animals, esp. rabbits.

Nhp.[1], e.An.[1] Suf. RAINBIRD *Agric.* (1819) 294, ed. 1849 ; Suf.[1] A long low net . . . placed upward by stakes along hedges . . . to prevent the transit of rabbits from side to side, when hunted by dogs. e.Suf. (F.H.) Ken.[1] A long net, often an old fish net, used in cover shooting to keep the birds and flick from running out of the beat.

[Haye a net for connes, *bourcettes a chasser*, PALSGR. (1530) ; Haye, nette to catche conys wythe, *Prompt.*]

HAYNISH, see Hainish, *adj.*[2]

HAY-REE, *int.* nw.Der.[1] Go on ! a carter's ad-dress to his horses.

[Cp. Fr. (Béarnais) *harri !* interjection pour exciter les bêtes, en avant ! (Catalan. *Arri ! arri !*) (LESPY). OFr. *harry !* RABELAIS *Garg.* I. 12.]

HAYRIFF, HAYRISH, see Hairif, Arrish.

HAYS, *sb. pl. Obs.* Sc. Also Cor. Also written hayes Kcb. Cor. ; heys Sc. The steps of a round country dance.

Sc. The beautiful time-piece . . . which . . . turns out, when it strikes the hour, a whole band of morrice-dancers to trip the hays to the measure, SCOTT *Nigel* (1822) xix ; I have some part of the silver candlesticks still dancing the heys in my purse, *ib.* Leg. *Montrose* (1818) viii. Kcb. Dance round the hayes like pipers at a wake, DAVIDSON *Seasons* (1789) 11. Cor. Mr. Noall's and other houses dancing hayes £1 15s. 6d., *St. Ives Borough Accts.* (1714).

[He taught them rounds and winding heys to tread, DAVIES *Orchestra* (1596) (NARES). Fr. *haye d'allemaigne*, the name of a dance in Marot ; see LA CURNE.]

HAY-SCALED, *adj.* Yks. [Not known to our corre-spondents.] Hare-lipped. (HALL.) Cf. hare, *sb.*[1] 1 (12).

HAYSING, *vbl. sb.* Cor. Also in form haizing. [ē·zin.] Following hares by night.

In many instances it would mean the same as poaching, if the latter word is divested of the idea of crime, *N. & Q.* (1854) 1st S. x. 318 ; Cor.[12]

HAYSTERS, *sb. pl.* n.Yks.[2] Haymakers.

HAYSUCK, *sb.* Wor. Glo. Som. Dev. Also in forms aizac se.Wor.[1] ; hay-sucker Som. Dev. ; hayzick Glo.[1] ; hazeck, hazock, Isaac Wor. [ē·-, e2·-sak.] 1. The hedge-sparrow, *Accentor modularis.* Cf. aichee.

Wor. SWAINSON *Birds* (1885) 29. se.Wor.[1] A small bird which builds its nest in the grass on the banks of hedges. Glo. *Horae Subsecivae* (1777) 207; Glo.[12]

2. The whitethroat, *Sylvia cinerea.*

Wor. SWAINSON *ib.* 23. Som. W. & J. *Gl.* (1873). Dev. SWAIN-SON *ib.* 23.

[1. Thou mordrer of the heysugge (*v. r.* heysoke) on the braunche, CHAUCER *Parl. Foules*, 612. OE. *hegesugge* (ÆLFRIC).]

HAYTY, *v.* War. Som. Cor. To move up and down ; to flicker about. Som. (W.F.R.) Cf. height, 8. Hence **Hayty-tayty,** *sb.* a see-saw. War. (J.R.W.) Som. (M.A.R.) ; W. & J. *Gl.* (1873). Cor.[1]

HAYVE, HAYVER, see Heave, Eaver, *sb.*[1]

HAYWARD, *sb.* Chs. Lin. Wor. Glo. Oxf. Bdf. Sus. Hmp. Dor. Som. Amer. Also in forms hayud se.Wor.[1] ; howard Bdf. Hmp.[1] [ē·wəd.] A manorial officer whose duty it is to see that fences are kept in repair, to look after the stock, and to impound stray cattle.

Chs.[1] The election of hayward takes place annually at the Court Leet of the township of Shocklach, *Chs. Courant* (June 27, 1883). Lin. At Wintringham, Lord Carrington has a man employed whose only business is to be constantly walking over every part of the estate in succession in order to see if the fences are in order ; if a post or rail is wanted and the quick exposed, he gives notice to the farmer, and attends again to see if the neglect is remedied, MARSHALL *Review* (1811) III. 119. n.Lin.[1] Wor. So well had the stock been looked after by the hayward that not a single case of pounding had occurred. . . That [repairs of fencing] being work which the hayward could do when there was no stock on the hills to look after, *Evesham Jrn.* (Oct. 17, 1896). s.Wor.[1], se.Wor.[1], Glo. (A.B.), Glo.[12] Oxf. From 1810 to 1852, the time of the Cowley Inclosure, he had frequently tended the cattle as hayward in these grazings, Oxf. *Chron.* (Apr. 8, 1892) 23 ; *N. & Q.* (1866) 3rd S. x. 74. Bdf. *ib.* 29. Sus.[1], Hmp.[1] Dor. He sometimes ' drives the common' ; i. e. drives all the stock in it into a corner, and pounds such as is not owned by those who have a right of common, BARNES *Gl.* (1863) ; Dor.[1] When the háyward come wi' all his men To dreve the common, 258. **Som.** So long as I be the hayward, RAYMOND *Love and Quiet Life* (1894) 109. **w.Som.**[1] [**Amer.** A township officer, whose duty it is to impound stray cattle (FARMER).]

[Canstow ... haue an horne and be haywarde, and liggen oute a nyghtes, And kepe my corn in my croft fro pykers and theeves? *P. Plowman* (c.) VI. 16. Hay, *sb.*[2] + *ward.*]

HAYZE, HAYZICK, see Haze, *v.*[3], Heaze, Haysuck.

HAZARD, *sb.* and *v.* Sc. Irel. Yks. Also in form **haizart** Sc. **1.** *sb.* A cab-stand.

Dub. Used occas. on Police Regulations (A.L.M.) ; Well in use in Dublin : ' Where is Jack 1 ' ' He is in the hazard ' (P.W.J.) ; What about providing a hazard at each arrival platform 1 . . . the public would then know it was beyond the power of a . . . cabman to refuse the first call, *Freeman's Jrn.* (Dec. 5, 1884).

2. *pl.* In phr. (1) *to gan upon the hazards on a thing,* (2) *to run hazards,* to run the risk.

(1) n.Yks.[2] I shall hae te gan upon t'hazards on't. (2) n.Yks. Ah'll run hazzuts (I.W.).

3. *v.* *Obs.* To venture to do something ; to venture a conjecture.

Sc. There is not a Scot's-man, but he'll haizart For to defend his countreyes right, MAIDMENT *Pasquils* (1868) 137 ; Give him a cuff, I'll hazard he'll be as ill as I am called, *Sc. Presby. Eloq.* (ed. 1847) 117.

HAZARDABLE, *adj.* Yks. Suf. Also in form **huzzudable** Suf. Hazardous, risky, uncertain.

e.Yks. (J.H.) Suf. Clover, for instance, is said to be ' a wonderful huzzudable crop,' (C.T.). e.Suf. Very common (F.H.).

[(It) were an hazardable peece of art, T. BROWNE *Hydriot* (1658), in *Wks.*, ed. Wilkin, III. 27.]

HAZARDOUS, *adj.* Rut. Sur. [æˑzədəs.] Dependent on chance, risky, uncertain.

Rut.[1] Pears is a hazardous thing, unless you gets 'em joost at the time. Sur.[1] A very hazardous crop.

HAZE, *v.*[1] n.Cy. Nhb. Yks. Lan. Lin. Wor. Suf. Also written **hase** w.Yks. [hēz.] **1.** To drizzle ; to be foggy.

N.Cy.[1] ; N.Cy.[2] It hazes, it misles or rains small rain. Nhb.[1] w.Yks. SCATCHERD *Hist. Morley* (1890) *Gl.*, ed. 1874 ; w.Yks.[1] Lin. STREATFEILD *Lin. and Danes* (1884) 236. n.Lin.[1] It haazed aboot five o'clock, bud noà watter cum'd to meàn noht. A man e' his she't sleeves wo'd n't hev gotten weet.

Hence **Hazy,** *adj.* drizzling. ne.Lan.[1], Wor. (J.R.W.)

2. To cover with hoar-frost.

e.Suf. The windows are all hazed up (F.H.).

Hence (1) **Hazer,** (2) **Haze-frost,** *sb.* hoar-frost. *ib.*

HAZE, *v.*[2] n.Cy. Yks. Lin. Also written **hase** n.Cy. (HALL.) [hēz.] **1.** To beat, thrash.

n.Cy. (HALL.) e.Yks. NICHOLSON *Flk-Sp.* (1889) 26 ; e.Yks.[1], m.Yks.[1] Lin. STREATFEILD *Lin. and Danes* (1884) 236. n.Lin. He's been hazing my lad shameful, *N. & Q.* (1889) 7th S. viii. 256 ; n.Lin.[1] sw.Lin.[1] Haze him well ; gie him a reiet good hiding.

Hence **Hazing,** *sb.* a thrashing.

e.Yks. NICHOLSON *Flk-Sp.* (1889) 26 ; e.Yks.[1] *MS. add.* (T.H.) Lin. STREATFEILD *Lin. and Danes* (1884) 236. n.Lin.[1]

2. To scold. m.Yks.[1] Cf. **hazen.**

Hence **Hazy,** *sb.* a scolding ; a quarrel ; abusive language. n.Yks.[12]

[2. To haze one, *perterrefacio,* COLES (1679). OFr. *haser,* ' irriter, piquer, fâcher, insulter ' (GODEFROI).]

HAZE, *v.*[3] Lin. Also written **hayze** Lin.[1] [ēz.] To bail water ; also used *fig.*

Hazing the food into the mouth, i.e. eating greedily and ravenously, STREATFEILD *Lin. and Danes* (1884) 236 ; Lin.[1], n.Lin.[1]

HAZE, *v.*[4] Sc. Lin. e.An. Hmp. [hēz.] To dry by exposure to the air, to half-dry, to dry on the surface.

Sc. (JAM. *Suppl.*) ; To half-dry clothes in the open air (JAM.). Lin. MILLER & SKERTCHLY *Fenland* (1878) iv. e.An.[1] Anything is said to be hazed, as rows of corn or hay, when a brisk breeze follows a shower. Nrf. Used of corn, when, under the influence of sunshine or a breeze, it is drying after a shower of rain, COZENS-HARDY *Broad Nrf.* (1893) 12 ; MORTON *Cyclo. Agric.* (1863) ; ' Ar the linen dry ! ' ' No, but they are good tid'ly hazed ' (W.W.S.). Suf. Land after ploughing is left to haze before being harrowed, RAINBIRD *Agric.* (1819) 299, ed. 1849 ; Suf.[1] Till 'tave hazed a little. e.Suf. (F.H.) Hmp.[1] The corn be'ant hazed enough.

[Cp. Norw. dial. *hesja,* frames on which hay or corn is put for drying (AASEN) ; Icel. dial. *hisjungr,* a soft air good for drying hay spread out on hesjar (VIGFUSSON).]

HAZE, HAZECK, see Hay, *sb.*[1], Heaze, Haysuck.

HAZE-BAZE, *sb.* Dur. A fool, 'ninny,' a stupid person.

Hoo he mi'ad a haze-baze o' ma. I, thoo may ca' ma green en silly ; b'd . . . Ah wez miad a bigger haze-baze on when thoo wedded ma, EGGLESTONE *Betty Podkin's Visit* (1877) 8.

HAZE-GAZE, *sb.* n.Cy. Nhb. Yks. A show in the sense of an exhibition of oneself ; a wonder.

N.Cy.[1] Nhb. [I] thought at their shippin see'd a haze-gaze, MIDFORD *Coll. Sngs.* (1818) 68 ; Nhb.[1] A country cousin makes a ' haze-gaze ' by staring about in the street. Yks. (HALL.)

HAZEL, *sb.*[1] and *v.* Sc. Irel. Nhb. Cum. Yks. Lan. Der. Lin. Nhp. Bck. Ess. Also written **hazle** n.Cy. n.Yks.[4] nw.Der.[1] ; and in forms **hasle** w.Yks.[1] ; **hazzel** nw.Der.[1] n.Lin.[1] ; **hensel** Ess. ; **hezal** n.Lan.[1] ; **hezel** w.Yks.[5] ; **hezzel** Cum.[1] n.Lan. sw.Lin.[1] ; **hezzle** Nhb.[1] n.Yks.[24] e.Yks.[1] w.Yks.[8] ne.Lan.[1] ; **hizzel** Cum.[4] ; **hizzle** Der.[2] nw.Der.[1] [(h)ēˑzl, h)aˑzl, h)eˑzl.] **1.** *sb.* In *comp.* (1) **Hazel-broth,** a flogging with a hazel stick ; (2) **-crottles,** the lungwort, *Sticta pulmonaria* ; (3) **-oil,** see (1) ; (4) **-rag,** (5) **-raw,** see (2) ; (6) **-rise,** a small hazel stick ; (7) **-scowb,** a hazel wand used in making traps for crabs ; (8) **-shaw,** an abrupt, flat piece of ground at the bottom of a hill, covered with hazels ; (9) **-twizzle,** a cluster of nuts grown together ; (10) **-wan,** a shoot of hazel.

(1) w.Yks.[8] (2) n.Ir. (B. & H.) (3) Sc. (JAM.) ; I'll present ye with a bottle o' hazel oil, if ye ken what that is, BLACK *Daughter of Heth* (1871) xvi. Nhb. Aa think some hezzle-oil 'll de ye good, me young man (R.O.H.) ; Nhb.[1], w.Yks.[1], n.Lan.[1], ne.Lan.[1] Nhp.[2] One of the common jokes, formerly prevailing on the first of April, was sending an inexperienced lad to a chymist for ' a penn'orth of hazel-oil.' (4) n.Ir. (B. & H.) (5) Sc. (JAM.) (6) n.Cy. (K.) (7) Nhb.[1] A strong hazel wand of some three or four years' growth for the purpose of making ' crab-creeves ' (traps for crabs). A ' creeve ' has a lattice woodwork bottom, and into holes burnt along the sides the scowbs are inserted, and bent over, arch-fashion, and then covered with a net. (8) Tev. (JAM.) (9) Der.[2], nw.Der.[1] (10) Nhb.[1]

2. Phr. (1) *oil of hazel,* a thrashing ; (2) *to give some hazel,* to give a beating.

(1) n.Lan. Oil o' hezzel's stuff to cure that complent, R. PIKETAH *Forness Flk.* (1870) 33. (2) n.Lin.[1]

3. *v.* To beat as with a hazel stick.

Nhb. Aa'll hezzle ye (R.O.H.). Cum.[14] I'll hezzel thee. n.Yks. Off Ah went, te hezzle 'em all out, TWEDDELL *Clevel. Rhymes* (1875) 48 ; n.Yks.[14], ne.Yks.[1] e.Yks. NICHOLSON *Flk-Sp.* (1889) 26 ; e.Yks.[1] Ah'll bezzle thi hide fo' tha. m.Yks.[1], w.Yks.[5], ne.Lan.[1], nw.Der.[1], nw.Lin. (B. & H.) Ess. I'll heusel your oad hide for you (W.W.S.).

Hence **Hazeling,** *sb.* a beating, flogging.

n.Yks.[124], ne.Yks.[1], e.Yks.[1], m.Yks.[1] w.Yks. GRAINGE *Nidderdale* (1863) 226 ; w.Yks.[5] To beat with a stick, not necessarily a ' hazel ' one. ' Tha'd du wi' a good hezeling, ah see thah wod ; thah's bin hinging on for't awalt' mornin'!' ne.Lan.[1], nw.Der.[1]

HAZEL, *sb.*[2] and *adj.* Sc. Irel. Nhb. Dur. Cum. Wm. Yks. Lin. Nhp. Ess. Also written **hazle** Nhb.[1] Dur. Ess.[1] ; and in forms **hezel** w.Yks.[2] ; **hezle** Wm.[1] ; **hezzel** Cum.[1] sw.Lin.[1] [(h)ēˑzl, h)aˑzl, h)eˑzl.] **1.** *sb.* A hard sort of sandstone.

Nhb.[1] *Gen.* of a kind too hard to work freely under the chisel, or a tough mixture of sandstone and shale in a pit. ' The sand-stones denominated hazles have a high crystalline and metamorphic appearance,' HOWSE *Nat. Hist. Trans.* (1890) X. 275. Nhb.[1], Dur. Underneath the hazle we find another slate bed, FORSTER *Strata* (1821) 97 ; Alternating beds of hazle and whetstone, *Borings* (1881) II. 12. Cum. HUTCHINSON *Hist. Cum.* (1794) I. App. 48.

2. *adj.* Of soil : stiff, clayey, loamy ; *gen.* in *comp.* **Hazel-earth** or **-mould.**

Dur. The soil is generally loamy, or what is called hazel mould, YOUNG *Annals Agric.* (1784-1815) V. 361. Nhp.[1] Hazel-earth, or hazel-mould, a loamy soil, which has a large portion of a rosin-like sand in it. In some places it is pretty full of small stones of the gravel kind. Ess. *Gl.* (1851) ; Ess.[1]

Hence **Hazely,** *adj.* loamy.

Ess.[1] Hazely brick earth, a kind of loam.

3. Of soil : light, friable, easily worked. Also in *comp.* **Hazel-mould.**

Cum.[1] Hezzel mowd, the fine powdery soil found about the roots of the hazel. Sick cattle are fond of this soil when recovering. **Wm.** (B.K.) **w.Yks.**[2] People speak of ' nice hazel land.' **sw.Lin.**[1] ' It's sort of hezzel land,' applied to land neither stiff nor light, from its usual colour.

Hence **Hazelly,** *adj.* of soil : poor, light, loose. **Banff.** Hazely ground being naturally loose and light will not admit of clear ploughing twice for one crop. . . Our own soil is . . . most part hazely and made up of sand and light earth, *Agric. Surv.* App. 37, 38 (JAM.\). **N.I.**[1] Light hazelly land.

HAZEL, *sb.*[3] Dev. Also written **hazle** Dev.[4] A haw, the fruit of the hawthorn, *Crataegus Oxyacantha.* (B. & H.), Dev.[4]

HAZEL, see **Hessle.**

HAZEN, *v.* Glo. Wil. Also written **hazon** Wil. ; and in form **hawzen** Glo.[1] [ē·zən.] To scold, to speak sharply ; with *at* : to speak impudently to. Cf. **haze,** *v.*[2] 2. Glo.[1] Doant thee 'awzen at I, or else I'll gi' thee the strap ; Glo.[2] To check a dog by the voice. **Wil.** BRITTON *Beauties* (1825); Wil.[1] Now dwoan't 'ee hazon the child for't. **n.Wil.** What d'ye kip hazoning I far? (E.H.G.)

[In older E. *hasen* meant to scare, terrify. Night . . . sent . . . fantasie for to hazan idle heads, *Hist. Evordanus* (1605) (N.E.D.).]

HAZEN, see **Halsen.**

HAZLE, *v.* Sc. Yks. Der. Not. Lin. Lei. Nhp. War. Oxf. Bck. Bdf. Hrt. Hnt. e.An. Also written **haisle** Ayr. (JAM. *Suppl.*) ; **hazel** Hrt. Ess. ; and in forms **aisle** Abd. Ayr. (JAM. *Suppl.*) ; **asol, assol** Ayr. (JAM. *Suppl.*) ; **azle** War.[2] ; **azzle** Lei.[1] ; **hazzle** w.Yks.[2] s.Der. Lin. Lei.[1] Nhp.[12] ; **hezzle** Not.[2] [h)ē·zl, h)a·zl.] To dry, mellow, season in the sun ; to dry on the surface. Cf. **haiser, haze,** *v.*[4]

Abd. (G.W.), Ayr. (JAM. *Suppl.*) **w.Yks.**[2] After the first harrowing of a field of newly-sown corn it is better, if the ground is damp, to let the sun hazle the surface of the land before the second harrowing. **Lei.**[1] If the clothes don't dry much, they'll hazzle. **Oxf.**, Bck., Bdf. (J.W.B.) **Hnt.** The surface of the earth is said to hazle, when it gets dry soon after being dug (T.P.F.). **e.An.**[1] **e.Suf.** I shall let this pitle hazle before I plant it (F.H.). **Ess.** Thou, who by that happy wind of Thine didst hazle and dry up the forlorn dregs and slime of Noah's deluge, ROGERS *Naaman* (1642) 886 ; I hung the linen out, and it nicely hazelled (S.P.H.).

Hence (1) **Hazel,** *adj.* half-dry ; (2) **Hazle,** *sb. (a)* drying by the sun ; the first process of drying linen ; (*b*) the dried appearance presented by the skin before it chaps ; (3) **Hazled,** *ppl. adj.* (*a*) half-dried ; (*b*) rough, chapped like the skin in frosty weather ; also *fig.* crabbed, sour, churlish ; (4) **Hazling,** *ppl. adj.* drying.

(1) Hrt. Hazel hay (H.G.). (2, *a*) Ayr. The claes 'll be getting a fine aisle the day. Run noo, an' set the claes to the asol (JAM. *Suppl.*). **Ess.** (W.W.S.) (*b*) Nhp.[2] (3, *a*) s.Der. (Miss P.) Not.[2] ' Are the clothes (before the fire) dry now?' ' No, but they are nicely "hezzled."' Lin. (M.D.H.) Hrt. That land is just nice hazelled for sowing (H.G.). **e.Suf.** (F.H.) **Ess.** ' Have you all your linen dry?' ' No, but it is hazelled ' (M.I.J.C.). (*b*) Lei.[1], Nhp.[1] War.[2] Now your hands are hazled. The child's skin is quite hazled. (4) Ayr. It's a gran' aislin day : see an put out a' the asolin' things first (JAM. *Suppl.*).

HAZLEY, *adj.* Sc. Also written **haslie** ; and in form **hazelly** Ayr. Clothed or covered with hazels. **Sc.** Frae out the haslie holt the deer Sprang glancing thro' the schaw, JAMIESON *Pop. Ballads* (1806) I. 197. Ayr. Thy burnie . . . trots by hazelly shaws and braes, BURNS *On Pastoral Poetry,* st. 8. Gall. Awa on the hazley brae, MACTAGGART *Encycl.* (1824) 257, ed. 1876.

HAZOCK, see **Haysuck.**

HAZY, *adj.* Sc. Also written **haizie** ; **hazzie** Rxb. (JAM.) 1. Dim, not seeing distinctly. **Gall.** Whan I grow auld wi' blinkers hazy, MACTAGGART *Encycl.* (1824) 353, ed. 1876.

2. Muddled ; crazy, weak in understanding. **Lth.** (JAM.) **Feb.** Ye're doitit, dais'd, an' haizie : Oh how drink degrades the man! AFFLECK *Poet. Wks.* (1836) 132. Rxb. (JAM.)

Hence **Hazie,** *sb.* a stupid, thick-headed person. Rxb. (JAM.)

HAZY-GAZY, *sb.* Lin. Also in form **asey-casey.** A window.

Es aw sat . . . lukking oot i' mi hazy-gazy, Aw sah a rueri run away. Es aw looked out i' my asey-casey, *Lin. N. & Q.* XI. 22.

HAZZICK, see **Hassock.**

HAZZLED, *adj.* Yks. Also written **hazled** n.Yks.[14] [a·zld.] Speckled red and white.

n.Yks. Hazzled coo, a roan-coloured cow (T.S.) ; **n.Yks.**[1] Speckled red and white, or rather with the hairs of these colours intermixed, so that it is hard to say in some cases which predominates. According to the preponderance of red or white the beast is ' dark-hazled ' or ' light-hazled ' ; n.Yks.[4], ne.Yks.[1]

HAZZY-TREE, *sb.* Bck. Also written **azzy-tree** s.Bck. The hawthorn, *Crataegus Oxyacantha.* (B. & H.)

HE, *pers. pron.* and *sb.* Var. dial. uses in Sc. Irel. Eng. and Amer. [Emph. h)ī ; unemph. h)i, ə. In the midl. and s. counties the unemph. form is *gen.* ə for all positions in the sentence ; but in the n. counties ə is *gen.* only used in interrogative and subordinate sentences, and i in affirmative sentences. See WRIGHT *Gram. Wndhll.* (1892) 116–21.] I. Dial. forms : (1) A, (2) Aɪ, (3) Aw, (4) E, (5) Ee, (6) Eɪ, (7) Ey, (8) Ɪ, (9) Ha, (10) Hĕ, (11) Hea, (12) Hee, (13) Hei, (14) Hey, (15) Hi, (16) Hi, (17) I, (18) I, (19) Hu, (20) U. [For further instances see II. below.]

(1) w.Yks.[1] Lin. 'A said, TENNYSON *N. Farmer, Old Style* (1864) st. 7. Nhp.[12] War.[2]; War.[3] A sez to me, sez a. m.Wor. (H.K.) w.Wor.[1] W'abr bin a? Shr.[12] Hrf. A dunna not lose not no toime, a don't, *N. & Q.* (1874) 5th S. ii. 197. Brks.[1] 6. Suf.[1], I.W.[12] Wil.[1] How a hackers an bivers, 124. w.Som.[1] Cor. A wudn't a gived in ef a 'adn't lost a lemb, *Longman's Mag.* (Feb. 1893) 988. [For further instances see A, V. 1.] (2) w.Som. Full aɪ', unemph. ai, ELWORTHY *Gram.* (1877) 33. (3) Cor. ' Allow me,' says maestur, an' aw fooched out hes arm, FORFAR *Jan's Crishp.* (1859) xx ; Aw fetched that boy a clout, THOMAS *Randigal Rhymes* (1895) 4. (4) Frf. In interrogatives the 'h' practically disappears (J.B.). w.Frf., e.Per. Unemph. ē kent fein, bət ē widnā tel. This ē is the short form of a close ē (W.A.C.). e.Yks. Unemph. (R.S.) m.Wor. (H.K.) w.Wor.[1] 'E 'anna, *Pref.* 26. Shr.[1] *Gram. Outlines,* 47. (5) e.Yks. Emph. (R.S.) s.Cha.[1] 66. Shr.[1] Emph., *Gram. Outlines,* 47. Sur. What ah 'ee sent they hops over there fur? BICKLEY *Sur. Hills* (1890) I. i. Suf. (F.A.A.) w.Som. Full ee' [=ī] ; unemph. ee [=ī] ; unconnected ee', ELWORTHY *Gram.* (1877) 33. e.Dev. Th' day ee was morried, PULMAN *Sng. Sol.* (1860) iii. 11. (6) m.Yks. Emph., ELLIS *Pronunc.* (1889) V. 524. s.Cha.[1] *ib.* 423. n.Stf. *ib.* 422. s.Stf. Emph. *ib.* 468. Der. *ib.* 433. Lei. *ib.* 490. Nhp. *ib.* 214. Suf. *ib.* 284. [A diphthong the first element of which is like the *e* in bet.] (7) s.Cha.[1] 64. (8) Dur. Unemph., ELLIS *ib.* 685. Cum. *ib.* 592. e.Yks. Unemph., *ib.* 534. m.Yks. Unemph., *ib.* 512. w.Yks. Unemph., WRIGHT *Gram. Wndhll.* (1892) 116. Lei. ELLIS *ib.* 470. Hrf. *ib.* 72. Glo. I teld, *ib.* 65. Brks. Unemph., *ib.* 88. e.An.[1] 138. n.Ken. Unemph., ELLIS *ib.* 138. Wil. *ib.* 490. s.Dev. *ib.* 163. w.Cor. *ib.* 173. (9) w.Som.[1] Thy missus is bad again idn ha? Dev. Ha brort ma ta tha bankitten houze, BAIRD *Sng. Sol.* (1860) ii. 4 ; Then ha took up es pipe, NATHAN HOGG *Poet. Lett.* (1847) 49. ed. 1865. sw.Dev.[1] (10) w.Frf., e.Per. Unemph. ; rarely (W.A.C.). (11) Wxf.[1] (12) Lin. MARSHALL *Review* (1811) III. 185. w.Wor. He bin a rum un, tho' heem [he is] not a bad un, S. BEAUCHAMP *N. Hamilton* (1875) I. 67. e.Wil. A zed heem dang if he Ood'un larn un ow ta zing, CALLOW *Joe's Blackbird* ; Heem dang if he did know, *ib. Courtship of Mister Clay.* (13) s.Sc. ELLIS *ib.* 717. Cum. Hei, *ib.* 670. (14) Sc. Accented, MURRAY *Dial.* (1873) 187, 189. Wxf.[1] s.Cha.[1] 64. (15) Sc. ELLIS *ib.* 689. w.Frf., e.Per. Hi diznā ken (W.A.C.). Nhb. Emph., ELLIS *ib.* 648. Dur. *ib.* 635. Cum., Wm. Emph., *ib.* 584. s.Lin. Emph., *ib.* 298. Oxf. *ib.* 117. Brks. *ib.* 97. Nrf. Emph., *ib.* 265. e.Suf. *ib.* 280. w.Suf. *ib.* 287. e.Dor. *ib.* 79. sw.Dev. *ib.* 164. w.Cor. *ib.* 172. [Almost *em.* (J.W.)] (16) Sc. *ib.* 689. Nhb. Unemph., *ib.* 648. Wm. Emph., *ib.* 584. s.Nrf. *ib.* 273. (17) e.Yks. Emph., *ib.* 534. m.Yks. *ib.* 524. w.Yks. WRIGHT *Gram. Wndhll.* (1892) 116. Lan. ELLIS *ib.* 335. w. & s.Cha. *ib.* 421. Lei. *ib.* 468. e.War. *ib.* 487. Hrf. *ib.* 73. Glo. *ib.* 63. Bdf. *ib.* 207. Hrt. *ib.* 198. Hnt. *ib.* 212. n.Ken. *ib.* 138. Wil. *ib.* 490. (18) Dur. Unemph., *ib.* 635. Cum. *ib.* 592. Wm. *ib.* 470. e.Yks. *ib.* 534. m.Yks. !Emph., *ib.* 512. w.Yks. Unemph., WRIGHT *Gram. Wndhll.* (1892) 116. Lan. ELLIS *ib.* 335. Stf. Unemph., *ib.* 470. s.Lin. *ib.* 300. Nhp. *ib.* 254. e.War. *ib.* 470. Shr.[1] Unemph., *Gram. Outlines,* 47. Oxf. ELLIS *ib.* 117. Bdf. *ib.* 207. Hrt. *ib.* 198. Hnt. *ib.* 212. e.Suf. *ib.* 280. w.Suf. *ib.* 288. n.Dev. *ib.* 158. (19) Glo. (S.L.) Dev. A cliver man tole mer hu vurily thort Thay sqweez'd up tha hawls uv thare stummiks ta nort, NATHAN HOGG *Poet. Lett.* (1847) 12, ed. 1865. (20) Shr.[1] Unemph., *Gram.*

Outlines, 47. **w.Som.** Unemph. and interrog. encl., ELWORTHY *Gram.* (1877) 33.

II. Dial. uses. **1.** *pers. pron.* in *comb.* **He-said** or **-say**, a rumour, hearsay ; *gen.* in *phr. to be neither he-said nor she-said.*

Wm. It's nowder he-said ner she-said, it's here i' print (B.K.). **w.Yks.** Used to affirm that a statement is not made from hearsay but from actual experience or observation. 'Ah saw it mysen, so it's nawther he say nor she say' (S.K.C.).

2. Used redundantly, esp. after proper names.

Bnff. If ye burn Auchindoun, Huntly he will head ye, GORDON *Chron. Keith* (1880) 303. **s.Wm.** Josee he's a yow dead, HUTTON *Dial. Storth and Arnside* (1760) l. 99. **w.Yks.** (J.W.) **nw.Der.[1]** Ned Wilson he said, &c. **n.Lin.[1]** Dr. P. he says to me, 'Mrs. D.,' he says, 'it's ovverharassment o' th' liver 'at yer sufferin' from.' **Wor.** (H.K.) **Nrf.** The king he ha' browt me into his charmbers, GILLETT *Sng. Sol.* (1860) i. 4. **Suf.[1]** Jack he go to skule. Mr. Johnson he have two sons (s.v. Have). **s.Cy.** (J.W.) **Sus.[1]** Master Tumptops, he's a man as you'll notice mostly happens along about anyone's dinner-time.

3. Used of fem. or inanimate objects : *she, it.* Also used *impers.*

Sh.I. He wis a bonny morning, HIBBERT *Desc. Sh. I.* (1822) 224, ed. 1891 ; Dere hit bides till he lichtens in da moarnin, CLARK *N. Gleams* (1898) 41. **a.Cbs.[1]** Wot)n yū thingk· ūbūw·t dhis gy·aa·rdin-aach' !—Ahy thingk ey(d dóo wi ū fresh kóout u pee·nt [What'n yō think abowt this garden-hatch !—I think hey'd do wi' a fresh cooat o' peent], 67. **St.[1]** Nhp.[2] ' A ' is used for 'he,' 'she,' and sometimes ' it,' 1. **War.[1]; War.[2]** ' She broke the winder.' ' Did ā I ' ' The cat's stole yo'r mate.' ' 'As ā I ' **w.Wor.[1]** Thar a [she, it] comes. **s.Wor.[1]** Most inanimate objects are spoken of as ' he,' the chief exceptions being a boat, a church-bell, a cricket-ball, a fire-engine, and a railway-train, which are always 'her.' ' He's a good lock,' 9. **Shr.[1], Hrf.** (R.M.E.) Glo. ' Ow does the twoad of a wife do ?' ' He lees a-bed loik a leddy,' LYSONS *Vulgar Tongue* (1868) 46 ; There is a prov. that everything in Glo. is 'he' except a tom-cat, and that is always 'she' (S.L.); **Glo.[1]; Glo.[2]** II. **Sur.** *N. & Q.* (1878) 5th S. x. 222. **Sus.** (R.B.), **Hmp.** (H.C.M.B.), **n.Hmp.** (E.H.R.) **s.Hmp.** That there moon ... he's hurrying away, VERNEY *L. Lisle* (1870) xx. **Wil.[1]** Marlborough folk are traditionally reputed to call everything 'he' but a bull, and that they always call ' she ' (s.v. Comical). Dor. ' He ' is used without much apparent distinction in Purbeck. I have heard it said of a gun-boat, ' He's just left Worbarrow.' Of a hen, ' He's now laying.' A cow also is ' he.' Of a picture, ' He did use to hang over yonder ' (C.W.) ; Things are taken as of two classes : (1) the personal class of formed individual things, as a man, a tree, a tool; and (2) the impersonal class, of unformed quantities of things, as a quantity of hair, or wood, or water. ' He ' is the personal pronoun for the personal class, and ' it ' for the impersonal. A tree is 'he,' and some water is 'it,' BARNES *Sng. Sol.* (1859) *Notes*, iii; They looked at the dairyman's cart, and he's got none neither! HARDY *Wess. Tales* (1888) II. 186-7. Som. Eze, he be their mother, WILSON *Dial.* (1855) 10 ; He idden in the drawer to-day, RAYMOND *Tryphena* (1895) 38. **w.Som.[1]** The universal nom. pronoun to represent all things living or dead, to which the indefinite article can be prefixed. ' He ' is used in speaking of a cow or a woman, but not of corn, water, wool, salt, coal, or such things as are not individual, but in the mass. Dev. He's a nice motherly shawl, LAWSON *Upton Gl.* (1884) 9. **n.Dev.** Ha [she] bed tha zet down, *Exm. Scold.* (1746) l. 167. **nw.Dev.[1]** [Amer. He's a whole team and the dog under the wagon, LOWELL *Biglow Papers* (ed. 1866) 199.]

4. Emphatic form of the acc. or dat. : *him, her, it.* Cf. **en,** *pron.*

Nhp. When him's busy us goes and does a day's work for he (F.P.T.). War. Us are going with he (N.R.). Wor. He said he'd bring he a canary and he was to get he a goldfinch (H.K.). **Hrf.** ELLIS *Pronunc.* (1889) V. 73. Oxf. 'Wurs my showel !' ' I aa got ee' (A.P.). **w.Oxf.** ELLIS *ib.* 93. Brks. *ib.* 97. Sur. But 'un proved 'ee frum Scripter, BICKLEY *Sur. Hills* (1890) I. v; He axes if we's nuthing hot to keep 'ee from starving, *ib.* i. **Suf.** If he hadn't ha' hit he harder than what he bit he, he'd ha' killed he instead of he killin' o' he (C.G.B.). **w.Suf.** ELLIS *ib.* 287. Ess. I had a long talk with he (W.W.S.). Wil. Yow can see he, PENRUDDOCKE *Content* (1860) 2 ; **Wil.[1]** 124. **n.Wil.** Have ye zeed he as my zowl do love ? KITE *Sng. Sol.* (1860) iii. 3. Dor. They tried Samuel Shane's waggon and found that the screws were gone from he, HARDY *Wess. Tales* (1888) II. 186. Som. I don't think much o' he, RAYMOND *Tryphena* (1895) 44 ; They wull always leave he

[the poker] sticking in the vire, WILSON *Dial.* (1855) 9. **w.Som.[1]** T'id'n no good to tris' to he. Dev. Ha anser'd an zed ontu hee thit told'n, BAIRD *S. Matt.* (1863) xii. 48. **n.Dev.** The better for he, CHANTER *Witch* (1896) 3. Cor. Have 'ee seed he what my sawl do love ? *Sng. Sol.* (1859) iii. 3 ; There's nothin' the matter weth he at all, TREGELLAS *Tales* (1868) 11.

5. Used instead of the *pron.* of the first person.

Suf. Used when the speaker wishes to be particularly polite and recognizes your superior position. Thus, instead of ' I will do it for yow with pleasure, I'm sure,' we have ' He will do it for him with pleasure, he's sure ' (C.G.B.).

6. Used for *you.*

n.Cy. (J.W.) **w.Yks.[1]** Freq. addressed to children. 'John, will he foch't kye.' Lan. Yo mey grope eh meh breeches in he win, TIM BOBBIN *View. Dial.* (ed. 1806) 40. **ne.Lan.[1]** ' Will he come an see us ?' [will you come]. Used to adults as well as to children. Suf. Used when the speaker wishes to be particularly polite and recognizes your superior position (C.G.B.).

7. Unemphatic form : *they.* See **A, V. 4.**

Lin. They knaws nowt, fur a says what's nawways true, TENNYSON *N. Farmer, Old Style* (1864) st. 2. **War.[2]** They broke the winder. Did ā I **Shr.[1]** *Gram. Outlines*, 47 ; **Shr.[2]**

8. Used by a woman to denote her husband ; also used to denote an important person whose name is supposed to be familiar to the person addressed.

ne.Yks.[1] The husband or wife would say, in speaking of the other, ' He (or sha) 's nut i' t'hoos,' neither the name nor the relationship having been previously mentioned, 24. **w.Yks.** Wenz ə bān tə kum !—Il bi iər inā (J.W.). **Sus.[1]** The devil always spoken of as 'he,' with a special emphasis. 'In the Downs there's a golden calf buried.' 'Then why dóänt they dig it up ?' 'Oh, it is not allowed ; he would not let them.'

9. *sb.* A male, man ; one, anybody.

Cai.[1] Abd. I b'lieve she thinks Bess match for ony he, SHIRREFS *Poems* (1790) 118 ; She well meith be, Gentle or simple, a maik to any he, ROSS *Helenore* (1768) 15, ed. 1812. Ayr. There wasna a he within the bounds of Scotland more willing to watch the fold, GALT *Ann. Parish* (1821) i ; I am as free as any he, BURNS *Here's to thy Health*, st. 3.

10. *Comp.* (1) **He-ane,** the male of any animal, a cock **;** (2) **-barfoot,** the bear-foot, *Helleborus foetidus* ; (3) **-body,** a woman of masculine appearance ; (4) **-brimmle, the** blackberry, *Rubus fruticosus* ; (5) **-broom,** the laburnum, *Cytisus Laburnum*; (6) **-der, Hedah,** or **Heeder,** the male of any animal, but *gen.* applied to sheep; occas. to plants **;** also used *attrib.* ; [lit. 'he-deer,' cf. **Sheder**] ; (7) **-holly** or **-hollin,** the prickly-leaved holly, *Ilex Aquifolium*; (8) **-wean,** (9) **-wife,** see (3) ; (10) **-witch,** a wizard ; (11) **-woman,** see (3).

(1) Edb. [Of a bantam] The bit he-ane was . . . a perfect wee deevil incarnate, MOIR *Mansie Wauch* (1828) xx. (2) **War.[2]** (3) **Wil.[1]** (4) Som. Applied to a bramble of more than one year's growth (B. & H.). (5) **Fif.** (JAM.) (6) **w.Yks.[2]** A male yearling sheep. **s.Not.** All animals have both he-ders and she-ders. That marrer flower's a he-der ; it waint bear noat (J.P.K.). Lin. The great mass of breeders in Lin. sell their heeder-lambs about old Michaelmas time, MARSHALL *Review* (1811) III. 185. **n.Lin.** SUTTON *Wds.* (1881); **n.Lin.[1]** Most commonly used of sheep. **s.Lin.** For sale, a flock of hedahs and shedahs (F.H.W.). **sw.Lin.[1]** Half on 'em were heders, and half sheders. He shewed a nice pen of heder hogs. (7) **Nhb.** (R.O.H.); HENDERSON *Flk-Lore* (1879) iii ; *Borderer's Table-bk.* (1846) VIII. 254. (8) **n.Yks.[2]** (9) **Cld.** She's an unco he wife (JAM.). (10) Lan. GROSE (1790) *MS. add.* (P.); **Lan.[1]** (11) **Wil.[1]**

HE, HEABLE, see **Hay,** *int.*, **Evil,** *sb.[2]*

HEAD, *sb., adj.* and *v.* Var. dial. and colloq. uses in Sc. Irel. Eng. and Amer. [h]ĕd, h]ĭd, iəd, ed, jed.] **I.** Dial. forms : (1) **Ad,** (2) **Ead,** (3) **Eead,** (4) **Haade,** (5) **Haid,** (6) **Heäd,** (7) **Heade,** (8) **Hed,** (9) **Hede,** (10) **Heead,** (11) **Heeade,** (12) **Heed,** (13) **Hehd,** (14) **Held,** (15) **Heoad,** (16) **Heyde,** (17) **Hid,** (18) **Hidd,** (19) **Hud,** (20) **Hyed,** (21) **Yead,** (22) **Yed,** (23) **Yedd,** (24) **Yeead,** (25) **Yod,** (26) **Yud.**

(1) Lan. LAHEE *N. Fitton*, 17. **Chs.[18]** (2) Lin. Break me a bit o' the esh for 'is 'eäd, lad, out o' the fence, TENNYSON *N. Farmer, New Style* (1870) st. 11. (3) **w.Yks.[2]** Glo. Her only had her petticoats over her 'eead, GISSING *Both of this Parish* (1889) I. 118. (4) **Wxf.[1]** (5) Dev. Es lift han es under ma haid, BAIRD *Sng. Sol.* (1860) ii. 6. (6) **w.Yks.[2]**, **ne.Lan.[1]** (7) **Wxf.[1]** (8) **s.Hmp.** VERNEY *L. Lisle* (1870) x. **I.W.[1]** (9) **N.Cy.[1]**, **Dur.[1]** (10) Cum.[1] Wm. A

wes wet throo an throo frae heead ta fooat, *Spec. Dial.* (1885) pt. iii. 2. n.Yks.[128], e.Yks.[1], w.Yks.[2], n.Lan.[1] (11) w.Yks. He threw it . . . an just miss'd pooer oade Dick heeade, Lucas *Stud. Nidderdale* (c. 1882) 257. (12) Cai.[1] nw.Abd. Set the bossy back again upon the bowie heed, *Goodwife* (1867) st. 37. N.Cy.[1], Nhb.[1] Dur. Thee heed atoppa the's leyke Carmel, Moore *Sng. Sol.* (1859) vii. 5. Lakel.[2], Cum.[1] Nrf. A sheep's heed, Darwood *Gl.* (1890) 13. Ken.[1] (13) ne.Sc. Gregor *Flk-Lore* (1881) 40. Bnff.[1] (14) Abd. Three hunner heids o' faimilies, Alexander *Johnny Gibb* (1871) vii. Cum. I'll batter their heids soft as poddish, Gilpin *Sngs.* (1866) 534. (15) Lan. Ey'd dee rayther than harm a hure o' her heoad, Ainsworth *Lan. Witches* (ed. 1849) bk. 1. ix. (16) e.Dev. My heyde ez a brim well o' deue, Pulman *Sng. Sol.* (1860) v. 2. (17) Nrf. She tossed up her hid, Spilling *Giles* (1872) 17 ; (W.W.S.) (18) Suf.[1] (19) Nhb.[1] (20) Lan. Walker *Plebeian Pol.* (1796) 30. (21) w.Yks.[25] Lan. If yo' wantn to kep the yeads on yo'r shoulders. Banks *Manch. Man* (1876) xx. Chs. I'll knock thy yead off (E.F.) ; Chs.[28], Der.[1] Nhp.[2] My yead's too big an' my wit's too small, 184. Hrf.[12] Glo. His yead it grow'd above his yare, Dixon *Sngs. Eng. Peas.* (1846) 201, ed. 1857. Brks.[1], Hmp.[1] Wil. Slow *Gl.* (1892) Som. Hiz lef'han' be oonder moi yeäd, Baynes *Sng. Sol.* (1860) ii. 6. n.Dev. Grose (1790). (22) Wm. Frae yed to fooat, *Spec. Dial.* (1877) pt. i. 42. w.Yks.[2], Lan.[1], e.Lan.[1], Chs.[123], s.Chs.[1], Stf.[1], Der.[2], nw.Der.[1], Not.[1], Lei.[1] War.[2], s.War.[1], w.Wor.[1], Shr.[1], Glo.[1] (23) Lei. I'd rayther wed a feller wi' a wooden leg, than one wi' a wooden yedd (F.P.T.). (24) n.Yks.[1] (25) s.Wor. (H.K.) (26) w.Wor.[1], s.Wor.[3], se.Wor.[1], Hrf.[2], Glo.[1], Brks.[1]

II. Dial. meanings. 1. *sb.* In *comb.* (1) Head-back, the rope which runs along the side of a herring-net, to which the cork buoys are attached ; (2) -band, (*a*) the band or rope fastening a cow to the stall ; (*b*) a band at the top of a pair of trousers ; (*c*) see (1) ; (3) -bolt, a road over a bog or morass, stopped at one end ; (4) -but(t (adbut, hadbut, hadebutt), the strip of land left at the sides of a ploughed field on which the plough turns, a 'head-land' ; (5) -cadab, a clever, sharp person, one quick of understanding ; (6) -clathing, head-dress, a covering for the head, a cap or bonnet ; (7) -collar, a halter or bridle worn by horses in the stable to fasten them to the manger, &c. ; (8) -corn, mixed corn ; (9) -cut, that cut of a fish which includes the head ; (10) -dyke, a wall dividing the green pasture from a farm ; (11) -end, (*a*) the beginning of a piece of cloth or silk ; (*b*) the mouth of a decoy pipe ; (12) -fall, a disease of children, see below ; (13) -filin', brains, mental power ; (14) -free, of a horse : unbridled ; (15) -gear, (*a*) see (6) ; (*b*) of harness : the blinders and bit ; (*c*) mental equipment, brains, good sense, ability ; (*d*) in phr. *to get one's head-gear*, to have an illness, to get one's death-blow, to be mortally injured ; (16) -grew, -grow, or -growth, (17) -grove, the aftermath ; (18) -hing, a droop of the head ; (19) -hurry, in phr. *to be in one head-hurry of*, to be in the thick of, in the midst of ; (20) -ice, a curling term : the ice at the heads or ends of a rink ; (21) -ill, jaundice in sheep ; (22) -lace, a narrow ribbon for binding the head ; (23) -ladder, a movable addition fixed to the front of a cart to increase its carrying capacities ; (24) -languager, a clever fellow, a prodigy ; (25) -lapped, dead and laid out for burial ; (26) -light, giddy, dizzy, light-headed ; also as *sb.* in form **Head-lightness** ; (27) -line, to attach a rope to the head of a bullock ; (28) -s-man or -man, (*a*) the head or chief of a clan ; a master, chief ; (*b*) the chief labourer on a farm ; (*c*) in mining : the elder of two boys who are employed together in 'putting' ; (*d*) a stalk of rib-grass, *Plantago lanceolata* ; (29) -mark, the natural characteristics of a person or animal, the countenance ; observation of the features of a person or animal ; esp. in phr. *to ken* or *know by head-mark*, to know by sight ; (30) -maud, a plaid covering the head and shoulders ; (31) -pence, a sum formerly paid to the sheriff of Northumberland, see below ; (32) -piece, the head ; *gen.* used *fig.* the brains, intellect, understanding ; (33) -ridge, the charlock, *Sinapis arvensis* ; (34) -rig, see (4) ; (35) -room, of ceilings, staircases, &c. : sufficient height overhead ; also used *fig.* ; (36) -salts, smelling-salts ; (37) -sheaf, the sheaf last placed on the top of a stack ; *fig.* the crowning point, finishing touch ; (38) -sheets, the

VOL. III.

sloping platform towards the stem of the keel of a boat ; (39) -stall, (*a*) see (7) ; (*b*) the head of a house, a father, husband, &c. ; (40) -stock, (*a*) the principal part of a self-acting mule ; a lintel ; (*b*) see below ; (41) -stone, (*a*) a gravestone, tombstone ; (*b*) a stone shaped like a head, see below ; (42) -stoop, headlong, in haste ; (43) -Sunday, the Sunday after old Midsummer day, see below ; (44) -swell, see (21) ; (45) -theeak, thick hair which hangs like thatch on the head ; a head-covering of any kind ; (46) -theekit, having the head covered ; (47) -tie, a collar used to tie horses' heads to the manger, &c. ; (48) -tire, (*a*) see (6) ; (*b*) see (15, *c*) ; (49) -tow, in a plough or other implement : the loop to which the 'short-chain,' or draft-chain,is attached ; (50) -tree, a lintel, a piece of wood set across the head of an upright prop to support the roof in a pit ; (51) -wark, -warch, -wartch, -yak, or -yik, (*a*) headache ; (*b*) the scarlet poppy, *Papaver Rhoeas* ; occas. the long smooth-headed poppy, *P. dubium* ; cf. headache, 1; (*c*) the cuckoo-flower, *Cardamine pratensis*, cf. headache, 3 ; (*d*) the red campion, *Lychnis diurna* ; (*e*) mental labour, thought, consideration ; studiousness ; (52) -washing, (*a*) a feast given to celebrate the birth of a child ; (*b*) an entertainment given to his comrades by one who has newly entered upon a profession or appointment, or who has made an expedition for the first time ; (53) -ways or -wis, (*a*) in a forward direction, onward ; (*b*) main arteries in a mine branching off on each side, passages leading to the crane or shaft ; also used *attrib.* ; (*c*) the direction of the cleat in a seam of coal ; (54) -ways course, a line of walls or holing extending from side to side of a panel of boards ; (55) -weir, a weir-head, the point where the water is diverted from the main channel ; (56) -y-peer or -a-peer, Heady-peer, equal in height ; equals, compeers.

(1) Bnff.[1] (2, *a*) Sh.I. Kye's head-bands, tethers, simmonds, *Sh. News* (Feb. 19, 1898). (*b*) His breeks were filled wi' Lilly's plash, Frae th' head-band to the knee, *Lintoun Green* (1685) 78, ed. 1817. (*c*) Bnff.[1] (3) Lan.[1] (4) Lan. My hat lay i' th' adbut, Lahee *N. Fitton*, 17 ; The same two acres are the hadebutts of the said acre, *Warrington in 1465*, in *Cheth. Soc. Publ.* (1872) 81. Chs.[18] (5) Ayr. That wily headcadab Geordie, Galt *Entail* (1823) lvi. (6) n.Dev. Thy gore coat oil a girred, thy head-clathing oll a foust, *Exm. Scold.* (1746) l. 155. (7) Chs.[1], s.Chs.[1] Shr.[1] An arrangement of leather straps, passing over the nose, under the throat, and round the neck of the animal. A rope—which is sometimes called the shank—is attached to the head-collar, and by it the horse is tied up in his stall. nw.Dev.[1] The ordinary bridle belonging to cart harness. (8) Yks. (Hall.) w.Yks. I am under the impression that this is used for a margin of barley sown around other kinds of grain to protect them (B.K.). (9) Sh.I. Twa hard sade, an' we hed da head cut o' da hidmist ane ta wir denner yesterday, *Sh. News* (Apr. 22, 1899). (10) Inv. The head dyke was drawn along the head of a farm, where nature had marked the boundary between the green pasture and that portion of hill which was covered totally or partially with heath, *Agric. Surv.* 180 (Jam.). (11, *a*) w.Yks. (J.M.) ; (S.A.B.) (*b*) Lin. Near the head-end . . . or mouth of the pipes, Miller & Skertchly *Fenland* (1878) xii. (12) Don. An infant at its birth is generally forced by the midwife to swallow spirits, and is immediately afterwards suspended by the upper jaw with her fore-finger ; this last operation is performed for the purpose of preventing a disease called head-fall. Many children die when one or two days old of the *trismus nascentium*, or 'jaw-fall,' a spasmodic disease peculiar to tropical climates, Mason *Par. Surv.* (1816) in Patterson *Gl.* (1880). (13) Lan. An' danged if he has na more head-fillin' than yo'd think fur, Burnett *Haworth's* (1887) iii ; I dunnot know wheer she getten her head-fillin' fro' unless she robbed th' owd parson, *ib.* Lowrie's (1877) xx. (14) Som. He . . . slipped of the bridle lest he should catch herself up, and let her go headfree, Raymond *Men o' Mendip* (1898) iii. (15, *a*) Sc. Miss Jennet's skill in the matter of head gear was ever a thing for a wifeless man to wonder at, Keith *Bonnie Lady* (1897) 36. Ayr. She was taking a glint at the head-gear ae Sabbath morning in the glass, Service *Dr. Duguid* (ed. 1887) 38. Nhb.[1] n.Yks.[12] ; n.Yks.[4] Did ti notish her head-gear ? It wur grand. w.Yks.[2] A cap and bonnet together are often so styled (s.v. Gear). (*b*) n.Yks.[4] He's putten t'heead-gear on afoor t'barfan. (*c*) n.Yks.[1] He's a knowfu' chap, yon. Ah wad lahk weel t' ha' 's stock o' headgear ; n.Yks.[2] ; n.Yks.[4] Ez far ez a bit o' heead-gear gans, he's ez sharp ez onny

P

on 'em. (*d*) Cum.[1] ' He's gitten his heedgeer,' he is so injured that he cannot survive. Wm. Mostly used in reference to those ailments that follow indiscretion (B.K.). (16) Chs.[1] Shr. MORTON *Cyclo. Agric.* (1863); Shr.[2] (17) Shr.[2] (18) Dmf. Dowie and dazed wi' a sair heid-hing, REID *Poems* (1894) 77. (19) Abd. Saunders Malcolmson in the 'heid-hurry' of oat-sowing, ALEXANDER *Ain Flk.* (1882) 35. (20) Lnk. Soopers [sweepers] are ready To keep baith the howe an' the head-ice in trim, WATSON *Poems* (1853) 72. (21) s.Sc. *Essays Highl. Soc.* III. 439 (JAM.). (22) Ags. (JAM.) (23) Mid. These carts, with the addition of movable head, tail, and side ladders or copps, carry hay, corn, and straw; and, when thus enlarged, are much more convenient than waggons, MIDDLETON *View Agric.* (1798) 87. (24) Yks. Any Flamburian boy was considered a brain-scholar and a head-languager when he could write down the parson's text, BLACKMORE *Mary Anerley* (1879) xi. (25) w.Yks. He's heead-lapped, *Leeds Merc. Suppl.* (Nov. 25, 1893). (26) Sh.I. Doo'll hae ta lift da kettle, dan, fir A'm faerd, A'm dat headlight, *Sh. News* (July 1, 1899) ; Man, da tought o' you maks me headlight, *ib.* (May 20, 1899) ; Whin da headlightness wōre aff o' me, I kent he widna wraet ony dis night, *ib.* (Jan. 6, 1900). (27) Som. (HALL.) (28, *a*) Lth. He ne'er parts wi' master, nor master wi' him, Gin sulky the headsman, the herdsman looks grim, BALLANTINE *Poems* (1856) 99. Nhb. A great number of gentlemen and headsmen of the neighbourhood appears to have come on the occasion to hear Bernard Gilpin, *N. Tribune* (1854) I. 198; Nhb.[1] (*b*) s.An.[1] Suf. RAINBIRD *Agric.* (1819) 294, ed. 1849; Suf.[1] (*c*) N.Cy.[1] The next stage above a 'half-marrow' amongst putters, needing a foal with him to put a corf of coals. Nhb. The heedsman little Dicky damns and blasts, WILSON *Pitman's Pay* (1843) 27; Nhb.[1] The heedsman was a lad of 16 or 17, the elder of two engaged to put a tram where a single hand was not strong enough to put it without assistance. This arrangement was called a ' tram of lads,' and the younger lad was called a ' foal '—or familiarly a ' foally.' One of these was yoked in front to the tram by short ropes, or ' soams.' Sometimes the heedsman was thus yoked whilst the 'foally' put behind ; and in other cases the positions were reversed. Nhb., Dur. GREENWELL *Coal Tr. Gl.* (1849). (*d*) Per. (JAM.) (29) Sc. I ken ye by heid-mark, but I canna be fash'd wi' frem'd names, KEITH *Prue* (1895) 274. Cai.[1] Edb. Never having seen him or his daughter before and not kenning them by headmark, MOIR *Mansie Wauch* (1828) xvii ; An intelligent shepherd knows all his sheep from personal acquaintance, called head-mark. Artificial marks he considers as very equivocal, PENNECUIK *Wks.* (1715) 52, ed. 1815. Peb. That characteristic individuality stamped by the hand of nature upon every individual of her numerous progeny, *Agric. Surv.* 191 (JAM.). Gall. This name of mine is no great head-mark, CROCKETT *Grey Man* (1896) 13. n.Yks.[2] ' He carries t'aud heeadmark about him,' he bears the family likeness. (30) Slk. (JAM.) (31) Nhb. The sum of £51 which the Sheriff of Nhb. antiently exacted of the inhabitants of that county, every third and fourth years, without any account to be made to the King, BAILEY (1721); Nhb.[1] (32) sw.Sc. A chiel wi' a rael lang tongue, an' nae an ill head-piece, GRANT *Keckleton,* 75. Ayr. His wig pu'd out hair by hair, Until they made his headpiece bare, *Ballads and Sngs.* (1847) II. 55. Edb. Your head-piece is a mint Whare wit's nae rare, FERGUSSON *Poems* (1773) 222, ed. 1785. Nhb. Noo, he hes a heed-piece, ma faith, thor is nowt But he kens a' aboot—he kin tawk aboot owt, ELLIOTT *Pitman gan to Parliament*; (R.O.H.) e.Yks.[1] What a heead-piece skeeal maysther must hev. w.Yks. (J.W.) Lan. My yeadpiece's noane what it were bi a long way, CLEGG *David's Loom* (1894) xvi. Midl. Ye're middlin' well had for a yokel, an' ye seeam to ha' a good head-piece, BARTRAM *People of Clopton* (1897) 77. nw.Der.[1] n.Lin.[1] You've gotten as poor a head-peäce for larnin' oht 'at 'll do you ony good as iver I seed. Nhp.[1], War.[2] Oxf.[1] 'E a got a good 'ead piece, an's upright and downstraight, *MS. add.* Hnt. (T.P.F.), Sus.[1] Dor. Her've 'a got a headpiece, her have ! HARE *Vill. Street* (1895) 153. Som. Joseph Piarce is a man wi' more headpiece an' heart, RAYMOND *Men o' Mendip* (1898) iii. w.Som.[1] He id'n no ways short, there's plenty o' headpiece 'bout he. (33) s.Pem. LAWS *Little Eng.* (1888) 420. (34) Sc. It's gude when a man can turn his ain head-rig (JAM.). Cai.[1] Per. Bide ahint the fence, an' glow'r—The headrig's no for bairns ava, HALIBURTON *Ochil Idylls* (1891) 102. Gall. A ploughman starts from one landen or headrig, plows to the other, and returns to where he broke off, MACTAGGART *Encycl.* (1824) 87, ed. 1876. Nhb.[1] Dur.[1] At right angles to the ridges of the field, and ploughed last of all. Lakel.[2] Cum. (J.Ar.); Hod up till t'heedrig, Dick, FARRALL *Betty Wilson* (1886) 131. n.Yks.[14], ne.Yks.[1], ne.Lan.[1] (35) Cai.[1] Abd. Tak' ye gweed care yersel' . . . that ye gi'ena 'er owre muckle heid room aboot the place, ALEXANDER *Ain Flk.*

(1882) 199. (36) n.Ir. Peggy had put a wee bottle o' heidsalts in my pokit whun a wuz comin' awa frae hame, an' a wuz mony a time thankfu' for it, LYTTLE *Ballycuddy* (1892) 32. (37) Ayr. I fear my business wi' Curwhang was the headsheaf o' her yirdly dool; AINSLIE *Land of Burns* (ed. 1892) 148. N.I.[1] (38) N.Cy.[1] Nhb.[1] The fore deck of a keel on which the keelmen worked their long oar. (39, *a*) Cai.[1] Buff.[1] That part of a halter that goes over the crown of the head. Ags. The band that forms the upper part of a horse's collar, bridle or branks (JAM.). Nhb. (R.O.H.) n.Yks.[1] The head-gear of a horse, by which it is secured in its stall, or led out to water, &c. ; made of hemp; n.Yks.[4] Usually made of hemp. ne.Yks.[1], Chs.[1], Not.[2], n.Lin.[1], War.[2], s.Wor.[1] Shr.[1] *Obsol.* Hrf.[2], Glo. (A.B.) [Amer. *Dial. Notes* (1895) 379.] (*b*) Cai.[1] (40, *a*) w.Yks. (J.M.), w.Yks.[2] n.Stf. The framework supporting the pulley or drum over which the rope works at the mouth of a pit (J.T.). (*b*) Sc. The schoolmaster would call on the boys to divide and choose for themselves. ' Head-stocks,' i. e. leaders for the yearly cock-fight, MILLER *Scenes and Leg.* (1834) 420, ed. 1858; I contributed in no degree to the success of the head-stock or leader, *ib. Schools and Schoolmasters* (1854) 50, ed. 1857. (41, *a*) Sh.I. The very few headstones rose sadly up as if to show how very few of those that pass away are kept in memory, BURGESS *Tang* (1898) 76. Abd. A ' headstone ' to mark the far-off grave of his deceased daughter and her husband, ALEXANDER *Ain Flk.* (1882) 79. Ayr. They were sitting under the lea of a headstone, near their mother's grave, GALT *Provost* (1822) xxiv. Lak. She often gaed to see her man's grave. She got a heidstane putten up, FRASER *Whaups* (1895) 166. Lth. A ghaist sat jabberin' on an auld heid-stane, SMITH *Merry Bridal* (1866) 52. Dmf. I've boo't my heid on the cauld heid-stane, REID *Poems* (1894) 243. Gall. The moss was trailing over the ' headstanes,' *Edb. Antiq. Mag.* (1848) 113. Nhb. (R.O.H.) Cum. He cud see Mally's heedsteäne nut far off, FARRALL *Betty Wilson* (1886) 140; A heed-aten they'll hev set up, min, ANDERSON *Ballads* (ed. 1840) 110; Cum.[1], n.Yks.[2], w.Yks. (J.W.) They'll get as much as t'others when there's a yed-stone o'er em ! *Cornh. Mag.* (Jan. 1894) 39. Der.[2], nw.Der.[1], I.W.[1] (*b*) s.Sc. Round [certain wells endowed with healing virtues'] lay stones resembling . . . different members of the human body, and these were called by the names of the members they represented, as the . . . hehd-stehn. The patient took a draught of the water of the well, washed the affected part of the body, and rubbed it well with the stone corresponding to it, GREGOR *Flk-Lore* (1881) 40. (42) Sh.I. Send him no head-stoop ta da deil, BURGESS *Rasmie* (1892) 93. (43) Nhb. Within my own recollection the yearly pilgrimage to Gilsland wells, on this Sunday and the Sunday after it, was a very remarkable survival of the ancient *cultus* of primitive times. Hundreds, if not thousands, used to assemble there from all directions. They were wont to walk or drive annually at the summer solstice . . . that they might take, unconsciously it may be hoped, their part in a heathen solemnity, HALL *Ancient Well Worship* in *Arch. Æliana,* VIII. 72; Nhb.[1] (44) s.Sc. There is a great swelling and falling down of the ears, and that when too long neglected, the head swells and the sheep dies, *Essays Highl. Soc.* III. 439, 441 (JAM.). (45) n.Yks.[2] (46) Lak. He was heid-theekit with a Kilmarnock bonnet, MURDOCH *Readings* (ed. 1895) II. 20. (47) w.Yks.[2] (48, *a*) n.Yks.[124] (*b*) n.Yks.[2] (49) nw.Der.[1] (50) Nhb.[1] Nhb., Dur. A piece of crown-tree, a foot long, placed upon a prop to support the roof; the head-tree being used to extend the bearance of the prop and prevent it cutting into the crown-tree. GREENWELL *Coal Tr. Gl.* (1849). m.Yks.[1], w.Yks.[2] (51, *a*) n.Cy. (K.), Nhb.[1], Dur.[1] Cum. Now full to the thropple, wi' headwarks and heartaches, ANDERSON *Ballads* (1805) 65 ; Cum.[1] Yks. I'd the yed wark bad enuf, FETHERSTON *T. Goorkrodger* (1870) 195. n.Yks.[234], e.Yks.[1] w.Yks. When I gate up with a heead-wark shoo stopped at home, CUDWORTH *Dial. Sketches* (1884) 9 ; WILLAN *List Wds.* (1811); w.Yks.[18] Lan. He's got a bad yed-warch, ASHTON *Basin o' Broth,* 123; He'd a bad yeadwartch, CLEGG *Sketches* (1895) 196; Lan.[1], n.Lan.[1], ne.Lan.[1], nw.Der.[1] (*b*) n.Cy. (K., s.v. Coprose) ; N.Cy.[2] e.Yks. NICHOLSON *Flk-Lore* (1890) 124 ; s.Yks.[1] Der. *Papaver Rhoeas* [and] *Papaver dubium* (B. & H.). (*c*) Cum. (B. & H.) (*d*) Lakel.[2] (*e*) n.Yks.[1] s.Yks.[1] Heead-waak's as laboursome as back-waak. n.Lin.[1] Ther's been a deäl o' heäd-wark putten into that carvin' sum time or anuther. (52, *a*) w.Yks. At the birth of a child, a party was usually given, and the ' heead-weshin' was the term given to the free-drinking which was carried on on such occasions (E.G.). e.Lan.[1] n.Lin.[1] Ther'll be sum heäd-weshin' to do this time, I reckon, noo that they've gotten a son at last. (*b*) Sc. (JAM.) (53, *a*) Nhb.[1] Thor's ne getten heedwis wid at awl (*b*) n.Yks.[1] n.Cy. In coal-mines the headways run in the same direction as the cleat (J.J.B.); N.Cy.[1] Excavations in a coal pit at right angles to the boards for ventilating and exploring the mine. **Nhb.** Ax'd Deddy to lay doun his pick, And help him to the heedwis end, Wilson *Pitman's Pay* (1843) 27 ; **Nhb.¹** They are driven with the 'cleat' of the coal. Winning Heedwis are exploratory headways ; and when two such are driven together they are called fore and back headways. **Nhb., Dur.** Driven parallel to the line of cleavage of the coal. 'A yard and quarter broad or wide for a Headways is full sufficient,' *Compleat Collier* (1708) 16, Greenwell *Coal Tr. Gl.* (1849). (*c*) **Nhb., Dur.** Greenwell *Coal Tr. Gl.* (1849). (54) **Nhb.** Greerley *Coal Mining* (1883). **Nhb., Dur.** Greenwell *Coal Tr. Gl.* (1849). (55) **Dev.¹** (56) **Abd.** Oor Liza an' you ees't to be heid-y-peers, Alexander *Johnny Gibb* (1871) vii ; To think ane's friends, and heady-peers, Scarce ken you in their ways, Shirrefs *Poems* (1790) 290. **Lnk.** (Jam.)

2. Phr. (1) *Head and a-bed*, a stone-digger's term, see below ; (2) *— and crop*, neck and crop, completely ; (3) *— and hange, henge*, or *hinges*, the pluck of an animal, the head, lungs, liver, and heart ; see **Hange** ; (4) *— and heels*, (5) *— and hide*, (6) *— and tail*, completely, altogether, without reserve ; with great earnestness ; (7) *— or harp*, heads or tails, the game of 'heads or tails' ; (8) *— over tip*, head over heels ; (9) *—over-hap*, headstrong, reckless ; (10) *heads and holls*, (11) *— and horns*, in confusion, pell-mell, topsy-turvy ; (12) *— and plucks*, the refuse of timber, the boughs, roots, &c. ; (13) *— and thrawarts*, see (11) ; (14) *— and thraws*, (*a*) lying alternately with the head of each article or person on a level with the feet of the other ; in disorder, in a confused heap ; unshapely ; (*b*) a game played with pins ; (15) *— and tails*, see (14, *b*) ; (16) *at the head on it*, to finish off with, at the end ; (17) *in head*, in view, purposed ; (18) *on the head(s of*, at the conclusion of, in confirmation of ; on account of, over ; (19) *over the head(s of*, on account of ; (20) *upon the heads of*, on the point of, purposing ; (21) *the head bigger*, or *less*, taller or shorter by a head ; (22) *to be in head and neck (hehdinex) with*, to be wholly engaged on, taken up with ; (23) *— in head of*, to fall foul of, to attack ; (24) *— out at head*, to be out of one's senses, half-crazed ; (25) *— taken by the head*, to be the worse for liquor ; (26) *to carry one's head along with one*, to have all one's wits about one, to be intelligent, quick ; (27) *— eat the head off some one*, to be very angry with some one ; (28) *— get a drop in one's head*, see (25) ; (29) *— go at head*, of bullocks : to have the 'first bite' in contradistinction to the 'followers' or those which are not for fattening ; (30) *— out of head*, to be forgotten ; (31) *to have a deal on one's head*, to have a great deal of responsibility ; (32) *— one's head on*, see (26) ; (33) *to ken by head*, to know by sight but to have no speaking acquaintance with ; (34) *— make neither head nor side of*, to make nothing of, not to be able to understand ; (35) *— no more head*, not to prosper or thrive ; (36) *to milk from the head*, of a cow : to give milk as she is fed ; (37) *— put one in the head of*, to remind one, cause one to recollect ; (38) *— run one in the head*, to occur to one ; (39) *— set one's heads together*, to consult or conspire ; (40) *— stand over the head of*, to warrant the quality or quantity of ; (41) *— take up*, or *learn, a thing of one's own head*, to teach oneself ; (42) *to take by the head*, of a horse : to lead by the bridle ; (43) *— one's head*, (*a*) to take one's fancy, captivate ; (*b*) of wine or spirits : to get into one's head ; (44) *to take*, or *ask, for a farm, &c. over a man's head*, to take or ask for a farm, &c. when the present tenant has not received notice to quit, to secretly offer a higher price and so dispossess the tenant ; (45) *to take the door over one's head*, to shut the door and depart ; (46) *— tell to one's head*, to tell to one's face ; (47) *— wash* or *wet the baby's head*, to drink the baby's health, treat one's friends with ale or spirits at the birth of a child ; cf. **head-washing** (*a*) ; (48) *weak in the head*, weak of intellect ; (49) *without a head*, of a woman : single and unprotected.

(1) **Nhp.²** A stone is said to rise with a head-and-abed, i. e. with an even side and surface, Morton *Nat. Hist.* (1712) 108. (2) **Lan.** Thrusting out a person, 'head and crop,' Gaskell *Lectures Dial.* (1854) 30. (3) **Cor.¹²** (4) **Lan.¹** His foot slipped, an' in he went, head-an-heels. He's th' reet sort of a chap ; when he starts he gwos in for it, head-an-heels. (5) **Dmb.** You wrought, baith head and hide, for the reward, Salmon *Gowodean* (1868)

103. (6) **Abd.** I'll tell the story head and tail, And how it did befa', Cadenhead *Bon Accord* (1853) 245. (7) **Ir.** You had better toss up, head or harp, for that, Barrington *Sketches* (1830) I. xxxvii ; A quarrel happened between two shoeblacks, who were playing at what in England is called pitch farthing, or heads and tails, and in Ir. head or harp, Edgeworth *Bulls* (1802) 128, ed. 1803. (8) **I.Ma.** Don't be tossing head over tip at the tail of the tourist, Caine *Manxman* (1894) pt. III. xxiii. (9) **Sh.I.** I wis young dan, .. bit a racklias, head-ower-hap deevil, Burgess *Sketches* (and ed.) 88. (10) **e.An.¹, Nrf.** (W.W.S.), **e.Suf.** (F.H.) (11) **Suf.** All heads and horns (C.L.F.). (12) **ne.Lan.¹** **Der.** Grose (1790) *MS. add.* (P.) ; **Der.², nw.Der.¹** (13) **Sc.** Yarn is said to be so when ravelled. Also corn cut down when disordered in the sheaf (Jam.). (14, *a*) **Sc.** Two persons are said to be lying heads and thraws in a bed, when the one lies with his head at the head of the bed ... while the other lies with his head at the bottom and his feet towards the head of the bed. Pins are said to lie heads and thraws when they are placed parallel to each other with the point of one directed towards the head of another (Jam.): I'll no ly wi' that unco woman indeed, if it binna heeds and thraws, the way that I lay wi' my mither, Graham *Writings* (1883) II. 15. **Cai.¹** w.**Sc.** He took the liberty of changing his position to that which in Scotland is termed 'heads and thraws,' Carrick *Laird of Logan* (1835) 188. **Ayr.** There they lay, heads and thraws, Hunter *Studies* (1870) 1. **Lnk.** He was, as he afterwards expressed it, pitched heids and thraws, Gordon *Pyotshaw* (1885) 40. **Edb.** Unshapely, uncouth in person, Ballantyne *Gaberlunzie* (ed. 1875) *Gl.* **Slk.** Ten hunder thousan' million thochts and feelins a' lie thegither, heads and thraws, in the great, wide ... bed o' the Imagination, Chr. North *Noctes* (ed. 1856) II. 267. **Dmf.** Happy weens Tumblin an' rowin heads an' thraws, Thom *Jock o' Knowe* (1878) 37. **Nhb.** (R.O.H.) **Cum.⁴** Lie heeds an' thraws like Jock an' his mither, *Saying.* Some heeds an' thraws war stretch't i' th' nuik, Stagg *Bridewain*, st. 48. (*b*) **Sc.** To play at heads and thraws (Jam.). **Cai.¹** (15) **Cai.¹** (16) w.**Yks.** Expectin' 'at Kana wad ax 'em to have summat to sup at th' heead on it, Hartley *Clock Alm.* (1896) 52. (17) **Bnff.** Sae we did gree, an' hame we gaed To tell auld Tam what was in head, Taylor *Poems* (1787) 62. (18) **Abd.** We concluded the bargain, an' shook han's, on the heads of it, *Deeside Tales* (1872) 173. **Gall.** (A.W.) n.**Ir.** Mony an argyment we hae had on the held o' it, Lyttle *Ballycuddy* (1892) 18. (19) **Sh.I.** He felt 'at he wid laek ta see if shü wis muckle upset ower da heids o't, Clark *Gleams* (1898) 59. **Ayr.** I am sae pleas'd that friendship is made up that I'll tak' a glass o'er the head o't, Hunter *Studies* (1870) 39. **N.I.¹** I got dismissed over the head of a letter the master got. (20) **Sh.I.** An' dey apo' da heads o' marriage in winter ! *Sh. News* (Sept. 23, 1899). (21) n.**Cy.** (B.K.) (22) **Bnff.¹** Gen. used in disapprobation. 'He's niver at paice ; he's eye in hehdinex wee something.' (23) **Abd.** (Jam.) (24) **Yks.** Ah's yamost oot 'at yed at t'news ah's getten, Macquoid *Doris Barugh* (1877) xv. (25) w.**Som.¹** To be a' took't by the head. (26) **Nhp.¹** She can't get on in service, unless she carries her head along with her. (27) **Sc.** (A.W.) **N.I.¹** He was like to ate the head off me. n.**Cy.** (J.W.) (28) **Sc.** Jock was a gae throughither chiel when he got a drap in his head, *Scotch Haggis*, 49. (29) **e.An.¹** e.**Nrf.** Marshall *Rur. Econ.* (1787). (30) **Rnf.** This gentleman ... Has been a feck o'twalmonths deid : And sin' he's maist gane oot o' heed, Neilson *Poems* (1877) 33. (31) **Glo.¹** (32) **Nhp.¹** She can't get on in service, unless she has her head on. (33) **Lakel.²** Ah've kent ye bi heed this many a year. (34) **Nhp.¹** He could make neither head nor side of it. **War.², Hnt.** (T.P.F.) (35) w.**Yks.** (I.W.) (36) **Sh.I.** The coo milks frae the head, Spence *Flk-Lore* (1899) 209. **Gall.** (A.W.) (37) **Dor.** He put me in the head on't (W.C.) (c. 1750) ; (A.C.) (38) s.**Chs.¹** (39) **ne.Lan.¹** **Dor.** Barnes *Gl.* (1863). (40) **N.I.¹** (41) w.**Yks.¹, ne.Lan.¹, nw.Der.¹, Nhp.¹, War.³, Hnt.** (T.P.F.) (42) w.**Som.¹** (43, *a*) **Ayr.** The wye that lassie toasted them ... fairly took my head, Johnston *Glenbuckie* (1889) 35. (*b*) **Gall.** Also used of drink taking effect on the brain (A.W.). (44) **Wgt.** Having fallen under scandal by taking his neighbour's ground over his head, Fraser *Wigtown* (1877) 120. w.**Som.¹** To ask for a farm over a man's heäd is to ask for another man's holding when he has not had notice to quit. (45) **Sh.I.** He wis blyde ta tak da door ower his head as fast as he cud, Stewart *Tales* (1892) 70. (46) **Brks.** I told him to his head, Grose (1790) ; *Gl.* (1852) ; **Brks.¹, e.An.¹** **Nrf.** Tellin' me to my hid t'was a story, Cozens-Hardy *Broad Nrf.* (1893) 34. e.**Suf.** (F.H.) **Ess.** *Trans. Arch. Soc.* (1863) 11. 183 ; She'd toad him to his head,—By none but one well tighted up To Tiptree she'd be led, Clark *J. Noakes* (1839) st. 60. **Hmp.** Holloway. **Sus.¹** I told him to his head that I wouldn't have such goings-on in my house any more.

P 2

(47) n.Yks. Wetting t'barn's head, *N. & Q.* (1890) 7th S. ix. 37. e.Yks. *MS. add.* (T.H.) w.Yks. *N. & Q.* (1889) 7th S. viii. 86. Lan. Very common in Liverpool and the neighbourhood, *ib.* (1890) 7th S. ix. 37. [Farmer A. was on his way from the house of Farmer B. where, said he, ' we have been washing the baby's head.' Farmer B. had just had a son born to him . . . and the ' washing ' referred to consisted in the two farmers drinking the baby's health, *ib.* (1888) 7th S. viii. 86. (48) Sc. (A.W.) w.Yks.² Strong i' th' back and weak i' th' yead. nw.Der.¹ Derbyshire born and Derbyshire bred, Strong i' th' arm, but weak i' th' yed. (49) Sc. It's no an easy thing, Mem, for a woman to go through the world without a head, MILLER *Schools and Schoolmasters* (ed. 1879) v.

3. The hair of the head.

Sh.I. Takkin' da redder shū gūde furt apo' da brig-stanes ta redd her head, *Sh. News* (June 17, 1899). Abd. ' To cut one's head,' to cut one's hair (A.W.). Yks. (J.W.) Lan. Combin my yead, LAYCOCK *Billy Armatage*, 6. w.Cy. It is usual to speak of combing the head instead of the hair. It is commonly said of a virago ' Her'll comb out his head vor'n.' . . Of a woman who is supposed to be capable of beating her husband, the usual saying is ' Her'd comb out 's head wi a dree-legged stool,' ELWORTHY *Wd-Bk.* (1888). Dev. Her'd comb out his head wi' a dree-legged stool, *Reports Provinc.* (188a) 15.

4. The mouth ; the stomach.

N.I.¹ Not a word out of your head. The doctor said he was never to have the milk away from his head. Nhb. He niver hes the pipe oot o' ees heed (R.O.H.). w.Yks. (J.W.) Nrf. I can't ate nothing. I hain't had nothing ' in my head ' all day (W.P.E.).

5. A bud ; the ears of grain upon a single stem of corn.

Fif. Pick ay, up quick ay, The heads the shearers leave, DOUGLAS *Poems* (1806) 124. Nhb. I wad like to . . . pick up heeds o' corn eftor him, ROBSON *Bk. Ruth* (1860) ii. 2. n.Wm. Oor rosy tree's o' full o' heeds. Can yan beg a heed er tweea ? (B.K.) Nhp.² If their seed be all of one head, as they call it, that is, of one particular sort, it sells the better, by sixpence or a shilling a bushel, for seed, MORTON *Nat. Hist.* (1712) 477.

Hence **Headlet**, *sb.* a bud. [Not known to our Wm. correspondents.] Wm. (HALL.), n.Yks.²

6. Of grass : the growth at any given time.

n.Lin. They have a tolerable head of grass in the spring, YOUNG *Lin. Agric.* (1799) 194.

7. The froth or foam of ale, porter, &c.

n.Cy. (J.W.) Lan. Margaret . . . slowly filled the beaker, a beautiful creamy ' head ' bubbling over the brim, *Longman's Mag.* (Apr. 1897) 547 ; Let's have it fresh drawn an' wi' a yead o' th' top on't, BRIERLEY *Out of Work*, i. Colloq. Some love to draw the ocean with a head Like troubled table-beer—and make it bounce, And froth, HOOD *Poems* (ed. 186a-3) *Storm at Hastings.*

8. Cream upon the surface of milk.

w.Som.¹ In reply to an application for milk in the forenoon, a farmer's wife's usual reply is—' I ont break my head vor nobody,' meaning that now the head or cream has begun to rise I will not disturb it. nw.Dev.¹

9. The upright post of a gate furthest from the hinges.

w.Yks. (J.J.B.), Hmp. (H.C.M.B.), Wil.¹, w.Som.¹, nw.Dev.¹

10. The doors of a clough or sluice, with the masonry belonging thereto. n.Lin.¹

11. Of a flail : the hood of raw hide ; see below.

Cai.¹ The hood of raw hide on the upper end of the soople by which it is attached to the Han'-staff by a thong called the Point.

12. A measure of wool or twine.

Rnf. This birkie bodie can . . . Temper yer ilka thrum and thread, Yea, whither they wimple thro' a head Or thro' a mall, WEBSTER *Rhymes* (1835) 152. Cum.⁴ Consists of 840 yards of twine when the material is fine, but in fine stuff it often contains from 10 up to 20 hanks ; it is used as often as hank by those who buy yarn by the bundle, but not when they buy a single hank ; a bundle of twine according to fineness, contains so many heads to the 28 lbs. ' No man can imagine, that twine, spun to sixty heads . . . in the dozen pound weight of hemp, should be as effectual in killing salmon, as the same hemp when spun only to twenty-six heads,' *Fisherman*, 10.

Hence **Yeddin**, *sb.* the first beginning of a warp, the portion woven at the beginning and end of a piece of cloth, which is cut off when the piece is taken out of the loom. w.Yks.², Chs.¹

13. The higher end of a place, the upper part of a street ; the upper part of a dale ; a hill or eminence.

Edb. Hills are variously named, according to their magnitude ; as . . . Hope, Head, Cleugh-head, PENNECUIK *Wks.* (1715) 50,

ed. 1815. Nhb. In Newcastle used to describe the higher part of a street, as ' Heed o' the Side.' Also applied to a commanding eminence (R.O.H.) ; Nhb.¹ Greenhead, at the watershade between the Irthing and the Tippalt. Cum. Ae neet we met, at our croft head, ANDERSON *Ballads* (ed. 1808) 85 ; Cum.⁴ Stair-heed, toon-heed, dale-heed. n.Yks.¹ The higher portion of the reclaimed part of a projecting spur of the moorland heights where it begins to verge on the unreclaimed part, or moor ; n.Yks.⁴

14. The source or spring of a stream or river ; also used *fig.* **in phr.** *a shower i' the heads.*

Slk. ' A shower i' the heads,' a flood of tears. Used . . . in a pastoral district and borrowed from the proof that rain is falling in the high grounds or at the heads of rivulets by their swelling below (JAM.) ; There's a shower i' the heads wi' Barny—his heart can stand naething—it is as soft as a snaw-ba', HOGG *Tales* (1818) II. 155 (*ib.*). n.Wil. Just at the edge there is water, the ' heads ' of the innumerable streams that make the Vale so verdant, JEFFERIES *Wild Life* (1879) 23.

15. The volume of water contained in a mill-pond or stream.

Sc. (A.W.) Lin. The one mill, by first raising the water from the mill drain, . . . lessens what is called the head of water, MILLER & SKERTCHLY *Fenland* (1878) vi. w.Som.¹ Applied to a mill-pond. If full, it is said ' There's a good head of water.' The pond or reservoir from which the water-wheel is driven is called the mill-head.

16. The surface of coal or perpendicular face of marl at the bottom of a pit.

Nhb. Sunk to the coal-head, *Borings* (1881) II. 57. Cha.¹ ; Cha.³ Head o' pit, the deepest part of the marl pit, the furthest from the space end ; also called ' Marl head.'

Hence (1) **Heading**, *sb.* the passage or drift driven into a mine in order to obtain coal ; (2) *to drive a head, phr.* to excavate a passage, or gallery in a mine, in the body of the work.

(1) n.Stf. The further end is ' blind,' i. e. does not lead forward into another gallery or roadway as does a ' thirling' (J.T.). (a) Shr.¹ (s.v. Drive) ; Shr.²

17. In curling : a division of the game in which both parties play all their stones ; see below.

Sc. A bonspiel is played according to time—a½ or 3 hours—or so many heads—usually 21 heads or ' 21 ends ' (G.W.). Ayr. You can . . . hear the roar of the channel-stane as it speeds on its mission of making or unmaking a decisive ' head,' BOSWELL *Poet. Wks.* (1803) *Mem.* 29, ed. 1871 ; The bonspiel fared on for four hours, by which time three of the rinks had finished their twenty-one heads, JOHNSTON *Kilmallie* (1891) II. 112. Gall. A ' head ' in curling is one single contest between a rink of players against their opponents on the rink-space. Twenty-one heads is the greatest number usually played in a match ; and the set which has most of the 21 is the victor in the match (A.W.).

18.— *adj.* **Chief, principal ; best, most excelling, superior to others ; freq. in** *superl.*

Abd. He's been ane o' the heid deesters, ALEXANDER *Johnny Gibb* (1871) xiii. Gall. The holy day o' the Sabbath was their head time for the evil wark, CROCKETT *Standard Bearer* (1898) 119. Nhb. Aa's heed man at the bellows (R.O.H.). w.Yks. He wor t'head customer at heed ever come across, BINNS *Vill. to Town* (188a) 38. Rut.¹ ' The head way,' the best method. Nrf. The first match was for cutter boats : £3 head prize, EMERSON *Son of Fens* (1892) 297 ; When they made up we was head boat that year, *ib.* 73. Suf.¹, Hmp. (H.E.) a.Hmp. And the eldest—that's Jesse, and he's the heddest on us too—he got the head lot, VERNEY *L. Lisle* (1870) x. w.Som.¹ Aay vrak'nz dhūsh yuur dh-ai·d roa·ud au·l ubaew·t [I consider this the head road in this neighbourhood]. Aew·t-n aew·t dh-ai·d au·s aew·t [Out and out the best horse out]. Head carpenter, head mason, head rat-catcher, i. e. best, not the foreman. Cant. Dy'e gin, Riley, the headest cuvva for creminor [best thing for worms] in horses! CAREW *Autob. Gipsy* (1891) x. [Amer. That's the head trick I ever see, *Dial. Notes* (1895) I. 372.]

19. *Comp.* **(1) Head-beetler**, the foreman beetler in a beetling-mill ; any foreman or man in charge of workmen ; (2) **-billie-dawkus**, one who has the chief charge, the presiding genius ; (3) **-bit**, a masterpiece, something surprising or astonishing ; (4) **-buil**, a manor-house, the best family residence on an estate ; the chief estate ; (5) **-bummer**, the head of a house, the chief representative of a family, the principal person ; (6) **-court**, a chief court of justice ; see below ; (7) **-doffer**, the principal or responsible ' doffer ' (q.v.) ; (8) **-go or -goo**, (a) the best of anything ; (b) the highest score in a game of skittles ;

(9) ·keep, the first bite ; the best keep a farm will afford ; (10) ·muck, one who takes the chief part in anything, a leader, person of consequence, master ; (11) ·piece, see (3) ; (12) ·sir-rag, ·serag, ·sha-rag, or ·sirag, see (10) ; (13) ·town, a county town.

(1) N.I.[1] Lan.[1] He wur a mak of a yed-beetler amung th' porters, up at th' railway-station, WAUGH *Chim. Corner* (1874) 146, ed. 1879. (2) Per. At coming hame o' bairns, an' at marriages an' kirns, She is head-billie-dawkus to be sure, FORD *Harp* (1893) 318. (3) Ess. (C.D.) (4) Sh.I. The principal mansion and estate that formed the share of the oldest son, HIBBERT *Desc. Sh. I.* (1822) 125, ed. 1891 ; S. & Ork.[1] Or.I. Alledgit that 6 mark land of Gruting was the heid-buil, and could not be gifdt nor disponit fra the principal air [heir], PETERKIN *Notes* (1822) App. 40. (5) Sc. (G.W.) e.Fif. An' honourable family . . . whaurof I . . . am at the present day head-bummer, LATTO *Tam Bodkin* (1864) i. (6) Sc. A head court of citizens is a special meeting called by the magistrates of a burgh or city for advice in unusual circumstances affecting the interests of the community (A.W.). Or.I. This meeting, being so thinly attended, adjourned to the Michaelmas head-court, PETERKIN *Notes* (1822) 175. Abd. The friends o' the slaughtered youth thought it best to have Forbes first condemned at a head court to be holden at the Foot o' Gairn, *Deeside Tales* (1872) 133. Rnf. In the olden time, before Heritable Jurisdictions were abolished in Sc., three several Head-courts were held in the County of Rnf.—the Head-court of the County, the Head-court of the Sheriffdom, and the Head-court of the Regality of Paisley, HECTOR *Judic. Records* (1876) 274. (7) w.Yks. Usually a lad about 13 to 15 years of age, employed to wind up the lifter of a spinning frame, and rap up or muster the doffers when a frame is stopped for doffing (F.R.). (8, *a*) l.W.[1] That's the head-goo on't aal. (*b*) Brks.[1] (9) e.Nrf. MARSHALL *Rur. Econ.* (1787). e.Suf. (F.H.) Sus. HOLLOWAY. (10) Ken. He is head-muck up there (D.W.L.). (11) Ess. (C.D.) (12) s.Chs.[1] Ée wŭz goo·in au·rdŭrin ŭn mes·tŭrin ŭbaay't, jŭs fŭr au· dhŭ wuurld ŭz iv ée)d bin top·aau·yŭr ŭn yed·sŭraag· ŭ dhŭ lot [He was gooin' orderin' an' mesterin' abaāt, just for aw the world as if he'd bin top-sawyer an' yed-sirag o' the lot]. s.Not. Yer man goo in Wrester Wright about gettin on the bede-housen ; he's 'ead Sir Rag o' that (J.P.K.). Nhp.[1] War.[2] Bob Walker's taken up wi' th' ranters, an' 'e's 'ead-sir-rag, I can tell yer ; War.[3] He likes to be head-serag. Oxf. Jack's sure to be head-sha-rag and bottle-washer wherever he goes (G.O.) ; Oxf.[1] *MS. add.* Nrf. Hid·se-rag, COZENS-HARDY *Broad Nrf.* (1893) 34. (13) Frf. Provost of the heid toono' the Coonty, LOWSON *Guidfollow* (1890) 101.

20. *v.* To behead, execute ; freq. in phr. *to head and hang*, to punish severely.

Sc. But the better the family the mair men hanged or heided, STEVENSON *Catriona* (1893) vii. Baff. If ye burn Auchindoun, Huntly he will head ye, GORDON *Chron. Keith* (1880) 303. n.Sc. O head me soon and head me clean, BUCHAN *Ballads* (1828) I. 21, ed. 1875. Abd. He was taken and headed, and his right hand set upon a stob, SPALDING *Hist. Sc.* (1792) I. 53. Per. Here are guards, Who will us either head or hang, SMITH *Poems* (1714) 3, ed. 1853. Lnk. When Cromwell took his prisoners, he neither headed them or hanged them as ye do, WODROW *Ch. Hist.* (1721) II. 57, ed. 1828. Edb. I'm sure the king wad gar hang him, or 'head him, PENNECUIK *Tinklarian* (ed. 1810) 9. N.Cy.[1] Lan. When hyeddet three queens, an won king, WALKER *Plebeian Pol.* (1796) 30.

Hence (1) **Heading**, *sb.* an execution, beheading ; (2) ·hill, *sb.*, obs., the hill of execution, the spot where criminals were beheaded ; (3) ·man, *sb.* an executioner, headsman.

(1) Sc. Has not heading and publickly affixing the head been thought sufficient for the most atrocious state crimes? MAIDMENT *Pasquils* (1868) 146. Gall. As for an ordinary heading, CROCKETT *Grey Man* (1896) 338. (2) Sc. They hae ta'en to the heiding hill His lady fair to see, AYTOUN *Ballads* (ed. 1861) I. 94. Or.I. To be tane to the Heiding-hill of Scalloway-Bankis and thair his held to be tane and struken fra his bodie, PETERKIN *Notes* (1822) App. 39. Peb. Stirling's heading-hill Adjoining to its castle, *Lintoun Green* (1685) 17, ed. 1817. s.Sc. The king who had covered with blood the 'heading hill' of Stirling, WILSON *Tales* (1836) II. 120. (3) Sc. Gar bid the heiding-man mak' haste ! AYTOUN *Ballads* (ed. 1861) II. 54.

21. To have as a head, or on the top.

Ayr. It was of the Indian cane, virled with silver, and headed with ivory, GALT *Gilhaize* (1823) xxii.

Hence **Heading-sheaf**, *sb.* the sheaf placed on the top of a stack ; *fig.* the crowning act. See Head-sheaf.

Baff.[1] The twa wives didna gree afore ; an' noo thir twa bairns hae lickit ane anither. . . That'll pit on the hehdin'-sheaf.

22. To put in the head of a cask.

Cor. The cask is 'headed,' marked, and is ready for exportation, HUNT *Pop. Rom. w.Eng.* (ed. 1896) 369.

23. Of plants : to bud ; of corn : to form a head, produce ears.

n.Wm. T'floor trees heeden up nicely (B.K.). Ess. Commonly used in these parts. 'The wheat is heading well, there will be a good crop' (H.H.M.) ; If the [wheat] crop is thin, it possesses the benefit of heading the better, YOUNG *Annals Agric.* (1784–1815) XXII. 174.

24. With *up* : to froth, foam ; *fig.* to excite, elevate ; of a wound : to suppurate, come to a head.

n.Yks.[2] It's heeaded him up. It heeaded up nicely. w.Yks.(J.W.)

25. With *in* : to cut a first swathe round a field with the scythe in order to prepare the way for the mowing or reaping machine.

s.Not. We was 'cadin' in yisterday for the mower (J.P.K.).

Hence **Heading**, *sb.* a first swathe thus cut. *ib.*

26. With *out* : to excavate a level or gallery in a mine in advance of the general workings ; to come to the head or surface. Shr.[1]

27. Phr. (1) *head him and cross him, headim and corsim, headum and corsum, or heedam a crossam, (a)* a game played with pins ; see below ; (*b*) in confusion and disorder, lying transversely, some with heads one way, others the other ; (2) *headamaneckum (head 'em and neck 'em)*, with great force ; recklessly, without consideration.

(1, *a*) s.Sc. Nanny and I have set us down on the greensward—played at chuck, 'head him and cross him,' or some such amusement, WILSON *Tales* (1836) III. 327. Gall. Pins are hid with fingers in the palms of the hands ; the same number is laid alongside them, and either headim or corsim called out by those who do so : when the fingers are lifted, if the heads of the pins hid, and those beside them be lying one way, when the crier cried headim, then that player wins ; but if corsim, the one who hid the pins wins, MACTAGGART *Encycl.* (1824). (*b*) Dmf. (JAM.), Cum.[1] (2) Lakel.[2] Ower he went, heed ower heals, an' landed I' t'gutter, heedamaneckum. n.Wm. Prob. a corruption of 'head 'em, or neck 'em', as horses in a race endeavour to win by a 'head' or a 'neck.' 'T'gurt feeal went heedamaneckum intult an' gat ehiselled' (B.K.).

HEADACHE, *sb.* Irel. Cum. Yks. Chs. Der. Not. Lin. Rut. Lei. Nhp. e.An. Sus. Hmp. Also in forms head-acher Nhp.[1] ; yed-ache s.Chs.[1] ; yeddock Not. **1.** The common red poppy, *Papaver Rhoeas* ; occas. applied to other species of poppy, esp. *P. Argemone* and *P. dubium* ; freq. in *pl.*

Wkl., Crl., Wxf., Wtf. The red poppies that grow in cornfields . . . are called Headaches, and are particularly obnoxious to females, the more so to unmarried young women, who have a horror of touching or of being touched by them, N. & Q. (1865) 3rd S. viii. 319. w.Yks. (W.F.) Chs.[1] It is a popular idea in Chs. that to smell the flowers of the poppy will cause headache ; Chs.[2], Der. (B. & H.) Not. We calls 'em yeddocks 'cause they make your yeddock [head ache], WORDSWORTH *Rutl. Wds.* (1891) (s.v. Headaches). s.Not. (J.P.K.), Lin.[1] n.Lin. Wi' th' field red cap he hes on shakin' like a heddaache o' a windy daay, PEACOCK *Tales* (1890) and S. 61 ; Prov. 'When headaches rattle Pigs will sattle,' i. e. fall in price, pigs being usually cheap in July (B. & H.) ; n.Lin.[1] 'More head-aches then arnin's,' said of bad sand land whereon these plants grow in such profusion as to eat away the corn. s.Lin. The wheat cloas 's chock full o' headaaches (T.H.R.). sw.Lin.[1] Rut.[1] 'Can that patch of red in yonder field be poppies?' 'No, sir, they are head-aches.' Lei.[1] Nhp.[1] Corn-poppies, that in crimson dwell, Call'd head-aches from their sickly smell, CLARE *Shep. Calendar* (1827) 47 ; Nhp.[2] e.An. N. & Q. (1865) 3rd S. viii. 274 ; e.An.[1] Nrf. What a lot of headaches there are in the wheat this year, N. & Q. (1878) 5th S. x. 78. Suf. *Science Gossip* (1882) 214. Sus.[1], Hmp.

2. *Comp.* **Headache-wine**, a drink made of the petals of the poppy. n.Lin.[1]

3. The cuckoo-flower, *Cardamine pratensis.* Cum.

4. The greater stitchwort, *Stellaria Holostea.* Cum.

5. The condition of a knife, corkscrew, &c., when the • blade or screw is loose in the haft.

s.Chs.[1] Dhis uwd nahyf ŭ dhahyn)z nóo gŭd : it)s got·n dhŭ yed·aik ; yŭ)kn ëëŭr it raat·l wen ahy shee·k it [This owd knife o' thine's noo good : it's gotten the yedache ; yŏ can hear it rattle when I sheek it].

HEADD, HEADEN, see Hide, *v.*², Haden.

HEADER, *sb.* Sc. Chs. Also in form **yedder** Chs.¹ A stone or brick in a wall having the head or end outwards. Clc. (G.W.), Chs.¹

HEADISH, *adj.* Bdf. Intelligent, clever, sharp. (J.W.B.)

HEADLAND, *sb.* In *gen.* dial. use in Eng. Also in forms **addle** Nhp.²; **addlun** Glo.¹; **adlan** s.Not. War.²; **adland** w.Yks.² Chs.² Stf.² Der.² s.Not. Rut.¹ Lei.¹ Nhp.¹² War.²⁸ w.Wor.¹ s.Wor.¹ se.Wor.¹ Shr.¹² Hrf.² n.Bck.; **adlant** Lan. Chs.¹ s.Chs.¹ nw.Der.¹ Lei.¹ War.⁸ Shr.¹; **haddlin** Glo.¹; **hadlan** Oxf.¹; **hadland** Nhp.¹ Shr.²; **hadloont** n.Cy. Lan.¹; **hedlen** Dor.¹; **hedlun** I.W.¹; **heeadland** e.Yks.¹ w.Yks.¹; **heeadlin** Cum.¹; **heedland** Nhb.¹; **heedlin** Cum.¹; **hidland,.hid-lond** Suf.; **hodland** s.Wor.; **yeadlan** Brks.¹ [h]ɪə·dlənd, a·dlənd, a·dlənt, e·dlən(d.]
1. The strip of land left unploughed at the ends of a field on which the plough turns, and which is afterwards ploughed at right angles to the rest of the field ; the grassy or waste borders of a field close to the hedge ; *gen.* in *pl.* Also used *fig.*
Nhb.¹ Sometimes across the middle of a field in like fashion, when the field is divided into two sheths, or divisions. Cum. A heedlin o' hemp or line, DICKINSON *Cumbr.* (1876) 243 ; Cum.¹, n.Yks. (R.H.H.), e.Yks.¹ w.Yks.¹ I presently spies him i' ouer hay claas, ont' heeadland, ii. 295 ; w.Yks.² Lan. Th' singers set at a lung teble doin th' reawhm and Lord Derby was on a adlant at th' end, *Manch. City News* (Feb. 26, 1881) in HOLLAND *Gl.* (1884) ; Lan.¹ Chs.¹ ; Chs.⁸ ' He's turned a narrow adland ' means that he's had a narrow escape. s.Chs.¹ To ' run a close adlant ' is to have a narrow escape. Stf.² When art goein plough th' adland ? Der.² nw.Der.¹ Thaa mŭn plŏo' th)aad·lŭnts dhis aaf·tŭrnŏo'n [Tha mun plow th)adlants this afternoon]. Not. I wish they'd keep to the headland, instead of gallivanting all over the wheat (L.C.M.) ; Not.², s.Not. (J.P.K.) n.Lin.¹ In the open fields these headlands are often the boundaries of property, and therefore headland is sometimes, though rarely, used as an equivalent for boundary. s.Lin. (T.H.R.), sw.Lin.¹, Lei.¹ Nhp.¹ The driving boy, glad when his steps can trace The swelling headland as a resting place, CLARE *Shep. Calendar* (1827) 99 ; Nhp.², War.²⁸⁴, s.War.¹, w.Wor.¹, s.Wor. (H.K.), s.Wor.¹, se.Wor.¹ Shr.¹ To ' turn on a mighty narrow adlant ' is a proverbial saying expressive of a very narrow escape. ' To plough the adlants afore the buts ' is to begin a matter at the wrong end; Shr.² Shr., Hrf. BOUND *Provinc.* (1876). Hrf.², Glo. (A.B.), Glo.¹, Oxf.¹, Brks.¹, n.Bck. (A.C.), Bdf. (J.W.B.), Hnt. (T.P.F.), Suf. (C.T.), e.Suf. (F.H.) Ken. They cut round the headlands for the reaper to come (D.W.L.). Sur.¹ Sus. (F.E.S.), Sus.¹, I.W.¹, Wil.¹, Dor. (C.W.), Dor.¹ Som. HERVEY *Wedmore Chron.* (1887) I. 187.
2. *Comp.* Had-loont-rean or -ryen, the gutter or division between the ' headlands.'
n.Cy. GROSE (1790). Lan. He fund an' urchon ith' hadloont-ryen, TIM BOBBIN *View Dial.* (1740) 6 ; Lan.¹
3. *Obs.* The fee given to an apparitor. [Not known to our correspondents.] Lin. *Gent. Mag.* LXIII. 843.

HEADLAND, *adj.* Glo. Wil. Dor. Also in form **hedlin** Dor. [e·dlən(d.] Headlong, precipitate, giddy ; also used *advb.*
Glo.¹ Wil.¹ To ' fall headland ' or ' neck-headland.' Dor. There's a hedlin chile, BARNES *Gl.* (1863).

HEADLANDS, *adv.* Suf. Headlong, precipitately.
I fare so dizzy, I nearly fell over headlands, *e.An. Dy. Times* (1892).

HEADLE, see Heald, *sb.*¹

HEADLESS, *adj.* Sc. 1. Thoughtless, heedless.
Sc. Some lassie young and headless Might to your vows say aye, *Shepherd's Wedding* (1789) 19. Gall. (A.W.)
2. Fatherless, orphaned.
Sh.I. Releeve da straets o' mony a needfil headless family, *Sh. News* (Nov. 18, 1899).

HEADLET, *sb.* Wm. Lan. The top of anything.
Wm., n.Lan. As we peep't ower t'headlet we cud see t'hoose war t'owd chap leeved (W.H.H.).

HEADLIN(G)S, *adv.* Obs. Sc. Suf. Headlong, precipitately.
Fif. Headlins hurryin' frae their doors [They] Out-ran in thousands to the Scores, TENNANT *Papistry* (1827) 135. e.Suf. (F.H.)

HEADLONG, *sb.* Wil.¹ A ' headland,' the strip of land at the ends of a field on which the plough turns.

HEADLONGS, *adv.* Stf. Lei. Headlong, precipitately.
n.Stf. That's the road you'd all like to go, headlongs to ruin, GEO. ELIOT *A. Bede* (1859) vi. Lei.¹

HEADMOST, *adj.* and *adv.* Sc. Glo. 1. *adj.* Topmost. Sc. (G.W.) ; (A.W.)
2. *adv.* Head-foremost, headlong.
Glo. And above that's a wite figur pitchin eadmost down a red devul's back, *Fairford Ch. Windows.*

HEADY, *adj.* Sc. Cum. Yks. Lan. Chs. Lin. War. Som. Dev. Amer. Also in forms **heddi-** Sh.I. ; **heedie** Cai.¹; **heedy** Cum.¹ Dev. ; **heeody** w.Yks.¹; **heidie, heidy** Sc. ; **yeddy** e.Lan.¹ s.Chs.¹ 1. Headstrong, impetuous, violent, self-willed, persistent.
Abd. They war baith owre heidie ye see, ALEXANDER *Johnny Gibb* (1871) xxxiv. w.Yks.¹, ne.Lan.¹, e.Lan.¹ n.Lin.¹ He's such a heady chap you can't talk wi' him for five minnits wi' oot his fallin' oot wi' you. [*Amer. Dial. Notes* (1895) 389.]
Hence **Headily,** *adv.* rashly, in a headstrong manner.
Lnk. The present government of the Church by presbytery was not . . . headily obtruded on this kirk, WODROW *Ch. Hist.* (1721) I. 124, ed. 1898.
2. Clever, having or giving proof of brains.
Lnk. The inside works were as fu' o' brains and mechanical understannin' as John's gifted heid could pang them ; and this was the programme o' heidy contrivances an' sleep-breakin' noises expected to be set agoing at half-past five o'clock, MURDOCH *Readings* (ed. 1895) II. 64. s.Chs.¹ Oa·, ée z ŭ yed·i yuwth; yoa· léeăv im ŭloo·ŭn ; ée dŭ)nŭ waan·t nee·dhŭr yoa·r elp nŭur mahyn [Oh, he's a yeddy yowth ; yo leeave him alooan ; he dunna want neither yo'r help nur mine].
3. *Comp.* (1) **Heady-craw,** (*a*) the hooded crow, *Corvus cornix*; cf. **hoodie** ; (*b*) a somersault ; also used *advb.* head-foremost ; (2) **·maud,** a plaid covering both head and shoulders ; see **Head-maud, s.v. Head, II. 1** (30) ; (3) **·peep,** the game of hide-and-seek ; to play hide-and-seek ; (4) **·whap,** a person with a preternaturally large head.
(1, *a*) Cai.¹ (*b*) Sh.I. Wisna doo sayin', Sibbie, 'at doo nearly guid headie craw coming frae da laamb-hoos ? *Sh. News* (Jan. 21, 1899) ; I gŭde fleein' heddicra' i' da burn, *ib.* (Aug. 20, 1898). S. & Ork.¹ (2) Slk. (JAM.) (3) Dev. Takin vokes hoff tu Gull Rock . . and other places ware thay wanted tu git away tu heedy-peep, *n.Dev. Jrn.* (Dec. 23, 1885) 6, col. 1. (4) War.²

HEAF, *sb.*¹ and *v.* n.Cy. Cum. Wm. Yks. Lan. Also written **heeaf** Wm. n.Yks.¹²; and in forms **haaf** n.Yks.²; **heave** n.Cy. w.Yks. [h)ɪf, h)iəf.] 1. *sb.* Accustomed pasture-ground of sheep; also used *fig.* Cf. **heft, sb.²**
n.Cy. GROSE (1790). Lakel.¹ The place where a mountain or fell sheep is born, and where it continues to live and pasture, is called its Heaf. Cum. All Helvellyn is divided into pastures which are stinted in the number of sheep allowed to graze on them. . . These separate pastures, though they have no walls to divide them, are very clearly marked out by usage and tradition in our minds, and are called ' heafs'; we all know our separate 'heafs,' and we train our flocks to know them too, *Cornh. Mag.* (Oct. 1890) *Helvellyn,* 381 ; Each flock has its separate heaf, or distinct walk, several miles perhaps in circuit, MARSHALL *Review* (1808) I. 201 ; He had right of heaf for four or five hundred sheep upon the Common, WATSON *Nature Wdcraft.* (1890) v ; It is often said the heaf is outstocked when too many of a family are kept at home, or an establishment is unwisely enlarged—' mair ner t'heaf'ill carry,' *N. & Q.* (1873) 4th S. xi. 58. Wm. Turns em oot ontet heeaf, *Spec. Dial.* (1880) pt. ii. 7 ; Some of the largest farms have most extensive 'heafs,' *Gent. Mag.* (May 1890) 528. n.Yks.² A scant heeaf. na.Yks. Common throughout the north-eastern moors, *N. & Q.* (1872) 4th S. x. 423. e.Yks. The haunt or habitual pasture of sheep, on a common, MARSHALL *Rur. Econ.* (1788). w.Yks. (J.W.) ; HUTTON *Tour to Caves* (1781). ne.Lan.¹
Hence **Heaf-ganging** or **-going,** (1) *vbl. sb.* of sheep: the act of returning to their native pasture when they have been taken away ; (2) *ppl. adj.* accustomed to keep to the particular ' heaf ' which has been assigned to them ; belonging to one flock on a certain portion of the fell.
(1) Cum. This love of home-going or heaf-ganging among the mountain sheep is as remarkable as is wonderful their knowledge of the just boundaries of their heafs or pasture-homes, *Cornh. Mag.* (Oct. 1890) *Helvellyn,* 382. (2) Lakel.¹ Heaf-going sheep

remain as one flock upon a certain portion of the fell, and are usually sold with the farm to which that portion of the fell is apportioned. **Cum.** Oor sheep are aw ' heaf-gaen ' sheep, *Cornh. Mag.* (Oct. 1890) *Helvellyn*, 380 ; Two or three thoosan heaf-gangen sheep, SARGISSON *Joe Scoap* (1881) 189 ; **Cum.¹ Cum., Wm.** It is now some years since the fell-flocks which in rustic speech were termed ' heaf-gangin sheep ' began to be styled in advertisements ' heath-going sheep. '..Their instinct is well known, —to preserve their place on the fell, the spot which by prescriptive right has been accorded to the farm they belong to, *N. & Q.* (1872) 4th S. x. 201.

2. Of persons : an abode, residence ; an habitual haunt.

n.Yks.¹ Nat at yamm! then mebbe he'll be at Willy N.'s. That's a noted heeaf o' hisn (s.v. Hofe) ; **n.Yks.²** A man's awn heeaf. **ne.Yks.** *N. & Q.* (1879) 4th S. x. 423.

Hence (1) **Heeaf-hod**, *sb.* the home or homestead ; the source of a spring, the fountain from which the stream runs ; (2) **-hooal**, *sb.* a place of shelter.

(1) **n.Yks.²** Hoore's his heeaf-hod? [where does he live?] (a) *ib.*

3. *v.* To settle a new flock of sheep on its own pasture, to accustom a flock to a certain pasture ; of sheep : to cling to the same spot ; also used *fig.*

Lakel.¹ Cum. A lamb that probably had not been more than six weeks upon the pasture where it was heafed or homed, *Cornh. Mag.* (Oct. 1890) *Helvellyn*, 382 ; If some one else who was a commoner chose to settle or heaf his sheep on my heaf I could not prevent him, but custom and good-fellowship prevent him, *ib.* 384. **Cum., Wm.** When a new flock is sent to find its own subsistence [in the fells] some person usually goes and stays for a time to see the sheep heafed ; for if disturbed by neighbouring sheep . . . or assailed by dogs at first ' the silly sheep ' might never afterwards be able to maintain their right, *N. & Q.* (1873) 4th S. xi. 58. **n.Yks.¹** ' Guinea-fowls is desper't' bad to heeaf.' In reference to their unwillingness to forsake the old home and adopt a new one. **ne.Lan.¹** Tending sheep or cattle on a mountain.

4. Of persons : to accustom or reconcile oneself to a place ; to settle down, make oneself at home.

Lakel.¹ People who cling to their home or birthplace, are said to heaf themselves to it ; **Lakel.²** They'll like when they get heafed. **Cum.** So, Miss, you have come to see your sister heafed in Westmoreland, *N. & Q.* (1873) 4th S. xi. 58. **Wm.** Amakly ta heeaf mesell, a sang naarly ot' wae, *Spec. Dial.* (1877) pt. i. 9 ; Nivver heed ye'll heaf tul't when ye gitten a barn or twea (J.M.). **n.Yks.²** Hae ye gitten heeaf'd to t'spot ?

· **5.** To lodge, reside, live.

n.Yks.¹ Deeavid ha' left t'au'd spot, an' hes heeaf'd wiv yoong John Garbutt at t'Grains sen Marti'mas (s.v. Hofe) ; **n.Yks.²** Where do you heeaf?

Hence **Heeafing**, *sb.* a lodging, abode.

n.Yks.² Hoor wilt thou be for heeafing ?

HEAF, *sb.²* **Ken.¹** The gaff-hook used by fishermen at Folkestone.

HEAGHMOST, see **Highmost.**

HEAGUE, *v.* **Sc.** Of cattle : to push with the head, to try their strength by the pressure of their heads against each other. **Mry.** *Gl. Surv.* (JAM.)

HEAH BACK, *phr.* **Oxf.¹** An exclamation used to call sheep from trespassing on the corn.

HEAKEN, HEAL, see **Hearken, Hale,** *adj.*

HEAL, *sb.¹* *Obs.* **Sc. Irel.** Also written **heel** Lnk. ; **hele Wxf.¹** Health, welfare.

Sc. I loe Mess John, Lord len' him heal, PENNECUIK *Coll.* (1787) 13. **Baff.** Gude heal' unto his Majesty, An' mony Fourths o' June, TAYLOR *Poems* (1787) 85. **Abd.** Was she scrimped of content or heal? Ross *Helenore* (1768) 53, ed. 1812. **Ayr.** My heal and weal I'll take a care o't A tentier way, BURNS *To Mr. Mitchell* (1795) st. 5. **Lnk.** I'll . . . aft in sparkling claret drink your heel, RAMSAY *Poems* (1721) 183. **Wxf.¹** ' Yer hele,' a toast.

[OE. *hǣlo, hǣl*, health, prosperity.]

HEAL, *v.¹* **Oxf.** e.An. **1.** In *comp.* **Heal-all**, (1) the wild valerian, *Valeriana officinalis.* **Oxf.** (B. & H.) ; (2) the rosewood, *Rhodiola rosea.* **e.An.** (*ib.*)

2. With *up* : to leave off raining.

Oxf.¹ Uuy thingks tuol ee·l uup prens'li [I thinks 'tull 'eal up prensly].

HEAL, *v.²* and *sb.³* In *gen.* dial. use in Sc. Irel. and Eng. Also written **heeal I.W.¹** ; **heel N.I.¹** Chs.²³ Shr.² Hmp.¹ Ken. Som. Dev. Cor. ; **hele w.Yks.⁸** Der. s.Wor.¹ Shr.² Glo.¹² Ken.¹² Sur.¹ Hmp. Wil.¹ Dor. w.Som.¹ Dev.¹

nw.Dev.¹ Cor.¹ ; and in forms **ail-** w.Som.¹ Cor.¹² ; **eel** Chs.¹³ s.Stf. ; **hael Cai.¹** ; **hail Dev.² Cor.¹²** ; **hale Hrt. Nrf. Hmp. w.Som.¹ Dev.⁸ Cor.²** ; **heald w.Yks.²** ; **heill w.Cy. ; hel(· Sc. S. & Ork.¹ Wxf.¹ Shr.¹ Oxf.** ; **hell-** Stf. Hrf. Dor. w.Som.¹ Dev.¹² nw.Dev.¹ Cor.¹²⁸** ; **?helon Sus.²** ; **hield Wil.** ; **yeal Chs.¹** ; **yeeld Wil.** [(h)īl, w.Cy. ēl, eəl.]

1. *v.* To hide, conceal ; to keep secret.

Sc. Wel helit in ane hude, JAMIESON *Pop. Ballads* (1806) I. 345. **S. & Ork.¹ Cai.¹** Dinna tell her, she canna heal a thing. **Abd.** Stoupfulls of crouds and ream she aft would steal, And could her souple tricks frae minny heal, Ross *Helenore* (1768) 52, ed. 1812. **w.Yks.⁸, Ken.¹, Sus.²** Som. JENNINGS *Obs. Dial. w.Eng.* (1825) ; **W. & J. Gl.** (1873). **w.Som.¹, Dev.¹, nw.Dev.¹, Cor.¹**

Hence (1) **Healer**, *sb.* one who hides or conceals anything ; a receiver of stolen goods, a thief's confederate ; esp. in prov. *the healer's as bad as the stealer* ; (2) **Heling**, *sb.* a hiding-place, cover, a sheltered spot ; (3) *to heal on a person, phr.* to keep any one's secrets, not to betray or reveal them.

(1) **Shr.¹** The heler's as bad as the heaver. **Glo.** *Horae Subsecivae* (1777) 209. Som. W. & J. *Gl.* (1873) ; JENNINGS *Obs. Dial. w.Eng.* (1825). **w.Som.¹** Dev. HEWETT *Peas. Sp.* (1892) 8. nw.Dev.¹ Cor. THOMAS *Randigal Rhymes* (1895) *Gl.* ; Cor.¹² (2) Dev. Even the wild deer came bounding from unsheltered places into any offering of branches, or of other heling from the turbulence of men, BLACKMORE *Slain* in *S. Low's Ann.* (1896) ; I ran up this very lane, over the plank-bridge, and up to this heling, *ib. Perlycross* (1894) vii. (3) **Sc.** O I hae heal'd on my mistress A twalmonth and a day, KINLOCH *Ballads* (1827) 5 ; O heal this deed on rue, *ib.* n.Sc. Altho' ye tauld upo' yourself Ye might hae heal'd on me, BUCHAN *Ballads* (1828) I. 74, ed. 1875.

2. To cover ; to wrap up, to tuck up the bed-clothes ; freq. with *in* or *up.* Cf. **hill**, *v.²*

Wxf.¹, N.Cy.², w.Yks.², Stf. (F.R.C.) Der. PEGGE *Gl.* (1736). **Nhp.** Used of covering a horse with a rug (H.K.). **s.Wor.** Sometimes to heal horses means to put their cloths on (H.K.). **Shr.², Glo.², Brks.** (W.W.S.), **Brks.¹** Hmp. ' To heel in the bed-clothes,' to tuck up the bed at the feet, GROSE (1790) *MS. add.* (M.) ; Hmp.¹ **Ken.** To heel one over with a rug (H.G.) ; To heal up a child in a cradle, or any other person in a bed, KENNETT *Par. Antiq.* (1695) ; **Ken.¹², Sur.¹ Sus.** To heal a person in bed, RAY (1691) ; **Sus.²** Som. JENNINGS *Obs. Dial. w.Eng.* (1825) ; W. & J. *Gl.* (1873). **w.Som.¹** Oh, 'tis nort but a thing I brought 'long to hale the 'osses way. Dev. The sheep was haled over, *Reports Provinc.* (1884) 20 ; *Horae Subsecivae* (1777) 209 ; Dev.¹ n.Dev. We've hailed tha neck, ROCK *Jim an' Nell* (1867) st. 3. Cor.¹

Hence (1) **Healer**, *sb.* a cover ; a horse-cloth, a coverlet ; (2) **Healing**, *sb.* a coverlet, bed-clothes.

(1) **w.Som.¹** Better nit put the haler 'pon th' 'oss gin he've a-colded a bit. Dev. Have you got the hailer, sir? *Reports Provinc.* (1884) 20. **nw.Dev.¹** (a) Chs.²⁸ Oxf. So called by our Oxford bed-makers, KENNETT *Par. Antiq.* (1695) ; (K.) Ken. I want more heleing (W.F.S.). **s.Ken.** It is very cold, will you have some more healing put on your bed? (G.G.) **Sus.** I'm terrible bad off for healin', sure-ly (S.P.H.) ; **Sus.¹** In the will of Rev. H. Marshall, he leaves ' 2 pillowberes and a healing.' **w.Som.¹, nw.Dev.¹**

3. To bind a book. War. (H.K.)

· Hence **Healing**, *sb.* the cover or binding of a book.

w.Yks. (J.T.), **Chs.²⁸ s.Stf.** They brought ' Uncle Tom's Cabin ' back wi' booth the eelins off, PINNOCK *Blk. Cy. Ann.* (1895). War. (H.K.), War.² Shr. *Reports Provinc.* (1887) 9 ; Shr.², w.Som.¹ Dev. *N. & Q.* (1853) 1st S. viii. 44 ; *Reports Provinc.* (1887) 9.

4. To cover over ; to cover with a slight layer of earth ; to harrow in seed ; also with *in*, *over*, or *up.* Cf. **hill**, *v.²*

N.I.¹ To plant young trees in a temporary way, to keep them safe till it is convenient to plant them permanently. **Wxf.¹** Heal the beans. **w.Yks.²** To heald up potatoes. **Wor.** We was wheat-planting yesterday till the snow came, and we 'ain't healed it yet (H.K.). **s.Wor.¹, Hrf.², Glo.¹ Hrt.** The barley will come in rows and be the better haled or covered from vermin, ELLIS *Mod. Husb.* (1750) II. ii. **Nrf.** Esp. of covering newly-made bricks with straw to protect them from the weather before they are burned, *N. & Q.* (1873) 4th S. xi. 393. **Ken.** To put a plant hastily in the soil when not convenient to plant it, so as to cover up the roots, is to hele it in (J.A.B.) ; **Ken.¹** All right ! I'll work 'im ; I've only just got this 'ere row o' taturs to heal. Sur.¹ Sus. (M.B.-S.) ; Sus.¹ I healed up the roots with some straw. Hmp. (H.E.), Hmp.² I.W.¹ That wheeat's well heeal'd in ; I.W.² To 'heal in' corn or potatoes. Wil. Used of covering or earthing up potatoes, &c., *Wil. Arch.*

Mag. XIV. 259; Wheat is said to be not well healed when not well covered with earth when sown, DAVIS *Agric.* (1813). Dor. (A.C.); (W.C.) (c. 1750); Dor.[1] To héal beåns. Som. (W.F.R.) w.Som.[1] Be sure 'n hale up the mangle way the greens, arter 'ee've a puild em, fear o' the vrost. Dev. (E.D.); There'll be a purty 'ard vrast tô-night, Bill; thee'st best ways hale up tha tatties, or they'll be spowiled. HEWETT *Peas. Sp.* (1892); Dev.[1]; Dev.[3] An old sexton said that his son dug the graves but he always haled them in himself.

Hence (1) **Heler**, *sb.* anything which is laid over as a cover, the cover of a wooden drain; (2) **Healing**, (*a*) *vbl. sb.* the process of covering potatoes, &c., with a layer of earth; (*b*) *sb.* a covering of earth laid over potatoes, &c.

(1) Ken.[1] (*a, a*) w.Cy. Every farmer or labourer ... will tell you that the second helling of potatoes is the covering them with earth a second time, *N. & Q.* (1852) 1st S. v. 16a. (*b*) w.Som.[1] Take off the helin off o' the tatee-cave, eens they mid airy a bit.

5. Of seed: to sink into the earth, to become covered over. Wil. When the newly sown corn does not 'heeld' or 'yeeld' it requires the harrow, JEFFERIES *Gt. Estate* (1880) viii; Wil.[1]

6. To besmear or daub with dirt.
Dev.[1] My coats was a dugg'd up and my shoes heal'd in mux, 19.

7. To roof in a building or rick; to cover with slates or tiles; occas. to thatch; also with *in*.
Hrf. The building was helled in (W.W.S.). Sur.[1] Ken. A woman, wishing to say she worked under cover, not in the open air, said the place where she worked was heled in (J.A.B.); Ken.[1] Sus. When the roofing of a house is completed it is said to be healed in. Horsham stone is much used (F.E.S.); They have nearly finished healing the church (S.P.H.); RAY (1691). Hmp. HOLLOWAY. Dev. MOORE *Hist. Dev.* (1829) I. 354; *N. & Q.* (1873) 4th S. xi. 393; Dev.[2] Routley hath'n' hailed his mews eet. w.Dev. MARSHALL *Rur. Econ.* (1796). Cor.*N.&Q.*(1874)5th S. i. 434; Cor.[1] w.Cor. This expression ... is being gradually restricted to such buildings as are covered with slate, *N. & Q.* (1873) 4th S. xi. 468.

Hence (1) **Healed**, *ppl. adj.* covered over with slate, having a slate roof; (2) **Healer**, **Hellier**, or **Helyer**, *sb.* a slater, tiler, one who lays on the slates or tiles of a roof; occas. a thatcher; (3) **Healing**, *sb.* (*a*) a slate used for roofing; a slate roof; (*b*) a garret under a sloping roof; (4) **Healing-stone**, *sb.* a flat slate used for roofing; occas. used as a tombstone.

(1) Sus. There is a 'Stone-healed House Farm' in Wivelsfield parish (F.E.S.). Cor.[3] (2) Wxf.[1] Wm. GROSE (1790) *MS. add.* (P.) s.Wor. (H.K.) Glo. *Horae Subsecivae* (1777) 209; Glo.[12] w.Cy. RAY (1691). Wil.[1] Dor. (A.C.); (W.C.) (c. 1750). Som. (F.R.C.); W. & J. *Gl.* (1873). w.Som.[1] A thatcher is never called a hellier. Dev. Slaters with us still retain that antique name ... for here they are called helliers, BRAY *Desc. Tamar and Tavy* (1836) I. lett. xvii. 306; Dev.[1], nw.Dev.[1] w.Dev. MARSHALL *Rur. Econ.* (1796). Cor.[123] w.Cor. *N. & Q.* (1873) 4th S. xi. 468. (3, *a*) Sus. (S.P.H.) Dev. He don't keep the haling on the roof as he should do, O'NEILL *Dimpses* (1893) 22; 1721-2. P[4] Charles Cary for one yeare repaireing the Church Helling' £4 0s. 0d., WORTH *Tavistock Rec.* (1887) 50; Dev.[2] Be you gwain ta ha' your new house datched or hellen hailed? nw.Dev.[1] w.Dev. MARSHALL *Rur. Econ.* (1796). Cor. The houses ... that were roofed with slates, had the hellins ... stripped off the roof by dozens at a time, PEARCE *Esther Pentreath* (1891) bk. I. iii; Cor.[123] (*b*) w.Yks.[3] (4) Dev. At one part, known locally as the 'Chapel Green,' were a lot of 'Hellan' stones, ... this spot being pointed out as the old churchyard or burial ground, n.*Dev. Herald* (Apr. 4, 1895) 8, col. 3; Dev.[1] n.Dev. ROCK *Jim an' Nell* (1867) Gl. nw.Dev.[1] To 250 Helling Stones 3s. 9d. s.Dev. 1690. For 200 and halfe of healing stones ... and y[e] carriage 04. 08, E. *Budleigh Chwarden's Acc.* Cor. For the covering of houses there are three sorts of slate which from that use take the name of heeling-stones, CAREW *Surv. Cor.* vi, in LEVESON-GOWER *Gl.* (1876); Cor.[12] w.Cor. *N. & Q.* (1873) 4th S. xi. 468.

8. To season an oven when first made. Chs.[18]
Hence **Eeling**, *vbl. sb.* the seasoning of an oven with fire when first made. Chs. (K.)

9. To take up a fire, to cover a fire. s.Cy. (HALL.) Sus. RAY (1691); (K.) **10.** *sb.* A hidden spot, an unseen place; shelter.
n.Wil. (G.E.D.) e.Dev. Keeping under hele with his oil-skins on, BLACKMORE *Perlycross* (1894) xxxvi. [RAY (1691) *MS. add.* (J.C.) 36.]

[OE. *helian, wv., helan, sv.*, to cover, hide, conceal.]

HEALD, *sb.*[1] Sc. Irel. n.Cy. Yks. Lan. Chs. Also Som. Also in forms evel w.Som.[1]; **headle** Dwn. w.Yks.; **heddle** Sc. N.I.[1] n.Cy. (HALL.) Lan.; **held** Yks.; **hevel** w.Som.[1]; **hiddle** Sc. (JAM.) Fif.; **yeald** w.Yks. Lan.; **yeld** w.Yks.[2] Lan.; **yell** Lan.[1] e.Lan.[1] Chs.[1] **1.** A series of loops knitted of twine upon two laths. In plain weaving a pair of these series is used, each series containing loops to half the number of threads in the warp. Through one series is threaded every other warp thread; through the other the alternate threads; *gen. in pl.*; see below.

Sc. The bed, loom, heddles, treadles, thrums, reeds, and pirn-wheel was a' brought and set up, GRAHAM *Writings* (1883) II. 211. Sh.I. A'm no tinkin' at Sandy Williamson 'ill set him apon a lûm, or grip a heddle, bi da time 'at we get waast an' yarn reddy, *Sh. News* (Feb. 26, 1898). w.Sc. Duncan after having dressed his web, went out. ... The goat made his way into the shop, ... scrambled up into the empty seat, and began to lick off the fresh dressing; in this act, his horns got entangled amongst the heedles, CARRICK *Laird of Logan* (1835) 157. Fif. Da [papa] is fairly oot o' hiddles, An' mither has nae mair to spin, EDWARDS *Mod. Poets*, 8th S. 161. Ayr. The brethren o' the heddles, SILLAR *Poems* (1789) 46; A puir blanket-weaver, wi' nothing but a set o' heddles between you and eternity, JOHNSTON *Glenbuckie* (1889) 77. Lnk. The reek o' the heddles an' treddles Might rise to the moon in a cloud, WATSON *Poems* (1853) 82. Gall. MACTAGGART *Encycl.* (1824) 259, ed. 1876. N.I.[1] Dwn. I went to my loom, to see she was in tune, But from her full soon I was obleeged to go, Neither headles, nor jacks, nor skays were correct, *Uls. Jrn. Arch.* (1857) V. 99. n.Cy. (HALL.) Yks. Thoo's tript me helds and meead me stop, *Spec. Dial.* (1800) 90. w.Yks. A series of fine cords, looped at each end to pass over a wooden shaft, and each bearing in its middle a metal eyelet [the 'mail'] through which an end of the warp is to pass. The shafts are raised or lowered in the motion of the loom, and thus the ends of the warp are lifted above, or depressed below, the level at which the shuttle passes (F.J.N.); Suspended from the top of the loom are two frames, or beadles, CUDWORTH *Worstedopolis* (1888) 52; w.Yks.[3] If it [the thread] breaks in front of the yeld it only wants once tying, otherwise twice, 10; At each end of the jack is a string; the one connects it with the lam below, the other with the yeld, *ib.* 70. Lan. He lets no lumpy yorn crash through his yells, CLEGG *Sketches* (1895) 232; DAVIES *Races* (1856) 268; Lan.[1], e.Lan.[1], Chs.[1] w.Som.[1] In this district the word is applied by weavers, only to the actual eye, if of steel, or loop, if of twine, through which the thread of warp is passed, and not to the whole heddle.—Each thread must have its own separate hevel. Hevel also means the string, or entire guide for each separate thread of warp, *ib.*

2. *Comb.* (1) **Heald-hook**, a hook used by weavers when drawing in their warps; (2) **knitting machine**, a machine used for knitting the 'healds'; (3) **-rug**, a rug made from the 'healds'; (4) **-twine**, the thread of which the 'healds' are made; a fine sort of twine; (5) **-yarn**, yarn made from the 'healds.'

(1) w.Yks. (D.L.) Lan. Mi linderins, shuttle, and yeald hook, HARLAND *Lyrics* (1866) 239; Aw've no moor use for a penknife nor Queen Victorey has for a yeld-hook, HARLAND & WILKINSON *Leg.* (1873) 190. Chs.[1] A hook for putting yarn through yells and reed. (2) Lan. Thir wur a heald-knittin misheen, FERGUSON *Preston Eggsibishun* (1865) vi. (3) w.Yks. (J.W.) Lan. That mess on th' new yeld rug, CLEGG *Sketches* (1895) 133. (4) Rnf. *Agric. Surv.* 257 (JAM.). Som. W. & J. *Gl.* (1873). w.Som.[1] (5) Yks. It may be stated that they were the first makers of worsted heald yarns in the Bradford district, CUDWORTH *Bradford* (1876) 250.

[1. An helde, *trama*, Cath. *Angl.* (1483). OE. *hefeld*, 'licium' (ÆLFRIC).]

HEALD, *v.*[1] and *sb.*[2] Sh.I. n.Cy. Yks. Lan. Chs. Pem. Glo. e.An. Also in forms **heeald** w.Yks.[1]; **heeld** Sh.I.; **heild** w.Yks.[1]; **held** n.Yks.[1]; **hild** Pem. Glo. e.An.[12]; **yeld** Chs.[1] s.Chs.[1] [h]ild, iald, jeld.] **1.** *v.* to bend downwards or to one side; to lean, incline, slope; also used *fig.* Cf. **heel**, *v.*[2]

Sh.I. Shü heeldid ower da kettle wi' his mooth ta da door ta ktile, *Sh. News* (May 28, 1898); He hed his shair heeldit back ower, BURGESS *Sketches* (2nd ed.) 77. N.Cy.[1] w.Yks. WILLAN *List Wds.* (1811); THORESBY *Lett.* (1703); w.Yks.[14]

Hence **Healding** or **Hilding**, *ppl. adj.* sloping, leaning, tilting.
w.Yks.[1] Gangin ower some heealdin grund, they welted t'cart ower yusterday, ii. 286. e.An.[12]

2. With *to*: to incline to, to be favourable to.

w.Yks.¹ He heealds au to yan side.

3. To rely on.

n.Cy. GROSE (1790). w.Yks. HUTTON *Tour to Caves* (1781). ne.Lan.¹

4. *Obs.* To incline or tilt a vessel in order to pour out; to pour out; also with *out*.

n.Cy. To heald the pot, GROSE (1790); N.Cy.² w.Yks. HUTTON *Tour to Caves* (1781). ne.Lan.¹ Glo. To hild out, *Horae Subsecivae* (1777) 213.

5. Of rain: to pour, to come down in torrents.

Pem. (W.H.Y.) s.Pem. Is it raining now?—Oh, 'tis hildin (W.M.M.).

6. *sb.* A slope, incline, declivity; a hill.

w.Yks.¹ Cha.¹ It's a foine bad place for wayter, is yonder yeld. s.Cha.¹ Used in more northern parts. Only appears in s.Cha. as a place-name; e. g. the Yeld (sometimes spelt Heald) is the name of a farm at Wrenbury.

7. Inclination, proclivity. n.Yks.¹ **8.** The act of pouring out. w.Yks.¹

[1. I hylde, I leane on the one syde, as a bote or shyp, *Je encline de cousté*, PALSGR. (1530). OE. *hieldan*, to bend, incline. 2. If þou thyn herte will to me helde, *York Plays* (c. 1400) 182. 4. [He] heeldide out as fyr his indignacioun, WYCLIF (1382) *Lam.* ii. 4. 6. *Clinium, i. discensum*, helde, burhsteal, *MS. Harl.* (c. 950), in Wright's *Voc.* (1884) 205.]

HEALD, *v.²* Yks. Wil. To heal.

w.Yks. (J.W.) n.Wil. 'Tis a healdin' up now nicely (E.H.G.).

HEALD, *sb.³* *Obs.* Wm. A shelter for cattle on the moors; a fence of earth or stones, 'a bield.' (J.H.)

[Cogn. w. ON. *hǽli*, a shelter, refuge (VIGFUSSON).]

HEALD, HEALE, HEALEY, see Heal, *v.²*, Hale, *adj.*, Heely, *adj.*

HEALING-LEAF, *sb.* Sc. The leaf of the orpine, *Sedum Telephium.*

Sc.' Mr. James Hogg . . . mentions the uniformly successful treatment of sheep affected with this disorder [Trembling Ill]—by giving them a decoction of the Dewcup and Healing-leaf boiled in butter-milk, *Essays Highl. Soc.* III. 389 (JAM.). Slg. Not known as a salve (G.W.).

HEALL, HEALLY, HEALO, see Hale, *adj.*, Heely, *adj.*, Heloe.

HEALTHSOME, *adj.* Sc. Yks. Healthy; wholesome, conducive to health.

Slg. Your meat and drink is made healthsome to your nurture by thanks to God, BRUCE *Sermons* (1631) xii, ed. 1843. n.Yks.¹² e.Yks. NICHOLSON *Flk-Sp.* (1889) 4; e.Yks.¹ It's a fahn healthsome bayne. A fahn healthsome spot, *MS. add.* (T.H.) m.Yks.¹

HEALTHY, *adj.* n.Cy. Nrf. 1. Of food: wholesome, conducive to health. n.Cy. (J.W.)

2. Phr. *healthy as trout*, perfectly healthy, in complete health.

Nrf. Now look at 'em with their red skins and dewy noses, healthy as trout, EMERSON *Yarns* (1891) 43.

HEALY, see Heely, *adv.*

HEAM, *v.* Dev. [ēm.] Also written aim nw.Dev.¹ With *up*: to save, lay by.

Dev. I've had five years of wool heamed up, BARING-GOULD *Spider* (1887) II. xxviii. nw.Dev.¹ 'I've 'aim'd up thucker viel' vor 'ay.' 'They zay he 'th a-got dree or vower years' shear o' wool 'aim'd up in shippen tallat.'

[Prob. repr. an OE. *hǽman*, to lay up at home, der. of *hám*, home. Cf. hame, *v.²*]

HEAM, HEAMSIES, see Hame, *sb.¹*

HEAN, *sb.¹* Nhb.¹ Also written heen. [hǐn.] The part of a plough which grips the land, also called the ' little heel.'

HEAN, *sb.²* Dor. The handle of a knife.

The knife's a-broke off up to the heän, BARNES *Gl.* (1863); Dor.¹ [Hean, the hilt of any weapon, HOWELL (HALL.).]

HEANLO, see Heloe.

HEAP, *sb.¹* and *adv.* Var. dial. and colloq. uses in Sc. Irel. Eng. and Amer. Also in forms aäpe w.Yks.; hape N.I.¹ Suf.; heeap Cum.¹ n.Yks.² e.Yks.; heep w.Sc. Nhb.; hep Nhp.² Sur.¹; heup N.Cy.¹ Nhb.¹ n.Lin.; yeap Som.; yep Lan. [h)ïp, h)iap.] I. *sb.* The accumulation of excavated material at the top of a pit.

Nhb. I'm wae for thy lads :—on the beap Nan, there's nane

half as raggie as thine, PROUDLOCK *Borderland Muse* (1896) 274; (W.G.); Nhb.¹

Hence (1) **Heap-keeper,** *sb.* the man who overlooks the cleaning of coals on the surface; (2) **-stead** or **-steed,** *sb.* the platform at a pit's mouth elevated above the surface level to allow the coals to be tipped over screens into wagons.

(1) Nhb.¹ *Mining Gl.* (1852). (2) Nhb. The back-shift men sprang frae their beds An' to the heapstead aff did rin—A heapstead noo rent into shreds, PROUDLOCK *Borderland Muse* (1896) 95; Nhb.¹ The tubs are landed on the heap-steed and run to the screens. [*Reports Mines.*]

2. *Comp.* **Heap-house,** a rubbish-house attached to a farm.

Dor. A rubbish or dirt house where things of no value or use are thrown—not manure, but simply rubbish (A.R.W.).

3. A small hillock or tump of earth.

nw.Dev.¹ Used in the words dung-heap, emmet-heap, wänt-heap, &c.

4. Of corn: the corn laid up by the thresher in a barn before it is cleaned. Sur.¹

5. A heaped measure, *gen.* a quarter of a peck; measure, the quantity measured.

Bwk. Six fills of the corn firlot, up to the edge of the wood or a little higher, called sleaks or streaks, or four fills, heaped by hand as high as they can go, called heaps, are counted as one boll, *Agric. Surv.* 448 (JAM.). Wgt. They sell their beir, malt, and oates by heap, and the vessel is so broad that the heap will be more than one third of the whole, FRASER *Wigtown* (1877) 90. n.Cy. GROSE (1790); N.Cy.¹ Nhb. Street vendors in Newcastle formerly pushed their sales of fruit, &c. by the cry ' Here's a heap an' lie on '—here's full measure and more laid on. This is now obs. (R.O.H.); Nhb.¹ n.Yks.¹; n.Yks.² ' They give shoort heaps,' an expression for bad measure of all sorts; n.Yks.⁴ e.Yk⁹. MARSHALL *Rur. Econ.* (1788). m.Yks.¹ Often half-peck or peck, also; not so much according to quantity, as appearance, as not being considered liberal, unless heaped to a point. ne.Lan.¹

Hence (1) **Heap-mete,** *sb.,* (2) *heap and thrutch, phr.* liberal measure, filled to overflowing; *fig.* excess.

(1) Keb. The covenant seeketh not heap-mete, nor stented obedience as the condition of it, RUTHERFORD *Lett.* (1660) No. 249. (2) Cha. It were Maxfield measure—heap and thrutch, CROSTON *Enoch Crump* (1887) 7.

6. *Obs.* A wicker basket. N.Cy.¹, Nhb.¹

7. A large number or quantity, a great deal, a great many; freq. in *pl.*

Cai.¹ A heap o' lees. Abd. There's a heap o' killin' i' a caird, ALEXANDER *Ain Flk.* (1882) 112. Frf. A heap o' the congregation couldna keep their seats, BARRIE *Minister* (1891) iii. w.Sc. A heep o' letters has been passing between Mr. Ochtertyre an' a Mr. Gibby Garrempy, MACDONALD *Settlement* (1869) 62, ed. 1877. Fif. A fearfu' heap o' lies, DOUGLAS *Poems* (1806) 125. Dmb. I . . . need a heap o' clippin' an' kaimin' before I can gang decently in the traces, CROSS *Disruption* (1844) v. Ayr⁴ It took a heap o' delvin' and shoolin before the stane was cleared, SERVICE *Notandums* (1890) 65. Lnk. I hae a heap o' drugget coais, Nae twa o' them's alike, THOMSON *Musings* (1881) 46. e.Lth. We thocht an awfu' heap o' him than, HUNTER *J. Inwick* (1895) 107. Edb. What heaps o' friends I hae got now, LIDDLE *Poems* (1821) 229. Ir. I git hapes to ate and a sup to dhrink, *Paddiana* (ed. 1848) II. 101; Not even for little Maggie that he always thought a hape of, BARLOW *Lisconnel* (1895) 211. N.I.¹ Boys, A had a hape o' dacency, When A first come among ye. N.Cy.¹ A heap of folks. Nhb. Aw dinnit leyke te gang amang a heep oh weyves o dressèt up, BEWICK *Tyneside Tales* (1850) 12; Thor wis heaps o' folks stannin sboot (R.O.H.). Dur.¹ Cum. He's git heaps o' money, ANDERSON *Ballads* (ed. 1840) 73; Cum.⁴ n.Yks. Ther was heaps o' foœaks on t'road, TWEDDELL *Clevel. Rhymes* (1875) 59; n.Yks.² I've walked it beeaps o' times. e.Yks. NICHOLSON *Flk-Sp.* (1889) 66; e.Yks.¹ Ah've been ti' Hull heeaps o' tahms, *MS. add.* (T.H.) w.Yks. They said ther was aäpes on 'em about, six or seven stoän (F.P.T.); w.Yks.¹ There wor, for seur, a heap o' folk; w.Yks.⁶ Lan. Thir wur sich o yep o numbers, SCHOLES *Tim Gamwattle* (1857) 41. I.Ma. A heap of sin, BROWN *Doctor* (1887) 19. Not.¹ n.Lin.¹ There was heäps o' rasin on Tho'sda'. s.Lin. Ah've heäps on 'em (T.H.R.). Rut.¹, Lei.¹ Nhp.¹ What a heap of apples there were on the tree! Nhp.², War.³ s.Oxf. Your poor ma, she thought a heap o' you both, ROSEMARY *Chilterns* (1895) 125. Hnt. (T.P.F.). e.An.¹² Suf. A ' hape ' of muck, of nonsense, RAVEN *Hist. Suf.* (1895) 265. Cmb.¹ And there's such a heap of baa-lambs

Q

a-coming down the road. Hmp., **Sus. Holloway.** **Som.** Yo got of fruit a yeap, **Agrikler** *Rhymes* (1872) 55. [*Amer. Dial. Notes* (1896) I. 376.]

Hence *a heap o' nought, phr.* anything that is worthless, rubbish, nonsense.

n.Lin. It's all a heap o' nowt, not worth talkin' on, **Peacock** *R. Skirlaugh* (1870) II. 122.

8. With *adj.* or *adv.* : much, a great deal, very many ; also in *pl.*

Cal.[1] A heap better. **Bnff.**[1] The doctor's a heap better the day. **Frf.** The airm-chair was a heap shinnier than the rest, **Barrie** *Thrums* (1889) xiv. **Per.** Gin they're no killed they're a heap waur than had they no striven, *Sandy Scott* (1897) 15. **Ayr.** I micht get waur than you—a guid heap waur, **Johnston** *Glenbuckie* (1889) 35. **Lth.** Ye've been a gude wife to me . . . better, a heap, than I've been a husband to you, **Strathesk** *More Bits* (ed. 1885) 235. n.Lin.[1] Kelton's heaps farther fra Gaainsb'r then Notherup is.

9. Phr. (1) *driven in heaps*, perplexed with a multiplicity of work or engagements ; (2) *to knock all of a heap*, to frighten, astonish ; (3) *to live at full heap*, of horses or cattle : to live in abundant food.

(1) **Nhp.**[1] (2) **Cor.**[1] When I heard it I was knocked all of a heap. (3) **Sus., Hmp. Holloway.**

10. Four cherry-stones.

Nhb. In com. use. Boys in reckoning cherry-stones in their play with them always count by so many heaps (R.O.H.) ; (W.G.)

11. A term of reproach applied to a slovenly woman.

Sc. Usually conjoined with some epithet—' A nasty heap ' (Jam.). **Abd.** Foul fa' the sly bewitchin' heap Cou'd turn hersel' in ony shape, **Cock** *Strains* (1810) II. 91. **Nhb.** She's just a movin' heap o' muck, **Wilson** *Pitman's Pay* (1843) 10 ; **Nhb.**[1] Usually in comb. with some other descriptive word.

12. *pl.* Turnips. **Cum.**[1]

13. *adv.* In a confused state, higgledy-piggledy. **Sc.** (Jam.)

HEAP, *sb.*[2] **Cor.**[1] The thigh.

HEAP, see Hap, *v.*[2] **Hoop,** *sb.*[1]

HEAPED, *ppl. adj.* **Shr. Som.** Also in form **yepped** **Shr.**[1] **1.** Having the contents piled above the brim, not levelled.

Shr. In other markets it means 2½ bushels, sometimes heaped, sometimes stricken, and sometimes a medium between both, **Marshall** *Review* (1818) II. 225 ; **Shr.**[1] I pût a yepped box o' coal o' the fire now jest.

2. With *up* : a term in building applied to a roof, ' hipped.'

w.Som.[1] I don't like they there heaped up ruvs, I zim th' old farshin gable's better by half.

HEAPING-STOCK, *sb.* **Dev.** [Not known to our correspondents.] A stepping-stone. (**Hall.**) See **Hip,** *v.*

HEAPLET, *sb.* n.Yks.[2] Written **heeaplet.** A small heap of hay, remaining to dry before being cocked. (s. v. Hipples.)

HEAR, *v.* and *int.* Var. dial. and colloq. uses in Sc. Irel. Eng. and Amer. [h)lə(r, iə(r), jə(r), w.Cy. also ai·ə(r).] **I.** Gram. forms. **1.** *Present Tense* : (1) Hare, (2) Heear, (3) Heer, (4) Heern, (5) Heir, (6) Hire, (7) Iə(r, 8) Year, (9) Yer, (10) Yerr, (11) Yi'h'r, (12) Yur. [For further instances see II. below.]

(1) **Nrf.** (W.R.E.) (2) **w.Yks.** Ah hed t'plessur o' heearin' a hextra crack, **Binns** *Orig.* (1889) No. i. 3. (3) **Wxf.**[1] (4) **Chs.**[1] Aw heern folks say. (5) **Sc. Murray** *Dial.* (1873) 205. **Wxf.**[1] (6) **Glo. Gibbs** *Cotswold Vill.* (1898) 83 ; **Glo.**[1] Wull. Let m' zee yer veace, let m' hire yer voice, **Kite** *Sng. Sol.* (1860) ii. 14 ; **Wil.**[1] (s.v. E). **Som. Jennings** *Obs. Dial. w.Eng.* (1825). **w.Som.**[1] Uy·ur. Not much used except by old people. The com. form is [yuur]. **Dev.** Dost hire Tom ? **White** *C'yman's Conductor* (1701) 127. n.**Dev.** Dist hire ma ? *Exm. Scold.* (1746) l. 31. (7) **w.Yks. Wright** *Gram. Wndhll.* (1892) 142. (8) **Lan.** An' dost year oi drop it deaun i' th' drawer, **Kay-Shuttleworth** *Scarsdale* (1860) II. 284. **Glo.** Thee know'st as thee wer main ager to year arl about et, **Buckman** *Darke's Sojourn* (1890) ii. **Som.** Let me year thoi voice, **Baynes** *Sng. Sol.* (1860) ii. 14. e.**Dev.** Deue let ai year'n teue ! **Pulman** *Sng. Sol.* (1860) viii. 13. (9) **Lan.** Aw like to yer at th' cookoo sing, **Harland** *Lyrics* (1866) 88. s.**Lan.** Yo'n then yer a roor o' weatur, **Bamford** *Traveller* (1844) 5a. **Chs.** It's worth a' the brass to yer that, **Banks** *Forbidden* (ed. 1885) xiv. **Brks.**[1] n.**Dev.** I yer a dap ta door, **Rock** *Jim an' Nell* (1867) st. 76. (10) **w.Som.**[1], nw.**Dev.**[1] (11) m.**Yks.**[1] *Introd.* 36. (12) **w.Som.** Yuur, **Elworthy** *Gram.* (1877) 44. **Dev.** Ha thit ith yurn ta yur, let min yur, **Baird** *St. Matt.* (1863) xi. 15.

2. *Preterite* : (1) Haerd, (2) Haird, (3) Hard, (4) Heärd, (5) Heeard, (6) Heerd, (7) Heered, (8) Hird, (9) Ind, (10) Yar, (11) Yarn, (12) Yeard, (13) Yerd, (14) Yi'h'd, (15) Yuurd.

(1) **Sc. Murray** *Dial.* (1873) 205. (2a) **Ken.** (G.B.) (3) **Sc. Murray** *ib.* **Cal.**[1] **Ir.** I hard thim—Molly Magee wid her batchelor, **Tennyson** *To-morrow* (1885). **Nhb.**[1] Aa hard ye wor comin. **Cum.**[3] It's varra weel we hård 'im though, 67. **Wm.** Lib hard t'aald chap clinkan throot faald, **Robison** *Aald Taales* (1882) 5. **w.Yks.**[1] **Lan.** l hard that fawse felly Dick o Yems o owd Harry's sey, **Tim Bobbin** *View Dial.* (ed. 1806) 57. **Ess.**[1] (4) n.**Yks.** I heärd Margery speakin', **Linskill** *Haven Hill* (1886) lvii. n.**Lin.**[1] (5) n.**Yks.** (T.S.) **w.Yks.** We hardly ivver heeard them, **Cudworth** *Dial. Sketches* (1884) 6. **Lan.** Madam Clough sent the tay an' sugar . . . when hoo heeard as feyther had axed for a holiday, **Banks** *Manch. Man* (1876) iii. **Sur.** And hee-ard 'em a yelping and howling, **Hoskyns** *Talpa* (1852) 44, ed. 1857. (6) **Cum.** Ah heerd t'cwoach wurl away, *Joe and Landlord*, 6. **Yks.** Well, I declare I never heerd t'like on't ! **Taylor** *Miss Miles* (1890) i. n.**Yks.**[1] ne.**Yks.**[1] 33. **Lan.** I heerd my gronny say, **Harland & Wilkinson** *Flk-Lore* (1867) 144. **Chs.**[1], sw.**Lin.**[1] **War.**[2], **Ken.** (G.B.) **Sur.** I heerd some'ut o' the kind, **Bickley** *Sur. Hills* (1890) II. xv. (7) **Lan.** I never heered nobry knock, *Longman's Mag.* (Aug. 1895) 389. (8) **Som. Jennings** *Dial. w.Eng.* (1869). (9) **w.Yks. Wright** *Gram. Wndhll.* (1892) 142. (10) **Not.** (L.C.M.), **Nhp.**[2] (11) **Nhp.**[2] I yarn as how you left bwuth them plazen. (12) **Lan.** An yeard so mich o what they'd bin saying, **Laycock** *Billy Armatage*, 3. **I.W.** I never yeard o' nobody returning thanks vur the buryen', **Gray** *Reproach Annesley* (1889) l. 109. **Dev.**[1] (13) **Lan.** I never yerd on't afore, **Waugh** *Chim. Corner* (1874) 22, ed. 1879. **Oxf.**[1] *MS. add.* **Brks.**[1], **Dev.**[6] (14) m.**Yks.**[1] *Introd.* 36. (15) w.**Som. Elworthy** *Gram.* (1877) 44.

3. *Pp.* : (1) Haad, (2) Haard, (3) Haerd, (4) Hard, (5) Heärd, (6) Hearn, (7) Heead, (8) Heeard, (9) Heeart, (10) Heerd, (11) Heern, (12) Hord, (13) Ind, (14) Yeard, (15) Yerd, (16) Yherd, (17) Yi·b'd, (18) Yi'h'n, (19) Yird, (20) Yuurd.

(1) e.**Yks.**[1] (2) **Wm.** Peggy hed haard o aboot t'cheeses, *Spec. Dial.* (1885) pt. iii. 6. (3) **Sc. Murray** *Dial.* (1873) 205. (4) **Sc. Murray** *ib.* **Cal.**[1] **Cum.** Sum mair pleaaces ab'd hard t'neaam on afooar, **Sargisson** *Joe Scoap* (1881) 14. **Per.** But yu mun ev hard tell on't, **Wilson** *Lile Bit ev a Sng.* 98. **w.Yks.**[1], n.**Lin.**[1] (5) n.**Lin.**[1] (6) **Lon.** If Tommy only heard what Shooel had hearn, **Barrie** *Tommy* (1896) 14. (7) e.**Yks.**[1] **w.Yks.** A vast ah hev beeath heead and seen, *Spec. Dial.* (1800) 44. (8) **n.Yks.** Ah've heeard it, **Tweddell** *Clevel. Rhymes* (1875) 11. **w.Yks.** A toathree moor cases nor heeard, **Yksman.** *Comic Ann.* (1890) 91, col. 2 ; **w.Yks.**[1] (9) **Lan.** Ther worn't a saand to be heeart, **Bowker** *Tales* (1882) 50. (10) ne.**Yks.**[1] 33. **Lan.** Hast heerd news, **Myles** ! **Fothergill** *Probation* (1879) i. **Der.** I've a heerd that Bessie Broom have a been very badly, **Verney** *Stone Edge* (1868) i. **Chs.** Ye an heerd it mony a time, **Croston** *Enoch Crump* (1887) 7. **Stf., War., Wor.** He an't heered from 'er since last summer (M.K.). **Wil.** Th' naise o' th' turtle uz heer'd in owr lond, **Kite** *Sng. Sol.* (1860) ii. 12. (11) **Sur.** I have heern say, **Jennings** *Field Paths* (1884) 3. (12) **Nhb.** When Rawfy Dagg . . . wis hord to growl and grane, **Robson** *Evangeline* (1870) 320. (13) **w.Yks. Wright** *Gram. Wndhll.* (1892) 142. (14) **Lan.** Yo' mowt a yeard hoo down to the town-hall, **Fothergill** *Probation* (1879) xv. **w.Som.**[1] (15) **Lan.** He were never yerd to grumble, **Clegg** *Sketches* (1895) 6. (16) **Lan.** Aw've yherd 'em rawt eawt, **Standing** *Echoes* (1885) 13. (17, 18) m.**Yks.**[1] *Introd.* 36. (19) e.**Dev.** Th' craw o' th' culver's a-yird vur an' naigh, **Pulman** *Sng. Sol.* (1860) ii. 12. (20) w.**Som. Elworthy** *Gram.* (1877) 44.

II. Dial. meanings. **1.** *v.* In phr. (1) *hearest thou but* (*eastabud, hearstobud*), (2) *hears to me*, (3) *hear ye but*, (4) *hear you*, or *thee*, exclamations expressive of surprise or emphasis ; (5) *to be heard for*, to be heard of, on account of, to be known for ; (6) *to hear a law-court*, to go to law ; (7) — *say*, (8) — *talk*, (9) — *tell*, to hear, to learn by report, be informed ; (10) *we'll be hearan*, we shall hear the result or issue by and by.

(1) **w.Yks.** ' Well George, what is the best news!' ' Eastabud, the best news I hear is—" This man receiveth sinners," ' *Leeds Merc. Suppl.* (1884) 8 ; **w.Yks.**[1] Oh, hearato bud, barn, how thou talks ! ii. 301. (2) **Lan.** So heors to meh yung mon, I mun quit thee as to this job, **Tim Bobbin** *View Dial.* (ed. 1806) 56 ; Scutcht with' seme rod wi' ther Clarks, hears to me ! *ib.* (3) w.**Yks.**[1], ne.**Lan.**[1] (4) **Lan.** ' Yer thee ! ' David whispered, **Clegg** *David's Loom* (1894) v ; Yer yo ! He's gettin up, *ib. Sketches* (1895) 184.

(5) Abd. Just in all his bargains, and never heard for his true debt, Spalding *Hist. Sc.* (1792) I. 5a. (6) Gall. Nor wad he step aside for mailin's : Ne'er preed anither but his wife,—Ne'er heard a law court in his life, Nicholson *Poet. Wks.* (1814) 39, ed. 1897. (7) w.Yks.[1] Sur. I have heard say that when anybody is going to die, Jennings *Field Paths* (1884) 86. (8) Sur. I've heerd talk of it so long, Hoskyns *Talpa* (1852) 183, ed. 1857. w.Mid. No, I never 'eer'd talk on it afore (W.P.M.). (9) Sc. Let me hear tell of her no more, Stevenson *Catriona* (1893) xxiii. Sh.I. He begood ta faer 'at his nicht's wark wid be heard tell o', Clark *Gleams* (1898) 58. Cai.[1] Frf. The deil a shot I e'er heard tell o' Cam' near't but ane, Sands *Poems* (1833) 84. Per. Sin she gaed awa, naebody kenned whaur, I hae na heard tell o' her ava, Cleland *Inchbrachn* (1883) 49, ed. 1887. s.Sc. It would vex me sair . . . to hear tell o' ye gettin ony fright about the glen, Wilson *Tales* (1839) V. 5a. Rnf. Did ye ever hear tell o' the like o't? Barr *Poems* (1861) 106. Ayr. It maybe grieves him to see and hear tell of so mony guid law pleas gaun bye his door to Dalry, Service *Dr. Duguid* (ed. 1887) 186. Edb. I've gien you the story leal, As I've heard tell, Liddle *Poems* (1821) 196. Dmf. Did ye ever hear tell o' a lanely wee toon? Reid *Poems* (1894) 46. Gall. Some gang daft when they hear tell, Nicholson *Poet. Wks.* (1814) 56, ed. 1897. Don. If I ever . . . hear tell of the lakes of such happenin', *Century Mag.* (Nov. 1899) 45. N.I.[1] Did ever ye hear tell o' the like ? Nhb. I heerd tell there was yan o' Fenwick's lads coom, Clare *Love of Lass* (1890) I. 26. Dur.[1] s.Dur. A' hear tell 'at thou's gannen te git wed (J.E.D.). Cum. He wad see a fella at hed beeath hard tell on't an seen't, Sargisson *Joe Scoap* (1881) 6a ; Cum.[1] I nivver hard tell o' sec a thing. Wm. Hev yah nivver hard tell on't ? *Spec. Dial.* (1880) pt. ii. 28. n.Yks. I heer'd tell on't (I.W.) ; n.Yks.[2] e.Yks. Ah say, Jim! hez tha heea'd tell what a dooment Navvy Bob had wi' that deead chap ? Nicholson *Flk-Sp.* (1889) 32 ; e.Yks.[1] w.Yks. Ah've heeard tell of a chap, Binns *Orig.* (1889) No. i. 4. Cha.[1], Not. (L.C.M.), Not.[1] n.Lin.[1] I don't think as I've heard tell o' ony body o' that naame e' this part. sw.Lin.[1], Nhp.[12] Lei.[1] Nivver 'eerd tell o' noo sooch a thing. War. We heard tell as he'd sold his own land, Geo. Eliot *S. Marner* (1861) vi ; War.[24], Hrf.[2] Glo. It makes a body's heart quop to hear tell of such a history, Gissing *Both of this Parish* (1889) I. 103. Oxf.[1] *MS. add.* Brks.[1], Hnt. (T.P.F.) Ess. Some were to be found who had 'heard tell as how' there was 'summat' to be seen, *Longman's Mag.* (Jan. 1893) 310. Sur. Tennyson? I never heered tell of that name, Jennings *Field Paths* (1884) 107; Sur.[1] n.Wil. I never heerd tell on't (E.H.G.). Dor. I heard tell as you mid be lef here all alone, Hare *Vill. Street* (1895) 108. Som. So your mind's a-made up, Sophia, as I've a-heard tell, Raymond *Sam and Sabina* (1894) 168. w.Som.[1] Well, I've a-yeard tell o' jis thing, but I never didn zee nother one avore. Dev. I dü yer tell that thy squire shüte a white coily yisterday, Hewett *Peas. Sp.* (1892) 64 ; Dev.[1] Dev.[2] I nivver yerd-tele ov ort likee to't. Cor.[2] I've heard tell as how old Tresawna is dead. w.Cor. I never heard tell of 'im before (M.A.C.). (10) Cai.[1]

2. With *till* or *to* : to listen to, hearken, to give heed to. **Sc.** Hear to that, ye sumph! the vera chairs seem as if they . . . hae taken to knockin ilkither, Whitehead *Daft Davie* (1876) 134, ed. 1894. Per. It diz a body gude to hear til ye whiles, Cleland *Inchbrachen* (1883) 73, ed. 1887. Ayr. Hear to me, Rabby, Gie me bonny Babby, Ainslie *Land of Burns* (ed. 1892) 325. Dev. I'd as lieve hear to her reading out a chapter as the passon himself, O'Neill *Idyls* (1892) 75. [*Amer. Dial. Notes* (1895) 389.] Hence *hear till him, phr.* an exclamation implying disbelief or ridicule. S. & Ork.[1] Cld. (Jam.) e.Lth. 'Hear til him,' says he, 'he downa be spoken to, he's that big,' Hunter *J. Inwick* (1895) 66. n.Yks.[2], m.Yks.[1]

3. To sound. Yks. It hears nicely (C.C.R.). n.Yks. 'It heard well ' ; of a flute, played together with several violins.

4. *Fig.* To understand. Nrf. (W.R.E.)

5. To treat. Sc. When conjoined with 'weel' or 'best,' expressive of favourable treatment (Jam.) ; ' Last in bed best heard,' spoken when they who lie longest are first serv'd, Kelly *Prov.* (1721) 238.

6. A sign of assent : yes. w.Yks. (S.K.C.)

7. *Phr. hear, hear!* an exclamation used by boatmen. Nrf. Used by the Lowestoft boatmen (A.S.-P.).

HEARDEN, *sb.* ? *Obs.* Bdf. A ' headland.' (Hall.)

HEARING, *sb.* Sc. Yks. Glo. Ken. Som. Dev. Also in form **yerring** w.Som.[1] nw.Dev.[1] **1.** Information, news ; a report, piece of news ; something to talk about.

Sc. That's fine hearing for me, and it ill sets your tongue, Keith *Indian Uncle* (1896) 4. Sh.I. He [it] wid be a job an' a hearing, *Sh. News* (Aug. 28, 1897). Yks. I got a hearing on it through him. A hearing went about that he was dead (C.C.R.). n.Yks.[2] We've had a good hearing. Glo.[1] That's not a good hearing.

2. A scolding, reproof. Sc. She aye ordered a dram or sowp kale, or something to us, after she had gien us a hearing on our duties, Scott *Old Mortality* (1816) xiv ; The aunt . . . had doubtless given him a hearing he would remember, Keith *Bonnie Lady* (1897) 71. Cai.[1] Frf. Mary had got a brisk hearin' on the occasion, Willock *Rosetty Ends* (1886) 54, ed. 1889.

3. A church service ; an opportunity of preaching to a congregation as a candidate for the pastorate. Cai.[1]

4. A trial, a charge in a court of justice. Ken. (G.B.) w.Som.[1] The yerrin idn avore next Monday. nw.Dev.[1]

HEARINGSEW, see **Heronsew.**

HEARKEN, *v.* Sc. Nhb. Dur. Yks. Lan. Chs. Der. War. Wor. Shr. Nrf. Wil. Also written **harken** Sc. Cai. Chs. ; and in forms **heaken** Yks. ; **herken** Lan. [(h)aˑrkən, äˑkən.] **1.** To listen, esp. to listen by stealth.

Abd. Johnny harkenin' 's gin he uner'steed it, Alexander *Johnny Gibb* (1871) xviii. Ayr. Do you think I'm to lie here on the braid o' my back . . . and hearken to thae cutty queans? Service *Notandums* (1890) 1. Yks. Heaken till her, Gaskell *Sylvia* (1863) 50, ed. 1874. w.Yks. He'd been hearkenin' to all they sed (J.T.). Lan. I'm tired o' hearkenin' to thee. Burnett *Lowrie's* (1877) viii ; It's a good job we herkent a bit, Parr *Minding the Baby,* 11.

Hence **Hearkener,** *sb.* a listener. Ayr. The tidings and bickerings to which he was a hearkener in the smiddy, Galt *Gilhaize* (1823) i.

2. *Phr.* (1) *hearken to the hinder end,* hear the end of the story, wait and see what the end will be ; (2) — *turn up, obsol.* an exclamation used to attract attention. (1) s.Dur., n.Yks. Often used in expressions of doubt as to the final success of an undertaking (J.E.D.). Yks. Grose (1790) *MS. add.* (P.) (2) s.Dur., n.Yks. (J.E.D.)

3. To be on the watch, to look out, listen for ; *gen.* with *out.* Chs. *Sheaf* (1879) I. 266 ; Chs.[1] Miss, oi wanted to ax yo if yo'd hearken aht for summat for ahr Polly. Dev. Ye mun hearken for a cottage, Verney *Stone Edge* (1868) xxi. War.[2] I expect the carrier's cart'll call ; you hearken out. Shr.[1] We'n 'eark'n-out, an' mebbe we shan 'ear o' summat.

Hence **Hearken-out,** *sb.* a listening ; a watch, look-out. s.Chs.[1] Ky'ee·p ü aa·rkn asyt for·)it [Keep a hearken-aht for it].

4. With *back* : to recall. Wil.[1]

5. With *down, in,* or *up* : to call in, pay a visit. Sc. For as Willie Gair harkened in to Sandy Corve, Tweeddale *Moff* (1896) 34. Chs.[1] If you canna give me a answer to neet, I'll hearken up i' th' morning. s.Chs.[1]

6. *Trans.* To listen to, hear. Abd. At kirk on Sunday we maun hearken sleepy stuff, Davidson *Poems* (1861) 87. Edb. Harken my sang, an' eke believe it, Maclagan *Poems* (1851) 149. w.Yks. ' Is baan to t'chappil?' ' Nay, A'm baan to hearken Pi Gow ' [Pigou]. ' What do you come to church for!' ' To hearken yo' (S.K.C.). s.Chs.[1] Ah went aaˑrkn)th Saalvee·shün Aaˑrmi [Ah went hearken th' Salveetion Army]. Wor. When us said to 'im, ' What be ye arter thur !' a said, ' A 'earkenin th' ornts ' (H.K.).

7. To hear a lesson, &c., repeated. Ayr. The mistress . . . ordered Nanny to hearken him the two double verses of the Psalm she had told him to learn, Johnston *Glenbuckie* (1889) 246 ; After dinner at four he was ' harkened ' as to his general knowledge of Scripture, ib. *Kilmallie* (1891) I. 5 ; ' Will ye hearken me!' said Andrew. And she took the book, and bad him begin, Galt *Sir A. Wylie* (1822) iii.

8. With *on* : to encourage, urge on, incite. Nrf. (W.W.S.). I have gone on for thirteen years, . . with Winifred by my side hearkening me on, Borrow *Lavengro* (1851) III. 140.

Hence **Hearkenin',** *sb.* encouragement. Abd. His father well can draw . . . six score o' lambs this year; That's harkening [heartning, ed. 1812] gueed, Ross *Helenore* (1768) 21 (Jam.). Nhb. He gat little hearkenin (R.O.H.).

9. To whisper ; with *in* : to prompt secretly. Cai.[1] Abd. He hearken't it intae ma lug (W.M.).

HEARN, see **Harden,** *sb.,* **Hear.**

HEARNSHAW, HEARNSHROW, see **Heronsew.**

HEARSE, *sb.* Sc. Yks. Lan. Chs. Lin. Hrf. Som. Dev.
I. Dial. forms : (1) **Hairse,** (2) **Herst,** (3) **Hesk,** (4)
Hess, (5) **Iest,** (6) **Yerst**.
(1) n.Sc. (JAM.) (2) e.Lan.¹, Chs.¹ (3) w.Som.¹ Coming down
Porlock Hill the drug-chain brokt, and over went the hesk, coffin
and all, rattle to rip ! n.Dev. Tha hesk es mostly vull, ROCK *Jim
an' Nell* (1867) st. 108. (4) s.Chs.¹, nw.Dev.¹ (5) w.Yks. (J.W.)
(6) Lan. ' But it's a berrin-coach.' ' A what ? ' ' A yerst. .. One
o' thoose coaches 'at they carry'n coffins in at funerals,' WAUGH
Ben an' th' Bantam (1866) 226; Lan.¹, e.Lan.¹
II. Dial. uses. 1. *Obs.* A lustre, a sconce with lights ;
a triangular frame for holding candles in a church. n.Sc.
(JAM.), n.Lin.¹ 2. *Obs.* A frame of wickerwork, timber,
or metal, placed over the body of a dead person for the
purpose of supporting the pall, while the funeral service
is being read. n.Lin.¹ 3. *Obs.* A frame attached to a
tomb for the purpose of supporting hangings and light. *ib.*
HEARST, *sb.* Som. Dev. [hēst.] A female deer,
between one and three years of age.
w.Som.¹ n.Dev. A hind and a hearst went down to Pixey
Coppice, and Tout with six couple followed them, *Rec. n.Dev.
Staghounds,* 79, in ELWORTHY *Gl.* (1888). [Hearse(among Hunters)
is a hind in the 2d year of his age, BAILEY (1721).]
[MHG. *hirs, hirss,* 'hirsch' (LEXER).]
HEART, *sb.* and *v.* Var. dial. uses in Sc. Irel. and Eng.
Also in forms art w.Yks.¹ War. ; har- Or.I. ; hart n.Yks.
I.W.¹ ; hehrt Bnff.¹ ; her- S. & Ork.¹ ; hert Sc. S. & Ork.¹
Cai.¹ 1. *sb.* In *comb.* (1) **Heart abeunn** or **abiun,**
continuing to hope, never despairing ; overjoyed ; (2) **-an-
guished, heart-sore** ; (3) **-axes,** the heartburn ; (4) **-break,**
(*a*) a great grief or disappointment ; (*b*) to break the heart
of, cause sorrow to ; (5) **-brossen, -brussen,** or **-brusten,** (*a*)
heartbroken, overwhelmed with grief; (*b*)exhausted, spent
with running, &c. ; (6) **-bun,** strongly attached to a place ;
having a great desire to accomplish something, ' set ' on
doing something ; (7) **-cruke,** an internal spasm often fatal
to sheep ; a cross in the affections ; (8) **-'s disease,** heart-
disease ; (9) **-ease,** (*a*) ease of the mind ; (*b*) to ease the
mind ; (10) **-'s-ease,** the wallflower, *Cheiranthus Cheiri* ;
(11) **-eased,** eased in mind, mentally relieved ; (12) **-eident,**
with a firm or fixed heart ; (13) **-eyt,** to envy ; (14) **-feared,**
afraid at heart ; (15) **-fever,** an illness or disease ; (16)
-fever grass, the dandelion, *Leontodon Taraxacum* ; (17)
-gone, (*a*) gone or diseased at the heart or core ; (*b*) fallen
in love ; (18) **-grace,** goodness of disposition ; (19) **-'s grace,**
delight ; (20) **-grief,** severe grief ; (21) **-groan,** a groan
from the heart, a groan of deep sympathy ; (22) **-groaner,**
a repiner ; (23) **-grown,** (*a*) strongly attached to a person
or thing ; set upon anything ; elated, sanguine ; (*b*) sickly,
puny, having spinal curvature from a supposed bewitch-
ment ; (24) **-guize,** dissimulation ; (25) **-gun,** a severe
internal pain, colic ; (26) **-heezer,** a comfort, that which
cheers the heart ; (27) **-heezing,** heart-cheering, encouraging ; (28) **-hod,** affection, hold upon the feelings ;
(29) **-hove,** of a sigh : heaved from the heart, deep ; (30)
-hunger, a ravenous desire for food ; (31) **-hungered,**
starved, hungry ; also used *fig.* ; (32) **-kittlin',** affecting ;
(33) **-lazy,** very lazy ; (34) **-loup,** a beat or palpitation of
the heart ; (35) **-noten,** envious ; (36) **-o' grace,** courage,
strength ; (37) **-o'-the-hearth** or **-earth,** the self-heal,
Prunella vulgaris ; (38) **-pansy,** the pansy, *Viola tricolor* ;
(39) **-rooted,** of a tree : self-sown ; (40) **-rovven,** having
the feelings lacerated ; (41) **-sair** or **-sehr,** (*a*) great vexation ; (*b*) sorrowful at heart, pitiful, distressing ; annoyed ;
(42) **-scald, -scad, -scaud, -scud,** the heartburn ; *fig.* a
great grief, disappointment, trouble ; (43) **-scalded,** troubled,
tormented, afflicted ; (44) **-scalding,** see (42) ; (45) **-seed,**
see (38) ; (46) **-seeds,** see (10) ; (47) **-shot,** (*a*) a burst of
laughter, a hearty fit ; (*b*) an exclamation used after
sneezing ; (48) **-sick,** (*a*) sad at heart, despondent, out of
spirits, wearied, disgusted ; (*b*) mortally ill, sick unto
death ; (49) **-skirt(s, -sket(s,** the pericardium or heart-bag,
the diaphragm, the fleshy appendages of the heart ; (50)
-skit, see (3) ; (51) **-slain,** exhausted by over-exertion ;
heart-broken ; (52) **-slay,** to kill with over-exertion ; (53)
-sluffed, -slufted, or **-sloughed,** see (48, *a*) ; (54) **-sluftin,**

heart-breaking ; (55) **-snares,** captivations ; (56) **-sound,**
having a good constitution ; (57) **-spoon,** the pit of the
stomach ; (58) **-spurn,** a tap-root ; (59) **-stangs,** mental
excruciations ; (60) **-stobb'd,** pierced to the heart ; (61)
-sunk, desponding, depressed ; (62) **-tree,** the upright post
of a gate to which the hinges are fixed ; (63) **-warm,** of a
kindly disposition ; feeling and showing kindness ; affectionate ; (64) **-wear,** an illness of the heart ; see below ; (65)
-well, in good general health and spirits ; (66) **-whole** or
-hale, (*a*) in good health and spirits ; sound-hearted, honest,
true ; (*b*) not in love, ' fancy-free ' ; (67) **-'s wind,** with the
utmost speed ; (68) **-work,** (*a*) sincerity, the work of the
heart morally ; (*b*) the heart-ache ; (69) **-worm,** see (3).
(1) Cum.¹ He hez a sair tue on't, bit he's heart abeunn still.
Wm. He was heart abiun when he gat hired (B.K.). (2) Fif.
Heart-anguish'd by vexation's sharpest stings, TENNANT *Anster*
(1812) 111, ed. 1871. (3) Lth. The common cure for it in the
country is to swallow sclaters or woodlice (JAM.). (4, *a*) Sh.I.
Dat wis my first hert-brak, *Sh. News* (Apr. 9, 1898). e.Sc.
What a heart-break to them ! SETOUN *R. Urquhart* (1896) vii.
Ayr. Leezock kent brawlies she was nae great heart-break hersel',
SERVICE *Dr. Duguid* (ed. 1807) 222. Gall. This is a sair heart-
break. But I ken I hae mysel' to thank for it, CROCKETT *Standard
Bearer* (1898) 326. (*b*) Ayr. I'll cross him and rack him Until I
heart-break him, BURNS *What can a Young Lassie do,* st. 4.
(5, *a*) Wm. T'waves blasht sea dowly that we warr fairly heart-
brossen, SOUTHEY *Doctor* (1848) 561. n.Yks.¹²⁴, w.Yks. (J.W.),
n.Lin.¹ (*b*) n.Lin.¹ (6) n.Yks.⁴ (7) n.Yks.² [Strikes them in
the inner parts, which is vulgarly called the heart-crook, KNOWL-
SON *Cattle Doct.* (1834) 25.] (8) N.I.¹ (9, *a*) m.Yks.¹ (*b*) Go and tell
him, now ; it'll maybe heart-ease him a bit, *ib.* (10) Cor. (B. & H.)
(11) n.Yks.¹²⁴, m.Yks.¹ (12) Dmb. With hands, heart-eident,
labourin' late and air, SALMON *Gowodean* (1868) 31. (13) e.Lan.¹
(14) n.Ir. I wuz heart-feared o' my ma, fur she haes a terble bad
tongue, LYTTLE *Paddy McQuillan,* 41. (15) N.I.¹ ' Measuring for
the heart fever,' a country charm. A tape is passed round the
chest. Don. In Don. women have what they call ' heart-fever,'
or a sort of ' all over-ness,' *Flk-Lore Jrn.* (1886) IV. 256. (16)
Don. She next hands the patient nine leaves of ' heart fever grass,'
or dandelion, BLACK *Flk-Medicine* (1883) vii. (17, 18) n.Yks.²
(19) Sc. The law o' the Lord is his hail heart's-grace, WADDELL
Psalms (1871) i. 2. (20) Xen.¹ (21, 22) n.Yks.² (23, *a*) n.Yks.¹ ;
n.Yks.² They were neea ways heartgrown about it ; n.Yks.⁴
ne.Yks.¹ They were despertly heart-grown on it. m.Yks.¹, w.Yks.¹,
Nhp.¹ (*b*) Nhb. At Stamfordham a sickly puny child is set down
as ' heart-grown' or bewitched, HENDERSON *Flk-Lore* (1879) vi ;
Applied to a sickly, puny child, which does not grow. Such a
child must be brought to a blacksmith of the seventh generation ;
this must be done before sunrise. The child is laid naked on the
anvil ; the smith raises the sledge-hammer as if he were going to
strike hot iron, but lets it come gently on the child's body.
This is done three times, and the child always thrives after this,
Trans. Tyneside Natur. Club (1860-62) V. 90 ; High-shouldered,
short-necked people, with a broad chest and slightly round-
shouldered—whilst the other parts of the body are not in due
proportion—are said to be ' heartgrowen.' (24) n.Yks.² (25)
w.Som.¹ *Obsol.* n.Dev. *Horae Subsecivae* (1777) 207 ; Jan does n't
me-an the bone-shave, ner the heartgun, *Exm. Scold.* (1746) l. 23.
(26) Ayr. There were three brief ' heart-heezers' that always
recurred to me in moments of desperation, AINSLIE *Land of Burns*
(ed. 1892) *Pref.* 32. (27) Per. Whiles a bicker o' swats—whiles
a heart-heezing gill, NICOLL *Poems* (ed. 1843) 131. Lnk. We cast
aff in fine style amid a lot of heart-heezin' hurrahs, MURDOCH
Readings (ed. 1895) II. 83. (28) n.Yks.² Full o' heart-hod. (29)
Per. The feckfu' grip, an' the heart-hove sigh Gae token o'
sanction enou', FORD *Harp* (1893) 319. (30) Sc. (JAM.) (31) Sc.
He never lets us go heart-hunger'd for a meal of love, KEITH
Bonnie Lady (1897) 154. n.Sc. (JAM.) (32) Ayr. This memorable
an' heart-kittlin' occasion, AINSLIE *Land of Burns* (ed. 1892) 76.
(33) N.I.¹ (34) Gall. Lag stood maybes three heart-loups in a
swither, CROCKETT *Raiders* (1894) xliv. (35) n.Yks. (T.S.) (36)
Sur. I was afeard to touch it at first, but at last I took heart o'
grace and did it, *N. & Q.* (1878) 5th S. x. 222. (37) Rxb.
Because it chiefly occurs on thin poor soils, where the farmers
give it the credit of eating away all the substance of the soil.
Nhb.¹, s.An. (38) Dev.⁴ (39) Chs.¹² (40) n.Yks.² (41, *a*)
Bnff.¹ It's a hehrt-sehr he winna seen cour it's sin'again' the black
gett. (*b*) *ib.* It wiz hehrt-sair to see the tinkler wife wee nae
a rag on, bit ae bit aul', torn quyttie. A wiz jist hehrt-sair fin a
got the news o' sic ill-deean. n.Yks.² Heartsair wi' gripe and

greed. (42) **Sc.** The first glisk that I got o' this slubberdegullion o' a maister gied me the heartscad at him, FORD *Thistledown* (1891) 296. **S. & Ork.**[1] Abd. 'Twere just as weel, And wad a heap o' heart-scads heal, CADENHEAD *Bon Accord* (1853) 171. **Rnf.** Grief such as only young mothers can feel at their first heart-scud, GILMOUR *Paisley Weavers* (1876) 93. **Ayr.** It has aye been a great heartscadd to me that I never forgathered with Robin, SERVICE *Dr. Duguid* (ed. 1887) 149. **Edb.** Tho' cholic or the heart-scad teaze us, FERGUSSON *Poems* (1773) 145, ed. 1785. **Gall.** MACTAGGART *Encycl.* (1824). Ir. A drunken husband is a great heart-scald (A.S.-P.); She thought what a heart scald it would be when the little boy ... would be fitting a vessel ... and that stone tumble down and kill him dead, KENNEDY *Fireside Stories* (1870) 10. **n.Cy.** *Border Gl.* (Coll. L.L.B.); **N.Cy.**[1], **Nhb.**[1] n.Yks.[2] 'It gae me a heartscawd.' 'There'll be a bonny heart-scawd about it.' Nhp.[1] (43) Ir. A person is said to be 'heart-scalded' with a drunken husband (A.S.-P.); Wurrah! wurrah! but it's me that's the heart-scalded crathur with that man's four quarters, CARLETON *Traits Peas.* (ed. 1843) I. 7. (44) Ir. The heart-scaldin' you're givin' both your mother and me! CARLETON *Traits Peas.* (ed. 1843) I. 351. (45) **s.Bcks.**, **Dev.**[4] (46) **w.Cor.** (M.A.C.) (47, a) **Sh.I.** Sizzie got inta a hertshot o' lauchin' at me, STEWART *Tales* (1892) 244. **S. & Ork.**[1] (b) **S. & Ork.**[1] (48, a) **N.I.**[1] I'm heart sick of your goin's on. **n.Yks.**[14] **m.Yks.**[1] He nagged at me till I was fair heartsick. **w.Yks.** Aw went an' left him lonely, and heartsick to travel, HARTLEY *Ditt.* (c. 1873) 71 ; **w.Yks.**[2] **Shr.**[2] (s.v. Heartwell). **Hrf.**[2], **Brks.**[1], **I.W.**[1] (b) aw.Lin.[1] She were real heartsick, the bairn was, sick for 'life and death. (49) **n.Yks.**[2] 'To tear one's heartskirt,' is to rend oneself with grief or vexation. **e.Yks.**[1], **w.Yks.**[1] **n.Lin.**[1] My bairns ewsed to pull at my goon-ske'ts once, bud thaay pull at my heart-sket's noo. (50) **Sh.I.** (Coll. L.L.B.), **S. & Ork.**[1], **Or.I.** (S.A.S.) (51) Lin. Of a horse that dies under too much work, *Cornh. Mag.* XLVI. 232. n.Lin.[1] He druv th' poor herse 'till it was clear heart-slaain. It was n't no illness that kill'd her, poor thing; she was heart-slaain. aw.Lin.[1] They got there, quite heartslain, on to midnight. (52, Lin. It's fit to heart-slay me a'most (R.E.C.). (53) Wm. Si' thi, Ah was heart-sluft when he telt mi (B.K.). **w.Yks.** Sho looked fair heart-sluffed, *Leeds Merc. Suppl.* (Mar. 30, 1889); An ther are times when a chap gets heartslufted, and feels like givin up life's struggle, HARTLEY *Clock Alm.* (1889) 60. **w.Yks.**[2] Of horses, &c. only. (54) **w.Yks.** Ther isn't a moor heart-sluftin an depressin seet to be met wi, HARTLEY *Clock Alm.* (1895) 50; If ther is owt at's heart-sluftin', *Yksman.* (1876) 22, col. 2. (55) **n.Yks.**[2] (56) **Chs.**[1] Heart sound as a cabbage. (57) **n.Yks.** It warks at his heart-speaun, MERITON *Praise Ale* (1684) l. 568. **e.An.**[1], **e.Suf.** (F.H.) (58) **Midl.** MARSHALL *Rur. Econ.* (1796). (59, 60, 61) **n.Yks.**[2] (62) **w.Yks.** (S.P.U.); (J.J.B.); **w.Yks.**[1] (63) **n.Yks.**[12], **w.Yks.**[1] (64) **Sh.I.** If the sufferer further complained of having 'lost dir stamack' they were supposed to be afflicted with the heart-wear. This disease assumed two forms, viz. the aaber and the feckless. In the former the heart was understood to be too big, and there was a voracious appetite without doing the body any good. In the latter—or feckless form—the heart was supposed to be wasting away under some trowie influence, and there was no desire for food, SPENCE *Flk-Lore* (1899) 156. (65) **War.**[28] **w.Wor.** [He] was still heart-well, S. BEAUCHAMP *Grantley Grange* (1874) I. 44; **w.Wor.**[1] Well, I be 'eart-well, thank yū, but I've got the rheumatics in my showlder mortial bad. **se.Wor.**[1] Shr.[1] I'm pretty 'cart-well, God be thankit, on'y in-firm'd; Shr.[2], **Hrf.**[12] (66, a) **Sc.** (JAM.) **Nhb.**[1] 'An' hoo are ye!' 'Oh, grand—just heart whole.' **n.Yks.**[4] Tak him all ends up he's a heart-w'oll, canny chap. **m.Yks.**[1], **w.Yks.**[1], **Der.**[2], **nw.Der.**[1] Lin.[1] Things turned up so well that he was heart-whole. n.Lin.[1] I thoht to hev fun' him doon-cast, but he's clear heart-whodle. **War.**[3] **s.Wor.** PORSON *Quaint Wds.* (1875) 13. **se.Wor.**[1] Lei.[1] She's quite well in health, she's heart-whole, but then she's stone-deaf. **Hrf.**[12], **Glo.**[1] (b) **Ayr.** Sound, heart-hale, an' free—Never thought o' marriage, AINSLIE *Land of Burns* (ed. 1892) 326. **Cum.**[8] I'll ho'd mysel' heart-heàl an free, 182. **n.Yks.**[12]; **n.Yks.**[4] Ah's heart-w'oll yet; ther's nowt aboot here 'at's ta'en mah fancy. **n.Lin.**[1] **w.Som.**[1] Well! I niver didn look to zee him come home therevrom heart-wole; but there, p'raps he idn, arter all. (67) **Cum.**[1] They wrought at heart's wind o' t'day. (68, a) **n.Yks.**[2] Yan's heead-wark, an't'others heart-wark. (b) ib. (69) **Rnf.** (JAM.)

2. Phr. (1) *Casting the heart* or *hearts*, a superstitious ceremony, see below; (2) *for the heart of*, 'for the life of,' for any consideration; (3) *soft at heart*, easily appeased, kindly disposed; (4) *to be heart and hand for a thing*, to be eagerly bent on accomplishing or obtaining a thing; (5)

to break the heart of a business, to do the greater part of, to nearly finish a business; (6) *to have one's heart in a nut-shell*, to act like a coward; (7) *to put one's heart away*, to cause one to faint; (8) *to tire one's heart out*, to be very troublesome and importunate; (9) *warm at heart*, see (3).

(1) **Sh.I.** It has long been a popular belief that when any person is emaciated with sickness, his heart is worn away... The patient seeks out a cunning woman, who ... melts some lead, and allows it to drop through an open sieve into cold water. If an image, bearing some faint resemblance to the heart, is after a certain number of trials, produced, it is an indication that the charm has been successful; but if no such figure appears, it is a sign that the decay of this organ is irremediable, HIBBERT *Desc. Sh. I.* (1822) 274, ed. 1891; A small quantity of lead was melted in a kollie, and the patient was set in the meat kettle before the fire. On the head was placed a blind sieve, in the centre of which a bowl of water was set. A pair of steel scissors or two keys were held in the hand of the operator in the form of a cross, and through the bool of the scissors or key the molten lead was poured into the water. The numerous shapes assumed by the lead were carefully examined, and the operation was repeated until a piece was found in form like the human heart. This was sewn in the left breast of some article of underclothing and worn by the patient for three moons. Further, the water used in this ceremony was made into porridge, of which the patient partook seated in the guit o' da door at the hour of sunset. In casting the heart attention was paid to the moon; for the aaber heart-wear the time chosen was the waning moon and the ebbing-tide, and for the feckless form the opposite was deemed the most fitting time, SPENCE *Flk-Lore* (1899) 156. (2) **Cum.** Ah couldn't git t'teaah leg by t'tudder for t'heart om meh, SARGISSON *Joe Scoap* (1881) 22. (3) **n.Yks.**[4] (4) **w.Yks.**[1] (5) **w.Yks.**[1] We've brokken t'heart of our hay-time. **ne.Lan.**[1] **Shr.**, **Hrf.** BOUND *Provinc.* (1876). **Sur.**[1] (6) **ne.Lan.**[1] (7) **Abd.** That stouns amo' my taes Will pit my heart awa! BEATTIE *Parings* (1801) 27, ed. 1873.' (8) **w.Yks.**[1] **Shr.**, **Hrf.** BOUND *Provinc.* (1876). (9) **n.Yks.**[4]

3. Comb. in exclamations of surprise and expletives: (1) By the heart, (2) Dear heart, (3) Dear heart alive, (4) Heart('s alive, (5) My heart.

(1) **w.Yks.** (J.T.); **w.Yks.**[8] 'By t'heart it's true.' On seeing a boat appear to founder one exclaimed, 'By t'heart they're gone.' (2) **n.Lin.**[1] **w.Som.**[1] Dear heart! whatever shall I do. (3) **Der.** Eh, dear heart alive, and here comes the rain, VERNEY *Stone Edge* (1868) iv. **n.Lin.**[1] Commonly of pain or sorrow. (4) **Not.**[1], **Lei.**[1] **Ken.**[1] Hearts alive! what ever upon earth be ye got at! **Som.** Heart alive! There was to be company to-night, then, sure enough, RAYMOND *Men o' Mendip* (1898) ii. **w.Som.**[1] Heart alive, soce! whatever b'ee about. (5) **Nrf.** My heart the sails do lash the air! EMERSON *Son of Fens* (1892) 357.

4. The stomach.

Sc. (JAM.) **Cai.**[1] Hid widna lie on his hert, it made him vomit. **w.Yks.**[1] I've a fearful pain at my heart. **ne.Lan.**[1] **e.An.**[1] 'A pain at the heart,' the stomach ache. **e.Suf.** (F.H.)

Hence *phr.* (1) *the heart gaes*, or *gangs*, *with a thing*, a thing suits the taste or liking, it is agreeable; (2) *to gae* or *gang against one's heart*, to dislike; (3) *to gae* or *gang with one's heart*, to be grateful to one's stomach, to be agreeable to one in any respect; (4) *to turn one's heart over*, to make one sick.

(1) **Sc.** (JAM.) (2) ib., **Cai.**[1] (3) **Sc.** (JAM.) (4) **s.Not.** The smell an' the sight was enough to turn their hearts ower (J.P.K.).

5. Strength, 'go'; spirits, cheer, courage.

Sc. (A.W.) **Uls.** The prince sailed away, in great heart, west-ward once more, *Uls. Jrn. Arch.* (1860) VII. 143. **w.Yks.** He is a poor creature, no heart in him (W.B.T.). **n.Yks.** He's in good heart (I.W.). **Dor.** Out o' heart, BARNES *Gl.* (1863).

Hence (1) *to have a bad heart*, *phr.* to be easily cast down; (2) *to have bad heart of*, *phr.* to be doubtful of, have little hopes of.

(1) **n.Lin.**[1] (2) ib. Well, it maay live, but I've a bad heart on it (s.v. Bad).

6. The inside, middle of anything; esp. in phr. *in the heart of*, in the midst of.

Sh.I. What wis I tinkin' aboot būits i' da hert o' paet-castin'! *Sh. News* (June 18, 1898). **Abd.** Mak' the cakes weet i' the hert, ALEXANDER *Johnny Gibb* (1871) viii. [That those in the heart, and near the bottom of the heap fermented, STEPHENS *Farm Bk.* (ed. 1849) I. 631.]

Hence **Heart-hole**, *sb.* the space in the middle of a fire, the centre of a fire.

Sh.I. Pit da kirnin stane i' da hert hole o' da fire, *Sh. News* (May 13, 1899); Sibbie spat i' da hert hole o' da fire, *ib.* (May 15, 1897); Ivery ee wis lack a hairst mûn as bright as da hert hole o' da lowin' fire, STEWART *Tales* (1892) 252.

7. The matured wood of a tree as distinct from the sap. Also in *comp.* **Heart-wood**.

Lin. The trees will be chilled to the heart-wood, MILLER & SKERTCHLY *Fenland* (1878) xv. Sur.¹ The heart of the beech is … the principal part of the beech. w.Som.¹ Thick there piece 'ont do; he's most all zape, id'n hardly a bit o' heart in un.

8. Of land: condition of soil, state of fertility, richness, strength; also used of hay or of cattle.

Sc. That bittie o' grun's in fine he'rt (G.W.). Per. My farm was in great heart, the other in miserable order, RAMSAY *Scotl.* (1888) II. 377. n.Yks. (I.W.) ne.Yks. MARSHALL *Rur. Econ.* (1796) II. 91. w.Yks. It is not uncommon to hear a farmer or dealer say of poor coarse hay, 'There's no heart in it' (W.B.T.). Chs.¹ Poor land is said to be 'in bad heart'; rich land 'in good heart.' nw.Der.¹ Nhp.¹ Used of land or cattle in a thriving state; land in good condition is said to 'plough up in good heart.' 'Out of heart' is the reverse, implying land impoverished and exhausted by over-cropping. War. That field is in good 'art. it had a rare mucking last year, *Leamington Courier* (Jan. 30, 1897); War.²⁸⁴ s.War.¹ There ain't no heart in this land. Shr.¹ It'll do mighty well this time athout muck, the groun' 's in good 'eart. Oxf. This land wants plenty of manure to keep it in good heart (G.O.); Oxf.¹ Dhis gruuwndz in sich bad aa·rt, chent noa eus tû sow wait nuur wuts [This ground's in sich bad 'eart, chent no use to sow whate ner wuts]. Hrt. For want of the grounds being in heart, ELLIS *Mod. Husb.* (1750) III. i. Hnt. (T.P.F.) w.Mid. The farm has been done so bad o' late years, there's no heart in the land (W.P.M.). Ken.¹ My garden's in better heart than common this year. Sur.¹ Sus.¹ I've got my garden into pretty good heart at last; Sus.² A common covenant is to leave the land 'in good heart and condition.' Hmp.¹ w.Som.¹ Always qualified by 'good,' or an adj. implying 'good.' 'Thick there field's in good heart now.' The word is not used to express the opposite condition. Dev.⁸ They'm jist in gûde heart vur work now.

Hence *to gather heart, phr.* of land: gradually to acquire fertility by being allowed to lie uncropped. Sc. (JAM.), Cai.¹

9. The bilberry, *Vaccinium Myrtillus.* Hmp.¹

10. *pl.* The wood-sorrel, *Oxalis Acetosella.*

Nhb.¹ [So called] from the shape of the leaf.

11. *pl.* The fossil-shells, *Pholadomyae.* Nhp.¹ 12. *v.* To encourage, 'hearten'; also with *up.* Sc. (JAM.), n.Lin.¹

13. To stun, to deprive of the power of breathing or of sensation by a blow near the region of the heart. Sc. (JAM.)

14. To sicken, nauseate, to make one sick.

Lth. Did ye really pit a thing like yon intil yer mooth? The sicht o't, na, the very thocht o't, fair hearts me yet, STRATHESK *More Bits* (1885) 93.

HEARTEN, *v.* In *gen.* dial. use in Sc. and Eng. Also written harten w.Yks.¹ 1. To cheer, comfort; to encourage, put heart into; to strengthen, invigorate; also with *on, up.*

Sc. It's a meeracle hoo a cup o' tea heartens a body, KEITH *Indian Uncle* (1896) 169. Sh.I. Gie Willie a corne oot o' da bottle afore he begins, hit'll heart'n him, *Sh. News* (Dec. 10, 1898). Per. This, ye'll find, Has heartened not a few, HALIBURTON *Ochil Idylls* (1891) 44. Ayr. My father was joyfully heartened by what he heard, GALT *Gilhaize* (1823) iv. Lth. Heart'ning thou com'st wi' modest grace, MACNEILL *Poet. Wks.* (1801) 231, ed. 1856. Gall. He came ower to hearten you in the day of your adversity, CROCKETT *Standard Bearer* (1898) 234. Nhb. Reach doon ma fiddle and gie's a bit tien to hearten us up, CLARE *Love of Lass* (1890) I. 31. Dur. I heartened her up till she agreed to go, *Longman's Mag.* (July 1897) 253. Cum.¹ n.Yks. It's hearten'd me up a bit (T.S.); n.Yks.¹⁴ m.Yks.¹ Tea is heartened with something stronger. The farmer heartens his land, or renders it more fertile, by various means. w.Yks. I found somewhat to say to hearten him, SNOWDEN *Web of Weaver* (1896) 79; w.Yks.¹, ne.Lan.¹, Chs.¹ n.Lin.¹ Well, I'm heart'd a good deäl by th' wāay theäse here elections is gooin', War.² Shr.¹ Come in an' 'ave a dish o' tay—it'll 'earten yo' on; Shr.² Hearten him on his journey. e.Suf. (F.H.) I.W. They thinks if only they lies hard enough, 'twill hearten up t'others to vote on the winning side, GRAY *Annesley* (1889) III. 19. n.Wil. Wants summut to hearten em on a bit (E.H.G.).

Hence **Heartening**, (1) *sb.* (a) encouragement, comfort, hope; (b) sustenance, food; (2) *ppl. adj.*, (a) lively, cheerful; (b) strengthening, sustaining.

(1, a) Sc. Nanny Meikle hung over him with fleeching and heartening, KEITH *Bonnie Lady* (1897) 38. Abd. Nae gryte heartnin till 'im, peer man, ALEXANDER *Johnny Gibb* (1871) xx. Ayr. There was something i' the fa'in' of the effigy o' King William, to gie us heartenin', JOHNSTON *Glenbuckie* (1889) 275. n.Yks.¹; n.Yks.² 'The doctor gave them good heartening.' 'Bad heartening,' discouragement. m.Yks.¹ (b) n.Yks.² (a, a) Cum.² An' few cud whyet hod the'r feet When Ben strack up his heartenin' reels, 58. (b) Ken.¹ Home-made bread is more heartening than baker's bread.

2. To incite; also with *on.* n.Yks.²

HEARTFUL, *adj.* Sc. Shr. Hrf. 1. In high spirits, cheery. Shr.² Hrf. BOUND *Provinc.* (1876); Hrf.¹

2. Sorrowful, sad-hearted.

Rnf. Dinna look sae sour an' heart-fu', NEILSON *Poems* (1877) 29.

HEARTH, *sb.*¹ and *v.* Var. dial. forms and uses in Eng. [h)arþ, āþ, eþ, jeþ.] I. Dial. forms: (1) Arth, (2) Eth, (3) Harth, (4) Heath, (5) Heth, (6) Heyath, (7) Yeath, (8) Yeth.

(1) Shr.² (2) Wil. BRITTON *Beauties* (1825). (3) Nhb.¹ (4) Som. SWEETMAN *Wincanton Gl.* (1885). (5) Wil. BRITTON *Beauties* (1825). Dor.¹ An' crickets roun' the bricken he'th did zing, 74. (6) I.W.¹ (7) n.Dev. Wan flinket cast a top tha yeath, ROCK *Jim an' Nell* (1867) st. 130. (8) e.Som. W. & J. Gl. (1873). w.Som.¹

II. Dial. uses. 1. *sb.* in *comp.* (1) **Hearth-cake**, a cake or loaf baked on the hearth; (2) **-ends**, particles of lead ore expelled by the blast in a lead-ore hearth; (3) **-muster**, the family circle at the fireside; (4) **-plate**, a blacksmith's tool used in connexion with the forge; (5) **-shovel**, a blacksmith's shovel; (6) **-staff**, a blacksmith's poker.

(1) Cum.¹ Let. A loaf baked without a tin mould. Such cakes used to be baked on the hot hearth (M.E.). (2) Nhb., Dur., Cum. PATTINSON *Trans. Nat. Hist.* (1851) II. 157. (3) n.Yks.² (4, 5) Shr.¹ (6) Nhb.¹ For drawing scar from the fire. Chs.¹ The Hearth Staff, to stir up the fire, and throw cinders out of it, *Academy of Armory*, bk. III. vii. Shr.²

2. The floor or pile of sticks on which wood is charred by charcoal-burners; the space on which a wood-fire is burnt.

Midl. MARSHALL *Rur. Econ.* (1796). Nhp.² MORTON *Nat. Hist.* (1712). w.Som.¹ The hearth does not include the space in front of a grate.

3. A file-maker's forge. w.Yks.²

4. Of reeds: a plantation or bed. [Not known to our correspondents.]

Nrf. Reed hearth, *Arch.* (1879) VIII. 17a.

5. *v.* To bake, to set on the bottom of an oven.

Nhp.¹ If tarts are not sufficiently soaked or browned, a servant would say, 'They had better be hearthed a little more.' Used only on the eastern side of the county.

HEARTH, *sb.*² Ken. Hearing, hearing distance.

Ken.¹ I called out as loud's ever I could, but he warn't no wheres widin hearth; Ken.²

[Þe vif wyttes of þe bodye be zyȝþe, be hyerþe, be smellinge, be ȝuelȝynge, and be takynge, *Ayenbite* (1340) 91.]

HEARTHSTONE, *sb.* Nhb. Cum. Wm. Yks. Lan. Der. Som. [h)a·rstan, ā·stan.] I. Dial. forms: (1) Aaston, (2) Arson, (3) Arstan, (4) Arston, (5) Arstun, (6) Haasten, (7) Hahst'n, (8) Harstan, (9) Harston, (10) Harstone, (11) Harstun, (12) Harstyen, (13) Harthstun, (14) Ha'stone, (15) Yethstone.

(1) nw.Der.¹ (2) w.Yks. (W.C.S.) (3) w.Yks. Thay sit up at arstan throo morn to neet, ROGERS *Nan Bunt* (1839) 11. (4) n.Yks. (I.W.) w.Yks. Dahn went broth uppat arston, BYWATER *Shef. Dial.* (1839) 8; w.Yks.²⁵, ne.Lan.¹, nw.Der.¹ (5) w.Yks. As ah went i' t'hahse Jim wor set o' t'arstun (Æ.B.). (6) w.Yks. Tlois to t'haasten, cheek to jawm, PRESTON *Poems, &c.* (1864) 18. (7) n.Yks. (I.W.) (8) w.Wm. Sally's meead up a girt lowan fire et harstan, *Spec. Dial.* (1880) pt. ii. 2. w.Yks. Ye cud see hoot o' t'top ont fra onny part o' t'harstan, LUCAS *Stud. Nidderdale* (c. 1882) 217. (9) Wm. Yer welcome tot harston again, BRIGGS *Remains* (1825) 181. w.Yks. Ther's th' harston to scaar, HARTLEY *Grimes' Visit* (1892) 15. nw.Der.¹ (10) w.Yks.¹ I will be maister o' my awn harstone. Lan. Happen ne'er to set foot on this harstone again, CLEGG *David's Loom* (1894) v. e.Lan.¹ (11)

Yks. My beginning to pray on my ain harstun, *Philip Neville*, i. **w.Yks.** Aw can't have thee sitting o' th' harstun. *Nidderdill Olm.* (1877). (12) **Nhb.**[1] (13) **w.Yks.** I sal hev done summat t'ards makkin' monny a breet harthstun, CUDWORTH *Dial. Sketches* (1884) 5. (14) **Lan.** A wot ha'stone, BRIERLEY *Layrock* (1864) v. (15) **e.Som.** W. & J. *Gl.* (1873).

II. Dial. uses. In *comb.* (1) **Harstone-rug,** a hearth-rug, a rug placed before the fireplace ; (2) **-talk,** boastful talk, promises made at night and not intended to be kept in the morning.

(1) **w.Yks.** (J.W.) **Lan.** Comin in at th' finish to make harstone rugs, CLEGG *Sketches* (1895) 59. (2) **Lan.**[1] Dunnot moind 'em, mon. It's o' harstone-talk. They'll do nowt i' th' morn.

HEARTLESS, *adj.* Sc. Yks. War. Wor. Gmg. Glo. Wil. Dev. [ä·tləs, Sc. he·rtləs.] 1. Disheartened, downhearted, hopeless ; without spirit.

Abd. Heartless ower thy fate I'll croon, An' sever'd ties, STILL *Cottar's Sunday* (1845) 85. **s.Sc.** Thrice owr Annie's name did blatter, Syne sank heartless on the yerd, T. SCOTT *Poems* (1793) 359. **Yks.** Don't make the lad heartless by giving him work he can't pass to (C.C.R.). **n.Yks.**[2]

2. Disheartening, discouraging.

n.Yks.[1] It's heartless wark, farming where ther's sikan a vast o' rabbits astor. **War.**[2] It's heartless work, trying to get this ground clear o' stones. **w.Wor.**[1] 'Tis 'artless to try an' kip yer 'ouse tidy w'en tharhr's such a lot uv mullock out in the yard. **Gmg.** It is very heartless that I can't wash a bit to-day (E.D.). **Glo.** (A.B.), **Glo.**[1] **Dev.**[5] I shant dū no moār tū this work, 'tez a most heartless job.

3. Forlorn, cheerless ; of the weather : wet, without hope of clearing.

Elg. The stibble field, Seems unco heartless round, COUPER *Poetry* (1804) I. 183. **Ayr.** And bird and beast in covert rest, And pass the heartless day, BURNS *Winter*, st. 1. **Wil.**[1] 'A heartless day' is a wet day with a strong south-west wind.

HEARTSOME, *adj.* Sc. Irel. Nhb. Cum. Yks. Nhp. War. I.W. Also written **hartsome** Gall. ; and in form **hertsome** Per. Lnk. [he·rt-, ha·rt-, ä·tsəm.] 1. Merry, cheerful, lively ; pleasant, genial, attractive ; also used *advb.*

Sc. The honest auld town of St. Ronan's, where blithe decent folk had been heartsome eneugh for mony a day, SCOTT *St. Ronan* (1824) ii. The heartsome lad that on the morn, MORISON *Poems* (1790) 15. **Per.** He was a heartsome merry chiel', FORD *Harp* (1893) 410. **Fif.** They took a horn wi' heartsome glee, DOUGLAS *Poems* (1806) 142. **s.Sc.** The heartsome smile that arrayed her still lovely features, WILSON *Tales* (1836) II. 114. **Dmb.** It's in a heartsome place on the ootside o' the town, CROSS *Disruption* (1844) vi. **Rnf.** 'Tis such a healthy heartsome place, McGILVRAY *Poems* (ed. 1862) 174. **Ayr.** It's the heartsomest grave in the kirkyaird, SERVICE *Dr. Duguid* (ed. 1887) 50. **Lak.** Hoo gleesum an' he'rtsum the time slippet on! HAMILTON *Poems* (1865) 294. **Lth.** Heartsome and healthfu' flew the hours, MACNEILL *Poet. Wks.* (1801) 242, ed. 1856. **Edb.** The Muse scuds ear' an' heartsome owr the dews, FERGUSSON *Poems* (1773) 137, ed. 1785. **Slk.** Laugh'd a heartsome laugh, HOGG *Poems* (ed. 1865) 311. **Dmf.** By my ain heartsome ingle, CROMEK *Remains* (1810) 53. **Gall.** A' nature's in a hartsome mood, LAUDERDALE *Poems* (1796) 52. **N.I.**[1], **N.Cy.**[1], **Nhb.**[1] **Cum.** Let's creep ower the heartsome turf ingle, ANDERSON *Ballads* (ed. 1820) 163 ; It's heartsome in t'summer sheen To lig, GWORDIE GREENUP *Rhymes* (1876) 7 ; An' the pint smiles wi' heartsome ale, BLAMIRE *Poet. Wks.* (c. 1794) 208, ed. 1842. **n.Yks.**[2], **Nhp.**[1], **War.**[3] **I.W.** 'Tis pleasant and heartsome up under tree where the primroses blows, GRAY *Annesley* (1889) l. 110.

Hence (1) **Heartsomely,** *adv.* cheerfully, merrily, heartily ; (2) **Heartsomeness,** *sb.* cheerfulness.

(1) **Per.** I might . . . heartsomely my penny free Spend frankly with good companie, NICOL *Poems* (1766) 38 ; To my frank neighbours heartsomelie I'll drink wi' hail good will, *ib.* 52. **Gall.** I am as heartsomely glad to see ye eat it as of a sunny morn in haytime, CROCKETT *Standard Bearer* (1898) 106. **Keb.** Take kindly and heartsomely with His cross who never yet slew a child with the cross, RUTHERFORD *Lett.* (1660) No. 299. (2) **N.I.**[1]

2. Encouraging, inspiring, cheering the heart.

Per. It's hertsome when they're wullin' tae wrestle aboot the Evangel, IAN MACLAREN *Brier Bush* (1895) 116. **Ayr.** It's heartsome to look owre The days sae firmly fixt In memory's map, AINSLIE *Land of Burns* (ed. 1892) 212. **Lnk.** It's heartsome aye tae see the bairns A' playin' roond sae fine, THOMSON *Musings*

(1881) 128. **Gall.** It was a heartsome sight to see the encampment of Silver Sand by the little burnside, CROCKETT *Raiders* (1894) vi.

HEARTY, *adj., sb.* and *adv.* Var. dial. and colloq. uses in Sc. Irel. and Eng. Also in form **herty** Cai.[1] [he·rti, h)a·rti, ä·ti.] 1. *adj.* In good health or spirits, in good circumstances ; lively, cheerful, high-spirited ; exhilarating ; also used *advb.*

Sc. Hale and hearty, ay, hale an' hearty eneuch, FORD *Thistle-down* (1891) 105. **Sh.I.** Lat da boy be. If he's no ta be hearty apo' a night laek dis whan wid ye bae him ta be? *Sh. News* (Dec. 10, 1898). **Per.** Me sae hale an' hearty lookin' on, Pooerless to help, HALIBURTON *Ochil Idylls* (1891) 67. **Rnf.** I always wish to see a hearty fire, FINLAYSON *Rhymes* (1815) 120. **Ayr.** Faithfu' servants ken the gate To mak sleek skin'd and hearty nags, THOM *Amusements* (1812) 38. **Lnk.** Blessings on the hearty maut, MURDOCH *Doric Lyre* (1873) 30. **e.Yks.**[1] **w.Yks.** 'Ha' gets ta on? ' 'O hearty, lass,' LISTER *Rust. Wreath* (1834) 30. **s.Pem.** LAWS *Little Eng.* (1888) 420. **Sur.**[1] Dor. Ye give me eight shillin' a week an' my keep, . . I was hearty enough then, *Longman's Mag.* (Nov. 1898) 47. **w.Som.**[1] 'Well, maister, how be you ?' 'Hearty, thank ee, how's all home to your house ?'

2. Merry, jovial from having taken too much of intoxicants, exhilarated by drink, the worse for liquor.

Sc. The pannel was hearty but knew what he was about and could walk very well, *Edb. Even. Cour.* (Oct. 8, 1818) (JAM.). **Lnk.** That nicht ye'd been uncommon heartie, MURDOCH *Doric Lyre* (1873) 13. **Cai.**[1] **Ir.** It'll make me hearty if I drink so much, CARLETON *Fardorougha* (1836) 21. **Ant.** *Ballymena Obs.* (1892). **Don.** The two gintlemen would get hearty at the potteen, *Harper's Mag.* (Sept. 1899) 510.

3. Having a good appetite, eager for food, hungry ; eating freely.

Sc. She's never hearty at her meat, KEITH *Lisbeth* (1894) xii. **w.Yks.**[1] Shoe's feaful hearty to her meat. **Cha.**[1] He's very hearty for an owd mon. **w.Der.**[1] **War.** 'You don't want cake again... He's wonderful hearty,' she went on, GEO. ELIOT *S. Marner* (1861) 73 ; **War.**[3] ; **War.**[4] You be allus hearty at your meals.

Hence **Hearty-etten,** *adj.* having a good appetite. **Lan.**[1] The poor woman said that her children were all ' hearty-etten,' especially the lads, WAUGH *Home Life* (1867) xix. **e.Lan.**[1]

4. Liberal, not parsimonious.

Sc. But as the truth is, I'm hearty, I hate to be scrimpit or scant, HERD *Coll. Sngs.* (1776) II. 137 (JAM.).

5. Of food : nourishing.

Bdf. Home-made bread is a deal heartier over baker's bread. Beans are the heartiest food you can give cattle (J.W.B.).

6. Plump, inclining to corpulence. n.Sc. (JAM.)

7. Of meal : swelling much when saturated with water. Nhb.[1]

8. Of land : fertile, in good condition. See Heart, 8. **Ayr.** A mailin cheap o' hearty lan', *Ballads and Sngs.* (1846) I. 190.

9. Of wood : full of ' heart,' having very little sap. n.Yks. (I.W.), Hmp.[1], w.Som.[1]

10. *sb.* A good fellow, *gen.* in phr. *my hearty,* a familiar form of address.

Abd. Reel, reel, my hearties, keep your partners wheelin', OGG *Willie Waly* (1873) 29. **Rnf.** Gin my auld hearty ye're ane o' the party, Ye'll baith see an' hear Rhymin' Rab, CLARK *Rhymes* (1842) 4. **Lnk.** My certie! auld heartie, But ye're a raucle dame, NICHOLSON *Idylls* (1870) 74. **Nhb.** Sae, say nought against it, Will Shuttle, my hearty! CRISPIN *Advice* (1803). **e.Yks.**[1] Hoo is thä, my hearty? **Nrf.** Stand by the winch, Jem. Now lower, my hearty, and let her go, PATTERSON *Man and Nat.* (1895) 67. **w.Som.**[1] Come on, my hearty, we'll show 'em the way. Colloq. And one of the party said ' Go it my hearty,' BARHAM *Ingoldsby* (ed. 1840) 64.

11. *adv.* Very.

Chs.[1]; **Chs.**[3] Oo's hearty fow [She is very ugly].

HEAS, *v.* Obs. ne.Lan.[1] To chill.

HEASE, *sb.* Obs. Chs.[1] In phr. *I'll do it at all hease,* I'll do it at all risks.

[The same word as ME. *hǣse,* command (*Ormulum*) ; OE. *hǣs.* So the phr. means lit. ' I'll do it in spite of every command.']

HEAT, *sb.* Var. dial. uses in Sc. and Eng. Also in forms **het** Hmp. Wil.[1] ; **yeat** w.Som.[1] Dev. ; **yet** s.Chs.[1] [(h)īt, iət, et.] 1. In phr. (1) *to be more het than wet,* of the weather : to be hot and cloudy ; (2) *to catch heat*, to get warm, become hot ; *fig.* to warm to a thing ; (3) *to come a heat*, see (2) ; (4) *to run o' the heat*, of cattle : to run about in hot weather when tormented with flies ; (5) *to take heat*, see (2).

(1) Hmp. In summer when the weather is hot and cloudy, and what moisture falls partakes more of heat than cold, indicating warm weather, it is a common expression [to say] ' There is more Het than Wet,' HOLLOWAY. (2) w.Som.¹ Wuul, Jùmz ! kùn-ee kaech yùt' s·mau·rneen—shaa·rp, ùd·-n ut ! [Well, James, can you catch heat this morning, sharp, is it not !] 'Spare work, could'n catch yit to it, *ib.* Dev. When ice glazed thee o'er [I] ev kitched yeat 'pon thy zlides, PULMAN *Sketches* (184a) 56, ed. 1853. e.Dev.' Can ee catch yeat ta day !' is a common mode of salutation, *ib.* 78. (3) Lth. Soop weel when I tell ye, an' ye'll soon come a-heat, STRATHESK *Morr Bits* (1885) 270. (4) Cai.¹ (5) Dor., Som. I took he·at comin' up th' hill (C.V.G.)

2. A warming ; *fig.* a thrashing.

Sc. (JAM.) e.Fif. Twa puir fizzenless han'less leukin' craiters ... but she wad gie them a heat afore the end o' the day, LATTO *Tam Bodkin* (1864) xxix. Edb. His shop was in a bleeze. Your arses then wad get a heat, Had ye not fled out to the street, CRAWFORD *Poems* (1798) 13.

3. An iron, in phr. *to have too many heats in the fire*, to have too many irons in the fire.

Sur.¹ I was proposing to my farm-man to work the steam-plough, and the thrashing-machine on the same day, and his answer was—' We shall get too many heats in the fire I doubt.'

4. A charge in a ' puddling ' or a ball furnace ; a pile in a furnace ready for the forgeman or a bar in a black-smith's fire ready to weld.

Nhb. We just had a heat oot when the buzzer went ; an' the shabby beggar clashed it doon wivoot strikin' a bat (R.O.H.) ; Nhb.¹ ' Sittin' doon atween heats,' that is, in the interval between the completion of one heat and the preparation of another.

5. A spell of time ; a round, bout ; a fit.

Sc. (A.W.', n.Cy. (J.W.) n.Lin.¹ He was dead bet th' fo'st heat. s.Chs.¹ Yoa)n aad' ù prit·i lùngg' yet on it dhis· tuurn [Yo'n had a pretty long yet on it this turn]. Wil.¹ A main het o' coughing. Hence *at a heat*, phr. at one time, 'at a go,' in a lump. s.Not. She's gen me fower shillings at a heat (J.P.K.)

HEAT, *v.* Var. dial. uses in Sc. Irel. Eng. and Amer. [h)ĭt, iət, et, hēt, jet.] I. Gram. forms. **1.** *Present Tense*: (1) Hate, (2) Heit, (3) Het, (4) Yeat, (5) Yet, (6) Yett. [For further instances see II. below.]

(1) Ir. There was Kit Flynn hating water, *Paddiana* (ed. 1848) I. 58. (2) Cai.¹ Hĕit. (3) Baff.¹ w.Yks. I'll bet the tea oop for yer (F.P.T.). Nhp.¹ Het me some broth. Dor. You ought to het a quart o' drink into 'ee, HARDY *Tess* (1891) 424, ed. 1895. (4) Yks. I is to gie notidge, that Joanie Pickersgill, yeats yewn to neit, *Spec. Dial.* (1800) 14. nw.Dev.¹ (5) Dev.⁸ (6) n.Dev. Yett theesel, Bob—Yen thick auther thicket, ROCK *Jim an' Nell* (1867) st. 9.

2. *Preterite*: (1) Hat, (2) Heited, (3) Het, (4) Hette.

(1) Shr.¹ I 'at the oven an' knad the bread. (2) Cai.¹ (3) Sc. I het it in the pan (JAM.). Lak. Oor fires were o' peats or o' faggots, And het the hoose better than coals, NICHOLSON *Kilwuddy* (1895) 158. N.I.¹ He over het himsel'. N.Cy.¹ Nhb.¹ He het it up till he set the place afire. w.Yks. (J.W.) Suf.¹, s.Suf. (F.H.) Ess. I het the water for brewing, *Trans. Arch. Soc.* (1863) II. 178. Cor.¹ [Amer. *Dial. Notes* (1896) I. 277.] w.Yks.¹

3. *Pp.*: (1) Hat, (2) Heited, (3) Het, (4) Hetted, (5) Hetten

(1) Midl. MARSHALL *Rur. Econ.* (1796). nw.Der.¹ (2) Cai.¹ (3) Sc. (JAM.) Edb. The house should be weel het, *Auld Handsel Monday* (1792) 20. w.Yks. T'iron were het, LUCAS *Stud. Nidderdale* (c. 188a). e.An.¹ I ha het the kittle. Nrf. Ha' yow het that there water yit ! (W.R.E.) e.Suf. (F.H.) [Amer. We must ollers blow the bellers Wen they want their irons het, LOWELL *Biglow Papers* (1848) 45; *Dial. Notes* (1896) I. 71, 216.] (4) Cor. THOMAS *Randigal Rhymes* (1895) *Gl.* (5) Nhb.¹ He'd just hetten the taings ready to start. w.Yks. To tell thee hah many times t'earth's hetten till it's brust itsen, HALLAM *Wadsley Jack* (1866) 6, ed. 1881; w.Yks.² I only know the word in the compound ' mow-hetten.'

II. Dial. uses. **1.** In phr. (1) *to be healed up in the bowels*, to be costive ; (2) *to heat the cheeks*, to cause to blush ; (3) *— the house*, to warm the house, to give an entertainment on entering a new house ; (4) *— the old broth*, to renew an old courtship.

(1) w.Yks. He's been het-up in his bowels (S.K.C.). (a) Lnk.

Nor heat my cheeks wi' your mad freaks, RODGER *Poems* (1838) 4, ed. 1897. (3) Sc. (JAM.) Lak. I proposed to John that we should hae a kind o' haunlin' by way o' heatin' the house, ROY *Generalship* (ed. 1895) 6. (4) Nhp.¹

2. To become hot.

s.Hmp. I hets and burns and smerts all night, VERNEY *L. Lisle* (1870) ii. Cor. I beginned to het and burn all ovver, TREGELLAS *Tales*, '*Lisberth Jane's Courtship*, 4.

3. Of hay or corn : to become hot in the stack through being carried when damp.

Sc. (A.W.) n.Yks. That haystack heated an' teeak fire (I.W.). w.Yks. (J.W.) Midl. MARSHALL *Rur. Econ.* (1796). nw.Der.¹ n.Lin.¹ Squire He&la's stacks got a fire thrif a fother stack'at heated.

4. With *on* or *upon* : to fly into a passion.

Bnff.¹ He het o' wir han', an' widna wirk at a'.

HEAT, see Hot.

HEATER, *sb.* Sc. Lakel. Yks. Lan. Wil. Som. Dev. Also in forms **hetter** Wil. Som. ; **heytter** Dev. ; **yetter** Lan.² e.Lan.¹ w.Som.¹ Dev. [h)ī·tər, iə·tə(r, e·tə(r), je·tə(r).]

1. A piece of iron made red-hot and used for heating a box- or tally-iron, or a tea-urn.

Sc. (A.W.) Lakel.² An iron ta heat t'iron, ta iron wi'. w.Yks. (J.T.) Lan. Her face wur as red as a yetter, WAUGH *Tattlin' Matty*, 25 ; Lan.¹, e.Lan.¹ w.Som.¹ Yút·ur, an iron to be made red-hot and then inserted into ironing box, tea-urn, or other article.

2. *Fig.* A triangular piece of land or of a wood ; the fork of a road.

e.An.¹ Nrf. Keep straight on till you come to the heater, COZENS-HARDY *Broad Nrf.* (1893) 88 ; Any triangle, or triangular ' piece ' of land, or wood, is called a ' heater '; from shape of heating iron, used for ironing linen (M.C.H.B.).

Hence (1) **Heater-bit**, *sb.* a small triangular field ; (2) -shaped, *adj.* of fields or pieces of land : shaped like the ' heater ' of a box-iron.

(1) e.Suf. (F.H.) (2) The roads run heater-shaped [i. e. into one], *ib.*

3. A flat iron.

Wil. SLOW *Gl.* (1892) ; Wil.¹ Som. SWEETMAN *Wincanton Gl.* (1885). Dev. Us shan't a finished i-oring tû-day. Thews blessed yetters won't yette ! HEWETT *Peas. Sp.* (1892).

4. A damper in an oven-flue. Lakel. (B.K.)

HEATFUL, *adj.* Lei.¹ Hot, scorching.

How heatful the fire is!

HEATH, *sb.* and *v.* Sc. Cum. Yks. Lan. Stf. Der. Nhp. Brks. Hmp. Dor. Som. Dev. Cor. Also in forms **heth** Hmp.¹ Dor.¹ ; **yeth** Lan.¹ e.Lan.¹ w.Som.¹ Dev.¹ nw.Dev.¹ ; **yirth** Lan.¹ [h)īþ, eþ, jeþ.] **1.** *sb.* In *comb.* (1) Heath-bell, the harebell, *Campanula rotundifolia* ; (2) -cropper, (a) an inferior kind of horse ; (b) an inferior breed of sheep ; (3) -hounds, a ghostly pack of hounds : see below ; (4) -poult, -polt, or -powt, the black grouse, *Tetrao tetrix*; (5) -shield fern, the shield-fern, *Aspidium Oreopteris* ; (6) -stones, gneiss ; see Heathens ; (7) -throstle, the ring-throstle, *Turdus torquatus.*

(1) Nhp. Blue heathbells tremble 'neath the sheltering furze, CLARE *Village Minst.* (1821) II. 135. (2, a) Hmp.¹ The small horses bred in Hmp., ' having scarcely anything to feed on but heath, have hence derived the appellation of heath-croppers,' DRIVER *View Agric.* (1794) 27. Dor.¹ w.Som.¹ Yaeth·-kraap·ur, a rough pony or horse turned out upon a common, and half starved. (*b*) Brks. A small breed, ill-shaped and of little value, MARSHALL *Review* (1817) V. 95. (3) Dev. They were heard in the parish of St. Mary Tavy several years ago by an old man. . . He was working in the fields when he suddenly heard the baying of the hounds, the shouts and horn of the huntsman, and the smacking of the whip, *N. & Q.* (1851) 1st S. iii. 404. Dev., Cor. The fairies pack of hounds, which the country people belive [sic] they sometimes hear in the night, pursuing their game over heaths and mores, with tongues hanging out of their mouths, as if all on fire, *Horae Subsecivae* (1777) 207. (4) Cum. *Gl.* (1851). m.Yks.¹ Hmp.¹ WISE *New Forest* (1883) 309. w.Som.¹ Dev. (W.L.-P.) ; BRAY *Desc. Tamar and Tavy* (1836) I. Lett. iv. s.Dev. (E.H.G.) Cor. Heathpoult, nor partridge, nay, nor pheasant, BARING-GOULD *Curgenven* (1893) xlix. (5) Edb. PENNECUIK *Wks.* (1715) 132, ed. 1815. (6) Ked. *Agric. Surv.* 3 (JAM.). (7) w.Yks. I find that the ring ouzel is so called with us in Craven, RAY *Corres.* (1676) 195.

2. Various species of ling or heather, esp. *Calluna vulgaris, Erica cinerea,* and *E. tetralix.*

.Lan.[1], Hmp.[1] w.Som.[1] In this district he~ther is unknown. 'The yeth's all ablow up t'hill,' *ib.* Dev. Bowring *Lang.* (1866) I. pt. v. 27; Dev.[1] n.Dev. Jefferies *Red Deer* (1884) x. nw.Dev.[1]

Hence **Heathy,** *adj.* abounding in heath.

Per. I long to see Thy heathy height and broomy lea, Spence *Poems* (1898) 1. Ayr. Farewell, old Coila's hills and dales, Her heathy moors, Burns *Author's Farewell,* st. 4.

3. *Comp.* (1) **Heath-bob,** a tuft of heather; (2) **-broom,** a broom made of heather; (3) **-curtained,** curtained with heather.

(1) Lan. Heaw arto gettin' on amung yon Yirth-bobs upo' Lobden Moor! Waugh *Yeth-Bobs* (1867) 16; Mr. Penrose, dun yo' think there'll be yethbobs i' heaven! Mather *Idylls* (1895) 30; Lan.[1], e.Lan.[1] (2) w.Som.[1] In distinction from a birch-broom. (3) Lan. As sweet and fresh as when it levs it yeth-curtained bed, Clegg *Sketches* (1895) 47.

4. The black crowberry, *Empetrum nigrum.* Der. (B. & H.)

5. A tough kind of coal; also in *comp.* **Heath-coal.**

Stf. The second measure of coal is called heath or tough coal (K.); Stf.[1]

6. *v.* To make into ridges. Som. *Wincanton Gl.* (1885).

HEATH, see **Hearth.**

HEATHEN-COAL, *sb.* Obs. Stf. A variety of coal. Cf. **heath, 5.**

The 12th [measure of coal] or lowest of all (K.) (s.v. Heath).

HEATHENS, *sb. pl.* Sc. Also in form **haethens** Abd. Gneiss.

Abd. It may be my luck to big wi' rock haethens in place o' dress't san'stane or polish't marble, Alexander *Ain Flk.* (1882) 167. Ked. *Agric. Surv.* 3 (Jam.).

HEATHER, *sb.* Sc. Irel. Nhb. Cum. Wm. Yks. Chs. Lin. Also Hmp. Also written **hether** Sc. (Jam.) N.Cy.[1] Nhb.[1] Lakel.[2]; and in forms **eather** Per. (Jam.); **hather** N.Cy.[1] Nhb.[1] n.Lin. [h]e·δə(r.)] **1.** Various species of heath or ling, esp. *Calluna vulgaris, Erica cinerea,* and *E. tetralix.* Cf. **hadder,** *sb.*[1]

Sc. *N. & Q.* (1873) 4th S. xi. 40; Grose (1790) *MS. add.* (C.) Ayr. Yon auld gray stane amang the heather, Burns *Tam Samson's Elegy* (1787) st. 12. n.Ir. (B. & H.) N.Cy.[1] Nhb.[1] In Coquetdale, and var. other parts of Nhb., it is applied to the common heath (*Calluna vulgaris*) only. *Erica tetralix* and *E. cinerea* are also known as heather, but when spoken of distinctively are invariably designated 'ling.' Cum., Yks., Chs.[1] n.Lin. The hather is in bloom at Twigmore (M.P.).

Hence (1) **Heathery,** *adj.* (a) abounding in heather, living amongst heather; (b) *fig.* rough, dishevelled, hairy; (2) **-headit,** *adj.* covered with heather; *fig.* having a rough, dishevelled head.

(1, a) Elg. Your heath'ry sons ha'e bluid aneugh To gild an honest crown, Couper *Poetry* (1804) I. 158. Peb. The bard lonedanderin gaes Thro' cowstlip banks and heatherie braes, Nicol *Poems* (1805) l. 98 (Jam.). (b) Sc. Gen. used as to the hair. In this sense 'heatherie head' is applied to one whose face being coarse, uncombed, or bristly, resembles a bunch of heath (Jam.). (2) Sc. *ib.* Lnk. Frae black heath'ry headed mountains sing, Ramsay *Poems* (1721) 369.

2. *Comb.* (1) **Heather-and-dub,** rough, poor, tawdry; (2) **-bell,** the flower of the heath; (3) **-bill,** the dragon-fly; cf. **ather-bill,** s.v. **Adder;** (4) **-birn,** the stalks and roots of burnt heather; (5) **-bred,** reared on the Fells, virile, vigorous; (6) **-buzzom,** a broom made of heather; (7) **-cat,** a cat become wild and roaming among the heather; *fig.* a wild, roaming person; (8) **-clu,** an ankle; (9) **-cow(e,** a tuft or twig of heather; a broom made of heather; (10) **-faced,** rough-faced, stubbly; (11) **-hook,** a hook used in cutting heather; (12) **-pillar,** the caterpillar of the emperor moth; (13) **-reenge,** the hydrangea, *Hydrangea hortensis;* (14) **-tap,** see (9); (15) **-theekit,** thatched with heather; (16) **-whin,** the moor-whin, *Genista anglica.*

(1) Abd. (Jam.); His want of voice, which was of a heatherand-dub order, was more than made up, Jolly *Life of J. Duncan* (1883) 487; (G.W.) (2) Sc. Gin heather-bells were corn and bere, They wad get grist aneugh, Chambers *Pop. Rhymes* (1870) 223. Ayr. Her moors red-brown wi' heather bells, Burns *To W. Simpson* (1785) st. 10. Lnk. Blew hether-bells Bloom'd bonny on moorland and sweet rising fells, Ramsay *Gentle Shep.* (1725) II. iv, ed. 1733. Bwk. On yonder hills the heather-bell Has lost its bonnie purple hue, Chisholm *Poems* (1879) 35.

VOL. III.

N.Cy.[1] (3) Baff.[1], Cai.[1] (4) Sc. (Jam.) Wgt. We'll be baith o' us starved, an' wi may gang an' eat heather-birns if we lake, Fraser *Wigtown* (1877) 377. (5) Nhb. Not used disparagingly, as in the slughorn 'Tarset and Tarret burn hard lads and heatherbred, Yet, Yet, Yet!' (R.O.H.) (6) N.Cy.[1], Nhb.[1] (7) Sc. He's ... here to-day and gone to-morrow; a fair heather-cat, Stevenson *Kidnapped* (1886) xvi. Gall. Hog turned like a heathercat, snarling with a flashing of white teeth, Crockett *Raiders* (1894) xxvii. (8) Ags. (Jam.) (9) Sc. Ralph Ronaldson that ... disna ken the colour of a heather-cowe, Scott *Rob Roy* (1817) xviii. Sh.I. Ill news is like a fitless heathercow, Spence *Flk-Lore* (1899) 220. Cai.[1] A twig of heather from which the leaves have been stripped. Slk. Wi her heather-cowe clean wiping, Hogg *Poems* (ed. 1865) 91. Gall. Mactaggart *Encycl.* (1824). (10) N.Cy.[1], Nhb.[1], Lakel.[2] (11) Hmp. (W.M.E.F.) (12) Cum.[4] (13) Frf., e.Per. (W.A.C.) Flf. Colville *Vernacular* (1899) 9. (14) Sc. Wi' e'en like diamonds, cheeks like roses, a head like a heather tap, Scott *St. Ronan* (1817) ii. (15) Frf. The little heathertheekit building, Inglis *Ain Flk.* (1895) 94. (16) Nhb.[1]

3. *Comb.* in names of birds: (1) **Heather-bleat** or **-bleet,** (2) **-bleater,** **-bluiter,** or **-blutter,** the common snipe, *Gallinago caelestis;* (3) **-cock,** the ring-ouzel, *Turdus torquatus;* (4) **-grey,** the mountain linnet or twite, *Linota flavirostris;* (5) **-lintie,** (a) the linnet, *Linota cannabina;* (b) see (4); (c) the meadow pipit, *Anthus pratensis;* (6) **-peep,** (7) **-peeper,** the common sandpiper, *Tringoides hypoleucus.*

(1) Sc. The heather bleet and corn-craik Sleep a' in a little holie, Chambers *Pop. Rhymes* (1870) 194. Rnf. The heather-bleat hath cour'd its wing, Allan *Poems* (1836) 58. Dmf. Shaw *Schoolmaster* (1899) 349. Gall. 'The laverock and the lark, The bawkie and the bat, The heather-bleet, the mire-snipe, How many birds be that!' The snipe is called the heather-bleet, from her loving wild heathery marshes, and when soaring aloft, 'bleating' with her wings, in the spring time, Mactaggart *Encycl.* (1824). N.I.[1], Cum.[1] (2) Sc. Forby moor-cocks, an heather-blutters, Scott *Monastery* (1820) iv. Per. (Jam.) Ayr. A bird which the people here call a hether blutter (it makes a loud roaring noise), built its nest on the island, ... but as some superstitious people suggested that its loud and uncommon cries forbode no good, it was soon either destroyed or banished, *Statist. Acc.* II. 72 (Jam.), s.v. Hedder-blutter). Slk. Hogg *Tales* (1898) 177, ed. 1866. Ir. Swainson *Birds* (1885) 192. Ldd. (J.S.) Nhb. Or hear the heather bleater hie Around my mountain hame, Armstrong *Wanny Blossoms* (1876) 12; Nhb.[1] (3) Lnk. 'Mang the bent the heathercock Cries tae his hen, Thomson *Musings* (1881) 93. Nhb.[1] (4) n.Ir. (J.S.), N.I.[1] (5, a) Sc. Swainson *ib.* 65. (6) Sh. & Or.I. *ib.* 66; Dunn *Ornith. Guide* in Yarrell *Birds* (ed. 1845) I. 571; S. & Ork.[1] a.Sc. Swainson *ib.* 66. Nhb.[1] (c) Cum., Wm. Swainson *ib.* 45. (6) Ayr. A bird, said to be peculiar to the mountains of Ayrshire, which continually emits a plaintive sound (Jam.). (7) Abd. Swainson *ib.* 196.

4. *Phr.* **to set the heather on fire,** to raise a disturbance, excite a tumult.

Sc. It's partly that whilk has set the heather on fire e'en now, Scott *Rob Roy* (1817) xxxv.

HEATHER, see **Edder,** *sb.*[1], **Hadder,** *sb.*[2]

HEATHERLING, *sb.* N.I.[1] The twite or mountain linnet, *Linota flavirostris.* Cf. **heather-grey,** s.v. **Heather.**

HEATSOME, *adj.* n.Yks.[2] Written **heeatsome.** Hottempered.

HEAUGH, see **Heugh.**

HEAVE, *v.* and *sb.* Var. dial. and colloq. uses in Sc. Irel. Eng. and Amer. [h]iv, eiv.] **I.** *v.* Gram. forms.

1. *Present Tense:* (1) **Ee'v,** (2) **Have,** (3) **Hayve,** (4) **Heeve,** (5) **Heighve,** (6) **Heive,** (7) **Heve,** (8) **Heyve,** (9) **Hive,** (10) **Hov,** (11) **Hove,** (12) **Hüve,** (13) **Yi'h'v.** [For further instances see **II.** below.]

(1) s.Cha.[1] 81. (2) Glo.[1] (3) Cha.[3], Dev.[2] (4) Cum.[1] (5) w.Yks. Com mon, just heighve a peawnd wilta (D.L.). (6) Sc. Murray *Dial.* (1873) 205. (7) Wxf.[1] (8) e.Lan.[1] (9) Sc. (Jam.) Som. W. & J. *Gl.* (1873). (10) Cor.[2] (11) Cai.[1] Per. To think on't, man, My bosom hoves, Ford *Harp* (1893) 346. I.Ma. (S.M.), Hrf.[2] (12) Sh.I. Yon ane is a midder. Hüve him by, Sh. *News* (July 9, 1898); S. & Ork.[1] (13) m.Yks.[1] *Introd.* 36.

2. *Preterite:* (1) **Ee'vd,** (2) **Haived,** (3) **Heeve,** (4) **Heft,** (5) **Heiv't,** (6) **Hove,** (7) **Huive,** (8) **Hüv'd,** (9) **Ov,** (10) **Uv,** (11) **Yi'h'vd.**

(1) s.Cha.[1] 81. (2) Cor. *T. Towser* (1873) 63. (3) Lan. Tim Bobbin

R

View Dial. (ed. 1740) 47. (4) Hrf.[1] He heft it. **Ess.** (W.W.S.) Cor.[1] Heft it upon the ground. (5) Sc. MURRAY *Dial.* (1873) 205. (6) Nhb.[1], w.Yks. (D.L.) **Lan.** He hove th' mug up to her, WAUGH *Tattlin' Matty*, 21. **I.Ma.** A handful of gravel I hove in the window, BROWN *Manx Witch* (1889) 34. Nhp.[1], Shr.[1], Hrf.[1], Pem. (E.D.), Cor.[1] [Amer. *Dial. Notes* (1896) I. 277.] (7) Sc. Obs., MURRAY *Dial.* (1873) 205. (8) Sh.I. He dan hüv'd da rig ta Berry, *Sh. News* (July 9, 1898). (9, 10) s.Chs.[1] 81. (11) m.Yks.[1] *Introd.* 36.

8. *Pp.*: (1) Ee·vd, (2) Heiv'd, (3) Hoaved, (4) Hove, (5) Hoved, (6) Hoven, (7) Hovven, (8) Huoven, (9) Huven, (10) Ov·n, (11) Uv·n, (12) Yi·h'vd, (13) Yi·hvu'n.

(1) s.Chs.[1] (2) Sc. MURRAY *Dial.* (1873) 205. (3) e.Fif. A little fat podsy body wi'. . . a paunch hoaved oot wi' roast beef an' maut liquor, LATTO *Tam Bodkin* (1864) xxx. (4) Nhb.[1], Nhp.[1], Glo.[1] [Amer. *Dial. Notes* (1896) I. 277.] (5) Sc. (JAM.), N.I.[1] (6) N.Cy.[12], Nhb.[1], w.Yks.[1], Cha.[1], s.Chs.[1], nw.Der.[1], n.Lin.[1] Shr.[1] 53. Glo. BAYLIS *Illus. Dial.* (1870). e.An.[1], Suf.[1] (7) **Lan.** I feld th' poke hovven off th' yurth, PAUL BOBBIN *Sequel* (1819) 11. e.Lan.[1] (8) Sc. MURRAY *Dial.* (1873) 205. (9) w.Yks. TOM TREDDLEHOYLE *Bairnsla Ann.* (1852) 7. (10, 11) s.Chs.[1] 81. (12, 13) m.Yks.[1] *Introd.* 36.

II. Dial. meanings. **1.** *v.* To lift, raise ; not confined to lifting a heavy weight ; freq. with *up.*

Nhb.[1] Nhb., Dur. Heave the crab.—A call from the shaft meaning that the weight attached to the crab is to be raised, NICHOLSON *Coal Tr. Gl.* (1888). w.Yks. Aw seed he wur deawn, soa aw went an' hove him up (D.L.) ; (J.T.) **Lan.** But for me heighvin' her to th' bedside, CLEGG *David's Loom* (1894) iii ; He heeve op his honds, TIM BOBBIN *View Dial.* (ed. 1740) 47. e.Lan.[1] Chs.[1] Cha.[2] I seed him heave the gun up. nw.Der.[1] Shr.[1] 'Aive that pot off the fire, them tatoes bin done. Pem. Pony hove up a's leg for to kick me (E.D.). Glo.[1] One day I was a havin up the lid of the paper box. I.W. He heft me up in bed and put some pillows round me, GRAY *Annesley* (1889) II. 196. Som. 'Fit to be heaved,' of a hive of bees (C.W.D.) ; I'm so weak, sir, I can't scarce heave my hand to my head (W.F.R.). w.Som.[1] Thick's t'eavy to car to anybody's back, can't heave'm, much more car'n. Dev.[2] Cor. She halved up the cover of un, T. TOWSER *Tales* (1873) 69 ; Heave-off the kittle there, Hannah, the water es all boilen' away, FORFAR *Pentowan* (1859) i.

Hence (1) **Heaver** or **Ever,** *sb.* (a) a collier who superintends the coal-pit, a banksman ; (b) a gate or stile made to open by lifting the gate or top rail from its sockets ; (c) a movable shutter across the doorway of a barn ; (2) **Heaving,** *vbl. sb.* a method of lifting a sack of corn or coal.

(1, a) n.Cy. GROSE (1790) *MS. add.* (P.) (b) Wor. He was y-lay just anent they heuvers (H.K.). w.Wor.[1], se.Wor.[1], Hrf.[2] Glo. The top-rail having an iron bolt driven through it, at one end, the other end falling into a notch in the opposite post, MARSHALL *Rur. Econ.* (1789) ; GROSE (1790) ; *Gl.* (1851) ; Glo.[1] A drop stile, the bar of which has to be lifted to make a passage. (c) Shr.[1] *Obsol.* A kind of vertical, sliding shutter across the doorway of a barn, made to fit into grooves in such a way that it can be lifted, or 'aived, out at pleasure. When grain was threshed on the barn-floor with a ' thrashal ' [flail], the heaver was employed to close up the lower part of the barn door-way, and so prevent the grain escaping by the—otherwise—open door of the barn. Glo.[1] A low board fitted into slots in the barn door to keep out poultry, &c. (2) Nrf. A term with corn- and coal-porters, for lifting a sack either by two men upon the shoulders of a third, or by means of a frame on which the sack is placed (W.W.S.).

2. *Comp.* (1) **Heave-gate,** a gate which has to be lifted out of the sockets or mortises, in order to open it ; (2) **-up,** a disturbance, fuss.

(1) Ken.[1] The sockets or mortises otherwise keep it in place, and make it look like a part of the fence ; Ken.[2] Sur.[1] A gate made entirely of wood without any iron about it, and so contrived that one end lifts off the post. These gates are fast disappearing, and are only met with in the Weald. Sus. (S.P.H.), Sus.[1] (2) Dev.[1] A huges heave-up truly if her had'n had a farding to marry such a stingy hunks, 6.

3. *Phr.* (1) **heave an' down thump,** bluntly, with emphatic directness ; (2) **to heave the hand,** to give alms, bestow charity ; *gen.* used *iron.* of one who gives in very small quantities.

(1) m.Yks.[1] He came out with it, heave-an'-down-thump. Aye, it's all heave-an'-down-thump with him. (2) n.Yks.[1] ; n.Yks.[2] Ay, ay, he has heaved his hand, he's a generous John. m.Yks.[1]

4. To lift a person from the ground in accordance with an old custom ; see below.

Lan. It is customary for the lasses on Easter Monday ti 'heave' the lads, i.e. ti lift them up from the ground in their arms. On Tuesday the lads heave the lasses, HENDERSON *Flk-Lore* (1879) ii. War.[2] Formerly a custom in Birmingham. 'A young man whom she was heaving fell.' Shr. On Monday the men 'heaved' the women and on Tuesday the women the men. . . Parties of young men went from house to house carrying a chair decorated with evergreens, flowers, ribbons, a basin of water, and a posy. . . The posy was dipped in water, and the young woman's feet sprinkled with it 'by way of a blessing,' while she was held aloft in the gaily-adorned chair. . . The chair must be lifted from the ground three times and turned round in the air, and the feet then sprinkled. . . The heaving party were rewarded by a kiss, and generally, when men were heaved, by a gift of money. Those who refused to be heaved had to pay forfeit, BURNE *Flk-Lore* (1883) 336, 337 ; Last week [Easter week, 1876] they'd holiday, it was wet, else i was to go out and see the wenches heaving the men o' the Tuesday—it seems they carry that on about here as much as ever, but they expect the men to give 'em money after and that looks bad, I doubt, *Lett.* in *N. & Q.* (1876) 5th S. v. 458. Hrf.[2] Orn Monday they hove the women, on Tuesday the men. A party would go round to the farmhouses and cottages, the youngest wench carrying a bunch of flowers. Entering the house the party would sing ' Jesus Christ is risen again.' Then seize the women one by one and putting them in a chair turn them round, while the girl with the flowers would dip them in a basin of water and sprinkle with them the women's feet.

Hence (1) **Heaving,** (a) *vbl. sb.* the custom of lifting or raising from the ground ; (b) *ppl. adj.* employed or engaged in 'heaving' ; (2) **-day,** *sb.* a day on which the custom of ' heaving' was carried out, e.g. Easter Monday or Tuesday ; (3) **-Monday,** *sb.* Easter Monday ; (4) **-Tuesday,** *sb.* Easter Tuesday.

(1, a) Lan. This singular custom formerly prevailed in Manchester, HARLAND & WILKINSON *Flk-Lore* (1867) 233. Lan., Chs. On the first day a party of men go with a chair into every house to which they can get admission, force every female to be seated in their vehicle, and lift them up three times with loud huzzas. For this they claim the reward of a chaste salute, which those who are too coy to submit to may get exempted from by a fine of one shilling, and receive a written testimony, BRAND *Pop. Antiq.* (ed. 1873) 155. n.Wal. The custom of heaving upon Monday and Tuesday in Easter week is preserved, *ib.* 156. Shr. Even in the collieries, where it has lingered longest, heaving is said to be very much on the decline, and elsewhere in the county it is, as a general public custom, dead, BURNE *Flk-Lore* (1883) 340. Hrf.[2] (b) Shr. The heaving party, BURNE *Flk-Lore* (1883) 337. (2) s.Stf. We did ha' some fun last hayvin-day, PINNOCK *Blk. Cy. Ann.* (1895). War.[2] The idea of 'lifting' seems to have been designed to represent our Saviour's Resurrection ; War.[2] Complainant pleaded that it was heaving day. Shr.[1] (3, 4) Hrf.[2]

5. To make an effort to raise or lift oneself ; to struggle, lift with difficulty.

Lan. So they hove, an' poo'd, an' grunted, WAUGH *Heather* (ed. Milner) I. 16a ; For when we'd'n mede shift to heyve an creep fro underth' hey, TIM BOBBIN *View Dial.* (ed. 1806) 61.

6. Of a coal-mine : to ' creep,' rise up owing to the insufficiency of coal left to support the roof. Nhb. (R.O.H.) Nhb., Dur. *Coal Tr. Gl.* (1888).

7. To rise up, to come into view.

Sc. His sins hove up before him, STEVENSON *Catriona* (1893) xv. Lnk. A bricht star o' guid luck ower yonner doth hove, EWING *Poems* (1892) 25. Nhb. (R.O.H.)

8. To throw ; with *away* : to throw away, waste, to sell too cheaply.

Sh.I. Havin' a lok o' banes an' truss ta Berry, *Sh. News* (Sept. 3, 1898). e.Sc. The tune's hoven awa', SETOUN *Sunshine* (1895) 335. Gall. I saw him heave up his hand, CROCKETT *Grey Man* (1896) 61. Nhb. He hove the ballas ower board. it's oney heavin money away to buy that (R.O.H.) ; Nhb.[1], Yks. (J.W.) Lan. Becose it had hovven him o'er its yed, BRIERLEY *Marlocks* (1867) 100. I.Ma. I hove a stone at him, and he hoves one back to me (S.M.). Chs.[1]; Chs.[2] O'il heave this stone at your head, if yo dunna shut up. n.Lin.[1] She was that mad wi' me, she heäv'd th' bread and butter up o' th' fire back. Ken.[1] w.Som.[1] Quiet ! heavin stones, you boys ! Confined to the fisher and seaside folk. Dev. Why ded'n 'e 'cave thickee theer stone arder ! PHILLPOTTS *rtmoor* (1896) 156. **n.Dev.** Until I'd killed it dead and heaved out on the dunghill, CHANTER *Witch* (1896) 42. **Cor.**[1] 'I hove y ball over the wall.' 'Why did you heave it so high?' [Amer. inally give in An' heft my arms away to git my leg safe back, in, LOWELL *Biglow Papers* (1848) 146.]

. In cards: to play a card. **Ken.**[1 2]

O. To winnow corn, to pour corn from the 'scuttle' so to expose it to a current of wind; to riddle, sift. **n.Yks.**[14] **ne.Yks.** MARSHALL *Rur. Econ.* (1796) I. 363; **ne.Yks.**[1], **Yks.**[1], **ne.Lan.**[1] **Shr.**[1] (s.v. Heaver).

Hence **Heaver,** *sb.* a kind of 'blower' or winnowing-achine used in threshing.

Shr.[1] A handle is turned that works a fan—from a box at the top the machine the grain falls over the thin edge of a board, and ing met by a blast of wind from the fan, the light grain and at are 'aived' out. **Wil.**[1] Van, heavier, caffin or caving rudder, e winnowing fan and tackle, DAVIS *Agric.* (1813). **Som.** Ames-ry heaver, SWEETMAN *Wincanton Gl.* (1885).

1. To swell, become swollen, distend; to puff up, *ause* to swell; of cattle: to become distended with *ating* too much fresh clover or succulent fodder.

Sc. Mr. J. Hog says that the whole body is hoved and swelled *e* a loaf, *Essays Highl. Soc.* III. 368 (JAM.). **S. & Ork.**[1] **Cai.**[1] *ap.* used of a distension of the stomach in cattle, after certain nds of fodder. **Abd.** The patient got hoven with the liberal *bations*, ALEXANDER *Johnny Gibb* (1871) V. 30. **Per.** Drink and *bacco* heaves him up with fat, NICOL *Poems* (1766) 77. **Ayr.** *ome* ill-brewn drink had hov'd her wame, BURNS *Death and Dr. *ornbook* (1785) st. 28. **Edb.** The gleg host . . . That travellers; *tes* with haggise heaves, *Carlop Green* (1793) 175, ed. 1817. *all.* Some [bees] crawl'd up and hov'd her doup, MACTAGGART *ncycl.* (1824) 96, ed. 1876. **Kcb.** Christ hiveth me a measured *eap* up, RUTHERFORD *Lett.* (1660) xxi. **N.I.**[1] **N.Cy.**[1] When cattle *re* turned into a fresh clover fog, especially in wet weather, they *re* sometimes hove, MARSHALL *Review* (1808) I. 89. **Nhb.** Me and's aal hove up. His fyes wis aal hove wi' tyuth wark (R.O.H.); *hb.*[1] When the bowels of cattle or sheep are distended the ani-als are said to be hoven. **Cum.** LINTON *Lake Cy.* (1864) 305. *m.* GIBSON *Leg. and Notes* (1877) 93. **w.Yks.**[1], **Cha.**[1], **s.Cha.**[1], *w.Der.*[1], **n.Lin.**[1], **Nhp.**[1] **Glo.** MARSHALL *Rur. Econ.* (1879); *Gl. *851*) **Glo.**[1], **e.An.**[1] **Cmb.** Lambs are found not to be so liable *e* be hoven by clover as sheep are, MARSHALL *Review* (1814) IV. 43. **Suf.** Turnips are hoven by rank and rapid growth in a *rong* wet soil, RAINBIRD *Agric.* (1819) 295, ed. 1849; **Suf.**[1]

Hence (1) **Hoven,** *ppl. adj.* swollen; (2) **Hoving** or **Hoven,** *sb.* of cattle: flatulence, distension from over-eating.

(1) **N.Cy.**[1] Hoven cattle. (2) **Fif.** The terror of bringing her *hoven*' . . . results from the gluttony of cattle, who sometimes *ll* themselves so full with food that in the fermentation which *ssues,* there is no room for the gases to escape, HAGGARD *'armer's Year* in *Longman's Mag.* (Nov. 1898). [ARMITAGE *Cattle 88a*) 163.]

12. *Fig.* To exalt, puff up with conceit; *gen.* in *pass.* *ith up.*

Sc. He hoves wi' nocht, WADDELL *Psalms* (1871) vii. 14. **Ayr.** wee deighle o' a puddock hoved up wi' its ain concate, SERVICE *Notandums* (1890) 26. **n.Dev.** Ay, ay, Kester Moreman wou'd *a* be hove up, *Exm. Scold.* (1746) l. 52.

13. Of bread, cheese, &c.: to rise unduly, to puff up, *ecome* swollen from fermentation; of milk: to curdle, *erment.*

Nbb.[1] Bread that is unduly 'raised' by fermentation and so *welled* up is hoven. **Cha.** If the milk has been set too near the *re,* it curdles the whole mass, making it 'go all to whig and *hey,*' and afterwards heave in the mug, YOUNG *Annals Agric. 784–1815*) XXVIII. 13; **Cha.**[1] The pent up gases often lift the *urface* until the cheese becomes almost spherical and bursts, *nless* the gas is liberated by pricking the cheese. **nw.Der.**[1] *hp.*[1] Badly made cheese, that rises in the middle, is said to be *ove* or heaved. **Shr.**[1] Of bread when 'laid in sponge'; or of *heeses* that rise up in the middle in consequence of the whey *ot* having been thoroughly pressed out. ' I doubt this bread'll *e* sad, it dunna 'aive well—the barm's bin fros'-ketcht, I spect.' Theer's won o' them cheese 'aivin' I see—we maun keep that *ur* ourselves.' **Glo.** If . . . the milk is too warm, it will cause the *heese* to 'heave' or ferment, MORTON *Glo. Farm* (1832) 31; *Ros* (1790); **Glo.**[1]

Hence (1) **Hove,** *sb.* in cheese: hollowness; (2) **Hoven-bread,** *sb., obs.,* leavened or fermented bread; (3) **-cheese,** **Heven-,** or **Hove-,** *sb.* cheese affected with 'hove,' cheese that is unduly puffed up; (4) **Hoving,** *vbl. sb.* the swelling or undue rising of cheese.

(1) **Hrt.** Hove in cheese is a hollowness with eyes [i. e. holes] caused by being made from clover, ELLIS *Pract. Farmer* (1750) *Gl.* (2) **N.Cy.**[2] **Cum.,** Wm. NICOLSON (1677) *Trans. R. Soc. Lit.* (1868) IX. [(K.)] (3) **N.Cy.**[2] **Chs.** MARSHALL *Review* (1818) II. 61. (4) **Ayr.** Hoving . . . is seldom met with in the sweet cheese of that county, *Agric. Surv.* 456 (JAM.).

14. To vomit, retch; also with *up.*

Peb. Bean, wi' her scout-mouth, gi'es gaffaws, As Ned heaves, *Lintoun Green* (1685) 62, ed. 1817. **Cum.**[1], **n.Yks.**[14], **Cha.**[1], **War.** (J.R.W.), **s.Wor.** (H.K.) **Som.** W. & J. *Gl.* (1873). **w.Som.**[1] To urge but not actually to vomit. 'The breath was that bad, nif did'n make me heavy to it.' **Dev.** A sick child 'hove up his little stomach,' *Reports Provinc.* (1882) 16.

Hence (1) **Heaving,** *ppl. adj.* causing to vomit, sicken-ing; (2) *to heave and throw,* *phr.* to vomit, retch.

(1) **n.Lin.** Biting them pups taals off was a heăvein' job (E.P.). (2) **n.Yks.**[14]

15. Of walls, stones, &c.: to give out moisture. Cf. **eve,** *v.* **Som.** This sort of stone heaves in a thaw (F.A.A.).

Hence **Heaving,** *ppl. adj.* damp, muggy.

Som. The kind of time when stones give out moisture (W.F.R.).

16. To supplant. **Dor.** *Gl.* (1851).

17. *sb.* A push, 'shove'; a heaving movement, throb.

Fif. Giein' Baudrons a no canny heeve aff the chair, McLAREN *Tibbie* (1894) 40. **Per.** Far frae yer love na callan thrives Ere faun' the slightest heave o't, QUINN *Heather* (1863) 227. **Gall.** Bumbees . . . May well lament for thee I ween, Wi' bibbling heaves, MACTAGGART *Encycl.* (1824) 501, ed. 1876.

18. A heap; a hillock, a mound of earth, a worm-cast.

s.Chs.[1] Püt dhŭ tai·tŭz i ee·vz [Put the tatoes i' heaves]. **Wor.** (H.K.) **Hmp.** Mole-heaves, wont-heaves (J.R.W.); **Hmp.**[1]

19. In a coal-mine: a 'creep,' the rising up of the 'thill' of a seam of coal; the 'thill' of the seam raised up by the pressure of the adjoining pillars. **Nhb., Dur.** NICHOLSON *Coal Tr. Gl.* (1888).

20. The displacement of a lode or vein of metal from its line of direction when coming in contact with a 'cross-course' or 'slide.'

Cor. The difficulties of mining are, in some Cornish districts, increased by faults or heaves, BURROW '*Mongst Mines,* 29; Could talk of slides, heaves, flookans, without end, TREGELLAS *Tales* (1865) 155.

HEAVE, see **Eve,** *sb.*[1], *v.,* **Heaf,** *sb.*[1]

HEAVELS, *sb. pl.* e.An.[1] Plain work in weaving.

HEAVELY-KEAVELY, see **Havey-cavey.**

HEAVEN, *sb.* Sc. n.Cy. Nhb. Yks. War. Oxf. Suf. Ken. Also written **heeaven** n.Yks.[2] In *comb.* (1) **Heaven-blest,** happy, fortunate; (2) **-born,** of a good or amiable disposi-tion; (3) **-'s hen,** the lark, *Alauda arvensis*; (4) **-rife,** ready for heaven; (5) **-water boundary,** (6) **-'s water provider,** a watershed; (7) **Heavens-hard,** (8) **-high,** of falling rain: heavily, very hard.

(1) **n.Yks.**[2] It's a heeavenblest bairn that dees iv its bairnheead. (2) *ib.* (3) **Rnf.** (JAM.) (4) **n.Yks.**[2] (5) **n.Cy.** It is often the limit of extensive property, PHILLIPS *Geol.* (1871) 42. (6) **Nhb.** *N. & Q.* (1855) 1st S. xi. 342. (7) **War.**[2] It's raining heavens-hard. **Oxf.** (G.O.), e.**Suf.** (F.H.), **Ken.**[1] (8) **w.Yks.** It rains heavens-high, *Prov.* in *Brighouse News* (Sept. 14, 1889).

HEAVENTHERS, *sb.* Irel. In *phr.* *by heaventhers,* an oath, exclamation.

' Be heaventhers,' thought Duffy, CARLETON *Fardorougha* (ed. 1848) xvii.

HEAVER, *sb.*[1] Ken. Sus. Also written **hever** Ken.[2] A crab. Cf. **haviler.**

Ken. GROSE (1790); **Ken.**[1] Folkstone. 'I've not catched a pung or a heaver in my stalkers this week'; **Ken.**[2] So called at Dover. **Sus.**[1]

HEAVER, *sb.*[2] Sus. Also in forms **aver, ēver.** [i·və(r).] A boar-pig. *N. & Q.* (1856) 2nd S. ii. 38; (G.A.W.) [OE. *eofor,* a boar; cp. G. *Eber.*]

HEAVGAR, *comp. adj.* Gmg. Heavier. COLLINS *Gow. Dial.* in *Trans. Phil. Soc.* (1848–50) IV. 222.

HEAVING-TIME, sb. Cor. The time of giving birth, the season of dropping calves, &c.

Cor.² Of infrequent use. w.Cor. Their rearing cattle, and working beasts as well, were so badly fed in winter that they came to heaving time, if not before, in the spring, BOTTRELL Trad. 3rd S. 159.

HEAVY, adj. Var. dial. uses in Sc. Irel. and Eng. [h)evi.] 1. In comb. (1) Heavy-arse or -ass, a hulking, lazy fellow, a sluggard; (2) -arsed or -assed, heavy, dull, lazy; (3) -cake, a rich cake made with cream and eaten hot; also used attrib.; (4) -cart, a strong two-wheeled cart used for carrying earth, bricks, &c.; (5) — charge, a heavy burden or trial, the maintenance of a number of young children; (6) -cream cake, see (3); (7) — end, the worst part; (8) — handful, see (5); (9) -headed, dull, slow of comprehension; (10) -hearted, of the weather: lowering, threatening rain; (11) -hunded, see (2); (12) — needs, straitened circumstances; pressure of business necessitating assistance; (13) -starned, see (2); (14) -tailed, having much wealth.

(1) w.Som.¹ Slang. FARMER. (2) Wm. (B.K.), w.Som.¹ Slang. FARMER. (3) Cor. It is a rich currant paste, about an inch thick, made with clotted cream, Flk-Lore Jrn. (1886) IV. 110; The two daughters . . . had coaxed their mother into 'a tea and heavy cake' party, HUNT Pop. Rom. w.Eng. (ed. 1896) 375; Cor.¹ A flat cake about an inch thick, made of flour, cream, currants, &c.; Cor.² Flavoured with lemon peel, and unleavened. (4) Ken. (D.W.L.) (5) Ant. Ballymena Obs. (1892). (6) Cor. A tea of Cornish 'heavy-cream cake,' Flk-Lore Jrn. (1886) IV. 234. (7) Sc. Is that the heavy en' o' your grief? Sc. Haggis, 39. (8) Fif. Worst trial of all was that heavy handfu', the helpless naitrel or harmless loonie, COLVILLE Vernacular (1899) 19. N.I.¹ 'She has a heavy handful': said of a widow who is left with a large family. Ant. Ballymena Obs. (1892). (9) Cal.¹ (10) Fif. (JAM.) (11) w.Yks. (B.K.) (12) e.Yks.¹ (13) w.Yks. Hull wor then a clecan, contrify'd, stupify'd, fortify'd, well-fed, heavy-starned, soart o' place, HALLAM Wadsley Jack (1866) 77, ed. 1881. (14) Lakel.² This refers to the magnitude of wealth a prospective bride may possess.

2. Phr. (1) heavy aback, of a cart: laden too heavily on the front part, so as to cause the weight to press upon the horse; (2) heavy on, (a) see (1); (b) to bear; (3) to be heavy on, to eat a great deal of; (4) to fall heavy, to die rich.

(1) N.I.¹ (s.v. Aback). (2, a) n.Yks. (I.W.), e.Yks.¹, Cha.¹, s.Cha.¹, n.Lin.¹ (s.v. Cart). (b) War. (J.R.W.) (3) N.I.¹ He's very heavy on the strawberries. (4) w.Yks. N. & Q. (1854) 1st S. x. 210.

3. Advanced in pregnancy; also in phr. heavy of foot.

Sh.I. Wir coo is heavy an' his ane is ield, Sh. News (Jan. 8, 1898). Ayr. James cam to me ae morning when she was heavy o' fit, SERVICE Dr. Duguid (ed. 1887) 146.

Hence Heavy-footed or -fitted, adj. pregnant. Gall. (A.W.), N.I.¹

4. Large, copious.

Ayr. Sandy sometimes took a gey heavy dram, JOHNSTON Glenbuckie (1889) 177.

5. Close-grained. Cor.²

6. Stern; also used advb. Shr.¹ Yo' look'n very 'eavy at me.

7. Hard to bear.

Abd. This captain Adam thought heavy, to be banished his own country, SPALDING Hist. Sc. (1792) I. 47.

HEAVYISH, adj. Nhb.¹ w.Yks.¹ nw.Der.¹ Also in form hivveyish Nhb.¹ Somewhat heavy.

HEAVYSOME, adj. Sc. n.Cy. Nhb. Yks. Lan. Also in form hivveysome Nhb.¹ Heavy, weighty; fig. low-spirited, dull, drowsy; of the weather: dark, lowering.

Sc. GROSE (1790) MS. add. (C.) N.Cy.¹, Nhb.³, n.Yks.² w.Yks.¹ Feaful heavisome it looked, ii. 285. ne.Lan.¹

HEAWE-EEL, sb. Sc. The conger, Conger vulgaris. Fif. Our fishers call it the Heawe eel, SIBBALD Hist. Fif. (1803) 121 (JAM.). [SATCHELL (1879).]

HEAWNGE, see Hunch, sb.¹

HEAZE, v. and sb. Sc. n.Cy. Nhb. Yks. Chs. Lin. Also written heaz n.Cy. e.Yks.; heeaze n.Yks.²; heeze Sc. n.Yks.¹⁴ ne.Yks.¹; and in forms haze Cum.⁴; hayze Lin.¹; hease N.Cy.² [h)īz.] 1. v. To breathe thickly and with difficulty, to wheeze; to cough or 'hawk.' Cf. hooze.

n.Cy. GROSE (1790). Nhb.¹, n.Yks.¹⁴, ne.Yks.¹ e.Yks. As cattle when they clear the windpipe, or force up phlegm, MARSHALL Rur. Econ. (1788). Cha.¹²³ [Hase (K.).]

Hence (1) Hazed, ppl. adj. hoarse; (2) Heazy, adj. hoarse, breathing with difficulty, wheezing; fig. creaking.

(1) Cum.⁴ (2) Lth. And some gat heezy chairs, SMITH Merry Bridal (1866) 12. n.Cy. GROSE (1790); (K.). N.Cy.² Nhb. As's as heazy as an aad coo thi day (R.O.H.). n.Yks.¹²⁴, ne.Yks.¹, w.Yks.¹ Cha.¹ He were that heazy, he could na spake a word, and you could hear him blowin like a pair o' bellus; Cha.²³

2. sb. Asthmatic breathing, wheeziness. n.Yks.², Lin.¹

3. A catarrhal disease, incident to cattle or pigs, causing difficulty in breathing.

n.Yks. That cow hez t'heeaze (I.W.); n.Yks.¹⁴

[1. Norw. dial. hæsa, to pant (AASEN). 2. ON. hæsi, hoarseness (VIGFUSSON).]

HEBBLE, sb. n.Cy. Yks. Lan. Lin. Also written heble w.Yks. [e'bl.] 1. The wooden hand-rail of a plank-bridge; also in comp. Hebble-tree.

n.Cy. GROSE (1790). n.Yks.¹² w.Yks. HUTTON Tour to Caves (1781). ne.Lan.¹ (1788); e.Yks.¹ w.Yks.

2. A narrow, short plank-bridge.

Yks. Macmillan's Mag. (Apr. 1889) 475. w.Yks. (S.J.C.), w.Yks.⁴, n.Lin.¹

HEBBLE, v. Obs. n.Cy. (HALL.) w.Yks.¹ To build up hastily; to cobble; gen. used with up.

HEBEN, sb. ? Obs. Sc. Ebony; gen. in comp. Hebenwood.

But there is the coffin. . . It is made of heben-wood, SCOTT Nigel (1822) vii; (JAM.)

[A curious coffer made of heben wood, SPENSER Ruines of Time (1599) 139. Lat. hebenus, ebony.]

HEBRUN, sb. Lnk. Lth. (JAM.) Also in form heburn. A goat of three years old that has been castrated.

HECCAT, see Hacket, v.¹

HECH, int. and v. Sc. Irel. Nhb. Also written heech Sh.I.; hegh Sc. Nhb.¹; heich Lnk.; and in forms heh Edb.; hich ne.Sc. [hex.] 1. int. An exclamation, gen. indicating surprise, contempt, sorrow, fatigue, or pain, freq. in phr. hech, sirs; also used subst. Cf. heigh.

Sc. Hegh, sirs! sae young and weel-favoured, SCOTT Antiquary (1816) xvi. Sh.I. Noo an' dan a wild 'heech' frae some o' da young chaps, BURGESS Sketches (2nd ed.) 114. Cai.¹ Elg. Hech! how they drive! COUPER Poetry (1804) I. 77. Abd. Hech! but it'll be sune eneuch, MACDONALD Sir Gibbie (1879) iii. Frf. Hech, sirs, but they would need a gey rubbing to get the rust aff them, BARRIE Minister (1891) xxv. Per. Hech sirse! but my hirdies are sair forfuchan, CLELAND Inchbrachen (1883) 13, ed. 1887. Fif. Hech! Surse, I've haen mony guid . . . offers in my time, but this dings them a', McLAREN Tibbie (1894) 10. Slg. At second pinch he graned, 'Hech, sirs!' TOWERS Poems (1885) 65. Rnf. But mony a hech! and howe! it cost, WEBSTER Rhymes (1835) 161. Ayr. 'Hech! man, Willie,' qu' I, 'is that possible!' SERVICE Notandums (1890) 76. Lnk. Heich! sit ye down, sirs, till ye cuil, Deil's Hallowe'en (1856) 28. Lth. The auld cripple beggar cam jumpin', jumpin', Hech how the bodie was stumpin', stumpin', BALLANTINE Poems (1856) 54. Edb. Heh! Sandie, lad, what dool's come owr ye now, FERGUSSON Poems (1773) II. 106, ed. 1785. Peb. Wild echo answered frae her cave, 'Hech! Satan's truly clever!' AFFLECK Poet. Wks. (1836) 36. Slk. Hech! are free men to be guidit this gait! HOGG Tales (1838) 20, ed. 1866. Rxb. Hech, but the thought o't is a horrid thing, A. SCOTT Poems (1808) 160. Gall. Hech, sirs! this war Will ruin us a', IRVING Lays (1872) 214. Wgt. Hech! sirs, . . A'm sorry A hae forgot tae bring the knife, FRASER Wigtown (1877) 980. N.I.¹ 'Hech man, but ye're dreigh o' drawin', i. e. faith man, but you have been slow in coming to call. Nhb.¹ The stroke groan uttered by a blacksmith or the expiration which emphasizes the delivery of a blow.

2. Comb. (1) Hech-hey, heigho! (2) -how, heigho! also used attrib. wearisome, causing one to cry 'hech-how'; in phr. in the old hech-how, in the same bad circumstances or state of health; (3) -how-aye, heigho! aye! (4) -how-hum, (5) -wow, an exclamation of despondency or regret.

(1) Sc. (JAM.) n.Ir. When his buttons came off he'd say 'Hech, hey!' Lays and Leg. (1884) 34. (2) Sc. I thocht he was in the auld hech-how aye pechin through Chronicles, HUNTER J. Inwick (1895) 125. Dmb. For the time to come he maun preach his dry,

shionless, hech-how sermons, Cross *Disruption* (1844) xxxix.
r. Hech-how, for sixty year . . . I have hung.up my hat on that
vidual same pin, Galt *Lairds* (1826) xxxviii. **Cld.** (Jam.) **Lnk.**
ech how, here I am, . . wi' no a leevin' soul tae speak a kindly
ord tae, Wardrop *J. Mathison* (1881) i. **Lth.** (Jam.) **Edb.**
ech-how, my day has long since passed, Moir *Mansie Wauch*
828) vi. **Gall.** Another [man] stretched himself . . . and said,
Hech how!' as though he were sleepy, Crockett *Raiders* (1894)
(3) **Gall.** Hech-how-aye! auld Drumglass has seen that,
rockett *Standard Bearer* (1898) 189. (4) **Per.** Fool that I was
refuse Auld Gagram . . . Hech-how-hum, Monteath *Dunblane*
835) 72, ed. 1887. **Gall.** Hechhowhum, granes auld Milha by
e cheek o' the caumer-door, Mactaggart *Encycl.* (1824) 28, ed.
76. **Keb.** Elder *Borgue* (1897) 28. (5) **Sc.** 'Hech wow!' he
ould say, when told of the death of any person, Ford *Thistledown*
891) 96. **Slk.** Hech-wow! but that is awesome, Hogg *Tales*
838) 333, ed. 1866.
3. *v.* To cry 'hech'; to make a sound resembling
ech'; to pant, breathe hard.
ne.**Sc.** There was . . . little art in their dances, but a tremendous
al of 'hooching' and 'hiching,' *Gordonhaven* (1887) 71. **Bnff.**
 cawm them a' John Ploughman heght, Taylor *Poems* (1787)
. **Per.** Heching and peching, Because I hae nae pith, Nicol
ems (1766) 124. **Ayr.** Yet aye she hechs and howes! and says,
e's never heard .complainin', Aitken *Lays* (1883) 138. **Lnk.**
r John sae pleas'd, he hech'd an' leugh, Watt *Poems* (1827) 44.
nf. Hech-kechan, making much ado about little, Shaw *School-
aster* (1899) 349. **Gall.** I laid on, and sae did he, till some o' us
heched again, Mactaggart *Encycl.* (1824) 26, ed. 1876.

HECH·HOW, *sb.* Sc. The hemlock, *Conium maculatum.*
all. Mactaggart *Encycl.* (1824) 259, ed. 1876.

HECHLE, *v.* Sc. Also written heghle (Jam.). [he'χl.]
. To breathe short and quick, as the effect of consider-
le exertion.
Sc. (Jam.) **e.Fif.** I hechle and clocher an' toyt, but an' ben,
ke a puir feckless gran'sire o' three score an' ten, Latto *Tam
odhin* (1864) xxi.
2. To exert oneself in climbing a steep incline, or in getting
ver any impediment; *gen.* used with *up.* Rxb. (Jam.)
3. With *on*: to advance with difficulty; applied either
 the state of one's health, or to one's temporal circum-
ances. s.Sc. (*ib.*)

HECHT, see Height, Hight, *v.*[1]

HECK, *sb.*[1] and *v.*[1] Sh.I. [hek.] 1. *sb.* A crutch.
Encumbered with a withered leg . . . our notable friend sub-
tuted for his recalcitrant, good-for-nothing crural appendage,
wooden 'heck,' *Sh. News* (Mar. 26, 1898); **S. & Ork.**[1]
Hence (1) Heckie, (2) Heckster, *sb.* a cripple, one who
ses a crutch in walking. S. & Ork.[1]
2. *v.* To limp, halt. *ib.* Cf. heckie, *v.*[2]

HECK, *sb.*[2] Lan. Chs. [ek.] 1. A euphemism for
hell,' in phr. *what the heck?* Cf. eck.
.**Chs.**[1] Wot dhŭ ek ŭ yŭ ŭp tóo! [What the heck are yŏ up to?]
2. Phr. *is it (will it) heck as like?* equivalent to saying that
thing is quite incredible.
Lan. *Manchester City News* (Oct. 28, 1899); Will it heck as loike!
 sez, Chapman *Widder Bagshaw's Visit,* 9.

HECK, *sb.*[3] Cai.[1] [hek.] A whore.

HECK, *v.*[2] Pem. Som. Also in form hack. [ek, æk.]
 hop on one leg; to play 'hackety oyster,' or 'hop-scotch.'
Pem. (W.H.Y.); (W.M.M.) **s.Pem.** Laws *Little Eng.* (1888)
0. Som. W. & J. *Gl.* (1873); Sweetman *Wincanton Gl.* (1885).
Hence Heck-shell, *sb.* the game *gen.* known as 'hop-
cotch' or 'pottle.'
Pem. (W.H.Y.) **s.Pem.** (W.M.M.); Laws *Little Eng.* (1888) 420.
om. W. & J. *Gl.* (1873).

HECK, *v.*[3] Nrf. [ek.] To make a noise with one's
roat. Cf. hack, *v.*[1] 80.
They had seen me, and they hecked when they come in,
merson *Son of Fens* (1892) iv.

HECK, *int.* and *v.*[4] Sc. Nhb. Dur. Cum. Yks. Also in
rms heik Sc. (Jam. *Suppl.*); hick Rxb. Dmf. (Jam.);
ke Sc. (Jam. *Suppl.*) N.Cy.[1] [h]ek.] 1. *int.* An ex-
amation used to order horses to come to the left or
ear side.
Sc. (Jam. *Suppl.*) Rxb., Dmf. (Jam.) **Nhb.** The well-known
heck' and 'gee,' Richardson *Borderer's Table-bk.* (1846) V. 71;
b.[1] Heck, or Heck-wo-heck. Dur.[1], e.Dur.[1], w.Yks.[1]

2. Phr. *neither heck nor ree,* (in carters' language) neither
left nor right; so *fig., he'll neither heck nor ree,* he'll not obey
the word of command, he'll not hear reason, he's unmanageable. Cf. ge(e, *int.*
N.Cy.[1], e.Dur. (J.E.D.), Cum.[1,4]
3. *v.* To turn a horse to the left.
Nhb.[1] Heck in husbandry, is to proceed in forming a rig by
turning the horses to the left hand, after it has been half-finished
by turning to the right. The first operation to the right is called
'to gether'; the second operation by turning to the left is called
to heck or 'felly oot' the rig.

HECK, *v.*[5] Or.I. To lay hold of hurriedly, to grab.
Hence Heckan, *adj.* nervous, fussy, apt to seize prematurely. (J.G.)

HECK, see Eck, Hack, *sb.*[12]

HECKABIRNIE, *sb.* Or.I. [Not known to our correspondents.] Any lean, feeble creature. S. & Ork.[1]

HECKAM-PECKAM, *sb.* Sc. The name of an angler's
fly; also in *comb.* Heckam-peckam-lass.
Lnk. Yon braw hare's lug I tied yestreen Should kill a trout or
twa; And here's a heckam-peckam lass, The best flee o' them a',
Penman *Echoes* (1878) 53.

HECKANODDY, *sb.* Dev. [e'kənodi.] The blue tomtit, *Parus caeruleus.*
Baring-Gould *J. Herring* (1888) 23; 'What is the name of that
bird?' 'Folks du ca'n a heckanoddy,' *Reports Provinc.* (1889).
s.Dev. (F.W.C.)

HECKAPURDES, *sb.* Or.I. The state of a person
when alarmed by any sudden danger or calamity; a
quandary. (Jam.), S. & Ork.[1]

HECKBERRY, HECKEMAL, see Hagberry, Hackmal.

HECKERY·PECKERY, *sb.* Sc. A boys' game. Lnk.
Glasgow Herald (Dec. 23, 1899).

HECKET, *sb.* Sc. [he'kit.] A hay-rack in a stable.
Gall. (A.W.)

HECKET·, see Hacket, *v.*[2]

HECKETT, *sb.* Dev. [Not known to our correspondents.] A fuss. n.Dev. Rock *Jim an' Nell* (1867) *Gl.*

HECKFOR, see Heifer.

HECK·HENS, *sb.* Obs. Cai.[1] An additional rent-
charge paid in fowls and eggs.
This fell into disuse early in the 19th century. It was revived
by the Earl of Caithness about 1850, but was dropped in a
year or two.

HECKIEBIRNIE, see Hecklebirnie.

HECKLA, *sb.* Sh.I. The dog-fish, *Squalus archiarius.*
S. & Ork.[1]

HECKLE, *sb.*[1] and *v.*[1] Sc. Irel. Nhb. Dur. Cum. Wm.
Yks. Lan. Lin. Shr. Oxf. Lon. e.An. Som. Also written
hekel Shr.[2]; and in forms hackle Nhb.[1] w.Som.[1]; hickle
e.An.[1] [h]e'kl.] 1. *sb.* A kind of comb with steel
teeth used for dressing flax and hemp; freq. in *pl.*
Sc. Lassie, lend me your braw hemp heckle, Ramsay *Tea-Table
Misc.* (1724) I. 35, ed. 1871. **Bnff.** Gordon *Chron. Keith* (1880)
68. **w.Sc.** He found [him] in a fearful state of trepidation, his
hair like a heckle, Carrick *Laird of Logan* (1835) 226. **Dmb.** A
lang-teethed heckle, Cross *Disruption* (1844) xxiii. **Ayr.** I wish
a heckle Were in their doup, Burns *Address to Toothache.*
Ant. *Ballymena Obs.* (1892). **Nhb.**[1], Cum., Wm. (M.P.), n.Yks.[2]
e.Yks. Marshall *Rur. Econ.* (1788); A rough coarse woman is
said to be 'as rough as heckles' (S.O.A.); e.Yks.[1], w.Yks.[2]
Lin. Streatfeild *Lin. and Danes* (1884) 337. n.Lin.[1], e.An.[12],
w.Som.[1]
2. *Comp.* (1) Heckle-pins, the teeth of a 'heckle,' in phr.
to come over the heckle-pins, to undergo a strict examination; to be severely handled during a course of probation;
(2) -shop, a shop or factory where flax or hemp is dressed;
(3) -teeth, see (1).
(1) **Sc.** (Jam.) **w.Yks.** Hiz hair stud on an end like heckle pins,
Leeds Comic Olm. 15. (2) **n.Yks.**[2] (3) **Sc.** I hae gotten a hunder
holes dung in my arse wi' the heckle teeth, Graham *Writings*
(1883) II. 17. **w.Sc.** My hair stood up like heckle-teeth, Carrick
Laird of Logan (1835) 164. **Dmf.** A hill o' heckle teeth for to climb
owre an' a', Cromek *Remains* (1810) 117. **n.Yks.**[2]
3. Phr. *to be a heckle to any one,* to be a thorn in his side.
Sc. He was a hedge about his friends, A heckle to his foes,
Aytoun *Ballads* (ed. 1861) II. 382. Cum., Wm. (M.P.)

4. *Fig.* Busy interference; intrusive meddling; impertinence. Yks. (HALL.)

5. *v.* To dress flax or hemp by separating it into its finest fibres. Also used *fig.*

Sc. 'The hemp's not sown that shall hang me.' 'It's sown, and it's grown, and it's heckled, and it's twisted,' SCOTT *Guy M.* (1815) liv. Cai.[1] Abd. He was half-witted, but was able to heckle hemp, ANDERSON *Rhymes* (1867) 203. Ayr. There be those of a coarse worldly grain and substance, coarse to heckle and ill to card, GALT *Sir A. Wylie* (1822) ciii. n.Cy. GROSE (1790); N.Cy.[1], Dur.[1] Cum. LINTON *Lake Cy.* (1864) 305. e.Yks.[1], w.Yks.[1] Lin. STREATFEILD *Lin. and Danes* (1884) 337. n.Lin.[1], Shr.[2], e.An.[1], w.Som.[1]

Hence (1) **Heckled**, *ppl. adj.* of flax: dressed; (2) **Heckler**, *sb.* (*a*) a dresser of flax or hemp; (*b*) a claw; (3) **Heckling**, *vbl. sb.* the process of dressing flax or hemp; also used *attrib.*

(1) Edb. Her hair is like the heckl'd Lint, PENNECUIK *Helicon* (1720) 160. (2, *a*) Sc. The weavers an' hecklers, they scamper'd like deer, VEDDER *Poems* (1842) 112. Abd. The shoemaker, the heckler, and weaver, ANDERSON *Rhymes* (1867) 194. Frf. Swipes farewell, and welcome rum, Hecklers an' the cash come, SANDS *Poems* (1833) 19. Ayr. Six and a half miles from Irvine, where he was a heckler, HUNTER *Studies* (1870) 17. Gall. MACTAGGART *Encycl.* (1824) 124, ed. 1876. Ant. *Ballymena Obs.* (1892). N.Cy.[1], Nhb.[1], Dur.[1], n.Yks.[1] e.Yks. MARSHALL *Rur. Econ.* (1788); e.Yks.[1], w.Yks.[1] Lin. STREATFEILD *Lin. and Danes* (1884) 337. n.Lin.[1] Lon. The hecklers or flax-dressers, can unfold 'a tale of woe' on this subject, MAYHEW *Lond. Labour* (1851) II. 306, ed. 1861. e.An.[12] (*b*) n.Yks.[2] (3) Bnff. Heckling was the chief business about 1770, when the neighbouring lanes . . . had abundance of heckling-shops, with small boles in the walls for the heckles, GORDON *Chron. Keith* (1880) 67. a.Sc. Wha was only making six shillings a week at the hecklin, THOMSON *Poems* (1819) 114. n.Yks.[2], w.Som.[1]

6. *Fig.* To examine searchingly; to pester with questions a candidate for Parliament, or for any municipal office.

Cai.[1] Abd. Sing baul'—nor dread the heckle, The Critic Lown will be a traicle, Wha seeks your native plumes to speckle, COCK *Strains* (1810) I. 19. Frf. He went on to the platform, at the time of the election, to heckle the Colonel, BARRIE *Thrums* (1895) v. Ayr. We'll heckle weel, and a' that, Baith Tories, Whigs, and a' that, WHITE *Jottings* (1879) 179. Lak. They were heckled by the maister about their knowledge, FRASER *Whaups* (1895) iii. Lth. Now shall each daurin' candidate Be heckled weel on Kirk an' State, LUMSDEN *Sheep-head* (1892) 88. n.Yks.[4]

7. To scold severely; to henpeck.

Bnff.[1] Abd. A couthie wife an' canty she has been. . . She never heckles me but for my guid, *Guidman Inglismaill* (1873) 33. Cld. (JAM.) w.Yks. Tha'll happen get one at tha connot heckle at as tha does me, HARTLEY *Clock Alm.* (1896) 54.

Hence (1) **Heckler**, *sb.* a female brawler or scold; a hard master; (2) **Heckling**, (*a*) *sb.* a severe scolding; a dispute; (*b*) *ppl. adj.* teasing, provoking to anger.

(1) Nhb.[1], Cum., Wm.(M.P.), n.Yks.[2] (2, *a*) Sc. Bargaining and heckling is a mean and damnable business, COBBAN *Andaman* (1895) v. Bnff.[1], Cld. (JAM.) Ayr. My word, ye'll get a heckling this time, JOHNSTON *Kilmallie* (1891) I. 118. n.Yks.[12] ne.Yks.[1] He gav him a good heckling. n.Yks.[1] Lan. The heckling they received at the hands of the clogger, ACKWORTH *Clog Shop Chron.* (1896) 197. (*b*) Sc. He answered with a heckling laugh, STEVENSON *Catriona* (1893) viii.

8. To fight; to flog, chastise.

n.Yks.[2] Oxf. I never did heckle such a wiry chap, BLACKMORE *Cripps* (ed. 1895) xlix; What, all on you afeard to heckle him? *ib.* lv.

Hence **Heckler**, *sb.* a good fighter; one who chastises.

Gall. If a melancholy mirky wight, Grim Heckler o' the feeling soul, MACTAGGART *Encycl.* (1824) 124, ed. 1876. Ant. *Ballymena Obs.* (1892).

HECKLE, *sb.*[2] S. & Ork.[1] *MS. add.* [Not known to our correspondents.] That part of a knife to which the handle is attached.

HECKLE, *sb.*[3] N.Cy.[1] Complexion. Hence **Heckled**, *ppl. adj.* complexioned, coloured.

'She's light heckl'd'—of a person of light hair.

HECKLE, *v.*[2] Sh.I. [he·kl.] To hobble. See Heck, *v.*[1]

Heckle noo! Flitt! BURGESS *Rasmie* (1892) 14.

HECKLE, see Hackle, *sb.*[12], Hickwall, Ickle, *sb.*

HECKLEBACK, *sb.* Sc. The fifteen-spined stickleback, *Spinachia vulgaris.*

Fif. SIBBALD *Hist. Fif.* (1803) 128 (JAM.).

HECKLEBIRNIE, *sb.* Sc. Nhb. Also written heckleburnie Nhb.; and in forms **heckiebirnie** Sc. (JAM.); **hecklebarney** Nhb. **1.** A substitute for the word 'hell' or the infernal regions. See Halifax, Hull.

Sc. The only account given of this place is that it is three miles beyond Hell (JAM.). Abd. If one says 'Go to the D—l,' the other often replies 'Go you to Hecklebirnie' (*ib.*). Lth. I dinna care though ye were at Heckiebirnie. As far as Heckiebirnie (*ib.*). Nhb. A' wish they'd been at Heckleburnie That ever mentioned Calleyforney, EMERY *Pitman's Return from California*; (R.O.H.); Nhb.[1] Gan to Hecklebarney wi ye.

2. A children's game; see below.

Abd. A play among children, in which thirty or forty, in two rows, joining opposite hands, strike smartly, with their hands thus joined, on the head or shoulders of their companion as he runs the gauntlet through them. This is called 'passing through the mires of Hecklebirnie' (JAM.).

[1. This word is prob. conn. w. the names of the mythical Wild Hunter known to Westphalian traditions. He is called *Hackelbärend* or *Hackelbernd*, also *Hackelberg* and *Hackelblock.* For details of these traditions, and discussion on the etym. of *Hackelbärend*, see GRIMM *Teut. Myth.* (tr. Stallybrass) III. 920–4. We may also compare the Danish saying: *gaa du dig til Hákkenfeldt, ib.* 1001, and Dan. dial. *Hakkelmand,* a name of the devil (FEILBERG).]

HECKLE-BISCUIT, *sb.* Sc. Also in form **heckled-**. A kind of biscuit.

Frf. So called because in process of manufacture they are punctured or perforated with a wooden disc full of spikes or heckles (J.B.); They have tried many ways of drawing Grizel, from heckle-biscuits and parlies, to a slap in the face, BARRIE *Tommy* (1896) 318; No tea-pairty was considered complete without 'heckled biscuits' and 'shortie,' INGLIS *Ain Flk.* (1895) x.

HECKLER, *sb.*[1] Nhb.[1] [he·klər.] A good eater; one with a good appetite.

HECKLER, *sb.*[2] Nhb.[1] [he·klər.] A boy's top when it spins unsteadily.

HECKS, *sb.* Not. Pain suffered through fear or passion. (J.H.B.)

HECKSLAVER, HECKT, HECKTH, see Hack-slaver, Hight, *v.*[1], Height.

HECKY, HECKWALL, HECLE, see Ecky, Hickwall.

HECTOR, *sb.* Lakel. Suf. **1.** In *comp.* Hector Hell-bones, an unruly boy. e.Suf. (F.H.)

2. *Phr. as sour as Hector*, a common saying. Lakel.[2]

HECTUM, *sb.* Lan. [e·ktəm.] An oath; *gen.* in phr. *by the hectum*, or *what the hectum?* See Heck, *sb.*[2]

It's hectum as like, WAUGH *Tufts* (ed. Milner) I. 208; What th' hectum are yo doin' up at this time? *ib.* II. 35; By the hectum, that wor a tide, *ib. Rambles Lake Cy.* (1861) ii; He'd bother no moore wi' it, would he hectum as like, WOOD *Hum. Sketches,* 31.

HED, HEDDER, see Heed, Hide, *v.*[2], Hadder, *sb.*[1]

HEDDERKIN-DUNK, *sb.* Sh.I. A see-saw; the game of see-saw. Also used *adv.*

Rig a hedderkin-dunk, BURGESS *Rasmie* (1892) 104; Twa lairge planks ridin' hedder-kindunk i' da shoor mil, *Sh. News* (Mar. 18, 1899); The game of see-saw, *ib.* (Apr. 15, 1899).

HEDDIWISSEN, HEDDLE, HEDER, see Have, Heald, *sb.*[1], He.

HEDGE, *sb.* and *v.* Var. dial. uses in Sc. Irel. and Eng. Also in forms **hadge** Dev.; **hadgy** Cor.[2]; **hedgy** nw.Dev.[1] Cor.[12]; **hydgy** Dev. Cor. **1.** *sb.* In *comb.* (1) **Hedge-accentor**, the hedge-sparrow, *Accentor modularis*; (2) **-and-bind**, in and out; (3) **-back** or **-backing**, the bank behind a hedge, or on which it grows; (4) **-Betty**, see (1); (5) **-bill**, a long-handled, hooked blade for cutting hedges; (6) **-boar** or **-a-boar**, a hedgehog; also a rough workman, a lout; (7) **-Bob**, see (1); (8) **-bote**, the right of cutting hedge-wood from the property of another; (9) **-brow**, see below; (10) **-brushings**, the clippings of hedges; (11) **-carpenter** or **-caffender**, a maker and repairer of hedges and rail-fences, &c.; a rough carpenter; (12) **-chat**, see (1); (13) **-chicker**, the wheatear, *Saxicola oenanthe*; (14) **-creep**, see below;

5) -creeper, see (1) ; (16) -cuckoo, see below ; (17) -dike, bank with a hedge on it ; (18) -dike-side, the part of the edge-bank on the water-channel side ; (19) -fathered, o) -got, of low birth, as if born in a hedge ; (21) -gripe, ditch at the foot of a hedge ; (22) -grubber, see (1) ; (23) ulling, a hollow ditch for the defence of the hedge ; (24) ug, the long-tailed tit, *Acredula rosea* ; (25) -knife, a long afted implement with a slightly curved blade, used in imming hedges ; (26) -lawyer, see below ; (27) -learned, educated ; (28) -looker, an official whose duty it is to e that the hedges on the boundary of the common are ept in repair ; (29) -man, one who trims hedges ; (30) arriage, a clandestine marriage ; (31) -mike, see (1) ; 2) -parson, an uneducated clergyman ; (33) -pick, see .) ; (34) -pig, see (6) ; (35) -plasher, see below ; (36) oker, see (1) ; (37) -popping, shooting birds as they fly ut of a hedge ; (38) -rise, underwood for making hedges ; 9) -row, see (21) ; (40) -row-timber, light varieties of ood that grow in hedges ; (41) -root or -rut, a hedge ; 2) -school, see below ; (43) -spick or -spike, see (1) ; (44) plasher, see (5) ; (45) -spurgie, see (1) ; (46) -tacker, see 9) ; (47) -tear, an angular rent ; (48) -trough, see (21) ; 9) -ward, see (28).

(1) e.An.[1] (2) w.Yks.[2] Others ran hedge and bind to and fro. 3) Lan. He dropp'd deawn into th' hedge backin' to see what 'ud appen next, Axon *Sketches* (1867) 25 ; Lan.[1] We'st ha' nowt to then i'th' summer, nobbut lie in hedge-backins, hearkenin' brids ing, Brierley *Ab-o'-th'-Yate* (1870) 94. Chs.[1], s.Chs.[1] (4) e.Wor.[1], s.Wor. (H.K.), s.Wor.[1], e.An.[1] Nrf. Cozens-Hardy *road Nrf.* (1893) 45. Ess. (H.H.M.) (5) s.Wor.[1] Shr.[1] Scythes ad sneads, hedge-bills, and broad hooks, *Auctioneer's Catalogue* 870). Hrf.[2] Glo. (A.B.) ; Glo.[1] A long two-handed tool used or stopping gaps in hedges. At the end of the pole is a straight nife with a slightly returned end, and with a hook projecting from ne back of the blade, and pointing towards its point, for pushing he cut-off bunch of thorns into the gap. It is also used for driving ap in. (6) Som. W. & J. *Gl.* (1873). w.Som.[1] Purty hedgeboar uller, he, for to set up for a doctor, better fit he'd take to farrin. ev. Making one's hair stand up leek queels Upon a hadgy-bore, eter Pindar *Wks.* (1816) IV. 196. n.Dev. A dinderhead hadge- oar, Rock *Jim an' Nell* (1867) st. 85. nw.Dev.[1] s.Dev. Fox *ingsbridge* (1874). s.Dev., s.Cor.,(Miss D.) Cor. The gipsies hat do live pon hedgy boors, Tregellas *Tales* (1865) 67 ; Cor.[12]] Cor.[2] (8) Cum.[14] n.Yks. Sufficient hedge-boote to be allowed repaire and mainteyne all the hedges and fences, &c., *Quart. ess. Rec.* in *N. R. Rec. Soc.* IV. 157 ; n.Yks.[2], ne.Lan.[1] n.Lin.[1] *bs.* To have . . . sufficient houseboot, hedgeboot . . . and stake- oot yearly, *Lease of Lands in Brumby* (1716). Wil. And that , shall be lawful for the s[d]. J. M. to cut lop and take . . . the nderwood of hedgerows for and towards necessary hedgebote nd haybote for the use of the premises, *Lease of property Cherhill* x783). (9) Hrt. Where bushes or other trumpery . . . which we call edge-brows, Ellis *Mod. Husb.* (1750) I. 37. (10) Chs.[1] (11) .Wor. (H.K.), Wil.[1] Dor. 'You may generally tell what a man a by his claws,' observed the hedge-carpenter, looking at his wn hands, Hardy *Wess. Tales* (1888) I. 29. w.Som.[1] (12) hp. Swainson *Birds* (1885) 29 ; No music's heard the fields mong, Save when the hedge-chats twittering play, Clare *Village finst.* (1821) I. 91 ; Nhp.[12] (13) Cor. Rodd *Birds* (1880) 314. r4) w.Yks.[6] A party of youths will make it up amongst themselves 'hedge-creep' a certain couple, i.e. follow two lovers along the alks which they frequent, but on the other side of the hedge, or all, for the purpose of listening to their conversation. (15) Nrf. *ature Notes*, No. 10. (16) Wil. We sometimes speak of our Vestern neighbours as Somerset hedge-cuckoes, in taunting allu- ion to their making a hedge round the cuckoo, to keep him from ying away (G.E.D.). (17) n.Yks.[14] (18) n.Yks.[1] ; n.Yks.[2] When he birth-place of a person is doubtful, it is jokingly said, 'he was orn on a hedge-dike side' ; n.Yks.[4] (19) Nrf. I'll go up to the orkhouse and see what I can do. So I goes and I sees a strap- ing young mawther with two bairns hedge-fathered, Emerson *arns* (1891) 47. (20) They're allust the best them hedge-got hildren, *ib.* (21) Cor.[1] (22) e.Suf. (F.H.) (23) Dev. *Horae ubsecivae* (1777) 209. (24) Lei.[1] (25) Nhb.[1], s.Not. (J.P.K.) (26) an. Jack was one of that unfortunate class of practitioners dis- aragingly denominated 'hedge lawyers,' who are supposed to ake up cases in a seemingly surreptitious manner, and lay them own when they are only fit to be decided by a jury of pick-

pockets, Brierley *Red. Wind.* (1868) vii. (27) Midl. Ye poor hedge-larned critter, Bartram *People of Clopton* (1897) 43. (28) Cum.[4] Hedge lookers and peat moss lookers. (29) Elg. Th' eternal hedgeman, balanc'd weel, Supports the balanc'd bill, Couper *Poetry* (1804) I. 6a. (30) n.Cy. (Hall.) (31) Sus. Swainson *ib.* 29 ; Sus.[1] (32) Sc. Then it fell under the dominion of a reformado captain, who . . . was deposed by a hedge parson, Scott *Nigel* (1822) xviii. (33) Sus.[1] I throwed a stone at a liddle hedge-pick a settin' on the heave-geat (s.v. Heen). (34) Glo.[1], e.An.[1] w.Nrf. He fed on nothin' 'cept hedge pigs, Orton *Beeston Ghost* (1884) 9. Ken. (D.W.L.) Sur. A gipsy, who has a taste for baked hedge-pig, *Forest Tithes* (1893) 23. Wil. (G.E.D.), w.Som.[1] n.Dev. Her coat stares like a hedge-pig's, Kingsley *Westward Ho* (1855) 39, ed. 1889. (35) Lin. One who 'plashes' or 'lays' a hedge, by cutting the stronger stems of the 'quick' half way through and forcing them into a horizontal position (M.P.) ; The run fox was headed back by a hedge-plasher, *Field* (Dec. 5, 1896) 915. (36) Brks.[1] Ken. *Science Gossip* (1882) 65 ; (G.E.D.) (37) Shr.[1] Of course the first stage in their progress was 'hedge-popping' at blackbirds, thrushes, and fieldfares, Davies *Rambles Sch. Field- Club* (1881) xxvii. Oxf. A favourite amusement with youths, armed with catapults, or with stones carefully selected and carried in the pocket. They first frighten birds out of the hedges, then 'pop' at them with the stones. Hedge-popping is generally carried on by small gangs of boys, some of whom act as 'drivers' (G.O.). (38) n.Cy. (Hall.) w.Yks.[1] It [a cart] wor crazy an wankle enif . . . wi' leadin' hedge-rise last spring, ii. 286. (39) Cor. Us druv' slap bang over 'eap o' stoanes, upset the geg an' sent us sprawlin' in the edge-raw, Pasmore *Stories* (1893) 4. (40) Chs. Hedge row timber is a prevailing product of the lower lands of Chs., Marshall *Review* (1818) II. 7. (41) Gall. My great sheep- skin coat . . . keeps me warm on the cauldest nicht in a hedge-root, Crockett *Raiders* (1894) xlvi. Nhb.[1] To ' sit in the hedge-rut,' is to sit under the shelter of a hedge. (42) Ir. When not even a shed could be obtained in which to assemble the children of an Irish village, the worthy pedagogue selected the first green spot on the sunny side of a quickset-thorn hedge. From this circum- stance the name of Hedge School originated, Carleton *Traits Peas.* (ed. 1843) I. 271 ; They arrived at the hedge school-house, *ib.* Fardorougha (1896) 229. (43) Nrf. Cozens-Hardy *Broad Nrf.* (1893) 45. Sus. Swainson *ib.* 29. (44) War.[2], s.Not. (J.P.K.) (45) Abd. Swainson *ib.* 28. (46) Dev. Varmer Bulley's acomed til zomtheng ; they say 'e's nort but a hadge-tacker now, an' work'th vur his dairyman that wuz, Hewett *Peas. Sp.* (1892) ; They wants a hadge-tacker tu a farm nigh by Crediton, I 'ear tell, Phillpotts *Dartmoor* (1895) 129, ed. 1896. n.Dev. Auld, northering, gurbed, hadge-tacker, Dick, Rock *Jim an' Nell* (1867) st. 75. (47) War.[3] Hedge-tear darning is taught in sewing classes. (48) w.Som.[1] Dev. Thay vownd ded in the hedgestraw, The best hoss in ther posseshun, *n.Dev. Jrn.* (Dec. 17, 1885) 2. nw.Dev.[1] (49) Lin. Marshall *Review* (1811).

2. *Comb.* in plant-names : (1) **Hedge-bells**, (*a*) the wild convolvulus, *Convolvulus arvensis* ; (*b*) the great bindweed, *C. sepium* ; (2) — **dead-nettle**, the hedge woundwort, *Stachys sylvatica* ; (3) **-feathers**, the Traveller's Joy, *Clematis Vitalba* ; (4) **-garlick**, the garlick mustard, *Alliaria officinalis* ; (5) **-grape**, the fruit of the white bryony, *Bryonia dioica* ; (6) **-horn**, the stink-horn, *Phallus impudicus* ; (7) **-lily**, see (1, *b*) ; (8) **-mushroom**, the horse-mushroom, *Agaricus arvensis* ; (9) **-nettle**, see (2) ; (10) **-nuts**, the fruit of the hazel, *Corylus Avellana* ; (11) **-peg**, the fruit of the sloe, *Prunus spinosa* ; (12) **-peeks** or **-picks**, see (11) ; (*b*) the fruit of the bullace, *Prunus insititia* ; (13) **-pigs**, see (11) ; (14) **-pink**, the soapwort, *Saponaria officinalis* ; (15) **-speaks**, **-specks**, or **-spikes**, (*a*) see (11) ; (*b*) the fruit of the wild rose, *Rosa canina* ; (16) **-strawberry**, the wood strawberry, *Fragaria vesca* ; (17) **-violet**, the dog-violet, *Viola sylvatica*.

(1, *a*) I.W.[1] (*b*) Cum., Stf., s.Eng. I.W. (C.J.V.) (2) Shr. (3) w.Yks. Lees *Flora* (1888) 111. (4) Cum. (5) Wor. (6) I.W.[1] (7) Hmp. (W.M.E.F.), Hmp.[1], I.W. (C.J.V.) (8) Chs.[1] (9) Shr.[1] (10) Dev. (W.L.-P.) (11) Brks., Hmp., Wil. (W.H.E.), Wil.[1] (12, *a*) Hmp. (W.M.E.F.), Hmp.[1], Wil.[1], Som. (W.F.R.), Cor. (M.A.C.) (*b*) Hmp. (W.M.E.F.), Som. (W.F.R.) (13) Glo.[1] (14) Hmp. (15, *a*) Glo. *Horae Subsecivae* (1777) 209. Wil.[1] At Huish, Slöns are large and Hedge-speaks small. (*b*) Glo. *Gl.* (1851). (16) s.Dev. (17) Dev.[4]

3. Phr. *to be on the wrong side of the hedge*, to be mistaken, to err. w.Yks.[1], nw.Der.[1]

4. A wall, *gen.* of granite, occas. of earth or turf.

I.Ma. One . . . had jumped to the top of the broad turf hedge, CAINE *Deemster* (1887) xvi. Dev. A group of little fellows amuse themselves with piling up loose stones, and making baby walls in imitation of those of granite, called hedges, on the borders of Dartmoor, BRAY *Desc. Tamar and Tavy* (1836) III. 385. Cor. Why do the giants show such a preference for granite? At Looe, indeed, the Giant's Hedge is a vast earthwork; but this is an exception, HUNT *Pop. Rom. w.Eng.* (1865) 43, ed. 1896; This place was hedged in with great rocks, which no ten men of these times could move. They call them the Giant's Hedges to the present day, *ib.* 56; Cor.[8]

5. *v.* To repair hedges; to build a stone fence.

nw.Der.[1] Cor.[8] I'm fit to hedgy against any one.

Hence (1) **Hedger**, *sb.* a man who trims and mends hedges; (2) **Hedging**, *vbl. sb.* (*a*) the process of trimming and repairing hedges; (*b*) beating a hedge in order to confuse and subsequently kill the birds in it; (3) **Hedging-bill**, *sb.* a bill with a long handle for brushing or cutting down hedges; (4) **Hedging-cuffs**, (5) **Hedging-mittens**, *sb. pl.* gloves with a division for the thumb only, used by the 'hedger' to protect his hands.

(1) Frf. His faither was a hedger roond aboot, an' made no that ill pay, WILLOCK *Rosetty Ends* (1886) 103, ed. 1889. Nhb. (R.O.H.), Yks. (J.W.) Oxf.[1] *MS. add.* se.Wor.[1] (*a*, *a*) Ayr. And sometimes a hedging and ditching I go, BURNS *Poor Thresher.* War.[8], Wor. (E.S.) (*b*) Brks.[1] A common sport, where boys go on either side of a hedge when the leaves have fallen, with long light poles. On seeing any bird fly into the hedge a-head, one gives the word, and both beat the hedge from opposite sides; the bird gets too confused to fly out and is generally killed by branches knocked against it; ten or twelve birds are often killed in an afternoon's 'hedgin',.' (3) Yks. (J.W.), e.Lan.[1], Chs.[1] (4) Oxf.[1] *MS. add.* (5) n.Yks. (I.W.)

6. *Obs.* To protect.

Edb. To hedge us frae that black banditti, FERGUSSON *Poems* (1773) 118, ed. 1785.

7. To shuffle in narration; to equivocate. Lth. (JAM.) Ant. *Ballymena Obs.* (1892).

HEDGEHOG, *sb.* and *v.* Sc. Nhb. Dur. Chs. Nhp. Ken. Sur. Sus. Wil. 1. *sb. in comp.* Hedgehog-holly, the holly, *Ilex aquifolium.* Edb. PENNECUIK *Wks.* (1715) 62, ed. 1815. **2.** The prickly seed-vessel of the corn crowfoot, *Ranunculus arvensis,* applied also to the whole plant. Ken., Sur., Sus., Wil.[1] **3.** The shepherd's needle, *Scandix pecten.* Sur.[1], Sus.[1] **4.** *pl.* Small stunted trees in hedgerows. Chs. (K.), Chs.[18] **5.** *v.* To open, divulge, or disclose anything.

Nhp.[1] A witness giving evidence in Assize Court, said, ' the prisoner hedge-hogged.' On being asked what he meant, he said that ' a hedge-hog when in water opened; and the man, when they gave him plenty of beer, opened, and told all he knowed.'

6. To break and turn up the ends of wire.

Nhb.[1], Nhb., Dur. The strand of a wire rope having broken is carried along the rope by coming in contact with the sheaves or rollers and forms a ravelled mass or ruffle on the rope which is then said to be hedgehogged, NICHOLSON *Coal Tr. Gl.* (1888).

HEDGY, *sb.* Nhb.[1] The hedge-sparrow, *Accentor modularis.*

HEDLEY, *sb.* Nhb. In phr. *the Hedley Kow,* the name of a 'bogle.'

RICHARDSON *Borderer's Table-bk.* (1846) VI. 60; The Hedley Kow, a Nhb. ghost story, *Denham Tracts* (ed. 1895) II. 78; Well known to me from traditional sources. The local name for a sprite or ' boggle ' possessing attributes common to such things. Hedley is a village in Nbb. The ' kow ' is a myth (R.O.H.).

HEDLOCK, see Hidlock.

HEE, *int.* Cum.[14] A call-note to a cur dog.

HEE, HEEA, HEEAD, see High, How, *adv.,* Hide, *v.*[2]

HEEAH, *int.* Yks. An exclamation of interrogation: ' what did you say?' e.Yks.[1] *MS. add.* (T.H.)

HEEAK, HEEAL(L, HEEAM, see Hake, *v.,* Hale, *adj.,* Hame.

HEEAMS, *sb. pl.* n.Yks.[2] [iəmz.] See below.

' She flings out her heeams,' said of a cow that protrudes the posterior parts, as showing signs for calving.

HEEAMSTER, *sb.* n.Yks.[2] Also in form **yamster.** A household provider; one of domestic habits.

HEED, *v.* and *sb.* Sc. n.Cy. Yks. Lan. Chs. Der. Rdn. Also in form **hade** w.Yks.; *preterite* **hed** e.Lan.[1] s.Lan. Der.[12] nw.Der.[1] [h]d.] **1.** *v.* To mind, attend, care for; to take notice, pay attention to. *Gen.* used with *neg.*

Fif. Never heed him, ROBERTSON *Provost* (1894) 109. Ayr. I think I'm no muckle heeded in this hoose, SERVICE *Dr. Dugnid* (ed. 1887) 148. Lnk. The Police chaps are nae that heedin' Or-'gainst sic tricks they'd been proceeding, WATT *Poems* (1827) 11. e.Lth. I'm no heedin muckle aboot growin figs, HUNTER *J. Inwick* (1895) 12. n.Yks.[12]; n.Yks.[4] Ah deean't heed mich ov owt 'at he sez. w.Yks. I'll nivver heed till dinner time, CUDWORTH *Dial. Sketches* (1884) 112; Never hade your feet, LUCAS *Stud. Nidderdale* (c. 1882) Gl. Lan. I ne'er hed thee all the while, BYROM *Poems* (1773) I. 120, ed. 1814. ne.Lan. Ne'er heed me, doctor, MATHER *Idylls* (1895) 219. e.Lan.[1] s.Lan. PICTON *Dial.* (1865). Chs.[1] Dunna heed him. Der. He hears better than he heeds, GROSE (1790) *MS. add.* (P.); Der.[1]; Der.[2] Ne'er heed him, lad. nw.Der.[1]

2. *sb.* Notice; attention, care.

Ayr. He drew the mortal trigger Wi' weel-aim'd heed, BURNS *Tam Samson* (1787) st. 11. n.Cy. (J.W.) Chs.[1] Tak no heed o'' what he sez. Tak heed. Rdn.[1]

Hence **Heedful**, *adj.* regardful. n.Yks.[2]

HEED, HEEDER, see Head, Hide, *v.*[2] He.

HEEDLIN, HEEDLY, see Headland, *sb.,* Eardly.

HEEGARY, *sb.* Lakel. Cum. [hīgē·ri.] A rage, passion, high temper; a disturbance; a whimsically dressed female. Cf. **fleegarie, fligary.**

Lakel.[2] A chap when he's hed a bit ov a tiff wi' his best lass, an' sets off an' 'lists, does it in a heegary. Many a yan leeves tea be sooary fer deein' things in a heegary. Cum.[4]

HEE-GRASS, see Ee-grass.

HEEL, *sb.* and *v.*[1] Var. dial. uses in Sc. Irel. and Eng. [h]īl.] **1.** *sb. In comp.* (1) Heel-calkers, heel-plates or irons to go round the heels of a boot; see Calker, *sb.*[2]; (2) -cap, to patch the heels of stockings with cloth; (3) -cutter, a shoemaker; (4) -hole, the hole in the handle of a spade; (5) -leathers, leathers formerly worn over stockings to prevent too rapid wear by the clog; (6) -shaking-dancing; (7) -shod, having iron guards on the heels of shoes, &c.; (8) -speck, the shoe-heel piece; (9) -strop, *obs.,* the finishing touch, parting kick; (10) -tap, (*a*) *see* (8); (*b*) to repair the heel of a boot or shoe; (*c*) the remains of liquor left in a glass after drinking; *gen. in pl.*; in *gen.* colloq. use; (*d*) the last or end of anything; (*e*) *fig., pl.* as term of contempt used when speaking of a scandal; (*f*) *pl.* fried slices of potatoes; (11) -tree, (*a*) the cross-bar to which the traces are fastened, a 'swingle-tree'; (*b*) a raised piece of wood or stone forming a kerb or edge of the ' groop ' behind the cows in a cow-house.

(1) n.Yks. A think yo'd betər put biath hīlkākərs ən tiakākərs əmai biuts (W.H.). (2) Abd. The Gaudman sits and toasts his nose, Or awkwardly heel-caps his hose, BEATTIE *Parings* (1801) 31, ed. 1873. (3) Sc. A slang name; the shaping-knife is the symbol of the craft (G.W.). Edb. Duncan Imrie, the heel-cutter in the Flesh-market, MOIR *Mansie Wauch* (1828) ii. (4) Sh.I. I pair'd oot o' da heel-hole o' da spaed heft wi' me knife, *Sh. News* (Apr. 1, 1899). (5) Cum.[4] Thin leather shaped like the posterior half of a boot or clog (without the sole) only not quite so high these were worn, fastened in front, over the stocking so as to preserve it from the heavy wear of the clog. ' Hankutchers, and heel-ledders,' SARGISSON *Joe Scoap* (1881) 11. w.Yks. (J.T.) (6) Frf. Oor ain bumble heel-shakin's in some empty barn, WILLOCK *Rosetty Ends* (1886) 64, ed. 1889. (7) Ayr. Heelshod or taeshod and tacket and pin, Shaemaker, shaemaker shoo ma-shoon, AITKEN *Lays* (1883) 118. (8) n.Yks.[2] (9) Sc. I've been letting you see this year and a half the ill of that idolatrous worship of the Church of England, and now I shall give it the heel-strop, and show plainly that all that of this communion are damned, unless they repent, CALDER *Presbyt. Eloq.* (1694) 157, ed. 1847. (10, *a*) n.Cy. GROSE (1790) *MS. add.* w.Yks.[1], Lei.[1] Nhp.[1], Cor.[12] (*b*) Cor.[2] (*c*) Ayr. Seize the bottle and push it about; Don't fill on a heel-tap, it is not decorous, BOSWELL *Poet. Wks.* (1803) 26, ed. 1871. Ir. A stray invalid or two completing his course of the waters . . . he dare not budge till he has finished his 'heel tap' of abomination, LEVER *A. O'Leary* (1844) xvi.

Nhb. There is a stupid custom which prescribes that each man should 'drink fair,' and hence the expression 'Nee heel taps, noo,' when one has been shirking his quantity by leaving a little in the bottom of his glass (R.O.H.). s.Lan. (T.R.C.), Der.², nw.Der.¹, Lei.¹, War.² **Shr.¹** Now, drink up yore 'eel-taps, an' åve another jug. **Hnt.** Clear off your heel-taps (T.P.F.). **I.W.¹** Take off your heeltaps. **w.Som.¹** Come, drink fair—no heel-taps! **Dev.** You shall dine on the leavings and drink the heel-taps for your trouble, BARING-GOULD Spider (1887) vii. **Cor.¹²** Slang. Nick took off his heel taps, BARHAM Ingoldsby (ed. 1864) Lay of S. Cuthbert. (d) **Wil.** I have got a little nest-egg of your mother's money for you, and a heel-tap of your father's, BLACKMORE Kit (1890) I. xix. (e) **s.Lan.** (T.R.C.) (f) **s.Pem.** We'll 'ave soom heel-taps for dinner to-day (W.M.M.). (11, a) **n.Lin.¹ sw.Lin.¹** Defendant was charged with stealing two heel-trees. (b) **Cha.¹, s.Cha.¹**

2. Phr. (1) *heel and fling board*, a spring-board; used fig.; (2) *to get by the heel*, to overreach; (3) *heels over body*, (4) *— over craig*, (5) *— over gowdie* or *gourie*, head over heels, topsy-turvy; in a state of confusion or disorder; (6) *— over head*, (a) see (5); (b) without distinction or particular enumeration; (7) *to get the heels of*, to trip up; (8) *to give heels to*, curling term: to accelerate the progress of a stone by sweeping the ice in front of its path; (9) *to have the heels of*, to have the best of, take the first place; (10) *to make the heels crack*, to make haste; (11) *to put in by the heels*, see below; (12) *to take heels away*, (13) *to take one's heels*, to run away, take to one's heels; (14) *to turn a commodity heels over head*, to double the purchase price in re-selling; (15) *to turn up the heels*, to die; (16) *to give the wind of one's heels*, to take a hasty or speedy departure; (17) *shaking of one's heels*, dancing vigorously; (18) *heels foremost*, dead; (19) *heels upwards*, contrary, the wrong way, out of temper.

(1) **Ayr.** He's a back like a spring board—a rale heel-and-fling board, AITKEN Lays (1883) 137. (2) **s.Ap.¹** You have got me by the heel. (3) **Gall.** The cow, that was a noted kicker, spilled me and the milking-pail heels-over-body, CROCKETT Raiders (1894) xviii. (4) **Sc.** Twa or three hours spinnin' aboot a wheen meeserable lang-nebbed bottles, is eneuch to cowp them heels ower craig, Sc. Haggis, 122. (5) **Sc.** Heels-over-gowdie Tumbled the dowdy, DRUMMOND Muckomachy (1846) 42. **Abd.** I wadna think it manly work To turn ye heels-oer-gowdy, Just here, the night, COCK Strains (1810) II. 131. **Frf.** My mind sae wanders at whate'er I be, Gaes heels o'er gowdie, when the cause I see, MORISON Poems (1790) 121. **Slg.** Gude help us a'! she turn'd up heels o'er gourie, GALLOWAY Luncarty (1804) 57. **Ayr.** Soon heels-o'er-gowdie l in he gangs, BURNS Poem on Life (1796) st. 7. **Gall.** He gaed heels twvre gowdy without a bough [bark], MACTAGGART Encycl. (1824) 26, ed. 1876. (6, a) **Cai.¹ Abd.** I coupet Mungo's ale Clean heels o'er head, ROSS Helenore (1768) 69, ed. 1812; The house is heels o'er head, ib. 94. (b) **Sc.** (JAM.) (7) **Sc.** I'm thinking human learning is likely to get the heels of his grace, KEITH Bonnie Lady (1897) 92. (8) **Ayr.** The second and third players were sooping up, or giving heels to laggard stones, JOHNSTON Kilmallie (1891) II. 110. (9) **Fif.** For expressiveness I maun say I think 'dam' has the heels o't, MELDRUM Margrdiel (1894) 151. **Lth.** Your mem'ry's fine, An' has the heels by far o' mine, THOMSON Poems (1819) 181. (10) **Not.²** (11) **Ken.** To put a plant hastily in the soil when not convenient to plant it, so as to cover up the roots, is to put it in by the heels (J.A.B.). (12) **Rnf.** A' the hens Wi' fricht took soople heels awa Tae their hen-pens, NEILSON Poems (1877) 32. (13) **Bch.** I . . . gart the lymmers tak their heels, FORBES Ulysses (1785) 19; This made my lad at length to loup, And take his heels, ib. Dominie (1785) 27. **Edb.** They took their heels and left the field, LIDDLE Poems (1821) 298. (14) **Abd.** 'They tell me 't he turn't a stirkie't he bocht a fyou ouks syne heels-o'er-heid i' the last market.' But turning animals heels-o'er-head, technically, by doubling the purchase price, was not always easy, however sincere a man's intentions in that direction might be, ALEXANDER Ain Flk. (1882) 100. (15) **w.Yks.¹** (16) **Dmb.** Forbye ither reasons for being in a hurry, we thocht it as weel for me to gi'e Whinnyside the wind o' my heels without loss o' time, CROSS Disruption (1844) v. (17) **Per.** Gaily linkin' through the reels, an' shakin' o' her heels, FORD Harp (1893) 317. (18) **N.I.¹** Never! till A'm taken heels foremost. (19) **s.Suf.** He got up heels upwards this morning. Everything goes heels upwards with me now-a-days (F.H.).

3. The ball of the thumb or the back part of the inside of the hand; gen. in phr. *the heel of the hand*.

Ir. Laying the heel of his hand upon her shoulther, Paddiana (ed. 1848) I. 60. **N.I.¹ Glo.¹** The part of the hand above the wrist, opposite the thumb; **Glo.²** **Dor.** Common (C.K.P.). **Som.** Wi' a gurt nugget o' bread in the heel of his hand (W.F.R.). **w.Som.¹** The part of the hand on which it rests in the act of writing. 'Bad an', zir, urnd a gurt thurn into the heel o' un, and now he do mattery.' **Cor.¹**

4. The bottom end of anything erect or capable of being set up on end.
w.Som.¹ The heel of a post. 'There must be a new hanch to the gate, the heel o' un's a-ratted.'

5. The vertical timber of a gate, which bears the hinges. **n.Yks.** (I.W.)

6. The thickest end of the scissors-blade. **w.Yks.** (C.V.C.)

7. That part of a scythe-blade which is furthest from the point.
w.Yks.², Glo.¹ Nrf. Do you try my scythe, and let me try your'n. . . We'll go and take her in a peg. Drop the heel down, EMERSON Son of Fens (1892) 172.
Hence (1) **Heel-ring,** sb. the ring by means of which the blade of a scythe is fastened to the pole. **w.Mid.** (W.P.M.), Dev.²; (2) **-wedge,** sb. the wedge driven between the 'heel-ring' and the pole of a scythe, whereby the blade is held firmly in its place. **w.Mid.** (W.P.M.)

8. That part of an adze into which the handle is fitted; that part of the head of a golf-club which is nearest to the shaft. **Sc.** (JAM. Suppl.), **Lnk.** (JAM., s. v. Hoozle).
Hence **Heel,** v. to strike or hit with the 'heel' of a golf-club. **Sc.** (JAM. Suppl.)

9. The rear point of a plough-sock.
Nhb.¹ In a plough, the little-heel, sometimes called the hean, is the part gripping the sheth. [Heel of the plough, STEPHENS Farm Bk. (ed. 1849) I. 150.]

10. The stern of a boat.
Sh.I. Set ye my waands i' da heel o' da boat, Sh. News (June 25, 1898).

11. The fulcrum of a lever. **Nhb.¹ w.Yks.** Leeds Merc. Suppl. (Nov. 8, 1884) 8.

12. The bottom remaining crust of a loaf; the top crust of a loaf cut off.
Sc. The heel o' the white loaf that cam frae the Bailie's, SCOTT Waverley (1814) lxiv. **Edb.** (A.B.C.) **Gall.** Used commonly for the bottom slice of a loaf of bread (A.W.). **Ir.** She took out of her pocket a battered-looking heel of a loaf, BARLOW Lisconnel (1895) 56. **N.I.¹, Nhb.¹, w.Yks.¹, Lan.** (T.R.C.), **ne.Lan.¹ s.Wor.¹** Uncommon. **Shr.¹** 'Cut a loaf through to sen' to the leasow, that 'eel öönna be enough.' A remaining corner is called the heel of the loaf at Clun; **Shr.², Glo.¹, Oxf.** (G.O.) **Dor.** Gl. (1851).

13. The rind of cheese; last part of a cheese.
Dmb. I wouldna like to lay the kebbuc-heel upon the board the day, SALMON Gowodean (1868) 108. **Ayr.** Dinna, for a kebbuck-heel Let lasses be affronted, BURNS Holy Fair (1785) st. 25. **Gall.** The last portion of a vanishing cheese (A.W.). **w.Yks.¹, ne.Lan.¹, Glo.¹ Dor.** Gl. (1851).

14. The remains of tobacco left in a pipe after smoking.
Nrf. COZENS-HARDY Broad Nrf. (1893) 62. **e.Suf.** (F.H.)

15. Obs. The grounds or dregs of a barrel of beer. **Nhp.** RAY (1691).

16. Fig. The end, finish, last part, esp. in phr. *the heel of the evening*, &c.
Per. Wha kens but what we've seen the heel O' Simmer in a last farewell, HALIBURTON Ochil Idylls (1891) 64. **Ayr.** Towards the heel of the evening, GALT Legatees (1800) ii. **Gall.** He had the whole cogfull lapped into his kyte; when they came up, he was just at the heels o't, MACTAGGART Encycl. (1824) 409, ed. 1876. **Nhb.** At the heel of the evening they often diverge into matter as miscellaneous as the contents of a newspaper, WILSON Pitman's Pay (1826) Introd.; (R.O.H.); **Nhb.¹ Lan.** For I'd good luck at heel of aw, TIM BOBBIN View Dial. (1740) 57.

17. v. To run off, take to one's heels. *Preterite:* held.
Bch. She didna bide to mend it But heel't that night, TARRAS Poems (1804) 68 (JAM.). **Gall.** This broke the charm—than Sawners held it, Down the moor wi' speed he flew, MACTAGGART Encycl. (1824) 6, ed. 1876.

18. To pull or haul forth by the heels.
Fif. Heel him forth reluctant to the day, TENNANT Anster (1812) 144, ed. 1871.

S

HEEL, *v.*[2] Irel. Lin. Glo. Hmp. Wil. Dor. Som. Also in forms **hele** Hmp.[1] Wil.[1] Dor.[1]; **hyle** Wxf.[1] 1. To slope or lean over on one side. Cf. **heald**, *v.*[1]
sw.Lin.[1] The ground heels down to the dyke. He felt the wagon heel over.
2. To upset or overturn a bucket.
Glo. Don't heel the bucket (H.T.E.); *Gl.* (1851); Glo.[1]
3. To pour out; to pour out of one vessel into another. Cf. **hale**, *v.*[1] **hell**, *v.*
Hmp.[1] Wil. BRITTON *Beauties* (1825); Wil.[1] n.Wil. Hele the beer out o' thuc bottle into t'other (E.H.G.). Dor. Shall I hele ye out another cup? BARNES *Gl.* (1863); Dor.[1] While John did hele out each his drap O' eäle or cider, 131. Som. W. & J. *Gl.* (1873).
4. Of liquor or rain: to pour. Wxf.[1] Cf. **heald**, *v.*[1] **5**, **hell**, *v.*

HEEL, *v.*[3] Glo.[1] Of crops: to yield.
How does your wheat heel?

HEEL, HEELD, see **Heal**, *v.*[2], **Heald**, *v.*[1]

HEELER, *sb.* Irel. n.Cy. Yks. Lan. Suf. 1. A quick, active runner; one who keeps close behind in a foot-race.
n.Cy. (HALL.), w.Yks.[1] e.Suf. He is the closest heeler I ever had (F.H.).
2. A sharp, prying, managing woman. N.I.[1] **3.** A poser, a silencer. ne.Lan.[1]

HEELIEGOLEERIE, *adv.* and *sb.* Sc. Also in forms **heldigoleery, hildegaleerie; hildegulair, hilliegulier** Per. (JAM.); **hilliegileerie.** 1. *adv.* Topsy-turvy, in a state of confusion.
Ags.[1] (JAM.) Fif. Barley-pickles flee round and round Hilliegileerie 'mang the bree, TENNANT *Papistry* (1827) 39. e.Fif. Doon aged the riders heeligoleerie abune a', LATTO *Tam Bodkin* (1864) ii. Lnk. Love is a gey queer sensation. . . It puts ane a' hildegaleerie, When ance it breaks oot in a lowe, THOMSON *Musings* (1881) 232. Lth. A' wad gang heeliegoleery, Gin ye wanted wee Tam an' his drum, BALLANTINE *Poems* (1856) 135. Edb. BALLANTINE *Gaberlunzie* (ed. 1875) *Gl.* Peb. Langsyne, what a heldigoleery, Ilk priest was the fae o' a ball; But now their [they're] grown learned and cheery, AFFLECK *Poet. Wks.* (1836) 51.
2. *sb. pl.* Frolicsome tricks.
Sc. She's ony thing but glaikit wi' a' her hilliegeleeris, *Saint Patrick* (1819) I. 97 (JAM.).
[1. Ir. *uile-go-leir*, altogether (O'REILLY).]

HEELING, *sb.* Dev. The allowance made in handicapping children for racing; the distance from the heel of a runner to him who follows. *Reports Provinc.* (1891).

HEEL-RAKE, *sb.* Chs. Lei. War. Wor. Shr. Hrf. Glo. Oxf. Brks. Mid. I.W. Also in forms **eldrake** Shr.[1]; **eller-rake** Chs.[1]; **ell-** Chs.[1] s.Chs.[1] War.[4] se.Wor.[1] Shr.[1] Hrf. Brks.[1] Mid.; **haul-** Glo.[1]; **hel-** War.[24] s.War.[1] Oxf.[1]; **hell-** Chs.[1] Lei.[1] War.[4] s.Wor.[1] Hrf.[2] Glo.[1] I.W.[1]; **hull-** Glo.[1] [i'l-, e'lrek.] A large rake, with curved iron teeth, used to clear the field in harvest after the greater part of the crop has been gathered.
Chs.[1] Usually drawn by two men. s.Chs.[1] Strong market-shandry with calf-cratches, set of thrill-gears, odd gears, shoval and yelve, heelrake, *Auctioneer's Cat.* (Apr. 9, 1887). Lei. Spring-teeth rakes ' by the lower class of people are called hell-rakes, on account of the great quantity of work they dispatch in a short time, *Reports Agric.* (1793-1813) 21; Lei.[1] War. MORTON *Cyclo. Agric.* (1863); War.[3] War.[4] Bring the ell-rake, Walt; us must carry the nine acre afore night. s.War.[1] s.Wor. PORSON *Quaint Wds.* (1875) 13; (H.K.); s.Wor.[1], se.Wor.[1] Shr. He used the 'ellrake in that field (K.P.); Shr.[1] Theer'll be mighty little lef' fur the laisers; they'n bin draggin' that ell-rake ever sence daylight. Shr., Hrf. BOUND *Provinc.* (1876). Hrf.[2] Glo. In this district (the Cotswolds) we *gen.* suppose the derivation to be from the rake being an ell in width. In the vale however (about Tewkesbury) they are called heel-rakes, from their being drawn at the heel of the person using them, instead of being used in front, as rakes ordinarily are, *N. & Q.* (1851) 1st S. iv. 260; Glo.[1], Oxf.[1], Brks.[1] w.Mid. We call them ell-rakes, but their proper name is heel-rake, most likely because they are drawn at one's heels (W.P.M.). I.W.[1]

HEELSTER-GOWDIE, *adv.* Bnff.[1] Head o'ver heels. Cf. *heel*-*over*-*gowdie*, s. v. **Heel**, *sb.* **2** (5).
The loon fell an' geed heelster-gowdie doon the brae.

HEELY, *adj.*, *v.*[1] and *sb.* Sc. Also written **healey** n.Sc.; **heally** Mry. (JAM.); **hehlie** Bnff.[1]; **heilie** Inv.

Bnff. Fif. [hi'li.] 1. *adj.* Haughty, proud, full of disdain; crabbed, ill-tempered. Cf. **heloe.**
Inv. (H.E.F.) Bnff. GREGOR *Notes to Dunbar* (1893) 195. Fif. (JAM.)
2. *v.* To look upon with disdain, to hold in slight esteem. Bnff.[1] Ye needna cast yir hehd that wye, an' hehllie the dress. It's our gueede for ye.
3. To take an affront in silence. Mry. *Gl. Surv.* (JAM.)
4. To abandon, forsake with disdain.
A bird forsaking her nest and eggs heallies it, *ib.*
5. *sb.* Consciousness of insult, dudgeon.
n.Sc. But he had a high spirit, an' just out o' the healey awa' he went, MILLER *Scenes and Leg.* (1853) xviii. Bnff.[1]
Hence **Heiliefow**, *adj.* full of disdain.
Bnff. She's a heiliefow limmer, GREGOR (*l.c.*); Bnff.[1]
[1. Hely (*v.r.* heilie) harlottis on hawtane wyiss, DUNBAR *Poems* (c. 1510), ed. Small, II. 118; Roboam quhilk throw his helie pride Tint all his lcigis hartis, DOUGLAS *Pal. Hon.* (1501), ed. 1874, 59.]

HEELY, *adv.* and *v.*[2] Sc. Also written **healy** n.Sc.
1. *adv.* Slowly, softly; also used as *adj.* Cf. **hooly.**
Sc. 'Healy, healy,' John cried, addressing one of the nuts, ROY *Horseman's Wd.* (1895) i. n.Sc. O healy, healy take me up, And healy set me down, BUCHAN *Ballads* (1848) I. 99, ed. 1875. Cai. Abd. Common in exclamatory use (H.E.F.)
2. *v.* To wait; *gen.* in *imper.*
Abd. Ye ees't to be gey gweed at garrin' the ba' row 's yer nain fit ca'd it; but heely till we see ye conter Maggie! ALEXANDER *Ain Flk.* (1882) 75; Heely, heely, Tam, *ib. Johnny Gibb* (1871) i.

HEEM. The same as **Aim**, *adj.* (q.v.)

HEEMER, *comp. adj.* Lakel. Also written **heemur** Wm. Higher.
Lakel.[2] A bit heemer up ner that. Wm. Ah'll tak t'heemur o' them tweea (B.K.).

HEEMEST, HEEN, see **Highmost, Eye,** *sb.*[1], **Hean,** *sb.*[1]

HEEMLIN, *adj.* Sc. Humiliating, 'humbling.'
Abd. A' this heemlin creengin to the Coort o' Session, ALEXANDER *Johnny Gibb* (1871) xxii.

HEEMLIN', *ppl. adj.* Bnff.[1] Applied to a continual, rumbling sound.

HEENESS, *sb.* Nhb. Height. 'It's nee heeness' (R.O.H.)

HEEP, see **Heap,** *sb.*[1]

HEEPIE-CREEP, *adv.* Sc. In a creeping, sneaking manner.
Lnk. No for that gang heepie-creep, But still wi' manly frame, MURDOCH *Doric Lyre* (1873) 47.

HEEPY, *sb.* Obs. Sc. 1. A fool; a stupid person. Also used *attrib.*
Lnk. Maggy ken'd the wyte, and sneer'd, Cau'd her a poor daft heepy, RAMSAY *Poems* (ed. 1800) I. 273 (JAM.).
2. A melancholy person.
Rnf. PICKEN *Poems* (1788) *Gl.* (JAM.)

HEER, see **Hair, Hier.**

HEERBREEADS, *sb. pl.* Yks. The back and front cross-bars in the frame of the bottom of a cart. w.Yks. (J.J.B.) See **Ear,** *sb.*[1] **2** (4).

HEERINSEUGH, HEERINSEW, see **Heronsew.**

HEERYESTREEN. The same as **ere yestreen,** s. v. Ere, *prep.* **2** (3).

HEESE, HEESEL, HEEST, see **Heeze, Hisself, Haste,** *v.*

HEESTERIN, *sb. Obsol.* Nhb. A handle for hoisting or lifting up.
They've putten a new heesterin on the pant (R.O.H.); Nhb.[1]

HEET, see **Hait.**

HEETHENBERRY, *sb.* Chs.[1] The fruit of the hawthorn, *Crataegus Oxyacantha.*

HEEVAL, HEEVE, see **Evil,** *sb.*[2], **Eve,** *v.*

HEEVIL, *sb.* Sc. The conger-eel, *Conger vulgaris.* Lth. NEILL *Fishes* (1810) 2 (JAM.).

HEEVY-SKEEVY, see **Havey-cavey.**

HEEZE, *v.* and *sb.* Sc. Irel. Nhb. Lakel. Cum. Yks. I.Ma. Also written **hease** Kcd.; **heese** Sc. n.Cy. Cum.[14]; and in forms **heis** Sc. (JAM.); **heise** Abd. I.Ma.; **heize** Fif.; **hease** Dmf.; **heyce** e.Yks.[1]; **hiese** Rxb.; **hise** Sh.I. Lnk.; **hize** N.I.[1]; **hyze** Bnff. [h)iz.] 1. *v.* To hoist, heave, raise, lift; also *fig.* to elevate, exalt. Cf. **hoise.**
Sc. The sailor wha's been lang at sea, On waves like mountains

heezed, *Shepherd's Wedding* (1789) 20. **Sh.I.** I wid staand an' luik ta da boats hisin' der sails, *Sh. News* (Nov. 5, 1898). **Elg.** Bunyan's louping-on-stane too, Whilk dreich-a—a'd Christians heez'd, COUPER *Poetry* (1804) II. 70. **Bnff.** How shall a Norlan' Bard, o' speech unkempt, To hyze remembrance to the bin attempt, TAYLOR *Poems* (1787) 136. **Abd.** Bind a laurel roun' her brow, An' heeze her to the sky, STILL *Cottar's Sunday* (1845) 152. **Frf.** High hoez'd by fame, MORISON *Poems* (1790) 99. **Per.** The friendly Bard Wha first should heese me up to fame, SPENCE *Poems* (1898) 146. **Fif.** Now, had the Sun's meridian chair Been heiz'd up heicher i' the air, TENNANT *Papistry* (1827) 8. **Slg.** Gude folk I like to heeze them, But rogues I ay will satirize them, GALLOWAY *Poems* (1792) 42. **Rnf.** When she saw our Johnnie's face, She set hersel' to please, And heezed him up wi' buttered scones, BARR *Poems* (1861) 162. **Ayr.** Still higher may they heeze Ye in bliss, BURNS *Dream.* st. 9. **Lnk.** Up to the starns I'm heezed, RAMSAY *Poems* (1721) 182. **e.Lth.** Heezin' hissel frae the tae leg on to the tither, HUNTER *J. Inwick* (1895) 27. **Edb.** Seyin' what he can To heeze up . . . A thocht o' ither days, McDOWALL *Poems* (1830) 221. **Slk.** It was heezing upon the tae side and myntyng to whommil me, HOGG *Tales* (1838) 110, ed. 1866. **Rxb.** The haly page abread he hiest, RUICKBIE *Wayside Cottager* (1807) 130. **Dmf.** His comrades . . . Heeze up his carcase on a chair, MAYNE *Siller Gun* (1808) 70. **Kcb.** John heez'd his cap An' gied the claith the ither chap, DAVIDSON *Seasons* (1789) 65. **N.I.**[1] **n.Cy.** *Border Gl.* (*Coll.* L.L.B.) ; **N.Cy.**[1], **Nhb.**[1], **Lakel.**[2], **Cum.**[14] **e.Yks.**[1] Roger lend us a hand to heyce this seck o' floor intl caat. **n.Yks.** (I.W.) **I.Ma.** I heis'ed a lil to one side to make room, RYDINGS *Tales* (1895) 38.

Hence **Heissing**, *sb.* a hoisting, lifting, shrugging. **I.Ma.** Givin' a lil heissin' wis his shouldars, lik he did in the pulfit, RYDINGS *Tales* (1895) 39.

2. To rock with a swinging motion ; to toss, dandle a child ; to dance. **Slg.** Nane can heeze the highland fling Like merry light Miss Drummond, GALLOWAY *Nelson* (1806) 16. **Nhb.**[1] Heeze a ba babby on the tree top. **Cum.** (M.P.)

Hence **Heezing**, *sb.* a rocking, tossing. **Nhb.**[1] Aa gat sic a heezin on the shuggy-shoe.

3. To carry, hurry ; to travel fast, push on. **Sc.** Aff they heezed her awa' to Glasgow, *Scotch Haggis*, 78. **Lnk.** How grim loom the mountains as onwards we heeze, NICHOLSON *Idylls* (1870) 20.

4. *sb.* A hoist, heave, lift up ; *fig.* aid, help, furtherance. **Bnff.** Robie after her did run To gie' r a hyze, TAYLOR *Poems* (1787) 92. **Abd.** Gi'en an auld wife a heise afore she wear awa, CADENHEAD *Bon Accord* (1853) 186. **Kcd.** He quickly gied the bags a heise, JAMIE *Muse* (1844) 102. **Ags.** (JAM.) **Frf.** Should plenty gie thy kyte a heeze, MORISON *Poems* (1790) 95. **Rnf.** It needs nae ither heeze To gar its fluid [flood] rin faster, PICKEN *Poems* (1813) I. 97. **Lnk.** It might rise, An' after by them get a hise, WATT *Poems* (1887) 8. **Edb.** Braid Claith lends fock an unco heese, FERGUSSON *Poems* (1773) 127, ed. 1785. **Rxb.** Business gets a noble heeze, A. SCOTT *Poems* (ed. 1808) 83. **Dmf.** Frae the Laird's han' gat mony a lad . . . A quiet hese up Fortune's brae, THOM *Jock o' Knowe* (1878) 56. **I.Ma.** Give me a heise with this, on to me back (S.M.).

5. A toss, twist, lift of the head, &c. **Wgt.** Cock yer lugs, if you please, Gie yer head a bit heeze, FRASER *Poems* (1885) 47. **I.Ma.** He gave me a Hm! and a heise of his neck, CAINE *Manxman* (1895) pt. v. iii.

6. A swing ; the act or instrument of swinging. **Lth.** We're just takin' a heeze on the yett, *Marriage* (1818) II. 392 (JAM.).

[1. Than all sammyn, with handis, feit, and kneis, Did heis thar sail, DOUGLAS *Eneados* (1513), ed. 1874, II. 274. Dan. *heise*, to hoist ; cogn.w.LG. *hisen* (Bremen dial. (*Wtb.*) ; EFris. *hisen* (*hisen*), 'hissen' (KOOLMAN).]

HEEZY, *sb.* Sc. Irel. Also written **heasie** Gall. ; **heisie** Sc. (JAM.) [hī′zɪ.] **1.** A hoist, heave ; a lift or help upwards. See Heeze, *sb.* 4. **Sc.** If he had stuck by the way, I would have lent him a heezie, SCOTT *Guy M.* (1815) xiii. **Rnf.** It yet will get its heezy, PICKEN *Poems* (1813) I. 148. **Lnk.** Hamilton the bauld and gay Lends me a heezy, RAMSAY *Poems* (1721) 189. **Lth.** My heart it gat a heezie Wi' joy, BRUCE *Poems* (1813) II. 70. **Gall.** His memory shall not perish ; it has got a famous heazie already, MACTAGGART *Encycl.* (1824) 33, ed. 1876. **Kcb.** Get a heezy o'er the sleugh o' want, DAVIDSON *Seasons* (1789) 9. **Ant.** 'Send him a heezie,' send him a lift ; used contemptuously, GROSE (1790) *MS. add.* (C.)

Hence **Blanket-heezie**, *sb.* one who tosses another in a blanket. This wark O' blanket-heezies stout and stark, TENNANT *Papistry* (1827) 130.

2. A tossing, anything that discomposes one. **Sc.** One is said to get a heisie in a rough sea (JAM.) ; They wad hae gotten an unco heezy, SCOTT *Bride of Lam.* (1819) xxiv. **Slk.** She's gi'en my heart an unco heezy, HOGG *Poems* (ed. 1865) 272. **Kcb.** To see ilk flegging witless coof Get o'er his thum' a heezy, DAVIDSON *Seasons* (1789) 16.

HEF, HEFFALD, HEFFUL, see Half, Hickwall.

HEFFER, *v.* Nhb. [he′fər.] To laugh vulgarly. **Nhb.**[1] Hence **Hefferin'**, *ppl. adj.* laughing in an imbecile fashion. He's a greet hefferin feul (R.O.H.) ; **Nhb.**[1]

HEFFLE, HEFFUT, see Haffle, *v.*, Evet.

HEFT, *sb.*[1] and *v.*[1] Sc. Irel. and midl. and s. counties of Eng. Also Amer. Also in forms **heifteen, heiftem** Wxf.[1]; **hift** e.An.[1] Dor. [h)eft.] **1.** *sb.* Weight, esp. the weight of a thing as ascertained by weighing it in the hand. Also used *fig.* **Wxf.**[1] Th' heiftem o' pley vell all ing to lug [The weight of the play fell into the hollow], 86. **Lin.** THOMPSON *Hist. Boston* (1856) 709 ; **Lin.**[1] The garthmen guessed it at ten stun heft. **Nhp.**[2] What's th' heft on't? **War.**[8] **w.Wor.**[1] That pan is real good iron, 'tis sold by heft. **s.Wor.** Feel th' 'eft on it, a's desput 'eavy (H.K.) ; **s.Wor.**[1] **Shr.**[1] A dead heft is a weight that cannot be moved ; **Shr.**[2], **Hrf.**[12] **Pem.** There's a heft in this (E.D.). **s.Pem.** There's a good heft in this 'ere block (W.M.M.) ; LAWS *Little Eng.* (1888) 420. **Glo.** I think the heft may be 4 lb. (A.B.) ; ELLIS *Pronunc.* (1889) V. 66 ; **Glo.**[12] **Brks.** That be a good heft (M.J.B.). **Ken.**[1] This here heeve 'll stand very well for the winter, just feel the heft of it. **Hmp.** The heft of the branches, WISE *New Forest* (1883) 188 ; I zee the gurt bell, too, and I was told the heft on 'un, *Forester's Miscell.* (1846) 166 ; **Hmp.**[1] **I.W.** 'Look at the heft of 'n,' said the proud father, ' entirely drags ye down, Miss Sibyl, 'e do,' GRAY *Annesley* (1889) I. 260 ; (J.D.R.) ; **I.W.**[1] 'Tes the deuce o' one heft ; ' it's a great weight. **Wil.** BRITTON *Beauties* (1825) ; SLOW *Gl.* (1892) ; **Wil.**[1] What heft is that parcel ? i. e. what weight is it ? **Dor.** A body plump's a goodish lump, Where reames ha' such a heft, BARNES *Gl.* (1869–70) 3rd S. 22 ; I cant maike it out How he can bear up sich a hift, YOUNG *Rabin Hill* (1864) 2. **Som.** Whatever tes, the heft es jest-the zame, AGRIKLER *Rhymes* (1872) 9 ; JENNINGS *Obs. Dial. w.Eng.* (1825) ; W. & J. *Gl.* (1873) ; SWEETMAN *Wincanton Gl.* (1885). **w.Som.**[1] The only word used to express ponderance. 'Weight' (q.v.) in the dialect means something quite different. ' You'll sure to catch a cold ! your things be so light's vanity, there id'n no. heft in em.' **Dev.** Dawntee vind thickee maid a purty gîide heft tû câr var ! HEWETT *Peas. Sp.* (1892) ; **Dev.**[4] **n.Dev.** Nell isn't a gurt fustîlugs O' cart-hoss heft, ROCK *Jim an' Nell* (1867) st. 62. [Amer. Constitoounts air hendy to help a man in, But arterwards don't weigh the heft of a pin, LOWELL *Biglow Papers* (1848) I. iv. 135 ; *Dial. Notes* (1896) 379.]

Hence **Hefty**, *adj.* heavy, weighty, ponderous ; also used *fig.* **Per.** She bein' a muckle denty wife, an' rael hefty, he coupet in himsel' an' got sair drookit, CLELAND *Inchbracken* (1883) 147, ed. 1887. **Brks.** (M.J.B.), **n.Wil.** (G.E.D.) **Som.** A hefty-lookin pictur—need hev a strongish naail, AGRIKLER *Rhymes* (1872) 59. [Amer. It was not a very hefty speech, *Dial. Notes* (1896) 379.]

2. The act of heaving ; an effort, heave, lift ; strength, heaving. **s.Chs.**[1] **Der.** Giving a sudden mighty heft that was intended to do the work, CUSHING *Voe* (1888) I. i ; It was a tremendous heft to raise the boat on to the wall, *ib.* II. x. **e.An.**[1] **Dev.** The sturdy parson . . . gave the stuck wheel such a powerful heft that the old cart rattled, BLACKMORE *Christowell* (1881) iii.

3. *Phr. at my heft, fig.* at my convenience or leisure. **Hrf.**[1], **Glo.**[1]

4. A shooting pain. **w.Wor.**[1] I've got such a heft in my side I canna scahrsely draw my breath.

5. *v.* To lift, raise, uplift. **Sc.** Mr. Paul hefted the wean, STEEL *Rowan* (1895) 129. **Kcb.** There to the beetling rock he hefts his prey, DAVIDSON *Seasons* (1789) 3. **War.**[2] **Wor.** It's too heavy to heft (W.B.). **m.Wor.** Heft this ! (J.C.) **w.Wor.** A bigger load than he could well heft, S. BEAUCHAMP *Grantley Grange* (1874) I. 30 ; **w.Wor.**[1] Do carr' this paay'l [pail] far mê, I canna heft it when it's full o' watter.

s.Wor. (H.K.), s.Wor.¹, Shr.², Hrf.² Glo. Ah! you know when you hefted one of thaay sheaves o' hissen, BUCKMAN *Darke's Sojourn* (1890) 197; ELLIS *Pronunc.* (1889) V. 66. Oxf.¹ Used in the sense of 'to lift' at Yarnton. Suf. (C.T.) Ess. But lor, he heft them peas up on his fork! DOWNE *Ballads* (1895) 29. Hmp. (H.E.); I can heft anything you like to name with any man of forty, GRAY *Heart of Storm* (1891) I. 37. I.W.¹ Som. W. & J. *Gl.* (1873). w.Som.¹ I don't think you be man enough vor to hef thick. Dev. Dñee, plaixe, tñ heft theãse flasket up 'pon my showlder; 'e's drefful 'eavy, HEWETT *Peas. Sp.* (1892).

6. To weigh in the hand; to lift in order to judge of the weight.

se.Wor.¹ Just heft this 'ere young un, yunt 'e a weight? Shr.¹ 'W'y, Betty, han yo' carried that basket all the way?' 'Iss, an' yo' jest heft it.' s.Pem. Poor 'l Jack is improvin' wonderful now laâtely; heft'n you (W.M.M.). Glo.¹² Oxf. ELLIS *Pronunc.* (1889) V. 128; Oxf.¹ Um bee prop·uur ev·i, dhee jest eft um ['Em be proper 'eavy, dhee jest 'eft 'em]. Brks. That basket is a weight, you just heft it then (W.H.E.); Brks.¹ A woman selling a turkey will say 'heft 'un.' Hmp. 'To heft the bee-pots,' is to lift them in order to judge how much honey they contain, WISE *New Forest* (1883) 188; Hmp.¹ I.W. (J.D.R.); I.W.² Jest heft it wull 'ee, you. Wil.¹ Som. Just you heft it, Sir—you'll see what a heft it is (W.F.R.). w.Som.¹ He's a very nice pullet, only please to hef'm—to try the heft o' your own zul. nw.Dev.¹ e.Dev. He took up a root or two here and there, and 'hefted it' (that is to say, poised it carefully to judge the weight, as one does a letter for the post), BLACKMORE *Perlycross* (1894) viii. [Nfld. *Trans. Amer. Flk-Lore Soc.* (1894).]

7. To throw, heave.

Dev. Take an' heft tha bagger intñ tha river. A gûde dowsing 'ull take tha liquor out o' 'n, HEWETT *Peas. Sp.* (1892); Heft they into the watter, BLACKMORE *Christowell* (1881) ii; Zober, passon, zober! or we'll heft 'un over tother zide, *ib.* iii.

8. Of bread, &c.: to rise.

Dev. My bread's hefting fine, O'NEILL *Idyls* (1892) 38.

Hence **Hefting**, *vbl. sb.* the rising of yeast or barm in bread, &c.

Dev. After I've paid for a drop of barm for the hefting, *ib.* 41.

[1. How shall my prince and uncle now sustain ... so great a heft? HARINGTON *Ariosto* (1591) xliii (NARES). 2. He cracks his gorge, his sides, With violent hefts, SHAKS. *Wint. T.* ii. i. 45.]

HEFT, *sb.*² and *v.*² Sc. n.Cy. Dur. Lakel. Cum. Also in forms haft Sc.; heff s.Sc. (JAM.) Slk. [heft.] 1. *sb.* An accustomed pasture; *fig.* a dwelling, place of rest, domicile; a haunt. Cf. heaf, *sb.*¹

Sc. She came to fetch her out of ill haft and waur guiding, SCOTT *Midlothian* (1818) xviii. Bch. When I found myself infeft In a young Jack, I did resolve to change the haft, FORBES *Dominie* (1785) 46. s.Sc. (JAM.) Slk. A weel-hained heff, and a beildy lair, HOGG *Brownie of Bodsbeck* (1818) I. 287 (JAM.). Rxb. The haunt which a sheep adopts, in the language of shepherds, is called its 'haft,' YOUNG *Annals Agric.* (1784–1815) XXVII. 185. N.Cy.¹

2. *v.* To accustom sheep to a new pasture.

Slk. (JAM.) Gall. I had been 'hefting' (as the business is called in our Galloway land) a double score of lambs which had just been brought from a neighbouring lowland farm to summer upon our scanty upland pastures. Now it is the nature of sheep to return if they can to their mother-hill, or at least to stray farther and farther off, seeking some well known landmark. So, till such new comers grow satisfied and 'heft' (or attach) themselves to the soil, they must be watched carefully both night and day, CROCKETT *Standard Bearer* (1898) 6; Animals are said to be hafted, when they live contentedly on strange pastures, when they have made a haunt, MACTAGGART *Encycl.* (1824).

Hence **Hefter**, *sb.* a man employed to watch sheep, when first taken to a new pasture, to prevent them breaking dike.

Gall. Ye'll no' dee like the hefter o' the Star, .. when he cam to heft hoggs, CROCKETT *Moss-Hags* (1895) xli.

3. To dwell, live; to cause or accustom to live in a place, to become domiciled. *Gen. in pp.*

Sc. Do not meet till he is hefted as it were to his new calling, SCOTT *Redg.* (1824) Lett. ix; HERD *Coll. Sngs.* (1776) *Gl.* Abd. Besides I'm tauld, the singin' lasses That heft sae aft about Parnassus, SKINNER *Poems* (1809) 43. Lnk. Ill nature hefts in sauls that's weak and poor, RAMSAY *Gentle Shep.* (1725) 33, ed.

1783; He is not yet properly hefted into the ways of the world, FRASER *Whaups* (1895) vii. Dmf. You will find yourself much more comfortable than you have been in your old place, if once you are fairly hafted to the new one, CARLYLE *Lett.* (1846) in *Atlantic Monthly* (1898) LXXXII. 681. Lakel.² He gat hissel fairly weel hefted in, an' nin o' them cud touch him.

Hence (1) **Heffing**, *sb.* keeping, maintenance, sustenance; (a) **Hefted**, *ppl. adj.* (a) accustomed, wonted; (b) of mountain sheep: let along with a farm and depastured on a particular part of the common or fell called their heaf (q.v.).

(1) Slk. (JAM.); Gin I had the heffing o' them, HOGG *Tales* (1898) 618, ed. 1866. (2, a) Dur. In a hefted manner (K.). '(b) Cum.¹⁴

HEFT, *sb.*³ and *v.*³ Sc. Cum. Wm. Yks. Lan. 1. *sb.* A pretext, excuse; deception, deceit, dissimulation.

Cum.⁴ n.Yks.¹; n.Yks.² 'That was t'heft on 'em,' their sly way of handling the matter. ne.Yks.¹ It's all heft. m.Yks.¹

2. *v.* To prevaricate. Cum.¹⁴

Hence **Hefter**, *sb.* a prevarication; a romancer or teller of incredible stories.

Cum.¹⁴ Lan. 'Thow's larnt me summat I duddent kna afooar, an' I'se obleegt ta the'; but I thowt ta mesell, 'That is a hefter,' R. PIKETAH *Forness Flk.* (1876) 11.

3. To nonplus, pose; to punish, vex.

Sc. GROSE (1790) *MS. add.* (C.) Cum.⁴ He did heft him.

Hence (1) **Hefter**, *sb.* an effective speech or operation; a poser, 'clincher'; anything very large; (a) **Hefting**, *sb.* a beating; *fig.* an effective and decisive attack.

(1) Cum.¹⁴ Wm. Thoo's a hefter mi lad, en better ner enny doctor, ROBISON *Aald Taales* (1882) 17. n.Lan.¹ (2) Lakel.² Ah gat a heftin wi tryin' ta carry that pig on mi rig. Cum.¹⁴

[1. A *fig.* use of haft, *sb.*¹]

HEFT, *v.*⁴ Sc. Irel. Nhb. Dur. Cum. Wm. Also in form haft N.I.¹ To confine or restrain nature; esp. to let a cow's milk increase until the udder gets large and hard, as is done with milch cows taken to market. *Gen. in pass.*

Sc. A cow's milk is said to be heftit, when it is not drawn off for some time. .. One is said to be heftit, when in consequence of long retention of urine, the bladder is painfully distended (JAM.)-Buff.¹ Flf. The terror of bringing her home heftet, .. the effect of grazing among wet clover, COLVILLE *Vernacular* (1899) 15. N.I.¹, N.Cy.¹ Nhb. A cow 'hefts well,' that is, gorges in the udder till it is distended. When the milk flows from the paps she 'will not heft' or she 'hefts ill' (R.O.H.); Nhb.¹ s.Dur. Her ure [udder] was ter'ble hefted (J.E.D.). n.Cum. ELLWOOD (1895)-Wm. If a cow's udder is loose and flaccid it is said 'she will not heft' or 'she hefts ill' (T.H.). [You also see the impropriety of hefting ... the milk in cows until the udder is distended, STEPHENS *Farm Bk.* (ed. 1849) I. 522.]

Hence **Hefted milk**, *phr.*, see below.

Nhb. A cow is put dry for some time before calving; and after calving the milk is called 'beasting' or 'hefted' milk (R.O.H.).

[Norw. dial. *hefta*, to bind, restrain (AASEN).]

HEFT, *v.*⁵ Yks. To hurry, hasten.

w.Yks. He did heft it (J.T.).

HEFT, see Haft, *sb.*¹, Heave.

HEFTIN, *ppl. adj.* Yks. Adhering, clinging to. See Heft, *v.*⁴

w.Yks. Great heftin chignons, *Nidderdill Olm.* (1880); LUCAS *Stud. Nidderdale* (c. 1882) *Gl.*

HEFTY, *adj.* e.An. Of wind or weather: rough; boisterous, wild.

e.An.¹ Nrf. Rum night this, hefty weather, don't it blow and snow, EMERSON *Lagoons* (ed. 1896) 98; A few flakes of snow and a hailstorm tore across the floods. 'An omen of hefty weather,' the keeper said, *ib.* 120; A hefty sea (A.G.). Suf. A hefty night (C.G.B.).

[Du. *heftigh*, vehement (HEXHAM); G. *heftig.*]

HEG, see Hag, *sb.*¹

HEG-BEG, *sb.* Sc. The nettle.

Sc. If ye touch Heg-beg, Heg-beg will gar you fyke, CHAMBERS *Pop. Rhymes* (1870) 109. Gall. An old riddle respecting the nettle runs this way—' Heg Beg adist the dyke—and Heg Beg ayont the dyke—Gif ye touch Heg Beg—Heg Beg—will gar ye byke, MACTAGGART *Encycl.* (1824) 10, ed. 1876.

HEG-BERRY, see Hagberry.

HEG(G, *v.* and *sb.* Nhb. Dur. Cum. Wm. [heg.]

1. *v.* To set the teeth on edge.

Cum. We caw them hegberries because they heg our teeth

(B. & H.). **Wm.** Eat those heg-berries and they will heg your teeth (B.K.).

2. To rue, repent of doing a thing. Nhb.[1]

3. *sb.* A spite, grudge.

a.Dur. She has a hegg at him [she spites him] (J.E.D.).

HEG(G, see Egg, *v.*

HEGGAN, *sb.* Cor. A hard, dry cough. THOMAS *Randigal Rhymes* (1895) *Gl.* Cf. hack, *sb.*[1] 18.

HEGGLE, HEGGR, HEGH, see Haggle, *v.*[1], **Higgle, Hagger,** *v.*[2], **Hech.**

HEGHEN, *sb.* Ayr. (JAM.) Also written hechen. The fireside.

HEGHLE, see Hechle, *v.*

HEGHT, *sb.* Obs. Sc. A heavy fall.

Gall. (JAM.) Keb. Laying the rosy weans upo' the floor Wi' donsy heght, DAVIDSON *Seasons* (1789) 28 (*ib.*).

HEGHT, HEGLE, see Hight, *v.*[1], **Higgle.**

HEGLET, HEGLUT, see Eglet.

HEG-PEG BUSHES, *phr.* Glo.[1] The blackthorn, *Prunus spinosa.*

HEGRIE, see Haigrie.

HEGRIL'S SKIP, *phr.* Sh.I. The heron, *Ardea cinerea.* SWAINSON *Birds* (1885) 144. Cf. skip hegrie.

HEGS, *int.* Sc. Also in form haigs e.Fif. [hegz.] An exclamation ; a petty oath, 'fegs.' Cf. halth.

Cai.[1] e.Fif. Haigs, it cheats me, LATTO *Tam Bodkin* (1864) ii. Rnf. Hegs, Jock, gin ye war here like me [Fegs, ed. 1813], PICKEN *Poems* (1788) 53 (JAM.). Lak. Hegs, when the Minister body cam' in The sorry a biddin' he needit but ane, WATSON *Poems* (1853) 35.

HEH, HEHLLIE, HEI, see Hech, Heely, *adj.,* **Aye,** *adv.*[1]

HEI, HEICH, HEICK, see He, Hech, High, Hike.

HEID, HEIDEN, see Head, Hide, *v.*[2], **Haden.**

HEIFER, *sb.* and *v.* Var. dial. forms and uses in Sc. Irel. and Eng.   **I.** Dial. forms : (1) Arfer, (2) Ayfer, (3) Haffer, (4) Haffer, (5) Harfer, (6) Heckfor, (7) Heifker, (8) Hiver, (9) Yaffer, (10) Yeffer, (11) Yeifer.

(1) ne.Ken. I've bought an â(r)fə(r) dis marnin' (H.M.). (2) se.Wor.[1], Glo.[1] (3) Sus.[1] (4) Shr.[1] (5) Sus.[1] (6) n.Cy. GROSE (1790). e.Nrf. MARSHALL *Rur. Econ.* (1787). (7) e.An.[1], Nrf. (HALL.) (8) Wxf.[1] (9) Dev. HEWETT *Peas. Sp.* (189a) ; Dev.[2] n.Dev. That prime yaffer That's down in Goiley Mead, ROCK *Jim an' Nell* (1867) st. 73. nw.Dev.[1] s.Dev., e.Cor. (Miss D.), Cor.[12] (10) w.Som.[1] A maiden yeffer. Cor.[2] (11) Dev.[1]

II. Dial. uses.   **1.** *sb.* In *comp.* Heifer-stirk, a one-year-old cow calf.

w.Yks. Theaze heifer stirks are worth £600 a peice, LUCAS *Stud. Nidderdale* (c. 1882) 32.

2. A young cow with its first calf.

e.Suf. A cow is so called till she has calved twice (F.H.). Som. (W.F.R.), Dev.[2]

3. *v.* To earmark castrated cows.

Gall. All castrated females [kine] are marked in the ear ; to mark them so is to heifer them, MACTAGGART *Encycl.* (1824) 432, ed. 1876.

[1. (6) Hekfere, beeste . . . *juvenca, Prompt.* ; Hekfere, *buccula, Pict. Voc.* (c. 1475) in Wright's *Voc.* (1884) 758. (7) A yonge hefker, *Found. St. Bartholomew's* (c. 1425) 41.]

HEIFFLE, *sb.* Fif. (JAM.) [Not known to our correspondents.] A 'toolyie' with a young wench.

HEIFTEEN, HEIFTEM, see Heft, *sb.*

HEIGH, *int.* and *v.* Sc. Irel. Nhb. Dur. Cum. Wm. Yks. Lan. Der. Not. Lin. Glo. Som. Dev. Also written hey Sc. e.Dur.[1] w.Yks.[1] e.Lan.[1] Der.[2] n.Lin.[1] Sus. Hmp. n.Dev.; and in forms ā Dev.[2]; high nw.Der.[1]   **1.** *int.* A call to attract attention ; an exclamation expressive of surprise, grief, &c. Cf. hech.

Sc. And 'heigh, Annie,' and 'how, Annie! O, Annie, winna ye bide!' JAMIESON *Pop. Ballads* (1806) I. 42; But hey! whar hae I got to now—My friend, I've maist forgotten you! GRAY *Poems* (1811) 85. Mry. Heigh, says breathless Willie, HAY *Lintie* (1851) 10. Frf. Heigh, when I think, A stane tied roon yer neck, nae doot, To gar ye sink, JOHNSTON *Poems* (1869) 120. Lak. Hey! but ye're early Robin, my man! ORR *Laigh Flichts* (1882) 62. Ir. And then heigh for the potsheen, and contrabands, BARRINGTON *Sketches* (1830) I. viii. e.Dur.[1] Hey! aa din-aa [really, I don't know]. Wm. Heigh Jack ! is te within ? WHITEHEAD *Leg.* (1859)

7, ed. 1896. Yks. (J.W.), w.Yks.[4] Lan. Hey Missis! let me gang wi' ye, HARLAND & WILKINSON *Flk-Lore* (1867) 60. Der.[2] Hey! how hoo did but syke! nw.Der.[1] An exclamation to arrest any one's progress, or to attract any one's attention at a distance. n.Lin.[1] Hey! but it was a big un.

2. Phr.(1) *Heigh go,* 'heigho,' an exclamation of surprise ; (2) — *gobet,* a call to horses to go more quickly ; (3) — *go-mago,* a virago, termagant ; (4) — *hey,* an exclamation expressive of weariness, sorrow, &c.; (5) — *ho* or *how(e,* (a) see (4) ; (b) to yawn ; (c) a charwoman ; (6) — *howe ham,* see (4) ; (7) — *jing-go-ring,* a girls' game ; (8) — *up,* an exclamation to attract attention ; also used to draw the attention of a person to move out of the way ; (9) — *willie-wine,* a fireside game ; see below ; (10) *to be in one's heigh-ohs,* to be in a state of exultation ; (11) *like hey-ma-nannie,* at full speed ; (12) *to play hay,* to be in a violent passion.

(1) w.Som.[1] Heighgo! here's a row! what's up! Hey go! here's a purty kettle o' fish. n.Dev. Hey go! What diayease dest me-an! *Exm. Scold.* (1746) l. 15. nw.Dev.[1] (2) Glo. GROSE (1790) *MS. add.* (M.) (3) Dev.[8] Thickee maid o' mine's a rigler âgo-mâgo. Her zwear'th and holler'th '2of her wuz the dowl hiszel. (4) Abd. 'Heigh hey,' quoth Bydby, 'this is unco hard,' Ross *Helenore* (1768) 72, ed. 1812. (5, a) Se. Heigh how is heavisome, An old wife is dowiesome, KELLY *Prov.* (1721) 156. Sc. *Monthly Mag.* (1800) I. 324. Frf. Hey how, my rumple sair does smart, MORISON *Poems* (1790) 107. Edb. I gap't, an' gae alang heigh-how, CRAWFORD *Poems* (1798) 47. Nhb. An exclamation, equivalent to 'well-well,' or to an expression of pity or regret (R.O.H.). Cum.[1] (b) n.Yks.[14], nw.Der.[1] (c) N.Cy.[1] So called from a notorious propensity to all kinds of low gossip and marvellous stories (s.v. Jar-woman. (6) Cum.[1] (7) Abd. Wi' their hey-jing-go-ring and their through-the-needle-e'e, CADENHEAD *Bon Accord* (1853) 251. (8) w.Yks. Heigh up lads, ther's a cah dahn, *Prov.* in *Brighouse News* (Sept. 14, 1889) ; BANKS *Whfld. Wds.* (1865) ; BURNLEY *Sketches* (1875) 321. e.Lan.[1] (9) Gall. There are many ways of drawing out the merry concern. . . One of the lasses . . . addresses one of the lads so—' Hey, Wullie Wine, an How Wullie Wine, I hope for hame ye'll no incline, Ye'll better light, and stay a' night, And I'll gie thee a lady fine.' Then he answers, 'Wha will ye gie if I wi' ye bide, To be my bonny blooming bride, And lie down lovely by my side ! ' Again, she— ' I'll gie thee Kate o' Dinglebell, A bonny body like yersell.' Then he—' I'll stick her up in the pear tree, Sweet and meek and sae is she, I lov'd her ance, but she's no for me, Yet I thank ye for your courtesy.' [And so on with alternate offers and refusals until one is accepted.] The lad, before the questions are put, whispers to another the girl he will stop with—so this one must be given before the dialogue ends. The chief drift . . . seems to be to discover the sweet-hearts of one another, MACTAGGART *Encycl.* (1824) 261, ed. 1876. (10) a.Not. When 'e wor on 'is heigh-oh's, 'e'd tek an' throw everything about the shop (J.P.K.). (11) Lak. GORDON *Pyotshaw* (1885) 158. (12) w.Yks.[2]

3. A call of encouragement to a dog when hunting rabbits. nw.Dev.[1]

Hence (1) **Heigh,** *v.* to urge on, incite, encourage; (2) *Heigh away,* (3) — *in,* (4) — *lads,* or *elats,* (5) — *there,* (6) — *up, phr.* a call of encouragement to dogs.

(1) w.Yks. I 'heigh'd' him an' clapped him, HALLAM *Wadsley Jack* (1866) viii. (2) Sus., Hmp. HOLLOWAY. (3) nw.Dev.[1] (4) n.Lin.[1] (5, 6) nw.Dev.[1]

4. *v.* To cry 'hey.'

Frf. He . . . played on his flute to the dancers while they 'hooch'd' and 'hey'd' till the rafters of the old Castle Keep rang again, LOWSON *Guidfollow* (1890) 227. Lak. They hooched, an' heyed, an' loupt an' flang, ORR *Laigh Flichts* (1882) 48.

HEIGH, HEIGHER, see Hie, *v.*[2], **High, Higher.**

HEIGH-GO-MAD, *adv.* and *sb.* n.Cy. Yks. Lan. Der. Also written heigomad w.Yks. heigo-mad n.Yks.[2] e.Yks. m.Yks.[1] e.Lan.[1] [(h)ei·gō-mad.]   **1.** *adv.* In excessively high spirits ; wildly, madly, furiously ; with great force. Also used as an *adj.*

n.Cy. (HALL.) e.Yks. They've played heygomad, MARSHALL *Rur. Econ.* (1796). m.Yks.[1] w.Yks. Sum we chimleys on em, an't smook putherin at tops like heigo-mad, TOM TREDDLEHOYLE *Trip ta Lunnan* (1851) 47 ; w.Yks.[124] Lan. Aw know naw what betook th' owd lad, He whirl'd his hat loike hey-go-mad, *Sngs. Wilsons* (1865) 50 ; Th' dandy-cock wur crowin' like heigh-go-mad lung afore dayleet, BRIERLEY *Day Out* (1859) 27. e.Lan.[1] The horse broke the traces and ran off like heygomad.

2. *sb.* Riotous frolic, tumult ; a state of great excitement, high spirits, rioting.

Yks. GROSE (1790). n.Yks.[1] ; n.Yks.[2] They went beyond all bounds, they played the very hey-go-mad. e.Yks. MARSHALL *Rur. Econ.* (1796) II. 325. m.Yks.[1], nw.Der.[1]

HEIGH'N, see Hain, *v.*[2]

HEIGHNE, *sb.* Lan. A lump ; a large piece of bread or other food. Cf. hunch, *sb.*[1]

Bobby give him a heighne o' that brade un cheese, STATON *B. Shuttle Bowtun,* 31.

HEIGHT, *sb.* and *v.* Var. dial. forms and uses in Sc. Irel. and Eng. **I.** Dial. forms: (1) **Eckth,** (2) **Haigth,** (3) **Hate,** (4) **Hecht,** (5) **Heckth,** (6) **Hecth,** (7) **Heet,** (8) **Heicht,** (9) **Heighth,** (10) **Height-th,** (11) **Heit,** (12) **Heith,** (13) **Hekth,** (14) **Heyt,** (15) **Hicht,** (16) **Hight,** (17) **Highth,** (18) **Higth,** (19) **Hith,** (20) **Hoith.** [For further examples see **II.** below.]

(1) w.Wor.[1] 'Ast ta bin a' the cathedral at 'Ööster? Eh ! 'tis a eckth to be sure ! se.Wor.[1] (2) e.Dev. In haigth laike a palm-tree, PULMAN *Sng. Sol.* (1860) vii. 7. (3) Chs.[1] (4) Sc. (JAM.), Nhp.[1] (5) m.Wor. (J.C.) Hrf. 'What a heckth he is now!' said of a balloon (N.G.). (6) Nhp.[2] War.[2] Poplars grow to a great heeth. s.Wor. (H.K.), Glo.[1], Hmp.[1] Wil. BRITTON *Beauties* (1825) ; Wil.[12] (7) Nhb. (R.O.H.) Cum. Cocker Willy lap bawk heet, GILPIN *Ballads* (1866) 303. Wm. Wi girt hee pows, sick a heet, *Spec. Dial.* (1885) pt. iii. 21. (8) Fif. Whilk raisit till ane unco beicht The crabbitness o' that guid knicht, TENNANT *Papistry* (1827) 177. Ayr. It's the heicht o' nonsense, SERVICE *Notandums* (1890) 4. Dmf. Ye're grown sic a maist awsom heicht, QUINN *Heather* (1863) 23. (9) Ken. Well, look what a heighth it is (D.W.L.). [Amer. *Dial. Notes* (1896) I. 418.] (10) w.Yks. (J.W.), s.Not. (J.P.K.) (11) nw.Der.[1] (12) Ken. (G.B.) (13) Oxf.[1] (14) e.Lan.[1] (15) Sc. (JAM.), Cai.[1] Per. Fra the hicht O' college ways an' college learnin', HALIBURTON *Ochil Idylls* (1891) 51. (16) Der.[1], s.Not., n.Lin.[1], sw.Lin.[1], Pem. (E.D.) (17) Lei.[1] Wil. What's the highth o' thuc doer? (E.H.G.) Som. Tha highth of happiness, AGRIKLER *Rhymes* (1872) 69. (18) War.[2] The rick is a good hight. (19) Dor. BARNES *Gl.* (1863). (20) s.Ir. He had the hoith o' fine language all about it, LOVER *Leg.* (1848) II. 461.

II. Dial. uses. **1** *sb.* A hill, elevation ; an elevated place. Also used *fig.*

Frf. At the smooth-skinned end [of the dog] were hichts an' howes, an' bare places whaur the banes stuck oot, WILLOCK *Rosetty Ends* (1886) 45, ed. 1889. Per. Haunted with anxiety lest any 'hicht' should end in a 'howe,' IAN MACLAREN *Brier Bush* (1895) 40. Rnf. Auld Hornie then forthwith 'gan scour By beicht and howe, THOM *Rhymes, &c.* (1844) 65. Edb. Hills are variously named, according to their magnitude, as . . . Scarr, Height, Shank, PENNECUIK *Wks.* (1715) 50, ed. 1815. Dmf. I hadna been oot on the heichts a mile, A mile on the heichts, REID *Poems* (1894) 160. Wm. Twind . . . Com bealen doon off Cross-fell heets, WHITEHEAD *Leg.* (1859) 12.

2. *Fig.* A help, lift up, assistance.

Lnk. I'se be doun some antrin' nicht To gie your furthy heart a hecht An' share your crack, MURDOCH *Doric Lyre* (1873) 56.

3. Pride. Brks. Oh, madam han't a bit o' height (W.W.S.).

4. The greatest degree of increase ; the greater portion.

Sc. The hicht o' the day, noon. The moon is said to be at the hicht, when it is full moon (JAM.). w.Yks. A geton t'eit at mak of (J.W.). Wor. I'll clear the hekth of it away and leave the rest for to-day (R.M.E.). s.Wor. The win' kips whiffling they leaves all over the place, but 'I swep' up the hecth on 'em. A's pretty nigh done ' ahy-makin,' th' hecth on it, 'owever (H.K.). Glo. Your umbrella was muddy, ma'am, but I've got the height of it off (A.B.) ; Glo.[1] I a cleared away the hecth on it.

5. Phr. (1) *to the height of music,* very much ; (2) *up a height,* up aloft.

(1) Rdn. *N. & Q.* (1878) 5th S. x. 105. (2) Nhb. ' Are ye gan up-a-heet !' are you going aloft, are you going to mount ! (R.O.H.) Cum. Dan gev yah greet lowp ebben up a heet, FARRALL *Betty Wilson* (1886) 141.

6. *v.* To raise, lift up ; to heighten. Also used *fig.*

Sc. Provisions are said to be hichted when the price is raised (JAM.). Abd. Naething can for his loss atone, Her heart to hight, SHIRREFS *Poems* (1790) 25. Per. It's nane o' yer orra bodies 'at's to hecht their tail on thae chairs, CLELAND *Inchbrachen* (1883) 28, ed. 1887. Rnf. These personal difficulties have been heighted with mighty changes in the posture of our Church affairs, WODROW *Corres.* (ed. 1843) I. 301. Lak. Some there are that sair misca',

---

Whilst ithers hecht an' roose ye, MURDOCH *Doric Lyre* (1873) 68. Edb. Weel may the shearers now pretend To height their fee ! *Har'st Rig* (1794) 40, ed. 1801. n.Lin. I just clam'd o'd o' th' owd mare mane an' highted my sen up (E.P.) ; n.Lin.[1] Hight th' barril-end, th' tap weänt run.

Hence (1) **Heighty** or **Highty,** *adj.* cheery, bright ; cheerful, well, healthy ; (a) **Hichtit,** *pp.* in great wrath, suggesting the idea of indignation approaching to frenzy.

(1) Pem. I found her real highty this morning. The sun do look highty coming in (E.D.). s.Pem. John is a bit more heightier to-day than a was isterday (W.M.M.) ; Laws *Little Eng.* (1888) 420. (2) Ags. (JAM.)

7. To toss or dandle a child up and down.

Der.[1] nw.Der.[1] To throw or toss up a child to give pleasure or produce quietness. n.Lin. (E.P.) sw.Lin.[1] Just hight it up and down a bit. He wants highting, his grandmother hights him.

Hence **Hightle,** (1) *v.* to dandle, move up and down ; (2) *sb.* a tossing or dandling of a child.

sw.Lin.[1] (1) She was hightling the bairn on her foot. They were hightling one another on a pole. (2) To a child: ' You want to be always on the hightle.'

8. To move up and down as children do on a see-saw ; to rise in the saddle in riding ; to walk jauntily with a high action. Also in form **highty.**

s.Not. Yer must larn to hight different to that before yer can ride. She's only been on a horse twice, but she highties very nicely. A tho't 'e'd hed a drop, by the way 'e went highting up and down (J.P.K.). n.Lin.[1]

Hence **Highty-tighty,** *sb.* a see-saw. n.Lin.[1]

HEIGHT, see Hait, Hight, *v.*[1]

HEIGHTS, *int.* w.Yks.[3] An exclamation used in the game of marbles when a boy wishes to shoot without the marble touching the ground, before it hits the other at which aim is taken. Cf. heist.

HEIGLE, HEIGN, HEIK, see Higgle, Hain, *v.*[2], Hike.
HEIKY, *adj.* Ken. Hmp. Smart, finely dressed.

Ken. Said by one woman of another, 'Aint she heiky !' (W.H.E.) Hmp. (ib.)

HEILD, HEILDED, see Heald, *v.*[1], Hold, *v.*
HEILIG, *sb.* Sh.I. Also in form **heilik.** A sloping rock dipping towards the sea. Cf. helyack.

He knew every stack and heilig and gro, and landing-place around the Ness, STEWART *Tales* (1892) 161 ; I'm been up an' doon ower dis heilik, an' roond aboot dis banks, fer da last tretty year o' my life, ib. 4.

HEILIT, HEILL, see Hold, *v.*, Heal, *v.*[2]
HEIM. The same as Aim, *adj.* (q.v.).
HEIMILT, *sb.* Sh.I. The pasture immediately adjoining an enclosure. S. & Ork.[1]
HEIN, see Hain, *v.*[1], Hine.
HEINOUS, *adj.* and *adv.* Cum. Yks. Dev. Also in forms **hayness** Cum.[1] ; **henjous** nw.Dev.[1] **1.** *adj.* Large, tremendous. nw.Dev.[1]

2. *adv.* Very, exceedingly, extraordinarily, used as an intensitive.

Cum.[1] Hayness fine. Hayness dirty. w.Yks.[3] Heinous cold. nw.Dev.[1] He hit ma most henjous hard.

HEIN-SHINNED, *adj.* Sc. Having projecting shin-bones or large ancles.

Sc. MACKAY. Ayr. She's bow-bough'd, she's hein-shinn'd, BURNS *Willie's Wife,* st. 3.

HEIR, *sb.* and *v.* Var. dial. uses in Sc. Irel. and Eng. Also written air Hmp.[1] ; heyr(e N.Cy.[2] w.Yks. **1.** *sb.* In comp. (1) Heir-looms, *obs.,* the fixtures in a house ; (2) -scap(e, (3) -ship, (4) -skip, inheritance ; (5) -word, a proverbial word, a by-word ; (6) Heirs-portioners, co-heirs, or co-heiresses.

(1) N.Cy.[2] Goods left in an house, as it were by way of inheritance ; some standing pieces of stuff that go with the house, RAY (1691). Cum., Wm. NICOLSON (1677) *Trans. R. Lit. Soc.* (1868) IX. (2) e.Fif. Ye be certain o' sic an heirscap as Jean Bodkin's fortune maun be, LATTO *Tam Bodkin* (1864) v ; Havin' come into the possession o' a fiddle by heirscape, ib. xi. Rxb. (JAM.) (3) Abd. She . . . Could write oot deeds an' settlements o' heirships an' entails, ANDERSON *Rhymes* (1867) 26. Per. I bequeathe, as heirship due, My whole estate and wealth to you, NICOL *Poems* (1766) 159. (4) Sc. This is the heir ; come, let us kill him, an' let us seize on his heirskip, HENDERSON *St. Matt.* (1862) xxi. 38.

N.I.[1] He got it by heir skip. (5) **Shr.**[1] (6) **Lnk.** She had three daughters . . . who . . . were served heirs-portioners to their mother in the above-mentioned subjects, LITHGOW *Poet. Remains* (ed. 1863) xxxviii.

2. A young timber-tree ; a young tree left standing when old trees are felled. *Gen.* in *pl.*

N.Cy.[2] **w.Yks.** *Leeds Merc. Suppl.* (July 11, 1896) ; (R.G.) **Sur.**[1] **Sus.** Young heirs—small elms so called in Chidham Manor (G.A.W.) ; **Sus.**[12] **Hmp.**[1] Universally applied to young trees.

3. *v.* To inherit, become heir to.

Sc. I stood a chance To heir her father's shop, VEDDER *Poems* (1842) 91. **Abd.** Wha it was, I dinna ken, That heir'd this queer an' antic aumrie, ANDERSON *Rhymes* (1867) 75. **Frf.** A niece, wha, as but richt, will heir a' her bawbees, WILLOCK *Rosetty Ends* (1886) 40, ed. 1889. **Ayr.** I'd rather be a tyrant's slave Than heir his will, LAING *Poems* (1894) 35. **Dmf.** Bring some weans to heir his farm, SHENNAN *Tales* (1831) 62. **Gall.** We shall heir her pursikie, MACTAGGART *Encycl.* (1824) 69, ed. 1876. **N.I.**[1] **n.Cy.** He heir'd his estate from his brother, GROSE (1790) *MS. add.* (M.) **Nhb.** (R.O.H.) **Cum.**[4] Dum' folk heirs nae lan', *Saying.* **w.Yks.** To heir an estate, is parlance as prevalent as it is intolerable, HAMILTON *Nugae Lit.* (1841) 321 ; **w.Yks.**[2], **Chs.**[3] **s.Chs.**[1] Dhür(z û prast'i shûv·lful û miin·i, ûn ey ae·rz it au· [There's a pretty shovelful o' money, an' hey heirs it aw]. **Der.**[2], **nw.Der.**[1] **n.Lin.**[1] He heir'd it all fra' his feyther. **e.An.**[1] His son will heir his estate. **Nrf.** He heired that estate from his father, in course (W.R.E.). **e.Suf.** (F.H.)

Hence (1) **Heirable**, *adj.* heritable, entailed ; (2) *Heired property, phr.* property under settlement.

(1) **Chs.**[1] Th' farm canna be sold ; it's heirable ; **Chs.**[3], **s.Chs.**[1] **sw.Lin.**[1] I thought it was heirable land. It's heirable land, or he'd have muddled it away long sin. (2) n.Lin.[1]

[3. Not one son more To heir his goods, CHAPMAN *Iliad* (1611) v. 161.]

HEIR, HEIR-OYE, HEIS(E, see Hear, Ier·oe, Heeze.

HEISAU, *sb.* Sc. A sea-cheer. FRANCISQUE-MICHEL *Sc. Lang.* (1882) 212.

HEISK, *adj.* Or.I. Also in form **hisk.** Heady, nervous, excited, crazy.

The creature gaed clean heisk (J.G.) ; (JAM. *Suppl.*)

Hence **Heisket,** *adj.* nervous, excitable. (J.G.)

HEIST, *int.* Der. Amer. A term used in the game of marbles which secures liberty to shoot the marble from the knee, instead of the ground. Also used *subst.* Cf. **heights.**

nw.Der.[1] Aeyst. [Amer. In marbles, 'I have heist,' I may raise my hand from the ground, *Dial. Notes* (1896) I. 61.]

HEIT, see Hite.

HEIYEARALD, *sb.* Lth. Rxb. (JAM.) Also written **high-year-old** Rxb. A heifer of a year and a half old. See **Ha,** *adj.*

HEIZE, HEK, HEKEL, see Heeze, Eck, Heckle, *v.*[1]

HEKKAH-PON-DOODLE, *sb.* Cor. [Not known to our other correspondents.] A blockhead. (F.H.D.)

HEKKAP, HEKTH, see Hiccup, Height.

HEL, *sb.* Cor. [el.] The passage leading from the door to the parlour. *Jrn. Royal Inst. of Cor.* (1886) IX.

[OCor. *hel,* 'aula,' STOKES *Gl.* in *Trans. Phil. Soc.* (1870) 191 ; cp. WILLIAMS.]

HEL, HELANGE, see Heal, *v.*[2]**, Elenge.**

HELDE, *sb.* Dev. Also in form **hilde.** A very small apple.

(HALL.) ; Some of the natives tell me that there is 'a zoart ov a awpel cal'd by thicky name, but they bain't very plentiful now, they be age out' (S.H.).

HELDER, *adv.* and *adj.* n.Cy. Yks. Lan. Der. Also in forms **eilder** n.Yks.[2] ; **elder** m.Yks.[1] w.Yks.[34] Lan.[1] Der.[2] nw.Der.[1] ; **either** Lan.[1] e.Lan.[1] ; **yelder** n.Cy. [e'ldə(r.]

1. *adv.* More ; rather ; preferable to.

n.Cy. (K.) ; GROSE (1790) *MS. add.* (P.) ; **N.Cy.**[2] **n.Yks.**[1] Ah wad helder gan an' feght an stay an' be ta'en by t'pollis ; **n.Yks.**[2], **m.Yks.**[1] **w.Yks.**[2] He'd helder go a begging than work. It's helder t'worst o' t'two ; **w.Yks.**[3] A flag stone wanting more packing, the mason said, 'It's elder slack yet' ; **w.Yks.**[4] **Lan.** Au'd elder goo for a begging, nur olis stop wheere aw wur born, *Eggshibishun* (1856) 11 ; **Lan.**[1] Aw'd go as fur as oather grace grew or waytur ran afore aw'd live amoon sich doins. One could either manage we't at th' for-end o' their days, WAUGH *Sketches*

(1857) 26. **e.Lan.**[1] **s.Lan.** PICTON *Dial.* (1865) 18. **Der.**[2] I'd elder goo to th' jail than th' Bastile [i. e. the work-house]. **nw.Der.**[1]

2. *adj.* Preferable.

n.Yks.[2] 'I'll tak t'eilder road,' I will take the most preferable road. 'T'eilder yan,' the one I prefer.

[1. My covetyng is helder The sadnesse of suche men þen swyftnes of childer, *Wars Alex.* (c. 1450) 1016. Norw. dial. *helder,* rather (AASEN) ; ON. *heldr,* Goth. *haldis.* In E. dials. the form *helder* is prop. a double compar. ; the phonological equiv. to ON. *heldr* is found in **helt.**]

HELDIGOLEERY, see **Heeliegoleerie.**

HELD-ON CAKE, *phr.* Yks. A particular kind of oat-cake. w.Yks. LUCAS *Stud. Nidderdale* (c. 1882a).

HELE, see Heal, *sb.*[1]**,** *v.*[2]**, Heel,** *v.*[2]

HELEGUG, *sb.* Wal. The puffin, *Fratercula arctica.* SWAINSON *Birds* (1885) 220.

HELIE, see Helly.

HELIER, *sb.* Sh. & Or.I. Also written **hellyer** Sh.I. ; **helyer** Sh.I. Or.I ; and in form **halier** Sh.I. [he·liər, he·ljər.] **1.** A cave into which the tide flows.

Sh.I. Natural caves and hellyers along the sea-coast were no doubt used by these early inhabitants as places of retreat, SPENCE *Flk-Lore* (1899) 38 ; The incessant operation of the waves indenting a calcareous rock has formed a deep halier, SCOTT *Pirate* (1822) xix ; Within the mouth of the helyer stood a man, *Chambers' Jrn.* (Oct. 23, 1886) 686 ; Right below the place where this dyke ends is a cave containing a beach, which place is called 'de hellyer o' Fivlagord,' JAKOBSEN *Dial.* (1897) 69 ; **S. & Ork.**[1] **Or.I.** The irresistible Atlantic rushing with inconceivable velocity into countless subterranean 'gios' or belyers, VEDDER *Sketches* (1832) 113.

2. *Comp.* **Helier-halse,** a cavern with a narrow entrance. S. & Ork.[1]

[1. Norw. dial. *hellar,* a cavern in a rock (AASEN). ON. *hellir,* a cave in rocks (*Orkney Saga*).]

HELK, *sb.* n.Cy. Yks. Lan. [h]elk.] **1.** A large, heavy person. w.Yks.[1], ne.Lan.[1] **2.** *pl.* Large detached crags ; a confused pile or range of rocks. n.Cy. (HALL.), w.Yks. (H.F.S.), w.Yks.[1], ne.Lan.[1] **3.** *pl.* Large white clouds, *gen.* indicating a thunderstorm. n.Cy. (HALL.), w.Yks.[1], ne.Lan.[1]

HELL, *sb.* Var. dial. uses in Sc. Irel. and Eng. Also written **hel** Wxf.[1] Dor. ; **helle** Sh.I. ; and in forms **ail** Bck. ; **hail** Hrt. ; **hale** Bdf. Hrt. ; **heel**-Brks. **1.** *In comb.* (1) **Hell-beck,** a rivulet, esp. one issuing from a cave-like recess ; (2) **-bind,** the greater dodder, *Cuscuta europaea* ; (3) **-bolter,** an untractable person ; (4) **-cat,** (*a*) a termagant, vixen ; (*b*) a thoroughly bad or coarse person ; (*b*) an oath ; (*c*) a small, troublesome black insect, a midge ; (5) **-dame** or **Heelden,** a bad woman ; (6) **-dyke,** a dark ravine ; (7) **-falleero,** see (9) ; (8) **-fire law,** summary proceedings against a debtor ; (9) **-for-leather** or **-for-leatherly,** at a great pace, recklessly ; (10) **-hole** or **-'s hole,** (*a*) a den of infamy ; (*b*) a dark nook supposed to be haunted ; (11) **-hound,** a ruffian ; (12) **-jay,** the razor-bill, *Alca torda* ; (13) **-kettle,** a pit full of water ; (14) **-mint,** unnatural and unseasonable growth ; (15) **-raker,** a wild, reckless fellow ; (16) **-root,** (*a*) the lesser broom-rape, *Orobanche minor* ; (*b*) the common Alexanders, *Smyrnium Olusatrum* ; (17) **-seed,** see (*a*) ; (18) **-spinner,** (19) **-sweep** or **-sweeper,** the common gnat, *Culex pipiens* ; (20) **-to-leather,** see (9) ; (21) **-wain,** a supernatural appearance seen in the sky at night ; (22) **-weed,** (*a*) see (2) ; (*b*) the lesser dodder, *Cuscuta Epithymum* ; (*c*) the Indian grass, *C. Trifolii* ; (*d*) the bindweed, *Convolvulus arvensis* and *C. sepium* ; (*e*) the corn crowfoot, *Ranunculus arvensis* ; (23) **-words,** words or spells of ill-omen.

(1) **Lakel.**[1] **n.Yks.** BAILEY (1791). (2) **Hrt.** (B. & H.) (3) **e.Suf.** (F.H.) (4, *a*) **w.Yks.** He's a hell-cat is yond (B.K.) ; **w.Yks.**[1] (*b*) **Suf.** (P.H.E.) (*c*) **n.Lin.**[1] (5) **Brks.** *Gl.* (1852) (6) **m.Yks.**[1] (7) **I.W.**[1] They be aal quarlun and fightun hell-falleero. (8) **w.Yks.** (S.K.C.) (9) **w.Yks.** We were gooen hell-faladerly when his tyre brast. Yon train was gooin' hell-fer-ladder throo t'tunnel (B.K.). **Midl.** Droives out on to the turnpike, an away hell-for-leather, BARTRAM *People of Clopton* (1897) 188. **War.**[3] **e.Suf.** Hell for luther (F.H.). (10, *a*) **n.Yks.**[2] (*b*) **Gall.** Nae boggles now to be seen about Hell's-hole and the Ghaist craft, MACTAGGART *Encycl.* (1824) 29, ed. 1876. (11) **Shr.**[1] A poor old

man whom a pack of ruffianly lads had hooted at and pelted, said of them, to a magistrate at Whitchurch, that ' they wun a paasle o' 'ell-'uns.' (12) Sh.I. SWAINSON *Birds* (1885) 217. (13) Dur. BAILEY (1721). (14) n.Ir. His heart full av hopes that in hellmint wir sloamin', *Lays and Leg.* (1884) 74. (15) Midl. A raal rantin' hell-raaker, I believe, but as good as gowld, BARTRAM *People of Clopton* (1897) 70. (16, *a*) Ken. (B. & H.) (*b*) Dor. w.*Gasetts* (Feb. 15, 1889) 7. (17) Hrt. ELLIS *Mod. Husb.* (1750) IV. i. (18, 19) Cum.⁴ (20) Nhb. So right across Towlerhirst Moor they galloped—hell-to-leather, PEASE *Tales* (1899) 37. (21) n.Cy. *Denham Tracts* (ed. 1895) II. 77 ; (HALL), (22, *a*) Nhp.² Brks. DRUCE *Flora* (1898) 358. Bdf. BATCHELOR *Agric.* (1813) 325. Hrt. ELLIS *Mod. Husb.* (1750) IV. i. Cmb., Sus. (*b*) Lak. From its destructive nature in suffocating plants, it has received the opprobrious names of hell-weed, and devil's-guts, PATRICK *Plants* (1891) 120. Nhp.¹, Cmb., Ken.¹, Sus. (*c*) n.Bck. (*d*) Nhp.¹² (*e*) Yks. (23) Abd. You came straight before the cow, and you cast an ill-ee upon her, muttering some hell-words about ' novum lac,' RUDDIMAN *Parish* (1828) 38, ed. 1889.

2. *Phr.* (1) *as hell kickt Betty*, (2) *at the hell o' one size*, at a great rate ; in a violent hurry ; (3) *hell to the rap*, never a bit ; (4) *like hell in a tow*, see (2) ; (5) *to go to hell as like*, to have no intention of doing a thing ; (6) *to make one smell hell*, to make one's life a hell on earth.

(1) w.Yks. He went by me on his bicycle as hell kickt Betty ta t'bottom o' t'rooad (B.K.). (2) LW.¹ That chap runs at the hell o' one size. (3) Ir. Hell to the rap of tythe-cess or hecuth-money, BARRINGTON *Sketches* (1830) II. v. (4) Sc. (G.W.) (5) w.Yks.² ' Are ta goin' to thy wark to-day ! ' ' To hell as like ; Ad guo to el oz laik (J.W.). (6) Ir. *Flb-Lore Rec.* (1881) IV. 106.

3. A hole, a hollow.
Wxf.¹ w.Yks. LUCAS *Stud. Nidderdale* (c. 1882) 258.

4. *Obsol.* A dark place in the woods.
Hmp. WISE *New Forest* (1883) 110, 283; Hmp.¹

5. A brick-kiln. n.Lin. (E.P.)

HELL, *v.* Nhb. Dur. Cum. Wm. Yks. Lan. Glo. Wil. Som. Dev. Also written helle N.Cy.¹ Cum.⁴ w.Yks.¹; and in form hill Glo. Wil.¹ [h]el.] 1. To pour out or down. Cf. heel, *v.*⁸

n.Cy. (K.), N.Cy.¹², Nhb.¹, Dur.¹ Cum. They drank in piggins, peynts, or quarts, . . An' some they helt it down sae fast, They suin could hardly stan', GILPIN *Pop. Poetry* (1875) 200 ? Till gush went the sickle into my hand : Down hell'd the bluid, RALPH *Misc. Poems* (1747) 2; Cum.⁴ *Obs.* Wm. (M.P.), n.Yks.²³, w.Yks.¹ Glo.(G.S.); ' To hill down,' to pour down as it were by pailfulls, spoken of rain pouring down like water spouts, *Horae Subsecivae* (1777) 213. Wil. Hill out some drink (K.) ; Wil.¹ Som. JENNINGS *Obs. Dial. w.Eng.* (1825); W. & J. *Gl.* (1873). n.Dev. Lewy, hell Bet a cup o' zider, ROCK *Jim an' Nell* (1867) st. 19.

2. With *on*: to pour water on dough in bread-making. w.Yks.¹, ne.Lan.¹

[To helle in, *infundere*, . . . To helle oute, *effundere*, *Cath. Angl.* (1483); Hell on þaim þi wreth, HAMPOLE *Ps.* (c. 1330) lxviii. 29. Norw. dial. *hella*, to pour down (AASEN); ON. *hella*.]

HELL, see Eel, Heal, *v.*⁸

HELLAM, HELLAR, see Haulm, Eller, *sb.*

HELLDOM, *sb.* Sc. Wretchedness.
s.Sc. There's mine awn wife, after leevin' wi' her in a state of helldom for four hale years, I was forced to drive forth out o' the castle, WILSON *Tales* (1836) II. 21.

HELLENSHAKER, see Hailanshaker.

HELLERED, *pp.* w.Yks.¹ Lan. [e·lǝd.] Swollen, inflamed.
Yks. (HALL.) w.Yks.¹ Her yowyer is seen heller'd wi' t'fellon, ii. 290. ne.Lan.¹

HELLERS, *sb. pl.* n.Yks.² Also in form ellers. [e·lǝrz.] The heels.

HELLICAT, *adj.* and *sb.* Sc. Also in forms hellicate Fif. Ayr. ; hellocat Dmf. (JAM.) [he·likat.] 1. *adj.* Wild, unmanageable, boisterous; giddy, light-headed; extravagant.
Sc. These hellicat quality, that lord it ower us like brute beasts, SCOTT *Bride of Lam.* (1819) xxxiv. Per. He huntit the ewes, an' he rade on the ram! Sic a hellicat deevil was Minister Tam, NICOLL *Poems* (ed. 1843) 95. Fif. Bethink ye on whom your hellicate cavalier may e'en the now be showering his ungodly kisses, GRANT *Six Hundred*, ix. e.Fif. There's naething wrang wi' the sneck if fouk wer'na sae sair hellicat and misleared, LATTO *Tam Bodkin* (1864) vi. Ayr. A ne'er-do-weel hellicate thing, that was the get of a son that was deid, SERVICE *Dr. Duguid* (ed. 1887) vii.

Lth. There's nane fear'd nor lo'ed like the hellicat loon, BALLANTINE *Poems* (1856) 99. Dmf. (JAM.) Gall. I wondered 'if it could be that hellicat lassie, who had called me a sheep,' CROCKETT *Raiders* (1894) iii.

2. *sb.* A wicked creature ; a villain.
Sc. Let us but get puir Grace out o' that auld hellicat's clutches, SCOTT *Blk. Dwarf* (1816) ix ; It's highly possible the hellicat would try and gar me marry her when he turned up, STEVENSON *Catriona* (1893) xxii. Frf. The hellicat says the rain's a dispensation to drown him in for neglect o' duty, BARRIE *Minister* (1891) xxxviii. Slk. (JAM.)

HELLIE-LAMB, *sb.* Cld. (JAM.) A ludicrous designation given to a hump on the back.

HELLIE-MAN, *sb.* Bnff.¹ 1. The devil. 2. *Comb.* Hellie-man's rig, a piece of land dedicated to the devil.

HELLIER, HELLIGAR, see Heal, *v.*⁸ 7 (2), Alegar.

HELLIGO, *adj.* w.Yks.² Also written heligo. [e·ligō.] Wild, romping. Cf. hellicat. ' They're just like heligo lads.'

HELLIKER, see Alegar.

HELLIN, *sb. Obs.* w.Yks.¹ Compacted soot.

HELLIN, see Eldern, *sb.*

HELLIO, *sb.* Or.I. A stone with a rim of clay about it used in parching corn for ' burstin.' (S.A.S.), S. & Ork.¹

HELLION, *sb.* Cmb.Amer. An inhabitant of hell, a devil. Cmb. *N. & Q.* (1873) 4th S. xii. 455. [Amer. Denizen of hell. Now common in Massachusetts, meaning ' a devil of a fellow.' It was used at least sixty years ago as a term of abuse (= devil's imp), *Dial. Notes* (1896) I. 61.]

HELLISH, *adv.* Yks. Wor. Applied to certain *adj.* to give an intensitive meaning.
Yks. (J.W.) s.Wor. PORSON *Quaint Wds.* (1875) 9.

HELLOCKY, see Hullocky.

HELLOYER, *int.* Ess. An exclamation meaning ' I see you,' 'hulloo you.' (J.M.), (H.H.M.)

HELLUM, see Haulm, Helm, *sb.*²

HELLY, *sb.* Sh.I. Also written helle S. & Ork.² [he·li.] The interval between Saturday evening and Monday morning ; also in *comp.* Helly-days.
I wis jõst tinkin at Bob Ertirson wid be comin haem dis Helly, BURGESS *Tang* (1898) iii ; Shelling bere, or barley, as a delicacy for belly days and Sunday dinners, SPENCE *Flb-Lore* (1899) 170 ; We need shuggar, an' I dunna den ken if we'll pit by da helly for tae, *Sh. News* (May 7, 1898) ; S. & Ork.¹

Hence Helys-cost, *sb.* food provided to last from Saturday evening to Monday morning. S. & Ork.¹

[Norw. dial. *helg*, a holiday, esp. the time between Saturday evening and Sunday evening (AASEN).]

HELLY, HELLYA, see Holy, Helyack.

HELM, *sb.*¹ Sc. Nhb. Cum. Wm. Yks. Also Suf. [h]elm.] 1. A covering; the top or head of anything.
n.Cy. BAILEY (1721). Nhb.¹ ' Helm o' the hill,' as it used invariably to be called, is a considerable eminence . . . a few miles south of Felton.

2. A heavy cloud which sometimes covers the top of a mountain, esp. Crossfell ; also in *comp.* Helm-cloud.
Lakel.¹ Sometimes, when the atmosphere is quite settled, with hardly a cloud to be seen and not a breath of air stirring, a small cloud appears on the summit of the mountain, and extends itself to the north and south. The helm is then said to be on, and in a few minutes the wind is blowing so violently as to break down trees, overthrow stacks, and occasionally throw a person from his horse, or overturn a horse and cart. When the wind blows the helm seems violently agitated, though on ascending the Fell and entering it there is not much wind. Sometimes a helm forms and goes off without a wind ; and there are essentially easterly winds without a helm. Cum. *Gl.* (1851) ; Cum.⁴ A rolling cloud, sometimes for three or four days together, hovers over the mountain tops, the sky being clear in other parts. This helm is not dispersed or blown away by the wind, but continues in its station although a violent roaring hurricane comes tumbling down the mountain, NICHOLSON & BURN *Hist. Antiq. Wm. and Cum.* (1777) I. 7. n.Wm. It is asserted that invariably if the ' helm remains for three consecutive days, that it will not leave before the end of nine days (B.K.). nw.Wm. *Denham Tracts* (ed. 1892) I. 218. Yks. SWAINSON *Weather Flb-Lore* (1873) 204.

3. A gale of wind which comes from the mountains with terrific force ; also used *fig.* ; also in *comp.* Helm-wind.
N.Cy.¹, Nhb.¹, Lakel.² Cum. What was it that distant noise

ke the roar of artillery,—it was the terrible Helm wind, CLARE *J. Armstrong*, 12 ; The helm wind has swept the fellside district, nd its rush has been felt and even heard as far as Carlisle, *Carlisle Patriot* (Nov. 9, 1888) 4 ; Cum.⁴ Wm. An t'blast o' the ugle, loud as t'wind o' the helm, WHITEHEAD *Leg.* (1859) 8. w.Wm. It is also spoken of a person in a furious passion, *Denham Tracts* (ed. 1892) I. 218. e.Wm. GIBSON *Leg. and Notes* (1877) 42.

Hence **Helm-bar**, *sb.* a strip of cloud which is thought o resist the progress of the 'helm.'

N.Cy.¹ Cum. HUTCHINSON *Hist.* (1794) I. 266 ; Cum.⁴ It must ave been the helm-wind for sure ; yet I cannot mind that I saw he helm-bar, CAINE *Shad. Crime* (1885) 102.

4. Phr. *helm of wet*, a great fall of rain. Ags. (JAM.)

Hence **Helmy**, *adj.* rainy. *ib.*

5. *pl. Obsol.* The sleeves to a waistcoat. e.Suf. (F.H.)

HELM, *sb.*² n.Cy. Yks. Lin. Also written **helme** Lin. ; nd in form **hellum** n.Yks.⁴ [h]elm.] A shed in the fields or the shelter of cattle when turned out to pasture ; a ovel or hut. Cf. **hemmel**, *sb.*¹

n.Cy. (K.), n.Cy.² Yks. Let's try if we can't drahve un inte 'helm, *Spec. Dial.* (1800) 24. n.Yks.¹²⁴, ne.Yks.¹ e.Yks. MAR-HALL *Rur. Econ.* (1788) ; e.Yks.¹ A long shed used as a shelter or cattle, *gen.* applied to those opening upon the fold-yard. It as a flat roof on which are built up stacks of straw or thorns, for uture use. m.Yks.¹ w.Yks. Many a seedy old performer has nade the 'helm' into a place of entertainment by fixing sheets up n front, BINNS *Vill. to Town* (1882) 45 ; w.Yks.¹⁴⁵ Lin. *Gent. Mag.* (1861) II. 507. n.Lin.¹ Stacked on the helm in the stack-ard 16 loads of short wheat, *Bottesford Farm Acc.* (Aug. 21, 1890).

HELM, see **Haulm**.

HELMA, *sb.* Sh.I. Grass growing among stubble. *Coll.* L.L.B.) Cf. **haulm**.

HELOE, *adj.* n.Cy. Yks. Lan. Chs. Der. Also in forms allo Lan. ; **ayla**, **aylo** Lan.¹ ; **hailow** Chs.¹²⁵ ; **hala** w.Yks.⁴ Lan.¹ ne.Lan.¹ nw.Der.¹ ; **halah** w.Yks.²⁴ ; **haler** Der. ; nalo w.Yks.¹ ne.Lan.¹ Chs.³ Der.¹ ; halow N.Cy.¹ Lan. Chs.¹²⁵ Der. ; healo w.Yks.¹ Lan.¹ ; heanlo s.Lan. ; helaw N.Cy.² ; heyloe Chs. ; yealo Lan. [h)e'lō, ē'lō, a lō.] Bashful, modest, awkwardly shy ; squeamish, scrupulous. *f.* heely, *adj.*

n.Cy. (K.), N.Cy.¹² w.Yks. HUTTON *Tour to Caves* (1781) ; w.Yks.¹² ; w.Yks.⁴ Why are you so halah ? Lan. Reitch to, an' lunnot be ailo—for I'm nobbut a poor hond at laithin, WAUGH *Chim. Corner* (1874) 229, ed. 1879 ; 'Don't be halow, you're very omely' (farmer's wife welcoming a handsome young lady) W.T.) ; DAVIES *Races* (1856) 233 ; Lan.¹, ne.Lan.¹ s.Lan. PICTON *Dial.* (1865) 16. Chs. 'Sit ye diown and dinna be heyloe' is common Chs. greeting, *N. & Q.* (1882) 6th S. v. 350 ; Chs.¹²³ Der. GROSE (1790) *MS. add.* (P.) Der.¹, nw.Der.¹

[It is prob. that this word was orig. a comp., being a orm of *hely how*, a name for a child's caul ; see JAM. (s.v. How, *sb.* 3).]

HELON, see **Heal**, *v.*²

HELOOR, *sb.* Sh.I. In phr. *lyin' up i' de heloor*, applied to a person half-awake and half-asleep in the norning before getting out of bed, and consequently sulky.

The word hel [Eng. hell] is in O.N. applied vaguely to the 'ealm of death or the world beyond the earth. A person in the leloor is thus properly speaking a half-dreaming person whose houghts are wandering away ; then it means a person who will not speak, of which unwillingness sulkiness is most often the ause, JAKOBSEN *Dial.* (1897) 39.

[Norw. dial. *helorar*, pl., confusion, heedlessness, also in whr. *Han laag i Hellioro*, he lies in the realm of death, he s dead to the things of this world (AASEN) ; see also AKOBSEN *Norsk in Shetl.* (1897) 145. ON. *hel*, the abode of the dead, Hades.]

HELP, *v.* and *sb.* Var. dial. uses in Sc. and Eng.

I. *v.* Gram, forms. **1.** *Present Tense*: (1) ? Help, (2) Hep-pen, (3) Hoap, (4) Holp, (5) Hope, (6) Houp, (7) Howp.

(1) ? **1.Ma.** That curious lek she couldn help, BROWN *Doctor* (1887) 11. (2) s.Yks.² (3) Eaa.¹ (4) Ken. (D.W.L.) Sur. *N. & Q.* 1874) 5th S. i. 517 ; Sur.¹ (5) Glo. HAVERGAL *Gl.* (1887) ; Glo.¹ 6, 7) Sc. GROSE (1790) *MS. add.* (C.)

2. *Preterite*: (1) Hælpit, (2) Hoap, (3) Hoaped, (4) Holp, 5) Holped, (6) Hoped, (7) Houp, (8) Howp, (9) *pl.* Holpen.

(1) Sc. MURRAY *Dial.* (1873) 205. (2) Eaa. John's arm long hoap Mary well, CLARE *J. Noakes* (1839) st. 85 ; *Gl.* (1851) ;

Eaa.¹ (3) Eaa.¹ I hoaped her along. (4) s.Stf. Esp. in the sense of serving. 'I holp him to the mustard,' PINNOCK *Blk. Cy. Ann.* (1895). Nhp.¹ I holp him to do it. Shr.¹ *Obsol.* I 'ō'p 'im ōōth that bag on 'is shūther. Glo.² Suf. Common (C.G.B.). Eaa. I holp load the waggon (W.W.S.). Ken.¹ Sus. An old farmer, speaking of some bottles for sale at an auction, said, 'I holp empty a good many o' they' (S.P.H.) ; Sus.¹ She . . . holp me to a cup of tea. Som. I holp get out all the graves here (W.F.R.). [Amer. He holp me out of the scrape, *Dial. Notes* (1896) I. 68.] (5) Ken. (D.W.L.) (6) Suf.¹ I hope him. (7) nw.Der.¹ (8) s.Chs. Uwp, 81. Nhp.² (9) Shr.¹ *Obsol.* Poor owd Tummas an' me wun al'ays good frien's, an' 'op'n one another as neighbours shoulden.

3. *Pp.*: (1) Hælpit, (2) Help, (3) Helpen, (4) Heppened, (5) Holp, (6) Holped, (7) Holpen, (8) Hope, (9) Hoped, (10) Houp, (11) Houpt, (12) Uw'pn.

(1) Sc. MURRAY *Dial.* (1873) 205. (2) Nrf., Suf., Sus. HOLLO-WAY. (3) e.Yks.¹ (4) n.Yks.² (5) Nhp.¹, e.An.¹ Suf. (C.T.), Ken.¹, Sus. (R.B.) (6) Nhp.¹, e.An.¹ (7) Rut.¹ Heard . . . in 1881, in the mouth of a cottager. Shr.¹ *Obsol.* They dunna ought to be bad off, they'n bin 'ōp'n more than anybody i' the parish. (8) Suf.¹ Ta cant be hope. I.W.¹ (9) I.W.² (10) Ken.² (11) Sc. It canna be houpt, GROSE (1790) *MS. add.* (C.) (12) s.Chs.¹ 81.

4. Used before another *v.*, esp. as gerund before the inf. of the principal *v.*, the inflexion passes from the auxiliary to the principal.

w.Som.¹ Instead of saying, 'I remember helping to load the cart,' we should always say, 'I mind help loadin the cart.' Instead of 'I helped to load the cart,' . . 'I help loaded the cart.' Dev. I can mind help cutting dōwn several trees, *Reports Provinc.* (1885) 96. nw.Dev.¹

II. Dial. uses. **1.** *v.* In phr. (1) *to help God away with any one*, to cause the death of a person by foul play ; (2) — *off*, (a) to attend during the last illness of a person ; (b) with the reflexive *pron.*, to go ; (3) — *to*, to refrain from ; (4) — *up*, (a) to support, assist ; (b) used iron. to encumber, hinder ; *pass.* to be in a difficulty, at one's wits' end, to be over-worked ; (5) *so help me never*, (6) *so help me later*, an oath.

(1) Ir. Some one helped God Almighty away with the crathur. Common (M.B.-S.). (2, a) LW. He've a helped dree on us off. . . Give me a dactor what hev seen all our volks off comfortable, GRAY *Annesley* (1889) I. 179. (b) w.Yks. (J.W.) n.Lin.Noo, noā moore wo'da, help thysen off! (M.P.) (3) Edb. Ere we parted [I] could na help To gie this upstart whalp a skelp, MACNEILL *Bygane Times* (1811) 35. (4, a) Yks. (J.W.), nw.Der.¹, e.An.¹ (b) Not.⁸ She seems so 'elped up with a.w that family o' little children. sw.Lin.¹ See how soon poor fellows get helped up! What wi' my lame arm, and the mester's rheumatis, and the childer all down wi' colds, we were well helped up! Nhp.¹ 'You're prettily holp up,' a common expression of derision. War. What with the missis bad and him out of work, they're well helped up (C.T.O.). e.An.² I am finely holp up. e.Suf. (F.H.) Ken.¹ I dunno as I shaānt purty soon look out another plaāce, I be purty nigh holp-up here, I think. Sus. Poor body, she be regler holp up with those six little lads ! (R.B.) I.W.¹ I am sadly hope up about this ; I.W.² She es terbul hoped up over it. (5, 6) Nrf. (E.M.) ; (M.C.H.B.)

2. To mend or repair anything.

Abd. I'll help the fire . . . An' gie the seethin' pot some bree, COCK *Strains* (1810) I. 117. n.Cy. GROSE (1790) *MS. add.* (P.)

3. To lift, take.

Lth. Frae aff his back he helpit his harp, N°NEILL *Preston* (c. 1895) 49.

4. To send, convey, pass on, deliver.

Nhp.¹ A butcher said to a lady, who purchased some steaks, he would help them up to her house directly. A very common use of the word. War.²³⁴ s.War.¹ Thankee, sir, I'll be sure and help the book back to you. Hnt. (T.P.F.) Ken.¹ 'What did you do with that letter I gave you to the wheelwright?' 'I holp it to his wife.' Sur. If you leave it with me, I'll holp it to him, *N. & Q.* (1874) 5th S. i. 517 ; Sur.¹ Sus. To help one to a thing, is to send it to one. 'Those are the books you holp me to' (S.P.H.) ; Sus.¹ I will help the letter to him if you'll write a few lines.

5. *Comp.* (1) **Help-ale**, *obs.*, a feast at which contributions were made for some one in distress ; (2) -**make**, a help-mate.

(1) Sus. I was a little while at the German's help-ale. I gave him as, MARCHANT *Diary* (1716) in *N. & Q.* (1879) 5th S. xi. 247. w.Eng. BRAND *Pop. Antiq.* (1777) 339. (2) Lan. GASKELL *Lectures Dial.* (1854) 19.

6.. *sb.* Muscular power.

n.Lin.[1] She's noá more help in her sen then a wooden body, poor thing.

HELPENER, *sb.* Sc. Also in form **helpender.** An assistant.

Sc. This new helpender, he's no ower muckle sense, ROY *Horseman's Wd.* (1895) vi. **Abd.** Maister Middleton . . . had been helpener afore to Ferdie, ALEXANDER *Johnny Gibb* (1871) xviii.

HELPER, *sb.* Sc. Nhb. Dur. Nhp. Hrt. **1.** A labourer. (R.O.H.) **2.** The largest hop-pole in a set of four. Hrt. ELLIS *Mod. Husb.* (1750) IV. iii. **3.** The stand or thrawl for a barrel. Nhp.[1] **4.** With *up*: a boy employed to assist the putters to bring coals up a dip or bank. Nhb. (R.O.H.) ; Nhb., Dur. GREENWELL *Coal Tr. Gl.* (1849). **5.** An assistant teacher ; an assistant preacher to a minister.

Sc. (A.W.) **Lth.** Mr. Sinclair was the 'helper'—for pupil teachers or certificated assistants were unknown in Blinkbonny, STRATHESK *More Bits* (ed. 1885) 12.

HELPLY, *adj.* Sc. Lakel. Cum. Helpful, ready and willing to assist.

Cai.[1] **Lakel.[2]** A helply mak ov a body's yan 'at'll deea a good turn when we're sair in need on't. **Cum.** A gud temper't swort ov a chap he was, ta be sure ; helply amang t'nabours, FARRALL *Betty Wilson* (1886) 5 ; **Cum.[4]**

HELPSOME, *adj.* Cum.[14] Ready and willing to help.

HEL-RAKE, HELSE, see Heel-rake, Halse, *sb.*[1]

HELSE, *v.* Sh.I. To have a liking for, to accept as a lover. S. & Ork.[1] Cf. halse, *v.* 9.

HELSIN, HELSUM, see Elsin, Halesome.

HELT, *adv.* Obs. Lan. Likely, easily. Cf. helder.

(HALL.) ; He moot as helt be forsworn, TIM BOBBIN *View Dial.* (1740) 39.

[The same word as ON. *heldr,* more, rather ; cp. OS. *hald,* MHG. *halt* ; see LEXER (s.v.).]

HELT. The same as Elt, *v.* (q.v.)

HELT, see Hold, *v.*

HELTER, *sb.* and *v.* Sh.I. Nhb. Dur. Cum. Wm. Yks. Lan. Not. Lin. Also written **helther** n.Yks. e.Yks. [h]e'lta(r.] **1.** *sb.* A halter ; a horse-collar made of hemp ; also used *attrib.*

S. & Ork.[1], **n.Cy.** (HALL.), **N.Cy.[1], Nhb.[1], Dur.[1], Cum.[14]** **Wm.** Pooin' away, at t'helter end, *Lonsdale Mag.* (1820) l. 512. **n.Yks.** He may ha' slipped his helther wiv a tug, BROWN *Yk. Minster Screen* (1834) 209 ; **n.Yks.[1][2][4], ne.Yks.[1]** **e.Yks.** *Dial.* (1887) 25. **w.Yks.** WATSON *Hist. Hlfx.* (1775) 539 ; **w.Yks.[1][2][4], e.Lan.[1], Not.** (J.H.B.), **Not.[1][2], s.Not.** (J.P.K.) **n.Lin.** A blood-foal fost time it's a helter putten on it head, PEACOCK *R. Shirlaugh* (1870) l. 194 ; **n.Lin.[1]** **sw.Lin.[1]** He's a strange pony to roll ; as soon as I get the helter off on him, he is down by that. **s.Lin.** Git haéf a dozen helters next Stamford Market daá (T.H.R.). **2.** *Comp.* (1) **Helter-head,** a halter ; (2) **-shank,** a cord or rope attached to a horse's head-stall.

(1) **Nhb.[1]** (2) **Sh.I.** Ane o' wir horses . . . wis knappid ane o' her helter shanks, an' staandin' i' wir best bit o' bere, Sh. *News* (Aug. 19, 1899). **Nhb.[1]** The rope from the 'halter-heed' to the balance weight that hangs below the manger, and runs through an iron ring therein fixed. **n.Yks.** *N. & Q.* (1869) 4th S. iv. 154 ; **n.Yks.[2]** The short rope attached to the halter for leading the horse to water. **ne.Yks.[1]**

3. *Phr.* (1) *Helter for helter,* a term used among the lowest class of horse-dealers to denote an exchange of horses without any money passing ; (2) *to slip the neck out of the helter,* to get out of a scrape, to escape from danger ; (3) *to swing in a helter,* to be hanged.

(1) **Nhb.[1], Cum.[14]** (2) **w.Yks.[1]** (3) **Cum.** Yen had as weel in a helter swing As luik at a bonny face, GILPIN *Sngs.* (1866) 297.

4. *v.* To put a halter on ; to break in young colts.

Nhb. When a colt is first caught and bridled, it is said to have been helter'd (R.O.H.). **Cum.** Then four men . . . heltert our nag, RITSON *Borrowdale Lett.* (1866) 3 ; **Cum.[4]** Thoo thinks to catch an' helter hur, RICHARDSON *Talk* (1871) 1st S. 79. **n.Lin.** Waait while I helter him (M.P.).

Hence **Heltering,** *vbl. sb.* the process of breaking in colts. **ne.Yks.[1]**

[1. *Hoc capistrum,* a heltyr, *Nom.* (c. 1450) in Wright's *Voc.* (1884) 727 ; Þe 3eolewe claÞ is Þes deofles helfter, *Hom.* (c. 1175), ed. Morris, I. 53. OE. *hælfter.*]

HELTER-SKELTER, *adv., adj.* and *sb.* Sc. Irel. n.Cy. Wm. Yks. Lan. Ess. Ken. Also written **helter-skelther** Don. ; and in forms **helter-kelter** Ess. Ken.[2]; **heltie-skeltie** Ayr. **1.** *adv.* Head-foremost, all together.

Ken. LEWIS *I. Tenet* (1736) ; **Ken.[2]**

2. With great speed ; without intermission.

Kcd. Couper Geordie sae hed drunken helter-skelter, nicht an' day, GRANT *Lays* (1884) 41. **Slg.** Oh! then to the sea helter-skelter, GALLOWAY *Luncarty* (1804) 77. **Ayr.** Heltie skeltie we gae scrievin', An' fash nae mair, AINSLIE *Land of Burns* (ed. 1892) 105. **Lth.** The supper came, when plate an' spoon Gaed there now helter skelter, BRUCE *Poems* (1813) II. 101. **Edb.** They kiss the cap, An' ca't round helter-skelter, FERGUSSON *Poems* (1773) 133, ed. 1785. **Don.** Brian Boru . . . turns, an' helter-skelther off in a new diraction he makes, MACMANUS *Billy Lappin* in *Cent. Mag.* (Feb. 1900) 606. **n.Yks.[4]** He went helter-skelter doon t'lonnin' leyke a scopperil, 396.

Hence **Helter-skeltering,** *sb.* hurrying.

Wgt. Nae helter-skeltering here an' there, FRASER *Poems* (1885) 9.

3. Vigorously, recklessly.

Yks. (J.W.) **Lan.** He went at it 'helter skelter' (S.W.).

4. *adj.* Confused ; careless, wild.

Fif. Stoups and jinglin' glasses thrang, Wi' helter-skelter cling-and-clang, TENNANT *Papistry* (1827) 23. **Wm.** Christ wad heve appeared a helterskelter Heroe, HUTTON *Bran New Wark* (1785) l. 183.

5. *sb.* Confusion, haste.

n.Cy., Yks. (J.W.) **Ess.** In sich a helter-kelter (W.W.S.).

HELTROT, see Eltrot.

HELVE, *sb.*[1] Sc. Chs. e.An. In phr. (1) *afraid of the hatchet lest the helve stick in his eye,* afraid of that which is unlikely to happen ; (2) *to fling the helve after the hatchet,* having adventured in a losing business, to engage further in it.

(1) **Chs.** RAY *Prov.* (1678) 224, ed. 1813. (2) **Sc.** 'This wretched estate . . . were it sold, I could start again, and mend my hand a little.' 'Ay, just fling the helve after the hatchet,' SCOTT *St. Ronans* (1824) x. **Chs.[12], e.An.[2]**

HELVE, *sb.*[2] Glo.[1] A stone pitcher.

HELVE, *sb.*[3] and *v.* Ken. Sus. [elv.] **1.** *sb.* A long gossip. Sus.[12]

2. *v.* To gossip.

Ken.[1] Where have you been helving? Sus.[12] **e.Sus.** HOLLOWAY. **HELVE,** see Halve.

HELWALLS, *sb. pl.* Oxf. The end outside walls of a gable house. (HALL.), (M.A.R.)

HELY, see Holy.

HELYACK, *sb.* Sh.I. Also written **heljack, hellyik ;** and in form **hellya.** A rock shelving to the sea ; a flat stone. Cf. hofsahellyika.

(Coll. L.L.B.) ; *Grn.* (but not always) at the sea-shore, JAKOBSEN *Dial.* (1897) 88 ; **S. & Ork.[1]**

[A der. of Norw. dial. *hella,* a flat stone (AASEN) ; ON. *hella,* a table-land of rocks (VIGFUSSON).]

HELYIES-AM, *sb.* Sh.I. A pleasant, agreeable person. S. & Ork.[1]

HEM, *sb.*[1] Yks. Lan. Dev. [em.] The edge of anything ; the border or skirting of a field or plot of ground.

Yks. (J.W.) **Lan.** A prattier wench niver nipt th' hem of a cake, BRIERLEY *Day Out* (1859) 18. **Dev.** *N. & Q.* (1879) 5th S. xi. 93.

[Hovande one þe hye waye þo þe holte hemmes, *Morte Arth.* (c. 1420) 1648.]

HEM, *sb.*[2] Obs. Som. A partition in an oven used for baking *Lapis calaminaris.*

The ovens wherein the *Lapis calaminaris* or *calamine* is baked have a hearth made on one side of the oven, divided from the oven itself by a partition open at the top, by which the flame passes over, and so heats and bakes the *calamine.* This partition is called the hem (K.).

HEM, *sb.*[3] and *adv.* Ken. Sur. Sus. Also written **em** Sus. [em.] **1.** *sb.* A euphemism for the devil, the infernal regions, &c.

Ken. Don't you be in such a terrible hem of a hurry, ELLIS *Pronunc.* (1889) V. 138. **Sur.[1]** I see a hem of a lot of sand mucked out there sure-ly. **Sus.** It was de very hem of a place for Pharisees, LOWER *S. Downs* (1854) 159 ; The six as be shut out, they just do make a hem of a noise, EGERTON *Flks. and Ways* (1884) 3 ; What de hem do you mean ? (F.W.L.)

2. *Comb.* (1) **Hem-a-bit,** never a bit, certainly not ; (2) **-and-all,** an intensitive *adv.*

(1) **Sus.**[1] 'Ah,' says he, ''tis better than no weather at all ; ' and hem-a-bit would he say any more ; **Sus.**[2] (2) **Ken.** My wife's brother's son is a hem-an-all fine shot with a rifle, they tell me, *Longman's Mag.* (Nov. 1891) 88. **Sus.** A liddle bowl full of summut dat smelt a hem-an-all better dan small beer, LOWER *S. Downs* (1854) 160 ; 'Twas em an all de nighest way, LOWER *Tom Cladpole* (1831) st. 100.

3. *adv.* Very, exceedingly.

Ken.[1] Hem queer old chap, he is ! **Sur.**[1] **Sus.** You be hem purty, my love ; there adnt a spot in ye, LOWER *Sng. Sol.* (1860) iv. 7 ; **Sus.**[2] Hem rum ol' fellow dat. **e.Sus.** A hem cold day (R.H.C.) ; Hem bad weather, HOLLOWAY.

HEM, *v.* Lakel. Yks. [(h)em.] With *in* : of winter days : to draw in.

Lakel.[1] **w.Yks.** The days hems in short, LUCAS *Stud. Nidderdale* (c. 1882) 258.

HEM, see Em, Hame, *sb.*[1]

HEMEL, *sb.* Dev. Also in form **hammel·.** [e·ml, æ·ml.] Frozen fog. Cf. hemple.

The cold was intense [on Dartmoor], and the frozen fog (locally known as the 'hemel') caused the paths and roads to become very slippery, *W. Morning News* (Jan. 22, 1897) ; *Reports Provinc.* (1897).

Hence **Hammelled,** *adj.* covered with frozen moisture.

The moisture on the twigs of bushes, &c., being frozen, is said to be hammelled. 'Everything is hammelled all over this morning ' (*ib.*).

HEMITORY, *sb.* Ken. The fumitory, *Fumaria officinalis.* (W.F.S.)

HEMLOCK, *sb.* Sc. Nhb. Dur. Cum. Yks. Chs. Not. Lin. e.An. **I.** Dial. forms : (1) Homleck, (2) Homlick, (3) Humblock, (4) Humleek, (5) Humlick, (6) Humloch, (7) Humluck, (8) Humluck, (9) Hummlock, (10) Humly, (11) Umlock, (12) Whumlick.

(1, 2) **Nhb.**[1] (3) **s.Not.** (J.P.K.) (4) **Nhb.**[1], **sw.Lin.**[1] (5) **N.Cy.**[1] **Nhb.** She's like sum holloo humlick grown a' puzzin the stem, ROBSON *Evangeline* (1870) 361 ; **Nhb.**[1] (6) **Rxb.** Na humlock hips she balanced sae weil, TELFER *Border Ballads, &c.* (1824) *Kerlyn's Broche.* (7) **Sc.** I couldna hae played pew upon a dry humlock, SCOTT *Bride of Lam.* (1819) xxiv. **Frf.** Skyters o' boortree, an' stout humlock shaws, WATT *Sketches* (1880) 58. **Nhb.** (B. & H.), **Dur.**[1], **Cum.**[1], **n.Yks.** (T.S.), **e.Yks.**[1], **w.Yks.**[22], **s.Not.** (J.P.K.), **Lin.**[1], **n.Lin.**[1], **sw.Lin.**[1], **e.An.** (B. & H.) (8) **n.Yks.** (I.W.) (9) **Bnff.**[1] (10) **Rxb.** *Science Gossip* (1876) 39. (11) **w.Yks.** BANKS *Wkfld. Wds.* (1865). (12) **Nhb.**[1]

II. Dial. uses. **1.** The chervil or cow-parsley, *Chaerophyllum sylvestre* (*Anthriscus sylvestris*).

n.Yks. (I.W.), **e.Yks.** (B. & H.), **w.Yks.**[1], **Chs.** (B.& H.), **sw.Lin.**[1] **2.** The cow-parsnip, *Heracleum Sphondylium.* Bnff.[1] **3.** Hollow-stemmed umbelliferous plants *gen.* **Lnk.** By the common people nearly all the Umbellate plants are called hemlock, PATRICK *Plants* (1831) 137. **Nhb.**[1] It's hollow as a homlick. **Yks.** *N. & Q.* (1878) 5th S. ix. 417. **w.Yks.** BANKS *Wkfld. Wds.* (1865). **e.An.** (B. & H.)

[**I.** (7) An humlock, *cicuta, Cath. Angl.* (1483). (10) OE. *hymlic* (*Leechdoms*).]

HEMM, see Hame, *sb.*[1]

HEMMA, *sb.* Sh.I. **1.** A home. S. & Ork.[1] **2.** A wife, housewife. *ib.*

HEMMEL, *sb.*[1] Sc. Nhb. Dur. Cum. Yks. Also Sus. Also written hemle Dur. Yks. ; hemmil Nhb. ; hemmle n.Yks.[2] ; and in forms hammel Bwk. (JAM.) Cum. ; hemble n.Cy. Dur. Yks. [(h)em·l.] **1.** A shed or covering for cattle, *gen.* in a field ; an out-building used for storage, &c. ; also used *fig.* for a group of children in one house. Cf. helm, *sb.*[2]

Bwk. *Monthly Mag.* (1814) I. 31 ; *Report,* 95 (JAM.). **n.Cy.** (HALL.) ; **N.Cy.**[1] **Nhb.** Shortly after this the Priest's Hemmel was burned, DIXON *Whittingham Vale* (1895) 276 ; Wor neybor hes a fine hemmel o' bairns (R.O.H.) ; **Nhb.**[1], **e.Dur.**[1] **Nhb.**[1] An outbuilding on a farm ; formerly made of upright posts, with whin or broom interlaced, and a thatched roof. Chiefly used in winter and the lambing season. The permanent hemmel, which forms a conspicuous feature in Northumberland farm buildings, is surrounded by a fold yard, and has in front an arcade of massive masonry, frequently surmounted by a granary. Dur. Any covered place, having open sides (K.) ; **Dur.**[1] An erection on pillars, with wooden cross-beams, so as to form a shed underneath, and made to support corn or hay. **e.Dur.**[1] The word, although still understood, is going out of use. **s.Dur.** Usually, a house where cattle run loose in, and adjoins a fold-yard (J.E.D.). **Cum.** Usually of rough unbarked posts, wickered in between with whin, a wide entrance, and no door (J.Ar.) ; **Cum.**[4] A shed contiguous to the dwelling house used as a storage for implements, bracken, &c. ; the word is current only in the outlying fell-dales. 'Two fields off . . . in a cattle hemel,' GRAHAM *Red Scaur* (1896) 77. **Yks.** A hovel or house for wains and carts (K.). **n.Yks.** (I.W.)

2. *Comp.* (1) **Hemmel-eye,** the archway leading to the covered arcade in fold-yards ; (2) **-thing,** a building having the appearance of a 'hemmel.'

(1) **Nhb.**[1] (2) **Nhb.** That hemmil thing that stan's upon tha heed, CHATER *Tyneside Alm.* (1869) 14.

3. A fold. n.Cy. GROSE (1790), N.Cy.[1], Sus.[1] **4.** A stage on posts to support corn or hay.

Bwk., Rxb. (JAM.), **Dur.**[1] **n.Yks.**[2] The wooden spars laid on the ground as a basis for the haystack. **ne.Yks.** (J.C.F.)

HEMMEL, *sb.*[2] Yks. [e·ml.] A hand-rail, such as is usually fitted on one side of a planked or wooden bridge.

Yks. With a 'hemmel' or hand rail on either side, HENDERSON *Flk-Lore* (1879) vi. **n.Yks.**[14], **ne.Yks.**[1]

[Cp. Sw. dial. *hammel,* a little bar or beam (RIETZ).]

HEMMEL, see Hamil.

HEMMIL, *sb.* and *v.* Sc. (JAM.) Also written **hemil** Ags. **1.** *sb.* A heap, crowd, multitude.

n.Sc. A hemmil of folk ; a hemmil of beasts.

2. *v.* To surround any beast in order to lay hold of it ; to surround with a multitude. Ags.

HEMMING AND SEWING, *phr.* Hmp. The yarrow, *Achillea millefolium.* (W.M.E.F.) ; *Nature Notes,* No. 3.

HEMP, *sb.* and *v.* Var. dial. uses in Sc. and Eng. Also in forms emp, impe, ympe Dur. **1.** *sb.* In *comp.* (1) Hemp-but, *obs.,* a garden plot, or a piece of field on which hemp was grown ; (2) -croft, a small paddock near a homestead ; (3) -dub, (4) -dyke, a small pond or pit in which hemp is steeped ; (5) -garth, a garden attached to a cottage, formerly used for growing hemp ; (6) -haugh, see (1) ; (7) -heckler, a flax-dresser ; (8) -land, a small piece of land set apart for growing flax for family use ; (9) -looking, fit for the gallows ; (10) -pit, *obs.,* see (4) ; (11) -riggs, ridges of fertile land on which hemp was formerly grown ; (12) -string, (*a*) a hangman's halter ; (*b*) to hang ; (13) -yard, see (5).

(1) **Shr.**[1] I have seene them pecking on the hemp-butt as if they did feed, GOUGH *Hist. Myddle* (1 1833) 47. (2) **Chs.**[1] Very common name for small paddocks near homesteads. **n.Lin.**[1] (3) **Cum.**[14] (4) **n.Lin.**[1] (5) **Cum.**[1] (s.v. Garth). **n.Lin.**[1] (6) **Ken.**[2] (s.v. Haw). (7) **n.Cy.** (HALL.), **n.Yks.**[2] **w.Yks.** WATSON *Hist. Hlfx.* (1775) 540 ; **w.Yks.**[4] (8) **Lan.**[1] **n.Lan.**[1] Although the practice has fallen into desuetude, the patches of land still retain the name. **e.An.**[12] **e.Suf.** Now that hemp is no longer cultivated here, the word is used for a poor man's paddock, a small field in which he grows vegetables. It is not an allotment (F.H.). (9) **Slk.** I never saw twa mair hemp-looking dogs in my life, HOGG *Tales* (1838) 7, ed. 1866. (10) **n.Lin.**[1] (11) **Gall.** When land is a praising for goodness it is said to be as strong as hemp-riggs, MACTAGGART *Encycl.* (1824) 259, ed. 1876. (12, *a*) **Frf.** In a' probability he wad form a bonnie tossil at the end o' a hemp string, WILLOCK *Rosetty Ends* (1886) 105, ed. 1889. (*b*) **Edb.** For rearing whiles a shilling or twa, They'll be hemp strung, LIDDLE *Poems* (1821) 153. (13) **Chs.**[1], **n.Lin.**[1]

2. A rope ; a small cord spliced on to a bell-rope.

Gall. Cows rattling at their hemps thro' the rings, CROCKETT *Grey Man* (1896) xviii. Dur. *N. & Q.* (1887) 7th S. iii. 268.

3. *Fig.* A rough, troublesome character ; one who is qualifying for the gallows.

Nhb. What to myek o' the lad, dear knaas, he's sic a hemp. Them bairns o' mine's hemps ; thor fair deevils wi' thor skylarking (R.O.H.) ; **Nhb.**[1], **e.Dur.**[1] **Lakel.**[2] Thoo's a gurt rough hemp. **Wm.** If ever there was a hemp of a lad that lad was Willie Mecca, JACKSON *Moor and Mead,* 123. **Cor.**[2] A proper hemp.

Hence **Hempy,** (1) *sb.* a rogue, a person deserving the gallows ; a giddy, wild, romping girl ; (2) *adj.* wild, riotous, giddy, idle, mischievous ; shabby-genteel.

T 2

(1) **Sc.** Where did ye get the book, ye little hempie! Scott *Midlothian* (1818) l. **Baff.** He was an exceedingly shy and bashful man, though he had been such a 'hempy' in his youth, Smiles *Natur.* (1876) ix. **Abd.** Murr's a leein'hempy, M¢Kenzie *Sketches* (1894) xi. **Frf.** Ye hempie, wad ye snore, An' try to gar me trow ye're sleepin'! Watt *Sketches* (1880) 102. **Per.** She was some thochtless young hempie 'at kenned na' weel what she was after, Cleland *Inchbracken* (1883) ix. **Dmb.** 'Gainst thae hempies on the lan' laid loose, Salmon *Gowodean* (1868) 29. **Rnf.** Think ye I'd rowt a name I like In ilka hempy's hearin? Picken *Poems* (1813) I. 155. **Ayr.** What na scamp or hempy is't that the cutty is gallanting wi'? Galt *Entail* (1823) lxxiii. **Lnk.** He had gather'd seven or aught Wild hempies stout and strang, Ramsay *Poems* (1721) 62, ed. 1733. **Edb.** Hempies thro' auld Reikie rantet, Crawford *Poems* (1798) 46. **Peb.** Aft thrawart hempies ... Laws human an' divine brick thro', Nicol *Poems* (1805) I. 52 (Jam.). **Slk.** Love them, giggling hempies! Hogg *Tales* (1838) 281, ed. 1866. **Gall.** She had been a big-boned 'hempie' at the Kirkland School for many a day, Crockett *Stickit Min.* (1893) 252. **Nhb.** A free-spoken Liddesdale hempy, Richardson *Borderer's Table-bk.* (1846) VII. 137; This hempie of a bird—the jackdaw (R.O.H.); Nhb.¹ Cum.¹; Cum.⁴ Eh, but she's a hempie is yon yen. (2) **Sc.** I was a daft hempie lassie then, Scott *Old Mortality* (1816) xlii. **Abd.** Syne a' the drochlin' hempy thrang Gat o'er him wi' a fudder, Skinner *Poems* (1809) 46. **s.Sc.** The hempie son, to get his horns shot out, Wad wiss his father yerdet hard an' fast, T. Scott *Poems* (1793) 366. **Lth.** Wha e'er wad hae thocht the weel-faur'd honest man as he is wad hae drawn up wi' sich a bit hempie hauflin lassie, Lumsden *Sheep-head* (1892) 94. **N.Cy.¹ Nhb.** Thor's elways luck iv a hempy lad (R.O.H.) ; But if like hempy lads they fight, We'll heh to keep them doon, Wilson *Tyneside Sngs.* (1890) 255. **e.Dur.¹ n.Yks.¹** ; **n.Yks.²** 'A hempy dog,' a youth whose course is likely to end in the hangman's hemp; **n.Yks.⁴, ne.Yks.¹** **Cor.²** A decayed gentleman who tries unsuccessfully to keep up an appearance is 'hempy.'

4. v. To beat, chastise. **Ess.** (W.W.S.) Hence **Hemping,** *sb.* a beating, thrashing. 'I'll give yow sich a hempin'' (*ib.*).

HEMPEN-HALTER, *sb.* **w.Som.¹** The ordinary rope head-stall for horses.

It is customary for the seller of a horse to provide [u ai·mpm-au·ltur], to enable the buyer to lead off his purchase.

HEMPERT, *sb.* **Obs. Shr.¹** Ground specially appropriated to hemp, a hemp-yard.

So I see Mr. Goff 'as let the 'empert into the stack-yurd—well, well, I s'pose as theer's more barley than 'emp wanted now-a-days.

HEMPIE, *sb.* **Sc. Yks.** [h)e·mpi.] The hedge-sparrow, *Accentor modularis.*

Sc. Swainson *Birds* (1885) 29. **Dmf.** Shaw *Schoolmaster* (1899) 349. **Yks.** Swainson *ib.*

HEMPLE, *sb.* **Dev. Cor.** Also written **hempel** Cor. [e·mpl.] A Scotch mist or drizzling rain. Cf. **hemel.**

Dev. It is only a hemple, *Reports Provinc.* (1884) 21. **Cor.** (J.W.)

HEMPLING, *sb.* **Cum.** [he·mplin.] **1.** A headridge sown with hemp-seed. **Cum.¹ 2.** The brown linnet, *Linota cannabina.* **Cum.¹⁴ 3.** The hedge-sparrow, *Accentor modularis.* **Cum.⁴**

HEMPSHIRE GENTLEMAN, *phr.* **Fif.** (Jam.) [Not known to our correspondents.] One who is qualifying for the gallows.

HEMPTON, *sb.* **Cum.** A succession of fairs, principally for horses, held at Carlisle between the 1st of Oct. and Martinmas.

Sullivan *Cum. and Wm.* (1857) 87; **Cum.⁴** Carlisle Head Hempton. . . The second of the October fairs was held on Saturday, *W. C. T.* (Oct. 29, 1898) 6, col. 4.

HEMSKIT, *adj.* **Sh.I.** Foolish. **S. & Ork.¹**

[ON. *heimskr* (neut. *heimskt*), foolish, silly.]

HEMUST, see **Hindmost.**

HEN, *sb.¹* Var. dial. uses in Sc. Irel. and Eng. Also in forms heyny Lnk. **Nhb.¹** e.Yks. w.Cor. ; **heny, heyn** e.Yks. ; **hin** Cor. **1.** In comb. (1) Hen-a-pecker, a miss ; (2) -baik or -boke, the rafter on which hens roost ; a henroost ; also used for a bed ; (3) -bird, the domestic fowl ; (4) -brains, few or no brains ; (5) -broth or -broo, chicken-broth ; (6) -('s care, care exercised without judgement ; (7) -caul or -coil, a hen-coop ; (8) -('s cavey, a hen-house ; (9) -chalk, a kind of gypsum ; (10) -chee, a hen-roost ; (11) -chick, a chicken as opposed to a duckling, 'duck-chick' ;

(12) -corn, a light, inferior grain, used for feeding poultry ; (13) -cote, a fowl-shelter, the rafters of the shed ; (14) -cower, to cower down as a hen sits ; to sit on one's haunches as pitmen do in mines ; (15) -('s croft, a portion of a corn-field frequented and damaged by fowls ; (16) -crow, the hooded crow, *Corvus cornix* ; (17) -egg, a hen's egg, as distinguished from a duck's egg ; (18) -fish, (a) a species of cod, *Morrhua minuta* ; (b) the pomfret, *Brama raii* ; (19) -flesh, the condition of the pores of the skin when they stand up through cold, making the skin rough like that of a plucked fowl ; goose-flesh ; (20) -('s gerse, a hen's keep ; (21) -hardy, the white female three-spined stickleback, *Gasterosteus aculeatus* ; (22) -harrier or -harrow, a species of kite, *Circus cyaneus,* very destructive to chickens ; (23) -headed, an epithet applied to a person who has acted foolishly ; (24) -hearted, timid, cowardly, 'chicken-hearted' ; (25) -hole, see (7) ; (26) -hoop, a female bullfinch, *Pyrrhula Europaea* ; (27) -hurdle, a hen-roost, esp. a loft over a pig-sty ; (28) -hussey or -huswife, a woman who looks after poultry ; also a meddlesome, officious person ; (29) -loft, the joists of a house ; also the space above them ; (30) -man, a poultry-tender ; (31) -meat, small, imperfectly formed grain, used as food for poultry ; (32) -minner, the female stickleback ; (33) -mould or -mouldy soil, light, dark loamy soil ; (34) -mouthed, toothless ; (35) -('s nap, a short nap ; (36) -('s nose-full, a very minute quantity ; (37) -pen, (a) see (7) ; (b) the dung of fowls ; sweepings from the fowl-house, of great manurial value ; (38) -penny, (a) money paid by the tenants to the lord of the manor instead of an original payment in hens ; (b) see (37) ; (39) -poller, -s' polly, or -s' pulley, a loft in which poultry roost ; (40) -race, see below ; (41) -rent, see (38, a) ; (42) -rip, see (7) ; (43) -scarts, -scrats, or -scratchings, certain kinds of fleecy clouds said to betoken wind or rain ; (44) -shoes, cloth shoes put on the feet of poultry to prevent them scratching in gardens ; (45) -sit, a long sitting like that of a hen upon her eggs ; (46) -stee, the board or ladder by which poultry ascend to the roost ; (47) -toed, having the toes turned in ; (48) -wife, (a) a woman in charge of poultry ; (b) a man who busies himself about matters usually left to women ; (49) -wifely, like a 'hen-wife' ; (50) -wile, a stratagem ; (51) Hens'-toes, a term applied to bad writing ; pot-hooks.

(1) **Nrf.** 'There's some eels here—keep your scoop low—I missed him.' 'You 'a 'made a henapecker o' that,' Emerson *Son of Fens* (1892) 117. (2) **Elg.** A' was thine, The marbl't ha's and painted bowr's, To hen-bauks and the swine, Couper *Poetry* (1804) II. 79. **Gall.** On the black henbauks i' the kirk, Crockett *Sunbonnet* (1895) xvi. **n.Cy.** (K.) ; **N.Cy.²,** **Nhb.¹, Cum.¹⁴ Yks.** A foomard gat croppen oop into t'hen-bawks, *Spec. Dial.* (1800) 24. **n.Yks.¹²⁴, ne.Yks.¹** **e.Yks.** Marshall *Rur. Econ.* (1796). **n.Lin.¹** (3) **Sc.** A chicken, properly one following its mother (Jam.). **Ayr.** The tane [cock] is game, a bludie devil, But to the hen-birds unco civil, Burns *Elegy on Year 1788.* **n.Yks.¹** 'Where t'partridges rase, Ah heered a cheeping lik' a young henbird' : a cry like that of a young chicken :—which it was, in fact, the hen partridge having by some chance sat on and hatched the egg of a common fowl. **ne.Yks.¹** Cocks and hens are distinguished as 'male bo'ds' and 'hen bo'ds.' (4) **w.Yks.** *Leeds Merc. Suppl.* (Jan. 26, 1884) 8.† (5) **Sc.** A simple decoction of two or three howtowdies (Anglice, fowls) thickened with black beans and seasoned with black pepper, Hislop *Anecdote* (1874) 52. **Ayr.** Kate sits i' the neuk Suppin' hen-broo, Burns *Gudeen, Kimmer,* st. 2 ; I got the lassock to fetch me a hue o' hen-broth, Service *Notandums* (1890) xl. (6) **Fif.** (Jam.) (7) **n.Cy.** Grose (1790) ; **N.Cy.²** **e.Yks.** Marshall *Rur. Econ.* (1788). (8) **Sc.** D'ye think you're to be free to plunder the faulds and byres of a gentle Elliot, as if they were an auld wife's hen-cavey? Scott *Blk. Dwarf* (1816) ix. (9) **n.Lin.¹** (10) **Ken.¹** (11) **Cor.** Thomas *Randigal Rhymes* (1895) *Gl.* (12) **e.Yks.¹** Refuse, or inferior grain, which falls from the hinder part of the thrashing or winnowing machine. **w.Yks.²** Poor, thin, ill-fed wheat ; corn which is not round and plump. 'It will grow nothing but hen corn.' When a farmer, instead of sowing corn which has been grown at a distance, sows, year after year, the corn which has been grown on his own land, it is apt to be poor and inferior stuff, and is called hen corn. **Chs.¹** The wheat was so badly down,

it were nowt bu' hen-corn when it were threshed. s.Chs.¹ (13) n.Yks.² Lan. Exploring some secret recess of the hencote, BRIERLEY *Irkdale* (1865) I. 119. (14) Dur. BROCKETT *Gl.* (1846) (s.v. Hunkers). s.Dur. Children slide in this position and call it hencowering. 'Let's gan down t'hill a-hencowerin'' (J.E.D.). Cum.⁴ (15) Per. (G.W.) (16) Ir. SWAINSON *Birds* (1885) 86. (17) Cum. I dunnet know why she gev' t'fry; It's t'hen egg for t'duck 'en, sed she. [A small present to secure the return of a larger], BURN *Border Ballads* (1877) 130. Som. Only a couple of little hen-eggs and a duck-egg; and that's the best tea he has eaten for months, RAYMOND *Misterton's Mistake* (1888) 368. (18, *a*) N.I.¹ (*b*) Ir. (C.D.) (19) Lth. My skin's a' hen's flesh (JAM.). Nhb.¹, Not.¹, Lei.¹, Nhp.¹, War.²³ (20) Bwk. For a hen's gerse They'll flit i' the Merse, HENDERSON *Pop. Rhymes* (1856) 32. (21) Cum.⁴ (22) N.Cy.² Nhb.¹ I have not seen a single individual for several years, HANCOCK *Birds of Nhb. and Dur.* 19. n.Yks.² w.Yks. THORESBY *Lett.* (1703); w.Yks.⁴ Bdf. BATCHELOR *Anal. Eng. Lang.* (1809) 135. (23) w.Yks. (F.K.) (24) Sc. Are you turned hen-hearted, Jack? SCOTT *Guy M.* (1815) xxviii. Sh.I. A fearder heart than thine, A more hen-hearted soul Dwells not afar, *Sh. News* (Sept. 10, 1898). Fif. Hen-hearted enough to renounce God, and his covenanted Kirk, and adhere to bishops and curates, GRANT *Six Hundred*, ix. e.Fif. Hen-hearted Neddy tane till's heels an' fled, LATTO *Tam Bodkin* (1864) xxx. Dmb. This is no the time for the like o' you to be hen-hearted, CROSS *Disruption* (1844) xxviii. Dmf. Quite sheepish, hen-hearted, and mean, JOHNSTONE *Poems* (1820) 129. Ir. He'd be a greater tyrant only he's so hen-hearted, CARLETON *Fardorougha* (ed. 1848) xvii. Cum. Ah mud be varra hen-heartit teh be freetent of a yurthquake, SARGISSON *Joe Scoap* (1881) 191. (25) w.Yks. T'man-i'-fact-hurry hed once been a hen hoil o' Tobias's, *Yksman. Comic Ann.* (1890) 31 ; w.Yks.⁵ (26) Som. W. & J. *Gl.* (1873). (27) Chs. (K.), Chs.¹², s.Chs.¹, nw.Der.¹ (28) Wil.¹ Som. W. & J. *Gl.* (1873). Dev.¹ He was sich a hen-huswife, wan couldu't turn a dish vor en, 11. [Amar. A man who meddles with women's affairs, *Dial. Notes* (1896) I. 74.] (29) Sc. Country-houses long ago were *gen.* of but one storey, with thatched roof and open ceiling. The joists . . . being the recognised place for the poultry to roost during night were called the hen-laft. . . Many a mother has brought order out of disorder by threatening to send the naughty ones 'to bide in the hen-laft' (JAM. *Suppl.*). (30) Ayr. I was ta'en oot to see James Beetle, the henman, SERVICE *Dr. Duguid* (ed. 1887) xxiii. (31) w.Cor. (M.A.C.) (32) Lan. (G.E.D.) (33) Nhp.¹ Bearn, in his 'Prize Essay on the Farming of Nhp.,' explains hen-mouldy-land as a moory or peaty soil, with gravelly and clay subsoil; Nhp.² War.² Land which is friable at the top (from exposure to the weather) but which is stiff beneath the surface. Oxf. A mixed soil, *Farmers' Jrn.* (Sept. 29, 1808). Bdf. Those parts which are upon high ground, and yet have little or no descent, are frequently what are denominated woodlands, or hen-mould earth, BATCHELOR *Agric.* (1813) 24; (J.W.B.) (34) Bnff. Ye're nae aul' eneuch yet to be hen-mouth'd, GORDON *Chron. Keith* (1880) 32. (35) Cor. Deddn sleep fitty for tha night; had nothin' but hin's naps (F.H.D.). (36) e.An.¹, e.Suf. (F.H.) (37, *a*) Rnf. A' the hens Wi' fricht took soople heels awa Tae their hen-pens, NEILSON *Poems* (1877) 32. (*b*) ne.Sc. Another ley was made of the droppings of the poultry and went by the name of hen-pen, GREGOR *Flk-Lore* (1881) 176; (J.Ar.) Cai.¹, Ags. (JAM.), N.Cy.¹, Nhb.¹, n.Yks.¹²⁴ (38, *a*) e.Yks. WILDRIDGE *Hist. Gleanings* (1886) 124. n.Lin.¹ (*b*) w.Yks.¹ (39) e.An.¹ Nrf. (HALL); COZENS-HARDY *Broad Nrf.* (1893) 27. e.Suf. (F.H.) (40) w.Yks.² An expression used to denote contempt in such sentences as, 'Au wodn't be seen at a hen-race wi' thee.' (41) n.Lin.¹ (42) w.Mid. He used to go about to all the sales, and buy all the old hen-rips, until he got his place chok full of 'em (W.P.M.). Sus.¹ (43) Sc. Hen scarts and filly-tails Make lofty ships wear low sails, CHAMBERS *Pop. Rhymes* (1870) 377. N.Cy.¹ Long pencilled clouds. Nhb.¹, Cum.¹⁴ n.Yks. *N. & Q.* (1883) 6th S. viii. 446; n.Yks.¹ Small streaky clouds of the *cirrus* form . . . deriving this name from some resemblance to the marks in dust or light soil left by a scratching hen; n.Yks.² Said to denote fine weather; as well as wind; n.Yks.⁴ w.Yks.¹ T'element wor feaful ful of filly-tails an hen-scrattins, ii. 286; w.Yks.²³, ne.Lan.¹ Chs.¹ Long, straggly clouds. Mid.l. MARSHALL *Rur. Econ.* (1790) II. Der.²(s.v. Filly-tails). n.Lin.¹ Small dappled clouds, or light thin clouds like torn locks of wool. Shr.¹ Filaments of white cloud crossing the sky like net-work. (44) Cum.¹⁴ (45) n.Yks. 'She'll sit a hen-sit,' she will sit till one gets tired of her company (T.S.). e.Yks. NICHOLSON *Flk-Sp.* (1889) 90; e.Yks.¹ When Jack gets tl yal-hoose [ale-house] he'll sit a nawd [an old]

hen-sit, *MS. add.* (T.H.) (46) n.Yks.², n.Lin.¹ s.Lin. Pick up that hen-stee and put it agen the hen-plaàce, the o'd hens wänt to go to roòst (T.H.R.). (47) Nhp.² Oxf.¹ *MS. add.* (48, *a*) Sc. A half-witted lad . . . who had charge of the poultry under the old hen-wife, SCOTT *Old Mortality* (1816) ii ; PENNECUIK *Coll.* (1787) 35. Cai.¹ Ayr. He heard from Jenny Sillishins, the henwife, JOHNSTON *Glenbuckie* (1889) xxii. (*b*) Cai.¹, Cld., Dur. (C.T.) (49) Abd. He rallied her on her henwifely qualifications and zeal, GREIG *Logie o' Buchan* (1899) 61. (50) Sc. Such courses as savoured of their old unhappy and unprofitable way of henwiles to make and increase parties among us, BAILLIE *Lett.* (1775) II. 80 (JAM.). (51) Abd., Ags. (JAM.)

2. *Comb.* in plant-names: (1) Hen and chickens, (*a*) the garden daisy, *Bellis perennis* ; (*b*) the London pride, *Saxifraga umbrosa* ; (*c*) the saxifrage, *S. sarmentosa* ; (*d*) the daffodil, *Narcissus Pseudo-narcissus* ; (*e*) the columbine, *Aquilegia vulgaris* ; (*f*) the bird's-foot trefoil, *Lotus corniculatus* ; (*g*) the ground-ivy, *Nepeta Glechoma* ; (*h*) the ivy-leaved toad-flax, *Linaria vulgaris* ; (*i*) the cudweed, *Filago germanica* ; (*j*) a variety of the garden Polyanthus, *Primula elatior* ; (*k*) the lady's fingers, *Anthyllis vulnaria* ; (2) -drunks, the fruit of the mountain ash, *Pyrus Aucuparia* ; (3) -gorse, (*a*) the rest-harrow, *Ononis arvensis* ; (*b*) the red Bartsia, *Bartsia Odontites* ; (4) -pen, (*a*) the yellow-rattle, *Rhinanthus Crista-galli* ; (*b*) the henbane, *Hyoscyamus niger* ; (5) -penny, (*a*) see (4, *a*) ; (*b*) see (4, *b*) ; (*c*) the crested cow-wheat, *Melampyrum cristatum* ; (6) -penny-grass, see (4, *a*) ; (7) -tails, the mat-grass, *Nardus stricta* ; also *fig.* worthless fellows ; (8) -ware, the edible fucus, *Fucus esculentus* ; (9) Hens-kaims, the spotted orchis, *Orchis maculata.*

(1, *a*) w.Yks.¹, Chs.¹ Nhp.¹ The large double daisy, with smaller ones growing round the same footstalk. War.²³, Shr.¹ Oxf.¹ *MS. add.* Sur., w.Som.¹, Dev.⁴ (*b*) Wil.¹, Dev.⁴ (*c*) Wil.¹ (*d*) Dev.⁴ (*e*) Nrf. From the resemblance of the spurs to chickens drinking. (*f*) Oxf. (*g*) s.Bck. (*h*) Ken.¹ (*i*) w.Yks. LEES *Flora* (1888) 289. (*j*) Sus. (*k*) Wor. (W.C.B.) (2) Cum.¹ Reputed to possess the property of intoxicating fowls; Cum.⁴ (3, *a*) n.Cy. (HALL), Chs.¹² Midl. MARSHALL *Rur. Econ.* (1796) II. (*b*) Chs.¹ (4, *a*) Nhb.¹, Cum.¹⁴, n.Yks. (I.W.) (*b*) Wm. It grows ower mich hen-pen (B.K.). (5, *a*) n.Cy. GROSE (1790). Nhb.¹, n.Yks.² e.Yks. MARSHALL *Rur. Econ.* (1788). w.Yks. LEES *Flora* (1888) 344. (*b*) Lakel.² (*c*) ne.Lan.¹ (6) Ir. (7) Cum. We'd hay-cruiks, an hentails, an hanniels, ANDERSON *Ballads* (1805) 170, ed. 1808 ; Cum.⁴ (8) Sc. (JAM.) (9) Nhb.¹

3. *Phr.* (1) *as busy as a hen with one chick*, unnecessarily active and fussy over trifles ; (2) *as fierce as hen-muck*, fierce but harmless ; (3) *as proud as a hen with one chick*, aggressively proud of an insignificant object ; (4) *like a hen on a hot griddle*, said of a very restless person ; (5) *to sell a hen on a rainy day*, to make a bad bargain.

(1) Nhp.¹, Oxf.¹ (2) n.Yks. (T.K.) (3) Oxf.¹ (4) Sc. She hirples like a hen on a het girdle, SCOTT *Blk. Dwarf* (1816) iii. N.I.¹ (5) Sc. KELLY *Prov.* (1721) 373 ; This is the price their indemnity must be purchased at. For the Devil is not such a fool as to sell his hen on a rainy day, M°WARD *Contendings* (1723) 328 (JAM.). Lth. John Hootsman is no' a man that'll sell his hens on a rainy day, LUMSDEN *Sheep-head* (1892) 293.

4. An opprobrious epithet applied to a woman.

Dmb. The aunt and oe, ilk just as slee a hen As e'er looped apron string round gowks o' men, SALMON *Gowodean* (1868) 85 ; Fegs, he's just ane o' the kind that wad seek sic a weel-gathered auld hen, CROSS *Disruption* (1844) vii.

5. A term of endearment.

Rnf. Dearest henie! Sweetest henie! Grown sae high I scarcely ken e'e, FINLAYSON *Rhymes* (1815) 119. Ayr. Tak' this frae me, my bonie hen, It's pretty beets the lover's fire, BURNS *Cy. Lassie*, st. 2. Lnk. O Kirsty, jist say that you'll be mine, my bonnie hen, my darlin' lamb, WARDROP *J. Mathison* (1881) 12. Lth. Come ower the burn, my bonnie hen, And wander wi' thy Chairley, M°NEILL *Preston* (c. 1895) 123.

6. A shell-fish, the *Cyprina Islandica.* s.Pem. LAWS *Little Eng.* (1888) 420.

7. A large pewter pot. Cf. grey-hen, s.v. Grey, *adj.*

Lon. The hens and chickens of the roguish low lodging-houses are the publicans' pewter measures; the bigger vessels are 'hens'; the smaller are 'chickens.' MAYHEW *Lond. Labour* (1851) I. 156.

8. *pl.* The spotted orchis, *Orchis maculata.* Nhb.¹

HEN, sb.[2] Cum. Wm. Yks. Lan. [h]en.] **1.** Money given by the bride or bridegroom on the evening after marriage, to enable their friends to drink their health.

e.Yks. On the evening of the wedding-day, the young men of the village call upon the bridegroom for a ' hen,' *Wit and Wisdom* (Aug. 1889) 163. **w.Yks.**[1]

2. *Comp.* (1) **Hen-brass,** money collected for drink at weddings; (2) **-drinking,** a wedding-feast, *gen.* provided by the bridegroom; (3) **-money,** money given by the bridegroom at the church door to his friends, or sent to poor neighbours; (4) **-silver,** money formerly given to the friends of the bridegroom for services performed, see below; now money begged at the church door after the wedding.

(1) w.Yks. When two get married they treat a company of their male friends, who are assembled at a public-house, to a quantity of ' drink.' When this is consumed, a hat goes round, and what is contributed is spent in the same way. The money thus collected is called ' hen-brass,' *N. & Q.* (1868) 4th S. i. 219. (2) w.Yks. (S.P.U.) ; A tea in honour of a bride (cost defrayed by subscription) (S.K.C.) ; It is a custom for the bridegroom to provide a hen-drinking, BURNLEY *Sketches* (1875) 71. (3) ne.Lan.[1] (4) Cum.[14] Wm. Formerly a gun was fired over the house of a newly married couple, to secure a plentiful issue of the marriage [probably to dispel the evil spirits that bring bad luck]. The firing party had a present given them [to drink the health and luck of the couple] and this was termed hen-silver, *Penrith Obs.* (Sept. 22, 1896). Yks. *N. & Q.* (1888) II. 10. n.Yks. Silver given by the bridegroom and also subscriptions of young people, who collect together to drink the health of the newly married pair, which is called drinking the hen-silver (W.H.). ne.Lan.[1]

HEN, adv. Obs. Yks. Lin. Hence. Lin. (HALL.) See Hine.

Hence **Hen-away,** adv. from a distance. n.Yks.[2] [Do now go hen fro me saton, *Cursor M.* (c. 1340) 18080. OE. (Nhb.) *heona,* ' hinc ' (*Luke* iv. 9).]

HEN(-, HENBERRY, see Hain, v.[16], Hindberry.

HENCE-AWAY, adv. n.Yks.[2] At a distance. Cf. hen, adv. ' They come frae some spot hence-away.'

HENCH, see Hainch, Hinch, v.[2]

HENCHIL, v. Sc. Also in form **hainchil.** To rock or roll from side to side in walking. Sc. (JAM.), Abd. (G.W.)

HENCHMAN, sb. Sc. Also in forms **hanchman** Sc.; **haunchman** Per. A personal attendant.

Sc. There is his hanchman or right hand man, SCOTT *Waverley* (1814) xvi ; Consider me your henchman ; I'm here to carry your basket, KEITH *Indian Uncle* (1896) 41. Abd. They brak in upon him, an' hangid him an' his henchman, *Deeside Tales* (1872) 140. Per. The haunchmen who stood by their leader in strife, To part from him only when parting from life, SPENCE *Poems* (1898) 173. w.Sc. On getting home, he called his faithful henchman, Donald Frisheal, and told him all that had occurred, MACDONALD *Settlement* (1869) iii. Fif. He soucht his henchman that did stand . . . Aye watchin at his yett, TENNANT *Papistry* (1827) 45. Dmb. Is Hance his henchman yet? SALMON *Gowodean* (1868) 14. Lnk. Monsieur at his back did prance Like a true henchman, MUIR *Minstrelsy* (1816) 95. Lth. A huge, shaggy, tousie collie dog at his heels, at once his henchman . . . and his surest guardian, LUMSDEN *Sheep-head* (1892) 266. Wgt. Who Wycliffe's valiant henchman stood—The noble-minded John of Gaunt, FRASER *Poems* (1885) 159.

HEND, adj. Obs. Sc. Also written **heynd. 1.** Dexterous, clever. GROSE (1790) *MS. add.* (C.) **2.** Courteous, gentle, a conventional epithet of praise in ballad poetry.

Sir Oluf the hend has ridden sae wide, JAMIESON *Pop. Ballads* (1806) I. 219. [L. Hary, Quha wes ane archer heynd, *Chrysts-kirk* (c. 1550) x, in *Evergreen* (ed. 1761) I. 7. **2.** Rouwenne þe hende sat bi þan kinge, LAȝAMON (c. 1205) 14357.]

HEND, see Hain, v.[6]

HENDE, sb. Obs. Sc. A young fellow. See Hind, sb.[1] **5.** When by there came a gallant hende, CHILD *Ballads* (1882) I. 71.

HENDER, see Hinder, adv.

HENDHOVEN-BREAD, sb. Lan. An oatmeal cake, much the same as **Riddle-cakes.** (K., s.v. *Riddle-cakes.*)

HENDON BENT, phr. Mid. The crested dog's-tail grass, *Cynosurus cristatus.*

The hay of Middlesex is often of good quality. Hendon, perhaps, produces the hay which has the best name in the market. The Hendon bent is well known to the dealers, and is seldom found except on good meadow-ground, *Jrn. R. Agric. Soc.* (1869) 25 (B. & H.).

HENG-, HENGE, see Hang-, Hainch.

HENGSIE, sb. Sh.I. [he·ŋsi.] A clownish, clumsy person. JAKOBSEN *Norsk in Sh.* (1897) 64 ; S. & Ork.[1] Hence **Hengsit,** adj. clownish, clumsy. S. & Ork.[1]

HENK, v. Sh.I. Also in form **hink.** [heŋk, hiŋk.] To limp; to dance awkwardly.

Henk is applied to the movements of trolls, particularly in a fairy dance, SPENCE *Flk-Lore* (1899) 39 ; ' Wha 'ill dance wi' me !' co Cuttie. Shö luked aboot an' saw naebody : ' Sae I'll henk awa mesel !' co Cuttie, *ib.* ; JAKOBSEN *Dial.* (1897) 116 ; S. & Ork.[1] Hence **Henkie,** sb. a person who limps or halts.

The word ' henki ' is sometimes applied to a troll or fairy. There are old legends in connection with these knolls [Henkis knowes], that the trolls used to dance there at night, and the trolls were always supposed to 'hink' or limp, when they danced, JAKOBSEN *Dial.* (1897) 116 ; Old people spoke of having seen numbers of puny beings dancing round a fairy knowe. These were spoken of as a 'scrae o' henkies,' SPENCE *Flk-Lore* (1899) 39; S. & Ork.[1]

[ON. *hinka,* to limp, hobble (VIGFUSSON) ; cp. G. *hinken.*]

HENK, HENKLE, see Hank, sb.[1], Hankle, v.

HENKY-PENKY, HENMOST, HENN, see Hanky-panky, Hindmost, Hain, v.[5]

HENNEL, sb. n.Yks.[2] The hen-roost.

HENOU, int. Cld. (JAM.) [Not known to our correspondents.] A command to a number of persons to pull or lift something all at once.

HENRIDGE, sb. Lan. Also written **hainridge** Lan.; [e·nridg.] A separate place for cattle, a ' haining.' DAVIES *Trans. Phil. Soc.* (1855) 268 ; Lan.[1]

HENSIGEM, sb. Cum.[14] In phr. a *Hensigem fortune,* a pair of pattens and a white apron.

[Hensingham, the name of a township and village near Whitehaven.]

HEN-STONES, sb. pl. w.Yks. Groups of stones on the ridge of high moors.

LUCAS *Stud. Nidderdale* (c. 1882) viii.

HENSURE, sb. Obs. Sc. [Not known to our correspondents.] A giddy young fellow.

Sc. (JAM.) a.Sc. Around them the younkers, 'hasty hensures' and wanton winklots, WILSON *Tales* (1839) V. 65.

[An hasty hensure callit Hary, *Chrysts-kirk* (c. 1550) x, in *Evergreen* (ed. 1761) I. 7.]

HENT, v.[1] Sc. Irel. Yks. Also written **hynt** Dmf. **1.** ? Obs. In pret. and pp. caught, laid hold of.

Sc. He hent the maiden by the hand, And thus bespak her meek, JAMIESON *Pop. Ballads* (1806) I. 239 ; Once again on his sturdy back Has he hente up the weary judge, SCOTT *Minstrelsy* (1802) IV. 104, ed. 1848; Red Rowan has hent him up, ATTOUN *Ballads* (ed. 1861) I. 101. Dmf. In his mitten'd hand He hynt up bluidie Cumberland, CROMEK *Remains* (1810) 167. Wxf.[1]

2. To catch a flying ball, to run in front of a ball and stop it. w.Yks. THORESBY *Lett.* (1703) ; w.Yks.[28] [L. Abute hir hals þan he hir hent (v.r. hint), *Cursor M.* (c. 1300) 3841. OE. *hentan* (pret. *hente*), to seize.]

HENT, v.[2] Sh.I. [hent.] To gather up and stow away; to collect, lay up ; also *refl.* to gather oneself up, to be off.

Girzzie wis geen i' da lodie ta hent up da denner tatties, *Sh. News* (Jan. 15, 1898) ; Ta see da wy 'at da folk hentit da broth . . . inta demsells, a body wid 'a' tought 'at dey wir sunteen guid aboot it, BURGESS *Sketches* (2nd ed.) 110; Oot o dis wi dee! Hent disell ! *ib.* *Rasmie* (1892) 14 ; S. & Ork.[1]

[Norw. dial. *hemta,* also *heimta* and *henta,* to gather, take up, pluck (AASEN) ; ON. *heimta,* to fetch home, to bring home the sheep in autumn from the summer pastures (VIGFUSSON).]

HENT, v.[3] Sh.I. To walk with a plunging motion. S. & Ork.[1]

HENT, v.[4] and sb. Sc. Irel. n.Cy. Cum. Yks. Lan. Glo. Oxf. Hrt. Hmp. Also in form **hint** Lnk. Gall. N.I.[1] Glo. [h]ent.] **1.** v. To plough up the bottom furrow between ridges ; also used *fig.*

nk. Steady action to proceed Thro' hintin' furs [furrows],
ATSON *Poems* (1853) 29. **Cum.** I'll rest content, To something
or sideway hent A character in plain black prent, DICKINSON
mains (1888) 145; **Cum.¹, w.Yks.¹**
Hence (1) **Henting,** *sb.* the furrow in a ploughed field
tween the ridges; the last sod of a ridge in ploughing;
Henty, *sb.* the opening between two ridges of ploughed
nd.
(1) **Gall.** Our ploughman ... Clean lifted the hinting of every
sh glass, KERR *Maggie o' the Moss* (1891) 93; These furrows ...
lifted out of the bottom of the same 'furr,' and are soil of a
ferent nature. The greatest difficulty young ploughmen have
surmount when learning the tilth trade, is the proper way to
ft hintins,' MACTAGGART *Encycl.* (1824) 270, ed. 1876. **N.I.¹**
on. SIMMONS *Gl.* (1890). **Wxf.¹** n.Cy. GROSE (1790). **w.Yks.**
UTTON *Tour to Caves* (1781). **ne.Lan.¹** The portions of subsoil
sed with the plough to cover seed sown. **Glo.** SMYTH *Lives
rkeleys* (1066–1618) III. 24, ed. 1885. **Oxf.** They have also a
ay of sowing in the Chiltern country, which is called sowing
ntings, which is done before the plough, the corn being cast in
straight line just where the plough must come, and is presently
oughed in, PLOT *Oxf.* (1677) 246. **Hrt.** Hentings or water fur-
ws, ELLIS *Mod. Husb.* (1750) I. i. 24. (2) **ne.Lan.¹**
. *sb.* A furrow; also used *attrib.*
N.I.¹ Hmp. Hent furrow is the last of a land, HOLLOWAY.
HENT, see **Hind,** *adj.*, **Hint,** *v.*¹⁴⁸
HENTING, *sb.* **Obs.** n.Cy. Also in form **hanting.** A
clownish fellow; one that lacks good breeding. (K.),
Cy.²
HEOGALDSRIG, *sb.* **Sh.I.** The part of a sheep's back
hich is nearest the neck.
Hjogalaarig, hjogalstørig, hovaldørig, JAKOBSEN *Norsk in Sh.
897) 53; **S. & Ork.¹**
HEP, see **Heap,** *sb.¹,* **Hip,** *sb.¹, v.*
HEPLEY, *adj.* **Obs.** or *obsol.* n.Cy. Yks. Lin. 1. Neat,
andsome. Cf. **heppen.**
n.Cy. GROSE (1816). **Yks.** (P.R.); GROSE (1790) *MS. add.* (P.)
. Dexterous, handy. n.Cy. (K.) Lin. SKINNER (1671).
[The same word as Norw. dial. *heppeleg,* lucky, fortunate
AASEN).]
HEPPEN, *adj.* n.Cy. Yks. Not. Lin. Also written
epen, hepn w.Yks.; and in forms epen s.Not.; heppem
Yks.¹ [e'pən.] 1. Tidy, neat; respectable; hand-
me. Cf. **hepley.**
n.Cy. GROSE (1790); BAILEY (1721). **Yks.** RAY (1691). **Yks.** He
he was heppener than t'other lasses (I.W.). **e.Yks.** Bessy, his
ife, thof i' nowt bud prent goons, Was heppenest woman you'd
nd i' ten toons, NICHOLSON *Flk-Sp.* (1889) 38; **e.Yks.¹** 'That
eaks [looks] heppener' is said when anything falling into
sorder is satisfactorily arranged. **w.Yks.** 'It's nice an' heppen.'
his word ... [is] applied to linen or cotton to describe the
enness of the texture, *Leeds Merc. Suppl.* (Dec. 20, 1890);
Yks.¹ I hedn't faun i sike a heppen way as a body mud a wished,
302; We can mack shift to live in a gradely, menceful, heppen
ay, *ib.* 306. **n.Lin.¹** All th' stacks is thack'd, an' th' plaace looks
al heppen noo.
Hence **Heppenly,** *adv.* neatly.
w.Yks.¹ Shoe's heppenly don'd.
. Handy, deft; able; clever at work.
n.Cy. (K.) **w.Yks.¹** If hee ... bee a heppen youth, BEST *Rur.
con.* (1641) 133; **e.Yks.¹** m.Yks.¹ He's very heppem in his
ings. **w.Yks.** LUCAS *Stud. Nidderdale* (c. 1882) *Gl.* **Not.¹** A's
eppen at owt. **s.Not.** In an ironical sense. 'This is a ep'n
ol, this is; a wouldn't own it' (J.P.K.). **Lin.** The housewife
erself is a heppen sort of body, STREATFEILD *Lin. and Danes
884) 264; SKINNER (1671). **Lin.¹** He's very heppen at teaming,
fact he's heppen at owt. **n.Lin.¹** Charlie's a heppen soort o' a
ap; he can do o'must oht that belongs to his traade, an' a lot
uther things an' all. **sw.Lin.¹** Bill Stirr is a heppen lad; he's
onderful heppen. He was a deal heppener than I was; I'd
ever done nowt o' sort. **s.Lin.** He's a heppen chap, that: he
n to'n his hand to owt that comes to it (T.H.R.).
[The same word as Norw. dial. *heppen,* lucky, fortunate
AASEN); ON. *heppinn,* lucky, also dexterous (VIGFUSSON).]
HEPPENSHAWS, *sb. pl.* n.Yks.² Pieces of land
dded to larger portions.
Only occas. heard in this part; our word being Intaks.
HEPPING-STOCK, *sb.* Som. Dev. Cor. Also in forms
ppen- Som.; epping- nw.Dev.¹ Cor.¹²; hipping- Cor.²

A horse-block; stones or steps for mounting a horse.
See Hip, *v.*
Som. SWEETMAN *Wincanton Gl.* (1885). **Dev.** 'There ye are,
my man,' said Farmer Pike, setting the crestfallen hero upright
on the epping stock, EVANS *Tavistock* (1847) 147, ed. 1875.
n.Dev. ROCK *Jim an' Nell* (1867) *Gl.* **nw.Dev.¹** Cor. And first, a
was bound to the old epping stock up to Churchtown, HUNT *Pop.
Rom. w.Eng.* (1865) I. 144; And overthraw'd as she fall'd down
A hepping-stock and cheer, J. TRENOODLE *Spec. Dial.* (1846) 40;
Cor.¹²
HEPS, see **Hasp,** *sb.¹*
HER, *pron.* Var. dial. forms and uses in Sc. and Eng.
I. Dial. forms: (1) **ur,** (2) **ɔr,** (3) **Er,** (4) **Har,** (5) **Hare,**
(6) **Hir,** (7) **Hire,** (8) **Hooar,** (9) **Hur,** (10) **Hur,** (11) **Ur.**
[For further instances see II. below.]
(1) **n.Shr.** ELLIS *Pronunc.* (1889) V. 453. (2) **a.Cy.** (J.W.) **Stf.**
ELLIS *ib.* 473. **e. & s.Der.** *ib.* 431. **s.War.** *ib.* 114. **Wor.** *ib.* 112.
Shr. *ib.* 476. **Hrf.** *ib.* 177. **Glo.** *ib.* 62. **w.Oxf.** *ib.* 92. **e.Dor.** *ib.*
77. **e.Som.** *ib.* 85. **n.Dev.** *ib.* 157. **e.Cor.** *ib.* 168. (3) **Wil.** SLOW
Rhymes (1889) *Gl.* **Dor.¹** **Som.** Er zidden, W. & J. *Gl.* (1873).
w.Som.¹ (4) **Ess.¹,** Ken. (G.B.) **Sus.** She is de dauling of har
dat brung her foorth, LOWER *Sng. Sol.* (1860) vi. 9. (5) **n.Dev.**
Exm. Crtshp. (1746) *Gl.* (6) **Sc.** GROSE (1790) *MS. add.* (C.)
ne.Lan.¹ (7) **Dev.** *Horae Subsecivae* (1777) 3. (8) **s.Yks.** (I.W.)
(9) **Nhb.¹, n.Yks.** (T.S.), **e.Yks.¹** Lan. Aw these fine folk coming
—and hor fresh fro' London, WESTALL *Birch Dene* (1889) II. 191.
(10) **Nhb.** Then she gat up wiv hur dowters-o'-law, ROBSON *Bk.
Ruth* (1860) i. 6. **e.Lan.¹,** Der.¹² War. (J.R.W.) **Glo.** SMYTH *Lives
Berkeley* (1066–1618) III. 24, ed. 1885. **e.Som.** W. & J. *Gl.*
(1873) (s.v. Ur). **Dev.** An hur shil bring vorrid a zin, BAIRD
St. Matt. (1863) i. 21. (11) **s.Chs.¹** 69. **Oxf.** (A.P.), **I.W.¹** **e.Som.**
W. & J. *Gl.* (1873). **w.Som.¹,** nw.Dev.¹
II. Dial. uses. 1. *Reflex.* : herself.
n.Cy. (J.W.) **w.Yks.** Tlas weət ər əfuə sə went ət (*ib.*). **Chs.¹**
Oo's cleaning her; **Chs.²** She got her ready. **s.Chs.¹** Aaɪˑóo uurt
ûr ! [Has she hurt herself?] 69.
2. Unemphatic form of the nom. : she.
a.Cy.¹ [Ur] is interchangeable with [óo] throughout the
district, but becomes more frequent the farther south one advances,
66. **Midl.** Her's a-comin' up the lane, NORTHALL *Wd. Bk.* (1896).
Stf. ELLIS *ib.* 473. **s.Stf.** Who'd ha thought it? her said an'
her went very white, PINNOCK *Blk. Cy. Ann.* (1895) 9. **Der.** Eh,
hur is a beauty, VERNEY *Stone Edge* (1868) vi ; Der.² Hur ta'es on
so. **n.Lin.¹** War. Her is a cousin to we (M.R.); War.¹ *Introd.*
14; War.⁴, s.War.¹ **Wor.** ELLIS *ib.* 112. **Shr.** I dunno what
hur's a settin' thar for, WHITE *Wrekin* (1860) vi ; **Shr.¹** Invariably,
Gram. Outlines, 47. **n.Shr.** ur, ELLIS *ib.* 453. **Hrf.** DUNCUMB
Hist. Hrf. (1804–1812); (R.M.E.) **Glo.** Her didn't tell me a dale
about the matter, GISSING *Vill. Hampden* (1890) I. vii ; Her aint
a calling we, LYSONS *Vulgar Tongue* (1868) 27 ; Glo.² Her y-'ent
sa' desperd bad a 'ooman as I've a knawed, 11. **Oxf.** Ur a got un
(A.P.); Oxf.¹ Her's up-stars. **Brks.¹** 'Mrs. Winburn is ill, isn't she ?'
...'Ees, her be—terrible bad,' HUGHES *T. Brown Oxf.* (1861) xxxii ;
ELLIS *ib.* 97. **Bdf.** Her are [she is], *ib.* 206. **Sur.** Her would say,
BICKLEY *Sur. Hills* (1890) III. vi. **Sus.** I did blow 'er but 'er
wouldn't bide blowed, EGERTON *Flks. and Ways* (1884) 137. **Wil.¹**
Her be a girt vule, that her be, 124. **w.Dor.** Her done it (E.H.G.).
e.Dor. ELLIS *ib.* 77. **e.Som.** W. & J. *Gl.* (1873). **w.Som.**
ELWORTHY *Gram.* (1877) 39 ; w.Som.¹ Hur núv·ur kaan dúe ut,
kan u ! 3. **Dev.** Where is hire gone ? *Horae Subsecivae* (1777)
3 ; Her's most gone mazed, *Mem. Rev. J. Russell* (1883) 275.
n.Dev. Hur mitched vro' schule, ROCK *Jim an' Nell* (1867) st. 12.
nw.Dev.¹ **s.Dev.** Her mitched vro' schule, ROCK *Jim an' Nell* (1867)
Sng. Sol. (1860) vi. 9. **sw.Dev.** Ər teld shii tə ɔt, ELLIS *ib.* 164.
Cor. Her is, *ib.* 167. **e.Cor.** *ib.* 168.
3. Unemphatic or interrogative form of *he* ; occas. *him.*
Shr. Used in a small district on the border, not far from Welshpool,
and another near Ellesmere, ROBERTS *Coll. Cambrica,* I. 359, in
GROSE (1790) *MS. add.* (M.) ; Shr.² **Hrf.** Near Wales 'her ' is
used for 'he' or 'him' (R.M.E.). **Glo.** Michael—'ev the figures;
ur'll make it up to 'e, GISSING *Vill. Hampden* (1890) I. i ; 'Good
morning, Mr. Bassut,' I says, ... an' er says, 'Marning,' BUCKMAN
Darke's Sojourn (1890) ii. I.W.¹ 'I axed meyastur.' 'Well: what
ded ur zay ?' 5t. **w.Sus.** SLOW *Gl.* (1892). **Dor.** The Lord hav'
been good to I, han' her ? (C.V.G.); (H.J.M.); **Dor.¹** **Som.** In
interrogations only ; as, 'Did 'er gi' 'em ort !' *Monthly Mag.*
(1814) II. 127; (F.A.A.); Used west of the Parret, JENNINGS
Obs. Dial. w.Eng. (1825). **w.Som.** Used interrogatively, except
when particular emphasis is required, as 'Ee oa·n dúe ut, wuol
ur!' [He will not do it, will he ?] ELWORTHY *Gram.* (1877) 35.

Dev. Why he zaid zo his-sul, did'n 'er? *Reports Provinc.* (1885) 97. !n.Dev. Ellis *ib.* 160. nw.Dev.¹ w.Cor. Ellis *ib.* 173.

4. Used for the masc. possess. *pron.* : his. Also in form **Hers.**

Sc. Houts! It's a' about her horse, ta useless baste, Scott *Leg. Mont.* (1818) x. Sc., Wal. The Highlanders, like the Welch, are apt to say her for his, *Monthly Mag.* (1800) I. 323. Glo. I starts fur to git ers pelt off, an' to dress un a bit, Buckman *Darke's Sojourn* (1890) xiv ; Ur've had her reward, Gissing *Vill. Hampden* (1890) III. xiii.

5. Used by Highlanders for the *pron.* of the first pers.

Sc. Ye'll ask her to gang nae farther, Scott *Rob Roy* (1817) xxx.

6. Of inanimate objects : it.

Abd. The Turriff post-runners took his mail-bag, asking, 'Is this her?' 'Yes, yes, that's her' (G.W.). Nhb. He' ye gettin' haad o' the styen there? Hoy bor up tiv us (R.O.H.). Hrf. Him's her [that's it] (R.M.E.). Glo. This be a queer start o' Master Michael's. . . Why shouldn't ur answer, mun? Gissing *Vill. Hampden* (1890) II. v. Sur. The House of Commons wants to let the sea take back its lands rather than pay so much to keep her out, Jennings *Field Paths* (1884) 3. Sus. ' Have her stopped?' a man would ask of a clock (R.B.). w.Som.¹ In interrogatory constructions. nw.Dev.¹

7. Unemphatic or interrogative form of *I, we, you, they,* or *one.*

w.Som. Ur is used interrog. for the nom. I, both instead of ' ées' when final, and when followed by other words, in which case ' ées' is seldom used, as Aa·l vach·n, shaa·l uur? [I will fetch it, shall I!] Muus·n ur goo? [Must I not go?] Elworthy *Gram.* (1877) 35 ; w.Som.¹ Wee kn goo tumaar·u, kaa·n ur? [We can go to-morrow, can we not?] An oa·vur dhu vuur·keen wül ur? [Hand over the firkin, will you?] Uneebau·dee wüdn düe ut vur noa·urt, wüd ur? [One would not do it for nothing, would one?] More commonly [wüd um?] Dhai düd·n düe ut dhoa· aar·dr au·l, düd ur? [They did not do it then after all, did they?] nw.Dev.¹

8. *Obs.* Their ; of them. ne.Lan.¹ [(K.)]

9. Used after nouns in place of the possess. 's.

w.Som.¹ Mary Jones her book (s.v. His).

10. *Comp.* Her-lane, herself alone. Sc. (Jam., s.v. Lane). [On the disjunctive use of *her*, see the Grammar.]

HER, see Har(r.

HERALD, *sb.* Sc. [he·rəld.] **1.** The diving-goose, *Mergus serrator.* Swainson *Birds* (1885) 164.

2. *Comp.* Herald-duck, (1) the diving-goose, *Mergus serrator* ; (a) the dun-diver, *M. merganser.*

(1) Sh.I. The beautiful red-breasted merganser or herald duck . . . is resident during the whole year, *Sh. News* (Jan. 14, 1899). Sh.I., Frf. Swainson *ib.* 164. (a) S. & Ork.¹

3. The heron, *Ardea cinerea.* Frf. Swainson *ib.* 144.

HERANGER, *sb.* Sh.I. Written haeranger S. & Ork.¹ A boat of fifteen or sixteen feet keel. (A.W.G.), S. & Ork.¹

HERB, *sb.* and *v.* Var. dial. uses in Sc. Irel. and Eng. Also in forms arb I.Ma. w.Som.¹ Dev.⁴ ; arby nw.Dev.¹ Cor. ; arib Ir. ; harby Cor.⁸ ; harb Cor.² ; yarb w.Yks.² Lan.¹ Chs.¹ s.Chs.¹ s.Stf. Der.² nw.Der.¹ War.² se.Wor.¹ Shr.¹ w.Som.¹ Dev. ; yarby w.Wor.¹ Cor.⁸ ; yebb Cum. ; yearb Cum. ; yerb Cum. n.Yks.² sw.Lin.¹ ; yirb Sc. [hərb, ēb, jarb, jēb, jərb, jēb.] **1.** *sb.* In comb. (1) Herb-beer, a decoction of balm or any other herb ; (2) -book, a herbal ; (3) -craft, botany ; (4) -flower, the bugle, *Ajuga reptans* ; (5) -of-grace or -grass, (a) the rue, *Ruta graveolens* ; (b) the yellow meadow-rue, *Thalictrum flavum* ; (6) -Peter, the cowslip, *Primula veris* ; (7) -pie, a pie containing herbs, see below ; (8) -pudding, a pudding made of herbs ; (9) -rabbit, the herb Robert, *Geranium Robertianum.*

(1) w.Yks.² I was gathering yarbs ' to mak yarb beer.' (2) w.Som.¹ A widow whose husband had been a ' worm-doctor ' came to me, and asked me to buy a Gerard's Herbal, which she said was ' his herb-book.' (3) n.Yks.² (4) Dor. (G.E.D.) (5, a) w.Yks. *N. & Q.* (188a) 6th S. vi. 408 ; w.Yks.²⁴, Der.², nw.Der.¹, n.Lin.¹ sw.Lin.¹ That's herbigrass ; it's good for fits ; we offens make tea on it. Mother wants to know if you've any herbigrass. w.Som.¹ (b) Dor. (G.E.D.) ; Sarum *Dioc. Gazette* (Jan. 1891) 14. (6) Chs.¹⁸ (7) nw.Dev.¹ Made of parsley, leeks, &c. Cor. They partake of pies stuffed with herbs which they call Harby pies, Tregellas *Tales* (1865) 153 ; Ded ax thum for a harby-pie, Daniell *Poems* ; Cor.³ A pie made of spinach, 'bits,' parsley, mustard-cress, pepper-cress, young onions, and lettuce, with some

---

slices of bacon, and a little milk, seasoned with pepper and salt; Cor.⁸ (8) Cum. A dish peculiar to Easter Sunday, made of the leaves of the plant Eastermann Giant, boiled in broth with barley-strained and served as spinach, the barley with it (J.Ar.) ; A dish of early spring, composed of young nettles and every wholesome vegetable that the garden affords, mixed with groats or oatmeal, or shilled barley, and boiled in a bag in broth. The great art in compounding this dish is to have much variety with no pre-dominating taste (E.W.P.) ; Gi'e me a yearb-puddin' o' t'oald-fashin't country mäk, meäd ó nowt bit Easter mergients—nettels, chives, curley greens, an' sec like, Farrall *Betty Wilson* (1886) 111. (9) w.Som.¹ Dev. *Reports Provinc.* (1884) 11 ; Dev.⁴

2. Phr. *like herbs for the pot*, in very small particles, like herbs prepared for cooking.

w.Ir. I'll chop you as small as aribs for the pots, Lover *Leg.* (1848) II. 511. se.Wor.¹

3. Any wild plant which has a medicinal use.

Ayr. The saw which my granny had made in secret from some yirbs she had gathered, Service *Dr. Duguid* (ed. 1887) 33. Lak. The plants that can kill, and the yirbs that can cuir, Nicholson *Kilwuddie* (ed. 1895) 134. n.Cy. (J.W.) Lan. But faith's a yarb to cure bad een, Bealey *Jottings* (1865) 36. I.Ma. Arbs and roots, Brown *Doctor* (1887) 8. Chs.¹ The country people of Cheshire are great herb doctors, and there are plenty of people, esp. in the manufacturing towns, who make their living by collecting yarbs in the fields. sw.Lin.¹ She boils some yerbs, and doctors it. War.² Shr.¹ ' The May-month's the best time to get yarbs ; I sid owd Lacy busy alung the diche-bonks the tother day.' ' Aye, 'e's mighty cliver, they tellen me, an' cures a power o' folks.' w.Som.¹ By this is meant ' simples,' or medicinal herbs, while those for cooking are always pot-herbs, such as thyme, sage, mint, organ, &c. ' I don't never go to no doctor ; nif any o'm be bad, I boils some yarbs down, and gives 'em to 'em, and they don't lack no doctor's stuff.' n.Dev. [She had] some skill in ' yarbs,' as she called her simples, Kingsley *Westward Ho* (1855) 33, ed. 1889.

Hence (1) Herbery, *sb.* a plantation of herbs for medicinal purposes ; (2) Herby, (a) *sb.* a shop for the sale of herbs and ' simples ' ; (b) *adj.* having a medicinal flavour.

(1) w.Som.¹ w.Dev. Marshall *Rur. Econ.* (1796). (2, a) Lan.¹ (b) w.Som.¹ Where d'ye buy this here tay, missus? I sim 'tis ter'ble arby.

4. *Comp.* (1) Herb-cure, a vegetable remedy ; (2) -doctor, a herbalist ; (3) -tea, a decoction of herbs ; (4) -ween, (5) -wife, a woman who deals in ' simples.'

(1) n.Yks.² It's some mak o' yerb-cure. (2) w.Yks. 'E's a yarb-doctor, an' 'e 'unts for yarbs all ovver t'hills (F.P.T.). Lan.¹ I bethought me of an old herbalist, or ' yarb doctor,' . . a genuine dealer in simples, Waugh *Sketches* (1855) 21. Chs.¹, s.Chs.¹ (3) w.Yks. (J.W.), Chs.¹ s.Stf. My feyther's got a rage for yarbs, we'm afraid to say we'm bad for fear o' the yarb tay, Pinnock *Blk. Cy. Ann.* (1895). w.Wor.¹ Dev.⁴ The oal people gathers it, an' lays' en up for winter, to make arb-tea. Cor. And harby tay of oall soorts, Tregellas *Tales* (1860) 21. (4) n.Yks.² (5) Gall. My famous yirbwives . . . think it an antidote against almost every distemper, Mactaggart *Encycl.* (1824) 18, ed. 1876.

5. A beer made of var. kinds of herbs. Cor.⁸

6. Hay-grass.

Lan. We'n the finest yarb i' yon top-meadow at ever I clapt een on, Waugh *Sketches* (1855) 228 ; Lan.¹

Hence Herbage, *sb.* the right of feeding or pasturing. e.An.¹

7. *v.* To gather herbs.

Lan.¹ w.Som.¹ Old women do vind 'em 'pon times, eens they be yarbing.

Hence (1) Yarber, *sb.* a gatherer of herbs ; (2) Yarbing, *vbl. sb.* the gathering of herbs.

(1) Lan.¹ (2) w.Som.¹ We've a-bin vor a riglur day's yarbin.

HERBAL BENNET, *phr.* Glo. The herb Bennet, *Geum urbanum.* (B. & H.), Glo.¹

HERBIVE, *sb.* ? *Obs.* Chs.¹⁸ The forget-me-not, *Myosotis arvensis* and *M. palustris.*

[*Ive arthritique*, Hearbe Iue, ground Pine, Forget-me-not, Cotgr. (1611).]

HERBOUR, see Harbour.

HERD, *sb.* and *v.* Sc. Irel. Nhb. Cum. Wm. Yks. Glo. Ken. Som. Amer. Also written hird S. & Ork.¹ ne.Sc. Lnk. Nhb.¹ w.Yks.¹ ; hurd Uls. Ant. Dwn. Lakel.¹ Cum. Wm. w.Yks.¹· ; and in forms haird Nhb. ; hard Nhb.¹ ; heord w.Yks.⁸ ; herid Nhb.¹ [(h)ərd, ēd.] **1.** *sb.* A shepherd ; a man or boy who tends cattle ; a farm servant; *fig.* a pastor ; also used *attrib.*

Sc. A puir herd callant, SCOTT *St. Ronan* (1824) xiv. n.Sc. The daft girl winks . . . at the herd laddie, GORDON *Carglen* (1891) v. ne.Sc. The hird used a stick for driving the cattle, GREGOR *Flk-Lore* (1881) 195. Elg. Dar'd ev'ry herd-loon keep a hound To chace the timid hare, COUPER *Poetry* (1804) I. 176. Abd. To the cham'er she wad steal, For the herdie's doublets dreepin', STILL *Cottar's Sunday* (1845) 35. Frf. Many granted that he could tell when a doctor went by, when a lawyer, . . when a herd, BARRIE *Tommy* (1896) 133. Per. I ken a place where the herd has as muckle to eat as the master here, *Sandy Scott* (1897) 10. Fif. Wi' a herd I did foregather, Singin' leanin' owre his crook, DOUGLAS *Poems* (1806) 99. Rnf. The herd, poor thing! thro' chillin' air, Tends, in the meads, his fleecy care, PICKEN *Poems* (1813) I. 76. Ayr. This New-Light, 'Bout which our herds sae aft have been Maist like to fight, BURNS *W. Simpson* (1785) st. 19. Lnk. How this creeshy rascal too was slain By a wee bird, BLACK *Falls of Clyde* (1806) 106. e.Lth. Tam Arnott, the herd at Wedderlairs, HUNTER *J. Inwick* (1895) 19. Edb. Her herdies playin' the pipe alane On muirlands bare, LEARMONT *Poems* (1791) 213. Bwk. She had a herd callant, or boy, who was engaged in tending her cows, HENDERSON *Pop. Rhymes* (1856) 50. Dmf. The stey peat-reek play swirl Abune the herd's auld bield, REID *Poems* (1894) 29. Gall. I was no more than a herd-laddie at the time, like David, keeping my father's flocks, CROCKETT *Standard Bearer* (1898) 1. N.Cy.¹ Nhb. (R.O.H.) ; Yauld herds on hale-some braxey fed, Wi' strang lang swinging strides, noo sped To join the sport, PROUDLOCK *Borderland Muse* (1896) 331 ; Nhb.¹, Lakel.¹ Cum. LINTON *Lake Cy.* (1864) 305. w.Yks. (J.T.); w.Yks.¹⁵, Ken. (J.A.B.) Som. JENNINGS *Dial. w.Eng.* (1869).

2. Comb. (1) Herd-club, the stick carried by a cattle-tender ; (2) **-man**, the common skua, *Stercorarius catar-rhactes* ; (3) **-man-of-the-sea**, the great Northern diver, *Colymbus glacialis* ; (4) **'s-maud**, the chequered plaid worn by a shepherd ; (5) **-widdiefows**, a name given to cattle-stealers.

(1) ne.Sc. By preference of ash in the belief that if of this wood it would neither break bones nor seriously injure a beast it might strike (J.Ar.) ; The carving on the hirdie club was very simple : it consisted of notches cut in a small piece of the club, smoothed for the purpose to show in what way the oxen were yoked, GREGOR *Flk-Lore* (1881) 195. (2) Or.I. It is believed to protect the young lambs from the attacks of the eagle, SWAINSON *Birds* (1885) 210. (3) Wil. It is also known as the ' Herdsman of the Sea ' from its habit of driving before it the fishes, which it pursues even to a very great depth, SMITH *Birds* (1887) 507 ; (É.H.G.) (4) Nhb.¹ (5) Sc. He . . . expressed his confidence that the herd-widdiefows could not have carried their booty far, SCOTT *Rob Roy* (1817) *Introd.*

3. Obs. A public pasture ; a road along which cattle are driven to water; the pen in which cattle are shut up at night.

Glo. GROSE (1790) *MS. add.* (M.) ; Such as the Herd at Tetbury . . . between the Warren and the Town, *Horae Subsecivae* (1777) 211.

4. In curling : a stone placed on the ice in order to prevent the principal stone being driven out.

Keb. Gib o' the Glen, a noble herd Behind the winner laid, DAVIDSON *Seasons* (1789) 166 (JAM.).

5. v. To tend cattle or sheep ; to watch over, take care of.

ne.Sc. Littlens wull tak' caulds, herd an' hap them hoo ye like, GRANT *Kechleton*, 95. Cai.¹ Abd. They were able now to herd the ewes, Ross *Helenore* (1768) 14, ed. 1812. Kcd. I can brawly see That but the house, an' ben the house, He herds ane wi' his e'e, GRANT *Lays* (1884) 173. Ayr. Will ye quat pappin' stanes at thae hens, sir, an' come an' herd this pat ! SERVICE *Dr. Duguid* (ed. 1887) 234. Edb. I . . . delv'd a' his garden, an' herdit his kye, FORBES *Poems* (1812) 131. Peb. The principles of herding are, to allocate to each particular flock separate walks upon the farm, *Agric. Surv.* 195 (JAM.). Gall. Our bairns shall herd, and gather slaes, Aroun' our cot, on Logan braes, NICHOLSON *Poet. Wks.* (1814) 171, ed. 1897. Ula., Ant., Dwn. (M.B.-S.) Nhb. (R.O.H.) ; When my father . . . herdit the Brockalaw, RICHARD-SON *Borderer's Table-bk.* (1846) VII. 137. Cum. Ah wad be likely teh git sum hogs to hurd at Chicago, SARGISSON *Joe Scoap* (1881) 25. [Amer. To take care of children, *Dial. Notes* (1896) I. 418.]

Hence **Herding**, *sb.* a 'herd's' place or work.

Sc. No one of them able to do anything . . . but the oldest lassie, who got a herding the other day, WHITEHEAD *Daft Davie* (1876) 155, ed. 1894. Frf. I'll send him straight to the herding, BARRIE *Tommy* (1896) 223. w.Sc. A boy, newly from the herd-

VOL. III.

ing, got admission into a gentleman's family, for the purpose of waiting table, CARRICK *Laird of Logan* (1835) 168. Dmb. At eight years I too a herdin' got, SALMON *Gowodean* (1861) 97. Lakel.² Herden t'kye i't looanens. Wm. A finer burth be hofe than hurden sheep, GRAHAM *Gwordy* (1778) l. 41.

6. To drive away, keep aloof.

Per. That herds us fra the joys o' earth, An' fain wad haud's fra heaven, HALIBURTON *Ochil Idylls* (1891) 56. Nhb. To ' herd craas' is to scare them off (R.O.H.). Cum. Ta hurd t'crows off t'wheet, FARRALL *Betty Wilson* (1886) 150.

7. To gather in the crop ; to keep, hold.

Sh.I. Hirdit mi sma crop, BURGESS *Rasmie* (1892) 38 ; JAKOBSEN *Norsk in Sh.* (1897) 24 ; S. & Ork.¹ e.Sc. The siller's no his : he's only herdin' it on trust for a friend, SETOUN *Sunshine* (1895) 289. w.Yks.¹

HERD, *v.²* Lin. [Not known to our correspondents.] To prostrate.

(HALL.); Lin.¹ They wired in a long while, and the last thump herded him.

HERDA, *sb.* Sh.I. Crush, confusion ; said of corn that has been trampled by animals.

(Coll. L.L.B.) S. & Ork.¹ They have laid it in herda. To tramp in herda.

HERDEN, see **Harden,** *sb.*

HERDER, *sb.* Hmp. [ə̄·də(r).] A sieve, a 'rudder.'

Sieve upon herder, One upon the other, WISE *New Forest* (1883) 185 ; Hmp.¹

[OE. *hridder*, an instrument for winnowing corn (ÆLFRIC); cp. G. *reiter*, a big sieve.]

HERDING-SPADE, *sb.* Lin. [Not known to our correspondents.] A narrow spade used in cutting dikes and small drains.

HERDS, HERDSEL, see **Hards, Hirsel,** *sb.*¹

HERDWICK, *sb.* Cum. Wm. [hə·rdwik.] **1. Obs.** The tract of land under the charge of a ' herd ' or shepherd.

Cum. The stock . . . have been from time immemorial farmed out to herds at a yearly sum. From this circumstance these farms have obtained the name of Herdwicks, i. e. the district of the herds, MARSHALL *Review* (1808) I. 199.

2. pl. The black-faced breed of sheep found on the fells, noted for their climbing powers and ability to live on bare pasture ; also used *attrib.*

Lakel.¹² Cum. MARSHALL *Review* (1808) I. 199 ; Cum.¹ ; Cum.³ He was summat akin tul a Herdwick tip, 2 ; Cum.⁴ ' He breaks bands like a herdwick tip ' is a proverbial saying . . . applied to a rustic scape-grace, GIBSON, 181. ' What were the sheep you bought ? ' Plaintiff. ' Herdwick hoggs,' *Carlisle Patriot* (Feb. 8, 1895) 3. Wm. He brag'd . . . aboot 'iz Herdwic hogs, BLEZARD *Sngs.* (1848) 42.

[l. Erleghecote haythe always beyn a hyrdewyke or pasture ground for the schepe of thabbottes of Furnes, LAMPLUGH (c. 1537) in BECK *Ann. Furnes.* (1844) App. 64 (N.E.D.).]

HERE, *adv.* Var. dial. uses in Sc. and Eng. Also written her.n.Yks. ; and in form yere Glo. [h)iə(r, w. and s.Cy. jə(r).] **1.** In *comb.* (1) Here-about(s, in the immediate neighbourhood, near by ; also used *attrib.* ; (2) **-anent,** concerning this ; (3) **-away(s,** hereabouts, belonging to this part of the country, in this direction ; in this present state ; also used *attrib.* ; (4) **-by,** here ; (5) **-fore,** hence, on this account; (6) **-from,** of place : hence ; (7) **-onward,** on this condition ; (8) **-right,** (a) of time : directly; of place : on this very spot ; (b) ? hence ; (9) **-under,** set down subsequently in the book or document.

(1) Fif. She'll marry a hereaboot man, or I'm cheated, MELDRUM *Margrédel* (1894) ix. Ayr. The Blair Museum, where a' kinds o' uncos from hereaboot and farawa are to be seen, SERVICE *Dr. Duguid* (ed. 1887) 60. e.Yks.¹ Isn't ther a yull-hoos sumwheear here-aboots ? w.Yks. (J.W.) Dev. There ain't no cot that I know by hereabouts, O'NEILL *Idyls* (1892) 3. Cor. The biggest maker [of cider] hereabouts, MORTIMER *Tales Moors* (1895) 122. (2) Fif. Hereanent [he] shall be subject to the tryall and censure of his owne Presbytery, SCOT *Apolog. Narration* (1644) 109, ed. 1846. Sig. If ye write hereanent to me again, I shall be ready to deliver it, BRUCE *Sermons* (1631) 198, ed. 1843. (3) Sc. That light is not here away in any clay body ; for while we are here, light is . . . broader and longer than our . . . obedience, RUTHERFORD *Lett.* (1765) II. ii (JAM.). Cai.¹ e.Sc. That's a heavy reproach to a man

U

hereawa, Setoun *R. Urquhart* (1896) viii. **Per.** I'se be hingin' round here-awa, Cleland *Inchbracken* (1883) 137, ed. 1887. **Fif.** 'Ye dinna belang here-a-wa'!' 'No, I don't live here,' Robertson *Provost* (1894) 182. **e.Fif.** We've nae use for gangrel bodies hereawa, Latto *Tam Bodkin* (1864) ii. **Rnf.** As lang as ye are here awa May health an' strength betide ye, Picken *Poems* (1813) II. 14. **Ayr.** It was here, or hereawa, that the famous Laird of the Linn and Jock o' the Scales leeved, Service *Dr. Duguid* (ed. 1887) 73. **Lnk.** The deil is surely hereawa, Watt *Poems* (1827) 65. **e.Lth.** Thae craps'll no dae up here-a-way sae nigh the hills, Hunter *J. Inwick* (1895) 12. **Edb.** I told him that we didna play at that game hereawa, Ballantine *Gaberlunzie* (ed. 1875) 336. **Gall.** You are not a hereaway man, Crockett *Grey Man* (1896) viii. **Lakel.²** We've neea bodder hereaway. **Cum.⁴** Ye ken as much as most ither lasses hereaways, *Pearl in Shell*, 77. **n.Yks.** (I.W.', ne.Lan.¹ n.Lin.¹ I hevn't seen him hereaways sin' June. **e.An.¹, e.Suf.** (F.H.) **Som.** Jennings *Obs. Dial. w.Eng.* (1825). (4) Glo. Er's harmless enow when he comes yereby, Buckman *Darke's Sojourn* (1890) 150. (5) Slg. Herefore it is that the devils are maist miserable, Bruce *Sermons* (1631) v, ed. 1843. (6) Glo. My veyther . . . set 'isself up in a pooblic on the road about twelve mile yerevrom, Buckman *Darke's Sojourn* (1890) 48. Dor. I brought it therefrom, and then he took it herefrom (C.W.). **Som.** If he should write a'ter you'd a-gone here-vrom, Raymond *Sam and Sabina* (1894) 112 ; I think, sir, 'tis the nigh'st way herefrom (W.F.R.). **w.Som.¹** I 'on't budge herefrom [yuur·vraum] gin you come back. 'Hence' is quite unknown. **Dev.** If Bets'll let mer go herevrom, Thee mayst uv kuse expek, N. Hogg *Poet. Lett.* (1847) 46, ed. 1858. **nw.Dev.¹** (7) **Chs.** Bailey (1721). (8, *a*) Glo.¹, Hmp.¹, Wil.¹ n.Wil. Let's have it hereright (E.H.G.). Dor.¹ Som. I'll bid ee eighteen hereright, Raymond *Sam and Sabina* (1894) 58 ; Jennings *Obs. Dial. w.Eng.* (1825). **w.Som.¹** No! let's settle it here-right. **Dev.** Let's hev it out here-right and a-donc o't, Pulman *Sketches* (1842) 105, ed. 1871. **nw.Dev.¹** (*b*) Wil.¹ (9) Gall. The result is appended hereunder, Crockett *Stickit Min.* (1893) 238.

2. **Phr.** (1) *here and there a one*, (*a*) very few and scattered ; one here and there ; (*b*) any one, any ; about *or* above the average ; (2) — *and there one*, see (1, *b*) ; (3) — *away, there away*, all in confusion ; (4) — *be I, where be you ?* an expression referring to a plum-pudding with the plums a long way apart ; (5) — '*s gone*, an expression used by the leader of a company of bellringers when he starts a peal ; (6) — ('*s to*, an expression used when drinking a person's health or proposing a toast ; (7) *heres and theres*, in various places.

(1, *a*) Ken.¹ There wasn't nobody in church to-day, only here and there a one. (*b*) Oxf. She managed as well as here and there a one (G.O.). (2) w.Yks. He can touch a fiddle as good as here and there one (S.K.C.) ; Otley Shivvin's abaht as nice a place as here an' theer one, Cudworth *Dial. Sketches* (1884) 28. Glo.¹ He knows as much about it as here and there one.' Sus.¹ He aint much of a boy I know, but he's quite as good a boy as you'll find here-and-there-one. Wil.¹ I wur mortal bad aal the way and as sick as here and there one. (3) **Sc.** Things are lying, here awa, there awa, Scott *Bride of Lam.* (1819) xi. (4) Oxf.¹ (5) s.Wor. (H.K.) (6) Sc. Here's to the Free Trade for ever! Vedder *Poems* (1842) 99. Cal.¹ Mry. Here's to the lass wha kens the way the hearts o' men to chain, Hay *Lintie* (1851) 53. Abd. She fills the mug, and till her head, Says 'Come, here's to ye,' Beattie *Parings* (1801) 42, ed. 1873. Per. Here's to them a' in reaming swat! Spence *Poems* (1898) 69. **e.Sc.** Here's to Hawick's bonnie lasses! Watson *Bards* (1859) 191. Ayr. Here's to oorsels, my Lord! Man, wha's like us! Service *Notandums* (1890) 29. Lnk. Here's to you an' yours, Lemon *St. Mungo* (1844) 51. Lth. He hadna a crony like me, Sayin', 'Here's t'ye' oure a drap yell, O! Ballantine *Poems* (1856) 114. N.Cy.¹, Dur.¹, Cum.⁴ e.Yks.¹ Hec'as tl yd. w.Yks.¹ When a Frenchman, returning from a temporary residence in London, was asked by his countrymen what was the usual beverage of the lower classes in Eng. [he] gravely answered 'Here's t'ye.' nw.Der.¹, e.An.² w.Som.¹ The commonest of all the forms of drinking health. The leader of a party of mowers always drinks first ; before putting the cup or firkin to his lips. he says, 'Come, soce! here's-tee.' (7) n.Lin.¹ Noo then, iv'rything is all heres and theäres, noht wheäre it should be. When we fost set up hoose-keäpin' I ews'd to get my shopthings heres and theäres, but noo I alus stick to one plaace.

3. With *this* or *these*: used to add emphasis, to denote the nearness of the object mentioned ; in *gen.* dial. use ; also used *subst.*

Sc. This here man, *Scoticisms* (1787) 45. **Rxb.** This here leg was almost battered to a jelly with a splinter of the ship, Ruickbie *Wayside Cottager* (1807) 8. n.Cy. (J.W.) w.Yks. Dis iər äs wonts ə lot ə tliənin, Wright *Gram. Wndhll.* (1892) 124 ; This here's getten fettled, Snowden *Web of Weaver* (1896) 12 ; Then, ha, hah fearse will Lunnon foaks Look, when dress't up e theaze here poaks, *Thowts, Joakes and Smiles* (1845) 29. s.Chs.¹ This here cal dunna doe upo' the same meat as that theer, 70. Lei.¹ 26. War.² These 'ere boots, *Introd.* 15. Shr.¹ *Gram. Outlines*, 50. Brks.¹ Theuz yer wuts be wuth double o' them ther, 7. Bdf. Batchelor *Anal. Eng. Lang.* (1809) 150. Sur. The sea used to wash right up to this 'ere precipice, Jennings *Field Paths* (1884) 3 ; Sur.¹ Wil.¹ Thic here, 124. w.Som. Elworthy *Gram.* (1877) 29.

HERE, see **Haar**, *sb.¹*

HERE AND WERE, *phr.* *Obs.* Fit. Rxb. (Jam.) Also written **hair and wair**. Contention, disagreement, as in phr. *they were like to come or gang to here and were about it,* they were very near quarrelling.

[*Here* is prob. conn. w. Sc. *herry*, to harry (Dunbar) ; see **Hare**, *v.* *Were* repr. Sc. *were* (*weir*), war.]

HEREAST, *adv.* Yks. Approximately in this place ; here as 'twere.

e.Yks.¹ *MS. add.* (T.H.) ; It happened sumwheere aboot hereast.

HEREFORDSHIRE WEEDS, *phr.* Hrf. Oaks. There is no lack of wood, or of 'Herefordshire weeds,' as oaks are called, White *Wrekin* (1860) xi.

HERENCE, *adv.* Hrf. Glo. Sus. Hmp. Wil. Dor. Som. Hence.

Hrf.¹, Glo.¹ Sus. Holloway. Hmp.¹ Wil. Britton *Beauties* (1825) ; Wil.¹ Dor. Barnes *Gl.* (1863). Som. Jennings *Obs. Dial. w.Eng.* (1825).

HEREYESTERDAY. The same as *Ere yesterday*, q.v., Ere, *prep.*

HEREYESTREEN. The same as *Ere yestreen*, q.v., Ere, *prep.*

HEREZELD, *sb.* *Obs.* Sc. The tribute, consisting of the best beast on the land, paid to the landlord on the death of the tenant.

Sc. He can trot ten mile an hour without whip or spur, and he's the young laird's frae this moment, if he likes to take him for a herezeld, as they ca'd it lang syne, Scott *Guy M.* (1815) lv ; Herrezelda is the best aucht ox, kow, or uther beast quhilk ane husbandman, possessor of the aucht part of ane dauach of land [four oxen-gang] dwelland and deceasand theirupon, hes in his possession the time of his decease, quhilk ought and suld be given to his landislord, or maister of the said land, Skene *Difficill Wds.* (1681) 63. Lnk. With court, plaint, herezeld, &c., Wodrow *Ch. Hist.* (1721) II. 77, ed. 1828.

[The same word as OE. *heregyld*, the war-tax, the Dane-gild (*Chron.* ann. 1052).]

HERIE, *sb.* Sc. Also written **heary** Abd. ; **heery** Dmf. 1. A term used by old women in addressing their husbands, and sometimes *vice versa.*

Sc. A well herie, she's yours as well as mine, Gie her to wha ye please, Graham *Writings* (1883) II. 13. Abd. Well, heary. quo' he, but fat do ye think o' 't? Ross *Helenore* (1768) 20, ed. 1812 ; (Jam.)

2. A term addressed to a female inferior. Dmf. (Jam.)

[1. A dim. of obs. Sc. *here* (*heir*), lord, master. Thiddir the heir with mony thowsand gan, Douglas *Eneados* (1513), ed. 1874, II. 241. OE. *hearra*, a lord (Cædmon).]

HERIF(F, HERINSHREW, see **Hairif, Heronsew.**

HERITOR, *sb.* Sc. A landed proprietor ; *gen.* one who has obtained his land by inheritance, and one who is liable in payment of public burdens.

Sc. His Grace, whose occasional residence in that county made him acquainted with most of the heritors, as landed persons are termed in Scotland, Scott *Midlothian* (1818) xxxviii. Or.I. The whole heretors, bishops, and dignified persons, Peterkin *Notes* (1822) 154. Per. My dear friends, and all well-wishers, You heritors, and all black-fishers, Smith *Poems* (1714) 29, ed. 1853. Rnf. Ilk gentleman, beritor, burgess, ten marks, Hector *Judic. Records* (1876) 77. Lnk. All heritors, landlords, and liferenters, who have granted tacks or rentals to their tenants, Wodrow *Ch. Hist.* (1721) II. 15, ed. 1828. Bwk. Coldingham Common was divided 'among those heritors proving right thereto,' Henderson *Pop. Rhymes* (1856) 101.

HERKLE, HERLE, see **Hurkle,** *v.*, **Harl(e,** *sb.¹*

HERLE, _sb._ Sc. Also in form **hurl** (JAM.). [herl, herɪl.] **1.** The heron, _Ardea cinerea._

Ags. The common name (JAM.). **Frf., Per.** Named Tammie herl, GREGOR _note_ to DUNBAR (l.c.).

2. A mischievous dwarf; an ill-conditioned child or small animal. Per. (JAM.)

[1. I thoght my self a papingay, and him a plukit herle, DUNBAR _Tua Mariit_ (1508) 382. This _herl-_ is found in Breton (Léon) _herligon,_ ' héron ' (DU RUSQUEC).]

HERLING, _sb._ Sc. Cum. Wal. Also written **herlyng** Wal.; **hirling** Dmf.; **hirrling** Gall. **1.** The salmontrout, _Salmo trutta_; also appl. to the whiting and the shad.

Sc. Herlings which frequent the Nith, SCOTT _Abbot_ (1820) xxiv. **Dmf.** A small kind of trout, a little bigger than a herring, and shaped like a salmon : its flesh is reddish, like that of the salmon or sea trout, but considerably paler, _Statist. Acc._ I. 19 (JAM.); The river Nith produces . . . a species somewhat larger than herrings, called hirlings, _ib._ V. 132. **Gall.** Get ye into water deep, Ye hirrlings, and therein sleep, MACTAGGART _Encycl._ (1824) 291, ed. 1876. **Kcb.** It [Tarff] abounds with trout . . . and in the summer and harvest there are sea-trouts called herlings, _Statist. Acc._ IX. 320 (JAM.). **Cum.**[4] A net was drawn ashore and two took out of it twelve herling or whiting, _Carlisle Patriot_ (Aug. 25, 1893) 3. **Wal.** The shad is by the Welsh called herlyng, herling, PENNANT _Zoology_ (1769) III. 350 (JAM.). [SATCHELL (1879).]

2. _Comp._ (1) **Herling-house,** (2) **·net,** a net in which ' herling ' are caught.

(1) **Bwk.** JARDINE _Nat. Club_ (1834) I. ii. (2) **Sc.** Ten men were arrested, . . small-meshed herling-nets being found in their possession, _Scottish Leader_ (July 10, 1893) 4.

HERMITING, _prp._ Hrf.[2] Keeping to oneself.

HERMS, _sb. pl._ Sh.I. In _comb._ **Herms and wallawa,** a noisy quarrel; a scolding, a disturbance. S. & Ork.[1] See **Harm,** _v._

HERN, _sb._ Sc. Irel. Nhb. Chs. Stf. War. Wor. Glo. Nrf. Wil. Cor. Also in forms **harn** Nrf.; **herny** Nhb.[1]; **yan** Stf. War. Wor. Glo.; **yarn** Chs.[128] s.Chs.[1]; **yern** Bch. Chs.[128] s.Wor. [hern, ən, jān.] **1.** The heron, _Ardea cinerea._

Ayr. The bern is a majestic bird, Comes sailin' owre the sea, SERVICE _Dr. Duguid_ (ed. 1887) 107. **Nhb.**[1], **Chs.** (E.F.), **Chs.**[128] **s.Chs.**[1] **Stf.** ' It's cold enough to frizzle a yan,' which will stand still in a pond in the coldest weather, NORTHALL _Flk.-Phr._ (1894). **Nhp.**[1] **War.** _N. & Q._ (1872) 4th S. ix. 514. **w.Wor.** _Berrow's Jrn._ (Mar. 3, 1888). **s.Wor.** (H.K.) **Wor., Glo.** NORTHALL _ib._ **Nrf.** SWAINSON _Birds_ (1885) 144. **Wil.** I see one of them herns vlee awver (E.H.G.). **Cor.** RODD _Birds_ (1880) 314.

2. _Comp._ (1) **Hern-bliter,** the common snipe, _Gallinago major_; (2) **-crane,** the heron.

(1) **Bch.** They had me up afore the . . . yern-bliter began to sing, FORBES _Jrn._ (1742) 9. (2) **N.I.**[1]

HERN, _pron._ Stf. Not. Lin. Lei. Nhp. War. Wor. Shr. Hrf. Glo. Oxf. Brks. Hrt. Mid. Ess. Sus. Hmp. Wil. Som. Amer. [ən, ə'rən.] Disjunctive possess. _pron._ : hers.

s.Stf. Her heerd a babby cry and knowed it was hern, PINNOCK _Blk. Cy. Ann._ (1895). **Not.** (J.H.B.) ; No daughter o' hern, PRIOR _Renie_ (1895) 192; **Not.**[1], **Lin.**[1], **n.Lin.**[1] **s.Lin.** Let that aloön, it's hern (T.H.R.). **Lei.**[1], **Nhp.**[1] **War.** (J.R.W.); **War.**[2] _Introd._ 14; **War.**[3] **Wor.** The child was one of hern (W.A.S.). **se.Wor.**[1] W'at's 'ern's 'is'n, an' w'at's 'isn's 'ern. **Shr.**[1] _Gram. Outlines,_ 49. **Hrf.**[1] **Glo.** Her've been ready enow to put down that thur voot o' hern, BUCKMAN _Darke's Sojourn_ (1890) xxii; **Glo.**[1] **Oxf.** It wa'n't hern (G.O.). **s.Oxf.** 'Twa'an't no fault o' hern, poor thing, ROSEMARY _Chiltern_ (1895) 64. **Brks.**[1] **Hrt.** ELLIS _Pronunc._ (1889) V. 202. **w.Mid.** (W.P.M.), **Ess.** (S.P.H.) **Sus.**[1] **Hmp.** So there were his'n, and her'n, and their'n, you see, VERNEY _L. Lisle_ (1870) viii. **Wil.** SLOW _Gl._ (1892); **Wil.**[1] 124. **Som.** W. & J. _Gl._ (1873); It's those doings of her'n, YONGE _Cunning Woman_ (1890) 102. [**Amer.** His heart kep' goin' pitypat, But hern went pity Zekle, LOWELL _Biglow Papers_ (1848) 10.]

HERNE, _sb._ Sc. Yks. Lin. e.An. Also written **hirn** n.Yks.[12] ; **hirne** Slg. ; **hurn** n.Yks.[1] **ne.Yks.** Lin.[1] ; **hurne** n.Yks. **ne.Yks.**[1] ; **hyrne** Nrf. ; and in form **hon** n.Yks.[2] **e.Yks.**[1] **1.** ? _Obs._ A corner, nook; esp. the recess by the wide chimney-firesides of old-fashioned houses.

Slg. Unto the all-seeing eye of God the maist secret hirne of the conscience is . . patent, cleare, and manifest, BRUCE _Sermons_ (1631) iv, ed. 1843. **n.Yks.** Clawt some cassons out o'th hurne, MERITON _Praise Ale_ (1684) l. 75 ; **n.Yks.**[1] A recess or shelved

cupboard ; a recess for the seats (of stone) at the wide chimney firesides of old-fashioned farm-houses ; **n.Yks.**[2] Tatey-hon, the nook in the barn where the potatoes are kept. **ne.Yks.** Wall space between chimney and roof, MARSHALL _Rur. Econ._ (1796) II. 327 ; **ne.Yks.**[1] _Obs._ Corner by the side of the ' hoodend ' in old houses, in which ' fire-eldin' was kept.

Hence **Hon-ends,** _sb. pl._ spaces for the stone seats at the wide firesides of old farm-houses. n.Yks.[2]

2. A corner or angular bit of land ; a nook of land projecting into another district, parish, or field.

n.Yks.[2] **e.Yks.**[1] Not in common use. **Lin.** THOMPSON _Hist. Boston_ (1856); Lin.[1], e.An.[1], e.Suf. (F.H.) **Nrf.** Which road leads to the corner of the furze hyrne ! _Nrf. Chron._ (Dec. 8, 1827) 3.

[1. Þe stane þat þe edifiand reprouyd here it is made in heuyd of hyrne, HAMPOLE (c. 1330) _Ps._ cxvii. 21. OE. _hyrne_ (_Matt._ vi. 5) ; OFris. _herne_ (RICHTHOFEN).]

HERO, _sb._ Yks. A person possessing any extraordinary quality ; a wilful person ; a child of a masterful disposition.

n.Yks. She's a hero of a woman (I.W.). **w.Yks.** (C.C.R.)

HERON-BLUTER, _sb._ n.Sc. (JAM.) The common snipe, _Gallinago major._ See **Bleater,** _sb._

HERONSEW, _sb._ Sc. Nhb. Dur. Cum. Wm. Yks. Not. Lin. Nhp. War. e.An. Ken. Also written **heerinseugh** Nhb.[1]; **heerinsew** w.Yks.; **herensew** Cum.[1]; **heronseugh** N.Cy.[1] Nhb.[1]; **heronsue** Lakel.[1] n.Yks.[2]; **herrensue** Wm.; **herrinseu** e.Yks.[1]; and in forms **anser** Nrf. ; **hahnser** Suf.; **hahnsey** Suf.[1]; **hancer** Nrf.; **handsaw** N.Cy.[1]; **hansa** e.Suf.; **hanser** e.An.[2]; **hansey** e.Suf.; **harnsa** Suf.; **harnsee** Nrf.; **harnser** Nrf. Suf.; **harnsey** e.An.[1]; **hearingsew** w.Yks.[1]; **hearnshaw** Ken.[1]; **hearnshrow** Ken.; **herinshrew** w.Yks.[2]; **hernseugh** Nhb.; **hernsew** n.Yks.[1] Nhp.[1]; **hernsey** e.An.[2]; **hernshaw** Not. Nhp.[12] War. Ess. Ken.[1]; **hernsue** Lin.; **hernshaw** Nhp.[1]; **heronsheugh** Nhb.[1]; **heronshew** Slk.; **heronshrew** Not.[2]; **heronshuf** Nhb.[1]; **heronsyueff** Nhb.[1]; **herringsew** w.Yks.[1]; **herringshaw** Lin.[1]; **herringsue** n.Yks.[2] m.Yks.[1]; **herrinsho** Cum.[14]; **hornsey** e.An.[1] The heron, _Ardea cinerea._

Slk. Ane shameful heronshew was sitting by the plashy shore, HOGG _Poems_ (ed. 1865) 329. **N.Cy.**[1] **Nhb.** The hern-seugh his eyrie for scaly fry quits, CRAWHALL _Coll. Garl._ (1857) 256; Nhb.[1], Dur.[1], Lakel.[12] **Cum.** I've seen many a heron-sew on our fell edge with a better pair, DICKINSON _Cumbr._ (1876) 291; Cum.[14] **Wm.** Nivver did hullet, herrensue, or miredrum, mak sic a noise before, HUTTON _Bran New Wark_ (1785) l. 337. **n.Yks.**[1]; **n.Yks.**[2] ' As lang and lanky as a herringsue,' tall and spare in body and limb ; n.Yks.[34], ne.Yks.[1], e.Yks.[1], m.Yks.[1] **w.Yks.** LUCAS _Stud. Nidderdale_ (c. 1882) _Gl._; **w.Yks.**[12] Not. There's that old hernshow again by the river-side (L.C.M.); **Not.**[2] **Lin.** _Horae Subsecivae_ (1777) 211 ; Lin.[1] n.Lin.[1] Heronsews hev built e' Manby Woods time oot o' mind. **sw.Lin.**[1], **Nhp.**[12] **War.** _N. & Q._ (1872) 4th S. ix. 514. **e.An.** (R.O.H.) ; **e.An.**[1] Hornsey, a young heron ; e.An.[2] **Nrf.** They [bitterns] fly like a harnsee, only a little quicker, EMERSON _Birds_ (ed. 1895) 205 ; He shot a hancer on the massh (W.H.); (H.J.H.) **Suf.** I shot a rare big harnser (M.E.R.); (C.T.) (G.E.D.); **Suf.**[1], **Suf.** (F.H.) **Ess.** He had seen an anser swallow an eel and fly away (H.H.M.). **Ken.** _N. & Q._ (1869) 4th S. iv. 134; Ken.[1]

Hence **Harnsey-gutted,** _adj._ lank and lean like a heron. e.An.[1], e.Suf. (F.H.)

[I wol not tellen of hir strange sewes, Ne of hir swannes, ne of hir heronsewes, CHAUCER _C. T._ F. 68 (see Skeat's note)_:_ AFr. _herouncel,_ a young heron (GODEFROY).]

HERPLE, see **Hirple.**

HERR, _sb._ Sh.I. A primitive wooden hinge.

Ta stramp wi' a' his weight apon a auld saem 'at wis been i' da herr, an' ran him ta da bone, _Sh. News_ (Feb. 3, 1900).

HERRET, _sb._ ? _Obs._ Wm. Also Som. [Not known to our correspondents.] A pitiful little wretch.

Wm. FERGUSON _Northmen_ (1856) 214. **Som.** W. & J. _Gl._ (1873).

HERRIDGE, HERRIF, see **Harriage, Hairif.**

HERRINBAND, _sb._ Sc. A string warped through the different skeins of yarn, to keep them separate when they are boiled.

Abd. Not common. ' See that ye tak' the richt en' o' yer yarn after brakin' the herrin-band, an' nae mak' a snort' [mess] (G.W.). **Ags.** (JAM.)

HERRING, sb. Var. dial. uses in Sc. Irel. Eng. and Aus. Also written herren Dor.[1]; and in form harrin Nhb. **1.** In comb. (1) **Herring-bairn,** the sprat, *Clupea sprattus*; (2) **-bone fern,** the hard fern, *Blechnum boreale*; (3) **-bone road,** see below; (4) **drewe,** a drove of herrings; used *fig.*, see below; (5) **-dub,** the sea; (6) **-fare,** the season for catching herrings, which begins about the end of harvest; (7) **-gant,** the gannet, *Sula bassana*; (8) **-gutted,** thin, bony, wiry, used of both man and beast; (9) **-gyte,** the herring-spawn found adhering to herring-nets during fishing operations; (10) **-hang,** a place where herrings are hung to dry; (11) **-hog,** (a) the bottle-nosed whale, *Ziphius Sowerbiensis*; (b) the porpoise, *Phocaena communis*; (12) **-piece,** a rushing sound in the air caused by the flight of the redwing, considered a good omen for fishing; (13) **-pool,** the English Channel; (14) **-riba,** a lanky, bony person; (15) **-signs** or **-siles,** the swarms of minute fish which come as forerunners of the herring-shoals; (16) **-soam,** the fat of herrings; (17) **-spear,** see (12); (18) **-spink,** the golden-crested wren, *Regulus cristatus*; (19) **-tack,** a shoal of herrings.

(1) Cor.[12] (2) Cum. An appropriate name, referring to the shape of the fertile fronds more especially (B. & H.). (3) Cha.[1]; Cha.[2] A few of these remnants of the pack-horse period, though rapidly disappearing, may still be seen. Stones placed like those coming from the backbone of a fish, and which support the narrow paved causeway; the first attempt at an improvement on a mere track since the time of those great road-makers, the Romans. (4) Abd. When a shoal of herrings appeared off the *e*. coast of Sc., all the idle fellows and bankrupts of the country ran off under the pretence of catching them; whence he, who ran away from his creditors, was said to have gone to the herring-drewe (JAM.). (5) Cum. Will ship o'er the herring-dub Charlie McGlen, GILPIN *Sngs*. (1866) 404. (6) Ken.[1] (7) Nrf. SWAINSON *Birds* (1885) 144. (8) e.Yks.[1], w.Yks.[2] Cha.[2] He's a herring-gutted wastrel, th' same soize all th' way up! Lin.[1] He'll weather a storm, there's nought of him,—he's herring-gutted. n.Lin.[1] w.Som.[1] A herring-gutted old son of a bitch. (9) Nhb. (R.O.H.) (10) Ken.[1] A lofty season brick room, made perfectly smoke-tight. Sus.[1] 134. (11, a) N.I.[1] (b) s.Dev. *N. & Q.* (1873) 4th S. xi. 138. (12) Ken. HENDERSON *Flk-Lore* (1879) iv. (13) Cor. A cargo brought across the herring-pool, FORFAR *Pentowan* (1859) iv. (14) Dor.[1] Zome ugly long-lagg'd herren-ribs Jump'd out, an ax'd en var his dibs, &c. (15) n.Yks.[2] e.Yks. White-bait is nothing but 'herring-sile, as it is called on the Yks. coast, *Newcastle Wkly. Chron.*; (I.W.) (16) Gall. Young girls throw this against a wall, and if it adheres to it in an upright manner, then the husband they get will also be so; if crooked, he will be crooked, MACTAGGART *Encycl.* (1824) 430, ed. 1876. (17) Ken. HENDERSON *Flk-Lore* (1879) iv; Ken.[1] (18) e.An.[1] Often seen during the herring fishery. Nrf. The herring-spink, as the North Sea fishermen call . . . the golden-crested wren—is rather rare about the Broad district, EMERSON *Birds* (ed. 1895) 33. e.Suf. SWAINSON *ib.* 25. (19) Gall. MACTAGGART *ib.* 422. I.Ma. A 'sea-spirit' that haunted the herring-tack, *Denham Tracts* (ed. 1892) I. 203.

2. Phr. *as dead as a herring,* quite dead.

Ayr. I'll nail the self-conceited Scot As dead's a herrin, BURNS *Death and Dr. Hornbook* (1785) st. 30.

3. The gar-fish, *Belone vulgaris*.

Cum.[4] [Aus. They were called herring, but had nothing of the herring in their character. They were about eighteen inches long, with large mouth and decided teeth, thin of body, greenish on the back and silvery underneath, and more like some descriptions of guard-fish [gar-fish] than herring, *Gent. Mag.* (Nov. 1880) 615.]

4. The sprat, *Clupea sprattus*. Sc. BUCKLAND *Fishes* (1880).

HERRISH, HERRY, see Arrish, Harry, v.[2]

HERSCHE, adj. Sc. Hoarse.

s.Sc. Hersche he grew, and then he blared Richt like ane cuddy asse, WATSON *Bards* (1859) 106.

HERSELF, pron. Sc. I.Ma. Wor. Hrf. Glo. Also in form **-sel)L 1.** In phr. *in herself*, in her general health. s.Wor.[1] 34. Hrf.[2] (s.v. In). Glo. (A.B.)

2. Used by Highlanders in speaking of themselves: himself; a name given to a Highlander.

Sc. The Lowlanders often jocularly call a Highlander 'her sel',' *Monthly Mag.* (1800) 323; Hersell wad do't wi' muckle mair great satisfaction than to hurt ta honest civil shentlemans, SCOTT *Rob Roy* (1817) xxxi; .'Hursel' be a puir Gregor lad, an' no doin' ony harm!' was his statement, CROCKETT *Raiders* (1894) xl.

---

8. A wife.

I.Ma. How is herself? [How is your wife?] Herself is gone to town (S.M.).

HERSEL(L, see Hirsel, sb.[1]

HERSHIP, sb. Sc. Also written hairship Abd.; hareship, heirship, herschip Sc.; and in form harship Sc. **1.** Obs. Plundering by an armed force, a foray.

Sc. The lawless thieves . . . had been in fellowship together . . . for the committing of divers thefts, reifs, and herahips upon the honest men of the low country, SCOTT *Waverley* (1814) xv; Dead [death] at the tae door, and heirship at the tither, FERGUSON *Prov.* (1641) 10; Herschip in the highlands! the hens are i' the corn, HENDERSON *Prov.* (1832) 76, ed. 1881. Abd. Riesing hairship was become a trade, Ross *Helenore* (1768) 10, ed. 1812.

2. Ruin, distress, mischief, harm.

Sc. Hareships sindle come single, KELLY *Prov.* (1721) 143; HERD *Coll. Sngs.* (1776) Gl. Per. It was juist a perfect hership upon 's (said of long-continued trouble) (W.A.C.). Ayr. She dreided some herschip in the byous weather to her auld guidman as he cam warplin' an' fanklin' owre the muirs by himsel', SERVICE *Dr. Duguid* (ed. 1887) 254.

3. Booty, prey, that which is carried off as plunder.

Slg. Even within the last century some of the Highlanders used to make predatory incursions into the Lowlands and either carry off the cattle or make the owners redeem them by paying a sum of money. This . . . was called lifting the hership, or corr. 'herschaw' (JAM.). Abd. And as he yeed [went] the track at last he found Of the ca'd hership on the mossy ground, Ross *Helenore* (1768) 49, ed. 1812.

[1. On Inglismen full gret herschipe thai maid, *Wallace* (1488) VIII. 942. 2. The landwart pepyll be thir waris war brocht to sic pouerte and heirschip that thair land was left vnsawin and vnlabourit, BELLENDEN *Cron. Scotl.* XI. xi (JAM.).]

HERSILL, see Hirsel, v.[2]

HERSKIN, adj. Or.I. Also in form herakit. Of material: rough, dry, harsh to the touch; of the skin or throat: rough, dry, parched; *fig.* rough-mannered, abrupt. (J.G.) See Hask, adj.[1]

HERSKING, sb. Hrf.[2] A hearse.

HERSKIT, HERST, see Heart, Hearse.

HERSUM, adj. Abd. (JAM.) [Not known to our correspondents.] Rank, coarse; strong.

This lamb is of a proper age; if it had been aulder the meat wou'd ha' been hersum.

HERTFORDSHIRE PUDDINGSTONE, phr. Hrt. See below.

Hertfordshire conglomerate, locally called 'Hertfordshire puddingstone,' composed of flint pebbles in a siliceous base, blocks of which are found scattered over the surface of the chalk district of Hertfordshire, RAMSAY *Rock Specimens* (1862) 178.

HERTS, see Hurts.

HERVEY, adj. Ags. (JAM.) [Not known to our correspondents.] Mean; having the appearance of poverty.

HESE, HESHIE-BA, see Heeze, Hush-a-ba(a.

HESHING, sb. n.Yks.[4] [e·ʃin.] A sound thrashing. See Ash, v.

HESHT, HESK, see Husht, Hearse, Hisk.

HESITATION, sb. Chs.[13] A half-promise.

There was a hesitation about a calf cote.

HESP, v.[1] ne.Lan.[1] To pick off the ends of gooseberries.

HESP, v.[2] Lakel.[2] To make a vigorous and determined effort.

'He was hespin intul't wi' a rattle.'

HESP, see Hasp, sb.[12]

HESPEL, v. Wor. Shr. Hrt. Also written hespall Hrf.[1]; hespil w.Wor.[1]; hesple Hrf.[2]; and in form hespel Shr.[1] Hrf.[2]; huspil Shr.[2] [e·spl.] To worry, harass, hurry, drive away, put to rout.

w.Wor.[1] Shr.[1] I'll 'uspel yo' childern off that causey, yo' jest like a kerry o' 'ounds up an' down. They dun 'espel poor wench shameful—er's on throm mornin' till night; Binnod a gween to be huspil'd a that'ns. Hrf. Obs., *Provinc.* (1876); Hrf.[1]; Hrf.[2] Don't hespel the pig. Don't hespel yourself.—Boys no longer hesple one another, *ib.* 3.

[Huspylyn or spoylyn, *spolio, dispolio, Prompt.* Fr. *houspiller,* 'maltraiter (qqn) en le secouant' (HATZFELD); *s'Houspiller l'un l'autre,* to tug, lug, tear one another, to shake or towse, as one dog doth another (COTGR.).]

HESPERT, HESPIN, HESPY, see **Haspert, Haspin,** *sb.*[2], **Hie-spy.**

HESS, *sb.* e.An.[1] [Not known to our correspondents.] A quantity of yarn containing two skeins.

HESS, see **Haise, Hearse.**

HESSEN, *sb.* Obs. Yks. Lin. Hessian, a coarse cloth ; canvas.

n.Yks. Tuke *Agric.* (1800) 136. e.Yks. Marshall *Rur. Econ.* (1796) II. 34. Lin.[1]

HESSLE, *sb.* Yks. Lin. Also written **hessel** Lin.; and in forms **hazel** e.Yks. Lin.; **hezzel** n.Lin. The name given to a particular variety of pear. Also in *comp.* **Hessle-pear.**

e.Yks. At Hull more people call it 'hazel' than 'hessle' (J.C.W.); Hessle, medium size, very juicy, abundant bearer, Sept. and Oct., *Catalogue of Messrs. Crowder and Sons, Horncastle* ; Hessle, fruit below medium size, turbinate, Hogg *Fruit Manual* (1860). n.Lin. Hezzel-pear i' frunt gardin bloomed i' back-end, Peacock *Tales* (1890) 2nd S. 101.

HEST, *sb.* Sh.I. [hest.] A horse ; pl. *hesten,* horses, used as a generic term. S. & Ork.[1] Hence **Hestensgot,** *sb.* an enclosure in which a number of horses are pastured. *ib.*

[Norw. dial. *hest,* a horse (Aasen), so Dan.; ON. *hestr.*]

HESTA, *sb.* Sh.I. A mare ; a female of any species. S. & Ork.[1]

HESTER, *v.* Sc. 1. To hesitate.

Per. Here heaps o' filth, there dubs o' mester: A grumphie at your door wad hester To enter in, Stewart *Character* (1857) 60.

2. To pester, bother, trouble.

Per. I was hestered [had too much to do]. Dinna hester me e'en-noo wi' yer questions (G.W.).

[*Hester* is for **hesiter,* fr. **hesite* (= Fr. *hésiter*) + *-er* (freq. suff.) ; for **hesite,* to hesitate.]

HET, *int.* Nhb.[1] Also in form **hets.** An exclamation of impatience.

HET, HET(T, see **Halt, Heat,** *sb., v.,* **Hight,** *v.*[1]**, Hit, Hot.**

HETCH, *sb.*[1] Suf. A thicket ; a hedge. (Hall.); e.Suf. (F.H.)

HETCH, *v.*[1] and *sb.*[2] Irel. Yks. Lin. Shr. [etʃ.] 1. *v.* To hatch.

e.Yks.[1] w.Yks. (J.W.) n.Lin. Th'owd betherd sits on her eggs an' hetches 'em like a hen (E.P.).

Hence **Hetching,** *sb.* a quantity, a litter.

Ant. A hetching of rabbits (W.H.P.).

2. *sb.* A brood of chickens. e.Yks.[1] *MS. add.* (T.H.),Shr.[1]

HETCH, *v.*[2] n.Cy. [Not known to our correspondents.] To turn upside down. (Hall.)

HETCH, see **Hitch,** *v.*[2]

HETCHEL, *sb.* and *v.* Shr. e.An. Ken. Amer. Also in form **hitchel** e.An.[12] Ken. [etʃl, i·tʃl.] 1. *sb.* A carding instrument for dressing hemp or flax. Cf. **heckle,** *sb.*[1]

Shr.[1] Obs. A board with rows of iron teeth set in it—the fibre was thrown across the hetchel and pulled through it. e.An.[12]

2. *v.* To comb hemp or flax.

Ken. Obs. (P.M.) [Amer. To tease, to call to account. Metaphor from the days of the domestic flax industry, *Dial. Notes* (1896) I. 382.]

Hence **Hitcheler,** *sb.* a hemp-dresser. e.An.[12]

[1. Hetchell for flaxe, *serancq, serant,* Palsgr. (1530). 2. I hetchyll, *Je cerance* (the same as I heckell flaxe), *ib.*]

HETCHEL, see **Hatchel,** *sb.*[2]

HETH, see **Haith, Hearth, Heath.**

HETHER, see **Eaver,** *sb.*[1]**, Edder, Ether,** *sb.,* **Heather, Hetter.**

HETHERIG, *sb.* Sc. (Jam.) The ridge of land at the end of a field on which the horses and plough turn. (s. v. Headrig.)

HETHERING, *sb.* Shr.[2] A pliant twig about six feet long, chiefly employed at the top of newly-laid-down hedges to keep under the loose, straggling shoots. See Edder.

HETHER-UP, *int.* Wil. A command to oxen when ploughing to go to the left. n.Wil. (E.H.G.) Cf. **come-hither.**

HETTED-BROTH, *sb.* Cor. Heated broth ; used *fig.* for a cast-off 'sweetheart' whom another man has taken up with. See Heat, *v.* II. 1 (4).

Thomas *Randigal Rhymes* (1895) *Gl.*; You may like hetted brath, Jan ; but I doant (M.A.C.) ; 'You will doubtless remain a bachelor.' 'I'd ruther do that than 'ave hetted broth,' Thomas *Rom. Cove* (1893) 100.

HETTE(D, HETTEN, see **Heat,** *v.*

HETTER, *sb.*[1] Cor. [Not known to our correspondents.] 1. A shackle. Thomas *Randigal Rhymes* (1895) *Gl.* 2. *Comp.* Hetter-pin, the pin of a shackle. *ib.*

HETTER, *adj., sb.*[2] and *v.* n.Cy. Nhb. Yks. Lan. Chs. Der. Lin. Lei. Nhp. Also in forms **ater** n.Yks. ; **etta** w.Yks. ; **hether** n.Cy. (Hall.) ; **hitter** w.Yks.[14] sw.Lin.[1] Lei.[1] ; **itter** Lei.[1] [(h)etə(r).] 1. *adj.* Cross, ill-tempered, spiteful, bitter ; hostile.

n.Cy. (Hall.), Nhb.[1] w.Yks. Watson *Hist. Hlfx.* (1775) 540 ; w.Yks.[24] ; w.Yks.[5] An hetter sort'n a body. Der.[2], nw.Der.[1] Lei.[1] I asked the overseers for a bit o' money, an' they were ever so hitter at me. A wur very 'itter agen 'er. Nhp.[2] He's allas been uncommon hetter agin me.

Hence (1) **Hettered,** *adj.* full of hatred, embittered ; (2) **Hetterly,** *adv.* bitterly.

(1) sw.Lin.[1] He's that hittered against him. They seem so hittered, they'd do anything at him. (2) w.Yks.[2]; w.Yks.[4] She wept hetterley. Der.[1] To cry hetterly.

2. Eager, keen, earnest ; of a dog : fierce ; of a horse : pulling with all its might ; also used *advb.*

n.Cy. (K.), n.Cy.[12], Nhb.[1] Yks. Grose (1790) *MS. add.* (P.) w.Yks. Thoresby *Lett.* (1703) ; The horse pulls hetter (W.W.P.); Leeds Merc. *Suppl.* (Dec. 20, 1890) ; w.Yks.[14] Lan. Davies *Races* (1856) 275 ; Grose (1790) *MS. add.* (C.) Der.[3] Obs., Der.[2], nw.Der.[1] 3. Rough, ugly, bearish. n.Cy. (Hall.) [Not known to our correspondents.] 4. *sb.* Eagerness. n.Yks. (I.W.) 5. *v.* To increase in intensity. s.Chs.[1]

[1. MLG. *hettere* (= *heter*), 'erbittend' (Schiller-Lübben).]

HETTER, see **Heater,** *sb.,* **Hotter,** *v.*

HETTLE, *sb.* Sc. 1. The name given by fishermen on the Firth of Forth to a range of rocky bottom lying between the roadstead and the shore.

Fif. The brassy is found in the summer months, on the hettle or rocky grounds, Neill *Fishes* (1810) 13 (Jam.).

2. *Comp.* Hettle-codling, a species of codling caught on the 'hettle.' Fif. (Jam.)

3. *Phr.* out of the hettle into the kettle, an expression used to impress a purchaser with the idea that the fish is perfectly fresh. *ib.*

HETTLE, *adj.* and *v.* Sc. Nhb. Dur. Yks. Also written **hetel-** Dur. [h)etl.] 1. *adj.* In *comb.* Hettle-tongued, foul-mouthed, ill-tongued, irascible in speech. Nhb.[1], Dur. (K.) 2. Hasty, eager. Cld. (Jam.), Nhb.[1], Yks. (Hall.) 3. *v.* To act in anger or haste.

Nhb.[1] A pitman charged with throwing his lamp down the pit shaft said, ' He nobbut hettled it away an' it stotted off the flat sheets an' ganned doon the shaft.'

[1. OE. *hetol (hetel),* full of hate, malignant (B.T.).]

HETTLE, see **Ettle,** *sb.*[1]

HEUCH, *int.* and *v.* Sc. 1. *int.* An exclamation, *gen.* used when dancing the Scotch reel. Cf. **hooch.**

Sc. Crying heuch, heuch ! when the dance warms, and the fiddler's arms are fleeing faster than a weaver's shuttle, Sc. *Haggis,* 157. w.Sc. There's nae clapping of hands, and whirling round, and crying ' heuch, heuch ! ' when the dance warms, Carrick *Laird of Logan* (1835) 279. Lth. Bang men cried ' heuch ! ' like warlocks driven Clean gyte this day, Lumsden *Sheep-head* (1892) 40.

2. *v.* To cry ' heuch.'

Lth. Wi' volte, an' caper, an' funk, They danced, they snappit, an' heuched awa, Lumsden *Sheep-head* (1892) 147.

HEUCH, HEUCHLE, HEUCKLE, see **Heugh, Huckle,** *sb.*[1]

HEUCK, *sb.* Sc. (Jam.) Also in forms **heuch, heugh.** 1. A disease of cows ; see below.

Ags. A disease of cows, supposed to proceed from want of water, or from bad water, which eventually inflames the eye, in which case it is accounted dangerous. But it primarily attacks the stomach or the belly.

2. *Comp.* Heuch-stone, blue vitriol with which the vulgar rub the inflamed eye. Sc.

HEUD, see **Heuld, Hold,** *v.*

HEUDD, HEUDIN, HEUE, see Hide, *v.*², Hooding, How.

HEUF, *sb.* Yks. A shelter; a home. (HALL.) See Howf(f.

HEUGH, *sb.* Sc. Irel. Nhb. Cum. Wm. Yks. Also written **heaugh** Yks.; **heuch** Sc.; and in forms **heuf** n.Yks.²; **hew** Sc. (JAM.) Nhb.; **hewe** Nhb.; **huwe** Sc. (JAM.) [hiux, hiu.] **1.** A crag, cliff, precipice, a steep bank.

Sc. They ... descended the broad loaning, which winding round the steep bank, or heugh, brought them in front of the ... farmhouse, SCOTT *Blk. Dwarf* (1816) iii. **Bch.** Gane backlench o'er the heugh, FORBES *Dominie* (1785) 39. **Abd.** Clippin' aff that lang heugh an' the bit burnside, ALEXANDER *Johnny Gibb* (1871) xlv. **Kcd.** She ... clam upon a heugh, GRANT *Lays* (1884) 12. **Frf.** There's game, I'm sure. I find the smell I' the park o' Ethie, neist the heugh, SANDS *Poems* (1833) 82. **Fif.** The rocks and braes a' thairabout Rang wi' the echo o' that shout, Till round the Kirk-heugh ... It ran to Ladie Buchan cave, TENNANT *Papistry* (1827) 80. **Ayr.** An' tho' yon lowin heugh's thy hame, Thou travels far, BURNS *Address to Deil* (1785) st. 3. **Slk.** And he's over the border And over the heuch, HOGG *Poems* (ed. 1865) 160. **Gall.** Down heuchs and craigs—and glens and hags, As fast as he cud flee, MACTAGGART *Encycl.* (1824) 24, ed. 1876. **Wgt.** Nae angry gust his coble neared That sune was moor'd aneath the heugh, FRASER *Wigtown* (1877) 212. **N.I.¹** ' The Gobbin Heughs,' precipitous rocks on the coast at the east of Ant. **N.Cy.¹ Nhb.** Oor weird wild hews, Oor cairns that mem'ry still embalms, Hae nursed my Muse, PROUDLOCK *Borderland Muse* (1896) 118; **Nhb.¹ Yks.** *N. & Q.* (1870) 4th S. v. 670. **n.Yks.** The entire Abbey cliff is essentially a 'heugh,' ATKINSON *Whitby* (1894) 80; **n.Yks.²; n.Yks.³** A grassy top or side of a mountain. **w.Yks.¹**

2. *Comp.* **Heugh-head,** the top of a cliff or precipice. Sc. GROSE (1790) *MS. add.* (C.)

3. *Phr.* *to coup one over the heugh, fig.* to undo, ruin a person.

n.Sc. (JAM.) **Abd.** This is hard enough, Against ane's will to coup him o'er the heugh, ROSS *Helenore* (1768) 100, ed. 1812.

4. A glen; a deep cleft in the rocks; a grassy ravine without water.

Sc. We 'ill stuff his stomach with English land, which is worth twice as much ... as these ... hills and beughs, SCOTT *Nigel* (1822) ix. **s.Sc.** I at the doup o' e'en Slide cannie owr the heugh alane, T. SCOTT *Poems* (1793) 319. **Lth.** He finds the same lambs he had cast in the heugh, BALLANTINE *Poems* (1856) 99. **Rxb.** Though snows be aff the heights and heughs, RIDDELL *Poems* (1871) I. 204. **Gall.** Yon carlin by the heugh and cairn, NICHOLSON *Poet. Wks.* (1814) 197, ed. 1897. **Nbb.** Ilk laverock that sprang Frae the heather an' green birky hewes, PROUDLOCK *Borderland Muse* (1896) 2; **Nhb.¹, Cum.¹⁴** Wm. A dry dell, as distinct from a cleugh, one through which a stream flows (J.H.).

5. A coal-pit; the shaft of a coal-mine.

Sc. It was mirk as in a coal heugh, GRAHAM *Writings* (1883) II. 54. **Fif.** A great fire of wood and coal from my Lord Sinclair's heughs blazed day and night on the stone hearth, GRANT *Six Hundred*, ix. **e.Frf.** A drucken collier chiel hailin' frae some o' the coal heuchs, LATTO *Tam Bodkin* (1864) ix. **Slg.** Steam That drives at heughs the wa'king-beam, O huge engines, to drain coal seam, MUIR *Poems* (1818) 11. **Dmb.** Sandy Tosh gaed to the heugh, TAYLOR *Poems* (1827) 71. **Ayr.** It was naething short of a miracle that we werena ... kilt in the auld heuch at Mossmulloch, as we raxed owre the mouth o't, to hear the stanes we flang doun stottin', SERVICE *Dr. Duguid* (ed. 1887) 28. **Lnk.** Lowin' like a heuch o' fire, MURDOCH *Doric Lyre* (1873) 12.

Hence (1) **Heughman,** (2) **Heughster,** *sb.* a pitman, coal-miner.

(1) **Fif.** The Dysart heughmen left their places O' darkness now, TENNANT *Papistry* (1827) 11. (2) **Sc.** And heughsters hard at heart and cruel, DRUMMOND *Muckomachy* (1846) 11.

6. A hollow made in a quarry. Lth. (JAM.)

[1. Ontill ane cave we went, Vndir a hingand hewch, DOUGLAS *Eneados* (1513), ed. 1874, II. 133. OE. *hōh*, a promontory, lit. a hanging (precipice), the same word as Goth. *hāh*, in *faúra hāh*, a hanging curtain; for the phonology cp. clough, *sb.*¹]

HEUGH, HEUK, HEUKS, see Heuck, Yonk, Yucks.

HEUKSTER, HEUL, see Huckster, Hewl.

HEULD, *adj.* Or.I. Also in form **heud.** **1.** Kindly, gracious. (JAM.)

2. *Comp.* (1) **Heuld-drink,** the grace-cup; see below; (2) **-horn,** the horn vessel in which the 'heuld-drink' was presented.

(1) Sometime after the guests retired to bed, the lady of the house made a round of the bed-rooms, offering every guest a drink of warm, spirituous liquor. This was called the 'heuld-drink,' *Or. Sketch-bk.* (1880) 63 (JAM.). (2) The vessel was smaller than the common drinking horn used at table, and held rather more than an ordinary tumbler, *ib.*

[1. Leche to þam was he ful hold, *Cursor M.* (c. 1300) 13364. OE. *hold*, kind, gracious; cp. G. *hold*.]

HEULLY, HEUNT, see Hooly, Want.

HEUP, HEUSAL, see Heap, *sb.*¹, Hoop, *sb.*¹, Hazel, *sb.*¹

HEUSIN, HEUTLE, see Hoosing, Wheutle.

HEUTTY-BACK, *sb.* Cum. A hunchback.

T'laal heuttyback rowlt his een aboot, SARGISSON *Joe Scoap* (1881) 183; **Cum.²**

HEUXTER, see Huckster.

HEVA, *int.* Cor. Also written **hevah** Cor.² A cry to warn fishermen of the approach of pilchards. Cf. hew, *v.*²

Shortly after daylight the cry of 'Heva! heva!' was heard from the hills. .. Heva is shouted from the hills, upon which a watch is kept for the approach of pilchards by the 'huer,' who telegraphs to the boats. 'If we have first stem when heva comes We'll the huer's bushes watch,' HUNT *Pop. Rom. w.Eng.* (1865) 370, ed. 1896; Aw, my dear, I should love for ee to hear a heva, TREGELLAS *Character* (1868) 11; Cor.¹; Cor.² The welcome sound of Hevah! was heard at St. Ives yesterday, and the boats on the look out for pilchards were instantly on the alert, *W. Morning News* (Oct. 14, 1881) (s.v. Hubba).

HEVE, HEVEL, see Heave, Heald, *sb.*¹

HEVEL, *sb.* Sh.I. Also written **hevil** S. & Ork.¹ [he·vl.] **1.** A handle for a pail. S. & Ork.¹

2. *Comp.* **Hevel-daffock,** a bucket with a handle across the top.

She ran to the hevel daffock for a little water, STEWART *Tales* (1892) 210.

[Norw. dial. *hevel*, a handle for a vessel without a top (AASEN).]

HEVER, HEVIOR, see Eaver, *sb.*¹, Haiver, Haver, *sb.*⁴

HEVVAL, HEVY-SKEVY, see Evil, *sb.*², Havey-cavey.

HEW, *v.*¹ Var. dial. uses in Sc. and Eng. **I.** Gram. forms. **1.** *Present Tense:* (1) Hoo, (2) Yaow, (3) Yaw, (4) Yo, (5) Yoe, (6) Yow.

(1) Not. (J.H.B.) (2) se.Wor.¹ (3) Hmp.¹, Dev.¹ (4) Chs.¹, Glo.¹ (5) Chs.³ w.Som.¹ 'Tis a gurt piece, t'll take us more'n quarter day to yoe [yoa] un. (6) Chs.¹ s.Chs.¹ [Yuw]. e.Som. W. & J. Gl. (1873). w.Dev. MARSHALL *Rur. Econ.* (1796) I. x 68.

2. *Preterite:* (1) Yaew, (2) Yoed, (3) Yowed.

(1) m.Yks.¹ *Introd.* 36. (2) w.Som. [Yao·d], ELWORTHY *Gram.* (1877) 47. (3) s.Chs.¹ [Yuw·d], 81.

3. *Pp.:* (1) Howen, (2) Yaewn, (3) Yoed, (4) Yowed.

(1) Per. Hae nae an emerald howen o' earth Like what ye see, STEWART *Character* (1857) 90. (2) m.Yks.¹ *Introd.* 36. (3) w.Som. [U-yao·d], ELWORTHY *Gram.* (1877) 47. (4) s.Chs.¹ [Yuw·d], 81.

II. Dial. uses. **1.** With *out*: to shape with an axe. w.Som.¹ Vuul·urz bee bad·r u-yoa·d aewt-n dhai bee· u-zae·d [felloes be better hewn out than they be sawn]. Sharp, Jim, and yoe out a laver [lever].

2. To cut with an effort; in salt-making: to dig marl; to break up the hard salt. Chs.¹, s.Chs.¹

Hence (1) **Yowing-knife,** *sb.* the tool with which slates are trimmed. Chs.¹; (2) **Yoings,** *sb. pl.* the hard salt broken off the flues of the hot-house. *ib.*

3. To work or dig coal.

Nhb. Aw kowk'd an' hew'd, aw toil'd an' tew'd, ROBSON *Evangeline* (1870) 332; I perceive you sinckers differ in judgment and methods from hewing or working coals, *Compleat Collier* (1708) 32; (R.O.H.); Nhb.¹, e.Dur.¹

Hence (1) **Hewer,** *sb.* a pitman who works coal; (2) **Hewing-double,** *sb.* the working together at one board by two 'hewers.'

(1) N.Cy.¹ Nhb. The lads are huntin' for their trams—The hewers for their picks and clay, WILSON *Pitman's Pay* (1843) 27; Nhb.¹ Nhb., Dur. In early life a hewer at Benton Colliery, WATSON *Hist. Newcastle* (1897) 100. e.Dur.¹, Lan. (HALL.) (2) Nhb. (R.O.H.)

4. To mow, *gen.* with one hand and with a reaping-hook ; to cut the stubble short.

  s.Chs.[1] Wen yŭ bin yuw·in ... in ŭ feyld, ŭn dhŭ sŭn puw·ŭrin daayn iz ĕeŭt ŭpon· yŭ, yoa bin dlaad· gy'et sŭm·ut dringk [When yŏ bin yowin' . . . in a feyld, an' the sun pourin' daïn his heeat upon yŏ, yo bin glad get summat drink] (s.v. Maul). **Hmp. Esp.** to cut corn, peas, or beans, WISE *New Forest* (1883) 288; Hmp.[1] **e.Som. W. & J.** *Gl.* (1873). **Som.** (W.F.R.)

  Hence (1) **Hewer,** *sb.* a mower; (2) **Hewing,** *vbl. sb.* the method of cutting wheat with one hand; (3) **Hewing-hook,** *sb.* a reaping-hook, *gen.* used for cutting wheat or beans.

  (1) **Som.** They reap very early, while the corn is green ; hewing the wheat ; one binder follows two hewers, YOUNG *Annals Agric.* (1784–1815) XXX. 310. (2) **Dev.** (HALL.) **w.Dev.** MARSHALL *Rur. Econ.* (1796) I. 168. (3) **Glo.**[1] **w.Dev.** The yowing hook, formed much like the common reaping hook, is larger. With this the corn is struck at (so that it is driven) against the standing corn, the workman taking a sweep round as much as will form a sheaf, supporting it with the left arm and leg until it is lifted to the band, MARSHALL *Rur. Econ.* (1796) I. 168.

  5. To knock one ankle against the other in walking. **w.Yks.**[1]

  HEW, *v.*[2] Dev. Cor. Also written **hu-** Dev. Cor.[12] To make signals from the cliffs to the fishermen in their boats to let them know in what direction the pilchards are. Wearne and he was out upon the cliffs waun day, a hewing, TREGELLAS *Tales* (1865) 196 ; Cor.[1]

  Hence (1) **Hewer,** *sb.* a person who makes signals from the cliffs ; (2) **Hewing-house,** *sb.* a shed, *gen.* on the highest cliff, to shelter the ' hewer.'

  (1) **Dev.** *Reports Provinc.* (1886) 96. Cor. The more general and successful method of enclosing fish is for the seine boats to receive their signals from a man called a ' huer,' stationed on the top of the nearest cliff, who, from this vantage ground, can have a much clearer sight of the fish. The huer has a furze bush or other signal in each hand, and by preconcerted movements can accurately guide the boats below, BUCKLAND *Fishes* (1880) 165 ; Cor.[1] (2) Cor.[1]

  [It shall ... be lawful ... for euery such watchmen, balcors, huors, condors, directors and guidors ... to balke, hue, conde, direct and guide the fishermen which shall be vpon the said sea and sea coasts, *Act* 1 *James I* (1603) c. 23. OFr. *huer*, ' crier ' (LA CURNE).]

  HEW, *v.*[3] e.An. Preterite of *to hoe*. See **How(e.**

  Nrf. GILLETT *Sng. Sol.* (1860) *notes* 4. **Suf.**[1] Hew hew them there tahnups—John Smith, he hew em. **e.Suf.** (F.H.)

  HEW, HEWAL, see **Hue, How,** *adv.*, **Evil,** *sb.*[2]

  HEWE, *sb.* Som. A corn or bunion. (HALL.)

  HEWE, HEW-HOLE, see **Heugh, Hickwall.**

  HEWIN, *sb.* Chs.[1] In phr. *Hewin or Dick,* ' Evan or Dick,' one thing or another.

  HEWING-CRY, *sb.* *Obs.* Rut.[1] A hue and cry.

  The usual spelling in constable's accounts in the eighteenth century for ' hue and cry.' ' Too hewing cries, 4*d.*' (1725).

  HEWL, *sb.* Sc. Nhb. Also in forms **heul** Nhb.[1]; **hewel** Nhb.[1]; **huel** Nhb.[1]; **hule** Sc. Nhb.[1]; **hyule** Gall. [hiuL.] **1.** An out-of-the-way person, one that acts in a headstrong and extraordinary manner.

  Fif. (JAM.) **Rxb.** A hule among the lasses (*ib.*). **Gall.** Gallovidians stood the spree, And o'ercam' the hules completely, MACTAGGART *Encycl.* (1824) 7, 8, ed. 1876 ; Auld Maminn, the hule for clubbing lees, *ib.* 85. **Nhb.** He's a hewel of a lad. He's a heul to spend money. He's a heul to drink. ' He swore he wad hang the wee huel,' ARMSTRONG *Trial of Wee Piper* ; (R.O.H.) ; Nhb.[1]

  Hence **Hewlish,** *adj.* reckless, lavish. Nhb.[1]

  2. Phr. (1) *to play hule,* to upset, disorganize ; (2) *what the hule?* what the deuce ?

  (1) **Nhb.**[1] He's played hule wi' the hyel consarn. (2) **Dmf.** What the hule's come on ye This mony a day ! QUINN *Heather* (1863) 99.

  3. A mischievous boy.

  Dmf. (JAM.) **Gall.** A word constantly used by my grandmother; still quite common (S.R.C.) ; He was usually referred to as ' that loon,' ' the hyule,' ' Wattie, ye mischeevious boy,' CROCKETT *Bog-Myrtle* (1895) 282 ; He's a terrible hule. He's a hule's boy. Saw ye the hule! MACTAGGART *Encycl.* (1824) 277, ed. 1876.

  4. A cross-grained person. Slk., Rxb. (JAM.)

  [A *fig.* use of ME. *hewell,* also *hewhall,* a hickwall, woodpecker (LEVINS) ; see **Hickwall.**]

  HEWLET, see **Howlet.**

  HEW-MACK, *sb.* w.Som.[1] The stock or stem of the wild rose, *Rosa canina,* used for budding or grafting upon. Always. ' D'ye please to want a nice lot o' hewmacks [yŭe·maaks] de year?'

  HEWNS, *sb. pl. Obs.* Cor. The sides of a calciner in a tin-burning house.

  The tops, bottom, and hewns of the calciner, PRYCE *Min. Cor.* ; Cor.[3] 70 or 80 years ago the word was common.

  HEWSICK, *sb.* War. [iu·sik.] The fly-catcher, *? Muscicapa grisola.*

  TIMMINS *Hist. War.* (1889) 213 ; *Trans. B'ham and Midl. Instit. Arch. Soc.* (Nov. 24, 1875) ; War.[2]

  HEWSON, *sb.*[1] n.Cy. Yks. [iu·sən.] In phr. *a blind hewson,* a term of reproach addressed to a person who cannot see what is plainly before his eyes, or who is apt to make mistakes from not using them properly. n.Cy. (HALL.), w.Yks.[1]

  HEWSON, *sb.*[2] Bdf. The leather which is placed on the top of a horse's collar. (HALL.)

  HEWSTRING, *adj.* Som. Dev. Wheezing, asthmatic, husky. See **Hooze,** *v.*

  w.Som.[1] Common. 'Tid'n no use vor to put a poor old hewstrin [ĕo·streen] old fellow like he 'bout no jich job's that there.' **n.Dev.** *Horæ Subsecivæ* (1777) 211 ; Ya gerred-teal'd, pauking, hewstring mea-zel ! *Exm. Scold.* (1746) l. 48.

  HEWT, *v.* ne.Lan.[1] To hit the heels and ankles together in walking. Cf. **hew,** *v.*[1] 5.

  HEX, *sb.* Yks. The rail or hurdle placed in front and behind a cart, used in housing hay. Cf. **hack,** *sb.*[2] 18.

  They fan it haat that too horses and a cart wi hex on wud karre as mich as heit pack horses, *Yks. Comet, MS. add.*

  HEXE, *sb.* Sc. [Not known to our correspondents.] A witch.

  Bwk. ' An old hexe,' means an old witch, and is often applied, in a bad sense, to females of the present day, HENDERSON *Pop. Rhymes* (1856) 43.

  [Du. and G. *hexe,* a witch.]

  HEXHAM, *sb.* Nhb. Yks. **1.** In phr. *(Go) to Hexham,* (go) to hell. See **Halifax.**

  Nhb. ' To Hexham wi' thy feythor,' ses she, *Keelmin's Ann.* (1869) 11 ; (R.O.H.) **m.Yks.**[1] I'll see him at Hexam first. He'll earn his salt, maybe—when he goes to live at Hexham.

  2. Comb. (1) **Hexham measure,** a generous measure; (2) **— tans,** brown leather gloves, formerly a speciality of the town.

  (1) **Nhb.** ' Hexham measure, heaped full an' runnin' ower,' was a proverb which Mr. J. P. Gibson points out to have originated in the circumstance that the ' beatment ' at Hexham had twice the capacity of the Newcastle ' beatment ' (R.O.H.). (2) *ib.*

  HEXT, *sb.* Nhp. Glo. The highest ; the top or principal part. Cf. **height,** *sb.* II. 1.

  Nhp.[1] ' I've taken the hext of the dirt off the table.' When any work is nearly completed, the hext of it is done. **Glo.** Take away the hext of it first, *Horæ Subsecivæ* (1777) 211. [When bale is hext boot is next, RAY *Proverbs* (1678) 96.]

  HEY, *v.* Yks. [Not known to our correspondents.] To play, gambol ; to kick about. (HALL.)

  HEY, see **He, Heigh, Hie,** *v.*[2], **High.**

  HEYAM, HEY-BA, see **Hame,** *sb.*[1], **Hay-bay.**

  HEYCE, HEYD(E, see **Heeze, Hide,** *v.*[2], **Heir.**

  HEYEL, HEYEM, see **Hade,** *adj.*, **Hame,** *sb.*[1]

  HEYGUS, HEYH, see **Haggis, Egg,** *v.*

  HEYHOWING, *sb.* e.An.[1] [Not known to our correspondents.] Thieving of yarn from the master-weaver. See **Hickwall.**

  HEYK, see **Hike.**

  HEY-KO-CUTTY, *sb.* Sh.I. A ludicrous dance performed by persons squatting on their haunches, to the tune of ' Hey-quo-cutty.' S. & Ork.[1] Cf. **curcuddie.**

  HEYLADS, *sb. pl.* sw.Lin.[1] In phr. *to be at* or *all of heylads,* to be at variance.

  HEYLOE, HEYMOST, HEYN, see **Heloe, Highmost, Hen,** *sb.*[1]

  HEYND, HEYNE, see **Hend, Hind,** *sb.*[1], **Hain,** *v.*[2]

  HEYPAL, HEYR(E, see **Hipple,** *v.*[2], **Heir.**

HEYRT, *adj.* Sc. Also written **heyrd** (JAM.). Furious, raging; in phr. *to gang* or *rin heyrd*, to fume, be in a violent rage.

Sc. Douce, cautious men aft fey are seen, Thai rin as thai war heyrt, SCOTT *Minstrelsy* (1802) III. 390, ed. 1806. Ang. (JAM.)

HEYSHIN, *sb.* w.Yks. A wooden receptacle for carrying liquids for dyeing. (R.S.) Cf. **ashen.**

HEYTIE, *sb.* Lth. (JAM.) The game of ' shinty.'

HEZ, *sb.* Cor.² [Not known to our correspondents.] A swarm of bees.

[OCor. *hez*, a swarm (WILLIAMS); Wel. *haid*; Breton (Léon) *hed-gwenan*, ' essaim d'abeilles ' (DU RUSQUEC); Ir. *saith beach*, a swarm of bees (O'REILLY).]

HEZARD, *v.* Sc. Also in form **hizard.** To dry clothes by bleaching. Rnf. SHAW *Schoolmaster* (1899) 325. See **Hazle, v.**

HEZEKIAH, *sb.* Sc. In phr. *as proud as Hezekiah*, excessively proud.

Edb. The piper. that played in the middle, as proud as Hezekiah, MOIR *Mansie Wauch* (1828) xiv.

HEZZEL, see **Hessle, Hazel,** *sb.*¹²

HEZZLE, see **Hazel,** *sb.*¹, **Hazle.**

HI, HIAM, see **Aye,** *adv.*², **Ha,** *adj.*, **He, Hie,** *int.*, **Hame,** *sb.*¹

HIAMSE, *adj.* Sh.I. Awkward, unwieldy; half-witted. S. & Ork.¹

[Dan. dial. *hiamsk*, half-witted (MOLBECH); MDan. *hemsk*, foolish (KALKAR).]

HIBBAL, *sb.* and *v.* Yks. Cor. Also written **hibble** Yks. [i·b'l.] **1.** *sb.* A small heap of anything, such as hay; anything loosely put together. Cor.² Cf. **hipple,** *sb.*¹ **2.** A knoll, hummock, tumulus. Cor. THOMAS *Randigal Rhymes* (1895) *Gl.* **3.** A turnip. *ib.* **4.** *v.* To heap up; to collect. Yks. (J.W.)

[1. Cp. EFris. *hubbel*, Unebenheit, Höcker, Erhöhung (KOOLMAN).]

HIBBIN, *sb.* I.Ma. Also written **hibben.** [i·bin.] The ivy, *Hedera Helix.* Cf. **ivin.**

She was dressing the house with hibben and hollin, CAINE *Deemster* (1889) 128; He's gone to the country to get some hibbin and hollyn [holly] for the church ones, they decorate it every Christmas (S.M.).

HIBBIT, *sb.* Dev. Cor. Also written **hibet** Cor. [i·bit.] A newt, a little eft. Cf. **evet.**

Dev. *N. & Q.* (1871) 4th S. vii. 510; Dev.⁸ Cor. THOMAS *Randigal Rhymes* (1895) *Gl.*

HIBBLED, *adj.* Fif. (JAM.) [Not known to our correspondents.] Confined.

HIBBLEDY-HOBBLEDY, *sb.* Suf. A confused mass, a muddle. RAVEN *Hist. Suf.* (1895) 263.

HIBBY, *sb.* Dev. A colt.

(HALL.); Dev.⁸ When a man is desirous of catching a horse which has been running free in a field, he often holds his hand out towards it . . . and murmurs ' Hib, hib hib, hibby, hibby ' in a persuasive tone.

HIC, HIC-BERRY, see **Hick,** *int.*, **Hag-berry.**

HICCUP-SNICKUP, *sb.* n.Cy. Nhb. Suf. Also written **hickup-snickup** N.Cy.¹ Nhb.¹ e.Suf. [h]i·kəp-snikəp.] The hiccups.

n.Cy.¹ Hickup—snickup, stand up, stick up, One drop, two drops—good for the hiccup. Nhb.¹ Suf.¹ Hiccup—sniccup—look up—right up—Three drops in a cup—is good for the hiccup. e.Suf. (F.H.)

HICE-PICE, HICH, HICHELE, see **Hie-spy, Hick,** *v.*⁸, **Hickwall.**

HICK, *v.*¹ and *sb.*¹ Sc. Also written **hic** Per. [hik.] **1.** *v.* To hesitate as in making a bargain; to chaffer. Fif., Bnff. (JAM.) **2.** To hesitate in speaking. Rxb. (*ib.*) **3.** *sb.* An expression of hesitation.

Sc. Hicks and hums, *Whistle Binkie* (1853) II. 232 (JAM. *Suppl.*). Per. Jamie began, wi' a ' hic' an' a stan', Like ony whase heart's ower fu', FORD *Harp* (1893) 319.

HICK, *int.*, *v.*² and *sb.*² Sc. Nhb. Lakel. Yks. Nhp. Also written **hic** Nhp.¹; **hik** m.Yks.¹ [h]ik.] **1.** *int.* A call to ducks. Nhp.¹ **2.** *v.* To make a clicking noise in the throat like the coming of a sharp sob; to hiccup. Ags.,

Per. (JAM.), m.Yks.¹ **3.** To cry intermittently; to whimper; to grieve; also with *on*.

s.Sc., Rxb. (JAM.) Nhb.¹ ' What a discontented bairn that is; it's constant hickin on.' A child pretending to cry is said to hick. m.Yks.¹

4. *sb.* A clicking noise in the throat; the hiccups. Ags., Per. (JAM.), m.Yks.¹ Hence **Hick-haw,** (1) *v.* to make a piteous noise; (2) *sb.* the braying of an ass.

(1) Yks. The poor creature did look piteous oop in the air, and hick-hawed like a good un, FETHERSTON *Farmer*, 131. (2) Lakel.⁸

HICK, *v.*³ Sc. Yks. Not. Lin. Also in form **hich** Sc. (JAM. *Suppl.*) [h]ik.] To hoist, hitch, lift with an upward jerk; gen. with *up*.

Sc. (JAM. *Suppl.*) e.Yks. Hick it up a bit higher, NICHOLSON *Flk-Sp.* (1889) 67. s.Not. Joost 'elp me to hick this oop on to my shou'der (J.P.K.). n.Lin.¹ sw.Lin.¹ He broke his body wi' hicking corn. Hicking's worse than carrying.

Hence (1) **Hicking-barrow,** (2) **Hicky-barrow,** *sb.* a small wooden handbarrow; a frame used for lifting sacks of corn, &c. on to a man's shoulder.

(1) e.Yks. NICHOLSON *Flk-Sp.* (1889) 34. w.Yks.², Not.² n.Not. A kind of small stretcher or cratch. It is so carried that the handles stand off the ground without legs (J.P.K.). n.Lin.¹ Hicking and running barrows, *Gainsb. News* (Apr. 8, 1876). m.Lin. Be quick and fetch the hickin'-barrer; it's time to begin wo'kkin' agen (T.H.R.). sw.Lin.¹ (2) n.Yks. (C.V.C.)

HICK, *v.*⁴ and *sb.*³ Yks. e.An. Dor. Som. Also in form **hickety** w.Som.¹ [ik.] **1.** *v.* To hop on one leg; to spring; to play hop-scotch. Cf. **heck,** *v.*⁴

w.Yks.², e.An.¹, Suf. (C.T.), e.Suf. (F.H.), Dor.¹ Som. JENNINGS *Obs. Dial. w.Eng.* (1825); W. & J. Gl. (1873). w.Som.¹

Hence (1) **Hickety-hackety,** (2) **Hickety-pound,** (3) **Hick-stone,** *sb.* the game of hop-scotch.

(1, 2) w.Som.¹ (3) Som. Little Jack Sandboy, in his smock, was playing hick-stone on the flags, RAYMOND *Love and Quiet Life* (1894) 35.

2. *sb.* A hop on one leg. Som. JENNINGS *Obs. Dial. w.Eng.* (1825). **3.** *Comb.* **Hick-step-and-jump,** hop-skip-and-jump. *ib.*

HICK, see **Hack,** *sb.*¹

HICKAMORE-'ACKAMORE, *sb.* Lin. The name for a cloud in an old riddle.

Hickamore, 'ackamore Sits over th' kitchen door; Nothing so long, and nothing so strong, As Hickamore, 'ackamore Sits over th' kitchen-door. Ans. A cloud, *N. & Q.* (1865) 3rd S. viii. 503.

HICKER, *adj.* n.Yks.² [i·kər.] Higher.

' Hicker lip,' the upper lip. ' I want t'hicker yan o' them,' the top one of the lot.

HICKER, HICKERTIE-PICKERTIE, see **Hacker,** *v.*, **Hickledy-pickledy.**

HICKERY-PICKERY, *sb.* Sc. Also written **hykerie-pykerie** Ayr. ' Hiera picra,' a drug composed of Barbadoes aloes and canella bark.

Sc. The leddy cured me wi' some hickery-pickery, SCOTT *Old Mortality* (1816) viii. Arg. Bring hickery-pickery—bring, Droshachs, to sooth my pain! COLVILLE *Vernacular* (1899) 7. Ayr. How to use hykerie pykerie and rue, and mony mae cunning cures, SERVICE *Dr. Duguid* (ed. 1887) 280.

[*Hiera picra*, Gr. ἱερὰ πικρά, the bitter remedy. In the medicine of the middle ages ἱερά freq. appears as an element in the names of drugs, in the sense of a nostrum or remedy; see *Alphita*, ed. Mowat, 195, n. 3, *Sin. Barth.*, ed. Mowat, 44, n. 2.]

HICKET, *v.* Ken.¹² Sur.¹ Also in form **hucket** Sur.¹ [i·kit.] To hiccup, gasp for breath, make a choking sound; to retch.

HICKET, HICKETY, see **Hacket,** *v.*¹, **Hick,** *v.*⁴

HICKETY-BICKETY, *sb.* Sc. A boys' outdoor game; see below.

One stands with his eyes bandaged and his hands against a wall, with his head resting upon them. Another stands beside him repeating a rhyme, whilst the others come one by one and lay their hands upon his back, or jump upon it : ' Hickety, bickety, pease scone, Where shall this poor Scotchman gang! Will be gang east, or will he gang west; Or will he gang to the craw's nest!' When he has sent them all to different places, he turns round and calls : ' Hickety, bickety !' till they have all rushed back to the place, the last in returning being obliged to take his place, when the game goes on as before. The 'craw's nest' is close beside the eye-bandaged boy, and is therefore an envied position, CHAMBERS *Pop. Rhymes* (1870) 122–3.

HICKEY, *sb.* Not.[1] [i·ki.] A name for the devil.

Let 'em go to owd hickey.

HICKLE, *v.*[1] Nrf. Suf. [i·kl.] **1.** To gather up one's effects into a little heap. Nrf. (A.G.) **2.** To make shift with indifferent lodgings or quarters, to put two beds into one room.

Suf.[1] To hickle one's self into lodgings—or a pig into a stye already sufficiently occupied. s.Suf. (F.H.)

HICKLE, *v.*[2] Nrf. Suf. [i·kl.] To bring up by hand; with *up* : to fatten slowly.

Nrf. *Arch.* (1879) VIII. 170. e.Suf. To hickle up fowls, pigs, &c. (F.H.)

Hence **Hickler,** *sb.* one who buys up fowls, eggs, and pork, or rears them himself, and sells them at the market. e.Suf. (*ib.*)

HICKLE, *v.*[3] and *sb.* Suf. **1.** *v.* To snare hares or rabbits. e.Suf. (F.H.) **2.** *sb.* A wire snare. *ib.*

HICKLE, see Heckle, *sb.*[1], Hickwall, Ickle, *sb.*

HICKLEDY-PICKLEDY, *adv.* Sc. Lakel. Cum. Yks. Also in forms hickertie-pickertie Abd. (JAM.); hikkelty-pikkelty Cum.[1] Higgledy-piggledy, one upon another.

Abd. (JAM.). Lakel.[2] He threw them in hickledy-pickledy, gurt an' lal, soond er unsoond. Cum.[1], Yks. (J.W.)

HICKLE-HACKLE, *v.* e.Lan.[1] To work unskilfully.

HICKLING, *adj.* Lin. [i·klin.] Of a cough : tickling, irritating. See **Hackling.**

s.Lin. I've got sich a nasty hickling cough, I keänt rest neëither night nor daä' for it (T.H.R.).

HICK-MALL, HICKOL, see Hackmall, Hickwall.

HICKORY, *adj.* Sc. Nhb. Also written hiccory Lnk. (JAM.) [hi·kəri.] Cross-grained ; ill-humoured. Lnk. (JAM.) Hence (1) Hickory-face, *sb.* an evil-looking, pockmarked face ; (2) Hickory-faced, *adj.* ill-visaged, pockmarked.

(1) Nhb. While Charley damns Jack's hoolet een, His hick'ryfyece and endless growl, WILSON *Pitman's Pay* (1843) II. 29. (2) Nhb.[1]

HICKSPICKIT, *sb.* w.Yks.[2] A child's name for the third toe.

HICKWALL, *sb.* In *gen.* dial. use in Eng. Also in forms acle Wor. ; eacle w.Wor.[1] Hrf.[2]; eakle Hrf. ; ecall Shr.[1]; eccle Wor. ; eckle Glo.[1] Oxf. ; eeckwall Glo.[1]; eecle Nhp.[2]; eekle War.[2] se.Wor.[1]; equal Glo.[1]; equaw Glo.[1]; ēqwal Hrf.[2]; etwall Chs.[18]; hakel Glo.[1]; heckle Glo. Oxf. Bck. ; heckwall Glo. ; hēcle Hrf.[2]; heffald w.Yks. ; hefful w.Yks.[1]; hew-hole Nhb. ; hichele War.[1]; hickle Nhp.[1] War.[2][3][4] s.War.[1] Oxf. ; hickol Hrf.[2]; hicwall Glo.[2]; hoodall, hoodawl Cor. ; hoodwall Dev. ; hufil e.Yks. ; iccol n.Cy. ; ickle, ickwell Nhp. ; icwell Nhp.[1]; yaffle Sur. ; yockel Shr.[1] **1.** The green woodpecker, *Gecinus viridis.*

s.Cy. *Poetry Prov.* in *Cornh. Mag.* (1865) XII. 35. Nhb. (R.O.H.) s.Yks. SWAINSON *Birds* (1885) 100. w.Yks. SCATCHERD *Hist. Morley* (1874) *Gl.* ; w.Yks.[1], Chs.[18] Nhp. SWAINSON *ib.* 99; Nhp.[1]; Nhp.[2] This bird may be said to be the countryman's barometer : when dead he hangs it up by the legs, and judges of the weather by the state of its tongue ; before rain it expands so much that it protrudes from the mouth, while in mild weather it remains shrivelled up in the head. War. *B'ham Whly. Post* (June 10, 1893) ; War.[1][2][3][4], s.War.[1] Wor. Ther'll be rain afore long, by the row o' them acles, *Berrow's Jrn.* (Mar. 3, 1888). m.Wor. (J.C.) w.Wor.[1] About Kidderminster this bird is called the stock-eacle. se.Wor.[1] Also called the stock-eckle. Shr.[1], Hrf. (W.W.S.), Hrf.[1][2], Glo. (A.B.), Glo.[12] Oxf. The woodpecker is the heckle or wood-heckle in this locality, *Science Gossip* (1870) 119 ; APLIN *Birds* (1889) 214 ; (M.A.R.) ; SWAINSON *ib.* 99. Bck. *Nature Notes,* No. 10. Sur. The yikeing laugh of the yaffle, *Forest Tithes* (1893) 30. Dev. When you hears the hood-wall calling, it's a sign of rain, *Reports Provinc.* (1889). s.Dev. Fox *Kingsbridge* (1874). Cor. For sartain there be a hoodall running up thickey oak tree, BARING-GOULD *Curgenven* (1893) xxxviii ; SWAINSON *ib.* 100; RODD *Birds* (1880) 314.

2. The lesser spotted woodpecker, *Dendrocopus minor.* Glo. SWAINSON *ib.* 99.

VOL. III.

8. *Comp.* **Eckle-** or **Hickle-hole,** a small hole in the trunk of a tree, usually made by a woodpecker.

Nhp. GROSE (1790) *MS. add.* (C.) se.Wor.[1]

[A hickwal (hickway), *Picus martius,* COLES (1679) ; Hickwal or Hickway, *Picus Martius,* SKINNER (1671). *Pic,* a Wood-pecker, Hickway, Greenpeak, COTGR.; An Hickwall or witwall, *Vireo,* BARET (1580). See NARES (s.v. *Hickway*).]

HID, see Head, Hide, *v.*[2], Hit, *pron.*

HIDANCE, *sb.* Sc. Shelter, a place of concealment.

Rnf. Into ilka hole an' bore, They rin for hidance by the score, YOUNG *Pictures* (1865) 139. Ayr. He at length got into hidance (J.F.).

HIDDER, HIDDIE-, see Hither, Hoodie.

HIDDIE-GIDDIE, *sb.* Bwk. (JAM.) [Not known to our correspondents.] A short piece of wood with a sharp point at each end for keeping horses asunder while ploughing.

HIDDILS, *sb.* Sc. Also written hiddles Fif. [hi·dilz.] A hiding-place.

Sc. In the hiddils of a dyke, under the cover or shelter of a stone wall (JAM.). Frf. The other yap his prey let drap, And to his hiddils drew, LOWSON *Guidfollow* (1890) 240. Fif. Croodle, bonnie, cuddle in : Da is fairly oot o' hiddles, EDWARDS *Mod. Poets,* 8th S. 161.

[He sittis in waitis with the riche in hidels that he sla the innocente, HAMPOLE (c. 1330) *Ps.* ix. 30. OE. *hўdels,* a hiding-place.]

HIDDLE, *v.* and *adv.* Sc. Lan. Also written hidle Sc. [h]i·dl.] **1.** *v.* To hide.

Per., Fif. (JAM.) Ayr. The double pieces that they are ! To think how the auld ane could receive us wi' open arms, while Beenie was hidling intended for the minister's wife into the press [cupboard], JOHNSTON *Kilmallie* (1891) I. 161. Rxb. The thing we need na hiddle, RIDDELL *Poet. Wks.* (ed. 1871) II. 196. Lan.[1]

2. *adv.* Mysteriously, secretly.

Sc. (JAM.) Ayr. Wha from his very inmost saul Did speak sae hiddle, SILLAR *Poems* (1789) 154.

HIDDLE, HIDDY, see Heald, *sb.*[1], Hide, *v.*[2]

HIDDY-GIDDY, *adv. Obs.* Sc. Nhb. Also written hiddie-giddie Fif. ; hiddy-giddie Sc. Hither and thither, topsy-turvy. Cf. **hirdy-girdy.**

Sc. The cart . . . flew backwards whummlet hiddy giddie, DRUMMOND *Muckomachy* (1846) 46. Fif. The Cross-kirk rang wi' scolds and flytes ; The Main-kirk rang wi' slaps and smites ; Pellmell, thwack ! hiddie-giddie! TENNANT *Papistry* (1827) 205. Lth. (JAM.) Nhb. To garr my joke run hiddy giddy, STUART *Joco-Serious Discourse* (1686) 44 ; (R.O.H.) ; Nhb.[1]

HIDE, *sb.*[1] and *v.*[1] Var. dial. uses in Sc. Irel. and Eng. Also written heyde Cum.[1]; and in forms holde w.Yks. Lei.[1]; hoyd, hoyde Lan. ; hyd(e Sc. (JAM.) [h)aid, oid.] **1.** *sb.* In *comp.* Hide-hook, an iron hook used to pull hides out of tan-pits. Lei.[1]

2. *Phr.* (1) *hide and hair,* the whole ; (2) *hide and hue,* the complexion, colour ; (3) *neither hide nor hair,* nothing at all.

(1) Ayr. Then farewell folly, hide and hair o't, BURNS *To Mitchell* (1795) st. 5. (2) Lth. It's sae dirty, it'll never come to hyd or hew (JAM.). (3) Sh.I. We'd nedder seen hide or hair o' dem, *Sh. News* (May 7, 1898) ; Dere win nedder hide nor hair o' da baste ta be seen, STEWART *Tales* (1892) 69.

3. The skin of a human being.

Sc. Each city in the nation Pours forth its dusky population To scrub and cleanse their dingy hides, VEDDER *Poems* (1842) 74. Sh.I. My claes wis dat wye steepid 'at da waitter ran doon ower my hide fil hit cam' oot at me feet, *Sh. News* (Aug. 27, 1898). Bch. Ajax sleeps in a hale hyde For a' his muckle crawin, FORBES *Ulysses* (1785) 22. Abd. It sae be That I may get a droukit hide Wi' her saut-bree, SHIRREFS *Poems* (1790) 263. Ked. A cudgel to wallop his hide, GRANT *Lays* (1884) 145. Frf. His hide was as hard as the horns o' rams, WATT *Post. Sketches* (1880) 26. Rnf. Fowks custe their slough just like a snake's, A fine new hide grew o'er the banes, PICKEN *Poems* (1813) II. 118. Ayr. Gae hame . . . in a hail hide, BOSWELL *Poet. Wks.* (1816) 165, ed. 1871. Dmf. Thae white-faced toon's fowk . . . maun look after their tender hides, REID *Poems* (1894) 197. e.Yks.[1] His hide's as rough as a badger. w.Yks.[2] In tipping of bumpers to loosen our hides. Lan. An I foryeat um agen, een raddle meh hoyd titely, sey I, TIM BOBBIN *View Dial.* (1746) xiii, ed. 1806 ; Lan.[1], Not.[1],

X

n.Lin.[1] Lei.[1] ' Moy hoide!' and ' Moy hoide an' limbs !' are very common as exclamations. War.[2] e.An.[1] To curry the hide. Suck that into your hide.

Hence **Hidesmatch**, *sb.* a disease indicated by a rank smell proceeding from the armpits. e.Lan.[1]

4. *Obs.* A contemptuous term applied to the females of domestic animals ; also to human beings, esp. to women. Lnk. (JAM.) Edb. Ye be sic an awfu' hide, CRAWFORD *Poems* (1798) 88. Rxb. (JAM.)

5. The nap of a hat. Xod. Ye'll get your hat baith haill and soun'. I'll raise a gloss upon its hide, JAMIE *Muse* (1844) 46.

6. *pl.* Entrails prepared to make sausages in. e.An.[12]

7. *v.* To beat, thrash ; in *gen.* colloq. use. Abd., Lnk. (JAM.), Nhb. (R.O.H.), Dur.[1], Cum.[1], s.Wm. (J.A.B.), n.Yks.[4], e.Yks.[1] w.Yks. Did they ivver hoide em, or thresh em, or mill em? *Shevvild Ann.* (1853) 7 ; w.Yks.[1], Lan.[1], Chs.[12] Der.[2] I'll hide thee, if I catch thee, thou rapscallion. nw.Der.[1], Not.[3] n.Lin. I nobut hided three or four on 'em for it this very mornin', PEACOCK *J. Markenfield* (1872) I. 132. Lei.[1], War.[3], Shr.[3], Hrf.[2], Brks.[1], e.An.[1] Suf. Yar father 'll hide ye for that (C.G.B.). Ess. For keepin' yow so late—(to hide)—He arter me may chevy, CLARK *J. Noakes* (1839) st. 172. Sus. I wish somebody would take one of these ... bats and hide me, EGERTON *Flks. and Ways* (1884) 13. I.W.[1] Dev. Mind, when I wance begin'h I'll hide thee tū this truth ov music, HEWETT *Peas. Sp.* (1892) ; Dev.[18]

Hence **Hiding**, *vbl. sb.* a sound thrashing. n.Sc. Geordie Peterson should, upon any future evidence of theft, get ' a raal guid hidin',' GORDON *Carglen* (1891) 171. Cai.[1] Abd. Sic a hiding as we s' a' get, MACDONALD *Alec Forbes* (ed. 1876) 73. Nhb. The hiding that he gae them, they've not forgot it yet, MARSHALL *Sngs.* (1823) 197 ; (R.O.H.) Dur.[1], Lakel.[2] Cum.[4] Fadder 'll mebbee give hem a hiding or mebbee he'll nobbut welt him, *W. C. T. H.* (1894) 12. Wm. Al gi ya o a reet good hidin, *Spec. Dial.* (1880) pt. ii. 10. n.Yks. (T.S.), e.Yks.[1], w.Yks.[12] Lan.[1], n.Lan.[1], m.Lan.[1], Chs.[123], Stf.[1], Not.[1] n.Lin.[1] If I iver catch thē agaain mislestin' that duck on her nest I'll gie thē a straange hidin'. s.Lin. (T.H.R.) Lei.[1] Ah gen 'im a good hoidin'. War.[23], se.Wor.[1], Shr.[3], Hrf.[2], Glo. (A.B.) Oxf.[1] *MS. add.* Brks.[1] Lon. MAYHEW *Lond. Labour* (1851) III. 76, ed. 1861. w.Mid. (W.P.M.), e.An.[1], Suf.[1] Sus. I was sure to get it whether it was a bull's eye or a hiding, EGERTON *Flks. and Ways* (1884) 73. I.W.[1] Wil. SLOW *Gl.* (1892). Dor. *Longman's Mag.* (Mar. 1889) 515. w.Som.[1] Let me catch thee again, you young seabird, and zee nif I don't gi' thee a d—n good hidin. Cor.[2]

HIDE, *v.[2]*, *sb.[2]* and *int.* Var. dial. uses in Sc. and Eng. [h]aid, oid, id.] **I.** Gram. forms. **1.** *Present Tense* : (1) Ad, (2) Hed, (3) Heed, (4) Heedy, (5) Heid, (6) Heyd, (7) Heyde, (8) Hid, (9) Hiddy, (10) Hidee, (11) Hidey, (12) Hidy, (13) Hod, (14) Hode, (15) Hoid, (16) Hoide, (17) Hud, (18) Huid, (19) Id, (20) Idy.

(1) m.Yks.[1] Aa'd, *Introd.* 36. (2) e.Yks.[1], w.Yks.[2] (3) nw.Dev.[1] Dant ren off, and heed away, PETER PINDAR *Dev. Hob's Love* (s.v. Heed-y-peep). Cor. How ded ee heed away up theere! TREGELLAS *Tales*, 40 ; Cor.[1] ; Cor.[2] 97. (4) nw.Dev.[1] (5, 6) s.Pem. (W.M.M.) (7) Sc. MURRAY *Dial.* (1873) 205. Cum. He meade some laugh, some heyde the feace, ANDERSON *Ballads* (ed. 1840) 51 ; Cum.[1] (8) Bnff. (W.G.), w.Yks. (S.K.C.), s.Lan.[1] (9) w.Yks.[2] w.Yks.[5] Aather hiddy theesen ur get the fiace wesh'd, 25. (10) Lth. (JAM.) Dev. *Reports Provinc.* (1893). (11) Som. Zo you ran away to hidey then when the clock struck midnight ! RAYMOND *Men o' Mendip* (1898) xiii. Cor. ' Q.' *Troy Town* (1888) xi. (12) Dor. Gl. (1851). Som. SWEETMAN *Wincanton Gl.* (1885). Dev. He [the kitten] is coming to hidy away from me, because I always put him to bed. Good example of the old w.Cy. affix to the infinitive mood when used *intr.* She would not have thought of saying ' to hidy the kitten,' *Reports Provinc.* (1893). (13) n.Sc. (JAM.) Frf. Esther Auld said she would hod ahint the tent, BARRIE *Tommy* (1896) x. (14) n.Sc. (JAM.) (15) Sh.I. Ta hoid her among da floss, JUNDA *Klingrahool* (1898) 25. Lan. Tam's wife kept hoidin her face, BRIERLEY *Adventures Blackpool* (1881) 30. (16) w.Wor. S. BEAUCHAMP *N. Hamilton* (1875) III. 95. (17) Sc. (JAM.) w.Yks. Aw seed her goa hud hursel i' th' hedge (D.L.). Lan.[1] Hud thisel' i' th' buttery theer, till hoo's gone, WAUGH *Chim. Corner* (1874) 186, ed. 1879. e.Lan.[1], Hmp.[1] Wil. SLOW *Gl.* (1892) ; BRITTON *Beauties* (1825). (18) Sh.I. Shū tried a' at shū could ta huid hit frae William an' me baith, *Sh. News* (Aug. 21, 1897). (19) m.Yks.[1] *Introd.* 36. w.Yks. WRIGHT *Gram. Wndhll.* (1892) 53. (20) m.Yks.[1] Id-i, *Introd.* 36.

2. *Preterite* : (1) Ādid, (2) Hade, (3) Haid, (4) Headd, (5) Hed, (6) Hedded, (7) Heead, (8) Heudd, (9) Hided or Hidet, (10) Hod, (11) Hodded, (12) Hoddit, (13) Hode, (14) Hoided, (15) Hud, (16) Huod, (17) Idid.

(1) m.Yks.[1] Aa'did, *Introd.* 36. (2) Ayr. Where she hade it I never could jaloose, SERVICE *Dr. Duguid* (ed. 1887) 15. (3) Sc. MURRAY *Dial.* (1873) 205. Slk. There was mony ane i' the days o' langayne, who haid weel, but never was back to howk again, HOGG *Winter Tales* (1820) I. 329 (JAM.). (4) Cum.[1] (5) w.Yks.[2] (6) e.Yks.[1] (7) Wm. He ran like a ridshank an' heead hisell sumwhares, *Spec. Dial.* (1877) pt. i. 13. (8) Cum.[1] (9) ne.Sc. Ma wife gied up t' the laft an' hidet hersel amo' the nets an' buoys, Gordonhaven (1887) 100. Abd. He hided the pose Securely and safe i' the sole o' his hose, ANDERSON *Rhymes* (1867) 198. Brks.[1] 12. (10) n.Sc. (JAM.), s.Wil. (G.E.D.) (11) Frf. ' My mother hodded it,' she explained, ' an' he winna speir nae questions,' BARRIE *Thrums* (1889) xix. (12) Per. He hoddit his feelings for fear o' makin' a fule o' himself afore the pairish, MACLAREN *Auld Lang Syne* (1895) 253. (13) The auld fouk in Drumtochty pit their siller in a pock and hode it ablow their beds, *ib.* K. *Carnegie* (1896) 365. (14) Sh.I. Hoided demsells awa at da ooter end o' da hoose, STEWART *Tales* (1892) 141. (15) w.Yks. He went upstairs and hud hissel, he're soa fear't o' bein licked (D.L.). Lan.[1] Mi feyther coom back wi' a greyt top-quot on ut welley hud him eawt o' seet, LAHEE *Charity Coat* (1875) 9. (16) Cum. Aw maks o' geer i' saicks they huod, STAGG *Misc. Poems* (ed. 1805) 117. (17) m.Yks.[1] *Introd.* 36. w.Yks. (J.W.)

3. *Pp.* : (1) Ādid, (2) Āden, (3) Hed, (4) Hedden, (5) Heead, (6) Hiddened, (7) Hided, (8) Hidit, (9) Hod, (10) Hodden, (11) Hoided, (12) Hoiddit, (13) Hood, (14) Hud, (15) Hudden, (16) Hydden, (17) Iden, (18) Idid.

(1, 2) m.Yks.[1] *Introd.* 36. (3) e.Yks. He'd monny a anksome lewk at his store, Noo carefully hed iv a newk ov a dhrawer, NICHOLSON *Flk-Sp.* (1889) 42. w.Yks.[2] (4) e.Yks.[1], w.Yks.[2] (5) Cum.[3] T'silver cup fund theear, Heead theear, girt like, o' purpose, 96. (6) n.Lin. They think you must be hidden'd in 'em, PEACOCK *R. Skirlaugh* (1870) II. 78. (7) n.Lin. Th' oud cat's hided th' kitlin's this to'n (M.P.). Brks.[1] 12. (8) Buff. Whan our day's wark we get done, And Phoebus hidit o'er the burn, TAYLOR *Poems* (1787) 72. (9) Frf. I speired at her whaur she had hud it, BARRIE *Thrums* (1889) xix. Per. Ford *Harp* (1893) 364. (10) Abd. An' thinks I, ' For as sharp's ye are, ye hinna hodd'n that, no,' ALEXANDER *Johnny Gibb* (1871) xxxviii. (11) Sh.I. He aye keeped da skin hoided fae her, STEWART *Tales* (1892) 35. (12) Sh.I. Da mooth o' da holl wis aye hoiddit, wi twartree muckle lumps o' stanes, BURGESS *Sketches* (and ed.) 90. (13) s.Lan. (S.B.) (14) w.Yks. Aw catcht hur hud i' th' barn (D.L.). Lan. Th' deep scent o' hud violets, CLEGG *Sketches* (1895) 1 ; Lan.[1], nw.Der.[1] n.Wil. He bin an' bud, I dun'naw wur a is (E.H.G.). (15) Cum.[1] Lan. Hudden amang t'steans bi t'road side, WAUGH *Rambles Lake Cy.* (1861) 145. (16) Sc. MURRAY *Dial.* (1873) 205. (17) m.Yks.[1] Id-un, *Introd.* 36. w.Yks. (J.W.) (18) m.Yks.[1] *ib.*

II. Dial. uses. **1.** *v.* In comb. (1) Hide-a-bo-seek, (2) -and-find, (3) -and-fox, the game of hide-and-seek ; (4) -and-peep, the game of Bo-peep ; (5) -and-seek, blind-man's buff ; (6) -and-wink, (7) -buck, (8) -coop, (9) -hoop, see (3) ; (10) -lose-my-supper, a Christmas game ; (11) -oh or Heddo, (12) -peep or Huddin-peep, see (3) ; (13) -pyke, a miser ; (14) -seek, (15) -up, see (3).

(1) Bwk. (JAM.) (2) Suf.[1] He's plahen at hide an find. (3) Ken.[12] (4) Dur. Some children play'd at hide and peep, Beneath their mother's apron, STEPHENSON *Gateshead Poems* (1832) 27. (5) Cai.[1] (6) Lei.[1] For he play'd with them at hide-and-wink, And where he was they could not think, YATES *Broadside Ballad* (1844). se.Wor.[1] 90. (7) Dor. Gl. (1851) ; Dor.[1] Som. SWEETMAN *Wincanton Gl.* (1885). (8) s.Pem. (W.M.M.) (9) s.Pem. Laws *Little Eng.* (1888) 420. (10) Lan. Many an evening was beguiled with ... hide lose my supper, HARLAND & WILKINSON *Flk-Lore* (1867) 255. (11) e.Yks. By and by there is a sound of children's voices, playing ' heddo' among the straw, and behind the stacks and buildings, NICHOLSON *Flk-Sp.* (1889) 13 ; Lan.[1] (12) w.Yks. (D.L.). Lan. Playin at huddin-peep i' big dark woods, CLEGG *Sketches* (1895). Dev. Jonas was constrained, as he termed it, to play ' hidey peep' on the moor so long as this turbulent crew held his premises, BARING-GOULD *Dartmoor Idylls* (1896) 150. nw.Dev.[1] Cor. Playin' hidey-peep in their clane pinnyfores 'mong the rocks, ' Q.' *Troy Town* (1888) xi. (13) Sc. (JAM.) Bnff. He's a real hiddie-pyke, he widd scraup hell for a bawbee gehn he wizna fleyt

for burnin's fingers (W.G.). (14) **w.Yks.** (S.K.C.) (15) **s.Pem.** Let's 'ave a gaâm of heideoop, lads (W.M.M.).

2. With *up* : to hide.

w.Yks. Hey, yo Munday idlers, yo may try ta hiddy yersenze up, but yor seen, TOM TREDDLEHOYLE *Bairnsla Ann.* (Jan. 23, 1861). **Nrf.** Soon as I got it, I nip off, egg and all, and runned and hid up, EMERSON *Son of Fens* (1892) 4.

3. To put by carefully ; to treasure.

Frf. Carefully put by ! Is it hod on the chimley ! BARRIE *Minister* (1891) xvii. **Per.** It ochtna to be han'led e'er, but hod aye in the wa', FORD *Harp* (1893) 364. **Lan.** Despised an' pointed at, but huddin brass, CLEGG *Sketches* (1895) 232.

4. To hide away ; consume.

w.Wor. Welly noigh full. Conna hoide no moore, S. BEAUCHAMP *N. Hamilton* (1875) III. 95.

5. *sb.* The game of hide-and-seek.

w.Yks. (S.K.C.) ; **w.Yks.[5]** Let mammy weah his flâce an' he sal lîâk at hiddy wi' Polly. **Wil.** A game of hud (G.E.D.). **n.Dev.** Sure I played ' Hidy ' well, you never saw me, CHANTER *Witch* (1896) xii.

6. A place in which smugglers used to conceal their goods. **Ken.[1]**

7. *int.* The cry given by the concealed person in the game of hide-and-seek.

Lth. The watchword of this last is hidee, *Blackw. Mag.* (Aug. 1821) 35 (JAM.). **Nhb.** (R.O.H.), **Yks.** (J.W.)

HIDEBIND, *sb.* Cld. (JAM.) The disease 'hidebound' to which cattle are subject, causing the skin to stick close to the bones.

[The hidebound, a sickness of cattel, *Coriago*, GOULDMAN (1678).]

HIDEBOUND, *adj.* Wm. Yks. Lan. Chs. Der. Lin. Hrf. Oxf. Hrt. Also in forms -bun Chs.[1] s.Chs.[1] nw.Der.[1]; ·bund Wm. ne.Lan.[1] **1.** A term for a tightness of the skin in animals, esp. cows, which is a frequent symptom of illness ; costive.

Wm. It's varra mich hide-bund (B.K.). **n.Yks.** (T.S.), **n.Yks.[2]**, **ne.Lan.[1]**, **Chs.[12]** **s.Chs.[1]** With tight-clipping hide ; a supposed mark of inferiority. nw.Der.[1] Oxf.[1] *MS. add.*

2. Of trees : with hard bark which does not open with the expansion of the tree.

Chs.[6] The . . . term is applied to a tree of which the bark, owing to accident or the grease of cattle or sheep that have been rubbing against it, cannot open with the expansion of the tree ; and the tree becomes dwarfed and unhealthy. **n.Lin.[1]** **Hrf.** When the trees are unkindly hide-bound they are scored by cutting the bark with the point of a knife, MARSHALL *Review* (1818) II. 293.

3. Of land : hard on the surface.

n.Yks.[2] **Chs.** Old pasture which a farmer wants to break up 'just for three crops' ; and which is not laid down again until exhausted, *Sheaf* (1879) I. 266; Applied to . . . land which carries a sod so tough, and old, and sour that it needs ploughing up, WORLIDGE *Dict. Rusticum* (1681); **Chs.[1]** **n.Lin.[1]** This land's that hide-boond ther's noâ gettin' a pleugh in till raain cums. **Hrt.** Land on both sides was full of moss and hidebound for want of moisture, MARSHALL *Review* (1818) II. 344.

4. Stingy. ne.Lan.[1]

HIDE NOR TIDE, *phr.* Dev. News ; tidings.

' Well, Bet, 'ows Jack a-gitting on by theäse time !' ' Aw, dawntee ax me nort about 'e ! I ant a-yerd hide-nur-tide aw'n vur a göddish bit,' HEWETT *Peas. Sp.* (1892) 88 ; I think it is not now in use (R.P.C.).

HIDERS-CATCH-WINKERS, *sb. pl.* Hmp. The game of hide-and-seek. (J.R.W.), Hmp.[1]

HIDEY, see Hide, *v.[2]*, Hidy.

HIDGE, *sb.* N.Cy.[1] The hip. Cf. **huggin.**

HIDGE, *v.* Nhp.[2] [idg.] To walk fast, or with increased speed ; *gen.* with *along.*

HIDGEL, *v.* Not. Lei. To sell retail ; to defraud on a petty scale. Not.[1], Lei.[1] See **Higgle, 3.**

Hence (1) **Hidgeler,** *sb.* a petty dealer ; (2) **Hidgeling,** *ppl. adj.* defrauding.

(1) **Not.[1]** Lei.[1] ' Theer warn't noo boyers theer,' i. e. at a horse-fair, ' oon'y pidgelers an' hidgelers.' (2) *ib.* Ah 'eet sooch hidgelin' pidgelin' tricks.

HIDING, *adj.* and *sb.* Sc. Yks. Lan. Also in form **hiddin** w.Yks. e.Lan.[1] **1.** *adj.* In *comp.* **Hiding-peep,** game of hide-and-seek.

w.Yks. *Leeds Merc. Suppl.* (Dec. 30, 1893). **e.Lan.[1]**

---

2. *sb.* A hiding-place.

w.Sc. If the French were once landed at Ayr, we'll hae you and mae o' your volunteers up amang us than we'll ken how to gie hidings to, CARRICK *Laird of Logan* (1835) 183. **Rnf.** [He] saw them frae out their hidins peep, PICKEN *Poems* (1813) I. 6.

HIDLANCE, *sb.* Sc. Lan. Chs. Der. Also in forms **hidlands** Lan.[1] ne.Lan.[1] Chs.[123]; **hudlance** s.Lan. s.Chs.[1] In phr. *in hidlance,* in secret ; in hiding. See **Hidlin(g)s, 2.**

s.Sc. And since I had naething in hidlance put by, I'll never be nocht but an auld broken farmer, ALLAN *Poems* (1887) 197. **Lan.[1]** He's not bin seen for mony a month. He's in hidlance somewheer. **ne.Lan.[1]** **s.Lan.** He has been in hudlance for three months (E.F.). **Chs.[1]** A man of a shaky character built a house in an out-of-the-way place. It was said he did so because he wanted rather to be ' in hid-lands '; **Chs.[23]** **s.Chs.[1]** Dhi)m trahy·inky'ee·p it i ùd·lûns,bû foa·ks noa·n móoùr)tn dhi thingk·n dhi dùn [They'm tryin'keep it i'hudlance, bu' folks known moor t'n they thinken they dun]. nw.Der.[1]

HIDLAND, see **Headland,** *sb.*

HIDLIN(G)S, *adv., sb.* and *adj.* Sc. Irel. Nhb. Lakel. Cum. Lan. I.Ma. War. Hrf. Also written **hiddleings** Lakel.[2]; **hiddlens** Ant. ; **hiddlin(g)s** Sc. ; and in forms **hiddlin**(g Sc. ; **hidlin**(g Sc. n.Cy. Hrf.[1] [h)i·dlin(z.]

1. *adv.* Secretly, stealthily.

Slg. The frichtsome tryst She hiddlins held yestreen, TOWERS *Poems* (1885) 57. **Rnf.** Colin . . . Right true, but hiddlins lang had lo'ed the Fair, PICKEN *Poems* (1813) II. 66. **Lnk.** Ye've to come and see me hidlins in the dark, FRASER *Whaups* (1895) xi. **Dmf.** Heedless o' his neighbour's pain . . . Hiddlins cadged away his grain, JOHNSTONE *Poems* (1820) 89. **Gall.** MACTAGGART *Encycl.* (1824) 269, ed. 1876. **N.Cy.[1]** **Nhb.[1]** *Obs.* **Cum.** (M.P.), **Cum.[1]**

2. *sb.* A place, or state of concealment ; *gen.* in phr. *in hidlin(g)s,* or *on the hidlin(g)s,* in secret. Cf. **hidlance.**

Sc. It wasna in hidlins I said it, nor in nae mark neuk o' the yirth, WADDELL *Isaiah* (1879) xl. 19. **Abd.** Nae hiddlins for a hungry ewe, They're sae beset wi' drift, BEATTIE *Parings* (1801) 35, ed. 1873. **Fif.** Craftilie their buschment set On ilk side o' the southern yett In hidlins near the wa', TENNANT *Papistry* (1827) 84. **Ayr.** What honour gets Christ, if thou be holy in hidlings ! DICKSON *Writings* (1660) I. 111, ed. 1845. **Lnk.** Skulk in hidlings on the hether braes, RAMSAY *Gentle Shep.* (1726) 40, ed. 1783. **Ant.** ' Hoo did he get the whusky !' ' Some yin has gi'en it tae him in hiddlens,' *Ballymena Obs.* (1892). **Lakel.[2]** T'lasses mead a gurdle ceak ta-day on t'hiddleings when t'mistris was et market. **Cum.** A man was in hidlins in the mysterious room, DICKINSON *Cumbr.* (1876) 141 ; **Cum.[14]** **Lan.** Hoo us't to lay i' hidlins behint th' door, FERGUSON *Moudywarp,* 27 ; **Lan.[1]** I.Ma. Yonder is the gully where Kitty kept in ' hidlins '—the Chartist outlaw, Ned Blake, RYDINGS *Tales* (1895) 15. **War.** (J.R.W.), **Hrf.[1]**

3. *adj.* Secret, stealthy, underhand.

Sc. I cannot abide hidling ways, KEITH *Bonnie Lady* (1897) 91. **Dmb.** Ye've been seen herding in a hiddling way wi' thief-catchers, CROSS *Disruption* (1844) xxviii, ed. 1877. **Rnf.** He ne'er kept up a hidlins plack To spend ahint a comrade's back, TANNAHILL *Poems* (1807) 282, ed. 1817. **Ayr.** That was Stair Whalbert, whom he never could byde with his hiddlin' kind of ways, SERVICE *Dr. Duguid* (ed. 1887) 91. **e.Lth.** The Tories are aye misca'in him for his joukry-pawkry, an' hiddlin ways, HUNTER *J. Inwick* (1895) 119. **Abd.** That will ding down yer hiddlin' heaps o' art, LEARMONT *Poems* (1791) 306. **Dmf.** Syne hiddlin' pranks appeared, QUINN *Heather* (1863) 57. **n.Cy.** *Border Gl.* (Coll. L.L.B.)

Hence (1) **Hiddlinsly,** (2) **Hidlingways,** (3) **Hidlin(g-wise,** *adv.* secretly, by stealth.

(1) **s.Sc.** Joseph her husban' was mindet to pit her awa hiddlinsly, HENDERSON *St. Matt.* (1862) i. 19. (2) **Slk.** Slippit that into the potato-pot hidling ways, HOGG *Tales* (1838) 363, ed. 1866. (3) **Sc.** I'll get in hiddling wise, when his back's turned, Sc. *Haggis,* 111. **Abd.** This her neebors manna ken—'Twas sippit hidlinwise, ANDERSON *Rhymes* (1867) 104.

[*Hide + -lings*; for the suff. cp. **backlings.**]

HIDLINGS, *adv.* e.An. [i·dlinz.] Headlong; at random. See **Headlin(g)s.**

e.An.[12] **e.Suf.** To fall down hidlings is to fall forward, fall on the face (F.H.).

HIDLOCK, *sb.* Hrf. Glo. Wil. Dor. Also in form **hedlock** n.Wil. [i·dlak.] A state of concealment.

Hrf.[1] **Glo.** He was in hidlock, LEWIS *Gl.* (1839) ; **Glo.[1]** **Wil.** A peart young owl . . . In a nook ov the paason's barn did dwell, In hidlock blinkin' the time away, HUGHES *Ashen Faggot,* iv ; (G.E.D.) ; **Wil.[1]** Her kep' it in hidlock aal this time ; **Wil.[2]** **n.Wil.**

X 2

He bin in hedlock this dree months (E.H.G.). **Dor.** BARNES *Gl.* (1863).

[*Hide*+-*lock* ; for suff. cp. **wedlock.**]

HIDMOST, *adj.* Sh.I. Also in forms -maist, -mist. Last, hindmost.

Frankie Broon's boat, ye may be shure, wisna hidmist, CLARK *N. Gleams* (1898) 34 ; Da hidmaist oot-gaein' o' him dat belanged ta me is as vieve as da ooer dat I heard dat he wis nae mair, SPENCE *Flk-Lore* (1899) 242.

HIDNES, *sb.* Chs.²⁸ [i‘dnəs.] In phr. *to be in hidnes,* to have got out of the way in order to avoid the consequences of some misdemeanour.

[OE. (*ge*)*hȳdnes,* security (B.T.).]

HIDY, *adj.* Sc. Nhb. Also written **hidey** Frf. Nhb. ; **hidie** Cai.¹ Gall. ; and in form **hoddy** Frf. [hai‘di.] In *comb.* (1) Hidy-corner, a cunning place in which to hide things ; (2) -hole, (*a*) a hiding-place ; (*b*) a subterfuge.

(1) Frf. I'm thinking as there's hoddy corners in manses as well as in—blue-and-white rooms, BARRIE *Tommy* (1896) xx. (2, *a*) Sc. But he had not been long in his hidy-hole before the awful Etin came in, CHAMBERS *Pop. Rhymes* (1870) 91. Cai.¹ Frf. He made a spring across the burn to reach his hidey-hole, WILLOCK *Rosetty Ends* (1886) 152, ed. 1889. Edb. We got James . . . hauled out of his hidy-hole, MOIR *Mansie Wauch* (1828) ix. Gall. Tim Kelly's hidie-holes where he kept the weapons of his craft, CROCKETT *Cleg Kelly* (1896) 18. Nhb. (R.O.H.) (*b*) Sc. (JAM.)

HIDY, see Hide, *v.*²

HIE, *int.* and *v.*¹ Sc. Nhb. Shr. Glo. Sus. Hmp. I.W. Som. Also written **hi** War.² ; **high** Lth. Bwk. ; **hy** Cai.¹ ; **hye** Nhb.¹ [h)ai.] 1. *int.* A call to dogs to encourage them to seek game ; also with *on* or *away.*

Cum.⁴ Hie! theh, git away by, Sharp—Sharp, hie! theh, git away by below, SARGISSON *Joe Scoap* (1881) 22. Sus., Hmp. HOLLOWAY. I.W.¹ w.Som.¹ Hie on, Dash.

2. A command to horses to turn to the left, or towards the driver.

Sc. MORTON *Cyclo. Agric.* (1863) (s.v. Horses). Cai.¹ Lth. ‘High! gee, wo!’ each ploughman cries, BALLANTINE *Poems* (1856) 295. s.Sc., n.Cy. STEPHENS *Farm Bk.* (ed. 1849) I. 160. Nhb.¹

3. *Comb.* (1) Hie-here, a command to horses to come towards the driver ; (2) -lag, go away ; (3) -up, a call to cows ; (4) -wo, a command to horses, (*a*) to turn abruptly to the left ; (*b*) to go to the right.

(1) n.Sc. *N. & Q.* (1856) and S. i. 395. m.Sc. STEPHENS *Farm Bk.* (ed. 1849) I. 160. (2) Glo. NORTHALL *Wd. Bk.* (1896) (s.v. Call-words). (3) Shr.¹ Common (s.v. Call-words). (4, *a*) Cai.¹, Rxb. (JAM.) (*b*) Bwk. *Monthly Mag.* (1814) I. 31.

4. *v.* To encourage a dog to hunt.

w.Som.¹ I zeed'n, my own zul, hiein o' the dog up in the hedge.

HIE, *v.*² and *sb.* Sc. Nhb. Cum. Wm. Yks. Lan. Chs. Der. Not. Nhp. Shr. Suf. Hmp. Som. Also written **heigh** ne.Lan.¹ ; **high** n.Yks. Shr.² Suf. ; **hy** Sc. Cum. w.Yks.¹ ; **hye** Chs.¹²⁸ Shr.² ; and in forms **eigh** Lan.¹ ; **hay** Fif. ; **hey** Nhp.² [h)ai.] 1. *v.* To hasten ; freq. with reflex. *pron.*

Sc. They were hying home after sunset, SCOTT *St. Ronan* (1824) xxv. Fif. Go hay thee hence to bed ! MELVILL *Autobiog.* (1610) Introd. 66, ed. 1842. Dmb. We'll catch the beacon as we round Lochrye, And then, wi' surer airt, mair swiftly hie, SALMON *Gowodean* (1868) 52. Ayr. I winna bide, but hie awa' To her that I lo'e best of a', LAING *Poems* (1894) 88. Gall. He hied him home to his wife and weans, CROCKETT *Moss-Hags* (1895) ix. Nhb. When songsters homeward are hieing, CHARNLEY *Fisher's Garl.* (1836) 7. Lakel.² Cum. Now hytha, an thu'll get back o' gud teyme (E.W.P.). Wm. Hie thi ways hiam (B.K.). n.Yks.² Thoo mun hie thee. w.Yks.¹ Go hie thee. Lan. Lady bird, lady bird, eigh thy way home, HARLAND & WILKINSON *Flk-Lore* (1867) 70. ne.Lan.¹ Chs.¹ Hie the, Sarah, hie the, and bring me a sope o' beer, aw'm welly kilt wi droot ; Chs.²⁸, Der.¹², nw.Der.¹ Not. HOLLOWAY. Nhp.² Hey an wi 'e. Shr.¹ Now then, 'ie away an' fatch me yore throck to pūt on ; Shr.² Suf. High to the holl, hinder come a dow (H.H.). Hmp. Hie off, HOLLOWAY. w.Som.¹ *Obs.*

2. *Comb.* (1) Hie-thee-really, (2) -tie-leather, quickly, at a great pace ; (3) -your-ways, hasten.

(1) e.Yks. If thoo's cum'd iv a quahter ov a noor, thoo's cum'd hietha-rally, NICHOLSON *Flk-Sp.* (1889) 91 ; e.Yks.¹ *MS. add.* (T.H.) (2) n.Yks. (S.K.C.) (3) Nhb.¹ Just hie yor ways, an' tell wor Jack 'at he's wantit (R.O.H.).

3. *sb.* Haste.

Yks. Make as much hie as you can, GROSE (1790) *MS. add.* (P.) Chs.¹⁶

HIE, *v.*³ Sh.I. In phr. *hie tongue,* hold thy tongue.

Hie tongue, lass, an' be na a fule . . . he's nae mair Johnny Smith den I am, STEWART *Tales* (1892) 154.

HIELD, *v.* Sc. To shield, protect.

Fif. Heav'n hielde us a' frae sic a drither, TENNANT *Papistry* (1827) 155.

HIER, *sb.* Sc. Also written **heer.** The sixth part of a ‘hesp’ of yarn, or the twenty-fourth part of a ‘spindle.’

Frf. The rock and the spindle were then used, by which a woman could spin at an average only 3½ hiers in a day. . . A hier is 240 threads, or rounds of the reel, each of them 91 inches long, *Lethnot Statist. Acc.* IV. 19 (JAM.). Frf. The crime of theft, or of reset, of a number of bobbins and some spindles and ‘beers’ of thread belonging to several manufacturers in town, HECTOR *Judic. Records* (1876) 252.

HIERSOME, *adj.* Abd. (JAM.) [Not known to our correspondents.] Coarse-looking.

HIE-SPY, *sb.* and *int.* Sc. Irel. Chs. Not. Nhp. Oxf. Brks. Lon. Ken. Hmp. Wil. and Amer. Also written **hispy** Frf. Gall. Amer. ; **hy-spy** Sc. N.I.¹ ; and in forms **heapy** Ayr. ; **hice-pie** Wil. ; **I-spy** Gall. Crk. Chs.¹ s.Not. Nhp. Oxf. Brks.¹ Lon. ne.Ken. Hmp.¹ Amer. [h)ai-spai.] 1. *sb.* A variety of the game hide-and-seek ; see below ; also in *comb.* Hie-spy-hie.

Sc. O, the curly-headed varlets!—I must come to play at Blind Harry and Hy Spy with them, SCOTT *Guy M.* (1815) lvii. Abd. Some to the buttons, bools or ba', Kee how or hy spy hy, ROSS *Poems* (1852) 130. Frf. Then, of course, there was ‘hi'-spy’ and many other games of a kindly social character, INGLIS *Ain Flk.* (1895) 100. Ayr. Callan's . . . keeking hespy round the auld turrets and the kirk, SERVICE *Dr. Duguid* (ed. 1887) 56; Skirling lassocks are playing at heapy on the stairs, *ib. Notandums* (1890) x. Rxb. The station which in Eng. is called Home is here the Den, and those who keep it, or are the seekers, are called the Ins. Those who hide themselves, instead of crying Hoop . . . cry Hy Spy ; and they are denominated the Outs. The business of the Ins is, after the signal is given, to lay hold of the Outs before they can reach the Den. The captive then becomes one of the Ins (JAM.). Gall. Bairns that had been skipping about the kirkyard and playing ‘I spy’ among the tombstones, CROCKETT *Standard Bearer* (1898) 166 ; We three played ‘tig’ and ‘hi-spy,’ and other games, *ib. Anna Mark* (1899) xiv. N.I.¹ Crk. Two sides are chosen for Spy ; one side hides while the other side hunts. When the hunters see one of the hidden players, they call out, ‘I spy —,’ and the child's name. The player called must run after the Spy and try to catch him before he reaches his Den ; if he succeeds, the one caught must go to the opposite side of players, then next time the spies hide, and those who have been hiding spy, GOMME *Games* (1894) I. 212. Chs.¹ s.Not. (J.P.K.) Nhp. The ‘I spy,’ ‘hallo,’ and the marble-ring, And many a game that infancy employs, CLARE *Village Minst.* (1821) I. 5. Oxf. The game takes its name from the cry uttered by those in hiding as a signal for the others to search (G.O.). Brks.¹, Lon. (A.B.C.), ne.Ken. (H.M.), Hmp.¹ Wil. SLOW *Gl.* (1892). [Amer. *Dial. Notes* (1896) I. 236.]

2. *int.* The call given by the players when ready in their hiding-places.

Ayr. To every secret haunt with speed they flie, Or watch with listening ear the scream, Hie spie, BOSWELL *Poet. Wks.* (1810) 53, ed. 1871.

HIESSEN, HIEVRE, see Haisen, Eaver, *sb.*¹

HIFFLE, HIFT, see Haffle, Heft, *sb.*¹

HIG, *sb.* Lakel. Yks. Lan. Not. Lin. Wor. Also written **ig** n.Yks. e.Yks.¹ w.Yks. m.Lan.¹ Wor. [ig.]

1. A fit of passion ; a petulant, offended state of mind, a ‘huff’ ; an attack of illness.

Lakel.² Ah went off i' a hig. n.Yks.¹⁴, ne.Yks.¹ e.Yks. She was iv a hig, 'cos Ah wadn't let her hev her new bonnit on, NICHOLSON *Flk-Sp.* (1889) 95 ; e.Yks.¹, m.Yks.¹ w.Yks. Foaks ats allas in a ig shews ignarance, TOM TREDDLEHOYLE *Bairnsla Ann.* (1872) 18; (J.T.) ; w.Yks.¹ What did shoe do . . . bud tack pet, and gang off in a girt hig, ii. 287 ; w.Yks.²³ Lan. Aw leep off, in a great hig, TIM BOBBIN *View Dial.* (1740) 36; Lan.¹, e.Lan.¹, m.Lan.¹ Not. He was much given to gawster, and to loup about, setting folks on the hig, HOLE *Memories* (1892) 192 ; Not.² n.Lin. Off he goas in a hig, PEACOCK *Tales* (1890) and S. 78 ; n.Lin.¹

sw.Lin.¹ He's gone to bed in his higs. We're all on us in our higs one while or other.

Hence (1) **Higged**, *adj.* angered, offended; (2) **Higly**, *adj.* passionate.

(1) **w.Yks.** He wor a bit higged (S.J.C.). (a) **Wor.** How can you live near that oman! er's that igly I would not live near 'er wotever (H.K.).

2. *Phr. to take the hig,* to take offence; to be in a pet.

n.Yks. Ah gess he'l finnd summat ta tack t'hig at gan wahr he will (W.H.) ; **n.Yks.²** They teuk t'hig at it; 'n.Yks.⁴ Tak neea notish, sha's nobbut ta'en t'hig. **ne.Yks.¹ w.Yks.⁶** Soin taks t'hig at owt. **ne.Lan.¹**

3. A temporary hurricane; a short shower of wind or rain.

n.Yks. 'Showery weather, missus.' 'Aye, the're March igs.' Common (R.H.H.). **ne.Yks.¹ w.Yks.** Ay, it's snowin', but it's nobbut a March hig, it'll soon be ovver (F.P.T.) ; **w.Yks.¹**

4. The main difficulty, the 'rub.' **ne.Lan.¹**

[1. The same word as ME. *hi3*, mind, disposition (*Ormulum*) ; OE. *hyge*, Goth. *hugs*, intelligence.]

HIG, *v.* Lin. Nhp. [ig.] **1.** To have a horse and cart and do odd jobs ; to go about with small wares for sale. Cf. **higgle.**

Lin. He has a horse and cart, and higs about (R.E.C.).

2. With *off*: to move away quickly. Nhp.²

HIGGIN, *sb.* s.Pem. [i·gin.] A child's nightdress.

Laws *Little Eng.* (1888) 490; Jaán, bring 'ere Willie's higgin, á moost go to bed (W.M.M.).

HIGGLE, *v.* In *gen.* dial. use in Sc. Irel. and Eng. Also written **higle** w.Yks.⁴ Der. e.Lin. War. Suf.¹ Som. ; and in forms **heggle** se.Wor.¹ ; **hegle** War. Som. ; **heigle** w.Som.¹ [h]i·gl.] **1.** To linger long over a bargain ; to beat down prices ; to chaffer.

N.Cy.¹ Cum.¹ ; Cum.⁴ Thuh'll just pay meh noo adoot enny mair higglin, **Sargisson** *Joe Scoap*(1881) 109. **n.Yks.² w.Yks.** Thoresby *Lett.* (1703) ; **w.Yks.⁴ n.Lin.¹** I'd rather traade wi' ony body then N—; he higgies soä, one can't get dun wi' him. **Shr.¹, Brks.¹, e.An.¹ Ess.** *Gl.* (1851). Som. There was no higgling when Christopher bought Sophia's litter of eleven little pigs, **Raymond** *Sam and Sabina* (1894) 38.

Hence (1) **Higgler,** *sb.* one who beats down a price ; (2) **Higgling,** *ppl. adj.* chaffering, bargaining.

(1) **n.Yks.²** (a) **Ayr.** Claud . . . was thriving as well as the prigging wives and higgling girls . . . would permit, **Galt** *Entail* (1823) iii.

2. To argue ; to demur, raise objections.

Slk. Laith wad I hae been to hae higgled wi' her, **Hogg** *Tales* (1898) 187, ed. 1866. **Cum.¹ w.Yks.** We higgled an' figgled till booath on us sware, *Pudsey Olm.* (1883) *Nov. Notes.* **Brks.¹**

3. To go about with small wares for sale ; to hire out a horse or cart, or one's personal services.

w.Yks. Yks. *Wkly. Post* (Apr. 10, 1897) ; **w.Yks.⁵, Chs.¹, s.Chs.¹ Lin.** He higgies, and has a herse, and ploughs for people (R.E.C.). **n.Lin.¹ s.Lin.** He higgies for his livin' (T.H.R.).

Hence **Higgler,** *sb.* an itinerant dealer ; *gen.* one who owns a horse and cart ; a man who carts materials for another.

Slk. A higgler for nits an' nest-eggs, **Hogg** *Tales* (1838) 160, ed. 1866. **Ir.** Took to carrying the remnant of his stock-in-trade about in a basket as a higgler, **Barlow** *Lisconnel* (1895) 53. **Yks.** He kept a public-house, had a small farm, and went out sometimes as a 'higgler,' i. e. a vendor of woollen cloth from house to house, **Henderson** *Flk-Lore* (1879) v. **n.Yks.² w.Yks.** Dealers in ready-made clothing who go with their wares in search of customers (B.K.) ; **w.Yks.³⁵ Lan.** Women who travel the country with mugs and other articles, which they exchange for eggs in Cum., &c. ; there are two or more higglers who follow this practice, **Marshall** *Review* (1808) l. 270. **Chs.¹ Midl.** Higgler and cottager the villagers called him, **Bartram** *People of Clopton* (1897) 9. **Der.** The occupation of a 'higler' . . . is a very old one, and before . . . the railways were made a great deal of coal was carried into Derby by this mode, and the men employed were called 'coal higlers,' *N. & Q.* (1894) 8th S. v. 178. **nw.Der.¹, n.Lin.¹, e.Lin.** (G.G.W.), **s.Lin.** (T.H.R.) **Rut.¹** A coal-higgler. Her son's a higgler, and oughtn't to let her come on the parish. **m.Wor.** (J.C.) **Bdf.** These ashes are carried by higglers on asses in sacks, **Marshall** *Review* (1814) IV. 593. **Suf.** A rag and bone man (C.L.F.) ; **Suf.², Sur.¹ Sus.** Another waggoner looks in, . . . next a higgler passing by, **Jefferies** *Hdgrow.* (1889) 79 ; **Sus.¹**

4. To buy and fatten up for market ; to practise the trade of a poultry-dealer.

e.An.¹ Higgling up a pig. **e.Suf.** (F.H.) **Sus.** Buying up chickens and fattening them for the market (F.E.S.). **w.Som.¹** What is your father doing now?—Well, mum, he do do a little to pork-butchin, and in the winter he [uy·glus]heigles; but he don't heig'y so ter'ble much.

Hence **Higgler,** *sb.* an itinerant middleman who buys up farm produce, and sells it at market.

N.Cy.¹, s.Chs.¹, War. (J.R.W.), **War.², m.Wor.** (J.C.), **se.Wor.¹, Shr.¹², e.Suf.** (F.H.), **Ken.** (D.W.L.), **Ken.¹, Sur.¹ Som.** W. & J. *Gl.* (1873). **w.Som.¹** A dealer in poultry only. Very com. 'Ter'ble rough lot, some o' they uy·glurz out about Langley Marsh.' **Dev.⁸** Cor. **Thomas** *Randigal Rhymes* (1895) *Gl.*

5. To work at anything slowly and laboriously ; to effect by slow degrees.

ne.Lan.¹ e.Lin. The old horse could only higle a bit (G.G.W.). **Nrf.** To work at anything carelessly and indifferently (G.B.R.B.).

6. To overwork ; to fatigue. **Cum.¹⁴**

7. To cut meat badly ; to play with one's food.

n.Lin.¹ If yé higgle yer meät e' that how you shan't hev noän.

8. To heap up earth round growing potatoes. **n.Lin.¹**

9. To play a game of chance.

w.Yks.⁵ 'Ah'll higgle thuh fur a meg,' says a youth, shaking two or three coppers within the hollow of his clasped hands.

HIGGLEDY-PIGGLEDY, *adv.* Chs. In *phr. higgledy-piggledy, Maupas shot,* serving all alike, making no difference between people.

Chs.¹ The following tradition accounts for the origin of the saying : 'King James I. was on a royal progress such as he was accustomed to make over various parts of his dominions. As he approached Malpas (which, be it observed, is on the high road between London and Chester) he sent forward to the Rector, as the principal person of the place, to require him to provide for his suitable entertainment. The Rector, whether, unlike his kind, disloyal, or like them, parsimonious, refused. The Curate saw his opportunity, and ordering the best viands the old "Lion" could produce, invited his Majesty to refreshment. . . . The rest of the story is less clear, and varies with different traditions. It appears, however, that at the end of the banquet there was some discussion as to settling the account. His Majesty, perhaps, desired to be generous ; the Curate insisted on the rights of hospitality. Eventually, however, the ancient custom of Malpas prevailed, even if it were against the King's wishes. Half-and-half, or Higgledy Piggledy, was the time-honoured rule of the "Lion." All who came should pay equal shares or 'stand the shot' alike. Accordingly, Curate and King divided the costs of the festival, and the Malpas proverb received the sanction of royal authority. But this was not the only thing divided. The monarch, who never said a foolish thing, had a good occasion for a practical joke. If "Higgledy Piggledy" was the rule of the "Lion," it might also be the rule of the Glebe and the Tithes. "Malpas Shot" was forced upon the unfortunate Rector, and the Curate received henceforth the mediety of the Benefice. . . . The chair in which the King is said to have sat is preserved at the "Lion." A variant of this tradition is: 'Before his invasion of England, William III. travelled in England incognito, with a view to certify himself of the state of the national feeling towards himself and his colleagues, and, coming to Malpas, betook himself to the inn for his dinner, a repast which he happened to share with the Rector and Curate of the parish. The meal over, the Curate proposed to the Rector to divide the payment of the "Shot," that of the stranger included, between them. To this the Rector, who enjoyed in the neighbourhood the reputation of being a miser, strenuously objected, exclaiming "Certainly not ; higgledy piggledy, all pay alike." "By all means," chimed in the future sovereign, "higgledy piggledy, all pay alike ;" and so it was arranged. But when William was seated on the throne, the Rector of Malpas, among others, made a journey to London to worship the rising sun. The King no sooner saw him than he reminded him of the incident, and compelled him to resign a moiety of the parish to his Curate, along with the title of Rector, on the principle embodied in his own apothegm 'Higgledy piggledy, all pay alike." And from that day forwards there have been two Rectors of Malpas.' The saying or proverb is frequently extended into 'Higgledy Piggledy, Malpas Shot ; let every tub stand on its own bottom.' **s.Chs.¹** Ig·ldi-pig·ldi, meu·pŭs shot·.

HIGGLEDY-PIGGLEDYNESS, *sb.* Nrf. Disorder ; want of arrangement.

(H.C.H.) ; There was a considerable degree of higgledy-piggledyness in the arrangements, **Gibbon** *Beyond Compare* (1888) II. x.

HIGGS, *sb. pl.* Yks. [igz.] White cumuli.

n.Yks. It'll rain to-morrow because of them higgs (E.L.).

HIGH, *adj., sb.* and *v.* Var. dial. uses in Sc. and Eng. Also written **hy** Sc.; and in forms **hee** Lakel.[2] Cum.[14] Wm. e.Lan.[1]; **heegh** Edb. Cum. n.Yks. Lan.; **heeh** Wm.; **heich** Sc.? Nhp.[1]; **heigh** Sc. w.Yks.[18]; **hey** e.Lan.[1] Der.[2]; **hie** Sc.; ? **hoich** Nhp.[1] [h]ai, h)ī, ei, Sc. also hīɣ.]

1. *adj.* In *comb.* (1) **High-bendit,** dignified in appearance; haughty, ambitious; (2) **-bo-leep,** a game; see below; (3) **-by-day,** in broad daylight; (4) **— change,** the time of greatest activity on the Exchange; see below; (5) **-cocked hat,** a hat with the brim thrice cocked; (6) **-cockledy,** pretentious; of an old house: rotten but still standing; (7) **-corned,** well-fed; (8) **— countries,** the hills about Towednack; (9) **-country cloth,** cloth made in Mer.; (10) **— daylight,** see (3); (11) **-de-lows,** boisterous merry-makings; (12) **-flown,** living above one's means; (13) **-fly,** conceited, boastful, 'set up'; (14) **-gate,** the highway; also *fig.* honesty; (15) **-go-life,** living upon one's capital; (16) **-henched,** having high or projecting thigh-bones; (17) **— horse,** in phr. *to be on the high horse,* see (13); (18) **— in the instep,** or to instep, proud, arrogant; (19) **-jail,** a disorderly room; (20) **— jinks,** *obs.,* a drinking game; see below; (21) **-jumper,** a parasite found in wool; (22) **-kept,** well-kept, highly fed; (23) **-kicked,** high-heeled; aspiring, conceited; (24) **-kilted,** wearing short petticoats; also *fig.* verging on indecency; (25) **-land doctrine,** the doctrine of the Church of Eng.; (26) **-learned,** highly educated, University taught, well-read; (27) **-light-day,** see (3); (28) **—, low, Jack and the game,** the game at cards *gen.* called 'all fours'; (29) **-lows,** men's heavy laced boots; 'ancle-jacks'; (30) **-main,** the best seam of coal on the Tyne; (31) **-minded,** inclined to grandeur; intellectually superior; (32) **-on-end,** expensive; (33) **-poll hat,** a hat high in the crown; a top hat; (34) **— pot hat,** a method of carrying a child; see below; (35) **-quartered,** of shoes; having the 'quarter' or back part of the shoe higher than the sides; (36) **-rigged,** of buildings with high, steep roofs; of land: see below; (37) **-run,** laxativeness in cattle [not known to our correspondents]; (38) **-shallow-sha,** the edge of paper cut in zigzags; *fig.* up and down in the world; (39) **-sniffingness,** airs of importance; (40) **-street,** the highway; (41) **-style,** bombastic; (42) **-surprises,** (*a*) high spirits; a show of temper; (*b*) extraordinary performances; (43) **-toltherum** or **-totherum,** (*a*) worthless, bombastic; (*b*) run to seed; (44) **-tops,** high shoes, covering the ancles; (45) **-town,** a hillside village; (46) **-twelve,** mid-day; (47) **-up,** (*a*) of high rank or position; (*b*) proud; 'stand-offish'; (*c*) aloud, distinctly; (48) **-way master,** a road surveyor; (49) **-ways,** the highway rate; (50) **— west,** close upon north; (51) **-year,** leap-year.

(1) Sc. She's a high-bendit lass that, ye needna speir her price (Jam.); If he had told her what a high-bendit, prickmadenty lady he had in his mind's eye, Keith *Bonnie Lady* (1897) 67. (2) Cum.[3] A very old game which is thus played: sides are chosen and stationed at opposite sides of a building; the ball is thrown over the roof, and whoever catches it runs round to the other side of the building and throws it at the players there; should anyone be hit, he must change sides and return with the thrower. 'There's some are playing hie baw leep,' *Random Rhymes,* 9. (3) w.Som.[1] Dev. The foxes . . . came down and car'd off some chicken all high-by-day, *Reports Provinc.* (1881) 12. Cor. The apparition of a huntsman and hounds, said to be often seen in the day-time getting over a hedge on the Land's End road, is called a high-by-day ghost (M.A.C.). (4) Lon. The Old Clothes Exchange . . . has its daily season of 'high change.' This is, in summer, from about half-past two to five, in winter, from two to four o'clock, Mayhew *Lond. Labour* (1851) II. 45, ed. 1864. (5) Gall. Mactaggart *Encycl.* (1824) 263, ed. 1876. (6) s.Wor. *Outis Vigor. Mon.* in *Berrow's Jrn.* (1896) xvi. (7) n.Yks.[2] A high-coorn'd fear-fickle horse. (8) Cor. Hunt *Pop. Rom. w.Eng.* (1865) 121, ed. 1896. (9) Shr. The webs that are made in Merionethshire are about ⅝ yards wide, and are called the strong, or high country cloth, Marshall *Review* (1818) II. 210. (10) Cum.[4] It was heegh dayleeght t'next mwornin, Sargisson *Joe Scoap* (1881) 242. Wm. (B.K.). (11) Dev. I can't abide sich high-de-lows.

Tidden modest like vur maidens an' bwoys tü go rumpsing about zo! Hewett *Peas. Sp.* (1892) 88; Dev.[1] Good-now, dame can't abide such may-games and highdelows sabbath days, 8. (12) n.Yks. What a heeghfloun woman yon iz. A guess sha'l eta [have to] cum doon (W.H.). (13) w.Cor. (M.A.C.). (14) Sc. Out the high-gate is ay fair play, downright honesty is both safest and best, Kelly *Prov.* (1721) 273. Abd. Wow! . . man, to tyn your feet, And tak' the gutter for hi'-gate, Cock *Strains* (1810) I. 131. Ayr. She watch'd me by the hie-gate side, Burns *Had I the wyte,* st. 1. e.Lan.[1] (15) Lin.[1] He'll have to strike the docket, for he's been high-go-life. (16) Ayr. Various animals in different conditions of equestrian decrepitude—high-henched, howe-backed, Johnston *Kilmallie* (1891) I. 87. (17) w.Cor. She is quite on the high horse (M.A.C.). (18) Hrf. Bound *Provinc.* (1876). Dev.[1] Volks zaid her was rather too high to instep. (19) Cor.[2] In a perfect high-jail. (20) Sc. The . . . company had begun to practise the ancient and now forgotten pastime of High Jinks. This game was played in several different ways. Most frequently the dice were thrown by the company, and those upon whom the lot fell were obliged to assume and maintain . . . a certain fictitious character, or to repeat a certain number of fescennine verses in a particular order. If they departed from the characters assigned, or if their memory proved treacherous in the repetition, they incurred forfeits, which were either compounded for by swallowing an additional bumper, or by paying a small sum towards the reckoning, Scott *Guy M.* (1815) xxxvi. Lnk. Aften in Maggy's at Hy-jinks We guzl'd Scuds, Ramsay *Poems* (1721) 11, ed. 1733; The . . . cup is filled to the brim, then one of the company takes a pair of dice, and after crying 'Hy-jinks,' he throws them out : the number he casts up points out the person that must drink; he who threw beginning at himself number one, and so round till the number of the person agree with that of the dice; . . then he sets the dice to him : . . he on whom they fall is obliged to drink or pay a small forfeiture in money, then throws, and so on. But if he forgets to cry 'Hy-jinks' he pays a forfeiture into the bank. Now, he on whom it falls to drink (if there be anything in the bank worth drawing) gets it all if he drinks; then with a great deal of caution he empties his cup, sweeps up the money, and orders the cup to be filled again, and then throws, for if he errs in the articles he loses the privilege of drawing the money. The articles are—(1) Drink, (2) Draw, (3) Fill, (4) Cry 'Hy-jinks,' (5) Count just, (6) Chuse your doublet, man—viz. when two equal numbers of the dice is thrown, the person whom you chuse must pay a double of the common forfeiture, and so must you when the dice is in his hand, *ib. note,* 21. (21) Gall. Some yarn is alive enough when it comes here—both with 'high jumpers' and 'slow bellies,' Crockett *Anna Mark* (1899) xiv. (22) s.Chs.[1] (23) Dev.[1] That was to show their high-kick'd loady heads, prink'd out in the tip of the mode, way a lamming wallige of hair bevore and a vumping beheend, and a race of rory-tory ribbons, stuff'd out leek so many pincushons, 8. (24) Sc. Carried home in compassion, by some high-kilted fishwife, Scott *Redg.* (1824) Lett. v. Ayr. His conversation, . . though aye stopping short of skulduddery itsel' was whyles . . . of a gey heich-kiltit kind, Service *Dr. Duguid* (ed. 1887) 281. Dmf. Tho' she may gang a wee thing high-kilted at times, Cromek *Remains* (1810) 13. (25) Cum. In the . . . fens there are a great number of Dissenters. . . On the higher lands . . . are the old parish churches; . . it is not uncommon to hear the tenets of the Church of Eng. described as High-land Doctrine, in contradistinction to the Low-land, or Dissenters' doctrine, *N. & Q.* (1850) 1st S. i. 187. (26) n.Yks.[4], ne.Yks.[1] Lan. Awm not hee-larnt hoo says, Staton *B. Shuttle,* 7. s.Chs.[1] n.Lin.[1] It isn't th' high-larntist men that's fittest fer business. Nhp.[1] I ar'nt high-larnt; I never had much schooling; Nhp.[2], War.[2], Hnt. (T.P.F.), e.An.[1] (27) Cum.[1] They drank and sang till hee leet day, Old *Sng.* Wm. An net tummal inta sick parrish pleeaces i heeh dae, *Spec. Dial.* (1885) pt. iii. 11. (28) Lakel.[2] Oxf.[1] MS. add. (29) Lakel.[2] Oxf. And laced-up boots, in vulgar parlance high, Rust *Old Times* (1888) No. vi. e.An.[1], Nrf. (E.M.) Sur. Bird *Agric.* (1819) 294, ed. 1849; (H.H.) (30) Nhb. To— high main, Wilson *Pitman's Pay* (1843) 60; (R.O.H.) (31) (J.W.) sw.Lin.[1] No one can get on with him, he's so— minded. s.Wor. (H.K.) ; s.Wor.[1] 'E was that 'igh-minded I couldn't understand 'is sermons no more nor nothin'. (32) Iv'ry thing now's at seea heigh an end; w.Yks.[8] At an on-end rāate. What will it be i' t'depth o' winter ah if things is so heigh-on-end now! (33) s.Dev. (F.W.C.) A high-poll hat, a bit rusted wi' Sunday observance, 'Q.' *Town* (1888) xi. (34) e.Suf. 'I carried my little boy all the way high pot ash,' i. e. astride of my neck, with his feet in front (F.H.) (35) Wor. The camp is in shape like a high-quartered shoe,

Antiq. (185a) 16a ; I can remember that shoes were very shallow, very low in the quarter. Later they were made higher in the quarter and often not level but highest at the back. These were called high-quartered shoes (H.K.). (36) e.**Yks.**[1] Lands, or the divisions of ploughing in a field, with a more than usually gradiented elevation in the middle, are said to be high-rigg'd. (37) **Nrf.** (W.W.S.) (38) n.**Yks.**[2] They're living high-sha-low-sha. (39) **Fif.** She being given rather to 'highsniffingness,' the idea was not very flattering to this daughter of the Hythe captain, **MELDRUM** *Margrédel* (1894) 79. (40) **Edb.** We live upon the king's highstreet, **PENNECUIK** *Wks.* (1715) 328, ed. 1815. (41) **Edb.** Some for fame, and some for fun, In high-style words mak' speeches run, **CRAWFORD** *Poems* (1798) 19. (42, *a*) e.**An.**[1] ; e.**An.**[2] He is all on his high-surprises to-day. e.**Suf.** The shanny maw cut up her high surprises one day, and was turned away from her place (F.H.). (*b*) **Nrf.** Marvellous performances in legerdemain, and sometimes it is applied to mean *Nisi prius*. In the *High si prius* Court (W.W.S.). **Ess.** I have only heard this once used, and then by a woman, and she was thus nick-named from her use of the word (M.C.H.B.). (43, *a*) **Lei.**[1] Yo' nivver heerd a sooch a lot o' high-toltherum stuff. **War.**[2] (*b*) **Lei.**[2] This hay is very high-toltherum. **War.**[2] (44) **Nhp.**[1] (45) ne.**Yks.** **MARSHALL** *Rur. Econ.* (1796) II. 80. (46) **Per.** At high-twal we rested aneath the same tree, **FORD** *Harp* (1893) 329. (47, *a*) n.**Yks.**[1] He's some desput high-up chap, a lord, or mebbe a duke, or such as that ; n.**Yks.**[4] (*b*) **Cum.** 'How do you like your new parson ?' 'Nobbut that much, he's varra hee ûp.' He's a hee-ûp mon (E.W.P.). (*c*) w.**Yks.** If ide a sed it heigh up foaks ad a thowt at ide hed a bottle or two, **TOM TREDDLEHOYLE** *Fr. Exhebishan*, 35. (48) n.**Yks.**[1] (49) w.**Yks.** Becos O wanted to borrow some to pay't highways we, *Gossips*, 14. (50) **Der.** The wind's high west to-day, **VERNEY** *Stone Edge* (1868) xxv. (51) **Nrf.** I was four-score year last Paschal Tuesday, whether this year be high 'un or low-'un, **ELLIS** *Pronunc.* (1889) V. 277.

2. Tall.

Sc. That boy's very heich o' his eild (JAM.). **Abd.** Ye're near as heich 's Peter, **ALEXANDER** *Johnny Gibb* (1871) vii. **Dmb.** Heigh as Saul amang the people, **TAYLOR** *Poems* (1827) 19. **Lnk.** Tell him that he can do nae wrang, That he's mighty, heigh, and strang, **RODGER** *Poems* (1838) 150, ed. 1897. **Edb.** O'er his carpet walks ilk day Wi' his heegh limber laud [son], *Carlop Green* (1793) 124, ed. 1817. **Cum.** I wondert 'at she didn't grow heer, *Borrowdale Lett.* in *Lonsdale Mag.* (Feb. 1867) 310. **Yks.** (J.W.) **Lan.** The heegher o mon o that mak gwos the moore e shows his tail, **ORMEROD** *Felley fro Rachde* (1851) iv.

3. Of an animal's ears : pricked, erect.

Edb. Hogs, wi' heegh or hingan' lugs, *Carlop Green* (1793) 130, ed. 1817.

4. Protuberant, big.

Fif. Bellies, the heicher they were and fatter, Were dunsched in and grus'd the flatter, **TENNANT** *Papistry* (1827) 86.

5. Of wind : north.

Sc. The wind's high, it'll be guid weather (W.G.). **Gall.** 'The wind's awa' heich,' the wind has veered to the north (*ib.*).

6. Proud, haughty ; aggressively aristocratic.

Per. Ye're rael heigh, are na ye : But ye gaed fleechin' to Miss Mary for a' that, **CLELAND** *Inchbracken* (1883) 188, ed. 1887. **Rnf.** Some . . . Whase line wad be as ill to trace, An' yet fu' heigh an' lordly carry't, **PICKEN** *Poems* (1813) I. 5. **Ayr.** Ony saucy quean That looks sae proud and high, **BURNS** *Tibbie*, st. 3. **Edb.** To pu' some heigh heads to the ground, **MACNEILL** *Bygane Times* (1811) 26. **Lan.** Some on um gett'n so gallus hee thi con ardly tutch the greawnd wi thir feet, **SCHOLES** *Tim Gamwattle* (1857) 37. n.**Lin.**[1] He's that high noo, he weänt move to poor foäks when he meäts 'em. sw.**Lin.**[1] Yon woman was very high, when they first married. **Oxf.**[1] *MS. add.* e.**An.**[1] **I.W.** Miss Alice is a vine-growed mayde . . . but she's powerful high . . . She's most too high vur work-a-days, **GRAY** *Annesley* (1889) I. 163–4.

Hence (1) **Highful**, *adj.* haughty ; (2) **Highfully**, *adv.* haughtily ; with a distant manner.

(1) **Shr.**[1] A 'ighful dame. (2) *ib.* I didna göö, 'cause 'er on'y axed me 'ighfully.

7. In high spirits, excited ; lively, playful.

e.**Fif.** I had never afore seen Andra si heich ; he was like to loup his lane wi' joy, **LATTO** *Tam Bodkin* (1864) xiv. **Ayr.** She was . . . at times a little unco and fey, and would come to the kirk dressed from tap to tae in scarlet robes. I never gaed to see her when she had ane of her heich turns, **SERVICE** *Dr. Duguid* (ed. 1887) 199. **Dmf.** Nae new-flown birds are sae mirthsome an' hie, **CROMEK** *Remains* (1810) 51. **Nrf.** We took 'em home to our old

women ; they went high and no mistake, **EMERSON** *Son of Fens* (189a) 217.

8. *sb.* A height, hill ; a slight elevation, knoll.

Sc. Amang such rugh rigs, highs an' hows as I hae to harl through, **GRAHAM** *Writings* (1883) II. 43. **Per.** The roads are graund the noo frae the heich, **MACLAREN** *K. Carnegie* (1896) 209. **Cld.** (JAM.) **Rnf.** Tho' snaw choke up baith heigh an' howe, **PICKEN** *Poems* (1813) I. 176. **Ayr.** There's heighs and there's howes in the wild Corsehill-Muir, **SERVICE** *Dr. Duguid* (ed. 1887) 72. **Lnk.** Heighs an' howes are clad wi' snaw, **THOMSON** *Musings* (1881) 4. **Edb.** Playing at boo-peep amang the heighs and howes, **BALLANTINE** *Gaberlunzie* (ed. 1875) 3. **Feb.** Ilk heigh has its howe, **AFFLECK** *Poet. Wks.* (1836) 111. e.**Lan.**[1], **Der.**[2]

9. *v.* To raise up. **Nhp.**[1]

HIGH, see **Heigh**, **Hie**, *int.*, *v.*[2]

HIGH-ANGELS, *sb. pl.* **Cor.** A common corruption of 'hydrangea.' (G.E.D.)

HIGHEN, see **Hain**, *v.*[2]

HIGHER, *v.* Yks. War. Lon. Also in form **heigher** w.Yks. To raise, heighten.

w.**Yks.** Heigher it a bit, *Leeds Merc. Suppl.* (Dec. 9, 1893) ; (J.W.) **War.**[2] That clothes-line's too low : go and higher it. **Lon.** I highered the rope in my yard, **MAYHEW** *Lond. Labour* (1851) III. 160, ed. 1864.

HIGHER QUARTER PEOPLE, *phr.* **Cor.**[2] People from the up-lands near a town.

HIGHGATE, *sb.* Yks. Der. **1.** Language akin to that of 'Billingsgate' ; also used *attrib.* m.Yks.[1] **2.** *Phr.* *he has been sworn in at Highgate*, used of a man who is very sharp or clever. n.Der. (S.O.A.) [The custom of swearing on the horns at Highgate near London is described in **HONE** *Everyday Bk.* (1827) II. 79–87.]

HIGH-GERANIUM, *sb.* nw.Dev.[1] The hydrangea.

HIGHHOE, see **Haihow**.

HIGHLAND, *adj.* Sc. Also in forms **hielan(d**, **hielint.** **1.** In *comb.* (1) **Highland blue**, Highland whisky ; (2) — **Donald**, a name given to a particular class of horses ; (3) — **fling**, (*a*) a Highland step-dance ; see below ; (*b*) to dance the Highland fling ; (4) -**man's burial**, a funeral which lasts more than a day ; (5) -**man's ling**, the act of walking quickly with a jerk ; (6) — **passion**, a violent but temporary ebullition of anger.

(1) **Edb.** Some Highland blue is unco gued, *New Year's Morning* (1792) 12. (2) **Ayr.** I have four brutes o' gallant mettle, . . The fourth's a Highland Donald hastie, **BURNS** *Inventory*, l. 22 ; A class of horses reared by the crofters in the Highlands and brought down to the Lowlands, where they were sold in large numbers. They were well known in Ayr. fifty years or so ago. On the breaking up of the Highland crofts they ceased to be known here. They were small, stout, sturdy animals, but very excitable and quick-tempered (J.F.). (3, *a*) **Sc.** Highlanders dance reels with great agility, and are fond of introducing the steps ordinarily called the Highland fling, which is of the character of dancing on each foot alternately, and flinging the other in front and behind the leg which is dancing, *Chambers' Information* (ed. 1842) 560. **Slg.** Raise the Highland fling swift in the reel, **GALLOWAY** *Luncarty* (1804) 14. **Gall.** **MACTAGGART** *Encycl.* (1824) 263, ed. 1876. (*b*) **Slg.** O ! to see them highland-fling in plaiden, **GALLOWAY** *Nelson* (1806) 14. (4) **Gall.** Whaever wished for a pouchfu' o' drink might tak' it. . . When we got tae the kirkyard . . . we put the coffin twice in the grave wrang. . . We got it to fit at last, and in wi' the moulds on't. The grave-digger we made a beast o'. Sic a funeral I was ne'er at afore ; surely I ay think that it was na unlike a Hielan'-man's burial, **MACTAGGART** *Encycl.* (1824) 263–5, ed. 1876. (5) **Fif.** (JAM.) (6) s.**Sc.** (*ib.*)

2. Silly ; clumsy.

Sc. We're no sae hieland, **FERGUSSON** *Village Poet*, 172. **Abd.** I'm no sae hielan' as a' that (G.W.). **Frf.** The excavators made no sic a hielint success in their labours, **WILLOCK** *Rosetty Ends* (1886) 7, ed. 1889.

HIGHLANDER, *sb.* Chs. Der. Nrf. Also in forms **highiarnder** Der. ; **highlonder** Chs.[1] **1.** A term of reproach for a rude man or boy ; a rough fellow.

Chs.[1] **Der.** 'Tha looks like a gret high larnder,' was said to a great rough fellow who had been sleeping under a stack all night, **ADDY** *Gl.* (1891) *Suppl.* 29.

2. *pl.* Cattle of the Highland breed. e.**Nrf.** **MARSHALL** *Rur. Econ.* (1787).

HIGHLE, v. Lnk. (JAM.) [Not known to our correspondents.] To carry with difficulty.

HIGHMOST, adj. superl. Irel. Dur. Lakel. Cum. Yks. Der. Also in forms heaghmost N.I.¹; beemest Lakel.² Cum.¹; heemost Dur.¹ Cum. nw.Der.¹: heighmost w.Yks.¹⁸; heymost w.Yks.¹ [h)ī·məs(t, w.Yks. ei·məs(t.] Highest.

N.I.¹, Dur.¹ Lakel.² It's t'heemest o' t'lot. **Cum.** Nimmy Nimmy Nack, Which haw will ye tack, Heemest or lowmest? (J.W.); Cum.¹ w.Yks. Leeds Merc. Suppl. (Dec. 9, 1893); w.Yks.¹; w.Yks.⁵ Tha'll find it i' t'farrest corner o't heighmost shelf. He's t'heighmost o' t'two. nw.Der.¹

HIGHRANGER, sb. Obsol. Shr.¹ The hydrangea, H. hortensis.

I put the 'ighranger out i' the garden to get the sun, an' the winde's wouted the pot o'er an' broke it all to pieces.

HIGHST, see Hoist.

HIGHSTY-TIGHSTY, sb. Som. A see-saw. Cf. hayty.

Alangside... was a empty cart an' a couple of buoys in it, playen' highsty-tighsty, one at each end o' a lang planch, LEITH Lemon Verbena (1895) 154.

HIGHT, v.¹ and sb. Obsol. Sc. n.Cy. Cum. Yks. Lan. Chs. Der. Also written height w.Yks.⁴; and in forms hecht, heght Sc.; pret. or pp. hecht, heckt Sc.; height w.Yks.⁴ Lan.; het Lan.; hight Sc. N.Cy.¹ Chs.¹ Der.

1. v. To promise; to vow; to offer.
Sc. But hope aye hechts his safe return, CHAMBERS Sngs. (1829) I. 40; And Rob my eem heckt me a stock, RAMSAY Tea-Table Misc. (1724) I. 175, ed. 1871. s.Sc. Fu' lang, my lads, I ha'e hecht ye sport, An' ye shall ha'e't the morn, WATSON Bards (1859) 106. Rnf. Ilka hill, an' haugh, an' plain, Scarce hechts that Spring will come again, PICKEN Poems (1813) I. 76. Ayr. The miller he hecht her a heart leal and loving, BURNS Meg o' the Mill, st. 3. Lnk. They hecht to get us cheaper fare, Yet we ha'e ne'er wan at it, WATSON Poems (1853) 6. Lth. Mony big loons hae hechted to wyle her awa', BALLANTINE Poems (1856) 92. Edb. They hecht him their fidelity To place him highest in their hall, PENNECUIK Wks. (1715) 398, ed. 1815. Slk. Willie's hecht to marry me, Gin e'er he married ony, BORLAND Yarrow (1890) 23. Gall. Four and twenty milk-white steeds Were hecht to set him free, NICHOLSON Hist. Tales (1843) 99. Cum. RAY (1691); Cum.²
2. Phr. hecht him weel, and haud him sae, promise much and perform little. Rxb. (JAM.)
3. To threaten.
Ayr. If Death, then, wi'skaith, then, Some mortal heart is hechtin', BURNS To Mr. Mackenzie, st. 2. e.Lth. Something, Athie, loors on me—That hechts death's comin' blow, MUCKLEBACKIT Rhymes (1885) 219. w.Yks. THORESBY Lett. (1703); w.Yks.⁴
4. To call or name a thing.
Gall. An' they hecht it the Galloway flail, HARPER Bards (ed. 1889) 50.
5. To be called or named; gen. as pp.
Sc. A large manor hight Nettlewood, SCOTT St. Ronan (1824) xviii. Abd. A derf young man, hecht Rob, SKINNER Poems (1809) 46. Lnk. Thy name. That still deorives all them that heght a Grahame, LITHGOW Poet. Remains (ed. 1863) A Conflict. n.Cy. GROSE (1790): N.Cy.¹² w.Yks. THORESBY Lett. (1703); w.Yks.⁴ Lan. A lawm fawse owd felley; het on Elder ot cou'd tell oytch think, TIM BOBBIN View Dial. (ed. 1806) Reader 12. Chs. Gough MS.; Chs.¹ Der. The first was a man hight Little John, JEWITT Ballads (1867) 100.
6. sb. A promise, offer; an engagement.
Sc. Fair hechts mak fools fain, HENDERSON Prov. (1832) 21, ed. 1881; Ye promise better than ye pay, yer hechts ye never brooked, RAMSAY Prov. (1737). Abd. Whilk, gin hights hadd, will be ere it be lang, Ross Helenore (1768) 34, ed. 1812. Slg. If all hichts had [hold] as the prophet hath said, BRUCE Sermons (1631) viii, ed. 1843. Ayr. (J.M.) Lnk. They'll Be blyth for silly heghts, for trifles grieve, RAMSAY Gentle Shep. (1725) 56, ed. 1783. e.Lth. If a' hechts haud, it's a' richt, HUNTER J. Inwick (1895) ii.
[1. They hir highten To been hir helpe, CHAUCER Tr. & Cr. II. 1623. OE. hátan (pret. hēht), to promise (GREIN). 4. Þu scald... bere knaue child, and haten hit helend, Hom. (c. 1175), ed. Morris, I. 77. 5. A cardinal, that highte Seint Ierome, CHAUCER C. T. D. 674. 6. Þis hight... was ful fals and fikel, Cursor M. (c. 1300) 785.]

HIGHT, v.² Obs. Sc. To trust, have recourse to.

Edb. His edge is gane, The taylor jeering bids him hight To grinding stane, Har'st Rig (1794) 23, ed. 1801.

[Cp. ME. hist, hope (Wars Alex.). OE. hyhtan, to hope, trust, rejoice.]

HIGHT, adj. Lakel.² [Not known to our correspondents.] Fickle, uncertain. Cf. highty-tighty.

HIGHT(H, see Height, Hite.

HIGHTY, sb. Dur. Yks. Cor. Also in forms highto Cor.¹; howghty m.Yks.¹ [ai·ti.] A child's name for a horse, also in comb. Highty-horse; a pony.

Dur.¹, n.Yks.¹², m.Yks.¹ w.Yks.¹ w.Yks. N. & Q. (1856) and S. i. 502; w.Yks.¹ Cor. N. & Q. (1854) 1st S. x. 480.

HIGHTY-TIGHTY, adj. Nhb. Lakel. Cum. Der. Not. Lin. Lei. War. Brks. Som. Dev. Also written hity-tity N.Cy.¹ Nhb.¹ nw.Der.¹ w.Som.¹ [h)ai·ti·taiti.]

1. Haughty; easily offended; also used subst. Cf. hoity-toity.
Nhb. He's a reg'lar hity-tity (R.O.H.). Cum.¹ (s.v. Hoyty-toyty). nw.Der.¹, Not.¹ s.Not. A wain't put up wi' sich highty-tighty ways (J.P.K.). n.Lin.¹, Lei.¹ War.² She is a highty-tighty lady. Brks.¹ w.Som.¹ They be ter'ble hity-tity sort o' vokes, I zim. Dev. Now he's a bin made superintendent of police, is that ighty-tighty, you wouldn't believe, DALZELL 'Anner in Cassell's Mag. (Apr. 1895) 334.
2. Flighty, jaunty; whimsically inclined; slightly crazy. N.Cy.¹, Lakel.², Cum.¹, nw.Der.¹ s.Not. She's too highty-tighty to mek 'im a good wife. He'd hed a sup, an' were a bit highty-tighty (J.P.K.). n.Lin.¹ Well, you see, he's not fit for th'sylum, maay be, bud he's highty-tighty like.
3. Fussy, undecided.
w.Som.¹ I never could'n get on way un, he's always so hity-tity like, don't know his own mind not dree minutes together.

HIGH-YEAR-OLD, see Heiyearald.

HIGLY-PIGLY, adv. w.Yks. (J.W.) s.Not. (J.P.K.) Higgledy-piggledy.

HIG-RIG-MA-REEL, adv. Sc. Obs. Higgledy-piggledy, confusedly.

Edb. Their theories run hig-rig-ma-reel Whan put in practice, LEARMONT Poems (1791) 178.

HIG TIG BIZZ, phr. Sc. A formula used by boys to startle cattle.

Abd. Cock a tailie, cock a tailie; hig, tig, bizz (G.W.).

HI-HOW, see Ha-ho.

HIKE, v. and sb. In gen. dial. use in Sc. Eng. and Amer. Also written heick Shr.²; heik Yks.; heyk Nhb.¹; hyke Gall. Nhb. Nrf. Suf.¹; and in forms hoick Nhb.²; hoik(e s.Chs.¹ Der.² nw.Der.¹ Lei.¹; hoyk Chs.¹²³ Nhb.²; ike Stf.¹ n.Lin.¹ Dev.; ixe Sus.; pret. huck Shr.² w.Cy. (HALL.) [h)aik.] 1. v. To hoist; to raise, lift out with a sharp instrument; to move with a jerk.
Gall. To move the body suddenly by the back joint, MACTAGGART Encycl. (1824). Nhb.¹, Chs.²³, Der.², nw.Der.¹ Nhp.¹ Hike this sack up. War.²
2. To toss up and down; to swing; of a cart: to jolt.
Sc. The hiking o' the boat (JAM. Suppl.). N.Cy.¹ Nhb. A niver imadgind the boat wad hike se, an the spray's myed us nearly wet throo, WILSON Tyneside Sngs. (1890) 153; Nhb.¹, Cum.² Dur. The nurse hikes the child (J.H.). Yks. (HALL.), n.Yks.²
Hence Hikey or Hikey-board, sb. a swing; a see-saw. N.Cy.¹ Nhb. Howay, see the hikeys, lads (R.O.H.); Nhb.¹, Yks. (HALL.), Nhp.¹, War.²
3. To throw; to throw up.
War.⁴ Will yer kindly hike me the ball, muster? Shr.² He huck it up. w.Cy. (HALL.) [Amer. Dial. Notes (1896) I. 397.]
4. With up: to pucker in sewing.
Dev. Now, dthee zee how yū've lked-up theäse zeam? I cūde sew better'n this when I wuz ten year old, HEWETT Peas. Sp. (1892) 90.
5. To push, or gore with the horns; to toss.
w.Yks.¹, ne.Lan.¹ Chs.¹ Timothy's goat cum behind him and hiked him o'er th' hedge; Chs.²³ s.Chs.¹ Yoa mun mahynd yaan'dur bül; ey)z ū naas'ti beg'ūr fūr ahykin [Yo mun mind yander bull; hey's a nasty beggar for hikin'].—Bull cooxn at me, ... but ah baulkt him o' hoikin', ib. (s.v. Clait). Midl. MARSHALL Rur. Econ. (1796) II. Stf.¹ s.Stf. The bull might ike the dog, PINNOCK Blk. Cy. Ann. (1895). Der.², nw.Der.¹ Lei.¹ Was he hoiked by a cow or kicked by a horse? The cow hiked at my dog. Nhp.² War. B'ham Wkly. Post (June 10, 1893); War.¹ War.² It is... applied to the practice of hikeing a toad, which is done thus : a narrow board, about a foot long, is balanced upon a convenient substance, with the toad laid upon one end of it. The opposite end is then smartly struck with a heavy stick, the effect

of which is to hike or raise the toad with considerable velocity into the air, whence it uniformly descends quite dead ; War.², Wor. (J.R.W.). Shr.¹ Theer com'd a bull, An' cracked 'is skull, An' 'iked 'im in a saw-pit. Hrf.¹

6. To pull ; to bring ; with *out* : to haul out roughly.
War.² e.Suf. Hike it down. Hike him to me (F.H.). Ess. They hiked him out of the way (M.I.J.C.). Ken. (G.B.) ; Ken.¹ He hiked 'im out purty quick. Sus.¹ He hiked me out of the pew. s.Hmp. I'd like to hike out the whole boiling o' um, VERNEY *L. Lisle* (1870) xxiii.

7. To snatch away ; to run off with anything, not necessarily with a felonious intention.
n.Lin. He iked off with it, *N. & Q.* (1880) 6th S. i. 193 ; n.Lin.¹ He's iked off wi' my shod tool, an' noo I want it it's noän here. Them bairns hes iked off wi' all th' band, ther isn't a bit left. Nhp.² Them tots be all hiked aff. Sus. Hunting for an article in the tool chest, my maid exclaimed, 'Somebody's gone and ixed that away,' *N. & Q.* (1880) 6th S. i. 76.

8. To dismiss a person peremptorily.
Nhb. Anither minute an' he'll hyke me aff, PROUDLOCK *Borderland Muse* (1896) 261. Nhp.² 'What has become of all these spirits !' . . 'Paasons all laid their yeads togither, and hiked 'em off to the Red Sea,' 141.

9. With *up* : to search for anything.
Nrf. If we lose an article we hyke it up, COZENS-HARDY *Broad Nrf.* (1893) 32. e.Suf. (F.H.)

10. To catch through some impediment.
Wil.¹ I hiked my foot in a root.

11. To beckon to a person with the lifted hand.
s.Stf. I iked Jim to foller me aboot ; PINNOCK *Blk. Cy. Ann.* (1895). War.² ; War.³ He hiked me, so I came back.

12. To move suddenly or hastily ; to go away.
Lin. MILLER & SKERTCHLY *Fenland* (1878) iv. Nhp.¹ I hiked down to Peterborough as soon as I heard the news. e.An.¹ 'Come, hike,' i. e. take yourself off ; begone. e.Suf. Hike after those sheep (F.H.). Sus.², Hmp.¹ Dev. Now an then up close I'd hike, NATHAN HOGG *Poet. Lett.* (1847) and S. 36, ed. 1866. [Amer. *Dial. Notes* (1896) I. 397.]

13. With *off* or *out* : to decamp ; slink away ; gen. in *imp.*
Yks. HOLLOWAY. n.Lin.¹ I said sum'ats to him aboot bein' laate in at neet, soä wi' oot ony moore to do he hiked off an' niver com by ageän. Oxf. If you don't be quick and hike off you'll hear from me (G.O.). Brks.¹ What be you bwoys at ther, hike aff that ther ladder an' be aff. Nrf. 'Hike you off,' my old woman say, 'and go to Critten's and see if you can't get a job,' EMERSON *Son of Fens* (1892) 27 ; Them old hogs will hike out, COZENS-HARDY *Broad Nrf.* (1893) 65. Suf.¹ e.Suf. Hike out of this 'ere (F.H.). Sus.², Hmp.¹, I.W.¹² Wil. SLOW *Gl.* (1892) ; Wil.¹ To sneak away dishonorably. Dor.¹ You shall hike out. Som. JENNINGS *Obs. Dial. w.Eng.* (1825). w.Som.¹ Jack agreed to go 'long way us, but come to last he hiked off. Now then ! hike out. Look sharp, else I'll hike thee ! Cor. What for be 'ee hikin' off like this , then ? PARR *Adam and Eve* (1880).

14. *sb.* A lift up.
Nhb. To famed Parnassus' topmost scar Some get a hyke, PROUDLOCK *Borderland Muse* (1896) 227.

15. A swinging gait ; a movement up and down ; a swing.
Nhb. Iv a vera douley hyke, Poor Dick went back his way, man, ROBSON *Pigeon's Milk* (1849) ; (R.O.H.) ; Nhb.¹

[5. Cp. EFris. *hikken,* 'mit einem schaufen od. spitzen Etwas auf ein anderes Etwas stossen u. schlagen, bz. überhaupt : stossen, aufstossen, etc.' (KOOLMAN).]

HIKE, see Heck, *int.*

HILCH, *sb.*¹ Slk. (JAM.) A shelter from wind or rain, a 'hield.'

HILCH, *sb.*² Lth. (JAM.) In phr. *hilch of a hill,* the brow or higher part of the face of a hill, whence one gets a full view, on both hands, of that side of the hill.
This term does not denote the ridge from which both the back and face of the hill may be seen.

HILCH, *v.* and *sb.*³ Sc. Irel. [hilʃ.] **1.** *v.* To limp, halt, hobble.
Cai.¹ Ayr. He'll hilch and stilt and jimp, BURNS *Ep. to Davie* (1784) st. 11. Ant. *Ballymena Obs.* (1892).
Hence (1) **Hilching,** *ppl. adj.* halting, limping ; (2) **Hilchy,** *sb.* a nickname given to a lame person.
(1) Ayr. He swoor 'twas hilchin Jean M'Craw, BURNS *Halloween* (1785) st. 20 ; SERVICE *Notandums* (1890) 122. (2) Ant. *Ballymena Obs.* (1892).

VOL. III.

---

2. *sb.* A halt, limp ; the act of halting.
Sc. (JAM.), Cai.¹ Gall. MACTAGGART *Encycl.* (1824).

HILCH, see Halsh.

HILD, *sb.* e.An. Also in forms **heeld** e.Suf. ; **hilding** c.An.² ; **hill** Suf.¹ [ild.] The sediment of beer, lees, dregs ; *gen.* in *pl.*
e.An.¹ Sometimes used as an imperfect substitute for yeast ; e.An.² Nrf. GROSE (1790) ; COZENS-HARDY *Broad Nrf.* (1893) 72. e.Nrf. MARSHALL *Rur. Econ.* (1787). Suf.¹ e.Suf. Used as a substitute for yeast (F.H.).

HILD, see Heald, *v.*¹, Hill, *v.*², Hold, *v.*, Hylt.

HILDE, HILDEGALEERIE, HILDER, see Helde, Heeliegoleerie, Elder, Eller.

HILDIE-GILDIE, *sb.* Rnf. (JAM.) An uproar.

HILDIN, *sb.* Sh.I. The fire. Cf. eldin(g.
Retained at the haaf as a lucky word, JAKOBSEN *Dial.* (1897) 30. [Dan. *ild,* fire, Norw. dial. *eld* (AASEN) ; ON. *eldr.* The *-in* in *hildin* is the suffixed def. art. ; cf. eldin(g.]

HILDING, *ppl. adj.* Nhp. Wor. [i·ldin.] **1.** Ailing, poorly. Wor. (H.K.)
2. Shuffling, shackling. Nhp.¹ We never apply it to females.

HILDING, see Hild.

HILDY-WILDY, *adj.* Nhp.¹ Fickle, changeable.
There's no good in such hildy-wildy doings.

HILE, *sb.*¹ e.Lan.¹ A cluster ; used in *combs.*
A cluster of whim-stalks is called a 'whimberry hile' ; an anthill is called a 'pisamoor hile.'

HILE, *sb.*² and *v.*¹ Hrt. Sus. Hmp. I.W. Wil. Dor. Som. Also written **hyle** Hrt. Hmp. w.Cy. Wil.¹ ; and in forms **aile** Wil. ; **aisle** Wil.¹ Dor. ; **hill** Wil. ; **hoyl** Sus. ; **ile** Som. [ail.] **1.** *sb.* A 'shock' of sheaves of corn (the numbers varying in different districts) ; used rarely of flax.
Sus. A shock of ten sheaves (S.P.H.). Hmp. Of flax, 10 sheaves, MORTON *Cyclo. Agric.* (1863). I.W.¹ A cock of wheat sheaves, usually eleven. 'The wheat's up in hile' ; I.W.² A double row of sheaves, *gen.* 12, set up in the field ready for carting. 'The wheeat in Corner Close es all up in hile.' w.Cy. Twelve sheaves of corn, GROSE (1790). Wil. The general custom of the district is to set up the sheaves in double rows (usually ten sheaves) together, for the convenience of the tithing-man, and the sheaves so set up are called an aile, or shock of corn, DAVIS *Agric.* (1811) vii ; Hile-a-whate, 10 sheaves in a pile, SLOW *Gl.* (1892) ; Wil.¹ The number of sheaves was formerly ten, for the tithing-man's convenience, but now varies considerably, according to the crop. In some parts the shape and size of a hyle will depend largely on the weather at harvest-time. Thus in a stormy season it will usually be built compact and round, while in a calm one it may sometimes form a line several yards in length. Dor. (C.W.) ; Ten sheaves of corn set up in the field, four on each side and one at each end, and forming a kind of roof, BARNES *Gl.* (1863) ; Dor.¹ Twer all a-tied an' zet upright In tidy hile, 158. Som. Twelve handsful of wheat put up, all leaning together at the top, SWEETMAN *Wincanton Gl.* (1885) ; There are ten sheaves in a hile (W.F.R.).

2. *v.* To place sheaves in a 'hile,' to pile up sheaves of corn.
Hrt. They hyle their barley . . . into one entire shock, ELLIS *Mod. Husb.* (1750) V. ii. Hmp.¹ Wil.¹ Wheat and rye are always hyled, and oats usually so, about Salisbury.

HILE, *v.*² Wor. Shr. Hrf. Glo. Also written **ile** Hrf.² [ail.] **1.** Of cattle : to strike with the horns, to butt, gore.
s.Wor. (H.K.), s.Wor.¹ Shr.¹ 'Our John's in a pretty way—them bollocks han 'iled 'is new plaiched 'edge.' 'Them cows 'll 'ile one another if they binna parted.' **2.** The attack of a savage bull consists of two processes ; he first hiles, or gores, and then hikes, or tosses. Hrf.¹ You had better take Fillpail out of the leasowes ; she do hile them young haifers unmerciful ; Hrf.² The cow's hiling the hedge down with her horns. Glo.¹

2. To thrash. Glo. (H.S.H.)

HILE, *v.*³ Lin. [ail.] To oppose, hinder.
MILLER & SKERTCHLY *Fenland* (1878) iv ; Lin.¹ The Duke of Northumberland is anxious to hile the Commissioners from taking his house.

HILE, *v.*⁴ Lin. [Not known to our correspondents.] To offer, to present. (HALL.)

HILE, see Ail, *sb.*²

Y

HILET, *sb.* Chs.[18] Also written hylet. A place of shade or shelter.

[Benadab forsothe drank drunken in his hilet (=schadewyng place, 1388), WYCLIF (1382) 3 *Kings* xx. 16.]

HILF, *sb.* Wil. Dev. Also in form hilth Wil. [ilf.] The haft or handle of such tools as an axe, mattock, &c., a 'helve.'

Wil. New hilth for the pickax, *ad., Chwarden's Acc.* (1614) *S. Edmund Sarum* (1896) 166. Dev. There now, the hilf be a-brokt, *Reports Provinc.* (1889). nw.Dev.[1]

HILL, *sb.*[1] and *v.*[1] Var. dial. uses in Sc. and Eng. Also written hyl Sus. [h)il.] **1.** *sb.* In *comp.* (1) Hill-ane, a fairy; (2) ·dyke, a wall dividing the pasture from the arable land; (3) ·folk, (a) the inhabitants of a hilly district; (b) the Covenanters or Cameronians; (c) the fairies; (4) ·gait, a hilly road; (5) ·head, the summit or top of a hill; (6) ·man, (a) a dweller among hills, an inhabitant of a hilly district; (b) a Covenanter or Cameronian; (7) ·trows, see (3, c); (8) ·water, water from a bog or moor; (9) ·wife, a fairy's wife; (10) ·worn, worn out or wearied with hills.

(1) n.Sc. Here is a man, bowed and crippled with rheumatism, who will tell how he was shot in the back by a 'hill-ane' when ploughing, *Longman's Mag.* (Nov. 1895) 39. (2) Or.I. The arable and waste land are divided from each other by what is here called a hill-dike, *Agric. Surv.* 35 (JAM.); S. & Ork.[1] *Gen.* of sods. (3, *a*) Ked. The eight o'clock bell is . . . to gar the hill-folk mak' theirsel ready for the Kirk win in, ANDREWS *Bygone Ch. Life* (1899) 43. Dmb. You're the long-lost son For whom the hill-folk's sorrow ne'er was done, SALMON *Gowodean* (1868) 98. Dmf. I've heard the hill folk say That the herds wad gang five mile aboot Tae pass this lanely brae, REID *Poems* (1894) 88. (*b*) Sc. Dinna be profane, you that had worthy ancestors among the hill-folk, KEITH *Bonnie Lady* (1897) 98; Still used, though the great bulk of the sect they founded is now incorporated with the Free Church of Scotland (A.W.). Gall. A tolerable Covenantman, and even a fairly consistent follower of the hill-folk, CROCKETT *Standard Bearer* (1898) 4; Kindly treated by the inmates, more particularly too by the Hillfowk, for the care he took in preserving the memories of their glorious brethren, MACTAGGART *Encycl.* (1824) 32, ed. 1876; They are called the hill-fowk, from their love of the primitive plan of worshipping the Creator . . . amongst the hills and mountains in the open air, *ib.* 269. (*c*) Sh.I. Robbie led the conversation gently round to all sorts of curious yarns about trows and hill-folk, BURGESS *Sketches* (2nd ed.) 58; Places that from time immemorial have been associated in the public mind with trows or hill-fowk, SPENCE *Flk-Lore* (1899) 39. Lan. The fairies, or 'Hill Folk,' yet live amongst the rural people, HARLAND & WILKINSON *Flk-Lore* (1867) 110. (4) Sh.I. Daandy was bidin' dan i' da Grind, tree mile o' hill-gait frae wir-hoose, BURGESS *Sketches* (2nd ed.) 66. (5) Abd. Now by this time the ev'ning's falling down, Hill-heads were red, ROSS *Helenore* (1768) 66, ed. 1812. (6, *a*) Gall. The warm smell of gathered sheep, ever kindly and welcome to a hill-man, saluted my nostrils, CROCKETT *Standard Bearer* (1898) 72. (*b*) Rnf. The first commotion that appeared was among the Hill-men or Cameronians, WODROW *Corrs.* (ed. 1842) I. 206. Dmf. The cry of the Hill-men, REID *Poems* (1894) 179. Gall. Weel, uncle, I shall never wed The Cameronian Hillman, MACTAGGART *Encycl.* (1824) 297, ed. 1876. (7) Or.I. (S.A.S.) (8) w.Som.[1] Tidn much account vor no meads, that there hill-water [ee·ul wau'dr]. (9) Sh.I. Wha sud shû meet bit da man o' da hill-wife dat shû wis aside, STEWART *Tales* (1892) 7. (10) Dmb. To rest my hill-worn feet he bade me stay, SALMON *Gowodean* (1868) 11.

2. *Comb.* in names of birds and plants: (1) Hill-bird, the fieldfare, *Turdus pilaris*; (2) ·chack, the ring-ouzel, *Turdus torquatus*; (3) ·cup, the bulbous buttercup, *Ranunculus bulbosus*; (4) ·hooter, the owl, *Strix flammea*; (5) ·linty, the twite, *Linota flavirostris*; (6) ·oat, a species of wild oat, *Avena nuda*; (7) ·plover, the golden plover, *Charadrius pluvialis*; (8) ·sparrow, the meadow-pipit, *Anthus pratensis*.

(1) Sc. SWAINSON *Birds* (1885) 5. (2) Or.I. SWAINSON *ib.* 8. (3) Dor. (B. & H.) (4) Chs.[18] (5) Or.I. SWAINSON *ib.* 66. (6) Nhb.[1] (7) Frf. SWAINSON *ib.* 180. (8) S. & Or.I. SWAINSON *ib.* 45.

3. Phr. (1) *hill and hole*, up and down, not level; (2) *to go down the hill*, to grow old; (3) — *set hills against slacks*, to equalize matters by giving and taking; (4) *to the hill*, in a

downward direction; (5) *up hill (and) down brae*, relentlessly, without stop; thoroughly.

(1) Midl. The road . . . was ' hill and hole ' all the way, BARTRAM *People Clopton* (1897) 227. (2) Ayr. Wi' learned lumber in their heads, Gaun doun the hill To get their wages for their deeds, In torments still, FISHER *Poems* (1790) 90. (3) Cum.[1] (4) Abd. He kaims his hair to the hill (JAM.). (5) Ayr. Misca'in' them up hill doon brae till he was oot o' breath, SERVICE *Dr. Duguid* (ed. 1887) 94; [He] cursed faither Euclid up hill and doon brae, *ib. Notandums* (1890) 89.

4. The district of the South Downs.
Sus.[1] Sur.[1] The Southdown country is always spoken of as 'The hill' by the people in the Weald. 'He's gone to the hill, harvesting.'

5. A piece of high ground entirely surrounded by water, a dry patch of elevated marsh.
e.An.[1] Nrf. If you watch them [yellow wagtails] building, you will see they have chosen a 'hill' where there is a scant crop of pin-rush and chate, EMERSON *Birds* (ed. 1895) 72; There are several channels marked out by posts, and they have a fair depth; but if you get out of them, you may get stuck on one of the 'hills,' as the natives term the shallow portions, DAVIES *Broads* (1884) 62.

6. A heap or mound of earth or rubbish, &c.
Cai.[1] Said chiefly of rubbish, or things in disorder. e.Lin. (G.G.W.). Ken.[1]
Hence *to do anything out of hill and heap, phr.* to fabricate or do anything out of one's own head.
e.Fif. D'ye really think at because ye've been sax moonths i' Edinbro' an' can coin a wheen lees oot o' hill an' heap, LATTO *Tam Bodkin* (1864) ix. Ayr. Gin thai ramstamphich, prick ma dainties . . . ware stentit to the makkin o' a tale out-o'-hill-an'-heap, I wadna fairly tho' it ware baith feckless an' fushionless, *Edb. Mag.* (Apr. 1821) 351 (JAM.).

7. A heap of sand *gen.* found by weirs. Cf. **flash**, *v.*[1] **7.**
s.Cy. The phr. run to hill means that the boat has run on a heap of sand found at the tail of most of the weirs, and called on the Thames a hill—indeed this word is used all the way to London, but on the Severn it is a Tump (S.S.B.).

8. The small mound on which hops are planted, a raised bank or mound of earth. Cf. **hill**, *v.*[1] **2.**
Ken.[1] Sur.[1] In planting a hop-garden, so many hills are reckoned to an acre.

9. A term applied to the oval side of a bat when it falls uppermost in tossing for an innings. e.Dur.[1]

10. A common.
w.Som.[1] Unenclosed land quite independent of its elevation. Vau·lee au·n dhu roa·ud gin ee kau·m tûe u ee·ul luyk [Follow on the road until you come to a sort of common]. In speaking of land, the climax of poverty is 'so poor's a hill.'
Hence Hill-ground, *sb.* unenclosed land; rough, uncultivated land.
I mind very well when 'twas all hill-ground here, so var's ever, you can zee, *ib.*

11. *Obs.* A land measure, amounting to half an acre.
Sus. In the manor of Rawkmer als Lavante, *Burrell MS.* [in Brit. Museum] 5701 *add.* 155.

12. *v.* Of birds: to assemble, collect together on a hill or piece of high ground.
Wil. These birds [the Ruff, *Machetes pugnax*] are polygamous, and like the Capercailie and Blackcock select a dry hillock in the breeding season on which to 'hill,' or take their stand in defiance of all rivals. Here . . . they proclaim their readiness to combat all opponents, and challenge such to fight for possession of the somewhat dowdy-looking females assembled around, SMITH *Birds* (1887) 424.

HILL, *v.*[2] and *sb.*[2] n.Cy. Yks. Lan. Chs. Flt. Stf. Der. Not. Lin. Lei. Nhp. War. Wor. Shr. Oxf. Wil. Also written hill e.Lan.[1]; hille w.Yks.; hyll N.Cy.[2] Chs. Oxf. and in forms hild w.Yks.[2]; ill Lan. Flt. Der.[2] nw.Der. [h)il.] **1.** *v.* To cover up or over; to wrap, cover with clothes, to tuck up; freq. with *up.* Cf. **heal**, *v.*[?] **hull**, *v.*[1]

n.Cy. GROSE (1790). w.Yks. Aw'll put th' childer i' bed an' hille 'em up warm (D.L.); w.Yks.[24] Lan. Sitch a floose o hey follut me, ot it . . . quite hill'd us booath, TIM BOBBIN *View Dial.* (1740) 45; A child in bed would say, 'Mother, hill me up' (S.W.); Th' owd lad had gotten croppen into bed; and he wur ill d up o'er th' yed, WAUGH *Th' Barrel Organ* (1867) 282; Lan.[1] Kan·d m.Lan.[1] Chs. Well hylled and filled [well clothed and fed], Sheaf

(1879) I. 168; Chs.¹; Chs.⁸ A sick person in bed says ' Hill me up.' s.Chs.¹ Naay, dhen, gy'et in·tū bed ūn ahy)l il· yū ûp [Nai, then, get into bed an' I'll hill yō up]. Flt. Ill it up (T.K.J.). Der. A noted toper was found one night asleep in a snowdrift, and when roused he called out, thinking that his wife was near, ' Hill me up, Meary! hill me up, good lass!' *N. & Q.* (1899) 9th S. iii. 285; Der.², nw.Der.¹, e.Lin. (G.G.W.), s.Lin. (T.H.R.) Lei.¹ Will you be hilled up? Nhp.¹ The old proverbial expression, where there is a large family, ' It takes a deal to hill and to fill.' War.² Shr.¹ Please, ma'am, shall I 'ill you up afore I gōō? [Ray (1691).]

Hence **Hilling**, *sb.* (1) bed-covering, a coverlet, bed-clothes; any loose covering; (2) the cover of a book; (3) the covering of a roof.

(1) n.Cy. Grose (1790); N.Cy.¹², m.Yks.¹, w.Yks.²⁴, ne.Lan.¹, e.Lan.¹ Chs.¹ Hast any hillin on the i' th' neet; art warm i' bed? Chs.²⁸, Stf.¹, Der.¹², nw.Der.¹ Lei.¹ Any loose covering such as a horse-cloth. Nhp.¹² War.²³, Oxf. (K.) (2) Chs.¹²⁸ Stf. Let me have one [hymn-book] with a red hillin, Whitx *Wrekin* (1860) xxvii; Stf.¹ Stf., Der. (J.K.) Der.², nw.Der.¹ War. Perhaps it is the hilling that makes it so expensive, Evans *Gl.* (1881); War.² The round back of a book; War.⁸, ne.Wor. (J.W.P.) Shr.¹ *Obsol.* Yo'd'n better pût some brown paper on them school-books, or else the 'illin's ōōn be spiled afore the wik's out; Shr.² (3) War.⁸ The wind blew the hilling off the cow-shed last night.

2. To cover with earth, raise a small mound of earth over potatoes, &c.; *freq.* with *up.*

w.Yks.² (s.v. Heald). Lan. A man burying potatoes or anything else in shallow ground would say 'I hill'd em up' (S.W.). ne.Lan.¹ Chs.¹ I put some manure in and hilled the soil atop of it, afore I put in th' seed; Chs.³ To hill a grave is an old term used by sextons, meaning to raise a mound over a grave. s.Chs.¹ Pût dhū tai·tōz i rùks ūn il· dhū sahyl ūtop)n ûm [Put the tatoes i' rucks an' hill the soil atop 'n 'em]. Der.², s.Not.(J.P.K.) Lin. Street-feild *Lin. and Danes* (1884) 338. n.Lin.¹, e.Lin. (G.G.W.) s.Lin. To-morrow we must hill the potatoes (T.H.R.). sw.Lin.¹ To ' hill up potatoes.' War. (J.R.W.); War.⁸ Have you hilled the celery up? Shr.¹ Mind an' 'ill them tatoes well ōōth feàrn w'en yo' tumpen 'em; Shr.² Ken. Holloway. Sus.¹ To hill-up hops is to raise small hills or heaps over the roots for the purpose of keeping them dry in the winter. Wil.¹

3. *sb.* A covering, esp. bed-covering.

Chs.¹ Aw dunna knaw wheer he'll get a hill, an' a fill, an' an o'erneet [a night's lodging].

[1. Vndire the shadow of this wenges hil me, Hampole (c. 1330) *Ps.* xvi. 10. ON. *hylja,* to cover, Goth. *huljan.*]

HILL, *sb.³* Abd. (Jam.) Husk. See Hull, *sb.¹*

HILL, see Hell, *v.,* Hild, Hile, *sb.²*

HILLA, *sb.* Cor.¹²³ Also written hillah Cor.² [i·lə.] The nightmare; also in phr. *to ride the hilla,* to have nightmare.

[Cp. Wel. *hunllef* and *hunllig,* the nightmare.]

HILLAN, *sb.* Sc. [hi·lən.] 1. A small hill or mound; a hillock, heap.

Sc. Every hollow and hillan was familiar to his feet, Keith *Bonnie Lady* (1897) 55. Gall. Pishminnie tammocks or hillans [are] ant-hills, Mactaggart *Encycl.* (1824) 383, ed. 1876. Kcb. And frae his hillan the poor mowdy whups, Davidson *Seasons* (1789) 6; An' fleggin, toss The moudy-hillan to the air in stoor, *ib.* 25.

2. *Comp.* Hillan-piet, the missel-thrush, *Turdus viscivorus.* Abd. Swainson *Birds* (1885) 2.

HILLER, *sb.¹* Sc. Shr. 1. *Obsol.* A dweller on a hill common; one who goes to the ' hills ' for the purpose of gathering 'wimberries.' Shr.¹ 2. A heap, a small mound, esp. of rubbish. Cai.¹

HILLER, *sb.²* Cai.¹ Also in form huller. A stout, untidy person.

HILLIEGILEERIE, see Heeliegoleerie.

HILLIER, *sb.* Chs. Nhp. War. Glo. I.W. Som. Also written hilliar Som.; hillyer Nhp.¹ 1. One who covers houses with any material but thatch; a 'hellier'; a slater; a tiler. See Hill, *v.²*

Chs.¹³, Nhp.¹, War.³ Glo. *Horae Subsecivae* (1777) 209. I.W.¹

2. A cover, cap.

Som. Free-stone mow caps with hilliars, *Sale-bill at Worle* (W.F.R.).

HILLING, *vbl. sb.* Sh.I. Grazing upon hill pastures.

In respeck o' da kye, I really tink 'at less hillin' wid 'a been better, *Sh. News* (Feb. 19, 1898).

HILLO, *int.* and *v.* Sc. Irel. Der. Pem. Also in forms hilloa Rxb.; hilln s.Pem. [(h)i·lō.] 1. *int.* An exclamation used to attract attention, ' hullo '; also used *subst.*

Rxb. A rap at the door, and a hilloa awakened me, Ruickbie *Wayside Cottager* (1807) 22. Der.² Hillo, gawky! s.Pem. Used in shouting at rabbits, crows, wood-pigeons, &c., to scare them away from a corn-field. ' Hillu there! hillu there! hillu there!' (W.M.M.)

2. *v.* With *on:* to cry ' hillo ' to, to call aloud to.

Don. The mornin' of the second day he hillooed on Shamus-a-Ruadh, an Shamus comed in, Macmanus *Billy Lappin* in *Cent. Mag.* (Feb. 1900) 607.

HILLOCK, *sb.* nw.Der.¹ [i·lək.] The ground, surface. Without any reference to its being elevated or otherwise. ' Throw it upo' th' 'illock.'

HILLOCKET, *ppl. adj.* Sc. Giddy, light-headed, wild. See Hallockit.

Half wittet hillocket sort o' creatures, Graham *Writings* (1883) II. 35.

HILLOCKY, *adj.* Yks. Lan. Midl. Nrf. Also written hilloky n.Lan.¹ [i·ləki.] Hilly, undulating, having small hills or mounds upon the surface.

n.Yks.², n.Lan.¹ Midl. Full of anthills, Marshall *Rur. Econ.* (1796). Nrf. The moles . . . are making the pathside hillocky with their landmarks, Patterson *Man and Nat.* (1895) 19.

HILLWARD, *adv.* and *adj.* Glo. Also written hillard Glo.¹² [i·ləd.] 1. *adv.* Towards the hills or high country. Glo.¹²

2. *adj.* From or belonging to the hills or high country. I could tell as 'e were one o' the hillard men, if I were as blind as a 'oont, Gissing *Vill. Hampden* (1890) II. v.

HILLY, *adj.* Sc. Of the sea: rough, having huge waves. Gall. A calm may lull the shore, my love, And smooth the hilly sea, Mactaggart *Encycl.* (1824) 504, ed. 1876.

HILLY HOWLEY, *phr.* e.Dur.¹ ' Hill and hole,' up and down.

HILP, *sb.* Wil.¹ [ilp.] 1. The fruit of the sloe, *Prunus spinosa.* 2. *Comp.* Hilp-wine, sloe-wine.

HILT, *sb.¹* Lin. Nhp. [ilt.] 1. The cross-piece on the top of the shaft of a spade. e.Lin. (G.G.W.)

2. A thatcher's instrument.

Nhp.¹ A curved or bowed piece of wood, with two staves and a hook, to affix it to the thatch, for the purpose of holding the yelm, or burden of straw, whilst thatching.

HILT, *sb.²* Sc. Irel. [hilt.] In phr. *hilt and hair, hilt or hair,* every particle, every jot; *freq.* used *neg.* nothing whatever. See Hair, *sb.¹* 2 (15).

Sc. I never saw hilt or hair of him that night, *Steam-boat* (1822) 267 (Jam.). Bch. 'Tis a' your ain, ye needna doubt, Ilk hilt and hair, Forbes *Dominie* (1785) 33. Abd. That ye were mine, ee'n ilka hilt and hair, Ross *Helenore* (1768) 90, ed. 1812. Frf. His traps an' snares wad be sittin' rampant wi' neither hilt nor hair o' a cat in them, Willock *Rosetty Ends* (1886) 18, ed. 1889. Fif. He kenned naething aboot him, had seen neither hilt nor hair o' him, Robertson *Provost* (1894) 51. Dmb. Here's ilk deed . . . That gies back your possessions hilt and hair, Salmon *Gowodean* (1868) 98. Rnf. Thou winna tell Or hilt or hair o't, Young *Pictures* (1865) 175. Ayr. Hilt or hair of Jeanie was not seen that night, Galt *Provost* (1822) xxxviii. Gall. The Maxwells may say ' Fare ye weel, Kilaivie,' to every hilt an' hair o' them, Crockett *Raiders* (1894) xvii. Arm. I have been looking for the cows and I can't see hilt or hair of them (D.A.S.).

[Cp. Sw. phr. *äta up något med hull och hår,* to eat up a thing entirely (lit. flesh and hair) (Widegren); Norw. dial. *hold,* flesh on the body, also the hide as opposed to the hair of an animal (Aasen).]

HILT, *sb.³* Midl. War. Wor. Glo. Oxf. Wil. Som. Dev. Also written ilt se.Wor.¹ Glo.² w.Som.¹ Dev.¹ n.Dev. [ilt.] 1. A young sow, *gen.* one that has not yet borne young. See Gilt, *sb.¹*; cf. elt, *sb.¹*

Midl. *Gen.* applied to the animal with a first litter of pigs, *Leamington Courier* (Jan. 30, 1897). War.⁴ Only five pigs in the farry! Well, what can yer more expect from that poor scribe of a hilt? s.Wor.¹ A young sow for breeding. se.Wor.¹ Glo. Lewis *Gl.* (1839); Glo.¹², Oxf.¹ w.Eng. Morton *Cyclo. Agric.* (1863). Wil. Britton *Beauties* (1825); Wil.¹

2. A spayed sow. Cf. elt, *sb.*[1]

a.Wor. PORSON *Quaint Wds.* (1875) 13. **w.Som.**[1] *Obsol.* **Dev.**[1] **n.Dev.** GROSE (1790); *Horae Subsecivae* (1777) 227; And to zar tha ilt and tha barra and melk tha kee, *Exm. Crtshp.* (1746) l. 409.

HILT, *v.* w.Yks.[2] [ilt.] To knead or mix dough. See Elt, *v.*

HILTED, *ppl. adj.* Sc. In *comb.* (1) **Hilted rung,** (2) — **staff,** a crutch.

(1) **Abd.** My hilted rung, A stick that never yet was dung, SHIRREFS *Poems* (1790) *To the Critics.* (2) **Abd.** (JAM.)

HILTER-SKILTER, *adv.* Sc. Also in forms **hiltie-skiltie, hilty-skilty.** 'Helter-skelter,' headlong, at full speed, in rapid succession. Also used as an *adj.*

Abd. Now we did not give them time to turn, but down the brae after them hilter skilter, *Deeside Tales* (1872) 87. **Ayr.** Then hiltie-skiltie, we gae scrievin', An' fash nae mair, BURNS *and Ep. to Davie,* st. 6. **Edb.** We'd enjoy but short time hilter skilter, LIDDLE *Poems* (1821) 36. **Slk.** Bonnie blinking, Hilty skilty lassie, HOGG *Poems* (ed. 1865) 428.

HILTER-WILTER, *adv.* Rut.[1] Also in form **hiltha-wiltha.** At all hazards, come what may.

HILTH, see Hilf.

HILTIE, *sb.* Obs. Sc. A crutch.

A hiltie drawn across their shanks, DONALD *Poems* (1867) 66.

HIM, *pron.* Var. dial. uses in Sc. and Eng. [Emph. h)im; unemph. im, əm.] I. Dial. forms : (1) Am, (2) Əm, (3) Em, (4) Heem, (5) Hem, (6) 'm, (7) Um. [For further instances see II. below.]

(1) **Cum.**[1] **c.Cum.** Let am kiss ma wid his mouth, DICKINSON *Sng. Sol.* (1859) i. 2. (2) **w.Frt., e.Per.** W.A.C.\ **Hrt.** Unemph., ELLIS *Pronunc.* (1889) V. 198. **e.Suf.** *ib.* 280. (3) **Cum.** Ah niver clappt een on em fra that day teh this, SARGISSON *Joe Scoap* (1881) 106; **Cum.**[1], **Suf.**[1] **Sur.** He . . . only bothers gentlefolk like you as canna give it 'em on his head if 'ee take a liberty, BICKLEY *Sur. Hills* (1890) I. iii. (4) **Dev.** Zaw ye heem wom ma zaul lov'th? BAIRD *Sng. Sol.* (1860) iii. 3. (5) **Som.** W. & J. *Gl.* (1873). (6) **w.Frf., e.Per.** Unemph. Fä telt 'm? I nevar hard tel ö'm (W.A.C.). (7) **Wm.** I laited him, but I dudn't find um, RICHARDSON *Sng. Sol.* (1859) iii. 1. **Suf.**[1] **Som.** I be come to meet Master Jack Poyntz, . . God bless 'um, JENKINS *Sec. Two Lives* (1886) 49.

II. Dial. uses. **1.** *Reflex.* : himself.

Sc. (A.W.) **Abd.** He bouns him to the house, And sits him down upo' the bink, BEATTIE *Parings* (1801) 24, ed. 1873. **n.Cy.** (J.W.) **w.Yks.** But he sat him down, SNOWDEN *Web of Weaver* (1896) 126; I lead im dãn i tfïld [he lay down in the field], WRIGHT *Gram. Wndhll.* (1892) 120; **w.Yks.**[2] He went to bathe him; **w.Yks.**[2] He has cut him. **Chs.**[2] (s.v. Her). **s.Chs.**[1] Less frequent in the third than in the other persons, 69.

2. *Comb.* Him lane, himself alone.

Sc. Lane . . . is frequently conjoined with the pronoun; . . sometimes as one word 'himlane' (JAM.). **Abd.** Speyk a word or twa to God him lane, MACDONALD *D. Elginbrod* (1863) I. 97. **Rnf.** Yet, quait, aside the fire himlane, Was harmless as the soukin' wean, PICKEN *Poems* (1813) I. 8.

3. Unemph. form of the nom. : *he.* See En, *pron.*

Nhp. When us is busy, him comes and does a day's work for we (F.P.T.). **War.**[1] **Hrf.** DUNCUMB *Hist. Hrf.* (1804-1812); Wen im də tʃok, ELLIS *ib.* 72. **Glo.** Had him? (H.S.H.); Im ə bin avən ə drap [he has been having a drop], ELLIS *ib.* 65. **w.Mid.** (W.P.M.) **Som.** If hem had hat hem as hem hat hem, hem 'oud a kill'd hem, W. & J. *Gl.* (1873).

4. Used of inanimate objects : *it.*

s.Chs.[1] Wot)n yū thingk˙ ŭbuw˙t dhis gy'aa˙rdin-aach˙? . . Wi mŭn gy'iv im ə greyn ŭn dhis tahym [What'n yō think abowt this garden-hatch? We mun give him a green 'un this time], 67. **War.**[12] **s.Wor.** My ooman put her bonnet there last year, and the birds laid their nest in it, PORSON *Quaint Wds.* (1875) 25. **se.Wor.**[1] **Shr.**[1] The Maister gid me this piece o' garden instead o' the other, an' I mucked 'im well, *Gram. Outlines,* 48. **Hrf.** ELLIS *ib.* 74; Him's her [that's it] (R.M.E.). **Oxf.** Wurs my showel? I aa got 'im (A.P.).

5. Used in addressing a superior for the acc. *you.*

Suf. When the speaker wishes to be particularly polite and recognizes your superior position. Thus instead of ' I will do it for you with pleasure,' we have ' He will do it for him with pleasure ' (C.G.B.).

[On the disjunctive use of *him* see the Grammar.]

HIMBER, HIMBEST, see Hindberry, Hindmost.

HIME, *sb.*[1] Yks. Lan. Der. Also written ime w.Yks.[1] ne.Lan.[1] Der.[1] [aim.] Hoar-frost when it hangs on the trees, rime. Cf. hind, *sb.*[2]

w.Yks. (E.G.); (J.T.); *Gen.* the mist of frost. Sometimes it is the hoar itself, HAMILTON *Nugae Lit.* (1841) 354; WRIGHT *Gram. Wndhll.* (1892) 80; **w.Yks.**[1234], **ne.Lan.**[1], **Der.**[1]

Hence Himy, *adj.* rimy, marked with hoar-frost.

w.Yks. (J.T.); **w.Yks.**[2] Himy frost [white frost].

[Norw. dial. *hīm,* a thin covering, esp. of hoar-frost or a thin covering of snow (AASEN).]

HIME, *sb.*[2] Sus. A wasp's nest. (S.P.H.)

HIME-BERRY, see Hindberry.

HIMP, *sb.* Sh.I. [himp.] The small bit of a hair-line or gut which attaches each hook to the principal line of a fishing-fly. S. & Ork.[1]

HIMP, *v.* e.An. [imp.] To limp.

e.An.[1] **Nrf.** The horse himps, COZENS-HARDY *Broad Nrf.* (1893) 25. **Suf.** A quarter of an hour himping down of the aisle, STRICKLAND *Old Friends* (1864) 250; **Suf.**[1] Poor fulla—'a go himpin about. **e.Suf.** (F.H.) [Lame of one leg, and himping all his dayes, UDALL *Erasmus Apoph.* (1542) 203 (DAV.).]

[Cp. Du. dial. *himp-* in *himphamp,* 'een hinkend persoon' (BOEKENOOGEN).]

HIMPLE, *v.* Obs. n.Cy. Lei. To halt ; to hobble, limp.

n.Cy. (P.R.); BLOUNT (1681) ; BAILEY (1721). **Lei.** *Trans. Phil. Soc.* (1858) 160.

[LG. *hümpeln,* ' hinken, auf Schwachen Füssen gehen ' (BERGHAUS).]

HIMS, *adj.* Sh.I. Also in forms **himst, hüms.** Hurried, hasty ; flighty in manner ; half-witted. S. & Ork.[1]

HIMS, *poss. pron.* Sc. Hrf. Also in form imz Hrf. His.

w.Sc. We wanted ta moon to gang till hims ped, CARRICK *Laird of Logan* (1835) 79. **Hrf.** Conjunctive, ELLIS *Pronunc.* (1889) V. 70, 74.

HIM-SAM, see Ham-sam.

HIMSELF, *pron.* Sc. I.Ma. Chs. Nhp. Wor. Hrf. Glo. Hnt. Also in form **himsel**(l Sc. **1.** In phr. (1) *at himself,* **in** the full possession of his mental faculties ; in a state of mental composure ; (2) *by himself,* beside himself, deprived of his reason, out of his mind ; (3) *in himself,* in his general health ; (4) *like himself,* (a) unchanged in appearance ; (b) consistent with his reputation ; (5) *not to be himself,* see (2) ; (6) *to be in himself,* to transact business on his own account ; (7) *weill at himself,* plump, fat, 'en bon point.'

(1) **s.Lan.** (J.W.) (2) **Sc.** (JAM.), **Cai.**[1] **Ayr.** But monie **a** day was by himsel, He was sae sairly frighted That vera night, BURNS *Halloween* (1785) st. 16. (3) **s.Wor.**[1] 34. **Hrf.**[2], Glo. (A.B.) (4, a) **Sc.** A dead person on whose appearance death has made no uncommon change is said to be ' like himself.' ' Nae like himsell,' applied to a person whose appearance has been much altered by sickness, great fatigue, &c. (JAM.) **Cai.**[1] (b) **Sc.** 'He's ay like him-sell.' Most *gen.* used in a bad sense (JAM.). **Cai.**[1] (5) **Sc.** (JAM.) **Cai.**[1], **Chs.**[2], **Nhp.**[1], **Hnt.** (T.P.F.) (6) **Abd.** (JAM.) (7) **Cld.** A vulgar phr. (*ib.*)

2. A term applied to the husband or master of the speaker.

I.Ma. The servant said 'himself was not at home.' His wife heard me asking after him and shouted that ' himself had gone to the herrings ' (S.M.).

HIN, *v.* e.Lan.[1] [in.] With *up* : to regain.

To recover lost time by working over hours is described as ' hinning up lost time.'

HIN, see En, *pron.,* Hen, *sb.*[1], Hind, *adj.*

HINCH, *v.*[1] and *sb.*[1] Lin. **1.** *v.* To be miserly. (HALL.) **2.** *sb.* Mean conduct, meanness.

Lin.[1] I cannot abide such hinch ; but he's a regular gnarlband. [These Romaines . . . did . . . bring in their mony and goodes, without hinching or pinching, to reliefe the charges of their common welth, AYLMER *Harb.* (1559) Pj2 (N.E.D.).]

HINCH, *v.*[2] and *sb.*[2] Sc. Also in forms **haincb** (JAM. *Suppl.*); **hench** (JAM.). **1.** *v.* To limp, halt ; with *away* : to move onwards in a halting manner.

Sc. To hench awa' (JAM.). **Buff.**[1] The aul' currack o' **a** carle cam hinchin' up the green. **w. & s.Sc.** A lame person hinches as he walks along (JAM. *Suppl.*). **Rxb.,** Gall. (JAM.)

Hence **Hincher**, *sb.* a lame person. w. & s.Sc. (JAM. *Suppl.*)

2. *sb.* A halt, limp, lameness. w. & s.Sc. (*ib.*)
[Cp. G. *hinken*, to limp; also EFris. (KOOLMAN).]
HINCH, *v.*[3] s.Chs.[1] In phr. *to hinch anything on to some one*, to make some one answerable for anything ; to put the responsibility of anything upon some one.
Dhaat·)l nev·ŭr bi in·sht on tŭ yoa· [That'll never be hinched on to yo].

HINCH, see Hainch.
HINCHY·PINCHY, *sb.* n.Cy. Nhb. A child's game ; see below.
N.Cy.[1] **Nhb.**[1] A game in which the play is begun gently, and gradually increased in intensity. Boy : ' Aa'll play ye at hinchy-pinchy.' Strikes gently his companion, who returns the blow, until it becomes a fight. The term is also employed in games of leaping, where the first player gives an easy leap, and each succeeding player exceeds the leap of his predecessor, until the game is left in the hands of the best jumper.

HIND, *sb.*[1] Sc. Nhb. Dur. Lakel. Yks. Lan. Der. Lin. Nrf. Suf. Sus. Som. Dev. Cor. Also written **hynd**(e Sc. ; and in forms **hain** Cor.[1] ; **heynd** Cum. ; **hiand** e.Yks.[1] ; **hine** Lakel.[1] w.Yks. w.Dev. Cor. ; **hyne** Sc. (JAM.) [h)ain(d.]
1. A farm-labourer or ploughman ; a farm-servant.
Sc. *Monthly Mag.* (1798) II. 435 ; Now restricted to a farm servant as distinguished from one employed in the house or in tending cattle (JAM.). **Abd.** A group of hinds were assembled, busily engaged in washing the fleeces of the sheep, RUDDIMAN *Parish* (1828) 60, ed. 1889. **Frf.** Hinds wha ha'e been labourin' hard preparin' the ground for anither crap, LOWSON *Guidfollow* (1890) 56. **Per.** Baith laird and tenant, herd an' hind, HALIBURTON *Ochil Idylls* (1891) 133. **Flf.** Hinds, plewmen, lands, and cottar callans, TENNANT *Papistry* (1827) 71. **Ayr.** Summons the hind to perform his appointed duties in the barn, WHITE *Jottings* (1879) 46. **Lnk.** The stalwart hind went to the door, HAMILTON *Poems* (1865) 248. **Lth.** The stout hind now whistles gay, BRUCE *Poems* (1813) II. 52. **Edb.** Hynds to the hamlet steer, GLASS *Cal. Parnassus* (1812) 17. **Bwk.** The circumstances of the country are such as to reward the toil of the hinds or labourers in this parish, with a very liberal share of the produce of the lands, *Statist. Acc.* XVI. 493 (JAM.). **Peb.** Loud ' Goosies !' everywhere resound Frae hizzy, hind, or weane, *Lintoun Green* (1685) 68, ed. 1817. **Slk.** Ministers, lairds, weavers, and poor hinds, HOGG *Tales* (1838) 8, ed. 1866. **Dmf.** Nae choice has thou o' hynde or peer, REID *Poems* (1894) 72. **Gall.** A kind of bold, self-respecting diffidence common among our Galloway hinds, CROCKETT *Standard Bearer* (1898) 188. **n.Cy.** GROSE (1790) ; N.Cy.[1] **Nhb.** Ralph Turnbull, hind to Mr. Thompson, RICHARDSON *Borderer's Table-bk.* (1846) V. 153. **e.Dur.**[1], **w.Yks.**[1] **Lan.** The household were summoned, Nathaniel, his son, and two hinds, KAY-SHUTTLEWORTH *Scarsdale* (1860) II. 109. **Sus.** The hind ploughs as his fathers ploughed, HOSKYNS *Talpa* (1852) 228, ed. 1857.

Hence (1) **Hindin·work**, *sb.* the work of a farm-servant or ploughman ; (2) **Hindish**, *adj.* rustic, clumsy, clownish.
(1) **Hdg.** Ye'll get wages like the lave when your hindin work begins, EDWARDS *Mod. Poets*, 10th S. 337. (2) **Gall.** Here I give . . . a few hindish speculations, MACTAGGART *Encycl.* (1824) 273, ed. 1876.

2. An upper farm-servant hired yearly and provided with a house ; a married farm-servant.
Lth. MORTON *Cyclo. Agric.* (1863). **se.Sc.** Farm labourers, engaged by the year, their wages being so much in money, with house, firing, milk, meal, and potatoes—all which things in kind go by the name of ' the benefit ' (A.W.). **Nhb.** Hinds, male and female, having now 'bound their bargains' with their masters, were coasting round the booths and stalls, *Newc. Dy. Leader* (June 1, 1897) 5, col. 2 ; **Nhb.**[1] A farm servant hired by the year at so much per week. Hinds formerly had ' corn wages,' and were mostly paid in kind by the produce of the farm, which included the pasturage of a cow. Money wages are now general. At present sixteen to eighteen shillings per week, with house free, coals carted, a garden, and generally some potatoes planted on the farm or ' found ' for him. At the hiring a stipulation is often made by the farmer that the hind must furnish a female field-worker at a stipulated price per day, with extra wage in harvest time. This extra hand is called a ' bondager.' **Dur.**[1] n.Yks.[1] Hired by the year or term, having a house rent-free in part remuneration and expected to find other labour besides his own—his wife's, or grownup daughter's, possibly—at certain seasons of the year. In some

instances, if not all, the hind has some of the responsibility of the bailiff, but works with his own hands, which the bailiff does not, or at least need not ; **n.Yks.**[4] A sort of bailiff, in fact, but of a lower degree. **ne.Yks.**[1] The hind lives rent-free, and manages all or a part of the farm under the owner, working at the same time with his own hands. A farmer renting two farms usually puts a hind into the house he does not occupy. **w.Yks.** (J.W.), **n.Lan.**[1] **ne.Lan.**[1] One entrusted with the charge of cattle. **Der.** A hind, therefore, engaging to work on one of the farms belonging to the estate, has a house assigned to him, HOWITT *Rur. Life* (1838) I. 165.

Hence **Hinding**, *sb.* an engagement, situation as a farm-labourer.
Nhb. He has tow dowters workin' oot and a full hindin' himsel', *Longman's Mag.* (Feb. 1897) 325.

3. A farm-bailiff or steward.
N.Cy.[1] **Lakel.**[1] A man put in to occupy a farmhouse where the farmer has more than one ; **Lakel.**[2] A farm manager who lives on the farm and carries it on as a farmer would. **Cum.** The squire and heynd, STAGG *Misc. Poems* (ed. 1805) 118 ; **Cum.**[1] A manager of an off-lying farm. **Yks.** Wanted, a situation as hind to manage a farm. Has part stock and implements, *Yks. Herald* (Mar. 13, 1886) in *N. & Q.* (1886) 7th S. i. 276. **n.Yks.** One end is occupied by a small dwelling-place for a ' hind ' or bailiff, TUKE *Agric.* (1800) 57. **e.Yks.** (Miss A.); MARSHALL *Rur. Econ.* (1788) ; **e.Yks.**[1] **w.Yks.** This hoose is whar mey hind bides, LUCAS *Stud. Nidderdale* (c. 1882) 83 ; **w.Yks.**[1], **ne.Lan.**[1] **n.Lin.** *N. & Q.* (1886) 7th S. i. 276; **n.Lin.**[1] Are you my cousin Thomas Peacock's hind ? **w.Som.**[1] He've a-got a very good place and a good maister : he's hind, you know, zir, to Squire Coles. **Dev.** (F.H.) **w.Dev.** MARSHALL *Rur. Econ.* (1796). **nw.Dev.**[1] Cor. The hind or general supervisor of farms and numerous other extensive farms, HUNT *Pop. Rom. w.Eng.* (ed. 1896) 156 ; Cor.[1]

4. A term of reproach, a rascal.
Nrf. COZENS-HARDY *Broad Nrf.* (1893) 84. **e.Suf.** (F.H.)

5. *Comp.* (1) **Hind-chiel**, (2) **-squire**, a youth, a young man, or squire.
(1) **n.Sc.** Twa gloves o' plate, a gowden helmet Became that hind-cheel well, BUCHAN *Ballads* (ed. 1875) II. 40. (2) The other was a young hynde squire, in rank, of lower degree, *ib.* 258.
[Formed fr. OE. *hī(g)na*, gen. pl. of *hīwa*, *hīga*, member of a family, servant. The *-d* is excrescent.]

HIND, *sb.*[2] Sh.I. Dur. Yks. Also in form **inde** s.Dur.
1. A thin slice of anything, a thin layer.
Sh.I. Shū begood ta straik aff da hind o' dust 'at wis fa'n frae da bent, *Sh. News* (Dec. 11, 1897) ; (*Coll.* L.L.B.)
2. Hoar-frost. s.Dur. (J.E.D.), m.Yks.[1] Cf. **hime**, *sb.*[1]
Hence **Indy**, *adj.* marked with hoar-frost, rimy.
s.Dur. It's a varra indy-morning (J.E.D.).
[1. Dan. dial. *hinde*, a thin coating, esp. the thin covering on milk (FEILBERG).]

HIND, *adj.*, *sb.*[3], *adv.* and *prep.* Sc. Nhb. Lakel. Cum. Yks. Not. Lin. Nhp. War. Glo. Oxf. Nrf. Suf. Ess. Wil. Som. Also in forms **hent** Sc. ; **hin** Sc. Bnff.[1] Cum.[14] Suf. Ess. ; **hine** Lin.[1] Som. ; **hint** Sc. Nhb.[1] Not. n.Lin.[1] ; **in-** w.Yks.[2] ; **ine** Wil. [ain(d, h)in(d, h)int.] **1.** *adj.* Belonging to or at the back, rearward, posterior. Cf. **hinder**, *adj.*[1]
Sh.I. A peerie white spot abūn his hint cliv ipa da left fit, STEWART *Tales* (1892) 244. **Abd.** Ye hinna on the hin shelvin' o' the cairt, ALEXANDER *Johnny Gibb* (1871) i. **e.Sc.** She has a bit dink i' the aff hent hoof, SETOUN *R. Urquhart* (1896) ii. **Nhb.** He wis ridin o' the hint waggon. Fetch yor hint hand forrit (R.O.H.). **Lakel.**[1] **n.Lin.**[1] Th' hint-wheels o' th' red waggon wants greåsin'. **Nrf.** We got the poles and be say, ' Where are you going ? hind or fore-poling ?' EMERSON *Son of Fens* (1892) 173. **Wil.** SLOW *Gl.* (1892). **Som.** (F.A.A.) ; JENNINGS *Obs. Dial. w.Eng.* (1825).

Hence **Hindling**, *sb.* one who falls behind others or who is on the losing side of a game.
Abd. A chiel came on him wi' a feugh Till a' the hindlings leugh At him that day, SKINNER *Christmas Ba'ing* (ed. 1805) (JAM.).

2. *Comp.* (1) **Hind-dore**, the back part of a box-cart ; (2) **-end** or **-ind**, (*a*) the further end, the rearward ; the latter part of anything ; (*b*) refuse or light corn blown out by the winnowing-machine ; cf. **hinder-end**, **5** ; (3) **-hand**, last, hindermost, esp. of the last player or last stone in a game of curling ; also used *subst.* ; (4) **-harvest**, the end of harvest, between harvest and winter ; also used *attrib.* ; (5)

-head, (a) the back of the head ; (b) a distant relationship, a 'German cousin'; (6) -heck, the back-end board of a cart ; (7) -heel, the tansy, *Tanacetum vulgare* ; (8) -lift, a joint of beef taken from the hind-quarters of the animal, the 'aitch-bone'; (9) -post, the post on which a gate hangs ; (10) -side, the back, rear-side ; (11) -yitt, *obs.*, the hinge of a barn-door.

(1) Bnff.[1] Always moveable. (a, a) Nhb. Pull the hint end roond a bit (R.O.H.). Cum.[1] Nhp.[2] Autumn is the hind-eend of the year. Suf. (C.T.) (b) Cum.[4] (3) Cld. The hindhand stane (JAM.). Lnk. Our hin'haun, unrivall'd at drawin', Sen's up a tee-shot to a hair—Game! game! WATSON *Poems* (1853) 64. Gall. Hin-hanplayers—For common the best players at the game of curling of their party ; they play after all the others have played and their throw is always much depended on, MACTAGGART *Encycl.* (1824). (4) Abd. The wan licht o' the hint hairst moon, *Guidman Inglismaill* (1873) 27. Gall. The bees are smuiked in the hinharrest time, MACTAGGART *Encycl.* (1824) 88, ed. 1876; Hin-harvest-time—That time of the year between harvest and winter, *ib.* 269. (5, a) Sc. (JAM.) (b) Lin.[1] (6) n.Cy. (HALL.) (7) n.Cy. (K.) (8) w.Yks.[3] (9) War.[2] (10) Abd. Whether he gaed wi' 's cwite [coat] hin'side afore or no, MACDONALD *Sir Gibbie* (1879) l. (11) Ess. *Gt. Bromley Chwarden's Accts.* (1638).

3. Spare, extra.

Cai. His hind or spare coat, his Sunday coat, ELLIS *Pronunc.* (1889) V. 696.

4. *sb.* The rear, back ; the hindermost, the very last.

Sc. To the hint (JAM.). Nhb. The hint o' a feast's better nor the forst o' a fray. Yor aawis at the hint (R.O.H.) ; Nhb.[1]

5. *Comp.* (1) Hind-afore or -before, (2) -first, the back part to the front, the wrong way round, backwards.

(1) Not. The man's got his 'at on hint-before! PRIOR *Renie* (1895) 51. Glo. It do blow cowld then, so I turns 'un hind-afore, BUCKMAN *Darke's Sojourn* (1890) iii. (2) Oxf.[1] Tuurn uuy'ndfust', uuy tel dhu, un dhen dhu kyanst kyaat 't [Turn 'indfust, I tell tha, an' then tha canst carr 't].

6. *adv.* Behind.

Frf. The mains are passed, baith slap and style, His troop o' Tartars hint a mile, SANDS *Poems* (1833) 75.

7. *prep.* Behind.

Sc. A discontented Fenian lot, Wha hint the hedge aft landlords shot, ALLAN *Lilts* (1874) 245. Bnff. Sally forth to scour the causeys, As yesterday 'hint tight-hough'd lassies, TAYLOR *Poems* (1787) 178. Cld. The sun, sae breem frae hint a clud, *Edb. Mag.* (Oct. 1818) 327 (JAM.). Ayr. 'Hint steekit door, Or door that's haflin's open, AINSLIE *Land of Burns* (ed. 1892) 318. Lnk. Nor scorn puir Johnny 'hint his back, WATSON *Poems* (1853) 9.

HINDBERRY, *sb.* Sc. Nhb. Cum. Yks. Lan. Stf. Also written hynd- Sc. ; and in forms hen- Stf. ; himber w.Yks. ; hime-berry w.Yks. e.Lan.[1] ; hine- Cum.[14] w.Yks.[24] ; ian- Cum.[1] [h]ai·n(d)bəri.] **1.** The wild raspberry, *Rubus Idaeus*.

Slg. Frae the rank blue-bells I skiff'd the clear dew That bloom on the Hynd-berry brae, MUIR *Poems* (1818) 89. s.Sc. What brambles did we not eat, and what hind or rasp-berries did we not convert into red wine, WILSON *Tales* (1839) V. 175. Cld. (JAM.) n.Dmf. *Garden Wk.* (1896) New S. No. cxiv. 112. Gall. The 'hip' and the 'hyndberry' . . . were gleaming there, *Edb. Antiq. Mag.* (1848) 113. n.Cy. GROSE (1790); (K.); N.Cy.[12], Nhb.[1], Cum.[1] w.Yks. (S.P.U.) ; (J.T.) ; THORESBY *Lett.* (1703) ; w.Yks.[1] They war feaful fain to pike amang t'shrogs some shoups, bummlekites, an' hindberries, ii. 296; w.Yks.[24], ne.Lan.[1], e.Lan.[1] Stf. RAY (1691) *MS. add.* (J.C.)

2. *pl.* Excrescences on the under-parts of cattle resembling raspberries. Cum.[14] Cf. anbury, angle-berry, sb.[1]

[OE. *hindbēriae*, acinum, SWEET *O.E. T.* 37.]

HINDER, *v.*[1] and *sb.*[1] Sc. Hmp. Dor. Also in form hin'er Abd. **1.** *v.* In phr. (1) *to hinder time*, to waste time ; (2) — *to do anything*, (a) to hinder from doing anything ; (b) to render unnecessary any act ; (c) to prevent from saying that one did anything ; a form of asseveration.

(1) Hmp. (H.E.), Dor. (G.M.M.) (2, a) Sc. *Scoticisms* (1787) 44. Abd. Ya sud hin'er him to gae, ALEXANDER *Johnny Gibb* (1871) vii. (b) Sh.I. Da sin is ower da waaster planticrub, dat's juist sax o'clock frae da know, an' hit'll hindir me ta waive apo' you, *Sh. News* (Sept. 3, 1898). (c) Sh.I. I tak's a guid look, an' ye'll no hinder me ta see da bow, SPENCE *Flk-Lore* (1899) 248; I wis up luikin' fir a grey yow o' wirse. . . Doo'll no hinder me ta fin her

lam'd [lambed] a bonnie black gimmer lamb, *Sh. News* (May 20, 1899).

2. To withhold from, keep back from.

Sh.I. I'm sure Mr. Shürtiends wid no hinder you da üse o' da kirk, STEWART *Tales* (1892) 11.

3. *sb.* Hindrance.

Or.I. An great hinder to His Majesty's princely resolutions, PETERKIN *Notes* (1822) App. 63. Abd. Without let or hinder, *Deeside Tales* (1872) 24.

HINDER, *adj.*[1], *sb.*[2] and *v.*[2] Sc. Nhb. Lakel. Cum. Yks. Lan. War. Shr. Som. Dev. Cor. Also in forms hinner Sc. ; hinther n.Yks. ; hoindur Lan. [h]ai·ndə(r, h)i·ndə(r.] **1.** *adj.* 'Hind', back, rearward ; remote. Cf. hind, *adj.*

Sh.I. Ta sit apon his hinder legs, *Sh. News* (July 23, 1898). Bnff. I . . . bought twa Brokie's hinner buttocks. TAYLOR *Poems* (1787) 68. Kcd. Couper Geordie loot his stick Drap on Foveran's hinner hurdies, GRANT *Lays* (1884) 43. n.Cy. BAILEY (1721). Nhb. The hinder part o' them wad fare badly ; there wis sic a scrudge (R.O.H.). Lakel.[1] w.Yks. LUCAS *Stud. Nidderdale* (c. 1882).

2. *Comb.* (1) Hinder-lan(d)s or -lins, (2) -lets, (3) -liths, the back part ; the hind-quarters, buttocks ; (4) -most, (a) the last ; (b) in arrears, behind-hand ; (5) -most o' three, a game played on village greens ; (6) -side, the back of any object.

(1) Sc. We downa bide the coercion of gude braid-claith about our hinderlans, SCOTT *Rob Roy* (1817) xxiii ; Tod sprang up frae his hinderlands and fell forrit on the wab, STEVENSON *Catriona* (1893) xv. Lnk. The candidates are those wha daily moil, An' harle at their hinderlins a cart, MUIR *Minstrelsy* (1816) 10. Gall. And doon Birsay fell . . . landin' on my hinderlands, CROCKETT *Moss-Hags* (1895) xxiii. (2) Sc. Her hinderlets being wickedly wet, in John Davie's well that morning, GRAHAM *Writings* (1883) II. 37. Rnf. On her hinderlets war seen The purpie an' the blue, Fu' gay, PICKEN *Poems* (1813) II. 91. (3) Gall. Animals of the lizard species are always considered to have poison somewhere about their hinnerliths, MACTAGGART *Encycl.* (1824) 22, ed. 1876. (4, a) n.Yks. (T.S.), n.Lan.[1] War.[4] Yes, there's Joe in as usual, the hindermost of all. (b) Cor. He'll go on paying—he's never got hindermost i' his paying, BARING-GOULD *Curgenven* (1893) xxi. (5) Cum.[4] (6) n.Yks. (T.S.), n.Yks.[2]

3. Last in point of time, latter.

Lnk. I dreamed a dreary dream this hinder night, RAMSAY *Gentle Shep.* (1725) 368, ed. 1733. Edb. Whilk happen'd on the hinder night, FERGUSSON *Poems* (1773) 173, ed. 1785. n.Cy. *Border Gl.* (Coll. L.L.B.) Nhb. (B.O.)

Hence **Hinnerly,** *adv.* at the last, finally.

e.Lth. He is juist the sort o' lad that hinnerly will ding the deil, MUCKLEBACKIT *Rhymes* (1885) 236.

4. *sb.* The buttocks ; the hind-quarters of an animal ; the back ; *gen.* in *pl.*

Bnff. Boasting of kissing, at their meetings the Devil's 'hinder,' GORDON *Keith* (1880) 55. Lth. A pull that brought the pony in a moment back upon its hinders, LUMSDEN *Sheep-head* (1892) 268. Lan. Thir is nah a barro e Smobruff uts big anouff fur iz hoindurs, SCHOLES *Tim Gamwattle* (1857) 20. Som. (G.S.)

5. *pl.* Fragments. Shr. (HALL.) Cf. hinder-end, 4.

6. *v.* To go backwards. [Not known to our correspondents.] Som. (HALL.)

HINDER, *adv.* and *adj.*[2] Bdf. e.An. Dev. Also in forms hender Bdf. ; hinter Nrf. **1.** *adv.* Yonder, in that direction. See Hin(n.

Bdf. (J.W.B.), e.An.[12] Nrf. (F.E.) ; Du yow see them whitebards hinder! PATTERSON *Man and Nat.* (1895) 27 ; To taake the faarm up hinder, SPILLING *Giles* (1872) 6. Suf. Hide in the holl 'bor, hinder come a doo (W.W.S.) ; (C.T.) ; Suf.[1] Hinder a go-Ess. That waiter hinder favours yow, CLARK *J. Noakes* (1899) st-141; Gl. (1851); Ess.[1] Dev. 'Hot's that dawn hinder!' 'It's zume mon a comin' along ter drangway,' MADOX-BROWN *Dwale Bluth* (1876) bk. IV. ii.

Hence (1) **Hindercome,** *adv.* in sight, but some way off. Suf. (H.H.) ; (2) **Hinderward(s,** *adv.* yonderwards, in that direction. e.Suf. (F.H.)

2. *adj.* Yon, yonder, that.

e.Suf. He live in hinder cottage (F.H.).

Hence **Hinderway,** *adj.* yonder, in that direction. *ib.*

HINDER-END, *sb.* and *adj.* Sc. Nhb. Dur. Cum. Wm. Yks. Lan. Der. Not. Lin. Nhp. Som. Also written hindor- Nhb.; hinnder- Cum.; and in forms hender- Sc.; hindher- e.Yks.[1]; hindrens Lin.; hindther- n.Yks.; hiner-Abd.; hinner- Sc.; hinter- Nhb.; hinther- n.Yks. 1. *sb.* The back part of anything, the rearward.

Sc. (A.W.), Nhb. (R.O.H.) n.Yks. Hinther end of cart (T.S.). e.Yks.[1] Shuv it in at hindher-end. m.Yks.[1] w.Yks. BANKS *Wkfd. Wds.* (1865). Lan.[1], ne.Lan.[1], e.Lan.[1] n.Lin.[1] Th' prickin' furk's e' th' hinderend o' th' barn. w.Som.[1] The hinder-end of the train.

2. The buttocks, breech.

Cai.[1] Fif. The Fisher-knicht, wi' halbert's prob, Their hobblin' hender-ends did job, TENNANT *Papistry* (1827) 160. Edb. Between ilk stenn she ga'e rift, Out frae her hinder end, FORBES *Poems* (1812) 164. w.Yks. He gat t'babby an reared it ov it hinder-end, *Yks. Wkly. Post* (Feb. 22, 1896). Lan. They both sprang onto their hinder-ends, WAUGH *Heather* (ed. Milner) II. 220; Lan.[1], ne.Lan.[1] w.Som.[1] Maister's bad again; he've a got a risin pon his hinder-end now, and 's fo'ced to have a 'oss-collar vor to zit pon.

3. The end, termination, extremity; the latter end, esp. the ultimate end of life; the latter part.

Sc. Weel, at the hinder-end, we saw the wee flag yirk up to the mast heid, STEVENSON *Catriona* (1893) xv; Falschood made ne'er a fair binder-end, FERGUSON *Prov.* (1641) 11. Sh.I. What will come o' da laek o' dat i' da hinder end! *Sh. News* (July 9, 1898). Cai.[1] Abd. There wud lickly be a ploy i' the hin'eren', ALEXANDER *Johnny Gibb* (1871) xl. Per. Read the deevil's books to ken The secret of their hinner en', HALIBURTON *Horace* (1886) 80. Kcd. She . . . thocht Her hinner-en' had come, GRANT *Lays* (1884) 14. Fif. His death came unco sudden at the hinderend, ROBERTSON *Provost* (1894) 34. Ayr. In the hinder-end of last year, SERVICE *Dr. Duguid* (ed. 1887) 7. Lnk. An' will be till the hinder-en', WATSON *Poems* (1853) 104. e.Lth. Just a pair still born at the hinner en', MUCKLEBACKIT *Rhymes* (1885) 6. Slk. This was the hinderend of all, HOGG *Tales* (1838) 283, ed. 1866. Gall. He was . . . reared in the hinder end o' the last century, CROCKETT *Stickit Min.* (1893) 103. Wgt. Truth may be warst at the first, bit its aye best at the hinner en', FRASER *Wigtown* (1877) 983. Keb. The hinder-end of the night, RUTHERFORD *Lett.* (1660) No. 321. Nhb. It wis at the hinderend o' the month (R.O.H.); Thoo's been kindor tiv us it the hinderend than it the furst, ROBSON *Bk. Ruth* (1860) iii. 10. Dur.[1] Cum. He . . . teaak off as hard as he could tull t'hinnder end eh t'steamer, SARGISSON *Joe Scoap* (1881) 48. Yks. (J.W.) n.Lin.[1] I was born at the hinderend of th' year.

4. The last remains of anything, the leavings, fragments; rubbish, refuse, riff-raff; the worst of anything. Also in *pl.*

n.Sc. The hinder-end o' aw trade, the worst business to which one can betake one's self. The hinder-end o' aw folk (JAM.). Abd. A drunken man's the hin'er-end o' a', SHIRREFS *Poems* (1790) 42. Lth. He's ane o' the rale auld stock . . . that ther's e'en noo but bits o' hinner ends an' shairds left o't, LUMSDEN *Sheephead* (1892) 294. Slk. They warna likit and the hinder-end o' them were in the catslack burn, *Blackw. Mag.* (Mar. 1823) 314. N.Cy.[1] Nhb. The broken meat of a feast. The last gathered corn from the fields at harvest-time is called the hinderends (R.O.H.). Cum. (E.W.P.) m.Yks.[1] The main feck of them went their way, but the hinder-end kept on.

5. *pl.* The refuse of corn after winnowing; the small, inferior grains of corn.

N.Cy.[1], Nhb. (R.O.H.), Dur.[1] s.Dur. It's ne better nor hinderends (J.E.D.). Cum. Fit only for hens meat (J.Ar.); Cum.[1] Wm. Give the cattle some hinder-ends (B.K.). n.Yks. (T.S.); Ise gin' the yawds some hinderends and caffe, MERITON *Praise Ale* (1684) l. 84; n.Yks.[4], ne.Yks.[1], e.Yks.[1] w.Yks. A corn-dealer's offal is the 'hinder ends,' the small, faulty, grub-eaten grains sold as 'beer corn,' *Leeds Merc. Suppl.* (May 23, 1896); w.Yks.[1][2], Not. (J.H.B.) s.Not. There's a lot o' hinder ends i' this flour (J.P.K.). Lin. MORTON *Cyclo. Agric.* (1863); Lin.[1] n.Lin.[1] So called because in winnowing it falls at the hinderend of the heap. 'We send forends to markit, seconds to th' miln for wer-sens, and chickens gets th' hinderends.' s.Lin. Gether up the hinder ends and put them in secks for the hens (T.H.R.). sw.Lin.[1] Kept for poultry. 'They cree'd all the hinder-ends for the herses.' Nhp.[1]

6. *adj.* Late in doing anything, behind others; hindmost. m.Yks.[1], nw.Der.[1]

HINDERLING, *sb.* Obs. Dev. A base fellow, a degenerate person; a groom, underling; a lower servant.

Horae Subsecivae (1777) 223, 224; BAILEY (1721); SKINNER (1671).

HINDERMENT, *sb.* Som. Dev. Cor. [i·ndəmənt.] A hindrance, obstacle.

w.Som.[1] Dev. They'm sinking the road, and I reckon that 'th a bin a hinderment, *Reports Provinc.* (1882) 15. n.Dev. 'Till be zum hinderment ta he, ROCK *Jim an' Nell* (1867) st. 118. nw.Dev.[1] w.Cor. The fire wouldn't burn, 'twas a terrible hinderment (M.A.C.).

HINDERSOME, *adj.* Sc. Nhb. Dur. Cum. Yks. Lan. Wor. Hrf. Glo. [(h)i·ndə(r)səm.] 1. Hindering, impeding, troublesome, esp. of the weather.

Cai.[1], N.Cy.[1] Nhb.[1] The bad weather's very hindersome for the harvist. Dur.[1], Cum.[1], n.Yks.[2], w.Yks. (J.W.), Lan.[1], n.Lan.[1], ne.Lan.[1], Wor. (W.C.B.) Hrf.[1] The weather is hindersome; Hrf.[2], Glo.[1]

2. Tedious, wearisome. Abd. (JAM.)

HINDLE-BAR, *sb.* War. An iron bar used for driving stakes. MORTON *Cyclo. Agric.* (1863).

HINDMOST, *adj.* and *sb.* Sc. Irel. Nhb. Dur. Cum. Yks. Lan. Also in forms hainmost Abd.; hemust Wxf.[1]; henmost Frf.; himbest Dur.; hindmaist, -mast, hinmaist Sc.; -mest Nhb. Cum.[1]; -most Sc. N.Cy.[1] Nhb. Dur.[1] ne.Lan.[1]; hintmest Cum. 1. *adj.* Last, latest, final; also used *adv.*

Sc. He was not hinmost on the fielde, ROGERS *Three Reformers* (1874) 110. Sh.I. So die'll be his hinmost nicht in wir 'oos, BURGESS *Sketches* (2nd ed.) 98. Cai.[1] Abd. I doot I've saired my hainmost day i' the garden noo, MᶜKENZIE *Cruisie Sketches* (1894) vi; [He] gars them pay the hindmost doit, Ye needna doubt, COCK *Strains* (1810) I. 138. Frf. The henmost time I saw him he was layin' doon the law aboot something, BARRIE *Thrums* (1889) xvi. Per. It's no an easy thing to speak to folk at the hindmost minute, *Sandy Scott* (1897) 57. Fif. It was ae nicht in the hinmaist week o' April, MᶜLAREN *Tibbie* (1894) 88. Rnf. Hindmaist, I've a poke o' siller Hauf as big's a knockin' mell, PICKEN *Poems* (1813) I. 105. Ayr. The hindmost Laird of Ardeer was certainly a vera wee droich o' a creatur himsel', SERVICE *Dr. Duguid* (ed. 1887) 253. Lnk. He took me up to the hindmost dance, ROY *Generalship* (ed. 1895) 30. Lth. The grave gudeman, the coo in hand, Cam' soberly an' hinmaist, LUMSDEN *Sheep-head* (1892) 72. Edb. Strip yon birkies o' their hindmaist sark, LEARMONT *Poems* (1791) 318. Bwk. The lav'rock his hinmaist sang had sung, CHISHOLM *Poems* (1879) 19. Slk. An' comfort till their hindmost day, HOGG *Poems* (ed. 1865) 98. Dmf. Stickt there in their hinmaist sleep, REID *Poems* (1894) 1. Wxf.[1], N.Cy.[1] Nhb. Hinmest pipe (R.O.H.). Dur.[1], w.Yks. (J.W.), ne.Lan.[1]

2. *Comb.* (1) Hinmost cut, the last cut of corn on the harvest-field; (2) — o' three, a game played on village greens; cf. hindermost, s.v. Hinder, *adj.*[1]

(1) Rxb. He or she who gets the last cut of the corn is to be first married (JAM.). (2) Cum.[1]

3. Youngest.

Nhb. He's the hinmest lad but he's the clivverest (R.O.H.). Dur. Ah ast fer a laken for t'himbest bairn, EGGLESTONE *Betty Podkin's Visit* (1877) 5.

4. *sb.* The last, the furthermost back; the end, close, the last remains.

Kcd. The week . . . was gettin' near its hin'most, GRANT *Lays* (1884) 110. Per. Tibbie Tirpie, sittin' awa back wi' the hindmost, took to the greetin, CLELAND *Inchbracken* (1883) 63, ed. 1887. Rnf. Some roar'd the hindmost was foremost, WEBSTER *Rhymes* (1835) 6. Ayr. Deil tak the hindmost, on they drive, BURNS *To a Haggis*, st. 4. Lth. The hindmost and the feeblest aft become the first and best, BALLANTINE *Poems* (1856) 58. Nhb. The last o' coffee's Nanny's share, And mine the hindmost o' the tea, WILSON *Pitman's Pay* (1843) 13; Deil tyek the hinmest (R.O.H.). Cum. T'varra hintmest eh thur velvet-plush chaps at we fell in wih pot us intull a girt room, SARGISSON *Joe Scoap* (1881) 165.

HINE, *adv.* Sc. n.Cy. Cum. Yks. Also written hein Cum.[4] n.Yks.[1]; hyne Sc.; and in forms hyn, hynd Sc. 1. *Obsol.* Hence; freq. used as *int.* hence, be off!

n.Cy. GROSE (1790); (K.) Cum. RAY (1691); BAILEY (1721); Cum.[4] n.Yks. Get up, mah bonny yan, an' hine away, ROBINSON *Whitby Sng. Sol.* (1860) ii. 10; n.Yks.[1]; n.Yks.[2] Hine away !

Hence **Hyne,** *sb.* a departure.

Abd. 'A merry hyne to ye,' a mode of bidding good bye to one when the speaker is in ill humour (JAM.).

2. Away, far away, to a distance.

Sc. And on it cam frae the Castle hyne, JAMIESON *Pop. Ballads* (1806) I. 234; A dyke that runs frae ahint the auld fauld hyne ower the way o' the loch, ROY *Horseman's Wd.* (1895) xxxi.

Elg. Hyne up in the glen he met Nell linking to the town, COUPER *Poetry* (1804) II. 74. **Abd.** They've gane hyne awa', ALEXANDER *Johnny Gibb* (1871) xv; Faith I wad thole a Murray ride, Tho' hine out o'er the raging tide, SHIRREFS *Poems* (1790) 354; It's in aneath the castle and hine ben a dark passage. GREIG *Logie o' Buchan* (1899) 147. **Ags.** Hyne far awa (JAM.). **Ayr.** Syne he has gane far hynd out o'er Lord Chattan's land sae wide. *Ballads and Sngs.* (1847) II. 42. **Edb.** Hyn awa' to E'inbrough scoured she, FERGUSSON *Poems* (1773) 108, ed. 1785.

Hence (1) **Hyne-awa**, *adj.* distant, far away; (2) ·till or ·to, *prep.* as far as, to the distance of.

(1) Abd. The wonders that lay 'neath the hyne-awa skies, CADENHEAD *Bon Accord* (1853) 206. (2) Abd. (JAM.)

3. *Obs.* From this time; ere long.

n.Cy. BAILEY (1721); To hine of a while [after a while or short time] (K.); (J.L.) (1783); N.Cy.² Hine of a while.

[1. Sped vs hyne, *Leg. Saints* (c. 1400), ed. Metcalfe, I. 159.]

HINE, HINE-BERRY, see Hind, *sb.¹, adj.*, Hindberry.

HING, *v.* and *sb.¹* Sc. Irel. and n. and midl. counties to Nhp. War. **I.** *v.* Gram. forms. **1.** *Preterite:* (1) Ang, (2) Eng, (3) Hang, (4) Hing, (5) Hung, (6) Ung. See Hang.

(1) m.Yks.¹ Aang', *Introd.* 33. (2) w.Yks. Eŋ, WRIGHT *Gram. Wndhll.* (1892) 132. (3) Sc. MURRAY *Dial.* (1873) 205. Sh.I. I took aff me kjaep, an' hang her apon a nail, *Sh. News* (Dec. 16, 1899). Cai.¹, ne.Yks.¹ 33. w.Yks. Doon't'chimler hang a gert chean, LUCAS *Stud. Nidderdale* (c. 1882) 257; w.Yks.¹ (4) Lin. I went and hing up my coat behind the door (C.L.F.). s.Lin. A hing my coat on yon nail (F.H.W.). (5) ne.Yks.¹ 33. (6) m.Yks.¹ Uong', *Introd.* 36.

2. *Pp.:* (1) Hing'd, (2) Hung, (3) Ung.

(1) na.Yks.¹ 33. (2) Sc. MURRAY *Dial.* (1873) 205. Cai.¹, Nhb.¹, n.Yks.², ne.Yks.¹ 33. w.Yks.¹ (3) m.Yks.¹ Uong', *Introd.* 36. w.Yks. Uŋ, WRIGHT *Gram. Wndhll.* (1892) 132.

II. Dial. uses. **1.** *v.* To hang, suspend; to hang down, droop, be suspended.

Sc. Na, na, he hings his sword on the cleek, SCOTT *Nigel* (1822) xxxvii. Cai.¹ s.Sc. It [gown] hings fine frae his shouthers, SETOUN *Sunshine* (1895) 332. nw.Abd. Hing on yer tatie bree, *Goodwife* (1867) st. 99. Frf. Her little leddyship was all hinging in gold and jewels, BARRIE *Minister* (1891) xxvi. Per. An' saft winds hing the plantin' booers Wi' leaves that rustle, HALIBURTON *Horace* (1886) 67. Fif. Garr'd his head hing like a doken, TENNANT *Papistry* (1827) 8. s.Sc. Wi' the blab frae my nose hinging doon, ALLAN *Poems* (1887) 93. Ayr. Come hing your heids an' mourn thegither, LAING *Poems* (1894) 9. Lnk. Whoever tak's her will just need to hing her up in a cage, FRASER *Whaups* (1895) vii. Edb. The deil ane wad hing on his kettle, LEARMONT *Poems* (1791) 168. Dmf. They were hinging down their heads, SHENNAN *Tales* (1831) 42. Gall. Them that steals hings in a tow, CROCKETT *Moss-Hags* (1895) xxiii. N.Cy.¹ Nhb. Whe's yon cumin' up ower the moor hingin' on hur sweetheart? ROBSON *Sng. Sol.* (1859) viii. 5; Nhb.¹, Dur.¹, e.Dur.¹ Cum. To gar thee sigh, luik sad, or hing thy head? GILPIN *Sngs.* (1866) 157. Wm. We've a flick a bacan hingan i't chimla, *Spec. Dial.* (1877) pt. i. 1. Yks. (K.) n.Yks. Thou stans an' hings the beead, TWEDDELL *Clevl. Rhymes* (1875) 21; n.Yks.¹²³⁴ e.Yks. We had ice-cannles a yahd lang, hingin fre' spoot end, NICHOLSON *Flk-Sp.* (1889) 95; e.Yks.¹ w.Yks. (J.W.); Ah'd rather hing hur up by t'neck, PRESTON *Poems* (1864) 6; w.Yks.¹²³, e.Lan.¹ Der.² This gate hings well and hinders none. nw.Der.¹ Not. It is a fat child, its cheeks fair hing (L.C.M.); Yer mustn't let your hair hing down like that, PRIOR *Renie* (1895) 101; Not.¹; Not.² Big foakes allus 'ings together, if yo offend one, yo offend the lot on 'em. Lin. I slep i' my chair agēān wi' my hairm hingin' down to the floor, TENNYSON *Owd Roä* (1889). n.Lin.¹ He'd said times many that afoore he'd marry her he'd hing hissen up o' th' highest tree e' Notherup. sw.Lin.¹ The berry-bushes are as full as they can hing. The jaw on one side seems to hing. s.Lin. The helter hings up on the naäle in the staäble (T.H.R.). Nhp. Dry up, ye dews, nor threat'ning hing, CLARE *Poems* (1820) 183; Nhp.¹² War. It's nothin' but contrairiness to make 'em hing down like a mastiff dog's, GEO. ELIOT *Floss* (1860) I. 42.

Hence (1) **Hinger-on,** *sb.* a toady, parasite, ' hanger-on.' n.Yks. (T.S.); (2) **Hingit,** *ppl. adj.* drooping, applied to flowers or plants. N.I.¹

2. *Phr.* (1) *to hing about,* (2) — *an a*—, to lounge, loiter about; to hang about; also used *fig.*; (3) — *back,* to be reluctant, unwilling; to hesitate; (4) — *in,* to work away,

go on, push on; to persevere, continue; (5) — *on,* (*a*) to linger, continue; to survive; (*b*) see (4); (6) — *to,* to have an inclination or affection for; to cling; (7) — *fire,* see (3); (8) — *hard for,* see (6); (9) — *the ears,* (10) — *the lugs,* to be crestfallen, abashed, taken aback; (11) — *by the breeirs o' the een,* to be on the eve of bankruptcy; (12) — *for rain or wet,* to threaten or portend rain; (13) — *in the bell-ropes,* a time of suspense; the time elapsing between the calling of banns in church and the wedding; (14) — *in the britchen,* to shirk work, like a lazy horse; (15) — *round,* to saunter about; to loiter, lounge; (16) — *one's hat upon,* to depend on for encouragement, to rely on.

(1) Sc. (JAM.), Cai.¹ Abd. A gryte squad o' them 't hed been hingin' aboot the manse door, ALEXANDER *Johnny Gibb* (1871) xviii. Frf. The memory o' that 'll hing about my death bed, BARRIE *Minister* (1891) xliii. ne.Yks.¹ Sha hings an' trails aboot. e.Yks.¹ w.Yks. While I wor hingin' abaht t'harse 'at shoo went into, CUDWORTH *Dial. Sketches* (1884) 2; w.Yks.¹ sw.Lin.¹ The bairns hing about one so. (2) w.Yks.¹ (3) e.Lth. There was nae hingin back, HUNTER *J. Inwick* (1895) 24. Nhb. He's hingin back (R.O.H.). Yks. (J.W.) (4) Inv. (H.E.F.) Abd. Hing-in, my lads, the day's our ain, SHELLEY *Flowers* (1868) 93; They hang in like grim death (G.W.). (5, *a*) Sc. After hinging on and teaching it a' the summer, SCOTT *Midlothian* (1818) v. n.Sc. (JAM.), Cai.¹, n.Cy. (J.W.) (*b*) Cum.¹ n.Yks.⁴ If t'droot hings on, to'nips 'll be ti neea good ti year. n.Lan. They ust et clout ther cleaths . . . as lang as they wod hing on, *Lonsdale Mag.* (Jan. 1867) 270. (6) n.Yks. They hing sair tl yam [They are very stingy]. Fooaks hings tl their dvarts i' ·. n.Yks.⁴ He's treated her warse 'an a dog, bud sha still hings tiv him. (7) Ayr. The man hung fire a wee, HUNTER *Studies* (1870) 39. e.Lth. Ye've been hingin fire for a gey while, HUNTER *J. Inwick* (1895) 183. n.Cy. (J.W.) (8) sw.Lin.¹ She hings hard for home. (9) w.Yks. We volunteers Will drop our crest, an' hing our ears, When t'Fenian banner waves, TWISLETON *Poems* (c. 1867) *Ep. to W. L.* (10) Bch. I dinna hing my lugs, like ane That has a riven breck, FORBES *Ulysses* (1785) 30. Cum. Theer mun be summat wrang when thou comes heäm hingin thy lugs that way, DICKINSON *Cumbr.* (1876) 115; Cum.¹ (11) Bnff.¹ (12) n.Yks.¹ Applied to the general appearance of the clouds and atmosphere when rain is evidently approaching. ' Ah aimed it wad be wet: it's bin hinging for raan ivver sen sunrise'; n.Yks.⁴ Common. ne.Yks.¹ w.Yks. Hingin for wet, TOM TREDDLEHOYLE *Bairnsla Ann.* (1857) 13; (J.W.) Lin. It hings for rain, BROOKES *Tracts Gl.* sw.Lin.¹ It seems to hing for rain. (13) Cum.³ We're hingin' i't bell reäps—to t'parson I've toak't, 39; Cum.⁴ Cha.¹ From the time the banns of a couple are completed asking in church, to the time they marry. they are said to ' hing i' th' bell ropes.' nw.Der.¹ (14) Nhb.¹ (15) Per. I'se be hingin' round here-awa, an ye maun fesh back the answer belive, CLELAND *Inchbracken* (1883) 197, ed. 1887. (16) n.Lin.¹ That's what I hing my hat upon, i.e. that is what encourages me.

3. *Comb.* (1) **Hing-benk,** the landing-place for ' kibbles '; (2) ·by, a dependent or adherent; a toady, parasite, ' hanger-on'; (3) ·lock, a padlock; (4) ·lug, a poor, lean horse or animal; a miserable, shiftless person; (5) ·lugs, a sullen fellow; (6) ·on, see (2); (7) ·on oven, an oven which is hung over the fire; (8) ·pillick, a slouching, slinking person; (9) ·post, (10) ·stohp, the post on which a gate or door hangs.

(1) Dur. GIBSON *Up-Weardale Gl.* (1870). (2) n.Yks.¹², ne.Yks.¹, w.Yks.¹ Nhp.¹ (3) Nhb.¹ Cum.¹; Cum.⁴ Fitted wid a strang door an' a hing lock, C. *Pacq.* (Apr. 20, 1893) 6, col. 1. n.Yks.⁴ w.Yks. (J.W.), n.Lin.¹ (4) e.Yks. A thoroughly forlorn despairing man is said to be a ' hing lug,' NICHOLSON *Flk-Sp.* (1889) 4; A poor lean miserable thing is termed a ' hing-lug,' ib. 67; e.Yks.¹ (5) w.Yks.² (6) w.Yks.¹ (7) n.Yks. They had a hing-on e-ærven (I.W.). (8) Cum.⁴ (9) n.Lin.¹, Lei.¹ (10) n.Lin.¹

4. *Fig.* To hang, be in suspense, be in a state of uncertainty.

Sc. (A.W.), n.Cy. (A.W.) s.Not. They hevn't raised the money, so the matter hings (J.P.K.).

5. To be beset with, hampered with. Used in *pp.*

n.Yks. He was hung wi' t'apples [he could hardly sell them] (I.W.); n.Yks.² ' I's sair hung wi 't,' I cannot sell the article.

Hence **Hinging,** *ppl. adj.* of a market or sale: stationary, not brisk.

Sc. (A.W.) n.Yks. He could hardly sell them for it was hingin' market (I.W.); n.Yks.²

6. Coal-mining term : to incline or dip. Nhb.[1]

7. With *on* : to start to draw coals.

Nhb. When corves and gins only were in use the men first ' set' each other down into the pit ; and in sending down the men and their gear, men only worked the gin. As soon as the pit hung on, that is, commenced to draw up coals, the labour was performed by horses (R.O.H.) ; **Nhb.**[1], **Yks.** (J.W.)

Hence (1) **Hinger-on**, *sb.* an onsetter in a pit ; (2) **Hinging or Hingen-on**, *sb.* (*a*) a place in a shaft where tubs are taken out and put in ; (*b*) the time at which the pit first begins to draw coal ; (3) **Hing-on**, *int.* a call from the banksman to the onsetter, after any stop, to recommence work.

(1) **Nhb.** Formerly so called from his having to ' hing on ' the corf to the clippers or hook by which it was attached to the winding rope (R.O.H.). (*a, a*) **Nhb.**, **Dur.** NICHOLSON *Coal Tr. Gl.* (1888). (*b*) **Nhb.** Frae hingin' on till howdy maw, Ye hardly knew if gawn or stannin', WILSON *Pitman's Pay* (1843) 29. (3) **Nhb.**, **Dur.** NICHOLSON *Coal Tr. Gl.* (1888).

8. *sb.* The way, fashion, or ' hang ' of a thing ; the way of putting a thing or telling a story.

Sh.I. Whin Eppie widna see da hing o' dis style edder, .. he wid turn practical in a meenit, BURGESS *Sketches* (2nd ed.) 87. **Per.** Ye hae na juist the hing o't as they had it, CLELAND *Inchbrachen* (1883) 65, ed. 1887.

9. Phr. *on the hing*, between times, in the intervals of work.

Banff. He also contrived to preserve his specimens ... in his idle time ' betwixt pairs,'—whilst, as shoemakers would say, they were ' on the hing, SMILES *Natur.* (1876) viii.

[From ON. *hengja* (pret. *hengða*), with change from *wv.* to *sv.*]

HING, *sb.*[2] Lakel.[2] Cum.[4] w.Yks. (C.W.D.) The male salmon, *Salmo salar*, or male trout, *S. fario.*

HINGE, *sb.*, *adj.* and *v.* Sc. Yks. Lan. Chs. War. Wor. Hmp. Also in form **inch** s.Wor.[1] [in̄j.] **1.** *sb.* In *comp.* (1) **Hinge-post** War.[2] ; (2) **-tree**, the upright post of a gate to which the hinges are attached. s.Wor.[1]

2. Phr. *to be off the hinges*, to be out of health. w.Yks.[1]

3. *pl.* *Fig.* Joints.

Lan. If I'd ha' been thirty younger, an' a bit less stiff i' th' hinges, BURNETT *Lowrie's* (1877) viii.

4. *adj.* Active, nimble ; supple, pliant.

Chs.[123] s.**Chs.**[1] Ey)z in-zh on lz legz für ün uwd mon [He's hinge on his legs for an owd mon].

5. *v.* *Fig.* To depend on.

Sc. (A.W.) **Chs.**[1] ; **Chs.**[2] What you say hinges upon what he did.

6. With *up* : to entangle.

Hmp. To be hinged-up, is to get so inclosed on all sides that one cannot get away, HOLLOWAY.

HINGED-BRIG, *sb.* Sc. A draw-bridge.

Per. Its ports and pends, hinged brigs an' slidin' doors, HALIBURTON *Dunbar* (1895) 89.

HINGER, *sb.* Sc. Nhb. Also written **hingar** Abd. ; and in forms **henger** S. & Ork.[1] ; **hingger** Sh.I. [hi'ŋər.]

1. A curtain, hanging.

Sh.I. Shü cam but ower da fluer carryin ane o' da bed hinggers apon her airm, *Sh. News* (Jan. 21, 1899) ; **S. & Ork.**[1]

2. A pendant ; a necklace.

n.Sc. I'll put gowd hingers roun' your cage, BUCHAN *Ballads* (1828) I. 49, ed. 1875. **Frf.** Till only five Remained at last, complete as hingers, Five goodly taes and just five fingers, SANDS *Poems* (1833) 101.

Hence **Hingar-at-lug**, *sb.* an earring.

Abd. Bein' a jeedge o' hingars-at-lugs [earrings] an' sic vanities, MACDONALD *Malcolm* (1875) II. 263.

3. A hinge. Nhb.[1] See **Hanger**, 3. **4.** A loop at the end of a whip-shank on which the whip is hung. *ib.*

5. *Fig.* A settler, a personal remark that takes effect. Nhb. (R.O.H.)

HINGING, *prp.* and *sb.* Sc. Irel. Dur. Cum. Yks. Lan. e.An. Also in form **hingan** Cai.[1] Edb. Cum.[1] **1.** *prp.* In *comb.* (1) **Hinging-chafted**, having hanging or pendulous cheeks ; (2) **-fashion**, in bad health, ill, out of health ; (3) **-lock**, a padlock ; (4) **-lugg**, a grudge ; dislike or enmity towards a person ; (5) **-lugged**, dull, dispirited ; out of humour, sulky ; (6) **-lugs**, hanging ears ; *fig.* crestfallen, abashed ; (7) **-mind**, an inclination or strong disposition to

VOL. III.

do anything ; (8) **-moot**, in low spirits ; (9) **-shouldered**, having sloping shoulders.

(1) **Edb.** Wi' hingan'-chafted Johnny Jow, Wi' nose on's face tae smell, *Carlop Green* (1793) 117, ed. 1817. (2) **w.Yks.** Tha knaws I've been At t'hingin feshun long, .. an I'd gie the wurld At I wur weel an strong, PRESTON *Poems* (1864) 21. (3) **N.I.**[1] (4) **Gall.** ' Such a one has a hinging-lugg at me,' means that one is not well disposed towards me. ' I ... have not a hinging-lugg at a living soul.' MACTAGGART *Encycl.* (1824) 269, ed. 1876. (5) **Cai.**[1] **Gall.** A person is said to be hinging-lugged when, having an ill-will at any one, and apparently sulky, MACTAGGART *Encycl.* (1824) 269, ed. 1876. (6) **Ayr.** I met four chaps yon birks amang, Wi' hingin' lugs and faces lang, BOSWELL *Poet. Wks.* (1803) 11, ed. 1871. (7) **n.Yks.**[1] Ay, he's had a hinging-mind tiv it, ivver syne his brither gaed furrin ; **n.Yks.**[2] (8) **Bnff.**[1] (9) **Edb.** Crouchy Car, wi's humpy gett, And 's hingan'-showthered Bess, *Carlop Green* (1793) 129, ed. 1817.

2. Sloping.

Cum. Hingin' ground, a road gently sloping downwards (J.Ar.) ; **Cum.**[1] A hingan field is one on the side of a hill ; **Cum.**[4] Yon rich hingin eworn-fields, ECHOES *Brokken Statesman*, st. 1.

3. *sb. pl.* Curtains, hangings.

Sc. I am ... winsome ... as the hingin's o' Solomon, HENDERSON *Sng. Sol.* (1862) i. 5. **Gall.** MACTAGGART *Encycl.* (1824) 269, ed. 1876. **Dur.**[1], **w.Yks.**[24]

4. A hinge.

w.Yks. T'door's dropt off t'hingins (Æ.B.). **ne.Lan.**[1], **e.An.**[1], **e.Suf.** (F.H.)

5. A place where clothes are hung to dry.

w.Yks. Ther's no hingin' to yond hahse (Æ.B.).

HINGKAPONK, *sb.* Lakel. Wm. Also written **hinkaponk** Wm. An impostor.

Lakel.[2] Wm. Still in use (W.H.H.). **n.Wm.** Thoo's a lal leein' hingkaponk (B.K.).

HINGLE, *sb.* and *v.*[1] Lan. Chs. Lin. e.An. Also written **hingel** e.An.[2] [i'ŋl, e.An. also i-ŋgl.] **1.** *sb.* A hinge.

e.Lan.[1] s.**Chs.** Irons with which to hang a door (A.G.F.). **e.An.**[12] Nrf. The door is blowed off the hingles, COZENS-HARDY *Broad Nrf.* (1893) 66. **e.Suf.** (F.H.)

2. A wire snare used by poachers. Cf. **hang**, 9.

e.An.[1] Moving easily, and closing like a hinge. **Suf.** (C.T.)

3. The handle of a pot or bucket by which it hangs ; the neck of a bottle. Lin.[1], sw.Lin.[1] **4.** *v.* To snare hares and rabbits, &c. e.An.[1] Hence **Hingling**, *sb.* a snare for pheasants, made with one or with two wires. *ib.*

HINGLE, *v.*[2] ? *Obs.* Sc. To loiter. Abd. (JAM.)

Hence **Hingling**, *ppl. adj.* loitering.

Abd. Artless tales an' sangs uncouth Shamm'd aff the hinglin hours, TARRAS *Poems* (1804) 16 (JAM.). **Flf.** (*ib.*)

HINGUM-TRINGUM, *adj.* Bnff.[1] **1.** In low spirits, in a weak state of health. **2.** Worthless, disreputable.

A doot they're nae the berrie. They hid sic a hingum-tringum horse an' cairt. The fouck it's taen the inn is a real hingum-tringum set.

HINGY, *adj.* Cum. Yks. Lei. Nhp. [(h)i'ŋi, i'ŋgi.]

1. Poorly, dull, heavy ; languid.

Cum.[1] Fadder's o' hingy to-day and nin reet at o' ; **Cum.**[4] Ah's hingy an twiny an' feckless an oot o' fettle. **n.Yks.** He leeaks a hingy leeak (I.W.) ; **n.Yks.**[2] In a hingy soort o' way.

2. Of beer : ' up,' fermenting, ' on the work.'

Lei.[1] ' Bless ye, m'm,' said a drayman of a beer-barrel showing symptoms of internal disturbance, ' it's on'y a bit hingy.' **Nhp.**[1] Particularly applied to beer that ferments in the cask from removal.

HINK, *sb.*[1] ? *Obs.* Hrt. Ken. Also written **hinck** Hrt. A hook used in cutting peas.

Hrt. By the hinck, whose wooden handle is about two feet long, they pull up the laid pease with one hand, ELLIS *Mod. Husb.* (1750) IV. iii ; MARSHALL *Review* (1817) V. 441 ; **Ken.**[1] A hook at the end of a stick, used for drawing and lifting back the peas, whilst they were being cut with the pea-hook. The pea-hook and hink always went together.

HINK, *v.*[1] and *sb.*[2] Sc. Lakel. **1.** ? *Obs. v.* To hesitate, pause.

Sc. Any that saw his strange deport Perceiv'd his maw to hink and jarr, CLELAND *Poems* (1697) 105 (JAM.). **w. & s.Sc.** Not yet quite *obs.* A stammerer hinks in his speech (JAM. *Suppl.*).

2. Phr. *hink, stride, an' lowp*, the game of hop, step, and a jump. Lakel.[2]

z

8. *sb.* Phr. *a hink in one's heart,* a hesitation, misgiving.
The doing of it . . . was a grait hink in my hart, and wrought sear remorse, MELVILL *Autobiog.* (1610) 423, ed. 1842 ; I have ay a hink in my heart about the Covenant, and I have ay a hink in my heart about the work of reformation, BRUCE *Serm.* (1668) in KIRKTON *Ch. Hist.* (1817) 273.
[1. EFris. *hinken,* 'claudicare' (KOOLMAN) ; Dan. *hinke,* to limp. 8. This may be a different word ; cp. ME. *hinke,* apprehension, misgiving (*Gen. & Ex.* 432).]

HINK, *v.*² Cor. Also written ink w.Cor. [iŋk.] With *up* : to cast in one's teeth.
Cor.² When she is vexed she inks it up what she has done for us. She often inks-it-up that she is better than we (M.A.C.).

HINK, HINKAPONK, see Hank, *sb.*¹, Henk, *v.*¹, Hingkaponk.

HINK-HANK, *adj.* and *v.* Gmg. **1.** *adj.* Said of neighbours who are constantly at variance, and provoking each other to quarrel.
They are hink-hank the one on the other all along (W.M.M.).
2. *v.* To be at variance, to be disagreeable, to taunt, to find fault with. (*ib.*)

HINKLIN, see Inklin(g.

HINK-SKINK, *sb.* Sc. A kind of malt liquor, very small beer.
There's first guid ale and syne guid ale, And second ale and some, Hink-skink, and ploughman's drink, And scour-the-gate and trim, CHAMBERS *Pop. Rhymes* (1870) 392.

HINKUM, *sb.* Sc. Also written hincum. **1.** Anything which is tied up into balls, as thread ; *gen.* used *fig.* a young and mischievous boy or girl.
Abd. Come oot o' that ye hinkum ; ye're makin' a' soss o' yer claes. The little hinkum put an en' to the readin' by blawing oot the can'le (G.W.).
Hence **Hinkum-sneevie** or **-snivie,** (1) *sb.* a silly, stupid person ; (2) *adj.* stupid, slothful, lounging.
(1) Abd. (JAM.) (2) Abd. To shame the hincum-sneevie louns wha aye holed on at hame, CADENHEAD *Bon-Accord* (1853) 259 ; You're nae a hincumsneevie slattern, Crouch'd in a corner, *ib.* 179.

HINKUMBOOBY, *sb.* Sc. A children's game ; see below.
The party form a circle, taking hold of each other's hands. One sings and the rest join. . . While doing so they move a little sideways and back again, beating the time . . . with their feet. As soon as the line is concluded, each claps his hands, wheels grotesquely round, singing . . . 'Hinkumbooby, round about.' Then they sing with the appropriate gesture—that is, throwing their right hand into the circle and the left out: 'Right hands in and left hands out,' still beating the time, CHAMBERS *Pop. Rhymes* (1870) 137.

HIN(N, *adj.* Suf. Ess. Yon. Cf. **hinder,** *adv.*
Suf. *s.An. Dy. Times* (1892) ; Suf.¹ A live a hinn house.
Hence **Hin-way(s,** *adv.* in that direction, yonderwards.
Suf. He live at that house up hin way (C.G.B.). e.Suf. (F.H.) Ess. I sweep that way, an' hin ways (S.P.H.).
[ON. *hinn,* that, yon (VIGFUSSON) ; cp. Dan. *hiin,* that, *hiinsides,* beyond, on the other side.]

HINNER, see Hinder, *adj.*¹

HINNIE-SPOT, *sb.* Sh.I. Also written hinnispot. [hi·ni·spot.] A three-cornered piece of wood connecting the gunwales with the stern of the boat.
He lint his breest apo' da boo o' da fowereen, a bit aeft by da hinnispot, *Sh. News* (Dec. 24, 1898) ; JAKOBSEN *Norsk in Sk.* (1897) 61 ; S. & Ork.¹
[Norw. dial. *hynne* and *honne,* a cross-beam (AASEN, s.v. *Hyrning*) + *spott,* a small piece (*ib.*) ; ON. *spotti,* a bit, piece (VIGFUSSON).]

HINNIE-WAAR, *sb.* Sc. A species of sea-weed, *Alaria esculenta.* Sh.I., S. & Ork.¹, Cai.¹
[Norw. dial. *hinna,* a membrane (AASEN) ; Dan. *hinde,* ON. *hinna* ; for *waar* see Ware.]

HINNY, *v.* Der.² nw.Der.¹ [iˑni.] To neigh, whinny.
[I hynnye as a horse dothe, *je hennis,* PALSGR. (1530).]

HINNY, see Honey.

HINT, *v.*¹ and *sb.* Sc. Irel. Also in form hent Or.I. [hint.] **1.** *v.* With *about* or *after* : to watch quietly ; to go about in a quiet, sly manner.

Bnff.¹ To go about having an eye to one's own interest. ' He's eye hintin' aboot, an' fa's in wee mony a gueede bargain.' ' She . . . hints aboot aifter 'im a' wye it he gangs t'keep 'im fae the drink.' Abd. Ye robins hintin teet aboot Fending the frost, TARRAS *Poems* (1804) 44 (JAM.).
2. To teach quietly, to suggest or indicate slightly.
Sc. The fear o' the Lord I sal hint ye, WADDELL *Psalms* (1871) xxxiv. 11.
3. *sb.* An opportunity, occasion ; a rôle.
Abd. Sae look about you ere the hint be past, Ross *Helenore* (1768) 114, ed. 1812. Ags. One asks a hint of a book or an opportunity of running over it (JAM.). Ir. At their first presentation it was their ' hint ' to fall up their knees and ask his blessing, *Paddiana* (ed. 1848) I. 285.
4. A moment of time, a minute.
S. & Ork.¹ Or.I. In a hent the grind-keepers Their grinds wide open threw, *J. Gilpin,* st. 30, in ELLIS *Pronunc.* (1889) V. 807. Cai.¹ Abd. He sprang, And in a hint he claspt her hard and fast, Ross *Helenore* (1768) 107, ed. 1812.

HINT, *v.*² Sc. **1.** To disappear quickly, to vanish ; in *pass.* to be lost.
Sh.I. Whin a body lays a thing oot o der haand i' dis boos, hit"s da sam' as if hit wis hinted, *Sh. News* (Jan. 8, 1898) ; S. & Ork.¹
2. With *back* : to start back.
Frf. While his lithe figure rose and fell as he cast and hinted back from the crystal waters, BARRIE *M. Ogilvy* (1896) 147; In *gen.* use (J.B.).

HINT, *v.*³ Cai.¹ To throw a stone in a peculiar way.
Practised by country boys, the hand holding the stone being struck sharply against the thigh.

HINT, *v.*⁴ Wor. Glo. Hmp. Wil. Also in form hent Glo. [int.] To carry and stow in a barn. See Hent, *v.*²
s.Wor. ' Well-hinted ' hay is such as has been ' well-caught,' ' well-harvested,' not such as has been badly caught by catching weather (H.K.). Glo. I have hented *or* hinted my corn well this year. This barley was well hented, *or* saved, *Horae Subsecivae* (1777) 210. Hmp.¹ Wil. DAVIS *Agric.* (1813) I. 36, ed. 1888 ; Wil.¹ Never zeed a better crop o' wheat, if so be [it] could be hinted well.

HINT, *v.*⁵ Som. Also in form hent. [int, ent.] To wither, to become slightly dry ; also used *trans.*
A man would be told to ' hint ' the vetches before giving them to cattle ; weeds are said to ' hint ' when exposed to the sun (W.F.R.); JENNINGS *Obs. Dial. w.Eng.* (1825) ; W. & J. *Gl.* (1873).

HINT, see Hent, *v.*⁴, Hind, *adj.,* Hunt.

HINTALS, *sb. pl.* n.Yks.² Also in form intles. [iˑntlz.] The heels.
He clicks up his hintals [lifts up his legs as he walks].

HINTER, HINTHER, see Hinder, *adv., adj.*¹

HIONICK, *sb.* Sh.I. **1.** A little, contemptible person. JAKOBSEN *Norsk in Sk.* (1897) 63 ; S. & Ork.¹ **2.** An emaciated person. JAKOBSEN (l. c.).

HIP, *sb.*¹ Sc. Nhb. Lakel. Yks. Lan. Chs. Der. Not Wor. Shr. Glo. Oxf. Wil. [h]ip, ep.] **I.** Dial. forms—
1. *Sing.* : (1) **Ep,** (2) **Epp,** (3) **Hap,** (4) **Hep,** (5) **Hepp,** (6) **Hyp,** (7) **Ip.**
(1) w.Yks. As red as a ep, *Yks. Wkly. Post* (Mar. 27, 1897) m.Lan.¹ (2) w.Yks. Getting stuff to eat—haegs and epps, SnowDEN *Web of Weaver* (1896) 6. (3) n.Sc. (JAM.) (4) Nhb. (R.O.H.) w.Yks.¹²; w.Yks.⁵ The hairy covering of the seeds, when dropped down the backs of persons, causes a disagreeable tickling sensation. . . Saturday afternoon is generally the time when juveniles go ' a gathering heps,' for the purpose of taking a supply with them to school on the Sunday. Lan.¹, e.Lan.¹, Chs.¹, s.Chs.¹, Der.², nw.Der.¹, Not. (J.H.B.), Shr. (B. & H.), Glo.¹, n. Wil. (G.E.D.) [Fie upon heps (quoth the fox), because he coul'd not reach them, RAY *Prov.* (ed. 1678) 142.] (5) w.Yks. Ther noon sees as red as hepps wi' t'keenness o'th frosty neet, BICKERDIKE *Doady Braan,* 17. (6) Lth. Ramblin', an' scramblin' Ower hedges, . . For brummels, hyps, an' haws, SMITH *Merry Bridal* (1866) 35. (7) Oxf.¹ Thur be so many ips an' aaz an the 'edges.
2. *Pl.* : (1) **Hipson,** (2) **Ipsis.**
(1) Oxf. *Science Gossip* (1882) 165. n.Wil. What a lot o' them hipsons there is about to year (E.H.G.). (2) Oxf.¹ MS. add.
II. Dial. meanings. **1.** in *comp.* (1) **Hip-boss,** the gall of the wild rose formed by the insect *Cynips rosae* ; (2) **-briar,** the wild rose, *Rosa canina* ; (3) **-gun,** a popgun

from which hips are fired; (4) -haws, the fruit of the hawthorn, *Crataegus Oxyacantha*; (5) -rose, (6) -tree, see (2).
(1) Shr.¹ (a) n.Cy. (B. & H.), w.Yks.¹, Chs.¹, se.Wor.¹, Glo.¹ (3) Chs.¹, s.Chs.¹ (4) Lakel.² (5) Glo.¹ (6) Nhb. (R.O.H.), Glo.¹
2. The berry of the hawthorn, *Crataegus Oxyacantha*. Not.²
3. *Fig.* A trifle, jot, particle, *gen.* in phr. *not worth a hip.*
Lan. I haven't a memory worth a hep now, WAUGH *Owd Cronies* (1875) v. s.Chs.¹ Ahy dú)nü ky'ae·r ü ep ¡í dunna care a hep].

HIP, *sb.*² Sc. Irel. Yks. e.An. Sur. Wil. [h)ip.] 1. In *comp.* (1) Hip-cloth, a baby's napkin, a cloth wrapped round the hips of infants; see Hippin(g; (2) -locks, the coarse wool which grows about the hips of sheep; (3) -shot or -shotten, halt, lame in the hip, having the hip-joint sprained or dislocated; (4) -strap, a strap which passes down near the hips of the horse to support and hold up the trace; (5) -striddled, girt about the hips.
(1) w.Yks.²⁸ (2) Gall. MACTAGGART *Encycl.* (1824). (3) Fif. Hip-shot they stood up, sprained with many woes, TENNANT *Anster* (1812) 64, ed. 1871. n.Wil. (G.E.D.) [BAILEY (1721).] (4) e.An.¹ (5) Ir. My hipstriddled little codger, CARLETON *Fardorougha* (1836) vi.
2. *Phr.* (1) *hip and hand*, (2) *— and hollion*, *obs.*, completely, entirely.
(1) Ayr. As things were gaun owre hip an' haun' Wi' wrath, baith butt and ben, LAING *Poems* (1894) 107. (2) Frf. O'er, baith hip an' hollion, She fell that night, MORISON *Poems* (1790) 24.
3. *Fig.* A protection, shelter.
Abd. I'll maybe gar ye wish 'at ye had na come so far from your mother's hip this mornin', ELLIS *Pronunc.* (1889) V. 773.
4. A round eminence situated towards the extremity or in the lower part of a hill; a shoulder or corner of a hill.
Sc. (JAM.) Dmf. Round the hip o' the hill comes the sweet Psalm tune, CROMEK *Remains* (1810) 51.

HIP, *v.* and *sb.*⁸ Sc. n.Cy. Nhb. Yks. Lan. Chs. Also in forms ep- Chs.¹; hep- w.Yks.² [h)ip.] 1. *v.* To hop, esp. to hop on one foot. N.Cy.¹, Nhb.¹, w.Yks.¹
Hence (1) Hippinable, *adj.* of stepping-stones: passable, capable of being crossed by jumping from stone to stone; (2) Hippings or Hippens, (3) Hipping-stones, *sb. pl.* stepping-stones across a river; (4) Hippy-beds, *sb.* the game of hop-scotch; see Hip-the-beds.
(1) w.Yks.¹ (2) n.Yks.⁸ w.Yks. (W.A.S.); w.Yks.⁴ E commin back ageean owert' slaap hippins, ii. 287; w.Yks.⁴ Lan.¹ There are two sets of stepping-stones—one known as the 'Pendle Hippings,' the other as the 'Duckpit Hippings,' *Burnley Gazette* (1879). e.Lan.¹, Chs.¹ (3) n.Cy. GROSE (1790); N.Cy.¹, Nhb.¹ n.Yks.⁴ w.Yks.¹ T' 'ippin-steäns doon by t'waither were coovered (F.P.T.); w.Yks.² Lan. He was surprised at dinner at Waddington Hall, and taken near Bungerley Hippingstones in Clitherwood, ROBY *Trad.* (1829) I. 439, ed. 1872; DAVIES *Races* (1856) 275; Lan.¹, ne.Lan.¹ (4) Nhb.¹ Played by hopping or hippin over 'beds' chalked out and kicking a broken crock, or 'playgin,' over the chalk marks with the foot on which the player hips.
2. *Comb.* (1) Hip-hop, with repeated hops; (2) -step-and-loup, the game of 'hop, skip, and a jump'; (3) -the-beds, the game of hop-scotch.
(1) Fif. Arnold's nakit ghaist was seen . . . Loupin hip-hop frae spire to spire, TENNANT *Papistry* (1827) 182. (2) N.Cy.¹ Nhb. Some one suggested 'to hev a bit . . . hip step an' loup,' DIXON *Whittingham Vale* (1895) 38; Nhb.¹ (3) Sc. (J.Ar.)
3. *Fig.* To miss; to pass over, skip.
Sh.I. Mony a time I firyat ta pit in da sets, an' sae whin da sprootins cam' up pieces o' furs wir hipped here an' dere a' ower da rig, STEWART *Tales* (1892) 249. Abd. Let's ilk daintie sip; An' ev'ry adverse bliffert hip, TARRAS *Poems* (1804) 28 (JAM.). Edb. For a' your penetration, Ye've hipt owre coin's depreciation, MACNEILL *Bygane Times* (1811) 9. Peb. The grace was hippit, NICOL *Poems* (1805) *The Run Supper*. ne.Yks. MARSHALL *Rur. Econ.* (1796) Il. 325. w.Yks.¹ s.Chs.¹ Almost exclusively used of passing over a word in reading which one cannot pronounce or understand.
4. *sb.* An omission, the act of passing over. Sc. (JAM.) [I. Suche . . . That hippe aboute in Engelonde, to halwe mennes auteres, *P. Plowman* (B.) xv. 557. LG. *hippen,* 'hupfen' (BERGHAUS).]
HIP, *sb.*⁴ Oxf. In phr. *to take the hip*, to sulk, to turn sulky. (G.O.) Cf. hipped, *ppl. adj.*² 2.
HIP, see Hup(p.

HIPE, *sb.*¹ and *v.*¹ Nhb. Cum. Wm. Yks. Also written hype Nhb. Wm. [h)aip.] 1. *sb.* A particular throw in wrestling.
Nhb. The throw across the hip (R.O.H.); It's hard te say whee's te hae the hype an' get the hoy, *Keelmin's Ann.* (1869) 31. Cum. Here's a parlish good pleaace for swingin hipe, SARGISSON *Joe Scoap* (1881) 21; The merits of his hipe won the applause of the wrestlers, *Carlisle Patriot* (Nov. 9, 1888) 6, col. 3; Cum.¹; Cum.⁴ The opponent is lifted off the ground and swung round to the right (left), at the same time the inside of his right (left) thigh is struck by the left (right) knee, and he is thrown by the hip. There are two forms of the hipe, the 'standing' and the 'swinging'; this last consists of a quick swing off the breast once round, or nearly so, and then a turn over the knee inside the thigh, *Wrestling*, 178. Wm. He threw him wi' t'hype (B.K.). Wm., w.Yks. (C.W.P.)
2. *v.* To throw with a 'hipe' in wrestling.
Cum. To hipe a chip (H.W.); Cum.⁴ Give him a sudden click—'kind o' bear him off his feet'—and then lift and hype, *Wrestling*, 46. Wm. At ivery tussel we hypt 'em an' aw! BOWNESS *Studies* (1868) 35. [Throwing, by lifting from the ground, and rapidly placing one of the knees between the thighs of the antagonist is provincially called hipeing, BLAINE *Encycl. Rur. Sports* (1870) § 462.]

HIPE, *v.*² and *sb.*² n.Cy. Wm. Yks. Lan. Lin. Nhp. Also written hype N.Cy.² Lakel. Wm. n.Yks.¹²⁸ m.Yks.¹ w.Yks.¹⁴⁸ n.Lin.¹; and in form hip w.Yks.⁸ [h)aip.]
1. *v.* Of cattle: to butt, to push with the horns, to gore.
n.Cy. (K.); GROSE (1790); N.Cy.¹, Lakel.² Wm. Sair hyp'd by her mischievous horn, WHITEHEAD *Leg.* (1859) 9; T'kye's hypin yan anudder (B.K.). n.Yks. (T.S.); She will nut mell Nor hipe, MERITON *Praise Ale* (1684) l. 15; n.Yks.¹²⁸⁴, m.Yks.¹ e.Yks. MARSHALL *Rur. Econ.* (1788). m.Yks.¹ w.Yks. (S.P.U.); w.Yks.¹⁸; w.Yks.⁸ Gotten hyped wi' that nasty bull. ne.Lan.¹ n.Lin. A bull 'a-hypin' an' a-hornin' at him thrif paales,' PEACOCK *Taales* (1890) and S. 72; n.Lin.¹, Nhp.¹
Hence Hipy, *adj.* disposed to gore. n.Yks. (I.W.)
2. *Fig.* To gird at, find fault with, to quarrel; to throw out insinuations, attack in reputation; to slander.
n.Cy. BAILEY (1721); N.Cy.² To do one a mischief or displeasure. n.Yks.¹² ne.Yks.¹ They're awlus hiping at ma. m.Yks.¹ He would hipe at the moon if there was nothing else to hipe at. w.Yks. (J.J.B.); Noan o' thee hyping ahaht Sally, sho's reight eniff (S.K.C.); w.Yks.¹ Thou's . . . ollas gnatterin an hypin at him, ii. 304; w.Yks.⁸
Hence Hipy, *adj.* disposed to backbite. n.Yks. (I.W.)
3. To make grimaces or ridiculous gestures; to make mouths at, to grin; to assume appearances, pretend.
n.Cy. (K.); GROSE (1790); N.Cy.², n.Yks.¹²⁴, m.Yks.¹
Hence Hiper, *sb.* (1) a mimic. n.Yks.¹²⁴; ne.Yks.¹; (2) a hypocrite. n.Yks.¹
4. *sb.* A push or poke, a stroke, blow. n.Yks.², w.Yks.⁸ [I. Sw. dial. *hypa*, to beat, strike (RIETZ).]
HIPE, *v.*⁸ and *sb.*⁸ Lin. Also written hype Lin.¹ n.Lin.¹ [aip.] 1. *v.* To limp or halt. n.Lin. SUTTON *Wds.* (1881). Cf. hip, *v.* 2. To go. n.Lin.¹ 3. To lift up or to reach down; to fetch forth anything hidden.
n.Lin.¹ 'He soon hyped it oot when I begun to question him.' The word is employed to indicate great muscular exertion.
4. *sb.* A person's gait. Lin.¹
HIPE, *adj.* Lin. Vexed, disappointed. Lin.¹ See Hipped, *ppl. adj.*
Hence (1) Hipish, (2) Hipy, *adj.* cross, out of temper. (1) sw.Lin.¹ I thought she were a bit hipish. (2) How hipy she is, *ib.*
HIP-HEI-DERRY, *int.* Pem. An exclamation of jollity.
s.Pem. Hip hei derry! round the skerrie, Loud the fiddel goes, *Wedding Song*; (W.M.M.)
HIPINCH, HIPPANY, see Hippin(g.
HIPPED, *ppl. adj.*¹ Sc. Nhb. Also in forms hippee Nhb.¹; hippet Sc.; hippit Sc. Nhb.¹ [hipt, hi·pit.]
1. Injured in the hip; having the muscles of the back and thighs overstrained, esp. from stooping.
Cai.¹ Edb. For we were hippet the morning parade, on account of our gallant men being kept so long without natural rest, MOIR *Mansie Wauch* (1828) xii. Peb. I never pretil onie where At midday, night or morn; And now I'm hippit like a hare, AFFLECK *Poet. Wks.* (1836) 60. Rxb. A term applied to reapers when in

consequence of stooping, they become pained in the back, loins, and thighs (JAM.). **Nhb.**[1]

2. *Comb.* Close-hipped, crouching, sitting close.

Bnff. Close-hipped I sat, thereby design'd to hide Some breekish holes, appearin' when I stride, TAYLOR *Poems* (1787) 4.

HIPPED, *ppl. adj.*[2] Sc. Cum. Yks. Chs. Not. Lin. Lei. Nhp. Hnt. Also in form hiped sw.Lin.[1] [h)ipt.]

1. Hypochondriacal, depressed, melancholy; disordered in intellect.

Sc. (A.W.), **Cum.**[1], s.**Chs.**[1] Nhp.[1] 'She's hipped to death,' she fancies she has all kinds of complaints. Hnt. (T.P.F.) [You are a little hipped, my dear fellow, DICKENS *Mutual Friend* (1865) bk. III. x; He said that W. Pen was the most hipt man in the world, BYROM *Remin.* (1737) in *Chet. Soc.* V. 100.]

2. Out of temper, vexed, cross.

w.Yks. (S.P.U.), Not.[1] sw.Lin.[1] He got quiet hiped about it. Lei.[1] I were quite hipped about it.

HIPPER, *sb.* Irel. Lan. Cor. A description of osiers used in coarse basket-making; *gen.* used *attrib.*

Ir. There were twenty-four hipper switches threshing tobacco, *N. & Q.* (1850) 1st S. ii. 280. Lan. A field in which hipper withies grow near the water side is called a hipper holm, *ib.* 397. Cor. Hipper withies fetch a higher price than common withies, *ib.* [Cp. Swiss dial. *hippe*, 'ein Stück Weidenrinde, von Knaben im Frühling zu einer Pfeife hergerichtet' (*Idiotikon*).]

HIPPETY, *adj.* and *adv.* Sc. Irel. Yks. Nhp. Glo. Suf. Hmp. Dor. Som. Cor. Also written hippity Sc. (JAM. *Suppl.*) Dor.[1]; and in forms hippa-dha s.Don.; hippedde Suf.[1]; hipperty Sc. (JAM.); ippity w.Yks.[2] [h)i'pəti.] In *comp.* (1) Hippety-clinch, (2) -haincher or -hincher, a lame person; (3) -hop, (a) a jumping kind of walk; (b) lamely, in a limping manner, unevenly; (4) -hoppety, a) see (3, a); (b) see (3, b); (5) -hoy, a hobbledehoy, a youth between the time of manhood and boyhood; (6) -pippity, an expression of contempt; (7) -skippertie, in a frisking manner; (8) -tippertie, (a) unstable, light, frivolous; (b) childishly exact or affectedly neat.

(1) s.Don. SIMMONS *Gl.* (1890). (2) Sc. (JAM. *Suppl.*) (3, a) Cor.[2] (b) w.Som.[1] (4, a) Cor.[2] (b) Nhp.[1], Glo.[1], Dor.[1] Som. JENNINGS *Obs. Dial.* w.*Eng.* (1825). w.Som.[1] Poor old fuller, he's a come vor to go all hippety-hoppety [eep'utee-aup'utee] like. Cor.[1] He goes hippety-hoppety. (5) Suf.[1] Hmp. HOLLOWAY. (6) w.Yks.[2] (7) Slk. (JAM.) (8, a) Rxb. A hipperty-tippertie lass ,JAM., s.v. Nipperty). (b) *ib.*

HIPPETY-HAW, *sb.* Shr.[1] **1.** The fruit of the hawthorn, *Crataegus Oxyacantha.* **2.** *Comb.* Hippety-haw tree, the hawthorn.

HIPPIE-DIPPY, see Hipsy-dipsy.

HIPPIN, *sb.* Yks. [Not known to our correspondents.] A cake.

w.Yks. Hippin out o' t'oven, *Nidderdill Olm.* (1874). [Cp. Swiss dial. *hippe*, 'gewürzhaftes, dünnes, in Form einer Röhre zusammen gerolltes Gebäck' (*Idiotikon*); Bavar. dial. *hippen*, 'oblatförmiger Kuchen' (SCHMELLER); MHG. *hipe*, 'hippe, waffel' (LEXER).]

HIPPIN(G, *sb.* Sc. Nhb. Cum. Wm. Yks. Lan. Chs. Der. e.An. Also written hippen Sc. N.Cy.[1] n.Yks.[2] e.Lan.[1]; and in forms hipinch Chs.[1]; hippany e.An.[1]; hippinch s.Chs.[1]; ippin m.Lan.[1] [h)i'pin.] **1.** A baby's napkin, a cloth wrapped round the hips of infants; also in *comp.* Hipping-clout.

Sc. They gae near my arse that steals my hippin', FERGUSON *Prov.* (1641) 33. Cai.[1] Abd. The first hippen to the green was flung, Ross *Helenore* (1768) 10, ed. 1812. Per. Was't a hippen that round our necks ye tucket? STEWART *Character* (1857) 40. Ayr. The only thing that livens up the gloom is the wavin' o' the hippin's owre heid, SERVICE *Notandums* (1890) 80. Rxb. Blankets A' to duds an' tatters torn For hippin clouts, A. SCOTT *Poems* (ed. 1808) 193. Gall. Seen your Granny's hippen clouts? CROCKETT *Grey Man* (1896) 132. Wgt. Meekly groaning under a load of unwashed hippens, FRASER *Wigtown* (1877) 374. n.Cy. GROSE (1790); N.Cy.[1] Nhb. He hawls doon wor hippins, ROBSON *Evangeline* (1870) 367; Nhb.[1] Cum.[4] T'fella at ah hed noo afooar meh waddent be far oot o' hippins when ah left heaam, SARGISSON *Joe Scoap* (1881) 6. Wm. (B.K.), n.Yks.[1234], e.Yks.[1] w.Yks. What wi' lewkin' after t'barns an' dryin' . . . hippins, CUDWORTH *Dial. Sketches* (1884) 11; w.Yks.[12345] Lan. Get thi hippins off

first, CLEGG *Sketches* (1895) 180; Bit of a snicket that's hardly done wearin' hippins, WAUGH *Hermit Cobbler*, vii; Lan.[1], s.Lan.[1], ne.Lan.[1], e.Lan.[1], m.Lan.[1], Chs.[13], s.Chs.[1], nw.Der.[1], e.An.[1]

2. The curtain of a theatre.

Nhb.[1] 'Hoist the hippin' is the common cry of an audience impatient of the delay in starting a performance.

3. *Comp.* Hippin-stall, a seat or recess with boarding at the back and sides.

n.Yks.[2] An old-fashioned seat or recess with solid boarding, in the arm-chair shape.

HIPPING-DAY, *sb.* Yks. The 10th of October; see below.

This festival is called ' hipping-day' from its connection with a confection of hips, HENDERSON *Flk-Lore* (1879) ii.

HIPPING-HOLD, *sb.* Obs. n.Cy. Yks. Also in forms -hawd N.Cy.[2]; -hod n.Yks.[1] A place of gossip, a loitering-place for lounging and gossiping.

n.Cy. (K.); GROSE (1790); N.Cy.[2], n.Yks.[12]

HIPPLE, *sb.*[1] and *v.*[1] n.Cy. Yks. [h)ipl.] **1.** *sb.* A small cock of hay set up to dry. Cf. hibbal.

n.Cy. GROSE (1790). n.Yks. (I.W.), n.Yks.[124] e.Yks. MARSHALL *Rur. Econ.* (1788).

2. *v.* To heap up hay into small cocks for drying. n.Yks.[2] [Damasch shal . . . be as an hypil of stones, WYCLIF (1382) *Isaiah* xvii. 1. OE. *hiepel*, a little heap; dim. of *heap*, heap.]

HIPPLE, *v.*[2] and *sb.*[2] Sc. Irel. Nhb. Also written hipel Ant.; hippal Cai.[1]; hypal(l Sc. (JAM.); hyple, hyppal Sc.; and in form heypal Sc. (JAM.) [hi'pl.] **i.** *v.* To limp, to go lame.

Rxb. (JAM.), N.Cy.[1] Nhb. He cam hipplin alang (R.O.H.); Nhb.[1] Hence (1) Hipplety-clinch, *sb.* a lame or halting person; cf. hippety-clinch, s.v. Hippety; (2) Hypald or Hypalt, (a) *ppl. adj.* lame, crippled; (b) *sb.* a cripple; an animal whose legs are tied; *fig.* a sorry-looking fellow or horse; (c) *sb.* a sheep which ' casts' its fleece as the result of some disease.

(1) Nhb.[1] (2, a) Rxb. (JAM.) (b) Slk. If their bit foggage was a' riven up by the auld raikin hypalts, HOGG *Tales* (1838) 23, ed. 1866. Rxb. (JAM.) (c) Ayr. (*ib.*)

2. *sb.* Sciatica; rheumatic pains in the upper part of the thigh. Cai.[1]

3. A term of contempt for any one; a good-for-nothing fellow.

Abd. I'm na to be o'ergone wi' you, nor ony foul hyppal like ye, ELLIS *Pronunc.* (1889) V. 773. Slk. One who is hungry or very voracious (JAM.). Dmf., Gall. A fellow with loose tattered clothes (*ib.*). Gall. He was as mean a hyple as ere graced fools, MACTAGGART *Encycl.* (1824) 176, ed. 1876. Ant. A lazy hipel, *Ballymena Obs.* (1892).

[1. Hesse dial. *hippeln*, 'hinken' (VILMAR).]

HIPPO, *sb.* Irel. Ipecacuanha; also used *attrib.*

Ir. Even chemists of repute label their bottles Hippo Wine (A.S.P.). N.I.[1]

HIPSEE-WEE, *sb.* Wor. In phr. *to get the hipsee-wee,* to be unable to work, to be in a state of complete idleness.

s.Wor. A con eat, an' drink, an' slip, but a con't work; a've got th' hipsee-wee (H.K.).

HIPSY-DIPSY, *sb.* Sc. Nhb. Also in form hipple-dippie Sc. A castigation; a 'skelping.'

Abd. ' In coorse he'll need hippie dippie'; and on the dog's return, he soon showed what was meant by hippie dippie, by the severe application of a heavy whip, PAUL *Aberdeenshire* (1881) 107. Nhb.[1]

HIRCH, *v.* and *sb.* Sc. **1.** *v.* To shrug the shoulders, Frf. (J.B.) Hence Hirch-and-kick, *sb.* a game formerly popular; see below.

So named because the competitor . . . had to toe the line and kick as high as he could without the aid of any impetus save that of a preliminary hirch or shrug of the shoulders, *ib.*

2. To shiver, to thrill from cold. Sc. (JAM.) **3.** *sb.* A shrug of the shoulders. Frf. (J.B.)

HIRCLE, HIRD, see Hurkle, *v.*, Herd, *sb.*

HIRDICK, *sb.* Som. Also written hirddick. A 'ruddock,' the robin redbreast, *Erithacus rubecula.*

W. & J. *Gl.* (1873). w.Som.[1] *Gen.* called Rabin hirdick. 'Rabin hirdick and Jenny Wren Be God Almighty's cock and hen.'

HIRDLE, HIRDSALE, -SEL, see Riddle, Hirsel, *sb.*[1]

HIRDUM-DIRDUM, *sb.* and *adv.* Sc. Lan. 1. *sb.* Confused, noisy mirth; uproar; also used *attrib.*

Sc. Sic hirdum, dirdum, and sic din, RAMSAY *Tea-Table Misc.* (1724) I. 9, ed. 1873. e.Fif. A lood reishil at the front door which...brochtoor hirdum-dirdum to a premature stan'-still, LATTO *Tam Bodkin* (1864) xi. Edb. O a' ye hirdum-dirdum chiels, Your kintry's shame, an' facs' best shield ! LEARMONT *Poems* (1791) 26. Rxb. (JAM.), ne.Lan.¹

2. *adv.* Topsy-turvy. Rxb. (JAM.)

HIRDY-GIRDY, *sb.* and *adv.* Sc. Nhb. 1. *sb.* A disorderly noise, a disturbance.

Sc. The contention, clamour, and uproar which form the prominent features of a hirdy-girdy (JAM. *Suppl.*). Nhb.¹ Obs.

2. *adv.* Topsy-turvy, in confusion, in a disorderly state. Cf. **hiddy-giddy.**

Sc. He ventured back into the parlour, where a' was gaun hirdy-girdie, SCOTT *Redg.* (1824) Lett. xi; The brains of those we have left behind are all astir, and run clean hirdie-girdie, *ib. Nigel* (1822) v. Fif. To the cross o' Anster ran hirdie-girdie, woman and man, TENNANT *Papistry* (1827) 50.

HIR(E, see Her.

HIRE, *v.* and *sb.* Sc. Nhb. Cum. Yks. Lan. Der. Lin. Wor. s.Wal. Glo. e.An. Also written hier s.Wal.; hyre Nhb. [hair, h)aiˀə(r.] 1. *v.* To engage as servant; *gen.* used *reflex.* : to engage oneself for service, to take service.

Ayr. Gif ye hired at Beltane, there would be ither words amang your win' afore auld Halla' day, AINSLIE *Land of Burns* (ed. 1892) 28. Lnk. Folk cam' in ... Some to hire an' some to fee, NICHOLSON *Kilwuddie* (ed. 1895) 71. Slk. Do you wish to hire, pretty maiden ! HOGG *Tales* (1838) 348, ed. 1866. Dmf. The lassie said she wasna willing To hire under fifty shillings, SHENNAN *Tales* (1831) 39. Gall. Ruddy was his face, and graceful', When first he hired wi' Laird Mane, NICHOLSON *Poet. Wks.* (1814) 113, ed. 1897. Nhb. Whae are ye thinkin' o' hirin' wi ! S. *Tynedale Stud.* (1896) *Courting of Tibbie Tamson*; 'The Bearer John Mather is at Liberty to hire with who he please to Enter the 12 of May' (1794)—'Lines' given to a friend on quitting the service of Jos. Fenwick (R.O.H.). s.Wal. If so be he can hier hisself to a place what has a cottage, *Longman's Mag.* (Dec. 1899) 143. Suf.¹

Hence (1) **Hired-man**, *sb.* a manservant; (2) **Hirer**, *sb.* a person engaged for farm work by the day or for a short period; (3) **Hiring**, *sb.* a statute-fair at which servants are hired; (4) **-day**, *sb.* the day of the hiring-fair; (5) **-Friday**, *sb.* a Friday on which the hiring-fair occurs; (6) **-money**, (7) **-penny**, *sb.* the sum of money given as earnest-money when hiring servants at the fair; (8) **-ship**, *sb.* service; the place of a servant.

(1) Suf. (F.H.) (a) Cai.¹ (3) N.Cy.¹ Nhb. Those who are in want of employment stand with a piece of straw in the mouth. As soon as an engagement has been made, the lads or lasses adjourn to the various attractions which attend a hiring. The usual proclamations are headed ' A hiring for hinds,' or ' A hiring for female servants will be held,' &c. (R.O.H.); Nhb.¹, Cum.² n.Yks.¹ A fruitful source of rustic demoralization ; n.Yks.²⁴, ne.Lan.¹, n.Lin.¹ (4) w.Yks. 'Tis the annual Hiring-day, LISTER *Rust. Wreath* (1834) 24. (5) e.Lth. Ae Hirin Friday I met in wi' Durie doun by, HUNTER *J. Inwick* (1895) 34. (6) s.Wor.¹ The shilling given at a Mop to engage a servant. Glo. (A.B.), Glo.¹ (7) n.Yks.¹ Usually a half-crown, given on concluding a hiring-engagement, by the master to his future servant, and which establishes the bargain ; n.Yks.²⁴ w.Yks. Since thou hast got no place to-day, Let me thy Hiring-penny pay, LISTER *Rust. Wreath* (1834) 32. (8) Abd. SHIRREFS *Poems* (1790) Gl.

2. *Comp.* (1) **Hire-house**, service ; the place of a servant ; (2) **-man**, a hired servant, a farm-labourer ; (3) **-quean**, a maidservant, a servant girl.

(1) Bnff.¹ A wiz sent t'the hire-hoose, fin a wiz bit aucht yer aul', an' nane o' ma maisters or mistresses took any trouble w' ma. (2) Sc. Awa wi' your slavery hiremen, Sic lads as ye ca' foremen, KINLOCH *Ballad Bk.* (1827) 14, ed. 1868. Abd. Hiremen their hats and bonnets pu' Upo' their face, KEITH *Farmer's Ha'* (1774) st. 62. Frf. The wages of a hireman, that is, a man-servant hired for the half year capable to hold the plough and work with horses were formerly 16s. 8d. ; such a man's wages now are £3 or £3 10s., *Statist. Acc.* IV. 15 (JAM.). (3) Sc. The hire-quean has tane my bed, And I am forc'd to flee, KINLOCH *Ballad Bk.* (1827) 24, ed. 1868.

3. *Obs.* To let on hire. Sc. SINCLAIR *Obs.* (1782) 87 (JAM.). Hence **Hirer**, *sb.* one who lets on hire, esp. a horse-jobber. Sc. *ib. Scoticisms* (1787) 43. 4. To rent a house or farm. e.An. (HALL.), Suf.¹ Hence **Hirement**, *sb.* a lease. e.Suf. (F.H.) 5. To borrow money at interest. nw.Der.¹, w.Wor.¹, e.An.¹, e.Suf. (F.H.) 6. To accept, welcome.

Abd. Wally fa' you, Willie, that Ye could nae prove a man, And taen the lassie's maidenhead, She would have hired your han', MAIDMENT *Garl.* (1824) 43, ed. 1868.

7. *sb.* A dealing, transaction, trade.

Edb. They little think they some day may, Get a lick o' sulphur vive, Frae clootie for sic hire in whisky, LIDDLE *Poems* (1821) 126.

8. A condiment or relish.

Cum. This meat wants a deal o' hire (J.W.O.). ne.Lan.¹ White fish is poor stuff without hire.

Hence **Hired** or **Hir't**, *ppl. adj.* seasoned, having condiments or seasoning.

Sc. I have heard inferiors say ' Nae faut but the gentles should sup parridge whan they maun be thrice hired ; wi' butter, and succre, and strong yill ' (JAM.). Abd. Weel hir't brose, ALEXANDER *Johnny Gibb* (1871) viii.

HIREN, *sb.* w.Cy. [Not known to our correspondents.] A peculiar sound like wind heard when the air is still.

Exceedingly mysterious, too, is the sound, as of wind, which is heard among the mountains when the air is still and calm, and which surely foretells a storm. It is known as the ' Hiren,' *Longman's Mag.* (Apr. 1898) 546.

HIRK, see Hurk, v.¹

HIRLING, *sb.* Wm. A thorough thrashing, or beating. (J.A.)

HIRLING, HIRM, see Herling, Harm, v.

HIRMAL, *sb.* Sh.I. A scrap, fragment.

What can be torn da fowl laek dis ! Dey're no da hirmal o' a maester pen left i' his tail, Sh. *News* (Nov. 6, 1897).

HIRN, see Herne, Run, v.

HIRP, *v.* n.Yks.⁴ To raise the back with cold. See **Hirple, 2.**

HIRP, see Harp, sb.¹

HIRPLE, *v.*, *sb.* and *adj.* Sc. Irel. Nhb. Dur. Cum. Wm. Yks. Lan. Chs. Not. Lin. Lei. Nhp. Also written herple Cum.¹ Wm. w.Yks. ; hirpil e.Fif. ; hurple n.Cy. Cum.¹ n.Yks.¹² e.Yks. m.Yks.¹ w.Yks.²⁶ n.Lin. Lei.¹ ; and in form urple w.Yks.² [hiˀrpl, h)əˀrpl, ə̄ˀpl.] 1. *v.* To walk lamely or with difficulty, to limp, hobble ; to move unevenly, esp. of the motion of a hare. Also used *fig.*

Sc. I'll e'en hirple awa there wi' the wean, SCOTT *Antiquary* (1816) xv. Cai.¹ Elg. His doggy hirpling at his heels, COUPER *Poetry* (1804) I. 114. Bch. An' hirplin' after the wil' birds, FORBES *Ajax* (1742) 7. Abd. Content to hirple far behind, SHIRREFS *Poems* (1790) 321. Kcd. Owre the hill he hitch't an' hirplet, GRANT *Lays* (1884) 114. Frf. He gabbled owre the sacred page, He hirpled throwe the prayer, INGLIS *Ain Flk.* (1895) 181. Per. He . . . Lang hirpled through the toun on crutches, SPENCE *Poems* (1898) 76. e.Fif. Mr. Squeaker hirpilt his wa's inbye to the lateran, LATTO *Tam Bodkin* (1864) xxiv. Slg. Nae midnight slipper cramps their taes When hirpling up Parnassus braes, MUIR *Poems* (1818) 7. Rnf. He hirpled in by wi' his cronies, WEBSTER *Rhymes* (1835) 83. Ayr. The hares were hirplin down the furrs, BURNS *Holy Fair* (1785) st. 1. Lnk. 'Twas now high time to hirple hame, MUIR *Minstrelsy* (1816) 28. Lth. Fu' lang had he hirpled about her, M°NEILL *Preston* (c. 1895) 85. Edb. She hirpled into the kitchen, MOIR *Mansie Wauch* (1828) xv. Peb. The hare hirpling slowly among the fern, AFFLECK *Poet. Wks.* (1836) *Introd.* 13. Slk. It hirpled on the bough and sang, HOGG *Poems* (1865) 359. Gall. The speech of the evening . . . ran, or rather hirpled, somewhat as follows, CROCKETT *Stickit Min.* (1893) 11. Kcb. Mawkins hirple owre the frosty lawn, ARMSTRONG *Ingleside* (1890) 151. N.I.¹ Uls. Goats sent out to graze on the grass of the roadside have their fore and hind feet fastened by a short bit of rope, and are said to hirple (M.B.-S.). Ant. *Ballymena Obs.* (1892). n.Cy. *Border Gl.* (*Coll.* L.L.B.); GROSE (1790) ; N.Cy.¹ Nhb. Te see them hirplin' cross the floor, WILSON *Pitman's Pay* (1843) 24 ; Nhb.¹ s.Dur. He hirples about on three legs [of a dog] (J.E.D.). Cum. He slipped and brak his left-leg shin, And hirpl'd sair about, ANDERSON *Ballads* (ed. 1808) 13 ; Tatter mud a bitten t'oald maister gayly sair teuh, for, thoo knoas, he hurpl't aboot t'scheul, SARGISSON *Joe Scoap* (1881) 3 ; Cum.¹ Wm. Ah can hardly hirple an' walk i' these lal shoes (B.K.); (E.C.) e.Yks.[1] w.Yks. HUTTON *Tour to Caves* (1781); WILLAN *List Wds.* (1811); w.Yks.[1] Shoe wor seea full o' pain, herpled an hobbled seea, ii. 288. ne.Lan.[1], Chs.[1 23] Not. There's old B. hirpling along the hedge side (L.C.M.). Lin. (J.C.W.), n.Lin. (M.P.) Nhp. Hirpling round from time to time, CLARE *Village Minst.* (1821) II. 117; Nhp.[1 2]

Hence **Hirploch**, *sb.* a lame creature. Rnf. PICKEN *Poems* (1788) *Gl.*

2. To raise the back from a sensation of cold; to contract the body with cold, crouch, cower down; to starve with cold.

n.Cy. As cattle under a hedge in cold weather, GROSE (1790). n.Yks.[1 2 4], ne.Yks.[1] e.Yks. What are yer hurpling about there for! (Miss A.); MARSHALL *Rur. Econ.* (1788). m.Yks.[1] w.Yks.[5] (s.v. Hurcle); w.Yks.[5] As an ill-clad person on a winter's morning. 'Goas hurpling abart fit to give a body t'dithers to luke at him!' n.Lin. (M.P.) Lei.[1] The feathered songsters, pensive and frigid, hurple from branch to branch, LILLEY *Village Musings.*

Hence (1) **Hurply**, *adj.*, (2) **Urpling**, *ppl. adj.* cringing or crippled with cold or pain, starveling. n.Yks.[2]

3. To be dull and inactive from the effects of severe cold or illness. n.Yks.[1]

4. *sb.* A limp, halt; the act of walking crazily.

Baff.[1] Per. Feent a hirple's in thy hurdy bane, STEWART *Character* (1857) 127. Ayr. Tak' grey hairs and wrinkles, and hirple wi' me, BOSWELL *Post. Wks.* (ed. 1871) 16. Edb. Wi' hirple and whost, frae ingle-side, CARLOP GREEN (1793) 131, ed. 1817.

5. A cripple.

Gall. I'm but a hirple Dick, an' it maitters little aboot me, CROCKETT *Raiders* (1894) xxxiv. Cum. (A.G.F.)

6. *adj.* Lame, limp, tender-footed. Wm. (E.C.)

[1. I saw the hurcheon and the hare In hidlings hirpling heir and thair, MONTGOMERIE *Cherrie* (c. 1600) iii, in *Evergreen* (ed. 1761) II. 99. **2.** Cp. ON. *herpast*, to be contracted as with cramp, *herpingr*, chilling, cramping, cold, *munn-herpa*, mouth-cramp, a contraction of the lips by cold.]

HIR(R, *v.* and *sb.* Sc. Lan. Also written **hur ne.**Lan.[1]; and in forms **hirrie** Sh.I.; **irr** Sc. **1.** *v.* To hound on a dog.

Ayr. Sharp at his heels auld Bawty sprang. Will hirr'd him on, AINSLIE *Land of Burns* (ed. 1892) 192. Gall. MACTAGGART *Encycl.* (1824).

2. In *imp.* an expression used in urging dogs to attack each other or any other animal.

Sh.I. Hirrie, hirrie, Berry, *Sh. News* (Nov. 6, 1897). ne.Lan.[1] Hir at him.

3. *sb.* The call of a shepherd to his dog to drive up cows or black cattle; also in *comb.* **Irrnowt.** Lnk. (JAM.)

HIRRIE-HARRIE, *sb. Obs.* Sc. Also written **hirie-harie.** An outcry after a thief; a broil, tumult; also used *advb.*

Fif. Then hirie-harie! folks did rusch; Then raged the scrimmage and strabusch, TENNANT *Papistry* (1827) 86. Ayr. (JAM.)

HIRRLING, HIRRO, HIRSCHLE, see Herling, Harro, Hirsel, *v.*[2]

HIRSEL, *sb.*[1] and *v.*[1] Sc. Irel. Nhb. Cum. Also written **hersel**(l Sc. Nhb.; **hirsell, hirsil, hirsle** Sc.; and in forms **hirsale** N.Cy.[1]; **hirdsale, hirdsel, hissel** Sc. [hi'rsl, ha'rsl.] **1.** *sb.* A flock or group of sheep; the stock of sheep on a farm; occas. used of cattle or swine; also *fig.* a spiritual flock.

Sc. Ae scabbed sheep will smit the hale hirdsel, RAMSAY *Prov.* (1737). Sh.I. I've seen a whole hirsel of sheep operated on, *Sh. News* (Aug. 7, 1897). Ags. (JAM.) Frf. As the tender herbage to the hungry hersel, LOWSON *J. Guidfollow* (1890) 171. Per. Whare savage hirsels ramp an' roar, FORD *Harp* (1893) 364. Ayr. The herds an' hissels were alarmed, BURNS *To W. Simpson* (1785) st. 24. e.Lth. We want nae scabbit sheep in oor hirsel! HUNTER *J. Inwick* (1895) 194. Hdg. [At Lammermuir] the hogs are not kept in a separate hirsel, and allowed to graze with the ewes, ARMITAGE *Sheep* (1882) 21. Bwk. On Cheviot, 'the flock or hirsel on a large farm forms itself into three, four, or more divisions called cuts, each keeping to its own range of pasture, and feeding gradually upwards to its resting place for the night near the top,' ELLIOTT *Hist. Bwk. Natur. Club*, VIII. 451. Rxb. As the sheep on the farm, or at least one hirsell of them, HOGG *Tales* (1838) 49, ed. 1866. Rxb. We are His hirsel, He does us feed, ELLIS *Pronunc.*

(1889) V. 715. Dmf. SHAW *Schoolmaster* (1899) 349. Gall. The herd left his hirsle amang the green taps, MACTAGGART *Encycl.* (1824) 78, ed. 1876. N.Cy.[1] Nhb. His master's 'hirsel' numbered some fifty score, PEASE *Borderland Stud.* (1893) 48; Nhb.[1] As bonny a hirsel o' sheep they war as ivver aa saa i' me life. Cum. *Gl.* (1851).

2. *Comp.* **Hirsil-rinning**, gathering sheep at a distance. Slk. HOGG *Tales* (1838) 418, ed. 1866.

3. The feeding-ground or place of gathering of a flock of sheep.

Sc. Like a poor lamb that has wandered from its ain native hirsel, SCOTT *Nigel* (1822) xxvi; HERD *Coll. Sngs.* (1776) 24; MORTON *Cyclo. Agric.* (1863). Lnk. I believe he had his ee on Gledshaw Mains ... it was the best hirsel in the parish, FRASER *Whaups* (1895) xiv. Nhb.[1]

4. *Fig.* A gathering, company; a large number of persons or things, a quantity, collection.

Ags. (JAM.) Ayr. Leezie Fizz was ane of a hirsell of braw hizzies, SERVICE *Dr. Duguid* (ed. 1887) 101. Lnk. Sum gaed in hirsells, sum in pairs, RAMSAY *Gentle Shep.* (Scenery ed.) 712. e.Lth. Thae impressions I note down o' the great human hirsel, MUCKLEBACKIT *Rhymes* (1885) 6. Peb. So in a hirsel, frae the north They a' the Cross gaed past, *Lintoun Green* (1685) 16, ed. 1817. Slk. Ye're just telling a hirsel o' eindown lees, HOGG *Tales* (1838) 26, ed. 1866. Wgt. The douce working man wi' a hirsel o' weans, FRASER *Poems* (1885) 177. Ant. A hirsel o' clothes. A hirsel o' weans, *Ballymena Obs.* (1892). Nhb. A great hirsel of wood (J.H.).

5. *v.* To arrange in separate flocks according to some peculiarity in the animals.

Sc. (JAM.) e.Lth. Their lordly and carnivorous chiefs wad hird an' hirsel, or war an' worry, MUCKLEBACKIT *Rhymes* (1885) 168. Dmf. The farms for breeding sheep are from 500 to 2500 acres. In these there is room to hirsel or keep separate different kinds of sheep which makes the want of fences the less felt, *Statist. Acc.* XIII. 573 (JAM.). [As we do not hirsel ... our sheep, ARMITAGE *Sheep* (1882) 63.]

6. Of persons: to arrange, dispose in order. s.Sc. (JAM.)

[1. The same word as ON. *hirsla* (*hirðsla*), safe keeping, custody.]

HIRSEL, *v.*[2] and *sb.*[2] Sc. Nhb. Cum. Yks. Chs. Also written **hersill** N.Cy.[1]; **hirsle** Sc. n.Cy. n.Yks.[1] w.Yks.[1]; **hursle** Cum.[4]; and in forms **hirachle** Bnff.[1]; **histle** s.Chs.[1]; **hurschle** Bnff.[1]; **hurstle** Sc.; **hurzle** Cum.; **huschle** Bnff.[1]; **hushel, hushle** Sc.; **hussel** Cum.[4] **1.** *v.* To move or slide with grazing or friction; to move in a creeping or trailing manner, with the idea of a slight grating noise; also *trans.* to move something with much friction or effort, to cause to slide, to push or roll down.

Sc. He sat himsel doun and hirselled doun into the glen, SCOTT *Guy M.* (1815) xiv; There is many a father, sir, that would have hirsled you at once either to the altar or the field, STEVENSON *Catriona* (1893) xxvii. Sh.I. Geed hiralin aroond lack da staen i da sling, BURGESS *Rasmie* (1892) 16. ne.Sc. He drappit into his chair again, hirsled it up to the side o' mine, GRANT *Kecklton*, 16. Baff.[1] Hurschle our a bit, an' lat ma lie doon. Cowp the cairt, an' hirschle oot the box. They hirschlet the trees down the face o' the hill. Abd. Peter hirsled off his seat, ALEXANDER *Johnny Gibb* (1871) vii. Ked. The bashfu' timid spinster ... Hirslin' back intil a corner Faur the sunlicht wis bit sma', GRANT *Lays* (1884) 86. Frf. He hirsled aboot on his seat, WILLOCK *Rosetty Ends* (1886) 69, ed. 1889. Per. Thrang hirslin' haunch-ways down a brae, SPENCE *Poems* (1898) 139; Thae shapeless, mony-nookit blocks ... Were hirsled frae the impending rocks By lichtnin' rent, STEWART *Character* (1857) 118. e.Fif. She also hirsled nearer to me, LATTO *Tam Bodkin* (1864) xi. Rnf. Ye'll no hirsle aff the stage Afore an ouk gangs o'er ye, PICKEN *Poems* (1813) II. 153. Ayr. They both ... hirsled down the rocks to conceal themselves, LNK. O'er mony a howe and knowe they have had hurstled hame, EWING *Poems* (1892) 12; I hirsled up my dizzy pow, RAMSAY *Poems* (1791) 90. Edb. A gude sheep's head ... And four black trotters ... Bedown his throat had learn'd to hirsle, FERGUSSON *Poems* (1773) 186, ed. 1785. Peb. Tae show her herd, all Satan slee, She's hirselled frae his girn, *Lintoun Green* (1685) 159, ed. 1817. Slk. Ye might hirsel yoursel' up to the corner o' the seat, HOGG *Tales* (1838) 360, ed. 1866. Rxb. When a' the nout gat hirsel'd right, A. SCOTT *Poems* (ed. 1808) 119. Dmf. Yer currie hirsle near Wi' tentie lug tae hear me, QUINN *Heather* (1863) 246. Gall. Some ill devil had, mayhap, long hirsled and harried an innocent body, CROCKETT *Raiders* (1894) xlvii. **n.Cy.** To move slowly and tamely, *Border Gl.* (*Coll. L.L.B.*); **N.Cy.¹** **Nbb.¹** ' Hirsel alang,' move along the seat.

Hence **Hirschlin**, *ppl. adj.* slightly grating.

Bnff.¹ A hear a hirschlin' soon. Faht can 't be ?

2. To move about restlessly, to fidget ; also *trans.*

Nbb.¹ ' Hirsel aboot,' to move restlessly about on a seat. **Cum.¹²;** **Cum.⁴** He'd been hussellan iv his chair fer a canny bit, SARGISSON *Joe Scoap* (1881) 244. **n.Yks.¹, ne.Yks.¹, w.Yks.¹, s.Chs.¹**

3. To work in a hurried, careless, or slovenly manner ; to dress slovenly. **w.** and **s.Sc.** (JAM. *Suppl.*)

Hence (1) **Hushloch**, *sb.* hurried, careless, slovenly work ; one who works in a hurried, careless, or slovenly manner ; (2) **Hushlochy**, *adj.* hurried, careless, slovenly ; also used *advb.* *ib.*

4. To shrug the shoulders.

Cum. *Gl.* (1851); And hurs'lt up his shou'ders, GILPIN *Sngs.* (1866) 275.

5. *sb.* A sliding or grazing motion ; the noise made by one body being dragged or sliding over another, a grating sound. Bnff.¹, Abd., Cld. (JAM.)

6. A confused mass, a heap of things fallen or thrown together carelessly.

Cai.¹ **Bnff.¹** A huschle o' streh cam off o' the hebd o' the sou. ' In a huschle,' in a confused mass ; as ' The aul' fehl dyke cam doon in a huschle aboot thir lugs.'

Hence (1) **Hushloch**, *sb.* a confused heap, tangled mass. **w.** and **s.Sc.** (JAM. *Suppl.*) ; (2) **Hushlochy**, *adv.* all of a heap. *ib.*

7. *Comp.* (1) **Huschle-muschle**, (*a*) a state of great confusion ; (*b*) to put into a state of great confusion ; (2) **Hushel-bushel**, an uproar.

(1, *a*) Bnff.¹ (*b*) Without any hope of reducing the confusion to order ; very often employed to indicate the confusion that may arise in money-matters, or when anything is done in which many people are concerned, *ib.* (2) Fif. A hushel-bushel sune began, *Ballad* (JAM.).

8. A sloven, one who is untidy in dress. **Cai.¹**

Hence **Hushly**, *adj.* disordered, untidy, dishevelled.

Ayr. His auld servant . . . was aye in a sort o' hushly state o' dress, HUNTER *Studies* (1870) 51.

9. A shrug of the shoulders.

Cum. Auld Deavie spak up wid a hursle, ANDERSON *Ballads* (ed. 1808) 116 ; **Cum.⁴** T'Oald'n was ledderan away oa t'time wid his powls, at nobbut wantit a hussel up noo an than teh keep them fra ower-balancen, SARGISSON *Joe Scoap* (1881) 73.

10. An old, worn-out vessel or implement ; *fig.* a worn-out, useless person.

Ags. An auld hushel (JAM.). **Rnf.** I'm but a hushle At ony trade, WEBSTER *Rhymes* (1835) 90. **Dmf.** He lies as straight as old Wull Moor, the Galloway hushel, CARLYLE *Lett.* (Feb. 1838).

11. An iron pen or auger used for boring when red-hot. Dmf. (JAM.)

[1. For on blind stanis . . . hirssillit we, DOUGLAS *Eneados* (1513), ed. 1874, II. 162. Cp. Dan. *ryste*, to shake ; ON. *hyrsta*.]

HIRST, *sb.*¹ Sc. A resting-place ; a small eminence on rising ground.

Abd. Wi' the help of haul' and hirst he joggit on, SHIRREFS *Poems* (1790) 219. **Slk.** He cross'd Murich's hirst nae mair, HOGG *Poems* (ed. 1865) 415.

Hence **Hirstin**, *sb.* a dwelling-place.

Sc. I maun rest an' tak thought in my auld hirstin', WADDELL *Isaiah* (1879) xviii. 4.

HIRST, *sb.*² Bnff.¹ Also in form **hist.** A great number ; a large quantity of anything.

There wiz a hirst o' fouck at the show.

HIRST, HIRSTLE, see Hurst, Hurstle.

HIRSTY, *adj.* w.Som.¹ ' Rusty.'

HIRTCH, *v.* and *sb.* Bnff.¹ [hirtʃ.] **1.** *v.* To move gradually or with jerks.

Hirtch the tuble a bittie nearer the fire. A he wiz unco bauch at the first, bit he shortly hirtcht in by amo' the laive.

Hence **Hirtchin-hehrie**, *sb.* a children's game.

They sit on their hams, and jump round and round, striking their hands alternately before and behind, and crying out ' Hirtchin-hehrie.'

2. To approach in a sly, wheedling fashion.

A kent the bodie wiz needin' something fae ma, fae the wye he cam hirtchin' up t' ma.

3. *sb.* A slight motion or jerk, a slight push.

Gee yir chair a hirtch till a side. Gi ma a hirtch up wee't.

HIRTLE, HIRTS, see Hurtle, *v.*, Hurts.

HIRY-HAG, *sb.* e.Yks.¹ A boys' game, see below.

Several joining hands, endeavour to catch another, who when caught is beaten with caps, the captors crying out—' Hiry—Hiry-hag, Put him in a bag,' &c.

HIS, *poss. pron.* Var. dial. forms and uses in Sc. and Eng. [emph. h)iz, unemph. iz, əz.] **I.** Dial. forms : (1) **As**, (2) **Ee's**, (3) **Es**, (4) **Ez**, (5) **Hee's**, (6) **Hees**, (7) **He's**, (8) **Hez**, (9) **Ho's**, (10) **Is**, (11) **Iz**, (12) **'z**.

(1) **w.Yks** Gret fat brussen gamekeepers at as heels, BYWATER *Sheffield Dial.* (1839) 2. (2) **Sur.** I'll trundle the mop round ee's head, BICKLEY *Sur. Hills* (1890) I. iii. (3) **Dev.** Es haid es as tha moast revin'd goold, BAIRD *Sng. Sol.* (1860) v. 11. **n.Dev.** A new fardelled Bible vrom es Gaffer, ROCK *Jim an' Nell* (1867) st. 66. (4) **w.Frf.,** **e.Per.** Unemph. Did yə sı ̃ez niu hors ? [Did you see his new horse ?] (W.A.C.). **e.Dev.** Let'n kees me wi' th' keeses o' ez meuth, PULMAN *Sng. Sol.* (1860) i. 2. (5) My young-man ez my awn, an' ai'm hee's, *ib.* ii. 16. (6) **Ken.** (G.B.) **Dev.** Ma beluvid es mine, an I am hees, BAIRD *Sng. Sol.* (1860) ii. 16. (7) **e.Lan.¹** **Sus.** Somehow he's head fell out of the manger, EGERTON *Flks. and Ways* (1884) 26. **Sus.** (F.A.A.) (8) **w.Frf.,** **e.Per.** Emph. Đat wε̨z hε̨z wei o'd [That was his version of it] (W.A.C.). (9) **Cum.** Ho's name in her mouth, SCOTT *Midlothian* (1818) xl. (10) **w.Yks.** It is used before voiceless consonants. Is koit [his coat], WRIGHT *Gram. Wndhll.* (1892) 116. (11) **Wm.** His fayce en 'iz head, BLEZARD *Sngs.* (1848) 34. **w.Yks.** Used before vowels and voiced consonants. Iz ās [his house] ; iz muđe(r) [his mother], WRIGHT *Gram. Wndhll.* (1892) 116. **Lan.** E lant us iz waggin, SCHOLES *Tim Gamwattle* (1857) 3. (12) **w.Frf., e.Per.** Rarely cut down to 'z even after vowels (W.A.C.).

II. Dial. uses. **1.** In *comb.* **His lane**, himself alone. Sc. (JAM., s.v. Lane).

2. Used without antecedent : God's.

s.Sc. His presence be aboot us a' to keep us frae evil, WILSON *Tales* (1836) IV. 101 ; This custom is due to reverence, or the superstitious dread of using the name of God in ordinary converse (G.W.).

3. Used of feminine objects : her.

w.Som.¹ How is the cow ?—Well, he idn no better ; I sim I do want to zee un chow 'is queed.

4. Used after proper names as a mark of the possessive instead of 's.

' John Smith his book,' is the commonest inscription in bibles and other books, even of the newest description. So firmly has this . . . taken root, that ' Mary Jones her book,' may also be seen, *ib.*

HIS, HISE, see Us, Heeze.

HISELL, HISEY-PRISEY, see Hisself, Hizy-prizy.

HISH, *v.* Sc. War. Nrf. [h)iʃ.] To make a hissing noise to hound on a dog ; *trans.* to drive away an animal by making a hissing sound ; also used as an *int.* See **Hiss, 3.**

Abd. Giving the cat a smart stroke on the nose [he] said, ' That's worth a score o' your " hish cats," sir,' PAUL *Aberdeenshire* (1881) 49. **Wgt.** The housewife observing him, shook out her apron, saying, ' Hish ! awa,' FRASER *Wigtown* (1877) 276. **War.** I might hish at him by th' hour together, before he'd fly at a real gentlewoman like you, GEO. ELIOT *Floss* (1860) bk. v. ii. **Nrf.** Just you hish them pigs out of my garden ! *Arch.* (1879) VIII. 170. [The Lord . . . ʒaf hem . . . in to hisshing, WYCLIF (1388) 2 *Chron.* xxix. 8. Cp. Du. *hisschen*, to hisse (HEXHAM).]

HISHI-BAW, HISHT, see Hush-a-ba(a, Husht.

HISHIE, *sb.* *Obs.* Sc. In phr. *neither hishie nor wishie*, not the slightest noise, profound silence.

Fif. (JAM.) **e.Fif.** I durst na . . . mak either hishie or wishie for fear o' back-fear, LATTO *Tam Bodkin* (1864) x.

HISK, *v.* and *sb.* n.Cy. Lakel. Yks. Lan. Also Wil. Som. Cor. Also in form **hesk** Wil.¹ w.Som.¹ w.Cor. [h)isk, w.Cy. esk.] **1.** *v.* To draw the breath with difficulty ; to breathe short through cold or pain ; to gasp.

n.Cy. GROSE (1790). **Lakel.¹** **Cum.** Black eh t'feeace an froathen eh t'mooth, an hisken fer wind, SARGISSON *Joe Scoap* (1881) 235 ; **Cum.¹** Used with reference to the difficulty a

person experiences in breathing on plunging into a cold bath. w.Yks. HUTTON *Tour to Caves* (1781); w.Yks.[1] Lan. Draggt lad in t'watter. He hisk't when he went in, R. PIKETAH *Forness Flk.* (1870) 6. ne.Lan.[1] Cor. *Randigal Rhymes* (1895) Gl. w.Cor. I've been hesking all the night (M.A.C.).
2. To draw breath through the closed teeth, making a hissing noise—a sign of alarm or fear.
Lakel.[2] Thoo fair maks yan hisk wi' thi tials aboot goasts.
3. *sb.* A kind of wheezing cough ; a hoarseness. Cf. hask, adj.[1] 7.
Wil.[1] A disease of the throat often fatal to calves. w.Som.[1] Very common in cattle. 'No! tid'n much, 'tis only a bit of a hesk.' Cor. Such a hisk, THOMAS *Randigal Rhymes* (1895) Gl. ; Cor.[2] A sore throat, in cattle or men. w.Cor. Give me something to stop this hesk (M.A.C.).

HISK, see Heisk.

HISKIE, *int.* and *sb.* Sc. Also in form **hisk** Abd. (JAM.) **1.** *int.* A call to a dog. Abd. (G.W.), (JAM.)
2. *sb.* A dog. Bnff.[1] **3.** A hissing sound. Abd. (G.W.)

HISN, *pron.* In *gen.* dial. use in ?Yks. Lan. Midl. and s. and w. counties. Also written **hisen** Glo. e.An.[1] ; **hiszen** Brks.[1] ; **isn** Shr.[1] ; **izən** Hrf. [i'zən.] **1.** Disjunctive possess. *pron.* : his.
† w.Yks. Mah luv is maine, an I is hisn, LITTLEDALE *Crav. Sng. Sol.* (1859) ii. 16. Lan. If that gomerl, Renny Potter, 'ud do his'n, CASTLE *Light of Scarthey* (1895) 77. e.Lan.[1] s.Cha.[1] 69. s.Stf. I honoured my father i' my day, an' I expect Job to do it in his'n, MURRAY *Rainbow Gold* (1886) 97. Not. (J.H.B.), Not.[1] s.Not. He's got mine an' I've got hisn (J.P.K.). Lin.[1] s.Lin. Whose is that ?—It's his'n (T.H.R.). Lei.[1] Nhp.[1] Tan't ourn, but his'n. War.[2] *Introd.* 14 ; War.[3][4], s.War.[1], se.Wor.[1] Hrf. ELLIS *Pronunc.* (1889) V. 75 ; Hrf.[1] It's one of his'n. Shr.[1] *Gram. Outlines,* 48. Glo. Our maister do do well by hisen an' we's trys t' accomadate 'ee as best us can, BUCKMAN *Darke's Sojourn* (1890) 105 ; Glo.[1] Oxf. It ain't his'n ; it's mine (G.O.). Brks. 'Tis na good to try thaay tunes o' his'n, miss, HUGHES *T. Brown Oxf.* (1861) xviii ; Brks.[1] Hrt. ELLIS *ib.* 202. w.Mid. The things 'av got mixt up, I don't 'ardly know what's yourn and what's 'isn (W.P.M.). e.An.[1] Suf.[1] Sur. The Lord don't forget them as looks after His'n, BICKLEY *Sur. Hills* (1890) III. vi. Sus.[1] Hmp. It's not mine, it's his'n (H.B.). s.Hmp. Then be generous with what isn't his'n! VERNEY *L. Lisle* (1870) vi. Wil. Thiccy there be hisn (K.M.G.) ; Wil.[1] 124. n.Wil. My beloved uz mine, an' I be his'n, KITE *Sng. Sol.* (1860) ii. 16. Som. In a prison like his'n a vly wer a rarity, AGRIKLER *Rhymes* (1872) 36. Dev. We mun ha' thik there pasture meådow o' his'n, *Longman's Mag.* (Dec. 1896) 156. [' Whose . . . Charley?' 'His'n, Miss,' DICKENS *Blk. House* (1853) xxxvi.]
2. Conjunctive possess. *pron.* : his.
Nrf. His'n old woman lives up the town, PATTERSON *Man and Nat.* (1895) 44.

HISS, *v.* and *sb.* Sc. Cum. Yks. Sus. Also written **his-** Cum.[1] ; and in forms **huss** Sus.[1] ; **iss** Lnk. (JAM.) [h)is.] **1.** *v.* Of insects : to buzz. Sus.[1] **2.** To express one's discontent ; to be cantankerous. n.Yks.[14]
3. To drive off an animal by making a hissing sound ; also used as an *int.* See **Hish.**
Lnk. I cried, hiss tae cat! plague on ye! hiss! BLACK *Falls of Clyde* (1806) 107.
4. *sb.* A sound used to incite a dog to attack. Sc. (JAM.), Lnk. (*ib.*) **5.** *Comp.* **His-stigh,** a term used in driving pigs. Cum.[1]

HISS, HISSEL, see Iss, Hirsel, *sb.*[1], **Hisself.**

HISSELF, *pron.* In *gen.* dial. use in Sc. Irel. and Eng. Also written **hiszelf** Brks.[1] s.Nrf. Som. ; **hizself** e.Suf. ; **hizzelf** Dor. ; and in forms **essael** Rxb. ; **eszul**(l w.Som.[1] Dev. ; **heesel** Nhb. ; **hisell** Wm. ; **hissel** Sc. Nhb. Cum.[8] Wm. n.Yks.[124] ne.Yks.[1] w.Yks.[1][25] Lan.[1] ne.Lan.[1] e.Lan.[1] m.Lan.[1] Chs.[1] ; **hisseli** w.Yks.[1] Chs.[2] nw.Der.[1] ; **hisseln** w.Yks.[1] **hissen** n.Yks.[14] ne.Yks.[1] e.Yks.[1] w.Yks.[2][3][5] Midl. Not.[12] n.Lin.[1] sw.Lin.[1] Lei.[1] War.[2] Sur. ; **hissens** Lei.[1] War.[2] ; **hisnn** n.Yks. ; **hizsel** Nhb. Dur. Cum. Wm. n.Yks. w.Yks.[2] ; **hizzen** w.Yks.[2] ; **hyssel** Sc. ; **iself** Brks. Ess. ; **issel** Nhb. Der. ; **issen** Der. Lin. ; **izel**(f Lan. Hrf. Glo. Wil. Dor. ; **izzaaf** n.Ken. ; **izzel**(f Nhb. m.Yks.[1] s.Stf. Nhp. Bdf. Suf. ; **izzen** e.Yks. m.Yks.[1] Lei. **1.** Refl. or emphatic : himself.
Sc. MURRAY *Dial.* (1873) 197. n.Sc. He couldna murder the

twa o' them hissel', MACDONALD *Settlement* (1869) 165, ed. 1877. Rxb. ELLIS *Pronunc.* (1889) V. 686. N.I.[1] Nhb. What for hes he not com heesel? (R.O.H.) ; Warmin his sel, BEWICK *Tyneside Tales* (1850) 11. Nhb., Dur. ELLIS *ib.* 646. Cum.[3] Jolly-jist as he co't his-sel, 3. Cum., Wm. ELLIS *ib.* 572. Wm. He thowt 'tle a gittan off be meeakin hisell badly, *Spec. Dial.* (1877) pt. i. 10. n.Yks. (T.S.), n.Yks.[124] ne.Yks.[1] His-sel is less com. in the *s.* Riding. 'He'll a'e ti gan wiv hissen.' e.Yks. ELLIS *ib.* 505 ; e.Yks.[1] m.Yks.[1] *Introd.* 25. w.Yks. Teld him ta cum in an sit hizsen daane, TOM TREDDLEHOYLE *Bairnsla Ann.* (1838) 20; He's a feeal that forgets hisseln, *Prov.* in *Brighouse News* (July 23, 1887) ; Ivery body else a little bit war cracked nor hissen, HARTLEY *Budget* (1867) 10 ; w.Yks.[3] He cares nut . . . seeabetide he can gain his ends an saav hissell, ii. 298 ; w.Yks.[2][3][5] Lan. Gwoan wi us izel, SCHOLES *Tim Gamwattle* (1857) 3 ; Aw wish Tom wur here neaw, to enjoy hisself wi' us, BANKS *Manch. Man* (1881) iii; Lan.[1], ne.Lan.[1], e.Lan.[1], m.Lan.[1] I.Ma. Lettin hisself too low, BROWN *Doctor* (1887) 12. Chs.[1] Midl. A lark . . . sung till oi thowt he 'ud split hissen to pieces, BARTRAM *People Clopton* (1897) 214. s.Stf. ELLIS *ib.* 466. Der. *ib.* 429. nw.Der.[1] Not. He hung hissen (J.H.B.) ; Let him answer hisself, PRIOR *Renie* (1895) 60 ; Not.[12] Lin. The Amoighty's a takkin o' you to 'issen, my friend, TENNYSON *N. Farmer, Old Style* (1864) st. 3. n.Lin.[1] s.Lin. I saw him do it his sen (T.H.K.). sw.Lin.[1] He was shutten up by his-sen. Lei. ELLIS *ib.* 466; Lei.[1] Nhp. ELLIS *ib.* 213. War.[23], se.Wor.[1] Hrf. ELLIS *ib.* 70. Glo. *ib.* 61; 'Ee has to look arter the bizness hisself, BUCKMAN *Darke's Sojourn* (1890) 6. Oxf. (G.O.) Brks. ELLIS *ib.* 95; Brks.[1] A wunt go by his-zelf. Bdf. ELLIS *ib.* 207. Nrf. He wanted to better hissell, JESSOPP *Arcady* (1887) ii. s.Nrf. ELLIS *ib.* 273. e.Suf. *ib.* 280. w.Suf. *ib.* 287. Ess. *ib.* 293. Ken.[1] When he's been married two or three weeks he won't scarcely know his-self. n.Ken. ELLIS *ib.* 137. Sur. It 'ud be a sight better if he kept they to hissen, BICKLEY *Sur. Hills* (1890) I. i; Sur.[1] He's got hisself into trouble over that job. Hmp. He took hisself off (H.C.M.B.). LW.[1] Wil. ELLIS *ib.* 45. Dor. He drove his ekkipage hisself and it was always hauled by four beautiful white horses, HARDY *Laodicean* (ed. 1896) bk. 1. v; He've a hurt hizzelf, BARNES *Gl.* (1863) 23. e.Dor. ELLIS *ib.* 77. Som. The very old Mirschey hizzelf must be in the maid, RAYMOND *Tryphena* (1895) 15. w.Som.[1] Neef ee ka·an dúe ut úz-zuul', Jüm mus uu·lp-m [If he cannot do it by himself alone, Jim must help him]. Dev. Let the genelman come vore and dry his-self, HARTIER *Evening with Hodge in Eng. Illus. Mag.* (June 1896) 254 ; Ole Nick es zul cude zed no wuss, NATHAN HOGG *Poet. Lett.* (1847) 55, ed. 1865.
2. Phr. *not to be hisself,* to be out of his mind, to be mentally deranged ; to be out of health. See **Himself.**
Sc. (A.W.) w.Yks. (J.W.) ; w.Yks.[1] Hee's not hissel. ne.Lan.[1], Chs.[2], nw.Der.[1]

HISSER, *sb.* Nrf. [Not known to our other correspondents.] A frying-pan. (A.G.F.)
HISSIE, HISSY, see Huss(e)y.
HISSING-OWL, *sb.* Wil. The barn-owl, *Strix flammea.* THURN *Birds* (1870) 12.
HISSOCKING, *vbl. sb.* n.Yks.[2] [i·sokin.] Clearing the throat, the attempt to expectorate with a hoarseness in the throat.
HIST, *sb. Obs.* Sc. Irel. A fist. Wxf.[1]
Hence **Histy-fisty,** *adj.* using the fists, with the fists.
Edb. A fa'en star Did spoil his histy-fisty game, An' gai rin'n mar, LEARMONT *Poems* (1791) 160.
HIST, *int.* and *v.* Sc. Irel. Cum. Lan. Lin. Brks. e.An. Ken. [h)ist.] **1.** *int.* in *comb.* (1) **Hist awa**, bye, (2) ~ **up,** (a) a command to a horse to lift up a foot; (b) a call to a horse when it stumbles ; (c) a warning given of a step or elevation ; (3) ~ **ye,** or **Hister, Hysta,** make haste, hurry on, be off.
(1) Lnk. What's the use o' sittin' sighin' here—hist awa bye, Rover! WARDROP *J. Mathison* (1881) 9. (2, a) Brks.[1], Ken. (W. F. S.) (b) Brks.[1] (c) e.An.[2] (3) Cld. (JAM.), Cum.[1], n.Lan.[1]
2. *v.* To make a hissing sound when driving geese or turkeys. Cf. hiss, 3.
w.Ir. Juggy Kelly . . . began, half awake, to hist and hoost vigorously, as if she were driving in geese or turkeys to roost, LAWLESS *Grania* (1892) II. pt. ii. 27.
HIST, see Hirst, *sb.*[2], **Hoist.**
HIST-HAST, *sb.* Cld. (JAM.) A confusion.
HISTIE, *adj. Obs.* Sc. Dry, barren.
Sc. O'er histy height and level plain, WILSON *Poems* (182— To

the Reader. Ayr. But thou, beneath the random bield ... Adorns the histie stibble-field, Burns *To a Mountain Daisy* (1786) st. 4.

HISTLE, see **Hirsel,** *v.²*

HISTORICALS, *sb. pl.* Sc. Historical statements, history.

Ayr. I have come across some bits o' notes and siclike that I had forgotten ... which I think may aiblins yet kythe ... to a purpose in the historicals, Service *Notandums* (1890) 8.

HIT, *v.* and *sb.¹* Var. dial. uses in Sc. Irel. Eng. and Amer. **I.** *v.* Gram. forms. **1.** *Present Tense* : (1) Hat, (2) Het, (3) Hot, (4) Hut. [For further instances see **II.** below.]

(1) Lakel.² w.Som.¹ Mind you don't aa't your head. Dev. The imps wiz vi-erin (be tha zoun) Ta hat ma auf ma pierch, Nathan Hogg *Poet. Lett.* (ed. 1866) and S. 17. (2) Glo.¹ Wil. Slow *Gl.* (189a). Som. Jennings *Obs. Dial. w.Eng.* (1825). nw.Dev.¹ (3) War. *B'ham Wkly. Post* (June 10, 1893) ; War.¹, Bdf. (J.W.B.) (4) Nhb.¹ Glo. 'Twur deark ... An' I cudn't zee to hut wi' the how, Buckman *Darke's Sojourn* (1890) xiii. n.Wil. I seed 'ee hut un I tull 'ee (E.H.G.).

2. *Preterite* : (1) At, (2) Hat, (3) Hatt, (4) Het, (5) Hot, (6) Hut.

(1) m.Yks.¹ Aat, *Introd.* 36. w.Yks. *Gram. Wndhll.* (189a) 137. (2) Sh.I. He hat hit for da hint legs o' wir broon mare, *Sh. News* (Feb. 12, 1898) ; S. & Ork.¹, Cai.¹ Bnff. I heezt the tricker ... an' hat the hallen A thump fu' sicker, Taylor *Poems* (1787) 62. s.Sc. Murray *Dial.* (1873) 205. Nhb.¹ Common. ' He hat him fair atwix the ees.' Dur.¹, Lakel.², Cum.⁴, w.Yks.¹² n.Lin. Sutton *Wds.* (1881) 113. w.Som.¹ Ee aup· wai uz vuy·s-n aat'-n daew·n [He up wi his vist and hat him down]. Dev. 'E henned a gert cob at 'er 'ead, an' hat 'er a dowst ov a whack in tha eye, Hewett *Peas. Sp.* (189a) 64. (3) Sh.I. He hokid da dottle oot o' his pipe, an' hatt hit i' da fire, *Sh. News* (Nov. 4, 1899). (4) s.Not. (J.P.K.) Sus. He's hind leg flew up and het agen t'other horse, Egerton *Flks. and Ways* (1884) 26. Wil. Slow *Rhymes* (1889) 59. Dor. They het me, an' bruised me, Barnes *Sng. Sol.* (1859) v. 7. Som. The little maid het the ho'se, they said, Raymond *Tryphena* (1895) ii. (5) Ir. I hot him that time (A.S.-P.). w.Ir. You just hot it, Lover *Leg.* (1848) I. 8. Dub. He hot me (P.J.M.). Cum.² 160 ed. 1873 ; Cum.⁴, Lei.¹, Nhp.¹² War.¹ ; War.² I up with a pear And hot him there, I up with another, And hot his brother ; War.⁴ s.War.¹ It was him as hot me. Glo.¹ Bck. I hot him a crack o' the head, Verney *Stone Edge* (1868) iv. Bdf. (J.W.B.), e.Suf. (F.H.) (6) Nhb. He hut me (R.O.H.) ; Nhb.¹ Glo. He hut me upon the head, *Horae Subsecivae* (1777) 222. Oxf.¹ Her 'ut I. Som. Jennings *Obs. Dial. w.Eng.* (1825).

3. *Pp.* : (1) A-hat, (2) A-hut, (3) Hatten, (4) Hitten, (5) Hittin, (6) Hot, (7) Hut, (8) Hutten, (9) Iten.

(1) w.Som.¹ He've u-aa't the tap of his vinger all abroad. Dev. 'E'th ahât 'is 'ead agin tha durn ov tha door, Hewett *Peas. Sp.* (189a) 75. (2) Som. (W.F.R.) (3) Nhb. He ɪɴuɴ he' been hatten on the left airm (R.O.H.) ; Nhb.¹ (4) S. & Ork.¹, Cai.¹ Nhb.¹ He gat hitten wiv a pantile. Cum.¹⁴, n.Yks.², e.Yks.¹, w.Yks.¹² Lei.¹ (5) Sc. (Jam. *Suppl.*) (6) Glo.², e.Suf. (F.H.) (7) Glo. Thuck 'un had hut thick 'un stead of thick 'un a hutting thuck 'un, Lysons *Vulgar Tongue* (1868) 46 ; Glo.² (8) Sc. Murray *Dial.* (1873) 205. Nhb.¹ He'd hutten him afore he'd ony chance ti fend. (9) m.Yks.¹ It'u'n, *Introd.* 36. w.Yks. Itn, Wright *Gram. Wndhll.* (189a) 137.

II. Dial. uses. **1.** *v.* In *comb.* with *prep.* and *adv.* : (1) to hit about, (*a*) to lie about ; (*b*) to agree ; (2) — across, to leave the road ; to strike across country ; (3) — away, to throw away ; (4) — back, (*a*) to hinder, injure pecuniarily ; to cause to relapse ; (*b*) to retaliate ; (5) — of, to meet with, come across ; (6) — off, to strike a bargain ; (7) — on, (*a*) to agree, come to terms ; (*b*) to meet ; (*c*) to keep on a peevish, continuous complaining ; (8) — out, to pour or throw out ; (9) — up, (*a*) to trip up ; (*b*) to put together hastily ; (*c*) to throw up ; also *fig.* to resign ; (*d*) to cast in one's teeth ; (10) — with, (*a*) to meet with ; (*b*) to agree with.

(1, *a*) Oxf.¹ I sin your clothes hittin' about the room, *MS. add.* (*b*) n.Yks.² We hit about it. (2) Dor. We be just walking round ... First we het across to Delborough, then athwart to here, Hardy *Woodlanders* (1887) III. xii. (3) Brks.¹ Hit it away, tent vit to yet. Hmp.¹ (4, *a*) w.Som.¹ Very com. Dhik dhae·ur aa·ruɪ aa·t-n baak· maa'yn luyk [That harvest injured him severely]. (*b*) Dev.² (5) w.Yks. Ah hit of a woman t'other daày ; an' ah says tiv 'er, 'Yow're nut a this-coontry woman' (F.P.T.). (6) n.Yks.²

VOL. III.

Hoo hae ye hit off ? (7, *a*) Lakel.² Cum. T'bottanist an' t'farmer hat on egsactly, Farrall *Betty Wilson* (1886) 110 ; Cum.¹ ; Cum.⁴ Ah doan't know who it was, bit we nivver hit on, *W. C. T. X.* (1894) 12. n.Yks.² They hit on varry badly. Hae ye hitton on yet ? e.Yks.¹ We couldn't hit-on at all aboot price for a lang whaal. (*b*) Lakel.² We hat-on at a public house. w.Yks. Just managed to hit on him (C.C.) ; I hit on wi' him on t'pier at Blackpool (M.F.). (*c*) Nhb.¹ (8) Hmp.¹ Wil.¹ Hit it out on the garden patch. (9, *a*) w.Som.¹ He hat'n op, 'bout putting his hand aneast'n—i. e. he tripped him up and made him fall, without touching with his hands. (*b*) *ib.* Here, Bill. take and hat up a bit of a box to put-n in. (*c*) Oxf. (G.O.) Brks. He hit up the farm (W.W.S.). Hmp.¹ Hit 'un up. (*d*) Oxf.¹ *MS. add.* Cor.¹ She het it up to hun that he was drunk last night. (10, *a*) w.Yks. It izzan't oft ta hez a chance Ta hit wi't barns an' me, Blackah *Poems* (1867) 241 ; (M.F.) ; (C.C.) (*b*) w.Yks. (M.F.)

2. *Comb.* (1) Hit-and-miss, a wooden window used in stables, granaries, &c., see below ; (2) -back, a hindrance, pecuniary injury ; a relapse ; (3) -on, an agreement, decision.

(1) sw.Lin.¹ A name given to a kind of wooden windows or shutters ... made in two frames fitted with bars or laths at intervals, and made to slide one in front of the other, so that when the bars coincide it is open, when they alternate it is shut. (2) w.Som.¹ Very com. Twuz u tuur·ubl aa·t-baak· vau·r-n haun ee broa·k-s lag· [It was a great loss to him when he broke his leg]. (3) n.Yks.² It was their own hit on.

3. *Phr.* (1) *to be a bit hit,* to be intoxicated ; (2) *to hit in the head,* to kill by a blow on the head ; (3) — *like a sledge-hammer,* to hit very hard ; (4) — *the eye,* to offend the eye ; (5) — *the road,* to walk fast.

(1) Nhb. (R.O.H.) (2) w.Som.¹ Aay kaecht u guurt kyat ügee·un z-maur·neen ... Aay aa·t-n een dhu ai·d pur·tee kwik [I caught a great cat again this morning ... I knocked it on the head directly]. (3) e.Suf. (F.H.) (4) War.³ I shall never like that drawing—the boat is badly drawn and hits my eye. (5) Nrf. I have been hitting the road something to get here quick, Emerson *Lagoons* (ed. 1896) 40.

4. To throw forcibly.

Sh.I. Fling him [it] ower da raep, or hit him inby da fire, *Sh. News* (Feb. 26, 1898). Brks. Maybe as your gardener just takes and hits it auver the top o' the ground and lets it lie, Hughes *T. Brown Oxf.* (1861) xxxiii.

5. Of a clock : to strike.

Glo. The klock hit ten, *Roger Plowman,* 77 ; Glo.¹ Wil. The clock het zix, tha clock het zeven, Nar zupper diden peer, Slow *Rhymes* (1889) 59 ; Wil.¹ A never stopped till the clock hut dree. Som. Soon as iver it hit three, we was up to milky of a morning (W.F.R.).

6. To knock up : to make.

Dev. Bezides vur nites long arter that, Zich noyze thit goats cud uny hat, Nathan Hogg *Poet. Lett.* (ed. 1866) and S. 49.

7. Of seeds or plants : to germinate ; to promise well for a crop.

n.Yks. ʋapples hit on weel this year (I.W.). nw.Der.¹ Glo. My trees hit well, or my orchard hits well this year, *Horae Subsecivae* (1777) 213. Hrt. This pirky wheat ... often hits well, Ellis *Mod. Husb.* (1750) II. ii. Hmp.¹ The corn hit well. Wil. Britton *Beauties* (1825) ; Wil.¹² w.Som.¹ The mangel didn't hat, so I put'n [the field] to turmuts. Nuudh·ur wau·n u dhai dhae·ur graa·fs ybe gid mee, düd-n aa·t [Neither one of those grafts you gave me, grew]. Dev. A farmer, aged about 25, said, ' The seed didn't 'et this year' (July 1896), *Reports Provinc.* (1897). nw.Dev.¹ [Amer. The peach trees didn't hit this year, *Dial. Notes* (1895) 372.]

8. To point out, indicate ; to discover.

Nhb. Your slaughter hat the way To devils that are in hell, Richardson *Borderer's Table-bk.* (1846) VII. 129 ; Lei.¹ A blot's no way of burning a lamp in fire-damp (R.O.H.). Lei.¹ A blot's no blot till it's hot, *Flk-saw,* 300. [A blot is no blot unless it be hit, Ray *Prov.* (1678) 103.]

9. To find ; to chance upon ; in phr. *to hit it* or — *it off,* to find the scent.

n.Cy. (Hall.) w.Yks. Awl goa too, an' th' weshin' can goa to whear it can hit, Hartley *Clock Alm.* (1881) 53 ; w.Yks.¹ I can hit t'gait. Lan. Grose (1790) *MS. add.* (C.) nw.Der.¹ War. The other side of the village I hit them, Mordaunt & Verney *War. Hunt* (1896) II. 246. Sus., Hmp. Holloway. w.Som.¹ The hounds then hit it up the river, and carried it on with more or less scent through Barton Wood, *Records n.Dev. Staghounds,* 65.

10. To pour out.

Wil.¹ You ought to het a quart o' drenk into 'ee.

A a

11. With *it*: to manage, succeed; to agree.

Sc. Gin I can hit it, nane sall shine Nor be sae braw as you, *Shepherd's Wedding* (1789) 23. **Ayr.** My friend to be, If I can hit it, Burns *To J. Lapraik* (Apr. 1, 1785) st. 14. n.Cy. (J.W.) **Nhb.** Him an' his wife had a bad time on't: they could nivver hit it together (R.O.H.). **n.Yks.²**, **w.Yks.** (M.F.)

12. *sb.* Phr. (1) *a hit in the teeth*, something said to make a man look foolish; (2) *more by hit than wit*, more by good luck than good management; (3) *to mind one's hits*, to embrace one's opportunities.

(1) **Glo.¹** (2) w.**Mid.** (W.P.M.) (3) **Cum.⁴** *Obs.* 'Twas at a feast (whoar youngsters mind their hits), Gilpin *Poetry*, 204. **w.Yks.¹**

13. An abundant crop of fruit or vegetables.

War.² There's a good hit o' taters this turn. **se.Wor.¹**, **s.Wor.¹** **Shr.¹** Theer's a perty good hit o' turmits this time; **Shr.²** **Hrf.¹** A good hit o' fruit; **Hrf.²** **Glo.** We have a hit this year. Grose (1790); **Glo.¹** **Sur.¹** They will say 'A good hit of seeds' for a good plant of clover. **Hmp.¹**

HIT, *pron.* and *sb.²* Sc. Nhb. Amer. Also in forms hed Cai.¹; hedt S. & Ork.¹; hid Or.I. Cai.¹ [hit, hid.]

1. *pron.* Emphatic form of the pron. *it.*

Sc. Hyt faell doon: did hyt faa† Murray *Dial.* (1873) 189. **Sh.I.** What a soss we wir in last year afore hit wis oot, *Sh. News* (Aug. 27, 1898): An mony a time hit's guided a boat safely ta da noost, Clark *N. Gleams* (1898) 41; **S. & Ork.¹** **Or.I.** Ellis *Pronunc.* (1889) V. 790. **Cai.** *ib.* 787; **Cai.¹** Hid's a fac'. **Abd.** Atween hit an' the tree it grippit a buik, Macdonald *Sir Gibbie* (1879) xlvi. w.**Frf.**, e.**Per.** I tuk ðə tiðər stik, ån hit wẹznä läng ənuf näðər [I took the other stick, and it wasn't long enough either] (W.A.C.). **Edb.** The vera smell o' hit They donna dree, Crawford *Poems* (1798) 53. **Nhb.¹** That's hit, noo. [**Amer.** A native on seeing a trolley car . . . asks, 'Does hit run hit, or hit run hit!' *Dial. Notes* (1896) I. 376.]

2. *sb.* The principal actor in certain games; the 'he.'

Nhb.¹ This is sometimes decided by a race to the playground, all crying out as they run, 'Last there's hit.' The boy who is hit has either to catch the others, give a back, or whatever may be required in the game. In the progress of a boys' game the inquiry is frequently heard, 'Whe's hit?' meaning who is the player.

HITCH, *sb.¹* Nhb. Wor. [hitʃ.] 1. A chest. **Nhb.¹**

2. The enclosure of hurdles in which sheep are penned while eating roots.

Wor. I have seen as many as a hundred sheep in a hitch about the size of this room. When they had bitten off the roots the hitch would be moved to a fresh place (E.S.).

[1. Whyche or hutche, *cista*, *Prompt.*]

HITCH, *v.¹* and *sb.²* Var. dial. uses in Sc. Irel. and Eng. Also in form itch w.Yks. Der.¹ Ken.¹ [hitʃ.] 1. *v.* To move about, *gen.* by a series of jerks; to make room, change places; to bestir oneself; also *fig.* to promote.

Ayr. Ainslie *Land of Burns* (ed. 1892) 45. **Peb.** Ilk ane near the fire was hitchin', Affleck *Poet. Whs.* (1836) 109. **Gall.** While his shanks after him he cud hitch, He keep'd up his glorious bonello, Mactaggart *Encycl.* (1824) 79, ed. 1876. **n.Cy.** (Hall.) **Lakel.** Ah cannot hitch Ah's that thrang (B.K.). **n.Yks.¹** **w.Yks.** Ah seem'd az if ah cuddant itch anuther peg, Tom Treddlehoyle *Trip ta Lunnun* (1851) 42; **w.Yks.⁴**; **w.Yks.⁵** Come, be hitching! Hitch along! **Der.¹** **n.Lin.¹** Hitch on a bit; ther's anuther to cum i'to this pew. **Nhp.¹** This sense is aptly illustrated by the distich, on the old beam which separated Bdf. from an insulated portion of Hrt., in the dining room of the late parsonage house, at Mappershall: 'If you wish to go into Hrt., Hitch a little nearer the fire.' When any one is promoted, 'he is hitched on a little.' **s.Wor.** 'E wuz used to sit o' the side o' the bed an' 'itch 'isself in (H.K.). **Hnt.** (T.P.F.) e.**An.¹** A man is often desired to hitch, in order to make room for another; . . to hitch any thing which happens to be in the way; e.**An.²**, **Nrf.** (E.M.) e.**Suf.** Don't keep hitching about (F.H.).

2. With *up*: to lift oneself up. **Dor.** (W.C.)

3. To move a heavy weight with difficulty; to jerk; to reach down.

w.Yks. Come bring it here; na, I can't hitch it, *Leeds Merc.* (Nov. 8, 1884). e.**An.¹** **Suf.** Hitch that er ladder a little more right upper (H.H.); **Suf.¹** Hitch it this waah. **Dev.** Hitch down thicky yeller dog from off the mantelshelf, Phillpotts *Dartmoor* (1895) 85, ed. 1896.

4. To hop on one leg; to spring.

Ked. Owre the hill he hitch't an' hirpled, Grant *Lays* (1884)

114. **N.Cy.¹**, **Nhb.¹** **Lakel.²** Hoo far can thoo hitch! **Cum.** He could ha' hitch't ower a five-bar't yat wi' just liggen ya hand on t'top on't, Richardson *Talk* (1871) 1st S. 50, ed. 1884; **Cum.¹⁴** **Wm.** Hoo far can thoo hitch withoot settin' doon? (B.K.). **n.Yks.¹²⁴** ne.**Yks.¹** Ah'll hitch tha ti yon yat (a boy's challenge). e.**Yks.** Marshall *Rur. Econ.* (1788). **Suf.¹**

Hence (1) **Hitch-a-pagy**, *sb.* [not known to our correspondents] a game; (2) **·hatch**, *sb.* a game similar to 'Drep-handkerchief'; (3) **·hob**, (4) **Hitchey-bed(s**, or **Hitchi-**, *sb.* the game of hop-scotch; (5) **Hitchey-dabber**, *sb.* the game of hop-scotch; the square piece of wood jerked by the foot in the game of hop-scotch; (6) **Hitchy-bay**, *sb.* the game of hop-scotch; in *pl.* the courts marked out for the game of hop-scotch; (7) **·cock-ho**, *sb.* [not known to our correspondents] a game; (8) **·pot**, *sb.* see (4).

(1) **Suf.** (Hall.) (2) **Lan.** All would lay hold of hands, a lad and a lass alternately, and a ring be formed. . . One of the maids then went round on the outside of the ring, with a handkerchief in her hand, which she applied to every pair of hands, and then took away again, repeating as she went round—' Hitch-hatch, hitch-hatch, I've a chicken undermi lap ; Heer I brew, an' heer I bake, An' heer I lay mi clap-cake,' laying the handkerchief at the same time on the arm of some youth or maiden, and running away, in and out, across the ring and round about, the one on whose arm the handkerchief was left following as quick as possible to catch her, and if he or she succeeded in doing so, she must begin and perambulate again, until she can contrive to slip into the vacant space left by her pursuer, when she keeps the station and her pursuer goes round as she did, Bamford *Early Days* (ed. 1849) 156, in *Manch. City News* (Dec. 30, 1899); We had a bout at 'hitch-hatch,' or 'drop napkin,' as some of them called the play, Brierley *Cast upon World* (1886) 122. (3) e.**Suf.** (F.H.) (4) **Nhb.¹** **Lakel.²** (s.v. Hitchi-pot). **Cum.** Some are by inclination led To 'skipping rope' or hitchey bed, *Random Rhymes*, 9; **Cum.⁴** **Wm.** Let's hev a lake at hitchi-bed (B.K.). **n.Yks.¹** (5) **Nhb.** A 'bed' is marked out, and the player throws a 'dabber' over its crossed lines. The dabber is jerked by the foot of the player, who must hop on one foot only. If the foot is put down or the 'dabber' touches a line the player is out. The top bed is marked 'pot,' and the player counts by getting the 'dabber' safely into this bed and calls it 'one-a-pot,' 'two-a-pot,' and so on (R.O.H.); **Nhb.¹**, e.**Dur.¹** (6) e.**Dur.¹** (7) **Suf.¹** (s.v. Move-all). (8) **Lakel.²** **Cum.** Hitchy-pot . . . requires ten divisions, the fourth, fifth, sixth and seventh being formed by sub-dividing the larger and central spaces into triangles. It is not possible to give here a full account of the game, of which there are variations besides those referred to above, which is played with a pot.

5. To run. **N.I.¹**

6. *Obs.* To creep; to linger.

Bch. I hitcht about Lyonessus' wa'as Till I my time cou'd see, Forbes *Ulysses* (1785) 19. **Ken.** (K.), **Lan.¹**

7. *sb.* A sudden movement; a jerk; a limp, a hop or spring from one foot.

Sc. (Jam.), **Cum.⁴** **Chs.¹** To have a hitch in one's gait is to be lame; **Chs.²³**, **Nhp.¹**, **Suf.¹** e.**Suf.** He made a hitch towards me (F.H.).

8. *Comb.* (1) Hitch, Jamie; hitch, Jamie, stride-and-loup, (2) —step-and-jump or —step-and-jump, (3) —stepping, (4) —stride-and-jump or —stride-and-loup, the game or movements of hop-skip-and-jump.

(1) **n.Yks.¹** (2) **N.Cy.¹** **Nhb.** Hitch, step, and loup, I sprang ashore, Gilchrist *Voyage to Lunnin* (1824); (R.O.H.); **Nhb.²** **Cum.** Hitch-step-an'-loup some tried for spwort, Stagg *Poems* (ed. 1805) 133; **Cum.⁴** (3) **Cum.¹** (4) **n.Yks.²⁴**, ne.**Yks.²**

9. A push, impetus; also *fig.* a little temporary assistance.

Sc. (Jam.) **Bch.** I'll gie his birn a hitch, an' help To ease him o' his pain, Forbes *Ulysses* (1785) 32. **Abd.** Both rapid manipulation and an occasional 'hitch' from a brother couper were needed to enable Sandy Mutch to meet his engagements, Alexander *Ain Flk.* (1882) 106. **Dmb.** Ablins the win in a hitch Will soughin blaw ye in the ditch, Taylor *Poems* (1827) 78. **Rnf.** Borrowing frae hope a hitch, Gude faith, they whyles grow vauntie, Webster *Rhymes* (1835) 207. **Ayr.** Come, gie your banes anither hitch Up Hudson's stream, Ainslie *Land of Burns* (ed. 1892) 278. e.**An.¹** Give your stool a hitch.

10. A throw in wrestling.

Cor. Tom proposed to try 'a hitch.' . . Jack knew nothing of wrestling. . . Tom put the tinkeard on his back at every 'hitch,'

UNT *Pop. Rom. w.Eng.* (1865) 63, ed. 1896; You an' me had hitch to wrestlin' once, over to Tregarrick feast, 'Q.' *Wandering Heath* (1895) 105.

11. An impediment; a flaw; a difficulty.

Edb. Fortune, she's a fickle b-t-ch, She's gien me mony a cursed itch, LIDDLE *Poems* (1821) 174. Ant. *Ballymena Obs.* (1892). um.⁴ Lan. Firm in danger's straitest hitch, KAY-SHUTTLEWORTH *carsdale* (1860) II. 296. Nhp.¹ A hitch, in a title to an estate. Wor. A got through Sunnay-School athout a 'itch (H.K.). Nrf. there's a hitch in that bargain, *N. & Q.* (1863) 3rd S. iv. 368.

12. Mining term : a small dislocation of the strata which oes not exceed the height of the coal-seam ; the broken oal found near such a dislocation; also used *attrib.*

Slg. The coal in this district is full of irregularities, stiled by e workmen coups, and hitches, and dykes, *Statist. Acc. Campsie,* V. 329 (JAM.). Ayr. The coal seams in this, as in other districts, re frequently intersected by dykes, hitches and troubles, *Agric. urv.* 50 (*ib.*). N.Cy.¹ Nhb. White stone like hitch, darker at ottom. . . The nature of the material is distinguished as ' hitch- oal,' or ' hitch-stone.' Soft hitch stone, mixed with post, 4 thoms. Soft blue hitch stone, *Borings* (1881) 8, 190; (R.O.H.); hb.¹ Nhb., Dur. Where the explosion occurred was a ' hitch ' r ' trouble ' in the seam of about 9 or 10 feet, *Newc. Leader* (Feb. 5, 1896) 6; A sudden elevation or depression of the strata to he extent of from a few inches to the thickness of the working eam of coal. When of a larger size it is called a dyke, GREEN- ELL *Coal Tr. Gl.* (1849). Dur. (J.J.B.), w.Yks. (S.K.C.)

Hence **Hitchy**, *sb.* coal or stone that is broken as by a 'hitch' ; also used *attrib.*

Nhb. Soft hitchy stone 6 fms. 5 ft., *Borings* (1881) 190; R.O.H.); Nhb.¹

13. A slight twitching pain. e.Suf. (F.H.)

HITCH, *v.*² and *sb.*³ Var. dial. uses in Sc. and Eng. Also in form **hetch** Wil. [h)itʃ.] **1.** *v.* To fasten ; to ttach loosely.

Sc. A brooch or a locket . . . An' mair than a poet can hitch in is metre, VEDDER *Poems* (1842) 204. I.Ma. Quilted and hemmed nd hitched and gored and eylotted and stitched, BROWN *Witch* 889) 21. Der.² Hitch the wheel. nw.Der.¹, Nhp.¹ Hrf. OUND *Provinc.* (1876). Oxf.¹ To hitch a dress is to sew a piece n the top of the skirt. Brks.¹ Hitch yer herse to the gaayte o-ast an' come an' help I get this nitch o' straa upon my back. en. (K.) Som. If old Mr. Gregg . . . had just tried to make isself a bit more pleasant like I'd a hitched the surplice on 'un vi' a deal more pleasure, PALMER *Mr. Trueman* (1895) 7. Dev.¹ or.¹ Don't put too many stitches ; hitch it together.

Hence (1) **Hitchel,** *sb.* a kind of halter for fastening a pony to a fence. e.An.¹; (2) **Hitcher,** *sb.* the 'chape' of buckle. Cor.¹

2. *Comb.* **Hitch-nail,** a strong nail, about two inches ong, with a flat point and a rose head. Nhb.¹

3. *Phr.* **to get hitched,** or **to get hitched up,** to be married.

w.Yks.² Glo. My lass wur sweet enow on I when er 'eard ow I'd-a-fought for 'er, an' 'twarn't long avore we got hitched up ogether, BUCKMAN *Darke's Sojourn* (1890) xxii.

4. To strike against an obstacle ; to entangle ; to catch.

Dor.¹ Zoo hitch'd her lag In brembles, 178. Som. I hitch'd my oot again the stone, RAYMOND *Men o' Mendip* (1898) xviii. n.Som.¹ Must have a boot, vor thick there 'oss he do hitch one oot gin tother, and he've a cut his vetter-lock sure 'nough. Cor. They run'd an' hitch'd me, *T. Towser* (1873) 80.

5. Of rope : to twist. e.An.¹

6. To eke out.

Hrt. To hitch out the penny, ELLIS *Cy. Housewife* (1750) 25.

7. With *in* or *on* : to harness a horse to a vehicle, plough, r harrow.

w.Mid. (W.P.M.) Wil. 'Shall I hitch the pony out vor 'ee, ur?' 'If you do, you'll only have to hitch un in again in five ainutes, Jim!' (G.E.D.) Dor. Hitch in the horses, BARNES Gl. (1863).

8. With *off* or *out* : to unharness, to release horses from work.

w.Mid. After dinner we 'itched off plough, and went on to arrow (W.P.M.). Hmp.(H.E.) Wil. SLOW *Gl.* (1892); Wil.¹ Som. As John hitched out his horse, RAYMOND *Gent. Upcott* (1893) 153.

9. With *up* : to hang up.

Dev. She hitched up the big tea-kettle to the chimney crook, O'NEILL *Idyls* (1892) 4. n.Dev. Cum, you buoys, hitch up yer aps, ROCK *Jim an' Nell* (1867) st. 14.

10. To depend upon.

Chs.¹ It aw hitches upon ahr John behavin hissel whether I come or not. s.Chs.¹ Not common.

11. To agree ; also with *on*.

Som. Very common. A mother will tell you that her maid has been trying for a place—but she and her missus could not hitch on. 'Black-smithing's a trade I never could hitch with' (W.F.R.); When volks relidgion didn't hitch, AGRIKLER *Rhymes* (1872) 63.

12. *pass.* To become entangled or hooked together ; with *in* or *up* : to be arm-in-arm.

Glo.¹ Hmp. HOLLOWAY. w.Cy. *N. & Q.* (1877) 5th S. viii. 156. Dor. They wer a-hitched up, BARNES *Gl.* (1863). Som. JENNINGS *Obs. Dial. w.Eng.* (1825) ; SWEETMAN *Wincanton Gl.* (1885).

13. *sb.* ? *Obs.* A noose ; a knot ; a turn of rope round anything ; a row of knitting.

Fif. Hitch on hitch succeeding fast Aff frae the gowden points were cast, And, sattlin' on the dazzlin' hose, Heigher and heigher still arose, TENNANT *Papistry* (1827) 16. Ayr. Upon her cloot she coost a hitch, An' owre she warsel'd in the ditch, BURNS *Death of Mailie,* l. 3. Gall. MACTAGGART *Encycl.* (1824) 271, ed. 1876.

HITCH, *v.*³ Lin. Oxf. Brks. Hrt. Wil. [itʃ.] **1.** *Obs.* To change crops in an open or common field.

n.Lin.¹ In fallow years no hitching is ever made in any of the fields, and consequently no clover or turnips are raised, *Surv. Kirton-in-Lindsey* (1787).

Hence **Hitching,** *sb.* part of a field ploughed and sown during the year in which the rest of the field lies fallow. Oxf. (HALL.) ; KENNETT *Par. Antiq.* (1695) *Gl.* (s.v. Inhoc).

2. *Comb.* (1) **Hitch-crop,** a crop grown on the best part of fallow land ; (2) **-land** or **-land-field,** see below.

(1) Hrt. We call such a barley crop a hitch crop, as not having a regular tilth made for the same, ELLIS *Mod. Husb.* (1750) VI. iii. (2) Wil. In this course of husbandry, the common-field farmers have thought some of the land too good to lie still for two years : instead, therefore, of sowing the whole of the barley field with clover, they have reserved one-third, or one-fourth of the best of it for vetches, pease, beans . . . for the two years during which the other parts of the fields are in clover ; but taking care to have it ready to come in course with the rest of the field for wheat. This part of the field is called a hookland or hitchland field, DAVIS *Gen. View Agric.* (1811) vii ; Wil.²

3. *Phr. hitching the fields* ; see below.

Brks. A kind of agreement among the parishioners to withhold turning stock out, whilst particular crops are growing, and by which means a few brush turnips, clover, and vetches are sown, *Reports Agric.* (1793-1813) 29.

HITCH, *v.*⁴ Dev.² [Not known to our correspon- dents.] [itʃ.] To beat, thrash.

I'll hitch thy back if the dis'n be quiet.

HITCHEL, see **Hetchel.**

HITCHER. *sb.* Dev.² [Not known to our correspon- dents.] Anything very large.

Was'n 'a a girt hitcher?

HITCHING, *adj.* Dev.² [Not known to our corre- spondents.] Very large. 'Thar' go'th a girt hitchin' rabbert.'

HITE, *v.* n.Cy. Yks. Wor. Shr. Also written **hyte** n.Cy. ; and in forms **ait** w.Wor.¹ ; **heit** Shr.² ; **hight** Wor. ; **hoit** Shr.² [ait.] **1.** To toss as a bull ; to toss as a mother tosses her baby ; to throw a stone. See **Height, 7.**

w.Yks. Ther muthers wor hitein em [the babies] up an daan, TOM TREDDLEHOYLE *Bairnsla Ann.* (1856) 45. Wor. That's right (as a lad picks up a stone), hight it at him ! (W.B.) w.Wor.¹ The lad aited a stoün, an' 'it the 'arse o' the yud. Shr.¹ The büll took after 'er an' ketcht 'er jest as 'er raught the whole . . an' then 'ited 'er clane o'er into the Drench Lane. We'd'n rar raps o' Sruv-Toosday ööth the bwoys tossin' thar poncakes ; Dick 'ited 'is right o'er 'is yed, an' Bob send 'is up the chimley ; Shr.² Hoit it up.

2. To raise the hand as a signal.

Shr.¹ I've bin to the top o' the bonk to call Jack ; the winde wuz so 'igh I couldna mak 'im 'ear, but I 'ited my 'ond at 'im.

3. To run about ; *gen.* in phr. *to hite up and down,* to run idly about.

N.Cy. To run hyting or gadding abroad (K.).

HITEM, *sb.* Cor.² [ai·təm.] Best clothes.

She'm some gay—she do wear hitem to the tea fight and hitem when she do trapesy—but law if you see'd her working in her scrubbs you'd know what a slut her really es.

A a 2

HITH, see **Height**.

HITHER, *adv., adj.* and *v.* Sc. n.Cy. Yks. Not. Nhp. e.An. Sus. w.Som. Also in forms **hatha** Suf.[1]; **hidder** Sc. 1. *adv.* In *comb.* (1) **Hither-and-yon** or **-and-yont**, here and there, backwards and forwards; in a state of confusion ; (2) **-away, hither** ; (3) **-come**, advent, descent ; (4) **-go-there**, a digression ; (5) **-thither**, here and there ; (6) **-toward(s**, towards the present time or place.

(1) **Sc.** (JAM.) **Ayr.** Noo that they're hither and yon frae ane anither, it behoves a' that wish them weel . . . to take tent that a breach is no opened that canna be biggit up, GALT *Sir A. Wylie* (1821) xxxv. **n.Cy.** GROSE (1790); **N.Cy.**[1], **Lakel.**[2], **Nhp.**[1] (2) **Sh.I.** Du cam hidderawa owre da sea, JUNDA *Klingrahool* (1898) 9. (3) **Abd.** An' I wat, for yer lords and ladies, it's no a' to their credit 'at's tauld o' their hither-come, MACDONALD *D. Elginbrod* (1863) I. 162. (4) **n.Yks.**[1] He's a dree au'd chap to talk wiv; his discoorse 's amaist nobbut hither-go-theres ; **n.Yks.**[2] (5) **Fif.** Knollie girdles queer and quaint, Lay hither-thither on the bent, TENNANT *Papistry* (1827) 90. (6) **e.An.**[1], **Suf.**[1], **e.Suf.** (F.H.)

2. To the left.

w.Som.[1] Common. ' Keep hither ' to the driver, ' km-aedh·ur ' [come hither] to a horse.

8. *adj.* Of the one of two objects or sides which is nearer the speaker.

Gall. Along the hither side of the inky pool, CROCKETT *Bog-Myrtle* (1895) 38. **w.Yks.** All down the hither side of the valley, *Leeds Merc. Suppl.* (Dec. 12, 1896) 56. **n.Yks.**[2] Hitherest, the nearest. Not. (L.C.M.) **Nhp.**[2] The hither delf, wung, &c., meaning the nearest to the homestead. **Sus.**[1] He's in the hither croft. **w.Som.**[1] The hither side is the left side—more commonly called the near side.

4. *v.* To assemble in the place where the speaker is.

n.Yks.[2] They come hithering frae all parts.

HITHERACS AND SKITHERACS, *phr.* n.Yks.[2] Odds and ends ; trifling amounts.

HITHERIDGE, *sb.* n.Yks.[2] In phr. *what is the hitheridge on't?* what comes hither in the shape of profit to yourself?

HITHIN, *sb.* Bnff.[1] The eye of the souple of a flail, the ' hooding ' ; see below.

The eye made of a piece of bent ash-wood, fixed to the end of the souple of a flail through which the midshackle passes to couple it with the handstaff.

HITTER, *sb.* Wil.[1] [i·tə(r).] In phr. *to be going off a hitter*, of a cow : to be ill and likely to die.

Hence **Hittery**, *adj.* of cows : suffering from looseness, ill.

HITTER, HITTERIL, see **Hetter**, *adj.*, **Hatterel**.

HITTER-A-BALL, *sb.* Der. A game for young men ; see below. Cf. **knur-and-spell**.

A hole is made in a stone fixed in the ground. A spell with a cup at the end is placed in the hole, and the projecting end of the spell is struck by a stick, ADDY *Gl.* (1891) *Suppl.* 29 ; Der.[2], nw.Der.[1]

HITTHERT, *pp.* Lan. [Not known to our correspondents.] Soiled.

Aw ne'er deeted mi honds yet wi' wark, Tho' they're hitthert wi' dirt an' wi' mire, *Cy. Wds.* (1867) No. xvii. 264.

HITTY-MISSY, *adv.* and *adj.* Sc. Nhb. Cum. Wm. Yks. Lan. Lin. Nhp. e.An. [h]i·ti-misi.] 1. *adv.* At random, haphazard ; accidentally, by chance, uncertain.

Sc. (A.W.) **Nhb.** He went at it hitty-missy (R.O.H.); **Nhb.**[1] **Lakel.**[2] Oor picnic 's a Setterda, an' it's hitty-missy fer a fine day for't, t'way t'glass is gaan doon. **Cum.**[1] The sign of an old inn at Pardshaw was a sportsman firing at a bird, and ' Hitty missy, luck's o' ' ; **Cum.**[4] It was aw hitty missy, . . they didn't oalas hit t'mark, *C. Pacq.* (Dec. 14, 1893) 6. **e.Yks.**[1] Sumtahms theease fooaks at fooakests weather's reet, bud of ther wrang—it's all hitty-missy, *MS. add.* (T.H.) **w.Yks.**[1], **n.Lan.**[1], **Nhp.**[1], **e.An.**[1] **Nrf.** Hitty-missy, as the blind man shot the crow, GLYDE *Garl.* (1872) ii. **e.Suf.** (F.H.)

2. *adj.* Undecided; promiscuous; irregular, unreliable.

Nhb. He can nivvor dee'd i' that hitty-missy way (R.O.H.). **Lakel.**[2] He's nobbut a hitty-missy customer, . . ye mun watch him. **Yks.** (J.W.) **n.Lin.**[1] Sum fooaks likes flooers set in pattrens, bud I like 'em all ony-how, hitty-missy like.

3. *Comb.* **Hitty-missy window** ; see below.

n.Lin.[1] A window made of upright bars of wood, one half of them attached to the frame, the other half to the slide. When the window is shut no light enters ; when open, the bars pass behind each other, and light and air are admitted.

HIUZ, see **Huzz**.

HIV, *sb.* Sc. A hoof.

Cai.[1] **Abd.** Very com. (G.W.) ; Ye had kent by mark o' hiv an' horn, MACDONALD *Malcolm* (1875) II. 287.

HIVAD, *sb.* Sh.I. Also in form **hivik**. A heap ; a lump.

As for da pones, dey'll laekly no geng, for dey're sowder'd tagedder in a sûtie, moorie hivik, *Sh. News* (Dec. 4, 1897) ; Der in wan hivik o' sprootens fir a' at I cleen'd dem only aught days sne syne, *ib.* (July 2, 1898) ; **S. & Ork.**[1]

HIVAROGUE, *sb.* Suf. A violent person, male or female ; lit. highway rogue. e.Suf. (F.H.)

HIVE, *sb.* and *v.* Sc. Glo. Suf. Som. [h]aiv.] 1. *sb.* A crowd, swarm of people.

Lnk. Lads an' lasses, men an' wives, Flock to the toddy-room in hives, WATT *Poems* (1827) 88.

2. The compartment in a pig-sty where the animal sleeps. e.Suf. (F.H.)

3. *v.* To go in crowds.

Peb. Frae the mob amang Within the ring (sae close they hived, O' them was sic a bang), He got that day, *Lintoun Green* (1685) 18, ed. 1817. **Gall.** They will just be hiving hame frae the conventicle, CROCKETT *Moss-Hags* (1895) xlvi.

4. To cherish ; to cover as a hen does her chickens. Glo.[12], Som. (W.F.R.)

HIVE, see **Heave**.

HIVEMAN, *sb.* Nrf. In phr. *as* or *like hiveman*, a term of comparison.

Nrf. Busy as hiveman (P.H.E.` ; Some on 'em swore like hive-men, EMERSON *Son of Fens* (1892) 54.

HIVEN, HIVER, see **Ivin, Heifer**.

HIVER-HOVER, *v.* and *adj.* Stf. War. Wor. Shr. [i·vər-ovə(r).] 1. *v.* To waver, be undecided.

s.Stf. He was just hiver-hoverin' on the pint o' jaggin' up, PIN-NOCK *Blk. Cy. Ann.* (1895) 9. **War.**[28] **w.Wor.**[1] I canna tell if I ought to go or no : I bin 'iver-'overin' over it this wik or more.

2. *adj.* Wavering, undecided.

War.[2] **Shr.**[1] ' Did'n yo' gôô!' ' No, I wuz 'iver-'over about it fur a bit, but as I said I ôôdna, I didna.'

HIVERS, see **Ivers**.

HIVES, *sb. pl.* Sc. Irel. Nhb. Cum. Yks. Lan. Hrf. Also written **hyves** Gall. [h]aivz.] 1. An eruption on the skin ; water-blobs or blisters ; rarely in *sing*.

Sc. Any eruption on the skin, when the disorder is supposed to proceed from an internal cause (JAM.) ; Superficial swellings accompanied with redness, but with little pain, which come on suddenly and go off without trouble, chiefly affecting children and young persons who are of a gross habit, GROSE (1790) *MS. add.* (C.) **Slg.** From hives on the outside to ulcers within, MUIR *Poems* (1818) 265. **Raf.** Hive, pock, an' measles a' at ance, PICKEN *Poems* (1813) II. 118. **Lth.** Hives is used to denote both the red and yellow gum (JAM.). **Gall.** Death . . . Stauk'd furth wi' a' his darts and scythes, In shape o' measles, kinks, and hives, NICHOLSON *Poet. Wks.* (1814) 40, ed. 1897 ; Rushes which come out at times on the skin of infants ; the most dangerous hives are those which come out in the interior, MACTAGGART *Encycl.* (1824). **N.I.**[1] Ant. *Bailymena Obs.* (1892). **s.Don.** SIMMONS *Gl.* (1890). **N.Cy.**[1] **Cum.**[4] Varieties of a skin disease called *Lichea strophulus*. I have seen cases of chicken-pox, *Urticaria* and *Impetigo*, called hives. **w.Yks.** WILLAN *List Wds.* (1811). **n.Lan.**[1]

2. A feverish complaint among children ; an inward feeling of enlargement. Cf. **bowel-hive**.

Inv. A disorder of the bowels in young children, loosely applied to any complaint where there is diarrhœa and wasting (H.E.F.). **Nhb.**[1] There are ' chest hives,' ' bowel hives,' &c., descriptive of an inward heaving or swelling. Hives are not usually outward eruptions, but when so they are commonly called het hives—hot heaves or hot spots. The term hives is also applied to a species of chronic diarrhœa, or feeling of such in the bowels, common in children. **Cum.** (M.P.) ; **Cum.**[4] Inward hives usually means a condition of low health accompanied with diarrhœa.

Hence **Hivy**, *adj.* sickly, weakly.

Cum. Life there was too hard and bleak for hivy children, LINTON *Silken Thread* (1880) 259 ; **Cum.**[4] Children with blue lips and general debility are hivy.

3. A windy distension of the belly in cattle. Hrf.[2]

HIVIE, *adj.* Sc. Also written **hyvie** Rnf. In easy circumstances, affluent.

Cld., Ayr. (JAM.) **Rnf.** Ilk wond'rin peasant saw that she was sweet, An' hyvie lairds e'en own'd that she was fair, PICKEN *Poems* (1813) II. 65.

HIVIK, see Havoc, Hivad.

HIVING-SOUGH, *sb.* Sc. A sound made by bees before they hive.

Gall. It is commonly heard the evening before their departure.
... It is a continued buzzing hum full of melancholy-like cadences, MACTAGGART *Encycl.* (1824) 271, ed. 1876.

HIVY-SKIVY, see Havey-cavey.

HIX, *v.* Sh. & Or.I. To hiccup. Or.I. (J.G.)
Hence **Hixie**, *sb.* a hiccup. S. & Ork.[1]

HIYAL, HIZ, HIZARD, HIZE, see Hale, *adj.*, Us, *pron.*, Hezard, Heeze.

HIZY-PRIZY, *sb., adj.* and *adv.* Nhb. Yks. Chs. Der. Som. Dev. Also in forms hizey-prisey Nhb. ; isie-prices Chs. ; izy-prizy nw.Der.[1] [h]ai·zi·praizi.] 1. *sb.* A corruption of ' Nisi prius,' a law-term.

Nhb. (W.G.), w.Yks.[1] Chs. The one [Judge], viz. my Lord Chief-Justice, sits upon Isie-prices, the other upon matters of misdemeanours and trials for life and death, BRERETON *Travels* (1634) in *Cheth. Soc. Publ.* (1844) I. 154. nw.Der.[1] Som. W. & J. *Gl.* (1873). w.Som.[1] ' We could'n get in to yur no prisoners a-tried, zo we went in the hizy-prizy.' Hence lawyer's tricks, and so any kind of chicanery or sharp practice. 'Come now! honour bright, none of your hizy-prizy.' Dev.[1]

2. Phr. *to be at hizy-prizy*, to be unsettled, quarrelsome, disagreeable.

Yks. A wadn't gan amang 'em, they're all at izy prizy. They're all at izy prizy amang ther's sells, they can't agree (W.H.).

3. *adj.* Quibbling, litigious ; tricky.

w.Som.[1] He's a proper hizy-prizy old fuller.

4. *adv.* At a venture, haphazard. e.Yks.[1] *MS. add.* (T.H.)

HIZZEL, HIZZLE, see Hazel, *sb.*[1]

HIZZY, see Huss(e)y.

HJAUDINS, *sb. pl.* Sh.I. Also in form hjodens. Remains, fragments ; the skeleton or carcase of an animal partly destroyed by decomposition or ravens.

Arty sood 'a' gotten da hjaudins o' him ta mak' tatie soap apon, *Sh. News* (May 22, 1897) ; Da dugs an' corbies . . . wid shûne a left naethin bit hir hjaudins, *ib.* (July 9, 1898) ; He's [a raven] awa ta feast apo' da hjodens o' som' o' da sheep 'at cam' ta demsels last ook, *ib.* (Apr. 29, 1899).

HJOAG, *sb.* Sh.I. A small height or hill.

Not so big as a fell, but usually above the size of the heights called 'hool,' for instance, 'de muckle and de peerie Hjoag (Unst),' JAKOBSEN *Dial.* (1897) 75.

[Norw. dial. *haug*, a height (AASEN) ; ON. *haugr*.]

HJOKFINNI, *sb.* Sh.I. An eccentric, odd-looking person ; also used *attrib.*

An odd-looking person is called in Unst and Yell a hjokfinni, which means properly ' somebody or something found in a burial mound,' JAKOBSEN *Dial.* (1897) 48 ; A person whose odd eccentric appearance and actions would lead to the supposition that ' they could dô mair dan maet demsels,' was termed a Hjok-finnie body, SPENCE *Flk-Lore* (1899) 26.

[Norw. dial. *haugfunnen*, an odd, somewhat deranged person, lit. ' hill-found' (JAKOBSEN *l. c.*).]

HO, *int.* and *sb.*[1] Sc. Irel. Cum. Yks. Chs. Stf. War. Wor. Glo. Oxf. Dev. Also written hoa Dev.[1] nw.Dev.[1] ; hoe Glo. [h(ō).] 1. *int.* A call to a horse to stand still.

Dev. *Horae Subsecivae* (1777) 179 ; GROSE (1790) *MS. add.* (M.) Hence (1) **Ho-back**, *int.* a call to a horse or an ox to step back ; (2) **-way**, *int.* a call to a horse to stop.

(1) Dev. *Horae Subsecivae* (1777) 179 ; GROSE (1790) *MS. add.* (M.) (2) Yks. (G.W.W.)

2. A call to a horse to come to the left. Also used *fig.* See Haw, *int.*[1]

Cum. Ah's nut hoat deunn yit, hooiver, bit ah finnd ah mun be fworcet teh hoa rayder, Gwordy, aboot an inch, or ah'll be a danger o' droonan t'miller eh t'offgang [refers to the fact that the sheet of paper on which the letter has been written is filled], SARGISSON *Joe Scoap* (1881) 5 ; Cum.[1] ; Cum.[4] Similar to Cumidder, which is *obs.*

3. A call to sheep to come to their food. Oxf.[1]

4. A call used in driving cattle. Also in *comp.* Ho-up. Chs.[1], nw.Dev.[1]

5. *sb.* Stop, delay, cessation ; moderation, self-restraint. *Gen.* with *neg.*

Keb. Love hath no ho, RUTHERFORD *Lett.* (1660) No. 166. s.Ir. The dirty scalpeen, there was no ho with him, CROKER *Leg.* (1862) 327. w.Yks.[1] There is ' no ho with him,' he is not

to be restrained. Stf., War., Wor., Glo. ' Out of all ho,' immoderately, NORTHALL *Flk-Phrases* (1894). Glo. A person who hath no hoe with him. There is no hoe with him, *Horae Subsecivae* (1777) 215. Dev.[1] Iv her was to begin to aggie way en there wid be no hoa, 5.

HO, *v.* and *sb.*[2] ? *Obs.* Yks. Brks. Sus. Hmp. I.W. Wil. Dor. Som. Also written hoe Sus.[1] Hmp.[1] ; and in forms haw Som. ; howe Yks. Wil.[1] Som. ; howe Wil.[1] ; oh e.Som. w.Som.[1] [ō, ǭ.] 1. *v.* To long for, desire greatly ; to care, heed, pay attention to. *Gen.* with *for*. See Hone, *v.*[2] 2.

e.Yks. Let us how it a while, *Lay-folks Mass-Bk.* 418 *note.* Brks. GROSE (1790) ; When people are extremely desirous or extremely solicitous for a thing, they very emphatically say that they ho for it (W.W.S.) ; *Gl.* (1852) ; Brks.[1], Hmp. (H.C.M.B.) s.Hmp. I didn't ho anything about what you was doing, VERNEY *L. Lisle* (1870) xiv. I.W.[1] How I do ho vor un! I.W.[2] I don't ho vor'n, I can tell ee. Wil.[1] I did hanker an' ho a'ter 'ee zo. Dor. I cannot understand Farmer Boldwood being such a fool at his time of life as to ho and hanker after thik woman in the way 'a do, HARDY *Madding Crowd* (1874) liii ; I don't know, an' don't ho, BARNES *Gl.* (1863) ; Dor.[1] Thy hills that I da ho about, 145. Som. JENNINGS *Obs. Dial. w.Eng.* (1825) ; W. & J. *Gl.* (1873). w.Som.[1] Pregnant women are said to oh for things. ' They auvis zaid how his mother oh'd vor strowberries, late in the fall.'

2. To provide for, take care of, see after ; to fuss. *Gen.* with *for*.

Sus. (M.B.-S.), Hmp.[1] I.W.[1] I.W.[2] Tes a good job the poor wold dooman's hoed vor now. Wil. BRITTON *Beauties* (1825) ; Wil.[1] Dor. To ho vor her motherless childern, BARNES *Poems* (1869–70) 3rd S. 11. Som. An haw'd vor my comfort, JENNINGS *Dial. w.Eng.* (1869) 83.

3. *sb.* Care, trouble, anxiety ; a state of fuss, worry, or excitement.

Sus. I doânt see as how you've onny call to put yurself in no sich tarrible hoe, JACKSON *Southward Ho* (1894) I. 200 ; Sus.[1] Hmp.[1] He made a great ho about it. Wil.[1] ' To be in a howe,' to be in a state of anxiety about anything. *Obs.* Dor. They must rise To their true lives o' tweil an' ov ho, BARNES *Poems* (1869–70) 3rd S. 83 ; Dor.[1] In happy daes when I wer young, An' had noo ho, 215.

[2. Ne scolde neuer yongmon howyen to swipe, *Prov. Alfred* (c. 1275) 135, in *O. E. Misc.*, ed. Morris, 110. OE. *hogian*, to be anxious (*Matt.* vi. 34). 3. The niʒtingale al hire hoʒe Mid rede hadde wel bitoʒe, *Owl & N.* (c. 1225) 701. OE. *hogu*, care, anxiety (B.T.).]

HO, HO', HOACH, see Hold, *v.*, How, *adv.*, Hall, *sb.*[1], Hawch.

HOAF, *int.* Sc. n.Cy. Nhb. Also Dor. Also written hofe- N.Cy.[1] ; and in forms hoof- Nhb.[1] ; hove Sc. (JAM.) Nhb. ; ove- Dor. A call to cows to come to be milked.

Bwk. In calling a cow to be milked, hove, hove, often repeated, is the ordinary expression, *Agric. Surv.* 503 (JAM.) ; *Monthly Mag.* (1814) I. 31. Rxb. Often hove-lady (JAM.). Nhb.[1]

Hence (1) **Hoafy**, (*a*) *int.* a call several times repeated to a cow to be milked ; (*b*) a pet name for a cow ; (2) **Ovey**, *int.* a call to sheep.

(1, *a*) N.Cy.[1] Nhb. (J.Ar.) ; Nhb.[1] ' Hovey! hove! hove!' the milkmaid says to the cow, advancing with her pail. (*b*) Nhb. She browt poor Hovey tiv hor pail, CHATER *Tyneside Alm.* (1869) 14. (*a*) Dor. Gabriel called at the top of his voice the shepherd's call, ' Ovey, ovey, ovey!' Not a single bleat, HARDY *Madding Crowd* (1874) v.

HOAFEN, HOAG, HOAK, see Halflin(g, Hogo, Howk, *v.*[1]

HOAKIE, *sb.* Ayr. (JAM.) A fire that has been covered up with cinders, when all the fuel has become red.

HOALM, HOAM, see Holm, *sb.*[1]

HOAL-PILTOCK, *sb.* Sh.I. A young coal-fish or piltock, *Merlangus carbonarius.* See Cooth, *sb.*[2]

In Unst and Fetlar a young piltock sometimes gets the name of a hoal-piltock, probably from its long cylindrical shape, JAKOBSEN *Dial.* (1897) 21.

HOAM, *sb.* Ags. (JAM.) The dried grease of a cod.

HOAM, *v.* Sc. (JAM.) 1. To give a disagreeable taste to food, by confining the steam in the pot, when boiling. Rxb. See Oam, *sb.*

2. To spoil provisions by keeping them in a confined place. Sc. Hence **Hoamed**, *ppl. adj.* applied to animal

food, when its taste shows that it has been kept for some time. Cld.

HOAM, see Holm, *sb.*[1]

HOAR, *adj.*[1] Sc. Chs. Also Hmp. I.W. Dev. Also in forms yar· Chs.[1] s.Chs.[1]; yer· Chs.[1] White, hoary. I.W.[1]

Hence (1) **Hoars**, *sb. pl., fig.* white hairs, old age ; (2) **Hoar-withy**, *sb.* the white bean, *Pyrus Aria* ; (3) **Hoary**, *adj.* covered with hoar-frost; (4) **Hoary-frost**, *sb.* a hoar-frost; (5)·**morning**, *sb.* (*a*) a species of apple ; (*b*) a morning when the ground is covered with hoar-frost.

(1) **Edb.** If auld age upon you draw, And poortith on your hoars do fa', LIDDLE *Poems* (1821) 154. (2) **Hmp.** WISE *New Forest* (1883) 283 ; From the white under-surface of the leaves (B. & H.); Hmp.[1] (3) **Chs.**[1] Th' edges are very yarry this morning. s.Chs.[1] (4) **Chs.**[1] Three yarry frosts are sure to end in rain, *Prov.* s.Chs.[1] It's a yaa'ri frost [It's a yarry frost]. (5, *a*) nw.Dev.[1] (*b*) Chs.[1] nw.Dev.[1]

HOAR, *adj.*[2] and *v.* Hrt. Som. **1.** *adj.* Mouldy. Som. (HALL.)

2. *v. Obs.* To become mouldy.

Hrt. Bread . . . will rope or hoar or mould, ELLIS *Cy. Hswfs.* (1750) 22.

[A hare that is hoar Is too much for a score, When it hoars ere it be spent, SHAKS. *R. & J.* II. iv. 143. Cp. obs. E. *hoary*, musty, mouldy ; *Chansi*, musty, fusty, mouldy, hoary, vinewed, COTGR.]

HOARD, *v.* and *sb.* Shr. Oxf. Dev. Cor. Written hoord· Oxf.[1] **1.** *v.* Used in forms (1) **Hoarded**, *ppl. adj.* in *comb.* **Hoarded eggs**, eggs preserved in lime or sawdust, for sale during the winter ; (2) **Hoarder**, *sb.* an apple in store for winter use ; (3) **Hoarding**, *ppl. adj.* suitable for keeping or storing.

(1) **Oxf.**[1] (*a*) Cor. Apples to chop for sauce, an' the hoarders no nearer away nor the granary loft, 'Q.' *Three Ships* (1890) ii. (3) s.Dev. 'Good hoarding apples,' sorts that will keep sound and well (G.E.D.).

2. *sb.* A heap. **Shr.**[2] A hoard of apples.

HOARDER, *v.* nw.Der.[1] e.An.[1] Written hoader nw.Der.[1] ; border e.An.[1] To hoard up or lay by.

HOARIN, *sb.* Sh.I. Also in form **horeng** S. & Ork.[1] The seal, *Phoca vitulina.*

(Col. L.L.B.) ; The seal was in the North Isles and Foula called 'de hoarin' (or woarin), which means 'the hairy one,' JAKOBSEN *Dial.* (1897) 28 ; *ib. Norsk in Sh.* (1897) 92 ; S. & Ork.[1]

[A der. of ON. *hár*, hair, so JAKOBSEN (*l. c.*).]

HOARSE, *sb.* Sc. Also Dor. A hoarse note ; a hoarseness, huskiness.

Edb. The liche fowle's hoarse Did fairly deave her ear, LEARMONT *Poems* (1791) 12. **Dor.** (W.C.) ; (A.C.)

HOARSGOUK, see Horsegowk.

HOAR-STONE, *sb.* Sc. Lan. Oxf. Also in form hairstane Sc. A boundary stone.

Wgt. Another possible purpose is preserved in the Scottish name of 'hair-stane,' or boundary-stone, by which they are occasionally known, *Chambers' Encycl.* (s.v. Standing-stones), in FRASER *Wigtown* (1877) 202. e.Lan.[1] Oxf. A large upright stone, 8 ft. high, formerly forming part of a cromlech, of which the other stones still remain near it. It is commonly known in the neighbourhood [Enstone] as the Hoar Stone, MURRAY *Handbk.* (1894) 218 ; Near Steeple Barton is a British earthwork called Maiden Bower, .. and hard by it ' Hoar Stones,' a ruined cromlech, *ib.* 159.

[OE. *hār stān* (lit. a hoar stone, i. e. a grey or ancient stone) often occurs in Charters in the part describing the boundary line; see *Charter* (ann. 847) in SWEET *O.E.T.* 433.]

HOASE, *v.* Cor.[2] [Not known to our correspondents.] To forbear.

HOAST, *sb.*[1], *v.* and *adj.* Sc. and n. and midl. counties to War. Also e.An. s.Cy. Also written hoazt Cum.[4]; and in forms haust N.Cy.[2] e.Yks.[1] w.Yks.[8] Lan. ; hawst e.Lan.[1] s.Lan. ; hoarst ne.Yks.[1] n.Lin.[1] sw.Lin.[1]; hoist Sc. (JAM.) Nhb.[1] e.An.[1] Nrf. ; hooast n.Yks.[2] e.Yks.[1]; host Sc. (JAM.) Cai.[1] n.Cy. Cum. Wm. w.Yks. Der.[2] nw.Der.[1] n.Lin.[1] ; hoste N.Cy.[2] w.Yks.[12]; houst w.Yks. ; howst Gall. ; hust Nhp.[2] Lei.[1] Nhp.[2] ; whust w.Yks. [hōst, oost.] **1.** *sb.* A cough. See Hose ; cf. also hoost.

Sc. Mony a sair hoast was amang them, SCOTT *Antiquary* (1816) vi. **Sh.I.** He gae a kind o' host, STEWART *Tales* (1892) 33. Cai.[1]

Baff. A scomfshing reek and a sair host, GORDON *Chron. Keith* (1880) 70. ne.Sc. He's had a sair cauld an' a hoast, GRANT *Chron. Kechleton*, 95. **Abd.** He . . . syn made a host, SHIRREFS *Poems* (1790) 90. **Frf.** I fought to keep my hoast down so as no to waken her, BARRIE *Tommy* (1896) 118. **Per.** Recommended the bottle which cured him of a hoast, IAN MACLAREN *Brier Bush* (1895) 62. e.Frf. She wad juist gie a hoast, LATTO *Tam Bodkin* (1864) iii. **Rnf.** Oh sic awfu' hosts he gie'd, CLARK *Rhymes* (1842) 31. **Ayr.** I canna expeck gude man that wi' your host ye'll come wi' me, GALT *Entail* (1823) xl. **Lnk.** If that host o' yours dinna gie me the shivers, GORDON *Pyotshaw* (1885) 38. **Edb.** Wi' hirple and whost, frae ingle-side, *Carlop Green* (1793) 131, ed. 1817. **Gall.** I'm whiles ta'en wi' the hoast, CROCKETT *Raiders* (1894) xxxiv. **Wgt.** When there a little she made a host, FRASER *Wigtown* (1877) 120. **n.Cy.** (K.) ; GROSE (1790) ; *Trans. Phil. Soc.* (1858) 160 ; N.Cy.[2], Nhb.[1], n.Yks.[1] w.Yks. WATSON *Hist. Hlfx.* (1775) 539 ; w.Yks.[124] Lan. I have sich a hoast. My throttle's as reawsty as a bone-house-dur-lock, WAUGH *Chim. Corner* (1874) 169, ed. 1879 ; Best ov owt for shiftin a hawst, CLEGG *Sketches* (1895) 399 ; DAVIES *Races* (1856) 271 ; Lan.[1], ne.Lan.[1], e.Lan.[1] Rut.[1] I can't get shoot o' my hoast. Lei.[1], Nhp.[2] War. Rare (C.B.). e.An.[1] Nrf. MILLER & SKERTCHLY *Fenland* (1878) iv.

Hence **Hoast-provoking**, *ppl. adj.* provocative of a cough. **Lnk.** Vile, stinkin', hoast-provokin' weed, THOMSON *Musings* (1881) 203.

2. A cough peculiar to animals, esp. cattle.

Nhb. *Gen.* applied to swine (R.O.H.). w.Yks.[2], nw.Der.[2], s.Not. (J.P.K.) Lei.[1] The mill-meado' allays gen the caows a hust. Nhp.[2]

3. A hoarseness, huskiness ; a cold on the chest or in the throat.

N.Cy.[1], n.Yks.[2] w.Yks. Hoast is a sore throat, HAMILTON *Nugae Lit.* (1841) 350; w.Yks.[1] s.Lan. BAMFORD *Dial.* (1854) Not.[8] 'E's 'ed that sort o' 'ust upon 'im for months past. Lin. STREATFEILD *Lin. and Danes* (1884) 338. n.Lin. SUTTON *Wds.* (1881) ; n.Lin.[1] I've gotten such a hoārst I can hardlin's speāk a wod. e.Lin. He's gotten a strāānge hoast (G.G.W.). s.Lin. I've sich a hoast I can hardly breāthe or speāk (T.H.R.).

Hence (1) **Hoasted-up**, *adj.* hoarse, closed up with cold ; (2) **Hoasty**, *adj.* hoarse, husky.

(1) e.Yks. Eiz austed up [I am closed up with cold] (Miss A.). (2) Rut.[1]

4. A hem, a vulgar mode of calling upon one to stop. Sc. (JAM.)

5. *Fig. Obs.* A thing or matter attended with no difficulty. **Sc.** It did na cost him a host, he made no hesitation about it (JAM.). **Abd.** In a host. Without a host, without delay or reluctance, SHIRREFS *Poems* (1790) Gl. ; The taiken shewn, that, but a host, was kent, Ross *Helenore* (1768) 136, ed. 1812. **Gall.** Through beef and bane, and wud and stane, Without a howst they whunner, MACTAGGART *Encycl.* (1824) 246, ed. 1876.

6. *v.* To cough.

Sh.I. 'Dat is leeker,' I said, as I hostid, an' rubbid me moot in wi' da back o' me haand, *Sh. News* (Dec. 3, 1898). Cai.[1] Inv. (H.E.F.) **Elg.** A wee bit mouse ran thort the floor, Sair hostira' and sair sneezin', COUPER *Poetry* (1804) 11. 58. **Abd.** The folk leugh as I hosted and flounder'd, CADENHEAD *Bon Accord* (1853) 214. **Kcd.** In simmer he hirplet an' hostit, GRANT *Lays* (1884) 172. **Frf.** Have you heard her hoasting! BARRIE *Tommy* (1896) 262. **Per.** Hoastin' on their haund-staffs And crynin' wi' the cauld, HALIBURTON *Ochil Idylls* (1891) 59. **Ayr.** They hoastit an' beighed tremendously, SERVICE *Dr. Duguid* (ed. 1887) 204. **Lnk.** Johnnie hooted and hoasted for about five minutes, WARDROP *J. Mathison* (1881) 11. **Lth.** He hirpled and hoastit, BALLANTINE *Poems* (1856) 54. e.Lth. The stour flew up in clouds an' set a'body hoastin, HUNTER *J. Inwick* (1895) 181. **Edb.** A' night lang he's hostin', grumblin', M[c]DOWALL *Poems* (1839) 199. **Gall.** He hoasts for breath, NICHOLSON *Poet. Whs.* (1814) 45, ed. 1897. **Kcb.** The gouk . . . hostin asks their leave to let him stay, DAVIDSON *Seasons* (1789) 43; (K.) ; N.Cy.[2] **Nhb.** Though nearly greetin wi' the reek, And sairly hoastin', STRANG *Earth Fiend* (1892) 6. **Cum.**, Wm. NICOLSON (1677) *Trans. R. Lit. Soc.* (1868) IX. w.Yks. I can't bear to hear ye houstin' like that, Lucas *Stud. Nidderdale* (c. 1882) Gl. Lei.[1] War.[2] Not heard except in rural War. e.An.[1] Nrf. MILLER & SKERTCHLY *Fenland* (1878) 129. s.Cy. (K.)

Hence **Hoasting**, (1) *vbl. sb.* the act of coughing; a cough ; (2) *prp.* in fits or gusts of coughing ; used *advb.* and *fig.*

(1) **Ayr.** Something gaed doon the wrang hass, and sic a fit o'

hoastin' cam on, Service *Notandums* (1890) 28. Lnk. With much 'hoasting' they rise to sing the doxology, Wright *Sc. Life* (1897) 15. Edb. Nae hostin now an' dowf excuse, McDowall *Poems* (1839) 220. Gall. Whan howstin' made me unco sair, Mactaggart *Encyl.* (1824) 18, ed. 1876. Lei.[1] Ah'd use to physic 'em for the hustin'. (2) Lnk. The gowlin' storm, as in 'twad come, Cam hoasting doun Kate Hyslop's lum, Murdoch *Doric Lyrs* (1873) 10.

7. To cough as a cow. Der.[2], War. (J.R.W.)

8. To belch up, bring forth. *Gen.* with *up*.

Sc. Host up, is said sarcastically to a child, who is crying, and who from anger brings on a fit of coughing (Jam.). Ayr. Some laird . . . may . . . host up some palaver, Burns *Willie Chalmers*, st. 5. Lnk. I couldna weel contain, Sae hoasted oot my chockin' mirth, Murdoch *Doric Lyrs* (1873) 20.

9. *Phr.* *to host out the craig*, to clear the throat by coughing.

Sh.I. He kind o' hostid oot his craig, *Sh. News* (Dec. 10, 1898).

10. To hem, to call upon one to stop. Sc. (Jam.)

11. *adj.* Hoarse, husky.

Cum. Bellart an rooart at them teh be whyet, till he was hoazt, Sargisson *Joe Scoap* (1881) 147; Cum.[4] ne.Yks.[1] Ah's that hoarst ah can hardlins talk. e.Yks.[1], m.Yks.[1] w.Yks. A hooast-coff, *Yks. Wkly. Post* (Apr. 17, 1897); (J.T.); w.Yks.[2]; w.Yks.[5] Ah mun ha' gotten cowd ah think, fur am gehring as hoast as hoast! l.Ma. ' Darlin,' he said, quite hoast, Brown *Doctor* (1887) 107, ed. 1891. Not. He war that hoast he could scarce speak (L.C.M.). s.Not. It couldn't hardly get 'cuckoo' out; it seemed hoast (J.P.K.). n.Lin. (E.S.) e.Lin. I'm very hoast to-day (G.G.W.). sw.Lin.[1] The pig's rather hoarst in its throat. Rut. I have a bad cold and am hoast all through them ash winds, *N. & Q.* (1876) 5th S. v. 364. Lei.[1]

HOAST, *sb.*[2] n.Yks.[2] [ōst.] Mist, frost haze.

HOAST, see Oast.

HOASTMEN, *sb. pl.* n.Cy. Nhb. An Incorporated Company of Newcastle Freemen; see below.

N.Cy.[1] Nhb. An ancient Gild or Fraternity at Newcastle-upon-Tyne, who deal in seacoal (K.); He was admitted to the freedom of the Hoastman's Company, Newcastle, Richardson *Borderer's Table-bk.* (1846) V. 4; Nhb.[1] The term hoastman has long ceased to describe the profession of coal-shipper or 'engrosser' of the commodities enumerated in the charter of incorporation. The Company of Hoastmen remains simply the premier Incorporated Company of Newcastle, and election to its membership is a much coveted honour.

[This corporation had orig. the function of receiving strangers (called (*h*)*ostes* or *oasts*) who came to buy coal and other commodities. ME. *hoste*, a guest (Gower *C. A.* (c. 1400) III. 205; so *oost*, *geste*, *Prompt.*; Fr. *hoste*, a guest (Cotgr.); see Hatzfeld (s. v. *Hôte*).]

HOATH, *sb.* Ken.[12] Also written both. A heath; only found in place-names.

HOATIE, *sb.* Sc. (Jam.) Also in form hots. A term used in the game of 'pearie' or peg-top; see below.

Lnk. A circle is drawn on the ground, within which all the tops must strike and spin. If any of them bounce out of the circle without spinning, it is called a hoatie. The punishment to which the hoatie is subjected, consists in being placed in the ring, while all the boys whose tops ran fairly have the privilege of striking, or as it is called 'deggin'' it, till it is either split or struck out of the circle. If [n]either of these take place, the boy to whom the hoatie belonged, has the privilege of playing again.

HOAVE, HOAVED, see Hauve, *v.*[12] Heave.

HOB, *sb.*[1] Var. dial. uses in Sc. and Eng. [(h)ob.]

1. A clown; a stupid, silly person; a greenhorn.

N.Cy.[1] Nhb.[1] ' De ye tyek us for a hob?'—do you take me for a greenhorn? s.Lan. Bamford *Dial.* (1854). Som. W. & J. *Gl.* (1873). [A hob [clown], *rusticus*, Coles (1679); *Vilenot*, a clown, peasant, boor, hob, or hinde of the country, Cotgr.]

2. *Comb.* (1) Hob Collingwood, the four of hearts in the game of whist; (2) 's-hog, see below.

(1) Tev. (Jam.), N.Cy.[1] Nhb.[1] Old ladies, in *gen.*, look upon it as proverbially unlucky. *Obs.* (2) Nhp.[1] When a person conjectures wrongly, he is commonly compared to Hob's hog, which, it is said, when the butcher went into the sty to kill him, fancied his breakfast was coming; Nhp.[2] You thought wrong, like Hob's-hog.

3. A sprite, hobgoblin. See Hob-gob, *sb.* 1.

Dur. Another sprite, called Hob Headless, infested the road between Hurzworth and Neasham, Henderson *Flk-Lore* (1879) vii. Lakel.[2] n.Yks.[1] Obtrush Rook, as well as Hob Hole and

the Cave at Mulgrave, is distinctly said to have been ' haunted by the goblin,' who being ' a familiar and troublesome visitor to one of the farmers, and causing him much vexation and loss, he resolved to quit his house in Farndale and seek some other home. Very early in the morning, as he was trudging on his way with all his household goods and gods in a cart, he was accosted by a neighbour with "I see you are flitting."—The reply came from Hob out of the churn, " Ay, we's flitting."—On which the farmer, concluding that the change would not rid him of his visitor, turns his horse's head homewards.' Hob of the Cave at Runswick was famous for curing children of the kink-cough, when thus invoked by those who took them to his abode : ' Hob-hole Hob! Mah bairn's getten t'kin'-cough : Tak' 't off! Tak' 't off!' Hob at Hart Hall, in Glaisdale, was, as the legend bears, a farm-spirit ' of all work,' thrashing, winnowing, stamping the bigg, leading, &c. Like the rest of the tribe who ever came under mortal eye, he was without clothes—nak't—and having had a harding-smock made and placed for him, after a few moments of—it would seem, ill-pleased—inspection, he was heard to say, ' Gin Hob mun hae nowght but a hardin' hamp, He'll come nae mair nowther to berry nor stamp'; n.Yks.[2] w.Yks. There are several localities in the township of Saddleworth, once, according to popular notions, invested with ' Old Hoba.' . . One of the parochial overseers kindly furnished me with . . . a list of the personal names and haunts, or reputed beats of the ' feorin' believed in when he was young. These comprise . . . 'Knott Hill Hob' and 'Narr Hob.' . . Hob of Knott Hill . . . was so designated on account of his having stood on that eminence on the approach of King Canute (Cnut or Knut), and ordered that monarch to march his army up the valley to the attack of Castleshaw, *N. & Q.* (1870) 4th S. v. 156. Der. They say giant Hobb hath ever a little un alongside o' him. . . The Hobb niver was knowed to come beyont the Dale. . . . T'other hole, where Hobb has his lodging, Verney *Stone Edge* (1868) ix.

4. *Comp.* (1) Hob-dross, (2) -man, a fairy, sprite, hob-goblin. Cf. hob-gob.

(1) Chs.[1] There were different kinds, having different habits. Some were called Hob-drosses, others Hob-gobs. There is a lane in Mobberley called Hobcroft Lane, and several adjacent fields called the Hobcrofts. These received their name from being the scene of the exploits of a noted Hob-dross. (2) n.Yks.[4] Each elf-man or hobman had his habitation, to which he gave his name.

5. A male ferret. Also in *comp.* Hob-ferret.

Chs.[1], s.Chs.[1] Midl. *N. & Q.* (1851) 1st S. iii. 461. Stf.[1], War.[8], w.Wor.[1], se.Wor.[1] Shr. The biggest coward of a ferret we ever had was a huge brown ' hob,' or male ferret, Davies *Rambles Sch. Field-club* (1881) xxviii; Shr.[1]

6. A male rat. Shr.[1]

7. A hog-sheep. Cor. *Horae Subsecivae* (1777) 213.

[1. To beg of Hob and Dick, Shaks. *Cor.* II. iii. 123. *Hob* is a familiar or rustic variation of the Christian name Robert or Robin. **8.** From elves, hobs, and fairies . . . From fire-drakes and fiends . . . Defend us, good heaven! Fletcher *Mons. Thom.* (c. 1625) IV. vi.]

HOB, *sb.*[2] and *v.*[1] Var. dial. uses in Sc. Irel. Eng. and Amer. Also in forms hab. Sc. Sus.[1]; hub Ant. n.Cy. Wm. n.Yks.[2] w.Yks.[12] e.Lan.[1] Not.[1] Lin.[1] Lei.[1] Nhp.[12] War.[2] s.Wor. Oxf. Bdf. Hnt. e.An.[1] Suf.[1] Amer.; ob Lin.[1] [(h)ob, h)ub, ub.] **1.** *sb.* *Obs.* The back of the chimney or grate. n.Cy. Grose (1790); N.Cy.[2]

Hence Habern, *sb.* the back of the grate.

Sus.[1] Why, whatever have you been a-doing with 'yourself! Your face is as black as a habern!

2. The flat-topped side or ledge on each side of a fire-place on which kettles, &c. can be placed; also *fig.* the fireside. In *gen.* colloq. use.

Sc. Stone or brick-work round a fire-place that projects so as to allow things to be placed on it, Grose (1790) *MS. add.* (C.) Ir. Same as if we had the ould kettle sittin' on the hob, Barlow *Idylls* (1891) 266, ed. 1892. Ant. Grose (1790) *MS. add.* (C.) N.Cy.[1] w.Yks. Tha'll find a drop o' hooam-brewd i' that pint up o' th' hob, Hartley *Ditt.* (c. 1873) 67; w.Yks.[1] Lan. Poo up to th' hob, Waugh *Winter Fire*, 18. nw.Der.[1], Not.[1], n.Lin.[1], Lei.[1] Nhp.[1] Called also the stock. War. *B'ham Wkly. Post* (June 10, 1893); (J.R.W.); War.[12] Glo. Baylis *Illus. Dial.* (1870). Hnt. (T.P.F.), e.An.[1], Suf.[1], Sus.[2] Som. W. & J. *Gl.* (1873).

Hence (1) Hob-end, *sb.* the flat-topped side of a fire-place, on which kettles, &c. can be placed; (2) Hub, *v.* to heat on the hob.

(1) n.Yks.⁶ w.Yks. He sits at th' hobend an' smooks his pipe (D.L.). Lan. Aw were pyerched at th' hobend reading politics, CLEGG *Sketches* (1895) 24 ; Push that arm-cheer up to th' hob-end, WAUGH *Heather* (ed. Milner) II. 130. e.Lan.¹, Chs.¹, Lin.¹, n.Lin.¹ (2) Lin.¹ Hub the frummery.

3. The mark at which things are aimed in quoits and other games ; the iron pin used in the game of quoits.

Nhb. With tent-pins for hobs, MIDFORD *Coll. Sngs.* (1818) 5 ; Nhb.¹, w.Yks.⁵, Lin.¹, e.An.¹ Suf.¹ A knife or fork or any such thing stuck into the ground, as a point to lay near in playing a ' pitch haapny ' or at quoits, is called a hub.

Hence Hobber, *sb.*, see below.

Nhb. ' A hobber,' or ' cock-hobber,' is when the ' shoe ' (or quoit) rests on the top of the hob (R.O.H.).

4. A stone or other mark set up as a boundary in var. games.

w.Yks. BANKS *Whfld. Wds.* (1865) ; This tree shall be one hob, that gate-post another (H.L.) ; w.Yks.³ ; w.Yks.⁵ A post. Assigned positions in a game.—At the game of ' Pize-ball ' . . . a number in succession run to different places called ' hobs,' where they remain till they have a chance of escape (s.v. Pize).

5. *Fig.* An aim, attempt.

w.Yks. Hoo nobbut made a poor hob at it (D.L.).

6. The hilt or guard of a weapon ; the point of insertion of the blade and handle of a knife. Also used *fig.*

e.An.¹ Up to the hub, as far as possible. Suf.¹ Up to the hub, a knife so [up to the point of insertion of the blade and handle] stuck into anything.

7. The nave or solid central part of a wheel from which the spokes radiate.

Midl. MARSHALL *Rur. Econ.* (1796). Lin. The ruts were . . . deeper than wagon-wheels, and the wheels didn't turn round, they only slid along on the hub, WHITE *Eng.* (1865) I. 260. Lel.¹, Nhp.¹², War.², s.Wor.¹(H.K.), Oxf.¹(K.) Bdf. BATCHELOR *Anal. Eng. Lang.* (1809) 199. Hnt. (T.P.F.), e.An.¹, e.Suf. (F.H.) [Amer. *N. & Q.* (1869) 4th S. vii. 524.]

8. A stake or pin in the ground or floor to keep a gate or door from swinging too far back, a short stake with which to secure a rat-trap set out of doors. e.Suf. (F.H.)

9. An uneven piece of ground in a wood. w.Yks.¹

Hence Hubbed, *adj.* lumpy, uneven, knobby.

Nhp.¹ A gardener said, when mowing a grass-plat, where the worms had thrown up numerous small protuberances, ' The grass is so hubbed, I can hardly tell how to cut it at all.' [Amer. BARTLETT (1859).]

10. *pl.* Large rugged stones that will not stand frost.

Nhp.² MORTON *Nat. Hist.* (1712).

11. A thick sod from the surface of peat ; the slaty adherent of inferior coal.

Ir. Others have bosses and many of them hobs—a light but compact kind of boggy substance found in the mountains, CARLETON *Traits Peas.* (ed. 1843) I. 301. n.Yks.² A thick sod pared off before cutting peat. w.Yks.¹ Used for fuel, but inferior to peat. Also called a basket. e.Lan.¹ Orig. the hard upper crust of peat.

12. A small haycock, a small stack of hay ; a pile. Also in *comp.* Hob-cock.

Cum. A strip across the field of 10 to 12 yards wide is raked together into seàngs or windrows ; from the seàngs hob-cocks, consisting of two or three small forkfuls of hay, are formed ; on the following day all is again spread out seànged, and then put into dry-cocks, which are three or four times larger than hob-cocks (E.W.P.) ; Cum.⁴, Wm. (B.K.), (E.C.), w.Yks. (F.P.T.), w.Yks.¹², Nrf. (H.P.E.)

13. A shoe. w.Yks.¹ Hence Hob-prick, *sb.* a wooden peg driven into the heels of shoes. n.Cy. (HALL.), w.Yks.¹

14. The shoe or sole of a sledge. Yks. (HALL.) e.Yks. MARSHALL *Rur. Econ.* (1788).

15. A hobnail.

Dor. He now wears shining boots with hardly a hob in them, HARDY *Madding Crowd* (1874) xlix.

16. A kick ; also in *comp.* Hub-up. e.Suf. (F.H.)

17. A fruit-stone. e.Yks. (W.W.S.), m.Yks.¹, n.Lin.¹

18. The berry of the hawthorn. War.⁸ Hence Hob-shooting, *sb.*, see below.

Wor. Hob-shooting is a favourite amusement with boys. When the berries are green and hard a berry is placed in a cleft stick which acts with pressure as a spring and ejects the berry forcibly at the person or object aimed at (E.S.).

19. An error or false step.

n.Cy. To make a hob, to make a false step, GROSE (1790) ; (HALL.) 20. *v.* To stud the sole of a boot or shoe with hobnails.

Dor. Then I went into Griffin's to have my boots hobbed, HARDY *Madding Crowd* (1874) xxxiii.

Hence (1) Hobbing-foot, *sb.* an iron foot or last used by shoemakers for holding the boot while it is being made or soled ; *fig.* a foot of the largest size, a very big foot ; see below ; (2) -iron, (3) -stob, *sb.* an iron foot or last used by shoemakers for holding the boot while the hobnails are being driven in.

(1) w.Yks. Thie fooit . . . weeant stear me—noa, not if it wor a hobbin fooit, an' it's moare loike that than owt else, HALLAM *Wadsley Jack* (1866) 40, ed. 1881 ; In the game of ' tip-cat,' after the stroke, the cat had to be at least three feet lengths from the ring. This measurement was naturally made by the boy who wore the largest clogs. The measuring was termed ' hobbing,' and the boys with big clogs were said to have ' hobbing feet ' (M.F.) ; (S.P.U.) (2) Cmb.¹ Reach me the hobbing-iron, and stand these clams in the corner. (3) Nhb.¹

21. To stop a marble with the foot.

Not.¹ Don't hob me. s.Not. Get out o' the road, or y'ull 'ob me [my marble] (J.P.K.).

22. To kick. e.Suf. (F.H.)

23. To make a small haycock.

w.Yks. To make two small haycocks into one larger one (F.P.T.) ; w.Yks.²

Hence Hubbing, *vbl. sb.* making up into haycocks.

w.Yks. Ah got very tired wi' hubbin' (F.P.T.).

HOB, *sb.*³ s.Wor.¹ se.Wor.¹ Shr.¹ Hrf.² Glo.¹ Also written ob Shr.¹ [ob.] The third swarm of bees in one season from the same hive, a ' bunt.' Cf. cast, *sb.*¹ 10.

HOB, *sb.*⁴ Shr.¹ In phr. (1) *hob and catch*, bit by bit, here and there, at odd times ; (2) *hobs and girds*, by fits and starts ; (3) *— and jobs*, see (1).

(1) Just as one can—as of getting in harvest in a bad season. (2) Theer's no 'eed to be took o' that fellow, 'e's all by 'obs an' girds—yo' never knowen w'en yo' han 'im. (3) We mun get that done by 'obs-an'-jobs.

HOB, *sb.*⁵ Hmp. A place where potatoes are covered over. WISE *New Forest* (1863) 163 ; Hmp.¹ Cf. hubble, *v.*

HOB, *v.*² Sur. Sus. Hmp. [ob.] To bring up or feed anything by hand. Freq. with *up.*

Sus. When they are a fortnight old, the calf is hobbed upon skim milk, *Reports Agric.* (1793-1813) 75 ; One hobs babies and pigs (S.P.H.) ; Sus.¹ A parishioner . . . came to complain that her husband had threatened to ill-use her on account of two little pigs which she was hobbing-up ; his objection rested on the fact that she was hobbing-up the pigs so carefully that she insisted on taking them to bed with her.

Hence Hob-lamb, *sb.* a pet lamb, brought up by hand.

Sur.¹, Sus.¹² Hmp. (W.M.E.F.) ; HOLLOWAY.

HOB, *v.*³ n.Cy. Nhb. Yks. Not. Lin. [h)ob.] To cut down or mow the thistles, coarse grass, &c., left by cattle.

w.Yks.² Hob the hedge bottoms. Go and hob the field round. Not.¹ Lin. THOMPSON *Hist. Boston* (1856) 710 ; Lin.¹ The sheep will not eat the bents, so the yardman must hob them. n.Lin.¹

Hence (1) Hobbing, *vbl. sb.* the act of mowing the high tufts of grass in a pasture ; (2) Hobbings, *sb. pl.* rough grass, &c., left by cattle in a pasture, converted into hay ; (3) Hobbing-scythe, *sb.* a scythe used to cut down the coarse tufts of grass left in a pasture.

(1) Lin. MORTON *Cyclo. Agric.* (1863) ; Graziers who attended much more to hobbing, which kept them fine, for nothing hurts marsh land so much as letting it run coarse, MARSHALL *Review* (1811) III. 190. (2) n.Cy. (HALL.), Nhb.¹ Lin. THOMPSON *Hist. Boston* (1856) 710 ; Lin.¹ (3) w.Yks.²

[LG. *hobben*, ' hauen ' (BERGHAUS).]

HOB, *v.*⁴ Som. To laugh loudly. (HALL.) ; W. & J. Gl. (1873).

HOB, *v.*⁵ Yks. Nrf. To throw up, heave ; also used as *int.*

n.Yks. He hobs up his ball on tl t'house top (I.W.). Nrf. Joe and me and the boy Derrick went carting—and Bob was our roller. He had to draw the barley with his rake up to the hind wheel and holler ' hob,' EMERSON *Son of Fens* (1892) 133.

HOBBAN, *sb.* Also in forms hobbin Cor.¹²³ ; hobbun. [o'bən.] 1. A cake made of dough and raisins baked in the form of a pasty. See Hoggan, *sb.*¹

Her dinner . . . was of saffron cake, or a figgy hobbun (a lump of dough with a handful of figs, as they call raisins, stuck into the middle of it and baked), *Longman's Mag.* (Feb. 1893) 378 ; Un Betty had made a figgy hobbun for Michael's dinner, TREGELLAS *Tales* (1868) 23 ; Cor.[128]

2. A miner's dinner-bag ; a piece of meat baked or boiled in paste. Also in *comp.* **Hobban-bag.**

A left . . . his hobban-bag jest by the door, TREGELLAS *Tales*, 8a ; Cor.[1]

HOBBEDY'S-LANTERN, *sb.* War. Wor. Glo. Also written **hobady's-, hoberdy's-** War. ; and in forms **hobany's-** War. ; **hobbady-lantern** se.Wor.[1] **1.** Will-o'-the-Wisp or *ignis fatuus.* Cf. **hob-lantern.**

War. TIMMINS *Hist.* (1889) 220 ; War.[2] Wor. In the district of Alfrick the *ignis fatuus* is called by the names of ' Hoberdy's Lantern,' ' Hobany's Lantern,' ' Hob and his Lantern,' ' Jack o' Lantern,' and ' Will o' th' Wisp,' to this day, ALLIES *Antiq. Flk-Lore* (1852) 412. w.Wor.[1], s.Wor.[1], se.Wor.[1], Glo.[1]

2. A hollowed turnip, with spaces cut to rudely represent eyes, nose, and mouth, with a lighted candle put inside. War.[2] Wor. ALLIES *Antiq. Flk-Lore* (1852) 423.

HOBBER-NOB, see **Hob-nob,** *v.*

HOBBIL, *sb.*[1] Sc. n.Cy. Yks. Lan. Also written **hobbie** Edb. ; and in forms **hobhald** n.Cy. w.Yks. ; **hobling** w.Yks.[2] [h)o'bil, h)o'bl.] A fool, a dull, stupid person ; a blockhead, dunce, idiot.

Edb. Altho' they are no worth a boddle, They'll mind you o' a Louden hobble, CRAWFORD *Poems* (1798) 121. n.Cy. GROSE (1790). w.Yks. What will th' old hobil say ? *Polly's Gaon* (1855) 24 ; HUTTON *Tour to Caves* (1781) ; w.Yks.[1] Girt hobbil at E war, ii. 289 ; w.Yks.[2] Lan. Thewd no may a hobbil on meh, TIM BOBBIN *View Dial.* (1740) 50 ; You're for makin som mak ov a hobbil on us, WAUGH *Owd Bodle,* 265 ; Lan.[1] s.Lan. BAMFORD *Dial.* (1854).

[An hobbel, a cobbel, dullard, *haebes, bardus,* LEVINS *Manip.* (1570).]

HOBBIL, *sb.*[2] and *v.* Yks. Stf. Der. Also in form **hubble-.** **1.** *sb.* A heap of hay, larger than a cock, but smaller than a ' coil ' (q.v.). Also in *comp.* **Hubble-row.** w.Yks.[2], Stf., Der. (J.K.), nw.Der.[1] Cf. **hob,** *sb.*[2] 12.

2. *v.* To make up into small haycocks. w.Yks.[2]

[Du. *hobbel,* a knot, a knobbe, or a bunch (HEXHAM).]

HOBBING, *prp.* Hrf.[2] Holloaing, whooping, making a noise.

HOBBIT, *sb.* Wal. Also written **hobit.** A measure of corn, beans, &c. ; see below.

Wal. *N. & Q.* (1850) 1st S. i. 470. n.Wal. Of wheat, weighs 168 lbs. ; of beans, 180 ; of barley, 147 ; of oats, 105 ; being 2½ bushels imperial, MORTON *Cyclo. Agric.* (1863).

HOBBLE, *v.*[1] and *sb.*[1] Var. dial. uses in Sc. Irel. Eng. and Amer. Also written **hoble** Sc. ; and in forms **habble** Rnf. ; **hubble** Sc. Uls. Wm. [h)o'bl.] **1.** *v.* To shake, jolt ; to dandle, toss ; to move unsteadily ; to walk with a quivering motion.

Sc. They disdain now to ride on pads as of old, or to be hobled on a horse's hurdies, GRAHAM *Writings* (1883) II. 151. Bnff.[1] He leuch till he hobblet. The pig wiz jist hobblin' in 'ts ain fat. Edb. O' a' the waters that can hobble, A fishing yole or sa'mon coble, FERGUSSON *Poems* (1773) 129, ed. 1785. Gall. MACTAGGART *Encycl.* (1824).

Hence (1) **Hobble-bog,** *sb.* a quagmire ; soft, wet, quaking ground. Bnff.[1] ; (2) **-quo,** (*a*) see (1) ; (*b*) *fig.* a scrape, dilemma. Slk. (JAM.) ; (3) **Hobblie,** *adj.* of ground : soft, quaking under the feet. Bnff.[1]

2. *Fig.* To be alive or astir with vermin ; to swarm with any kind of living creatures, esp. insects.

Bnff.[1] The pot [deep pool] wiz hobblin' wee salmon. The kebback wiz hobblin' wee mites.

Hence **Hobble,** *sb.* a swarm of any kind of living creatures, esp. insects. *ib.*

3. To move or walk with difficulty ; to limp, shuffle.

Abd. Yee'd to rise and tak' the way To hobble home, SHIRREFS *Poems* (1790) 219. Per. At that age he could not run ; he only hobbled when he tried, HALIBURTON *Fields* (1890) 92. Rnf. Some habblin' on without a leg, Was tholin muckle wrang by't, PICKEN *Poems* (1813) II. 96. Ayr. Tho' now ye dow but hoyte and hoble, BURNS *To his Auld Mare,* st. 7. n.Yks.[1] To move as a hare or rabbit does, when undisturbed, with desultory hopping movements.

and almost as if with its hindlegs tied together ; n.Yks.[4], w.Yks. (J.W.) Lan. Yo'dn o thaut as heaw hoo'd getten th' rheumatis, hoo hobbelt so, ORMEROD *Felley fro Rachde* (1864) iv. Not.[1], n.Lin.[1], War. (J.R.W.)

Hence **Hobbling,** *ppl. adj., fig.* awkward, clumsy ; overgrown, shambling.

w.Yks. (J.W.) Lan. He'd grown into a greight hobblin' lad, WOOD *Hum. Sketches,* 9a ; Two gret hobblin' lads, STANDING *Echoes* (1885) 9.

4. *Fig.* To hamper, embarrass ; to be in a difficulty or predicament. *Gen.* in *pp.*

Cai.[1] ' I'm no muckle hobbled aboot 'id,' it gives me little concern. Uls. It will hubble him to do it (M.B.-S.). s.Don. SIMMONS *Gl.* (1890). Nhb. But Ah hobbled him a bit, and the lads had nae difficulty in catchin' him, *Tynedale Stud.* (1896) No. 6. Lan. Loike most young folks 'ot goes a courtin' th' fust toime, I wur terrebly hobbled for t'find summut to say, GASKEL *Sngs.* (1841) 88. Nhp.[1] She was quite hobbled with her work. If I sell my fruit to the little gardeners, I am so hobbled to get the money. Ken.[12]

5. To tie an animal's legs together to prevent it straying ; *fig.* to confine, keep in one place. Cf. **hopple.**

Per. I was sair hobbled wi rheumatics. I was fairly hobbled to my bed wi' my last ill turn (G.W.). Wm.[1] Chs.[1] Animals are said to be hobbled when their forelegs are tied loosely together to prevent them straying. s.Chs.[1] To fasten the hind legs of a horse with hobbles. Der.[2], nw.Der.[1] Not.[1] To fasten a piece of wood to the foot of a horse or cow to prevent it straying from the field. Hrf. (W.W.S.) Nrf. Jist you go and hobble that there old dicky (W.R.E.). Suf.[1] A horse is said to be hobbled when . . . a hind and forefoot of the same side are connected by a rope or thong. When feet of different sides are so brought somewhat closer together, the beast is said to be ' yangled.' s.Suf. (F.H.), Dor.[1], w.Som.[1], Cor.[1]

6. *sb.* A shake, toss.

Sig. When I tak ye [child] oot o't [out of the cradle], A hobble ye've to get, TAYLOR *Poems* (1862) 52.

7. A limp. w.Yks. (J.W.), n.Lin.[1] Hence **Hobbly,** *adj.* lame, limping.

n.Yks. T'awd man's varry hobbly (I.W.).

8. *pl.* Rough places on a road or path.

e.An.[1], Suf.[1] (H.H.), e.Suf. (F.H.) [Amer. Esp. when a road is frozen after being cut into ruts, *Dial. Notes* (1896) I. 379.]

Hence **Hobbly,** *adj.* of a road : rough, uneven, full of stones.

n.Cy. It's a hobbly road, as the man said when he fell over a cow, *Denham Tracts* (ed. 1895) II. 65 ; N.Cy.[1], Nhb.[1], Lakel.[2] w.Yks.[1] This is a feaful hobbly road. Der.[12], nw.Der.[1] Nhp.[1] Applied to newly-made roads, when the stones are irregularly broken. e.An.[1] Suf. Applied to ground dried and hardened by sun or frost, RAINBIRD *Agric.* (1819) 294, ed. 1849 ; Suf.[1], e.Suf. (F.H.) Ess. 'Tis so hobbly, too, whene'er we'd walk, To stumble we bargin, CLARK *J. Noakes* (1839) st. 105 ; *Trans. Arch. Soc.* (1863) II. 185.

9. *Fig.* A difficulty, predicament ; trouble, perplexity. See **Habble.**

Sc. Will you, or will you no, help us out o' our present hobble ? *Campbell* (1819) I. 40 (JAM.) ; In a sad hobble, at a nonplus (JAM.) Cai.[1] Ayr. It's no doot a most unfortunate hubble for a man of your active habits to have gotten into, SERVICE *Notandums* (1890) 2. Dmf. Tom is in a great hubble at this time : you will know he has to begin to lecture the first of May, and has no time to prepare, CARLYLE *Lett.* (1897) in *Atlantic Monthly* (1898) LXXXII. 901. Ir. We'd never have got into the hobble we did, only that he was no more fit for knocking about in the bush than —well, than you are yourself, BARLOW *Kerrigan* (1894) xi. s.Ir. My man, you're in a pretty hobble, CROKER *Leg.* (1862) 288. n.Cy. (J.W.), Cum.[2] s.Wm. When ony o' them gat into a hubble we' ther wark, SOUTHEY *Doctor* (ed. 1848) 559. n.Yks.[1] ; n.Yks.[4] Throw what ah've tell'd Bob ah've gitten mysel intiv a gret hobble. e.Yks.[1] He's getten his-sen intiv a pratty hobble. w.Yks. He'll be soon to finnd hissen in a hobble befoor long, HARTLEY *Clock Alm.* (1877) 11 ; w.Yks.[125] Lan. But in a strange hobble I fun myself soon, For I're singing a song to a different tune, GASKEL *Sngs.* (1841) 85 ; Aw wur very near gettin' into a similar hobble myself, DOTTIE *Rambles* (1898) 95. m.Lan.[1] I.Ma. That's where the Doctor got in hobbles, BROWN *Doctor* (1887) 26, ed. 1891. s.Chs.[1] Yoa')m in ŭ ob'l, naay [Yo'm in a hobble, nai]. Stf.[1], Not.[1] Lin. If I've got you into a hobble I'll stand by you, FENN *Dick o' Fens* (1888) xv. s.Lin. He's gotten hissen into a hobble (T.H.R.). Nhp.[1] You've got into a pretty hobble now. War.[2]

B b

Gmg. He's got a fine old hobble, i.e. he has a difficult task (J.B.). Oxf. (G.O.), Hnt.(T.P.F.), e.An.¹ Nrf. HOLLOWAY. Snf.(H.H.), Suf.¹ Ess. A joulterhead... Had gut John in this hobble, CLARK *J. Noakes* (1839) st. 145. Ken.¹ I'm in a reg'lar hobble. Sus., Hmp. HOLLOWAY. Dor.¹ He's got into a hobble. w.Som.¹ We got into a purty hobble over thick job. Dev. Es dreem'd thit tha Vrench was a com'd in tha town, .. Wen es waked up an voun merzel out uv tha hobble, N. HOGG *Poet. Lett.* (1847) 31, ed. 1865. Cor. Described St. Just feast . . . as ' A hobble, a squabble, and a hub "babullion" altogether,' *Flb-Lore Jrn.* (1886) IV. 112. w.Cor. I'm in no end of a hobble (M.A.C.).

10. A confused fight. See Habble, 2.

11. A doubt, an uncertainty.
e.An.¹ Nrf. HOLLOWAY. Sus. ' De devil is in de hoss! ' ' Dere bent no hobble ov dat,' JACKSON *Southward Ho* (1894) I. 389. Sus.¹ Sus., Hmp. HOLLOWAY.

12. A rope, strap, clog, or other apparatus used for ' hobbling ' a horse or other beast; also used *fig. Gen.* in *pl.*
Wgt. When he heard of the proclamation in order to marriage of any couple, ' Guid be thankit, Peggy '; there's anither pair intae the hobble,' FRASER *Wigtown* (1877) 330. s.Don. SIMMONS Gl. (1890). Nhb.¹ Two straps with chain between used for hobbling a horse. s.Cha.¹ The term hobbles is confined to the hind-legs, fetters being the word used in the sense of a ' fastening on the fore-legs.' Not.¹, War.², Brks.¹, e.An.², e.Suf. (F.H.) Dor. A wooden instrument to confine the legs of a horse while he is undergoing an operation, BARNES Gl. (1863). w.Som.¹ Dev. The carrier's horse . . . was sometimes turned out on Broadbury, with hobbles on its feet, BARING-GOULD *Red Spider* (1889) iii; Cor.²

HOBBLE, *v.²* and *sb.²* I.Ma. Pem. Ken. I.W. Som. Cor. [o'bL] 1. *v.* To assist in bringing a vessel to anchor or out of harbour. w.Som.¹ Cf. hovel(l, *v.*

Hence Hobbler, *sb.* (1) a boatman or unlicensed pilot employed to assist in bringing a vessel into or out of harbour; (2) a light boat used to run out quickly and land passengers; also called Hoveller (q.v.); (3) *obs.*, a sentinel posted at a beacon to give warning of the approach of an enemy.
(1) s.Pem. A man who drags vessels up the river Cleddy with a warp or rope, Laws *Little Eng.* (1888) 420. Ken. A coastman, an unlicenced pilot, one towing a vessel, a watchman, ANSTED *Sea Terms* (1898). Som. Men who go out to sea in boats for the purpose of meeting homeward-bound vessels and engaging with the captain to unload them when they have entered the harbour (W.F.R.); JENNINGS *Obs. Dial. w.Eng.* (1825). w.Som.¹ Always known by this name in the little ports of the Bristol Channel. Cor.¹ A man who tows in a vessel with ropes. Two or three *gen.* own a boat between them; Cor.² (2) Ken. Applied to the light boats at Deal, Dover, and other parts, which are always on the watch to run out, at the first signal, to land passengers, *N. & Q.* (1873) 4th S. xi. 35. (3) I.W. In the Isle of Wight they have centinels who keep watch and ward at the Beacons, and their Posts or Runners who presently give intelligence to the Governor, and these by an old name are still called Hoblers, LEIGH *England*, 85 (K.); I.W.¹, Cor.²

2. To act as a guide or boatman.
Cor. He's gone hobbling, THOMAS *Randigal Rhymes* (1895) Gl.
Hence Hobbler, *sb.* a boatman who lets out small boats for hire; a ferryman, boatman; a guide, touter.
I.Ma. We waited till the packet started And the hobblers there was terr'ble divarted, BROWN *Doctor* (1887) 226; *N. & Q.* (1873) 4th S. xi. 35. Cor. THOMAS *Randigal Rhymes* (1895) Gl.

3. *sb.* The sum of money received by a ' hobbler ' for helping to bring a vessel into harbour; a ship requiring to be brought into harbour.
Cor. I went down on the wharf ... to see whether there was any ' hobble,' that is found a sloop . . . in the bay, bound for Hayle, HUNT *Pop. Rom. w.Eng.* (1865) 357, ed. 1896; One night, a gig's crew was called to go off to a ' hobble ' . . . each one being eager to get to the ship as she had the appearance of a foreign trader, *ib.* 358; Cor.¹²

4. A casual piece of work, a job.
Gmg. A casual labourer on obtaining employment is said to have got a hobble (J.B.).

5. A party of tourists under the charge of a boatman or guide. Cor. THOMAS *Randigal Rhymes* (1895) Gl.

HOBBLE, *sb.³* Suf. A kind of pig-sty; see below.
MORTON *Cyclo. Agric.* (1863); RAINBIRD *Agric.* (1819) 294, ed. 1849; Suf.¹ A ' hobble ' differs from a sty in this, that it is not a place for either fatting or farrowing—but a lodge, without a door, for swine to run in and out at pleasure. e.Suf. (F.H.)

HOBBLE-BOBBLE, *sb.* Suf. Confusion. (HALL), e.Suf. (F.H.)

HOBBLEDEHOY, *sb.* Var. dial. forms in Eng.: (1) Aubety-oy, (2) Hobbadehoy, (3) Hobbady-hoy, (4) Hobberdehoy, (5) Hobbettehoy, (6) Hobbety-hoy, (7) Hobbidy, (8) Hobbity-hoy, (9) Hobbledyhoy, (10) Hobble-hoy, (11) Hobble-te-hoy, (12) Hobblety-hoy, (13) Hobbly-hoy, (14) Hobbotyhoy, (15) Hobby de hoy, (16) Hober de hoy, (17) Hoberdy-hoy, (18) Hobidehoy.

(1) Glo.¹ (2) Lei.¹ 901. Hrf. (W.W.S.) (3) se.Wor.¹ (4) Midl. A lot o' them hobberdehoys o' Bilham set behind me, BARTRAM *People of Clopton* (1897) 54. Not.¹, War.², s.An.² (5) Bdf. BATCHELOR *Anal. Eng. Lang.* (1809) 135. (6) n.Cy. GROSE (1790). Chs.², Shr.¹ (7) s.Nrf. MARSHALL *Rur. Econ.* (1787). (8) w.Yks.¹, Chs.¹² (9) N.Cy.¹, Nhb. (R.O.H.), Nhp.¹, Hrf.², Hnt. (T.P.F.), e.Ken. (G.G.), Dor.¹ (10) Wil. SLOW Gl. (1892). (11) n.Yks. (T.S.) (12) N.Cy.¹ s.Lan. BAMFORD *Dial.* (1854). Der.², nw.Der.¹ (13) Dor.¹ (14) w.Yks. BANKS *Whfld. Wds.* (1865). War. (J.R.W.) (15) Hrt. ELLIS *Mod. Husb.* (1750) V I. i. (16) [A hober de hoy, half a man and half a boy, RAY *Prov.* (1678) 73.] (17) War.² Wor. A hobling or awkward gaited country lad is called a hoberdy-hoy, ALLIES *Antiq. Flb-Lore* (1852) 412. (18) e.An.¹, Nrf. (W.R.E.)

HOBBLE-DE-POISE, see Avoirdupois.

HOBBLE-GOBBLES, *sb. pl.* Nhp. Ken. 1. Turkeys. Nhp.¹ A name allusive to the voracious manner in which they eat their food.
2. The cuckoo-pint, *Arum maculatum.* Ken. (G.E.D.)

HOBBLESHOW, *sb.* Sc. Nhb. Dur. Cum. Wm. Yks. Lan. Also written hobbleashow, -ahew Sc.; and in forms habbleashow Peb.; hobbleashue Slk.; hubbeashow w.Yks.²; hubbiashow Dur.; hubbledeashew N.Cy.¹; hubbleshow Sc. n.Cy. Nhb. n.Yks.¹ e.Yks.; hubbleshoo Lnk. n.Yks.¹⁴ ne.Yks.¹ e.Yks.¹ m.Yks.¹ w.Yks.⁵; hubbleshow Sc. Wm. ne.Lan.¹; hubbleshue Shl.I.; hubble-te-ahives Cum.; hubby-shew, -shoo N.Cy.¹; hubly-shew, -shoo Nhb.¹ Cum.⁴ A tumult, hubbub, disturbance, row; confusion, commotion; a noisy tumultuous gathering or assembly; a rabble.
Sc. If that silly man would stop till all this hubbleshow's past, FERRIER *Destiny* (1831) III. v; Tir'd wi' the hobbleschow and clutter, DRUMMOND *Muchomachy* (1846) 49. Sh.I. Da hubbleashue o' oot door wark tak's a' his time, STEWART *Tales* (1892) 27. Abd. Fan ance the merry job is wrought, The De'il's to pay! And in sic hobblesho' ye're brought, As I'll no say, COCK *Strains* (1810) l. 86. Fif. Sic hubbub and sic hubble-shew, As scrim per't aff the frichtet crew, TENNANT *Papistry* (1827) 87. Dmb. Bauumie sleep fled like a dream, Sic a hobbleshew was never seen, TAYLOR *Poems* (1827) 22. Ayr. A' this stracmash and hobbleshow that fell out last Sabbath in Embro', GALT *Gilhaize* (1843) xiii. Lnk. Sic a terrible hubbleshoo' o' folk rinnin' up and doon, FRASER *Whaups* (1895) xv. Edb. I saw the hobble shaw coming fleeing down the street, MOIR *Mansie Wauch* (1828) v. Slk. I littl e wist how sic a hobbleashue might end, HOGG *Tales* (1838) 51, ed. 1866. Peb. By habble-shows inflamed Whan in his way, *Lintoun Green* (1685) 154, ed. 1817. Dmf. The hubbleshaw Wi' neeves and staff and rugging hair Sae awsome grew, MAYNE *Siller Gun* (1808) 73. N.Cy.¹, Nhb.¹ n.Nhb. Thor's a fine hubbleyshoo gan on up the street (R.O.H.). sw.Nhb. Heard but once, when it was used by a man, a newcomer into the parish, who when I said ' I am going to call on you,' replied, ' Come anither day, we're ahl in a hubble-shew ' (J.M.M.). s.Dur. (J.E.D.) Cum. LINTON *Lake Cy.* (1864) 306; Cum.⁴ What a hubby-shoo thoo's mekin ! ' I cannot dush wi' fwok mekin' a hubby-shoo aboot nowt,' *Rosenthal,* 137. Wm. ' Ey, ther' skiftin', an' ther' is a fine hubbleshow on': said of neighbours moving to a new house (J.M.). n.Yka.¹²⁴, ne.Yks.¹ e.Yks. MARSHALL *Rur. Econ.* (1788); e.Yks.¹ The's been a feyn [fine] hubbleshoo l' the public-hoos te neet. m.Yks.¹ w.Yks.(R.H.H.); w.Yks.¹; w.Yks.⁵ ' Ther's a bonny hubbleshoo l ' in front of the hustings during election time. A mother ' no soiner gets her back turned 'an shoo's at it, an' ther's a grand hubble-shoo of a house to come back tul !' ne.Lan.¹
[An hubbleshowe, *tumultus,* LEVINS *Manip.* (1570); Hubbilschow ! DUNBAR *Poems* (c. 1510), ed. Small, II. 314]

HOBBLY-ONKER, see **Hoblionker**.

HOBBUCK, *sb.* Cum. A field.

Not uncommon, in conjunction with some other word (E.W.P.); Girt cobbles hofe t'size eh t'leeath oot of oor Steaan-rays an Beunn hobbuck, SARGISSON *Joe Scoap* (1881) 225.

HOBBY, *sb.*[1] and *v.* Yks. Lin. Wor. e.An. w.Cy. Som. Dev. [oˑbi.] **1.** *sb.* A small horse or pony ; a roadster, hack.

Lin. A small hardy horse, such as used to be raised in the Fens, and called Wildmore hobbies, or tits, THOMPSON *Hist. Boston* (1856) 710 ; MILLER & SKERTCHLY *Fenland* (1878) iv ; Lin.[1], n.Wor. (H.K.), e.An.[1 2] Nrf. Used for a horse of any size (A.G.) ; (E.M.) ; COZENS-HARDY *Broad Nrf.* (1893) 40. e.Nrf. MARSHALL *Rur. Econ.* (1788). Suf. He come along on his hobby (C.G.B.) ; I know of a right pretty white hobby that would carry you nicely, STRICKLAND *Old Friends* (1864) 323 ; RAINBIRD *Agric.* (1819) 294, ed. 1849 ; Suf.[1], e.Suf. (F.H.)

Hence **Hobby-colt**, *sb.* a colt.

Dev. Aye, four and a half, it's time the little hobby-colt should be put to work (W.F.R.).

2. A child's name for a horse ; a pet name for a pony or small horse. w.Yks. (C.C.R.), w.Som.[1] **3.** Phr. *to play the hobby*, said of a woman who romps with men. w.Cy. HOLLOWAY.

4. *v.* Of women : to romp with men in a wanton, lewd manner.

w.Som.[1] Very common. ' Her'll hobby wi' any fuller.' n.Dev. Thee wut steehoppe, and colty, and hobby, and riggy, wi' enny Kesson zoul, *Exm. Scold.* (1746) l. 296.

HOBBY, *sb.*[2] Sh.I. Dur. Nhp. Nrf. Wil. [h)oˑbi.] **1.** *Obs.* The cuckoo, *Cuculus canorus.*

Nrf. It [the hobby bird] comes either with, or a little before, the hobbies (i. e. cuckoos) in the spring, SIR T. BROWNE in SWAIN-SON *Birds* (1885) 103 ; *Athenaeum* (Mar. 19, 1887).

2. The wryneck, *Jynx torquilla.* Wil.[1]

3. The merlin, *Falco aesalon.* Sh.I. SWAINSON *Birds* (1885) 140.

4. A goose. Dur. (HALL.)

5. *Comp.* (1) Hobby-bird, *obs.*, the wryneck, *Jynx torquilla* ; (2) -owl, the barn-owl, *Strix flammea.*

(1) Nrf. SIR T. BROWNE in SWAINSON *ib.* 103 ; COZENS-HARDY *Broad Nrf.* (1893) 51. (2) Nhp. SWAINSON *ib.* 125 ; Nhp.[1]

HOBBY, *sb.*[3] Chs.[13] [oˑbi.] An overlooker or bailiff.

HOBBY, *sb.*[4] Nhb.[1] The tool held by a 'holder-up' to press and keep a rivet in its hole, while its end is being hammered up by the riveter.

HOBBY, *adj.* Ess.[1] Rough, uneven. Cf. hobbly, s.v. Hobble, *v.*[1] 8.

HOBBY-DE-POIS, *sb.* Suf. Uncertainty, doubt. Cf. avoirdupois.

e.Suf. I am in a hobby-de-pois whether I should do so (F.H.).

HOBBY-HORSE, *sb.* Sc. Cum. Yks. Lan. Der. Lin. Also Som. Dev. Cor. **1.** In *comb.* Hobby-horse day, a festival held in Padstow on May 1st.

Cor. *Flk-Lore Jrn.* (1886) IV. 226 ; Cor.[1] A hobby-horse is carried through the streets to a pool called Traitor's Pool, a quarter of a mile out of the town. Here it is supposed to drink ; the head is dipped in the water, which is freely sprinkled over the spectators. The procession returns home singing a song to commemorate the tradition that the French having landed in the bay, mistook a party of mummers in red cloaks for soldiers, and hastily fled to their boats and rowed away.

2. *Fig.* A hoyden, romp, tomboy ; an offensive term applied to a woman.

w.Som.[1], Dev.[1] n.Dev. As thee art a colting Hobby-horse, *Exm. Scold.* (1746) l. 46.

3. A child's toy, like a horse on wheels ; a rocking-horse.

nw.Der.[1] Wooden horses for children and others to ride upon at fairs and other pastimes. n.Lin.[1]

4. A hobby, favourite pursuit or avocation.

Frf. To drive dull care away, or kill the time, Commend me to the hobby horse of rhyme, SMART *Rhymes* (1834) 1. Gw.Cy. Shew me ane that disna keep A Hobby-Horse, to ride on, FINLAYSON *Rhymes* (1815) 68. Dmf. A hobby-horse ye ride yersel', And mayna some ride theirs as weel ! QUINN *Heather* (1863) 28.

5. *Fig.* An exhibition, show, sight ; a butt, object of ridicule. Also in form hobby.

w.Yks. You're not going to have me for your hobby (S.O.A.). Lan. ' While thae'rt makin a hobby-horse o' thi-sel i'th inside.'

' Aw'm noan beawn to make a hobby-horse o' mysel',' said Ben, WAUGH *Snuch-Bant* (1867) 88.

6. A dragon-fly.

Cum. *Gl.* (1851). n.Lin.[1] It is believed there that ' three on 'em will tang a hoss to dead.' A neighbour of the author's affirms that when he lived in the ' Isle ' (q.v.), a hobby-herse stung a horse of his so badly that it caused its death.

HOBBY JACKSON, *phr.* Nhb.[1] When a person coming from the pit is carried over the pulleys.

HOBBY-LANTERN, see **Hob-lantern**.

HOBBYNAGGY, *sb.* n.Yks.[2] An ignorant, clownish fellow.

HOBBY-TOBBY, *sb.* Sc. (JAM.) [Not known to our correspondents.] A term used to describe the dress, personal appearance, manners, &c., of an awkward, tawdry woman.

[Cp. Du. *hobbel-tobbel*, in mingle-mangle wise, without order, confusedly (HEXHAM).]

HOBE, *int.* w.Som.[1] [ōb.] The call to a cow, several times repeated ; a call used in driving oxen. Cf. hoaf.

Also in driving oxen the plough-boys use ' hobe !' in a sort of sing-song way, but at the same time shout it angrily when using the gore to prod them, or to cause them to back ; then it is [Hoaˑbaak !]

HOB-GOB, *sb.* Yks. Lan. Chs. War. Shr. Suf. **1.** A hobgoblin, sprite, elf. See Hob, *sb.*[1] 3.

w.Yks. All t'Hob-gobs, an that short-horned brace [*sic*], SENIOR *Rhymes* (1882) 72. Lan. There may be scores o' those hobgobs, DONALDSON *Rossendal Beef-neet*, 14. Chs.[1]

2. A fool, idiot ; an awkward, uncouth person. w.Yks.[2], War.[2] **3.** Silly, empty talk ; gossip, chat. w.Yks. (S.P.U.), e.Suf. (F.H.)

4. *pl.* Small hillocks of dirt or refuse, &c. from the gutters scraped together by roadmen ; odds and ends ; inequalities of surface. Also in form Hobs-and-gobs.

War.[2] Shr.[1] Theer's some difference betwix them two turmit-fallows—the one's all 'obs-an-gobs like 'orses' yeds, an' the tother's as fine as a tnion-bed.

HOBGOBBIN, *sb.* *Obs.* n.Cy. A fool, simpleton, idiot. GROSE (1790) ; (HALL.)

HOB-GOBBLE, *sb.* Irel. The noise made by a goose when angry.

Th' ould gander let one hob-gobble at him, BARLOW *Kerrigan* (1894) v.

HOBHALD, see **Hobbil**, *sb.*[1]

HOBHOUCHIN, *sb.* Oxf. Bck. Hrt. Also written hobowchin Oxf. **1.** *Obs.* The owl, *Strix flammea.* See Houchin.

Hrt. With us the owl is called Hobhouchin, ELLIS *Mod. Husb.* (1750) V. ii.

2. A butterfly. See below.

Oxf. A native of these parts distinguishes between the *Pieridae*, as represented by the ' Whites,' and the *Vanessidae*, as far as the Peacock and Red Admiral are concerned. The former are ' butterflies,' the latter ' hobowchins,' *Science Gossip* (1869) 140: Bck. Heard applied to the Peacock and Red Admiral butterflies, but not to the common white one, ELLIS *Mod. Husb.* (1750) *note*.

HOB-JOB, *sb.* and *adv.* Nhp. Shr. [oˑb-dgob.] **1.** *sb.* A clumsy, awkward job.

Nhp.[1] A servant dropping a cup and saucer, without breaking them, exclaimed, ' That was a lucky hob-job ! '

2. *adv.* Off-hand, without deliberation.

Shr.[1] 'E did 'ob-job at a ventur.

HOBKNOLLING, *vbl. sb.* *Obs.* n.Cy. (HALL.) w.Yks.[1] Saving one's own expenses by living with others on slight pretences.

HOB-LANTERN, *sb.* n.Cy. Wor. Hrt. e.An. Hmp. Wil. w.Cy. Also in forms hob and lantern Wor. ; hob and lanthorn n.Cy. ; hoble-lantern w.Cy. ; hob o' lantern Hrt. ; hobby-lantern Hrt. e.An.[1] Nrf. Suf. Will-o'-the-Wisp or *ignis fatuus.* Cf. hobbedy's-lantern.

n.Cy. Hob-and-lanthorns, gringes, boguests, *Denham Tracts* (ed. 1895) II. 78. Wor. In the district of Alfrick, the *ignis fatuus* is called ' Hob and his lantern,' ALLIES *Antiq. Flk-Lore* (1852) 412. Hrt. They are called ' hob o' lanterns ' or ' hobby-lanterns,' *N. & Q.* (1855) 1st S. xii. 290. e.An.[1] Nrf. COZENS-HARDY *Broad Nrf.* (1893) 99. Suf.[1], e.Suf. (F.H.), Hmp.[1] Wil. BRITTON

Beauties (1825); **Wil.[1]** **w.Cy.** The will-o'-the-wisp is the ' hobie lantern' still, *Longman's Mag.* (Apr. 1898) 546.

HOBLING, *sb.* Yks. Hnt. [o'blin.] **1.** A haycock ; a small temporary heap of hay in size between a 'ricklin' and a 'haycock,' into which hay is raked in unsettled weather. **w.Yks.[8]** Cf. hobbil, *sb.*[2] **2.** *pl.* A scanty crop of hay formed by the skimmings of the aftermath or second mowing. Hnt. *N. & Q.* (1866) 3rd S. x. 145.

HOBLING, see Hobbil, *sb.*[1]

HOBLIONKER, *sb.* War. Wor. Hrf. Rdn. Glo. Also written hobbley-honker War.[2] ; hobbly-onker Wor. ; obbly-onker Wor. s.Wor.[1] Glo.[1] ; oblionker Wor. Hrf. [o'bli-onkə(r).] **1.** *pl.* A game played with horse-chest-nuts threaded on a string. See Cobbler, *sb.*[1] 4, Conker, *sb.*[1] 2.

War.[8] Wor. The name 'Hobbly-onkers,' or 'Obbly-onkers,' given to chestnuts pierced through and threaded upon a string, and used in some parts as the subjects in a children's game, *Berrow's Jrn.* (Mar. 4, 1897). **w.Wor.[1]** Played in autumn with horse-chestnuts strung together. The following rhyme [is] used in this game here : 'Hobley, hobley Honcor, My first conkor. Hobley, Hobley ho, My first go. Hobley, hobley ack, my first smack.' **s.Wor.[1]** Hrf. Heard at Ledbury, *N. & Q.* (1878) 5th S. x. 105, 378. Glo. (S.S.B.), Glo.[1]

2. A horse-chestnut, the fruit of the *Aesculus Hippo-castanum.* See Conker, *sb.*[1] 3.

Wor. A common and well-known word, *N. & Q.* (1878) 5th S. x. 177; The word oblionker seems a meaningless invention to rhyme with conker, but has gradually become applied to the fruits themselves (B. & H.). **s.Wor.** The pigs likes they obley-onker things, they picks 'em out (H.K.). **se.Wor.[1]** Wor., Hrf., Rdn. Common as the name of horse-chestnuts, esp. when pierced and threaded and used in a children's game (H.K.). Glo. (S.S.B.)

3. *Comp.* Oblionker-tree, a horse-chestnut tree, *Aesculus Hippocastanum.*

Wor. (B. & H.) ; *N. & Q.* (1878) 5th S. x. 177. Glo. (S.S.B.)

HOBNAIL, *sb.* Glo. In phr. *Hobnail's wake,* a fair held at Tewkesbury. Hone *Table-bk.* (1827) 23 ; (S.S.B.)

HOB-NOB, *v.* In *gen.* dial. and colloq. use in Sc. and Eng. Also in forms habber-nab Sc. (Jam.) ; hob and nob Ayr. N.Cy.[1] Der.[2] nw.Der.[1] ; -a-nob w.Yks. ; -or-nob N.Cy.[1] Suf.[1] ; hobber-nob Lth. To drink together ; to consort with, be on very friendly terms. Also used *attrib.*

Sc.(Jam.) Ayr. On Freedom's richts we'll tak oor stand, And hob and nob, in smiles sae bland, Wi' brithers free, White *Jottings* (1879) 182. **Lnk.** Hob-nobbing with the het mineral water as if it had been toddy, Roy *Generalship* (ed. 1895) 92. **Lth.** Some hobber-nob, fu' cosh, did souk, In corners, out their glasses, Bruce *Poems* (1813) II. 68 ; The Burgh Sires and Councillors . . . Are all his rage, his hob-nob friends, Lumsden *Sheep-head* (1892) 102. **N.Cy.[1]** **w.Yks.** He hob-a-nobbed with tinklers and gipsies, Dixon *Craven Dales* (1881) 162 ; (J.T.) ; **w.Yks.[1]** Lan. Aw seed oth' lot hob-nobbin' te-gether, Dottie *Rambles* (1898) 98. Der.[2], nw.Der.[1] Not. To share equally (J.H.B.). Suf.[1], e.Suf. (F.H.) Dor. She ought to hob-and-nob elsewhere, Hardy *Woodlanders* (1887) I. x. **w.Som.[1]** They was hob-nobbin together down to Clock [Inn] last Zadurday night. Colloq. Agreed to hob-nob, Barham *Ingoldsby* (1840) 102.

HOB-NOB, *adv.* n.Cy. Chs. Offhand, at a venture, rashly. See Hab-nab, s.v. Hab, *adv.*

n.Cy. Grose (1790). **s.Chs.[1]** Wi)n goa· aat· it· ob·-nob· ūt ū ven·chūr [We'n go at it hob-nob at a venture].

HOB-NOBBLE, *v.* Yks. Not. [o'bnobl.] To hob-nob; to talk intimately and confidentially together.

w.Yks. (J.W.) **s.Not.** They're hob-nobbling ower summat. A seed wut both i' th' road, hob-nobbling together (J.P.K.).

HOBOWCHIN, see Hobbouchin.

HOBRAN, *sb.* Sh.I. Written hobrin S. & Ork.[1]; hoeborn. [hō·brən.] The blue shark, *Squalus glaucus.* Also used *fig.* of persons.

A muckle hōbran, a great ugly hōbran, is in some places in Shetland (for instance N. Roe) applied to a big repulsive looking person, but ' hōbran' really means a ' shark,' in which sense it is still used in other parts of the country, Jakobsen *Dial.* (1897) 51 ; (W.A.G.) ; Muckle hoeborn slunges, a lock o' years younger den mysel', Stewart *Tales* (1892) 249; S. & Ork.[1]

[Norw. dial. *haabrand,* a kind of shark, *Lamna cornubica* (Aasen) ; see Ho(e, *sb.*[1]]

HOBRECK, *sb.* Or.I. A straw basket or 'cassie.' (S.A.S.)

HOBSHACKLED, *adj.* Lan. Chs. Also written ob-shackled Chs.[18] [o'bʃakld.] Lame, limping ; hampered, fettered ; embarrassed.

Lan. Aw'll be hobshackl't wi thee no longer, Clegg *David's Loom* (1894) xxi ; May thy bed clooas lie leet on thee, so ut theau winno' be hobshackled in 'em when theau'rt wanted somewheere else, Brierley *Red Wind.* (1868) 90. **e.Lan.[1], Chs.[18]**

HOBSHANKS, *sb. pl.* Sc. Knees.

He shall have his lugs tacked to the muckle trone . . . until he down of his hobshanks and up with his muckle doube, *Prod. of Langholme Fair in N. & Q.* (1851) 1st S. iii. 56 ; Still in common use, *ib.* 156.

HOB-THRUST, *sb.* Nhb. Dur. Cum. Wm. Yks. Lan. Der. Also in forms hob-throas Cum. ; -thrush n.Cy. Nhb.[1] Cum.[14] n.Yks.[8] e.Yks.[1] w.Yks.[1] ; -thurst Lan.[1] Der.[2] nw.Der.[1] ; -trush Dur. Cum. n.Yks.[1] ; hog-thrush n.Yks. [h)o'b-þrust.] **1.** A hobgoblin, sprite, elf, 'thurse' ; see below.

n.Cy. In the farm houses a cock and bacon are always boiled on Fassens eve (Shrove Tuesday), and if any person neglect to eat heartily of this food Hobthrust amuses himself at night with cramming him or her up to the mouth with big-chaff (J.L.) (1783) ; A spirit, supposed to haunt woods only. Called sometimes Robin Goodfellow, Grose (1790) ; **N.Cy.[1]** **Nhb.[1]** 'The hobthrush of Elsdon Moat' was a browney or sprite who performed drudgery of all kinds during the night season. As he wore a tattered old hat a new one was placed for him in his accustomed haunt. Instead of propitiating hobthrush, this action broke the spell ; and the sprite disappeared, uttering a piteous cry : 'New hat, new hood, hobthrush'll do no more good.' **Dur.** 'N' hob-trushes, 'n' meg-wu-mony-feet leaikin' things 're pop'd in here 'n there, Egglestone *Betty Podkin's Visit* (1877) 9. **Cum.** T'some oot o' t'way pleaces hobthrushes dud aw maks o' queer pranks, Richard-son *Talk* (1876) 153 ; I's weel seer, Hob Throas 'll ne'er Ha' thee to chowk wi' caff mun, Gilpin *Pop. Poetry* (1875) 72 ; **Cum.[1]** A hobgoblin having the repute of doing much useful work unseen and unheard during the night, if not interfered with ; but dis-continuing or doing mischief if crossed or watched, or if endeavours are made to coax or bribe him to work in any way but his own ; **Cum.[4]** Wm. Or, as he was more generally called, Throb thrush was a being distinct from the fairies, *Lonsdale Mag.* (1822) II 254. **n.Yks.[1]** Hobtrush Hob, a being once held to frequent a certain cave in the Mulgrave Woods, and wont to be addressed, and to reply, as follows :—' Hob-trush Hob ! Where is thou ? ' ' Ah's tying on mah left-fuit shoe ; An' Ah'll be wiv thee—Noo ! ' **e.Yks.[1]** **w.Yks.** Hutton *Tour to Caves* (1781) ; **w.Yks.[8]** When a man boasts of being a good workman, as of the great number of things which he can make in a day, some one will say, ' Ah, tha can mak' 'em faster nor Hob Thrust can throw shoes out o' t'window.' **Der.** Ye mun tak' heed to the Hobbthursts, . . the big boggatas robs the mills, Verney *Stone Edge* (1868) ix ; Der.[2], nw.Der.[1]

2. An ungainly dunce ; a fool, an awkward or clumsy fellow. Also used *attrib.*

Cum. ' Walk in . . . and see ' Exclaims a hobthrust fellow, Stagg *Misc. Poems* (ed. 1807) 137. **Lan.** Whot a hob-thurst he lookt wi o' that berm obeawt him ! Tim Bobbin *View Dial.* (1740) 26 ; Thir wur some quare lewkin hobthrusts omung um forshure, Scholes *Tim Gamwattle* (1857) 56 ; Lan.[1] Der.[1] *Obs.*

3. A wall-louse. Also in *comp.* Hobthrush-louse.

n.Cy. Hobo' t'hurst-lice. Prob. what we call in the south wood-lice, from their living in old wood, Holloway. **n.Yks.** Hog-thrush-louse. Also called lobster louse and old sow (T.K.); **n.Yks.[8], w.Yks.[1]**

[1. Our own rustical superstition of hobthrushes, fairies, goblins, and witches, Steele *Guardian* (1713) No. 30; *Lutin,* a Goblin, Robin-good-fellow, Hob-thrush, Cotgr.]

HOBURN SAUGH, *phr.* Sc. (Jam.) The laburnum, *Cytisus Laburnum.*

HOCE, see Halse, *sb.*[1], Hose, *adj.*

HOCH, *sb.* Sc. In phr. *on hoch,* on the run.

ne.Sc. 'He is like the dogs o' Keith, he's aye on hoch.' This saying is applied to one who is much given to going about in an idle way, Gregor *Flk-Lore* (1881) 112.

HOCH, *int.* Sc. Mtg. **1.** An exclamation expressive of var. emotions.

Sc. Hoch! had I drank the well-water, Whan first I drank the wine, Kinloch *Ballads* (1827) 23; Hoch! it's owre an oor syne, Ford *Thistledown* (1891) 220. **Lak.** Hoch, I could sing an' dance wi' perfect joy, Gordon *Pyotshaw* (1885) 174.

Hence (1) *hoch anee, phr.* an exclamation of grief; (2) — *hey,* (3) — *wow, phr.* an exclamation of weariness.

(1) Gall. Sad, sad news—Hoch Anee! MACTAGGART *Encycl.* (1824) 272, ed. 1876. Kcb. Sad wark, man. Hoch anee! ELDER *Borgue* (1897) 30. (2) Sc. Hoch hey, will I never win out o' this weery'd life, GRAHAM *Writings* (1883) II. 49. Abd. Resting his two elbows on his knees, [he] gave utterance to a prolonged 'Hoch-hey,' ALEXANDER *Ain Flk.* (1882) 217. Lnk. 'Twill save you frae many a dreary hoch-hey, LEMON *St. Mungo* (1844) 22. (3) Kcb. Hoch, wow! I'm unco dune the nicht, ARMSTRONG *Ingleside* (1890) 139.

2. An expression used to indicate a taint on bacon or on meat imperfectly salted. Mtg. (E.R.M.)

HOCHEN, *sb.* Ayr. The fireside. *Gl. Surv.* 69a (JAM.); (J.M.)

HOCHIE, *sb.* Sc. [ho·χi.] A keg or cask; a small barrel.

e.Fif. Their zeal had been rewardit by the discovery o' that hochie o' brandy stowed awa in the broom-buss, LATTO *Tam Bodkin* (1864) vii.

HOCHLE, *v.* and *sb.* Sc. Also in forms **hoichel** Ayr. (JAM.); **hoichle** Rnf.; **hoighel** Knr. (JAM.) [ho·χl, hoi·χl.] **1.** *v.* To walk with short steps; to scramble or shuffle in one's gait; to walk clumsily and with difficulty. Cf. **hockle,** *v.*[1]

Fif. (JAM.) Rnf. Puir cheels that canna pay for hacks Maun use their ain strong arms and backs, An' 'tis, I trow, a queer conceit To see them hoichlin' 'lang the street, YOUNG *Pictures* (1865) 166. Slk. (JAM.)

Hence **Hochling,** *ppl. adj.* sprawling, shambling, walking with difficulty.

Lnk. I mind when a wee hochlin' laddie, NICHOLSON *Kilwuddie* (ed. 1895) 155.

2. To do anything clumsily or awkwardly. Used in *prp.* Knr. (JAM.) Hence **Hochlan,** *ppl. adj.* awkward, clumsy; untidy in dress.

Arg. Thou'rt not a hochlan scleurach, dear, As many trooshlach be, COLVILLE *Vernacular* (1899) 6.

3. To tumble lewdly with women in open day. Gall. MACTAGGART *Encycl.* (1824). **4.** *sb.* A person who pays no attention to dress; a sloven. Ayr. (JAM.)

HOCK, *sb.*[1] and *v.*[1] Var. dial. uses in Irel. and Eng. Also written hoc Nhp.[1] e.An.[1]; and in forms **hawk** N.I.[1]; **huck** Lin. n.Lin.[1] w.Som.[1] Dev.[1] Cor.; **hug-** w.Yks.[1]; *pl.* **hucksen** Cor.[12]; **huckson** Dev.; **hux** n.Dev.; **huxen** Dev.[1]; **huxon** Ken.[12] [h)ok, uk, ʉk.] **1.** *sb.* The thigh, hip, ham, leg. See **Hough,** *sb.*[1]

e.Yks.[1] Lin. I thowt he'd broken all his bones . . . He mud ha' putten out his huck, BROWN *Lit. Laur.* (1890) 49 ; STREATFEILD *Lin. and Danes* (1884) 338. n.Lin.[1] When I was a sojer e' Egypt, I was wouhded e' th' huck. s.Lin. Ah'm fairly well fur an o'd man 'cept a lot o' paån i' my hûck (T.H.R.). Ken.[12] W.L. SLOW *Gl.* (1892). Som. SWEETMAN *Wincanton Gl.* (1885). w.Som.[1] Dev. *Horae Subsecivae* (1777) 219; Dev.[1] Muxen up to the huxen. n.Dev. Tha mux A·tap the draxel's up ta hux, ROCK *Jim an' Nell* (1867) st. 2. Cor. A woppin g'eat huck a beef, HIGHAM *Dial.* (1866) 18; Cor.[1] Muck [dirt] up to the hucksen; Cor.[2]

Hence (1) **Hockadois,** *sb. pl.* large, ungainly, sprawling feet; (2) **Huckaheens, -shins,** or **Huxens,** *sb. pl.* the undersides of the thighs just above the bend of the knee; (3) **Hug-bone,** *sb.* the hip-bone.

(1) m.Lin. Eh, what hockadois! (T.H.R.) (2) w.Som.[1] Dev. Th' parson's g'eat stug i' th' plid agin. . . Ers stratted ter th' huxens! MADOX-BROWN *Dwale Bluth* (1876) bk. 1. ii; Dev.[1] To trounch in the mux arter the hosses,—squash, squash,—shatted up to the huxens in plid, 15. n.Dev. Thy hozen muxy up zo vurs thy gammerels to the very hucksheens, *Exm. Scold.* (1746) l. 154; *Horae Subsecivae* (1777) 219. (3) w.Yks.[1] Mally . . . grazes her hug-baan, il. 288.

2. A pig's foot, esp. in phr. *hocks and hoes,* the feet and leg-bones of swine, cut off at the ankle.

Nhp.[1] With us, the thigh is certainly not included. Nrf., Suf. 'Feet and hocks' is the name given to those parts of a dead hog which are below the knee-joints, with the feet of the fore legs, and below the stifle, with the feet of the hind legs, HOLLOWAY. e.Suf. (F.H.), I.W.[1]

3. A knuckle of pork or bacon.

w.Yks. Here ah sat, gettin me dinner off an a pig hock, TOM TREDDLEHOYLE *Trip ta Lunnan* (1851) 12. Lei.[1], War.[2] Glo.

Horae Subsecivae (1777) 213. Mid. There's a bit of cold hock of bacon in the cupboard, BLACKMORE *Kit* (1890) I. xxii.

4. *v.* To throw stones, &c. from under the thigh or ham. N.I.[1]

5. To make an incision in one hind leg of a hare or rabbit, so that the other leg may be passed through it, for the purpose of suspension.

War. (M.D.H.) Nhp.[1] ' Hock ' is another word for the same operation [as ' harkle ' or ' hartle '], and in much more *gen.* use. Oxf. (M.A.R.) ; Oxf.[1] Ave ee 'ocked the rabbut! *MS. add.*

HOCK, *sb.*[2] Yks. Also Brks. Sus. Hmp. Also in form **hockney-** Brks. [ok.] In *comp.* (1) **Hock-day,** the second Tuesday after Easter Day ; (2) **·Monday,** the second Monday after Easter ; (3) **·tide,** the time or season of the hock-days, an annual rejoicing or festivity ; also used *attrib.*

(1) Brks. On ' Hockney-day '—which is the Tuesday following Easter week—they [the tithing-men or ' tuttimen '] have to visit each house in the borough [of Hungerford] and demand a coin of the realm from each male. . . Tuesday, Hockney Day, is ushered in by the blowing of John of Gaunt's horn from the balcony of the town-hall, *Chambers' Jrn.* in LOWSLEY *Gl.* (1888) 169. (2) Sus.[1] Kept as a festival in remembrance of the defeat of the Danes in King Ethelred's time. ((K.)) (3) w.Yks.[2] A Sheffield man, who was much respected by his neighbours, having died, an old lady, aged about 80, said, ' They will not make hock-tide over him.' Upon being asked what she meant, she said that when she was a girl it was occasionally the custom in Sheffield to keep the anniversary of a person who was disliked by having 'sports ' on the day of his death, such as races, cricket, &c. The games were played as near as possible to the house in which the dead person lived. Brks. The proceedings of Hocktide are of a very festive character and begin on the Friday preceding Hockney day by the holding of what is called the ' Audit Supper ' at the ' John o' Gaunt Inn.' . . The following Tuesday, Hockney Day, is ushered in by the blowing John of Gaunt's horn. . At nine o'clock the Hocktide jury having been summoned, assemble in the town-hall . . . the ancient rules and regulations of the court are read over by the town clerk. . . The whole of the Hocktide proceedings come to an end on Sunday, *Chambers' Jrn.* in LOWSLEY *Gl.* (1888) 169. s.Hmp. At the Hocktide games, VERNEY *L. Lisle* (1870) xiv. [A popular festival which commenced the fifteenth day after Easter, or the second Tuesday after Easter, HONE *Every-day Bk.* (1826) I. 476; (K.).]

[*In quindena Paschae, quae vulgariter* Hoke-dai *appellatur,* MATT. PARIS *Chron.* ann. 1255 (Rolls Ser. V. 493).]

HOCK, *sb.*[3] Cum. Slang. In phr. *old hock,* sour ale sold at a cheap rate for harvesters.

Cum. It was esteemed superior for ' slockenin' than the higher-priced article (W.H.). Slang. Stale beer, swipes (FARMER).

HOCK, *sb.*[4] Lei.[1] [ok.] A shock or mop of hair.

They're laffin' at the man wi' the heery hock.

HOCK, *v.*[2] Ess. [ok.] To jeer. Also with *at.*

This word occurs freq. in the *Times* report of an Ess. libel case tried at the last Assizes before Mr. Justice Hawkins, *N. & Q.* (1879) 5th S. xi. 245 ; Ess.[1]

HOCK, *v.*[3] Cmb. With *up* : to snap up, seize, hook, used *fig.*

'Hocked her up for her son,' said of a clever mother who brought about a somewhat unequal match (W.M.B.).

HOCK, *v.*[4] Sc. To scoop out ; to dig. Cf. **howk,** *v.*[1]. Sc. Hock a holl, dig a pitt, FLEMING *Scripture* (1726). S. & Ork.[1]

Hence **Hocking,** *vbl. sb.* scraping out a hole with the hands or with a hoe. S. & Ork.[1]

HOCK, see **Hack,** *sb.*[1]

HOCKATTY KICK, *phr.* Ken. A lame person. (G.B.), Ken.[1]

HOCKEN, *adj.* Sh.I. [ho·kən.] Keen or greedy for food. (JAM.), S. & Ork.[1]

[Cogn. w. Norw. dial. *hæken,* greedy (AASEN); see JAKOBSEN *Norsk in Sh.* (1897) 89.]

HOCKER, *v.*[1] Sc. Lakel. Cum. Lan. Also written **hoker** Sc. (JAM.) [(h)o·kə(r.] To bend, stoop ; to crouch or sit over the fire.

s.Sc. To sit as if the body were drawn together, as those who brood over the fire in cold weather (JAM.) ; The auld wife cam in, and hoker'd herself down By the ingle that bleez'd sae finely, *Old Sng.* (JAM.) Lakel.[1], Cum.[4], ne.Lan.[1]

Hence **Hocker,** *sb.* one who stays at home. ne.Lan.[1]

[ON. *hokra,* to go bent, to crouch or creep (VIGFUSSON).]

HOCKER, *v.*[2] Nhb. Cum. Wm. Yks. Lan. Lin. [h)o'kə(r.] 1. To clamber or scramble awkwardly over or up anything ; to walk awkwardly. Also used *fig.*

Lakel.[2] A chap 'at izzant ower lish 'll hocker ower a wo er on ta a nag back as weel as he can. An' sometimes if ye ass a nebbur hoo he's gaan on he'll say, 'Ah's hockeren on as weel as Ah can,' an' ye know at yanse 'at that izzant as weel as he could like. **Cum.** When ah'd gitten hockert up a lock o' girt hee steps, SARGISSON *Joe Scoap* (1881) 14 ; **Cum**[4] **Wm.** He hockers an' crammels like an auld man (B.K.). **n.Yks.**[2] 'Hockering along,' jolting on a rough track. To get 'hocker'd up,' to climb, for instance, the rugged sides of a cliff ; **n.Yks.**[8] Applied esp. to cattle climbing on cach other's backs. **w.Yks.** WILLAN *List Wds.* (1811).

Hence (1) **Hockered,** *ppl. adj.* crippled, disabled ; stiff, lame ; *gen.* with *up* ; (2) **Hockery,** *adj.* of a road or pavement : uneven, rough, ill-kept.

(1) **n.Lin.**[1] I've gotten th' frost e' my feät, an' I hev to goä cram'lin' aboot ; I'm sorely hocker'd up. **sw.Lin.**[1] He was hockered up before they'd haef got thruff the harvest. What wi' my corns, and what wi' my bad knee, I'm quiet hockered up. (2) **n.Yks.**[1] 'It's a despert hockery bit o' road ;' of the line between Grosmont and Whitby, passing over which in the train was, owing to its badly-kept condition, accompanied with much jolting and shaking ; **n.Yks.**[2] A hockery road.

2. To do anything in an awkward, clumsy manner ; to dance about roughly and awkwardly. w.Yks. (R.H.H.), w.Yks.[1], ne.Lan.[1]

3. To stammer, hesitate, grow confused in speaking, esp. when about to tell an untruth. Cf. **hacker,** *v.* 2.

w.Yks. *Hlfx. Courier* (May 15, 1897) ; SCATCHERD *Hist. Morley* (1874) 170 ; **w.Yks.**[8] I hockered long about it ; **w.Yks.**[8]

4. To ride or swing on a gate, on a person's back, and such like.

Nhb. To hocker and ride on a gate. Hockering and climbing on one's back (R.O.H.) ; **Nhb.**[1] Wm. To hocker on a gate, on a person's back (J.H.).

[1. Norw. dial. *hokra,* to hobble or shuffle along as if with tender feet (AASEN).]

HOCKER, *adj.* n.Cy. Ken. Sus. Hasty, testy ; passionate. Sus. RAY (1691).

Hence **Hocker-headed,** *adj.* fretful ; passionate.

n.Cy. (HALL.) Ken. GROSE (1790) ; LEWIS *I. Tenet* (1736) ; Ken.[1] [2]

HOCKERIE-TOPNER, *sb.* Dmf. (JAM.) The houseleek, *Sempervivum tectorum.*

HOCKERTY-COCKERTY, *adv.* Obs. Sc. With one leg on each shoulder.

Bch. The carlen was riding hockerty-cockerty upo' my shoulders, FORBES *Jrn.* (1742) 14. Abd. (JAM.)

HOCKET, *sb.* Obs. Glo. A large lump, esp. of bread or cheese.

'A great hocket,' a great lump of bread or cheese, GROSE (1790) *MS. add.* (M.) ; *Horae Subsecivae* (1777) 214 ; *Gl.* (1851) ; Glo.[1]

HOCKET, *v.* e.An. [o'kit.] To laugh in a loud, vulgar manner ; to romp about foolishly.

e.An.[1] Nrf. There they wor, lots on 'em, on the back o' dickeys, laughing and hocketting and galloping about, SPILLING *Molly Miggs* (1873) vi ; All the paaple bust out a hocketin' and a laughin', *ib. Johnny's Jaunt* (1879) ii. Ess. Used all over Ess. (H.H.M.)

Hence **Hocketing,** *ppl. adj.* laughing in a loud, vulgar manner.

Nrf. They burst out into a great hocketing hoss-laugh, SPILLING *Daisy Dimple* (1885) 8a ; Them trolloping mawthers bust out into a hocketting laugh, *ib. Molly Miggs* (1873) 15.

[Prob. the same word as Fr. *hoqueter,* to have the hickup or hickock (COTGR.).]

HOCKETIMOW, *sb.* War. [o'kətimou.] An instrument to cut the sides of a rick with. Cf. **hoggerdemow.**

B'ham Wkly. Post (June 10, 1893) ; War.[1] *Gen.* formed of a scythe blade fixed to a pole or staff ; War.[28]

HOCKEY, *sb.*[1] Irel. Yks. Hrt. e.An. Also in forms hawkey e.An.[1] ; hawkie Cmb. Suf. ; hooky Ir. ; horkey e.An.[12] ; horky Hrt. [o'ki, ọ̄'ki.] 1. A harvest-home or supper ; the last load in harvest.

Ir. The game also called 'Hooky' and 'Crying the mare' (G.M.H.). e.Yks.[1] The last load in harvest ; formerly in use about Hornsea, but not much used now. It was followed by the men and boys shouting at intervals : 'We hev her ; we hev her ; A coo in a tether ; At oor toon end ; A yow an a lamb ; A pot an a pan ;

May we get seeaf in Wiv oor harvest yam ; Wiv a sup o' good yal, An sum haupence ü spend.' Hrt. (H.G.) e.An. GROSE (1790) *MS. add.* (P.) ; e.An.[1] Cmb. (J.W.B.) ; In common parlance (A.H.D.H.) ; At the Hawkie, as it is called, I have seen a clown dressed in woman's clothes, decorated with ears of corn, carried in a waggon. The people [said] that they were drawing the Harvest Queen, CLARKE *Travels* in BRAND *Pop. Antiq.* (ed. 1870) II. 15. Nrf. MORTON *Cyclo. Agric.* (1863) ; COZENS-HARDY *Broad Nrf.* (1893) 61. Suf. The completion of the whole is crowned by a banquet called the Horkey, to which the wives and children are also invited. In Suf. husbandry the man who . . . goes foremost through the harvest with the scythe or the sickle, is honoured with the title of ' Lord,' and at the Horkey, or harvest-home feast, collects what he can for himself and brethren, *Garl.* (1818) 338 ; Wheat harvest is finished by a little repast given by the farmer to his men. And the completion of the whole is crowned by a banquet, called the hockey, to which the wives and children are also invited, CULLUM *Hist. Hawsted* (1813) ; Chiefly used in High Suffolk of late years, SPURDENS *Gl.* (1840) ; (A.H.D.H.) ; (C.T.) ; (H.H.) ; Suf.[1], e.Suf. (F.H.), Ess. (H.H.M.)

2. *Comp.* (1) **Hockey-cake,** a cake distributed to the poor at harvest-home ; (2) -**cart,** the cart which carries the last load of harvest ; (3) -**load,** the last load of harvest ; (4) -**supper,** a harvest-supper.

(1) Hrt. The Cart that brings in yᵉ last of yᵉ Harvest is still called yᵉ Hockey Cart and yᵉ Cake then distributed yᵉ Hockey Cake, SALMON *Surv.* 169. (2) Hrt. The Hockey Cart is that which brings the last corn, and the children rejoicing with boughs in their hands, with which the horses are also attired, BRAND *Pop. Antiq.* (1813) I. 444. (3) e.An. (HALL.) ; e.An.[1] The last load of the crop, which was always led home on the evening of the hawkey, with much rustic pageantry ; the load and the horses being gaudily decorated with flags, streamers, and garlands ; and attended by a troop of masquers in grotesque disguises. (4) Cmb. (D.W.L.)

[Prob. conn. w. LG. *hokk* (pl. *hokken*), a heap of sheaves (BERGHAUS) ; see KLUGE (s.v. *Hocke*). Cp. obs. E. *hock-cart,* the cart which carries the last sheaves home. The harvest swains and wenches bound, For joy to see the Hock-cart crowned, HERRICK *The Hock-cart* (1648) 14.]

HOCKEY, *sb.*[2] n.Cy. Wor. Bck. Lon. 1. The game of ' bandy ' (q.v.) or ' doddart ' (q.v.). N.Cy.[1], se.Wor.[1]

2. A game similar to golf ; see below.

Lon. The name given to the game of golf. It seems to be the game called Not in Glo., the name [i. e. Not] being borrowed from the ball, which is made of a knotty piece of wood, HONE *Year-bk.* (1832) col. 1448.

3. See below.

Bck. The boys at Olney have a very entertaining sport, which commences annually upon this day [Nov. 5] ; they call it hockey, and it consists in dashing each other with mud and the windows also, COWPER *Lett.* (Nov. 5, 1785) in *Wks.* V. 174, ed. Southey.

HOCK-HOLLER, *sb.* Som. The hollyhock, *Althea rosea.* (B. & H.), w.Som.[1]

HOCKLE, *sb.* w.Yks. A stew or broth made of the hocks or houghs of cattle. *Leeds Merc. Suppl.* (Sept. 21, 1895). Cf. **houghle,** *sb.*[1]

HOCKLE, *v.*[1] Nhp. War. Wor. Glo. Brks. [o'kl.] To shuffle along, walk with difficulty ; to hobble along quickly. Cf. **hochle,** *v.,* **hocker,** *v.*[2], **hotchel, houghle,** *v.*

Nhp.[1] War.[2] ; War.[8] *Gen.* used of people who kick their feet together when walking. Wor. He was club-footed and could hardly hockle along (E.S.). s.Wor. 'Er [a cow] sims despret wik ov 'er 'ind legs, 'er gooes hocklin' alung (H.K.). se.Wor.[1] We sh'll a some wet I be afeard ; my carns plagues mū so as I caunt 'ardly 'ockle along. Glo.[1]

Hence (1) **Hockling,** *ppl. adj.* awkward, shambling ; (2) **Hockly,** *adj.* awkward, helpless, having no notion how to do a thing properly.

(1) War.[1] s.War.[1] He's a hocklin' sort of walker. (2) War.[1]

HOCKLE, *v.*[2] Nhp.[1] [o'kl.] To tie a horse's legs together and throw him down to prevent kicking while being shod. [To hockle, *Poplites seu suffragines succidere,* SKINNER (1671).]

HOCKLE, *v.*[8] ? Obs. Wor. [o'kl.] To cut up stubble. We pay about 4s. per acre for reaping wheat, and diet if they set it up and hockle it, YOUNG *Annals Agric.* (1784-1815) IV. 108.

HOCKLE, v.⁴ Lin.¹ To cast lots for sides in a game, with a coin or other article.

HOCKLIN, vbl. sb. Sh.I. Gutting fish. S. & Ork.¹

HOCKNEY·, HOCKNIE, see Hock, sb.², Hackney.

HOCKS, v. Nhp. War. Hrf. Glo. Oxf. Brks. Bdf. Hrt. Mid. Sus. Hmp. Wil. Also written aux Brks.¹; hox Nhp.¹ War.³ Glo.¹² s.Oxf. e.An.¹ Sus.¹; ox War.⁴ Oxf.¹ Bdf. Hrt. Mid. [oks.] 1. To cut the hamstrings; to cut the sinews of a rabbit or hare's hind leg and put the other foot through it, in order to hang it up.

Brks. In common use (B.L.); Brks.¹, e.An.¹, Sus.¹

2. To knock the feet together in walking.

Glo. To cut behind, and dirt one's stockings by such an irregular motion of the feet, *Horae Subsecivae* (1777) 219; *Gl.* (1851); Glo.¹

3. To trample or tread earth into a muddy, miry condition; to clatter the feet, walk noisily. Gen. in *prp.*

Nhp.² To go hocksin about. Oxf. Now then, clumsy, what are you hocksing about like that for? (G.O.) s.Oxf. ' I boords wet,' repeated the shepherd; ' the ewes 'a bin a-fightin' an' the lambs a-hoxin' all over the fold,' ROSEMARY *Chilterns* (1895) 96. Brks.¹ When I scawlded un a went hoksin' awaay wi'out a-stoppin' to year what I was a-zaayin'. w.Mid. ' Don't come a oxing over these stones what I've jest cleaned, with them dirty shoes o' yorn.' ' E's bin a oxin' all through the mud, an' made 'is self in a nice mess ' (W.P.M.). Hmp.¹ Hocksing, walking rudely, trespassing. Wil.¹ n.Wil. Don'ee get hocksing it about so (E.H.G.).

Hence *oxed about, phr.* trodden about by the hoofs of cattle.

Oxf.¹ Spoken of soft mould or grass, where the marks of their feet would show.

4. To hack or cut clumsily or in an unworkmanlike manner.

Glo.¹² Hrf.¹ Principally in reference to cutting underwood. The 'stubs are hocksed,' i. e. split and cut unevenly and irregularly by a person not used to cutting them. Wil. BRITTON *Beauties* (1825); Wil.¹

5. *Fig.* To fret, harass, worry; to put in a state of perplexity or embarrassment. Gen. in *pp.*

Nhp.¹ ' She does hox me uncommon.' A butter woman in the market, the other day, said, ' I've left my wench at home to-day; and I'm so hoxt without her, I don't know how to get on ; I've nobody to go of an errand but myself; I never was so hoxt.' War. I was just that oxt at what you told me, a feather would have knocked me down, *Leamington Courier* (Feb. 27, 1897) ; War.³⁴ Brks. Bdf. It regularly oxed him. It oxed him uncommon (J.W.B.).

6. To annoy a person by constantly following about ; to seek after, hunt.

Hrt. He hocksed me about all day. Hocksing birds' nests, CUSSANS *Hist. Hrt.* (1879–1881) III. 320.

7. To remove, carry off.

Nrf. A master speaking of a servant who had behaved very ill, his neighbour replied : ' If he had been my servant I'd have hox'd him off to Bridewell ' (W.W.S.).

Hence (1) Aux or Hocks, *int.* a call used in the game of hockey; see below ; (2) Hocksey, *int.* a call to a person to move off.

(1) Oxf. When a boy unfairly strikes the shins of another player with his stick, the boy struck exclaims ' Hocks your own,' and gives him a rap in return (G.O.). Brks. If your opponent is in the way of your swipe, you shout the warning ' aux ! ' and if he does not at once jump out of your way, you have a right to hit him on the leg with your hockey-stick. The word ' aux ' so used has nothing to do with the word ' hockey,' because hockey is a new term for the game here. ' Bandy ' was and still is, in villages, the name used (B.L.). (2) Nhp.²

[1. Thou schalt hoxe the horsis of hem, WYCLIF (1388) *Josh.* xi. 6.]

HOCKSING UP, *phr.* Hmp.¹ Throwing down.

HOCKSY, *adj.* Glo. Oxf. Brks. Wil. Also written hoxy Glo.¹ Oxf.¹ Brks. Wil.¹; oxy Glo. Oxf.¹ [o·ksi.] Dirty, muddy, miry, soft, sticky. See Hocks, v. 3.

Glo. Ground is hoxy when it is a regular staux, a muddy gateway with pools of water ; and ground into which the feet sink is hoxy (S.S.B.); Glo.¹ Oxf. You will find it oxey, ma'am, to-day (M.A.R.); It was hocksy walking after the rain (H.R.); Oxf.¹ ' It's oxy,' i. e. the dirt sticks to one's feet. Brks. ' Hoxy and gamsy,' dirty and sticky (W.W.S.); Brks.¹ Wil. It's about two miles in vine weather ; but when it's hocksey, like this, we allows

a mile for zlippin' back, AKERMAN *Tales* (1853) 179; BRITTON *Beauties* (1825); Wil.¹

HOCUS, sb. Sc. (JAM.) A stupid fellow, fool, simpleton.

HOCUS-POCUS, *adv.* Suf.¹ Higgledy-piggledy, intermixed, indiscriminately.

HOD, sb.¹ Yks. Not. Nhp. Lei. War. Hnt. e.An. Wil. [h]od.] 1. A wooden box or trough used for carrying coals, bricks, &c. ; a receptacle, flask.

n.Yks.² A powder-hod. w.Yks.², Not.¹ Nhp.¹ ' A coal-hod,' or ' cinder-hod.' Lei.¹ A box for coals set in a room. War. MORTON *Cyclo. Agric.* (1863). Hnt. (T.P.F.), e.An.¹ Nrf. Brick hod, mangold hod, COZENS-HARDY *Broad Nrf.* (1893) 84. Suf.¹ e.Suf. Made of wood, and tapering towards the bottom (F.H.).

2. A wooden measure for corn, meal, &c. e.Suf. (F.H.), Wil. (K.M.G.)

3. A cup or vessel for holding liquid.

e.Suf. A hod [cup] of tea. A hod [a glass] of liquor (F.H.).

HOD, sb.² and v.¹ Wor. Shr. Nrf. w.Cy. Also written od Wor. [od.] 1. sb. A heap of potatoes or turnips covered with straw and soil to protect them from frost.

Shr.¹ Nrf. Mangel-hod or beet-clump (F.H.). w.Cy. (HALL.)

2. v. To cover potatoes, &c. with straw and soil.

Shr. I see they'n got them mangels hodded up (A.J.M.) ; Shr.¹

Hence **Hodding**, *vbl. sb.* the covering of potatoes with straw and earth.

Wor. It would not be safe to wash potatoes if they were gathered for ' oddin'—they would perish. Odding is placing the potatoes in long rows in the field, covering them with straw and then earth, leaving straw to come through the earth at the top of the earth at intervals for ventilation (E.S.).

HOD, sb.³ e.Suf. In phr. (1) *to be in a hod with,* to be in a rage or angry with ; (2) *to give any one the hod,* to anger any one. (F.H.)

HOD, v.² Sc. [hod.] To jog along ; to ride badly.

Kcd. Hoddin' on through Tullynessle . . . Wi' a seat nae unco sicker, GRANT *Lays* (1884) 43. Ayr. Here farmers gash in ridin graith Gaed hoddin by their cotters, BURNS *Holy Fair* (1785) st. 7.

HOD, see Hide, v.², Hood, sb.¹, Hud, sb.¹

HOD-BOW-LUD, sb. se.Wor.¹ Also written 'od-bowlud. A large moth.

HODDAMADOD, HODDED, see Hodmandod, Hide, v.²

HOD-DEEA, sb. Lakel. 1. A hobby.

Lakel.² Wm. He wad mak a walkin stick er garden a bit mair as a hod-deea ner owt (B.K.).

2. A hindrance.

Lakel.² Sista come oot o' t'way, thoo's nowt but a hod-deea.

HODDEN, sb. and *adj.* Sc. n.Cy. Lakel. Cum. ? Der. Also in forms hoddin Sc. Der. ; hoden Sc. ; hodin Sc. n.Cy.; hudden Abd.; huddin n.Sc.; huddun Abd. [hɔ·dən.] 1. sb. Homespun cloth made of wool of the natural colour ; a coarse thick cloth worn by the peasantry ; also used *attrib.*

Sc. My lad . . . forsook his sonsie lassie with the homely hoddin coat, CUNNINGHAM *Sngs.* (1813) 73 ; The rost was teugh of raploch hodin, RAMSAY *Tea-Table Misc.* (1724) I. 176, ed. 1871. n.Sc. Mr. Merrison Dean . . . put on his ' hoddin ' overcoat of darkest gray, GORDON *Carglen* (1891) 295. Kcd. Claid was he in honest hodden Woven in his ain true leem, GRANT *Lays* (1884) 38. Frf. Of the wool . . . is manufactured almost every kind of cloth worn in the parish ; hodden, which is mostly used for herd's cloaks, and is sold at 1s. 8d. the yard, *Statist. Acc.* IV. 242 (JAM.). Per. The hodden web was swirled out o' its fauld For cleedin' to the childer, STEWART *Character* (1857) 175. Rnf. His coat o' guid hodden, had ne'er been afiel', PICKEN *Poems* (1813) II. 134. Lak. I had cuist my hodden coat, MURDOCH *Doric Lyre* (1873) 17. Dmf. Till they maist brunt my hoddin-breeks, CROMEK *Remains* (1810) 91. Gall. Trudging afoot in hodden, CROCKETT *Grey Man* (1896) 351. Der. ADDY *Gl.* (1891) ; Hoddin start-ups warm'd above the fire, FURNESS *Medicus* (1836) 20.

Hence **Hodden-clad**, *adj.* clad in homespun.

Fif. Tenant, laird, and hedger, hodden-clad, TENNANT *Anster* (1812) xxi.

2. *Comb.* **Hodden grey**, grey homespun; also used *attrib.* and *fig.*

Sc. Exchanging my hoddin-grey coat of my mother's spinning, SCOTT *Redg.* (1824) xiv. Or.I. Hamlets in tartan kilts, and Norvals in hodden gray inexpressibles, VEDDER *Sketches* (1832) 105. Abd. Meg hersel' began the play, Clad in a bran-new hudden-grey,

SHIRREFS *Poems* (1790) 213. **Frf.** Hodden-grey, undy'd or drest, Was sonsy weeds to busk the best, *Piper of Peebles* (1794) 5. **Per.** Dressed generally in a suit of 'hodden-gray,' MONTEATH *Dunblane* (1835) 10, ed. 1887. **Dmb.** I hae seen my grand-father in hodden-grey Weaving his stockings, TAYLOR *Poems* (1827) 89. **Rnf.** Nae hodden gray can now be seen, PICKEN *Poems* (1813) I. 124. **Ayr.** He was dressed in hodden-grey, mealy, dirty, and sair worn, HUNTER *Studies* (1870) 73. **Lnk.** Our fathers wore the hodden gray, WATT *Poems* (1827) 87. **e.Lth.** A broadcloth . . . suit of the royal hodden grey of Auld Scotland, MUCKLEBACKIT *Rhymes* (1885) 168. **Edb.** Ane clad in hoden grey, LIDDLE *Poems* (1821) 23. **Gall.** Douce, grave, hodden-grey men every one of them, CROCKETT *Standard Bearer* (1898) 260. Lakel.[2] **Cum.** T'men fwok hed cwoats o' hodden gray, RICHARDSON *Talk* (1871) 58, ed. 1876; A very old-fashioned suit of home-spun hodden gray, DALBY *Mayroyd* (1880) I. 200, ed. 1888.

3. A covering made of ' hodden.'

n.Sc. Make us a bed o' green rashes And covert wi' huddins sae grey, BUCHAN *Ballads* (ed. 1875) II. 103.

4. *adj.* Clad in homespun ; *fig.* homely, coarse.

Abd. A huddun hynd came wi' his pattle, As he'd been at the pleugh, SKINNER *Misc. Poems* (ed. 1805) *Christmas Ba'ing* (JAM.). **n.Cy.** *Border Gl.* (*Coll.* L.L.B.)

HODDEN, see Hide, *v.*[2]

HODDENLY, *adv.* Cum. Also in form **hoddingly.** [ho'dənli.] Continuously, persistently, without intermission. See Hold, *v.* 27.

If t'eah sud bud before t'yek Our feyne summer wedder 'ill hoddenly brek ; But if t'yek bud be t'suiner cummer We'll sartanly hev a drufty summer, *Prov.* (E.W.P.) ; **Cum.**[2] He's hoddenly been a gud husband to me, 45 ; ' Does your pain come and go ! ' ' It nayder cūms ner ga's, it's theear hoddingly,' *ib. Gl.*

HODDER, *sb.*[1] Nrf. [o'də(r).] A spade shaped so as to take up a considerable quantity of earth entire. See Hodding-spade, s.v. Hodding (2).

Nrf. Next day morning he met me and say . . . Have you brought your hodder? EMERSON *Son of Fens* (1892) 109.

HODDER, *sb.*[2] w.Yks.[1] A heat-mist. Cf. **hadder,** *sb.*[2]

HODDIE, HODDIN, see Hoodie, Hooding.

HODDING, *vbl. sb.* Chs. Lin. e.An. [o'din.] In *comp.*
(1) Hodding-scythe, *obs.*, an implement used in clearing land from rushes ; (2) **-spade,** a spade used in the fens.

(1) **Cha.** The sneath or sneyd to which the blade is fixed is about 3½ ft. long, and has one scythe-like handle, placed about 18 ins. from the top ; when the work is performed one hand is placed upon the top of the sneath, and with the handle in the other the crown of the rush roots is scooped out by the convex part of the blade, MARSHALL *Review* (1818) II. 34 ; **Chs.**[1] The implement is nothing more than a short, strong scythe. The blade is about twenty inches in length, but curves in a different way to the common scythe; the edge is nearly one way of it in a straight direction from heel to point; but the flat part of the blade forms a curvature, which varies about four inches from a straight line. . . The crown of the rush roots by a smart stroke of the implement, is scooped out by the concave part of the blade, HOLLAND *View Agric.* (1808) 116. (2) **Lin.** MORTON *Cyclo. Agric.* (1863). **e.An.**[1] **Nrf., Suf.** MORTON *Cyclo. Agric.* (1863). **Suf.** So shaped as to take up a large portion of earth entire, RAINBIRD *Agric.* (1819) 294, ed. 1849.

HODDINS, *sb. pl.* Per. (JAM.) [Not known to our correspondents.] Small stockings such as are used by children.

HODDLE, *v.* and *sb.*[1] Sc. Lan. Also in form **hodle** Sc. [h)o'dl.] 1. *v.* To waddle ; to walk awkwardly or quickly.

Sc. Play us up 'Weel hoddled, Luckie,' SCOTT *Redg.* (1824) Lett. xi. **Abd.** Wattie gaed hoddlin' to the mill, *Gwidman Inglismaill* (1873) 39. **Lnk.** URE *Hist. Rutherglen* (1793) 95 (JAM.). **Edb.** [She] round her a' her servants made to hoddle, An' paid them a' their wages to a boddle, LEARMONT *Poems* (1791) 194. **Dmf.** Ye vain coquettes wha flirt aboot, An' scarce for pride can hoddle, QUINN *Heather* (1863) 238. **e.Lan.**[1]

Hence (1) **Hodler,** *sb.* one who moves in a waddling way ; (2) **Hodling,** *ppl. adj.* waddling.

(1) **Lnk.** She who sits next the fire, towards the east, is called the Todler ; her companion on the left hand is called the Hodler. These terms occur in a curious account of the baking of what are denominated 'sour cakes' before St. Luke's Fair, URE *Hist. Rutherglen* (1793) 95 (JAM.). (2) **Sc.** Thy half-shut een and hodling air, RAMSAY *Tea-Table Misc.* (1724) I. 24, ed. 1871.

2. *sb.* A waddle, jog-trot ; a step, pace ; also used *fig.*

Sc. I teuk up my tail ower my rigging, And ne'er hun't my hoddle, HISLOP *Anecdote* (1874) 544 ; Ta'en ane anither's word, a kiss, and a hoddle, at the hillock side, GRAHAM *Writings* (1883) II. 63 ; To hune one's hoddle, to slack one's pace (JAM. *Suppl.*).

HODDLE, *sb.*[2] Rxb. (JAM.) [Not known to our correspondents.] A clumsy rick of hay or corn.

HOD-DOD, see Hoddy-doddy.

HODDY, *sb.*[1] Bdf. Bck. Also written **oddy** Bck. [o'di.] A snail ; the shell of a snail.

Bdf. The hoddy is the shell of the snail, not the snail itself. If a child finds an empty snail-shell, he says, ' I have found a small hoddy ' (J.W.B.). **Bck.** (W.H.Y.) ; (J.W.B.)

HODDY, *sb.*[2] Nrf. [o'di.] The uppermost breadth of a herring-net.

Herring-nets are usually made in four parts or widths—one width when they are in actual use being fastened above the other. . . . The uppermost of them (connected by short ropes with a row of corks) being called the ' hoddy,' *N. & Q.* (1850) 1st S. i. 387.

HODDY, *adj.* Sc. Der. Glo. e.An. s.Cy. Ken. Dor. Som. [h)o'di.] In good condition generally ; well-disposed, pleasant, in good humour, in good spirits ; well in health.

Sc. BAILEY (1721). **Der.**[1] Pratty hoddy. *Obs.* **Glo.**[1] Hoddy pretty, pretty well. **e.An.**[1] **s.Cy.** I'm pretty hoddy, GROSE (1790). **se.Cy.** RAY (1691). **Ken.** (K.) **Dor.** HAYNES *Voc.* (c. 1730) in *N. & Q.* (1883) 6th S. vii. 366. **Som.** W. & J. *Gl.* (1873).

[A der. of ME. *hod* (OE. *hád*), state, condition (*Ayenbite*).]

HODDY, *int.* N.Cy.[1] Nhb.[1] [ho'di.] A call to geese.

HODDY, see Hidy.

HODDY-DODDY, *sb.* and *adj.* Irel. Nhp. Oxf. Bdf. e.An. Dev. Also in forms **haddy-daddy** Dev. ; **hodd-idod** Ess. Dev. ; **hod-dod** Nhp.[1] ; **hoddy-dod** Bdf. e.An. ; **huddle-duddie** Oxf. ; **oddie-dod, oddie-doddie** Cmb. 1. *sb.* A snail, *gen.* the garden snail ; a snail-shell.

Nhp.[1] Oxf. *Science Gossip* (1869) 140. **Bdf.** (J.W.B.) **e.An.**[1] *N. & Q.* (1875) 5th S. iii. 166. **Cmb.** (J.D.R.), **Ess.** (W.W.S.), **Dev.** (J.W.B.)

2. A revolving light.

s.Ir. The wheels spinning round like hoddy-doddies, CROKER *Leg.* (1862) 298. **Dev.** The circumvolution of a firebrand, so as to make the appearance of a continual lucid circle to please children, *Horae Subsecivae* (1777) 214, 197 ; GROSE (1790) *MS. add.* (M.)

3. *adj.* Short and stout, squat.

Nhp.[1] A short, lusty, squat-looking person is said to be ' all hoddy-doddy.' With us it is restricted to females.

4. Giddy, drunk. Dev. GROSE (1790) *MS. add.* (M.)

HODDY-TABLE, *sb.* Sc. A small table which goes under a larger one when not in use.

Frf. So called because it goes beneath the larger one at night, like a chicken under its mother, BARRIE *Tommy* (1896) 189.

HODE, see Hide, *v.*[2]

HODENING, *sb.* Ken. Also in forms **hoodening** Ken.[1]; **hooding** Ken.[2] The name formerly given to a mumming or masquerade on Christmas Eve, still applied to the singing of carols.

'Hodening ' still goes on . . at Deal and Walmer. . . We were warned of the arrival of this creature by a very loud clapping noise, and on rushing to the street-door, saw a horse's head, supported on a pole by a man in a crawling position so as to resemble an animal, and covered in front by a coarse cloth. Nothing was done or sung by the small crowd around ; and the clapping caused by the opening and shutting of the mouth continued, till the creature having been satisfied with money was driven away, *Church Times* (Jan. 2, 1891) 20, col. 1 ; The custom of ' going a hodening ' at Ramsgate is now discontinued, but the singing of carols is still called ' hodening,' BRAND *Pop. Antiq.* (ed. 1848) L 474 ; **Ken.**[1] Formerly the farmer used to send annually round the neighbourhood the best horse under the charge of the wagoner, and that afterwards instead, a man used to represent the horse, being supplied with a tail, and with a wooden figure of a horse's head, and plenty of horse-hair for a mane. The horse's head was fitted with hob-nails for teeth ; the mouth being made to open by means of a string, and in closing made a loud crack. The custom has long since ceased ; **Ken.**[2]

[The word *hoodening* is locally associated with *wooden*, from the wooden figure of the horse's head.]

HÖDER, *sb.* Sh.I. Also in form **hoodik**. The staff used by fishermen to strike the fish.

De huggistaff : the staff with which the fisherman strikes into the fish, was called at the haaf by the North Isles fishermen ' de hoodik ' or 'hoder,' meaning : the threatener, JAKOBSEN *Dial.* (1897) 98.

[*Höder* lit. the threatener, a der. of Norw. dial. *höta*, to raise the arm in a threatening way (AASEN) ; see JAKOBSEN (l.c.) and *Norsk in Sh.* (1897) 87.]

HODGE, *sb.*[1] Chs. Der. Not. Lin. War. Shr. Cmb. [odg.] **1.** The paunch of a pig ; see **Roger**. Also by extension the stomach, belly (generally).

Chs.[1] The stomach of a cow, cleaned out and eaten as tripe. s.Chs.[1] Not. A cow's stomach (J.H.B.). sw.Lin.[1] The inside of a pig's stomach ; [it] is very bitter. ' Like the old woman who was told that nothing about a pig was lost, so she tried a bit of the hodge, but that bet her.' War.[2]; War.[3] He has a biggish hodge. Shr.[1] Cmb.[1] The flat portion of the ' chidlins.' ' When you go for the chidlins, ask for a piece of hodge.'

2.. The iron last used by cobblers. Der.[2] ; nw.Der.[1]

HODGE, *v.*[1] and *sb.*[2] Sc. n.Cy. Nhb. Yks. Lan. Nhp. War. Hmp. Wil. Also in form **hudge** War.[2] Hmp.[1] Wil.[1] [h)odg.] **1.** *v.* To move with a heaving or awkward motion, to trot ; to stagger, shake, esp. in phr. *to hodge and laugh,* to shake with laughter.

Bnff.[1] Abd. Sae he took gate to hodge to Tibb An' spy at hame some faut, SKINNER *Misc. Poems* (ed. 1805) *Christmas Ba'ing* (JAM.) ; They gar'd him hodge and jump Upon the jaggit pole, CADENHEAD *Bon-Accord* (1853) 247. Edb. The body hodged and leuch as if he had found a fiddle, MOIR *Mansie Wauch* (1828) xiv. n.Cy. To ride gently (HALL.) ; N.Cy.[1] Nhb. He hodg'd off the moor, like a sheep gyen astray, MARSHALL *Sngs.* (1825) 183 ; Nhb.[1] Hodgin' an' laughin'. n.Yks. (I.W.)

Hence **Hodgin**, *ppl. adj.* walking in an ungainly, heaving manner. Bnff.[1]

2. To advance the hand unfairly when discharging a marble. War.[2] Cf. **fudge**, *v.* 5. **3.** With *about* : to carry constantly and with difficulty or awkwardness. Bnff.[1]

4. To raise, lift up, to hitch up ; to push roughly.

Sc. He hodged up his breeches, MESTON *Poet. Wks.* (1767) 125. Bnff.[1] Hodge that stane doon the brae. Nhp.[1] Hodge this sack up.

5. *sb.* A push, ' shove ' ; a shake, jolt.

Bnff.[1] Abd. Nineteen hodges fairly given, To help a sinner on to heaven, SHIRREFS *Sale Catal.* (1795) 10. Nhb. Here comes the aad mear wi' Geordy on her back hodge for hodge (R.O.H.).

6. A big, awkward person, a fool ; a ' bunch', huddle.

Bnff.[1] Lan. Me blud wur kend, gredely, ut sich un awkurt cretur us him, ut I'd sin i' th' lone, munt think to mak o hodge o' me, PAUL BOBBIN *Sequel* (1819) 9. Nhp.[1] When one child is carrying another and drives the clothes in heaps, it is very commonly said, ' What a hodge you are making of that child.' War.[3]

Hence **Hudgy**, *adj.* thick, clumsy ; short. Hmp.[1], Wil.[1] **7.** Phr. *all of a hodge,* in a bunch, in an awkward, huddled manner.

Nhp.[1] An ill-made dress, when the fulness is irregular, and driven too much to one place, sits ' all of a hodge.' War.[2] ' All of a hudge.' Usually applied to the clothing of a child or woman, if greatly rucked ; War.[3]

HODGE, *v.*[2] Nhp. [odg.] To patch or sew clumsily. Nhp.[2]

HODGELL, see **Hodgil**, *v.*

HODGEN, *sb.* Shr.[1] [o'dgin.] A hedgehog, an ' urchin.'

HODGERKIN, *prp.* Cmb. Also in form **hodgekin**. Working, pottering, bothering, fretting over work.

She was hodgerkin about (W.M.B.).

HODGIL, *sb.*[1] Sc. A dumpling.

Rxb. An oatmeal hodgil (JAM.) ; But should a hodgil, in sweet rolling gleam, Be seen to tumble in the scalding stream, What prospects fair when stomachs keenly crave, A. SCOTT *Poems* (1805) 40 (*ib.*).

HODGIL, *v.* and *sb.*[2] Sc. Lei. Also in form **hodgell** Lei.[1] [h)o'dgl.] **1.** *v.* To move by slight jerks and with difficulty ; with *about* : to carry about constantly.

Bnff.[1] He hodgilt the muckle stane up the brae. She hodgils aboot that littlin' o' hirs a' wye it she gangs.

2. To move slowly and clumsily, to hobble. Bnff.[1], Lei.[1]

Hence **Hodgilin**, *ppl. adj.* walking in an awkward,

VOL. III.

---

hobbling manner. Bnff.[1] **3.** *sb.* A push. Bnff.[1] **4.** A stout, clumsy person. *ib.*

HODGING, *vbl. sb.* Der.[2] nw.Der.[1] Bad nursing.

HOD-HOLE, *sb.* Chs. A hollow formed by cutting up rushes by the root with a scythe. See **Hodding-scythe**, s.v. **Hodding**.

The hod holes or cavities should be filled level to the surface of the land with soil, MARSHALL *Review* (1818) II. 35 ; Chs.[1]

HODIN, see **Hodden**.

HODLACK, *sb.* Slk. (JAM.) [Not known to our correspondents.] A rick of hay. Cf. **hoddle**, *sb.*[2]

HODLAD, *sb.* ne.Lan.[1] The bedstraw, var. species of *Galium.*

HODLAND, see **Headland**, *sb.*

HODLE, *sb.* Bnff.[1] A small roadside inn.

HODMAN, *sb.* *Obs.* Oxf. A term of contempt applied by undergraduates of Christ Church, who were Kings' Scholars of Westminster School, to those who were not, and hence to men of other colleges.

Not chosen immediately from Westminster School, but recommended by one of the canons, and therefore consider'd as a sort of novice, *Horae Subsecivae* (1777) 214 ; GROSE (1790) *MS. add.* (M.) ; The men [of Christ Church] gave themselves airs. . . Those of other colleges were 'squils' and 'hodmen,' AMHERST *Terrae Fil.* (1721) No. 1.

[Hodman, *advena, alienigena,* COLES (1679).]

HODMANDOD, *sb.* and *adj.* ?n.Cy. Nhp. War. Wor. Glo. Brks. Hrt. Hnt. e.An. Hmp. I.W. Wil. Dor. Som. Cor. Cant. Also in forms **hoddamadod** Cmb.[1] ; **hoddy-mandoddy** Cor.[12] ; **hodmadod** n.Cy. Glo.[1] Suf. Ess.[1] Dor. ; **hodman** Suf. ; **hodmedod** Nhp.[1] Brks.[1] Hrt. Hnt. e.An.[1] Suf. Ess. Wil.[1] Som. ; **hodmidod** Suf. ; **hudmedod** War.[8] Wor. ; **hudmedud** Hmp.[1] Wil.[1] ; **odmedod** Brks.[1] **1.** *sb.* A snail with its shell ; the shell of a snail. Cf. **dodman**.

Hrt. (H.G.) Hnt. Empty snail shells (T.P.F.). e.An.[12] Cmb.[1] The boys at Wisbech used to recite some words commencing ' Hoddamadod, hoddamadod, draw in your horns.' Nrf. (P.R.) ; *Horae Subsecivae* (1777) 139, 214. Suf. A certain number of ' hodmidods' or small snails . . . were passed through the hands of the invalids and then suspended in the chimney on a string, in the belief that as they died the hooping-cough would leave the children, *New Suf. Garl.* (1866) 171 ; (C.T.) ; (M.E.R.) ; Suf.[1] e.Suf. Children here will take a snail, shake it, and repeat the lines : ' Hodmadod, hodmadod, pull out your horns ; Here comes a beggarman to cut off your corns' (F.H.). Ess. (R.G.C.), Ess.[1] e.Cy., s.Cy. RAY (1691). Wil.[1] Cant. *Life B. M. Carew* (1791) Gl. [The slugs or dew-snails are snails [hodmandods] without a shell, COMENIUS *Jan. Ling.* (1650) 216.]

2. An ill-shaped, deformed person ; a ' bunchy,' clumsy thing ; an overgrown stupid boy, a simpleton.

?n.Cy. JAGO *Gl.* (1882) (s.v. Hoddy-mandoddy). Suf. Now I fares like a hodmadod, what wi' my poor leg and back, HEYGATE *Poems* (1870) 186. I.W.[1] Any strange animal ; a nondescript. Dor. I han't a rod An can't in think there hodmadod, BARNES *Poems* (1863) 133. Cor. I'd rather be toarned to a hoddymandoddy, J. TRENOODLE *Spec. Dial.* (1846) 35 ; Cor.[12]

3. A scarecrow.

War.[3], Wor. (E.S.) Glo. *Horae Subsecivae* (1777) 214 ; Glo.[1] Brks. *Gl.* (1852) ; Brks.[1], Hmp.[1] Wil. He do be for all the world like a hudmedud, without the usefulness of un, EWING *Jan Windmill* (1876) xviii ; Its sutch a cusnashun rum looking hudmedud of a theng, AKERMAN *Tales* (1853) 79 ; Wil.[1] In common use in n.Wil. 'That nimity-pimity odd-me-dod ! ' JEFFERIES *Greene Ferne Farm* (1880) iii.

5. Old or very poor clothes, rags.

n.Wil. I've got my hudmeduds on (G.E.D.).

6. *adj.* Short and clumsy, squat.

Nhp.[1] Wil. BRITTON *Beauties* (1825) ; Wil.[1] Som. JENNINGS *Obs. Dial. w.Eng.* (1825).

HODMAN-HOB, *sb.* e.An.[1] A snail-shell.

HODS, *sb. pl.*[1] n.Yks.[2] [odz.] Pains, twinges, esp. in phr. *crukes and hods.* Cf. **crook**, *sb.*[1] 11.

HODS, *sb. pl.*[2] Nhp.[2] Pieces of turf cut into a quadrangular shape.

HODS-BOBS, *int.* Not. Also in form **hobs-bobs**. An exclamation used to give additional emphasis to a remark ; also in phr. *hods-bobs and buttermilks.*

THROSBY *Hist.* (1797) 455 ; Not.[3] Quite common. ' Hods-bobs

C C

and buttermilks! if you do so, I'll be after you!' addressed to a child in mischief.

HOE, see Ho, *int.*, How, *sb.*¹, How(e, *adj.*

HO(E, *sb.*¹ Sh. & Or.I. e.An. 1. The piked dog-fish, *Squalus acanthias* or *Acanthias vulgaris.* Also in *comp.* Hoe-fish.

Sh.I. Du's laek a whaal wi little faer For dis, or twice as mony mair O siccan hoes, Burgess *Rasmie* (1892) 36; Noo da hoes an' skate rumples boiled fir da grice, Stewart *Tales* (1892) 42; Da first time 'at ye can get a haud o' a hoe or twa tak' in [and] cut aff da tails an lug fins, *Sh. News* (July 30, 1898); (W.A.G.); S. & Ork.¹ Or.I. More freq. called dog (Jam.). The piked dog-fish,— here known by the name of hoe, Barry *Hist.* (1805) 296 (Jam.).

2. *Comp.* (1) Hoe-egg, the egg or spawn of the 'hoe'; (2) -mother or Homer, the basking shark, *Squalus maximus*; (3) -tusk, the smooth-hound, *S. mustelus.*

(1) S. & Ork.¹ (2) *ib.* Or.I. The basking-shark has here got the name of the hoe-mother, or homer, that is, the mother of the dog-fish, Barry *Hist.* (1805) 296 (Jam.). e.An.¹ (3) Sh.I. Edmonston *Zetl.* (1809) II. 304 (Jam.); S. & Ork.¹

[1. Norw. dial. *haa*, the dog-fish, *Acanthias vulgaris* (Aasen); Dan. dial. *hå* (Feilberg). 2. (2) MDan. *hâmær*=hâbrand (Kalkar). See Hobran.]

HO(E, *sb.*¹ Sc. n.Cy. *pl.* hone n.Cy. [hō.] A single stocking; a soleless stocking. Also used *fig.*

Sc. Herd *Coll. Sngs.* (1776) *Gl.*; A mach and a horse's hoe are baith alike, Ferguson *Prov.* (1641) 147; Very seldom used, Grose (1790) *MS. add.* (C.) Cai.¹ Lnk. The bride was now laid in her bed, Her left leg ho was flung, Ramsay *Christ's Kirk* (1715) ii. 163, in *Poems* (ed. 1733) 55. Slk. On ilka leg a ho had he, Hogg *Poems* (ed. 1865) 274. Gall. The left leg hoe they now prepare, Nicholson *Poet. Wks.* (1814) 43, ed. 1897. n.Cy. Grose (1790) *MS. add.* (P.)

[*Ho* is a sing. fr. *hose*; cp. *pea* fr. *pease.*]

HOEG, *sb.* Sh. & Or.I. Also written hög. Or.I. A sepulchral mound or tumulus. S. & Ork.¹

Hence Hög-folk, *sb.* elves, hobgoblins.

Or.I. A portion of these elves were known as Hill-people or Högfolk, who resided in grassy knowes and within caves by the sea, Fergusson *Rambles* (1884) 195.

[Norw. dial. *haug* (*hog*), a mound (Aasen); ON. *haugr* (Vigfusson).]

HÖER, HOES, HOESHIN, HOFE, HOFF, see Hover, *v.*¹, Hose, *sb.*¹, Hoshen, Hoaf, Howf(f.

HOFF, *v.* Lin. [of.] To scoff at; to laugh at; to imitate. (Hall), Lin.¹

HOFF, HOFFIL, see Hough, *sb.*¹, Hovel, *sb.*²

HOFFLE, *sb.* Nhb.¹ [ho·fl.] A stake on which salmon-nets are dried.

In a row of hoffle stakes one is higher than the others, and is called the bosom-hoffle.

HOFFLE, *v.* Nhb. Yks. Also e.An. Also in form houfle Nhb.¹ [b)o·fl.] To shuffle, walk haltingly, limp. See Houghle.

Nhb.¹ n.Yks.¹; n.Yks.² I can hardly get hoffled home; n.Yks.⁴ e.Yks. Marshall *Rur. Econ.* (1796) II. 325. e.An.¹

Hence Hoffling, *ppl. adj.* lame, limping, walking haltingly. Nhb. (R.O.H.)

HOFFLE, see Houghle, *sb.*¹

HOFSAHELLYIKS, *sb. pl.* Sh.I. Eave-stones, the flat stones laid along the lower edge of the roof under the straw for running off the water, Jakobsen *Dial.* (1897) 88.

[(*H*)*ofsa* (Norw. dial. *ufs*, eaves of a roof) + *helyack* (q.v.).]

HOFT, see Ought.

HOG, *sb.*¹ and *v.*¹ Var. dial. uses in Sc. Irel. and Eng.

1. *sb.* In *comb.* (1) Hog-backed, round-backed; (2) -berry or -bare, a wooden stretcher used for carrying the carcase of pigs or hogs from the place where they are killed to where the carcases are to be dressed; (3) -form, a bench on which pigs are laid to be killed and dressed; (4) -grubber, a Thames waterman, licensed by the Trinity House; (5) -grubbing, 'swinishly' sordid; (6) -headed, pig-headed, obstinate; (7) -house, a pig-stye, piggery; (8) -jet, a small bucket with a long handle, by which the food for pigs is taken out of the tub; (9) -loom, a sunk receptacle, *gen.* of brick, for the wash and refuse food for

pigs; (10) -meat, pork; (11) -mouse, the shrew or little-snouted mouse, *Mus araneus*; (12) -pat, a trough made of boards; (13) -pig, a barrow or castrated pig; (14) -pound, see (7); (15) -(a pudding, a pork sausage; a black pudding or sausage of blood and meat; (16) -seam, pig's fat or lard; (17) -seel, the thick skin on the neck and shoulders of a hog; (18) -taturs, bad potatoes of a blue colour, fit only as food for pigs; (19) -trou, a confusion, litter, an untidy scene; (20) -trough, a trough-like hollow; used *fig.*; (21) -tub, a large tub or tank into which all the refuse is thrown for the pigs; (22) -wash, the refuse given to pigs.

(1) Bnff.¹ Ken. (G.B.); Ken.¹ Applied to a vessel when, from weakness, the stem and stern fall lower than the middle of the ship. (2) Ken. (P.M.) (3) Sus.¹ (4) Lon. Among other privileged classes are the 'hog-grubbers' (as they are called by the other watermen), but their number is now only four. These hog-grubbers ply only at the Pelican stairs; they have been old sailors in the navy, and are licensed by the Trinity house. No apprenticeship or freedom of the Waterman's Company in that case being necessary, Mayhew *Lond. Labour* (ed. 1861) III. 329. (5) e.An.¹ Nrf. Holloway. (6) Ken.¹ He's such a hog-headed old mortal, 'taint no use saying nothing to him. Sur. (T.S.C.) (7) Wgt. Discharge any of the inhabitants of this Burgh to keep any swine from the date hereof in all time coming, unless they be confined in a hog-house, Fraser *Wigtown* (1877) 39. (8) Sus.¹ (9) Nhp.¹ (10) Sus. (S.P.H.) (11) Nhp.¹ The name has obviously been suggested from its long nose like a pig's. It is superstitiously looked upon with disgust, probably from the erroneous idea that its bite is venomous. The labourers . . . consider this little mouse prognosticates in which quarter of the heavens the wind will prevail during the winter, by making the aperture of its nest in a contrary direction. (12) Nhp.¹ (13) n.Cy. Holloway. Yks. (W.H.) n.Yks.² Pigs of both sexes which cannot be bred from. e.Yks. Marshall *Rur. Econ.* (1788). Cha.¹ (14) Sus.¹ Ab! many's the time as we've stood over the hog-pound together, and looked 'em over, and reckoned 'em up, whiles people was in church. (15) War.⁴ Don't forget the hog's puddings, and put plenty of fat in them. se.Wor.¹ Chitterlings stuffed with cutlins seasoned with herbs, &c. Oxf. (G.O.); Oxf.¹ If it has blood in it, it is called black hog-puddin', *MS. add.* Sur. (L.J.Y.); Sus. (S.P.H.) Hmp. The entrail of a hog, stuffed with pudding, composed of flour, currants, and spice, Holloway. Dev. In a¹ the countryzide there beant 'er equal at 'ogs-pudden, Salmon *Ballads* (1899) 56. nw.Dev.¹, s.Dev. (G.E.D.), Cor.⁸ (16) s.Cy. (K.) Same\. (17) e.An. (Hall.) (18) Bdf. (Hall.) (19) Nhb.¹ (s.v. Howstrow). (20) Ess. I did not see one false furrow, or any tendency to a hog through upon his whole farm, Young *Agric.* (1813) I. 200. (21) Oxf.¹ *MS. add.* Brks.¹ The 'hog-tub' has stock of barley meal, and at feeding time the pigs assemble eagerly at the call of 'shug,' 'shug,' 'shug,' and the mixture is then bailed out by means of a sort of bucket, with a very long wooden handle. (22) Brks.¹ Lon. The trade in hogs'-wash, or in the refuse of the table, is by no means insignificant, Mayhew *Lond. Labour* (ed. 1861) II. 192.

2. *Comb.* in plant-names: (1) Hogails or Hogils, (2) -arves,the fruit of the hawthorn, *Crataegus Oxyacantha*; (3) -bean, the black henbane, *Hyoscyamus niger*; (4) -'s-bean, the sea starwort, *Aster Tripolium*; (5) -berries, the fruit of the bird-cherry, *Prunus Padus*; (6) -gazels, (7) -gosses, see (2); (8) -grass, the wart-cress, *Senebiera Coronopus*; (9) -haws, see (2); (10) -knives, the common garden iris, *Iris germanica*; (11) -weed, (a) the cow-parsnip, *Heracleum Sphondylium*; (b) the knot-grass, *Polygonum aviculare*; (c) the common sow-thistle, *Sonchus arvensis* (more prob. *S. oleraceus*); (d) the upright hedge-parsley, *Torilis Anthriscus*; (e) the coltsfoot, *Tussilago Farfara*; (f) the scarlet poppy, *Papaver Rhoeas.*

(1) I.W. (B. & H.); I.W.¹² (2) Sur.¹, Sus.¹ (3) Cum. Hutchinson *Hist. Cum.* (1794) II. 316. (4) Ess. (5) Hmp. (J.R.W.), Hmp.¹ (6, 7) Sus. (8) War. (9) s.Cy. Hmp. Holloway; Hmp.¹ (10) Suf. The leaves are supposed to resemble the knives used for slaughtering pigs (M.P.). (11, a) Cum., n.Yks. (I.W.) Stf. Hog-weed, a good plant for neat beasts, which they are fond of, Marshall *Review* (1814) IV. 42. s.Bck. Hrt. Ellis *Mod. Husb.* (1750) III. i. Nrf., Suf., Ken., Sus. [Stephens *Farm Bk.* (ed. 1849) II. 582.] (b) Bdf. Bud's knot-grass (*Polygonum aviculare*) or hog-weed—frequently abounds on sandy, gravelly, and loamy soils, Batchelor *Agric.* (1813) 321; Though much hog-weed was left near this row, *ib.* 318. e.An.¹ Nrf.

Cozens-Hardy *Broad Nrf.* (1893) 101. e.Nrf. Marshall *Rur. Econ.* (1787). (c) Nhp.¹ (d) Glo.¹ (e) n.Yks. (f) e.An.¹

3. Phr. *to come from Hog's Norton*, to snore. Lei.¹ 301.

4. A young sheep of about a year old, before it has been shorn.

Sc. It retains this name [hog] till it be a year old. Then it is called a dimmond, if a wedder; and a gimmer if a ewe (Jam.); A shepherd, whose whole stock was forty sheep, whereof fifteen were hogs, *Scoticisms* (1787) 120. Sh.I. One or two 'gimmers' or fat 'hogs' were found to be amissing, Stewart *Tales* (1892) 120. Bnff. Sure as foxes worry hogs, Taylor *Poems* (1787) 10. Bch. I was lying tawin an' tumblin' like a sturdy hoggie, Forbes *Jrn.* (1742) 15. Abd. James Stevens saw her meeting John Donaldson's 'hoggs' in the burn of Green Cottis, and casting the water out between her feet backward, in the sheep's face, and so they all died, Andrews *Bygone Ch. Life* (1899) 179. Twd. The names of sheep are—1st, ewe, wedder, tup, lambs, until they are smeared. and, ewe, wedder, tup, hogs, until they are shorn, *Statist. Acc.* I. 139 (Jam.). Slk. How could we turn our hand wi' our pickle hoggs i' winter if their bit foggage war a' riven up? Hogg *Tales* (1838) 23, ed. 1866. Rxb. That our croaks and our hoggs in the spring time might dee, Riddell *Poet. Wks.* (ed. 1871) II. 202. Dmf. What gars ye tatter At a dead sheep amang the water. I'm sure at hame ye may get bettir Than a dead hog? Hawkins *Poems* (1841) V. 24. Gall. (H.M.) n.Cy. Grose (1790); N.Cy.¹² Nhb. I'm flaid yon hogs beside the cairn Are drifted up, Proudlock *Borderland Muse* (1896) 85; Nhb.¹ s.Dur. A' lost a lot o' hogs in t'Blackwatter last backend (J.E.D.). Lakel.¹ A lamb for twelve months after weaning (J.P.); Cum.⁴ Wm. He brag'd ... aboot his Herdwic hogs, Blezard *Sngs.* (1848) 42; (E.C.) n.Yks. A gelded sheep is simply a hog (R.H.H.); n.Yks.¹²⁴ ne.Yks.¹ Young sheep from weaning till first shearing-time. Hogs are distinguished as wether- and gimmer-hogs, according to sex; after shearing they are called shearlings. e.Yks. The hogges went snuffinge and snookinge, Best *Rur. Econ.* (1641) 74; e.Yks.¹ A yearling male sheep. m.Yks.¹ w.Yks. Hutton *Tour to Caves* (1781); A young male sheep (S.P.U.); w.Yks.¹ Neen gimmer mugg'd hogs, ii. 289; w.Yks.² Lan. The sheep are separated and sorted, viz. the wethers aged, ewes one year old (provincially hogs), Marshall *Review* (1808) I. 323. Chs.¹² Stf., Der. (J.K.), Der.¹², nw.Der.¹, Not.¹², s.Not. (J.P.K.) Lin. Thompson *Hist. Boston* (1856) 710; (J.C.W.) n.Lin. Sutton *Wds.* (1881); n.Lin.¹ A lamb, separated from its mother, but unshorn. s.Lin. (T.H.R.) sw.Lin.¹ Amongst the sheep the bulk were hogs, there being few ewes and lambs. Lei. Ray (1691); Lei.¹ Nhp. Ray (1691); Nhp.¹ A yearling sheep, which has only been shorn once; Nhp.², War. (J.R.W.), w.Wor.¹ Shr.¹ A male sheep of the first year. Rdn.¹, Glo.¹², Hnt. (T.P.F.), e.An.¹ Suf. The male sheep in its second year, Rainbird *Agric.* (1819) 291, ed. 1849; Suf.¹ Lamb, male or female, between one and two years old. I.W.¹ Dor. Lambs after weaning up to the time they have shed their first or sucking teeth, usually about 15 months (C.V.G.); The men were proceeding with the shear- lings and hogs, Hardy *Madding Crowd* (1874) xxii; *Reports Agric.* (1793-1813) 8; Dor.¹ Som. Fourteen ewe hogs, *Auctioneer's Advt.* (Nov. 1890); W. & J. Gl. (1873); Jennings *Obs. Dial. w.Eng.* (1825). w.Som.¹ Hogs, simply, would be understood to mean sheep of a year old of either sex; these would be more parti- cularly described as [yoa'augz] ewe hogs, [wadh·ur augz] wether hogs, or [aug raa·mz] hog rams. '150 splendid fat sheep, nearly all wether hogs,' *Wellington Wkly. News* (Dec. 2, 1886). Dev.¹ w.Dev. Marshall *Rur. Econ.* (1796). Cor.¹; Cor.² Only applied to sheep, and to them only before knowledge of the other sex. [After a lamb has been weaned, until the first fleece is shorn from its back, it receives the name of hogg, which is also modified according to the sex and state of the animal, Stephens *Farm Bk.* (ed. 1849) L. 213.]

Hence **Hogging**, *sb.* a place where sheep, having ar- rived at the state of 'hogs,' are pastured. s.Sc. (Jam.)

5. *Comp.* (1) Hog-chapped, deformed in the mouth, having the upper jaw longer than the lower, as sheep often have; (2) -ewe, a female sheep of a year old; (3) -fence, a feeding-ground for sheep; a fence for enclosing sheep; (4) -fold, a fold of young sheep; (5) -gap, a small opening or aperture left in a wall or dry stone fence, to allow sheep to get through from one pasture to another; (6) -garth, an inclosure to fold lambs in; (7) -ham, hung mutton of a year-old sheep, that has died of disease or been smothered in the snow; (8) -hole, see

(5); (9) -house, Hoggas, or Hoggast, an out-house or pen for wintering lambs in after weaning on the mountain-side; (10) -lamb, a young sheep of about a year old; (11) -mutton, meat of a year-old sheep; (12) -pox, the pox in sheep; (13) -ram, a male sheep of about a year old; (14) -reek, *fig.* the light fleecy patches of mist which float away on hillsides with the rising sun; (15) -sheep, see (10); (16) -wool (also called Hog), wool taken from year-old sheep.

(1) Nrf. *Arch.* (1879) VIII. 170. (2) Cor.² (3) Sc. A proper hog-fence ought to consist of a variety of pasture, Young *Annals Agric.* (1784-1815) XXVII. 66. e.Lth. The ewes are milked for about 8 weeks after the weaning ... and are then put out with the lambs, into the hog-fence, for the winter, *Agric. Surv.* 19a (Jam.). Peb. In a hog-fence or pasture capable of keeping thirty score of hogs, there is some years a loss of from three to four score, *ib.* 393. Slk. It's our hogg-fence, that's the hained grund like, Hogg *Tales* (1838) 23, ed. 1866. (4) Hmp.¹ (5) Cum.⁴ (6) ne.Lan.¹ (7) Twd. (Jam.) (8) Lakel.¹² Cum. T'feul a hog- whoal through hed croppen, Richardson *Talk* (1876) and S. 143; Cum.² It wosn't seeaf ut let him climm t'wo's, I meead him creep t'hog-hooals, 87; Cum.⁴ Wm. Sooa Betty dreeave im on be t'side et woe while thar com et a hog-hooal, *Spec. Dial.* (1880) pt. ii. 27. ne.Lan.¹ (9) Lakel.², Cum. (J.W.O.), Cum.¹⁴ Wm. (E.C.); They're carting hay to t'hoggus (B.K.). n.Lan.¹ ne.Lan.¹ A shed for sheep and young cattle. (10) Sc. The warst blast of the borrowing days couldna kill the three silly poor hog-lams, Scott *Midlothian* (1818) xxviii. Cor.¹²⁸ [Tup-lamb, and this last is changed to hogg-lamb, when it undergoes emasculation, Stephens *Farm Bk.* (ed. 1849) L. 213.] (11) n.Yks.² 'Hog-mutton,' last year's lamb. Lan. Hoo browt meh some hogmuttn an special turmits, Tim Bobbin *View Dial.* (1740) 26; Davies *Races* (1856) 278; Lan.¹ (12) Hrt. Ellis *Shepherd's Guide* (1750) 324. (13) w.Som.¹, Cor.⁸ (14) Nhb.¹ From the resemblance to the fleece of the 'hog' or young unshorn sheep. (15) Yks. Thou art as wairm and comfortable as a hog sheep in winter neights, Fetherston *T. Goorkrodger* (1870) 84. Glo. Grose (1790) *MS. add.* (M.) Hmp.¹ Dev. The ewes and lambs, with the preceding year's hog sheep, Vancouver *Agric.* 346, in Pengelly *Provinc.* (1875) 93. (16) ne.Lan.¹, s.Chs.¹ Glo. Hogs wool, long wool, tagg, *Horae Subsecivae* (1777) 215. e.An. (Hall.), e.Suf. (F.H.) w.Som.¹ The wool of a hog sheep which had not been shorn as a lamb, and consequently it is the growth of about eighteen months instead of twelve, the ordinary growth of the fleece. Hog-wool is, by reason of its age, of greater length of staple, and *gen.* of more value per lb. than the fleece of the same animal if it had been shorn as a lamb at six months old. Dev. *Horae Subsecivae* (1777) 215.

6. Phr. (1) hog and score, a term formerly used in buying sheep, one being allowed in, in addition to every score; (2) — and tatoe, 'braxy' mutton stewed with potatoes, onions, salt, and pepper; (3) — in har'st, a young sheep, that is smeared at the end of harvest, when it ceases to be a lamb; (4) a Hampshire hog, a country simpleton; (5) to lose a hog for a ha'porth or pennyworth o' tar, prov., to be niggardly or over-economical in farming.

(1) Tev. (Jam.) (2) *ib.* It is customary with those who have store-farms to salt the 'fa'en meat' (i.e. the sheep that have died of 'the sickness') for the use of servants during the winter (*ib.*). (3) Sc. The central dish was a yearling lamb, called 'a hog in har'st,' roasted whole, Scott *Waverley* (1814) xx; (Jam.) (4) Hmp. Ellis *Pronunc.* (1889) V. 103. (5) e.Yks. Let's not loase a hogg for a hawporth of tar, *Spec. Dial.* 42. Not. (L.C.M.) Nhp.² To conclude with the old proverbe, hee that will loose a sheepe (or a hogge) for a pennyworth of tarre, cannot deserve the name of a good husband, *Cyman's Instructor* (1636).

7. The first fleece clipped from a sheep. w.Yks. (S.P.U.), Nhp.¹

8. A horse of a year old.

War. (J.R.W.) Som. W. & J. Gl. (1873). w.Som.¹ A sale of 'Live Stock,' among which is a 'black hog cart mare,' *Wellington Wkly. News* (Mar. 14, 1878).

Hence **Hog-colt**, *sb.* a colt or filly of a year old.

Glo.¹ Hmp. Grose (1790); Hmp.¹ Som. One hog colt. Sale bill, *Weston Merc.* (Mar. 4, 1876); (W.F.R.); Morton *Cyclo. Agric.* (1863). w.Som.¹ w.Dev. Marshall *Rur. Econ.* (1796).

9. Any animal of a year old.

Wil. Originally meant a castrated animal, .. now used for any animal of a year old, as a hog bull, a chilver hog sheep, Davis *Agric.* (1813); Wil.¹ *Wilts Arch. Mag.* XVII. 303.

10. A shilling.

Ir. I'll pay five shillings a week... Here's five hogs to begin with, Lever *O'Malley* (1841) xii ; Before the English and Irish currency were assimilated in 1825, a white hog meant an English shilling or twelve pence, and a black hog the Irish shilling of thirteen pence, *N. & Q.* (1851) 1st S. iv. 240 ; Grose (1790) *MS. add.* (C.) Dub. 'Till you pay me a hog for the pike, Barrington *Sketches* (1830) III. xxv. Lon. A sixpence is a ' tanner '; a shilling a ' bob ' or a ' hog,' Mayhew *Lond. Labour* (1851) I. 473. Ken. A score of hogs, Nairne *Tales* (1790) 47, ed. 1824. Slang. ' What's here!' cried he, searching the attorney's pockets ... ' one quid, . . three hogs, and a kick,' Ainsworth *Rookwood* (1834) bk. III. xiii.

11. Curling term : a stone which does not pass over the distance score.

Sc. The stone neglects the rank And stops midway; . . ev'ry mouth Cries ' Off the hog,' Græme *Poems* in Anderson *Poets*, XI. 44 (Jam.); (G.W.) n.Sc. It seems to be denominated from its laziness. It is thrown aside, as of no account in the game (Jam.). Lth. Allan's first stone was a 'hog,' Strathesk *More Bits* (ed. 1885) 271 ; Tak' him aff—he's a hog, *ib.* Gall. The trimling player stells his tramps Wi' mony a stamping stay; Af gangs his stane, and ay it clamps, But hoh portule, a hog—It grunts that day, Mactaggart *Encycl.* (1824) 81, ed. 1876 ; If the bottom of a stone gets over this ' score,' and its upper bulb not, still that stone is no hogg. If the stones come not over this line, they are flung out of the game, *ib.* 274. Wgt. The willing rink watch how each stone is sent, And with deft brooms the lazy hog prevent, Fraser *Poems* (1885) 202 ; We'll soop up the stanes wi' the greatest o' pains, An' strive tae ha'e nae hogs ava, *ib.* 210.

Hence **Hogged**, *ppl. adj., fig.* fallen behind in substance or trade.

Rnf. The ballast o' every business has shifted; an' there's no a merchant amang us that's no hogged mair or less, *Blackw. Mag.* (Sept. 1822) 307 (Jam.).

12. The distance-line in the game of curling. *Gen.* in *comp.* **Hog-score**; also in form **Hogging-score.** Also used *fig.*

Sc. It was wholly hidden into the butcher's stone back at the hog-score, Tweeddale *Moff* (1896) 161 ; The score short of which your stone is a ' hog ' is sometimes called the hoggin' score— usually the hog-score. So the player is ' a hog,' the score is ' the hog,' the stone is ' a hog' (G.W.) ; O'er far to either side Or lag ahint the hoggin' score, *R. Caled. Curling Club Ann.* (1887-88) 379. Frf. Feech, man, ye're no owre the hog score, Inglis *Ain Flk.* (1895) 96. Per. The nineteenth century has proved, in the language of curlers, a hogscore to not a few old Scottish customs, Haliburton *Fields* (1890) 1. Ayr. But now he lays on Death's hog-score, Burns *Tam Samson* (1787) st. 5. Lnk. Stan' back at the hog wi' a besom, Watson *Poems* (1853) 63. Peb. Yont the hog-score, straight in the way, [He] warns, o' his flock, ilk chiel His stane to lay, Lintoun *Green* (1685) 38, ed. 1817. Gall. They are made in the form of a wave, and are placed one fifth part of the whole rink from either witter; that is to say, if the rink be fifty yards long from tee to tee, the hog-scores of that rink are thirty yards distant from [each other]. ... Sweeping is not allowed until the stone comes over the ' hogg,' unless by the person who played, Mactaggart *Encycl.* (1824) 274, ed. 1876. n.Ir. A shot we try at ' chap an' lie,' At ' hogs ' we luk sae dreary, O ; Then fling the stane wi' micht an' main, Lyttle *Robin Gordon*, 96.

Hence *to lie at the hog-score, phr.* not to be able to get over some difficulty in an undertaking. Cld. (Jam.)

13. A term used in the game of peg-tops; see below. Cf. **hoges.**

e.Yks.[1] When a boy throws his top down, and it spins round on its side, instead of on its peg, it is called a hog ; if it becomes entangled in the string it is called a hog in a band. In either case he has to put it into the ring, to be aimed at by the other players, and it is often split up, to the great grief of the owner, *MS. add.* (T.H.)

14. v. To cut short the mane of a horse or pony, so that it stands straight up like a brush.

Nhp.[1] ' To hog a horse's mane,' is to cut it up on both sides to a point. War. It may sometimes but rarely happen that a hunter's mane grows so badly ... it may be necessary to hog it, Mordaunt & Verney *War. Hunt* (1896) I. 293. s.Wor.[1] Sus., Hmp. Holloway. Wil.[1], w.Som.[1]

Hence (1) **Hog-mane**, *sb.* a horse's mane, cut quite short, so as to stand erect ; (2) **-maned**, *ppl. adj.* having the mane cut quite short.

(1) Shr.[1] Sus., Hmp. Holloway. I.W.[1] (2) n.Lin.[1] w.Som.[1] Used by auctioneers in their advertisements.

15. To cut or trim a hedge by sloping it to the top.

nw.Der.[1], Der.[2], Shr.[1], Hrf.[1], Wil.[1]

Hence **Hog'd**, *ppl. adj.* cut, clipt.

Wil. A hog'd thorn hedge, Davis *Agric.* (1813).

16. To clip or make pollards of trees.

Per. To cut them over about the place where the branches begin to divide. In this case they are said to be hoggit (Jam.)

17. To hack, cut off roughly. s.Wor. (H.K.)

HOG, *sb.[2]* and *v.[2]* Wm. Yks. Lan. Chs. Flt. Wor. Shr. Also Dev. [og.] **1.** *sb.* A mound or heap of earth in which potatoes, &c. are stored to keep out the frost.

s.Wm. (J.A.B.) Lan. I laid up 17 half bushels of [seed potatoes] in one hog and 6 half bushels of little ones in another, Walkden *Diary* (ed. 1866) 56; The 'hog' was the nook where the potatoes were put and covered over, and the word was after-wards transferred to the more convenient pit, Davies *Races* (1856) 233. ne.Lan.[1] Chs. Morton *Cyclo. Agric.* (1863) ; Chs.[1] A potato hog is a heap of potatoes covered with straw and soil to keep out the frost. The potatoes are then said to be ' hogged up' or ' in the hog '; Chs.[2] ; Chs.[3] A heap of potatoes, in form either conical or roof shaped. It is covered with earth and either straw fern or the wizells of the potatoes, to keep the root from frost ; such is the usual mode in Chs. for storing potatoes, mangolds, and turnips in winter. s.Chs.[1], Flt. (T.K.J.), Shr.[12], Dev.[1]

2. v. To earth up potatoes, &c. in a heap.

w.Yks. (J.T.) Lan. Davies *Races* (1856) 233 ; Lan.[1] I put off at present, being throng hogging up some of my potatoes, Walker *Diary* (1730. 23. ne.Lan.[1], Chs.[12], s.Chs.[1] Wor. Oggin is placing the potatoes in long rows in the field, covering them with straw and then earth, leaving straw to come through the earth at the top of the earth at intervals for ventilation (E.S.). Shr.[1]

HOG, *sb.[3]* Stf. Som. In phr. *hog, dog, or devil*; see below. Cf. hob, *sb.[1]*

s.Stf. I'd fight this as lung as I could stand again, hog, dog, or divil, Murray *Rainbow Gold* (1886) 159. w.Som.[1] 'I 'ont hark to,' or ' I don't care vor hog, dog, nor devil.' Prob. an alliterative change from hob or devil.

HOG, *v.[3]* Yks. [og.] To spy after people who are courting.

w.Yks. To go ' oggin ' is to go watching courters (S.P.U.); (J.W.)

HOG, *v.[4]* Suf. To tumble.

e.Suf. They never have a bed made ; they hog out and **hog** in as best they can (F.H.).

HOG, see **Hug**, *v.*

HOGA, *sb.* Sh.I. A hill-pasture.

Your young horse is up i' da hoga, *Sh. News* (Mar. 18, 1899); Hoga [hag] is a piece of hill or uncultivated land enclosed for pasture, or in a more general sense, hill-pasture, Jakobsen *Dial.* (1897) 108.

[ON. *hagi*, a pasture : Icelanders dist. betw. *túrs* and *engjar*, for haymaking, and *hagar* for grazing (Vigfusson).]

HOG-A-BACK, *sb.* Cum.[4] The blue scabious, *Scabiosa succisa.* Also called **Blue-buttons** (q.v.).

HOGALIF, *sb.* Sh.I. Also written **hagalef, hoga-leave** [ho'gəlif.] The privilege given to a man to use another's distant field for cutting peat, also, the payment for such a privilege.

Hoga-leave ... liberty either to cut peats or to have a animals grazing for a certain payment in another skattald, and then secondly : payment for this liberty to make use of another skattald, and hence the phr. to pay hoga-leave, Jakobsen *Dial.* (1897) 108 ; If there be no moss in the scatthold contiguous to his farm, the tenant must pay for the privilege to cut peat in some other common and this payment is called hogalif, Edmonston *Zell.* (1809) I. 149 (Jam.) ; S. & Ork.[1]

[ON. *hagalýfi*, leave, permission for cutting (Jakobsen, *l. c.*).]

HOGAMADOG, *sb.* Nhb.[1] The huge ball of snow made by boys in rolling a snowball over soft snow.

HOGA-WE, *sb.* Nhp.[2] A boys' game, in which the chief feature is tickling or gently striking.

HOG-BOAT, *sb. Obsol.* Sus. A small kind of fishing-boat formerly in use at Brighton.

Going out of use. There were only two on the beach in 1862 (F.E.S.) ; Merrifield *Nat. Hist. Brighton* (1864) 102.

HOGE, *int.* w.Yks.[2] [ōg.] A cry used by shepherds to call sheep to be fed.

HOGER, *sb.* Sh.I. Condition, circumstances.
To come till a puir hoger, JAKOBSEN *Norsk in Sh.* (1897) 36; S. & Ork.[1] ' To come to an ill hoger,' to come to an ill end.

HOGES, *sb. pl.* N.I.[1] A boys' game played with peg-tops. Cf. hog, *sb.*[1] 13.
The victor is entitled to give a certain number of blows with the spike of his ' peerie ' to the wood part of his opponent's.

HOGEY, see **Huggerie**.

HOGG, *sb.* War. Pem. [og.] Subsoil ; the red soil on the layers of limestone.
War. Certain limestone beds of the Lower Lias are so called by the quarrymen near Stratford-on-Avon, PHILLIPS *Geol.* (1871) 109. s.Pem. (W.M.M.)

HOGG, *v.* Obs. Sc. To ' shog,' jolt. Cf. hog-shouther.
Aga. You'll hogg your lunach in a skull [shog your child in a basket made for a cradle], *Old Ballad* (JAM.).

HOGGAN, *sb.*[1] Cor. Also written hogan-, hoggen ; and in forms agan Cor.[3] ; haggen-, hugging-. [o·gən.]
1. A pork pasty ; a flat cake, *gen.* with a piece of salt pork in the centre. Cf. fuggan, hobban.
Tom Trevarton had a piece of hoggan weth un, HIGHAM *Dial.* (1866) 14 ; A passel of good things, flesh and fowl and figgy hoggens, T. *Towser* (1873) 4 ; (J.W.) ; Cor.[1] A cake made of flour and raisins, often eaten by miners for dinner. Sometimes called figgy hoggan or fuggan. A pork pasty ; Cor.[2] ; Cor.[3] A large bun ; a ' plum ' [raisin] bun, rather heavy baked piece of dough, often baked with a slice of pork pressed into the top before baking.
2. *Comp.* Hoggan-bag, a miner's bag in which he carries his provisions ; mutton or beef boiled or baked in pie-crust.
(H.E.) ; Eggs, clidgy, traade, and hoganbags, J. TRENOODLE *Spec. Dial.* (1846) 39 ; GROSE (1790).
3. The stomach of a pig. Cor.[3]
[1. OCor. *hogen*, a pork pasty, a der. of *hoch*, a pig (cp. Wel. *hwch*, a sow) (WILLIAMS).]

HOGGAN, *sb.*[2] Cor. Also written hogan. [o·gən.]
The fruit of the hawthorn, *Crataegus Oxyacantha.* See Hog, *sb.*[1] 2 (2).
Cor. (B. & H.) w.Cor. A haws is also called a ' hoggan,' BOTTRELL *Trad.* 3rd S. 158.

HOGGARD, *sb.* s.Sur. [o·gəd.] One who looks after pigs, a hog-herd. (T.T.C.)

HOGGER, *sb.* Sc. Irel. Nhb. Dur. Cum. Wm. Lan. Stf. Nhp. Also written hoger Ant. ; hoger Sc. (JAM.) ; hoggar Sc. Nhb. Dur. ; and in forms hooger Lnk. ; hugger Per. Ayr. Ant. ; hugger Sc. Stf.[1] [h)o·gə(r.]
1. A stocking with the foot cut off, used as a gaiter. See Cockers, *sb.*[1] 2.
Sc. Some had hoggars, some straw boots, Some uncovered legs and coots, MAIDMENT *Pasquils* (1868) 232 ; And there she washed her foul face clean, And dried it wi' a huggar, CHILD *Ballads* (1884) I. 303. Abd. A pair of grey hoggers well clinked benew, ROSS *Helenore* (1768) *Sng.* (JAM.) Per. Lest their limbs should catch cold, they are securely encircled with ample huggars, MONTEATH *Dunblane* (1835) 84, ed. 1887. Rnf. Aff his huggars Watty drew, PICKEN *Poems* (1813) II. 47. Ayr. Whyles, on a blusterous nicht, he would draw on a pair o' huggers to hap his legs, SERVICE *Notandums* (1890) 71. Lnk. Hoogers—that is, old stockings minus the feet, worn to protect the limbs during harvest operations from the weather, stubbles, and thistles, HAMILTON *Poems* (1865) 183. Edb. His limbs encased in strong gray rig-and-fur hoggers, BALLANTINE *Gaberlunzie* (ed. 1875) 21. Slk. Stockins that are in fack huggers, CHR. NORTH *Noctes* (ed. 1856) IV. 38. Dmf. SHAW *Schoolmaster* (1899) 349. Gall. Knitted gaiters worn by boys over their shoes and above the knees, were so called (A.W.). Ant. *Ballymena Obs.* (1892) ; N.Cy.[1] Nhb. Wi' sark and hoggers, like maw brothers, WILSON *Pitman's Pay* (1843) 23 ; Nhb.[1] Footless stockings worn by pitmen at work. Hoggers were sometimes used for riding stockings instead of gaiters by country people ; and they are variously called looags, scoggers, hoggers, and gamashers. Nhb., Dur. There is my hoggara, likewise my hoggers, Bishoprick Garl. (1834) 54. e.Dur.[1] The coal-hewer formerly wore his stockings with the ' feet ' cut off, so that when small coals got into the stocking-foot, he had only to pull off this, and not the whole stocking ; consequently his ankles were bare, while the stocking-leg covered his calf. He still swears by his

hoggers, as, ' Dash mi hoggers ! ' s.Dur. Stockings worn over the shoes in snowy weather to keep the feet dry. ' T'snaw was that deep she had te put on hoggers te keep hersel dry ' (J.E.D.). Cum.[1] (s.v. Beutt stockins) ; Cum.[4], Wm. (J.H.), ne.Lan.[1], Stf.[1], Nhp.[1]
Hence (1) Hoggart, *ppl. adj.* of stockings: footless, having no feet ; (2) Hugert, *ppl. adj.* clothed with hoggers or footless stockings ; (3) Huggerful, *sb.* a stocking-leg full.
(1) Sc. Her tawny face was furrowed ower Like a beggar's hoggart hose, VEDDER *Poems* (1842) 224. (2) Rnf. While herdies sing wi' huggert taes, WILSON *Poems* (1816) *Ep. to Mr. W. M.* (3) Sc. I've a huggerfu' o' saut, CHAMBERS *Sngs.* (1829) I. 130. Ayr. A wee callan is swappin' a soocker for a huggerfu' o' boola, SERVICE *Notandums* (1890) 74.
2. An old stocking used as a purse. Also used *fig.*
Sc. I have a bit auld hogger an' something in't, thou's get it when I die, GRAHAM *Writings* (1883) II. 56. Per. A rich man is here said to possess a lang hugger (G.W.) ; I heard one stone-mason say to another, ' Ye'll draw the hugger for this ! ' [tip me]. Stockings were formerly largely used by the peasantry as purses —hence ' draw the hugger' means, take out the purse and pay something, *ib.* ; Your hugger and my hugger coupit intil ane wad be sure to keep us comfortable as lang's we leeve, MONTEATH *Dunblane* (1835) 92, ed. 1887. Cld. A ' hugger ' cam doon the lum and fell at his feet. He . . . finding it very heavy opened it. His astonishment was great when he fand it fu' o' goud pieces, Edb. *Antiq. Mag.* (1848) 40. Dmb. A' that she has in the hugger may be his ain, if he just tak' her alang wi't, CROSS *Disruption* (1844) vii. Ayr. I hae maybe a hogger and I ken when I die wha sall get the golden guts o't, GALT *Entail* (1823) xxxix. Lnk. Nae millstane o' debt roun' the neck, but something laid by in a hugger, NICHOLSON *Kilwuddie* (ed. 1895) 156.
3. A short pipe of leather, metal, &c., used as a con-nexion.
Nhb. A short length of pipe, esp. the lead-away pipe from the top length of a pumping set. Also the short length of pipe at the suction end. In old locomotive engines, the flexible tube used for insertion and withdrawal in the feed tank. In modern locomotives, the india-rubber pipe connecting the tender feed with the engine delivery pipe. Also the india-rubber connection pipes for the Westinghouse and for the vacuum brake between carriages (R.O.H.) ; Nhb.[1] The receptacle at the top of a delivery pipe of a pump to receive the water before its discharge into the conduit. A spout and pipe lead away the discharged water. This arrange-ment is sometimes called a collar-lander. Nhb., Dur. GREENWELL *Coal Tr. Gl.* (1849). Dur. GIBSON *Up-Weardale Gl.* (1870). e.Dur.[1]
4. *Comp.* (1) Hogger-pipe, the uppermost length in a pumping set, with an attachment cast on it for the hogger. Nhb. (R.O.H.) ; (2) -pump, the top pump of a set, with a short pipe cast on to it at right angles near the top. Nhb., Dur. GREENWELL *Coal Tr. Gl.* (1849).

HOGGERDEMOW, *sb.* and *v.* War. Glo. Oxf. Also in forms hoggerimaw War.[2] ; hoggery-maw Glo.[1] ; hoggerymore, oggery-maw War. ; oggery-mow Oxf.
1. *sb.* A bill for cutting hedges. War.[12] See Hocketi-mow.
2. A very long-handled knife or scythe used for trim-ming ricks or corn-stacks.
War. (R.P.C.) ; (L.M.) ; War.[2] This tool is often made from an old scythe blade with the end filed off and the cutting edge curved upwards at the end of the blade. Glo.[1], Oxf. (J.W.)
3. *v.* To work in an awkward, bungling manner ; to hack or cut a thing clumsily.
Glo. On course we cud a-go in and a-hoggerymaw ut aff and leäve 's many yeds on the ground as was in the sheiff, BUCKMAN *Darke's Sojourn* (1890) xxii ; Glo.[1]

HOGGET, *sb.*[1] Irel. Nhb. Cum. Yks. Chs. Not. War. Shr. e.An. Sus. Hmp. Wil. Som. Dev. Cor. [h)o·git, -ət.] 1. A young sheep of about one year old. See Hog, *sb.*[1] 4.
Ir. This seems to be a word imported by the English as it has no Irish signification. It is now, however, common both with the English and Irish speaking people, *Flk-Lore Rec.* (1881) IV. 125. Nhb.[1] Cum.[4] A sheep more than one year old. ' Cross Down hoggs to 27s. 6d., cross hoggets to 26s. 6d.,' *Carlisle Patr.* (Jan. 27, 1899) 2, col. 4. e.Yks. The fleeces of the wethers, ewes, hogs or hoggits, MARSHALL *Reports* (1818) I. 521. n.Chs.[1], Not.[12], War. (J.R.W.), Shr.[12] e.An.[1] A sheep a year old, after its first shearing. Nrf. The fleeces of hoggets, that is year-old sheep which have never been shorn before, HAGGARD *Farmer's Year*,

viii, in *Longman's Mag.* (Apr. 1899) 502; Year old sheep not sheared, YOUNG *Annals Agric.* (1784–1815) XVI. 45. **Suf.** The female sheep in its second year, RAINBIRD *Agric.* (1819) 291, ed. 1849; Lambs kept for the recruit of the flock, and so called till after their first shearing, which in this flock [on Hardwick Heath] is when they are about sixteen months old, CULLUM *Hist. Hawsted* (1813); Lambs of last yeaning, YOUNG *Annals Agric.* (1784–1815) XI. 197; (C.T.) **e.Suf.** (F.H.) **Sus.¹** A little hogget what she'd hobbed-up (s.v. Holp). **Wil.** A wether sheep not 2 yrs. old (E.H.G.). **Som.** W. & J. *Gl.* (1873). **Dev.** In very gen. use, *Lin. N. & Q.* 145. **Cor.¹** A two-year-old ewe; **Cor.²**

Hence **Hogget-wool**, *sb.* wool from a one-year-old sheep. e.Suf. (F.H.) See Hog-wool, s.v. Hog, *sb.¹* 5.

2. A colt of a year old.

War. (J.R.W.) **Hmp.** GROSE (1790); *Wheeler's Hmp. Mag.* (1828) 481; **Hmp.¹** **Som.** W. & J. *Gl.* (1873).

HOGGET, *sb.²* Sc. Irel. Also written **hoggat** N.I.¹; **hoggit** Ayr.; and in forms **hoggart** N.I.¹; **hogyet** Gall.; **hugget** Rnf. [ho·git, ·ət.] **1.** A hogshead, a large cask or barrel.

Rnf. The lass wi' hakit hands an' feet, An' like a hugget roun' the waist, M'GILVRAY *Poems* (ed. 1862) 48. **Ayr.** Loaded seemingly with a hogget of tobacco and grocery wares, but the hogget was empty and loose in the head, GALT *Gilhaize* (1823) xxi. **Lnk.** To buy their hogget for my gill, COGHILL *Poems* (1890) 108. **Gall.** 'He spak right how, My name is Death.' Country folk say of those who speak this way, 'that they speak as if the soun' cam out o' a hogyet,' MACTAGGART *Encycl.* (1824) 276, ed. 1876.

2. *Obs.* A dry measure containing ten bushels. N.I.¹

HOGGIN, see Huggin.

HOGGING SHIRT, *phr.* Yks. Wor. A very coarse sort of shirt.

w.Yks.² A man who had torn his shirt whilst working, said, 'Way, it's nobbut my hoggin' shirt,' meaning apparently his working shirt. **Wor.** He had an old coarse shirt, patched both at the neck and hand, of that very coarse sort which in that county goes by the name of ' Hogging ' shirts, *Wil. Arch. Mag.* XXVI. 14.

HOGGINS, *sb. pl.* Ess. [o·ginz.] Gravel out of which the largest stones have been sifted. Occas. in *sing.*

'No 'm, this aint siftins—they've left the medium stones in this —this is hoggins.' Spoken by a gardener who had just brought a load of gravel (F.P.); Hoggin, 2s. 9d. per yard (A.S.P.); **Ess.¹** The sand sifted from the gravel before the stones are carted upon the roads.

HOGGINS, *sb.* Oxf. An ' innings ' in the game of cricket or other similar game.

The captain of a side will say, ' Let's hit up for hoggins.' Or a boy will protest against the premature drawing of stumps by saying, ' Not till I've had my hoggins ' (G.O.).

HOGGISH, *adj.* Der. Not. Wor. Glo. Ken. [o·giʃ.] **1.** Greedy, grasping.

n.Not. She's not hoggish—she'll gie, if she has oat (J.P.K.). **Ken.** A boy was asked the meaning of the command ' Thou shalt not covet.' The answer was that we were not to be 'oggish (A.L.M.).

2. Obstinate.

Der. He's so queerish and snappish, and hoggish as niver were, VERNEY *Stone Edge* (1868) viii. **w.Wor.¹, Glo.¹**

HOGGLE, *sb.* Ess. A bump, sudden jolt or jerk.

An old woman here, said, ' I came down with a hoggle ' (H.H.M.).

HOGGLE, *v.* Som. [o·gl.] To pick over the refuse from a ' mindry ' for the sake of the small particles of ore.

At Shipham women would earn often £1 10s. a week by ' hoggling ' (W.F.R.).

HOGGLER, *sb.* Obs. Som. Sidesmen or kind of assistants to the churchwardens ; see below.

Freq. occurring in early churchwardens' accounts of the parish of Banwell. It is explained to mean ' sidesmen,' or some kind of assistants to the churchwardens. They seem to have been responsible for collecting certain rates. Two seem to have been appointed, one for the upland, the other for the lowland or marsh (W.F.R.).

HOGGLING, *vbl. sb.¹* Pem. [o·glin.] The begging and receiving of alms or New Year's gifts ; see below.

s.Pem. Lime-burners go round to beg of the farmers who employ them ; this is hoggling, *Laws Little Eng.* (1888) 420; (W.M.M.)

HOGGLING, *vbl. sb.²* Som. Clumsy, awkward work.

The word ' hoggling ' for clumsy work is still a living expression in the neighbourhood of Cheddar, *Antiquary* (1892) XXV. 25.

HOGGLING, *prp.* Sc. (JAM.) In phr. *hoggling and boggling*, unsteady, moving backwards and forwards.

HOGGREL, *sb.* Sc. Nhb. Lei. Nhp. Nrf. s.Cy. Also written **hogrel** Sc. (JAM.) ; and in forms **hoggerel** Nhb.¹ Lei.¹ ; **hoggeril** Lei.¹ [h)o·gril.] A young sheep of about a year old. See Hog, *sb.¹* 4, Hogget, *sb.¹* 1.

Tev. (JAM.) **Nhb.** Male sheep from weaning, or taking from the ewes, to the shearing or clipping for the first time, are called hogs, or hoggerels, or lamb-hogs, CULLEY *Live Stock* (1801) 18; (R.O.H.); **Nhb.¹** **Lei.** RAY (1691) ; (K.) ; **Lei.¹** **Nhp.** RAY (1691) ; (K.) **Nrf., s.Cy.** HOLLOWAY. [A Hogrell, a sheepe two yeres old, *Bidens*, BARET (1580).]

HOGGY, *adj.* w.Wor.¹ [o·gi.] Clumsy, ugly.

The parish 'as give poor little Bill this 'ere pa'r o' boots. I should like far you to saay, miss, did you ever see a hoggier pa'r ? Why the poor lad canna lift 'is fit up 'ardly, thaay be so lombersome.

HOGH, HOGHLE, see How, *sb.¹*, How(e, *adj.*, **Houghle,** *sb.¹, v.*

HOGLIN(G,*sb.* e.An. [o·glin.] A baked apple dumpling.

e.An.¹ A homely sort of pastry, made by folding sliced apples with sugar in a coarse crust, and baking them without a pan. Otherwise called a ' flap-jack,' an ' apple-hoglin,' &c. (s.v. Applejack). **Nrf.** (F.H.), **Ess.¹**

HOG-LIQUOR, *sb.* Chs. The liquor produced in the course of cheese-making.

The hog-liquor of the Cheshire dairy farms, MARSHALL *Review* (1818) II. 64.

HOGMANAY, *sb.* Sc. Nhb. Cum. Wm. Yks. Also written **hoghmanay** Lnk. ; and in forms **hagmana** Sc. Lakel.² Cum. ; **hagmanay** Nhb. ; **hagmanheigh** Yks. ; **hagmena** N.Cy.¹ Nhb. n.Yks. ; **hagnuna** Cum. ; **hogamanay** Nhb.¹ ; **hogmanae** Edb. ; **hogmanee** Ayr. ; **hogmena** Bnff. ; **hogmenay** Sc. (JAM.) ; **hogminae** Lth. ; **hogminay** ne.Sc. ; **hogmonay** e.Sc. ; **hogmynae** Lnk. ; **hoguemennay** Sc.

1. The 31st of December, New Year's Eve. Also used *attrib.*, and in *comb.* Hogmanay day, night, &c.

Sc. It is ordinary among some plebeians to go about from door to door upon New Year's eve, crying Hagmana, a corrupted word from the Greek Hagia-mana, which signifies the holy month, CALDER *Presbyt. Eloq.* (1694) 193, ed. 1847 ; Base popish angels, which first keept that day [Christmas] And with the herds sung the first Hoguemennay, MAIDMENT *Pasquils* (1868) 269; The schoolboys in those days were all expected to bring a game-cock to the annual ' main,' or fight, which was usually held on the earthen floor of the village school on Hogmanay, WRIGHT *Sc. Life* (1897) 42. **n.Sc.** Hogmanay was another of the days to be remembered it in this wise. . . Our sports did not begin until the evening. We would form a party of four or five, thoroughly disguise ourselves, and then sally forth, going from house to house. We boldly entered the kitchen, shouting lustily—' Rise up, good wife, and shak' yer feathers, Dinna think that we are beggars: We are guid folks come to play, Rise up, an' gie us Hogmanay.' Then we boldly insisted upon kissing every unmarried female in the room, claiming at the same time from the ' guid-wife ' . . . hogmanay more specifically, in the form of refreshment, GORDON *Carglen* (1891) 292. **Banff.** About Yule-time an' Hogmenai, TAYLOR *Poems* (1787) 44. **Abd.** Jist last Hogmanay Nicht, as usual a gay nicht, OGG *Willie Waly* (1873) 41. **Frf.** Hogmanay is the mighty winter festival of Thrums, BARRIE *Tommy* (1896) 77 ; About fifty years ago, it was a common custom for the youths in the country villages to go round amongst their better-off neighbours on Hogmanay night, disguised as guisers, partly for sport and also for the purpose of getting something nice to eat. The version of the rhyme then employed by them in the parish of Kirkden was as follows :—' Get up, guideman, and be na sweer, And deal your bread as lang 's you're here; The day will come when you'll be dead, You'll neither care for meal nor bread,' *N. & Q.* (1878) 5th S. x. 278. **Per.** I cam' to remind you That this is Hogmanay, STEWART *Character* (1857) 160. **w.Sc.** On the 31st Dec., all household work was stopped, rock emptied, yarn reeled and hanked, and wheel and reel put into an outhouse. The house itself was white-washed and cleaned. A block of wood or large piece of coal was put on the fire about ten p.m. so that it would be burning briskly before the household retired to bed. The last thing done by those who possessed a cow or horse was to visit

byre or stable, and I have been told it was the practice with
ne, twenty years before my recollection, to say the Lord's Prayer
ing this visit, NAPIER *Flk-Lore* (1879) 159. **Fif.** Saunders was
ing in his easy chair at the side of a blazing fire on Auld
gmanay night, ROBERTSON *Provost* (1894) 92. **Rnf.** 'Twas fear
y micht forget themsels, Puir me sae anxious made, That on
t scowlin' Hogmanay At hame they wad ha' stayed, YOUNG
turs (1865) 19. **Ayr.** Blithe and ree frae New 'er's day to
gmanae, GALT *Gilhaise* (1823) v. **Lnk.** We renounce Hallow-
n, Hogmynae night, Valentine's even, WODROW *Ch. Hist.*
n1) III. 351, ed. 1848. **Lth.** Neist Hogminae, to Scotsmen
r, Comes smiling in fu' dainty, BRUCE *Poems* (1813) II. 16 ;
ildrife Rab last Hoghmanay Cam' tae try his hand at wooin',
NEILL *Preston* (c. 1895) 92. **Edb.** We first canty held our
g-ma-nae, LEARMONT *Poems* (1791) 192. **N.Cy.¹ Nhb.** He
ely forgets 'twas on Hogmanay day That he found me half
d 'mang the snaw, PROUDLOCK *Borderland Muse* (1896) 347 ;
e Hagmena is still preserved amongst them [at Newcastle],
g, Hagman-heigh,' DIXON *Sngs. Eng. Peas.* (1846) 186, ed. 1857.
  The offering for which children go round and beg on
w Year's Eve ; a New Year's gift.
Sc. Hogmanay trollolay, Give us of your white bread and none
your grey, Get up and gie's our hogmanay, CHAMBERS *Pop.
mes* (1870) 165. **ne.Sc.** On the last night of the year the
ldren . . . went into the houses asking their hogminay, GREGOR
-Lore (1881) 162. **Frf.** We are bairns come to play— Get up
gie's oor Hogmanay, INGLIS *Ain Flk.* (1895) 107. **w.Sc.** Rise
gudewife, and shake your feathers, Dinna think that we are
ngars, We're girls and boys come out to-day, For to get our
d hogmanay, Hogmanay, trol-lol-lay. Give us of your white bread,
i not of your grey, Or else we'll knock at your door a' day, NAPIER
-Lore (1879) 154. **a.Sc.** At one time [the custom was] very pre-
ent in Sc., not on New Year's Day, but on Old Year's Day, under
e name of Hogmanay. In the south of Scotland it has greatly
en off, but in various rural districts it is still observed to a limited
tent. The children go in companies, chiefly to houses of people
he better class, and repeat the simple rhyme:—' My feet's cauld,
' shoon's thin, Gie's my cakes an' let's rin.' . . . It was not money
t was given and expected, but a cake and perhaps a bit of cheese
sometimes, no doubt, oat cake, but more *gen.* a bit of wheat-flour
ce baked with currants and raisins. On Dec. 30 last I saw a
aket containing perhaps 50 currant rolls, about the size of an
linary penny roll, ready to give to the children who might call
at day on their hogmanay errand, *N. & Q.* (1878) 5th S. x. 59.
y.¹ Nhb. The New Year's offering for which children beg.
eir common inquiry is, ' Please will you give us wor hoga-
nay !' Or, varying this, they chant : ' Hogamanay, hogamanay,
a wor breed-an'-cheese, an' set's away' (R.O.H.) ; **Nhb.¹** In n.Nhb.
e hogmanay is a small cake given to children on Old Year's
y ; or the spice bread and cheese, with liquor, given away, on
e same day. **Lakel.²** Ah've come ta lait mi hag-ma-na. **Cum.**
some parts of Cum., a number of boys and girls, on the eve of
w Year Day, go about from house to house, singing a sort
carol, of which the following lines are the first couplet :
agnuna, Trolola, Give us some pie, and let us go away.'
hen they receive their present of pie, they depart peaceably,
ishing the donor a Happy New Year, SANDERSON *Essay*, 59, in
nDERSON *Poems* (ed. 1820) I. Cum., Wm. NICOLSON (1677)
n. R. Lit. Soc. (1868) IX. **Yks.** Hagman-heigh, a local New-
ar's custom, of demanding a Christmas box ; formerly on behalf
the hagman, or wood cutter, in consideration of an extra supply
fuel at Christmas. ' To-night it is the new year's night,
morrow is the day, Sing, fellows, sing, Hagman-Heigh,' HONE
ble-bk. (1827) 8.

'l. Of Fr. origin. Cp. Norm. dial. *hoquinano, haguinelo,*
es on New Year's Eve ; *hoguilanno* (at Caen), a New
ar's gift, see DUMÉRIL (s.v. *Hoguinètes*).]

HOG-ME-DITHERUM, *sb.* Lin. A confused mass ; a
xture of many things.
THOMPSON *Hist. Boston* (1856) 710 ; Lin.¹

HOGMINNY, *sb.* Dev. [Not known to our correspon-
nts.] A very depraved young girl. (HALL.)

HOGMONAY, HOGMYNAE, see Hogmanay.

HOGNEL, *adj.* Hrf.² Uneven ; awkward, surly.

HOGO, *sb.* Irel. Nhb. Yks. Nhp. Hrt. e.An. Ken. Hmp.
V. Wil. Som. Amer. Also written **haugo** n.Yks.¹² ;
goh I.W.¹ ; and in forms **hoag** N.I.¹ ; **hoogo** e.An.¹²

Ken.¹ [(h)ō̆·gō.] **1.** A strong disagreeable smell or
odour. Also used *attrib.* Cf. fogo, *sb.¹*
Ir. Such as meat has when ' high' or tainted (A.S.P.). **N.I.¹
Nhb.¹** A very common expression is ' The meat' is hogo.' **Nhp.¹
Hrt.** Coleseed oil is mixed with fresh oil to lessen its hogo or
stinking scent, ELLIS *Mod. Husb.* (1750) IV. iii. **e.An.¹² Ken.¹**
A gamekeeper, noticing a horrible stench, exclaimed : ' Well,
this is a pretty hoogo, I think !' **Sus.¹² Hmp.** HOLLOWAY ;
Hmp.¹, I.W.¹ Wil.¹ Still freq. used of tainted meat or strong
cheese. **s.Wil.** *Monthly Mag.* (1814) II. 114. **Som.** W. & J. *Gl.*
(1873). **w.Som.¹** Well, Soce, this here's a pretty hogo, sure
enough ! [**Amer.** *Dial. Notes* (1896) I. 389.]

Hence **Haugoed,** *ppl. adj.* tainted like over-kept meat or
game. n.Yks.¹²

2. A disease, imaginary or otherwise, caused by a disagreeable smell.
e.Suf. That stink is enough to give one the hogo (F.H.).

[Fr. *haut goût*, high flavour.]

HO-GO, *sb.* Brks. Lon. A children's game played with
marbles ; see below.
Brks.¹ The first holds up a number in closed hand and says,
' Ho-go' ; the second says ' Hand full' ; the first then says ' How
many !' The other guesses. If he should guess correctly he is
entitled to take them all ; but otherwise he must give the difference between the number he guessed and the number actually
held up to ' make it so.' **Lon.** Also called ' How many eggs in a
basket !' GOMME *Games* (1894) 218.

HOG-OVER-HIGH, *sb.* e.An.¹ Suf.¹ e.Suf. (F.H.) The
game of leap-frog.

HOGSHEAD, *sb.* Wor. Hrf. Glo. Dor. Cor. **1.** A cask
or butt containing about 100 gallons of cider.
se.Wor.¹ Wor., Hrf. Of cider, 110 gallons, MORTON *Cyclo.
Agric.* (1863). **Hrf.²** The oak casks containing cider, usually 100
to 112 gallons. All other vessels for cider are casks. **Glo.¹** Pronounced Hockshet.

2. A dry measure of varying capacity ; see below.
Dor. Of lime, 4 bushels, MORTON *Cyclo. Agric.* (1863). **Dev.** Of
lime, sometimes 36 level pecks, or 40 ; sometimes 11½ heaped
bushels, Winchester, *ib.* **Cor.** Nine imperial bushels of lime, *ib.*

HOG-SHOUTHER, *sb.* and *v.* ? *Obs.* Sc. **1.** *sb.* A
game in which the players jostle or push each other with
the shoulders. **Sc.** (JAM.) **Ayr.** BURNS *Poems Gl.*, Globe ed.

2. *v.* To push or jostle with the shoulders.
Ayr. The warly race may drudge an' drive, Hog-shouther, jundie,
stretch, an' strive, BURNS *To W. Simpson* (May 1785) st. 16.

Hence **Hog-showthering,** *ppl. adj.* pushing, jostling.
Fif. A howdle o' hog-showtherin' freirs, Augustines, Carm'leits,
Cordeliers, But bauldly left ahent, To be that altar's body-guard,
TENNANT *Papistry* (1827) 203.

HOG-THRUSH, see Hob-thrust.

HOGWELLY, *adj.* Hrf.² Large, hoggish.

HOH, see How, *sb.¹*

HOHLE, *sb.* Lin. Also in forms **howl, owle.** A
wooden tunnel under a bank or road for the conveyance
of water.
Lin. In common use. ' We shall be glad to build howl at Bottesford 20 ft. long, 3 planks deep' (E.P.). **n.Lin.¹** ½ hundred nales
for a owle, 6*d.* ; crooks & bands for an howl, 2*s.* 6*d.* ; to Wm.
Stainforth for an howl, £1 1*s.* 0*d.*, *Bottesford Moors Acc.* (1809).

HOICHLE, HOIGHEL, see Hochle.

HOICK, *v.* Lin. To hoist, lift up.
Tha joompt in thysen, an' tha hoickt my feet wi' a flop fro' the
clady, TENNYSON *Spinster's Sweet-arts* (1885) ; Lin.¹ Now then, hoick.

HOID, see Hide, *v.²*

HOIDE, *v.* Sh.I. To conceal, hide.
Man, dü's gane fae bad ta wirse, Dy letter just but hoides a
curse, *Sh. News* (Oct. 16, 1897) ; (K.I.) ; (J.I.)

HOIDE, HOIDED, see Hide, *v.¹²*

HOIDEEN, *sb.* Sh. & Or.I. Also written **hoiddin** ;
hoyddeen S. & Ork.¹ [hœ̄·din.] A ' haaf' term for a
clergyman or minister.
Sh.I. (*Coll.* L.L.B.) ; He [the minister] had many other names,
such as, for instance, .. de hoideen, JAKOBSEN *Dial.* (1897) 26 ; **S. &
Ork.¹** Or.I. FERGUSSON *Rambles* (1884) 165.

[Lit. 'the threatener,' see Höder.]

HOIDER, *sb.* Lakel. Yks. Written **hoyder** Cum.¹⁴
[(h)oi·də(r).] Injury, mischief, in phr. *to play hoider,* (1) to
take severe measures to injure or harm a person or enter-

prise; (2) to complain or scold violently because anything has gone wrong.

(1) Cum.¹ Stop! you're gaan to play hoyder wi' me; Cum.⁴ w.Yks. (S.P.U.) (2) Lakel.² Ah threw t'cart ower at t'gap steed an' t'maister play'd hoider ower't. w.Yks. (S.P.U.)

HOIDLE, v.   Yks.   [oi·dl.]   **1.** To idle, loiter; to lose or waste time. n.Yks.¹²⁴   Hence (1) **Hoidler,** sb. a loiterer, idler: n.Yks.²; (2) **Hoidling,** ppl. adj. ib.; (3) **Hoidly,** adj. loitering, idling. n.Yks. (I.W.)   **2.** To compliment or flatter. n.Yks.²

HOIK(E, see Hike.

HOIL, v.   Yks.   To expel.

w.Yks. Hoil him out (S.P.U.); (HALL.)

HOIL(E, HOILIE, see Ail, sb.², Hole, sb.¹, Hooly.

HOILK, sb.   Sh.I.   See below.

In Unst a wooden oil vessel, broader at the bottom than at the top, is called 'a ôli hoilk,' JAKOBSEN Dial. (1897) 34.

[Norw. dial. holk, a small vessel for butter, cheese, or milk (AASEN).]

HOILY COAL, phr.   w.Yks.   Coal-tar; black grease or dirty oil, &c.   (S.P.U.), (M.F.)

Hence **Hoily coild,** ppl. adj. covered with coal-tar, grease, &c.

Great bokes runnin' across t'top, t'chimley jome hoily coild, HALLAM Wadsley Jack (1866) vi.

HOIN, v.   Yks. Lan.   Also written hoine m.Yks.; and in forms hooin ne.Yks.¹ w.Yks.⁶; hoon w.Yks.¹⁸ ne.Lan.¹; oine Yks.; ooin w.Yks. ne.Lan. e.Lan.¹; oyne e.Lan.¹; yooin w.Yks.⁶ [uin.]   **1.** To ill-treat, ill-use, esp. by starvation and chastisement. Cf. hone, v.⁸

w.Yks. Doant ooin him, Hlfx. Courier (May 29, 1897); T'wife vowed shoo'd stop no longer wi' sich a beast, ... shoo'd been ooined long eniff, CUDWORTH Dial. Sketches, 99; WRIGHT Gram. Wndhll. (1892) 51; w.Yks.¹ I's as waa to see 'em hoined as thou can be, ii. 350. ne.Lan. Everybody wur ooined at their house but Oliver an' th' dog, MATHER Idylls (1895) 210; ne.Lan.¹, e.Lan.¹

Hence (1) **Hoined,** ppl. adj. ill-used, maltreated; half-starved; (2) **Hoined-looking,** ppl. adj. ill-looking, as from sickness or bad treatment; (3) **Ooin,** sb. ill-treatment.

w.Yks. (1) My poor hooined bairns! Yksman. Comic Ann. 8; Poor oined thing, Leeds Merc. Suppl. (Oct. 26, 1895). (2) Hlfx. Courier (May 29, 1897). (3) So regg'd, an' so pale, an' hooined-leukin' wor he, Wol Ah pitied t'poor lad i' mi heart, Wilsden Alm. (1892) 30.

2. To overwork, overdo; to fatigue, oppress; to harass. Gen. in pp.

Yks. It's too hard work for him, he seems fair oined when he comes home of a neet (M.N.). ne.Yks.¹ m.Yks. Tak' care tha doosn't hoine thisel (F.P.T.). w.Yks. Fur rayther nur he sud be hoined, Shoo'd wheel him in a barra, PRESTON Poems (1864) 12; He wor fair hooined wi't'job (J.T.); w.Yks.¹ It hoins t'galloway fecafully, ii. 286; w.Yks.⁵⁴; w.Yks.⁵ 'Hooined to death.' 'It's fair hooining.' One returning from a crowded place of assembly declares that she 'ne'er wur so hooined i' her life afoar.' A man 'hooined ' his horse by over-working it, or, rather, in the act of over-working it. Also, to be neglected and put upon, as applied to a baby, who, having been left in the care of children, has not had its wants attended to. ' Come thee wâays to me doy!—it's bin fair hooined am sûre.' 'Ower-yooin'd,' over-fatigued. Lan. Oyned an' harrished whol life were a harebargain, CLEGG Sketches (1895) 397.

Hence **Hoined** or **Hooyned,** pp. overdone, over-pressed; low-spirited, harassed, depressed.

w.Yks. Stur abat, thal get reglar hooyned sitting there (W.H.); This lovin' wife, Hard-ooined although shoo be, CUDWORTH Dial. Sketches (1884) 107; w.Yks.⁸⁴

[1. The same word as ME. hônen in for-hônen, to despise (STRATMANN); MDu. hoonen, to ill-treat (OUDEMANS); cp. OFr. honnir, couvrir de honte publiquement (HATZFELD).]

HOIN, see Hone, v.²

HOIND, v.   ? Obs.   Chs.   Also written hoynd. To make a hard bargain; to screw up.

Chs.¹ Chs.² A landlord who behaves in this manner with his tenants, is said to hoynd them; Chs.⁸

HOINDUR, see Hinder, adj.¹

HOINS, sb. pl.   Sh.I.   [Not known to our correspondents.] The latest time of the night.   (Coll. L.L.B.)

HOINTIKLOK, sb.   Sh.I.   A beetle.

Oh gûd gad ! a hointiklok. . . Come an' shak' him aff or A'll be oot o' me head, Sh. News (Aug. 27, 1898); K.I.); (J.I.)

HOISE, v. and sb.   Sc. Irel. Cum. Yks. Lan.   Also written hoice ne.Lan.¹; hoize Edb.; hoyse Sc. Cum.¹⁴; and in form hoish e.Yks.¹ [h)oiz.]   **1.** v. To hoist, lift on high; to raise, elevate, lift. Cf. **heeze.**

Sc. They boysed their sails on Monenday morn, SCOTT Minstrelsy (1802) I. 301, ed. 1848. Or.I. Men at the top of the rock, who hoise up the net till it be over against the place where the young fowls sit, WALLACE Desc. Or. I. (1693) 43, ed. 1883. Rnf. The growlin' fish wives hoise their creels, PICKEN Poems (1813) I. 89. Ayr. I'm hois'd a wally wipe indeed, But I'm sae dizzy i' the head, I'll no stay lang up there, FISHER Poems (1790) 95. Lak. Ye are hoisin' Yer flags on heights, frae shore tae shore, THOMSON Musings (1881) 75. Edb. They . . . wad hoize our isle aboon the sky, LEARMONT Poems (1791) 169. Slk. Gin I could get a cleik o' the bane . . . I might hoise it gently up . . . and then pu' it out o' his mouth, CHR. NORTH Noctes (ed. 1856) II. 349. Rxb. Whan in her scales does Libra hoise The day an' night in equal poise, A. SCOTT Poems (ed. 1808) 93. Dmf. Treadna on worth, yersel' to hoise Up into view, QUINN Heather (1863) 23. Gall. It was you that . . . hoised him oot o' the wicket . . . when his lordship . . . cam' on us ower quick, CROCKETT Raiders (1894) xxxiii. N.I.¹ s.v. Hize. Cum.⁴ e.Yks.¹ s.v. Heyce. ne.Lan.¹

Hence **Hoising,** vbl. sb. a hoisting, lifting on high ; a kicking into the air.

Ir. The result was a severe hoising, KENNEDY Fireside Stories (1870) 148. Wxf. Won't you call me to hold up John Dunne the next time he desarves a hoising ? ib. Banks Boro (1867) 257.

2. Fig. To brag, vaunt; to bluster, rant; to talk, gossip.

Abd. (JAM.); The hinds did wi' the hizzies hoise, An' a' the country news Recount that day, ANDERSON Poems (1826) 100.

3. sb. A hoist, lift upwards; a kick upwards. Also used fig.

Ayr. They gie her on a rape a hoyse, BURNS Ordination (1786) st. 13. Edb. He ... gies them a' a hearty hoyse Wi's bacchanalian muse, BALLANTINE Gaberlunzie (ed. 1875) 210. Gall. So we e'en gied him a bit hoise and ower he gaed intil the water, CROCKETT Moss-Hags (1895) xl. a.Ir. The little man gave him one hoise, CROKER Leg. (1862) 330. Wxf. Ay, and ourselves get a hoise, and maybe fall down on the top of Castleboro and be kilt, KENNEDY Banks Boro (1867) 189. Cum. ' Ah'll let yeh see a hoise.' Ah turn't in t'buttick, an fetcht me greasy gentlemas reeght ower me heid, SARGISSON Joe Scoap (1881) 130; Cum.¹⁴

[1. We'll quickly hoise Duke Humphrey from his seat, SHAKS. 2 Hen. VI, i. i. 169; I hyse up the sayle, as shyp-men do, Je haulce, PALSGR. (1530).]

HOISPEHOY, HOIST, see Ho-spy, Hoast, sb.¹

HOIST, v.¹ and sb.   Var. dial. forms and uses in Sc. and Eng.   **I.** Dial. forms: (1) **Heist,** (2) **Highst,** (3) **Hist,** (4) **Hoost,** (5) **Hyste,** (6) **Oost.** See **Heeze, Hoise.**

(1) Sh.I. We'll heist up da sail, STEWART Tales (1892) 92. Gbl.¹ Dor. An' heist his zacks, BARNES Poems (1879) 81. (2) Midl. (E.S.) Glo. The Cotswold native does not talk of hoisting a ladder, but 'highsting ' is the term he uses, GIBBS Cotswold Vill. (1898) 84 ; Glo.² Wil. Slow Gl. (1892). (3) Ken. (G.B.) Som. Hev fresh cask ready histed, AGRIKLER Rhymes (1872) 17. Oxf., Brks. They were a-hoostin' the cask when the rope broke W. B.T.). Brks. Gl. (1852); Brks.¹ Hoost up thee end o' plank a bit. (5) Sh.I. The ship is noo come, an' her sails hysted up, STEWART Tales (1892) 238. Ken. Gie me a hyste up wid dis meäte (W. G.P.). (6) w.Mid. Oost up a minuit, I want that paper you're sitting on. Just oost up that end a bit (W.P.M.).

II. Dial. uses.   **1.** v. intrans. To rise.

e.An.¹ The river is hoisted or risen.

2. To raise a person sitting in a chair, as high as the arms can reach. Hence **Hoisting,** vbl. sb. an Easter custom; see below. See **Heave, v. II. 4.**

Chs.¹ Formerly practised throughout Chs. but now fast dying out. The custom is sometimes called Heaving and occas. Hoisting (s.v. Lifting); Chs.³ Raising up a person sitting on a chair decorated with ribbons and flowers, as high as the arms can reach, at Easter. This is done by the women of a household on Easter (also called lifting) Monday, and by the men to the women on Easter (lifting) Tuesday. A slight fee is paid by the lifted to the lifters, afterwards spent in a feast.

Hence (1) **Hoisting-days,** sb. pl. Easter Monday and Tuesday. Chs.¹; (2) **Hoisting-the-glove,** sb. a custom of carrying a hand with the first two fingers erect, and surrounded by flowers, formerly practised at Lammas fair. Dev. (HALL.)

3. *sb.* Phr. *to give the hoist*, to give the 'cold shoulder.'

Dev. For the maidens they gave them the hoist more than ever, through Nance having picked them out for them, CHANTER *Witch* (1896) iv.

HOIST, *v.[2]* Hrf.[2] To keep still. (s.v. Hice.)

HOISTER, *sb.* Irel. A bundle of things put together without any order.

Ant. A boister of clothes, *Ballymena Obs.* (1892).

HOISTER, *v.* Obs. Ess. To support. *Gl.* (1851) ; Ess.[1]

HOISTING, see Hosting.

HOIT, *sb.[1]* and *v.[1]* Sc. n.Cy. Nhb. Dur. Yks. Lan. Also written hoyt N.Cy.[1] Nhb.[1] e.Yks. w.Yks. ; hoyte Sc. (JAM.); and in forms hoity n.Yks. e.Yks.[1]; hout Nhb.[1]; oit w.Yks. [h]oit.] **1.** *sb.* A foolish, awkward, clumsy person ; a fool, simpleton ; a lazy, good-for-nothing fellow.

Ags. A clumsy and indolent person always conjoined with an epithet expressive of contempt. 'Nasty hoit' (JAM.). n.Cy. GROSE (1790) ; N.Cy.[1] Nhb. Thoo bubbly hoit, thoo (R.O.H.) ; Nhb.[1] Ye greet lazy hoit. e.Dur.[1] Ye mucky hoit. n.Yks.[1][2][4] ne.Yks.[1] He's a hoit. e.Yks. MARSHALL *Rur. Econ.* (1788) ; e.Yks.[1], m.Yks.[1] w.Yks. A gurt silly oit, he's nooa gumption (B.K.) ; w.Yks.[1] An ill-taught, spoilt child ; w.Yks.[5] 'A gurt fond hoit.' One least fit to be seen yet who is fondest of showing herself ; for the word is more often applied to females. n.Lan.[1]

2. A hobbling or awkward motion.

n.Sc. One to whom this motion is attributed is said to be at the hoit (JAM.).

3. A shrug, a motion of the shoulders.

Sh.I. 'Weel dan, why spaeks doo laek yon !' Sibbie axed wi a kind ill hoit apon her, *Sh. News* (Oct. 30, 1897) ; (K.I.) ; (J.I.)

4. *v.* To act or play the fool.

n.Yks.[1] With a sort of implication of ostentatiously. To engage in some evident absurdity ; n.Yks.[2] 'Hoiting and toiting,' trifling away time ; playing the fool ; n.Yks.[4], ne.Yks.[1], m.Yks.[1]

Hence **Hoyting,** *sb.* riotous and noisy mirth. N.Cy.[1], Nhb.[1]

5. To move in an awkward or clumsy manner ; to run or walk clumsily.

Sc. Do ye think I have naething a-do, but come here every other day hoiting after you! GRAHAM *Writings* (1883) II. 62; Often used to denote the attempt made by a corpulent person to move quickly (JAM.). Ayr. Tho' now ye dow but hoyte and hoble, BURNS *To his Auld Mare*, st. 7.

Hence **Hoited,** *ppl. adj.* clumsy, awkward ; clumsily made or shaped.

Sh.I. A'll wush me haands i' dy hert blûde, doo ill hoitid fat üseless lump at doo is, *Sh. News* (June 17, 1899); He's [a foal] a weelhoited craeter, an' weel at himsel', *ib.* (Dec. 4, 1897).

[4. Let none condemn them [the girls] for Rigs, because thus hoiting with boys, FULLER *Pisgah* (1650) II. iv. vi. Prob. cogn. w. MDu. *hoetelen*, to play the fool, *hoeteler*, one who plays the fool, a good-for-nothing fellow (OUDEMANS); cp. EFris. *hôtelen* (KOOLMAN).]

HOIT, *sb.[2]* Bck. A newt. (HALL.)

HOIT, *sb.[3]* Sh.I. A small, uncomfortable dwelling or house ; a hut, hovel.

Der shürely nane bit da puir folk here in Shetlan' 'at bide in siccan hoits as dis, *Sh. News* (Dec. 11, 1897) ; (J.I.) ; (K.I.)

HOIT, *v.[2]* Irel. **1.** To persuade or goad any one on to do a thing. Ant. *Ballymena Obs.* (1892).

2. To turn cattle out of a field. Ant. (S.A.B.)

HOIT, *adj.* Sh.I. [Not known to our correspondents.] Ill- or well-behaved. Hence **Hoitafick,** *adj.* applied to good or bad behaviour. (*Coll.* L.L.B.)

HOIT, *int.* Dev.[2] A call to cows.

HOIT, HOITH, see Heit, Hoyt, Height.

HOITHER, *v.* e.Yks.[1] [oi·ðər.] To talk in a foolish or imbecile manner. Hence **Hoithering,** *ppl. adj.* silly, blundering ; fatuous.

HOITINA, *sb.* Sh.I. Also written hoitana, hoitena, hüitina. The end or finish of anything ; *fig.* a time of rest and quietness.

Noo, Sibbie, dis is Hoitina, Gude be tankit, *Sh. News* (Apr. 22, 1899) ; Tanks ta Gud your koo hûvd oot her feet da last year. Dat wis hoitana. Da folk 'ill no loss der butter noo, *ib.* (May 7,

VOL. III.

1898) ; A'm düne no sae ill, bit dis will be hüitena wi' me dis year, *ib.* (Aug. 7, 1897) ; The last load of peats when they are being brought from the hill, or the last of any heavy piece of work, is called ' hoitena ' in some parts, but it is not common everywhere in Shetland (K.I.) ; (J.I.)

HOITY-TOITY, *int., adj.* and *sb.* Sc. n.Cy. Nhb. Cum. Yks. Lan. Lei. Nhp. Hnt. e.An. Hmp. Dev. Cor. Also written hoyty-toyty Cum. ; and in forms hoit-a-poit e.An.[12]; hoity-poity e.An.[2] [h]oiti-toiti.] **1.** *int.* An expression used to soothe cows when they are being milked ; also used as *v.*

nw.Dev.[1] Hoity-toity wi' min [fondle or soothe them].

2. *adj.* Giddy, frolicsome, flighty. Cf. **highty-tighty.**

N.Cy.[1], Cum.[1], w.Yks.[1], ne.Lan.[1], Lei.[1] Nhp.[1] An epithet applied to giddy, thoughtless young females. Hnt. (T.P.F.) e.An.[1]; e.An.[2] [Assuming] important airs, high spirits. e.Suf. (F.H.) Hmp. HOLLOWAY.

3. Haughty, proud, 'uppish'; somewhat ruffled in temper.

N.Cy.[1], Nhb. (R.O.H.), n.Yks.[4] Lei.[1] A hoity-toity sort of a body. e.Suf. (F.H.) Cor.[1] She's a hoity-toity thing [capricious, haughty].

4. *sb.* A fuss, commotion, ' to-do.'

Dev. Humph! what a pretty hoity toity's here, PETER PINDAR *Whs.* (1816) I. 211.

5. An awkward, tawdry appearance. Per. (G.W.)

HOITY, HOKE, see Hoit, *sb.[1]*, Howk, *v.[1]*

HOKE, *v.[1]* w.Cy. [Not known to our correspondents.] To gore with the horns. (HALL.)

HOKE, *v.[2]* Som. [Not known to our correspondents.] To romp or play ; to gambol. (HALL.)

HOKER, see Hocker, *v.[1]*

HOKEY, *int., sb.* and *adj.* Sc. Irel. Lin. Cor. Slang. Also written hoakie Ayr. (JAM.); and in forms hookey Lin.[1]; hookie Edb. ; hooky Cor. **1.** *int.* A meaningless exclamation or expletive. Also in *comb.* Hokey oh !

N.I.[1] s.Don. SIMMONS *Gl.* (1890). Lin.[1] An expression signifying ' Catch me at it,' ' See me do it,' and the like.

2. *sb.* Phr. *by the hokey* or *hokeys*, a meaningless exclamation or mild expletive.

Ayr. (JAM.) Edb. By the hookie! if ye think I at your teasings here do wink, M[c]DOWALL *Poems* (1839) 54. Ir. By the hokey, such sport you never saw, CARLETON *Traits Peas.* (ed. 1843) I. 106; Be the hokey, it's herself has more gumption and comprehension in her than the half of yous all rowled together, BARLOW *Idylls* (1892) 113. n.Ir. By the hokey, I'll fish no more here—it won't pay, *Lays and Leg.* (1884) 15. w.Ir. By the hokey, this is too bad intirely, LOVER *Leg.* (1848) II. 436. Myo. Aye, an' be the hokey, the shquire himself sez that it was a good day for him whin he set eyes on her first, STOKER *Snake's Pass* (1891) vii. Qco. Ough, by the hokys ! BARRINGTON *Sketches* (1830) I. i. s.Ir. By the hokey, this is too bad intirely, LOVER *Leg.* (1848) II. 436. Lin. ' By the hookeys,' an unmeaning adjuration, supposed to have reference to the fairies, THOMPSON *Hist. Boston* (1856) 710. Cor. By the hooky! but they'm givin' t us hot, PARR *Adam and Eve* (1880) III. 143. Slang. What sound mingles too! By the hokey—a drum! BARHAM *Ingoldsby* (1840) *Dead Drummer*.

3. *adj.* Phr. *by the hokey farmer*, a meaningless exclamation or expletive.

Ir. O, be the hoky-farmer, but that was the hair! YEATS *Flk-Tales* (1888) 110.

HOKEY, HOKKEN, see Hawkie, Howkan.

HOKNER, *sb.* Sh.I. A ' haaf' term for a dog. SPENCE *Flk-Lore* (1899) 121.

HOKY-POKY, *sb.* Sc. Nhb. Cum. I.Ma. Lon. Slang. Also in forms hokery-packery Sc. ; hokery-pokery Sc. Cum. **1.** Hocus-pocus, anything mysterious or underhand ; ' sharp practice,' ' hanky-panky.' Also used *attrib.*

Sc. Managed them weel eneuch wi' nane o' that kind o' hokery-packery, ROY *Horseman's Wd.* (1895) v. Nhb.[1], Cum. (J.Ar.) I.Ma. No keepin back, no sneaking hoky-poky ways, With yandhar fellow, BROWN *Witch* (1889) 35.

2. Ice-cream.

Lon. A curious delicacy known as 'hokey-pokey,' a kind of sublimated ice-cream frozen into small solid blocks and wrapped in highly-coloured papers at two a penny, *Tit-bits* (Aug. 8, 1891) 277, col. 2. Slang. He had been earning a precarious living by the sale of penny ices—or ' hoky-poky,' as the substance is called by many, *Sat. Review* (1890) 366, col.·2.

D d

HOL, *v. Obs.* Wxf.[1] To bawl.

HOL, HOLAP, see Holl, *adj.,* Hollop.

HOLD, *sb.* Var. dial. uses in Sc. Irel. and Eng.

I. Dial. forms: (1) **Had,** (2) **Hadde,** (3) **Haowt,** (4) **Haut,** (5) **Hawlt,** (6) **Hoad,** (7) **Hoal,** (8) **Hoald,** (9) **Hote,** (10) **Hoult,** (11) **Hout,** (12) **Howlt,** (13) **Howt,** (14) **Odd,** (15) **Olt,** (16) **Oud,** (17) **Owlt,** (18) **Owt.** [For further forms see Hold, *v.* I. 1 and II. below.]

(1) **Sh.I.** He took a had o' her, *Sh. News* (Dec. 2, 1899). **Cai.**[1] (2) **Sh.I.** *Sh. News* (Jan. 22, 1898). (3) **se.Wor.**[1] Now then lay haowt o' this 'ere shuppick. (4) **Hrf.**[2] (5) **Brks.**[1] (6) **Nhb.**[1] Wm. I gat hoad ev hes hand, CLOSE *Satirist* (1833) 155. (7) **Cum.**[1] (8) **Cum.**[14] (9) **Glo.**[1] (10) n.Ir. A gruppit hoult o' him, LYTTLE *Paddy McQuillan,* 22; **N.I.**[1] **I.Ma.** The docther slacked the hoult, BROWN *Doctor* (1887) 94. **Chs.**[13] **Glo.** He catched hoult of my leg, BUCKMAN *Darke's Sojourn* (1890) vii. (11) **Chs.**[2], nw.Der.[1], **Shr.**[12] (12) Ir. It's a . . . good howlt of the floore she's got too, *Paddiana* (ed. 1848) I. 251. **Glo.**[1] (13) **Chs.**[1], s.**Chs.**[1] (14) w.**Yks.** Hittha, David, tak odd, CUDWORTH *Dial. Sketches* (1884) 17. (15) **Wor.** ELLIS *Pronunc.* (1889) V. 112. (16) w.**Yks.** Sooa yo seen Dame Flatback ger oud a won leg, BYWATER *Sheffield Dial.* (1877) 33. (17, 18) **Glo.**[1]

II. Dial. uses. **1.** In phr. (1) *a hold of health,* a symptom, sign of health; (2) *sleek haud,* a term of encouragement used in setting dogs to fight; (3) *to drop hold of,* to come across, light upon, find; (4) — *get* or *take a hold of* or *on,* to get or take hold of; (5) — *get hold,* to recover; (6) — *get hold of,* to become possessed of; (7) — *go by the holds,* to be in leading-strings, to go by the help of another; (8) — *had haul,* to offer sufficient resistance, to be firm, strong, hard; (9) — *hold one's hold,* (a) to adhere, keep what one has got; (b) to hold fast, to stop or go gently; (10) — *plough with a hold,* to plough deeply; (11) — *take holds,* to take hold.

(1) Ayr. Ony ha'd o' health he has is aye at meal time, and yet he puts a' in an ill skin, GALT *Lairds* (1826) i. (2) **Nhb.** (R.O.H.) (3) Wor. Where 'er'll very likely drop olt o' that old drunken deaf Tom, ELLIS *Pronunc.* (1889) V. 112. (4) n.Sc. Here, my laddie, tak' a haud o' the reins, GORDON *Carglen* (1891) 9. **Cai.**[1] He gote a had o'm. Frf. The very bairns at the Sabbath-School got a haud o' the story, WILLOCK *Rosetty Ends* (1886) 53, ed. 1889. Rnf. God's common-sense, as we have it i' the Book, if we only got a haud o't, GILMOUR *Pen-Flk.* (1873) 21. **Nhb.**[1] Stop till aa get ahad on't. If aa get ahad on ye, aa'll warm ye (s.v. Ahad). (5) w.**Yks.**[1] My lad begins to git hod. (6) n.**Lin.**[1] Sally's that setten up wi' her bairn onybody wo'd think she was fo'st woman as hed larnt how to get hohd o' childer. (7) **Sc.** To gae be the hadds (JAM.). (8) **Cai.**[1] 'E last rope brook but 'iss ane 'ill had haul.' Things hard to chew 'had haul' to the teeth. A thrifty mother in getting clothes for her boys wishes to get material that will 'had haul' to them. (9, a) n.**Yks.**[1]; n.**Yks.**[2] They'll hod their hod. m.**Yks.**[1] (b) **Shr.**[1] (10) **Nhb.** (R.O.H.) (11) **Nhb.** There—tak hauds, lad, and lets gan in, CLARE *Love of Lass* (1890) I. 19.

2. A tenure of land; a 'holding,' property held upon a certain tenure; a home, habitation, resp. in phr. *house and hold.*

Sc. And I'm your Annie of Lochroyan, Turned out frae house and hald, JAMIESON *Pop. Ballads* (1806) I. 46. Abd. A wuddiefu', wi' nedder hame nor haul' o' 's nain, ALEXANDER *Ain Flk.* (1882) 18. Fif. Scarce house or hald to screen frae cauld, DOUGLAS *Poems* (1806) 49. Rnf. It seem't to be the hale Life's ain hoo best they micht defraud Him oot the payments o' his haud, YOUNG *Pictures* (1865) 153. Lnk. Ye may be reft o' house and hald, RODGER *Poems* (1838) 167, ed. 1897; They thrust them out of house and hould, LITHGOW *Poet. Rem.* (ed. 1863) *Scotland's Welcome.* e.Lth. The ministers turned oot o' hoose an' hauld, HUNTER *J. Inwick* (1895) 158. Edb. I now hae neither house nor hauld, And maun wander far awa, MᶜDOWALL *Poems* (1839) 129. Slk. While I hae house or hauld on earth, HOGG *Poems* (ed. 1865) 99. Dmf. Rentit their hauld frae the Laird o' the Peel, REID *Poems* (1894) 76. Cum. God help them widout house or hauld This dark and stormy neet, ANDERSON *Ballads* (ed. 1808) 33; Cum.[1] They've nowder house nor hoald to draw teeb. n.**Yks.**[1]; n.**Yks.**[2] 'A wankle hod,' an uncertain tenure. 'He has his land under a good hod'; n.**Yks.**[4] If thoo dizn't mak thi ho'd paay thi owt. ne.**Yks.**[1], e.**Yks.**[1] m.**Yks.**[1] He has his land under a good hod. ne.**Lan.**[1]

3. A haunt, resort, a place of rendezvous.

Sh.I. The 'Summer-set' was . . . a hadde for old soldier pensioners and man-of-war's men, *Sh. News* (Jan. 22, 1898). **Cor.**[2]

4. A place of retreat or shelter, a hiding-place; the den, hole, or lair of an animal, esp. the lurking-place of fish in streams.

Sh.I. 'Had,' the den of a wild beast, *Chambers' Jrn.* (Oct. 23, 1886) 685; The word 'hadd' is applied particularly to the hole made by a burrowing animal. Even the earth dwelling of man might be termed a hadd or hiding place, SPENCE *Flk-Lore* (1899) 19; **S. & Ork.**[1] **Nhb.** Terriers . . . are necessary to make the otter bolt from his 'hover ' or 'holt,' DAVIES *Rambles Sch. Field-club* (1881) xxxvi; Thrusting the hand and naked arm up rat holes, or below the brae edges under water (called haads), whilst lying flat on the burn side, and gumping the trout there concealed (R.O.H.); **Nhb.**[1], **Cum.**[1] **Wm.** That's a likely hauld fer a troot er tweea (B.K.). n.**Yks.** A rabbit hod (T.S.). w.**Yks.**[1] There's nut a finer hod i' au'th' beck. ne.**Lan.**[1] Fish haalds. **Nhp.**[1] When a pike has taken its bait, he is often said to run to his holt or home. The retreat of the otter is frequently called his holt. **War.**[12] **Wor.** The sport was worked from holt to holt, *Evesham Jrn.* (Apr. 29, 1899). **Shr.**[12] **Hrf.**[1]; **Hrf.**[2] You canna get at 'im, he's in 'is hoult. **Glo.** (W.H.C.); **Glo.**[1] A rabbit's burrow; a badger's earth. **Sur.**[1] Such a wood is a good holt for a fox. **Dev.** Thee was glad tu kom tu holt, Ov the cold thee'st had a taste, *n.Dev. Jrn.* (Dec. 17, 1885) 2, col. 5. **Cor.**[12]; **Cor.**[2] Badger's holt; otter's holt. w.**Cor.** Commonly implying secrecy as well as security, *N. & Q.* (1854) 1st S. x. 319. [The lurking place of a fish, especially of a trout, MAYER *Spitsmn's Direct.* (1845) 63.]

5. The goal in a game; a temporary stopping-place in games of chase. n.**Yks.** (I.W.), e.**Yks.**[1] Cf. **holt,** *sb.*[2]

6. A prison, lock-up; confinement; *gen.* in phr. *in hold.*

Qco. We have your husband in hoult, BARRINGTON *Sketches* (1830) I. ii. w.**Yks.** They've getten 'o'd on 'im, and putten 'im in hold (F.P.T.). Midl. Tom is in the hold of Bumbledon, BARTRAM *People of Clopton* (1897) 20. **War.**[3] 168a. Served a warrant on Will. Clark and going to justise with him and keeping him in hould, *Ansley Par. Accounts* in *Trans. Arch. B'ham Institute* (1890).

7. A wrestling term: a wrestle, tussle; a grip, embrace; *gen.* in phr. *in holds.*

N.I.[1] When I first seen them they were in hoults,' i. e. they were grappling with each other. **Nhb.** 'To tyek had,' to get into grips (R.O.H.); **Nhb.**[1] Let's hev a haad together. **Cum.**[4] Used when the wrestler gets hold of his own two hands. Hoalds may be 'slack' or 'close.' 'It teeak a fella wid t'grip of a dancen bear teh keep Bob fra twisten that girt roond back eh his oot eh hoalds,' SARGISSON *Joe Scoap* (1881) 75. 'When they were in haud s the comical sight provoked a burst of laughter,' *C. Patr.* (June 30, 1893) 3, col. 4. **Wm.** To secure some advantage in the game great caution is displayed in taking. After the umpire has declared 'hauld' the contestants are compelled to wrestle. 'They war a lang time gitten hauld' (B.K.). **Hrf.**[1] When two men are grappling with one another, they are said to be in holt. **Glo.** LEWIS *Gl.* (1839).

8. An argument, dispute, wrangle.

Not.[1] **Lei.**[1] I had several arguments and holts with him. **Nhp.**[1] We'd such a holt over it; **Nhp.**[2], e.**Suf.** (F.H.)

9. A support, something to lean against, esp. in *comb.* **Back-hold.** Also used *fig.* and *advb.*

Sc. I'm old and faild, And cannot walk without a hald, GRAHAM *Writings* (1883) I. 237. Bnff.[1] A'm a' richt noo: a've gotten mu back till a haul. Abd. Wi' the help o' haul' and hirst, He joggit on, SHIRREFS *Poems* (1790) 219. Wm. Wait a minute till Ah mend mi back-hauld (B.K.); In wrestling where one of the contestants is much superior in skill and strength, he will allow the other to embrace him from behind, with a view to equalizing the disparity—this is called 'wrusslin' back-hauld' or '-back-hod.' 'Ah can wrussle thee back-hauld' (ib.). e.**Yks.** Ah's tired oot o' sitting here, wivoot a bit o' back-hod, NICHOLSON *Flk-Sp.* (1889) 92; e.**Yks.**[1], w.**Yks.** (J.W.)

10. A handle to lay hold upon, a holder. n.**Yks.**[2]

11. A mortgage on property. *ib.* **12.** A hobby, favourite pursuit. *ib.*

13. Anything nursed, a source of care or trouble.

My bairn's my hod. My bad leg's my hod, *ib.*

14. Restraint, power of retention.

Ayr. Applied with the negative to denote prodigality (JAM.); My people . . . dealt round shortbread and sugar-biscuit with wine . . . as if there had been no ha'd in their hands, GALT *Ann. Parish* (1821) xlvi.

15. Trust, faithfulness; dependence on a person or thing. s.**Chs.**[1] Dhŭr)z nŏo uwt ŭ dhaat· mon [There's noo howt o' that mon]. **Nhp.**[1] We have no holt on him, i. e. we have no security that he will keep to any promises of amendment. **Hrf.**[1] Glo. **Lewis** *Gl.* (1839). ['There is no hold in him,' said of a false and treacherous person (K.).]

16. Ability, intellect.   n.**Yks.**[2] Has he a good hod?

17. Force, energy; strength, body, substance.
e.**Yks.**[1] We gå job sum hod when we gat ageeat on't, *MS. add.* (T.H.) Glo.[1] Used of cider, hay, &c. 'I didn't think there was no owt in bran.' Cor.[8] The stew is sloppy—no holt in it.

18. Punishment, a beating, flogging; a scolding; pain; also used *fig.*
n.**Yks.**[2] 'They gave 'em some 'od;' as we say, 'held them to the mark.' e.**Yks.**[1] Ah'll gi tha sum hod afooar lang, **Nicholson** *Flk-Sp.* (1889) 26; e.**Yks.**[1] *MS. add.* (T.H.) m.**Yks.**[1] I'll give him some ho'd when I get hold of him. Of a blister, it will be said, 'It gave me some hold.' w.**Yks.** (J.W.)

19. A crick in the neck.
n.**Cy.** (Hall.) w.**Yks.**[1] I've gitten a hod i' my neck.

HOLD, *v.* Var. dial. uses in Sc. Irel. Eng. and Amer.

I. Gram. forms. **1.** *Present Tense*: (1) Ald, (2) Haad, (3) Haald, (4) Had(d, (5) Hald, (6) Haud, (7) Haul, (8) Hauld, (9) Hawld, (10) Heeld, (11) Ho, (12) Hod, (13) Hode, (14) Hohd, (15) Hole, (16) Holld, (17) Holt, (18) Houd, (19) Houl, (20) Hould, (21) Houle, (22) Howd, (23) Howld, (24) Hud, (25) Hull, (26) Hyld, (27) Oald, (28) Od, (29) Ole, (30) Owd. [For further instances see **II.** below.]

(1) Shr.[1] (2) Nhb.[1](R.O.H.), ne.Lan.[1] (3) ne.Lan.[1] (4) Sc. As good hads the stirrup as he that loups on, **Ferguson** *Prov.* (1641) 7. Cai.[1] nw.Abd. We hae an unco canny laft For haddin orra trock, *Goodwife* (1867) st. 6. N.Cy.[1], Nhb.[1], Cum.[1], n.Yks.[4] (5) Sc. *Obs.*, **Murray** *Dial.* (1873) 205. Lakel.[1], n.Lan.[1] (6) Sc. Haud my naig, **Scott** *Nigel* (1822) xxvii. Bnff.[1], N.I.[1], N.Cy.[1], Nhb.[1], Dur.[1], m.Yks.[1], w.Yks.[18], e.Lan.[1], Not.[1] (7) Abd. *Deeside Tales* (1877) 213. Dmf. (Jam.) (8) Dmf. (Jam.) Cum. **Relfe** *Misc. Poems* (1847) *Gl.* (9) Brks.[1] (10) Abd. **Alexander** *Johnny Gibb* (1871) xv. (11) Cum.[14], Wm. (B.K.) (12) n.Cy. (Hall.), Lakel.[2], Cum.[1], n.Yks.[124], ne.Yks.[1] 33, e.Yks.[1], m.Yks.[1], w.Yks.[188], ne.Lan.[1], Der.[2], Lin.[1], n.Lin.[1] (13) Nhb.[1], Chs.[1], Der.[2] (14) n.Lin.[1] (15) e.Yks. *E. Morning News* (Aug. 3, 1896), (16) w.Yks. Hey, dog! Hey, Wolf, holld him, holld him! **Brontë** *Wuthering Hts.* (1847) ii. (17) Nhp.[1], Glo.[1], Sur.[1], Sus.[12], Hmp.[1], w.Som.[1], nw.Dev.[1] [Amer. *Dial. Notes* (1896) I. 50.] (18) Yks. Hou'd thy tongue, mother, **Gaskell** *Sylvia* (1863) 43, ed. 1874. e.Lan.[1], Lin. (M.P.), Shr.[1] (19) N.I.[1] (20) Ir. Kitty was houlding the door, *Paddiana* (ed. 1848) I. 99. Nhb.[1], I.Ma. And you ... houldin on, **Brown** *Doctor* (1887) 11. (21) Wxf.[1] (22) w.Yks.[2], Chs.[18] Der. I'd a hole big enow to howd my fist, **Cushing** *Voe* (1888) II. vii. Lin. For whoâ's to howd the lond ater meâ? **Tennyson** *N. Farmer, Old Style* (1864) st. 15. Nrf. A large charch big enow to howd a dozen o' the rector's in, **Spilling** *Giles* (1872) 7. Suf.[1] (23) Ir. **Barrington** *Sketches* (1830) III. vi. (24) e.Sc. **Setoun** *R. Urquhart* (1896) iii. (25) Nhp.[1] (26) s.Pem. Laws *Little Eng.* (1888) 420. (27) w.Som. **Elworthy** *Gram.* (1877) 47. (28) Wm. Ez lang ez yer wind ur yer taael 'll od out, *Spec. Dial.* (1880) pt. ii. 29. m.Yks.[1] *Introd.* 28. w.Yks. **Wright** *Gram. Wndhll.* (1892) 140. Not.[2] (29) Nhp. *N. & Q.* (1883) 6th S. vii. 18. (30) Lan. Owding t'varmint by it neck, **Kay-Shuttleworth** *Scarsdale* (1860) I. 149.

2. *Preterite*: (1) Hadded, (2) Haded, (3) Haeld, (4) Hald, (5) Heed, (6) Heilded, (7) Heilit, (8) Helt, (9) Heud, (10) Hewd, (11) Hild, (12) Hilt, (13) Hodded, (14) Hoddit, (15) Hoded, (16) Hold, (17) Holted, (18) Howded, (19) Howdud, (20) Howld, (21) Howlded, (22) Hude, (23) Hued, (24) Huild, (25) Oald, (26) Oddad, (27) Odid.

(1) Nhb. Aw hadded him, an' waddent let him gan, **Forster** *Newc. Sng. Sol.* (1859) iii. 4; Nhb.[1] (2) Nhb. An' when she haded it, **Robson** *Bk. Ruth* (1860) iii. 15. (3) Sc. **Murray** *Dial.* (1873) 205. (4) Sc. **Grose** (1790) *MS. add.* (C.) Nrf. (W.R.E.) (5) Cai.[1] (6, 7) Sc. **Grose** (1790) *MS. add.* (C.) (8) Lan. Whol e helt o greyt sloice o bam, **Scholes** *Tim Gamwattle* (1857) 40. Not.[1], Lel.[1] Nhp.[1] He helt it up. War.[2], Oxf. (G.O.) [Amer. *Dial. Notes* (1896) I. 233.] (9) Nrf. I heu'd him, and wudn't ler 'im go, **Gillett** *Sng. Sol.* (1860) iii. 4. (10) Suf.[1] A nivva hewd up a's hid aater. (11) Suf.[1] [Amer. *Dial. Notes* (1896) I. 277.] (12) Oxf.[1], Cmb. (J.D.R.) [Amer. *Dial. Notes* (1896) I. 233.] (13) n.Yks. (I.W.), e.Yks.[1] (14) Cum. He teùkk hod o' t'reakk, an' hoddit t'oot (E.W.P.); Cum.[1] (15) Cum. I hoded up my neef, **Graham** *Gwordy* (1778) 72. ne.Yks.[1] 33. (16) e.Dev. Ai hold'en, an' eud'n leyve geu, **Pulman** *Sng. Sol.* (1860) iii.4. (17) Ant. (W.H.P.) (18) Lan. Aw howded him, un wouldn't let him gooa, **Staton** *Sng. Sol.*

(1859) iii. 4. (19) Lan. Thi bwoath howdud thir honds eawt tu mi, **Scholes** *Tim Gamwattle* (1857) 5. (20) Cor. I howld un, and wudn't lev un go, *Sng. Sol.* (1859) iii. 4. (21) Wil. I howlded un, an' keep'd un, **Kite** *Sng. Sol.* (1860) iii. 4. (22) Frf. When dark December's tempest hurl'd, She hude unholy feasts, **Lowson** *Guidfollow* (1890) 232. (23) e.Suf. (F.H.) Ess. For still she hued it toight, **Clark** *J. Noakes* (1839) st. 85; Ess.[1] (24) Slk. (Jam.) (25) w.Som. **Elworthy** *Gram.* (1877) 47. (26) w.Yks. Yo'de see at e oddad it undar hiz chin like, **Tom Treddlehoyle** *Ben Bunt* (1838) 12. (27) m.Yks.[1] w.Yks. **Wright** *Gram. Wndhll.* (1892) 140.

3. *Pp.*: (1) Hadden, (2) Haddin, (3) Haddn, (4) Haden, (5) Halden, (6) Halt, (7) Hauden, (8) Haudin, (9) Helt, (10) Hilt, (11) Hodded, (12) Hodden, (13) Hoddn, (14) Hoden, (15) Holden, (16) Holt, (17) Holten, (18) Houden, (19) Hoult, (20) Howd'n, (21) Howlded, (22) Howt, (23) Hudden, (24) Hued, (25) Huld, (26) Oald, (27) Oaldud, (28) Odid, (29) Odn.

(1) Sc. An ill wife and a new kindled candle shou'd ha'e their heads hadden down, **Ramsay** *Prov.* (1737). Cai.[1], Nhb.[1] (2) Sc. (Jam.) (3) Sh.I. Da frost [ice] wis very tick, an' wid a hadd'n wiz a' up, *Sh. News* (Jan. 21, 1899). (4) Sh.I. *Sh. News* (Dec. 4, 1897). Edb. *Har'st Rig* (1794) 25, ed. 1801. (5) Sc. *Obs.*, **Murray** *Dial.* (1873) 205. (6) Wxf.[1] Vaate apan vaate a met-borde was ee-halt, 98. (7) Sc. Better hae hauden her tongue, **Scott** *Leg. Mont.* (1818) iv. Dur.[1] Cum. At Skinburness ... This weddin' it was hauden, **Stagg** *Misc. Poems* (ed. 1807) 3. (8) Sh.I. Da coo wis dat wye gluff'd 'at I couldna get her haudin, *Sh. News* (Oct. 9, 1897). (9) Not.[1], Lei.[1] War.[2] [Amer. *Dial. Notes* (1896) I. 233.] (10) [1] Oxf.[1], Cmb. (J.D.R.) [Amer. *Dial. Notes* (1896) I. 233.] (11) n.Yks.[2] w.Yks.[2] Hah long's he hodded it? (12) Lakel.[2] Cum.[2] If t'doctor he went tull, hed hodden his tung, 165; Cum.[4], n.Yks.[2] ne.Yks.[1] 33, m.Yks.[1], e.Yks.[1], w.Yks.[123], ne.Lan.[1] Der. That's yan thing to be hodden i' mind, **Ward** *David Grieve* (1892) III. bk. iv. vi. (13) Wm. T'king's hodd'n i' t'galleries, **Richardson** *Sng. Sol.* (1859) vii. 5. w.Yks. Hodd'n cloise to t'pipe, **Binns** *Orig.* (1889) No. i. 6. (14) w.Yks.[2] (15) Or.I. Holden under thraldom and tyranny, **Peterkin** *Notes* (1822) 116. Abd. A head court to be holden at the Foot o' Gairn, *Deeside Tales* (1872) 133. Ayr. A person holden in great respect and repute, **Galt** *Gilhaize* (1823) v. n.Yks.[2] (16) Hnt. (T.P.F.) [Amer. *Dial. Notes* (1896) I. 233.] (17) Lel.[1] 28. (18) w.Yks. *Pogmoor Olm.* (1869) 24. (19) I.Ma. **Brown** *Doctor* (1898) 138. (20) Lan. Johnny went to a perty howd'n at a public-heawse, **Staton** *Loominary* (c. 1861) 50. (21) Wil. Th' king uz howlded in th' galleries, **Kite** *Sng. Sol.* (1860) vii. 5. (22) s.Chs.[1] (23) Sc. You'll wish you'd hudden your hands aff ane, **Roy** *Horseman's Wd.* (1895) xv. (24) e.Suf. (F.H.) (25) Dev. Tha king es huld en tha gallerys, **Baird** *Sng. Sol.* (1860) vii. 5. (26, 27) m.Yks.[1] w.Som. **Elworthy** *Gram.* (1877) 47. (28) m.Yks.[1] w.Yks. **Wright** *Gram. Wndhll.* (1892) 140. (29) w.Yks. **Wright** *Gram. Wndhll.* (1892) 140.

II. Dial. meanings. **1.** *Comb.* with *prep.*, *adv.*, &c. (1) **To hold again**, to resist, withstand; to stop, arrest; (2) — **at**, to persist in; keep on at; not to spare; (3) — **away**, (a) to keep away, hold off; (b) to go on one's way, to go on or away; *gen.* in *imper.* as a term of encouragement; (4) — **by**, (a) to go past, to pass; (b) to stand or get out of the way; (c) to refrain from, abstain; (d) to esteem, to have an opinion of; (5) — **forrust**, to lead the first horse in a team; (6) — **forward** (forrit), to go forward; (7) — **in**, (a) to restrain; to confine, keep from spreading; (b) of vessels, &c.: not to leak, to contain any liquid; (c) not to expend, to save; also used *fig.*; (d) to supply; (8) — **in about**, to curb, check, keep in order; (9) — **in with**, to keep on good terms with, curry favour with; (10) — **off**, or — **aff**, (a) to keep off, keep away from, not to befall; esp. of rain, &c.; (b) to keep back or away; *gen.* in *imper.*; (11) — **off of**, or **affen**, to protect or defend; (12) — **on**, (a) to stop, wait, pause; *gen.* in *imper.*; (b) to continue, persevere; (c) in sewing: to keep one side of two pieces to be sewn together fuller than the other; (13) — **out**, (a) to pretend, allege, to persist in a lie; (b) to dwell, live; (c) to present a gun; (d) to extend to the full measure or weight; (e) to attend regularly; to frequent; (14) — **so**, to cease, give over, *gen.* in *imper.*; (15) — **till**, to persist in anything; (16) — **to**, (a) to keep to, stick to, maintain; (b) to go on one's way; (c) to keep shut; (d) to keep hard at work, to keep going; (17) — **up**, (a) to keep fine; to leave off raining ; (b) to endure, bear up against illness or trouble, not to give way to despondency ; to keep up and about, not to take to one's bed from illness; (c) to hold, cause to take place, observe ; (d) to resist ; (e) to occupy the attention of; (f) of a woman : not to be confined so soon as was expected; (18) — up to, to court, woo, make up to ; (19) — up with, to keep pace with ; (20) with, (a) to agree with, be of the same opinion as, to approve of, side with ; (b) to consume, take.

(1) Sc. (Jam.) (a) Sc. Pete wadna let me. He hauds at me mornin', nune, an' nicht, Swan Gates of Eden (1895) iii. Cai.¹ Elg. Ye're ahin wi' the wark, a lang waay behind, Haud the cidenter at it, Tester Poems (1865) 134. (3, a) n.Sc. And ye'll had far away frae me, Buchan Ballads (1828) l. 111, ed. 1875. Bch. They had awa' frae you: they ken Ye're but an useless folp, Forbes Ulysses (1785) 24. Abd. Toot, haud awa', don't shake me thus, Ogg Willie Waly (1873) 50. Gall. I'm no sae sonsie To haud away the wights unchancie, Nicholson Poet. Wks. (1814) 54, ed. 1897. (b) Abd. Ye maun jist haud awa' ower to Kirkbyres, Mac-donald Malcolm (1875) III. 181. Ayr. Beneath the moon's unclouded light I held awa to Annie, Burns Rigs o' Barley, st. 1. N.I.¹, N.Cy.¹ Nhb. Hadaway, get yor coat on, lad. 'Hadaway Harry, lad ; hadaway Harry! Pull like a good 'un, through storm or through shine' (R.O.H.); Nhb.¹ Dur.¹ When used to another man implies that the speaker will accompany the one spoken to (A.B.). Cum. 'Hold away' was the common phr. used by sportsmen to encourage their dogs to take a wider and quicker range in search of game, or as a signal to the dog to start off after the down charge (J.Ar.). n.Yks.²⁴ (4, a) Sc. (Jam.) nw.Abd. Haud by the lun-cart, by the strype It's no a bit, Goodwife (1867) st. 54. (b) Cum. Mak a ring, mak a ring ; iverybody [ho bye] hob-bye, an let's ha fair-play, Sargisson Joe Scoap (1881) 123; Cum.¹ (c) Abd. 'Come roun' to Luckie's, an' we'll weet oor mou'.' 'Na ; I think I'll need to try an' haud by't some the day,' Guidman Inglismaill (1873) 37. (d) Sc. I haud unco little by the Parliament House, Scott Midlothian (1818) xii. (5) Oxf.¹ I wants a bwoy t' 'old forrust, MS. add. (6) Slk. He had hodden forrit a' the way wi' our wife, Hogg Tales (1838) 297, ed. 1866. (7, a) Edb. Whenever they begin The deil's nae fit to had them in. Learmont Poems (1791) 60. Gall. They ran on the braes sae sunny That haud in the river Dee, Mactaggart Encycl. (1824) 272, ed. 1876. (b) Sc. That lume [vessel] doesna hald in (Jam.). Cai.¹ Nhb. The kit winna had in ; it's runnin' like a siv (R.O.H.). (c) Sc. Little wats the ill-willy wife what a dinner may had in, Ferguson Prov. (1641) 23 ; He hauds in the siller weel (Jam.) ; Ilk presbyter had given up the names of the disaffected ministry within their presbytery—whilk held in their travels frae coming to Turriff, Spalding Hist. Sc. (1792) II. 195 (ib.). (d) Sc. 'Hald in eldin,' supply the fire with fuel, spoken of that kind which needs to be constantly renewed, as furze, broom, &c. (ib.) (8) Sc. (ib.) (9) Sc. (ib.), Cai.¹ Abd. To help 'im wi' that he heeld in wi' Johnny Gibb, Alexander Johnny Gibb (1871) xv. (10, a) Per. Haud aff the daddin' wind an' weet, An' bless the bread, an' mak' it sweet, Haliburton Ochil Idylls (1891) 28. n.Yks.¹ Of something probably impending, as a fall of rain, a change of weather, a fit of illness or pain; n.Yks.⁴ Ah think t'rain's gahin' ti ho'd off. If he can nobbut ho'd off fra drinkin' he'll cum roond. w.Yks. (J.W.) Lan. Howd on, Harry! see the, Jim! there's sommat yon, Donaldson Rossendel Beef-neet, 14 ; Howd on, lad, Aw want thee, Ackworth Clog Shop Chron. (1896) 50. I.Ma. But hould on, you'll hear, you'll hear, Brown Witch (1889) 17. nw.Der.¹ Uu:öd onn. e.Suf. (F.H.), Ken. (D.W.L.) (b) Abd. Up there, . . . I' the bow o' the Baa, Haud skirlin' on as gien a' war new, Macdonald Sir Gibbie (1879) lxii ; Hadd on a cow till I come o'er the gate, Ross Helenore (1768) 70. Per. 'It may be a' discharged for the past, but ye'll never haud on.' 'Never haud on !' says I, Sandy Scott (1897) 66. (c) Sc. (Jam.) (13, a) Sc. (Jam.), Cai.¹ Bnff.¹ Will' ye haud oot sic a lee i' ma face ! (b) Edb. A far away cousin . . . that held out among the howes of the Lammermoor hills, Moir Mansie Wauch (1828) xvii. (c) Sc. When Sir Edgar hauds out, down goes the deer, Scott Bride of Lam. (1819) iii. (d) Sc. 'Will that claithe hald out !' will it be found to contain the number of yards men-tioned ? (Jam.) (14) Sc. I think I'll haud sae for a' night (Jam.). Edb. Had sae, and let me get a word in, Fer-gusson Poems (1773) 176, ed. 1785. Nhb.¹ 'Fill up [the glass] an' hadsee,' fill up a sufficient quantity. (15) Sc. (Jam.) (16, a) n.Yks. Ah sall hod teab as lang as Ah live, Sketches Broad Yks. 6 ; n.Yks.⁴ Thoo mun ho'd ti what thoo's sed. (b) Ayr. O, he held to the fair, Burns Rattlin', Roarin' Willie, st. 1. (c) Sc. Hald to the door (Jam.). Cai.¹ (d) Edb. They've been right sair haden to, And kept their place wi' great ado, Har'st Rig (1794) 25, ed. 1801. (17, a) n.Yks.² It isn't boun te hod up. w.Yks.², Not.¹ n.Lin.¹ Will it hohd up to-daay, I wonder ? Th' glass is droppin' fast. Oxf.¹ The rain 'ilt up. w.Som.¹ I hope t'll hold up zoon, or I can't think whatever we shall do about the wheat sowing. Please God t'll hold up' gin to-marra night, all our hay'll be up in rick. (b) n.Yks.¹ Match'd t'ho'd up ; n.Yks.⁴ Noo deean't gi'e waay, thoo mun ho'd up. Things isn't seea bad, noo ho'd up. e.Yks.¹ Cha.¹ Hode-up. Said to . . . a man who is inclined to ' give in ' to any misfortune. Lin. Aw, lad, I can't houd it up noä moore (M.P.). Oxf. (G.O.) (c) Lan. Th' witches are howdin up their devulment, Brierley Waverlow (1863) 174, ed. 1884. (d) n.Yks. Ah hodded him up (I.W.). (e) n.Yks. He hodded her up wi talk [he kept her in conversation so as to take her attention off something else] (I.W.). (f) nw.Lin. When a woman is not con-fined so soon as is expected, esp. when her friends have reason to wish the event to be delayed, she is said ' to hold up well.' 'She held up well, I will say that, but they fool'd about so as not to get married till the week afore the bairn was born ' (E.P.). (18) Fif. Wha's yon lassie he's tryin' to haud up to? McLaren Tibbie (1894) 193. (19) Sc. (Jam.) (20, a) Sc. (ib.) Sh.I. Da mair I toucht ipun hit, da mair I wis inclin'd ta haud wi' Captain Henderson, Clark Gleams (1898) 95. Per. Gley'd Andro Toshack held wi' Pate, Ford Harp (1893) 156. e.Sc. But I dinna hud wi' ye there, Setoun R. Urquhart (1896) iii. n.Yks.⁴ Whya noo, Ah ho'd wi' t'main o' what thoo sez. w.Yks. (J.W.) Lan. Tha knows aw've never howden wi this loom-makkin', Clegg David's Loom (1894) v. ne.Lan.¹, nw.Der.¹ Not.¹ Ah don't haud with such goings on. n.Lin.¹ It's no ewse talkin' noä moore, I shall niver hod'd wi' you aboot them theäre things. Oxf.¹ MS. add. Suf. I don't hold with that by no manner o' means, s.An. Dy. Times (1892). Sur.¹ I don't hold with these new-fashioned ploughs. Sus. Good prin-ciples, Sir, good principles—I hold wi' them, Egerton Flks. and Ways (1884) 82 ; (J.W.B.) w.Mid. I don't hold with walloping children (W.P.M.). Wil. Well, wi' yer mother I don't hold, Slow Rhymes (1870) 35. Dor. I doant hold wi' all that there school larnen, Hare Vill. Street (1895) 149. w.Som.¹ I do hold wi' letting volks do eens they be a minded to. Dev. You do not hold with the Dissenters, then ? (J.W.B.) ; Vather doant hold wi none o' sich vo'k, Longman's Mag. (Dec. 1896) 158. (b) Abd. Fining both parties, and advising them to ' haud wi' less drink neist time,' Alexander Ain Flk. (1882) 113.

2. Comb. in horse-calls : (1) Hold back, a ploughman's call to the horses of his team to turn to the left ; (2) — in, keep in the furrow ; (3) — off or aff, (a) turn to the right, away from the driver ; (b) see (1) ; (4) — oot, a call to the near horse when it gets too far from the far horse ; (5) — to the right, see (3, a) ; (6) — towards, see (1) ; (7) — up, (a) go forwards a little ; (b) a command to a horse to lift up its foot for the purpose of shoeing, &c.

(1) Sc. (G.W.) (2) Lakel.², Cum.⁴, Wm. (B.K.) (3, a) n.Sc. N. & Q. (1856) 2nd S. i. 395. Midl. Stephens Farm Bk. (ed. 1849) I. 160. Lakel.², Cum.⁴ (b) Sc. (G.W.) (4) Cum.⁴ (5, 6) w.Mid. (W.P.M.) (7, a) Nhp.¹ A waggoner's caution to a horse at starting. w.Mid. (W.P.M.) (b) e.Yks.¹, Cha.¹

3. Comb. (1) Hold-again, a check, opposition ; (2) -dog, a sheep-dog ; (3) -dune, a hindrance, interruption to any kind of work ; (4) -fash, a trouble, bother ; a troublesome person, a ' plague ' ; (5) -fast, (a) possession, hold ; (b) a stone in a field held fast in the ground and difficult to dig out ; (c) part of a plough ; (d) an iron hook for supporting a rain-water spout ; (e) sure, certain ; (f) honourable ; (6) -fire, putrid blood [not known to our correspondents]; (7) -on, a thrashing, beating ; (8) -over, (a) see below ; (b) a temporary licence given to a publican before he obtains a full licence when taking to a public-house ; (9) -plaster, plaster of Paris ; (10) -poke, a churl, beggar ; (11) -pot, one who detains the circling bottle or drinking vessel ; (12) -sae, a sufficiency, a due allowance ; (13) -stock, a culvert under a road; a small bridge over a stream of water crossing a road; (14) ·talk, a chat, gossip, commonplace talk; (15) ·to-dea, useless employment; (16) ·tyul, (a) see (3); (b) to hold on to, keep fast to; to hamper, hinder; (17) ·weel, a miserly person.

(1) Abd. (Jam.) (2) Sh.I. When a flock is in sight the Shetlander seizes hold of his had-dog . . . and points out to him a particular sheep, HIBBERT *Desc. Sh. I.* (1822) 184, ed. 1891. (3) Cum.[1] (4) N.Cy.[1] Sic a hadfash. Nhb. Had away, bairn, ye'r a fair hadfash. He led me sic a hadfash as aa nivvor did see (R.O.H.); Nhb.[1] Cnm.[1] He's a fair hodfash, for he niver lets yan aleànn. Wm. (B.K.) (5, a) Wm. HUTTON *Bran New Wark* (1785) l. 443. (b) n.Yks. This steean's a hod-fast (I.W.). (c) Bdf. Shar-hook and holdfast, 2s. 6d., BATCHELOR *Agric.* (1813) 162. (d) Lakel.[2] (e) w.Yks.[3] Au'm varry hodfast on it. (f) n.Yks.[2] (6) n.Cy. (HALL.) (7) w.Yks. T'company ax'd him if't owd lass had been giin him sum 'howd-on,' HALLAM *Wadsley Jack* (1866) xvii. (8, a) War.[3] A sheriff's officer or Court bailiff taking possession of property under an execution sometimes withdraws from possession for a stated period on receiving from a responsible person a guarantee that his position shall not be thereby prejudiced, or that if it is the guarantor will be personally responsible for the amount distrained for. 'Mr. So-and-so has given me a holdover.' (b) Wor., Glo. Applied for a holdover of the licence, *Evesham Jrn.* (Apr. 10, 1897). Oxf.[1] A paper given to a publican authorizing him to sell beer in the name of the former occupant. (9) Cum.[4] Wm. Them ornaments is meead o' ho' plaster (B.K.). (10) Sc. GROSE (1790) *MS. add.* (C.) (11) Cnm.[1] (12) Rxb. Ye've gotten your haud-sae (JAM.). (13) e.Yks. He dreamed that he saw a dog coming out of a holestok . . . This holestok is near to where the body was found, *E. Morning News* (Aug. 3, 1891) 3, col. 6; e.Yks.[1] (14) n.Yks.[1] (15) Cum.[1] It's fair hod te dea. (16, a) Nhb.[1] He's a reg'lar had-tyul; aa wish he'd stop at hyem. (b) ib. Whe are ye haddin-tyul? Wm.[1] (17) Nhb.[1] Ane o' Hadweel's kind, *Prov.*

4. Phr. (1) *Hold away from*, except, with the exception of; (2) — *fast*, an expression used to warn the man on the top of a wagon of hay or corn that the cart is about to be moved on; (3) — *the rake*, the creeping buttercup, *Ranunculus repens*; (4) — *thee*, see (2); (5) — *thee by the wall*, (a) a kind of thin gruel sweetened with treacle; (b) an expression used when any one sneezes violently; (6) — *thy lail in water* or — *tail o' watty*, a term of encouragement: persevere, stick to it; (7) — *ye, yer*, or *you*, see (2); (8) *to be howt on anything*, to have hold of anything; (9) — *hold a care*, to take care, beware; (10) — *an ear to*, to listen, attend; (11) — *a hard cheek*, to keep a thing secret; (12) — *the heart in one*, to keep in good spirits, cheer up; (13) — *a hough*, to assist at a confinement; (14) — *a wark with*, to be fond of, familiar with; (15) — *aff oneself*, to go ahead, go on; (16) — *foot or feet (with, (a)* to keep pace with, to equal; (b) to keep to one's point, to do what is right; (17) — *going*, to continue, go on; (18) — *good with*, to agree; (19) — *hard*, (a) to stop, wait; (b) to hold fast, keep hold; (c) to pay attention; (20) — *in a cheek of*, to help to bury; (21) — *in the mouth*, to feed by hand; (22) — *light*, to esteem but little; (23) — *mending*, to mend slowly, recover; (24) — *on anything to the mast-head*, to keep on with, endure to the end; (25) — *one by the wall*, to intoxicate; (26) — *one lack*, to keep one close to the point; (27) — *one unthought*, to keep one from thinking, to hold engrossed; (28) — *one's bit*, to retain health, station, or position; (29) — *one's feet*, to keep one's feet; to walk straight; (30) — *one's loof*, to hold out one's hand; (31) — *one's own*, (a) to keep one's health; (b) to persist in the same conduct; (32) — *pace*, to slacken one's speed; (33) *to hold plough*, to plough, drive the plough; (34) — *pross*, to have a gossip; (35) — *slack*, to relax the pressure or tension of one's grasp; to relax one's attention, wile away time; (36) — *soft*, to keep still, control oneself; (37) — *still*, to keep still, be quiet; to be at rest; (38) — *strong*, of liquor: to be strong, see below; (39) — *talk*, see (34); (40) — *the crack*, to keep up the conversation; (41) — *the pudden reeking*, to 'keep it up,' to keep up, continue dancing or merriment; (42) — *thy bother*, intoxicating liquor sold on unlicensed premises; (43) — *thy bother shop*, the unlicensed premises where intoxicating liquor can be

obtained; (44) — *way*, to keep pace with others; (45) — *way by*, to get out of the way.

(1) e.Fif. Her word was a law to a' the women fouk i' the parish; haud awa frae the meenister's wife, an' maybe the Dominie's, LATTO *Tam Bodkin* (1864) ii. (2) Yks. (J.W.), nw.Der.[1] I.W.[1] Used for the horses to move from one cock of corn to the next, as well as to caution the man on the load to be careful and hold on. (3) Cum. In raking up hay in fields where this plant grows the teeth of the rakes are pulled over its creeping and rooting stems with great difficulty (B. & H.); Cum.[1] (4) Chs.[1], nw.Der.[1] (5, a) Lan. Wee'n . . . had nout for 'live on boh a little howd-te-beh-th'-wooes, mede ov a bit o' mele, aw saut an wetur, like gruel, WALKER *Plebeian Pol.* (1796) 10, ed. 1801; (S.W.); We'd nothin' to fence eawr cowd bodies 'gen th' cowd But creep-o'ers, an howd-teh-bi-th'-wohs, BRIERLEY *Spring Blossoms* (ed. 1893) 114. s.Lan. (F.E.T.) (b) w.Yks.[2] Heigh up; howd thi by t'wall, lad! (6) Cum. Hod thy tail in the watter, lad, and there's hope for thee yit, CAINE *Shad. Crime* (1885) 215'; An anudder cried, Hod tail o' watty, ANDERSON *Ballads* (ed. 1840) 2; Cum.[1], n.Yks. (I.W.) (7) nw.Der.[1], Not. (L.C.M.), s.Not. (J.P.K.) Nhp. Ole jer, *N. & Q.* (1883) 6th S. vii. 18. Shr.[1], Bdf. (J.W.B.), e.An.[1] (8) s.Chs.[1] We say indifferently, 'I had howt on it' or 'I was howt on it.' (9) Sc. Haud a care, haud a care, Monkbarns! SCOTT *Antiquary* (1816) viii. (10) Per. An old man told me he was going 'to haud an ear to' the minister of a neighbouring parish next Sunday. I lately heard a man say, 'Ye sudna haud an ear to gossip' (G.W.). (11) Ir. Jist a girl we're bringin' off, an' to hould a hard cheek about it, CARLETON *Fardorougha* (1836) 246. (12) Abd. Jist haud the hert in her till I come back, MACDONALD *D. Elginbrod* (1863) I. 191. (13) Abd. She could, . . giu wives were to cry [in travail], Haud a hough on occasions, ANDERSON *Rhymes* (1867) 32. (14) Abd. When we were at the schule Willie held a wark wi' me, SHELLEY *Flowers* (1868) 267. (15) Ayr. Ay! ay! doctor, noo ca' awa and haud aff ye, SERVICE *Notandums* (1890) 3. Lnk. Weel, then, jist ca' awa' an' haud aff ye! GORDON *Pyotshaw* (1885) 128. (16, a) Sc. (JAM.), Cai.[1] Cum.[1] I can hod fit wi' that chap. Wm. Ah's flait ah's nivver hod feut wi yon lad (B.K.). (b) n.Yks.[2] (17) Sc. (JAM.), Cai.[1] (18) w.Wor. I holds good ooth that, and approves o' it too, S. BEAUCHAMP *Grantley Grange* (1874) I. 205. (19, a) Lakel.[2] Hod hard, Thomas, mi fuit's gitten hankled i' t'car riap. It's a good thing i' life ta know when ta hod-hard a bit and lisk aroond. Yks. (J.W.), Chs.[1] w.Mid. Hold hard there! Don't run over me. Let's hold hard a bit, till we see which way it's coming (W.P.M.). Ken. (D.W.L.) Colloq. 'No; hold hard a bit, Joe,' he said imperatively, BLACK *Three Feathers*, xxii. (b) Brks.[1] There is a game commonly played about Christmas time where a number hold a piece of a handkerchief. One then moves his hand round the handkerchief, saying, 'Here we go round by the rule of Contrairy. When I say "hawld hard," let go, and when I say "let go," hawld hard.' (c) Ken. (D.W.L.) (20) Lnk. When they brought out the corps John told the people they were welcome, to haud in a cheek o' his auld mither wast the gate, GRAHAM *Writings* (1883) II. 40. (21) Sh.I. If dey're [lambs] no haden i' da mooth o', dey'll hae a' da less shance, *Sh. News* (Dec. 4, 1897). (22) Ayr. If he hasna siller an' gude claes, he is held light amang the lasses, HUNTER *Studies* (1870) 19. (23) Lei. She holds mending, but nows and thens she hurls up, *N. & Q.* (1858) 2nd S. vi. 186. (24) Abd. He'll haud on the manure to the mastheid fat ever it may cost, ALEXANDER *Johnny Gibb* (1871) xi. Per. (G.W.) (25) Stf. *Monthly Mag.* (1816) I. 494. (26) e.An.[1] (27) Sc. To haud him unthought lang, JAMIESON *Pop. Ballads* (1806) I. 94. (28) Cum.[1] 'Hoo's Peggy?' 'Nobbet waekly and pinch't to hod her bit.' (29) Abd. A drunken jeet, Unable amaist to haud his feet, Reelin' frae side to side o' the street, ANDERSON *Poems* (1826) 71. (30) N.I.[1] An expression used in bargaining at markets. (31, a) Lei.[1] Bdf. 'I hold my own,' was the reply of a woman who wished to say that she was as she had been—neither better, nor worse. It was declared of a child that he would grow up as stout as his elder brother, 'if he held his own' (J.W.B.). e.An.[1] (32) n.Yks.[2] (33) Oxf. Wanted at once, a strong boy to hold plough, *Oxf. Times* (Mar. 14, 1896). (34) ne.Yks.[1] (35) n.Yks.[1]; n.Yks.[2] 'Hod slack,' slacken the rope you have hold of. m.Yks.[1] (36) Lin.[1] Sometimes she couldn't ho'd her soft When we got up ta bed, 230. (37) Sc. (JAM.) Lth. Haud still thy tongue, SMITH *Merry Bridal* (1866) 65. Nhb. Had still (R.O.H.). w.Yks. Hod t'still er ah'll gie the' a twanck, LUCAS *Stud. Nidderdale* (c. 1882) 30. (38) Suf. 'It don't hold strong enough,' an excuse for not drinking, meaning 'I can't afford it' (R.E.L.). (39) n.Yks.[1][2]; n.Yks.[4] Sha'll ho'd talk wi' onnybody; aye, sha's a champion at ho'ding talk. ne.Yks.[1] e.Yks.[1] Ah like ti hod talk wi Bessy a bit, sha

knaws all news ! toon, *MS. add.* (T.H.) **m.Yks.**[1] (40) Lnk. They'd come stappin' yont that nicht, An' haud the crack till mornin' licht, MURDOCH *Doric Lyre* (1873) 8. (41) **e.Fif.** As for the lads an' lassies they ' held the pudden reekin ' till four o'clock the followin' mornin', LATTO *Tam Bodkin* (1864) xxix. (42, 43) **s.Lan.** Very common (F.E.T.). (44) **n.Yks.**[2] (45) **Cum.**[1]

5. To keep, maintain ; to look after, preserve.
Sc. Foulks hae need o' a wee puckle sense, juist to haud the world gangin' straucht, KEITH *Prue* (1895) 274. **Sh.I.** Ye hae nae wife at hame ta haud you oot o' langer wi'. STEWART *Tales* (1892) 4. **nw.Abd.** Fae green bogs haud free, *Goodwife* (1867) st. 51. **Per.** Haud him on the richt road, IAN MACLAREN *K. Carnegie* (1896) 96. **Lnk.** Blythely roun' the board that nicht, I held the story passing licht, MURDOCH *Doric Lyre* (1873) 26.

6. To nurse. n.Yks.[2]

7. To hold the plough, direct, guide the plough.
w.Yks. ' Ah can't boath hod and drive,' i. e. hold the plough and drive the cattle, BANKS *Wkfld. Wds.* (1865)

8. To uphold. **Sc.** GROSE (1790) *MS. add.* (C.)

9. Of vessels : to be sound, not to leak.
w.Som.[1] Thick there cask 'ont hold, tidn no good to put it in he. The wall o' the leat don't hold, the water's all hurnin away.

10. To occupy, give employment to ; to keep busy, engage.
Ayr. Hughoe, the great bluiter, hauds her wi' his clavers, SERVICE *Notandums* (1890) 3. **Slk.** Nae doubt, she's hadden busy, HOGG *Poems* (ed. 1865) 94. **Dmf.** Gousty winter . . . is hadden thrang a manufacturing storms, JOHNSTONE *Poems* (1829) 113. **n.Yks.**[1] A job at'll hold him mair an yah year, or tweea owther ; **n.Yks.**[4] T'job at t'church 'll ho'd him foor lang eneeaf. **Lan.** But I have moneys to get in and pay which holds me in employ at present, WALKDEN *Diary* (ed. 1866) 67.

11. To oppress, burden ; to afflict with trouble or illness ; to suppress, tread down ; *gen.* in *pass.* and with *down* ; also in phr. *to be hadden and dung.*
Sc. My lassie's . . haddin an' dung, daresna speak to them that I'm sure she anes liket, *Campbell* (1819) I. 334 (JAM.) ; An auld and honourable name, for as sair as it has been worried and hadden down and oppressed, SCOTT *Rob Roy* (1817) xxvi. **Cai.**[1] **Ayr.** Would they be hauden doon by kings or governments ! JOHNSTON *Glenbuckie* (1889) 41. **e.Lth.** He tell't us we had been lang eneuch hadden an' dung, livin on doug's wages, HUNTER *J. Inwick* (1895) 88. **Edb.** Wae-worn fock dung doil'd, an' haddin down, LEARMONT *Poems* (1791) 195. **Rxb.** She's been sairly hauden doon in mony ways, MURRAY *Hawick Sngs.* (1892) 30. **Nhb.** He's sair hadden a fash (R.O.H.) ; **Nhb.**[1] **Dur.**[1] Thou was hauden just like me. **Cum.**[4] Said of ground trodden down by walking. ' Ah was hard hodden ta keep mi tongue atween mi teeth, an' keep frae tellin mi mind,' *Pen. Obs.* ' Thoo's maist as sair hodden as moother,' *Rise of River,* 281. **n.Yks.**[4] He's laam'd foor leyfe ; 't'll ho'd him ti t'end ov his daays. -

Hence (1) **Hodden** or **Hadden-doon,** *ppl. adj.* oppressed, troubled ; kept under, suppressed, downtrodden ; (2) **Hodden-up,** *ppl. adj.* frail.
(1) **Sc.** He's a peer hauden-doon man b' that vyaag o' a wife o' his (W.G.). **ne.Sc.** We're a lot o' poor folk, sair hadden doon wi' big families, bad seasons, and sma' prices for oor fish, *Gordonhaven* (1887) 119. **Abd.** A gweed aneuch servan', but sair haud'n doon naitrally, ALEXANDER *Ain Flk.* (1882) 229. **w.Yks.** They came fro men hard hodden, SNOWDEN *Web of Weaver* (1896) 9. **Hnt.** (T.P.F.) (2) **m.Yks.**[1]

12. To restrain, hold in check ; to prevent, detain ; to govern.
Sc. But cold they not have holden me when I was in all that wrath, JAMIESON *Pop. Ballads* (1806) I. 15 ; The wizard made sic a terrible wark to haud fowk frae meddlin, ROY *Horseman's Wd.* (1895) vii. **Slg.** Discharged of my ministry, holden from my family, BRUCE *Sermons* (1631) 94, ed. 1843. **w.Yks.** Such folks are fitter to hang than to hold, *Prov.* in *Brighouse News* (July 23, 1887). **I.Ma.** Aw, they would' be hoult, BROWN *Doctor* (1887) 138, ed. 1891.

Hence phr. (1) *to be neither to hold nor to bind, to neither hold nor bind,* to be ungovernable, unmanageable, to be beyond control ; see Bind, *v.* 5 ; (2) *to hold one's bother,* (3) — *din,* (4) — *gab* or *gob,* to be quiet, keep silent ; *gen.* used in *imper.* ; (5) — *hand,* to stop, desist, stay ; (6) — *jaw,* (7) — *noise,* (8) — *whisht, husht,* or *hush,* see (4).
(1) **Sc.** Neither to haud nor to bind, SCOTT *Rob Roy* (1817) xiv. **Sh.I.** He wis nedder ta had nor binnd, bit wis aff ower da hill laek a shot, BURGESS *Sketches* (2nd ed.) 65. **ne.Sc.** When the gudeman

wis tel't, he wis naither to haud nor bin' wi' anger, GRANT *Kechleton,* 147. **Cai.**[1] **Abd.** When this he heard he wadna ha'd nor bin', SHIRREFS *Poems* (1790) 73. **Frf.** The curlers were neither to haud nor bin' wi' joy, WILLOCK *Rosetty Ends* (1886) 73, ed. 1889. **Dmb.** Mr. Bacon will miss his mark, and he'll be neither to haud nor bin', CROSS *Disruption* (1844) xxvi. **Ayr.** Whan the luckies they fannd out the trick. They were neither to haud nor bin', AINSLIE *Land of Burns* (ed. 1892) 244. **Edb.** Our laird wad neither haud nor bind, M'DOWALL *Poems* (1839) 130. **n.Ir.** He's nether tae haud nor tae bin' aboot, LYTTLE *Paddy McQuillan,* 74. **Nhb.** He wis nowther ti had nor to bin' (R.O.H.). (2) **Qco.** BARRINGTON *Sketches* (1830) III. vi. **Cum.** O Jack, hod thy bodder ! I can't sleep a wink, ANDERSON *Ballads* (ed. 1840) 64 ; **Cum.**[1] (3) **Yks.** Cannot ye hod yer din ! TAYLOR *Miss Miles* (1890) i. **w.Yks.** When they'd houden their din, *Pogmoor Olm.* (1869) 24 ; **w.Yks.**[5] Hod thi din, wilt ta ! **w.Yks.**[5] **Lan.** HAMERTON *Wenderholme* (1869) v. **Der.**[2] (4) **Edb.** Wha kens na whan to haud his gab, Or whan to speak, M'DOWALL *Poems* (1839) 35. **Nhb.** An' thurs nivver a one o' them offers to speak, For it tells them to had aw thur gobs, man, BAGNALL *Sngs.* (c. 1850) 10 ; **Nhb.**[1] (5) **Bch.** I wonder how they held there [sic] hands, They girnt at me sae sair, FORBES *Ulysses* (1785) 21. **Abd.** When hunger now was slak'd a little wee . . . she hads her hand, ROSS *Helenore* (1768) 30, ed. 1812. **N.I.**[1] **n.Cy.** GROSE (1790). **Nhb.** Had yor hand ! *Keelmin's Ann.* (1869) 32. **e.Dur.**[1] An expression to be heard every day in playing games. **Yks.** (J.W.), **Chs.**[1] (6) **Abd.** Haud yer jaw, min, ALEXANDER *Johnny Gibb* (1871) iii. **Nhb.** Just haud yer jaw, an' sit doon on that steul, BAGNALL *Sngs.* (c. 1850) 23 ; Hout, hinny, had thy blabbin' jaw, WILSON *Pitman's Pay* (1843) 12. **Cum.**[4] **n.Yks.** Hod the jaw, TWEDDELL *Clevel. Rhymes* (1875) 68. **w.Yks.** (J.W.) **Der.**[2] (s.v. Jaw). **Cor.** For genteel talking, thee must knaw, Waent do for thee, so hould thy jaw, TREGELLAS *Farmer Brown* (1857) 7. (7) **ne.Yks.**[1] **e.Yks.** Hod thee noise an' bundle oot, WRAY *Nestleton* (1876) 69 ; **e.Yks.**[1] Hod thi noise. **w.Yks.** ' Hod thi noise! ' cries a voice, hez'nt ta seld enew! *Bradford Life,* 5. **Not.**[2] **Lin.** Ho'd yer noise, bairns, can't ye, *Gilbert Rugge* (1866) I. 35. (8) **Sc.** ' Haud your whist ! ' said Jean, ROY *Horseman's Wd.* (1895) xx. **N.I.**[1] **Nhb.** Thou'd best had thy whisht about warik, *N. Minstrel* (1806–7) pt. iv. 76 ; (R.O.H.) **Cum.**[4] Oh ! haud yer whisht ! Haud yer whisht, Geordie ! *Pearl in a Shell,* 107. **w.Yks.** Hod thy wist, the' tiresome brat (W.F.). **Lan.** He couldn't booath sup and tawk, so he howded his husht, STATON *Loominary* (c. 1861) 100 ; ' So howd thi hush,' aw sez, ' an behave thysel dacent,' *Widder Bagshaw's Trip* (c. 1860) 7. **Chs.**[3] Howd yer hush.

13. To arrest. Ant. (W.H.P.) See Hold, *sb.* 6.

14. To withhold, refuse to give ; to retain.
Kcd. O Fortune . . . haud or gie whate'er ye will Sin' ye hae gi'en me Lizzie, GRANT *Lays* (1884) 180. **n.Yks.**[1] T'au'd roan coo ho'ds her milk. We'll hev to quit 'r. **w.Yks.**[1] T'cow hods her milk. **ne.Lan.**[1] The cow hods her milk.

15. To snatch. n.Cy. (HALL) [Not known to our correspondents.]

16. To consider, have as an opinion, maintain, to think ; to agree.
Rnf. It holds that Mr. Kennedy . . . came from Spain to the rebels and encouraged them, WODROW *Corresp.* (1843) II. 446. **n.Yks.**[4] Ah ho'd 'at he's i' t'wrang. **Bdf.** (J.W.B.), **Suf.** (F.A.A.), (H.H.)

17. To owe, be indebted to ; used only in *pret.*
w.Yks. I knew how much I held him, *N. & Q.* (1884) 6th S. x. 386 ; He said that he held everything to his mother (S.O.A.) ; ' He held me twenty pound.' Peculiar to Sheffield, *Sheffield Indep.* (1874) ; **w.Yks.**[2]

18. To wager, bet.
Sc. ' What will you hold, master, but I'll steal that calf from the butcher before he goes two miles off?' ' Why, . . I'll hold a guinea you don't,' GRAHAM *Writings* (1883) II. 77 ; I'll haud ye the gill on the table that there's no a word about the Patterraw in a' Paul's history, DICKSON *Auld Preentor* (1894) 101. **Lnk.** I'll haud ye a saxpence ye'll lauch on the wrang side o' yer mooth before ye're dune wi' this job, MURDOCH *Readings* (ed. 1895) II. 48. **Ir.** I'll howld ye a quart, *Paddiana* (ed. 1848) 18. **n.Ir.** A'll haud ye it's yin o' them new sort o' preechin' buddys that's gaun aboot the country, LYTTLE *Ballycuddy* (1892) 11. **Cum.** Now I'll hod t'ee a bit of a weager, ANDERSON *Ballads* (ed. 1808) 15. **n.Yks.**[1] Ah's ho'd thee a crown on't. **Chs.**[1] ; **Chs.**[3] I'll hold thee sixpence.

19. To accept as a bargain, to ratify an engagement, esp. in *pp.* or in phr. *hadds you.*

Abd. A pair of kissing-strings and gloves fire new . . . shall be your due. Says Betty, Hadds you, Ross *Helenore* (1768) 34, ed. 1812 ; Betty might have said 'hadden': in such way boys complete a bargain or ratify an engagement (G.W.). **Rnf.** Clooty leuch an' shook his head, An' says, 'My lad, I'll haud ye,' CLARK *Rhymes* (1842) 39. **Lnk.** I'll mak ye a propine . . . a tartan plaid. . . Weel, hald ye there, RAMSAY *Poems* (ed. 1733) 371.
20. To preserve for stock. See Holding, 11.
Sc. (JAM.) m.**Yks.**[1] Of a calf—to hod which, is to rear it for milking.
Hence **Hodden-ewe,** *sb.* a ewe kept for stock and not for slaughter. w.**Yks.**[1]
21. Of animals : to conceive, be with young.
n.**Yks.**[1] 'She's been te t'bull, bud Ah quesshun ef she ho'ds.' Sometimes, 'ho'ds t'bull.' n.**Lin.**[1] If she [a mare] hobds we can't work her next spring. nw.**Dev.**[1]
22. Of seeds : to keep to the ground ; to come up, shoot.
Sc. Most of these planted under the second turf have held, and made good shoots, MAXWELL *Sel. Trans.* (1743) 101 (JAM.).
23. To contest or resist strongly, to be a match for. Also in phr. *to hold one a good one.* n.**Yks.**[1], w.**Yks.**[1]
24. In *pass.* : to be inclined to, to favour.
n.**Yks.**[4] Ah war gretly held i' t'seeam waay.
25. To go on one's way, to proceed ; of things : to go on, take place ; to turn out.
Sc. Ye should hae hadden eassel to Kippletringan, SCOTT *Guy M.* (1815) i ; Ho thy way, my bonny bairn, Ho thy way upon my airm, Ho thy way, thou still may learn To say dada sae bonny, *N. & Q.* (1881) 8th S. iv. 29. **Sh.I.** Haddin' fur wir 'oos, BURGESS *Sketches* (2nd ed.) 107. **Brks.** One man told him to 'gang east a bit, then turn south, syne haud wast,' SMILES *Natur.* (1879) iv. **Abd.** He and I sall hae a horn, Gin ilka thing had right, BEATTIE *Parings* (1801) 36, ed. 1873. **Ayr.** She held o'er the moors to spin, BURNS *There was a Lass,* st. 1. **Edb.** Near Edinbrough a fair there hads, FERGUSSON *Poems* (1773) 131, ed. 1785. **Wm.** Heel git it hot . . . if he dusn't . . . git ta kna fer hissel hoo things is hodden, *Kendal Cy. News* (Oct. 22, 1888). m.**Yks.**[1] Thou must hod on the lane, till thou comes to the old wooden bridge.
26. To fare, progress, to be (as regards health) ; to retain one's state of health. Also used *reflex.* and in *pass.*
Fif. How hauds your health ? DOUGLAS *Poems* (1806) 88. **Lnk.** An' hoo are ye haudin yersel, Peggy ? MURDOCH *Readings* (ed. 1895) III. 9. **Cum.** T'doctor com' an' examin't him ower, an' enquir't hoo he was hodden, RICHARDSON *Talk* (1871) and S. 74, ed. 1876 ; **Cum.**[1] **Wm.** A went tull her fadther an a telt him hoo a wes hodden et heeam, *Spec. Dial.* (1877) pt. i. 28. **Yks.** (J.W.) **Rnt.** 'How do you hold ?' implying that the inquirer hopes you are quite well, though he feels some little anxiety about the state of your health (P.G.D.); **Rnt.**[1] How do you hold yourself, mister ? **Lei.**[1] A'll git to wook agin, if a 'oo'd's better. **Nhp.**[1] 'How d'ye hold ?' A common mode, amongst old people, of inquiring after each other's health ; **Nhp.**[2] **Nrf.** 'How is your husband ?' 'Well, sir, I am sorry to say he hald werry sadly' (W.R.E.). **Suf.** With regard to condition of health, denotes an unchanged state. 'Thank ye, sir, I hould right purely,' RAVEN *Hist. Suf.* (1895) 264.
Hence *how are you hadden till'd ?* phr. how are you ? Cai.[1]
27. To continue, last, esp. of the weather.
Frf. The ice never held again that winter, WILLOCK *Rosetty Ends* (1886) 77, ed. 1889. e.**Sc.** It'll no howd muckle langer, but Ah quesshun an it'll ho'd fair while neeght ; n.**Yks.**[1] Better weather now ; but Ah quesshun an it'll ho'd fair wi'sher hay. ne.**Yks.**[1], w.**Yks.** (J.W.) n.**Lin.**[1] If th' raain hohds like this I shall not goä to Brigg. **Lei.**[1] Way shall git the corn if it hoolds foine. s.**Pem.** Esp. of rain, Laws *Little Eng.* (1888) 420. **Oxf.**[1] I hope t'ull hold fine, *MS. add.* **Suf.** 'That hood dry, Jim !' 'That that du, Tom bor !' ['It keeps dry, Jim !' 'Yes it does, Tom, bor !'] FISON *Merry Suf.* (1899) 33.
28. To stay, remain, keep.
Sc. Better haud with the hound than rin with the hare, RAMSAY *Prov.* (1737). **Ayr.** Gif ye'd keep dry, in back or wame, Hap ye weel, or haud at hame, AINSLIE *Land of Burns* (ed. 1892) 13. **Slk.** Haud out o' my gate, aßld wife, HOGG *Tales* (1838) 351, ed. 1866. m.**Yks.**[1] Hod here a bit.
29. To restrain oneself, refrain from ; to cease, stop ; *gen.* used in imper. as an *int.*
Sc. Enough of this, therefore I'll had Lest all the Poland dogs go mad, CLELAND *Poems* (1697) 112 (JAM.). **Abd.** Winna ye haud ! Ye're surely mad ! MACDONALD *Sir Gibbie* (1879) lxii. **Nhb.**[1] w.**Yks.** I could not hold from stroking her hair, SNOWDEN *Web of Weaver* (1896) xviii ; T'doctor . . . laft as hard as he cud bide, He cuddant

hod, *T. Toddles' Alm.* (1875) 2 ; w.**Yks.**[1] I cudn't hod fray laughin, ii. 288. **Lan.** Houd ; what mak ov a nick dun yo meon ! WAUGH *Tim Bobbin* (1858) iii. **Nhp.**[1] **Sur.**[1] At a country cricket match an incautious batsman, on attempting a run, will be met by a chorus of 'Holt ! Holt !' from the bystanders. **Sus.**[1,2], **Hmp.**[1] **Wil.** SLOW *Gl.* (1890) ; BRITTON *Beauties* (1825). w.**Som.**[1] Always used by a man to his mate or mates working with him, when he desires to stop. Among sawyers, blacksmiths, and handicrafts, where two or more men have to work in concert, the expression is invariable. It is never used in speaking to horses or cattle. nw.**Dev.**[1]
Hence (1) **Hodsta, Hod-ta, Hod-to,** or **Holter,** *int.* (*a*) stop, wait ; (*b*) come back ; (2) *hold ye there,* phr. stop, that will do ; (3) *holt-a-blow,* phr. give over fighting.
(1, *a*) m.**Yks.**[1] w.**Yks.**[1] Hodto a bit, hodto a bit. I'll tell the au enow, ii. 301. ne.**Lan.**[1] (*b*) **Brks.**[1] (2) s.**Sc.** ' Haud ye there, cummer,' interrupted Mrs. Cruickshanks, not a little piqued at the air of incredulity assumed by her visitor, WILSON *Tales* (1836) II. 1. (3) **Som.** JENNINGS *Obs. Dial. w.Eng.* (1825).
30. To take care, beware. ne.**Lan.**[1], nw.**Der.**[1]
31. Of fish : to get under stones for shelter, to lurk, hide under rocks.
Abd. He knew every stone for miles along the river where the salmon were likely to 'haul,' *Deeside Tales* (1872) 213. **Dmf.** The trout has haul't under that stone (JAM.).
HOLDER, *sb.* **Sc. Nhb. Lakel. Der. Lin. Glo. Som.** Also in forms **hadder** Dmf. (JAM.) ; **halder** Abd. Dmf. (JAM.) Lin.[1] ; **hauder** Abd. (JAM.) ; **hodder** Lakel.[2]; **houder** Der. ; **houlder** nw.Der.[1] **1.** One who never leaves go of a thing, one who sticks to a thing or perseveres. Lakel.[2]
2. *Comp.* **Holder-up,** the workman who holds up a 'set' or 'hobby' against the head of a hot rivet at one side of a plate whilst its red-hot end is clinched by the riveter at the other. Nhb.[1] **3.** A niggard ; also in *comp.* **Holder-in.** Abd. (JAM.) **4.** A plough-handle. Lin.[1]
5. Part of a flail ; *gen.* in phr. *hadder and pelter.*
Dmf. The hadder or halder is that part which the thrasher lays hold of ; the pelter, that which is employed for striking the corn (JAM.).
6. A needle-cushion.
Sc. The first job that he gied me was to mak a holder to mysel', FORD *Thistledown* (1891) 296.
7. *pl.* Sheaves placed as a temporary covering for corn-stacks.
Der. Sheaves placed as ridges on corn-stacks to hold the corn down before the thrashing takes place, GROSE (1790) *MS. add.* (P.) ; **Der.**[2], nw.**Der.**[1]
8. *pl.* 'Sprinklings' used in thatching. nw.Der.[1]
9. *pl.* The fangs of a dog. Glo.[1], w.Som.[1]
HOLDIN(G, *ppl. adj.* **Som. Dev.** Beholden.
w.**Som.**[1] I'd zoonder work my vingers to bones, than I'd be holdin [oa-ldeen] to they. **Dev.** I ban't holding to you vor ort I've a-got, PULMAN *Sketches* (1842) 105, ed. 1871.
HOLDING, *sb.* and *ppl. adj.* **Sc. Irel. Nhb. Cum. Yks. I.Ma. Chs.** Also in forms **hadden** Sh.I. ; **haddin**(g Sc. N.I.[1]; **hadin**(g Sc. ; **hauddin** Kcd. ; **haudin**(g Sc. Nhb. Cum. ; **hoddin**(g n.Yks.[2] e.Yks. ; **hodin** Bnff. ; **houldin** N.I.[1] I.Ma. ; **howdin** Chs.[1] **1.** *sb.* A house or land held upon lease ; a farm, tenement. Also used *attrib.*
Sc. Sae swift away hame to your haddin', The mair fule ye e'er came awa, CHAMBERS *Sngs.* (1829) II. 361. **Sh.I.** In her hoose an' her hadden been sairly distressed, STEWART *Tales* (1892) 113. **Bnff.** Came chearfu' to us for a biddin As Peggy to her Patie's hodin, To fish for fadges frae the night, TAYLOR *Poems* (1787) 176. **Abd.** Gushetneuk, a two-horse 'haudin' on the property of Sir Simon Frissal, ALEXANDER *Johnny Gibb* (1871) i. Per. We'll a' get meat and claith enough, A croft and haudin' braw, SPENCE *Poems* (1898) 66. **Rnf.** A wee bit housie to my mind . . . Is a' I'd seek o' haddin' kind, PICKEN *Poems* (1788) 168 (JAM.). **Ayr.** An' he get na hell for his haddin', BURNS *The Election,* II. Lnk. Ye hae siller, An' aiblins a haddin fu' braw, THOMSON *Musings* (1881) 45. **Slk.** Are we to be habbled out o' house and hadding ! HOGG *Tales* (1838) 323, ed. 1866. **Gall.** The beggar, free from tax or charge, Sighs for a house and haddin', NICHOLSON *Poet. Wks.* (1814) 196, ed. 1897. **Ir.** His 'little houldin', as he called some five hundred acres of bog, mountain, and sheep-walk, LEVER *H. Lorrequer* (1839) xix. **N.I.**[1] **Nhb.** An' ravaged wi' fire Peel, hau'din' an' byre, DIXON *Whittingham Vale* (1895) 192. **Cum.** Our haudin', wi' its sma' kail yard, GILPIN *Ballads* (1874) 201. **Chs.**[1,2]

2. Possessions, means of living, property.

Sc. I wad fain marry that lass, but I fear I haena haddin for her (Jam.); A puir lad like himself, . . that had nae hauding but his penny fee, Scott *Rob Roy* (1817) xxiv. **Cai.**¹ ' House an' haddin,' all that one possesses. **Kcd.** Ye ken my hauddin' an' mysel', Mak' it an' me yer ain, Grant *Lays* (1884) 90. **Rnf.** When John and me were married Our hading was but sma', Tannahill *Poems* (1807) 200, ed. 1817. **Lnk.** The haill o' my haudin' an' warldly plack Button'd beneath the coat on my back, Murdoch *Doric Lyre* (1873) 96. **Kcb.** This wee creepie stuil that I noo hae my fit on, Has been in the haudin' for mony a year, Armstrong *Ingleside* (1890) 69.

3. Furniture, equipment, trappings; the stock of a farm.

Dmb. It was owre little to gang far in the way o' house plenishin, or house haudin', no to speak o' stockin' a farm, Cross *Disruption* (1844) v. **Rnf.** A gude bein house, wi' haudin neat an' fine, Picken *Poems* (1788) 104 (Jam.). **Ayr.** Ye maun just let me ride my ain horse wi' my ain ha'ding, Galt *Sir A. Wylie* (1822) xxv. **Rxb.** The haddin o' a farm, the quantity or number of scores of stock, i. e. sheep which a farm is reckoned to maintain or graze (Jam.).

4. *pl.* Savings, money laid by. **n.Yks.**² Yan's bits o' hoddings.

5. The holding of an entertainment, a party, feast.

Lnk. At ilk haddin' in the kintra She was still the reignin' queen, Nicholson *Kilwuddie* (ed. 1895) 44.

6. The act of embracing.

Lnk. Sic haudin' and drawin', sic daffin' and fun, Nicholson *Idylls* (1870) 21.

7. *Comp.* Holding-brass, the money or stake of a wager. **n.Yks.**² Wheea hods t'hodding-brass ?

8. *ppl. adj.* Lasting, enduring; also with *out*.

n.Yks. Luckily it was not a ' hoddin' storm,' for the snow ceased in less than half an hour. Atkinson *Moorl. Parish* (1891) 377. **I.Ma.** 'Deed he was as active as a cat, was Cain—and skilful, and houldin out, Brown *Yarns* (1881) 263, ed. 1889.

9. Phr. *with a holding stroke*, without intermission. **Che.**¹ With a howdin stroke.

10. Sure, certain.

Sc. This and many other things about them and amongst them are holding evidences and sad swatches of anti-gospel spirits, Walker *Life of A. Peden* (1727) 75 (Jam.) ; One of the holdingest signs or marks, *ib.* 79.

11. Of animals : preserved for stock, not intended for sale; *gen.* in *comp.* Holding-calf, -stock, &c. Cf. hold, *v.* 20.

Sc. A haudin cawf (Jam.). **Peb.** The whey is used . . . sometimes instead of water for drink to weaned calves for holding stock, *Agric. Surv.* 82 (*ib.*). **n.Yks.** Three tenants who might . . . send up their holding-stock, viz. young horses, young cattle, and perhaps a few sheep, Tuke *Agric.* (1800) 216 ; **n.Yks.**¹ Holdingewes, holding-stock ; **n.Yks.**² ' Hodding cawvs,' kept for growing up to full-sized cattle. ' In hodding order,' in a condition for retaining as stock.

12. Of corn : not fully ripe.

e.Yks.¹ ' Ah likes tł cut mah wheeat hoddin ; it tons oot betther,' i. e. yields more when threshed, *MS. add.* (T.H.)

HOLE, *sb.*¹ and *v.*¹ Var. dial. uses in Sc. Irel. and Eng. Also in forms haul w.Yks. Dev. ; hawle Cor. ; hoil Yks. w.Yks.²⁸⁵ ; hoile Yks. ; hooal Cum.⁸ n.Yks.² e.Yks.¹ ; hoyle Lan. ; hul- Wxf.¹ ; hyell Nhb. ; oil w.Yks. ; whoal Cum.⁸ ; wholl Cum. [h)ōl, h)oəl, w.Yks. oil.] **1.** *sb.* An opening, an empty space or cavity ; *gen.* used with a qualifying prefix.

w.Yks. Gate-hoil, door-hoil, window-hoil (J.T.) ; Wreng chimley hoil, *w.Yks. Alm.* (1881) 21 ; **w.Yks.**⁵ Draught-hoil, pickin-hoil, &c. **Dev.** Ma beluvid put in es han be tha haul uv tha dore, Baird *Sng. Sol.* (1860) v. 4. **e.Dev.** My leuve putt in es han' by th' deur-haul, Pulman *ib.*

Hence *to put boards i' t'hoil, phr.* to shut the door. **w.Yks.** (S.P.U.), (J.W.)

2. A house ; a room ; a corner, recess ; a coal-hole.

Yks. A house full, a hoile full. ' Ya' canna' fetch a bowl full.' *Answer,* Reek, *Riddle* in *N. & Q.* (1865) 3rd S. viii. 325. **n.Yks.** In contempt. ' I wish I was out o' this hooal ' (I.W.). **w.Yks.** They meeade sike a row iw hooal, that Bob gat up off a creeal, Nicholson *Flk-Sp.* (1889) 34. **w.Yks.** There's not another hoile to lig down in i' th' hahse! Brontë *Wuthering Hts.* (1847) xiii ; He works i' t'combin' hoil (J.T.) ; **w.Yks.**² O'll clear t'hoil a yond set ; **w.Yks.**⁵ We've bowt t'owd hoil twice over, 21. **Lan.** Thea'st have a quart o'th best ale i' this hole, Waugh *Owd Bodle,* 259 ; They mun be somwhere i' th' hoyle, Westall *Birch Dene* (1889) I. 292.

Hence **Hoilful,** *sb.* a houseful, room-full.

w.Yks. There's a hoilful below, an' t'steps is full waitin' to cum up, Cudworth *Dial. Sketches* (1884) 17 ; An' a rare hoilful ther wor, Hartley *Pudden* (1876) 31.

3. A gallery in a mine or quarry ; the opening in which gunpowder, &c. is placed when blasting is necessary.

Nhb. Though still they're i' the hyell a ' hewin,' Wilson *Pitman's Pay* (1843) 59. **n.Yks.** (C.V.C.) **Cor.** Stopped the owld hop, an' jumped out like as ef a hawle wor going off, Tregellas *Tales,* 33 ; (M.A.C.) ; **Cor.**⁸ An everyday word with miners and quarrymen. When the explosion occurs the ' hole ' is said to have ' gone off.'

4. A gaol, prison.

w.Yks. Three or four custom-hawse officers pahnced on us, an' tuk us to't hoile, Hallam *Wadsley Jack* (1866) xiii ; They'l other foin us, or else send us to't oil, Bywater *Sheffield Dial.* (1839) 9 ; **w.Yks.**² But wot's to become on us families when we gooan to t'hoil ; **w.Yks.**⁸⁵ **Lan.** Eawr Dick 'll ha' to goo i' th' hole, Brierley *Irkdale* (1868) 164.

5. A grave.

e.Yks.¹ We put him intiv hooal, and happed him up, and that's end on him.

6. *Obs.* Shelter, cover, esp. in phr. *to take hole.*

Flf. They landit at Balmernie : And there he took hole like a rabbit, Tennant *Papistry* (1827) 67.

7. *Obs.* A hole dug in the surface of a vein to denote the right of a miner to the vein which he has found.

Der. Manlove *Lead Mines* (1653) l. 268 ; A miner by digging a hole, and cutting a cross upon the surface of a vein first found by him, thereby gained by custom a perfect right to such vein. . . It was the duty of the miner to fence in his holes and groves in order that cattle might not fall into them, Tapping *Gl. to Manlove* (1851).

8. A sheep-mark.

Sh.I. These 'sheep-marks' received such names as a shear, a slit, a hole, Hibbert *Desc. Sh. I.* (1822) 185, ed. 1891.

9. *sb. pl.* A game of marbles ; also in form Holie.

Bnff.¹ Played by running the marbles into holes, three in number. **Rnf.** ' Holie ' is his favourite game, Hoo he birls them in, Neilson *Poems* (1877) 92 ; Play of three round cup-shaped holes (at equal distances in which the ' bools' or marbles have to be rolled (A.W.).

Hence (1) Hoilakes, (2) Hoil-taw, (3) Hole-and-taw, *sb.* a game of marbles.

(1) **w.Yks.**⁸ The marbles are cast into a hole in the ground. Lit. ' Hole lake,' hole play (J.W.). (2) **w.Yks.** Can tah laik at hoil-taw ! Wyke *Yks. Cousins* (1895) 272. (3) **N.I.**¹

10. Phr. (1) *a hole in the* or *one's coat*, a flaw or blemish in character or conduct ; (2) *by the hole of one's coat*, an expletive : (3) *to make a hole in the water*, to commit suicide by drowning ; (4) *to make holes in anything*, to empty.

(1) **Ayr.** It was like butter in the black dog's hass for Jenny to get haud of a hole in my coat like this, Service *Dr. Duguid* (ed. 1887) 102 ; If there's a hole in a' your coats I will you tent it, Burns *Grose's Peregrinations* (1789) st. 1. **n.Cy.** Holl-coway. **n.Yks.** (I.W.) **w.Yks.**¹ ' To have a hole in his coat,' to know of some blemish in another's character. **nw.Der.**¹ ' Poo a hole in his coat,' disparage him. **Nhp.**¹ **n.Cy.** To pick a hole in one's coat, Holloway. (2) Ir. By the hole o' my coat, there's some thing alive in it ! Yeats *Flk. Tales* (1888) 190. (3) **w.Yks.** If it hedd'ant a been at ah wor affread on hur mackin a hoyle i t'wattar ah sud a brockan t'conneckshan off, Tom Treddlehoyle *Bairnsla Ann.* (1859) 28. (4) **Lan.** Took hold of the proffered pot, and to use his own expression, 'made holes in it,' Brierley *Marlocks* (1867) 88.

11. *Comp.* (1) Hole-ahin, a term of reproach ; (2) -gitten, of obscure origin ; (3) -pits, vestiges of ancient British dwellings.

(1) **Kcb.** Her tittas clap'd their pips an' hooted Ah, hol-e—ahin ! Davidson *Seasons* (1789) 178 (Jam.). (2) **n.Yks.**² (3) *ib.* Each pit having had heightened sides of stones and earth above ground, with a roof formed, doubtless, of branches and sods. Originally conical or hive-shaped, some exhibit a paved flooring; and stand in a line like a street between parallel walls of earth.

12. *v.* To perforate, to drill a hole ; to pierce, gnaw; also used *fig.*

Gall. Those a-gnawing with hunger, are said to be ' holin wi' hunger,' or that the worms are holing their bodies, Mactaggart *Encycl.* (1824). **Nhb.**¹ **Cha.**¹ Salt-mining term. Cutting with a chisel holes in various directions from twelve inches to thirty or forty inches deep, and about one inch in diameter for the purpose of blasting the rock-salt.

Hence (1) Holed, *ppl. adj.* suddenly pierced; (2) Holed-stone, *sb.* a stone having a hole in it. Cf. holey-stone. s.v. Holey.

(1) **N.I.**[1] (a) **Nhb.** Holed stones are hung over the heads of horses as a charm against diseases. Horses that sweat in their stalls are supposed to be cured by the application of this charm. The stone must be found naturally holed. If it be made it has no efficacy (J.H.). **Cor.** [An] ancient custom which prevails to the present day at the 'holed stone,' near the village of Lanyon, **Black** *Flk-Medicine* (1883) iii.

13. In mining: to excavate a passage-way; to undermine a seam of coal.

Nhb.[1] **Nhb., Dur.** They frequently hole or cut through from one board to another, *Compleat Collier* (1708) 18; Holing, making a passage of communication between one place and another, **Nicholson** *Coal Tr. Gl.* (1888). **w.Yks.** (D.T.); To open into or make a communication with a working place (S.J.C.). **Shr.**[1] To cut round a block of coal in such a way as to detach it for removal; **Shr.**[2] [To undercut, *Reports Mines.*]

Hence (1) hole to grass, *phr.* to work a vein of metal to the surface; (2) Holers, *sb. pl.* in a colliery: men employed in 'kirving' where 'getters' and fillers are employed; men who 'hole'; (3) Holing, *sb.* the depth of coal displaced by one blasting; (4) Holing about, *phr.* driving in a pit with 'bratticed' air after a seam of coal has been won; (5) Holing-shots, *sb. pl.* in blasting: shots nearest the floor.

(1) **Cor.**[1] (2) **Nhp.**[1] **Nhb., Dur.** **Nicholson** *Coal Tr. Gl.* (1888). **Shr.**[1] (3) n.Ayr. *N. & Q.* (1870) 4th S. vi. 339. (4) **Nhb.**[1] In order to establish the air communication between the downcast and upcast shafts and to form off the shaft pillars and walls. (5) **w.Yks.** (T.T.)

14. To dig, delve; with *out*: to dig out; *fig.* to expel.

Abd. To go down one evening to Craiguise to hole some fir to make blazes, *Deeside Tales* (1872) 147. **Frf.** Willum was hol'ing, and I was lifting, **Barrie** *Tommy* (1896) 342. **Dmb.** I'll hole out McCorkle before I be mony days aulder, **Cross** *Disruption* (1844) xxix.

15. To bury, inter; to make away with, murder.

s.Ir. Keep yourself from being holed as they holed Muster Bingham the other day, **Trollope** *Land Leaguers* (1885) 13. **Wxf.**[1] 84.

Hence Hooald or Hulth, *ppl. adj.* buried, interred. **Wxf.**[1], n.Yks.[2]

16. To put in prison, send to gaol.

w.Yks. Tell'd em abaht bein boiled an fined, *Yksman.* (1877) 5, col. 1; **w.Yks.**[1]

17. To claim possession of, to secure, 'bag.'

Cum.[2] Thou thinks th'u's hooal't our lile bit grund, 97; A great hulking fellow thrust it into his pocket, exclaiming, ' I've hooal't that an',' *ib. Gl.*

18. To wear into holes; to have holes.

Lnk. When a shoe begins to hole, Be't upper-leather, or the sole, **Watson** *Poems* (1853) 23. **Cum.** His shoon war wholl't, beath nebs and heels, **Gilpin** *Ballads* (1874) 175.

Hence Holed, *ppl. adj.* having holes, worn into holes. **N.I.**[1] **w.Yks.** Ah can't bear a woman wi' a hauled stockin' (F.P.T.).

19. To hide; to take shelter, get under cover.

Nhb. The ryaing moone . . . holed ahint a cloude, **Richardson** *Borderer's Table-bk.* (1846) VII. 139. **w.Yks.** If it's bahn to rain Ah think we'd better hoil, hed we n't? (S.K.C.); Wet to t'skin! What didn't ta hoil in somewhear for? *Leeds Merc. Suppl.* (Mar. 3, 1894). **Lan.** ' How leets thou didn't hole? ' ' Hole! wheer mut I hole, at th' top o' Rooly Moor?' **Waugh** *Chim. Corner* (1874) 169, ed. 1879; **Lan.**[1], ne.**Lan.**[1]

Hence Hooal'd, *ppl. adj.* concealed. n.Yks.[2]

20. To earth as a fox; *fig.* to stay at home lazily; also with *on.*

Abd. To shame the hincum-sneevie louns wha aye holed on at hame, **Cadenhead** *Bon-Accord* (1853) 259. **w.Yks.**[1] ne.**Lan.**[1] 'He's holed,' he's gone into the house.

Hole, *sb.*[2] Irel. A bad, wicked person. s.Don. **Simmons** *Gl.* (1890).

Hole, *v.*[2] Sh.I. To run down, pour. Cf. hale, *v.*[1], heel, *v.*[2]

He wis yarkin oot da paets an' da swaet holin' aff o'm, *Sh. News* (Nov. 25, 1899).

HOLE, HOLEN, HOLEYN, see Hold, *v.*, Holl, *adj.*, Hollin.

VOL. III.

HOLEY, *adj.* Nhb. Lakel. Yks. Lei. Also Som. Also written holy N.Cy.[1] Lakel.[2] n.Yks.[124] w.Yks.[1] w.Som.[1]; and in form hooaley n.Yks.[2] [h)ō·li, oə·li.] In *comp.* (1) Holey-flint, a flint with a natural hole through it; (2) -stone, or Holstone, Hosten, Hoston, (a) a stone with a natural hole through it, supposed to act as a charm; (b) a large upright stone.

(1) **w.Som.**[1] It is better even than a horse-shoe to keep off the pixies, or the witches, or the evil-eye. (2, a) n.Cy. **Brand** *Pop. Antiq.* (ed. 1777) 97; **N.Cy.**[1] A charm against diseases. **Nhb.**[1] The stone must be found already perforated, or it has no virtue. These are very commonly hung behind house doors as charms. A sanctity or superstition appears to have been attached to stone implements with holes. They were supposed to have been perforated by snakes.—Within recollection no fishing boat was without a 'holey-stone' suspended from the inwiver, *ib.* (s.v. Inwiver). **Lakel.**[2] n.Yks.[1] Supposed to have peculiar virtues in propitiating luck, and efficacy as against witch-power and mischief. Suspended by a string from the bed-tester, or attached to the key of the house-door for the safety of the inmates; hung above the standing of the cow, or over the stall of a horse, especially one that is found to sweat much at night, for the several security of those animals; n.Yks.[2] The perforated fragments of the grey alum shale found on our beach, the round holes being viewed as the work of the shell-fish called the 'borer'; though tradition assigns the punctures to the sting of the adder (s.v. Haggomsteeans); n.Yks.[4] w.Yks.[1] Frequently suspended by a string from the tester of a bed, or from the roof of a cow house. (b) n.Yks.[2] Holy-stones are those artificial formations connected with the oracular ceremonies of past ages; and it is recorded that one of these up-rights, called the Needle, stood in the vicinity of the west pier at Whitby, through the eye of which rickety children were drawn in order to strengthen them; a custom practised in some parts to this day. Lovers also pledged themselves by joining hands through the hole, esp. in the case of young mariners bound on their voyage; and where the holes were large enough people crept through them 'so many times' to cure pains in the back (s.v. Haggom-steeans). **Lei.** There is a parish called Humberstone wherein is a stone called Holstone, Hoston, or Hosten, **Nichols** *Hist. Lei.* III. pt. ii. 981.

HOLGHE, *sb.* Obs. Wxf.[1] Also in forms haoleghey, holgave. Shrove Tuesday.

HOLIDAY, *sb.* Yks. Lan. Bdf. Cor. Also in forms haliday n.Yks.[2] Lan.[1] e.Lan.[1]; hallidey Lan. [o·li-, a·lidə.] 1. In *comp.* (1) Holiday-folks, people without the ties of business; (2) -Jack, a man fond of holidays and the display of clothes; (3) -turned, intent upon pleasure.

(1) n.Yks.[2] (2) Lan.[1] Look at him neaw. He's a bonny holiday-jack—isn't he?—wi' his mester's foine shirt on. (3) n.Yks.[2]

2. *phr. to ride, gallop, &c., as if the devil had bad holiday,* to ride, gallop, &c., fiercely, wildly.

Lan. I heard some fock cummink after meh o gallop, o gallop os if the Deel had bad hallidey, **Tim Bobbin** *View Dial.* (ed. 1806) 48.

3. A pastime; a party, esp. one given for the sake of dancing. e.Lan.[1], Bdf. (J.W.B.)

4. *pl.* Parts left untouched in dusting, sweeping, painting, &c.

Cor. Plenty of holidays on that door, **Thomas** *Randigal Rhymes* (1895) *Gl.*; **Cor.**[2] Don't leave any holidays.

HOLIE, *sb.* Sh.I. In *phr. hōlie be with you,* an exclamation.

Hōlie be wi you, dere I fan hit! *Sh. News* (Sept. 11, 1897); Jeemie Willie guid saft ta shut da rudder, bit hōli be wi' you, diel rudder wis inside her, *ib.* (Mar. 25, 1899).

HOLIE, *adj.* Sc. In *comb.* Holie-pie things, patterns of sewing or knitting; small holes cut out of linen and stitched round.

Abd. This is a little bun'lie 't my mither bad's gie ye; there's holie-pie thingie's in't 't ye made yersel', **Alexander** *Ain Flk.* (1882) 21. **Per.** (G.W.)

HOLIMAUL, *v.* Som. [Not known to our correspondents.] To beat. (Hall.)

HOLING, *vbl. sb.* and *ppl. adj.* Som. Dev. Also written hoaling n.Dev. 1. *vbl. sb.* Picking holes, fault-finding.

n.Dev. Oll vor whistering and pistering, and hoaling and halzening, or cuffing a tale, *Exm. Scold.* (1746) l. 297; 'Hoaling and halzening,' picking holes, and suggesting the worst that can happen, *Horae Subsecivae* (1777) 213.

E e

2. *ppl. adj.* Ready to pick holes, fault-finding.

w.Som.[1] A purty holin old thing her is!

HOLIS-BOLIS, see Holus-bolus.

HOLL, *adj., sb.*[1] and *v.*[1] Sc. n.Cy. Yks. Lan. Der. e.An. Also written hol n.Yks.[2] e.Nrf.; and in forms hole N.Cy.[1] w.Yks.[1] e.Lan.[1] Glo. ; hooale.Yks.[1] [h]ol, h)ôl.] 1. *adj.* Hollow, deep, concave. Cf. how(e, *adj.*, howl, *adj.*

n.Cy. Opposed to shallow, GROSE (1790); N.Cy.[2] An ' hole dish.' n.Yks.[1]; n.Yks.[2] ' Hol spots,' depressions in the ground. e.An.[1]

2. Empty, hungry.

e.Yks.[1] Of cattle ; empty of meat, MARSHALL *Rur. Econ.* (1788); e.Yks.[1] Let's hé summat tí eeat ; Ah's as holl as a dhrum.

Hence **Holl-kited,** *adj.* with an empty stomach ; also in phr. *a holl-kited set,* a penurious lot. n.Yks.[2]

3. *sb.* A hollow or depression in the surface of the ground, a deep or narrow valley, a ravine.

n.Yks.[1] A deep narrow depression in the surface of the land or place, of no great longitudinal extent; n.Yks.[2][4], ne.Yks.[1] e.Yks. MARSHALL *Rur. Econ.* (1788); e.Yks.[1], m.Yks.[1], e.Lan.[1] Nrf. (E.M.) ; (R.H.H.\

4. *pl.* The hollow or concave parts : the groin, legs, &c.; esp. in phr. *heads and holls,* heads or tails.

e.An.[1][2] e.Suf. Children, here, will throw up a stone, or anything else, and cry out : ' Heads and holls ! God Almighty only know [*sic*] where it falls' (F.H.).

5. A ditch, *gen.* a dry one; a moat.

e.An.[1][2] Nrf. He'd . . . bundle me and my spades and traps off his back into some holl or deek, STRICKLAND *Old Friends, &c.* (1864) 324 ; I see the mare fall into the holl myself (W.R.E.) ; A wide ditch of water, COZENS-HARDY *Broad Nrf.* (1893) 2. e.Nrf. The hollow of the ditch, in distinction to the ' dick ' or bank of the hedge, MARSHALL *Rur. Econ.* (1787). Suf. *e.An. Dy. Times* (1892\ Suf.[1], e.Suf. (F.H.)

6. *Fig.* The depth, middle of winter or of the night, &c. Also in comp. Holl-time. Cf. how(e, *sb.*[1] 10.

n.Yks. A fire was to be made as the ' holl time of the night ' drew on, ATKINSON *Moorl. Parish* (1891) 104 ; n.Yks.[1]; n.Yks.[2] The holl of winter ; n.Yks.[4], m.Yks.[1] w.Yks.[1] T'hole o' winter. ne.Lan.[1] Holl o' winter, holl o' neet.

7. *v.* To hollow out, to dig ; to pierce, penetrate.

Sc., Abd. (JAM.\ Kcb. Communion feasts, the remembrance whereof . . . holleth my heart, RUTHERFORD *Lett.* (1660) No. 177. n.Yks.[1] n.Der. Farmers speak of holling out land for drain-pipes (S.O.A.)

8. To make hollow or lean by starvation, to emaciate.

n.Yks.[1]; n.Yks.[2] Holling, pining or pinching with cold or hunger. m.Yks.[1]

Hence **Holl'd,** *ppl. adj.* starved, puny, without growth or power. n.Yks.[1][2], m.Yks.[1]

[1. Of the holl grave law, A gret eddir slydand gan furth thraw, DOUGLAS *Eneados* (1513), ed. 1874, II. 228 ; Hol, as pypys, or percyd thyngys, *cavus,* Prompt. OE. *hol,* hollow (*Leechdoms*). 2. Holle, *inanis,* Cath. Angl. (1483). 3. *Lustra,* wilddeora holl and denn, *Voc.* (c. 1050) in Wright's *Voc.* (1884) 187. 5. Þe holl of wyntir, BARBOUR *Troy-Bk.* (c. 1375) II. 1695.]

HOLL, *v.*[2] and *sb.*[2] Sc. [hol.] 1. *v.* To stay in a place without occupation ; to frequent a place in a lazy, idle manner ; to loaf ; also with *aboot.* Cf. hole, *v.*[1] 20.

Bnff.[1] Twa or three o' thim hollon at the corner o' the street.

Hence **Hollin** or **Hollin-aboot,** *ppl. adj.* lazy. *ib.*

2. To be contented with mean work ; to be working hard and accomplishing little ; also with *aboot.*

Bnff.[1] He's built the hail simmer castin' peets i' the moss. Abd. To employ oneself in a sluggish, low, dirty manner ; to satisfy oneself with any occupation, however mean and dishonourable; in this sense commonly ' to howk and holl ' (JAM.\

Hence **Hollin** or **Hollin-aboot,** *ppl. adj.* unskilful, awkward. Bnff.[1]

3. *sb.* A lazy, idle meeting or gossiping.

Bnff.[1] They keep an unco holl in that chop.

HOLL, *v.*[3] Yks. Chs. Der. Not. Lin. Lei. Nhp. Hrt. Hnt. Ken. Sus. Hmp. [ol.] To throw, hurl. Cf. hull. *v.*[3]

e.Yks. (W.W.S.), e.Yks.[1] w.Yks.[2] He's holling stones at him! Chs. He holl'd a stone, *Sheaf* (1878) No. 125. I. 37 ; Chs.[1], Der.[2], nw.Der.[1], Not.[1] s.Not. Holl a stun at 'im (J.P.K.). Lin. Holl it to me, THOMPSON *Hist. Boston* (1856) 710 ; Lin.[1] Holl the tennis ball to me. Lei. GROSE (1790) *MS. add.* (P.) Nhp.[1] Holl it away.

Hrt. (E.G.), Hnt. (T.P.F.) Ken. I . . . holl'd her pattens to de top An dragged her through de quick, MASTERS *Dick and Sal* (c. 1821\ st. 39 ; Ken.[1][2], Sus.[1][2], Hmp.[1]

HOLLAN, see Hallan, *sb.*[1][2], Holland, Hollin.

HOLLAND, *sb.* Sc. Lin. Nrf. Cor. Also in forms hollan Sc. (JAM. *Suppl.*); hollen Cor. [h)oˑlǝn(d.] In *comb.* (1) Holland('s bools, Dutch marbles ; (2) -duck, the scaup, *Fuligula marila* ; (3) -goose, the solan-goose or gannet, *Sula bassana* ; (4) -hawk, the great northern diver, *Colymbus glacialis* ; (5) -smock, the sea-campion ; (6) — wait, a frog.

(1) Sc. Striped or variegated bowls greatly prized by boys (JAM. *Suppl.*); Grannie ! Mysie's ta'en my ba' . . . And flung my Hollan's bools awa'. SMART *Whistle Binkie,* II. 377 (*ib.*\. (2) Prf. SWAINSON *Birds* (1885) 159. (3) Nrf. COZENS-HARDY *Broad Nrf.* (1893) 45. (4) Ayr. SWAINSON *ib.* 213; She . . . could hae run wi' the win' an' took the sea like a hollan' hawk, AINSLIE *Land of Burns* (ed. 1892\ 127. (5) Cor. Where hollen-smoks and fragrant tags, And britons were in blowth, THOMAS *Randigal Rhymes* (1895) 15. (6) Lin. Frogs swarmed everywhere, and because of their croaking were called Holland waits. WHITE *Eng.* (1865\ I. 280.

HOLLARD, *sb.* Som. The alder, *Alnus glutinosa.* w.Som. (B. & H.)

HOLLARDS, *sb. pl.* Sus.[1][2] [oˑlǝdz.] The dead branches of trees.

HOLLARDY-, HOLLEE, see Holyrood, Hollo.

HOLLER, *sb.* and *v.* Nhb. Cum. Also in form huller Nhb.[1] Cum. [hoˑlǝr, huˑlǝr.] 1. *sb. pl.* A great number, a great quantity.

Nhb. Aa've seen hollers on them (R.O.H.) ; Nhb.[1]

2. *v.* To heap on indiscriminately. Nhb.[1]

Hence **Huller't,** *ppl. adj.* of blood : clotted, coagulated.

Cum.[3] At last some barns peep't in, an' so' some huller't bleud on t'flooar, 71.

HOLLEY, see Hully, *sb.*

HOLLIBUBBER, *sb.* Cor. [oˑlibʷbǝ(r).] A man employed to clear away refuse from a slate quarry.

The old man had once . . . made his living as a ' hollibubber,' or one who carts away the refuse slates, 'Q.' *Three Ships* (1890) viii; Cor.[1] A man who, unattached to the works, makes a living out of the refuse of the slate quarries at Delabole ; Cor.[2]

HOLLICK, *sb.* Cor.[1][2] Also written ollick Cor.[1][2] [oˑlik.] The house-leek, *Sempervivum tectorum.*

[Apparently the same word as *holleke,* used by 16th c. writers for the Welsh onion, *Allium fistulosum* ; *cp.* COTGR. : *Ciboule,* a chibol, or hollow leek.]

HOLLIE, *adj.* Sh.I. Holed, having holes. See Holey, *adj.*

Hit's dis hollie yakle o' mine. Der been a staangin' intil hi an di hale day, *Sh. News* (Oct. 29, 1898).

HOLLIE, see Hollo.

HOLLIN, *sb.* Sc. Nhb. Lakel. Cum. Yks. Lan. I. Ma. Chs. Der. Not. Lin. Shr. Also written holen Sc. ; hol eyn w.Yks.[8] ; hollan Sc. ; hollen Sc. n.Cy. e.Lan.[1] Shr.[2]; holleyn Chs.[2][8]; hollyn w.Yks.[1] Shr.[2]; holyn e.L.th. ; and in forms holland Sc. (JAM.) Nhb.[1]; hollond n.Lin. ; ollen w.Yks. [hȯˑlin, -ǝn.] 1. The holly, *Ilex Aquifolium*; also used *attrib.* Cf. holling.

Sc. He lies never but when the holen is green, RAY *Prov.* (1678) 374; *Garden Wk.* (1896\ New S. No. ciii. 100. Abd. The body of the devise was a hollin or lawrell branch, TURREFF *A Antiq. Gleanings* (1859) 288. Rnf. Willie first made love to me Bern cath my daddy's hollan tree, FINLAYSON *Rhymes* (1815) 82. e.Lth. J. man . . . that never lees but whan the holyn's green, HUNTER R Inwick (1895\ 165. Edb. Wi' mealy bags and hollan kent, To help him on his way, LIDDLE *Poems* (1821) 23. Slk. The picture of a knight, and a ladye bright, And the grene hollin abune their hollin BORLAND *Yarrow* (1890) 34. N.Cy.[1] Nhb.[1] In s.Nhb. he hout and she-hollin are discriminated. The latter is the kind with prickles, and is used for fortune telling. Lakel.[1] Cum. Within a hundred yards o' t'hollin' buss, FARRALL *Betty Wilson* (1886) 124. John White o 't'Hollins, DICKINSON *Lamplugh* (1856) 8. n.Yks. ne.Yks.[1] e.Yks. MARSHALL *Rur. Econ.* (1788). w.Yks. Some ollen twigs. wi berries on, SENIOR *Smithy Rhymes* (1882) 38. w.Yks. Lan. Meh mind moot os weel o line . . . in o rook o hollins or gorses, TIM BOBBIN *View Dial.* (ed. 1806) 39 ; Lan.[1], n.Lan.[1] ne.Lan.[1], e.Lan.[1] I.Ma. Uncle carried me down some hibbins and hollin this mornin', from the farrim (S.M.); The last bunch of the hibben and hollin, CAINE *Deemster* (1887) 130, ed. 1889. **Chs.** Frames o' green and red hollin' berries, CROSTON *Enoch Crump* (1887) 12; Chs.[123], s.Chs.[1], Der.[12], nw.Der.[1] Not. It lays just there by the hollin hedge (L.C.M.); Not.[2], n.Lin.[1] sw.Lin.[1] Sometimes called Prick-hollin. **Shr.[2]**

2. *Comp. Obs.* Hollin-rent, rent paid for the holly-trees growing upon a certain portion of ground in the commons of the manor of Sheffield. w.Yks.[2]

[OE. *hole(g)n*.]

HOLLIN, see Hallan, *sb.[1]*

HOLLING, *sb.* Wm. The eve of the Feast of Epiphany, Twelfth Night, Jan. 5; also called **Holling Day.** See Hollin.

So called at Brough, where there is an annual procession of an ash-tree lighted on the top of its branches, to which combustible matter has been tied. This custom is in commemoration of the Star of the wise men of the East (HALL.); *N. & Q.* (1899) 9th S. iii. 108; For a full account of the ceremonies by which 'Holling' or 'Holly Night' are celebrated at Brough see HONE *Table-bk.* (1838) III. 26; Wm.[1] The last time it was observed 'was the year of the Crimean War': 1854 or 1855). An ash-tree, with suitable branches, was peeled, and to each branch was attached a torch made of rushes dipped in oil. At 8 o'clock in the evening this tree, lighted, was carried in procession from the 'Swan' Inn twice round the town, by one of the strongest men, and brought to the central bridge. Here, in the presence of hundreds of spectators, a fierce struggle for the possession of the tree took place between two parties, one for the 'Swan,' the other for the 'Black Bull.' Whichever house won supplied free drink for a while. The ceremony ended in Bacchanalian disorder. The tree was formerly associated with the Star of Bethlehem. The night on which the ceremony took place was called 'Hol(l)in-night.' [Holling Day, Jan. 5, in the *Purse Almanack* (1898) (Crane & Co.).]

HOLLO, *v.* and *sb.* In *gen.* dial. and colloq. use in Sc. Eng. and Amer. Also written **hollow** Hmp.[1] Dev. Cor.[1]; and in forms **holl** w.Som.[1] Dev.[1] Cor.[2]; **holla** Dev.[2] Cor.[2]; **hollah** e.Yks.[1]; **hollar** Som.; **hollee** Dev.; **holler** Lan. Der. War. Wor. Oxf.[1] Brks.[1] Sus. Hmp. w.Som.[1] Amer.; **hollie** Wil. Som.; **holloa** n.Lin.[1]; **holly** Dor.[1]; **holo** Sc.; **yoller** Cum. [(h)o'lə.] **1.** *v.* To call loudly, shout, halloo; to cry out, scream; of animals: to make a loud noise, to neigh, low, bark, &c.

Cum. He yoller'd out for Cursty Bell, GILPIN *Pop. Poetry* (1875) 109. **Yks.** (J.W.) Lan. I'd holler now, an' mak' thee coom back an' change 'em, *Longman's Mag.* (Nov. 1897) 66. Not.[1], Lin.[1] **Lei.[1]** 'Ah picked him [a jackdaw] opp, an' a 'ollered an' a 'ollered.' 'The doogs begoon a-'ollerin'.' Freq. intensified by the addition of 'boller.' 'They was a-'ollerin' an' a-bollerin', yo' moight 'a 'eern 'em a moile off.' War. (J.R.W.); War.[2] He thrashed him so that you might have heard him holler for a mile. Wor. I does it for Christmas boxes; and I doesn't go hollering and bawling nights (H.K.). Oxf.[1] Brks.[1] In the rhyme sung by boys going their rounds on Guy Fawkes' Day we have—' Holler bwoys, holler bwoys, maayke yer bells ring, Holler bwoys, holler bwoys, God zaayve the Quane.' Hmp.[1] I heard the mare hollowing. That cow was hollowing. **s.Hmp.** I heerd ye hollering and squealing, VERNEY *L. Lisle* (1870) viii. Wil. SLOW *Gl.* (1892). Som.[1] Where zellers buold to buyers shy Did holly roun' us, 186. **Som.** SWEETMAN *Wincanton Gl.* (1885); Never a soul on earth to hear you when you did hollar, RAYMOND *Men o' Mendip* (1898) ii. **w.Som.[1]** I yeard em hollin mackerell s'morning, but I didn ax how they was zellin o'm. **Dev.** I graps-en za 'ard, I made 'en hollee tö't, HEWETT *Peas. Sp.* (1892). A puffin an blawin, .. A screechin an hollin, as if ha cude veel, NATHAN HOGG *Poet. Lett.* (1847) 1st S. 15, ed. 1858. **nw.Dev.[1], Cor.[2]** [Amer. *Dial. Notes* (1896) I. 341.]

Hence (1) **Hollering** or **Hollowing,** *ppl. adj.* shouting, noisy; (2) **-bottle,** *sb.* a bottle of strong beer, sent to the labourers at the end of harvest; see below; (3) **-owl,** *sb.* the tawny owl, *Syrnium aluco*; (4) **-time,** *sb.* a hop-picker's term for five o'clock; (5) *hollowing the apple-tree*, *phr.* a custom carried out on old Christmas Day; see below; (6) — *the neck*, *phr.* the customary rejoicing when the 'neck' of corn is brought home; see *crying the neck*, s.v. Cry, **12** (19).

(1) **Der.** This craze for 'shoutin' hollerin' people,' WARD *David Grieve* (1892) I. x. (2) **Hmp.** At the end of harvest, some forty years ago, it was the custom to have what was called the

---

Hollowing Bottle. This was a bottle of strong beer containing seven or eight gallons, which was sent out to the field. The head carter then recited these lines: 'Well ploughed—well sowed, Well reaped—well mowed, Well carried and never a load overthrowed.' After which he gave the sign and all cheered, *N. & Q.* (1872) 4th S. x. 408; It was understood that if one load or more had been overthrown the last line was altered to suit the circumstances, *ib.* 524. (3) **Sus.** SWAINSON *Birds* (1885) 129. (4) **se.Cy.** 'Why do you call it hollering time!' I asked a picker once. 'Why, sir, they hollers "no more poles," at five,' BLACKLEY *Wd. Gossip* (1869) 164. (5) **Dev.** The custom is still very prevalent. Toasted bread and sugar is soaked in new cider made hot for the farmer's family, and the boys take some out to pour on the oldest tree and sing, 'Here's to thee, Old apple-tree, from every bough Give us apples enough, Hat fulls, Cap fulls, Bushel, bushel boss fulls. Hurrah, hurrah.' The village boys go round also for the purpose and get some half pence given them for their hollering, *N. & Q.* (1852) 1st S. v. 148. (6) **Cor.** 'Hollaing the neck' is in some parts still heard, *Flk-Lore Rec.* (1879) VII. 202.

2. *Comp.* (1) **Holla-balute,** a shouting or cheering; (2) **-mouth,** a foul-mouthed ruffian; (3) **-mouthed,** noisy, swearing, abusive, foul-mouthed; (4) **-pot,** a loud-talking person, a rude, noisy fellow.

(1) **Dev.[2]** (2) **w.Som.[1]** A gurt holler-mouth [aul·ur-maewdh]. (3) Why, there id'n no gurt holler-moutheder fuller 'thin twenty mild, *ib.* (4) **Cor.[12]**

3. *sb.* A halloo, a loud shout; in hunting: the cry given when the quarry is seen. Also in *comb.* **Holo-hoi.**

Sc. The Chess-windows they were broke, Sir, .. With a convoy of holo hoi Unto the sheets were sent, Sir, MAIDMENT *Ballads* (1844) 65, ed. 1868. **n.Lin.[1]** When a person holloas to any one at a great distance, a person near him often says: 'Holloa's dead An' I'm cum in his stead.' At other times: 'Holloa's dead, an' his wife lives at Hull, Kept a coo but milk'd a bull.' **Som.** JEN-NINGS *Obs. Dial. w.Eng.* (1825). **w.Som.[1]** The deer's gwain vor Horner, I yeard a holler down the bottom.

HOLLOCK, *sb.* w.Yks.[2] [o'lək.] A hollow, valley. A house is said to be 'down in a hollock' when it stands low down in a valley.

HOLLOCK, HOLLOK, HOLLOND, see Hallock, Hallan, *sb.[2]*, Holland.

HOLLOP, *v.* Hrf. Also written **holap-.** [o'ləp.] To scoop out the inside of an apple, turnip, &c. Hrf.[2]

Hence **Holaper,** *sb.* an apple-scoop. (W.W.S.), (N.G.)

HOLLOU, *int.* Yks. [olọu'.] An exclamation of surprise; a call to stop.

e.Yks.[1] w.Yks. 'He's trapped,' he said. 'Hollou!' And his mate fell back, SNOWDEN *Web of Weaver* (1896) 104.

HOLLOW, *sb.*, *adj.* and *adv.* Var. dial. uses in Sc. and Eng. Also written **hollah** Yks.; **holler** n.Lin.[1] Nrf. w.Som.[1]; **hollo** n.Yks.; **owler-** s.Chs.[1] [h)o'lə.] **1.** *sb.* A deep lane, a road or lane through a cutting or between high banks. *Gen.* in *comp.* **Hollow-way.** s.Wor.[1], Glo. (A.B.), Glo.[1], Wil. (K.M.G.)

2. A carpenter's tool, a plane, *gen.* used in *comb.* with 'Rounds.'

Sc. Casements used in making any kind of moulding, whether large or small in wood. 'Hollows and Rounds, per pair to 1⅛ inch, o-34,' ARTHUR *List of Tools* (JAM.). n.Lin.[1] Used for making hollow trenches in wood. w.Som.[1] A small plane having a concave or hollow cutting iron with which to plane a convex surface. 'Th' old Tamlin . . . 'd a got a wole set o' rounds and hollers.'

3. *adj.* In *comp.* (1) **Hollow-back,** (*a*) easily, completely, thoroughly; (*b*) a stiff back, an attitude of pride; a term of derision to an idle person too lazy to stoop; (2) **-blocks,** sabots; (3) **-gouge,** a gouge, a hollow chisel; (4) **-headed,** foolish, silly, shallow-pated; (5) **-meat,** poultry, fowls as opposed to butcher's meat; (6) **-time,** winter; (7) **-tool,** (*a*) a spade used in digging earth; (*b*) a cooper's drawing knife; (8) **-ware,** (*a*) see (5); (*b*) turned bowls, cups, and other hollow vessels; (9) **-work,** in embroidery: open work.

(1, *a*) **n.Yks.** They ran togider A while, b't just at last he bet him hollo-back (W.H.); n.Yks.[2] Beaten them all hollow-back. (*b*) **w.Yks.** As I an' he had a hollah back whoile he wor tellin' me this, HALLAM *Wadsley Jack* (1866) xv; Occasionally heard (B.K.). (2) **Nrf.** Brendy, holly golone [Eau de Cologne], hollow blocks, gin, &c., EMERSON *Wild Life* (1890) 108; I bought one of them glass holler-blocks, more for images than for use, *ib. Son of Fens* (1892) 54. (3) Lin.[1] A curved chisel of unusual length, a gouge which will make a round hole. n.Lin.[1] (4) s.Chs.[1] Gamblers are called 'owlery edded gawnies.' (5) Sc. GROSE (1790) *MS. add.* (C.) Nhb. A' the kinds o' hollow meats That greasy cuicks se oft are speetin', WILSON *Pitman's Pay* (1843) 25; Nhb.[1], n.Yks.[2], w.Yks.[1] e.Suf. Applied to fowls, hares, rabbits (F.H.). w.Som.[1] A man said to me of another who was suspected of stealing fowls : 'Jim was always a tartar for holler meat.' (6) n.Yks.[2] This hollow-time sholls on [the winter is sliding over] (s.v. Holl). (7, *a*) n.Yks. The symmetrical pieces of clay raised by employment of the navvy's 'hollow-tool'—seven or eight inches in the blade by about six wide, and with convex back and concave front, ATKINSON *Moorl. Parish* (1891) 191. n.Lin.[1] A hollow wooden spade shod with iron used on the Trent-side for digging warp and other soil that is free from stones (s.v. Tool). (*b*) w.Som.[1] Bent into a shape suitable for shaving out the inner surfaces of casks. (8, *a*) Cor. THOMAS *Randigal Rhymes* (1895) *Gl.* (*b*) Hrt. Maple is approved of by the turner for making hollow-ware, ELLIS *Mod. Husb.* (1750) VII. ii. (9) Cor.[1]

4. Of wood : concave.

w.Som.[1] Technical. Kaa'n dùe noa·urt wai dhaat dhae·ur boo·urd, tez z-au·lur [Can't do anything with that (lot of) board, 'tis so hollow].

5. Having a dismal sound, moaning ; speaking in hollow tones. Also used *advb.*

Ayr. The wind blew hollow frae the hills, BURNS *Lament for Glencairn*, st. 1. Edb. The hollow Dempster, with an ugly gloom, Pronounc'd the bloody word, PENNECUIK *Helicon* (1720) 28. n.Lin.[1] The wind sounds low and hollow, As a watchdog howls in pain. s.Wor. The church bell sounds hollow, PORSON *Quaint Wds.* (1875) 19. Glo.[1] Of the wind or a church bell.

6. One-sided, not closely contested.

War.[2] It was a hollow race, i. e. 'Eclipse was first and the rest nowhere.'

7. Deceitful, double-faced.

nw.Der.[1] Ée)z ûz old ûz û chu°:rn [He's as hollow as a churn].

8. *adv.* In phr. (1) *to carry a thing hollow*, to carry a thing off triumphantly, without difficulty, or completely ; to proceed exultingly. n.Yks.[2], w.Yks.[1] ; (2) *to chip up hollow*, a cry used by boys when sliding on the ice. Dur.[1] See Chip, *v.*[1] **2.**

HOLLOW, see Hallow, *sb.*[1], Hollo.

HOLLY, *sb.* Nhb. Wm. Yks. Pem. Ken. In *comp.* (1) Holly-beating, *obs.*, an old custom at Tenby on St. Stephen's Day; (2) -boy, ? *obs.*, a figure made of holly burnt by girls upon Valentine's Day; (3) -brash, a bright transient flame; (4) -bussing, the custom of fetching holly from a wood with music and dancing on Easter Tuesday; (5) -dance, a dance at Christmas; (6) -night, Twelfth Night; see below ; (7) -tree, a tree having lighted torches on each branch, carried in procession on Twelfth Night; see below.

(1) Pem. *N. & Q.* (1872) 4th S. x. 267; The custom was for men and boys to parade the streets of Tenby with branches of holly wherewith to beat the bare arms of any chance females, who usually chanced to be domestic servants. It was purely a local custom and did not obtain elsewhere in the county (H.O.) ; At Tenby, 50 years ago, all maid-servants wore short sleeves, pulling linen slips over their bare arms when waiting at table, &c. On St. Stephen's Day the boys used to cut branches of holly and with these belabour such maids as they found in the streets with bare arms. This custom may have the same origin as the blooding of horses on St. Stephen's Day, i. e. shedding blood in honour of the Protomartyr (E.L.). (2) Ken. *N. & Q.* (1880) 6th S. i. 129; Ken.[1] It was the custom on Shrove Tuesday in West Kent to have two figures in the form of a boy and girl, made one of holly, the other of ivy. A group of girls engaged themselves in one part of a village in burning the holly-boy, which they had stolen from the boys, while the boys were to be found in another part of the village burning the ivy-girl, which they had stolen from the girls, the ceremony being, in both cases, accompanied by loud huzzas; Ken.[2] (3) w.Yks.[1] Such as that caused by burning holly. (4) Nhb. A very ancient custom that still obtains at Netherwitton. On Easter Tuesday the lads and lasses of the village and vicinity meet; and ... proceed to the wood to get holly, with which some decorate a stone cross that stands in the village, while others are 'bobbing around' to 'Speed

the Plough' or 'Birnie Bouzle,' *N. & Q.* (1857) 2nd S. iii. 344; BRAND *Pop. Antiq.* (ed. 1870) I. 101. (5) n.Yks.[2] When the holly-bough is a decoration. (6) Wm. [So called from] the ancient custom of carrying the 'Holly-tree' on Twelfth Night at Brough, HONE *Table-bk.* (ed. 1898) 26. (7) Wm. Formerly the 'Holly-tree' at Brough was really 'holly,' but ash being abundant the latter is now substituted... The ... townspeople mostly lend their assistance in preparing the tree, to every branch of which they fasten a torch. About eight o'clock in the evening it is taken to a convenient part of the town, where the torches are lighted, the town band accompanying and playing till all is completed, when it is removed to the lower end of the town, and after divers salutes and huzzas from the spectators is carried up and down the town in stately procession, usually by a person of renowned strength, named Joseph Ling, *ib.*

HOLM, *sb.*[1] Sc. Nhb. Cum. Wm. Yks. Lan. Der. Not. Lin. Nhp. e.An. se.Cy. Ken. Som. Also written holme s.Sc. n.Cy. Cum.[4] Wm. w.Yks.[2] ne.Lan.[1] sw.Lin.[1] Nrf. Ken. ; and in forms hoalm Lin. ; hoam Gall. ; home Sc. (JAM.) Ken. ; houm Sc. ; howm Sc. Nhb.[1] n.Yks.[2] ; oam e.An.[1] e.Nrf. ; om- N.Cy.[12] Nhp.[1] e.An.[1] Nrf. ; owm n.Yks. [h]oum.] **1.** A small island or islet, esp. an island in a lake or river ; an isolated rock.

Sh.I. Every holm and rock in the sea ... has its own distinctive name, JAKOBSEN *Dial.* (1897) 58 ; Seeing that to attempt reaching the holm ... was useless, he ... laid in one of the oars, NICOLSON *Aithstin' Hedder* (1898) 45. S. & Ork.[1] Or.I. A little isle for the most part desart, and only employed for pasturage, WALLACE *Desc. Or. I.* (1693) 109, ed. 1883; The several isles ... are divided into such as are inhabited and so are more commonly called Isles; and such as are not inhabited, which they call Holms, only useful for pasturage, BRAND *Desc. Or. I.* (1701) 28 (JAM.) ; A rock surrounded by the sea which has been detached from the adjoining rocks or from the mainland (JAM.). N.Cy.[1], Lakel.[1], Cum.[24] Wm. (J.H.) ; *Appleby Monthly Messenger* (Apr. 1891). n.Yks.[2] e.Yks. MARSHALL *Rur. Econ.* (1788). ne.Lan.[1] Holme Island near Grange. n.Lin.[1] Nhp. Or padded holm, where village boys resort, Bawling enraptur'd o'er their evening sport, CLARE *Village Minst.* (1821) II. 76. se.Cy. RAY (1691). Som. Two islands in the mouth of the Severn are called the Holms : one flat-holm, lying low and flat; the other steep-holm, lying high and surrounded with cliffs (K.). w.Som.[1]

2. Low-lying level ground on the borders of a river or stream. Also in *comp.* Holm-land.

Sc. Dauner doon the lanely howm, whaur flow'rs Wi' sweets are laden, ALLAN *Lilts* (1874) 373. Per. Fair moon, light up thy beams And silver holms and lea, SPENCE *Poems* (1898) 108. e.Fif. The laverock frae the grassy howm Hoo joyfully he springs ! LATTO *Tam Bodkin* (1864) xiv. Rnf. I'll cross the bura and gowan howm, CLARK *Poet. Pieces* (1836) 8. Ayr. A flat alluvial piece of ground along the Fail, opposite the mouth of the bloody burn, is still called 'The Dead-mens-holm,' probably from its having been the burial place of the warriors, *Ballads and Sngs.* (1846) I. 23. Lnk. A flowrie howm between twa verdant braes, RAMSAY *Gentle Shep.* (1725) 27, ed. 1783. s.Lth. Broom-clad knolls and ravines, with the ... greenest of haughs and howms between, MUCKLEBACKIT *Rhymes* (1885) 291. Edb. Green knolls and grassy holms ... come unexpectedly on the eye at every bend of the stream, BALLANTINE *Gaberlunzie* (ed. 1875) 270. Peb. On t'other side of this bright howm, The Lyne runs circling round, *Lintoun Green* (1685) 17, ed. 1817. Slk. The plough was standing idle on the houm, HOGG *Tales* (1838) 186, ed. 1866. Dmf. Green an' bonnie is the holm lan', THOM *Jock o' Knowe* (1878) 86. Gall. Ripin' up the green hoams, and forcing wheat to grow whar Providence never intended it, MACTAGGART *Encycl.* (1824) 28, ed. 1876. n.Cy. GROSE (1790) ; N.Cy.[1], Nhb.[1], Lakel.[2] Cum. The best grazing land we saw ... were the holm lands on both sides the Eden near Carlisle, MARSHALL *Review* (1808) I. 193 ; Cum.[12] ; Cum.[4] That lown-liggin' onset by fair Eden side ; Aw its green holms an ings, POWLEY *Echoes*, 148. Wm. Then doon by Crosby thro' the holme She gangs a gentle pace, WHITEHEAD *Leg.* (1859) 22 ; (J.H.) Yks. The Howms, a green piece of ground near Thrustre, lying between the river Codbeck and the brook Sewell (K.). n.Yks.[1] Low-lying land which in time of flood may become more or less insular ; n.Yks.[284] ne.Yks.[1] Land which is or has been liable to be surrounded by water at times. e.Yks.[1] A sort of peninsula, bounded by swamps or streams of water on the three sides. m.Yks.[1] A piece of ground entirely, or in great part, bounded by a water-course. w.Yks. WILLAN *List Wds.* (1811) ; w.Yks.[124] Lan. Across moor an' bog, howt an howm, CLEGG *Sketches* (1895) 242. **ne.Lan.**[1] **Der.**[1] *Obs.* Not. (J.H.B.) **Lin.** Wi' aâf the cows to cauve an' Thurnaby hoâlms to plow! TENNYSON *N. Farmer. Old Style* (1864) st. 13. **sw.Lin.**[1] Freq. in place names, signifying land rising from a plain or marsh. **Nhp.**[1] **Nrf.** Holmes abound in the valleys and flats of the Bure, MUNFORD *Local Names* (1870) 37. **Ken.** A low flat pasture in Romney Marsh is yet called the Holmes or the Homes (K.).

Hence (1) **Holming**, *sb.* low-lying level ground on the borders of a stream; (2) **Holmlet**, *sb.* a little 'holm'; (3) **Holmy**, *adj.* (*a*) of land: level, having flat spaces; rich, fertile, mellow; (*b*) light, porous, floury.

(1) **Sc.** MAXWELL *Sel. Trans.* (1743) 9 (JAM.). (2) **Lth.** Ilk lown grassy holmlet and snell heathy brae, BALLANTINE *Poems* (1856) 309. (3, *a*) **n.Cy.** GROSE (1790); **N.Cy.**[12] **Cum.** In some low, an' holmy land, RICHARDSON *Talk* (1871) 106, ed. 1876. **n.Yks.** This is a howmy field (I.W.). **Nhp.**[1], **Nrf.** (W.W.S.) (*b*) **e.An.**[1] Omy land, land just brought into cultivation, and requiring clay or marl to give it firmness. **e.Nrf.** MARSHALL *Rur. Econ.* (1787).

3. A depression, hollow; a narrow and deep glen.

Abd. (G.W.) **Nhb.** It lies rather in a howm, OLIVER *Rambles* (1835) 229; **Nhb.**[1]

4. A hill; *obs.* except in place-names. **Nhb.** (R.O.H.), **n.Lin.**[1]

[1. OE. *holm*, land rising from water, an island in a river. 2. Holm, place be-sydone a watur, *hulmus*, *Prompt.*]

HOLM, *sb.*[2] Glo. Sus. Hmp. Dor. Som. Dev. Cor. Also written **holme** Hmp.; and in forms **holn** Dev.[4]; **hôm** Dor.[1]; **home** Dor. Som. Dev.[24] e.Cor.; **hoom** Dev.; **hum** Cor.[2] [ôm.] **1.** The holly, *Ilex Aquifolium*; also used *attrib.*

Sus. (S.P.H.) **Hmp.** To nattle like a boar in a holme bush, WISE *New Forest* (1883) 179; **Hmp.**[1] **Dor.**[1] Esp. the low and more prickly holly. **Som.** The clump of holm, RAYMOND *Love and Quiet Life* (1894) 219. **w.Som.**[1] Mind you bring some Christmasin, a good bush o' holm [oa·m], and a mestletoe, s'now. Dev. We an't a cut down none of thick holm bush, *Reports Provinc.* (1881) 12; **Dev.**[4] w.Dev. MARSHALL *Rur. Econ.* (1796). **Cor.**[12]

Hence **Holmen**, *adj.* made of holly, consisting of holly.

Dor.[1] Holmen bushes, in between The leafless darns, 211. **Som.** A wayside inn near the village of Blagdon was called in my remembrance Holmen Clavel, from its having originally had a clavel or clavel-tack [a chimney-piece] of holly (F.A.A.); JENNINGS *Obs. Dial. w.Eng.* (1825). **w.Som.**[1]

2. *Comp.* (1) **Holm-berry**, a holly-berry; also used *attrib.*; (2) -**cock**, the missel-thrush, *Turdus viscivorus*; (3) -**frith**, a wood of holly; (4) -**screech** or -**scritch**, (*a*) see (2); (*b*) the jay, *Garrulus glandarius*; (5) -**thrush**, see (1).

(1) **Dor.** Let me put one little kiss on those holmberry lips, *Tess*, HARDY *Tess* (1891) 66, ed. 1895. (2) **Dor.**, **Dev.**, **Cor.** From the fondness of this bird for the berries of the ... holm, SWAINSON *Birds* (1885) 1. (3) **Hmp.**[1] BLACKMORE *Cradock Nowell* (1866) II. 6a. (4, *a*) **Glo.**[1] **Dor.** (C.V.G.); *w.Gazette* (Feb. 15, 1889) 7. **Som.** A home-screech came flying out of the apple-tree, RAYMOND *Gent. Upcott* (1893) 105; JENNINGS *Obs. Dial. w.Eng.* (1825). **w.Som.**[1] **Dev.** HEWETT *Peas. Sp.* (1892); **Dev.**[1], **nw.Dev.**[1] **s.Dev.** FOX *Kingsbridge* (1874). **s.Dev.**, **e.Cor.** (Miss D.) **Cor.** RODD *Birds* (1880) 314; **Cor.**[12] (*b*) **Dev.**[2]; **Dev.**[8] The usual name throughout the county. (5) **Dor.**, **Dev.**, **Cor.** SWAINSON *ib.* **Cor.** RODD *Birds* (1880) 314; **Cor.**[8]

[1. Holme or holy, *hussus*, *Prompt.*]

HOLM, *sb.*[3] Cum. Yks. Also in forms **ome** Cum.[1]; **owm**· n.Yks. The elm, *Ulmus campestris* and *U. montana*. **Cum.**[1] **w.Yks.** LUCAS *Stud. Nidderdale* (c. 188a) 259.

Hence **Owmy**, *adj.* consisting of elm, made of elm.

n.Yks. This is a owmy wood (I.W.).

[Holme, *Ulmus*, *Prompt.*]

HOLMBY, *sb.* Nhp.[1] In phr. *to shine like Holmby*, to shine very brightly.

A comparison that may have originated in the glittering appearance which Holdenby House presented, when gilded with the rays of the sun. The situation being elevated, it was visible from the surrounding country.

HOLME, see **Hame**, *sb.*[1]

HOLMOGEN, *sb.* *Obs.* Irel. Dor. Also in forms **homogen** Dor.; **hulmogee** Wxf.[1] A small cupboard in the wall; a cabinet.

Wxf.[1] **Dor.** A lady once had an old oak cabinet which she called the homogen or holmogen, POOLE *Forth Gl.* (1867).

HOLN, see **Holm**, *sb.*[2]

HOLROD, *sb.* Dor. The cowslip, *Primula veris. w.Gazette* (Feb. 15, 1889) 7, col. 1.

HOLSH, see **Halsh,** *v.*

HOLSIE-JOLSIE, *sb.* Rxb. (JAM.) [Not known to our correspondents.] A confused mass of food, swine's meat, &c.

HOLSTER, *sb.*[1] and *v.*[1] Som. Dev. Cor. Also in forms **hulster** Cor.[1]; **olster** s.Dev. e.Cor. [o·l-, u·lsta(r).] **1.** A hiding-place, a harbouring place.

s.Dev. (Miss D.) **Cor.**[1] This rubbish es only a hülster for snails; **Cor.**[2] (s.v. Holt'.

2. *Comb.* **Holster-iron**, *sb.* the iron socket inserted in the 'summers' into which the 'stud' is fastened. Som. (W.F.R.)

3. *v.* To harbour; to gather together into one close company. **Cor.**[1] How dare you hulster my daughter here! w.Cor. *N. & Q.* (1854) 1st S. x. 319.

[1. OE. *heolstor*, a place of concealment (B.T.). 2. There I hope best to hulstred be, *R. Rose* (c. 1400) 6146.]

HOLSTER, *v.*[2] and *sb.*[2] *Obs.* Dev. **1.** *v.* To make a noise or racket; to hustle and bustle.

n.Dev. *Exm. Scold.* (1746) *Gl.*, ed. 1879; To make a confounded rattle, *Horae Subsecivae* (1777) 215.

2. *sb.* A noise, racket, disturbance.

n.Dev. Rather than tha wudst ha' enny more champ and holster, *Exm. Scold.* (1746) l. 219.

HOLT, *sb.*[1] Sc. Nhb. Cum. Yks. Lan. Not. Lin. Rut Lei. Nhp. War. Glo. e.An. se.Cy. Ken. Sus. Som. Also in forms **haut** Dmf. (JAM.); **ho't** s.Not.; **howt** Lan. [h]olt, h]out, ot.] **1.** A wood, grove, or plantation; a wooded hill or knoll.

Sc. Frae out the haslie holt the deer Sprang glancing thro' the schaw, JAMIESON *Pop. Ballads* (1806) I. 197. **Ayr.** Both hill and holt, and moore and fenne, *Ballads and Sngs.* (1846) I. 26. **Bwk.** It died away o'er holt an' lea, CHISHOLM *Poems* (1879) 21. **Slk.** And there was ... riding O'er holt and lea, HOGG *Poems* (ed. 1865) 29. **Dmf.** Ne'er on heath or holt, by wood or river, REID *Poems* (1894) 51. **N.Cy.**[1] A peaked hill covered with wood. **Nhb.**[1], **Cum.**[4] w.Yks. THORESBY *Lett.* (1703); Peaked hills covered with wood, WILLAN *List Wds.* (1811†; **w.Yks.**[4] **Lan.** Across moor an' bog, howt an' howm, CLEGG *Sketches* (1895) 242. **ne.Lan.**[1] **Lin.** SKINNER (1671); **Lin.**[1] n.Lin. SUTTON *Wds.* (1881). **sw.Lin.**[1] **Rut.**[1] He lets the cherry-bolt separate. **Lei.**[1], **Nhp.**[1], **War.**[4], **s.War.**[1], **Glo.**[12] **e.An.**[1] We have gooseberry-holts, cherry-holts, nut-holts. **Cmb.**[1] Stag's Holt is about 8 miles from Wisbech, on the Low Road to March. **Nrf.** (E.M.) **se.Cy.** RAY (1691). **Ken.**[1] Much used in names of places, as Bircholt, Knockholt, &c.; **Ken.**[2] **Sus.** LOWER *S. Downs* (1854) 152; **Sus.**[1]; **Sus.**[2] Esp. on a side hill, thus Jevington Holt, Wilmington Holt, &c. **w.Som.**[1]

2. An osier-bed or plantation. Also called **Osier-holt**. **s.Not.** (J.P.K.), **Lin.**[1] n.Lin.[1] If anyone talked of a plantation of willows instead of a willow-holt he would be laughed at. **sw.Lin.**[1] They fun in an osier holt. **Lei.**[1] **Nhp.** Osier holts by rivers near, CLARE *Poems* (1827) 4; **Nhp.**[1] **War.** *B'ham Wkly. Post* (June 10, 1893); **War.**[18], **e.An.**[1]

3. Poor land covered with furze or ling; a field in a rough, weedy condition; a name for a field.

Nhp.[1] In Canons Ashby they have Thistly Holt, and Rushy Holt; **Nhp.**[2] A common name for a field.

4. A small haycock; a small quantity of manure before it is spread. **Dmf.** *Statist. Acc.* XIII. 568 (JAM.). Cf. **hut.**

[OE. *holt*, copse, wood; timber; G. *Holz*.]

HOLT, *sb.*[2] Chs. Also in form **hoult.** In games: a 'holing,' putting the ball into a hole. Cf. **hold,** *sb.* 6. **Chs.**[1]; **Chs.**[2] I gained three points at one hoult; **Chs.**[3]

HOLTLESS, *adj.* Hrf. Also in form **holdless** Hrf.[1] Careless, heedless, random. BOUND *Provinc.* (1876); Hrf.[1]

HOLTS, see **Halts,** *sb. pl.*

HOLUMS-JOLUMS, *adv.* War. All at once. (J.R.W.)

HOLUS-BOLUS, *adv.* Sc. Irel. Lan. Chs. Lin. Shr. Brks. Som. Dev. Also in forms **holis-bolis** Ant.; **hollis-bollis** Sc.; **hollos-bollos** Ayr.; **holuns-boluns** s.Chs.[1] **1.** Completely, entirely, all at once; also used as *subst.*

Sc. Precious little would tempt me tae lift my lines and gang ower tae the Auld Kirk hollis-bollis, TWEEDDALE *Moff* (1896) 55.

Kcd. It wad cost my wob o' wincey Holus-bolus, warp an' waft, GRANT *Lays* (1884) 37. Ayr. We wad leave it 'hollos-bollos' had we claes to rin away, AITKEN *Lays Line* (1883) 40. Lnk. A sort o' twa-hunder-year-auld shepherd's but . . . tooken doon, holus bolus, frae the hillside, MURDOCH *Readings* (ed. 1895) II. 61. Lth. At fifteen she left my school for good and carried off my heart—holus bolus—along with her, LUMSDEN *Sheep-head* (1892) 251. Ant. The whole lot, *Ballymena Obs.* (1892). ne.Lan.[1], Lin.[1] nw.Dev.[1] He swallowed the cherries holus bolus.

2. Impulsively, without consideration, recklessly.
Chs.[1] s.Chs.[1] Öo wü:nū stop tū bi tuwd, óo goz aat' it oa·lūns-boa·lūns [Hoo wunna stop to be towd, hoo gos at it holuns-boluns]. Shr.[1] 'E never thinks 'ow it's gwein to end, but gwuz at it 'ölus-bólus. Brks. Having resolved to 'sar' it out, as we say in the Vale, 'holus bolus,' just as it comes, HUGHES *T. Brown* (1856) i.

3. Without asking leave, ' nolens-volens.'
w.Som.[1] They come and tookt th'osses, holus-bolus, and never so much as axed or zaid thank ee.

HOLY, *adj.* Var. dial. uses in Sc. Irel. and Eng. Also written **holie** Abd. e.An.[1]; and in forms **hali·** Som.[1]; **halli·** e.Yks.[1]; **hally** Sc. ; **haiy** Sc. (JAM.) ; **helly, heiy** Sc. (JAM.) ; **höli(e** Sh.I. ; **holly** Lns. In comb. (1) **Holy band,** the Kirk-session ; (2) — **bizen** or **by·zont,** a show, spectacle, a conspicuous or ridiculous object ; (3) — **dabbies,** a species of cake or shortbread, freq. used instead of bread at Holy Communion ; (4) — **dance,** a name given to the proceedings of certain religious sects, owing to the excitement and extravagance shown ; (5) ·**day tolls,** *obs.,* customs paid for all manner of provisions sold on holy-days ; (6) — **doupies, see** (3) ; (7) — **eve,** All Hallows' Eve ; (8) — **fair,** *obs.,* a summer gathering held on a Communion Sunday ; (9) — **falls,** trousers buttoned with ' flap ' instead of ' fly ' fronts ; (10) — **friar,** a liar ; (11) — **how,** a membrane on the head, with which some children are born ; (12) ·**mass,** All Saints' Day ; (13) — **mokers,** an exclamation of surprise ; (14) — **palmer,** the palmer-worm ; (15) — **poker, see** (13) ; (16) — **pokers,** the great reedmace, *Typha latifolia* ; (17) — **post, ?** a ghost, ' boggle ' [not known to our correspondents] ; (18) — **show,** see (2) ; (19) — **Sunday,** Easter Day ; (20) — **tavern.** see (13) ; (21) — **thorn,** the Glastonbury thorn, *Crataegus Oxyacantha,* var. *praecox*; (22) — **Thursday,** (*a*) Ascension Day ; (*b*) Maundy Thursday, the day before Good Friday ; (23) — **verd,** holly used in the Christmas decoration of churches ; (24) — **wake,** *obs.,* a bonfire ; (25) · **water,** in phr. *to like as the devil likes holy water,* to hate mortally.

(1) Sc. The blear-ein'd bell-man . . . summoned him and her before the hally-band, a court that held in the kirk on Saturday morning, GRAHAM *Writings* (1885) II. 295. (2) n.Cy. GROSE (1790). Nhb.[1] Applied to an idolized and over-dressed person. ' Yor myekin a fair holy-bizen on that bairn.' Also used menacingly : ' Aa'll myek a holy-bizen on ye, ye slut.' n.Yks.[1] (3) Lnk. (JAM.) Edb. A species of cake baked with butter, otherwise called Petticoat-tails (*ib.*), s.v. Dabbies). Dmf., Gall. The designation still given to the bread used in the Sacrament of the Lord's Supper. This is not baked in the form of a loaf but in cakes such as are *gen.* called shortbread (*ib.*). Gall. I saw these about 32 or 33 years ago used in a neighbouring parish at the Communion, for the Bread. They were cakes of shortbread. That have not now used I think in any church in Gall. (A.W.) (4) n.Yks.[1]; n.Yks.[2] We've been at a holy dance. (5) Suf. GARDNER *Dunwich* (1754). (6) Frf. (JAM.) (7) Lns. It's neither Holly Eve, nor St. John's Eve, CROKER *Leg.* (1862) 248. (8) Per. Ostensibly it was a gathering of Christians convoked at some rural central spot for the purposes of religious exercises, preparatory to a celebration of the Lord's Supper. The religious exercises took place in the open air, and were continued without intermission throughout the day, while the more sacred ordinance of the Sacrament was dispensed to communicants, coming and retiring in relays, under the roof of the little adjoining church, HALIBURTON *Fields* (1890) 3, 4. Ayr. I'm gaun to Mauchline Holy Fair To spend an hour in daffin, BURNS *Holy Fair* (1785) st. 5. Edb. By my faith they drank it rare As ony at the holy fair, LIDDLE *Poems* (1821) 232. Gall. The ' holy fair ' is long defunct as an institution (A.W.). (9) Stf. NORTHALL *Flk-Phr.* (1894). War.[2] Wor., Glo. NORTHALL *Flk-Phr.* (1894). (10) War.[2] You are a holy-friar. (11) Sc. This covering is carefully preserved till death, first by the mothers and afterwards by those born with it ; from the idea that the loss of it

would be attended with some signal misfortune (JAM., s.v. How); They give out that children so born will be very fortunate, RUDDIMAN *Gl.* (1773) (JAM.). '12) e.An.[1] (13) Ant. (S.A.B.) (14) Som. W. & J. *Gl.* (1873). w.Som.[1] (15) Myo. Oh holy poker ! BARRINGTON *Sketches* (1830) III. xvi. (16) n.Dev. (B. & H.) (17) Sur. A young servant-girl . . . told me that she was afraid to go into the garden after dark for fear of seeing ' a holy post,' *Flk-Lore Rec.* (1878) I. 246. (18) N.I.[1] He made a holy show of himself. Wxf. ' Oh, you impostor,' says he, ' if ever you rise out of that, I'll make a holy show of you,' KENNEDY *Banks Boro* (1863) 214 ; He became a holy show and gazabo to the entire world, *ib. Evenings Duffrey* (1869) 305. Lon. He wasn't a going to make a holy show of his-self, MAYHEW *Lond. Labour* (ed. 1861) II. 377, col. 2. (19) Sus.[1] There is a tradition that the sun always dances on the morning of Holy-Sunday, but nobody has even seen it because the devil is so cunning that he always puts a hill in the way to hide it. (20) Ant. (S.A.B.) (21) War.[2] (22, *a*) n.Yks.[2] e.Yks.[1] Halli-thesdā fair, held at Beverley. Oxf. (G.O.) Hrt. ELLIS *Mod. Husb.* (1750) III. i. (*b*) Not. My mother did use to say as she wouldn't hang out a pair o' sheets if 'twere iver so, for if you did so a' Holy Thursday you'd have a corpse in t'house afore a year wer out, *N. & Q.* (1897) 8th S. xi. 485. (23) e.An.[1]; e.An.[2] (s.v. Hulver). (24) Glo. GROSE (1790) ; *Gl.* (1851) ; Glo.[1] (25) w.Yks.[1] He likes him as the Devil likes holy water.

HOLYROOD, *sb.* Yks. Lin. Wil. Som. Also in forms **hally-loo·** n.Lin.[1]; **hollardy·** Wil.[1] Som. In comp. (1) **Holyrood-day,** the Festival of the Invention of the Holy Cross, May 3 ; (2) ·**morn,** the Festival of the Exaltation of the Holy Cross, Sept. 14.

(1) n.Lin. *Obs.* (E.P.) ; n.Lin.[1], Wil.[1] Som. The third of May, JENNINGS *Obs. Dial. w.Eng.* (1825). (2) n.Yks.[2] If the buck rises with a dry horn on Holyrood morn, it is the sign of a Michaelmas summer.

[(1) Any time between Martilmas and holyrode-day, FITZHERBERT *Husb.* (1534) 86. (2) On Holy-rood day, the gallant Hotspur there, Young Harry Percy and brave Archibald . . . At Holmedon met, SHAKS. 1 *Hen. IV,* i. i. 52 ; Þe holi Roode was i-founde, as ȝe witeþ, in May, Honoured he was seþþe in Septembre, þe holi Rode day, *Leg. Holy Rood* (c. 1300), ed. Morris, 49.]

HOM, see Ham, *sb.*[1], Holm, *sb.*[2]

HOMAGE, *sb.* and *v.* Yks. Lin. Nhp. Bdf. e.An. Sus. Also in form **hommidge** n.Yks. [ō·midg, o·midg.] L. *sb.* Attention, deference, respect.

n.Yks. Te men ov honerubbel neeam, Refuse that homm edge 'at their titles claim ! CASTILLO *Poems* (1878) 52. sw.Lin.[1] They want such a deal of homage, them inspectors.

2. *v.* To respect, to show deference to.
e.Suf. (F.H.) Ess. ' I do homage you, sister, for that you have done so well for poor father.' · I don't think but what he would homage a poor person as much as he would a rich one ' (H.M. M.). Sus. I've always homaged my betters, O'REILLY *Stories* (c. 1880) I. 240.

Hence **Homaging,** (1) *vbl. sb.* flattery ; (2) *ppl. adj.* respectful, deferential.

(1) n.Lin.[1] Ther's noā gettin' on wi' her she wants soā much homaagein' ; it's that she lives on. (2) Nhp. What makes you 'neath the maples creep, In homaging surprise ? CLARE *Poems* (1820) 184.

3. To make a bow to, curtsey to. Bdf. (J.W.B.)
HOMANY, *sb.* Som. Noise, disturbance. W. & J. *Gl.* (1873).

HOMBER, see Hamburgh, Hammer, *sb.*[1]
HOMBLE, *sb.* Dor. [o·mbl.] A duck. *Gl.* (1851) ; Dor.[1]
HOMBLE, *v.* Oxf.[1] [o·mbl.] With *about*: to pull about.
HOMBLE, HOME, HÖMEEN, HOMELLS, see Hamble, Hame, *sb.*[1], Holm, *sb.*[12], Humin, Hommells.

HOME, *sb.*[1], *adv., adj.* and *v.* Var. dial. uses in Sc. Irel. and Eng. Also in forms **hame** Sc. Bnff.[1]; **heamm** Cu. n.[1]; **heeam** n.Yks.[2]; **heyem** Nhb.[1]; **hiam** Lakel.[2]; **hoam** n.Yks.[2]; **hoame** w.Yks. ; **hom** Dev.[2] Cor.[1]; **hooam** I.W.[12]; **hum** Not.[1] s.Not. Lei.[1] Nhp.[2] Hmp.[2] Cor. ; **hwum** Dev.[2]; **hyem** Nhb.[1]; **whoam** Wil. ; **whome** Shr. ; **whum** n.Dev.[2]; **yam** n.Yks.[2] [ō·m, oəm, h]ēm, h]iəm, wom, wum.]

1. *sb.* In comb. (1) **Home-airted,** directed homewards ; (2) ·**along** or ·**long,** homewards, towards home ; (3) ·**born,** belonging to the family ; (4) ·**bred,** a calf bred on the premises ; *pl.* cattle of the Norfolk breed ; (5) ·**bringer, a**

ousehold provider; (6) ·bringing, the act of bringing ome; (7) ·close, the enclosure in which a farm-house is uilt, the field nearest the farm-house; (8) ·come, (9) coming, an arrival at home; a return, the festivities or reception on returning home, the time of return; (10) draughtit, (11) ·drawn, selfish, looking after one's own nterest; (12) ·dwellers, people accustomed to live in ouses as opposed to tramps; (13) ·fare or ·fair, the removal of a bride from her own or her father's house to hat of her husband; the home-coming of a newly-married ouple; (14) ·field, see (7); (15) ·given, of a present: given by a relation or one of one's own home; (16) ·going, a) a return, a return journey; the act of going home; b) returning home, homeward-going; (17) ·harvest, a arvest-home, the supper at the close of the harvest; (18) head, the head of a family or house; (19) ·lan', applied o farm-servants who live in the farm-house; domestic; 20) ·leg goose, the greylag goose, *Anser cinereus*; (21) livier, a person belonging to the immediate neighbour-ood, a local inhabitant; (22) ·over or ·owre, (a) see (2); b) homely, humble, rustic, unpolished; home-keeping; 23) ·sang, a song of home or country; (24) ·spot, a house, he situation of a house; (25) ·spun, see (22, b); (26) ·stall, a) a farm-house and adjacent buildings, a farm-yard and ts appurtenances; (b) the place of a mansion-house, the nclosure of ground immediately connected with a mansion-ouse; (27) ·sucken, (a) the crime of assaulting a person n his own house; (b) greatly attached to home; (c) see 11); (28) ·teuny, *obs.*, a stronghold, a place of security; (29) tried, of lard: made at home; (30) ·water, a cordial made rom horsemint; (31) ·went, to go home; (32) ·with, (a) see (2); (b) homeward; (c) self-interested, esp. in phr. *to be ay to the hamewith*; (33) ·work, work done at home instead of at a mill or factory; (34) ·yard, see (7).

(1) **Slg.** I pray ilka nicht let your thochts be hame-airted, TOWERS *Poems* (1885) 180. (2) Dor. He've clinked off home-along, depend upon't, HARDY *Greenwood Tree* (1872) I. 6a. Dev. Now than, sose, 'tez time vur us tŭ shett away homalong, HEWETT *Peas. Sp.* (1892); Trim, my lil 'earty, I've comed 'ome-along to 'e, PHILLPOTTS *Dartmoor* (1896) 238. Cor. Just as I turned back home-long, I see a man leanin' against thicky post, 'Q.' *Noughts and Crosses* (1891) 109; Cor.³ (3) n.Yks.² He's heeam-boorn; you may see he's gying his father's geeat. (4) e.Nrf. MARSHALL *Rur. Econ.* (1787). Suf.¹, e.Suf. (F.H.) (5) n.Yks.² '6) Sc. A debt owing . . . for home bringing Queen Ann out of Denmark, SPALDING *Hist. Sc.* (1792) I. 331 (JAM.). (7) Lin. The farmer thought it more advisable to remove his barn further into his fields, or home close, MARSHALL *Review* (1811) III. 57. n.Lin.¹ Rut.¹ There are two home-closen and twenty homesteads in the Glaston parish map attached to the tithe award. Nhp.² (8) Cai.¹, Nhb.¹ n.Yks.¹ He'll be here about from home-come. (9) Sc. During the week between Miss N.'s homecoming and the wedding, SWAN *Aldersyde* (ed. 1892) 121. Sh.I. We'll get a hamecomin' 'at 'ill be dreary i' da hearin' o, *Sh. News* (July 17, 1897). Cai.¹ Frf. She did not tell the story until Jamie's home-coming had become a legend, BARRIE *Thrums* (1889) xxii. Flf. This is a sad hame-comin' for ye, ROBERTSON *Provost* (1894) 185. e.Lth. To see if it wasna time for my hame-comin, HUNTER *J. Inwick* (1895) 179. Nhb.¹ They hed sic a hyem-comin as nivver was. Cum.¹ I whope thou'll hev a hearty heàmm comin'. n.Yks.² The evening tide for returning home after the labours of the day. 'I shall hev a bonny heeamcoming about it with my wife'; n.Yks.⁴ m.Yks.¹ The time for return after the day's work. w.Som.¹ The arrival of the bride at her husband's home. This used to be celebrated with much estivity, but now it is mostly confined to a peal on the church bells. 'A purty home-coming that, sure 'nough, vor to slink in to he back door, 's off they was asheeamed to show therzuls.' (10) Snff.¹ Abd. Fowk's files mair hame-drauchtit than they wid like ill alloo, GREIG *Logie o' Buchan* (1899) 10. (11) Bnff.¹ (12) Sus.¹ A good many of these people who've come harvesting this rear, look like home-dwellers. (13) Sc. (JAM.) Abd. Their merry omefair I remind, When their blythe tenantry convened . . . To welcome them With signs of joy, ANDERSON *Poems* (1826) 36. (14) n.Lin.¹ Rarely used. When it is employed in this connection an error s made. w.Som.¹ (15) n.Yks.² (16, a) Sc. My Auntie K. would only consent to stay another aight on the home-going, WHITE-HEAD *Daft Davie* (1876) 204, ed. 1894; The masters being under fear hat the committee . . . would come and visit their college in their

home-going, SPALDING *Hist. Sc.* (1792) I. 110 (JAM.). Cai.¹ Ags. It is said iron. when one meets with something very disagreeable on one's return, 'I gat a bonny walcom for my home gàin' (JAM.). Ayr. In the hame-gaun we took a shorter road, SERVICE *Notan-dums* (1890) 25. n.Yks.² Lnk. The hame-gaun wearied busy bees Flee by on bummin' wings, THOMSON *Musings* (1881) 127. (17) Lin. (HALL.) I.W.¹ ; I.W.² I ben at all the hooam harvests all they years. (18) n.Yks.² He'll be a heeam-heead by noo. (19) Edb. The hamelan' servants tak' the lead; The cottars next come on wi' speed, *Har'st Rig* (1794) 9, ed. 1801. (20) Nrf. COZENS-HARDY *Broad Nrf.* (1893) 52. (21) e.Dev. Tell us the full names of this man, gentleman or ploughboy, gipsy or home-liver, BLACK-MORE *Perlycross* (1894 \ ix. (22, a) Frf. Cadge the craps, fan cuttit down In hairst, hame o'er unto the town, *Piper o' Peebles* (1794) 5. Flf. The weel kend gate They're on the nick o' takin' Hame owre this night, DOUGLAS *Poems* (1806) 152. Edb. Deil ane o' them . . . wad be fit to take a dance Hame o'er, to tell the news in France, CRAWFORD *Poems* (1798) 91. (b) Sc. I hadna weel begun to play Some hameowre lilt, ALLAN *Lilts* (1874) 40. Abd. Mak' nae words to speak in a gey hameo'er place, ALEXANDER *Johnny Gibb* (1871) xvii. Ags. Will ye tak' a cup o' tea ' for ye'll no like our hame-ower meal, I doot, *St. Kathleen* (1800) III. 232 (JAM.). Frf. What hame o'er foulk whiles ca' a keeking-glass, MORISON *Poems* (1790) 158. Lnk. Geography . . . was . . . perfect nonsense for hame ower folk, FRASER *Whaups* (1895) 34. Edb. Hame-o'er langsyne you hae been blyth to pack Your a' upon a sarkless soldier's back, FERGUSSON *Poems* (1773) 181, ed. 1785. (23) Lnk. Oh ! for the lilt o' an auld hame-sang, THOMSON *Leddy May* (1883) 111. (24) n.Yks.² (25) Dmb. In consideration of having such a homespun visitor in the place, CROSS *Disruption* (1844) vi. Rnf. This feeble, plain, Rough hame-spun dirge, may flow in vain, FINLAYSON *Rhymes* (1815) 110. Edb. Gar auld-warld wordies clack In hamespun rhime, FERGUSSON *Poems* (1773) 224, ed. 1785. Dmf. Ye're thinkin' I'm rough, an' lackin' o' lear, Hame-spun, THOM *Jock o' Knowe* (1878) 25. Gall. My house is fu' baith butt and ben, Of hyplock hame-spun gentlemen, LAUDERDALE *Poems* (1796) 35. Lakel.² Cum.¹ He's a real heàmm-spun an. n.Lin.¹ She's a hoàmespun un; she is that. Glo. We be but plain, home-spun folk, GISSING *Vill. Hampden* (1890) I. iv. (26, a) Nhb. These huts are built a short distance from the home-stall, MAR-SHALL *Review Agric.* (1818) I. 40. Nhp.¹ Not very gen... It occurs in notices of sale : ' To be sold, a close lying contiguous to the home-stall.' Oxf.¹ MS. add. Suf.¹ (b) Ken.¹² (27, a) Sc. I have evited striking you in your ain house . . . because I am ignorant how the laws here may pronounce respecting burglary and hame-sucken, SCOTT *Nigel* (1822) xxvi; Explained the nature of the various crimes, assault, robbery, and hamesucken, FORD *Thistle-down* (1891) 211 ; It is still a capital offence, although, as a matter of fact, the infliction of the extreme penalty has long fallen into desuetude. . . Nowadays hamesucken is seldom charged, but occa-sionally cases occur, and such a case has just been tried in the Dumfries Sheriff Court, *Carlisle Jrn.* (Jan. 3, 1899). (b) Cld. (JAM.) Lnk. Like some hamesucken weaver that had never been twa mile west o' Camlachie in his life, MURDOCH *Readings* (ed. 1895) II. 76. (c) Ayr. (JAM.) (28) Cum.¹ (29) e.Suf. (F.H.) (30) Hmp. WISE *New Forest* (1883) 283 ; Hmp.¹ s.Hmp. Could ye gi'e her a pinch of bishopswort, for to make humwater ! VERNEY *L. Lisle* (1870) x. (31) Sur. If the snow had been any deeper nobody couldn't home-went (H.J.M.). (32, a) Abd. We thocht it time to be stappin hamewuth, ALEXANDER *Johnny Gibb* (1871) xviii. Per. As hamewith he cam' wi't he paikit a bairn, NICOLL *Poems* (ed. 1843) 95. (b) Abd. And now the squire his hamewith course intends, ROSS *Helenore* (1768) 137, ed. 1812. n.Sc. He's ay to the hamewith (JAM.). Bnff.¹ (33) w.Yks. Not heard so frequently now. ' Ah've seen 'em swop hand-looms fer pahr-looms, . . hoame-wark fer miln-wark,' *Yks. Wkly. Post* (Apr. 18, 1896). (34) n.Lin.¹ In the home-yards two sorts of hemp were grown, MACKINNON *Acc. of Messingham* (1825) 12.

2. Phr. (1) *at home*, (a) at no great distance, not out of town ; (b) of servants, &c. : out of situation, not in em-ployment ; (2) *in home*, indoors ; (3) *up home*, upstairs ; (4) *to be called home*, to have the banns of marriage published ; (5) — *be not all at home*, to be wanting in intellect ; (6) *to come home*, (a) to be born ; (b) of a servant : to arrive at a new situation, to come to her mistress's or master's house ; (7) — *go home*, (a) of a servant : to go to a new situation ; (b) to die ; to decay, perish ; to be ex-tinguished ; (8) — *put home*, to escort home ; (9) — *spring home*, to be born ; (10) — *take home*, to cause to die, to call to heaven.

(1, *a*) Sc. ' Is Mr. Such-a-one at home?' ' Yes, sir, he is at home, but he is not within,' *Monthly Mag.* (1800) I. 323. (*b*) Abd. A tolerably lively recollection of her experiences in having previously had one or two of her sons ' at home ' during the winter season, ALEXANDER *Ain Flk.* (1882) 212. n.Cy. (J.W.) (2, **Yks.** (*ib.*) Dev. You bide here, us be goin' in home for a minnit, *Reports Provinc.* (1887) 9. (3) ' Where's your bonnet, Polly?' ' He's up home on the bed,' *ib.* (4) Wil.[1] They tells I as 'ow Bet Stingymir is gwain to be caal'd whoam to Jim Spritely on Zundy. Dor. You was not called home this morning, HARDY *Tess* (1891) xxxii. (5) ne.Lan.[1] He's net o' at heyam. (6, *a*) Abd. A richt protty gate-farrin bairnie. . . Fan cam't hame no! ALEXANDER *Ain Flk.* (1882) 219. Rnf. Janet had her firstlin' baby, In September cam' he hame, NEILSON *Poems* (1877) 37. (*b*) Ked. A sonsie pawkie quean Cam' hame to keep his house, GRANT *Lays* (1884) 92 ; (A.W.) (7, *a*) Sc. (JAM.) ; (A.W.) (*b*) a.Not. Them taters never did no good · they went hum after they were flooded. Th' owd jackass hes gone home (J.P.K.). sw.Lin.[1] I'm sure it would be a blessing if it went home again. e.Suf. Used of whatever has animal or vegetable life, and of a lamp, candle, or fire (F.H.). Dev. Poor Sam's gwâyne hwum, PULMAN *Sketches* (1842) 105, ed. 1871. (8) Cor.[1] (9) Slg. Twa waly chaps sprung hame, twa lovely boys, GALLOWAY *Luncarty* (1804) 58. (10) sw.Lin.[1] If it would please the Lord to take it home.

3. A parish consisting of several hamlets or townships.

Shr. A very large and populous parish containing at least twenty hamlets or townships. . . The inhabitants of this large district are said to live ' in Worfield-home,' and the adjacent . . . parishes (each of them containing in like manner many townships or hamlets) are called Claverly- or Clarely-home, Tatnall-home, Womburn-home or 'whome,' HONE *Table-bk.* (1827) 23.

4. Household furniture.

w.Yks. People in Sheffield speak of having got a home together, when they have got enough furniture together for housekeeping (S.O.A.). Not. I have been in the house a fortnight, but I wont be comfortable till my home arrives (A.S.P.).

5. *adv.* Close, near by, to the extreme point, quite, freq. in phr. *to make* or *shut home*, to close, shut. Also used *fig.* closely, urgently.

e.An.[1] The nail is driven home. ' I pressed him home ' upon the subject. Suf.[1] Is the nail home? I gave it him home. e.Suf. (F.H.) Wil. For generosity to their comrades in trouble ' I cannot speak them home,' SWINSTEAD *Par. on Wheels* (1897) 203. Som. They hauled the waggon home beside the rick, RAYMOND *Tryphena* (1895) 14. w.Som.[1] Her and her mother do live home beside o' we. Dev. Hur drap'd bothe tha cans . . . An val'd . . . hom pin tap a tha vlore. NATHAN HOGG *Poet. Lett.* (1847) 2nd S. 14. ed. 1866. nw.Dev.[1] Cor. Take the niddle and crafe home that great squard in thy skirt, THOMAS *Randigal Rhymes* (1895) 22 ; Lev us shut hum our eyes, T. TOWSER *Tales* (1873) 12 ; Cor.[1] Make hom the door ; Cor.[3]

6. *Comb.* (1) Home-by, close to, near by ; (2) -done, of meat : well-cooked ; (3) -to, (*a*) up to, as far as, close to ; (*b*) all but, excepting only.

(1) w.Som.[1] The house id'n ezactly in the street, but he's home by. Dev. Jenny Brook's 'ouze is homeby ours, HEWETT *Peas. Sp.* (1892). n.Dev. I wiz born whum by es side, PULMAN *Sketches*, 6, in ELWORTHY *Wd. Bk.* (1888). (2) e.An.[1] Nrf. COZENS-HARDY *Broad Nrf.* (1893) 41 ; I like my meat home-done; but my husband like his in the main (W.R.E.). Suf.[1] Do you love your meat home-done or rare? (3, *a*) Som. W. & J. *Gl.* (1873). w.Som.[1] The routs was up home to the nuts o' the wheels. 'Home to door' is a very common idiom. ' We went 'long way un all the way, right home to door.' Dev. He'th a-urned the nive intû 'is leg right up 'ome tû tha hannel, HEWETT *Peas. Sp.* (1892) ; Dev.[2] 'Where's my glasses?' ' We thar' they be hom' to 'ee.' nw.Dev.[1] (*b*) w.Som.[1] Dhai·v u kaar·d uwai· au·l aay-d u·gau·t, oa·m tu dhee·uz yuur [They have stolen all I had, excepting this one alone]. Dev. I have carried away everything, home to this, *Reports Provinc.* (1882) 15. nw.Dev.[1]

7. *adj.* To the point, direct, close ; decisive; also used *fig.* Lnk. The paper was very home and close, WODROW *Ch. Hist.* (1721) III. 342, ed. 1828. Nhp.[1] ' I gave him a home stroke.' A figurative expression for completion. Nrf. A ' home-stroke,' HOLLOWAY. Sus. It won't be long afore you have homer things to think of than politics, BLACKMORE *Springhaven* (1887) xxix. Hmp. HOLLOWAY.

Hence Home-dealing, *sb.* plain-dealing, close application to a man's conscience or feelings on any subject.

Sc. The interest of precious truth, and your great confidence,

makes plain and home-dealing with you in the case indispensably necessary, M'WARD *Contendings* (1723) 196 (JAM.).

8. *v.* To go homewards ; *fig.* to die.

Cum. We'll heame to driving ploughs, RAYSON *Poems* (1899) 42. n.Yks.[2] He's heeaming fast.

9. With *in* : of the tide, to flow in, come in. n.Yks.[2] Hence Homer, *sb.* the seventh wave. Cf. home, *sb.*[2]

Suf. Every seventh wave is a heavy one, and when a boat is coming in, or a bather wanting to land, it might be said, ' Let's wait for a seventh wave, that'll be a " homer " ' (A.L.M.).

10. With *to* : to live with, be domesticated with.

Not.[1] Lel.[1] She hums to us now her mother's dead.

11. To assign a particular pasture to a particular flock.

Cum. There is no rule which can oblige me to heaf or home my flock on any particular pasture, *Helvellyn* in *Cornh. Mag.* (Oct. 1890) 384.

12. Of corn : to carry, harvest. Cor. (J.W.)

HOME, *sb.*[2] Suf. A swell on the beach, esp. a well-marked swell, rolling in independently of any blowing. Cf. homer, s.v. Home, *sb.*[1] 9.

There's no wind, but a nasty home on the beach, *N. & Q.* (1896) 8th S. x. 432.

HOMELY, *adj.* Sc. Cum. Yks. Lan. Ess. Amer. Also in forms hamely, hamly Sc. ; haumly Ess.[1] ; heamly Cum. ; hemly Sh.I. ; humly w.Yks. 1. Friendly, familiar, ' at home,' free; regarded as one of the house and not as a stranger.

Sc. The Captain's sae hamely, he gars ane forget himsell, SCOTT *Guy M.* (1815) lv ; Hame is a hamely word, KELLY *Prov.* (1721) 132. S. & Ork.[1] Keb. Now I am homely with Christ's love, so that I think the house mine own, RUTHERFORD *Lett.* (1660) No. 134. Cum. They mead ther-sels beath cumfurtabel an' heamly, FARRALL *Betty Wilson* (1886) 83. Yks. (J.W.) Lan. Don't be balow, you're very homely (W.T.).

Hence Homeliness, *sb.* familiarity, intimacy, fellow-feeling.

Sc. O'er mickle hameliness spills courtesy, KELLY *Prov.* (1721) 270. Ayr. Is there not some hameliness betwixt the work and the workman? DICKSON *Writings* (1660) I. 30, ed. 1845.

2. Phr. *to take so homely upon one*, to be at home with, treat in a familiar, easy way.

Sh.I. Noo, bairns, 'at I sall tak sae hamely apo' you, saet you in, an' Loard grant His blissin, *Sh. News* (July 3, 1897).

3. *Comp.* Homely-spoken, plain-spoken, unaffected.

Sc. She is sae plain put on, and sae hamely spoken I kent every word she said, *Saxon and Gael* (1814) I. 34 (JAM.).

4. Ugly. Ess.[1] [Amer. (A.S.P.)]

HOMER, *adj.* Cor.[1] Homeward. ' The homer fields.'

HOMER, see Ho(e, *sb.*[1], Oumer.

HOMERKIN, *sb.* *Obs.* Wil. A measure of beer. One Homerkin of Beere, 12s., *Churden's Acc. St. Thomas, Sarum* (1662-3) 335, ed. 1896.

HOMESOME, *adj.* Sc. Yks. Also in forms hamesSc. ; heeam- n.Yks.[2] 1. Native, home-like, arousing associations of home.

n.Yks.[2] ' That sounds varry heeamsome,' said of hearing one's own dialect when abroad. ' T'seeght o' t'aud church was varry heeamsome.'

2. Homely.

Dmb. Braw in his beuk, and hamesome in his ways, SALMON *Gowodean* (1868) 25. m.Yks.[1]

HOMEY, *sb.* w.Yks. [u·mi.] A term used in children's games : a rendezvous, ' home.' (J.T.)

HOMIL, see Hummel, *adj.*

HOMING, *adj.* Wm. [Not known to our correspondents.] Ridiculous. (HALL.)

HOMINY, *sb.* Wm. Lan. Shr. Also written hominy ne.Lan.[1] [o'mini.] A homily ; a tale, story ; a long, uninteresting story or recitation ; a proclamation.

Wm.[1] ' He's been tellin ma a girt lang hominy.' ' What a hominy!' Freq. used. ne.Lan.[1] Shr.[1] Theer's no end to that fellow's story, 'e's jest like somebody readin' a 'ominy.

HOMLECK, HOMLICK, HOMM, see Hemlock, Ham, *sb.*[2]

HOMMAGED, *ppl. adj.* Chs. Shr. [o·midgd.]

1. Harassed, overworked.

Chs. *Sheaf* (1879) I. 298 ; Chs.[1] a.Chs.[1] Óo)z des·purt oo·n·ijd wée·ûr ôo iz [Hoo's despert hommaged wheer hoo is].

1. Severely censured.

Shr.¹ 'E wux badly 'ommaged about it, an' 'e wunna do it agen a 'urry.

HOMMEL, see Hummel, adj.

HOMMELIN, sb. Sc. The rough ray, *Raia maculata.*

e.Sc. NEILL *Fishes* (1810) 28 (JAM.). [Homlin, Homelyn Ray, Omelyn Maid, SATCHELL (1879).]

HOMMELLS, sb. pl. War. Hrf. Also written **homells** **'ar.** Large feet. BOUND *Provinc.* (1876).

HOMMER, see Hammer, sb.¹

HOMMERED, ppl. adj. Yks. [Not known to our corre-ondents.] Decayed, mouldy. (HALL.)

HOMMOCK, sb. and v. Yks. Chs. Not. Lin. Nhp. War. 'or. Shr. Hrf. Oxf. Bck. Bdf. Ken. Dev. Also written **imock** Nhp.²; and in forms **aumox** s.Not.; **hammick** **ev.²;** hammock w.Yks.² n.Lin.¹ War.²⁴ se.Wor.¹; **immack** War.² Shr.¹; **hommak** Shr.; **hommox** Hrf.²; **immuck** War.² se.Wor.¹ Ken.¹; **homuk** Bdf.; **omuck** **ot.²;** omux. [o'mək, a·mək.] **1. sb.** A heap; a large **ece** or slice; an untidy mess; gen. in phr. all of a **immock.** Cf. **hummock.**

w.Yks.² 'I'm all of a hammock!' 'Now, then, throw it all **to** a hammock!' **Nhp.¹** Always restricted to a female who, **im** an excess of ill-made clothing, that sits in heaps or ridges, **oks** disproportionally stout. 'She is all of a hommock.' **War.²** **ll** of a hommock,' uneven, lumpy; **War.²** What a hommuck **ur** clothes are in. **Wor.** A've maade a fine 'ommock o' that. **'s** a' ov a 'ommock (H.K.). **Dev.²** What a hammick of meat **ey** gave me!

Hence **Hommocky, adj.** rough, uneven.

Wor. Rough hommocky ground (H.K.).

2. An awkward, clumsy person, esp. a tall, slatternly or **imping** girl; gen. in pl. form.

Not. Not restricted to females (W.H.S.). **s.Not.** Can't yer go **a** cheear, yo gret aumox, wi'out knockin' it ower? (J.P.K.) **ev.²** A great hommocks. **War.²** **Bdf.** You're a great hommocks **,W.B.).**

3. A large, awkward foot or leg; gen. in pl.

s.Chs.¹ Tree'd of wi dhem om·ŭks [Treed off wi' them hom-**ocks].** 'To shift one's hommocks' is to show a clean pair of **eels.** **Nhp.¹²** **War.²** Keep your great hammocks outside—**an't**come traepsing all over the clean floor. **Wor.** Shift your great **immocks,** 'ull 'a! (H.K.). **se.Wor.¹** Keep thee great 'ommucks off **y** toes ŏŏt, thy fit be like two great barges. **Bdf.** BATCHELOR **nal.** *Eng. Lang.* (1809) 136. **Ken.** (G.B.), **Ken.¹**

4. Comp. **Hommock-plough,** a short, strong plough used **for** rough maid ground. **Wor.** (H.K.), se.Wor.¹

5. v. To huddle, heap together; to mess, spoil by rough **sage.**

War.² He has hommucked these apples together anyhow. **Shr.¹** **aid** chiefly of dress. 'Look at that wench, 'ow 'er's 'ommacked **r** new bonnet.' **Hrf.²** What's the cow hommoxing with it?

Hence **Hommocking, ppl. adj.** untidy, confused.

War.² What a hommucking mess this straw, is in.

6. To hurry a person away with one unceremoniously.

ne.Wor.¹ He don't give me no peace, he hommucks me off **own** to the Lion with him (J.W.P.).

7. To walk with a clumsy, awkward gait; to tread upon **ith** large heavy feet; to romp; to hobble.

s.Chs.¹ Aay dhal om·ŭks on dhŭr feyt [Ha! they hommocken **n** their feit]. **n.Lin.¹** Ther's been sum herses hammockin' aboot **Mr.** Sorsby's barley. **War.⁴** I be so lame I can but just ham-**ock** to church. **n.Bck.** (A.C.) **Bdf.** A rude, romping, boisterous, **nmannerly** girl is said to go ' hommocking' (J.W.B.).

Hence (1) **Hommocking** or **Hommocksing, ppl. adj.,** (2) **lommocky, adj.** clumsy, awkward.

(1) Not.² Yo' gret omŭckin' brute. **Nhp.¹** She is a great hom-**ocking** thing; **Nhp.²** **War.²;** **War.³** A hammocking walker. **(2)** A big hommakin fellow, **ound** *Provinc.* (1876); **Shr.¹** 'Er's a great 'ommakin', on-gain **okin'** wench. **Oxf.** A gret hommocksing gal (G.O.). **(2) s.Chs.¹**

HOMNITHOM, sb. s.Chs.¹ Also in form **hopmithom.**
1. dwarf, 'hop-o'-my-thumb.'

Ŭ reg·ŭlăr lit'l om·nithom ŭv ŭ fel·ŭ; wot kŭn ey dóo wi ŭ **ae't** baa·rj ŭv ŭ wŭm·ŭn lahyk dhaat· für, ŭ weyf? [A regular **tle** homnithom of a fellow; what can hey do wi' a grăt barge **f** a woman like that for a weife?]

HOMOGEN, see Holmogen.

VOL. III.

HOMOLOGATE, v. ? *Obs.* Sc. To express agreement with or approval of; to countenance; to ratify, confirm.

Sc. Whilk I was altogether unwilling to homologate by my presence, SCOTT *Leg. Mont.* (1818) ii; It might be confidently affirmed by the judge who tendered them, that the subscriver hade homologate the present government, civil and ecclesiastick, KIRKTON *Ch. Hist.* (1817) 267; MITCHELL *Scotticisms* (1799) 44.

Hence **Homologation, sb.** a confirmation, ratification.

Sc. So going to the presbytery should be a homologation of episcopacy, KIRKTON *Ch. Hist.* (1817) 297. **Rnf.** I am much straitened in anything that may import a homologation of prelacy, even in England, WODROW *Corresp.* (ed. 1842) I. 130.

HOMPEL, sb. *Obs.* n.Cy. A kind of jacket. (HALL.)

HOMPER, HOMPLE, HOMSCHACKLE, see Hamper, v.¹, Humper, Hamble, Hamschackle.

HON, adv. w.Som.¹ When.

Usual form. 'I can't mind hon I zeed zo many volks to fair avore.' 'I'll lef the kay o' the door, and vetch 'n hon I come back along.'

HON, see Herne.

HONE, sb.¹ Wor. Hrf. Also written **one·** Wor. [ōn.] In phr. *to have the hone,* to be lazy.

Hrf. Occas. used (H.C.M.); **Hrf.²** Thee hast got the hone.

Hence **Honey** or **Oney, adj.** idle, lazy.

w.Wor.¹ ' My son an't able to work d'yŭ saay!' ' E con if 'e's a mind, but 'e allus was oney.'

[The same word as ME. *hone,* delay, tarrying (*Cursor M.* 8413); cp. *hone* (*hoyne*), to delay, tarry (*York Plays*).]

HONE, sb.² *Obs.* Dev. A long, flat piece of dry bread.

GROSE (1790) *MS. add.* (M.); *Horae Subsecivae* (1777) 215. [Prob. an extended use of *hone* (a whetstone for razors), see Hone, v.¹]

HONE, sb.³ Pem. A lean horse.

s.Pem. I moost put my hone in the trap an' car' yea (W.M.M.).

HONE, v.¹ and **sb.⁴** Sc. Irel. Wor. Amer. **1. v.** To sharpen on a hone or whetstone.

Per. He . . . could hone yer auld razor, FORD *Harp* (1893) 235. **s.Wor.** The 'ook waunts 'onin(g (H.K.). [Amer. Mr. Green . . . brought out a jack-knife, and commenced honing it on his shoe, TROWBRIDGE *Coupon Bonds,* 286 (C.D.).]

2. sb. A whetstone.

Dwn. A few strokes upon his hone made the razor all right, LYTTLE *Betsy Gray* (1894) 20.

HONE, v.² Sc. n.Cy. Lin. Stf. War. Wor. Shr. Dev. Amer. Also in forms **hoin** Lin.; **hoon** Slk.; **hune** Ags.; on s.Wor.¹ [h)ōn, oən.] **1.** To whine, complain, murmur.

Sc. Thou awakest to hone, and pine, and moan, as if she had drawn a hot iron across thy lips, SCOTT *Fair Maid of Perth* (1828) v. **Ags.** (JAM.) **Ayr.** I honed on at my grandfather to take me to see it, SERVICE *Dr. Duguid* (ed. 1887) 58. **Lin.** A dog hoins for his master, THOMPSON *Hist. Boston* (1856) 710.

Hence (1) **Hoining, vbl. sb.** moaning, complaining; (2) **Hooning, ppl. adj.** murmuring.

(1) Lin.¹ I don't like to go to see her because of her hoining. **(2) Slk.** I heard a kind o' hooning sound, HOGG *Tales* (1838) 175, ed. 1866.

2. With *after* or *for*: to repine for want of; to long or pine for. Cf. **hunge, v.**

n.Cy. (HALL.) **Stf.** RAY (1691) *MS. add.* (J.C.) **War.²** I think he's gettin' better—he's a beginning to hone arter his vittles. **w.Wor.¹** Thahr's on'y one thing 'e 'ones far, an' that's a drap o' cider. **Shr.¹** That poor cow's 'onin' after 'er cauve an' lowin' pitiful. 'E canna do no good at school, 'e does so 'one fur 'ome; **Shr.²** This word was appropriately used in the following way, by a poor person towards his rector who was in the constant practice of rigorously exacting the utmost of his tithes: ' One would think thee didst want thy money, for thee meetily honst after it.' **Dev.** LYE (1743) (HALL.). [Amer. He des nat'ally hone fer ter be los' in de woods some mo', HARRIS *Nights with Uncle Remus* (1884) 54; GREEN *Virginia Flk-Sp.*]

[L. Fr. (Norm. dial.) *hoigner,* 'hogner, geindre, pleur-nicher, se lamenter ' (MOISY).]

HONE, v.³ Wor. Shr. Hrf. Pem. [ōn.] To ill-use, beat; to punish a child. Cf. **hoin.**

s.Wor. (H.K.) **Shr.** BOUND *Provinc.* (1876). **Hrf.²** A boy speaks of honing another for getting him punished. **s.Pem.** (W.M.M.)

Hence **Honing, vbl. sb.** a beating.

s.Wor. (H K.) **s.Pem.** That fellow ought to 'ave a good honing for 'is trick (W.M.M.).

F f

HONE, see Ho(e, *sb.*[2]

HONE LAD, *phr.* Nhb.[1] A cry of encouragement to a dog.

HONES, *sb. pl.* Yks. Lan. Shr. Also in forms **oans, oons** Shr.[1] [ōnz, ūnz.] Lumps in the udder of a cow consequent upon the milk-ducts having been overcharged.

Shr.[1] Betty, yo' mun rub that cow's elder, theer's oáns in it as 'ard as a stwun. [I saw Mistris Vrsula Leigh ... wife to W. M. Schoolemaster of Petersfield ... gather it [Hone-wort] in the wheat eershes about Mapledurham, who told me it was called Hone-wort, and that her Mother, late of Brading in the Isle of Wight taught her to use it for a swelling which shee had in her left cheeke. . . This swelling her mother called by the name of a Hone, GERARDE *Herb.* (ed. 1633) 1018.]

Hence **Honed,** *adj.* having the udder swollen and hard, as a cow after calving.

w.Yks.[1], n.Lan.[1] Shr.[1] That brind'ed cow's elder's badly oaned. The cow's elder is honed.

HONEST, *adj.* and *adv.* Sc. n.Cy. Yks. Lan. Nrf.

1. *adj.* In *comb.* (1) **Honest hour,** the hour of death; (2) **-like,** well-looking, respectable in appearance; good, substantial; liberal.

(1) Rnf. I tauld him ... that he had come to the honest hour, and that if there was onything on his mind ... it behooved him to make confession before he appeared at the judgment bar of the Lord, GILMOUR *Pen-Flk.* (1873) 12. (2) Sc. Honest like has in some cases the same meaning with purpose-like—it *gen.* however implies something of fulness—thus, an honest-like man, means a jolly man, and an honest-like piece of beef, is a good substantial joint, *Monthly Mag.* (1798) II. 435; Everything in the house was honest-like (JAM.). Abd. (*ib.*), N.Cy.[1]

2. Honourable; respectable, in good repute.

Sc. I'll warrant it's some idle dubskelper frae the Waal, coming after some o' yoursells on nae honest errand, SCOTT *St. Ronan* (1824) xxviii. Or.I. William Neip, Fold [Fowd], accompanied with three honest men, to minister justice betwixt thame, PETERXIN *Notes* (1822) App. 31.

3. A kindly epithet, *gen.* applied to an inferior.

Sc. Collector Snail, honest man, that never fashes ony body, SCOTT *Guy M.* (1815) ix; Honest woman, what garr'd ye steal your neighbour's tub! RAMSAY *Remin.* (ed. 1872) 114. Ayr. When twilight did my Grannie summon, To say her pray'rs, douce, honest woman, BURNS *Address to Deil* (1785) st. 6. Edb. MOIR *Mansie Wauch* (1828) ix. N.Cy.[1] Well, my honest man, you have been convicted of a felony.

4. Chaste.

Sc. She saith herself she is an honest woman, but I trow scantly, Sc. *Presby. Eloq.* (ed. 1847) 115.

5. Phr. *to make an honest woman of any one,* to marry a woman whom one has previously seduced. Sc. (JAM.), w.Yks.[1] 6. Open, artless, engaging. Yks. (C.C.R.) 7. Well-informed.

n.Lan. He was the only honest man there (W.S.).

8. *adv.* Honestly, fairly.

Per. Helenot noo! Wad ye raelly pet's a' out e'y dark this nicht! CLELAND *Inchbracken* (1883) xxxiv. Nrf. 'It will be all honest your time.' Said to a person when they happen to be passing, and are asked to take a message if not inconvenient, COZENS-HARDY *Broad Nrf.* (1893) 34.

9. *Comb.* **Honest-come,** honestly obtained; well-earned; used *attrib.*

Abd. My honest-come gear I earn'd with the sweat of my brow, COCK *Strains* (1810) II. 79.

HONESTISH, *adj.* Yks. Honest.

w.Yks. O think if a body's honestish, BYWATER *Gossips,* 6; (J.W.); (C.C.)

HONESTLY, *adv.* Obs. Sc. Decently, respectably.

Dame Elizabeth Gordon . . . was buried honestly out of her own native soil, SPALDING *Hist. Sc.* (1792) II. 58, 59 (JAM.).

HONESTY, *sb.*[1] Obs. Sc. 1. Honour; respectability; that which is becoming to one's station in life.

Beggarly pride is devil's honesty, and blusheth to be in Christ's common, RUTHERFORD *Lett.* (1765) No. 50 (JAM.); 'Honesty is no pride.' Spoken to them that go too careless in their dress; intimating that it is no sign of pride to go decently, KELLY *Prov.* (1721) 48.

2. Kindness, liberality.

I'll hide nae man's honesty (JAM.); Why should I smother my husband's honesty, or sin against his love, or be a niggard of

---

giving out to others what I get for nothing? RUTHERFORD *Lett.* (1765) No. 86 (*ib.*).

3. A handsome, valuable gift; a thoroughly good article of its kind, worthy of the giver. Abd. (A.W.)

HONESTY, *sb.*[2] Lakel. Yks. War. Wor. Hrf. Glo. Oxf. Brks. e.An. Wil. The traveller's joy, *Clematis Vitalba.*

Lakel.[2], w.Yks.[2], War.[2] se.Wor.[1] A creeping plant, common in old hedges. s.Wor.[1], Hrf.[2], Glo. (G.E.D.), Glo.[1], Oxf. (G.O.), Oxf.[1] Brks.[1] Always. Cmb., Nrf., n.Ess. (B. & H.), Wil.[1]

HONEY, *sb.* and *adj.* Var. dial. uses in Sc. Irel. Eng. and Amer. Also written **honie** Rxb. n.Yks.[2]; **huney** Wm.; **hunny** n.Yks.; and in forms **hiney** Lnk.; **hinney** Sc. N.Cy.[1] Nhb.[1] Cum.[4]; **hinnie** Sc. S. & Ork.[1]; **hinny** Sc. N.Cy.[1] Nhb.[1] e.Dur.[1] Cum.[14]; **honny** Nhb.; **hooney** e.Dur.[1] w.Yks. [u·ni, ᴜ·ni, h)i·ni.] 1. *sb.* In *comb.* (1) **Honey and joe,** (2) **— and muck,** kindness; sweetness; (3) **— and nuts,** anything peculiarly agreeable; (4) **-bee,** a working bee as contrasted with a drone; (5) **-bike,** a hive of honey; (6) **-blob,** the contents of a bee's honey-bag; also used as a term of endearment; (7) **-bread,** bread and honey; (8) **-butter-cake,** a slice of bread on which both honey and butter are spread; (9) **-comb-bag,** the second stomach of a ruminating animal, whence the cud is returned to the mouth; (10) **-comb work,** the ornamental stitching on a smock-frock; (11) **-crock,** the earthen vessel in which honey is kept; (12) **-dew,** a kind of blight which covers the leaves of plants with a viscous covering something like honey; (13) **-drink,** a beverage made from honey; see below; (14) **-drop,** a mole on the skin; (15) **-fall,** (a) see (12); (b) an unexpected piece of good fortune; a 'windfall'; (16) **-good-gracious,** an exclamation of surprise; (17) **-(s how,** an exclamation of glad surprise; (18) **-mead,** see (13); (19) **-month,** the honeymoon; (20) **-mug,** a vessel containing honey; (21) **-pig**(s, (a) see (11); (b) see (22, c); (22) **-pot**(s, (a) the vessel into which savings are put; (b) a term of endearment; (c) a child's game, see below; (23) **-spot,** see (14); (24) **-sweet,** (a) perfectly sweet; (b) sweetly, pleasantly; (25) **-work,** endearments, fine speeches.

(1) Sc. (JAM.) Slk. Unless it come frae her ain side o' the house, and then she's a hinny and joe, HOGG *Tales* (1838) 67, ed. 1866. (2) s.Yks. He's all honey an' muck (I.W.). (3) Nhp. Common. The most *gen.* use of the phr. is when a person hears another, who is no favourite, rebuked for his meanness or pride, he would say, 'Oh, it was honey and nuts to me!' (4) Sc. I wer I were a hinny-bee, That I awa' might sing, NICOLL *Poems* (ed. 1843) 139. Ags. This term occurs in a ... proverb, expressive of the little dependance that can be had on mere probabilities... 'Maybe was neer a gude hinny-bee' (JAM.). Lak. The honeybee [should] sip the reward o' his toil, the drone suit his wants to his winning o't, RODGER *Poems* (1898) 101, ed. 1897. Cum.[4] Industrious as the hinny bee, ANDERSON *Advyce to Nanny,* st. 1. (5) Abd. Nae honey-byke that I did ever pree Did taste so sweet and smervy unto me, Ross *Helmore* (1768) 119, ed. 1812. Dur. (K.) (6) Lnk. A tear, like a pure hinny-blab, Was shed o'er the wretched by Jamie M'Nab, RODGER *Poems* (1898) 32, ed. 1897. Gall. A honey-blob ay, unto me ye doth prove, MACTAGGART *Encycl.* (1824) 323, ed. 1876. (7) Sus.[1] (8) Lan. Ga' me a honey-butter-cake, TIM BOBBIN *View Dial.* (1746) 10, ed. 1806. (9) Dor. BARNES *Gl.* (1863) (s.v. Read). (10) Dor. HARDY *Madding Crowd* (1874) ix. (11) Sc. (JAM.) Keb. The little feckless bee, pantry toom, And hinny crock ev'n wi' the laggin lick'd, DAVIDSON *Seasons* (1789) 1, 2 (JAM.). (12) s.Not. This rain 'll wesh the honey-dew off o' the trees (J.P.K.). War.[2] I cut the tree down finding that the honey-dew from the leaves was such a nuisance on the flower border. se.Wor.[1] (13) w.Yks.[1] After the honey is melted from the combs they are put into a pancheon or vessel, and water is poured upon them, in order to extract the remainder of the honey. The liquor thus produced is allowed to ferment and then bottled. When old it is intoxicating (s.v. Honey-mead). (14) Sc. My sister Maisy, Wi' the hinny-draps on her chin, CHILD *Ballads* (1886) IV. 383. (15, a) Lakel.[2] Lan. YOUNG *Annals Agric.* (1784-1815) III. 319. Chs.[1], a.Chs.[1] s.Not. There's bin a honey-fall on my currans (J.P.K.). (b) Lakel.[2] n.Yks.[1]; n.Yks.[2] 'They have had a brave honey-fall lately,' a great deal of property bequeathed to them. n.Yks.[4] w.Yks. Ah gate a honey-fall this mornin' i' t'shap. s.Yks. A fifty pund 'at's been owing this thirteen year (S.K.C.). Chs.[1] A

man who had made several good speculations was described as having had 'two or three good honey-faws.' **a.Cha.**[1] It)l bey ū rae'r ūn'ifau· for)ûm, wen dh)uwd mon deyz [It'll be a rare honey-faw for 'em, when th'owd mon deys]. (16) **e.Yks.**[1] (17) **N.Cy.**[1] **Nhb.** Hinneys-how! efter aal we'll not fret, *Sng.* (R.O.H.) ; **Nhb.**[1] (18) **w.Yks.**[2] (19) **Frf.** The honey month's done, and she won't be control'd, MORISON *Poems* (1790) 188. (20) **Frf.** All you fair maids . . . Beware of evil-doing; Lest dipping in the honey-mug, An' that 'll be a snare, *N. & Q.* (1869) 4th S. iii. 95. (21, *a*) **Sc.** (JAM.) **e.Lth.** Ye're a' after this Bill o' Tod-Lowrie's like flees to the hinny-pig, HUNTER *J. Inwick* (1895) 199. **Gall.** MACTAGGART *Encycl.* (1824). (*b*) **Gall.** The boys who try this sport sit down in rows, hands locked beneath their hams. Round comes one of them, the honey-merchant, who feels those who are sweet or sour, by lifting them by the arm-pits, and giving them three shakes; if they stand these without the hands unlocking below, they are then sweet and saleable, fit for being office-bearers in other ploys, *ib.* 270, ed. 1876. (22, *a*) **m.Yks.**[1] A certain field is called Honeypot Field, because a vessel containing spade guineas was ploughed up there. (*b*) **w.Yks.** Aw, it's mi little honey-pot (Æ.B.). (*c*) **Ir.** Several children squat down clasping their hands under their hams, and are then carried by others from place to place by their arms as handles, to the jingle 'Honey-pots, honey-pots, all in a row' (A.S.P.). **Nhb.**[1] **n.Yks.** Two lads carrying another on their arms clasped together (I.W.). **e.Yks.**[1] Two carry a third, as a pot of honey to market. **w.Yks.**[2] **Lan.** THORNBER *Hist. Blackpool* (1837) 90. **Cha.**[1] The game consists in one child sitting down and clasping its hands together under its knees. Two others then lift it up by its arms and swing it backwards and forwards, whilst they count twenty; if its hands give way before twenty is counted it is a bad honey-pot, if not it is a good one. **Lon.** Sometimes we has a game of 'honey-pots' with the girls in the court, MAYHEW *Lond. Labour* (1851) I. 15a. **Sur.** (L.J.Y.), **Wil.**[1] [For further information, see GOMME *Games* (1894) 219 ff.] (23) **S. & Ork.**[1] *MS. add.* (24, *a*) **Som.** There's nothing on earth so honey-sweet as a Papist in disguise, RAYMOND *Love and Quiet Life* (1894) 58. **Dev.**[3] The clayne cloäthes, I've a jist tûcked in vrom the line, 's whit 's za drip, and honey sweet. (*b*) **Dor.** I heard um tell, they did catch a sheep—just sweeale th' behur off o' un, down wi' un honey-sweet (C.W.B.). **w.Som.**[1] Usually applied to hay or straw. ' Well, tidn very good hay, but I mixes their corn 'long way it, and puts a little bit o' salt in 'long way it, and then they eats it honey-sweet.' ' I was afeard o' un [the rick], 'cause 'twas out so long, but howsomever, he cuts out honey-sweet.' (25) **n.Yks.**[2]

2. Comp. in plant-names : (1) **Honey-ball**, the orange ball-tree, *Buddlea globosa*; (2) **-bind**, the honeysuckle, *Lonicera Periclymenum*; (3) **-blob**, a variety of gooseberry, *Ribes Grossularia*; (4) **-bottle**, (*a*) the cross-leaved heath, *Erica Tetralis*; (*b*) the furze, *Ulex europaeus*; (5) **-cherry**, a sweet variety of cherry, *Prunus Avium*; (6) **-crach**, a small plum; (7) **-flower**, (*a*) the bee-orchis, *Ophrys apifera*; (*b*) any flower which yields honey; (8) **-knobs**, (9) **-pear**, a variety of the pear, *Pyrus communis*; (10) **-pin**, a peculiar sweet apple; (11) **-pink** [not known to our correspondents] ; (12) **-plant**, a sweet-scented garden plant; (13) **-stalks**, the blossoms of the white clover, *Trifolium repens*; (14) **-stick**, the traveller's joy, *Clematis Vitalba*; (15) **-sweet**, the meadowsweet, *Spiraea Ulmaria*; (16) **-ware**, a species of edible sea-weed, *Alaria esculenta*; (17) **-wort**, the sweet Alysson, *Alyssum maritimum*.

(1) **w.Som.**[1] (2) **Oxf.** *Science Gossip* (1882) 165. (3) **Sc.**, **Ant.** (W.H.P.) (4, *a*) **Wil.** Moor-like lands, beautiful with heaths and honey-bottle, JEFFERIES *Gt. Estate* (1880) i; **Wil.**[1] (*b*) **Wil.**[1] (5) **Rnf.** Her lips were a hinney-cherrie, Sae tempting to the sight, *Harp* (1819) 288. **Dmf.** Her lips were a cloven hinnie-cherrie, CROMEK *Remains* (1810) 7. **Hrt.** ELLIS *Mod. Husb.* (1750) III. ii. 151. (6) **e.An.**[1] Of luscious sweetness, but little flavour. (7, *a*) **Ken.** (*b*) **Ayr.** All sorts of honey-flowers, marigolds, pansies, roses, clover, and what not, SERVICE *Dr. Duguid* (ed. 1887) 36. **Som.** 'Tis a ztrange thing that where they honey vlow'rs blaw, there d' graw the pizen blossoms, LEITH *Lemon Verbena* (1895) 100. (8) **War.**[2] **Wor.** A pear known as Honey Knobs is grown for perry and cider making (E.S.). (9) **Lak.** Her wee mou' as red as June roses, An' ripe as a sweet hiney-pear, NICHOLSON *Idylls* (1870) 76. (10) **Cor.**[12] (11) **Dor.** Here's rath'ripes here, enuff methink, But I do like a honeypink, *Eclogue* (1863) 25. (12) **I.W.** Sibyl bent over a honey plant encrusted with pink-scented blossom, about which the bees from Raysh Squire's hives were humming —an old-fashioned cottage plant, GRAY *Annesley* (1889) I. 119.

Wil. She watched the bees busy at the sweet-scented honey-plant, JEFFERIES *Gt. Estate* (1880) 25; **Wil.**[1] Some old-fashioned sweet-scented plant, perhaps the dark Sweet Scabious, which used to be known as 'Honey-flower' in some counties. (13) **War.** (G.E.D.) (14) **War.**[3], **Glo.**[1] (15) **Som.**, **w.Som.**[1] (16) **Sc.** (JAM.) **Sh.I.** A twal fit plank . . . wi' da 'clacks' hingin' frae him laek hinniwirs, *Sh. News* (Mar. 18, 1899). **Or.I.** (17) **Hmp.** (W.M.E.F.)

3. A pet; a sweetheart; a term of endearment, gen. addressed to women and children; also used *attrib.*

Sc. For mony a bein nook . . . has been offered to my hinny Willie, SCOTT *Redg.* (1824) Lett. x; Just twa o' my old joes, my hinny dear, STEVENSON *Catriona* (1893) iii. **n.Sc.** O open the door, my honey, my heart, BUCHAN *Ballads* (1867) 27. **Sh.I.** Quat says du, hinnie! BURGESS *Rasmie* (1892) 25. **Per.** Rise, my bonny hinny, Dance to Donald Ker, FORD *Harp* (1893) 159. **Fif.** Here, my honey, ye've bonnie red cheeks, ROBERTSON *Provost* (1894) 108. **Dmb.** Whist, hinny, bide a blink, SALMON *Gowodean* (1868) 30. **Lnk.** Sweet hinney, come ye ben, NICHOLSON *Idylls* (1870) 81. **Lth.** Come to my arms, my sweet wee hinny, Fair image o' thy bonny minny, BALLANTINE *Poems* (1856) 49. **e.Lth.** Bide a wee hinnies, an' ye'll get a' thae bonny-dies for naething, HUNTER *J. Inwick* (1895) 91. **Rxb.** The cits . . . That durst not to their betters speak Are all grown jolly honies, WILSON *Poems* (1824) 24. **Edb.** Will ye come down a wee, hinnie, and keep the shop ! BALLANTINE *Gaberlunzie* (ed. 1875) 133. **Gall.** Think weel, hinny ! Hae ye nane that ye love! CROCKETT *Moss-Hags* (1895) li. **Ir.** But spake to me, honey—spake to me, acushla, LEVER *C. O'Malley* (1841) lxxx. **n.Ir.** Betty, me honey, tak care av the money, *Lays and Leg.* (1884) 47; **N.I.**[1] **Wxf.** 'Ah! then, Sir, honey,' said Shan, KENNEDY *Banks Boro* (1867) 27. **N.Cy.**[1] Ironically said of a light woman, 'She's a canny hinny,' she's a bad woman. Used contemptuously of a man. **Nhb.** Heigho, heigho, my honny, Heigho, heigho, my own dear love, RITSON *Garl.* (1810) I. 43; **Nhb.**[1] The kye are come hame, but I see not my hinnie; . . I'd rather lose all the kye than lose my hinnie, *Old Sng.* **Dur.** And do you ken Elsie Marley, honey ! *Bishoprick Garl.* (1784) 49, ed. 1834. **e.Dur.**[1] The standing epithet of endearment to children, and used in the *n.* in much the same unrestrained way that 'my dear' is used in the *sw.* 'Hooney hinney' is sometimes heard. 'Behave, hinny,' the stock admonition to a child at table. **Lakel.**[2] **Cum.** And Etty is the hinny fowt Of aw the country roun, ANDERSON *Ballads* (ed. 1808) 74 ; **Cum.**[1] ; **Cum.**[4] Whey, hinney, if that's the best thou hes it's not worth the money. **Wm.** I, then, drink ey, drink yersels full, hineys, RICHARDSON *Sng. Sol.* (1859) v. 1. **n.Yks.**[1] Often used also by the aged in addressing those they feel both respect and regard for: a kindly clergyman or lady-visitor often gets the appellative honey; **n.Yks.**[2] ' My blessed honies !' is a kindred exclamation [of surprise] (s.v. Honey Feathers) ; **n.Yks.**[4] Gan thi ways, honey dear. **ne.Yks.**[1] Cum thi ways, hunny. **e.Yks.** It's noän him 'ats made me cry, honey, LINSKILL *Exchange Soul* (1888) xvii ; **e.Yks.**[1], **m.Yks.**[1] **w.Yks.** LUCAS *Stud. Nidderdale* (c. 1882) Gl. **Cha.** Dunna cry, honey (E.F.). **n.Lin.**[1] **s.Pem.** Come, honey ! LAWS *Little Eng.* (1888) 420. **Hrt.** *Hrt. Merc.* (May 26, 1888). **w.Som.**[1] Common. ' Sally my honey ! Take care o' your money.' [Amer. Anything well approved. Also, the person sought, as ' you're my honey,' i. e. the one I am looking for. A fine fellow, *gen.* ironically, CARRUTH *Kansas Univ. Quar.* (Oct. 1892) I. No. 2.]

Hence (1) **Honey-bairn**, *sb.* a dear child ; (2) **-dove**, *sb.* pet, sweetheart ; (3) **-fathers**, *sb. pl.* the sweet saints, used as an expression of surprise.

(1) **n.Cy.** GROSE (1790). **Nhb.** (R.O.H.) **n.Yks.**[3] [2] ; **n.Yks.**[4] ' Oh, mah sweet honey bairn !' said as a mother picked up a fallen child. **n.Yks.**[1] (*a*) **Lth.** My ain pet ! my honey-doo ! My trootie o' the burn, SMITH *Merry Bridal* (1866) 50. (3) **n.Yks.**[2] Honey feathers ! is that you ! **m.Yks.**[1]

4. Phr. *to be honey to,* to do one good, cheer one up.

Sh.I. Güd lat yon [whisky] be hinny 'ithin dee, Girzzie, *Sh. News* (Jan. 20, 1900).

5. adj. Honeyed ; sweet as honey.

Sc. Stottie ba', hinnie ba', tell to me How mony bairns am I to hae, CHAMBERS *Pop. Rhymes* (1870) 115. **Abd.** Fu' fain to pree her hinny lip, STILL *Cottar's Sunday* (1845) 172. **Per.** I played amang her gouden hair, And preed her hinny mou', EDWARDS *Lyrics* (1889) 28. **Slg.** In the sweet hinny hours o' the gloamin', TOWERS *Poems* (1885) 196. **Rnf.** O! her hinney breath lift her locks, As through the dance she flew, *Harp* (1819) 288. **Ayr.** My hinny bliss, BURNS *Gowden Locks*, st. i. **Lnk.** And hinny breath o' heather bells Comes glaffin on the breeze, HAMILTON *Poems* (1865) 51. **Edb.** Ah, fleechin' Jamie ! had your hinny tale, LEAR-

F f 2

MONT *Poems* (1791) 268. **Slk.** Wi' hinny word I row'd my tongue, HOGG *Poems* (ed. 1865) 276.

HONEYSUCK, *sb.* Yks. Nhp. War. Hmp. Dor. Som. Also in forms **honeysouk** n.Yks.[4]; **honeyzook** Som.; **honeyzuck** Dor.[1] 1. The honeysuckle, *Lonicera Periclymenum.*

n.Yks.[4], Hmp.[1] Dor. There be rwoses an' honeyzucks hangèn among The bushes, BARNES *Poems* (1879) 72; Dor.[1] Som. The hawthorn wasn't arl off th' hedges, an' yet the honey-zooks and dag rhoses was out, LEITH *Lemon Verbena* (1895) 38.

2. The flowers of the red clover, *Trifolium pratense.*

Nhp.[1], War. (J.R.W.), Hmp. w.Som.[1] Uun-ee-zèok. Common.

HONEYSUCKLE, *sb.* Yks. Chs. Midl. Lin. Nhp. War. Oxf. Bdf. Hrt. Sus. Hmp. Wil. Som. Dev. 1. The purple clover, *Trifolium pratense.*

Yks. Lin. SKINNER (1671). Nhp.[1], War. (J.R.W.), War.[284], s.War.[1], Oxf. Hrt. ELLIS *Mod. Husb.* (1750) III. i. 46. Wil.[1] Som. JENNINGS *Obs. Dial. w.Eng.* (1825); Common (W.F.R.).

2. The white clover, *T. repens*; also in *comb.* **Honeysuckle clover.**

Midl. MARSHALL *Rur. Econ.* (1796) II. Bdf. Watering into sections the moss of dry pastures, and promote the growth of the white honeysuckle, BATCHELOR *Agric.* (1813) 492. Wil.[1]

3. The bird's-foot trefoil, *Lotus corniculatus.* Chs.[1]

4. The dwarf cornel, *Cornus suecica.* n.Yks. (B. & H.)

5. The great bindweed, *Convolvulus sepium.* Dev.[4]

6. The white dead-nettle, *Lamium album.* Wil.[1] 7. The lousewort, *Pedicularis sylvatica.* Hmp. (J.R.W.), Hmp.[1]

8. The blossoms of the willow, *Salix.* Sus.

HONEYSUCKLED, *adj.* e.Yks. Twisted by honeysuckle; of ash saplings. (W.W.S.)

HONG, see **Hang.**

HONISH, *v.* Lan. Also in form **hunnish** ne.Lan.[1]; **unnish** Lan.[1] To ill-treat; to starve a person for want of food. Cf. **hoin.**

Hoo wur a bad un and her bairns wur fair honisht (J.D.): Th' puir bairns wur fair honished, aw uphowd yo, *N. & Q.* (1878) 5th S. x. 164; Lan.[1], ne.Lan.[1]

Hence **Honished,** *ppl. adj.* wearied, tired out. Lan.[1], n.Lan.[1]

[Nis no mon him neih his nuy to amende, Bote honesschen him as a hound, *P. Plowman* (A.) xi. 48. OFr. *honnir* (*hunir*), 'déshonorer' (LA CURNE).]

HONK, *sb.* and *v.* Lakel. Lan. [h)oŋk.] 1. *sb.* A lazy, idle fellow.

Lakel.[2] Thoo gurt idle honk. Cum.[14] Wm. Twa girt guzzlan honks, *Spec. Dial.* (1885) pt. iii. 33.

2. *v.* To idle about.

Lakel.[2] Thoo'll honk aboot anyway afoor thoo'll buckle ta some wark. Cum.[4] Lan. Oalas honkin about yam when he sud be at wark, R. PIKETAH *Forness Flk.* (1870) 38; Aw kept honkin un hoverin abeawt, STATON *Loominary* (c. 1861) 109.

HONK, see **Hank,** *sb.*[1]

HONKA-DONKA, *sb.* e.An. Also in form **hunka-donka** e.Suf. Thick, heavy boots.

Nrf. (M.C.H.B.), Nrf., Suf.(P.H.E.) e.Suf. In common use (F.H.).

HONKAZIN, *prp.* Chs. Idling, lounging; 'hankering.' See **Honk.**

s.Chs.[1] Ahy mai· ndo ůky'aay·nt ův ů mon lahyk dhaat·; ey důz nuwt bů goa· ongk·ůzin ůbuw·t [I may noo accaïnt of a mon like that; hey does nowt bu' go honkazin abowt].

[For the freq. suff. *-as* (*-us*) see s.Chs.[1] *Introd.* 8.]

HONNERIL, *sb.* Cld. (JAM.) A foolish, talkative person.

HONOUR, *sb.* Sc. Irel. Yks. Pem. Also written honor Irel. s.Pem. A title given to the younger sons of Earls, Viscounts, or Barons; a term of address used to a superior.

Ayr. His Honour maun detach, Wi' a' his brimstone squadrons, Fast, fast this day, BURNS *Ordination* (1786) st. 10. Ir. BARRINGTON *Sketches* (1830) vi. s.Ir. I suppose your honor will be for startin' in the mornin', LOVER *Leg.* (1848) II. 406. w.Yks.[2] His Honour Wortley. s.Pem. If your honor will please to take the turning to the village, LAWS *Little Eng.* (1888) 420.

HONOUR-BRIGHT, BET WATT, *phr.* Nhb. A protestation of honour.

Nhb.[1] Often made use of by the common people in Newcastle. It originated with, and is still retained in commemoration of, a late well-known Newcastle worthy, DENHAM *Flk-Lore Newcastle* (1855) 6.

HONTISH, *adj.* Dor. Haughty. Cf. **hountish.**

In case you should be hontish with him and lose your chance, HARDY *Tess* (1891) xii; Now there's a better-looking woman than she that nobody notices at all, because she's akin to that hontish fellow Henchard, *ib. Mayor of Casterbridge* (1886) xxxvii; Dor.[1]

[Perh. the same word as ME. *hontous,* bashful, ashamed (with change of suffix). I am ashamed and hontouse to lyue, CAXTON *Jason* (c. 1477) 42. OFr. *hontos, honteux,* 'modeste' (LA CURNE).]

HONTLE, see **Hantle.**

HOO, *sb.*[1] and *v.*[1] Sc. Yks. Lan. Chs. Also written **hooh** Ayr.; **hou** Sc. (JAM.); **huie** Bnff.[1] [h)ū.] 1. *sb.* A cry to frighten away birds; a call to attract attention.

Bnff.[1] Gee a hoo t'yir father t'cum haim till 's dainner. Cld. (JAM.) Ayr. Then Clootie ga'e a horrid hooh, *Ballads and Sngs.* (1846) I. 99.

Hence **Hoo-shoo,** (1) *int.* a word used in driving away fowls; (2) *v.* to drive or frighten away fowls. s.Chs.[1]

2. *v.* To frighten away birds; to drive away generally.

Bnff.[1] ' Awa' is often added. 'The ooster cam a nicht or twa in the gloamin', bit the hird-loons huiet 'im awa.' Cld. (JAM.)

3. To hollo, shout. Cld. (JAM.)

Hence **Hooing,** *vbl. sb.* shouting, holloing.

Ked. And noo the hooing it began, JAMIE *Muse* (1844) 103. Lnk. Foxy frae 'mang the whins steals peulin', Syne sic a hooin', sic a youlin', WATT *Poems* (1827) 98.

4. To howl; to jeer at, hoot.

w.Yks. *Yks. Wkly. Post* (Apr. 17. 1897). m.Lan.[1] s.Chs.[1] Dhùr wůz ů mon i)dhů au· ůz waan tid mai· ů speych; bů dhai ood im daayn [There was a mon i' the haw as wanted may a speich; bu' they hoo'd him daïn].

5. Of an owl: to hoot.

Sc. The houlet hou't through the riftit rock, *Edb. Mag.* (May 1820) (JAM.). s.Sc. The hoolet frae his garret gray Hoos up the glen at close o' day, WATSON *Bards* (1859) 142. Dmf. When the gray howlet has three times hoo'd, CROMEK *Remains* (1810) 276.

6. Of the wind: to moan, sigh, howl in a melancholy manner. Cld. (JAM.)

Hence (1) **Houan,** *ppl. adj.* of the wind: howling, moaning; (2) **Houin,** *vbl. sb.* the dreary whistling of the wind.

(1) Cld. Will sang the houan' win', *Edb. Mag.* (Oct. 1818) 320 (JAM.). (2) Cld. (JAM.)

HOO, *v.*[2] and *sb.*[2] Ken. Hmp. Also written **oo** Ken.[1] [ū.] 1. *v.* To simmer, boil. Hmp.[1] 2. *sb.* A simmer, boil, in phr. *on the hoo.* Hmp. (J.R.W.), Hmp.[1]

3. *Fig.* in phr. (1) *all in a hoo,* all in confusion and disorder; (2) *all of a oo;* see below.

(1) Hmp. BLACKLEY *Word Gossip* (1869) 167. (2) Ken. (G. B.); Ken.[1] ' I feel all of a oo,' I feel ill; or, ' That's all of a oo,' that is all in confusion.

HOO, *int.* Cum. Yks. Chs. Der. Lin. Nhp. Shr. Oxf. Hnt. Also in forms **hoo'e** Nhp.[1] Hnt.; **hooy** e.Yks.[1] w.Yks.; **hoûy** sw.Lin.[1]; **huigh** n.Lin.[1] [ū, ū·i.] A call used in driving pigs.

e.Yks.[1] n.Lin. *N. & Q.* (1852) 1st S. v. 375; n.Lin.[1], sw.Lin.[1] Nhp.[1] ' Hoo'e, hoo'e, hoo'e.' Used to drive away pigs, as ' Tig, tig, tig,' is to call them together; Nhp.[2] Oxf.[1] *MS. add.* Hnt. (T.P.F.)

Hence **Hoo-away,** *int.* go along. Cum.[14]

2. A call of encouragement to a dog, &c. Also used *fig.*

w.Yks. They all seemed as keen as dogs, yet specially one man, that went dancing among them doing nought that I could see but shout ' Hooy, lads ! Nah, then ! At him !' and such like little barks, SNOWDEN *Web of Weaver* (1896) i. Der. Hoo [hùu], go rive them (T.H.).

3. *Comb.* (1) **Hoo in,** an exhortation to zeal or energy in any kind of work; (2) **Hoo-leg,** (*a*) a call used in driving geese; (*b*) a call to go away.

(1) s.Chs.[1] (*a, a*) Shr.[1] (*b*) Shr. NORTHALL *Wd. Bk.* (1896) (s.v. Call-words).

HOO, *pron.* nw.Cy. Yks. Lan. Chs. Flt. Dnb. Stf. Der. Not. Wor. Glo. Also in forms **ho** Wor.; **how** Der.; **hu** Lan.; **oo** Chs.[123] s.Chs.[1]; **ou** Glo.; **ū** Der. Not.[2] [ū.] 1. She.

nw.Cy. RAY (1691); (K.) w.Yks. Huddersfield, Halifax, and those parts of w.Yks. bordering on Lan. and Der. (J.W.); Eh! but hoo is a bonnie lass (D.L.); w.Yks.[1] Seldom used except on the borders of Lan. ; **w.Yks.**²⁸ ; **w.Yks.**⁴ Rarely heard. **Lan.** Hoo'd had to nurse the poor thing, WAUGH *Rambles Lake Cy.* (1861) 3 ; An' hoo're yore second chilt, BRIERLEY *Layrock* (1864) v ; Hu could talk quoite foine, YELLOND *Triumph* (1860) 8 ; **Lan.**¹ **ne.Lan.** Hoo were some protty, bless her. MATHER *Idylls* (1895) 21 ; **ne.Lan.¹, e.Lan.¹, m.Lan.¹ aw.Lan., Chs.** Oo ossed to fattle a poi (T.C.). **Chs.** But oo did no' say owt, CROSTON *Enoch Crump* (1887) 8 ; Œu, ELLIS *Pronunc.* (1889) V. 411; Cha.¹²⁸ **s.Chs.¹** Oo sez tū, mi, 65. Fit., Dnb.? Iu, ELLIS *ib.* 453. Stf. (K.) e.Stf. Œu, ELLIS *ib.* 444. **Der.** Of hur head hoo had, as I since hard, A bone-lace cost full fourteen pence a yard, M. A. *Poems* (1668) 28 ; Molly sed how didna keer, ROBINSON *Sammy Twitcher* (1870) 9 ; Ū, eu, ɔ, ELLIS *ib.* 319 ; Der.¹ ; Der.² How's a rare firk (s.v. Firk). **nw.Der.¹** **w.Der.** wu, ELLIS *ib.* 446. **Not.², Wor.** (K.)

2. *Comp.* (1) Hoo-cat, a female cat ; (2) -Jew, a Jewess ; (3) -justice, the wife of a justice of the peace.

(1) **e.Lan.¹** (2) **Lan.** Thou'd ha' bin as rich as a hoo-Jew now, BRIERLEY *Fratchingtons* (1868) Frop i. (3) **Lan.** That th' hoo Justices awlus did mooast o th' wark, TIM BOBBIN *View Dial.* (ed. 1806) 27.

3. *He.*

w.Yks.¹ Lan. Theer's th' owd parson…Hoo's goin'to teach some one summat I warrant, BURNETT *Lowrie's* (1877) iii ; As hoo does when hoos tawkin, BRIERLEY *Layrock* (1864) vi. **ne.Glo.** 'I axed thee wheer he wur.' 'An' I towld thee ou hadn't come in… I knooaw nowt, but that ou was like to goo any day,' *Household Wds.* (1885) No. 217, 141. [GROSE (1790).]

[1. I am in drede Lest ho turne her testament, *P. Pl. Crede* (c. 1394) 412 ; Ho watʒ me nerre þen aunte or nece, *Pearl* (c. 1325) 233, in *Allit. P.* 7. OE. *hēo*, she. **2.** & ay þou meng with þe maleʒ þe mete ho-besteʒ, *Cleanness* (c. 1360) 337, in *Allit. P.* 46.]

HOO, see Hew, *v.*¹, How, *sb.*¹², *adv.*

HO(O, *int.* Cum.¹⁴ [hō.] A preliminary expletive used as some use the word ' well.'

HOOAK, HOOAL, see Hawk, *v.*, Hole, *sb.*¹, Holl, *adj.*

HOOANT, *ppl. adj.* and *sb.* **Lan.** [uǝnt.] **1.** *ppl. adj.* Swollen, hard in the flesh, fastened in the flesh.

He ses, ut I two hard hoo-ant spots ut he cun plenely feel ur goinkt o sprewt fro boouth sides o' me nob, PAUL BOBBIN *Sequel* (1819) 4 ; GROSE (1790) *MS. add.* (C.)

2. *sb.* Flesh swelled and hard from inflammation ; a swelling from inflammation.

DAVIES *Races* (1856) 234. **s.Lan.** PICTON *Dial.* (1865) 11.

HOOAR, see Her.

HOOB, *sb.* **Sh.I.** [hœb.] The ebb-shore at the head of a bay over which a rivulet spreads itself ; *gen.* used in *pl.*

Hoob is applied to a small shallow bay or bight, JAKOBSEN *Dial.* (1897) 98 ; (*Coll.* L.L.B.) ; **S. & Ork.¹**

[ON. *hōp,* a small shallow bay (FRITZNER).]

HOOCH, *int., v.* and *sb.* **Sc. Irel.** Also written **hoogh** Lnk. Dwn. ; **hough** e.Sc. Ayr. [hūχ.] **1.** *int.* An exclamation of joy, &c. ; a shout, esp. a shout used in the dancing of a reel.

Cai.¹ Elg. Hooch, Sammy, hooch, man, there's naething like siller, TESTER *Poems* (1865) 108. **Abd.** Hooch! reel, ye kitties, keep yer ribbons reelin', OGG *Willie Waly* (1873) 29. **Per.** Ha, ha ! a deuran bla', Hooch ! gars a body loup again, STEWART *Character* (1857) 21. **Ayr.** ' Hooch, hooch,' said David laughing, HUNTER *Studies* (1870) 95. **Lnk.** Then hoogh for her bonnie young Queen, RODGER *Poems* (1838) 34, ed. 1897.

2. *v.* To cry ' hooch,' to shout.

Sh.I. Dey … began at ence ta irp an' flite Ipa da folk for hoochin twartree times a Yûl-day, *Sh. News* (Jan. 29, 1898). **Frf.** A' day lang he hooched an' shooed till he was as dry as a whistle, WILLOCK *Rosetty Ends* (1886) 182, ed. 1889. **Per.** Gran'faither is hoochin' an' crackin' his thooms, FORD *Harp* (1893) 217. **Flf.** Tom and Elshin were in the middle o' the floor, hoochin' and whirlin' aboot on their taes like mad, McLAREN *Tibbie* (1894) 111. **Slg.** Those that canna dance or sing, 'ill clap their hands and hooch, TOWERS *Poems* (1885) 187. **Ayr.** The lads hooched and loupit, JOHNSTON *Glenbuckie* (1889) 176; Telt them sleely ne'er to hough Till safe frae oot the wood, WHITE *Jottings* (1879) 237. **Lnk.** They hooched an' heyed, an' loupt an' flang, ORR *Laigh Flichts* (1882) 48. **Lth.** Even when looking on they capered and 'hooched' (i.e. shouted merrily). 'Tammas, Tammas! ye're forgettin' yersel',' STRATHESK *Blinkbonny* (ed. 1891) 37.

Hence **Hooching**, *vbl. sb.* the shouting or crying of ' hooch.'

---

ne.Sc. There was … little art in their dances, but a tremendous deal of ' hooching' and ' hiching,' *Gordonhaven* (1887) 71. **e.Sc.** Now there is little heart in the ' houghing,' SETOUN *Sunshine* (1895) 20. **Rnf.** Wi' hoochin' and crackin' his whup, The youngsters around him cam staring, WEBSTER *Rhymes* (1835) 83. **Lth.** Whan the prodigal came hame, there was not only dancin', but there maun a' been hoochin', STRATHESK *More Bits* (ed. 1885) 295.

3. *sb.* The exclamation used in dancing reels ; a shout, hollo.

Sh.I. He could noo hear da hoochs an' skreichs, o' da folk, an' da barkin' o' da dugs, *Sh. News* (July 31, 1897). **Abd.** The gentlemen taking the change of time as the signal to snap their thumbs rapidly over their heads, and utter a wild ' hooch,' ALEXANDER *Ain Flk.* (1882) 246. **Dwn.** Mat … every now and then uttered a ' hoogh !' which could be heard above the noise of the stamping feet upon the earthen floor, LYTTLE *Betsy Gray* (1894) 25.

4. The sound made by narrowing the lips and blowing the breath ; a smell, savour.

Frf. ' I jist took the drappie masel',' but he hastened to add, ' I gied her the booch o't,' INGLIS *Ain Flk.* (1895) 159; (G.W.)

HOOCH, HOOD, see Hootch, Hide, *v.*²

HOOD, *sb.*¹ and *v.*¹ Var. dial. uses in Sc. Irel. and Eng. Also in forms **heud** Cum.¹⁴; **hod** Dmf. n.Cy. w.Yks.²; hud Sc. (JAM.) N.I.¹ N.Cy.¹ Nhb.¹ Cum.¹⁴ n.Yks. Yks.¹ w.Yks.²⁸⁴ Chs.¹ n.Lin.¹ Lei.¹ Wil.¹ Som. ; **hudd** Sc. (JAM.) Gall. Cum. ; **hudde** e.Yks. ; **hude** Sc. (JAM.) ; ud w.Yks. [h]ud, h]ʉd, uid.] **1.** *sb.* In phr. *to have one's hood on*, to take offence, be angry.

n.Lin.¹ Harry got i'to truble on Frida', an' his muther's hed her hood on iver sin'.

2. A large calico bonnet worn by women when working in the fields.

n.Yks. (I.W.) **Brks.¹** It is a poke bonnet which shades the face from the sun, and which has an enormous flap covering the neck, shoulders, and upper part of the back.

3. *Comp.* Hud-lark, the skylark, *Alauda arvensis.*

Chs.¹ So called from its crest or hood.

4. A game ; see below.

Lin. At Haxey, a game called ' the hood ' is played annually on Jan. 6, in commemoration, it is said, of the loss and recovery of her hood by a certain lady of the Mowbray family many centuries ago. … The hood, which consists of a stiff roll of leather, is thrown up in the middle of the open field, on the borders of which are posted four official players, called ' boggans' … whose office it is to prevent the carrying away of the hood from the field, *N. & Q.* (1883) 6th S. vii. 147; In the parish of Epworth a similar game is played under the same name but with some variations. The hood is not here carried away from the field, but to certain goals, against which it is struck three times and then declared free. This is called ' wyking' the hood, which is afterwards thrown up again for a fresh game, *ib.* 148 ; GOMME *Games* (1894) 221. **n.Lin.¹** Played at Haxey, in the Isle of Axholme, on the sixth of January. ' The hood is a piece of sacking, rolled tightly up and well corded, and which weighs about six pounds. This is taken into an open field, on the north side of the church, about two o'clock in the afternoon, to be contended for by the youths assembled for that purpose. When the hood is about to be thrown up, the plough bullocks or boggins, as they are called, dressed in scarlet jackets, are placed among the crowd at certain distances. Their persons are sacred, and if amidst the general row the hood falls into the hands of one of them the sport begins again. The object of the person who seizes the hood is to carry off the prize to some public-house in the town, where he is rewarded with such liquor as he chooses to call for,' STONEHOUSE *Isle of Axholme*, 291.

5. A finger-stall or finger of a glove.

Wil. If you cuts your finger bad, you ought to put a hud upon it to prevent the dirt getting in (W.C.P.) ; SLOW *Gl.* (1892) ; **Wil.¹ Som.** He've a-got huds to his fingers (W.F.R.) ; SWEETMAN *Wincanton Gl.* (1885).

Hence (1) **Huddick**, (2) **Hudkin**, *sb.* the finger of a glove ; a finger-stall.

(1) **Wil.** SLOW *Gl.* (1892); **Wil.¹ Som.** SWEETMAN *Wincanton Gl.* (1885). (2) **Nrf.** (E.M.), **Suf.¹,** e.**Suf.** (F.H.)

6. The skin or outer shell of a walnut. **Wor.** (W.C.B.)

7. A sheaf of corn placed on the top of a ' stook ' to keep off the rain. Also in *comp.* Hood-sheaf. See Hooder.

Sc. (JAM.), **Nhb.¹, Cum.¹⁴ Wm.** Tak a bit o' pains wi' t'hoods as it'll likely rain (B.K.). **n.Yks.** Wheat and rye are set up in shocks of twelve or ten sheaves each, two of which are invariably used as hood-sheaves, Tuke *Agric.* (1800) 115. e.Yks. Marshall *Rur. Econ.* (1796) I. 350. w.Yks.[1] s.Chs.[1] The two end sheaves of the hattock are used as hoods for the remaining six. Midl. Marshall *Rur. Econ.* (1796) II. Shr.[1], Hmp. (H.E.) [These last inclining sheaves are called hood-sheaves, and are intended by their drooping position, to ward off the rain from the corn in the body of the stook, Stephens *Farm Bk.* (ed. 1849) II. 324.]

8. The 'hob' or shelf at the side of a fireplace on which pots, &c. are put to boil.

Dmf. The flat plate which covers the side of a grate (Jam.). N.Cy.[1], Nhb.[1] Cum. Auld Wulson...Clwose by th' huddsat gruntin, Gilpin *Sngs.* (1866) 282 ; Ye've gien it [chimney] ower mickle draft, yan can trust nought on t'hud for 't, Dickinson *Cumbr.* (1876) 282 ; Cum.[14], Wm. (B.K.), n.Yks. (I.W.) ne.Yks.[1] Sometimes now applied to the hobs of an ordinary iron fire-grate. e.Yks. 'As black as hud.' Hud is the hob of a fireplace, Nicholson *Flk-Sp.* (1889) 16. m.Yks.[1] w.Yks. Willan *List Wds.* (1811) ; w.Yks.[24] n.Lin.[1] The flat-topped side of a fire-place, on which a tea-kettle or small pan can be placed.

9. *Comp.* (1) Hood-end, the flat surface or 'hob ' at either side of a fireplace on which the kettle, &c. is placed ; (2) -nook, the corner beside the fireplace ; also used *fig.* ; (3) -stone, see (1).

(1) n.Yks.[1] ; n.Yks.[2] Prob. so called from their situation beneath the old-fashioned chimney vent which projected like a hood into the room. n.Yks.[4], ne.Yks.[1], m.Yks.[1], e.Yks.[1] w.Yks. Put that pan on t'ud end (Æ.B.) ; w.Yks.[1] Squat thysel down a bit i' th' langsettle, by th' hud-end, ii. 309 ; w.Yks.[45], n.Lin.[1] (2) s.Sc. Nae mair we by the biel hud-nook Sit hale fore-sippers owr a book, T. Scott *Poems* (1793) 317. Wm. He was sittin i' t'hud-neuk (B.K.). (3) n.Cy. Grose (1790) *MS. add.* (P.) Nhb. Jack Roe was . . . leanin on the hud steahyn, Bewick *Tyneside Tales* (1850) 10. w.Yks.[2]

10. The back of a fireplace ; a stone at the side of a fire-place used as a seat.

Sc. There is a species of clay which the smiths use for fixing their bellows in their furnaces and of which the country people make what they call, Hudds, to set in their chimnies behind their fires, *Statist. Acc.* II. 289 (Jam.). Slk., Dmf. The back of a fire-place, made of stone and clay, built somewhat like a seat. Also called the cat-hud (Jam.). Dmf. The back of the fire-place built of stone or clay, somewhat like a seat ; applied now to the spaces [shelves] on each side, Shaw *Schoolmaster* (1899) 349. Tev. The seat opposite to the fire on a blacksmith's hearth (Jam.). Gall. (W.G.) n Cy. Grose (1790) ; (K.) ne.Yks.[1] Ends or corners of old-fashioned open fireplaces, holding space for seats. e.Yks. They take the stickes and sette them up an ende, slanttinge against the hudde ; and keep a good fire under them, Best *Rur. Econ.* (1641) 122 ; Marshall *Rur. Econ.* (1788) ; w.Yks.[1]

11. *Comp.* Hud-stone, a flag-stone set on edge as a back to a fire on a cottage hearth.

Rxb. Heard the cricket chirp ahint the black hud-stane, Telfer *Ballads* (1824) *Auld Ringan.* Tev., Dmf. (Jam.)

12. A small enclosure or shelf built at the side of a fire-place ; see below.

Sc. There was the cutty still lying on the hud, *Blackw. Mag.* (Nov. 1820) 203 (Jam.). Dmf. A small enclosure at the side of the fire, formed by means of two stones set erect, with one laid across as a cover, in which a tobacco-pipe, or any other small object, is laid up, in order to its being properly preserved and at hand when there is use for it (Jam.). Nhb.[1]

13. A portion of a wall, built with single stones or with stones which go from side to side.

Gall. He . . . invented also snecks or hudds, i. e. spaces built at short intervals, *Agric. Surv.* 86 (Jam.).

Hence Hud-stone, *sb.* a stone used in building a 'hud.'

Gall. One hudd-stone will do at the grass ; but the more the better. When a double dyke between the hudds is built as high as the first hudd-stone, a stone sufficiently long is placed so that one half of it may cover the hudd, and the other half the double dyke, *Agric. Surv.* 86 (Jam.).

14. *v.* To cover corn 'stooks' with two sheaves.

Sc. (Jam.) Slk. The crop . . . all standing in tight shocks, rowed and hooded, Hogg *Tales* (1838) 48, ed. 1866. Ir. They were hooding stooks below at Hilfirthy's, Barlow *Idylls* (1892) 210. n.Yks. (I.W.) w.Yks.[2] To hood corn is to cover it in the shock with sheaves so that the rain may fall off. Lei.[1] To ' hud' corn is to put it up in shocks, the lower sheaves being hooded by the upper ones, which are placed with the ears downwards.

Hence Hooden- or Hudden-sheaves, *sb. pl.* the sheaves placed on the top of a ' stook ' of corn to turn off the rain. N.I.[1]

HOOD, *sb.*[2] Nhp. Hrf. Glo. Wil. Som. Dev. Cor. Also written ood Hrf.[2] Glo.[12] Wil.[1] Cor.[2]; and in form hude Dev.[2] [ud.] **1.** Dial. form of ' wood.'

Nhp.[2], Hrf.[2], Glo.[12], Wil.[1] Dev. Tha happle-tree among tha trees uv tha hood, Baird *Sng. Sol.* (1860) ii. 3 ; A goed to the hood, and a got a crooked steck, Bowring *Lang.* (1866) L 37 ; Dev.[2] s.Dev. Fox *Kingsbridge* (1874). s.Dev., e.Cor. (Miss D.) Cor. I was going through a hood, Tregellas *Tales*, 69 ; Cor.[2]

Hence (1) Hoodwood, *sb.* a forest ; (2) Hoodycock, *sb.* the woodcock, *Scolopax rusticula* ; (3) Hude-wahl or Hoodle, *sb.* (a) the green woodpecker, *Gecinus viridis* ; (b) the nightingale, *Daulias luscinia.*

(1) Cor. Thomas *Randigal Rhymes* (1895) Gl. (2) s.Dev., e.Cor. (Miss D.) (3, a) Dev.[2], n.Dev. (C.L.-P.) (b) Glo.[2] 53.

2. Underwood, brushwood ; firewood made up into faggots. Som. (W.W.S.), Cor.[3]

Hence Hooding, *prp.* gathering sticks for fuel. Nhp.[2]

HOOD, *v.*[2] Yks. [ūd, uid.] With *up*: to hoard up, keep, treasure. n.Yks. (I.W.), w.Yks. (J.W.)

HOODALL, HOODAWL, see **Hickwall.**

HOODED, *ppl. adj.* Sc. Also Nrf. **1.** In *comb.* (1) Hooded crow, (a) the black-headed gull, *Larus ridibundus* ; (b) the carrion crow, *Corvus corone* ; see **Hoodie** ; (2) — mew, see (1, a).

(1, a) Or.I. The Pewit Gull . . . here called the hooded crow, Barry *Hist.* (1805) 303 (Jam.) ; In summer, the head and upper part of the neck are a deep dark brown, hence the name, Swainson *Birds* (1885) 208. S. & Ork.[1] e.Lth. Swainson *ib.* (b) Sc. (Jam.) ; Edmonston *Gl.* (1866). Nrf. Only one species of bird appears really contented, and that is the hooded crow, Patterson *Man and Nat.* (1895) 12. (2) Or.I., e.Lth. Swainson *ib.* [Morris *Birds* (1857).]

2. Tufted, having a hood or tuft on the head.

Gall. Soon an ingle was brought ben, And soon they plucked the hoodet hen, Nicholson *Poet. Wks.* (1814) 74, ed. 1897.

HOODENING, see **Hodening.**

HOODER, *sb.* and *v.* Yks. Chs. Der. Shr. Also written hudder w.Yks.[2] Chs.[1] [u·də(r).] **1.** *sb.* A sheaf of corn placed on a ' stook ' to keep off the rain. *Gen.* in *pl.* See Hood, *sb.*[1] 7.

w.Yks.[12] Chs.[1] The two sheaves which are placed, corn downwards, on the top of the stooks or riders, to throw off the rain ; Chs.[2] nw.Der.[1], Shr.[1]

2. *v.* To place protecting sheaves on the corn 'stooks.' Chs.[1], s.Chs.[1]

HOODICK, see **Höder.**

HOODIE, *sb.* Sc. n.Cy. Nhb. Yks. Nrf. Also in forms hiddie- ne.Sc. ; hoddie Sc. ; hoddy s.Sc. ; huddie n.Cy.; huddy Per. (Jam.) Lnk. **1.** The hooded crow, *Corvus cornix.* Also applied to the carrion crow, *C. corone.*

Mry., Per. So called from its black head and throat, contrasted with the grey plumage of back and belly, Swainson *Birds* (1885) 85. Per. There are also carrion crows (hoddies, as they are called here), *Statist. Acc.* XIX. 498 (Jam.) ; It . . . hunts the hoodies frae the bog, Spence *Poems* (1898) 98. s.Sc. Swainson *ib.* 83. Lth. I was as hoarse as a hoodie for a whole week afterwards, Lumsden *Sheep-head* (1892) 229. e.Lth. ' As hoarse as a hoodie' with speechifying, Mucklebackit *Rhymes* (1885) 130. Feb. Like corby craw, or hoody gray, Lintoun *Green* (1685) 39, ed. 1817. Slk. Scrauchin like pyats on the leads or a hoodie wi' a sair throat, Chr. North *Noctes* (ed. 1856) III. 11. Kcb. Upon an ash above the lin, A hoody has her nest, Davidson *Seasons* (1789) 4. n.Cy. Smith *Birds* (1887) 237. Nhb.[1] Called also the grey-back'd craa and the corby. Yks. *Yks. Whly. Post* (Dec. 31, 1898). Nrf. Cozens-Hardy *Broad Nrf.* (1893) 45.

2. *Comp.* Hoodie-crow, the hooded and carrion crow, *C. cornix* and *C. corone.*

Sc. Deil a black cloak will be there, Robin, but the corbies and the hoodie-craws, Scott *Rob Roy* (1817) xxiii. n.Sc. Wi' a face like a hoodie-craw, Gordon *Carglen* (1891) 54. ne.Sc. The guile, the Gordon, an the hiddie-craw Is the three worst things that Moray ever saw, Gregor *Flk-Lore* (1881) 111. Mry. Thy Lawyers—plentiful as slaes, or as the hoodie-craw, Hay *Linsie* (1851) 54. Elg. The hoody-craws perch on the porch, Couper *Poetry* (1804) II. 91. Frf. The gullet of a hoodie craw, Beattie

Arnha (c. 1820) 37, ed. 1882. **Per.** Howlets, Kaes, and huddy-craws Haud consultations, STEWART *Character* (1857) 97. **Ayr.** A cushie-doo would croodle frae its nest in the firs, or a hoodie-craw skraik far up in the lift, SERVICE *Notandums* (1890) 63; Some bewilder'd chicken Scar'd frae its minnie and the cleckin By hoodie-craw, BURNS *Verses at Selkirk* (May 13, 1787). **Lnk.** Swarm like nests o' huddy craws, NICHOLSON *Kilwuddie* (ed. 1895) 25. **e.Lth.** A hoodie-craw, sittin on a dyke by a fa'n yowe, an' shairpenin its beak to pike her bones, HUNTER *J. Inwick* (1895) 126. **Slk.** The hoody-craw dursna pick there, HOGG *Tales* (1838) 16, ed. 1866. **Dmf.** The gled pykes the banes o' the auld hoodie craw, CROMEK *Remains* (1810) 118. **Gall.** I'll gie the hoodie craws a drap drink o't, CROCKETT *Moss-Hags* (1895) xli ; Carrion, or grey, crows, called 'hoodicraws'; for when they get old they become white in colour, all but the feathers of the head ; these keep black, and look as if the bird had on a cowl or hud [hood], MACTAGGART *Encycl.* (1824) 275, ed. 1876.

3. *? Obs.* A hired mourner.

Sc. This designation seems to have originated from their wearing hoods (JAM.).

HOODING, *sb.* Sc. Irel. Nhb. Dur. Lan. Nhp. Also in forms **heudin** N.Cy.[1] Nhb.[1] Nhp.[1]; **hoddin** ne.Lan.[1]; **hooden** N.I.[1] The leather strap or thong connecting the handstaff and the souple of a flail.

Lth., Rxb. (JAM.) **N.I.**[1] Called also the Mid-kipple. **N.Cy.**[1] **Nhb.** He left nae mare skin on her aw Then wad been a heudin to a flail, BELL *Rhymes* (1812) 149 ; **Nhb.**[1] A piece of cow-hide lashed on to the end of the soople, or swingle of a flail in the form of an eye. A piece of leather called a couplin passes through the heudin and connects the movable arm, or soople, with the handstaff. *Obsol.* **Dur.**[1], ne.Lan.[1], Nhp.[1]

HOODLE, see **Huddle.**

HOODLE-CUM-BLIND, *sb.* Nhp.[1] The game of 'blind-man's buff.'

HOODLING HOW, *phr.* *Obs.* Sc. A kind of cap. See **How,** *sb.*[2]

An auld band, and a hoodling how, HERD *Coll. Sngs.* (1776) II. 144 (JAM.).

HOODOCK, *adj.* *Obs.* Sc. Like a 'hoodie' or carrion crow, foul and greedy.

Ayr. The harpy, hoodock, purse-proud race, BURNS *Ep. to Maj. Logan* (Oct. 30, 1786).

HOODWALL, see **Hickwall.**

HOODWINK, *sb.* Lakel. Chs. Shr. **1.** In phr. *in hood-wink,* in hiding. **Lakel.**[2] They've a few cotters i' hoodwink.

2. *pl.* Two sheaves of corn inverted over a 'stook' of corn to keep out the rain. Chs.[1], Shr.[1] See **Hooder.**

HOODY, *sb.* Wm. [hū·di.] A country girl or woman.

Sir Alan's daughter donned herself like a country hoody, BRIGGS *Remains* (1825) 158 ; (E.W.P.)

HOOF, *sb.* and *v.* Wm. Yks. Lan. Chs. Lei. War. Shr. Glo. Amer. Also in forms **hof**· s.Chs.[1]; **hoove** w.Yks.[123] ne.Lan.[1] **1.** *sb.* In *comp.* (1) **Hoof-band,** a hair-rope used to tie the legs of a kicking cow ; (2) **-lock,** the fetlock of a horse ; also used *fig.*

(1) s.Chs.[1] (2) **Shr.**[1] Whad 'uflocks 'er 'as !—bif to the anclers like a Lancashire bullock.

2. *pl.* The coltsfoot, *Tussilago Farfara.*

Wm. (J.H.) **Glo.** In allusion to the shape of the leaves (B. & H.) ; **Glo.**[1]

3. Hard skin on the hands caused by hard work.

w.Yks.[2]; **w.Yks.**[5] Sometimes hurriers in coal pits will have hooves on their heads, from constantly pushing the carts.

Hence **Hoofed** or **Hooved,** *ppl. adj.* callous, hard, horny. Also used *fig.*

w.Yks.[1]; **w.Yks.**[2] 'He's hoofed to it,' hardened or accustomed to it. **ne.Lan.**[1]

4. *v.* To walk, trudge, go on foot.

Lan. The frost being quite thawed, it was more troublesome hoofing, BYROM *Remin.* (1744) in *Cheth. Soc.* XLIV. 373. **Lei.**[1] Way mut hoof it. 'Hoof it !' is often used for 'begone !' **War.**[2] [Amer. *Kansas Univ. Quar.* (1892) I.]

HOOF, HOOG, HOOGER, HOOGO, HOOGY, see **Hoaf, Howf(f, Hug,** *v.,* **Hogger, Hogo, Howgy.**

HOO-HOO, *sb.* Nhb. A prostitute ; a wicked person.

A greet fat chep, wi' horns a pair, Was dancin' wi' some hoo-hoos there, ROBSON *Bards of Tyne* (1849) 36 ; Aw'll nut let a hoo-hoo ippeer a sweet saint, *Keelman's Ann.* (1869) 6.

HOOI, *v.* and *sb.* Hmp. w.Cy. [ūi.] **1.** *v.* Of the wind : to whistle, moan, sigh.

Hmp. WISE *New Forest* (1883) 186. **w.Cy.** The west-countryman says the wind 'hooïs' when it soughs among the trees, *Poetry Provinc.* in *Cornh. Mag.* (1865) XII. 37.

2. *sb.* The sound made by the wind whistling round a corner or through a keyhole.

Hmp. (J.R.W.) ; WISE *New Forest* (1883) 186 ; **Hmp.**[1]

HOOIE, *v.* and *sb.* Sc. [hū·i.] **1.** *v.* To exchange, barter, 'swop.'

Fif. Properly where no 'boot' is given (JAM.) ; Only of exchanging knives. In use among boys in Dundee (W.A.C.).

2. *sb.* An exchange, barter. Fif. (JAM.)

HOOIN, HOOISHT, see **Hoin,** *v.,* **Husht.**

HOOK, *sb.*[1] and *v.*[1] Var. dial. uses in Sc. Irel. and Eng. Also in forms **heak** m.Yks.[1] ; **heuck** Sc. N.Cy.[1] Cum. ; **heuk** Sc. Cai.[1] N.Cy.[1] Nhb. Cum.[14] n.Yks.[48] ; **hewk** e.Yks. ; **heyuk** Nhb.[1] ; **huck** Nhb. Wor. Hrf. ; **huik** Sc. ; **huke** Sc. (JAM.) N.Cy.[1] Dur.[1] n.Yks.[124] ne.Yks. e.Yks. ; **hyeuck** Abd. ; **hyeuk** N.I.[1] ; **hyuck** S. & Ork.[1] Fif. ; **hyuk** Nhb.[1] ; **yuck** Cum.[4] e.Yks.[1] ; **yuk** n.Yks. ne.Yks.[1] [uk, iuk, hŏk.] **1.** *sb.* In *comp.* (1) **Hook-a-back,** the bush vetch, *Viccia cracca* ; (2) **-busser,** a person who dresses fly-hooks ; (3) **-fingered,** thievish, dishonest ; (4) **-finnie,** lucky, fortunate ; (5) **-fishes,** fishes caught by hooks ; (6) **-ful, see** (3) ; (7) **-lug,** a long slender pole with a hooked end, for shaking the branches of trees in order to get the fruit ; (8) **-seams,** hooks or panniers to carry turf, lead, &c.

(1) **Cum.**[4] (s.v. Hug-a-back). (2) **s.Sc.** I never see auld Isaac Fletcher, the huik-busser, .. but I think on him, CUNNINGHAM *Sketches* (1894) xiv. (3) **N.Cy.**[1] **Nhb.** Aw jump'd there wiv heuk-finger'd people, MIDFORD *Coll. Sngs.* (1818) 70 ; (R.O.H.) **n.Yks.**[2], **Nhp.**[1] (4) **S. & Ork.**[1] (5) **Lin.** (HALL.) (6) **n.Yks.**[2] (7) **Hrf.** (W.W.S.) (8) **n.Cy.** (HALL.) **w.Yks.**[1] Now nearly extinct.

2. *Phr.* (1) *hook and eye,* arm in arm ; (2) *to have a hook at every finger,* said of a greedy, avaricious person ; (3) *to lift off the hook,* to marry ; (4) *by the hooks,* an exclamation or mild oath ; (5) *to be off the hooks,* to be out of health ; to be in a bad temper, unsettled ; (6) *to draw the hooks over the eyes,* to captivate, transfix.

(1) **Suf.** (F.H.) (2) **Nhb.** (M.H.D.) (3) **Lnk.** She had never been, up till date, lifted off the hook... Not but what she could have been, often enough. Oh no! The offers she had refused in her day were many, MURDOCH *Readings* (ed. 1895) III. 9. (4) **Der.** Aye, by the hooks (S.O.A.). (5) **n.Lin.**[1] is oht wrong, missis, maaster seems clear off th' hooks to-daay. **Nhp.**[1] (6) **Lnk.** He's drawn the heuks owre my puir lassie's e'en, HAMILTON *Poems* (ed. 1885) 201.

3. *Fig. pl.* Anxieties, annoyances.

n.Yks.[2] 'Poverty's yan o' my heuks,' one of my adherents.

4. The hinge of a field-gate on which the staple or gudgeon works. Yks. (J.W.), Chs.[1]

5. A downward bend given to the ends of the axle to make them fit properly into the nave of a wheel.

Chs.[1] Formerly carts had wooden arms, the arms being the ends of the axle or bed, thinned and tapered to work in the naves of the wheels, and it required a skilful workman to work the arms properly and give them the proper hook or downward bend (s.v. Cart).

6. A wooden shoulder-yoke for carrying pails. e.Yks.[1]

7. A bend or turning in a river ; the land enclosed by such a bend.

Bwk. The hooks and crooks o' Lambden Burn, Fill the bowie and fill the kirn, HENDERSON *Pop. Rhymes* (1856) 11. **n.Lin.**[1] Th' packit pick'd up th' body just agaïn th' Hook.

8. A piece of land situated on a slope. Nhp.[2], Pem. (E.D.)

9. A reaping-hook, a sickle.

Sc. If a wench quean rin away from her hairst ye'll send her back to her heuck again, SCOTT *Redg.* (1824) vii ; *Scoticisms* (1787) 44. **Cai.**[1] **Elg.** Ilka day that shines, Smiles for the plough, or for the hook, COUPER *Poetry* (1804) L 102. **Abd.** Scythes and heuks for the shearers, ANDERSON *Rhymes* (1867) 138. **Fif.** Rapidly gleamed the hyucks in sturdy hands, COLVILLE *Vernacular* (1899) 13. **Rnf.** Ilka heuk, an' auld pleugh pettle, WEBSTER *Rhymes* (1835) 31. **Ayr.** [She] daunered with her heuck and pock at the dyke-sides scutching a wheen nettles for her swine, SERVICE *Dr. Duguid* (ed. 1887) 67. **Lth.** Nae hooks are noo, ava,

ava, But muckle machines hae a', hae a', LUMSDEN *Sheep-head* (1892) 237. **Edb.** The master looks To see gin a' his fowk ha'e hooks, *Har'st Rig* (1794) 9, ed. 1801. **N.I.[1], N.Cy.[1] Nhb.** When coorn cam forrit fast, it gav us muckle grief, For 'twas cutten up wi' heuks, and gether'd wi' the neif, CHATT *Poems* (1866) 86; Distinguished from a sickle, which is broad-bladed, with a knife edge, the hyuk is a narrow crescent, with fine saw like teeth at the edge. 'A bad shearer nivvor gat a good hyuk,' *Prov.* (R.O.H.) ; **Nhb.[1]** A ' cruck' is bent to a right angle ; a hyuk is bent round like a loop. **Dur.[1] Cum.[4]** Armed wid a sickle or a heuk, C. Pacq. (Aug. 31, 1893) 6. **w.Yks.** (R.H.H.), **nw.Der.[1], Ken.[1] Dev.** Each holds aloft his hook, BRAY *Desc. Tamar and Tavy* (1836) I. 330. **nw.Dev.[1]**

Hence (1) **Hook-penny**, *sb.* a penny per week given to reapers in addition to their wages ; (2) *throwing the hooks, phr.*, see below.

(1) **Lth.** (JAM.) **Edb.** 'Hook-penny,' which each shearer is in use to ask and receive weekly over and above their pay, *Har'st Rig* (1794) 37, ed. 1801. (2) **Lth., Tev.** This is done immediately after 'crying the kirn.' The 'bandster' collects all the reaping-hooks ; and, taking them by the points, throws them upwards: and whatever be the direction of the point of the hook, it is supposed to indicate the quarter in which the individual, to whom it belongs, is to be employed as a reaper in the following harvest. If any of them fall with their points sticking in the ground, the persons are to be married before next harvest ; if any one of them break in falling, the owner is to die before another harvest (JAM.).

10. *Fig.* A reaper ; a shearer.

Abd. Their 'hyeucks' had 'kempit' side by side through the hairst. . . At the hour appointed, Eastie's 'hyeucks' had gone out to take 'klyock' by the light of the moon, ALEXANDER *Rur. Life* (1877) iii. **Edb.** What think ye they were gien for hooks [shearers]? . . A shillin's gaen, *Har'st Rig* (1794) st. 127, ed. 1801.

11. A bill-hook ; a cutting implement ; a chopper.

Suf. (C.T.), (H.H.), **Suf.[1] Ken.[1]** An agricultural tool for cutting, of which there are several kinds. **w.Som.[1]** A bill-hook for chopping wood. All other kinds of hooks have a descriptive prefix. A carpenter pointing out bad work in some sash frames, said, ' Nif I widn chop em out way a hook, and stick em way a board-nail better-n that there is, I'd ate em 'thout zalt!' **nw.Dev.[1]** Applied only to a cutting instrument.

Hence **Hooked**, *pp.* applied to a saw when its teeth are so pointed as to catch the wood instead of cutting smoothly. **w.Som.[1]** In other districts the saw is said to be 'too rank,' here it is always 'too hooked.'

12. *Comp.* **Hook-bill**, a hatchet. **War.[24]**, s.**War.[1]**

13. The hip of a man or animal. Cf. **hock,** *sb.[1]*

n.Cy. GROSE (1790). **Lakel.[2] Cum.** Of a cow: 'She's rare and wide across t'heuks.' 'To slip his heuk,' dislocation (of a person). A not uncommon accident to a cow or a horse by which a morsel of the projecting hip bone is knocked out of place under the skin (J.Ar.); Girt bags, stufft weh nowt, on ther heucks, SARGISSON *Joe Scoap* (1881) 17 ; **Cum.[14] Wm.** Strayed, two Herdwick ewes ; marked red pop near shoulder and near hook, *Advt., Wm. Gazette* (Feb. 3, 1900) ; A pain catches me fair across t'hiux (B.K.). **n.Yks.** (T.S.) ; **n.Yks.[1]** ; **n.Yks.[2]** ' I've nivver crook'd my huke to-day,' never bent myself to sit down or rest myself ; **n.Yks.[3]**, **ne.Yks.[1]** ; **e.Yks.** MARSHALL *Rur. Econ.* (1788). **m.Yks.[1]**

Hence (1) **Hook-bone**, *sb.* the hip-bone ; (2) **Huke-sore**, *adj.* sore or stiff in the hips.

(1) **n.Sc.** (JAM.) **Fif.** Heukbanes and shrine were now nae miss't, TENNANT *Papistry* (1827) 153. **Edb.** Lamb, beef, mutton . . . in roasting and boiling pieces—spar-rib, jigget, shoulder and heuk-bane, MOIR *Mansie Wauch* (1828) xix ; By huke-bane fleshers always understand the haunch-bone (JAM.). **N.Cy.[1]**, **n.Yks.[1][2][4]** (2) **n.Yks.[2]**

14. *Fig.* A pile, heap.

w.Yks. Look theer whot a greyt hewk o' wool they han ready fur th' cart (D.L.).

15. *v.* In *phr.* (1) *to hook on with,* (2) *— together,* to associate with ; to marry ; (3) *— off,* to leave off work.

(1) **e.Yks.[1]** MS. *add.* (T.H.) (2) **w.Wor.** To huck 'em togither, S. BEAUCHAMP *Grantley Grange* (1874) II. 283. (3) **Chs.** *Sheaf* (1879) I. 266 ; **Chs.[1]**

16. To grab, seize hold of.

Cum.[4] She heuks his lugs wid yah fist an' a kebby wid t'udder an' gaes for him pell-mell, *W. C. T. X.* (1895) 3, col. 4.

Hence **Heuking, Heuksome, Heuky,** *adj.* avaricious, restless ; urgent.

n.Yks.[2] 'Of a heuking turn.' 'As heuksome as a dog's hairy,' anxious all over, as the wretch who said he felt a desire for money in every pore of his skin. Also, ' a heuky sort of a body,' who ' hooks on,' or takes you by the button to detain you for gossip.

17. To tighten a girth, strap, or chain. e.**Yks.[1]**

18. *Fig.* To cheat, deceive, hoax.

s.Not. A think a hooked 'em pretty well, for all their cleverness (J.P.K.).

19. To cut with a hook or sickle.

Bdf. Beans, though reaped like wheat with a sickle, are said to be hooked (J.W.B.).

Hence **Hooker**, *sb.* a reaper, a worker with a hook or sickle.

Per. He convened and hired hookers or shearers on the Sabbath in time of harvest, PARKER *Bk. of Perth* (1847) 249.

20. To pick out, extricate, poke out ; to jerk ; to lift up. Cf. **huck,** *v.[2]*

e.Yks.[1] I.W. Not necessarily with a hook (J.D.R.).

21. To carry along.

Yks. I'm tired of hooking this willow bough (S.K.C.).

HOOK, *v.[2]* and *sb.[2]* In *gen.* dial. and slang use in Sc. and Eng. **1.** *v.* To run away, make off, esp. in *phr. to hook it.*

Sc. (G.W.) ; (A.W.) **Sh.I.** We hookit hit as hard as we could oot aroond da hoose, BURGESS *Sketches* (2nd ed.) 86. **Lakel.[2] w.Yks.** Robert thowt his best plan was to hook it, HARTLEY *Dial.* (1868) 90 ; **w Yks.[2] Lan.** He's hookin' it, BRIERLEY *Out of Work,* iii. **s.Lan.** (F.R.C.) **I.Ma.** You'd better be hookin, BROWN *Witch* (1889) 43. **Midl.** Gi' the whistle an' hook it, BARTRAM *People of Clopton* (1897) 188. **Not.[1], n.Lin.[1], War.[2] Lon.** And so he hooks it, MAYHEW *Lond. Labour* (1851) I. 425. **e.Ken.** (G.G.) **Wil. SLOW** *Gl.* (1892). **Som.** We very zoon hooked out o' that, FRANK *Nine Days* (1879) 32. **Cor.[2]** Hook-it, you young imp. **Slang.** I'd wish, if you please, for to hook it away, GILBERT *Bab Ballads, Precocious Baby* ; He give me . . . four half bulls . . . and ses Hook it! DICKENS *Blk. House* (1853) xlvi.

2. *sb.* Phr. *to take* or *sling one's hook,* to run away, make off.

w.Yks. Awl gi thee one on th' nooase if tha doesn't tak thi hook, *Yksman.* (1890) 168 ; **w.Yks.[2], s.Lan.** (F.R.C.) **Cha.** You take your hook and be off (*ib.*). **Lin.** He admitted taking his hook with the half-sovereign (R.E.C.). **n.Lin.** An' soä he teks his hook back agaain, PEACOCK *Tales* (1886) 106 ; **n Lin.[1]** He heärd p'liceman cumin' coomin' soä he took his hook, an' I seed noä moore on him. **War.[2] Wor.** When he saw the policeman he slung his hook, *Evesham Jrn.* (Nov. 6, 1897). **Cant.** When I was about fourteen I slung my 'ook and joined some travellin' Barks, CAREW *Autob. Gipsy* (1891) xxxv.

HOOK, *sb.[3] Obs.* Rut. A term in land measuring.

Rut.[1] One Hooke at Wynge Dike, *Glaston Terrier* (1635).

HOOK, *v.[3]* Hmp. I.W. Wil. Dor. Som. Dev. Also in forms **hoak** Som. ; **hoke** w.Som.[1] n.Dev. ; **uck** Wil. To thrust with the horns, to gore, applied to horned cattle. Cf. **huck,** *v.[2]*

Hmp. Cows are said to 'hook' a person down (J.R.W.); **Hmp.[1] I.W.[2]** Mind the wold cow don't hook ee. **Wil.** The cow ucked the fogger with her horn, JEFFERIES *Gt. Estate* (1880) 78, ed. 1881 ; **Wil.[1] Dor.** That bull o' yourn, do 'e hook now? (C.V.G.) ; **Dor.[1]** They toss Ther heads to hook the dog, 175. **Som.** W. & J. *Gl.* (1873) ; JENNINGS *Obs. Dial. w.Eng.* (1825). **w.Som.[1]** Hoa'k. This word rather implies the playful thrusting of the horns. **n.Dev.** Rock *Jim an' Nell* (1867) *Gl.*

HOOK, *v.[4]* Yks. To crouch or sit over the fire.

n.Yks. He sat hooking in t'cooarner (I.W.); *Obsol.* Oor lass heeaks an' shawms ower t'fire whahl sha'll b' on her 'arse some day (R.B.).

[E Fris. *huken, hukken,* 'mit zusammengebogenen Knieen u. gekrümmtem Rücken sitzen ' (KOOLMAN).]

HOOK, see **Howk,** *v.[1]*

HOOKATIE, *adj.* Sh.I. Bowed, bent.

Huk-oti, kruk-oti, hwar rins du? JAKOBSEN *Norsk in Shet.* (1897) 112 ; **S. & Ork.[1]**

HOOK-EM-SNIVEY, *sb.* Irel. See below.

An indescribable, though simple, machine, employed by boys in playing at head and harp, EDGEWORTH *Irish Bulls* (ed. 1803) 131 ; ' Billy,' says I, ' will you sky a copper?' ' Done,' says he. . . With that I ranged them fair and even with my hook-em-snivey —up they go, *ib.* 129.

HOOKEM-SNIVEY, *adj.* Dev. Deceitful, tricky, sly.
I tellee 'onesty is tha best policy. Niver yū be up tū hookem-snivey ways, twant answer in tha long-rin! HEWETT *Peas. Sp.* (1892); The boy was full o' hookemsnivey ways, an' cunnin' as a stoat, PHILLPOTTS *Dartmoor* (1896) 43; That'll larn 'e to whine prayers 'ere, you black-'earted, 'ookem-snivey beast! *ib.* 197.

HOOKER, *sb.*[1] Sc. Yks. Lin. Shr. **1.** In *comb.* Hooker in, a traveller or person who stands outside merchants' warehouses to invite customers to enter. w.Yks.[8]
2. A large quantity; a large size.
a.Lin. Ah've bin ha'ing a look at the tonups and cabbages. What hookers they ar', sure-ly (T.H.R.). Shr.[1] *Gen.* employed in combination with 'pretty.' 'My eye! we'n got a pretty 'ooker o' tail-ends fur the fowl—the Maister hanna furgot us this time.'
3. Whisky, a 'dram.'
Elg. Sandy liket a hooker, an' brawlie I kent, The drap creatur' wad set him a speakin', TESTER *Poems* (1865) 133. w.Sc. He found the liquor so good that he took another 'hooker,' MAC-DONALD *Settlement* (1869) 223, ed. 1877.

HOOKER, *sb.*[2] Irel. A one-masted fishing-smack.
Having failed during the past three days to get from the islanders a hooker to bring himself and the cattle seized to the mainland, *Standard* (Apr. 2, 1888).

HOOKERS, *sb. pl.* Sc. Bended knees or hams, esp. in phr. *to sit on one's hookers.*
Sh.I. Settin' her doon apon her hookers apo' da flüer, *Sh. News* (Feb. 5, 1898); Ye shårely wirna tinkin' 'at I wis ta sit apo' me hookers apo' da green, *ib.* (Aug. 20, 1898); S. & Ork.[1], Cai.[1]

HOOKET, *sb.* Glo.[1] [u·kit.] A kind of axe for cutting faggots.

HOOKEY, see Hokey.

HOOKINGS, *sb. pl.* Shr.[1] [u·kinz.] Two long spells of work, with an interval of rest between.
A man who works by hookings, i. e. early and late, with an intervening 'siesta,' is said to do two days' work in the twenty-four hours. An arrangement corresponding to this, is known to miners as ' double-shift.'

HOOKLAND, *sb.* Obs. Wil. A portion of the best land in a common field, reserved for potatoes, vetches, &c., instead of lying fallow for two years. Also called Hitchland field (s.v. Hitch. *v.*[3]).
DAVIS *Agric.* (1811) vii; Wil.[1] Parts of some fields are still known as Hooklands in s.Wil., though the system has died out. Sometimes defined as 'land tilled every year.' [Hook-land, land tilled and sowed every year, WORLIDGE *Dict. Rust.* (1681).]

HOOL, *adj.* Obs. Sc. Beneficial; kind, friendly; used in prov.; see below.
'You are any [ay] hool to the house, you drite in your loof, and mool't to the burds.' Spoken to pick-thanks, who pretend great kindness to such a family, KELLY *Prov.* (1721) 383.
[Norw. dial. *holl*, kind, friendly, gracious (AASEN); ON. *hollr*, gracious, wholesome (VIGFUSSON); cp. OE. *hold*.]

HOOL, *v.* Obs. ne.Lan.[1] To shiver with cold. Cf. hurl, *v.*[2]

HOOL, see Hull, *sb.*[1], *v.*[2]

HOOLACHAN, *sb.* Sc. Nhb. Also in forms hoolakin Nhb.[1]; hullachan Sc. [hū·ləχən.] A Highland reel or Scotch dance.
Per. Dancing a Hoolachan and Jig Amang the rocks, STEWART *Character* (1857) 94. w.Sc. You may reasonably expect to find John in the Highlands, dancing the reel of Hullachan, MACDONALD *Settlement* (1869) 122, ed. 1877. Slg. Gar the rafters ring Wi' rousing reel and hullachan, TOWERS *Poems* (1885) 188. Rnf. Play up the reel o' Hullachan, BARR *Poems* (1861) 219. Nhb.[1] A reel in great favour in n.Nhb.

HOOLER, *sb.*[1] nw.Dev.[1] A roller at the back of a hay-cart, used for tightening the cart-ropes.

HOOLER, *sb.*[2] Cor.[2] Mining term: a bundle of blunt borers.

HOOLET, see Howlet.

HOOLIE-GOOL-OO-OO, *sb.* Sc. The cry of an owl, a hooting.
Banff. The quick eye or ear of the owl detected me, and I was at once greeted with his hoolie-gool-oo-oo, SMILES *Natur.* (1876) 124.

HOOLOCH, *sb.* Obs. Sc. Also in form hurloch. A falling or rolling mass; an avalanche or fall of stones, &c.
Gall. The yellest craigs for you boud yeal'd, What hoolochs down ye clanterin' reel'd, At ae gude prize, MACTAGGART *Encycl.*
VOL. III.

HOOLY, *adv., v.* and *adj.* Sc. Nhb. Dur. Cum. Wm. Also in forms heully N.Cy.[1]; hoilie Abd.; hoolyie Fif.; huelly Nhb.[1]; huilly N.Cy.[1]; hulie Sc.; huly Sc. (JAM.) Frf. Dur.[1] s.Dur. [hū·li, hö·'li.] **1.** *adv.* Slowly, carefully, gently, cautiously. Also used *attrib.* and as *int.* Cf. heely, *adv.*
Sh.I. (*Coll.* L.L.B.) Abd. But hooly, nor let your conclusions impose, ANDERSON *Rhymes* (1867) 56; Up the kirkyard he fast did jee, I wat he was na hoilie, SKINNER *Poems* (1809) 9. Frf. O hooly there, ma bonnie bairns, BEATTIE *Arnha* (c. 1820) 16, ed. 1882; Huly throw the frichtsom how His form a ghaist uprear'd,' LOWSON *Guidfollow* (1890) 239. Per. But, hoolie! an' let's understand Whaur's this new goshen! HALIBURTON *Horace* (1886) 86. Fif. Nae man did spare his faeman's bacon: Nae man cry'd, Hoolyie! Hoolyie! TENNANT *Papistry* (1827) 196. s.Sc. But, hooly, I needna say sae, T. SCOTT *Poems* (1793) 338. Rnf. Wi' awkward step she onward drited. Hooly enough, WEBSTER *Rhymes* (1835) 88. Ayr. But still the mair I'm that way bent, Something cries, 'Hooly!' BURNS *To J. Smith* (1785) st. 7; (J.M.) Lak. 'Hooly! ye silly goats!' quo' he, *Deil's Hallowe'en* (1856) 35. Lth. Tired ae e'ening, stepping hooly, Pondering on his thraward fate, MACNEILL *Poet. Wks.* (1801) 159, ed. 1856; 'A hooly prize fair won, my lad! A hooly prize!' the king cried he, LUMSDEN *Sheep-head* (1892) 32. Edb. Something cries hooly, And bids the muse to cour awee, LIDDLE *Poems* (1821) 112. Slk. I walked hooly doun to the bank, CHR. NORTH *Noctes* (ed. 1856) IV. 180. Dmf. O hooly and wae I laid her doun, REID *Poems* (1894) 128. Nhb.[1] Cum., Wm. NICOLSON (1677) *Trans. R. Lit. Soc.* (1868) IX.
Hence Huliness, *sb.* slowness, tardiness.
Lak. The trauchl't stag i' the wan waves lap, But huliness or hune, *Edb. Mag.* (May 1820) (JAM.).
2. *Phr.* (1) *hoolie and fair*, (2) — *and fairly*, fair and softly, slowly and gently.
(1) Sc. Hulie and fair, men rides far journeys, RAY *Prov.* (1678) 370; Hooly and fair goes far in a day, KELLY *Prov.* (1721) 125. (2) Sc. Let the chair down and draw it up hooly and fairly, SCOTT *Antiquary* (1816) viii; Hooly and fairly men ride far journeys, FERGUSON *Prov.* (1641) 15. w.Sc. I comforted my stamack with a leetle brandy toddy, and sooked it aff hooly and fairly, CARRICK *Laird of Logan* (1835) 275. s.Sc. Hooly an' fairly's far the best plan, WATSON *Bards* (1859) 194. Edb. 'Hooly and fairly,' quoth Thomas, MOIR *Mansie Wauch* (1828) xviii. Dmf. The laird maun ha' wished, baith hooly an' fairly, That Nick the auld had brunt the law, THOM *Jock o' the Knowe* (1878) 22.
3. Tenderly. n.Cy. GROSE (1790); (J.L.) (1783).
4. *v.* To go softly or slowly; to pause.
Per. Then's the time for you to hoolie And cram your wallet wi' the spoolie, SPENCE *Poems* (1898) 188. Ayr. If you'll only hooly a wee, I'll tell ye a' aboot it, SERVICE *Notandums* (1890) 17; Here I maun hooly a wee, and let Willie tell it again, *ib.* 263. Cum. 'They will all hooly away,' said he; 'but where are we to hooly to!' HOWITT *Rur. Life* (1838) I. 138.
5. *adj.* Delicate, sickly, tender, weak; nervous, complaining, peevish, fretful.
N.Cy.[1], Nhb.[1] Dur. To be huly. A huly-man (K.); Dur.[1] s.Dur. 'She's varra huly.' Spoken often of a person who is nervous about her health and complains of slight ailments (J.E.D.).
Hence Huel, *sb.* a delicate or ailing person, esp. one who is nervously morbid or 'hipped.'
Nhb.[1] An expostulation to one talking too freely in presence of an invalid is 'Had yor tongue: he's nobbut a huel.'
[**1.** My God, cum not holy, HAMPOLE (c. 1330) *Ps.* xxxix. 24. ON. *hōgliga*, gently (VIGFUSSON); Dan. dial. *hovlig* (pron. *houle*), quietly, gently (MOLBECH). **2.** (1) Hully and fair on to the cost I swam, DOUGLAS *Eneados* (1513), ed. 1874, III. 32.]

HOOLYBUSS, *sb.* Cor.[2] A noise, tumult, uproar.
Thai cheldurn are maakan some hoolybuss.

HOOM, *sb.* Rnf. (JAM.) [Not known to our correspondents.] A herd, flock.

HOOM, see Holm, *sb.*[2]

HOOMAGE, *sb.* Suf. A homestage. (C.T.) Cf. home, *v.*11.

HOOMER, *sb.* Yks. The grayling, 'umber,' *Thymallus vulgaris.* n.Yks. Obs. or obsol. (R.B.) ne.Yks.[1]

HOOMER, see **Oomer.**

HOOMET, *sb.* Sc. Also written hoomit Bnff. ; humet (Jam.) ; and in form howmet (Jam.). [hū·mit.] 1. A large flannel nightcap.

Abd. *Gen.* worn by old women (Jam.).

Hence **Hoometed,** *pp.* having the head covered with a ' hoomet.'

Sc. Witches hoometet in fright In flanen rags, and wousey, Anderson *Poems* (1813) 82 (Jam.).

2. A child's under-cap. Mry. (Jam.)

3. A man's Kilmarnock bonnet.

Bnff. There were usually several broken panes stopped up with our Kilmarnocks, or, as we called them, ' Hoomits,' Gordon *Chron. Keith* (1880) 71.

HOON, *v.* Obs. Sc. With *off* : ? to put off, postpone. Cf. hune, *v.*[1]

Bwk. ' Hoon aff ! hoon aff ! ' quo' Robin Tait, Henderson *Pop. Rhymes* (1856) 164 ; Hoon aff, dear Kate, till comes the day, *ib.* 165.

HOON, see **Hoin,** *v.*[1]

HOONCE, *v.* e.Yks.[1] [ūns.] To drive off unceremoniously.

HOONSKA, *sb.* Sh.I. A pudding made of the blood of an ox mixed with meal. S. & Ork.[1]

HOONT, see **Want,** *sb.*

HOONY, *adj.* Nhb. Cum. Also in form howney Cum.[14] [hū·ni.] Gaunt, ghostly ; dismal, empty.

Nhb.[1] Cum.[4] Applied to a house depleted of furniture; Cum.[4] [Cp. Norw. dial. *hundeleg,* ill-looking, unpleasant (Aasen).]

HOOP, *sb.*[1] and *v.*[1] Var. dial. uses in Sc. and Eng. Also in forms heǎp ne.Lan.[1] ; heup N.Cy.[1] Nhb.[1] Cum.[4] ; hop Yks. ; hupe Lin.[1] ; h)ūp, h)iap.) 1. *sb.* In *comp.* (1) Hoop-drift, a cooper's tool used for tightening the hoops of a barrel ; (2) -driving, bowling or trundling a hoop ; (3) -headed, of a stag : see below ; (4) -pins, the two pins used for securing the ' hal ' of a ' timbern zole ' to its ' chip.'

(1) s.Wor. (H.K.), s.Wor.[1] (2) [The boys go hoop-driving, never bowling, Jefferies *Hdgrw.* (1889) 189.] (3) w.Som.[1] A stag whose horns are curved upwards, and between which the space narrows towards the points, is said to be hoop-headed, Collyns, 41. (4) Dev. *Reports Provinc.* (1893).

2. *Phr.* (1) *to go through the hoop,* to become bankrupt ; (2) *to go a hoop,* to go where one likes ; to go to the bad.

(1) Glo.[1] (2) Hmp. He is going a hoop, Wise *New Forest* (1883) 283 ; Hmp.[1]

3. A plain finger-ring. w.Yks.[23] Stf.[1] 4. The tire of a wheel. w.Yks. (J.J.B.), w.Yks.[2] 5. The woodwork projecting from the sides of a wagon so as to form an arch over the hind wheels. Wil.[1] 6. The circular wooden frame which surrounds the mill-stones and preserves the meal from being lost. Lth. (Jam.) 7. A broad band of tin used for raising the sides of a cheese-vat when the curd is first put to press. Also called Fillet (q.v.). Chs.[1] 8. A species of cheese-vat.

Midl. The cheese-vats of this country are merely hoops of ash, with a boarden bottom, Marshall *Rur. Econ.* (1796) I. 319.

9. A measure varying from a quarter of a peck to four pecks.

n.Cy. A measure, containing a peck, or a quarter of a strike, Grose (1790) ; A measure containing ⅓ of a peck (J.L.) (1783) ; N.Cy.[1] A measure rather less than a peck. Nhb. (R.O.H.) ; Nhb.[1] A measure of ½ peck. Dur. ¼ peck, Morton *Cyclo. Agric.* (1863). Cum. He peel'd (potatoes) fer hissel a full heup an a hawf, Anderson *Ballads* (ed. 1840) 95 ; Cum.[4] A six-quart measure, formerly made of a broad wooden hoop; quarter of a Carlisle bushel. Yks. A measure containing a peck, or quarter of a strike, Ray (1691) ; Kennett *Par. Antiq.* (1695) ; A measure containing 2 pecks or a halfs of a strike (K.). ne.Lan.[1] The quarter of a peck. nw.Der.[1] A measure of four pecks, or a strike. Shr. The quarter bushel is called a hoop or peck, Marshall *Review* (1818) II. 225 ; Shr.[1] *Obsol.* The pars bin so thep, they binna wuth twopence a 'oop. Mtg. 5 gallons, Morton *Cyclo. Agric.* (1863).

10. *v.* Of drapery, &c. : to fall unevenly, loop up.

Nhp.[1] If the skirt of a dress is so tight in any part, that it does not fall easily, and requires more fullness, it is said to hoop ; or when lace or other trimming is set on so scantily, that it will not fall properly, it also hoops, i.e. it assumes the form of a hoop.

11. *Fig.* ? To speed, hurry.

Sc. My lord wants a coach : now he may get an Anstruther bark, and hoop o'er to Versailles, Pitcairn *Assembly* (1766) 6.

HOOP, *sb.*[2] War. Wor. Hrf. Glo. Wil. Dor. Som. Dev. Cor. Also in forms hope War.[2] Dor. Som. Dev. Cor. ; up Dev. [ūp, ŏp, ūp.] The bullfinch, *Pyrrhula vulgaris* or *Europaea.* See Alp.

War.[2], s.Wor.[1], Hrf.[12] Glo. (J.S.F.S.) ; Glo.[1] Common ; Glo.[2] So called from the white marks on his neck. Wil. Thurn *Birds* (1870) 33 ; Britton *Beauties* (1825) ; Wil.[1] Dor. (C.V.G.) ; w.Gazette (Feb. 15, 1889) 7, col. 1. Dor., Som. Swainson *Birds* (1885) 66. Som. (W.F.R.) w.Som.[1] They hoops (e·ops) be beating out the bud again ter'ble, we must burn some more powder 'bout em (shoot at]. Dev. The hoop is a bird of the same family, who makes more noise than he does work, Bray *Desc. Tamar and Tavy* (1836) I. 390 ; 1670-1. To Richard Sweatland for an ups head, *East Budleigh Chwarden's Acc.* ; Dev.[12] n.Dev. Us fourn° . . . A copperfinch an' hoop's nest, Rock *Jim an' Nell* (1867) st.. 123. nw.Dev.[1] s.Dev. Fox *Kingsbridge* (1874) ; (F.W.C.) s.Dev., e.Cor. (Miss D.) Cor. Rodd *Birds* (1880) 314 ; Cor.[12]

HOOP, *sb.*[3] and *v.*[2] Lin. 1. *sb.* Vain, ostentatious boasting. Lin.[1] 2. *v.* To boast or brag. (Hall.)

HOOP, *v.*[2] Nhp. Glo. Hnt. Som. [ūp, Som. ŏp.] To cry or call out ; to shout, whoop.

Glo. (J.S.F.S.) Som. I hoopit to he—but he didn' hear ! (W.F.R.) ; A lad hoop'ed fire ! *Spectator* (Feb. 16, 1895) 230 ; (F.A.A.) ; Sweetman *Wincanton Gl.* (1885). w.Som.[1] Used gen. with 'holler.' 'I yeard-n hoopin and hollering ever so long avore I zeed-n.' ' There was purty works way em ; you never year'd no jis hoopin and hollerin in all your live, 'twas fit to wake the very dead.'

Hence **Hoop** or **Hoopit,** *int.* a call or signal in children's games.

Nhp.[1] When a child is playing at the game of ' Hide and seek,' and has concealed herself, she calls out ' hoop! hoop!' to signify to her playmates that they may begin to search for her. Nhp.[1] The signal in the children's game of tig : thus, to ' cry hoop it ' is to exercise the lungs pretty lustily. Hnt. (T.P.F.)

HOOP, *int.* w.Som.[1] [ūp.] A call used by carters to their horses to move on.

It is never used when the horses are already in motion, nor is it used except to heavy teamsters ; but it is the regular word among farm carters to start their ' plough,' whether drawing sull, harrows, or wagon.

HOOPEE', *int.* Nhp.[1] Also in form hoopa'h. A call to a child to make an effort to raise itself, when it is taken by the arms to lift it.

HOOPER'S HIDE, *phr.* Obs. Hrt. A game. Ellis *Shep. Guide* (1750) 199.

HOOREN, *sb.* Or.I. A disgust. (Jam.), S. & Ork.[1]

HOORIKOORIS, *sb.* Sh.I. In phr. *in the hoorikooris,* in a sulky, offended state of mind.

' He's lying i' de hoori-kooris ' is originally applied to a person half-awake and half-asleep in the morning, before getting out of bed, and as he is then generally sulky, the expression is most often applied in this latter meaning. We find both words also in the expression : ' To sit oorin-koorin (nodding, half-asleep) ower de fire,' Jakobsen *Dial.* (1897) 39.

[*Oor* or *ouri,* ON. *örar,* a senseless state, see oorie + *hoor,* a state between waking and sleeping, Jakobsen (*l.c.*).]

HOORIP, *adv.* s.Chs.[1] At a great rate or speed. Also used *subst.* and *attrib.*

Commonly used of boiling water—bey'lin óo·rip [beilin' hoorip]. The phr. ' at the hoorip,' ' with a hoorip,' are also frequent. Or, as *adj.,* ' at th' hoorip gallop.' Uwd ― z os kóo·m tae·rin alüngg üt)dh óo·rip· gy'aal·ŏp [Owd ―'s hoss coom tearin' alung at th' hoorip].

HOO-ROO, *sb.* Yks. Lan. Chs. Der. War. Also in form howrow Lan. [ū·rū.] 1. A hubbub, noise, tumult. w.Yks.[2] You never heard such a hooroo in all yer life. Lan. They used to feaw eawt un kick up the dule's own howrow, Staton *Loominary* (c. 1861) 112. s.Lan. Bamford *Dial.* (1854). Chs.[1], nw.Der.[1] War. Hoo-roo, the devil's to do, *Prov.* (Hall.) ; War.[4] What a hooroo they be making, and all about nothing, I be sartain.

2. A fête, public rejoicings of any kind.

s.Chs.[1] Aas·t ey·ūrd ŭ dhis· óo·róo ŭz iz góo·in bey ŭt Aak·n ! [Hast heeard o' this hooroo as is gooin bey (= take place) at Acton!]

3. A kind of cake, baked in a pan, prepared for special occasions.

  s.Cha.¹ Wi')m góo·in in fūr ū reg·īlūr jūngk·itin, ūn fūr aav·in ū o·róo bai·kt i dhū pon, ūn aby noa·)nū wot els [We'm gooin' in or a regilar junkettin', an' for havin' a hooroo baked i' the pon, an' I knowna what else].

HOORRO, *int.* Sh.I. In phr. *like hoorro,* with spirit, spiritedly.

  He . . . brook inta 'Da sailer ower da roff tree' like hoorro, BURGESS *Sketches* (and ed.) 113.

HOOSACK, *int.* Shr.¹ [ū·sak.] An exclamation used upon finding or recovering a thing lost; 'Eureka.'

  Dick fund 'is knife w'en we wun gettin' the barley-stack in – I eard 'im cry ' 'oosack !' an' I said, ' W'ast'ee fund, Dick !'

HOOSAMIL, *sb.* Sh.I. [hū·samil.] A road between or past houses. S. & Ork.¹

  Hence **Hoosamillya,** *adv.* from house to house.

  ' To geng hoosamillya ' is to go among the houses, carrying gossip from the one to the other, JAKOBSEN *Dial.* (1897) 43 ; The young lads [at Hallowmas] banded themselves together in squads and went hoosamylla (from house to house) as maskers, commonly called grōliks, SPENCE *Flk-Lore* (1899) 189.

  [*Hoosa,* houses + *millya, milli,* between, among, JAKOBSEN *l.c.*). *Millya,* a form of Norw. dial. *millom,* for the numerous variants of which see AASEN.]

HOOSAPAAIL, *sb.* Sh.I. The head. S. & Ork.¹ Cf. *ushapan.*

  [*Hoosa,* ON. *hausa-* (in comp.), *hauss,* the skull, cranium, the head of beasts (VIGFUSSON) ; *paail,* Norw. dial. *paale,* a pole, stake, post (AASEN).]

HOOSBIRD, see **Hosebird.**

HOOSET, *sb.* and *v.* Brks. Wil. Also written **housset** Wil.¹; **husset** n.Wil.; and in form **wooset** Wil.¹ **1.** *sb.* A horse's head curiously dressed up and carried about by men and boys. Brks. *Gl.* (1852) ; Brks.¹ Cf. **hodening.**

  Hence *Hooset hunt, phr.,* see below.

  Brks.¹ When persons are believed to be guilty of incontinence, men and boys assemble for a ' Hooset Hunt '; they take with them pots or pans or anything wherewith to make discordant noise, and this they call ' Rough Music,' they also carry the ' Hooset ' on a pole. On arrival at a house to be visited. the ' Rough Music ' is vigorously played, and the ' Hooset ' shaken in front of all the windows, and even poked into them if any be open.

2. A serenade of rough music, got up to express public disapproval of flagrant immorality, or of marriages where there is great disparity of age.

  Wil.¹ n.Wil. 'What's that noise ?' 'Oh, there's a hoosset going up the street !' (E.H.G.).

3. *v.* To take part in a ' hooset.'

  Wil.¹ n.Wil. 'What's thuc noise ?' 'Aw, they be a hussetting up street ' (E.H.G.).

  Hence **Woooseting,** *vbl. sb.,* see below.

  Wil. The ceremony of ' wooseting ' is the same as in a ' skimmeting,' and expresses popular disapproval of adultery, *N. & Q.* (1873) 4th S. xi. 295.

HOOSH, *sb.* and *v.*¹ Irel. [hūʃ.] **1.** *sb.* A lift, heave, push upwards.

  ' To give one a hoosh ' is to help him to mount a wall or height by a push or propulsion *a tergo.* ' I can get over this wall if you'll give me a hoosh ' (A.S.P.).

2. *v.* To lift up, heave, raise. (*ib.*)

HOOSH, *int.* and *v.*² Suf. Dor. **1.** *int.* A cry used to scare or drive away fowls, pigs, &c. Cf. **howsh(e, hush,** *sb.*⁸

  e.Suf. 'Hoosh !' go away (F.H.). Dor. Saying ' Hoosh !' to the cocks and hens when they go upon your seeds, HARDY *Madding Crowd* (1874) x.

2. *v.* To scare or drive away fowls, pigs, &c. e.Suf. (F.H.)

HOOSHT, see **Hushed.**

HOOSIE, *sb.* Cum.⁴ The house-sparrow, *Passer domesticus.*

HOOSING, *sb.* n.Cy. Cum. Wm. Yks. Lan. Also in forms **heusin** Cum.⁴; **huzzin** n.Cy. w.Yks. ne.Lan.¹; **yuzin** Wm. [(h)ū·zin, h)u·zin.] The husk of a nut. Cf. **oase,** *sb.*¹ **3.**

  n.Cy. GROSE (1790). **Cum.** Ah coh across sum eh thur girt furpple things . . . wih heuzzins o' them stickan oot oa roond like eid-horse-heucks for size, SARGISSON *Joe Scoap* (1881) 232 ;

Cum.²⁴ Wm. When nuts is ripe they come oot o' t'hyuzin (B.K.). w.Yks. HUTTON *Tour to Caves* (1781) ; w.Yks.¹, ne.Lan.¹

  [In *Lind. Gosp.* (c. 950) *Luke* xv. 16 we find *pisum hosum* glossing ' siliquis.']

HOOSK, see **Husk,** *sb.*¹

HOOST, *sb., v.*¹ and *adj.* Irel. Also Shr. Som. Dev. Cor. Also in forms **houst·** Irel. ; **oost** Cor.¹² [hūst, w.Cy. ōst.] **1.** *sb.* A cough, esp. a cough peculiar to cattle ; a hoarseness. Cf. **heaze, hoast,** *sb.*¹

  Shr.¹ The cows han gotten a bit'n a 'oost. Som. (W.F.R.) Dev. Wan farmer Ham had got som kows, . . wis bad way hoost an koff, *n.Dev. Jrn.* (Nov. 12, 1885) 2, col. 4. nw.Dev.¹ A wheezing cough in cattle. s.Dev. Fox *Kingsbridge* (1874). Cor.¹ A disease of cattle, a symptom or cause of which is the presence of worms in the windpipe and bronchial tubes ; Cor.²

  Hence **Housty,** *sb.* a sore throat.

  Dev. One of the children had a ' housty,' KINGSLEY *Westward Ho* (1855) 122, ed. 1889.

2. *v.* To cough. Hence **Hoosting,** *vbl. sb.* coughing.

  Ir. It's destroyed entirely I am with the hoosting and screeching, *Paddiana* (ed. 1848) II. 85.

3. *adj.* Hoarse. Cor.²

  [OE. *hwōsta,* a cough ; *hwōstan,* to cough.]

HOOST, *v.*² Irel. To make a sound as if driving fowls, &c. Cf. **hoosh,** *int.*

  w.Ir. Juggy Kelly . . . began, half awake, to hist and hoost vigorously, as if she were driving in geese or turkeys to roost, LAWLESS *Grania* (1892) II. pt. III. iii.

HOOSTER, *sb.* Stf.¹ Refuse from the furnaces.

HOOSUCK, see **Hussock.**

HOOT, *sb.* Cor.¹ [ūt.] A business, affair, concern.

  ' A bad hoot,' a bad job. ' That's a bad hoot, says Madison.'

HOOT, *v.*¹ and *int.* Nhb. Yks. Midl Not. Lei. Nhp. War. Wor. Hrf. Glo. Brks. Ken. Hmp. Som. Dev. Cor. Also in forms **hout** Dev. ; **howt** Som. (HALL.) ; **yewt** Lei.¹ [h)ūt.] **1.** *v.* To call out, shout, bawl.

  Midl. A boy hootin' birds [a boy shouting at birds while ' birdtending'], BARTRAM *People of Clopton* (1897). Not.¹ Lei.¹ A ewted 'em to coom in an' hev a glass. Shay's ollus a-ewtin' affter me [said a mother of a child]. War. A girl carried on in the train beyond her destination said, ' I never heard them hoot Coventry ' (A.J.C.) ; War.⁸ I made him hoot. How those lads are hooting. I hooted after him. Hrf.², s.Wor.¹, se.Wor.¹

  Hence (1) **Hooting,** *vbl. sb.* (*a*) the noise made by a wheel which requires greasing, when in motion ; (*b*) blubbering, crying ; (*c*) see (4) ; (2) **Hooting-bottle,** *sb.* the reapers' or haymakers' beer-keg ; (3) **-cough,** *sb.* whooping-cough ; (4) **-owl,** *sb.* the tawny owl, *Syrnium aluco* ; (5) **-pudding,** *sb.* a pudding in which the plums are very few and far between, as if within shouting distance of each other ; (6) **Hoot-owl,** *sb.,* see (4).

  (1, *a*) se.Wor.¹ (*b*) Cor. Stop tha hootin', dew. (*c*) Som. (HALL.) (*a*) Lei.¹ When emptied by the last drinker, he is expected to shout for more to be fetched. (3) s.Dev., e.Cor. (Miss D.), Cor.¹ (4) e.Yks. *Leeds Merc. Suppl.* (Apr. 5, 1884). (5) Nhp.¹, War.⁸, s.Wor. (R.L.) (6) Nhb.¹ w.Yks. SWAINSON *Birds* (1885) 129.

2. Of dogs : to bark, yelp. Of birds : to sing.

  Not.¹ Lei.¹ Ah 'eerd 'em a-ewtin' in the spinney [the hounds after a fox]. The boo'ds are a-ewtin' beautiful this mornin'. Ah 'eerd the doogs yowtin'.

3. To bray like a donkey. Cor.¹

4. *trans.* To drive or urge onwards, to hurry up, drive.

  Ken. He hoots him about. They hooted him about too much (D.W.L.).

5. *int.* A driver's call to his horse ; see below.

  Nhp.² A term used to a horse when he is required to turn from the driver ; opposed to ' or ' (s.v. Woot). Glo.¹ Call to a cart horse to bear to the right. Brks.¹ Hmp. 'Oot seems to answer to ' stop ' (H.C.M.B.). Dev. GROSE (1790) *MS. add.*

HOOT, *v.*² s.Chs.¹ To peep, used only in phr. *hooting and tooting.*

  Ée wūz ōo·tin ūn tōo·tin ūbuw·t au· dhū weyl wi wūn tau·kin [He was hootin' an' tootin' abowt aw the wheil we wun talking] (s.v. Toot).

HOOTCH, *v.* Shr. Hrf. Also written **hooch** Hrf.¹² [ūtʃ.] To crouch, sit huddled up.

  Shr.¹ ' Come out—'ootchin' i' the cornel theer.' *Gen.* used with

                      G g 2

reference to a corner. **Hrf.** Bound *Provinc.* (1876); **Hrt.**[1]; **Hrf.**[2] Hoo-ching over the fire.

HOOTCHER, *sb.* Brks. [ū·tʃə(r).] A hooked stick used to pull down branches when gathering fruit. *Gl.* (1852); **Brks.**[1]

HOOTER, *sb.*[1] Chs. Flt. War. Wor. Oxf. Brks. [ū·tə(r).] 1. An owl.

Chs. ·E.F.); **Chs.**[1] Some cows which had been turned out of a good pasture into a poor one were described to me as having ' exchanged a hen for a hooter'; **Chs.**[2], s.**Chs.**[1], Flt (T.K.J.)

2. A steam whistle.

War. In Birmingham we find the steam hooter . . . quite enough of a trial, *B'ham Dy. Mail* (Dec. 1, 1896); **War.**[3], Wor. (H.K.), Oxf. (L.J.Y.), (G.O.), **Brks.** (G.O.)

HOOTER, *sb.*[2] War. Wor. Glo. Oxf. [ū·tə(r).] A cone-shaped tin vessel used for heating beer, &c. Also called a Hastener (q.v.).

War.[23], se.Wor.[1] Glo. BAᵗLɪs *Illus. Dial.* (1870). Oxf.[1] Called a ' Joram ' at Begbrook.

HOOTHOO-AN·NOOTHOO, *adv.* Yks. Alternately, first one and then the other.

n.Yks. Our lads ran efther em, an' it wur hoo thoo and noo theo a greeat whahl (T.S.). e.Yks. NICHOLSON *Flk-Sp.* (1889) 95 ; e.Yks.[1] They're two reglar scally-brats [scolds] an went at 'it hoothoo-an-noothoo for a-noor an mare.

HOO-TREE, *sb.* Nhb.[1] The top framing of a coal-wagon.

HOOT(S, *int.* and *v.* Sc. Irel. n.Cy. Nhb. Cum. Yks. Also written huts Sc. ; and in forms hout Sc. (JAM.) N.Cy.[1] Nhb.[1] n.Yks.[14] ne.Yks.[1]; howt(s Sc. (JAM.) Nhb.[1]; hut(s N.I.[1] Nhb.[1] Cum.[24] [h]ūt(s.] 1. *int.* An exclamation expressive of dissatisfaction, incredulity, irritation, annoyance, &c.

Sc. ' Hout wi' your fleeching,' said Dame Martin, SCOTT *Redg.* (1824) Lett. xii ; Hute, daft laddie, GRAHAM *Writings* (1883) II. 56. Bnff. Hout, hout, said Mam, ye're sure in jest, TAYLOR *Poems* (1787) 64. Abd. Hoot, 'oman, ye sudna vex yersel', ALEXANDER *Johnny Gibb* (1871) viii. Frf. Hoots, doctor, don't lose your temper, BARRIE *Minister* (1891) xi. Per. ' Hoot!' responded the housekeeper, ' it's just Dr. Brown's daughter', CLELAND *Inchbracken* (1883) 12, ed. 1887. w.Sc. Hoot, I dinna want to buy ony thing, CARRICK *Laird of Logan* (1835) 71. s.Sc. Hout, hout! hae done, ye'll never gree, T. SCOTT *Poems* (1793) 333. Dmb. Hoots, kimmer, but you're syboe short the day, SALMON *Gowodean* (1868) 26. Rnf. Wi' face as grave as ony priest [he] Says hoot, gae wa, WEBSTER *Rhymes* (1835) 136. Ayr. Hout, Laird, ye're like a tap o' tow, AINSLIE *Land of Burns* (ed. 1892) 189. Lnk. Hoots, that's naething tae be wondered at, WARDROP *J. Mathison* (1881) 37. Lth. Hoot, whisht· ye, my dame, BALLANTINE *Poems* (1856) 206. Edb. Hoot ! hoot !—ye're wrang ! MACNEILL *Bygane Times* (1811) 3. Slk. ' Hout,' quo he, ' ye crazy gawkie,' HOGG *Poems* (ed. 1865) 9a. Dmf. Hout, Jenny, bogles fley'd me nought, SHENNAN *Tales* (1831) 72. Gall. The word which sometimes prefaces one thing, sometimes another, such as, howts—nonsense ; howts—ay ; and so howts means a something between yes and no, which is not easy to express, MACTAGGART *Encycl.* (1824) 29, ed. 1876. Ir. ' What . . . could keep him so long out ! ' . . . ' Hut, he's gone to some neighbour's,' CARLETON *Fardorougha* (1848) v. n.Ir. ' Hoots, woman ! ' sez I, LYTTLE *Paddy McQuillan*, 19. n.Cy. A negative; as nay, GROSE (1790) ; N.Cy.[1] Exclamation of disapprobation or disbelief, of irritation or contempt. Nhb. Howt ! is a most expressive word, signifying, according to intonation, a negative, both the quip courteous, and the lie direct ; incredulity ; wonder ; disinclination (R.O H.) ; Nhb.[1] An expression of impatience. Cum. She answers ' Huts ! I'll nut !' BURN *Ballads* (1877) 125 ; Cum.[1] Hoot it was nea sec thing ; Cum.[2] Hut, Jwohnny, git oot ! 40; Cum.[4] n.Yks.[1] Strongly expressive of incredulity or dissent : not so! nothing of the sort ! impossible ! n.Yks.[4] ne.Yks.[1] Denoting incredulity, as 'nonsense,' 'surely not.'

Hence **Houttie,** *adj.* of a testy humour, irritable. Fif. (JAM.)

2. *Phr.* (1) *hoot(s awa,* an expression of disbelief or incredulity, ' get away,' nonsense ; (2) — *ay,* a strong affirmation : indeed, to be sure ; (3) — *fie,* an expression of dissatisfaction or expostulation ; (4) — *no,* a strong negative ; (5) — *shaff,* an expression of impatience ; (6) — *toot(s,* an exclamation expressive of dissatisfaction, irritation, &c.; (7) — *toot-toot,* an exclamation expressive of annoyance; (8) — *ye,* an exclamation expressive of surprise.

(1) Sc. Hout awa' wi' the daft Sassenach, SCOTT *Leg. Mont.*

(1818) x. Per. Hoot, awa ! Peter Malloch, ye maunna judge sae hard, CLELAND *Inchbracken* (1883) 20, ed. 1887. w.Sc. Hoots ! awa', man, hae ye nae sense ! MACDONALD *Settlement* (1869) 20, ed. 1877. s.Sc. Hoot awa, thae words are like the gravings on kirkyard stanes, WILSON *Tales* (1836) II. 269. Lnk. Hout awa', Johnny lad ! what mak's ye flatter me ! RODGER *Poems* (1838) 53, ed. 1897. Lth. Hout awa ! our stoupie's dune ! BRUCE *Poems* (1813) II. 178. Ayr. Hoot-awa ! Laird, ye maunna ban the Earl, ye ken, SERVICE *Notandums* (1890) 2. Gall. Hoot awa', twa young folk, CROCKETT *Sunbonnet* (1895) vii. Nhb. Hoot awa', lads, hoot awa', RICHARDSON *Borderer's Table-bk.* (1846) VII. 404. (2) Sc. ' I will never look on him again.' ' Hoot ay, my lord, hoot ay,' said the king, SCOTT *Nigel* (182a) xxxii ; Hout, ay, I'm thinking Jemmy means to live and blaw the last trumpet, RAMSAY *Remin.* (1872) 26. Frf. Hoot aye; what's to hender ye ! BARRIE *Licht* (1888) viii. (3) Sc. Hout fye—hout fye—all nonsense and pride, SCOTT *Redg.* (1824) xi. Flf. They'll cry to us. Hout, fy ! TAYLOR *Markinch Minst.* (1811) 19, ed. 1870. Ayr. Hout fy, man Ringan, SILLER *Poems* (1789) 118. Lnk. Hout fy ! ye're fairly wrang, WATT *Poems* (1827) 56. (4) Sc. ' I wonder, can there be onything wrang wi' Sandy ! ' ' Hoots no ! ' answered Susan, SWAN *Gates of Eden* (1895) ix. Lnk. Hoot no ! I want nae mair eat, BLACK *Falls of Clyde* (1806) 110. Gall. Hoot na, Portmark, it was yirsel' he was hittin' at, CROCKETT *Bog-Myrtle* (1895) 19. (5) Nhb.[1] Cum.[4] ' Ye've fettlet him, Becka ! ' ' Hoot, shaff, no wurt o' t'mak,' says Becka. *W. C. T. X.* (1893) 4, col. 2. (6) Sc. Hout, tout, man, SCOTT *Nigel* (1824) xxxv. Flf. Hoot-toots, I had nae thoughts o' this, ROBERTSON *Provost* (1894) 67. Ayr. Hoot toot, friend, ye're owre hasty, GALT *Gilhaize* (1823) xxii. Lnk. Hoot toot, Johnnie, you're shurely in a reverie, WARDROP *J. Mathison* (1881) 25. Lth. Hoots, toots—dinna kiss ony mair, LUMSDEN *Sheep-head* (1892) 260. Edb. But, hout-tout, one thing and another coming across me almost clean made me forget, MOIR *Mansie Wauch* (1828) iii. Keb. How't tow't, the young lasses get nae men now sic as they are either as they gat lang syne, ELDER *Borgue* (1897) 30. N.I.[1] An exclamation of impatience. Cum.[14] (7) Abd. Hoot-toot-toot, ye're wrang i' the up-tak', ALEXANDER *Johnny Gibb* (1871) x. (8) Bwk. (JAM.), N.Cy.[1]

3. *v.* To pooh-pooh, discredit, disbelieve, to cry ' hoots' at. Also used *fig.*

Ayr. When ance her chastity took leg, When she spoke o't he houted, FISHER *Poems* (1790) 83. Lnk. Johnny hooted and boasted for about five minutes afore he would or could gi'e a rusty an answer, WARDROP *J. Mathison* (1881) 11. Pmb. When young I hootit lads away, For this I live unhappy, AFFLECK *Post. Wks.* (1896) 137.

HOOV, *v.* and *int.* s.Chs.[1] 1. *v.* With *at:* to throw oneself with energy into.

It)s a big· job, laad-z; but wi)n 6ov aat· it [It's a big job, lads; but we'n hoov at it].

2. *int. Phr. hoov at ye,* an exclamation of surprise or pleasurable emotion ; a greeting.

HOOVE, *sb.* and *v.* War. Wor. Som. Also in form hove War.[234] s.War.[1] Som. w.Som.[1] [ūv, ōv.] 1. *sb.* A hoe.

se.Wor.[1] Som. To hove turmits with an auld hove, W. & J. *Gl.* (1873). w.Som.[1]

Hence **Hoove-plate,** *sb.,* see below.

Wor. A labourer, describing to me a convertible agricultural implement, said he could use it either with a 'hoove-plate,' a moulder, scuffle feet, or a 'scratter' (E.S.).

2. *v.* To hoe.

War.[234], s.War.[1] Wor. He was hooving early and late, and didn't earn above fifteen-pence (C.W.). w.Wor.[1], s.Wor. (H.K.), a.Wor.[1], se.Wor.[1] Som. W. & J. *Gl.* (1873). w.Som.[1] For hoving o' turmuts, did'n ought to have your hove no less'n nine inches wide.

HOOVE, see Hoof, *sb.*[1], Hove, *v.*

HOOZE, *sb., v.* and *adj.* n.Cy. Dur. Lakel. Yks. Lan. Chs. Not. Lin. Wor. Also Dev. Cor. Also in forms heuz(e Cum.[14]; hewse n.Yks.; hiuz Lakel.[2]; hoose Cum.[4] s.Chs.[1] hooyze w.Yks.[4]; house m.Yks.[1]; houze w.Wor.[1]; huse N.Cy.[1] Dur.[1]; ooze w.Yks.[2] [h]ūz, w.Yks. uiz.] 1. *sb.* A hoarseness, dry cough, esp. a difficult breathing or cough peculiar to animals. Cf. heaze, hoast, *sb.*[1]

N.Cy.[1] Lakel.[2] That coo hez a nasty hiuz wi't. Cum. (J.W.-O.); Cum.[1]; Cum.[4] That coo hez a nasty hiuz wi 't ; it's a bit o' turnip i' t'throat, *Penrith Obs.* (Feb. 15, 1893). Wm. I don't like sound of that hyuz (B.K.). w.Yks. THORESBY *Lett.* (1703); w.Yks.[14], ne.Lan.[1], s.Chs.[1] n.Lin. SUTTON *Wds.* (1881).

One of the pigs has gotten a strange hooze on it. s.Wor. (H.K.), Cor.[2] [Asthma... This disorder is attended with a shortness of breath, and a frequent hoose, Knowlson *Cattle Doctor* (1834) 29.]

Hence **Hoozy** or **Husy,** *adj.* hoarse, wheezy, asthmatical. Dur.[1] s.Dur. He's all husy iv his windpipe (J.E.D.). Dev. This yer east wind 'ath a-gied me a zoar droat, an' I be gitting hoozee, Hewett *Peas. Sp.* (1892). Cor. But I've ben a bit hoozy sence, J. Trenoodle *Spec. Dial.* (1846) 59 ; Cor.[1] I'm oisy, so that I can hardly speak; Cor.[2]

2. *v.* To breathe with difficulty ; to wheeze.
Cum.[4] n.Yks. That barn must a gitten coud [cold], it hewses badly. That hoss must be brockenwinded, it hewses varra bad (W.H.) ; n.Yks.[12] m.Yks.[1] How he does houze and êaze, to be sure ! w.Yks.[2] s.Not. Hark 'ow the sow hoozes in 'er sleep (J.P.K.). n.Lin.[1] w.Wor.[1]

Hence **Houzing,** *vbl. sb.* wheezing, hoarseness.
w.Wor.[1] The child's got a reg'lur bad cowd : 'e's such a 'ouzin' on 'is chest as is quite terrifyin'. s.Wor. (H.K.)

3. *adj.* Hoarse. Cor.[2]
[1. Hoose or cowghe, *tussis, Prompt.* **2.** OE. *hwōsan*, to wheeze.]

HOOZEN, *sb.* Dev. The windpipe, the 'weasand.'
An old woman complained that she had 'a pain across the hoozen,' placing her fingers on her wind-pipe, *Reports Provinc.* (1877) 192.

HOOZER, *sb.* Cum.[4] [hū·zər.] Said of anything unusually large.

HOOZLE, *sb.*[1] Sc. Irel. Nhb. Also written **hoosel** Ant. ; **hoosle** Sh.I. ; and in forms **housel** Sc. (Jam.) s.Don. Nhb.[1] ; **houzle** Nhb.[1] [hū·zl] **1.** A socket ; the eye or hole where the shaft or handle is inserted in an axe, hoe, &c. Lnk., Rxb. That part of an axe, shovel, pitchfork, &c., into which the handle is fitted (Jam.). Bwk. (*ib.*) s.Don. The eye or opening of a hatchet made for the insertion of the handle, Simmons *Gl.* (1890). Nhb.[1]

2. The head or top of a hatchet, &c.
Sh.I. Dey strak dem doon wi' a hammer, or da hoosle o' a eech [adze]... Hit wis nae winder 'at da ox fell, fir da hoos'l o' da eech guid cleen trow her skult, *Sh. News* (Oct. 4, 1899). Ant. (W.H.P.)

3. A slip of paper fastened round a number of papers to keep them together. Rxb. (Jam.)

HOOZLE, *v.*[1] and *sb.*[2] Sc. Also in forms **houzle** Per. ; **huzle, huzzle** (Jam.). [hū·zl] **1.** *v.* To wheeze ; to breathe with a wheezing noise as when out of breath. Rxb. (Jam.) Cf. **hooze.**
Hence **Huzling,** *ppl. adj.* wheezing, breathing hard.
Bwk., Rxb. A puir huzlin bodie (Jam.).

2. *sb.* Heavy breathing ; a deep breath or inhalation ; a pinch of snuff.
Per. Talk of a pinch of snuff ! phoo—my new acquaintance knew of no such quantity—it was houzle after houzle for about two minutes, with a corresponding thankful pech to each, Stewart *Character* (1857) *Mem.* 96.

HOOZLE, *v.*[2] Sc. (Jam.) **1.** To perplex, puzzle, nonplus. Ayr. **2.** To drub or beat severely. Lnk. Hence **Hoozlin,** *vbl. sb.* a severe drubbing. *ib.*

HOP, *sb.*[1] and *v.*[1] Sc. Nhb. Yks. Wor. Hrf. Glo. e.An. Ken. Sur. Sus. Hmp. Wil. Dev. Cor. [h)op.] **1.** *sb.* In *comp.* (1) Hop-acre, the space of ground occupied by a thousand hop-plants, *gen.* half a statute acre ; (2) -bind, the stem of the hop, whether dead or alive; (3) -cat, a caterpillar which infests hop-plants, esp. the larva of the *Dayschira pudibunda* ; -clover, (*a*) the yellow clover, *Trifolium procumbens* ; (*b*) the sainfoin, *Medicago lupulina* ; (5) -dog, (*a*) see (3) ; (*b*) an instrument for drawing hop-poles out of the ground for the purpose of carrying them to the hop-pickers ; (*c*) the pointed iron bar used to make holes for setting the hop-poles; (6) -horse, a short ladder used by hop-pickers ; (7) -lees, a row of trees planted to shelter a hop-garden ; (8) -mand, a vessel used in a brewhouse ; (9) -mass, the medlar, *Mespilus germanica* ; (10) -medic, see (4, *b*) ; (11) -oulud, a moth found in hop-gardens in May; (12) -pitcher, see (5, *c*) ; (13) -pole marriage, a marriage just in time to save the legitimacy of a child ; (14) -poles, in phr. *to rain hop-poles,* to rain 'cats and dogs'; (15) -sack, a kind of loosely-woven cloth ; (16) -spud, a three-pronged fork, with which hop-gardens are

dug ; (17) -temse, a hop-sieve ; (18) -wagon, a little cart used by hop-pickers, see below ; (19) -yard, a hop-garden.
(1) Hrf. Marshall *Review* (1818) II. 313 ; Bound *Provinc.* (1876). (*a*) Ken.[1] (3) Ken. (F.R.C.) (4, *a*) Bwk. Sometimes two pounds of white clover, and a pound or two of yellow clover, ... called provincially hop clover, are added to the mixture, *Agric. Surv.* 305 (Jam.). Glo. Grose (1790) *MS. add.* (M.) Wil. Hop clover, and ray-grass sown together—a very common and good custom, Davis *Agric.* (1813). Dev.[4] (*b*) s.Wil. Marshall *Review* (1818). (5, *a*) w.Wor.[1] Hrf.[2] A white striped grub. Ken. A caterpillar rather more than an inch in length and covered with yellow hair (W.H.E.) ; Ken.[1] A beautiful green caterpillar. Sur.[1] Sus. A 'hop-dog,' a handsome green caterpillar marked with black velvet stripes and downy bands between, Jefferies *Hdgrow.* (1889) 81 ; Sus.[1], Hmp. (W.M.E.F.) (*b*) Ken.[1] Ken., Sus. It is made of a long piece of wood, with a piece of iron at the lower part standing out a few inches, so as to clasp the pole when it is raised out of the ground; the iron is grooved so as to have teeth, from whence perhaps its name, Holloway. Sus.[12] (*c*) Ken.[1] (s.v. Hop-pitcher). (6) Ken., e.Sus. Holloway. Sus.[1] (7) Ken. (G.B.) (8) Sus.[1] (9) Cor. Thomas *Randigal Rhymes* (1895) *Gl.* (10) Nhb. With these some people mix hop-medic, Marshall *Review* (1818) I. 88. (11) w.Wor.[1] (12) Ken.[1] (13) s.An.[1], e.Suf. (F.H.) (14) Ken. It has been 'raining hop-poles' for a week, Jefferies *Hdgrow.* (1889) 188 ; Raining hop-poles sharp ends downwards (A.E.C.). (15) w.Yks. So called from its resemblance in texture to a hop-sack (S.K.C.). (16) Ken.[1] (17) w.Yks.[2] (18) Ken. A vehicle consisting of a rectangular car—often an old box—on four very low wheels, with a handle sloping upwards in front to a convenient height and fitted near the end with a cross-piece, by which the carriage is drawn along. This vehicle is used by hop-pickers for carrying children, or things which they require, to and from the hop-gardens (W.H.E.). (19) w.Wor.[1] (s.v. Hop-oulud).

2. *Phr. as thick as hops,* said of things very close together.
Nhb. To see the keels upon the Tyne As thick as hops, a' swimmin, Allan *Tyneside Sngs.* (ed. 1891) 189.

3. The white bryony, *Bryonia dioica.* Glo. (B. & H.), Glo.[1]

4. Wood fit for hop-poles.
n.Yks. *Quart. Sess. Rec.* in *N. R. Rec. Soc.* IV. 159. Ken. (Hall.), Ken.[1]

5. *v.* To pick hops. Ken.[1] Hence (1) **Hopper,** *sb.* (*a*) a hop-picker; (*b*) a hop-bin ; (2) **Hopper-house,** (3) -hut, *sb.* a wooden hut inhabited by non-native hop-pickers ; (4) **Hopping,** *sb.* the season of hop-picking.
(1, *a*) Ken. We never go out after dark when the hoppers are about (D.W.L.) ; Ken.[1] I seed the poor hoppers coming home all drenched. Sur.[1] Ken. 'Well you see, sir,' he said, 'we are "hoppers," and we don't want to be stopping about here after hops are done,' Egerton *Flks. and Ways* (1884) 96. (*b*) Ken. (G.B.) (2, 3) Ken. (D.W.L.) (4) Ken.[1] A fine harvest, a wet hopping, *Eastry Prov.*

HOP, *v.*[2] and *sb.*[2] Var. dial. uses in Sc. Irel. and Eng. Also in form **hap** Sc. Irel. [h)op, Sc. also **hap.**] **1.** *v.* In *comb.* (1) Hop-about, an apple dumpling ; (2) -and-go-one, a one-legged man ; a lame man who uses a crutch ; (3) -crease, the game of hop-scotch ; (4) -frog, (*a*) a frog ; (*b*) a game, see below ; (5) -frog-over-the-dog, the game of leap-frog ; (6) -my-fool, a game of chance ; (7) -o'-dock, a lame person ; (8) -o'-my-thumb, a fop, dandy ; (9) -over, a stile; see below ; (10) -over-cap, a children's game [not known to our correspondents] ; (11) -score, (12) -scratch, (13) -scrawl, see (3) ; (14) -step-and-loup, to play at hop-skip-and-jump ; (15) -the-beds, see (3) ; (16) -thrush, the wood-louse ; (17) -to, a grasping fellow.
(1) Hrf.[1], Glo.[1], Hmp.[1] Wil. Britton *Beauties* (1825) ; Wil.[1] Probably from its bobbing about in the pot. (*a*) e.An.[1] (3) e.An.[1] Nrf. We played hop-crease or Scotch-hop—as Jim called it, Emerson *Son of Fens* (1892) 8. Sus., Hmp. Holloway. (4, *a*) Hmp. (J.R.W.), Hmp.[1] Wil. Never used without the pref. (K.M.G.) (*b*) Dor. The players bend as though about to sit on a very low stool, then spring about with their hands resting on their knees, *Flk-Lore Jrn.* VII. 234, in Gomme *Games* (1894) I. 229. (5) Lin. Gomme *ib.* (6) Ayr. The slouched and the slovenly... wrangled at skittles and toss-my-luck, and bent eagerly over the hop-my-fool tables, Galt *Rothelan* (1824) II. iii. (7) w.Yks.[1] w.Som.[1] (9) Chs.[1] It is made by nailing a plank on to two short posts, at right angles to the hedge. If the fence to be got over is high, two planks are placed one above the other,

and crossing each other; the hop-over then consists of two steps up and two steps to descend. (10) w.Yks.⁶ (11) n.Cy., Yks. The game has always, I believe, been called in Yks. and the n. counties 'hop-score,' *N. & Q.* (1890) 7th S. ix. 296. w.Yks.²⁴ (12) Wil. Slow *Gl.* (1892). (13) s.Not. (J.P.K.) (14) Ruf. He swore he wad hap, stap, and loup, Ay or fecht ony man i' the parish, Webster *Rhymes* (1835) 83. (15) Gall. Hap the beds, Mactaggart *Encycl.* (1824). (16) m.Yks.¹ (17) Suf. LW. (C.J.V.)

2. Phr. (1) *to hop the twig*, to elude one's creditors; (2) *to hop the wag*, to play truant.

(1) w.Yks.¹ (2) Lon. When I used to hop the wag from school I went there, Mayhew *Lond. Labour* (1851) III. 113, ed. 1861.

3. To dance; to caper. Sc. (Jam.), n.Cy.¹, Nhb. (R.O.H.)

Hence (1) **Hopper**, *sb.* one who dances at a country dance; (2) **Hopping**, *sb.* a country wake; a dance.

(1) Nhb.¹ (2) n.Cy. In many villages in the north of England these meetings [wakes] are still kept up under the name of Hoppings, Brand *Pop. Antiq.* (1813) II. 7. ed. 1870; N.Cy.¹ Nhb. A hopping, my lord, is a ball, Richardson *Borderer's Table-bk.* (1846) VI. 235; Nhb.¹ An annual festival, at which shows, roundabouts, and stalls of all descriptions attract the holiday-makers. In Newcastle the Easter hoppin was the most famous. But the hoppin of present day memory was but a relic of a former greatness. Nhb., Dur. Hoppings, fairs, vigils ... or Whitsun ales are anniversary feasts, Denham *Tra-ts* (ed. 1895) II. 3. n.Yks.²

4. To jump; to jump with the feet together.

n.Ir. Mister Davison's horse happit ower iverythin', jist as easy as oor dug jumps throo a hoop, Lyttle *Robin Gordon*, 88. e.Suf. (F.H.) Som. Hop out [of a cart] an' open the gate, there's a good maid, Raymond *Gent. Upcott* (1893) 101.

Hence **Happer**, *sb.* a jumper, in *comb.* **Counter-happer**, a shopman, counter-jumper.

n.Ir. Yin o' them coonter-happer buddies wuz tryin' tae tak a rise oot o' me, Lyttle *Paddy McQuillan*, 29.

5. To revolve.

Ayr. We came to a mill that stood in the hollow of the glen, the wheel whereof was happing in the water with a pleasant and peaceful din, Galt *Gilhaize* (1823) xx.

6. Of tears: to trickle, drop fast.

Sc. The big tears happit down her cheeks as fast as they could run, Sc. *Haggis*, 79. Elg. The tear haps oure thy chin, Couper *Poetry* (1804) I. 102. Ayr. Tears hap o'er her auld brown nose, Burns *To H. Parker* (1795) l. 22. Lnk. The silent tears o' deep emotion happing in quick succession oure John's cheeks, Roy *Generalship* (ed. 1895) 62. Lth. Johnie took a parting keek, Saw the tears hap owre her cheek, Macneill *Poet. Whs.* (1801) 210, ed. 1856. Edb. Gart tears hap owre our Laird's wan cheek, *ib.* *Bygane Times* (1811) 42. Slk. Till tears cam happing like rain, Hogg *Poems* (ed. 1865) 358. Gall. Wi' the water happin' off her cheeks, Crockett *Bog-Myrtle* (1895) 174.

7. To die. w.Yks.¹

8. *trans.* To make hop; to cause anything to crack by sudden heat.

Sc. A poacher may ... hap ye out of ae county and into anither at their pleasure, Scott *St. Ronan* (1824) viii. w.Som.¹ Mind you don't hop the glass.

Hence **Hopped**, *ppl.adj.* cracked, as a boiler by heat. Wil.¹

9. *sb. Comb.* (1) **Hop-skip-and-jump pudding**, a pudding in which the plums are very far apart; (2) **-step-and-jump**, (*a*) a game, see below; (*b*) a hopping movement; (3) **-step-and-loup**, (*a*) see (2, *a*); (*b*) at full speed; (4) **-stride-and-loup**, (*a*) see (2, *a*); (5) **Hops-and-girds**, (*a*) fits and starts; (*b*) as well as a person can, to the best of one's ability.

(1) Brks.¹ (2, *a*) Wxf. And tried each others powers leaping the brook, or seeing how far we could go in a hop, step and jump, Kennedy *Banks Boro* (1867) 5. Oxf. (G.O.) Hrt. The games appertaining to the play-ground consisted of prisoners' base ... hop, step, and jump, Wickham *Recollections* (1841) x. w.Sus. A well-known game in some parts, the trial being who, out of a number of boys, can cover the most ground with a hop, a step or stride, and then a jump with both feet together, Holloway (s.v. Hick, step and jump). (*b*) Edb. Aff he [a crow] hirples ... Hap, stap, and jump, Forbes *Poems* (1812) 110. (3, *a*) Ayr. Gars them dance hap-stap-an-loup, Sillar *Poems* (1789) 40. (*b*) Sc. Forrit she gade, hap, stap, and loup: and what for no ! Sc. *Haggis*, 111. Ayr. The third cam up, hap-stap-an'-lowp, As light as ony lambie, Burns *Holy Fair* (1785) st. 3. Lnk. On I sped, hap-stap-an'-loup, Alang the road wi' pace tremendous, Murdoch *Doric*

Lyre (1873) 23. Peb. Fu' thick, at ance a shoal Wi' weapons cam', hap, stap, and loup, Lintoun *Green* (1685) 14. ed. 1817. (4) w.Yks.¹ (5) w.Yks. (J.W.), s.Lin. (T.H.R.) (6, *a*) Shr.¹, Nig. (E.R.M.)

10. Phr. (1) *all of a hop*, suddenly; (2) *not to care a hop*, to care nothing at all; (3) *on the hop*, in a lively condition; (4) *to catch* or *have a person on the hop*, to surprise a person in some mischief; (5) *to take a hop at any one*, to take a mean advantage.

(1) Dev. Thay aul uv a hop Stude outside uv Kenhoods, Nathan Hogg *Poet. Lett.* (1847) 22, ed. 1865. (2) s.Not. I don't care a hop (J.P.K.). (3) Nhb. Sae wiv some varry canny chiels, All on the hop and murry, Aw thowt aw'd myek a voyage to Shiels, Thompson *Sngs.*; (R.O.H.) (4) Gmg. He caught me on the hop; at a moment of rumours and serious warnings, Blackmore *Maid of Sker* (1872) xxv. Wm. (B.K.), e.Suf. (F.H.) (5) Ant. (W.H.P.)

11. A dance, *gen.* of a rustic nature.

Sc. They danced as weel as they dow'd Wi' a knack o' their thumbs and a happie, Jamieson *Pop. Ballads* (1806) I. 313. Lnk. Then for a hap ... they did their minstrel bring, Ramsay *Poems* (1721) 50, ed. 1733. N.Cy.¹, Nhp.¹, Hnt. (T.P.F.) Dor. The younger vo'k That got up vor a hop, Barnes *Poems* (1879) 79.

HOP, *int.* Dur. Cum. Wm. Yks. **1.** A command to horses or oxen, directing them to turn to the right or off side; also with *off* or *up*.

Cum. Bon bon, ger on, will ta; Dick ... hop up beath, Farrall *Betty Wilson* (1886) 131; I niver cried woah, hop, or gee, Anderson *Ballads* (ed. 1808) 197; Cum.¹⁴, Wm. (B.K.), n.Yks.¹

2. *Comb.* (1) **Hop-back**, a command to horses to turn to the left. Dur.¹; (2) **-nor-ree**, right nor left. Cum. (B.K.)

HOP, see **Hope**, *sb.¹*, **Hoop**, *sb.¹*

HOPE, *sb.¹* Sc. n.Cy. Nhb. Dur. Yks. Glo. Som. Also in form *hop* Sc. (Jam.) [hōp.] **1.** A hollow among the hills; a valley through which a brook runs.

Sc. A sloping hollow between two hills, or the hollow that forms two ridges on one hill (Jam.). Slk. There is a little snug sheep house in our hope, Hogg *Tales* (1838) 68, ed. 1866. Rxb. Long wearily he wandered on Among the hollow hopes and hills, Riddell *Poet. Whs.* (ed. 1871) I. 189. Gall. A country of wide green holms and deep blind 'hopes,' or hollows among the mountains, Crockett *Moss-Hags* (1895) ix. n.Cy. Gross (1790) *MS. add.* (M.) Bailey (1721); N.Cy.¹ (s.v. Hogh). Nhb.¹ A smaller opening branching out from the main dale, and running up to the mountain ranges as the burns branch out, or are tributaries to the main stream, Egglestone *Weardale Names*, 50. The upland part of a mountain valley. Dur. (J.H.), s.Dur. (J.E.D.)

2. *Comb.* (1) **Hope-head**, the highest part of the 'hope'; (2) **-foot**, the lower part of the 'hope.'

(1) Abd. The water ran doon frae the heich hope-heid, Macdonald *Malcolm* (1875) II. 280. (1, 2) Lth., Twd., Dmf. (J.A.M.)

3. A hill.

Edb. Hills are variously named, according to their magnitude; as ... Kaim, Bank, Hope, Pennecuik *Whs.* (1715) 50, ed. 1815. Nhb.¹ Freq. applied to mere eminences, and is then usually pronounced 'up.' w.Yks. (J.W.), Glo.¹² Som. Hervey *Wedmor Chron.* (1887) I. 385.

[**1.** Ouer hil and hoip, bank and bra, Dalrymple *Leslie's Hist. Scotl.* (1596) I. 103; And so pai come till a cause ... Be-twene twa hillis in a hope, *Wars Alex.* (c. 1450) 5390.]

HOPE, *sb.²* Sc. Also Ken. **1.** A small bay; a haven.

Sc. It was a little hamlet which straggled along the side of a creek formed by the discharge of a small brook into the sea ... It was called Wolf's-hope (i.e. Wolf's Haven), Scott *Bride of Lam.* (1819) ix. S. & Ork.¹, Lth. (Jam.)

2. A place of anchorage for ships. Ken.¹

[**1.** Norw. dial. *hop*, a small creek (Aasen); so ON. *hōp* (Fritzner).]

HOPE, HOPED, see **Hoop**, *sb.²*, **Help**.

HOPED, *pp.* Sc. In phr. *to be better hoped*, to be more hopeful.

Frf. The Dr. says this morning that he is better hoped now, Barrie *M. Ogilvy* (1896) ii.

HOPES, *sb. pl.* Nrf. The queen stock, *Mutthiola incana.* (B. & H.)

HOPKEN, *sb.* Ken. Also written *hopkin* Ken.¹² [o'pkən, -kin.] **1.** A supper given to the workpeople when the hop-picking is over. Cf. **huffkin**.

N. & Q. (1877) 5th S. vii. 56; Ken.¹ Not often given in East

Kent now-a-days, though the name survives in a kind of small cake called huffkin, formerly made for such entertainments ; Ken.²
2. A small present given by the hop-pickers to a popular overseer. ne.Ken. (H.M.)

HOPMITHOM, HOPPEE, see Homnithom, Hoppy.
HOPPER, sb.¹ Sc. Nhb. Dur. Cum. Wm. Yks. Lan. Chs. Der. Not. Lin. Rut. Lei. Nhp. Shr. Hrt. Also in form happer Sc. [h)oˑpǝ(r, Sc. also haˑpǝr.] 1. In comb. (1) **Hopper-a-e,** resembling in gait the motion of a hopper; (2) ·balk, the beam on which a hopper rests; (3) ·frees, obs., tenants who had the right of grinding corn at the lord's mill free of payment; also the corn so ground ; (4) ·trough, a box into which grain is put to be brought between the mill-stones.

(1) w.Yks.¹ (2) Sc. (Jam.) (3) w.Yks.²⁴ (4) Shr.¹ The grain runs out of the trough, through the hopper, into the 'eye ' of the upper mill-stone. Com. ; Shr.²
2. A seed-basket, slung over one shoulder, used in sowing corn by hand. Cf. hoppet, sb.¹ 2.

Nhb.¹, Lakel.², e.Wm. (J.A.B.), n.Yks. (I.W.), n.Yks.¹²⁴, ne.Yks.¹ e.Yks. Lay [the lambe] in an hopper or baskett, Best Rur. Econ. (1642) 11. w.Yks.²³ Lan. For a wood seed hopper and a pair of trappings I bid 5¼d., Walkden Diary (ed. 1866) 57. Chs.³ Der. One hand in the hopper, the other in the bag, Flk-Lore Jrn. (1883) VI. 385. Not.², s.Not. (J.P.K.), n.Lin.¹ e.Lin. Brown Lit. Laur. (1890) 102. Rut.¹, Lei.¹ Nhp. What once were kernels from his hopper sown, Now browning wheat-ears and oat-bunches grown, Clare Village Minst. (1821) II. 106 ; Nhp.¹ Called more commonly seblet or siblet. Shr.¹ Obsol. It . . . usually rests on his left hip, being hollowed ; Shr.² [S. Mattho, take thy hopper and sow, Ray Proverbs (1678) 52.]

Hence **Happered,** adj. shrunken, as the hips from the pressure of the ' hopper.'
Lnk. On happer't leg The waefu' woman comes to beg the pickle meal, Murdoch Doric Lyre (1873) 55.
3. **Comb.** (1) **Hopper-arsed,** (a) shrunken about the hips; (b) with protuberant buttocks ; (2) ·balk, a blank space in growing corn caused by unequal sowing ; (3) ·balked, see below ; (4) ·cake, a seed-cake with plums in it given by farmers to their men at the end of seed-time ; (5) ·cake-night, the evening on which ' hopper-cakes ' are distributed ; (6) ·eared, of corn with small ears and few grains ; (7) ·galled or ·gawed, see (3); (8) ·gaw, (a) see (2) ; (b) to sow grain unevenly ; (9) ·hipped, see (1) ; (10) ·rowed, see (3); (11) ·shaker, a scamp, a worthless fellow.

(1, a) Rnf. Happer-arsed Nancy, Motherwell Harp (1819) lxiii. Lnk. A vast number of city ricketty hopper-arsed beaux who had been padded up, Graham Writings (1883) II. 128. Nhb. There was knack knee'd Mat, wiv's purple suit, An' hopper-a—s'd Dick, a' yellow-o, Bell Rhymes (1812) 45. (b) n.Cy. Grose (1790) (s.v. Hoppet). (a) Der. Wood, in his Hist. Eyam 46, mentions the hopperbaulk as an omen of death, Addy Gl. (1891) 30. (3) w.Yks.² A field of corn is said to be hopper-balked . . . when each track made by the sower is afterwards found to be ' short of plant.' This is caused by the sower not making his right and left casts join properly together in front of his hopper. (4) w.Yks.² Der. Grose (1790) MS. add. (P.) ; Der.², nw.Der.¹, Not.³ n.Lin.¹ Between sixty and seventy years ago, hopper-cakes or offer-cakes, as they were sometimes called, were given away accompanied by spiced beer, at Scotter, by the farmers when the last seed was sown. Obs. e.Lin. Brown Lit. Laur. (1890) 102. sw.Lin.¹ It was the custom to place them, and hand them round, in the empty Hopper or seed box, whence the name. Rut.¹ (5) sw.Lin.¹ (6) Hrt. An hopper eared crop or . . . a little ear with few kernels, Ellis Mod. Husb. (1750) III. i. 19. (7) s.Lth. (Jam.) Nhb.¹ When every ' cast' or handful is distinctly marked it is termed hopper-gawed. n.Yks.² e.Yks. Such a seedsman doth overstride his cast, and thereupon cometh the lande to bee hopper-galde, Best Rur. Econ. (1641) 50. (8, a) Bwk. (Jam.) (b) Sc. This species of bad sowing is named in the country laddering or happergawin, Stephens Farm Bk. (ed. 1849) I. 539. Rxb. (Jam.) (9) Rxb. My cauldrife muse, wi' age decripit, Looks e'en right lean, and happer-hippit, Ruickbie Wayside Cottager (1807) 175. Nhb. There was knack-kneed Mat, wiv's purple suit, An hopper hipp'd aw yellow, O, Allan Tyneside Sngs. (ed. 1891) 94. (10) w.Yks.² (11) e.Yks.¹
4. A large boat or keel which receives mud from the harbour-dredger, and refuse material from factories, and carries them out to sea.

Nhb.¹ Cum.⁴ The hopper which was in tow of the tug, w.Cum. Times (Oct. 22, 1898) 3.
5. An automatic feeder to the carding-machine into which wool is put before it passes through the rollers. w.Yks. (S.A.B.) 6. A large box to contain coals. Nhb., Dur. Nicholson Coal Tr. Gl. (1888).

[2. He heng an hoper on his bac in stude of a scrippe, P. Plowman (c. 1362) A. vii. 57.]
HOPPER, sb.² Irel. Cum. Chs. Wor. Oxf. Brks. Wil. Som. Cor. [h)oˑpǝ(r.] 1. A small maggot which infests bacon and cheese.

Oxf.¹ MS. add. Brks.¹ w.Som.¹ These have the power of curling and suddenly straightening themselves, thereby they are able to hop or leap several inches. Cor.²
Hence **Hoppery,** adj. abounding in ' hoppers '; also of ground full of hares and rabbits.

Cum. (J.Ar.), Cum.⁴ Oxf.¹ MS. add.
2. A grasshopper. Wil.¹ 3. The three-bearded rockling, Motella vulgaris. Ant. (W.H.P.) 4. A piece of crackling coal in a fire. Som. Sweetman Wincanton Gl. (1885). 5. Salt-making term : a salt crystal that forms at the top of a pan.

Chs.¹ Skeleton salt-crystals, in shape like a hollow, inverted pyramid, that form and float for a time on the surface when coarse salt is being made. w.Wor.¹
HOPPER, sb.³ n.Cy. Lakel. Yks. Lan. Chs. Der. Not. Lin. Lei. Also written hoppett w.Yks. ; hoppit w.Yks.¹³ Chs.¹³ s.Chs.¹ Not. Lei.¹ [h)oˑpit.] 1. The hopper of a mill.

w.Yks. Thoresby Lett. (1703) ; w.Yks.⁴, Chs.¹, s.Chs.¹
2. A small basket, esp. one used by husbandmen to carry seed-corn in sowing time. Cf. hopper, sb.¹ 2.

n.Cy. Grose (1790) ; N.Cy.², Lakel.², n.Yks.¹, m.Yks.¹ w.Yks. Leeds Merc. Suppl. (May 9, 1885) 8 ; w.Yks.¹²³⁴⁵ Lan. Peg had hur hoppet ov hur arm, Scholes Tim Gamwattle (1857) 98 ; Lan.¹ s.Lan.¹ A hopper or wooden vessel in which seed-corn is carried. Chs.¹³, s.Chs.¹ Der. Pope then whirl'd his hoppet round, Furness Medicus (1836) 32 ; Der.¹ A little handbasket. Obs. Not. (J.H.B.) Lin. Ray (1691); Lin.¹ A fruit basket. sw.Lin.¹ A small hand-basket with lids. ' She has ta'en a hoppet with her lunch.' Lei. The basket which a labourer carries on his back when going to his daily work, and which contains his food (C.E.) ; Lei.¹ Gen. oval, with a lid, in which labourers carry out their victuals for the day.
3. A cone-shaped iron ' skep' for carrying materials in the sinking shaft of a coal-mine. w.Yks. (T.T.) 4. Salt-making term : the tub in which rock-salt is raised to the surface. Chs.¹ 5. A beehive. Yks. (J.W.) See Bee-hoppet, s.v. Bee, sb.¹
HOPPET, sb.² Yks. Ess. Also written hoppit Ess.¹ [oˑpit.] 1. A small, square, enclosed field, gen. one near a house.

Ess. Used as a place [hospital] for a sick beast. ' He don't look very fierce [lively], hirn him into the hoppit (M.W.) ; Ess.¹
2. A gaol, prison.
n.Yks. The lower part was made the hoppet or prison, Atkinson Whitby (1894) 204 ; n.Yks.¹² w.Yks. Mi mates wer all e ther 'hoppits' like so menny haufe-fledg'd canaries e ther rearin boxes, Tom Treddlehoyle Bairnsla Ann. (1892) 55.
HOPPET, v. Sc. Yks. Chs. War. Brks. Ken. Som. Cor. Also in forms happit Sc.; hoppety w.Som.¹ [h)oˑpit.] To hop. Som. W.& J. Gl. (1873) ; w.Som.¹
Hence (1) **Hoppetty,** (a) sb. a man with a club-foot ; (b) adj. lame ; (2) **Hoppetty-bed,** sb. the game of hop-scotch ; (3) ·clench or ·clink, (4) ·hick, sb. the uneven gait of a lame person or horse ; (5) ·kick, sb. (a) see (4) ; (b) ? an ill-assorted couple ; a couple ill-assorted as to walking together.

(1, a) Per. (G.W.) (b) Sc. I hae a hen wi' a happitie-leg, Chambers Sngs. (1829) I. 134. Brks.¹ I hev a-bin a bit hoppetty zence the hammer veil on my voot. (a) Cor.² (3) s.Chs.¹ Som. Then he departed without delay, hoppety-hick, all the way to Langport market, Raymond Sam and Sabina (1894) 61. (5, a) w.Yks.² He goes with a hopperty-kick. War.² Spoken of a person whose gait exhibits a sort of hopping movement, followed by a kicking or swinging motion of the rear leg. Ken. (G.B.) w.Som.¹ You don't zay her's gwain to have thick there hoppety-kick fuller ! (b) Edb. A bonny happie-ti-kick ye'll mak o't atween ye, Ballantine Gaberlunnie (ed. 1875) 47.

HOPPETOT, see Hopping-toad.

HOPPIL, *adj.* m.Yks.[1] [Not known to our correspondents.] [o·pil.] Convenient.

Thou'll find a hoppil end for them somewhere.

HOPPING, *ppl. adj.* and *sb.* Irel. Yks. Nhp. Glo. e.An. Som. [h)o·pin.] 1. *ppl. adj.* In *comb.* (1) **Hopping-block**, a stone or steps from which to mount a horse; (2) -derry, a diminutive lame person; (3) — **Giles**, a person who limps; (4) -jack, a frog; (5) -mad, violently angry; (6) -stock, see (1).

(1) **Wxf.** What should I see but masther Billy sitting on the hopping-block, KENNEDY *Banks Boro* (1867) 283. (2) n.Cy. (HALL.) (3) **Nhp.**[1] **e.An.**[1] St. Giles was reputed the especial patron of cripples. Churches dedicated to him were always on the boundaries of towns or cities; and near them, or rather in the neighbouring fields, were lazar-houses or hospitals. e **Suf.** (F.H.) (4) **e.Suf.** (F.H.) (5) Glo. *Gl.* (1851); Glo.[1] (6) w.Som.[1] Called also Upping-stock.

2. *sb.* The game of prison-bars, in which the persons who play hop throughout the game. Brks. (HALL.)

HOPPING, *prp.* Glo. Also in form a-hopping. Fretting. (W.H.C.), Glo.[1]

HOPPING-TOAD, *sb.* e.An. Also in forms **hoppentoad** Nrf. Suf.[1]; **hoppetot** Suf.; **hoppintoad** e.An.[1] 1. A toad, esp. the natterjack, *Bufo calamita*.

e.An.[1] Nrf. COZENS-HARDY *Broad Nrf.* (1893) 7. **Suf.** A toad crawled out of the flowers, and the gardener promptly raised his hoe, and exclaiming, 'I'll larn ycon to be a hoppin' toad,' hewed it in pieces, *e.An. Dy. Times* (1892); **Suf.**[1]

2. A frog.

Nrf. (E.T.B.) **e.Suf.** A frog after it has shed its first skin. Frogs and toads are here confounded, very generally (F.H.).

3. *Comb.* **Hoppen-toad's cap**, a toadstool. e.Suf. (F.H.)

HOPPING-TREE, *sb.* Yks. The stumps in front of a wagon when the shafts have been pulled out; the pole of a coup-cart (q.v.).

n.Yks.[1] **e.Yks.** See that the hoppinge-tree of the first [wagon] standeth under the body of the second, BEST *Rur. Econ.* (1641) 137.

HOPPIT, *sb.*[1] *Obs.* Yks. An infant.

Yks. (HALL.), **n.Yks.**[1] [A young child danced in the arms, KENNETT *Par. Antiq.* (1695).]

HOPPIT, *sb.*[2] *Obs.* w.Yks. A hassock.

To cash pd. for two straw hoppits to kneel on, 1s. 6d., *Bradford Par. Acc.* (1707).

HOPPLE, *v.* and *sb.* Sc. Nhb. Cum. Wm. Yks. Lan. Der. Not. Lin. Lei. Nhp. War. Hrf. e.An. [h)o·pl.] 1. *v.* To tie together two legs of an animal to prevent it straying. Cf. **hobble**, *v.*[1] 5.

Rxb. (JAM.), **N.Cy.**[1], **Nhb.**[1] **Dur.** Cotherstone, where they hopple lops and knee-band spiders, *Prov.* The allusion is to the practice (or supposed practice) in that neighbourhood of hoppling very small cattle (W.H.H.). **Lakel.**[2] **Wm.** T'nag wor hoppled (B.K.); **Wm.**[1] We hoppled em tagedder soa es the cuddent git soa far awaa. **n.Yks.** (I.W.), **n.Yks.**[1 2 4], **ne.Yks.**[1] **e.Yks.** Hopple and sidelange their tuppes, BEST *Rur. Econ.* (1642) 28; **e.Yks.**[1], **m.Yks.**[1], **w.Yks.**[1], Der.[2], nw.Der.[1], Not. (J.H.B.), **Not.**[1 8], **e.Lin.** BROWN *Lit. Laur.* (1890) 68. **sw.Lin.**[1] We used to hopple them just above the cambrils. **Lei.**[1], **Nhp.**[1 2], War.[2], Hrf.[1], e.An.[1], **e.Suf.** (F.H.)

Hence **Hoppled**, *ppl. adj.* having the feet fastened together. **n.Cy.** GROSE (1790). **Nhb.**[1] **n.Yks.** Ah's be nae mair use an a hoppled jackass, ATKINSON *Lost* (1870) xxvi. **m.Yks.**[1] In a leaping match, competitors will sometimes engage each other with 'hoppled legs.' **w.Yks.** HUTTON *Tour to Caves* (1781).

2. To hobble, walk unsteadily; to trot.

Nhb. She wad nowthor drive, hopple, nor leed, ROBSON *Evangeline* (1870) 349; Nhb.[1] **n.Yks.**[2] To 'hopple sair,' to walk badly as with corns on the feet. **w.Yks.** Hardlins hopple along, *Nidderdale Alm.* (1875). **sw.Lin.**[1] I couldn't hopple about hardly. **e.Suf.** (F.H.)

Hence (1) **Hoppled**, *ppl. adj.* lame, crippled; (2) **Hoppling**, *ppl. adj.*, (3) **Hopply**, *adj.* hobbling, limping, tottering; lame.

(1) **w.Yks.** I'se sadly hoppled o mi feet wi corns (J.W.). **sw.Lin.**[1] Some was very nimble, and some seemed very hoppled. (2) **ne.Yks.**[1] He gans hopplin' aboot. **sw.Lin.**[1] He's so hoppling he can't get about. **e.An.**[1] Freq. applied to children. (3) **sw.Lin.**[1] What, you're a bit hopply then !

3. To fetter; also *fig.* to hamper, impede.

Nhb. Faith ! I've been hopp'ld to a prize! PROUDLOCK *Borderland Muse* (1896) 339; Nhb.[1], Cum.[14] **n.Yks.**[4] It's neea ewse his endivering when he's hoppled wiv a weyfe leyke yon ; sha's nowt bud a clog tiv his foot. **w.Yks.** Water and the soft ground hoppled me, SNOWDEN *Web of Weaver* (1896) ix ; **w.Yks.**[2] **Lan.** It's true, as I'se hoppelt here fast i' this dock, BOWNESS *Studies* (1868) 47 ; **Lan.**[1] **s.Lin.** Sin I were hoppled to my loss, BROWN *Lit. Laur.* (1890) 68.

4. *sb.* The rope or strap used to confine the legs of animals; the piece of wood tied to the legs of oxen to prevent them straying.

Rxb. (JAM.), **N.Cy.**[1], **Nhb.**[1], **n.Yks.** (I.W.), **ne.Yks.**[1], **w.Yks.**[2], **Not.**[1] **n.Lin.**[1] Cords made of horse-hair. **sw.Lin.**[1] **s.Lin.** Put the hopples on the hind legs of the filly while we dress the sore on her shoulder (T.H.R.). **Lei.**[1] Blame the gel ! shay's ollus slippin' her hopples an fallin' to pieces. **Nhp.**[1 2], War.[2], e.An.[1], **e.Suf.** (F.H.)

HOPPS, *sb. pl.* Cor.[2] [Not known to our correspondents.] Small bits of anything.

HOPPY, *adj.* and *sb.* Cum. Yks. Mid. Also written **hopy** w.Yks.[8] [h)o·pi.] 1. *adj.* Lame. Also used *advb.*

w.Mid. 'To go hoppy' is to walk rather lame. Among the working classes, lame persons are often nicknamed 'Oppy,' as 'Oppy Smith,' which denotes a certain Smith who is somewhat lame (W.P.M.).

2. *sb.* A child's name for a horse ; a toy horse. **Cum.**[14], **w.Yks.**[8] ; also in *comp.* **Hopy-dob**. w.Yks.[8] Cf. **houpy**.

3. *Comb.* **Hoppy-bed**, a simple form of the game of hopscotch, in which the plan marked out has only five to eight divisions. **Cum.**[4]

HOPPY, *v.* Glo. Som. Dev. Also written **hoppee** n.Dev. [o·pi.] To caper, jump.

Glo.[1] **w.Som.**[1] Aa·l mack dhee aup·ee lau·ng, ah-uur· mee, neef dus·n muuv·ee [I'll make you get on, dost hear me ? if dost not make haste]. **n.Dev.** Chell make thy kep hoppee, *Exm. Scold.* (1746) l. 94.

Hence **Hoppy-gallows**, *sb.* a bar set up for jumping over. nw.Dev.[1]

HOPPY, see **Houpy**.

HOPRICK, *sb.* Rxb. (JAM.) [Not known to our correspondents.] A wooden pin driven into the heels of shoes.

HOP-SHACKLE, HOR, see **Hap-shackle, Her**.

HORBLE, *v.* Wm. To join ; to gather together.

A miser was said to 'horble' money. A patient said of a dislocated shoulder, after very painful unsuccessful manipulations, 'Oa, let it horble up' (J.M.).

Hence **Horbling**, *ppl. adj.* closely united, hard, knotty. Com. used of tumours under the skin, usually of movable tumours. A cancerous breast was described as a 'nasty girt horblen lump' (*ib.*).

HORBLED, *adj.* Cum. Stunted, not freely grown. **Cum.**[4] (s.v. Knur't.)

HORCH, *v.* Som. Dev. Also in form **ortch** Dev.[8] [ō·tʃ.] To push or gore with the horns.

w.Som.[1] 'Ton't do for they bullicks for to be a-dring'd up too much, they'll sure t'horch one or tother.' Common. **Dev.** 'The cow horched John.' It is quite common to hear, 'The bullocks be horchin' about, we be gwain t'have rain,' when they push or butt each other with their heads, *Reports Provinc.* (1889) ; 'Er wuz coming up Smalworthy 'ill when Varmer Tapper's bull urned out an' ortched 'er in the zide, HEWETT *Peas. Sp.* (1892) ; Dev.[8] Tha bûle 'th a-ortched Feddy How in es stummick an' us be afeared 'e'll die.

HORCLE, HORD, HORENG, see **Hurkle, Hear, Hoarin**.

HORIE GOOSE, *phr.* Sh. & Or.I. Also in form **horra** goose S. & Ork.[1] The brent-goose, *Bernicla brenta*.

Sh.I. SWAINSON *Birds* (1885) 149. Or.I. On the . . . shores of Deerness are seen myriads of plovers . . . and a large grey bird with a hoarse cry, called by the inhabitants 'Horra Goose,' *Statist. Acc.* X. 203 (JAM.); **S. & Ork.**[1]

HORK, *v.* n.Yks.[4] [ork.] To trail about. Cf. **hawk**, *v.*[1]

HORKEY, HORKLE, HORL, see **Hockey**, *sb.*[1], **Hurkle**, *v.*, **Harl, Hurl**, *v.*[1]

HORN, *sb.* and *v.* Var. dial. uses in Sc. Irel. Eng. and Amer. Also written **hooan** n.Yks.; **hoarn** Nhb.[1]; **hoorn** n.Yks.[2]; and in form **orn** w.Yks. [h)orn, ɔən.] 1. *sb.* In *comb.* (1) **Horn-and-hoof fair**, a fair principally for horses and cattle ; (2) -arred, branded on the horns ; (3) -beam, (4) -beech, the witch-elm, *Ulmus montana* ; (5)

·blŏd, a form of cupping ; (6) ·book, *obs.*, a child's primer ; (7) ·bouet, a hand-lantern ; (8) ·burn, (*a*) a mark branded upon horned sheep, &c. ; (*b*) to brand the horns of cattle ; (9) ·coot, the long-eared owl, *Asio otus* ; (10) -cutty, a short spoon made of horn ; (11) ·daft, quite mad, foolish, outrageous ; (12) ·dry, dry, empty, thirsty for drink ; (13) -eel, the garfish, *Belone vulgaris* ; (14) ·end, the best or parlour end of a house ; (15) ·fair, see below ; (16) ·fish, see (13) ; (17) ·garth, a fence round horned stock ; (18) ·garth service, the annual setting up of a hedge of wicker-work on the *e.* shore of Whitby harbour ; (19) ·geld, a form of rent, the amount of which is settled by the number of horned cattle possessed by the tenant, 'cornage' ; (20) ·golach, the earwig ; (21) ·grey, a variety of pea ; (22) ·haft, a haft or heft made of horn ; (23) ·hard, (*a*) very hard ; (*b*) soundly, profoundly ; (24) ·head, with full force ; without stopping ; (25) ·idle, quite idle ; (26) ·mad, raving mad ; outrageously vexed ; (27) ·mark, see (8, *a*) ; (28) ·ouzel, see below [not known to our correspondents] ; (29) ·pane, the pane of a horn window ; (30) ·pie, (*a*) the lapwing, *Vanellus vulgaris* ; (*b*) the plover, *Charadrius pluvialis* ; (31) ·shoot, crooked, twisted out of the straight line ; (32) ·spoon, a spoon made of horn ; (33) ·tammie, a butt, a laughing-stock ; (34) ·top, in phr. *as slow as a horn-top*, excessively slow ; (35) ·wink, see (30, *a*) ; see Hornywink.

(1) Chs. MARSHALL *Review Agric.* (1818) II. 122 ; At Chester there are three very considerable fairs in the year. The first, held on the last Thursday in Feb., is principally for cattle and horses, and is called Horn and Hoof fair, HOLLAND *View Agric.* (1808) 313 ; Chs.[1] (a) n.Yks.[2] (3) w.Som.[1] The usual name. (4) Sur.[1] (5) Sh.I. For sprains and bruises, and affections of an inflammatory nature, a form of cupping called horn blŏd was very frequently employed, and even yet is not quite obs. . . . The blŏd-horn was commonly made of the horn of a quey or young cow, SPENCE *Flk-Lore* (1899) 159. (6) Gall. Wull ye sit doon lake Hennypenny in the hornbuik wi' your finger in your mooth? CROCKETT *Stickit Min.* (1893) 148. n.Lin.[1] Hornbooks were used here in dames' schools until about a hundred years ago. Cor. His earliest education was at the dame's school, where . . . he learned from his horn-book, COUCH *Hist. Polperro* (1871) 4. (7) Edb. The watchmen that guarded us . . . in blue dreadnoughts with red necks, and battons, and horn-bouets, MOIR *Mansie Wauch* (1828) vi. (8, *a*) Cum. *Helvellyn in Cornh. Mag.* (Oct. 1890) 388. w.Yks. (J.J.B.) (*b*) n.Yks.[2], w.Yks.[1] (9) Dar.[2], nw.Der.[1] Hrt. ELLIS *Mod. Husb.* (1750) V. ii. 105. (10) n.Sc. Put far awa' your siller speens, . . And bring to me my horn cutties, BUCHAN *Ballads* (1828) II. 95, ed. 1875. (11) n.Sc. Tibby Stott's no that far wrang there, . . horn daft as she is, HOGG *Winter Evening Tales* (1820) I. 314 (JAM.). Cai.[1] Ayr. Horn daft is he wha greens to gie A liferent to some gipsy, AINSLIE *Land of Burns* (ed. 1892) 253. (12) Cai.[1], Twd. (JAM.) n.Yks.[2] ' Thou's hoorn-dry,' your glass is empty. (13) N.I.[1] (14) Abd. He would himself . . . walk . . . solemnly along to the ' horn en' ' to seek repose, ALEXANDER *Ain Flk.* (1882) 208. (15) Ken. The sternly virtuous cottagers . . . held a ' Horn Fair.' Some erring barmaid at the inn . . . aroused their righteous ire . . . with cow's horns, poker and tongs, and tea-trays . . . [They] collected night after night by the tavern, and made [a] fearful uproar, JEFFERIES *Hdgrow.* (1889) 69 ; Ken.[1] An annual fair held at Charlton, in Kent, on St. Luke's Day. . . It consists of a riotous mob, who, after a printed summons, disperse through the adjacent towns, meet at Cuckold's Point, near Deptford, and march from thence, in procession, through that town and Greenwich to Charlton, with horns of different kinds upon their heads ; and, at the fair, there are sold ram's horns, and every sort of toy made of horn ; even the ginger-bread figures have horns. It was formerly the fashion for men to go to Hornfair in women's clothes. Sus.[1] Rough music with frying pans, horns, &c., generally reserved for persons whose matrimonial difficulties have attracted the attention of their neighbours. (16) Cor.[2] (17) n.Yks. ATKINSON *Whitby* (1894) 52. (18) n.Yks.[2] (19) Cum.[4] (20) Ags. (JAM.) (21) Bdf. The horn-grey is sometimes sown in mixture with beans, BATCHELOR *Agric.* (1813) 399. (22) Kar. In Kinross was I made, Horn-haft and blade, HALIBURTON *Furth in Field* (1894) 198. (23, *a*) Sc. The hearty shake of Mr. Girder's horn-hard palm, SCOTT *Bride of Lam.* (1819) xxv. Cum. He wink't horn hard when he fir't his gun, CLARK *Survey* (1787) 32 ; Cum.[14] (*b*) Abd. The lads are sleeping horn-hard, Ross *Helenore* (1768) 56, ed. 1812. (24) Slk. (JAM.) (25) Sc. I

fell into a bit gruff sure enough, sittin' horn idle, wi' my hand aneath my haffit, *Saxon and Gael* (1814) I. 189 (JAM.). Lnk., Lth. (JAM.) Peb. Through the day ye gang horn idle, How I fend ye never think, AFFLECK *Poet. Wks.* (1836) 132. (26) Sc. The man is mad, horn-mad, SCOTT *Nigel* (1822) xxvi ; Well, I tell ye fairly, I'm horn-mad, STEVENSON *Catriona* (1893) Ix. Lth. By yonder horned moon It's clear ye're a' horn-mad, MACNEILL *Poet. Wks.* (1801) 175, ed. 1856. Nhb.[1], nw.Der.[1] (27 ' Ayr. A' the lug and horn marks o' my staigs and stots, SERVICE *Notandums* (1890) 5. (28) N.I.[1] A bird mentioned by Harris (1744) as found in Dwn. (29) Wxf. There came on his mind at times, a glimmering as it were through a horn-pane, KENNEDY *Evenings Duffry* (1869) 56. (30, *a*) s.An.[1] The long tuft of feathers on its head confers on it the first syllable of this name. Nrf. Here, 'bor, hornpies, or pe-weeps, as some calls 'em, gin'rally lead this time o' the year, PATTERSON *Man and Nat.* (1895) 106. Suf. (C.G B.), Suf.[1] e.Suf. *e.An. Dy. Times* (1892) ; (F.H.) (*b*) Suf. (H.H.), e.Suf. (F.H.) (31) w.Yks.[1] w.Som.[1] Very com. ' Thick there board 'on't do ; can't never get-n true, he's a'horn shut's a dog's hind leg.' (32) s.Sc. Sowens . . . was then set down, Sae ilk auld Billie chang'd his bad-ane For a horn-spoon, T. SCOTT *Poems* (1793) 341. Ayr. The medium o' conveyance a horn spoon, HUNTER *Studies* (1870) 156. Dmf. Tureens o' reekin' kail. At whilk carls would wag the lang horn spoon, THOM *Jock o' the Knows* (1877) 39, ed. 1878. (33) Abd. (JAM.) (34) s.Cur.[1], n.Yks. (I.W.) (35) Dev.[2]

2. Phr. (1) *as dry as a horn*, very dry ; (2) *as fond as a horn*, very foolish ; (3) *as hard as a horn*, very hard ; (4) *horn, corn, and wool*, all the stock and crops of a farm ; (5) *horn and spoon*, drink and food ; (6) *in a horn*, an expression of incredulity, used in reference to an event which is never likely to happen ; (7) *old in the horn*, old ; (8) *so crooked as a horn*, very crooked ; (9) *to be deaf in the horn*, to be dull, stupid ; (10) *to bear away the horn*, to win the prize in any contest ; (11) *to be nicked in the horn* or *to have many nicks in one's horn*, to be advanced in years ; (12) *to blow a good horn*, to look well and hearty ; (13) *to have a soft horn*, to be a simpleton ; (14) *to have the horn in one's hip*, to have the mastery over one ; (15) *to have got the horn*, to be lustful ; (16) *to have got the horn in one*, to be slightly tipsy ; (17) *to have too much horn*, to be impudent ; (18) *to make a blow horn of a thing*, to proclaim it everywhere ; (19) *to sleep as sound as a horn*, to sleep very soundly ; (20) *to take off the horn*, to drink off a 'horn' of ale ; (21) *all horns to the lift*, a game ; see below ; (22) *to draw in one's horns*, to retract one's opinions ; to retrench ; (23) *to get the horns*, to be made a cuckold.

(1) Cai.[1], Lth. (JAM.), n.Yks. (T.S.) (2) n.Yks. (I.W.) (3) Cai.[1] (4) Abd. Things are deein' gran'—horn, corn, and woo', *Guidman Inglismaill* (1873) 37. (5) Per. Sorn on them for horn and spune, HALIBURTON *Ochil Idylls* (1891) 46. (6) Suf.[1] Dev. *Horae Subsecivae* (1777) 71 ; 'Yes, in horn, Master Franky, I should think you would.' As much as to say, ' I think I see you doing it,' *Reports Provinc.* (1887) 9. [Amer. Now common, used to qualify a falsehood. . . A boy will say, 'I saw a man jump over the house,' and add *into voce*, 'In a horn,' meaning thereby directly the reverse. ' Tie the boat up!' says Jim, 'I'll lie her up, in a horn! Do you reckon I can't run her in such a fog as we'll have to-night?' *N. Y. Spirit of the Times*.] (7) Per. A'm ower auld in the horn to change noo, IAN MACLAREN *Brier Bush* (1895) 43. (8) w.Som.[1] (9) Gall. O but wi' scholar-craft my ain, To see this whurlie-birlie. But hech! I am unco deaf i'e horn, A shauler gow was never seen, MACTAGGART *Encycl.* (1824) 476, ed. 1876. (10) Sc. He that blows best bear[s] away the horn, KELLY *Prov.* (1721). (11) Lnk. I'm owre weel nicket in the horns by this time to let a Cockney tak' a laugh oot o' me, MURDOCH *Readings* (ed. 1878) III. 108. Edb. ' Hegh sirs, does she expect to be Lady Nairn?' ' There's ower mony nicks in her horn, I doot,' BALLANTINE *Gaberlunzie* (ed. 1875) 172. (12) Wm. Thoo blows a rare good horn (B.K.). (13) w.Ir. My horn's not so soft, all out, as to repair your auld goose for nothin', LOVER *Leg.* (1848) I. 9. (14) Abd. In his hip they ha'e their horn An' push him headlong to the foot, Wi' the brutality o' nowt, ANDERSON *Poems* (1826) 77. (15) s.Suf. He has got the horn (F.H.). (16) N.I.[1] (17) Lakel.[2] Thoo's ower mich horn fer me. (18) Cai.[1] (19) Cai.[1] (20) Lth. Gin ye tak' nae aff yer horn, They're no right weel contented, BRUCE *Poems* (1813) II. 19. (21) Sc. A circle is formed round a table, and all placing their fore fingers on the table, one cries. 'A' horns to the lift, cats' horns uppost.' If on this anyone lift his finger, he owes a wad [forfeit], as cats have no horns. In the same

manner, the person who does not raise his finger, when a horned animal is named, is subject to a forfeit. The wads are recovered by the performance of some task, as kissing, at the close of the grme, the person named by the one who has his eyes tied up (JAM.). **(aa)** Sc. He 'drew in his horns,' to use the Bailie's phrase, on the instant, professed no intention whatever to disoblige, Scott *Rob Roy* (1817) xxvii. n.Cy. (J.W.), **Nhp.[1]**, **War.[2]**, **Hnt**. (T.P.F.) **Dor.** I draw in the horns of my mind and think to myself, Hardy *Ethelberta* (1876) i. **(23)** Gall. A smith, may be ye kend him, That's got the horns, Lauderdale *Poems* (1796) 67.

3. A drinking-vessel; a draught of ale or whisky; a tin vessel used for warming drink, a 'hastener.'

Sc. He . . . ca'd in at the change-house, an' took a gude horn, Vedder *Poems* (1842) 206. **Elg.** Welcome at morn a weel-filled horn, When drouthy dogs are dry, Tester *Poems* (1865) 121. **Abd.** He and I sall hae a horn, Beattie *Parings* (1801) 36, ed. 1873. **Frf.** The Captain . . . drew his bottle an' gie'd me a guid muckle horn . . . o' the real Glenferrichan, Lowson *Guidfollow* (1890) 55. **Per.** They'll reach the howff by fa' o' nicht, In Poussie Nancy's cowp the horn, Haliburton *Ochil Idylls* (1891) 22. **Fif.** Welcome, childer, tak' a horn O' my rare highland whisky, Douglas *Poems* (1806) 141. **Rnf.** He . . . Can tak' a hearty horn at e'en, Picken *Poems* (1813) I. 154. **Ayr.** That merry night we get the corn in! O sweetly, then, thou reams the horn in! Burns *Sc. Drink* (1786) st. 9. **Lnk.** Twa hours confab Owre a horn o' gude yill, Rodger *Poems* (1838) 32, ed. 1897. **Edb.** They toutit aff the horn, Which wambles thro' their weym Wi' pain, Ferguson *Poems* (1773) 157, ed. 1785. **Shr.[1]** Hrf.[2] Fast going out of use. **Oxf.** To have a 'half horn' is a very common phr., meaning to have half a pint of beer (G.O.).

Hence **Horning**, *sb.* a supply of drink.

Lnk. Cam' the drouths to get their bornin', Nicholson *Kilwuddie* (ed. 1895) 71. **Edb.** He reels hame . . . An' pours out the effects o' hornin', Learmont *Poems* (1791) 172.

4. A spoon made of horn.

Ayr. Horn for horn they stretch and strive, Burns *To a Haggis*, st. 4.

Hence **Horner**, *sb.* a maker of horn spoons.

Abd. (Jam. *Suppl.*) **Bwk.** They are known 'either as horners, muggers, or besom and basket-makers,' Henderson *Pop. Rhymes* (1856) 124.

5. A snuff-box in form of a sheep's horn.

Mry. A native of Dallas, who carried several snuff-mulls about him, and to almost every person he met, offered his horn to take a pinch, Hay *Lintie* (1851) 75. **Lnk.** Ay the ither pinch (they) were takin' O' gude Scots snuff frae out a' horn, Muir *Minstrelsy* (1816) 41. **Peb.** It was his doom, Whan takan' o' a sneesh, Auld Sawny's horn on's croon tae toom, *Lintoun Green* (1685) 57, ed. 1817.

6. A vessel used for cupping.

Sh.I. I houp Arty tell'd you ta tak' da horn, Sh. *News* (Sept. 11, 1897). **Or.I.** For a cupping glass they have a horn with a small thin skin at the lesser end: the way how they use it is thus, the physician with the point of his knife gives three or four small cuts or gashes on the place where he proposes to set the horn, and having set the broadest end on the wounds, he sucks the small end a little and then lets it stand, till the abundance of blood that it draws make it full off. Wallace *Desc. Or. I.* (1693) 39, ed. 1883.

7. Hard skin on the foot; a corn.

n.Sc. (Jam.) **Abd.** Your edge sometimes has touched the horn, Or men't a pen, or cut a corn, Anderson *Rhymes* (1867) 116.

8. A comb for the hair.

Ayr. In some beggar's haffet squattle; . . Whare horn nor bane ne'er dare unsettle Your thick plantations, Burns *To a Louse*, st. 3. **Lan.[1]** Tak how o' this horn, an' ready thi yure a bit, Waugh *Chim. Corner* (1879) 168.

9. The continuation of the stern of a boat. S. & Ork.[1]

10. The nose; also used *fig.* of things.

Sc. I wad like ill to wait till Mr. Harrison and auld Gudyill cam to pu' us out by the lug and the horn, Scott *Old Mortality* (1816) vii. **Lth.** Tea-pots wi' baith lug an' horn, Thomson *Poems* (1819) 73. **Gall.** There ye [a teapot] set, wi' lug an' horn, My joy an' comfort, e'en an' morn, Lauderdale *Poems* (1796) 85.

11. Part of a bell.

Ayr. The model bell o' a' the laun', Twal' hunner wecht jist as ye staun', Tongue, lip, an' horn, Laing *Poems* (1854) 79.

12. A corner.

Nhb.[1] It occurs in place-names. **Ken.** The horn of an apple pasty (K.); Ken.[1]

13. A legal term; *gen.* in phr. *put to the horn*, declared a criminal; see below.

Sc. To 'put to the horn' was almost a proverbial expressicn,

and came from one of the recognised statutory Acts. . . The theory of law which gave rise to this process of horning was that the debtor who failed to obey the Royal summons to pay his debt was to be treated as a rebel against authority, and when he had been 'put to the horn' he could be thrown into prison, though he had to be maintained there not by the State, but by the creditor. This could not be done, however, until the debtor was duly warned and given a certain time to pay. If that was overrun the Horning Office officials proceeded to the cross of the burgh or county town, read letters of denunciation against the debtor, and then followed that up by three blasts on a horn, and by the affixing of the letters to the cross. This practice . . . has long since fallen into desuetude, *Scotsman* (June 28, 1899). **Bnff.** 'At the horn,' on the verge of bankruptcy (Jam.). **Abd.** She rung the bell instantly on her servants to put him to the horn, Shirrefs *Poems* (1790) 305. **Dmb.** Glad to catch him with your poind and horn, Salmon *Gowodean* (1868) 63. **Ayr.** I'll be put to the horn whenever it's kent, Service *Notandums* (1890) 60. **Lnk.** [They] Will be harry't wi' taxes, an' put to the horn, Hamilton *Poems* (1865) 46. **Edb.** Your horn and caption and sic gear, Liddle *Poems* (1821) 243. **Gall.** I had been put to the horn—that is I had been proclaimed rebel and outlaw at the Cross of Edinburgh with three blasts of the king's horn, Crockett *Grey Man* 1896) vi.

Hence **(1) Horner**, *sb.* one who is sent to Coventry; **(2) Horning**, *sb.* the legal process of 'putting to the horn'; *gen.* in *comb.* **Letters of horning**, or **Horning and caption**, an order requiring a debtor to pay his debt on pain of being declared a rebel; a letter of amercement.

(1) n.Sc. (Jam.) **(2)** Sc. If he was freed o' his hornings and captions, Scott *Rob Roy* (1817) xxvi. **Sh.I.** 'Horning,' or 'putting to the horn,' was the method of enforcing the decrees of the civil courts, Willcock *Minister* (1897) 27. **Abd.** Ralph Boswell the officer . . . threatened the parishioners with charges, hornings, poindings, distrainings, &c., Ruddiman *Sc. Parish* (1828) 43, ed. 1889. **Per.** Summonses, hornings, and poindings for debtors, Stewart *Character* (1857) 35. **w.Sc.** If I'm alive, I will, to-morrow morning, Protest his bill, and get a charge o' horning, Carrick *Laird of Logan* (1835) 200. **Fif.** It is desyred that by speciall Act of Parliament, horning and caption be decerned aganis excommunicats, Row *Ch. Hist.* (1650) 64, ed. 1842. **Slg.** The council resisted still threatened with letters of horning, Bruce *Sermons* (1631) 119, ed. 1843. **Ayr.** However strict in the harsh offices of caption and horning, he had the friendly spirit of the poor man among the poor, Galt *Sir A. Wylie* (1822) vii; 'Horning' and 'caption' were forms of diligence. 'Letters of caption,' which ran in the name of the sovereign and were authenticated by his signet, ordered the judges and officers of the law to incarcerate a debtor who had disobeyed the charge given him on 'letters of horning' to pay a debt or perform an act, *ib. note A*. **Lnk.** The ither mornin', wi' a' caption an' hornin', The auld janitor—deathseiz'd on Johnny the Laird, Lemon *St. Mungo* (1844) 84. **Lth.** In Session Courts and Admiralty Till tired o' horning and memorial, Ye turn frae tricks to things corporeal, Macneill *Poet. Wks.* (1801) 168, ed. 1856. **Edb.** As if he had been an Edinburgh Parliament House lawyer, studying his hornings, Moir *Mansie Wauch* (1828) xxiv. **Slk.** Never went to bed without sayin his prayers to escape a charge o' hornin, Chr. North *Noctes* (ed. 1856) III. 285. **Gall.** This is not a horning but a hanging job, Crockett *Moss-Hags* (1895) xvi. **Kcb.** If I had that pawn I would bide horning and hell both, ere I give it again, Rutherford *Lett.* (1660). No. 134.

14. *pl.* The awns of barley. e.An.[1], e.Suf. (F.H.)

Hence **Horny**, *adj.* of barley: abounding in 'horns.'

e.An.[1] It is applied to a sample of barley, from which the awns have not been properly separated in the process of winnowing. e.Suf. (F.H.)

15. The old name for 'outlets,' wooden frames used to enlarge the carrying surface of a wagon. Ken. (D.W.L.)

16. *v.* To gore, push with the horns.

Ir. They kicked and they horned, so that she was afraid to come near them, Kennedy *Fireside Stories* (1870) 35. **N.I.[1]** n.Lin. He horn'd th' poor thing to dead (M.P.). **Oxf.** If thee goest in old Dan'l Kearsey's close, his bull 'll horn thee, Ellis *Pronunc.* (1889) V. 126. **e.Nrf.** Marshall *Rur. Econ.* (1787). **e.Suf.** (F.H.)

17. To publish anything abroad as by blast of a horn.

Dor. 'I'm afeard your labour in keeping it close will be throwed away,' said Coggan. . . 'Labe Tall's old woman will horn it all over parish in half-an-hour,' Hardy *Madding Crowd* (1874) lvii.

Hence **Horning**, *vbl. sb.* trumpeting.

Do hold thy horning, Jan! Hardy *Madding Crowd* (1874) xlii.

18. To saw the horns off cattle. N.I.[1] Hence **Horned,** *adj.* of cattle : having the horns sawn off. *ib.*
19. To pour drink down a person's throat ; to drench a beast.
n.Yks. (I.W.) ; n.Yks.[2] 'We hoorn'd it intiv her,' said of liquid medicine for the cow, poured through a natural horn. w.Yks. Nurse 'ad fairly to 'orn the brandy into her (F.P.T.).
20. To cup.
Sh.I. Kirstin is [has] horn'd mam's shooder. . . Hornin' an' kuppin' wis maistly da cûre for a', *Sh. News* (Sept. 11, 1897).
21. Curling term ; see below.
Sc. When the stone has not pith to cross the score, which the sweepers wish—the opposite side cry out in derision 'horn him, horn him'—draw it up by the handle, which of course takes it out of play (G.W.).
22. *Obs.* To cuckold.
Sc. By those that do their neighbour [*sic*] horn, COLVIL *Whigs Supplication* (1796) I. 64 ; He cherish'd one himself to horn, *ib.* 342.
Hence **Horning,** *vbl. sb.* cuckolding.
Edb. Let auld Jock a horning dree . . . And she'se ne'er be blam'd by me, M⁰DOWALL *Poems* (1839) 199.
HORNA, *sb.* Sh.I. A ewe.
I wis gotten mee ee apo' wir horna an' her lamb, so I says . . . 'Fist haud o' yon lamb at horna's side,' *Sh. News* (July 31, 1897).
[Cp. Norw. dial. *hyrna,* a horned animal, esp. a sheep, also called *hornsaud* (AASEN).]
HORNBILL-BUNTING, *sb.* Irel. The corn-bunting, *Emberiza miliaria.* SWAINSON *Birds* (1885) 69.
HORN-DOON, see **Undern.**
HORNECKS, *sb. pl. Obs.* Sc. The roots of a plant, probably the earth-nut, *Bunium flexuosum.* Cf. **gourlins.**
Gall. The black bulbous roots of an herb with a white bushy flower, good to eat, called hornecks in some parts of Scotland, MACTAGGART *Encycl.* (1824) 234, ed. 1876.
HORNED, *ppl. adj.* Sc. Yks. Not. Lei. Nrf. Hmp. Wil.
1. Furnished with horns ; used *fig.* of a cuckold.
Frf. Our horn'd master (waes me for him) Believes that sly boots does adore him, MORISON *Poems* (1790) 112.
2. *Comb.* (1) **Horned cattle,** domestic animals having horns ; (2) — **owl,** the long-eared owl, *Asio otus.*
(1) Not.[1], Lei.[1] (2) w.Nrf. COZENS-HARDY *Broad Nrf.* (1893) 45. Wil. THURN *Birds* (1870) 11.
3. Hard as horn ; also with 'up' : of land ; see below. ·
n.Yks. Our hands are horned [ooand] (I.W.). Hmp. When land gets very dry and hard so as to be unworkable it is what is called 'horned up' (H.C.M.B.).
HORNEL, *sb.* Fif. (JAM.) A name given to the sand-eel, *Ammodytes tobianus* or *A. lancea,* when of large size.
HORNEN, *adj.* e.An. Hmp. Wil. Som. Also written **hornin** Som. ; and in forms **harnen** Hmp.[1] Wil.[2] ; **harnin** Som. Made of horn.
e.An.[1] A hornen spoon. e.Suf. (F.H.) Hmp.[1] If a horse's skin [is] coarse, it is called harnen. Wil. SLOW *Gl.* (1892) ; Wil.[2] n.Wil. Thus knife got a harnen handle to un, have'n a ? (E.H.G.) Som. W. & J. *Gl.* (1873) ; JENNINGS *Obs. Dial. w.Eng.* (1825). w.Som.[1] A hornen lantern is in every farm stable.
Hence **Hornen-book,** *sb.* the horn-book. e.An.[1] Som. JENNINGS *ib.*
HORNER-SCORNER, *sb.* Nrf. A term used by boys for the game of prisoner's base. (W.W.S.)
HORNET, *sb.* Nhp. Dor. **1.** The common wasp. Dor. (C.W.) **2.** The large dragon-fly, *Libellula vulgatissima.* Nhp.[1]
HORNICLE, *sb.*[1] Suf. Ken. Sus. [ō·nikl.] A hornet. Suf. BAILEY (1721). Ken.[12] Sus. RAY (1691) ; Sus.[12]
HORNICLE, *sb.*[2] Suf. [Not known to our correspondents.] A little hand-basket. (P.R.)
HORNIE, *sb.* Sc. Irel. n.Cy. Nhb. Yks. Also written **hoorny** n.Yks.[2] ; **horney** N.I.[1] N.Cy.[1] Nhb.[1] ; and in form **hornock** Lnk. **1.** The devil.
Elg. It smells o' Hornie's herrin' pickle, TESTER *Poems* (1865) 147. Frf. Newd doin' bodies . . . Wad amaist as soon send for auld Hornie himsel', WATT *Poet. Sketches* (1880) 74. Per. Hornie did present himsel' ; I didna like his seety smell, FORD *Harp* (1893) 95. Slg. Auld Hornie Wha serves them as their chief attorney, GALLOWAY *Poems* (1792) 42. Rnf. A waggon sae rare That e'en to auld Hornie cou'd venture, PICKEN *Poems* (1813) II. 44. Ayr. Should Hornie, as in ancient days, 'Mang sons o' God

present him, BURNS *Holy Fair* (1785) st. 12. Lnk. In auld Hornock's drear dominions, He scarce had wind to lift his pinions, *Devil's Hallowe'en* (1856) 12. Lth. Auld Hornie is maist like to be burned and blazed aff at the hinder end, LUMSDEN *Sheep-head* (1892) 206.
2. *Comp.* **Hoorniman,** the devil. n.Yks.[2]
3. A slang word for a constable.
N.I.[1] Dub. Look out, boys—the horney's comin' (A.S.P.).
4. An untruth ; a hoax, delusion ; also in *comp.* **Horney-way.**
N.Cy.[1] Nhb. Begox ! it's all a horney, ROBSON *Sngs. of Tyne* (1849) 25 ; Nhb.[1]
5. *Phr.* (1) *fair horney(s,* fair play ; (2) *to believe a thing horney-way(s,* to recognize that it is a hoax.
(1) Fif. 'Fair Hornie !' was the general appeal for honesty in games, COLVILLE *Vernacular* (1899). e.Lth. Fair hornie ; if I'm to gang up the brae, ye'll hae to come doun, HUNTER *J. Inwick* (1895) 39. N.Cy.[1] Nhb. What will ye tyek for the beast ? Come noo,. fair horneys (R.O.H.). (2) Nhb.[1]
HORNPIPES IN FETTERS, *phr.* Lon. A dance.
The other dances are jigs, 'flash jigs '—hornpipes in fetters, MAYHEW *Lond. Labour* (1851) I. 12.
HORNSEY, see **Heronsew.**
HORNTA, *adj. Obs.* Wxf.[1] Also written **hoornta.** Horned.
HORNY, *adj.* and *sb.* Sc. Nhb. Dur. Lakel. Lan. Bck. Bdf. Also written **horney** N.Cy.[1] Nhb.[1] ; **hornie** Sc.
1. *adj.* In *comb.* (1) **Horny-corn,** (2) **-dorney,** a snail with a shell ; (3) **-golach,** the earwig ; (4) **-holes,** a game for four persons ; see below ; (5) **-hoolet** or **-oolet,** the long-eared owl, *Asio otus* ; (6) **-rebels,** a children's game ; (7) **-tram,** a tram with four upright arms or horns of iron used for leading timber or rails ; (8) **-worm,** a grub ; see below.
(1) Bdf. (J.W.B.) (2) Bck. (H.K.) (3) Sc. (A.W.) (4) Rxb. A. stands with his assistant at one hole, and throws what is called a cat (a piece of stick and frequently a sheep's horn) with the design of making it alight in another hole at some distance, at which B. and his assistant stand ready to drive it aside. The bat or driver is a rod resembling a walking-stick. The following rhyme . . . is repeated by a player on the one side, while they on the other are gathering in the cats ; and is attested by old people as of great antiquity : 'Jock, Speak, and Sandy, Wi' a' their lousie train, Round about by Errinborra We'll ne'er meet again. Gae head 'im, gae hang 'im, Gae lay 'im in the sea ; A' the birds o' the air Will bear 'im companie. With a nig-nag, widdy- [or worry-] bag, And an e'endown trail, trail ; Quoth he ' (JAM.). (5) e.Lth. SWAINSON *Birds* (1885) 128. (6) Ayr. (JAM.) (7) Nhb.[1] Nhb., Dur. NICHOLSON *Coal Tr. Gl.* (1888). e.Dur.[1] (8) Fif. A grub, or thick, short worm with a very tough skin, inclosing a sort of chrysalis, which in June or July becomes the long-legged fly called by children 'Spin-Mary' (JAM.).
2. With horns, strong, fortified.
Gall. They dunch down strengths like wiggiewams, And hornie wa's roun towns, MACTAGGART *Encycl.* (1824) 247, ed. 1876.
3. Noisy as a horn.
Slg. Confound that horny trumpet cock, TOWERS *Poems* (1885) 18.
4. Amorous ; fond of drink. Ayr. (JAM.)
5. *sb.* A ball made of horn. ne.Lan.[1] **6.** A boy's top made from the tip of a cow's horn ; freq. in *comp.* **Horney-top.** N.Cy.[1], Nhb.[1], Lakel.[2]
Lth. A game among children, in which one of the company runs after the rest, having his hands clasped and his thumbs pushed out before him in resemblance of horns. The first person whom he touches with his thumbs becomes his property, joins hands with him, and aids in attempting to catch the rest ; and so on till they are all made captives. Those who are at liberty, still cry out ' Hornie, hornie !' (JAM.)
8. *pl.* Horned cattle. Rxb. (JAM.)
HORNYWINK, *sb.* Dev. Cor. Also written **horney-wink** Cor.[1] ; **horniwink** Dev. Cor. ; and in forms **horny-wick** Dev. ; **hornywig** n.Dev. ; **hornywinky** Cor.[2] ; **horrywink** Cor.[1] **1.** The lapwing, *Vanellus vulgaris.*
Dev. The horniwinks have left the moor, BARING-GOULD *Dartmoor Idylls* (1896) 101. Dev. *Hand-bk.* (1877) 258, 4th ed. nw.Dev.[1] Gen. called Bradery horny-wink. At Combmartin this bird is called Challacombe horny-wink. Cor. From the long crest

like a horn projecting from the back of its head, SWAINSON *Birds* (1885) 184: If I was to hear a horniwink whistle outside o' the winder I'd up . . . and away I'd go out o' the winder and away after the horniwink, BARING-GOULD *Curgenven* (1893) xxxviii; Cor.[12]

Hence **Hornywinky,** *adj.* desolate, outlandish, like a moor where ' hornywinks ' resort.

Cor. (J.W.) ; Cor.[1] An old tumble-down house has been revilingly described as an old shabrag horny-wink place ; Cor.[2]

2. ? A toad. Cor.[12] **3.** A slug. Cor.[2] [Not known to our correspondents.]

HORRA, *sb.* Cor.[8] [o·rə.] A prostitute.

[OCor. *hora,* ' meretrix,' STOKES *Gl. in Trans. Phil. Soc.* (1870) 192.]

HORRA GOOSE, see Horie goose.

HORRALS, *sb. pl.* Sc. Very small wheels, casters.

Slk. So ye contrive to rin upon horrals, halting before a darling 'dish and then away on a voyage o' new discovery, CHR. NORTH *Noctes* (ed. 1856) III. 287.

HORRID, *adj.* and *adv.* Sc. Irel. Ken. **1.** *adj.* Great, extraordinary.

Sh.I. Da sheep an' lambs ir sellin' weel, some o' dem gaun at horrid prices, *Sh. News* (Oct. 29, 1898). Cav. That horrid yield of flax will surely pay the rent (M.S.M.).

Hence **Horridly,** *adv.* very much, exceedingly.

s.Ir. He's horridly improved in his preaching, CROKER *Leg.* (1862) 30.

2. *adv.* Used as an intensitive.

Ayr. My life's near done—I'm horrid ill, FISHER *Poems* (1790) 66. Gall. A horrid good man is a very good man (A.W.). Wmh. He is a horrid clever man. It's a horrid fine day. She's a horrid nice lady (A.S.P.). Crk. *Flk-Lore Jrn.* (1883) 318. Ken.[2] Horrid bad.

HORRIS, see Arris, *sb.*

HORROCK, *sb.* Lakel. Wor. [(h)o·rək.] **1.** A collection, quantity.

Cum.[4] Used in the expression ' a horrock o' beans,' a skeleton. Wor. Horrocks of winds, hurricanes (H.K.).

2. *Phr. to play* or *make horrock,* to play old gooseberry, Mag's diversion.

Lakel.[2] He gat on t'spree an' played horrock wi' his wage. Wm.[1] Tho me·ad sad horrack amang 't.

HORROCKS, *sb.* Glo. [o·rəks.] A large, fat woman.

Gl. (1851) ; Glo.[1]

HORRORS, *sb. pl.* Som. In phr. *to put the horrors on any one*; see below.

' I put the horrors on him.' Said by W. R. à propos of a highwayman whose knuckles he broke with his loaded whip-stock on the Bristol road (W.F.R.).

HORROR-SLAIN, *adj.* n.Lin.[1] Killed by fright.

She was o'must horror-slaain by what happen'd; we noan o' us thoht she'd get oher it.

HORRY, *sb.* e.An. Hoar-frost.

Suf. (HALL.), e.Suf. (F.H.), Ess. (H.H.M.)

HORRY, *adj.* Obsol. Lin. Som. Dev. Also written horey Lin. Filthy, foul ; mouldy. Cf. **howery.**

Lin. It's strange mucky horey weather, ELLIS *Pronunc.* (1889) V. 298. w.Som.[1] Old people know the word. Dev.[1] n.Dev. *Horae Subsecivae* (1777) 217; And oll herry zo vurs tha art a vorked, *Exm. Scold.* (1746) l. 47 ; Thy waistcoat all berry, *ib.* 155.

[Hit nis bote a hori felle, *E. E. Poems* (c. 1305), ed. Furnivall (1862a) 19. OE. *horig* (ÆLFRIC).]

HORRY, HORRYWINK, see Harry, *sb.*[1], Hornywink.

HORSAM, *sb.* Obs. n.Yks. A small tax ; see below.

A small tax which is still paid (though the intention of it has long since ceased) by the townships on the north side of the vale, and within the lathe or wapentake of Pickering, for horsemen and hounds kept for the purpose of driving off the deer of the forest of Pickering from the cornfields which bordered upon it. When that field of a given township which lay next the forest was fallow, no tax was due from it that year; and though this forest has long been thrown open, or disforested, and the common fields now inclosed, the 'sauf year' (calculating every third year) is still exempt from this imposition, GROSE (1790) ; MARSHALL *Rur. Econ.* (1788).

HORSE, *sb.* and *v.* Var. dial. uses in Sc. Irel. Eng. and Aus. Also written hors Cor. ; and in forms harse Som.; herse n.Lin.[1]; hos Not.[8]; hoss n.Yks.[4] e.Yks.[1] MS. add. s.Chs.[1] s.Not. n.Lin.[1] Hmp.[1] I.W.[1] Wil.[1]

Dor.[1] Som. Dev. Cor.[28] [(h)ors, ōs, os.] **1.** *sb.* In *comb.* (1) Horse-adder, the dragon-fly, *Libellula vulgatissima*; (2) -and-crooks, pack-saddle carriage ; (3) -and-jockey, a name for the George III sovereign, which had St. George and the dragon on the reverse side ; (4) -back, on horseback ; (5) -back carriage, a method of carriage on a horse's back by means of pack-saddles ; (6) -balk, a portion of the roof or floor of a pit which obtrudes into the coal ; (7) -baze, a wonder ; (8) -beans, salt-making term : broken marl in which the brine frequently runs; (9) -beast, a horse ; (10) -bee, (a) the horse bot-fly, *Gasterophilus equi* ; (b) the cleg, *Tabanus bovinus* ; (11) -bitter, see (1); (12) -boggart, an industrious, yet mischievous imp, a kind of ' lubber-fiend ' ; (13) -box, a high boarded compartment in a stable in which a sick horse or a mare and foal are confined ; (14) -buckie, the white whelk, *Purpura lapillus*; (15) -causey, a paved road for pack-horses ; (16) -clothes, harness ; (17) -cock, a small variety of snipe, ? *Limnocryptes gallinula*; (18) -cod, a horse-collar ; (19) -comber, a rude, boisterous girl ; (20) -corn, (a) bruised oats given to horses ; (b) the small corn which is separated by sifting ; (21) -couper, a horse-dealer, *gen.* of a low type, dealing in inferior horses ; (22) -coupering or -couping, horse-dealing ; (23) -course, to beat ; (24) -eel, an eel of uncommon size ; (25) -elf-stone, a petrified sea-urchin ; (26) -emmet, a large ant ; (27) -fair, in phr. *to make a horse-fair*, to make a game or jest of a person or thing ; (28) -feast, a dinner without water, or drink of any kind ; (29) -fettler, the man who has care of horses in a pit ; (30) -flesh, fibrous carbonate of lime ; (31) -flesh ore, variegated copper ; (32) -foal, a colt ; (33) -gan, the circular track for horses when driving a threshing-machine ; (34) -gang, the fourth part of a piece of land which is ploughed by four horses belonging to four separate tenants ; (35) -gate, (a) a way for horses in coal workings ; (b) a horse's journey; (36) -gawk or -gowk, the green sandpiper, *Helodromas ochropus* ; (37) -gear, harness, saddlery ; (38) -gell, the horse-leech, *Haemopsis sanguisorba* and *Aulastroma gulo*; (39) -gentler, a horse-breaker ; see Gentle, *v.* 8 ; (40) -godmother, a tall, ungainly, masculine woman ; (41) -gold, the tinsel spread on a banner carried at a rush-bearing ; (42) -grace, see below ; (43) -graith, see (37); (44) -'s head, (a) a wooden ventilator used in a mine ; (b) the foot of a boot with the sole and heel and part of the front ; (c) *pl.* the small portions into which the wind rows are broken up in hay-making; (45) -hirer, one who lets out saddle-horses ; (46) -hoe, (a) a hoe drawn by a horse ; (b) to hoe with a horse ; (47) -hole, (a) an entrance into the shaft of a coal-mine, where horses are put in or out; see below ; (b) a place for watering horses ; (48) -hove, see (46, a) ; (49) -keeper, (a) a groom ; (b) see (29) ; (50) -kiss, a pretended kiss which is really a bite ; (51) -knacker, one who kills and cuts up old horses ; (52) -knave, *obs.*, an hostler ; (53) -ladder, see below; (54) -lark, the corn-bunting, *Emberiza miliaria* ; (55) -laugh, loud, rude laughter, ' guffaws ' ; (56) -lease, meadow ground, unploughed and kept for horses ; (57) -('s leg, a musical instrument ; a bassoon ; (58) -leg dumpling, rowly-powly pudding ; (59) -limpet, a coarse, unedible limpet ; (60) -load, as much as a horse can carry ; (61) -lock, a fetter for a horse ; a padlock ; (62) -long-cripple, see (1) ; (63) -loping, horse-dealing; (64) -louse, the wood-louse ; (65) -mackerel, the scad, *Caranx trachurus* ; (66) -magog, a boisterously frolicsome clown ; also used *attrib.*; (67) -mallison, a person who treats his horse cruelly; (68) -man, (a) a servant who has charge of a pair of horses on a farm ; (b) a man who attends to, and travels with a stallion ; (69) -manship, a circus ; (70) -marine, a stout, clumsy person ; (71) -match, the red-backed shrike, *Lanius collurio* ; (72) -matcher, the stonechat, *Saxicola rubicola* ; (73) -mill, a mill driven by a horse ; (74) -mixen, a horse-midden ; (75) -monger, a dealer in horses ; (76) -morsel, a coarse woman ; (77) -mount, a stone or steps for mounting a horse ; (78) -musher, the wheatear, *Saxicola oenanthe* ; (79) -mussel, a large mussel, esp. *Modiola modiolus* ; (80)

ail, (a) a tadpole; (b) in phr. *to make a horse-nail of a ~ing*, to do anything in a clumsy, imperfect manner; (81) ·eedle, see (1); (82) ·nest, an oft-told story; an idle tale; 3) ·net, (a) a net for lowering horses into, and drawing em out of a mine; (b) a net for catching sea-trout; see ·low; (84) ·of-knowledge, a person who knows everything, and who is always ready with advice; (85) ·path, e (15); (86) ·pit, a coal-pit worked by a horse-engine; 7) ·poke, a horse's nose-bag; (88) ·pot, a round wooden ·essel, about the size of a peck measure, used for holding ·rn in a stable; (89) ·protestant, a person indifferent to ·ligion; (90) ·provven, stable food; (91) ·rake, a hay-rake ·awn by horses; (92) ·ribbon day, May-day; see below; 3) ·road, the roadway for wheeled traffic; (94) ·rod, rod with which to strike a horse; (95) ·setter, a horse-·ealer; one who lets out horses; (96) ·sheet, a horse-cloth; 7] ·shoe(s, the game of quoits; (98) ·shoe stubs, horse-shoe ·ails; (99) ·smatch, see (78); (100) ·snake, see (1); (101) ·natcher, see (78); (102) ·'s spurs, the callosities on the ·ner side of a horse's leg; (103) ·steps, see (77); (104) ·ting, ·stang, or ·stinger, (a) see (1); (b) the gad-fly; (c) ·e hornet; (105) ·stobs, peculiar nails used in shoeing ·orses; (106) ·stone, see (77); (107) ·stopples, holes made ·y horses in wet land; (108) ·suppering, a horse's evening ·ed; (109) ·tailor, ? a saddler [not known to our corre-·pondents]; (110) ·tang, see (104, b); (111) ·teng, see (1); 12) ·thrush, the missel-thrush, *Turdus viscivorus*; (113) ·ied, of land: kept for grazing land for horses; (114) ·om, in phr. *to horse-tom the roads*, to play the tomboy on ·e roads; (115) ·tooth, quartz spar; (116) ·tosser, an ·iplement for tossing hay, drawn by horses; (117) ·tree, ·e piece of wood to which the swingle-tree of a pair of ·arrows is attached, the swingle-tree; (118) ·trod, ·bridle-road; (119) ·trough, a drinking-trough for horses; 20) ·ware, (121) ·wash, a roadside pond where horses ·e watered and their feet washed; (122) ·yard, an en-·osure into which cart-horses are turned for the night.

(1) Dor. *w. Gazette* (Feb. 15, 1889) 7. Cor.¹ So called because is supposed to sthng horses; Cor.²³ (a) Cor. Touches lightly ·'horse-and-crooks,' or packsaddle carriage, MARSHALL *Review* ·817) V. 599. (3) Chs.¹² (4) Yks. (J.W.) s.Not. He war hoss-·ack. A shall ride hoss-back (J.P.K.). (5) Dev. Some account f pack-saddle furniture, used in horse-back-carriage, MARSHALL *eview* (1817) V. 576. (6) Nhb.¹ (7) Nhb. (HALL.), Nhb.¹ (8) ·as.¹ (9) ne.Sc. Maybe the horse beast at Greenslack had grown ·aur, GRANT *Kackleton*, 45. Abd. It's ower fifty awcre—we need ·va horse beasts, ALEXANDER *Ain Flk.* (1882) 51. Gall. The kye ·d the horse-beasts within the bounds of my parish, CROCKETT *tandard Bearer* (1898) 199. Don. A studdy responsible lump iv horse-baste, MACMANUS *Pathrick's Proxy in Pearson's Mag.* (Mar. ·900) 31a. (10, a) Cum. T'horse-bees com buzzin' roond, RICHARD-·on *Talk* (1876) and S. 26; Cum.⁴ Hrt. If the fly, dar, or horsebee ·ould blow your sheep, ELLIS *Mod. Husb.* (1750) IV. i. 132. ·rt. I had an opportunity of watching a botfly, or horse-bee, at ·ork. . . It is an insect greatly resembling a bee, with an arched ·il, or egg depositor, and very large transparent eyes, HAGGARD ·armer's Year in *Longman's Mag.* (June 1899) 156. (b) Cum.⁴ 1) Chs.¹ (12) Lan. Of boggarts the Rev. William Thornber ·serves, that there were several different kinds, having their ·aunts in that part of the Fylde near Blackpool; as for instance ·. the lubber fiends, the horse-boggarts, and the house-boggarts, ·· industrious, yet mischievous imps, haunting dwellings, HARLAND ·· WILKINSON *Flk-Lore* (1867) 58, 59. (13) n.Lin. (E.P.) (14) ·Sc. (JAM.) Mry. *Zoologist* (1854) XII. 4428. (15) Chs.¹ In ·veral of the old Chs. lanes, which were formerly either covered ·ith grass or were nothing but sand, and full of deep ruts, axle ·eep in mud in the winter, a narrow road about three or four ·et wide was paved along one side. This was intended for the ·ack-horses or for foot passengers, and to prevent the farmers' ·arts using them they had frequently mounds of earth thrown up ·· each side, *Chs. Sheaf*, I. 291. Several of these ancient horse ·ads still exist. (16) War.² (17) Lth. (JAM.) (18) N.Cy.², ·Yks.², Der.¹ (19) Wil. *N. & Q.* (1881) 6th S. iv. 106. (20, a) ·· Yks. (J.T.) (b) Dev.¹ (21) Sc. I was bred a horse-couper, ·ott *Waverley* (1814) xxxix. Bnff. Valiantly we strade shanks-·aigie, As glib horse-coupers do a staigie, TAYLOR *Poems* (1787) ·7. Per. But the. horse-couper that tried to play upon their ·mplicity did not boast afterwards, IAN MACLAREN *Auld Lang Syne*

(1895) 9. s.Sc. Horse-cowpers were a numerous band in Hawick tryst that day, ALLAN *Poems* (1887) 79. Rnf. There'll be carriers, horse-coupers, and cadgers, WEBSTER *Rhymes* (1835) 194. e.Lth. (A great horse-coper he) . . . I'll swap your horse, MUCKLEBACKIT *Rhymes* (1885) 75. Edb. What cairds and tinklers come, An' ne'er-do-weel horse-coupers, FERGUSSON *Poems* (1773) 132, ed. 1785. Bwk. The horse couper . . . spirit is to be found in ten thousand instances, besides in those respectable persons who deal in horses, HENDERSON *Pop. Rhymes* (1856) 103. Slk. An heiress who has broken the hearts of three horse-coupers, HOGG *Tales* (1838) 283, ed. 1866. N.Cy.¹² Nhb. Old Jack Campbell (the horse-couper) [is] still fresh in the mind of the writer, DIXON *Whittingham Vale* (1895) 184; Nhb.¹ Cum. There were smug-glers, excisemen, horse-cowpers, ANDERSON *Ballads* (ed. 1808) 100. n.Yks. (T.S.), n.Yks.¹² Midl. He won't have that gipsy horse-coper up there wi' him, BARTRAM *People of Clopton* (1897) 172. n.Lin. A lot o' nor' country horse-coupers, PEACOCK *R. Skirlaugh* (1870) I. 37; n.Lin.¹ Thŷ faather was noht bud a horse-cohper. War.² One who prepares inferior horses for sale. Lon. Horses are stolen by a low unprincipled class of men, who travel the country dealing in them, who are termed 'horse coupers,' MAYHEW *Lond. Labour* (ed. 1862) IV. 325. n.Som.¹ 'Twas a very purty lot o' 'm, I 'sure 'ee. There was Tom Saffin the heigler, and Gypsy George the horse-coper, and tailder Jones. Cor. A tall, olive-faced young man, in a horse-coper's coat, MORTIMER *Tales Moors* (1895) 163. (22) Abd. A horse cowpin doctor, ALEX-ANDER *Johnny Gibb* (1871) xxv. n.Lin. Horse couperin' is a better trade then farmin', PEACOCK *R. Skirlaugh* (1870) II. 113. (23) n.Lin.¹ I'll hoss-course ony o' you lads I find ony moore e' my otcherd. It wo'd hev been a vast sight better to hev gen him a good horse-coursin', an' not to hev hed noā justice do aboot it. (24) w.Ir. Instead of a throut, it was a thievin' horse-eel, LOVER *Leg.* (1848) I. 15. (25) N.I.¹ (26) Ken. (G.B.), Ken.¹ (27) s.Suf. (F.H.) (28) Sc. (JAM.), n.Yks. (T.K.) (29) Nhb.¹ (30) Dor. It occurs in beds or thin laminae, termed . . . 'horseflesh' in the Isle of Portland, RAWSAV *Rock Spec.* (1862) 143; Sandy limestone, with surface markings . . . from the 'horseflesh' beds, *ib.* (31) Cor. Purple-ore, or variegated copper ('horse-flesh ore' of the Cornish miners), SMYTH *Mineral Coll.* (1864) 14. (32) Sh.I. She hed a horse-foal wi' a white snie atween his een, STEWART *Tales* (1892) 244. (33) Nhb.¹ (34) n.Sc. (JAM.) (35, a) w.Yks. (T.T.), (J.P.) (b) Lan. James Bleasdall sent me pay for my horse-gate to Preston, WALKDEN *Diary* (ed. 1866) 79. (36) Sh.I. Da nicht whin I wis maetin' da lambs da horse-gouk wis cryin' up i' da lift, *Sh. News* (Jan. 29, 1898). Sh.I., Or.I. SWAINSON *Birds* (1885) 197. (37) Ayr. Besides his traffic in the polished garniture of horse-gear, my grandfather's father was also a farrier, GALT *Gilhaize* (1823) i. n.Yks.¹ (s.v. Gear). n.Yks.² w.Yks.² Horse-gear may either mean the trappings complete of a horse or only a portion (s.v. Gear). n.Wil. Hoss gear is used of the harness for use with an elevator or other machine of the kind, but not for cart or wagon harness (E.H.G.). Som. Horse-gear work, *Auctioneer's Advt.* (1895). (38) Frf. Of filthy gar his e'e-brees war, With esks and horse-gells lin'd, LOWSON *Guidfollow* (1890) 239. e.Fif. He clappit his mooth to the gimlet hole and sookit like a horse-gelly, LATTO *Tam Bodkin* (1864) vii. (39) Lin. *N. & Q.* (1900) 9th S. v. 104. (40) Ir. *N. & Q.* (1856) and S. ii. 499. N.Cy.¹, Nhb. (R.O.H.) n.Yks.¹ ; n.Yks.² Horse is here used as a prefix to signify huge, as we say 'Horse quantities.' m.Yks.¹, Der.², nw.Der.¹, Not.², n.Lin.¹, Nhp.¹, War. (J.R.W.) Som.W. & J. *Gl.* (1873). (41) Lan. HONE *Year-bk.* (1832) col. 1106; GROSE (1790) *MS. add.* (M.) (42) ne.Sc. What was called the Horse Grace was in the following words: 'It's up the brae ca' me not, It's doon the brae ca' me not, It's in fair road spare me not, An in the stable forget me not,' GREGOR *Flk-Lore* (1881) 131; Up the hill spare me, Down the hill bear me, On the level let me trot, And never give me water when I'm hot, *Eng. version* (J.Ar.). (43) n.Yks.² (44, a) Der. MAWE *Mineralogy* (1802). (b) Lon. MAYHEW *Lond. Labour* (1851) II. 40. (c) Hnt. (T.P.F.) (45) Se. The . . . horse-hirers, to use a Sc. expression, who attended him in his journey, MacNICOL *Remarks* (1779) 90. (46, a) Mid. Horse-hoes in such a soil, in a dry season, would have so unsteady a motion, as to cut up part of the rows without being able to raise any mould towards earthing up the plant, MARSHALL *Review* (1817) V. 135. (b) Edb. If horse-hoed, the drills should cross the last ploughing, PENNECUIK *Wks.* (1715) 56, ed. 1815. Nrf. Yesterday we horse-hoed the five acres of winter beans, HAGGARD *Farmer's Year in Longman's Mag.* (Nov. 1898). (47, a) Nhb.¹ Formerly applied to a passage way hewn out of the coal inbye at the flat for the purpose of bringing the horse round from the head of the flat to the outbye end, instead of passing by the side of the tubs as at the present day, *Newcastle Wkly. Chron.* (Sept. 12, 1891). **Nhb., Dur.** An entrance into the shaft, level with the surface, where horses are netted and put in or landed when drawn out; timber, rails, &c., are also put in at the same place, NICHOLSON *Coal Tr. Gl.* (1888). (*b*) **n.Ir.** She dookit Wully Gunyin in the horse hole, LYTTLE *Robin Gordon,* 9. (48) **w.Som.**[1] (49, *a*) **Ken.**[2] (*b*) **Nhb.**[1] (50) **w.Yks.** *Leeds Merc. Suppl.* (Mar. 17, 1894). [A rude kiss, able to beat one's teeth out, RAY *Prov.* (1678) 74.] (51) **Lon.** GROSE (1790) *MS. add.* (P.) (52) **n.Yks.**[2] (53) **w.Mid.** It was formerly usual to employ a horse to tread down the corn when building the mow. Sometimes an inquisitive boy or stranger would want to know how the horse was to be got off from the mow when it was finished. Such persons would be sent to the blacksmith, to borrow his 'horse-ladder' for the purpose. The smith, knowing that it was a hoax, took up his stoutest horse-whip and drove them from the amithy (W.P.M.). (54) Cor. RODD *Birds* (1880) 314; SWAINSON *Birds* (1885) 69. (55) **w.Yks.** Wot the deuce are yo all settin up yer horse-laffs at! TOM TREDDLEHOYLE *Bairnsla Ann.* (1861) 46; But t'slaughter butchers didn't forget to mak' a skare wi' horse laffs, HALLAM *Wadsley Jack* (1866) vii. (56) **Hmp.**[1] (57) **w.Yks.** A gooid noation a playin' a horse-leg, *Yksman. Comic Ann.* (1879) 34. **Lan.** That played a horse-leg aboon forty year, CLEGG *Sketches* (1895). **n.Lin.**[1] **War.**[2] The horse's leg was an essential instrument in village churches when two or three instrumentalists were responsible for leading the church music before organs became general. These church bands were frequent in War. down to near 1840, and the name of horse's leg survived long after—even if it is now *obs.* **Wil.**[1] (58) **n.Lin.**[1] (59) **nw.Dev.**[1] (60) **Sc.** A servant-man sent from a worthy and charitable lady with a horse-load of meal, cheese, and beef, VEITCH *Memoirs* (1680) 144, ed. 1846. **n.Cy.** (J.W.) (61) **Lan.** WALKDEN *Diary* (ed. 1866) 44. **Ken.**[1] (62) **nw.Dev.**[1] **s.Dev.** FOX *Kingsbridge* (1874). (63) **Hrf.**[2] (64) **Nhb.**[1] (65) **Bwk.** JOHNSTON *Nat. Club* (1838) I. No. vi. 171. **Sus.** (F.E.S.) (66) **Ayr.** We approached towards the rampant horse-magog, GALT *Lawrie T.* (1830) I. iii. **n.An.**[1] Applied to a clumsy clown playing extravagant gambols, all agog for fun! as a dray-horse might be supposed to attempt cantering. (67) **Cld.** (JAM.), **Cum.**[1] (68, *a*) **n.Sc.** 'Weel, man, what's yer fee!' 'Aye, but what for, ye ken!' 'Ou, jest second horseman,' GORDON *Carglen* (1891) 69. **Abd.** He's a rash chap the secon't horseman owre by, ALEXANDER *Ain Flk.* (1882) 50. **Nrf.** The wife of one of my horsemen is engaged in singling the mangolds, HAGGARD *Farmer's Year* in *Longman's Mag.* (May 1899) 35. (*b*) **n.Lin.**[1] (69) **Lin.** (W.W.S.), **Ken.** (G.B.) **Dev.** Tha tother night I went to zee Tha hossminship, lor wat a spree! NATHAN HOGG *Poet. Lett.* (1847) 5, ed. 1865. (70) **Cor.**[3] Like a gaait hoss-marine. (71) **Oxf.** APLIN *Birds* (1889) 214. (72) **Wil.** THURN *Birds* (1870) 55; SMITH *Birds* (1887) 150; **Wil.**[1] **n.Wil.** 'Horse matchers' or stonechats also in summer often visit the rickyard, JEFFERIES *Wild Life* (1879) x. (73) **Lan.** Went to view the new horse-mill, WALKDEN *Diary* (ed. 1866) 75. (74) **Wor.** (W.C.B.) (75) **I.W.**[1] (76) **Glo.** GROSE (1790) *MS. add.* (M.) **Dev.** *Horae Subsecivae* (1777) 218. (77) **n.Yks.**[1] (78) **Hmp.** SWAINSON *Birds* (1885) 9. (79) **Abd.** They [pearls] are found in a kinde of shell-fish called the horse muskle, TURREFF *Antiq. Gleanings* (1859) 113. **Frf.** For his een, with dowie sheen, Twa huge horse-mussels glar'd, LOWSON *Guidfollow* (1890) 239. **Lnk.** In deep still pools are found a large bivalvular shell-fish, known here by the name of the horse muscle. They are not used as food, but in some of them are found small pearls, HAMILTON *Statist. Acc.* II. 179 (JAM.). **Ant.** *Modiola vulgaris* (W.H.P.). **n.Lin.**[1] The large fresh-water mussel. (80, *a*) **Ken.**[1] Probably so called because, in shape, they somewhat resemble large nails, **Ken.**[2] (*b*) **Fif.** (JAM.) (81) **Bdf.** (J.W.B.) (82) **Glo.** Let me hear no more of your horsenest, *Horae Subsecivae* (1777) 217; **Glo.**[1] (83, *a*) **Nhb.**[1] (*b*) **Nrf.** The horse net is used by night to take them (sea trout). A man mounts a strong cart-horse, and rides out with one end of the net into the shallow sea. The other end is held by the fishermen on shore, who walk along parallel with the horse. The net drags behind in a big curve, and from time to time the horse is ridden ashore, the net hauled, and any fish that may be caught extracted, *Cornh. Mag.* (June 1899) 320. (84) **Cor.**[3] (85) **Yks.** Before carriage roads were formed of hard materials, these horse-paths were common in the *n.* of Eng.... for the use of pack-horses and travellers on horseback in the winter season, MARSHALL *Review* (1808) I. 352. (86) **w.Yks.**[2] A piece of wast[e] near the horse-pit. (87) **n.Yks.** (I.W.) (88) **w.Dor.** (C.V.G.) (89) **Ant.** (W.H.P.) (90) **n.Yks.**[2] (91) **Nrf.** The horse-rake ... rakes it into lines, the man seated on the machine from time to time freeing the roll of hay from the hollow of his rake by means of a lever at his side, which lifts all the prongs simultaneously, to be dropped again immediately the line is cleared, HAGGARD

Farmer's Year in *Longman's Mag.* (May 1899) 35. (92) **n.Yks.**[2] They [May-day fêtes] are here no otherwise observed, than by the stable-boys and draymen garnishing their horse's heads with ribbons which are usually begged at the shops;—hence the designation 'horse-ribbon day' (s.v. May). (93) **Not.**[1], **Lei.**[1] **War.** In Birmingham the common name for the central section of a street where vehicles pass is the 'horse-road,' not simply 'road' (C.T.A.O.); **War.**[2] **Ken.** Thus in time of snow one person will say to another who is walking on the footpath, 'Come out into the horse-road, as it is better walking here' (W.F.S.); **Ken.**[1] In Ken. a road is not divided as elsewhere, into the carriage-road and the footpath; but into the horse-road and the foot-road. (94) **w.Yks.**[1] (95) **Sc.** The horsesetter in Kilpallat to palm off an inferior animal, HUNTER *Armiger's Revenge* (1897) vi. **Ayr.** One Tobit Balmuto, a horse-setter, of whom my grandfather had some knowledge by report, GALT *Gilhaise* (1823) i. (96) **Sc.** 'Thou maun do without horse-sheet,' he said, addressing the animal, SCOTT *Blk. Dwarf* (1816) x. (97) **N.Cy.**[1] **Nhb.** Old horse-shoes were used for quoits in the country (R.O.H.). **Lakel.**[2] **Lan.** Engaged in the games of ... horse shoe, HARLAND & WILKINSON *Flk-Lore* (1867) 255. (98) **n.Yks.** Nail t'clog heel wi hoshy stubs (I.W.). (99) **Hmp.** SWAINSON *Birds* (1885) 9. (100) **Dev.**[2] (101) **Wil.**[1] **n.Wil.** SMITH *Birds* (1887) 159. (102) **n.Lin.**[1] A cancer in the breast... Take horses'-spurs and dry them by the fire till they will beat to a powder; sift and infuse two drams in two quarts of ale; drink half a pint every six hours, new milk warm. It has cured many, WESLEY *Primitive Physic* (1755) 38. (103) **n.Yks.**[1], **w.Yks.**[2] (104, *a*) **Cld.** (JAM.), **n.Lan.**[1], **n.Lin.**[1], **Lei.**[1] **Nhp.**[1], **se.Wor.**[1], **Glo.** (A.B.), **Oxf.** (G.O.), **Ken.** (G.B.) **Sur.** The farmers' lads all call the great dragon-fly the hoss-stinger, *Forest Tithes* (1893) 22. **Hmp.**[1] Rather the horse-fly (W.H.C.). **Wil.** SLOW *Gl.* (1892); **Wil.**[1,2] **Dor.** *N. & Q.* (1877) 5th S. viii. 45; **Dor.**[1] **Som.** JENNINGS *Obs. Dial. w.Eng.* (1825). **w.Som.**[1] The common dragon-fly of all varieties is known only by this name. (*b*) **Lan.**[1], **Glo.**[1] **Oxf.**[1] *MS. add.* (*c*) **Hrf.**[2] (105) **Nhb.** (M.H.D.) (106) **Nhb.**[1], **n.Yks.**[4] **Lan.** Hoo seet up o yeawll, clapt th' tele between hur legs on crope into o hoyle ith horse-stone, TIM BOBBIN *View Dial.* (1746) 43, ed. 1806. (107) **I.W.**[1] (108) **e.Frf.** It was wearin' near horse-supperin' time, LATTO *Tam Bodkin* (1864) xiii. (109) **Lnk.** Horse tailors, smiths, an' clockies, MUIR *Minstrelsy* (1816) 8. (110) **w.Yks.** Ah think e me heart at sum on em must a been yung horse-tangs. for they tang'd an bate me noaze, TOM TREDDLEHOYLE *Bairnsla Ann.* (1856) 41. **aw.Lin.**[1] (111) **n.Yks.**[2,4], **m.Yks.**[1] **w.Yks.** BANKS *Whfld. Wds.* (1865); **w.Yks.**[2] (112 **Nhp.** SWAINSON *Birds* (1885) 2; **Nhp.**[1] (113) **War.** On lands which have been horse-tied, which is the term applied, they never fail from reaping abundant crops of wheat; insomuch, that on seeing heavy wheat crops it is a common exclamation, 'This was horse-tied,' YOUNG *Annals Agric.* (1784–1815) XXXVII. 488. (114) **e.Suf.** (F.H.) (115) **Dev.** Look at that great hunch of suet in it, like a horse-tooth in granite, BARING-GOULD *Spider* (1887) xxix. **Cor.** The granite is so full of horseteeth that he can make nothing of it, *ib. R. Cable* (1889) 316. (116) **Nrf.** After the hay has lain a while to dry, comes the hay-tosser, breaking up the wisps and airing it, HAGGARD *Farmer's Year* in *Longman's Mag.* (May 1899) 35. (117) **Ayr.** Weel yoked in a twa horse tree, FISHER *Poems* (1790) 193. **n.Lin.**[1] **e.An.**[1] **Nrf.** MARSHALL *Rur. Econ.* (1787). (118) **n.Yks.**[1] **e.Yks.**[1] *MS. add.* (T.H.) (119) **Frf.** Gie them a bit steep in the nearest horse-troch, WILLOCK *Rosetty Ends* (1886) 154, ed. 1889. (120) **Bdf.** BATCHELOR *Anal. Eng. Lang.* (1809) 136. (121) **Cha.**[1] **s.Cha.**[1] Goa' ùn tel Jim· ey moth tak· ùn waat·ùr)th ky·ey ùt)dh os·wesh [Go an' tell Jim hey mun tak an' watter th' kye at th' hoss-wesh]. (122) **e.Suf.** (F.H.)

2. *Comb.* in plant-names: (1) **Horse-beech,** the hornbeam, *Carpinus betulus*; (2) **-blob,** the marsh-marigold, *Caltha palustris*; (3) **-bramble,** the dog-rose, *Rosa canina*; (4) **-break,** a kind of whin; (5) **-'s breath,** the rest-harrow, *Ononis arvensis*; (6) **-buckle,** the cowslip, *Primula veris*; (7) **-buttercup,** see (2); (8) **-clog,** a very inferior, ungrafted plum; (9) **-cress,** the brooklime, *Veronica Beccabunga*; (10) **-daisy,** (*a*) the ox-eye daisy, *Chrysanthemum Leucanthemum*; (*b*) the stinking may-weed, *Anthemis Cotula*; (*c*) the corn feverfew, *Matricaria inodora*; (11) **-thistle,** the green endive, *Lactuca virosa*; (12) **-gogs,** a variety of the plum, *Prunus domestica*; (13) **-gold,** the buttercup, esp. the crowfoot, *Ranunculus arvensis*; (14) **-gollan, -gowan,** or **-gowlan,** a name applied to most of the larger Compositae, esp. to the ox-eye daisy, *Chrysanthemum Leucanthemum*; (15) **-hardhead,** the black knapweed, *Centaurea* *nigra*; (16) ·hoof, the coltsfoot, *Tussilago Farfara*; (17) ·jags, see (12); (18) ·jessamine, the coarse-flowered jessamine; (19) ·jug, a small red plum; (20) ·knobs or ·knops, (a) see (15); (b) the great knapweed, *Centaurea Scabiosa*; (21) ·knot, see (15); (22) ·may, leaves of the witch-elm, *Ulmus campestris*; (23) ·mint, a name applied *gen.* to all wild mints, esp. *Mentha hirsuta* and *M. rotundifolia*; (24) ·mushroom, the hedge-mushroom, *Agaricus arvensis*; (25) ·pease, the wood-bitter vetch, *Vicia Orobus*; (26) ·pen, the yellow-rattle, *Rhinanthus Crista-galli*; (27) ·pennies, (a) see (26); (b) see (10, a); (28) ·peppermint, the common mint, *Mentha sylvestris*; (29) ·pipe, (a) the great horse-tail, *Equisetum maximum*; (b) the ' colt's tail,' *E. arvense*; (30) ·piping, see (29, b); (31) ·plum, see (19); (32) ·prickle, a dwarf variety of gorse, growing in poor pastures; (33) ·saving, the common juniper, *Juniperus communis*; (34) ·shoe, the sycamore, *Acer Pseudo-platanus*; (35) ·snap, see (15); (36) ·tail oats, a variety of oats, *Avena orientalis*; (37) ·thristle, the bur, ? *Carduus lanceolatus*; (38) ·thyme, the wild thyme, *Thymus Serpyllum*; (39) ·tongue, the hart's-tongue fern, *Scolopendrium vulgare*; (40) ·violet, (a) the dog-violet, *Viola canina*; (b) the wood-violet, *V. sylvatica*; (c) the wild pansy, *V. tricolor*; (41) ·well-grass, see (9); (42) Horses-and-carriages, the monkshood, *Aconitum Napellus*.

(1) Ken., Sus.¹² e.Sus. HOLLOWAY. Hmp.¹ (2) a.Not.(J.P.K.), Lei. Nhp. 'Neath the shelving bank's retreat, The horse-biob swells its golden ball, CLARE *Village Minst.* (1821) II. 120; Nhp.¹, Wor. (E.S.), Snr. (3) e.An.¹ Nrf. MARSHALL *Rur. Econ.* (1787). (4) Ken. YOUNG *Annals Agric.* (1784-1815) II. 70. (5) Wor. (6) Ken. *N. & Q.* (1869) 4th S. iii. 242; Ken.¹ (7) w.Som.¹ Very common. Dev.⁴ (8) Not. Also called a wind-sor (J.P.K.). (9) e.Yks. (10, a) Nhb.¹, Nhp.¹, Hrf., Bck., Hnt. (T.P.F.) Ken. *Science Gossip* (1881) 211. Sus.¹, Wil.¹, w.Dor. (G.E.D.) Som. The meads that year was white as milk wi' harse daisies, LEITH *Lemon Verbena* (1895) 39. w.Som.¹ Always. Dev. Our bishop ain't th' kind o' individual fur to b'leive 'is clergy frequaints th' turf in order fur to gather wild vlowers, even if them zame vlowers do 'appen to be 'oss-daisies, STOOKE *Not Exactly*, ii; Dev.⁴, Cor. (b, c).Bck. (11) Dev. Zum zmooth es dies, zum like hoss-dishels rough, DANIEL *Bride of Scio* (1842) 177. (12) Wm.(B.K.) n.Yks.¹ A fair-sized but highly astringent blue plum which grows abundantly in the district, and sometimes even in the hedge-rows; n.Yks.² Plums of a coarse bitterish kind; n.Yks.⁴ A common, astringent, purple brown plum. ne.Yks.¹ Yellow plum which hangs till nearly Christmas. e.Yks. NICHOLSON *Flb-Lore* (1890) 227; e.Yks.¹ Used about Hornsea. m.Yks.¹ A large wild plum, yellow in colour, and very late in ripening. w.Yks.¹, ne.Lan.¹ (13) Nhp.¹ Hrt. ELLIS *Mod. Husb.* (1750) III. i. 43. (14) Sc. *Garden Wk.* (1896) No. cxiii. 100. Cai.¹, Cld. (JAM.) Bwk. As to the horse-gowans, we never saw this plant so abundant anywhere else, HENDERSON *Pop. Rhymes* (1856) 105. Nhb.¹ (15) Dev.⁴ (16) Nhp.¹ (17) Yks. (18) Dev. I had that horse-jessamine from Mrs. ——, *Reports Provinc.* (1885) 98. (19) Cha.¹ (20, a) n.Cy.¹², Nhb.¹ Cum.¹ Cum.⁴ He saw a single pair of goldfinches feeding on horse knops, *Fauna*, 134. n.Yks.¹² e.Yks. MARSHALL *Rur. Econ.* (1788); e.Yks.¹, Lan.¹, n.Lan.¹, ne.Lan.¹, Nhp.¹ (b) Cum., n.Yks. (21) Ags. (JAM.) sw.Sc. *Garden Wk.* (1896) No. cxiv. 112. n.Cy., Nhp.¹, Ken.¹ (22) Cor. Coarse kinds of elm leaves are called Horse May, to distinguish them from the small-leaved kind, FRIEND *Plant-Names* (1882) s.v. Horse-violet. (23) Nhb.¹, e.Yks., n.Lin., War.³ Glo.¹, I.W., w.Som.¹ (24) Cum.⁴ Poisoning from eating red dogberries and horse mushrooms, *Carlisle Patriot* (Sept. 2, 1898) 4. Yks. Mid. Mingling with the true Agaric some very fine 'horse-mushrooms,' and even one or two poisonous toadstools, BLACKMORE *Kit* (1890) xlvii. (25) Cum.⁴ (26) Cum.¹⁴ (27, a) Yks. w.Yks. *Leeds Merc. Suppl.* (Mar. 17, 1894); w.Yks.¹, se.Lan.¹, nw.Der.¹ (b) Der. (28) Ken.¹ (29, a) N.I.¹, Ant. (b) Stf. YOUNG *Annals Agric.* (1784-1815) IV. 431. (30) n.Yks. (31) Cha.¹ (32) Ken. (P.M.) (33) Cum.⁴ (34) Wil.¹ (35) Dev.¹, n.Dev. (36) Bdf. The Tartarian, or horse-tail oats, have been sown by various farmers, BATCHELOR *Agric.* (1813) 395. (37) Gall. MACTAGGART *Encycl.* (1824) 104. (38) Nhp.¹² (39) Dor. The hart's-tongue fern took its name from the shape of the fronds; in Dor. it is called hoss (or horse) tongue, *Science Gossip* (1869) 29; BARNES *Gl.* (1863). (40, a) Ess., Dev.⁴ (b) Ess. (W.W.S.) (c) Dev.⁴ (41) Sc. (JAM.) (42) Hmp. (W.M.E.F.)

3. Phr. (1) *as big* or *as ugly as a horse's head*, a simile for anything very big, awkward, or shapelessly ugly; (2) *Black Jack rides a good horse*, a phr. used by miners when zinc ore gives good promise for copper; (3) *horse and foot*, wholly; (4) *like a horse a-kicking*, a simile for anything strong and vigorous; (5) *if two ride upon a horse one must sit behind*, if two are engaged in a contention one must ' go to the wall '; (6) *that is a horse of a very different colour*, that is quite a different matter; (7) *to hitch, put, or set one's horses together*, to be friendly; to agree after a difference; (8) *to ride* or *to be on the high horse*, to assume a haughty manner; to take a high tone with any one; (9) *to work on a dead horse*, to draw money on account before work is finished; (10) *to skin off all dead horses*, to finish work paid for; used *fig.*

(1) n.Lin.¹ Alfred Stocks hes putten sloäns upo' th' Scalla' laane as big as hoss-heäds. w.Som.¹ I never didn zee the fuller place o' it for stones; why I've a tookt out stones out o' thick there gutter, so big and so ugly as a horse's head. (2) Cor. HUNT *Pop. Rom. w.Eng.* (1865) I. 214. (3) Lnk. 'We'll be baith teetotally ruined!'.. 'Ruined, horse an' foot!' GORDON *Pyotshaw* (1885) 151. (4) w.Wor. He talked to him that powerful, sir, it were like a horse a-kickin, S. BEAUCHAMP *Grantley Grange* (1874) II. 186. (5) Glo. SMYTH *Lives Berkeleys* (1066-1618) III. 3a, ed. 1885. (6) e.An.¹ (7) n.Yks.⁴ w.Yks.¹ They don't put up their horses together. Nhp.¹, Hnt. (T.P.F.) Ken.¹ Muster Nidgett and his old 'ooman can't set their horses together at all, I understan'. Dor. Not to hitch woone's hosses together, BARNES *Gl.* (1863). w.Som.¹ (8) Not.¹ Lei.¹ A rood the 'oigh 'oss all the toime as if a'd run ovver ye, as praoud as praoud. Nhp.¹, War.², Hnt. (T.P.F.) Dev. You might have learned before now 'tis a waste of time to ride the great horse with me, WHYTE-MELVILLE *Katerfelto* (1875) xxvi. (9) w.Yks. (J.W.), Oxf. (G.O.¹, e.An.¹ (10) Slg. So we vow'd at the parting kiss, to skin off all dead horses, And mak' a wife o' ilka lass, GALLOWAY *Poland* (1795) 20.

4. Used for *pl.* horses.
Sc. 'Three or four horse' is an expression, as common in the mouth of a farmer or a ploughman, as 'three or four squadrons of horse' is in that of a general officer, *Monthly Mag.* (1800) I. 238. Kcd. Horse, pigs, an' kye were droont, GRANT *Lays* (1884) 2.

5. A wooden trestle used for var. purposes; see below; a mason's hod.
Sc. (JAM.) Cai.¹ A mason's large trestle. Dmf. A hod or tray used by masons for carrying lime (JAM.). w.Yks. The seat on which a grinder sits to work, with his legs on each side. Usually made of wood and shaped var., but *gen.* somewhat like a trestle (J.S.). Chs.¹ Salt-mining term. Tressels [sic] of wood on which to fix plank-runs or stages. w.Mid. Used for supporting the shafts of laden carts when the real horse is detached (W.P.M.). w.Som.¹ A cross-legged frame, on which logs are laid to be sawn up.
Hence Horsing, sb. the seat on which a grinder sits astride while at work.
w.Yks. In a 'hull' there may be several grinding-troughs; at each trough works one grinder, who sits astride a wooden seat called a ' horsing' (J.S.); T'rattens has hetten all't hofe-pahnd at wer left uppat horsin t'last neet, BYWATER *Sheffield Dial.* (1839) I. 6; w.Yks.²

6. Comp. Horse-tree, (1) the beam on which timber is placed previous to sawing. w.Yks.¹; (2) a trestle on which cloth is put to drain, after being dyed. w.Yks.(H.H.),(R.S.)

7. A frame; a rack.
Lth. That sort of 'trees' which is used for supporting a frame for drying wool (JAM.). Nhb.¹ The frame with a cross-piece atop, against which cut boards are rested in a timber yard. w.Yks. A frame upon which wet cloth pieces are placed, hanging down on each side as if thrown across the back of a real horse (M.T.); A piece of wood not unlike the letter Y fixed upright into one end of the cam stock. Over this hook the sliver ends were laid, the body of the wool being on the stock. Also known as the Judy-hook (J.T.). Nrf. Rack on which spits of herring hang to drain, COZENS-HARDY *Broad Nrf.* (1893) 100. Ken.¹ The arrangement of hop-poles, tied across from hill to hill, upon which the pole-pullers rest the poles, for the pickers to gather the hops into the bins or baskets.

8. A screen, or frame on which to air linen before a fire; a clothes-horse; also in comp. Horse-maiden.
Sc. Her mantle was steaming upon the wooden horse before the kitchen fire, KEITH *Bonnie Lady* (1897) 173. n.Lin.¹, Lan., Chs. (F.E.), Dev.¹

9. An iron stool used for setting things on before a fire. n.Lin.¹ **10.** A beer tram. Glo.¹ **11.** A plank or faggot to stand upon when digging in wet ditches, moved forwards by a knobbed stick inserted through it. Dor. BARNES *Gl.* (1863) ; Dor.[1]

12. A fault in a rock ; a piece of ' dead ' ground or ' matrix,' rising in a lode of metal, throwing it out of its course ; *gen.* in phr. *the lode has taken horse, or a horse is in the lode.* w.Yks.[1] Glo. There is a remarkable instance of what is called a ' Horse ' in this coal field [Forest of Dean], which resembles a channel cut amongst a mass of vegetable matter ; in fact it appears to be an old river-channel filled with mud, WOODWARD *Geol. Eng. and Wal.* (1876) 103. Cor. Cappen, we've got a horse come into our lode, TREGELLAS *Tales* (1865) 147 ; Cor.[12] [Aus. What we thought was the ' hanging-wall ' caved in, and showed us the true reef again, and a nice little fortune too on the other side of a ' horse,' VOGAN *Blk. Police* (1890) vii.]

13. A spinning-machine, somewhat different from a ' mule.' w.Yks. (S.C.H.) **14.** A fault in warping, when the warp is passed twice over the same pin or when a pin is missed, a cloth-making term. w.Yks. (M.T.) **15.** A faucet, a wooden instrument for drawing off liquors ; a reed or straw introduced into a cask by means of which the liquor is stolen. n.Sc. (JAM.), e.An.[1] **16.** A vacant space in a chartered ship ; ' dead freight.' e.An.[1] **17.** A cruel method of putting a frog or toad to death by placing it on the end of a balanced stick, and striking the other end smartly, so that the animal is sent high into the air and killed by the fall. Hmp.[1]

18. A leech.

Lan. She was ' boiling two horses for their Philip.' The doctor came the day after and asked if the leeches had bitten, and was answered . . . ' He took 'em i' gruel,' *N. & Q.* (1869) 4th S. iii. 594.

19. A boy who holds another on his back while the latter is being flogged.

Wxf. Sometimes an obdurate little delinquent would . . . keep a pin in his mouth and while the birch was doing duty, and he was in agony, stick it into the neck of the unfortunate youth who acted as horse in the exciting little drama, KENNEDY *Banks Boro* (1867) 262.

20. *v.* To mount ; to ride a horse.

Sc. Upon this all within horsed and chased Carstaires and his party, KIRKTON *Ch. Hist.* (1817) 381 ; There was horsing, horsing in haste, SCOTT *Minstrelsy* (1802) II. 118, ed. 1848 ; He that is mann'd with boys and hors'd with colts will have his meat eaten and his work undone, *prov.*, GREGOR *The Horse,* 9. Fif. Quietlie the Esquyre and he horsed, and were gone toward the Queenes-ferrie, Row *Ch. Hist.* (1650) 453, ed. 1842. Lakel.[2]

Hence (1) **Horsing-bench,** (2) -block, *sb.* steps or a stone to assist persons to mount a horse ; (3) -clog, (4) -dog, *sb.* a log of wood used in mounting horses ; (5) -steps, (6) -stock, (7) -stone, *sb.,* see (2).

(1) nw.Der.[1] (2) n.Lin.[1] (3, 4) e.Yks.[1] (5) Lakel.[2], n.Yks.[4], m.Yks.[1], w.Yks. (C.C.) (6) Lan. The defendant had got upon the ' horsing-stock ' and harangued the mob, BRIERLEY *Tales* (1854) II. 38. (7) Nhb.[1], Lakel.[12], Cum.[14], n.Yks.[12], e.Lan.[1]

21. Phr. (1) *horse and away,* a command to mount one's horse and be off ; (2) *horse and hattock,* the flitting words of fairies and witches ; a command to ride off ; (3) *to horse the heels of a person,* see below.

(1) Lakel.[1] (2) Sc. HISLOP *Anecdote* (1874) 445 ; Away with you, sirs, get your boots and your beasts—horse and hattock, I say, SCOTT *Fair Maid of Perth* (1828) vii ; Now horse and hattock speedilie, ib. *Blk. Dwarf* (1816) viii. Ayr. Then they [witches] would put a strae between their legs, cry—' Horse and hattock in the Devil's name ! ' and flee awa owre the muirs and fells, SERVICE *Notandums* (1890) 101. (3) Ayr. Ye who . . . count it your contentment to plot his overthrow : to be above him and about, and count it your gain to horse his heels, DICKSON *Sel. Writings* (1660) I. 160, ed. 1845.

22. To punish by striking the buttocks on a stone. Sc. (JAM.) **23.** To tie the upper branches of the hop-plant to the pole. Ken.[1] e.Sus. HOLLOWAY. **24.** Salt-making term : to set the lumps of salt upon the top of each other in the hot-house. Chs.[1]

HORSE, see **Halse,** *sb.*[1]

HORSE-GOWK, *sb.* Sh. & Or.I. Also in forms -gawk, -gook, and hoars-gouk (JAM.). The common snipe, *Gallinago major.*

The snipe, which is here named the hoarsgouk, BARRY *Hist.*

(1805) 307 (JAM.); SWAINSON *Birds* (1885) 192; S. & Ork.[1] [Hoarse Gowk, the snipe, JOHNS *Birds* (1862).] [Cp. Sw. *horsgök,* the common snipe (WIDEGREN) ; Dan. dial. *horsegjög* (FEILBERG) ; MDan. *horsegög* (KALKAR) ; ON. *hrossagaukr* (FRITZNER).]

HORSEWARD, *adj.* Som. Dev. Also in forms **horse-head** Som. ; **horsewood** Glo. ; **hossed** w.Som.[1] Of a mare : *maris appetens.* Cf. **bullward.**

Som. (HALL.) w.Som.[1] Au·seed. Dev. *Horae Subsecivae* (1777) 67. nw.Dev.[1]

HORSING, *ppl. adj.* Chs.[1] Of a mare : *maris appetens.* Cf. **horseward.**

HORSISH, *adj.* w.Som. Horsey. ELWORTHY *Gram.* (1877) 18.

HORSLY, *adj.* Lan. Exaggerated, fictitious.

The towd'n o thoos horsly tales abeawt th' jakobins o'er turnink th' government, WALKER *Plebeian Pol.* (1796) 47, ed. 1801. s.Lan. (S.W.)

HORST, HORT(EN, HORTLE, see **Hurst, Hurt, Hurtle,** *v.*

HORVE, *v.* Dor. To be anxious, to worry about trifles ; to vacillate, be doubtful, undecided about a small matter.

She did horve about fur foive minutes ur better whether it shud be red ribbon ur blue (H.J.M.) ; (HALL.) ; *Gl.* (1851).

HORVE, see **Hauve,** *v.*[1]

HORVEN, *sb.* Sh.I. The kraken, a mythical sea-monster.

The kraken or horven, which appears like a floating island, sending forth tentacula as high as the masts of a ship, HIBBERT *Desc. Sh. I.* (1822) 260, ed. 1891.

HOSE, *sb.*[1] Sc. n.Cy. Lan. Midl. Lei. Glo. Hrt. e.An. Sus. Som. Dev. Cor. Also written **hoes** Sh.I. ; and in forms **hosen** Gall. (JAM.) ; **hoy's-** Slk. (JAM.) [hōz.]

I. Gram. forms : *pl.* (1) **Hosen,** (2) **Housen,** (3) **Hozen.**

(1) Dmf. Weel darned hosen, CROMEK *Remains* (1810) 101. Gall. Cross-gartered hosen, CROCKETT *Anna Mark* (1899) xliii. Lan. You'll not want no jacket, nor yet shirt and hosen, WESTALL *Birch Dene* (1889) I. 289. Cor.[1] (2) Dev. Now and then they use the form of the old Saxon plural, for they sometimes talk about their housen and their shooen, BRAY *Desc. Tamar and Tavy* (1836) I. 26. (3) w.Som. I have heard that shüern [shoes] and oa zn [hose] were used in this district quite within 'the memory of the oldest inhabitant,' ELWORTHY *Gram.* (1877) 7. Dev. WHITE *Cyman's Conductor* (1701) 127.

II. Dial. meanings. **1.** A single stocking, esp. a stocking without a foot or sole. Cf. **hoshen, hoe,** *sb.*[2]

Cai.[1] Stockings without soles formerly worn by people who went barefoot. The wearing of hose in summer by boys and girls in country districts was very common till about the middle of the 19th century. Abd. In a hose . . . lay Just fifty crowns, ANDERSON *Rhymes* (1867) 19. Gall. Hosen sometimes used in the sing. (JAM., s.v. Hoeshins).

2. Women's drawers. Lei.[1] 302.

3. The sheath or vagina of corn. Cf. **hoosing.**

Ked. The daisy did bloom, and the corn in the hose, JAMIE *Muse* (1844) 68. Frf. The disease of smut is found in the ears before they have burst from the hose or seed-leaves, *Agric. Surv.* 299 (JAM.). n.Cy. (HALL.) Midl. MARSHALL *Rur. Econ.* (1796) II. Hrt. (The honey dews) glew up the tender hose of the ear, ELLIS *Mod. Husb.* (1750) II. i. e.An.[1] In long and severe drought, at the time when barley should come into the ear, it is apt to 'stick in the hose ' and perish. e.Suf. (F.H.)

4. A socket in an implement for receiving a handle or shaft.

Sc. You make an iron instrument, . . with a hose or socket, as a fork is made for holding of a pole or shaft ; which being fixed into the hose it may be thrust down into the earth, MAXWELL *Sel. Trans.* (1743) 96 (JAM.). Sh.I. I tried ta prise up da hoes o' da tusker wi' da blade o' da limpit pick, *Sh. News* (May 13, 1899). [The prongs are connected with a hose, into which a wooden helve, with a short cross handle, is fastened, STEPHENS *Farm Bk.* (ed. 1849) II. 36.]

5. A faucet. e.Suf. (F.H.)

6. Comb. (1) **Hose-doup,** the medlar, *Mespilus germanica,* (2) -fish, the cuttle-fish, *Sepia loligo* ; (3) -grass, the meadow soft-grass, *Holcus lanatus* ; (4) -in-hose, a variety of the polyanthus, *Primula elatior,* or primrose, *P. acaulis* ; (5) -net, *obs.,* a small net affixed to a pole and used for rivulet fishing ; also used *fig.*

(1) Rxb. (Jam.) (2) Sc. Sibbald *Scotia* (1684) 26. (3) Ayr. Hose-grass or Yorkshire fog is next to rye-grass the most valuable grass, *Agric. Surv.* 287 (Jam.). (4) Glo.[1] The calyx becomes petaloid, giving the appearance of one corolla within another. e.An.[1] A primrose or polyanthus with one corolla within another. e.Sus. (B. & H.) (5) Sc. They had made a fine hosenet for me, Scott *Rob Roy* (1817) xxxiv ; Some tarred sticks once brought Hannibal and his host out of a terrible hose-net, *Magopico* (ed. 1836) 26. Abd. They were all drawn in an hose-net, frae the whilk they could not fly, Spalding *Hist. Sc.* (1792) II. 206. Slg. Be your awin words ye have drawne your selfes in a hose-net, and crucified your messe, Bruce *Sermons* (1631) iii. Ayr. Here is the very hosenet wherein Satan catches the civilians of this world, Dickson *Writings* (1660) I. 16a, ed. 1845. Slk. Some o' thae imps will hae his simple honest head into Hoy's net wi' some o' thae braw women, Hogg *Perils of Man* (1822) III. 386 (Jam., s.v. Hois).

HOSE, *v.*[1] n.Cy. To embrace, 'halse.'

He hose her hourly to my heart, Child *Ballads* (1884) I. 285.

HOSE, *adj., sb.*[2] and *v.*[2] Rut. Som. Dev. Also in forms hoaze Rut.[1]; hoaze n.Dev.; hoce Dev.; hoze n.Dev. [ōᵊ, ōᵤ, oᵊs, oᵤz.] 1. *adj.* Hoarse. Cf. hoast, *sb.*[1]

Dev. I thort I shude railly a laff'd mezul hose, Nathan Hogg *Poet. Lett.* I. 44, in Pengelly *Verbal Pron.* (1875) 95.

2. *sb.* Hoarseness, huskiness of the throat; a cough. Cf. hooze, *sb.*

Rut.[1] w.Som.[1] A well-known local cattle specific professes to cure in various animals—'yearlings or calves: husk or hose, scour, chills, worms in throat.' A clergyman found the sexton on the Saturday night walking up and down the river Barle. He said he was trying to get a bit of a hose, because he had to sing bass in church next day. Dev. Then ha took up es pipe, an ha kauff'd auff tha hoce, Nathan Hogg *Poet. Lett.* (1847) 53, ed. 1858 ; I be troubled wi' such a hose in my throat, Tom, that I can scarce quilty, *Eng. Illus. Mag.* (June 1896) 256. n.Dev. Uur'dh u·guut u tuur·ubl oa·uz [she has a terrible hoarse], *Exm. Scold.* (1746) l. 261. nw.Dev.[1]

3. *v.* To die, cease to breathe. Only used in *pp.*

w.Som.[1] A cant phrase for 'died,' like 'croaked.' n.Dev. He must a hozed in a little time, *Exm. Scold.* (1746) l. 290.

[1. OE. *hás*, hoarse.]

HOSE, see **Halse,** *sb.*[1]

HOSEBIRD, *sb.* Wor. Oxf. Sus. Hmp. Wil. Dor. Som. Dev. Also in forms hoosbird Hmp.[1]; hozeburd Dev.; husbird Wil. Dor.[1] Som. ; husbud s.Wor.; huzburd Som.; oosbird se.Wor.[1]; osbūd w.Wor.[1] 1. An illegitimate child. w.Wor.[1] se.Wor.[1]

2. A term of abuse, a rascal; a lazy, clumsy person; also used *attrib.*

†Oxf. That there hose-bird have a been in jail, Blackmore *Cripps* (1876) xvi. †Sus. Doubt the young hosebird were struck last moon, *ib. Springhaven* (1887) ix. Hmp.[1] Wil. (K.M.G.) ; Slow *Gl.* (1892). Dor. The husbird of a fellow, Sam Lawson, .. took me in completely, Hardy *Greenwood Tree* (1872) ii ; Dor.[1] Som. Lef the little maid alone, young huzburd, Raymond *Love and Quiet Life* (1894) 21 ; A man of bad omen, Sweetman *Wincanton Gl.* (1885). w.Som.[1] Let me catch the young hosebird [oa·zburd, hoa·zburd, wuuz·burd], that's all, aa'll make'n know. Dev. A term of mild and playful abuse. 'Dūee zee whot thickee young hozeburd's about !' 'E'th broked awl tha eggs Polly zot upon, tū let tha chicken out !' Hewett *Peas. Sp.* (1892). nw.Dev.[1] [They'd set some sturdy whore's-bird to meet me, *Plautus made English* (1694) 9 (Dav.).]

HOSEMEVER, see **Howsoever.**

HOSH, *sb.* s.Pem. A mixture of beer, eggs, butter, and sugar, taken to promote perspiration. (W.M.M.)

HOSHEN, *sb.* Sc. Also written hoeshin Ayr. (Jam.) ; and in form hushion Ayr. Lnk. 1. A stocking without a foot ; *gen.* in *pl.*

Ayr. She dights her grunzie wi' a hushion. Burns *Willie's Wife,* st. 4 ; (Jam.) ; A hushion is the last stage of a stocking, which, when entire, is a scabbard for the leg and foot ; when the sole of

the stocking is worn off it becomes a hugger; when the leg is sore worn and darned past redemption for footing, and the foot cut off, it then takes the name of a hushion, and used to be worn on the legs of women and boys at country work to keep their legs frae hacking—what refinement calls chapping or gelling, Hunter *Studies* (1870) 29. Lnk. Hushions on her bare legs, Bauchels on her feet, Nicholson *Kilwuddie* (ed. 1895) 164. Dmf. Stocking-legs used as gaiters in snowy weather, Shaw *Schoolmaster* (1899) 349. Gall. My spawls hae ne'er a hoshen now, my pouches ne'er a plack, Mactaggart *Encycl.* (1824) 69, ed. 1876. Kcb. Some wi' wallets, some wi' weghts, An' some wi' hoshens cap'rin, Davidson *Seasons* (1789) 118 (Jam.).

2. *Phr.* throwing the hoshen, *obs.*, a wedding custom ; see below.

Gall. At weddings, when the time of bedding comes on, the young folk are surrounded by the people at the wedding, to witness the ceremony ; one part of which is, that the bride takes the stocking off her left leg, and flings it at random amongst the crowd, and whoever it happens to hit will be the first of them who will get married, Mactaggart *Encycl.* (1824) 447, ed. 1876.

3. *Fig.* A term of abuse.

Gall. It wad be a lang time or ever he howkit a dreel o' my tawties. He's fitter at eatin' them, great fushionless hoshen that he is ! Crockett *Raiders* (1894) xxi.

HO-SHOW, *sb.* s.Cy. The 'whole' show; everything exposed to sight. (Hall.)

HOSIE, *sb.* Bnff.[1] The cuttle-fish, *Sepia loligo.* Cf. hose-fish, s.v. Hose, *sb.*[1]

HOSK, *sb.* Pem. The long-bracteated sedge, *Carex divisa.*

s.Pem. Yea better not cross the path ; yea canna see the gorse for hosk (W.M.M.).

[Wel. *hesg,* sedges, Ir. *seisg,* sedge, bog-reed (O'Reilly).]

HOSK, see **Hask,** *adj.*[1]

HOSKIN, *sb.* e.Yks.[1] [o·akin.] A 'land' or division in the ploughing of a field, narrower than the rest.

HÖSLIG, *sb.* Sh.I. A house, home.

Hunger an' wark ir aye ill met, an' never gree. Com' on. Lat's mak' fir da höslig, *Sh. News* (Sept. 3, 1898) ; We'll pit aff nae mair time wi' da playin' dis night, Willie. I tink he's time 'at ye, and da boys, wis tinkin aboot da höslig. *ib.* (Mar. 19, 1898) ; (J.I.)

HOSPITAL, *sb.* w.Yks. A place in a warehouse where damaged lengths of cloth are put, previous to disposal. (J.M.)

HOSPITALITY RESIDENCE, *phr.* Dur. The residence of one of the canons of the cathedral church.

At the public dinners given by the canons, in what is there called 'hospitality residence,' one of the choristers comes in after dinner dressed in his official costume, and taking his station behind the canon in residence reads . . . eight verses of the 119th Psalm, *N. & Q.* (1851) 1st S. iii. 308.

HO-SPY, *sb.* Sc. Also in forms hoispehoy Bnff. (Jam.) ; hospie Bnff. The game of 'hy-spy,' a variety of hide-and-seek.

Bnff. The pronunciation about Keith is 'hospie,' with the accent on the first syllable, Francisque-Michel *Lang.* (1882) 249 ; (Jam.) Lth. Ho, spy! is chiefly a summer game. Some of the party . . . conceal themselves ; and when in their hiding-places, call out these words to their companions : and the first who finds has the pleasure of next exercising his ingenuity at concealment, *Blackw. Mag.* (Aug. 1821) 35 (*ib.*).

HOSS, see **Oss.**

HOSSACK, *sb.* Sh.I. A knot tied on a stranded line by fishermen to strengthen it. S. & Ork.[1]

HOSSACK, HOSSOCK, see **Hussock, Hassack.**

HOSSEN-POT, *sb.* Dor. [Not known to our other correspondents.] A 'horse-pot' or basket. (C.W.B.)

HOST, *sb.* and *v.* n.Cy. Nhb. Yks. Lan. Lin. Also Sus. Also written hoste Sus.[12] ; and in forms hoast Nhb.[1]; oast N.Cy.[1] Nhb.[1] [h]ōst, n.Yks. wost.] 1. *sb.* A vendor of articles out of shops or houses.

Sus.[1] So used at Hastings ; Sus.[2] Every person not lotting or shotting to the common charge of the Corporation, who should be a common hoste in the fish-market, *Hastings Corporation Rec.* (1604).

2. *Comp.* Host-house, (1) an inn, ale-house, esp. that at which farmers and countrymen put up on market days ; (2) a place of rendezvous, or resort, a cottage where young men and women meet in the evening.

(1) n.Cy. Grose (1790) ; N.Cy.[1] Nhb.[1] The inns where farmers

i i

put up in coming to market have oast-hooses attached. They are the waiting rooms used by wife and daughters, and the reception place for parcels or goods sent in by tradesmen to go by the farmers' carts. n.Yks.¹² s.Yks. They have hoast-howses wheare they dine, Best *Rur. Econ.* (1642) 100 ; Marshall *Rur. Econ.* (1788 . Lan. Who took me down to their host-house and gave me a treat, Walkden *Diary* (ed. 1866) 66. (2) n.Lin.¹ No good'll cum to her ; her's is a reg'lar host-hoose.

3. *v.* To frequent ; to 'put up.'
N.Cy.¹ He oasts at the Half-Moon. n.Yks.² Where do you wost at ! (s.v. Wost-house).

HOST, HOSTA, HÖSTAK, see **Hoast,** *sb.*¹, **Oast, Husta, Hustack.**

HOSTER, *sb.* Dev: [Not known to our correspondents.] A kind of jug without a handle. (Hall.)

HOSTILLAR, *sb. Obs. Sc.* Also written **hostellar.** A hostelry, an inn.
Sc. Francisque-Michel *Lang.* (1882) 367. Fif. They ... spers'd about in search o' beds Throu' houses, hostillars, and sheds, Whairon to rest their heavie heads, Tennant *Papistry* (1827) 125.

HOSTING, *vbl. sb. Obs. Sc.* Also in form **hoisting** (Jam.). The raising or assembling of an army or host.
Being obliged to follow Sir Robert in hunting and hosting, watching and warding, Scott *Redg.* 1824) Lett. xi ; *ib. Monastery* (1820) xiii; *ib. Old Mort.* (1816) v; (Jam.) [The annual value of the services, commonly called personal attendance, hosting, hunting, watching and warding . . . shall be paid in money annually instead of them, *Act* 1 *Geo. I* (1715 .]

HOSTLE, *v.* Cum. Yks. Also in form **ossle** Cum. [o·sl, n.Yks. wo·sl.] **1.** To lodge, put up at an inn.
n.Yks.¹²; n.Yks.⁴ Only used in connexion with an inn. We ' put up ' and ' hostle ' at an inn, and ' lowse out ' at a friend's.

2. To act as hostler, perform the duties of hostler.
Cum. He osslt fer oald Mally Piell eh t'Croon an Mitre, Sargisson *Joe Scoap* (1881) 157.

HOSTLER, *sb. Obs. Sc.* Also Nrf. Also in forms **hosteler** Nrf. ; **hostilar** Abd. ; **hostiler** Sc. ; **ostler** Abd. **1.** An innkeeper.
Sc. Impowering hostlers and common innkeepers, to impose oaths upon all passengers and travellers, Sc. *Presb. Eloq. Answer,* 34. Abd. He lodges in Andrew Haddentoun's at the yett-cheek, who was an ostler, Spalding *Hist. Sc.* (1792) I. 17 ; That na tavernar nor hostilar within the samen mak onie flesche reddie during the said tyme of Lentrone, Turreff *Antiq. Gleanings* (1859) 183

2. *Comp.* (1) **Hostler-house,** a house of public entertainment, a hostel ; (2) **-wife,** a landlady, an innkeeper's wife.
(1) Sc. Upon the doores of tavernes, hostlier houses, and mercat crosses, Wodrow *Sel. Biog.* (1847) I. 267. Per. See ye, Sir, yon hostler-house. . . This very day have landed in it Full fifteen Englishmen, Ford *Harp* (1893) 19. (2) Sc. Donald Caird can drink a gill Fast as hostler-wife can fill, Chambers *Sngs.* (1829) I. 57 ; Syne paid him upon a gantree As hostler-wives should do, Ramsay *Tea-Table Misc.* (1724) I. 100, ed. 1871 ; We alighted at the door of a jolly hostler-wife, as Andrew called her, Scott *Rob Roy* (1817) xix.

3. *pl.* A name given to those who lodged fishermen in Yarmouth. Nrf. (H.J.H.)

HOSTRY, *sb.* w.Yks. A long stool used for ' cuttling ' (q.v.) on. (S.K.C.)

HOT, *adj., sb.* and *v.* Var. dial. uses in Sc. Irel. and Eng. Also in forms **heat** Cai.¹ n.Yks. ; **heeat** n.Yks.²⁴ ; **het** Sc. Bnff.¹ N.Cy.¹ Nhb.¹ Dur.¹ Lakel.² Cum.¹⁴ Wm. ; **hoat, hote** Wxf.¹ ; **oot-** Shr.¹ ; **ot-** War.⁸ ; **yat** n.Yks.²⁴ e.Yks.¹ m.Yks.¹ [h)ot, h)lat, het, yat, w.Yks. ut.] **1.** *adj.* In *comb.* (1) **Hot-ache,** the tingling sensation and pains caused by sudden warmth after extreme cold ; (2) **-bitch,** a bitch in the rutting season ; (3) **-brained,** hot-tempered, hot-headed ; (4) **-broan,** a firebrand ; (5) **-chills,** the fever accompanying ague ; (6) **-drinks,** warm drinks of a cordial nature ; (7) **-evil,** fever [not known to our correspondents] ; (8) **-flares,** accesses of heat in sickness ; (9) **-foot,** (10) **-foot-hot,** at once, immediately, full speed, in great haste ; (11) **-gingerbread,** gingerbread having in it a mixture of ginger and cayenne ; (12) **-hands,** a children's game, see below ; (13) **-hive,** an eruption or small boil ; (14) **-house** (**-us**), the stove in which salt is dried in salt-making ; (15) **-loof,** a game ; (16) **-millo,** a boys' game, see

below ; (17) **-pickles,** a scolding, trouble ; (18) **-pint,** a hot beverage composed of ale, spirits, and other ingredients, and drunk esp. on New Year's eve or early morning ; (19) **-posset,** hot milk and bread ; (20) **-pot,** (*a*) a mixture of warmed ale and spirits, with other ingredients ; (*b*) a dish of meat and potatoes baked together ; an Irish stew ; (*c*) a melting-pot ; (21) **-seed, early** grain or peas ; (22) **-skin,** a thrashing, beating ; (23) **-skinned,** irascible, hot-tempered ; (24) **-spoken,** sharp of speech ; (25) **-spurred,** see (10) ; (26) **-stoup,** see (18) ; (27) **-trod,** *obs.,* the pursuit of Border marauders ; the signal for the pursuit ; also used *fig.* ; (28) **-tuik,** a bad taste ; (29) **-wardens,** pears ; (30) **-waters,** spirits ; (31) **-weeds,** annual weeds, such as field-mustard, &c. ; (32) **-whittle** or **-whissel,** a borer or skewer heated red-hot for the purpose of boring a hole through wood.

(1) w.Yks.², Not.¹ n.Lin. Sutton *Wds.* (1881); n.Lin.¹ sw.Lin.¹ I oftens get the hotache in my foot, and very bad it is ; it comes on when my foot's starved with binging out the clothes. Nhp.¹, Lei.¹, War.⁸ Bdf. My hands have got the hot-ache (J.W.B.). Hnt. (T.P.F.) Nrf. Common (M.C.H.B.). (2 Gall. Mactaggart *Encycl.* (1824). (3) n.Yks. I alias knew 'at sha was a heeatbrain'd 'en (W.H.). (4) Wxf.¹ (5) Sus.¹ (6) Gall. Mactaggart *Encycl.* (1824). (7) Dev. (Hall.) (8) Hmp. I have nasty hot-flares (T.L.O.D.). (9) Sc. But to go to him hot-foot from Appin's agent was little likely to mend my own affairs, Stevenson *Catriona* (1893) i. Abd. Rin awa noo het-fit an' bring him here. Rin het-fit, I'm sayin' (G.W.). w.Sc. Burns heard of the elopement with surprise and followed the pair ' hot foot ' to Killie, Carrick *Laird of Logan* (1835) 49. Ir. I can run on hot foot, Barrington *Sketches* (1830) I. xii ; Set off hot-foot to the wake, Croker *Leg. Killarney* (1829) I. 83, in Grose (1790 · *MS. add.* (M.) N.Cy.¹, Lakel.² Cum. He's geaan het feutt efter a fella they co Arch, Sargisson *Joe Scoap* (1881) 64 ; Cum.⁴ Wm. Ah set off het fiut i mi majesty (B.K.). m.Yks.¹ Lan.¹ He coom deawn hot-foot, bent on havin' a quarrel. n.Lin.¹ As soon as she heàrd on it she went off hot-foot to oor Tom's, an' tell'd him what foäks was saäyin'. Brks. ' Now's your time, Billy,' says I, and up the hedge I cuts, hot-foot, to get betwixt he and our bounds, Hughes *T. Brown Oxf.* (1861) xxxvi. Mid. They made off, hot foot, for the cart, Blackmore *Kit* (1890) II. viii. Cor. ' I'll ha' 'ee ! ' cries the Squire ; an' wi' that pulls hot foot roun' the hill, ' Q.' *Troy Town* (1888) xix. (10) Dur.¹ s.Dur. She ran het foot het to met off hot-foot to oor Tom's, an' tell'd him what foäks was saäyin'. with any piece of gossip she got hold of, *Weardale Forest Ann.* ne.Lan.¹ (11) Lan. [When ' pace-egging '] children . . . go up and down from house to house ; at some receiving pence, . . . at others gingerbread, some of which is called hot gingerbread, . . causing the most ridiculous contortions of feature in the unfortunate being who partakes of it, Harland & Wilkinson *Flk-Lore* (1867) 230. (12) Rxb. A number of children place one hand above another on a table till the column is completed, when the one whose hand is undermost pulls it out and claps it on the top, and thus in rotation (Jam.). (13) Nhb.¹ (14) Chs.¹ (15) Ir. The first play we began was hot-loof, Carleton *Traits Peas.* (ed. 1843) I. 106. (16) War.² A kneels with his face in *B's* lap, the other players standing in the background. They step forward one by one, at a signal from *B,* who says of each in turn, ' 'Otmillo, 'Otmillo, where is this poor man to go ? ' *A* then assigns each one to a place. When all are dispatched, *A* removes his face from *B's* lap, and, standing up, exclaims, ' Hot ! Hot ! Hot ! ' The others then rush to him, and the laggard is blindfolded instead of *A.* (17) Lin.¹ (18) Sc. I took a rest at Pepper-mill, A het-pint and a double gill, Pennecuik *Collection* (1787) 16 ; The hot beverage which it is customary for young people to carry with them from house to house on New-Year's-eve, or early in the morning of the New Year ; used also on the night preceding a marriage and at the time of child-bearing. . . This is made of spirits, beer, sugar, and eggs (Jam.). Frf. A het pint in a cup maun neist be made To drink the health o' her that's brought to bed, Morison *Poems* (1790) 191. Raf. The first fit bauldly fronts the storm. The maudlin' het pint's heavenly power Has rais'd a flame that brings the shower, Picken *Poems* (1813) I. 78. Lnk. I'd toddle butt, an' I'd toddle ben, Wi' the hearty het pint an' the canty black hen, Rodger *Poems* (1838) 56, ed. 1897. Lth. The kettle then on ingle clear, Boils fu' o' ale an' whisky; Wi' eggs an' sucker, . . To mak a birkie frisky. ... Fu' o' het pints he'll bauldly dash, Bruce *Poems* (1813) ll. 17. Edb. I agreed to a cupful of het-pint, Moir *Mansie Wauch* (1828) xix ; Among the lower classes of the people, it is customary for some person in each family to rise very early in new year's morning, and prepare a kind of caudle, consisting of ale mixed with

eggs, beat up with sugar and a little spirits, prepared hot, which is carried through every apartment in a stoup containing a Scots pint ; and a cup of this is offered to each person when in bed. This beverage is technically called het pints, *New Year's Morning* (1792) 7. **Dmf.** Until twelve o'clock announces the new year, when people are ready at their neighbours' houses with het-pints, and buttered cakes, Cromek *Remains* (1810) 46. **N.Cy.¹, Nhb.¹** (19) **Wm.** She'd give a het-posset her belly to warm, Whitehead *L{g.}* (1859) 7. **Yks.** (J.W.) (20, *a*) **N.Cy.¹** **Dur.** An aged fisher woman . . . tells me that at her wedding there were seventy hot pots, Henderson *Flk-Lore* (1879) i. **n.Yks.** (C.A.F.) ; **n.Yks.¹** Pots of hot spiced ale brought out by the friends of a newly-wedded couple to be partaken of by the bridal party as they return from church ; **n.Yks.²⁴** **Nhp.¹** Spiced, sweetened, and thickened with eggs and flour. **e.An.¹, Nrf.** (W.R.E.) **w.Nrf.** He . . . is too comfortable with his 'hot pot' to quit his present quarters, Orton *Beeston Ghost* (1884) 5. **e.Suf.** (F.H.) **Lon.** Sponsors at low christenings pretty far advanced in liquor, by too plentiful a drinking of common beer, hot-pots, and Geneva punch, *Low Life* (1764) 98. **Sus.¹²** **Hmp.¹** Not very common. (*b*) **ne.Lan.¹, Chs.¹, s.Chs.¹, War.³** (*c*) **War.²** A hot-pot is so called because it is always kept at smelting heat. It is kept ostensibly for purposes of trade, but is usually regarded as being kept for the convenience of thieves. To be known as a hot-pot is to be regarded with opprobrium. The name has in some instances stuck to a man for life, e.g. 'Hot-pot Smith,' or 'Hot-pot Jones.' (21) **Bwk.** These [oats] are distinguished into hot seed and cold seed, the former of which ripens much earlier than the latter [*sic*], *Agric. Surv.* 243 (Jam.). **Rxb.** Peas are sown of two kinds. One of them is called hot seed or early peas, *Agric. Surv.* 87 (Jam.). **Nhb.** Young *Annals Agric.* (1784–1815) XXI. 225. (22) **Sc.** I'll gie ye a guid het skin (Jam.). (23) **Sc.** (*ib.*), **Cai.¹** (24) **n.Yks.²** (25) **Dmb.** I'm aff, het spurred, to gain the prize, Salmon *Gowodean* (1868) 117. (26) **Peb.** Het stoups an' punch around war sent, Nicol *Poems* (1805) I. 147 (Jam.). (27) **s.Sc.** The pursuit of Border marauders was followed by the injured party and his friends with blood-hounds and bugle-horn, and was called the hot trod, Scott *Lay Last Minst.* (1806) 308 n. (Jam., s.v. Futehate) **N.Cy.¹ Nhb.** Richardson *Borderer's Table-bk.* (1846) VII. 97 ; **Nhb.¹** A wisp of straw or tow mounted on the top of a spear and set on fire and carried through the Border country. Its display was the signal for every man to arm and follow the pursuit on the track of a marauder, the 'war path' of the Borderers. **Cum.** A thief might be pursued into the opposite realm within six days, and the chace carried on, as the term is, in hot trod, with hound and horn, with hue and cry, Hutchinson *Hist. Cum.* (1794) I. 24 ; **Cum.¹** He follo't the reivers on the het trod. (28) **Lnk., Lth., Rxb.** When meal is made from corn that has been heated in the stack, the peculiar taste is denominated the het tuik (Jam., s.v. Teuk). (29) **Lon.** Mayhew *Lond. Labour* (1851) I. 8. (30) **Sc.** (A.W.), **n.Cy.** (Hall.) (31) **Bnff.¹** (32) **Cum.⁴** Sow Ah's garn to mak a burtri gun, len us thi het-whittle (B.K.).

2. Phr. (1) *hot and hot*, (2) *hot as hot*, (3) — *as a piper*, very hot, as hot as can be ; (4) — *beans and butter*, a children's game, similar to 'hunt the thimble' ; (5) *a hot cup of tea*, (*a*) a bad bargain ; an unexpected loss or accident ; (*b*) an unruly, troublesome girl ; (6) — *in the pepper*, 'hot,' uncomfortable, of a dangerous situation ; (7) — *rows and butter baiks*, a boys' game ; see below ; (8) *to be hot ahame*, to have a comfortable domestic settlement ; to be comfortable at home ; (9) — *hot in the house*, a saying used of those who come out in inclement weather without reason ; (10) — *kept in hot water*, to be in a constant state of anxiety or suspense ; (11) — *in hot water*, to be at variance or on ill terms with ; (12) — *o'er hot*, to make a change for the worse from restlessness or folly ; (13) *to carry hot water with one*, to bring ill-will with one, to quarrel ; (14) — *hold one in hot water*, to keep one in a state of constant uneasiness or anxiety ; (15) — *make anything with a hot needle and burning thread*, to sew very slightly.

(1) **Der.** As for the pikelets . . . butter 'um as folks want 'um, hot and hot, Verney *Stone Edge* (1868) iii. (2) **n.Cy.** (J.W.), **Nhp.¹, Hnt.** (T.P.F.) (3) **e.Suf.** (F.H.) (4) **Rxb.** One hides something and another is employed to seek it. When near the place of concealment, the hider cries 'Het,' i.e. hot on the scent ; when the seeker is far from it, 'Cald.' . . He who finds it has the right to hide it next (Jam.). (5) **e.Suf.** (F.H.) (6) **w.Wor.** Whin he begins it gits rayther too hot i' the pepper fur me, S. Beauchamp *N. Hamilton* (1875) I. 91. (7) **Frf.** One boy stood against the hillside or against a wall, and another boy, putting his head against

the first one's stomach, made a 'backie,' which was immediately mounted by one of the boys from the crowd, who was not supposed to be known to the one he bestrode. The captain of the game would now address the bowing lad, . . 'Lanceman, lanceman, lo ! Where shall this poor Scotchman go ? Shall he go east, or shall he go west, Or shall he go to the huddie craw's nest ?' If he was sent to the hooded crow's nest, he ranged himself alongside number one. If otherwise he had to go to some indicated post and there remain until all engaged in the game were placed in their various positions. The three chief actors and all who had remained in 'the crow's nest' ranged themselves in line, and . . . the captain now yelled out 'Het rows and butter baiks,' whereupon all those that had been banished to the outposts came rushing in, attempting to touch number one, who was surrounded by his legion of bonneters, who smacked and thrashed the invaders. When the 'draiglers,' as the invading party were called, had touched number one, they in turn became the defending party, Inglis *Ain Flk.* (1895) 110. (8) **Gall.** (Jam.) ; It is said of those who wander abroad when they have no need to do so, and happen to fare ill, that they were het ahame, Mactaggart *Encycl.* (1824). (9) **N.I.¹** You were hot in the house. (10) **Nhp.¹, Hnt.** (T.P.F.) (11) **Not.¹, Lei.¹, War.³** (12) **Cai.¹** He wiz o'er heat. (13) **Not.¹ Lei.¹** A carries 'ot water wi' 'im wheriver a goos. **War.³** (14) **Sc.** That bairn hauds me ay in het water ; for he's sae fordersum (Jam.). (15) **Oxf.¹, Sur.** (L.J.Y.)

3. Warm, comfortable.

Sc. The jinketing and the jirbling wi' tea and wi' trumpery that brings mony a het ha' house to a hired lodging in the Abbey, Scott *St. Ronan* (1824) x.

4. sb. Heat.

S. & Ork.¹ What a hot it is. **Wxf.¹** **s.Chs.¹** Aay red yŭr aa'rmz bin, Em'ŏ ! Iz it wi kuwd ? Wel, it i)n'd wi ot [' Hai red yur arms bin, Emma ! Is it wi' cowd ?' ' Well, it inna wi' hot ']. **Dev.** Wull then in es gose, bit moast daid way that hot, Nathan Hogg *Poet. Lett.* (1847) 15, ed. 1865.

5. v. To make hot, to heat, warm, esp. to warm up cooked food. Also *with up*.

e.Yks.¹ Yatten, *pp., MS. add.* (T.H.) **m.Yks.¹, w.Yks.** (T.H.), **w.Yks.²** **Chs.¹** I've hotted the water ; **Chs.³** **s.Chs.¹** Tŭ ot dhŭ ŏon [to hot the oven]. Tŭ ot kuwd tai'tŭz ŭp ŭgy'en'. **Der.²**, **nw.Der.¹, Not.¹** **n.Lin.¹** Hot me this iron Alice, my lass, an' bring it by ageän as soon as ta can. **sw.Lin.¹** She hotted up his dinner for him. **Rut.¹** I hot her a few broth. **Lei.¹** There's no hot water, but I'll hot some. **Nhp.¹, War.²³⁴, s.War.¹** **Shr.¹** Draw some drink an' 'ot it fur the men's suppers. **Glo.** (F.H.), **Glo.¹** **Oxf.** (G.O.) ; **Oxf.¹** *MS. add.* **Bdf.** (J.W.B.), **Hnt.** (T.P.F.), **Lon.** (F.H.) **Sur.¹** We jist lit a fire to hot our kettles. **Sus.¹** I was that cold when I got indoors that gaffer hotted up some beer for me. **Wil.** A piece of roast beef, that had been, as the housekeeper explained, 'hotted up,' Riddell *The Senior Partner*, i. **Dev.** If yŭ widden mind a scrap-dinner yŭ cŭde have tha cold beef hotted up intŭ a hash tŭ-day, Hewett *Peas. Sp.* (1892) ; I never can get a plate hotted through, Sharland *Ways and Means* (1885) 45.

Hence (1) **Hotted**, *ppl. adj.* warmed up, made hot ; (2) **Hotter**, *sb.* a heater, a long funnel-shaped tin vessel put into the fire to warm a liquid quickly ; also called **Hastener** (q.v.).

(1) **n.Yks.² w.Yks.¹** Hotted meat. **Der.²** Hotted ale. **nw.Der.¹** (2) **Shr.¹**

HOT, HO'T, see **Hit,** *v.*, **Hurt, Holt,** *sb.¹*

HOTAGOE, *v.* ? *Obs.* **s.Cy. Sus.** Also in form **hotague Sus.** In phr. *to hotagoe the tongue*, to move the tongue nimbly ; to babble.

s.Cy. Grose (1790). **Sus.** He do hotague he's tongue, Jackson *Southward Ho* (1894) I. 289 ; You hotagoe your tongue, Ray (1691) ; **Sus.¹ ; Sus.²** I believe disused now.

HOTCH, *v.* and *sb.* **Sc. Nhb. Dur. Cum. Wm. Yks. Lan. Der. Lin. Lei. Nhp. War. Glo. Nrf. Ken. Wil. Dev.** Also in forms **hatch Sc.** ; **hotchen Ayr.** [(h)otʃ, Sc. also hatʃ.]

1. v. To jerk, move awkwardly, lurch ; to fidget, heave, shrug ; to hitch ; to shake, esp. to shake with laughter. Also used *fig.* Cf. **hutch,** *v.²*

Sc. The laird changed colour and hotched in his chair, Tweeddale *Moff* (1896) 178. **Elg.** He hotch'd, he fidg'd – the foul fiend leugh, Couper *Poetry* (1804) II. 72. **Abd.** The haggis e'en hotched to the piper its lane, *Guidman Inglismaill* (1873) 43. **Fif.** Garrin' him scream a hideous rippet ; As aye they hotcht and laucht, Tennant *Papistry* (1827) 128. **s.Sc.** He hotched an' leuch, An' clawed his tawtie heid, Watson *Bards* (1859) 106. **Slg.** I've seen it . . . Gar a' the hillocks heave an' botch, Muir *Poems* (1818) 9.

Rnf. Had ye seen the auld hash how he hotched and he smil'd, WEBSTER *Rhymes* (1835) 164. **Ayr.** Even Satan glowr'd and fidg'd fu' fain, And hotch'd and blew wi' might and main, BURNS *Tam o' Shanter* (1790) l. 285; (J.M.) **Lnk.** To keep awa' the thocht o't yet aft gars me hotch an' blaw, NICHOLSON *Kilwuddie* (ed. 1895) 97. **e.Lth.** Hootsman was hotching with half suppressed laughter, MUCKLEBACKIT *Rhymes* (1885) 126. **Peb.** Some wi' their ribs 'maist like tae crack, As hotching, in a fry, . . He row'd toward his sty, *Lintoun Green* (1685) 68. ed. 1817. **Slk.** It was beginning to trummle, and crummle, and sigh, and groan, and heave, and hotch, like the earlier stages o' some earthquack, CHR. NORTH *Noctes* (ed. 1856) III. 87. **Rxb.** An' to mysel I hotch'd, an' leugh good speed, A. SCOTT *Poems* (ed. 1808) 162. **Dmf.** Ill-folk how they giggle and hotch, man, SHAW *Schoolmaster* (1899) 196. **Gall.** Brawly kenned I that they were hotchin' for me to gie them the presbytery, CROCKETT *Stickit Min.* (1893) 22. **N.Cy.¹ Nhb.** Lord, ye'd hae hotch'd had ye been there. PROUDLOCK *Borderland Muse* (1896) 174; **Nhb.¹** Aa fairly hotch'd agyen. **Dur.** GIBSON *Up-Weardale Gl.* (1870). **Cum.** First yan an' than anudder tel't a gud teal, an' Bob hotch't an' laff't till nine o'clock, FARRALL *Betty Wilson* (1886) 75. **m.Yks.¹, w.Yks.¹**

2. To shift one's position so as to make room for another, to sit closer; *gen.* with *up*.
Sc. 'Are ye sure ye hae room aneugh, sir!' ' I wad fain hotch mysell farther yont,' SCOTT *St. Ronan* (1824) xv. **Lakel.²** A chap 'll hotch-up ta mak room on a seat without gitten up. **w.Yks.²** To move on a seat without moving oneself. **Nhp.¹** Hotch a little further and give me a little more room. **Nrf.** ' Come, hotch up,' applied to some one of a party sitting round the fire when the person was required to move a bit, *N. & Q.* (1883) 6th S. vii. 217.

3. To limp, walk lamely or in an awkward manner; to trot slowly and jog along; to jump like a frog.
Slk. (JAM.) **Cum.** Now fit up a pillion for maister and deàmm, To hotch off t'town amang t'rest, DICKINSON *Cumbr.* (1876) 217. **m.Yks.¹ w.Yks.** He'd a hotched off thinkin he was so smart, *Dewsbro Olm.* (1865) 15; **w.Yks.¹ Lan.** GROSE (1790) *MS. add.* (C.) **e.Lan.¹ Lin.¹** To get upon a pillion. **n.Lin.¹ sw.Lin.¹** He went first and the old woman hotched along after him. **Ken.¹** ' He hotched along on the floor to the top of the stairs.' When a man walking with a boy keeps him on the run, he is described as keeping him hotching.

4. To swarm.
Sc. Our Sannock's head is a' hotchen, and John's is little better, GRAHAM *Writings* (1883) II. 106. **Nhb.¹** Hotchin wi' maggots. The place is fair hotchin wi' rabbits.

5. To botch, bungle; with *up*: to contrive to bring about in an irregular way.
n.Yks.⁴ Ken.¹ I lay he'll hotch up a quarrel afore long.

6. To cause to jerk, to hitch, heave; to move with a jerking motion; to hoist, lift up, raise; to pitch, throw. Also used *fig.*
Sc. He clenched his neives an' hotched himsel', ALLAN *Lilts* (1874) 5. **e.Lth.** Their sleeves hotched up ower their shouthers, HUNTER *J. Inwick* (1895) 148. **Gall.** That disease . . . hotch'd out his breath, MACTAGGART *Encycl.* (1824) 265, ed. 1876. **Cum.** He hotches his shooders, RICHARDSON *Talk* (1871) 176, ed. 1876. **Wm.** See'sta Ah've forked hay tell mi shirt's o' hotcht-up under mi oxters (B.K.). **m.Yks.¹, w.Yks.¹** Lel.¹ Hotch it ower your shoulder. **Nhp.¹** Hotch this up for me. He talks of five pounds, but if you don't bind them down, he'll hotch it up to twenty pounds. **War.²** A large bag of corn grasped round the neck of it and pushed by the knee a few inches at a time, or a heavy weight or tree moved along the ground or up an inclined plane by levers, would be hotched along. **Glo.¹ Wil.** Hotch it up into the dung-pot (W.H.E.).

7. To shake up, esp. to shake lead ore together in a bucket in the process of washing and sifting.
Nhb.¹ The bucket containing the ore is suspended from a long lever by which a boy jerks or hotches it in the water. **Dur.** *Lead Mine Lang.* (1866). **Lin.** When they shake potatoes in a bag so that they may lie the closer, they are said to hotch them (HALL.); **Lin.¹**

Hence (1) **Hotching**, *vbl. sb.* the process of sifting; (2) **-tub**, *sb.* a machine for washing ore.
(1) **Nhb.** 'Buddling' and 'hotching,' which may be described as a kind of sifting with sieves suspended in water, WHITE *Nhb.* (1859) 46. (2) **w.Yks.** A large square tub filled with water, over which a shallow tub is suspended. This tub has a wire bottom, and is worked up and down in the larger tub by means of a long handle; by this means the lead is washed and separated from the

soil or earth (J.E.); Another washing in the hotching tub, GRAINGE *Nidderdale* (1863) 193.

8. To examine wheat by shaking it in a sieve ; to dress and clean in a peculiar manner with a riddle.
w.Yks.² Lin. MORTON *Cyclo. Agric.* (1863).

9. To separate beans from peas after they ar threshed. **Der.², nw.Der.¹**

10. To cook cockles by heating them in a pan.
n.Cy. (HALL.), **n.Lin.¹ e.Lin.** Oh, you've gotten some cockles, hev ya! We mun 'ev 'em 'otched (J.T.F.).

11. To drive cattle. **n.Cy.** (HALL.), **Dev.¹** [Not known to our correspondents.]

12. *sb.* A jerk, jolt ; a shove, push, shrug. Also used *fig.*
Sc. Give her one hatch, all is done, KELLY *Prov.* (17a x) 79. **Lnk.** Put a spectacle glass to his ee, gied a bit hotch nearer me and opened oot wi' his impidence, FRASER *Whaups* (1895) xv. **Edb.** Uncanny hotches Frae clumsy carts or hackney-coaches, FERGUSSON *Poems* (1773) 176, ed. 1785. **Gall.** He gave his showthers a hotch, and answered, MACTAGGART *Encycl.* (1824) 163, ed. 1876. **m.Yks.¹ Lei.¹** Gie us a hotch up.

13. A market-day trot. **Cum.¹**

14. A job, business ; a bout, occasion, time ; a bungle, a mismanaged affair, a ' botch.'
n.Yks.¹; n.Yks.² They made a poor hotch on't. I gat a sair hotch [a severe tumble]; **n.Yks.⁴ e.Yks.** Thou's meead a bad hotch on't, MARSHALL *Rur. Econ.* (1796) II. 306. **m.Yks.¹ w.Yks.** I am ut bound to go wi' him this hotch (S.P.U.); **w.Yks.²**

15. A big, unwieldy person.
Ayr. A fat muckle hotch with a screw of dirty weans at her fit, SERVICE *Dr. Duguid* (ed. 1887) 101 ; The muckle fat hotchin ! she should been sotten doon on her ain fire till her spittle biled't, ib. *Notandums* (1890) 22.

[1. With old bogogers, hotching on a sped, MONTGOMERIE *Poems* (c. 1600), ed. Cranstoun, 122. OFr. *hocher*, ' secouer, ébranler ' (LA CURNE).]

HOTCH, *int.* n.Yks. A call for sheep. (R.H.H.)

HOTCHEL, *v. and sb.* Sc. Not. Lin. Rut. Lei. Nhp. War. Wor. Bck. Also written **hotchell** Rut. ; **hotchle** Sc. [h)o·tʃl.] **1.** *v.* To walk in an awkward, ungainly manner ; to hobble, limp. Cf. **hockle,** *v.*¹
Lnk. I hotchled alang in my grandeur, ROY *Generalship* (ed. 1895) 56. **Not.²** She can just hotchel about the house (J.P.K.). **n.Lin.¹** I'm that bad wi' rewmatics I can hardly hotchle along. **Rut.** I'm that bad wi' roomatis, that I can barely hotchel backard and forards, *N. & Q.* (1882) 6th S. vi. 513. **Lei.¹** Ah cain't but joost hotchel. **Nhp.¹; Nhp.²** It's as much as I can do to hotchel along. **War.** He goes hotcheling along (J.B.). **se-War.¹, n.Bck.** (A.C.)

2. To be gone, be off ; used as an *int.*
Not.⁵ Cum, 'otchel—d'ye 'ear.

3. *sb.* A jerk, hitch.
e.Fif. Gi'en his sparticles a hotchle up on's nose, LATTO *Tam Bodkin* (1864) xix.

HOTCHERTY-HOY, *sb.* m.Yks.¹ A hobbledehoy ; awkward, clumsy boy, a half-grown lad.

HOTCHERY-CAP, *sb.* Lakel. Also in form **hotchey-cap** Lakel.² Cum.⁴ A boys' game played with caps.
Lakel.² A lads' gam wi' a bo' an' ther hats o' set in a row ta throw intul. **Cum.** Played about 1830. ' While others start " bellied Scot," and hotchery-cap is not forgot ' (J.H.); **Cum.⁴** A row of caps being laid on the ground, each boy in turn hops over each cap, finally picking up his own cap in his mouth and throwing it over his shoulders ; should he fail in this, he is chased by the others and brayed with their caps.

HOTCHIE, *sb.* ? *Obs.* Sc. A general name for puddings.
Bch. *Gl.* (JAM.) **Abd.** The hotchie reams, the girdle steams, TARRAS *Poems* (1804) 12 (*ib.*).

HOTCH-POTCH, *sb.* Sc. Nhb. Yks. e.An. [h)o·tʃ-potʃ.] **1.** A mutton broth, made with meat and vegetables boiled together ; a stew, a dish composed of various ingredients cooked together, Irish stew.
Sc. A dish of broth, made with mutton, or lamb cut into small pieces, together with green peas, carrots, turnips, and sometimes parsley or celery, served up with the meat in it (JAM.) ; A favourite Scotch dish, *N. & Q.* (1880) 6th S. i. 394. **Lnk.** Mak' his glorious lordship dine On good sheep-head and haggis fine, Hotchpotch too, RODGER *Poems* (1838) 152, ed. 1897. **Nrf.** COZENS-HARDY *Broad Nrf.* (1893) 84. **e.Suf.** (F.H.)

. *Fig.* A medley, a confused jumble. Also used *attrib.*
Abd. I never yet saw . . . Sic a hotch-potch a' thegither, Cock *rains* (1810) I. 129. **Rnf.** Question this queer hotch-potch—'hich down our throats is cramm'd, McGilvray *Poems* (ed. 1862) 3. **Ayr.** Yon mixtie-maxtie queer hotch-potch, The Coalition, urns *Author's Cry* (1786) st. 21. **Lnk.** Wi' haughty pride he 'er was douted, Or high-floun style o' mix'd hotch-potch, Hunter *rms* (1884) 12. **Edb.** [He] made sic a hotch potch story of it, ddle *Poems* (1821) 203. **Nhb.** When English, Irish, Welsh and rotch, Promiscuous form a mere hotch-potch (W.G.). **w.Yks.** anks *Wkfld. Wds.* (1865).

HOT-COCKLES, *sb.* Irel. Yks. Lan. Lon. A children's ame ; see below.
Crk. At Cork a handkerchief is tied over the eyes of one of the mpany, who then lays his head on a chair and places his hand a his back with the palm uppermost. Any of the party come hind him and give him a slap on his hand, he in the meantime ying to discover whose hand it is that strikes, Gomme *Games* 894) I. 229. **w.Yks.** At Sheffield a boy is chosen for a stump id stands with his back against a wall. Another boy bends his ack as in ' leap-frog ' and puts his head against the stump. The sp of the boy who bends down is then taken off and put upon his ack upside down. Then each of the other boys . . . puts the first iger of his right hand into the cap. When all the fingers are it into the cap [certain] lines are sung. . . Then the boy whose ckle is bent jumpe up and the others run away crying out ' Hot ockles.' The boy who is caught by the one whose back was st bent has to bend his back next time, and so on, *ib.* **Lan.** lany an evening was beguiled with snap-dragon, . . hot cockles, arland & Wilkinson *Flk-Lore* (1867) 255. **Lon.** The felons in ewgate . . . playing at hunt the slipper, hot-cockles, and blind-an's buff, *Low Life* (1764) 83. [For further information see omme *Games* (1894) I. 229.]

HOTE, see Hold, *sb.,* **Hot.**

HOTES, *int.* e.Dur.¹ Also written hoats. Hush, e silent.

HOTHEN, *int.* Irel. An exclamation of surprise or issent.
' What'll I do if ye're drowned on me?' ' Hothen, what a notion have o' gettin' drownded !' Francis *Fustian* (1895) 49.

HOTH, HOTIL, see Hawth, Hottle, *sb.²*

HOTNESS, *sb.* n.Lin.¹ e.An.¹ Heat.

HOTS, see Hoatle.

HOT(T, *sb.* Sc. Nhb. Cum. Wm. Yks. Lan. Chs. e.An. lso in forms haut Lan.¹ ; ott Chs.² ; hut Dmf. [h)ot.]
1. A square basket or pannier used for carrying manure, tc. ; *gen.* in *pl.* Also called **Muck hot.**
Dmf. Shaw *Schoolmaster* (1899) 349. **Gall.** (Jam.) **n.Cy.** ' A air of hots,' two hampers of wood to lay cross a horse (K.) ; To arry turf or slate in, Grose (1790) ; **N.Cy.¹ Cum.** We carry't muck i' hots, Richardson *Talk* (1871) 57, ed. 1876 ; Muck's to e carry't in hots or in creels, Dickinson *Cumbr.* (1876) 244; *l.* (1851) ; **Cum.¹** Muck hots; **Cum.²** Wm. Used for carrying nanure into fields of steep ascent, one being hung on each side of pack-saddle. The bottom being opened by two wooden pins mptied the contents (J.H.). **w.Yks.** Hutton *Tour to Caves* 781) ; **w.Yks.¹,** ne.Lan.¹
2. A ' hot(t-load,' a heap of manure or lime in a field ; a mall heap of any kind carelessly put up.
Sc. There was hay to ca' and lint to lead, A hunder hotts o' uuck to spread, Chambers *Sngs.* (1829) I. 269. **Slk.** Will then aid his arm over the boy and the hott o' claes and fell sound sleep, Hogg *Perils of Man* (1822) II. 255 (Jam.). **Rxb.** ' A hot of uuck,' as much dung as is laid down from a cart in the field at one lace in order to its being spread out. ' A hot of stones,' &c. (Jam.) **n.Cy.¹** When persons or things are huddled or clumped together, hey are said to be ' all in a hott.' **Cum.¹**
3. A finger-stall or cover used to protect a cut or sore ; small bag to hold a poultice to protect a sore finger. an.¹, **e.Lan.¹, Chs.¹²,** s.**Chs.¹** Cf. **hottle,** *sb.¹,* **hut,** *sb.³*
Hence **Hotkin,** *sb.* a case for a sore finger. e.An.¹
[L OF. *hotte,* a pannier or creel.]

HOTT, *v.* Fif. (Jam.) To move by sudden jerks, to hake with laughter. ' He hottit and leuch.' Cf. **hotch,** *v.*

HOTTED, HOTTEN, HOTTEL, see Hurt, Hottle, *sb.¹²³*

HOTTER, *v.* and *sb.¹* Sc. Nhb. Dur. Cum. Yks. Lan. lso in forms **hetter** w.Yks.¹ ; **other** e.Yks.¹ ; **otter** .Yks. [h)o'tə(r.] **L** *v.* To move unsteadily or awk-

wardly, to hesitate ; to hobble, totter, walk lamely ; to shake with laughter. Cf. **hatter,** *v.,* **hotch,** *v.*
Sc. The humbler functionary . . . bottered and leuch in a semi-suppressed manner, Ford *Thistledown* (1891) 92. **Abd.** Hale be yir crowns, ye canty louns, Tho' age now gars me hotter, Tarras *Poems* (1804) 73 (Jam.). **Per.** To be gently shaken in the act of laughing (Jam.). **Peb.** A muir-hen . . . was rinnin hotterin round about, Nicol *Poems* (1805) *Man and Muir-fowl.* **Gall.** On the scent awa wad hotter, And sae hae at the roast a snack, Mactaggart *Encycl.* (1824) 135, ed. 1876. **Wgt.** He hotters about the clachans, and a troop of boys in his train, Fraser *Wigtown* (1877) 231. **Nhb.¹ Lakel.²** A body's sair hodden when they can hardly hotter an' walk. **Cum.** Than hotter to heàmm, through bog and wet syke, Dickinson *Cumbr.* (1876) 253 ; **Cum.¹ n.Yks.¹** Hottering on, nae better an a lamiter. **e.Yks.¹** To be decrepit ; to work feebly. ' Otherin-aboot,' going about in a stupid blundering way. **m.Yks.¹, Lan.** (C.W.D.), **e.Lan.¹**
Hence **Hottery,** *adj.* tottering in walking. Nhb.¹
2. To shudder, shiver. Abd., Per. (Jam.)
3. To shake, jolt ; to vibrate in moving over a rough surface.
Banff. In doing a melder, the primitive mill hottered away at the rate of six bolls of meal ground in a week, Gordon *Keith* (1880) 148. **Rxb.** A cart or other carriage, drawn over a rough road, is said to hotter (Jam.). **N.Cy.¹** ' I'm all hottered to pieces,' said of a jumbling ride on an uneasy vehicle. **Nhb.¹ Dur.** Gibson *Up-Weardale Gl.* (1870). **s.Dur.** A' feel sadly hotter'd wi ridin' i' t'cart (J.E.D.). **n.Yks.¹²⁴ e.Yks.** Marshall *Rur. Econ.* (1796) II. 326. **m.Yks.¹**
Hence **Hottery,** *adj.* jolting ; rough, uneven.
Nhb.¹ This is a tarrible hottery cairt. **n.Yks.¹** ; **n.Yks.²** ' A hottery journey,' said of a course over uneven tracks ; a hazardous one ; **n.Yks.⁴ e.Yks.** Marshall *Rur. Econ.* (1796) II. 326. **m.Yks.¹**
4. To boil slowly, to simmer ; to seethe, bubble, make a bubbling noise.
Abd. Twa pots soss'd in the chimney nook, Forby ane hott'rin' in the crook, Beattie *Parings* (1801) 4, ed. 1873. **Abd., Per.** (Jam.), **w.Yks.¹, Lan.** (C.W.D.)
5. To stir up, vex ; to harass, weary ; to boil with anger, rage. **N.Cy.¹ Lan.** Grose (1790) *MS. add.* (C.)
Hence (1) **Hottering,** *ppl. adj.* raging, trembling with anger ; (2) **Hottering mad,** *phr.* mad with anger, raging.
(1) **w.Yks.¹ Lan.** Hoo wur fayr hotterin' wi' vexashun, Scholes *Tim Gamwattle* (1857) 28 ; **Lan.¹** (2) **w.Yks.¹** I war then seea hotterin mad at I could bide na langer, ii. 293. **Lan.¹, e.Lan.¹**
6. To crowd together, to jumble, throw into confusion ; to romp.
Sc. Conveying the idea of individual motion (Jam.). **n.Yks.¹²** ne.Yks.¹ They were all hotthered tigither.
7. To swarm.
Nhb.¹ The dog wis fair hotterin o' fleas.
8. To rattle, clatter, make a loud noise. Sc. (Jam.)
Hence **Hottering,** *ppl. adj.* clattering, rattling.
Athwart the lyft the thun'er rair'd Wi' awfu' hottrin din, Laing *Coll. Ballads* (1823) 13 (Jam.).
9. To talk indistinctly ; to mumble, mouth ; to talk wanderingly or foolishly.
e.Yks. (W.W.S.) ; Nicholson *Flk-Sp.* (1889) 76 ; **e.Yks.¹**
Hence (1) **Othering,** *ppl. adj.* slow-witted, stupid ; (2) **Other-kite,** (3) **-poke,** (4) **-skeat,** *sb.* a silly blundering person ; one who talks foolishly.
(1) **e.Yks.** The village of Ottringham is often said by sarcastic neighbours to have got its name from its otherin inhabitants, Nicholson *Flk-Lore* (1890) 105; **e.Yks.¹** (2) **e.Yks.¹** *MS. add.* (T.H.) (3) **e.Yks.** Ah felt buggy mad, Ti think at oor ottherpooak clunch ov a ass Sud mak sike a April-daft watty o' lass, Nicholson *Flk-Sp.* (1889) 46 ; **e.Yks.¹** (4) **e.Yks.¹**
10. *Comp.* (1) **Hotter-bonnet,** a person overrun with vermin. Gall. Mactaggart *Encycl.* (1824) ; (2) **-dockin,** (a) a nursery term for a child learning to walk ; (b) a help-less, feeble person. **Cum.¹**
11. *sb.* A jolting ; a shaking-up, romp.
Abd. I've stan't mony a roch hotter, Alexander *Johnny Gibb* (1871) xliii. **ne.Yks.¹** Dog-hotter, game of romps with a dog.
12. A shaking, heaving mass ; a swarm, a crowd of small animals in motion ; the motion made by such a swarm.
Rnf. ' It's a' in a hotter.' Applied to a very fat person whose

skin upon the slighest exertion appears as moving : 'He's in a hotter o' fat' (JAM.). **Bwk.** Loury Lauder is a' in a hotter. A hotter of lice, HENDERSON *Pop. Rhymes* (1856) 34.

[1. Flem. *hotteren*, to totter, shake, wag, jolt (SCHUER-MANS).]

HOTTER, *sb.*[2] n.Lin.[1] Also written **otter.** 1. A half-circle of iron attached to the upper side of the axle-tree of a cart or wagon to hinder the wheels from having too much play.

HOTTIE, *sb.* Edb. (JAM.) A name given to one who has something pinned to his back of which he knows nothing.

A High School term. His sportive class-fellows call after him ' Hottie ! Hottie.'

HOTTIL, see **Hottle,** *sb.*[1]

HOTTISH, *adj.* Sc. Nhb. Cum. Yks. Wor. Also in forms **hettish** Nhb.[1] Cum.[1] ; **yattish** n.Yks.[2] Rather hot, warm ; also used *fig.*

Sc.(A.W.) **Nhb.** Hettish wark (R.O H.). **Cum.**[1], n.Yks.[2], w.Yks. (J.W.) **Wor.** At a hottish pace, *Evesham Jrn.* (Jan. 22, 1898).

HOTTLE, *sb.*[1] n.Cy. Yks. Lan. Der. Not. Lin. Lei. War. Also written **hottel** w.Yks.[2] e.Lan.[1] ; **hottil** w.Yks.[2] nw.Der.[1] ; and in form **hattil** nw.Der.[1] [h]o·tl.] A finger-stall, a cover for a sore or cut finger. Cf. **hot(t,** 3.

n.Cy. GROSE (1790) *MS. add.* (P.) **w.Yks.**[2], **e.Lan.**[1], **Der.**[2], nw.Der.[1], Not. (J.H.B.), Not.[12], s.Not. (J.P.K.) **n.Lin.** Why, missis, wots ivver this i' th' floor ? Why dang me if it isn't my hottle (E.P.). **sw.Lin.**[1] She can't bear a hottle on. **Lei.**[1], **War.**[2]

HOTTLE, *sb.*[2] n.Cy. Yks. Der. Also written **hottel** w.Yks.[2] ; **hotil** Der.[1] ; and in form **uttil** w.Yks. [o·tl, u·tl.] A piece of wire or iron heated in order to bore a hole through anything ; a heated iron.

n.Cy. (HALL.) **w.Yks.** Heat a uttil, heat a coil, Weear mun I buddle a hoil ? *Nursery rime* (Æ.B.) ; w.Yks.[1] Wad E hed a . . . rid hoat hottel in his throttle, ii. 306. Der.[1] *Obs.*

HOTTLE, *sb.*[3] Sc. The bubbling sound of anything boiling. Cf. **hotter,** *v.* 4.

Raf. The hottle o' stiff parritch, pechin' an' dune [boiled], . . beats a', sirs, NEILSON *Poems* (1877) 109.

HOTTLE, *sb.*[4] Sc. Also written **hottel** Frf. [ho·tl.] An hotel.

Sc. They maun hae a hottle ; maun they ! And an honest public canna serve them, SCOTT *St. Ronan* (1824) i. **Frf.** In the best o' inns or hottels, SANDS *Poems* (1833) 118. **Ayr.** Getting a hue o' toddy when we gaed hame to the hottle we were staying at in the Trongate, SERVICE *Dr. Duguid* (ed. 1887) 167.

HOTTLE, *v.* and *sb.*[5] Sc. Cum. [ho·tl.] 1. *v.* To totter, to walk feebly. Cum.[1] 2. *sb.* Anything which has not a firm base, anything tottering. Gall. MACTAG-GART *Encycl.* (1824).

HOTTS, *sb. pl. Obs.* w.Yks.[1] 1. Water gruel. 2. The hips or 'huggans.'

HOU, see **Hoo,** *sb.*[1], **How,** *int.*

HOUCHTY-POUCHTY, *adj. Obs.* Sc. High and mighty, haughty, consequential.

Edb. Your houchty-pouchty factors sour Do sairly prick us, LEARMONT *Poems* (1791) 180.

HOUCK, HOUD, see **Howf(f, Howd,** *v.*[1]

HOUDEE, *sb.* Rxb. (JAM.) Also in form **howdoye.** A sycophant, flatterer. 'She's an auld houdee.'

HOUD(EN, HOUDER, HOUF(F, HOUFFLE, see **Hold,** *v.,* **Howder,** *v.*[2], **Howf(f, Hoffle,** *v.*

HOUGH, *sb.*[1] and *v.*[1] Sc. Irel. Nhb. Cum. Wm. Yks. Lan. Also Glo. Suf. Ken. Dev. Also written **haugh** Sc. (JAM.) Sh.I. ; and in forms **hoch** Sc. (JAM.) Cai.[1] Bnff.[1] N.I.[1] N.Cy.[1] ; **hoff** N.Cy.[1] Nhb.[1] Lakel.[2] Wm. e.Yks. w.Yks.[1] ne.Lan.[1] ; **howf** Nhb.[1] [h]of, uf, Sc. Ir. hox.]

1. *sb.* The hock of an animal ; the leg or lower part of the thigh of a man ; the ham, thigh, hip. See **Hock,** *sb.*[1]

Sc. His poor wizened houghs as blue as a blawart, SCOTT *St. Ronan* (1824) xx ; Lord cut their houghs and stay their running ! HISLOP *Anecdote* (1874) 620. Cai.[1] **Bnff.** Garterless, my thrummy-wheelin hose O' my lean houghs haf hap, an' haf expose, TAYLOR *Poems* (1787) 4. **Abd.** The bare houghs o' ony heelan' rascal, MACDONALD *Malcolm* (1875) I. 169. **Per.** Boo your backs an' crook your hochs Afore your sovran leddy, HALIBURTON *Ochil Idylls* (1891) 60. **Fif.** Glad to unbend

their stiffened houghs and backs, TENNANT *Anster* (1812) 39, ed. 1871. **e.Fif.** We were a' sittin' roon' a stook resting our hochs, LATTO *Tam Bodkin* (1864) xxix. **Lnk.** Land up to the hochs in a dib, MURDOCH *Readings* (1895) III. 24. **Bwk.** A man that is lame o' the leg or the spauld, Or short o' the houghs, HENDERSON *Pop. Rhymes* (1856) 77. **Rxb.** Though houghs grow thin and chafts fa' in, MURRAY *Hawick Sngs.* (1892) 28. **n.Cy.** (K.) ; If you send to a butcher for a hough, you get what in s.Eng. would be called a shin of beef (J.Ar.). **Nhb.** The warst of meat, Bad bullock's liver, houghs and knees, WILSON *Pitman's Pay* (1843) 10 ; Nhb.[1] The back of the knee where the hough sinews are. **Lakel.**[2] Ah's as sair as sair aboot t'hoffs wi' mowin. **Cum.**[4] **Wm. & Cum.**[1] Leyle tyelleyer How was spwort o' th' hough, 199. **Wm.** Up ta t'hoffs i muck (B.K.). **Yks.** (K.) **n.Yks.**[2] Also applied to a man's dirty shoes or clumsy feet. **e.Yks.** MARSHALL *Rur. Econ.* (1796). **w.Yks.**[1] **Lan.** It had nother y-ed nor tele, hont nor hough, TIM BOBBIN *View Dial.* (1740) 7 ; Bo-uth o' me houghs shotun ewt, PAUL BOBBIN *Sequel* (1819) 13. **ne.Lan.**[1] **Nrf.** The lower portion of a leg of pork (M.C.H.B.). **e.Suf.** A fore-leg of a pig—leg and foot, excluding the thigh (F.H.).

Hence (1) **Houghed,** *ppl. adj.* having legs or thighs ; *gen.* in *comb.* with an *adj.* ; (2) **Hough up,** *phr.* to the height of the ' hough ' or leg.

(1) **Sh.I.** Aet girse, doo ill triv'n slootid haugh'd haeth—n, *Sh. News* (Aug. 13, 1898). **Bnff.** Handsome weel-hough'd lassies, TAYLOR *Poems* (1787) 175 ; Tight-hough'd lassies, *ib.* 178. **Edb.** A clean-hough'd nimble little man, *Har'st Rig* (1794) 22, ed. 1801. (2) **Frf.** The dirt hough up has flown ; The lads will see may legs Sae black this day, MORISON *Poems* (1790) 14.

2. *Comp.* (1) **Hough-band,** (a) a strap or band placed round the hough of an unruly cow or other animal to prevent it from kicking or from straying ; (b) to tie a band round the leg of a cow or horse, to prevent it from straying ; (2) **-bund,** impeded in gait ; (3) **-deep,** as deep as the thighs ; up to the thighs ; (4) **-hicht,** to stand on one leg, and put the other over any object ; (5) **-hiech,** as tall as a full-grown man's leg ; (6) **-magandy,** (a) fornication ; (b) an awkward person ; a person of hobbling gait ; (7) **-sennen,** the hock sinew, the sinew of the lower back part of the thigh ; (8) **-strakert,** lame, limping.

(1, a) **Cai.**[1] A band on a cow's leg to prevent her from kicking when being milked. **Rxb.** (JAM.) **Gall.** It passes reund the neck and one of the legs, MACTAGGART *Encycl.* (1824) 273, ed. 1876. **Nhb.**[1] *Obs.* **Cum.**[14], **Wm.** (B.K.) (b) s.Sc. (JAM.) (2) **Nhb.** A person who is unable to take long steps is termed hough-bund (M.H.D.). (3) **Per.** At the very trons in toons It's [snow] hoch-deep lyin', HALIBURTON *Ochil Idylls* (1891) 65. (4) **Bnff.** 'A hich eneuch to hoch-hicht that dyke.' It is a notion amongst boys that if a taller one hoch-hicht a smaller one, the smaller one is stinted in his growth. (5) **Bnff.**[1] (6, a) **Sc.** Ye . . . plaid me Houghmagandy, SHARPE *Ballad Bk.* (1823) 28, ed. 1868. **Ayr.** Monie jobs that day begin, May end in Houghmagandie, BURNS *Holy Fair* (1785) st. 27. **Slk.** As she hersel cam to ken by cruel experience, it a' 'ends in houghmagandy,' CHR. NORTH *Noctes* (ed. 1856) III. 102. **Gall.** Be not sair on hough-magandie, As it's a fit o' friendly passion, And vera muckle now in fashion, LAUDERDALE *Poems* (1796) 50. (b) **Uls.** (M.B.-S.) **s.Don.** SIMMONS *Gl.* (1890). (7) **Nhb.**[1] (8) **Chs.**[1]

3. *Phr.* (1) *to crook a hough,* to sit down, bend the knees ; (2) *to lift a hough,* to dance ; (3) *the last hough in the pot,* the last of anything, esp. of anything to eat.

(1) **Sc.** That ony ane . . . should ever daur to crook a hough to fyke and fling at piper's wind and fiddler's squealing, SCOTT *Mid-lothian* (1818) x. **e.Lth.** Come ower to your auld place, an' crook your hough an' say what ye'll tak, HUNTER *J. Inwick* (1895) 226. **Edb.** Having a timber leg he could not well creuk his hough to the shopboard for our trade, MOIR *Mansie Wauch* (1828) xvii. **Slk.** I'd sooner see you a' . . . hung up . . . than that ony o' ye sal crook a hough or break bread wi' me, HOGG *Tales* (1838) 68, ed. 1866. **Nhb.**[1] (2) **Abd.** When I lift my hough, and fling, There's few will dance completer, SHIRREFS *Poems* (1790) 280. (3) **N.I.**[1]

4. *v.* To hamstring, cut the houghs.

Sc. (JAM.) **Per.** He and others houghed, mangled, and destroyed 36 stots, *Edb. Antiq. Mag.* (1848) 47. n.Cy. (K.), N.Cy.[1], **s.Lin.**[1]

Hence (1) **Houghed,** *ppl. adj., fig.* used as a meaningless expletive ; (2) **Hought,** *pp., fig.* overthrown, confounded.

(1) **Ken.** Snuffboxes, shows, and whirligigs, An houghed sight o' folks, MASTERS *Dick and Sal* (c. 1821) st. 9 ; Ken.[1] (2) **Sc.**

I am not like to get reprieve, But truly I am hought, PENNECUIK *Coll.* (1787) 17. **Abd.** Fatrakes o' that, there's naething tint, Tho' ye ware fairly bought, COCK *Strains* (1810) I. 106.

5. To throw a stone or missile under the thigh or 'hough.'
n.Sc. (JAM.), N.I.¹, N.Cy.¹ **Ant.** ' To hough a stone,' to chuck a stone to a distance under the ham, GROSE (1790) *MS. add.* (C.) Nhb.¹ Glo. GROSE (1790) *MS. add.* Glo., Dev. *Horae Subsecivae* (1777) 218.

6. Phr. *to hough an oar*, to place the handle of an oar under the thigh, in order to rest oneself after rowing.
Sh.I. Houghin' his aer, an' hüvin' aff his waeskit, *Sh. News* (Apr. 23, 1898); I hough'd me aers ta draw on me mittens, *ib.* (June 3, 1899); **S. & Ork.¹**

7. *Fig.* To tramp, trudge, use the legs.
Per. When naething could be done, We houghed the glen awa to Scone, SPENCE *Poems* (1898) 168.

HOUGH, *sb.²* *Obs.* Lan. [Not known to our correspondents.] A fog. GROSE (1790) *MS. add.* (C.)

HOUGH, *v.²* Yks. Also s.Cy. Hmp. I.W. [uf, ɐf.] To breathe hard; to breathe over anything. Cf. **huff,** *v.¹*
w.Yks.¹, s.Cy. (HALL) Hmp. Don't hough all over the window and make it dirty, HOLLOWAY; Hmp.¹ It made me hough going up hill. I.W.¹

HOUGH, see **How,** *sb.¹,* **How(e,** *adj.,* **Huff,** *sb.¹*

HOUGHAMS, *sb. pl.* Tev. (JAM.) Bent pieces of wood, slung on each side of a horse, for supporting dung-panniers.

HOUGHANY, *adj.* *Obs.* Wxf.¹ Vulgar, stupid.

HOUGHEN-MOUGHEN, *adj.* *Obs.* Nhb.¹ Also written hoghen-moghen. Greedy, ravenous.

HOUGHER, *sb.* *Obs.* Nhb. **1.** The public whipper of criminals; the executioner of felons in Newcastle.
N.Cy.¹ Nhb. *Gent. Mag.* (1794) 14, ed. Gomme; The hougher of 1705 was appointed to be ' common executioner in hanging of felons, putting persons in the pillory, clearing the streets of swine, and to doe and perform all other matters belonging to the place and duty of the hougher.' As whipper, too, there appertained to the post the duties of whipping at the cart-tail, leading round the inebriate in his ' drunkard's cloak,' and following the scolding woman in her ' branks,' or iron bridle (R.O.H.).
2. An inferior officer appointed by the Corporation of Newcastle-on-Tyne.
Nhb.¹ He is called hougher from the power he is said to have had formerly of cutting the houghs, or sinews of the houghs of swine that were found infesting the streets of the town, BRAND *Hist. Newcastle* (1789) I. 365, *note.* The hougher was still in 1827 a regular officer of the town with a yearly salary of £4 6s. 8d.

HOUGHLE, *sb.¹* Yks. Lan. Der. Also in forms hoffle ne.Lan.¹ Der.¹; hoghle ne.Lan.¹ The hough or shank of an animal, esp. a shank of beef. Cf. **hockle,** *sb.*
w.Yks.¹ A favourite dish with farmers. Lan. Then bought twelve flooks, cost 1d., and a houghle at 10d., WALKDEN *Diary* (ed. 1866) 66. e.Lan.¹, ne.Lan.¹, Der.¹

HOUGHLE, *v.* and *sb.²* Sc. Irel. Nhb. Also written hoghle Sc. (JAM.); houghel N.I.¹; and in form hughyal Lnk. (JAM.) **1.** *v.* To walk with a hobbling or limping gait; to hobble. Cf. **hochle, hockle,** *v.¹,* **hoffle,** *v.*
Sc. (JAM.), Lnk. (*ib.*) **Ant.** To walk as a person encumbered by having his breeches loose and hanging about the hocks, GROSE (1790) *MS. add.* (C.) Ldd. *N. & Q.* (1874) 5th S. i. 91. s.Don. SIMMONS Gl. (1890).
Hence (1) **Hougheling,** *sb.* lewd tumbling, sexual intercourse; (2) **Houghling,** *vbl. sb.* (a) walking in an awkward, clumsy manner; (b) *ppl. adj.* limping, hobbling, shuffling.
(1) Gall. Twa'r-three months after did swaul i' the wame, Wi' hougheling at the bonello, MACTAGGART *Encycl.* (1824) 79, ed. 1876. (2, a) **Ant.** GROSE (1790) *MS. add.* (C.) (b) Nhb. A houghlin' body (R.O.H.); Nhb.¹
2. *sb.* An awkward, splay-footed clumsy person or animal.
n.Ir. *N. & Q.* (1873) 4th S. xii. 479; N.I.¹ He's a sore houghel of a craithur. **Ant.** Houghle also signifies a person who goes about in a slovenly manner with his breeches half off his haunches, GROSE (1790) *MS. add.* (C.) Ldd. *N. & Q.* (1874) 5th S. i. 91.

HOUGHY, HOUK, see **Howgy, Howk,** *v.¹*

HOUKA, *sb.* Nhb. The plant ' baldmoney,' *Meum athamanticum.*
Nhb.¹ Found ' on the basaltic ridge a quarter of a mile north of the village of Throckrington,' *Nat. Hist. Trans.* (1867) II. 180.

HOUL, see **Howl,** *adj.*

HOULAT, *v.* Sc. (JAM.) [Not known to our correspondents.] **1.** To reduce to a hen-pecked state. Per.
2. To go about in a downcast and peevish state; to look miserable. Cld.

HOULAT, HOULET, HOULIT, see **Howlet.**

HOULDER MOULDER, *phr.* Som. To brood over. SWEETMAN *Wincanton Gl.* (1885).

HOULT, see **Hold,** *sb.,* **Holt,** *sb.²*

HOULTERED, *pp.* Nhb.¹ Shattered.
In a pit, when a shot has fissured the stone, the cracked and shattered place is said to be houltered.

HOUNCE, *sb.* e.An. Also in forms houncer e.An.¹ e.Suf.; houncing e.An.² [euns.] The red and yellow worsted ornament spread over the collars of horses in a team. Gen. in *pl.* Cf. **housing,** *sb.²*
e.An.¹² Suf. RAINBIRD *Agric.* (1819) 294, ed. 1849; Suf.¹, e.Suf. (F.H.) **Ess.** That part of the furniture of a cart-horse which lies spread upon his collar, RAY (1691); (K.); High square leathern flaps on horse-collars, MORTON *Cyclo. Agric.* (1863); Gl. (1851); Ess.¹
[A nasalized form of Fr. *housse,* a foot-cloth for a horse (COTGR.); for the phonology cf. **caunsey.**]

HOUND, *sb.¹* and *v.* Var. dial. uses in Sc. and Eng. Also in forms hahnd w.Yks.; heawnt Lan.; hoond Nhb.¹ Cum.²⁴ Wm. e.Yks.¹; hun' Cai.¹ Cum.¹; hund Sc. (JAM.) Sh.I. Or.I. Nhb.¹ n.Yks.¹ **1.** *sb.* In *comp.* (1) **Hound-hunger,** the ravenous appetite of a dog or a hound; (2) **-hungry,** ravenous as a dog; (3) **-trail,** a dog-trail or drag-hunt.
(1, 2) n.Sc. (JAM.) (3) Nhb.¹ There was a hoond-trail at Alwinton Races in Upper Coquetdale each year until the last race there in 1853. Cum.²; Cum.⁴ The programme included a hound trail in the morning, *Carlisle Patr.* (May 26, 1893) 3. Wm. T'hoond-trail wes ower—ther titter folk, Ets theear when t'dogs begin, *Spec. Dial.* (1880) pt. ii. 51; (B.K.)
2. A large, ill-favoured dog.
Sh.I. He's clappid on yon üseless hund o' his apon his black hug, *Sh. News* (July 24, 1897); **S. & Ork.¹** *MS. add.*
3. *Fig.* A low, mean fellow, a rascal; a term of reproach applied esp. to a dirty, idle person.
Or.I. A contemptuous expression still used, as instead of 'O you dog,' it is 'O you hund' (S.A.S.). Nhb.¹ Wm. Yah lile gallas hoond, *Spec. Dial.* (1880) pt. ii. 50. n.Yks. Commonly used to mischievous or dirty children, as 'Ahl gi tha't thoo mucky hund ' (W.H.). e.Yks.¹ Thoo hoond! tl talk i' that way tl th' awn muther. w.Yks. I may be thowt a brazzened hahnd, CUDWORTH *Dial. Sketches* (1884) 13; w.Yks.⁵ Ther's Tommy here, t'head an' shoulthers less, an' sharper behorf 'an what thou art; isn't tuh 'shäamed o' theesen?—gurt idle hound! Lan. He's a very impident, dirty-looking heawnt, WAUGH *Owd Blanket* (1867) 13. nw.Der.¹ Tha gret idle hound. s.Lin. You tiresome young hound, do clear out o' my way (T.H.R.). Shr.² w.Som.¹ *Gen.* applied to boys. 'You lazy, good-for-nort young hound, I'll skin yer backzide vor ee, I will!'
4. A greedy, avaricious person, eager to seize all he can.
Sc. (JAM.), Cai.¹
5. *v.* To hunt, drive with dogs or hounds. Also used *fig.*
Sc. There were dougs, nae doot, to hund them Frae the shelter o' the trees, *Ballads and Poems* (1885) 143. Sh.I. She hunds her here an dere, BURGESS *Rasmie* (1892) 52. Dmf. The mawkin, houn'd wi' fear, Gaed like a glouf the bracken through, REID *Poems* (1894) 60. Cum. Jinkinson hoondin' on t'fell, RICHARDSON *Talk* (1876) 19; Cum.¹ Wm. He usta gang oot ontet fells . . . an hoond fooaks sheep, *Spec. Dial.* (1877) pt. i. 22; Sarran the coves, er hoondan the sheep, *Gooardy Jenkins;* Wm.¹ Hoondan t'sheep is ' driving the sheep by dogs away from one part of the fell to another.'. . . 'We say a shepherd is hoondan up t'sheep, when he's driving them up on t'fell.' sw.Lin.¹ He's fit to hound one to dead. War.² He is a bad fellow, and ought to be hounded out of the parish.
6. Phr. (1) *to hound fells,* to hunt or drive sheep on the fells; (2) — *the tyke,* to put the law in motion; (3) — *off,* to drive off unceremoniously.
(1) Cum. If one of our dogs takes to houndin' fells we put him down, *Helvellyn* in *Cornh. Mag.* (Oct. 1890) 384; We were soon sitting with the Helvellyn shepherds, . . learning the various incidents of the day's ' hounding' of the fells for ' the gethering,' as it is called, *ib.* 384. (2) Nhb.¹ (3) e.Yks.¹ *MS. add.* (T.H.)

7. To urge on, encourage, incite, instigate, esp. to encourage to do mischief.

Rxb. To hund mischief, to incite some other person to work mischief, while the primary agent stands aside and keeps out of the scrape (Jam.). n.Cy. 'To hound a dog at a beast,' to set him on (K.). Nhb. He hoonded his tarrier at the beggar (R.O.H.); Nhb.[1] A shepherd is said to hund his dog when he directs it. Cum. Collies ... can be hounded for miles—as far as they can see the action of the shepherd directing them, Watson *Nature and Wdcraft.* (1890) xl ; Cum.[2] He'll niver dee of his-sel' sa lang as ther's any wark to hoond yan on tull, 8. n.Yks.[1]; n.Yks.[2] When one person is introduced to another by the stratagem of a third party, as a man to a match he is desirous of making, he is said to have been hounded to the woman; n.Yks.[4] Them 'at hounded him on war t'fo'st ti bleeam him. Neeabody's hounded him on mair 'an what Ah 'ev an' yet he wadn't stick up tul him. ne.Yks.[1] Jack was au'd eneeaf ti knaw better, bud he nobbut hoonded t'others on. e.Yks.[1] *MS. add.* (T.H.)

Hence **Hounding**, *sb.* an advantage obtained for another person by recommendation, or by creating an opportunity for him.

n.Yks.[1]; n.Yks.[2] A sideaway recommendation in any one's behalf is called a hounding for another's benefit (ed. 1855).

8. To urge, worry, importune.

sw.Lin.[1] She almost made me cross wi' hounding at me so. They hound me to go gleaning. She's hounding after her bottle and her titty. My lass housads my belly out.

HOUND, *sb.*[2] Sc. Nhb. Sus. Wil. Dor. Som. Amer. Naut. Also in forms **heughn** Nhb.[1]; **hune** S. & Ork.[1] 1. *pl.* Those projections at the lower part of a mast-head which carry the trestle-trees, shrouds, stays, &c.; in *sing.* the upper end of a 'keel's' mast.

S. & Ork.[1] *MS. add.* Nhb.[1] [Amer. The ice ... in the tops and round the hounds of the lower masts, Dana *Bef. Mast* (1840) xxxiii. Naut. Ansted *Sea Terms* (1898).]

2. *pl.* The extreme ends in the couples of a house, where they join at the pitch of the roof. S. & Ork.[1]

3. One of the wooden bars, of which there are two or more, connecting the fore-carriage of a springless waggon. Sus.[1], Wil.[1] Dor. Barnes *Gl.* (1863). w.Som.[1] One of the two or more pieces which are morticed through the poll-piece of the fore-carriage, and which carry the sweep-piece. This latter permits the carriage to turn upon the main-pin without causing undue strain upon it. Not used in spring wagons. [Amer. Hounds, a pair of side-bars or horizontal braces for strengthening parts of the running-gear of a waggon, Green *Virginia Flk-Sp.* (1899).]

[L. Fr. *hune,* the scuttle of the mast of a ship (Cotgr.); OFr. *hune,* 'plate-forme au sommet d'un mât' (La Curne). ON. *hûnn,* the knob at the top of the mast-head (Vigfusson).]

HOUNDER-OUT, *sb. Obs.* Sc. An instigator, setter-on.

Abd. The lords demand whether he was at part, and part, or on the counsel, or hounder-out of their gentlemen ... to do such open oppressions and injuries as they did daily, Spalding *Hist. Sc.* (1792) I. 43.

HOUNTISH, *adj.* Dor. Som. [eu·ntiſ.] Boorish, unmannerly. Cf. **hontish.**

Dor. Zed Rabin in his hountish way, Young *Rabin Hill* (1867) 5. Som. Sweetman *Wincanton Gl.* (1885).

HOUP, *sb.*[1] and *v.* Sc. Also written **howp** Per.

1. *sb.* A mouthful of any drink; a taste of any liquid; a mouthful of food.

Bfry. (Jam.) Per. Come up the brae an' bide a week, .. An' get a howp in ilka cheek O' halesome livin', Haliburton *Horace* (1886) 29.

2. *v.* To drink by mouthfuls. Hence **Houpan**, *vbl. sb.* the act of drinking by mouthfuls.

Bnff.[1] He hauds an unco preean an' houpan at that ale. He's surely (or seerly) nae plaist wee't.

HOUP, *sb.*[2] Sc. Hops.

Abd. Nor did we drink a' gilpin water, But reemin nap wi' houp weel beardit, Tarras *Poems* (1804) 24 (Jam.).

HOUPY, *sb.* Yks. Lan. Der. Also written **howpey, howpy;** and in forms **awpy, hoppy, oapy-** w.Yks.; **oppy** e.Lan.[1]; **owppy-** nw.Der.[1] [ou·pi, o·pi.] 1. A child's name for a horse.

w.Yks. A little black Shetland pony, hardly bigger than a Newfoundland dog was standing at the door... 'O, what a hoppy!

Is it alive, uncle? Bring it in!' Yks. *Post Xmas Ann.* (1890); Hlfx. *Wds.* (1865); (J.T.); w.Yks.[1] Only used by children; w.Yks.[5]

Hence (1) **Howpy-beef**, *sb.* horse-flesh; (2) **-dick**, (3) **-gee**, (4) **-horse**, *sb.* a child's name for a horse.

(1) w.Yks. Wibsey is noted for its inhabitants' love of 'howpey beef,' Binns *Vill. to Town* (1882) 87; A bit of 'howpey' beef was a necessary dish at the Sunday dinner of a Wibsey family, Cudworth *Bradford* (1876) 18. (2) w.Yks. Look at the oapy-dick! (S.O.A.) (3) w.Yks. (J.H.), w.Yks.[5] (4) w.Yks.[5]

2. A child's name for a cow. Also in *comp.* **Houpey-cow.** e.Lan.[1], nw.Der.[1]

HOUR, *sb.* Sc. Also Cor. Also written **oor** Sc. 1. **In phr.** (1) *a blue hour,* a bad time; a time of quarrelling or ill-will; (2) *in good hour,* in good time; appropriately, suitably; (3) *this hours,* for some hours, for a long time.

(1) Abd. Some while after this the lairds met in the morn, an' there was like to be a blue hour between them, *Deeside Tales* (1872) 119. (2) Fif. In guid hour you're come, fersay, To gie our filthy freirs a fray, Tennant *Papistry* (1827) 81. (3) Cor. They both ben in bed this hours, Hunt *Pop. Rom. w.Eng.* (1865) 350, ed. 1896.

2. *pl.* O'clock, time of day.

Sc. Thursday about ten hours we went to take some meat, Thomson *Cloud of Witnesses* (1714) 46, ed. 1871; What hour what o'clock? (Jam.) Abd. By the morn at ten hours, Spalding *Hist. Sc.* (1792) I. 39. Per. At ten and eleven hours at even, Spottiswoode *Miscell.* (1844) II. 285. Fif. Sanct Salvador's lang strappan steeple Had peltit five hours to the people, Tennant *Papistry* (1827) 134. Ayr. 'What's your oors, doctor?' 'Wed,' said I, 'Hugh, it's exactly two minutes to two with me,' Service *Dr. Duguid* (ed. 1887) 154. Lak. Ane-hours, one o'clock (Jam.). Edb. At five-hour's bell scribes show their faces, Ferguson *Poems* (1773) 149, ed. 1785.

HOUSE, *sb.*[1] and *v.* Var. dial. uses in Sc. Irel. Eng. and Amer. Also in forms **haase, hahse** w.Yks.; **hause** s.Chs.[1]; **hause** w.Yks.; **hawwse** Cum.[14]; **hem, wse** Lan.[1]; **hooas** Cum.[14]; **hooase** Lakel.[1]; **hoos** e.Yks.[1]; **hoose** Sc. Cai.[1] Bnff.[1] Nhb.[1] Cum.[14] n.Yks.[2]; **houe** Oxf.[1] Suf.[1] Wil. Som. Cor.; **howze** I.W.; **oose** ne.Sc.; **owze** Dev.[8] [aus, Sc. n.Cy. hûs, w.Yks. âs, Lan. âs, s.Cy. eus.] I. Gram. forms. 1. *sb. sing.* ? **Housen.**

Glo. My father's grandfather lived in that 'ere housen, Gibbs *Cotswold Vill.* (1898) 388. s.Wil. 'Yan housen,' yonder house, *Monthly Mag.* (1814) II. 114.

2. *pl.* **Housen.** [Not known to our correspondents n. of Yks.]

Dmb. Wrathfu' waters, hurlin' wi' their shock The very housen fra' the rifted rock, Salmon *Gowodean* (1868) 40. Rnf. O lassie, will ye tak' a man? Rich in housen, gear an' lan? Tannahill *Poems* (1807) 13 (Jam.). Nhb.[1], n.Yks.[12] ne.Yks.[1] Aback o' t'hoosen. w.Yks.[2] Lan. Housen and castles and kings decay, Roby *Trad.* (1872) II. 121. Chs. (E.F.) Stf. It's nine or ten housen up, Murray *Joseph's Coat* (1882) 100. s.Stf. Some praichers bin mighty particler what housen they gone to dinner to, Pinnock *Blk. Cy. Ann.* (1889) 63. Not. (J.H.B.), Not.[1] s.Not. Still in use (J.P.K.). Lin.[1] n.Lin.[1] Rare. s.Lin. Common (T.H.R.). Rut.[1], Lei.[1] War. B'ham Wkly. Post (June 10, 1893); War.[1234] s.War.[1] Still very commonly used. m.Wor. (J.C.), se.Wor.[1], Nhp.[12] Shr.[1] 'Ousen bin despert scase about cheer' Shr.[2], Hrf.[12], Rdn.[1] Glo. Spends more time in their neighbours' housen nor iver thay doos in their own, Buckman *Darke's Sojourn* (1890) xv; Glo.[12], Oxf.[1] Brks. *Gl.* (1852); (W.H.Y.) P.F., H.G.); Ousen, Ellis *Pronunc.* (1889) V. 208. Hnt.[1] s.An.[12], Cmb. (J.D.R.) Nrf. Still often used by quite old people (E.M.); I niver knew housen had naames, A.B.K. *Wright's Fortune* (1885) 32. Suf. Yet used freq. (C.G.B.); Ellis *sb.* 285 Suf.[1] e.Suf. Very common (F.H.). Ess. (S.P.H.); Them housen, sir, is harnted, Downe *Ballads* (1895) 17; Ess.[1] Sus. (J.L.A.), Hmp.[1] n.Hmp. I remember as a boy hearing the *N.* 'housen,' but I never meet with it now (E.H.R.). s.Hmp. It was not down to housen gay, that Christ a Child came for to stay, Verney *L. Lisle* (1870) III. 34. I.W.[1] Wil. (K.M.G.); Slow *Gl.* (1892); Wil.[1] 52. n.Wil. Thur beant nobody in these yer housen, Jefferies *Gl. Estate* (1880) ix. Dor. The bright-shod veet vrom housen round, Barnes *Poems* (1869-70) 3rd S. 9. Som. Jennings *Obs. Dial. w.Eng.* (1825); W. & J. *Gl.* (1873). e.Dev. Pulman *Sng. Sol.* (1860) *Notes,* 3. Cor. Fram our houzen and hoam, J. Trenoodle *Spec. Dial.* (1846) 33; Cor.[2] Nearly obs.; Cor.[3] Obsol. [Amer. *Dial. Notes* (1896) I. 331.]

II. Dial. uses. 1. *sb.* In *comp.* (1) **House-arse**, the sea anemone; (2) **-ball**, a girls' game of ball; (3) **-body**, a dwelling-room; (4) **-boggart**, an imp or goblin supposed to haunt houses or dwellings; (5) **-boot(e** or **-bote**, *obs.*, the right of getting wood to repair houses; (6) **-carles**, *obs.*, household servants; (7) **-cat**, *fig.* a stay-at-home; (8) **-dame**, the mistress of the house; (9) **-devil**, a 'devil at home, a saint abroad'; (10) **-dirt**, the dust of a house; (11) **-dove**, a person who is constantly at home; (12) **-dowly**, a tenderly brought up person; (13) **-dweller**, a householder; (14) **-end**, (*a*) the gable or end of a house; (*b*) the parlour in a house; see End, *sb.*[1] 3; (*c*) used as a simile for anything very large; (15) **-fare**, household provisions; (16) **-fast**, confined to the house by illness, &c.; (17) **-fasten**, to confine to the house by illness; (18) **-fellow**, (*a*) a fellow-servant; (*b*) a wife; (19) **-fending**, household management; (20) **-folk(s**, (*a*) the inmates of a house; (*b*) the house-servants; (21) **-gear**, household furniture; (22) **-green**, the house-leek, *Sempervivum tectorum*; (23) **-haddin**, house-keeping; (24) **-handsel**, the convivialities on taking possession of a new dwelling; (25) **-head**, (*a*) the head of the house; (*b*) the ridge of the house roof; (26) **-heat**, (27) **-heating**, a 'house-warming' or festivity given on coming to a new house; (28) **-hicht**, (*a*) applied to a person of small stature; (*b*) in a state of excitement or anger; (29) **-hold**, ordinary; of bread: common as distinguished from fancy; (30) **-hold goods**, see (21); (31) **-holdments**, households, tenements; (32) **-holdry**, household utensils; (33) **-keep**, to keep indoors or in the house; (34) **-keeper**, (*a*) used of any one staying at home in charge of a house; (*b*) see (7); (*c*) an heirloom, an old piece of family furniture; (*d*) a bumbailiff; (35) **-kept**, confined to the house owing to some preventing cause, other than illness; (36) **-lamb**, a lamb set aside for feeding for the table; (37) **-leek (Houzlick, Huslock)**, (*a*) the plant, *Sempervivum tectorum*; (*b*) the biting stonecrop, *Sedum acre* or *S. reflexum*; (38) **-maill**, *obs.*, house-rent; (39) **-master**, see (25, *a*); (40) **-midges**, common house-flies; (41) **-money**, a wife's allowance for household expenditure; (42) **-nook**, an ingle-nook; (43) **-plat**, the ground on which a farm-house is built, with its immediate surroundings; (44) **-proud**, proud and fond of one's house or home; taking pride in having one's house nice and well kept; (45) **-provven**, see (15); (46) **-rearing**, *obs.*, a feast given when the roof of a new house was put on; (47) **-ridding**, changing houses, moving; (48) **-rigg**, (49) **-riggin**, the ridge at the top of the roof; (50) **-row**, in phr. *by house-row*, (*a*) from house to house, taking the houses as they come; (*b*) see below; (51) **-side**, a big, clumsy person; (52) **-snail**, the common shell-snail; (53) **-stead**, (*a*) the site of a house; (*b*) the kitchen, *gen.* occupied by the farmer and his family; (54) **-tendered**, said of a person that has become delicate by confinement to the house; (55) **-things**, articles of furniture; (56) **-verdeen**, a servant who has charge of the outdoor work on a farm; (57) **-wallah**, one who inhabits a house in contradistinction to a tent; (58) **-warming**, a wedding gift or present made on first keeping house; (59) **-wean**, a female servant; (60) **-wifery**, (61) **-wifeskep**, house keeping; (62) **-worthy**, said of an article of sufficient value to be taken care of, or stored by.

(1) Cum.[4] (2) Lth. The 'lassies games' were skipping on the 'jumpin'-rope,' the 'house ba',' the 'pickies,' STRATHESK *More Bits* (ed. 1885) 33. (3) w.Yks. (E.G.) (4) Lan. The house-boggarts, or industrious yet mischievous imps haunting dwellings, HARLAND & WILKINSON *Flk-Lore* (1867) 59. (5) Nhb.[1], n.Yks.[2], w.Yks.[2] Lin. STREATFEILD *Lin. and Danes* (1884) 338. n.Lin.[1] Cor. The prior gave 'privilege and freedom' to the poor of Bodmin for gathering, for 'fire-boote and house-boote,' such boughs and branches of oak-trees in his woode . . . as they could reach to . . . with a 'hook and a crook,' HUNT *Pop. Rom. w.Eng.* (1865) 434, ed. 1896. (6) Gall. How many sons and limber house-caries can you spare, Ardarroch, . . to march with me! CROCKETT *Standard Bearer* (1898) 68. n.Yks.[2] (7) Dev.[1] I wish her was'n such a house-cat, but wud go more abroad; 'twid do her good, 5. (8) n.Yks.[2] (9) Peb. Causey saint an' house devil, Wi' your wife ye

canna gree, AFFLECK *Poet. Wks.* (1836) 128. (10) Lnk. I'm wadin ankle-deep in stoor and boose-dirt, MURDOCH *Readings* (ed. 1895) II. 96. (11) w.Cy. (HALL.) (12) s.An.[1] (13) Stf.[1] (14, *a*) Abd. Whaur was he! Saumerin' at his ain hoose-end, *Guidman Inglismaill* (1873) 60. Per. He vanish'd in a flash o' fire an' smoke, Vanish'd, an' took the house-end wi' him near! HALIBURTON *Dunbar* (1895) 86. Ayr. There would come twa or three birkies . . . snoakin' after her at the hoose-en', SERVICE *Notandums* (1890) 111. Lth. Mind ye yon aik that grew at our house-end! BALLANTINE *Poems* (1856). Gall. The herd-lads and ploughmen were gathered at the house-end when I came up the loaning, CROCKETT *Standard Bearer* (1898) 187. n.Cy. (J.W.) (*b*) w.Yks. Andrew Law and the child had, in dale-phrase, 'taken the house-end at Gibb's Ha''; that is, the little parlour at Gibb's Ha', with the chamber over it, HOWITT *Hope On* (1840) vi. (*c*) Not.[1] Lei.[1] Beard! Ah, as big as a 'acuse-end! A een't a man wi' a beard, a een't! A's a beard wi' a man ahoint it. (15) n.Yks.[2] (16) Sc. O' ither wives wha ne'er were keepit hoose-fast Like what she was, ALLAN *Lilts* (1874) 153. n.Yks.[124], ne.Yks.[1], m.Yks.[1] (17) an.Yks.[1] (18, *a*) w.Yks.[2] (*b*) Lan. He came back and told me that his house-fellow had gone out, WALKDEN *Diary* (ed. 1866) 58. (19) n.Yks.[2] A poor hand at house-fending. (20, *a*) n.Yks.[124] (*b*) Lakel.[2] T'hoose fooak's them at stops at hiam an' du't gah oot ta work i' t'fields. Cum. T'hoose-fwok gat mair help, DICKINSON *Lamplugh* (1856) 5. n.Yks.[1] (s.v. Folk). (21) Sc. She has held the house-gear well together, SCOTT *Pirate* (1821) v. n.Yks. (T.S.), n.Yks.[2] Dor. How still do all the housegear stand Around my lwonesome zight, BARNES *Poems* (1869–70) 3rd S. 94. (2a) Chs.[1], Nhp. (B. & H.), War.[3] (23) Sh.I. Wissin' an' waddin' are pôr hoose haddin', SPENCE *Flk-Lore* (1899) 216. (24) n.Yks.[2] Before occupying a fresh house, a person should go into every room, bearing a loaf and a plate of salt, for luck to the new place. (25, *a*) Ayr. She was up on the household, *Ballads and Sngs.* (1846) I. 74. (*b*) Frf. There lichtit a corbie on oor hoose-heid, WATT *Poet. Sketches* (1880) 19. (26) Dmf. At brydal shaw, or new hoose heat, We thraw auld age awa, Jo! CROMEK *Remains* (1810) 48. (27) Sc. The foondin', the hoose-heatin', the foy, the maiden, FORD *Thistledown* (1891) 124. ne.Sc. When the house was taken possession of, there was a feast, the hoose heatin or fire kinlin, GREGOR *Flk-Lore* (1881) 51. Cai.[1] s.Sc. There's to be a hanlin' at Bracehead the nicht—a hoose heatin, WILSON *Tales* (1836) II. 292. Ayr. Flitting in at the back end, we had our house-heating on Hogmanay, SERVICE *Dr. Duguid* (ed. 1887) 119. (28, *a*) Bnff.[1] He's nae twa hoose-hicht mair nor I am [or me]. (*b*) *ib.* He wiz hoose-hicht at the factor fin he set's fairm bye 'im. (29) w.Som.[1] Aew-zl brai-d. (30) *ib.* Furniture of a house is scarcely ever called by any other name. 'I would not mind giving up the house if I could tell what to do with my household-goods' [aew·zl gèodz]. (31) n.Yks. With some other odd householdments within the said township, *Quart. Sess. Rec.* (Jan. 12, 1724-5) in *N. R. Rec. Soc.* IV. 171. (32) Ayr. To judicate that leddies would be flinging householdry at ane anither's heads. GALT *Lairds* (1826) xiv. (33) n.Yks.[2] 'Mun we hoose-keep her!' that is, the sickly cow; must she remain indoors, or be let out? (34, *a*) n.Lin.[1] There's no housekeepers at home, is there, missis! My daughter's at home, so I've a housekeeper. Charles has stayed at home to be housekeeper a bit. (*b*) n.Lin.[1] I'm a real hoose-keâper noo, I hevn't been to Brigg markit for oher a twel' munth. She's a good hoose-keâper, niver runs clartin' efter th' lads. (*c*) Chs.[1] An old oak chest in a cottage was spoken of by its owner as 'a nice old housekeeper.' s.Chs.[1] Such a piece of furniture is often spoken of as a 'good owd halse-keeper.' (*d*) Hrf.[2] (35) n.Yks.[14] (36) Mid. Some of these barns are fitted with deal linings, partitions, and floors for the purpose of suckling house lambs, MARSHALL *Review* (1817) V. 128. Dor. The breed of sheep which is remarkable for supplying the metropolis with house-lamb at a very early season, *ib.* 279. (37, *a*) Wm. Hoose leek is good fer sair spots (B.K.). n.Yks. (T.S.) ne.Yks.[1] Usually planted on the ridge of thatched houses. e.Yks.[1] w.Yks. It's only a bit o' house-leek, you can get plenty at t'pooblic-'ouse ovver t'waäy (F.P.T.). Nhp.[1] This plant is traditionally regarded as a preservative from lightning; whence arises its frequency on the roofs of our rural cottages. Suf.[1] (*b*) Nhp. Its thatch with houseleek blooms was yellow o'er, CLARE *Jockey and Jenny*; Close beneath the houseleek's yellow flower, *ib.* (B. & H.) (38) Abd. The tenth penny of ilk house maill within the town was also uplifted, SPALDING *Hist. Sc.* (1792) I. 290. Fif. Ane thousand merks monie, with ane hundreth merkis of housmaill, Row *Ch. Hist.* (1650) 44, ed. 1842. (39) n.Yks.[2] Is t'hoose-maisther at yam? (40) *ib.* (41) Lan.[1] 'Does he turn up his wages?' 'Nawe, he gies me what he loikes for th' heawse-money, an' keeps th' rest for hissel.' Sur. (L.J.Y.) (42) w.Yks. (S.P.U.) (43) w.Yks.

Mem. Rev. J. Gregory (1876) 13. (44) **n.Yks.** Sha's sa hooseprood noo 'at sha caht bide ta see a thing ather dusty er oot ov t'pleeas (W.H.). **w.Yks.** You are what you call house-proud ; you like to have everything handsome about you, Brontë *Shirley* (1849) xviii. **Lan.** Hoo was very house-proud, was mother, hoo was that, *Longman's Mag.* (July 1896) 254 ; **Lan.**[1] We had some talk with that class of operatives who are both clean, provident, and heawse-proud, as Lancashire folk call it, Waugh *Factory Flk.* (1867) vi. **n.Lin.**[1] She's not a bit hoose-prood. iv'rything is alus at sixes and sevens. (45) **n.Yks.**[2] (46) **n.Lin.**[1] Spent at ye houses rearing as., *Lea Overseer's Acc.* (1752). (47) **Dor.** Are you house-ridding to-day like every one else ? Hardy *Tess* (1891) 467, ed. 1895. (48) **Cum.** They have a saying . . . that when bairns reach a certain age, they are thrown on the house-rigg, and that those who stick on are made thatchers of, while those who fall off are sent to St. Bees to be made parsons of, *Cassell's Tech. Educ.* (1879) IV. 366. **w.Yks.** There cat . . . jump't up . . . an away she went ovver t'hause-rigs like wildfire, Tom Treddlehoyle *Bairnsla Ann.* (1843) 14. (49) **Sc.** Heap them as high as the house-riggin', Scott *Antiquary* (1816) xxxiii. (50, *a*) **s.Not.** 'E took an' distributed the bills by 'ouse-row (J.P.K.). **n.Lin.**[1] To call at every house in a street or village. as rate-collectors and distributors of handbills do, is to go by house-row. (*b*) **s.Not.** The labourers who, being out of work, were formerly sent by the overseer of the poor to work for the different farmers in succession, were said to go by house-row. They were called house-row men ; rounds-men in other parts of the country (J.P.K.). **s.Lin.**[1] Before the Act of Parliament was passed for rating poor-law unions as a whole, it was customary for the farmers, instead of giving a pauper direct relief, to let him go by house-row, that is, each farmer employed him at a low rate of wages for a time proportionate to the land which he occupied. **s.w.Lin.**[1] The old plan of keeping men employed, when work was scarce, by finding them so many days' work at each house in the parish in turn. ' It used to go by house-row.' ' They used to go by house-row when feyther was agate.' (51) **n.Sc.** Sic a house-side o' a wife (Jam.). (52) **nw.Dev.**[1], **s.Dev.** (F.W.C.) (53, *a*) **n.Yks.**[2] (*b*) **n.Cy.** Holloway. (54) **n.Yks.**[2] (55) **Lnk.** They had gathered twa-three hoose-things thegither, Murdoch *Readings* (ed. 1895) II. 53. (56) **S. & Ork.**[1] (57) **Hmp.**[1] Used commonly by the gypsy-tribes in n.Hmp. (58) **Cor.**[1] (59) **n.Yks.**[2] (60) **Per.** Your skill in house-wif'ry is widely known, Stewart *Character* (1857) 175. (61) **Sc.** My hand is in my housewifeskep, *Old Sng.* (Jam.) ; I wadna affront your housewifeskep, gudewife, Scott *Bride of Lam.* (1819) xii. **Per.** Wi' that she sent some blankets on before, Turn'd to her huswifeskep, and no words more, Haliburton *Dunbar* (1895) 101. (62a) **n.Yks.**[2]

2. Phr. (1) *house and hall*, entirely, completely ; a clean sweep ; (2) — *of industry*, the workhouse ; (3) — *of Keys*, the Manx House of Parliament ; (4) — *of ore*, an accumulation of rich ore in a mine ; (5) — *of water*, an old working in a mine, full of water ; (6) *all the house*, the whole household ; (7) *in house*, indoors ; (8) *to be at the house-top*, to be in a great rage ; (9) *to bring the house* or *old house over the head*, to bring a calamity by carelessness or improvidence ; (10) *to get on like a house on fire*, to get on very rapidly or well ; (11) *to put* or *throw the house out at the windows*, to cause great disorder and confusion.

(1) **Fif.** Root, root her out o' house and ba', Tennant *Papistry* (1827) 27. **Gall.** A very common phr. in connection with a person's losing all his property and being left homeless as well as poor (A.W.). (*a*) **Shr.** In addition to the house of industry at Shrewsbury, Marshall *Agric.* (1818) II. 212. **Oxf.** The House of Industry for the reception of the poor of eleven of our fourteen parishes, Peshall *City* (1773) 221, in Clark *Wood's City* (1889) I. 393. (3) **I.Ma.** He is one of the 24 keys. He sits for Peel ; as member of the House of Keys, he is entitled to write M.H.K. after his name (S.M.). (4) **Cor.**[2] (s.v. Carbonas). (5) *ib.* Old workings that are full of water are sometimes called ' gunnies of water,' yet more commonly, ' a house of water ' (s.v. Gunnies). (6) **ne.Sc.** Part of the invitation to attend a wedding was, ' Come our and fess a' yir oose wi' ye,' Gregor *Flk-Lore* (1881) 98. (7) **Som.** I couldn't speak when I came in house (T.K.L.). (8) **w.Yks.**[1] (9) **Nhp.**[1], **War.**[2], **Hnt.** (T.P.F.) (10) **Nhp.**[1], **War.**[2], **Hnt.** (T.P.F.), **Sur.** (L.J.Y.), **Cor.** (L.C.A.T.) (11) **w.Yks.**[1] **nw.Der.**[1] Yo'n put th' house out at th' windus. **Nhp.**[1], **War.**[2]

3. pl. House property.
N.Cy.[1], **n.Yks.**[1][2] **Wor.**[1] He gave him some housen,' bequeathed some house property to him (E.S.).

4. The workhouse. In *gen.* colloq. use.
Lnk. Many old people . . . have to enter the ' house,' as it is nick-named, like humble suppliants, Gordon *Pyotshaw* (1885)

163. **w.Yks.** They think we'd best go into t'house, Fletcher *Wapentake* (1895) 21. **Oxf.** They were at last safely housed in the new House, Stapleton *Parishes* (1893) 162 ; **Oxf.**[1] *MS. add.* **Brks.** They would ha' liked to ha' seen me clean broke down, that's wut they would, and in the house, Hughes *T. Brown Oxf.* (1861) xxxix. **Lon.** She died in the house in Birmingham, Mayhew *Lond. Labour* (ed. 1861) II. 378. **Ken.** If you or me, Dimmick, was to be took with a stroke, or a fit, or any sich thing, off to the house they'ld bundle us, sure as my eye, *Cornh. Mag.* (Jan. 1894) 56. **Sur.**[1] He most always goes into the house in winter. **Sus.** Feeling I suppose aggrieved by being obliged to go into 'the house,' Egerton *Flks. and Ways* (1884) 11. **Dor.** Who's a-goin' to take you on as a new hand if you leave me ! It'll be the House, man, *Longman's Mag.* (Nov. 1898) 48. **Colloq.** The respectable poor have a natural repugnance to 'the House,' *Standard* (Sept. 6, 1887) 5.

5. The portion of a building, consisting of one or more rooms, occupied by one tenant or family.
Sc. Among the working classes . . . even in modern legislation the word ' house ' is used for any separately occupied portion of a building, while the word ' tenement ' represents the whole edifice, *and Rep. R. Comm. Housing Wkng. Classes* (1885) 4.

6. A room ; a room in any building.
w.Som.[1] **Dev.** Hewett *Peas. Sp.* (1892) 109. **n.Dev.** In answer to my inquiry Lizzie was summoned from the ' back houze,' when she emerged grinning broadly as usual, E.E.D. *Dev. Village* in *Outlook* (Apr. 16, 1898) 332 ; Jan, clare tha 'cess in t'other houze, Rock *Jim an' Nell* (1867) st. 4. [Amer. This grew up from the custom of having houses of one room, or two, connected by a porch, each of which rooms was called a house, *Dial. Notes* (1865) I. 372.]

7. The kitchen or general living-room in a farm-house or cottage.
Ant. *N. & Q.* (1893) 8th S. iv. 93. **n.Cy.** Grose (1790) ; **N.Cy.**[2] **Cum.**[1] The apartment or living room into which the front door opens. The ground floor consists of house, parlour, kitchen, and milk-house ; **Cum.**[4] Wm. The door, . . leading into what Westmoreland folk call the ' house ' or sitting-room of the farm, was open, Ward *R. Elsmere* (1888) 133. **n.Yks.**[2] ; **n.Yks.**[4] Deean't set it doon i' t'hoos, tak it inti t'parlour. **ne.Yks.**[1] Sha's nut i' bed, sha's i' t'hoos. **e.Yks.** Marshall *Rur. Econ.* (1788) ; **e.Yks.**[1] The better room of a farm-house. **m.Yks.**[1] **w.Yks.** A cottage often consists of a ' house ' and two chambers [a living-room and two bedrooms] S.P.U.) ; **w.Yks.**[2][3][4] ; **w.Yks.**[5] Always the room on the ground floor, in which the family take their meals, and use throughout the day. ' Awaay wi' thuh up i' t'house [from the kitchen] an' fotch muh t'long brush darn.' **n.Lan.** (W.S.) **s.Lan.** **Not.** (L.C.M.), **Not.**[1][2], **Der.**[1], **nw.Der.**[1], **n.Lin.**[1] **sw.Lin.**[1] The floor of the house is worse than the kitchen. Some would ha' putten him in the kitchen, or in a chamber, but I ha' kep' him in the house. **Rut.**[1] The best kitchen or inner living room in a farm or good-sized cottage. A stranger is often invited to ' Joost step into the house ' when he is under the impression that he is in the house already. **Lei.**[1] **Nhp.**[1] So *gen.* adopted, that houses are so described in the advertisements in our local papers. 1832. ' To be let, a dwelling comprising a parlour, house, kitchen, and back-kitchen ' ; **Nhp.**[2] **War.**[2] Any ground-floor room as opposed to the kitchen. **Glo.** He stepped into the ' house,' the large inhabited kitchen so-called, Gissing *Vill. Hampden* (1890) I. **Oxf.**[1] My missis ent in the house, but I knows er's indoors some-ur, *MS. add.* **Bdf.** Batchelor *Anal. Eng. Lang.* (1809) 135. **e.An.**[1], **Ess.** (H.H.M.) **sw.Eng.** The living room is nearly always called the house, while the second room is the ' back-house,' *N. & Q.* (1893) 8th S. iv. 93. **w.Som.**[1] The living room ; the ground floor *gen.* Dhu vloo·ur-z u·wae·urd aew·t, eens üz u guurt oa·l rai·t-n dhu müd·l u dh-aew·z [The floor is worn out, so that there is a great hole right in the middle of the living room.]

Hence (1) **House-place,** *sb.* (*a*) the kitchen or general living-room in a farm-house or cottage ; (*b*) the parlour of a farm-house, containing the best furniture and seldom used ; (2) **-room,** see (1, *a*).
(1, *a*) **n.Cy.** Grose (1790). **n.Yks.** He ushered her into the kitchen or house-place, Simpson *Jeanie o' Biggersdale* (1893) 177 ; **n.Yks.**[1][2] **w.Yks.** Crunch can rooam abaat booath i' th' room an th' haase place, Hartley *Clock Alm.* (1887) 90 ; (J.T.) **Lan.** What an amount of comfort did his house-place present, Gaskell *M. Barton* (1848) ii ; **Lan.**[1] Come, my wench, let's have this heawse-place cleaned up. **Chs.**[1], **s.Chs.**[1] **Stf.**[1] A room with a quarried floor, used as a kitchen and sitting-room. **Der.**[2], **Not.**[1][8], **s.Not.**

(J.P.K.), sw.Lin.[1] Lei. A messuage at Market Harborough . . . consisting of a houseplace fronting the street with two chambers and garret over the same, *Particulars of Sale* (1803); Lei.[1], Shr.[1] s.Wal. The mistress sat feathering in the doorway of the house-place, *Longman's Mag.* (Dec. 1899) 143. (*b*) Chs.[2] (*2*) Cum. He's in t'house-room, DALBY *Mayroyd* (1880) II. 12.

8. Curling term : the circle round the tee within which the stones must lie to count.

Sc. Frae bristles, dottles, an' the like, Aye sweep the hoosie clean; May nane gang roarin thro' the hoose, *Royal Caled. Curling Club Ann.* (1894-5) 101 ; There's no a stane in a' the hoose, *ib.* 348. Ayr. 'Stand wide, men,' cried William Sorby, for the eager onlookers were crowding uncomfortably close to the 'house,' JOHNSTON *Kilmallie* (1891) II. 113. Lth. After the stone had passed between the two [other stones], David swept behind the tee, and 'saw him out o' the house,' STRATHESK *More Bits* (ed. 1885) 272.

9. *Obs.* A deep bing broader at the top than at the bottom, used in smelting tin.

Der. (HALL.) Cor. The black tin is smelted . . . with charcoal only, first throwing on charcoal, then upon that black tin, and so interchangeably into a very deep bing (which they call the house), RAY *Blowing of Tin* (1691) 12 ; (K.)

10. *v.* To go indoors, go into the house.

Nhb.[1] 'Have you seen the clergyman ?' 'No; he mun be hoosed.'

11. To go gossiping from house to house. Used in *prp.*

Cor. THOMAS *Randigal Rhymes* (1895) Gl.

Hence **Houser,** *sb.* one who goes from house to house gossiping.

Cor.[2] She'm always making mischief—she'm a reglar houser.

12. To shelter, take into the house ; to hide.

Lth. E'en when weary warkmen hose, Their sair forfoughen spunks to rouse, BALLANTINE *Poems* (1856) 69. Nhb.[1], Yks. (HALL.), n.Yks.[2] w.Yks.[2] If a chap comes wi' a cart looad o' coils . . . my fayther 'll haase em, HARTLEY *Clock Alm.* (1883) 13. Lan. The hinds say they were carefully heawsed an' fettled, KAY-SHUTTLEWORTH *Scarsdale* (1860) II. 84.

13. Of hay or corn : to get under cover, either in rick or barn.

Gall. At ev'ry stack we meand to house, There with the curra he happed crouse, MACTAGGART *Encycl.* (1824) 400, ed. 1876. Cum. We wor hoosin' a stack, FARRALL *Betty Wilson* (1886) 135 ; When fwok hed hoose't hay aw t'day, RICHARDSON *Talk* (1876) and S. 155. nw.Der.[1] Oxf.[1] MS. add. s.Cy. (HALL.) Ken.[1] We've housed all our corn. Sur.[1] w.Som.[1] All the corn's a-housed in our parish. Dev.[2] Be yū agwaine tū owze yer corn tū-day, maister ?

Hence (1) **Housed,** *pp.* covered over ; (2) **Housing,** *vbl. sb.* the act of getting in, corn, &c. under cover ; (3) **Housing-supper,** *sb.* a harvest-supper.

(1) Der.[1] *Obs.* (2) Lan. When th' heawsin wur done, eh, We had some rare fun, LAYCOCK *Sngs.* (1866) 53. e.Lan.[1] (3) Lan. Simon and his daughther were axed to th' heausin supper, CLEGG *Sketches* (1895) 9.

14. Of corn, hops, &c. : to grow thick and compact. *Gen.* in *pp.*

e.An.[1], s.Suf. (F.H.) Sus.[1] When hops have a great deal of bine, and the poles are thickly covered over the top, so as almost to shut out the light and sun, they are said to be 'housed.' Ken. HOLLOWAY.

HOUSE, *sb.*[2] *Obs.* Dev. A child's blanket ; a coverlet, wrapper, mantle.

Horae Subsecivae (1777) 218 ; GROSE (1790) *MS. add.*

[Fr. *housse,* a coverlet, or counter-point for a bed (COTGR.).]

HOUSE, *sb.*[3] Chs.[12] The act of a cow or bull when turned out of the 'shippon,' throwing itself on a hedge or hedge-bank to have a satisfactory scratch, working away violently with the horns and often kneeling down to the work.

HOUSE, see **Houst.**

HOUSEL, *sb.* and *adj.* Sc. Yks. Lan. Der. Lin. Shr. Ess. Ken. Sus. Cor. Also in forms **haasel** w.Yks. e.Lan.[1] **housal** Sc. nw.Der.[1] ; **housil** m.Yks.[1] ; **houssel** n.Lin.[1] ; **hussel-** Der.[2] **1.** *sb.* Household goods or furniture.

w.Yks. (J.R.), e.Lan.[1], nw.Der.[1] n.Lin.[1] If in caase 1 was to dee behoot a will would my missis get th' houssels ? Shr.[1] I 'ear as theer's to be two days' sale at the 'George'—one fur live stock,

an' another fur 'ousel. Ess. (H.H.M.) Ken.[1] I doānt think these here new-comers be up to much ; leastways, they didn't want a terr'ble big cart to fetch their housel along ; Ken.[2] 'An old housel,' i.e. household, meaning household stuff or furniture. Sus.[1] Whose housel is that up on the wagon ?

Hence **Husselments,** *sb. pl.* household goods or chattels. Der.[2]

2. *Phr. housel of goods,* a furnished house, a houseful. Cor.[1]

3. *adj.* Household, belonging to the house.

Sc. FRANCISQUE-MICHEL *Lang.* (1882) 424. Rnf. In sicken housal wark she bure a skair, PICKEN *Poems* (1813) II. 63. m.Yks.[1] Housil-stuff, household articles in general. w.Yks. So Sam gat shut at haasel gooids, PRESTON *Poems* (1864) 23.

HOUSELINGS, *sb. pl.* n.Cy. Tame animals, animals bred up by hand. (HALL.)

HOUSELLING, *adj.* Shr. Dor. In *comb.* **Houselling cloths** or **towels,** white cloths spread on the altar-rails during the administration of the Holy Communion.

Shr. In Much Wenlock Church last Easter Day I observed that a white cloth was laid along the chancel rails for the Holy Communion. Upon inquiry from the vicar afterwards I learnt that the use of 'Houselling' cloths is a very old custom at Wenlock as it has been from time immemorial, and is practised not only at the great festivals, but every time there is an administration of the sacrament, DAVIES *Shreds and Patches.* Dor. At Wimborne Minster a white cloth is spread on the altar rails while the eucharist is being administered to the communicants, *N. & Q.* (1869) 4th S. iii. 174.

HOUSEN, *v.* Der. War. Sus. Dev.   **1.** To put into a house ; to house, harbour. Also used *fig.*

Der. Ye thought fit to housen thy own secret in thy own heart, CUSHING *Voc* (1888) II. vii. Sus. An' ax'd me uf a swarm o' bees Was housen under dat, LOWER *Tom Cladpole* (1872) st. 60. nw.Dev.[1] *Obsol.* 'Tis time to houzen they there bullocks.

2. To muffle, encumber.

War.[2] Don't ouzen yer neck wi' that great comforter.

HOUSEN, see **Halsen, Hose,** *sb.*[1]

HOUSEY, *adj.* Sur.[1] Also in form **housed.** [eu·zi.] Used of hops ; see below.

Hops are said to be housey when the fruit is mixed up with the leaves, and is, in consequence, difficult to pick. The word housed occurs in the same sense.

HOUSEY, *adv.* Cor.[2] Suffering from too much confinement in the house.

HOUSING, *sb.*[1] Nhb. Cum. Yks. Lan. Chs. Also written **houseing** Chs.[1] ; **housen** m.Yks.[1] ; **housin** Nhb.[1] ; and in forms **hoosin'** Cum.[14] ; **hoozin** w.Yks.   **1.** A set of buildings, esp. those belonging to a farm.

Cum.[14], w.Yks.[2], Chs.[1] *Obs.*

2. *Comp.* (1) **Housing-sticks,** (2) **-stuff,** household goods or furniture.

(1) n.Yks.[4] (2) n.Yks. (T.S.), n.Yks.[124], m.Yks.[1] w.Yks. Com in and teeak me lass away, An hoozin stuff, *Spec. Dial.* (1800) 45.

3. *Fig.* A capacity for holding much, esp. food or drink ; feeding, eating.

Nhb.[1] He has a good housin for drink. Lan. What must be th' state of his inside after sich housein as he's dooin ! BRIERLEY *Ab-o'th-Yate Yankeeland* (1885) v ; Before one hauve o'th' mess had been put out o'th' seet, th' housein began a-bein very slow, *ib.* vi.

4. *pl.* The lower edges of a roof or eavesing. w.Yks.[2]

5. *pl.* The iron framework which supports machinery in a mill, &c. w.Yks.[2]

HOUSING, *sb.*[2] Yks. Chs. Der. Not. Lin. Lei. Nhp. Wor. Shr. Oxf. Bdf. Nrf. Som. Also in forms **housen** Lin.[1] Lei.[1] Bdf. Nrf.[1] ; **housin** Nhp.[2] ; **houzen** Nhp.[1] ; **houzin** se.Wor.[1] ; **ousing** Chs.[1] [au·zin, eu·zin.] **1.** The piece of leather attached to a draught-horse's collar, standing erect on the shoulders of a horse. Cf. **hounce.**

w.Yks. Yks. *Wkly. Post* (July 21, 1883) ; w.Yks.[2], Chs.[1], nw.Der.[1], Not. (J.H.B.) Lin. THOMPSON *Hist. Boston* (1856) 710 ; Lin.[1], Lei.[1] Nhp.[1] *Gen.* ornamented with red fringe, and in olden time with bells, to give notice of the approach of the waggon, when the roads were so narrow that two were unable to pass ; Nhp.[2], se.Wor.[1] Shr.[1] *Obsol.* The large leather cape attached to the collar of a waggon-horse's gears, which can be raised or lowered at will ; when laid down, it serves to protect the horse's neck from wet ; Shr.[2] Oxf.[1] Us mus' take the 'ouzen, it boords rain, *MS. add.* Bdf. BATCHELOR *Anal. Eng. Lang.* (1809) 139.

Nrf. (C.W.B.N.) w.Som.¹ A broad leather flap which is fastened to the top of a horse's collar. In fine weather it stands upright ; in wet weather it is turned down (its true use) to keep the horse's shoulders dry. The word also includes many kinds of ornaments erected over the collar of the ' vore-horse.' [MORTON Cyclo. Agric. (1863).]

Hence Housing-thungs, sb. a long strap curled at the end pendant from the ' hames ' of a horse's gear. Shr.²

2. A petticoat. Lin. (HALL.), Lin.¹

HOUSING, adj. m.Yks.¹ Very large.
A great housing fellow.

HOUSSACK, see Hussock.

HOUST, v. Wil.¹ Also in form house. [eus(t.] To grow stout. ' Lor, ma'am, how you've a-housted !'

HOUSTER, v. and sb. Sc. Also written howster ; and in form huister. 1. v. To gather together confusedly. Fif. (JAM.)

Hence (1) Houstrie, sb. (a) soft, nasty, bad food ; (b) fig. trash, trumpery ; (2) Houstring, ppl. adj. bustling but confused.

(1, a) Rxb. Gen. a mixture of different sorts of meat (JAM.). (b) Fif. Let us practice for the trial ;—Cast coat, an' hat, an' ither houstrie, LIEUT. C. GRAY Poems (ib.). (a) Fif. A huistrin' body (JAM.).

2. sb. One whose clothes are ill put on. Fif. (ib.)

HOUT, HOUTHER, see Hait, Hoit, sb.¹, Hold, sb.², Hoot, v.¹, Hoot(s, Howder, v.²

HOUTIE CROUTIE, phr. Sc. The haunches, hams.
I sat upon my houtie croutie, I lookit owre my rumple routie, CHAMBERS Pop. Rhymes (1870) 185.

HOUTS, sb. pl. e.An. Written house [sic] e.An.¹ A contemptuous name for feet, always in comb. with ' great,' ' clumping,' &c. e.An.¹, e.Suf. (F.H.)

HOUXIE, int. Cai.¹ [hau·ksi.] A call to a cow.

HOUY, HOUZLE, see Hoo, int., Hoozle, sb.¹, v.¹

HOVE, sb. Nrf. A floating island in the Broads. DAVIES Broads (1884) 104. See Hover, sb. 14.

HOVE, v. Sc. Nhb. Chs. Der. Also Som. Also in form hoove Sc. 1. Obs. To stay, tarry, wait.
Tev. (JAM.), Nhb. (R.O.H.) Der. I myselfe will hove on the hill, JEWITT Ballads (1867) 50.

2. To take shelter. Chs.¹²³ 3. To move. Som. (HALL.)
[1. Quhair of I hovit ... in dowt, DUNBAR Poems (c. 1510), ed. Small, II. 308 ; Ye houe stille, Dest. Troy (c. 1400) 3531. 3. Hove out of my soune And lete it shine into my toune, GOWER C. A. (c. 1400) I. 323.]

HOVE, see Half, Hauve, v.³, Heave, Hoaf.

HOVED, ppl. adj. Sc. Of light, loose soil : puffed up.
Lnk. Such a mixture, however, renders the soil too light, and too much disposed to become loose and hoved, PATRICK Plants (1831) Pref. 20.

HOVED UP, phr. Obs. w.Cy. Dev. A phr. implying that the person spoken of is in some great difficulty.
w.Cy. GROSE (1790) Suppl. n.Dev. You are finely hoved up, ib. MS. add. (P.)

HOVEL, sb.¹ and v. Irel. n.Cy. Yks. Chs. Lei. Nhp. War. Shr. Bdf. Hrt. e.An. Sus. Wil. [h)o·vl.] 1. sb. A shed for cattle or pigs, an out-house of any kind, a coal or wood shed, a tool-house.
n.Cy. GROSE (1790) MS. add. (P.) Chs.¹²³ Lei. I can get ti my howel without going out of doors (G.H.G.). War. MORTON Cyclo. Agric. (1863). Shr.¹ Dun'ee call that a 'ouse to live in! W'y it's no better than a 'óvil for cattle to 'erd in. e.Suf. The compartment of a pig-sty in which the pig sleeps (F.H.). Wil. Not meant in a dirty or ill-conditioned sense (H.M.M.). Wil. (K.M.G.) n.Wil. ' Wurs the showl ?' ' In th' hovel ' (E.H.G.).

2. The compartment of a smithy where the horses stand to be shod, as distinguished from the forge. Chs.¹, s.Chs.¹

3. A building roofed with dead wood laid on cross-beams, instead of upright rafters ; also called Dead-hovel. Nhp.¹

4. Comp. (1) Hovel-posts, a sarcastic term for thick legs ; (2) -pricks, short flexible sticks, used in thatching.
(1) Nhp.¹ (2) ib. Pointed at one end, and hooked at the other ; used to confine the rod which secures the straw or yelm, at the eaves and ridge of a roof, when thatching.

5. The frame or stand upon which a stack of corn is built ; a corn-rick.

N.I.¹ Lei. MORTON Cyclo. Agric. (1863). Bdf. A stack of wheat raised upon a frame is so called. One never hears of hay-hovels ; but that is because hay is not so kept (J.W.B.). Hrt. Others place their corn on a framework of wood, which they call a hovel, ELLIS Mod. Husb. (1750) V. ii. Sus. (J.W.B.)

Hence (1) Hovel-cap, sb. a broad stone or piece of iron laid on the top of each pillar of a ' hovel ' ; (2) -frame, sb. the wooden frame or platform on which stacks or ricks are built up.
(1) N.I.¹ To prevent rats, &c., from climbing up to the grain. (2) Lei.¹

6. Obs. The brickwork cover surrounding an old-fashioned pottery kiln.
w.Yks. One of the master brick-layers hurrying up one of the tall hovels (as they are called) too expeditiously, when the top fell in, Leeds Merc. (Aug. 28, 1770).

7. v. To place corn on a ' hovel ' or frame for stacking.
Hrt. A hand that can hovel, ELLIS Mod. Husb. (1750) V. i.

Hence Hovelled, ppl. adj., fig. laid flat ; the condition of corn after a storm of wind or rain. Nrf. COZENS-HARDY Broad Nrf. (1893) 14.

HOVEL, sb.² Nhb. Dur. Cum. Yks. Lan. Lin. Also in forms hoffil ne.Yks.¹ ; huffel w.Yks.² ; huffil n.Yks.¹⁴ ne.Yks.¹ e Yks. m.Yks.¹ ; huffle Nhb.¹ Dur. Cum.⁴ n.Yks.¹ w.Yks.² ; huval w.Yks. ; huvel Cum.⁴ ; huvil w.Yks. ; huvvel Cum.¹ w.Yks. ; huvvil n.Yks.¹³ m.Yks.¹ ; hauvvle e.Yks.¹ w.Yks.² ; ooavl ne.Lan.¹ [h)o·vl, h)u·vl ; o·fl, h)u·fl.] 1. A finger-stall ; a cover for the protection of a sore or cut finger. Also in comp. Hovel-poke.
Nhb.¹ A clout tied round a hurt finger (s.v. Haffle). Dur. GIBSON Up-Weardale Gl. (1870). Cum.¹⁴, n.Yks.¹²⁴, m.e.Yks.¹ e.Yks. MARSHALL Rur. Econ. (1788) ; n.Yks.¹ m.Yks.¹ Usually of leather. It will be said of a wounded finger : ' I've got a finger-poke for it ; now I want a huvvil.' w.Yks. (H.L.) ; Leeds Merc. Suppl. (Mar. 24, 1894) ; w.Yks.²³, ne.Lan.¹, s.Lin.¹

2. A nosebag.
w.Yks. Bless me wot trubble yo hev we that noaze a yors, if I wor yo ide hev a huval for it, TOM TREDDLEHOYLE Bairnsla Ann. (1852) 46 ; I't winter time ta wear a wesh-leather huvil on ta keep t'frost off an it, ib. (1868) 28.

Hence Huvil, v. to enclose in a nosebag.
w.Yks. Ivvery noaze Sal huvill'd be wi leather, TOM TREDDLE-HOYLE Bairnsla Ann. (1858) 23.

[1. A der. of OE. hūfe, a head-covering ; cp. ME. houfe, 'tena,' Cath. Angl. ; Norw. dial. huva (AASEN), ON. húfa (VIGFUSSON) ; see How, sb.³]

HOVEL(L, v. and sb. Ken. Sus. [o·vl] 1. v. To render assistance to ships requiring help, for payment ; to carry on the trade of ' hoveller.' Cf. hobble, v.²
Ken. They are going hovelling (D.W.L.) ; Ken.¹

Hence Hoveller, sb. (1) a boatman who gains a living by assisting vessels in distress, landing passengers, or piloting, &c. ; (2) a bargeman, one who tows barges ; cf. huffler, 2 ; (3) a light boat sent out to land passengers, &c.
(1) Ken. He es a hoveller in the winter (D.W.L.) ; (G.B.) ; N. & Q. (1852) 1st S. vi. 412 ; One that carries off fresh provisions to ships, GROSE (1790) ; At the Cinque Ports, a name for pilots. As an old term it means those who range the seas around the coast in the chance of falling in with ships in distress, ANSTED Seas Terms (1898) ; Ken.¹ A Deal boatman who goes out to the assistance of ships in distress. The hovelers also carry out provisions, and recover lost anchors, chains and gear. They are first-rate seamen, and their vessels are well built and well manned. Sus.¹ Men who go out to sea in boats for the purpose of meeting homeward-bound vessels, and engaging with the captain to unload them when they enter the harbour. A pilot ; Sus.² Used at Rye, as well as at Dover, for the pilot, who frequently looks out for vessels in distress. (2) Ken. The men who pull or tow flats or lighters or barges up Faversham creek were known up to very lately as hovelers (H.M.). (3) Ken. The light boats at Deal, Dover, &c., which are always on the watch to run out, at the first signal, to land passengers, &c., and when the weather permits often ply about for that purpose far out at sea, N. & Q. (1852) 1st S. vi. 388 ; (H.M.)

2. sb. Assistance rendered for payment by boatmen to vessels in distress ; a paying job of ' hovelling,' a piece of good luck.
Ken. The greater and more terrible the storm, the greater and more likely their chances of 'a good hovel,' as the term goes to

press a job that pays, GATTIE *Mem. Goodwin Sands* (1890) 96; n.[1] In some families, the children are taught to say in their ayers, 'God bless father and mother, and send them a good vel to-night.' e.**Ken.** They got a good hovel (D.W.L.).

HOVEN, *sb.* Lin. A fee paid for marking stock when ey are turned into the commons. e.Lin. WHEELER *Fens* ppend. 8.

HOVER, *v.*[1] *sb.* and *adj.*[1] Sc. n.Cy. Nhb. Yks. Lin. rf. e.An. Brks. Bck. Mid. Sur. Wil. Som. Dev. Also in rms auver n.Lin.[1]; höer Lin.; hovver w.Yks.[1] e.An.[12]; iver Dev.[1]; huvver e.An.[12]; hyver Nrf.; iver, over rf.[2]; ovver n.Yks.[2] [h]o·və(r, s.Cy. ɐ·və(r).] 1. *v.* To dulate, wave, shake.

e.**Suf.** Said of a table-cloth, carpet, hay, &c., raised by the wind's tting under it (F.H.).

Hence (1) **Hovering,** *ppl. adj.*, (2) **Hovery,** *adj.* tremulous, aky, unsteady.

(1, 2) e.**Suf.** The old woman is growing very hovery (*ib.*).

2. To go about in an awkward, aimless manner.

s.**Lin.**[1] He neádn't come auverin' aboot after oor Mary.

3. To hesitate, waver, to be uncertain in mind or action.

m.**Yks.**[4] Ah hovered a larl bit afoor Ah bowt it. m.**Yks.**[1] w.**Yks.** .W.); It was dark, and when he got to the top of the stairs he gan hovering there. One with an impediment of speech ' hovers his talk' (C.C.R.). n.Lin.[1], Hrf.[2] w.Som.[1] A man is said to ver about when considering a bargain before completing it.

4. To wait, stay; to delay, linger, take time; esp. in phr. *ver a blink*.

Sc. But, Andra man, just hover for a blink, LEIGHTON *Wds.* 869) 17. **Sh.I.** Come, men, Foò lang ir ye gaun ta hover] *Sh. ews* (Sept. 24, 1898). **Frf.** Jist hover a blink till I cheenge ma eeks, INGLIS *Ain Flk.* (1895) 157. **Per.** But hover a blink, I'd e ye to think, FORD *Harp* (1893) 334. **Lnk.** They'll no gie us ense to hover a blink, WATSON *Poems* (1853) 67. **Edb.** Hover blink, my Jessie dear, M^cDOWALL *Poems* (1839) 28. n.Cy. GROSE 790). **Nhb.**[1] n.**Yks.**[2] I rather hover'd a bit. ne.**Yks.**[1] Hower nahl they come up. Thoo mun 'ower a bit. o.**Yks.** MARSHALL *ur. Econ.* (1788). m.**Yks.**[1] w.**Yks.**[1] 'I mun endays.' .. 'Nay, an, hovver a bit,' ii. 290. **Lin.** Tittn up t'sprunt mun höer a bit, aown *Lil. Laur.* (1890) *Pref.* 15.

5. Of the weather: to be inclined to, to threaten, gather o for; to be uncertain.

n.**Yks.**[1]; n.**Yks.**[2] It hovers for wet; n.**Yks.**[4] Ah doot it's hover-g foor raain. m.**Yks.**[2]

Hence **Hovering,** *ppl. adj.* of the weather: uncertain, iny and fickle in turns. n.**Yks.**[2]

6. To stay, suspend in action.

n.**Yks.**[1]; n.**Yks.**[2] 'Hover your hand,' as in the act of pouring ater. m.**Yks.**[1]

7. Of a hen: to cover with her wings.

w.**Mid.** Look how the old hen hovers her chicken! The chicken e cold and want the hen to bover them. 'Hover' rimes with over' (W.P.M.).

8. With *over*: to lean or bend over from behind.

e.**Suf.** Don't keep hovering over me so (F.H.).

9. To clean out a ditch or dike; see below.

Nrf. 'I mean that partable deek.' 'What do you think of having one to it! hovered or bottomfyed or what!' EMERSON *Son of ns* (1892) 104; To 'hover a dike' is a term applied to the treat-ent of 'grown-up' dikes, and the operation consists in cutting e sides clean with a 'meag' or shore-cutter, and drawing the ttings out with a 'crome' and piling them on the shore. No ud is removed as far as 'bottom-fying' (P.H.E.).

10. *Comp.* (1) **Hover-fly,** a dipterous insect of the order *mbyliidae*; (2) **-hawk,** the kestrel, *Tinnunculus alaudarius.*

(1) **Wil.** Yellow-barred hover-flies, JEFFERIES *Hdgrow.* (1889) ; The wasp-like hover-flies, that are generally past all thought counting, *ib.* 96. (2) n.**Yks.** What had that to do with the ver-hawk not doing any hurt among the game! ATKINSON *oorl. Parish* (1891) 331. Brks., Bck. SWAINSON *Birds* (1885) 140.

11. *sb.* A slackening of pace, a pause, wavering.

e.**Yks.** Sha gans up t'hill withoot a hover, bud meeast on 'em aks a bit ov a whibble (M.C.F.M.).

12. Suspense, hesitation, uncertainty; of the weather: uncertain state.

Sc. 'In a hover' is applied to the weather, when from the state the atmosphere, one is uncertain whether it will rain or be fair AM.). **Abd.** Her heart for Lindy now began to beal An' was in ver [swidder, ed. 1812] great to think her leal, Ross *Helenore*

(1768) 64 (JAM.). n.**Lin.**[1] I was all in a hover when he cam' up whether I should say noh or speak to him.

13. A cover, shelter, 'hold,' esp. a hiding-place for fish.

Nhb. Terriers . . . are necessary to make the otter bolt from his 'hover' or 'bolt,' DAVIES *Rambles Sch. Field-club* (1881) xxxvi. w.**Som.**[1] Any overhanging stone or bank under which a fish can hide is so called. Also any kind of overhanging shelter, especially hollows in the side of a hedge. 'Be sure and keep your eye 'pon the hovers [uuv·urz] along thick side o' the hedge.' **Dev.** Every bolt and hover which could harbour a fox, *Cornh. Mag.* (Nov. 1887) 515; The word is the regular one for such a hollow under a bank as a rabbit loves to squat in, *Reports Provinc.* (1897); Dev.[1], nw.**Dev.**[1]

14. A floating island, or bed of reeds.

e.**An.**[1] **Nrf.** COZENS-HARDY *Broad Nrf.* (1893) 77; They [bitterns] sleep on the hovers round the broads, EMERSON *Birds* (ed. 1895) 205; I think there's a hover there, *ib. Son of Fens* (1892) 120.

15. Dried flags or peat cut for fuel.

e.**An.**[1]; e.**An.**[2] Differing from turves, in being the upper cut with the grass, reeds, &c. **Nrf.** We used to burn dry cow dung an' hovers, PATTERSON *Man and Nat.* (1895) 61; Peat cut into blocks 4 in. sq. and 2 ft. deep, *Leg. Broads*, iv; COZENS-HARDY *Broad Nrf.* (1893) 12.

Hence **Hover-spade,** *sb.* a tongue-shaped spade for cutting turf. e.**An.**[1]

16. *adj.* Of the wind: blowing up for rain. Sur.[1]

HOVER, *adj.*[2] and *v.*[2] s.Cy. Ken. Sur. Sus. Hmp. Also in form huvver Ken. Sus. [o·və(r), ɐ·və(r).]

1. *adj.* Light, puffy, raised; not pressed down.

Ken. Used of bread, also of hops just gathered and not pressed down (J.A.B.); Ken.[1], Sur.[1]

2. Of soil: light, loose, *gen.* in *comp.* **Hover-ground.**

s.**Cy.** GROSE (1790). se.**Cy.** RAY (1691). **Ken.** As the land on the upper part of the island (Thanet) is generally light and hover, the wheat, especially in a dry season, is apt to be what they call root-fallen, YOUNG *Annals Agric.* (1784–1815) XXVII. 516; Ken.[2], Sus.[12]

3. Cold, shivery, hunched up; of birds or animals: having the coat or feathers ruffled from cold; poorly, unwell.

Ken. Sur.[1] His coat is so hover. Sus.[1] Some of the children looked middlin' hover as they went along to school this morning through the snow. [Birds [in frost] creep about with all their feathers starting and ruffled—'hover,' as the country people call it, *Sat. Review* (1891) LXXI. 99.]

4. *v.* To spread lightly or loosely; in hop-picking: to pack hops lightly, to measure them lightly into the basket.

Ken. 'To hover ground,' to lay it on lightly (K.); Have they been hovered! (S.H.); To pack lightly, in order to defraud in measure. The hop pickers, who are paid by the basket, lay them lightly in for that purpose, GROSE (1790); Ken.[1] In e.Ken. it is the custom to pick, not in bins, but in baskets holding five or six bushels. The pickers gather the hops into a number of small baskets or boxes, until they have got enough to fill the great basket; they then call the tallyman; .. one of the pickers ... then comes to bover the hops; this is done by putting both hands down to the bottom of the great basket, into which the hops out of the smaller ones are emptied as quickly but gently as possible, the woman all the while raising the hops with her hands; as soon as they reach the top, they are quickly shot out into the green bag before they have time to sag or sink. Thus, very inadequate measure is obtained, as, probably, a bushel is lost in every tally; indeed, hovering is nothing more than a recognized system of fraud. **Sus.** To spread hay loosely (F.E.S.); Sus.[12]

5. With *in*: to cover with straw or matting, &c. Hmp. (H.C.M.B.) 6. To huddle.

Ken. Huvvered up under the wall. All huvvered together (D.W.L.).

HOVERA, *num. adj.* *Obs.* Cum. In sheep-counting: eight.

Used 50 years ago in Borrowdale (J.S.O.); LUCAS *Stud. Nid-derdale* (c. 1882) 39; Cum.[4]

HOVIE, *sb.* Sh.I. A small limpet-creel.

Liftin' up his head to rake ower his hovie, STEWART *Tales* (1892) 32.

HOVREL, HOVVER, see Haverel, Hover, *v.*[1]

HOW, *sb.*[1] Or.I. Nhb. Cum. Wm. Yks. Lan. I.Ma. Not. Lin. Nhp. War. Bdf. Bck. Nrf. Som. Dev. Also written houe n.Yks.[14]; howe Or.I. Cum. Yks. s.Lan.; and in forms ha w.Yks.[1]; hauf e.Yks.; haugh n.Cy. w.Yks.[1];

haw w.Yks.[1]; hoe N.Cy.[1] Nhb.[1] Not. n.Lin.[1] Bdf. Bck. Nrf. w.Som.[1] Dev. ; hogh N.Cy.[1]; hoh, boo Nhp.[2]; hough Yks. Lan. I.Ma. ; howack Or.I. ; howie Or.I. S. & Ork.[1] [h)ou, h)ō.] A small detached hill or mound, *gen.* a tumulus or barrow ; a hillock, knoll ; almost *obs.* except in place-names ; also used *attrib.*

Or.I. (S.A.S.) ; Another beautiful tumulus . . . distinguished by the name of Mesow or Mese-how. In this country, ' how ' . . . is applied to elevated hillocks, whether artificial or natural, *Statist. Acc.* XIV. 130 (JAM.) ; It was a matter of common occurrence for the Norsemen to break open a howe in the expectation of finding treasure, FERGUSSON *Rambles* (1884) 47 ; S. & Ork.[1] n.Cy. *Trans. Phil. Soc.* (1858) 160 ; GROSE (1790) ; N.Cy.[1] Nhb.[1] In place-names, as Cambhoe. Lakel.[1] Originally a grave-mound, then a gentle eminence or mound, freq. in proper names. . . Silver How, Fox How. Cum. Croppins of esh mun be foddert on t'howes, DICKINSON *Cumbr.* (1876) 245 ; Cum.[12] Wm. *Appleby Monthly Messenger* (Apr. 1891). Yks. If Brayton bargh, and Hambleton hough, and Burton bream Were all in thy belly 'twould not be team, RAY *Prov.* (1678) 339. n.Yks. The heights of Swart Houe, ATKINSON *Moorl. Parish* (1891) 39: n.Yks.[1] [2] [4] e.Yks. Sometimes natural, *gen.* artificial, MARSHALL *Rur. Econ.* (1788) ; e.Yks.[1] *Obs.* except in place-names, MS. *add.* (T.H.) w.Yks. GRAINGE *Nidderdale* (1863) 221; w.Yks.[1] Lan. Yonder at th' Hough, where yeow seen th' leeghts there, SHADWELL *Witches* (1682) 30. ed. 1718. ne.Lan.[1] A gentle eminence near a vale. s.Lan. Howe-side, BAMFORD *Dial.* (1854). I.Ma. After church, we went for a walk to the houghs (S.M.). Not. Hoe-hill, Row How (L.C.M.). Lin. *Obs.* as a single word, but very common in local names, STREATFEILD *Lin. and Danes* (1884) 338. n.Lin. A place full of sand hoes, PEACOCK *R. Skirlaugh* (1870) I. 255; n.Lin.[1] Freq. in names of places. Nhp.[2] An elevated site : a frequent name for a field in such situations. War. That there be a how or hows laid over our bodies to prevent our remains being disturbed, *Deeds at Southam* (1792). Bdf., Bck. A range of eminences. . . Two spurs of these are termed respectively Ivinghoe and Totternhoe, *N. & Q.* (1872) 4th S. x. 172. Nrf. Forehoe or Feorhou, i.e. Four Hills, BLOMEFIELD *Hist. Nrf.* II. 374, in *N. & Q.* (1872) 4th S. x. 507 ; Grenehow, i.e. green hills or tumuli, *ib.* vi. 1. w.Som.[1] Dev. Trentishoe, Martinhoe, and Mortehoe are each connected with an eminence or promontory, *N. & Q.* (1872) 4th S. x. 172.

[The shadow of it couyrd howis (=montes), HAMPOLE (c. 1330) *Ps.* lxxix. 11. Norw. dial. *haug*, an eminence with a rounded top (AASEN) ; ON. *haugr*, a ' how,' mound (VIGFUSSON).]

HOW, *sb.*[2] Sc. Also written hoo. [hū.] 1. A coif, head-dress ; a nightcap.

Sc. There occurs how or hoo, nightcap, FRANCISQUE-MICHEL *Lang.* (1882) 87 ; He breaks my head and syne puts on my hoo, FERGUSON *Poems* (1641) 19 ; Break my head and draw on my hoo, KELLY *Prov.* (1721) 61 ; Still used (JAM.). n.Sc. (*ib.*) Per. The heads of the matrons are enveloped in large pieces of cloth of a tawny colour, which they term hoos, MONTEATH *Dunblane* (1835) 84, ed. 1887.

2. A membrane or ' caul ' on the head with which some children are born ; used in *comb.* Happy how, Hely how, Sely how.

Sc. The women call a haly or sely how (i.e. holy or fortunate cap or hood,) a film or membrane stretched over the heads of children new born, . . and they give out that children so born will be very fortunate, RUDDIMAN *Gl. to Douglas* (s.v. How) in BRAND *Pop. Antiq.* (ed. 1813) II. 451 ; (JAM.) Rxb. He will be lucky, being born with the helie-how on his head (*ib.*). [Great conceits are raised of the involution or membranous covering, commonly called the silly-how, . . which midwives were wont to sell unto credulous lawyers, who had an opinion it advantaged their promotion, T. BROWNE *Vulgar Errors* (1646) bk. v. xxiii. § 15.]

[1. Thair haris all war tukkit wp on thar croun, That baith with how and helm wes thristit down, DOUGLAS *Eneados* (1513), ed. 1874, II. 257; Howe, heed hyllynge, *sidaris, Prompt.* ; OE. *hūfe*, (' cidaris ' (ÆLFRIC). 2. Those who are born with a caul about their head are popularly believed to be lucky children. Such a membrane is called in Germany *Glückshaube, Wehmutter-haüblein*, and is carefully treasured up, GRIMM *Teut. Myth.* (tr. Stallybrass) II. 874; Hove that a chylde is borne in, *laye*, PALSGR. (1530).]

HOW, *sb.*[3] Sc. Irel. Also written hoe Ir. ; hoo Sc. s.Don. ; hou Sc. (JAM.) ; hōu Sh.I. [hū.] A piece of wood used in building the couple of a roof.

Sc. A piece of wood which joins the couple-wings together at the top, on which rests the roof-tree of a thatched house (JAM.). Sh.I. Da wattermills is no one aboot . . . an' da maist o' dem ye can see da hōus o' da couples, *Sh. News* (Mar. 12, 1898). ne.Sc. The couples were placed first and consisted of five or six parts— two upright posts resting on the ground, the two arms of the couple, called hoos, fixed to the top of the upright posts, GREGOR *Flk-Lore* (1881) 50. Lnk. Clam up the mow, Where was an opening near the hou, RAMSAY *Poems* (1800) II. 523 (JAM.). s.Don. SIMMONS *Gl.* (1890).

[Norw. dial. *huv*, the timber for the roof of a house (AASEN) ; ON. *hūfa* (also *hūa*), part of a church in the old timber churches (VIGFUSSON).]

HOW, *adv.* and *sb.*[4] Var. dial. uses in Sc. Irel. and Eng. I. Dial. forms. 1. (1) Foo, (2) Fou, (3) Fow, (4) Fu, (5) Ha, (6) Haa, (7) Haaw, (8) Hah, (9) Hau, (10) Haw, (11) Hea, (12) Heaw, (13) Heea, (14) Heue, (15) Hew, (16) Ho, (17) Hoo, (18) Hu, (19) Ya, (20) Yaa, (21) Yah. [For further instances see II. below.]

(1) Sh.I. Lat me ken foo ye mak' dis busk, *Sh. News* (July 30, 1898). Cai.[1] Abd. I cudna say foo the fees 'll be rinnin, ALEXANDER *Johnny Gibb* (1871) viii. Kcd. But foo do I, alang the Feugh Sae sadly, lanely stray ? GRANT *Lays* (1884) 18. (2) S. & Ork.[1] Kcd. He . . . shortly speired ' fou they were a',' JAMIE *Muse* (1844) 107. (3) Wxf.[1] Shoo pleast aam all, fowe ! 90. (4) Bnff. I said, my Meg, an' fu' are ye ! TAYLOR *Poems* (1787) 58. e.Fif. Fu' wad ye like to hae sic a weel lined wallet ! LATTO *Tam Bodkin* (1864) iv. (5) w.Yks. *Yks. Wkly. Post* (Apr. 10, 1897). Lan. Tell meh ha theese lung nemes leet'n, TIM BOBBIN *View Dial.* (ed. 1806) 33. (6) w.Yks.[2], e.Lan.[1] (7) Lan. Hae coom yo to speer fur me meaustur ! KAY-SHUTTLEWORTH *Scarsdale* (1860) II. 154. (8) w.Yks. I once read of hah a 'deead donkey towt a lesson,' CUDWORTH *Dial. Sketches* (1884) 1. (9) Wm. WHEELER *Dial.* (1790) 114, ed. 1821. (10) Wm. Haw dus awe at heaam dea ! WHEELER *Dial.* (1790) 114, ed. 1821. (11) Lan. HARLAND & WILKINSON *Leg.* (1873) 197. (12) Lan. Good Lord, heaw they trembled between, HARLAND *Lyrics* (1860) 135. e.Lan.[1] (13) Lan. Heea art tuh cummin on ! *O Bit oo o Chat* (1844) pt. i. 2. (14) e.Dev. Heue grassy's our beyde, PULMAN *Sng. Sol.* (1860) i. 16. (15) Lan. Hew's that ! BRIERLEY *Layrock* (1864) iv. (16) Cum. Thare's nea matter ho menny o' them, *Lonsdale Mag.* (Feb. 1867) 312. Lin.[1] (17) Sc. Hoo's Katie ! SWAN *Gates of Eden* (1895) i. Nhb.[1], Cum.[14], n.Yks.[24], e.Yks.[1] w.Yks. LUCAS *Stud. Nidderdale* (c. 1882). n.Lin.[1] Ken. LEWIS *I. Tenet* (1736) 50. (18) Sc. GROSE (1790) MS. *add.* (C.) (19) w.Yks. And ya sho thought, A. L. *Forty Years Ago*, 113. (20) w.Yks.[2] (21) w.Yks. If they nobbut knew yah clever he wor, A. L. *Forty Years Ago*, 9.

2. Var. contractions or elliptical phr. : (1) Fousticait, Fushica'd, or Howsticaad, lit. ' how is it you call it,' a term used to denote anything the name of which has been forgotten, ' what d'ye call it ' ; (2) Fushica'im, lit. ' how is it you call him,' ' what d'ye call him ' ; (3) Hoo's, How's, Foo's, Fou's, or Fu's, (*a*) how is *or* how are ; (*b*) how hast *or* how has ; (*c*) how does ; (4) Hoost, Howst, or Hah'st, how is the . . . ; (5) Hoosta or Howsta, (*a*) how doest thou ; (*b*) how hast thou ; (*c*) how art thou ; (6) Hoo't or Heaw't, (*a*) how that ; (*b*) how it ; (7) Howsa, how are you ; (8) Yamdy, how many. [For further instances see II. below.]

(1) Sc. (JAM.) ; As I cam near hand I thought it was a market an' put my hand i' my fushica'd for something to the custom wife, BLYD *Contract*, 3 (JAM.). Nhb.[1] Bring us yor howsticaad. (2) Sc. Up by comes Fushica'im that dwells at the briggen, BLYD *Contract*, 3 (JAM.). Ant. (W.H.P.), N.Cy.[1] e.Yks.[1] Hoo's all bayns ! MS. *add.* (T.H.) w.Yks. Az je faθə(r) ! (J.W.) (*b*) e.Yks.[1] Hoo's thā deean it ! MS. *add.* (T.H.) ; Hoo's he deean't ! *ib.* w.Yks. (J.W.) (*c*) e.Yks.[1] Hoo's he deeah't ! MS. *add.* (T.H.) w.Yks. Az i diut ! [How does he do it ?] (J.W.) (4) Cum. I hwope ya mend nicely, Betty. Wat howst barn ! *Lonsdale Mag.* (July 1866) 25. Wm. Wat hoost barn ! BRIGGS *Remains* (1825) 181. w.Yks. An hah'st lad ! BYWATER *Gossips* (1851) 6. (5, *a*) w.Yks.[2] Howsta think o' going ! (*b*) Howsta done that, pretha ! *ib.* (*c*) Wm. Sowgers com up butt him an sed ' Hoosta gaan on noo ! ' *Spec. Dial.* (1877) pt. i. w.Yks.[2] Howsta fur wark like ! (6, *a*) Abd. ALEXANDER *Johnny Gibb* (1871) viii. (*b*) Lan. Bur thae'st sing to neet as heawt leets, KAY-SHUTTLEWORTH *Scarsdale* (1860) II. 214. (7) Dor. Howsa going haven cooked, John ! *Flk-Lore Rec.* (1880) III. 111. (8) w.Yks.[2]

Inkum jinkum, Jeremy buck, Yamdy horns do Au cock up! *Rhyme in boys' game.*

II. Dial. meanings. 1. *adv.* In phr. (1) *about how,* near the matter, about it, sufficiently near the right way of doing anything ; (2) *as how,* (a) that ; (b) in any case ; (3) *as how it is* or *leets,* as it happens, as the case is ; how ever it comes about ; (4) *how and about,* about, concerning ; (5) *— are you coming on ?* a greeting, salutation ; 'how are you?' 'how do you do?' (6) *— came you so,* slightly intoxicated ; (7) *— do ye ?* (8) *— do you come on ?* (9) *— do you get your health ?* (10) *— fend ye ?* (11) *— go(es ?* (12) *— goes it?* see (5) ; (13) *— it be,* however, nevertheless ; (14) *— leets* or *licht?* (15) *— lish* or *lysh ?* how comes it ? how is it ? (16) *— preev ye ?* (17) *— 's a' ?* (18) *— 's a' wi' ye* or *you ?* (19) *— 's yourself?* see (5) ; (20) *— so be,* however ; (21) *— soon, obs.,* as soon as ; (22) *— at* or *that,* how was it that, why was it ; (23) *— thou talks,* an exclamation of surprise.

(1) **Ken.²** That's about how. (2, a) **s.Stf.** He said as how the gaffer came down the pit, PINNOCK *Blk. Cy. Ann.* (1895). (b) **w.Yks.** I'm bound to Bradforth as how 'tis, *Longman's Mag.* (Nov. 1895) 69 ; Thee'rt too good to burn, as hea't be, HARLAND & WILKINSON *Leg.* (1873) 197 ; We'nn burn him to neet as heaw't leet, KAY-SHUTTLEWORTH *Scarsdale* (1860) II. 108. (4) **e.Suf.** I'll tell you all how and about it. He told me how and about it all (F.H.). (5) **N.I.¹** (6) **Stf.** *Monthly Mag.* (1816) I. 494. (7) **Nhb.** Te ax a frind 'Hoo de ye !' WILSON *Poems* (1843) 113. (8, 9) **N.I.¹** 100 ; **Cum.¹⁴** (11) **n.Yks.** How go, John ! (I.W.) **w.Yks.²,** **Lin.¹, War.²,** Oxf.(G.O.) (12) **Cum.¹, e.Yks.¹** **w.Yks.** BANKS *Whfld. Wds.* (1865). **Lan.** The common greeting, GASKELL *Lectures Dial.* (1854) 26. (13) **w.Yks.** They fought well, how it be, SNOWDEN *Web of Weaver* (1896) i. (14) **w.Yks.** How leets tha doesn't pay thy club when tha's t'chonce ? (S.K.C.) **Lan.** Wel, aw sed, heaw leetes theaw didn't speyke afore ! ORMEROD *Felley fro Rachde* (1851) v ; How leets you couldn't ha aunt'er sooner ! BRIERLEY *Daisy Nook* (1859) 35, ed. 1881 ; How leets thou artnt at schoo ! WAUGH *Chim. Corner* (1874) 100, ed. 1883. **Chs.¹,** **Der.²** (15) **Lan.** (S.W.) (16) **Cum.** Heo preuv ye o ! DICKINSON *Lamplugh* (1856) 6 ; **Cum.¹** (17) **Abd.** Ay! man, hoo's a' ! Na! Mains ; you there ! *Guidman Inglismaill* (1873) 36. **Per.** Fair lass, good e'en ! How's a' the nicht ! SPENCE *Poems* (1898) 10. **Nhb.** How's a' the day, Willie M°Nair ! WEBSTER *Rhymes* (1885) 4. **Gall.** MACTAGGART *Encycl.* (1824). **Nhb.** Hoo's a' at Dilston ? CLARE *Love of Lass* (1890) I. 28. **Wm.** Haus awe friends ? WHEELER *Dial.* (1790²) 114, ed. 1821. (18) **Sh.I.** Fu's a' wi' you, an' fu's a' da rest ! STEWART *Tales* (1892) 134. **S. & Ork.¹, Cai.¹** **Rnf.** Hoo's a' wi' ye, dear Gowan Ha'! BARR *Poems* (1861) 151. **Ayr.** How are ye, Tam ! and how's a' wi' ye, Bob ! BOSWELL *Poet. Wks.* (1810) 50, ed. 1871. **Dmf.** How's a' wi' you? Ye'll hae some news to gi' me, SHAW *Schoolmaster* (1899) 330. **Ant.** (W.H.P.), **N.Cy.¹** (19) **Nrf.** (A.G.F.) (20) **Cor.** How so be we must lop up the swit, weth the sour, DANIEL *Bride of Scio* (1842) 231 ; 'Tis that, Jutson. Howzobe, you'm vound a better half than me, MORTIMER *Tales Moors* (1895) 105. (21) **Sc.** Those who were present ... undertook to cause the other princes how soon they could meet with them, *Scoticisms* (1787) 117 ; How soon I got home, *Monthly Mag.* (1798) II. 436 ; (W.C.) (c. 1750). **Or.I.** To burie thair deid bow shone ony sall happin to die, PETERKIN *Notes* (1822) *App.* 32. **Abd.** Mortimer, with his muskatyres, how soonne they saw them, makes a halt, TURREFF *Antiq. Gleanings* (1859) 58. **Fif.** How soon he was espyed to rise... one was sent to him, SCOT *Apolog.* (1644) 163, ed. 1846. (22) **Cum.** Hoo 'at thoo couldn't hod t'noise on the ! GWORDIE GREENUP *Anudder Batch* (1873) 14 ; **Cum.⁴** (23) **w.Yks.** Why! how thou talks ! (F.P.T.)

2. Why ? how comes it ?

Frf. How are you greeting so sair ! BARRIE *Minister* (1891) xxiv ; How will you no look at me ! *ib.* vii. **Lan.** Well, an ha didneb gooa on with him ! TIM BOBBIN *View Dial.* (ed. 1806) 33. **Pem.** How didn't you tell'n I would come ! He've a runned off, nobody knows how (E.D.). **Cor.** Well, how caen't Zacky think a bit Before begin to spaik ! FORFAR *Poems* (1885) 11 ; **Cor.²** How ded 'ee go there ?

3. Used redundantly after *that* ; also in phr. *that how that.*

Abd. She said 't hoo 't sbe cudna help it, ALEXANDER *Johnny Gibb* (1871) viii. **Nrf.** He say that how he din't know (E.M.).

4. *sb.* A way, method, style of doing anything.

w.Yks. (J.W.) **s.Not.** Do it a this 'ow (J.P.K.). **Lin.** Thou'st talked to me this how, FENN *Cure of Souls* (1889) 35 ; I'll teach you to go and break and smash i' this how, *Gilbert Rugge* (1866) I. 310. **n.Lin.¹** See bairn, thoo shou'd do it e' this how. **sw.Lin.¹** It is better that how than any ways else. He can't do it no how else. **s.Lin.** What ar' you a doin' it a that how for ! (T.H.R.) **w.Som.¹** I can't do it no how : no, not to save my life.

HOW, *int.* and *v.* Sc. Nhb. Dur. Cum. Wm. Yks. Lan. Chs. Der. Lin. Also written hou nw.Der.¹ ; **howe** Sh.I. Rnf. ; and in form **ha-** Nhb.¹ Cum.¹ [h]ou.] **1.** *int.* An exclamation used to attract attention ; a salutation, 'hullo'; freq. in *comb.* **How there.**

Sc. And hey Annie! and how Annie (JAM.). **Sh.I.** Whin he ... wanted da hill-folk ta lave him at wance, he wid a just strucken his staff ipa da ert, an' said—'Skeet howe hame, göid folk !' STEWART *Tales* (1892) 89. **N.Cy.¹** **Nhb.** How! Geordy man ! cum here, MARSHALL *Sngs.* (1819) 10 ; How! marrows, I'se tip you a sang, MIDFORD *Coll. Sngs.* (1818) 10 ; **Nhb.¹** 'How there, lads !' The ordinary formula of the salute is 'How there, marra !' with the reply, interrogative, of 'What cheer, hinney !' **w.Yks.⁵** 'How Bil !' 'How my lad !'

Hence **How-way** or **Howay,** *int.* (1) a term of encouragement: come or go away, come on ; (2) in mining: a call to the braksemen to lower the cage or to quicken its movement.

(1) **N.Cy.¹** Used by rustic auctioneers. **Nhb.** How'way, Dicky, how'way, hinney, There's the tooting o' the horn, WILSON *Oiling o' Dicky's Wig* (1826) 1 ; Howay, Geordie ! sprint, man, like the devil, howay ! PEASE *Mark o' the Deil* (1894) 103; **Nhb.¹** In n.Nhb. the call 'haway !' is given to the farm hands by the woman-steward at starting or yoking time, so that all the women start together. **Dur.¹ s.Dur.** How-way wi' me (J.E.D.). **Cum.** He ... set it off galloping, saying, 'Howway wu the,' SILPHEO *Billy Brannan* (1885) 6 ; **Cum.¹** ; **Cum.³** 'Heway wid tha, Joe,' sez fadder to me, 2. **Wm.** How-way hame, honey, afoor it's dark (B.K.). (2) **Nhb.¹** **Nhb.,** Dur. NICHOLSON *Coal Tr. Gl.* (1888).

2. An exclamation of joy or sorrow.

Sc. Monie a lady fair siching and crying, Och how ! CHILD *Ballads* (1889) III. 392. **Rnf.** Mony a hech ! and howe ! it cost—The cripple flea that Janet lost, WEBSTER *Rhymes* (1835) 161. **Gall.** O ! sing how for the Binwud tree, MACTAGGART *Encycl.* (1824) 70, ed. 1876.

Hence **How-hum,** *int.* an exclamation of grief, alas !

Gall. It's altered days wi' us. How-hum ! we're a' gaen to the de'il, MACTAGGART *ib.* 69.

3. A call used in driving cattle.

Cum. (J.Ar.) **e.Yks.** THOMPSON *Hist. Welton* (1869) 171 ; **s.Yks.¹** A soothing call to horses or cattle, when inclined to stray or be obstinate, 'How, then, how, awd oss,' *MS. add.* (T.H.) **n.Lin.¹**

Hence (1) **How-sheep,** *int.* a call to a dog used in driving sheep; (2) **-up,** (a) *int.* a call to cattle; (b) *sb.* a child's name for a cow ; (3) **-way,** *int.,* see (2, a) ; (4) **-way-bye,** *int.* a call to a dog used in driving cattle, sheep, &c.

(1) **Lnk.** A call given by a shepherd to his dog to incite him to pursue sheep (JAM.). (2, a) **Chs.¹ s.Chs.¹** (3) **Lakel.², Wm.** (B.K.), **ne.Lan.¹** (4) **Lakel.²** **Wm.** 'How-way-bye! How-way-bye !' is the term used to urge a dog on to get in front of and turn cattle, sheep, &c. (B.K.)

4. *v.* To cry 'how !' with pain or grief.

Sc. What need ye hech and how, Ladies ? What need ye how for me ! CHILD *Ballads* (1889) III. 392.

5. To call sheep or cattle ; to shout 'how'; to quicken the speed of cattle. Also with *up.*

Cum. I began howin' an' shootin' at t'sheep, RICHARDSON *Talk* (1871) 30, ed. 1876 ; **Cum.⁴** Begins to how them to the fold, RAWNSLEY *Life* (1899) 98. **Shr.¹**

6. To hurry away.

Nhb. Now, fra this show aw hows away, ALLAN *Tyneside Sngs.* (ed. 1891) 356; **Nhb.¹**

HOW, HOWACK, see Who, How, *sb.¹*

HOWANABEE, *adv.* Sc. Also written **howanawbee.** However.

Sc. Howanawbee there was ae chiel there, HISLOP *Anecdote* (1874) 302. **Slk.** Dinna think, howanabee, that I care for you, HOGG *Tales* (1838) 18, ed. 1866.

HOWANEVER, *adv.* Sc. Irel. Nhb. Also in forms **hooanivvor** Nhb.¹; **how-an'-divir** N.I.¹; **howane'er, how-an-iver** Ir.; **howiniver** n.Ir. However.

Cai. Fö)ən)evər, ELLIS *Pronunc.* (1889) V. 685. **Ir.** Howane'er,

I knew it's distressed you were, BARLOW *Lisconnel* (1895) 58; Hownanever, he went of a suddint, *ib. Bogland* (1892) 183, ed. 1893; How-an-iver they laid this body they foun' an the grass, TENNYSON *Tomorrow* (1885). n.Ir. 'Howiniver, achree! whin I'm breathless,' sez he, 'I must hev a wake,' *Lays and Leg.* (1884) 45; Hooaniver, a pluckit up heart an' went oot, LYTTLE *Paddy McQuillan,* 10; N.I.¹, Nhb.¹

HOWARD, HOWCH, see Hayward, How(e, *adj.*

HOWD, *sb.*¹ Bnff.¹ A great quantity.

The aul' wiffie hard she wiz gettin' sic a howd o' siller.

HOWD, *v.*¹ and *sb.*² Sc. n.Cy. Also written **houd** Sc. [houd, haud.] 1. *v.* To sway, rock, to move from side to side; to wriggle; to bump up and down, move by jerks. Cf. **howdle, *v.***

Sc. She saw something howd down the water like a green bunch o' potato shaws, CHAMBERS *Pop. Rhymes* (1870) 70; The coffin came houdin' down the water in great haste, *ib.* 933. *Cai.*¹ As on a galloping horse, or in a small boat at sea. *Bnff.*¹ *Frf.* Auld horny thought to gar him howd Upo' the gallows, for the gowd, *Piper o' Peebles* (1794) 20. *Lth.* (JAM.) *Slk.* They were aye gaun out o' sight an' comin' howdin' up again, HOGG *Tales* (1838) 150, ed. 1866. *Rxb.* A boat, tub or barrel, sailing about in a pool, is said to houd (JAM.); Then houding owre gaed mony a tub To cowe the town, A. SCOTT *Poems* (ed. 1808) 69.

2. *sb.* A motion from side to side; a swaying or jerking; the act of wriggling. n.Sc. (JAM.), Cai.¹

3. A sudden gale of wind.

*Bnff.*¹ A howd o' ween raise, an' shook the corn. The ween got up wee a howd.

4. A strain. n.Cy. (HALL.) [Not known to our correspondents.]

HOWD, *v.*² Sc. To hide.

e.Sc. Wi' his e'en glistenin', an' the master aside him howdin' his in his hankey, SETOUN *Sunshine* (1895) 339. *Frf.* (JAM.)

Hence **Howdlins** or **Hoddlins,** *adv.* in secret, clandestinely. Sc., Rnf. (JAM.)

HOWD, *v.*³ Sc. (JAM.) To act the part of a midwife, to deliver a woman in labour. See **Howdie.**

HOW-DEE-DOW, *sb.* Nhb.¹ A regular namby-pamby.

HOWDER, *v.*¹ and *sb.*¹ Sc. Irel. n.Cy. Nhb. Dur. Yks. Also in forms **howther** Nhb.¹ s.Dur.; **hudder** Lnk.; **huther** Rnf. Ant. Dur.¹ 1. *v.* To heap together in a disorderly manner; to crowd, swarm, huddle.

Sc. Like swarms o' bees hungry hordes may howder, DONALD *Poems* (1867) 147. *Rnf.* Huthrin' in a thrang, Out frae their hole, at unco rate They driftit wi' a bang, PICKEN *Poems* (1813) II. 88 Ayr. Our greenwood tree Where wives an' weans are howdering, AINSLIE *Land of Burns* (ed. 1892) 250. *Lnk.* Howder'd wi' hills a crystal burnie ran, RAMSAY *Poems* (1800) II. 8 (JAM.). *Gall.* MACTAGGART *Encycl.* (1824). *Edb.* Menzies o' moths an' flaes are shook, An' i' the floor they howder, FERGUSSON *Poems* (1773) 167, ed. 1785. *Ant.* It's a gatherin' up an' hutherin'-like, *Ballymena Obs.* (1892). n.Cy. *Border Gl.* (Coll. L.L.B.). s.Dur. T'kitchen was all howthered up till ane could hardly git a seat (J.E.D.). n.Yks.²

Hence **Howthery, Howthery-towthery,** *adj.* untidy, slovenly. *Nhb.*¹ She myeks oney a howthery kind o' wife.

2. With *on:* to put on hurriedly, and in a disorderly fashion. *Lnk.* When at len'th she wauchels up, her claes she hudders on, NICHOLSON *Kilwuddie* (ed. 1895) 93.

3. *sb.* A heap of stones or rubbish. Dur.¹, n.Yks.²

HOWDER, *v.*² and *sb.*² Sc. Lakel. Lan. Also in forms **houther** Slg. Ayr.; **howdther** Wm.; **howther** Sc. (JAM.); **howthir** Bnff.¹; **hudder, hudther** Lan. 1. *v.* To push. *Bnff.*¹ Often with the notion of rudeness. 'Howthir that stane doon the brae.' 'The twa ill-contrivet geets bowthirt the peer gangeral our the dyke.'

Hence **Houthering,** *sb.* rough, clumsy romping.

Ayr. Are there touslin's on the hairst-rig, An' houtherin's 'mang the hay! AINSLIE *Land of Burns* (ed. 1892) 334.

2. Of wind: to blow fitfully.

Lan. The tempest 'huddered' about the chimney-top, BRIERLEY *Irkdale* (1865) 247, ed. 1868.

3. *sb.* A push, a sudden shock.

*Bnff.*¹ Gee 'im a howthir on o' the horseback. The little ill-trickit hurb ran in ahin 'im an' ga' 'im a howthir doon aff o't. *Lan.* I wondered what wur up, when ther a hudther, ut shook the vessel as if there'd bin a saequake, BRIERLEY *Ab-o'th-Yate Yankeeland* (1885) ii.

4. A rocking motion, swaying; the act of fornication; a violent tossing.

*Bnff.*¹ The ween raise, an' they got a howthir or they cam in. *Abd.* The howder of the boat made her quite sick (G.W.). *Slg.* The breeks he woo'd and wed in Maggy Tudor, When first he blest her with a highland houther, GALLOWAY *Luncarty* (1804) 55. *Lnk., Lth.* (JAM.) *Gall.* MACTAGGART *Encycl.* (1824).

5. Confusion, havoc.

Abd. I tint my bonnet in the howder, DAVIDSON *Poems* (1861) 100. *Lakel.*² T'frost's played howder wi' berry trees. *Wm.* 'He did play howdther wi' 'em,' said of a batsman who had just passed the score of the other side off his own bat (J.M.).

6. A blast of wind.

ne.Sc. That's a gey howder, noo. A wiss oor folk war a' weel hame again, herrin' or no herrin', *Gordonhaven* (1887) 52. *Abd.* A howder o' win'. Common (G.W.); (JAM.)

HOWDER, *v.*³ Som. Dev. Also written **houder** Dev.¹ [au'də(r).] Of the weather: to be overcast or cloudy; to look threatening. *Dev.*¹ It is houdering for rain.

Hence (1) **Howdering,** *ppl. adj.,* (2) **Howdery,** *adj.* cloudy, overcast, threatening.

(1) w.Som.¹ These yere howderin [uw·dureen] days like be good vor the turmuts, but they be bad vor the corn. *Dev.* The weather is changing. It looks howdering, *Reports Provinc.* (1884) 21. (2) **Dev.**¹

HOWDER, see Huthir.

HOWDIE, *sb.* Se. Nhb. Dur. Cum. Wm. Yks. Der. Also written **houdie** Sc. Dur.; **houdy** Sc. [h]ou'di, h]au'di.] 1. A midwife. Also in *comp.* **Howdie-wife.**

Sc. The laird's servant . . . rade express by this e'en to fetch the houdie, SCOTT *Guy M.* (1815) i. *Cai.*¹ *Elg.*¹ 'Na, na,' quo Howdie Hucks, . . . 'For my pairt, I'd prescribe a little bleedin', TESTER *Poems* (1865) 119. *Bnff.* Triformis Howdie did her skill, For the blyth-meat exert, TAYLOR *Poems* (1787) 37. *Bch.* A toothless houdy, auld and teugh, FORBES *Dominie* (1785) 99. *Abd.* Ae Sunday mornin', atween three an' four . . . gaen for the howdie wife down to the shore, ANDERSON *Rhymes* (1867) 21. *Kcd.* Aye the howdie eest to brag . . . Hoo bravely she rade through the spate, GRANT *Lays* (1884) 11. *Frf.* The howdie for a dose will keenly cry, MORISON *Poems* (1790) 191. *Per.* Assisted in her function as howdie in bringing many children into the world, HALIBURTON *Fields* (1890) 53. *Dmb.* Ne'er to sing the howdies' sang, TAYLOR *Poems* (1827) 43. *Rnf.* Three times be for his mistress flew, And brought the howdie, McGILVRAY *Poems* (ed. 1862) 246. *Ayr.* Nae howdie gets a social night, Or plack frae them, BURNS *Sc. Drink* (1786) st. 12. *Lnk.* When he brought east the houdy under night, RAMSAY *Gentle Shep.* (1725) 50, ed. 1783. *Lth.* To perform the duties and evince the peculiar skill of howdies, LUMSDEN *Sheep-head* (1892) 176. *Edb.* I ran up and down like mad for the howdie, MOIR *Mansie Wauch* (1828) viii. *Bwk.* The howdie on the auld grey mare, HENDERSON *Pop. Rhymes* (1856) 165. *Peb.* The howdy had the doctor brought, *Lintoun Green* (1685) 60, ed. 1817. *Slk.* It's unco like bringing the houdy, HOGG *Tales* (1838) 326, ed. 1866. *Rxb.* Nor cause him creash a bowdie's loof For boy or girl, A. SCOTT *Poems* (ed. 1808) 65. *Dmf.* The howdie lifts frae the beuk her ee, CROMEK *Remains* (1810) 78. *Gall.* MACTAGGART *Encycl.* (1824). *Wgt.* Bell's wife was brought to bed, when the howdie exclaimed, 'The bairnie's clepped!' FRASER *Wigtown* (1877) 153. n.Cy. The web belonged to . . . the howdie, or old village nurse, *Monthly Pkt.* (June 1862) 630; GROSE (1790); N.Cy.¹ Nhb. Aw so Jack Gorfoot galloppin by on the oad grey meer, wiv Mragery the howdy bebint him, BEWICK *Tyneside Tales* (1850) 10; Nhb.¹ s.Dur.¹ 'Thoo's niver been weshed since the howdie weshed th',' — sometimes said to a very dirty person. *Cum.* The parish howdy, Greacy Peel, ANDERSON *Ballads* (1805) 13; Her mudder was a howdy, *ib.* 75. *Wm.* (J.H.), n.Yks.¹²³ w.Yks. Yhs. *Whly. Post* (Apr. 17, 1897). *Der.*², nw.Der.¹

Hence (1) **Howdy-fee,** *sb.* the fee given to a midwife; (2) **-horse,** *sb.* a pit-horse kept on the surface for use in case of emergency; (3) **Howdying,** *sb.* confinement, childbed; (4) **-fee,** *sb.,* see (1).

(1) Dmf. I creeshed kimmer's loof weel wi' howdy fee, Else a cradle had never been rocked for me, *Blackw. Mag.* (June 1820) 277 (JAM.); MACKAY. (2) Nhb.¹ (3) Ayr. As to their howdyings, there were juist the twa kinds of them, — the ane that sent for me five meenonts owre late, and the ither ane that was hauf a day owre sune, SERVICE *Dr. Duguid* (ed. 1887) 156. (4) Dmf. I creeshed weel kimmer's loof wi' howdying fee, CROMEK *Remains* (1810) 61.

2. *Obs.* A name given to the last corf of coals drawn to the bank of a pit in any current year ; see below.

Dur. In the days when coals were brought up in corves. The houdie had numerous lighted candles stuck on it with clay, sometimes as many as 40 or 50, and this ceremony was known as ' bussing the houdie ' (A.B.).

Hence **Howdy-ma(w,** *sb.* the last corf or the last but one ; *fig.* the conclusion of the day's labour.

Nhb. Frae hingin'-on till howdy-maw, WILSON *Pitman's Pay* (1843) 29 ; Nhb.¹ The last corf. **Dur.** The last corf but one (A.B.).

[1. An appellative (like *brownie*, &c.) from *hold*, friendly, benevolent, kind ; cf. Fr. *sage-femme* (N.E.D.).]

HOWDIE, see **How-towdie.**

HOWDLE, *v.* and *sb.* Sc. Also written **houdle** Fif. (JAM.) [hou'dl, hau'dl.] **1.** *v.* To move up and down, to sway, rock ; to rock to sleep. Bnff.¹ See **Howd,** *v.*¹

2. To crowd together, swarm, to move hither and thither. Fif. (JAM.) **3.** To limp, halt, walk with a heaving, clumsy motion. Bnff.¹ Hence (1) **Howdler,** *sb.* one who walks in a limping, heaving manner ; (2) **Howdlin',** *ppl. adj.* limping, walking awkwardly.

(1) *ib.* (2) The elephant hiz a howdlin' kyne o' a step, *ib.*

4. With *about*: to carry in a clumsy manner.

Ye've nae manner o' yse in howdlin' aboot that big basket, *ib.*

5. *sb.* A swarm, a huddle, wriggling mass ; the motion of a mass of swarming creatures.

Sc. (JAM.) Fif. A howdle o' bog-showtherin' freirs, Augustines, Carm'leita, Cordeliers, TENNANT *Papistry* (1827) 203 ; The simultaneous motion of a great number of small creatures which may be compared to an anthill (JAM.).

HOWDON-PAN-CANT, *sb.* n.Cy. Nhb. Cum. An awkward fall ; an upset, overturn.

N.Cy.¹ Nhb. The world wasn't gannin sae cliver—It had gettin a Howdon-Pan cant, GILCHRIST *Sngs.* (1824) 5 ; Nhb.¹

Hence (1) **Howdon-can-Panter,** *sb.* an ungraceful rider ; (2) **-pan-canter,** *sb.* a slow, ungraceful way of riding.

(1) **Cum.** LINTON *Lake Cy.* (1864) 305. (2) **N.Cy.¹**

HOWDTHER, HOWDY-TOWDY, see **Howder,** *v.*², **How-towdie.**

HOW(E, *adj.*, *sb.*¹ and *v.*¹ Sc. Nhb. Cum. Wm. Yks. Lan. Also in forms hoo N.Cy.¹ ; hogh N.Cy.¹ Nhb.¹ ; hough Sc. (JAM.) n.Cy. Nhb.¹ w.Yks. ; houh Peb. ; howch Sc. (JAM.) ; you- Nhb.¹ [hou, h)au.] **1.** *adj.* Hollow, deep, concave. Also used *advb.* Cf. **holl, howl,** *adj.*

s.Sc. Ye cowr and howk sae howe Till art can scarce gar can'les lowe, T. SCOTT *Poems* (1793) 321. **Rnf.** I saw them reach the howe loan-head, YOUNG *Pictures* (1865) 15. **Lnk.** The wilcat yow't through its dowie vouts Sae goustie, howch and dim, *Edb. Mag.* (May 1800) (JAM.). **e.Lth.** Yon spruce-pine tap, Spearin' the howe sky, MUCKLEBACKIT *Rhymes* (1885) 31. n.Cy. (K.), Nhb.¹, Lakel.², w.Yks.¹

2. *Comb.* (1) **How(e-backed,** hollow-backed, bent in the back ; (2) **-cow,** a peat-hole ; (3) **-doup,** the medlar, *Mespilus germanica* ; (4) **-drill,** the hollow between two drills in a field ; (5) **-foor,** the track of the plough, a hollow furrow ; (6) **-gait,** a hollow or sunken way or path ; (7) **-hole,** a hollow, valley ; a depression, hole ; (8) **-house,** a dwelling below the level of the street, an area-dwelling ; (9) **-howm,** a vale, a low-lying plain ; (10) **-meal seeds,** the husks of oats ; (11) **-necked,** of animals : long and hollow in the neck ; (12) **-rush,** a hollow rush ; (13) **-seeds,** see (10) ; (14) **-way,** see (6) ; (15) **-wecht,** a circular implement of sheepskin stretched on a hoop.

(1) **Ayr.** Tho' thou's howe-backit now, an' knaggie, BURNS *To his Mare,* st. 1 ; Ye'll ne'er be howe-backit In carrying yer friens, WHITE *Jottings* (1879) 279. Nhb.¹, Lakel.² (2) w.Yks. Sticks frae t'wood or turves frae heaf how cow, *Spec. Dial.* 9. (3) Lth. (JAM.) (4, 5) Nhb.¹ (6) w.Yks.¹ (7) Sc. It's a' scabbit i' the how hole o' the neck, HISLOP *Anecdote* (1874) 124. **Bwk.** In the howe hole o' the Merse A' the folk are bannock fed, HENDERSON *Pop. Rhymes* (1856) 34. (8) Sc. She took me . . . down a dark stair to ane o' the how houses beneath the yird, GRAHAM *Writings* (1883) II. 54. (9) Dmf. I' the howe-howms o' Nith my love lives an' a', CROCKETT *Remains* (1810) 112 ; The howe-howms of Nith is a romantic vale, of near ten miles diameter, at the bottom of which stands Dumfries, *ib. note.* (10) Cum.¹ (11) Nhb.¹ A yow-neckeet horse. (12) w.Yks.¹ (13) n.Cy. GROSE (1790). Lakel.² Cum. For sale, how seeds and mill dust, very cheap, *Penrith Obs.* (Apr. 1898). Wm. (J.H.);

VOL. III.

Thaed send im ta coont t'how seeds a topat mill hill, *Spec. Dial.* (1885) pt. lii. 30. w.Yks. HUTTON *Towr to Caves* (1781). ne.Lan.¹ (14) Nhb. The old track from Newham to Bamburgh is called Newham Howe-way (R.O.H.) ; Nhb.¹ A term applied to certain ancient trackways. (15) Gall. Used about barns and mills to lift grain and such like things with, MACTAGGART *Encycl.* (1824).

3. Empty ; *fig.* hungry, famished.

Sc. This is the how and hungry hour, HERD *Coll. Sngs.* (1776) II. 198 (JAM.). Bnff.¹ A doot 's purse is growin' how by this time. The mehl-bowie's gettin' how. **Abd.** His duds o' breeks, he ca's nankeen. Are unco teem an' how, COCK *Strains* (1810) II. 129. **Fif.** Stech their how hungry stammachs fou, TENNANT *Papistry* (1827) 216. **Ayr.** His back an' wame had near han' met, He grew sae how. FISHER *Poems* (1790) 72. n.Cy. (J.L.) (1783) ; N.Cy.¹ How-i'-the-wame [hungry]. Nhb.¹ A hough belly. Lakel.² Ah've hed neea breakfast, an' Ah's as how as Ah can be for 't. **Cum.** A house luiks howe widout a weyfe, ANDERSON *Ballads* (1805) 110 ; We're aw as howe as hunters, GILPIN *Pop. Poetry* (1875) 71. **Wm.** A wes sa varra how an dry a thowt asta nivver a filt mi kyte, *Spec. Dial.* (1877) pt. i. 11.

4. Of sounds or of the voice: hollow, deep, low, guttural ; also used *advb.*

Sc. Wha ga'e you yon howe hoast ? FORD *Thistledown* (1891) 97 ; The black man's voice was hough and goustie, GLANVILLE *Sadduc.* (1726) 393 (JAM.). **Sh.I.** Oot spak the ghaist wi' a voice right howe, STEWART *Tales* (1892) 239. **Or.I.** The selkie [seal] mither gae a groan sae dismal an' how, an' sae human like, FERGUSSON *Rambles* (1884) 246. **Elg.** Howe and fearfu' grows the voice, COUPER *Poetry* (1804) I. 209. **Abd.** He was startled by a voice that spoke 'richt howe'—' Follow me,' *Deeside Tales* (1872) 182. **Ayr.** It spak right howe—' My name is Death,' BURNS *Death and Dr. Hornbook* (1785) st. 9. **Lnk.** (JAM.)

Hence **How-speaking,** *sb.* speaking in a low, deep voice, speaking like a ventriloquist. Gall. MACTAGGART *Encycl.* (1824).

5. Bleak, exposed. Lakel.¹

6. Poor, humble, mean ; dejected, in low spirits, in bad health ; *gen.* in phr. *how(e enough.* Also used *advb.*

Sc. Hough enough is often used to denote that one is in a poor state of health (JAM.). Bnff.¹ He wiz aince weel upon 't, but he's how eneuch noo. **Bnff., Abd.** Dejected, through poverty, misfortune, or failing health (JAM.). **Per.** He was bred but howe enough to a ' mean trade,' HALIBURTON *Puir Auld Sc.* (1887) 65. **Lnk.** Now when thou tells how I was bred But hough enough to a mean trade, RAMSAY *Poems* (1800) II. 581 (JAM.). **Peb.** Now I'm auld and houh, AFFLECK *Poet. Wks.* (1896) 61.

7. *sb.* A hollow, depression ; a hollow space ; a hole, abyss, depth. Also used *fig.*

ne.Sc. I hae often wisst that I had been born wi' an e'e in the howe o' my neck, MACDONALD *Sir Gibbie* (1879) xlvi. **Frf.** At the smooth-skinned end there were hichts an' howes, an' bare places whaur the banes stuck oot, WILLOCK *Rosetty Ends* (1886) 44, ed. 1889. **Per.** Smooth as the howe o' her loof or her cheek, STEWART *Character* (1857) 27. **Ayr.** Whare got ye sic a pow ? Did it . . . on your shouthers, i' the how, Light wi' a dad? FISHER *Poems* (1790) 93. **Lnk.** In the bonnie green howes of the sea, MOTHERWELL *Mermaiden* (1827). **Lth.** The ship's i' the howe o' a roarin wave, SMITH *Merry Bridal* (1866) 28. **e.Lth.** Up i' the howe o' the April sky, MUCKLEBACKIT *Rhymes* (1885) 5. **Edb.** Gang your wa's thro' hight an' how, FERGUSSON *Poems* (1773) 196, ed. 1785. **Slk.** I gat the end o' my stick just i' the howe o' his neck, HOGG *Tales* (1838) 7, ed. 1866. **Dmf.** An ill-cuisten crap in the howe o' the burn, REID *Poems* (1894) 46. **Gall.** The drifts will be sax flit in the howes o' the muir-road, CROCKETT *Bog-Myrtle* (1895) 237. Nhb.¹ The how of the neck is the hollow at the back of the neck. w.Yks.¹

8. A hollow, valley, glen ; a flat plain or tract of land.

Sc. Mony a cummer lang syne wad hae sought nae better horse to flee over hill and how, SCOTT *Bride of Lam.* (1819) xxiii. **Elg.** His snaw sleeps in the howe, COUPER *Poetry* (1804) I. 42. **Bnff.** We . . . sat down In a green howe, near by the town, TAYLOR *Poems* (1787) 62. **Abd.** There's a bonnie howie ower here below the rocks, *Deeside Tales* (1872) 173. **Kcd.** The howes were in a soom. GRANT *Lays* (1884) 2. **Frf.** A cottage in a howe between Twa verdant hills, MORISON *Poems* (1790) 117. **Per.** Lest any hicht should end in a howe, IAN MACLAREN *Brier Bush* (1895) 40. **Slg.** Ae white sheet o' milk-white flame Filled a' the fiery howe, TOWERS *Poems* (1885) 54. **Dmb.** Ye can bring water owre heights and howes, TAYLOR *Poems* (1827) 109. **Rnf.** Tho' anaw choke up

LL

baith heigh an' howe, Picken *Poems* (1813) I. 176. Ayr. At howes or hillocks never stumbled, Burns *Ep. to H. Parker* (1795) l. 25. Lnk. Gae farer up the burn to Habbie's how, Ramsay *Gentle Shep.* (1725) 27, ed. 1783. Lth. Among the hills . . . An' bonnie green howes, MᶜNeill *Preston* (c. 1895) 108. Edb. A far away cousin, that held out amang the howes of the Lammermoor hills, Moir *Mansie Wauch* (1828) xvii. Bwk. In mirksome howes, they reel'd and squall'd, Henderson *Pop. Rhymes* (1856) 55. Peb. Ilk heigh has its howe, Affleck *Poet. Wks.* (1836) 111. Slk. I ken a howe amang the hills, Chr. North *Noctes* ed. 1856) IV. 72. Rxb. Grassy howes, and fairy knowes, Murray *Hawick Sngs.* (1892) 98. Dmf. Unresting he wan'ered by hill-side an' howe, Thom *Jock o' Knowe* (1878) 1. Gall. Hughie Kerr brings it over the hill from the howe of the Kells, Crockett *Moss-Hags* (1895) xl. n.Cy. *Border Gl.* (Coll. L.L.B.); A green plot in a valley (K.); N.Cy.¹ A depression on the top of a hill ; a sloping hollow between hills. Nhb. 'Mang the ferney hows, Proudlock *Borderland Muse* (1896) 307; Nhb.¹ w.Yks. (J.W.); Willan *List Wds.* (1811) ; w.Yks.¹

9. *pl.* Phr. (1) *in the howes*, obs., out of spirits, depressed, 'in the dumps'; (2) *to cast* or *ding in the hows*, obs., to overturn, upset an arrangement, plan, &c., to render unavailing.

(1) Sc. Sair did my heart fa' in the hows, Pennecuik *Coll.* (1787) 13. Cld. (Jam.) Ayr. I'm i' the hows, To die an' be laid i' the till, Indeed's nae mows, Fisher *Poems* (1790) 63. (2) Sc. The great law business, for which I came south, . . was at once casten in the hows, Wodrow *Sel. Biog.* (1847) II. 195 ; Thomas Goodwin and his brethren . . . carried it so, that all was dung in the howes, Baillie *Lett.* (1775) II. 59 (Jam.).

10. A curling term : the path or run of the stone to the tee.

Sc. By turning his little finger 'out' . . . Sandy's stone made its passage down the 'howe,' Tweeddale *Moff* (1896) 159; The skip could never see till now The pace the stanes came up the howe, Caled. Curling Club *Ann.* (1893–94) 115. Lnk. The soopers are ready To keep baith the howe an' the head ice in trim, Watson *Poems* (1853) 72.

11. The depth or middle (of the night, &c.), mid-time.

Sc. How o' the year (Jam.) Abd. Aft-times at dreary howe o' nicht, In thought I'm daunderin' by thy side, Shelley *Flowers* (1868) 158. Fif. How o' winter, from November to January (Jam.). Ayr. In the dead howe o' winter, Ainslie *Land of Burns* (ed. 1892) 126. Slk. Ye ken fu' weel, gudeman, ye coortit me i' the howe of the night yoursel, Hogg *Tales* (1838) 3, ed. 1866. Rxb. How o' the night, how o' winter (Jam.). Gall. At the roaring linn in the howe o' the night, Nicholson *Hist. Tales* (1843) 84. n.Cy. (J.W.)

Hence (1) **How-doup**, *sb.* the depth or worst part of winter ; (2) **-dumb-dead**, *sb.* the depth, middle ; (3) **-night**, *sb.* the dead of night.

(1) Cum. Linen, 'At keep'd her feckly thro' th' how doup, Gilpin *Ballads* (1866) 240 ; Cum.² 181. (2) Ayr. That's no a guid bed for a sick body in the how-dumb-dead o' a caul' ha'rst night, *Blackw. Mag.* (Nov. 1820) 202 (Jam.). (3) Rxb. (Jam.), Cum.¹

12. Reduction, diminution. Abd. (Jam.) **13.** *v.* To reduce, to drain, thin, to diminish in number or quantity. *ib.*

HOW(E, *sb.²* and *v.²* Sc. Irel. Nhb. Lakel. Yks. Shr. Glo. Brks. Nrf. [(h)ou, h)au.] Dial. form of hoe.

Sc. O' howin the gairden, Swan *Aldersyde* (ed. 1892) 60. Sh.I. Hid wid set dee better ta be furt howin' a bit o' da taties, *Sh. News* (June 19, 1897). Cai.¹ Rnf. Howe, or rake, or delve the soil, Picken *Poems* (1813) II. 41. Wgt. Can ye now whuns f Fraser *Wigtown* (1877) 295. Wxf.¹ n.Cy. Grose (1790). Nhb.¹, Lakel.², Cum.⁴ n.Yks. How that land wi't shuv how (I.W.). e.Yks.¹, w.Yks. (J.W.) Shr.¹ Some like sowin', some like mowin'; But of all the games that I do like, Is the game of turmit-owin', *Local Doggerel Verse.* Glo. I cuddn't bee to how, Buckman *Darke's Sojourn* (1890) xiii. Brks. (W.W.S.) Nrf. Cozens-Hardy *Broad Nrf.* (1893) 35. [Ray (1691).]

Hence **Hower**, *sb.* a hoe.

Glo. I tuck up my turmut hower, Gibbs *Cotswold Vill.* (ed. 1899) 97.

HOW(E, see Ho, *v.,* Haw, *sb.¹*

HOWELLED, *ppl. adj.* Lin. Splashed, dirtied, muddy; of the weather : wet, dirty, unpleasant. Cf. howery.

Lin.¹ sw.Lin.¹ See how howell'd they look.

HOWEN, see Hew, *v.¹*

HOWERY, *adj.* Lin. Also in forms howerly n.Lin.¹; howry, oury sw.Lin.¹; owery s.Lin.; owrie Lin. [ou'(ə)ri.]

Muddy, dirty, filthy ; foul, indecent ; of the weather : wet, damp, 'soft.' Cf. howelled ; see Horry, *adj.*

How when it came a 'howery' daay and 'teemed and siled' wi' raāin, Brown *Lit. Laur.* (1890) 64 ; Very common (J.C.W.); Lin.¹ The weather is cazzelty and howery. n.Lin. Sutton *Wds.* (1881) ; n.Lin.¹ I'd a real howerly jo'ney to Gaainsb'r, it raain'd all th' waay theāre an' by ageān. If ye' talk e' that howerly waay when we're gettin' wer vittles, I weānt gie the noān. s.Lin. This is what I call a howery soort of a daā (T.H.R.). sw.Lin.¹ She's the howriest woman as ever I seed. It's oury work this wet weather.

HOWES, *sb. pl.* Suf. [Not known to our correspondents.] The time of oats coming into ear.

Rainbird *Agric.* (1819) 295, ed. 1849.

HOWEVER, *adv.* Var. dial. forms and uses in Eng.

I. Dial. forms : (1) Arver, (2) Awever, (3) Awiver, (4) Awivver, (5) Hahivver, (6) Harver, (7) Havver, (8) Hawivver, (9) Heawever, (10) Hoolver, (11) Hoviver, (12) Howivver, (13) H'wevr, (14) Oavver, (15) Wuvver. [For further instances see **II.** below.]

(1) Lin. (W.W.S.) (2) Oxf.¹ (3) n.Yks. Awiver A wetid til A was tired (W.H.). w.Yks. (J.W.), n.Lin.¹ (4) Cum.¹ (5) w.Yks. Hahivver mich we addled, Cudworth *Dial. Sketches* (1884) 1. (6) s.Lin. Harver I will, now I come to think about (T.H.R.). (7) Havver I'll do it this once (*ib.*). (8) Wm. We er somat maar merciful hawivver, Hutton *Bran New Wark* (1785) l. 272. Yks. Ha-wivver, ah will deeah mi best, *Spec. Dial.* 32. e.Yks. Hawivver he went on graping aboot, Nicholson *Flk-Sp.* (1889) 36. (9) Lan. Aw'll goo an' see heawever, Brierley *Layrock* (1864) v. (10) Nhb. I'se not that black hooiver, Clark *Love of Lass* (1890) I. 20. Cum. Hooiver it disn't maffer much, Mary Drayson (1872) 17. n.Yks. (W.H.) (11) ne.Lan.¹ (12 Wm. Howivver that lad a Tomson's, Robison *Aald Tales* (1882) 3. n.Yks. Howivver scant ther meeals may be, Tweeddell *Clevel. Rhymes* (1875) 8. (13) s.War. *Why John* (Coll. L.L.B.). (14) w.Yks. Oavver, were quoite sure, Bywater *Gossips* (1851) 1. (15) Cum.¹

II. Dial. uses. **1.** Used as an emphatic expletive: indeed, in fact, truly. *Gen.* used to end a sentence.

Cum. I will—however I will. He's mad' a fin' mess o' that job, however (J.Ar.); Cum.¹ w.Cum. 'What a windy night!' 'It is however' (S.K.C.). w.Yks. Ah thowt ta may'r sen 'thoo's a feal ' hooiver, Lucas *Stud. Nidderdale* (c. 1882) Gl. ; Becos. if thah weeant believe the awn eyes, thah't a rattler, oavver, *Shevvild Ann.* (1851) 20. n.Lin.¹ Well, awiver, I niver seed sich a sight e' all my born daays. Woy, herse, woy, herse, awiver, herse, thoo'll be tired afoore ta gets hairf a mile, herse. Nhp. It is not a bad crap, it is a good one, however (P.G.D.). s.Wor. I'd like to have been in the river, however (H.K.) ; s.Wor.¹, Hrf.² Glo. 'T be a-smoking still—was doing as I comed by, however, Gissing *Vill. Hampden* (1890) I. vi ; Glo.¹

2. At least, at any rate ; anyhow, in any case.

n.Cy. (J.W.) s.War. H'wevr 'ur tell'd me, *Why John* (Coll. L.L.B.). s.Wor. You have some nice plants, however, Porson *Quaint Wds.* (1875) 8 ; s.Wor.¹, Hrf.² Glo. He don't seem a bad man, not by appearance however, Gissing *Vill. Hampden* (1890) I. i.

HOWF, *sb.* Rxb. (Jam.) A severe blow on the ear given with a circular motion of the arm.

HOWF, see Hough, *sb.¹*

HOWF(F, *sb.* and *v.* Sc. n.Cy. Nhb. Yks. Also written houf(f Sc. n.Cy. ; and in forms hauf Gall. ; hofe n.Yks.¹ ne.Yks.¹; hoff n.Yks.²; houck Bnff.¹ [(h)ouf, h)auf, of.] **1.** *sb.* A place of resort, a meeting-place ; a haunt, resort ; a much-frequented tavern.

Sc. He'll no likely gang back to ony o' his auld howffs, Scott *Midlothian* (1818) xvi ; Just by way o' takin' a freendly glass in her canny howff, *Sc. Haggis*, 123. Elg. Through a' their weelken'd houffs and haunts they prance wi' muckle glee, Couper *Poetry* (1804) I. 184. Bnff.¹ He keeps a sad houck at the still. Abd. In Charlie's bit howff a' the laddies wad meet, Anderson *Rhymes* (1867) 10. Frf. To ransack every houff, Beattie *Much Ado, &c.* (c. 1820). Per. They'll reach the howff by fa' o' nicht, Haliburton *Ochil Idylls* (1891) 22. w.Sc. To this howf, then known as the 'Race Horse,' the trusty agent proceeded, Carrick *Laird of Logan* (1835) 49. Fif. Thir twa bangsters . . . row'd the surge o' weir Aff frae the Papish houffs, Tennant *Papistry* (1827) 171. Slg. I hous'd him in a houf, Galloway *Sutor's Mag.* (1810) 16. Dmb. Weir's scant houf, as cute if no sae braw, Salmon *Gowodean* (1868) 68. Rnf. He . . . challeng'd a' the beagle tribe Gif they his howffs cou'd learn him, Clark *Rhymes* (1842) 31. Ayr. The oury rafters of an auld bigging ... a perfect howf of cloks and biders, GALT *Gilhaize* (1823) xvi. **Lnk.** Drink-howffs raise in ilka ne, NICHOLSON *Kilwuddie* (ed. 1895) 58. **Lth.** The howffs whaur ' thae arts grew great, BALLANTINE *Poems* (1856) 11. **Edb.** And andering about all my old haunts and houffs, MOIR *Mansie Wauch* (1828) xxviii. **Peb.** Wha's best aff we'll soon See, whan t' our owfs we murch, *Lintoun Green* (1685) 64, ed. 1817. **Slk.** The orby left her howf in the rock, HOGG *Poems* (ed. 1865) 35. **Gall.** hat's a graund hauf o' smugglers and gypsies, CROCKETT *Raiders* 1894) xvii. **Wgt.** (S.R.C.) **n.Cy.** *Border Gl.* (*Coll.* L.L.B.) bb.[1], n.Yks.[1]

Hence **Houffie**, *adj.* snug, comfortable. **Rxb.** (JAM.)
2. An abode, residence ; a stay or residence at a place ; shelter.
Bnff.[1] A continued stay in one place in idleness. **Slg.** Housed howff in cold December, While her children cry for bread, OWERS *Poems* (1885) 129. **s.Sc.** A' the wandering. houseless an Got aye some howf at Little Billy, WATSON *Bards* (1859) 9. **yr.** Mony a gallant family, Sin' my last howff was here By rtune's fell and fickle blasts Been scattered far an' near, AINSLIE *Land of Burns* (ed. 1892) 100. **Lth.** Wearily he socht afar Some ary howff to pass the nicht, SMITH *Merry Bridal* (1866) 82. Yks.[12] an.Yks.[1] Whether of man or beast, esp. sheep.
3. A cemetery or burial-place.
Abd. A private mausoleum or walled-in burial-place (A.W.). rf. A cemetery in Dundee, now disused, goes by this name ecause it formerly served as the merchants' exchange (H.L.L.) ; JAM., s.v. Hoif).
4. *v.* To haunt, frequent ; to lodge, abide, live ; to take helter. Also with *about*.
Sc. The hopes and fears that houff the springtime o' our years, WILSON *Poems* (1822) *To the Reader*. **Bnff.[1]** The drunken swab oucks on in the public-hoose. He's a sweer filsch o' a cheel, or nan he wid . . . nae houck-aboot at hame is he diz. **Kcd.** He's ome to howff in my kailyard, Or scramble up a tree, GRANT *Lays* 1884) 14. **s.Sc.** She had nei'rly flung the sportsmen a', An' owffed i' the howdie's biggin', WATSON *Bards* (1859) 110. **Ayr.** Ve hoist our creels, tak' to our heels, An' howff where less they en us, AINSLIE *Land of Burns* (ed. 1892) 251. **Lth.** There was a ttle tailor . . . Houf'd wi' auld Eppie Johnstone, M°NEILL *Preston* . 1895) 112. **Rxb.** He drave doun the maukins to howff mang ne whins, RIDDELL *Poet. Wks.* (ed. 1871) II. 20. **n.Yks.[12]**

Hence **Houckin'-aboot**, *ppl. adj.* lazy, idle, lounging about.
Bnff.[1] He's a houckin'-aboot cheel, that ; he niver diz ony thing t a'.
5. To lodge, house, cause to live ; to shelter ; to accustom sheep to a pasture.
Sc. Yont our hallan he's houft till the gurl gaed past, EDWARDS *Modern Poets*, 1st S. 325 ; 'Where did you gae'f' ' I was houff'd' (JAM.). **Lnk.** Oor auld grey smiddy ... Is howff'd a mile ayont the len, MURDOCH *Doric Lyre* (1873) 25. **n.Yks.[1]** **ne.Yks.[1]** Sheep, ssigned to a pasture on the moors, were said to be ' hoofed ' to it.
6. *Fig.* With *up* : to bury.
Sc. The Bedral, who houfs up the best in the land, VEDDER *Poems* (1842) 79.

HOWFFIN, *sb.* Sc. Also written **howfin** (JAM.). A lumsy, foolish person.
Abd. That aul' greedy, sneeshinie howffin, ALEXANDER *Johnny Gibb* (1871) xii ; He's a sweir howffin ; that's fat he is, *ib. Ain Flk.* 1882) 94.
[My new spanit howffing (v.r. howphin) fra the sowk, DUNBAR *Poems* (c. 1510), ed. Small, II. 248.]

HOWGATES, *adv.* Yks. Lin. [ū'gəts.] In what manner, how.
Yks. She'd tell you both how-gates it were, and when it were, ELLIS *Pronunc.* (1889) V. 508. **m.Yks.[1]** ' Howgates did he go !' He took the old yau'd ' [horse]. **Lin.** SKINNER (1671).
[Howgates? *quomodo* ? LEVINS *Manip.* (1570) ; Howe-gates bought schall he be, *York Plays* (c. 1400) 229.]

HOWGY, *adj.* War. Wor. Shr. Hrf. Glo. Sus. Also written **hoogy** War.[2] ; **houghy** Sus. ; **hougy** s.Wor. ; ougy Hrf. [ū'dgi.] 1. Huge, large, bulky ; great. Cf. augy.
War.[2] These are 'ougy boots. **s.Wor.** PORSON *Quaint Wds.* 1875) 13. **Shr.[1]** 'E fat a great 'owgy stwun an' pūt agen the gate. Hrf. The yungest son hizzelf—a big oujy boy o' nin, *Why John Coll.* L.L.B.) ; Hrf.[1] ; Hrf.[2] Did you ever see such howgy great tones the flood did bring down ! Glo.[1] **Sus.** We met sich houghy ight-ov folks, LOWER *Tom Cladpole* (1831) st. 79.

2. *Fig.* Great, valuable, rich.
Shr.[1] An old man at Clun said that the living of the place was not very 'owgy.
3. Intimate, friendly, ' thick.'
War.[2] Wor. They be very howgy together, very close friends (sometimes desperate folks) (H.K.) ; William Grubb an me, us wuz allus despret folks an' howgy, OUTIS *Vig. Mon., Berrow's Jrn.* (1896) ; He be very hougy along of so-and-so (R.M.E.). **Shr.[1]** They bin gotten mighty 'owgy.

HOW-HOW, *sb.* Nhb. A charwoman ; an untidy, slovenly woman. (R.O.H.), Nhb.[1]

HOWICK, *sb.* Sc. A small rick. Bnff., Abd. MORTON *Cyclo. Agric.* (1863).

HOWIE, see How, *sb.*[1]

HOWIN, *sb.* Yks. [Not known to our other correspondents.] A turn, occasion, time, ' doing.'
w.Yks. A man who had had the influenza twice said he 'didn't want a third howin'.' Gi' me as many on 'em as you can at one howin' (S.O.A.).

HOWISH, *adj.* Lin. Having a vague sense of indisposition ; out of sorts.
e.Lin. I've had some tea for I felt a bit owish (probably ' not knowing how I felt ') (G.G.W.). [(She) feels, as she says, quite howish and vapourish, *Minor* (1787) 39 (N.E.D.).]

HOWK, *v.*[1] and *sb.* Sc. Irel. Nhb. Dur. Cum. Wm. Yks. Lan. Lin. Nhp. Oxf. Brks. Sus. Wil. Also in forms **hoak** Wgt. s.Don. Nhb.[1] ; **hoke** Sc. N.I.[1] s.Don. ; **hok(k** Sh.I. ; **hook** Per. Wil. ; **houk** Sc. Cai.[1] ; **oke** n.Yks. ; *pret.* **huck** Nhb.[1] [h)ouk, h)auk.] 1. *v.* To hollow out by digging ; to excavate, dig out or up ; to burrow, scratch up earth, grub. Also with *out* and *up*.
Sc. Folks say this place was howkit out by the monks langsyne, SCOTT *Antiquary* (1816) xxi. **Sh.I.** Wi pick and shŭl hok for his bread, BURGESS *Rasmie* (1892) 92 ; William hokid oot o' his pipe, shŭ wis dat wye furr'd up, *Sh. News* (Sept. 17, 1898). Cai.[1], **Mry.** (JAM.) **Bnff.** Whare some o' his gear he'll howk, I canna tell, TAYLOR *Poems* (1787) 11. **Bch.** He howk'd the gou'd which he himself Had yerded in his tent, FORBES *Ajax* (1742) 7. **Abd.** In a hole howkit oot o' a green foggy brae, ANDERSON *Rhymes* (1867) 35. **Frf.** She would howk them up as quick as I could plant them, BARRIE *Minister* (1891) xxv. **Per.** When wi' shools they hookit for't, Darkness cam' on, HALIBURTON *Horace* (1886) 79. **Fif.** Tam . . . wi' a set o' gowffin' sticks . . . howkin' for the lost ba's, M°LAREN *Tibbie* (1894) 80. **Slg.** Howk the sweet earth-nuts on Dorrator braes, TOWERS *Poems* (1885) 145. **Rnf.** He, weary, winds his road, an' slaw, To howk them out frae 'mang the snaw, PICKEN *Poems* (1813) I. 76. **Ayr.** Whyles mice and moudiewarts they howkit, BURNS *Twa Dogs* (1786) l. 40 ; (F.J.C.) **Lnk.** She howks unchristen'd weans out of their graves, RAMSAY *Gentle Shep.* (1725) 47, ed. 1783. **Lth.** To get folk to howk holes in their ain plots to fill their pats, STRATHESK *More Bits* (ed. 1885) 147. **Edb.** Howking up the bodies from their damp graves, MOIR *Mansie Wauch* (1828) x. **Bwk.** Out o' their graves, below the stanes They houkit skulls, wi' grievous granes, HENDERSON *Pop. Rhymes* (1856) 57. **Slk.** A vultur rug-ruggin—gnaw-gnawin . . . howk-howkin at his miserable liver, CHR. NORTH *Noctes* (ed. 1856) III. 146. **Dmf.** Twa-three men cam' here, Syne howkit a hole and hid the deid, REID *Poems* (1894) 88. **Rxb.** So they houkit a pint o' worms, and biled them in fresh water, HENDERSON *Flk-Lore* (1879) v. **Gall.** We'll howk holes in the sand, CROCKETT *Cleg Kelly* (1896) 87. **Kcb.** She howks the gutters huntin' preens, ARMSTRONG *Ingleside* (1890) 142. **Wgt.** She ... hoakit awa' the boards wi' her nose, FRASER *Wigtown* (1877) 364. **n.Ir.** He was pickin' an' hokin there still, *Lays and Leg.* (1884) 91. **N.I.[1]** To hollow out anything, such as a toy boat. A dog hokes out the earth from a rabbit hole. **Ant.** You hoke a hole by picking or digging it out roughly. Pigs hoke the ground with their noses, *Ballymena Obs.* (1892). **s.Don.** SIMMONS *Gl.* (1890). **n.Cy.** GROSE (1790) ; N.Cy.[1] To make a hole in the earth in a bungling way. **Nhb.** For gowld ye may howk till ye're blind as a bat, MIDFORD *Coll. Sngs.* (1818) 68 ; Nhb.[1] If ye howk mair anunder't ye'll fetch the waal doon. He huck up the rose bush. Nhb., Dur. NICHOLSON *Coal Tr. Gl.* (1888). **e.Dur.[1]** He's howked all the flowers up. **s.Dur.** He's howken' stanes out o't dyke (J.E.D.). **Lakel.[12]** **Cum.** He's howkin' mawks oot o' a deed dŏg (E.W.P.) ; Where Geordie Girdwood many a lee-lang day, Howkit for gentles' banes the humblest clay, WILLIAMSON *Local Etym.* (1849) 110 ; T'aud man's off howkin' taties (J.Ar.) ; Cum.[1] **Wm.** An things howked oot o' cairns, WHITEHEAD *Leg.* (1859) 43. **s.Wm.** A big potato pie was put on the table, and the

L l 2

host said to the guest, 'Now then, help yersel'; howk in!' (J.A.B.) **n.Yks.**[124] **w.Yks.** WILLAN *List Wds.* (1811). **Lan.** Howk, hack, and dig spade, ROBY *Trad.* (1829) II. 121, ed. 1872. **n.Lin.**[1], **Sus.**[1] s.Wll. 'To hook taters,' to hoe potatoes (G.E.D.).

Hence (1) **Howked,** *ppl. adj.* hollowed out, excavated, dug out; unearthed; (2) **Howker,** *sb.* a digger; (3) **Howking,** (*a*) *vbl. sb.* the act of digging or burrowing; an excavation, mining; (*b*) *prp.* digging, burrowing; (4) **Howky,** *sb.* a pitman, miner.

(1) **Ayr.** Let warlocks grim, an' wither'd hags, .. in kirk-yards renew their leagues, Owre howkit dead, BURNS *Address to Deil* (1785) st. 9. **Lth.** Certain opprobrious epithets, such as 'Howkit-out mowdies,' STRATHESK *More Bits* (ed. 1885) 253. **Rxb.** An' no like boss houk'd gutless hills i' Lowden, A. SCOTT *Poems* (ed. 1808) 34. **Gall.** Roomy howket graves, MACTAGGART *Encycl.* (1824) 334, ed. 1876. **Cum.** Here in this newly howked grave, STAGG *Misc. Poems* (ed. 1807) 81. (*a*) **Ayr.** There was a wheen tattie howkers in a field, SERVICE *Notandums* (1890) 43. **Peb.** Mean howkers in a ditch, AFFLECK *Poet. Wks.* (1836) 68. (3, 4) **Sc.** His houkings and minings for lead and copper, SCOTT *Antiquary* (1816) xii. **Abd.** It's a michty howkin! MACDONALD *Malcolm* (1875) II. 133. **Per.** Thank Heaven! his howkin' cam' to nocht, HALIBURTON *Ochil Idylls* (1891) 149. **Fif.** Strivin' wi' howkin' and wi' diggin', TENNANT *Papistry* (1827) 191. **Lnk.** The nooks where arnits are to be had for the howking, WATSON *Poems* (1853) *Pref.* 11. **Slk.** Slacks will be sleek, a hogg for the howking, HOGG *Tales* (1838) 141, ed. 1866. **Nhb.** Then he and she to howkin fell, DONALDSON *Poems* 1809) 176. (*b*) **Per.** Ye've seen a boar by moonlight snoukin', Pounce on a moudy-wort thrang houkin, SPENCE *Poems* (1898) 197. (4) **Nhb.** Before two hours had passed the 'Howkies' occupied Morpeth in overwhelming force. Some of the burghers of that town have contemptuously invented for them the nickname of 'Howkies,' which the miners have accepted with a certain grim dignity, *Dy. News* (Sept. 30, 1872); Though Tommy's a Howkie, he'll show them he can Discuss wi' the wisest, behave like a man, ELLIOTT *Pitman gans te Parliamint*; **Nhb.**[1]

2. To pull or draw out; to pull up by the roots; to clear, disentangle; to lift or push violently. *Gen.* with *out*.

Peb. Frae her pouch a crown she houkit, AFFLECK *Poet. Wks.* (1836) 132. **n.Yks.**[4] He gat at t'back o' ma an' howk'd ma inti t'carridge afoor Ah' ken'd wheear Ah war. **n.Lan.**[1] **n.Lin.**[1] If I was him I should hev them ketlocks howk'd oot o' yon barley. **Nhp.**[2] Howk it out. **Oxf.** He howked it out in a second [said of a tooth] (W.B.T.). **Sus.** To howk out a ditch or hedge (E.E.S.). **Wil.** I howked 'em out as fast as I could bait and put in [said of fish] (W.B.T.).

3. *Fig.* To rummage, to look through for the purpose of finding something, to hunt up, root out.

Sh.I. He's aye houkin among yon aald prophecies, BURGESS *Sketches* (2nd ed.) 10. **Frf.** You can howk ony mortal thing out o' the original Hebrew, BARRIE *Minister* (1891) x. **Per.** It's a peetifu' job howking thro' the Bible for ill words tae misca yir fouk wi', IAN MACLAREN *Brier Bush* (1895) 75. **Ayr.** Ye will ne'er howk a quarrel oot o' Sawney McGraw, AITKEN *Lays Line* (1883) 63. **Lnk.** When mem'ry houks auld stories up, THOMSON *Musings* (1881) 179. **e.Lth.** He was . . . howkin' his harns for a sermon, HUNTER *J. Inwick* (1895) 44. **Gall.** He was howkin' up in the garret twa afternoons last week, CROCKETT *Stickit Min.* (1893) 101. **Lakel.**[2] Howken aboot for owt he can git.

Hence **Howking,** *vbl. sb.* the act of sounding or 'pumping' any one.

Ayr. There was owre muckle of the howking and speering at me on the roadsides, SERVICE *Dr. Duguid* (ed. 1887) 122.

4. To punish. **Cum.**[1]

Hence **Howking,** *vbl. sb.* punishment, a beating, thrashing. **Nhb.** (H.M.) **Cum.**[4] Aal ge thee a howkin, as lay.

5. *Comp.* (1) **Howk-back,** a bent back; a hump back; cf. **how(e-backit,** s.v. How(e, *adj.*; (2) **-backit,** having a bent back, hump-backed; (3) **-chowk,** to make a noise as if poking among decayed mud. Bnff.[1]

6. *sb.* The act of digging, an excavation; an indentation; a dint, blow.

Sc. (JAM.) **Keb.** The chirp O' wand'ring mouse or moudy's carkin hoke, DAVIDSON *Seasons* (1789) 62. **s.Don.** Indentations made in the head of one pegging top by the spike of another, SIMMONS *Gl.* (1890). **Nhb.** He gat a howk i' the guts (R.O.H.); **Nhb.**[1] 'What a howk they've myed there.' Also used for the dint or impression

caused by a heavy blow. **Cum.** The Howk is a water-fall in a narrow gill, or dell, HUTCHINSON *Hist. Cum.* (1794) II. 388.

[1. 3onder wther sum the new havin holkis, DOUGLAS *Eneados* (1513), ed. 1874, 11. 45; To holke, *palare,* Cath. Angl. (1483). EFris. *holken,* 'hohlmachen' (KOOLMAN); cp. Sw. *hålka,* to make hollow (WIDEGREN).]

HOWK, *v.*[2] Stf. War. Wor. Glo. Also in form **yowk**. To howl. NORTHALL *Flk. Phr.* (1896).

HOWK, *int.* m.Yks.[1] An exclamation used to attract the attention of horses running loose in a field. Hence **Howky,** *sb.* a pet name for a horse.

HOWK, see **Hawk,** *v.*[1], *sb.*[2]

HOWKAN, *ppl. adj.* Sh.I. Cum. Also in form **hokken** Sh.I. Large, great, 'hulking'; freq. used as a term of contempt.

Sh.I. Da muckle sheeld swall yon useless hokken hund o' dine, *Sh. News* (May 29, 1897); Yon hokken lipper o' a dug o' Arty's is begun to sloom aboot da doors agen, *ib.* (Aug. 20, 1898). **Cum.**[4] It's a howkan lee.

HOWKER, *sb.* Cum.[14] Anything large or great, a 'whopper.'

HOWKES! HOWSHE! *phr.* w.Som.[1] An exclamation used in driving pigs.

Usually in connection with 'Turr!' Tuuru! aew·ks! tuur! aew·shu!

HOWKY, *adj.* Nhp.[1] Husky, chaffy. See **Hulk,** *sb.*[1] 8. When the outer skin or integument of corn, called the chaff, adheres to the grain after it is winnowed and dressed for market, it is said to be howky.

HOWL, *adj.* and *sb.* Nhb. Dur. Yks. Lan. Chs. Lin. Also written **howle** Lan.[1] Chs.[18] n.Lin.; and in form **houl** n.Yks.[14] w.Yks.[1] [h)oul, h)aul.] **1.** *adj.* Hollow, deep; empty, hungry. Cf. **holl, how(e,** *adj.*

N.Cy.[1], **Nhb.** (W.G.), **Nhb.**[1] **Dur.** GIBSON *Up-Weardale Gl.* (1870). **s.Dur.** As howl as a hunter (J.E.D.). **n.Yks.** That coo leuks varra howl, sha must hev had next ta nowt to yeat (W.H.); And lse seay howl, I knaw nut what to deau, MERITON *Praise Ale* (1684) l. 214. **w.Yks.**[1] A howl dish. **Lan.** 'He must be varra howle when he's hungry.' .. 'Howle! why he'll be like a two-legged drum, about t'middle o' t'forenoon,' WAUGH *Jannock* (1874) iv; **Lan.**[1], **Chs.**[18]

Hence (1) **Howl-hamper,** (2) **-kealop,** (3) **-kite,** *sb.* an empty stomach.

(1) **m.Yks.**[1] **w.Yks.**[1] They cadged ther houl-hampers, ii. 300. (2) **N.Cy.**[1], **Nhb.**[1] (3) **N.Cy.**[1] **Nhb.** Very oft wi' howl kites and torn duds, MIDFORD *Coll. Sngs.* (1818) 15.

2. *sb.* A hollow, a depression in the surface of the ground.

Elg. He's passed thro' death's dark valley's howl, TESTER *Poems* (1865) 95. **N.Cy.**[1] Wherever there's a hill, ther's sure to be a howl. **n.Yks.**[1] Of no great lateral extent or length; scarcely amounting to a valley, and not rugged or precipitous like a gill; **n.Yks.**[2]; **n.Yks.**[4] Varying in length but never extensive.

3. A tunnel or culvert under a road or bank.

Lin. A wooden trunk or tunnel under a bank or road used for conveying water. [In] a bill dated 1809 occur . . . 'Crooks and bands for an howl, 2*s.* 6*d.*,' *N. & Q.* (1881) 6th S. iv. 493. **n.Lin.** He would . . . then hide his sen a bit in a clew or a howll, PEACOCK *R. Skirlaugh* (1870) II. 87.

4. The middle or depth of anything. Also used *attrib.*

N.Cy.[1] The howl quarter of the year. **Nhb.** Aw was up at the Mistrisses, .. ith th' howl oh wounter, BEWICK *Tyneside Tales* (1850) 9; **Nhb.**[1] Howl-o'-wounter. **n.Yks.**[4], w.Yks.[1]

HOWL, *v.* Nrf. In phr. *to howl along on the wind,* to be 'in the wind,' to be rumoured.

You've heard what's howlin' along on the wind... I would rather he had been the first to tell us, GIBBON *Beyond Compare* (1888) l. vi.

HOWLD(ED, see **Hold,** *v.*

HOWLER, *sb.* Yks. Lan. Chs. Lin. Also in form **owler** Yks. Lan. Chs.[1] The same word as **Aller,** *sb.*[1](q.v.) **Yks., Lan.** To send a boy 'nutting among the howlers,' is to put him on a fool's task, *N. & Q.* (1852) 1st S. v. 250. **Chs.**[1], nw.Lin. (B. & H.)

HOWLER, *v.* Chs.[1] s.Chs.[1] Also written **owler** s.Chs.[1] [au·lə(r).] To howl; to shout out, hollo.

HOWLERS, *sb. pl.* Sus. Boys who go round 'howling' or wassailing orchards. See **Howling,** *vbl. sb.* **Sus.**[1] Now nearly *obs.* On the eve of the Epiphany, the howlers went to the orchards, and there encircling one of the best bearing trees, drank the following toast, ' Here's to the, old apple tree, May'st thou bud, may'st thou blow, May'st thou bear apples enow! Hats full! Caps full! Bushel, bushel, sacks full! And my pockets full, too! Huzza!' *Sus.*⁶ On New-year's eve.

HOWLET, *sb.* and *v.* Sc. Nhb. Dur. Cum. Wm. Yks. Lan. Chs. Stf. Der. Not. Lin. Nhp. Wor. Shr. Hrf. Sus. Som. Also written howlat(e, howlit Sc. ; and in forms hewlet Dur.¹ Cum. n.Yks.² ; hiulet Lakel.² ; hoolet Sc. Nhb.¹ Cum.¹ Not. Nhp.² Hrf.¹² ; hoolit Sc. ; houlat Sc. w.Yks. ; houlet, houlit Sc. ; hulert Cum.¹ ; hulet n.Cy. Wm. e.Yks. ; hull- ne.Lan.¹ ; hullart m.Yks.¹ Chs.¹²² nw.Der.¹ Som. (HALL.) ; hullat Or.I. w.Yks.¹ n.Lan.¹ ; hullert Cum. ; hullet n.Cy. Lakel.¹ Cum.¹ Wm. w.Yks.¹⁴ Lan.¹ m.Lan.¹ n.Lin.¹ Lin.¹ ; hullot w.Yks.⁶ Chs.¹²³ ; hulote Or.I. ; oolat Hrf.² ; oolert Shr.¹ ; oulud w.Wor.¹ ; owlard Shr.¹ ; owlert Chs.¹² ; owlet s.Stf. Sus.¹ ; owlud se.Wor.¹ ; ullard Chs.¹ ; ullat w.Yks.² Der.² ; ullert Lan.¹ Chs.¹² ; ullet(t w.Yks. Lan.¹ Chs.¹² ; ullot w.Yks. e.Lan.¹ ; ulyet Lan. [h)ū·lət, h)u·lət.] 1. *sb.* An owl, an owlet.

Sc. I hae sat mony a time to hear the howlit crying out of the ivy tod, SCOTT *Antiquary* (1816) xxi ; Loud rair'd the wind frae rock to cave, Sad yowts the howlate ga'e, JAMIESON *Pop. Ballads* (1806) I. 24t. Or.I. SWAINSON *Birds* (1885) 125. **Elg.** The howlet howls within, COUPER *Poetry* (1804) II. 91. **Frf.** It's now forhow't And left the houlat's prey, LOWSON *Guidfollow* (1890) 238. **Per.** A curran hoolets wi' their muckle blinkin' e'en, CLELAND *Inchbracken* (1883) 203, ed. 1887. **Dmb.** It's no the hawk which dis thee fright, Or howlet in the dead o' night, TAYLOR *Poems* (1827) 67. **Rnf.** Rab lookit as blear't as a houlit When tryin' to glour at the sun, BARR *Poems* (1861) 89. **Ayr.** Ravens and howlets are the only singing-birds she can bide to hearken to, GALT *Sir A. Wylie* (1822) xlvii ; (F.J.C.) **Lnk.** Howlet-like, my e'e-lids steek, RODGER *Poems* (1838) 5, ed. 1897. **Lth.** The houlets gie me a' the latest news, SMITH *Merry Bridal* (1866) 54. **Edb.** The howlet screamt, LEARMONT *Poems* (1791) 12. **Bwk.** The wak'nin' hoolets cam' doon, CHISHOLM *Poems* (1879) 19. **Peb.** Ye howlets, herons, come and see, AFFLECK *Poet. Wks.* (1836) 62. **Slk.** We huntyd the hoolet out of brethe, HOGG *Poems* (ed. 1865) 13. **Rxb.** Hoolets houted then guid-bye, RIDDELL, *Poet. Wks.* (ed. 1871) I. 173. **Dmf.** Gleds and hoolits work their will, REID *Poems* (1894) 179. **Gall.** There sat the minister, .. blinkin' an no weel pleased, juist like a hoolet, CROCKETT *Stickit Min.* (1893) 130. **Wgt.** The lonely hoolets eldritch cry, FRASER *Poems* (1885) 234. **n.Cy.** GROSE (1790) ; **N.Cy.**¹ **Nhb.**¹ The barn owl (*Strix flammea*) is called hoolet, gilli hoolet. The tawny owl (*Syrnium aluco*) is called Jenny hoolet. **Dur.**¹, **Lakel.**¹² **Cum.** That screechan sound Sprang frae her hulert and her breed, DICKINSON *Cumbr.* (1876) 258. * **Wm.** A skirling hullet, HUTTON *Bran New Wark* (1785) l. 337 ; Dreayve back the hulet to his haunts, WHITEHEAD *Leg.* (1859) 12. **s.Wm.** (J.A.B.), **n.Yks.²** **e.Yks.** MARSHALL *Rur. Econ.* (1788). **m.Yks.¹** **w.Yks.** His een were as sharp as a houlat's, SNOWDEN *Web of Weaver* (1896) v ; Hullats seghen la stur aght a ther nooks abaht dusk, TOM TREDDLEHOYLE *Bairnsla Ann.* (1847) 19 ; **w.Yks.¹** Gloarin wi' her een like onny hullet in a loup hole, ii. 288 ; **w.Yks.²⁴⁵** **Lan.** Bit bats an' ulyets fly here neaw, CLEGG *Sketches* (1895) 403 ; Whether th' ullerts ar worth shot or do', TIM BOBBIN *View Dial.* (1740) 3 ; **Lan.¹**, **n.Lan.¹**, **e.Lan.¹**, **m.Lan.¹** **Chs.** There were a brood o' hullarts shakin' their feathers, CROSTON *Enoch Crump* (1887) 10 ; **Chs.¹²** ; **Chs.²** ' He swapped his hen for a hullert,' he made a bad exchange. **Der.¹²**, **Not.** (L.C.M.), **Lin.¹**, **n.Lin.¹**, **Nhp.²** **w.Wor.** He be as lazy as a gowk or a howlet, as don't make no nest, *Berrow's Jrn.* (Mar. 3, 1888) ; **w.Wor.¹**, **se.Wor.¹** **Shr.¹** A saying—' I live too nigh the ōōd to be afeard of a ōōlert.' Hrf.¹², **Som.** (HALL.)

Hence (1) Howlety, *adj.* like an owl ; (2) -hoo or Hully-hoo, *sb.* an owl ; the cry or hoot of an owl.

(1) **Slk.** To scare the howlaty face o' him away, HOGG *Tales* (1838) 45, ed. 1866. Hrf.² A moping hoolety creature. (2) **Lth.** An eerie ugly skraigh that I like waur than a hoolet's 'hoolety-hoo,' STRATHESK *More Bits* (ed. 1885) 182. **Edb.** The guid grieve ayont the dyke, The lang hoolety-hoo, The whawp, frae the south, *Carlop Green* (1793) 125, ed. 1817. ne.Lan.¹

2. *Comb.* (1) Howlet-blind, blind as an owl ; (2) -een or -'s een, eyes like those of an owl, large staring eyes ; (3) -faced, having a face like an owl ; (4) -haunted, frequented by owls ; (5) -hole, a hole left in the gable of a building to admit owls ; (6) -'s quid, the remains of a mouse, bird, &c., disgorged by an owl after having eaten the fleshy portion.

(1) **Lnk.** 'Tis ten to ane she's houlet-blin' An a' thing tapsalteerie,

COGHILL *Poems* (1890) 89. (2) **Rxb.** Close her howe sunk howlet's een, A. SCOTT *Poems* (ed. 1808) 21. **Nhb.** While Charley damns Jack's hoolet-e'en, WILSON *Pitman's Pay* (1843) 29 ; **Nhb.¹** (3) **Ayr.** How daur ye ca' me howlet-faced, BURNS *Impromptu*, l. 1. (4) **Sc.** This howlit haunted biggin, DONALD *Poems* (1867) 1. **Ayr.** By some auld houlet-haunted biggin, GROSE *Grose's Peregrinations* (1789) st. 3. (5) **Chs.¹** (6) **se.Wor.¹** A compact mass somewhat in the shape of the finger. ' Finger biscuit ! Why I cun remember the time w'en 'er ōōdn't a knaow'd a finger biscuit from a owlud's quid.'

3. *Fig.* A term of reproach : a fool ; a noisy or dirty person.

Sc. O, the most egregious night-howlets ! SCOTT *Rob Roy* (1817) xxxiv. **N.Cy.¹ Cum.** What's t'matter wid the, thoo silly wooden hewlet ? FARRALL *Betty Wilson* (1886) 80. **Yks.** Tha owd starin ullat goa wesh tha, BINNS *Tom Wallop* (1861) 11. **w.Yks.** ' Tha mucky ullot,' you dirty thing, *Leeds Merc. Suppl.* (Jan. 3, 1891) ; **w.Yks.⁵** A nasty stinking hullot. Whisht ! yuh noisy hullots, an' doan't let's hev a house like Lee-gap fair. **nw.Der.¹** Tha'rt a lyin' 'ullart. Hrf.² A regular howlet.

4. A moth ; also in *comp.* Oolert-moth.

s.Stf. We wun catching owlets _in the garden, PINNOCK *Blk. Cy. Ann.* (1895). **w.Wor.¹ Shr.¹** Ōōlert-moth, one of the order *Lepidoptera Noctuidae*, believed to be *Plusia gamma*, Gamma Moth. The local name of ' ōōlert ' is probably given to this moth from its nocturnal habits. **Sus.** Any night-flying moth, the larger ones more especially (R.P.C.) ; **Sus.¹**

5. *v.* To travel or go anywhere by night.

Hrf.² Why can't you go by daylight instead of hooleting about the country ?

[L. Lizard's leg *and* howlet's wing, SHAKS. *Macb.* IV. i. 17 ; An hulet, *vtula,* LEVINS *Manip.* (1570). Fr. *hulotte,* a madge-howlet (COTGR.) ; Walloon *houlott,* ' espèce de gros hibou ' (REMACLE).]

HOWLING, *vbl. sb.* Sus. In *comb.* Apple-howling. The custom of ' wassailing ' orchards ; see below. Cf. apple-owling, *sb.*, howlers.

The custom of wassailing the orchards still remains. It is called apple-howling. A troop of boys visit the different orchards and encircling the apple-trees they repeat the following words: ' Stand fast root, bear well top, Pray the God send us a good howling crop. Every twig, apples big, Every bough, apples enow, Hats full, caps full, Full quarters, sacks full.' They then shout in chorus, one of the boys accompanying them on the cow's horn ; during the ceremony they rap the trees with their sticks, *N. & Q.* (1852) 1st S. v. 293.

Hence Howling-boys, *sb. pl.* the boys who carry out the custom of ' howling.'

1670, Dec. 26. I gave the howling boys 6d., *Arch. Coll.* I. 110, in SAWYER *Flk-Lore* (1883) 20.

HOWLING, *adj.* Sus. Slang. A general intensitive : big, first-rate.

Sus. Pray God send us A good howling crop, *Flk-Lore Rec.* (1878) I. 13 ; *N. & Q.* (1852) 1st S. v. 293. **Slang.** A howling lie (FARMER).

HOWLY, *sb.* Yks. [hūlī·.] A boys' game ; a cry used in the game of ' howly ' ; see below.

n.Yks.¹ A street game played by boys in a town, one of them hiding behind a wall or house-end and crying ' Howly ' to the seekers ; **n.Yks.²** How-ly [*y* long], a street play among boys resembling ' hide and seek ' ; **n.Yks.⁴**

HOWM, *sb.* n.Yks.² A hovel ; an open shed for cattle in a field. See Helm, *sb.²*

HOWMET, HOWP, HOWROW, see Hoomet, Houp, *sb.¹*, Hoo-roo.

HOWRY, *adj.* Cum.¹ Hollow, empty.

HOWSE, *v.* Lan. [ouz.] To stir up, as a fire by poking ; to rouse from sleep.

Lan. GROSE (1790) *MS. add.* (C.) ; DAVIES *Races* (1856) 234. e.Lan.¹ a.Lan. PICTON *Dial.* (1865) 11.

HOWSH(E, *int.* Dor. An exclamation used in driving swine, a call to move on. *Gl.* (1851) ; Dor.¹

HOWSHIES, *sb. pl.* Nrf. Boots or feet.
Wipe yar howshies (E.M.).

HOW-SKROW, *sb.* Lakel. Also written -scrow. Disorder, a state of confusion ; also used *advb.* See How-strow.

Lakel.² Wm. It's cleenin time an we're o in a how-skrow (B.K.) ; Net gat teavan how scrow intet middle ont, seeam es swine in a taety bed, *Spec. Dial.* (1877) pt. i. 30.

HOWSOEVER, *adv.* Sc. Irel. Nhb. Yks. Lin. Bdf. Suf. Also in forms asiver Lin.; howsaye e.Yks.; -seer n.Yks.; -sever Sc. e.Suf.; -aiver, -aivor Nhb.; -aivver Nhb.[1] n.Yks.[14]; -zeer n.Yks.; -ziver Edb. N.I.[1] Bdf.; -zivver n.Yks.[2] [For further variations cf. how, *adv.* I. 1.] However, any way; indeed, in fact.

Ayr. Hoosever, in the end, we got a terr'ble lickin', SERVICE *Notandums* (1890) 24. Lnk. I kenna, hows'ever they gaedna the-gither, WATSON *Poems* (1853) 31. Lth. Hoosoever wise they seem, LUMSDEN *Sheep-head* (1892) 70. Edb. ELLIS *Pronunc.* (1889) V. 685. N.I.[1] Nhb. Bud hoosivor thoo's yen nighor akin te the' nor me, ROBSON *Bk. Ruth* (1860) iii. 12; 'Yor mistyeken,' says Geordy, 'hoosiver,' HORSLEY *Ride Upon the Swing Bridge* (1882); Nhb.[1] n.Yks. (T.S.); Hooseer ah'll try and deea mi best, *Broad Yks.* (1885) 10; n.Yks.[124] e.Yks. I have done it, howsaye! MARSHALL *Rur. Econ.* (1796). Lin. ' Will you do this for me!' 'No; asiver I can't do it' (J.C.W.). Bdf. ELLIS *ib.* 207. Suf. Howsivir the last day o' the last month he takes her, FISON *Merry Suf.* (1899) 11. e.Suf. ELLIS *ib.* 280. [Hows'ever he looked neither out to sea nor towards Coverack, 'Q.' *Wandering Heath* (1895) 10.]

HOWSOME, *adj.* Lan. 'Wholesome,' healthy.

Wenches . . . lookin' as free an' as howsome as th' leets and shadows ut rowled o'er th' country, BRIERLEY *Cast upon World* (1886) 156; Hoo's us ard o worchin, howsom, farrently, daysunt o bodi us is ti bi fund, SCHOLES *Tim Gamwattle* (1857) 14.

HOWSOMEVER, *adv.* In *gen.* dial. use in Sc. Irel. Eng. and Amer. Also in forms ahsomdivver Not.[1] War.[6]; ahsomivver War.[9]; amiver, amsumivver w.Yks.; ar-sumivver, a's'mivver w.Yks.[5]; asumiver w.Yks.; erm-sumivver, ersumivver w.Yks.[5]; hamsever Sur.; ham-sumivver, harmsumivver, horsomivver w.Yks.[5]; hosem-ever Wil.; howmswever n.Lin.[1]; howmiver n.Lin.; -simiver Dev.; -smever Brks.; -smiver w.Yks.; -som-dever Or.I. w.Yks.[3] ne.Lan.[1] s.Oxf. Nrf. Ken.[1] w.Som.[1] n.Dev. Cor.[2]; -somdiver Nhp.[1]; -somdivver w.Yks.[5]; -somedever Ir.I.Ma. Glo. Ken.[12] Dev.Amer.; -somedivver s.Lin.; -some'er Ir. Der.[1]; -somer Cor.; -some-ever Frf.; -somiver Sh.I. Wm. ne.Lan.[1] Som.; -somivver n.Yks.[14] m.Yks.[1] w.Yks.[15]; -sumdever Ir. War.[24] s.War.[1] Brks. s.Nrf. Sus.[1]; -sumdiver e.Yks.[1]; -sumever Wor. Nrf. Cor.[2]; -sumiver n.Yks.[4] w.Yks.; -summider n.Yks.; -zomivver n.Yks.[2]; -zumever Som.; humsumivver, om-somdivver, omsomivver, o's'mivver, ossumivver w.Yks.[6]; owdzimiver Dev.; smivver w.Yks.[5] [For further varia-tions cf. how, *adv.* I. 1.] However, nevertheless; at all events, in any case.

Sh.I. Da Crofter's Ack, hoosomiver, is da foremist o' dem a', *Sh. News* (May 29, 1897); Howsomdever d'ye see, it has turned out for the worst for me this time, SCOTT *Pirate* (1822) xl. Abd. Hoosomever, ye're away, *Deeside Tales* (1872) 27. Frf. How-some-ever I daur say we could arrange to fling the grounds open to the public, BARRIE *Thrums* (1889) xvii. Fif. I've seen the day hoosomever, ROBERTSON *Provost* (1894) 20. Dmb. Hoosomever, I'll gang wi' ye, CROSS *Disruption* (1844) xviii. Ayr. Howsomever no doubt ye did your best, GALT *Lairds* (1826) xiii. Lnk. Hoo-somever, gie's anither screed, FRASER *Whaups* (1895) viii; Hoo-sumever . . . I'll risk it, MURDOCH *Readings* (1895) I. 190. Rxb. ELLIS *Pronunc.* (1889) V. 685. Ir. Howsomedever, at first we thried puttin' the best face we could on the matter, BARLOW *Bog-land* (1892) 8, ed. 1893; Howsome'er, Quality this is, sure enough, *ib.* Kerrigan (1894) 59. w.Ir. Howsomiver, the king never re-covered the loss iv his goose, LOVER *Leg.* (1848) I. 16. n.Cy. (J.W.) Wm. Hawsomiver, as niver thowt naw mair aboot it, WARD *R. Elsmere* (1888) bk. i.ii. n.Yks. Howsumivver Ah manisht te say, TWEDDELL *Clevl. Rhymes* (1875) 62; n.Yks.[124], ne.Yks.[1], e.Yks.[1] m.Yks. ELLIS *ib.* 504; w.Yks. But hawsum-ivver, it seems at tha's made up thi mind, HARTLEY *Seets i' Yks. and Lan.* (1895) ii; But amsumivver shoo diddant wait ta tell him, TOM TREDDLEHOYLE *Bairnsla Ann.* (1846) 7; Hahsumivver ah gat him persuaded, BANKS *Whfld. Wds.* (1865); WRIGHT *Gram. Wndhll.* (1892) 166; w.Yks.[125] Lan. Well, heawsomever, moi name propper is Sam Swindles, OWEN *Good Oud Toimes* (1870) 5; ELLIS *ib.* 333. ne.Lan.[1] I.Ma. Howsomedever, that's the why they thought the child was terrible high, BROWN (1881) 66, ed. 1889. s.Stf. ELLIS *ib.* 465. Der.[1], nw.Der.[1], Not.[1] Lin. I can't do it in any way howsomever (J.C.W.). n.Lin. It wakken'd 'em up homeniver, PEACOCK *J. Markenfield* (1874) I. 135; Howmsewever, just when he got about a hundred yards past Mottle-Esh Turnin', *ib. R. Shir-laugh* (1870) I. 37; n.Lin.[1] s.Lin. Howsomedivver if you'll promise

me nivver to do it agen ah weänt tek eny noätice on it (T.H.R.). Nhp. ELLIS *ib.* 213; Nhp.[1], War.[234] s.War. Owsumdevr thees be the faks o' the ca-ase, *Why John* (*Coll.* L.L.B.); s.War.[1] Wor. *Why John* (*Coll.* L.L.B.). Hrf. ELLIS *ib.* 70. Glo. Howsomedever th' passon coouldn't allow un to call un that thur, BUCKMAN *Darke's Sojourn* (1890) 9; Glo.[1] Oxf. ELLIS *ib.* 117. s.Oxf. 'Owsomdever, we must 'ave our teas now, ROSEMARY *Chilterns* (1895) 35. Brks. Hows'mever, sir, I hears as they found it, HUGHES *Scour. White Horse* (1859) v; ELLIS *ib.* 95; Brks.[1] A wunt never do't howsom-ever a med try. Hrt. ELLIS *ib.* 198. Hnt. (T.P.F.) Nrf. How-somdever, I goes arter 'em, PATTERSON *Man and Nat.* (1895) 123; Howsumever you want to know too much, sir, EMERSON *Lagoons* (ed. 1896) 69. s.Nrf. Heu'samde'va, ELLIS *ib.* 273. e.Suf. (F.H.) Ess. Some, howsomever, so jubb'd on, CLARK *J. Noakes* (1839) st. 86 Ken.[1] But howsomdever, doänt rान it down tight; Ken.[2] Sur. Howsomever they didn't give him a chance to stab any more, JENNINGS *Field Paths* (1884) 7; Hamsever, I has some coûld tea i' this bottle, BICKLEY *Sur. Hills* (1890) i; Sur.[1] Sus. Well I shall keep you to your promise, sir, howsomever, HOSKYNS *Talpa* (1852) 140, ed. 1857; Sus.[1] Wil. SLOW *Gl.* (1892). e.Dor. ELLIS *ib.* 77. Som. (J S.F.S) ; Howzumever we got in the trane, FRANK *Nine Days* (1879) 29. w.Som.[1] Dev. Howsimiver hur didn, N. HOGG *Poet. Lett.* (1847) and S. 15, ed. 1866; 'Owdzimiver, I brished tha mucks off 'er gownd, HEWETT *Peas. Sp.* (1892) 141. n.Dev. But howsomdever us ded wull, ROCK *Jim an' Nell* (1867) st. 16. Cor. Howsomer a tram-road from Levvurpool here, DANIEL *Bride of Scio* (1842) 229; Cor.[12] [Amer. Howsomedever I pulled over to the shanty, ADELER *Elbow Room* (1876) 270.]

[The same word as ME. *hou sum euir,* in whatever manner, however (*Cursor M.* 2339). A parallel formation to *howsoever,* with the ON. conj. *sem* (Norw. dial., Da., Sw. *som*), as, that.]

HOW-STROW, *sb.* Nhb. Dur. Cum. Wm. Also written -strowe Dur.; howe-strowe Cum.[6] Wm. Confusion, dis-order, an untidy state of things; also used *attrib.* and *advb.*

Nhb. What wi' byeth weshin' an' beyekin', sic a howstrow the kitchen's in (R.O.H.); They leeved a kind o' howstrow life, ROBSON *Sngs. of Tyne* (1849) 157; Nhb.[1] s.Dur. T'house was in terrible howstrow (J.E.D.). Cum. (H.W.); Thy plew-gear's aw liggin how-strow, ANDERSON *Ballads* (ed. 1808) 182; Cum.[1]; Cum.[2] If t'cobble steeäns wor left liggin howe-strowe, 80. Wm. (B.K.)

HOWSUMBE, *adv.* Wor. In phr. *howsumbe however,* however.

w.Wor. Howsumbe howivver they slipped inter the thrashin' quickest, S. BEAUCHAMP *N. Hamilton* (1875) I. 24.

HOWT, HOWTHER, HOWTHIR, see Hold, *v.,* Holt, *sb.*[1], Howder, *v.*[12], Huthir.

HOWTIE, *adj.* Sc. Apt to wax angry and sulky.

Cld. (JAM.) Lnk. Some like to figure in the van In howtie expectation, That we wha toddle as we can May see with admiration, WATSON *Poems* (1853) 69; Her kin were owre lordly for tellin' An' I was owre howtie to speer, *ib.* 79.

Hence (1) **Howtilie,** *adv.* in an angry and sulky manner; (2) **Howtiness,** *sb.* anger and sulkiness. Cld. (JAM.)

HOW-TOWDIE, *sb.* Sc. n.Cy. Also written howtoudie Peb.; and in forms howdie Frf.; howdy-towdy n.Cy.; 'toudie Peb. [hau'-taudi.] A young hen, one that has never laid; also used *fig.* of a young unmarried woman.

Sc. Howtowdies took their flight, Turkies bade the board good night, VEDDER *Poems* (1842) 158; My gentleman tell't the king that he wadna gie a gude Scotch howtowdie for a' the puir like gear in his poultry yàrd, *Petticoat Tales* (1823) II. 163 (JAM.); Peat-reek an' paitricks, het toddy, howtowdies, EDWARDS *Modern Poets,* XII. 283. Frf. The weeng o' a guid fat howdie, LOWSON *John Guidfollow* (1890) 55. Ayr. Fosy monks stechin' wi' how-towdies and rumbledethumps, SERVICE *Dr. Duguid* (ed. 1887) 258. Lth. ' My honey-doo! my auld howtowdie!' Cried Rory to a canker'd howdie, SMITH *Merry Bridal* (1866) 20. Edb. Bargain-ing with the farmers for their ducks, chickens, gaislings, geese, turkey-pouts, howtowdies, &c., MOIR *Mansie IVauch* (1828) vi. Peb. Chanticleer . . . Wi's hens an' 'toudies by his side, LINTOUN *Green* (1685) 40, ed. 1817; She at him flies, And her howtoudies brings, *ib.* 41. Slk. At leeterary soopers I like to see a blue-stockin playin the how-towdie, CHR. NORTH *Noctes* (ed. 1856) III. 192. n.Cy. *Border Gl.* (*Coll.* L.L.B.)

HOWT'S, HOWZE, see Hoot(s, House, *sb.*[1]

HOX, see Hocks.

HOXTER, *sb.* Nhb.[1] One who hoaxes others; an impostor.

HOXTER-POXTER, *adv.* Sc. In great confusion, 'higgledy-piggledy.'
Elg. Rowdy dowdy, hoxter poxter—Ower the chair they tumbled baith, TESTER *Poems* (1865) 148.

HOY, *sb.*[1] Ken. [oi.] A small vessel employed in carrying passengers and goods, particularly in short distances on the sea-coast.
A barge-like sloop. Two were used at Faversham before the railway was opened to bring shop-keepers' goods from London. They were flat-bottomed and had lee-boards; but they had no sprit-sail and carried the main-sail and gaff top-sail of a sloop or cutter (H.M.); Still in use for a species of lighter, ANSTED *Sea Terms* (1898). [To hire a Margate Hoy, PEPYS *Diary* (June 16, 1661).]
[Du. *heu, heude*, a boate or a ship, fit to transport passengers (HEXHAM).]

HOY, *v.*[1] and *sb.*[2] Nhb. Dur. Cum. [hoi.] **1.** *v.* To throw, heave.
N.Cy.[1] **Nhb.** He hoys hissel ower the prissypis, *Keelmin's Ann.* (1869) 31; Hoy a hap'ney, canny man (H.M.); His backers they hoyed up the sponge, ROBSON *Coll. Tyneside Sngs.* (1872) 38; **Nhb.**[1] **e.Dur.**[1] Let's see wee'll [who will] hoy the far-est. **2.** *sb.* In wrestling: the throw of an adversary. Nhb. (R.O.H.) **3.** A lift. Dur. GIBSON *Weardale Gl.* (1870). **4.** A single-horse cart; *gen.* in *comp.* **Hoy-cart.** N.Cy.[1], Dur.[1] Cum. *Gl.* (1851).

HOY, *int.* and *v.*[2] Sc. Lan. Not. Lei. Ken. Dev. [h]oi.] **1.** *int.* An exclamation used to attract attention; also used *subst.* a shout, cry.
Sc. Baldie man! hoy Baldie! gae wa' an' clod on a creel fu' o' ruh-heeds, St. Patrick (1819) II. 313 (JAM.). **Cai.**[1] **Bnff.**[1] Gee 'im a hoy to cum back. **Per.** On the Terrey they did cry A hoy for Roy come over the Water, SMITH *Poems* (1714) 9, ed. 1853. **e.Lan.**[1], **Lei.**[1], **Ken.** (G.B.). **n.Dev.** I'll gie tha 'ouse, hoy, an' badge roun', ROCK *Jim an' Nell* (1867) st. 44. [I give him a Hoy! DICKENS *Mutual Friend* (1865) bk. i. viii.] **2.** A call to pigs to go on. **s.Not.** (J.P.K.) **3.** *v.* To call to, shout, summon, hail.
Sc. Hoy till 'm to keep aff the sawn grun (JAM.). **Cai.**[1] **Bnff.**[1] Mack ready, an' a'll rin an' hoy till 'im t'wyte for ye. Hoy aifter 'im t'fess the newspaper wee 'im fin he comes haim. **Per.** Providence ... Discover'd him ... Far on the road that's sair ajee, An' hoy'd him hame, STEWART *Character* (1857) 75. **Lnk.** There was a cab passing, which John hoyed, ROY *Generalship* (ed. 1895) 25. **4.** To urge on, incite, provoke, to set on dogs, &c.
Sc. This young birkie that ye're hoying and hounding on the shortest road to the gallows, SCOTT *Rob Roy* (1817) xxiii; The Crails-men hoyin' their daft Barber! DRUMMOND *Muchomachy* (1846) 57; *Gen.* used with respect to dogs (JAM.). **Dur.** To him the dogs may then be hoyt Wi' a' their force, TAYLOR *Poems* (1787) 8. **Ayr.** They hoy't out Will, wi' sair advice, BURNS *Halloween* (1785) st. 23.

HOYD, *sb.* Sh.I. A fishing-lodge. JAKOBSEN *Dial.* (1897) 30.

HOYD(E, see Hide, *sb.*[1]

HOYDEN, *adj.* and *v.* Sc. Ken. Also written **hoiden** Ken. **1.** *adj.* Inelegant, homely, commonplace.
Edb. Delightfu' flower! the richest kingly vest, Is hoyden to the glowin' o' thy breast, LEARMONT *Poems* (1791) 119. **2.** *v. Obs.* With *about*: to romp, act in a hoydenish manner. Ken. (K.)

HOYDER, HOYK, HOYL(E, see Holder, Hike, Hile, *sb.*[2], Hole, *sb.*[1]

HOYLENS-VOYLENS, *adv.* Cum. Nolens volens, 'willy-nilly.'
He cam hoylens voylens an' threep't a big lee in my face (E.W.P.).

HOYND, HOY'S, see Hoind, Hose, *sb.*[1]

HOY-SCOTCH, *sb.* Yks. [oi'skotʃ.] The game of hop-scotch.
w.Yks. A number are playing at hoy scotch, *Rambles in Wharfedale*, 123.

HOYSE, see Hoise.

HOYT, *sb.* ? *Obs.* Lan. Also written **hoit** (HALL.). A long rod or stick.
(J.D.); (HALL.); GROSE (1790) *MS. add.* (C.); Awth' rest on

um had hoyts, TIM BOBBIN *View Dial.* (1740) 14; **Lan.**[1] A long road [*sic*]. **e.Lan.** BAMFORD *Dial.* (1854).

HOYTE, see Hoit, *sb.*[1]

HOYTTIN-GENG, *sb.* Sh.I. The completion of any kind of work. **S. & Ork.**[1] The hoyttin-geng o' peats.

HOZE(E, *v. Obs.* Dev. Also in form **hawze. To be badly off. Cf. **hoved up.**
n.Dev. GROSE (1790); Hozed, 'male multatus,' *Horae Subsecivae* (1777) 219.

HOZEN, see Hose, *sb.*[1]

HU, *int.* Sc. Glo. Bdf. An exclamation.
Slk. Hu! tear him limb from limb! HOGG *Poems* (ed. 1865) 81. **Glo.** A term of address to an equal whether man or woman—often used for emphasis. 'Doant thee go for to draw I no more hu!' (S.S.B.) **Bdf.** Implying either anger or acquiescence, BATCHELOR *Anal. Eng. Lang.* (1809) 136.

HU, see He, Hew, *v.*[2], How, *adv.*

HUAM, *sb.* Sc. The moan of an owl in the warm days of summer.
Gall. It retires into the darkest recesses of woods and continues repeating with a moaning air 'huam,' MACTAGGART *Encycl.* (1824) 277, ed. 1876.

HUB, *sb.* Nhp.[1] [ʊb.] A secret signal or hint; a nudge.
Given *gen.* by a gentle touch with the elbow, to call the attention of a next neighbour to anything.

HUB, *v.* Sh.I. [hʊb.] To blame or hold guilty of a crime. S. & Ork.[1]

HUB, see Hob, *sb.*[2]

HUBBA, *sb.* Cor. [ʊbə.] **1.** A cry given to warn fishermen of the approach of pilchards. See **Hew, *v.*[2]**
The cry of Hubba! rang through the town, and quantities of pilchards were reported to be passing through the stems, *Cornishman* (Oct. 13, 1881); Cor.[2] **2.** A noise, disturbance. THOMAS *Randigal Rhymes* (1895) *Gl.*
[1. OCor. *ubba*, in this place, here (WILLIAMS).]

HUBBADALION, *sb.* Cor. Also in forms **hubbab-dullion, hubbadullion.** A noise, disturbance; a 'row.'
Flk-Lore Jrn. (1886) IV. 11a. **w.Cor.** St. Just Feast is a hobble, a squabble, and a hubbadullion all together, Cor. *Teleg.* (Nov. 2, 188a); (M.A.C.)

HUBBIE, *sb.*[1] Or.I. [hʊ·bi.] A short jacket worn by women when performing household work; a 'bed-gown.' (J.G.), S. & Ork.[1]

HUBBIE, *sb.*[2] Rxb. (JAM.) [Not known to our correspondents.] A dull, stupid, slovenly fellow.

HUBBIN, *sb.* Shr. w.Cy. [ʊ·bin.] A small anvil used by blacksmiths in making nails. Shr.[2], w.Cy. (HALL.)

HUBBINS, *sb. pl.* Hrf. Chips, small pieces of wood for burning.
Still known but seldom heard now. 'Get some nice hubbins for the fire' (J.B.); (W.W.S.)

HUBBISHOW, see Hobbleshow.

HUBBISTEW, *sb.* Sh.I. A hubbub, stir, tumult; a flurry, excitement.
I' da 'hert o' dis hubbisten [*sic*] in cam' Sibbie, *Sh. News* (Apr. 30, 1898); Sibbie 'ill be in a hubbistew aboot da rig (J.I.).

HUBBLE, *sb.* Sc. Cum. [hʊ·bl, hu·bl.] A stir, bustle, confusion, a noise, tumult; a crowd.
Sh.I. Dey wir sic hubble wi' boys, jaagers, an' men, 'at I cam' awa as shūne as I wis gien daa his braed, *Sk. News* (July 15, 1899). **Rnf.** But the [race] Corse it was a' in a hubble O' confusion and perfect uproar, WEBSTER *Rhymes* (1835) 5; The sodger too for a' his troubles, His hungry wames an' bludy hubbles, TANNAHILL *Poems* (1807) 109 (JAM.). **Ayr.** Should there e'er spring up a hubble Like yon most famous water squabble, LAING *Poems* (1894) 6a. **Dmf.** When they do get up a hubble, The purses hardly pay the trouble, SHENNAN *Tales* (1831) 30. **Gall.** The ragabash were ordered back, And then began the hubble, MACTAGGART *Encycl.* (1824) 267, ed. 1876. **Cum.**[1] A hubble o' fwok.
Hence **Hubblebub**, *sb.* the rabble, riff-raff.
Gall. Caper on a tub, At market-crosses, to attract The ragged hubblebub, MACTAGGART *ib.* 41.

HUBBLE, *v.* Wor. [ʊ·bl.] To cover seeds with earth; with *up*: to cover up.
They are hubbling parsnips [pushing with the feet the earth into the drills in which parsnip seed had been sown]. Hubbling is also done with a harrow following a drill (E.S.). **ne.Wor.** (J.W.P.)

HUBBLE-, HUBBLESHOW, see Hobbil, *sb.*[1], Hobble, *v.*[1], Hobbleshow.

HUBBLING, *prp.* w.Yks.[2] Stuttering.

HUBBON, *sb.* Lan. [u·bən.] The hip or hip-bone. Cf. huggin.

Wi' mi cooatts brad eawt o yard un o hauve across th' hubbons, Scholes *Tim Gamwattle* (1857) 23; Grose (1790) *MS. add.* (C.); Lan.[1] e.Lan.[1] *Obs.*

HUBBUBBOO, *sb.* and *int.* Irel. Also written hubbuboo.   1. *sb.* An uproar, a 'to-do.'

w.Ir. Och, Mary Queen of Heaven, but that was a hubbuboo! Lawless *Grania* (1892) I. pt. ii. 248.

2. *int.* An exclamation of wonder.

s.Ir. 'Hubbubboo,' cries Jack, 'now I see how it is,' Croker *Leg.* (1862) 140.

The same word as *hubbabowe*, a confused crying or yelling; cp. Spenser *Ireland* (1596), ed. 1886, 632. *Abowe* or *aboo* was the war-cry of the ancient Irish (so Spenser *l.c.*), Ir. *abu* (O'Reilly). Cp. *Butler-aboo!* the war-cry of the Butlers.]

HUBBY-SHEW, see Hobbleshow.

HUBGRUBBING, *adj.* Nrf. Dirty, piggish, 'grubby.' Still in use (M.C.H.B.); *Arch.* (1879) VIII. 170.

HUBLY-SHEW, see Hobbleshow.

HUBS, *sb. pl.* e.An.[12] [ubz.] Hoofs.

HUBSTACK, *sb.* w.Yks.[1] [u·bstak.] A clumsy, fat person.

HUCCANER, *sb.* Cor.[12] [u·kānə(r).] Lit. a wood corner. See Hood, *sb.*[2]

HUCH, *v.* Sc. [hūx.] To warm the hands by breathing on them.

Lnk. They huch them, and rub them, and shake them wi' pain, Till the dinnelin' gaes aff them, Lemon *St. Mungo* (1844) 31.

[MHG. *hüchen*, 'hauchen' (Lexer).]

HUCH, see Hutch, *v.*[2]

HUCK, *sb.*[1] Sus.[12] [uk.] A hard blow or rough knock.

HUCK, *sb.*[2] and *v.*[1] Ken. Sus. Hmp. Wil. [uk.] The husk, pod, or shell of vegetables or nuts.

Ken. (G.B.); Ken.[1] The husk, pod, or shell of peas, beans, but esp. of hazel nuts and walnuts. Sus.[1] Children get the pods [of peas] and cry to each other : 'Pea-pod hucks, Twenty for a pin ; If you doänt like 'em I'll take 'em back again '; Sus.[2] Hmp. Husk of corn (H.E.). Wil.[1] The chaff of oats.

2. *pl.* Grains of wheat which have the chaff still adhering to them after threshing, only fit for feeding poultry. Wil.[1]

3. *v.* To shell peas ; to extract walnuts from the outer covering.

Ken.[1] 'Are the walnuts ready to pick ?'   'No, sir, I tried some and they won't huck.'

HUCK, *v.*[2] Glo. Wil. Dor. Dev. [uk.] To bargain, cheapen ; to haggle, beat down in price.

Glo. 'Doest huck ?'   'Aye, ard enow to bate the cloas af me back,' Lysons *Vulgar Tongue* (1868) 46 ; Glo.[1] Wil.[1] 'I hucked un down vrom vive shillin' to vower an' zix.' Formerly used at Clyffe Pypard, but not known there now. e.Wil. Still in use at Deverill (G.E.D.). Dor. (A.C.); (W.C.) (c. 1750). Dev. *Horae Subsecivae* (1777) 221.

[I love nat to sell my ware to you, you hucke so sore, Palsgr. (1530) ; *Auccionor*, to hukke, *Trin. Coll. MS.* (c. 1450) in Wright's *Voc.* (1884) 566. Cp. MHG. *hucke*, 'kleinhändler' ; *hucke*, verkaufsladen oder platz der 'hucker' (Lexer).]

HUCK, *v.*[3] Oxf. Brks. Sus. Wil. Dor. Also written uck Wil.[1] [uk.] 1. To stir or pick out with a pointed instrument ; to clear ; to spread about manure. Cf. hook, *v.*[1] 20, howk, *v.*[1] 2.

Oxf.[1] I'll lend ee a spade, an' you can 'uck the worms up for yourself. Brks. A man·' hucks out ' a ditch, or ' hucks ' his potatoes (M.J.B.) ; Brks.[1] To poke, as by inserting a stick under anything and on pushing it to give a lifting motion. Sus.[1] Wil. Uck the stable-dung out with a fork, Jefferies *Gt. Estate* (1880) 78, ed. 1881 ; Wil.[1] Stable-litter is ucked about with a fork in cleaning out ; weeds are ucked out of a gravel path with an old knife.

2. *Fig.* To turn out of work, to oust from one's place.

Dor. You hucked me out, and I'll huck you out [spoken by an offcast workman to a foreman] (W.B.).

HUCK, *v.*[4] s.Chs.[1] [uk.] With *up* : to raise the shoulders and back ; to hunch up. Cf. hook, *v.*[4], huckle.

Uwd dhisel· streyt, laad· ; iv dhaa ùks dhi baak· ùp ů)dhaa·n dhaa)l bi raaynd-shóo·dhūrd au· dhi dee·z [Howd thysel straight, lad ; if tha hucks thy back up a-that-n tha'll be raïnd-shoothered aw thy deez].

[Cp. Du. *huck-schouderen*, to bowe or shugg with the shoulders ; *hucken*, to stoope or to bowe (Hexham).]

HUCK, *v.*[5] *Obs.* Wxf.[1] To come, draw near ; to hitch. Huck nigher ; y'art scuddeen, 84.

HUCK, see Hike, *v.*, Hock, *sb.*[1], Hook, *sb.*[1], Howk, *v.*[1]

HUCKER, *v.*[1] Yks. Glo. Dev. Also written huker n.Yks.[14] To bargain, barter. n.Yks.[14] *Obs.* Glo., Dev. *Horae Subsecivae* (1777) 221. See Huck, *v.*[2]

[Du. *heukeren*, to sell by retail (Sewel) ; Dan. *høkre*, to huckster.]

HUCKER, *v.*[2] and *sb.* e.An. [u·kə(r).] 1. *v.* To stammer. e.An.[1], e.Suf. (F.H.) Cf. hocker, *v.*[2] 3.

Hence **Huckerer,** *sb.* a stammerer. e.Suf. (F.H.)

2. *sb.* A stammer. e.Suf. (*ib.*)

HUCKER, *v.*[3] Suf. With *down* : to .stoop down. e.Suf. (F.H.) Cf. hocker, *v.*[1], huckle.

HUCKERMUCKER, *sb.* and *adj.* Chs. War. [u·kəmukə(r).] 1. *sb.* Confusion, disorder, a disorderly condition. See Huckmuck, *sb.*[2], Hugger-mugger, 4.

s.Chs.[1] Mi plee·siz bin au· i sich· ū ůk·ūrmuk·ūr ahy)m rae'li ůshee·md ū aan·ibodi gôo·in in ům [My pleeces bin aw i sich a huckermucker I'm rtily asheemed o' annybody gooin' in 'em].

2. A miserly churl. War. (J.R.W.) 3. *adj.* In confusion, disorderly. s.Chs.[1], War. (J.R.W.)

Hence **Huckermuckerin,** *adj.* disorderly, confused ; inconvenient.

s.Chs.[1] Ahy wùd)nū goa· liv· i sich· ū ůk·ūrmůkūrin oa·i [I wudna go live i' sich a huckermuckerin' hole]. So it is huckermuckerin' to work without proper tools, &c.

HUCKET, see Hicket.

HUCKFAIL, *v.* Sh.I. To like or fancy any thing or person. S. & Ork.[1]

HUCKIE, *sb.* Rnf. (Jam.) [Not known to our correspondents.] The pit in which ashes are held under the fire. Cf. howk, *sb.* 6.

HUCKIE-BUCKIE, *sb.* Sc. In phr. *huckie-buckie down the brae,* a children's game.

Lth. A play in which they slide down a hill, sitting on their hunkers (Jam., s.v. Hunkers). [The well-known custom at Greenwich is probably the same game, and there are examples at Tumbling Hill, a few miles from Exeter, at May Pole Hill near Gloucester, and other places, Gomme *Games* (1894) 239.]

HUCKLE, *sb.*[1] Sc. Nhb. Yks. Lin. e.An. Sur. Sus. Dor. Som. Also in forms heuchle, heuckle Fif. [h)u·kl, u·kl.] The hip.

n.Yks.[14], e.An.[1], e.Suf. (F.H.) Dor.[1] Breeches button'd roun' his huckles, 250. Som. I've got the rheumatics so in my huckle all the while (W.F.R.) ; My huckle pains I ter'ble (W.B.T.) ; He stood up and limped out in front the better to rub his hurt huckle, Raymond *Men o' Mendip* (1898) ii.

Hence (1) **Huckle-bone,** *sb.* (*a*) the hip-bone or joint ; (*b*) a small bone found in the joint of the knee of a sheep ; a knucklebone ; in *pl.* a game played with such bones ; cf. dib, *sb.*[3] ; (2) **-strings,** the tendons of the thigh.

(1, *a*) Fif. [She] maist dislocate her heuchle-bane, Tennant *Papistry* (1827) 49 ; Yon heuchle-bane, though mouldie, may Be a Palladium in a fray To guard baith you and me, *ib.* 91. n.Yks.[2], e.An.[12], Suf.[1], Som. (F.H.) Som. Some sort of weakness which had het into his huckle-bones, Raymond *Gent. Upcott* (1893) 59. w.Som.[1] Uuk·l-boa·un. (*b*) Nhb. Huckle-bones is played in Hexham, Gomme *Games* (1894) 239. n.Lin.[1] Used by children for playing a game called in some parts of England, ' dibs.' The floors of summer-houses used frequently to be paved with these huckle-bones. Sur. Gomme *ib.* Sus.[1] [*Bibelots,* hucklebones ; or the play at hucklebones (Cotgr.).] (2) Som. Well known (W.F.R.).

HUCKLE, *sb.*[2] Sus. [u·kl.] A shock of corn consisting of ten sheaves, a ' hile.' (S.P.H.)

HUCKLE, *v.* Lan. Chs. Lin. Lei. Oxf. e.An. [u·kl, u·kl.] 1. To stoop, bend from weakness or age ; to crouch ; with *off* or *on* : to go with a slow, halting pace ; to jog along. See Huck, *v.*[4] ; cf. hurkle.

Lan. Gaskell *Lectures Dial.* (1854) 13; Lan.[1] s.Chs.[1] Dh)uwd mon wůz snee·pt, ůn bigůn· ůk·l of ůz soft ůz mi pok·it [Th' owd mon was sneeped, an' begun huckle off as soft as my pocket]. Lin. Started leatherin' the old ass an' made 'im huckle on above a bit, Ellis *Pronunc.* (1889) V. 298. Lei.[1], s.An.[12]

Hence **Huckle-backed,** *adj.* stooping, hunchbacked. Lan. Gaskell *Lectures Dial.* (1854) 13.

2. Of a hen: to cover her chickens with her wings. Oxf.[1] *MS. add.* Cf. **hurkle,** 2.

HUCKLE-MY-BUFF, *sb.* Sus. Slang. A beverage composed of beer, eggs, and brandy.

Sus.[12] [Slang. 'Huckle my buff,' beer, egg, and brandy, made hot, *Lex. Balatronicum* (1811).]

HUCKMUCK, *sb.*[1] Glo. Sus. Hmp. Wil. Som. Dev. [s·kmŭk.] A wicker strainer used in brewing.

Glo. An unshapely kind of wicker basket made use of to prevent the grains running out with the wort, *Horae Subsecivae* (1777) 219; Glo.[1] A strainer of peeled osier for straining the wort from the goods in the mash-tub. It is made somewhat in the shape of a quarter of a sphere. A neck is formed at lower angle into which the tap of the tub is fitted. Sus.[1] Sus., Hmp. Holloway. Wil. A tapwaies or tap used in brewing (K.); Britton *Beauties* (1825); Wil.[1], s.Wil. (G.E.D.) Som. Placed before the faucet in the mashing-tub, Jennings *Obs. Dial. w.Eng.* (1825); W. & J. Gl. (1873). w.Som.[1] It consists of a bundle of twigs, *gen.* part of an old broom which is placed at the bottom of the mashing-keeve or vat, to prevent the grains running out when the wort is drawn off. n.Dev. *Horae Subsecivae* (1777) 219.

[Cp. *hosemocke* (a strainer used in brewing), *Cellerarian's Roll* (1498) in *Obedientiary Rolls S. Swithun, Winchester,* ed. Kitchin (1892) 388.]

HUCKMUCK, *sb.*[2] Glo. Wil. Som. Dev. [s·kmŭk.]
1. A dwarf, a small ill-shaped man or woman, a hunchback; a dirty, untidy person.

Glo. *Horae Subsecivae* (1777) 219; Glo.[1] Wil.[1] A very dirty untidy old woman is 'a reg'lar huckmuck.' Dev. A short man with big shoulders and humped back, and more commonly for a mis-shapen woman. Also, spoken of a little man covered with mud to the knees, Grose (1790) *MS. add.* (M.); Dev.[1] A sort of stick-i'-the-mud. n.Dev. *Horae Subsecivae* (1777) 219; Grose (1790).

2. A mean shuffling person, a humbug.

w.Som.[1] Ya huck-muck son of a bitch, thee't ha my tools again in a hurry, aa'll warn thee! n.Dev. The old Mag Dawkins es bet a huckmuck to tha, *Exm. Scold.* (1746) l. 118.

3. The long-tailed titmouse, *Parus caudatus.* Wil. Smith *Birds* (1887) 173; Wil.[1]

HUCKMUCK, *sb.*[3] and *v.* Brks. Hmp. Wil. Dor. Dev. [s·kmŭk.] **1.** *sb.* Confusion caused by all things being out of place, a muddle; also used *attrib.*

Brks.[1] On visiting a small house on cleaning day the apology comes 'E vinds us in a gurt huck-muck to-daay, zur.' Hmp.[1], Wil.[1], n.Wil. (G.E.D.), Dor.[1] Dev. I niver did zee sich a huck-muck place in awl my born days, Hewett *Peas. Sp.* (1892).

2. *v.* To mess or muddle about. Wil.[1]

HUCKSEN, HUCKSON, see **Hock,** *sb.*[1]

HUCKSTER, *sb.* Sc. Irel. Nhb. Cum. Yks. Lan. War. Som. Also written **huxter** Sc. Ir.; and in forms **heukster** Cum.[1]; **heuxter** Nhb.; **hucksther** e.Yks.[1]; **uxter** w.Yks. [h]ŭ·kstə(r, u·kstə(r.] A petty tradesman, a small shopkeeper.

Abd. Come, Mains, will ye put too yer hand, We're nae to keep a huxter's stand, Beattie *Parings* (1801) 8. Frf. The canty huxter wives I see Wi' kindness blinkin' in her e'e, Smart *Rhymes* (1834) 86. Uls. A grocer in a small way, Uls. *Jrn. Arch.* (1858) VI. 46. Nhb. Ye heuxters aw resent it, Oliver *Sngs.* (1824) 16. Cum.[1] e.Yks.[1] Dealers in farm produce, who hold the position of middlemen between the producers and consumers. w.Yks. This they kept repeatin', wal Uxter Billy hed ta cum in, Tom Treddlehoyle *Bairnsla Ann.* (1864) 43. Lan. Persons whose business it is to go about buying one commodity and selling another. 'He was counting them out to the hucksters,' Marshall *Review* (1808) I. 270. War. Hucksters' shops, as they are locally called, abound, White *Wrekin* (1860) xx; War.[2] The hucksters are not to forestall the market in buying up things, *Par. Accts. St. Martin's* (1709) in Bruce *Old St. Martin's* (1875). w.Som.[1] They do keep a little huckster's shop, an' zells can'ls, and bacca-pipes, and that.

Hence **Huxtry,** (1) *sb.* a general shop, a shop where small articles of all sorts are kept; also used *attrib.*; (2) *adj.* such as is used by a huckster.

(1) Ayr. Mrs. Firlot, that kept the huxtry in the Saltmarket, Galt *Ann. Parish* (1821) vi; A decent elderly carlin that kept a huxtry shop close by, *ib. Gilhaize* (1823) xii. (2) Ayr. Ye wad never write your letters on huxtry tea-paper, *ib. Lairds* (1826) xxix.

[Forr þatt te33 turrndenn Godess hus Inntill huccsteress boþe, *Ormulum* (c. 1200) 15817. Cp. MDu. *hoecster,* fem. of *hoeker,* a petty tradesman (Verdam).]

HUCKSY-BUB, *sb.* Dev. [Not known to our correspondents.] The female breast. (Hall.)

HUCRIN, *sb.* Dur. [hu·krin.] A cutter or chisel. Gibson *Up-Weardale Gl.* (1870).

HUD, *sb.*[1] and *v.*[1] War. Wor. Hrf. Glo. Oxf. Brks. Mid. e.An. Wil. Dor. Som. Dev. Cor. Also written **hudd** Cor.[1]; and in forms **hod** e.An.[1] Som.; **od** w.Som.[1] [ŭd, od.] **1.** *sb.* The shell of seed-bearing plants; the husk of hard fruit and of corn; the skin of a gooseberry; the calyx of a strawberry; also used *fig.*

War.[23] w.Wor.[1] W'en thee'st done shellin' them peasen, pŭt the 'uds far the pigs. se.Wor.[1], s.Wor. (F.W.M.W.), s.Wor.[1], Hrf.[2] Glo. (A.B.); Glo.[1] Common. Oxf.[1], Brks.[1] w.Mid. We used to ridder the corn to get the uds out of it (W.P.M.). e.An.[1] Potato hod. Wil.[1] n.Wil. They beant ripe—the huds won' coom off (E.H.G.). Dor.[1] Som. Jennings *Obs. Dial. w.Eng.* (1825). w.Som.[1] 'Tid'n a good sort o' peas, there's too much hud to 'em. Billy, be you eating the hud of the gooseberries? Dev. Gie awl they pea-huds tů tha pegs bimbye, Hewett *Peas. Sp.* (1892). Cor. Thomas *Randigal Rhymes* (1895) Gl.; Take off your huds from your strawberries (M.A.C.); Cor.[1]; Cor.[2] The dry crust or scab on a sore.

2. The stone of a cherry.

w.Som.[1] 'Tommy, be sure you don't rwaller th' ods.' Boys play a kind of pitch-and-toss game with cherry-stones, which they call 'playing cherry ods.'

3. *v.* To shell peas; to remove the husk from beans or walnuts.

se.Wor.[1] I a bin a'uddin some bannits, an' they makes my 'onds pretty nigh black. s.Wor. (F.W.M.W.), Glo. (A.B.) Brks.[1] Get them warnuts hudded agin I comes back. e.An.[1] Hodding peas. Wil.[1] Beans are hudded and peas shelled for cooking. n.Wil. I be gwain walnut-hudding this aaternoon (E.H.G.). Som. Holloway.

HUD, *v.*[2] and *sb.*[2] Chs. Shr. Wil. Also in form od· Wil.[1] **1.** *v.* To collect, gather together. Cf. **hood,** *v.*[2] Chs.[1] Occasionally. Shr. Bound *Provinc.* (1876); Shr.[1] Oh! 'e'll be sure to 'ud it all up; Shr.[2] Hudding up fitches.

2. *sb.* A small heap. Shr.[2] **3.** A lump or clod of earth. Wil.[1] Hence **Huddy,** *adj.* full of lumps and clods. *ib.*

HUD, see **Head, Hide,** *v.*[2], **Hold,** *v.*, **Hood,** *sb.*[12]

HUDDACK, *sb.* Sh.I. [Not known to our correspondents.] A knot in a fishing-line fastening two parts together. S. & Ork.[1]

HUDDER, see **Hooder, Howder,** *v.*[12]

HUDDERIN, *sb.* Abd. (Jam.) [Not known to our correspondents.] Meat condemned as unwholesome.

[Transporting and carrying foorth of this Realme, of Calue-skinnes, huddrounes, and Kid-skinnes, *Acts Jas. VI* (1592) c. 155.]

HUDDERING, *sb.* and *adj.* e.An. [ŭ·derin.] **1.** *sb.* A well-grown lad; a young man grown awkwardly tall, a hobbledehoy. Cf. **hutherin.**

e.An.[1] If a Suf. farmer be asked how many male servants he keeps, his answer may probably be, 'Two men and a hudderin.' He may be, and often is, a handsome, well-formed, and decently clothed lad. Suf.[1], e.Suf. (F.H.)

2. *adj.* Overgrown, ungainly, loutish.

e.An.[1] Nrf. Great huddering boys standing with their backs to the walls, and their hands in their pockets, Spilling *Molly Miggs* (1873) ii. e.Suf. Always qualified by 'great' (F.H.).

HUDDERON, *sb.* and *adj.* Sc. Also in forms **hudderen** Bch.; **huddroun** Bnff.; **huderon** Sc. [hu·daran.] **1.** *sb.* A dirty, ragged person; also used *attrib.* Cf. **huther-my-duds.**

Sc. A morning-sleep is worth a foldful of sheep to a huderon, duderon daw, Kelly *Prov.* (1721) 14. Gall. Mactaggart *Encycl.* (1824).

2. A big, fat, flabby person, commonly applied to a woman. Bnff. Gregor *Notes to Dunbar* (1893) 199.

3. *adj.* Hideous, ugly.

Sc. (Jam.) Bch. The great hudderen carlen was riding hockerty-cockerty upo' my shoulders in a hand-clap, Forbes *Jrn.* (1785) 3.

HUDDERY, *adj.* Sc. Also in form **huddry** Abd. [hʊ̆ʹd(ə)ri.] Rough, shaggy, dishevelled.

Abd. His head was seen to be huddry, ALEXANDER *Johnny Gibb* (1871) xv. Kcd. Smooth yer huddery head, GRANT *Lays* (1884) 84. w.Sc. *Gl. Sibb.* (JAM.)

HUDDICK, *sb.* Som. Cor. [wʹdik.] **1.** A pea-pod. Som. SWEETMAN *Wincanton Gl.* (1885). See **Hud,** *sb.*[1]

2. *pl.* Grains of wheat not separated from the husks.

w.Cor. So I throwed down a kayer of huddicks, THOMAS *Randigal Rhymes* (1895) 8.

HUDDIE-DUDDIE, see **Hoddy-doddy.**

HUDDIMUK, *v.* Shr.[1] Also in form **uddermuk.** [wʹdimək.] To do things on the sly.

I dunna know about 'em bein' so poor, .. it strikes me they'n 'uddimuk an' junket by tharselves, an' al'ays looken poor to get all they can.

Hence **Huddimukery,** *adj.* close, sly, underhand.

I fund a bran'-new shillin' in a noud canister; .. I 'spect Jim 'ad pūt it theer—I dunna like sich uddermukkery ways.

[Cp. ME. *hodymoke,* concealment. Huyde hyt not in hodymoke, MYRC *Inst. Par. Priests* (c. 1450) 2031.]

HUDDIN, *sb.* Per. A cap or covering for a child's head. (G.W.)

HUDDIN, see **Hodden.**

HUDDLE, *v.* and *sb.* Sc. Irel. Cum. Wm. Yks. Lan. Chs. Der. Not. Lin. Mid. e.An. Som. Also written **huddel** Som.; and in forms **hoodle** Suf.; **oodle** Irel. [h)wʹdl, uʹdl.] **1.** *v.* To gather together greedily.

Edb. Some fuck . . . thieve and huddle crumb by crumb, FERGUSSON *Poems* (1773) 215, ed. 1785.

2. With *up* : to draw together all of a heap ; to tuck up.

Chs.[18] ' To huddle up corn ' is to make it up into sheaves. **Suf.** I hoodled him up in bed, *e.An. Dy. Times* (1892).

3. To crowd together uncomfortably ; to get close together.

Lth. At mid-day the gloamin' grey O'ershadows the hame that she buddies in, BALLANTINE *Poems* (1856) 59. Dmf. Doon calmly huddle in amang Oor kindred dust, QUINN *Heather* (1863) 69. Yks. (J.W.), Not. (J.H.B.), n.Lin.[1], Suf.[1]

4. To embrace, hug.

Cum.[4] Wm. Fowk says he huddles thee a bit, WHEELER *Dial.* (1790) 57. w.Yks. If a chap meets a lass it street, an begins a huddlin her, an sitch loike, BYWATER *Sheffield Dial.* (1839) 262; w.Yks.[145], ne.Lan.[1], nw.Der.[1] s.Not. Ah could a huddled 'im, ah were that pleased (J.P.K.).

Hence **Huddle-me-close,** *sb.* the side bone of a bird. e.An.[1]

5. *sb.* A mass of things, a heap ; a confused heap.

Ir. They'll be gettin' oodles o' money on at the fair afore Lent, BARLOW *Idylls* (1892) 57. Mid. The sharp merry shouts of boys and men dashing at the hockey-bung in the jagged slippery huddle, BLACKMORE *Kit* (1890) xxvii. e.Suf. She fell down all in a huddle (F.H.). Som. (HALL.)

6. An embrace, hug.

s.Not. Gie me a huddle, mother (J.P.K.).

[3. Cp. LG. (Göttingen) *hudern,* 'von Hühnern u. anderen Vögeln die die Küchlein unter ihre Flügel nehmen, um sie so zu wärmen, bisweilen auch von Menschen die einen anderen an sich drücken und so wärmen ' (SCHAMBACH).]

HUDDLEBERRY, *sb.* Sus. The whortleberry, the fruit of *Vaccinium Myrtillus.* FRIEND *Plant Names* (1882) 31.

HUDDLE-ME-BUFF, *sb.* w.Yks.[2] Hot ale and rum. Cf. **cuddle-me-buff, huckle-my-buff.**

HUDDLE-MUDDLE, *adv.* Obs. Sc. Secretly.

Frf. Syne huddle muddle o'er the bent, To fill the clerk's seed kist it went, MORISON *Poems* (1790) 110.

HUDDOCK, *sb.*[1] n.Cy. Nhb. Dur. Also written **huddick** N.Cy.[1] Nhb.[1] Dur. [huʹdak.] **1.** The cabin of a 'keel' or coal-barge.

N.Cy.[1] Nhb. I huik'd him an hawl'd him suin into the keel, an' o' top o' the huddock aw rowl'd him aboot, ALLAN *Sngs.* (ed. 1891) 73 ; The huddock is entered by a scuttle in the after deck and is of such small proportions that when a keelman stands upright in it, his head and shoulders appear through the scuttle, and in cold weather he can handle the tiller whilst in this position (R.O.H.); Nhb.[1] Nhb., Dur. NICHOLSON *Coal Tr. Gl.* (1888).

2. A small wooden hut or hutch.

Nhb. Huddock is at times applied to any small and cosy apartment, but jocularly and invariably with a reference to its original sense as the cabin of a keel (R.O.H.) ; (J.Ar.)

HUDDOCK, *sb.*[2] Dor.[1] Also written **huddick.** [wʹdak.] A covering for a sore finger ; a finger-stall.

HUDDOCK, *sb.*[3] Obs. e.Lan.[1] [uʹdak.] The least of a number of estates or pastures.

HUDDOCKS, *sb. pl.* Pem. Brushwood.

s.Pem. Sweep away these huddocks and set fire to them (W.M.M.).

HUDDUN, see **Hodden.**

HUDDY-BOX,'*sb.* Dor. In phr. *to lie in huddy-box,* to lie in ambush.

HAYNES *Voc.* (c. 1730) in *N. & Q.* (1883) 6th S. vii. 366 ; Still in use (H.J.M.).

HUDDY-DROCH, *sb.* Cld. (JAM.) [Not known to our correspondents.] A squat, waddling person.

HUDEIN, *adj.* Sh.I. Chiding, scolding. S. & Ork.[1]

HUDERON, *adj.* Or.I. Also in form **hudderin,** Empty, ill-filled. S. & Ork.[1]

They've jist gotten a hudge o' money.

HUDGE, *sb.*[1] and *v.*[1] Bnff.[1] **1.** *sb.* A great quantity.

2. *v.* To amass, heap up. ' The're jist hudgin' up siller.'

[1. *Hudge,* a form of lit. E. *huge.* Hudge is 3our fais within this fals Regioun, *Sat. Poems,* ed. Cranstoun, I. 147. The word *huge* is used as a *sb.* for a mass, a quantity, by Sc. writers. More than euer Rome could comprehend In huge of learned books that they ypend, HUDSON *Judith* (c. 1600) I. 102 (DAV.).]

HUDGE, *v.*[2] and *sb.*[2] Bnff.[1] **1.** *v.* To speak in a suppressed manner ; to spread abroad an evil report.

The're beginnin' to hudge it the banker's puschin' 'im some hard. He's gefn far ahin wee's cash-accoont.

2. *sb.* A suppressed talking. See **Hudge-mudge.**

HUDGE, see **Hodge,** *v.*[1]

HUDGE-MUDGE, *sb., adv.* and *v.* Sc. Yks. **1.** *sb.* Concealment, secrecy, ' hugger-mugger '; a suppressed talking, a side-talk in a low tone.

Bnff.[1] Bch. Bat fat use will they be to him, Wha in hudge mudge wi' wiles, Without a gully in his hand, The smeerless fae beguiles ? FORBES *Ajax* (1785) 11.

2. *adv.* Secretly, underhand. Sc. GROSE (1790) *MS. add.* (C.) w.Yks.[1]

3. *v.* To talk in a suppressed manner, to whisper.

Bnff.[1] The twa began to hudge-mudge wee ane anither in a corner. The hail pairies heeld a hudge-mudgan aboot thir mairrage lang afore it cam on. Per. For a' his wiles, an' his hudgemudgin', He'll be nae fainer, FORD *Harp* (1893) 97.

HUDGER, *sb.* Sur. [Not known to our other correspondents.] A bachelor. (H.W.)

HUDGIE-DRUDGIE, *sb., v.* and *adj.* Sc. **1.** *sb.* A drudge ; a person who toils unceasingly.

Per. That lassie's a hudgie-drudgie (G.W.).

2. *v.* To toil, drudge.

She's been hudgie-drudgin' here a' day (*ib.*).

3. *adj.* Toiling, drudging, slaving.

Lnk. There's naething for us women folks But hudgie-drudgie toil, MURDOCH *Doric Lyre* (1873) 38.

HUDJUCK, *sb.* and *v.* Wor. Hrf. Also written **hudyeuck** s.Wor. [wʹdgak.] **1.** *sb.* A mess, litter ; an untidy heap.

s.Wor. 'E fell down a' ov a hudyeuck [all of a heap]. It conveys the notion of slovenliness, laziness, &c. (H.K.) Hrf. Not heard lately (R.M.E.) ; Hrf.[2] The house be in such a hudjuck.

2. *v.* To go about in a slovenly, untidy manner.

s.Wor. ' 'E gooes hudyeuckin' alung as if 'e 'adn't got no life in 'im,' said of a man with a slouching, idle gait (H.K.).

HUDLANCE, HUDMEDOD, see **Hidlance, Hodmandod.**

HUDSKIN, *sb.* n.Cy. [Not known to our correspondents.] A kind of hobgoblin.

Seventy or eighty years ago . . . when the whole earth was so overrun with ghosts, boggles, .. hudskins, nickers, *Denham Tracts* (ed. 1895) II. 78.

HUE, *sb.* and *v.* Sc. Also written **hew** Sc. ; and in form **hy** Sh.I. [hiu.] **1.** *sb.* Look, appearance.

Abd. Tho' we were dress'd, this creeshy woo' Wou'd soon rub out the mangle hue, BEATTIE *Parings* (1801) 31, ed. 1873.

2. A slight quantity, a ' soupçon.'

Sc. The storm kicked up by the dancers was like to mak' maist of us on-lookers a wee hue hearse, Sc. *Haggis*, 160. Sh.I. JAKOBSEN *Norsk in Sh.* (1897) 68. Abd. Give me a hew o' meal to bait the mouse-trap. Pit in a huie o' whisky amo' yer water (G.W.). Rnf. (JAM.) Ayr. I'll hae to whummle't through my wame the nicht wi' a hue o' toddy, SERVICE *Notandums* (1890) i; (J.F.) Lnk. And for beauty, pray, what's a' her share o't? Like me she could thole a hue mair o't, RODGER *Poems* (1838) 36, ed. 1897. Rxb. (JAM.)

3. *v.* To colour ; *gen.* in *pass.*

Edb. Its back was hue'd like a grey nag, LIDDLE *Poems* (1821) 101. [1. Godess Gast Inn aness cullfress heowe, *Ormulum* (c. 1200) 12605. OE. *hiw* (CYNEWULF *Crist* 721). 2. Yee leuedis ... studis hu your hare to heu, hu to dub and hu to paynt, *Cursor M.* (c. 1300) 28013. OE. *hiwian,* 'colorare,' *Voc.* (c. 1050) in Wright's *Voc.* (1884) 178.]

HUE, HUED, HUEL, see **Whew, Hold,** *v.,* **Hull,** *sb.*[1], **Wheal.**

HUEL, *sb.* N.Cy.[1] A gluttonous, greedy fellow. Cf. **hewl.** 'He's a huel for fish.'

HUER, *sb. Obs.* ne.Lan.[1] Hail.

HUETA, see **Husta.**

HUFF, *sb.*[1] Hnt. e.An. Also written **hough** Nrf. [**uf.**] **1.** A dry, scurfy, or scaly incrustation of the skin ; a furred condition of the tongue. See **Hurf.**

Hnt. (T.P.F.), e.An.[1] Nrf. Arter the fàver, the skin came off my poor gal's hands all in a huff (W.R.E.) ; Still in use (M.C.H.B.) ; COZENS-HARDY *Broad Nrf.* (1893) 53.

2. *Obs.* Fungus appearing on pickles or jam when in a fermenting state. Nrf. COZENS-HARDY *Broad Nrf.* (1893) 53 ; (M.C.H.B.)

HUFF, *sb.*[2] Hmp. [**uf.**] A drove or herd of cattle.

The cattle in huffs came belloking to the lew of the boughy trees, BLACKMORE *Cradock Nowell* (1866) xxxi ; WISE *New Forest* (1883) 185 ; Hmp.[1]

HUFF, *v.*[1], *sb.*[3] and *adj.* In *gen.* dial. and colloq. use in Sc. Irel. Eng. and Amer. [h)uf, h)uf.] **1.** *v.* To blow, puff ; to breathe heavily, to pant. Cf. **hough,** *v.*[2]

Sus. After repeating some words to herself huffed or breathed quickly on it, HENDERSON *Flk-Lore* (1879) v ; Of sheep (S.P.H.) ; So I come huffen off, ya see, The blood was bilen hot, LOWER *Jan Cladpole* (1872) 124. I.W.[2] Gwyne up hill makes me huff.

2. To swell, puff up ; to rise in baking ; *gen.* with *up* ; also used *trans.*

Sh.I. Shûs gotten a sair brûse i' da open o' her head, an' hit's blue an' huff'd up, *Sh. News* (Aug. 28, 1897) ; Da bakers hae some shilpit thing 'at dey pit i' da flooer ta mak' hit huff up, an' be white, *ib.* (Mar. 24, 1900). n.Yks. T'wound huff't up (I.W.) ; n.Yks.[1] Her eye huffed oop in a minute ; n.Yks.[2][4], Lei.[1] Nhp. [Of] the stomach being distended with flatulence, GROSE (1790) *MS. add.* (C.) War.[2] The milk huffs one up so.

Hence (1) **Huffing,** *sb.* a swelling, distention ; (2) **Huffy,** *adj.* puffy, not firm.

(1) Nrf. The people speak of suffering from ' a huffin' o' the lights ' (S.P.H.). (2) Glo.[1]

3. To become angry, to rage ; to take offence.

Bnff. She hufft at me, the saucy limmer, TAYLOR *Poems* (1787) 55. Frf. (J.B.) Ayr. They'd scarce deserve the name of men Wha wadna at sic nonsense huff, THOM *Amusements* (1812) 40. n.Cy. (J.W.) n.Ir. Dinnae be huft wi' me, Paddy, LYTTLE *Paddy McQuillan*, 75. Lakel.[2], n.Lan.[1] I. Ma. Sniffs and snuffs, and sulks and sulks, and huffs and huffs, BROWN *Witch* (1889) 62.

Hence **Huffy,** *adj.* quick-tempered, apt to take offence, ' touchy' ; angry, offended ; also used *advb.*

Sc. There's three brave chins as any man may see, air—There's huffie chin, and muffie chin, and chin of gravitie, MAIDMENT *Pasquils* (1868) 326. Rnf. In case your Highland heart gets huffy, WEBSTER *Rhymes* (1835) 167. Lnk. Ye needna leuk huffie at me, WRIGHT *Life* (1897) 75. Nhb. If aa said no, 'twud seem as if aa bore malice an' wes huffy aboot the lickin', PEASE *Mark o' the Deil* (1894) 45 ; He's a varra huffy chep (R.O.H.). Yks. (J.W.) Lan. If I'd told Miss Gerrard what I suspected ... she might have been huffy, BRIERLEY *Cotters*, ii. Chs.[1] Brks.[1] A be a huffy zart o' chap. Sus. I be dubersome wether dey loike foreigners, an

dey be rite huffy, JACKSON *Southward Ho* (1894) I. 289 ; Sus.[1] w.Som.[1] Her's a huffy old thing, nif her id'n a keep plaised. [Amer. Don't get huffy, *Dial. Notes* (1896) I. 397.]

4. To offend, affront ; to put in a bad temper.

Abd. I kenna how the Quean's sae huff'd, SHIRREFS *Poems* (1790) *Introd.* 21. Frf. In common use (J.B.). Ayr. For fear that he should chance to huff The fouk that's gentle, FISHER *Poems* (1790) 69. Gall. He had called at Whitehaven, a town that had once huffed him, MACTAGGART *Encycl.* (1824) 375, ed. 1876. Nhb.[1], Dur.[1], Lakel.[2] Cum. Dan was terrably hufft at this, FARRALL *Betty Wilson* (1886) 27 ; Cum.[14], n.Yks.[24] n.Yks.[1] Don't huff him now, if thou can help it. n.Lan.[1], ne Lan.[1], Nhp.[1], w.Wor.[1] s.Wor. 'E 'uffed 'is missus, an' 'er gen 'im the sack (H.K.). se.Wor.[1] Shr.[1] ; Shr.[2] Now you have huff'd him. Glo.[1] Wil. BRITTON *Beauties* (1825). Cor. He is huffed (M.A.C.). [They broke my pitcher, And spilt the water, And huff'd my mother, And chid her daughter, HALLIWELL *Rhymes* (ed. 1886) 95.]

5. To treat scornfully ; to bully ; to scold, reprimand, reproach.

Sc. They have several times huff'd and hiss'd us out of the college like so many Jesuits, PITCAIRN *Assembly* (1766) 58. Ayr. To see how ye're negleckit, How huff'd an' cuff'd an' disrespeckit! BURNS *Twa Dogs* (1786) l. 87. Lnk. They wha hae nane are huft an' howted Wi' jybes an' jeerin', WATT *Poems* (1827) 73. Cum.[1] They huff't it as if it hed been dirt. n.Yks.[2] Lan. DAVIES *Races* (1856) 234. ne.Lan.[1], e.Lan.[1] Nhp.[1] He huft her well. e.An.[1], Nrf. (W.R.E.), Sus.[1] Hmp. HOLLOWAY. Dev. Our neighbour Flail, That huffith his wive, and kickth her tail, PETER PINDAR *Wks.* (1816) III. 253.

6. With *off* or *out:* to get rid of by bullying or hectoring.

Edb. I ... had not the heart to huff her out, MOIR *Mansie Wauch* (1828) xx. e.Suf. (F.H.)

7. *Obs.* With *away:* to get on smartly with one's work.

Peb. Wi' gooly sticks pig, soo, and boar, Wi' frock their blood besmears, He'll huff away, *Lintoun Green* (1685) 84, ed. 1817.

8. *sb.* A fit of anger or ill-temper ; a pet, 'tiff' ; offence, dudgeon ; *freq.* in phr. *to take the huff.*

Sc. I never knew Jane in a huff yet ... that she didn't alter her will, KEITH *Lisbeth* (1894) xviii. Sh.I. Der nae gude iver gotten be gettin' in a huff ower triflin' maitters, *Sh. News* (Dec. 11, 1897). Abd. 'Twad pit the wife in sic a huff, To liken it to scaun stuff, SHIRREFS *Poems* (1790) 331. Ked. Some huff at me he's taen, JAMIE *Muse* (1844) 90. Frf. Syne he began to loup an' ban, When out the wife flew in a huff, SMART *Rhymes* (1834) 207. Rnf. Fools who left her in a huff, Says may be cheeping, M°GILVRAY *Poems* (ed. 1862) 264. Ayr. ' Noo dinna ye be obstropalous, or tak the huff,' quo' he, SERVICE *Notandums* (1890) 38. Lnk. Wi' nae word o' explanation, Aff an' left her in the huff, NICHOLSON *Kilwuddie* (ed. 1895) 60. Edb. They gang by ye wi' sic a huff, LEARMONT *Poems* (1791) 2. Rxb. Her jibes I canna bear, She gars me tak the huff, WILSON *Poems* (1824) 20. Dmf. When e'er I tak' the huff, My fair opponents skelp me aff, QUINN *Heather* (1863) 131. Gall. Jean at length took up the huff, Because neglected o' her due, LAUDERDALE *Poems* (1796) 58. Lakel.[2] Cum. I oft send her off in a huff, RICHARDSON *Talk* (1876) and S. 19 ; Cum.[1] n.Yks.[1] ; n.Yks.[2] ; n.Yks.[4] He's ta'en huff, an' sha's ta'en t'hig, an' tha've baith gitten t'hump tigither. m.Yks.[1] w.Yks. Vowed shoo'd nivver tak t'huff, TOM TREDDLEHOYLE *Bairnsla Ann.* (1883) 29 ; Shoo's taen t'huff at what tha said (J.T.). ne.Lan.[1], m.Lan.[1], Chs.[1], Stf.[1] nw.Der.[1] He's gon away in a huff. Not.[1] Lin.[1] I told him he had a hanged-gallows-look and he went off in a huff. n.Lin.[1] I tell'd him one or two things aboot his sen, soä he went awaay in a huff. w.Wor.[1], se.Wor.[1] Shr.[1] ; Shr.[2] Gone away in a huff. e.An.[1] He is in a huff. ne.Ken. He's gone off in a huff (H.M.). Sus., Hmp. HOLLOWAY. Wil. SLOW *Gl.* (1892). w.Som.[1] Her was in a purty huff about it. Cor. He is in a huff (M.A.C.). Colloq. Lady Macbeth looks uncommonly cross, And says in a huff, It's all ' Proper stuff,' BARHAM *Ingoldsby* (1840) 105.

Hence **Huffishness,** *sb.* offence, dudgeon, ' hauteur.'

Yks. After a brief pause, she replied with a touch of huffishness, HOLMES *Farquhar Frankheart*, 4.

9. Haste, hurry.

Sh.I. What's da raison 'at da folk is in sic a huff to get da tatties oot o' da grund ! *Sh. News* (Oct. 16, 1897).

10. Light pastry or pie-crust.

Glo. Light paste, inclosing fruit or meat whilst stewing ; so called from its huffing or puffing up in the operation. *Gen.* made with yeast, GROSE (1790) ; BAYLIS *Illus. Dial.* (1870) ; *Gl.* (1851) ; Glo.[1]

M m 2

11. Strong beer.

Hmp.¹ Very strong (Winchester) College ale. Wil. Grose (1790); Britton *Beauties* (1825).

12. *adj.* In a bad temper. Lakel.², Lin.¹

HUFF, *v.*² and *sb.*⁴ Fif. (Jam.) [Not known to our correspondents.] 1. *v.* To humbug, illude, disappoint.

2. *sb.* A humbug, disappointment.

HUFF, *int.* Sc. An exclamation expressive of surprise or suddenness.

Ayr. Aft to my sighing, I've thought her complying, Whan, huff! aff she's flying, Flaff, like a flee, Ainslie *Land of Burns* (ed. 1892) 325.

HUFF-CAP, *sb.* Wor. Hrf. Glo. e.Cy. Suf. w.Cy. Som. [u·f-kæp.] 1. Anything good or strong in the way of drink. Suf.¹

2. A brand of perry ; a pear used for perry.

Wor. Little is exported excepting the prime sorts such as real taynton squash, huffcap, Marshall *Review* (1818) II. 367. Glo.¹, w.Cy. (Hall.)

3. A swaggering fellow. e.Cy. (Hall.) [Not known to our correspondents.] 4. The white couch-grass, *Triticum repens.* Hrf. (Hall.) Som. (W.F.R.); (B. & H.); W. & J. *Gl.* (1873). 5. A mound of coarse grass. Som. (J.S.F.S.), (F.A.A.)

[1. The best nippitatum in this town, which is commonly called hufcap, it will make a man looke as though he had seene the devill, *Art of Flattery* (Nares). 3. Was not this huff-cap once the Indian emperour ? Clifford *Notes on Dryden* (1687) (ib.).]

HUFFEL, HUFFIL, see Hovel, *sb.*²

HUFFKIN, *sb.* Ken. Sus. Also written hufkin, uffkin Ken. [u·fkin.] A kind of muffin. See Huff, *sb.*⁸ 10.

Ken. (G.B.) ; Grose (1790) *MS. add.* ; Ken.¹ A kind of bun or light cake, which is cut open, buttered, and so eaten. e.Ken. *N. & Q.* (1869) 4th S. iv. 76. Sus. *ib.* (1859) and S. viii. 483.

HUFFLE, *sb.*¹ e.An.¹² [u·fl.] A rattling in the throat in breathing ; also used in *pl.* and in form Hufflins. See Huff, *v.*¹ 1.

HUFFLE, *sb.*² Ess. A quantity, a large amount of anything.

Gen. used ironically. 'Well, that's a huffle to bring anybody' (J.F.).

HUFFLE, *v.*¹ and *sb.*³ Dor. Dev. Cor. Also written huffel Dev.⁸ [u·fl.] 1. *v.* Of the wind: to blow unsteadily, to shift, waver ; to blow up in sudden gusts, to raise by blowing. See Huff, *v.*¹ 1.

w.Cy. (Hall.) Dor. Where sharp-leaved ashès' heads did twist In huffeln wind, an' driftèn mist, Barnes *Poems* (1869-70) 3rd S. 126. Dev.¹ The weend huffled an' hulder'd et in wans eyes, 18; Dev.⁸ nw.Dev. The wind huffled up the dust rather (R.P.C.). Cor. The wind huffles, Thomas *Randigal Rhymes* (1895) *Gl.*

2. *sb.* A sudden change of wind ; a wailing or hollow sound of wind.

Dev. At the huffle of the gale, Here I toss and cannot sleep, Baring-Gould & Sheppard *Sngs. of West* (1889) 9 ; Dev.⁸

[1. To swage seas surging or raise by blusterus huffling, Stanyhurst *Aeneis* (1583) I. 75 (Dav.).]

HUFFLE, *v.*² and *sb.*⁴ Yks. Shr. e.An. Ken. Also in form huvel e.An.¹ e.Suf. [u·fl, u·fl.] 1. *v.* To shuffle.

m.Yks.¹ To shuffle painfully, in a sitting or recumbent position. e.An. (W.W.S.) ; e.An.¹ I've just cleaned the place, and you've come huvelling about.

2. *Comp.* Huffle-footed, (2) -heeled, clumsy-footed, shuffling in gait.

(1) Shr.¹ (a) *ib.* 'E'll mak' a prime militia-mon—w'y 'e's 'ump-backed an' 'uffle-'eeled !

3. To rumple ; in *pass.*, with *up* : to be in a tangled, confused mass.

Suf. (Hall.) e.Suf. The wind has blown the (cut) barley so that it's huvelled up anyhow—some standing, some half-down, some prone (F.H.).

4. *sb.* A shuffling. m.Yks.¹

5. A merry meeting, a feast.

Ken. Lewis *I. Tenet* (1736) ; Grose (1790) ; Ken.¹²

HUFFLE, see Hovel, *sb.*²

HUFFLE-BUFFS, *sb. pl.* Rxb. (Jam.) [Not known to our correspondents.] Old clothes.

HUFFLED, *ppl. adj.* Hmp.¹ Angry, offended. See Huff, *v.*¹ 8.

HUFFLER, *sb.* Ken. Also written uffler. [u·flə(r).] 1. One who gains a living by carrying fresh provisions, &c. to ships. Grose (1790), Ken.⁸ Cf. hoveller (1), s.v. Hovel.

2. A bargeman, one who is employed to tow barges. Cf. hoveller (2), s.v. Hovel.

Used on the banks of the Medway (W.F.S.); A class of person about Maidstone . . . who are men in the barging line out of employ, who attend as extra help to get the craft home in our inland navigation, *Gent. Mag.* (Aug. 1824) 111 ; Grose (1790) *MS. add.* (M.)

HUFFLING, *ppl. adj.* Lon. Confining, oppressive, thick.

Used of a garment which confines the movement of the limbs and especially of the head. Of a shawl—'Don't put it so high up on my neck ; put it lower down ; it's so huffling' (W.H.E.).

HUFFLIT, *sb.* Fif. (Jam.) [Not known to our correspondents.] A blow with the hand on the side of the head, a box on the ear. See Haffet, 4.

HUFFOCK, *sb.* Stf.¹ [u·fək.] A large foot.

HUFIL, see Hickwall.

HUFT, *v.* Chs. Not. [uft.] To offend; only in *pp.* See Huff, *v.*¹ 4.

s.Chs.¹ Ey;z ver·i sóon uf·tid [Hey's very soon hufted].

Hence (1) **Hufted,** *adj.* sullen ; (2) **Hufty,** *adj.* in a 'huff,' offended, angry.

(1) Chs.¹ (2) s.Not. When 'e knows it's broke, 'e'll be very hufty about it (J.P.K.).

HUFTY, *sb.* Yks. [Not known to our correspondents.] A swaggerer. (Hall.)

HUFUD, *sb.* n.Sc. (Jam.) [Not known to our correspondents.] A blow with the hand on the side of the head, a box on the ear. See Haffet, 4.

HUG, *sb.*¹ Sh.I. [hug.] A young sheep, a 'hog.'

He's clappid on yon fieless hund o' his apon his black hug, *Sh. News* (July 24, 1897).

Hence **Huggie,** *adj.* young (used of sheep).

Da grey huggie lamb, an' dy shaela ane wis as nakid is da back o' my haand (ib.).

HUG, *sb.*² Som. [ug.] 1. The itch, the 'you k.'

Commonly, but not always applied to brutes, Jennings Obs. *Dial. w.Eng.* (1825) ; W. & J. *Gl.* (1873). w.Som.¹ Called also the Welshman's hug.

2. *Comp.* Hug-water, water to cure the itch. Jennings Obs. *Dial. w.Eng.* (1825).

HUG, *v.* Sc. Nhb. Dur. Lakel. Cum. Yks. Lan. Der. Lin. Nhp. War. Shr. e.An. Ken. I.W. Dor. Cor. Also in forms hog n.Cy. w.Yks.; hogg s.Lan. ; hoog n.Yks.; huggy e.An.¹ [hug, ug.] 1. In *comb.* (1) Hug-a-bed, a sluggard, one who is fond of his bed ; (2) -a-mă-tug, the scapula of a fowl with the coracoid bone attached ; (3) -me-close or Huggy-me-close, (a) the merry-thought or clavicle of a fowl ; (b) the goose-grass, *Galium Aparine.*

(1) sw.Lin.¹ Eleven will do better for us hug-a-beds. I doubt he's a bit of a hug-a-bed. (2) Shr.¹ (3, a) ne.Lan.¹, Nhp.¹, e.An.¹ Ken. Holloway. (b) Dor. (G.E.D.)

2. *Phr.* (1) *to hug one's whelps,* to sit with the arms folded; (2) *huggin' an' luggin',* nursing and suckling an infant.

(1) Cor.⁸ Has'n the' nothing to do but set theare huggin your whelps ? (2) Lakel.² Wm. Hoo can t'woman git on huggin an' luggin a gurt fat barn like yon ? (B.K.)

3. To cherish, to cling to with fondness.

I.W. A plot He cultures as garden, and as freehold bug, Moncrieff *Dream* (1869) 22.

4. To kiss. n.Lin.¹

5. To keep close to, to cling to ; to run closely side by side.

Sc. As whan dark clouds the fair sky fill, An' smokin' hug ilk distant hill, Allan *Lilts* (1874) 5. Lan. Gan on by t'track, an hug t'beck weel till ye cum to Floutern Tarn, Waugh *Rambles* 124. Cy. (1861) v. ne.Lan.¹, War. (J.R.W.) [A good dog must not hug, Mayer *Sptsmn's Direct.* (1845) 47.]

6. To carry on the back or in the arms, to carry with difficulty, to 'lug.'

n.Cy. Grose (1790) ; N.Cy.¹, Nhb.¹ Dur. A singl' man cudn't x ; huggd aboot wuv em, Egglestone *Betty Podkin's Lett.* (187 ?) a Gibson *Up-Weardale Gl.* (1870). n.Yks. They picked up near a hoondred weeight ov paving staanes an' hooged 'em a' th' rooad whooame, Fetherston *Smuggins Fam.* 72; n.Yks.¹; n.Yks.² I's brussen wi' hugging on't; n.Yks.³⁴ ne.Yks. (J.C.F.); ne.Yks.¹ Used to express every kind of carrying, whether e. g. carrying out for burial, or holding any light article, like a stick. ' Sha'll nivver cum oot na mair whahl sha's bugg'd oot.' ' Wheea hugs t'kei [key]!' e.Yks. Marshall *Rur. Econ.* (1788); e.Yks.¹ Can thä hug a seck o' wheeat up granary steps? m.Yks.¹ w.Yks. Hutton *Tour to Caves* (1781); 'Ah'll hug her it up,' being said very rapidly, sounded like one word, 'huggerytup,' *Leeds Merc. Suppl.* (Jan. 5, 1889); w.Yks.¹²⁸⁴; w.Yks.⁵ Am tired mammy; hug muh a bit! Lan. Aw could hug a chap a mile if he wurno drunken, Brierley *Irkdale* (1865) 132, ed. 1868; Shou'd they naw be hugg'd oth' seme back! Tim Bobbin *View Dial.* (ed. 1806) 57. ne.Lan.¹, e.Lan.¹ s.Lan. Ta' th' chylt, an' hogg it (S.B.). nw.Der.¹ Lin. Hugging a sack on his back (J.C.W.). n.Lin.¹ Can ta hug a seck o' beåns? He's gotten moore then he can hug [he is drunk]. s.Lin. Neer mind, mester, I'll hug 'em for yur into the barn (T.H.R.). sw.Lin.¹ They hugged it right a top of the seed stack. The pig always hugs the straw out into the yard.

Hence (1) **Hugger**, *sb.* a porter or carrier; (2) **Huggin**, *sb.* an armful, a load; *fig.* a share, amount; (3) **Hugging-sticks**, *sb. pl.* the poles on which a coffin is carried to the grave.

(1) n.Yks.² w.Yks.⁵ ' Rod-hugger,' teazle-rod carrier at a dressing-mill. (2) Lakel.² Some fooak er said ta be huggin an' pooin thersels ta death fer t'siak o' siaven brass. w.Yks. (J.W.) Lin.¹ This is hugging work. (3) n.Yks.² w.Yks.⁵ 'Rod-hugger,' teazle-rod carrier at a dressing-mill. (2) Lakel.² As mich streea, er hay, er owt o' that sooart as yan can carry at yance, that's a huggin. As mich yal as a chap can carry an' walk streck; that's a huggin, ano. Cum.⁴ w.Yks. A stock o' patience . . . an' a gooid huggin o' determination to be pleased, Hartley *Clock Alm.* (Jan. 1872). (3) w.Yks. Lucas *Stud. Nidderdale* (c. 1882) Gl.

7. To tire as with a heavy burden.
Lakel.² Some fooak er said ta be huggin an' pooin thersels ta death fer t'siak o' siaven brass. w.Yks. (J.W.) Lin.¹ This is hugging work.

8. To urge, incite, to persuade to do anything.
w.Yks. Tha's hugged him on to it, *Leeds Merc. Suppl.* (Nov. 8, 1884).

9. Phr. *to hug one a bill on something*, to send one in a bill for something. n.Yks.² We hugg'd 'em a bill on't.

HUG, HUG-A-MUG, see **Hock**, *sb.¹*, **Hugger-mugger**.

HUGE, *adv.* Lan. Ken. Also in form **hugy** Ken.¹² Very.
Lan. *Obs.* I was huge sleepy at duty y⁰ night, Newcome *Diary* (1661) 10, in *Chet. Soc.* (1849) XVIII. Ken.¹ The saying 'hugy' for 'huge' is merely the sounding of the finale; Ken.² I'm not huge well.

HUGEOUS, *adj.* Sc. Nhb. Nhp. Hnt. Dev. Also written **hugious** Nhb.¹; and in form **huges** Dev.¹

1. Huge, large; also used *advb.*
Sc. A hugeous conch he in his left Held, like a bugil horn, Jamieson *Pop. Ballads* (1806) I. 243. Nhb.¹ Nhp. We met three or four hugeous ugly devils, Dryden *Wild Gallant* (1669); Nhp.¹, Hnt. (T.P.F.) Dev. What thoff Iss ban't so hugeous smurt, Peter Pindar *Wks.* (1816) III. 252; Dev.¹ A huges heave-up truly if her had'n had a farding to marry such a stingy hunks, 6.

2. Used to express great intimacy between friends.
Nhp.¹ They are hugeous folks. Hnt. (T.P.F.)

HUGGABACK, *sb.* Cum. Yks. Also written **huga-back** Cum.⁴ [h]u·gəbak.] 1. A strong linen fabric, huckaback, ' hag-a-bag.' w.Yks.² 2. The tufted vetch, *Vicia cracca.* Cum.¹⁴

HUGGA-MABUFF, *sb.* Hrt. Also written **hugger-merbuff.** [ʊ·gəməbʊf.] The second growth of grass, the aftermath. (H.G.); *N. & Q.* (1853) 1st S. viii. 102.

HUGGAN, *sb.* w.Yks. The fruit of the dog-rose, *Rosa canina*, hips. (B. & H.)

HUGGAR, HUGGER, see **Hogger**.

HUGGER, *sb.¹* Nhb.¹ [hu·gər.] A line of cleavage in coal, a 'back' or 'cleat.'

HUGGER, *v.¹* and *sb.²* Sc. [hʊ·gər.] 1. *v.* To shudder, shiver; to be bent down with cold or disease, to crouch with cold. Bnff.¹, Abd. (Jam.) Hence **Huggerin**, *ppl. adj.* bent down with cold or disease.
Bnff.¹ It wiz behrt-sair to see the peer huggerin' bodie oot i' the caul' an weet.

2. To crowd together from cold.
ib. A' the nout wir huggerin' the geethir at the lythe side o' the dyke.

3. *sb.* A shivering and crouching condition due to cold or disease. *ib.*

[1. A freq. of obs. E. *hugge*, to shudder, shiver. It is good sporte to se this lytle boye hugge in his bedde for colde, Palsgr. (1530).]

HUGGER, *v.²* Yks. Brks. 1. With *up* : to wrap up. n.Yks.² Hugger't up onny hoo, I's clash'd for time.
2. To hoard. Brks.¹ Cf. **hugger-mugger**, *v.* 9.

HUGGERIE, *adj.* Sc. Also in forms **hogry** Lth. (Jam.); **huggrie, hugrie** Bwk. Rxb. (Jam.) [hʊ·g(ə)ri.] 1. Awkward and confused in behaviour or dress. Bwk., Rxb. (Jam.)
2. *Comp.* **Huggry-muggry** or **Hogry-mogry**, in a confused state, disorderly, untidy, slovenly. Cf. **hugger-mugger.**
Per. I'm wae to see a puir man's chucky Turn out a huggry-muggry lucky, Stewart *Character* (1857) 61. Ayr. In common use (J.F.). Lth., Bwk., Rxb. (Jam.)

HUGGER-MUGGER, *sb., adv., adj.* and *v.* In *gen.* dial. use in Sc. and Eng. Also in forms **hug-a-mug** Cor.; **hug-mug** Nhp.²; **hugger-smugger** Sh.I. 1. *sb.* Concealment, secrecy, stealth; esp. in phr. *in hugger-mugger*, in secret, clandestinely.
Sh.I. Lasses, what is a' dis 'at ye're haein' in hugger-smugger? *Sh. News* (Oct. 8, 1898). w.Yks. *Leeds Merc. Suppl.* (1884). Dev.¹ My dame was abu (!) doing ort in hugger-mugger, 13.

2. A secret conclave, a suspicious meeting together.
w.Yks.² 3. A miser. Der.², nw.Der.¹ Som. Sweetman *Wincanton Gl.* (1885).

4. Confusion, disorder, untidiness; esp. in phr. *in (a) hugger-mugger*, in disorder.
n.Yks.⁴ I.Ma. Every place as nate as a pin, and couldn stand no hugger-mugger about, Brown *Doctor* (1887) 36. Not. (J.H.B.) Nhp.¹ They live all in a hugger-mugger; Nhp.² All in a hug-mug. s.War.¹, Brks. (W.H.Y.) I.W.¹ Anything done badly and carelessly.

5. One who talks fast and cannot tell the truth. s.Lan. (W.H.T.)

6. *adv.* Clandestinely, in a sneaking way; also used as *adj.* underhand.
Sh.I. I kent Bawby wid laek ta come oot wi' suntin' 'at da tedder sheelds wis tryin' ta keep hugger-smugger, *Sh. News* (Mar. 5, 1898). Nhb. (R.O.H.), Cum.¹ w.Yks. Cooper Gl. (1853). Der. *Monthly Mag.* (1815) II. 297. Suf.¹ Dev.¹ In huggermugger fashion. n.Dev. Jones, you've condiddled they, Just in your huggermugger way, Rock *Jim an' Nell* (1867) st. 113. Slang. *Lex. Balatronicum* (1811).

7. In confusion, disorder; also used as *adj.* untidy, slovenly.
Nhb. Wors weren't hugger-mugger things, Wilson *Pitman's Pay* (1843) 54; Whatn a kine iv a hugger-mugger way's that yor deein! They aall leev'd hugger-mugger (R.O.H.). Cum. (H.W.); Cum.¹; Cum.⁵ I'd gitten sumat to eat, iv a hugger-mugger mak of a way, 18. Yks. (J.W.) Lan. Let alone his meals being all hugger-mugger, Gaskell *M. Barton* (1848) x. Cha.¹ Used chiefly to express an untidy, unsystematic way of living. Der.², nw.Der.¹ Lin. Hugger-mugger they lived, but they wasn't that easy to pleäse, Tennyson *Vill. Wife* (1880) st. 18; Lin.¹ I dislike having my meals in such hugger-mugger ways. n.Lin.¹ War.⁴ It's a sha'am to put a carriage like this into a hugger-mugger place like that. Sus.¹; Sus.² There was no system; it was all hugger-mugger. Hmp. Holloway. w.Som.¹ 'Tis a shockin poor hugger-mugger [uug·ur·mugg·ur] concarn way em, I 'sure ee. Dev. They be a hugger-mugger lot, I can tellee; they live awl ov a heap like pegs, Hewett *Peas. Sp.* (1892). Cor. They be all a-gwain to sea, hug-a-mug, bang! Baring-Gould *Vicar* (1876) I.

8. *adj.* Stingy. e.An.¹

9. *v.* To act in an underhand manner; to conceal; to stow away carefully, to hoard.
Sh.I. The dyke . . . was erected . . . as a barrier to hugger-smugger the debris, *Sh. News* (Mar. 12, 1898). Ayr. They continue whispering and whispering, and hugger-muggering, as if they were smuggling something awa', Galt *Sir A. Wylie* (1822) civ. Gall. Doing business not openly, quibbling about trifles and raising misunderstandings, Mactaggart *Encycl.* (1824). N.Cy.¹, Cum.¹ n.Yks. He huggermuggers his brass (T.S.). Brks.¹ A ke-ups his money pretty much hugger-muggered up an' dwoant spend none hardly.

10. To act in a confused manner; to spend time unprofitably.
Cum.¹ Hugger-muggeran about heåmm. Lan. A taggelt hugger-mugg'rin about, R. Piketah *Forness Flk.* (1870) 31.

Hence **Hugger-muggerer**, *sb.* one who spends his time unprofitably.

Cum.[4] Nin o' thur eight-page ditties, et hugger-mugerers sec as us er fworc'd to lissen tui, ANDERSON *The Cram.* 61.

[1. These heretyques teche in hucker mucker, MORE *Dyalogue* (1529) ii. 52 (N.E.D.).]

HUGGET, see **Hogget**, *sb.*[2]

HUGGIE, *sb.* Sh.I. [hɐ·gi.] **1.** A blow. S. & Ork.[1]

2. *Comp.* **Huggie-staff**, a wooden pole, furnished with a strong iron hook, used for striking fish into the boat.

Die ye mind da roar 'at Jeemie Aerterson gae for you ta fling him da huggie-staff? Hit wis a turbot, . . . an' dey twa huggie-staaves intil him, forby Paetie's haand in his gills, afore he cam' i' da boat, *Sh. News* (Sept. 17, 1898); His skône, huggie-staff, and karel-tree are at hand, SPENCE *Flk-Lore* (1899) 134 ; (*Coll.* L.L.B.); JAKOBSEN *Norsk in Sh.* (1897) 30 ; **S. & Ork.**[1]

[1. A der. of Norw. dial. *hogg*, a blow, stroke (AASEN); Dan. *hug*, ON. *högg.*]

HUGGIN, *sb.* Lakel. Yks. Lan. Der. Lin. Also written huggan ne.Yks.[1] e.Yks. w.Yks.[1] ne.Lan.[1]; huggen w.Yks.[8]; hugging n.Yks.; huggon e.Yks.[1] w.Yks.[45] Der.[1]; and in form hoggin s.Lan. [h)u·gən.] The hip or hip-bone, 'hock-bone,' esp. of a horse or cow ; also in *comp.* **Huggin-bone.** Cf. **hubbon.**

Lakel.[2] She'd t'barn astride ov her huggin an' a canful o' watter e' tudder hand. **n.Yks.** [Of a fat cow] She squared at the huggings three feet five inches, TWEDDELL *Hist. Cleveland* (1873) 97. **ne.Yks.**[1] Mind thou disn't knock a huggon off, gannin wi awd meear thruff that narrow deearsteed. **w.Yks.** Shoo rested her neives on her huggens, HARTLEY *Clock Alm.* (1894) 28 ; **w.Yks.**[1] Clappin baath kneaves to my huggans, ii. 294 ; **w.Yks.**[2] He's lame of his huggin ; **w.Yks.**[345], **Lan.**[1], **ne.Lan.**[1], **e.Lan.**[1], **s.Lan.** (S.W.), **Der.**[1], **n.Lin.**[1] **sw.Lin.**[1] He's gotten a strange lump on his huggin, where he fell on the gasfaulting. I was always a poor shortwaisted thing, my huggins come up so high.

Hence **Huggan-slipt**, *adj.* of a horse : having the thigh-bone out of joint. e.Yks. *Leeds Merc. Suppl.* (Mar. 31, 1894).

HUGGING-, see **Hoggan**, *sb.*[1]

HUGGLE, *v.* Der. Not. Lin. Lei. Nhp. War. Wor. Hnt. [ʊ·gl, ɐ·gl.] To hug, cuddle, embrace.

Der.[2], nw.Der.[1] Not. He saw that great biped putting out his arm to huggle his mother round the neck, HOOTON *Bilberry Thurland* (1896) ; Not.[1] **s.Not.** 'E catched ho'd on me an' huggled me an' tried to throw me down (J.P.K.). **sw.Lin.**[1] Do huggle me, mammy, I'm so starved. Lei.[1], Nhp.[1], War.[2], s.Wor. (H.K.), Hnt. (T.P.F.)

HUGH, *int.* Irel. An exclamation of disgust.

Don. Hugh! small obligement, indeed, to help a craithur in distress, *Century Mag.* (Oct. 1899) 958.

HUGHYAL, **HUG-MUG**, see **Houghle**, *v.*, **Hugger-mugger.**

HUGO, *sb.* Cor. Also in form **huggo**. A cavern. See **Fogo**, *sb.*[2]

In many a huggo, dark and damp, Where oft the wild waves roar, THOMAS *Randigal Rhymes* (1895) 16 ; Cor.[2] (s.v. Vugg).

HUGY, *adj. Obs.* Sc. Huge.

Fif. He grip'd his hugy gnarl'd staff in hand, TENNANT *Anster* (1812) 144, ed. 1871.

HUH, *adj.* Nhp.[1] e.An.[2] w.Som.[1] Awry, out of the perpendicular ; the same word as **Ahuh** (q.v.).

HUH, *int.* Nhb.[1] [hū.] The stroke groan uttered by a blacksmith ; the expiration which emphasizes the delivery of a blow.

Two men were engaged in working a heavy pavior's mell. One of them was asked if he did not find it very heavy work. ' Yis,' he replied, 'it tyeks the two on us aal wor time. Me mate dis the mell an' **aa** de the huh ! '

HUI, *int.* Sc. Also written **huuy. 1.** Begone! Abd. (JAM.) Cf. **hoy**, *int.*

2. *Comb.* **Hui-hoi**, a cry used by fishermen when heaving all together to launch their boats.

ne.Sc. With a succession of 'hui-hoi,' 'hurrah-ooings,' they pushed and shoved, *Gordonhaven* (1887) 31.

HUIA, *sb.* Sh.I. Also written **huya.** A height, a hill. S. & Ork.[1]

HUICK, *sb.* Sc. A small rick of corn.

Bnff. (JAM.) Abd. I was jist gyann awa' to tirr that bit huickie that we wus takin' into the barn to thrash, ALEXANDER *Johnny Gibb* (1871) xxxii.

HUID, HUIE, HUIGH, HUIL-, see **Hide**, *v.*[2], **Hoo**, *sb.*[1], *int.*, **Yule.**

HUILK, *sb.* Sh.I. A small vessel for holding oil. S. & Ork.[1]

[Norw. dial. *hylke*, a vessel for holding water (AASEN); ON. *hylki*, a hulk of an old tub or vessel.]

HUILLY, HUISHT, see **Hooly, Husht.**

HUISK, *sb.* Rxb. (JAM.) [Not known to our correspondents.] An untidy, dirty, unwieldy woman.

HUIST, *sb.* Cld. (JAM.) [Not known to our correspondents.] A heap ; also *fig.* an overgrown and clumsy person.

HUISTER, see **Huster.**

HUIT, *sb.* Sc. (JAM. *Suppl.*) A heap.

HUIT, *v.* Cum. [Not known to our other correspondents.] To urge ; to instigate. (M.P.)

HUIVE, HUL, see **Heave, Hole**, *sb.*[1]

HULBIE, *sb.* Lnk. (JAM.) [Not known to our correspondents.] A large, clumsy object.

A hulbie of a stone, a large unwieldy stone.

HULCH, *sb.*[1] Chs. [uḻʃ.] In phr. (1) *by hulch and stulch*, by hook or by crook ; (2) *hulch and stulch*, pell-mell, confusedly.

(1) **Chs.**[2] **s.Chs.**[1] Ey'z fūr lee·in uwt bi ùlsh ūr bi stúlsh [Hey's for leein' howt by hulch or by stulch]. (2) *ib.* A man who was stacking a load of hay complained to the one who was handing it up, 'Yoa· throa·n it ùp ùlsh ūn stùlsh ; kon)d yū taak· noa·tis wëeūr yū bin chùk·in it !' [Yo thrown it up hulch an' stulch ; conna yō tak notice wheer yō bin chuckin it ?]

HULCH, *sb.*[2] e.An. Dev. Also in form **hullchin** e.An.[1] [ʊltʃ.] A thick slice. Cf. **hulge.**

e.An.[1] Dev. I be most mortal 'ungry. I can ayte a güde hulch ov burd an' cheese ; wan za big's my tū vistes, HEWETT *Peas. Sp.* (1892).

[The same word as obs. E. *hulch*, a hump on the back. Hulch, *bosse*, *gibbe* (SHERWOOD).]

HULDER, *sb.* and *v.*[1] Dev. [ɐ·ldə(r).] **1.** *sb.* A deafening noise or din.

nw.Dev.[1] I could'n yur nort at all, there waz zich a hulder in the room.

2. *v.* Of wind : to blow violently, drive along ; to howl.

Dev.[1] The weend huffled and hulder'd et in wans eyes, 18. nw.Dev.[1] The win' hulder'd in the chimley.

HULDER, *v.*[2] Som. Dev. [ɐ·ldə(r).] To conceal, harbour.

Som. W. & J. *Gl.* (1873) ; Bit Jan did'n hulder long iz thawts, JENNINGS *Dial. w.Eng.* (1869) 86. n.Dev. I can't hulder haff zich bliss, ROCK *Jim an' Nell* (1867) st. 94.

HULDIE, *sb.* Gall. [Not known to our correspondents.] A nightcap. MACTAGGART *Encycl.* (1824).

HULE, HULERT, HULET, see **Hewl, Hull**, *sb.*[1], **Yule, Howlet.**

HULE AND HULE-BAND, *phr.* Sh.I. Bag and baggage.

SPENCE *Flk-Lore* (1899) 239 ; JAKOBSEN *Norsk in Sh.* (1897) 35 ; **S. & Ork.**[1] He's gane, hule and hule-band.

[*Hule* prob. repr. Norw. dial. *hogold* (*holda, holl*), a curved piece of wood fixed to the end of a rope (AASEN); *hule-band* will then mean the rope to which the 'hule' is fastened ; see JAKOBSEN (*l.c.*).]

HULGE, *sb.* Irel. [hɐlg.] A large irregular mass of anything. Cf. **hulch**, *sb.*[2]

N.I.[1] 'A hulge of a horse,' a loose-limbed horse. Ant. *Ballymena Obs.* (1892).

HULGIE, *adj.* Sh.I. Roomy, convenient. S. & Ork.[1]

HULGIN, *sb.* Sh.I. [hʊ·lgin.] A big mass. See **Hulge.**

A big and stout fellow is called 'a hulgin o' a fellow,' JAKOBSEN *Dial.* (1897) 49.

HULGY, *adj.* ? *Obs.* Sc. Having a hump. n.Sc. (JAM.)

Hence (1) **Hulgy-back**, *sb.* a humpbacked person ; (2) **Hulgie-backed**, *adj.* humpbacked.

Abd. (1) My bairn will now . . . of a wardly hulgy-back get free, That dad design'd his wedded wife to be, ROSS *Helenore* (1768) 85, ed. 1812. (2) An ugly hulgie-backed canker'd wasp, And like to die for breath at ilka gasp, *ib.* 36.

[The same word as obs. E. *hulchie*, humpbacked. Hulchie, *gibbeux* (SHERWOOD).]

HULK, *sb.*[1] n.Cy. Nhb. Nhp. Som. Dev. [hulk, ɐlk.] **1.** A cottage ; a temporary shelter in a field for the shepherd during the lambing-season, or for the turnip-cutter.

n.Cy. (K.), Nhb.¹ Nhp. We may rest us then, In the banish'd herdsman's den ; Where the wattled hulk is fixt, CLARE *Vill. Minst.* (1821) I. 204 ; Nhp.¹²

2. A hull or husk of fruit, grain, &c. Som. (W.F.R.)

Hence **Hulkage,** *sb.* husks, bran.

Dev. She . . . pointed to the great bock of wash and riddlings and brown hulkage (for we ground our own corn), BLACKMORE *Lorna Doone* (1869) xxxii.

8. Seed or grain when mixed with the chaff, after being threshed, but before it is winnowed.

w.Som.¹ Dev. We draws in the hulk into the barn, eens we do drash it, fear o' the rain, *Reports Provinc.* (1881) 13.

[1. As an hulke in a place where gourdis wexen, WYCLIF (1388) *Isaiah* i. 8. OE. *hulc,* 'tugurium' (ÆLFRIC). **2.** The hulk, hull, or pill is . . . any covering of fruit that is thin skinned or easily cut, HOLME *Armory* (1688) 85.]

HULK, *sb.*² Cor.² [Not known to our correspondents.] [ʋlk.] A kick.

HULK, *sb.*³ and *v.*¹ e.An. [ʋlk.] **1.** *sb.* A heavy fall. Cf. **hulker,** *sb.*²

Suf.¹ I came down such a hulk. e.Suf. (F.H.) Ess. If toddlers 'ood but mine their path, They'd seldom have a hulk, CLARK *J. Noakes* (1839) st. 106 ; Ess.¹

2. *v.* To fall. e.Suf. (F.H.)

HULK, *v.*² and *sb.*⁴ Var. dial. uses in Sc. Irel. and Eng. Also in form **hulks** s.Lin. War.² Cmb. [h]ʋlk, ulk.]

1. *v.* To skulk about as though too lazy to work ; to hang about a place ; freq. with *about.*

ne.Sc. Birdie Briggs . . . comes hulking into my shop, GRANT *Chron. Keckleton,* 65. Cai.¹ Bnff.¹ That lazy cheel's eye hulkin' at haim. Cld. (JAM.), Lakel.², Com.⁴, w.Yks.² Lan. Aw've hulked i' th' smithy till my yead's gone dazed, DOHERTY *N. Barlow* (1884) 56. nw.Der.¹ Wot art hulkin' en dooin', makkin' dh1 time away. Nhp.¹ War.² See that everything is made fast before you come in—a tramp has been hulking about this afternoon. Shr.², Glo.¹ e.An.¹ It is said of a lazy lout, who has nothing to do, and desires to have nothing, that he goes hulking about from place to place, seemingly watching for opportunities to pilfer. e.Suf. (F.H.), Som. (HALL.) Cor. To sit down idly, without moving, usually in a dirty manner, *N. & Q.* (1854) 1st S. x. 319.

Hence (1) **Hulking,** (*a*) *sb.* a lazy, shambling, overgrown fellow ; (*b*) *ppl. adj.* loutish, skulking, idle ; bad-tempered ; (2) **Hulky,** (*a*) *sb.* a big, loutish fellow ; (*b*) *adj.* lazy, clumsy, unwieldy, heavy, stupid.

(1, *a*) Lakel.² Wm. He is an idle hulkin (B.K.). Suf.¹ (*b*) Sc. (JAM.) Bnff.¹ He's a hulkin' swab o' a cheel that. Frf. Yon hulking man of sin, BARRIE *Minister* (1891) iii. Nhb. A greet hulkin chep (R.O.H.). w.Yks. He wor a big hulkin chap, HARTLEY *Clock Alm.* (1886) 42. n.Lin.¹ s.Lin. He's a gre't, lazy, hulking feller that nobudy would gi'e a day's wo'k to (T.H.R.). War.² Common. se.Wor.¹ Bdf. A great (hulkin lobutin ; fellow, BATCHELOR *Anal. Eng. Lang.* (1809) 136. Nrf. A loose hulkin' rascal, COZENS-HARDY *Broad Nrf.* (1893) 5. w.Som.¹ I never zeed no such gurt hulking (uul·keen] fuller. Dev.¹ (*a, a*) Dev.¹ (*b*) Der.², nw.Der.¹ Nhp.¹ He's a great, hulky, idle fellow, always loitering and lolloping about. War. *B'ham Wkly. Post* (June 10, 1893) ; War.¹², Shr.¹²

2. To obtain by importunity ; to hunt for.

e.Suf. The fellow hulked me out of sixpence (F.H.) ; To hulk about for a thing (*ib.*).

8. To cut uneven, as bread, cheese, &c. e.Suf. (F.H.)

4. *sb.* A lazy, clumsy fellow ; an idle, good-for-nothing lout ; a beggar.

Sc. He's gien the lazy hulke, the mither o't, baith meal and groats to maintan't, GRAHAM *Writings* (1883) II. 25. Gall. Think shame o' yersel', ye great hulk, CROCKETT *Raiders* (1894) v. Ant. A dirty lazy hulk, *Ballymena Obs.* (1892). N.Cy.¹ Nhb. An idle hulk (R.O.H.). Lakel.² Git oot o' mi rooad, thoo gurt idle hulk thoo, fer thoo's nowt else. Cum. A lang hulk of a miller, ANDERSON *Ballads* (ed. 1808) 80 ; Cum.¹⁴, e.Yks.¹ w.Yks. Ther's a gooid deeal o' lazy hulks ith' world, *Yks. Wkly. Post* (Apr. 17, 1897) ; w.Yks.⁵ A gurt hulk of a beggar, as åable to work as onnybody ! n.Lan.¹, e.Lan.¹ s.Lin. The gre't hulks, lungin' about, ah keånt abeår to see 'im (T.H.R.). Nhp.¹ War. (J.R.W.) ; War.² Keep off me, you great hulks. Shr., Hrf. BOUND *Provinc.* (1876). e.An.¹ Cmb.¹ You great hulks ! can't you wipe your feet when you come in ? Nrf. HOLLOWAY. e.Suf. (F.H.) Sus., Hmp. HOLLOWAY.

Hmp.¹ w.Cy. Gurt lazy hulks they'm bound to be, rolling about in a carriage, BAYLY *J. Merle* (1890) xxxvii. Wil. SLOW *Gl.* (1892). Som. SWEETMAN *Wincanton Gl.* (1885). Dev. He was a hulk of a man, MORTIMER *Tales Moors* (1895) 85. Cor. Barker—that was this hulk's name, HUNT *Pop. Rom. w.Eng.* (1865) 88, ed. 1896.

5. Of food : a large piece ; a hunch.

e.An.² A hulk of bread, of meat, of cheese. A great hulk of a piece. e.Suf. (F.H.)

HULK, *v.*³ and *sb.*⁵ Der. Not. Nhp. e.An. Cor. [ulk, ʋlk.] **1.** *v.* To take out the entrails of a hare or rabbit. See Howk, *v.*¹ **2.**

Not. The lad's got all them rabbits to hulk afore dinner time (L.C.M.). Nhp.¹² e.An.¹ It does not appear to be applied to the exenteration of any other animal. Nrf. COZENS-HARDY *Broad Nrf.* (1893) 72 ; (M.C.H.B.) Suf.¹ e.Suf. Rarely, of a pig (F.H.). Ess. (W.T.)

2. To clear out the 'gouge' or softer part of a lode before blasting or breaking down the harder part. Cor. WEALE. See Howk, *v.*¹ **1.**

3. *sb.* An old excavated working in a mine. nw.Der.¹, Cor.²

HULK, *v.*⁴ War. Slang. To skulk about. War.² (s.v. Hullock). FARMER.

HULKEN, *sb.* ? *Obs.* Suf.¹ [Not known to our correspondents.] A piece of skin chafed off the hand by hard work. See Hulk, *sb.*¹ **2.**

'A worked 'till hulkens came off of his hands.

HULKER, *sb.*¹ Dev. Also written **ulker.** Something big and heavy.

That's a whacking gert ulker, Idden et ? HEWETT *Peas. Sp.* (1892) ; Still in common use. A big heavy man would be called ' a reg'lar 'ulker.' Only applied to a man or animal, not to an inanimate object. It implies awkwardness or loutishness as well as great size and weight (R.P.C.).

HULKER, *v.* and *sb.*² e.Suf. [ʋlkə(r).] **1.** *v.* To dash down. (F.H.) Cf. **hulk,** *v.*¹

2. *sb.* A violent fall. ' To come down a hulker ' (*ib.*).

HULL, *sb.*¹ and *v.*¹ In *gen.* dial. use in Sc. and Eng. Also in forms **heul** N.Cy.¹ ; **hool** Sc. ; **huel** N.Cy.¹ Nhb.¹ ; **hule** Nhb.¹ Suf. [h]ʋl, ul, Sc. also hül.] **1.** *sb.* A husk ; a pod ; the outer skin of fruit ; the shell of a nut ; the rind of cheese.

Sc. There is little sap in dry pea-hools, FERGUSON *Prov.* (1641) 32 ; Every land has its ain laugh, Ilk kind of corn it has its hool, RAMSAY *Tea-Table Misc.* (1724) I. 110, ed. 1871. S. & Ork.¹ Per. I bo'ed gie them for a treat A hool o' cheese, Or dry cod fish, FORD *Harp* (1893) 347. Frf. I cleaned them out, baith pea and hool, SANDS *Poems* (1833) 24. Rnf. Buy in slump, so much the stack, Grain, straw, and hools, M°GILVRAY *Poems* (ed. 1862) 66. Lth. So ' freethought ' horn'd, these later bulls, Wha reive auld Nature to the hools, LUMSDEN *Sheep-head* (1892) 117. Dmf. Life's corn was spent, an but the hulls—The thowless hulls were left, THOM *Jock o' Knowe* (1878) 22. Gall. Maist like to cast his hoole, HARPER *Bards* (ed. 1889) 238. N.Cy.¹ Nhb. Beans eaten with the hulls be hard to defy and breed much swelling ; but the clean beans when the hull is always cleansed. Legumina be not gendered in hulls, but in cods (J.H.) ; (R.O.H.) ; Nhb.¹, Wm. (J.H.) n.Yks.¹ Pea-hulls ; nut-hulls ; n.Yks.² ³ ⁴, ne.Yks.¹ w.Yks. Hulls are the husks of the filberts, HAMILTON *Nugae Lit.* (1841) 356 ; w.Yks.¹ A potato hull. Lan.¹ Esp. the husk of the pea. Chs.¹³ s.Stf. Them bean hulls bai' much good for pigs (T.P.). s.Not. Ah uster bang the wheat about in a bag to separate the hull from the kernel (J.P.K.). Lin. Husks of turnips, eaten close to the ground, MORTON *Cyclo. Agric.* (1863) ; Lin.¹, n.Lin.¹, e.Lin. (T.H.R.), sw.Lin.¹, Nhp.¹, War.¹²³, se.Wor.¹ Shr.¹ Chuck them beån-'ulls o'er to the pigs afore yo' gin 'em the wesh ; Shr.² Shr., Hrf. BOUND *Provinc.* (1876). Hrf.¹ Glo. Ewes . . . are admitted into the fold to clear up the ' hulls,' or those bits of the turnips which have been left by the lambs, MORTON *Farm* (1892) 16 ; (A.B.) ; Glo.¹, Brks.¹ Hrt. ELLIS *Mod. Husb.* (1750) III. i. 85. e.An.¹², Nrf. (E.M.), Suf.¹ Ken.¹ After we have sheel'd them we throw the hulls away. Sus.¹², Hmp.¹ Dor. BARNES *Gl.* (1863). w.Som.¹, Cor.¹²

Hence (1) **Hulling,** *sb.* the shell or pod of seeds or nuts ; the husk of grain ; (2) **Hullspoke,** *sb.* a bed made with oat-flites.

(1) n.Yks.⁴ ne.Yks.¹ Thoo mun braay it weel ti get t'hullins off. e.Yks.¹, m.Yks.¹ (2) e.An.¹

2. *v.* To remove the outer husk of any vegetable or fruit; to shell peas; to thresh seed from the pod or sheath; to take out a kernel; to shed one's teeth.

Per. Hull that orange. I was hullin' the taties (G.W.). **Cld.** (JAM.) Nhb.[1] She's hyullin' the peas. n.Yks.[1 2 4], ne.Yks.[1], m.Yks.[1] w.Yks. HAMILTON *Nugae Lit.* (1841) 356; w.Yks.[1 2] Lan. GASKELL *Lectures Dial.* (1854) 15; Lan.[1], Chs.[1 2 3] Not. I've hulled the peas (J.H.B.); Not.[1], Lin.[1] n.Lin. Th' little lad is hulling his milk-teeth (M.P.); n.Lin.[1] e.Lin. She never hulled her first teeth (G.G.W.). sw.Lin.[1] I had just set me down to hull the peas. Nhp.[1] Hull them there walnuts. War. *B'ham Wkly. Post* (June 10, 1893); War.[1 2] Shr.[1] I've bin 'ullin walnuts all day, so I shanna want a par o' gloves fur Sunday. Gie Jim the side-basket o' pase, an' 'e'll 'ull 'em afore 'e gwuz to church, an' throw the pessum to the pigs; Shr.[2], Hrf.[2], Glo. (A.B.), Hnt. (T.P.F.) e.An.[1 2] To hull the banes. e.Suf. (F.H.) Ken. On the same day I heard a controversy between two rustics as to which was the proper term to designate this process [of stripping the outer coats of walnuts]. One insisted on the phrase 'husking,' the other 'hulling,' *N. & Q.* (1867) 3rd S. xii. 203. Sus.[1] w.Som.[1] They be coming way th' ingin a Monday, vor to hull thick there rick o' clover-zeed. They there pays [peas] on't never pay vor hullin. n.Dev. With that Jones hulled out a kern, ROCK *Jim an' Nell* (1867) st. 113.

Hence **Huller**, *sb.* a drum or apparatus belonging to a threshing-machine, used to break up the 'hull' of peas, beans, clover, &c., without injuring the seed. w.Som.[1]

3. To take off the crust of a pie, to lift up the meat in it in order to get to that which lies beneath.

Shr.[1] Yo' bin 'ullin' an' ortin' that pie as if it wunna fit to ate.

4. To pick out with a pickaxe.

Suf. She up an' took the pick and huled out the brick fast enough, FISON *Merry Suf.* (1899) 60.

[1. Hoole of pesyn, or benys, or oþer coddyd frute, *Prompt.* OE. *hulu*, husk (B.T.). 2. Take Whyte Pesyn, and hoole hem in þe maner as men don Caboges, *Cookery Bk.* (c. 1430), ed. Austin, 33.]

HULL, *v.*[2] and *sb.*[2]   Sc. Nhb. Dur. Cum. Wm. Yks. Lan. Stf. Der. Nhp. Shr.   Also in forms **hooil** Sh.I.; **hool** Sc.; **hyul** Nhb.[1] [h]ul, ul, Sc. also **hûl**.]   **1.** *v.* To conceal; to cover, wrap up. See Hill, *v.*[2]

Abd. This ane tells that, and that ane tells anither, Nor wad they hool't, on sister, or on brither, SHIRREFS *Poems* (1790) 67. n.Cy. 'To hull into bed'—to get into bed and be covered up (K.). Lan.[1] n.Lan.[1] Potatoes covered for the winter are hulled. Stf.[1] Der. I'd use to hull 'em up so mony a time, WARD *David Grieve* (1892) I. xi.

Hence **Hulling**, *sb.* the binding of a book. Shr.[1]

2. To house animals or poultry for the night; to drive a trout into its hole.

Dur.[1] To hull geese. e.Dur. Hes' ta' hulled t'geese? (J.E.D.) Cum.[1 4]

3. *sb.* An outer covering; clothes; the membrane surrounding the heart, or the head of a child; the scrotum; the body.

Sc. Her heart out o' the hool maist lap, WILSON *Poems* (1822) *Maggie Waring.* Sh.I. Mi very hert felt for dem comin' ta da byre wi' a hooil apo' der backs, an' trimblin' wi' cauld, *Sh. News* (Dec. 4, 1897); S. & Ork.[1] My heart is out o' hule. n.Sc. (JAM.), Cai.[1] Abd. But O the skair I got into the pool, I thought my heart had couped frae its hool, ROSS *Helenore* (1768) 45, ed. 1812. Per. Riven hose and raggit hools, FORD *Harp* (1893) 64. Fif. (JAM.) s.Sc. Aften in a jiffie to auld Nick Sen' ane anither dunner-in' saul an' hool, T. SCOTT *Poems* (1793) 365. Ayr. Poor Leezie's heart maist lap the hool, BURNS *Halloween* (1785) st. 26. Lnk. The buttons burstin thro' their hools, Jist bits o' airn red roostit, NICHOLSON *Kilwuddie* (ed. 1895) 36. Lth. While he dawted and kissed, though I ken he's a fool, Lord! I thought that my heart wad hae loupt-out o' hool, MACNEILL *Poet. Whs.* (1801) 207, ed. 1856. Edb. Gar your sauls maist quat their hools, LEARMONT *Poems* (1791) 4. Nhb.[1], w.Yks.[1], n.Lan.[1]

4. A covered outbuilding; a hovel; a place in which animals are kept to be fattened; a pig-sty.

N.Cy.[1 2] Nhb.[1] A swine hull; a duck hull. Dur.[1], s.Dur. (J.E.D.), Lakel.[2] Cum. An' bags fower geese 'at he fand in a lâl hull, FARRALL *Betty Wilson* (1886) 138; Cum.[1] Cum.[4] A sow was turned out of the hull into the stackyard, *Carlisle Patriot* (Jan. 5, 1894) 3. Wm. Where are the pigs!—In the hull (B.K.). n.Yks.[2], m.Yks.[1] w.Yks. A pig gat aht ov it hul, TOM TREDDLE-

---

HOYLE *Bairnsla Ann.* (1850) 31; w.Yks.[1 2 4], n.Lan.[1], ne.Lan.[1], Der.[1], Nhp.[1]

5. The room in which one or more grinding-stones are worked.

w.Yks. In a hull there may be several grinding-troughs; at each there works one grinder: he sits astride a wooden seat called a horsing, and leans forward over the grinding-stone, which revolves away from him and which is kept wet by passing through water contained in a wooden trough at each revolution. The grinding hull is usually a lofty, airy place, the windows being open, and not having glass in them (J.S.); Patty's front room lets for more than a hull, MATHER *Sngs. Sheffield* (1862) lv; w.Yks.[2] Two steps there go up to his hull.

6. *Comp.* **Hull-arston**, the fireplace in the 'hull.'

w.Yks. Discussion uppa ahr Hull Arston between Jack Wheels-warf an the Reverend Jabez Ruleall, BYWATER *Shevvild Ann.* (1853) 17.

[1. Hov hertily þe herdes wif hules þat child, *Wm. Pal.* (c. 1350). 4. An hul for hogs, *porcile*, LEVINS *Manip.* (1570).]

HULL, *sb.*[3] e.An.[1] [Not known to our correspondents.] A thick piece of bread and meat or other food.

HULL, *sb.*[4] Yks. Lin. [ul.] **1.** In *comp.* Hull-cheese, the strong ale of Hull.

Yks. 'You have eaten some Hull cheese' means that you are intoxicated, *Flk-Lore Rec.* (1878) I. 162; Hull is famous for strong ale, GROSE (1790). e.Yks. NICHOLSON *Flk-Lore* (1890) 105.

2. *Phr.* (1) *as strong as Hull*, very strong indeed; (2) *from Hull, Hell, and Halifax, good Lord deliver us*; see below.

(1) n.Lin.[1] The allusion is to the fortifications of that town, which were formerly much renowned in these parts. (2) Yks. At Hull all vagrants found begging in the streets, were whipped and set in the stocks; and at Halifax persons taken in the act of stealing cloth. were instantly, and without any process, beheaded, with an engine called a maiden, GROSE (1790). n.Lin.[1] Hull II, in the beginning of the great Civil War, refused to admit Charles I; Halifax was notorious for its stern gibbet law; they are, therefore, bracketed with the place of torment.

HULL, *v.*[3] Yks. Chs. Stf. Der. Not. Lin. Rut. Lei. Nhp. War. Shr. Bdf. Hrt. Hnt. e.An. Ken. Sus. Hmp. Som. Also written **hul** Bdf. Ess.[1] [ul, ul.] **1.** To throw; used *fig.* Cf. holl, *v.*[3]

w.Yks.[2] (s.v. Holl). Chs.[1 2 3] s.Stf. We'n get some st—one ready to hull at 'em (T.P.). nw.Der.[1] Not. Oid ma'y that hull mysen i' th' Trent (J.H.B.); Not.[1 2] sw.Lin.[1] If she was away for a day, it would hull her back so. Rut.[1] David... pulled the little cat out of yewr loft. Lei. Why don't you hull yoursell on the parish and go a-begging? (C.E.); Lei.[1] Nhp.[1] Look, mother, how he hulls the hulls away; Nhp.[2] Hull th' orts to the hoog. War. (J.R.W.), War.[1 2 3], Shr.[2] Bdf. BATCHELOR *Anal. Eng.* (1809) 135. Hrt. CUSSANS *Hist.* (1879–81) III. 320. Hnt. (T.P.F.) e.An.[1] He hulled it into the holl. Nrf. Let him as is without fault hull the first stone, PATTERSON *Man and Nat.* (1895) 93. Suf.[1] took and hulled a tater at her (M.E.R.); Just you leave off a-hull-ing them ston's at that daug (H.H.); Suf.[1], e.Suf. (F.H.) Ess. If they'd their shells away but hull, CLARK *J. Noakes* (1839) st. 140; Ess.[1] Hul it away. Ess.[1] Ha! there, leave off hulling o' stones. Sus.[1] Hmp. I just hulled it a'into the pig-wash, VERNEY L. Lisle (1870) ii. Som. W. & J. *Gl.* (1873).

2. *Fig.* To relinquish, throw up.

Hrt. If he don't give in I shall hull it up (H.G.). e.Suf. To hull up one's occupation (F.H.).

3. With *up*: to invest in a mountebank's lottery; see below.

e.An.[1] To put into the mountebank's lottery, which is done by tying up a shilling in the corner of a pocket-handkerchief, and hulling it on the stage.

4. With *up*: to vomit.

Not.[1] Rut.[1] Now, child, I've done hulling-oop; yewr mother's a new woman [recovering after nausea]. Lei.[1] Shay 'ooled oop blood wonderful. War.[2] e.An.[1] Nrf. I can't kape noothin down—as soon as I ate my brakefast this mornin, I hulled it up agin (W.R.E.). Suf. I ha' hulled up my wittles ivry morning, *Dy. Times* (1892). e.Suf. (F.H.)

Hence **Hull-up**, *sb.* the operation of an emetic. e.An.[1]

5. To bring sheaves up to the ridges for the 'shocker' to make up.

Nrf. Some on 'em shocking up, whilst others hulled in above, EMERSON *Son of Fens* (1892) 138.

6. To fell a tree.

Rnf.¹ When [the tenant] hulls his trees, you must set a man to kid-up the tops, an' get 'em carried away. Will you have the opple hulled !

[**1.** *Contretirer*, to hull, throw, fling against, Cotgr.]

HULLA-BALLOO, *sb.* In *gen.* dial. and colloq. use in Sc. Irel. and Eng. Also written **hulli-baloo** Rnf. ; **hulli-ullew** e.An.² ; **hully-baloo** Frf. ; and in forms **alla-baloo** Pem. ; **halapaloo** Sh.I. ; **halla-baloo** Sh.I. N.Cy.¹ Der.² w.Der.¹ Suf.¹ ; **hallar-baloo** Ess. ; **halle-bulloo** Dev. ; **alli-bulloo** Dev. ; **halHe-balloo** Rnf. (Jam.) ; **hallo-baloo** hp.¹ ; **halloo-baloo** Rnf. (Jam.) I.W.¹ Wil. ; **hallow-alloo** Hmp. Dev. ; **hallow-baloo** ; **hally-balloo** Bnff. (Jam.) ; **hally-baloo** Fif. ; **haloo-balloo** Rnf. (Jam.) ; **hille-uloo** N.Cy.¹ ; **hillie-balow** Cai.¹ Abd. ; **hillie-balow** Rxb. (Jam.) ; **hillie-belew** Fif. ; **hillie-bullow** Fif. (Jam.) ; **hillie-uloo** Ags. (Jam.) ; **hilly-baloo** Rnf. ; **holla-beloo** Som. ; **olloo-balloo** I.W.¹ ; **hullie-bullie** ; **hullie-bulloo** Sc. (Jam.) ; **hurla-baloo** Nhp.¹ ; **hurley-bulloo** Sus.¹ ; **ulla-baloo** Yks. ; **whulabaloo** n.Ir. A noisy tumult ; an outcry ; commotion.

Sh.I. Wi' da halapaloo o' da folk, an' da yarmin' o' da yows an' lambs, deil wird could I mak' oot, *Sk. News* (July 31, 1897). **Cai.¹** **g.** Willa-wins, willa-woo, sic a hullabaloo, Tester *Poems* (1865) 41. **Abd.** Siccan a hilliebaloo as the factor kicket up for want o' rent (G.W.). **Ags.** (Jam.) **Frf.** Thinkin' him fu', [she] raised a ullybaloo, Whilk waukened the neebours around, Watt *Poet. Sketches* (1880) 96. **Per.** Gin ye heard sic a hullabaloo ! Sic a aterwaulin' amang the crew ! Stewart *Character* (1857) 192. **Lf.** Bra thing it was, perfay, to view Sae blithe and brisk a hally-aloo, As intill ither's arms they flew, Tennant *Papistry* (1827) 3. **Rnf.** Hech, sirs, sic a hullibaloo ! Frae taverns and tents they were rinning, Some sober, and ithers blin' fou, Webster *Rhymes* (1835) 6. **Ayr.** A terr'ble hullabaloo got up at the ither end of the table, Service *Notandums* (1890) 27. **Lth.** When fanners was first introduced, there was a great hullabaloo about them, Strath-Esk *Mora Bits* (ed. 1885) 63. **Rxb.** (Jam.) **Wgt.** What a hulla-alloo is in Wigtown toon On the Cattle Show day, Fraser *Poems* (1885) 51. **Ir.** Baker *Gl.* (1854). **n.Ir.** The maist tremenjus hulabaloo iver ye heerd, Lyttle *Ballycuddy* (1892) 60. **N.Cy.¹** **nb.** Thor wis sic a hullabaloo on as aa nivvor seed (R.O.H.). **Yks.** Ha dear what a hullabaloo ther waz ; it waz mar like a edlam ner howt a can think ov (W.H.). **e.Yks.¹** **w.Yks.** Ther for sich a hullabaloo 'at aw thowt mi heead 'ud split, Hartley *Tales*, and S. III. 50. **Lan.** What ever's o' this hullabaloo abeawt ! Waugh *Rambles Lake Cy.* (1861) iii. **Der.²** **nw.Der.¹** **Nhp.¹** What a hallobaloo they are making. **War.⁸** **s.Pem.** There was grand allabaloo there betwain am (W.M.M.). **Brks.¹, Hnt.** (T.P.F.), **e.An.²**, **Suf.¹**, **e.Suf.** (F.H.) **Ess.** Sich a hallarbaloo did on In our pair's aers resoun', Clark *J. Noakes* (1839) st. 87. **ua.¹** Hmp. Grose (1790) *MS. add.* (M.) **I.W.¹** **Wil.** Britton *Beauties* (1825). **Dor.** Fie upon ye all for making such a hulla-lloo, Hardy *Trumpet-Major* (1880) ix. **Som.** Jennings *Obs. Dial. w.Eng.* (1825). **Dev.** They zet zich a hallebulloo, Close by e palace doors ! Peter Pindar *Wks.* (1816) IV. 175 ; **Amongst** e derty, lowzy crew, There's zich a touse and hallibulloo, feaw atun ould Nick, ib. 182.

HULLACHAN, HULLART, see **Hoolachan, Howlet.**

HULLCOCK, *sb.* Or.I. The smooth-hound fish, *squalus galeus*. S. & Ork.¹ [Buckland *Fishes* (1880).]

HULLER, *v.* e.Suf. In phr. *to huller largess*, to shout or alms. (F.H.), (C.L.F.)

HULLER, see **Hiller,** *sb.²*, **Holler.**

HULLERIE, *adj.¹* Sc. [hʌ·ləri.] **1.** Erect, bristling. **Rxb.** 'A hullerie hen,' a hen with its feathers standing on nd (Jam.).

2. Of a head after hard drinking : confused. ib. **3.** Slovenly. Slk. (ib.) [Not known to our correspondents.] Of walls : ill-built, crumbling, friable. Cai.¹, Slk. (Jam.)

HULLERIE, *adj.²* Sc. (Aasen.) [Not known to our orrespondents.] Of the weather : raw, damp, and cold. **Rxb.** That's a hullerie day.

HULLERT, *ppl. adj.* Cum. Of blood : coagulated, clotted.

Cum.⁸ T'huller't bleud laid an inch thick on t'flooer (ed. 1873) 3 ; **Cum.⁴**

HULLERT, HULLET, see **Howlet.**

VOL. III.

HULLETT, *sb.* e.An.¹ [Not known to our correspondents.] [ʊ·lət.] A brook with woody banks.

HULL-FOOTED, see **Whole-footed.**

HULLION, *sb.* Sc. **1.** Wealth, goods, property. **Abd.** The half o' my hullion I'll gie to my dear, *Old Sng.* (Jam.) ; Ye'll get a hullion (or hullion o' bawbees) wi' Jessie, I'm thinkin'. I didna need to brak in on the hullion ; I had siller eneuch on me to pay him (G.W.).

2. A burden ; a heap. **Abd.** A hullion o' claes (G.W.).

HULLION, see **Hallion.**

HULLOCK, *sb.* and *v.* Chs. War. Wor. Shr. Glo. Also written **hullack** ; **ullack** Chs.¹ [u·lək, ʊ·lək.] **1.** *sb.* A lazy, worthless fellow. **Chs.¹** 'He's an idle ullack.' The word is only applied to a man. **War.², Shr.¹**

2. *v.* To go about in a lazy manner. Cf. **hulk,** *v.⁴* **War.²** He goes hullocking about.

Hence **Hullocking,** *ppl. adj.* overbearing, 'hulking.' w.Wor.¹, Glo.¹

HULLOCKIT, see **Hallockit.**

HULLOCKY, *int.* Wil. Also written **hullucky** Wil. ; and in form **hellocky** Wil.¹ [ʊ·ləki.] An exclamation to denote surprise, or to call attention to anything : hullo ! look here !

Slow *Gl.* (1892) ; **Wil.¹** n.Wil. Hullucky, he bin an caught un (E.H.G.).

HULLOP, *int.* Shr. Dev. Also written **hullope** Shr.¹ A loud call, used to attract attention : hullo !

Shr.¹ If a horseman rode up to a house at nightfall, he would cry ' 'Ullope !' [uloa·p]. **Dev.** Hullop! to mezul vur zoftly I zess, Nathan Hogg *Poet. Lett.* (1847) 44, ed. 1865.

HULLOT, HULL-RAKE, HULLUCKY, see **Howlet, Heel-rake, Hullocky.**

HULLY, *sb.* Nhb. Yks. Som. Cor. Also written **hulley** Som. ; and in form **holley** Som. [h]u·li, ʊ·li.] **1.** A peculiarly shaped, long wicker trap used for catching eels.

Som. W. & J. *Gl.* (1873) ; An hullies too an jitch, Jennings *Dial. w.Eng.* (1869) 124.

2. A perforated box in which fishermen keep lobsters and crabs in a live state ; a hole in the rocks often used as a store for shell-fish.

Nhb.¹ **Yks.** Much like a great chest, bored full of holes to let in the sea, which at high water always overflows it, where are kept vast quantities of crabbs and lobsters, which they put in and take out again all the season according to the quickness or slow-ness of their markets, Brome *Travels* (ed. 1700) 160 (Hall.). **w.Cor.** There was an awful pop and towse just now down by the hully, Thomas *Randigal Rhymes* (1895) 3.

HULLY, *adj.* Sc. **1.** Having a husk or outer shell or skin. See **Hull,** *sb.¹* **Per.** These potatoes are hully (G.W.).

2. Husky, hoarse.

Lth. [He] will sit an' hear his best freend on earth grow hully an' hairse, as a mootered hoody-craw, an' never say—Sam lat abee, Lumsden *Sheep-head* (1892) 287.

HULLY-BUTTERFLEE, *sb.* Lan. [u·li-butəfli.] The tiger-moth, *Euprepia caja*, whose larvae are known as ' woolly bears ' ; also any heavy-bodied night-flying moth. Lan.¹, n.Lan.¹

HULMOGEE, HULOTE, see **Holmogen, Howlet.**

HULSTER, *v.* and *sb.* Bnff.¹ [hʊ·lstər.] **1.** *v.* To carry a burden with difficulty, and in an awkward manner ; freq. with *about* ; to walk with an ungraceful, heavy step.

Gee ma birn a hulster on a ma back.

2. *sb.* The pushing up of a burden.

3. A big, awkward person.

[**1.** Cp. Norw. dial. *holstra*, to go gropingly as in the dark (Aasen.)]

HULSTER, see **Holster, Hulter,** *sb.¹*

HULT, *v.* Nhp.¹ To take out the entrails of a hare or rabbit. Cf. **hulk,** *v.⁸*

HULTER, *sb.¹* Sh.I. Also in form **hulster** S. & Ork.¹ [hʊ·ltər.] **1.** A shapeless block of stone, a loose block of rock.

(Coll. L.L.B.) ; Jakobsen *Norsk in Sh.* (1897) 64 ; **S. & Ork.¹**

N n

2. A big, unwieldy person. JAKOBSEN (*l.c.*). **3.** A huge mass or heap. *ib.*

[1. A der. of Norw. dial. *holt*, a rough, stony hill (AASEN); so Mod. Icel. (VIGFUSSON).]

HULTER, *sb.*² e.Suf. A head-stall. (F.H.)

HULTER-CORN, *sb.* Sc. Grain that has passed through the mill, and been freed from the husk.

Abd. Another absurdity is, that shillen, i. e. . . . hulter corn, is measured by the tacksman of the mill, and is paid . . . in meal, *Statist. Acc.* XV. 117 (JAM.).

HULVE, *v.* Som. Dev. To turn over; to turn upside-down.

Som. JENNINGS *Obs. Dial. w.Eng.* (1825). **n.Dev.** May . . . ploughman's vell Hulve not wan turf where they two dwell, ROCK *Jim an' Nell* (1867) st. 98.

[Cp. ME. *whelve* in *over-whelve*, to turn over, to agitate. The horrible wind Aquilon moeveth boilinge tempestes and over-whelveth the see, CHAUCER *Boethius*, bk. 1. met. iii. 13.]

HULVER, *sb.* e.An. Also written hulva Suf.¹ [u·lə(r).] The holly, *Ilex Aquifolium*.

e.An.¹² **Nrf.** He [the greenfinch] chooses a glossy prickly hulver tree. EMERSON *Birds* (ed. 1895) 93. **Suf.** Helver [*sic*] (B. & H.); (H.H.); **Suf.**¹

Hence **Hulver-headed,** *adj.* stupid, muddled, confused. e.An.¹, e.Suf. (F.H.)

[Hulwur, tre, *huscus*. *Prompt.*; An hulfere, LYDGATE *Compl.* (c. 1430) 129. ON. *hulfr*, ' aquifolium ' (FRITZNER).]

HULY, see Hooly.

HULYIE, *adj.* Sh.I. Lasting; economical. S. & Ork.¹

HUM, *sb.*¹ Ags. (JAM.) [Not known to our correspondents.] The milt of a cod-fish; used as a dish and esteemed a great delicacy.

[Du. *homme*, the milt of a fish (HEXHAM), now *hom* (FRANCK).]

HUM, *v.*¹ and *sb.*² Sc. n.Cy. Nhb. Cum. Yks. Lan. Chs. Der. Nhp. War. Suf. Ken. [h)um, h)um.] **1.** *v.* Of a cow: to low softly from pleasure; of a cat: to purr. Cf. **hummer,** *v.* 2.

s.Chs.¹ Aa·rkn aat· ūr ūm·in; 6o)z pley·ūzd ūt aav·in ūr kau·f widh ūr [Hearken at her hummin'; hoo's pleeased at havin' her cauf with her]. **Suf.** (C.G.B.)

2. To stammer, murmur; to speak hesitatingly or evasively, to prevaricate, dally; *gen.* in phr. *to hum and haw*.

Sc. I hope never . . . to be hum'd or haw'd with, I know not what, out of this persuasion, M°WARD *Contendings* (1723) 20 (JAM.). **Frf.** I hummed an' I haed, till I finally said, JOHNSTON *Poems* (1869) 177. **Per.** I stood bare-headit, hummin', hayin', STEWART *Character* (1857) 44. **Slg.** At the gown ye hum an' ha' Till 'tis threadbare, GALLOWAY *Crichton* (1802) 78. **Ayr.** Ne'er claw your lug an' fidge your back An' hum an' haw, BURNS *Author's Cry* (1786) st. 6. **Lnk.** Will said little, but hum'd and hae'd, WATT *Poems* (1827) 63. **Wgt.** I humm'd an' I ha'd till I'm sure she was stawed, FRASER *Poems* (1885) 64. **Nhb.** He oney humm'd an' haa'd, an' gat ne farther endways wiv his speech (R.O.H.); Aw . . . humm'd and haw'd te little use Aboot somethin' aw had te say, WILSON *Pitman's Pay* (1843) 49. **Cum.**¹ **w.Yks.** BANKS *Whfld. Wds.* (1865); (J.W.) **nw.Der.**¹ **Nhp.**¹ He does nothing but hum and haw; you can get nothing out of him. **War.**³

3. To whip a top; to beat, flog; to strike.

Edb. The guillotine, wi' weight o' lead, An' edge as sharp's a lance, Hum'd him yon day, FORBES *Poems* (1812) 33. **e.Yks.**¹ **Ken.** To hum a gig. I'll hum your gig [I'll whip you soundly] (K.); **Ken.**¹

4. To throw anything, as a stone; to throw violently.

n.Cy. (HALL.); GROSE (1790). **w.Yks.** HUTTON *Tour to Caves* (1781). **ne.Lan.**¹

5. *sb.* The sound made by a missile in the air.

Nhb. He sent it wiv a hum (R.O.H.).

6. Hesitation, indecision; an evasive or hesitating answer; *gen.* in phr. *hum and haw*. Also used *fig.*

Bnff. Tho' I wou'd like your sols an' fa's, I'll may be get but hums an' haws, TAYLOR *Poems* (1787) 90. **Per.** He gart them a' behave and work, And mak' nae mony hums and haws, NICOLL *Poems* (ed. 1843) 91. **s.Sc.** Some Will tell ye plain without a hum, T. SCOTT *Poems* (1793) 317. **Rnf.** Aff loof he tauld his min' sae free, Wi' neither hum nor haw anent it, CLARK *Rhymes* (1842) 15. **Lth.** New-fangled schules hae ither laws, Wi' mony English hums

an' haws, BALLANTINE *Poems* (1856) 198. **Yks.** The Quaking sect, Who would seem to act by merit Of yeas and nays, and hums and hahs, DIXON *Sngs. Eng. Peas.* (1846) 173, ed. Bell. **w.Yks.**¹ Let's hev naan o' yer hums and hahs.

7. See below.

e.Yks. A punishment inflicted by boys on an obstinate player. They lug his hair, or strike him with their caps, saying ' Hum, hum, hum,' long drawn out. Such pulling or striking being continued until their leader cries ' Off ! ' when all must at once desist or be subject to a like punishment themselves, NICHOLSON *Flb-Sp.* (1889) 26.

HUM, *v.*² and *sb.*³ In *gen.* dial. and colloq. use in Sc. and Eng. [h)um, h)um.] **1.** *v.* To deceive, cheat, impose upon; to ' humbug.'

Gall. Though they hum the gazing youth, A near encounter shows the truth, NICHOLSON *Poet. Wks.* (1814) 85, ed. 1897. **n.Cy.** (J.W.) **Nhb.** But sum chep aw seun fand was hummin, *Tyneside Sngstr.* (1889) 44. **w.Yks.**³ **Lan.** Theaw knew at same time, ot theaw'r humink her, WALKER *Plebeian Pol.* (1796) 6, ed. 1801. **Bdf.** BATCHELOR *Anal. Eng. Lang.* (1809) 136. **Lon.** Young males . . . humming one another, as they term it, *Low Life* (1764) 76. **Ken.** [He] hums as highly with a serious face as any one, NAIRNE *Tales* (1790) 6a, ed. 1824. **Dev.** Yow make us stare ! 'Squire Rolle, why yow be hummin ! PETER PINDAR *Wks.* (1816) III. 371. **Slang.** While you hum the poor spoonies with speeches so pretty, *Tom Crib's Mem.* (1819) 2.

Hence **Hummer,** *sb.* a lie, falsehood.

e.Suf. (F.H.) **Dev.** All is not Gospel ; People tell hummers ev'ry hour, PETER PINDAR *Wks.* (1816) IV. 194. **Cant.** *Life B. M. Carew* (1791) *Gl.* **2.** *sb.* A cheat, sham, ' humbug'; a lie, a false report ; a foolish trick.

Sc. Often applied to a story told in jest (JAM.). **Frf.** Screw weel your pins an' banish hums, MORISON *Poems* (1790) 93. **Edb.** His honour will turn out a hum, CRAWFORD *Poems* (1798) 74. **n.Cy.** (J.W.), **Suf.** (C.G.B.) **w.Som.**¹ Don't 'ee believe it, 'tis all a hum. **Dev.** He zaid he did not care a lowze . . . But that, my lord's, a hum, PETER PINDAR *Wks.* (1816) IV. 174. **Slang.** It's no go! it's gammon! it's 'all a hum,' BARHAM *Ingoldsby* (ed. 1864) *Row in an Omnibus*.

[A shortened form of ' humbug.']

HUM, *v.*³ and *sb.*⁴ Sc. Irel. Wm. Yks. [hum, h)um.] **1.** *v.* To feed by the mouth as a bird feeds her young ; to transfer food from one's mouth to that of an infant.

Sc. A nurse is said to hum to her child when she gives it food from her mouth (JAM.). **S. & Ork.**¹ *M S. add.* **Cai.**¹, **Lnk.** (JAM.), **N.I.**¹

Hence **Humming,** *sb.* (1) a quid of tobacco after it has been chewed ; (2) anything that has been gnawed and then left by rats, &c.

(1) **Wm.** What mack o ket is ta amiuken?—Auld hummins (B.K.). **s.Wm.** He smooks owt, tea-leaves and bacca hummins (J.A.B.). **w.Yks.** He used to keep his hummins and dry them to smoke (L.M.S.). (2) **Dmf.** SHAW *Schoolmaster* (1899) 349.

2. *sb.* A morsel of masticated food given to a child.

Cai.¹ **Dmf.** ' Give the wean a hum,' chew a piece and feed it therewith, SHAW *Schoolmaster* (1899) 349. **Gall.** Mouthfuls of chewed matter, MACTAGGART *Encyd.* (1824). **N.I.**¹

HUM, *v.*⁴ Sh.I. To grow dark, to darken in the evening. S. & Ork.¹

[Norw. dial. *hyma*, to grow dusk (AASEN) ; a der. of ON. *húmr*, overcast, murky (FRITZNER).]

HUM, *adj.* ? *Obs.* Sc. Out of humour, sullen.

Abd. Saw ye e'er a tear rin frae my e'e? Or wantin plaid, or bonnet, leukit hum, TARRAS *Poems* (1804) 115 (JAM.).

HUM, see **Em,** *pron.*, **Holm,** *sb.*², **Home,** *sb.*¹

HUMACK, *sb.* Som. [ə·mək.] **1.** The dog-rose, *Rosa canina*. (B. & H.), (F.T.E.) **2.** *pl.* Wild briar stocks used to graft roses upon. W. & J. *Gl.* (1873).

HUMAN, *sb.* Sc. Amer. A human being.

Sh.I. If dis is no wark mair fir a horse as fir a human dan I sall haud me tongue, *Sh. News* (Apr. 22, 1899). **Abd.** Gibbie fell to . . . hugging him [a dog] as if he had been a human, MACDONALD *Sir Gibbie* (1879) ix. [**Amer.** Swallowing up thirteen houses an' four humans, *Sharpe's Jrn.* XIII. 290; Humans ain't got no business up this yere creek, *Dial. Notes* (1896) I. 372.]

HUMANIST, *sb.* *Obs.* Sc. A classical scholar, a teacher of the classics, esp. of Latin.

Sc. Mr. William Wallace, an good man and a learned humanist,

HUMMEL, *sb.*[2] ne.Lan.[1] A shortened form of 'humble-bee.'

HUMMELD, *ppl. adj.* Gall. Chewed in a careless manner. MACTAGGART *Encycl.* (1824). Cf. hum, *v.*[8]

HUMMEL-DRUMMEL, *adj.* Sc. Morose, taciturn.
Per. Well known. 'What's wrang wi ye, man ! ye're awfu' hummel-drummel' (G.W.). **Rxb.** (JAM.)

HUMMEL-JUMMEL, *sb.* Cum. Yks. [(h)u·ml·dguml.] Confusion, 'jumble '; also used *advb.*
Cum.[1] n.Yks. Manners vulgar an' refahn'd, Was i yah hummel-jummel join'd, CASTILLO *Poems* (1878) 57.
Hence **Hummel-jummelt,** *ppl. adj.* mixed together in confusion, jumbled together.
Cum. Croas an cocksparras, an' jack-dohs an sec like, oa hummel jummelt tegidder, SARGISSON *Joe Scoap* (1881) 89.

HUMMEL-STONE, *sb.* Yks. Lan. Also written hummle-w.Yks. ; ummel- Lan. [u·ml-.] A small pebble of quartz or calliard.
w.Yks. Found in coal districts (J.J.B.) ; (J.T.) **Lan.** Found in millstone grit (J.S.J.).
[Norw. dial. *humul* (*hummel*), a stone, pebble (AASEN) ; ON. *hōmul* in *hōmul-grȳti* (VIGFUSSON).]

HUMMELTY COUR, *phr.* Cum.[4] In a crouched position. Cf. humly, *adv.* ; see Cower, *v.*[1]

HUMMEN, *v.* ne.Lan.[1] [u·mən.] To make a low rumbling noise. See Hummer, *v.*

HUMMER, *sb.*[1] Sc. Yks. Suf. **1.** A steam whistle or ' hooter.' w.Yks. (C.A.F.), w.Yks.[2] **2.** A small top. Bnff.[1], Cld. (JAM.) **3.** A hard blow. e.Suf. (F.H.) Cf. hum, *v.*[1] **3.** **4.** Anything extraordinarily large in size. e.Yks.[1]

HUMMER, *sb.*[2] *Obsol.* Lakel.[1] A grassy slope by the side of a river ; wet, swampy land.
[A der. of ON. *hvammr*, a grassy slope or vale, freq. as a local name (VIGFUSSON) ; see **Wham.**]

HUMMER, *sb.*[3] Lakel. Yks. Also in form ummer e.Yks.[1] A euphemism for the devil, the infernal regions, &c. Also used as *v.* in phr. *hummer it!* Cf. hem, *sb.*[3] See **Buckhummer.**
Lakel.[2] Thee gah ta hummer, an' tak' thi auld nag wi' tha. Hummer it. Ah've knock't mi' finger nail off. **e.Yks.** Thoo gan ti hummer, NICHOLSON *Flk-Lore* (1890) 105 ; **e.Yks.** Hah the hummer did ta do it ? *N. & Q.* (1897) 8th S. xi. 25 ; Well, I'll go to Hummer Nick, *ib.* ; To hummer ! wi th' 'flittin ! let's have a pint, HARTLEY *Clock Alm.* (1884) 49.

HUMMER, *v.* Sc. n.Cy. Yks. Chs. Der. Lin. e.An. s. & e.Cy. [(h)u·mə(r), u·mə(r).] **1.** To hum, murmur, to make a low, rumbling noise ; to grumble.
Slk. (JAM.) **n.Cy.** GROSE (1790) ; **w.Yks.** HUTTON *Tour to Caves* (1781) ; **w.Yks.**[2] A man said to a child, ' What are you hummering about there ? ' **n.Lin.**[1], **e.An.**[1] **2.** Of a horse : to neigh gently ; of a cow : to make a soft, lowing noise. Cf. hum, *v.*[1]
Chs.[1] As a cow does when she sees her calf ; or as she does sometimes when the man who usually feeds her goes into the shippon. **nw.Der.**[1] **e.An.**[1] The gentle and pleasing sound which a horse utters when he hears the corn shaken in the sieve, or when he perceives the approach of his companion, or groom. **Suf.** (C.T.). **Ess.** The horse hummered (W.W.S.). **s. & e.Cy.** RAY(1691).

HUMMER-BEE, *sb.* Yks. Lan. Chs. Der. Also written hum-a-bee Lan. ; humma- w.Yks. Lan.[1] e.Lan.[1] ; hummo-Lan. Chs.[1] nw.Der.[1] ; and in forms humber- Chs. ; umma- w.Yks. [u·mə-bī.] The humble-bee, *Apis lepidaria.*
w.Yks. BANKS *Whfld. Wds.* (1865); Ther's a humma bee i' t'hahse (Æ.B.). **Lan.** Thou's bin agate o' buzzin' for this last hauve hour like a hum-a-bee in a foxglove, WAUGH *Owd Cronies* (1875) vii ; As thick as wasps in a hummobee-neest, TIM BOBBIN *View Dial.* (ed. 1806) 20 ; Lan.[1], e.Lan.[1], m.Lan.[1] **Chs.** I have crutches for lame ducks, spectacles for blind humber-bees, *St. George Play* (1890) ; Chs.[1], nw.Der.[1]

HUMMERS, *int.* Not.[3] Also in form oomers. [u·məz.] An exclamation of delight.
When eating something especially juicy, as a mellow plum. ' 'Ummers, Sarrey, it is sum jewcety.'

HUMMERY, *int.* Lakel.[2] An expletive or mild oath. Cf. hummer, *sb.*[3] ' Oh, hummery ta seck as thee.'

HUMMICK, *sb.*[1] Dev. [u·mik.] A large piece or slice, a hunch. Cf. hommock, *sb.* **1.**
He's carried down a great hummick of bread to the pony, *Reports Provinc.* (1887) 9 ; Let 'un ate a hummick, BLACKMORE *Kit* (1890) ix ; I 'ates tû zee tha breyde awl up in hummicks, HEWETT *Peas. Sp.* (1892). **nw.Dev.**[1] *Gen.* applied to bread or cheese.
Hence **Hummicking,** *adj.* large and clumsy.
Dev.[2] What a hummickin' piece of bread they gave me.

HUMMICK, *sb.*[2] Dor. Heat, sweat. *N. & Q.* (1883) 6th S. viii. 157 ; Dor.[1]

HUMMIE, *sb.*[1] Sc. Also Lon. [(h)u·mi.] A hump.
Lth. A brass-banded box filled wi' uncas an' braws, Smooths the hummie o' Patie the Packman, BALLANTINE *Poems* (1856) 107. **Edb.** *ib. Gaberlunzie* (ed. 1875) *Gl.* **Lon.** A growth on the back of the neck called a ' hummie,' the result of long friction, is needful to enable a man to balance a plank [in discharging cargoes] with any degree of comfort, *19th Cent.* (1887) 486.

HUMMIE, *sb.*[2] and *v.* Sc. n.Cy. Nhb. Also in forms humma Slk. Rxb. (JAM.) N.Cy.[1] Nhb.[1] ; hummock Sc. (JAM.) Gall. [hu·mi, hu·mi.] **1.** *sb.* A grasp taken by the thumb and four fingers placed together ; the space thus included, to the exclusion of the palm of the hand.
Ags. Hummock is occas. used towards the coast (JAM.). **Lth.** The hummock denotes a smaller space than the goupin (*ib.*). **Slk.** To make one's hummie, to compress the points of the fingers of one's hand all at once upon the point of the thumb. ' Can ye mak your hummie ? ' is a question often asked in a cold day (*ib.*). **Rxb.**, **Dmf.** (*ib.*) **Gall.** When the hand is cold, it is impossible to fling the fingers into this form. People in frosty weather try who stands cold best, by the way the hummock can be made, MACTAGGART *Encycl.* (1824) 277, ed. 1876.
2. *Comp.* **Hummie-fou,** (1) a pinch of anything, a small quantity. Cld., Dmf. (JAM.) ; (2) to lift up the ' hummies.' Bnff.[1]
3. A pinch of anything, as much as can be taken up between the thumb and fingers, a small quantity.
Lth., **Slk.**, **Rxb.**, **Dmf.** (JAM.) **N.Cy.**[1] As much as can be held between the finger ends and the thumb. ' A humma of sage.' **Nhb.**[1]
4. *v.* To lift up the ' hummies,' or the thumb and fingers. Bnff.[1]

HUMMIE, *sb.*[3] Sc. [hu·mi.] **1.** The game of ' shinty,' a variety of hockey.
Lth. The shinty, or hummy, is played by a set of boys in two divisions, who attempt . . . to drive with curved sticks a ball, or, what is more common, part of the vertebral bone of a sheep, in opposite directions, *Blackw. Mag.* (Aug. 1821) 36 (JAM.).
2. The hooked stick used in the game of ' shinty.' Lth.(JAM.)
3. A cry used in the game of ' shinty ' ; also in phr. *hummie your stick.*
s.Sc. This cry is raised at the game of shinty when a player crosses to his opponents' side although still striking the ball in the direction contrary to his opponents. By doing this he renders himself liable to knocks from the enemy's shinty-sticks until he returns to his proper side (J.F.). **Edb.** In Fif. the cry hereabouts of ' hummie your side ' is expressed in the one word ' karshab,' *Edb. Even. Dispatch* (Nov. 18, 1897). **Slk.** If one of the adverse party happens to stand or run among his opponents, they call out ' Hummie,' i.e. ' keep on your own side ' (JAM.).

HUMMING, *ppl. adj.* Var. dial. and colloq. uses in Sc. and Eng. [(h)u·min, u·min.] **1.** In *comp.* (1) **Humming-bird,** the golden-crested wren, *Regulus cristatus*; (2) -**bumming,** a humming sound ; (3) -**clock,** the humming flying beetle ; (4) -**fly,** the hoverer fly, *Eristalis tenax.*
(1) **Wil.**[1] ' We always calls 'em humming-birds here, and they *are* humming-birds ! ' said the school-children at Huish, . . when cross-examined as to the Gold-crest. **Dev.** The golden-crested wren mentioned by Polwhele is probably the humming bird noticed by Martin, in the environs of Tavistock, BRAY *Desc. Tamar and Tavy* (1836) II. 146. (2) **Ayr.** What humming bumming's this ye had ? The fiddle's either drunk or mad, FISHER *Poems* (1790) 114. (3) **e.Lan.**[1] (4) **Oxf.** *Science Gossip* (1882) 165.
2. Of ale or liquor : strong, heady, foaming.
Sc. I drink . . . devoutly wishing it were Rhenish wine or humming Lubeck beer, SCOTT *Leg. Mont.* (1818) xiii. **Lth.** Three times in humming liquor llk lad deeply laid his lugs, MACNEILL *Poet. Wks.* (1801) 130, ed. 1856. **Nhb.**[1] An earthen pot with humming beer Stood on a little table near, *Collier's Wedding*

(1735). **w.Yks.**[1] Der. With humming strong liquor likewise, JEWITT *Ballads* (1867) 89. **Dev.** Herself must have good cheer, Herself drink humming beer, BARING-GOULD *Dartmoor Idylls* (1896) 187. **Slang.** A silver flagon of 'humming bub,' BARHAM *Ingoldsby* (ed. 1864) *Leech of Folkestone.*

3. Of large size. **e.Yks.**[1]

HUMMLE, see Humble, Hummel, *adj.*

HUMMOCK, *sb.* and *v.*[1] Sc. n.Cy. Yks. Lan. Chs. Hrf. Glo. Brks. Nrf. Hmp. I.W. Wil. Som. Cor. Also written **hummick** Brks. Hmp. Wil. Som.; **hummuck** Chs.[2]; and in form **umack** N.Cy.[1] [h)ʊ·mək, h)ʊ·mək.] **1.** *sb.* Rising ground, a hillock or mound of earth; a boulder; a tumulus, barrow.

Per. What's in your head To lat thae hummocks lie intil yer bed? FERGUSSON *Vill. Poet.* (1897) 140. **n.Yks.**[2] Hillocks of sea-ice. **Lan.** The road which approached it from the uplands over a huge hummock of moor, KAY-SHUTTLEWORTH *Scarsdale* (1860) I. 272. **ne.Lan.**[1], **Hrf.**[1], **Glo.**[1], **Brks.**(M.E.B.), **Brks.**, **Hmp.** (W.H.E.) **I.W.** The path by a founder of hummock was shut, MONCRIEFF *Dream* (1863) l. 6. **Cor.** (M.A.C.); **Cor.**[3] A big pile.

Hence (1) **Hummocked,** *ppl. adj.* covered with hillocks or mounds; (2) **Hummocky,** *adj.* lumpy, uneven, rough.

(1) Cor. Hummocked as it was in every direction with deads [refuse] from a bal [mine], PEARCE *Esther Pentreath* (1891) 314. (2) Nrf. I saw a large bird beating over the hummocky warrens, EMERSON *Birds* (ed. 1895) 185. **sw.Som.** (W.H.E.)

2. *Comp.* **Hummock-grass,** the hassock-grass, *Carex paniculata.* w.Yks. ARNOLD *Flora* (1888) 461.

3. A stout, unwieldy woman. **Cor.**[12]

Hence (1) **Hummocksing,** *adj.* clumsy, awkward, loutish; (2) **Umackly,** *adj.* ill-shapen.

(1) Wil. She had a lover, but he was 'a gurt hummocksing noon-naw,' JEFFERIES *Gt. Estate* (1880) iv; Wil.[1] (2) N.Cy.[1]

4. *v.* Of trees or plants: to earth up. Chs.[2]

HUMMOCK, *v.*[2] s.Chs.[1] To pester, harass.

A man talked to me of 'ʊmˈʊkin dhū foaˑks ūbuwˑt dhūr voaˑts' [hummockin the folks abowt their votes], in the sense of using undue influence.

HUMMOCK, see Hummle, *sb.*[2]

HUMOROUS, *adj.* Obsol. Sc. Yks. Lan. Chs. Capricious, full of whims, inconstant; pettish, in a bad temper.

Sc. A pleasant gentleman, but I will warrant him an humorous, SCOTT *Monastery* (1820) xx; Of more value than a popular vogue from an humorous silly multitude, KIRKTON *Ch. Hist.* (1817) 361. **Lnk.** To expose them to the hatred of the magistrat as ane humorus unpeaceable pack, WODROW *Ch. Hist.* (1721) I. Pref. 31, ed. 1828. **w.Yks.** (C.C.R.) **Lan.** I discoursed Sarah Seed, but she was passionate and humorous, and I saw no good could be done, WALKDEN *Diary* (ed. 1866) 25. **Chs.**[18]

Hence **Humourousness,** *sb.* caprice, pettishness, 'temper.'

Lnk. The numbers and humourousness of those who are gone up, has done all they could to shake loose all the foundations of authority here, WODROW *Ch. Hist.* (1721) II. 451, ed. 1828.

HUMOUR, *sb.* and *v.* Sc. Nhb. Yks. Chs. Not. Lin. Lei. Nhp. War. Wor. Oxf. Som. Dev. Also in forms **hümber** s.Wor.; **yummer** Nhb.[1] n.Yks. w.Som.[1] Dev. [h)ɪuˑmə(r, juˑmə(r.] **1.** *sb.* Matter or pus from a wound or sore.

Sc. (A.W.) **n.Yks.** There's some yummer at t'wound (I.W.). **Oxf.**[1] *MS. add.* **w.Som.**[1] He 'on't be no better till all the yuumˈurˑz [humour's] a draw'd out.

Hence **Humoury** or **Hümbery,** *adj.* full of matter, eruptive.

s.Wor. 'E's legs be despret humbery (H.K.). **Oxf.** (L.J.Y.)

2. A sore, boil, or gathering; in *pl.* spots, a rash.

Nhb.[1] It's the yummers 'at's the maiter wiv her. **n.Yks.** He hez spots on his feeace; its yummers 'at he hez (I.W.). **Lin.** Sores caused by peculiar states of the skin or flesh, THOMPSON *Hist. Boston* (1856) 710; Lin.[1], n.Lin.[1] **s.Wor.** O! this hümber acrass muh 'ere, a could scrat it (H.K.). **w.Som.**[1] Can't think hot ailth maister's hackney mare, her'th a-got a yummer a-brokt out all over the zide o' her.

Hence (1) **Humourless,** (2) **Humoury,** *adj.* subject to eruptions of the skin; liable to boils.

w.Som.[1] (1) Ter'ble yuumˈurlees [humourless] horse—always somethin or nother the matter way un. (2) Of the condition of a horse or other animal.

---

3. Ill humour, bad temper; also in *pl.*

Elg. The little cobweb which unthinkingness and humour had spread over our friendship, COUPER *Tourifications* (1803) ll. 139. **Yks.** (J.W.), **n.Lin.**[1]

Hence **Humourless,** *adj.* humorous, frolicsome, joking. **w.Som.**[1] So good-tempered humourless a young fellow as you shall vind in a day's march.

4. Advice, opinion, 'mind.'

Frf. Thank you kindly, Tammas, for your humour, BARRIE *Minister* (1891) xvii; Rare (G.W.).

5. *v.* To cajole, coax; to make much of, indulge.

Chs.[3] **w.Som.**[1] You never 'ont do nort way thick there young 'oss nif you don't yummer'n. **Dev.** Ef 'er shūde diddle Jack an' come along tū yŭmmer me, SALMON *Ballads* (1899) 62.

6. To ease; to accommodate a thing to its position, to work in the best or easiest way; to do anything gently.

e.Yks. Noo, deean't let it cum doon wiv a soss; humour it doon, NICHOLSON *Flk-Sp.* (1889) 91; **e.Yks.**[1] To stretch or contract a little, as in making the pattern meet in joining carpets, paperhangings, &c., MS. add. (T.H.) **w.Yks.** In the case of a piece of timber, not to work against the grain. 'Tha can't plane that smooth bah't tha humours it a bit' (J.T.). **Not.**[1] **s.Not.** Ah should like to ha' put the bars in mysen, then sh could a humoured 'em a bit (J.P.K.). **LeL.**[1] You can bring in that side of the seam if you humour it a bit. **Nhp.**[1], **War.**[2], **Oxf.** (G.O.)

HUMOURSOME, *adj.* Sc. n.Cy. Yks. Lan. Chs. War. Wor. Shr. Hrf. Glo. Hrt. Ess. Ken. w.Cy. Also written **humersome** Hrf.[2]; and in form **hŭmbersome** s.Wor.

1. Eruptive on the skin. n.Yks.[2], s.Wor. (H.K.) See Humour, 2.

2. Capricious, full of whims, fanciful; spoilt, peevish.

Lnk. Some of us are so humoursome that we neither agree with our brethren that are indulged, nor could agree among ourselves in any possible demand, WODROW *Ch. Hist.* (1721) II. 489. ed. 1828. **N.Cy.**[1], **Yks.** (J.W.), **ne.Lan.**[1], **Chs.**[1], **War.**[3], **s.Wor.** (H.K.), **s.Wor.**[1] **Shr.**[1] The child's well enough, but 'e's spiled till 'e's that 'umoursome 'e dunna know whad to do ōōth 'isself. **Hrf.**[2], **Glo.** (A.B.), **Glo.**[1] **Hrt.** If he has too much his own way he'll get so humoursome (G.H.G.).

3. Humorous, droll, witty.

Sc. Amongst the most humoursome effusions in the native tongue, FORD *Thistledown* (1891) 193. **Rnf.** This humoursome, honest man struck down, FRASER *Chimes* (1853) 69. **Lnk.** Of a somewhat humorsome turn, MURDOCH *Readings* (ed. 1895) II. 10. **Edb.** For he is a clever humoursome man as ye ever met with, MOIR *Mansie Wauch* (1828) ix. n.Cy. (J.W.), n.Yks.[2], w.Yks. (J.W.), **Ken.** (G.B.) **w.Cy.** If he veel humoursome he do speak vunny, *Cornhill Mag.* (Sept. 1898) 384.

4. Complaisant, courteous, kind, good-tempered.

Shr.[1] **Ess.** Ye jockeys, with your hosses, why More humoursome ain't yow! CLARK *J. Noakes* (1839) st. 117; Lan.[1]

HUMP, *sb.* and *v.* Var. dial. and colloq. uses in Sc. Eng. and Aus. Also in form **humph** Sc. Bnff.[1]; **umph** Stf.[3] [h)ʊmp, h)ump.] **1.** *sb.* In *comp.* (1) **Hump-backed,** of things: crooked, awkwardly shaped; (2) **-shouldered,** high-shouldered, humpbacked; (3) **-stridden,** astride.

(1) w.Som.[1] This here's a proper hump-backĕd [uump-baakˈud] old thing, why, he's so crooked's a horn. Said of a piece of timber. (2) Gall. A little wizened hump-shouldered man, CROCKETT *Standard Bearer* (1898) 136. (3) Lan. GROSE (1790) *MS. add.* (P.); Nick may ride hump-striddn a' beggin, TIM BOBBIN *View Dial.* (1740) 2; Boh I leet hump stridd'n up o' summot ot feld meety bewry, *ib.* 62, ed. 1806; Lan.[1]

2. A curved or arched back.

Fif. Mew and yell, And shoot yer humph sae prude and spruce, JOHNSTON *Poems* (1869) 129.

3. A hillock, mound; a protuberance, knob, or irregularity of surface.

Sc. Just one o' the sort wi' a hump somewhere. I kenna whaur the fashion'll put it then, STEEL *Rowans* (1895) 391. **Frf.** Roofs were humps in the white blanket, BARRIE *Licht* (1888) ii. **War.** Ant-hump (W.C.B.). **Bdf.** Humps and pumilz, BATCHELOR *Anal. Eng. Lang.* (1809) 135. **Dor.** I don't want to break my limbs running over the humps and hollows of this wild country, HARDY *Tales* (1888) I. 42.

Hence *humps and holls, phr.* pell-mell, topsy-turvy, in promiscuous confusion. e.An.[1]

4. A lump or hunch of anything. Glo.[1], w.Cy. (HALL)

5. A contemptible quantity, a poor pittance ; *fig.* a thankless task.

Wor. That would be a hump of a thing, to go for subscriptions and receive nothing (W.A.S.). **e.An.**[1], **Nrf.** (HALL.) **s.Suf.** Used of food, &c. (F.H.)

6. *Fig.* The temper ; ill-humour, an offended, sulky mood, the ' sulks ' or ' blues ' ; *gen.* in phr. *to get,* or *have, the hump,* to be offended, angry, or sulky. Also used in *pl.*

Lnk. When they grew nettled an' set up their humph, NICHOL-SON *Kilwuddie* (ed. 1895) 173. **Nhb.** He flang maw hump se out o' joint, Se, smash ! aw thowt aw'd hev a pint ! MIDFORD *Coll. Sngs.* (1818) 38 ; **Nhb.**[1] He's getten his hump up. **Stf.**[1] **s.Not.** Don't say much to the mester; 'e's in a hump (J.P.K.). **War.**[2] **Wor.** It arose from what was said to me, and that got my hump up, *Evesham Jrn.* (July 9, 1898). **Glo.**[1], **Oxf.** (L.J.Y.) **e.An.**[1] He has got the hump. **e.Suf.** Enough to give me the hump (F.H.). **w.Cor.** (A.L.M.) Colloq. 'Arry . . . has got the blooming hump, JEROME *Idle Thoughts* (1886) 14, ed. 1888.

7. *v.* To be dissatisfied with, to grumble ; to be in an ill-temper, to sulk ; to cry.

Bnff.[1] Fin gueede-made-ready cabbitch wiz setten doon till 'im, he humpht at thim. He humpht an' glumcht sae muckle a' day aboot nae gettin' t' the market. Lakel.[2] What's ta humpin aboot? **s.Wor.** (H.K.), **s.Wor.**[1], **e.An.** (HALL.) **e.Suf.** To hump and grump, to complain querulously (F.H.).

Hence (1) **Humped,** (2) **Humping,** *ppl. adj.* sulky.

(1) n.Yks.[4] (a) Bnff.[1] He's a humphin' an' grumphin' cheel o' a maister, that o' yours.

8. To offend.

Chs.[1] You know it does not do to hump folks when you're in business.

9. To carry on the back or shoulders.

Lnk. O' ' humphin ' my kit I grew weary, COGHILL *Poems* (1890) 91. [**Aus.** We humped our saddles and swags ourselves, BOLDREWOOD *Robbery* (1888) II. i. **N.Z.** We have had to hump on our backs and shoulders every blessed thing that we have imported or exported, HAY *Brighter Britain* (1882) I. 119.]

10. To live with, to be domesticated with.

Lel.[1] My own mother died soon after I came, an' my father soon after her, so I allays humped to these (s.v. Hum).

11. To insinuate, to make an obscure, defamatory hint.

w.Yks.[1] Come, man, speak out, an dunnot hump soa. ne.Lan.[1]

HUMPER, *v.* Chs. Also in form **homper** s.Chs.[1] To limp, hobble. *Gen. in prp.*

Chs.[1] ; Chs.[2] Jim came humpering along. **s.Chs.**[1] Tŭ sey im om'pūrin of/th bongk, yŭ)d thingk' ey mid· ŭ uurt imsel· ve·ri baad·li [To sey him homperin' off th' bonk, yo'd think hey mid ha' hurt himsel very badly].

HUMP-GUTTERAL, *sb.* Slk. (JAM.) The flesh of a sheep that has died a natural death, as distinguished from braxy, which intimates that the animal has died of disease.

[Norw. dial. *hump* (*hupp*), a piece of flesh (AASEN).]

HUMPH, *sb.*[1] and *v.* Sc. Nhb. [hwmf, humf.] **1.** *sb.* A bad smell or flavour.

Bnff.[1] Abd. That's a fine tea, but hasna't a humph o' burnt heather ! (G.W.) Nhb.[1]

Hence (1) **Humphed,** *ppl. adj.,* (2) **Humphy,** *adj.* tainted, having a bad smell or flavour.

(1) Sc. Humph'd beef (JAM.). **Edb.** And to another wife, that, after smell-smelling at it, thought it was a wee humphed, he replied, &c., MOIR *Mansie Wauch* (1828) xxiii. **Slk.** I wish he had fawn aff the tap o' his humphed ill-smelled hides, HOGG *Perils of Man* (1822) III. 283 (JAM.). **Gall.** Food of any kind, but particularly fresh meat, is said to be humph'd when it has a putrid taste or smell, MACTAGGART *Encycl.* (1824). (2) Nhb.[1]

2. *v.* To sniff, as one detecting a foetid odour. Bnff.[1]

HUMPH, *sb.*[2] w.Sc. (JAM.) The name given to coal, when it approaches the surface and becomes useless.

HUMPH, see Hump.

HUMPHREY-ROW, *sb.* Nhp.[2] A violent dispute.

HUMPLE, *sb.* Obs. Sc. A hillock, mound.

Edb. Ne'er stan' at mountain, hill, or humple, 'Tween you an' fame, CRAWFORD *Poems* (1798) 109.

[LG. *humpel* (*hümpel*), ' ein kleiner niedriger Erdhügel' (BERGHAUS).]

HUMPLE, see Hamble.

HUMPLOCK, *sb.* Sc. Irel. A hillock, mound, knoll ; a small heap ; a protuberance, lump. See **Humple,** *sb.*

Sc. Nae howe or humplock, wet or dry, Should ever daunton him, *Ballads and Poems* (1885) 211 ; Tae be stoiterin' an' fa'in o'er the first bit clod or humplock it taks your fit, *St. Patrick* (1819) III. 200 (JAM.). **w.Sc.** The howes and the humplocks, CARRICK *Laird of Logan* (1835) 257. **Rnf.** The dirt is clautit into humplocks (JAM.). **Ayr.** The fit rowed up wi' a great humplock o' clouts, HUNTER *Studies* (1870) 51. **Lnk.** He glowered at me like a weasel frae a humplock o' stanes, FRASER *Whaups* (1895) xv. **N.I.**[1] Applied to a badly-built hayrick.

HUMPSY, *adj.* Der. Ken. Also in form **humpsty-**Ken. [u·msi, w·msi.] In *comp.* (1) **Humpsy-backed,** (2) **-crumpsy,** humpbacked, deformed.

(1) Ken. (G.B.) ; No, not my humpsty-backed aunt ; the other one (D.W.L.). (2) Der.[2], nw.Der.[1]

HUMPTY, *adj.* Yks. Stf. Der. Nhp. e.An. Dor. Also in form **humpety** Stf.[1] [u·mti, w·mti.] **1.** Hunchbacked ; short, thick-set. nw.Der.[1], Nhp.[1], e.An.[1]

2. *Comp.* (1) **Humpty-dumpty,** (*a*) short, thick-set, clumsy; (*b*) a shapeless mass ; (2) **-jumpety,** uneven, irregular.

(1, *a*) w.Yks.[1] He's a lile humpty dumpty fellow. nw.Der.[1], Nhp.[1] (*b*) Dor.[1] (2) Stf.[1]

HUMPY, *adj.* and *sb.* Sc. Nhb. Cum. Yks. Chs. Not. Nhp. War. Wor. Wil. Dor. Dev. Also in forms **humphie** Sc. ; **humphy** Sc. Nhb.[1] [h)u·mpi, h)u·mpi.] **1.** *adj.* Hunchbacked, having a hump, deformed ; also used *fig.*

Rnf. Straight as a rash was humphy Hare, When dancing with the bride, MᶜGILVRAY *Poems* (ed. 1862) 157. **Ayr.** Auld humpy thing, hoo can it be THat I sae fondly cling to thee [of a bridge with a high and narrow arch], WHITE *Jottings* (1879) 190. **Lnk.** Makin' ane humpy, anither ane dumpy, Like the trees o' the wood, LEMON *St. Mungo* (1844) 62. **Edb.** Crouchy Car, wi's humpy gett, *Carlop Green* (1793) 129, ed. 1817. **War.** (J.R.W.)

Hence (1) **Humphy-back,** *sb.* a humped back; (2)**-backit,** *adj.* having a hump-back, hunchbacked.

(1) Edb. Her humphy back is sax times bow't, MACLAGAN *Poems* (1851) 95. (2) Sc. Dougal had the misfortune to be ' humphie backit,' GRAHAM *Writings* (1883) I. 24. **Ayr.** He was sheevil-shot, bumphy-backit, reel-fitted, and gleeyed, SERVICE *Dr. Duguid* (ed. 1887) 253. **Edb.** To mend his sins He's wed the humphy-backet howdie, MACLAGAN *Poems* (1851) 317. Nhb.[1]

2. Full of humps, rough, uneven.

Dor.[1] Zoo whether 'tis the humpy groun' That wer a battle viel, 277.

3. *Comp.* (1) **Humpy-down-dap,** a children's game ; see below; (2) **-scrumples,** the cow-parsnip, *Heracleum Sphondylium.*

(1) nw.Dev.[1] A game consisting in throwing stones at a large triangular stone set up on end. Each boy before throwing usually calls out: ' Humpy down dap, Knack'n down vlat.' If he does not call out something, he is out. (2) Dev. My donkey will eat humpy scrumples, *Reports Provinc.* (1885) 98.

4. Sulky, offended ; discontented, grumbling, cross, peevish. See **Hump,** *sb.* **6.**

n.Yks.[4] A wakely humpy bairn (I.W.). Chs.[1] What makes you so humpy ? s.Chs.[1] s.Not. 'E's allus 'umpy when there's oat to pay (J.P.K.). ne.Wor. A humpy ol' fella (J.W.P.). s.Wor. (H.K.) Wil. SLOW *Gl.* (1892).

Hence **Humpy-grumpy,** *adj.* grumbling ; complaining from indisposition. Nhp.[1], War.[2]

5. *sb.* A hunchback.

Per. Wae's heart for the back that this bushel was tied on ! A humphy for ever the owner maun be, SPENCE *Poems* (1898) 77. Cum. (J.Ar.), Cum.[4]

HUMS, *sb.* Sh.I. Also in forms **homsk, hooms.**

1. Dusk. Cf. **húmin.**

He's comin to de hums o' de night, JAKOBSEN *Dial.* (1897) 37. Hence **Homsi (Hoomsi),** *adj.* of the sky : slightly obscured. *ib.*

2. Haze ; also in forms **homak, hoomaker.**

JAKOBSEN (*l. c.*) ; *ib.* *Norsk in Sh.* (1897) 71.

[1. A der. of Norw. dial. *hum,* obscurity in the clouds, an overcast sky (AASEN). ON. *hūm,* dusk, twilight (FRITZNER) ; see JAKOBSEN *Norsk in Sh.* (*l. c.*).]

HUMSTRUM, *sb.*[1] Obs. Abd. A slight fit of peevishness. SHIRREFS *Poems* (1790) *Gl.* See **Strum.**

HUMSTRUM, *sb.*[2] and *adj.* Nhp. War. Oxf. Wil. Dor. Slang. [**ɐ·m-strɐm.**] **1.** *sb.* A rude kind of musical instrument.

Nhp.[1] Sometimes applied to the [piano] when crazy, or out of tune. **Wil.** [A] home-made fiddle, SLOW *Gl.* (1892); Wil.[1] Sometimes applied also to a large kind of Jew's-harp. **Dor.** At Christmas tide . . . The humstrums here did come about, A-sounden up at ev'ry door, BARNES *Poems* (1869-70) 101 ; Dor.[1] **Slang.** A musical instrument made of a mopstick, a bladder, and some packthread. . . It is played on like a violin, which is sometimes ludicrously called a humstrum ; sometimes instead of a bladder a tin canister is used, GROSE *Dict. Slang* (1811).

Hence **Humstrumming**, *sb.* a singing, or playing on an instrument, in a monotonous way.

Oxf. Oh stop that humstrumming ; I can't stand any more of it (G.O.).

2. *adj.* Dull, dreary, lagging ; unskilful in doing anything.

Nhp.[1] Applied to playing on a piano. ' She's a poor humstrum performer.' **War.**[2] A humstrum job.

Hence **Humstrumming**, *ppl. adj.* lounging about in enforced idleness. War.[2]

HUMSUMIVVER, HUN, see **Howsomever, Hunt.**

HUN-BARROW, *sb.* Wil. Also written -barrer Wil.[1] [**ɐn-bɛrə.**] A tumulus. SLOW *Gl.* (1892) ; Wil.[1]

[LG. *hünenbarge*, prehistoric barrows near the North Sea coast (BERGHAUS) ; EFris. *hünen-bed, hünengraft* (KOOLMAN). For a discussion on the etym. of EFris. *hüne* (a giant) see GRIMM *Teut. Myth.* (tr. Stallybrass) II. 522.]

HUNCH, *sb.*[1] n.Cy. Yks. Lan. Chs. Not. Lin. Rut. Lei. Nhp. War. Hrf. Brks. Bdf. e.An. Sus. Hmp. I.W. Dev. Cor. Also in forms **haunch** s.Not. ; **haunge** s.Chs.[1] ; **heawnge** Lan. [**unʃ, ɐnʃ.**] **1.** A lump ; a large slice, esp. of victuals. Cf. **hunk,** *sb.*[1]

w.Yks.[1] **s.Lan.** Cut thesel a good heawnge, BAMFORD *Dial.* (1854). **s.Chs.**[1] Yoa·)n gy'en mi sich· û au·nj û raap·it·pahy ; ahy shaa)nû bi fit fûr nóo púd·in ût aaf·tûr. Not.[1] ; Not.[2] A hunch of bread and cheese. **s.Not.** 'E wor gnawin' a gret haunch o' bread (J.P.K.). **n.Lin.**[1], Rut.[1], Lei.[1] **Nhp.**[1] A misshapen piece, in contradistinction to a slice. A solid piece of meat or cheese would be called ' a great hunch ' ; a ' hunch of bread ' is a large irregular piece, generally cut angularly from the corner of a loaf. **War.**[2], Hrf.[1,2], Brks.[1] Oxf. (G.O.) **Bdf.** BATCHELOR *Anal. Eng. Lang.* (1809) 135. **e.An.**[1], Nrf. (W.R.E.), Suf.[1], Sus.[2], Hmp.[1], Dev.[1], Cor.[1,2]

2. A bunch, a confused heap.

Nhp.[1] Your things are all of a hunch.

3. *Comb.* **Hunch-rigged,** humpbacked. n.Cy. (HALL), w.Yks.[1]

4. Of thunder : a deep, heavy peal. I.W. (J.D.R.), I.W.[1]

HUNCH, *v.*[1] and *sb.*[2] Sc. Yks. Lan. Der. Lin. Nhp. Brks. Bck. Hrt. e.An. Sus. Hmp. Wil. Also written **hunsh** S. & Ork.[1] ; and in forms **hunge** Bdf. Hrt. ; **hungs** Sh.I. [**h)unʃ, unʃ.**] **1.** *v.* To hoist up, heave, lift, shove.

Sh.I. Shû hungsd da lamb farder up apon her neck, *Sh. News* (Aug. 21, 1897). Nhp.[1] Hunch the sack on his back. **e.An.**[1] **Nrf.** HOLLOWAY. **e.Suf.** (F.H.) **Sus.,** Hmp. HOLLOWAY.

2. To push, *gen.* with the shoulder or elbow ; to gore or butt with the horns ; to maul ; freq. with *about.*

Sh.I. He hunches wi pooer, BURGESS *Rasmie* (1892) 17. **Lan.** *N. & Q.* (1878) 5th S. x. 164. Der.[2], nw.Der.[1] **sw.Lin.**[1] I shouldn't like to be hunched about, now I'm old. **Nhp.**[2] **Brks.**[1] The cow tried to hunch muh. **Bck.** (W.H.Y.) **Bdf.** BATCHELOR *Anal. Eng. Lang.* (1809) 135. **Hrt.** The lambs hunching and butting her bag, ELLIS *Shepherd's Guide* (1750) 272 ; [The ewe] will hunge and beat the lambs with both her feet and horns, *ib. Mod. Husb.* (1750) IV. i. 117. **Hmp.**[1], Wil.[1], s.Wil. (G.E.D.)

3. To shrug the shoulders up.

S. & Ork.[1] **Wil.** But Tiney winced, and Tiney hunched, And Tiney cocked her nose, AKERMAN *Spring-tide* (1850) 118.

Hence **Hunched-up,** *ppl. adj.* having a stooping posture like a hunchback.

w.Yks. I just gat a glimpse at her, . . a hunched up little body, SNOWDEN *Web of Weaver* (1896) x.

4. *sb.* A push, shove, hoist up. Cf. **hunk,** *sb.*[2]

Nhp.[1] Give him a hunch on the horse. **e.An.**[1] ' Give me a hunch, Tom,' said an elderly e.An. matron, somewhat corpulent, to her stout footman, who stood grinning behind her, while she was endeavouring to climb into her carriage. **Nrf.** HOLLOWAY. **e.Suf.**

(F.H.) **Sus.**[1] I thought they were sweethearts, because I see him give her a hunch in church with his elbow. **Hmp.** HOLLOWAY.

5. An awkward bending movement of the body.

Fif. What an awkward hunch the fellow makes As to the priest he does the bow repay, TENNANT *Anster* (1812) 7, ed. 1815.

HUNCH, *v.*[2] and *sb.*[3] Yks. Lin. **1.** *v.* To snub.

Lin. BROOKES *Tracts Gl.* ; Lin.[1] Did they hunch her ! **sw.Lin.**[1] Don't hunch her, poor little thing ! She shan't be hunched.

2. To set a person's back up, to ' huff.'

m.Yks.[1] Thou shouldn't say naught of the sort to him ; thou'll hunch him if thou doesn't mind. **n.Lin.** I thought the old man had turned huncht about this wedding, PEACOCK *M. Heron* (1872) III. 14.

Hence **Huncht,** *ppl. adj.* bad-tempered.

n.Lin.[1] A——'s a straange huncht an' queer man, he weänt let noäbody cum along side on him wi'oot slaatin' 'em.

3. *sb.* A huff, a fit of ill-temper.

Yks. T'awd hoit's geean aaf i' a hunch, MACQUOID *Patty* (1877) xix. **sw.Yks.**[1]

HUNCH, *adj.* Lin. Nhp. e.An. Also in form **hunchy** Lin.[1] [**unʃ, ɐnʃ.**] **1.** *adj.* Harsh, unkind.

Lin. (HALL) **sw.Lin.**[1] Sons and daughters are oftens so hunch to old folks.

Lin.[1] **sw.Lin.** It's been a cold hunch March (R.E.C.). **sw.Lin.**[1] If there comes a cold hunch winter.

2. Cold, frosty.

Lin. One cold slate-coloured morning towards the end of March (' hunch-weather,' as I have heard it termed in Lincolnshire, because, I suppose, a sense of starvation has a tendency to set one's back up), HOLE *Roses* (ed. 1896) 12. **Nhp.**[1] **e.An.**[1] Which makes men hunch up their shoulders, and animals contract their limbs, and look as if they were hunch-backed. *Suf. e.An. N. & Q.* (1866) II. 327.

3. *Comb.* **Hunch-weather,** damp, cold, foggy weather.

HUNCHED-UP, *pp.* I.W. [**ɐnʃt.**] Of a crop of apples, potatoes, &c. : diminished in size. (J.D.R.), I.W.[1] See **Hunch,** *sb.*[1] **2.**

HUNCHEON, *sb.* Lan. e.An. [**u·nʃən.**] A thick slice of bread with some other food. See **Hunch,** *sb.*[1]

Lan. He gan me a great huncheon o' [denty] snig poy, *N. & Q.* (1868) 4th S. ii. 100. **e.An.**[1] Nrf. I used to get a huncheon of bread and cheese, EMERSON *Son of Fens* (1892) 17 ; I cut her a pretty good huncheon off the loaf, SPILLING *Johnny's Jaunt* (1879) i. **e.Suf.** (F.H.)

HUNCHERY-MUNCHERY, *sb.* n.Yks.[2] The habit of eating at any time of the day instead of making stated meals.

HUND, HUNDER, see **Hound,** *sb.*[1], **Hundred.**

HUNDERSHILLEN, *sb.* Hrt. A small hammer used by a thatcher. (H.G.)

HUNDG(E, *v.* Sh.I. [**hɐndg.**] To drive or chase away. S. & Ork.[1]

HUNDRED, *num. adj.* and *sb.* Var. dial. uses in Sc. Irel. Eng. and Amer. **I.** Dial. forms : (1) **Hondred,** (2) **Hunder,** (3) **Hunderd,** (4) **Hundert,** (5) **Hunderth,** (6) **Hundort,** (7) **Hundredth,** (8) **Hundreth,** (9) **Huner,** (10) **Hunner,** (11) **Huntherd,** (12) **Hunthert,** (13) **Oonderd.**

(1) **n.Lan.** Wi'in a hondred yirds o' yam, *Lonsdale Mag.* (July 1866) 8. (2) **Sc.** Twa hunder merks, SCOTT *Leg. Mont.* (1818) iv. Or.I. (JAM. *Suppl.*) **Frf.** Lochiel has twa hunder spearsmen, BARRIE *Tommy* (1896) xxi. **Ayr.** Snaw-white seventeen hunder linnen, BURNS *Tam o' Shanter* (1790) l. 154. **Edb.** *Tint Quey* (1796) 22. **Yks.** He'll be worth his two hunder a year, GASKELL *Sylvia* (1863) II. vi. (3) **w.Yks.** Poisonin' hunderds o' lads, *Yksman Comic Ann.* (1890) 31. **Stf.** A hunderd pownd, MURRAY *Joseph's Coat* (1882) 304. **s.Not.** (J.P.K.), n.Lin.[1] **Glo.** Take a hunderd of it, GISSING *Vill. Hampden* (1890) I. viii. **n.Wil.** Ye . . . must haä a thousan', an' thoy as keeps th' vruit on un two hunderd, KITE *Sng. Sol.* (1860) viii. 12. **Som.** There's mebby now a hunderd, AGRIKLER *Rhymes* (1872) 55. **Dev.** Too hunderd, BAIRD *Sng. Sol.* (1860) viii. 12. [Amer. *Dial. Notes* (1896) I. 7.] (4) **Lan.** Have a hundert wi bur, BRIERLEY *Layrock* (1864) xvi. (5) **Wxf.**[1] (6) **Nhb.** Twe hundort, ROBSON *Sng. Sol.* (1859) viii. 12. (7) **Sc.** The thirtieth and first verse of the hundredth, fortieth, and ninth Psalm, *Monthly Mag.* (1800) I. 299. **Or.I.** Four thousand six hundredth sixty six pound, PETERKIN *Notes* (1822) 155. **Ref.** In ane hundredth pounds, HECTOR *Judicial Records* (1876) 56. (8) **Abd.** Many hundreth yeares before, FORBES *Rec. of Kirk* (1606) 491. (9) **n.Sc.** The noise . . . Would fear'd five huner men, BUCHAN *Ballads* (1828) I. 138, ed. 1875. (10) **Abd.** In scores an'

hunners, ALEXANDER *Johnny Gibb* (1871) xviii. Lnk. Hunners ran at ither's heels, WATSON *Poems* (1853) 11. Dmf. A hunner lairds an' mair besides, THOM *Jock o' Knowe* (1878) 19. n.Ir. There wuz hunners that cudnae get in the daur [door], LYTTLE *Ballycuddy* (1892) 35. (11, 12) e.Lan.[1] (13) Lin. Haäte oonderd haacre, TENNYSON *N. Farmer, Old Style* (1864) st. 11.

II. Dial. uses. **1.** *num. adj.* In *comb.* (1) **Hundred-fald**, the yellow bedstraw, *Galium verum* ; (2) **-leaved grass**, the yarrow, *Achillea Millefolium* ; (3) **-legged worm**, or **-legs**, a centipede ; (4) **-thistle**, the field eryngo, *Eryngium campestre.*

(1, 2) Nhb.[1] (3) Glo.[1] w.Som.[1] Uun·durd, or uun·düd-ligz, usual name. (4) Nhp. (B. & H.); Nhp.[2] MORTON *Hist.* (1712).

2. Phr. *a hundred words won't fill a bushel :* '*it's all the same to Sam,*' you talk to no purpose. e.Suf. (F.H.)

3. *sb.* Of land: a hundred acres; a hundred square yards. Lei.[1] Dor. 'A large farm?' she inquired. ' No; not large. About a hundred.' (In speaking of farms the word ' acres ' is omitted by the natives), HARDY *Madding Crowd* (1874) iii.

4. Phr. *out of one's hundred*, strange, out of one's element. e.An.[1]

5. The **long hundred**, six score ; a number varying according to the articles counted ; a measure of ground large enough to grow six score plants.

Or.I. A measure of garden-ground in Orkney 15 ft. by 18 ft. in extent : ground sufficient for the growth of a hundred plants of kail. In each plot or hundred the plants are set 18 inches apart, or in ten rows of twelve each. Hundred, therefore, means the long hundred or six score (JAM. *Suppl.*). a.Wor.[1] Long, by machine weight, 112 lb. ; by count, six score = 126 ; e.g. a hundred of asparagus, of oranges, of walnuts, &c., would be 126. Nrf. Six score ' casts ' (or pairs) of crabs, i.e. 240, are called a hundred, JARROLD *Guide to Cromer*, 39; Six score go to the hundred, RYE *Hist. Nrf.* (1885) xv. Sus. In counting fish 128 herrings make a hundred and 132 mackerel according to Brighton measure, but the reckoning is by warps of 4 fish (F.E.S.). w.Som.[1] A long hundred is six score... In markets, when buying by tale, unless ' the hundred of five score ' is specially mentioned, the hundred is understood to be one hundred and twenty, now often called '·a long hundred.' [Of balks, deals, eggs, faggots, bunches, &c., *gen.* 120, MORTON *Cyclo. Agric.* (1863) ; STEVENSON in *Arch. Review* (Dec. 1889) 313 ff.]

Hence **Hundredweight**, *sb.* a measure, *gen.* of 120 lb., but varying in different districts according to the article weighed.

Lan. 100, 112, 120 lbs., MORTON *Cyclo. Agric.* (1863). Chs. Of cheese and hay : 120 lbs., the long hundred, *ib.* ; Cha.[1] Formerly the long hundredweight of 120 lbs. was in *gen.* use in Cheshire ; and I can recollect the time when the sets of weights at farm-houses were 60 lbs. and aliquot parts of 60. Even now many things are reckoned and sold by the score which is the sixth of the old hundredweight. Many things are sold by the load of 240 lbs. or *pack*, a term which is frequently heard, and which is in reality two long hundredweights. I think the only article which is still sold by the long hundredweight is cheese ; and in weighing cheese a rather curious and ingenious method was adopted which still prevails amongst old-fashioned people. The method was perhaps invented because, before the introduction of weighing machines, it was almost impossible to weigh more than one or two hundredweight at a time on an ordinary pair of scales ; perhaps also, because farmers were not very good scholars, and to work a long compound addition sum involving many lines of cwts. qrs. and lbs. would have been a difficult task. The scales, large wooden ones, hung by strong chains, were fixed up in some convenient place, and two 60 lb. weights were put into one scale—representing a hundredweight. Cheeses to equal this as nearly as possible were placed in the other scale, and ' 1 ' was scratched upon the wall, or chalked up on the door to show that 1 cwt. of cheese had been weighed. Of course the cheeses might be a few pounds over or under the hundredweight, and to ascertain the difference small paving stones were used instead of small weights. If the cheeses weighed more than one cwt. stones were added to the weights until the scales balanced. These stones were then called cheese and were placed on the floor near the cheese scale. If the cheeses weighed less than 1 cwt., stones were put in the cheese scale until the two scales balanced ; these stones were called weights and were put on the floor near the weight scale. This process went on until all the hundredweights of cheese had been weighed; but to avoid having large piles of stones it was

VOL. III.

customary to add to or deduct from the stones representing cheese as the weighing went on. At the last the stones were weighed against each other, and the difference added to or subtracted from the number of hundredweights recorded on the wall. Occas. 2 cwt. instead of 1 cwt. were weighed at each weighing ; but the principle was the same. Stf., Der., Lei. Of cheese, MORTON *ib.* Shr. Of cheese, Bridgenorth 113 lbs., Shrewsbury 121 lbs., *ib.* Hnt. Of Leicester cheese, 120 lbs., *ib.* Cmb. Of cheese, 120 lbs., *ib.* Ess. Of potatoes, 120 lbs., *ib.* Ken. Of filberts, 104 lbs., *ib.* w.Som.[1] One hundred pounds.

6. *pl.* A game of marbles ; see below.

w.Yks.[2] The name of a game at marbles which is carried on till one of the players scores 100, or some higher number agreed upon ; at that stage a change takes place in the proceedings. Two or more can play. First they 'taw' up to a hole ; if they both get in, they repeat the process till one is left out ; the other counts 10 ; if both fail the nearest goes first. *A* may now lay his taw about the hole, or fire at the other, on hitting which he counts another 10. He now goes for the hole again, and failing, lies where he happens to stop. If he misses, *B* from his present position tries to get into the hole, and failing, lies still ; but if he reaches the hole he counts 10 and proceeds as *A* had done. The one who first gets the 100 (or other number) now goes in for his 'pizings,' which performance takes place thus :—The loser, so far, is lying about, and the winner goes back to ' drakes,' and again tries to lodge in the hole, and if he succeeds the game is up. If not, he lies still, and the loser tries for the hole ; if he gets in he counts another 10, or if he should succeed in hitting the winner, he scores his adversaries' hundred to his own number, and then goes in for his pizings, as the other had done. In failure of either securing the game thus, the process is repeated at drakes. When, however, the one who is on for his pizings manages to taw into the hole, the game is concluded.

HUNDYCLOCK, *sb.* Sh.I. A large black beetle. See **Clock**, *sb.*[2]

JAKOBSEN *Norsk in Sh.* (1897) 25 ; S. & Ork.[1] *MS. add.*

HUNE, *sb.*[1] w.Som.[1] [ən.] A handle, ' haft.'

Not common. ' The hune o' me knive's a-brokt.'

HUNE, *v.*[1] and *sb.*[2] Sc. [hœn, hün.] **1.** *v.* To loiter ; to stop. Cld., Ayr. (JAM.)

2. *sb.* Delay.

Sc. The trauclit stag i' the wan waves lap But huliness or hune, *Edb. Mag.* (May 1820) 422 (JAM.).

3. A loiterer ; one who delays ; a lazy, silly person. Cld. (JAM.)

[1. Petre þan gan to hone, *Cursor M.* (c. 1300) 19867. **2.** With-outyn hone (*v. r.* forouten hoyne), BARBOUR *Bruce* (1375) XIV. 182.]

HUNE, *v.*[2] and *sb.*[3] Cld. (JAM.) **1.** *v.* To stammer from shyness, or from a sense of guilt. **2.** *sb.* One who stammers.

HUNE, HUNER, see **Hone**, *v.*[3], **Hound**, *sb.*[3], **Hundred.**

HUNG, *ppl. adj.* Sh.I. Yks. Lin. [huŋ, uŋ.] In *comb.* (1) **Hung-beef**, salted beef hung up to dry ; (2) **-milk**, see below ; (3) **-teap**, a ram ; a male sheep.

(1) n.Lin.[1] (2) S. & Ork.[1] Milk coagulated by the heat of the weather, placed in a linen bag and suspended until the whey, &c., has dripped from it, leaving a thick creamy substance. (3) n.Yks.[2] s.Yks. MARSHALL *Rur. Econ.* (1796) II. 327.

HUNG, HUNGE, see **Hing**, *v.*, **Hunch**, *v.*[1]

HUNGE, *v.* sw.Lin.[1] [uŋg.] To long for, regard wistfully. See **Hone**, *v.*[2] **2.**

The herses stand hunge-ing about. He comes hunge-ing after money.

HUNGELL, *sb.* Sh.I. [hwŋgl.] The greenbone or garfish, *Belone vulgaris.* JAKOBSEN *Norsk in Sh.* (1897) 25 ; S. & Ork.[1]

[Norw. dial. *horngjæla*, the garfish, ' Belone vulgaris ' (AASEN) ; ON. *horn-gæla*, ' Esox Belone' (VIGFUSSON); see JAKOBSEN (*l. c.*).]

HUNGE-PLUNGE, *sb.* and *adv.* Not. Also in form **hunge-splunge**. [uŋg-pluŋg.] **1.** *sb.* A plunging movement.

s.Not. He went such a hunge-plunge to the tother side the road (J.P.K.).

2. *adv.* With a plunging movement.

Into the dike 'e went, hunge-splunge (*ib.*).

o o

HUNGER, *sb.*[1] and *v.* Var. dial. uses in Sc. Irel. and Eng. Also written **hungar** Cor.; **hungher** Wxf.[1]; and in form **honger** N.Cy.[1] Hrf.[1] Glo.[1] [h]ʊ'ŋgə(r, u'ŋə(r.]

1. *sb.* In *comb.* (1) **Hunger-bane**, *obs.*, to starve to death; (2) **-bit** or **-bitten**, half-starved; (3) **-groin**, a hungry-looking fellow; also used *attrib.*; (4) **-house**, a place where animals are kept without food the night before they are slaughtered; (5) **-like**, starved, stunted; (6) **-poisoned**, (*a*) starving, unhealthy from want of food; (*b*) miserly, stingy; (7) **-rot**, a penurious, griping wretch; (8) **-slain**, (9) **-starved**, pined to the bone; having a famished appearance; also of land : impaired for want of manure; (10) **-stone**, a quartz pebble; a stone honeycombed by the pholas, and considered unlucky as ballast; (11) **-weed**, (*a*) the corn crowfoot, *Ranunculus arvensis*; (*b*) the slender foxtail grass, *Alopecurus agrestis*.

(1) Wil.[1] At Bradfield and Dracot Cerne is such vitriolate earth . . . [which] makes the land so soure, it bears sowre and austere plants. . . At summer it hunger-banes the sheep, AUBREY *Hist.* 35. (2) Per. The ape, hunger-bitten, was moved with envy 'Gainst puss, NICOL *Poems* (1766) 117. Lnk. Some hungerbit, or stomacksick at least, Convert tobacco in Duke Vmphraes feast, LITHGOW *Poet. Rem.* (ed. 1863) Sc. *Welcome.* n.Yks. He hez a hungerbitten looak (T.S.). (3) w.Yks. (S.P.U.) (4) n.Yks. (I.W.) (5) Abd. Dry graively hills a' aboot it, an' naething upo' them but a wheen short hunger-like gerse, MACDONALD *Sir Gibbie* (1879) xlvi. (6, *a*) n.Cy. *Poetry Provinc.* in *Cornh. Mag.* (1865) XII. 31. e.An.[1] ' A poor star-naked, hunger-poisoned creature!' said of a ragged and emaciated vagrant, by the constable who brought her before the magistrate. e.Suf. (F.H.) (*b*) e.An.[1], e.Suf. (F.H.) (7) n.Cy. (HALL.), w.Yks.[1] (8) n.Yks.[2] A poor hunger-slain spot. m.Yks.[1] Freely applied where hardly applicable, as to a family living in a large house, without suitable attendance. ' A poor hungerslain lot.' (9) n.Yks.[2] (10) ne.Sc. A stone bored by the pholas was rejected as ballast; such a stone bore the name of the hunger steen, GREGOR *Flk-Lore* (1881) 198. w.Yks.[1], Lin. (HALL.) (11, *a*) Glo.[1] Glo., Nrf. From being an indication of poor land or from impoverishing crops amongst which it grows (B. & H.). (*b*) Chs.[1]

2. *Phr.* (1) *a hunger and a burst*, a period of privation alternating with one of excess; (2) *hunger is a sharp thorn*, hunger is hard to bear.

(1) Cai.[1] We say of the improvident poor that their life is ' a hunger and a burst,' i. e. that when they get a little money they at once arrange for a ' big feed ' or ' great drink ' and then for a time are in a state of starvation. (2) w.Yks. Hunger, they say, is a sharp thorn, an' begow it's true, CUDWORTH *Dial. Sketches* (1884) 15.

3. *v.* To starve : to withhold necessary food.

Sc. I will put her in cold prison, And hunger her till she die, KINLOCH *Ballads* (1827) 79. Lnk. She's ay flyting on her lasses, hungers her servant lad, GRAHAM *Writings* (1883) II. 140. Slk. He wad hae hungered the lad to death, HOGG *Tales* (1838) 298, ed. 1866. Gall. I hunger my wyme and my back I keep duddy, MACTAGGART *Encycl.* (1824) 109, ed. 1876. n.Cy. GROSE (1790) *MS. add.* (P.) n.Yks.[1] 'Twur a cruel act, hungerin' thae poor bairns, as she did, fra yah week's end tiv anither; n.Yks.[4] He hungers ivverything aboot t'pleeace. ne.Yks.[1] T'pigs is beealin seea, ah lay you've been hungerin' em. w.Yks.[1] He hungers t'barn.

Hence **Hungered**, *ppl. adj.* (1) ill-fed, starved; (2) scanty, ill-provided.

(1) Ayr. Hungered Highland boors, BURNS *Address of Beelzebub* (1786) l. 2. Wxf.[1], N.Cy.[1] Wm. She niver thought of leaving her cabin till she was hungered out, BRIGGS *Remains* (1825) 57. s.Wm. We wer safe to ha' been hungert, SOUTHEY *Doctor* (ed. 1848) 560. n.Yks.[1] Ah's about hungered to deid; n.Yks.[4] Ah war hungered past my bahdings. ne.Yks.[1] Ah's that hungered whahl ah can hardlins bahd. Hrf.[1], Glo.[1], Dor.[1] Cor. Why, how are 'ee so late, soas? Arn't 'ee hungar'd? FORFAR *Pentowan* (1859) i. (2) Per. Whyles a simmer cauld an' green Has left a hunger'd hairst ahint it, HALIBURTON *Ochil Idylls* (1891) 52. Edb. Never dree a hungert day, FERGUSSON *Poems* (1773) 150, ed. 1785.

4. *Phr. to hunger the hook*, to spare the bait.

Sh.I. Fish or no fish, Magnie, 'ill no hae sin for hungerin' da huiks, *Sh. News* (Apr. 23, 1898); I wisna lang fir we hed a nebbard an' a half, an' I didna hunger da huik, *ib.* (Dec. 9, 1899).

HUNGER, *sb.*[2] Sh.I. [Not known to our correspondents.] A kettle for broiling. (*Coll.* L.L.B.)

HUNGER, *sb.*[3] Cum.[4] Crystallized carbonate of lime. Also called **White hunger**.

[It] is found as ' white threads ' in the backs or cleets of the

coal seam. It is much used by miners for polishing the brass of their lamps.

HUNGERSOME, *adj.* Sc. Also written **hungersum** Cai.[1] Bnff.[1] [hʌ'ŋərsəm.] **1.** Hungry.

Dmb. Ye ken luive makes me desperate hungersome, CROSS *Disruption* (1844) xv.

2. Causing hunger.

Cai.[1] Bnff.[1] Hairstan's hungersum work.

HUNGE-SPLUNGE, see **Hunge-plunge**.

HUNGE-STONE, *sb.* Lin.[1] [Not known to our correspondents.] A quartz pebble. Cf. **hunger-stone**.

HUNGIL-MONEY, *sb. Obs.* Yks. A small payment; see below. Cf. **horsam**.

A small tax, which is still paid . . . by the townships on the north side of the Vale . . . of Pickering, for horsemen and hounds kept for the purpose of driving off the deer of the forest of Pickering from the corn-fields which bordered upon it, GROSE (1790) (s. v. Horsam); MARSHALL *Rur. Econ.* (1788).

[OE. *hundgild*, dog-payment.]

HUNGKLECK, *sb.* Sh.I. The rhinoceros-beetle, *Dynastes tityus.* JAKOBSEN *Norsk in Sh.* (1897) 25. See **Clock**, *sb.*[3]

[ON. *horn-klukka*, see JAKOBSEN (*l. c.*).]

HUNGRELS, *sb. pl. Obs.* Chs. The rafters.

Commonly made of poles split in the middle to support a covering of thatch (K.); Chs.[1]

HUNGRISOME, *adj.* Sc. Also written **hungrisum** Cld. (JAM.) Voracious, eager.

Cld. (JAM.) Gall. Thirty [psalms] would not suit this hungrisome Quintin of ours. He must needs learn the whole hundred and fifty by rote, CROCKETT *Standard Bearer* (1898) 99.

Hence (1) **Hungrisomelike**, *adv.* somewhat voraciously; (2) **Hungrisomeness**, *sb.* the state of hunger. (JAM.)

HUNGRY, *adj.* Var. dial. uses in Sc. Irel. Eng. and Aus. Also in form **hongry** se.Wor.[1] **1.** In *comb.* (1) **Hungry-grass**, a magic grass; see below; (2) **-ground**, an enchanted tract of country supposed to cause hunger to the person who passes over it; (3) **-gut**, a penurious person; (4) **-heart**, an empty, craving stomach; (5) **-hillock**, see (2); (6) **-land**, poor, unproductive soil; (7) **-poisoned**, miserly, stingy; lean, starved-looking; (8) **-worm**, a worm supposed to cause hunger.

(1) Ir. Tafts of a peculiar grass that grows on the mountains, on which if anyone tread he immediately becomes faint and hungry and incapable of walking, *Flk-Lore Rec.* (1881) IV. 109. N.I.[1] Uls. If one treads on hungrygrass—which is said to grow up where persons dining in a field have not thrown some of the fragments to the fairies—he will be seized with what the Irish call *feargartha* or *fairgurtha*, hungry disease, BLACK *Flk-Medicine* (1883) i. Don. *Fairgorta, fairgarta,* or hungry-grass. . . Any one who chances to put their foot on it is immediately seized with weakness and sleepiness, *Flk-Lore Jrn.* (1886) IV. 362; Mountain and moory places chiefly abound with hungry-grass, MACMANUS *Oiney Kittack* in *Century Mag.* (Oct. 1899) 956. (2) Bnff.[1] w.Sc. Some tracts of country are believed to be so much under the power of enchantment, that he who passes over any one of them, would infallibly faint, if he did not use something for the support of nature. It is therefore customary to carry a piece of bread in one's pocket, to be eaten when one comes to what is called the hungry ground (JAM.). (3) e.Suf. (F.H.) (4) N.I.[1] (5) ne.Sc. If one was rather suddenly seized with a craving for food accompanied with a feeling of faintness, or if one seemed to eat more heartily than usual, it was attributed to going over what was called a hungry hillock, GREGOR *Flk-Lore* (1881) 30. Bnff.[1] A'm sae yaap, a've surely gehn our a hungry-hillock. (6) N.I.[1] Cha.[1] Barren soil which requires constant manuring is said to be hungry land. Nhp.[1] Land on a gravelly and sandy subsoil, which soon absorbs the manure, and exhausts its fertilizing properties. War.[4] You may put as much muck as you loikes on that field, and it will be gone in one year. It's hungry land. (7) e.Suf. (F.H.) (8) n.Sc. Gie the bairn a bit piece, for fear the hungry worm cut its heart (JAM.).

2. *Phr.* (1) *a hungry dog will eat dirty pudding*, ' hunger is the best sauce '; (2) *a hungry eye sees far*, necessity sharpens the wits; (3) *as hungry as a hunter*, excessively hungry; (4) *hungry folk's meat*, food which takes longer than usual to cook.

(1) se.Wor.[1] Glo. SMITH *Lives Berkeleys* (1066-1618) III. 31,

ed. 1885. (2) N.I.[1] (3) w.Yks. HARTLEY *Tales*, 2nd S. 149. (4) ne.Sc. In cooking any dish, if the cooking seemed to require longer time than usual it was said that there was hungry folk's meat in the pot, GREGOR *Flk-Lore* (1881) 30.

3. Of soil : poor, barren ; requiring constant manuring. n.Cy. (HALL.), w.Yks.[1], Cha.[1], War.[4] Cmb. Norfolk's a very hungry country (W.M.B.). e.Suf. (F.H.)

4. Greedy ; stingy, covetous, mean. ne.Lan.[1], War. (J.R.W.), e.Suf. (F.H.) w.Som.[1] Main near, hungry old feller, proper old skin-vlint. Dev.[1] ; Dev.[8] They be that bungry, they'd skin a vlint tū save a penny and spowl a vowerpenny knive tū dū't. Cor.[1] He's as hungry as the grave; Cor.[2] [Ans. They . . . have been the very first to kick against cooking for poor swaggers, and . . . have given stations a hungry name, FERGUSON *Bush Life* (1891) vii.]

HUNGS, see Hunch, *v.*[1]

HUNK, *sb.*[1] In *gen.* dial. use in Sc. Eng. and Amer. Also in form nunk Som. [hʊŋk, h)ʊŋk.] A mis-shapen lump ; a large, thick piece of food ; also used *fig.* Cf. hunch, *sb.*[1]
Frf. There were three bridies, an oatmeal cake, and a hunk of kebbock, BARRIE *Tommy* (1896) ix. Nhb.[1] A hunk o' breed. Cum. Ah saw a gurt hunk of a fellow ledderan away, SARGISSON *Joe Scoap* (1881) 6 ; Cum.[4], w.Yks. (J.W.), Lan. (F.R.C.) Midl. The two hunks of fat, BARTRAM *People of Clopton* (1897) 4. Der.[2], nw.Der.[1], Not.[1], n.Lin.[1], Lei.[1], Nhp.[1], War. (J.R.W.), War.[2], Brks.[1] Mid. I had brought some bread and a hunk of bacon, BLACKMORE *Kit* (1890) III. iv. Nrf. PATTERSON *Man and Nat.* (1895) 63. Ken. (G.B.) Sus.[2] A gurt hunk o' bre'n cheese. Hmp. COOPER *Gl.* (1853). Wil. A huge hunk of bread and cheese in his left hand, AKERMAN *Tales* (1853) 30 ; SLOW *Gl.* (1892). Som. SWEETMAN *Wincanton Gl.* (1885). w.Som.[1] He'd a got a hunk o' burd'n cheese fit to make a farmer's heart ache. Dev. Dawntee cut sich gert hunks ov mayte 's that: tha chillern can't ayte um, HEWETT *Peas. Sp.* (1892). n.Dev. 'Tis thick gurt hunk. I tell'e all, Auver tha passon's desk I'll vall Avore I wool be kist, ROCK *Jim an' Nell* (1867) st. 40. e.Dev. Laike hunks o' pomegranate's yer temples in under yer locks, PULMAN *Sng. Sol.* (1860) iv. 3. Cor. A hunk o' cold beef as salt as Lot's wife's elbow, ' Q.' *Troy Town* (1888) v ; Cor.[123] [Amer. *Dial. Notes* (1896) I. 341.]
[WFlem. *hunke* (eene hunke brood, eene hunke vleesch), a hunk of bread or meat (DE Bo).]

HUNK, *sb.*[2] Sc. Also in form hunks Edb. A sluttish, indolent woman.
Edb. BALLANTINE *Gaberlunzie* (ed. 1875) *Gl.* Rxb. A nasty hunk. A lazy hunk (JAM.).

HUNK, *sb.*[3] Sh.I. A lift ; a push. Cf. hunch, *sb.*[2] **4.** Hyst him wi a hunk, BURGESS *Rasmie* (1892) 104.

HUNKER, *v.* Sc. Irel. n.Cy. Nhb. Nhp. Hrf. Amer. [h)ʊŋkə(r, hʊˈŋkər.] **1.** To squat with the haunches, knees, and ankles acutely bent so as to bring the hams near the heels ; also used *fig.*
Sc. Hob, that was the eldest, hunkered at the door-sill, STEVENSON *Weir* (1896) v. Bnff. Hunker down upo' her hurdies, TAYLOR *Poems* (1787) 190. Abd. I can see . . . Lily hunkert doon in that dark neuk, GREIG *Logie o' Buchan* (1899) 147. Frf. In a sharp frost children hunker at the top and are blown down with a roar and a rush on rails of ice, BARRIE *Licht* (1888) 9. Per. We'll hunker doon to nane, FORD *Harp* (1893) 306. Rnf. A wee bit cot, Bare, hunkerin' on some lanely spot, WILSON *Poems* (1790) 210 (JAM.). Ayr. Hunkert doon, aside the dais, He seemed a bunch o' dirty claes, AINSLIE *Land of Burns* (ed. 1892) 192. Lth. Hunkerin' there in a corner, LUMSDEN *Sheep-head* (1892) 287. Edb. Hunk'ring down upon the cauld grass, PENNECUIK *Tinklarian* (ed. 1810) 8. Hdg. Then hunkering down upo' her knees, Poor Hornie o' her milk to ease, TINT Quey (1801) l. 187. Gall. Bending his hams and laying his hands upon his knees in the attitude which we of Moreham call 'hunkering,' CROCKETT *Anna Mark* (1899) xxxix. Keb. I hunker'd down, sae did the hizzy, DAVIDSON *Seasons* (1789) 179. N.I.[1] To crouch on the ground with the heels under the hams. Ant. GROSE (1790) *MS. add.* (C.) s.Don. SIMMONS *Gl.* (1890).
Hence (1) Hunkered, *ppl. adj.* knee-bent, elbowed, bowed, crooked ; (2) Hunkering, *ppl. adj.* of cattle : crowding.
(1) N.Cy.[1] This wheat is sadly hunkered. Nhb.[1], Nhp.[1] (2) Hrf.[2] **2.** *Comb.* (1) Hunker-slide, (*a*) to slide on the ice, sitting on one's hunkers ; (*b*) *fig.* to do anything in a mean, unmanly way ; (2) -tottie, in a ' hunkering ' position ; (3) Hunkertys (Hunkert-wise), in a squatting position.

(1, *a*) Gall. MACTAGGART *Encycl.* (1824). s.Don. SIMMONS *Gl.* (1890). (*b*) *ib.* [Amer. No hunkersliding here, *Dial. Notes* (1896) I. 379.] (a) Fif. Slides on which in gleeful rows the boys careered, erect or hunker-tottie, COLVILLE *Vernacular* (1899) 14. (3) Frf. Doon they gaed, . . some staunin', some hunkertys, WILLOCK *Rosetty Ends* (1886) 74, ed. 1889 ; A lang coorse o' sittin' hunkertys, an' wearin' breeks had maybe worn oor tails oot o' sicht, *ib.* 178.

HUNKERS, *sb. pl.* Sc. Irel. n.Cy. Nhb. Dur. Cum. Yks. Suf. Amer. [(h)ʊˈŋkə(r)z, hʊˈŋkə(r)z.] In phr. *on one's hunkers*, in a squatting position ; also *fig.* ' on one's last legs,' in reduced or desperate circumstances.
Sc. I'll eat my bonnet if she wadna hae flappit hersel' doon on her hunkers, FORD *Thistledown* (1891) 129. w.Sc. Bailie commanded the workmen . . . to get down on their knees or hunkers, CARRICK *Laird of Logan* (1835) 94. Rnf. Like all petty tyrants he meanly can cour, Kneel on his bare hunkers for favour and power, McGILVRAY *Poems* (ed. 1862) 58. Ayr. Wi' ghastly ee, poor tweedle-dee Upon his hunkers bended, BURNS *Jolly Beggars* (1785) l. 211 ; Oor cheese is on its hunkers, but yoū'll hae a preein' o't for a' that, SERVICE *Dr. Duguid* (ed. 1887) 298. Lnk. Twenty or thirty colliers usually sat on their hunkers and discussed the situation, WRIGHT *Sc. Life* (1897) 7. Edb. Crouching on his hunkers, MOIR *Mansie Wauch* (1828) xix. Rxb. The twasome on their hunkers there, Upon the green sward as they sat, A. SCOTT *Poems* (ed. 1808) 157. Dmf. On his hunkers sat the blin' man's doggie, THOM *Jock o' Knowe* (1878) 37. Gall. [He] would . . . crouch there on his hunkers, CROCKETT *Moss-Hags* (1895) liii. Ir. I seen an auld woman sittin' on her hunkers, YEATS *Flk. Tales* (1888) 109. N.I.[1] Uls. Jist sittin' at home on yer hunkers, Uls. *Jrn. Arch.* (1853–62) VI. 45. Ant. *Ballym ena Obs.* (1892). Dwn. (C.H.W.) w.Ir. Up sits the fox an his hunkers, LOVER *Leg.* (1848) I. 233. N.Cy.[1] Nhb. Aa teuk the chance to sit doon on me hunkers to leet me pipe, HALDANE *Other Eye* (1880) 6 ; Nhb.[1] e.Dur.[1] ' Sitting on the hunkers ' means squatting, as miners do in the streets (sitting on the toes, with the thighs resting on the calves). Cum.[4] He sat doon on his hunkers ahint t'dyke. w.Yks. (S.J.C.) Suf.[1] A dog sitting up on its hind legs, would be described as ' sitting on its hunkers.' [Amer. *Dial. Notes* (1896) I. 419 ; *N. & Q.* (1870) 4th S. vi. 249.]

HUNKLE, *v.* and *sb.* Sh.I. [hʊˈŋkl.] **1.** *v.* To lift oneself up ; to shrug one's shoulders. See Hunk, *sb.*[3]
An hunkled himsell, for his cott wis geen swint, BURGESS *Rasmie* (1892) 12.
2. *sb.* A shrug of the shoulders. 'Gae himsell a hunkle,' *ib.* 87.

HUNKS, *sb.* Sc. Wm. Lin. Ess. Sus. Hmp. Som. Dev. Cor. Slang. Also written hunx Wm. [h)ʊŋks, h)ʊŋks.] A miserable, niggardly old person ; a miser.
Lth. [They] might think him a beggar, and her an auld hunks, BALLANTINE *Poems* (1856) 122. Wm. A griping covetous hunx, HUTTON *Bran New Wark* (1785) l. 122. n.Lin.[1] Ess. John tipp'd the blunt for 't, for No hunks e'er seemèd he, CLARK *J. Noakes* (1839) st. 158 ; Ess.[1] Sus., Hmp. HOLLOWAY. w.Som.[1] He's a rigler old hunks, mid so well try to git blid out of a vlint-stone, as to get a varden out o' he. Dev.[1] A huges heave-up truly if her had'n had a farding to marry such a stingy hunks : such a purse-proud hectoring braggadocia, 6. Cor. There was a covetous old hunks in St. Just, HUNT *Pop. Rom. w.Eng.* (1865) 98, ed. 1896. Slang. FARMER. [Hunks, as a meer hunks, i. e. a base covetous wretch, a pitiful niggardly fellow, PHILLIPS (1706).]

HUNKS, see Hunk, *sb.*[2]

HUNKSIT, *adj.* Sh.I. [hʊˈŋksit.] High-shouldered ; having the head sunk between the shoulders.
JAKOBSEN *Norsk in Sh.* (1897) 64 ; S. & Ork.[1]

HUNNER, HUNNIEL, HUNNISH, see Hundred, Hanniel, Honish.

HUNSE, *v.* Sh.I. To search, hunt for.
An hunsd, an hunsd, wi baid mi haands Trou boady, skirt, an linin, BURGESS *Rasmie* (1892) 108 ; Ta redd oot kin ye maun be wice ; It tak a pooer o hunsin, *ib.* 85.

HUNSH, see Hunch, *v.*[1]

HUNSIL, *v.* Sh.I. To search, hunt for.
Shū wis hunsilin' i' da kist for da [fishing] flee, *Sh. News* (June 18, 1898) ; Hit'll be Mr. M'Leod's time ta hunsil troo da dicksahinar noo, bit I faer he'll luik twise or he fins some o' dy wirds, *ib.* (Nov. 12, 1898).

HUNT, *v.* and *sb.* Var. dial. uses in Sc. Irel. Eng. and Aus. Also in forms hint Fif. ; hun Lakel.[2] Cum.[14] w.Yks.[12] [h)ʊnt, h)unt.] **1.** *v.* In *comb.* (1) Hunt-a-gowk, or

-the-gowk, (a) a person sent on a fool's errand ; also used *attrib.* ; (b) a fool's errand ; (c) to go on a fool's errand ; (2) — heel, to follow scent backwards ; (3) -the-fox, a variation of the game of hare and hounds ; see below ; (4) -the-glaiks, see (1, c) ; (5) -the-hare, see (3) ; (6) -the-slipper, a game ; see below ; in *gen.* use ; (7) -the-squirrel, a sort of country dance ; (8) -the-stag, (9) -the-staigie, a boys' game ; see below ; (10) -up, an additional stake in the game of Loo ; see below ; (11) -you-shin-you, the game of shinty, q. v.

(1, a) Sc. It wad look unco-like, I thought, just to be sent out on a hunt-the-gowk errand wi' a land-louper like that, Scott *Guy M.* (1815) xlv. Fif. Tibbie still was as positive as ever that Tam meant to elope, but a wheen o' the news-laddies seemed to think different, for . . . thae began shouting, Hint-a-gowk ! Hint-a-gowk ! Hint-a-gowk ! April, McLaren *Tibbie* (1894) 60. e.Lth. We had seen ower mony o' their dodges in oor time, to let the Tories mak a hunt-'e-gowk o' us noo, Hunter *J. Inwick* (1895) 177. N.I.[1] (b) Sc. I never got sic a huntiegouke in a' my days [the speaker had been invited to a funeral but found it had already taken place], *Jokes*, 1st S. (1889) 99. n.Cy. This . . . is called a 'gowk's errand,' 'an April errand,' 'hunt the gowk,' *Flk-Lore Rec.* (1879) II. 85. (c) Sc. (Jam.) (2) n.Dev. At these breaks of the scent the hounds are checked and sometimes the young hounds will begin to run it back the wrong way ; they are then said to 'hunt heel.' The ancient term was to 'hunt counter,' Jefferies *Red Deer* (1884) viii. (3) Wxf. Played hunt the fox, Kennedy *Banks Boro* (1867) 5. Wal. The fox has a certain time given him for a start, the other players then go after him, Gomme *Games* (1894) I. 191. Oxf. Played as a street-game. An occasional cry is raised by the fox to assist the hunters (G.O.). (4) Sc. We did nothing but hunt the glaiks, Colvil *Whigs' Supplication* (ed. 1796) l. 1091. (5) N.Cy.[1] Child's game played on the ice as well as in the fields. [In this game one boy is permitted to run out, and having law given to him—that is, being permitted to go to a certain distance from his comrades before they pursue him—their object is to take him, if possible, before he can return home, Gomme *ib.* 241.] (6) Sc. (Jam.) Sh.I. They amused themselves with such games as hunt-da-slipper, wads, and haand-de-kroopin, Spence *Flk Lore* (1899) 189. w.Yks. Gomme *ib.* 242. Lan. One Lan. version reverses the characters by making the cobbler run round the ring, and the children requiring the shoe to be mended, call out, 'Blackie, come mend my slipper,' *ib.* Shr., Sur. *ib.* Sus., Hmp. Now almost out of fashion. A number of girls and boys sit on the floor in a circle, while one stands in the middle. Those who sit have a slipper which they pass from one to the other, concealing it underneath them : it is the business of the one in the middle to find it, when the person beneath whom it is found has to stand up in turn till it is again discovered. The chief amusement arises from the one in the circle who has the slipper striking the one who stands up, while he or she is steadily looking for it, in an opposite quarter, Holloway. Dor. Gomme *ib.* Som. Jennings *Obs. Dial.* w.Eng. (1825). (7) Som. Uncle Granger triumphed over his anckles so far as to dance Hunt the Squirrel with Mrs. Toop, Raymond *Gent. Upcott* (1893) 138 ; They had 'Hunt the squirrel' and the handkerchief dance, *ib. Men o' Mendip* (1898) xiii. (8) w.Mid. We labouring men's children hadn't time to have a regular paper-chase by day, so we used to play 'Hunt the stag' of an evening. The 'stag' carried an old cow's horn which he blew at all the corners so that the 'hunters' followed him by the sound (W.P.M.). (9) Bnff. One is chosen to be the staigie (little stallion). The other players scatter themselves over the play-ground. The staigie locks his fingers into each other. He then repeats the words—'Hunt the Staigie, Huntie, untie, staig[i]e, Ailleman, ailleman, aigie,' and rushes off with his hands locked, and tries to touch one of the players. He must not unlock his hands till he has caught one. When he has captured one, the two join hands and hunt for another. When another is caught he joins the two. This goes on till all are hunted down, Gomme *ib.* 242. (10) Cum.[4] At a certain stage in each round of Lant (Loo) every player has to put a stake into the pool in addition to the stake he has to pay ordinarily,—this is called 'hunt-up.' (11) w.Yks.[2] During the game the players shout 'Hunyou, shinyou.'

2. To drive by force ; to drive away, to send a person about his business.

Ayr. Leezie comes down the stair, . . wi' a cannle in her hand, to hunt me to the bed, Service *Notandums* (1890) 4. Uls. (M.B.-S.) [Aus. A supernumerary for some travelling stock caravan, who had been 'hunted' for drunkenness or inefficiency, Boldrewood *Colon. Reformer* (1890) II. xxiii.]

3. To search for.

Keb. She howks the gutters huntin' preens, Armstrong *Ingleside* (1890) 142. n.Yks. They are hunting watter up (I.W.). w.Yks. (J.W.), Chs.[1] s.Chs.[1] Ahy)v bin ŭn'tin mi weyf au'l oa·т dhŭ taayn [I've been huntin' my weife all o'er the taīn]. Shr.[1] 'Han yo' sin the kay . . . o' the one-w'y-drink ! I've bin 'untin' it up an' down—likely an' onlikely—an' canna find it now'eer.' 'Yo' mun 'unt till yo' find'n it, an' then yore labour ŏŏnna be lost.'

4. To frequent, resort to ; to visit frequently. Cf. haunt, v. 3.

Abd. It was buntin' aye the ale-house, Anderson *Poems* (1826) 26.

5. *sb.* *Comb.* (1) Hunt-lands, hunting grounds ; (2) -'s-up, (a) an old pipe tune, esp. used by the waits on Christmas eve or Christmas morn ; (b) a tumult, outcry ; (c) to scold, rate, abuse.

(1) Nhb.[1] The huntlands of Tindale are often spoken of in ancient deeds and grants. A large proportion of these lands are Huntlands to this day, as far as regards grouse and black game ; but goodly flocks of Cheviot sheep have replaced the red deer and roe that formerly tenanted these wastes, Charlton *N.Tyne-dale* (1871) 15. (2, a) Nhb.[1] Cum.[1] Hunsep through the wood, hunsep through the wood, Merrily goes the day, sir ; Get up old wives and bake your pies, To-morrow is Christmas day, sir, &c.; Cum.[3] 'Thŭnt's up' of a Kersmas mworn . . . Wad roose us, 57 ; Cum.[4] (b) Cum. A bonny hunsup, faith, he'll mek, Anderson *Ballads* (ed. 1808) 28; Cum.[14], w.Yks.[1] (c) Lakel. He'll hunsip thi fer thi pains (B.K.) ; Lakel.[2] Cum. *Gl.* (1851) ; Cum.[14]

6. *Phr.* *neither hunt nor hare,* absolutely nothing.

Lak. There's neither hunt nor hare tae be seen o' the auld plenishin' except the picturs, Wardrop *J. Mathison* (1881) 17.

HUNTER, *sb.* Irel. n.Cy. Of a cat : a good mouser. N.I.[1] 'Her mother was a right hunter :' said of a kitten. n.Cy. (J.W.)

HUNTING, *sb.* and *adj.* Sc. Yks. Der. Shr. Glo. Som. 1. *sb.* A game ; see below.

w.Yks., n.Lin. 'O have you seen the Shah, O have you seen the Shah ! He lights his pipe on a star-light night, O have you seen the Shah ! For a-hunting we will go, A-hunting we will go ; We'll catch a fox and put him in a box. A-hunting we will go.' . . The children range themselves in double rank at one end of the room . . . and march down to the other end hand in hand. At the bottom they loose hands and divide, the first rank turning right, the second left, and march back in two single files to the other end again, where they reform as at first, and repeat their manœuvre, singing the verses alternately, Gomme *Games* (1894) I. 244. Der. *Flk-Lore Jrn.* I. 386, in Gomme *ib.* Lin. 'Hunting we will go, brave boys, Hunting we will go ; We'll catch an old fox And put him in a box, For a-hunting we will go. Halt ! shoulder arms ! fire !' . . The . . . game is played by the children walking two and two in a circle round one of their companions, singing. The players then stand facing the child in the centre, and place their hands on their partner's shoulders. After the lines are sung the centre child cries out, 'Halt ! Shoulder arms ! Fire !' at which words each child kisses his partner. If the commander sees anyone hesitate, or avoid kissing, he runs forward and takes the defaulter's place, leaving him to fill the middle position, Gomme *ib.* Shr. Burne *Flk-Lore* (1883) 514. Som. 'Oh, a-hunting we will go, a-hunting we will go ; We'll catch a little fox and put him in a box, And never let him go.' . . The Bath game is played by the children standing in two rows facing each other, and clapping hands and singing the verse. At the same time the two children facing each other at the top of the lines join hands and trip down and up between the lines. Their hands are unclasped, and the two children run down the outside of the lines, one running on each side, and meet at the bottom of the lines, where they stand. The two children now standing at the top proceed in the same way : this is continued until all the children have done the same. A ring is then formed, when the children again clap and sing, Gomme *ib.*

2. *adj.* In *comb.* (1) Hunting-hawk, the peregrine falcon, *Falco peregrinus.* e.Lth., Rxb. Swainson *Birds* (1885) 139 ; (2) — ten, a game at cards. w.Yks.[2]

HUNTSMAN, *sb.* Sc. Irel. Lan. Cor. In *comb.* (1) Huntsman's cap, the water figwort, *Scrophularia aquatica*; (2) — moon, the October moon.

(1) Cor. From the shape of the corolla (B. & H.). (2) s.Sc., s.Ir., Lan. Harland & Wilkinson *Flk-Lore* (1867) 250.

HUNTY, sb. Sc. A boys' game; see Hunt, v. 1. (9).

Abd. The hail at 'Shinty,' and the dell at 'Hunty' and 'Kee-how,' CADENHEAD Bon-Accord (1853) 192; One or more boys get a good start, and the others follow in full cry. The 'stags' turn and double until caught by their pursuers (A.W.).

HUOD, HUOVEN, see Hide, v.², Heave.

HUP, sb. e.Dur.¹ A whip.

HUPE, sb. Lakel.² 1. The hip. 'He's gay middle no' hiup.'
2. Comp. (1) **Hupe-band,** an old-fashioned trousers-band; (2) **-bun,** stiff from unusual exercise.

HUPH, sb. Obs. Nhb. A measure for corn or dry goods.

GROSE (1790) MS. add. (P.); Gent. Mag., ed. Gomme (1886) 16.

HUP(P, int. and v. Sc. Irel. Nhb. Dev. Also in form **hip** Sc. [h)up, hup.] 1. int. A call to a horse to go to the right or off-side; also in comb. **Hup-hup.**

Sc. MORTON Cyclo. Agric. (1863); In towns Haap is used where wynd is heard, and Hip bears a similar relation to wane, STEPHENS Farm Bk. (ed. 1849) I. 160. Cai.¹, N.I.¹, Nhb.¹ s.Cy. N. & Q. (1856) and S. i. 395. Dev. Horae Subsecivae (1777) 179.
2. A call to a horse or cow to go on.

Mry. 'Jee! hup!' cried Sir Robert, an' sprang to the back O' that fierce-lookin' charger, HAY Lintie (1851) 57. Gall. Rob ... brought down his hand with a surprising 'flap' upon each cow's flank, and said in a loud, stable-yard voice, 'Hup, you beast!' CROCKETT Kit Kennedy (1899) xvii. N.I.¹
3. Comb. (1) **Hup-howay,** a drover's cry to urge on cattle. Nhb.¹; (2) **-hup,** a car-driver's cry to get out of the way. N.I.¹
4. v. To cry 'hup' to a horse.

Sc. The clown ... was soon heard hupping and geeing to the cart, SCOTT St. Ronan (1824) xvii. Lth. He hyted, he huppit—in vain, O! He ferlied what gaured his horse stand like a stock, BALLANTINE Poems (1856) 114.
5. To go forward.

Rnf. My muse will neither hup nor wind, M°GILVRAY Poems (ed. 1862) 176.

[2. Swiss dial. hüpp! 'Ruf des Fuhrmanns oder Reiters zum Antreiben der Pferde' (Idiotikon).]

HUPS, int. s.Chs.¹ [ups.] Fie! Cf. yaps.

HUPSTITCH, sb. e.Dur.¹ In phr. every hupstitch, every now and again.

She bakes every hupstitch. He does it every hupstitch, . . i.e. constantly, or oftener than seems to be required.

HURB, sb. Sc. An awkward fellow; a puny, dwarfish person.

Abd. (JAM.); He's a queer-leukin hurb, ALEXANDER Johnny Gibb (1871) iii.

HURBISHED, ppl. adj. Obs. Chs.¹ Pulled down, distressed, harassed.

HURBLE, sb.¹ n.Sc. (JAM.) [Not known to our correspondents.] A lean or meagre object.

HURBLE, sb.² Wm. An irregular lump.

Wm. Obs. (B.K.) s.Wm. The result of superfluous material or clumsiness in disposing of it, e.g. an uncomfortable boss in a badly-made bed (J.A.B.).

HURCH, v. Shr. Som. Also in form **hurchen** Shr.² [ətʃ.] To keep close together; to cuddle up.

Shr.² Hurchenen clos up i' th' chimlay cornel. Som. (HALL.) [Hurchyn togeder, collido, Prompt. (ed. Pynson).]

HURCH, adj. Chs.¹² [ətʃ.] Tender, touchy.

HURCHED, ppl. adj. Lin. Ajar. (HALL.), Lin.¹

HURCHENT, HURCHEON, HURCLE, see Urchin, Hurkle, v.

HURD, sb. and v. Sc. Yks. Glo. [hərd, ōd.] 1. sb. A hoard.

Sc. Craftie heidis sall na mair hyde The hurde of thair hypocrisie, ROGERS Three Reformers (1874) 95.
2. v. To hoard; to store. w.Yks.¹, Glo.¹

[1. He ... had me hard by the hand quhair ane hurd lay, DOUGLAS Eneados (1513), ed. 1874, iii. 147. 2. Preiss nevir to hurde the kirkis gude, DUNBAR Poems (c. 1510), ed. Small, II. 306.]

HURD, v. Lin. [ōd.] To clip the dirty, 'clagged' wool off sheep. THOMPSON Hist. Boston (1856) 710; Lin.¹

HURD, HURDEN, see Herd, sb., Red, Harden, sb., v.

HURDER, sb. Obs. n.Cy. Yks. A heap of stones.

n.Cy. GROSE (1790). w.Yks. HUTTON Tour to Caves (1781).

HURDIK, sb. Sh.I. Also in form **hurdin.** A big boulder; a piece of rock; used fig. of a big, clumsy woman.

JAKOBSEN Dial. (1897) 48, 91; ib. Norsk in Sh. 65.

HURDLE, sb. and v.¹ Chs. Der. Wor. Brks. I.W. Wil. Dor. Dev. [ō·dl.] 1. sb. In comb. (1) **Hurdle-bumper,** a sheep's head; (2) **-footed,** club-footed; (3) **-herse,** a hurdle frame, see below; (4) **-shore,** (5) **-staff,** a stake driven into the ground to support a hurdle, a 'foldshore.'

(1) s.Wor.¹ (2) Wil.¹ (3) Brks.¹ The frame fixed on the ground having holes for the uprights of hurdles; the brushwood used in making 'vlaayke hurdles,' is woven horizontally between these uprights. (4) Wil.¹ (5) Dor. With hurdle-staves in their hands, they poured out of the door, HARDY West. Tales (1888) I. 40.
2. A substitute for a gate; gen. having a movable top bar which is lifted into a square hook at each end. nw.Der.¹, I.W. (HALL.) **3.** Salt-making term: a table or platform of wood planks running along each side of the pans, for the purpose of receiving the salt when drawn out of the pans. Chs.¹
4. v. To confine sheep within the fold.

Dev. They use flakes for hurdling sheep. When they hurdle sheep, Reports Provinc. (1891).

HURDLE, v.² Sc. 1. Obs. To crouch; to contract the body as a cat, hedgehog, or hare. Abd. SHIRREFS Poems (1790) Gl. Cf. hurtle, v. 2. To curtsey, bow. Per. (G.W.)

HURDLE, v.³ e.An. Also in form **huddle.** To couple the hind-legs of a rabbit by threading one leg through the hamstring of the other. (M.C.H.B.) Cf. harl, v. 3.

HURDLER, sb. Dor. [ō·dlə(r).] A hurdle-maker.

To visit her sister, who was married to a thriving hurdler, HARDY Madding Crowd (1874) xxxi.

HURDLE-SHELL, sb. I.W.² Tortoiseshell; gen. used attrib. of colour, lit. reddle-shell.

I got zummet like a cat now, a hurdle-shell one.

HURDON, sb. Sc. [hərdən.] A woman with large hips. See Hurdy, sb.¹

Abd. Am I to lea' the keyes wi' yon hurdon! MACDONALD Malcolm (1875) II. 299. Gall. MACTAGGART Encycl. (1824).

HURDS, see Hards.

HURDY, sb.¹ Sc. Irel. n.Cy. Nhb. [hərdi.] 1. pl. The buttocks; the hips and parts adjacent.

Sc. How cou'd ye ca' my hurdies fat! RAMSAY Tea-table Misc. (1724) II. 130, ed. 1871. Elg. Sidlins upon the mare's hurdies he sat, Abd. Wkly. Free Press (June 25, 1898). Bnff. Blethrin sic wordies, As d— your hurdies, TAYLOR Poems (1787) 26. Bch. A bit o' a bacon haam, that is the hinder hurdies o' an auld swine, FORBES Jrn. (1742) 18. Abd. She kent by the pains in her hurdies ... We micht look for a storm, ANDERSON Rhymes (1867) 31. Kcd. Geordie loot his stick Drap on Foveran's hinner hurdies, Wi' an unexpected lick, GRANT Lays (1884) 43. Frf. Their wither'd hurdies wallop, BEATTIE Arnha (c. 1820) 49, ed. 1882. Per. His spunk-flask at his hurdies hung, MONTEATH Dunblane (1835) 122, ed. 1887. Flf. They douce her hurdies trimly Upo' the stibble-rig, DOUGLAS Poems (1806) 128. Slg. The sweat ran o'er their hurdies flowing, GALLOWAY Poems (1792) 33. Rnf. Ower their hurdies They neither had wylie coats nor jackets, WEBSTER Rhymes (1835) 23. Ayr. His gawcie tail, wi' upward curl, Hung owre his hurdies wi' a swirl, BURNS Twa Dogs (1786) l. 35. Lnk. Aff his hurdies her fit she took, And sent him sprawling in the gutter, STEWART Twa Elders (1886) 5. Lth. He sat on his hurdies, and looked Patience herself, LUMSDEN Sheep-head (1892) 9. Edb. With bottles at his hurdies hung, MACLAGAN Poems (1851) 127. Bwk. Its 'hurdies like a distant hill,' HENDERSON Pop. Rhymes (1856) 24. Peb. It micht befriend her hapless lot, And half her hurdies hide Frae open day, Lintoun Green (1685) 61, ed. 1817. Rxb. The taws that on thy hurdies play, A. SCOTT Poems (ed. 1808) 13. Dmf. If I were at ye, . . I wad your hurdies rightly tan, SHENNAN Tales (1831) 54. Gall. A rouch curry tyke, seated . . . on his ain twa tashellie hurdies, MACTAGGART Encycl. (1824) Introd. 9, ed. 1876. n.Cy. (HALL.), Nhb.¹
2. Comp. (1) **Hurdy-bone,** the thigh-bone; (2) **-caikle,** a pain in the loins commonly felt by reapers, and occasioned by stooping.

(1) Per. Feent a hirple's in thy hurdy bane, When dancing 'Gillie-Callum,' STEWART Character (1857) 127. s.Don. SIMMONS Gl. (1890). (2) Rnf. (JAM.)

[1. Of hir hurdies scho had na hauld, LYNDESAY Sat. (1535) 4363.]

HURDY, sb.[2] Nhb.[1] [hə·rdi.] A mischievous or abandoned person.

HURDY-GURDY, sb. and adj. Sc. Glo. **1.** sb. Obs. A rustic instrument, consisting of a single string and a bladder fastened to a bent stick. Glo. *Horae Subsecivae* (1777) 221.
2. adj. A contemptuous epithet applied to a harp.
Elg. 'Tis like a puppy's whine. A hurdy-gurdy thing, I wat, Unfit for you to play, TESTER *Poems* (1865) 193.

HURE, sb. Lan. [Not known to our correspondents.] [jō(r), iuə(r).] A covering for the head. ELLIS *Pronunc.* (1889) V. 345.
[Hwyr, cappe [v.r. hure], *tena, Prompt.*]

HURE, see **Hair.**

HURF, sb. Yks. Also in forms orf n.Yks.[12] m.Yks.[1]; urf n.Yks.[2] [ərf, ŭf.] **1.** Scurf; esp. on a horse's skin after the application of a blister. Cf. **huff,** sb.[1]
n.Yks.[1] Yon sheep fleece is full of orf as can be : it's had a desper't shrift i' t'winter. That bairn's heead's as full o' orf as ivver it can ho'd ; n.Yks.[2] We hear of a 'wet orf' on the animal skin, as sweat, or a lea-like exudation from other causes. 'Orf,' however, is dry scurf *gen.* 'A dry orf.' m.Yks.[1]
Hence **Hurfy,** adj. scurfy.
n.Yks. His hair is orfy (I.W.) ; n.Yks.[2] 'An urfy smell,' the scent of a mangy animal.
2. A running sore on cattle. m.Yks.[1]
[1. ON. *hrufa,* the crust or scab of a boil or the like (VIGFUSSON).]

HURGHILL, sb. Chs.[1] A little stunted person.

HURGIN, ppl. adj. Yks. Also in form **orgin** n.Yks. [ə·gin.] Fat, stout, unwieldy.
Yks. (HALL.) n.Yks. A great orgin lad (I.W.\ w.Yks. The rough hairy Good-fellow . . . lying 'like a hurgin bear' . . . before the fire, EWING *Lob Lie-by-the-Fire,* 30 ; w.Yks.[2]

HURIL, see **Herle.**

HURK, v.[1] and sb. Sc. Nhp. War. Also written **hirk** War.[2] [hərk, ŭk.] **1.** v. To crouch, cower ; contract the body. Cf. **hurkle.**
Nhp.[1] 'How you sit hurking ower the fire !' is often said to one who sits with the feet on the fender, and the elbows on the knees. War.[2] The cows are hurking under the hedges—they do not like this cold weather.
2. To stay idly in one place ; to do little ; with *about* : to go about in a lazy, underhand fashion. Bnff.[1] Hence **Hurkie,** adj. lazy, careless, slovenly ; of work : troublesome, unpleasant, unmanageable. w.Sc. (JAM. *Suppl.*) **3.** sb. A temporary shelter in the field for young lambs, formed of hurdles wattled with straw. Nhp.[1], War.[2]
[1. EFris. *hurken,* 'kauern, sich zusammen biegen u. krümmen, bz. mit zusammengebogenen knieen u. gekrümmtem Rücken sitzen' (KOOLMAN) ; so MLG. *hurken* (SCHILLER-LÜBBEN).]

HURK, v.[2] Nhp.[1] To take out the entrails of a hare or rabbit. Cf. **hulk,** v.[2]

HURKER, sb. Rxb. (JAM.) [Not known to our correspondents.] A semicircular piece of iron, put on an axletree, inside of the wheel, to prevent friction on the cart-body.

HURKIE, sb. Bnff.[1] [hə·rki.] The bib, *Morrhua lusca.*

HURKLE, sb. Slk. (JAM.) [Not known to our correspondents.] A 'horse-hoe' used for cleaning turnips.

HURKLE, v. Sc. n.Cy. Nhb. Lakel. Yks. Lan. Der. Not. Lin. Lei. Nhp. War. Wor. Wil. Also written **herkle** w.Yks.[1] s.Not. ; **hircle** Lei.[1] War.[2] ; **hurcle** w.Yks.[2] ; **hurkel** Gall. ; and in forms **erkle** s.Not. ; **hørcle** Nhb.[1] ; **horkle** Nhb. ; **irkle** w.Yks. ; **urcle** Yks. Der.[2] nw.Der.[1] [h]ə·rkl, ŏ·kl.] **1.** To crouch, cower, stoop, squat down ; to huddle together ; also *fig.* to submit. See **Hurk,** v.[1]
Sc. Grant and Mackenzie and Murray, And Cameron will hurkle to nane, CHAMBERS *Sngs.* (1829) I. 163. Sh.I. He sees a auld man sittin' hurklin i' da chimley neuk, STEWART *Tales* (1892) 70. ne.Sc. Lizzie's been hurklin' an' grainin' owre the fire a' day, GRANT *Chron. Keckleton,* 43. Bnff. The loon gyd 'im a dunt o' the riggin' an' he cam hurklin' ben the fleer roarin' like a stickit bill, GREGOR *Notes to Dunbar* (1893) 48. Frf. He hurkled him[self] doon like a beast i' its sta', WATT *Poet. Sketches* (1880) 80. Ayr. Mournin' . . . That he, when stalwart bands were gane, Fourscore,

maun hurkle there his lane, BOSWELL *Poet. Wks.* (1816) 166, ed. 1871. Luk. Nicht hurkles doon at the back o' the gloamin, THOMSON *Musings* (1881) 145. Feb. Hurklan' down, he scarce cou'd stand, Wi' dool that gard him girn, *Lintoun Green* (1685) 58, ed. 1817. Slk. Then down he hurkled by her side, HOGG *Poems* (ed. 1865) 277. Gall. Hurkeling in glen abodes, MACTAGGART *Encycl.* (1824) 266, ed. 1876. Nhb. (R.O H.) ; Nhb.[1] He horcled doon ahint the waa. n.Yks. A'v been i't lngs to see t'beos an' they we all urcling under t'hedge (W.H.). w.Yks. Yor hommast suar ta find hur hurkling befoar t'fiar, ROGERS *Nan Bunt* (1839) 13 ; w.Yks.[2] ; w.Yks.[3] Animals that appear poorly, or have been out on a cold night, hurcle. Lan.[1], n.Lan.[1], Der.[2], nw.Der.[1] s.Not. Come off erklin on the fire ; the more yer erkle, the more yer may. Now then ! don't stop erklin in bed (J.P.K.). Lin. A hare hurkles behind a bush (J.C.W.). n.Lin. Rest on 'em was hurklin' under th' hedge-side (M.P.). Lei.[1] Doon't sit theer, hurclin. Nhp. The hare . . . Behind the dead thistle hurkles from the view, CLARE *Vill. Minst.* (1821) II. 23; Nhp.[12], War.[2], ne.Wor. (J.W.P.), Wil.[1]
Hence (1) **Hurkles,** sb. one who shrinks from the cold, or crouches near the fire ; (2) **Hurkling,** ppl. adj. misshapen, drawn together.
(1) s.Not. Oh, she is a herkles (J.P.K.). (2) e.Sc. He is a hurklin gnarled carl, WILSON *Tales* (1839) V. 322. Slk. The tane was a wee bit hurklin' crile of an unearthly thing, HOGG *Tales* (1838) 3, ed. 1866.
2. trans. Of a hen : to cover the chickens with the wing.
ne.Wor. Of a hen : 'She's a bad mother, she won't hurkle the chickens well ' (J.W.P.).
3. To shrug the shoulders ; to set up the back ; to contract the body and become motionless ; to shudder.
Cai.[1] To move the shoulders as if in discomfort about the back. n.Cy. GROSE (1790). Wm. What for does thoo hurkle thi back up like that ! Thoo'll gang hutty backt if thoo doesn't mind (B.K.). n.Yks. T'sheep i't holme yonder wer all urcling up ther rigs oaf stahv'd to death, an't hosses wed a been a lot better i't steeabl if they'd nowt to yet [eat] ner urcling up ther rigs i' yon way—they'l be like eneuf to git ther deeath o' coad ; an' it meead me urcle up my rig an all, fer all a wer nocking aboot sea (W.H.). w Yks. He's begun to herkle of late years, and gets less (M.N.); He seemed to irkle when he saw t'rope (J.B.) ; w.Yks.[12], ne.Lan.[1], Der.[1], Nhp.[1], ne.Wor. (J.W.P.)
Hence **Hurkled,** ppl. adj. wrinkled, contracted ; laid flat.
Feb. With shoes, each like a hurkled snail, *Lintoun Green* (1685) 37, ed. 1817. Nhb.[1] Applied to growing grass or corn that has been flattened in the field by rain or wind.
4. Comb. (1) **Hurkle-backed,** hunchbacked ; **crook-backed** ; having stooping shoulders ; (2) **-bone,** the hipbone ; (3) **-durkle,** (a) laziness, sluggishness ; (b) to lie long in bed ; to lounge.
(1) Sc. If he's hurklebackit and frail, it is God's pleasure alone that puts the difference between him and the strong and the straight, KEITH *Bonnie Lady* (1897) 247. Luk. I'm an auld canty carle . . . Hurkle-backit, sairly rackit wi' rheumatic pains, NICHOLSON *Idylls* (1870) 43. Slk. Hurkle-backit Charlie Johnson, HOGG *Tales* (1838) 71, ed. 1866. (2) Sc. She . . . falls down on her hurkle-bones, MESTON *Poems* (1767) 133 (JAM.). Abd., Rnf. (JAM.) (3, a) Sc. Lang after peeping greke o' day, In hurkle-durkle Habbie lay.—Gae tae ye'r wark, ye dernan murkle, And ly nae there in hurkle-durkle, *MS. Poem* (JAM.). (b) Fif. (ib.)
5. To walk with difficulty because of rickety legs ; to limp. Bnff.[1], Lakel.[2] (s.v. Hirpie).
6. Fig. To sidle or make up to.
Lakel.[2] He wad hurkle up tull her if he bed t'least lal bit ov a chance (s.v. Hirple).
[1. Þen come þar-in a litill brid, in-to his arme floʒe, And þar hurkils & hydis, as scho were hand-tame, *Wars Alex.* (c. 1450) 504.]

HURKLIN, sb. Sh.I. The peculiar sound made in breathing when there is phlegm in the throat or breast S. & Ork.[1]

HURL, sb.[1] Sh.I. [hərl.] A kind of Dutch tobacco.
He produced a large tin crammed full of Dutch 'hurl,' CLARK *Gleams* (1898) 48 ; No foryattin' da swig oot o' da Dutch crook, an' twartree fills o' hurl, *Sh. News* (Aug. 20, 1898).

HURL, sb.[2] Ken. A 'hurdle.'
(HALL.) ; A hurl made of small hazle-rods, LEWIS *I. Tenet* (1736) (s.v. Ruddle).

HURL, *v.*[1] and *sb.*[3] Sc. Irel. n.Cy. Nhb. Dur. Cum. Lei. Also Cor. Also in form horl Nhb.[1] [hərl, əl.] **1.** *v.* To drive, convey in a cart or carriage ; to draw ; to wheel, to trundle ; also *intr.*

Sc. They disdain now to ride on pads as of old, or to be hobled on a horse's hurdles, but must be hurled behind the tail, safely seated in a leather conveniency, GRAHAM *Writings* (1883) II. 151 ; I remember the General . . . when he was hurling a barrow fu' of turnips, HISLOP *Anecdote* (1874) 404. **Or.I.** Tə hərl əp tee də duur, ELLIS *Pronunc.* (1889) V. 805. **Cai.**[1] **Bch.** And hurl'd me awa to Portsmouth, FORBES *Jrn.* (1742) 18. **Abd.** The fishers gettin' the muckle boats hurl't doon to the water, ALEXANDER *Johnny Gibb* (1871) vi. **Frf.** Cummers sled, an' hurl'd as weel On ice, as ony vady chiel, *Piper of Peebles* (1794) 7. **Per.** Several girls hunker down on the ice, cling to one another, and are pushed along by one who ' hurls the truck' (G.W.). **Flf.** They had to hurl him hame in a cart, ROBERTSON *Provost* (1894) 121. **Rnf.** I hurl'd my milk and butter Doun by the banks o' Levern water, WEBSTER *Rhymes* (1835) 178. **Ayr.** If on a beastie I can speel Or hurl in a cartie, BURNS *To* —— (1786) ll. 7, 8. **Lnk.** If ever you're sae venturesome as to hurl in a train, FRASER *Whaups* (1895) xv. **Lth.** A spankin gig-hack . . . seen to and frae the kirk, Hurlin' his maisters wi' a birr That gart the sooplest roadster stir, LUMSDEN *Sheep-head* (1892) 98. **Edb.** Her dochter then—'tween you and me, Her coach may hurl, M'DOWALL *Poems* (1839) 35. **Nhb.** We'll horl wor paste eggs i' the fad. Get inti the barra an' aa'll horl ye (R.O.H.) ; Nhb.[1] Where ye gan ti horl yor gords ? Nhb., Dur. That which was at the low end is hurled to the cutting washers, FORSTER *Section Strata* (1821) 343.

Hence **Hurler,** *sb.* one who wheels a barrow.

Edb. It [the peat] is taken up by the women wheelers [hurlers], who lay a number of them upon a wheelbarrow without sides, and lay them down, side by side, upon some contiguous dry ground. Two hurlers commonly suffice to spread the peat dug by one man, PENNECUIK *Whs.* (1715) 71, ed. 1815.

2. *Comp.* Hurl-barrow, a wheelbarrow.

Sc. It is kittle for the cheeks when the hurl-barrow gaes o'er the brig o' the nose, RAMSAY *Prov.* (1737). **Per.** Every one present was drunk as a piper, And Bilzy carried hame in a hurl-barrow, MONTEATH *Dunblane* (1835) 105, ed. 1887. **w.Sc.** It looked like a hurl-barrow on end, making its way without the trupel, CARRICK *Laird of Logan* (1835) 164. **e.Flf.** Garrin' them creak an' quiver like an auld gizzen't hurl-barrow under the wecht o' a bow o' petawties, LATTO *Tam Bodkin* (1864) vii. **Slk.** A man could drive on a hurlbarrow, HOGG *Tales* (1838) 327, ed. 1866. **N.Cy.**[1], **Nhb.**[1]

3. With *up* : to ' pull up,' to come to a stop.

Lei. She holds mending, but nows and thens she hurls up, *N. & Q.* (1858) and S. vi. 186.

4. To whirl ; to rush ; to roll.

Per. The thunner tout Far rumlin' hurls, STEWART *Character* (1857) 106. **Ayr.** Dinna ye see the callans slidin' on the mill-dam already, and hurlin' in their stools doon the Corsehill-brae? SERVICE *Notandums* (1890) 115. **Lth.** Ilk clear burnie purlin, and dark torrent hurlin', BALLANTINE *Poems* (1856) 309. **Edb.** How the bowls for me may hurl, I dinna ken, M'DOWALL *Poems* (1839) 32. **Slk.** He fell, and hurling down with great celerity soon reached the bottom of the steep, HOGG *Tales* (1838) 410, ed. 1866.

Hence **Hurling,** *ppl. adj.* quickly passing ; rushing.

Sc. The hurling stream was still'd therewi' Sae fast afore that ran, JAMIESON *Ballads* (1806) I. 226. **Per.** Who with laughing merriment Beguile the hurling minutes so, NICOL *Poems* (1766) 37. **Ayr.** Like the hurling and the drifting ice, found no effectual obstacle to its irresistible and natural destination, GALT *Gilhaize* (1823) xvii.

5. To fling, toss ; used *fig.* Cf. **hull,** *v.*[3]

Lei. Is it true that the squire has taken those closen from you, and hurled them to Sims ? *N. & Q.* (1858) and S. vi. 186.

6. To toy ; to dally amorously. Dmf. (JAM.) Hence **Hurling,** *vbl. sb.* dalliance, esp. that practised at the ' hair'st rig.' (J.)

7. *sb.* A drive ; a lift on the road ; a journey in a train.

Sc. A tailor and his wife . . . coming to the car terminus . . . the tailor proposed a ' hurl ' a wee bit, *Jokes* (1889) and S. 100 ; An I had ken't ye were gaun till Rottenstocks I could hev given ye a hurl, OCHILTREE *Redburn* (1895) v. **Cai.**[1] **w.Sc.** The weans and me wad be a' the better o' a bit hurl to the town, CARRICK *Laird of Logan* (1835) 85. **Ayr.** If a frien' hire a chaise, and gie me a hurl, am I to pay the hire? GALT *Sir A. Wylie* (1822) xii. **Lnk.** If ever you tak' a hurl on the railway, FRASER *Whaups* (1895) 210.

e.Lth. If a man stan's ye a nip, . . or gies ye a hurl in a hired machine, he loses his seat, HUNTER *J. Inwick* (1895) 198.

8. A confused mass of any material, thrown, or falling down with violence.

Cai.[1] **Bnff.**[1] A hurl o' stanes cam doon on's back, an' hurtit 'im geyan sehr. ' In a hurl,' means in a confused mass, accompanied with noise. **Lnk.** Frae the house riggin' hurls o' snaw Gart fock believe they'd killed be a', WATT *Poems* (1827) 12.

9. The noise caused by the violent fall of any hard material, or by the passage of one hard substance over the surface of another.

Cai.[1] **Bnff.**[1] A heard the hurl o' the trees gain' oot our the rocks in o' the river. A heard the hurl o' the cairts comin' in the rod.

10. A large oblong standing sieve against which earth, lime, or any other material is to be sifted is thrown ; also called **Hurler.** Cor. THOMAS *Randigal Rhymes* (1895) *Gl.* ; Cor.[3]

11. A tempest.

Cum.[1] 'Storm's cumman, John.' ' Ey, an' it'll be a hurl'; Cum.[4]

12. *Comp.* Hurl-bassey, a star which, when seen near the moon, foretells stormy weather. N.I.[1]

13. A scolding ; freq. in phr. *a hurl of a flyte.*

Sc. (JAM.); I gaed in by, thinking she was gan' to gi' me cheese and bread, or something that woudna speak to me, but she ga' me sic a hurl I never gat the like o't, BLYD *Contract*, 6 (*ib.*).

[**4.** Flodis camen, and wyndis blewen, and thei hurliden in to that hous, WYCLIF (1382) *Matt.* vii. 27. **9.** I herd mony hurlis of . . . stanis that tumlit doune, *Compl. Scotl.* (1549) 39.]

HURL, *v.*[2] and *sb.*[4] Irel. Also Cor. [hərl, əl.] **1.** To play the game of ' hurling.'

Ir. Sometimes one barony hurls against another, but a marriageable girl is always the prize, YOUNG *Tour Irl.* (1780) I. 365.

Hence (1) **Hurler,** *sb.* a player in a ' hurling' match ; (2) **Hurling,** (*a*) a game played with a ball ; see below ; (*b*) a form of hockey.

(1) **s.Ir.** The best hurler in the village, CROKER *Leg.* (1862) 150. **Cor.** The three circles, which are seen on the moors not far from the Cheesewring, . . are called the ' Hurlers,' and they preserve the position in which the several parties stood in the full excitement of the game of hurling, when, for the crime of profaning the Sabbath, they were changed into stone, HUNT *Pop. Rom. w.Eng.* (1865) 178, ed. 1896 ; ' Fair play is good play,' is the hurlers' motto, *Flk-Lore Jrn.* (1886) IV. 128 ; Cor.[1] s.v. Hurling. (*a*, *a*) **Cor.** ' Hurling matches ' are peculiar to Cor. . . The success depends on catching the ball dexterously when thrown up, or dealt, and carrying it off expeditiously, in spite of all opposition from the adverse party ; or, if that be impossible, throwing it into the hands of a partner, . . to convey it to his own goal, HUNT *Pop. Rom. w.Eng.* (1865) 400, ed. 1896 ; A trial of skill between two parties of forty or more men, each striving to carry off a wooden ball to its own goal, which is sometimes three or four miles distant, HONE *Every-day Bk.* (1826) II. 1008 ; On Quinquagesima Sunday, an annual hurling-match is held on the sands, *Flk-Lore Jrn.* (1886) IV. 128 ; Cor.[1] The players are divided into two equal parties, each of which tries to secure and keep the ball in their possession. The prize is one made of cork covered with silver ; Cor.[2] A game in which a silvered or silver-gilt ball is thrown or hurled towards the opponents' goal. (*b*) **Wkl.** The 'hurling-green where the famous match was played by the people of Wxf. against those of Cather, . . and where the former got the name of yellow bellies, from the colour of the scarfs they wore round their waist, is a sunny flat on the w. side of n.Wkl. Gap, *Flk-Lore Jrn.* (1884) II. 266, in GOMME *Games* (1894) I. 246. **Wxf.** We appointed to meet at Gath-na-Coologe, and exhale our superabundant animal spirits in a hurling match, KENNEDY *Banks Boro* (1867) 89.

2. *Comp.* Hurl-bat, the crooked stick used in the game of ' hurling'; also called Hurlet.

Ir. At my bed-foot decaying My hurl-bat is lying, CALLANAN *Convict* (c. 1825) in HAYES *Ballads*, I. 347 ; HONE *Table-bk.* (1827) I. 692.

3. The game of ' hurling.' Ir. *Flk-Lore Jrn.* (1884) II. 265. **4.** The crooked stick used by the ' hurler.'

Ir. He would give his ball a stroke of his hurl, . . he would throw his hurl at it, O'CURRY *Manners Anc. Irish* (1873) II. 359.

HURL, *v.*[3] Yks. [əl.] **1.** To be chilled ; to be pinched with cold. **w.Yks.**[1]

2. Of cold weather : to pinch, nip.

m.Yks.[1] Don't go out ; it will hurl thee, honey.

HURLE, *sb.* *Obs.* Yks. In phr. *holes and hurles*, odd dark blind holes in a house.

n.Yks. There is seay monny holes and hurles to seek, MERITON *Praise Ale* (1684) l. 205.

HURLE, see Harl(e, *sb.*[1]

HURLED, *ppl. adj.* n.Yks.[2] Warped, crooked ; mottled, as cattle. Cf. **harled**, *ppl. adj.*

HURLESS, *adj.* Sh.I. Also in form **hurraless.** Deafened with noise. S. & Ork.[1]

HURLEY, *sb.* Irel. Also written **hurly.** [həˈrli.]

1. The game of 'hurling.' See **Hurl,** *v.*[2] **l.**

Ir. It's hurley the dead people do be playing, and Maurice brings them the hurley-ball, *Spectator* (Oct. 26, 1889). n.Ir. A game called hurly, similar to hockey, and the rules similar to Association football, is played here occasionally, principally by the pure Celtic race (A.J.I.) ; **N.I.**[1]

2. The crooked stick used in a 'hurling' match.

Ir. The players . . . are arranged . . . in two opposing ranks, with their burleys crossed, to await the tossing up of the ball, HALL *Irel.* (1841) I. 257.

HURLEY-HOUSE, *sb.* ? *Obs.* Sc. A large house fallen into disrepair or nearly in ruins.

I now wish . . . that I could have left Rose the auld hurley-house, SCOTT *Waverley* (1814) lxvii ; His old hurley-house of a castle, *ib. Leg. Mont.* (1818) xx ; (JAM.)

HURLING, *sb.*[1] Cum. w.Cy. Also in form **urlin** Cum.[1]

l. A young perch, *Perca fluviatilis.* Cum. (E.W.P.), w.Cy. (HALL.)

2. A term of contempt : a dwarf ; a dwarfish thing.

Cum. He turnt on t'urlin no at ah still held be t'neck an telt em he was reet sarrat, SARGISSON *Joe Scoap* (1881) 107 ; Cum.[1]

[l. Cp. Swiss dial. *hürling,* 'was im laufenden Jahr erzeugt ist, junges Wesen oder Gewächs, spec. : junger, kleiner Fisch ' (*Idiotikon*) ; *Percula, perca minima,* ' ein Heurling, i.e. hornus,' WAGNER (1680), quoted in *Idiotikon.* **2.** Swiss dial. *hürling,* 'unerfahrener Mensch, unartiger, schlimmer Mensch ' (*ib.*).]

HURLING, *sb.*[2] w.Cum. (S.K.C.) Also in form **erling.** That part of a field which is too near the wall to be ploughed.

HURLING, *prp.* Chs.[18] [əˈlin.] Harrowing a field after a second ploughing.

HURLING WEATHER, *phr.* Cor. Dry, fine weather ; weather suitable for drying things.

Cor. They'd a lot of hurling weather when they got the corn together, THOMAS *Randigal Rhymes* (1895) 18 ; Cor.[5] ' The roads are wet but will soon be dry again this hurling weather.' Well known in sw.Cor. but not in this district [Redruth]. w.Cor. Prob. because corn cannot be winnowed through a sieve unless the weather is fine, with a slight breeze blowing (M.A.C.).

HURLOCH, see Hooloch.

HURLOCK, *sb.* Bdf. Hrt. Also written **hurluck** Hrt. ; **hurluk** Bdf. [əˈlək.] ' Bastard ' chalk ; hard chalk lying near the surface of hills ; lime.

Bdf. BATCHELOR *Anal. Eng. Lang.* (1809) 135 ; The farmers in the chalky district are careful not to plough so deep as to bring up the 'noxious hurlock,' which is frequently very near the cultivated soil, *ib. Agric.* (1813) 277 ; Lime is usually known by the name of hurlock, MARSHALL *Review Agric.* (1814) IV. 572. Hrt. The downs skirting the county towards Cmb. are for the most part a continued bed of hurlock, or bastard chalk, *ib.* (1817) V. 7 ; A shallow chalky surface whose bottom is a stony hurlock, ELLIS *Mod. Husb.* (1750) II. i.

Hence **Hurlucky,** *adj.* chalky.

Hrt. The bottom . . . of this field is a whitish hurlucky stony earth, ELLIS *ib.* i. 50.

HURLS, *sb. pl.* Lei. Also in form **hurs.** A peculiar kind of limestone found at Barrow and elsewhere.

Still well known (C.E.) ; Lei.[1]

HURLY, *sb.*[1] Sc. Irel. Also written **hurley** Rnf. Lnk. Edb. ; **hurlie** Cai.[1] e.Fif. [həˈrli.] **l.** A wheel. (JAM. *Suppl.*) See Hurl, *v.*[1] l.

2. A two-wheeled barrow used by porters and hawkers ; a large wheelbarrow ; a cart for light goods.

Cai.[1], Bnf.[1] Per. From the light hurlie to the heavy cowp, HALIBURTON *Fields* (1890) 25. Rnf. A cuddie cart or porter's hurly Sune whups them aff, YOUNG *Pictures* (1865) 164. Edb. Hurleys fu' o' cherry-cheekit apples, BALLANTINE *Gaberlunsie* (ed. 1875) 9. **N.I.**[1]

3. A truckle-bed ; a trundle-bed ; a bed set on wheels and pushed under another ; also in *comp.* **Hurly-bed.**

Sc. In the houses of the working-classes the hurly-bed is an important piece of furniture. During the day it stands under a larger bed : at night it is hurled out to receive its occupants (JAM. *Suppl.*). Lnk. Aye the first thing when she waukens, E're she lea' her hurley bed, Is to clasp her han's and pray, NICHOLSON *Idylls* (1870) 30.

4. *Comp.* (1) **Hurly-barrow,** a barrow with two large wheels ; (2) **-cart,** a toy-cart ; (3) **-hacket,** (*a*) see below ; (*b*) a term of contempt for an ill-hung carriage ; (*c*) a game, see below.

(1) Rnf. Noo hies he aff to Micky Sparrow, His coalman, for a hurley-barrow, To get their heavy things transported, YOUNG *Pictures* (1865) 161. (2) Lnk. O' you they mak a hurly-cart, an' kytch ye owre the flair, NICHOLSON *Kilwuddie* (ed. 1895) 93. (3, *a*) Sc. 'Hurley-hackets,' small troughs or sledges in which people used formerly to slide down an inclined plane on the side of a hill, *Gl. to Waverley Novels.* (*b*) Sc. I never thought to have entered ane o' their hurley-hackets, SCOTT *St. Roman* (1824) xv. (*c*) Edb. A courtly amusement . . . which consisted in sliding, in some sort of chair it may be supposed, from top to bottom of a smooth bank. The boys of Edb. about twenty years ago, used to play at the hurly-hacket on the Caltonhill, using for their seat a horse's skull, SCOTT *Lady of the Lake* (1810) V. st. 20, *note.*

[**4.** (3, *c*) Sum hurlit him to the hurlie-hakket, LYNDESAY *Works* (ed. 1592) 265 (JAM.).]

HURLY, *sb.*[2] Sc. Cum. Also written **hurley** Ir. ; **hurlie** Bwk. (JAM.) [həˈrli.] **1.** A noise, tumult. See Hurl, *sb.*[2] **9.**

Per. The wa' gie'd a hurly an' scattered them a', FORD *Harp* (1893) 111. Cum. They make a hurly to be heard over the whole parish, LINTON *Lizzie Lorton* (1867) xxiii.

2. *Comb.* (1) **Hurlie-go-thorow,** a racket, a disturbance ; (2) **-gush,** the bursting forth of water ; (3) **-hacket,** see (1).

(1) Bwk. (JAM.) (2) Rxb. (*ib.*) (3) e.Fif. The divots tint their grip and doon we row'd them an' me thegither wi' an awful hurlie-hacket, LATTO *Tam Bodkin* (1864) x.

HURLY, *adv.* Sc. Also written **hurley** Per. Dmf. [həˈrli.] **1.** Last.

Bch. If I was hurly, there was cause, Believe me as ye like, FORBES *Ulysses* (1785) 30.

2. *Comb.* (1) **Hurly-buck-out,** (2) **-burley,** (3) **-hindmost,** the last, the hindmost.

(1) Mry. ' The hurly-buck-out o' the school is my fee,' Cried Satan, HAY *Lintie* (1851) 56. (2) Per. When a number of young people are all engaged doing something—say a sum—to induce them to hurry up, it is asked ' Which o' ye'll hurley-burley ? ' A lagging one would be admonished, ' Ca' awa, an' nae haad them cryin' hurley-burley at you.' The child last in dressing might be called ' hurley-burley ' to spur it on (G.W.). (3) Bnf.[1] Employed when speaking to children.

HURLY, *int.* Sc. [həˈrli.] In phr. *Hurly Hawkie !* a milkmaid's call to her cows. See **Hawkie.**

Dmf. SHAW *Schoolmaster* (1899) 349. Gall. I'll let her cry, ' Hurly Hawkie,' and wize the kye hame to the milking loan, ' Hurly, Hurly, Hawkie,' MACTAGGART *Encycl.* (1824) 257, ed. 1876.

HURLY-BURLY, *sb., v.* and *adj.* Sc. Irel. Nhp. Wor. Cor. **1.** *sb.* A storm of wind ; a thunderstorm.

Per. The hurly-burly's stunnin' rattle Grows wild an' dread, STEWART *Character* (1857) 107. Wor. An atmospheric hurly-burly, ALLIES *Antiq. Flk-Lore* (1840) 462, ed. 1852.

2. A scramble. Cor.[1] A hurly-burly for nuts.

3. A boys' game.

Ir. A boy called the ' cow ' bends his back, placing his head against the stomach of another boy called the ' master.' The boys standing around place a hand one by one on the ' cow's ' back, and the ' master ' then repeats the following : ' Hurly-burly, trumpy trace, The cow stands in the market-place ; Some goes far and some goes near, Where shall this poor sinner (French-man) steer ? ' The cow then directs each boy to various places in the neighbourhood, the object being to create an even race as far as possible. When the master and the cow are satisfied that each boy has taken up his allotted position they cry—' Hurly-burly, trumpet early, The cow stands in the market-place ; Come from east and come from west, Come back to the old crow's nest.' The boys then rush in from all points of the compass. The last in then becomes the ' cow,' the first is the ' master,' and so on, *Manch. City News* (Feb. 3, 1900). N.I.[1]

4. *v.* To play 'hurly-burly.'

Nhp. Where we, when children, 'hurly-burly'd' round, Or blindman-buff'd some morts of hours away—Two games . . . Jane dearly loved to play, CLARE *Vill. Minst.* (1821) II. 89.

5. *adj.* Tumultuous, tempestuous.

Sc. Little kens the wife that sits by the fire, how the wind blaws on hurlyburly swire, FERGUSON *Prov.* (1641) No. 608. **Rnf.** This same Twenty-aucht o' May, This hurly-burly flittin' day, YOUNG *Pictures* (1865) 16a.

HURLY-GURLY, *sb.* Wil. A hand-organ, hurdy-gurdy. SLOW *Gl.* (1892).

HURN, see Herne, Run.

HURNYEAD, *sb.* Lan. [Not known to our correspondents.] [ŝ·njed.] A blockhead.

Wheay, th' Falls o' Niagara, thou hurnyead! BRIERLEY *Ab-o'th-Yate Yankeeland* (1885) vii.

[The same word as obs. E. *horn-head*, a cuckold. And Vulcan a limping horn-head, for Venus his wife was a strumpet, FLETCHER *Love's Cure* (c. 1625) II. i.]

HUROOSH, *sb.* and *v.* Sc. Irel. **1.** *sb.* A disturbance, tumult. Cf. hoo-roo.

Per. Heard occas. (G.W.) **s.Sc.** Our puir, thochtless maister has joined thae infernal rebels that are kickin up sic a huroosh in the country enow, WILSON *Tales* (1839) V. 330. [There was a wild hurroosh at the Club, KIPLING *Plain Tales* (1891) 31.]

2. *v.* To make a noise in order to drive animals away.

Ir. Run and huroosha th' ould ass a bit down the bog. Ody had to spend a considerable time in catching Jinny, as the boys had done their hurooshing with much enthusiasm, BARLOW *Idylls* (1892) 123–4.

HURPLE, see Hirple.

HURR, *v.*[1] and *sb.*[1] Sh.I. Glo. **1.** *v.* To whir round; *gen. in prp.*

Sh.I. Auld granny in the corner sits Her spinnin' wheel fast hurrin', STEWART *Tales* (1892) 97; Ipo his hurrin spinnie, BURGESS *Rasmie* (1892) 28.

2. *sb.* Obs. A thin flat piece of wood tied to a string and whirled round in the air.

Glo. *Horae Subsecivae* (1777) 221; So called from the noise it makes, GROSE (1790) *MS. add.* (M.)

[L. Norw. dial. *hurra*, to whirl round so as to make a dull sound (AASEN). A hurre, *giraculum*, *Cath. Angl.* (1483).]

HURR, *v.*[2] and *sb.*[2] Sc. n.Cy. Lan. Der. Lin. Also in form harr n.Cy. nw.Der.[1] [har, ŝ(r).] **1.** *v.* To snarl like a dog.

Sc. Poetaster parasites . . . who . . . Where no hope of gain is, huffe and hur, and bark against the moon, as doth a cur, ADAMSON *Muses Threnodie* in CANT *Hist. Per.* (1774) (JAM.). **n.Cy.** GROSE (1790). **Lan.**[1], nw.Der.[1]

2. To purr as a cat. e.Lan.[1]

3. *sb.* Rough breathing; hoarseness.

Sh.I. That spak agen wi crex an hurr, BURGESS *Rasmie* (1892) 24. **n.Lin.**[1] I've gotten such a hurr on me I can hardlin's speak.

[Hurron, or bombon as bees, and other lyke, *bombiso*, *Prompt.*]

HURR, *v.*[3] Lakel. Yks. To go along in a crouching attitude with the shoulders raised, as though to avoid recognition. *Gen. in prp.*

Lakel.[2] A shoolen, slenken, shaffien sooart ov a chap gahs hurren by fooak wi' his heed doon. **w.Yks.** (R.H.H.)

[Cp. Swiss dial. *hüren*, 'kauern, geduckt sitzen' (*Idiotikon*).]

HURR, *adj.* and *sb.*[3] Lin. Ken. Sus. [ŝ(r).] **1.** *adj.* Tart, astringent, rough-tasting.

n.Lin.[1] **Ken.**[1] These 'ere damsons be terr'ble hurr. **Sus.**[1] The doctor's ordered me to drink some of this here claret wine, but I shall never get to like it, it seems so hurr.

2. *sb.* A rough taste; tartness.

n.Lin.[1] That beer hes gotten a hurr wi' it.

HURRACK, *sb.* Sh.I. Also written hurrik. [hŝ·rŝk.] The part of a boat between the sternmost seat and the stern.

The [haf] boat was divided into six compartments, viz. fore-head, fore-room, mid-room, oost-room, shott, hurrik or kannie, SPENCE *Flk-Lore* (1899) 127; **S. & Ork.**[1]

[The men that were within schip thei killid, save o boy that fled to on of the Flemysch shippis, and hid him in

VOL. III.

the horrok (*v.r.* hurrok), CAPGRAVE *Chron.* (1460), Rolls ed., 234; On helde by þe hurrok, *Jonah* (c. 1360) 185, in *Allit. P.* 94.]

HURRALESS, see Hurless.

HURR-BURR, *sb.* Lei. Shr. Also written hur- Lei.[1] The burdock, *Arctium Lappa.* Lei.[1], Shr. (B. & H.)

HURRIED, *ppl. adj.* and *adv.* Sc. Also written hurrlet Ayr. **1.** *ppl. adj.* In phr. **hurried enough**, having enough to do, 'having one's work cut out before one.'

Rnf. You reached the street, Hurried enough to keep your feet, McGILVRAY *Poems* (ed. 1862) 170. **Ayr.** I asked him if he thought his works would save him, and he replied in an offhand manner, that he thought they would be 'hurried enough,' JOHNSTON *Glenbuckie* (1889) 142.

2. *adv.* Quickly, in a hurry.

Ayr. I cam hame geyan hurriet, JOHNSTON *ib.* 225.

HURRIFUL, see Hurryful.

HURRION, *sb.* Obs. Yks. A slut.

Yks. (HALL.) **w.Yks.** So called from hurrying on things, or doing them so hastily, and carelessly, that they are not well done, WATSON *Hist. Hlfx.* (1775) 540; **w.Yks.**[4]

HURRISH, *v.* Wor. [ŝ·rij.] To drive cattle.

The Major put up his hands to hurrish her out, as we say in Worcestershire by the cows, WOOD *Johnny Ludlow* (1874) 81. **s.Wor.**[1]

HURRISH-THURRY, *int.* N.I.[1] A call to pigs.

HURROCK, *sb.* n.Cy. Nhb. Dur. Wm. [h]ŝ·rŝk.] A piled-up heap of loose stones or rubbish; a collection of anything in a loose state.

n.Cy. King James to Sir Harry Vane: Did thou na say that Raby Castle was only a hurrock of stanes! Ah! mon, I hae nae sic anither hurrock in a' ma' dominions, *Denham Tracts* (ed. 1892) I. 105. **Nhb.**[1], **Dur.** (HALL.) Wm. GIBSON *Leg. and Notes* (1877) 93.

[A der. of Norw. dial. *horg* (*horv*, *hurv*), a heap, a confused mass (AASEN).]

HURROO, *int.* and *sb.* Sc. Also written hurro Fif. [hŝ·ru.] **1.** *int.* Hallo! hurrah!

Fif. Cry, Hurro! Down wi' the mass and monkish squad, TENNANT *Papistry* (1827) 28.

2. *sb.* A hallo; a murmuring noise as of the sea on a pebbly shore. Gall. MACTAGGART *Encycl.* (1824). **3.** A hurly-burly; a noisy commotion. *ib.* Cf. hoo-roo.

HURRY, *sb.*[1] and *v.*[1] Var. dial. uses in Sc. Irel. and Eng. Also written hurrie e.Fif. [h]ŝ ri.] **1.** *sb.* In *comb.* (1) **Hurry-bob,** a smart blow; (2) **-burry,** (*a*) confusion, noise; extra hurry with noise and confusion; (*b*) in confusion; (3) **-cart,** *obs.,* the cart at the tail of which culprits used to be whipt; (4) **-gurry,** hurry, confusion; a mad frolic; (5) **-push,** (*a*) bustle, confusion; (*b*) in haste, bustling; (6) **-scurry,** a tumult, an uproar.

(1) **n.Cy.** (HALL.) (2, *a*) **Cai.**[1] **Abd.** The burry-burry now began, . . Wi' routs and raps frae man to man, Some getting, and some gieing, SKINNER *Poems* (1809) 43. **e.Fif.** I' the midst o' the general hurrie-burrie I glidit to the door like a ghaist, LATTO *Tam Bodkin* (1864) x. **Rnf.** In hurry-burry, yet in order, Big trains frae baith sides o' the border . . . Or gaun or comin' still are birlin', YOUNG *Pictures* (1865) 169. **Lnk.** I'll just tak' ye at your word, An' end this hurry-burry, RODGER *Poems* (1838) 3, ed. 1897. **e.Lth.** Tod-Lowrie wull fin' that oot for himsel, gin he steers up ony sic hurry-burry, HUNTER *J. Inwick* (1895) 163. Ant. *Ballymena Obs.* (1892). **Nhb.**[1] (*b*) **Abd.** Dashy bucks, and ladies trippin, . . But hurry burry runnin', loupin', As till red fires, ANDERSON *Poems* (1813) 116 (JAM.). (3) **Lin.** THOMPSON *Hist. Boston* (1856) 220. (4) **Fif.** Ever in a hurry gurry Frae mornin's peep to gloamin gray, EDWARDS *Modern Poets*, 8th S. 160. **Cor.**[2] I doan't hould wei nos sech hurry-gurries. (5, *a*) **Som.** Life's all such a hurry-push these times, RAYMOND *Love and Quiet Life* (1894) 26. (*b*) **w.Som.**[1] Her's always alike, no rest wi' her, all hurry-push [uur'ee-pěo·sh]. You can't expect to hab'm so well a made all hurry-push, as off I'd a got time for to do un vitty like. (6) **Ags.** (JAM.)

2. *Phr.* (1) **take your hurry,** or **take your hurry in your hand,** take your time; (2) **what is your hurry?** why are you going? (3) **you shouldn't do nothing in a hurry but catch fleas,** there are only a very few occasions when 'more haste' is not 'less speed'; (4) **in a hurry,** suddenly; (5) **in a couple of hurries,** instantly, in great haste.

(1) **N.I.**[1] (2) **n.Cy.** (J.W.), **Cor.**[1] (3) **Oxf.**[1] Yoo shuod·nt doo

P p

nuth'n in u uur i but kech flaiz. (4) Elg. Did he dee in a hurry ! TESTER *Poems* (1865) 141. (5) Edb. Off Nanse brushed in a couple of hurries, MOIR *Mansie Wauch* (1828) xix.
3. A press of work.
Abd. I thocht I would tak' a step owre noo that your hurry's feckly by, GREIG *Logie o' Buchan* (1899) 286. Dmb. I lend a hand there whiles when the smith has a hurry, CROSS *Disruption* (1844) xiii.
4. A period of time. Rdn.[1]
5. A riot, commotion; a quarrel, scolding; a bout of fighting.
Abd. Raither nor conter 'im or rin the chance o' a hurry wi' 'im, Sandy wud maist face his nain gweed-mither aiven, wi' 'er birse up, ALEXANDER *Ain Flk.* (1882) 180. Fif. (JAM.) Ayr. Or ere the hurry it was o'er, We scrambled up the brae, *Ballads and Sngs.* (1846) I. 94. Peb. 'Tween stick and wa' they keep their feet, The hurry heats their blood, *Lintoun Green* (1685) 5, ed. 1817. Dmf. Soon we heard an unco hurry, And saw twa men in dreadfu' fury, Pushing, drawing, striking, swearing, SHENNAN *Tales* (1831) 40. N.I.[1] w.Yks. Tha nivver cums theas doors within Bud tha mun curse and swear, An try ta bring ma ta me grave Wi breedin hurries hear, PRESTON *Poems* (1864) 8. Chs.[1 2 3] Hrf.[1] We shanna finish it this hurry.
6. A spasm; a fit; a sharp attack of illness; a fright; an outburst of temper.
Lan.[1] Hoo's had a bad cryin' hurry (said of a passionate child). Dev.[8] Ya've put me in a rigler hurry, I du shake like a leaf.
7. A small load of corn or hay got up in haste from apprehension of rain.
e.An. *N. & Q.* (1866) II. 52; e.An.[1] e.Nrf. MARSHALL *Rur. Econ.* (1787). Suf. The quantity is not defined. Ess. No inhabitant of this towne shall ... cutt any grasse in any of the comon meadows ... vpon the penaltie of forfeiting tenn shillings for euery londe or hurry of haye so cutt, *Dedham Rec.* (1659) IV. 5, ed. 1894.
8. A drawing, dragging. n.Cy. GROSE (1790) *MS. add.* (P.)
9. *pl.* A name given to the Irish Rebellion of 1798. N.I.[1]
10. *v.* To trouble, vex; to flurry, frighten; *gen.* in *pp.*
Not.[1] Lei.[1] I've been very much hurried this morning, for I've just heard of the death of my old friend. Nhp.[1] Don't burry your head about that. Hnt. (T.P.F.) Cor.[1] I was bra'ly hurried when I heard of it; Cor.[2] Tell, if you mind to. I aren't hurried.
11. To quarrel. Yks. (HALL.) **12.** To shove, to push. w.Yks.[1] **13.** To subsist; to shift. *ib.*

HURRY, *v.[2]* and *sb.[2]* n.Cy. Cum. Yks. Lan. Der. [h]ə·ri.] **1.** *v.* To transport or convey; esp. to transport the coal from the face of the working to the bottom of the shaft.
w.Yks. (S.J.C.); w.Yks.[2] A horse hurries coals; w.Yks.[4] Lan. GROSE (1790) *MS. add.* (C.) nw.Der.[1]
Hence **Hurrier,** *sb.* a person, *gen.* a boy who pushes the coal 'corves' along the colliery roads.
w.Yks. *Leeds Merc. Suppl.* (May 9, 1885) 8; w.Yks.[2 3]
2. *sb.* One of the 'spouts' which allow coal to rush down from cars (running on a timber framework) into the hold of a ship; *pl.* the whole framework or 'stathe.'
Cum. Gat to Whitehebben, a girt sea-side town, whare sea-nags eats cwoals out o' rack-hurrys, *Borrowdale Lett.* in *Lonsdale Mag.* (Feb. 1867) 309; Cum.[4] Concealed in a hurry on the Lonsdale Dock, *W. C. T.* (July 2, 1898) 3. [Hurries, stages or frames at the sides of a quay for the convenience of tumbling coals from the waggons right into the holds of sea-going vessels, STORMONTH *Dict.*]

HURRYFUL, *adj.* Shr. w.Cy. Also written hurriful Shr.[1] [ə·rifl.] Quick; hasty; hurried.
Shr.[1] It inna the 'urriful sort o' folk as bringen the most to pass, fur they runnen about athout thar yed ööth 'em; Shr.[2] He was very hurryful and could not wait. w.Cy. (HALL.)

HURRYSOME, *adj.* and *adv.* Cum. Wor. Hrf. Nrf. Dev. Cor. Also written hurrisome Nrf. Dev.[1] Cor.[1 2] [ə·risəm.]
1. *adj.* Hurried, confused; quick, hasty; passionate.
Cum.[14] Wor. HOLLOWAY. Nrf. Provided you beant hurrisome, JESSOPP *Arcady* (1887) ii. Dev.[1] Cor. THOMAS *Randigal Rhymes* (1895) Gl.; Cor.[1 2]
2. *adv.* In haste, fast. Hrt.[2] The rain comes hurrysome.

HURSCHLE, HURSEL, HURSH, see Hirsel, *v.[2]*, Herself, Rush.

HURSLING, *ppl. adj.* Dev. 'Rustling.'
Th' hurslin' leaves, PULMAN *Sketches* (1842) 22, ed. 1853.

HURST, *sb.* Sc. n.Cy. Nhb. Yks. Lan. Chs. Der. Not. Shr. Nrf. Ken. Sus. Hmp. Dor. Also written hirst Sc. (JAM.) Abd. Frf. N.Cy.[1] Nhb.[1] w.Yks. ne.Lan.[1]; and in forms horst Ken. Sus.; hus Nrf. Sus.[2] Hmp.[1] [hirst, ðət.] **1.** A small wood; a wooded eminence; nearly *obs.* except in place-names.
Sc. *Gl. Sibb.* (JAM.) N.Cy.[1] Nhb.[1] [It] enters into the names of three parishes and townships, and into that of eleven other inhabited places in Nhb. 'Scroggy hirsts of hazel,' HODGSON *Nhb.* (1827) pt. 11. I. 100, *note.* w.Yks. Mostly in place-names (J.W.). Chs.[1] Old, freq. used in place names. Der.[2] (s.v. Hob-hurst). Shr.[1], Sus.[1 2], Hmp.[1]
2. *Comp.* Hurst-beech, the hornbeam, *Carpinus Betulus.*
Nrf., Ken., Sus. From its growth in hursts, and some resemblance of its leaves to those of the beech tree (B. & H.); Sus.[1 2] (s.v. Horse-beech). Hmp.[1] (s.v. Horse-beech).
3. *? Obs.* A bank; a little hill; a ridge; a barren height; the bare and hard summit of a hill.
Sc. We are bound to drive the bullocks, All by hollows, hirsts and hillocks, SCOTT *Waverley* (1814) xxxviii, *note*; Ower hirst an scaur, DONALD *Poems* (1867) 11. Abd. Down she leans her birn upon a hirst, SHIRREFS *Poems* (1790) 89. Frf. But up ... I'll o'er the hirst, MORISON *Poems* (1790) 158. n.Cy. GROSE (1790). w.Yks. HUTTON *Tour to Caves* (1781). ne.Lan.[1] Dor. HAYNES *Voc.* (c. 1730) in *N. & Q.* (1883) 6th S. vii. 366.
4. A sand-bank on the brink of a river; a shallow; a shelf in a river-bed.
n.Sc. Being asked, If these dykes were removed, there would be a ford or hirst in the river, .. depones, That he does not know whether if these dykes were removed, there would be fords or shallows at the place where they stand, *State, Fraser of Frasersfield* (1805) 192 (JAM.); The current of water removed a sand bank or hirst that lay on the margin of the river ... and placed it in the mouth of ... Allochy Grain, and thereby occasioned the rising or hirst above described, *State, Leslie of Powis*, 6a (*ib.*). Not. There are in the channel of this river [the Trent] divers hursts or shelves, which in summer time lye dry, DEERING *Hist. Not.* 164. Shr. That part of a ford in the Severn over which the water runs roughly, BOUND *Provinc.* (1876); Shr.[1] A bed of shingle in the Severn is called a hurst; Shr.[2]
[1. OE. *hyrst*, a copse, wood (B.T.). LG. (Pomerania) *horst*, 'ein erhöheter Ort im Walde' (DÄHNERT). 3. EFris. *hörst* (*horst*), 'eine sandige Anhöhe' (KOOLMAN). 4. LG. (Göttingen) *horst* (*host*), 'eine bewachsene kleine Erhöhung im Sumpfe' (SCHAMBACHI.)]

HURSTLE, *sb.* Sc. Irel. Also written hirstle Abd. The sound of rough breathing caused by mucus in the air-passages. N.I.[1]
Hence **Hurstling,** (1) *sb.* the sound of rough breathing; (2) *adj.* wheezing.
(1) Gall. (A.W.), N.I.[1] (2) Abd. The sound of the tiny voice was accompanied by a slight 'hirstling' noise, ALEXANDER *Ain Flk.* (1882) 184.

HURSTLE, *v.* n.Yks.[2] To struggle, wrestle.

HURT, *v.*, *sb.* and *adj.* Var. dial. uses in Sc. Irel. and Eng. [h]ərt, ðt.] **I.** *v.* Gram. forms. **1.** *Present Tense:* (1) Hort, (2) Hot, (3) Yurt.
(1) Cai.[1], Nhb.[1], Ken.[2], Sus.[2], Hmp.[1] (2) s.Yks.[14] ne.Yks.[1] 33. e.Yks.[1] m.Yks.[1] *Introd.* 36. w.Yks.[5] Glo. N.other tuppence a leave yain't much to yurt un, BUCKMAN *Darke's Sojourn* (1890) vi.
2. *Preterite:* (1) Hort, (2) Horted, (3) Hot, (4) Hotted, (5) Hurted, (6) Hurtet, (7) Hurtit.
(1) Ken.[1] (2) Cai.[2] (3) ne.Yks.[1] 33. m.Yks.[1] *Introd.* 36. n.Lin.[1] (4) m.Yks.[1] *Introd.* 36. (5) w.Yks.[5], Glo.[1] Brk ... i 12. a.Wil. Th' watchmen as went about th' zitty vound m'; - tha' hurted m', KITE *Sng. Sol.* (1860) v. 7. (6) Sc. Whase feet thaye hurtet wi' fettirs, RIDDELL *Ps.* (1857) cv. 18. (7) s.Sc. MURRAY *Dial.* (1873) 205.
3. *Pp.:* (1) Hat, (2) Hort, (3) Horted, (4) Horten, (5) Hot, (6) Hotten, (7) Hurted, (8) Hurten, (9) Hurtid, (10) Hurtit.
(1) Nrf. Are yow hat, mor! A. B. K. *Wright's Fortune*, 19 ... (2) Wm. Sall hes hort her heel, WHEELER *Dial.* (1790) 112. ed. 1821. (3) Cai.[1] (4) Nhb.[1] He's horten his heed. (5) n.Lin.[1] Th' bairns hed been climbin' an' ... hot it sen. (6) ne.Yks.[1] 33. e.Yks.[1] Aot'n. m.Yks.[1] *Introd.* 36. w.Yks.[5] Nobbud luke how they've hotten that poor barn! n.Lin.[1] Ther's two men been hotten at th'

fo'nises. (7) **Sh.I.** Spence *Flb-Lore* (1899) 154. Ir. Were ye hurted, sir? *Paddiana* (ed. 1848) I. 17. **w.Yks.²**, Glo.¹ Brks.¹ 12. Ken. She set to and cried like as if she'd been the one hurted, *Cornh. Mag.* (Jan. 1894) 64. Cor. It was Harry that was ' hurted,' *Longman's Mag.* (Feb. 1893) 386 ; Cor.¹ Murder committed, but nobody hurted. (8) **Nhb.¹** He's hurten his hand. **n.Yks.²**, **w.Yks.²** n.Lin.¹ I've hurten my sen wi' clootin' my head agean a bauk. (9) **Sh.I.** Nane can be mair hurtid wi' tales o' da loss o' life ... den me, *Sh. News* (Apr. 9, 1898). (10) **s.Sc.** Murray *Dial.* (1873) 205.
II. Dial. uses. **1.** *v.* In *comb.* Hurt-sickle, the black knapweed, *Centaurea nigra.* Wor. (B. & H.)
2. Phr. *hurt from the ground*, injured in health by supernatural agents. See Ground, *sb.* 14.
Sh.I. Most forms of illness were supposed to be either an ' evil onwaar,' or ' hurted frae da grund.' .. The latter was the supernatural influence of trows or hillfolk, Spence *Flb-Lore* (1899) 154-5.
3. To matter, signify.
Sus. A man cannot find a strap or buckle he *gen.* uses, and says ' It won't hurt about the strap ' (he can do without it) (G.A.W.).
4. *sb.* Phr. (1) *no hurt*, no matter ; never mind ! (2) *to be hurt done*, to be bewitched.
(1) **Dev.** I made a mistake, zo et zim'd, bit no hurt, Nathan Hogg *Poet. Lett.* (1847) 44, ed. 1865. (2) **n.Cy.** (Hall.) **Yks.** The child's hurt done, Henderson *Flb-Lore* (1879) vi. **w.Yks.¹** Is waa to hear at Joan Shepherd's hurt done.
5. *adj.* Down-hearted.
n.Dev. Hur layv'th us all, 'e zee, to-day, An' veelth a littul hurt, Rock *Jim an' Nell* (1867) st. 55.

HURTER, sb.¹ Nhb. Dur. Yks. Nhp. Wor. Shr. Also written hurtur Dur. ; and in form hurter Nhb.¹ [hə˙rtər, ə˙tə(r).] The shoulder of the axle against which the nave of the wheel knocks.
N.Cy.¹, Nhb.¹ Dur. Raine *Charters* (1837) ccxcix. **w.Yks.¹** A ring of iron in the axis of a cart. Nhp.¹ so.Wor.¹ A thick piece of iron fastened to a wooden axle, against which the back of the wheel works. **Shr.¹** An iron plate edged with steel, fastened—by 'langets ' or stays—on to the axle of a ' tumbrel ' to keep the wheel from wearing into the axle-tree : the steel edge works against the ' boukin.'

HURTER, sb.² Sus. Hmp. A calf which runs with the dam for seven or eight months. Sus. Young *Annals Agric.* (1784–1815) XI. 220. Sus., Hmp. (G.A.W.)

HURTFUL, adj. Bdf. In a dangerous condition.
In parts of Bdf. this word is used only in a passive sense. A person is said to be ' not hurtful this morning,' when no apprehensions are entertained that his disease will occasion him hurt (J.W.B.).

HURTLE, sb.¹ Hrf.¹ [5˙tl.] A spot.
[Cp. Fr. *heurt*, ' coup donné en heurtant contre quelque chose, la marque que le coup a laissée ' (Littré).]

HURTLE, v. and *sb.²* Sc. Irel. n.Cy. Nhb. Yks. Der. Lin. Nhp. Also written hirtle Nhb.¹ ; hurtel Nhp. ; and in form hortle Nhb.¹ [h)ə˙rtl, 5˙tl.] **1.** *v.* To crouch on the ground as young birds do when alarmed ; to contract the body into a round form as through pain or severe cold. Cf. hurkle, *v.*
N.Cy.¹, Nhb.¹ **w.Yks.** Willan *List Wds.* (1811). Der.¹ Used in the form ' hurtle up ' (s.v. Hurkle). Lin.¹, n.Lin.¹, nw.Lin. (M.P.)
2. To crowd together in confusion. N.Cy.¹, Nhp.¹
3. To move with violence ; to hasten.
Gall. Loch Enoch with the snowdrift hurtling across it, Crockett *Raiders* (1894) xliii. Nhb.¹ The clud's gan hirtlin alang the hill side. Lin.¹ Nhp. An arrow hurtel'd e'er so high, Clare *Remains* (1873) 270.
4. *sb.* A falling mass of anything.
Ir. She forced herself to look up, and at once descried them through the hurtle of the pelting shower, Barlow *Idylls* (1892) 186.

HURTLEBERRY, sb. Som. Dev. [ə˙tl-bəri.] The whortleberry, fruit of the *Vaccinium Myrtillus.* Cf. hurts.
w.Som.¹ A little ' fine ' talk. **Dev.** Bray *Desc. Tamar and Tavy* (1836) II. 254 ; Dev.¹ [A hurtle berry, *Vaccinium*, Coles (1679).]
HURTLESS, adj. Yks. Harmless, uninjurious. n.Yks.³, m.Yks.¹

HURTS, sb. pl. Cth. Pem. Glo. Sur. Sus. Hmp. Som. Dev. Cor. Also written herts Sus. Hmp. Cor.² ; hirts Dev.⁴ ; and in form horts s.Pem. Dev.⁴ [əts.] Whortleberries, the fruit of the *Vaccinium Myrtillus.*
Cth. (W.W.S.) **s.Pem.** There any 'mount of hurts in Cresselly

Wood (W.M.M.). **Glo.¹** **Sur.** [Children] stained from head to feet with the deep purple juice of the ' hurts,' *Forest Tithes* (1893) 49 ; Sur.¹, Sus.¹ **Hmp.** Children's all gone to Hind Head hertgathering (W.M.E.F.). **w.Som.¹** Common. The cry ' Hurts ! hurts ! ' may be heard daily in the season, in most towns and villages of the district ; but now, alas ! the Board schools are corrupting the old name into ' worts ' (s.v. Hurtle-berry). **Dev.** Oftentimes during summer she goes to Dartmoor to gather hurtleberries, called by the country people ' hurts,' Bray *Desc. Tamar and Tavy* (1836) II. 254 ; Dev.⁴, Cor.¹²
Hence Hurting, *prp.* gathering ' hurts.'
n.Dev. Whorts are ' hurts ' among the labouring people, and to go gathering whortleberries is to go ' a hurting,' Jefferies *Red Deer* (1884) x.
[Rawe crayme vndecocted, eaten with strawberyes or hurtes, is a rurall mannes banket, Boorde *Dyetary* (1542), ed. Furnivall (1870) 267.]

HURTSOME, adj. Sc. Nhb. Yks. Also in form hortsome Nhb.¹ Hurtful, harmful.
Sc. Their entry was hurtsome to the cause, *Society Contendings*, 108 (Jam.). **Ayr.** Wi' sic knowledge I felt it was hurtsome to speak, Laing *Poems* (1894) 10a. N.Cy.¹, Nhb.¹ n.Yks.² ' It's owther hurtsome or puzzomous,' either dangerous, or poisonous outright. m.Yks.¹

HURZLE, HUS, see Hirsel, *v.²*, Hurst, Us, *pron.*

HUSBAND, sb. Sc. Nhb. Dur. Cum. Yks. War. Oxf. Ken. Dev. Also in form hoosband Yks. [h)v˙zbən(d, h)u˙zbən(d.] **1.** In *comb.* (1) Husband's candle, a long candle lit by the master of the house at Christmas, round which the household sit ; (2) -land, a division of land, *gen.* containing from twenty to thirty acres ; (3) -man, an agricultural labourer ; (4) -'s tea, poor, weak tea ; (5) -work, household work.
(1) **Yks.** And sit roond the lang hoosband's cannal with 'em, Fetherston *T. Goorkrodger* (1870) 166. (2) **Sc.** Husbandland conteines commonlie 6 aikers of sok and syith land : That is of sik land as may be tilled with an pleuch, or may be mawed with a syith. .. I find na certaine rule prescrived anent the quantitie and valour of ane husband land, Skene *Difficill Wds.* (1681) ; Commonly containing twenty-six acres of soc and syith land (Jam.). **Hdg.** Yt [that] everie twa husband-lands of yᵉ parische suld furnish out ane man, Ritchie *Churches of St. Baldred* (1883) 152. **Nhb.** The manor of Lorbottle and of twelve husband lands, and twelve cottages there (1407), Dixon *Whittingham Vale* (1895) 145 ; Nhb.¹ The husbands of land, mentioned so frequently in deeds respecting Northumberland, contained twenty acres, and at times twenty-four or thirty. (3) N.Cy.¹ Dur. A skilful husbandman by frequent ploughings, Marshall *Review* (1808) I. 145. Cum. (J.P.) ; Don't you know the difference between a farmer and a husbandman ? *Penrith Obs.* (1896). **w.Yks.** *Spec. Dial.* 6. (4) War.² Oxf.¹ The wife is supposed to have drunk all the strong tea herself, and then filled the teapot with water for her husband, *MS. add.* Dev. *Reports Provinc.* (1877) 132. (5) **Sc.** A muckle lazy useless jade, she can do naething but work at husband wark, Graham *Writings* (1883) II. 54 ; The women about fishing communities differed, and do still, from their sisters further inland, regarding house-work, or ' husband-work,' *ib. note.*
2. A pollard. Ken.¹

HUSBANDLY, adv. Obs. Yks. Thriftily, economically, to good purpose.
n.Yks. And that two gentᵉ. see the money husbandly employed for the country's advantage, *Quarter Sess. Rec.* (Oct. 3, 1671) in *N. R. Rec. Soc.* VI. 161.

HUSBIRD, HUSBUD, see Hosebird.

HUSCEN, pp. Cor.¹² Scolded.

HUSELACK, sb. Sh.I. A small stone hut for drying fish. S. & Ork.¹

HUSH, v.¹, sb.¹ and *adj.* Sc. n.Cy. Yks. Lan. Chs. Glo. Cor. Also written husch Bnff.¹ ; and in forms hishie Fif. (Jam.) ; hushie, huzzh Sc. *ib.* [h)vʃ, uʃ.] **1.** *v.* To lull to sleep, to sing a lullaby to ; used in *imper.* as an *int.* ' go to sleep.'
Sc. Hush and baloo, babie, Hush and baloo ; A' the lave's in their beds—I'm hushin' you, Chambers *Pop. Rhymes* (1870) 19. **w.Sc.** (Jam.) **Lth.** She had little time to ' hush ' any of them. They were smartly stripped, night-gowned, and tumbled one by one into the box-bed, Strathesk *More Bits* (ed. 1885) 186.

2. Phr. (1) *Hush a bit*, go gently ; (2) *hushta* or *-to*, (*a*) hold your tongue, be quiet ; (*b*) hold fast, take care, go gently.

(1) Cor.¹ (*a, a*) w.Yks.¹ (*b*) Yks. (K.) n.Yks. Hushta. good lad! Tack teaum and gome thy feet, MERITON *Praise Ale* (1684) l. 381.

3. *sb.* In phr. *hold thy hush*, hold thy tongue, be quiet. See Hold, *v.* II. 12.

Lan. So howd thi hush an' let's get on wi' t'essay, *Essay on Dreams*, 4. s.Lan. Very common (F.E.T.). Chs.³ (s.v. Howd).

4. A whisper, the slightest noise. Ags. (JAM.)

Hence **Hush-musch**, (*a*) *sb.* a secret talking, a rumour; a state of bustling disorder; (*b*) *v.* to speak much in a suppressed manner ; (2) *hush or mush*, (3) *hushie or whishie*, *phr.* the slightest intimation given in the most cautious manner, a single whisper ; *gen.* with *neg.*

(1, *a*) Bnff.¹ Thir's a sair hush-musch aboot fa's deen sic an ill deed. Lth.¹ (JAM.) (*b*) Baff.¹ (2) Ags. Neither hush nor mush (JAM.). (3) Sc. Ye maun just excuse me, my Lady, but Jeanie ne'er let on hushie or whishie o' your visit, *Saxon and Gael* (1814) I. 133 (JAM.). Flf. Neither hishie nor wishie (JAM.).

5. Ale or spirits sold without license.

Lan. He wur taen up for sellin' hush, WAUGH *Chim. Corner* (1874) 30, ed. 1879. s.Lan. Common (F.E.T.).

6. *Comp.* **Hush-shop**, an unlicensed house where spirituous liquors are sold, a house in which an illicit trade in beer, &c. is carried on.

Lan. The Jolly Jumper originally sprang from the kernel of a ' hush-shop,' BRIERLEY *Irkdale* (1865) i ; ' Hush' signifying that the company frequenting such places were expected to conduct themselves as orderly as possible that no alarm might be given to parties in authority, *ib. note.* s.Lan. (F.E.T.) ; BAMFORD *Dial.* (1854). Chs.¹²

7. *adj.* Quiet, still, hushed.

Sc. The owl has seen him and is hush, SCOTT *Rokeby* (1813) c. vi. st. 3. Abd. And winds are hush, DAVIDSON *Poems* (1861) 93. Frf. All hush around on every side, I heard a sound, MORISON *Poems* (1790) 29. n.Cy. (J.W.) Glo. Wee shim all hush at home, SMYTH *Lives Berkeleys* (1066-1618) III. 25, ed. 1885.

HUSH, *sb.*² and *v.*² Sc. Nhb. Dur. Cum. Yks. Lan. Lin. [huʃ, h)uʃ.] **1.** *sb.* A sudden gush or rush, the sound of rushing water ; a low, murmuring wind, a gust of wind.

Sc. In came the neighbours in a hush, dinging ither down in the door, GRAHAM *Writings* (1883) II. 39. **S. & Ork.**¹ A low murmuring wind. Sik. (JAM.) Nhb. There was a hush of falling waters in the air, CLARE *Love of Lass*, 71, in PREVOST *Gl.* (1900) ; Nhb.¹ Cum.¹ ; Cum.⁴ Expresses the feeling as it were of wind coming. A rumbling and hissing in a mine, due to the cracking of the roof and escape of gas. w.Yks.³ A gust of wind.

2. A swell, a rolling motion of the sea.

Sh.I. We wir andowin' ahead fir saith, wi' a hush o' a sea on, STEWART *Tales* (1892) 242 ; It wis a raem calm, wi' a hush an' a caa aboot da shore, *ib.* 260.

3. In mining : water used to wash away earth from the surface of rock or mineral. Also in *comp.* **Hush-water.**

Nhb.¹ This is produced artificially so as to bare the surface of the rock in order to discover indications of ore in the face of a hill side. s.Dur., n.Yks. The dirty water from the lead mines which having been used to wash the ore pollutes the streams it falls into, at times causing annoyance to anglers and harm to fish. 'Th'ush is comin' down— ye need'nt gan a fishin' to-day' (J.E.D.).

4. A part in a mine or quarry which has been cleared for excavation by an artificial flow of water.

Cum.⁴ He worked . . . in what is called a hush connected with the mines, *Wrestling*, 37.

5. *Comp.* **Hush-cush**, a wet, marshy condition.

s.Lin. The water stood in the field, it was all of a hush-cush (G.G.W.).

6. Abundance, great plenty, a quantity.

Abd. A thriftless hush (G.W.). **Rxb.** The only thing wi' yon there's luck o' Is bush o' strae for makin muck o', A. SCOTT *Poems* (ed. 1808) 90. Nhb.¹ Cum. I scworn to vex mysel ; When I've a hush o' gud strang yell, ANDERSON *Ballads* (1805) 95; Cum.¹ Sec a hush o' fwoak.

7. *v.* To rush, gush forth.

Lth.¹ To hush in, to make one's way with force and haste (JAM.). Edb. We heard the water . . . roaring and hushing over the rocks. MOIR *Mansie Wauch* (1828) xv. Cum. On the fluir, bluid an punch now hush't leyke a stream, ANDERSON *Ballads* (ed. 1840) 96 ; Cum.¹ ; Cum.⁴ Bleud hush't out like watter.

8. To cause to rush, to force forward. Lth. (JAM.)

9. To separate earthy particles from minerals by the force of running water. Dur.¹, Cum.¹, w.Yks.¹, ne.Lan.¹

Hence **Hushing**, *vbl. sb.* the production of a rush of water for the purpose of carrying away the surface débris in mines and quarries, the process of washing away earthy particles from minerals.

Nhb., Dur. Hushing is by far a more effectual method, FORSTER *Strata* (1821) 285; Hushing, in lead-mining is practised : (1) for baring rock-faces in prospecting for ore ; (2) in working alluvial deposits for detached and water-worn ore ; (3) in working over again the sediment which has been carried away in the process of washing and become deposited in the bed of the stream (R.O.H.).

HUSH, *sb.*³ and *v.*³ Sc. Irel. Suf. Cor. Also written husch, husah ; and in form hysch Bnff.¹ **1.** *sb.* A cry used to frighten and drive away birds, &c. ; also used as an *int.* Cai.¹, Bnff.¹, e.Suf. (F.H.) Cf. hoosh, *int.*

2. *v.* To drive away birds or animals by making a slight noise ; also used *fig.*

Cai.¹ Bnff.¹ See, laddie, rin an' husch the craws fae the tares. He wis unco ill aboot the aulest dother, an' soucht her ; bit she huscht 'im awa. Per. Thou was husht out to the door When thou (like Hell) began to roar, SMITH *Poems* (1714) 36, ed. 1853. N.I.¹ To drive a flock of fowl, saying at the same time, ' Hush, hush.' e.Suf. Less common than Hoosh (q.v.) (F.H.). Cor.¹ They hushed the hen out of the nest.

Hence **Huschou**, (1) *v.* to drive away birds, to frighten away. Bnff.¹; (2) *sb.* a cry used to frighten and drive away anything ; also used as an *int. ib.*

HUSH, *sb.*⁴ Sc. The lump-fish, *Cyclopterus lumpus.* (JAM.) [SATCHELL (1879).]

HUSH-A-BA(A, *int.* and *v.* Sc. Lan. I.Ma. Also in forms **a-hishi-baw** Lnk.; **heshie-ba** Elg.; **hushee-bow** I.Ma.; **hushie-ba**(a Or.I. Gall. ; **hushy-ba**(a Flf. ; **hushy-baa** Flf. ; **huzzhie-baw** Sc. (JAM.) **1.** *int.* An expression used in lulling a child to sleep ; also used *sbst.* a lullaby.

Sc. (JAM.) Sh.I. A ramished bairn, which she soothes by singing : ' Husha baa baet dee, Minnie is gaen ta saet dee,' SPENCE *Flk-Lore* (1899) 180. Or.I. Trowies canna tak' thoo, Hushie-ba, lammie, FERGUSSON *Rambles* (1884) 168. Elg. Heshie ba—sleep awa, Dinna wauken mammy, TESTER *Poems* (1865) 182. Flf. O my lovely charming boy, Hushy baa ! ly still and sleep, DOUGLAS *Poems* (1806) 83. Ayr. His sermons in the warm summer after-noons were just a perfect hushabaa, GALT *Provost* (1822) viii. Lnk. Hush-a-ba', my sweet wee dearie, Sleep fu' soun' till morn-in's daw', M°LACHLAN *Thoughts* (1884) 63 ; And aye she sung, ' A-hishi-baw, babby! ' And aye she kiss'd it, *Deil's Hallowe'en* (1856) 50. Edb. Shouggie shou, shouggie shou ! Hush-a-ba my dearie ; Hech surae! but a waukrife bairn Aye mak's a mither weary ! *Scots Poems and Ballants*, 91. Gall. In the old song of Rocking the Cradle, ' hushie baa babie lye still ' is a line much used, MACTAGGART *Encycl.* (1824).

2. *v.* To lull to sleep ; also in form **Hushee-bowbabby.**

Flf. A mither huzhy-baa-in' a bairn to sleep, ROBERTSON *Provost* (1894) 11. Lan. Hushabying a babby as wouldn't be hushabied, GASKELL *M. Barton* (1848) ix. I.Ma. She had her up and in her lap, and hushee bowbabbied and on the tree top in a minute, BROWN *Witch* (1889) 85.

HUSHAPAN, *sb.* Sh.I. Also written **hôshapan.** The skull, cranium. Cf. **hoosapaail.**

Doo haes Him ta tank 'at mi hushapan is no laid in mummie, *Sh. News* (Aug. 28, 1897) ; (J.I.) ; JAKOBSEN *Dial.* (1897) 16.

[Norw. dial. *haus* (*hause*), the cranium + *panna*, the brain-pan (AASEN) ; ON. *hauss* (*hausa-*).]

HUSHEL, see **Hirsel**, *v.*⁵

HUSHION, *sb.* Obs. Nhb. Yks. Also written **hus-sian** Nhb. A cushion, a ' wishin.'

Nhb. Had I as many hussians, shusians, chairs and stools, RICHARDSON *Borderer's Table-bk.* (1846) VIII. 379. Yks. *N. & Q.* (1877) 5th S. vii. 56. w.Yks. WATSON *Hist. Hlfx.* (1775) 540.

HUSHION, see **Hoshen.**

HUSHO, *v.* Irel. To sing a lullaby to, to lull to sleep. See **Hush**, *v.*¹

s.Ir. My mother was hushoing my little sister, CROKER *Leg.* (1862) 296; The stream kept up a continued cronane like a nurse hushoing, *ib.* 298.

HUSHOCH, v. and sb. Sc. [hʊ·ʃɒx.] 1. v. To work in a hurried, careless, or slovenly manner ; to dress slovenly. w. & s.Sc. (JAM. Suppl.) See Hirsel, v.² 3.

Hence Hushochy, adj. hurried, careless, slovenly ; also used advb. ib.

2. To heap up loosely.

Gall. The millers did hushoch their melders in sacks, MAC-TAGGART Encycl. (1824) 78, ed. 1876.

3. sb. Hurried, careless, or slovenly work ; one who works in a hurried, careless, or slovenly manner. w. & s.Sc. (JAM. Suppl.)

4. A confused heap, a tangled mass ; a loose quantity of anything.

w. & s.Sc. (JAM. Suppl.) Gall. MACTAGGART Encycl. (1824).

HUSHT, int., v. and sb. Sc. Lan. Yks. Chs. Der. Shr. Hrf. Pem. Also in forms heaht Shr. ; hisht Hrf.² s.Pem. ; hooisht ne.Lan. e.Lan.¹ ; hooaht Cai.¹ ; huisht Hrf.

1. int. Hush, be silent.

Cai.¹ Bch. A toothless houdy, auld and teugh, Says, Cummer, husht, we ha'e enough, FORBES Dominie (1785) 39. w.Yks. J.W.) Lan. Molly, husht, BRIERLEY Layrock (1864) v. ne.Lan. Th' conductor—said ' Hooisht,' MATHER Idylls (1895) 49. e.Lan.¹, s.Chs.¹, nw.Der.¹ Shr. An old nurse used to use the word ' Hesht' when we made a noise (R.M.E.). Hrf.², s.Pem. (W.M.M.)

2. v. To be silent, become quiet.

w.Yks. (J.W.) Lan. Awm cummin to that very peighnt, if theaw'll husht, STATON B.Shuttle, 7 ; Just thee husht, BRIERLEY Layrock (1864) x. Hrf. A man was riding close up to the window and telling them to huisht, but they would not huisht for all that, Longman's Mag. (Apr. 1899) 564.

3. To order silence. Cai.¹

4. sb. In phr. to hold one's husht, to be silent. See Hold, v. II. 12.

Lan. He couln't booath sup and tawk so he howded his husht, STATON Loominary (c. 1861) 120.

5. Exciseable goods, esp. liquors sold without license. e.Lan.¹ See Hush, sb.¹ 5.

HUSHTER, HUSIF, see Hashter, Huss(e)y.

HUSK, sb.¹ and adj. Lakel. Yks. Lin. Hrf. Glo. Sus. Wil. Som. Dev. Also in form hooak Hrf.² Dev. [(h)usk, usk.] 1. sb. A dry cough, hoarseness ; esp. a wheezing cough or disease of the throat among animals. Cf. hask, usk.¹ 7.

Hrf.² Glo. A disease in calves caused by thread-worms in the windpipe making a dry cough. A barking cough made by pigs (S.S.B.). Sus. They sometimes lose calves by a distemper they call the husk, which is occasioned by little worms in the small pipes on the lights, YOUNG Annals Agric. (1784-1815) XI. 182, 193. Wil.¹ Often fatal to calves. w.Som.¹ On a building in Wellington is a large inscription—Manufactory, Devonshire Oils. Devonshire compound for husk and scour (s.v. Hesk) ; A well-known cattle specific sets out the various ailments it professes to cure, . . and inter alia reads thus : ' Yearlings or calves : husk, or hose, scour chills, worms in throat,' ib. (s.v. Hose).

Hence Hooaky, adj. hoarse, having a wheezing cough. Dev. I be aveared that tha mare's bad ; 'er's oncommon hooaky to-night. I thenk I'll gie 'er a bran mash, HEWETT Peas. Sp. (1892).

2. adj. Hoarse.

Lakel.² Ah've a bad cauld, an' Ah've bin as husk as husk fer ower a week. w.Yks. (J.W.) sw.Lin. I'm very husk to-day (R.E.C.).

3. Dry, parched. Lin. (HALL.), sw.Lin. (R.E.C.) See Hask, adj.¹ 1.

HUSK, sb.² and v. Yks. Lan. Lin. Also Ken. Wil. [usk, usk.] 1. sb. pl. The chaff of oats. Wil.¹

2. Fig. Clothes, garments.

w.Yks. Hah menny ar ther at tays ther Sunday husks ta me uncle's throo habit, TOM TREDDLEHOYLE Bairnsla Ann. (1874) 64.

3. A blow, smack, rap.

Lan. I could like to give him a good husk i' th' earhole, BRIERLEY Out o' Work, iii.

4. v. To take off the husks or outer coats of walnuts.

Ken. I heard a controversy between two rustics as to which was the proper term. One insisted on the phrase ' husking,' the other ' hulling,' N. & Q. (1867) 3rd S. xii. 203.

5. To thrash, beat.

Lin.¹, n.Lin.¹ sw.Lin.¹ The Newton lads reckoned they were going to husk us.

HUSKIN(G, prp. and sb. n.Cy. Lan. Lin. Dev. Also in forms hask- n.Cy. ; hush- n.Dev. [u·skin.] 1. prp. Obs. Creeping stealthily about, creeping with bent shoulders and slow steps ; walking idly about.

n.Cy. GROSE (1790). Lin.¹ Dev. Horae Subsecivae (1777) 222. n.Dev. GROSE (1790).

2. sb. A clownish fellow, a ' clodhopper.'

ne.Lan.¹ Lin. MILLER & SKERTCHLY Fenland (1878) iv ; Lin.¹ That husking axes too much for his pokes.

[1. Cp. Norw. dial. huska, to rock or pitch as a boat (AASEN).]

HUSKIT, ppl. adj. Sc. Husky, hoarse.

Lth. But he cries in tones sae huskit, BALLANTINE Poems (1856) 102.

HUSKY, adj. Lin. [u·ski.] Hard, dry, coarse.

Lin. Producing sour, coarse, husky, sedge or sword grass, Reports Agric. (1793-1813) 74. n.Lin.¹ [Free from the defect that wool staplers call husky and pinny, that is, dry and brittle, STEPHENS Farm Bk. (ed. 1849) I. 236.]

HUSPEL, HUSPIL, see Hespel.

HUS-PUSH, sb. m.Yks.¹ [u·s-puʃ.] A busy time.

It will be time for going in an hour. We'd better have the hus-push now as then.

HUSS, sb. Ken. Sus. [us.] The dog-fish, esp. the lesser-spotted dog-fish, Scyllium caniculo.

Ken.¹ Sus. The lesser-spotted dog-fish is skinned and eaten at Brighton (F.E.S.). [SATCHELL (1879).]

HUSS, v.¹ Sus. [us.] To caress, fondle.

Sus. ' Ah, Tom,' ses she, a bussin an a hussin ov un, JACKSON Southward Ho (1894) I. 339 ; Sus.¹ The children play a game, which is accompanied by a song beginning : ' Hussing and buss-ing will not do, But go to the gate, knock and ring,—Please, Mrs. Brown, is Nellie within ? '

HUSS, v.² Glo. Som. [us.] To incite, urge on a dog ; also used in the imper. as a term of encouragement to a dog.

Glo.¹ If thee dost come near me I'll huss the dog at tha. ' Huss dog, buss, allow ! ' in putting a dog at a rabbit, cat, &c. Som. To huss a dog on (W.F.R.).

HUSSEL, see Hirsel, v.², Housel, Hustle, v.¹

HUSSER, sb. ? Obs. Sus. In phr. husser and squencher, a pot of beer with a dram of gin in it. GROSE (1790) ; Sus.¹

HUSSET, see Hooset.

HUSS(E)Y, sb. Var. dial. uses in Sc. Eng. and Amer. Also in forms hissie Sc. (JAM.) ; hissy Sc. ; hizzey Lnk. Cum. ; hizzie Sc. Cai.¹ Nhb. ; hizzy Sc. ; husif w.Yks. ; hussif Lakel.¹ w.Yks.² Not. n.Lin.¹ War.² Suf.¹ ; hussyfe Sc. ; huswife War.² Shr.¹ ; huzzaf Cum.¹⁴ ; huzzey w.Yks. Not.¹ ; huzzie Cai.¹ Dur.¹ ; huzzif(f Dur.¹ Wm. w.Yks.¹ Lan. ne.Lan.¹ s.Chs.¹ nw.Der.¹ ; huzzy Sc. Nhb.¹ n.Yks. w.Yks. Lan.¹ Stf. w.Som.¹ Dev.¹ ; hyzzie Edb. [h)u·si, h)u·zi, h)u·si, h)u·zi, h)u·sif, h)u·zif.] 1. A housewife, a woman of any age, but gen. applied to a young girl, a ' lass,' wench.

Sc., Gen. used in a jocular way of ' a lively strapping wench,' with no ill signification (J.Ar.) ; If 'e ask me, she is a gui' well-faured hizzie, TWEEDDALE Moff (1896) 71. ne.Sc. Some o' them can go to balls an' dance wi' young hizzies, Gordonhaven (1887) 85. Mry. Strapping, braw, good-looking hizzies, HAY Lintie (1851) 13. Elg. Sorra tak' my gowkit muse, The hizzie's mad, TESTER Poems (1865) 97. Baff. The birth O' the maist bloomin hissy o' the earth, TAYLOR Poems (1787) 75. Abd. She's a fell ticht, gweed leukin hizzie tee, ALEXANDER Ain Flk. (1882) 210. Frf. When a man o' forty tak's up wi' an auld hizzy o' sixty, WILLOCK Rosetty Ends (1886) 37, ed. 1889. Per. A clever huzzy and a furthy quean, MONTEATH Dunblane (1835) 96, ed. 1877. w.Sc. She's a steerin' hizzy, but disna want for sense aithers, MACDONALD Settlement (1869) 62, ed. 1877. Fif. Canty Tibbie Sma', a sonsy mettle hizzy, DOUGLAS Poems (1806) 93. Dmb. To see the hizzies rank and file, Gawn thro' the dreel wi' a' their might, TAYLOR Poems (1827) 99. Rnf. A buxom hizzie . . . To make his butter, M°GIL-VRAY Poems (ed. 1862) 42. Ayr. An' buirdly chiels, and clever hizzies, Are bred in sic a way as this is, BURNS Twa Dogs (1786) l. 85. Lnk. A smart, clever bizzy she was, ROY Generalship (ed. 1895) 5. Lth. O honesty! my winsome hizzie, BRUCE Poems (1813) II. 30. Edb. A' the hyzzies round the place . . . Was stryvand sae that ony ane Wa'd danss wi' hym fu' faynly, RAMSAY Gentle Shep. (1725) 711, Scenery ed. Bwk. Our hind's daughters —most of them clever hizzies, HENDERSON Pop. Rhymes (1856) 80. Peb. Loud ' Goosies ' everywhere resound Frae hizzy, hind, or weane, *Lintoun Green* (1685) 68, ed. 1817. **Slk.** O the selfish hizzie, CHR. NORTH *Noctes* (ed. 1856) III. 157. **Dmf.** They'll be richt winsome hizzies Whan fed on beef, QUINN *Heather* (1863) 101. **Gall.** Hizzies gaen spangin' and flaiperin' about wi' white muslin frocks on, MACTAGGART *Encycl.* (1824) 27, ed. 1876. **Nhb.** Twae young lish clever hizzies, RICHARDSON *Borderer's Table-bk.* (1846) VII. 137; **Nhb.**¹ **Cum.** Monie a cliver lish hizzey was there, ANDERSON *Ballads* (ed. 1808) 66. **w.Yks.** A careless hussie maks mony thieves, *Prov.* in *Brighouse News* (July 23, 1887). **Lan.** Other folk wi' ther bits o' huzzies reawnd 'em an' noane o' ther own for t'mak 'em even, BRIERLEY *Irkdale* (1865) i; **Lan.**¹ **Dev.**¹ A comely bowerly woman her was, ... and a thorra paced huzzy, 6.

Hence (1) **Hizzie-fallow**, *sb.* a man who interferes with domestic management, a man who undertakes women's work; (2) **Huzzy-skep** or **-skip**, *sb.* (a) housewifery; (b) a workbasket or box; (c) in phr. *to have one's hand(s in one's huzzy-skep*, to be very busy, to be fully occupied in some household matter.

(1) Sc. HISLOP *Anecdote* (1874) 127. **w.Sc.** (JAM.) **Ayr.** There is a sort of false odium attached to men milking cows. His companions would call him hizzy-fallow and other nicknames, and offer him a petticoat to wear, *Agric. Surv. (ib.)* **Lth.** (JAM.) (2) **n.Sc.** 'Mair by chance than guid hissieskip,' a prov. phr. signifying that a thing happens rather by accident than proceeds from proper management (JAM.). (b) **Lin.** (J.T.F.) (c) **Sc.** My hand is in my hussyfe skep, Gudeman, as ye may see, CHAMBERS *Sngs.* (1829) I. 122. **Lin.** I've gotten my hands in my huzzy-skep (J.T.F.).

2. *Fig.* Applied to horses: a mare, a 'jade.'
Sc. The death of the grey mare, puir hizzie, was naething till't, SCOTT *Guy M.* (1815) xv. **Ayr.** I'se ne'er ride horse nor hizzie mair, BURNS *Inventory* (1786) l. 64.

3. A term of contempt or reproach for a woman or girl; a woman of bad character.
Sc. A set of impudent hizzies, too lazy to work, KEITH *Lisbeth* (1894) xviii. **Cai.**¹ **Abd.** She's a rude, vulgar hizzie, ALEXANDER *Johnny Gibb* (1871) xiii. **Kcd.** Nor ever ane could liken them to sic a forward hizzy, GRANT *Lays* (1884) 93. **Per.** An' there's that hizzie, her dochter! CLELAND *Inchbracken* (1883) 76, ed. 1887. **Fif.** The severest criticism of conduct indeed was directed to the frailer sex, progressively characterised by the epithets—'gilpy,' 'besom,' 'hizzie,' 'harry,' 'randy,' 'limmer,' COLVILLE *Vernacular* (1899) 18. **Rnf.** Ye thrawn, cauld-bluidit hizzie! PICKEN *Poems* (1813) I. 151. **Lnk.** [He] boozed wi' some fat-hippit hizzey, RODGER *Poems* (1838) 149, ed. 1897. **Dmf.** Gossip, the leesing auld hizzie, THOM *Jock o' Knowe* (1878) 31. **Slk.** Hoy, Heaster! thou fusionless hussey, HOGG *Poems* (ed. 1865) 372. **Gall.** Ill-tongued hizzy! CROCKETT *Raiders* (1894) v. **Wgt.** Said a loodspoken hissy, 'My word but he's spruce,' FRASER *Poems* (1885) 88. **Nhb.**¹ Only a term of reproach when a qualifying adjective makes it so. 'An ill-demised huzzy,' 'a bad huzzy.' **Dur.**¹ **Cum.** What'n manishment's 'tis That tou's gaen ti dee for a hizzy, GILPIN *Sngs.* (1866) 256. **n.Yks.** Thoo mucky huzzy (W.H.). **w.Yks.** Tha huzzy, tha's been actin summat at's nowt wi this bacca, *Dewsbre Olm.* (1865) 7; **w.Yks.**⁵ **Gen.** preceded by a strong adjective, and, frequently, by a string of them. **Lan.** A nasty huzzy, as hoo is, BRIERLEY *Fratchingtons* (1868) Frap i; You come of an ill stock, ye saucy hussy, AINSWORTH *Witches* (ed. 1849) bk. I. ix. **Stf.** Is it young Joe Bushell as made a huzzy o' you? MURRAY *Joseph's Coat* (188a) 35. **Not.**¹ Go on, you brazen-faced hussey. **War.** (J.R.W.) **Wil.** SLOW *Gl.* (189a). **Som.** SWEETMAN *Wincanton Gl.* (1885) An impudent young huzzy. **Dev.**¹ Mall hath'n [her peer], I'm sure, for a mirchivus hizzy, 7.

4. A needlecase, a cloth or leather case for needles, thread, &c.
Sc. For the hussy itself ... was a very valuable thing for a keepsake, SCOTT *Midlothian* (1818) xxxviii; Did I never see my mither makin' a hussey? FORD *Thistledown* (1891) 296. **Cai.**¹ **e.Lth.** He coft me a bonny hussie to mind me o' the day, HUNTER *J. Inwick* (1895) 149. **Gall.** A woman's purse, MACTAGGART *Encycl.* (1824). **Dur.**¹ **Lakel.**², **Cum.**¹⁴ **Wm.** Hannah's head is like her huzziff, full of all sorts of recollections, CLOSE *Lag.* (186a) 99. **w.Yks.** (J.T.), **w.Yks.**¹² **Lan.** A new-fleawered huzzif aw browt eaut o' th' teawn, BRIERLEY *Marlocks* (1867) 59. **ne.Lan.**¹, **s.Chs.**¹ **nw.Der.**¹ An article made of print or other textile fabric, from 5 to 6 inches wide and 12 to 18 inches long, with a number of pockets for needles and other small articles appertaining to sewing; and hung against the wall. **Not.** (J.H.B.), **Lin.** (J.T.F.), **n.Lin.**¹, **War.** (J.R.W.), **War.**², **Shr.**¹, **Oxf.**¹, **Suf.**¹ **Hmp.** GROSE (1790) *MS. add.* (M.) **Som.** SWEETMAN *Wincanton Gl.* (1885). **Dev.**¹ [Amer. *Dial. Notes* (1896) I. 389.]

HUSSIAN, HUSSICK, HUSSIF, see **Hushion, Hassock, Huss(e)y.**

HUSSLE, *v.* Ken.¹ [w⋅sl.] To wheeze, to breathe roughly or thickly. 'Jest listen to un how he hussles.'
Hence **Hussling,** *sb.* a wheezing, thick, heavy breathing. 'He had such a hussling on his chest.'

HUSSLE, see **Hustle,** *v.*¹

HUSSLEMENT, *sb.* Yks. [u⋅slment.] An' uproar; the crushing of a crowd. **e.Yks.**¹ *MS. add.* (T.H.)

HUSSOCK, *sb.* and *v.* Lei. Wor. Hrf. Glo. Ess. Also in forms **hassick-** Ess.; **hoosuck** Hrf.² Glo.¹; **hossack** Lei.¹; **houssack** w.Wor.¹ [w⋅sk.] **1.** *sb.* A hard, dry cough; a bad cold.
Wor. The pig had got a hussock (W.C.B.); A bit uv a hussock (H.K.). **w.Wor.**¹ **Hrf.²** I've got a hoosuck. **Glo.**¹
2. *v.* To cough in a peculiar dry way. **Hrf.²**
Hence (1) **Hussocked-up,** *ppl. adj.* choked with phlegm; (2) **Hussocking,** (a) *sb.* hoarseness, huskiness; (b) *ppl. adj.* of a cough: hacking, wearing; (3) **Hussocky,** *adj.* hoarse, husky.
(1) **Glo.**¹ (2, a) **Lei.**¹ **Wor.** 'Er 'ave a bad cough and a hussocking (H.K.). (b) **Wor.** (H K.) **Ess.** She has a hassicking cough—a very hassicking cough indeed! (A.S.P.) (3) **s.Wor.** *Berrow's Jrn.* (July 10, 1897).

HUSSOCK, see **Hassock.**

HUSSY, *v.* Ken.¹ [w⋅si.] To chafe or rub the hands when cold.

HUSSYFE, HUST, see **Huss(e)y, Hoast,** *sb.*¹

HUSTA, *int.* Sc. Also written husto; and in forms **hosta** Ags. (JAM.); **hueta** Abd. (*ib.*) [hu⋅sta.] An exclamation of surprise and hesitancy; 'see here,' 'see to it.'
Sc. 'Hech husto!' quo Habbie, 'I chaps ye,' JAMIESON *Pop. Ballads* (1806) I. 299. **Abd.** SHIRREFS *Poems* (1790) *Gl.* Abd., **Ags.** (JAM.)

HUSTACK, *sb.* Sh.I. Also written **hustak;** and in form **höstak.** A big, fat, clumsy woman. JAKOBSEN *Dial.* (1897) 48; S. & Ork.¹
[Prop. a hay-stack, Dan. *hÿ-stak,* see JAKOBSEN *Norsk in Sh.* (1897) 65.]

HUSTED, *pp.* Chs.¹² A term applied to the seed or seeding of the penny-grass, *Rhinanthus Crista-galli.*

HUSTER, *sb.* ? *Obs.* Rxb. (JAM.) Also in form **huister.** An uncomplimentary term for a woman.
'An auld huister o' a quean.' Supposed to include the idea of lasciviousness.

HUSTLE, *v.*¹ and *sb.* Var. dial. uses in Sc. Eng. and Amer. Also written **hussel** Nhb.¹ Glo. Hmp.; **hussle** Cum. e.Yks.¹ w.Yks.⁵; and in forms **isel** Hrt.; **osale** n.Yks.; **yessel** Dev.²; **yestle** Dev. [h)w⋅sl, h)u⋅sl.] **1.** *v.* In *comb.* (1) **Hustle-farrant,** one who is clothed in tattered garments. Lth., Rxb. (JAM.); (2) **Pitch and hussel,** a game of 'pitch and toss.' Glo. *Horae Subsecivae* (1777) 222.
2. To drive off, to drive away roughly; also with *off.* e.Yks.¹ Hrt. CUSSANS *Hist. Hrt.* (1879) III. 320. **3.** To scatter abroad, as apples among boys to be scrambled for. ne.Lan.¹
4. With *in*: to push forward.
Lth. Hustle in by your creepy and bustle your toes at the ingle, ELLIS *Pronunc.* (1889) V. 724.
5. With *up*: to wrap up.
Lan. Then, hustlin mysel up ith cloas, aw wurnt monny minnits afore aw fell into a seawnd sleep, STATON *Loominary* (c. 1861) 17.
6. To hasten, move quickly; with *off*: to retreat precipitately.
e.Yks.¹ **Nhp.** Then ere the parting moments hustle nigh, CLARE *Vill. Minst.* (1821) II. 80; Haymakers, hustling from the rain to hide, *ib.* 84. [Amer. *N. & Q.* (1890) 7th S. x. 53.]
7. To work hard, bustle about.
Ayr. He had to hustle for a living, AINSLIE *Land of Burns* (ed. 1892) *Pref.* 23. [Amer. FARMER.]
8. To bustle, to move about restlessly, to fidget.
Dev. I cud'n zlaip at all. A kipt on yestlin' about zo [in bed], *Reports Provinc.* (1893); **Dev.²** Do sit still, don't keep yesselin' about so.
Hence **Hustly** or **Osaly,** *adj.* restless.
n.Yks. He was varry ossly on his seat (I.W.); **n.Yks.²**

9. To shrug the shoulders.

Rxb. To move the clothes, particularly about the shoulders like a person who is itchy (JAM.). n.Cy. What macks thee hustle? (K.). Lakel.² What for does thoo hussle like that? Fooak 'll say thoo's t'scab. Cum. What's t'husslan at? yan med think thoo was swarmen (J.D.). n.Yks. What macks thee hustle? thou's mare fawse then silly, MERITON *Praise Ale* (1684) l. 480.

10. To make shift.

m.Yks.¹ Well, we must e'en hustle without it.

Hence Hussely-farrant, *adj.* strange, ill put together, uncommon-looking. Nhb.¹

11. To vex, annoy.

Not.¹ Lei.¹ Shay wur ivver so hustled ovver it.

12. *sb.* A crowd.

Nhp.¹ There was a wonderful hustle of people. The people were all of a hustle.

13. Rubbish.

w.Yks.² Before Au turned it into a garden, there was nowt but hustle there.

HUSTLE, *v.*² Ags. (JAM.) To emit a cooing sound, as an infant when pleased ; of a cat : to purr.

HUSTLEMENT, *sb.* Yks. Chs. Der. Lin. Also written husselment nw.Der.¹ ; hussalment n.Lin.¹ [u'slment.]

1. Household goods, furniture.

nw.Der.¹ n.Lin.¹ Th' landlord's ton'd ivery bit o' husselement they hed oot into th' bare streåt.

2. Odds and ends, a miscellaneous collection of persons or things.

n.Yks.², m.Yks.¹ w.Yks. GROSE (1790) *MS. add.* (P.) Chs.¹ In lumber or hustlements, as. 6d., *Township Bks. Pownal Fee* (1773).

[1. Precious ostelments, CHAUCER *Boethius*, bk. ii. pr. v. 85. OFr. *ostilement* (GODEFROY).]

HUSWIFE, see Hussa(e)y.

HUT, *sb.*¹ n.Lin.¹ [ut.] A small hovel, such as a dog-kennel or rabbit-hutch.

HUT, *sb.*² Der. Also written hutt nw.Der.¹ [ut.] The hob of a grate. Der.², nw.Der.¹

HUT, *sb.*³ Yks. Lin. e.An. [ut, ʊt.] A covering for a sore finger ; a finger-stall. See Hot(t, *sb.* 3.

e.Yks.¹ Lin. STREATFEILD *Lin. and Danes* (1884) 338. Lin.¹, n.Lin.¹ s.Lin. Hev y'h seën owt o' the hut that ah've dropt off 'n my finger? (T.H.R.)

Hence Hutkin, *sb.* a covering for a sore finger ; a finger-stall.

e.An.¹² Cmb.¹ That there cut on your finger's rare and angry ; you'd better put a hutkin on. Nrf. 'What's the matter with your finger?' 'Oh! I jammed it with the door, and am forced to wear this old hutkin' (W.R.E.). e.Suf. (F.H.)

HUT, *sb.*⁴ and *v.* Sc. Nhb. Yks. Also Wil. [h)ʊt, h)ut.]

1. *sb.* A heap. See Hot(t, *sb.* 2.

s.Sc., Cld. A hut of snow. A hut of dung, i. e. a heap of dung laid out in the field (JAM.). Nhb.¹ A muck hut is a heap of manure. A hut of turnips.

2. A lump of earth ; a ridge of clay in a river-bed. ne.Yks.¹, Wil.¹ Hence Hutty, *adj.* lumpy, as ground that does not break up well. Wil.¹ **3.** A fat, overgrown person ; a slattern. Ags., Cld. (JAM.)

4. A small stack built in a field.

Sc. (JAM.) Rnf. Hiding himself behind or beneath ane hutt of corn standing upon ye field, HECTOR *Judicial Records* (1876) 194.

5. *v.* To pile in heaps ; to put up grain in the fields ; to stack peats ; see below.

Sc. (JAM.) Nhb.¹ Wor busy huttin wor tormits. w.Yks. The peats are laid to dry and harden on the moor. . . After about a fortnight the cutters 'set' them, which is standing three pieces together, one piece on its side edge, slightly leaning over towards two others resting end-ways against it. After another fortnight they 'hut' them, which is setting six or eight more peats round these, and laying two or three flat on the top to shoot the rain off, LUCAS *Stud. Nidderdale* (c. 1882) 119.

HUT, *int.* Sc. A call to a careless horse. *N. & Q.* (1856) 2nd S. i. 395.

HUT, see Hit, *v.*, Hot(t.

HUTCH, *sb.*¹ and *v.*¹ Var. dial. uses in Sc. and Eng. [h)ʊtʃ, h)utʃ.] **1.** *sb.* A chest or coffer in which things are stored ; *fig.* a coffin.

n.Cy.¹ Nhb.¹ Specially applied to the town treasure chest, which was called 'the toon hutch.' At Morpeth 'each of the aldermen keeps

a key of the town's or corporation's hutch or box, on which there are seven different locks, and in which box is contained all the cash, books, papers, and records belonging to the borough, so that without the consent of the seven aldermen this box can never be opened,' MACKENZIE *Hist. Nhb.* (1825) II. 193, *note.* The Morpeth hutch now stands in the town clerk's office. Nhp.¹², Hnt. (T.P.F.) e.An.¹ An iron chest in which the registers are kept ; e.An.² Now chiefly used for the 'meal hutch' in the pantry, and the 'corn hutch' in the stable. Gen. . . it is any large chest with a falling lid. Suf. Usually one of those oaken chests with a lid, still to be seen in Suf. cottages, e.An. *Dy. Times* (1892) ; I keep that safe in my oud mingen hutch, FISON *Merry Suf.* (1899) 48 ; Suf.¹, e.Suf. (F.H.) Ess. A bran-new suit He'd claa'd out of his hutch, CLARK *J. Noakes* (1839) st. 57 ; A church hutch (H.H.M.) ; Ess.¹, w.Som.¹ Dev. I shall not sleep in peace within my hutch, PETER PINDAR *Whs.* (1816) I. 57.

2. A cupboard, esp. one in a wall.

n.Lin.¹, Nrf. (G.E.D.) Dev. She have two hundred good shillings in a bag, in my hutch, *Gent. Mag.* (1733) 331, ed. Gomme, 1886.

3. A hoard, esp. of money.

n.Cy. GROSE (1790). w.Yks. HUTTON *Tour to Caves* (1781) ; w.Yks.² Lan. He's piled a hutch o' brass up, BRIERLEY *Ab-o'th-Yate's Xmas Dinner* (1886) 4. ne.Lan.¹ The field-mouse makes a hutch of nuts for the winter. Der. A hutch of money, *Monthly Mag.* (1815) II. 297.

4. A covered recess in a barn, adjoining the 'floor,' into which the grain is shovelled as fast as it is threshed to await the winnowing. Also called Scuttle-hatch. w.Som.¹

5. A coop or cage for any animal. Nhp.¹² Hrf., Shr. BOUND *Provinc.* (1876).

6. A cottage.

Sc. GROSE (1790) *MS. add.* (C.) Lan. Keep yor own hutch clen, CLEGG *Sketches* (1895) 68. Cor. Sleepless from his hutch the lover stole, w.*Eclogue* in *Gent. Mag.* (1762) 287.

7. A trap, esp. of a box kind, used for catching fish, animals, or vermin bodily, in contradistinction to a gin.

Sus. A wooden trap for vermin, MORTON *Cyclo. Agric.* (1863). w.Som.¹ A rat-hutch, eel-hutch, salmon-hutch ; so also a big ugly carriage is a booby-hutch.

8. A half-door or 'hatch' to a barn, stable, or house. See Hatch, *sb.*¹ 1.

w.Som.¹ Many cottages have a hutch outside the door proper, often called the half-hutch.

9. A covering for a cut finger, a finger-stall. n.Lin.¹

10. The kind of basket or small wagon in which coals are brought from the pit.

Rnf. (JAM.) Lnk. 'Any men up yet?' he said to the man . . . who was in the act of drawing a loaded hatch, or 'hutch,' as it is commonly called, off the cage. . . 'Fetch my things from the engine-house, Jim,' he called over to a boy greasing the wheels of the 'hatches.' . . The coal is emptied out of the 'hutches' over a large iron screen set at an angle of about forty-five degrees into waggons, GORDON *Pyotshaw* (1885) 84. Dur. (A.B.) [Hutches or tubs, small waggons into which the miner loads his coal, *Gl. Lab.* (1894).]

11. A measure of coals, &c.

Sc. The coal hutch is two Winchester bushels (JAM.). Rnf. The price of these pyrites or copperas stones, by old contract, was a½d. per hutch of two hundred weight, *Agric. Surv.* 26 (*ib.*).

12. The upper part of a wagon ; a small cart ; also in *comp.* Hutch-wagon.

Hrt. They carry [pease] home on a hutch waggon, ELLIS *Mod. Husb.* (1750) IV. iii. 142. Ken. GROSE (1790) ; The large barrel on wheels, used for carrying away the contents of a cesspool (W.F.S.) ; Ken.¹ The hutch, or open box (sometimes enlarged by the addition of floats) which carries the corn or other load, and is supported by the wheels ; Ken.² e.Ken. We usually draw our corn to market in boarded carriages, here called hutches, YOUNG *Annals Agric.* (1784–1815) XXVIII. 419.

13. A miner's wash-trough in which he washes the ore from its refuse.

Der. MANLOVE *Lead Mines* (1653) (s.v. Wash-trough).

14. *Comp.* Hutch-work, small ore washed by a sieve. Cor.¹ **15.** An embankment to hinder the water from washing away the soil ; *fig.* an obstruction. Rxb. (JAM.), e.Yks.¹

16. A sluice for keeping back water.

w.Som.¹ Somebody . . . vor mirschy [mischief] pulled up the hutch, and let go'd all the mill-head.

17. A deep pool in a river underneath an overhanging bank. Rxb. (Jam.)

18. *v.* To lay up in a hutch or chest, to hoard ; to confine in a close place ; to cover.

Wm. We laid trimmiling an' hutched oursells ower heead e' bed, Southey *Doctor* (ed. 1848) 560. Lan. There's mony a pund theere . . . An' the little kangaroo has hutched o' this by without anybody knowin', Brierley *Cast upon World* (1886) iii ; We cawn't olez be hutched up i' th' dog kennels we're forced to live in, Clegg *Sketches* (1895) 207 ; Lan.[1]

19. To wash ore free from refuse in a water-trough.

Der. Manlove *Lead-Mines* (s.v. Wash-trough).

[1. Fr. *huche*, a hutch or binne (Cotgr.) ; MLat. *hutica*, 'cista' (Ducange).]

HUTCH, *v.*[2] and *sb.*[2] Wm. Yks. Lan. Der. Not. Lin. Wor. Ken. Also in forms huch Not.[2] ; outch w.Wor.[1] [h]utʃ, ʊtʃ.] **1.** *v.* To move anything as with a jerk ; to raise or lift with a jerk ; also *intr.* to move with a jerk or succession of jerks. See **Hitch,** *v.*[1]

e.Yks.[1] w.Yks. It's too low down. Tha'll nivver carry it like that. Hutch it up a bit (H.L.) ; So as it wodn't hutch up into mi neck-boil, it ud be better, Hartley *Clock Alm.* (1896) 44 ; w.Yks.[2] Lan. Hutching my chair near to the hob, Waugh *Tattlin' Matty,* 11 ; Let's be hutchin a bit nar whoam ! *ib.* Besom Ben, 10. Der. *Monthly Mag.* (1815) II. 297. nw.Der.[1] Not. (J.H.B.) ; Not.[2] 'Huch' yersen up a bit, I've got no rowm 'ere. s.Not. The child don't creep about the flooer; it hutches (J.P.K.). Lin. Streatfeild *Lin. and Danes* (1884) 338 ; Lin.[1] See how you've hutched up your under-clothes. n.Lin.[1] sw.Lin.[1] He sat on the pole, and hutched hisself across. The mare hutched him on to her shoulders. s.Lin. What ar' yur hutchin' about ! Why keànt yah keèp quiet (T.H.R.). Ken. He hutches himself along. Always hutchin' about in his chair (D.W.L.).

Hence **Hutching,** *ppl. adj.* fidgeting, in *comb.* **Hutching-fain,** restlessly glad.

Lan. Aw peped into my cot last neet, It made me butchin fain, Waugh *Sngs.* (1866) 19, ed. Milner.

2. To move nearer, to get closer together ; to lie close.

w.Yks. Tha's seen Jim ! He hutch'd cloise to me in a bit, Hartley *Ditt.* (1863) 25. Lan. Let's hutch together, Mally, wolfe, Bealey *Field Flowers* (1866) 34 ; Th' cottage were hutched up under elm, beech, and saplin branches, Clegg *Sketches* (1895) 2 ; Lan.[1], e.Lan.[1], m Lan.[1] s Lan. A conductor of an omnibus or tram might say to the passengers, 'Hutch a bit closer there' (S.W.). Not. Hutch up to me (W.H.S.).

3. To shrug the shoulders.

w.Yks.[1] Lan. Davies *Races* (1856) 234 ; At Bury, if a small boy refuses to obey and rounds his shoulders to show his obstinacy, his mother will say, 'What art tha hutchin' at !' (G.H.H.) ne.Lan.[1], nw.Der.[1]

4. To crouch down ; also used *fig.*

Lan. Fortin hutches at mi feet, Clegg *David's Loom* (1894) v ; Th' poor freeten't brid hutchin itsel into t'fur corner, *ib. Sketches* (1895) 41. w.Wor.[1] A hare is said to 'outch on 'er farm.'

Hence **Hutched,** *ppl. adj.* bent ; huddled together.

I wonder how thou can for shame . . . sit keawerin' theer, hutch't of a lump, like garden-twod, Waugh *Chim. Corner* (1874) 151, ed. 1879. Der. Hutched together like an owd man o' seventy, Ward *David Grieve* (1892) vi.

5. In a vague sense : to be.

Lan. He's as ill-tempert an' cross-graint as he con hutch, Wood *Sketches,* 34.

6. Phr. *to hutch and abide,* to bear, endure.

Lan. I could hardly hutch an' abide while he wur agate o' talkin', Waugh *Heather* (ed. Milner) II. 289 ; Boh e con ardly hutch un aboide, iz so stark wi' th' kronikle, Scholes *Tim Gamwattle* (1857) 3.

7. *sb.* A jerk ; a hoist ; also in phr. *on the hutch,* on the fidget.

s.Not. Gie 'im a hutch up. They were all on the hutch, when they thought you was goin to leave (J.P.K.).

8. Phr. *to warm one's hutch,* to give one a thrashing.

Lan. Aw'll warm his hutch for him to-morn . . . Aw'll knock him deawn as flat as a pancake when aw catch him agen, Wood *Hum. Sketches,* 22 ; At Bury a mother will say to an obstinate child, 'What art the hutchin' at ! Aw'll warm thi hutch for thi, if tha doesn't do as aw tell thi' (G.H.H.).

9. A bout, turn. w.Yks.[2]

HUTCH, *sb.*[3] Sc. Yks. Lan. [hʊtʃ, ʊtʃ.] **1.** A small heap ; a small rick or temporary stack of corn. Sc. (Jam. Suppl.) **2.** Comb. (1) **Hutch-backed.** e.Lan.[1] ; (2) **rigged,** humpbacked. w.Yks.[1] **3.** An opprobrious term applied to ill-favoured persons, esp. women. m.Yks.[1]

HUTCH, see **Which.**

HUTCH-CROOK, *sb.* Yks. **1.** A crooked stick. (Hall.) **2.** The two beams which tie at a gable end. w.Yks. (J.S.)

HUTCHIN, *sb.* Chs.[13] A large slice of bread or lump of meat.

HUTHER, *sb.*[1] Lin.[1] [Not known to our correspondents.] The state of fermentation.

The berry wine is in a huther.

HUTHER, *sb.*[2] and *v.* n.Sc. (Jam.) [Not known to our correspondents.] **1.** *sb.* A slight shower; a wetting mist. **2.** *v.* To fall in slight showers ; to rain intermittently.

HUTHER, see **Howder,** *v.*[1], **Whether.**

HUTHERIKIN-LAD, *sb.* ? *Obs.* n.Cy. Dur. Nhp. A ragged youth ; an uncultivated boy ; a hobbledehoy. N.Cy.[1] Dur. Grose (1790). Nhp.[1] Cf. **hudderon.**

HUTHERIN, *sb.* Sc. **1.** A young heifer ; a beast between the state of cow and calf. Ags., Lth. (Jam.) **2.** A stupid fellow. Or.I., S. & Ork.[1] Cf. **huddering,** *sb.* **3.** A stalk of greens raised from the seed of common greens and cabbages when they grow too near together ; also in *comp.* **Hutherin-stock.** Fif. (Jam.)

HUTHER-MY-DUDS, *sb.* Sc. [Not known to our correspondents.] A ragged person ; a tatterdemalion. Fif. (Jam.) Cf. **hudderon.**

HUTHIR, *v.* and *sb.* Sc. Irel. Cum. Also in forms howder Cum. ; howthir Bnff.[1] **1.** *v.* To walk in a clumsy, hobbling manner.

Sc. (Jam.) Bnff.[1] 'He cam howthirin' an cloutherin' up the rod.' Most commonly applied to women. 'She cam hutherin' up the rod.' Joined with such words as carry, lift, &c. 'She needna be howthirin' and cairryin' that muckle bairn.' Cum. Linton *Lake Cy.* (1864) 305 ; Gl. (1851).

2. To do work in a hasty, slovenly manner.

Bnff.[1] Rnf. Picken *Poems* (1813) Gl.

Hence (1) **Huthering** or **Hutheron,** *adj.* confused ; awkward; showing haste in walking, or in working ; of a stout woman : slovenly in dress ; (2) **Huthery,** *adj.* untidy.

(1) Sc. Unco wary should we be To leuk before we loup ; Nor e'er, in huth'ron haste, advance. Wilson *Poems* (1790) in *Lit. Prose* (1876) II. 40. Cai.[1], Bnff.[1] Rnf. Now I'se be doon wi' huthran fumle, As I'm aye unca redd to bumle, Picken *Poems* (1788) 98 (Jam.); Aff the bank in huth'rin' hurry, Heels-o'er-head he tumml'd in, *ib.* (ed. 1813) II. 47. (2) N.I.[1]

3. *sb.* An awkward, hasty walker ; a slovenly worker ; a slattern.

Bnff.[1] Per. Thou clorty huther o' a wife, Thou doun draught o' thy husband's life, Stewart *Character* (1857) 61.

4. Unbecoming haste. Bnff.[1]

HUTICK, see **Utick.**

HUTIE-CUITTIE, *sb.* Rxb. (Jam.) [Not known to our correspondents.] A copious draught of any intoxicating liquor.

HUTN-TRUTN, *adj.* Sh.I. Surly, ill-tempered. (W.A.G.), S. & Ork.[1]

[Norw. dial. *truten,* angry, ill-tempered (Aasen).]

HUT(S, see **Hoot(s.**

HUTTER, *sb.* Sh.I. A mass ; a heap. S. & Ork.[1]

HUTTER, *v.* n.Cy. Yks. [u·tə(r). To stammer, stutter ; to speak with difficulty. n.Cy. (Hall.), n.Yks.[124], w.Yks.[1] Cf. **hotter,** *v.* 9.

HUTTOCK, see **Hattock,** *sb.*[1]

HUTTON, *sb. Obs.* or *obsol.* Lin. [u·tən.] A fingerstall. (M.P.) ; Lin.[1] Cf. **hut,** *sb.*[1]

HUTTY-BACK, *sb.* Lakel. A hunchback, a hunchbacked person.

Wm.[1] E canna du mitch, pooer chap, es nobbet a hutty-back.

Hence **Hutty-backed,** *adj.* hunchbacked, round-shouldered ; having a curved spine.

Lakel.[2] Cum. Still used amongst old people and country folk (J.A.). Wm. He's gian sadly hutty-backt (B.K.) ; Wm.[1] Well known here and in freq. use.

HUUY, HUVAL, HUVEL, HUVER, see Hui, Hovel, *sb.*², Huffle, *v.*², Hover, *v.*¹

HUVIE, *sb.* Or.I. A large straw basket used as a bag-net for trout. (JAM. *Suppl.*)

HUVIL, -VEL, -VER, see Hovel, *sb.*², Hover, *v.*¹, *adj.*²

HUVVERS, *sb. pl.*¹ Suf. A disease to which pigs are subject. **Suf.** (S.P.H.) **e.Suf.** In common use (F.H.).

Hence **Huvvery,** *adj.* of a pig: affected with the 'huvvers.' **e.Suf.** A pig affected with huvvers is said to be huvvery, as is a person unsteady on his legs, or a load of corn that looks as if it would fall off the cart, &c. (F.H.)

HUVVERS, *sb. pl.*² Lin. [u·vəz.] Ridges of land separating, in unenclosed lands, one tenant's fields from another's.

The space between the land of different proprietors or occupiers, in an uninclosed field, the grass of which is mown for hay, THOMPSON *Hist. Boston* (1856) 710 ; **Lin.**¹

HUVVIL, HUWE, HUX, HUXEN, HUXON, see Hovel, *sb.*², Heugh, Hock, *sb.*¹

HUY, *sb.* Sh.I. Thin hair. S. & Ork.¹

[Norw. dial. *hy*, the down on the cheek, fine small grass (AASEN) ; ON. *hý*, 'lanugo' (VIGFUSSON).]

HUY, *int.* Suf. Ken. Also in form **hwee** Suf. A cry used in driving pigs. e.Suf. (F.H.), Ken.²

HUYA, see Huia.

HUYLLE. Sh.I. A word applied to anything which does not justify appearances. S. & Ork.¹

HUYT, HUZ, HUZBURD, HUZHY-BAA, see Hait. Us, *pron.*, Hosebird, Hush-a-ba(a.

HUZZ, *v.* and *sb.* Lakel. Yks. Lan. Chs. Der. Lin. Shr. Also written huz w.Yks. Chs.¹ Shr.¹ ; and in form **hiuz** Lakel.² [h)uz.] **1.** *v.* To buzz, hum, make a whirring noise.

w.Yks. To snert and titter and huz, SKIPTON *Farmer Giles* (1834) Pref. **s.Chs.**¹, nw.Der.¹ **Lin.** Summun 'ull come ater meä mayhap wi' 'is kittle o' steäm, Huzzin' an' maäzin the blessed feälds wi' the Divil's oän teäm, TENNYSON *N. Farmer, Old Style* (1864) st. 16. **n.Lin.**¹

Hence **Huzzer,** the grasshopper warbler, *Locustella naevia.* Lan. *Science Gossip* (1882) 164.

2. Comb. Huzz-buzz, (1) the common cockchafer, *Melolontha vulgaris.* Chs.¹, s.Chs.¹, Shr.¹ ; (2) a buzz ; a tumult. Chs.¹²

3. Of a liquid : to come rushing through some outlet.

Lakel.² Water'll fair huzz throo a lal whol ; seea will bliud oot ov a pig throoat. **w.Yks.** (J.W.)

4. *sb.* A buzz, hum ; a clamour, tumult.

w.Yks. (J.W.) **Lan.** The huzz of the bobbin wheel, BRIERLEY *Layrock* (1864) i. **Chs.**³ There were a pretty huzz i' th' house.

HUZZAF, HUZZEY, HUZZIN, HUZZLE, HUZZOCK, see Huss(e)y, Hoosing, Hoozle, *v.*¹, Hassock.

HWEE, HWICK, see Huy, *int.*, Quick.

HWIDD, *sb.* Sh.I. In phr. *to have taken a hwidd*, to be sulky. JAKOBSEN *Dial.* (1897) 39.

[Norw. dial. *kvida*, dislike, disgust (AASEN).]

HWINKLED-FACED, *adj.* Or.I. Lantern-jawed. S. & Ork.¹

HWRINKET, *sb.* and *adj.* Ayr. (JAM.) [Not known to our correspondents.] **1.** *sb.* Unbecoming language.

2. *adj.* Perverse, stubborn.

HWUM, HY, HYAL, see Home, Hie, *int.*, *v.*², Hale, *adj.*

HYAN, *sb.* Obs. n.Cy. (HALL.) w.Yks.¹ ne.Lan.¹ A fatal disease among cattle, in which their bodies instantly become putrid.

HYANK, *v.* and *sb.* Sc. **1.** *v.* To cut in large slices. Per. (G.W.), Slk. (JAM.) **2.** *sb.* A lump, a big piece or slice. Per. (G.W.)

HYAUVE, *adj.* Sc. That kind of colour in which black and white are combined, or appear alternately ; grey. Cf. **chauve,** *adj.* **Bnff.** A hyauve cow (JAM.).

HYCHLE, *v.* Lnk. (JAM.) To walk, carrying a burden with difficulty. Cf. **hechle.**

HYDE, *sb.* Sc. A disagreeable fellow.

Bnff. He's a naisty hyde o' a chiel, GREGOR *Notes to Dunbar* (1893) 52.

VOL. III.

HYDGY, HYE, HYEL, HYELL, see Hedge, *sb.*¹, Hay, *sb.*², Hie, *int.*, *v.*², Hale, *adj.*, Hole, *sb.*¹

HYEMMELT, HYESTY, see Hamald, Hasty, *adj.*

HYKE, HYKERIE-PYKERIE, HYLD, see Hike, *v.*, Hickery-pickery, Hold, *v.*

HYLDEN, *sb.* Obs. Glo. A term of contempt : a great, foul, hulky, filthy creature such as a butcher or hangman ; a mean, base fellow ; also a forward wench, apt to turn up her heels. *Horae Subsecivae* (1777) 223.

[Hilding, hylding, an idle jade (K.) ; *Caguemaille*, a greedy wretch, covetous hilding, COTGR. ; Une lasche godde, a slothful hylding, *ib.* ; Out on her, hilding, SHAKS. *R. & J.* III. v. 169.]

HYLE, HYLET, see Heel, *v.*¹, Hile, *sb.*², Hilet.

HYLT, *pp.* Obs. Glo. Ken. Also in form **hild** Glo, Flayed, skinned.

Glo. Y w'ood t'wert hild, SMYTH *Lives Berkeleys* (1066-1618) III. 93, ed. 1885. **Ken.** (K.)

[I will as soone be hylt, As waite againe for the mooneshine in the water, HEYWOOD *Prov.* (1546), ed. 1867, 36. OE. *hyldan* (*Lev.* i. 6).]

HYMENANNY, *sb.* I.Ma. A large shell.

A bullet as big as a hymenanny fit to drop the devil's granny, BROWN *Witch* (1889) 107.

HYMNLER, *sb.* Sc. A singer of hymns.

Five's the hymnlers o' my bower, Four's the gospel-makers, CHAMBERS *Pop. Rhymes* (1870) 45. [' Hymnlers ' prob. the authors of Job, Psalms, Proverbs, Song of Solomon, and Lamentations.]

HYN, HYNAIL, HYND(E, see Hine, Hanniel, Hind, *sb.*¹

HYND-WYND, *adv.* Sc. [Not known to our correspondents.] Straight ; by the nearest way.

Rxb. He went hynd-wynd to the apples, just after I forbade him (JAM.).

HYNE, see Hind, *sb.*¹, Hine.

HYNNY-PYNNY, *sb.* Som. Dev. A game of marbles ; see below.

A hole of some extent was made in an uneven piece of ground, and the game was to shoot the marbles at some object beyond the hole without letting them tumble into it (HALL.).

HYNT, HYPAL(L, see Hent, *v.*¹, Hipple, *v.*²

HYPAL, *sb.* Sc. Also written **hyple.** A badly-dressed person. Cf. **hipple,** *sb.*² **3.**

Abd., Per. Common. He's a throughther hypal (G.W.).

HYPE, *sb.* Sc. A big person of a not very comely appearance, used sometimes by way of approval, and sometimes as a mark of disrespect.

Bnff.¹ She's nae an ill hype o' dehm aifter a'. He's a cantakarous hype o' a cheel. **Abd.** (G.W.)

HYPE, see Hipe, *sb.*¹, *v.*²²

HYPOCREETIES, *sb. pl.* Sc. Hypocrisies, shams.

Lnk. You've nae doobt come wi' mair o' yer infernal hypocreeties, but I winna listen to them, GORDON *Pyotshaw* (1885) 156.

HYPOCRIP, *sb.* Sc. Sus. [h)i·pəkrip.] **1.** A hypocrite.

Lnk. He's a deceitfu', twa-faced hypocrip, GORDON *Pyotshaw* (1885) 131. **Sus.** EGERTON *Flks. and Ways* (1884) 13.

2. A lame person. Cf. **hypocrite, 2.**

Sus. The master calls me a hypocrip (a lame person) he does. Now if I be a hypocrip (a hypocrite), I wish somebody would take one of these bats, and hide me bang out, EGERTON (*l. c.*).

HYPOCRITE, *sb.* Suf. Sus. **1.** One who is indisposed, unwell.

e.Suf. I've been a real old hypocrite for more than a week (F.H.).

2. A lame person. Cf. **hypocrip, 2.**

Sus.¹ Yes, she's a poor afflicted creature ; she's quite a hypocrite ; she can't walk a step without her stilts.

HYPOCRITING, *ppl. adj.* Suf. Deceptive ; crippling.

I ha' been hully pa'ad over with the rheumatic ; that fare a wonnerful hypocriting disease, *e.An. Dy. Times* (1892a).

HYPOTHEC, *sb.* Sc. **1.** A pledge or legal security for payment of rent or money due.

Sc. As we hold your rights, title-deeds, and documents in hypothec, shall have no objection to give reasonable time—say till next money term, SCOTT *Antiquary* (1816) xli.

2. *Obs.* The landlord's claim to the property of a tenant, which is prior to that of any other creditor.

Sc. MORTON *Cyclo. Agric.* (1863) ; The landlord's hypothec over

Q q

the crop and stocking of his tenants is a tacit legal hypothec provided by the law itself. . . It gives a security to the landlord over the crop of each year for the rent of that year, and over the cattle and stocking on the farm for the current year's rent, BELL *Law Dict.* (1807-8) (JAM.). Lth. Cumbrous restraints frae tacks he'll weed, An' root out auld hypothec, LUMSDEN *Sheep-head* (1892) 160.

Hence **Hypothecate**, *v.* to impose a pledge for payment.

Sc. The rule in regard to the crop is, that each crop stands hypothecated to the landlord for the rent that year of which it is the crop, BELL *Law Dict.* (1807-8) (JAM.).

3. Phr. *the whole hypothec,* the whole concern.

Abd. Johnny . . . got the whole 'hypothec' into the cart, ALEXANDER *Johnny Gibb* (1871) i. Kcd. In his vain opinion kept 'The hale hypothec richt,' GRANT *Lays* (1884) 56. Frf. Ye've drucken the haill hypothec, INGLIS *Ain Flk.* (1895) 9. Per. We've juist tae find anither, and that's the hale hypothec, IAN MACLAREN *Auld Lang Syne* (1895) 100. Luk. Gin she had her ain sweet will, she'd gie the haell hypothec awa' to Tam, Dick, and Harry, GORDON *Pyotshaw* (1885) 14. Lth. It wad either poison the whole hypothec, or blaw them up, or maybe baith, STRATHESK *More Bits* (ed. 1885) 63.

HYPPAL, HYRNE, HYSCH, see **Hipple,** *v.*², **Herne, Hush,** *sb.*⁸

HYSE, *v.* and *sb.* Sc. **1.** *v.* To romp; to banter. Bnff.¹ **2.** To brag, vaunt; to bluster, rant. Abd. (JAM.) **3.** *sb.* An uproar; a wild riot; a frolic.

Bnff.¹ Abd. There was ane in the poopit haudin a terrible hyse, ALEXANDER *Johnny Gibb* (1871) xviii.

4. A vaunt; a cock-and-bull story; a practical joke. Bnff.¹, Abd., Cld. (JAM.)

HY-SPY, see **Hie-spy.**

HYSSY-PYSSY, *sb.* Som. Dev. The game of 'hynny-pynny,' q.v. (HALL.)

HYSTE, *sb.* Ken.¹ [eist.] A call; a signal.

Just give me a hyste, mate, when 'tis time to goo.

HYSTE, see **Hoist,** *v.*¹

HYTE, *adj.* Sc. Also written **hite** Abd.; and in form **hyt** Sc. [hait.] **1.** Mad, raging; 'gyte'; freq. in phr. *to gae hyte,* to act as if one were mad.

n.Sc. (JAM.) Abd. If ye be angry, Bessy may gae hyte, Gin

ony's blam'd, she's sure to get the wyte, SHIRREFS *Poems* (1790) 66. Frf. May a' rin hyte that mean to tease him, MORISON *Poems* (1790) 8. w.Sc. The tongue as lang as a cow's tail, and wags as weel as when they gang hyte in simmer, CARRICK *Laird of Logan* (1835) 252. Rnf. They cast up my pickle snuff, An' pit me hyte, PICKEN *Poems* (1813) I. 132. Ayr. What the deevil mak's you sae hyte about the fellow! GALT *Sir A. Wylie* (1822) xciv. Luk. Bodies like hyte A' wrang it, WATSON *Poems* (1853) 44. Peb. Wi' me gae hame 'Ore hunger mak's me hyt, *Lintoun Green* (1685) 64, ed. 1817.

2. *Comb.* **Hyte-styte,** (1) acting as if mad, in a state of madness; (2) arrant nonsense; (3) utter ruin. Bnff.¹

HYTER, *v.*, *sb.* and *adv.* Bnff.¹ **1.** *v.* To walk with tottering steps; to work in a weak, unskilful manner.

Hence **Hytering,** *ppl. adj.* weak; stupid; unskilful.

2. *sb.* The act of working in a weak, confused manner; the act of walking with tottering steps; a state of confusion; ruin. **3.** Nonsense. **4.** A weak, stupid person. **5.** *adv.* With weak, tottering steps. **6.** In a state of ruin.

He did weel a filie, but he's a' hyter noo, an hiz taen't the sellan o' spunks an' cabbitch.

7. *Comb.* (1) **Hyter-skyter,** (a) the act of walking with tottering steps; (b) a great deal of arrant nonsense; (c) to walk with tottering steps; (d) with weak steps; in a state of ruin; (2) **-styte,** (a) nonsense; stupidity; (b) utter ruin; (c) silly, stupid, like one mad; (d) stupidly, madly; (e) an exclamation of dissent or disbelief; (3) **-styter,** (a) to walk with tottering steps; (b) with weak, tottering steps; in a state of ruin.

HYTERPRITES, *sb. pl.* Nrf. Antics. (E.M.)

HYTER-SPRITE, *sb.* e.An.¹ A beneficent fairy.

HYUCK-FINNIE, *adj.* Sh.I. Used of anything rare or curious.

Auld bjok faqi tings [old curiosities, curious old things], JAKOBSEN *Norsk in Sh.* (1897) 63.

[Repr. ON. *haugfunnit,* found in a 'how' or barrow; see JAKOBSEN (*l.c.*).]

HYUK, HYUL, HYULE, see **Hook,** *sb.*¹, **Hull,** *v.*², **Hewl.**

HYVER, *v.* Sh.I. To saunter, lounge; to idle. S.& Ork.¹

Hence **Hyveral,** *sb.* a lounger; an idle, lazy person. *ib.*

HYVER, HYZE, see **Hover,** *v.*¹, **Heeze.**

I

I. Apart from the influence of neighbouring sounds OE. ĭ has remained unchanged in the modern dialects.

II. OE. **y** (i-umlaut of **u**) has generally become **i** except that it has become **e** in those dialects where OE. ȳ̆ has become ī.

III. The normal development of OE. ī is:—

1. ai in Dur. (rarely), Cum. (see 3), Wm., n.Yks., w.Yks. (also ǫi, especially in those parts bordering on Lan. and Der.), I.Ma., nw.Der., n. and m.Lin., Rut. (also ai), Nhp. (also ǫi), n.Wor., m.Shr., Cmb., e.Suf., w.Suf., s.Sur., w.Sus., w.Som., n.Dev., sw.Dev., Cor. **2.** əi in sw.Nhp., s.War., s.Wor., s.Shr., Mon., Hrf., Rdn., Glo., Oxf., Brks., Bck. (see **4**), Nrf., n.Ken., Hmp., I.W., Wil., Dor., e.Som. **3.** ei in Sc. (rarely ai), Nhb., Dur. (see **1**), Cum. (rarely), e.Yks. (also ā), n.Stf., Pem. **4.** ǫi in w.Yks. (see **1**), Lan., Chs., Flt., Dnb., Stf., Der., Not., s.Lin., Rut. (see **1**), Lei., Nhp. (also ai), War. (see **2**), Shr. (see **1, 2**), n. and s.Bck., Hrt., Hnt., Ess., e.Ken., Sur. (see **1**), e.Sus. **5.** ā in ne., e. and m.Yks., se.Lan. (also ǭ).

IV. The normal development of OE. **y** (i-umlaut of ū) has been the same as that of OE. ī with the following exceptions:—

It has become (1) ī in Glo., Bdf., Cmb., Nrf., Suf., Ess., Ken., e.Sus., Dev., Cor.; (2) ei in nw.Der., Chs.; (3) ai in s.Lin.

I-, *pref.* Irel. w.Cy. Before *pp.* repr. OE. **ge-.** See **A,** *pref.*

w.I. Ilet, HALL *Irel.* (1841) II. 161. **w.Som.**[1] Used by writers indifferently with *a.* . . Very freq. the use of the prefix in the dialect supplants the ordinary past inflection, whether strong or weak, as in u-bee, u-baeg, for been, begged. 'We hant i-bake no cakes to-day.' 'They zaid how twidn be i-know by nobody 'vore the votes was all a-told, and then twidn on'y be i-know by they that told em.'

I, *pron.* Var. dial. uses in Sc. Irel. and Eng. [The unemphatic or unstressed forms are printed in italics. Sh.I. ai, *a*, ə; Or.I. ai, ə; Cai. Elg. a; Bnff. Abd. ai, *a*; Kcd. ai (ei), ə; Frf. ai (ā), *a*, ə; Per. ai, *a*; Fif. a, ə; s.Sc. ā, *a*; Ayr. Lnl. a; Lth. ai, *a*, ə; Edb. ā, *a*; Hdg. Bwk. Rxb. Dmf. Gall. Wgt. ā (a), *a*; Ir. ai, *a*; Nhb. Dur. ā, *a*; Cum. ā (ai), *a*, ə, enclitic *i*; Wm. ā (ǭ), *a*, ə; n.Yks. ā (ai), *a*, enclitic *i*; ne.Yks. e.Yks. m.Yks. ā, *a*; w.Yks. ai (ǭ), ǫ, *a*, enclitic *i*; ne.Lan. ǫi (ai), ǫ, *a*; m.Yks. s.Lan. ǫi, ǫ; se.Lan. ǭ, ǫ; I.Ma. ǫi, ǫ; Chs. Stf. ǫi, ǫ; Der. ǫi (ǭ), ǫ; Not. ǫi, ǫ; n.Lin. ai, *a*, ə; m.Lin. ǫi, ə; s.Lin. ǫi, *a*; Rut. Lei. Nhp. e.War. w.War. ǫi; s.War. ǫi (əi); n.Wor. ǫi (ai); m.Wor. ai, *a*; s.Wor. ǫi (əi); Shr. ai (əi); Hrf. əi; Pem. ei; Glo. ai; Oxf. əi, ǫ; Brks. əi; Bck. əi (ǫi); Bdf. Hrt. Hnt. Cmb. ǫi; Nrf. n.Suf. əi; e.Suf. ai, ə; w.Suf. ǫi, ə; Ess. əi; n.Ken. əi; e.Ken. ǫi; Sur. ǫi, ə; Sus. ǫi, ə; Hmp. Wil. Dor. e.Som. āi; w.Som. āi (ā), *ai, a, ə*; Dev. Cor. ai.]

I. Dial. forms: (1) A, see A, *pron.* IV ; (2) Aa, (3) Ah, (4) Ai, (5) Au, (6) Aw, (7) Aye, (8) Ch, (9) Che, (10) E, (11) Ee, (12) Eea, (13) Eh, (14) Eigh, (15) Ea, (16) Ez, (17) Ha, (18) Hah, (19) Hi, (20) Ich, (21) Iché, (22) Ichy, (23) Ice, (24) Ia, (25) Ise, (26) Iah, (27) Iss, (28) Ize, (29) O, (30) Oi, (31) Utch, (32) Utchy. [On the forms under numbers 12, 15, 16, 23-28 see ELWORTHY *Gram. w.Som.* (1877) 35 note,

PRINCE L. L. BONAPARTE *Trans. Lond. Phil. Soc.* (1875-6) 581.]

(1) **Sc.** If not emphatic (D.N.). **Sh.I.** A'm [I have] shūrely shakken me inside loose, *Sh. News* (Aug. 27, 1898). **Elg.** A got a fricht the ither nicht, TESTER *Poems* (1865) 106. **n.Ir.** A saw naebuddy that a kenned till a got tae Bilfast, LYTTLE *Paddy McQuillan*, 9. **Dur.**[1] **Cum.** A's fain to see thee, an a's laith to part, GRAHAM *Gwordy* (1778) l. 4. **w.Yks.** (J.W.) **Chs.**[8] All [I'll]. **n.Lin.** (M.P.), m.Wor. (H.K.) (2) **Nhb.** Aa mind yen day at Aa went alang, HALDANE *Geordy's Last* (1878) 6; **Nhb.**[1] **Cum.** Aā was at yan o' ther girt yearly Club days, DICKINSON *Cumbr.* (1875) 5; **Cum.**[1] **Wm.**[1] Aa's vary glad to see tha. (3) **ne.Sc.** Ah hid a strange dream, *Gordonhaven* (1887) 50. **Nhb.** Ah'll tell thee, though, fayther, CLARE *Love of Lass* (1890) I. 53; **Nhb.**[1] **Dur.** B'd Ah cudn't sleep, EGGLESTONE *Betty Podkin's Visit* (1877) 3. **Cum.** When I is emphatic (E.W.P.). **n.Yks.** Ah'll trust i' God, TWEDDELL *Clevel. Rhymes* (1875) 33. **ne.Yks.**[1] **e.Yks.**[1] Before consonants, for euphony's sake ; frequently becomes I before vowels. **w.Yks.** Ah'm fit to think there's nobbud here an' there one, CUDWORTH *Dial. Sketches* (1884) 12. **Chs.**[1] When not emphatic. **Stf.** Ah couldn't groind without un, *Good Wds.* (1869) 171. **Not.** No, ah wain't, PRIOR *Renie* (1895) 12. **n.Lin.** (M.P.) (4) **e.Dev.** Deue let ai year'n teue! PULMAN *Sng. Sol.* (1860) viii. 13. (5) **Lan.** It's as mich as au con offord, BRIERLEY *Daisy Nook* (1859) 24. **Der.** Au have iten mon, HOWITT *Rur. Life* (1838) I. 150. (6) **Abd.** It's a caul' up-throu place, aw b'lieve, ALEXANDER *Ain Flk.* (1882) 34. **Nhb.** Aw think, WILSON *Pitman's Pay* (1843) 3 ; **Nhb.**[1] **Dur.**[1] **Wm.**[1] Aw've gitten a terrible cowld. **w.Yks.** If aw new a barn o' mine Wur born ta leead my life, PRESTON *Poems, &c.* (1864) 6. **Lan.** Aw've done, CLEGG *David's Loom* (1894) ii ; **Lan.**[1] **e.Lan.**[1] **Chs.**[12] **nw.Der.**[1] (7) **w.Yks.**[1] (8) †**Obs.** Wor. 'Ch 'oonder.' Constantly used by Farmer Hemns of Broomhall (H.K.). (9) **Dev.** Che know not what you mean by numicate [communicate] it to me, *Obliging Husband* (1717) 9 ; Ther'll be vine messings an' muckings avore zennet, che'll warndy ! MADOX-BROWN *Dwale Bluth* (1876) bk. 1. i. [For further information see Ch.] (10) **ne.Yks.**[1] Mun ē cum ! **w.Yks.** A! what ivver mun e do ! BYWATER *Gossips*, 21. **nw.Der.**[1] (11) **Cum.** An' I's cum't to advise thee,—'at is ee, GILPIN *Ballads* (1866) 256. **w.Yks.** 'All well at the Heights!' 'Eea, f'r owt ee knaw,' BRONTË *Wuthering Hts.* (1847) xxxii. (12) **w.Som.** Aa'y kn ab-m, kaa'n ëes! [I can have it, can I not!] Bee gwaa'yn, bae·ŭn ëes! [I am going, am I not!], ELWORTHY *Gram.* (1877) 34 ; Ēes is only used interrogatively and finally, *ib.* 35. **Dev.** GROSE (1790). (13) **Lan.**[1] Aw'm donnin this lad as fast as eh con, WAUGH *Sneck-Bant* (1868) iii. (14) **w.Yks.**[1] (15) **w.Som.**[1] Enclitic. **Dev.** *Monthly Mag.* (1810) I. 435; GROSE (1790) *MS. add.* (M.) (16) **w.Som.**[1] Enclitic. (17) **w.Yks.** Am full a noan sich stuff at ha naw on, Ben, TOM TREDDLE-HOYLE *Ben Bunt* (1838) 4. (18) **n.Yks.**[2] Hah's boun. (19) **m.Wor.** (H.K.) (20) [For the use of Ich see Ch.] (21) **Som.** JENNINGS *Obs. Dial. w.Eng.* (1825) s.v. Utchy. (22) **Dor.** Gi' ichy a bit ! *Longman's Mag.* (Mar. 1889) 523. (23) **Som.** As Ice ztood thare, HALLIWELL *Zummerset Pieces* (1843) 3. (24) **w.Cor.** *N. & Q.* (1854) 1st S. x. 319. (25) **Shr.,** Hrf. BOUND *Provinc.* (1876). **Som.** *Horae Subsecivae* (1777) 4. **w.Som.** JENNINGS *Obs. Dial. w.Eng.* (1825). **Dev.** GROSE (1790) ; *Monthly Mag.* (1810) I. 435. (26) **Dev.** *Monthly Mag. ib.* ; GROSE (1790) *MS. add.* (M.) (27) **Dev.** Iss can't but zay, PETER PINDAR *Royal Visit* (1795) pt. i. st. 8. (28) **Wil.** SLOW *Rhymes* (1889) *Gl.* **Som.** W. & J. *Gl.* (1873). **Som.**[1] (29) **w.Yks.** But O reckon be ment, BYWATER *Gossips*, 1. (30) **Lan.** Oi'm mista'en, KAY-SHUTTLEWORTH *Scarsdale* (1860) II. 89. **Chs.**[1] **Der.**[2] Oi'm very craitchy this morning. **War.** (J.R.W.) **Sur.** Here am oi fit to drop wi' heat, BICKLEY *Sur. Hills* (1890) I. i. (31, 32) [For the use of Utch, Utchy, see Ch.]

II. Dial. uses. **1.** In *comb.* **I-dree-I-dree—I-droppit-it**, a children's game.

Frf. The grandchildren spinning the peerie and hunkering at I-dree-I-dree—I-droppit-it—as we did so long ago, BARRIE *Thrums* (1889) i.

2. Emphatic form of the acc. or dat. : *me.*

Glo. 'Er up and shook I in the bed, BUCKMAN *Darke's Sojourn* (1890) xi ; Glo.[1] Doaut thee 'awzen at I, or else I'll gi' thee the strap. **Oxf.** ELLIS *Pronunc.* (1889) V. 126 ; Oxf.[1] Her's a gwain wi' I. **Brks.**[1] Gie I one o' them apples. **Sur.** Let I catch she a foolin', BICKLEY *Sur. Hills* (1890) I. xiii. **n.Wil.** This here 'ull make I sweat (E.H.G.). **Dor.** She twoid it to I, *Why John* (*Coll.* L.L.B.) ; Him said to I (A.C.). **w.Som.** ELWORTHY *Gram.* (1877) 33. **e.Dev.** Aupen, my sister, ta ai, PULMAN *Sng. Sol.* (1860) v. 2. **Cor.** Billum was behind I, TREGELLAS *Tremuan*, 9.

3. *Reflex.*: myself.

Som. I first catched a hold o' the hathern, so I jissy saved I (W.F.R.).

I, *adv.* **Yks. Som.** Yes, aye. See **Aye**, *adv.*[2]

w.Yks. He asked her if she had the paper, and she answered, ' I, I,' *Yksman.* (Oct. 27, 1894) XXXVI. **Som.** JENNINGS *Obs. Dial. w.Eng.* (1825).

I, see In, *prep.*

IANBERRY, *sb.* **Cum.**[1] Same word as **Anbury**, q.v.

IANKEN, *prp.* **Cor.** Walking quickly.

Cor.[2] **w.Cor.** BOTTRELL *Traditions*, 3rd S. *Gl.*

IARTO, ICCLE, ICCOL, see Jarta, Ickle, *sb.*, **Hickwall.**

ICE, *sb.* and *v.* Var. dial. uses in Sc. and Eng. **1.** *sb.* In *comb.* **(1) Ice-bell, (2) -candle**, an icicle ; **(3) -cold**, very cold ; **(4) -creeper**, a contrivance fixed below the instep of a boot, for walking securely in slippery weather ; see below ; **(5) -dangle, (6) -dirk,** see **(1)** ; **(7) -meers, ground-ice ; (8) -plant,** a name given to var. garden plants, esp. to the *Mesembryanthemum crystallinum* ; **(9) -stone**, a curling-stone.

(1) Sur.[1] **(2) e.Yks.** Las' Kesmas, we had ice-cannles a yahd lang, hingin fre' spoot end, NICHOLSON *Flk-Sp.* (1889) 95 ; **e.Yks.**[1] **Lin.** STREATFEILD *Lin. and Danes* (1884) 339. **n.Lin.** Bairns begin to look up at barn-eavins fer ice-can'les, PEACOCK *Tales* (1890) and S. 147 ; **n.Lin.**[1] **Ken.** LEWIS *I. Tenet* (1736). **Hmp.** Here's the poor Robin redbreast approaching our cot, And the ice-candles hanging at our door (J.R.W.) ; Hmp.[1], Dor.[1] **(3) Nhb.** He's icecaad (R.O.H.). **Yks.** (J.W.) **(4) Nhb.** The points of the ice-creeper should not project quite a quarter of an inch below the level of the sole of the boot, otherwise it will be uncomfortable. Shod with this little article the most timorous pedestrian might almost walk down an iceberg, *Newc. Dy. Chron.* (Dec. 29, 1886) ; (R.O.H.) ; Nhb.[1] It is made of a single piece of sheet iron, two pieces of which are turned up at the sides to form ears, whilst four points are turned down so as to touch and grip the surface of the ice below the foot. **(5) ! Sc.** STREATFEILD *Lin. and Danes* (1884) 339. **(6) s.Sc.** Long gleaming ice-dirks hanging from the eaves, ALLAN *Poems* (1887) 56. **(7) Oxf., Brks., Sc.**[1] **& O.** (1856) and S. i. 216. **(8) w.Som.**[1] There are many new kinds, but each is known as ' one of the ice-plants.' **Dev.**[4] A name vaguely applied to garden plants with fleshy leaves, especially to such as are glossy, or look as though they had hoar frost on them —house-leek, stonecrops, &c. **(9) Ayr.** Your ice-stanes in your gray plaids fauld, And try on lochs a pingle, BOSWELL *Poet. Whs.* (ed. 1871) 195. **Lnk.** (JAM.)

2. *v.* To freeze.

Ken.[1] The pond iced over, one day last week.

ICE-BONE, *sb.* **Yks. Lan. e.An. Sus. Hmp.** The share-bone, or some other bone of the pelvis or haunch ; in cookery the ' aitch-bone.' Cf. **izle-bone.**

w.Yks.[1], ne.Lan.[1], e.An.[1] **Nrf.** RAY (1691). **Sus.**[1] **Sus., Hmp.** HOLLOWAY.

[Bremen dial. *is-been*, ' das Hüftbein ' (*Wtb.*) ; Du. *is-been*, the haunch (HEXHAM) ; MLG. *isbēn*, ' Eisbein ' (SCHILLER-LÜBBEN).]

ICELAND, *sb.* **Sh.I. Yks.** **1.** In *comb.* **Iceland scorie**, the glaucous gull, *Larus glaucus.*

Sh.I. A name only applied to the young gulls while speckled ; they lose the speckled appearance after the first year. In Shetland the name ' scorie ' or ' scaurie ' is given to the young of any kind of gull, SWAINSON *Birds* (1885) 207 ; **S. & Ork.**[1]

2. *pl.* A loosely-knitted muffler of mohair, or some other glossy hair or wool. **w.Yks.** (M.F.)

ICELET, *sb.* **Sc. Hmp. Wil.** An icicle.

Frf. From mountains west, Upon whose breast The icelets kill The frail and ill, LOWSON *Guidfollow* (1890) 115. **Hmp.** (J.R.W.); Hmp.[1] Rare. **Wil.** (J.R.W.)

ICE-SHOCKLE, *sb.* **Sc. Nhb. Dur. Cum. Wm. Yks. Lan. Chs. Nhp.** Also in forms **-shackle** m.Yks.[1] w.Yks.[15] Chs.[1] ; **-shog** n.Yks. m.Yks.[1] ; **-shog(g)le** Sc. N.Cy.[1] Nhb.[1] Dur. Cum.[1] n.Yks.[124] **Nhp.**[1] ; **-shogglin** n.Yks.[4] ; **-shoglin** n.Yks.[12] ne.Yks.[1] m.Yks.[An icicle, an ' ickle.'

Sc. Bid iceshogles hammer red gauds on the studdy, RAMSAY *Tea-Table Misc.* (1724) I. 56, ed. 1871. **Lnk.** Up the glen the linn Was hung wi' kirstal iceshoggles, A' skinklin' in the sin, LEMON *St. Mungo* (1844) 50. **Slk.** Enough to turn the heart of flesh to an iceshogle, HOGG *Tales* (1838) 43, ed. 1866. **N.Cy.**[1] **Nhb.** Ice-shoggles, te, is sharp an breet ! but then they're stiff an caud, ROBSON *Sngs. of Tyne* (1849) 171 ; Nhb.[1] **Dur.** Brack like ice-shoggles, EGGLESTONE *Betty Podkin's Lett.* (1877) 13; Dur.[1] **Cum.** As plentiful as ice-shokkels in a frosty December, FARRALL *Betty Wilson* (1886) 123 ; Cum.[1] **Wm.** Aw was cauld as an ice-shockel —weel mud he shak, BOWNESS *Studies* (1868) 26. **n.Yks.**[124], ne.Yks.[1], m.Yks.[1] **w.Yks.** Whisky, cream, and ice shackles were handed round, DIXON *Craven Dales* (1881) 176 ; w.Yks.[1] He war parfitly as coud as an iceshackle, ii. 287 ; w.Yks.[3] n.Lan.[1] And lang ice-shockles danglin' doon, BIGG *Alf. Staunton* (1861) 20. Chs.[1], Nhp.[1]

[Our craggis . . . Hang gret isch schoklis lang as ony spere, DOUGLAS *Eneados* (1513), ed. 1874, III. 76; As men may se in wyntre Ysekeles (*v.r.* iseyokels) in eueses, *P. Plowman* (B.) XVII. 228, see Skeat's *Gl.* (E.E.T.S.) Norw. dial. *isjøkul*, an icicle (AASEN) ; ON. *jøkull*, an icicle (VIGFUSSON) ; cp. EFris. *is-jøkel* (KOOLMAN) ; MLG. *jokel* (SCHILLER-LÜBBEN).]

ICET(-, **see Iset, Ist**.

ICH, *v.* n.Cy. (HALL.) Same word as **Eke**, *v.* (q.v.)

ICH, *int.* Sh.I. Eh !

Ich ! oot o' a wa' clay'd as slight as a egg ! Na, na, *Sh. News* (Dec. 24, 1898).

ICH, see Ch, I, *pron.*

ICHET, *sb.* ? Som. The itch. (HALL.)

ICHIE, see Eechie.

ICHILA-PEA, *sb.* ? *Obs.* Wil.[1] The missel-thrush, *Turdus viscivorus.*

ICHON, see Each, *adj.*

ICILY, *sb.* **Ken.** [ei·sili.] An icicle. (HALL.), Ken.[1]

ICKER, *sb.* **Sc.** Also in forms **acher** Sc. (JAM. *Suppl.*) ; **acre** Sh.I. [i·kər.] An ear of corn.

Sc. (JAM. *Suppl.*) ; It was waesome to look at the bonnie yellow ickers lookin' up here and there in aboot three fit o' snaw, OCHILTREE *Redburn* (1895) x. **Sh.I.** (*Coll.* L.L.B.) **Ayr.** A daimen-icker in a thrawe 'S a sma' request, BURNS *To a Mouse* (1785) st. 3. **Dmf.** Fient an icker rowthly sawn Cam' stowlins tae the sieve, REID *Poems* (1894) 56. **Gall.** MACTAGGART *Encycl.* (1824).

[Echirris of corn thik growing, DOUGLAS *Eneados* (1513), ed. 1874, III. 133. OE. (Merc.) *æchir* (Nhb. *eher*, *æhher*), an ear of corn (*Matt.* xii. 1). Cp. Swiss dial. *acher*, ' Ähre ' (*Idiotikon*) ; MHG. *echer* (LEXER, s.v. *eher*).]

ICKERY, ICKERY, HOCK, *phr.* **Yks.** Also in forms **ikery, dickery-hock** ; **ickima, dickima, dock.** A child's game ; see below.

n.Yks. ' Ickima dickima-dock, The mouse ran up the clock, The clock struck one, The mouse is gone, So ickery-ickery-hock.' Children make on a slate a drawing somewhat like a clock-face with figures on it, and shutting their eyes, say ' Ickery, &c.,' and strike a number, and rub it out, and put it in a place of winnings. If a place is struck outside of the bounds, or not belonging to a number, the striker is out. Two or several can play. When done add up the several persons' figures and the highest wins (I.W.) ; The infants' game of running one's fingers upwards on a child and slightly knocking on its nose, saying, ' Ikery, ikery hock, The mouse ran up the clock ; The clock struck one (striking nose of child, who opens its mouth, when a finger is inserted, and then verse goes on), The mouse was gone, Ikery, dickery-dock ' (R.H.H.).

ICKITTY-PICKITTY, *adv.* **Dev.**[2] Moving with a jerky action.

'Er wawkth all ickitty-pickitty jumpy-jumpy, like a lame gūze.

ICKLE, *sb.* n.Cy. **Nhb. Yks. Lan. Chs. Stf. Der. Not. Lin. Lei. Nhp. War. Shr.** Also written **iccle** n.Cy. Nhb.[1] w.Yks.[4] Lan.[1] e.Lan.[1] Der.[2] nw.Der.[1] ; **ikil** Nhb.[1] ; and in forms **ecle** Shr.; **eecle** Shr.[18]; **eekle** s.Chs.[1]; **heckle** sw.Lin.[1]; **hickle** w.Yks.; **ieker** (*pl.* **ickas**) Chs.[1]; **iggle** Lel.[1] War.[8] [**i·kl.**] **1.** An icicle.

n.Cy. Grose (1790). Nhb.[1], n.Yks.[124] w.Yks. He snapt t'shaft oo a besom clean i' two wi his teeth, az eazy az if it hed been a 'hickle, Tom Treddlehoyle *Bairnsla Ann.* (1859) 33; w.Yks.[1234] Lan. As cowd as iccles, Waugh *Birthplace Tim Bobbin* (1858) 14; Lan.[1], e.Lan.[1] Chs.[1] It wer so cowd that it froz ickas at his chin eend. s.Chs.[1], Stf.[1], Der.[12], nw.Der.[1], Not. (J.H.B.) sw.Lin.[1] There were heckles hinging from· the pump spout, and from the tiles. Lel.[1], Nhp.[1], War.[2] Shr. Bound *Provinc.* (1876); Shr.[1] It's bin a snirpin' fros' sence it lef' off ralnin'; theer's eecles at the aisins a yard lung; Shr.[2]

2. Comb. Ickle-rod, a long pole with an iron cross-piece, used to remove icicles from the sides and roof of a railway-tunnel. w.Yks. (B.K.)

[Ickles, *stiriae*, Levins *Manip.* (1570). OE. *gicel.*]

ICKLE, *v.* w.Wor.[1] [Not known to our correspondents.] To long for.

ICKLE WOVEN BASKET, *phr.* Yks. Also written **icle-**. A small basket; see below.

w.Yks. T'orphan is fun laid up a yer door-stan it icle-woven basket, Tom Treddlehoyle *Bairnsla Ann.* (Jan. 1854); The ickle-woven basket was a small basket that would hold about six spools; these were steeped in water for some hours; when wanted for [hand-loom] weaving they were placed in a small hemispherical basket, with a string attashed about 3 feet long, and swung round·by means of a stout rod, at an enormous speed, in order to expel superfluous moisture by centrifugal force (M.F.).

ICKLE, ICKWELL, ICWELL, see Hickwall.

I-CO, *sb.* Cum. A children's game of ball; see below.

A game played by children by throwing a ball on a low house-top and calling out the name of one of the players, who must catch the ball or otherwise bear on his back the caller, who·immediately on calling the name, runs backwards. The name 'I-co' is prob. a corruption of 'I call' (J.Ar.).

ICYBELLS, *sb. pl.* s.Dev. Icicles. Fox *Kingsbridge* (1874).

ID, IDDEN, see Hide, *v.*[2], Be, *v.*, In, *prep.*, It, Will, Would.

IDDY-IDDY-ALL, *sb.* Oxf. A game of ball; see below. Cf. **I-co.**

One boy throws a ball on the slates or the side wall of a house, shouting at the same time, 'Iddy-iddy-all, catch my fine ball, Jack Horner'—or any other boy's name. The boy called tries to catch the ball: if he succeeds he throws it up again for some other boy to catch; if he fails to catch the ball, he picks it up from the ground and throws it at one of the other boys. If he hits·a boy, that boy pays a penalty; if he misses, the thrower pays the penalty (G.O.).

I·DENT, *adj.* Irel. Same word as **Eident** (q.v.).

N.I.[1] Ant. He's very ident at his books, *Ballymena Obs.* (1892).

IDENT, IDER, IDGET, see Eident, Either, Edget.

IDGETS, *sb. pl.* Sus. [Not known to our other correspondents.] Very little things. (S.P.H.)

IDIOT, *sb.* Irel. A species of 'natural fool'; see below.

Idiots and innocents . . . are nearly alike, but not quite, the first being generally more or less deformed; both however are considered lucky, *Folk-Lore Rec.* (1881) IV. 113.

IDIOTICALS, *sb. pl.* Sc. Foolish things, nonsense; cheap, trashy news.

Per. Newspapers are characterized as idioticals (G.W.). Ayr. No to summer and winter on idioticals, the laird told me he wouldna be at hame to a living soul, Galt *Lairds* (1826) i.

IDIOTRY, *sb.* Sc. Idiocy, folly.

Ayr. Far frae the carfuffle and idiotry of a thechtless worl', Service *Dr. Duguid* (ed. 1887) 244.

ID JIT, *sb.* Dev. Cor. Also in form **idiot Cor.** A particular form of toothed instrument used in the cultivation of land. See **Edget.**

nw.Dev.[1] It consists of a square frame, which carries 16 short tings [tines] having small triangular feet. It has no wheels, and is drawn from one corner. It is a modern implement, but I think it is only made by local smiths. w.Cor. *N. & Q.* (1876) 5th S. v. 129.

IDLE, *adj.*, *sb.* and *v.* Var. dial. uses· in Sc. Irel. and Eng. **1.** *adj.* In *comb.* (1) **Idle-back**, (a) an idle fellow, a 'lazy-bones'; (b) soft stone, or broken lumps of plaster casts, used for whitening stone floors, &c.; (c) a loose piece of skin about the finger-nail; (2) **·man**, (a) a man

living on his means, without any employment; (b) a man employed on a farm to do odd jobs; (3) **·pack**, a bad woman; (4) **·rope**, a rope which carries empty 'corves' into the coal-workings; (5) **·set**, (a) idleness; (b) without work, idle; (6) **·wart** or **·wort**, (7) **·welt**, (8) **·wheal**, see (1, c).

(1, *a*) n.Cy. (Hall.) w.Yks. That's the way to help sitch idle-backs as thee ont'road, *Yksman. ComicAnn.* (1878) 48: w.Yks.[1] Lan. Heaw leets tha couldn't fot 'em thisel, idleback! Clegg *Sketches* (1895) 350. s.Chs.[1], nw.Der.[1] (b) w.Yks. Gave th' hearthstun another dooas o' idleback, Hartley *Puddin'* (1876) 137; Chalk or pipe clay used to whiten the floor . . . is rapidly going out of use. . . . Formerly idleback was the only thing the poor could afford to take the cold, bare look off the flagged floors of their humble dwellings (D.L.). Lan. He's scrubbin brushes, idle back, Laycock *Sngs.* (1866) 33. e.Lan.[1] Chs.[1] Broken lumps of plaster casts upon which plates have been moulded. They are sold by itinerant vendors, and are used for whitening stone floors. This is only a comparatively mod. term; the old Chs. women did not use the material, and the name was applied to the new-fangled whitening for floors in contempt. nw.Der.[1] (c) e.Yks.[1] Popularly supposed to be found only on the fingers of non-workers or idle people. s.Not. (J.P.K.), Lin.[1] (2, a) Som. (Hall.) w.Som.[1] Nif I was on'y a idle man, same as you be, I'd zee whe'r they should have it all their own way, or no. (b) n.Lin.[1] The title 'idle man' does not imply that his time is wasted. (3) s.Pem. *Laws Little Eng.* (1888) 420. (4) w.Yks. (J.P.) (5, a) Sc. Idleset is at the bottom of many matches, Whitehead *Daft Davie* (1876) 200, ed. 1894. Abd. She had not come to her years, she said, to learn idleset, Macdonald *Sir Gibbie* (1879) xxiv. Per. Her only choice in spending the day was between idleset and poaching, Haliburton *Furth in Field* (1894) 76; (G.W.) e.Fif. To me the period of bridegroomhood was onything but a time o' idleset, Latto *Tam Bodkin* (1864) xxiv. Ayr. Isna idleset the wark o' a gentleman! What could he do more? Galt *Lairds* (1826) v. Lnk. The bailies are no subject to idle-sets, like puir working men, Murdoch *Readings* (ed. 1895) I. 88. Edb. He kens that idle-set is sinful, Moir *Mansie Wauch* (1828) xxvi. Gall. Mactaggart *Encycl.* (1824). N.I.[1] There wasn't much idleset since you went away. (b) Sc. (Jam.) N.I.[1] The horse was kept idleset. Ant. You hae been lang enough idleset, *Ballymena Obs.* (1892). (6) Lin. Thompson *Hist. Boston* (1856) 710; Lin.[1], Nhp.[1] (7, 8) Nhp.[1]

2. Mischievous, full of fun; saucy; flippant; restless.

e.Suf. (F.H.), Sus. (F.E.) Hmp. He's a tiresome, idle boy (H.C.M.B.); De Crespigny *New Forest* (1895) 111. I.W.[2] That maade is jest about idle: she wants taking down a peg or two. Wil. Slow *Gl.* (1892); Wil.[1] Dor. 'Those children of X's are such idle boys!' said a village schoolmistress. I said in answer that I found the young scamps apt at lessons but a bit mischievous; it needed some explanation before she could understand that 'idle' meant lazy in some benighted places. An old man who had been rebuking some children for misbehaving in the church reported to me, 'I tell them they've all the week to be idle, without being idle on the Sabbath.' Half a choir resigned when a lady told them they were idle. They believed that she had accused them of vicious life (C.W.).

Hence **Idleness**, *sb.* mischief.

Nhb. A mischievous person is said to be 'full of idleness' (R.O.H.). w.Yks. (J.W.)

3. Handy, useful.

Hmp. I don't want my child to go to school; she is so idle about the house, I can't spare her. Common in New Forest (A.J.C.).

4. *Phr. an idle hussy*, an immoral woman. Nhb.[1], Cum.[8] Hence **Idleness**, *sb.* wantonness, wickedness. Nhb.[1]

5. Of young cattle: playful, frolicsome.

Cum. Specially of horses fresh from want of work (J.Ar.).

6. Of plants: barren; only occasionally bearing a good crop.

s.Not. The Blenheim orange is rather an idle bearer (J.P.K.). †Glo. Ellacombe *Garden* (1895) x.

7. Of a clock: not going.

w.Cor. The clock is idle to-day. Common (M.A.C.).

8. *sb.* The cuckoo. War.[8]

9. *v.* To make idle.

Ir. 'Don't idle me—I've a great deal to do.' 'He'd idle a parish,' said of an engaging child (A.S.P.). Don. Next day it was Nancy's turn to feed the pigs, and she did not meet with any company to idle her, *Flk-Lore in Cornh. Mag.* XXXV. 180.

IDLED, *ppl. adj.* Lin. [ai·dld.] **1.** Idle.

n.Lin.[1] Ira was the idledist chap that iver cum'd aboot a hoose.

2. *Comb.* **Idled-back,** (1) an idle person ; (2) a stand with projecting forks placed before the fire for toasting bread ; (3) a piece of loose skin by the finger-nail. n.Lin.[1]
3. *Phr. not to have an idled bone in one's skin,* to be very industrious. n.Lin. (J.T.F.)

IDLEDOM, *sb.* Cai.[1] Idleness.

IDLETON, *sb.* ? *Obs.* Som. An idle fellow.
The Soliloquy of Ben Bond the Idleton is printed in the dialect of Zummerset (1843) 6 (HALL.); W. & J. *Gl.* (1873). w.Som.[1] This word is given in the glossaries, but I cannot find that it exists in the spoken dialect. [The old merry monosyllable is quite obliterated, and in its stead, each idleton and loitering school-boy with a previous d—n, writes B—ng, COLLINS *Misc.* (1762) 27 (HALL.); When I see idletons, as Jack Townsend can overcome all yr good resolutions, MRS. SHERIDAN *Lett.* to Sheridan, in Rae's *Sheridan* (1896) (*Guardian,* Oct. 7, 1896).]
[For the suff. *-ton,* cp. *simpleton.*]

IDLETY, *sb.* Sc. Lan. **1.** Idleness.
Abd. (JAM.) Lan. He're a bit gan to idlety, BRIERLEY *Irkdale* (1868) 141.
2. *pl.* Idle frolics. Abd. (JAM.)

IDOCITY, *sb.* nw.Dev.[1] The same word as Docity (q.v.). Commoner than 'docity.'

IDY, IE, IEEN, IELA, see Hide, *v.*[2], Ea, *sb.,* Eye, *sb.*[1], Eela.

IELD, *adj.* Sh I. Of a cow: not giving milk. See Geld, *adj.* 2.
Wir coo is heavy, an' his ane is ield, *Sh. News* Jan. 8, 1898); Ivery body 'at haes a hog, or a ield craetir, is gotten der 'oo', *ib.* (July 1, 1899).

IER-OE, *sb.* Sc. Also in forms **heir-oye, jeroy** S. & Ork.[1] A great grandchild.
Sc. There was also one Laurentius in the parish of Waes, whose heir-oyes do yet live there, BRAND *Descr. Ork.* (1701) 71. **S. & Ork.**[1] Ayr. May health and peace, with mutual rays, Shine on the evening o' his days ; Till his wee, curlie John's ier-oe . . . The last, sad, mournful rites bestow ! BURNS *To G. Hamilton,* ll. 108–13.
[Gael. *iar-ogha,* a great grandchild (M. & D.).]

IF, *conj.* Irel. Yks. Lan. Chs. Lin. Nhp. War. Wor. Hrf. Oxf. Brks. Hnt. Nrf. Sur. Dor. Dev. Also in form **ef** Dev. **1.** In phr. (1) *if Goddil,* an exclamation : if God will; (2) *if I can speak,* an expression used in correcting some slip of the tongue ; (3) *if I know,* I don't know ; (4) *if or but,* let or hindrance ; (5) *if so be as, — as how, — that,* or *if so being,* an intensitive of 'if'; in *gen.* colloq. use ; (6) *if stands stiff in a poor man's pocket,* see below ; (7) *ifs and ands,* hesitation, prevarication.
(1) Lan. 'I think lunger ot fok liv'n an' th' moor mischoances they han.'. . . 'Not awlus, o Goddil,' TIM BOBBIN *View Dial.* (1746) 16, ed. 1806: Lan.[1] s.Lan. BAMFORD *Dial.* (1854) *Gl.* (2) Chs.[1] I went last Tuesday—no, Wednesday, if I can spake. (3) N.I.[1] Deed if I know when he's commin'. (4) Chs.[1] He'll come, tha may depend on't, witheawt oather if or but. (5) n.Yks.[4], ne.Yks.[1] Nhp.[1] If so be as how I get on with my marketings, I'll call. War.[2] If so be as how I've done my work in time, I'll come across; War.[3] Wor. If so be as he had tried, *Evesham Jrn.* (Jan. 30, 1897). Hrf.[2] Brks.[1] If zo be as you can come an' hev tay wi' we to-morrow, I hopes you 'ooll. Hnt. (T.P.F.) Nrf. If so bein' yow luck to find my beloved, GILLETT *Sng. Sol.* (1860) v. 8. s.Suf. If so bein' yow can't go, yow must stop at home (F.H.). Sur.[1] If so be as you should have e'er a cottage to let, I should be glad of the offer of it. Dor. If zo be as 'mis'ess can spare I, HARE *Vill. Street* (1895) 230. Dev. It ef so be thee goes wey . . . Jist see . . . what you gits, DANIEL *Bride of Scio* (1842) 178. (6) Oxf.[1] Used to imply the difficulty poor people find in obtaining their wishes where money is concerned. If some one should say 'I would buy a new dress if I had the money to spare,' somebody might answer 'If stands stiff in a poor man's pocket,' i. e. the want of money, *MS. add.* (7) w.Yks.[1] Let's hev naan o' yower ifs an ans. n.Lin.[1]
2. Used redundantly before *in case, supposing,* &c. Cf. an, *conj.*[1]
n.Yks.[1]; n.Yks.[2] If-in-sera-keease that I wer te tummle ; n.Yks.[4], ne.Yks.[1] n.Lin.[1] If suppoäsin' she hed dun it, he'd no call to ewse her e' that how.

IFE, *sb.* Suf. The yew, *Taxus baccata.*
(HALL.); (B. & H.) e.Suf. Heard from the old, but only very rarely (F.H.).
[Fr. *if,* a yew (COTGR.).]

IFF, *sb.* and *v.* Ken. [if.] **1.** *sb.* A fishing-gaff.
Marsh was kept fairly busy with his 'iff' (as gaffs are called at Deal), *Fishing Gazette* (Nov. 29, 1890) 289.
2. *v.* To use a gaff-hook in landing fish.
For two hours I kept Marsh busy with baiting hooks and 'iffing' fish. *ib.*

IFING, *prp.* Chs. War. Wor. Shr. Glo. Som. Also written **iffin** Chs.[1] s.Chs.[1]; **iffing** War.[2] w.Wor.[1] se.Wor.[1] Glo.[1]; and in form **iftin** Shr.[1] [i·fin.] In *comb.* (1) **Ifing-and-anding,** (a) hesitating ; (b) hesitation ; (2) **-and-buttings,** invalid excuses ; hesitation combined with unwillingness ; (3) **-and-offing,** (a) in a state of indecision ; (b) indecision.
(1, a) w.Som.[1] I likes to hear anybody zay ees or no, to once, and not bide if-in-and-andin gin anybody can't tell whe'r they be going to do it or no. (b) Shr.[1] I axed the ōōman about the weashin', an' after a good bit o' iftin'-an'-andin' 'er said 'er'd come —but 'er didna seem to car' about it. (2) Chs.[1] Dunna mak so many iffins an' buttins ; we can do beawt thee. s.Chs.[1] Naay, wun yū tel mi streyt, baayt aan·i if·inz ūn būt·inz ? [Naï, wun yo tell me streight, baït anny iffins an' buttins !] (3, a) War.[2], se.Wor.[1] (b) War.[2] Make up your mind, don't let's have any iffing-and-offing. w.Wor.[1], Glo.[1]

IFLE, *v.* Hrt. To drive away roughly ; to hustle.
CUSSANS *Hist. Hrt.* (1879–81) III. 320.

IFT, *sb.* n.Lin. [ift.] Way ; habit ; manner.
PEACOCK *Tales* (1890) and S. 117 ; n.Lin.[1] I knawed he'd soon be at th' ohd ift agëan ; ther's no moore chanch o' keäpin' him fra that thing then ther is a sheäp-worryin' dog fra mutton.

IGG, IGGLE, see Egg, *v.,* Ickle.

IGNAGNING, *sb.* *Obs.* Lan. Also in form **ignagics.** A name given to a morris or sword-dance.
In the Fylde on the afternoon of Easter Sunday the young people . . . performed a kind of Morris or Moorish dance or play, called 'Ignagning,' HARLAND & WILKINSON *Flk-Lore* (1867) 236; *ib.* *Leg.* (1873) 153; Ignagning has almost fallen into disuse, and a band of boys, called Jolly Lads, has succeeded, THORNBER *Hist. Blackpool* (1837) 99 ; Lan.[1] Common in the Fylde some fifty years ago.

IGNORANT, *adj.* and *sb.* Sc. Irel. Not. Lin. Oxf. Wil. Som. Also written **ignerint** Sh.I. ; and in forms **highnint** Dev.; **igerant** Oxf.[1]; **ignoran** Wil. [i·gnǝrant.] **1.** *adj.* Ill-mannered.
N.I.[1] s.Not. It looked so ignorant of 'er to be staring like that (J.P.K.). sw Lin.[1] I thought it would be so ignorant to stop yon. Oxf.[1] *MS. add.* w.Som.[1] The usual description of a rough, uncouth lout. 'There idn a hignoranter gurt mump-head athin twenty mild, he idn fit vor no woman's company.' Dev. 'No, Jan,' zeth her, 'sic highnint sets Thay wishes thay wis me !' NATHAN HOGG *Poet. Lett.* (1847) 36, ed. 1865.
2. *sb.* An ignorant person.
Sc. What poor ignorants sustain Who've much of fear and very little brain, PENNECUIK *Coll.* (1787) 37. Sh.I. Man, doo is a auld ignerint, *Sh. News* (Oct. 15, 1898). Per. Whilk places were furnished by the bishops by ignorants and insufficient persons, WODROW *Sel. Biog.* (ed. 1845–7) I. 73. Wil. When I was about twenty or so, a poor ignoran, PENRUDDOCKE *Content* (1860) 57.

I'GODLIN, *int.* Lan. Der. Also in form **i'gadlin** Lan.[1] A petty oath.
Lan. I'godlin, he's done a good stroke at that, hissen ! WAUGH *Jannock* (1874) iv ; I'gadlin, we's never look beheend us after this, *ib. Old Cronies* (1875) iii ; Lan.[1], nw.Der.[1]

IGSY-PIGSY, *adj.* Dev. Confused, 'higgledy-piggledy.'
I'm passelled quite a score o' ways an' led an igsy-pigsy dance, SALMON *Ballads* (1899) 62 ; Dev.[3] In constant use.

I'GY, *int.* Yks. [i·goi.] An exclamation. See Egow.
w.Yks. I'gy it is a blazer ! INGLEDEW *Ballads* (1860) 276.

IKE, see Hike.

IKEY, *adj.* Ken. [ei·ki.] Proud. (G.B.), Ken.[1]

IKIL, see Ickle, *sb.*

IKINS, *sb. pl.* War. In phr. *my ikins,* an exclamation.
'Ikins !' went out of use some 30 years ago, to be replaced by 'My eye !' (G.F.N.); HOLLOWAY.

IKY-PIKY, *sb.* n.Lan.[1] A corruption of 'ipecacuanha.'

IKY-PIKY, *int.* Lan. An exclamation of surprise or astonishment. (S.W.)

ILD, *v.* n.Cy. Nhp. Shr. [ild.] To yield, 'eald.'
n.Cy. (HALL.) Shr.[1] 'Ow does the corn ild, William ?' 'Well, but mighty middlin', the ears bin lathy.'

Hence **Ildy**, *adj.* fruitful, abundant, yielding. Nhp.¹

[Herein I teach you How you shall bid God 'ild us for our pains, SHAKS. *Macb.* I. vi. 13.]

ILDER, *sb.*¹ Sh.I. Fire. JAKOBSEN *Dial.* (1897) 30. *f.* hildin.

ILDER, *sb.*² n.Lin.¹ The same word as Elder, *sb.*¹

ILE, *sb.*¹ Cai.¹ [ail.] The fishing-ground inside the main tidal current, in the space between two points where there is a counter current.

In such a space fishing may be carried on irrespective of the de, but in the main current, only at slack water.

ILE, *sb.*² Cai.¹ [ail.] A wing of a church ; a half transept. See Aisle, *sb.* 2.

ILE, *sb.*³ Cor. [ail.] 1. The liver ' fluke,' *Distoma* *epaticum*, productive of rot in sheep. Cor.¹²

2. The plant *Rosa solis* (?).

Cor.² The name given to a plant, *Rosa solis*, by eating which was supposed the disease was caused. The plant is not in-urious until it becomes infested with the ova of the ' fluke.'

ILE, see Ail, *sb.*², Hile, *sb.*², Oil.

ILK, *sb.* Sc. Irel. Lakel. War. Glo. Som. [ilk.] 1. In hr. *of that ilk*, of the same name, place, or nature.

Sc. Mungo Marsport of that ilk, SCOTT *Midlothian* (1818) xii. r.I. Hugh Halcro of that ilk. PETERKIN *Notes* (1822) 185. **Elg.** hammel-spun coat o' the vera same hue, Wi' breeks o' that ilk, n' queetikins too, *Abd. Wkly. Free Press* (June 25, 1898). **Baff.** he young Laird of Glengerrack met and engaged the fellow, nd the sword of that ilk had again freed the country from nother of those pests, GORDON *Chron. Keith* (1880) 144. **e.Sc.** any relation to Sir Patrick of that ilk, SETOUN *R. Urquhart* (1896) i. **Abd.** John Udney of that ilk, SPALDING *Hist. Sc.* (1792) II. 6. **Fif.** We have also Spittal of Lickspittal and that ilk, GRANT *Six Hundred*, ii. **Rnf.** The farm o' Scartclean o' that ilk, *NEILBON Poems* (1877) 110. **Ayr.** The only son of Fatherlans of that ilk, GALT *Entail* (1823) xiv. **Lnk.** The Boyds of Greenend, ainers of that ilk, WRIGHT *Sc. Life* (1897) 42. **Edb.** The Penny-ooks of that ilk, PENNECUIK *Wks.* (1715) 4, ed. 1815. **Ir.** Never-heless he was . . . one of the real old O'Tooles, lineally escended from the famous king of that ilk, FRANCIS *Fustian* (1895) 5. **¹Glo.** I remember a cow which was for many years called Harry ' because of its fancied resemblance to a man of that ilk, *BUCKMAN Darke's Sojourn* (1890) 38.

2. Family ; breed ; kind.

Ayr. Ilk ane a cap an' cloak o' silk Has got, as if she was lady, An' that indeed, o' nae sma' ilk, FISHER *Poems* (1790) 155. **Lakel.**² He's yan o' t'siam ilk. War. The horses most famous for marvellous exploits must have blood as well as bone, but only ertain districts of the Green Isle can produce this ilk, *Evesham rn.* (June 29, 1897). **Som.** SWEETMAN *Wincanton Gl.* (1885).

[1. King James, the fyfte of that ilke, DALRYMPLE *Leslie's Hist. Scotl.* (1596) I. 126. ME. *þat ilke*, the same (*Cursor M.* 1284) ; OE. *þat ilc(e* (*Chron.* an. 1135).]

Sc. Dancing ilk night, SCOTT *Pirate* (1822) ix. **Sh.I.** Let ilk fad iss his dearie, STEWART *Tales* (1892) 97. **Elg.** Ilk eager hand preads oure the field, COUPER *Poetry* (1804) I. 48. **Abd.** He vill ilk friend, in a fit manner, thank, SHIRREFS *Poems* (1790) 78. **Frf.** Ilk glower'd at Myse, an' bock'd an' spat, WATT *Poet. ketches* (1880) 22. **Per.** Aye he growled the other growl, As ilk ad been his last, SPENCE *Poems* (1898) 55. **Fif.** Breathin' ilk hers' breaths for twa mortal hours, ROBERTSON *Provost* (1894) o. **s.Sc.** They hae cleared o' ilk buss, WATSON *Border Bards* 859) 5. **Dmb.** Winter . . . Dis cover ilk brae and hill, TAYLOR *oems* (1827) 9. **Ayr.** Faithless snaws ilk step betray Whare she as been, BURNS *Vision*, st. 1. **Lnk.** Ilk glen an' bosky dingle, HAMILTON *Poems* (1865) 94. **Lth.** Ilk lad faulds his arm round is ain lassie's waist, BALLANTINE *Poems* (1856) 99. **Peb.** In aste frae ilk' direction, AFFLECK *Poet. Wks.* (1836) 35. **Rxb.** Ilk rcumstance I've mentioned, WILSON *Poems* (1824) 9. **Dmf.** Ilk our o' the day, THOM *Jock o' the Knowe* (1878) 2. **Gall.** She ould . . . Crimp up ilk ruffle, NICHOLSON *Poet. Wks.* (1814) 41, d. 1897. **Keb.** Ilk sturdy stroke, ARMSTRONG *Ingleside* (1890) 97. **Vgt.** We'll show then Ilk yin's his neebour's brither, FRASER *Poems* ,885) 240. **n.Cy.** Ilk other house, GROSE (1790) ; **N.Cy.**¹ **Nhb.** k playful tike, GRAHAM *Moorland Dial.* (1896) 50 ; Nhb.¹ Chiefly now sed in N. Nhb. and Redesdale, but freq. heard south of the Tweed. **um.** Ilk thing that leeves can git a mate, ANDERSON *Ballads* d. 1808) 30 ; **Cum.⁴** **n.Yks.** An' mebbe mair deed o' th' ilk

soort wad be heered on afore a' war deean, ATKINSON *Lost* (1870) cxix ; **n.Yks.**¹ ; **n.Yks.**² Ilk other day, every alternate day. **e.Yks.** MARSHALL *Rur. Econ.* (1788). **w.Yks.**¹ Now extinct.

Hence **Ilk ane** (**Ilk-ane**, **Ilkin**), each one.

Sc. (A.W.) Rnf. Affliction mak's Ilk ane o' Adam's seed the sibber grow, YOUNG *Pictures* (1865) 12. **Edb.** Bids ilk ane come fast awa, *Auld Handsel Monday* (1792) 18. **N.Cy.**² **Cum.** *Gl.* (1851). **Lan.** Let ilk yen fancy what they will, WAUGH *Heather*, I. 137, ed. Milner.

[Ilk knew vthir weil, DALRYMPLE *Leslie's Hist. Scotl.* (1596) I. 77. OE. (Anglian) *ylc*, 'omnem', *Ps.* lxxvii. 51 (Vesp.).]

ILKA, *adj.* Sc. Nhb. Yks. Also written **ilky** Lnk.

1. Each ; every.

Sc. Ilka penny on't, SCOTT *Bride of Lam.* (1819) xii. **ne.Sc.** The young man looks owre at you in the kirk ilka Sunday, GRANT *Chron. Kechleton*, 36. **Cai.**¹ **Elg.** Ilka chiel look'd sad an' dour, TESTER *Poems* (1865) 93. **e.Sc.** Ane in ilka pouch, SETOUN *Sunshine* (1895) 7. **Bch.** Syne ilka a thing gaed widdersins about wi' us, FORBES *Jrn.* (1742) 15. **Abd.** On ilka side, the trees grew thick and strang, ROSS *Helenore* (1768) 21, ed. 1812. **Kcd.** At ilka jolt She lookit unca scare, GRANT *Lays* (1884) 5. **Frf.** To muck the riggs in ilka field, *Piper of Peebles* (1794) 5. **Per.** Ilka man hes a richt tae his ain thochts, IAN MACLAREN *Auld Lang Syne* (1895) 30. **Fif.** Ilka nicht he's oot on the hunt, M'LAREN *Tibbie* (1894) 11. **Rnf.** Down ilka paw sae saftly set. PICKEN *Poems* (1813) I. 6. **Ayr.** Ilka thing, BURNS *Thou art sae Fair*, st. 2. **Lnk.** Ilky month, RAMSAY *Poems* (1721) 25. **Lth.** Ilka day brought joy, MACNEILL *Poet. Wks.* (1801) 127, ed. 1856. **Edb.** What ilka ane had wared his pay on, MOIR *Mansie Wauch* (1828) xviii. **Bwk.** Ilka bairn, HENDERSON *Pop. Rhymes* (1856) 16. **Slk.** Ilka spring, CHR. NORTH *Noctes* ed. 1856) II. 3. **Rxb.** It sweetens care at ilka hand, WILSON *Poems* (1824) 9. **Dmf.** Sic joy appeared In ilka face, REID *Poems* (1894) 30. **Gall.** Ilka time they gang oot, CROCKETT *Sunbonnet* (1895) iv. **Keb.** Ilka day, ARMSTRONG *Ingle-side* (1890) 139. **Nhb.** Tak ilka ane a hand. RICHARDSON *Borderer's Table-bk.* (1846) VII. 333 ; **Nhb.**¹ **Cum.⁴** And the twelve nogs on ilka side, GILPIN *Sngs.* (1866). **n.Yks.**¹ ; **n.Yks.**² Ilka yan on 'em.

2. *Comb.* (1) **Ilka-body's** body, a universal favourite ; a time-server ; (2) **-day**, week-day ; (3) **—deal**, every whit ; (4) **-where**, everywhere.

(1) **Ayr.** Get ye that bra' wallie name, O' ilka body's body, FISHER *Poems* (1790) 64. (2) **Sc.** When ye are in your auld ilka-day rags, SCOTT *Midlothian* (1818) xvi ; Alike ilka day makes a clout on Sunday, FERGUSON *Prov.* (1641) No. 104. **e.Sc.** He donned his ilka-day attire, SETOUN *Sunshine* (1895) 253. **Abd.** The bellman meant his 'ilka-day's' coat, ALEXANDER *Ain Flk.* (1882) 46. **Frf.** Knick-knacks that a tradesman hasna to bather wi' for ilkaday wear, WILLOCK *Rosetty Ends* (1886) 192, ed. 1889. **Lnk.** Twa hours wi' pleasure I wad gic to heaven, On ilka days, on Sundays sax or seven, BLACK *Falls of Clyde* (1806) 134. (3) **Abd.** I hae heard your tale And were fairly at it ilka deal, ROSS *Helenore* (1768 99, ed. 1812. (4) **Abd.** Chairs, tables, an' cradles were ilkawhere sittin', ANDERSON *Rhymes* (1867) 8. **Rnf.** This system, I remember weel, . . Was scorned an' laucht at ilkawhere, YOUNG *Pictures* (1865) 140. **Lth.** His faither daunders in at e'en, An' ilkawhere looks he, McNEILL *Preston* (c. 1895) 64. **Peb.** Embro town. and ilka where, AFFLECK *Poet. Wks.* (1896) 53.

3. *Phr. no ilka body*, no common person.

Abd. He thinks himsell nae ilka body (JAM.).

[1. Ilka day, *cotidie*, Cath. *Angl.* (1483) ; OE. (Anglian) *ylc ān.*]

ILL, *adj., adv., sb.* and *v.* Var. dial. uses in Sc. Irel. and Eng. I. *adj.* Gram. forms. 1. *Comparative.* **Iler.**

w.Yks. It war ilo(r) nor i þout on (J.W.). **e.An.**¹ More iller.

2. *Superlative.* **Illest.**

Fif. This reception's the illest part of 't, MELDRUM *Margrédel* (1894) 21. **n.Cy.** (J.W.)

II. Dial. uses. 1. *adj.* and *adv.* In *comb.* (1) **Ill-æble**, unable, hardly able ; (2) **-becoming**, unsuitable, unbecom-ing ; (3) **-best**, the best of a bad lot or job ; (4) **-bind**, of an article of dress : a bad shape or form ; (5) **—bit**, a euphemism for hell ; (6) **-blained**, (7) **-blended**, morose, ill-tempered, irritable ; (8) **-boden**, insufficiently stocked ; (9) **-brew**, an unfavourable opinion ; (10) **-brought-up**, badly trained ; (11) **-cankered**, evilly disposed ; (12) **—chance**, bad luck ; (13) **—cheer**, grief ; (14) **-cleckit**, misbegotten, base-born ; (15) **-clepped**, ill-conditioned, surly, churlish ; (16) **-coloured**, discoloured ; (17) **-contricked**, knavish ; (18)

·contrived or ·contriving, (a) ill-tempered, badly behaved, tricky, mischievous; (b) awkward, badly constructed; (19) ·convenience or ·conveniency, (a) inconvenience; (b) to inconvenience; (20) ·convenient, inconvenient; (21) ·cuisten or ·kessen, (a) badly sown; (b) badly decided; (22) ·curponed, see (15); (23) ·deed, ill-luck, misfortune; evil proceedings; (24) ·deeded or ·deedie, mischievous, evilly disposed; (25) ·demised, malevolent; (26) ·dereyt, disorderly, untidy; (27) ·designed, see (11); (28) ·digestion or ·diagestion, indigestion; (29) ·divvadged, ill-arranged, slovenly; (30) ·doed, lean, ill-fed, not thriving; (31) ·doer, (a) an evil-doer; (b) an animal which does not thrive; see Dow, v.¹ 4; (32) ·doing, (a) badly behaved; (b) in a bad condition, sickly; (33) ·done, wrong, mischievous, ill-advised; (34) ·done-to, ill-used; (35) — dread, an apprehension of evil; (36) ·dreaded, ? expecting evil; (37) ·dreader, one who anticipates evil; (38) ·eased, see (20); (39) — ee, the evil eye; also used fig. dislike; (40) — end, a bad end, a miserable death; (41) ·faced, having an evil countenance; (42) ·faired, ill-favoured; (43) ·fare, (a) to fare badly, meet with ill-success; (b) a state of need or discomfort; (44) ·fared, unlucky, unsuccessful; (45) ·farrant, ugly; ill-conditioned; (46) ·fashed, troubled, worried; (47) ·fashioned, (a) badly shaped; (b) ill-mannered; quarrelsome; (48) ·favoured, (a) unbecoming, unmannerly; out of place; (b) unpleasant; (c) not looking well in health; (d) ill-tempered, ill-natured; mean; (e) clumsy; (f) see (30); (49) ·favouredly, (a) clumsily, ungracefully; (b) meanly; (50) ·fearing, fearing the powers of evil; (51) ·fleyed, scared, frightened; (52) ·flitten, of a scolding, when it is as applicable to the scolder as to the person scolded; (53) ·foot, a foot supposed to bring ill-luck; (54) ·footer, the person having the 'ill-foot'; (55) ·gab, (a) insolent, impudent language; the power to use such language; (b) to use abusive, insolent language; (56) ·gabbed, foul-tongued; (57) ·gain, see (20); (58) ? ·gainshoned, (59) ·gaishoned, mischievous; (60) ·gait or ·gate, (a) a bad habit, an evil way; (b) an awkward manner of walking; (61) ·gaited or ·gated, (a) see (32, a); (b) clumsy in walking; unable to walk far; (62) ·given, (a) niggardly; (b) evil-minded, ill-tempered; prone to speak or do evil; (63) ·giveness, ill-nature; (64) ·gotten, illegitimate; good-for-nothing; (65) ·gritted, of a bad, obstinate temper; (66) ·grun or ·grunyie, a bad, knavish disposition; (67) ·grunyiet, having a bad disposition; (68) ·guide, (a) to mismanage; (b) to ill-treat; (69) ·guided, ill-treated; ill-advised; (70) ·hadden, ill-mannered; (71) ·hained, saved to no good purpose; (72) ·hairt, see (15); (73) ·hap, misfortune; (74) ·happit, ill-clothed; (75) ·haudden-in, see (71); (76) ·hear, to chide, scold; (77) ·hearted, malevolent, illiberal; (78) ·heartedness, malevolence; (79) ·hearty, ailing, delicate; (80) ·heired, inheriting bad qualities; (81) ·helt or ·healt, a euphemism for 'the devil'; (82) ·helty-hair, never a bit; (83) ·heppen, see (42); (84) ·hoited, (85) ·hued, fig. ill-favoured; (86) ·hung, of a tongue: impudent, insolent; (87) ·hung-on, dissatisfied at or with any occurrence; (88) ·hyver, (a) awkward behaviour; (b) ill-humour; (89) ·hyvered or ·hivard, (a) awkward, abusive; (b) ill-looking, ill-skinned; (c) ill-tempered; (90) ·jaw, (a) bad language; an abusive tongue; (b) see (55, b); (91) ·jawt, see (56); (92) ·kenning, hardly knowing; (93) ·laid-on, ill-served; (94) ·learned, badly taught; inexperienced; (95) ·legged, having unshapely legs; (96) ·less, harmless, having no evil designs; (97) ·like, ugly; not looking well in health; (98) ·liked, (a) unpopular; (b) see (42); (99) ·likken, to give a bad and false impression of any one; (100) ·liver, one who leads an immoral life; (101) ·living, immoral conduct; (102) ·lucked, unlucky; (103) ·made-on, of a child: neglected, badly brought up; (104) ·maired, cross-grained, intractable; (105) ·making, mischief-making; (106) ·man, the devil; (107) ·marred, badly spoilt; (108) ·marrowed, badly matched, awkwardly arranged; (109) ·measure, ill-usage; (110) ·minded, ·minted, or ·mynt, evil-minded; ill-meant; (111) ·mindings, forgetfulness; (112) ·mite, (a)

see (15); (b) an ill-natured person; (113) ·mouth, (a) (55, a); (b) see (55, b); (114) ·mouthed, see (56); (115) — my common, see (2); (116) — name, a bad name; (117) ·named, misnamed; (118) ·nature, bad temper; (119) ·natured, peevish; (120) ·off, (a) poor, miserable, ill-used; (b) perplexed in mind; (121) — one, a bad character; (122) ·paid, very sorry; (123) ·paired, see (108); (124) ·part, (a) see (5); (b) ill-temperedly; (125) — payment, a bad debt; (126) ·pegged, (127) ·pictured, see (15); (128) — place, see (5); (129) ·prat, a mischievous trick; (130) ·prattie, (131) ·protted, roguish, mischievous; (132) ·put-on, (a) of a person: badly or carelessly dressed; (b) see (34); (133) ·red-up, in a state of disorder; (134) ·relished, of a person: disagreeable; (135) ·saired or ·ser'd, (a) badly served; not having sufficient food; (b) impudent; (136) ·sar'd, unsavoury; (137) ·scraped, of a tongue: rude, abusive; (138) ·set, (a) to become badly; also used fig.; (b) see (15); (c) placed in a difficulty, 'hard put to'; (139) ·set-ness, opposition; (140) ·set-on, foully attacked; (141) ·shaken-up, uncomely, ungraceful, disordered in dress; (142) ·shaped, see (32, a); (143) ·side, a defect, blemish; (144) — sight, in phr. ill sight be seen upon anything, an imprecation; (145) ·sitten, ungainly from long sitting; (146) ·sket, rude, unmannerly; (147) ·some, see (11); (148) ·sorted, dissatisfied; (149) ·speaker, an evil speaker, a slanderer; (150) ·speaking, evil speaking, slandering; also used attrib.; (151) ·spent, misspent; (152) ·spoken, see (56); (153) ·spued, see (32 a, b); (154) ·taken, taken amiss; (155) ·tasted, see (48, b); (156) ·tended or ·tented, neglected, badly nursed, little cared for; (157) ·tethed, see (25); (158) ·teul, a person of evil habits; (159) — thief, see (106); (160) ·thing, erysipelas; (161) ·thoughted, suspicious, malevolent; (162) ·thriven, ·throdden, or ·throven, see (30); (b) see (15); (163) ·tied, engaged; (164) — tongue, (a) see (149); (b) see (90, a); (165) ·tongued, (a) see (56); (b) ? difficult to pronounce; (166) ·toward, see (146); (167) — trick, see (129); (168) ·tricked or ·tricky, see (131); (169) ·trodden, badly worn; also fig. evil, wicked; (170) — turn, a turn for the worse; (171) ·twined, see (7); (172) — upon't, in bad health, fatigued, spiritless; poor; (173) ·used, put to a wrong use; (174) ·vaamed, ? ill-sounding; (175) ·vicked, see (18, a); (176) ·vuxen, ill-grown, ill-shaped; (177) ·vynd, a bad shape; bad manners; (178) ·vyndit, badly made, ill-shaped; ill-mannered; (179) ·waled, badly chosen; (180) ·wan, a faint hope; (181) ·wared or ·wared-out, badly bestowed, foolishly expended; (182) ·washing, badly washed; (183) ·ween, (a) see (90, a); (b) news; (c) see (55, b); (184) — will, (a) to wish evil to; (b) in phr. to have an ill-will at, to take a dislike to; (185) ·willed or ·willied, sulky, ill-tempered; reluctant; (186) ·willer, one who wishes evil to befall another; (187) ·willing, disobliging; (188) ·willy, (a) bad-tempered, spiteful; grudging, disobliging; (b) grudgingly; (189) ·win, (a) ·won; (190) ·wind, a slander; evil report; (191) ·wish, (a) an imprecation, witch's curse; (b) to bewitch.

(1) Sh.I. Da crew . . . wir nearly a' auld men, ill-able ta fecht da gale, CLARK N. Gleams (1898) 37. n.Yks.² 'Ill-yabble o' feeat,' lame. 'Ill-yabble o' t'pocket,' poor. w.Yks. As bi il eobl ta kum [I shall hardly be able to come] (J.W.). (2) Suf. It would be a very ill-becoming thing for the likes of you, STRICKLAND Old Friends (1864) 68. (3) Sc. Let . . . such wicked men be put from about him, and the ill-best there be taken into his service, BAILLIE Lett. (1775) II. 290 (JAM.). Abd. Left me to mak an ill best o't wantin' him, MACDONALD Sir Gibbie (1879) xxvii. (4) w.Sc. (JAM. Suppl.) (5) Kcb. The deil . . . took him awa' to the ill bit, ye ken, To hae a' nicht's swatlin' o' toddy, ARMSTRONG Ingleside (1890) 215. (6) Hrf.² He's so illblained. (7) War.⁶ Shr.¹ E's a ill-blended, down-looking, hang-dog fellow. Hrf.² I never see sich an ill-blended ooman i' my life. (8) Sc. His pantry was never ill-boden, JAMIESON Pop. Ballads (1806) I. 299. (9) Rnf. Glasgow bailies had an illbrew o' the Hielanders, GRAHAM Writings (1883) I. 90. (10) Sh.I. Home wi' dee! home! doo ill-brought up lepper! Sh. News (July 24, 1897). (11) Bwk. Ill-canker't fiddle-doup, leaving ay her trail, HENDERSON Pop. Rhymes (1856) 98. Yks. (J.W.) (12) Lnk. Ill chance on you stir [sir],

nd out he goes, cursing like a madman, GRAHAM *Writings* (1883)
I. 215. (13) n.Yks.² They made neea ill-cheer on't. (14) Sc. Ye
I-cleckit gude for nought, SCOTT *Bride of Lam.* (1819) xii. **Frf.**
’s that ill-cleakit witch, BARRIE *Minister* (1891) xxxviii. (15)
.Yks.¹² (16) Sh.I. His haand an’ airm . . . wis swall’d oot o’ a’
kate, an’ awfil ill-coloured, *Sh. News* (Feb. 17, 1900). (17) **Bnff.¹**
8, a) Sh.I. Doo wisna sae ill contrived ta him, whin we wir a’
kaen ta da schule togedder, *Sh. News* (July 17, 1897); **S. & Ork.¹**
*al.*¹ **Bnff.** All . . . vowed vengeance on the ill-contrived loons,
GORDON *Chron. Keith* (1880) 19; **Bnff.¹ Gall.** The ill-contriving
hiel, CROCKETT *Moss-Hags* (1895) xl. **n.Yks.** He’s an ill-contrived
llow (I.W.); **n.Yks.¹** (s.v. Ill-clep’d). **w.Yks.** He’s an ill-con-
rived bairn, I cannot constree him, *Prov. in Brighouse News* (Sept.
4, 1889); **w.Yks.¹, Chs.¹ s.Chs.¹** Aay il·-kŭntrahy·vd yŭ bin!
(*ŭthin)z reyt ſo)yŭ* [Hai ill-contrived yŏ bin! Nothin’s reight for
ŏ]. **nw.Der.¹ War.²³; War.⁴** He’s the most ill-contrived boy in
he whole school. **Shr.¹** Yo’ bin as contrairy an’ ill-contrived as
ꞓ’ knowen ’ow to be. **w.Som.¹** Usually applied to a woman. ‘I
nows her, a zour-lookin, ill-contrived old bitch, but I never didn
now no good by her.’ **Dev.** ’Er’s bad tempered, an’ no mistake ;
niver zeed zich a tatchy, ill-contrived little twoad in awl my life,
iꞃwɛʈʈ *Peas. Sp.* (1892) 132. **nw.Dev.¹** (b) Sh.I. I hate a lang
hit mak’s a body’s burden dat ill contriv’d, *Sh. News* (July
5, 1899). **Gall.** The folk couldna tell whether he was gi’en them
uid Scots or ill-contrived Laitin, CROCKETT *Standard Bearer* (1898)
ꞩo. (19, a) **Yks.** (J.W.) **War.** Great ill-conveniences have
tended, BUNCE *Old St. Martin* (1875); **War.⁴, e.Suf. (F.H.)**
.Som.¹ I hope we shan’t put you to no ill-convenience. We must
ut up way th’ ill-conveniency o’ it. (b) **Rut.¹** I don’t want to Ill-
onvenienceyou. (20)Sc.Whilkwadbeill-convenienttoyourfathers
ffairs, SCOTT *Rob Roy* (1817) xxvi. **N.I.¹, Yks.** (J.W.) Der. All the
nings . . . seemed foolish and ill-convenient, VERNEY *Stone Edge*
(1868) iv. **Not.¹, sw.Lin.¹, Rut.¹, Lei.¹, Nhp.¹ War.²³; War.⁴**
himp.¹ s.Hmp. If so be it ain’t ill-convenient, VERNEY *L. Lisle*
(1870) x. **w.Som.¹** ’Tis ter’ble ill-convenient, not vor t’ have nother
it of a oven. (21, a) **Dmf.** Like an ill-cuisten crap in the howe o’
he burn, REID *Poems* (1894) 46. (b) **n.Yks.²** (22) **Fif.** A figure
orrowed from a horse that will not bear to be touched under the
ail or crupper (J.M.). (23) **n.Yks.⁴** Ill-deed nivver thrives. He’s
ꞁd nowt bud ill-deed fra t’ startin’. (24) Sc. That ill-deedy hempy,
ꞩOTT *Redg.* (1824) vii. **Cai.¹ Abd.** Ill-deedie fowk wud aye
wre-gang you, *Poems in Abd. Dial.* 35. **Frf.** An ill-deedy younker
ꞏd plundered his nest, WATT *Poet. Sketches* (1880) 29. **e.Fif.** Ill-
eedie vaig that he was, LATTO *Tam Bodkin* (1864) iii. **s.Sc.** The
I-deedie wratch, WILSON *Tales* (1836) III. 82. **Ayr.** I told you
hat the ill-deedy pyet would bring you into baith skaith and
corn, GALT *Sir A. Wylie* (1822) iii. **Lnk.** Ill brocht up, ill deedie
veans, HAMILTON *Poems* (1885) 56. **n.Yks.²** An ill-deedy body.
a5) **Nhb.** Ye ill-demised wretch (R.O.H.); **Nhb.¹** (26) **Bnff.¹** A’
hing wiz unco ill-dereyt i’ the hoose. He wiz weel eneuch claid,
it he wiz ill-dereyt amo’ the sheen. (27) **Per.** No a cratur’ ill-
esign’d, HALIBURTON *Ochil Idylls* (1891) 133. (28) **Not.¹, Lei.¹**
.Som.¹ Her’ve a got th’ ill-disgestion so bad. (29) **S. & Ork.¹** (30)
ꞏChs.¹ (31, a) **Per.** It’s the ill doer ’at fears the ill word, CLELAND
nchbracken (1883) 191, ed. 1887. **Dmb.** I cannot understand how
ou needed to rin awa frae Embro like an ill doer, CROSS *Disruption*
1844) xxxii. **Ayr.** A foul friar made my mother an ill-doer, GALT
ꞏilhaias (1823) vii. (b) **n.Lin.¹** As soon as a grazier is convinced
hat he has a beast which is not kindly disposed to take on fat, or
s an ill-doer, . . he should dispose of the unthrifty animal, *Treatise*
Live Stock (1810) 128. (32, a) **Abd.** Ill-doin’ blackguards,
ᴀNDERSON *Rhymes* (1867) 91. **Per.** Wadna . . . belike ane o’ the
raesome Psaulms o’ penitence be fitter baith for the puir bairn an’
s ill-doin’ faither! CLELAND *Inchbracken* (1883) 188, ed. 1887.
If. The ill-doin waffie . . . found no favour, COLVILLE *Vernacular*
1899) 18. **Rnf.** Tormented wi’ wasterfu’ ill-doing wives, M⁽ᴳILV-
AY *Poems* (ed. 1862) 47. (b) **Lan.¹** (33) **Sh.I.** Kens doo no ’at
it’s ill dŭn ta cry after a man whin he’s apon his gaet ta da
ea! *Sh. News* (Oct. 2, 1897). **Frf.** It was real ill-dune o’ ye,
ᴏBERTSON *Provost* (1894) 126. **N.I.¹** It was very ill done of you
ꞩo go there. **Nhb.** ’Twas an ill-dyun thing on thame laddies ti gan
n’ styen the poor dukes (R.O.H.). (34) **w.Yks.², Lan.¹ s.Lan.¹**
here’s a lot o’ fooak as thinks they’re ill done to when they just
ꞏd wod they deserve. (35) **Sc.** I kent richt weel it boded nae
ᴜde, an’ had an ill dread that Kenny widna wait to meet his end

in a contented manner, *St. Kathleen* (1820) IV. 144 (JAM.). (36)
Bwk. That nae guid will be his end Gin he no’ tak’ thocht an’
mend, Puir, ill-dreaded Yiddum, CALDER *Poems* (1897) 123. (37)
Sc. It is the ill-doers are ill-dreaders, SCOTT *Guy M.* (1815) liii ; A
common Sc. prov. (JAM.) **Cai.¹** (38) Sc. (JAM.) (39) Sh.I. Doo
shŭrely kens at Sholma is hed a ill e’e ta Rigga, sin dey wir calves,
Sh. News (Sept. 4, 1897). **n.Sc.** The power of the evil eye was
possessed by some. It was supposed to be inherent in some
families, and was handed down from generation to generation to
one or more members of the families. The power was called into
use at the will of the possessors and was exercised against those
who had incurred their displeasure, or on behalf of those who
wished to be avenged on their enemies and paid for its exercise. . .
To avert the influence . . . Go to a ford where the dead and the
living cross, draw water from it, pour it into a cog with three girds
over a crosst shilling, and then sprinkle the water over the victim
of the ill ee in the name of the Father, the Son, and the Holy
Ghost, GREGOR *Flk-Lore* (1881) 34, 35, 42. **Mry.** When bairns we
were a’ douk’d thegither, To take aff the ill e’e o’ a witch, HAY
Lintis (1851) 14. **Abd.** You came straight before the cow, and you
cast an ill ee upon her, muttering some hell-words about ‘ novum
lac,’ RUDDIMAN *Sc. Parish* (1828) 38, ed. 1889. **a.Per.** All was
ascribed to witch-craft. ‘ ill e’en,’ and Auld Donald o’ Jerah, MON-
TEATH *Dunblane Traditions* (1835), ed. 1887. **Ayr.** The blighting
blink o’ an ill e’e has lighted upon you, GALT *Gilhaize* (1823) xvii.
Lnk. They would be thick enough if ill hands and ill e’en baed
awa’ from them, GRAHAM *Writings* (1883) II. 102. **Gall.** Some
people are yet suspected of having an ill e’e, otherwise, having an
eye hurtful to everything it looks on. Blacksmiths pretend to know
many of this way, and will not allow them to stand in their forges,
when joining or wielding pieces of iron together, as they are sure
of loosing the *wauling lunt*, if such be present, MACTAGGART *Encycl.*
(1824) 278, ed. 1876. (40) **Ayr.** They had baith of them an ill end,
and indeed, from their way of leeving, it was a thing to be looked
for, SERVICE *Dr. Duguid* (ed. 1887) 115. **n.Cy.** (J.W.) (41) **Nhb.**
An ill-fyeced leukin chep (R.O.H.); **Nhb.¹** (42) **Nhb.** He’s an
ugly body, a bubbly body, An ill-faired, ugly loon, *Sandgate Girl’s*
Lamentation (R.O.H.). (43, a) **n.Yks.¹²⁴, m.Yks.¹** (b) **n.Yks.²**,
m.Yks.¹ (44) **n.Yks.²** An ill-fared lot. **n.Lin.¹** (45) **Cum.** The
vile ill-farrant randy, RAYSON *Poems* (1839) 46 ; **Cum.¹⁴ Lan.** He
was ‘ ill-farrant’ and revengeful, BURNETT *Lowrie’s* (1877) viii. (46)
Edb. We were very ill-fash’d with the English landloupers, PENNE-
CUIK *Tinklarian* (1810) 6. **Wm.** When t’man com back ta whar
he left his cofe, an’ cudn’t find it, he wes gradely ill-fasht aboot it,
Spec. Dial. (1890) pt. ii. 34. (47, a) **War.⁸** It is an ill-fashioned house.
(b) Abd. A vulgar, ill-fashion’t set, ALEXANDER *Johnny Gibb* (1871) viii.
Fif. (JAM.) (48,a) Sc. Gosh woman. A wad be ill-far’d to see, GRAHAM
Writings (1883) II. 13. **Bch.** Oftentimes there is no help but to commit
Some ill-far’d crimes, FORBES *Dominie* (1785) 32. **w.Sc.** He needit the
help o’ that ill-faured loon, MACDONALD *Settlement* (1869) 165, ed.
1877. **Fif.** Ye ill-faured loon! ROBERTSON *Provost* (1894) 95.
Dmb. Partly for this ill-faur’d affair o’ yours, CROSS *Disruption*
(1844) xxviii. **Ayr.** ‘ Whereas’ is an ill-farr’d beginning to a billy
doo, GALT *Lairds* (1826) xi. **Lnk.** That’s just his ill-fart crime,
WATT *Poems* (1827) 56. **Edb.** They never stand to say wi’ speed
Some ill-far’d name, *Har’st Rig* (1794) 21, ed. 1801. **Slk.** Ye sudna
swear that gate for it’s unco ill-faured, HOGG *Tales* (1838) 21, ed.
1866. **Dmf.** He left aff the ill-faurt pranks, QUINN *Heather* (1863)
22. (b) **Gall.** I forgot the ill-fared memory of the two girls,
CROCKETT *Grey Man* (1896) 56 ; There cursed clamour queemly
sleeps, The wicked ill-fared din, MACTAGGART *Encycl.* (1824) 166,
ed. 1876. (c) **Abd.** He insisted on my lookin’ at his leg, which he
said was very ill-faurt twa or three days syne, but wasna that oon-
bonny noo, PAUL *Abd.* (1881) 111. (d) **Sc.** It wad be a sair misery
if oor ill-faured tongues suld make the young maister worse,
REDDEN M⁽ᶜlellan (1895) 352. **s.Yks.¹** *MS. add.* (T.H.) (e) **Sc.**
(JAM.) (f) **n.Yks.⁴** (49, a) **Sc.** (JAM.) **Abd.** Wha has a heart
sae borne down wi’ wae, Will but ill-far’dly owther sing or say,
SHIRREFS *Poems* (1790) 100. (b) **Sc.** Kend my minny I were wi’
you Ill-fardly wad she crook her mou’, HERD *Coll. Sngs.* (1776)
II. 51 (JAM.). (50) **n.Yks.²** They’re nowther God-fearing nor ill-
fearing. (51) **w.Yks.** (J.W.) **Lan.** Yo’ wanted me to tell yo’ why
I were so ill-fleyed o’ Sunday neet, FOTHERGILL *Healey* (1884) viii.
(52) **Sc.** (JAM., s.v. Flyte). (53) **Sc.** Keep off my boat; . . you have
an ill-fitt, ROY *Horseman’s Wd.* (1895) xv. **Sh.I.** When a fisherman left his house to proceed to his boat . . . he was very particular
as to meeting a person by the way, lest they should have an ‘ evil
eye,’ or an ‘ ill fit,’ SPENCE *Flk-Lore* (1899) 110. **n.Sc.** GREGOR
Flk-Lore (1881) 194. (54) **Sc.** He’ll be sayin’ they want nae ill-
fitters there, ROY *Horseman’s Wd.* (1895) xvi. (55, a) **Cai.¹, Bnff.¹,**
Cld. (JAM.) (b) **Bnff.¹** The twa loons ill-gabbit ane anither, till a’

thocht muckle black shame o' thim. Cld. (Jam.) (56) Cai.¹, Baff.¹, Cld. (Jam.) Gall. Till every ... ill-gabbit mim-mooed hizzie had a lick at puir Birsay, Crockett *Moss-Hags* (1895) xxiii. (57) sw.Lin.¹ It's an ill-gain place. (58) Fif. Skail that mad ill-gainshon'd byke O' Test'ment-men that doth us fyke, Tennant *Papistry* (1827) 103. (59) Fif. (Jam.) (60, *a*) Sc. (Jam.) Baff.¹ 'That bavin hiz an ill-gait o' throwin' stehns.' Often used in the *pl.* 'A thocht he wiz gain't'dee weel, bit he's back till a's ill-gaits.' Lnk. He's brocht curses enow on the hoose wi' his ain ill-gates, Hamilton *Poems* (1865) 26a. (*b*) m.Yks.¹ (61, *a*) Sc. (Jam.) Abd. He's a coorse ill-gate't ablach, Alexander *Johnny Gibb* (1871) xix. Lnk. She's an ill-gaeted body, Hamilton *Poems* (1865) 282. Gall. Mactaggart *Encycl.* (1824). n.Yks.², m.Yks.¹ (*b*) n.Yks.¹²⁴ (62, *a*) Cai.¹ (*b*) Sc. (Jam.) Edb. He's been an ill-gien chiel indeed, Learmont *Poems* (1791) 46. Bwk. Ill-gien witches, Henderson *Pop. Rhymes* (1856) 59. Cum. Ye'd think to see her ill-gean feace, Rayson *Poems* (1839) 52 ; Cum.¹ ; Cum.⁴ Ill-gien gossips, Richardson, 159. Wm. (B.K.) (63) Cum. Ah bully-rag't a lock eh t'warst end o' them fer ther ill-geeness, Sargisson *Joe Scoap* (1881) 167 ; Cum.⁴ (64) Frf. Some hundreds o' ill-gotten, unchristened weans, Watt *Poet. Sketches* (1880) 75. Lnk. Wae be to thee an' that ill-gotten gett o' thine, Graham *Writings* (1883) II. 32. Lan. That ill-getten whelp, Waugh *Tattlin' Matty*, 20. (65) Hrf. (W.W.S.) (66, 67) Baff.¹ (68, *a*) Sc. The thing was ill-guided, Stevenson *Catriona* (1893) xv. n.Sc. Through grief, and ill diet, and ill-guiding, I took a bloody flux, Wodrow *Sel. Biog.* (ed. 1845–7) II. 97. (*b*) Sc. Ne'er a bit will I yield my consent to his being ill-guided, Scott *Rob Roy* (1817) xxv. Abd. Ye tak' mair drink than's good for you, and come home drunk, an' vex an' ill-guide your wife, Paul *Abd.* (1881) 6a. (69) Abd. To his puir, foul, ill-guided bairns a mither's kindness shaw, Anderson *Rhymes* (1867) 48. Frf. Leavin' the ill-guided loon to the soothin' sympathy o' ane or twa wha had stuid their grund, Willock *Rosetty Ends* (1886) 13, ed. 1889. (70) Abd. That ill-hadden gaist, Skinner *Poems* (1809) 97. (71) Cai.¹ Baff.¹ The siller, it's keepit in upon squeelin's ill haint. Edb. Binna swear To ding a hole in ill-hain'd gear, Fergusson *Poems* (1773) 217, ed. 1785. (72) Cld. (Jam.) (73) n.Yks.⁴ (74) Frf. I may have given a present of an old top-coat ... he looked ill-happit. Barrie *M. Ogilvy* (1896) vi. n.Cy. (J.W.) (75) Baff.¹ Cld. (Jam.) (76) n.Sc. (Jam.) (77) Cai.¹, Baff.¹ Abd. The puir rascal's nae that ill-hearted, *Deeside Tales* (1872) 26. Per., Cld. (Jam.) Ayr. Fient hae't o' them's ill-hearted fellows, Burns *Twa Dogs* (1786) l. 180. Gall. A fair-faced, hard-natured, ill-hearted woman, Crockett *Standard Bearer* (1898) 103. (78) Sh.I. Arty o' Uphoos repents na his ill-hertidness la Willa Ridland, *Sh. News* (Aug. 21, 1897). Per., Cld. (Jam.), Baff.¹ (79) w.Som.¹ Her's a ill-hearty, wisht poor bild a come. n.Dev. Thee tack me, ya unlifty, ill-hearty, untidy meazel, *Exm. Scold.* (1746) l. 103. (80) w.Yks. He's a reight ill-heired un (Æ.B.). (81) Sh.I. On I gaed laek da very Ill helt, Burgess *Sketches* (2nd ed.) 66 ; I felt da Ill-helt risin' up 'ithin me, Clark *N. Gleams* (1898) 100. Or.I. The devil [is called] da auld chield, da sorrow, da ill-healt, or da black tief, Fergusson *Rambles* (1884) 165. (82) Sh.I. Clip aff as muckle or as little as doo tinks fit, ill helty hair I care, *Sh. News* (July 1, 1899). (83) n.Yks.² (84) Sh.I. Dey [lambs] wir maistly a' sair illhoitlt, an' nae winder, whin der midders wis just skin an' bane, *Sh. News* (May 29, 1897). (85) Slk. The ill-hued carlin, Hogg *Tales* (1838) 153, ed. 1866. (86) Abd. That ill-hung tongue o' yours, Alexander *Ain Flk.* (1882) 97. (87) Nhb.¹ (88, *a*) S. & Ork.¹ (*b*) Or.I. (J.G.) (89, *a*) S. & Ork.¹ Cai.¹ An ill-hyvered tongue. (*b*) S. & Ork.¹ *MS. add.* (*c*) Or.I. (J.G.) (90, *a*) Cai.¹, Baff.¹ Abd. Fat's the eese o' a lawyer gin he hinna a gweed moufu' o' ill jaw, Alexander *Ain Flk.* (1882) 98. Cld. (Jam.) Gall. (He) was just a grabbing, shyling cuif, Fu' fit to gie ill jaw The lee-lang day, Mactaggart *Encycl.* (1824) 93, ed. 1876. (*b*) Baff.¹ (91) Baff.¹ (92) Sh.I. I wannder'd aboot da hoose a fore-nûn, ill-kennin'whatta dû, Clark *N. Gleams* (1898) 96. (93) m.Yks.¹ (94) Gall. I was not so ill learned in the ways of maids, Crockett *Standard Bearer* (1898) 107. Keb. I keep house-room amongst the rest of the ill-learned bairns, Rutherford *Lett.* (1660). (95) Per. He is pock-pitted, ill-legged, in-kneed, and broad-footed, *Edb. Antiq. Mag.* (1848) 47. (96) Sc. Why should a young ill-less thing like this be made to suffer! Keith *Bonnie Lady* (1897) 51. S.& Ork.¹ Abd. A most gracious ill-less prince, having no mind of such plots, Spalding *Hist.* Sc. (1792) I. 317. Ayr. The ill-less vanity of being thought far ben with the great is among others of her harmless vanities, Galt *Provost* (1822) xxxv. (97) N.I.¹ Ant. 'A ha'e been gye an' bad this while.' 'A jest thocht that ; you're very ill-like,' *Ballymena Obs.* (1892). n.Yks.², w.Yks. (J.W.) (98, *a*) Sh.I. Nae winder 'at doo's ill-laekit bi a' 'at iver kent dee, *Sh. News* (July 31, 1897). (*b*) e.Yks.¹ *MS. add.* (T.H.) ; Bess isn't

at all a ill-like't lass. (99) n.Yks.² They ill-likken'd her sair. (100) Per. Think o' me to be taen by the folk for an ill liver, Cleland *Inchbracken* (1883) 149, ed. 1887. (101) Per. It's a daft-like story o' ill livin' 'at they're wantin' to pruive on him, *ib.* 232. (102) Sh.I. Puir ill-luckid Willa, Shû hassna a man body ta tak her pairt, *Sh. News* (June 17, 1899). (103) m.Yks.¹ (104) Yks. (C.W.D.) (105) Sh.I. Dat inquisitive ill-makin' lipper. Her time is spent in vitchin, an' carryin' stories frae wan neebor till anidder, *Sh. News* (Jan. 8, 1898). (106) Sc. 'Give a thing, and take a thing, Is the ill man's goud ring.' A cant among children, when they demand a thing again, which they had bestowed, Kelly *Prov.* (1721). (107) w.Yks. (E.G.) ; *Leeds Merc. Suppl.* (Apr. 28, 1894). (108) m.Yks.² (109) Lakel.² Ther war tween or three ugly liuken thieves darken aboot, an' he was flait o' gitten ill-mezzur frae them gaan hiam. (110) Or.I. (Jam. *Suppl.*) Cai.¹, Baff.¹ w.Sc. (Jam. *Suppl.*) (111) Abd. An noo, for a' oor wrang-duins an' ill-min'in's, for a' oor sins and trespasses, Macdonald *D. Elginbrod* (1863) I. 6. (112, *a*) Cum.¹ (*b*) Cum.⁴ (113, *a*) Baff.¹ (Jam.) (*b*) Baff.¹ The ill-mouan, it they ga' the aul' man, wiz past a' spykan. (114) Baff.¹ (Jam.) (115) Ir. He knows it's ill my common, Carleton *Traits* (ed. 1843) I. 6. (116) Abd. For a' the ill name they bear, Cadenhead *Bon-Accord* (1853) 118. Lnk. To thraw the mouth, to ca' ill-names, Is surely very bad, Rodger *Poems* (1898) 130, ed. 1897. (117) Per. Ye lawwers, lay aside your briefs ; Ill-named, they ne'er have endin', Haliburton *Ochil Idylls* (1891) 61. (118) Sh.I. Juist set dee doon agen laek a gûde boy ... as doo'll pit me in ill-nature, *Sh. News* (Oct. 8, 1898). Abd. Nane o' yer ill-natur', Alexander *Johnny Gibb* (1871) xxv. n.Cy. (J.W.) (119) Sc. He has a very kind heart; but O! it's hard to live wi' him, he's sae ill-natured (Jam.). n.Cy. (J.W.) (120, *a*) ne.Sc. If there was ony ill-aff creatur' that had been gien owre by the ither doctors, he never refused them his services, Grant *Chron. Keckleton*, 38. Cai.¹ Baff.¹ She's ill-aff amon' sic a hard-hehrtit crew. Ayr. They let him spend as much siller ... as would keep an ill-off family for weeks, Johnston *Kilmallie* (1891) I. 175. n.Lan.¹ (*b*) Cld. (Jam.) (121) Ayr. Or else, I fear, some ill ane skelp him, Burns To G. Hamilton, l. 20. w.Yks. Eh, but he's an ill en, *Yks. Wkly. Post* (Apr. 17, 1897) ; w.Yks.¹ Thou munnot forgit how there wor ya illan amang twelve, ii. 314. (122) Abd. I was rael ill-pay't for 'im, peer stock, Alexander *Ain Flk.* (1882) 219. Rnf. I was ill-paid to hear't (Jam.). (123) Cai.¹, Baff.¹, Cld. (Jam.) (124, *a*) Sc. They had a great fire ; .. it minds me o' the ill part, Graham *Writings* (1883) II. 54. (*b*) w.Som.¹ Her did'n ought to a tookt it ill-part like. nw.Dev.¹ (125) Lnk. Out of which was to be deduced [deducted] some ministers' stipends ... and ill payments, with all public dues, Wodrow *Ch. Hist.* (1721) I. 146, ed. 1828. (126) w.Yks. At first I used to be varry ill-pegged, Burnley *Girlington Jrn. Alm.* (1875) 3. (127) Bdf. (J.W.B.) (128) Sc. I trust, if ayont to the ill place she win, They'll be able to bear wi' her flytin' an' din, Nicoll *Poems* (ed. 1843) 134. Baff. Donald, pardon thae, Or to an ill place ye maun gae, Taylor *Poems* (1787) 118. Abd. Dinna sen' me to the ill place. Ye loot the deils gang intil the swine, lat me tee, Macdonald *Sir Gibbie* (1879) vi. Per. Hell and heaveu were pulpit words ; in private life we spoke of the ill place, Ian Maclaren *Brier Bush* (1895) 182. Ayr. He thocht he was deid, and sinking doon, doon, to the hettest neuk of the ill place, Service *Dr. Duguid* (ed. 1887) 135. Gall. She must gang to the Ill Place her ain gate, Crockett *Anna Mark* (1899) viii. (129) n.Sc. (Jam.) (130) Sc. (*ib.*) (131) Cai.¹ (132, *a*) Frf. They were gey ill put on, Willock *Rosetty Ends* (1886) 25, ed. 1889. N.I.¹, n.Yks.¹²⁴, m.Yks.¹ (*b*) m.Yks.¹ (133) Sc. An awfu' thing it is to see sic an ill-red-up house, Scott *St. Ronan* (1824) xvi. Cai.¹ (134) Hrf.¹ (135, *a*) Sc. (Jam.), Cai.¹ (*b*) Ant. A gied him an ill-ser'd answer, *Ballymena Obs.* (1892). (136) Sc. Fresh fish and poor friends become soon ill-sar'd, Kelly *Prov.* (1721) 106. (137) Sc. (Jam.), Cai.¹ Bch. Wha' for's ill-scrappit tongue, Forbes *Ulysses* (1785) 24. Abd. The ill-scrapit tongue o' you! Ruddiman *Sc. Parish* (1828) 37, ed. 1889. Frf. The brunt o' her ill-scrapit tongue, Willock *Rosetty Ends* (1886) 35, ed. 1889. Per. Haud yer lang, ill-scraipet tongue, Cleland *Inchbracken* (1883) 188, ed. 1887. (138, *a*) Sc. Thae blae wishy-washy colours ill set an old skin, Keith *Bonnie Lady* (1897) 112 ; it ill-sets me to be thinkin' such a thought, *ib. Lisbeth* (1894) vii. Sh.I. Isna some o' da boy's claes awfil ill-settin'! *Sh. News* (Apr. 28, 1900). (*b*) Sc. My lady ... is an ill-set body, and inhadden too in the matter of hospitality, *ib. Bonnie Lady* (1897) 98. Abd. Ye're o'er ill-set, As ye'd hae measure, ye sud met, Keith *Farmer's Ha'* (1774) st. 38, ed. 1801. Fif. The ill-set rascal, the ill-doing, Colville *Vernacular* (1899) 18. Dmb. He may be an ill-set thief, Cross *Disruption* (1844) xv. Rnf. A' that ill-set men will say Shall dae nae harm, Fraser *Post-Chimes* (1853) 174. Ayr. It's neither because I'm sour nor ill-set, Ainslie

Poems (ed. 1892) 70. **Lnk.** Ye ill-set imp l NICHOLSON *Kilwuddy* (1895) 161. **Gall.** Ill-set customs duties, CROCKETT *Standard Bearer* (1898) 119. **Ant.** A biting dog will be called ' ill-set,' *Bally-mena Obs.* (1892). (c) w.**Yks.** Their parents are ill set to knaw what they are javvering about, SKIPTON *Dial.* (1834) *Pref.*; w.**Yks.**[1] He's ill-set to git a living. **Lan.** Folk 'll be as ill set to believe witch tales as th' Heawse o' Lords to pass a reform bill, STANDING *Echoes* (1885) 10. e.**Lan.** Said of a lame man. ' He seemed very ill-set to walk,' *N. & Q.* (1874) 5th S. i. 6; e.**Lan.**[1] (139) **Gall.** Frustrated of my intention by the ill-setness of others, CROCKETT *Grey Man* (1896) ii. (140) m.**Yks.**[1] (141) **Cai.**[1], **Bnff.**[1], **Abd.** (JAM.) (142) **Ayr.** There's o'er muckle o' the auld sojer in yon deevil—an ill-shapet, ungratefu', impertinent blackguard, HUNTER *Studies* (1870) 189. (143) **Ayr.** Ye'll search lang and vain for an ill-side in the life-work o' Betsey M'Nabb, AITKEN *Lays* (1883) 48. (144) **Sh.I.** Da brown kidneys wis da first brak' 'at iver I got—ill sicht be seen apon hit frae my hert, *Sh. News* (Aug. 28, 1897) ; Ill-sight be seen apo' der sanitary laws, *ib.* (Mar. 3, 1900). (145) **Edb.** An ill-sitten, shanglan' sutor, he, Wi' bairnly squeaking voice, *Carlop Green* (1793) 129, ed. 1817. (146) **Sh.I.** Nae lass could staand his ilsket fun, *Sh. News* (May 15, 1897). (147) n.**Yks.**[1] (148) **Sc.** Ye'll be ill-sorted to hear that he's like to be in the prison at Portanferry, SCOTT *Guy M.* (1815) xlv. e.**Sc.** (JAM.) (149) **Sh.I.** Ill-spaekers, leers, an' clashers ir kebbie at ony time for suntin' ta spaek aboot, *Sh. News* (May 28, 1898). (150) **Rnf.** She's a very ill-speakin' woman, BARR *Poems* (1861) 112. **Ayr.** The sough of their ill speaking fallowed them and was forgotten, SERVICE *Dr. Duguid* (ed. 1887) 115. **Lnk.** Their leein', ill-speakin' and clashes Are ill to put up wi' nae doot, NICHOLSON *Idylls* (1870) 65. (151) **Gall.** It was ill-sorten on men like these, CROCKETT *Standard Bearer* (1898) 249. (152) n.**Yks.**[1] (153) e.**Yks.**[1] *MS. add.* (T.H.) (154) **Ayr.** Jenny sees the visit's no ill-ta'en, BURNS *Sat. Night* (1785) st. 8. **Gall.** [He] tauld his erran' pat and plain, And saw it was na that ill-ta'en, NICHOLSON *Poet. Wks.* (1814) 62, ed. 1897. n.**Yks.**[4] It war nobbut ill-ta'en what thoo sed. (155) **Sh.I.** Doo widna need ta tell them dat, daa, or den doo wid get a ill-taestid answer, *Sh. News* (Feb. 5, 1898). (156) n.**Yks.**[1 2 4], e.**Yks.**[1] *MS. add.* (T.H.), m.**Yks.**[1] w.**Yks.** Ther's a lot o' fowk as thinks they're ill-tented when they just get what they desarve, *Yks. Wkly. Post* (Apr. 17, 1897) ; w.**Yks.**[2] Poor barns, ain' ther' mother deed thuh been ill-tented eniff. w.**Som.**[1] Her was that ill-tended, could'n never expect her to get on. They sheep do look as off they was ill-tended, I zim they be gwain back. (157) **Fif.** (JAM.) (158) **Cum.** It was a teaal at just suitit that ill-teull, SARGISSON *Joe Scoap* (1881) 8 ; **Cum.**[1] He's been an ill-teüll o' his life ; **Cum.**[4] **Wm.** Thoos an ill-teul [lit. ill-tool] min, thoo'll deea neea dow (B.K.). (159) **Sc.** We sudna speak o' the ill thief in the kirk, GRAHAM *Writings* (1883) II. 26. **Ayr.** The ill-thief blaw the Heron south ! BURNS *Dr. Blacklock* (1789) st. 2. **Lnk.** By the ill thief, What was't that fetch't ye hither ! WATT *Poems* (1827) 63. (160) w.**Som.**[1] Also applied to any spontaneous sore. ' Plaise, sir, they zen us home from school, 'cause they would'n let'n come to school, 'cause he've a got a ill thing in his neck.' *Dev. Horae Subsecivae* (1777) 227; **Dev.**[1] An inflammation of the finger. (161) **Sc.** Speak you him fair, and dinna be ill-thochtit, ROY *Horseman's Wd.* (1895) iv. **Sh.I.** I wis ta blame fir bein' sae ill-toughted, Girzzie, bit ... whin a lad laeks a lass right, he's most awfil suspicious, *Sh. News* (Nov. 26, 1898). (162, a) **Sh.I.** Doo ill-triv'n slootid baugh'd haeth'n, *Sh. News* (Aug. 13, 1898). **Nhb.**[1], **Cum.**[14] n.**Yks.** ' Thou puts the meat intu an ill-throvven skin,' your meat does you little good (T.S.); n.**Yks.**[1 2 4], e.**Yks.**[1] ne.**Yks.**[1] Feebly or imperfectly developed. m.**Yks.**[1] Stunted or uncultivated. w.**Yks.** He's an ill-thriven little tyke (J.J.B.). **Lan.**[1] Don't let that ill-thriven humble-bee chisel you. n.**Lin.**[1] (b) **Nhb.** He is an awd ill-throven thief, WILSON *Pitman's Pay* (1843) 46 ; **Nhb.**[1], n.**Yks.**[12], e.**Yks.**[1] (163) **Chs.**[2] I'm ill tied at home. (164, a) **Cum.** I hear a voice flyte—waur ner ill-tongues could tell, ROWLEY *Echoes Cum.* (1875) 149. (b) **Bch.** And very loud they me mischiev'd Wîth their ill tongues, FORBES *Dominie* (1785) 43. **Wgt.** A heard ya gi'en my wife a lot o' ill tongue an' abuse the ither day, FRASER *Wigtown* (1877) 258. (165, a) na.**Sc.** Wisht, Poppy, ye ill-tongued jaud, *Gordonhaven* (1887) 95. **Abd.** Ill-tonguet, ill-tricket little anes, ALEXANDER *Ain Flk.* (1882) 10. **Per.** Ye ill-tongued limmer, CLELAND *Inchbracken* (1883) 188, ed. 1887. **Ayr.** Yon ill-tongued tinkler, BURNS *Cry and Prayer* (1786) st. 19. **Lnk.** Ser's yee weel For a' yer ill-tongued slander, NICHOLSON *Kilwuddy* (1895) 38. **Edb.** A Randy race Of ill-tongued lim-mers, that exceed In want o' grace, *Har'st Rig* (1794) 9, ed. 1801. **Gall.** Ill-tongued loons hae scal'd me, KERR *Maggie o' the Moss* (1891) 75. (b) **Gall.** He wad whiles gie them swatches o' the auld ill-tongued Laitin, CROCKETT *Standard Bearer* (1898) 119. (166) e.**Yks.**[1] Ah niver seed sike a lot ov ill-toward brewts as Bess

Johnson bayns is, *MS. add.* (T.H.) (167) **Sh.I.** Sae fou o' nonsense an' ill tricks 'at ye can dö little idder bit budder folk, *Sh. News* (Sept. 9, 1899). (168) **Sh.I.** Aless he laeves his ill-trickid wyes, *Sh. News* (Oct. 1, 1898). n.**Sc.** (JAM.) ne.**Sc.** The child of their old age—a black-heidit, ill-trickit nickum, *Gordonhaven* (1887) 23. **Cai.**[1] **Abd.** Like ill-tricket nickums, we leuch at them a', OGG *Willie Waly* (1873) 75. (169) n.**Yks.**[2] 'An ill-trodden geeat,' a life of evil habits. ' Ill-trodden shoes.' (170) **Ayr.** The neebor woman took an ill-turn and deed, SERVICE *Dr. Duguid* (ed. 1887) 68. n.**Cy.** (J.W.) (171) **N.Cy.**[1], **Nhb.**[1] (172) **Bnff.**[1], **Ags.** (JAM.) (173) **Lnk.** When it [drink] 's ill used lts sting is keen, its mischief great, M'LACHLAN *Thoughts* (1884) 49. (174) **Sh.I.** De ill-vaamed wirds wir lang an' nebblt, An' wirna dine, *Sh. News* (Sept. 11, 1897). (175) **Sh.I.** The ill-vicked coo haes short horns, SPENCE *Flk-Lore* (1899) 229; Ye sood a' mak fewer illvickit remarks, *Sh. News* (June 12, 1897); **S. & Ork.**[1] (176, 177, 178) **S. & Ork.**[1] (179) **Ayr.** My ill-wal'd words, master, excuse, FISHER *Poems* (1790) 119. (180) **S. & Ork.**[1] (181) **Sc.** I thought no travel ill-wared, or any hazard too great on any occasion, whereby I might propagate this despised interest among you, *Cloud of Witnesses* (ed. 1720) 96 (JAM.). **Cai.**[1], n.**Yks.**[2], e.**Yks.**[1] *MS. add.* (T.H.), w.**Yks.** (J.W.) (182) **Sh.I.** A lot o' soor yoags an' ill-washin' scags, i' da shot o' his boat, STEWART *Tales* (1892) 14. (183 a, b, c) **Bnff.**[1] A hinna seen ye sin ye cam haim. Come our bye some forenicht, an' gee's yir ill-ween. (184. a) **Sc.** A' that illwul me whuspir thegither agayne me, RIDDELL *Ps.* (1857) xli. 7. **Gall.** A' my neibours to ill-will I thought it best, LAUDERDALE *Poems* (1796) 60. (b) **Rnf.** Did she no tak an ill will at me For saying her man was sae greedy, BARR *Poems* (1861) 112. **Ayr.** Onybody she took an ill will at—dod l she wrocht them dreeofully, they said, SERVICE *Dr. Duguid* (ed. 1887) 218. (185) **Sh.I.** l see her inunder da flee, bit shö's ill willied, *Sh. News* (Feb. 4, 1899) ; Ae ill-willied coo braks up a hael byre, *ib.* (Jan. 15, 1898). **Cai.**[1], **N.Cy.**[1] (186) **Sc.** (JAM.), **Cai.**[1] **Abd.** He wasna weel advis l by some o' Mully's ill-willers, ALEXANDER *Ain Flk.* (1882) 180. **Kcd.** Plague on Fortune ! a' my life I've found in her a sair ill-willer, GRANT *Lays* (1884) 191. **Lnk.** Our ill-willers would have it who believed that some of us are so humoursome that we neither agree with our brethren that are indulged, nor could agree with our brethren in any demand, WODROW *Ch. Hist.* (1721) II. 489, ed. 1828. (187) **Nhb.**[1] w.**Som.**[1] I can't abear to ask Jims to do nothin, he's always s' ill-willin. (188, a) **Sc.** An illwilly cow shou'd ha'e short horns, RAMSAY *Prov.* (1737) ; Little wats the ill-willy wife what a dinner may haud in't, *ib.* ; Then, Maggie, bena sae ill-willy, JAMIESON *Ballads* (1806) I. 310. **Abd.** Ye're as ill-willy a madam as ever I had to do wi', M'KENZIE *Cruisie Sketches* (1894) viii. **Per.** The auld ill-willy cow Wha weirded them nae good, SPENCE *Poems* (1898) 55. **Fif.** Baith the Bears now shine ill-willie Growlin' at our carouse, TENNANT *Papistry* (1827) 194. **Rnf.** That droll daugeon ca'd the deil Must be a base ill-willie chiel, WEBSTER *Rhymes* (1835) 25. **Ayr.** Your native soil was right ill-willie, BURNS *On a Sc. Bard*, st. 10. s.**Lth.** An ill-willy auld jaud o' a deacon's wife, HUNTER *J. Inwick* (1895) 62. **N.I.**[1] **Ant.** *Ballymena Obs.* (1892). **Lei.**[1], **War.**[2] (b) n.**Lan.**[1] (189) **Sc.** An ill win penny will cast down a pound, FERGUSON *Prov.* (1641) No. 69. (190) **Abd.** The laird wud hear ony o' his ill-win 'aboot respectable fowk, ALEXANDER *Johnny Gibb* (1871) xix. (191, a) **Ayr.** Bessie jawed a cuitty-boyneful of sapples on her neebor, muttering some ill-wish aboot her at the same time, SERVICE *Dr. Duguid* (ed. 1887) 68. **Cor.** The most common results of the witch's malice, or, as it is termed, 'the ill-wish,' are mis-fortunes in business, BRAND *Pop. Antiq.* (ed. 1870) III. 101. (b) n.**Lin.** Thaay gets up talk 'at Tommy hes ill-wished 'em, PEACOCK *Tales* (1890) and S. 37. e.**Suf.** (F.H.) **Dor.** Not quite satisfied he had been ill-wished, HEATH *Eng. Peas.* (1893) 82. w.**Som.**[1] It is common to say, of the pig is taken ill, or any other like calamity happens, 'I be safe he's a-ill-wished by somebody.' **Dev.** She'd ill-wish you if she could, BARING-GOULD *Spider* (1887) xx. **Cor.** The gossips of the parish . . . insisted . . . that the child had been ill-wished, and that she never would be better until ' the spell was taken of her,' HUNT *Pop. Rom. w.Eng.* (1865) 211, ed. 1896; **Cor.**[1] The common people still believe if they have a sudden illness that they are ill-wished, and pay a visit to the conjuror (white witch) to try and find out who has done it ; **Cor.**[2]

2. Phr. (1) *an ill servant will never make a good master*, he that cannot obey, cannot rule ; (2) *an ill shearer never got a good hook*, ' bad workmen complain of their tools '; (3) *as ill as a witch*, very ill; (4) *ill beef never made good broo*, one cannot make a good thing out of bad materials ; (5) *ill mat ye do that*, an imprecation : may evil attend you if you do that ; (6) *ill to follow*, (a) difficult to understand ;

R r 2

(b) hard to equal ; (7) *ill to learn*, hard to teach ; (8) *ill yetto comin*, a malediction : may evil return ; (9) *not that ill*, not so badly ; (10) *to be ill about anything*, (a) to be desirous of it ; (b) to be angry about it ; (11) *to be ill at anything*, to be displeased ; (12) *to be ill for anything*, to have a vicious propensity to a thing ; (13) *to be ill in oneself*, to have a derangement of the bowels, or a slight fever ; (14) *to be ill of anything*, ? to be grudging of, adverse to ; (15) *to be ill put to it*, to be in straitened circumstances ; (16) *to be ill to any one*, to treat any one unkindly ; to drive a hard bargain with any one.

(1) w.Yks. *Prov.* in *Brighouse News* (July 23, 1887). (2) Sc. FERGUSON *Prov.* (1641) No. 41. (3) s.Chs. (A.G.F.) (4) Sc. KEITH *Bonnie Lady* (1897) 66. (5) n.Sc. (JAM.) (6, a) Cai.¹ (b) w.Yks.¹, Nhp.¹ (7) N.I.¹ I wasn't ill to learn when I was young. (8) S. & Ork.¹ (9) Abd. She can ... vreet nae that ill, ALEXANDER *Ain Flk.* (1882) 192. Raf. [I] Could read my Bible no that ill, YOUNG *Pictures* (1865) 151. Ayr. Even the ploughman ... answered not that ill, JOHNSTON *Glenbuckie* (1889) 142. (10, a) Abd. (JAM.) (b) Ags. He was very ill about it (JAM.). Lnk. I kenna how I'll do without it ; An' faith I'm michty ill aboot it, NICHOLSON *Idylls* (1870) 298. (11) Sc. I was ill at my folk, WADDELL *Isaiah* (1879) xlvii. 6. Cai.¹ (12) Abd. (JAM.) (13) Hrf.¹ His arm be better, but he is ill in hisself and canna eat his victuals. (14) Sc. He that is ill o' his harbory is good o' the way-kenning, FERGUSON *Prov.* (1641) No. 347. (15) w.Yks. *Leeds Merc. Suppl.* (Apr. 28, 1894). (16) Sc. I jist didna like to see him ower ill to ye, FORD *Thistledown* (1891) 98. Cai.¹ Fif. She was ill to the bairn, and he couldna stand that, HEDDLE *Marget* (1899) 206. Ayr. The ne'er a bit they're ill to poor folk, BURNS *Twa Dogs* (1786) l. 184. Gall. I'se be na ill to thee, Billie, MACTAGGART *Encycl.* (1824) 66, ed. 1876.

3. adj. Evil, vicious, immoral.

Sc. Nane of your deil's play-books for me, it's an ill world since sic prick-my-dainty doings came in fashion, SCOTT *St. Ronan* (1824) xii. Bch. I dinna like to tell ill tales Upo' my neiper man, FORBES *Ulysses* (1785) 27. Abd. Ill bairns mend whiles by the lash, SHIRREFS *Poems* (1790) 349. Per. Thae hafflin callants ... dinna need it [toddy], an' it's an ill trick to learn them, CLELAND *Inchbracken* (1883) 106, ed. 1887. Ayr. The Laird of Linn wasnae the ill chiel that mony ane believed him to be, SERVICE *Dr. Duguid* (ed. 1887) 74. Lnk. Soon wi' ill neebors she fell in, NICHOLSON *Idylls* (1870) 123. Dmf. They sent ill Tam to fight the French, SHENNAN *Tales* (1831) 57. Gall. She is no that ill after a', CROCKETT *Cleg Kelly* (1896) 379. Nhb. (R.O.H.), Lakel.¹² Cum.⁴ Thy ill sinister look, RICHARDSON *Talk* (1886) 1st S. 68. n.Yks.⁴ An ill deed as ivver Ah kenn'd ; n.Yks.⁴ He's queer, bud sha's an ill un. w.Yks. Any man can guid a ill-wife but him at hez her, *Prov.* in *Brighouse News* (July 20, 1889) ; w.Yks.¹ Oliver war ill enif, ii. 306. Lan. Folk at's elected to go to heaven heawever ill they'n bin, STANDING *Echoes* (1885) 7.

4. Bad ; noxious ; hurtful ; insufferable.

Sc. The crop has turned no that ill after a', Sc. *Haggis*, 46. ne.Sc. Nae an ill head-piece, GRANT *Chron. Keckleton*, 75. Abd. The gait was ill, our feet war' bare, KEITH *Farmer's Ha'* (1774) st. 36. Frf. The town's ill smell and smoke, SANDS *Poems* (1833) 70. Per. The Trees are ill, but worse the Fruit, SMITH *Poems* (1714) 39, ed. 1853. Dmb. The cause o' his death was ill drink, TAYLOR *Poems* (1827) 18. Raf. Ill trade, ill prices, keep him under, FINLAYSON *Rhymes* (1815) 55. Ayr. Ill har'sts, BURNS *Toothache*, st. 4. Edb. This ill spring ye ken we're mony dead, LEARMONT *Poems* (1791) 268. Slk. The she 's ill, but no nae ill's the he, CHR. NORTH *Noctes* (ed. 1856) IV. 77. Dmf. There never was a good horse had ill color, CARLYLE *Lett.* (1844) in *Atlantic Monthly* (1898) LXXXII. 678. Nhb. It's an ill way o' thankin' a wife, s. *Tynedale Stud.* (1896). ne.Yks.¹ Sparrow-feathers dizn't mak an ill bed. w.Yks. (J.W.) Lan. When it's [a shirt] getten so ill whol 't weant stick together, STANDING *Echoes* (1885) 13. Chs.¹ ' It's as ill as scutch,' said of some weed difficult to eradicate.

5. Grieved, sorrowful. Ags. (JAM.)

6. Stormy.

Sh.I. I'm feared it's gaen ta be a ill nicht, an' sae I tink we'll a' just mak fir hame, STEWART *Tales* (1892) 144.

7. Hard, difficult.

Sc. Lazy folk are ill to kill, WHITEHEAD *Daft Davie* (1876) 61, ed. 1894. Sh.I. Dey [old customs] are ill ta sinder frae, I ken, *Sh. News* (Feb. 19, 1898). Abd. He's ill to please, KEITH *Farmer's Ha'* (1774) st. 12. Ked. Foreign dainties, Ill to get in Scottish glens, GRANT *Lays* (1884) 69. Frf. They winna be ill to mak, BARRIE *Thrums*

(1889) xiv. Per. Youth-head is wild, and ill to manage aft, NICOL *Poems* (1766) 178. Fif. It's no ill to understand hoo John wrote sae i' the Revelation, ROBERTSON *Provost* (1894) 22. Raf. Your impudence was ill to thole, M°GILVRAY *Poems* (ed. 1862) 101. Ayr. Hard work's no for him, and saft's ill to get, GALT *Sir A. Wylie* (1822) vi. Lnk. She's ill to please, NICHOLSON *Idylls* (1870) 30. Edb. State knaves are unco ill to catch, LEARMONT *Poems* (1791) 51. Bwk. Pride was aye a fractious yaud, An' unco ill to ride, CHISHOLM *Poems* (1879) 67. Slk. People were ill to know, HOGG *Tales* (1838) 132, ed. 1866. Dmf. Greet on, your sorrow's ill tae bide, THOM *Jock o' the Knowe* (1878) 82. Gall. Bairns were sma' and ill to rear, NICHOLSON *Poet. Wks.* (1814) 116, ed. 1897. Keb. He is not ill to be found, RUTHERFORD *Lett.* (1660) No. 78. N.I.¹ That stuff's ill to grind. Nhb. It's ill gettin a byen frev a dog (R.O.H.). Yks. (J.W.)

8. adv. Badly.

Sc. She's sprained her hand so ill that she cannot get to the shearing, WHITEHEAD *Daft Davie* (1876) 59, ed. 1894. Abd. Nae ill he limped, BEATTIE *Parings* (1801) 14, ed. 1873. Raf. Tho' [siller's] ill divided, NEILSON *Poems* (1877) 28. Ayr. Ye hate as ill's the very deil The flinty hearts that cannot feel, BURNS *J. Kennedy*, st. 5. Edb. Villas and Trade gree ill thegither, MACNEILL *Bygane Times* (1811) 54. n.Cy. (J.W.) w.Yks. Two men wor varry ill flay'd one neet, *Saunterer's Satchel* (1875) 15. Lan. Aw wantud to slek mi sum ill, *Sam Sondnokhur*, pt. v. 19. Chs.¹ Ill hurt, ill vexed.

9. sb. Evil, misfortune, injury ; harm ; misunderstanding.

Sc. Wad there be ony ill in getting out o' thae chields' hands? SCOTT *Old Mortality* (1816) xiv. ne.Sc. I'm sure some ill has happened to my faither, GRANT *Chron. Keckleton*, 45. Abd. I watna gin she's yet forgi'en him For a' his ill, COCK *Strains* (1810) l. 133. Fif. Bluidie fiend and ill To the vile Strumpet on the Hill! TENNANT *Papistry* (1827) 77. Ayr. May ill befa' the flattering tongue, BURNS *My Nanie*, st. 3. Lnk. I'm feer't that he'll dae himsel' ill, GORDON *Pyotshaw* (1885) 112; Gen. a reference to suicide in ' do oneself ill ' (A.W.). Bwk. In a' ill they took the lead, HENDERSON *Pop. Rhymes* (1856) 59. Nhb. What ill hes he deun ye? (R.O.H.) Yks. (J.W.) n.Yks.⁴ Thoo's warked him all t'ill 'at ivver thoo c'u'd.

10. Phr. (1) *ill take me*, may mischief befall me ; (2) *ill thram ye*, a malediction ; (3) *to cast ill on one*, to bewitch one ; (4) *to have got ill*, to have been bewitched ; (5) *to have ill at any one*, to bear any one ill-will.

(1) Ayr. Ill tak me gin I hae the like, GALT *Gilhaize* (1823) iii. (2) Cai.¹ (3) Sc. Apprehensions are sometime entertained, that witches by their incantations may cast ill upon the couple [recently married], particularly the bridegroom, if the bride has a rival. To counteract these spells, it is sometimes the practice for the bridegroom to kiss the bride immediately after the minister has declared them married persons, Edb. *Mag.* (Nov. 1818) 412 (JAM.). (4) Sc. He's gotten ill (JAM.). (5) Sh.I. Der Flekka an' wir Sholma haes ill at een anidder, *Sh. News* (Jan. 8, 1898).

11. Illness, pain ; disease ; difficulty.

Ked. Those who nursed him Through his sair and weary ill, GRANT *Lays* (1884) 46. Raf. Nae ill was e'er sae wickit, That the cure o't ever stickit, PICKEN *Poems* (1813) II. 118. Ayr. I have ill getting down and worse getting up, HUNTER *St. Mocha* (1870) 73. Nhb. The ' quarter-ill ' was a disease formerly prevalent among cattle (not sheep). It is now practically extinct (R.O.H.) ; Nhb.¹ n.Yks.² Cow-ills ; horse-ills. w.Som.¹ Usually applied to some local disease.

12. v. To harm ; to reproach, rail at ; to speak evil of. N.Cy.¹² Cum.¹ Don't ill a body if ye can't weel o' yaa ; Cum.⁴ n.Yks. You ill my farme, for you have said to some, Your undeaun and beggar'd, aine you com, MERITON *Praise Ale* (1684) ll. 519-20.

ILL-BISTIT, *adj.* Sh.I. Ill-natured, wicked. S. & Ork.¹

ILLECK, see Elleck.

ILLEGAL, *sb.* and *adj.* Sc. Suf. 1. *sb. Obs.* An illegality.

Abd. Whatsoever illegals hath been used against his friends and subjects, by imprisoning them without law, SPALDING *Hist. Sc.* (1792) II. 72.

2. A bastard. e.Suf. (F.H.)

3. *adj.* Illegitimate. e.Suf. In common use here (F.H.).

ILLEGIBLE, *adj.* and *sb.* e.An. 1. *adj.* Illegitimate. e.An.² An illegible child. e.Suf. In common use (F.H.).

2. *sb.* A bastard. e.Suf. (F.H.) Cf. illegal.

ILL-FIT, *sb.* Shr. A large vessel used in brewing.
(HALL.); **Shr.²** If it innod worked cool i' th' illfit, it wunna mak good drink.
[OE. *ealofæt*, an ale vat (*Leechdoms*, 142).]

ILLIFY, *v.* Lakel. Cum. Yks. Lan. Stf. Lin. [i·lifai.]
To vilify, slander, depreciate.
Lakel.¹; **Lakel.²** He dud iv'rything 'at laid i' his poor ta illify me at mi spot. **Cum.¹⁴** n.Yks. Sha's allas fun' sum'at oot sea 'at sha can illify this body er that (W.H.); n.Yks.¹²; n.Yks.⁴ Sha illifies onnybody an' evverybody, sha spares nowt na neeabody. ne.Yks.¹ They're awlus illifyin' yan anoother. e.Yks.¹, m.Yks.¹ w.Yks. Thare they ar, illifyin' an' backbitin ivvry boddy, Tom TREDDLEHOYLE *Bairnsla Ann.* (1862) 45; w.Yks.¹⁵, ne.Lan.¹, n.Stf. (J.T.) n.Lin. She should ha' kep' her-sen fra illifying you an' yours, PEACOCK *Tales* (1890) and S. 21; n.Lin.¹ Dick's been illifying my foäl, soä as I can't sell him fer hairf what he's wo'th, *Messingham* (1873).
Hence (1) **Illified**, *ppl. adj.* scandalized; (2) **Illifier**, *sb.* a slanderer. n.Yks.²

ILLIGHTEN, *v.* Obs. Sc. To enlighten.
Fif. Some of the Princes of Germanie, illightened by that same Holy Spirit and Word of God, Row *Ch. Hist.* (1650) 5, ed. 1842.

ILLION, *sb.* Lakel. Yks. [i·lian.] The waxed thread used by cobblers, a 'lingel'; also in *comp.* **Illion-end.**
Lakel.², n.Yks.² e.Yks. Coblers ... are to bringe with them ... thrid whereon to make illions, BEST *Rur. Econ.* (1641) 142.
[Lynyolf or inniolf, threde to sow wythe schone or botys, *Prompt.*; A lynȝelle, *licium*, Cath. Angl. (1483). Fr. *ligneul*, shoomakers thread, or, a tatching end (COTGR.).]

ILL-MUGGENT, *adj.* Obs. Sc. Evil-disposed.
Bch. Nor do I fear his ill chaft taak, Nor his ill-muggent tricks, FORBES *Ajax* (1785) 30.

ILLNESS, *sb.* Yks. Lin. An epidemic, as distinguished from a non-infectious disease.
Yks. (J.W.) sw.Lin.¹ I don't think it's a cold, I think it's an illness; we've all had it. She's gotten a cold; I don't know if it's an illness or not.

ILLUSTRATED, *ppl. adj.* Lon. Coloured.
Coloured, or ' illustrated shirts,' as they are called, are especially objected to by the men, MAYHEW *Lond. Labour* (1851) I. 51.

I-LORE, *int.* Sc. Also in form **elore.** Woe is me!
Gl. Sibb. (JAM.)

ILT, *sb.* Dev. (HALL.) The same as **Elt**, *sb.*¹ (q.v.)

ILTA, *sb.* Sh.I. Or.I. Also written **ilty** Or.I. [i·lta.]
1. Malice, anger. S. & Ork.¹, Or.I. (S.A.S.) **2.** *Comb.* **Ilta-foo**, full of malice and anger. *ib.*
[Cogn. w. Norw. dial. *ilt*, angrily (AASEN).]

IMAGE, *sb.* Sc. n.Cy. Lon. Nrf. Som. Cor. Also written **eemage** Sh.I. [i·midȝ.] **1.** A plaster figure.
w.Som.¹ The plaster figures carried about for sale by Italians are always 'images.'
2. A wooden figure carved by the fairies in the likeness of a certain person intended to be stolen.
ne.Sc. A man in the parish of New Deer was returning home at night. On reaching an old quarry ... he heard a great noise... He listened and his ear caught the words, ' Mak' it red cheekit and red lippit like the smith of Bonnykelly's wife.' He knew at once what was going on and what was to be done, and he ran with all his speed to the smith's house and ' sained ' the mother and her baby—an act which the nurse had neglected to do. No sooner was the saining finished than a heavy thud, as if something had fallen, was heard outside the house opposite to the spot where stood the bed on which the mother and her baby lay. On examination a piece of bog-fir was found lying at the bottom of the wall. It was the image the fairies were to substitute for the smith's wife, GREGOR *Flk-Lore* (1881) 62.
3. A figure of clay or wax used in witchcraft.
w.Sc. It is a very old belief that those who had made compacts with the devil could afflict those they disliked with certain diseases, and even cause their death, by making images in clay or wax of the persons they wished to injure, and then, by baptising these images with mock ceremony, the persons represented were brought under their influence, so that whatever was then done to the image was felt by the living original. The custom, not yet extinct, of burning persons in effigy is doubtless a survival of this old superstition, NAPIER *Flk-Lore* (1879) 77.
4. A thing supposed to adorn a room.
Nrf. I bought one of them glass boller-blocks more for images than for use, EMERSON *Son of Fens* (1892) 54.

5. A pitiful object; an oddity; a ' sight.'
Sh.I. What sees-doo ailin' da calf, man? Could doo noo a geen ta da eemage till I cam? *Sh. News* (Aug. 27, 1898); I da first dimrivin' dey swöped dis eemage oot among da ase, STEWART *Tales* (1892) 90. **Frf.** Wear absurd hats ... an' otherwise mak' images o' themsel's—the puir ignorant wretches, WILLOCK *Rosetty Ends* (1886) 65, ed. 1889. **n.Cy.** (J.W.) **Lon.** One boy, whose young woman made faces at it, .. got quite vexed and said, ' Wot a image you're a-making on yourself!' MAYHEW *Lond. Labour* (1851) I. 193. **Nrf.** Go on, you fond image, EMERSON *Son of Fens* (1892) 222. **Cor.²** You owld image.

IMAKY-AMAKY, *sb.* Slk. (JAM.) [Not known to our correspondents.] The ant. Cf. **emmet.**

IMBER, *sb.* and *v.* e.An. **1.** *sb.* A number.
e.An.¹ e.Suf. I should think she would soon have her imber of children (F.H.).
2. *v.* To number.
e.Suf. Hev you imbered them ship [sheep] to-day, bor? (F.H.)

IMBER, see **Ember.**

IMBOG, *v.* Obs. Sc. To engulf as in a bog.
Fif. Imbogg'd amid my biting mire I lay, TENNANT *Anster Fair* (1812) 148, ed. 1871.

IMBRANGLE, *v.* Chs. Lin. [imbra·ŋ(g)l.] To confuse, entangle; to embroil. See **Brangle**, *v.* **2.**
Chs.¹ He geet imbrangled wi' a woman; **Chs.³** An imbrangled affair. **Lin.** THOMPSON *Hist. Boston* (1856) 711; **Lin.¹**

IME, *sb.¹* Sc. Cum. [aim.] Soot; a thin scum or coating deposited on a surface.
Sh.I. Geordie Moad wis goin' at rubbin' da deid kirst wi ime an' watter, *Sh. News* (Dec. 31, 1898); 'At spunks sae bricht sood faa ta ime, BURGESS *Rasmie* (1892) 94; S. & Ork.¹ The sooty exhalation that forms a coating on kettles. **Cai.¹**, **Cum.¹⁴**
Hence (1) **Imey**, *adj.* sooty, black; (2) **Imin**, *sb.* a thin scum or covering.
(1) **S. & Ork.¹** (2) **Cum.¹**; **Cum.⁴** By this time it bed a good imin' of cream ower it, *C. Pacq.* (Aug. 17, 1893) 6, col. 1.
[ON. *ím*, dust, ashes, embers (VIGFUSSON).]

IME, *sb.²* Som. [Not known to our correspondents.] The tip of the nose. (HALL.)

IME, see **Hime**, *sb.¹*

IMEZ, *adv.* War. [i·mæz.] Near.
(HALL.); **War.⁴** Where's Warwick, d'ye say?—Why it's imez Barford where I was born.
[The same word as *eemest*, nearest, superl. of *eem*, near. See **Aim**, *adj.*]

IMFERENCE, *sb.* Hrf.² Sauciness; impertinence.

IMHIM, see **Impham.**

IMITATE, *v.* Chs. War. Shr. Oxf. e.An. Wil. Dor. [imitē·t.] **1.** To resemble, correspond to, match; *gen.* with *of.*
Wil.¹ ' The childern be immitatin' o' their wather about the nause.' Participle only so used. **w.Dor.** This here line ought to imitate that (C.V.G.).
2. To attempt, endeavour.
e.Chs.¹ It)s nóo yóos imitai·tin aat· it [It's noo use imitatin' at it]. **War.³** **Shr.¹** 'E's bin imitatin' at drivin' the 'orses the las' wik or two, but 'e inna-d-up to much. **e.An.¹** A child, or a sick person ' imitated to walk,' or to do something else, which he' proves unable to accomplish. **Nrf.** That hoss kick, sir? I never see him imitate to kick in my life (W.R.E.). **Suf.** That'll larn yow not to imitate gitten up there agin! *e.An. Dy. Times* (1892). **e.Suf.** Don't yow imitate hittin me, or yow'll find it won't pay (F.H.).
Hence **Imitation**, *sb.* an attempt.
e.Chs.¹ ' A very good imitation,' a very fair attempt at performing any given task.
3. To think about, feel inclined for; to consider how to do.
s.Oxf. ' Well, folks are a-sayin' as you be sweetheartin'.' ' It's a lie, mother! I never imitated of such a thing!' ROSEMARY *Chilterns* (1895) 145. **Suf.** I don't imitate to do it (C.L.F.). **Ess.** How do you imitate doing that? (H.H.M.)
4. To just miss doing or suffering a thing.
Nrf. He imitated to fall (W.W.S.).

IMMEDIENT, *adj.* Sc. Irel. I.Ma. Som. Cor. Also in forms **immadient, immajant** I.Ma.; **immaydiant** N.I.¹; **immedant** Abd.; **immedjunt** Cor. Immediate. Also used *advb.*
I.Ma. Bout ship, sir! aye immedient, BROWN *Witch* (1889) 8; There wasn' any train back immajant, RYDINGS *Tales* (1895) 70. **Cor.** So

they made a clear roo-ad, and I pass'd up between, And got tended immedjunt, by coose, FORFAR Poems (1885) 6.

Hence **Immediently,** adv. immediately.

Abd. The tither ane, they tell me, 's to be a bridegreem immedantly, ALEXANDER Ain Flk. (1882) 151. n.Ir. Immediantly there a cock gave a loud crow, Lays and Leg. (1884) 23 ; N.I.¹ I.Ma. And whipped af coorse immadiently, BROWN Doctor (1887) 158. w.Som.¹ Always. 'Nif tidn a teokt in hand [eemai·juntice], better let it alone.'

IMMENSE, adj. n.Yks.⁴ Exactly, precisely the thing required.

IMMER, see Ember.

IMMICK, sb. Sc. Also in form imok. The ant. See Emmet.

Its on-dwallers a' are but imoks afore Him, WADDELL Isaiah xl. 22 ; (JAM.) Per. Still in use here (G.W.).

IMMIE, IMMIS, see Emmet, Emmis.

IMODST, adj. Or.I. Also in form imoast. Unwilling, reluctant ; hindering. (JAM. Suppl.)

[Cp. Dan. imod, contrary.]

IMP, sb. and v. Sc. Irel. n.Cy. Nhb. Dur. Cum. Yks. Lan. Shr. Hrf. Rdn. e.An. Dev. [imp.] **1.** sb. A shoot from a tree or fence ; a sucker ; an ingrafted slip.

Sc. The imp or scion revives when the stock reviveth, BROWN Romans vi. 5 (JAM.). Shr.¹² Hrf.¹ A bud or a young shoot of a coppice that has been felled to bud. Rdn.¹ Dev. A friend of mine, who wished to improve the fences of some property he had purchased, was told by his labourer, 'he must dig up all the imps,' N. & Q. (1857) and S. iii. 195.

Hence **Impish,** adj. consonant to nature.

m.Yks.¹ Of a child, it will be said, ' He's impish enough : he's dad all over' [he's father all over ; bears a complete resemblance in disposition`]... Of the rosemary-tree, it will be said, that it is ' an impish thing,' and will not grow on any soil. Hence the common country saying, that it is only to be found about a house where the mistress is master.

2. A child.

Ir. It's starved wid the could the imp of a crathur does be, BARLOW Idylls (1892) 39. e.An.¹ I was afraid the poor imp would have been frizzled.

3. An additional ring of straw or other material, of varying size, placed under a bee-hive to enable the bees to add to their combs. Cf. eke, sb.¹

N.Cy.¹, Dur.¹, Cum.² n.Yks.¹ If of three folds or plies in height, it is a three-wreathed imp ; if four, a four-wreathed imp, and so on; n.Yks.²⁴, ne.Yks.¹ e.Yks. MARSHALL Rur. Econ. (1788) ; e.Yks.¹ w.Yks. Put an imp on it, BANKS Wkfld. Wds. (1865); w.Yks.¹

4. A length of hair twisted and forming part of a fishing-line.

e.Sc. Whether will ye put five or six hairs in the imp ? (JAM.) N.Cy.¹, Nhb.¹

5. v. To graft.

Sc. Believers are so closely united to Christ, as that they have been imped into him, like an imp joined to an old stock, BROWN Romans vi. 5 (JAM.).

6. To lengthen by the addition of something else ; to add 'imps' to a bee-hive.

n.Yks.² We're imping a bee-skep. e.Yks.¹ w.Yks. Our Fan's dress doose want impin' (F.P.T.) ; w.Yks.¹, ne.Lan.¹

7. To deprive of ; to rob.

Lan. GROSE (1790) MS. add. (P.) ; DAVIES Races (1856) 234.

[1. I was ... þe couentes gardyner for to graffe ympes, P. Plowman (B.) v. 137. OE. impa, a sucker, scion (SWEET). 5. Impe on an ellerne, P. Plowman (B.) IX. 147. OE. impian, to graft.]

IMPARFIT, adj. Nhb. Faulty, vicious.

Nhb.¹ Always used to denote a dirty, untidy woman.

[Al reson reproueþ such imparfit puple, P. Plowman (c.) IV. 389. OF. imparfait, imperfect (HATZFELD).]

IMPE, see Hemp.

IMPEDIMENT, sb. Irel. A physical defect.

N.I.¹ There was a man who had an impediment ; he had lost more than the half of his hand.

IMPER, v. Sh.I. To be so bold, ' imperent.'

I houp doo wid hae mair sense. I widna imper ta ax sic a thing, Sh. News (Oct. 14, 1899).

IMPERENCE, sb. Sc. Irel. I.Ma. Chs. War. Lon. Suf. Dor. Som. Cor. Also written imperance Don. Chs.¹⁸; and in form emprence Cor. [i·mpərəns.] A corruption of the word ' impudence.'

Frf. My certie, Hughie, what an imperence ye ha'e, Lowson Guidfollow (1890) 98. n.Ir. The imperence o' the fellow tae axe me wha sent it! LYTTLE Paddy McQuillan, 26. Don. Ye're too knowledgable a man for me have imperance to tell ye what ye're to do afther, MACMANUS Billy Lappin in Century Mag. (Feb. 1900) 604. I.Ma. 'Well, the imperence!' says Kelly's wife, BROWN Doctor (1887) 113. Chs.¹ Very common. War.⁴ I'll stand none of your imperence. Lon. 'Let me alone, imperence,' said the young lady, DICKENS Pickwick (1837) xiv. e.Suf. (F.H.) Dor. It be like her imperence, Windsor Mag. (Feb. 1900) 387. w.Som.¹ Eem·puruns. Cor. It was owing to the pride and emprence of the people, Tim. Towser (1873) 31.

IMPERENT, adj. Irel. I.Ma. Glo. Suf. Som. Dev. Cor. Also in forms emperent Cor.² ; emprent, hemparunt Cor. ; imprint I.Ma. [i·mpərənt.] A corruption of the word ' impudent.'

n.Ir. Half a dizen o' imperent wee fellows, LYTTLE Robin Gordon, 94. I.Ma. You're as bould as brass and as imprint as ain (S.M.). Glo. But I could talk to you, if you oodn't think it imper'ent, GISSING Vill. Hampden (1890) II. iii. e.Suf. (F.H.) w.Som.¹ Fap. prone to take liberties. 'Go 'long y' imperent young osebird.' Dev.⁸ Cor. But the people are nothen but hemparunt tra-ade, FORFAR Jan's Crtshp. (1859) st. 8 ; The emprent, saucy dog, HUNT Pop. Rom. w.Eng. (1865) 460, ed. 1896 ; Cor.²

IMPERIOUS, adj. Chs.¹⁸ Impetuous.

IMPERSOME, adj. Ken. Sus. Impertinent, 'imperent.' ne.Ken. (H.M.), Sus.¹

IMPERT, adj. Rut.¹ [i·mpət.] Pert, impertinent, 'imperent.' ' I don't think I was at all impert to him.'

IMPET, sb. Suf. An imp.

' Noo t'ain't,' said the impet, Suf. Chron. (1893). e.Suf. ' An impet of a boy, or girl,' very diminutive. ' What an impet thet gal hev turned out to be !' (F.H.)

IMPHM, int. Sc. Also in forms imhim Ayr. ; imph Lnk. ; imphim Sc. Sh.I. Kcd. An exclamation, gen. of assent.

Sc. Never got mair frae him ... than just a shak' o' the head, and maybe ay or imphm, ROY Horseman's Wd. (1895) v ; 'Imphim' wuss Susan Bethune's sole comment, SWAN Gates of Eden (1895) ii. Sh.I. 'Imh'm,' Sibbie said, as shü held ane o' her waers [wires] in her lips, Sh. News (Aug. 12, 1899). e.Sc. 'Imphm !' he sneered, 'it's easy dealin' whangs aff other folk's leather,'SETOUN Sunshine (1895) 289. Kcd. Dinna say a word at present. .. Gin it's 'imphim' Littlefirlot Sall mak' a' the rest his care, GRANT Lays (1884) 87. Ayr. Im-him! I see—then there'll be news, I don't misdoubt, JOHNSTON Kilmallie (1891) I. 160. Lnk. I gloom'd, and said 'Imph-m.'.. I was ... owre dour to say 'A-y-e!' NICHOLSON Idylls (1870) 50; 'Ay, imph!' sneered the unassured husband, MURDOCH Readings (ed. 1895) I. 190. Bwk. 'Aye, no, an' imphm,' was a' that I spak', CALDER Poems (1897) 288.

IMPIDENT, adj. Cum.⁴ [i·mpidənt.] In good spirits.

The idea intended to be conveyed is much weaker than that of impertinence or insolence, for it is used with reference to a person recovering his spirits after illness.

IMPINGALL, sb. Som. Dev. Also in forms impigang w.Som.¹; impingang Dev. ; nippigang w.Som.¹ An ulcer, cancer, abscess, 'amper' ; a sore, gathering.

w.Som.¹ Eem·pigang. Rare. 'I got a nippi·gang 'pon my 'an'-wrist ; and he do ache ... and I be feared there's another comin' tap my thumb. Dev. Horae Subsecivae (1777) 229.

IMPITTENCE, sb. Nhb. Impudence, forwardness, impertinence.

'Where's yor impittence to taak te me like that?' Phr. equivalent to—How dare you talk to me?' (R.O.H.)

IMPLEMENT, v. Obsol. Sc. To fulfil, perform.

Sc. To implement a promise, Scoticisms (1787). Per. I went to Finningand To implement your kind command, SMITH Poems (1714) 99, ed. 1853. Ayr. I come in ... neist market day and get them implemented, GALT Entail (1823) xviii.

IMPLIFY, v. e.Yks.¹ MS. add. (T.H.) [i·mplifai.] To implicate.

IMPOSE, v. w.Som.¹ With upon : to overcharge.

Hence **Imposing,** ppl. adj. high-charging.

A high-charging tradesman is an 'imposing fellow,' of the [eempoa·zeens]—i.e. the imposingest.

IMPOSSIBLE, *adj.* n.Yks.[2] Unsurpassable.

'An impossible being,' an 'out of the way' individual; an oddity.

IMPOSURY, *sb.* Irel. Imposition.

Ant. It was naethin' but a piece o' imposury, *Ballymena Obs.*
(1892).

IMPRESTABLE, *adj.* Obs. Sc. Impracticable.

Sc. Counting the cost, and seeing the cost of themselves imprestable, THOMSON *Cloud of Witnesses* (1683) 316, ed. 1871. Lak.
It is imprestable, because the number of the nonconformists is very
great, WODROW *Ch. Hist.* (1721) II. 393, ed. 1828.

IMPROVE, *v.* Nhb. Lin. Rut. War. Hrf. Nrf. Dev.
[imprū'v.] 1. To learn one's trade as an apprentice.

Rut.[1] He has to go out with the meat and that, and to improve
killing and such (s.v. Improver).

Hence **Improver,** *sb.* a deacon; one who is learning
the profession of a clergyman.

Dev. He had two with him who weren't proper parsons, but
improvers, *Reports Provinc.* (1885) 98.

2. To grow larger.

n.Lin.[1] Sam is n't long for this wo'ld; th' tumour's improved
that much this weak 'at he weän't hohd oot a deäl longer.

3. To approve; *gen.* with *upon.*

Nhb.[1], Hrt.[2] Nrf.[1] I don't improve of such conduct, I don't
(W.R.E.).

4. To reprove.

War.[4] You be too aisy with your children; you should improve
them when they are so ill-mannered.

IMPROVEMENT, *sb.* w.Yks.[2] A specimen of writing
brought from a school to show a boy's progress in writing.

Every such specimen would not be called an improvement; only
large sheets of paper ornamented at the borders with engravings
were so called. Now, it is believed, out of use.

IMPSE, *sb.* Dor. [Not known to our other correspondents.] Image, model.

The very impse o' 'im (C.W.B.).

IMPUDENCE, *sb.* Hrf. Indecency.

This deponent, blushing to see soe much impudence betwixt
the said persons, immediatly went out of the same chamber, *Hrf.
Dioc. Reg.* (Oct. 9, 1682); Hrf.[2]

[Taxe of impudence, A strumpet's boldness, SHAKS.
All's Well, 11.i. 173. Fr. *impudence,* shamelessness (COTGR.).]

IMPUNE, *sb.* Sc. Impunity.

Nane shall touch them with impune, JACKSON, in EDWARDS *Sc.
Poets,* 7th S.

IMPY, *adj.* n.Yks.[2] Wor.(H.K.) [i'mpi.] Mischievous.

IMRIGH, *sb.* Sc. Also in forms **eanaruich** Sc.;
imrie Gall. 1. A kind of soup.

Three cogues . . . containing eanaruich, a sort of strong soup
made out of a particular part of the inside of the beeves, SCOTT
Waverley (1814) xvii; (JAM.)

2. The scent of roasted meat.

Gall. Various viands of luscious dainties, the imry of which
went up the noses of the red-coated lads like electricity, MACTAG-
GART *Encycl.* (1824) 451, ed. 1876.

[1. Gael. *eanraich,* a kind of soup, flesh-juice (M. & D.);
Ir. *eanbhruith,* soup (O'REILLY).]

IMSOEVER, *adv.* Obs. Not. Howsoever, 'howsomever.' THROSBY *Thoroton's Not.* (1797) III. 455.

IN, *prep., adv., sb.* and *v.* Var. dial. uses in Sc. Irel. Eng.
[Eng. dial. forms. 1. (1) E, (2) En, (3) He,
(4) I, (5) Id, (6) Ih, (7) Ing, (8) Inn, (9) Iv. [in, i; iv is
gen. used when the next word begins with a vowel.]

(1) w.Yks. At we ma bake all us bread e won, *Gossips,* 23;
w.Yks.[1] Lan. Iv mi cwoat wur rent eteaw, SCHOLES *Tim Gamwattle* (1857) 27. nw.Der.[1] (a) S. & Ork.[1] Dev. Tha king es
huld en tha gallerys, BAIRD *Sng. Sol.* (1860) vii. 5. (3) n.Lin.[1]
You'll find it he th' carpenter's shop. (4) Wxf.[1], N.Cy.[1] Nhb.[1]
Used before a consonant. 'Where i' the warld are ye gannin ?'
Dur.[1] This pear grew i' my garden. Cum.[1] n.Yks.[12]; n.Yks.[4]
'I' is used before a consonant. 'I' t'boddum o' t'box.' ne.Yks.[1],
w.Yks.[1], w.Yks.[25], Lan.[1], e.Lan.[1], ne.Lan.[1] Cha.[1] The *n* is very
seldom sounded, either before a vowel or a consonant. Der.[1]
When not under stress; even before a vowel; Der.[2] I' good
saddens, 162. nw.Der.[1] I'taaw. Not. (J.H.B.), Shr.[1] Glo. What
be i' your fancy now, John ? GISSING *Both of this Parish* (1889) I.
307. Sur. I has some coûld tea i' this bottle, BICKLEY *Sur. Hills*
(1890) I. i. (5) e.Yks.[1] Before a vowel [1in the]. (6) Nhb. Aw
stept up an begun ih maw turn, BEWICK *Tyneside Tales* (1850) 14.
(7) Wxf.[1] (8) Sc. (JAM.), w.Yks. (S.K.C.), I.W.[1] (9) N.Cy.[1]

Nhb.[1] Used before a vowel. Dur.[1] The apple grew iv our orchard.
Cum.[1] He's lishest lad iv o' Brumfell parish. n.Yks.[1] Before a
vowel. 'Tolf iv all'; n.Yks.[24], ne.Yks.[1] e.Yks.[1] Before vowels.
m.Yks.[1] w.Yks.[1] He's iv our house.

2. Var. contractions: (1) Et; (2) Id, in the; (3) Imma,
in me; (4) Imme, in my; (5) Int, (*a*) in it; (*b*) see (2);
(6) It or I't', (7) Ith or I'th', see (2).

(1) Wm. Fowk et cuntra hes gitten ta dress thersell, GIBSON
Leg. and Notes (1877) 70. (2) Dur. Ah'll . . . gan aboot t'city id
streets, an id bracad ways ah'll seek 'im, MOORE *Sng. Sol.* (1859)
iii. 2. Not.[2] He's id garden. (3) Cum.[1], Yks. (J.W.) (4) Cum.
Aw 'at iver was imme way, *Borrowdale Lett.* in *Lonsdale Mag.*
(Feb. 1867) 311; (E.W.P.) w.Yks. (J.W.) (5, *a*) Nhb. Awn
warn a keahm hes-int been int this twee months, BEWICK *Tyneside
Tales* (1850) 10. Wm. This seck wi' Tomson int, ROBISON
Aald Taales (1882) 4. w.Yks. They fan a hoil in't (Æ.B.).
Lan. Th' Owd Lad's hed a hand int, BOWKER *Tales* (1882) 65.
(*b*) w.Som.[1] (6) Wm. Reet it middle et rooad, *Spec. Dial.* (1885)
pt. iii. 2; She mun ha shining shoon et sit it hoos in, BRIGGS
Remains (1825) 162. n.Yks. It's i't waanhuss [wagon-house]
(T.S.); n.Yks.[1] I' t'thick on't. w.Yks. Worn a greeat hoyle it
hause-floar, TOM TREDDLEHOYLE *Ben Bunt* (1838) *Int Publick.*
(7) Cum. Them twea fellows ith bwoat, *Borrowdale Lett.* in *Lonsdale Mag.* (Feb. 1867) 310. Wm. I'th loft, BLEZARD *Sngs.* (1848)
42. w.Yks.[12], Lan. (J.W.), Chs.[2], s.Not. (J.P.K.)

II. Dial. uses. 1. *prep.* In *comb.* (1) In-a-doors, in the
house; (2) — calf, of cows: with young; (3) -calver, a
cow with young; (4) -calving, see (2); (5) -chorn, the
inner pocket or pouch of a fishing-net [not known to our
correspondents]; (6) — co, in company, in partnership,
in league; also used *attrib.*; see Co, *sb.*; (7) — coose,
ready, prepared; (8) — dress, dressed in one's best
clothes; (9) — drink, drunk; (10) — facks, faiks, or
fakins, (11) — fechlings, an asseveration: in faith, indeed, certainly; (12) — fere, together; (13) — go, in the
fashion; (14) — godsnam, an oath: in God's name; (15)
-hand meag, a scythe-shaped tool used in the operation
of 'bottomfying' and ditch-draining; (16) — hill, down
hill; (17) — home, up to the hill; (18) — house, indoors;
(19) — kindle, of rabbits and small animals: with young;
(20) — kittle, of cats: with young; (21) -kneed, knock-
kneed, having the knees bent inwards; (22) — lamb, of
ewes: with young; (23) — life, alive; (24) -liftin, of
animals: so weak as to be unable to rise without assistance; (25) — (n)use, usually; (26) — plat, on the ground;
(27) — print, very neat and orderly; (28) — sma', briefly;
(29) -taed, having the toes turned inward; (30) -taes, toes
which turn inward; (31) — traath, see (11).

(1) Oxf.[1] My missis yent in-a-doors jest now. (2) Som. Three
in-calf dairy cows, *Auctioneer's Advt.* (Nov. 1895). w.Som.[1]
Mostly when speaking of them collectively and not severally.
'Most all my cows be in calf but thick there, her's barren, we
couldn't get her way calve' (s.v. In lamb). (3) n.Yks. He sell'd
me a in-cawver (I.W.); Great numbers of in-calvers, within a
month or six weeks of calving, are now brought up to the vale of
York, TUKE *Agric.* (1800) 258. (4) n.Lin.[1] For sale, one in-calving
cow, *Gainsb. News* (Mar. 23, 1867). (5) War. (HALL.) (6) n.Cy.
(J.W.), n.Lin.[1] sw.Lin.[1] There was two on 'em in co. together. It was
an in co. concern. Sus.[2], Hmp.[1] (7) Cor. Get in coose avore they
come, THOMAS *Randigal Rhymes* (1895) Gl. (s.v. Coose); Cor.[2] Es
everything in coose ! (8) Cum.[4] Lizzie is soon ' in dress,' *Rosenthal,* 245. (9) w.Yks. (J.W.), Chs.[1] (10) n.Cy. GROSE (1790);
N.Cy.[1], Nhb.[1], w.Yks.[2] Cor. A crokeing timdoodle i' facks, J.
TRENOODLE *Spec. Dial.* (1846) 17; Cor.[12] (11) Wm. These er
sad duings, efechlings, HUTTON *Bran New Wark* (1785) l. 153.
(12) Sc. In which there stood three chests in-fere, AYTOUN *Ballads*
(ed. 1861) II. 347. (13) w.Yks. Blouse bodices are all i' go just
nah (S.K.C.). (14) Lan. An' who were they, i' godsnam ! WAUGH
Heather (ed. Milner) II. 111; Lan.[1] Let um speyk greadly, os we
dun, e' godsnum, TIM BOBBIN *View Dial.* (ed. 1750) 35. (15) Nrf.
I want an in-hand meag about five foot staff, EMERSON *Son of
Fens* (1892) 97. (16) Cum.[14] (17) Dev. 'E 've a-urned tha knive
into his thigh, inhome tů bone, HEWETT *Peas. Sp.* (1892) 140.
(18) Som. Is anybody in house! RAYMOND *Sam and Sabina* (1894)
136. w.Som.[1] Common in the Hill district. 'There her'll bide
in 'ouze over the vire all the day and all the wik long.' 'I baint
safe wher missus is in 'ouze or no.' Dev. I zee'th her hom ta
door—Zomtimes es go'th in houze, NATHAN HOGG *The Milshy,* 1st
S. 37, in ELWORTHY *Gl.* (1888); HEWETT *Peas. Sp.* (1892).

nw.Dev.[1] (19) s.Chs.[1], nw.Der.[1] (20) s.Chs.[1] Der. Th' owd cat's i' kittle agen (H.R.). nw.Der.[1] (21) Per. Ill-legged, in-kneed, 'and broad-footed, *Edb. Antiq. Mag.* (1848) 47. Edb. Sittin' gies them sic a thraw, They're ay in-kneed, *The Complaint* (1795) 5. (22) n.Lin.[1] 170 lambed and inlamb ewes, *Gainsb. News* (Mar. 23, 1867). Som. Twenty down ewes. forward in lamb, *Auctioneer's Advt.* (Nov. 1895). w.Som.[1] 70 Nott ewes in lamb and with lambs by their side, *Wellington Wkly. News* (Feb. 1881). nw.Dev.[1] (23) Sc. He is still in life, *Scoticisms* (1787) 52; *Glasgow Herald* (Apr. 3, 1899). (24) S. & Ork.[1] (25) Oxf.[1] What In nuse is the price of nutmegs ! (26) ne.Lan.[1] T'peāts is i·plat yet [spread out on the ground]. (27) Oxf.[1] 'Er's all in print. (28) Abd. This is jist my opingan aboot it in sma', MACDONALD *D. Elginbrod* (1863) I. 95. (29) Sc. (JAM.), Cai.[1] (30) Bnff.[1] She hiz a ticht eneuch fit, bit she hiz in-taes. (31) w.Yks.[1] Etraath, there nivver wor' t'marrow to him, ii. 286.

2. *Comb.* with *adv.*, &c.: (1) **In-about,** into the immediate neighbourhood, thereabouts, near ; (2) — **almost,** almost ; (3) — **anunder,** underneath ; (4) — **at,** to, at; (5) — **atween,** between ; (6) — **between,** a sandwich made of sponge-cake, having jam between; (7) — **betwixt,** see (5); (8) — **by(e,** (a) in, inside, within the house; near, close, towards the speaker ; (b) with omission of the verb of motion : come in, come near ; (c) in mining : in the direction of the workings away from the shafts ; (d) beside, close to ; (e) lying close at hand, on the premises, near the house or farm ; (f) low-lying ; (g) an inner room ; (9) — o(f, av, or iv, in, into, inside ; (10) — **o'er,** ower, or owre, (a) see (8, a); (b) over ; (c) in phr. *in-ower* and *out-ower,* backwards and forwards, thoroughly ; *fig.* violently, with complete mas-tery ; (d) in phr. *to take in owre,* to take advantage of; (11) -**sunders,** asunder ; (12) — **through,** throw, or trow, (a) see (8, a) ; (b) through, from the outside to the centre ; *fig.* in phr. *to gae in-throw* and *out-throw anything*; to examine or try in every direction ; (c) within, in the interior of; (d) through, by means of ; (13) — **to,** near, towards ; (14) — **to oneself,** silently, not aloud ; (15) — **under** or **onder,** (a) under, underneath ; (b) in phr. *to lay inunder one's feet,* to keep secret ; (16) — **with,** (a) down-hill, inclining down-wards ; low-lying ; (b) a slope, angle ; (c) see (8, a) ; (d) seized with, affected by ; (e) self-interested.

(1) Abd. Just as I entered in-about, my Aunt by chance was lookin' out, BEATTIE *Parings* (1801) 2, ed. 1873. (2) Wil.[1] It inamwoast killed our bwoy Sam, AKERMAN *Tales* (1853) 145. (3) Lakel.[2] Dud thoo see that gurt whelken rattan gah in anunder t'coorn kist ! w.Yks. (J.W.) (4) Ayr. He had been in at Glasgow, GALT *Ann. Parish* (1821) x. (5) Nbb.[1] Ye'll find him inatween the cairt an' the barn. Yks. (J.W.) (6) w.Yks. Reyk us some o' that 'in-between' (B.K.). (7) w.Som.[1] I've a-catch my vinger in-betwixt the door and the durn. (8, a) Sc. Come in by and we'll see to get you some breakfast, SCOTT *St. Ronan* (1824) xiv. Sh.I. At lent dey got dem set doon inbe at da fire, BURGESS *Sketches* (2nd ed.) 74. Cai.[1] Abd. 'Come awa in by, auld man,' cried the farmer from the ingle-neuk, GREIG *Logie o' Buchan* (1899) 9. Ked. The gard'ner came inby, BURNESS *Garron Ha'* (c. 1800) l. 343. Frf. Draw your chair in by, an sit An' pay attention, SANDS *Poems* (1833) 23 ; He had been in-by at me after lowsin'-time to get the measure o' his feet, WILLOCK *Rosetty Ends* (1886) 26, ed. 1889. Per. 'Come in by.' . . Ebenezer unlocking the door invited Joseph to enter, CLELAND *Inchbracken* (1883) 147, ed. 1887. Arg. And the two went round to the ditch-brig and in-by, MUNRO *Lost Pibroch* (1896) 273. Fif. Come awa in bye, there's somebody here wants to speak wi' ye, ROBERTSON *Provost* (1894) 39. Rnf. He hirpl'd in by wi' his cronies, WEBSTER *Rhymes* (1835) 83. Lnk. 'Come in by,' quo' Neil, 'an' I'll tell ye a' aboot it,' WARDROP *J. Mathison* (1881) 17. e.Lth. Come awa in by, Jims, HUNTER *J. Inwick* (1895) 225. Gall. It was an awsome peety that ye werena inby this afternoon, CROCKETT *Bog-Myrtle* (1895) 200. Nbb. My lad's inbye wi' thine, PROUDLOCK *Borderland Muse* (1896) 99 ; Nbb.[1] Is thee fether in-by, hinney ! Cum.[4] He went in bye again, W. C. T. (May 6, 1899) 8, col. 1. (b) Sh.I. In by, dog, or doo said to da waur o' hit ! *Sh. News* (Apr. 30, 1898). e.Fif. Inbye an' warm ye an' gie's the news, LATTO *Tam Bodkin* (1864) x. (c) Nbb. In bye they bunn'd me in a crack, WILSON *Pitman's Pay* (1843) 27; The fore shift wis gan in-by, HALDANE *Geordy's Last* (1878) 5; Nbb.[1] Nbb., Dur. GREENWELL *Coal Tr. Gl.* (1849). w.Yks. There's a fall on the inbye side of No. 7 ending (S.J.C.). [*Reports Mines.*] (d) Sh.I. A speet 'at wis stikkid in a hole i' da wa' inby da fire, *Sh. News* (Sept. 17, 1898).

(e) Bnff.[1] s.Sc. The in-bye band Jock would emerge from his bed in the stable loft, CUNNINGHAM *Broomieburn* (1894) vi. Nbb.[1] In the fields a man ' oot-by ' is a way off and ' in-by ' he is about the premises. Cum.[4] Said of cultivated lands near a town, having means of communication. (f) Slk. Inby land (JAM.). (g) N.Cy.[1] Nhb. Behind the beds was a small space called the ' in-bye,' DIXON *Whittingham Vale* (1895) 32 ; Nhb.[1], Cum.[4] (9) Abd. Stap yer feet in'o some bits o' auld skushles, ALEXANDER *Ain Flk.* (1882) 25. Ayr. I laid them in a my kings-hood Wi' gude fresh butter, FISHER *Poems* (1790) 112. Rnf. Hey for the kintry o' cakes, Hey for the heroes that's in o't, WEBSTER *Rhymes* (1835) 20. Nhb.[1] Yor in iv a greet horry. Cum.[1] He leevs in av Ackton parish ; Cum.[4] (10, a) Sc. ' Come in ower ' is an invitation to a person to come over the distance between him and the person speaking (A.W.). Sh.I. Yon ane guid inower whin shū might a geen whaur shū cam frae, *Sh. News* (June 25, 1898). Elg. Tak' in ower yer chair, an' sit doon, TESTER *Poems* (1865) 107. e.Sc. Come in by inower to 'e body o' 'e kirk, SETOUN *R. Urquhart* (1896) iii. Abd. Hand me in o'er the maund yonder, anent ye, BEATTIE *Parings* (1801) 9, ed. 1873. Frf. Ye'll gang anower, noo, mother,' . . meaning that it was Jess's bed-time, BARRIE *Thrums* (1889) xx. Per. Stappin' richt in ower o' my house, CLELAND *Inchbracken* (1883) 244, ed. 1887. Fif. He drew in-owre, an' took a piece, DOUGLAS *Poems* (1806) 96. s.Sc. We'll juist cowp him inowre in oor ain warm bed, WILSON *Tales* (1839) V. 95. Rnf. I obey thy warm request To ' stap in owre,' YOUNG *Pictures* (1865) 33. Lnk. Johnnie drew his chair in ower tae the fire, an sat doon, WARDROP *J. Mathison* (1881) 24. (b) Abd. She wad tak' a peep in o'er the dyke, SHIRREFS *Poems* (1790) 89. Per. The willin' han's an' feet To get in ower their faither's seat, FORD *Harp* (1893) 313. Lnk. [She] tumbled in owre the bed just as she was, ROY *Generalship* (ed. 1895) 79. n.Yks.[2] It was inower on us. (c) Sc. The lady carried it in-ower and out-ower wi' her son, SCOTT *Antiquary* (1816) xxvi. Rxb. (JAM.) (d) Abd. We've baith been weel aneuch ta'en in-owre, ALEXANDER *Johnny Gibb* (1871) xliii. (11) Ken. (G.B.), Ken.[1] (12, a) Sh.I. Come in trow, Tirval, NICOLSON *Aithstin' Hedder* (1898) 32 ; Haud your tongue, man, an' come introw, an' dip you doon, *Sh. News* (June 18, 1898). Cld. (JAM.) (b) Sc. I gaed inthrow that field (JAM.). Ags. (ib.) (c) Sc. I would rather have one of yon sufferers that is bred in Christ's school in throw Clydesdale yonder, *The Lord's Trumpet,* 7 (JAM. *Suppl.*). (d) Cai.[1] He got the place inthrough his under. Abd. It was inthrow him that I got that berth (JAM.). (13) Sc. Come in to the fire, MITCHELL *Scotticisms* (1799) 48. Sh.I. Noo, lasses, slip aff o' your feet, an' set you in ta da fire, *Sh. News* (Oct. 23, 1897). e.Lth. Draw aff your buits, an' come in to the fire, HUNTER *J. Inwick* (1895) 186. (14) Sh.I. A'll read hit in ta mesel, mam, if doo canna hear it, *Sh. News* (Mar. 3, 1900). (15, a) Sh.I. It's ill ta sit inonder drap, lat alane wi' under watter, SPENCE *Flk-Lore* (1899) 226. N.I.[1] w.Yks. Close to the Beck, where it grumbled all night in-under the rock, SNOWDEN *Web of Weaver* (1896) x. [*Amer. Dial. Notes* (1896) I. 419.] (b) Sh.I. My wirds min be laid inunder your fit—keepit da sam' hit been blue murder, *Sh. News* (June 17, 1899). (16, a) n.Sc. Applied to a low culti-vated situation as opposed to an uninterrupted range of high land (JAM.). Abd. Is the road steep or inwith ? (G.W.) ; She the east hand took, The inwith road by favour of the brook, Ross *Helenore* (1768) 49, ed. 1812. (b) Slk. Laid them down a groof wi' their heads at the inwith, HOGG *Tales* (1838) 150, ed. 1866. (c) s.Per. ' Come inwith,' an invitation to come nearer the fire in the house (W.A.C.). (d) Sh.I. I wiss he bena middlin' in wi' da vinster-sickness, *Sh. News* (Oct. 15, 1898). (e) Bnff.[1]

3. *Phr.* (1) *in all,* at all ; (2) — *a manner of speaking,* so to speak, as it were ; (3) — *a mistake,* by mistake ; (4) — *a twitter,* soon, quickly ; (5) — *a way of speaking,* see (2) ; (6) — *and in,* of sheep or cattle : bred from the same stock, without crossing ; see **Breed, 4** (3) ; (7) *in and out,* (a) in-doors and outdoors, inside and outside ; (b) now and again, intermittently ; not regularly ; not to be depended upon ; (c) inside out ; (d) out of a straight line ; (e) a wrestling term, see below ; (8) — *and outer,* a fisherman who does not venture out in stormy weather ; (9) — *for it,* in danger of punishment, in a difficulty ; unexpectedly engaged in a transaction from which there is no retreating ; (10) — *hazard to,* in danger of ; (11) — *it,* there, present ; (12) — *lieu,* instead, in exchange ; (13) — *o' bant,* of the same mind, in league ; (14) — *or over,* near about any fixed date or exact quantity ; (15) — *place of,* instead of ; (16) — *sae meickle,* insomuch ; (17) — *so far,* inasmuch ; (18) — *spite of my* teeth, in spite of myself, against my will ; (19) — *that'n*, the same as **Athatn(s** (q.v.) ; (20) — *the inside of an hour*, within an hour ; (21) — *the straw*, lying in ; (22) — *the suds*, downcast, 'in the dumps'; (23) — *the way*, (*a*) near at hand, close by ; (*b*) on one's way ; (24) — *this'n*, the same as **Athisn(s** (q.v.) ; (25) — *toil* or i' *foil*, having one's attention engaged or occupied ; in an equable state of mind ; (26) — *two*, (*a*) in pieces, broken ; see **Atwo** ; (*b*) in phr. *to fall in two*, to be brought to bed, be confined ; see **Fall**, *v.* 16 (9) ; (27) *not to be in one's own mind*, to be distracted with grief ; (28) *to be in hands with*, to treat as to terms with ; (29) — *in him*, to be something internal or mental ; (30) — *in hopes*, to hope ; (31) — *in one's ten, twenty*, &c., to be in one's tenth, twentieth, &c. year ; (32) — *in to*, of ground : to be in cultivation for, in crop ; (33) — *in use to*, to be accustomed to ; (34) — *no in*, to be in a fit of abstraction, to be absent-minded ; (35) — *used in*, to be used to ; (36) *to belong in*, to belong to, pertain to ; (37) *to come in*, to come short, to alter one's method in the way of diminution ; (38) *to have it in for*, to harbour resentment towards, to contemplate some revenge upon ; (39) *to meet in with*, to fall in with, meet ; (40) *to put in place*, to replace ; (41) *to sit in* or *in to the table*, to take a seat at table, to take one's place for a meal ; (42) *to value in*, to value at ; (43) *a day in remark*, a memorable or notable day.

(1) **Nhb.** And Bold Archy, he too was ne'er seen iv a, *Coronation Sngs.* (1822) 14 ; That would ne'er done iv aa, *Sng., Newcastle in an Uproar* (1821) ; (R.O.H.) (2) **Cha.¹** Som. An' 'eet you mid zay thirty, to be zure, in a manner o' speaken, RAYMOND *Love and Quiet Life* (1894) 107. (3) **s.Pem.** (E.D.) (4) **Cum.¹; Cnm.⁴** In a state implying fear or doubt. (5) **w.Yks.** (J.W.) **Cha.¹** In a way o' spakin', one may say it has ne'er raint sin May coom in. (6) **Dmb.** No regular system of crossing is followed, and the more ordinary practise is to breed in and in, *Agric. Surv.* 224 (JAM.). **Ayr.** Tups are allowed to couple even with their own progeny, which is called breeding in and in, *ib.* 485 (JAM.). **w.Yks.¹ Midl.** MARSHALL *Rur. Econ.* (1796) II. n.Lin.¹ **Shr.** MARSHALL *Review* (1818) II. 253. **Brks.¹, w.Som.¹** [The white shows the symptoms sooner than any of the other colours of breeding in-and-in, STEPHENS *Farm Bk.* (ed. 1849) II. 712.] (7, *a*) **Gall.** Sandy was a clever chiel . . . Had thoughts on things baith in and out, NICHOLSON *Poet. Wks.* (1814) 51, ed. 1897. (*b*) **e.Suf.** She's as in and out as a dog's hinder leg [not to be depended on] (F.H.). **Dev.** He've a worked to Woodgate in and out's ten year, *Reports Provinc.* (1886) 97. (*c*) **w.Som.¹** Neef mee oa·l uumbruul·ur waud·n u·bloa·d een·-un-aewt zu zôo·n-z üv·ur aay puut mee ai·d aewtzuy·d dhu doo·ur [If my old umbrella was not blown in-and-out so soon as ever I put my head outside the door]. (*d*) **Wm.** Seck plewin ! It's o' in an' oot (B.K.). (*e*) **Cum.⁴** This auxiliary movement is performed by striking the opposite leg of the opponent in such a manner that the knee is outside his knee, and the foot inside his ankle ; thus the shins cross. (8) **Cor.¹** (s.v. Busker). (9) **n.Yks.** Tbou rascal ! thou's in for 't (I.W.). **w.Yks.** (J.W.) **Lan.¹** Tha'rt in-for-it, neaw, owd mon ; aw wouldn't be i' thy shoes for summut. **Nhp.¹, War.²**, **Hnt.** (T.P.F.) **Dev.³** Now thee'rt in-vor-'t, Polly ; you've a tored yer frock. **Colloq.** Paul was encouraged by a remark from Tozer that he was ' in for it ' now, DICKENS *Dombey* (1848) xii. (10) **Sc.** I am in hazard to rob the poor as well as my sister, SCOTT *St. Ronan* (1824) x. (11) **w.Ir.** Light the candle thin, and see who's in it, LOVER *Leg.* (1848) I. 172. **Glw.** As we did in the owld times, . . as when the squire was in it, BARRINGTON *Sketches* (1830) III. xvii. **Wm.** Were there many in it ? Who's in it ? (M.S.M.) (12) **Shr.¹** The Maister said 'e'd gie me the top adlant i' the ' Red-buts ' fur tatoe ground, an' 'e mun 'a a couple o' days work i' the 'arrôost in lieu. (13) **Lan.** I durst no begin cose I knew they'rn aw in o' bant, PAUL BOBBIN *Sequel* (1819) 34. (14) **N.I.¹** (15) **Sc.** They, in place of assisting, only laughed at him, *Scoticisms* (1787) 119. (16) **Sc.** There rase up an unco tempest insaemeikle that the ship was cover't wi' the waves, HENDERSON *St. Matt.* (1862) viii. 24. (17) **n.Yks.²** (18) **Slk.** In spite of my teeth, I turned eiry, HOGG *Tales* (1838) 53, ed. 1866. n.Cy. (J.W.) (19) **Not.** (J.H.B.) (20) **N.I.¹**, n.Cy. (J.W.) (21) **n.Lin.¹** (22) **Suf.** Very favourable weather must occur, or the farmer is in the suds, YOUNG *Annals Agric.* (1784–1815) XXXIX. 89. (23, *a*) **w.Som.¹** He 'appened to come to the house, when ah wor i' the way (J.P.K.). (*b*) **Suf.** They were in the way (C.L.F.). (24) **Not.** (J.H.B.) (25) **w.Yks.** Thess various improvements, as he called 'em, kept him i' toit a while longer, *Yksman.* (1880) 167 ; Ah thowght it wor t'man ah

wanted, and so ah gat somedy to keep him i' toit whal ah wor suer, BANKS *Whfld. Wds.* (1865) ; **w.Yks.⁵** Thah's kept him i't' oit rarely awalt' neet lad ! ' He's like to ha' summat to keep him i't' oit,' says a mother of a squalling child. (26, *a*) **w.Yks.¹ Lan.** GROSE (1790) *MS. add.* (C.) **e.Lan.¹** (*b*) **Rnf.** She fell in twa wi' little din, PICKEN *Poems* (1788) 50 (JAM.). **w.Yks.¹, ne.Lan.¹** (27) **Yks.** (J.W.) **Lin.¹** When I said so I was not in my own mind, as my master was only just lapped up. (28) **Ayr.** I was in han's wi' the Laird at that very time for a tack o' his house, AINSLIE *Land of Burns* (ed. 1892) 66. (29) **Nhb.¹** ' It's in 'im 'at ails him '—some mental or occult trouble that is going on. (30) **Ken.¹** I'm in 'opes he's better. I'm in 'opes she'll like herself and stay. (31) **Rut.¹** (s.v. Age). **Oxf.¹** Dhis iz muuy burth·dai— is·tuurdi uuy wuz un·i in mi ten, bt tû dai uuy bee ugwai·n an fuur leb·n [This is my birthday—isterday I was uny in my ten, but to-day I be agwain an for leben]. **Ken.** She's just in her twenty (D.W.L.). (32) **nw.Dev.¹** (33) **Sc.** I am in use to ride, *Monthly Mag.* (1798) II. 438 ; He is in use to rise early, *ib.* (1800) I. 322 ; He was in use to walk every day, *Scoticisms* (1787) 98. (34) **Ayr.** Jean used to say to her brother sometimes when watching the large dreamy eyes . . . ' She's no in,' JOHNSTON *Glenbuckie* (1889) 149. (35) **Sc.** Bring to me the linsey clouts, I hae been best used in, KINLOCH *Ballads* (1827) 23. (36) **Shr.¹** That tub belungs i' the brew-hus, *Introd.* 82. (37) **Sc.** (JAM., s.v. Ind). (38) **s.Don.** SIMMONS *Gl.* (1890). (39) **Ayr.** When they meet in wi' an every day shock They imagine it maun be the drain, LAING *Poems* (1894) 72. **e.Lth.** The first time I met in wi' An'ra, HUNTER *J. Inwick* (1895) 65. (40) **w.Som.¹** Things be zoonder a brokt 'n they be a put in place again. (41) **Sc.** (A.W.) **Ayr.** The gude wife bade Andrew sit in and partake, GALT *Sir A. Wylie* (1822) x. (42) **Dev.** I bant agwaine tû peart wi' 'n. I vallee 'n in vifty pound, HEWETT *Peas. Sp.* (1892) 141. (43) **Sh.I.** Dis is gaen ta be a day in remark, *Sh. News* (Feb. 24, 1900).

4. Used pleonastically.

I.Ma. The sweet soft coo there was in, ye said, it was music fit to wake the dead, BROWN *Witch* (1889) 96.

5. In the midst of, occupied with.

Sh.I. Das, rise an' haand her da eel muggie aff o' da wa' ; my haands is i' da supper, *Sh. News* (Nov. 13, 1897).

6. Near, close.

Abd. Yer light casts little shine,—Had in the candle, sir, BEATTIE *Parings* (1801) 26, ed. 1873.

7. Into.

Sh.I. A'm no tinkin' 'at da makin o'm in a elder 'ill hinder him ta curse, *Sh. News* (July 23, 1898) ; Risin' shû took a can, an' guid i' da barn for da baess' supper, *ib.* (Mar. 19, 1898). **Per.** The folk hae taen't i' their heids to think the ither thing, CLELAND *Inch-brachen* (1883) 145, ed. 1887. n.Cy. (J.W.)

8. On, upon.

Sh.I. His lang tail wabblin' an' wirlin' dis wy an' dat wy laek a conger-eel in a cavil, STEWART *Tales* (1892) 253. **Per.** I'll gie ye a gouff i' the lug'll gar't stound the next half-hour, CLELAND *Inch-brachen* (1883) 136, ed. 1887. **Rnf.** At length we fell s' to the prancing, And louping like fools in the floor, WEBSTER *Rhymes* (1835) 7. **Ayr.** Got ye ony drink, Jamie, in the gait hame ? GALT *Entail* (1823) lxx. **e.Lth.** John H. is no' a man that'll sell his hens in a rainy day, MUCKLEBACKIT *Rhymes* (1885) 236. n.Cy. (J.W.) **Lan.** Oi dunnot think as they'n knocked onybody it t'yed, KAY-SHUTTLEWORTH *Scarsdale* (1860) I. 94. n.Lin.¹ Put it in th' floor, Mary, for th' cat to lap. **w.Som.¹** Thick old ladder's so wake I be most afeard to go up in un.

9. Of.

War. *Leamington Courier* (Mar. 13, 1897) ; **War.¹** Her cut a bit out in it ; **War.²⁴** **s.War.¹** They be just come out in school. **Suf.** I had to get out in bed (M.E.R.). **Dev.** Bill didn't take much stock in him, PHILLPOTTS *Bill Vogwell in Blk. and White* (June 27. 1896) 824.

Hence In course, *phr.* of course.

Frf. In coorse she's grand by the like of me, BARRIE *Thrums* (1889) vii. **Ir.** Barrin', in coorse, that Mad Bell's bound to keep on the dhry land, BARLOW *Lisconnel* (1895) 10 ; (A.S.P.) **N.I.¹ Yks.** Why, in course he will, TAYLOR *Miss Miles* (1890) xviii. **Not.¹, Lei.¹ Nhp.¹** In course I shall go. **War.** Not every week, in course, GEO. ELIOT *S. Marner* (1861) 71 ; **War.³**; **War.⁴** ' You understand me now !' ' Yes, in-course, in-course, I do.' **Hnt.** (T.P.F.) **w.Som.¹** In coose you'll have your wages. **Dev.** Ma paper's vill'd up, so in kuse I mist stap, NATHAN HOGG *Poet. Lett.* (1847) 10, ed. 1865. **Cor.²**

10. With.

Sc. I will serve you in ten thousand at the same rate, SCOTT *St.*

Roman (1804) xviii. **Abd.** Their een were tied up in a napkin, ANDERSON *Rhymes* (1867) 2.

11. As ; in phr. *in a present.*

Sc. A half-choked duck which he had gotten in a present, FORD *Thistledown* (1891) 51 : A pound in a present, *Glasgow Herald* (Apr. 3, 1899). **Slk.** I'll give you fifty guineas in a present, HOGG *Tales* (1838) 163, ed. 1866. **Ir.** After you a-givin' her to us in a present that way, BARLOW *Lisconnel* (1895) 23. **Dev.** I've brought 'ee something in a present, O'NEILL *Idyls* (1892) 12.

12. adv. Within, inside, in the house.

Sc. Is he in! MITCHELL *Scotticisms* (1792) 47. **Frf.** They had haen a guid supply o' meat in afore the storm come on, WILLOCK *Rosetty Ends* (1886) 72, ed. 1889. **n.Cy.** (J.W.) **w.Yks.** Iz ði muðər in ! (*ib.*)

13. Of a gathering or meeting : assembled, met together ; held, going on.

Sc. The kirk's in (A.W.). **Lnk.** We would be stopped by a shout, 'The schule's in,' FRASER *Whaups* (1895) 27. **Edb.** On Saturday, nae school being in, FORBES *Poems* (1812) 95.

14. In prison, in gaol.

Lon. She was in the first time for robbing a public, MAYHEW *Lond. Labour* (1851) IV. 237, ed. 1862.

15. With omission of a verb of motion : to go or come in.

Sc. He is in to her brother, As fast as gang cou'd he, JAMIESON *Pop. Ballads* (1806) l. 74. **Ked.** A sturdy chap . . . Cam to the door and wanted in, JAMIE *Muse* (1844) 86. **Per.** Doun to the braehead wi' your mooth, An' cry them in, HALIBURTON *Ochil Idylls* (1891) 42. **Lak.** But if you please we'll in, BLACK *Falls of Clyde* (1806) 168. **Lth.** Let's in, Will, and syne we'll see, MACNEILL *Poet. Wks.* (1801) 130, ed. 1856. **Yks.** (J.W.) **Oxf.** 'All in,' a cry to boys to go into school (G.O.). **w.Som.¹** Ee·n wai·ee [In with you].

16. With *with* and omission of the verb : to put, push, get, &c. in.

Per. He juist in wi' her an' sticket the door, CLELAND *Inchbracken* (1883) 63, ed. 1887 ; Aff wi' yer bannet an' in wi' ye ! Juist hap up weel, *ib.* 268. **Cum.⁴** He in wid it as hard as he cud. **w.Yks.** (J.W.) **w.Som.¹** I in way my hand vore he could turn, and catcht hold o' un by the neck.

17. Having the harvest gathered in ; of corn : harvested, stacked.

Sh.I. Ir ye fairly in wi' a'! *Sh. News* (Nov. 6, 1897). **Frf.** The hay crop will be in, an' a' thing snug, MORISON *Poems* (1790) 118. **Lth.** But ye're all in, Sam, . . and in tolerable order, too, LUMSDEN *Sheep-head* (1892) 304. **Edb.** There's little time wi' them to spare Till corn's a' in, and fields are bare, CRAWFORD *Poems* (1798) 43. **Gall.** His harvest in, his grain well sold, LAUDERDALE *Poems* (1796) 10.

18. Shrunken, fallen in, hollow.

Lnk. Gluttony's flabby sides were in, *Deil's Hallowe'en* (1856) 18. **Edb.** Elritch Girn-again, Goblin, Wi' back out, and breast in, *Carlop Green* (1793) 128, ed. 1817.

19. Of the sea : at high tide.

Per. The sea's in the nicht, an' there's five feet o' water on the sands, CLELAND *Inchbracken* (1883) 14, ed. 1887.

20. Of the wind : blowing from the south or west.

Ken. *N. & Q.* (1852) 1st S. vi. 388.

21. Friendly, on good terms, associated with ; approving of ; *gen.* in phr. *to be* or *keep in with any one.*

Sc. 'I'm no in wi' ye.' Common among the vulgar and with children (JAM.). **Sh.I.** Wir folk wisna in wi' keepin' da quaik i' da barn a' night even, *Sh. News* (July 9, 1898). **Ayr.** However keen I may be for reform, I'm no in wi' the French, JOHNSTON *Glenbuckie* (1889) 42. **Gall.** There's nane exempit frae life's cares; . . . A' whiles are in, and whiles are out, For grief and joy come time about, NICHOLSON *Poet. Wks.* (1814) 76, ed. 1897. **n.Don.** SIMMONS *Gl.* (1890). **Cum.¹** He gat in wi' t'oald fwok, and he keeps in. **n.Yks.** He keeps in wi' t'maister (I.W.) ; **n.Yks.⁴** Jack's weel in wi' t'Squire. **w.Yks.¹** To keep in with a person. **ne.Lan.¹**, **nw.Der.¹** **n.Lin.¹** He's in with squire an' th' missis, an' that maks a lot o' difference. **Nhp.¹**, **War.²**, **Brks.¹** **w.Som.¹** He's in wi' all the roughest lot about ; there id'n a worser proacher no place.

22. Stocked, furnished, provided, 'off.'

n.Yks.² How are you in for brass ! **e.Yks.¹** 'Hoo are yă in fo cooals !' 'Whah, we're pratty weel in, just noo,' *MS. add.* (T.H.)

23. Permissible, allowable.

Lakel.² Nay, come noo, that izzant in at neea price.

24. sb. An entrance.

Abd. Nae an in cud we win for near an oor, till we got an aul' ledder an put it up to the en' o' the hoose, ALEXANDER *Ain Flk.* (1882) 209.

25. pl. Phr. *ins and oots,* (1) zig-zags ; (2) changes of opinion.

(1) **Cum.¹⁴** (2) **n.Yks.** Of a fickle or unstable person : ' Ya see thar's nea depending on him, he's had his ins an' oots afoor.' A member of a church : ' A'v had mi ups an' doons i't wo'ld, but A'v niver had mi ins an' oots ' (W.H.).

26. pl. Additions to make full weight ; articles 'thrown in,' makeweights ; freq. in double *pl.* form **Insees.**

n.Yks.¹ No doubt from the expression ' a dozen and one in' and the like ; **n.Yks.²** Short candles to make up the pound, or rolls at the bakers where they give insees to the dozen.

27. v. To enclose.

Sus. (M.B.-S.) ; **Sus.¹** ; **Sus.²** I inned that piece of land from the common. **I.W.²** The first part of Bradinge Haven was inned, when Yarbridge was made.

Hence **Innings,** *sb. pl.* land recovered from the sea by draining and banking.

Ken. (H.M.) **Ken.**, **e.Sus.** HOLLOWAY. **Sus.¹**

28. To bring or gather in ; to get in the harvest, to house corn.

Cum.¹⁴, Yks. (K.) **w.Yks.²** The corn was all inned before Michaelmas day ; **w.Yks.⁴** Hrt. He employs eight harvest men and two boys to inn his harvest corn, ELLIS *Mod. Husb.* (1750) II. i. **Sur.¹, Sus.¹², Hmp.¹**

Hence (1) **Inning,** *vbl. sb.* the act of bringing in corn from the field to the barn ; (2) **Inning-goose,** *sb.* an entertainment given when all the harvest has been got in ; (3) **-time,** *sb.* harvest-time.

(1) **Sc.** We have heard the song and the laugh of those engaged with inning even at the hour of midnight, *Caled. Merc.* (Oct. 25, 1823) (JAM.). (2) **w.Yks.** When all the corn is got home into the stackyard, an entertainment is given called the Inning Goose, BRAND *Pop. Antiq.* (ed. 1870) II. 15. (3) **Yks.** (K.)

29. Of a clock : to gain. **w.Yks.³**

30. With *up* or *up with* : to catch up, overtake.

w.Yks. To 'in it up' is to overtake any work which has been suspended, HAMILTON *Nugae Lit.* (1841) 352 ; Nah 'at he's gotten back to t'schooil he'll sooin inn up wi' t'others (S.K.C.).

IN, *conj.¹* Sc. n.Cy. Lan. Der. [in.] If. Cf. **an,** *conj.¹*

S. & Ork.¹, Cai.¹, Buff.¹ **Ayr.** In't werena just aiblins to cure the cholick, BOSWELL *Poet. Wks.* (1803) 9, ed. 1871. **n.Cy.** Intle [if you will] (HALL.). **s.Lan.** BAMFORD *Dial.* (1854). **Der.¹** In God ill [if God will].

IN, *conj.²* Lan. Than. Cf. **an,** *conj.²*

s.Lan. Moor in bargain [more than the bargain]. ' There's bin moor t'do in a gonnor t'muck.' PICTON *Dial.* (1865) 24 ; More brass inney [than you] hadd'n, *ib.* 27.

IN(·, see **Eye,** *sb.¹,* **Hind,** *adj.,* **Ing.**

INACTIOUS, *adj.* Lei. [Not known to our correspondents.] Anxious. (HALL.)

IN ALL, *phr.* Nhb. Chs. Also, too, et caetera. See **And all.**

Nhb.¹ Him aw'r his brother wis there in aa. **Chs.¹** ; **Chs.³** 'He's coming in all.' 'He's gathered the rabbidge in all.' The omission or presence of ' in all,' makes no difference in a phrase. Sometimes used for ' et caetera,' often following the recapitulation of different things. 'He sould his cows, his horses, his pigs, in all.'

INARCHED, *ppl. adj.* Lin. Of a monument or tomb : placed in an arch in the wall on the north side of the chancel.

An inarched monument, *gen.* supposed to be the tomb of the founder or of a person who contributed largely to the building or repairs (W.W.S.).

INAWE, *v.* Obsol. Sc. Also in form **inawn** Lnk. (JAM.) To owe.

Sc. (JAM. *Suppl.*) **Lnk.** He inawns me ten pund (JAM.). **Dmf.** Spurn the honest chiel inawin A stane o' meal, QUINN *Heather* (1863) 67.

INBANK, *adv.* and *sb.* Cum. Wm. Yks. Also in form **in-ban'** Cum. [i'nbaŋk.] **1.** *adv.* Down hill, descending or inclining ground ; downwards.

Lakel.² It's o' inbank frae Pe'rith. **Cum.** It's aw in-ban', FARRALL *Betty Wilson* (1886) 147 ; Tak time, oald lass—it's o' in-bank, DICKINSON *Cumbr.* (1876) 298 ; **Cum.¹** **Wm.** Thaed naedthre naggs, ner reeaps, ner owt ato ta poo-em, gaan bi theirsells, an it wossant inbank naedthre, *Spec. Dial.* (1885) pt. iii. 28. **n.Yks.²** **w.Yks.¹** I did dirl away inbank, ii. 302.

2. *sb.* A working in a pit, driven to the dip of the coal. **Cum.⁴**

INBARK, *v.* and *sb.* Chs. 1. *v.* Used of the bark of certain trees ; see below.

Chs.¹ ; Chs.² Used to express the way in which the bark of some trees (yews, &c.) not only grows on the outside, as bark commonly does, but also fills up interstices.

2. *sb.* Bark which grows in the above manner. *ib.*

IN-BARN, see Embarn.

INBEARING, *ppl. adj. Obs.* Sc. 1. Officious, meddlesome, prone to seize every opportunity of ingratiating oneself.

Sc. (JAM.) n.Sc. Then out it speaks an auld skipper, An inbearing dog was hee, BUCHAN *Ballads* (1828) I. 3, ed. 1875.

2. Persuasive, eloquent, impressive.

Sc. Get able men, with soul-refreshing and in-bearing gifts to do duty to her, PITCAIRN *Assembly* (1766) 14 ; Men that . . . have an in-bearing gift, speaking home to their hearts, CALDER *Presbyt. Eloq.* (1694) 49, ed. 1847.

INBIGGIT, *ppl. adj.* Sh.I. Also written inbigit S. & Ork.¹ [inbi'git.] Selfish, morose, reserved. (JAM.), S. & Ork.¹

[Dan. *indbygge*, to enclose with buildings.]

INBREAK, *sb.* Sc. Also in forms inbreck, inbrek Or.I. (JAM. *Suppl.*) [i·nbrēk, ·brek.] 1. An inroad, a breaking in.

Edb. I aye hated lying as a poor cowardly sin, and an inbreak on the ten commandments, MOIR *Mansie Wauch* (1828) xvii.

2. A portion of 'in-field' pasture-land newly broken up or tilled. Or.I. (JAM. *Suppl.*)

INBRED, *adj.* Sh.I. Som. 1. Native. Som. (HALL.) [Not known to our correspondents.]

2. *Comb.* Inbred fever, a disease similar to influenza.

Sh.I. The most serious forms of disease were 'mort-caald' and 'inbred fever,' SPENCE *Flk-Lore* (1899) 157.

INBRING, *v. Obs.* Sc. To bring in ; to pay in.

Sc. All merchands sall inbring and pay in all time coming, for ilk last of hydes, six ounces bullion, SKENE *Difficill Wds.* (1681) 27. Sh.I. Your moveabil goods escheat and inbrought to his Majesty's use, HIBBERT *Desc. Sh. I.* (1822) 286, ed. 1891. Or.I. Inbring all yair moveabill gudis to or. use, for yair contemptioun, *Edb. Antiq. Mag.* (1848) 62. Abd. He should have 18,000 merks for inbringing of the Marquis of Huntly to the estates quick or dead, SPALDING *Hist. Sc.* (1792) II. 203

INBU, *sb.* Sh.I. Welcome.

S. & Ork.¹ I'se warrant ye didna get muckle inbû.

INCALL, *v. Obs.* Sc. To invoke, pray.

Slg. Of force he man bow down, and earnestly incall for the Spirit, BRUCE *Sermons* (1631) iii, ed. 1843.

Hence (1) Incaller, *sb.* a petitioner, invoker ; (2) Incalling, *vbl. sb.* invocation, the act of calling upon.

(1) Slg. Ye man be diligent incallers for mercie, *ib.* v. (2) Abd. After incalling of God, Agnes Gray . . . compering in presence of the magistrattis and sessioun was accusit, TURREFF *Gleanings* (1859) 34. Per. By incalling on the great name of God, LAWSON *Bk. of Per.* (1847) 184. Fif. Efter incalling of the name of God, entring in the doctrine, MELVILL *Autobiog.* (1610) 245, ed. 1842. Slg. In this holy action suld we begin with God, and at the incalling upon his name, BRUCE *Sermons* (1631) iii, ed. 1843.

INCAST, *sb.* Sc. [i·nkast.] A quantity given over and above legal measure or sum.

Slk., Rxb. A pound in a stone of wool, and a fleece in a pack, usually given above measure, MORTON *Cyclo. Agric.* (1863). Rxb. It is still usual in several places to give a pound of incast, . . to every stone of wool, and a fleece to every pack sold, a sheep or lamb to every score, and an additional one to every hundred. Part only of this incast is allowed by many sheep farmers, *Agric. Surv.* 357 (JAM.).

INCENSE, see Insense.

INCEP, *prep.* and *conj.* Sh.I. [inse·p.] Except.

Yes sir, incep bit be for some folk 'at's left Shetlan', *Sh. News* (Aug. 14, 1897) ; Incep fir ta kind i' haud i' da paet, I can dû you little gûde, *ib.* (Apr. 8, 1899) ; S. & Ork.¹

INCH, *sb.*¹ and *v.* Sc. Yks. Chs. Lin. War. Wor. Shr. Hrf. Glo. Dor. Dev. Cor. Also in form ins- Shr.¹ [inʃ.] 1. *sb.* In *comp.* (1) Inch-meal, ·mil, or ·mull, inch by inch, little by little ; minutely ; all over ; (2) ·more, inch by inch ; (3) ·muckle, a piece as small as an inch ; (4) ·pieces, very small fragments ; (5) ·small, see (1).

(1) Chs.¹ s.Chs.¹ We speak of killing an animal 'by inch-meal.' The word is formed on the model of 'piece-meal.' War. (HALL.), s.Wor.¹, se.Wor.¹ Shr.¹ Well, it conna be theer, I've looked it inch-meal ; Shr.² Hrf.² His head is broken out inchmull. I've searched the paper inchmull. Glo.¹ (2) Shr.² (3) Bnff.¹ He cuttit it in inch-muckles. (4) n.Lin.¹ I'd raather be cutten e' to inch peâces then do what thaay want. I've fun it at last, but it's to noâ mander of ewse ; it's all brok e' to inch peâces. (5) Chs.¹ Shr.¹ I've sarched the 'ouse ins-small, an' canna find it 'igh, low, nor level.

2. Phr. (1) *an inch of time*, the least moment of time ; (2) *to be at inches with*, to be very near ; (3) *to pay within an inch of any one's life*, to thrash soundly, give a good beating to.

(1) Lnk. It's precious seldom we hae got An inch o' time to spare, MURDOCH *Doric Lyre* (1873) 38. Yks. (J.W.) (2) Dev. (HALL.) (3) w.Yks.¹ I'll pay within an inch o' thy life.

3. *Obs.* A youth, boy ; *gen.* in *comb.* Goad-inch (q.v.).

Dev. The plough boy, who has the goad, and is called the goard inch, *Horae Subsecivae* (1777) 179, 229; GROSE (1790) *MS. add.* (M.)

4. *v.* To encroach gradually ; to move little by little.

Yks. (J.W.) Cor. THOMAS *Randigal Rhymes* (1895) *Gl.*

Hence Inchin', *vbl. sb.* encroaching gradually.

Dor. We might drive in by inching and pinching, HARDY *Tower* (ed. 1895) 2. Cor. No inching there, THOMAS *Randigal Rhymes* (1895) *Gl.* ; Cor.² Boys cried out at play, 'No inchin, no inchin.'

[1. (1) Make him By inch-meal a disease ! SHAKS. *Temp.* II. ii. 3.]

INCH, *sb.*² Sc. Irel. Also in form insh Abd. [inʃ.] A small island ; low-lying land near a river or stream.

Sc. The river becomes narrower ; and there are some beautiful islands which are called Inches, *Statist. Acc.* VIII. 597 (JAM.). Abd. There are some inshes within the harborie, of small worth, not overflowed by the tyde, TURREFF *Gleanings* (1859) 109. Frf. On the north side of the Loch of Forfar, there is a peninsula called the Inch, LOWSON *Guidfollow* (1890) 256. Fif. There is two Inches at the same [Perth], Upon the south and north, TAYLOR *Markinch Minst.* (1811) 39, ed. 1870. Gall. On the green inch of Dalrymple, CROCKETT *Grey Man* (1896) 93 ; Such as the 'Inch o' the Isle,' well known to wild ducks ; and 'Inch Keith,' as well known to the natives about the Firth o' Forth, MACTAGGART *Encycl.* (1824) 279, ed. 1876. s.Ir. Opposite the big inch near Ballyhefaan ford, CROKER *Leg.* (1862) 60. Wxf. The green inches by Boro's side, KENNEDY *Banks Boro* (1867) 295.

[Gael. *innis*, an island ; Ir. *inis*, Wel. *ynys* (MACBAIN).]

INCH, see Hinge.

INCHOR, *sb. Obs.* Som. A sucker or young sprout growing from the root of a tree.

For the most part these grow from the inchors or suckers of the neighbouring trees, BELLINGSLEY *Agric.* (ed. 1798) 285; (W.F.R.)

INCHY-PINCHY, *sb.* War.² [i·nʃi-pinʃi.] The boys' game of progressive leap-frog ; see below.

A makes a back : *B* pitches and makes a back : *C* pitches over *A* and *B* and makes a back. *A* then rises and pitches over *B* and *C*, &c. The formula is 'Inchy-pinchy, last lie down.' The player who first cries this is entitled to wait until all the players are 'down,' before he leaps.

INCLE, see Inkle, *sb.*¹

INCLINABLE, *adj.* Sc. Sur. Som. Inclined to, having regard or desire for.

Rnf. Ministers . . . that are much more inclinable than once was thought, to fall into every thing that may recommend them to the Church, WODROW *Corrs.* (1842-3) I. 91 ; Many are very much inclinable to new schemes, *ib.* 255. Sur.¹ It don't seem no ways inclinable for rain this year. w.Som.¹ No, her would'n let'n come aneast her, her wad'n no way inclinable [eenkluy·nubl].

INCLINATE, *v.* Lin. To incline to, be disposed to.

s.Lin. Noâ, I doônt feel inclinâtted that waâ (T.H.R.).

INCLINE, *sb.* and *v.* Sc. Nhb. Dur. Yks. Shr. [i·nklain, inklai·n.] 1. *sb.* An inclined plane on a rolley-way or on an underground roadway ; also in *comb.* Incline-bank.

Nhb.¹ Nhb., Dur. Used underground, either worked by an engine when to the dip, or self-acting when to the rise. Where the inclination of the seam is sufficient to admit of a self-acting plane being employed, it is an economical mode of transit, especial motive power being thus dispensed with, GREENWELL *Coal Tr. Gl.* (1849). Yks. (J.W.) [Incline man. Person attending to work on an inclined plane, *Reports Mines.*]

2. *v.* To be inclined for, be disposed for.

Edb. Fit to cheer and mak' ye merry When a bottle ye incline, FORBES *Poems* (1812) 19.

3. To decline. Shr.[2]

INCLIN(G, see **Inklin(g.**

INCOME, *sb.* and *ppl. adj.* Sc. Irel. Nhb. Cum. Yks. Lin. [i·nkɐm, ·kum.] **1.** *sb.* Advent, arrival, entrance; an influx.

n.Sc. The income of spring (JAM.). **Ayr.** Frae the settle o' the night To the income o' the light, AINSLIE *Land of Burns* (ed. 1892) 33. **w.Yks.** Much used in relation to the mind. 'I had such an income of fear.' The word is a favourite with old Methodist people, in relating their spiritual experiences. 'I had such sweet incomes all that day' (C.C.R.); 1683. In candles for y⁰ ringers at y⁰ income of Andrews flare, 1*d.*, *Bradford Par. Chwardens' Accts.*

Hence (1) **Incomer,** *sb.* a new-comer, an arrival; a stranger, visitor; (2) **Incoming,** (*a*) *sb.* an arrival, entrance, approach; an introduction; a conversion or accession to the Church; (*b*) *ppl. adj.* ensuing, succeeding; entering upon a farm, &c.

(1) **Sc.** Many of the new incomers were men of corrupt principles, KIRKTON *Ch. Hist.* (1817) 456. **Sh.I.** Shü'd no been a penny ower a half o' croon yit if hit no been fir incomers, *Sh. News* (Aug. 19, 1899). **ne.Sc.** Any real or supposed injustice on the part of the 'incomers' was certain to be resented, GORDON*haven* (1887) 101. **Cai.**[1] A new tenant of a farm, &c. **e.Sc.** It's no every nicht we meet to welcome an incomer, SETOUN *R. Urquhart* (1896) iii. **Ayr.** Thomas was nae a hereawa man, being an incomer frae Piper's Haugh or the Saltcoats, SERVICE *Dr. Duguid* (ed. 1887) 116. **e.Lth.** Ye're but an incomer ye ken. Ye haena been abune four year in the pairish, HUNTER *J. Inwick* (1895) 231. **n.Yks.**[2] **e.Yks.**[1] (*a, a*) **Sc.** With whom he might consult anent the way of his incoming to hold the assembly and parliament in person, GUTHRY *Mem.* (1747) 61 (JAM.). **Cai.**[1] Entry, settlement in a place. **Abd.** The Covenanters understanding their haill proceedings, laid compt before the incoming of this general assembly to bear down episcopacy, SPALDING *Hist. Sc.* (1792) I. 81; Till the incoming of the service-book at Edinburgh, *ib.* II. 25. **Ayr.** On account of the neglect of the Breadland the incoming of Major Gilchrist was to be deplored, GALT *Ann. Parish* (1821) iii. **Edb.** Tell us a' the outgauns, incomings, dounpoorins, and affcoupins in the parish, BALLANTINE *Gaberlunzie* (ed. 1875) 23. **n.Yks.**[4] The taking possession by a new tenant. (*b*) **Sc.** The incomin ook (JAM.). **Sh.I.** What wid ye say ta wis casin' some day da incomin' ook, *Sh. News* (July 10, 1897). **Cai.**[1] The incoman week. The incoman tenant. **Fif.** There's a chance o' the Queen comin' to this toon this incomin' summer, ROBERTSON *Provost* (1894) 168. **Lnk.** It will . . . prevent ony reduction in wages this incomin' winter, GORDON *Pyotshaw* (1885) 14. **N.Cy.**[1] The incoming week. **Nhb.**[1]

2. A new-comer, an arrival.

Abd. When a young man in the real fishing village pays court to the daughter of a crofter or a tradesman, the women of the fishing community rise in revolt against the newcomer, or 'income,' as they term her, *Abd. Wkly. Free Press* (Mar. 12, 1898); Nor are they to incomes I own new fangie, ANDERSON *Poems* (1826) 8; The New Year comes. . . Lat's try this income, how he stands, An' eik us sib by shakin hands, TARRAS *Poems* (1804) 14 (JAM.). **w.Yks.**[1] 'Income of the fair,' arrivals the evening before the fair.

3. Phr. *to be its own income*, to be its own cause, to arise from itself. **n.Yks.**[2] It's all its own income.

4. An internal disease, a bodily infirmity not due to accident or contagion, an ailment without apparent external cause; freq. an abscess, boil, or running sore. Cf. ancome.

Sc. She had a great income, and her parents were then too poor to take her south, RAMSAY *Remin.* (ed. 1872) 118. **Cai.**[1] Disease in a joint, usually knee or elbow, which causes it to be permanently bent. **Fif.** Grown-up people spoke more gravely of an inward trouble, an income, COLVILLE *Vernacular* (1899) 18. **s.Sc.** Ye'll aiblins ken what an income is! Weel, ye maun ken that the bairn's fashed wi' a maist tremendous ane in the heuch o' his knee, WILSON *Tales* (1836) II. 7. **Ayr.** She had got an income in the right arm, and couldna spin, GALT *Sir A. Wylie* (1822) xciii. **Lnk.** Nor a' the skill they can comman' Can heal the income in his haun', HAMILTON *Poems* (1865) 37. **Edb.** Ill with an income in her leg, MOIR *Mansie Wauch* (1828) xvi. **Gall.** It was then that I got the income in my back, CROCKETT *Raiders* (1894) xxiii. **N.I.**[1] 'What makes you lame!' 'A tuk' it first wi'

an income in ma knee.' **Uls.** (M.B.-S.) **Dwn.** An abscess, KNOX *Hist. Dwn.* (1875). **N.Cy.**[1] (s.v. Ancome). **Nhb.**[1] An ulcer; something that has come in from an outside cause as distinguished from a 'gathering' caused by internal bad blood, which is called 'bred-venom.' **Cum.**[1], **n.Lin.**[1]

5. Of things weighed or measured: deficiency from the stated quantity or amount expected.

Cai.[1] Herrings of very poor quality shrink so much in the process of curing, that the result may be a less number of barrels of cured fish than of crans of green fish. Those of best quality usually give a considerable ootcome.

6. That which is thrown in by the sea; also in *comb.* Income ware.

Sc. What I have hitherto observed is only of ware thrown in by the sea, which the farmers call income ware, MAXWELL *Sel. Trans.* (1743) 116 (JAM.).

7. *ppl. adj.* Introduced, come in.

Abd. Not before our ordinary justice or sheriff court, . . but before a new income court, SPALDING *Hist. Sc.* (1792) I. 316 (JAM.).

INCOMPOOT, *sb.* Chs.[1] A 'nincompoop,' a fool, trifler.

INCONSISTENT, *adj.* Nhp. Wor. Hnt. [inkonsi·stənt.] **1.** Reprehensible.

Nhp.[1] He beat his wife and starved his children; it was quite inconsistent! Hnt. (T.P.F.)

2. Phr. *to be inconsistent*, to have a child before marriage. **s.Wor.** PORSON *Quaint Wds.* (1875) 20.

INCONTINENT, *adv.* Obs. or obsol. Sc. Immediately, forthwith, at once.

Sc. The Scots laundry-maid from neighbour Ramsay's who must speak with you incontinent, SCOTT *Nigel* (1822) viii. **Abd.** Charging the haill inhabitants incontinent to bring to the tolbooth the haill spades, shovels, SPALDING *Hist. Sc.* (1792) I. 220. **Per.** Incontinent the trumpets loudlie sounded, FORD *Harp* (1893) 6; He dived incontinent into some profound bole of the High Street, HALIBURTON *Furth in Field* (1894) 58. **Arg.** He commanded incontinent to put fire to the house, SPOTTISWOODE *Miscell.* (1844) II. 363. **Slg.** Incontinent I was sent for by the Provost and Council of Edinburgh, BRUCE *Sermons* (1631) 9, ed. 1843. **Ayr.** The waves come on the shore a great deal, and incontinent run back, DICKSON *Writings* (1660) I. 58, ed. 1845. **Lnk.** We charge you strictly, that incontinent, thir our letters seen, you pass to the market-cross of Edinburgh, WODROW *Ch. Hist.* (1721) I. 399, ed. 1828. **Gall.** I backed the Highlandman into the crack of the door, and discharged him incontinent upon the floor, CROCKETT *Standard Bearer* (1898) 96.

Hence **Incontinently,** *adv.* immediately, forthwith.

Sc. When the woman saw her treasured bink thus laid waste, she relented incontinently, SC. *Haggis*, 61. **Ob.Yks.** They sall be holdin incontinentlie to close the samin [grinds] again, *Edb. Antiq. Mag.* (1848) 6. **n.Sc.** Incontinently the wind was up very boisterous, WODROW *Sel. Biog.* (ed. 1845-7) II. 114. **Per.** Treating himself incontinently to a huge pinch of snuff, HALIBURTON *Furth in Field* (1894) 11. **Fif.** They . . . did all incontinently flic in disorder and disband, Row *Ch. Hist.* (1650) 519, ed. 1842.

INCONVENE, *adj.* Sc. Inconvenient. *Glasgow Herald* (Apr. 3, 1899).

INCONVENIENT, *sb.* Obs. Sc. Inconvenience.

Sc. Fearing the insolency showld bursth furth wnto some worser inconuenient, SPOTTISWOODE *Miscell.* (1844) I. 261. **Fif.** Fearing that it might bring with it some inconvenients, SCOT *Apolog.* (1644) 189, ed. 1846. **Slg.** To see a youth pass over his young years without a notable inconvenient either to body or soul, or to both, BRUCE *Sermons* (1631) xv, ed. 1843.

INCORMANT, *sb.* Bnff.[1] A share, portion.

INCREASE, *sb.* and *v.* Irel. n.Cy. Lin. Nrf. Sur. **1.** *sb.* Interest on money.

n.Lin.[1] He niver taks less increase then five pund e' th' hundred.

2. The birth of a child, an addition to a family by the birth of a child.

n.Cy. (J.W.) **Nrf.** They tell unto me there's an increase up at the Hall this morning (W.R.E.).

Hence **Increasement,** *sb.* the pains of labour. Sur.[1]

3. *v.* To grow fat.

Ir. Sure he do lu picking up and increasing, *Paddiana* (ed. 1848) I. 121.

INCREED, *sb.* n.Yks.[2] Internal persuasion.

INCREEDIT, *v.* n.Yks.[2] To credit, to reason oneself into believing. 'I can't increedit that.'

IND, *sb.* Nhp.[1] Hrf.[2] An inn, public-house.

IND, *v.* Dmf. (JAM.) To bring in, to house corn. See **In,** *v.* **28.** ' Inding the corn,' leading the corn.

INDE, see **Hind,** *sb.*[2]

INDECENT, *adj.* Sc. Irel. Lin. Som. Dev. Also in forms **ondacent** Sc. n.Ir. w.Som.[1] Dev.; **ondaicent** N.I.[1]; **ondecent** Lin. [indi·sənt, ondē·sənt.] **1.** Unbecoming, unseemly; disreputable; also in *comp.* **Indecent-like.**

Sc. Two very ragged indecent-like Highlandmen, STEVENSON *Catriona* (1893) i. **Ayr.** I allow mysel' that was an ondacent-like thing, JOHNSTON *Kilmallie* (1891) I. 179. **n.Ir.** It's rether ondacent to fecht wi' the clargy, *Lays and Leg.* (1884) 6. **Lin.** A haxin' me hawkard questions, an' saiyin' ondecent things, TENNYSON *Spinster's Sweet-arts* (1885). **w.Som.**[1] There's he an' her and all they vower gurt maaidens, and zometimes a lodger too, an' on'y two chimmers. I will zay it, 'tis downright ondacent [aun·dai·sunt]. **Dev.** He graws beet-red, naturally enough 'fore such an ondacent speech, *Red Rose* in *Pall Mall Mag.* (Apr. 1900) 440.

2. Unfair. N.I.[1]

INDEED, *adv.* Sc. Irel. Yks. Pem. [indī·d.] In phr. (1) *indeed-an'-doubles,* a strong asseveration; (2) — *aw nawther,* indeed I did not; (3) — *indeed and doubles,* (4) — *in-double-deed,* see (1); (5) — *no,* no indeed.

(1) **N.I.**[1] (2) **w.Yks.** 'Tha mended mi jacket all reight!' 'Nay, indeed aw nawther,' HARTLEY *Clock Alm.* (1872). (3) **Dwn.** (C.H.W.) (4) **a.Pem.** Usually the prefix to a lie, LAWS *Little Eng.* (1888) 420. (5) **Sc.** MITCHELL *Scotticisms* (1792) 47; *Monthly Mag.* (1798) II. 436.

INDEL, *adv.* Dev. [i·ndl.] Indoors, *gen.* in phr. *indel and oudel,* indoors and outdoors. Also used *attrib.*

Goe indel till hare an try, parson, nif tha dust! MADOX-BROWN *Dwale Bluth* (1876) bk. i. ii; Indel and oudel, *n.Dev. Hand-bk.* (ed. 1877) 258; **Dev.**[1] Who ha zo much indel and oudel work to do, 3; **Dev.**[2] Tez winderful fainty indel and oudle [it is wonderfully hot both indoors and out].

INDENT, *v.* Obs. Sc. To bind by contract, to pledge, make a compact; to engage, warrant.

Fif. I indented with the King for the staying of that decreit, MELVILL *Autobiog.* (1610) 422, ed. 1842. **Rnf.** The day will come yet, I'se indent, Experience sad will teach us, PICKEN *Poems* (1813) II. 151. **Ayr.** For Britain's guid his saul indentin, BURNS *Twa Dogs* (1786) l. 148. **Edb.** For towmonths twa their saul is lent, For the town's gude indentit, FERGUSSON *Poems* (1773) 170, ed. 1785. **Kcb.** Rouse up your conscience, and begin to indent and contract, RUTHERFORD *Lett.* (1660) No. 173.

INDEPENDENCE, *sb.* Sc. In phr. *the Independence set,* Independents, Congregationalists.

Dmb. Are ye for trying the Burgher, or the Relief, or the Independence set o't? CROSS *Disruption* (1844) xl.

INDEPENDENT, *adj.* Sc. n.Cy. Lin. Oxf. [indipe·ndənt.] **1.** Rich, in easy circumstances.

Sc. An independent man; a man of an independent fortune, MITCHELL *Scotticisms* (1792) 48. **n.Cy.** (J.W.)

2. Uncourteous, unobliging.

n.Lin.[1] Sarvants are soä independent noo a daays, ther' is no gettin' on wi' 'em at all. A baker once said to the author, 'I alus strive niver to shaw myself independent, that's how I keäp my customers together.' **Oxf.**[1] 'Er's very well for work, but 'er's too independent for I, *MS. add.*

INDER, *sb.* e.An. [i·ndə(r).] A great number or quantity of persons or things, esp. of money.

e.An.[1] He is worth an inder of money; **e.An.**[2] He is worth an inder. **Nrf.** I have laid an inder of loads of gravel in my yard, GROSE (1790). **Suf.** CULLUM *Hist. Hawsted* (1813); **Suf.**[1] *Gen.* in reference to money or property. 'We'av sitch an inder of poor.'

INDERMER, see **Innermore.**

INDETRIMENT, *sb.* Yks. Lin. Som. Also in forms **indeterment** w.Som.[1]; **indethriment** e.Yks.[1]; **indetterment** n.Lin.[1] [inde·triment.] Detriment, loss, injury; a stumbling-block. Cf. **detriment.**

e.Yks.[1] **n.Lin.** An' it wasn't noa indetterment to onybody else, PEACOCK *Tales* (1890) and S. 67; **n.Lin.**[1] **sw.Lin.**[1] It'll be no indetriment to him. I never felt no indetriment wi' it. **w.Som.**[1] Nif you could spare me some o'm, 'thout no indeterment to yourzel, I should be uncommon 'bleege t'ee.

INDIA, *sb.* Sc. Irel. Chs. Glo. Suf. Som. Also in forms **Indee** e.Suf.; **indy** Chs.[1] Glo.[1]; **ingy** w.Som.[1] [i·ndiə.]

1. In *comp.* (1) **India-buck,** meal or porridge made from Indian corn. N.I.[1]; (2) ·**pink,** (*a*) the ragged robin, *Lychnis Flos-cuculi.* Glo.[1]; (*b*) the clove-pink, *Dianthus Caryophyllus.* *ib.* **2.** Phr. *as rich as Indee,* very wealthy. e.Suf. (F.H.)

3. India-rubber.

w.Som.[1] They be the best sort o' balls, they way a bit o' ingy [een·jee] in the inside o'm. Hast a-got other bit o' ingy vor to rub out this here black-lead.

Hence **Chewing-india,** *sb.* india-rubber chewed until it becomes soft.

Lnk. I . . . begged as a great favour that he would lend me his slab of chewin' india for the rest of the day, FRASER *Whaups* (1895) 25; India rubber chewed enough to admit of air bells being formed in it and exploding with a crack (A.W.).

4. Ground maize. Chs.[1]

INDIAN, *adj.* Irel. Glo. Som. Dev. In *comb.* (1) **Indian fog,** var. species of stonecrop, esp. *Sedum reflexum* and *S. glaucum*; (2) ·**pink,** (*a*) the ragged robin, *Lychnis Flos-cuculi*; (*b*) the clove-pink, *Dianthus Caryophyllus*; (*c*) the Chinese pink, *D. chinensis*; (3) ·**rubber,** india-rubber.

(1) **Don.** (B. & H.) (2 *a, b*) **Glo.**[1] (*c*) **w.Som.**[1], **Dev.**[4] (3) **Dev.** If the indian-rubber tube happen to choke, you must blow through it, BARING-GOULD *Dartmoor Idylls* (1896) 7.

INDICATOR, *sb.* Nhb. Dur. In mining: an apparatus attached to the engine by means of which the brakesman can tell the position of the cages in a shaft. NICHOLSON *Coal Tr. Gl.* (1888).

INDICTED, *ppl. adj.* Sh.I. Nhb. [indi·ktid.] Inclined, addicted.

Sh.I. Yunsin in da first of his time, was indicted ta drink, BURGESS *Lowra Biglan* (1896) 54. **Nhb.**[1]

INDIFFERENT, *adj.* Sc. n.Cy. Yks. Lin. Lei. Nhp. War. Hnt. e.An. [indi·f(ə)rənt.] **1.** Tolerable, passable, pretty good; middling, mediocre; also used *advb.*

Sc. He was supposed to make an indifferent good thing of it, SCOTT *St. Ronan* (1824) iii. **N.Cy.**[1] **w.Yks.**[1] If I ask a Craven peasant how his wife does, he replies 'indifferent, thank ye;' then I conclude that she is in tolerably good health. **Lei.**[1] It's an indifferent crop. 'How are you to-day?' 'Well, Ah've indifferent well.' 'There seems to be a great number of them!' 'Ah, indifferent!' **Nhp.**[1], **War.**[2], **Hnt.** (T.P.F.)

Hence **Indifferently,** *adv.* tolerably. w.Yks.[1]

2. Poorly, bad, ill, esp. in phr. *very indifferent.*

w.Yks.[1] I's seure Joan's vara unfit to be oute lat; for hees lang been vara indifferent, ii. 286. **n.Lin.**[1] 'How's your wife to-day?' 'Oh, she's nobbut indifferent thank you.' Oor Jaane's gotten an uncommon indifferent place; I shall tell her to gie warnin'. **Nhp.**[1] When 'very' is added it implies severe indisposition. **Hnt.** (T.P.F.) **e.An.**[1] It was rather an indifferent match for Miss B. Mr. C. had very indifferent success in his attempt, he was totally disappointed.

Hence **Indifferently,** *adv.* ill, poorly. e.An.[1]

INDIGESTER, *sb.* Wor. Digestion.

a.Wor. Old Mr. Rasler 'e 'ave allus said as my indigester werc out of order (H.K.).

INDIGNIFY, *v.* Obs. Sc. To disgrace.

Edb. That immoral, indignifies the man, Sinks him far neath the brute creation, LIDDLE *Poems* (1821) 210.

INDING, *adj.* Obs. Sc. Unworthy, shameful.

Sc. GROSE (1790) *MS. add.* (C.) **Fif.** The mem'rie o' that wicket thing, And cruel martyrdom inding, TENNANT *Papistry* (1827) 198.

[1, maist wrachit synfull catyve inding, DOUGLAS *Eneados* (1513), ed. 1874, III. 276. Fr. *indigne,* unworthy (COTGR.).]

INDISCREET, *adj.* Obs. Sc. Uncivil, rude.

Sc. Others . . . gave me indiscreet, upbraiding language, calling me a vile old apostate, WALKER *Life Peden* (1727) 3 (JAM.). **n.Sc.** The first night he was so indiscreet as to put me into a gousty, cold, wide, dark, filthy, smoky room, WODROW *Sel. Biog.* (ed. 1845-7) II. 357.

Hence **Indiscreetly,** *adv.* uncivilly, rudely.

Sc. (JAM.) **Fif.** I hope you will not use me so indiscreetlie as did one Mr. David Calderwood, Row *Ch. Hist.* (1650) 212, ed. 1842. **Lnk.** Upon this the bishop went off, as indiscreetly as he came up, WODROW *Ch. Hist.* (1721) IV. 458, ed. 1828.

INDISCRETION, *sb.* Obs. Sc. Incivility, impoliteness. Cf. **discretion,** s.v. **Discreet.**

Lnk. I am told he treated the chancellor with indiscretion abundance, WODROW *Ch. Hist.* (1721) I. 384, ed. 1828.

INDISGESTION, *sb.* e.Lan.[1] Chs.[1] Sur.[1] [indisdge·ʃən.] Indigestion.

INDOOR, *adj.* Sc. Lin. e.An. Som. Dev. In *comb.* (1) Indoor face, the face of one not exposed to the weather; (2) — servant, a farm-servant living in his master's house.

(1) **Lnk.** He has an unco han'-me-doon look, an indoor face, no tashed wi' the weather, FRASER *Whaups* (1895) 189. (2) **Lin.**[1] **n.Lin.**[1] A farm servant who does not work out of doors. **e.An.**[1] A servant in the country who is entirely within doors. **w.Som.**[1] In all cases the term 'indoor' refers to the board and lodging and not to the work done. **nw.Dev.**[1]

INDOORS, *adv.* Som. Of a servant: with board and lodging in the master's house.

Man (trustworthy) wanted, indoors, who understands sheep, and will make himself generally useful, *Auctioneer's Advt.* (1895). **w.Som.**[1] I be working to Mr. Venn's to Dykes, indoors [I work for Mr. Venn on his farm, and live in his house]. 'Wanted at once, a man, indoors, to drive horses and make himself useful on a farm,' *Wellington Wkly. News* (Jan. 13, 1887).

INDRAIN, *sb.* n.Yks.[2] [i·ndrēn.] A whirlpool; *fig.* a place of attraction or resort. Cf. indraw.

INDRAUGHT, *sb.* Sc. [i·ndrǟxt.] 1. Suction of air.

Sc. So slight was the indraught of air, that the reek ... descended cloud after cloud to the very floor, *Blackw. Mag.* (June 1820) 281 (JAM.). **Cai.**[1]

2. A strong current, a vortex.

Or.I. The other part [of the flood-tide] slips down by Sandwick shore till it gets in to the indraught of Hoy Sound, *Statist. Acc.* XIV. 315 (JAM.).

INDRAW, *sb.* n.Yks.[2] A whirlpool; *fig.* a place of attraction or resort. Cf. indrain.

INDRINK, *sb.* Sc. A diminution, shrinkage.

Rnf. There has been a great indrink of communicants in many places in this country-side this summer, WODROW *Corres.* (1842–3) I. 30.

INDUMIOUS, *adj.* Sh.I. Very bad; of the weather: extraordinarily rough or stormy.

Da wadder is juist bȫn indūmious fir a lang time noo, *Sh. News* (May 7, 1898).

INDURING, *prep.* Obs. Sc. During.

Sc. Ane bastard ... may in his lige pousty, and induring his lifetime, annalie and diapone his landes, gudes and geare, SKENE *Difficill Wds.* (1681) 17. **Abd.** Any maister quhatsumever that teiches Inglische induring the will and plesure of the Counsaill, MELVILLE *Commonplace Bk.* (1640) xxxii, ed. 1899. **Per.** Give yearly to the said Archibald Steedman five merks induring his service in tempering of the knock, SPOTTISWOODE *Miscell.* (1844) II. 269. **Fif.** We haiff fund of God's guidnes this fruict, that induring sa manie yeirs na heresie hes sprung up in our kirks, MELVILL *Autobiog.* (1610) 155, ed. 1842.

[Pensionis ... Induring his gude will, *Sat. Poems* (1573), ed. Cranstoun, I. 319.]

INDUSTHER, *v.* Irel. [indu·sþər.] To work hard, be industrious.

He was allaways industherin'at somethin' or other, BLACKBURNE *Stories,* 8.

INDUSTRIOUS, *sb.* N.I.[1] An industrious person.

He was a good industrious.

INDWELL, *v.* Sc. Also in form indwall Kcd. [indwe·l.] To reside in, inhabit; to possess as a habitation.

Sc. We aw him nought but a grey groat, The off'ring for the house we indwell, HERD *Coll. Sngs.* (1776) II. 46 (JAM.); He hath thought it fit that some relicts of sin ... should indwell, DURHAM *X. Command.* (1675) *Ep. Ded.* (JAM.)

Hence (1) **Indweller,** *sb.* an inhabitant; (2) **Indwelling,** *sb.* a habitation, dwelling.

(1) **Sc.** This old, black city, which was for all the world like a rabbit-warren, not only by the number of its indwellers, STEVENSON *Catriona* (1893) i; A poor Trojan ... had been ten months or thereby, an indweller in Sparta, *Scoticisms* (1787) 118. **Abd.** The drum went through the Oldtown, commanding and charging the baill indwellers thereof, SPALDING *Hist. Sc.* (1792) I. 160. **Kcd.** An indwaller i' the parish o' Stra'an, GRANT *Lays* (1884) 1. **Lnk.** Christian Fyfe, late indweller in Fife, WODROW *Ch. Hist.* (1721) III. 409, ed. 1828. **Gall.** My father ... had been all his life 'indweller' in the hill farm of Ardarroch, CROCKETT *Standard Bearer* (1898) 1. **Wgt.** Anthony Conning, 'indweller in Wigtoun,' FRASER *Wigtown* (1877) 34. (2) **Sc.** MITCHELL *Scotticisms* (1792) 47; *Scoticisms* (1787) 47.

INDY, INE, see India, Hind, *adj.*

INEAR, *sb.* n.Cy. Yks. Also written innear m.Yks.[1] A kidney, 'ear.' n.Cy. GROSE (1790). n.Yks.[124], m.Yks.[1] See Near, *sb.*

INFAIR, see Infar(e.

INFALL, *sb.* Obs. Sc. An invasion, attack, onslaught.

ne.Sc. This infall (known afterwards commonly by the name of 'the Trott o' Turra' in derision) fell out May fourteenth, 1639, GREGOR *Flk-Lore* (1881) 114. **Abd.** Having been provocked by a party of the Aberdeen's garrison, ther infall into his quarters in the night tyme, TURREFF *Gleanings* (1859) 96. **Lnk.** The rebels were at Drumclog, the first of June being Sunday, upon Monday at the infal upon Glasgow, WODROW *Ch. Hist.* (1721) III. 89, ed. 1828.

[Norw. dial. *innfall,* an invasion (AASEN); Sw. *infall,* Dan. *indfald.*]

INFANG, *v.* Obs. Sc. To cheat, gull, 'take in'; to get into one's clutches. See Fang, *v.* 1.

s.Sc. I hope ye are na Just infang't i' love sae sair, T. SCOTT *Poems* (1793) 361. Cld. (JAM.)

INFANT-HARROW, *sb.* War.[2] A rake-harrow.

A small light harrow used to cover seeds after drilling or dibbling, and drawn by hand, or by cord fastened round the workman who drills and harrows at one operation.

INFAR(E, *sb.* Sc. Irel. Cum. Amer. Also written infair N.I.[1] Cum.[4]; and in form infore Ayr. [i·nfər.] The home-coming of a bride; the entertainment given for the reception of a bride in the bridegroom's house; the reception after a wedding.

Sc. (JAM.) **Abd.** He brought over his wife to his own house in the Oldtown, where there was a goodly infare, SPALDING *Hist. Sc.* (1792) II. 54. **Ags.** The name of the day succeeding a wedding, including the idea of the entertainment given to the guests (JAM.); The day after the wedding is the infare... This may be considered a second edition of yesterday, only the company is less numerous and the dinner is commonly the scraps that were left at the wedding feast. On this occasion every one of both sexes who has a change of dress appears in a garb different from that worn on the preceding day, *Edb. Mag.* (Nov. 1818) 414 (*ib.*). **Ayr.** A dull bridal and a scrimp infore bodes quench'd love or toom pantries, GALT *Lairds* (1826) xx. **Ir.** A dangerous compliment is paid to the bride-party, at what is called the infair or bringing home. They are saluted with shots from muskets and pistols at every village, Flk-Lore Jrn. (1884) II. 212. **N.I.**[1] **Cum.** Sec an infair I've been at, STAGG *Misc. Poems* (ed. 1807) 2; **Cum.**[4] The holding of a marriage feast for the purpose of receiving assistance was subsequently termed 'infair,' but this expression was more commonly applied to a festivity held in a public-house at other than the stated and regular dates for 'Merry nights' (s.v. Bridewain). [Amer. CARRUTH *Kansas Univ. Quar.* (Oct. 1892) I; *Dial. Notes* (1896) I. 383.]

Hence **Infar·cake,** *sb.* a cake broken over the head of a bride on her home-coming.

Sc. The guests assembled at the door, on the threshold of which a sieve containing bread and cheese was held over her head, and, as she entered the house, a cake of shortbread was broken over her head, the young folk scrambling for the fragments, ANDREWS *Bygone Ch. Life* (1899) 224. **Lth.** It makes nae matter about the infar-cake: it's jist an' auld superstition aboot it's no' bein' lucky not to hae't richt broken, or about dreamin ower bits o't to ken wha's to marry you, STRATHESK *Blinkbonny* (ed. 1891) 176; The infar-cake was only broken over Bell's head, *ib.* 176.

[He thoucht for till mak Infair, And till mak gud cher till his men, BARBOUR *Bruce* (1375) XVI. 340. OE. *in-far,* an entrance (*Gen.* iii. 24).]

INFARING, *adj.* Som. In-lying, lying within or near home.

'An infaring tithing,' a tithing within a borough, W. & J. *Gl.* (1873). **w.Som.**[1] The opposite of outlying. 'I mean to keep all the infaring [eenfae·ureen] ground in hand.

INFATUATE, *adj.* Sc. Infatuated, mad, foolish.

Sh.I. Though we had several shipmasters and a double crew on board, they were as infatuate as to mistake their reckoning, WILLCOCK *Minister* (1897) 59. **Lnk.** So infatuate in their thirst after blood have some people been, WODROW *Ch. Hist.* (1721) I. 158, ed. 1828.

INFEFT, *v.* Sc. [infe·ft.] To put into legal possession, to legally or formally invest with property, &c.; to enfeoff. Gen. with *in.*

n.Sc. I would infeft your son this day In third part o' my

land, Buchan *Ballads* (1828) I. 82, ed. 1875. **Bch.** When I found myself infeft In a young Jack, I did resolve to change the haft For that mistak, Forbes *Dominie* (1785) 46. Abd. I hope they're now infeft, by law, To bar objections, Cock *Strains* (1810) I. 132. Per. She were infeft in her future husband's lands, Lawson *Bk. of Per.* (1847) 190. **Dmb.** In the mailin get our Kirst infeft, Salmon *Gowodean* (1868) 88. **Slg.** I had denuded my hands of some lands and casualties that I was infefted in, Bruce *Sermons* (1631) 9, ed. 1843. Ayr. In houses an' mailins I'll soon be infeft, Ainslie *Poems* (ed. 1892) 225. **Lnk.** The major's lady was happily infeft in a part of his lands, Wodrow *Ch. Hist.* (1721) II. 49, ed. 1828. **Wgt.** The said Burgh has been more freely infefted by our predecessors, Fraser *Wigtown* (1877) 10.
　Hence **Infeftment,** *sb.* investiture, legal possession.
　Sc. The Earl wished to resign all his lands into the King's hands for new infeftments, Kirkton *Ch. Hist.* (1817) 157. **Sh.I.** Lands ... of which ... the vassals were not seised by infeftment from the Crown, Hibbert *Desc. Sh. I.* (1822) 139, ed. 1891. Or.I. A new infeftment in favour of his Lordship, Peterkin *Notes* (1822) 111. Per. Our holy fathers who ... left to us, as it were, in haereditate infeftment, a pure forme of worshipping God, Wodrow *Sel. Biog.* (ed. 1845–7) I. 99. Ayr. If there is aught in this life that may be regarded as the symbols of infeftment to the inheritance of Heaven, Galt *Gilhaize* (1823) xii. **Lnk.** To pass infeftments under the great seal, Wodrow *Ch. Hist.* (1721) I. 258, ed. 1828. **Slk.** Taking infeftment of some new grants of land, Hogg *Tales* (1838) 195, ed. 1866. **Wgt.** According to their ancient infeftment belonging as hitherto to the same persons, Fraser *Wigtown* (1877) 10.
　INFELL, *v.* s.Chs.[1] To hem down the inside of a seam. Run)th see·m ûlôngg·, tin dhen in·fel it [Run th' seam alung, an' then infell it].
　INFESTUOUS, *adj.* Sc. Extraordinary. Dmf. Wallace *Schoolmaster* (1899) 349.
　INFIELD, *sb.* ? *Obs.* Sc. Cum. Chs. Arable land which receives manure and is perpetually in crop. Also used *attrib.*
　Sc. With the ... tofts, crofts, mosses, muirs—outfield, infield, &c., Scott *Waverley* (1814) xlii. **Sh.I.** The land lying near the homestead was kept for successive years in tillage, and under the name of Infield received all the manure, mixed with earth, which the farm afforded, Hibbert *Desc. Sh. I.* (1822) 202, ed. 1891; Da infield corn is no ta be compeaned apon, an' da tatties is luikin' weel, *Sh. News* (Aug. 14, 1897); A glebe o' guid infield land, Stewart *Tales* (1892) 26. Abd. The ancient division of the land was into infield, outfield, and fauchs. The infield was dunged every three years for bear; and the two crops that followed bear were oats invariably ... Since the introduction of turnips the farmers make it a general rule not to take more than one and never more than two crops of oats in succession in their infield grounds, *Statist. Acc.* II. 533 (Jam.). Per. That non of the tennents of wester Tullineddies cast up any of the grein or infield grass of West-Tullineddies in time comeing, *Edb. Antiq. Mag.* (1848) 55. **Edb.** Whose ancient crofts, or infield lands contiguous to their steadings, were equal to their rents and sustenances, Pennecuik *Wks.* (1715) 67, ed. 1815. **N.Cy.[1]** Cum. Ah wad hev as fine a stock eh hogs as yeh ivver leuckt gaan eh t'infields, Sargisson *Joe Scoap* (1881) 189; Fell lambs are wintering well on the in-fields, *Carlisle Patriot* (Dec. 14, 1888) 3, col. 6; **Cum.[3]** They'd rayder part wi' life Ner sell or swap a single yird of infield land or fell, 95; **Cum.[4]** Ancient enclosed land, and commonly the best. **Chs.** The obsolete system of infield and outfield—of occasionally plowing and cropping the inferior lands situated at a distance from the homestead, and bringing home the produce to enrich the better land, Marshall *Review* (1818) II. 30. (The nearer portion of the land, which bore the grain and vegetables for the cultivators and their families and dependents, and the fodder for the cattle in winter, was called the infield, Stephens *Farm Bk.* (ed. 1849) II. 555.)
　INFIRM, *adj.* Glo. [infē·m.] Silly, foolish.
　A man must be an infirm creatur, Philip, to talk as ye do, to a certainty, Gissing *Vill. Hampden* (1890) II. v.
　INFIT, *sb.* Bnff.[1] [i·nfit.] 1. An introduction.
　2. Influence.
　He's sure t' get 's fairin agehn. He hiz a gey gueede infit wee the laird.
　Hence **Infittan,** *sb.* influence.
　He hiz great in-fittan at behid quarters.
　INFOORCE, *sb.* n.Yks.[2] Internal agency or action; fermentation.
　INFORE, see Infar(e.

INFORMATION, *sb.* Lin. Sus. Som. Dev. Also in form infamation n.Lin.[1] [infəmē·ʃən.] Inflammation.
　n.Lin.[1] Th' ohd hoss deed o' infamation, though we fermented him all neet. **Sus.[1]** She was took with the information (s.v. Dunnamany). **Som.** Old Gabriel still laments the days o' his youth, when if you suffered from 'information' you were 'blooded,' Raymond *Misterton's Mistake* (1888) 370. **w.Som.[1]** His leg don't get no better, and th' information's that bad, he's a-swelled so big's two. **Dev.** Betty reproved me by saying she didn't know much of faith that couldn't put down an 'information,' Peard *Mother Molly* (1889) 204.
　INFUSE, *v.* War.[4] [influ·z.] To inform.
　I wish I could infuse you more accurately, but that's just what I can't do.
　ING, *sb.* Nhb. Dur. Cum. Wm. Yks. Lan. Not. Lin. Nhp. e.An. Ken. Sur. Sus. Also in form inge Nhb.[1] Cum. Ess.[1]; in Nhb.[1] [iŋ.] 1. A meadow, pasture, esp. low-lying land by the side of a stream or river, &c.; freq. in *pl.* Also used *attrib.* and in place-names.
　n.Cy. (K.); Grose (1790); N.Cy.[12] **Nhb.** A great flood swept them away into the inges below, Hodgson *Arch. Æliana,* I. 269; **Nhb.[1]** **s.Dur.** Now only used in place or rather field names, as Hard Ings, Broad Ings (J.E.D.). Lake.l.[1]; Lake.l.[2] A field and place name—Wood Ing, Main Ing. **Cum.** None shall ride ... through Wilson's Inge, Hodgson *Water Mellock* (ed. 1883) 30; I've lost a fat wether, and David's lost twa—all oot o' t'ings, Dalby *Mayroyd* (1880) I. 251, ed. 1888; The fields with us so named mostly retain their meadowy character, lying low and too near the rivers to be safely ploughed, *N. & Q.* (1873) 4th S. xii. 401. **Wm.** Poor Maggy ! the Pride of the Ings ! Blezard *Sngs.* (1848) 22; Esp. [a meadow] that is moist or liable to be flooded (J.H.). **Yks.** Morton *Cyclo. Agric.* (1863). **n.Yks.** If it consists of ings or low-land adjoining a river refrain from sowing hay-seeds grown on up-land, Marshall *Review* (1808) I. 483; **n.Yks.[1]** A name for some field or other in a farm, which field originally was a low-lying, wet or marshy meadow, although now it may have been long drained and become arable; **n.Yks.[2][3][4]** **ne.Yks.[1]** The *sing.* is never used ; a double *pl.* 'ingses' is frequent. 'T'watther's gitten all ower t'ingses.' **e.Yks.** Marshall *Rur. Econ.* (1788); **e.Yks.[1]** **m.Yks.[1]** The low ing pasture. **w.Yks.** That ing at back of our 'ouse (A.L.K.); We had seen the ings first from the rig of it, Snowden *Web of Weaver* (1896) 90; **w.Yks.[1234]** **Lan.** The level Ings are flooded into lakes, Kay-Shuttleworth *Scarsdale* (1860) III. 305. **ne.Lan.[1]**, **Not.** (L.C.M.) **Lin.** Before the common land in this parish—Springthorpe—was enclosed, there was a part of the common called 'The Ings,' where the inhabitants had a right to pasture cattle, *N. & Q.* (1873) 4th S. xii. 482; The unenclosed Ings, or open meadows, of this neighbourhood, Thompson *Hist. Boston* (1856) 676; Ray (1691). **n.Lin.[1]** 1000 acres of ings or common meadow, Young *Lin. Agric.* (1799) 179. **sw.Lin.[1]** They're soughing the great ing agen Skellingthorpe Wood. **Nhp.[2], e.An.[1]** **Ess.** White *Eng.* (1865) II. 293; **Ess.[1]** The salt 'inges.' **ne.Ken.** (H.M.) **Sur.** Little Ing, near Godalming, *N. & Q.* (1884) 6th S. x. 225. **Sus.** (M.B.-S.); Sus.[1]; Sus.[2] A meadow on a side hill, as 'The Ings' near Kingston.
　2. Mould rayzed by moles, mole-hills, esp. in phr. *to dress the ing,* to spread the mole-hills and dung in a field.
　w.Yks. Thoresby *Lett.* (1703) (s.v. Durse); **w.Yks.[4]**, Lin. (W.W.S.)
　3. *Comp.* **Ing·rake,** a meadow or hay-rake, a rake used in dressing 'ings.' **w.Yks.** Thoresby *Lett.* (1703).
　[ME. *eng,* a medew, *Cath. Angl.* (1483); ON., Dan. *eng.*]
　INGAIN, *sb.* e.An.[1] [i·ngēn.] Profit in buying and selling.
　IN-GAITHERAN, *vbl. sb.* Bnff.[1] The act of gathering or collecting together.
　The lassies are a' oot at the in-gaitheran o' the claise.
　INGAN, *sb.* Sc. Also Suf. Also in forms ingun, ingyun e.Suf. [i·ŋgən.] An onion; also used *attrib.*
　Sc. Our Spanish colonel, whom I could have blown away like the peeling of an ingan, Scott *Leg. Mont.* (1818) ii. n.Sc. A *prov.* is used expressive of high contempt as addressed to one who makes much ado about trifles : ' Ye're sair stress'd stringing ingans ' (Jam.). Per. An ingan, too, maks them sae nice, Stewart *Character* (1857) 185. **Lnk.** He could ... cut the ingans, minsh the shooet, and saut and pepper the stew to perfection, Murdoch *Readings* (ed. 1895) I. 10. **Edb.** The auldest man alive Ne'er saw sae ill their ingans thrive, Thomson *Poems* (1819) 122. **Gall.** My wee yaird is like a desert, Ingans, leeks, and carrots fail, Kerr *Maggie o' the Moss* (1891) 73. **Suf.[3], e.Suf.** (F.H.)

INGANG, *sb.* n.Sc. (JAM.) Lack, deficiency; prop. a going in, a contraction.

INGANGERS, *sb. pl.* n.Yks.[2] People assembling or coming in.

INGANGING, *sb.* Nhb. Yks. A recess, the entrance to a house, &c. Cf. ingo.

Nhb.[1] He fell doon just at the ingannin o' wor entry. n.Yks.[2]

INGANGS, *sb. pl.* ? *Obs.* Sc. The intestines, entrails.

Gall. At that season of the year called Michaelmas, he [the devil] is said to touch the black-berries, or to ' throw his club over them,' none daring after that period to eat one of them, or the ' worms will eat their ingangs,' MACTAGGART *Encycl.* (1824) 167, ed. 1876.

[Sw. *ingång,* an entry, passage (WIDEGREN).]

INGATE, *sb.* Sc. Nhb. Cum. Wm. Yks. Lan. Also in forms **ingaate** Wm.; **ingeat** Cum.[4]; **ingeatt** Cum.[1] [i·ngět, -giat.] **1.** An entrance, ingress, a way in; the act of entering. Cf. gate, *sb.*[2] 7.

n.Cy.[1] Entrance to a working place in a coal mine; the inlet for a current of air in the working of a pit. Nhb.[1] Specially applied to the way into a mine at the bottom of a shaft, or at any point in a shaft where the cages are stopped to enter a seam; or to the way by which the air enters the workings of a pit. Cum.[4] n.Yks.[1]; n.Yks.[2] Right both of ingate and outgate. ne.Yks.[1] m.Yks.[1] If applied to a pathway, a short, more or less enclosed one, is indicated. Of the outlets of divergent paths within a wood, it will be said, ' There is only one ingate; all the rest is [are] outgates.' w.Yks.[1], ne.Lan.[1]

2. Phr. (1) *ingate and outgate,* within and without, completely; (2) — *or outgate,* (*a*) within or without, *gen.* used *neg.* not at all, nothing; (*b*) willy-nilly, by any means whatever.

(1: Gall. May they burn back and front, ingate and outgate, hide, hair, and harrigals, CROCKETT *Standard Bearer* (1898) 301. (2, *a*) w.Yks.[1] Mostly used when speaking of something that is lost, which, after the most diligent search, cannot be found. Thus a person will say, ' I lost a sheep last week, bud I can mak nayther ingate ner outgate on't '; w.Yks.[2] Of a child who had fallen down an old chambered well, but could not be discovered, it was said that she ' couldn't be fun, nAather ingate nur out.' (*b*) Wm. He wad hev her, ingaate er ootgaate, ROBISON *Auld Taales* (188a) 3.

3. An inroad, attack. Cum.[14] **4.** The time when the post comes in. Cum.[1]

INGE, see Ing.

INGENURIOUS, *adj.* Sus.[1] Ingenious.

For my part I consider that King Solomon was a very ingenurious man.

INGER'S POCK, *phr.* Lth. (JAM.) [Not known to our correspondents.] A quantity of all kinds of grain dried in a pot and ground into meal.

INGETTING, *vbl. sb.* *Obs.* Sc. The act of gathering in or receiving.

Lnk. That . . . all obstructions [be] removed that may hinder the ingetting of what is resting [owing], WODROW *Ch. Hist.* (1721) I. 339, ed. 1828.

INGINE, *sb.* ? *Obs.* Sc. Also written **ingyne, injine.** **1.** Ingenuity, quickness of intellect, ability; knowledge, invention. See Engine.

Sc. Joannes Barclaius thought my ingine was in some measure inspiration, SCOTT *Nigel* (182a) xxvii; Whose craft, ingyne, and policy, AYTOUN *Ballads* (ed. 1861) II. 221. Abd. Devysit ane instrument of his awin ingyne, TURREFF *Gleanings* (1859) 177. Per. Endowed to an unusual degree with the perfervid 'ingyne' of the Scot, HALIBURTON *Furth in Field* (1894) 191. Fif. Maun I see yon bairns o' mine Sae bown on deeds divine, And I na help their weak ingyne? TENNANT *Papistry* (1827) 17. Ayr. Then a' that ken'd him round declar'd He had ingine, BURNS *Ep. to Lapraik* (Apr. 1, 1785) st. 5. Edb. To cramb their minds wi' grit ingine, LEARMONT *Poems* (1791) 141. 'Keb. O for an ingine to write a book of Christ, RUTHERFORD *Lett.* (1660) No. 96.

2. An ingenious person, a genius, a person of ability.

Gall. We say of any one with a dungeon of a head, that that person is a great injine, MACTAGGART *Encycl.* (1824) 279, ed. 1876.

INGLE, *sb.*[1] Sc. Nhb. Cum. Wm. Yks. Lan. Lin. Also Sus. [i·ŋ(g)l.] **1.** Fire, flame; a fire in a room; the furnace of a kiln. Also used *attrib.*

Sc. Let him that's cauld blaw up the ingle, RAMSAY *Prov.*

(1737); From some superstitious notion, the kiln men insist that their fire shall be called ingle, *Monthly Mag.* (1800) I. 325. ne.Sc. GRANT *Kecklston,* 176. Cai.[1] The fire which heats a kiln. The fire of a house, &c., is not called ' ingle ' in Cai. ' To put fire to a kiln,' would mean to set the kiln on fire; but ' to put ingle to it,' would mean to light the ingle. Elg. Join thy comrades a' Around the ingle char, COUPER *Poetry* (1804) l. 87. Baff. TAYLOR *Poems* (1787) 43. Bch. FORBES *Jrn.* (1742) 13. Abd. COCK *Strains* (1810) I. 117. Frf. That brimstone belsh, or bock up ingle, BEATTIE *Arnha* (c. 1820) 41, ed. 1882. Per. Beet the ingle, mend the fire (JAM.). Fif. DOUGLAS *Poems* (1806) 151. Slg. Fresh turf I will lay in a heap on my ingle, MUIR *Poems* (1818) 64. Dmb. The ingle weak, the cruizie out, TAYLOR *Poems* (1827) 21. s.Sc. Tibbie's clean fireside And ingle bleezing bonnilie, WATSON *Bards* 1859) 71. Rnf. The lassie had stown frae a braw bleezing-ingle, WEBSTER *Rhymes* (1835) 12. Ayr. And peacefu' rose its ingle reek, BURNS *Verses,* st. 4. Lnk. It's easier frae the door . . . Than frae the ingle edge to drive the deil, BLACK *Falls of Clyde* (1806) 110. Lth. The kettle then on ingle clear, Boils fu' o' ale an' whisky, BRUCE *Poems* (1813) II. 17. Edb. Gathering round Their neighbour's blazing ingle, M‘DOWALL *Poems* (1839) 94. Bwk. Auld Jock by the ingle, his pipe in his cheek, CALDER *Poems* (1897) 68. Peb. AFFLECK *Poet. Wks.* (1836) 79. Slk. The wee bit ingle blinkin bonnily, CHR. NORTH *Noctes* (ed. 1856) III. 35. Rxb. Afore the ingle, RUICKBIE *Wayside Cottager* (1807) 172. Dmf. We unskaithed may toast our soles by ingle bricht, QUINN *Heather* (1863) 292. Gall. NICHOLSON *Poet. Wks.* (1814) 74, ed. 1897. Kcb. The pingle pan Is on the ingle set, DAVIDSON *Seasons* (1789) 6. Wgt. The yill they quaff'd By the ingle's cheery bleeze, FRASER *Wigtown* (1877) 209. n.Cy. GROSE (1790); N.Cy.[1] Nhb. When seated by the ingle, DONALDSON *Poems* (1809) 31. Cum. Let's creep owre the heartsome turf ingle, ANDERSON *Ballads* (ed. 1800) 163; To aither nut I gave a neame, and baith i' th' ingle put, RELPH *Misc. Poems* (1747) 95. n.Yks. How mun I leet my pipe, Whaugh! here's nea ingle, MERITON *Praise Ale* (1684) l. 674; n.Yks.[12], ne.Yks.[1], m.Yks.[1] w.Yks. Ayont the ingle, LUCAS *Stud. Nidderdale* (c. 188a) 24; HUTTON *Tour to Caves* (1781). Lan. HARLAND *Lyrics* (1866) 199. ne.Lan.[1]

Hence **Inglin,** *sb.* fuel. Dmf. (JAM.)

2. A hearth, fireplace, or fireside; a chimney-corner.

Fif. She sat in the ingle by the hall fire, GRANT *Six Heenndrid.* ix. Rnf. He crap to his ingle like ane gaun to steal, PICKEN *Poems* (1813) II. 196. Ayr. No longer do we see the old gaber-lunzie sitting by the farmer's cosy ingle, WHITE *Jottings* (1879) 46. Gall. A fire blazed in a wide ingle, CROCKETT *Raiders* (1894) xxvii. n.Cy. *Border Gl.* (Coll. L.L.B.) Lakel.[2] It's set doon at some ov oor auld ingles hed hed a fire allus burnen i' them fer generations, but it's a fashion 'at's deein oot. Yks. (R. H. H.) n.Yks.[1] A body's ain ingle; n.Yks.[4] 'Ah tell'd my taal o' luv by t'ingle glow.' m.Yks.[1] Lan. I' th' ho' an' cottage ingle, KAY-SHUTTLEWORTH *Scarsdale* (1860) II. 228. n.Lin.[1] nw.Sus. In use about Lynchmere (G.A.W.).

3. A faggot or bundle of fuel, a burning coal, peat, or log.

Sc. GROSE (1790) *MS. add.* (C.) Abd. Tibby was back jusst in a gingle, An' soon set on a bleezin' ingle, BEATTIE *Parings* (1801) 4. Cum.[2] An ' ingle of fire sticks '; Cum.[4] The farmer leaves the ingle-seyde, STAGG *Misc. Poems* (1805) 118.

4. *Comp.* (1) **Ingle-biel,** fireside shelter; (2) **-bole,** a chimney-cupboard; (3) **-bred,** home-bred; (4) **-cheek,** the fireside, hearth; (5) **-end,** the side of a room where the fire is; (6) **-fleeak,** a wooden slab suspended by the ends above a fireplace for a mantelshelf; (7) **-gleed,** (9); (8) **-lighted,** lighted by the fire; (9) **-lowe,** the flames or blaze of a fire, firelight, a blazing fireside; (10) **-lug,** see (4); (11) **-mids,** the centre ofa fire; (12) **-nook** or **-nooking,** a chimney-corner, a corner by the fireside; also used *fig.* and *attrib.*; (13) **-ring,** the fireside circle; (14) **-side,** see (4); (15) **-stone,** the hearthstone.

(1) Edb. Husbandmen had bent their way Towards their homes . . . To rest them by their ingle biels, LIDDLE *Poems* (1822) 186. (2) Sc. And then she took frae the ingle-bole, *Ballads* (1885) 235. (3) Rnf. Mony an ingle-bred auld wife, Has baith na mair wit an' senses, Than me this day, PICKEN *Poems* (1788) 112 (JAM.). (4) Sc. Ye'll readily find him at his ingle cheek, *Shepherd's Wedding* (1789) 14. Abd. To cheer the winter's ingle-cheek, CADENHEAD *Bon-Accord* (1853) 203. Frf. A welcome guest at the ingle cheek ' of many a farmer's kitchen, LOWSON *Guidfollow* (1890) 29. Per. FORD *Harp* (1893) 202. s.Sc. Ilk ane by the ingle cheek Cours the down, T. SCOTT *Poems* (1793) 323. Ayr. There, lanely, by my ingle-cheek, I sat and ey'd the spewing reek, BURNS *Vision* st. 3.

Lnk. Orr *Laigh Flichts* (1882) 36. **Lth.** At the lown ingle-cheek in the lang winter night, Ballantine *Poems* (1856) 99. **Edb.** Placed cozie by our ingle-cheek, Macneill *Bygane Times* (1811) 54. **n.Ir.** Enscons'd behind the ingle-cheek, *Lays and Leg.* (1884) 63. (5) Dmf. E'enin' cranreuch airts her Tae her couthie ingle-en', Reid *Poems* (1894) 148. (6) n.Yks.[2] (7) Ayr. Cheerlie blinks the ingle gleed, Burns *Lady Onlie*, st. 2. (8) Slg. Points his seat across the ingle-lighted floor, Muir *Poems* (1818) 170. (9) Sc. I saw the cheery ingle lowe Blink thro' the peens, Coghill *Poems* (1890) 25. Abd. To share the ingle lowie, Baudrins ligs wi' streckit collie, Cadenhead *Bon-Accord* (1853) 252. Per. Stewart *Character* (1857) 3. Ayr. And by my ingle-lowe I saw, Now bleezin bright, A tight, outlandish hizzie, braw, Burns *Vision*, st. 7. Edb. I sat down bi the ingle low, Crawford *Poems* (1798) 117. Dmf. Shrivel like a threid That's held abune the ingle lowe, Reid *Poems* (1894) 60. (10) Rnf. This bonnie young lassie ... maks me sae blyth by my ain ingle lug, Clark *Rhymes* (1842) 30. Ayr. A snug berth within rax o' the ingle-lug, Ainslie *Land of Burns* (ed. 1892) 45. (11) Abd. A burning ccal with the het tangs was ta'en, Frae out the ingle-mids, Ross *Helenore* (1768) 20, ed. 1812. (12) n.Sc. Snug an' cantie by the ingle neuk, Gordon *Carglen* (1891) 148. Abd. He was seated in the ingle-neuk, Macdonald *Sir Gibbie* (1879) xxvi. Kcd. A sat in the ingle neuk, Jamie *Muse* (1844) 109. Frf. Barrie *Minister* (1891) xxiv. Per. It was just the powerfu' ca' o' duty 'at garred me ... steer frae the ingle neuk this nicht, Cleland *Inchbracken* (1883) 9, ed. 1887. e.Fif. Flingin' doon his cutty i' the ingle-neuk, Latto *Tam Bodkin* (1864) ii. Rnf. By the bleezin' ingle neuk, Young *Pictures* (1865) 10. Ayr. The cosy ingle-neuk of some auld farm hoose, Service *Dr. Duguid* (ed. 1887) 130. Lnk. The ingle-nook, whaur aft he played, McLachlan *Thoughts* (1884) 33. e.Lth. Hunter *J. Inwick* (1895) 143. Edb. The ingle-nook supplies the simmer fields, Fergusson *Poems* (1773) 111, ed. 1785. Slk. The auld man asleep by the ingle-neuk, Chr. North *Noctes* (ed. 1856) II. 53. Dmf. The ingle-neuk, the heartsome ha', Reid *Poems* (1894) 180. Gall. Crockett *Standard Bearer* (1898) 4. Kcb. Jock sat up drinkin' yill Fu cosy in the ingle neuk, Armstrong *Ingleside* (1890) 41. Nhb. When he had finished his supper, Robbie pushed back his chair into the 'ingle-neuk,' s.*Tyneside Stud.* (1896) Robbie *Armstrong*. Lakel.², Cum.⁴ Wm. An as he sat by t'ingle neuk, Whitehead *Leg.* (1859) 31. n.Yks.¹²⁴, ne.Yks.¹, m.Yks.¹ w.Yks. Another feller 'at wor sittin i' th' ingle-nuk, Hartley *Clock Alm.* (1887) 34 ; (W.M.E.F.) Lan. To sit twiddlin' her thumbs i' th' ingle neuk wan half of her time, *Longman's Mag.* (Nov. 1895) 65; Lan.¹, n.Lin.¹ (13) Gall. Amongst the many amusements of the ingle ring one is, who shall say a certain saying quickest, Mactaggart *Encycl.* (1824) 404, ed. 1876. (14) Sc. My sisters wad sit peengin' at the ingle-side, Scott *Blk. Dwarf* (1816) x. Elg. I'll e'en step to the ingle side, Tester *Poems* (1865) 191. Frf. Watt *Poet. Sketches* (1880) 16. Per. But you, puir woman, need to hide Tongue tied aboot the ingle-side, Haliburton *Horace* (1886) 74. Dmb. Aft they toast their ingle-side, Taylor *Poems* (1827) 20. Rnf. Sit gleefully down by our ain ingle-side, Webster *Rhymes* (1835) 9. Ayr. I canter'd her hame to my ain ingle side, *Ballads and Sngs.* (1846) I. 118. Lnk. Wardrop *J. Mathison* (1881) 10. Lth. By the cheerful ingleside I sat the ither day, McNeill *Preston* (c. 1895) 25. Edb. By th' ingle-side they clank them down, *Har'st Rig* (1794) 28, ed. 1801. Bwk. Chisholm *Poems* (1879) 36. Rxb. And beak by the kitchen-ha' ingleside, Riddell *Poet. Wks.* (ed. 1871) I. 37. Dmf. Play roun' yer ingle side, Quinn *Heather* (1863) 202. Wgt. Fraser *Wigtown* (1877) 291. Cum. As Sawney's bacco spred by th' ingle side, Relph *Misc. Poems* (1747) 13. Sus. Oh come, come to the ingle side, For the night is dark and drear, Heath *Eng. Peasant* (1893) 184. nw.Sus.(G.A.W.) (15) Abd. 'Mang the sheaves his flail he shot it, Sighin', sought the ingle stane, Still *Cottar's Sunday* (1845) 44. Dmb. Round the ingle-stane Sat wife and wean, Salmon *Gowodean* (1868) 11. Ayr. White *Jottings* (1879) 281.

[1. Cp. Gael. *aingeal*, light, fire.]

INGLE, sb.² and v. Glo.¹² [i·ŋgl.] 1. sb. A favourite, fondling. 2. v. To fondle, cherish.

[1. Call me your love, your ingle, *Honest Whore*, III. 260 (Nares). 2. We must ingle with our husbands, *Roaring Girl*, vi. 89 (ib.).]

INGLEANINGS, sb. pl. n.Yks.² The residue after the main harvest has been gathered.

INGLE-BERRY, sb. Sc. A fleshy growth upon the bodies of oxen. See Angle-berry, sb.¹

Gall. Fleshy wens, which grow on the tender parts of oxen ; they are of a fiery nature, Mactaggart *Encycl.* (1824) 279, ed. 1876.

INGLE-DOG, sb. Dor. An earthworm. (W.C.); w.*Gazette* (Feb. 15, 1889) 7, col. 1. See Angle-twitch.

INGLOORING, prp. n.Yks.² Staring a person 'through and through.' See Glore, v.

* **INGLUNSHIRE, sb.** Lan.¹ England.

INGO, v. Sc. n.Cy. Lan. Also in form inga Sc. To go in. ne.Lan.¹

Hence (1) **Ingaand-mouth, sb.** the mouth of a coal-pit, which enters the earth in the horizontal position; (2) **Ingoing, (a) sb.** an assembling, entering; an entrance; (b) ppl. adj. entering, taking possession of; (3) **Ingoing-ee, sb.** an opening in the ground, the mouth of a pit or well.

(1) Cld. (Jam.) (2, a) Sc. The ingâin of a kirk, the assembling of the people in a church for public worship (ib.). Cai.¹, ne.Lan.¹ (b) Sc. The ingâin tenant, he who enters on possession of a farm or house when another leaves it (Jam.). n.Cy. (J.W.), ne.Lan.¹ (3) Ayr. Forbye them [two new coal-pits] there was an ingoing e'e at the Goldcraig, Service *Dr. Duguid* (ed. 1887) 168.

INGOT, sb. Yks. Cor. [i·ŋ(g)ət.] 1. A block of cast or unwrought metal. s.Yks. (W.S.) 2. Tin cast in a small oblong iron mould. Cor.¹

[1. Cp. Fr. *lingot*, an ingot, lump, or masse of mettal (Cotgr.).]

INGOTHILL, phr. Dmf. (Jam.) ' An God will,' ' God being willing.'

INGRAM, adj. Nhb.¹ [i·ŋgrəm.] Ignorant.

[An ingrame, *ignarus*, Levins *Manip.* (1570).]

INGRATE, adj. Sc. Irel. Nhb. Sur. Also written ingrat Sc. Nhb.¹ [ingrē·t.] Ungrateful; also used as sb.

Sc. 'Why thou ungracious and ingrate knave,' said Dame Ursley, Scott *Nigel* (1822) xxi. Fif. I was maist ingrat if I could forget my guid, godlie, and maist courteus lady, Melvill *Autobiog.* (1610) 221, ed. 1842. Ayr. Whilst I here, must cry here, At perfidy ingrate ! Burns *Despondency*, st. 4. Lnk. If not ingrate I must recall thy worth, Lithgow *Poet. Rem.* (ed. 1863) *To Lord Sheffield*. Gall. I wad be an ingrate to say onything else, Crockett *Stickit Min.* (1893) 56. Ir. It shan't be said ... that the anointed priest of the parish was left to starve by an ingrate, McNulty *Misther O'Ryan* (1894) xvii. Sur.¹

Hence **Ingratsow, adj.** ungrateful. Nhb.¹

[Al them that ar ingrate of the benefecis of gode, *Compl. Scotl.* (1549) 20.]

INGRINDEET, ppl. adj. Nhb.¹ Ingrained; esp. of dirt.

INGROSSER, sb. Cor.² One who buys wheat at eighteen gallons the bushel and delivers it at sixteen gallons the bushel.

INGROUND, sb. Yks. Som. Also in form ingrund w.Yks.¹ 1. Descending or inclining ground. w.Yks.¹ Cf. inbank.

2. Enclosed land as opposed to ' hill-ground,' which is unenclosed common. w.Som.¹

INGROWTH, sb. Sc. Increase.

Ayr. With the ingrowth o' turnip-farming there has aye been a corresponding smasherie amang the looms and sugar-hoggits, Galt *Lairds* (1826) xxxv.

INGY, v. Cai.¹ [i·ŋi.] To bring forth lambs.

[Norw. dial. *yngja*, to bring forth young, to breed (Aasen).]

INHABLE, v. Obs. Sc. To disable, prevent, disqualify.

Slg. Sik faults as inhables the person of the giver to be a distributor of the sacrament .. So, quhen the person of the giver is this way inhabled, na question, it is not a sacrament, Bruce *Sermons* (1631) i, ed. 1843.

Hence **Inhability, sb.** inability, unfitness.

Sc. That parliament which took upon them to judge of the habilitie of these sixty, and of the inhability of other Presbyters to govern, Calder *Presbyt. Eloq.* (1694) 94, ed. 1847. Slg. To help our belief, our weaknes, and inhabilitie that is in us, Bruce *Sermons* (1631) i, ed. 1843. Rnf. The estates of this kingdom have always asserted and often practised a constitution-right of setting aside the next immediate successor in case of inhability, Wodrow *Corres.* (1842-3) I. 599.

INHADDEN, INHADDIN, see Inholding.

INHERITAGE, sb. w.Som.¹ Inheritance.

Well, 'tis hard vor the poor young fuller to lost his inheritage [eennur·itae·uj] ; but there, th' old man was always agin un like.

INHOLDING, sb. and ppl. adj. Sc. Also in forms inhadden, -haddin Sc.; -hauddin Bnff.¹; -haudin Abd.

1. *sb.* Frugality, parsimoniousness.

Sc. (Jam.) Keb. In-holding and sparingness, RUTHERFORD *Lett.* (1660) No. 169.

2. *ppl. adj.* Frugal, penurious, parsimonious.

Sc. My lady, as we say, is an ill-set body, and inhadden too, in the matter of hospitality, KEITH *Bonnie Lady* (1897) 28. Bnff.¹

3. Selfish; fawning, cringing, given to flattery.

Bnff.¹ Abd. Jist like im'; inhaudin scoonrel, ALEXANDER *Johnny Gibb* '1871) xiv.

4. *Comp.* Inhaddin eldin, fuel which needs constant renewal.

n.Sc. That kind of fuel ... which must be constantly held in to the fire because so quickly consumed, as furze, thorns, &c. (Jam.)

INIQUOUS, *adj.* *Obs.* Sc. Iniquitous.

Sc. The beginning of his history; where ... he condescends upon other iniquous proceedings; not unlike the crime of Paris, *Scoticisms* (1787) 118. Lnk. Well knowing nothing, how iniquous soever, would be blamed, WODROW *Ch. Hist.* (1791) III. 263, ed. 1828.

IN JIST, *adv.* w.Cy. (HALL.) Dor.¹ Also in form injest w.Cy. [indgi·st.] Almost, very nearly.

IN JURY, *sb.* Dev. In phr. *to do an injury to,* to cast an evil eye on, to bewitch.

An old woman, suffering from rheumatism, was heard to aver that the cause was traceable to some one having ' done her an injury,' PAGE *Explor. Dartmoor* (1889) ii.

INK, *sb.* Var. dial. uses in Sc. and Eng. [iŋk.] In *comp.* (1) Ink-holder, a vessel for containing ink; (2) ·horn, (*a*) an inkstand, inkbottle; also used *fig.* and *attrib.*; (*b*) a flatterer, one who curries favour; (3) ·pud, see (1); (4) ·spew·er, the cuttle-fish, *Sepia officinalis*; (5) ·standish, ·standage, ·stanch, or ·stange, see (2, *a*).

(1) Sc. Of what materials soever a vessel for holding ink is made, it is very properly called an ink-holder, MITCHELL *Scoticisms* (1792) 47. (2, *a*) Sc. There is my own daughter, but just now overturned my ink-horn and broke my spectacles, *Magopico* (ed. 1836) 31. Fif. Being molested by a condisciple, wha cutted the stringes of my pen and ink-horn with his pen-knyff, MELVILL *Autobiog.* (1610) 21, ed. 1842. Nhb.¹ Still in *gen.* use. Cum.¹ This term is used for any pocket vessel holding ink, but the original was of cow's or sheep's horn. Wm. (K.); Ink-horn words, to be honest, we knaw lile abaut, HUTTON *Bran New Wark* (1785) l. 18. n.Lin.¹ *Obsol.* Lei.¹ Sus.¹ Fetch me down de inkhorn mistus; I be g'wine to putt my harnd to dis here partition to Parliament. Dor. The steward saw her put the inkborn—' horn,' says I in my old-fashioned way—the inkstand, before her uncle, HARDY *Wess. Flh.* in *Harper's Mag.* (June 1891) 127. w.Som.¹ (*b*) n.Cy. (J.W.) (3) Lth. (Jam.) (4) ne.Lan.¹, Ken.¹ (5) Sc. He dipped his pen once or twice into his snuff-box instead of the ink-standish, SCOTT *St. Ronan* (1824) xvii. Nhb.¹, e.Yks.¹, w.Yks.¹

INK, see Hink, *v.*²

INKEEP, *sb.* and *v.* Suf. **1.** *sb.* A pound for cattle.

e.Suf. Used at Dunwich, Yoxford, &c. Going out of use (F.H.).

2. *v.* To put cattle in the pound. *ib.*

INKER, *sb.* Lakel.² [iˑŋkər.] The eatable contents of a beggar's wallet.

INKER-PINKER, *sb.* Sc. Small beer. See Hink-skink.

I have a little bottle of inker-pinker in my pocket, CHAMBERS *Pop. Rhymes* (1870) 174.

INKERPUNK, see Intepunk.

INKET, *sb.* Suf. A market.

e.Suf. Used only by the old, and seldom by them (F.H.).

INKLE, *sb.*¹ n.Cy. Nhb. Cum. Yks. Lan. Chs. Lin. Nhp. War. Shr. Dev. Cor. Also written incle Nhb.¹ w.Yks. Chs.¹² [iˑŋkl.] **1.** *Obsol.* An inferior, coarse kind of tape; also called Beggar's Inkle. See Beggar.

N.Cy.¹ A sort of coarse tape wove by beggars and other itinerants. Nhb.¹ Cum. He selt beggar-inkle, caps, muslins and cottons, RAYSON *Poems* (1839) 62; A strong coarse tape formerly much used. It was made in the country, of thread, spun at home (M.P.); Cum.² Coarse narrow tape used for shoe-ties. n.Yks.¹ A narrow linen fabric, or kind of tape, formerly used for shoe-ties, apron-strings, and the like; n.Yks.²⁴ e.Yks. Beggar's inkle, a coarse unbleached linen tape or binding of much strength (H.E.W.). m.Yks.¹ w.Yks. 1689. In inkle for strings for ye bagg in which the pulpit cloth is put, 2d., *Bradford Chwardens' Accts.* ne.Lan.¹, e.Lan.¹ Chs. Paide for incle, thread, and making

the little bag, £0 0s. 3d., *Chwardens' Accts. Whitegate* (1656) in Chs. *Sheaf* (1891) I. 134; Chs.¹², Lin.¹ n.Lin.¹ Used for shoe-ties. Nhp.¹ Penny inkle. War. WISE *Shakespere* (1861) 153; War.² Rarely used now. Shr.¹ If yo' bin gweïn to markit, be so good as bring me a pen'orth o' inkle fur my linsey apparn—nod w'ite —if yo' canna get it striped, bring blue caddas. Dev. It. for ynkell for the Comunion bocke—ij⁴, *Woodbury Chwardens' Accts.* MS. (1577). n.Dev. Zum inkle, gurts vor bliddy pots, ROCK *Jim an' Nell* (1867) st. 70. Cor.¹ Narrow webbing. [Inckle, or Beggar's Inckle, is a kind of coarse tape used by cooks to secure meat previous to being spitted, and farriers to tie round horses' feet, &c., *N. & Q.* (1855) 1st S. xi. 351.]

2. *Comp.* (1) **Inkle-frame,** a frame used in weaving ' inkle'; (2) ·maker, a weaver of ' inkle,' *gen.* in phr. (*as*) thick as inkle-makers, very friendly or intimate together; cf. inkle-weaver.

(1) Cum. (M.P.) (a) Nhb. ' As thick as inklemakers ' is a very widespread prov. (R.O.H.) Cor. (A.L.M.); Cor.¹ As thick as inkle-makers; Cor.² They be so thick as inkle-makers.

INKLE, *v.* and *sb.*² Yks. [iˑŋkl.] **1.** *v.* To form notions, guesses, or projects.

n.Yks.¹; n.Yks.⁴ He's awlus inklin' summat, but it nivver cums ti nowt. w.Yks.⁵ He's inkling upo' nowt 'at's good, I'm sãre !

2. To form wishes or inclinations for this or that gratification.

n.Yks.¹ ' He inkles after this an' that, and can take nane iv 'em when it cooms till '; of an invalid ; n.Yks.⁴ He maistly inkles efther what he can't git. m.Yks.¹ A person inkles after riches or after a better life. w.Yks.⁵ An invalid inkles after all sorts o' things.

3. *sb.* A notion, hint, suspicion, 'inkling.'

Yks. No inkle in your mind who it is, or wouldst have told me ! BLACKMORE *Mary Anerley* (1879) xiv. n.Yks.² ' A bit of an inkle anent it,' a hint on the subject. w.Yks. (J.W.)

INKLE-WEAVER, *sb.* In *gen.* dial. and colloq. use in Sc. Irel. and Eng. Also written incle· Chs.¹ s.Chs.¹

1. In phr. *as thick (great, kind, &c.) as inkle-weavers,* very friendly or intimate together. See Inkle, *sb.*

Sc. We were as loving as inkle-weavers, SCOTT *Nigel* (1822) xxiii. Ayr. Twa or three bodies in their brats, confabbin' thegither as thick as inkle weavers, SERVICE *Notandums* (1890) 74. Uls. To be as thick (or great) as inkle-weavers, Uls. *Jrn. Arch.* (1857) V. 105. Ant. As great as inkle-weavers, HUME *Dial.* (1878) 28. Nhb.¹ Lakel.² They're as thick as inkleweavers. Cum. Aw as busy as inkle weavers, *Borrowdale* (1869) 2; Cum.² Stump't away togidder as thick as inkle weavers, 15. Wm. He mud ga wi er an stick as clooas es inkle weavers, *Spec. Dial.* (1880) pt. ii. 12. n.Yks.¹ Weavers of the fabric, on account of the narrowness of the web they produced, were able to sit very close, thus giving origin to the proverbial expression ' as kind ' or ' as thick as inkleweavers '; n.Yks.² As kind as inkle-weavers; n.Yks.⁴ ; e.Yks. NICHOLSON *Flb-Sp.* (1889) 21. m.Yks.¹ w.Yks. They wor as thick as incle weyvers, TOM TREDDLEHOYLE *Bairnsla Ann.* (1853); w.Yks.² Lan. Thick! We're as thick as a pair o' owd reawsty inkle-weyvers, WAUGH *Sneck-Bant* (1868) i ; Lan.¹, e.Lan.¹ Chs.¹ They're allus together, ne'er seen too beawt tother; they're as thick as incle-waivers. s.Chs.¹, Der.², Nhp.¹, War. (J.R.W.), Shr.¹ Brks. Oh, they are as thick as inkle-weavers just at present, *N. & Q.* (1878) 5th S. ix. 7. Wil. (E.H.G.), Dor.¹ w.Som.¹ When tapes had to be hand-woven, a single tape to a loom, the weavers had naturally to work very close together, and hence the common saying to express crowding together, ' So thick as inkle weavers.' Dev.² Jessie Sage and Billy Grose be so thick 's inkleweavers, can't keep um 'part dû whats will. Cor.¹ Slang. As great as two inkle-weavers, *New Cant. Dict.* (1725); FARMER.

2. See below.

se.Yks.¹ Used as an opprobrious epithet to those who cause trouble. ' They're all inkleweavers tigither is that lot.'

INKLIN(G, *sb.* In *gen.* dial. and colloq. use in Sc. and Eng. Also written inclin n.Yks.² Nrf.; incling N.Cy.¹; ynckling N.Cy.²; and in form hinklin Cai.¹ Fif. Dev. [iˑŋklin.] **1.** A faint or half-concealed desire or inclination.

Edb. I never kenned that he had ony inkling for the seafaring line, MOIR *Mansie Wauch* (1828) xx. n.Cy. GROSE (1790); N.Cy.¹ n.Yks.¹; n.Yks.³ I've neea inclin for t'spot. m.Yks.¹ One of those words used effectively in the pulpit by the lay exhorters who labour among a sect of Dissenters. ' Come now, has none of you an inkling for Jesus ?' w.Yks.¹ I've an inkling to gang to't'fair to-morn; w.Yks.⁴⁵, ne.Lan.¹, Der.², nw.Der.³, Nhp.¹ s.Wor. A've 'ad a inklin' ahter 'er this lung time, an' now 'em walks out together (H.K.). Hnt. (T.P.F.) Nrf. He have an inclin for that mauther (W.W.S.). Som. Young Zam have a-caught a bit of a inklin' a'ter our Sabina, RAYMOND *Sam and Sabina* (1894) 44. w.Som.¹ Will Hookins would'n never come up here every whip's while for nothing; I can zee very well he've a got a bit of a inkling a'ter our Sue. Dev. I've got a girt hinklin ta zee ma ole gal, NATHAN HOGG *Poet. Lett.* (ed. 1865) 8.

2. A slight conjecture or suspicion; a faint idea, a 'soupçon'; a slight hint or intimation.

Sc. His parishioners had got an inkling of his bonny behaviour at Edinburgh, *Magopico* (ed. 1836) 25. Sh.I. Dem 'at's for makin' ill gets an inklin ta spaek, da news spreads laek fire, *Sh. News* (Jan. 15, 1898). Cai.¹ Abd. Your advice comes an inklin too late at present, RUDDIMAN *Sc. Parish* (1828) 21, ed. 1889. Frf. I heard indeed an inklin' o' your love for Susan, MORISON *Poems* (1790) 163. Per. She . . . had an inkling o' the trick, SPENCE *Poems* (1898) 194. Fif. Never so lytle a hinkling of ther pen till haiff born out his course, MELVILL *Autobiog.* (1610) 154, ed. 1842. s.Sc. For deil a bit o' me ever could see the least inklin o' onything past ordinar between them, WILSON *Tales* (1839) V. 237. Ayr. Thoughtful he was that he had given no inkling to any one in the house, GALT *Gilhaize* (1823) iv. Lnk. If you were just to give your friends an inkling of your willingness to take office, ROY *Generalship* (ed. 1895) 112. Edb. It was absurd to suppose that we should know any inkling about the matter, MOIR *Mansie Wauch* (1828) xvii. n.Cy. GROSE (1790); N.Cy.¹², Dur.¹ s.Dur. A' just gat an inklin' on't (J.E.D.). Cum.¹; Cum.⁴ Them black-smith fellas gat an inklin eh t'stwory, SARGISSON *Joe Scoap* (1881) 2. Wm. Thae gemma a bit ov an inklin et thae'd raedther ad stop wiem, *Spec. Dial.* (1885) pt. iii. 15. n.Yks.¹; n.Yks.² No inkling of what was going on; n.Yks.⁴ Ah've gi'en her a bit ov an inklin' o' what's gahin' on. m.Yks.¹ w.Yks. (E.G.); w.Yks.¹⁴; w.Yks.⁵ He's an inkling on't al be bun for't; it's easy guessing eggs when thuh see shells. Lan. *Monthly Mag.* (1815) I. 197. ne.Lan.¹, Cha.¹, Stf.¹ Not. He's got an inkling (J.H.B.). Nhp.¹, s.Wor. (H.K.), Hnt. (T.P.F.) Suf.¹ Cant yeow gi me an inklin' 'a what 'as coming about?

[1. OFr. *enclin*, 'action de pencher, inclination' (LA CURNE).]

INKLOGS, *sb. pl.* Yks. Heavy pieces of wood forming the lintel of a door to carry the masonry. w.Yks. (J.J.B.)

INKS, *sb. pl.* Sc. [iŋks.] Low-lying land on the banks of a river, freq. overflowed by the sea in high tides. Cf. ing.

Gall. On muddy, level shores there are pieces of land overflowed with spring tides, and not touched by common ones, according to the laws of nature; on these grow a coarse kind of grass, good for sheep threatened with the rot. This saline food sometimes cures them, MACTAGGART *Encycl.* (1824) 280, ed. 1876. Wgt. Extent 240 acres or thereby of coarse land of excellent quality, together with a very large extent of 'inks' or shore pasture, *Gall. Advertiser* (July 27, 1899); I owned quite a fleet O' wee boats o' ilk rig, .. An' the inks where they voyaged scarce drooned my bare feet, FRASER *Poems* (1885) 57.

INKUM-JINKUM, *int.* w.Yks.² A meaningless word used in the game of 'Buck, buck'; see below.

A rhyme used at Lepton. A boy, jumping on another's back, holds up some fingers and says: 'Inkum jinkum, Jeremy buck, Yamdy horns do Au cock up!' If the boy beneath guesses wrong, the first proceeds: '(Two) tha' sès, and (three) there is; Au'll leán thee to lake at Inkum jinkum,' &c.

INLAID, *pp.* w.Yks.¹ Laid up in store.
We're weel inlaid for coals.

INLAIK, *sb. and v.* ?*Obs.* Sc. Also written **inlake**; and in forms **inlack** Slg.; **inleak** Fif. Gall. 1. *sb.* A deficiency, lack.

Sc. Sic great inlack amang the butter, RAMSAY *Tea-Table Misc.* (1724) II. 188, ed. 1871; There would have been inlake among the peerage, if the master had not whipt in, SCOTT *Bride of Lam.* (1819) iii. Abd. Great men and men o' worth, Whose inlake did frae countless een Gaur grief's saut tears gush forth, DAVIDSON *Poems* (1826) 123; Often used to denote the deficiency of liquor in a cask (JAM.). Fif. Their inlaiks were supplied and doubtes opened up to them, Row *Ch. Hist.* (1650) 16, ed. 1842. Slg. The abounding murders and oppressions daily multiplied, through impunity and inlack of justice, BRUCE *Sermons* (1631) 27, ed. 1843. Edb. Inlakes o' brandy we can soon supply By whisky, FERGUSSON *Poems* (1773) 184, ed. 1785. Gall. MACTAGGART *Encycl.* (1824).

2. *v.* To be deficient, to lack.

Per. If your knives inlakes, My durk, let no man lack it, Will soon supply, NICOL *Poems* (1766) 48; What shall be said of other martial games? None was inlaking from whence bravest stemmes, FORD *Harp* (1893) 3. Fif. Whow the Parliament sould nocht in-leak the spirituall esteat, bischopes being removit, MELVILL *Auto-biog.* (1610) 118, ed. 1842. Ayr. If he grant he hes inlaiked, and would be helped of yow, WODROW *Sel. Biog.* (ed. 1845-7) II. 24. Edb. FERGUSSON *Poems* (1773) 170, ed. 1785.

Hence **Inlacking,** *sb.* want, deficiency.

Sc. So great an inlacking was in the ministers to come out with the regiments, BAILLIE *Lett.* (1775) II. 10 (JAM.).

3. To die.

Sc. He inlakit this morning (JAM.); Afore his perfect age it micht happin the witnessis to deceis or inlaik, BALFOUR *Practicks* (1754) 333. Bch. I was fley'd she had taen the wytenon-fa an' inlakit afore sipper, FORBES *Jrn.* (1742) 7. Abd. Without sayin' mair, he inlaket that nicht, ANDERSON *Rhymes* (1867) 68.

[1. All thing perteineng to the dignitie of a Bischope, that na inlaik war, DALRYMPLE *Leslie's Hist. Scotl.* (1596) I. 327. 2. Helpe, and graunt hap, gud Hemene! Lat not thy pairt in hir inlaik, MONTGOMERIE *Poems* (c. 1600), ed. Cranstoun, 215.]

INLAND, *sb. Obsol.* Yks. Enclosed and cultivated land as opposed to common or waste land. Also used *attrib.*

s.Yks. During the winter the cattle would be enfolded in the pens upon the 'inland,' ATKINSON *Whitby* (1894) 14; n.Yks.¹ w.Yks. It's a bit of as good inland land as ever was trodden (C.C.R.).

INLEAK, see **Inlaik.**

INLER, *sb. Obs.* Sc. One who is in office; the Government and its party.

Edb. At length the Outlers grew sae mad Against ilk Inler purse-proud blade, LEARMONT *Poems* (1791) 160.

INLESS, *conj.* I.W. [inle·s.] Unless. (J.D.R.), I.W.¹

[*In less*, for the older *on lesse*, on a less supposition that; see SKEAT *Etym. Dict.* (s.v. *Unless*).]

INLET, *sb.* Sc. Lin. [i·nlet.] 1. A branch drain used for conveying water from a warping-drain to the land to be warped. n.Lin.¹

2. An entrance, a road leading into.

Wgt. To charge a groat for going round the Square, and up the vennels, and inlets into the town, FRASER *Wigtown* (1877) 84.

INLUTE, *sb.* Nhb.¹ A wooden bar in a boat.

INLY, *adv.* Sc. Yks. Brks. [i·nli.] Inwardly, internally.

Sc. Vile is the wretch, wha inly feels His life to be a road, ALLAN *Lilts* (1874) 382. Fif. At his fate he inly grumbl'd, DOUG-LAS *Poems* (1806) 108. Ayr. What warm poetic heart but inly bleeds, BURNS *Brigs of Ayr* (1787) 38. Gall. A dart thrown at random, which sticks and is lost, yet inly rankles, CROCKETT *Standard Bearer* (1898) 144. n.Yks.², Brks.¹

INLYING, *sb.* Sc. A lying-in, confinement in childbed.

Sc. The many absurd and sometimes unseemly ceremonies . . . practised by the 'canny wives' and gossips, when attending at inlyings, *Edb. Mag.* (Mar. 1819) 219 (JAM.); The castle of Edin-burgh being thus pitched upon—as the most commodious place for her Majesty's inlying, KEITH *Hist.* (1734) 335 (*ib.*). Cai.¹

INMEAT, *sb.* Sc. n.Cy. Yks. Lan. Lin. Also in forms **inmaet** Sh.I.; **inmeyt** e.Lan.¹ 1. The edible viscera of any animal; freq. in *pl.*; also used *fig.*

Sc. The hide, head, feet and in-meat were given for attendance, MAXWELL *Sel. Trans.* (1743) 275 (JAM.). Peb. Part of the entrails, or in-meat of cattle, *Lintoun Green* (1685) 92, ed. 1817. N.Cy.¹ n.Yks.¹; n.Yks.² The gizzard, heart, liver,—from the insides of poultry; n.Yks.⁴ ne.Yks. MARSHALL *Rur. Econ.* (1796) II. 328. e.Lan.¹ Encased machinery, as the works of a clock or watch. n.Lin.¹

2. Food given to animals within doors.

Sh.I. If whaiks [queys] revive no at da hill noo i' da mont o' May, hit'll no be lyin' i' da byre, an' in-maet is noo oot o' da whistin, *Sh. News* (May 13, 1899).

INN, *sb. and v.* Sc. Irel. Yks. Also written **in** S. & Ork.¹ [inn.] 1. *sb.* A dwelling; *gen.* in *pl.*

S. & Ork.¹ Abd. Mony ane . . . scoup'd hame at e'en Maybe to hungry inns, SKINNER *Poems* (1809) 52; Still used (JAM.).

2. *pl.* An inn.

Sc. (JAM.) Ayr. They came to the inns [inn, ed. 1895] to their dinner, GALT *Ann. Parish* (1821) 294 (JAM.). N.I.¹ He went to the horse show, and stayed at the inns. Uls. I put up at the heed inns, *N. & Q.* (1877) 5th S. vii. 107.

3. *pl.* In games : the goal, the spot held by the winning side.

Gall. To obtain the inns, is the object of these games, MACTAGGART *Encycl.* (1824) 280, ed. 1876.

4. *v.* To sojourn.

w.Yks.² The traveller likes them because they're genteel, And sings of their merit wherever he inns.

IN'NEAW, see Enow, *adv.²*

INNER, *adj.* Sc. Lin. In *comp.* (1) Inner-girl, (2) -maid, a housemaid in a farm-house, a kitchen-maid ; (3) -water, water entering a house through the foundations.

(1) Lin.¹ He's spoony on the inner-girl. n.Lin.¹ (2) n.Lin.¹ (3) Cai.¹

INNERLY, *adj.* Sc. [i·nərli.] **1.** Situated in the interior part of a district ; not exposed, snug ; of land : fertile. Cld., Slk. (JAM.) Dmf. WALLACE *Schoolmaster* (1899) 349.

2. Towards the shore, keeping near land.

Sh.I. ' Don't ye tink men 'at were innerly !' . . ' I doot afore a' is dune, doo'll fin' at doo's fram eneugh,' *Sh. News* (Apr. 23, 1898).

3. In a state of near neighbourhood. Slk. (JAM.)

4. Pleasant, cheerful, sociable ; kindly, affectionate, compassionate.

Sc. Johnie's queer bits o' says, an' his innerly ways, We'll mind a' oor days, EDWARDS *Mod. Poets*, 11th S. 294. Slk., Rxb. She's an innerlie creature (JAM.). Rxb. (H.C.)

Hence **Innerly-hearted,** *adj.* of a feeling disposition. Gall. MACTAGGART *Encycl.* (1824).

INNERMORE, *adj. Obs.* n.Cy. Yks. Lan. Also in forms indermer w.Yks.¹ ne.Lan.¹ ; indermore n.Cy. ; innermer w.Yks.¹ ne.Lan.¹ Inner, more within, interior. n.Cy. An Indermore chamber, GROSE (1790) *Suppl.* ; (HALL.) w.Yks.¹, ne.Lan.¹

INNO, *prep.* Sc. In, into, within, close beside.

Sc. (A.W.) Bch. Or e'en to sit ben inno the guidman upo' the best bink o' the house, FORBES *Jrn.* (1742) 13. Abd. He's inno the town. He's inno his bed. I'm inno my wark (JAM.). Cld. (*ib.*)

INNOCENT, *adj.* and *sb.* Var. dial. uses in Sc. Irel. and Eng. Also written innercent Ken. ; innicent Lan. n.Lin.¹ ; and in form hinnocent Wor. [i·nisənt.] **1.** *adj.* Halfwitted, silly. Chs.¹, n.Lin.¹, e.An.¹ Sus., Hmp. HOLLOWAY.

2. Small, pretty, unobtrusive ; *gen.* applied to flowers. Also used *advb.*

Chs.¹ Lin.¹ The crocus is an innocent flower. n.Lin.¹ Sometimes to the patterns on women's dresses, hangings, and wall papers. sw.Lin.¹ It's a pretty innocent flower. It looks so innocent. War.⁴ Where did yer get that flower, Sal ! It's so sweet and innocent-like. s.Wor. That plant be what we calls gill. It is a hinnocent thing for all it runs about so (H.K.). Ken.¹ I do always think they paigles looks so innocent-like. Sus.¹ Wil.¹ A innocent little primrose.

3. *sb.* A person of weak intellect, an imbecile, idiot ; a fool.

Sc. Waverley learned . . . that . . . a natural fool [was called] an innocent, SCOTT *Waverley* (1814) ix. Abd. Lord preserve's, it's Rob Grant's innocent ! MACDONALD *Sir Gibbie* (1879) xxxvi. Ayr. Burns has only said that he was a half-witted innocent, HUNTER *Studies* (1870) 24. Ir. Idiots and innocents are very nearly alike, but not quite, the first being generally more or less deformed ; both however are considered lucky, *Flk-Lore Rec.* (1881) IV. 113 ; N.I.¹, N.Cy.¹, Nhb.¹, w.Yks.²⁴ Not. Andrew got more an innocent than ever, *Norman Abbey*, II. 329. Hrf.¹ e.An.¹ He's a rare simple innocent. w.Som.¹ Poor little fellow, he'll never be no better-n a innocent. Well, nif thee art-n a rigler innocent ! Cor. HUNT *Pop. Rom. w.Eng.* (ed. 1896) 81.

Hence **Innocence,** *sb.* idiocy, weakness of intellect.

s.Ir. The poor creature is sadly afflicted with innocence, CROKER *Leg.* (1862) 30.

4. *Obs.* A name given to the ' Small People ' ; see below.

Cor. The Small People are believed by some to be the spirits of the people who inhabited Cor. many thousands of years ago, . . . They were not good enough to inherit the joys of heaven, but . . . too good to be condemned to eternal fires. They were said to be ' poor innocents,' HUNT *Pop. Rom. w.Eng.* (ed. 1896) 80.

INNOM-BARLEY, *sb. Obs.* n.Cy. Barley sown for the second crop after the ground is fallowed. GROSE (1790) ; BAILEY (1721) ; (K.) ; N.Cy.²

INOBEDIENT, *adj.* Sc. n.Cy. Som. Disobedient.

Sc. The skreigh of duty which no man should hear and be in

obedient, SCOTT *Rob Roy* (1817) xxiii. n.Cy. (J.W.) w.Som.¹ I told you not to go out, you're a very bad, (een·ubai·junt) boy.

[Adam inobedyent, *Cleanness* (c. 1360) 237, in *Allit. P.* ed. Morris, 43. OFr. *inobedient,* 'désobeissant' (LA CURNE).]

INOFFENSIVE, *adj.* Hrf.² Innocent, pure-minded.

INOO, INOW, see Enow, *adv.²*, *adj.*

INPUT, *sb.* Sc. Yks. Also in form in-pit Bnff.¹ [i·nput.] **1.** A contribution to a collection ; help, assistance.

Sc. An ilka friend wad bear a share o' the burden, . . ilka ane to be liable for their ain input, SCOTT *Midlothian* (1818) xxix. Bnff.¹ Abd. Ye's hae my input, to gar him comply, ROSS *Helenore* (1768) 100, ed. 1812. n.Yks.²

2. Balance, in change of money. Sc. (JAM.)

3. A setting up in business, settlement.

Bnff.¹ His father ga' 'im a fair in-pit t'that chop [shop].

4. That which one is instructed by another to do. Abd. (JAM.)

INQUEST, *sb. Obs.* Sc. A formal inquiry or investigation.

Sc. The schireff is judge to the brieve of inquest, SKENE *Difficill Wds.* (1681) 116. Abd. Quhill sche be put to the tryall of ane inquest of hir nicht-bowris, TURREFF *Gleanings* (1859) 34. Per. He is ordained to be warded, and sustain an inquest of neighbours, SPOTTISWOODE *Miscell.* (1844–45) II. 242.

INQUIRATION, *sb.* Suf. Ess. [inkwaiˈrējən.] An inquiry.

Suf. I was axed some stounds agon . . . to make inquiration a' yeow, *New Suf. Garl.* (1866) 271 ; Suf.¹ Ha' yeow made inquiration ! e.Suf. (F.H.) Ess. If they their inquirations maake In winter-time, some will condemn that place, CLARK *J. Noakes* (1839) st. 5 ; Ess.¹

INREADY, *adv.* Irel. [inreˈdi.] Already.

Myself's over head and ears in love with him inready, CARLETON *Fardorougha* (ed. 1848) i ; Why, man alive, it's through the whole parish inready, *ib. Traits Peas.* (ed. 1843) I. 394.

INRING, *sb.* Sc. [i·nriŋ.] **1.** Curling term : a particular movement of the curling-stone ; see below. Cf. **inwick.**

Sc. A powerful movement of a stone that either carries off the winner, taking its place or lies within the ring which surrounds the tee (JAM.) ; Should a treacherous bias lead Their erring steps ajee, man, Some friendly inring may they meet To guide them to the tee, man, R. *Caled. Curling Club Ann.* (1869) 276. Ayr. Now, Willie, here's a fine inring, Play straught, and rub him like a king, BOSWELL *Poet. Wks.* (ed. 1871) 197. Kcb. Here stands a winner by a bottle hid, Immoveable, save by a nice inring, DAVIDSON *Seasons* (1789) 171.

2. That segment of the surface of a curling-stone which is nearest the tee.

Gall. Old wary curlers sail them past the sentinels, nigh wutter length, obtains a Inring, plays on it, and not infrequently drives out the winner, MACTAGGART *Encycl.* (1824) 65, ed. 1876.

INSCALES, *sb. pl. Obs.* Sc. The racks at the lower end of a pen for live stock.

The Court . . . found . . . that the Saturday's slap, viz. an ell wide of a sluice in each cruive, from six o'clock on Saturday evening till Monday at sunrising, was and ought to be observed, and that during that space the inscales, . . in all . . . the cruives ought to be taken out, and laid aside, *Petition of T. Gillies* (1806) 3 (JAM.).

INSEAM, *v.* and *sb.* Sc. Chs. **1.** *v.* To hem down the inside of a seam. s.Chs.¹

2. *sb.* The seam attaching the welt to the insole and upper of a shoe or boot.

Sh.I. Sibbie brook me bit o' inseam alishen da last day wirkin wi da wharles o' her wheel, *Sh. News* (Aug. 20, 1898). Per. Bent owre a last, at an in-seam hard toiling, FORD *Harp* (1893) 235 ; (G.W.) Ayr. Shoemaker . . . Gie us an inseam that winna gang wrang, AITKIN *Lays Line* (1883) 118.

INSEAT, *sb.* Sc. Also in form inset (JAM. *Suppl.*). [Not known to our correspondents.] The kitchen in a farm-house.

Slg. The morn I shall speak to my father To big us an inset an' spence, WATSON *Poems* (1877) 67 (JAM. *Suppl.*). Ayr. Another apartment—which entered through the inseat, was called the spense, *Agric. Surv.* 114 (JAM.). Lak. Corresponding to the ben or inner apartment (JAM.).

INSENSE, *v.* In *gen.* dial. use in Sc. Irel. and Eng. Also written incense Nhb.¹ Chs. Hrf. Hnt. [inseˈns.] **1.** To cause to understand ; to explain, inform ; with *into* or *with*: to drive anything into a person's head, to instil, impress upon; to enlighten as to; lit. to put sense into.

Sc. Wha insenses mankind wi thought, WADDELL *Ps.* (1871) xciv. 10. Ayr. We'll do the best we can to insense the bit cratur into its mither tongue, SERVICE *Notandums* (1890) 125. Gall. (A.W.) Ir. *N. & Q.* (1865) 3rd S. viii. 37. n.Ir. It wuz a guid while afore he wuz able till insense me intil the wae gas wuz burnt, LYTTLE *Ballycuddy* (1892) 71; N.I.¹ Come here, and I'll insense you into it. Wxf. I'll insense you who is wrong, KENNEDY *Evenings Duffrey* (1869) 327. Wtf. I insensed him into it, *N. & Q.* (1873) 4th S. xi. 467. n.Cy. *ib.* (1865) 3rd S. vii. 425. N.Cy.¹ Nhb. Aa tried ti incense't intiv him (R.O.H.); Nhb.¹ Nhb., Dur. This word means more than to explain: it means the making the person, to whom the explanation is given, thoroughly understand such explanation, GREENWELL *Coal Tr. Gl.* (1849). e.Dur.¹ You didn't insense me what your name is, did you? We insensed him intid. Cum. A pen and ink sketch at the foot of the pages will insense you into the matter (E.W.P.); It was acose ah wasn't up teh that mak o' wark at he wadn't be yabble teh insense meh intull oa t'ins an' oots, SARGISSON *Joe Scoap* (1881) 202; (J.Ar.); Cum.¹⁴ Wm. Dud thoo insense it intul him, fer thoo knows what a mem'ry t'man hez? (B.K.) n.Yks. (R.H.H.); n.Yks.² Ah couldn't insense him intiv it, dee what Ah wad; n.Yks.²; n.Yks.⁴ Ah varra seean insens'd it intiv him. ne.Yks.¹ Ah'll seean insense tha inti t'yal ti deea. He'll gie tha t'brass hard eneeaf nobbut he's reetly insensed. e.Yks. Ah thried mi best ti insense it intiv him, NICHOLSON *Flk-Sp.* (1889) 95; e.Yks.¹, m.Yks.¹ w.Yks. Aw connut insense hur do whot aw will (D.L.); RAY (1691); w.Yks.¹²³⁴⁵ Lan. Aw con show yo th' machine an insense yo into th' action, CLEGG *David's Loom* (1894) xvi; Lan.¹ It's no mak o use me troyin' for to insens yo into o us aw seed, ORMEROD *Felley fra Rachde* (1862). ne.Lan.¹, e.Lan.¹ Chs. Aw mun trey and incense thee gradely abaht these pattens, CLOUGH *B. Bresshitle* (1879) 5; Chs.¹ Aw conna insense 'im, no how; Chs.²³ s.Chs.¹ Ahy insen'st ûr wel in'tü wot óo)d aa)tü ekspek't, ûn óo sed óo)d dóo ûr best [I insensed her well into what hood'd ha' to expect, an' hoo said hood'd do her best]. Stf. (J.T.), Stf.¹ s.Stf.¹ hadner time to insense him what her was drivin' at, PINNOCK *Blk. Cy. Ann.* (1895). Der. (J.K.), Der.², nw.Der.¹ Not. I expect his father has insensed him about it (L.C.M.). Lin.¹ I was incensed to do it by my gaffer. n.Lin. We tried to insense him about things, PEACOCK *Tales and Rhymes* (1886) 77; n.Lin.¹ sw.Lin.¹ I shall wait while I get further insensed. Lei.¹ I've insensed Mr. A. that his flour is unsound. Nhp.¹ War. *B'ham Wkly. Post* (June 10, 1893); War.¹²³⁴ w.Wor. To incense 'em into it, S. BEAUCHAMP *Grantley Grange* (1874) II. 78; w.Wor.¹ 'E insensed me into the manin' of it. s.Wor.¹ Shr.¹ If 'e dunna bring the things right I canna 'elp it—I insensed 'im well into it; Shr.² Y' told him sodidenye, but y' didna insense him. Hrf. DUNCUMB *Hist. Hrf.* (1804–12); Hrf.¹² Glo. (E.D.); (A.B.); Glo.¹ Hnt. During the past ten days he has 'incensed' me on the sanative properties of goose-grass, *N. & Q.* (1866) 3rd S. x. 268. Cmb. I doubt but insense you (W.M.B.). Som. W. & J. *Gl.* (1873). w.Som.¹ The paa'son took care i' insense 'em what time they'd a got to come. In common use. Cor.¹ I'll insense him into it; Cor.²

Hence **Incensing**, *sb.* instruction, explanation.

ne.Lan.¹ n.Lin.¹ Thoo taks as much insensin' as a naail duz dingin' into a oák plank wi' a dish-cloot.

2. Tounderstand. w.Yks.⁵ He's a good un to insense abartowt.

INSE-TEZ, see Eena, *adv.* 2.

INSETT, *ppl. adj.* Sc. Chs. **1.** Substituted for a time in place of another.

Abd. In came the insett Dominie Just riftin frae his dinner, SKINNER *Poems* (1809) 45.

2. Phr. *Obs. Insett stuff*, household furniture. Chs.¹³

INSETTEN, *pp.* n.Yks.² Inserted; inducted.

INSHAVE, *sb.* N.I.¹ A cooper's tool, similar to a drawing-knife but curved.

INSHORING, *vbl. sb.* Nrf. The coming in of herrings towards the shore.

That in-shorin' of herrins is a wonderful thing, PATTERSON *Man and Nat.* (1895) 126.

INSHOT, *ppl. adj.* and *sb.* Cum. [i·nʃot.] **1.** *ppl. adj.* Of a sickness: established inwardly, which does not come out. Cum.⁴ **2.** *sb.* A recess. Cum.¹

INSIDE, *sb.*, *adj.*, *adv.* and *prep.* Var. dial. uses in Sc. Irel. and Eng. Also in form **insi-** w.Som.¹ Cor.¹ [i·nsaid.]

1. *sb.* The inner parts of the body, the stomach, entrails, &c.; the digestion. Also in *pl.*

Sc. They country doctors—bits o' laddies, a' for expeerimentin' on ither folk's insides, KEITH *Indian Uncle* (1896) 170. Sh.I. 'Eh! my inside,' pressing both her hands on her sides, STEWART *Tales* (1892) 42. Per. I'se bring ye a drap toddy to het yer insides, CLELAND *Inchbracken* (1883) 103, ed. 1887. Ayr. JOHNSTON *Glenbuckie* (1889) 44. Wgt. His wife had put an open basket containing the 'inside of a sheep' partly under the bed, FRASER *Wigtown* (1877) 294. Cum.¹ He's bad of his inside. n.Yks.¹ A desper't' pain i ma' insides; n.Yks.⁴ w.Yks.¹ Ise feaful ill i my inside. Lan.¹ Th' lad had bin wrang in his inside a while, WAUGH *Manch. Critic* (1876). n.Lin.¹ I'm straange an' bad o' my inside, squire: I wish you'd gie me a drop o' gin. Cmb. (W.M.B.) w.Som.¹ Ter'ble fuller vor his inside. I've a yeard em zay he don't make nort of a leg o' mutton, and half a peck o' cider. Dev. 'Tis 'most all over wai um; he an't a had the use of his inside this vortnight, *Reports Provinc.* (1889) 16.

2. *adj.* *Comb.* (1) **Inside click**, a 'chip' in wrestling; see below; (2) **-clothes**, underclothing; (3) **-coat**, an undercoat, a petticoat; (4) **-lining**, a dinner; (5) **-servant**, a labourer who boards and lodges in the family.

(1) Cum., Wm. It consists of a sharp stroke, or 'click' brought to bear on the inside of the ancle or foot, by which it is sought to bring one's opponent to the earth (B.K.). (2) Sh.I. Doo needed inside claes ta shift dee, *Sh. News* (Dec. 25, 1897). (3) w.Som.¹ [Een·zi-koa·ut], only applied to a female's garment. Cor.¹ (4) Lon. When one o'clock struck, a lad left, saying, he was 'going to get an inside lining,' MAYHEW *Lond. Labour* (1851) I. 18, col. 1. (5) Ir. CARLETON *Fardorougha* (ed. 1848) xiii.

3. *adv.* In the house, indoors; in an inner room, in the next room.

Ir. Where is Jack?—He's inside. Where is the book?—You'll find it inside, where I left it (A.S.-P.).

4. *prep.* Within; also in phr. *inside of.*

Keb. O' a' the braw lasses inside o' my ken There's no' ane amang them like sweet Jessie Ghen! ARMSTRONG *Ingleside* (1890) 155. n.Cy. (J.W.) War.² I can do it inside two days.

5. Phr. *to be, go, inside any one's door*, to call, visit any one.

Ayr. A minister's wife should do the feck o' the visiting, but I'm told she's seldom inside onybody's door, JOHNSTON *Kilmallie* (1891) I. 53. n.Cy. (J.W.)

INSIGHT, *sb.* Sc. n.Cy. Nhb. Lin. Shr. Also in form **insicht** Sc. (JAM.) Or.I. **1.** Intelligent appreciation.

n.Lin.¹ It makes a deal o' difference, I alus saay, whether folks gohs for sight or insight. If I can't do nos good I can gos for insight.

2. *Comp.* **Insight-kennage**, knowledge, information. Rxb. (JAM.)

3. *Obs.* The furniture of a house; household goods. Also used *attrib.*

Sc. They not only intromitted with their whole goods . . . outsight and insight plenishing, . . but moreover made prisoners, SCOTT *Waverley* (1814) xiv. Or.I. Casting doun of ye saids housses and spoliatioun of yair insicht and gudis being yrintill, *Edb. Antiq. Mag.* (1848) 61. Abd. Dr. Guild . . . violently breaks doun the insight plenishing within the bishop's house, SPALDING *Hist. Sc.* (1792) II. 26 (JAM.). Ayr. I saw nae wanworths gaun either in the outsight or insight plenishin', AINSLIE *Poems* (ed. 1892) 68. N.Cy.¹ H. Hume, reft of two neices and all his insight geare, to the valewe of £5. Nhb.¹

4. Implements or utensils of husbandry kept within doors. Abd. SPALDING *Hist. Sc.* (1792) *Gl.* (JAM.)

5. Mining term: the entrance into the workings from the bottom of the shaft. n.Cy. (HALL), Shr.¹²

INSIGNIFICANT, *adj.* Suf. Immaterial, indifferent.

e.Suf. It is perfectly insignificant to me whether you go or stay (F.H.).

INSIST, *v.* *Obs.* Sc. **1.** To persevere; to continue in a discourse.

Sc. He insisted lang [he gave a long sermon] (JAM.); The person went out and he insisted, yet he saw him neither come in nor go out, SCOTT *Minstrelsy* (1802) III. 405, ed. 1803 (JAM.). Per. He insisted continually in praying for him, and in spirituall exercise, WODROW *Sel. Biog.* (ed. 1845–7) I. 110.

2. With *for*: to insist upon having.

Sc. He insisted for it, *Monthly Mag.* (1800) I. 324.

INSLEEP, *sb.* Irel. [i·nslip.] An itching.

Ant. Taken as a prognostication. For instance that some one will call. If the insleep is in the right arm it will be a man, if in the left a woman, *Ballymena Obs.* (1892).

INSNORL, *v.* Sc. To entangle, inveigle; the same word as Ensnarl, q. v.

Abd. Lat aleen tryin' to insnorl the peer guileless lad in ony sic menner, ALEXANDER *Ain Flk.* (1882) 169; Get that minaister insnorl't wi' 'er dother, *ib. Johnny Gibb* (1871) xliii.

INSOOK, *sb.*[1] Cai.[1] 1. Of frost: a slight amount, a touch. 2. Of the tide: an inrush.

INSOOK, *sb.*[2] Sc. A bad bargain; a 'suck in,' fraud.

Abd. That horse I bought was a complete insook [I was taken in by the bargain] (G.W.).

INSOULING, *sb.* ? *Obs.* Lin. The outfall of a ditch or drain; a drain; a 'soak-dike.'

n.Lin. Evrie man within Messingham and Butterwicke shall make ther becke and insowlinge before All Sowles Day nexte, SCOTTER *Manor Rec.* (1581); n.Lin.[1] There is a soak-dyke in Ashby called the Insouling.

INSPECTOR, *sb.* Nhb. Dur. Mining term: see below.

A man who has charge of the workmen engaged on the heapstead and screens and who is responsible for the proper cleaning and screening of the coals. Where an underground inspector is employed his duty is to attend to the working of the coals and to see that proper pains are taken to make them large and good. He is also required to attend to the straight driving or holing of the places, and to set on compass marks for the purpose, GREENWELL *Coal Tr. Gl.* (1849).

INSPRAITH, *sb. Obsol.* Sc. Nhb. Also in forms **inspreght** Sc.; **inspress** Nhb.[1] Furniture, household goods.

Sc. Inspreght and other household plenishing, 9 merks, *Acct. of the Depredations committed on the Clan Campbell* (1686) 37 (JAM.). **Ayr.** He makes Satan fall from heaven like lightening, he robs him of his armour, and inspraith, DICKSON *Writings* (1660) I. 125, ed. 1845. **Nhb.**[1] In com. use at Spital, more particularly amongst old people.

[Heir all the inspraich he proydit, *Bp. of St. Androis* (c. 1590) 925, in *Sat. Poems*, ed. Cranstoun, I. 384. Gael. *spreidh*, booty (MACBAIN).]

INSTANCE, *sb.* w.Som.[1] An event, occurrence; curiosity.

Twuz jish ee·nstuns uz aay nùv·ur dúd·n zee uvoa·ur, een au·l muy bau·rn dai·z ['Twas such (an) event as I never saw before, in all my born days].

INSTANCY, *sb.* Sc. [i·nstənsi.] Eagerness.

Sc. You will bear me out with what instancy I besought you to depart, STEVENSON *Dynamiter* (1885) 146. **Gall.** Silver Sand snatched it from me with great instancy, CROCKETT *Raiders* (1894) xxxv.

[Those heavenly precepts which our Lord and Saviour with so great instancy gave, HOOKER *Eccles. Polity* (1594) bk. I. x (C.D.). Fr. *instance*, earnestnesse (COTGR.).]

INSTANT, *adj.* Sc. [i·nstənt.] Urgent, pressing, persistent.

a.Sc. O Mr. Reid, ye're sae instant, man. Can ye no gie a body time to think? WILSON *Tales* (1839) V. 85.

[Instant in praier, *Rheims Version* (1582) *Rom.* xii. 12.]

INSTEAD, *adv.* Yks. In forms **esteead** w.Yks.[1]; **isteead** w.Yks. [əstiəd.] With *on*: instead of.

w.Yks. HOWSON *Guide to Craven* (1850) 110; Gi mə ðat əstiəd ont (J.W.); w.Yks.[1]

INSTEP, *sb.* w.Yks.[1] ne.Lan.[1] Nhp.[1] In phr. *to be high in the instep*, to be proud and haughty.

INSTERS, *sb. pl.* n.Yks.[2] [i·nstərz.] The people who have come in. Cf. **inler.**

INSTORE, *v. Obs.* Sc. To store up.

Rnf. The silly knave, wha goud instores, 'Mang haughty sons o' wealth to shine, CLARK *Poet. Pieces* (1836) 14.

INSTROKE, *sb.* Nhb. Dur. [i·nstrōk.] 1. The entry from one mining royalty into another. Nhb.[1]

2. *Comp.* **Instroke-rent**, a rent charged by the lessor of a royalty for allowing a lessee whose pit is in another royalty to break the barrier between the two. Nhb.[1] Nhb., Dur. NICHOLSON *Coal Tr. Gl.* (1888).

INSTRUCT, *v. Obs.* Sc. To prove clearly.

Sc. I can instruct what I say, *Scoticisms* (1787) 47; After having ... heard Menelaus ... adduce evidence sufficient to instruct his assertions, *ib.* 116; It was also a day of very astonishing apparitions ... which I can instruct the truth of, WALKER *Life Peden* (1727) 12 (JAM.). **Abd.** The continuance of the consanguinity ... to the

Prestones of Formartine, though changed in name, is certain and well instructed by charters, TURREFF *Gleanings* (1859) 284.

INSTRUMENT, *sb.* Sc. Legal term: a written document given in proof of any deed of a court or transaction of an individual in that court; *gen.* in phr. *to take instrument(s)*, to protest against a decision, to appeal to a higher court.

Sc. This term, in ecclesiastical courts at least, is now *gen.* used in an improper sense. In consequence of a decision, any one who has interest in the court is said to take instruments, either when he means to declare that he claims the benefit of that decision... or as confirming a protest. As it is customary ... to throw down a piece of money to the clerk of the court, it is *gen.* understood that he takes instruments who gives this money (JAM.); The commissioners then required instruments in my Lord Register's hands of his protestation, BAILLIE *Lett.* (1775) I. 104 (JAM.). **Abd.** Whereupon they took instrument in the hands of two notars, SPALDING *Hist. Sc.* (1792) I. 63. **w.Sc.** Taking instruments simply means handing the clerk of the Presbytery the sum of one shilling for every protest and appeal taken, MACDONALD *Settlement* (1869) 89, ed. 1877. **Ayr.** Albeit God took instruments that he had taken thee in the fang, yet I speir, where is thy new life? DICKSON *Writings* (1660) I. 104, ed. 1845. **Lnk.** The lawyers for the marquis ... took instruments. When the pannel and his advocates were removed, the king's advocate, in order to intimidate and frighten the marquis' lawyers, got the parliament to refuse to record their instrument, WODROW *Ch. Hist.* (1721) I. 135, ed. 1829. **Wgt.** FRASER *Wigtown* (1877) 116.

INSULT, *sb.* and *v.* Lin. 1. *sb.* An assault. Lin.[1] n.Lin.[1] 2. *v.* To assault. Lin.[1] He first insulted me. n.Lin.[1]

INSURE, *v.* Yks. Suf. [insiu·ə(r).] To assure, pledge (one's word); to make sure.

w.Yks. I'll insure you my word for it (C.C.R.). **s.Suf.** I have insured that job [made sure of having it to do] (F.H.).

INSUSGESTION, *sb.* Not.[1] Indigestion.

INTAK(E, *sb.* and *v.* Sc. Nhb. Dur. Cum. Wm. Yks. Lan. Chs. Der. Lin. Nhp. War. Shr. Ess. Sus. Also in forms **intack** Sc. Bnff.[1] N.Cy.[1] Dur.[1] Cum. Wm. w.Yks.[124] Lan.[1] n.Lan.[1] Chs.[123] Der.[2] nw.Der.[1]; **intick** Bnff.[1]; **intock** n.Cy. [i·ntěk, i·ntak.] 1. *sb.* An inhalation, a drawing in of the breath.

Gall. With a hurried intake of the breath he nerved himself for that which was before him, CROCKETT *Anna Mark* (1899) xxvi. 2. The bringing in of the crop. Sc. (JAM.) 3. Gain, profit; anything gathered in or obtained.

n.Yks. 'His intake weeant pay for t'intak,' i. e. the produce of the 'intak' will not pay for the cost of enclosing the land. 'T'intak 'll need a seet o' mannishment, afoor t'intake stops t'hoal iv his pocket.' 'When t'intak's good.' 'T'intake's better' (R.B.). **e.Yks.** The Hamborough fishermen talk about their 'intak,' meaning their receipts after the fishing season, or after working at a rent, &c. (J.R.B.)

4. That which the occupier of land introduces when he changes his land. n.Yks.[2]

5. A rental, land or houses rented.

w.Yks. They have a cottage intake at Baildon (S.K.C.).

6. A contraction; the place in a seam where the dimensions are narrowed. Sc. (JAM.), Cai.[1]

7. A piece of land enclosed from a moor, common, or road; a fell-side pasture; land reclaimed from a tidal river or the sea.

Cld. That portion of a farm which has been recently taken in from moor. As it *gen.* retains this designation afterwards it is common to distinguish this part of a farm as the intack (JAM.). n.Cy. KENNETT *Par. Antiq.* (1695); **N.Cy.**[1] **Nhb.**[1] The Town Moor at Newcastle has intaks, where portions of the land are fenced in and let for stated periods. **Dur.**[1] **s.Dur.** (J.E.D.), **Lakel.**[1] **Cum.** Taking our stand by the margin of the valley stream, we have, first, the meadow slip, then the 'intacks' or fell-side pasture, the 'grassing heads,' and, finally, the mountains, WATSON *Nature Wdcraft.* (1890) iv; Nut far fra t'intack boddom, RICHARDSON *Talk* (1876) and S. 142; Afooar we war weet throo t'intak, SARGISSON *Joe Scoap* (1881) 12; **Cum.**[2] They wor o' trailin' away varra slã an' varra whishtly, down Willy Garnett girt intak, 79. **Wm.** The crofts, the intacks of the north, HUTTON *Bran New Wark* (1785) l. 44; Sooa he set ma throot intack fell-yet reet ontet fell, *Spec. Dial.* (1885) pt. iii. 11. **n.Yks.**[1] Applied in the case of small plots taken up at will, and without any reference to, or power derived from, any general enclosure act; n.Yks.[2] ' Benty intak,' one of ose enclosures where the grass at first grows coarse or rush-like; **Yks.⁴ ne.Yks.¹, e.Yks.¹ w.Yks.** We can gan up o' this side 'y t'Intaks, Lucas *Stud. Nidderdale* (c. 1882) 32; (C.W.D.); **Yks.¹** Gang down ... through Harrison Intack, ii. 295; **w.Yks.²⁴** an. To which were attached large intacks of half reclaimed pas-re, Kay-Shuttleworth *Scarsdale* (1860) II. 125; **Lan.¹ n.Lan.¹** .Lan.¹ Part of a common enclosed and planted or sown while e other part lies wild and unimproved. **e.Lan.¹ Chs.¹** A not scommon name for a field which, at some period or other, has sen enclosed or taken in from the waste, or from the common oughing or meadow lands of the village community; **Chs.²⁸,** Chs.¹, Der.², nw.Der.¹ n.Lin.¹ Land taken in from a common r] land taken from a tidal river. There was a field in Wintering-m called the intake, which had been taken from the Humber in 881; it has been almost entirely washed away again. **Nhp.¹,** Var. (J.R.W.), War.² Shr.¹ An acre or thereabouts of reclaimed aste land, enclosed and taken into a farm. ' I 'ad for'casted to laid the new in-tak down this time.' **Eas.** Through the whole of e marsh islands ... the corresponding levels, or those intakes fected at the same period of time, are found to consist of a perfectly milar surface... Those intakes which have been accomplished in ore modern times, are from the additional quantity of animal or sgetable remains which the sea-water ... has deposited upon sem, become so far abundant and generally fruitful in their produce, *oung Agric.* (1813) I. 17.

Hence **Intaking, sb.** that portion of a farm which has een recently taken in from moor.

Baff. The reason of ebb-ploughing, at intaking, are [sic] to retain se dung as near the surface as possible, *Agric. Surv. App.* 49 (Jam.). **8.** A canal, that part of a body of running water which a taken off from the principal stream.

Sc. Water-wraiths an' in-tack drear Wi' eerie yamour, Tarras *oems* (1804) 40 (Jam.); The intake of this water is within the ounds of the cruive-fishing property, *State Leslie of Powis, &c.* 57 (ib.); A passage across the intake to allow the fishers to go p the side of the river above it, *ib.* 158. **Bnff.** A coble was chained nderneath this Bridge for ..., when juveniles, to row in the Earl's-kill 'intak,' Gordon *Chron. Keith* (1880) 51.

9. A dam across a stream, to turn off water from a mill. nff.¹

10. The air-way along which the fresh air is conducted nto a mine or ' district.'

Nhb. The air-way from the bottom of the downcast shaft going a-bye, along which the fresh air is conducted to the inner work-igs (R.O.H.); **Nhb.¹** Nhb., Dur. Greenwell *Coal Tr. Gl.* (1849). ur. (J.J.B.)

11. A cheat, deception, fraud, swindle.

Sc. She characterised the action of the great Scottish preacher a ' a perfect intake,' Dickson *Auld Min.* (1892) 110. **Sh.I.** Dat's een wan intak, an' I widna 'a' cared, bit hits da first time at he's een in wattir, *Sk. News* (Oct. 22, 1898). **Cai.¹** Abd. Declaring Lob's proposed charge to be a ' perfeck intak,' Alexander *Ain 'lk.* (1882) 142. **Raf.** Gif ye'll no class them without swither A et o' intacks a'thegither, Young *Pictures* (1865) 160.

Hence **Intackin', ppl. adj.** fraudulent. Bnff.¹

12. A swindler, cheat.

Cai.¹ Abd. Some even made so bold as to call him an intak and n adventurer, *Edinborough,* II. 118 (Jam.).

13. Work undertaken which cannot be accomplished at he stipulated price. Shr.²

14. v. Obs. To take a fortified place.

Sc. No artillery at all fit for intaking any strong house, Baillie *tt.* (1775) II. 265 (Jam.). **Abd.** They heard sermon, and gave nanks to God for the intaking of this strong house with so little aith, Spalding *Hist. Sc.* (1792) I. 221.

15. To understand, comprehend, 'take in.'

Sus. I were fool enough to laugh about it, not intaking how it ould be, Blackmore *Springhaven* (1886) xxix.

[7. Norw. dial. *inntak,* a taking in (Aasen); Sw. *intaga,* n enclosed space that formerly was part of a common Widegren).]

INTAKER, sb. Obs. Sc. Nhb. A receiver of stolen coods, an accomplice of thieves.

Sc. Persons on the borders of Sc., who were the receivers of uch booty as their accomplices, called out-partners, used to bring n, Bailey (1721). **Nhb.¹**

INTELL, sb. n.Yks.² [i·ntel.] What is brought to ne's knowledge from information received.

According to mah awn intell.

INTELLECTS, sb. pl. Sc. Dev. Written **intellecks** Dev. Intellect, wits; also in phr. *to have one's intellects,* to have the full use of one's senses.

w.Sc. This was considered a mad freak; a girl who knew her, was asked ' if she had her intellects,' Carrick *Laird of Logan* (1835) 56. **Dev.** I niver did profess such power o' intellecks as some, Salmon *Ballads* (1899) 81.

INTELLECTUALS, sb. pl. Sc. Intellect, understanding, mental capacity.

Sc. Many men in all ages, otherwise of good intellectuals, Thom-son *Cloud of Witnesses* (1714) *Pref.* 17, ed. 1871. **Abd.** My intel-lectuals were so forjasket wi' that terrible visitation, Ruddiman *Sc. Parish* (1828) 94, ed. 1889. **Ayr.** I could see the body was fashed and somewhat dotrified in the intellectuals, Service *Notan-dums* (1890) 16.

INTEN, sb. Not. [Not known to our other correspon-dents.] Enclosed land. (J.H.B.) Cf. intak(e, 7.

INTEND, v. Sc. Yks. Also in form **intent** Sc. [inte·nd.] **1.** To expect, hope, wish for.

w.Yks.² Used to express desire or expectation in matters beyond one's own control. ' I had intended our rector to be a bishop.'

2. In law: to prosecute legally, raise an action, litigate.

Sc. Ye see I intented the process ... before the Quarter Ses-sions, Scott *St. Ronan* (1824) viii. **Per.** The actions intended before them by Robert Marr, Spottiswoode *Miscell.* (1844) II. 242. **Fif.** That they intend na actioun civill without the said advys, Melvill *Autobiog.* (1610) 351, ed. 1842. **Lnk.** A process is in-tended against some very worthy presbyterian ministers, Wodrow *Ch. Hist.* (1721) III. 405, ed. 1828. **Hdg.** If he did not amend they wald assist the woman to intend process against him befor the Comissers, Ritchie *Churches of St. Baldred* (1883) 221. **Wgt.** The Session of Minigaff intented a process against him, Fraser *Wigtown* (1877) 115.

INTEPUNK, sb. Yks. Also in form **inkerpunk** e.Yks.¹ [i·ntə-, i·ŋkəpuŋk.] A child.

e.Yks. Nicholson *Flk-Sp.* (1889) 95; **e.Yks.¹** God bless the maysther of this hoose, The mistheress also; An all the lahtle intepunks, That round the table go, &c., *Xmas Carol of the Beasle-cup-women.*

INTERCEDE, v. Glo. Ken. [intəəi·d.] **1.** To speak on behalf of.

Ken.¹ Mrs. Moper kindly interceded for her, and so Em'ly got the place.

2. With *into*: to inquire or look into a matter. Glo.¹

INTERCEDING, adj. Hrf.² Ready to take the lead, prominent.

' An interceding man ' is one who is a prominent person, ready to take the lead.

INTERCOMMUNE, v. Obs. Sc. Also in form **inter-common** Or.I. To hold intercourse in any way with proscribed persons; to lay under sentence forbidding all intercourse.

Sc. These, together with a considerable number of gentlemen and others they intercommune, which was the greatest length they could goe, Kirkton *Ch. Hist.* (1817) 363. **Or.I.** The said Adam ... intercommoned with his own servant, the actual doer of the slaughter, Peterkin *Notes* (1822) App. 39. **Abd.** The said marquis was charged ... not to intercommune with Haddo, help nor supply him, Spalding *Hist. Sc.* (1792) II. 123. **Lnk.** A good many ministers are intercommuned, and several gentlemen and others are persecuted, Wodrow *Ch. Hist.* (1721) II. 278.

Hence (1) **Intercommuner, sb.** (a) one who holds inter-course with a proscribed person; (b) one who treats between parties at variance; (2) **Intercommuning, sb.** (a) intercourse with proscribed persons; (b) in phr. *letters of intercommuning,* letters prohibiting all intercourse with proscribed persons.

(1, a) **Fif.** Speciallie the intercommuners and resetters of jesuits, Row *Ch. Hist.* (1650) 270, ed. 1842. (b) **Sc.** We agreed, on con-dition that Haddington, Southesk, and Lorn, the intercommuners, should engage their honour, Baillie *Lett.* (1775) I. 59 (Jam.). (2, a) **Sc.** Declare his repentance publicly ... for his inter-communing with the Earl of Angus, excommunicated Papist, Spottiswoode *Miscell.* (1844) II. 274. **Lnk.** Are encouraged to continue in their rebellion, by the reset, supply, and intercom-muning which they have with several of their friends and acquaintances, Wodrow *Ch. Hist.* (1721) II. 288, ed. 1828. **Gall.** Lest the strict laws against intercommuning should lay him by the heels in the gaol of Kirkcudbright, Crockett *Standard Bearer*

(1898) 5. (b) Abd. Letters of intercommuning were proclaimed against them, whereby, as they were lawless, so made friendless, and might not bide together, SPALDING *Hist. Sc.* (1792) I. 42. **Lak.** These letters of intercommuning were the utmost our managers would go upon non-appearance, WODROW *Ch. Hist.* (1721) I. 394.

INTERFERE, *v.* Ken.[1] To cause annoyance or hindrance.

I was obliged to cut my harnd tother-day, that's what interferes with me.

INTERLEAN, *adj.* Dev. Of bacon: 'streaky,' having layers of lean and fat alternating. HEWETT *Peas. Sp.* (1892) 129. The same word as Enterlean, q.v.

INTERLOPER, *sb.* Nrf. A person of no regular employment. (P.H.E.)

INTERMELL, *v.* *Obs.* ne.Lan.[1] To intermeddle.

INTERMENT, *adj.* w.Som.[1] Intimate, friendly, 'thick.' 'Twas on'y tother day they was like the devil and holy water, and now they be all s'interment [ee·nturmunt].

INTERMINED, *ppl. adj.* Nhb. Yks. I.Ma. Also Cor. Also in forms intahmined Yks.; intarmined n.Yks. I.Ma.; intarmint I.Ma.; intormin'd Nhb. Determined.

Nhb. She wis fair intormin'd te gan, ROBSON *Bk. Ruth* (1860) i. 18. **Yks.** Franck is intahmined on't te tak az here, *Spec. Dial.* 16. n.Yks. (T.S.) **I.Ma.** Got him home—intarmined she wud —intarmined, BROWN *Witch* (1889) 20; I was intarmint to purr a stoppar on that, RYDINGS *Tales* (1895) 105. w.Cor. I intermined to do it (M.A.C.).

INTERMIT, *v.* Rut.[1] To admit, allow to enter.

They allus intermits 'em of-a Tuesday [patients at the Infirmary].

INTERMITTING, *sb.* *Obs.* n.Cy. The ague.

He has gotten an intermitting, GROSE (1790).

INTERRUPT, *v.* Ken. Sur. Sus. [intərrəpt.] To annoy, cause discomfort to, to disagree with; to interfere with, attack, pursue.

Ken. A drunken man stopping or attacking a person in the street interrupts him (W.F.S.); **Ken.**[1] It does interrupt me to think you can't run your right side; what a thick head you must have! **Sur.**[1] 'If I eat any heavy food it interrupts me so.' To attack or pursue, as of a dog or any other animal. **Sus.**[1] Used to express all kinds and degrees of assault.

INTERVAL, *sb.* Sc. The time between the hours of public worship.

Sc. Common (A.W.). **Raf.** The boys ... stated very explicitly that the 'intervals' were more to their liking than 'kirk-time,' GILMOUR *Pen-Flk.* (1873) 22.

INTICK, see Intak(e.

INTIL(L, *prep.* Sc. Irel. Nhb. Dur. Cum. Wm. Yks. Lan. Der. Also in forms atil Sh.I.; intul Cum.[1] Wm. n.Yks.[4] ne.Yks.[1] e.Yks.[1] w.Yks.[1] ne.Lan.[1]; intull Cum. Lan. [inti·l, intu·l.] 1. Into.

Sc. Deil anither body's fit should gang intill't, SCOTT *St. Ronan* (1824) xx; He's taen his harp intil his hand, JAMIESON *Pop. Ballads* (1806) l. 94. **Sh.I.** Shü shook da tae laeves oot o' da pot atil a peerie pan, *Sh. News* (Oct. 29, 1898). **ne.Sc.** Well done, Goodman. That's intil him. Hit him again, *Gordonhaven* (1887) 125. **Bnff.** I'm no gaun intill a hole like a wild beast, SMILES *Natur.* (1876) xviii. **e.Sc.** He kent as weel as ony what to put intill't, SETOUN *Sunshine* (1895) 20. **Abd.** As ye are born intil the war!', MACDONALD *Sir Gibbie* (1879) xxvii. **Frf.** Jumpt quick intil his Sunday's claes, SANDS *Poems* (1833) 71. **Per.** She's gotten Miss Mary's lug, an' says what she likes intil't, CLELAND *Inchbracken* (1883) 64, ed. 1887. **e.Fif.** An auld horn lantrin wi' a bit cawnel doup stuck intil't, LATTO *Tam Bodkin* (1864) ii. **Ayr.** We were obligated ... to come intil Glasgow, GALT *Entail* (1823) ii. **Slk.** The langer you gazed intil't, the deeper it grew, CHR. NORTH *Noctes* (ed. 1856) II. 6. **Gall.** I'll pit my wee knife intil ye, CROCKETT *Cleg Kelly* (1896) 34. n.Ir. Close to his ear the Devil came, And slipped intil his breast, ALEXANDER *Stumpie's Brae*; Fur brekin' intil the squire's clover, LYTTLE *Ballycuddy* (1892) 54; **N.I.**[1] Uls. *Uls. Jrn. Arch.* (1853–1862). **Nhb.** An' wi' sorrow the teardrop crap intil his e'e, PROUDLOCK *Borderland Muse* (1896) 25; **Nhb.**[1] Put them in till a poke. Lakel.[1] **Cum.** I gat intul a great feeld, *Borrowdale Lett. in Lonsdale Mag.* (Feb. 1867) 311; **Cum.**[1] **Wm.** T'aald fella gat intul a sweeat, ROBISON *Aald Taales* (1882) 3. **n.Yks.**[124] ne.Yks.[1] There's neea spot ti put t'gallowa intul. e.Yks.[1] Rarely used. m.Yks.[1] w.Yks. Dosey went intuik back kitchen to see abaht t'dinner, CUDWORTH *Dial. Sketches* (1884)

26; w.Yks.[1] ii. 305. **Lan.** Thou ïed her first intul t'Park wood, HARLAND & WILKINSON *Flk-Lore* (1867) 60. ne.Lan.[1] Der. Thee mun help me to stack what I've got intil th' cart, VERNEY *Stone Edge* (1868) x.

2. In, within.

Sc. Ilka ee intil her head Was like a rotten ploom, SHARPE *Ballad Bk.* (1823) 84, ed. 1868. **Sh.I.** Da füde o' ivery laand is da best ... for da folk 'at's born an' brought up intil hit, *Sh. News* (Mar. 12, 1898). **ne.Sc.** There's ane intill the ladye's bower, GREGOR *Flk-Lore* (1881) 109. **Abd.** Like stars intil a frosty nicht, *Guidman Inglismaill* (1873) 48. **Kcd.** An hoor intil Achallie's neuk Wi' Jess, GRANT *Lays* (1884) 16. **Frf.** He had sic power intil his tail O' magnetism, SANDS *Poems* (1833) 90. **Per.** Maybe there's a knack intil't, *Sandy Scott* (1897) 20. **Fif.** The swine ... drown't themselves intill the sea, TENNANT *Papistry* (1827) 45. **Raf.** Intill the wainscot kitchen press, Ye'll find some lamb, an' something else, PICKEN *Poems* (1813) I. 62. **Ayr.** He wonner'd what wad be intilt, HUNTER *Studies* (1870) 51. **Dmf.** He sat intil this room, THOM *Jock o' Knows* (1878) 23.

INTIMATED, *adj.* Lin. Som. Intimate.

n.Lin.[1] He's been clear different sin' him an' her hes been intimsated together. **w.Som.**[1] Ees, I knows'n well enough to pass the time o' day, but we baint very much intimated [ee·ntimae·utud].

INTIMMERS, *sb. pl.* Sc. [i·ntimərz.] The intestines.

Bnff.[1] Frf. Had your intimmers keepit richt, JAMIE *Emigrant's Family* (1853) 51. **Gall.** His intimmers are of the best kind, he can be drunk and sober three times a day, MACTAGGART *Encycl.* (1824) 376, ed. 1876.

INTIRE, *adj.* *Obs.* Sc. Intimate, heart and soul with.

Sc. He and Argyle became so very intire that they feasted daily together, GUTHRY *Mem.* (1747) 117 (JAM.). **Slg.** The Marquese of Argyle, who of ane long time had been very intire with William Murray and Sir Andrew Murray, WODROW *Sel. Biog.* (ed. 1845-7) I. 170.

INTLES, INTOCK, see Hintals, Intak(e.

INTO, *prep.* Var. dial. uses in Sc. Eng. and. Amer.

1. In *comb.* Into-the-house, the up-stroke of a pumping engine. Nhb.[1]

2. *Phr.* (1) *into that,* (a) as well as; (b) nevertheless; (2) *out into,* out of, out from; (3) *to be into a person,* to find fault with any one.

(1, a) Som. (F.L.N.) (b) Shr. That plant doesn't flower, but into that it has fine leaves (ib.). (a) Sc. Gif onie ladie wad borrow me Out into this prison strang, KINLOCH *Ballads* (1827) 131. (3) Yks. (J.W.)

3. In, within.

Sc. Say, ye left him into Kirkland fair, Learning the school alone, JAMIESON *Pop. Ballads* (1806) I. 62. **Sh.I.** Dat's no ita me pooer, NICOLSON *Aithstin' Hedder,* 5. **Abd.** I met a frien' or twa into the Fair, SHIRREFS *Poems* (1790) 41. **Kcd.** Tradition says, into this Pot A golden vessel lies, JAMIE *Muse* (1844) 23. **Frf.** Mair hae died into their shoon than what hae died in bed, LOWSON *Guidfollow* (1890) 236. **Per.** Gin ye list to lig into the laft, there"s a braw flure-head, HALIBURTON *Dunbar* (1895) 100. **Ayr.** There was three kings into the East, BURNS *J. Barleycorn* (1781) st. 2. **Edb.** The lasses met into a barn, LIDDLE *Poems* (1821) 295. **Keb.** The sparks and flaughens of this love shall fly up and down this bed so long as I lie into it, WODROW *Sel. Biog.* (ed. 1845-7) I. 40x. w.Yks.[2] The horse is into the stable. **Stf.**[1] Som. They'd a-starve'd her maid into thick there hospital, ELWORTHY *Evil Eye* (1895) 4. **Dev.** We live into the village (H.S.H.); I was seized into church, *Reports Provinc.* (1877) 132. **Cor.** I seed un ... sittin' into my cousin Joe's, PARR *Adam and Eve* (1880) I. 83. [Amer. Is there any milk into that pail? CARRUTH *Kansas Univ. Quar.* (Oct. 1892) I. **Nfd.** There is nothing into the man (G.P.).]

4. Of distance: within, short of.

Hrf. He came into a yard of it, BOUND *Provinc.* (1876); Hrf.[1] It is not far into a mile.

5. Of age: approaching, in.

w.Som.[1] 'How old are you?' 'I bee into my twelve year old.'

6. Of time: to, as regards.

s.Wor. You never knows when he'll come, he's not pertikler into an hour; a'most any time (H.K.).

INTOWN, *sb.* Sc. Also written intoon Sc. Bnff.[1] [i·ntün.] 1. The land or pasture adjacent to a farmhouse. Also used *attrib.* Cf. infield.

n.Sc. (JAM.) **Sth.** The milk cows are fed on the intown pasture until the farmer removes them by the end of June to distant shealings, *Agric. Survey,* 62 (JAM.). **Abd.** The first intowns that we came to, The captain was sick and weary, O; And the next intown that we came to We got our captain to bury, O, GREIG *Logie o' Buchan* (1899) 115; To graze . . . on the intoon rigs, during the early forenoon, ALEXANDER *Ain Flk.* (1882a) 91.

2. *Comp.* In-toon-weed, an annual weed. Bnff.[1]

INTRESS, *sb.* n.Cy. Som. [i·ntrəs.] Interest upon money.

n.Cy. (J.W.) w.Som.[1] Always. ' I have sent by the barer £20 the Intress Due the 12th of this Month.'

[Not the worth of any living wight May challenge ought in Heavens interesse, SPENSER *F. Q.* (1596) bk. VII. vi. 33; The laste day is ende of myn intresse, CHAUCER *Minor Poems*, x. 71. Fr.'dial.(Béarnais) *interesse*, 'intérêt' (LESPY).]

INTROMISSION, *sb.* Sc. Intermeddling; in *pl.* goings on with a person.

Ayr. They said that the expulsion of the players was owing to what I had heard anent the intromission of my nephew, GALT *Provost* (1822) xxxvii. Gall. Supposing that you are satisfied with my present intromissions, CROCKETT *Anna Mark* (1899) lii.

INTROMIT, *v.* Sc. [intrəmi·t.] To meddle with, interfere; to associate.

Sc. Forbear from intromitting with affairs thou canst not understand, SCOTT *Midlothian* (1818) v. Abd. Div ye tell me that Jean was intromittin' wi' thae drawers? MACDONALD *Malcolm* (1875) III. 194; A' out o' the way creatures intromit wi' that unprofitable art of poem-making, RUDDIMAN *Parish* (1828) 96, ed. 1889. Ayr. When the country gentry, with their families, began to intromit among us, we could not make enough of them, GALT *Provost* (1822) xxxiv.

INTRUST, *sb.* Rut. e.An. Amer. [i·ntrəst.] Interest upon money.

Rut.[1] A year's intrust. e.An.[1] e.Suf. That's heavy intrust to pay (F.H.). [Amer. What is the intrust on that amount? *Dial. Notes* (1896) I. 68.]

INTURN, *adv.* Shr. [intə·n.] Instead.

Bound *Provinc.* (1876); Shr.[1] I'll do it inturn o' yo'; Shr.[2] Tak this inturn o' that'n.

IN-TY(E, *phr.* Sus. Som. [intəi·.] After a neg. assertion: not I.

Sus. I don't know nothing about it, in tye, for I never seen none an 'em, LOWER *S. Downs* (1854) 157. w.Som.[1] 'I don't know hot to zay 'bout it, in-ty.' The expression is one of every-day use, and rather implies indecision or doubt. [A country fellow, scratching his head, answered him, ' I don't know measter, un't I,' FIELDING *Tom Jones* (1749) bk. IV. viii.]

INVADE, *v.* Obs. Sc. To assail, attack.

Per. He came and invaded her openly on the street, and spulziet her of her silver belt, SPOTTISWOODE *Miscell.* (1844) II. 280. Slg. This man . . . had offered to invade Mr. Bruce's person, BRUCE *Sermons* (1631) 146, ed. 1843. Lnk. Christian Fyfe . . . is indicted for invading a minister, WODROW *Ch. Hist.* (1721) III. 409, ed. 1828.

INVEETORS, *sb. pl.* Sc. [invi·tərz.] Articles taken over by inventory at a valuation on taking a farm.

Abd. Afore ye pay yer inveetors an' ae thing wi' anither, ye'll be workin' upo' paper again for maist part, ALEXANDER *Ain Flk.* (1882a) 136.

INVENTION, *v.* Irel. To invent.

n.Ir. Afore them things mentioned wor known, or inventioned, *Lays and Leg.* (1884) 16.

INVIE, *v.* Obsol. e.Suf. To value, set store by. (F.H.)

INVIGOR, *v.* Obs. Sc. To invigorate, strengthen.

Elg. Th' invigour'd stem wi' a' its flow'rs Embalm the rising day, COUPER *Poetry* (1804) I. 98. s.Sc. It will invigor ev'ry limb, Unclog your vitals a', T. SCOTT *Poems* (1793) 376.

INVITE, *sb.* Sc. Oxf. Som. Also in form inveet Abd. [invəi·t.] An invitation.

Abd. He's aye some shy o' comin' in wantin' an inveet, MACDONALD *Sir Gibbie* (1879) xxxiii. Ayr. The Earl of Killie . . . complimented me with a special invite delivered by the hand of his own serving-man, JOHNSTON *Glenbuckie* (1889) 180. Lnk. Like me, wha had come there alane Without invite, COGHILL *Poems* (1890) 11. Dmf. I leuch to hear the kind invite She gied the lads to woo, REID *Poems* (1894) 41. Oxf. (G.O.) w.Som.[1] The paa'sn 've a zend a [ee·nvuyt, eenvuy·t] t'all they hot belongth to the club.

INVITORY, *sb.* n.Lin.[1] Also written invittery. [invi·təri.] **1.** An inventory. **2.** Tenant right on going out of a farm.

INVYFULL, *adj.* Sc. Also in form invy-fu' Cai.[1] [invəl·, i·nvi-.] Envious.

VOL. III.

Cai.[1] Fit. To close the mouthes of invyfull sklanderars, MELVILL *Autobiog.* (1610) 265, ed. 1842.

INWARD, *adj.*, *sb.* and *adv.* Var. dial. uses in Sc. and Eng. Also in forms inard m.Yks.[1] Lan. n.Lin.[1] Nhp.[1] e.An.[1] Sur.; innard n.Yks.[4] e.Yks.[1] w.Yks.[2] Lan. I.Ma. s.Stf. War.[4] s.War.[1] w.Wor. Glo.[12] Oxf.[1] Suf.[1] Ken.[1] Som.; innerd Cum.[14] Not. Nhp.[2] Brks.[1] e.An.[2] Nrf. Ken. Sus. Hmp.[1] I.W.[1] Wil. Dor. Cor.[12]; inniard e.Yks.[1]; innod War.[4]; innud se.Wor.[1] [i·nərd, i·nəd.] **1.** *adj.* In *comb.* (1) Inward fits, an infant disorder, a mild convulsive fit; (2) — maid, the housemaid in a farm-house, who has no work in the dairy, &c.; (3) — meat, the edible parts of the entrails of an animal; (4) — trouble, an internal disease or illness.

(1) n.Yks.[1], w.Yks. (J.W.) (2) e.An.[1], Suf. (HALL.) (3) Lei.[1] 'Will you take a kidney?' 'No, thank you, I don't like any inward meat.' (4) Sc. A poor Trojan . . . much distressed with an inward trouble, *Scoticisms* (1787) 118.

2. Living within.

Abd. Contrary to the foundation of that college, forbidding marriage to any of the inward members serving therein, SPALDING *Hist. Sc.* (1792) II. 67.

3. Silent, reserved.

Sus.[1] I can't abear going to work along ud Master Meopham, he be so inward. Hmp.[1]

4. *sb. pl.* The inner parts of the body, the inside; the entrails, intestines, &c. of animals, esp. of pigs. Occas. in *sing.*

Sh.I. Da morn we can hae some o' da inwards o' da ram, *Sh. News* (Oct. 9, 1897). N.Cy.[1], Cum.[14], n.Yks.[14], e.Yks.[1] w.Yks. It pierceth into the inwards, and goes down into the bowels of the belly, WALES *Mount Ebal* (1658) 27; w.Yks.[2] Lan. I feel as if I had summat i' my in'ards, FRANCIS *Daughter of Soil* (1895) 30; One o' theese savidges i' th' bird tribe seems to be mekkin' a herty meal off th' innards ov a rabbit, FERGUSON *Moudywarp's Visit*, 17. I.Ma. Some could granny's innards routin, BROWN *Doctor* (1887) 4. s.Stf. He'd got a awful gnawin' in hes innards, PINNOCK *Blk. Cy. Ann.* (1895). Der.[2], nw.Der.[1] Not. He's got hurt i' the innards I'm afraid (L.C.M.); Not.[1] n.Lin.[1] I'd a strange paain e' my in'ards, so I went an' boht sum stuff an' took it. Lei.[1] A's so bad of his innards. Nhp.[12], War.[234] s.War.[1] I'm that bad in my innards. w.Wor. It be summat i' his innards or his yud, S. BEAUCHAMP *Grantley Grange* (1874) I. 29. se.Wor.[1] Shr.[1] The heart, liver, &c. of a pig or lamb. Glo. (A.B.); Gl. (1851); Glo.[12] Oxf. He's got something the matter with his innards (G.O.); Oxf.[1] Brks.[1] 'Chitterlings' as frequently go by the name of ' peg's innerds.' e.An.[12] Nrf. A basin o' hot tea 'ud du my innerds good, PATTERSON *Man and Nat.* (1895) 117. e.Nrf. MARSHALL *Rur. Econ.* (1787). Suf.[1], Ken. (G.B.), Ken.[1], Sur.[1] Sus.[1] He did not know what he meant by saying so much about the innards of an hog. Hmp.[1], I.W.[1] Wil. SLOW *Gl.* (1892); BRITTON *Beauties* (1825). n.Wil. What be gwain to do wi' they pig's-innerds? (E.H.G.) Dor. I shall ask to be let carry half of these good things in my innerds—hee, hee! HARDY *Wess. Tales* (1888) II. 12. Som. (F.A.A.) w.Som.[1] 'I be ter'ble sick, and do keep on bringin up, and I do suffer ter'ble pain in my inwards.' The intestines of any slaughtered animal. The liver, lungs, and heart are not included in this term. Used only in the *sg.* in this sense. In the plural, the viscera of more than one animal would be referred to. ' I never did'n kill nother pig way such a beautiful fat inward avore.' Dev. I'm terrible boller in my in'erds, BARING-GOULD *Dartmoor Idylls* (1896) 193. Cor.[1] A pain in my innerds; Cor.[2] w.Cor. I ca·ant skippy, I should jostle my innerds (M.A.C.).

5. *pl.* The ins and outs, the inner details of a case.

Cum.[4] Those acquainted with the 'inwards' of the affair, *W. C. T.* (July 30, 1898) 4, col. 5.

6. An innings at cricket.

Ken. (G.B.); Ken.[1] They bested 'em first innards.

7. *adv.* Within, inside; also in form Inards.

m.Yks.[1] Sur. Well, let 'ee com, or let 'ee stop, us 'ull go in'ards, BICKLEY *Sur. Hills* (1890) III. xvii.

INWARD, *v.* Obs. Sc. Also in form invaird. To imprison, to put in ward. Gl. Sibb. (1802) (JAM.).

INWARDLY, *adv.* Oxf. Ken. Sur. Sus. Hmp. Cor. Also in forms innardly Ken.[1] Sus.[1]; innurdly Oxf. [i·nədli.] **1.** Inaudibly, in a low tone.

Oxf.[1] Her laughs innurdly, *MS. add.* Ken.[1] He says his words innardly. s.Ken. He speaks so inwardly (G.G.). Sur.[1] Sus.[1]

U U

This new parson of ours says his words so innardly. **Hmp.**[1] He spoke so inwardly I couldn't rightly understand him.

2. *Phr. to be inwardly given*, to be pious, spiritual.

w.Cor. She's not inwardly but outwardly given. Com. (M.A.C.)

INWAVER, see Inwiver.

INWICK, *sb.* and *v.* Sc.   **1.** *sb.* Curling term: a particular cast of the stone. Cf. **inring**.

Sc. A station, in curling, in which a stone is placed very near the tee after passing through a narrow port (JAM.); (G.W.) AYR. By a clever ' inwick ' put a pot-lid on the tee, JOHNSTON *Kilmallie* (1891) II. 109. GaIl. To take an inwick is considered by all curlers the finest trick in the game, MACTAGGART *Encycl.* (1824) 280, ed. 1876.

2. *v.* In curling : to play the stone in a particular manner; see below.

Gall. To inwick a stone, is to come up a port or wick and strike the inring of a stone seen through that wick, MACTAGGART *Encycl.* (1824) 280, ed. 1876.

INWINDING, *adj.* se.Wor.[1] [inwai·ndin.] Uneven, twisting.

INWIVER, *sb.* Nhb.[1] Also in form **inwaver**. A bar of wood put inside a ' coble ' (q.v.) for the seats or thofts to rest upon.

INWORK, *sb.* Sc. Indoor or domestic work.

Ayr. His regret·that a bonny Ayrshire lass should, instead o' handling the inwork o' a house, .. be condemned to mak' her bread by such unluesomelike thumping and kicking, AINSLIE *Land of Burns* (ed. 1892) 34.

INYA, *adv.* Irel. Forsooth.

Wxf. What a purty squire and estated gentleman we are inya, KENNEDY *Evenings Duffrey* (1869) 285 ; Jealous inya ! to be sure you are, *ib. Banks Boro* (1867) 240.

INYABY, *sb.* S. & Ork.[1] A defeated cock driven away and kept at a distance by the ruler of the dunghill.

[Norw. dial. *einrgjabue*, a dweller alone (AASEN).]

IODINE, *sb.* s.Lin. [Not known to our other correspondents.] The greater celandine, *Chelidonium majus*. (I.W.)

ION, *sb.* Abd. (JAM.) [Not known to our correspondents.] A cow a year old.

[Cp. Norw. dial. *kviginde*, a young cow (AASEN) ; ON. *kvigendi*, a der. of *kviga*, a young cow before she has calved (VIGFUSSON) ; cp. Sc. *whye*, a pron. of *quey* (q.v.).]

IPER, *sb.* Or.I. Any foul liquid, ooze, mud, or sewage.

A' draigled ower wi' iper, DENNISON *Sketch-bk.* (1880) 125 (JAM. *Suppl.*).

IPSON, IR, see Yaspen, Or.

IRBY·DALE GRASS, *phr.* Lin. The sun-spurge, *Euphorbia Helioscopia*.

So called at Irby-dale, near Laceby, where it is abundant, and used by the poor people as a cure for warts, and ' applied as a poultice to venomed wounds with good effect ' (B. & H.).

IRE, *sb.*[1] and *adj.* Brks. Hmp. I.W. Wil. Dor. Som. Dev. Cor.   [ai·ə(r).]   **1.** *sb.* Iron.

Brks. For iron they say ire, NICHOLS *Bibl. Topog. Brit.* (1783) IV. 56, ed. 1790 ; Brks.[1], Hmp. (H.E.)   I.W.[1] ; I.W.[2] Pick up that bit o' ire under hedge. n.Wil. In common use. That's a girt piece o' ire (E.H.G.).   Som. JENNINGS *Dial. w.Eng.* (1869). w.Som.[1] Uy·ur. In the dial. [uy·urn] is the *adj.* form. Cp. Iron-bar with Bar-ire.   Dev. *Horae Subsecivae* (1777) 230. nw.Dev.[1] e.Dev. A ire thing, moore smart by half, PULMAN *Sketches* (1842) 55, ed. 1853.   Cor. I'm rud as the smith makes the pieces of ire, J. TRENOODLE *Spec. Dial.* (1846) 34 ; Cor.[2]

2. *Comb.* (1) Ire·gear, ironwork ; ironware ; plough-gear ; (2) -monger, an ironmonger ; (3) — or mire, stiff, clay soil ; (4) -stuff, ironwork.

(1) Dor.[1] Som. JENNINGS *Obs. Dial. w.Eng.* (1825). w.Som.[1] [Uy·ur gee·ur] would mean all kinds of ironmongery, and completed iron-work, including machinery of all kinds. (2) Hmp. (H.E.) (3) Som. W. & J. *Gl.* (1873). (4) w.Som.[1] The ironwork of a cart, carriage, gate, or of any construction in which iron is used with other material. ' He'd [the cart] a been a finished avore now nif ad'n a been a fo'ced to woit [*sic*] for the ire stuff.'

3. An iron stand, on which dishes, pots, &c. are put to cook.

Cor. The dough was put in a tin dish and this was placed on an ire, as she called it, or iron stand (J.W.).

4. Ironstone ; iron-ore.

Hmp.[1] That ire is not good.   Som. (W.F.R.)

5. *adj.* Made of iron. Wil. SLOW *Gl.* (1892).

[1. Ne mon mid stele ne mid ire, *Owl & N.* (c. 1225) 1026.]

IRE, *sb.*[2] Sh.I. A passion ; a fit of wrath.

Shū wis in sic a ire o' wraeth 'at shū'd no tought a eetim o' laein him caald, *Sh. News* (Oct. 15, 1898).

IRE, *sb.*[3] Som. [Not known to our correspondents.] An onion. JENNINGS *Obs. Dial. w.Eng.* (1825).

IREFUL, *adj.* n.Yks.[2] Angry ; stormy ; inflamed.

' It leuks varry ireful,' said of a wound. ' It leuks ireful ower sea,' the clouds are darkening, and the sea beginning to surge.

IRENESE, *sb.* Som. [Not known to our correspondents.] Rennet. (HALL.)

IRIE, *adj.* Obs. Sc. Also written **irey** Edb. Melancholy, gloomy ; causing fear. Cf. **eerie**.

Sc. And irie is, and sair forfairn Thy bodin' dark to hear, JAMIESON *Pop. Ballads* (1806) I. 237.   Lnk. I've been tald—an irie tale to tell—Ilk seven year they [fairies] pay a teind to hell, BLACK *Falls of Clyde* (1806) 121 ; I'm unco irie and dirt-feart, RAMSAY *Poems* (ed. 1733) 102.   Edb. Death in all his irey pride, Devoid of fear behold, LEARMONT *Poems* (1791) 186.

IRISH, *adj.* and *sb.*[1] Sc. Irel. Nhb. Yks. Chs. Rut. War. Lon. Sur.   [ai·riʃ.]   **1.** *adj.* In *comb.* (1) Irish black-guard, a variety of snuff ; (2) — cry, the lamentation of mourners attending a funeral ; (3) — daisy, the dandelion, *Leontodon Taraxacum* ; (4) — lemons, potatoes ; (5) — mahogany, the common alder, *Alnus glutinosa* ; (6) ·man, the work of the ' hay-harvest' ; (7) ·man's fire, ? a fire which burns only on the top; (8) ·man's harvest, the orange season ; (9) — moss, pearl-moss, *Chondrus crispus*; see **Carrageen** ; (10) — nightingale, the sedge-warbler, *Acrocephalus phragmitis*; (11) — ortolan, the stormy petrel, *Procellaria pelagica* ; (12) — stone, see below ; (13) — vine, the honeysuckle, *Lonicera Periclymenum*.

(1) Lnk. Two pinches in one, of Irish blackguard and taddy snuff mixed, WRIGHT *Life* (1897) 5. GaIl. His snuff-box ... always well filled with the best Macabaa, or with the smartest Irish Blackguard, MACTAGGART *Encycl.* (1824) 491, ed. 1876. (2) Ir. What is termed the Irish cry, is keening on an extensive scale. BARRINGTON *Sketches* (1830) I. v. (3) Yks. (B. & H.) (4) War.[2] (5) Wtf. (B. & H.) (6) Rut.[1] (7) Sur. How bad this fire burns ! It's like an Irishman's fire, all atop, *N. & Q.* (1878) 5th S. x. 222. (8) Lon. The orange season is called by the costermonger the ' Irishman's harvest,' MAYHEW *Lond. Labour* (1851) I. 79. (9) Chs. Imported from Ir. Occas. used for feeding calves (B. & H.). (10) Ir. It continues its song after dusk and through the night, SWAINSON *Birds* (1885) 28. (11) Ker. In 1756 this bird of all others was esteemed a delicacy for the table and was named the Irish ortolan, SMITH *Birds* (1887) 546. (12) Nhb. Mrs. R., of Kyloe House, had a sore leg. Her servant ... was despatched ... to borrow an Irish stone. This is a stone brought from Ireland, and never permitted to touch English soil. The stone was put in a basket and carried to the house where the patient resided ; the leg was rubbed with it, and it was cured. They all considered it would have been more efficacious if it had been brought and used by an Irish person, *Trans. Tyneside Field Club* (1860–62) V. 90 ; These stones were at one time common in the dales of Northumberland, and were used as charms to deter frogs, toads, and the whole of the serpent tribe from entering the dwelling-house of their possessor. In size the stone is three and a quarter inches in diameter, of a cake form, is of a pale brown or dark drab colour, and about three-quarters of an inch thick in the middle, where it is the thickest. It is unperforated, DENHAM *Flk-Lore* (1852) 16 ; (R.O.H.) (13) Don. (B. & H.)

2. *Phr. you are Irish and the top of your head's poison*, a jocular gibe. War. (G.F.N.), War.[1]

3. *sb. pl.* Obs. Irishmen.

Sc. The Frenches and Irishes are a' coming here, SHARPE *Ballad Bk.* (1823) 110, ed. 1868.   Fif. Throche the persecution and oppression of the Ireshes, Row *Ch. Hist.* (1650) xvii, ed. 1842.

IRISH, *sb.*[2] Yks. Passion, anger, rage, fury.

e.Yks. Very common. ' Deen't show thi irish, lad ' (J.N.) ; e.Yks.[1] Mau wod ! bud didn't he shew his irish. w.Yks. Iz airis wor up i nuo taim (J.W.).

IRISHER, *sb.* Sc. Irel. An Irishman.

Gall. A panic story, that the wild Irishers had landed, CROCKETT *Standard Bearer* (1898) 85.   Qco. What would the poor Irishers have done in owld times ! BARRINGTON *Sketches* (1830) III. iii.

IRK, *v.* and *sb.* Sc. Yks. Lei. War. Also in form **nirk**-Lei.[1]   [irk, 5k.]   **1.** *v.* To annoy, harass, weary ; also *intr.* to grow weary.

Sc. Father Peter, whose lessons did not irk me, Lang *Monk of Fife* (1896) 5; Yet when she irks to Kaidly birks She rins and sighs for sorrow, Ramsay *Tea-Table Misc.* (1724) I. 190, ed. 1871. Edb. All others they began to irk, Pennecuik *Wks.* (1715) 385, ed. 1815. w.Yks.[4] Used as an *impers.* ' it irks me.' War. Wise *Shakespeare* (1861) 153.

Hence (1) **Irked,** *ppl. adj.* teased ; forced to become a foe ; (2) **Irker,** *sb.* a finishing stroke, a ' clencher ' ; something that will 'irk' an opponent to beat ; (3) **Irking,** *ppl. adj.* irritating, troublesome ; (4) **Irksome,** *adj.* painful, uncomfortable, worrying.

(1) **Gall.** Mactaggart *Encycl.* (1824). (2) **Lei.**[1] That's a nirker ! (3) **Gall.** I could hear the irking and waesome yammer of my lady's supplication, Crockett *Standard Bearer* (1898) 299. (4) **Ayr.** Sirs, what I hae seen ! I had a very irksome dream, Fisher *Poems* (1790) 65.

2. *sb.* Weariness ; pain.

Gall. Say nought o' hell, that hole o' irk, Lauderdale *Poems* (1796) 8a.

[1. Ioy that we yrk noght in godis 30ke. Hampole (c. 1330) *Ps.* ii. 11. Sw. *yrka,* to urge, press (Widegren).]

IRKLE, see **Hurkle,** *v.*

IRM, *v.* Sc. Also in form **yirm** (Jam.). To whine, complain ; to question querulously and continuously. (Jam. *Suppl.*)

[Thou doost my herte to erme, Chaucer *C. T.* c. 312. Cp. OE. *geyrman,* to make miserable.]

IRON, *sb.* and *v.* Sc. Irel. Nhb. Cum. Yks. Lan. Chs. Nhp. Shr. Oxf. Bdf. Hrt. e.An. Wil. Som. Cor. Also written **airn** Sc. Lnk. Gall. N.I.[1] ; and in forms **ern** Slk. Cum.[1] ; **irn** Sh.I. ; **irne** Abd. See **Ire,** *sb.*[1] [airn, ai·ən.] 1. *sb.* In *comb.* (1) **Iron-back,** a large iron plate set against the back of the chimney ; (2) **-balls,** nodules of iron, 'cat-heads' ; (3) **-bar,** a crowbar ; (4) **-dish,** a frying-pan ; (5) **-eer** or **-ever,** iron-ore ; also used *attrib.* ; (6) **-eer-spot,** a spot on linen caused by oxide of iron ; (7) **-eery,** impregnated with iron-ore, chalybeate ; (8) **-flower,** the sheep's bit scabious, *Jasione montana* ; (9) **-fork,** a pitch-fork ; (10) **-grass,** (a) var. species of sedges growing in poor, clay pastures, esp. the spring sedge, *Carex praecox* ; (b) the bent-grass, *Aira caespitosa* ; (c) the common knot-grass, *Polygonum aviculare* ; (11) **-heater,** a cooking utensil, *gen.* made of iron wire or slender rods ; (12) **-house,** *obs.,* a room in prison where prisoners were put or kept in irons ; (13) **-knobs,** the hard-head, *Centaurea nigra* ; (14) **-moulded,** of potatoes : rusty-coloured and porous ; (15) **-moulds,** yellow lumps of earth or soft stone found in chalk ; (16) **-near,** see (5) ; (17) **-pear,** the white beam-tree, *Pyrus Aria* ; (18) **-sick,** see below ; (19) **-sided,** hardy, rough, unmanageable ; impudent, defiant ; (20) **-stone,** compact greenstone ; (21) **-stone-balls,** see (2) ; (22) **-tings,** fire-tongs ; (23) **-ub'n,** a flat-bottomed pan for baking in ; (24) **-weed,** (a) see (13) ; (b) the viper's bugloss, *Echium vulgare.*

(1) w.Som.[1] For the purpose of shielding the wall from the blows of logs thrown on the fire, and from the fire itself. These iron-backs were frequently ornamental in character. (2) Nhb.[1] (3) w.Som.[1] Plai·z tu lai·n Jŭmz yur uy·urn-baar. (4) w.Yks. (J.T.) (5) Cai.[1] Bog-iron ore. Iron-ever water, water impregnated with iron. Abd. D'ye think the water is less clear Comes frae my spoot ! Or is't because the iron eer Is a' run oot, Cadenhead *Bon-Accord* (1853) 158. (6) Abd. (Jam.) (7) Abd. (Jam.) Per. That water's awfu' ironeery. That's a fine drink o' ironeery water (G.W.). (8) Chs.[1] (9) Cum.[1] (10, a) Chs.[1] (b) Shr.[1] e) Hrt. (B. & H.) (11) Edb. When the [oat] cake is so hardened as to stand on edge, it is placed on an iron-heater, linked upon a bar of the grate, where it toasts leisurely, till it is perfectly dry, Pennecuik *Wks.* (1715) 85, ed. 1815. (12a) Lnk. In the iron-house he was robbed of all his money sent him by his friends, Wodrow *Ch. Hist.* (1721) IV. 177, ed. 1828. (13) Chs.[18] (14) Suf. Young *Annals Agric.* (1784–1815) V. 251. (15) Oxf. (Hall.) (16) Per. (G.W.) (17) Wil.[1] (18) n.Yks.[2] As when the metal bolts of a ship's timbers are worn with rust, so as to have little hold of the wood. 'She's iron-sick.' (19) e.An.[1] A boy who fears nobody, and plays all sorts of mischievous tricks, is called an iron-sided dog. e.Suf. That boy's a reglar iron-sided young devil. She be an iron-sided hussy. Not used of animals (F.H.). (20) Cor. Ramsay *Rock Spec.* (1862) 278. (21) Nhb. Grey thill, with iron-

stone-balls, *Borings* (1881) 203 ; (R.O.H.) ; Nhb.[1] (22) Slk. Carrying you out like a taed in the erntings, Hogg *Tales* (1838) 234, ed. 1866. (23) Cum.[14] A fire being placed on the lid as well as below the pan. Now superseded by cast-iron and sheet-iron ovens. (24, *a*) Nhp.[1] And iron-weed, content to share The meanest spot that spring can spare, Clare *Shep. Calendar* (1827) 47. (*b*) Bdf. Batchelor *Agric.* (1813) 321.

2. A sword.

Sc. Here stand up, out with your airn, Stevenson *Catriona* (1893) xii.

3. A horse-shoe.

Lnk. I there had stuid my waukit legs on, An' ca'd new airns a gey wheen naigs on, Murdoch *Doric Lyre* (1873) 26.

4. A steel implement used for boring a cheese. s.Chs.[1]

5. An oven or ' girdle ' for baking. Sh.I. (A.W.)

6. *pl.* Spurs. N.Cy.[1], Nhb.[1]

7. The coulter, sock, &c. of a plough.

Gall. It is never those who gain prizes . . . who are most useful ploughmen. . . They are . . . always running to the forge with their airns, Mactaggart *Encycl.* (1824) 270, ed. 1876. N.I.[1]

8. Thin plates of iron fastened on to the edges of the wooden soles of clogs to make them last longer.

Fif. The word 'swine' was considered unlucky among fisher folk ; as a counter-spell they touched the iron heels of their boots, crying, 'touch cauld airn,' Edwards *Mod. Poets,* 12th S. 54. w.Yks. (J.W.) Lan. Aw punced him weel wi these very clogs, nobbut they'n had new irons sin', Clegg *David's Loom* (1894) xix.

9. Phr. *to be new off the irons,* to have just finished one's course of study.

Sc. It had been originally applied to workmanship. . . Its determinate application seems to have been to money newly struck, which retained not only the impression but also the lustre (Jam.). Cai.[1]

10. *v.* To bore a cheese with an iron or scoop for the purpose of tasting it ; to taste a cheese. n.Cy. (Hall.), Chs. (C.J.V.), Chs.[1], s.Chs.[1]

11. To make cheese.

Lan. A farmer is said to begin ironing when he begins to make curd for cheese (W.H.T.) ; Bamford *Dial.* (1854) *Gl.*

IRONEN, *adj.* Som. Dev. Made of iron.

w.Som.[1] Very common. This use is emphatic—i.e. of iron and of nothing else. 'Aay nûv·ur dûd·n zee noa jis voaks vur tae·ureen u tloa·m-z aaw·urz bee ; wee shl bee u-foo·us t-ae·u uy·urneen dee·-shez un kuup·s neef wee bee u muy·n vur tu kee·p oa·urt.' nw.Dev.[1]

IRONY, *adj.* Sc. Also written **airny** Gall. Hard or strong as iron.

Sc. Their irony soles do never tire On stony ground, dub or mire, Graham *Writings* (1883) I. 107. Edb. Break the tyrant's ir'ny rod That desolates the plain, Learmont *Poems* (1791) 106. Gall. Thy airny joints what time can fade, . . My darling auld arm-chair, Mactaggart *Encycl.* (1824) 351, ed. 1876.

IRP, see **Erp.**

IRRESPONSAL, *adj. Obs.* Sc. Unable to respond to the claims of one's creditors.

But they shall prove irresponsal debtors, Rutherford *Lett.* (1765) I. No. 153 (Jam.).

IRY, *sb.* e.Yks.[1] [Not known to our correspondents.] Passion, anger, rage, fury.

IS, *conj.* Sh.I. Than. Cf. **as,** *conj.*

Mony a time we hae mair ta dū is we're fit for, *Sh. News* (Oct. 29, 1898).

ISAAC, *sb.* War. In phr. *to look like a throttled Isaac,* to look as if one couldn't move. See **Haysuck, 2.**

Might be applied to a man with a high collar on, or to any one very much 'got-up' (C.T.O.).

ISAAC, see **Haysuck.**

ISABELLA, *sb.* Yks. Stf. Der. Not. Lin. Brks. Lon. Ken. Sur. Sus. Hmp. Wil. Also in form **Isabellow** Yks. Not. Lin. A game played by young people. See below.

[Var. verses are sung while the game is being played, varying slightly from those given under **Wil.**] Yks. Gomme *Games* (1894) I. 253. Stf. The centre child pretends to be weeping ; another child stands outside the ring and goes to it ; when the two meet they kiss, *ib.* 255. n.Der. A ring is formed of young men and women, a young man being in the centre. He chooses a young woman at the singing of the fifth line, and then joins the ring, the girl remaining in the centre, *ib.* Lin. *ib.* 253. Brks. A ring is formed by the children (boys and girls) joining hands. Another child stands in the centre. The ring of children walk round while singing the verses. The singing is confined to the ring. When the centre child is told to 'choose' she selects a boy from the ring, who goes into the centre and they stand together. At the next verse these two children walk out of the ring arm-in-arm. When the next verse is sung they return, and again stand in the centre. At the next verse the boy pretends to put a ring on the girl's finger. They walk out of the ring when told to go to church (two children in the ring unclasping hands to let them walk out, and again clasping hands after they return), and kiss each other and shake hands when the two next verses are sung. The child who was first in the centre then joins the ring, and the game proceeds in the same way with the second child, who chooses in his turn. In the Fernham and Longcot version the one child leads the other out of the ring at 'go to church' with a graceful half-dancing motion, and back again in the same way, *ib.* 255. **Lon.** A handkerchief was laid on the ground and the two children stood on each side of it and clasped hands across it, *ib.* **Ken.** [Name Arabella used instead of Isabella], *ib.* 251. **Sur.** *ib.* 255. **Sus.** *ib.* 250. **Hmp.** [Name Elizabella], *ib.* 250, 253. **Wil.** ' Isabella, Isabella, Isabella, Farewell! Last night when I departed I left her broken-hearted ; Upon the steep mountain There stands a young man. Who'll you choose, love? [repeated three times] Farewell! Go to church, love,' &c. ' Say your prayers, love,' &c. ' Put your ring on,' &c. ' Come back, love,' &c. ' Roast beef and plum pudding,' &c. ' For our dinner to-day Kiss together, love,' &c., H. S. May *ib.* 249 ; The two children in the centre sing the verse ' Roast beef and plum-pudding.' They stand face to face, take hold of each other's hands, and sway their arms from side to side. The ring then sing the concluding verse. In those versions where ' say your prayers' and ' kneel down' occur, the two centre children kneel, and hold their open hands before them to imitate a book, *ib.* 255.

ISCA, *int.* Sc. n.Cy. Nhb. Also written **iska** N.Cy.[1]; **iskey** Frf. ; **iskie** Sc. (Jam.); and in forms **isk** Lnk.; **iskiss** Per. Gall. [i·aka, i·aki.] A call to a dog.
Sc. (Jam.) Frf. ' Puir doggie !' ' Doon, sir !' ' Fine fellow !' ' Iskey, iskey,' an' a' ither blandishments that mak' dogs friendly, Willock *Rosetty Ends* (1886) 136, ed. 1889. Per. *Obsol.* ' Iskis' was called to a dog by an old woman who placed a dish for him to lick (G.W.). Lnk. I cry'd ' Isk ! isk ! poor Ringwood, sairy man.' He wagg'd his tail, cour'd near, and lick'd my han', Ramsay *Poems* (ed. 1800) II. 9 (Jam.). Gall. Mactaggart *Encycl.* (1824). N.Cy.[1], Nhb.[1]

ISEL, ISERUM, see **Hustle,** *v.*[1], **Easle, Izle,** *sb.*[2], **Isrum.**
ISET, *adj.* Sh.I. Also written **iset-.** Of a bluish-grey colour ; also in *comp.* **Iset-gray.**
A skubby hask hings, icet-gray, Junda *Klingrahool* (1898) 22 ; Jakobsen *Norsk in Sh.* (1897) 110.

ISHAN, *sb.* Cor. [i·ʃən.] The dust or husks from winnowed corn.
Cor.[1] Take up the ishan and put it in the costan ; Cor.[2]
[OCor. *us*, the husk of corn, pl. *usion, ision,* Wel. *usion* (Williams).]

ISHE, *v. Obs.* Wxf.[1] To ask. 'Dinna ishe mee a raison.'
ISH-WISH, *int.* Sc. A call to a cat to come to its food. Gall. Mactaggart *Encycl.* (1824).

ISIL, see **Easle.**
ISING, *sb.* Sc. [ai·zin.] The silvering of a looking-glass.
Slk. Ae single lookin-glass in a' the house, gey an sair cracket, and the ising rubbed aff, Chr. North *Noctes* (ed. 1856) II. 53.

ISK, ISKA-BEHAGH, ISKEY, ISKIE, ISKISS, see **Isca, Usquebaugh.**
ISLAND, *sb.* Yks. Ken. 1. The Isle of Thanet.
Ken.[1] He lives up in the island, som'er.
2. A piece of land nearly surrounded by water. n.Yks. (I.W.)

ISLE, *sb.*[1] and *v.* Bnff.[1] 1. *sb.* Anger.
He wiz in an isle at 'im for deein' that.
2. *v.* To be angry.
He wiz jist islin' at 'im fin he widna dee fat he bade 'im.

ISLE, *sb.*[2] Lin. The Isle of Axholme.
n.Lin.[1] At Butterwick, in the Isle, Young *Agric.* (1799) 145 ; The Isle a reputation had, For Tory votes secure, *Election Sng.* (1852).
Hence **Islonian,** *sb.* a native of the Isle of Axholme.
n.Lin.[1] The Islonians destroyed his crops, Stonehouse *Hist. Axholme,* 110.

ISLE, see **Easle.**

ISLE-OF-WIGHT, *sb.* Hmp. I.W. In *comb.* (1) **Isle-of-Wight dog,** a fit of laziness ; (2) **—parson,** the cormorant, *Phalacrocorax carbo;* (3) **—rock,** a particular kind of very hard skim-milk cheese ; (4) **—vine,** (*a*) the white bryony, *Bryonia dioica;* (*b*) the black bryony, *Tamus communis.*
(1) I.W. You'v got the Isle of Wight dog (H.C.M.B.). (2) Hmp. (J.R.W.), Hmp.[1] (3) Hmp. (Hall.); Hmp.[1] Warner *Hist. I.W.* 292. (4) I.W. (B. & H.)

ISNET, *sb.* Wil. [i·znit.] ? The small bugloss, *Anchusa* (*Lycopsis*) *arvensis.* Davis *Agric.* (1813) ; Wil.[1]

I-SPY, see **Hie-spy.**
ISRAEL, *sb.* Suf. A fool, idiot.
e.Suf. I must be an Israel, if I could do that. He's a downright Israel (F.H.).

ISRUM, *sb.* Lin. Also written **izram** Lin.[1]; **izrosn-** n.Lin. ; and in form **iserum** Lin.[1] [i·zrəm.] A long, tedious tale.
Them's real owd isrums! *Lin. N. & Q.* II. 23 ; Lin.[1] I was surfeited with his iserum. n.Lin. Sutton *Wds.* (1881).

ISS, *adv.* War. Wor. Shr. Hrf. Glo. Suf. Wil. Som. Dev. Cor. Also written **hiss** Wil. Cor. [is.] 1. Yes.
War.[2], se.Wor.[1], Shr.[1] Hrf.[2] You shouldna say aye, Jemmy, you should say Iss. Glo. Iss, Miss—but 'ere her be, Gissing *Vill. Hampden* (1890) I. i. Suf.[1] s.Wil. Hiss sure mum, *Monthly Mag.* (1814) II. 114. Som. Aw iss, Agrikler *Rhymes* (1872) Title-page. Dev. Iss, iss, he'll do the feat, Peter Pindar *Royal Visit* (1795) II. 157, ed. 1824. Cor. ' Why, hiss,' zes Aant, Hunt *Pop. Rom. w.Eng.* (1865) 461, ed. 1896 ; Cor.[2] Iss a es.
2. *Comb.* **Iss faith, fay,** or **fie,** in good faith, certainly.
n.Dev. ' Iss fye, to-night,' saith Liz, Chanter *Witch* (1896) 37. Cor. And had a sweetheart too—iss fie! Forfar *Poems* (1885) 3 ; Cor.[2]

ISSE, ISSEL, ISSEN, see **Easse, Hisself.**
ISSLE, *adj.* Lin. [Not known to our correspondents.] [i·sl.] Quarrying term : near the stone.

ISSOL, see **Izle,** *sb.*[2]
IST, *sb.* Yks. Lan. Chs. Der. Ken. Also in forms **awst** w.Yks.[2] ; **icet** Chs.[1] [aist.] Ice.
w.Yks.[2] (s.v. Slurring ice). Lan. (S.W.), Chs.[1], nw.Der.[1], Ken. (G.B.)

ISTICK, *sb.* Sh.I. Also in form **jestick.** A slight, temporary frost ; cold weather with rain ; the same word as **Eastick.** (Coll. L.L.B.), S. & Ork.[1]

IT, *pron.* and *sb.* Var. dial. uses in Sc. Irel. Eng. and Amer. I. Gram. forms : (1) 'D, (2) Et, (3) Het, (4) Id, (5) 'T, (6) Ut. See **Hit.**
(1) Sc. After a verb. Still in common use on both sides of the Tweed (Jam. *Suppl.*). Cai.[1] When not at the beginning of a phr. or not emphatic. ' Hiv ye deen'd !' Nhb. (Jam. *Suppl.*) (2) n.Lan. Et went nineteen times round, *Lonsdale Mag.* (Jan. 1867) 269. Sur. He'll do et, Miss, dunno fear, Bickley *Sur. Hills* (1890) II. i. Dev. I know who'th a dood et, *Flk-Lore Jrn.* (1883) I. 334 ; Dreeskaur valyint men are about et, Baird *Sng. Sol.* (1860) iii. 7. (3) Som. Jennings *Obs. Dial. w.Eng.* (1825). (4) Cai.[1] When not at the beginning of a phr. or not emphatic. ' He leuch at 'id.' e.Lan.[1], m.Lan.[1] (5) n.Yks. In certain parts . . . the abbreviation ' 't ' for ' it ' is always made, e.g. ' he brak 't two ' ; ' fettle 't up.' The usage is not so common in other districts, Morris *Flk-Talk* (1892) 24. ne.Yks.[1] ' It ' is *gen.* abbreviated to ' 't,' esp. at the end of a word, as ' on't,' ' wi't.' w.Yks. (J.W.) w.Som.[1] When used as an abstract pronoun. ' Túd'n muy dhingz.' (6) Glo. I disproved o' ers doing ut at the time, Buckman *Darke's Sojourn* (1890) iv. Dor. Zilas well knows ut, *Windsor Mag.* (Mar. 1900) 418.
II. Dial. uses. 1. *pron.* In phr. *on it,* of it, its.
Shr.[1] In speaking of the smaller animals as of inanimate objects ; ' the track, hole, or marks on it ' ; ' the legs on it,' *Introd.* xlix.
2. *Possess.* Its.
n.Cy. (J.W.) Cum. As like it fadthur as owt can be, *Lonsdale Mag.* (July 1866) 25 ; Cum.[1] Wm. It fadther varra een, Briggs *Remains* (1825) 181. e.Yks. He tewk off his hat and put keea pot on iv it pleeace, Nicholson *Flk-Sp.* (1889) 36 ; e.Yks.[1] Tub hez a hooal iv it boddam, *MS. add.* (T.H.) w.Yks. If it tail heddn't been too long, Eccles *Leeds Olm.* (1877) 14 ; A so it faßta(r) jastado (J.W.). Lan.[1] If he can catch howd o' that dog he'll have it life, as what comes on it. e.Lan.[1] Chs.[1] The country people always use the neuter pronoun in speaking to little chil-

dren or pet animals. **s.Chs.**[1] It lit·l aan·ds bin dhaat· thin; yŭ)kn wel·i sey thróo ŭm [It little hands bin that thin, yŏ con welly sey through 'em] (s.v. Bark). **nw.Der.**[1] **Not.** It wouldn't tak' it food, not at no price (L.C.M.). **s.Not.** What es it got in it mouth? (J.P.K.) **sw.Lin.**[1] The bairn's hurten it arm. **Nhp.**[2] **Lei.**[1] It little face is ever so bad. [*Amer. Dial. Notes* (1896) I. 419.]

3. Used impersonally to introduce a statement, the specific subject being added subsequently ; see below.

Sc. (A.W.) **Lakel.** It is a pretty valley, this Longaleddale. It runs remarkably well, does that horse, BRIGGS *Remains* (1825) 185.

4. *Obs.* Used impersonally for 'there.'

Sc. O out it spak a bonny boy, JAMIESON *Pop. Ballads* (1806) I. 77 ; Then out it spak the lady, As she stood on the stair, *ib.* 179. **n.Sc.** Then out it speaks him, sweet Willie, And he spake aye thro' pride, BUCHAN *Ballads* (1828) I. 100, ed. 1875.

5. Used of persons of either sex, esp. of infants or as a term of contempt.

n.Cy., w.Yks. (J.W.) **m.Lan.**[1] Some fooak says id as iv they were tawkin' abeawt a hinseckt when they mecan their husband, child, wife, or parent. **n.Lin.**[1] What a bawbaw it is to call itsen a parson. What a gib it is to hev a babby. **Oxf.** (G.O.) **Dev.** 'Twas weeks and weeks afore the Squire got about again, .. and when he did, it was a changed man, CHANTER *Witch* (1896) iii.

6. Used of impersonal or collective things.

Oxf. (A.P.) **Dor.** [Used of] the impersonal class of unformed quantities of things, as a quantity of hair or wood or water, BARNES *Sng. Sol.* (1859) Notes iii. **w.Som.**[1] 'It' frequently takes the place of 'them,' when many animals or objects are referred to collectively.

7. *Interrog.* referring to a previous statement ; see below.

Wil.[1] We'm best be gwain, hadn't it? We can aal on us ha' a holiday to-day, can't it?

8. *sb.* In games: the 'he' or central figure, the person who has the innings. See Hit, **2.**

Sc. (A.W.) **Nhb.**[1] Now you're it ; gan on wi' ye. **s.Not.** Let's play at Willy Wancey ; I'll be it (J.P.K.).

IT, *dem. pron.* and *conj.* Nhb. Also in forms 'd, 't Nhb.[1] **1.** *dem. pron.* Used to give emphasis after an assertion : That. See **At,** *dem. pron.*

Ye can di'd yorsel ; it can ye. Aa had it here this minit ; it had aa (R.O.H.) ; Nhb.[1] Aa'l tell yor muthor ; it will aa.

2. *conj.* That. See **At,** *conj.*

It thaw [that thy], ROBSON *Sng. Sol.* (1859) Notes.

ITALIAN, *adj.* Dur. Yks. Nrf. Also in form (a)**tallion** e.Dur.[1] w.Yks. [ita·lian.] In *comb.* (1) **Italian iron,** an iron for crimping cap-frills ; (2) — **rat,** a small, red rat.

(1) **e.Dur.**[1] An iron tube about 6 in. long and pointed at one end. Into the tube is inserted a heater. .. Still to be seen in many cottages. **w.Yks.** (C.C.) (2) **Nrf.** These rats ... go by the name of 'Italian rats,' and 'ship rats' ; for old fenmen say they come from foreign ships wrecked on the coast, EMERSON *Birds* (1895) 361.

ITCHING, *ppl. adj.* Lan. Stf. Lin. War. Wor. Glo. [i·tʃin.] **1.** In *comb.* **Itching-berries,** the fruit of the dog-rose, *Rosa canina.*

Lan. (B. & H.) **Stf.** **War., Wor., Glo.** NORTHALL *Flb-Phr.* (1894). **War.**[2] So called because children put them down their playmates' backs, to induce irritation.

2. *Phr. may you have perpetual itching without ever scratching,* a humorous form of curse used by women when they quarrel. **n.Lin.**[1]

ITCH, IT(E, ITE, see Hitch, *v.*[1], **Eat, Out.**

ITEM, *sb.* n.Cy. Yks. Lan. Chs. Der. Lin. War. Wor. Shr. Hrf. Sus. Som. Dev. Cor. Also in form **nitem** Chs.[1] [ai·təm.] **1.** In phr. *to care not an item,* to care nothing at all. **w.Yks.** (A.C.), (J.W.)

2. A hint ; a signal ; a cue.

n.Cy. GROSE (1790). **w.Yks.** HUTTON *Tour to Caves* (1781). **Lan.** I'll gi' yo th' item when we're ready, WAUGH *Heather* (ed. Milner) I. 25. **Chs.**[1] Oo gen him th' item. **s.Chs.**[1] Oo gy'en mi dhŭ ahy tŭm tŭ see· nŭth·in [Hoo gen me the item to see (= say) nothin']. **nw.Der.**[1] **Lin.** He gave me an item of it, THOMPSON *Hist. Boston* (1856) 711 ; **Lin.**[1] When I got the item, I bought the shares. **War.**[2] ; **War.**[4] I can 'zoon manage to give you an item or two as to what he's about now. **s.Wor.**[1] I whistled to Tim to give 'im an item as the gaffer were a-comin'. **Shr.**[1] I sid the Maister comin', so I gid 'im the item. **Hrf.** *N. & Q.* (1853) 1st S. vii. 544. **Sus.**[1] **Sus.** HOLLOWAY.

3. An intention, purpose ; a crafty design ; a trick ; a fancy, fad.

w.Som.[1] Dhaat wuz dhur uy·tum. He've a got th' item now,

vor to zee whe'r he can't save a lot o' coal way doin something to the furnace door. **Dev.** They urned out o' the gate and back under the hedge to the very same place where we vound 'em at first. That was their item [of a covey of partridges], *Reports Provinc.* (1887) 10 ; Her's za vull ov items as a egg's vull ov mayte, HEWETT *Peas. Sp.* (1892). **nw.Dev.**[1]

4. *pl.* Fidgets, antics.

w.Som.[1] 'Nŭv·ur oa·n buyd kwuy·ut, gau̇t̄·moa·ur uy·tumz-n u daan·seen bae·ur.' One of the commonest of sayings. 'All full of his items.' **Dev.**[1] Thee cast'n think what hanticks and items a had, **2.** **n.Dev.** ROCK *Jim an' Nell* (1867) Gl. **nw.Dev.**[1]

Hence (1) **Iteming,** (a) *prp.,* and *ppl. adj.* fidgeting, trifling ; (b) *sb.* trifling, nonsense ; (2) **Itemy,** (a) *adj.* trifling ; tricky, fidgety ; of horses : frisky, restless ; (b) *sb.* a trifle.

(1, *a*) **Som.** I'd be about little iteming partridges (L.K.L.). **w.Som.**[1] Why's-n mind thy work, and not bide itemin there? **Dev.** They stood there iteming with one another, *Reports Provinc.* (1897). **nw.Dev.**[1] **n.Dev.** Had 'e bin always iteming, ROCK *Jim*'*an*' *Nell* (1867) st. 90. (*b*) **Cor.** A bit outspoken, but I liked un the better ; there wasn't no iteming with 'im, QUILLER-COUCH *J. Vernos,* 12. (2, *a*) **w.Som.**[1] I don't like thick mare 't-all, her's zo uncommon itemy. **Dev.** Night an' day her'm talking 'bout her old itemy things, PEARD *Mother Molly* (1889) 90 ; My measter ... he's a bit itemy when he's about the place hisself, HARTLEY *Evening with Hodge* in *Eng. Illus. Mag.* (June 1896) 256. **nw.Dev.**[1] (*b*) **Dev.** And how many other itemies—as Tabby Tapscott calls them—the Lord only knoweth, who made them, BLACKMORE *Kit* (1890) xiv.

5. *pl.* Trifles, finery. Cf. **hitem.**

Cor. Dressed out with flowers and such items (M.A.C.).

ITERIDAN, *sb.* Stf. A trivial occasion ; the same word as **Aitredan.**

s.Stf. Her dolls her best cloos on at ivery iteridan, PINNOCK *Blk. Cy. Ann.* (1895).

ITHER, *sb.* Sc. Lin. [i·ðə(r.] The udder of a cow, mare, or goat. Cai.[1] Lin.[1] n.Lin. SUTTON *Wds.* (1881). [Iddyr or vddyr of a beeste, *ulcer*, *Prompt.*]

ITHER, see **Other.**

ITLE, *v.* Lin. [ai·tl.] To have an uncertain footing ; to sway to and fro.

s.Lin. See how he itles? The bains wor itlin' on them high rails in sich a wai they ommost maide mi heart come i' mi mouth (T.H.R.).

ITS, *poss. pron.* Sc. Irel. In *comb.* **Its lane** or **lone,** alone, by itself.

Sc. (JAM., s.v. Lane.) **Abd.** I see a house it's lane, ROSS *Helenore* (1768) 82, ed. 1812. **n.Ir.** It began to play its lone, *N. & Q.* (1870) 4th S. v. 23 ; **N.I.**[1] Can the chile go it's lone?

ITSELF, *pron.* Irel. Yks. Nhp. **1.** Himself or herself. **w.Yks.**[1]

2. As a term of endearment : yourself.

w.Yks.[1] Freq. used when addressed to a child, 'Tak care on jtsell.' **Nhp.**[1] To a little child, chiefly when attempting to walk. 'Take care of itsell, there's a little dear.'

3. *Phr. to be disguised itself,* to be drunk.

w.Ir. But, if I'm disguised itself, I'll make you know the differ, LOVER *Leg.* (1848) I. 197.

IT(T, ITTER, see **Yet, Etter, Hetter,** *adj.*

IULGA, *sb.* Sh.I. (JAM.) An uneasy, rapid motion of the waves.

IV, see **In,** *prep.,* **Of.**

IVELL, *v.* War.[2] [i·vl.] To pilfer, rifle.

IVEN, IVER, see **Ivin, Eaver,** *sb.*[1], **Uver, Hover,** *v.*[1]

IVERLY, *adv.* Dur. Cum. The same word as **Everly.**

s.Dur. She's at it iverly. He was iverly doing it, *Weardale Alm.* (J.E.D.) **Cum.**[4] 'How often do you take your ale?' 'Yall? I tak it iverly!' 'Iverly!' 'Ey, ebben endways away,' GIBSON, 183.

IVERS, *sb. pl.* Dev. Also written **hivers.** [i·vəz.] In phr. *My ivers!* My eyes! an exclamation of surprise. Cf. **eyemers.**

'My ivers!' ejaculated Tom, STOOKE *Not Exactly,* i ; My hivers! hur zot too, an holler'd an skritch'd, NATHAN HOGG *Poet. Lett.* (1847) 48, ed. 1865. **nw.Dev.** The commonest expression of surprise. 'My hivers, 'ot a booty' (R.P.C.).

IVERSOME, *adv.* Lakel.[2] [i·vəsəm.] Always, 'ever-some.' 'Iversome at yan aboot it.'

IVIGAR, *sb.* *Obs.* Or.I. The sea-urchin, ? *Echinus marinus.*

(JAM.) ; There is one Shell-fish of a round figure, the skine above the shell being thick set with prickles, they call them Ivigars, WALLACE *Desc. Or. I.* (1693) 17, ed. 1883 ; The common people reckon the meat of the Sea Urchin or Ivegars, as they call them, a great rarity, and use it oft instead of butter, *ib.* 186.

IVIN, *sb.* n.Cy. Nhb. Cum. Yks. Lan. Chs. Der. Lin. Also written **iven** n.Cy.; **ivine** n.Lin.; and in forms **hiven** Nhb.[1]; **hyvin** n.Cy. Cum.[1] e.Yks.; *pl.* **ivvens** Chs.[18]; **ivvins** e.Lan.[1] [ai·vin, i·vin.] The ivy, *Hedera Helix.*

n.Cy. GROSE (1790) ; (J.H.); Nhb.[1], Cum.[1] n.Yks. Green ivin i' lang narra glasses, LINSKILL *Betw. Heather and N. Sea* (1884) lvi ; n.Yks.[123] e.Yks. MARSHALL *Rur. Econ.* (1788). m.Yks.[1] w.Yks. T'ivin weeant mak t'hahse damp if yeh nobbud cut it cloisish to t'wall, BANKS *Wkfld. Wds.* (1865) ; w.Yks.[1235] Lan. It's groon o'er wi' ivin, BRIERLEY *Red Wind.* (1868) ii ; Lan.[1] e.Lan.[1] Clusters of ivy bushes. Chs.[18], nw.Der.[1] Lin. They niver 'ed seed sich ivin' as graw'd hall ower the brick, TENNYSON *Owd Rod* (1889). n.Lin. *Lin. N. & Q.* I. 91 ; n.Lin.[1]

Hence **Ivind,** *adj.* ivied. n.Yks.[2]

[OE. *ifegn*, 'hedera' (*Corpus*) ; see SWEET *O. E. T.* 59.]

IVOLE, see **Evil,** *sb.*[2]

IVORY, *sb.* Irel. Not. Lin. Rut. Hrt. e.An. Also written **ivery** n.Lin. sw.Lin.[1] [ai·v(ə)ri.] The ivy, *Hedera Helix.*

N.I.[1], Not.[1] n.Lin. *Lin. N. & Q.* I. 91 ; n.Lin.[1] s.Lin. *Lin. N. & Q.* I. 49. sw.Lin.[1] The ivery had grown thruff the roof. Rut.[1] I can't attend to you now, miss: I'm got to coot the ivory. Hrt. (H.G.), e.An.[1] Nrf. Soon the little nest is begun . . . in an ' ivory bush,' EMERSON *Birds* (ed. 1895) 56. Suf. (C.T.) e.Suf. One very rarely hears anything but Ivory from the common people (F.H.). Ess. (B. & H.)

IVRY, *adj.* Cum.[4] In phr. *ivry whupwhile,* every now and then. Cf. **every.**

Cum.[4] He hed teh gah for't ivery whupwhile, SARGISSON *Joe Scoap* (1881) 73.

IVVEN, IVVENS, IVVINS, IVVERLY, see **Even, Ivin, Everly.**

IVVY, *sb.* Yks. [Not known to our correspondents.] A sheep's heart.

w.Yks. Picking up the ' ivvy,' as old Clay used to call it, BINNS *Vill. to Town* (188a) 110.

IVY, *sb.* Sc. n.Cy. Nhb. Glo. Ken. Hmp. Wil. Dev. Also in form **hivy** Dev. [ai·vi.] In *comp.* (1) **Ivy-drum,** the stem of an ivy-bush which grows round the trunk of another tree ; (2) **-flower,** the common hepatica, *Anemone Hepatica* ; (3) **-girl,** *obs.,* a figure in human shape made of ivy or corn ; see below ; (4) **-owl,** the tawny owl, *Syrnium aluco* ; (5) **-tod,** an ivy-bush.

(1) Hmp.[1] Dev. How thick those ivy drums are, *Reports Provinc.* (1884) aa. (a) Glo. (B. & H.) ; Glo.[1] (3) Ken. A figure in human shape composed of some of the best corn ears, which is brought home with the last load of corn, and is supposed to entitle the harvesters to a supper, BRAND *Pop. Antiq.* (ed. 1870) II. 14 ; Ken.[1] It was the custom on Shrove Tuesday in w.Ken. to have two figures in the form of a boy and girl, made one of holly, the other of ivy. A group of girls engaged themselves in one part of a village in burning the holly-boy, which they had stolen from the boys, while the boys were to be found in another part of the village burning the ivy-girl which they had stolen from the girls, the ceremony being, in both cases, accompanied by loud huzzas (s.v. Holly-boys) ; Ken.[2] (4) Nhb.[1] Wil. SMITH *Birds* (1887) 111. (5) Sc. Look out from amang your curls then like a wild cat out of an ivy-tod, SCOTT *Rob Roy* (1817) xxxv. N.Cy.[1], Nhb.[1] ! ne.Glo. You look like an owl in an ivy-tod, *Household Wds.* (1885) No. 217, 144. Dev. Stained and time-bitten, wi' hivy-tods in the winder-'oles, PHILLPOTTS *Dartmoor* (1895) 192, ed. 1896.

IWIS, *adv.* ? *Obs.* Sc. Also in form **awis.** Certainly. Yie'll nae do that, awis, GROSE (1790) *MS. add.* (C.)

[*I-wis,* certainly, DOUGLAS *Eneados, Gl.* OE. *gewis,* certain, so EFris. (KOOLMAN).]

IX, IXE, see **Ax,** *sb.*[1], **Hike.**

IXEY-PIXEY, *adj.* Sc. Equally matched.

Per. Not uncommon. 'Ixey pixey, barley straw, Nine nips is the law ; Nip me now, nip me then, Nip me gin I f—t again.' This saved the misbehaving boy from punishment. *Local Rime* (G.W.). Fif. It's about ixey-pixey. The French girl's gotten the features ; Jean's a ' strapper,' MELDRUM *Margrédel* (1894) 191.

IZED, IZEL, see **Izzard, Easle, Izle,** *sb.*[2]

IZEY-TIZEY, *sb.* and *adj.* Dev. 1. *sb.* Uncertainty. (HALL.) [Not known to our correspondents.]
2. *adj.* Uncertain, wavering, undecided.

Dev.[5] Used when speaking of persons of hesitating character. ' Tidden wan bit ov use to ask he ort,—he's that izey-tizey you nivver knawth what he maynth tû dû.'

IZLE, *sb.*[1] n.Cy. Cum. Wm. Lan. [ai·zl] 1. A hoar-frost. N.Cy.[1], Wm. & Cum.[1] 2. An icicle. e.Lan.[1]

[L. Du. *ijsel,* sleet, glazed frost, rime.]

IZLE, *sb.*[2] Sc. Cum. Yks. Chs. Der. Lin. Also written **izel** w.Yks.[2] sw.Lin.[1]; **issol** Cum.[14]; **izel** Slk. Cum.[1] n.Lin. sw.Lin.[1] [ai·zl.] 1. A smut or flake of soot from a chimney ; a hot cinder ; *gen.* in *pl.* See **Easle.**

Dmf. She lay 'mang the black izles, CROMEK *Remains* (1810) 174. Slk. Bryht til ane izel reide, HOGG *Poems* (ed. 1865) 173. Cum.[14], n.Yks.[2], w.Yks.[2], s.Chs.[1] Der. The furniture is covered with izles, *Monthly Mag.* (1815) II. 297. Lan. MILLER & SKERTCHLY *Fenland* (1878) iv. n.Lin. SUTTON *Wds.* (1881) ; n.Lin.[1] sw.Lin.[1] My word, how the isels come down ! What wi' the smoke and the isels, things soon get ditted up in a market-town. It's not only the smoke, it's the isels from the straw.
2. *pl.* Vapoury spots which float before the eyes when they are weak or the health is out of order ; *fig.* blemishes.

n.Yks.[2] s.Chs.[1] An old man suffering from cataract told me ' won ahy wûz klee'n gon, ûn dhûr wûz ahy·zlz ûfoa·r tûdh·ûr.'

IZLE-BONE, *sb.* n.Yks.[2] The share-bone, ' ice-bone.'

IZRAM, IZROM, see **Isrum.**

IZZARD, *sb.* and *adj.* Sc. Nhb. Dur. Cum. Yks. Lan. Chs. Der. Lin. Nhp. Glo. Suf. Wil. Amer. Also in forms **huzzat** w.Yks.; **huzzet** Lan.; **ized** Glo. ; **izot** w.Yks.; **izzad** e.Yks.[1]; **izzart** n.Yks.[2]; **izzat** Per. ; **izzed** w.Yks.; **izzert** Cum.[14]; **izzet** Per. N.Cy.[1] w.Yks.[124]; **izzit** Per. w.Yks.; **uzzard** s.Chs.[1] Nhp.[12]; **uzzit** Lan.[1] nw.Der.[1] [i·zəd, i·zət.] 1. *sb.* The letter *z* ; also *fig.* an oddity.

Per. Wee curly Mary is puzzled at D, . . But Charlie's . . . forrit at izzit, STEWART *Sketches* (1857) 19 ; For he was a' thrawn cast an' wast like an izzat, HALIBURTON *Fields* (1890) 132. Ayr. Crumple us up like ony izzard, An' then devour us, AINSLIE *Poems* (ed. 1892) 215. N.Cy.[1], Nhb.[1], Dur.[1] Cum.[14] Old. n.Yks.[2], e.Yks.[1] w.Yks. Which wor a A, or which wor a huzzat, it ad a capt a antequarian toa nawn, TOM TREDDLEHOYLE *T'French Exhebishan* (c. 1856) 15 ; w.Yks.[124], Lan.[1], s.Chs.[1], nw.Der.[1], Lin.[1] Nhp.[1] ' Izzard, Izzard, Izzard, I. Izzard, Izzard, izzard, I.' Often repeated among school-boys as a Tell, to decide who is to commence a game ; Nhp.[2], Suf.[1] Wil. SLOW *Gl.* (189a) ; Wil.[1] Still in use in s.Wil. ; Wil.[2] [Amer. From a to izzard, from beginning to end, from first to last, GREEN *Virginia Flk-Sp.* (1899).]

Hence **Izzardly,** *adv.* to the last degree.

Glo. The bull frightened him most izedly (E.S.).
2. *Phr.* *as crooked as an izzard,* deformed in person ; perverse in disposition.

n.Yks.[2] w.Yks. Rhumatiz creeps inta foaks' elbows an' knees an' macks em az crook't as huzzats, TOM TREDDLEHOYLE *Bairnsla Ann.* (1856) 31 ; (J.T.) Lan. When I're th' age o' yon lass, I're as straight as a pickin-peg. But now . . . I'm as croot as a huzzet, BRIERLEY *Red Wind.* (1868) ii. s.Chs.[1] Still occas. used.
3. *adj.* Zig-zag.

Per. But let a shark . . . Soom round him, shawin' izzet teeth, HALIBURTON *Horace* (1886) 8.

J

JA(A, JAAGER, JAALE, JAAP, see Jaw, *sb.*[1], *v.*[2], Jagger, Jail, *v.*[2], Jaup, *v.*[1]

JAAMBLE, *v.* Sc. Also in form jaumle. To jumble; to shake; to mix by agitation. GROSE (1790) *MS. add.* (C.)

JAB, *v.*[1] and *sb.* Sc. Nhb. Cum. Yks. Also Nrf. ? Dev. Amer. Also in form jaub Ayr. [dɡab, dɡæb.] 1. *v.* To prick sharply; to thrust, pierce, stab; to peck as a bird. Cf. job, *v.*[1]

Slk. (JAM.) Nrf. He'd [the bittern] a jabbed my eyes out if he'd got at 'em, EMERSON *Birds* (ed. 1895) 205. [Amer. If your butcher is going to stab Markley, you'll oblige me by telling him that I want him to jab him deep, ADELER *Elbow Room* (1876) xxv.] 2. To crush, squeeze.

n.Yks.[4] Ah've gitten mah finger sadly jabbed wi' t'yat.

3. *Fig.* To ' shut up,' embarrass.

Lnk. Shoving into her plate the toughest bits o' girsle he could pick out o' the dinner stew, so as to effectively 'jab up' her clackin' tongue, MURDOCH *Readings* (1895) I. 10.

4. *sb.* A sharp thrust or stab; a prick, peck; a slight blow which frightens rather than hurts. Also used *fig.*

Ayr. I've seen yer screed, oh guid forgie Yer harden'd heart for jaubs at me! WHITE *Jottings* (1879) 226. Slk. (JAM.) Nhb. A jab i' the eye (R.O.H.); Nhb.[1], Cum.[4] ?Dev. A jab in the back with a Spanish dagger, MORTIMER *Tales Moors* (1895) 237.

JAB, *v.*[2] Cum.[1] [dɡab.] To spill. Cf. jabble, *v.* 2. She brought milk in a can, and jab't it ower at iv'ry step.

JABART, *sb.* Sc. Also in form jaabard Cai.[1] [dɡaˑbət, -əd.] 1. A lean, worthless horse; any animal in a feeble, weak condition.

n.Sc. (JAM.), Cai.[1] Mry. Jabart, a starved horse, and unfit for service, *Gl. Surv.* (JAM.) 2. A lean fish of one of the larger kinds, esp. a large, lean cod.

Cai.[1] Mry. Fish out of season, as a haddock in January, *Gl. Surv.* (JAM.)

JABB, *sb.*[1] ? *Obs.* Sc. A fishing-net; see below.

Inv. The best and most expeditious way of catching the cuddie . . . is with a sort of creel, called jabb. The jabb commonly consists of three or four strong rods, from 8 to 10 feet long, laid across each other in the middle, and gently bent upwards, till they are fixed at the ends to a large hoop, from 4 to 6 feet in diameter, which forms its mouth; on the inside it is lined with a narrow net, made for the purpose to retain the fish and let out the water, tightly tied to its ribs and mouth, *Statist. Acc.* XVI. 150 (JAM.)

JABB, *v.* and *sb.*[2] Sc. [dɡab.] 1. *v.* To weary, tire out, exhaust.

Bnff.[1] He dreeve the nout our fast, an' jabbit thim or they wan t' the market. He traivelt abeen forty mile yesterday, an' jabbit himsel' athegeethir. Abd. SHIRREFS *Poems* (1790) *Gl.* (JAM.) 2. *sb.* A big, lean, uncomely person; a big-boned, lean animal, with its strength nearly exhausted. Bnff.[1]

JABBER, *v.*[1] and *sb.* In *gen.* dial. and colloq. use in Sc. and Eng. Also in form jaubber Per. [dɡaˑbə(r, dɡæˑbə(r).] 1. *v.* To chatter, talk idly; to talk rapidly and indistinctly. Cf. gabber.

Per. (G.W.) Lth. A ghaist sat jabberin' on an auld heid-stane, SMITH *Merry Bridal* (1866) 52. n.Cy. (J.W.) Lan. He's jabberin all th' day o'er (S.W.). Chs.[13] Hrf. Them as jabbers too fast iz niniamerz (*Coll.* L.L.B.). Hmp., Sus. HOLLOWAY. Som. Jabberen' every language as was ever heard, LEITH *Lemon Verbena* (1895) 131. w.Som.[1]

Hence (1) Jabbering, *ppl. adj.* chattering, talking idly; (2) Jabberknowl or ·nowl, *sb.* a prating blockhead; a term of contempt for an ignorant person; cf. jobbernowl; (3) Jabberment, *sb.* idle talk, chatter.

(1) Sc. Hoot! jabberin bodies, wha could understand them, RAMSAY *Remin.* (1872) 109. (2) n.Cy. GROSE (1790) *Suppl.* Dur. It's nee oads whether ye meet wuv a jabernowl er a biak towght en, EGGLESTONE *Betty Podkin's Visit* (1877) 6. (3) w.Som.[1] There wadn not one bit o' sense in it, I 'sure 'e 'twas nort but a jabberment from fust to last.

2. To scold; to 'jaw.'

War. If she jabbers at me, I can't abide it, GEO. ELIOT *F. Holt* (1866) I. 202.

3. *sb.* Chatter, idle talk.

Frf. The puir foreign bodies couldna understand onything but their ain ill-faured gibberish, an' only screamed back a lot o' jabbers, WILLOCK *Rosetty Ends* (1886) 188, ed. 1889. Per. (G.W.) N.Cy.[1] Lakel.[2] Ther jabber's nivver diun. Cum.[2] Yks. Then, will ye stop yer jabber an' go yer ways! *Farquhar Frankheart*, 67. w.Yks.[4], Chs.[3], s.Lin. (T.H.R.), Nhp.[1], Brks.[1], Hnt. (T.P.F.), Suf.[1] s.Cy. HOLLOWAY. w.Som.[1], Cor. (J.W.)

4. The jaw; the under-jaw of a fish.

w.Som.[1] When you hook 'em in the jabber you can catch 'em. Cor. (J.W.); Cor.[3] The upper jaw.

JABBER, *v.*[2] Cum. To bespatter or splash with mud. *Gen.* in *pp.* Cf. jabble, *v.* 2, jarble, *v.*

' Thou'l be jabbered up to the arse' was said to an old lady who was going to walk up a dirty lane (W.K.).

JABBLE, *v.* and *sb.*[1] Sc. Irel. n.Cy. Nhb. Cum. Also in form jaible N.Cy.[1] Nhb.[1] [dɡaˑbl.] 1. *v.* Of water: to ripple, break in small waves. To agitate or shake the liquid contents of a vessel.

Bnff.[1] (s.v. Geeble). Cld. (JAM.) Gall. The tide that came . . . jabbling along the side of the boat, CROCKETT *Raiders* (1894) xxxiii. Ant. *Ballymena Obs.* (1892). N.Cy.[1], Nhb.[1]

Hence Jabbled, *ppl. adj.* agitated, stormy.

ne.Sc. The Gordonhaven men would . . . hold fearlessly out to the fishing ground, and from its jabbled waters oft return with a goodly catch of prime haddocks, *Gordonhaven* (1887) vii.

2. To spill; to bespatter, wet, bedew. Also with *up* and *oot our.* Bnff.[1] (s.v. Geeble). N.Cy.[1], Cum.[4] Cf. jarble, *v.*

3. To cook badly or with a want of skill. Bnff.[1] (s.v. Geeble). 4. To use constantly as an article of food. *ib.*

5. *sb.* A slight movement or ripple on the surface of water; a sea with small broken waves.

Or.I. The short leaping of waves in conflicting tides is a 'jabble' (S.A.S.). Cai.[1] Abd. The jabble o' the jaws [waves] again the rocks, MACDONALD *Sir Gibbie* (1879) l. Gall. The wavelets broke on my back and upon the raft at my chin with a little jabble of sound, CROCKETT *Standard Bearer* (1898) 51; MACTAGGART *Encycl.* (1824). N.I.[1], Cum.[4]

6. A confused mixing of a liquid with its sediment; *fig.* turmoil, confusion.

Cai.[1] Per. Carmichael's mind was in a 'jabble' that day, IAN MACLAREN *K. Carnegie* (1896) 307. Frf. There was a terrible jabble of emotions, MELDRUM *Margrédel* (1894) 101.

7. A quantity of liquid or half-liquid food; a quantity of any kind of liquid; soup.

Bnff.[1] When a large quantity is spoken of 'jabble' is used (s.v. Geeble). Abd. Meg saird them first wi' some jabble To ground their wame, SHIRREFS *Poems* (1790) 211.

Hence (1) **Jabblick**, *sb.* a quantity of worthless liquid or half-liquid food ; used as a dim. of 'jabble' ; (2) **Jabblin**, *ppl. adj.* of liquids : weak, washy ; (3) **Jabbloch**, *sb.* a quantity of liquid or half-liquid food ; weak, watery, spirituous liquor.

(1) **Bnff.**[1] (s.v. Geeblick). (2) **Gall.** We had nae jabblin thing like scaud ava to sipple wi', MACTAGGART *Encycl.* (1824) 27, ed. 1876. (3) **Bnff.**[1] (s.v. Geebloch). **Gall.** MACTAGGART *Encycl.* (1824).

JABBLE, *sb.*[2] Sc. [Not known to our correspondents.] A large, blunt needle or knife.

Sc. MACKAY *Gems of Sng.* (1883) *Gl.* **Rnf.** PICKEN *Poems* (1788) *Gl.* (JAM.)

JABBY, *adj.* Yks. [dʒaˑbi.] Saucy, insolent.

e.Yks. *Leeds Merc. Suppl.* (May 19, 1894) ; **e.Yks.**[1] *MS. add.* (T.H.)

JABERS, *sb.* Irel. Slang. Also written **jabbers** ; and in form **japers.** [dʒēˑbə(r)z.] An exclamation or quasi-oath.

Ir. But be Japers, I got sick of it, CARLETON *Fardorougha* (1848) xvi ; Bejabers, you've got it now, BARLOW *Lisconnel* (1895) 58 ; A head wind, be jabbers ! NISBET *Bail Up* (1890) 265 (FARMER) ; Arrah, be jabbers ! but that's the foinest song I have listened to since I left Ould Oirland, *ib. Bushranger's Sweetheart* (1892) 152. **n.Ir.** Neighbours (an sthrangers, be jabers!), *Lays and Leg.* (1884) 44. **Ant.** Oh japers Cripes [Christ] (S.A.B.). **Slang.** BAUMANN *Londonismen* (1887).

JACE, *sb.* ? *Obs.* Dev. [Not known to our correspondents.] A kind of fringe. (HALL.)

[The same word as older E. *jess*, used in *pl.* of the silken straps attached to the legs of a hawk (SHAKS. *Oth.* III. iii. 261). Iesses for a hauke, *get* (pl. *ges*), PALSGR. (1530).]

JACEY, see **Jersey.**

JACHELT, *pp.* Sc. [dʒaˑx̣lt.] Bent, blown to one side by the wind. Cf. **jaffled.**

Ayr. That farm ye see wi' the trees jachelt a' to the tae side, JOHNSTON *Kilmallie* (1891) I. 84.

JACK, *sb.* Var. dial. uses in Sc. Irel. and Eng. Also in forms **jaak**- Nhb.[1] ; **jag**- w.Yks.[2] ; **jaik**- Lnk. [dʒak, dʒæk.] **1.** In *comb.* (1) **Jack-about**, a person not engaged in any particular business ; a 'Jack of all trades' ; (2) — **Adams**, a noodle, simpleton ; (3) **-alally**, a foolish person ; (4) **-baal**, a boys' game resembling 'rounders' ; (5) **-band**, a *fig.* expression for the course of the year ; (6) — **Blunt**, a person who speaks his mind freely ; (7) **-bolts**, potatoes ; (8) **-boot**, a long boot, reaching above the knee ; (9) **-catch**, a catch used to prevent corves running back ; (10) **-chain**, (*a*) the endless chain by which the spit is driven ; see (18) ; (*b*) a peculiar chain made of thin links of iron ; (11) — **durnals** or **durnils**, the tubers of the pig-nut, *Bunium flexuosum* ; also called **Jacky-jurnals** (q.v.), s.v. **Jacky** ; (12) **-end**, a fragment or small remainder ; (13) **-engine**, the engine for raising men, débris, &c., in a sinking pit ; (14) **-head**, the high set of pumps in a coal-mine, in the arrangement when the pumping-engine has a back beam ; (15) **-head-set**, the set of pumps in the jack-head-staple (q.v.) ; (16) **-head-staple**, a small pit in which the feed set for the boilers is *gen.* placed ; (17) **-idle**, a crook with a swivel in it ; see below ; (18) — **Jennet**, see (11) ; (19) — **Jesums**, see below ; (20) **-jumper**, the breast-bone or 'merry-thought' of any poultry or edible bird ; see below ; (21) — **jurnals**, see (11) ; (22) **-man**, (*a*) the game of 'follow my leader' ; (*b*) a cream-cheese ; (23) **-neck**, the top or ridge tile of a sandstone roofing slate ; (24) **-pit**, a shallow pit-shaft in a mine, communicating with an overcast, or at a fault ; (25) **-plane**, a coarse plane used to take off the roughest points from timber ; also used as *v.* ; (26) **-pudding**, a merry Andrew, a clown ; (27) **-rag**, an individual, *gen.* in phr. *every jack-rag* ; (28) **-roll**, a windlass ; (29) **-roll rope**, the rope used on a windlass or jack-roll ; (30) **-rot**, a disease among sheep ; (31) **-rowler**, a machine to tighten wire fencing ; (32) **-sharp**, (*a*) a smart, tingling frost ; (*b*) the holly ; (33) **-sprat**, a dwarfish, insignificant-looking person ; (34) **-steel**, a game of jumping on the backs of others ; (35) **-stone** or **-stones**, (*a*) a children's game played with stones, pebbles, &c. ; (*b*) small pebbles or stones, &c., used in the game of **Jack-stones** ; see **27** ; (*c*) small cobbles of coal ; (36) **-straw**, (*a*) a straw elevator ; a man who carries straw

from the threshing-machine to the stack ; (*b*) a thing of the least value ; (37) **-straws**, the ribwort plantain, *Plantago lanceolata* ; (38) **-tiles**, roofing-tiles ; (39) **-tooth**, a back tooth ; (40) **-towel**, a long narrow towel, with the ends joined together and suspended on a roller ; a coarse linen towel ; see **19** ; (41) **-weaver**, the coloured dancing reflection of sunlight cast by a swinging prism ; (42) **-weed**, the corn crowfoot, *Ranunculus arvensis* ; (43) **-weight**, the weight by which a spit was turned ; see **18** ; (44) — **West**, a sty on the eye-lid ; (45) **-whore**, a strong Amazonian sailor's trull.

(1) **w.Yks.**[2 5] (2) **e.Suf.** (F.H.) (3, 4) **Nhb.**[1] (5) **w.Yks.**[3] 'When the jackband is turned,' means after the 21st June or Dec. (6) **e.Suf.** (F.H.) (7) **Dor.** *N. & Q.* (1875) 5th S. iii. 424. (8) **Wm.** Wide jackbeuts ower their shins, WHITEHEAD *Leg.* (1859) 4. **n.Lin.**[1] Now used to indicate any boot, not a top-boot, which is bigger than a Wellington. **Hmp.** Large boots, reaching above the knees, worn by fishermen, when they go into the water to haul up their nets or their boats, HOLLOWAY. (9) **w.Yks.** A catch working on a pin which allows of the mine-car to pass over it but cannot pass back again, grips the axle of the mine-car, and holds it there till a sufficient number of cars are got together to form a train to send to the pit bottom (J.H.B.) ; (J.P.) (10, *a*) **War.**[3], **w.Som.**[1] (*b*) **n.Lin.**[1] **w.Som.**[1] It is made of twisted wire links, and is of the description used formerly for turning the spit. A country ironmonger asked for jack-chain would at once know the kind required. (11) **Cum.**[1 4] (12) **n.Yks.**[2] **w.Yks.** *Leeds Merc. Suppl.* (May 19, 1894). (13) **Nhb.** GRESLEY *Gl.* (1883) ; (R.O.H.) (14) **Nhb.**, **Dur.** GREENWELL *Coal Tr. Gl.* (1849) s.v. Staple. (15) **Nhb.** *Mining Gl. Newc. Terms* (1852). (16) **Nhb.** *ib.* (17) **Wm.** This crook hangs on the crane from which a girdle with handle to it is suspended : it can be turned round without lifting it off (E.W.P.) ; This girdle was also occasionally suspended from the ratten-crook in a jack-idle, made to supply the place of the brandreth, *Lonsdale Mag.* (1822) III. 290. (18) **n.Yks.** (B. & H.) (19) **Dev.** Small children, who studiously searched for what was commonly termed Jack Jesums—a small button-like growth gathered from a herb that grew on the side of the embankment, *n. Dev. Herald* (Mar. 11, 1897) in *Reports Provinc.* (1897). (20) **w.Yks.**[2] The breast bone of a goose, which being fixed before a fire, with a piece of wood underneath, can be made to jump in a somewhat startling way. **w.Som.**[1] So called from its often being made into a toy. A piece of fine string tied across the two ends, a little piece of wood, as a lucifer match, stuck in to twist the string, and a morsel of cobbler's wax at the bifurcation. The stick is then brought over with another twist and the end stuck in the wax. On being placed on the floor, after a few seconds the wax 'lets go,' and jack jumps a considerable height. (21) **Cum.** (22, *a*) **Nhb.**[1] (*b*) **w.Cy.** (HALL.) (23) **Nhb.**[1] It is a squared slate about fifteen inches deep by eight inches wide, with a deep notch cut on each side near the upper end. Jack-necks are arranged alternately on each side of the roof ridge, laid on with each notch fitting into its neighbour, and so cut in size that, when fitted close, they form a continuous self-supporting ridge with a cock's-comb-like apex, *Proc. Newc. Soc. Antiq.* V. 98. (24) **Nhb.** GRESLEY *Gl.* (1883). (25) **n.Cy.** (HALL.), **w.Yks.**[1], **Chs.**[1], **s.Chs.**[1], **n.Lin.**[1], **Shr.**[1] **w.Som.**[1] A plane of medium length, having a projecting handle in the form of a bent peg. With this the rougher part of the work is done, to be finished as required by the long trying-plane or the short smoothing-plane. Used also as a *v. t.* To roughly plane over any board. 'Must jack-plane un over a bit, I 'spose.' (26) **Sc.** The man of mirth or the Jack Pudding to the company, SCOTT *St. Roman* (1824) iii. **War.**[3] Colloq. Meanwhile his attendant Jack Pudding was busily employed on the proscenium, doing his best to attract attention by a practical facetiousness, BARHAM *Ingoldsby* (ed. 1864) *Leech of Folkestone.* (27) **I.W.**[2] Every jackrag on 'em's gone, you. **Dor.** Every Jack-rag and Tom-straw that drops the knee, HARDY *Tower* (ed. 1895) 173 ; Every jack-rag o'm, BARNES *Gl.* (1863). (28) **n.Cy.** (HALL.) **Nhb.**[1] A winch, consisting of a cylinder of wood with a handle at each end, such as is seen in old draw wells. It is used in shallow shafts for winding and in other places where hand power only is available. **Nhb.**, **Dur.** GREENWELL *Coal Tr. Gl.* (1849). **w.Yks.** *Leeds Merc. Suppl.* (Nov. 8, 1884) 8. **Hrt.** The earth and chalk is raised by a jack-rowl on a frame, MARSHALL *Review* (1817) V. 16. (29) **Nhb.**[1] (30) **Hrt.** When Jack rot comes he generally takes nineteen sheep out of twenty, ELLIS *Shepherd's Guide* (1750) 155. (31) **n.Yks.** (I.W.) (32, *a*) **w.Som.**[1] Mornin, maister! this is what I calls Jack sharp s'mornin. (*b*) **Cum.**[4] (33) **Sur.** (L.J.Y.) **w.Som.**[1] What, thick little Jack-sprat of a fellow ! why he idn no higher'n a twopenny loav ! (34) **Som.** SWEETMAN *Wincanton Gl.* (1885). (35, *a*) **Ir.** A domestic game is

played with five pebbles, or five small bones, which are thrown up into the air, and caught as they fall on the back of the hand. ... The pastime is called ... Jack-stones, *N. & Q.* (1865) 3rd S. vii. 34. **Con.** Jack-stones, played with three or four small stones that are thrown up in the air and caught again, seems to have been a very ancient game, *Flk-Lore Jrn.* (1884) II. 266. **e.Yks.** Several more boys are about the place, playing at 'merrills,' or 'Jack steean,' NICHOLSON *Flk-Sp.* (1889) 10. **Lan.** Many an evening was beguiled with snapdragon, bobbing apples, Jack stones, THORNBER *Hist. Blackpool* (1837) 90; **Lan.¹ s.Lan.** The name given to the game of Bobber-and-Kibbs (q. v.) when played with small stones instead of 'kibbs,' i. e. the knucklebones of a sheep (F.E.T.). **s.Chs.¹** The game consists in throwing up white stones—usually five in number —and catching them again. War.², Shr.¹ (*b*) **s.Chs.¹, n.Stf.** (J.T.), War.², Shr.¹ (*c*) Nhp.¹ (36, *a*) Lin.¹, e.Lin. (J.C.W.), s.Lin. (T.H.R.) (*b*) **s.Ir.** The story ... is the only thing about the place that's worth a jack-straw, CROKER *Leg.* (1862) 327. (37) **Yks.** We used to call the spikes 'Jack straws,' and many a good game I have had with them, fighting my fifty against my neighbour's fifty, PLUES *Wild Flowers*, 239, in (B. & H.). (38) Shr.¹ So called from the place where they are made—Jack-field. (39) **w.Cor.** (M.A.C.) [If she's only got one hollow rum tum serum tum old jack tooth in the back of her head, *Mummers Play* in *Flk-Lore Jrn.* (1886) IV. 100.] (40) **Chs.¹, Not.¹ Lei.¹** Sarmunt! ah, it wur a sarmunt an' all! All the same o'er agen, an' niver an end, jack a jack-towel. Nhp.¹, War.²³, Oxf. (G.O.), Hnt. (T.P.F.) (41) **w.Som.¹** (42) Oxf. (43) **w.Som.¹** (44) Hmp. It is common to hear a stye on the eye-lid called a Jack West, *N. & Q.* (1856) and S. ii. 289. (45) Hmp., GROSE (1790) *MS. add.* (M.) Cor. Curse Mall Rosevear, I says, a great jack wh-re, *Cornwall*, *W. Ecologue* in *Gent. Mag.* (1762) 287.

2. *Comb.* in the names of birds, fishes, &c.: (1) **Jack-baker,** (*a*) the red-backed shrike, *Lanius collurio*; (*b*) an owl; (2) **-bandy,** the stickleback, *Gasterosteus aculeatus*; (3) **-bannel** or **-a-barnell,** (*a*) the minnow, *Leuciscus phoxinus*; (*b*) see (2); (4) **-bannial,** a tadpole; (5) **-bannock,** (*a*) see (2); (*b*) see (3, *a*); (6) **-barrel,** see (3, *a*); (7) **-bird,** the fieldfare, *Turdus pilaris*; (8) **-blay** the bleak, *Cyprinus alburnus*; (9) **-craw,** the jackdaw, *Corvus monedula*; (10) **-curlew** or **-curley,** (*a*) the whimbrel, *Numenius phaeopus*; (*b*) the curlew, *Numenius arquata*; (11) **-doucker** or **-douker,** the lesser grebe, *Podiceps minor*; (12) **-e-stop,** a kite; (13) **-hare,** a male hare; (14) **-hearn** or **-hern,** the heron, *Ardea cinerea*; (15) **-ickle,** the green woodpecker, *Gecinus viridis*; (16) **-jaw,** see (9); (17) **-nicker** or **-a-nickas,** (18) **-nicol,** the goldfinch, *Fringilla carduelis*; (19) **-noup,** the tomtit or blue titmouse, *Parus caeruleus*; (20) **-rabbit,** a half-grown rabbit; (21) **-sharp,** (*a*) see (2); (*b*) see (3, *a*); (22) **-sharpling,** see (2); (23) **-sharpnails,** (*a*) see (2); (*b*) a hedgehog; (24) **-shewall,** the redwing, *Turdus iliacus*; (25) **-snag,** the snail; (26) **-snipe,** (*a*) the snipe, *Limno-cryptes gallinula*; (*b*) the dunlin, *Tringa alpina*; (27) **-squall,** the wryneck, *Jynx torquilla*; (28) **-squealer,** the swift, *Cypselus apus*; (29) **-star,** *Cuculus canorus*; (30) **-straw,** the blackcap, *Sylvia atricapilla*; (*b*) the white-throat, *Sylvia cinerea*; (*c*) the stonechat, *Pratincola rubicola*.

(1, *a*) **m.Wor.** 'Whatn' yer think I telled oud kill-cauf—our butcher!' 'Dunno.' 'Why, as he wan a shrike, a Jack Baker, ecos he alleys hangs up what he slaughters,' *Berrow's Jrn.* (Mar. 10, 1888). Sur.¹ Sur., Sus., Hmp. SWAINSON *Birds* (1885) 47. (*b*) **s.Cy.** (HALL.) (2) Nhp.¹ (3, *a*) War. B'ham *Wkly. Post* (June 10, 1893). n.War. *N. & Q.* (1867) 3rd S. xi. 466; War.¹; War.² For they've filled up poor old Pudding Brook Where in the mud I've often stuck, Catching Jack-banils near Brummagem, *Old Sng.* (*b*) War. When us wants Jack Bannels us allus goes to that stream of yourn, *Leamington Courier* (Jan. 30, 1897); War.²⁴, ne.Wor. (J.W.P.) (4) War.⁴, s.War.¹ (5, *a*) s.Stf. PINNOCK *Blk. Cy. Ann.* (1895). (*b*) War. NORTHALL *Flk-Phr.* (1894). (6) War. (HALL.) [SATCHELL (1879).] (7) w.Wor. *Berrow's Jrn.* (Mar. 3, 1888). [(So called) from its cry, SWAIN-SON *ib.* 6.] (8) Oxf. *Science Gossip* (1882) 165. (9) Nhb.¹ (10, *a*) Cum.⁴, Lin., e.An. (R.H.H.) (*b*) Shr. SWAINSON *ib.* 200. (11) Shr. *ib.* 216; Shr.¹ (12) Cum. A glead or kite they call Jack-e-stop, HUTCHINSON *Hist. Cum.* (1794) II. 210. (13) Midl. Handin' over a Jack-hare, BARTRAM *People of Clopton* (1897) 52. s.Not. (J.P.K.), War.⁸, se.Wor.¹, Brks.¹ Hrt. ELLIS *Cy. Hswf.* (1750) 293. w.Mid. Common (W.P.M.). Hmp. (W.M.E.F.) Dor. You may do as you like for all I care, I'll never fry a dry Jack hare, *Flk-Lore Rec.* (1880) III. 98. w.Som.¹ The male hare is always so called, while a male rabbit is invariably a buck. The

females are doe-rabbit and doe-hare. (14) Glo.¹, w.Mid. (W.P.M.) **Ken.** He [a marshman] moves over the flats with the deliberation of one of his own Jack-her'ns, *Ann. Fishing Vill.* (ed. 1892) 5. Sus. SWAINSON *ib.* 144; Sus.¹ Always spoken of as 'a gurt old jack-hearn'; Sus.², Hmp.¹, I.W. (HALL), I.W.¹² Wil.¹ (15) Nhp. SWAINSON *ib.* 99; Nhp.¹ (s.v. Dicky-bird). (16) Nhb.¹, e.Dur.¹, Yks. (J.W.) (17) Chs. (HALL.), Chs.¹²³, s.Chs.¹ Wal. Common (H.R.). Nhp.¹ Nearly obs. Nhp., Shr. SWAINSON *ib.* 58. (18) Shr.¹ (19) Chs. *Sheaf* (1879) I. 266; Chs.¹ (20) n.Lin.¹ (21, *a*) Lan. He mun larn to tak' care on himself th' next toime he mar-locks [gambols] among th' Jacksharps, BANKS *Manch. Man* (1876) v; He flasker't about i' th' bruck after jack-sharps, WAUGH *Chim. Comer* (1874) 159, ed. 1879. e.Lan.¹, Chs.¹²³, s.Chs.¹, nw.Der.¹ (*b*) w.Yks.⁵, Lan. (F.R.C.) (22) Chs.³ War. B'ham *Wkly. Post* (June 10, 1893); War.¹²³, Nhp.¹ (23, *a*) Der. GROSE (1790): Der.² (*b*) Stf.¹ (24, 25) Cor.⁸ (26, *a*) Gall. The brown moorland began where the ... jacksnipe swooped sidelong, CROCKETT *Stickit Min.* (1893) 230. Giw. The d—d duns, like a flock of jack snipes, BARRINGTON *Sketches* (1830) III. viii. Nhb.¹, Chs.⁸ Nhp.¹ (s.v. Dicky-bird). War. Nearly as large as a jack snipe, *Proc. Nat. and Arch. Field Club* (1894) 5. Nrf. COZENS-HARDY *Broad Nrf.* (1893) 45. w.Som.¹ The smaller of the two common kinds of snipe. The term has no reference to sex. (*b*) Sh.I. SWAINSON *ib.* 193. (27) w.Brks. (W.H.Y.) (28) Lei.¹ War. TIMMINS *Hist.* (1889) 213; War.²⁸ w.Wor. Like them swifts, them Jack-squealers, *Berrow's Jrn.* (Mar. 10, 1888); w.Wor.¹, s.Wor.¹ Shr.¹ This bird's loud piercing cry has obtained for it the name of 'squealer'; Shr.², Glo. (A.B.) (29) w.Wor. He come down ooth a crash like Jackstars on reeds, when they settles you know of a evenin', *Berrow's Jrn.* (Mar. 10, 1888). (30, *a*) Shr.², Som. (HALL.) (*b*) Shr.¹ The name of Jack-straw is given to this bird from the straw-like material with which it builds its nest; Shr.², Hmp. (H.W.E.) (*c*) Hmp. So called from its nest being formed of dry hay and straw (J.R.W.); Hmp.¹

3. *Phr.* (1) *Jack and Gill,* a figure composed of the last blades of corn cut from the harvest-field; (2) *— and his lantern,* a Will-o'-th'-Wisp or *ignis fatuus*; see Jack-a-lantern; (3) *— and his team,* (4) *— and his team going to pit,* (5) *— and his wagon,* (6) *— and his wain,* the constellation *Ursa major*; (7) *— amongst the maidens,* one who is always after women's society, and who likes to be made much of by them; (8) *— at the hedge,* the goosegrass, *Galium Aparine*; (9) *— at a pinch,* a useful man, one who is ready on emergency; one who is made useful on occasion but ignored at other times; (10) *— at the wat* or *Jacket-the-wat,* the small bag of a pig's intestines; (11) *— behind the garden gate,* the pansy, *Viola tricolor*; (12) *— by the hedge,* (*a*) the garlic mustard, *Alliaria officinalis*; (*b*) the goat's-beard, *Tragopogon pratensis*; (*c*) the red campion, *Lychnis diurna*; (*d*) the small toad-flax, *Linaria minor*; (13) *— by the hedgeside,* see (12, *a*); (14) *— in the box* or *in box,* (*a*) the cuckoo-pint, *Arum maculatum*; (*b*) a hose-in-hose variety of garden primrose or double poly-anthus, *Primula vulgaris*; (15) *— in the bush,* (*a*) the navel-wort, *Cotyledon Umbilicus*; (*b*) see (12, *a*); (16) *— in the cellar, obs.,* an unborn child; also called *Hans in Kelder* (q.v.), s.v. Hans; (17) *— in green doublet,* a variety of *Primula vulgaris* in which the calyx is transformed into leaves; (18) *— in the green,* (*a*) var. kinds of garden polyanthus; (*b*) the pheasant's eye, *Adonis autumnalis*; (*c*) a chimney-sweep enclosed in a frame of green leaves shaped like a bower, who perambulates the streets on May-day; (19) *— in the hedge,* (*a*) see (12, *a*); (*b*) see (12, *c*); (*c*) see (12, *d*); (*d*) the red or white bryony, *Bryonia dioica*; (20) *— in irons,* a supernatural being of great stature, wearing clanking chains, who may at any moment spring out on a passer-by in the dark; (21) *— in prison,* the 'love-in-a-mist,' *Nigella damascena*; (22) *— in the pulpit,* see (14, *a*); (23) *— in the water,* a sailor; (24) *— o' both sides,* (25) *— o' two sides,* the corn crowfoot, *Ranunculus arvensis*; (26) *— of the hedge,* see (12, *a*); (27) *— on both sides,* one who plays for both sides in a game; (28) *— up the orchard,* a threat; (29) *— upon the mopstick,* a boys' game; see below; (30) *— a boney,* see (27); (31) *— a dandy,* (*a*) a conceited, empty-headed little fellow; (*b*) a light thrown by the reflection of the sun on a looking-glass or other bright surface, on to a wall or ceiling; (32) *— a lent* or *o' lent,* (*a*) a figure, made up of straw and cast-off clothes, carried round and burnt at the beginning of Lent; a scarecrow; (b) a dirty, slovenly person; (c) a simple, stupid fellow; (33) — *a loon*, a term of abuse; (34) — *a nods*, see (32, *c*); (35) —*'s alive*, (*a*) a game; see below; (*b*) a game at cards played by children; (36) — *churn-milk*, a boy who works the churn; (37) — *go to bed at noon*, (*a*) the Star of Bethlehem, *Ornithogalum umbellatum*; (*b*) see (12, *b*); (38) — *jag the flae*, a tailor; (39) — *jump about*, (*a*) the goutweed, *Aegopodium Podagraria*; (*b*) the bird's-foot trefoil, *Lotus corniculatus*; (*c*) the wild angelica, *Angelica sylvestris*; (40) — *a-making pancakes*, see (31, *b*); (41) — *run along by the hedge*, see (12, *a*); (42) — *run in country*, the great bindweed, *Convolvulus sepium*; (43) — *run the dyke*, see (8); (44) — *strike up a light*, a boys' game played at night; see below; (45) —, *Jack, the bread's a-burning*, a children's game; see below; (46) — *had i' wist or wiss*, an expression of disapprobation; see below; see **Have**, v. III. 2 (27); (47) — *Harry's lights*, phantom lights, *gen.* seen before a gale, taking the form of a vessel sure to be wrecked; (48) —*'s land*, little odds and ends of unused land; (49) *a good Jack makes a good Jill*, a good husband makes a good wife; (50) *to be John at night and Jack in the morning*, to boast of one's intentions overnight and leave them unfulfilled next day; (51) *wind-up Jack*, a game; see below.

(1) Bdf. BRAND *Pop. Antiq.* (ed. 1870) II. 16. (2) se.Wor.[1] (3) Shr.[1] Obs.[1] Glo.[1], Wil.[1] (4) Wil.[1] Also Jack-and-his-teamgoin'-to-pit, the constellation's motion seeming to be from Deverill towards Radstock collieries, as if it were a farmer's team going by night to fetch coal thence. (5) se.Wor.[1], Shr.[1] (6) Shr.[1] (7) w.Som.[1] Jaak-umang·s-dhu-maa·ydnz. The term is applied to some parsons who cultivate female worshippers; it is, of course, depreciatory. nw.Dev.[1] (8) Don. (9) Dor.[2], nw.Der.[1], Nhp.[1], War.[2] Suf.[1] Well—if I be'ent set tew regular don't come Jack at a pinch. e.Suf. (F.H.) (10) Nhb.[1] (11) Suf. (12, *a*) n.Yks., w.Cha., Mer., Sus., Dev.[4] (*b*) e.Sus. (*c*) Sus. (*d*) Brks. (13) Dor. Daisies, an' jil-cups, an' Jack-by-the-hedgezide, HARE *Vill. Street* (1895) 235. (14, *a*) N.I.[1], Bck. w.Som.[1] Jaak-n-dhu-bau·ks. (*b*) Nrf., Ken.[1] (15, *a*) Rxb. (JAM.) (*b*) Glo.[1] (16) n.Yks.[2] A toast to Jack in that situation, was formerly drunk to the family matron by her company; it being a custom to gather a lot of intimates together for 'a take-leave party' at a house where hospitalities would necessarily be suspended until the prospective Christening day. (17) Stf. (18, *a*) Hmp. (J.R.W.), Hmp.[1], Wil.[1] Dor. *w.Gazette* (Feb. 15, 1889) 7, col. 1. (*b*) Wil. At South Newton Pheasant's eye bears the ... descriptive name of Jack-in-the-Green, *Sarum Dioc. Gazette* (Jan. 1891) 14; Wil.[1] (*c*) Oxf. Common so or 25 years ago; now seldom seen. Often used *fig.* 'He looked for all the world like a Jack-in-the-green' (G.O.). (19, *a*) n.Lin.[1], Lei.[1] Hrt. Jack-in-the-hedge ... stinks like onions, ELLIS *Cy. Hswf.* (1750) 129. I.W.[1], Dor. (G.E.D.) (*b*) Sus.[1] (*c*) Brks. (*d*) Hmp.[1] (20) Yks. Thou mun look sharp or Jack-in-irons 'ill be after ye (W.M.E.F.). (21) n.Lin.[1], Sus.[1] (22) n.Lin.[1] (23) Lon. I ran away and tried my hand as a Jack-in-the-water, MAYHEW *Lond. Labour* (ed. 1861) II. 224. (24) Not.[1] Lei.[1] So called from having a few bristles on each side of its flattened carpels. (25) Shr.[1] (26) Cha.[1] (27) Oxf. (G.O.) (28) Shr.[1] If yo' dunna tak' car' I'll shewn yo' Jack-up-the-orchot. (29) War. Sometimes two parties play this game. The boys that are cast for 'down' dispose themselves as follows. One stands upright, setting his back against a wall or tree, .. the rest bend in file, holding on to each other's sides to make the bridge as strong as possible ... as the other party leap on one by one... The leaping part must maintain their position whilst their leader says—'Jack upon the mopstick, One, two, three, four, five, six, seven, eight, nine, ten, Count 'em off again,' NORTHALL *Flk-Rhymes* (1892) 401. Oxf. (G.O.) (31, *a*) n.Cy. (HALL.) n.Yks.[1], Nhp.[1] n.Cy. HOLLOWAY. w.Som.[1] Be sure, you don't never take no notice of a whipper-snapper Jack-a-dandy like he! why I widn [vuy'n un] find him! (*b*) Not.[1], War.[2], Shr.[1] (32, *a*) Nhp.[2] Now only used as a reproachful epithet. Dor. BARNES *Gl.* (1863); Dor.[1] Cloaz in slents An' libbets, jis' lik' Jack-o'-lents, 179. Cor. In the eastern part of this county at the beginning of Lent a straw figure dressed in cast-off clothes, and called Jack-o'-Lent, was not long since paraded through the streets, and afterwards hung. .. The figure is supposed to represent Judas Iscariot, *Flk-Lore Jrn.* (1886) IV. 132; Cor.[1] (*b*) Hmp. The raggedeat jack-o'-lent had a crust an' cheese for the asking o' it, *From Paddington to Penzance*, xiii. Cor. *Flk-Lore Jrn.* (1886)

IV. 132; Cor.[22] (*c*) Dor. Can a Jack-o'-lent believe his few senses on such a dark night, or can't he! HARDY *Wessex Tales* (1888) II. 65. (33) Dev. A Jack-a-loon! thinkin' to trick an ould maid out o' t'bit o' monney her father worked an' toiled to lay by, DALZELL '*Anner in Cassell's Fam. Mag.* (Apr. 1895) 332. (34) n.Cy. (HALL.) (35, *a*) Tev. A piece of paper or match is handed round a circle, he who takes hold of it saying 'Jack's alive, he'se no die in my hand.' He, in whose hand it dies or is extinguished forfeits a ' wad'; and all the ' wads' are recovered only by undergoing a kind of penance (JAM.). w.Yks.[2] A number of people sit in a row, or in chairs round a parlour. A lighted wooden spill or taper is handed to the first, who says—' Jack's alive, and likely to live; If he dies in your hand you've a forfeit to give.' The one in whose hand the light expires has to pay the forfeit. nw.Der.[1] s.Wor. From the merry character of the game the expression passed into a proverb; and if there were any noisy gathering held anywhere, and laughter cracked his sides, people would say, 'They're having "Jack's alive" there' (H.K.). w.Som.[1] A burning stick whirled round and round very quickly so as to keep up the appearance of a riband of fire. e.Cor. *Flk-Lore Jrn.* (1886) IV. 124. (*b*) Nhp.[1], Hnt. (T.P.F.) (36) e.An.[2] (s.v. Churn-milk). (37, *a*) Cha.[1] The plant closes its flowers very early in the day. (*b*) Wil.[1] (38) Lnk. That'll dae; Nae mair o't, lang Jaik-jag-the-flae, MURDOCH *Doric Lyre* (1873) 13; He was a tailor lad—Lang Jaik-jag-the-Flae they ca'd him, *ib. Readings* (1895) I. 76. (39, *a*) Nhp.[1], War. Hrt. A poor woman ... gathered a herb that grew in the hedge called Jack-jump-about, ELLIS *Cy. Hswf.* (1750) 150. (*b*) Nhp. (*c*) Nhp.[1] Called also Eggs and bacon. (40) Midl. (A.L.M.), se.Wor.[1] (41) Wil.[1] (42) Yks. (43) Nhb.[1] (44) Nhb.[1] It is a kind of nocturnal 'fox and hounds.' The ' fox,' after getting away, strikes a light, generally with flint and steel, at short intervals, and the chase is continued until the ' fox' is captured. (45) War. ' Jack, Jack, the bread's a-burning All to a cinder, If you don't come and fetch it out We'll throw it through the winder.' These lines are chanted by players that stand thus. One places his back against a wall, tree, &c., grasping another, whose back is towards him, round the waist; the second grasps a third, and so on. The player called Jack, walks apart, until the conclusion of the lines. Then he goes to the others and pokes at or pats them, saying, ' I don't think you're done yet,' and walks away again. The chant is repeated, and when he is satisfied that the bread is ' done,' he endeavours to pull the foremost from the grasp of the others, &c., NORTHALL *Flk-Rhymes* (1892) 390. Oxf. (G.O.) (46) Cum. It related to imperfect knowledge, or consideration, or want of a proper understanding between persons associated, or intended to meet, in some way. Of late I have heard, ' Now, know what you are going about. Don't run Jack Haddewas' (M.P.). (47) Cor. The phantom lights are called ... ' Jack Harry's lights,' because he was the first man who was fooled by them, HUNT *Pop. Rom. w.Eng.* (1865) 359, ed. 1896; Cor.[12], w.Cor. (A.L.M.) (48) w.Yks.[2] (s.v. Jack-flatt). (49) Nhp.[1] (50) Shr. BURNE *Flk-Lore* (1883) 596. (51) Shr. This is the closing game of any play-time and was played before ' breaking-up' at a boys' school at Shrewsbury. The players form a line hand in hand, the tallest at one end, who stands still; the rest walk round and round him or her, saying, ' Wind-up Jack! Wind-up Jack!' till ' Jack' is completely imprisoned. They then ' jog up and down,' crying, ' A bundle o' rags, a bundle o' rags,' *ib.* 521.

4. A familiar, half-contemptuous term for an individual, esp. in phr. *every Jack man*.

Gall. Every canting Jack may fling away the white rose and about for the Orange lily, CROCKETT *Standard Bearer* (1898) 78. Tip. There was once a lad whose name was Jack, *Flk-Lore Jrn.* (1883) I. 54. n.Cy. (J.W.) w.Yks. Drew 'em ivvery Jack-man away throo me, BICKERDIKE *Beacon Alm.* (1874) 43; Ivvery man jack on yo, TOM TREDDLEHOYLE *Thowts* (1845) 5. s.Stf. Every Jack one, *Leeds Merc. Suppl.* (Dec. 6, 1890). s.Not. Every Jack on uz got summat. Every Jack man wor drunk (J.P.K.). Nhp.[1] Brks.[1] A child whose face is begrimed with dirt is reproached by being called ' Jack nasty vaayce.' e.An.[2] Every farming lad, also, whose name is not known, is familiarly called Jack. ' Well! Jack, borh!' Ken.[2] (s.v. Tamsin). Dev. Rade them there banns out loud, so as every jack-man an' woman in th' congregashun kin hear 'ee distinct, STOOKE *Not Exactly*, xii.

5. A young workman.

Ken. There's nobody to marry there [in the village] but the jacks (D.W.L.).

6. A police officer or detective in plain clothes.

War. A couple of men who were in plain clothes in the tap-room of a public-house, and were suspected by the 'gaffer' of being 'Jacks,' *B'ham Dy. Mail* (Nov. 1, 1899).

7. The knave at cards. In *gen.* colloq. use.

Gall. Now, what's the cut? The Jack, by jing; O, if they hae the Ten, the game we lose, MACTAGGART *Encycl.* (1824) 376, ed. 1876. n.Cy. (HALL.), w.Yks.[12], Chs.[1], nw.Der.[1], Not.[1], Lei.[1], e.An.[2] w.Som.[1] Always so called. Cor. When Mr. Simpson had spoken of the 'Jack of Oaks' [meaning the Knave of Clubs] . . . we had pretended not to notice it, ' Q.' *Troy Town* (1888) xii.

8. The male of an animal; see also **Jack-hare.** Brks.[1], w.Cy. (HALL.)

9. The pike, *Esox lucius*, esp. a young pike.

Lan. I had a jack to supper, BYROM *Remin.* in *Chet. Soc.* (1729) V. 385. Chs.[1], Not.[1], n.Lin. (T.H.R.), Lei.[1] Nhp.[1] A young male pike; also applied indiscriminately to the whole species of pike of whatever size. War.[2], Shr.[1] Oxf. Pyke, i. e. old jack; pykerell, young jack, WOOD *City of Oxf.* (c. 1662) I. 399, ed. 1889. e.Suf. (F.H.) Ken.[2] (s.v. Tamsin). [SATCHELL (1879).]

10. The jackdaw, *Corvus monedula*.

Sc., Eng. SWAINSON *Birds* (1885) 81. Nhb.[1], Shr.[1] Ken.[2] 'Caw, Jack,' we say to a jackdaw (s.v. Tamsin).

11. The heron, *Ardea cinerea*. Also called **Jack-hern** (q.v.). Wil.[1] **12.** The tawny owl, *Syrnium aluco*. sw.Cum. (E.W.P.) **13.** A turnip-fly; a black caterpillar produced by the turnip-fly; *gen.* in *pl.* form. Suf. (HALL.), (C.T.), Suf.[1], e.Suf. (F.H.) **14.** A newt. Wil.[1]

15. A machine for lifting heavy weights, esp. a hand-engine for drawing up water from a mine.

Nhb.[1] Nhb., Dur. The engine or gin used in the engine shaft, or, in sinking two pits or a pit and a staple simultaneously by means of two gins, one of them, to prevent mistakes, is called the jack, NICHOLSON *Coal Tr. Gl.* (1888). Stf. (K.), Stf.[1], se.Wor.[1] Ken.[2] (s.v. Tamsin). Dev. What is here called a jack, an engine for lifting, BRAY *Desc. Tamar and Tavy* (1836) I. 362.

16. A contrivance, consisting of a lever and fulcrum, used for supporting the axle-tree of a cart, &c., so that the wheel may run round freely.

n.Lin.[1], Brks.[1], Hmp.[1] w.Som.[1] Sometimes called a 'carriage-jack.'

17. A frame to hold the 'yelm' for the thatcher. Nhp.[1] **18.** A machine for turning a spit in roasting; a meat-jack; see below.

w.Som.[1] A kind of clock-work driven by a heavy weight, to which was attached an endless chain; by this the spit was turned before the fire. These were very common before the days of kitchen-ranges, and might be seen fixed upon the right side of the high chimney-shelf in most kitchens of the better sort. Known also as 'roasting-jack.' Cor.[2]

19. A roller for a kitchen towel. Sc. (A.W.), Not.[1], Lei.[1], Nhp.[1], War.[2]

20. *pl.* The woodwork between the shafts of a wagon where they are attached to the fore-shears. n.Lin.[1], e.Suf. (F.H.)

21. The crossbar in a loom from which cords are attached to raise and lower the 'healds.' *Gen.* in *pl.*

N.I.[1] Dwn. I went to my loom to see she was in trim. . . Neither headles, nor jack, nor slays were correct, BURNS *Poem* in *Uls. Jrn. Arch.* (1857) V. 99. w.Yks. Stands at the top of the loom connected with the healds; enables a larger pattern to be made than is possible with ordinary tappets (J.M.); Short pieces of wood used to hold up the upper portions of the healds and control their working (D.L.); w.Yks.[2]

Hence (1) **Jack-ladder,** *sb.* a wooden frame to hold the 'jacks' in position; (2) **-rods,** *sb. pl.* rods, the width of the loom, which regulate the pile-rods.

w.Yks. (1) (D.L.); (2) The arrangement for working the healds up and down. This was effected by means of rods affixed to treadles, worked by the feet of the weaver (J.T.); (S.A.B.)

22. A machine for spinning, driven partly by hand and partly by power, used for spinning coarse, heavy woollen yarns. w.Som.[1]

23. A drinking vessel; a large copper can. Also in *comb.* **Black jack.**

Sc. Overturned pitchers, and black jacks, . . still encumbered the large oaken table, SCOTT *Bride of Lam.* (1819) vii. Shr.[1] *Obs.* A drinking vessel of leather. A jack of this kind was preserved until quite a recent period at Corra, not far from Whitchurch. A local tradition was formerly current at Corra that a certain traveller, half dead with fatigue, being helped on his way by a

refreshing draught of nut-brown ale at that place, by way of thank-offering, charged his estate with a sum of money yearly, to provide a Jack of ale at a cost of 1d. for future wayfarers in Corra. Nhp.[1] A large copper can; a japan tin jug is called a black jack. Suf.[1], Hmp.[1] Cor. To bring down to the mill . . . a jack of the strongest beer she had in the cellar, HUNT *Pop. Rom. w.Eng.* (1865) 243, ed. 1896. [Treene dishes be homely, and yet not to lack, Where stone is no laster take tankard and Jack, TUSSER *Husb.* (1580) 175.]

24. A liquid measure of a quarter or half of a pint.

Yks. Half a pint. GROSE (1790). n.Yks. (I.W.). n.Yks.[124], ne.Yks.[1], m.Yks.[1], e.Yks.[1] w.Yks.[2]; w.Yks.[5] 'A jack o' gin, an' it's to be good, 'cos' it's for a poorly body!' A measure perhaps confined to dram-shops. Der.[1] Now used for 'a quarter of a pint.' n.Lin.[1] The quantity of fluid contained in a jack. 'I'll tell you a tale Of a jack of ale.'

25. A counter resembling in size and appearance a sovereign.

Lon. The slang name for these articles is 'Jacks' and 'Half Jack.' . . They are all made in Birmingham and are of the size and colour of the genuine sovereigns and half-sovereigns, MAYHEW *Lond. Labour* (1851) I. 387.

26. A small bowl thrown out as a mark in the game of bowls.

Ayr. Just tak' the jack clean thro': Awa' it gaes! Weel play'd my lad! WHITE *Jottings* (1879) 236. Dur.[1], War.[2]

27. *pl.* Small bones, pebbles, or dice-shaped pieces of earthenware, &c., used in a children's game; the game itself. Also called **Jack-stones** (q.v.).

Gall. Playing at quoits, tops, marbles, tic-tac-toc, jacks, knuckle-bones, CROCKETT *Anna Mark* (1899) 415. N.I.[1] A children's game played with five white pebbles, called 'Jack stones.' Ant. The small bones of sheep's feet, ground flat on two sides, and used by little girls to play at a game which they call by the same name (jacks), but which in England is called 'cochel.' The game consists in setting upright, arranging in a certain order and going through certain motions with three or four of the bones, during the time another of them is thrown up to be caught in its descent, as the movement is performed. And the person who goes through all the steps with the fewest failures wins the game, GROSE (1790) *MS. add.* (C.) Cum.[4] 'Pebbles,' a game among school-girls, played with small pebbles and sometimes with plum or cherry-stones (s.v. Jacky steans). e.Yks.[1], n.Stf. (J.T.)

Hence *Jacks and Bouncer, phr.* a girls' game played with little 'checks' and a large marble. See **Check,** *sb.[2]*

w.Yks. They bounce the marble while the jacks are picked up and put down again in a variety of ways, catching the bouncer repeatedly at the same time, *Hlfx. Courier* (May 22, 1897).

28. A garden variety of the polyanthus.

Lon. One of the forms of the so-called 'hose-in-hose' Polyanthus —having the calyx more or less coloured, and partly assuming the character of the corolla, *Garden Chron.* (1868) 438 (B. & H.).

29. *pl. Obs.* The chimes or tunes struck on bells.

w.Yks.[4] So called from little figures who struck the tunes on the bells.

30. A large fissure or crack in the roof of a mine; a portion of stone in the roof of a mine.

Nhb.[1] Nhb., Dur. A portion of stone in the roof of a coal-mine easily detachable and thus of highly dangerous character to the miner beneath. A jack is also called a cauldron-bottom (q.v.) (R.O.H.). [*Reports Mines.*]

31. A whit. Som. (HALL.) [Not known to our corre-spondents.]

JACK, *v.[1]* In *gen.* dial. and colloq. use in Eng. and Aus. Also in form **jag** s.Stf. [dʒak, dʒæk.] **1.** To give up suddenly; to withdraw or back out of anything; to relinquish, abandon, esp. to leave off or throw up work. *Gen.* with *up.*

Nhb. If there's ony mair fash myed, aa'll jack up the job (R.O.H.). w.Yks. Hiz mester tell'd him he'd better jack it up altogether, TOM TREDDLEHOYLE *Bairnsla Ann.* (1892) 29; Thee jack it (J.T.); w.Yks.[2] Lan. Aw jack'd th' contract up, DOHERTY *N. Barlow* (1884) 90; Another batch o' th' bigger end Are jackin' o'er ther wark, STANDING *Echoes* (1885) 5. Chs.[1] It rather conveys the idea of giving up after continuous effort, or when there is no chance of success. A card player, if his hand does not suit him, will say, 'I think I shall jack it up.' It also implies failure in business. 'He tried hard for t'mak his farm do, bur he could na, an at last he had to jack up.' s.Chs.[1] s.Stf. Well, I'm gooin to jag up, I can work no longer, PINNOCK *Blk. Cy. Ann.* (1895). Not.[1] s.Not.

Nay, it's all jacked up; they aren't coming (J.P.K.). **n.Lin.**[1] **sw.Lin.**[1] She used to go wi' that young Smith, but she jacked him up. **Rut.**[1], **War.**[2 8 4] **w.Wor.**[1] Bill, 'e's reg'lar dahnted; 'e's jacked-up 'is plack, 'e canna stand it no longer. **s.Wor.**[1] **Glo.** If it weren't for the cursed loss I'd jack up the place altogether and take another, GISSING *Vill. Hampden* (1890) II. ix. **Oxf.** I'm going to jack this job up; I've had enough of it (G.O.). **s.Oxf.**, **Bck.**, **Brks.** I've done all I can for you, and there's no reason you should jack now. I got him part up Stokenchurch Hill, and then he jacked-up—couldn't do anything with him [said of a jibbing horse] (W.B.T.). **Nrf.** COZENS-HARDY *Broad Nrf.* (1893) 55. **e.Suf.** 'She has jacked him up,' jilted him (F.H.). **Ken.** (D.W.L.); (G.B.); **Ken.**[1] Give up anything from pride, impudence, or bad temper. 'They kep' on one wik, and then they all jacked-up!' **Sur.**[1] That spring 'most always jacks up in autumn time. **Sus.** (F.E.S.); **Sus.**[1] We've all been a-practising together, and now they're properly jacked up. **I.W.**[2] I jacked it up sharp and left it. **Dor.** I din't know as Bill were going to jack out of the choir (C.V.G.). **w.Som.**[1] A man said to me of a farmer,' Gwai·n tu jaak aup faa·rmureen u blee·v, ad· nuuf oa ut' [(He is) going to give up farming, I believe, (he has) had enough of it]. **nw.Dev.**[1] He'll sure to jack out o't eef he kin. **Cor.** Ould Sammy jacked up rayther soon, *T. Towser* (1873) 102 ; **Cor.**[2] He've jacked up drinking and took to praiching lstead. [**Aus.** We . . . decided to 'jack up' or thoroughly abandon work at our present claim, BOLDREWOOD *Miner's Right* (1890) I. iv.]

2. To become bankrupt or insolvent; to ruin. *Gen.* with *up.*

Yks. lv my buk shud jaack oop Coompany, FETHERSTON *T. Goorkrodger* (1870) 179. **s.Chs.**[1] It,s û ter·ûbl pùsh ùpon· ùm dheyz aa·rd tahymz ; dhai)n bi gy'et·in tû,th wuurldz end veri sôon ; ah dôo daayt dhai)n aa jaak· up· [It's a terrible push upon 'em theise hard times ; they be gettin' to th' world's end very soon ; ah do daît they'n ha' jack up]. **Stf.**[1], **Not.**[1] **Lei.**[1] A wur jacked-up a month agoo.

3. To wear out ; to tire, exhaust. *Gen.* with *up.*

s.Chs.[1] **Sus.** My fowls are so jacked up they will not lay (J.L.A.).

4. To beat. **w.Yks.** (HALL), **w.Yks.**[1]

JACK, *v.*[2] Sh. & Or.I. [dgak.] To take off the skin of a seal.

S. & Ork.[1] Or.I. One party . . . set to jacking, i. e. cutting off the skin, together with the blubber on it, Low *Faun. Orcad.* (1813) 17 (JAM.) ; FRANCISQUE-MICHEL *Lang.* (1882) 425.

JACK, *v.*[3] War. Wor. To project.

War.[2] Wor. A farmer in describing a mediaeval dove-cote to me told me that rows of bricks were jacked out from the wall to afford footing for the examination of the nests (E.S.).

JACK, *int.* Yks. Der. Lin. [dgak.] A call to pigs.

n.Yks.[1] The invariable call or summons to the pigs (while as yet suffered to ramble about in the day-time) to come to their food at nightfall is ' Jack, Jack,' many times repeated in a high-pitched and sustained note (s.v. Hog). **nw.Der.**[1], **n.Lin.**[1]

JACK-A-LANTERN, *sb.* Sc. Irel. n.Cy. Nhb. Yks. Lan. Der. Not. Lin. Nhp. War. Shr. e.An. Hmp. I.W. Wil. Som. Dev. Cor. Also in forms **Jack-and-the-lantern** Gall. ; **-l'-the-lantern** Dev.[1]; **-in-the-lanthorn** Hmp. Som. ; **-o'-lantern** Not.[1] War.[2] Hmp.[1] n.Wil. Cor.[2] ; **-o'-lanthorn** Som. ; **-o' lattin** Nhb. ; **-o'-the-lanthorn** Shr.[1]; **-the-lantern** Cor. ; **-wi'-a-lanthorn** n.Lin.[1] ; **-with-lanthorn** Lan. ; **-with-the-lanthorn** nw.Der.[1] Cor.[2] ; **Jacky-lanthorn** s.Ir.

1. *Ignis fatuus* or Will-o'-th'-Wisp.

Gall. Some fancy that Jack and the Lantern, alias Will o' the Wisp, has his habitation in the Quaking-quaw, MACTAGGART *Encycl.* (1824) 390, ed. 1876. **s.Ir.** Maybe . . . you are only a Jacky lanthorn, CROKER *Leg.* (1862) 286. **n.Cy.** (J.W.) **w.Yks.** (J.T.) ; **N. & Q.** (1870) 5th S. 156. **Lan.** The flickering flame of the Corpse Candle, ' Will-o'-th'-Wisp,' or ' Jack ' or ' Peg-a-Lantern,' performed his or her fantastic and impossible jumps in the plashy meadows near Edge Lane, HARLAND & WILKINSON *Flk-Lore* (1867) 53 ; Occasionally in the plashy meadows ' Jack-or Peggy-with-lanthorn ' was visible after dark, dancing and gambolling away in impossible jumps, and folks there were who . . . ' had been kept at bay, By Jack-with-lanthorn till 'twas day,' *N. & Q.* (1869) 4th S. iv. 508. **nw.Der.**[1], **Not.**[1], **n.Lin.**[1] **Nhp.** They steal from jack-a-lantern's tails A light, whose guidance never fails To aid them in the darkest night, CLARE *Shep. Calendar* (1827) 73 ; **Nhp.**[1], **War.**[2] **Shr.**[1] *Obs.* **e.An.**[1] Also called lantern man. **Hmp.**[1], **I.W.**[1] **Wil.** BRITTON *Beauties* (1825). **n.Wil.** The *Ignis fatuus* is almost extinct—so much so that Jack o' the Lantern has died out of village folk lore, JEFFERIES *Wild Life* (1879) 385. **Som.** JENNINGS *Obs. Dial. w.Eng.* (1825) ; (W.F.R.)

w.Som.[1] The only name known in the district. The phenomenon only occurs in certain parts of the boggy moorland of Brendon Hill and the Exmoor district. **Dev.**[1] Cor. Jack the lantern, Joan the Wad, That tickled the maid and made her mad, Light me home, the weather's bad, *Flk-Lore Rec.* (1879) II. 203 ; **Cor.**[1 2]

2. A bright spot of reflected light, such as is produced by a small mirror or a tin or lantern reflector.

Nhb. It is played by boys as a practical joke to startle the passer-by. ' Let's myek a jack o' lattin, lads !' (R.O.H.) ; **Nhb.**[1]

3. A hollowed turnip cut into the semblance of the human face and lighted within by a candle. Not. (J.H.B.), Hmp. HOLLOWAY.

4. A term of abuse.

Dev. A dri&avin' back to Tawboro wi' that Jack-a-lantern's arm roun' 'er waist a-pretendin' to hold 'er in at the back o' the shay, DALZELL '*Anner,* in *Caswell's Family Mag.* (Apr. 1895) 335.

5. *Phr. to carry jack-a-lantern,* to carry on the shoulders. Nhp.[2]

JACKALEGS, *sb.* Nhb. Dur. Cum. Wm. Yks. Lan. Also Glo. Also in forms **jackilegs** Lakel.[2] Cum.[4]; **jack-o-legs** n.Cy. n.Yks.[2]; **jackylegs** Nhb. s.Dur. w.Yks. ; **jockalegs** N.Cy.[1] ; **jockelegs** w.Yks. ; **jockylegs** Cum.[1 4] [dga·kslegz.] **1.** A pocket-knife, a large clasp knife. Also in *comb.* **Jackalegs knife.** Cf. **jockteleg.**

n.Cy. GROSE (1790) ; **N.Cy.**[1] **Nhb.** A word of freq. use, *Monthly Chron.* , 1887) 282 ; **Nhb.**[1] A large, single-bladed clasp-knife, *gen.* with a broad and square-edged blade. **Dur.**[1] When a boy has a tumble from a horse, he is tauntingly reproached with having got off to 'take up t'jackalegs.' **s.Dur.** *Obsol.* (J.E.D.) **Lakel.**[2] Ah've a famish good jackilegs at Ah'll gie thi for't, if thoo'l cowp mi. **Cum.** A girt huzzefful eh Jackylegs knives, SARGISSON *Joe Scoap* (1881) 12 ; **Cum.**[1 4] **Wm.** Ah've gitten a new jackilegs for thi (B K.). **n.Yks.**[2] **w.Yks.** It's like carving wood with the back of a jackalegs knife, is honest advice, *Jabez Oliphant* (1870) bk. I. vi ; He went on sharpening his jacky-legs knife, CUDWORTH *Dial. Sketches* (1884) 126 ; **w.Yks.**[1], **ne.Lan.**[1]

Hence **Jack-lag-knife,** *sb.* a clasp knife.

Glo. *Horae Subsecivae* (1777) 227 ; *Gl.* (1851) ; **Glo.**[1]

2. *Fig.* A tall, long-legged man, used as a term of opprobrium.

n.Cy. (HALL.) **w.Yks.**[1] Roberts wad let aike a lousith-heft, jack-a-legs, come ower t'door-stons, ii. 297.

JACKANAPES, *sb.* Sc. Nhb. Dur. Lakel. Yks. Nhp. Hnt. e.An. I.W. Slang. Also in forms **jackanepes** I.W.[1]; **jack-a-nips** Suf.[1] Ess. ; **jackanyeps** Nhb.[1] **1.** A conceited coxcomb ; an affected, puppyish young man. In *gen.* slang use.

Sc. (A.W.), **Dur.**[1] **Lakel.**[2] He's a young jacki-napes ta be sewer. **w.Yks.** Some good man ought to give such a conceited young jacka-napes a horse whipping, HARR *Love for an Hour*, 66. **Nhp.**[1], **Hnt.** (T.P.F.), **Suf.**[1] **Ess.** Oft some jackanips we wine A-handlin' e'en their class, CLARK *J. Noakes* (1839) st. 127. **I.W.**[1] **Slang.** It's little good you'll learn of a Jackanapes like that, SMEDLEY *H. Coverdale* (1856) 209. [More to do with one Jack-an-apes than all the bears, RAY *Prov.* (ed. 1890) 106.]

2. A clownish fellow, one easily gulled. **w.Yks.**[5]

3. Small rollers between the rope-rolls and pulleys of a whim on which a pit-rope runs. Nhb.[1]

JACKASS, *sb.* and *v.* I.W. Som. **1.** *sb.* A term of contempt prefixed to some other epithet.

Som. And we all a-zot [seated] round like jackass-vools, RAYMOND *Sam and Sabina* (1894) 25. **w.Som.**[1] You jackass fool, what's a bin and a do'd now! A gurt jackass toad, d—n un ! that ever I should zay zo !

2. *v.* With *about:* to be occupied with trifles, to be busy to no purpose.

I.W.[2] I ben jackassen about like that all the mornen.

JACKDAW, *sb.* Yks. In phr. *jackdaw tricks,* odd pranks, vagaries. **n.Yks.** He's on wiv his jackdaw tricks (I.W.).

JACKER, *sb.* Chs.[1] Salt-making term : the name given by the boilers to a cheap tar oil.

JACKERDAW, *sb.* Yks. The jackdaw, *Corvus monedula.* **Yks.** *Wkly. Post* (Dec. 31, 1898).

JACKET, *sb.* and *v.* Var. dial. uses in Sc. and Eng. [dga·kit, dga·kit.] **1.** *sb.* In phr. (1) *jacket and waistcoat,* see below ; (2) — *o' muck,* a good covering of manure on a field ; (3) *jackets and petticoats,* the ' hose in hose ' polyanthus.

(1) **Cum.** Each [breed of sheep] wears what the hill farmer terms a 'jacket and waistcoat'—that is, long wool without, with a soft, thick coating beneath, WATSON *Nature and Wdcraft.* (1890) xi; Cum.[4] (*a*) **Chs.**[18] (3) **Cum.** (B. & H.)

2. A waistcoat.

Nhb. Maw shinin' coat o' glossy blue, .. Maw posy jacket, a' bran new, WILSON *Pitman's Pay* (1843) 43. Dur.[1]

3. The skin of a potato.

s.Sc. They cast their jackets in the pot, Ilk ane o' Jamie's tatties, WATSON *Bards* (1859) 75. Dmf. Routh o' potatoes—champit an' hale I' thin ragged jackets, THOM *Jock o' Knowe* (1878) 39. Lakel.[2] **w.Yks.** Potatoes boiled wi' ther jackets on, *Yks. Wkly. Post* (Nov. 28, 1896). Lan. Dun yo' allus ha' taters boiled i' their jackets ! *Longman's Mag.* (Nov. 1895) 71. e.Lan.[1], Oxf. (G.O.)

Hence **Jackutty-taters,** *sb. pl.* potatoes boiled with their skins on. Oxf.[1] *MS. add.*

4. *v.* To flog, thrash, beat.

Nhb.[1] n.Lin.[1] I'll jacket you, young man, next time I light on you. **sw.Lin.[1]** By guy, young man, but I'll jacket you. **Sur.[1]** **Sus.[1]** I'll jacket him when he comes in. **w.Som.[1]** To thrash with some weapon other than the hand. 'He hold'n vast, gin he come out in the churchyard, and then he tookt his stick, and my eye-mers, how he did jacket'n ! '

Hence **Jacketing,** *vbl. sb.* (1) a beating, thrashing, flogging ; (2) a severe scolding or rating ; (3) a hard day's work.

(1) **Nhb.[1], Not.** (J.H.B.) **s.Not.** I gave him a good jacketing before I let him go (J.P.K.). **n.Lin.[1]** **sw.Lin.[1]** He wants a solid good jacketing. **s.Lin.** He gev the young rackapelt sich a jackettin' as he'll not forgit for many a long daā (T.H.R.). **Sur.[1], Sus.** (K.L.), **w.Som.[1]** (2) **Lon.** 'I've got a good jacketing many a Sunday morning,' said one dealer, 'for waking people up with crying mackerel,' MAYHEW *Lond. Labour* (1851) I. 52. **Sur.[1]** I'd sooner hev a jacketin' from th' old Squire, *Blackw. Mag.* (1890) 462. **w.Som.[1]** The judge gid Turney . . . a purty jackettin, sure 'nough ; a zaid, never did'n ought to a braat no such case avore he. (3) **Sus.[1]**

5. Phr. (1) *to jacket it,* to leave a place without warning ; (2) *to be jacketed,* to hear a charge or bear reproof ; to be closeted with.

(1) **Lin.[1]** King said if he didn't suit us he'd jacket-it. (2) **n.Yks.[4]** He's been jacketed wi' t'gaffer i' t'parlour ower an hour noo. Ah'll lay he's gi'en him t'lines properly.

JACKO, *sb.* w.Sc. (JAM. *Suppl.*) Also in forms **gekgo, jecko.** 1. The jackdaw, *Corvus monedula.* See Jack, *sb.* 10. 2. The magpie, *Pica rustica.*

JACKSON, *sb.* and *v.* Lakel. Chs. Nhp. [dʒa‧ksən.] 1. *sb.* In phr. *Jackson's pig,* see below.

Nhp.[1] It's gone over Borough Hill [an extensive Roman encampment near Daventry] after Jackson's pig.' A common phr. in that neighbourhood when anything is lost.

2. *v.* Used only in forms (1) **Jacksoned,** *pp.* thrashed ; (2) **Jacksoning,** *vbl. sb.* a thrashing ; a knocking up, tiring.

(1) **Lakel.[2]** (2) *ib.* He gat amang a lot o' potters at Brough Hill, an' they gev him sec a Jacksonin as he'll nivver fergit. **s.Chs.[1]** Dhaat' koa'l-pit juu·rni gy'en mahy os·iz ū reg·ilŭr Jaak·snin [That coal-pit journey gen my hosses a regular Jacksonin].

JACKY, *sb.* and *adj.* Var. dial. uses in Sc. and Eng. Also written **jakey** Suf. ; **jakky** Wil. ; and in form **jecky-** Cai.[1] 1. *sb.* In *comb.* (1) **Jacky-bread,** currant cake ; (2) **-breezer,** the dragon-fly, *Libellula trimaculata* ; (3) **-crane,** the heron, *Ardea cinerea* ; (4) **— Dinah,** the wood-warbler, *Sylvia sylvicola* ; (5) **-dowker,** the lesser grebe, *Podiceps minor* ; (6) **-forty-feet,** a centipede ; the grub of certain beetles of the species *Elater* ; (7) **-hullot,** a young male owl ; (8) **-jurnal,** the earth-nut, *Bunium flexuosum* ; (9) **-lo',** see (1) ; (10) **-long-legs,** a large gnat, *Tipula oloracea* ; (11) **-nick,** a narrow passage between buildings ; (12) **-pig,** a young pig ; cf. Jack, *int.* ; (13) **-pit,** a shallow pit-shaft in a mine, communicating with an overcast, or at a fault ; cf. Jack-pit ; (14) **-ralph,** the fish wrasse, *Labrus maculatus* ; (15) **-slope,** the kite, *Milvus ictinus* ; (16) **-stones,** (*a*) pebbles ; a game played by children with pebbles, small stones, bones, &c. ; see Jack-stones, s.v. Jack, *sb.* ; (*b*) rather small and extremely hard fossilated shells common in red gravel ; (17) **— Tar,** a sailor's hornpipe ; (18) **-toad** or **Jacket-a-twad,** an *ignis fatuus* or Will-o'-th'-Wisp ;

see Jack-a-lantern ; (19) **-wobstraw,** the blackcap, *Sylvia atricapilla.*

(1) **s.Dev.** Fox *Kingsbridge* (1874). (2) **e.An.[12]** (3) **Cum.** Our food till now was good and cheap ; Poor Jacky Cranes ! DICKINSON *Lit. Rem.* (1888) 160 ; **Cum.[4]** (4) **Wil.[1]** (5) **Chs.[1]** (6) **Cai.[1]** (7) **w.Yks.[5]** (8) **Cum.** The earth-nut I know as 'Jacky jurnal,' *Science Gossip* (1876) 116. (9) **s.Dev.** Fox *Kingsbridge* (1874). (10) **Lin.[1]** Hmp. GROSE (1790) *MS. add.* (M.) **Dev.** BOWRING *Lang.* (1886) I. pt. v. 18 ; **Dev.[1]** (11) **Cum.[4]** (12) **Yks.** (R.S.) **Wil.** *N. & Q.* (1881) 6th S. iv. 106. (13) **Nhb.[1]** (14) **Cor.[12]** (15) **Cum.** LINTON *Lake Cy.* (1864) 306 ; **Cum.[4]** (16, *a*) **Lakel.[2]** **Cum.** A group of girls may be seen with jackey-steans upon the green, SILPHEO *Random Rhymes* (1893) 9 ; **Cum.[1]** A game played amongst school girls with round pebbles, plum or cherry stones ; **Cum.[4]** **Cum., Wm.** Quite common, *N. & Q.* (1865) 3rd S. vii. 250. (*b*) **ne.Wor.[1]** (17) **Rnf.** He not only . . . danced a reel, but . . . actually volunteered 'Jacky Tar,' GILMOUR *Pen-Flk.* (1873) 28. (18) **Dev.** Noa more 'n Jackie-twoad can live away from the marsh an' the bogs, PHILLPOTTS *Dartmoor* (1896) 142 ; I bant coming acrass the moor awl be myzel tū-night. I be aveāred ov the Jackie-twoads, HEWETT *Peas. Sp.* (1892) ; *Horae Subsecivae* (1777) 227 ; **Dev.[1]** n.Dev. GROSE (1790). (19) **w.Wor.[1]**

2. Phr. *one by one like Jacky Lingo's sheep,* one after another, in single file.

w.Yks. They cam one by one like Jackey Lingo's sheep (H.L.).

3. A frog. Cf. Jacob, 3.

Suf. We call it a jakey because we use young frogs as bait to catch the jack with, *N. & Q.* (1877) 5th S. viii. 208.

4. English gin.

Nhb. While rum an' brandy soak'd each chop, We'd Jackey an' fine Ginger Pop, MIDFORD *Coll. Sngs.* (1818) 6 ; An' fine Fardin Pants runnin whisky an' jackey, ROBSON *Bards of Tyne* (1849) 70 ; (R.O.H.) **e.Suf.** (F.H.) Slang. *Household Wds.* (1854) VIII. 75.

5. The game of 'hide-and-seek' or 'I spy.' War.[3]

6. *adj.* Having too much 'Black Jack' or 'blende' in the ore. **Cor.[2]** For the ore was walk and jacky in the stoan.

JACOB, *sb.* Var. dial. uses in Sc. and Eng. [dʒē‧kəb, dʒeə‧kəb.] 1. In phr. (1) *Jacob's chariot,* the monk's-hood, *Aconitum Napellus* ; (2) *—'s ladder,* (*a*) the plant Solomon's seal, *Polygonatum multiflorum* ; (*b*) a garden species of *Gladiolus* ; (*c*) a *gen.* name for *Polemonium coeruleum* ; (*d*) the greater celandine, *Chelidonium majus* ; (*e*) the orpine, *Sedum Telephium* ; (*f*) the wild larkspur, *Delphinium Consolida* ; (*g*) the belladonna, *Atropa Belladonna* ; (*h*) the hole or gap made by a dropped stitch having run down in knitting ; (*i*) a flight of steps running up from a lane into a raised field ; (*j*) a small ladder ; (*k*) see below ; (3) *—'s staff,* the great mullein, *Verbascum Thapsus* ; (4) *—'s stee,* (*a*) see (2, *g*) ; (*b*) see (2, *k*) ; (5) *—'s stones,* see below.

(1) **Ess.** (B. & H.) (2, *a*) **n.Stf.** She did not like the Jacob's Ladder and the row of hollyhocks . . . better than other flowers, GEO. ELIOT *A. Bede* (1859) I. 231. **Lei.[1]** **Brks.** [So called from the alternate leaflets.] **Wil.[1]** **Som.** Coming down the garden path . . . between . . . red Jacob's ladders . . . an' blue love-in-a-puzzle, LEITH *Lemon Verbena* (1895) 208. (*b*) **Glo.[1]** **Suf., Dev.** [So called] from the long spike of alternate flowers (B. & H.). **Dev.[4]** Always so known at Ippleden. (*c*) **e.An.[2], e.Suf.** (F.H.) **Sus.** FRIEND *Gl.* (1882). **Dev.[4]** (*d*) **Shr.** (*e*) **Ken.** (*f*) **Dev.** (*g*) **Ayr.** (JAM.) (*h*) **Lin.** (W.W.S.) **Nhp.[1]** Called also Loose-lather or Louse-ladder. **Cor.[1], Sur.** (L.J.Y.) (*i*) **s.Stf.** On the Beacon-Hargate road was what the country-people thereabouts call a Jacob's ladder, a stile with ten or a dozen steps to it, leading from the low-lying lane to fields on a higher level, MURRAY *John Vale* (1890) i ; Below a Jacob's ladder lay a man of uncommonly large proportions, *ib. Rainbow Gold* (1886) 66. (*j*) **Lon.** A time-keeper of a building society gave evidence that the workmen had left a ladder known as a 'Jacob's ladder' standing against a hut, *Times* (Jan. 29, 1889) 8, col. 1. (*k*) **Lei.[1]** The appearance presented by the rays of the sun falling through an opening in the clouds in hazy weather, the pathway of the ways, generally lighter than the surrounding atmosphere, but more opaque, often having a fanciful resemblance to a ladder. This phenomenon is sometimes called also 'the sun drawing water,' and is considered a sure sign of rain. War.[3] (3) **Cum.[14]** (4) **n.Lin.[1]** (5) **Wal.** In the Caradoc Sandstone (of the Cambrian Series) remains of fossils are often so abundant as to render some of the beds sufficiently calcareous to be burnt for lime. These beds are known to the workmen as Jacob's Stones, WOODWARD *Geol. Eng. and Wal.* (1876) 46.

2. A silly fellow. Dev. *Reports Provinc.* (1889). **3.** A frog. e.An.[1], Ess.[1] **4.** The starling, *Sturnus vulgaris.* Chs.[8] (s.v. Jack Nicker). Nhp.[1] (s.v. Dicky-bird). [SWAINSON *Birds* (1885) 73.]

5. A round black plum, in considerable demand in the local markets. Chs.[1]

JACOBINES, *sb. pl.* ? *Obs.* Lin.[1] Loose, disorderly persons; malcontents.

[Fr. *Jacobins,* a name applied to a famous revolutionary club in Paris in 1789.]

JAD, *sb.* Glo. Som. [dʒæd.] Stone-quarrying term: a narrow groove picked out at the top of the freestone.

Som. A narrow gap [groove] picked out by the quarrymen at the top of the freestone, the first operation in removing blocks. Commencing with a heavy pick 7½ lbs. and finishing with a light one 4½ lbs. on a 6 ft. handle, a graduated series of picks being used, WINWOOD *Excur. to Corsham, Prov. Geol. Assoc.* (July 1896) XIV. 8.

Hence (1) **Jadder,** *sb.* a stone-cutter; (2) **Jaddings,** *sb. pl.* the marks on the stone which show where a 'jad' has been cut.

(1) Glo. (H.T.E.); *Gl.* (1851); Glo.[1] (2) Som. WINWOOD *ib.*

JADDER, *v.* Lakel. Also written **jaddur** Lakel.[2] [dʒa·dθər.] To shake, vibrate; of the teeth: to chatter.

Lakel.[2] Du't clash t'door teea like that, thoo maks iv'ry pot i' t'hoose jaddur. Wm. Mi teeth faer jaddthred i mi heead, *Spec. Dial.* (1885) pt. iii. 9; His teeth jadder'd in his heed wi t'cauld wind (B.K.).

JADDER, *adj.* e.An. [Not known to our correspondents.] Shaky; infirm. (HALL.) Cf. **jouder,** *v.*

JADDY, *sb.* Yks. [dʒa·di.] A cake made with flour and lard or dripping; 'fatty-cake' (q.v.).

w.Yks. We'll hev sum rum-an'-tea an' jaddy after t'christenin' (S.K.C.).

JADE, *sb.* Sc. Nhb. Lakel. Yks. Hrt. e.An. I.W. Wil. Also in forms jad Fif. Ayr.; jaud(e Sc. Yks.; jawd Sc.; jed Wil.; jeead I.W.[1]; yaad Hdg.; yad Sc. (JAM.); yade Abd. s.Sc. (JAM.); yaud s.Sc. (JAM.) [dʒēd, Sc. also jad, jād.] **1.** A mare; a horse; an old worn-out horse; also used *fig.*

Sc. Ye'll tak' the grey yad an' gang to the toun on Monday, FORD *Thistledown* (1891) 245; If wads were yads, beggars would ride, RAMSAY *Prov.* (1776) 42 (JAM.). Abd. The yade has turn'd sae baul' As dare to hit, SHIRREFS *Poems* (1790) 218. Lnk. Pleasure is a fickle jaud, MURDOCH *Doric Lyre* (1873) 24; Haud the auld jade till I loup on, GRAHAM *Writings* (1883) II. 32. Edb. I'm mounted on a jade That winna speel, M^cDOWALL *Poems* (1890) 30. Dmf. Country lads (Their joes abint them on their yads), MAYNE *Siller Gun* (1789) 13. Hdg. A meer ... Fat, sleek, and sonsy, slow—but sure; And yet a sicker jaud and dour . . . A pawky yaad, LUMSDEN *Poems* (1896) 13. Nhb.[1], Yks. (K.) Hrt. She proved a jade in the collar, ELLIS *Mod. Husb.* (1750) III. i. e.An.[1] We do not always use it in a contemptuous sense. A clown will sometimes call a fine hunter, 'a brave jade.' Cart horses are very commonly called so. A horse that will not work well up to the collar. e.Suf. A refractory or jibbing horse (F.H.). I.W.[1]

2. A worthless woman; a giddy young girl, used in a playful sense.

Sc. The auld jaud is no sae ill as that comes to, SCOTT *Midlothian* (1818) xiii; Jaude is often used in a kind, familiar way in speaking of or to a smart growing girl. A mother will say with evident pride, 'Our Meg's growin' a ticht, braw jaude, so she is!' (JAM. *Suppl.*). Abd. I own I ance had liking for the yade, But couk to think o't since she turn'd a bawd, SHIRREFS *Poems* (1790) 51. Frf. Since a wheen rough jauds cam' in, WATT *Poet. Sketches* (1880) 22. Per. Though Nance is an ill-natured jaud, HALIBURTON *Horace* (1886) 75. Fif. Down wi' the mass and monkish squad, Down wi' the jad in scarlet clad, TENNANT *Papistry* (1827) 28. Rnf. Haud your tongue, ye scoldin' jaud, BARR *Poems* (1861) 10. Ayr. The bardy jaud gaed awa, lauchin' to hersel', SERVICE *Notandums* (1890) 43; But clear your decks, and here's the sex! I like the jads for a' that, BURNS *Jolly Beggars* (1785) st. 290. Lnk. Baith canker'd auld carle, an' raucle-tongued jaudie, Hae aye a kind word for the Puir's-hoose laddie, NICHOLSON *Idylls* (1870) 46. Lth. Bess, pawky Jaud, is aye smirkin' an' jeerin', BALLANTINE *Poems* (1856) 57. e.Lth. I tell't Jess no to fash hersel for an ill-willy auld jaud o' a deacon's wife, HUNTER *J. Inwick* (1895) 60. Dmf. The younglin' jauds, were they never sae shy, Aye buskit

their best when the Laird gaed by, REID *Poems* (1894) 77. Bwk. When younger jauds brisked up to lads An' tripped it by the hour, CALDER *Poems* (1897) 94. Nhb.[1] Lakel.[2] A gay lish jade, not meaning anything but approval, of an active, stirring woman. 'A gurt idle jade' has the opposite meaning. I.W.[1]

3. A term of contempt applied to a person of either sex. Wil. Only in the phr. 'You be a comical jade' (W.C.P.).

JADED, *ppl. adj.* n.Yks.[1 4] Placed in circumstances of almost inextricable difficulty, straitened on all sides.

JADIN, *sb.* ? *Obs.* Sc. The stomach of a cow. See **Jaudie.**

Fif. I had rather eat Sow's jadin aff a plotter-plate, *MS. Poem* (JAM.).

JADSTANE, *sb.* Sc. The common white pebble, found on the sand, or in beds of rivers.

Lth. (JAM.) e.Lth. They say, bile jadstanes in butter, the bree'll be guid, HUNTER *J. Inwick* (1895) 79.

JAFFLE, *sb.*[1] Cor. Also in forms jeffull, jerffel Cor.[2]; yaffle Cor.[1]; yafful Cor.[2] [dʒæˑfl, jæˑfl.] A handful.

Cor.[1] *Gen.* applied to a bunch of flowers. 'A jaffle of flowers.' 'Jeffulls of hay'; Cor.[2] w.Cor. Holding on to its tail until it could stand steady enow to devour the little jerffel of straw put before it, BOTTRELL *Trad.* 3rd S. 159.

JAFFLE, *sb.*[2] e.An.[1] e.Suf. (F.H.) [dʒæˑfl.] Idle discourse of an indecent or malicious character. Cf. **jiffle, 3.**

JAFFLED, *ppl. adj.* Gall. Fatigued looking, down in body and clothes. MACTAGGART *Encycl.* (1824). Cf. **jachelt.**

JAFFLER, *sb.* Obsol. Cum. A careless, idle man.

Wi' Harry, Jack, an' Symie, com', An' monny jafflers leyke his sell, STAGG *Misc. Poems* (ed. 1807) 89; Cum.[4]

JAFFLING, *adj.* e.An.[1] e.Suf. (F.H.) Fidgety. See **Jiffle.**

JAFFOCK, *v.* Chs.[1] [dʒaˑfək.] To argue, dispute.

JAFFSE, *v.* S. & Ork.[1] To make a noise with the jaws in eating.

[Cp. Norw. dial. *kjeft (kjaft),* the jaw (AASEN); ON. *kjaptr.*]

JAG, *sb.*[1] Nhb. Cum. Wm. Yks. [dʒag.] A small watery 'blush' or blister; *gen.* in *comb.* **Water jag.**

Nhb.[1], Cum. (M.P.) n.Wm. 'Watter jags' is the term used for a complaint most children have, and which is in the nature of a large rash, *Yks. Wkly. Post* (Jan. 28, 1899). m.Yks.[1] The face of a person in the first stage of the small-pox is covered with 'water-jags.'

JAG, *sb.*[2] Oxf. Wil. [dʒag.] The awn and head of the oat; the large head of a flower.

Oxf.[1] My wuts be out in jag, *MS. add.* Wil. The oats were coming out in jag. . . In jag means the spray-like drooping awn, JEFFERIES *Gt. Estate* (1881) 8; Wil.[1] Oats are spoken of as 'having a good jag,' 'coming out in jag,' &c. 'Wull, to be shower, they chrysantums is beautiful! They be sal in a jag !'

Hence **Jagged,** *ppl. adj.* of oats: coming out in heads. Wil.[1] n.Wil. Oats ... sown early on good ground promises to be well jagged, *Devizes Gazette* (June 22, 1893) 5; (E.H.G.)

JAG, *sb.*[3] ? *Obs.* Sc. Calf-leather.

Jack or hunter fashion of boots, *Gl. Sibb.* (JAM.); His boots they were made of the jag, RAMSAY *Tea-Table Misc.* (1724) I. 298, ed. 1871; This term still signifies the best part of calf-leather (JAM.).

JAG, *sb.*[4] ? *Obs.* Sc. Fatigue.

Abd. Ne'er thinkin't ony jag or pingle, Till I was clankit at your ingle, TARRAS *Poems* (1804) 26 (JAM.).

JAG, *v.* and *sb.*[5] Sc. n.Cy. Yks. Not. Suf. [dʒag.]

1. *v.* To jerk roughly; to jolt; to move with a sharp, jerking motion; to 'jog.'

Cai.[1] Bnf.[1] Tho rod wiz sae rough, an' the cairt jaggit sae muckle, it a thocht ma vera bodie wid hae been jaggit out o' it her. Abd. As through the thrang we push our way We're jagged back an' fore, MILNE *Sngs.* (1871). e.Not. Niver jag the reins a that how (J.P.K.). e.Suf. We jagged on very pleasantly (F.H.).—

2. With *off* or *over:* to fall or 'jog' over, as a load of corn may do.

n.Cy. In some districts a displaced load would be said to have 'jagged ower o' ta yah side,' *Yks. Wkly. Post* (Jan. 28, 1898). e.Yks.[1] It varry near jagged off, just as we com thruff yatstead.

3. *sb.* A sharp jerk or jolt.

Cai.[1], Bnf.[1] n.Not. He gen the chain no end of a jag (J.P.K.).

Hence **Jaggie,** *adj.* having a jerking or jolting motion. Bnf.[1] The cairrige is unco jaggie the day. Faht can ail't?

4. A rut. Bnf.[1] The rod's fou o' jags.

Hence **Jaggie,** *adj.* full of ruts. *ib.*

JAG(G, *sb.*[1] and *v.*[1] Sc. n.Cy. Lakel. Yks. Lan. Chs. Der. Lin. Lei. Nhp. Shr. Hrf. Glo. Bdf. e.An. Also in forms **jaug** Sc.; **jog** Nhp.[1] Glo.[1] Bdf. [dʒag, dʒæg, dʒog.]
1. *sb.* A small load of coal, hay, &c.

n.Cy.[1] Lakel.[2] We've nobbut a lile jagg left. n.Yks. Let's hev a little jag of hay (I.W.). ne.Yks.[1] w.Yks. PIPER *Dial. Sheffield* (1824); w.Yks.[1] A large cart-load of hay; w.Yks.[2] Lan. So aw went to th' coalpit. . . an' we temd two jags o' coal by breakfast time, BRIERLEY *Red Wind.* (1868) 109; The ass and cart with their modest 'jag' of timber, *ib. Irkdale* (1868) 174. Chs.[1] 'An yo done le-adin curn l' 'Yah, aw bur abaht a jag'; Chs.²⁸ s.Chs.[1] Fatch a jag o' coal. Der.[1] s.Lin. He's just brought the last loaad, a jag o' raakin's (T.H.R.). Nhp.[1] Shr.[1] Tak' the light waggin an' fatch them tuthree rākin's, they'n on'y be a bit o' a jag. Hrf.[1]; Hrf.[2] I drawed three jag of tinnit. Glo.[1], Bdf. (J.W.B.). e.An.[1] An indefinite quantity, but less than a load, of hay or corn in the straw. Nrf. A parcel or load of anything, whether on a man's back, or in a carriage, GROSE (1790). Suf. In an account dated Sept. 1700, is the item : 'Carried the widow Smith one jag of thorns, 12s.,' CULLUM *Hist. Hawsted* (1813); (G.F.J.); Suf.[1], s.Suf. (F.H.) w.Ess. A jag of wood, hay, straw, manure, &c., is intended to mean a little less than a one-horse cartload, *N. & Q.* (1893) 8th S. iii. 95. [MORTON *Cyclo. Agric.* (1863).]

2. A journey ; the carrying or carting of a load.

Lakel.² We'll gang anudder jagg. n.Wm. 'Another jag' would mean not only a load, but implies the journey for it, as in loading hay, corn, manure, &c., Yks. *Wkly. Post* (Jan. 28, 1899). Shr.[1] 'So John Ivans is turned jagger, I 'ear l' 'Aye, an' it's a poor jag 'e'll mak' on it, fur I dunna know w'ich is the biggest drum-mil, 'im or the owd 'orse.'

3. A leather bag or wallet ; a pocket ; *pl.* saddle-bags.

Sc. There's nae room for bags or jaugs here, SCOTT *St. Ronan* (1824) ii ; The bearer of a wallet or leather bag called a 'jag,' Yks. *Wkly. Post* (Dec. 24, 1898). Per., Fif., Cld., Rxb. (JAM.), n.Yks.²

4. Ale in a bottle in common among miners. Der.², nw.Der.[1]

5. A fill of drink, esp. in phr. *to have one's jag*, to be drunk.

n.Wm. A man with 'a fairish jag on,' would be one with rather more intoxicants inside him than he could 'carry streck,' Yks. *Wkly. Post* (Jan. 28, 1899). Nrf. 'He has got his jag,' i.e. as much drink as he can fairly carry, Garl. (1872) ii. [RAY *Prov.* (1678) 87.]

6. A branch of broom or gorse ; a large bundle of briars, used for breaking the clods in ploughed fields.

Lei.[1] Called also, a 'clothing harrow.' 'Tek the caart, an' fetch a jagg o' thorns.' Shr.[1]

7. *v.* To cart or carry a load of anything, esp. hay ; to act as a carman or carrier.

Chs. I once asked a servant girl in Chester, who her father was. She replied, 'John Vaughan, what jags.' He was a sort of town carman in a small way, *N. & Q.* (1877) 5th S. viii. 266. s.Chs.[1], nw.Der.[1] Shr.[1]; Shr.[2] To jag him a load of hay. Shr., Hrf. *Provinc.* (1876).

JAG(G, *v.*² and *sb.*² Sc. Irel. Nhb. Yks. Amer. Also written jog w.Yks.; and in form jog Sc. Uls. [dʒag.]
1. *v.* To prick or pierce with some sharp instrument ; to throb or prick painfully.

Sc. He bade her ride, And with a spur did jag her side, WATSON *Coll. Sngs.* (1706) I. 39 (JAM.); HERD *Coll. Sngs.* (1776) Gl. Cai.[1] Per. Lang hae I trod in folly's path, Sair jogged wi' thorns and nettles scaudie, SPENCE *Poems* (1898) 72. Ayr. A preen has been jaggin' the dowp o't, SERVICE *Notandums* (1890) 94. Lnk. He tak's a preen And jags the very weans, RODGER *Poems* (1898) 133, ed. 1897. Lth. He couldna eat a hedgehog ; it would jag his tongue, STRATHESK *More Bits* (ed. 1885) 83. Edb. A thistle on the grave jagged her, PENNECUIK *Tinklarian* (ed. 1810) 8. Bwk. Thistles that could jag fu' sair, CALDER *Poems* (1897) 95. Dmf. But our thristle will jag his thumbs, CROMEK *Remains* (1810) 144. Gall. MACTAGGART *Encycl.* (1824). Kcb. Cauld Willie Winter, Comin' wi' your needle nose to jag the bonnie bairn, ARMSTRONG *Ingleside* (1890) 24. n.Ir. There maun be a pin jaggin' him, a think, LYTTLE *Paddy McQuillan*, 70 ; N.I.[1] A wee bit o' spruce fir jagged me in the sight o' the eye. Uls. (M.B.-S.), Nhb.[1] [Amer. He went up and jagged a pin into the baby's leg, ADELER *Elbow Room* (1876) ii.]

Hence (1) **Jagger**, *sb.* (*a*) a prickle ; (*b*) a good used for urging on a donkey ; (*c*) a staff with an iron prong used for lifting turnips ; (2) **Jaggit**, *ppl. adj.* pierced ; (3) **Jag-the-flea**, *sb.* a term of contempt for a tailor ; see **Jack**, 3 (38).

(1, *a*) Fif. (JAM.) (*b*) Nhb. It is made by inserting a sharpened horse stob nail into the end of a staff (R.O.H.) ; Nhb.[1] Seldom seen now. (*c*) Nhb.[1] (*a*) Bwk. The thrissels Their jaggit tassels reared, CALDER *Poems* (1897) 81. (3) Ayr. Gae mind your seam, ye prick-the-louse, An' jag-the flae, BURNS *Post. Ep., to a Tailor*, st. 2. Lnk. I'll let him ken—'vile jag the flea'—'That I'm no made o' common mettle, NICHOLSON *Idylls* (1870) 35.

2. *Fig.* To vex, irritate, annoy, trouble ; to pain, rankle.

Frf. Easie Haggart jagged the minister sorely, BARRIE *Licht* (1888) iii. Fif. He's planted a thorn in his breist that will jag him a' his days, ROBERTSON *Provost* (1894) 51. w.Yks. I had a terrible rough way at that time if ought jagged me, SNOWDEN *Web of Weaver* (1896) 76 ; Albeit this jagged against my pride, *ib.* 8.

3. *sb.* A prick or tear made by a sharp instrument, thorn, &c. ; a thorn. Also used *fig.*

Sc. Affliction may gie him a jagg, SCOTT *Midlothian* (1818) ix. Cai.[1] Frf. A girl gives him the jag, and it brings out the perspiration, BARRIE *Tommy* (1896) 65. Per. Mustard had gotten a lang jag in's forepaw, CLELAND *Inchbracken* (1883) 209, ed. 1887. Ayr. Whatever bliss it brag, In the hinny there's a jag, AINSLIE *Poems* (ed. 189a) 46. Lnk. There's jags on ilka path o' life, MACDONALD *Poems* (1865) 19. s.Lth. An'ra Wabster never missed a chance o' haein a jag at me, HUNTER *J. Inwick* (1895) 124. Bwk. A jag frae the thorn, CALDER *Poems* (1897) 250. Gall. Ye gied Duke Wellwood's lads some most unmerciful jags aneath the ribs, CROCKETT *Moss-Hags* (1895) xxxiii. Ir. He gize him a jagg of a pin under the desk, CARLETON *Traits Peas.* (ed. 1843) I. 307. n.Ir. Ivery time that a gied her a wee jag wi' them a thocht she was that fu' o' spirit that she riz on her hin' legs, LYTTLE *Robin Gordon*, 79 ; N.I.[1] Ant. GROSE (1790) *MS. add.* (C.)

Hence (1) **Jag-armed**, *ppl. adj.* armed with a sharp point or sting ; (2) **Jaggy**, *adj.* prickly ; sharp-pointed, piercing.

(1) Fif. Jag-arm'd nettles soon, I trow, The passer-by shall sting, TENNANT *Papistry* (1827) 73. (a) Inv. (H.E.F.) Baff. Their ain doups rather shou'd be kickit Wi' something jaggy, TAYLOR *Poems* (1787) 9. Fif. (JAM.) Lnk. The gowden bloom o' the jaggy whins, WRIGHT *Life* (1897) 28. Nhb.[1]

JAG(G, *sb.*³ and *v.*³ n.Cy. Dur. Cum. Yks. Lan. Chs. Hrf. Suf. Ess. Som. Dev. Amer. Also in form jeg w.Yks. [dʒag, dʒæg.]
1. *sb.* A rag or shred of raiment ; *gen.* in *pl.* rags, tatters ; splinters.

n.Cy. (HALL.) Cum.²; Cum.⁴ I met an old man all rags and jags. w.Yks. (J.W.), e.Lan.[1], Ess.[1] w.Som.[1] Brokt his coat all to jags. Dev.[2], nw.Dev.[1]

2. A bit of anything.

Hrf.² A tidy jag left yet. [Amer. CARRUTH *Kansas Univ. Quar.* (189a) I.]

3. *v.* To cut roughly or unevenly ; to make notches ; also used *intrans.* Cf. **jaggle**, *v.* **1.**

w.Yks. (J.W.) e.Suf. When a saw is not properly set, and sawdust collects in its teeth, it is said to jag (F.H.). w.Som.[1] I told you, Mary, to cut it straight, and you've been and jagged the cloth right across. Aay oa'n lai'n dhee muy' nuy·v ugee·un. Lèok·ee zee, aaw dhee-s ubûn' un u jag'n [I will not lend you my knife again. Look see, how you have been and notched it].

Hence (1) **Jag**, *sb.* the sawdust collected in the teeth of a saw which 'jags.' e.Suf. (F.H.); (2) **Jagged**, *ppl. adj.* applied to edges uneven or denticulated irregularly, frayed or worn at the edges, used only of raiment. Dur.[1], w.Yks. (J.W.); (3) **Jagging-iron**, *sb.* a circular instrument with teeth used in making ornamental pastry. w.Yks.[1]

4. To trim up the small branches of a tree or hedge. n.Cy. (HALL.), Chs.¹²³

JAG(G, see **Jeg**.

JAGG, *sb.* Sc. See below. Also called **jougs** (q.v.).
The jägg or jougs consisted of an iron collar fastened by a padlock, which hung from a chain secured in the church wall near the principal entrance. An offender sentenced to the jagg was compelled to stand locked within this collar for an hour or more before the morning service on one or more Sundays, ANDREWS *Bygone Ch. Life* (1899) 113.

JAGGER, *sb.* Sc. Nhb. Dur. Cum. Wm. Yks. Chs. Der. Lin. Shr. Also in forms jauger, jager Sh.I. ; jigger Der.² nw.Der.[1]; yaager Sc. (JAM.); yagger Sh.I. (JAM.) [dʒa·gə(r, Sh.I. also jä·gər.] **1.** A travelling pedlar ; a hawker, esp. a fish-hawker.

Sc. The name 'jagger' is applied to a pedlar, or the bearer of a wallet or leather bag called a 'jag,' Yks. *Wkly. Post* (Dec. 24,

1898); (JAM.) Sh.I. ' I am a jagger,' .. replied ... a stout, vulgar little man, who had indeed the humble appearance of a pedlar, called jagger in these islands, SCOTT *Pirate* (1822) v; The word ... properly signifies a person who purchases goods, chiefly fish, contracted for by another (JAM.) ; Dey wir sic a hubble wi' boys, jaagers, an' men, *Sh. News* (July 15, 1899).

2. A boat, which takes the first catch of herrings to land in the deep-sea fishing.

Sh.I. The doggers attached to them [herring busses], named also Jaggers or Yaggers, were swifter sailers, being intended to run home with the herrings first caught. After the Jaggers are all dispatched, the busses continue fishing till they make up cargoes, HIBBERT *Desc. Sh. I.* (1822) 215, ed. 1891.

Hence **Jager-steamer**, *sb.* a steamer for the transport of herrings.

Sh.I. There might have been from 100 to 120 of the Dutch craft in. No Germans at that epoch, and no booms, nor jager steamers, *Sh. News* (June 25, 1898).

3. A carter or carrier, esp. a man who makes his living by carting for other people ; one who sells coals in small loads. See **Jag(g**, *v.*[1] 7.

n.Cy. (HALL.) Cum. A carrier, when loads were carried on the backs of horses. The word was never applied to a carrier in carts here. It is seldom heard now; but a road on Stanemore by which pack-horses used to travel is still called 't'jagger rwoad' (M.P.). Chs. A poor labourer that carries coal from the pits in Flintshire to Chester market, on a small horse (K.) ; Chs.[12] s.Chs.[1] For the horse in best condition owned by huxters or coal-jaggers residing at Threapwood, Worthenbury, or Shocklach, *Advt. of Flower Show* (1886). n.Lin. You're the best jagger that ever run'd round Wivilby Green, PEACOCK *R. Skirlaugh* (1870) III. 229. Shr.[1] So John Ivans is turned jagger, I 'ear ! Shr.[2]

4. A pack-horse driver.

Dur. GIBSON *Up-Weardale Gl.* (1870). n.Yks.[2] Der. *N. & Q.* (1876) 5th S. v. 474 ; Der.[2], nw.Der.[1]

Hence **Jagger-horse**, *sb.* a pack-horse.

n.Yks.[2] Der. *N. & Q.* (1876) 5th S. v. 474.

5. A carrier of ore from the mine to the smelting-mill.

Der. Until the introduction of wheel carriages in the Peak ... the only mode of conveying goods and merchandise from one part of this country to a distance was on the back of pack-horses, or, as they were here called, 'jagger-horses,' and the drivers or conductors, 'jaggers.' These jaggers were employed in conveying lead ore from Eyam, and mines in the locality, to the smelting-houses in the neighbourhood of Sheffield, returning at night loaded with sacks of coal, *N. & Q.* (1876 5th S. v. 474 ; GROSE (1790) *MS. add.* (M.) ; Der.[12], nw.Der.[1]

Hence **Jagger-galloway**, *sb.* a pony with a peculiar saddle for carrying lead, &c.

N.Cy.[1], Nhb.[1] Obs. Cum., Wm. A ' jagger-galloway ' may yet be heard of as employed in the mining districts (M.P.).

6. A small dealer in hay.

Der. The word 'jagger' is used in the Peak, not confined to a person who sells cartloads of coals. I have heard it *gen.* applied to men who purchased hay, and then carted it for sale to Manchester or Stockport—such a man is called a 'hay jagger,' *N. & Q.* (1877) 5th S. viii. 518 ; Der.[2], nw.Der.[1]

JAGGET, *sb.* n.Sc. (JAM.) [Not known to our correspondents.] A full sack or pocket, hanging awkwardly, and dangling at every motion.

JAGGLE, *v.* Yks. Shr. Also in form **jiggle** w.Yks.[5] [dga·gl, w.Yks. dge·gl, dgi·gl.] **1.** To cut badly and unevenly. Cf. **haggle**, *v.*[1]

w.Yks.[5] Shr.[1] Them scithors mun gōō to Soseb'ry to be grond —jest look 'ow they jagglen the stuff—somebody's bin nōsin' an' taflin' faib'ries ōōth 'em.

2. To shake ; to move from side to side.

w.Yks.[2] When machinery gets loose and begins to jaggle it is time to fetch the engineer.

3. To quarrel, jangle.

w.Yks. Ta set things square wi ivvriboddy, an save onny hagglin an jagglin at mud spring up ameng em, TOM TREDDLEHOYLE *Bairnsla Ann.* (1868) 3 ; w.Yks.[2] I don't like your hagglin', jagglin' ways.

JAIBLE, see **Jabble**, *v.*

JAIL, *sb.* and *v.*[1] Sc. Also in form **jile** Abd. **1.** *sb.* In phr. *a month of the jail*, a month's imprisonment.

Ayr. Only gied the creature a month o' the jail. HUNTER *Studies* (1870) 24.

2. *v.* To put in prison.

Abd. Fat'll they dee wi' 'im ? Will they jile 'im ? ALEXANDER *Ain Flk.* (1882) 121 ; To apprehend and jail me, I gi'e ye 'llowance, ANDERSON *Poems* (1826) 90. Slg. Bess, Who jail'd her eighteen years, GALLOWAY *Poems* (1792) 58. Rnf. Jail him till his hindmost plack Is paid to them, M'GILVRAY *Poems* (ed. 1862) 104. Lnk. Ye can jail me, banish me, hang me gin ye please, but naething will jale me, FRASER *Whaups* (1895) 122. Gall. They can only tak' an' jail me, KERR *Maggie o' the Moss* (1891) 73.

Hence **Jailing** or **Jileing**, *sb.* imprisonment.

Abd. An' wud it be a fine or jilein than ? ALEXANDER *Johnny Gibb* (1871) xxiii. Edb. Gie them routh for toilin' for it, Ye'll see less jailin', LIDDLE *Poems* (1821) 81.

JAIL, *v.*[2] Cor. Also written **jaale** Cor.[2] ; **jale**. [dgēl.] To walk fast, hurry along.

He ran up the granite-strewn hillside ' like wan jailin' off to a wreck,' PEARCE *Esther Pentreath* (1891) bk. 1. iii ; I jaaled after un. He keeped on jaalin hum, HIGHAM *Dial.* (1866) 11 ; But I must be jaleing-along, O'DONOGHUE *St. Knighton* (1864) xiii ; Cor.[1] Where be 'ee jailing ? Cor.[28] w.Cor. They were leading and jailing uplong (A.L.M.).

JAIL, *v.*[3] ne.Lan.[1] [Not known to our correspondents.] To crack ; to spill.

JAIMMINTY, *sb.* Irel. In phr. *by Jaimminty*, an exclamation or quasi-oath.

Don. ' By Jaimminty yis !' says Billy, clappin' his hands, MAC-MANUS *Billy Lappin*, in *Century Mag.* (Feb. 1900) 605.

JAIP, JAIRBLE, see **Jaup**, *v.*[1], **Jirble**, *v.*[2]

JAISTER, *sb.* n.Cy. Nhb. Dur. [dgē·stər.] Swagger, pride of manner and gait. See **Gester**.

n.Cy. Aw's gat a canny maister, Ayon, Ayon, Aw ken him by his jaister [gesture], Ayon, Ay (W.T.). s.Dur. He hes a lot o' jaister about him (J.E.D.).

Hence **Jaistering**, *ppl. adj.* swaggering, gesturing, gesticulating.

N.Cy.[1] It is common to call a person of an airy manner, if a male, 'a jaistering fellow ' ; and, if a female, 'a jaistering jade.' Nhb.[1], Dur.[1]

[The same word as lit. E. *gesture*.]

JAKE, see **Jauk**.

JAKES, *sb.* Som. Dev. Cor. [dgēks.] **1.** Human excrement.

w.Som.[1] Very common. ' Zee where you be going, else you'll sure to tread in the jakes.' The word rather implies a considerable quantity, such as that found at the back of a privy ; not the privy itself. nw.Dev.[1]

2. A state of dirty mess or untidiness ; a mess, confusion. Also used *fig.*

w.Som.[1] The snow have made a proper jakes of my work to-night. Dev. Ef yü'd azeed tha jakes 'er made wi' thickee there pudden, yü widden ayte wan mossel aw'n, HEWETT *Peas. Sp.* (1892) ; Zich a jakes (such a mess) as never was seen, fit to make my flesh crip ess fay it is ! LYALL *Donovan* (1887) xx ; Dev.[2] The rawds be in a reg'lar jakes. n.Dev. If ha lov'th jakes, why let un beckon Hagegy Bess, ROCK *Jim an' Nell* (1867) st. 89. nw.Dev.[1] s.Dev. 'Tis a proper jakes (F.W.C.). Cor.[1]

[**1.** The older meaning of *jakes* was 'latrina.' There was a goddess of idleness, a goddess of the draught, or jakes, BURTON *Anat. Mel.* (1621), ed. 1896, II. 13.]

JAKLE, *sb.* Som. Dev. Written **jaykle** Dev.[1] [dgē·kl.] In phr. *by jakle* ! or *O jakle !* a disguised oath.

w.Som.[1] Dev.[1] O Jaykle ! this was but a vlee-bite, 15.

JALE, see **Jail**, *v.*[2]

JALLISHY BUFF, *phr.* Cor. [dgæ·liʃi bœf.] Yellowish buff.

Adm'ral Buzza in full fig, and a row o' darters in jallishy buff, ' Q.' *Troy Town* (1888) viii ; Cor.[1] I want a bit of jallishy buff prent, to make a frock for my cheeld ; Cor.[2] (s.v. Jaller).

JALLUP, *sb.* Sc. n.Cy. A brisk purgative; also used *fig.* Edb. They will chance to get some jallup Frae the laird o' Jelly Ben, FORBES *Poems* (1812) 164 ; (G.W.) n.Cy. (J.W.)

JALOUSE, *v.* Sc. n.Cy. Dur. Yks. Der. Lin. Suf. Also written **jaloose** Sc. ; and in forms **jealous**(e Sc. N.Cy.[1] Dur. n.Yks.[2] Lin. Suf. ; **jelouse** Fif. Ayr. [dgalū·z.] To suspect, be suspicious of ; to guess, imagine, suppose. Cf. **jealous**, *adj.*

Sc. It's my puir thought, that he jaloused their looking into his letters, SCOTT *Antiquary* (1816) xvi. Cai.[1] Abd. Jalousin that something was going on, ALEXANDER *Johnny Gibb* (1871) xli. **Kcd.** I jalouse he is a wooer, GRANT *Lays* (1884) 84. **Frf.** I daresay you can jalouse the rest, BARRIE *Tommy* (1896) 334. **Per.** A'm jalousing that nae man can be a richt father without being sib tae every bairn, IAN MACLAREN *Brier Bush* (1895) 160. **w.Sc.** As ye may jalouse there were few in our house could tak ony denner that day, CARRICK *Laird of Logan* (1835) 275. **Fif.** Ye needna be feared, for Tibbie 'll be the last to jalouse onything, MᶜLAREN *Tibbie* (1894) 54 ; When I cam' back Tammas had awakened, and he jeloused, HEDDLE *Marget* (1899) 61. **e.Fif.** Never aince jealousin' what was what, LATTO *Tam Bodkin* (1864) x. **Dmb.** 'Twould make some folks jalouse that Sandie Fry Had got his sooty finger in the pie, SALMON *Gowodean* (1868) 90. **Ayr.** Where she hade it I never could jaloose, SERVICE *Dr. Duguid* (ed. 1887) 15. **Lnk.** Joy may come when we least jalouse, THOMSON *Laddy May* (1883) 11. **Lth.** I . . . muckle 'jalouse 'tis a theme To crack a jest on, LUMSDEN *Sheep-head* (1892) 119. **e.Lth.** A' body jaloused wha it was meant for, HUNTER *J. Inwick* (1895) 16. **Edb.** I jealoused at once what they were after, MOIR *Mansie Wauch* (1828) xvi. **Bwk.** Her lad—I ne'er jaloused she'd ane, CALDER *Poems* (1897) 203. **Slk.** I thought it was the young fallows ye jaloosed her wi', HOGG *Tales* (1838) 3, ed. 1866. **Gall.** D'ye no jaloose what for it disna gang straight forrit ? CROCKETT *Raiders* (1894) xxiv. **Wgt.** I began to jealouse some evil design towards me, FRASER *Wigtown* (1877) 190. **N.Cy.¹** **s.Dur.** A' jealous he's about nowt [no good or of no use] (J.E.D.). **n.Yks.** They jealous'd him of having set the shed on fire (C.V.C.) ; n.**Yks.²** 'I jealous'd it,' I had my suspicions about it. **Der.** I dunna want him to jalouse his sister, VERNEY *Stone Edge* (1868) vii ; **Der.²,** nw.**Der.¹** n.Lin. He said he jealous'd that a billy biter had gotten a nest in it (E.P.). **s.Lin.** I jealoused him from the fost (T.H.R.). **e.Suf.** Used of both persons and actions (F.H.).

Hence **Jalousings,** *sb. pl.* suspicions.

Sc. If 'e don't ken yersel', it's no expected I can hae ony jaloosins, TWEDDALE *Moff* (1896) 199. **w.Sc.** I had ma ain jalousings when Jan telt me, MACDONALD *Settlement* (1869) 77, ed. 1877.

[OFr. *jalouser,* 'devenir jaloux' (LA CURNE).]

JALP, see **Jaup,** *v.*¹

JAM, *v.* Sc. n.Cy. Cum. Yks. Lan. Der. Lin. Brks. e.An. Hmp. Som. Dev. Cor. Also written **jamb** e.An.¹ Dev.; and in form **jaum** w.Yks. n.Lin.¹ [dʒam, dʒæm.]

1. To squeeze tightly ; to press together ; to wedge ; to bruise or crush by compression.

Sh.I. Shü used ta . . . draw da door, an' jam it wi' somethin' sae 'at it couldna slide, BURGESS *Sketches* (2nd ed.) 87. **Dmb.** 'There's mair folk just come wi' clamour loud.' ' And us already jammed wi' sic a crowd,' SALMON *Gowodean* (1868) 82. **e.Lth.** We had been a' jammed thegither like herrin in a barrel, HUNTER *J. Inwick* (1895) 184. **Gall.** There's somebody ringing the front-door bell and it's jammed wi' the rain forbye, CROCKETT *Bog-Myrtle* (1895) 265. **n.Cy.** (J.L. 1783), **Cum.¹,** w.**Yks.¹⁴,** nw.**Der.¹** **Brks.¹** Jam down the zugar zo as to get ut all into the baaysin. **e.An.²** He jamm'd his funger in the door. **Nrf.** When he come on deck, he must go splodding into the little boat, and jam athwart our things, EMERSON *Son of Fens* (1892) 84. **Ess.** Must I jam the bones with the hammer ? I have jammed [mashed] the potatoes (J.B.). **Hmp.** GROSE (1790) *MS. add.* (M.) **w.Som.¹** Th' old horse muved on, and the body of the butt valled down, and he [the hand] was a jammed in twixt the body o' un and the sharps. **Hor. Subsecivae** (1777) 227. **Cor.¹**

Hence (1) *Jam cram,* (2) *— cram full,* (3) *—full,* phr. very full, full to overflowing.

(1, 2) **Lan.** (F.R.C.) (3) w.**Yks.** Ah filled it ram jam full, *Leeds Merc. Suppl.* (May 19, 1894); (J.W.)

2. *Fig.* To press upon ; to put about or cause inconvenience ; to corner or press in argument.

Sh.I. Ye'll be come aboot your tedders. . . Ir ye been jammed for want o' dem ? I houp no, *Sh. News* (June 11, 1898). **Abd.** They're jammin tae at their heels, ALEXANDER *Johnny Gibb* (1871) xviii. **Rnf.** Ye jamm'd them so, They saw no way to cut you short, MᶜGILVRAY *Poems* (ed. 1862) 158.

3. To tread heavily ; to render firm by treading.

e.An.¹ Some one has been jambing here afore us [Some one has walked on these ronds before us, looking for snipe] ; **e.An.²** The stock have jamm'd up the midder [meadow]. **Nrf.** They speak of jamming their land with bullocks, in a tone of peculiar satisfaction, MARSHALL *Review* (1817) V. 211 ; 'Tis healthy, I think, a-jamming about the snow (W.R.E.) ; (E.M.) **e.Nrf.** MARSHALL *Rur. Econ.* (1787). **e.Suf.** (F.H.)

4. *Phr. to jamb the ronds,* to hunt for eggs, snipe, &c. e.An.¹

5. To slam, shut with a bang.

w.Som.¹ What a rattle her do make wi' jamming thick door.

6. To strike the head against any hard object.

w.Yks. (J.W.) n.**Lin.** I tum'l'd oher th' heåp o' kelterment [accent on *mmt*] she'd feyed oot, an' left i' th' door-steåd, an' did n't I jaum mÿ heåd agen wall ! (M.P.) ; n.**Lin.¹**

JAM(B, *sb.* Nrf. Dor. A vein or bed of marl or clay ; a layer or stratum of earth ; a large block of stone.

Nrf. GROSE (1790) ; For sale—freehold brick tower windmill, with going gear, dwelling-house and garden ; a jamb of good brick earth runs under same, *e.Dy. Press* (Oct. 31, 1894) ; m.**Yks.¹** *Rur. Econ.* (1787). **Dor.** To break down a large jam of it, MARSHALL *Review* (1817) V. 243. [Jam, Jamb, a thick bed of stone, which hinders the miners in their pursuing the veins of ore, BAILEY (1721).]

JAMB, *sb.* Sc. Irel. Nhb. Dur. Lakel. Yks. Lan. Chs. Der. Not. Lin. Nhp. Wor. Shr. e.An. s.Cy. Som. Cor. Also written **jam** Sc. (JAM.) **Bnff.¹** **Lnk.** **Bwk.** **N.Cy.¹** **Dur.¹** **Lan.**; and in forms **jaum** N.Cy.² **Lakel.²** w.**Yks.¹** **Chs.³** n.**Lin.¹** nw.**Der.¹** **Nhp.¹** ; **jaumb** N.Cy.¹ m.**Yks.¹** ; **jawm** w.Yks. **Lan.¹** e.**Lan.¹** **Chs.¹³** s.**Chs.¹** **Shr.¹** ; **jime** se.Wor.¹ ; **joam** m.Lan.¹ ; **jomb** w.Yks. ; **jome** Cum.¹ w.Yks. n.Der. ; **jorm** Not. [dʒam, dʒǎm, dʒŏm, dʒoəm.]

1. The side-post of a door or window.

Sh.I. He strak da snaw aff o' his shün apo da jam o' da door, *Sh. News* (Jan. 21, 1899). **Ayr.** What wi' your drawing-rooms, and your new black jambs and your wings ! GALT *Entail* (1823) lx. **n.Cy.** GROSE (1790) ; The jaum of the door (K.) ; **N.Cy.²,** **Dur.¹,** **Lakel.²,** **Cum.¹,** m.**Yks.¹** w.**Yks.** A short pipe in his maath, reared agean th' door jawm or th' haase end, HARTLEY *Clock Alm.* (1896) 3 ; w.**Yks.¹²³,** **Lan.¹,** e.**Lan.¹,** **Chs.¹,** **Not.** (J.H.B.) n.**Der.** ADDY *Sheffield Gl.* (1891). aw.**Der.¹,** n.**Lin.¹,** **Nhp.¹** w.**Som.¹** The jamb of a window is no part of the woodwork, but the side of the opening in the wall ; hence it is usual to talk of the 'splay of the jamba.' The side of the frame of a doorway. This is a technical word in the West, and is never used to express the door-post or durn-blade. When the frame to which a door is fastened is made of square, solid wood, the whole frame is called a pair of durns (q.v.) ; but when it is of flat shape, or, as it is sometimes called, 'linings,' then the whole door-frame is a pair of jambs, of which each side is a jamb. 'Will you have the doors fixed with jambs or durns !' **Cor.** The house could be entered on hands and knees alone, between granite jambs under a granite lintel, BARING-GOULD *Curgenven* (1893) xlvii.

Hence **Jamb-stone,** *sb.* the side-stone of a door or window.

Nhb.¹ w.**Yks.** He's fit to pail his heead agean th' jaumstooan for bien sich a fooil, HARTLEY *Ditt.* (1868) 84 ; w.**Yks.²**

2. The upright support of a fireplace ; the projecting side of a fireplace.

Fif. For cheese-making the stomach of a calf was held in reserve, filled with salt and hung up over the cruck in the jambs, to make rennet, or 'ernin,' COLVILLE *Vernacular* (1899) 15. **Per.** Whase dux is preferr'd to a seat near the jambs, STEWART *Character* (1857) 19. **Lnk.** On nail beside the jam, .Like . . . reekit braxy ham, NICHOLSON *Kilwuddie* (1893) 89. **Gall.** The mistress allows me to put my feet on the jambs, which is the only way to get warmed up, CROCKETT *Bog-Myrtle* (1895) 204. **s.Dur.** He propped his'sel up again t'jambs (J.E.D.). **Lakel.²** w.**Yks.** Shoo then went heead first agean t'chimney jaum, *Pudsey Olm.* (1885) 26 ; w.**Yks.⁸** **Lan.** It's ter'ble hard, owd wife, to ceawer bi' th' chimley jam, HARLAND *Lyrics* (1866) 304. m.**Lan.¹,** **Chs.¹³** s.**Chs.¹** The cross-beam over an old-fashioned kitchen fireplace. **Nhp.¹,** **Shr.¹** s.**Cy.** RAY (1691). w.**Som.¹** The chimney-jambs are the side walls of the fireplace, while the jambs of the chimney-piece are the usual upright parts of the structure, whether wood, marble, or other material, forming the front on each side of the fireplace from the floor to the shelf.

Hence (1) **Jamb-corner,** *sb.* a chimney corner ; (2) -friends, *sb. pl., fig.* intimate or fireside friends ; (3) -stone, *sb.* the side-stone of a fireplace ; (4) -wall, *sb.* the wall between the fireplace and the outer door of a kitchen.

(1) w.**Yks.** That office belong'd to one at sat at t'jome corner, HALLAM *Wadsley Jack* (1866) viii. (2) **Lnk.** On the day the laird was kisted, A wheen o' his jamb freens insisted That they'd come stappin' yont that nicht, MURDOCH *Doric Lyre* (1873) 8. (3) **Bwk.** I take my keelievine an' on the jam-stane draw a horse or hoose, CALDER *Poems* (1897) 299. **Nhb.¹,** w.**Yks.⁸** se.**Wor.¹** Thee say that agyun, look ; un I'll knock thee yud agyunst the jimestone. (4) s.**Don.** SIMMONS *Gl.* (1890).

3. A projection or buttress of a building; an addition to a building. Also used *attrib.*

Sc. A building is often enlarged by carrying an addition out from the back wall, set at right angles with the rest of the house, the gable of the projection being parallel with the side wall of the main building. This is styled a back-jam (JAM.); A projection, a wing, a word applied also to the aisle of a church. The word 'jam' was at times applied to a large house having a wing, and is yet applied to a large rambling house, or even to a large cupboard, FRANCISQUE-MICHEL *Lang.* (1882) 28. **Dmb.** Rubble work is what they use for gavles, back wa's, and back jambs in the best o' houses, CROSS *Disruption* (1844) xi. **Rnf.** How pleasing it was to see in this humble dwelling the 'back-jamb parlour' neatly furnished and carpeted, HECTOR *Judicial Records* (1876) 156. **Dmf.** It [the church] has a large jam, very commodious for dispensing the Sacrament of the Lord's Supper, *Statist. Acc.* VIII. 311 (JAM.). **e.An.[1]** A mass of masonry in a building, or of stone or other mineral in a quarry or pit, standing upright, and more or less distinct from neighbouring or adjoining parts.

4. A corner made by a projection.

Gall. His highness [fox] places himself so in a jamb or chink that they [terriers] cannot get behind him, MACTAGGART *Encycl.* (1824) 256, ed. 1876.

5. Anything large and clumsy; a big, ugly animal. Cf. jum, *sb.*[3]

Bnff.[1] A jam o' a hoose. He's bocht an aul' jam o' a coo. **Abd.** It's [the house] sic a muckle jamb, an' mair nor the tae half o't 'll hae to stan' teem, ALEXANDER *Ain Flk.* (1882) 194; Common (G.W.).

JAMBLE, *v.* Som. To pull a bell rapidly.

The clerk tells me he always jambles the fifth bell when he thinks it is about five minutes to service time, and when he sees Sam in the vestry he jolls the lenis bell. This 'jolling' is slower than the jambling which precedes it (W.F.R.).

JAMBLES, *sb. pl.* Lan.[1] The 'hames'; the part of the collar by which horses draw.

JAMBREADS, *sb. pl.* Sus.[1] Slices of bread and jam.

JAMES, *sb.* Cum. Yks. Shr. Also in form **Jams** Cum.[14] w.Yks.[1] In phr. (1) *James mass,* the festival of St. James. w.Yks.[1]; (2) —*'s weed.* Shr. (B. & H.), (3) —*wort,* the ragwort, *Senecio Jacobaea. ib.*; (4) *St. James' fair,* a fair held at Ravenglass on Aug. 5. Cum.[14]

JAMIE, *sb.* Sc. A peasant, rustic.

Slg. He made complaint to Jamies, Jocks, and Megs, GALLOWAY *Luncarty* (1804) 55.

JAMMER, *sb.* w.Yks.[5] [dga·mə(r).] A term of address from one boy to another.

Boys address one another as 'Jammer.' 'Hey up! jammer!' one will give voice to another at a distance; and he, in his turn, will put the question, upon being over-taken,—' Whear's thah for, jammer!'

JAMMER, see Jimmer, *sb.*[1], Yammer.

JAMMIE, *v.* w.Yks. [dga·mi.] To wall loosely and carelessly without mortar; to do anything in a slovenly manner. (R.H.H.)

JAMMOCK, *v.* and *sb.* Shr. Hrf. e.An. Also written jammuck Nrf. [dgæ·mək.] **1.** *v.* To squeeze, press; to beat, crush, or trample into a soft mass. Also used *fig.* Cf. jam, *v.* 1.

Shr., Hrf. BOUND *Provinc.* (1876). **e.An.** (HALL.), **e.An.[1]**, **e.Suf.** (F.H.)

Hence **Jammocked,** *ppl. adj.* worn out, exhausted.

Nrf. I have heard of a donkey purchased for little money on account of some injury, but it was not so malahacked as to be jammucked for all that, COZENS-HARDY *Broad Nrf.* (1893) 54. **e.Suf.** Said esp. of cattle. Also jammocked [bruised] fruit (F.H.).

2. To mumble food. e.Suf. (F.H.)

3. *sb.* A soft, pulpy substance.

e.An.[1], **e.Suf.** Don't make such a jammock of the food on your plate (F.H.).

JAMMOCK, see Jannock, *sb.*[2]

JAMMY, *sb.* Wm. Lan. [dga·mi.] **1.** The heron, *Ardea cinera.* s.Wm. (J.A.B.)

2. *Comb.* (1) Jammy-crane, (2) ·long-neck, *sb.* the heron, *Ardea cinera.*

(1) Lan.[1], n.Lan.[1] (2) Wm. Foomarts, magpies, and jammy-lang-necks, *Spec. Dial.* (1885) pt. iii. 8; I yance kilt a Jammy-lang-neck we a staen fleein ower oor hoose, TAYLOR *Sketches* (1882) 6.

JAMMY, *v.* Lakel.[2] To sway to and fro; to stagger. Yan jammies a bit sometimes when yan's mair ner yan can carry streck.

JAMMY-MARSE, *sb.* Cor.[2] Bread spread with jam.

JAMPER, *sb.* Slk. (JAM.) A tool for boring holes.

JAMPH, *v.*[1] and *sb.* Sc. Also written jamf(f; and in form jaumph Rnf. Slk. [dgamf.] **1.** *v.* To make game of; to mock at, jeer, sneer. Cf. gamp.

Sc. Ye manna tell the nibours, for the chields wad aye jamf me wi 't, GRAHAM *Writings* (1883) II. 50. **Abd.** She but jamphs me, telling me I'm fu', Ross *Helenore* (1768) 129, ed. 1812. **Ayr.** Bell tell't her aboot the dirdum in the byre, and she was aye jamphin' me wi't when we met, SERVICE *Notandums* (1890) iii. **Edb.** The grit fock jamph an' jeer at ye, LEARMONT *Poems* (1791) 2. **Slk.** And the bonny May scho jaumphit and jeerit, HOGG *Tales* (1898) 119, ed. 1866.

2. To shuffle, make false pretences; to act the part of a male jilt. Sc. (JAM.), MACKAY.

Hence (1) **Jampher,** *sb.* a male jilt; (2) **Jamphing,** (*a*) *ppl. adj.* jilting, making false pretences of courtship; (*b*) *vbl. sb.* the acting of jilting or making false pretences, applied to a male.

Abd. (1) It was well waird, Let never jamphers yet be better saird, Ross *Helenore* (1768) 62, ed. 1812. (2, *a*) He had naething but a jamphing view; But she in gnapping earnest taks it a', *ib.* 98. (*b*) For, for my coat I wadna wish 't were said, That I o' jamphing maidens made a trade, *ib.* 197 ; For Lindy did na look like ane to cheat, For onie lass wi' jamphing sae to treat, *ib.* 50.

3. To trifle, spend time idly; to walk in a slow, idle manner.

Sc. (JAM.) **Banff.[1]** The twa loons jampht o' the rod, an' pat thimsel's ahin the squeel. **Abd.** (G.W.) **Rnf.** High rais't wi' hope, baith late an' air I've jaumph't to houble at 'er [her], PICKEN *Poems* (1788) 159.

Hence **Jampher,** *sb.* an idler. Bnff.[1], Abd. (G.W.)

4. *sb.* A mock, jeer, sneer.

Sc. The Laird of Bamffe he's gotten the jamffe, And so did Gight ane other, MAIDMENT *Pasquils* (1868) 104.

5. Trifling over work; an habitual idler. Bnff.[1]

JAMPH, *v.*[2] Sc. [dgamf.] **1.** To tire, fatigue; to exhaust by toil.

Sc. Freq. used to denote the fatigue caused by continued motion of a shaking kind, as that of riding, esp. if the horse be hard in the seat. One is thus said to be 'jampht with riding' (JAM.). **Ayr., Slk.** (*ib.*)

2. To destroy by jogging or friction; to chafe; to drive to difficulties. Sc. (JAM.), Lnk. (*ib.*)

Hence **Jamphit,** *pp.* pinched, reduced to straits. Lnk.(*ib.*)

3. To travel with extreme difficulty, as one trudging through mire.

Sc. To trudge, plod, to make way laboriously, MACKAY. **Cld., Ayr.** (JAM.) **Rnf.** Jaumph, to travel with exertion as if on bad roads, PICKEN *Poems* (1813) Gl.

JAMPHLE, *v.* Lnk. (JAM.) Also written jamfle. To shuffle in walking, as if in consequence of wearing too wide shoes. See Jamph, *v.*[1] 2.

JAMRAG, *sb.* and *v.* Cum. Wm. Lan. Chs. Not. War. Oxf. Also in forms jim-rag s.Chs.[1] s.Not. War.[23]; jimrig s.Chs.[1] [dga·mrag, dgi·mrag.] **1.** *sb. pl.* Rags, tatters, shreds.

Cum.[4] Wm. T'coo's bin chowin thi shirt an' she's rovvent o' ta jamrags (B.K.). **Lan.** Th' bakehouse wur blaired to jamrags, WAUGH *Heather* (ed. Milner) I. 145; **Lan.[1]**, **n.Lan.[1]**, **s.Lan.[1]** **s.Chs.[1]** Dhai mai·dn ũ fŭt·-bau· ũ mi aat', ŭn nokt it au· tũ jim-raagz [They maden a foot-baw o' my hat, an' knocked it aw to jimrags]. **s.Not.** Ma cooat's all in jim-rags (J.P.K.). **War.[2]** My ankēcher's all to jimrags; **War.[3]** His clothes are all in jim-rags. This meat has been boiled to jim-rags. **Oxf.** I'm not fit to be seen, my clothes are all jam-rags (L.J.Y.).

2. *v.* To render useless; to destroy, knock to pieces.

s.Chs.[1] Wen foa·ks bor·ũn ũdh·ŭr foa·ksiz thing·z dhi shũd tai·ky'ae·r on ũm; ahy lent uwd Stoa·ks mahy baar·ũ, ũn ah diklae·r iv dhi aan·)ũ jim·rigd it ũmũngg· ũm, ũz it'l nev·ŭr bi gũd nuwt ũgy'en· [When folks borrow'n other folks'es things they should tay care on 'em; I lent owd Stokes my barrow, an' ah declare if they hanna jimrigged it among 'em, as it'll never be good nowt agen].

JAMS, sb. pl. w.Cy. Dor. [dgæmz.] Wire shirt-buttons, formerly made near Blandford.

w.Cy. (HALL.) Dor. The making of thread buttons, .. once a flourishing trade in Dor., has now almost ceased to be. . . . The more common sorts of buttons were jams, shirts, sprangles, and mites, N. & Q. (1894) 4th S. vii. 94 ; BARNES Gl. (1863).

JAN, IANBERRY, see John, Hindberry.

JANCE, v. and sb. Yks. Also Sus. Also in form jaunce Sus.[1] [dgans, dg̣o͞ns.] 1. v. With about : to knock about, expose to circumstances of fatigue.

n.Yks.[1] 'Thoo's been sair janced about, Ah's seear'; to one who had been compelled to take two or three sudden long and harassing journeys.

2. sb. A weary or tiring journey.

Sus.[1] I do͝ent justly know how far it is to Hellingly, but you'll have a middlin' jaunce before you get there.

[1. Spurr'd, gall'd and tired by jauncing Bolingbroke, SHAKS. Rich. II, v. v. 94. Fr. jancer, to stirre a horse in the stable till he be swart with-all (COTGR.). 2. Fie, how my bones ache ! what a jaunce have I had ! SHAKS. R. & J. II. v. 26.]

JAN-CHIDER, sb. Wil. [dgæn-tʃaidə(r).] The sedge-warbler, Salicaria phragmitis. Also called Johnny-chider (q.v.). SLOW Gl. (1892); WIL.[1] So called 'because it scolds so.'

JANDER, v. Yks. [dgandə(r).] To shake, rattle.

w.Yks. T'wind med our windas jander and dither all neet (J.W.). Hence **A-jander,** adv. on the shake.

He stamped and louped till he set all t'pots a-jander (ib.).

JANDERS, see Jaundice.

JANE-JAKES, sb. Cor.[1] Also in form Jean-Jakes. A snail.

JANET JO, phr. Sc. A children's game ; see below. Cf. Jenny Jo or Jones, s.v. Jenny, sb.[1] 1 (22).

w.Sc. Flk-Lore Rec. IV. 274, in GOMME Games (1894) 261. a.Sc. One version represents Janet as at the well instead of upstairs, and afterwards at the mill, &c., CHAMBERS Pop. Rhymes (1890) 141. Edb. Janet lies on her back behind the scenes. The father and mother stand up to receive the visits of the lover, who comes forward singing : ' I'm come to court Janet jo . . . How's she the day ?' Mother and father : 'She's up the stair washin'. . . Ye canna see her the day.' The lover retires and again advances and . . . receives similar evasive answers from Janet's parents, who successively represent her as bleaching, drying, and ironing clothes. At last they say : ' Janet jo's dead and gane,' &c. She is then carried off to be buried, the lover and the rest weeping. She sometimes revives, and sometimes not, as Janet herself chooses, ib. 140. Kcb. In the Stewartry of Kcb. ' Janet Jo ' is a dramatic entertainment amongst young rustics. Suppose a party has met in a harvest or winter evening, . . and it is resolved to fiave ' Janet Jo' performed. Two undertake to personate a good-man and goodwife ; the rest a family of marriageable daughters. One of the lads, the best singer of the party, retires, and equips himself in a dress proper for representing an old bachelor in search of a wife. He comes in, singing : . . ' I'm come to court Janet jo,' &c. The goodwife sings : ' What'll ye gie for Janet jo ?' &c. Wooer : ' I'll gie ye a peck o' siller,' &c. Goodwife says : ' Gae awa', ye auld carle.' . . The wooer hereupon retires, . . but soon re-enters singing : ' I'll gie ye a peck o' gowd,' &c. . . . At his next entry he offers ' three pecks o' gowd,' at which the goodwife sings : ' Come ben beside Janet jo,' &c. The suitor then advances gaily to his sweetheart, and the affair ends in a scramble for kisses, ib. 141-2.

JANGLE, v.[1] and sb.[1] Sc. Lakel. Yks. Lan. Chs. Lin. War. Shr. Oxf. e.An. Som. [dga·ŋl, dgæ·ŋ(g)L] 1. v. To quarrel, wrangle, argue angrily.

Sc. And other some do stiffly jangle, That they and thighs make a quadrangle, COLVIL Whigs Supplication (1796) I. 211 ; GROSE (1790) MS. add. (C.) w.Sc. Ye jangle an' skirl when ye fa' in wi' ither and grow pack ; but the colour o' a ribbon . . . 'll mak ye jangle in earnest (JAM. Suppl.). Cum. Sum o' t'rest began ta git rayder ower full, an gat ta janglin like owt, DICKINSON Lamplugh (1856) 8 ; Cum.[1][3], n.Lin.[1] War.[2] ' Wrangling and jangling ' is a common phr. Oxf. Those two are for ever wrangling and jangling (G.O.). Nrf. COZENS-HARDY Broad Nrf. (1893) 72. e.Suf. (F.H.)

Hence (1) **Janglement,** sb. an angry disputation ; angry dispute, altercation ; (2) **Jangler,** sb. a quarreller, wrangler; (3) **Janglesome,** adj. quarrelsome ; noisy, boisterous ; (4)

Jangling, (a) sb. domestic discord ; (b) ppl. adj. quarrelling, wrangling.

(1) Cum.[14] e.Yks.[1] MS. add. (T.H.) w.Som.[1] Vas·tree meet·een! ees! un u pur·tee jang·ulmunt twau·z dhur; aay zeed dhur wüd·n bee noa soe·urt u gree·munt, un zoa aay wüd·n buy'd noa laung·gur [Vestry meetin! yes! and a nice disputing it was there; I saw there would be no kind of agreement, and so I would not stay any longer]. (a) Sc. GROSE (1790) MS. add. (C.) (3) Suf. (HALL.), e.Suf. (F.H.) (4, a) Lakel.[2] Will te drop thi janglin', Jinnet ? (b) Cum.[4]

2. To prattle, chatter, prate ; to talk incessantly.

Sc. FRANCISQUE-MICHEL Lang. (1882) 369. w.Sc. (JAM. Suppl.) Fif. Tongues never wi' sic clitter-clatter Did jangle and did jarr, TENNANT Papistry (1827) 108. Edb. 'Tis cuffin' wind to wrangle Wi' ane wham pride maks ay to jangle, LEARMONT Poems (1791) 44. Chs.[1], s.Chs.[1] Shr.[1] Them women bin al'ays janglin'—it o͝od look better on 'em to mind thar own business, an' let other folks mind thars. e.Suf. (F.H.) w.Som.[1] Not necessarily in a quarrelsome manner, though dispute is rather implied. ' Ter'ble umman to jangly.' ' Why, they'd jangle anybody to death.' This was said of a number of washerwomen.

Hence **Jangling,** sb. confusion of tongues, chatter, idle talk.

w.Som.[1] Here drop it, there's to much janglin by half, anybody can't year theirzul spake. **3.** To cry. Cmb. The child is jangling again (W.M.B.). **4.** sb. A quarrel, wrangle, altercation, dispute.

Cum.[4] Lan. She mud as weel hex o' t'jangle tul herself, R. PIKETAH Forness Flk. (1870) 37. e.Suf. (F.H.) **5.** A chat, gossip. e.Suf. (F.H.)

[1. OFr. jangler, 'medire, bavarder, railler' (LA CURNE).]

JANGLE, v.[2] and sb.[2] n.Cy. Yks. Lan. Suf. [dga·ŋl.] 1. v. To rove about, to lead a disorderly life ; to trifle, idle. Cf. bangle, v. 2.

n.Cy. (HALL.), w.Yks.[1], e.Lan.[1] s.Chs.[1] Tŭ jaangg·l wŭnz tahym ŭwee· [To jangle one's time awee].

2. Of hay or straw on a cart : to hang loose on the outside. e.Suf. (F.H.) Cf. bangle, v. 3.

3. sb. Phr. on the jangle, ' on the loose.' s.Chs.[1]

JANIVEER, see January, sb.[1]

JANJANSY, sb. Cor. [dgæ·ndgænsi.] A two-faced person. Also used attrib.

All agreed the new eye gave'n a janjansy kind o' look, ' Q.' Troy Town (1888) xi ; Cor.[1] I don't like her ; she's a janjansy ; Cor.[3]

JANK, sb.[1] War.[2] Excrement. Hence **Jankhole,** sb. a ' privy,' ' latrina.'

JANK, v. and sb.[2] ? Obs. Sc. [dgaŋk.] 1. v. To trifle. Lth. Now he's rewarded for such pranks, When he would pass, it's told he janks, CLELAND Poems (1697) 19 (JAM.).

2. Phr. (1) to jank the labour, to trifle at work ; also used sb. a trifler at work ; (2) — off, to run off.

(1) Fif. A common phr. (JAM.) (a) Lth. (ib.)

3. sb. A shuffling trick ; the act of giving another the slip. Sc. His pretending to bring witnesses from the East Indies, seem'd liker a fair jank than any proper defence, Observator, No. iv. 22 (JAM.).

[The same word as Norw. dial. janka, to waver, totter (AASEN).]

JANKEN, prp. Cor. [Not known to our correspondents.] Walking quickly.

JANKER, sb. Obs. Sc. A long pole, on two wheels, used for carrying wood, the log being fixed to it by strong clasps.

Lth. As a janker [a timber machine] was passing along with a log of wood, a fine boy . . . attempted to get on the log, but fell, Edb. Courant (July 26, 1803) (JAM.).

JANKIT, pp. Obs. Sc. Fatigued, jaded.

Fif. My Muse is jankit now and jadit, TENNANT Papistry (1827) 148. Lth. (JAM.)

JANNEK, sb. Cor. Also written jannak Cor.[1] [dgæ·nək.] An overgrown, blundering bully.

Cor.[1] The great jannek tho͝oht he could thrash his tenant, but the tenant fought him out afore the door, and beat him rarely.' Mem. The J. was a lout 6ft. 4in. high ; Cor.[3]

JANNER, sb. Cor.[3] [dgæ·nə(r).] The jay, Garrulus glandarius.

JANNER, see Jaunder.

JANNERD, *sb.* Cor.² The redwing or winnard, *Turdus iliacus.*

JANNOCK, *adj., adv.* and *sb.*¹ In *gen.* dial. use in Sc. and Eng. Also Colon. Also in forms **gennick** Ayr.; **janic** Nhb.¹; **jannack** e.Yks. Chs.² Lin. s.Lin.; **jannak** e.Yks. n.Lan.¹; **jannic** Cum.²; **jannick** N.Cy.³ Cum.¹⁴ Not.² s.Not. n.Lin.¹ sw.Lin.¹; **jenic(k** Nhb.¹; **jennick** N.Cy.¹; **johnnick** w.Cor.; **jollick** e.An.¹; **jonach** s.Pem.; **jonic** Dev. w.Cor.; **jonick** Som.; **jonnack** Chs.¹ s.Chs.¹ War.² Shr.¹ Oxf.; **jonnacks** Oxf.; **jonnick** s.Not. Nhp.¹ War. Oxf. e.An.¹ I.W.² Wil.¹ Dor. w.Som.¹ Cor.²⁸; **jonnock** m.Lan.¹ Not. War.² Shr.² Hrf.² Pem. Glo.¹ Oxf.¹ Dor.; **jonnok** Hmp.; **jonnox** Cor.; **jonnuck** se.Wor.¹ [dʒaˑnək, dʒæˑnək, dʒoˑnək.] 1. *adj.* Fair, honest, straightforward, upright, genuine, 'square.' *Gen.* with a *neg.* Also used *adv.*

Ayr. The uncos, both spurious and gennick, which I possessed, Service *Dr. Duguid* (ed. 1887) 80. **N.Cy.¹** 'To be not jennick,' to act improperly or shabbily. **Nhb.** De thoo what's jenick iv Ephrath, Robson *Bk. Ruth* (1860) iv. 11; Nhb.¹, Dur.¹. **s.Dur.** (J.E.D.) **Cum.¹**; **Cum.²** Thoo hes ower mickle jaw to be jannic, 183; **Cum.⁴** Wm. I don't think it's jannock! a don't think it's reet! *Spec. Dial.* (1880) pt. ii. 32. **n.Wm.** (B.K.), **n.Yks.¹²³⁴**, **ne.Yks.¹** **e.Yks.** Sike a click iv her back, an sa jannack an tall, An highly beliked an rispected bi all, Nicholson *Flk-Sp.* (1889) 38. **m.Yks.¹** **w.Yks.** Awm nooan gooin to tell whear we went, that wodn't be jannock, Hartley *Clock Alm.* (1892) 53; He's a jannock chap, Hamilton *Nugae Lit.* (1841) 354; **w.Yks.¹²³⁵** **Lan.** Mary, also, was nothing if not jannock, Fothergill *Probation* (1879) ix; Lan.¹ **n.Lan.** Alack-aday! sur, our nebburs it's sartain are not jannock, Thornber *Penny Stone* (1845) 43; n.Lan.¹, ne.Lan.¹, m.Lan.¹ **Chs.¹** I told them I thought it wasn't hardly jannock for me to rid up the roots till my landlord had put up the fence; **Chs.²** **s.Chs.¹** Dŭs noaˑ uwd Aarˑi Mŭm·fŭt! Wotˑ)s ey thuwt on i yairˑr kŭn·trî!—Oaˑ, eyˑz verˑi jon·ŭk—nóo mon faeˑrŭr tŭ déeŭl widh ['Dost know owd Harry Mumford! What's hey thowt on i' yay'r country!' 'Oh, hey's very jonnock—noo mon fairer to deeal with']. **Stf.¹** Der. 'Can you rely on his support!' 'Ya, lad, oi'm sartin he's jonnock,' N. & Q. (1882) 6th S. vi. 213; Der.², nw.Der.¹ Not. (J.H.B.); Not.² Such treatment is not jannick. **s.Not.** Yo'n tryin' to back out o' yer bargain, mester, an' it een't jonnick. He didn't charge me ower much neither; he were pretty jannick (J.P.K.). **Lin.** Streatfeild *Lin. and Danes* (1884) 339. **s.Lin.** (T.H.R.), War. (J.R.W.), War.² **Shr.¹** Bill said 'e ŏŏdna. an' 'e didna, 'e's al'ays jonnack; **Shr.²** When a person seems unlikely to yield or retract, the fiat he pronounces, is said to be 'jonnock'; there's no appeal that can avail when a man utters this decisive word : 'That's jonnock.' **Shr.**, **Hrf.** Bound *Provinc.* (1876). **Hrf.²** One labourer would say to another, 'Come, be jonnock,' i. e. drink your share of cider, pay your share, do your proper amount of work. In use in Bishop's Frome 70 years ago. **Pem.** (W.H.Y.) **s.Pem.** Laws *Little Eng.* (1888) 420; (W.M.M.) Oxf. It isn't jonnacks (M.A.R.); (M.W.) **e.An.¹** That's not jollick. **Nrf.** I don't deal with him because he don't act jannock, *Arch.* (1879) VIII. 170; And tell you she thinks her very 'dis-improved' as she is not 'jannock' now, Rye *Hist.* (1885) xv. **Hmp.** (T.L.O.D.) **I.W.²** He's acted very jonnick about it. **Wil.** Slow *Gl.* (1892); Wil.¹ Dor. If he did not act up jonnock, she would renew the summons, *Bridport News* (Oct. 31, 1892); His jonnick face as white as his clothes with keeping late hours, Hardy *Laodicean* (ed. 1896) bk. i. 34. **Som.** If she be jonick and true . . . I'll larn to put up wi her temper, Agrikler *Rhymes* (1873) 8; W. & J. *Gl.* (1873); Sweetman *Wincanton Gl.* (1885). **w.Som.¹** He's a proper jonnick old fellow. **Dev.** God be gude tu un—er's jonic I promise 'e, Phillpotts *Dartmoor* (1896) 159; Yŭ may trist 'she.' I teliee 'er's jonic tŭ tha back-bone! Hewett *Peas. Sp.* (1892). Cor. If you'll be jonnox to me, I'll be jonnox to you (J.W.); Cor.² Used only of events, or things, not of persons. An honest man's conduct is jonnick, not himself. **w.Cor.** 'He's not johnnick,' does not act fairly, said by boys when playing (M.A.C.). [**Nfld.** *Trans. Amer. Flk-Lore Soc.* (1894). **Aus.** There was a wildness about that fellow's look that made me feel certain he was not jonick, Ferguson *Bush Life* (1891) xx.]

Hence **Jonnocky**, *adj.* equitable, fair.

s.Not. But shall yer be jonnocky ower the job! (J.P.K.)

2. Even, level.

n.Yks.¹ T'cloth deean't lig Jannock. Draw yon end your-hand way. ne.Yks.¹

3. Satisfactory, fit, proper; pleasant, jolly, agreeable, easy to get on with.

ne.Lan.¹ n.Lin.¹ Well, this is real jannick. sw.Lin.¹ 'Well, that's just jannick,' said by anyone doing a thing correctly. War.² Shr.² Sometimes we hear an independent, lawless living fellow described as jonnock; 'he's jonnock.' The word must assuredly be tralatitious, and is very likely most limited in circulation. s.Pem. (W.M.M.) Glo.¹ Now be jonnock. Oxf.¹ Tha's jonnock, *MS. add.* w.Som.¹ We always got on jonnick enough vore thick there keeper come here. Dev. I thought we should a-got on very well, but he wad'n no way jonnick, *Reports Provinc.* (1884) 22; She ban't jonic for sartain, though God forbid as I should so much as think ill of her, *Pall Mall Mag.* (Feb. 1900) 151. Cor.²

4. Liberal, kind, hospitable.

Nhp.¹ 'I went to see him, and he was quite Jonnick.' The circulation of this word is very limited; I believe it is confined to the *ne.* part of the county.

5. *adv.* Phr. *to go jonnocks*, to take fair and equal shares; to be partners.

w.Yks. (J.W.) s.Not. Don't let's quarrel; let's put our money together and go jonnocks (J.P.K.).

6. *sb.* Fair play, fair treatment. *Gen.* in *pl.* form.

Lakel.² w.Yks. To say that a proceeding is 'not jannocks' is equivalent to saying that it is not on the square, *Leeds Merc. Suppl.* (Dec. 19, 1896); Let's have jannocks, and we'll not grumble (M.N.); (R.H.H.); w.Yks.² I say, owd lad, that's not jannocks; w.Yks.⁵ 'That isn't jannocks;' said on one person tendering another an unequal share of anything, when such an one had the right of an equal share.

7. One who always pays his full share in a reckoning for beer, &c. se.Wor.¹

8. Phr. *to make a jannak of it*, to make a fit and suitable union. e.Yks.¹

[2. Of Scand. origin. A der. of Norw. dial. *jamn*, even, level (Aasen); so Sw. dial. (Rietz); ON. *jafn* (*jamn*).]

JANNOCK, *sb.²* Sc. n.Cy. Cum. Wm. Yks. Lan. Chs. Der. Hrt. e.An. Cor. Also in forms **jammock**, **jannacks** w.Yks.; **jannek** Cor.² [dʒaˑnək, dʒæˑnək.] 1. A loaf of leavened oatmeal, a 'bannock.'

Sc. Mattie gae us baith . . . ane o' her thick ait jannocks, Scott *Rob Roy* (1817) xiv. N.Cy.¹², Cum.⁴ Wm. A piece of mouldy jannock, Hutton *Bran New Wark* (1785) l. 403; Wm.¹, n.Yks.² w.Yks. Hutton *Tour to Caves* (1781); (G.R.); w.Yks.¹² Lan. Aw see theaw's done me as breawn as a jannock, Brierley *Marlocks* (1866) iii; On Good Friday . . . white jannocks, introduced by the Flemish refugees, . . . were also then eaten, Harland & Wilkinson *Flk-Lore* (1867) 237; Lan.¹ A dark-coloured bread or cake made of oatmeal, or of coarse wheat-meal. ne.Lan.¹ Bread made of rye and oatmeal. s.Lan.¹, Chs.¹², nw.Der.¹ Hrt. This cake is called a jannock or crumpet, Ellis *Mod. Husb.* (1750) III. i. e.An.¹; e.An.² A cake baked on the hearth. Both the name and the cake nearly *obs.* e.Suf. *Obsol.* (F.H.) Cor.² A soft cake made of oaten flour.

2. *Comp.* Jannock-bread, oaten bread made into coarse and hard large loaves. Lan. (K.)

[1. The cake is prob. so called from its flatness; cp. jannock, *adj.* 2.]

JANNY, *int.* Lan. [dʒaˑni.] See below.

A cry raised at the interruption of a game at marbles when each player tries to secure some of those remaining on the ground (H.M.).

JANT, see Jaunt, *sb.¹*

JANTY, *adj.* Sc. n.Cy. Dur. Nhp. Also Hmp. Also written **jaunty** Nhp.¹ [dʒaˑnti, dʒăˑnti.] 1. Smart, showy. See Genty, *adj.* 2.

N.Cy.¹, Dur.¹ Nhp.¹ A little jaunty body. Hmp.¹

2. Cheerful.

Fif. The scraighs o' lauchter there, And janty faces shinin' fair, Tennant *Papistry* (1827) 140; To gar the lazy hours slide by, Feil janty jokes the shearers try, Douglas *Poems* (1806) 124; Fu' janty an' canty, I trow they're a' thegither, *ib.* 131. N.Cy.¹

JANUARY, *sb.¹* In *gen.* dial use in weather lore. Also in forms **Janiveer** Sc. Cum.; **Janniwerry** Shr.¹; **Jiniver** Sur.¹; **Janwar** Hdg. 1. See below.

Sc. A January spring is worth naething, Inwards *Weather Lore* (1893) 10; If the grass grow in Janiveer, 'Twill be the worse for't a' the year, Chambers *Pop. Rhymes* (1870) 363. Hdg. Janwar's day creeps in, Just like a peevish auld gray man, Lumsden *Poems* (1896) 67. Cum. 'Janiveer, freeze the pot o' the fire. Februaire, fill dyke, black or white.' In common use 50 years ago (J.Ar.). **Yks.** January 14th, St. Hilary. The coldest day of the year, INWARDS *ib.* 12. **w.Yks.**[2] From June to Januäry, To nature it's contráry. **Shr.**[1] Janniwerry-freeze-the-pot-by-the-fire. **Bck.** If the calends of January be smiling and gay, You'll have wintry weather till the calends of May, NORTHALL *Flk-Rhymes* (1892) 431. **Sur.**[1] Jiniver poults never come to no good. [Janiveer freez the pot by the fire. If grass grows in Janiveer It grows the worse for't all the year, RAY *Prov.* (1678) 43 ; March in Janiveer, Janiveer in March I fear, INWARDS *ib.* 11 ; Jack Frost in Janiveer Nips the nose of the nascent year. The blackest month in all the year Is the month of Janiveer, SWAINSON *Weather Flk-Lore* (1873) 19 ; Who in Janiveer sows oats, Gets gold and groats, *ib.* 24.]

2. *Comp.* January-butter, mud. **Sus.**[1] It is considered lucky to bring mud into the house in January.

JANUARY, *sb.*[2] Ess. [Not known to our correspondents.] A name given to a horse or beast of burden.

' Whoa, January!' ejaculated that ancient functionary as he pulled up Strawberry close to John Short. Why the natives of Essex . . . habitually address their beasts of burden as 'January' is a matter best left to the discrimination of philologers, CRAWFORD *Tale of Lonely Parish* (1886) xix.

JANUS, *sb.* **s.Chs.**[1] A contemptuous term used of a man or woman, being an ironical use of the word 'genius.'

Wel, 60)z ū praat-i jai-nūs [Well, hoo's a pratty janus].

JAP, see **Jaup,** *v.*[1] **Jump,** *v.*

JAPE, *sb.* and *v.* Sc. Yks. Also Cor. Also written jaip Sc. ; and in form jawp n.Yks.[2] [dŋep.] **1.** *sb.* A jest ; a jeer, mock.

Per. A collection of japes at Scottish ways, IAN MACLAREN *K. Carnegie* (1896) 65. **Fif.** All hail, sweet son of Nox ! Father o' daffin, jaips, and jokes ! TENNANT *Papistry* (1827) 20.

2. *pl.* A jester or buffoon; a jackanapes. n.Yks.[2], Cor.[12]

3. *v.* To mock, jeer ; to jest, act the mountebank, play antics.

Fif. Auld folks, that scarce could girn or gape, At Papistry did gleek and jaip, TENNANT *Papistry* (1827) 109. **n.Yks.**[2] **Cor.** Th' ould bird had got ha'f-way round, a-mincin' an' japin', an' throwin' out hes legs this way an' that, ' Q.' *Troy Town* (1888) xi. [1. A lape, bourde, *iocus,* LEVINS *Manip.* (1570). Fr. *jappe,* ' caquet, bavardage ' (LITTRÉ). **2.** And thanne . . . helde [Lyf] Holynesse a Iape, and Hendenesse a wastour, *P. Plowman* (B.) xx. 144. **3.** Our hoste Iapen tho bigan, CHAUCER *C. T.* B. 1883.]

JAPERS, see **Jabers.**

JAPPLE, *v.* and *sb.* Sh.I. [dga-pl.] **1.** *v.* To step or stamp on clothes in the process of washing them ; to get the feet wet through.

Tak yon chair, an' tak aff o' dy feet. Der shūrely japplin', *Sh. News* (May 14, 1898); A'll hae ta get a pair o' new shūn. My feet is juist japplin' noo ivery day, *ib.* (Oct. 23, 1897) ; **S. & Ork.**[1] To japple clothes — to stamp upon them in a tub.

2. *sb.* A liquid mess.

A'm gien ower me bäit i' dis japple o' gutter, *Sh. News* (Nov. 11, 1899); I faer der foon flōers bit what's in a japple wi' dis, *ib.* (Feb. 17, 1900).

JAR, *sb.* Nhb. Also w.Cy. Som. [dgä(r.] **1.** In *comp.* Jar-handles, a colloq. name for large or prominent ears. Nhb.[1]

2. A stone bottle having a handle on one side near the top — often enclosed in wickerwork.

w.Som.[1] John Gilpin's famous ' stone bottles' would be jars in w.Som. ' Be sure they 'an't a-drinkt out all that there cider a'ready ! why, I zend up the eight quart jar and the zix quart virkin to ' leb'm [eleven] o'clock, and 'tis on'y but half arter two now ! ' ' Mr. Kemp called in vor to zay, must zend on a jar o' gin and a jar o' brandy, cause they be gwain to hold the revel next week.'

3. A vessel containing 20 gallons of oil. w.Cy. (HALL.) [A jarr, an earthen vessel, containing of oil from 18 to 26 gallons, BAILEY (1721).]

JARAM, see **Gearum(s.**

JARBLE, *sb.* Gall. An old tattered garment. MAC-TAGGART *Encycl.* (1824).

JARBLE, *v.* Nhb. Dur. Cum. Wm. Yks. Lan. Also in form jargle s.Dur. [dga-rbl, dgä-bl.] To bespatter or besmear with mud or dirt ; to wet, bedew, bemire.

n.Cy. GROSE (1790). **Nhb.**[1] **Dur.**[1] It is a custom with boys to turn up their trowsers at the ankle, to prevent them from being jarbelled by the wet grass. **s.Dur.** Her frock was all jargled wi' muck (J.E.D.). **Lakel.**[2] **Cum.** What gars t'gowky gang through t'garth to jarble o' her cleäzz, DICKINSON *Cumbr.* (1876) 121 ; **Cum.**[4] **Cum., Wm.** NICOLSON (1677) *Trans. R. Lit. Soc.* (1868) IX. **Wm.** He'll turn oot as jarbled as Bobby Grime's dog, BOWNESS *Studies* (1868) 3 ; She has jarbled all her petticoats (B.K.) ; **Wm.**[1] Thoo must a beean rowlin iv a dub i' 't rod thoo's si jarb'lt ower wi' mud. **s.Wm.** (J.A.B.) **n.Yks.** Tibb is all jarbil'd, and Ise basely mired, MERITON *Praise Ale* (1684) l. 636. **w.Yks.** WILLAN *List Wds.* (1811) ; HUTTON *Tour to Caves* (1781). **n.Lan.**[1], **ne.Lan.**[1]

Hence **Jarbled,** *ppl. adj.* (1) jumbled, disordered ; (2) dirtied, bespattered, bemired.

(1) **n.Yks.**[2] (2) **Cum.** The muddy syke it ower-ran the wear — The jarbelt lasses, sairy things, were spent, GILPIN *Pop. Poetry* (1875) 207 ; **Cum.**[4] **Wm.**[1] What a jarbled seet thoo is, to be sewer.

JARG, *v.* and *sb.*[1] Sc. Chs. [dgarg, dgäg.] **1.** *v.* To make a harsh, shrill noise like a door creaking on its hinges ; to ' chark.' See **Girg.** **Sc.** The door jargs (JAM.).

2. To jar.

Chs.[1] A heavy timber carriage going past would be said ' to jarg the whole house.' If one strikes the ' funny bone' it jargs the whole arm. **s.Chs.**[1]

3. To fall out, quarrel.

Chs. They rayther jarg'nt, *Sheaf* (1879) I. 168 ; **Chs.**[1] **s.Chs.**[1] Dū)nū jaa-rg sū, fūr gūd-nis see-k ; dhūr)z nōo pee-s i)dh aays fo)yi [Dunna jarg sō, for goodness' sake ; there's noo peace i' th' halse for ye].

4. *sb.* A harsh, grating sound. **Slk.** (JAM.)

5. A jolt, jar.

s.Chs.[1] Aby ky'echt mi el-bū ūgy'en- dhū weyl, ūn it gy'en mi aa-rm sich ū jaa-rg [I ketched my elbow agen the wheil, an' it gen my arm sich a jarg].

JARG, *sb.*[2] Cld. (JAM.) [Not known to our correspondents.] In *phr. to play the jarg on one,* to play a trick on one, to make game of one.

JARGLE, *v.*[1] Sc. To make a sharp shrill noise time after time in quick succession.

Per. That band has kept on jarglin' a' day. Johnny's jarglin' on his tin whistle (G.W.). **s.Sc.** (JAM.)

JARGLE, *v.*[2] w.Som.[1] [dgä-gl.] To gargle or gurgle with liquid in the throat.

Ee tos-l mee aew aay waz- vur tu jaar-gl mee droa-ut wai vin'-igur un puop-ur, bud dhae-ur, ded-n dūe- un waun bee-t u gēo-d [He told me that I was for to gargle my throat with vinegar and pepper, but there, (it) did not do it the slightest good].

JARGLE, see **Jarble,** *v.*

JARGON, *v.* Wm. [dga-rgon.] To scold, rate, 'slang.' Sooah Geordie coh tull me, an' rated an' jargoned, *Spec. Dial.* (1880) pt. ii. 30.

[Fr. *jargonner,* to jangle, chatter, babble confusedly (COTGR.).]

JARGONELLY, *sb.* Cor.[8] [Not known to our correspondents.] A large vessel, such as a pitcher, pan, bath, &c.

JAR-HOLE, see **Jaw-hole.**

JARIE, *sb.* Sc. [dga-ri.] A boy's marble.

Rnf. Sic a pock o' bools he's won — Redies, jaries, marbles blue, yellow, green, an' grey, NEILSON *Poems* (1877) 93.

JARL, *v.* and *sb.* Wor. Oxf. Wil. [dgäl.] **1.** *v.* To quarrel, ' have words.'

s.Wor. I heard 'em jarling (H.K.). **Wil.**[1]

2. *sb.* A quarrel, dispute.

Oxf. ' What's up now !' ' Oh, only another family jarl ' (G.O.).

JARLER, *sb.* Chs.[1] Anything out of the common way. A bricklayer who came from the neighbourhood of Winsford used to say of a brick that was above the common size, ' It's like one o' owd Matty Tasker's jarlers.' I presume Matty Tasker was some local celebrity who was given to telling very wonderful stories.

JARMAN, *sb. Obsol.* Som. A thin kind of gingerbread ; a ' brandy-snap.' See below.

It is (or was) also the word employed in the unlicensed houses for sale of beer or cider which used to be so common. A habitué would ask for a big or a little jarman, meaning either a quart or a pint of liquor. The ' jarman ' of course was sold — and the liquor given with it (W.F.R.).

JARME, *v.* Yks. [Not known to our correspondents.] To bawl, cry. (HALL.)

JARMER, *sb.* Sus. [dg͞a·mə(r).] An uncouth person. Children are warned not to behave like 'a country jarmer,' or 'a Sussex jarmer,' *N. & Q.* (1884) 6th S. ix. 40a.

JAR-NECKED, *adj.* m.Yks.[1] Wry-necked.
[Fr. dial. (Languedoc) *jar,* 'tortu, difforme, contrefait' (BOUCOIRAN).]

JARNESS, *sb.* Fif. (JAM.) [Not known to our correspondents.] A marshy place, or any place so wet as to resemble a marsh.

JAR(R, *v.* and *sb.* Sc. Yks. Not. Der. Nhp. Wor. Ess. Hmp. Also in form **jaur** Rnf. [dgar, dg͞a(r).] 1. *v.* To make a harsh whirring or grating noise.
w.Yks. (J.W.), nw.Der.[1] n.Not. A could mek the stockin-frame jarr i' them days (J.P.K.).
2. *Fig.* To quarrel, fall out; to ruffle, disturb, discompose. With *on*: to be continually at variance.
Fif. Tongues never wi' sic clitter-clatter Did jangle and did jarr, TENNANT *Papistry* (1827) 108. Rnf. When they in their reveries began for to jaur, WEBSTER *Rhymes* (1835) 142. n.Yks.[4]
Hence **Jarring,** *ppl. adj.* contending, quarrelling.
Edb. Rino gilds its jarring wights Them to his side to draw, LEARMONT *Poems* (1791) 104.
3. To scold, 'jaw.'
Ess. An' so he jarr'd no more, CLARK *J. Noakes* (1839) st. 71; 'Don't stand jarrin' there,' i.e. talking loudly or disputing; also used of talking idly, without disputing (W.W.S.); Ess.[1]
4. *sb.* In *comp.* (1) Jar-bird, (2) -owl, the goatsucker or nightjar, *Caprimulgus Europaeus*; (3) -peg, the woodpecker, *Gecinus viridis*.
(1) Hmp. WISE *New Forest* (1883) 187; Hmp.[1] e.Hmp. A bird that makes a clatter with its bill against a dead bough, or some old pales, calling it a jar-bird, WHITE *Selborne* (1788) 40, ed. 1853. (2) w.Wor. *Berrow's Jrn.* (Mar. 3, 1888). [SWAINSON *Birds* (1885) 97.] (3) Nhp. SWAINSON *ib.* 100; Nhp.[1] This bird often takes its station on an old oaken stump, and strikes with its beak on a hard knot or peg, so that the jar is heard in the stillness of the evening for a considerable distance around.

JARSENT, JARSEY, see **Jazzen, Jersey.**

JART, *v.* and *sb.* Yks. Lan. [dg͞at.] 1. *v.* To jerk; to throw quickly. See **Jert.**
e.Yks.[1] Hoo far can thā jart that steean ? e.Lan.[1]
Hence **Jarty,** *adj.* jerky. n.Yks. (I.W.)
2. To whip, punish. w.Yks. I'll jart tha (J.R.).
3. *sb.* A jerk, a sudden throw. e.Yks.[1]

JARTA, *sb.* Sh.I. Also in forms **iarto** S. & Ork.[1]; jarto, yarta (JAM.). A term of endearment: my dear. Also used *attrib.*
She could hear the strong voice of the Udaller ... call, in a tone of some anxiety, 'Tak heed, Jarto,' SCOTT *Pirate* (1822) xxvii; You forget, Jarto Claud, .. that the factor was only counting over the money for my Lord the Chamberlain, *ib.* xxx; My jarta ! JAKOBSEN *Norsk in Sh.* (1897) 30; S. & Ork.[1]
[Norw. dial. *hjarta* (*jarta*), heart (AASEN); see JAKOBSEN (*l.c.*).]

JARUM, see **Gearum)s.**

JARVALLY, *adv.* Sh.I. [Not known to our correspondents.] Actively. (*Coll.* L.L.B.)

JAR-WOMAN, *sb.* N.Cy.[1] Nhb.[1] An occasional assistant in the kitchen; a charwoman. See **Char(e,** *sb.*[1] 4 (1).

JARWORM, *sb.* s.Cy. (HALL.) I.W.[1] [dg͞a·wöm.] An ugly insect found in wet, marshy places.

JASAY, JASEY, see **Jersey.**

JASKIN, *sb.* Lth. (JAM.) [Not known to our correspondents.] A person occasionally employed in work to which he has not been regularly bred. Cf. **joskin.**

JASKIT, *ppl. adj.* Bnff.[1] [dga·akit.] Jaded, worn out, exhausted. See **Disjaskit,** 2.

JASNACK, see **Jazzen.**

JASP, *sb.* Slk. (JAM.) [Not known to our correspondents.] A particle; a spot, blemish. Cf. **jesp.**

JASPER, *sb.* Chs. Lin. Sus. 1. A name given to Brighton fishermen. Sus. *N. & Q.* (1884) 6th S. ix. 342.
2. A louse. Lin.[1] See **Dicky,** *sb.*[1] 5. 3. *Comp.* **Jasper-crab,** a kind of apple. Chs.[1]
[1. *Jasper* was formerly a common Christian name. Jasper [a man's name], *Gasparus*, COLES (1679). LG. *Jasper,* 'der Vorname Kaspar, cfr. Gaspar' (BERGHAUS).]

JASS, *sb.* and *v.* Sc. [dgas.] 1. *sb.* A violent throw; a dash; a heavy blow; the noise made by a heavy blow or fall. See **Joss,** *sb.*[2] 7.
Bnff.[1] He threw 'im our wee a jass. He got a jass o' the back it knockit 'im on 's nose. 'Jass' is a stronger term than 'joss.' Cld. (JAM.)
2. *v.* To throw with violence; to dash.
Bnff.[1] The ae loon jasst the ither our on 's back. Cld. (JAM.)

JASTER, see **Gaster.**

JATTER, *v.* Sc. Yks. Lan. e.An. [dga·tə(r).] 1. To break into small pieces; to shiver to atoms, to 'shatter.' e.Lan.[1], e.An.[1], Suf. (HALL.), e.Suf. (F.H.)
2. To shake, vibrate; to jolt; of the teeth: to chatter.
Sc. His teeth jatterin' and his face blue wi' cauld, ROY *Horseman's Wd.* (1895) v. w.Yks. The window jatters (J.R.). e.An.[1] Nrf. I ha' just sneezed, that du jatter my hid [head], that that du (A.G.F.); His teeth reglar jattered in his head. The things on the tray jattered up agin one another. That window do jatter so (M.C.H.B.). e.Suf. (F.H.)

JAUB, JAUBBER, see **Jab,** *v.*[1], **Jabber,** *v.*[1]

JAUCHLE, *v.* and *sb.* Lnk. (JAM.) [dg͞a·χl.] 1. *v.* To walk like one who has feeble joints, to 'bauchle.'
2. *Fig.* To make a shift, to do a thing with difficulty.
3. *sb.* A shift. 'He'll mak an unco jauchle.'

JAUD, see **Jade.**

JAUDIE, *sb.* Sc. n.Cy. Nhb. Written **jawdy** N.Cy.[1] Nhb.[1] [dg͞a·di, dgö·di.] 1. The stomach of a pig; the first stomach of an animal. The same word as **Chawdy** (q.v.).
Lth. Ilk oily leary, Ilk midden mavis, wee black jaudie, A' dread an' fear ye, BALLANTINE *Poems* (1856) 68. Rxb. Several superstitious ideas prevail among the vulgar with respect to the jaudie... The black spot, with which this stomach is marked, is carefully avoided by persons of both sexes who are conscious that they have lost their virtue. The thief is afraid to touch it; the glutton also, though ever so hungry (JAM.). N.Cy.[1] Nhb.[1] The term is applied to the edible entrails of the pig, ox, and sheep, especially to the large bag of a pig.
2. A pudding; see below.
Sc. A pudding of oatmeal and hog's lard, with onions and pepper, inclosed in a sow's stomach; formerly used as a supperdish at entertainments given by the country people on Fastren's Even, *Sibb. Gl.* (JAM.) s.Sc., Lth. *Gen.* used; often as equivalent to pudding; as, a bloody jaudie, a pudding made of blood (JAM.).

JAUG, see **Jag(g,** *sb.*[1]

JAUK, *v.* and *sb.* Sc. Also in form **jaik(e.** [dg͞ak.] 1. *v.* To trifle, dally, spend one's time idly.
Sc. (JAM.) Fif. And akaralie when they haid iaked on manie days gott sa mikle as a fear [fair] answer, MELVILL *Autob.* (1610) 435, ed. 1842. Lak. My mither ... wadna alloo me to jauk or rebel, HAMILTON *Poems* (1865) 145.
Hence (1) **Jaukan,** *vbl. sb.* the act of trifling over work; (2) **Jauker** or **Jaker,** *sb.* an idler, trifler; (3) **Jaukery,** *sb.* joking, trifling; (4) **Jauking,** (a) *vbl. sb.* idling, trifling, dallying; flirting; (b) *ppl. adj.* having a habit of trifling over work.
(1) Bnff.[1] A' mornin' they keepit a jaukan at the cuttan; an' the rain wiz on afore they got cliack. (2) Sc. The down-sittin o' lowse jaukers, WADDELL *Ps.* (1871) i. 1. Bnff.[1] Ayr. Get up my muse, ye lazy jaker, FISHER *Poems* (1790) 85. (3) Slk. She wad hae flown i' my face wi' her gibery and jaukery, HOGG *Tales* (1838) 322, ed. 1866. (4, a) Ayr. An' aye she win't, an' aye she swat, I wat she made nae jaukin, BURNS *Halloween* (1785) st. 19; Nor mair o' love be talking, We've fools an' beggars' brats enew; Sae, youngsters, quit your jauking, AINSLIE *Poems* (ed. 1892) 253. Lak. Nae stannin' still nor jaukin', Oor wark's ahin, HAMILTON *Poems* (ed. 1885) 55. (b) Bnff.[1]
2. To walk slowly; to waste time in walking.
Bnff.[1] A sent 'im an airran; bit he jauckit sae lang o' the rod, it a wiz forcet to gang an' fess 'im hame.
3. *sb.* Trifling over work; an idler, one who trifles over work. *ib.*

JAUL, *v.*[1] Ken. [dg͞ol.] To throw the earth about and get the grain out of the ground, when it is sown, as birds do. See **Jowl,** *v.*[1] 4.
Ken.[1] The bothering old rooks have jauled all de seeds out o' de groun'; Ken.[2]

JAUL, $v.^2$ n.Cy. [Not known to our correspondents.] To scold or grumble. (HALL.)

JAUL, JAUM, JAUM(B, see Jowl, $v.^1$, Jam, Jamb.

JAUMPH, JAUNCE, see Jamph, $v.^1$, Jance.

JAUNDER, $v.$ and $sb.$ Sc. Also in forms **jander** Rxb. (JAM.); **janner** Rxb. (JAM.) Dmf. Gall.; **jauner** Ayr. e.Lth.; **jawner** Cld. (JAM.) [dȝā·n(d)ər.] 1. $v.$ To talk idly or foolishly; to 'maunder.'

s.Sc., Cld. (JAM.) Lnk. To death You haze me, jawnering ay o' faith! faith! faith! BLACK *Falls of Clyde* (1806) 133. e.Lth. Ye may jaun'er on as lang as ye like for me, HUNTER *J. Inwick* (1895) 93. Slk. They war just jaundering wi' the bridegroom for fun, HOGG *Tales* (1838) 155, ed. 1866. Dmf. All which poor Irving is pleased . . . to janner about at great length, CARLYLE *Lett.* (1891). Gall. Ae glass brought anither; him and me to jawner, and whan I gat hame, Lord knows, MACTAGGART *Encycl.* (1824) 159, ed. 1876.

Hence **Jannerer**, $sb.$ one who talks foolishly or incoherently. Gall. MACTAGGART *Encycl.* (1824).

2. Phr. *to jaunder about*, to go about idly from place to place without having any proper object in view. Bwk. (JAM.)

3. $sb.$ Idle talk; rambling conversation.

Sc. (JAM.) Ayr. O haud your tongue and jauner, BURNS *Lass of Ecclefechan*. Rxb. What but harm can come of this senseless jauner? *Blackw. Mag.* (Dec. 1821) 321 (JAM.); We've had a gude jaunder this forenoon (JAM.).

4. One who talks incoherently or foolishly. Slk. (ib.)

JAUNDICE, $sb.$ Var. dial. forms in Sc. Irel. and Eng. I. (1) **Jaanders**, (2) **Jaandice**, (3) **Jaanis**, (4) **Janders**, (5) **Jandhers**, (6) **Jandies**, (7) **Jandrers**, (8) **Jaunas**, (9) **Jaunders**, (10) **Jaunis**, (11) **Jaunus**, (12) **Jawnas**, (13) **Jenis**, (14) **Joanas**, (15) **Jonas**. [dȝā·ndəz, dȝō̄·nəs.]

(1) Chs.[1], Ken. (G.B.) (2) Chs.[1] (3) Nhb.[1] (4) n.Lan.[1] Lei.[1] Almost always qualified as the 'yaller janders.' The 'black janders' designates its more malignant form. Brks.[1], ne.Ken. (H.M.), Hmp.[1], w.Cy. (HALL.) Wil. Slow *Gl.* (1892) [1] BRITTON *Beauties* (1825). n.Wil. They tells me as Jack Smith have got the yaller janders (E.H.G.). Dor.[1], Cor.[12] (5) w.Ir. Is it the jandhers you have? LOVER *Leg.* (1848) II. 492. (6) Per. Our Davie was ta'en down wi' the jandies, CLELAND *Inchbracken* (1883) 209, ed. 1889. (7) Ken. To find poor Peter ill in bed. He said it was only the 'jandrers,' *Longman's Mag.* (Nov. 1891) 83. (8) w.Yks. WATSON *Hist. Hlfx.* (1775) 541; w.Yks.[4] (9) Chs.[1], Not.[1] n.Lin.[1] Black-jaunders, jaundice of a more than usually severe kind; so called from the dark colour of the skin and fœces, and perhaps also from its highly dangerous character. Lei.[1], War.[24], s.Wor. (H.K.) Shr. The jaundice, commonly called the jaunders or yallow-wort, BURNE *Flk-Lore* (1883) xiv; Shr.[1] Poor owd mon! 'e's bin bad a lungful time, an' now they sen it's turned to the black jaunders. Hrf.[2], Hrt. (H.G.) s.Cy. HOLLOWAY. Som. JENNINGS *Obs. Dial. w.Eng.* (1825). w.Som.[1] Jau·nderz, jaa·ndurz, jaa·rndurz. Always so, prob. because in the dial. nearly all diseases are *pl.* nouns. Cor.[1] (10) N.Cy.[1], Nhb.[2] (11) N.Cy.[1], n.Yks. (I.W.), w.Yks.[1] (12) e.Yks.[1] (13) Nhb.[1] (14) e.Lan.[1] (15) Nhb.[1] Cum. Sin laid up i' th' jonas, he's niver been reght, ANDERSON *Ballads* (ed. 1840) 73. e.Yks.[1] Is it yallow jonas, or black, she's getten? w.Yks.[4]

II. Dial. use. In *comp.* **Jaundice-tree**, the common barbary, *Berberis vulgaris*.

w.Som.[1] From the yellow colour of the wood. Cor. From a' belief (on the 'doctrine of signatures') that the yellow under-bark indicated its value as a cure for the yellow disease (B. & H.).

JAUNT, $sb.^1$ and $v.^1$ Sc. Irel. Nhb. Cum. Wm. Lan. Also Oxf. Brks. I.W. Also in forms **jaant** Oxf.[1] Brks.[1] I.W.[1]; **jant** Nhb. Lakel.[2] Cum.[14] Wm. [dȝǫnt, dȝānt, dȝant.] 1. $sb.$ A pleasure-trip, an excursion, expedition, journey.

Frf. Has . . . E——d C——d taen his last jaunt? SANDS *Poems* (1833) 40. Fif. I wonner hoo Mysie Chalmers 'll look when she hears I'm gaun sic a lang jaunt, M°LAREN *Tibbie* (1894) 64. Ayr. Too short seemed the day For a jaunt to Downpatrick, Or a trip on the sea, BOSWELL *Poet. Wks.* (1803) 17, ed. 1871. Lnk. A thocht cam' in his min' Tae gang wi' her a jaunt, STEWART *Twa Elders* (1886) 11. Edb. On their waddin jaunt they drive, M°DOWALL *Poems* (1899) 35. Peb. Idle jaunts to me were pain, AFFLECK *Poet. Whs.* (1896) 61. Gall. Allan and the wife were at Drumquhat overnight on their marriage jaunt, CROCKETT *Stickit Min.* (1893) 107. Nhb. (R.O.H.) Lakel.[2] We'll hev a jant oot efter tea. Cum.[1]; Cum.[4] He myad up his mind 'at he'd hev a jant off, W. C. T. (July 16, 1898) 4. I.W.[1]

2. $v.$ To go on a pleasure-trip or excursion.

Frf. Like maukins thro' the fields they're jauntin', MORISON *Poems* (1790) 7. Per. A mettled, but canny young yaud for the yokin', When ye gae a jauntin' wi' me, FORD *Harp* (1893) 164. Lnk. I micht hae been rowin' in gear, An' jauntin' aboot in my carriage, M°LACHLAN *Thoughts* (1884) 80. Cum. There's our 'squire, wi' his thousands, jant jantin' about, ANDERSON *Ballads* (1805) 99. Wm. We'd meant ta gah on t'sly an' jant an' spree aboot, *Spec. Dial.* (1880) pt. ii. 47. Lan. Rambling through fields and meadows in a cheerful light-hearted way (S.W.). Oxf.[1] Jauntin about, going off on pleasure. *MS. add.* Brks.[1]

Hence (1) **Jaunting-bottle**, $sb.$ a pocket-flask; (2) **-car**, $sb.$ an Irish car, esp. a car used for pleasure excursions.

(1) Lnk. Drawin' oot his jauntin' bottle [he] says, 'Will ye tak' a bit taste!' WARDROP *J. Mathison* (1881) 41. (2) Ir. The journey was to be performed in a jaunting car hired for the occasion, *Paddiana* (ed. 1843) I. 246; GROSE (1790) *MS. add.* (M.) n.Ir. There wusnae less nor twunty horses an' jauntin' cars, LYTTLE *Paddy McQuillan*, 10.

3. To trip along, go jauntily.

Per. Through arch an' aisle they jouk an' jaunt, STEWART *Character* (1857) 99. Rnf. With big hand-basket in his mouth To shops he jaunted, M°GILVRAY *Poems* (ed. 1862) 245.

Hence **Jauntingly**, $adv.$ jauntily.

Per. Whaur water-bobbies jauntin'ly Bow to their shadows in the stream, EDWARDS *Strathearn Lyrics* (1889) 59.

JAUNT, $v.^2$ Not. [dȝǫnt.] To jolt, shake.

s.Not. It did jaunt me goin' ower them stones (J.P.K.).

JAUNT, $v.^3$ and $sb.^2$ Fif. (JAM.) 1. $v.$ To taunt, gibe, jeer. 2. $sb.$ A gibe, taunt.

JAUNT COAL, $phr.$ *Obs.* Sc. A species of coal.

Lnk. Coal called jaunt coal, URE *Hist. Rutherglen* (1793) 290 (JAM.).

JAUNTY, see Janty.

JAUP, $v.^1$ and $sb.$ In *gen.* dial. use in Sc. Irel. and n. counties to Lin. Also written **jawp** Sc. (JAM.) Lin.; and in forms **jaap** Sc. (JAM.) Nhb.[1]; **jab** Cum.[4]; **jaip** Nhb.[1]; **jalp** Sc. (JAM.); **jap** Sh.I. Fif. Edb. N.I.[1] Ant. Don. Nhb.[1] Cum.[4]; **joap** Cum. Wm.; **jop** w.Yks.; **jope** Nhb.[1] Cum.[4] n.Lan.[1] ne.Lan.[1]; **joup** n.Cy. w.Yks.[1]; **jowp** n.Yks.[12] e.Yks.[1] m.Yks.[1] [dȝāp, dȝǫp, dȝǫup, dȝap.] 1. $v.$ Of water: to dash and rebound, in waves. Also used *fig.*

Sc. (JAM.) Per. Stinking ware that jaups in lugglies clean out of caup and market, HALIBURTON *Furth in Field* (1894) 4. Fif. Like swallin' waves on rough shores jappin', TENNANT *Papistry* (1827) 168. s.Sc. The wind . . . maks the water jaw, an' jawp, an' foam like a cauldron, WILSON *Tales* (1836) V. 91. Dmb. The steem-bott . . . snoovt awa and snoovt awa tho' the water was jaupin till the Lum tap, CROSS *Disruption* (1844) xxix. Ayr. She wished it would blaw sic ane tempest as would soop the sea out of the sea, and jawp the sea oure the hills, SERVICE *Dr. Duguid* (ed. 1887) 255. m.Yks.[1] To wash or dash about in mass, like water, when shaken. Waves are said to go jowping up against the stones on the beach, or sea-wall. w.Yks.[1]

Hence (1) **Japper**, $sb.$ a billow, broken wave; (2) **Jauping**, $ppl. adj.$ dashing, breaking in waves.

(1) Fif. Beside the shore Whairon th' Aegean's jappers roar, TENNANT *Papistry* (1827) 3. (2) Ayr. The jauping weet, the sentrid sheet, AINSLIE *Poems* (ed. 1892) 132. Bwk. Green wi' the dew o' the jauping main, HENDERSON *Pop. Rhymes* (1856) 108.

2. To splash; to bespatter with mud or water; to spill, throw water, &c. over anything.

Sc. Ride fair and jaap nane, KELLY *Prov.* (1721) 283. s.Fif. He wad persist in carvin' the chickens, . . wi' the result that he jaupit wi' the jice a' the young leddies' white goons, LATTO *Tam Bodkin* (1864) xxv. Rnf. I'll gar your dull, foostit brains Jaup on Heaven's causie stanes, FINLAYSON *Rhymes* (1815) 57. Ayr. A wheen callans wi' their leather breeks, jawpin' through the glaur, SERVICE *Notandums* (1890) 79. Lnk. Jouk atween their stumpy legs, dinna jaup the dears, NICHOLSON *Kilwuddie* (1895) 104. s.Lth. Ye'll hae to tak unco care that ye dinna jaup yoursel, HUNTER *J. Inwick* (1895) 63. Edb. Poor Saundie, frae his doughty wark, Came hame a' jappet i' the dark, TINT *Quey* (1796) 13. Gall. MACTAGGART *Encycl.* (1824). N.I.[1] s.Don. SIMMONS *Gl.* (1890). Cav. Yon boy running past japped you (M.S.M.). Nhb.[1] Cum. I'd jaup This quart a' yell about your scope, STAGG *Misc. Poems* (ed. 1807) 91; Cum.[1]; Cum.[4] Don't jope t'flooer wid t'whitewesh, noo. Anyone in the way when a bucketful of water is thrown down with force,' is liable to get japped. 'She brought milk in a can, an' jab't it ower at ivery step.' Cum., Wm. Nicolson (1677) *Trans. R. Lit. Soc.* (1868) IX. n.Lan.¹, ne.Lan.¹

Hence **Jopina**, *sb. pl.* anything spilled. Cum.¹⁴

3. Phr. (1) *to jawp the water*, to spend time on any business, without the least prospect of success ; — *waters with one*, to play fast and loose.

(1) Sc. A' that ye do 'ill be just jawpin the water (Jam.). (2) Fif. 'I'll no jawp waters wi' you,' said to a person who has made a bargain with another, and wishes to cast it (*ib.*).

4. To shake up, toss to and fro ; to shake up the sediment at the bottom of a liquid ; to beat up eggs.

n.Cy. Grose (1790). Nhb. Anything thrown sharply and suddenly into the water is said to jap it about (R.O.H.); Nhb.¹ n.Yks.¹; n.Yks.² 'We com jowping alang,' knocking one against another in the vehicle. 'Jowp'd up,' shaken up, as the sediment in a liquid; n.Yks.⁴ If thoo jaups t'milk leyke that, thoo 'll finnd butter i' t'can when thoo gits yam. ne.Yks.¹ Deean't jaup it aboot. e.Yks. Deean't jowp coffee-pot an stor all gruns up, Nicholson *Flb-Sp.* (1889) 93 ; Marshall *Rur. Econ.* (1788) ; e.Yks.¹ Thoo leeak at taties, while Ah jaup this egg. w.Yks. Hutton *Tour to Caves* (1781) ; w.Yks.¹, ne.Lan.¹

Hence **Jowpment**, *sb.* a mixture of viands; a hash. n.Yks.²

5. To make a splashing noise like liquid agitated in a bucket or barrel.

n.Cy. Grose (1790) ; N.Cy.¹ The water went jauping in the skeel. Dur.¹ s.Dur. A rotten egg is said to jaup when shaken (J.E.D.). n.Yks.¹ e.Yks. Marshall *Rur. Econ.* (1788). sw.Lin.¹ How it jaups aboot.

6. To strike together ; to smash by a sudden blow.

N.Cy.¹ 'Jauping paste-eggs' at Easter is a game at Newc. Two boys give blow for blow with their eggs, and whichever is broken is forfeited. Nhb.¹ Nhb., Dur. On Easter Monday the children have a festival entitled 'paste-egg day,' on which dyed eggs, boiled hard, are bowled along the grass and jaaped to see which will break first (J.H.B.). Dur. To test the relative strength of various articles by hitting them together. At Easter men and boys 'jap' paste eggs, striking one against another, to test which is the stronger (F.P.). n.Yks.⁴ Ah'll jaup tha eggs.

Hence (1) **Jaaper**, *sb.* one who strikes the egg of an opponent ; (2) **Japin**, *sb.* a jerk, a smart stroke.

(1) Nhb. At Easter time the relative merits of the dyed ' paste-eggs ' are settled by the arbitrament of ' jaapin.' One holds his egg, exposing the small end, and the ' jaaper ' knocks the end of his egg against it. The egg remaining unbroken is the conqueror, and an egg which has come off entire after many such trials is considered prizeworthy (R.O.H.). (2) Fif. (Jam.)

7. To beat, thrash.

n.Lin.¹ Noo then, Bill, I shall jaup thÿ jacket for thê if thoo dux n't mind.

8. *sb.* A dash of water, a broken wave ; a cross, short sea. Also used *fig.*

Sc. That portion of water which is separated from a wave, when it is broken by its own weight, or by dashing against a rock, ship, or any other body that resists its force and causes part of it to fly off (Jam.). Sh.I. Sair daddit wi' life's jap, Burgess *Rasmie* (1892) 32 ; Hit makes a jap ipo da shaald, Junda *Klingrahool* (1898) 22 ; (Coll. L.L.B.) Abd. Gien yer lordships hed hed as mony . . . jaups o' could sea watter, Macdonald *Malcolm* (1875) II. 24. Fif. Again the crowd, like water-jaup, Thegither rush'd, Tennant *Papistry* (1827) 141. Ayr. Dash the gumlie jaups up to the pouring skies, Burns *Brigs of Ayr* (1787) l. 126 ; Gie me the jaup o' the dear auld saut [sea], Ainslie *Poems* (ed. 1892) 315.

9. A spot or splash of mud or dirty water ; a spurt of water.

Sc. Properly that which is thrown on one's clothes, by the motion of the feet, or of a horse or carriage, when the road is wet or miry (Jam.). Per. See til the jaups o' glaar about yer guttery trotters, Cleland *Inchbracken* (1883) 263, ed. 1887. Ayr. He bad got a jaup o' glaur on his specks, Johnston *Kilmallie* (1891) II. 140. Edb. Ay the jawps flee frae the whiel That quirlis at the end o't, Ramsay *Gentle Shep.* (1725) 708, Scenary ed. Bwk. Ye needna be feared for a jaup o' glaur, Calder *Poems* (1897) 209. N.I.¹ Ant. A person after walking on a wet day will complain of being covered with ' japs,' *Ballymena Obs.* (1892) ; Grose (1790) *M.S. add.*(C.) s.Don. Simmons *Gl.* (1890). Nhb. My father cam hame a' covered wi japs o' glair ; Nhb.¹

10. A quantity of liquid ; the dregs of anything.

Sc. Canty war we ower your kale, Toddy jugs and jaups o' yill, Chambers *Sngs.* (1829) I. 46. s.Sc. Come ! whurl the drumlie dregs o't rown ; . . Gie then the jaups anither twirl, Nicol *Poems*

(1805) II. 60 (Jam.). Raf. Jaups o' milk and pails o' whey, Barr *Poems* (1861) 199. Gall. Awa' ye foreign jaups and gills, Ye're brought auld Scotlan' mony ills, Nicholson *Poet. Wks.* (1814) 130, ed. 1897.

11. The sound produced by liquid shaken in a half-empty vessel, *fig.* senseless talk.

N.Cy.¹ w.Yks. Willan *List Wds.* (1811). Lin. Streatfeild *Lin. and Danes* (1885) 339. n.Lin.¹ Ho'd the jaup wi' thê ; dos't ta want ivery body to knaw how soft thoo is ?

12. The sound made by shoes when full of water. Per. (G.W.)

13. A slap, a slight blow, which frightens rather than hurts ; a cut, blow.

Cai.¹ Ayr. Wi' bluid upon his beak and claw, And jaups on ilka wing, *Ballads and Poems* (1885) 190. Cum.⁴ Hittin' Abe a jope under t'chin, W. C. T. H. (1893) 10 ; I simply meant to give it two or three japs to frighten it, *Carlisle Patr.* (May 25, 1894) 3. LMa. A jap in the mous he should have got, Rydings *Tales* (1895) 106; I give him the jap on the mouth for his imperence (S.M.).

14. *Fig.* Ruin, destruction, wreck.

Sc. Mony a day as I hae been guid til you, ridden you canny and never skelpit the hide o' you, to put sic a jawp on me noo, Roy *Horseman's Wd.* (1895) xi. Dmf. Their fine balloon journey a' knockit tae jaup, Reid *Poems* (1894) 48. Kcb. The farm gaed to jap, an' the bummers cam' in, An' hoisted puir Tam to the causey, Armstrong *Ingleside* (1890) 218.

JAUP, *v.²* Bnff.¹ To fatigue, weary.

JAUPIE, *v.* Sc. Also written **jauppie**. [dȝā'pi.] To spill, scatter, separate into small portions of liquid, &c. See **Jaup**, *v.*¹ 2.

Edb. Thou gar'st the hidden treasure jaupie A' in the air, Ballantine *Wee Raggit Laddie*, st. 11 (Jam. *Suppl.*) ; *ib.* Gaberlunnie (ed. 1875) Gl.

JAUR, JAUR-HOLE, see **Jar(r, Jaw-hole.**

JAURNOCH, *sb.* w.Sc. (Jam.) Filth ; washings of dishes, &c.

JAVE, *sb.* Sc. [Not known to our other correspondents.] The upper crust of a loaf of bread. (F.H.)

JAVE, see **Jeve.**

JAVEL, *v.* Yks. Also written **javvle** e.Yks.¹ [dȝa·vl.] To wrangle, quarrel, dispute. Yks. (Hall.), e.Yks.¹, w.Yks.²²

JAVELIN, *sb.* Cum. [Not known to our correspondents.] A crowbar. Easther *Gl.* (1893).

JAVVER, *v.* and *sb.*¹ n.Cy. Yks. Der. Also written **gavver** w.Yks. Der.² nw.Der.¹ [dȝa·və(r.] **1.** *v.* To talk idly ; to be garrulous, talkative. Cf. gabber, jabber, *v.*¹

m.Yks.¹ w.Yks. He may do pratta weel to bawl to t'Oirishmen, or javver abaht chetch rates, Bywater *Sheffield Dial.* (1839) 98, ed. 1877 ; w.Yks.¹ Their parents er ill set to ken what ther barns er javverin about, i. xix. Der.², nw.Der.¹

Hence (1) **Gavering**, *ppl. adj.* w.Yks. (J.T.); (2) **Javversome**, *adj.* noisy, talkative, garrulous. n.Yks.²

2. *sb.* Idle talk ; impudence, ' jaw.'

n.Cy. (Hall.), n.Yks.¹²⁴, m.Yks.¹ w.Yks.¹ Let's hey naan o' thy javver ; w.Yks.², nw.Der.¹

JAVVER, *sb.²* Yks. Food. The same word as **Chavver** (q. v.).

w.Yks. Average price oo wheat wor 133s. for 8 bush. ; it wor dear javver at that day, *Dewsbre Olm.* (1866) 4.

JAW, *sb.¹* and *v.¹* Var. dial. and colloq. uses in Sc. Irel. Eng. and Amer. Also in forms **ja** w.Cy. Dor.¹; **jaa** Sh.I. Nhb.¹ Cum.¹⁴; **jah** Ess.¹; **jo** Cum.¹⁴ [dȝ̄ō, dȝā.]

1. *sb.* In *comb.* (1) **Jaw-bit**, food carried out in the fields by labourers, to be eaten about 10 or 11 o'clock ; (2) -**blades**, the jaws, chafts; (3) -**bone yat-steads**, gateways with pointed arches made of whales' jaw-bones ; (4) -**breaker**, (5) -**cracker**, a long word, difficult to pronounce ; (6) -**hole**, a fissure or opening in the land, as the mouth of a stream ; the arched entrance to a cavern ; (7) -**lock**, **lockjaw**; (8) -**locked**, lock-jawed ; (9) -**work**, talk.

(1) Wil.¹ (2) Nhb.¹ (3) e.Yks.¹ In the neighbourhood of Hull, formerly the chief port for Greenland whalers, it was customary to set up over gate-ways, whales' jaw-bones in the form of a pointed arch, many of which may still be seen. (4) Nhb.¹, e.Yks.¹, w.Yks. (J.W.) n.Lin.¹ Thaay mak ewse on sich jaw-breakers when thaay talk aboot the'r flooers, 'at I can't tell a wo'd thaay saay, nor tung it efter 'em. s.Lin. He preaached a sarmon as wor nist and short

and wi'out any jawbrakers (T.H.R.). Oxf.[1] *MS. add.* Lon. 'I can't tumble to that barrikin,' said a young fellow; ' it's a jaw-breaker,' MAYHEW *Lond. Labour* (1851) I. 25. (5) e.Yks.[1] (6) n.Yks.[2] (7) Ayr. The gun burst and blew aff his thoomb : he dee'd of jaw-lock in a week, SERVICE *Dr. Duguid* (ed. 1887) 115. w.Yks. T'wife hezzant hed t'jawlock yet, *Pudsey Ann.* († 1875) *Pref.* 3. (8) w.Yks. Wi' my mathe woide oppen, an' neearly jaw-lock'd, HALLAM *Wadsley Jack* (1866) xvi. (9) Lan. Le's ha' less jaw-work an' more paw work fro' th' gentry, BURNETT *Haworth's* (1887) vii.

2. *Fig.* Talk, chatter; abusive or insolent talk, ' cheek.' In *gen.* colloq. use.

Sh.I. Man, howld dy jaw, *Sh. News* (Aug. 13, 1898). Cai.[1] Elg. I'll gar ye haud yer jaw yet, TESTER *Poems* (1865) 118. Abd. Fat's the eese o' a lawvyer gin he hinna a gweed moufu' o' ill jaw ! ALEXANDER *Ain Flk.* (1882) 98. Frf. Come now, mum, no jaw, WILLOCK *Rosetty Ends* (1886) 166, ed. 1889. Flf. Ne'er gie them surly jaw, nor jeer Whan they for fauts reprove you, DOUGLAS *Poems* (1806) 82. Rnf. Mungo Martin had grown dry Thro' extra jaw and jobbin', WEBSTER *Rhymes* (1835) 11. Ayr. A very good sort of a town—plenty of punch and plenty of jaw, GALT *Lairds* (1826) xxvii. Lnk. If ye treat me to ony mair o' yer sma' jaw, I'll rise an' wring the bit neck o' ye, MURDOCH *Readings* (1895) I. 122. Edb. Plagu'd wi' jails and lawwer's jaw, LEARMONT *Poems* (1791) 62. Gall. MACTAGGART *Encycl.* (1824). Wgt. Ye lawyers ... Wha deaved his lugs wi' learned jaw, FRASER *Poems* (1885) 227. N.I.[1], Nhb.[1], Dur.[1], Lakel.[2] Cum.[1]; Cum.[4] Hod theh jo. Wm. (B.K.), Yks. (J.W.), e.Yks.[1] Lan. Bur aw conno' the'r jaw un' the'r gam', HARLAND *Lyrics* (1866) 137; Lan.[1] Esp. talk which annoys or aggravates. ' Come, let's have none o' thy jaw.' Der.[2], nw.Der.[1], Not.[1] n.Lin.[1] N—— hed been warkin' doon at th' boddom o' a well, soä I ax'd him, at dinner-time, for jaw like, if he'd seed oht o' ohd Sam. s.Lin. (T.H.R.), Lei.[1], War.[2], Suf.[1] w.Som.[1] Kau'm naew ! noa'un u dhuy jaa', uls dhee-t bee u-puut· tu doo·urz een u kwik stik [Come now ! (let us have) none of your abusive language, otherwise you will be put to doors (turned out) very quickly]. Ee·! wai, u-z au·l jaa', lig u sheep's aid ! [He ! why, he is all jaw, like a sheep's head !] A very common description of an empty talker. Slang. Desiring him to do his duty without further jaw, SMOLLETT *P. Pickle* (1751) xxxii. [Amer. 'Twould save holl hay-cartloads o' fuss an' three four months o' jaw, LOWELL *Biglow Papers* (1848) 136.]

3. A jest. Lan. (HALL.) [Not known to our correspondents.] **4.** The open-ended tenon for a mortice. Glo.[1], w.Cy. (HALL.), Dor.[1] **5.** *pl.* The breaking part of a stone-crushing machine. s.Yks. (S.K.C.)

6. *v.* To talk, chatter.

Abd. Jawin' wi' the ither lasses, MACDONALD *R. Falconer* (1868) 105. Rnf. Priests may preach and scribes may jaw, WEBSTER *Rhymes* (1835) 8. Edb. Ither people jaw away About politica o' the day, CRAWFORD *Poems* (1798) 108. W.I. To talk in an offensive way; to give saucy answers. Cum. Lantie laugh't An' jaw't an' chaff't, RICHARDSON *Talk* (1876) 86. Yks. (J.W.), Lan. (S.W.) n.Lin. If I stan' jawin' wi' a . . . yawnax like you she'll maybe be deud afore I get to her, PEACOCK *R. Skirlaugh* (1870) II. 88. s.Lin. Nobody heer'd sich jawin' and argyin' i' all the'r born dais as wor carri'd on (T.H.R.). Nrf. Mind yow don't go loafing and jawing about, HAGGARD *Col. Quaritch* (1888) I. vi. Ess.[1] She's in a jahing yumer to-day. Slang. They jawed together, fore and aft, a good spell, SMOLLETT *R. Random* (1748) xxiv.

Hence (1) **Jawing-shop**, *sb.* a debating society; (2) **.tacks**, *sb.* the mouth ; jaws.

(1) Brks. Worth more than all the chaps at that jawing shop of yours, HUGHES *Scour. White Horse* (1859) viii. (2) Cor. He gives a shake o' the head to set hes jawin'-tacks loose, ' Q.' *Troy Town* (1888) xi.

7. *Phr. to jaw over,* (1) to talk over, to persuade; (2) to talk about a person or thing in a loud or offensive manner.

n.Lin.[1] I doän't want to hev my lass's naame jaw'd oher e' ivery public-hoose e' all th' cuntry side.

8. To scold, vituperate, abuse ; to grumble, complain ; to taunt. *Pret.* jew. In *gen.* colloq. use.

Sh.I. Get 'is friends ta start an' jaa me, *Sh. News* (July 30, 1898). Flf. She jaw'd them, misca'd them For clashin' claikin' haips, DOUGLAS *Poems* (1806) 125. n.Cy. (J.W.) Lakel.[2] He jaw'd me rarely when A spak tull him fer his awn good. w.Yks.[2] LMa. The master was jawin' beastly enough, RYDINGS *Tales* (1895) 114. Der. I wish I was here when you jawed cousin, LE FANU *Uncle Silas* (1865) I. 299; Der.[2], nw.Der.[1], Lei.[1], War.[2] Lon. Because he kept jawing me, MAYHEW *Prisons* (1862) 550. Suf. He jew good tightly about it (C.G.B.); e.An. *Dy. Times*

(1892). e.Suf. (F.H.) Ken. He did jaw when he heard it (D.W.L.). e.Ken. (G.G.) Sus., Hmp. HOLLOWAY. n.Dev. Tamzen and thee be olweys . . . jawing, *Exm. Scold.* (1746) l. 307.

JAW, *v.*[2] and *sb.*[2] Sc. Irel. n.Cy. Nhb. Cum. Also in forms jaa Nhb.[1]; jae Sc. (JAM.) [dʒǭ, dʒ ̅a.] **1.** *v.* Of water : to dash, surge, splash. Cf. jow, *v.*[1] 6.

Sc. A naked craig wi' a bure jawing ower 't, SCOTT *Rob Roy* (1817) xxi ; The stately tower Whilk proud defies the jawing wave, *Lass of Roch Royal,* 7, in CHILD *Ballads* (1885) II. 223. Frf. The billows around him micht jaw, WATT *Poet. Sketches* (1880) 105. Per. Aye I faucht wi' the jawin' wave, FORD *Harp* (1893) 342. Rnf. A burn ' whiles jawin' like a sea,' GILMOUR *Pen-Flk.* (1873) 50. Lnk. Sheughs an' deep fur-drains were jawin' To spate the burns, WATSON *Poems* (1853) 26. Ant. (W.H.P.)

2. To pour or dash about a quantity of water.

Sc. When it [the elephant] drinks, it sucks up the water with its trunk,—and then putting the low end of the trunk in its mouth, by wynding it in, it jaes in the water in its mouth as from a great spout, Law *Memorialls* (1818) 177 (JAM.). Ayr. [They] jawed a-stowpfu' o' water on his heid, SERVICE *Notandums* (1890) 35 ; (F.J.C.) Lnk. Bletherum bore her to the vestry, Jaw'd some water in her face, NICHOLSON *Kilwuddie* (1895) 80. n.Lth. Nae need to jaw watter on a droun'd moose, HUNTER *J. Inwick* (1895) 194. Gall. ' Jaw,' in some of the ancient tongues, means ' pour' ; we use it yet for that in ours, MACTAGGART *Encycl.* (1824) 281, ed. 1876.

3. *sb.* A wave, billow, breaker. Also used *fig.*

Sc. Ugly, ugly were the jaws That rowd unto their knee, *Sir Patrick Spens,* 8, in CHILD *Ballads* (1885) II. 21. Bnff. Jouk till o'er you gang the jaw, TAYLOR *Poems* (1787) 97. Abd. Weet to the skin wi' the splash o' a muckle jaw, MACDONALD *Malcolm* (1875) II. 13. Kcd. [He] Took the wiser coorse to 'jook, An lat the jaw gang by,' GRANT *Lays* (1884) 57. Frf. A craft . . . That . . . Jinket the jaws On the briny breist o' the main, WATT *Poet. Sketches* (1880) 20. Flf. Lampin' alang . . . frae jaw to jaw athort the sea, TENNANT *Papistry* (1827) 3. Lnk. Drink gaed roun' like jaws o' water, NICHOLSON *Kilwuddie* (1895) 72. Lth. Scores o' our sturdiest farmers fail To jouk the jaw, An' broken-hairted families haill Gae to the wa', LUMSDEN *Sheep-head* (1892) 164. Edb. Upo' the briny Borean jaws to float, FERGUSSON *Poems* (1773) 198, ed. 1785. Gall. I had ye baptized, . . and never a whinge or a greet did ye gae when he slappit ye into the thickest o' the jaw, CROCKETT *Standard Bearer* (1898) 326. N.Cy.[1], Nhb.[1]

4. A dash or spurt of water ; a quantity of water thrown out with a jerk.

Sc. A gush of water, &c., such as takes place when we suddenly overset a tub or bucket of water, GROSE (1790) *MS. add.* (C.) nw.Abd. The trance is in a jaw [flood], *Goodwife* (1867) st. 44. Frf. Anither day he wad be dashed frae head to feet wi' great jaws o' cauld water, WILLOCK *Rosetty Ends* (1886) 80, ed. 1889. Per. Doon wad thud my ravelled snood, Creatin' sic a jaw, man, FORD *Harp* (1893) 149. Peb. The nauseous mixture fell Wi' jaws upon the sprawling hash, *Lintoun Green* (1685) 62, ed. 1817.

5. A large quantity of any liquid.

Sc. The cow has gi'en a gude jaw the day, i. e. a large quantity of milk (JAM.). Bnff.[1] Jaws of milk, a large quantity of milk (s.v. Haul). Flf. Fisher-Willie and the lairds . . . wash't their gebbies and their beards In sparklin' jaws o' claret, TENNANT *Papistry* (1827) 82. Rnf. Drown dull care in jaws o' liquor, PICKEN *Poems* (1813) I. 80. Ayr. He was gaun to be very big, and order in a great jaw of drink for the company, SERVICE *Dr. Duguid* (ed. 1887) 195. Lnk. Wee draps gar sense its mettle feel, Grit jaws gar wit an' reason reel, WATT *Poems* (1827) 109. s.Lth. It poored on maist o' the month o' September, wi' awfu' jaws an' skelps o' rain, HUNTER *J. Inwick* (1895) 9. Cum. Wi' jaws o' yell some durty beutts Pat loft suin in a slatter, GILPIN *Sngs.* (1866) 275 ; A certain slight rollick in his voice and accent, perhaps due to the jaws o' yell, LINTON *Lizzie Lorton* (1867) II. 233 ; Cum.[4]

[1. Cp. Norw. dial. *jaga,* to dash or sweep along (AASEN); ON. *jaga,* to move to and fro (VIGFUSSON). 3. I am God Tibris . . . wyth mony jaup and jaw, DOUGLAS *Eneados* (1513), ed. 1874, III. 153.]

JAW, see **Jay,** *sb.*

JAWBATION, *sb.* In *gen.* dial. and colloq. use in Eng. Also in forms jaabation Nhb.[1]; jobation n.Lin.[1] Nhp.[1] War.[2] Oxf. Hnt. Nrf. Sus.[2] Hmp.[1] w.Som.[1]; jubation n.Lin.[1] [dʒǭbē·ʃən, dʒobē·ʃən.] A long and tedious harangue ; a scolding, severe lecture or reprimand.

Nhb.[1], n.Yks. (T.S.), e.Yks.[1], Not.[1] Lin.[1] She nearly drove me scranny with her jawbation. n.Lin.¹, Nhp.¹, War.³ Oxf. GROSE (1790) MS. add. (M.) Hst. (T.P.F.), Nrf. (E.M.), Sus.² Sus., Hmp. HOLLOWAY. Hmp.¹ w.Som.¹ A preachment, or any continued speaking—not necessarily a scolding. A long sermon would often be spoken of as 'a rigler jobation' [joabae·urshun]. Colloq. Don't be angry at my jobation ; but write me a long answer of your own free will, HUGHES T. Brown Oxf. (1861) xlii.

Hence **Jawbatious**, adj. loquacious. n.Yks.²

JAW-BOX, sb. Sc. Irel. [dgō·-boka.] A sink under a tap ; an indoor sink for refuse water. Also used fig. See Jaw, v.² 2.

Sc. (W.G.R.) e.Sc. The half-way house?. . The place is little else than a jaw-box itsel'—the jaw-box o' the parish, SETOUN R. Urquhart (1896) xviii. Ayr. Posies which cam oot from some of the jaw-boxes and reeking closes and stairs in the High Street, SERVICE Dr. Duguid (ed. 1887) 87 ; (F.J.C.) Lnk. Duly chronicled in the local paper—the 'jawbox,' as Doghip called it, GORDON Pyotshaw (1885) 297. Dmf. The sewerage, never good in rural town, becomes abominable—instead of the flower pot a rank jaw-box at the stair-head, WALLACE Schoolmaster (1899) 41. N.I.¹ Jaw tub, jaw box, a scullery sink.

JAWD, JAWDY, see Jade, Jaudie.

JAW-HOLE, sb. Sc. Also in forms jar-, jaur- Ayr. (JAM.) A place into which dirty water, &c. is thrown ; a cesspool, midden, sewer. Also used fig. See Jaw, v.² 2.

Sc. That gulf ycleped in Scottish phrase, the jaw-hole, in other words an uncovered common sewer, SCOTT St. Ronan (1824) xxviii ; Fig. any society that is viewed as a receptacle for persons of a worthless or doubtful character (JAM.). Frf. Playin' clyte owre into his ain jawhole, WILLOCK Rosetty Ends (1886) 183, ed. 1889. Per. Ae scabbit ewe will smit a flock, Ae jaw-hole splutter fifty folk, SPENCE Poems (1898) 196. e.Fif. Defendit in front by a fortification o' muck, an' moated by a jawhole o' fulzie, LATTO Tam Bodkin (1864) i. Ayr. All the old houses had a jaur-hole, i. e. a hollow perforated stone built into the wall for carrying off dirty water (JAM.). Bwk. Such a disaster as a plunge in the jaw-hole, HENDERSON Pop. Rhymes (1856) 77. Slk. He was forced to take shelter in his own jaw-hole, HOGG Poems (ed. 1865) 71. Gall. Set their head thro' the round jaw-holes, CROCKETT Grey Man (1896) 2.

JAWL, see Jowl, v.¹

JAWLED, ppl. adj. Yks. Also Sur. Sus. Hmp. Also in form jowled n.Yks. 1. With out : excessively fatigued, exhausted, tired out. Sur.¹, Sus.¹², Hmp.¹

2. Weak, overdone.

n.Yks. 'Watther jawled muck,' over-watered grog (T.S.).

JAWLS, sb. pl. Obs. e.Lan.¹ Jaws. The same word as Chawl, sb. (q. v.)

JAWLTER, JAWM, see Jolter-head, Jamb.

JAWMAS, sb. Yks. [dgō·məs.] A talkative, chattering person ; a conceited person.

w.Yks. Ah'm stalled o' t'clatter ov a jawmas like thee, Leeds Merc. Suppl. (May 26, 1894) ; Ah can happen afford ta keep a pony as weel as thee, as big a jawmas as tha art, FRANKLAND Gammer Grown in Leeds Sat. Jrn. (1895) X'mas No. 10.

JAWMATREES, JAWNER, see Geometries, Jaunder.

JAWP, v. n.Cy. Yks. Also written jaup n.Yks.²⁴ w.Yks.¹ [dgǭp.] To gape, yawn.

n.Yks.² 'It jawps sair,' it gapes very much, as an open seam, or a wide mouth.

Hence **Jawping** or **Jaupen**, ppl. adj. gaping, yawning, open-jawed ; wide, spacious, roomy.

n.Cy. (HALL.) n.Yks.¹ ; n.Yks.² 'A great jawping firestecad,' a wide old-fashioned fire-place, where the family group can seat themselves beneath the chimney-vent, with the hearth-fire in the centre ; n.Yks.⁴, m.Yks.¹ w.Yks.¹ A girt jaupen room.

JAWP, see Jape.

JAWSY, adj. Ken.¹² [dgǭ·zi.] Talkative.

JAWTHER, v. and sb. Sc. (JAM.) 1. v. To be engaged in idle or frivolous conversation. 2. sb. pl. Idle, frivolous discourse, implying a weak mind.

JAWTHERUM, see Joathrum.

JAY, sb. Sc. Irel. n.Cy. Nhb. Cum. Wm. Yks. Midl. Lin. Rut. Lei. War. Wor. Glo. Oxf. e.An. Wil. Dev. Cor. Also in forms jaw- Wil. ; jee- w.Yks. [dgē.] 1. In comp. (1) Jay-bird, the jay, Garrulus glandarius ; (2) -fulfer, the fieldfare, Turdus pilaris ; (3) -pie, see (1) ; (4) -piet or ·pyet, (a) see (1) ; (b) the magpie, Pica rustica ; (5) -teal, the common teal, Querquedula crecca.

(1) Yks. Yks. Wkly. Post (Dec. 31, 1898). sw.Lin.¹, Rut.¹, Lei.¹ (2) e.An.¹ (3) Midl. SWAINSON Birds (1885) 75. War.⁴ w.Wor. Berrow's Jrn. (Mar. 3, 1888). Glo. The screaming 'jay-pies,' as the local people call the jays, GIBBS Cotswold Vill. (1898) 374. Oxf.¹ MS. add. Wil. (K.M.G.) Dev., Cor. SWAINSON ib. Cor. A reg'lar little dandy-sprat, an' so pert as a jay-pie in June, ' Q.' Troy Town (1888) xi ; RODD Birds (1880) 315 ; Cor.¹ Swset as a jay-pie sang a Cornish song ; Cor.² (4, a) Ags. Per. (JAM.) Per. SWAINSON ib. 75. e.Fif. If we dinna chatter awa like a wheen jay-pyats, LATTO Tam Bodkin (1864) xv. Gall. It was the patch of blue sky on a jay's wing. They call it the jay piet hereabouts, CROCKETT Bog-Myrtle (1895) 420. N.Cy.¹, Nhb.¹, Cum. (H.W.), (J.Ar.), Cum.⁴ Wm. That's a bonny feddur, it's oot ov a jay-pyatt wing (B.K.). (b) Cum.⁴ (5) Kcb. SWAINSON ib. 158.

2. The missel-thrush, Turdus viscivorus. Also in comp. Jay-pie.

n.Ir. [So called from] the harsh note it utters when alarmed, SWAINSON ib. 2 ; N.I.¹ Wil. SWAINSON ib.

JAY, int. Dev. Also in form jayly. [dgē.] A disguised form of ' Jesus' ; also in phr. laur jayly! Lord Jesus ! used as a mild imprecation.

Dev. Jay faather how i glazed! DANIEL Bride of Scio (1842) 184; Jay, I zwear I'd sooner kiss our maister's owld blind mare, ib. 176; Zeth es wurship, laur jayly ! my ivers! now be ! NATHAN HOGG Post. Lett. (ed. 1866) and S. 18. nw.Dev.¹ 'Jay, but I wull then.' Now rarely heard.

JAYKLE, JAYL, see Jakle, Geal, v.²

JAY-LEGGED, adj. Nhb. Small or feeble in the legs. The jay-legg'd bodies frae the toon, WILSON Dicky's Wig (1843) 83 ; Nhb.¹

JAYVEL, v. Cum.¹⁴ Also written gayvel Cum.⁴ [dgē·vl.] To stagger ; to walk loosely or ungainly like a cow.

JAYWEED, sb. Sus. The stinking chamomile, Anthemis Cotula. (B. & H.)

JAZACK, sb. Yks. [dgē·zak.] A disguised form of ' Jesus,' used in imprecations.

e.Yks.¹ ' By Jazack,' a prefix to a threat, or an expression of anger or annoyance, MS. add. (T.H.)

JAZY, adj. w.Wor.¹ Also in form jazyfied. [dgē·zi.] Tired out; flagging.

JAZZEN, sb. Lin. Also in forms jarsent ; jasnack Lin.¹ ; yarsent. A donkey. Cf. jessop.

N. & Q. (1873) 4th S. xi. 323 ; Lin.¹ Do not lallop the jazzen. Two pence more and up goes the jasnack.

JAZZUP, JEAL, see Jessop, Geal, v.¹

JEALOUS, adj. Sc. Yks. Lan. Lin. War. Cmb. Cor. Also in form jillous n.Yks.⁴ [dge·ləs, w.Yks. also dgiə·ləs.] 1. Suspicious, apprehensive. Cf. jalouse.

Ayr. The French guards . . . were instructed to be jealous of all untimeous travellers, GALT Gilhaize (1823) iv. Slk. As he picked his herbs out of the churchyard . . . the owld wives . . . grew jealous of him, HOGG Tales (1838) 384, ed. 1866. n.Yks.¹ Ah's jealous he's efter nae guid ; n.Yks.⁴ Ah war a bit jillous 'at he wad splet on uz. m.Yks.¹ Ah's jealous he weean't cum. w.Yks. I am jealous we are going to have some wet (C.C.R.); w.Yks.⁵ Au'm jealous he's not baan to carry on long ; w.Yks.⁵ ' D'yuh think it al rīan to dāay māaster ? ' ' Am jealous it will missis.' Lan. Bein' jealous 'at hoo' I nitch her pots, STANDING Echoes (1885) 8. Lin. ' Will it keep fine to-day, John ? ' ' I'm somehow jealous of it, sir ' (J.C.W.). n.Lin.¹ I'm very jealous that th' corn weänt to'n oot well t'year. e.Lin. I wer jealous she wouln't get better (G.G.W.). War. I was very jealous of that tramp that came to the door (L.M.). Cor. I had a jealous thoft [thought], THOMAS Randigal Rhymes (1895) Gl. ; I was jealous that he was not doing what he ought (M.A.C.) ; Cor.² The baby's ill. I'm jealous it's going to die. I'm jealous of the result.

Hence **Jealousy**, sb. suspicion.]

Sc. It would never do if the Lord Advocate were to get any jealousy of our acquaintance, STEVENSON Catriona (1893) ii. Rnf. I couldna help some jealousy ; Thought at the time that it might be Merely a hoax, WEBSTER Rhymes (1835) 134. Ayr. My colleagues all approving of it I had no jealousy or suspicion that a design . . . would meet with any other opposition, GALT Provost (1822) xxvi. Lnk. Having a jealousy in my mind that I should be troubled, WODROW Ch. Hist. (1721) II. 54, ed. 1828.

2. Perplexed, 'staggered.'

w.Yks.² Well, I am jealous ; I don't know where them dogs has got to.

3. Fragile. Cmb. (W.W.S.)

JEALOUSE, see Jalouse.

JEALOUSY, *sb.* and *adj.* Shr. Ken. 1. *sb.* The St. Vincent's Rock stonecrop, *Sedum rupestre.* Shr.[1] 2. *adj.* Jealous. Ken.[2]

JEANIE, *sb.* Sc. A generic name for a country damsel. Cf. **Jenny**, *sb.*[1] 3.

Mry. Smit, smit—honest man—wi' our Jockies an' Jeanies, HAY *Lintie* (1851) 49. Frf. Supplyin' green kail an' whisky an' beef to the Jockies and Jeannies wha hae assembled, WILLOCK *Rosetty Ends* (1886) 158, ed. 1889. Bwk. The lads an' lassies hameward speed, Ilk Jock an' Jeanie as agreed, CALDER *Poems* (1897) 115.

JEAREM, see **Gearum(s.**

JEARN, *adj.* Hrf.[2] Raw, cold, severe. The same word as **Dern**, *adj.*[2]

JEAT, JEBBER, see **Jet**, *sb.*[1], **Jibber**, *v.*

JECK, *v.* Sc. To neglect. Cf. **jack**, *v.*[1]

Dmf. Jeck any piece of work (JAM.).

JED, *adj.* Chs. Stf. Der. Lei. War. Shr. Also written **ged** nw.Der.[1] [dged.] 1. Dial. form of *dead.*

Chs.[2] Jed as a dur nail. Stf. Him an me's been fatched out for jed five-six times, MURRAY *Nov. Note Bk.* (1887) 53. Der.[2], nw.Der.[1] Lei.[1] Ah'm welly jed. War.[24], Shr.[1]

2. Phr. *to go jed,* to die.

s.Chs. Ur two sons an' ur uwd mon wun gone jed, DARLINGTON *Bk. Ruth,* i. 5.

JEDBURGH, *sb.* Sc. n.Cy. Nhb. Also in forms **Jeddart** Sc.; **Jethart** Nhb.[1] In *comb.* (1) **Jedburgh-cast,** a legal trial after the infliction of punishment; (2) — **jug,** a brass jug containing about eight gills, used as a standard of dry and liquid measure; (3) — **jury,** a jury that tries a case after punishment has been inflicted; (4) — **justice,** (*a*) see (1); (*b*) wholesale punishment or acquittal; (5) — **law,** see (1); (6) — **staff,** *obs.,* a kind of battle-axe; also in phr. *to rain Jeddart staves,* to rain 'cats and dogs.'

(1) Sc. I canna but be that in the life ye lead you suld get a Jeddart-cast ae day, SCOTT *Rob Roy* (1817) xxxvi. (2) Rxb. Kept by the Dean of Guild (JAM.). (3) Lnk. John appeals to a Jedburgh jury, if it be not easier to deal wi' fools, than headstrong fashious fouks, GRAHAM *Writings* (1883) II. 216. (4, *a*) Sc. The memory of Dunbar's legal proceedings at Jedburgh, is preserved in the proverbial phr. Jeddart Justice, which signifies trial after execution, SCOTT *Border Minstrelsy* (1803) *Pref.* lvi (JAM.). s.Sc. Jeddart justice—hang first, and judge after, WILSON *Tales* (1836) II. 137. Slk. 'To Jeddart they hauled the auld miller wi' speed, An' they haught him dead on a high gallows tree; An' afterwards they in full counsel agreed That Rob Riddle he richly deserved to die.' This alludes to an old and very common prov., 'That such a one will get Jeddart Justice,' HOGG *Poems* (ed. 1865) 67. N.Cy.[1] (*b*) Sc. I have a different account given of Jeddart Justice. It is said to signify either a general condemnation, or a general acquittal. Twenty or thirty persons . . . having been brought to trial here at once, it was previously resolved that they should have a common fate. One of the assize, to whose lot it fell to give the casting voice, having fallen asleep, as he was rather in a bad humour at being disturbed, on the question being put to him, is said to have replied to the Judge, 'Hang them a'' (JAM.). (5) Gall. Ye shall never dee, auld lad, By 'Jeddart law,' KERR *Maggie o' the Moss* (1891) 51. Nhb.[1] (6) Sc. If men are to break the peace under pretence of beating them, why it will rain Jeddart staves in our very antechamber, SCOTT *Nigel* (1822) xxxiii; Breaketh bones as well as a Jeddart staff, *ib.* *Abbot* (1820) iv. Abd. That they be furnished with halberts, Lochaber axes, or Jedburgh staves and swords, SPALDING *Hist. Sc.* (1792) II. 101. Rxb. It is commonly called Jeddart staff, and understood to denote the same kind of weapon which is still carried before the magistrates of that burgh, or in other processions. Some of these resemble the halbert on one side, having a short kind of bill or sharp hook on the other. There are others which exhibit the hatchet-form on both sides. They are in length from seven to eight feet (JAM.).

JEDDER, *v.* and *sb.* Cum. Lan. Also in form **jidder** Cum. [dge·dǝ(r, dʒi·dǝǝr.] 1. *v.* To tremble, shake, 'dither.'

Cum. Na mair you'll hear the hammer-bleats Flee jedd'rin ow'r your heids at neets, DICKINSON *Rem.* (1888) 161; Cum.[14], n.Lan. (C.W.D.), n.Lan.[1]

Hence **Jidderty-jadderty**, *adv.* of a wheel which has become loose in the 'bush': moving irregularly.

Cum. It gǝ's jidderty-jadderty (E.W.P.).

2. *sb.* A jar, jarring; a discord. Cum.[14]

JEDDY-CUM-JIDY, *sb.* n.Cy. Cum. Also in form **jiddi-cum-jidy** n.Cy. [Not known to our correspondents.] A see-saw. n.Cy. (HALL.) Cum. LINTON *Lake Cy.* (1864) 306.

JEE, JEEACK, JEEG, JEEGIT, JEEGLE, see **Ge(e, ini.,** *v.*[2], **Gike,** *v.,* **Gig,** *sb.*[24], *v.*[24], **Jig,** *sb.*[1], **Jiggit, Giggle,** *v.*[2]

JEEGLER, *sb.* Sc. [dgī·glǝr.] A half-fledged bird, a 'cheeper.'

Lth. (JAM.) e.Lth. But we were ower auld birds to be catched wi' ony sic caff. We werena a wheen jeeglers wha had chippit oor shell yestreen, HUNTER *J. Inwick* (1895) 177.

JEEL, see **Geal,** *v.*[1], **Jeill.**

JEEPS, *sb.* N.Cy.[1] Nhb.[1] [dgīps.] A severe beating.

JEER, *v.* and *sb.* Sc. [dgīr.] 1. *v. trans.* To mock, make fun of, scorn.

Dmb. It's ill dune o' you to jeer me in that way, CROSS *Disruption* (1844) xx. Ayr. The vintner's wife . . . jeered him, and would fain have been jocular, GALT *Gilhaize* (1823) ii. Lth. She jeers them, BALLANTINE *Poems* (1856) 92. Edb. Aye she jeers me air and late, M'DOWALL *Poems* (1839) 29.

2. *sb.* Derision.

Edb. I there should be . . . A jeer to all my neighbours, *Carlop Green* (1793) 139, ed. 1817.

Hence **Jeery,** *adj.* jesting.

Frf. To crack their jeery jock, MORISON *Poems* (1790) 6.

JEESTIE, *sb.* Sc. A jesting matter.

Abd. Dancin' wasna jeestie to them that try't it, ALEXANDER *Johnny Gibb* (1871) xl.

JEET, *sb.* Sc. [dgīt.] A low term of contempt, a worthless person; a brat.

Abd. You'll often see a drunken jeet Unable amaist to haud his feet, ANDERSON *Poems* (1826) 71; Yer shameless praise o' siclike jeets, SHELLEY *Flowers* (1868) 177. Per. 'He's a low drunken jeet.' 'He keeps company wi ony orra jeet he can pick up.' All but unknown (G.W.).

JEETY, *adj.* Sc. 1. Resplendent, bright.

Abd. For a' that's noble, grand, an' jeety, I point you to the Granite City, OGG *Willie Waly* (1873) 82. Per. That's a jeety star (G.W.).

2. Neat. Also used *fig.* and *advb.*

Abd. That's a jeety parcel. That's jeety done (G.W.).

JEEZY, see **Gizz.**

JEF, *sb.* w.Yks.[5] [dgef.] The master. Cf. **gaff,** *sb.*[8]

Where's 't'jef? He'll be coming jef ower thuh if thah doesn't mind. Ah'll tak care on him; av awalus bin me awan jef an' awalus mean to be.

JEF(F, see **Geff.**

JEFFERY, *sb. Obs.* Yks. In phr. *St. Jeffery's day,* never. GROSE (1790) *MS. add.* (P.)

JEFFULL, see **Jaffle,** *sb.*[1]

JEG, *sb.* and *v.* Lakel. Yks. Lan. Also in forms **jag(g** Lakel.[2] w.Yks.; **jig** Lakel.[2] w.Yks. [dgeg, dgag.] 1. *sb.* Share; esp. in phr. *to go jegs.*

Lakel.[2] Ah'll stand mi jagg. w.Yks. Thah'll gooa jegs ah'st think, *Yks. Wkly. Post* (Jan. 28, 1898); w.Yks.[2]; w.Yks.[5] Principally in juvenile use. When two are in company, and either happens to find something of any value, if the one who had not the good fortune of seeing and picking it up can say 'Jegs!' before the finder has time to say 'No Jegs!' he is entitled to equal shares, and an equal right of disposing of what is found, it becoming common property. 'Shabby jegs,' a poor share. A railway carrier gets 'a good jeg' when trade is brisk.

2. *v.* To join; to share. w.Yks.[5]

3. In games: to be able to play; to 'go.'

Lan. As in domino playing—'I conno jeg this time,' *Yks. Wkly. Post* (Jan. 28, 1898).

JEGGING, *adj.* Sc. Creaking. Cf. **gig,** *v.*[8]

Syne wi' the jeggin' wheel Roun' in a rummlin' reel, EDWARDS *Sc. Poets,* 3rd S. 396.

JEGGLE, JEHO(E, see **Giggle,** *v.*[2], **Gehoe.**

JEILL, *sb.* I.Ma. Also written **jeel.** [dgīl.] Damage. Eyes that played the very mischief wis the boys—but then! I won't thry to tell you what they were lads. You will hear from the 'jeill' they done further on, RYDINGS *Tales* (1895) 29; 'What's the jeel now!' said Pete, CAINE *Manxman* (1894) pt. I. vi. [Gael. *diobhail,* damage, loss (MACBAIN).]

z z 2

JEISSLE, *sb.* Slk. (Jam.) A multitude of things thrown together without order. Cf. **jossle**.

JEIST, JEISTIECOR, see **Just, Justicoat**.

JELDER, *v.* e.Suf. Also in form **jilder**. To flog soundly, to thrash, maul. Also with *up*. (F.H.)

JELDERED, *adj.* e.An.[1] [Not known to our correspondents.] With *up*: severely bruised.

JELL, *sb.* Chs.[28] Stf.[1] Nhp.[1] War.[24] Also written gell Chs.[2] Nhp.[1] [dgel.] The same word as **Deal**, *sb.*[1] (q.v.)

JELL, see **Deal**, *sb.*[1], **Geal**, *v.*[1]

JELLICK, *v.* Dor. [dge·lik.] To throw a stone in a peculiar manner. Cf. **jelt**.
We used the term 'jellick' . . . to denote a mode of projecting a stone as the arm came suddenly against the ribs, or by a more fantastic trick still, against the thigh of the lifted right leg, *Longman's Mag.* (Mar. 1889) 516.

JELLY, *v.* Chs. Also in form **jilly** Chs.[1] To congeal. Chs.[1] Blood jellies when it stands. When black-puddings are made the pig's blood is stirred with a stick for some time to prevent it jellying. s.Chs.[1]

JELLY, *adj.* ? *Obs.* Sc. Also written **gelly** Rnf. Pleasant, agreeable; upright, worthy.
n.Sc. Stand back, stand back, ye jelly bridegroom, Buchan *Ballads* (1828) II. 58, ed. 1875. Abd. Fan Will an' me were at our dinner, By chance came in a jelly tanner, Cock *Strains* (1810) II. 106, Rnf. To the West, thy gelly mouth Stood wide to a', Picken *Poems* (1788) 180 (Jam.).
Hence **Jellily**, *adv.* merrily, gaily.
Sc. And jellily dance the damsels, Jamieson *Pop. Ballads* (1806) I. 189.
[The woddes . . . are verie jocund and jellie, Dalrymple *Leslie's Hist. Scotl.* (1596) I. 7. Fr. *joli*, gay, handsome (Cotgr.).]

JELLY-DOG, *sb.* w.Som.[1] A harrier.

JELLY-FLOWER, JELOUSE, see **Gillyflower, Jalouse**.

JELT, *v.* and *sb.* Sc. Not. Nhp. Also in form **jilt** Per. Fif. (Jam.) Not. Nhp.[1] [dgelt, dʒilt.] **1.** *v.* To throw underhand with a quick and suddenly arrested motion. Cf. **jerk**, *v.*, **jert**, and **jet**, *v.*
Not.(W.H.S.), Not.[1] s.Not. To throw underhand across the body in such a manner that the thrower's arm is stopped by his body with a jerk at the moment that the missile leaves it; *gen.* when the intention is to cast gently or to a short distance, but the action is made use of by some otherwise capable athletes, who from some weakness of the proper muscles are unable to throw vigorously from the shoulder. 'Cock Selby was no thrower; he allus used to jelt the ball' (J.P.K.). Nhp.[1] And larks, that fly above the corn, Frit by a jilted stone, Clare *MS. Poems.*
2. To throw water over any one. Fif. (Jam.) **3.** *sb.* A jerk; a suddenly arrested throw. s.Not. (J.P.K.) **4.** A dash of water. Per., Fif. (Jam.)

JEMIMA, *sb.* Glo. A term of reproach applied to a boy.
I thrown a stwun at Earny Mustoo akez 'e did call oi ' Jemima,' *Longman's Mag.* (May 1900) 43.

JEMMAL, JEMMER, see **Gimmal**, *sb.*[1], **Jimmer**, *sb.*[1]

JEMMIES, *sb. pl.* Sc. [Not known to our correspondents.] A species of woollen cloth.
Abd. Clothes manufactured from the above wool-shafts, . . jemmies and striped apron stuffs, *Statist. Acc.* XIX. 208 (Jam., s.v. Shafts).

JEMMY, see **Jimmy**, *sb.*[14]

JEN, *sb.* Sc. Cum. Lin. Also in form **jin** n.Lin.[1] sw.Lin.[1] [dgen, dʒin.] **1.** A generic name for a country girl. Cf. **Jenny**, *sb.*[1] 8.
Edb. Siccan fun, I neer did see, Wi' Jocks and Jens, in sicca glee, Liddle *Poems* (1821) 227. Cum. Every Jack mun have his Jen, Rawnsley *Remin. Wordsworth* (1884) vi. n.Lin.[1] To call a woman Jin is an insult.
2. *Comb.* (1) **Jen-ass**, a female ass. n.Lin.[1]; (2) **on-the-ground**, the ground-ivy, *Nepeta Glechoma*. sw.Lin.[1]

JENDL, *v.* Sh.I. To be jealous of any one. S. & Ork.[1]

JENIC(K, JENIS, JENK, see **Jannock**, *adj.*, **Jaundice, Jink**, *v.*[1]

JENKIN, *sb.* and *v.* n.Cy. Nhb. Dur. [dʒe·nkin.]
1. *sb.* A narrow passage driven up the middle of a pillar of coal when it is about to be excavated; a slice taken off a pillar.

N.Cy.[1], Nhb.[1] Nhb., Dur. A fast jenkin is a narrow place, driven lengthways in a pillar of coal, but unholed into the board at either side of the pillar. A loose jenkin is a similar place, driven along the side of a pillar, and open to the board along that side, Greenwell *Coal Tr. Gl.* (1849).
2. *v.* To drive a board within a pillar of coal; to reduce the size of a pillar.
Nhb. They jenkin a' the pillars doon, Wilson *Pitman's Pay* (1843) 59; Nhb.[1]

JENKIN'S HEN, *phr.* Sc. Also in forms **Jinkam's** — Sc. (Jam.); **Jinken's** —, **Jinkings** — Gall. **1.** A hen that never knew the cock; used *fig.* for an old maid; *gen.* in phr. *to live the life*, or *die the death of Jenkin's hen*, to live or die an old maid.
Sc. I ance had sweethearts nine or ten, . . But oh ! the death of Jenkin's hen, I shudder at it, A. Scott *Poems* (1805) 87 (Jam.); She may gie owre her stertlin for she'll die the death of Jinkam's hen (Jam., s.v. Stertlin). n.Sc. She never may get sic an offer again, But pine away bit an' bit like Jenkin's hen, *Wee Pickle Tow* (*ib.*). Abd. I loor by far, she'd die Jenkin's hen Ere we again meet yon unruly men, Ross *Helenore* (1768) 102, ed. 1812. Per. By this time Bessy's hopes of a husband had become very faint, and . . . she had been heard to mutter that even ' the Bob o' Dunblane' was preferable to 'the Life of Jenkin's hen,' Monteath *Dunblane* (1835) 73, ed. 1887. Rxb. (Jam.) Gall. She pines awa like 'Jinken's hen'; Yet still she sighs for youthfu' sport, Nicholson *Poet. Wks.* (1814) 86, ed. 1897.

JENNAPIE, *sb.* Sh.I. A dwarfish person or animal. S. & Ork.[1]

JENNET, *sb.* Dur. Suf. Som. Dev. Also written gennet w.Cy.; and in forms **jenneton** Dur.[1]; **jenneting** w.Som.[1] Dev.; **jennetten** Suf.[1] [dge·nət.] A kind of apple that ripens early; also in *comp.* **Gennet-moyle**.
Dur.[1], Suf.[1] w.Cy. Nice promise of apples. . . Now, if I could have my wish, I should like a splendid crop of foxwhelps and gennet-moyles, Fenn *Crown and Sceptre*, xix. w.Som.[1] Jún-ut, jún·uteen. Dev. Under the shadow of a big jenneting tree, O'Neill *Dimpses* (1893) 149. [Trees grafted on a gennet-moyl or cider-stock, Worlidge *Dict. Rust.* (1681) 181.]

JENNY, *sb.*[1] Var. dial. uses in Sc. Irel. and Eng. Also written Jeni Der.[1]; and in form Jinny Bnff.[1] Ayr. Ant. N.Cy.[1] Nhb. Dur.[1] Lakel.[2] Cum.[2] Wm. n.Yks.[24] e.Yks.[1] w.Yks.[15] Lan.[1] n.Lan.[1] e.Lan.[1] Chs.[1] s.Chs.[1] Nhp.[2] Oxf.[1] Suf. Cor.[2] [dge·ni, dʒi·ni.] **1.** In *comb.* (1) **Jenny-balk**, a small beam near the roof of a house; (2) **-bun-tail, -bun-tain, or -burnt-tail**, the Will-o'-th'-Wisp; (3) **-coat**, a skirt; a petticoat; a child's bedgown; (4) **-crane**, (5) **-crow**, the heron, *Ardea cinerea*; (6) **-crudle**, the wren, *Troglodytes parvulus*; (7) **-cut-throat** or **-cut-throater**, the whitethroat, *Sylvia cinerea*; (8) **-dab**, a small fish, see below; (9) **-flucker**, the flounder, *Pleuronectes flesus*; (10) **-foster**, the long-tailed duck, *Harelda glacialis*; (11) **-fuddler**, see (6); (12) **-goat**, a cowrie-shell; (13) **— green-teeth**, (a) the green scum on ponds, esp. the lesser duck-weed, *Lemna minor*; (b) a 'boggart' haunting wells and ponds, whose presence is indicated by such scum; (14) **-heron**, see (5); (15) **-hole**, the ventilating hole in the gable of a barn made use of by owls; (16) **-hooker**, an owl; (17) **-howlet**, an owl, esp. the barn-owl, *Strix flammea*, and the tawny owl, *Syrnium aluco*; (18) **-hummer**, the cockchafer, *Melolontha vulgaris*; (19) **-hunting**, bird-catching; (20) **-idle**, (a) a pot of tallow with a wick in the centre, used as a lamp; (b) a frame for holding 'spunks' at the fireside; (21) **-jay**, the jay, *Garrulus glandarius*; (22) **— Jo or Jones**, a singing game; see below; (23) **-longlegs**, the daddy-longlegs, *Tipula oleracea*; (24) **-long-neck**, the hen heron, *Ardea cinerea*; (25) **— Mac**, a game, see below; (26) **-many-feet** or **-with-the-many-feet**, a species of centipede; (27) **-nettle**, (a) see (23); (b) the stinging-nettle, *Urtica dioica*; (28) **-ninny**, a simpleton; (29) **-owl**, see (17); (30) **-pig**, see (6); (31) **-quick**, (a) an ' Italian iron '; (b) to iron with an ' Italian iron '; (32) **-rain**, see (6); (33) **-redtail**, the redstart, *Ruticilla phoenicurus*; (34) **-run-by-** (or **-in**) **-the-ground**, the ground-ivy, *Nepeta Glechoma*; (35) **-spinner**, (a) see (23); (b) the cockroach, *Blatta orientalis* [not known to our correspondents]; (c) a teetotum; (36) **-squit**, see (6); (37) **-tit**, the blue titmouse,

Parus caeruleus; (38) **·wagon**, a little 'tip wagon' used in collieries and railway works; (39) **·wallops**, a mechanic's instrument for measuring the inside dimensions of a groove or collar; (40) **·with-the-lantern** or **·with-the-wisp**, see (2); (41) **·wren**, (*a*) see (6); (*b*) see (37); (*c*) the herb Robert, *Geranium Robertianum*.

(1) n.Cy. Grose (1790). w.Yks. Hutton *Tour to Caves* (1781). (2) Nhp.[1]; Nhp.[2] Believed in Nhp. to proceed from a dwarfish spirit, who takes delight in misleading 'night-faring clowns,' not unfrequently winding up a long series of torments by dragging his victims into a river or pond. Oxf. *Science Gossip* (1882) 165; Oxf.[1] *MS. add.* (3) Shr.[2] w.Som.[1] The word, though not uncommon, is rather used jokingly or derisively than as a sober term. (4) n.Cy. Holloway. (5) n.Cy. Swainson *Birds* (1885) 144. (6) s.Cy. Grose (1790); (Hall.) (7) Rxb. Swainson *ib.* 23. Nhb.[1] (8) n.Yks. The beck was carefully swept with a net sufficiently close in the mesh to take the smallest minnow, stickleback, and 'jenny-dab,' Tweddell *Hist. Cleveland* (1873) 44. (9, 10) Nhb.[1] (11) Oxf. *Science Gossip* (1882) 165. (12) Nhb. (R.O.H.) (13, *a*) n.Lan.[1] Lan., War. (B. & H.) War. *Science Gossip* (1865) 258. (*b*) w.Yks. *Leeds Merc. Suppl.* (June 2, 1894). Lan.[1], s.Lan.[1] Cha. A clerical friend ... states that he remembers being threatened more than once with 'Jenny Greenteeth.' But in that case, probably as there was no pond near the house, she was said to perch in the tops of trees, at least after night-fall... He was led into the garden and bade to listen to the sighing of the night-wind through the branches, and then told it was the moanings of Jenny Greenteeth, *N. & Q.* (1870) 4th S. v. 157; Cha.[1] Often used as a threat or warning to children to prevent them going near the water, lest 'Jinny Green-teeth should have them.' s.Cha.[1] Der. *N. & Q.* (1870) 4th S. v. 157. Shr. Burne *Flk-Lore* (1883) 79. (14) Kcb. Swainson *ib.* 145. (15) Cum.[14] (16) n.Cy. (Hall.) (17) n.Cy. (J.L.), N.Cy.[1], Nhb.[1], Dur.[1] Cum. (H.W.); Cum.[4] Ye can't mak game cocks oot of jinny-hoolets. Wm. Let's gah lait a jinny hewlet nest e't'gill (B.K.). n.Yks.[1234] ne.Yks.[1], e.Yks.[1], m.Yks.[1] w.Yks. He beard wot he thowt wor a Jenny-ullatt, Tom Treddlehoyle *Bairnsla Ann.* (1895) 63; w.Yks.[18] n.Lin. (E.P.) w.Wor. *Berrow's Jrn.* (Mar. 3, 1888). (18) ne.Lan.[1] (19) w.Yks.[2] (20, *a*) Nhb. (R.O.H.) (*b*) *ib.* It is a flat board having a nail-hole in the top for suspension. Two parallel strings, passed through holes, are kept taut by a suspended holey-stone, and the stock of spunks are held in place ready for use behind the lines of tightened strings. (21) n.Yks. Swainson *ib.* 75; n.Yks.[2] (22) Ant. In playing this game the children form themselves into two parties. The first consists of Jinny with her father and mother. Jinny, who is a very small child, is concealed behind her parents. All the other children form the party of suitors. The children retire some little distance off, and then approach Jinny's 'house,' saying: 'We've come to court Jinny Jo, Jinny Jo, Jinny Jo, We've come to court Jinny Jo, Is she within?'.. The father and mother ... sing in answer: 'Jinny Jo's washing clothes, washing clothes, washing clothes, You can't see her to-day.' The visiting party, who are holding hands, retire slowly, walking backwards, while all sing: 'So fare ye well ladies, O ladies, O ladies, So fare ye well ladies, and gentlemen too.' The suitors return immediately singing as before, and this is repeated a number of times: each time they receive an excuse that Jinny is 'drying clothes,' 'starching clothes,' 'ironing clothes,' &c., till at last the parents ... announce ... that: 'Jinny Jo's lying dead, Lying dead, lying dead, Jinny Jo's lying dead, you can't see her to-day... So turn again ladies,' &c. But instead of going to their own homes again, the suitors remain and sing: 'What shall we dress her in! Dress her in, dress her in! What shall we dress her in! Shall it be red!'.. The ... parents answer: 'Red's for the soldiers, The soldiers, the soldiers, Red's for the soldier's, And that will not do.' Various other colours are suggested ... but found unsuitable, ... till at last white is named, and the parents sing: 'White's for the dead people, The dead people, the dead people, White's for the dead people, And that will just do.' Then the father and mother step aside, and Jinny is seen lying quite still... The funeral must be arranged; when suddenly Jinny comes to life again, and springs up, when the play ends amid wild rejoicing, *N. & Q.* (1891) 7th S. xii. 492. [The words and actions vary slightly in the different counties. In no other version except that of Hmp. does Jinny return to life.] Dwn., Ldd., Wtf., e.Yks., Nhp., Shr., Brks., Mld., Cmb., Nrf., Gomme *Games* (1894) I. 260-83. Ess. And then they go to the meadow and play 'Jenny Jones' with renewed zest, *Flk-Lore Rec.* (1880) III. 173. Ken. Sur. Gomme *ib.* Hmp. In the Southampton version, after the carrying of Jenny by her head and feet to the grave, and the other children following and standing round, Jenny Jones rises up and pursues the children.

She is called the Ghost. .. Whoever she catches becomes Jenny Jones in the next game. [This incident is also played in Ldd., Nhp., Brks., Sur.] An additional incident occurs in the Liphook version which represents her as being 'swung to life again,' Gomme *ib.* 278-9. I.W. *ib.* 278. (23) Ayr. There was a Jenny-langlegs bumming at the corner o' the window, Wilson *Tales* (1836) xxv. Yks. (J.W.) (24) Cum. [The hawk] a dart at t'Jenny langneck meäde, Richardson *Talk* (1876) 2nd S. 26; Cum.[4] (25) Sc. 'Jenny Mac, Jenny Mac, Jenny Macghie, Turn your back about to me, And if you find an ill baubee, Lift it up, and gie 't to me!' Two girls cross their arms behind their backs, and thus taking hold of each other's hands, parade along together, by daylight or moonlight, occasionally turning upon their arms as indicated in the rhyme, Chambers *Pop. Rhymes* (1870) 123. (26) Banff.[1] Ayr. There cam only frae't a muckle Jenny-mony-feet and a pluff o' bad air that put the cannle oot, Service *Notandums* (1890) 56. (27, *a*) s.Sc. You are as het in the temper as a jenny-nettle, Wilson *Tales* (1836) II. 323. Lak. Jenny Nettle, spinnin' low, Dancin' on the kitchen wa' Wi' yer legs sae lang an' sma', Nicholson *Idylls* (1870) 9; (Jam.), s.v. Jenny-spinner. Dmf. Wallace *Schoolmaster* (1899) 349. (*b*) I.Ma. A sort of scrub of jenny-nettles, Brown *Yarns* (1881) 211, ed. 1889. (28) Cor.[2] e.Cor. If her's made a jinny-ninny of, there's only herself to thank for it, Parr *Adam and Eve* (1880) xv. (29) w.Wor. *Berrow's Jrn.* (Mar. 3, 1888). (30) Oxf.[1] *MS. add.* (31, *a*) Dev. (Hall.), Cor.[123], w.Cor.(G.F.R.) (*b*) Cor.[1] (32) Nhb.[1] (33) Cum.[14] Wm. *Penrith Obs.* (May 11, 1897). n.Yks. Swainson *ib.* 12. (34) n.Lin. (B. & H.), sw.Lin.[1] (35, *a*) Rxb. (Jam.) Dmf. Wallace *Schoolmaster* (1899) 349. Gall. Mactaggart *Encycl.* (1824). N.Cy.[1], Nhb.[1], Dur.[1], Lakel.[2], Cum.[14], n.Yks.[124], m.Yks.[1] w.Yks. They wor regelarly run ovver we jinny-spinners, &c., Tom Treddlehoyle *Thowts* (1845) 39; w.Yks.[1], Lan.[1], s.Lan.[1], ne.Lan.[1], Nhp.[1], Wor. (J.R.W.) (*b*) I w.Yks.[5] (*c*) Gall. Mactaggart *Encycl.* (1824). Nhb.[1], Cum.[14] (36) Brks.[1] (37) Suf. Swainson *ib.* 34. (38) Stf., War. (W.B.T.) (39) w.Yks. Jinny-wallops are callipers turned the contrary way (B.K.). (40) Nhb.[1] n.Yks. They saw in the swampy, undrained 'swang' ... a will-o'-the-wisp, or in local nomenclature, a 'Jenny-wi'-t'-lant'ren,' Atkinson *Moorl. Parish* (1891) 70. Lin.[1] (41, *s*) Lth. The jenny-wren an' the sedge-singer, Lumsden *Sheephead* (1892) 76. Wm. It o' ekes, as t'jinny-wren said when it pissed e' t'sea, *Saying* (B.K.). w.Yks.[1] An opinion prevails amongst some people in Craven, that this diminutive bird is the female of the Robin Redbreast; w.Yks.[2] s.Lan.[1] The female wren. s.Cha.[1], Der.[1], Not. (J.S.H.), Lin. (E.P.) Lei.[1] It is thought sacrilegious to kill a robin or a wren, and even to take their eggs is a profanity certain to bring ill-luck, because 'The Robin and the Jennywren Are God Almighty's cock and hen.' Nhp.[1], War.[2], Oxf.[1] *MS. add.*, Hnt. (T.P.F.), e.An.[2] Suf. s.An. *Dy. Times* (1892); Suf.[1] e.Suf. (F.H.), Ken. (P.M.) Wil. Thurn *Birds* (1870) 42. w.Som.[1] (*b*) w.Yks. Swainson *ib.* 34. (*c*) w.Som.[1] The most usual name in the vale district.

2. Phr. *Jenny-a'-thing shop*, a general dealer's shop.

Lak. William Campbell ... owned a thriving wee Jenny-a'-thing shop at the head of the auld Sautmarket. Willie kept everything saleable in stock, Murdoch *Readings* (1895) II. 12.

3. A generic name for a country girl.

Frf. A' the Jockies an' Jennies for twa or three miles roon wad be schemin' hoo to get a holiday, Willock *Rosetty Ends* (1886) 158, ed. 1889. Dmb. Nae lass gaed hame her lane, For ilk kindly lad saw his Jenny hame, Taylor *Poems* (1827) 93. Ayr. Many a whinging lover mourns His saucy Jenny, Thom *Amusements* (1812) 28. s.Ir. Priests and publicans, and Jockeys and Jennys, Croker *Leg.* (1862) 231.

4. A female ass.

w.Yks. *Yks. Wkly. Post* (Apr. 17, 1897); w.Yks.[5], e.Lan.[1] w.Som.[1] Is it a 'oss dunkey, or a jenny, you've a-lost!

5. The wren, *Troglodytes parvulus*. War.[24], s.War.[1]

JENNY, *sb.[2]* Sc. Cum. Yks. Lan. Shr. Som. Also in form jinny Cum.[4] w.Yks. [dge·ni, dgi·ni] **1.** A machine for spinning cotton or yarn; a spinning-wheel.

Lnk. O Steam! .. The jenny and loom thy minuteness attest, Rodger *Poems* (1838) 109, ed. 1897. Cum.[4], w.Yks. (J.W.) Lan. The 'jenny' was getting at the 'stretch,' Brierley *Waverlow* (1863) 31, ed. 1884. Shr. The manufacture in Wal., by means of jennies introduced into farm-houses, is four times as great, Marshall *Review* (1818) II. 211. w.Som.[1] A machine for spinning various yarns, and also for twisting two or more yarns into one thread. It was always a hand machine.

2. *Comp.* (1) Jenny-broach, (2) ·gate, the passage or space between two 'jennies.' Cf. gate, *sb.[2]*

(1) w.Yks.[2] In form like a pencil pointed at both ends, and

thicker towards the bottom. (2) **Lan.** Ned came flapping down the 'jenny gate' on his bare feet, BRIERLEY *Cast upon World* (1886) 48; (S.W.)

8. A snare for partridges; an illegal instrument for taking fish, consisting of a casting-line with two or three hooks tied together back to back.

Cum.[4] The wound was that of a jenny. There was no hook mark about the fish's mouth, *Whitehaven Free Press* (Oct. 31, 1896).

JENNY-LIND, *sb.* Yks. Lon. **1.** *Obs.* A wide-awake hat.

Lon. The fashionable dress of the trade is the 'Jenny Lind,' or 'wide-awake' hat, MAYHEW *Lond. Labour* (1851) I. 162.

2. *Comp.* Jenny-Lind-pie, a bone pie. m.Yks.[1] [Not in common use (J.W.).]

JENTY, *sb.* Der. Not. Lin. Also in form jintey n.Lin.; jinty Not.[1] n.Lin. [dgeˑnti, dgiˑnti.] **1.** The wren, *Troglodytes parvulus.* Cf. Jenny, *sb.*[1] **5.**

Not. That there young youth's found a jinty's nest (L.C.M.); (J.S.H.); **Not.**[1] **s.Not.** A've fun a jinty's ness wi' three eggs in't (J.P.K.). **n.Lin.** An' jinteys deed by handfuls together, cluther'd i' th' haay-stacks, PEACOCK *Tales* (1890) and S. 54; (E.P.)

2. *Comp.* Jenty-hunting, hunting wrens to death with sticks and stones. Der. *N. & Q.* (1872) 4th S. ix. 25.

JEOPARTY-TROT, *sb.* Dmf. (JAM.) [Not known to our correspondents.] **1.** A quick motion between running and walking, when one, on account of fear or weakness, runs as if in jeopardy of his life. **2.** A contemptuous term for a person who runs in this fashion; a coward, poltroon.

JEOPERD, *sb.* Sc. (JAM.) Also in form joperd. A hazardous enterprise; a bold adventure; a battle.

JERCOCK, *sb.* Wm. The missel-thrush, *Turdus viscivorus.* Cf. chereock.

The harsh note it utters when alarmed has caused it to receive the name, SWAINSON *Birds* (1885) 1.

JERDAN, see Jordan, *sb.*[1]

JERDLE, *v.* ne.Lan.[1] [Not known to our correspondents.] To dance.

JEREMIAH, *sb.* e.Suf. A donkey. (F.H.)

JEREMY, *sb.* Cor.[2] [dgərimaiˑ.] A latrine.

Aint theer no law 'gainst a man sticking his jeremy right under my winder?

JERFFEL, JERG, see Jaffle, *sb.*[1], Girg.

JERK, *sb.*[1] Lei.[1] Also in form juck. A coat. Cf. jerkin, *sb.*[1]

JERK, *v.* and *sb.*[2] Sc. Lakel. Yks. Chs. Lei. Nhp. Glo. Suf. Sus. Hmp. Dev. Also written gherk n.Yks.; jirk Sc.; and in form jowk s.Chs.[1] [dgərk, dgirk, dgōk.]

1. *v.* To throw underhand; to hurl anything forcibly; with *out:* to eject a person.

n.Sc. Jerk him oot; nae mair shall he drink in this hoose, GORDON *Carglen* (1891) 209. **Lakel.**[2] **n.Yks.** Can't ye gherk it up? (W.H.) **w.Yks.** (J.W.) **s.Chs.**[1] Aay faaˑr kŭst juwk? [Ha! far cost (canst thou) jowk?] **Glo.** *Horae Subsecivae* (1777) 227. **Hmp., Dev.** GROSE (1790) *MS. add.* (M.)

2. To fidget, romp; to walk or drive smartly.

Elg. Down by the Hospital [he] jerkit fu' trig, As supple as futherer could be, *Abd. Wkly. Free Press* (June 25, 1898). **Nhp.**[2] How you keep jerking about! **Nhp.**[2]

3. To move; with *up:* to rise suddenly.

Lth. His Hielant dirk Nae clansman plied mair stuffy, Than did our lads their wapons jerk Among the creesh an' taffy, LUMSDEN *Sheep-head* (1892) 99; I abruptly jerked up and yerked them off a blaud about 'Auld Castled Hailes,' *ib.* 215.

4. To make a splashing noise.

nw.Abd. The watter's jerkin i' my sheen, *Goodwife* (1867) st. 17.

5. Of a covey of partridges: to settle for the night on the ground. **Lei.**[1] They're just a-gooin' to jerk.

6. As a smart blow; also *fig.* a stroke of fortune.

Fif. Gie the Pape a jerk, And in his droddum clap the dirk O' reformation richt, TENNANT *Papistry* (1827) 27. **Dmb.** Think you I'll lose by sic left-handed jirk What I've made ripe by years o' anxious work? SALMON *Gowodean* (1868) 90. **Rnf.** Tho' as stupid as a dunky, Yet by accidental jerk Donald rides before a flunky, WEBSTER *Rhymes* (1835) 97. **Suf.**[1]

7. *Obs.* A trick.

Gall. Ye ken yersel' how ye did play Your jirks just here the ither day, LAUDERDALE *Poems* (1796) 24. **Sus.** I wol for once Have jest a merry jerk, LOWER *Tom Cladpole* (1831) st. 14.

8. *Phr. in a jerk*, in an instant.

Lth. In a jerk, Jean was in the room with an armful of white robes, LUMSDEN *Sheep-head* (1892) 279.

JERKIN, *sb.*[1] and *v.* Sc. Wm. Yks. Nhp. Brks. Also written jerking Sc. [dgəˑrkin, dgōˑkin.] **1.** *sb.* A short coat; an under-waistcoat.

Sc. Ay time cloak and jerkin were through my hands, SCOTT *Nigel* (1822) xxxi. **Gall.** One saw underneath the sailor's jerkin of rough cloth, CROCKETT *Moss-Hags* (1895) xix. **Wm.** Thick leather jerkins hap'd their sides, WHITEHEAD *Leg.* (1859) 4; A loose linen jacket (B.K.). **Yks.** Thoo must be rang, Thus to cut short my jerkin, *Spec. Dial.* (1800) 29. **w.Yks.**[1] **Nhp.**[1] A flannel jerkin. **Brks.**[1]

Hence **Jerkined,** *adj.* wearing or possessing a 'jerkin.'

Gall. Though I am a jerkined man and handle the mattock in another man's kailyaird, CROCKETT *ib.* xxxiii.

2. *Fig.* A beating, thrashing, 'jacketing.'

Sc. My lady's favour stood between your skin and many a jerking, SCOTT *Abbot* (1820) xix.

3. *v.* To beat. w.Yks.[1]

[1. With dutchkin dublets, and with Jerkins iaggde, GASCOIGNE *Steel Glass* (1576) l. 1161.]

JERKIN, *sb.*[2] ? *Obs.* Sc. A gathering of people for some particular purpose.

Dmf. A kind of pic-nic meeting among the low Irish (JAM.). **Gall.** At waddings, raffles, jerkins, balls, Blyth Tammie ay attended, MACTAGGART *Encycl.* (1824) 165, ed. 1876; A poor woman, such as a widow, gets some tea and whisky; she then awakens the country to her meaning; some fling in the mite to her jerkins, but go not thither, as jerkins are truly meetings of the low vulgar, *ib.* 262.

JERKS, *sb. pl.* Shr. [dgōks.] The heart, liver, and lights of a lamb. In daily use still (W.B.); Shr.[1]

JERNISS, *sb.* Fif. (JAM.) Also written gernia. [Not known to our correspondents.] The state of being soaked with rain or water. 'I was just in a jerniss wi' rain.'

JEROBOAM, *sb.* Sc. Lan. e.An. Som. Slang. **1.** A capacious bowl or goblet; a large bottle; the contents of such a bowl or bottle.

Sc. Make a brandy jeroboam in a frosty morning, SCOTT *Blk. Dwarf* (1816) xiii. **Per.** in the shape of toom bottles and defunct Jeroboams, HALIBURTON *Fields* (1890) 33. **Lan.** (F.R.C.) **e.An.**[1] The contents of the Jeroboam, the nut-brown ale, with toast and sugar and spice, is sometimes called by the same name. **Slang.** A four-fold measure of wine, one esp. apt to 'make Israel to sin,' see 1 *Kings* xv. 34 (FARMER).

2. A chamber utensil. w.Som.[1]

[1. The same word as the name of the famous son of Nebat. For another instance of the der. of the name of a drinking-vessel fr. a Scripture proper name see Jorum.]

JERRIME, *sb.* Yks. [dgəˑrəmi.] A boys' game; see below.

w.Yks. 'Jerrime, jerrime buck, ha mony horns do aw cock up?' One makes a back on which the other jumps. Holding up a number of fingers, he repeats the line until the number is guessed, *Hlfx. Courier* (May 22, 1897).

JERRY, *sb., v.* and *adj.* Var. dial. uses in Eng. Also written jerree w.Yks. [dgəˑri.] **1.** *sb.* In *comb.* (1) Jerry('s burial, in phr. *to go to Jerry's burial*, to go on a bootless errand; cf. burying, *vbl. sb.* 8; (2) -bury, to take in, swindle; to go on a bootless errand; (3) -burying, (*a*) *obs.*, a quarryman's term; see below; (*b*) see (1); (4) -cum-foggle, to cheat; (5) -cummumble, (*a*) nonsense; (*b*) to shake, or tumble confusedly; (6) -go-nimble, a circus; (7) -me-diddler, an ignorant, good-for-nothing fellow; (8) -pattick, a simpleton.

(1) **w.Yks.** On one occasion the intended victim, to use his own phrase, had been to 'Jerry's burial' before, *Yks. Character*, 59. (2) **Yks. Yhs. Wkly. Post** (Apr. 17, 1897). **w.Yks.** (S.P.U.); **w.Yks.**[5] Jerry-burrying abart thro' morn to neet, an' ther's nowt at t'end on't after awal. (3, *a*) **w.Yks.** By the use of the steam crane the phr. 'jerry buryin',' once in common use among quarrymen, has been done away with. This phr. was applied to the custom of carrying large landings on men's backs, a practice often resulting disastrously, CUDWORTH *Bradford* (1876) 267. (*b*) **Yks.** Been to jerry-burrying, *Yks. Wkly. Post* (Apr. 17, 1897). **w.Yks.**[5] 'Thenk yub, bud av been to Jerry-burring once,'—a delicate intimation that it is hard to catch a weasel asleep. (4) **Stf.**[1] (5, *a*) **War.** It's all jerricummumble, and that's my opinion on it, *Leamington Courier* (Jan. 30, 1897); **War.**[4] (*b*) **nw.Der.**[1] (6) **Dor.** A great

large jerry-go-nimble show, where there were women-folk riding round—standing upon horses, HARDY *Madding Crowd* (1874) viii. (7) Glo.[1] (8) Cor.[18]

2. A public-house ; *gen.* one without a licence where home-brewed ale is sold ; poor ale such as is sold in such a house.

Lake.[2] Cum.[4] A public house in which only beer, ale and porter may be sold. 'That neighbour keeps a public house, doesn't he ?' 'A jerry,' *W. C. T.* (Apr. 29, 1899) 2. s.Wm. (J.A.B.), Lan.[1], Chs.[1] Lon. But 1s. of this went to pay off an advance of 5s. made to him by the keeper of a beer-shop, or, as he called it, a 'jerry,' MAYHEW *Lond. Labour* (1851) II. 227, ed. 1861.

3. *Comp.* (1) **Jerry-beer**, inferior beer ; (2) **-hole** or **-oil**, (3) **-house**, a beer-house ; a low public-house ; (4) **-lord**, the proprietor of a 'jerry' ; (5) **-shop**, (a) see (3) ; (b) a shop where provisions were formerly supplied in part-payment of wages.

(1) Lan. Jerry beer, malt liquor I cannot call it, debilitated their constitutions, THORNBER *Hist. Blackpool* (1837) 84. (2) Lake.[2] w.Yks. E used to get tut jerree hoil befoar it oppand it mornin an' stop wile nine or ten o'clock at neet, *Frogland Olm.* (1856) 14 ; w.Yks.[5] Monny shillins' slaaved through t'public-harses an' jerry-oils, 45. (3) War.[2], w.Wor.[1], Glo.[1] (4) w.Yks. If a jerry-lord can be said to have one, *Yksman.* (Mar. 17, 1877) 13. Lan.[1] don't care neaw for jerrylords, WOOD *Sngs.* (1879) 41. (5, a) Wm. Slempin' yam of an ibb'ning efter a lile rest i' t'jerry-shop, *Spec. Dial.* (1880) pt. ii. 41. w.Yks.[2] ; w.Yks.[5] Underneath the distinguishing sign of these (there are very few now) is the name of the proprietor, duly 'licensed,' but with the intimation that the ale and beer is 'not to be drunk on the premises.' Lan. A jerry shop, . . with a board announcing 'to be drunk on the premises,' THORNBER *Hist. Blackpool* (1837) 72 ; Lan.[1], e.Lan.[1], m.Lan.[1] Chs. Tha'd spend it aw at th' jerry shop, CLOUGH *B. Bresshittle* (1879) 7 ; Chs.[1] n.Lin.[1] A public-house that has not a licence to sell spirits. War. (J.R.W.), Glo.[1] w.Som.[1] Well there, I widn'a gid up a good place vor to g'in such a house as that, why, twad'n never no other'n a jerry-shop. Dev.[2] (b) Wil.[1] A 'Tommy-shop,' conducted on the truck system, now illegal. Much used about Swindon at the time the railway was being made there. *Obs.*

4. A chamber utensil. w.Som.[1], Cor.[2]

5. *Comb.* **Jerry-go-nimbles**, a disorder of the stomach ; diarrhœa.

s.Wor. Poor Bill's got a touch of the jerry-go-nimbles, PORSON *Quaint Wds.* (1875) 27.

6. A soft felt hat. Nrf. *Arch.* (1879) VIII. 170.

7. Noise, clamour ; ironical applause.

Oxf. A 'jerry' is often given to one who makes some extravagant statement, or otherwise brings down upon himself the disapproval of his mates (G.O.).

Hence **Jerried**, *adj.* jeered at, teased.

w.Yks. I gat rayther jerried abaht bein' henpecked, CUDWORTH *Dial. Sketches* (1884) 7.

8. A machine which removes all the rough portions of cloth. w.Yks.[2] **9.** *v.* To cheat. Lan.[1] **10.** *adj.* Bad, defective ; unsubstantial ; *gen.* of bricklayers' or joiners' work.

Lan. The butcher understood What property was 'jerry,' what was good, DOHERTY *N. Barlow* (1884) 32 ; Lan.[1], Chs.[1]

JERRYMANDER, *sb.* Chs.[1] The germander speedwell, *Veronica Chamaedrys*. A corruption of 'germander.' 'Jerrymander tay' is a favourite remedy for convulsions.

JERSEY, *sb.* Sc. Nhb. Dur. Lan. Chs. Der. Lin. Nhp. Shr. e.An. Som. Also in forms jacey s.Sc. ; jarsey Chs.[1] s.Chs.[1] nw.Der.[1] Nhp.[1] Shr.[1] ; jarsy e.Lan.[1] ; jassy Nhb.[1] ; jassey Nhb.[1] Dur.[1] ; jaysey Chs.[28] **1.** *In comb.* **Jersey lily**, the Scarborough lily, *Vallota purpurea*. w.Som.[1]

2. *Obs.* Wool which has been combed but not spun into yarn.

Chs.[18], nw.Der.[1] Nhp.[1] It is first drawn from the comb in slithers, and afterwards gathered into large hanks ready for spinning. Shr.[1]

3. *Comp.* (1) *Obs.* **Jersey-comb**, a comb for combing 'jersey' ; (2) **-hilling**, *obs.*, a bed-cover quilted with refuse wool-combings between the double-fold material ; (3) **-school**, a place where 'jersey' is spun ; a prison where work is done under compulsion ; (4) **-spinner**, one who spins 'jersey' ; (5) **-spinning**, the practice of spinning

'jersey' ; (6) **-wheel**, a wheel for spinning 'jersey' ; (7) **-yarn**, wool spun with a lint wheel.

(1) Chs.[1] (2) Shr.[1] I think yo' bin prepar'd fur the winter ôôth two par' o' blankets an' a jarsey-'illin'. (3) Lin. THOMPSON *Hist. Boston* (1856) 711 ; Lin.[1] The Old Grey Friars, in Lincoln, was used as a jersey-school at the close of the last, and early in the present century. (4) Chs.[1], Nhp.[1] (5) Chs.[1] It was spun by the pound by those who made a trade of jarsey-spinning, and when the pound was spun it could be taken home and the money for spinning it obtained. (6) *ib.* (7) Nhb. (R.O.H.)

4. Yarn ; worsted ; any coarse woollen fabric.

s.Sc. White lambs-wool or blue jacey are both alike to me, WILSON *Tales* (1836) II. 322. Nhb.[1] Dur.[1] A sort of yarn of wool and lint ; an article not much used now. Yks. (J.W.) e.Lan.[1] Yarn spun from blue and white wool. s.Chs.[1] Oa·, it)s nuwt bû sûm û dhis rhf jaa·rzi stûf [Oh, it's nowt bu' some o' this rough jarsey stuff]. Lin. THOMPSON *Hist. Boston* (1856) 711 ; Lin.[1] Shr.[1] *Obs.* A coarse fabric of loose texture. 'As coå'se as jarsey' is a proverbial saying still extant, and applied to any material of inferior quality.

5. *Comp.* (1) **Jersey-net-cap** or **-night-cap**, a knitted cap made of worsted ; (2) **-road**, see below ; (3) **-woolsey**, a dress material.

(1) Nhb. Aw so him stannin wouv his Jassay neetcap on, BEWICK *Tales* (1850) 10 ; Nhb.[1] Not unlike the conventional smuggler's cap. (2) Lan. The roads are to this day known as 'Jersey roads,' that is, paths used by the collectors of the woollen thread spun for the flannel baize or blanket loom and called 'Jersey,' KAY-SHUTTLEWORTH *Scarsdale* (1860) III. 129. (3) Shr.[1] *Obs.* Woven of fine worsted yarn and linen thread—warp and woof often of diverse colours, as of dark blue and orange, or brown—a pretty fabric of changing hue and serviceable quality, entirely 'home-made.' 'Aye, theer's nuthin' wars like the owd-fashioned jarsey-ôôlsey, it beåts yore merinoes out o' sight.'

6. A blue woollen waistcoat with sleeves. Lin.[1]

7. A contemptuous term for a head of hair.

Chs.[1] A rough head of hair ; Chs.[2] A contemptuous term for a lank head of hair, as resembling combed wool or flax. 'He has got a fine jaysey' ; Chs.[8] Shr.[1] *Obsol.* Yo' wanten yore jarsey cropt. e.An.[1]

JERT, *v.* and *sb.* Sc. Nhb. Dur. Cum. Yks. Lan. Chs. Der. Also written jirt Cai.[1] Ayr. Gall. Nhb.[1] w.Yks. Chs. ; and in form jort Nhb.[1] [dgərt, dgət.] **1.** *v.* To jerk.

Nhb.[1] Dur. GIBSON *Up-Weardale Gl.* (1870). Cum.[4], w.Yks. (S.P.U.), w.Yks.[2], m.Lan.[1], Der.[1]

Hence **Jerty**, (1) *adj.* jerking, slipping about. Der.[1] Cf. cherty ; (2) *sb.* a see-saw. w.Yks. (M.A.)

2. To throw a stone by a sudden movement of the arm against the hip. Lake.[1] Cum.[14], n.Yks.[4], w.Yks. (C.W.D.), Chs.[1] Cf. jerk and jelt. **3.** To squirt, 'chirt.' Cai.[1] Gall. MACTAGGART *Encycl.* (1824).

4. To walk quickly.

Lan. Aw seed Jammie jertin' deawn to-art th' mangle, BRIERLEY *Treadlepin,* vi.

5. *sb.* A jerk. Cf. jart, *sb.* 3.

Ayr. She's gien me monie a jirt an' fleg, BURNS *Ep. J. Lapraik* (Apr. 21, 1785) st. 9. Dur. GIBSON *Up-Weardale Gl.* (1870). Cum.[1] Chs. *Sheaf* (1879) I. 141.

JERTY, *adj.* Yks. [dgə̄·ti.] Of meat : tough.

w.Yks. Still in use to denote meat that is stringy or tough through too much fibrous or sinewy material, and is esp., on this account, applied to leg-meat (J.S.) ; w.Yks.[2]

JERUM, see Gearum(s.

JERUSALEM, *sb.* and *adj.* Cum. Yks. Chs. Nhp. War. Shr. Glo. Oxf. Bck. Lon. e.An. Som. Dev. [dgərū·-, dgərū·sələm.] **1.** *sb.* *In comb.* (1) **Jerusalem cowslip**, the lungwort, *Pulmonaria officinalis* ; (2) **-cuckoo**, (3) **-pony**, a donkey ; (4) **-seeds**, see (1) ; (5) **-star**, the large-flowered St. John's wort, *Hypericum calycinum.*

(1) Cum.[4], Chs.[1], Glo.[1], Oxf., Bck., Nrf. (B. & H.) (2) War.[2] (s.v. Jerusalem Pony) ; War.[3] (3) w.Yks. BURNLEY *Sketches* (1875) 16a. Nhp.[1], War.[23], Oxf.[1] *MS. add.* Lon. Sometimes a party of two or three will be seen closely examining one of these 'Jerusalem ponys,' MAYHEW *Lond. Labour* (1851) I. 28. (4) w.Som.[1] Jurûe·sulûm zee·udz. Dev. My mother used to be very much over they Jerusalem seeds as an arb, *Reports Provinc.* (1884) 22. (5) Shr. (G.E.D.), Shr.[1]

2. A donkey. e.Suf. (F.H.)

3. *adj. Obs.* Of a meal : superlatively good.

Cum. 'And was't a well trett !' 'Aye man ! it was a fair Jerusalem feast we were setten down to I' (J.Ar.) ; Cum.⁴

JERUSALEMER, *sb.* Yks. A donkey.

w.Yks. Well, I gi'd Jerusalemer away, for I'd had enuff o' his antics, HALLAM *Wadsley Jack* (1866) xiv.

JESH, *adj.* I.Ma. [dʒeʃ.] Neat, spruce ; active.

He's a jesh man to have about the house, can turn his hand to anything. She's very jesh in her clothes. She's upstairs making herself jesh (S.M.).

[Gael. *deas*, right, handsome, trim (M. & D.).]

JESOOITER, *sb.* e.Suf. A tiresome, empty talker. (F.H.)

JESP, *sb.* Sc. n.Cy. Nhb. Also in form jisp Sc. (JAM.) Gall. [dʒesp, dʒisp.] A hole or flaw in a texture ; a seam in one's clothes.

Sc. There's no a broken jisp in it (JAM.). n.Sc. Slip shod, wi' no a hale jesp aboot him, WILSON *Tales* (1836) II. 166. Gall. MACTAGGART *Encycl.* (1824). N.Cy.¹ Nhb.¹ Spots of dirt and signs of wear are also termed jesps.

JESSAMINE, *sb.* War. [Not known to our other correspondents.] The cuckoo orchis, *Orchis mascula.* (J.R.W.)

JESSAMY, *sb.* e.An. Som. Dev. Also in forms jessama, jessame Dev.⁴ ; jeshamy e.An.² e.Suf. The jessamine, *Jasminum officinale.*

e.An.², e.Suf. (F.H.) Som. She was putting a nail to the jessamy by the porch, RAYMOND *Sam and Sabina* (1894) 87. Dev.⁴

JESSOP, *sb.* Lin. Glo. Also in forms jazzup Lin.¹ ; jessops n.Lin.¹ [dʒesəp.] 1. A donkey.

Lin. (HALL.), Lin.¹ Glo. At Dumbleton Jessop is still the only word in common use for a donkey. In Stroud it appears to have quite died out, though it was known to a very old native, as used in her childhood (H.S.H.).

2. An ill-conditioned woman. n.Lin.¹

JESSUP, *sb.* Chs. Nhp. War. Wor. Shr. Also in forms jezzup War.³ ; jissop s.Chs.¹ ; jizzup ne.Wor. [dʒesəp, dʒe·zəp, dʒi·səp, dʒi·zəp.] Juice, syrup ; gravy.

s.Chs.¹, Nhp.¹, War. (HALL.), War.²³, ne.Wor. (J.W.F.) se.Wor.¹ Uncommon. Shr.¹ W'en the rûbub's so young it grouz all to jezzup, an' w'en the puddin's cut it's nuthin' but duff.

JESTICK, see **Istick.**

JET, *sb.¹* Sc. Nhb. Dur. Also in forms jead, jeat, jit Nhb.¹ 1. In *comp.* Jet-tribe, crows.

Edb. Dissonant heard, were the jet-tribe On ilka towering tree, LIDDLE *Poems* (1821) 23.

2. Cannel coal, bituminous shale.

Nhb.¹ Nhb., Dur. It burns with a bright flame but loses little bulk in the fire, GREENWELL *Coal Tr. Gl.* (1849).

JET, *sb.²* Hrf. [dʒet.] A descent ; a declivity.

Coming down a jet, BOUND *Provinc.* (1876) ; Hrf.¹ A bit of a jet to go down.

JET, *sb.³* w.Som.¹ A very short distance or space.

Muuv aun u jŭt, wŭl· ur ! Jûs dhu lais·tees jŭt moo·ur.

JET, *v.* and *sb.⁴* Sc. Lakel. Yks. Not. Lin. War. e.An. Ken. Hmp. Wil. Dor. Som. Dev. Cor. Also written jett Sc. (JAM.) s.Not. ; and in forms jīt Som. Dev. ; jut Ken.¹ Som. Wil.¹ Dor.¹ ; *preterite* jot Som. [dʒet.] 1. *v.* To throw ; to throw a stone by bringing the elbow into contact with the side, instead of the usual over-arm method of throwing ; to throw with a jerk. Cf. jelt, jert.

Lakel.² Ah cud varra near jet it as far as thoo can throw't. Wm. The hand is drawn behind the body and hangs downward ; by a sharp movement the arm is brought into contact with the side, and the jerk gives the momentum. 'Let's see hoo far thoo can jet' (B.K.). n.Yks. If I cud tell wheay's cutt our band fra'th sneck, Next time they come, Ise mack them jet the heck, MERITON *Praise Ale* (1684) l. 202. e.Yks.¹ MS. *add.* (T.H.) s.Not. In them days cricketers uster jett ; they never throwed (J.P.K.). n.Lin.¹ sw.Lin.¹ The boys were pelting and jetting. Dev.¹ I'll eat none o' at : and away a jet the cow-heels in a pet, 13.

2. To knock, push ; to nudge, jog. Cf. jot, *v.²*

Lakel.² Children's rhyme, as follows : 'Shak hands lal kind cousin, Lang sen we met ; A cup o' good ale, Jet, Jet, Jet.' Wil. SLOW *Gl.* (1892) ; Wil.¹ Dor. HAYNES *Vocab.* (c. 1730) in *N. & Q.* (1883) 6th S. vii. 366 ; Dor.¹ She jutted 'en. w.Som.¹ How can anybody do it nif you will jet the table ? Dev. An old woman said she ' was afraid they would jet her arm,' *Reports Provinc.* (1877) 132 ; Dev.¹ n.Dev. If Death jet'th one, Ha must obey es call, ROCK *Jim an' Nell* (1867) st. 100. nw.Dev.¹ s.Dev. Don't

ye jit me (F.W.C.). Cor. I'd zoonder be clunk'd by a dragon, ur tiger, Ur be jet in ma pots weth a spaar ur a dagger, DANIEL *Bride of Scio* (1842) 231.

3. To empty a cistern with a 'jet' or ladle. e.An.¹

4. To strut, jerk oneself about ; to turn round.

Sc. To jett up and down, *Gl. Sibb.* (1802) (JAM.). n.Cy. (HALL.) sw.Lin.¹ Jetting and jumping. War. WISE *Shakespere* (1861) 153.

5. *sb.* A nudge, push, slight blow.

Som. SWEETMAN *Wincanton Gl.* (1885). Dev. I ant a-hurted tha bwoy. I only gied 'n a jit in tha niddick, HEWETT *Peas. Sp.* (1892) ; Dev.¹ He geed the table zich a jet, 7. Cor. Zo the guard give'd me a jit and zaid, ' Us be come,' PASMORE *Stories* (1893) 4.

6. A huge ladle affixed to a long pole, used to empty a cistern or pond.

Lin. THOMPSON *Hist. Boston* (1856) 711 ; Lin.¹, e.An.¹ Cmb. See him lifting the jet (W.M.B.). Nrf. HOLLOWAY ; The long-handled ladle or bale with which a water-cart is filled (U.W.). Suf. (C.T.), Suf.¹, e.Suf. (F.H.) Ken. (HALL.) ; Ken.¹ A pail with a long handle. Hmp. HOLLOWAY.

[1. Fr. *jetter,* to throw (COTGR.). 4. I jette, I make a countenaunce with my legges, *Je me jamboye* ; I pray you, se how this felowe jetteth, PALSGR. (1530) 589.]

JET, *int. Obs.* w.Yks.¹ A call used by milkmaids when they wish a cow to turn on one side.

JETH, *sb.* Chs. War. Shr. [dʒeþ.] 1. Dial. form of ' death.' s.Chs.¹ Welly clemt jeth (s.v. Clem). War.², Shr.¹

2. *Comp.* Jeth-pinch, death-pinch (q. v.). Shr.¹

JETHART, see **Jedburgh.**

JETHER, *v.* Fif. (JAM.) [Not known to our correspondents.] To talk idly. Cf. jawther.

JETTICS, *sb. pl.* n.Yks.² The cliffs and places where jet is found.

JETTY, *v.¹* and *sb.¹* Not. Lin. Lei. Nhp. War. Glo. Hnt. Also in forms jitty Not. sw.Lin.¹ Lei.¹ Nhp.¹ War.² Hnt. ; jitway Nhp.¹ [dʒe·ti, dʒi·ti.] 1. *v.* To protrude, jut out. Glo.¹²

2. *sb.* A raised footpath by the side of a road ; a path between two walls or hedges ; a narrow passage.

Not. A've begun to sweep the jitty (L.C.M.). s.Not. Esp. a back-way to a row of houses, or a short hedged foot-way leading up to a field path (J.P.K.). Lin.¹ s.Lin. Ton up the fost jitty, an' it's the last door (T.H.R.). sw.Lin.¹ It's bad in market towns, when the wind catches you in them jitties. They went into a narrow jetty, leading to Chapel Lane. Lei.¹ A passage common to two houses. Nhp.¹ An alley or narrow passage communicating from one street to another, as distinguished from an entry, which is generally a covered passage between houses leading into an open court or yard. War. There go Bill and Sal a racing along the jetty, *Leamington Courier* (Jan. 30, 1897) ; An open jetty between property, *Evesham Jrn.* (Nov. 25, 1899) ; War.²⁴, Hnt. (T.P.F.)

JETTY, *v.²* and *sb.²* Lan. Chs. Stf. Shr. Also written getty Chs.² ; and in forms gitty Chs. ; jiddy Lan.¹ ; jitty Chs.¹ s.Chs.¹ Stf.¹ ; jutty Chs.¹ [dʒe·ti, dʒi·ti.] 1. *v.* To agree.

Lan.¹ They never jiddy together. Chs. They gitty very well together (C.J.B.) ; Chs.¹ They dunna seem to jetty ; Chs.³ s.Chs.¹ Wae·rin)th blóo ŭn braan·di-dringk·in dûn·)ŭ jit·i ['Wearin' th' blue an' brandy-drinkin' dunna jitty]. Stf.¹ Shr.¹ The new cow jetties reet well alung wuth the others.

2. A state of evenness and uniformity.

Shr.¹ ' The new buildin' an' the 'ouse bin all of a jetty,' i. e. not detached—all under one roof.

JETTY, *v.³* Nhb. [dʒe·ti.] To hoist up. (R.O.H.)

JETTY, *v.⁴* Der. [dʒe·ti.] With *about*: to do odd jobs about a house. Der.², nw.Der.¹

JEUK, see **Jouk, Juck,** *sb.¹*

JEVE, *v.* and *sb.* ? *Obs.* Sc. (JAM.) Also in form jave Fif. 1. *v.* To push hither and thither. Fif. 2. *sb.* A push with the elbow. Sc.

JEVEL, *sb.¹* Sc. [dʒe·vl.] A rascal, ne'er-do-weel.

Sc. (JAM.) s.Sc. He had no more honour than ony auld jevel wha ever cheated the world, WILSON *Tales* (1836) III. 69.

[Let be, quoth Jok, and cawd him Jevell, *Chrysts-kirk* (c. 1550) vii, in RAMSAY *Ever Green* (ed. 1761) I. 6 ; Iavel, *joppus, gerro, Prompt.*]

JEVEL, *v.* and *sb.*² Sc. (JAM.) Also written jevvel Lnk. **1.** *v.* To joggle; to shake. Ags. **2.** To spill a large quantity of any liquid at once. Slk. **3.** To move obliquely. Lth. **4.** *sb.* The dashing of water. Lnk.

JEVVEL, JEW, see Jevel, *v.*, Jue.

JEW, *sb.* and *v.* Sc. Cum. Yks. Lan. I.Ma. Chs. Stf. Der. Lin. Nhp. Lon. Hnt. Suf. Ken. Hmp. Som. Dev. Cor. and Aus. [dʒū, dʒiu.] **1.** *sb.* In *comp.* (1) Jew(s'-bowels, small pieces of smelted tin found in old smelting works; (2) -('s-ears, (a) some species of fungi, esp. *Peziza coccinea* and *P. cochleata*; (b) the tomato, *Lycopersicum esculentum*; (c) a species of lichen; (3) -('s-eye, in phr. *worth a Jew's eye*, of great value; (4) -(s'-fish, the halibut, *Hippoglossus vulgaris*; (5) -s'-house, a very ancient smelting place; (6) -s'-leavings, mine refuse; (7) -'s-myrtle, the butcher's broom, *Ruscus aculeatus*; (8) -(s'-offcast, see (6); (9) -s'-pieces, very ancient blocks of tin; (10) -s'-poker, a person employed to light the fires of Jews on their Sabbath; (11) -('s-roll, a penny loaf rounded on top, and with a reddish-brown glaze; (12) -(s'-tin, block tin found in ancient smelting houses; tin ore left by ancient tin-workers; (13) -('s-trump or -trunk, a Jew's-harp; also *fig.* a dowdy; (14) -whidn, see (5); (15) -s'-works, ancient places for raising and washing tin ore.

(1) Cor.¹ Tradition always connects Jews with tin in Cor. (2, *a*) Cum., Yks. (B. & H.) Suf.¹ A bright red fungus found adhering to sticks. Dev. (B. & H.), Cor.¹² (b) Hmp.¹ (c) Bnff.¹ (3) I.Ma. A drop of the rael stuff is worth a Jew's eye, CAINE *Demster* (1887) 28, ed. 1889. Chs.¹ s.Chs.¹ Oo mai·z ū rae·r weyf; 60)z woth ū Jóoz ahy [Hoo mays a rare weife; hoo's woth a Jew's eye]. Nhp.¹, Hnt. (T.P.F.), Suf.¹ Som. She's one in a thousand for management. She'd be wo'th a jew's-eye in any house, RAYMOND *Men o' Mendip* (1898) viii. w.Som.¹ Taek-ee·ur oa un, un put·-n uwai·, ee·ul bee u waeth u Jūe·z uy, zau·m dai. (4) Dev.² A favourite part of the Jews' diet. [Aus. The jewfish . . . is salmon-shaped, and quite as silvery as that royal fish, with lovely dark violet tints over the head and back. . . [It] comes from the sea in large shoals, *Gent. Mag.* (June 1878) 723-4.] (5) Dev. After the Conquest . . . the Jews . . . farmed the mines, and to them, perhaps, may be attributed the erection of that smelting-house near the confluence of the e. and w. Dart, which Mr. Pearse describes as Phœnician, though he adds . . . 'called by the miners Jews' houses,' PAGE *Explor. Dartmoor* (1889) ii. Cor. That the Jews farmed the tin mines of Cornwall and Devonshire is an historical fact . . . Hence the terms 'Jews' houses,' given to old and rude smelting works, HUNT *Pop. Rom. w.Eng.* (1865) 346, ed. 1896; Cor.² (6) Cor. HUNT *Pop. Rom. w.Eng.* (1865) 343, ed. 1896. (7) Ken. It is the popular belief that the crown of thorns . . . was composed of its branches, *N. & Q.* (1856) and S. i. 432. (8) Cor.² (9) Cor.² (10) Lon. A miserly woman who got her living by lighting the Jews' fires on Saturday, and was known as a 'Jew's poker,' died from sheer want in Whitechapel, *Marlborough Times* (June 20, 1891) 6. (11) Gall. The solid and enduring charms of a penny Jew's roll unsettled his mind, CROCKETT *Bog-Myrtle* (1895) 197; (S.R.C.) (12) Dev. Not far from this place there was found a block of Jews' tin, supposed to be the most ancient in existence, BRAY *Desc. Tamar and Tavy* (1836) III. 255. Cor. HUNT *Pop. Rom. w.Eng.* (1865) 346, ed. 1896; Cor.² (13) Cum. And played on twee jew trumps together, ANDERSON *Ballads* (1805) 45; Cum.⁴ w.Yks. *Hlfx. Courier* (May 22, 1897); w.Yks.²⁵ Lan. Playing the fiddle and jewtrump, ROBY *Trad.* (1829) II. 359, ed. 1872. n.Lan.¹, Stf.¹, nw.Der.¹ n.Lin.¹ 'What an ugly noise that thing makes, Sarah!' 'O, Master Edward, you should not say so; don't you know it's a jew-trump like what King David played his Psalms with.' (14) Cor. HUNT *Pop. Rom. w.Eng.* (1865) 476, ed. 1896. (15) Cor.²

2. Phr. *to wander like a lost Jew*, to wander aimlessly. s.Chs.¹

3. A black field beetle.

Cor.² Because it exudes a bloody or pinkish froth, they call to it while holding it in the hand, 'Jew, Jew, spit blood.'

4. *v.* To cheat, defraud.

Per. The'll not jew us—we're no sae hieland, FERGUSSON *Vill. Poet* (1897) 172. Ayr. Some had hinted that this bad report was to jew the Colonel out of a great treasure, HUNTER *Studies* (1870) 8. Keb. 'Twad tak' them to be early up Whae'er micht think to jew him, ARMSTRONG *Ingleside* (1890) 141. Cum.⁴ w.Yks. I doan't like ta be jewed aght ov ma reights, *Yksman. Comic Ann.*

(1878) 30; (J.W.) m.Lan.¹, Chs.¹, e.Suf. (F.H.) w.Som.¹ They do say that Bob Hellings have a jewed his brother out of all the money the old man left em.

JEWBERRY, *sb.* Wil. Som. **1.** Dial. form of 'dewberry,' *Rubus caesius*.

Wil. (J.M.), Wil.¹ Som. The hedges 'ud be ripe wi' black jew-berries, LEITH *Lemon Verbena* (1895) 86.

2. *Comp.* Jewberry-hunter, a gatherer of dewberries. Wil. (J.M.)

JEWBUS, JEWDICOW, see Jubious, Judy-cow, s. v. Judy.

JEWEL, *sb.*¹ and *v.* Sh.I. Irel. n.Cy. Hrf. Bck. Dev. **1.** *sb.* A term of endearment.

Sh.I. Rin dee wis oot, jewel, BURGESS *Sketches* (2nd ed.) 3; Come in trow, my jewels, *Sh. News* (Sept. 3, 1898). s.Ir. Go on, Jewel, . . if you dance I'll pipe, CROKER *Leg.* (1862) 4. N.Cy.¹

2. Phr. *Jewel run the ground*, the ground-ivy, *Nepeta Glechoma*. Bck. *Nature Notes*, IX.

3. *v.* To put a ring in a pig's snout. Hrf.²

4. To value highly, regard with affection.

Dev. The ladies perfeckly jewels that cat, *Reports Provinc.* (1887) 10; She jewels that chair, *ib.* (1893).

JEWEL, *sb.*² *Obs.* n.Cy. Yks. The 'starling' of a wooden bridge. Cf. jowel, *sb.*¹.

n.Cy. GROSE (1790). n.Yks. Thus in the memorandum of repairs of How Bridge payments are recorded for 'timber for making fower paires of jewells and one odd jewell,' *Quart. Sess. Rec.* in *N. R. Rec. Soc.* I. *Introd.* 7. e.Yks. MARSHALL *Rur. Econ.* (1788).

JEWITT, *sb.* w.Yks.⁵ A term of reproach.

If a landlady presumes too much upon her position, in dealing with her tenants, either one of her consequential visits, when her back is turned, she is called 'a silly owd jewitt.'

JEW-LIMESTONE, *sb.* Nhb.¹ A bed of limestone lying below the whin-sill in the lead-mining district.

JEWSLE, *v.* Lei.¹ [dʒiu·zl.] To cheat.

JEW-STONE, *sb.* Hrf. Som. The technical name for a hard grey stone used for mending roads.

Hrf. (E.M.W.) Som. A kind of lias-stone found at Wedmore. This kind of stone is found in large blocks, locally called 'Jews.' They will not bear cutting, or take a face of any kind, but break with a conchoidal fracture when struck (W.F.R.); WOODWARD *Geol. Eng. and Wal.* (1876) 440.

JEYCE, JEYKE, see Gist, Gike, *v.*

JEZABANEEAK, *sb.* e.Yks.¹ [Not known to our correspondents.] A word expressive of evil personal qualities generally. *MS. add.* (T.H.)

JEZZOP, see Jessup.

JIB, *sb.*¹ and *v.*¹ Shr. Som. Dev. Also written gib Shr.¹² Dev.; jibb Dev. [dʒib.] **1.** *sb.* A wooden stand for a barrel.

w.Som.¹ Dev. *Horae Subsecivae* (1777) 227; Dev.¹ n.Dev. Slat the keeve and tha jibb, *Exm. Scold.* (1746) l. 249.

Hence *Jibbing*, *sb.* a continuous row of stands for casks; a number of loose stands.

w.Som.¹ For sale, a quantity of empty casks and jibbing, *Local Advt.*

2. A rack in which the raw cream coolers stand in the dairy.

Som. Milk pans, pails, jibs, *Wellington Wkly. News* (Apr. 29, 1896).

3. A wooden prop used to support the coal when being 'holed.'

Shr.¹; Shr.² A piece of wood about ten inches long, used in supporting the roof of a coal mine.

4. A piece of iron used in connecting machinery together in collieries.

Shr.¹ Of a peculiar shape—not unlike the half of a hollow square.

5. *v.* To place a cask upon its stand.

w.Som.¹ Aay-v u-yuur·d um zai· aew ee kud júb u auk·seed u suy·dud pun uz tūe nee·z [I've heard tell how that he could jib a hogshead of cider upon his two knees].

JIB, *sb.*² and *v.*² Lakel. Yks. Lan. I.Ma. Stf. Rut. Shr. Hrf. e.An. Sus. Som. Dev. Also written gib e.Suf. [dʒib.] **1.** *sb.* The under-lip; the mouth.

Lan. The lower jaw, sometimes including the mouth (S.W.). e.Lan.¹ The lower lip when it hangs loose. s.Stf. He'd got the ugliest jib I ever see, PINNOCK *Blk. Cy. Ann.* (1895). Shr., Hrf.

3 A

BOUND *Provinc.* (1876). e.An.[1] e.Suf. The babe makes a gib : it wants its mother (F.H.); Used esp. of a child working its mouth before it begins to cry, so that its under-lip trembles or drops. ' The little fellow wholly dropped his jib.' ' The girl pulled such a jib!' (*ib.*) Sus.[1] Som. AGRIKLER *Rhymes* (1872) 7. Dev.[1]; Dev.[8] Zee how white her is about the jib, I be sartin her's bad. Lûkee zee tû the jib aw'n 'e hang'th down like a slatterpûch 'oss. **2.** Phr. *to hang the jib*, to look cross.

Shr.[2] Shr., Hrf. BOUND *Provinc.* (1876). e.An.[1] Nrf. Oh! I could see he didn't like it much; he hung his jib a bit (W.R.E.). e.Suf. (F.H.) Sus. But de gal, hanging de jib, said de mistus ool huff an hang de jib an be hem nunty, JACKSON *Southward Ho* (1894) I. 339 ; Sus.[1]

3. *Fig.* Talk, 'jaw'; scorn, sarcasm, ridicule.

w.Yks. (J.W.) Lan. They care for no color, they fear no jib, COLLINS *Poems* (1859) 45 ; 'Hold your jib' is not uncommon (S.W.).

4. ? A mouthful.

Rut.[1] He comes in here for a jib of tea ; and that's better than going to the public-house.

5. The face.

Lakel.[2] Hod up thi jib tell Ah wesh't. w.Yks. Fouks a' fooit wi' ther different shap'd hats an' jibs, TOM TREDDLEHOYLE *Fr. Exhibition* (c. 1856) 14. m.Lan.[1] I.Ma. He has a jib on him, as sharp as a hatchet (S.M.).

6. *v.* To draw down the mouth (as a child beginning to cry). e.Suf. (F.H.)

JIB, *sb.*[3] Lin.[1] [Not known to our correspondents.] Butter-scotch ; toffee.

JIB, *v.*[2] and *sb.*[4] War. Lon. Suf. **1.** *v.* In phr. *to jib at the collar*, to shirk work. War.[2]

2. *sb.* A horse that jibs.

Lon. Frequently young horses that will not work in cabs—such as ' jibs '—are sold to the horse-slaughterers as useless, MAYHEW *Lond. Labour* (1851) I. 181. e.Suf. (F.H.)

JIB, *v.*[4] Sc. Also written jibb (JAM.). [dgib.] **1.** To milk closely.

Dmf. They jib their kye, feed them on 'orts' and locks, WALLACE *Schoolmaster* (1899) 339. Gall. MACTAGGART *Encycl.* (1824).

Hence **Jibbings,** *sb. pl.* the last and richest milk drawn from a cow's udder.

e.Sc. *N. & Q.* (1882) 6th S. vi. 54. Gall. MACTAGGART *Encycl.* (1824).

2. To fleece. Lnk. (JAM.)

JIBB, JIBBAL, see Jib, *sb.*[1][2], *v.*[4]

JIBBER, *sb.*[1] Nhp. Oxf. Suf. Sus. Som. Dev. Also written gibber Oxf.[1] [dgi·bə(r).] A horse that jibs.

Nhp.[1], Oxf.[1], e.Suf. (F.H.) e.Sus. HOLLOWAY. w.Som.[1] Ee·u jûb·ur! daar·nd eef ee oa·un pŏo·l tüe u dai·d laef· gin dhu buul·ee oa un du thich dhu graew'n, voaur ee·ul gee aew't tüe ut [He a jibber! darned if he will not pull at a dead lift until his belly touches the ground, before he will give up]. Dev.[8]

JIBBER, *sb.*[2] War. A sweetmeat, lollipop. Also in *comb.* Jibber-and-jumbles.

Jibbers were long, thin, flat sticks, about an inch wide. ' The Squire gave us a penny and we went to buy some jibbers' (W.S.B.); War.[2]

JIBBER, *v.* and *sb.*[3] Sc. Som. Also in form jebber Dmf. (JAM.) [dgi·bə(r).] **1.** *v.* To chatter, talk nonsense. Cf. gibberish.

Sc. The jackanape . . . jibbered and cried as if it were mocking its master, SCOTT *Redg.* (1824) Lett. xi. Abd., Per. What are ye jibberin' at there ! (G.W.) s.Sc. (JAM.)

2. *Comb.* Jibber-jabber, (1) noisy, nonsensical talk ; (2) to talk foolishly.

(1) Banff.[1], Cld. (JAM.) w.Som.[1] Jûb·urjab·ur. (2) Banff.[1], Cld. (JAM.)

3. *sb. pl.* Silly talk, idle chatter.

Abd., Per. Ye're speaking only a lot o' jibbers. Nane o' yer jibbers (G.W.). Dmf. (JAM.)

JIBBERIDGE, see Gibberish.

JIBBER UGLY'S FÜLE, *phr.* Dev. A selfish person. 'Er is like jibber-ugly's-fûle—'er knaws whot's gûde vur erzel, 'er dû, HEWETT *Peas. Sp.* (1892).

JIBBET, *sb.* Irel. Hmp. Wil. Also written gibbet Ir. [dgi·bit.] **1.** A small load of corn or hay.

Hmp. A jibbet of corn or hay (J.R.W.); Hmp.[1]

2. *pl.* Morsels, small pieces, 'mincemeat.'

Ir. Guards woke up, clashed their arms, and were going to make gibbets of the foolish boy, KENNEDY *Fireside Stories* (1870)

53. Wxf. They'd have made gibbets of him only for Tommy Whitty, *ib. Evenings Duffrey* (1869) 81. Wil.[1] You never did see such a slut! her gownd a-hangin' in dirty jibbets [rags] aal about her heels!

[L. Cp. OFr. *gibe*, ' paquet, ballot' (LA CURNE).]

JIBBET, *v.* Suf. To sprain.

e.Suf. ' I have jibbeted my ankle.' Used by the old only (F.H.).

JIBBET, see Gibbet.

JIBBLE, *v.*[1] Lei.[1] To jingle, rattle.

JIBBLE, *v.*[2] e.Suf. [dgi·bl.] To make a face (as a child about to cry). (F.H.) Cf. jib, *sb.*[2]

JIBBLE, *v.*[3] Nrf. [Not known to our correspondents.] To pick out with a sharp tool.

A mason said to his server, ' You must jibble the mortar out of them joints ' (W.W.S.).

JIBBLE, see Geebal(l, Geeble, Gibble.

JIBBLY, *sb.* Lan. [dgi·bli.] A giblet ; a fragment, odd piece.

Jibbly pie is a pie made of odds and ends (S.W.). e.Lan.[1]

JIBBY, *sb.* Obsol. e.Cy. e.An. [dgi·bi.] **1.** A giddy, flaunting girl, dressed in showy finery, and full of affectations. e.Cy. (HALL.), e.An.[1], e.Suf. (F.H.) **2.** *Comb.* Jibby-horse, a showman's horse decked out with particoloured trappings ; also used of a human being. *ib.*

3. A jibbing horse. e.Suf. (F.H.)

JIBE, *v.*[1] Ant. [Not known to our other correspondents.] To coax. (S.A.B.)

JIBE, *v.*[2] and *sb.* e.Suf. **1.** *v.* To excoriate. (F.H.) **2.** *sb.* An excoriation. (*ib.*)

JIBE, see Gibe.

JIBES, *sb.* Dev. An eccentrically-dressed woman.

Mrs. Snooks is a rummee old jibes : 'er cloase is za old's Aldon an' awl tha colours ov tha rainbow, HEWETT *Peas. Sp.* (1892).

JIB-FORK, *sb.* e.An.[1] A two-pronged fork of the length used in harvest.

e.An.[1] Nrf. Still in use here (M.C.H.B.). e.Suf. Rare (F.H.).

JIB-JOB-JEREMIAH, *sb.* Suf.[1] [Not known to our correspondents.] A children's game. (s.v. Move-all.)

JIBS, *sb. pl.* Cor. [dgibz.] Small, waste pieces of cloth. THOMAS *Randigal Rhymes* (1895) *Gl.* ; Cor.[3]

JICCOP, *v.* e.An.[1] [Not known to our correspondents.] [dgi·kap.] To move; to disturb a seat.

JICCUPS, *sb. pl.* Cor.[12] [dgi·kaps.] The hiccoughs.

JICE, *sb.* Suf. Ess. [dgais.] A very small quantity, esp. of powder. The same word as Chice.

Suf.[1] A pinch of snuff. Ess. Jest a little jice, CLARK *J. Noakes* (1839) st. 152 ; Ess.[1]

JICE, see Joist, *sb.*[1]

JICK, *sb.*[1] and *v.*[1] Cor. Also in form juck Cor.[2] [dgik.] **1.** *sb. pl.* The hiccoughs. Cor.[1] Cf. jiccups.

2. *v.* To hiccough. Cor.[2]

JICK, *v.*[2] and *sb.*[2] Sc. (JAM.) [dgik.] **1.** *v.* To avoid anything by a sudden jerk of the body; to elude.

Lak., Twd., Bwk., Slk. It is said of a hare, that she has 'jickit the hunds.'

2. Phr. *to jick the school*, to play truant. Lnk. **3.** *sb.* A sudden jerk; the act of eluding. Slk. Hence Jicky, *adj.* of a horse: startling. Slk.

JICKER, *v.* Obs. Sc. To walk smartly.

Dmf. (JAM.) Gall. On their taptaes what couples did jicker and spang, MACTAGGART *Encycl.* (1824) 78, ed. 1876. Kcb. In sweat and snow they did jicker! DAVIDSON *Seasons* (1789) 89.

JICKERING, *ppl. adj.* Sc. [Not known to our correspondents.] Of a woman : more smartly dressed than she should be. Gall. MACTAGGART *Encycl.* (1824).

JID, *sb.* Nhb. Also written gid. The Jack-snipe, *Limnocryptes gallinula.*

Nhb. (R.O.H.) [SWAINSON *Birds* (1885) 193.]

JIDDER, JIDDY, see Jedder, Giddy, Jetty, *v.*[2]

JIDGETT, *v.* e.An. [dgi·dgit.] To wriggle, fidget. Cf. jigget.

Nrf. Children jidgett about, COZENS-HARDY *Broad Nrf.* (1893) 55. e.Suf. (F.H.)

JIE, *v.* Sc. To cast aside. See Ge(e, *v.*[1]

Ayr. Auld Halbert jied his wig aside, FISHER *Poems* (1790) 151.

JIE, see Ge(e, *int.*

JIFF, *sb.* Stf. War. Oxf. Ken. Som. [dʒif.] 1. The shortest possible lapse of time. Stf.[1] Cf. jiffy.

2. Phr. (1) *in a jiff*, (2) *in half a jiff*, with the least delay possible.

(1) War.[2] Common. Oxf. I'll be there in a jiff (G.O.). Som. Joe zinged 'Nancy Lee,' which vetched an audiens in a jiff, FRANK *Nine Days* (1879) 39. (2) Ken. Off again in half a jiff, NAIRNE *Tales* (1790) 49, ed. 1824.

JIFFING, *sb. Obs.* Sc. In phr. *in a jiffing*, in an instant. Cf. jiffy.

Rnf. Watty . . . in a jiffin' Row'd his fecket like a clew, PICKEN *Poems* (1813) II. 47.

JIFFLE, *v.* and *sb.* Sc. Der. Lin. e.An. Wil. Also written giffle e.An.[1] [dʒi·fl.] 1. *v.* To fidget, be restless; to shuffle; also *trans.* to make restless.

Per. (JAM.), n.Lin.[1] sw.Lin.[1] Children are always jiffling about. e.An.[1] Nrf. There, child; don't keep a jiffling about like that. Why can't ye sit still? (W.R.E.); (M.C.H.B.) Suf. (C.T.); Suf.[1] Don't jiffle about so. e.Suf. (F.H.) Wil.[1] Used in connexion with a horse, when a bad rider who was pulling its head about was told not to jiffle it.

2. *sb.* A fidget; a shuffling movement; ? confusion.

Per. (JAM.) n.Lin.[1] He's alus up o' th' jiffle an' flit, like a ill-sittin' hen. Wil.[1] An old bell-ringer was recently heard to accuse the younger men of having got into a regular 'jiffle' while ringing.

Hence **Jiffley**, *adj.* unsteady, restless.

sw.Lin.[1] If the cow's a bit jiffley.

3. Idle talk; idle, disputative talk. Also in *comp.* Jiffle-jaffle. Der.[2], nw.Der.[1], Nrf. (M.C.H.B.) Cf. jaffle, *sb.*[2]

JIFFY, *sb., v.* and *adv.* In *gen.* dial. and colloq. use in Sc. Eng. and Irel. Also written giffey w.Yks.; giffy Nhp.[1] Hnt. e.An.[12] Nrf. Sus. Hmp.; jiffey Sc. Ir. n.Yks. w.Yks. Lan. se.Wor.[1] Nrf. Sus. Hmp. Som. Dev.; jiffie Sc. Bnff.[1] [dʒi·fi.] 1. *sb.* The shortest possible lapse of time.

Lth. Sae weel our tusks an' talons work In this wee glorious jiffy, LUMSDEN *Sheep-head* (1892) 39. Hdg. The mirkiest hour . . . Precedes the daw'—A jiffey ere god Sol abune O'erwhelms it a', *ib. Poems* (1896) 94. Uls. Uls. *Jrn. Arch.* (1853–62). n.Cy. (J.W.), Dur.[1], n.Yks.[1], nw.Der.[1], Not.[1], Lei.[1], Nhp.[1], War.[3], Oxf. (G.O.) Brks.[1] 'Twunt taayke I moor'n a jiffy to clim to that ther bird's ne-ast. Hnt. (T.P.F.) Nrf. COZENS-HARDY *Broad Nrf.* (1893) 55. Sus., Hmp. HOLLOWAY. Wil. BRITTON *Beauties* (1825). Dor.[1] Som. JENNINGS *Dial. w.Eng.* (1869). Dev.[1]

2. Phr. (1) *in a jiffy*, (2) *in half a jiffy*, (3) *in a brace* or *couple of jiffies*, with the least possible delay.

(1) Sc. He was out in the road in a jiffy, KEITH *Bonnie Lady* (1897) 68. Sh.I. In a jiffey comes back wi' da claes, STEWART *Tales* (1892) 34. ne.Sc. Lizzie will be wi' you in a jiffie, GRANT *Kackleton*, 41. Abd. I s' tak ye hame in a jiffey, MACDONALD *Sir Gibbie* (1879) xlii. Ked. I'll be wi' 'lm in a jiffy, GRANT *Lays* (1884) 85. Per. He'll smell out the rogue in a jiffy, STEWART *Character* (1857) 36. s.Sc. Wad often in a jiffie to auld Nick Send ane anither dunnerin' saul and hool, T. SCOTT *Poems* (1793) 365. Dmb. I'll tell you my errand in a jiffy, CROSS *Disruption* (1844) xxxiv. Ayr. In a jiffy the whole market-place was as white . . . as . . . snow, GALT *Provost* (1822) xiii. Lnk. We'll prise the lid open in a jiffey, MURDOCH *Readings* (1895) I. 111. Lth. In bopes that in a jiffy he cou'd stechin to his belly gie, BRUCE *Poems* (1813) II. 165. Edb. We'll be aff in a jiffy, BALLANTINE *Gaberlunzie* (ed. 1875) 328. Slk. The Gentles will be here in a jiffey, CHR. NORTH *Noctes* (ed. 1856) II. 270. Dmf. The wee servant lassie came in, in a jiffy, WALLACE *Schoolmaster* (1899) 331. Ir. They'll be at the door in a jiffey, CARLETON *Traits Peas.* (ed. 1843) I. 22. Nhb. They popp'd us in a jiffy down, WILSON *Pitman's Pay* (1843) 25. s.Dur. He was out o' seet iv a jiffy (J.E.D.). Cum.[14] Wm. It seeam wae o in a jiffy, *Spec. Dial.* (1885) pt. iii. 25. n.Yks. We were there iv a jiffey, TWEDDELL *Clevel. Rhymes* (1875) 64. w.Yks.[12] Lan. Tha'll be i' th' wayter in a jiffey, WOOD *Hum. Sketches*, 12. m.Lan.[1], nw.Der.[1] Not. I'll dut in a jiffy (L.C.M.). n.Lin.[1] s.Lin. He hed it ready in a jiffy (T.H.R.). Nhp.[2], War.[2] Brks.[1] n.Bck. (A.C.), e.An.[1], Suf.[1] Wil. SLOW *Gl.* (1892). Dev. Auver hur went in a jiffey, BENNETT *Stable Boy* (1888) viii. Cor.[1] (2) se.Wor.[1] I'll be there in half a jiffey. w.Som.[1] Yue goo au'n, un aa-l oa·vurgit· yue ugee·un een aaf· u jüfee. (3) Lan. My owd dame con tell yo' where hoo is in a couple o' jiffies, BRIERLEY *Waverlow* (1863) 207, ed. 1884. e.An.[12]

---

3. A hurry.

Bnff.[1] Y'er in an unco jiffie. I.W.[1] He's off in a jiffy.

4. *v.* To hurry. Bnff.[1] He jiffiet haim.

5. *adv.* With haste. *ib.*

JIG, *sb.*[1] and *v.*[1] Sc. Irel. n.Cy. Cum. Yks. Nhp. War. Hnt. Som. Dev. and Amer. Also written gig Bnff.[1] Bch. Ayr. (JAM.) m.Yks.[1] w.Yks.[5]; and in forms geg w.Yks.[1]; jeeg Cai.[1] Ayr. [dʒig.] 1. *sb.* In phr. *all on the jig*, or *in a jig*, 'all agog,' in a state of flurry or expectation.

m.Yks.[1] He's on the gig to be off. In a gig to go [in a state of flurry to go]. w.Yks.[5] All on the gig fur going.

2. An illegal instrument for catching fish, composed of a number of wires with fish-hooks attached. N.I.[1] 3. A jerk, tilt, shake, rock, swing; a sudden pull. Sc. (JAM. *Suppl.*), Cai.[1]

4. *v.* To dance briskly or boisterously.

Frf. Ye needna houp, That I, like some bit puppet thing, Will e'er consent to jig an' loup Whan ony coof sall pu' the string, WATT *Poet. Sketches* (1880) 32. Frf. See her [Aurora] jiggin' truttie-trottie Without her jupes or little-coatie, TENNANT *Papistry* (1827) 132. Lnk. Set your flingin' tree a jiggin' Till streams o' sweat rin owre your riggin', WATSON *Poems* (1853) 14. Dev. All jiggin up and down I caan't tell bow, Jist like the tail o' thecky Jarsey cow, DANIEL *Bride of Scio* (1842) 176.

Hence (1) **Giggle**, *adj.*, (2) **Giggin**, *ppl. adj.* brisk, hearty, lively; (3) **Gig-trot**, *sb.* habit; (4) **Jigger**, *sb.* a small spinning-top.

(1) Bch. Sprush i' their graith, the ploughmen loons, To see their joes fu' giggie, TARRAS *Poems* (1804) 64 (JAM.). (2) Bnff.[1] She's gotten a fine codgie giggin' bodie for a man. (3) *ib.* (4) w.Yks.[5] The smallest size made, known amongst juveniles as 'fardin' jiggers.'

5. To play the fiddle.

Dmf. Jock Willison . . . who for the fiddle left his trade, Jigg'd it far better than he sped, MAYNE *Siller Gun* (1808) 42 (JAM.).

6. To trot; to walk briskly; to work in a lively, hearty manner.

Bnff.[1] The wiffie for ass aul's she is, cam giggin' up the road wintin' ony help. Bnff., Ayr. (JAM.) Lakel.[2] Thoo's jiggen aboot i' good time ta-day. w.Yks.[1] w.Som.[1] Faster than to jog. Dev. Of some horses, 'They only jigged off at the bottom of the road,' *Reports Provinc.* (1882) 16; (HALL.) w.Yks.[1]

7. *Comb.* Jig-to-jog, the slow pace of a horse, just faster than a walk; also used of a person.

w.Som.[1] Wuy·s-n muuv· au·n, neet buyd dhae·ur jig-tu-jaug· jis dhu vuur·ee sae·um·z wuop u snaa·yul? [Why dost not move on, (and) not stay there jig-to-jog just like whip(ping) a snail?] nw.Dev.[1]

8. To go gadding and gossiping about.

Nhp.[1] You're never easy only when you're jigging about. War.[2] She's never right on'y when she's jigging about. Hnt. (T.P.F.)

9. To run away, rove; to play truant from school, 'play the wag'; sometimes with *it*. Also used *subst.* in phr. *to play jig*.

n.Cy. (HALL.) e.Yks.[1] Let's all jig-it tl-day, lads. w.Yks.[1] To rove, to make frequent idle excursions from home. [Amer. 'Play jig,' to play truant from school, *Dial. Notes* (1896) I. 379.]

10. To jerk, tilt, shake, rock; to give a sudden pull.

Cai.[1] Ayr. I maun sit the lee-lang day And jeeg the cradle wi' my tae, BURNS *Duncan Gray*, 1st version.

11. To dandle a baby. N.I.[1]

12. To take herrings by means of an illegal instrument.

N.I.[1] To jig for herrings is to catch herrings by means of an apparatus composed of a number of wires with fish-hooks attached. The jig is lowered into the sea where the fish are numerous, and is jigged up and down. Any herrings that come in contact with the hooks are caught and pulled into the boat.

Hence (1) **Jigger**, *sb.* a snatch made of two or three hooks tied together back to back; cf. jenny, *sb.*[2] 3; (2) **Jiggering**, *prp.* taking fish by means of a 'jigger.'

(1) Cum.[4] There was no bait or gut on the line, . . Blood was oozing from the jigger marks, *Whitehaven Free Press* (Oct. 31, 1896) 4. (2) *ib.* The watchers never mentioned jiggering.

JIG, *sb.*[2] Yks. Lan. Der. [dʒig.] 1. Colliery term: a self-acting incline so arranged that the full 'corves' travelling down pull the empty ones up. w.Yks. (S.J.C.), Lan. (C.B.C.) Hence **Jigger**, *sb.* the man who works the 'jig.' Lan. (C.B.C.) 2. *Comp.* (1) Jig-brow, a self-

3 A 2

acting incline. w.Yks. (T.T.); (2) -pin, a pin used to stop the machine in drawing. nw.Der.[1]

JIG, sb.[2] Obsol. Nhp.[1] e.An.[1] Nrf.[1] e.Suf. (F.H.) [dʒig.] In phr. *jig by jowl*, very close together; 'cheek by jowl.' See **Cheek**, sb. 2.

JIG, v.[2] n.Cy. Yks. Lan. Shr. Cor. [dʒig.] 1. Of hand wool-combing: to comb wool for the first time.

w.Yks. We came upon a live comber, probably the last of his race, 'jigging' away for life and death, CUDWORTH *Bradford* (1876) 218. e.Lan.[1]

Hence (1) **Jigger**, sb. the comb used in hand wool-combing; (2) **Jigger-lad**, a boy who combs the wool; (3) **Jiggin-sliver**, sb. the result of the first combing over.

w.Yks. (1) (J.T.) (2) Jigger lads an' bobbin turners, ECCLES *Leeds Olm.* (1875) 21. (3) (E.G.)

2. To separate ore from the refuse by means of a sieve.

Cor. The singing of the bucking and jigging maidens, TREGELLAS *Tales* (1868) 5; Cor.[1] To separate the ore from the refuse by means of a sieve; so placed in a box of water that by the continuous action of a brake-staff the ore is precipitated to the bottom of the sieve; Cor.[2]

Hence (1) **Jigger**, sb. (a) an ore-sifter; (b) a rough kind of sieve; (2) **Jiggin-sieve**, sb. a fine cloth which sifts the dust from oats or wheat when they are ground.

(1, a) n.Cy. (HALL.) Cor. The news of the accident spread like wildfire among the buddlers and jiggers, PEARCE *Esther Pentreath* (1891) bk. I. i; Cor.[1] The work is done by girls called jiggers. (b) Come ... will ee go and see the jiggers? TREGELLAS *Tales* (1865) 146. w.Cor. Took her meal with no other sifting than what it had in the jigger, BOTTRELL *Trad.* 3rd S. 60. (2) Shr.[2]

JIG, v.[3] s.Chs.[1] [dʒig.] 1. To wear out; gen. with *up*. Yoa·)n sóon jig· ydrsel· up ût dhaat· ree·t [Yo'n soon jig yursel up at that rate]. Dhis· misheyn)z gy'et·in jig-d [This machine's gettin' jigged].

Hence **Jigged up**, phr. bankrupt.

2. Of horses: to hurt the back or spine.

This mare's jigged her back. That hoss is jigged.

JIGE, see **Gig**, v.[2]

JIGGAMY, sb. Brks.[1] A name given to an implement, tool, &c., the proper name of which cannot be recalled at the moment; a 'thingamy.'

Gie us the jiggamy as stans' to yer han' ther.

JIGGATE, sb. Obs. Sc. A sail shaped like a leg of mutton. The same word as Gigot (q.v.).

Abd. We hope she'll prove a Lively Frigate ... And that she winna gee her jiggate To ilk weak blast, SHIRREFS *Poems* (1790) 252.

JIGGER, sb.[1] Sc. n.Cy. Nhb. Hmp. Cor. [dʒig(ə)r.] 1. A contemptuous term applied to a human being.

Bnff.[1] He's a queer jigger. Abd. 'He's a queer jigger.' 'The tailor's a coorse jigger.' It may be contemptuously applied to women. 'Jean Findlay's a strange jigger.' 'Did ever you see such a jigger o' a woman in a' yer life?' (G.W.) Cld. (JAM.) n.Cy. (HALL.), N.Cy.[1] An airy, swaggering person. 'A comical jigger.' Nhb.[1] Applied as a cant phrase to an out-of-the-way person.

2. A policeman. Hmp. (G.E.D.), (HALL.) 3. An ill-made thing. Cor.[1]

JIGGER, sb.[2] Irel. Wor. Glo. [dʒig(ə)r.] 1. A leg of mutton; a man's leg or thigh. See **Gigot**.

s.Wor. The flood come into our kitchen, very high. I went down to get summut out of the cubbard, and smack I went in up to my jiggers, PORSON *Quaint Wds.* (1875) 24. Glo. (S.S.B.)

2. A sail that projects over the stern of the boat. See **Jiggate**. N.I.[1] Set on a short mast called the 'jigger mast.'

JIGGER, sb.[3] Lan. [Not known to our other correspondents.] An entry; a narrow passage between houses. (S.K.C.)

JIGGER, sb.[4] Sc. Ken. Sus. [dʒigə(r).] An open vehicle for carrying trees from the forest; also in comp. **Jigger-wheels**.

Cai.[1] ne.Ken. A vehicle consisting of two wheels, a small frame, and a pole (called a dyster) for fastening the horse to it. 'Get the jigger for that tree' (H.M.). Sus. MORTON *Cyclo. Agric.* (1863).

JIGGER, sb.[5] Wm. Not. Oxf. Suf. Ken. [dʒigə(r).] 1. A shoemaker's tool.

Wm. Run t'jigger roond t'welt—it'll set it off (B.K.). e.Suf. For polishing the edge of the sole of a boot (F.H.). Ken. (H.M.)

2. A small notched wheel with which to cut pastry. Not.[2], Oxf.[1] *MS. add.*

JIGGER, sb.[6] Wor. [dʒigə(r).] A horizontal lathe used in china-making.

se.Wor.[1] s.Wor. A horizontal lathe on which flat ware such as plates and dishes are made. Still in use (H.K.).

JIGGER, sb.[7] Som. [dʒigə(r).] A vessel of potter's ware used in toasting cheese. (HALL.); W. & J. *Gl.* (1873).

JIGGER, sb.[8] s.Wm. A large kettle with a tap, for suspending over the fire. (J.A.B.)

JIGGER, sb.[9] Lon. Amer. [dʒigə(r).] 1. An illicit distillery.

The 'private' distilleries are the illicit ones; 'jiggers,' we call them, MAYHEW *Lond. Labour* (1851) I. 186.

2. Comp. **Jigger-worker**, a person who carries about spirits made at an illicit still.

Two, and sometimes three, female lace-sellers are also 'jigger-workers.' They carry about their persons pint bladders of 'stuff,' or 'jigger stuff' (spirit made at an illicit still), ib. 387.

3. One who works an illicit still.

'Jiggers' defrauding the Excise by working illicit stills, ib. (ed. 1862) IV. 24. [Amer. A small glass of whisky as dealt out to railroad hands, CARRUTH *Kansas Univ. Quart.* (Oct. 1890) l.]

JIGGER, v.[1] Cum.[4] [dʒigər.] To play truant. Cf. jig, v.[1] 9.

He gangs t'scheul i' t'mwornins, an' jiggers i' t'efterneuns.

JIGGER, v.[2] Glo. [dʒigə(r).] To put out of joint. Glo.[1]; Glo.[2] I'll jigger thee neck.

JIGGER, see **Giggot**, **Jagger**.

JIGGERED, pp. Wm. Yks. Lan. I.Ma. Not. [dʒigəd.] 1. Exhausted, tired; hard up; gen. with *up*.

Wm.[1] w.Yks. T'chap wor reight jiggered, *Yks. Wkly. Post* (June 6, 1896); (J.R.); w.Yks.[5] Av tramp'd a matter o' fotty mile to-daay, an' am fair jigger'd up. Lan. A generation or two would see it jiggered up if it wurno' for th' fresh blood ut's bein sent into it, BRIERLEY *Ab-o'th-Yate Yankeeland* (1885) v. Not.[2] I'm clean jiggered ûp.

2. With *up*: shut up, confined in prison.

I.Ma. Poor Mastha Dan had been nabbed ... and jiggered up in Peel Castle, CAINE *Deemster* (1887) 216, ed. 1889.

JIGGERMAROLE, sb. Lan. A rigmarole.

Th' landlord ... beginn'd a-kwestiunin' yung Bobber, who towd him aw th' jiggermarole, *New Wkly.* (Jan. 12, 1895) 7; When a person is full of pranks and 'marlocks,' they say he is full of 'jig-maroles' (S.W.).

JIGGEROO, sb. s.Chs.[1] [dʒigərü.] A kind of rot which affects potatoes, showing itself in brown marks on the surface.

Hence **Jiggeroo'd**, adj. affected with 'jiggeroo.'

JIGGER-PUMP, sb. Sus.[1] A pump used in breweries to force the beer into the vats.

JIGGER-SAW, sb. e.Suf. A kind of frame-saw, used for 'trenching.' (F.H.)

JIGGERY-POKERY, sb. Oxf. Wil. Suf. Also in form **jiggery-poke** Wil.[1] 1. Unfair dealing; deception.

Oxf. I was fair took in with that fellow's jiggery-pokery over that pony (G.O.). Wil. SLOW *Gl.* (1892); Wil.[1] n.Wil. 'There's jiggery-poke about!' 'That's all jiggery-poke.' Occas. used (G.E.D.).

2. Trifling, fooling. e.Suf. (F.H.)

JIGGET, v. and sb. Sc. Irel. Lan. War. Oxf. Brks. Wil. Som. Dev. Cor. Also written **jiggot** Oxf.[1]; and in form **jeeggit** Sc. (JAM.) [dʒi·git.] 1. v. To ride or walk at a jog-trot; to shake, jog; to dance up and down.

Sc. Here you stand jiggeting and sniggling and looking cunning, SCOTT *Abbot* (1820) xix; (JAM.) Ir. His car went jiggeting back empty to Ardnacreagh, BARLOW *Kerrigan* (1894) 39. Oxf.[1] *MS. add.* Brks.[1] Jiggettin' is moving up and down quickly, as in riding a child on the knee: this is always called jiggettin the child. Wil.[1] Here we go a jiggettin' along. Som. The fiddles was zcrapin' an' the village vok a' jiggeten', LEITH *Lemon Verbena* (1895) 75.

Hence (1) **Jiggeting**, ppl. adj. jolting, shaking; (2) **Jiggetty**, adj. (a) see (1); (b) fidgety; (3) **Jiggetty-jig** or **-jog**, a jog-trot style of travelling.

(1) ne.Lan.[1] (2, a) Wil.[1] This be a ter'ble jiggetty train. (b) SLOW *Gl.* (1892); Wil.[1] (3) Brks.[1] To markut, to markut, to buy a vat hog, Whoam agin, whoam agin, jiggetty jog. Dev.[2] Theäse yer ol' trap is awl jiggety-jig as us draves along. Cor.[2] Gwain jiggety-jig.

2. To gad or flaunt about.

War.² A jiggeting young hussy. w.Som.¹ Usually said of women with a distinctly depreciatory implication. 'Wuy· doa·n ur buy'd au·m, un neet bee au·vees jig·uteen ubaew·t !' [Why does she not stay at home, and not be always gadding (or dancing) about ?] **Dev.** A woman always jiggiting about the place, HARTIER *Evening with Hodge*, in *Eng. Illus. Mag.* (June 1896) 259.

3. sb. A dancing movement.

Lan. I ha' learnt th'.way now ; it's two jiggits and a shake, GASKELL *M. Barton* (1848) ix.

[1. Fr. *gigotter*, ' remuer vivement les jambes ' (LITTRÉ).]

JIGGET, see Gigot.

JIGGIN, int. Lei. Shr. [dʒi·gin.] **1.** A call of the wagoner or ploughman to the fore-horse to go to the off-side. Lei.¹ **2.** An address to a wagon-horse bidding him proceed. Shr.¹² Cf. **chiggin.**

JIGGIT(T, see Giggot.

JIGGLE, v. Yks. [dʒi·gl.] **1.** To contradict.

w.Yks. We higgled an' jiggled till booath on us sware, *Pudsey Olm.* (Nov. 1889).

2. To swindle, defraud. w.Yks. (S.P.U.)

JIGGLE, see Giggle, v.², Jaggle.

JIGGLE-JUGGLE, sb. w.Yks.⁵ A game ; see below. A lot of children get together and play at ' jiggle-juggle '— cluster together with their arms round each other's waists, and then dance about wildly till they all come to the ground, one upon the other.

JIGGOT, see Giggot, Gigot, Jiggit.

JIGGS, sb. pl. Obsol. e.An.¹ Suf.¹ e.Suf. (F.H.) [dʒigz.] Small dregs or sediment.

[Of Scand. origin ; cp. Norw. dial. *tjukk* (*tykke*), thick, used esp. of liquids (AASEN).]

JIGS, sb. e.Suf. In phr. by Jigs / a disguised oath. (F.H.)

JIKE, JILAFFER, see Gike, v., Gillyflower.

JILE, JILL, see Jail, sb., Gill, sb.²·⁴·⁷⁸

JILLBOW, JILLERY, see Gilbow, Gillery.

JILLET, sb. Sc. n.Cy. Cum. Also written **gillet** Sc. (JAM.) Per. (ib.) ; and in form **jilly** Sc. [dʒi·lit.] **1.** A giddy young woman, a jilt.

Sc. Gen. conjoined with some epithet, as ' idle jillet ' (JAM.) ; She's nae gilter jilly, MAIDMENT *Ballads* (1844) 14, ed. 1868. **Per.** The wiles o' knaves, and gillets' lures, Blackguards and cheats, STEWART *Character* (1857) 102. **e.Fif.** But since she's greinin' for't, the jillet, Sic like's it is she's welcome till it, LATTO *Tam Bodkin* (1864) xxvii. **Ayr.** A jillet brak his heart at last, BURNS *Sc. Bard*, st. 6. Lth. The ither night the jillet spak Right cheery owre a glass, MACNEILL *Poet. Wks.* (1801) 175, ed. 1856. **Edb.** Look at our wives, and jillets, linking, Foul day or fair, about the street, MACNEILL *Bygane Times* (1811) 28. **Peb.** They're jillets baith, their skin's a token, AFFLECK *Poet. Wks.* (1836) 80. **n.Cy.** *Border Gl.* (Coll. L.L.B.) Cum. Thou cannot act a jillet's part, GILPIN *Sngs.* (1866) 383 ; Cum.¹

2. A young woman entering on the state of puberty. Per. (JAM.)

[1. Prob. a dim. of the ME. proper name *Gille*, Jill (CHAUCER).]

JILL-FLIRT, JILL-HOOTER, see Gill-flirt, Gill-hooter.

JILL-HOOTER, sb. e.Suf. An old man or woman, given to grumbling or complaining. (F.H.) See **Gill-hooter.**

JILLING-BO'OR, see Julian bower.

JILLIVER, JILLOUS, see Gillyflower, Jealous.

JILLY-, JILLY-HOOTER, see Jelly-, v., Gill-hooter.

JILLY-HOOTING, vbl. sb. Nrf. ? Cheating ; deception. I'm awake to your jilly-huting, *s.An. N. & Q.* (1860) I. 76.

JILLY-JOG, sb. w.Yks. The game of ' Jenny Jones ' (q.v.). GOMME *Games* (1894) I. 280.

JILP, see Gilp, sb.¹, v.

JILT, sb.¹ Der.¹ War.² [dʒilt.] An opprobrious term for a girl ; a slattern, a prostitute. See **Jillet.**

JILT, sb.² Stf. War. Wor. Glo. [dʒilt.] A state of rags and jags and tatters.

War.² Her shawl was all of a jilt. Stf., War., Wor., Glo. In a jilt of rags, NORTHALL *Flk-Phr.* (1894).

JILT, see Jelt.

JIM, sb.¹ e.An. [dʒim.] A vehicle composed of an axle, two wheels, and a pole for moving timber. See **Gill, sb.³**

---

e.An.¹, Nrf. (W.W.S.) Suf. MORTON *Cyclo. Agric.* (1863) ; Suf.¹ So as the rolling Jim did me control, The Lord above have mercy on my soul, *Epitaph in Hoxne Churchyard.* e.Suf. (F.H.)

JIM, sb.² Yks. Glo. Lon. Suf. In *comp.* (1) **Jim-cat,** a tom-cat ; (2) **-crake,** a ridiculous person ; (3) **-crow,** (a) a disreputable hat ; (b) a street-actor.

(1) e.Suf. (F.H.) (2) m.Yks.¹ (3, a) Glo. ' Look at this 'ere owld Jim-crow o' mine,' he cried, .. plucking off his hat, BUCKMAN *Darke's Sojourn* (1890) xvi. (b) Lon. The street-actors—as clowns, ' Billy Barlows,' ' Jim Crows,' and others, MAYHEW *Lond. Labour* (1851) I. 4.

JIM, adj. Sc. Lan. e.An. Ken. Also written **gim** Fif. e.An.¹ e.Suf. Ken. ; **jimm** Lan. [dʒim.] Neat, spruce. See **Jimp,** adj.

Sc. (JAM.) Fif. Gay as May-morning, tidy, gim, and clean, TENNANT *Anster* (1812) 28, ed. 1871. **Lan.** GROSE (1790) *MS. add.* (C.) ne.Lan.¹ s.Lan. PICTON *Dial.* (1865). e.An.¹, Nrf. (W.W.S.) w.Nrf. She is a timid woman, not at all 'jim,' with a doleful 'whuling' air, ORTON *Beeston Ghost* (1884) 5. e.Suf. (F.H.) Ken. (K., s.v. Gimmes).

[The payntit povne pasand with plomys gym, Kest vp his taill, a provd plesand quheil rym, DOUGLAS *Eneados* (1513), ed. 1874, IV. 85.]

JIM-BANG, JIME, see Jing-bang, Jamb.

JIMES, sb. pl. Obs. Irel. Also written **jhimes** ; and in form **jhemes.** Pieces.

Wxf.¹ Amang wefty jhemes, 'cha jeist ee-rid apan, 98.

JIMMANY, JIMMENY, see Gemminy.

JIMMER, sb.¹ Nhb. Dur. Cum. Wm. Yks. Lan. Lin. e.An. Also written **gimmer** Nhb.¹ Wm. w.Yks.² ne.Lan.¹ e.An.¹ ; and in forms **gemmer** w.Yks.⁵ ne.Lan.¹ ; **jamer** Cum.¹⁴ ; **jammer** w.Yks. ; **jemmer** Cum.¹⁴ n.Yks. Lan. n.Lan.¹ ; **jymer** Cum.⁴ [dʒi·mə(r).] **1.** A hinge, esp. a small hinge for a closet or desk-door ; gen. in pl. ; also in comp. **Jimmer-hinges.** See **Gimmal,** sb.¹

n.Cy. GROSE (1790) ; N.Cy.¹² Nhb.¹, Dur.¹ s.Dur. She's brokken t'gimmers off t'closet door (J.E.D.). Lakel.² T'door jimmers wants greasin'. Cum.¹⁴ Wm. The door hangs loose on its gimmers (B.K.). n.Yks. (R.H.H.), n.Yks.² ne.Yks.¹ T'decar beeals oot on t'jimmer. e.Yks. (R.H.H.) w.Yks. The door's off t'jimmers (J.W.D.) ; w.Yks.¹²³⁴, Lan. (C.W.D.), n.Lan.¹, ne.Lan.¹, n.Lin.¹, e.An.¹ e.Nrf. MARSHALL *Rur. Econ.* (1787). Suf.¹ e.Suf. It is unlucky to sit opposite the 'jimmers' of the table when playing at cards, *Flk-Lore Rec.* (1880) III. pt. i. 127 ; (F.H.)

Hence **Jimmerly,** weak, ill-jointed. Cum.¹⁴

2. Phr. *to be loose i' (on) t'jimmers,* to work loosely, move easily.

w.Yks. This knife-blade's lowse i' t'jimmers (Æ.B.) ; His tongue wor hung sa laus on t'jimmers wol he cuddant control it, TOM TREDDLEHOYLE *Bairnsla Ann.* (1881) 17.

3. pl. Broken pieces, fragments.

m.Yks.¹ A plate much cracked, but still unbroken, will be said to be 'all in jimmers.' w.Yks.² A plate is said when badly broken to be broken all to jimmers.

Hence *hung i' jimmers,* phr. to be ready to fall to pieces at any moment.

w.Yks. Owd Jim Batley's varry owd nah, he's hung i' jimmers (S.K.C.) ; A setpot hung i' jimmers, TOM TREDDLEHOYLE *Exhebishan* (1857) 4.

4. The fork of a tree, one of the pairs of a forked branch.

Nhb.¹ 'Tyek off that gimmer,' a common expression used by woodmen for ' Take off one of the forks only.'

JIMMER, v. and sb.² ? Obs. Sc. **1.** v. To make a disagreeable noise on a violin. Rxb. (JAM.)

2. sb. The sound made by a violin when not well played.

Rxb. O sweet bewitching piece o' timmer—Could I but claw your wame, ye limmer, Like W——y M——s, There wad be mony a jimmer, I'm sure, atween us, A. SCOTT *Poems* (1805) 2 (ib.).

JIMMERY, int. Dev. Cor. [dʒi·məri.] **1.** An exclamation : a form of Gemminy (q.v.).

Cor. Awh, Jimmery ! wasn't there a kick-up, PARR *Adam and Eve* (1880) II. 143 ; Cor.²

2. Comb. **Jimmery-chry** or **-cry,** an exclamation of surprise.

Dev. Aw ! jimmery cry ! Whot's thur adðed now, than ! HEWETT *Peas. Sp.* (1892). Cor. 'Oh, jimmery-chry !' Esther burst out laughing, BARING-GOULD *Curgenven* (1893) xxxviii ; Cor.²

JIMMY, *sb.*[1] Wil. Dor. Som. Dev. Also written gimmy Dor.[1]; and in forms **gimmace** (prop. a *pl.*) Wil. w.Som.[1]; **jemmy** Som.; **jemy** Dev. [dʒi·mi.] **1.** A hinge of two parts working on a joint, a 'jimmer'; *gen.* in *pl.* See **Gimmal,** *sb.*[1] **2.**

Wil. *Obs.* (G.E.D.), Dor.[1] **Som.** *Gent. Mag.* (1794) 110; A pair of jimmies, *ib.* (1793) 1083; When a criminal is gibbetted, or hung in irons or chains, he is said to be hung in gimmaces, most prob. because the apparatus swings about as if on hinges, JENNINGS *Obs. Dial. w.Eng.* (1825). **Dev.** Tha jimmies ov they new doors craketh ; yü'd best ways graise [grease] um! HEWETT *Peas. Sp.* (1892); *Horae Subsecivae* (1777) 229.

2. *pl.* Handcuffs. w.Som.[1]

JIMMY, *sb.*[2] n.Yks. [dʒi·mi.] A sort of hooked fork with two prongs for drawing together the rails on which the tubs run, used in whinstone quarries. (C.V.C.)

JIMMY, *sb.*[3] *Obs.* or *obsol.* w.Yks. A nightdress, a 'shimmy,' a chemise. *Leeds Merc. Suppl.* (June 2, 1894); (S.P.U.)

JIMMY, *sb.*[4] and *adj.*[1] Irel. Dur. Lakel. Yks. Lan. Stf. Lin. War. Shr. Lon. e.An. Ken. Wil. Cor. Also in form **Jemmy** ne.Lan. Lin.[1] Lon. Cmb. Ken. [dʒi·mi, dʒe·mi.]

1. *sb.* In *comb.* (1) **Jimmy-burty,** a Will-o'-th'-Wisp ; (2) **-labbet,** a liar ; (3) **-longlegs,** (4) **-neck,** the heron, *Ardea cinerea* ; (5) **-swiver,** a state of trembling ; (6) **-twitcher,** an insect ; see below.

(1) Cmb. (HALL.) (2) Cor.[2] (3, 4) ne.Lan. SWAINSON *Birds* (1885) 145. (5) Wil.[1] 'Lor, Miss, how you did froughten I! I be all of a jimmy-swiver,' and she visibly trembled, which was what she meant, JEFFERIES *Greene Ferne Farm* (1880) vii. (6) Lakel.[2] A wire-worm wi' as many feet o' them as thers days in a year. Wm.[1] Called also a Crackel-neck. It is a small hard-backed black insect (about ¼ of an inch long) which springs up suddenly when disturbed.

2. Phr. *Jimmy Johnson squeeze me,* an exclamation expressive of surprise.

War. Commonly used (J.W.R.); War.[2] Common between fifty and sixty years ago. 'But a Brummagem lad Is not to be had; If he is, Jimmy Johnson squeeze me.'

3. A generic name for a silly person.

w.Ir. Mr. —— meeting Jimmy one morning on the road, LOVER *Leg.* (1848) I. 107. e.Suf. (F.H.)

4. A sheep's head ; also used of a large human head.

n.Dur. *N. & Q.* (1894) 8th S. v. 437. w.Yks. They called sheep-heeads Jimmys at that market, HARTLEY *Tales,* and S. 106. Lin.[1] Buy a jemmy and pluck. Lon. They clubbed together for a good supper of tripe, or had a 'prime hot Jemmy a-piece,' MAYHEW *Lond. Labour* (1851) II. 42. e.Suf. (F.H.), Ken. (W.F.S.) Wil. SLOW *Gl.* (1892); Wil.[1]

5. The nose. e.Suf. Don't turn up your jimmy at me (F.H.).

6. *adj.* Silly ; half-witted.

Stf., Shr. All for my jimmy old nose, *Flk-Lore Jrn.* (1886) IV. 260. e.Suf. (F.H.)

JIMMY, *adj.*[2] Sc. Dur. Yks. Lei. Nhp. Wor. Shr. Lon. e.An. Sus. Hmp. Som. Amer. Also written gimmy Nhp.[1] e.An.[1]; **jemmy** Lei.[1] Nhp.[1] Lon. [dʒi·mi, dʒe·mi.] **1.** Neat, spruce, smart ; neatly made ; dexterous ; also used as *adv.* See **Jim,** *adj.*

Sc. (JAM.), Abd. (*ib.*), Dur.[1], w.Yks.[1], Lei. (W.W.S.), Lei.[1] Nhp.[1] 'He's a gimmy little man.' Never I believe applied to females. w.Wor. As jimmy as a two-year-old, S. BEAUCHAMP *N. Hamilton* (1875) III. 46. Shr. Comin' along right jimmy, BURNE *Flk-Lore* (1883) vi; Shr.[1] The owd mon an' ôôman wun comin' alung together as jimmy as yo' plässen. Lon. Dressing themselves up in the Jemmy taste, with half caps, many ribbons, *Low Life* (1764) 63. e.An.[1], e.Suf. (F.H.) Sus., Hmp. HOLLOWAY. w.Som.[1] Oh, that's jimmy, and no mistake. They got on jimmy like together, 'vore thick there up-country 'osebird comed along. [Amer. GREEN *Virginia Flk-Sp.* (1899).]

2. Slight, flimsy, ill-made.

w.Yks.[2] Usually applied to badly-made furniture.

JIMP, *sb.* Sc. (JAM.) A thin slip of leather put between the inner and outer soles of a shoe, to give an appearance of thickness.

JIMP, *adj., adv.* and *v.* Sc. Irel. Nhb. Dur. Lakel. Yks. Lan. Not. Nhp. Brks. Also written **gimp** Sc. Ant. N.Cy.[1] Nhb.[1] [dʒimp.] **1.** *adj.* Slender, small ; neat, elegant. Cf. **jump,** *adj.*[2]

Sh.I. His airm he's pat roond her middle sae jimp, STEWART *Tales* (1892) 237. n.Sc. His bonny jimp middle, BUCHAN *Ballads* (1828) I. 186, ed. 1875. Cai.[1] Frf. Wi' his airm roon' the by nae means jimp waist o' the leddy, WILLOCK *Rosetty Ends* (1886) 37, ed. 1889. w.Sc. She was as jimp as a young girl, NAPIER *Flk-Lore* (1879) 88. Fif. Waist sae jimp, ane might it span, GRAY *Poems* (1811) 198. Rnf. She was sae jimp and sma', ALLAN *Hours* (1896) 26. Ayr. Thy waist sae jimp, BURNS *Parnassus' Hill,* st. 2. Lak. I was yince on a time jimp enough aboot the waist, MURDOCH *Readings* (1895) I. 71. Lth. Thy wee feet, sae jimp an' tender, BALLANTINE *Poems* (1856) 72. Edb. Wi' waist drawn in, sae tight and jimp, M'DOWALL *Poems* (1839) 118. Slk. He was jimp an' gay, HOGG *Poems* (ed. 1865) 110. Dmf. Nae mair wi' kilted coats we see Thy middle jimp and sma', JOHNSTONE *Poems* (1820) 78. N.Cy.[1] Nhb. Let me clasp that girdle jimp, RICHARDSON *Borderer's Table-bk.* (1846) VI. 353; Nhb.[1] Cum. Jimp lively black fustin britches, ANDERSON *Ballads* (ed. 1808) 191 ; Cum.[1,4] n.Yks.[1]; n.Yks.[4] Sha's gitten ez jimp a waist ez onny lass. w.Yks. WILLAN *List Wds.* (1811). Lan. (J.A.P.), Lan.[1], ne.Lan.[1] Not. She's jimp waisted (J.H.B.). Brks.[1]

Hence (1) **Jimpey,** *sb.* a short gown without skirts reaching only to the middle, worn by cottage women ; (2) **Jimpsey,** *adj.* neat, smart ; cf. **dimpsey** ; (3) **Jimpy,** (*a*) *adj.* slender ; (*b*) *adv.* slenderly ; tightly.

(1) Sc. To mak me a coat and a jimpey, JAMIESON *Ballads* (1806) I. 310. (2) Nhp.[1] (3, *a*) Sc. Ye're a jimpy black body, no like the Nesbit lads, who hae aye been stoot and fair, SWAN *Aldersyde* (ed. 1892) 30. Per. Lizzy laced her genty waist, Sae jimpy neat an' sma', MONTEATH *Dunblane* (1835) 116, ed. 1887. Rnf. Her jimpy waist, it was sae sma', ALLAN *Hours* (1896) 34. Ayr. Sae jimpy lac'd her genty waist, BURNS *Bonie Ann,* st. 1. Edb. With his arm round her jimpy waist, MOIR *Mansie Wauch* (1828) xvii. Dmf. CROMEK *Remains* (1810) 130. Nhb. As her jimpy waist be spanned, RICHARDSON *Borderer's Table-bk.* (1846) VI. 374. (*b*) Sc. Clasp her waist sae jimpy sma', NICOLL *Poems* (ed. 1843) 139. Lth. Bawbee dolls the fashions apit, Sae rosy cheekit, jimpy shapit, An' wee bit lasses gazed an' gapit Wi' mouth an' ee, BALLANTINE *Poems* (1856) 9. Dmf. Sae jimpy laced an' sma', CROMEK *Remains* (1810) 6.

2. Scanty ; tight ; narrow ; deficient in quantity.

Cai.[1] Abd. A jimp full o' the timmer ladle, ALEXANDER *Johnny Gibb* (1871) xxxviii. Per. The captain o' the Tarshish boat was just on the jimp side o' ceevility, *Sandy Scott* (1897) 78. Fif. Jimp time he took to steek his mou', TENNANT *Papistry* (1827) 120. Dmb. Wi' it the jimpest nook Would ser' To bed and blanket half a score and mair, SALMON *Gowodean* (1868) 83. Rnf. Spurn the imp wi' soul sae jimp, WEBSTER *Rhymes* (1835) 128. Ayr. Weel I wat that your ellwand would hae been a jimp measure, GALT *Entail* (1823) xxxi. Lnk. Wee toddlin' breekums Tak' ye the jimpest road, MURDOCH *Doric Lyre* (1873) 59. Wgt. The evidence was 'a wee jimp,' FRASER *Wigtown* (1877) 259. Ant. Gimp measure, *Ballymena Obs.* (1892). N.Cy.[1] n.Yks.[1]; n.Yks.[4] 'It's jimp i' t'paper, an' jimp i' pot,' i.e. light both as to weight and measure.

Hence **Jimply,** *adv.* scarcely ; straitly ; smoothly.

Sc. Bid them agree on an income that could jimply afford braws for one, KEITH *Bonnie Lady* (1897) 9. Frf. There's jimply enough for ourselves, BARRIE *Minister* (1891) iii. Per. Wha's snouts and chins in friendly greetin' Were jimply twa strae braidths frae meetin', SPENCE *Poems* (1898) 189. Ayr. Jimply a mile frae this spot, AINSLIE *Poems* (ed. 1892) 76. Lnk. I fear he jimply has a share O' common brains, RODGER *Poems* (1898) 178, ed. 1897. Gall. She jimply 'scapit frae a swoon, NICHOLSON *Poet. Wks.* (1814) 72, ed. 1897. n.Yks.[2] It fits ower jimply. Lan.[1]

3. *adv.* Scarcely.

Sc. She had been married to Sir Richard jimp four months, SCOTT *Antiquary* (1816) xxiv. Fif. What wi' swesch-trump, what wi' bells, The Anster folks were jimp themsells, TENNANT *Papistry* (1827) 49. Ayr. In stature he was jimp the ordinary size, GALT *Gilhaize* (1823) vi. Lnk. He wasna blin', but jimp could see, THOMSON *Musings* (1881) 118. Lth. I doot this dream Is jimp fit matter for my whim, LUMSDEN *Sheep-head* (1892) 119. Gall. Jimp a yard (A.W.). Dur. GIBSON *Up-Weardale Gl.* (1870).

4. *v.* To contract, curtail ; to make too narrow ; to give too little measure, weight, or room.

Bnff.[1] The taylor gimpit's quyte i' the mackan. He gimpit 'im in the mizer. He gimpit the weight an unce or mair. His father gimps 'im gey sair wee siller. A bocht our mony nout this weentir, an' gimpit masel' o' siller t'get sheep. Lth. The nappie ale to warm the bluid, Gaun roun', trowth was nae jimpit, Nor sma' that night,

BRUCE *Poems* (1813) II. 101. **Edb.** On Saturday the night's no lang, But unco jimpet, FORBES *Poems* (1812) 82. **Lakel.²** Thoo's jimp't it off far ower short at t'back.

Hence (1) **Jimped-in,** *ppl. adj.* tightly laced ; (2) **Jimped-up,** *ppl. adj.* affected in dress and manners.

(1) **Dur.¹** **s.Dur.** When a woman tight-laces she is said to be 'jimped in at t'waist' (J.E.D.). (2) **n.Yks.²**

JIMP, JIMPSEN, see Gimp, Jump, *sb.¹, v.,* Gimson.

JIM-RAG, JIN, see Jamrag, Gin, *sb.¹⁸,* Jen.

JINCH, *adj.* *Obs.* **Sc.** Neat, spruce, 'jimp.'

Abd. Right jinch he was and fell weel fawr'd, SKINNER *Poems* (1809) 10.

JINDERING, *prp.* **Lan.¹** [Not known to our correspondents.] Seeking a mate, 'gendering.'

JINDING, *prp.* **Nrf.** A corruption of 'adjoining.'

But for us [wherrymen] many of the willages jindin' the rivers would find freightage rather awk'ard, PATTERSON *Man and Nat.* (1895) 43 ; (M.C.H.B.)

JINDY, JING, see Gindy, Ging, *v.²*

JING, *sb.* **Sc. Chs.** Also in form **jings s.Chs.¹** [dȝiŋ.] In phr. *by jing !* a common oath : by jingo !

Abd. In a wee the chiel, by jing, Clapt her on Mungo's pate, COCK *Strains* (1810) II. 140. **Frf.** By jing, you look as brave as Hector, MORISON *Poems* (1790) 177. **Ayr.** While Willie lap, and swoor by jing, BURNS *Halloween* (1785) st. 9. **Lnk.** Noo, by jing ! MURDOCH *Doric Lyre* (1873) 74. **Peb.** Anither jug or twa, by jing, .AYFLECK *Poet. Wks.* (1836) 90. **Gall.** Now, what's the cut ? The Jack, by jing, MACTAGGART *Encycl.* (1824) 459, ed. 1876. **s.Chs.¹** (s.v. By).

JING, *v.* I.Ma. To crowd, push ; to move along.

'Jing over,' move up. 'Jing in, can't you?' 'I've jung in as far as I can get.' What are you jinging people like that for ! (S.M.) ; We can get in without such jingin' and scrunchin', RYDINGS *Tales* (1895) 63.

[Ir. *ding,* a wedge (FOLEY) ; Gael. *dinn,* to press, squeeze (MACBAIN).]

JING-BANG, *sb.* **Sc. Irel. Aus. Amer.** Also written **ging-bang** Sc. Don.; and in form **jimbang** Aus. [dȝi·ŋ·baŋ.] In phr. *the whole jing-bang,* the whole party ; the whole affair.

Sc. The officer was supposed to protect ... 'the hale ging-bang of the processionists,' WRIGHT *Life* (1897) 7. **Bnff.¹, Cld.** (JAM.) **Lnk.** It's no aboot ane or anither, But the hale jing-bang, EWING *Poems* (1892) 30. **N.I.¹** I don't care a pin about the whole jing-bang of them. **s.Don.** A number, a party, as 'the whole ging-bang,' SIMMONS *Gl.* (1890). [Aus. The best thing you can do is to leave the whole jimbang in his hands, BOLDREWOOD *Colon. Reformer* (1890) II. xvi. **Amer.** To use an expressive Americanism, all the whole 'jing-bang'—could teach the ignorant jackass of a farmer, JEFFERIES *Hodge* (1880) 18.]

JINGLE, *sb.¹* **Sc. Irel.** 1. Gravel, shingle, 'chingle.' Dmf. (JAM.), **N.I.¹** 2. The smooth water at the back of a stone in a river. **Ags.** (JAM.)

JINGLE, *sb.²* and *v.* **Sc. Irel. n.Cy. Yks. Lan. Lin. Lei. Nhp. War. Dev. Cor. Aus.** Also written **gingle Abd.** [dȝi·ŋ(g)L] 1. *sb.* In *comb.* (1) **Jingle-brains,** a wild, noisy, talkative person ; (2) -**cap,** see (4) ; (3) -**harrows,** harrows the bulls of which are curved so as to run free of each other ; (4) — **the bonnet,** a game ; see below ; (5) — the key, the cry of the yellow-ammer.

(1) **w.Yks.¹, s.Lan.¹, Nhp.¹** (2) n.Cy. (HALL), **N.Cy.¹** (3) n.Lin.¹ (4) **Rxb.** A game in which two or more put a half-penny each, or any piece of coin, into a cap or bonnet. After jingling or shaking them together, they are thrown on the ground ; and he who has most heads when it is his turn to jingle, gains the stakes which were put into the bonnet (JAM.). (5) **Lnk.** There aften the yawkie sang 'Jingle the key,' At least it seemed sae to wee laddies like me, NICHOLSON *Idylls* (1870) 38.

2. Phr. *to play jingle,* to jingle, rattle.

Edb. Made skelf and plates, a' things play jingle, LIDDLE *Poems* (1821) 196.

3. Noisy mirth ; a merry, noisy party.

Edb. Mak' the cottage resound Wi' hamely, heartfelt jingle, M°DOWALL *Poems* (1839) 94. **Lei.¹**

4. A covered two-wheeled car ; a gentleman's jaunting-car.

Dub. The maimed attorney was now thrown across a horse and carried to a jingle, BARRINGTON *Sketches* (1830) III. xxvi. **s.Ir.**

(C.D.) [Aus. Once common in Melbourne, still used in Brisbane and some other towns (MORRIS).]

5. An instant.

Abd. Tibby was back just in a gingle, BEATTIE *Parings* (1801) 4, ed. 1873.

6. *pl.* The spangles or beads attached to a lacemaker's bobbins.

Nhp.¹ An appropriate name, from the sound produced by the movement of the bobbins. Not altogether useless ornaments, as is *gen.* imagined, as they give additional weight to the bobbins, and thereby tighten the stitches and give firmness to the texture of the lace ; **Nhp.²** These jingles are more for ornament than use, and are adopted from an ambition to make the pillow look smart. Old coins are frequently used for this purpose ; hence that eyesore to antiquaries, the perforation through the rim.

7. A string of glass beads. Dev., Cor. (R.H.H.)

8. *v.* Phr. *to jingle and jangle,* to wrangle, quarrel.

War. They kept jingling and jangling (A.F.F.).

JINGLED, *ppl. adj.* **Bdf.** Mingled, blended, confused together. (J.W.B.)

JINGLING, *ppl. adj.* **Sc. Yks. Not. Lei. Nhp. War. Wor. Brks.** Also written **gingling** Sc. 1. In *comb.* (1) **Jingling Johnnie,** a hurdy-gurdy ; (2) -**match,** a game or dance ; see below.

(1) **w.Yks.** It wor play'd we a swape like a box-organ or jinglin' Jonny, TOM TREDDLEHOYLE *Trip ta Lunnan* (1851) 29. (2) **se.Wor.¹** A kind of dance. **Brks.** Master Tom mounts on Benjy's shoulders and beholds a jingling match in all its glory. It is a quaint game immensely amusing to look at. . . A large roped ring is made, into which are introduced a dozen or so of big boys and young men who mean to play ; these are carefully blinded and turned loose into the ring, and then a man is introduced, not blindfolded, with a bell hung round his neck and his two hands tied behind him. Of course every time he moves, the bell must ring, as he has no hand to hold it, and so the dozen blindfolded men have to catch him, HUGHES *T. Brown* (1856) ii.

2. Noisy, chattering ; nonsensical.

Sc. Prelates spend their short glass, with gingling pyebald orations, SR. *Presby. Eloq.* (ed. 1847) 86. **Not.** Mr. W—'s allus so jinglin' and discursive (L.C.M.).

3. Rattling, wild, leading a disreputable life ; careless ; slipshod.

Not.¹ A's a jinglin' feller. **Lei.¹** A goos about it in a jinglin' sort o' wee ! **Nhp.¹** A sad jingling chap. **War.²**

JINGO-RING, *sb.* and *v.* **Sc. Nrf.** 1. *sb.* A children's game ; see below ; also part of the game of 'Merry-ma-tanzie,' q.v.

ne.Sc. Not infrequently joining hands like a company of school children at jingo-ring—leaping and shouting by way of accompaniment to the hymn, *Gordonhaven* (1887) 92. **Elg.** He is dancing a Highland fling, Or a sort of Spanish jingo-ring, TESTER *Poems* (1865) 43. **Fif.** Girls chose the quieter sports—'merry-my-tanzie, jing-a-ring,' COLVILLE *Vernacular* (1899) 13. **Slg.** The last at nicht in jingo-ring, TOWERS *Poems* (1885) 161. **Ayr.** At jing-ga-ring, buttons, the bat or the ba', LAING *Poems* (1897) 11. **Lnk.** Children in Glasgow have a favourite game, in which a number join hands, and go round slowly in a circle, singing what may be written—'Here we go by jingo ring, By jingo ring, by jingo ring ; Here we go by jingo ring And round about Mary matan'sy,' *N. & Q.* (1868) 4th S. ii. 324. **Lth.** Wi' paips, an' bools, an' jingo-ring, An' 'Through the needle-e'e !' SMITH *Merry Bridal* (1866) 35. **Nrf.** The children form a ring and dance round singing. At the last word they all fall down, GOMME *Games* (1894) I. 284.

2. *v.* To encircle, as though dancing 'jingo-ring.'

Per. Here a fairy band of blue bells Jingo-ring an aged boulder, HALIBURTON *Ochil Idylls* (1891) 158.

JINGUMBOB, *sb.* **Lan. I.W.** [dȝi·ŋəmbob.] A knick-nack.

Lan. Sum mak ov a jingumbob ur anuther, SCHOLES *Tim Gamwattle* (1857) 6. **I.W.¹**

JINGY-JOG, *sb.* **w.Yks.** The game of 'Jenny Jones' (q.v.). GOMME *Games* (1894) I. 280.

JINIFER, JINIPPEROUS, see Ginifer, Jinniprous.

JINK, *sb.¹* ? *Obs.* **Sc.** A long and narrow aperture, a 'chink.'

Ayr. Just open a wee bit jinkie o' this window, GALT *Gilhaize* (1823) xxiii. **Edb.** The back-window being up a jink, I heard the two confabbing, MOIR *Mansie Wauch* (1828) xxv.

JINK, $v.^1$ and $sb.^2$ Sc. n.Cy. Nhb. Cum. Yks. Dor. Nfld. Also in form **jenk** n.Sc. (JAM.) Elg. N.Cy.¹ Nhb.¹ [d**ʒiŋk**, d**ʒeŋk**.] 1. *v.* To elude ; to swerve quickly aside ; to dodge.

Sc. Blinking and jinking in, in that fashion, SCOTT *Antiquary* (1816) xxv. n.Sc. (JAM.) e.Sc. Ye're safest to jink them, SKTOUN *Sunshine* (1895) iv. Kcd. Lang he watched the belles and beaux . . . Hoo the former jinkt their joes, GRANT *Lays* (1884) 113. **Frf.** He had a craft o' his ain, That, like the white sea-mew, jinket the jaws On the briny breist o' the main, WATT *Poet. Sketches* (1880) 20. **Per.** Black-a-viced care . . . There's some think to jink him by crossin' the sea, HALIBURTON *Horace* (1886) 49. **Fif.** Unto a wife he ne'er was linket ; The bonnie lasses ay he jinket, GRAY *Poems* (1811) 74. **Dmb.** I can ne'er bide there again without some kind o' subterranean passage up the garret whaur I can jink the beagles, CROSS *Disruption* (1844) xxviii. **Rnf.** Some steal through life just wi' jinkin', Whase dealings are no very straught, WEBSTER *Rhymes* (1835) 20. **Ayr.** Rab slips out an' jinks about, Behint the muckle thorn, BURNS *Halloween* (1785) l. 48. **Lnk.** In spirit I'll be there Gin I can jink Saint Peter's care, COGHILL *Poems* (1890) 114. e.Lth. I made ready to jink him, for I couldna ha' strucken him back, HUNTER *J. Inwick* (1895) 193. **Edb.** If ye think . . . my vengeance aye ye'll jink, You're wrang indeed, McDOWALL *Poems* (1839) 54. **Slk.** I didna see the queen o' the fairies jink by the corner, HOGG *Tales* (1838) 232, ed. 1866. He nippet the blossom and jinkt the thorn, REID *Poems* (1894) 127. **Gall.** What's jinking, and slinking, and crouching night and day, MACTAGGART *Encycl.* (1824) 334, ed. 1876. n.Cy. *Border Gl.* (Coll. L.L.B.) **Nhb.** Roun' the gudeman swift went jinkin', And by him slippit, STRANG *Earth Fiend* (1892) II. st. 5. 2. To move quickly ; to dance ; to jaunt ; to ramble about.

Sc. And see the lammies jinkin' about their mithers, ROY *Horse-man's Wd.* (1895) ix. **Sh.I.** Dey whirled, an' cleekit, an' jinket sae lichtly, it wis a graand sicht ta see dem wi' a bricht mûnlicht nicht, STEWART *Tales* (1892) 89. **Bch.** Then ilka wanter wudlins jinks To hear a tune, TARRAS *Poems* (1804) 12 (JAM.). **Abd.** Through ilk dirty corner jink, Your wig to please, CADENHEAD *Bon-Accord* (1853) 178. w.Sc. (JAM.) **Slg.** He gard us nimble kiss an' jink At dancing Bob at the Bowster, GALLOWAY *Luncarty* (1804) 67. **Rnf.** An jinken 'bout the hallan wa', ALLAN *Hours* (1836) 14. **Ayr.** Guid auld Scotch Drink, Whether thro' wimplin worms thou jink, BURNS *Sc. Drink* (1786) st. 2. **Lnk.** Aye chirpin' an' jinkin' as onward ye fly, TENNANT *Wayside Musings* (1872) 67. **Lth.** She gazit doon the glen where the burnie jinks, LUMSDEN *Sheep-head* (1892) 145. **Slk.** Rinnin jinking after fok's dochters, HOGG *Tales* (1838) 239, ed. 1866. **Gall.** Jink aroun' wi' airy wheel To hide the bareness o' your keel, NICHOLSON *Poet. Wks.* (1814) 83, ed. 1897. n.Cy. (J.L. 1783) ; N.Cy.¹ **Nhb.** Oh ! were my limbs as ance they were to jink across the green, CHARNLEY *Fisher's Garland* (1841) 6. **Cum.** Ritson Joe can cap them aw For jinkin' an' careerin', GILPIN *Sngs.* (1866) 271.

Hence (1) **Jinker**, *sb.* a fast horse; (2) **Jinking**, *ppl. adj.* wriggling, quickly moving ; *fig.* dexterous, crafty, evasive.

(1) **Ayr.** That day ye was a jinker noble, BURNS *To his Auld Mare*, st. 7. (2) **Per.** Lawyers ana [! an' a'] a jinkin' band, Maun' tak' their summons from that hand, HALIBURTON *Dunbar* (1895) 36. **Lnk.** Tiny jinking eels, which he captures in his outspread palms, WATSON *Poems* (1853) xi. **Dmf.** Doon the jinkin' burn I'd dauner when the mune was fu', REID *Poems* (1894) 57. 3. To play tricks ; to frolic ; to be gay and thoughtless.

Bch. Jove did jink Arcesius Upo' a noble lady, FORBES *Ulysses* (1785) 15. **Dmb.** They who would wi' Gibbie clink or jink Maun ken to soop the ice to ony rink, SALMON *Gowodean* (1868) 74. n.Cy. (HALL.), Nhb.¹

Hence (1) **Jinker**, *sb.* a giddy girl ; an immoral woman; a wag ; (2) **Jinking**, (*a*) *sb.* a frolic, trick ; a quick movement ; (*b*) *ppl. adj.* gay, sportive.

(1) **Sc.** I am a genteel jinker, RAMSAY *Tea-Table Misc.* (1724) I. 99 ; Wanton jinkers, MAIDMENT *Pasquils* (1868) 297. **Rnf.** Frae dark close mou' the jinkers craw, ' Ha !—will ye gie's a gill, sir!' PICKEN *Poems* (1813) I. 97. **Ayr.** Ochon for poor Castalian drinkers, When they fa' foul o' earthly jinkers, BURNS *Ep. to Maj. Logan*, st. 10. **Lnk.** Where mates some greedy, some deep drinkers, Confound with thriftless mates or jinkers, RAMSAY *Poems* (1800) II. 489 (JAM.). [**Nfld.** An unlucky fellow, one who does not succeed at anything (G.P.).] (2, *a*) **Sc.** I have not forgotten the jinking we used to have about the mill, *Petticoat Tales* (1823) I. 398 (JAM.). **Bnff.** He's no pe Minister to flyte 'Pon fowk for youthfu' jinkin, TAYLOR *Poems* (1787) 133. **Ayr.** There's mair

ways an' fair ways, To tak' an honest heart Than winkin's and jinkin's O beauty spic'd wi' art, AINSLIE *Poems* (ed. 1892) 89. Where are a' your jinkings and prancings now ! HOGG *Tales* (1838) 313, ed. 1866. (*b*) **Ayr.** Jinkin' hares in amorous whids Their loves enjoy, BURNS *To W. Simpson* (1785) st. 12. **Slk.** Just a jinking, Bonnie blinking, Hilty skilty lassie yet, HOGG *Poems* (ed. 1865) 428. 4. To make short movements with the arm as in fiddling ; to play a tune smartly.

Sc. Raithie on his fiddle jinks Till all the trees dance round him. MAIDMENT *Pasquils* (1868) 341. **Abd.** Troth the fiddler's jinked lang, An' tired our lasses, BEATTIE *Parings* (1801) 14, ed. 1873. e.**Fif.** He wad seize heads o' the fiddle an' rin up an' doon the gamut like lichtnin', garrin' his elbock jink and diddle, LATTO *Tam Bodkin* (1864) ix. **Ayr.** Hale be your fiddle ! Lang may your elbuck jink and diddle, BURNS *Ep. to Maj. Logan*, st. 3. **Slk.** Jinks away at the muckle wheel as she war spinning for a wager, HOGG *Tales* (1838) 362, ed. 1866. **Rxb.** To dance with her where jinkin fiddles play, A. SCOTT *Poems* (ed. 1811) 96 (JAM.). **Nhb.¹**

5. *Phr.* *to jink off and on the dram*, to have sudden fits of drinking.

Lnk. Ben'-leather Tammie, Wha jinkit aff an' on the dram, MURDOCH *Doric Lyre* (1873) 8.

6. *sb.* A sudden turn ; a slip ; an escape ; avoidance.

Sc. They played the game of jinks with a good deal of skill, each avoiding the other if he could, KEITH *Bonnie Lady* (1897) 139. **Ayr.** At this jink o' their controversy who should come into the house . . . but Winterton, GALT *Gilhaize* (1823) v ; Our billie's gi'en us a' a jink, An' owre the sea, BURNS *Sc. Bard*, st. 1. **Lnk.** Fickle fortune's jinks Are like to drive us mad, ORR *Laigh Flichts* (1882) 118. **Nhb.¹**

7. A game ; a playful trick ; a frolic ; freq. in *pl.* Cf. gink, *sb.* 2.

Sc. What jinks we could play ! KEITH *Indian Uncle* (1896) 50. **Abd.** Sic fiddlin' an' pipin', Sic dancin' an' jinks, *Guidman Inglismaill* (1873) 43. **Per.** Stack-yard jinks, an' fireside joys, HALIBURTON *Ochil Idylls* (1891) 134. **Slg.** GALLOWAY *Sutor's Mag.* (1810) 17. **Edb.** Wi' ither moles I'm never seen, Wi' a' their jinks an' jirks, FORBES *Poems* (1812) 56. **Slk.** I ken your pawky jinks an' jeering, HOGG *Poems* (ed. 1865) 383. w.**Yks.²** **Dor.** He was the star of good company 40 years ago. I remember him in the height of his jinks, HARDY *Laodicean* (1881) bk. i. v.

JINK, *v.²* and *sb.²* n.Cy. Nhb. Yks. Lan. I.Ma. Der. Not. Lei. Nhp. War. Hrt. Hnt. Suf. Ess. [d**ʒiŋk**.] 1. *v.* To jingle ; to ' chink '; to try money by ringing it.

N.Cy.¹ **Nhb.¹** They jinked thor glasses. e.**Yks.¹**, w.**Yks.¹**, nw.Der.¹, Not. (J.H.B.), s.Not. (J.P.K.) **Lei.¹** It jinks like glass. **Nhp.¹** The money jinks, or it does not jink well. **War.³** **Hnt.** (T.P.F.), e.**Suf.** (F.H.) **Ess.** *Monthly Mag.* (1814) l. 498 ; **Ess.¹**

2. *sb.* A chinking noise ; a sharp rattle.

N.Cy.¹, **Nhb.¹** **Lan.** There was neither the jink nor the glitter of gold, BRIERLEY *Cast upon World* (1886) xvi. s.Not. (J.P.K.) 3. Money, property.

I.Ma. A nice little lump of jink—wasn she heiress to the Ballachrink! BROWN *Yarns* (1881) 191, ed. 1889. 4. A smooth, water-worn pebble.

Hrt. CUSSANS *Hist.* (1879-1881) III. 320. 5. *pl.* Part of the game of ' snobs ' (q.v.).

s.Not. One of the divisions of the game of snobs is called jinks that is, when the snobs have to be caught with a chink (J.P.K.).

JINK, *v.³* Yks. e.Cy. Suf. 1. To sprain.

e.Suf. To jink one's wrist or ankle. To jink one's back. Used of both man and beast (F.H.).

Hence (1) **Jinked**, *ppl. adj.* of an animal : hurt in the loins or back ; (2) **Jinked-backed**, *ppl. adj.* having a weak back, incapable of bearing heavy burdens.

(1) e.Cy. (HALL.) (2) w.**Yks.** It's an owd jink'd-back'd horse (Æ.B.).

2. Of the links of a chain : to entangle. e.Suf. (F.H.)

JINKEN'S HEN, see Jenkin's hen.

JINKER, *v.* Chs. To jingle, rattle. Cf. jink, *v.²* Yo mun always put plenty of strea i'th bottom o'th shay ; then, when the gentlefolk drop a shilling or a sixpence, it doesna jinker, *Sheaf* (1880) II. 27.

JINKERS, *sb. pl.* N.Cy.¹ In phr. *by jinkers*, an oath.

JINKET, see Junket.

JINKETING, *vbl. sb.* Irel. Jingling.

s.Ir. I hear the jinketing of their swords, CROKER *Leg.* (1862) 352.

Publications of the English Dialect Society.

[NOTE.—*All the prices are net.*]

LONDON: PUBLISHED FOR THE ENGLISH DIALECT SOCIETY BY HENRY FROWDE.
OXFORD UNIVERSITY PRESS WAREHOUSE, AMEN CORNER, E.C.